INTERNATIONAL LAW

Sixth edition

Malcolm Shaw's engaging and authoritative *International Law* has become the definitive textbook for instructors and students alike, in this increasingly popular field of academic study. The hallmark writing style provides a stimulating account, motivating students to explore the subject more fully, while maintaining detail and academic rigour. The analysis integrated in the textbook challenges students to develop critical thinking skills. The sixth edition is comprehensively updated throughout and is carefully constructed to reflect current teaching trends and course coverage. The International Court of Justice is now examined in a separate dedicated chapter and there is a new chapter on international criminal law. The detailed references and reliable, consistent commentary which distinguished previous editions remain, making this essential reading for all students of international law whether they be at undergraduate level, postgraduate level or professional lawyers.

MALCOLM N. SHAW, QC is the Sir Robert Jennings Professor of International Law at the University of Leicester. One of the world's leading international lawyers, he has been awarded the decoration of 'Officier de l'Ordre de la Valeur' by the Republic of Cameroon. He is a member of the Advisory Council of the British Institute of International and Comparative Law and a founding member of the Curatorium, Xiamen Academy of International Law. He is also a practising barrister at Essex Court Chambers.

INTERNATIONAL LAW

Sixth edition

MALCOLM N. SHAW QC

Sir Robert Jennings Professor of International Law
University of Leicester

CAMBRIDGE
UNIVERSITY PRESS

CAMBRIDGE UNIVERSITY PRESS

Cambridge, New York, Melbourne, Madrid, Cape Town, Singapore, São Paulo,
Delhi, Tokyo, Mexico City

Cambridge University Press
The Edinburgh Building, Cambridge CB2 8RU, UK

Published in the United States of America by Cambridge University Press, New York

www.cambridge.org
Information on this title: www.cambridge.org/law/shawsixthedition

Fourth edition first published by Cambridge University Press 1997
Reprinted 1999, 2000, 2001 (twice), 2002
Fifth edition 2003
Sixth edition 2008
5th printing 2011

Printed in the United Kingdom at the University Press, Cambridge

A catalogue record for this publication is available from the British Library

Library of Congress Cataloguing in Publication data
Shaw, Malcolm N. (Malcolm Nathan), 1947–
International law / Malcolm N. Shaw. – 6th ed.
p.   cm.
Includes index.
ISBN 978-0-521-89929-1
1. International law.   I. Title.
KZ3275.S53   2008
341 – dc22   2008037228

ISBN 978-0-521-89929-1 Hardback
ISBN 978-0-521-72814-0 Paperback

For my wife Judith

CONTENTS

PREFACE

The fifth edition of this book that appeared in 2003 has been extensively revised. To mark the growing importance of the international prosecution of alleged war criminals and others accused of egregious crimes, a new chapter on Individual Criminal Responsibility in International Law has been introduced. The chapter on Air and Space Law has had to be removed, with the section on Outer Space being moved to the chapter on Territory. The increasing significance of the International Court of Justice is recognised by devoting a separate chapter to it. The section on the International Tribunal for the Law of the Sea has been moved to the chapter on the Law of the Sea. The other chapters in the book have been re-examined, updated and, where necessary, rewritten. I have also been able to correct some errors. I am particularly delighted that the book has been translated into, among other languages, Chinese, Polish, Hungarian and Portuguese and I am very grateful for the work of all those involved.

I would especially like to thank Sinead Moloney of Cambridge University Press for her encouragement, assistance and above all patience. Particular gratitude is owed to Merel Alstein for her meticulous research assistance and for updating the web reference section. I am, once again, very grateful to Diane Ilott for her careful and thorough copy-editing and to Maureen MacGlashan for so carefully preparing the index and tables respectively. A debt remains to Sir Elihu Lauterpacht QC for his encouragement in the early development of this work. I also remain grateful to my many colleagues from many countries for their advice and encouragement, while reassuring them that all responsibility for the end product rests squarely with me.

As ever, the real and deepest thanks are due to my wife Judith and my children, Talia, Ilan and Daniella. They have borne the brunt of my travails over the years and endured the inevitable pressures and have done so in a caring and loving manner. Their support remains the indispensable foundation of this work.

Malcolm N. Shaw QC
Faculty of Law
University of Leicester
Spring 2008

TABLE OF CASES

ABBREVIATIONS

AC	Law Reports, Appeal Cases
AD	Annual Digest and Reports of Public International Law Cases (now International Law Reports)
AFDI	Annuaire Français de Droit International
AJIL	American Journal of International Law
All ER	All England Law Reports
ALR	Argus Law Reports (1895–1959); Australian Argus Law Reports (1960–73); Australian Law Reports (1973–)
Annuaire	Annuaire de l'Institut de Droit International
AU	African Union
Australian YIL	Australian Yearbook of International Law
B & C	Barnewall Cresswell (English Reports)
BCLC	Butterworths Company Law Cases
BFSP	British and Foreign State Papers
BPIL	British Practice in International Law
Bull.	Bulletin
Burr.	Burrow's Reports
BYIL	British Year Book of International Law
Cal	California Reports
Canadian YIL	Canadian Yearbook of International Law
Cass. Crim.	Cour de Cassation, France, Criminal
CCC	Canadian Criminal Cases
Cd, Cmd or Cmnd	UK Command Papers
Ch.	Law Reports, Chancery Division
Cl. Ct.	US Court of Claims Reports
CLJ	Cambridge Law Journal
CLR	Commonwealth Law Reports
CMLR	Common Market Law Reports

Co.Litt.	Coke on Littleton (First Institute)
COMECON	Council for Mutual Economic Assistance
Cr App R	Criminal Appeal Reports
Cranch	Cranch Reports, United States Supreme Court
Crim. L. Forum	Criminal Law Forum
Crim. LR	Criminal Law Review
C.Rob.	C. Robinson's Admiralty Reports
Dall.	Dallas, Pennsylvania and United States Reports
Dir. Mar.	Diritto Marittimo, Italy
DLR	Dominion Law Reports
Dod.	Dodson's Admiralty Reports
DUSPIL	Digest of US Practice in International Law
EC	European Communities
ECHR	European Convention on Human Rights
ECOSOC	Economic and Social Council
ECR	European Court Reports
ECSC	European Coal and Steel Community
EEC	European Economic Community
EJIL	European Journal of International Law
Encyclopedia	Encyclopedia of Public International Law
ER	English Reports
Euratom	European Atomic Energy Community
EWCA Civ.	England and Wales, Court of Appeal, Civil
EWHC Admin.	England and Wales, High Court
Ex.D.	Law Reports, Exchequer Division
F.2d	Federal Reporter (Second Series)
Fam.	Law Reports, Family Division
FAO	Food and Agriculture Organisation
FCO	Foreign and Commonwealth Office
FCR	Federal Court Reports (Australia)
Finnish YIL	Finnish Yearbook of International Law
F.(J.)	Faculty of Advocates
FLR	Family Law Reports
F.Supp.	Federal Supplement
GAOR	General Assembly Official Records
GDR	German Democratic Republic
German YIL	German Yearbook of International Law
HC Deb.	House of Commons Debates

HLC	House of Lords Reports (Clark)
HL Deb.	House of Lords Debates
HMSO	Her Majesty's Stationery Office
HR	Hague Academy of International Law, Recueil des Cours
HRJ	Human Rights Journal
HRLJ	Human Rights Law Journal
HRQ	Human Rights Quarterly
ICAO	International Civil Aviation Organisation
ICJ	International Court of Justice
ICLQ	International and Comparative Law Quarterly
ICR	Industrial Cases Reports
ICRC	International Committee of the Red Cross
ICSID	International Centre for the Settlement of Investment Disputes
ICTY	International Criminal Tribunal for the Former Yugoslavia
IJIL	Indian Journal of International Law
ILA	International Law Association
ILC	International Law Commission
ILM	International Legal Materials
ILO	International Labour Organisation
ILR	International Law Reports (see also Annual Digest and Reports of Public International Law Cases)
Iran–US CTR	Iran–United States Claims Tribunal Reports
ITU	International Telecommunications Union
KB	Law Reports, King's Bench Division
L.Ed.	US Supreme Court, Reports, Lawyers' Edition
LL. R	Lloyd's Law Reports
LNOJ	League of Nations Official Journal
LNTS	League of Nations Treaty Series
LQR	Law Quarterly Review
LR A&E	Law Reports: Admiralty and Ecclesiastical
MLR	Modern Law Review
NATO	North Atlantic Treaty Organisation
NE	Northeastern Reporter
Netherlands YIL	Netherlands Yearbook of International Law

—

NGO	Non-governmental organisation
NILR	Netherlands International Law Review
NLM	National Liberation Movement
NQHR	Netherlands Quarterly of Human Rights
NY	New York Reports
NYS	New York Supplement
NZLR	New Zealand Law Reports
OAS	Organisation of American States
OAU	Organisation of African Unity
OECD	Organisation for Economic Co-operation and Development
OECS	Organisation of Eastern Caribbean States
OR	Ontario Reports
P.	Law Reports, Probate, Divorce and Admiralty Division, 1891–
PAIGC	Partido Africano da Independencia da Guine e Cabo Verde
PASIL	Proceedings of the American Society of International Law
PCA	Permanent Court of Arbitration
PCIJ	Permanent Court of International Justice
PD	Law Reports, Probate, Divorce and Admiralty Division, 1875–90
Pet.	Peter's United States Supreme Court Reports
PLO	Palestine Liberation Organisation
QB	Law Reports, Queen's Bench Division
RecChl	Recommendation of the Committee of Ministers on the European Charter for Regional or Minority Languages
RFDA	Revue Française de Droit Administratif
RGDIP	Revue Française de Droit International Public
RIAA	United Nations Reports of International Arbitral Awards
R (J)	Justiciary cases in vols. of Session Cases, 1873–98
SA	South African Reports
SC	Supreme Court
SCOR	Security Council Official Records
SCR	Supreme Court Reports (Canada)

S. Ct.	Supreme Court Reporter
SR (NSW)	New South Wales, State Reports
Stat.	United States Statutes at Large
TFSC	'Turkish Federated State of Cyprus'
TRNC	'Turkish Republic of Northern Cyprus'
UKHL	United Kingdom, House of Lords
UKMIL	United Kingdom Materials in International Law
UNCESCR	United Nations Committee on Economic, Social and Cultural Rights
UNCIO	United Nations Conference of International Organisation
UNCLOS	United Nations Conference on the Law of the Sea
UNESCO	United Nations Educational, Scientific and Cultural Organisation
UNHRC	United Nations Human Rights Committee
UNJYB	United Nations Juridical Yearbook
UNTS	United Nations Treaty Series
US	United States Reports (Supreme Court)
US Av R	United States Aviation Reports
US and C Av R	United States and Canadian Aviation Reports
USC	United States Code
USLW	United States Law Weekly
Va. JIL	Virginia Journal of International Law
Ves. Jun.	Vesey Junior's Chancery Reports
VR	Victoria Reports
Wheat	Wheaton, United States Supreme Court Reports
WHO	World Health Organisation
WLR	Weekly Law Reports
Yale JIL	Yale Journal of International Law
YBWA	Yearbook of World Affairs
ZACC	South African Constitutional Court
ZaöRV	Zeitschrift für ausländisches öffentliches Recht und Völkerrecht

The nature and development of international law

In the long march of mankind from the cave to the computer a central role has always been played by the idea of law – the idea that order is necessary and chaos inimical to a just and stable existence. Every society, whether it be large or small, powerful or weak, has created for itself a framework of principles within which to develop. What can be done, what cannot be done, permissible acts, forbidden acts, have all been spelt out within the consciousness of that community. Progress, with its inexplicable leaps and bounds, has always been based upon the group as men and women combine to pursue commonly accepted goals, whether these be hunting animals, growing food or simply making money.

Law is that element which binds the members of the community together in their adherence to recognised values and standards. It is both permissive in allowing individuals to establish their own legal relations with rights and duties, as in the creation of contracts, and coercive, as it punishes those who infringe its regulations. Law consists of a series of rules regulating behaviour, and reflecting, to some extent, the ideas and preoccupations of the society within which it functions.

And so it is with what is termed international law, with the important difference that the principal subjects of international law are nation-states, not individual citizens. There are many contrasts between the law within a country (municipal law) and the law that operates outside and between states, international organisations and, in certain cases, individuals.

International law itself is divided into conflict of laws (or private international law as it is sometimes called) and public international law (usually just termed international law).[1] The former deals with those cases, *within* particular legal systems, in which foreign elements obtrude, raising questions as to the application of foreign law or the role of foreign courts.[2]

---

[1] This term was first used by J. Bentham: see *Introduction to the Principles of Morals and Legislation*, London, 1780.

[2] See e.g. C. Cheshire and P. North, *Private International Law*, 13th edn, London, 1999.

For example, if two Englishmen make a contract in France to sell goods situated in Paris, an English court would apply French law as regards the validity of that contract. By contrast, public international law is not simply an adjunct of a legal order, but a separate system altogether,[3] and it is this field that will be considered in this book.

Public international law covers relations between states in all their myriad forms, from war to satellites, and regulates the operations of the many international institutions. It may be universal or general, in which case the stipulated rules bind all the states (or practically all depending upon the nature of the rule), or regional, whereby a group of states linked geographically or ideologically may recognise special rules applying only to them, for example, the practice of diplomatic asylum that has developed to its greatest extent in Latin America.[4] The rules of international law must be distinguished from what is called international comity, or practices such as saluting the flags of foreign warships at sea, which are implemented solely through courtesy and are not regarded as legally binding.[5] Similarly, the mistake of confusing international law with international morality must be avoided. While they may meet at certain points, the former discipline is a legal one both as regards its content and its form, while the concept of international morality is a branch of ethics. This does not mean, however, that international law can be divorced from its values.

In this chapter and the next, the characteristics of the international legal system and the historical and theoretical background necessary to a proper appreciation of the part to be played by the law in international law will be examined.

Law and politics in the world community

It is the legal quality of international law that is the first question to be posed. Each side to an international dispute will doubtless claim legal justification for its actions and within the international system there is no independent institution able to determine the issue and give a final decision.

Virtually everybody who starts reading about international law does so having learned or absorbed something about the principal characteristics of ordinary or domestic law. Such identifying marks would include the

---

[3] See the *Serbian Loans* case, PCIJ, Series A, No. 14, pp. 41–2.
[4] See further below, p. 92.
[5] *North Sea Continental Shelf* cases, ICJ Reports, 1969, p. 44; 41 ILR, p. 29. See also M. Akehurst, 'Custom as a Source of International Law', 47 BYIL, 1974–5, p. 1.

existence of a recognised body to legislate or create laws, a hierarchy of courts with compulsory jurisdiction to settle disputes over such laws and an accepted system of enforcing those laws. Without a legislature, judiciary and executive, it would seem that one cannot talk about a legal order.[6] And international law does not fit this model. International law has no legislature. The General Assembly of the United Nations comprising delegates from all the member states exists, but its resolutions are not legally binding save for certain of the organs of the United Nations for certain purposes.[7] There is no system of courts. The International Court of Justice does exist at The Hague but it can only decide cases when both sides agree[8] and it cannot ensure that its decisions are complied with. Above all there is no executive or governing entity. The Security Council of the United Nations, which was intended to have such a role in a sense, has at times been effectively constrained by the veto power of the five permanent members (USA; USSR, now the Russian Federation; China; France; and the United Kingdom).[9] Thus, if there is no identifiable institution either to establish rules, or to clarify them or see that those who break them are punished, how can what is called international law be law?

It will, of course, be realised that the basis for this line of argument is the comparison of domestic law with international law, and the assumption of an analogy between the national system and the international order. And this is at the heart of all discussions about the nature of international law.

At the turn of the nineteenth century, the English philosopher John Austin elaborated a theory of law based upon the notion of a sovereign issuing a command backed by a sanction or punishment. Since international law did not fit within that definition it was relegated to the category of 'positive morality'.[10] This concept has been criticised for oversimplifying and even confusing the true nature of law within a society and for overemphasising the role of the sanction within the system by linking it to every rule.[11] This is not the place for a comprehensive summary of Austin's

---

[6] See generally, R. Dias, *Jurisprudence*, 5th edn, London, 1985, and H. L. A. Hart, *The Concept of Law*, Oxford, 1961.

[7] See article 17(1) of the United Nations Charter. See also D. Johnson, 'The Effect of Resolutions of the General Assembly of the United Nations', 32 BYIL, 1955–6, p. 97 and below, chapter 22.

[8] See article 36 of the Statute of the International Court of Justice and below, chapter 19.

[9] See e.g. *Bowett's Law of International Institutions* (eds. P. Sands and P. Klein), 5th edn, London, 2001, and below, chapter 23.

[10] See J. Austin, *The Province of Jurisprudence Determined* (ed. H. L. A. Hart), London, 1954, pp. 134–42.

[11] See e.g. Hart, *Concept of Law*, chapter 10.

theory but the idea of coercion as an integral part of any legal order is a vital one that needs looking at in the context of international law.

The role of force

There is no unified system of sanctions[12] in international law in the sense that there is in municipal law, but there are circumstances in which the use of force is regarded as justified and legal. Within the United Nations system, sanctions may be imposed by the Security Council upon the determination of a threat to the peace, breach of the peace or act of aggression.[13] Such sanctions may be economic, for example those proclaimed in 1966 against Rhodesia,[14] or military as in the Korean war in 1950,[15] or indeed both, as in 1990 against Iraq.[16]

Coercive action within the framework of the UN is rare because it requires co-ordination amongst the five permanent members of the Security Council and this obviously needs an issue not regarded by any of the great powers as a threat to their vital interests.

Korea was an exception and joint action could only be undertaken because of the fortuitous absence of the USSR from the Council as a protest at the seating of the Nationalist Chinese representatives.[17]

Apart from such institutional sanctions, one may note the bundle of rights to take violent action known as self-help.[18] This procedure to resort to force to defend certain rights is characteristic of primitive systems of law with blood-feuds, but in the domestic legal order such procedures and

---

[12] See e.g. W. M. Reisman, 'Sanctions and Enforcement' in *The Future of the International Legal Order* (eds. C. Black and R. A. Falk), New York, 1971, p. 273; J. Brierly, 'Sanctions', 17 *Transactions of the Grotius Society*, 1932, p. 68; Hart, *Concept of Law*, pp. 211–21; A. D'Amato, 'The Neo-Positivist Concept of International Law', 59 AJIL, 1965, p. 321; G. Fitzmaurice, 'The Foundations of the Authority of International Law and the Problem of Enforcement', 19 MLR, 1956, p. 1, and *The Effectiveness of International Decisions* (ed. S. Schwebel), Leiden, 1971.

[13] Chapter VII of the United Nations Charter. See below, chapter 22.

[14] Security Council resolution 221 (1966). Note also Security Council resolution 418 (1977) imposing a mandatory arms embargo on South Africa.

[15] Security Council resolutions of 25 June, 27 June and 7 July 1950. See D. W. Bowett, *United Nations Forces*, London, 1964.

[16] Security Council resolutions 661 and 678 (1990). See *The Kuwait Crisis: Basic Documents* (eds. E. Lauterpacht, C. Greenwood, M. Weller and D. Bethlehem), Cambridge, 1991, pp. 88 and 98. See also below, chapter 22.

[17] See E. Luard, *A History of the United Nations*, vol. I, *The Years of Western Domination 1945–55*, London, 1982, pp. 229–74, and below, chapter 22.

[18] See D. W. Bowett, *Self-Defence in International Law*, Manchester, 1958, and I. Brownlie, *International Law and the Use of Force by States*, Oxford, 1963.

methods are now within the exclusive control of the established authority. States may use force in self-defence, if the object of aggression, and may take action in response to the illegal acts of other states. In such cases the states themselves decide whether to take action and, if so, the extent of their measures, and there is no supreme body to rule on their legality or otherwise, in the absence of an examination by the International Court of Justice, acceptable to both parties, although international law does lay down relevant rules.[19]

Accordingly those writers who put the element of force to the forefront of their theories face many difficulties in describing the nature, or rather the legal nature of international law, with its lack of a coherent, recognised and comprehensive framework of sanctions. To see the sanctions of international law in the states' rights of self-defence and reprisals[20] is to misunderstand the role of sanctions within a system because they are at the disposal of the states, not the system itself. Neither must it be forgotten that the current trend in international law is to restrict the use of force as far as possible, thus leading to the absurd result that the more force is controlled in international society, the less legal international law becomes.

Since one cannot discover the nature of international law by reference to a definition of law predicated upon sanctions, the character of the international legal order has to be examined in order to seek to discover whether in fact states feel obliged to obey the rules of international law and, if so, why. If, indeed, the answer to the first question is negative, that states do not feel the necessity to act in accordance with such rules, then there does not exist any system of international law worthy of the name.

The international system[21]

The key to the search lies within the unique attributes of the international system in the sense of the network of relationships existing primarily, if not exclusively, between states recognising certain common principles

---

[19] See below, chapter 19. See also M. Barkin, *Law Without Sanctions*, New Haven, 1967.

[20] See e.g. H. Kelsen, *General Theory of Law and State*, London, 1946, pp. 328 ff.

[21] See L. Henkin, *How Nations Behave*, 2nd edn, New York, 1979, and Henkin, *International Law: Politics and Values*, Dordrecht, 1995; M. A. Kaplan and N. Katzenbach, *The Political Foundations of International Law*, New York, 1961; C. W. Jenks, *The Common Law of Mankind*, London, 1958; W. Friedmann, *The Changing Structure of International Law*, New York, 1964; A. Sheikh, *International Law and National Behaviour*, New York, 1974; O. Schachter, *International Law in Theory and Practice*, Dordrecht, 1991; T. M. Franck, *The Power of Legitimacy Among Nations*, Oxford, 1990; R. Higgins, *Problems and Process*, Oxford, 1994, and *Oppenheim's International Law* (eds. R. Y. Jennings and A. D. Watts), 9th edn, London, 1992, vol. I, chapter 1.

and ways of doing things.[22] While the legal structure within all but the most primitive societies is hierarchical and authority is vertical, the international system is horizontal, consisting of over 190 independent states, all equal in legal theory (in that they all possess the characteristics of sovereignty) and recognising no one in authority over them. The law is above individuals in domestic systems, but international law only exists as between the states. Individuals only have the choice as to whether to obey the law or not. They do not create the law. That is done by specific institutions. In international law, on the other hand, it is the states themselves that create the law and obey or disobey it.[23] This, of course, has profound repercussions as regards the sources of law as well as the means for enforcing accepted legal rules.

International law, as will be shown in succeeding chapters, is primarily formulated by international agreements, which create rules binding upon the signatories, and customary rules, which are basically state practices recognised by the community at large as laying down patterns of conduct that have to be complied with.

However, it may be argued that since states themselves sign treaties and engage in action that they may or may not regard as legally obligatory, international law would appear to consist of a series of rules from which states may pick and choose. Contrary to popular belief, states do observe international law, and violations are comparatively rare. However, such violations (like armed attacks and racial oppression) are well publicised and strike at the heart of the system, the creation and preservation of international peace and justice. But just as incidents of murder, robbery and rape do occur within national legal orders without destroying the system as such, so analogously assaults upon international legal rules point up the weaknesses of the system without denigrating their validity or their necessity. Thus, despite the occasional gross violation, the vast majority of the provisions of international law are followed.[24]

---

[22] As to the concept of 'international community', see e.g. G. Abi-Saab, 'Whither the International Community?', 9 EJIL, 1998, p. 248, and B. Simma and A. L. Paulus, 'The "International Community": Facing the Challenge of Globalisation', 9 EJIL, 1998, p. 266. See also P. Weil, 'Le Droit International en Quête de son Identité', 237 HR, 1992 VI, p. 25.

[23] This leads Rosenne to refer to international law as a law of co-ordination, rather than, as in internal law, a law of subordination, *Practice and Methods of International Law*, Dordrecht, 1984, p. 2.

[24] See H. Morgenthau, *Politics Among Nations*, 5th edn, New York, 1973, pp. 290–1; Henkin, *How Nations Behave*, pp. 46–9; J. Brierly, *The Outlook for International Law*, Oxford, 1944, p. 5, and P. Jessup, *A Modern Law of Nations*, New York, 1948, pp. 6–8.

In the daily routine of international life, large numbers of agreements and customs are complied with. However, the need is felt in the hectic interplay of world affairs for some kind of regulatory framework or rules network within which the game can be played, and international law fulfils that requirement. States feel this necessity because it imports an element of stability and predictability into the situation.

Where countries are involved in a disagreement or a dispute, it is handy to have recourse to the rules of international law even if there are conflicting interpretations since at least there is a common frame of reference and one state will be aware of how the other state will develop its argument. They will both be talking a common language and this factor of communication is vital since misunderstandings occur so easily and often with tragic consequences. Where the antagonists dispute the understanding of a particular rule and adopt opposing stands as regards its implementation, they are at least on the same wavelength and communicate by means of the same phrases. That is something. It is not everything, for it is a mistake as well as inaccurate to claim for international law more than it can possibly deliver. It can constitute a mutually understandable vocabulary book and suggest possible solutions which follow from a study of its principles. What it cannot do is solve every problem no matter how dangerous or complex merely by being there. International law has not yet been developed, if it ever will, to that particular stage and one should not exaggerate its capabilities while pointing to its positive features.

But what is to stop a state from simply ignoring international law when proceeding upon its chosen policy? Can a legal rule against aggression, for example, of itself prevail over political temptations? There is no international police force to prevent such an action, but there are a series of other considerations closely bound up with the character of international law which might well cause a potential aggressor to forbear.

There is the element of reciprocity at work and a powerful weapon it can be. States quite often do not pursue one particular course of action which might bring them short-term gains, because it could disrupt the mesh of reciprocal tolerance which could very well bring long-term disadvantages. For example, states everywhere protect the immunity of foreign diplomats for not to do so would place their own officials abroad at risk.[25] This constitutes an inducement to states to act reasonably and moderate

---

[25] See *Case Concerning United States Diplomatic and Consular Staff in Tehran*, ICJ Reports, 1980, p. 3; 61 ILR, p. 502. See also the US Supreme Court decision in *Boos v. Barry* 99 L. Ed. 2d 333, 345–6 (1988); 121 ILR, p. 499.

demands in the expectation that this will similarly encourage other states to act reasonably and so avoid confrontations. Because the rules can ultimately be changed by states altering their patterns of behaviour and causing one custom to supersede another, or by mutual agreement, a certain definite reference to political life is retained. But the point must be made that a state, after weighing up all possible alternatives, might very well feel that the only method to protect its vital interests would involve a violation of international law and that responsibility would just have to be taken. Where survival is involved international law may take second place.

Another significant factor is the advantages, or 'rewards', that may occur in certain situations from an observance of international law. It may encourage friendly or neutral states to side with one country involved in a conflict rather than its opponent, and even take a more active role than might otherwise have been the case. In many ways, it is an appeal to public opinion for support and all states employ this tactic.

In many ways, it reflects the esteem in which law is held. The Soviet Union made considerable use of legal arguments in its effort to establish its non-liability to contribute towards the peacekeeping operations of the United Nations,[26] and the Americans too, justified their activities with regard to Cuba[27] and Vietnam[28] by reference to international law. In some cases it may work and bring considerable support in its wake, in many cases it will not, but in any event the very fact that all states do it is a constructive sign.

A further element worth mentioning in this context is the constant formulation of international business in characteristically legal terms. Points of view and disputes, in particular, are framed legally with references to precedent, international agreements and even the opinions of juristic authors. Claims are pursued with regard to the rules of international law and not in terms of, for example, morality or ethics.[29] This has brought into being a class of officials throughout governmental departments, in

---

[26] See *Certain Expenses of the United Nations*, ICJ Reports, 1962, p. 151; 34 ILR, p. 281, and R. Higgins, *United Nations Peace-Keeping; Documents and Commentary*, Oxford, 4 vols., 1969–81.

[27] See e.g. A. Chayes, *The Cuban Missile Crisis*, Oxford, 1974, and Henkin, *How Nations Behave*, pp. 279–302.

[28] See e.g. *The Vietnam War and International Law* (ed. R. A. Falk), Princeton, 4 vols., 1968–76; J. N. Moore, *Law and the Indo-China War*, Charlottesville, 1972, and Henkin, *How Nations Behave*, pp. 303–12.

[29] See Hart, *Concept of Law*, p. 223.

addition to those working in international institutions, versed in international law and carrying on the everyday functions of government in a law-oriented way. Many writers have, in fact, emphasised the role of officials in the actual functioning of law and the influence they have upon the legal process.[30]

Having come to the conclusion that states do observe international law and will usually only violate it on an issue regarded as vital to their interests, the question arises as to the basis of this sense of obligation.[31] The nineteenth century, with its business-oriented philosophy, stressed the importance of the contract, as the legal basis of an agreement freely entered into by both (or all) sides, and this influenced the theory of consent in international law.[32] States were independent, and free agents, and accordingly they could only be bound with their own consent. There was no authority in existence able theoretically or practically to impose rules upon the various nation-states. This approach found its extreme expression in the theory of auto-limitation, or self-limitation, which declared that states could only be obliged to comply with international legal rules if they had first agreed to be so obliged.[33]

Nevertheless, this theory is most unsatisfactory as an account of why international law is regarded as binding or even as an explanation of the international legal system.[34] To give one example, there are about 100 states that have come into existence since the end of the Second World War and by no stretch of the imagination can it be said that such states have consented to all the rules of international law formed prior to their establishment. It could be argued that by 'accepting independence', states consent to all existing rules, but to take this view relegates consent to the role of a mere fiction.[35]

---

[30] See e.g. M. S. McDougal, H. Lasswell and W. M. Reisman, 'The World Constitutive Process of Authoritative Decision' in *International Law Essays* (eds. M. S. McDougal and W. M. Reisman), New York, 1981, p. 191.

[31] See e.g. J. Brierly, *The Basis of Obligation in International Law*, Oxford, 1958.

[32] See W. Friedmann, *Legal Theory*, 5th edn, London, 1967, pp. 573–6. See also the *Lotus* case, PCIJ, Series A, No. 10, p. 18.

[33] E.g. G. Jellinek, *Allgemeine Rechtslehre*, Berlin, 1905.

[34] See also Hart, *Concept of Law*, pp. 219–20. But see P. Weil, 'Towards Relative Normativity in International Law?', 77 AJIL, 1983, p. 413 and responses thereto, e.g. R. A. Falk, 'To What Extent are International Law and International Lawyers Ideologically Neutral?' in *Change and Stability in International Law-Making* (eds. A. Cassese and J. Weiler), 1989, p. 137, and A. Pellet, 'The Normative Dilemma: Will and Consent in International Law-Making', 12 Australian YIL, 1992, p. 22.

[35] See further below, p. 88.

This theory also fails as an adequate explanation of the international legal system, because it does not take into account the tremendous growth in international institutions and the network of rules and regulations that have emerged from them within the last generation.

To accept consent as the basis for obligation in international law[36] begs the question as to what happens when consent is withdrawn. The state's reversal of its agreement to a rule does not render that rule optional or remove from it its aura of legality. It merely places that state in breach of its obligations under international law if that state proceeds to act upon its decision. Indeed, the principle that agreements are binding (*pacta sunt servanda*) upon which all treaty law must be based cannot itself be based upon consent.[37]

One current approach to this problem is to refer to the doctrine of consensus.[38] This reflects the influence of the majority in creating new norms of international law and the acceptance by other states of such new rules. It attempts to put into focus the change of emphasis that is beginning to take place from exclusive concentration upon the nation-state to a consideration of the developing forms of international co-operation where such concepts as consent and sanction are inadequate to explain what is happening.

Of course, one cannot ignore the role of consent in international law. To recognise its limitations is not to neglect its significance. Much of international law is constituted by states expressly agreeing to specific normative standards, most obviously by entering into treaties. This cannot be minimised. Nevertheless, it is preferable to consider consent as important not only with regard to specific rules specifically accepted (which is not the sum total of international law, of course) but in the light of the approach of states generally to the totality of rules, understandings, patterns of behaviour and structures underpinning and constituting the international system.[39] In a broad sense, states accept or consent to the general system of international law, for in reality without that no such system could possibly operate. It is this approach which may be characterised as consensus

---

[36] See e.g. J. S. Watson, 'State Consent and the Sources of International Obligation', PASIL, 1992, p. 108.

[37] See below, chapter 3.

[38] See e.g. A. D'Amato, 'On Consensus', 8 Canadian YIL, 1970, p. 104. Note also the 'gentleman's agreement on consensus' in the Third UN Conference on the Law of the Sea: see L. Sohn, 'Voting Procedures in United Nations Conference for the Codification of International Law', 69 AJIL, 1975, p. 318, and UN Doc. A/Conf.62/WP.2.

[39] See e.g. J. Charney, 'Universal International Law', 87 AJIL, 1993, p. 529.

or the essential framework within which the demand for individual state consent is transmuted into community acceptance.

It is important to note that while states from time to time object to particular rules of international law and seek to change them, no state has sought to maintain that it is free to object to the system as a whole. Each individual state, of course, has the right to seek to influence by word or deed the development of specific rules of international law, but the creation of new customary rules is not dependent upon the express consent of each particular state.

The function of politics

It is clear that there can never be a complete separation between law and policy. No matter what theory of law or political philosophy is professed, the inextricable bonds linking law and politics must be recognised.

Within developed societies a distinction is made between the formulation of policy and the method of its enforcement. In the United Kingdom, Parliament legislates while the courts adjudicate and a similar division is maintained in the United States between the Congress and the courts system. The purpose of such divisions, of course, is to prevent a concentration of too much power within one branch of government. Nevertheless, it is the political branch which makes laws and in the first place creates the legal system. Even within the hierarchy of courts, the judges have leeway in interpreting the law and in the last resort make decisions from amongst a number of alternatives.[40] This position, however, should not be exaggerated because a number of factors operate to conceal and lessen the impact of politics upon the legal process. Foremost amongst these is the psychological element of tradition and the development of the so-called 'law-habit'.[41] A particular legal atmosphere has been created, which is buttressed by the political system and recognises the independent existence of law institutions and methods of operation characterised as 'just' or 'legal'. In most countries overt interference with the juridical process would be regarded as an attack upon basic principles and hotly contested. The use of legal language and accepted procedures together with the pride of the legal profession reinforce the system and emphasise the degree

---

[40] See e.g. R. Dworkin, *Taking Rights Seriously*, London, 1977.
[41] See e.g. K. Llewellyn, *The Common Law Tradition*, Boston, 1960, and generally D. Lloyd, *Introduction to Jurisprudence*, 4th edn, London, 1979.

of distance maintained between the legislative–executive organs and the judicial structure.[42]

However, when one looks at the international legal scene the situation changes. The arbiters of the world order are, in the last resort, the states and they both make the rules (ignoring for the moment the secondary, if growing, field of international organisations) and interpret and enforce them.

While it is possible to discern an 'international legal habit' amongst governmental and international officials, the machinery necessary to enshrine this does not exist.

Politics is much closer to the heart of the system than is perceived within national legal orders, and power much more in evidence.[43] The interplay of law and politics in world affairs is much more complex and difficult to unravel, and signals a return to the earlier discussion as to why states comply with international rules. Power politics stresses competition, conflict and supremacy and adopts as its core the struggle for survival and influence.[44] International law aims for harmony and the regulation of disputes. It attempts to create a framework, no matter how rudimentary, which can act as a kind of shock-absorber clarifying and moderating claims and endeavouring to balance interests. In addition, it sets out a series of principles declaring how states should behave. Just as any domestic community must have a background of ideas and hopes to aim at, even if few can be or are ever attained, so the international community, too, must bear in mind its ultimate values.

However, these ultimate values are in a formal sense kept at arm's length from the legal process. As the International Court noted in the *South-West Africa* case,[45] 'It is a court of law, and can take account of moral principles only in so far as these are given a sufficient expression in legal form. Law exists, it is said, to serve a social need; but precisely for that reason it can do so only through and within the limits of its own discipline. Otherwise, it is not a legal service that would be rendered.'[46]

International law cannot be a source of instant solutions to problems of conflict and confrontation because of its own inherent weaknesses

---

[42] See P. Stein and J. Shand, *Legal Values in Western Society*, Edinburgh, 1974.

[43] See generally Henkin, *How Nations Behave*, and Schachter, *International Law*, pp. 5–9.

[44] See G. Schwarzenberger, *Power Politics*, 3rd edn, London, 1964, and Schwarzenberger, *International Law*, 3rd edn, London, 1957, vol. I, and Morgenthau, *Politics Among Nations*.

[45] ICJ Reports, 1966, pp. 6, 34.

[46] But see Higgins' criticism that such a formulation may be question-begging with regard to the identity of such 'limits of its own discipline', *Problems*, p. 5.

in structure and content. To fail to recognise this encourages a utopian approach which, when faced with reality, will fail.[47] On the other hand, the cynical attitude with its obsession with brute power is equally inaccurate, if more depressing.

It is the medium road, recognising the strength and weakness of international law and pointing out what it can achieve and what it cannot, which offers the best hope. Man seeks order, welfare and justice not only within the state in which he lives, but also within the international system in which he lives.

Historical development[48]

The foundations of international law (or the law of nations) as it is understood today lie firmly in the development of Western culture and political organisation.

The growth of European notions of sovereignty and the independent nation-state required an acceptable method whereby inter-state relations could be conducted in accordance with commonly accepted standards of

---

[47] Note, of course, the important distinction between the existence of an obligation under international law and the question of the enforcement of that obligation. Problems with regard to enforcing a duty cannot affect the legal validity of that duty: see e.g. Judge Weeramantry's Separate Opinion in the Order of 13 September 1993, in the *Bosnia* case, ICJ Reports, 1993, pp. 325, 374; 95 ILR, pp. 43, 92.

[48] See in particular A. Nussbaum, *A Concise History of the Law of Nations*, rev. edn, New York, 1954; *Encyclopedia of Public International Law* (ed. R. Bernhardt), Amsterdam, 1984, vol. VII, pp. 127–273; J. W. Verzijl, *International Law in Historical Perspective*, Leiden, 10 vols., 1968–79, and M. Koskenniemi, *The Gentle Civilizer of Nations: The Rise and Fall of International Law, 1870–1960*, Cambridge, 2001. See also W. Grewe, *The Epochs of International Law* (trans. and rev. M. Byers), New York, 2000; A. Cassese, *International Law in a Divided World*, Oxford, 1986, and Cassese, *International Law*, 2nd edn, Oxford, 2005, chapter 2; Nguyen Quoc Dinh, P. Daillier and A. Pellet, *Droit International Public*, 7th edn, Paris, 2002, p. 41; H. Thierry, 'L'Evolution du Droit International', 222 HR, 1990 III, p. 9; P. Guggenheim, 'Contribution à l'Histoire des Sources du Droit des Gens', 94 HR, 1958 II, p. 5; A. Truyol y Serra, *Histoire de Droit International Public*, Paris, 1995; D. Gaurier, *Histoire du Droit International Public*, Rennes, 2005; D. Korff, 'Introduction à l'Histoire de Droit International Public', 1 HR, 1923 I, p. 1; P. Le Fur, 'Le Développement Historique de Droit International', 41 HR, 1932 III, p. 501; O. Yasuaki, 'When was the Law of International Society Born? An Inquiry of the History of International Law from an Intercivilisational Perpective', 2 *Journal of the History of International Law*, 2000, p. 1, and A. Kemmerer, 'The Turning Aside: On International Law and its History' in *Progress in International Organisation* (eds. R. A. Miller and R. Bratspies), Leiden, 2008, p. 71. For a general bibliography, see P. Macalister-Smith and J. Schwietzke, 'Literature and Documentary Sources relating to the History of International Law', 1 *Journal of the History of International Law*, 1999, p. 136.

behaviour, and international law filled the gap. But although the law of nations took root and flowered with the sophistication of Renaissance Europe, the seeds of this particular hybrid plant are of far older lineage. They reach far back into history.

Early origins

While the modern international system can be traced back some 400 years, certain of the basic concepts of international law can be discerned in political relationships thousands of years ago.[49] Around 2100 BC, for instance, a solemn treaty was signed between the rulers of Lagash and Umma, the city-states situated in the area known to historians as Mesopotamia. It was inscribed on a stone block and concerned the establishment of a defined boundary to be respected by both sides under pain of alienating a number of Sumerian gods.[50] The next major instance known of an important, binding, international treaty is that concluded over 1,000 years later between Rameses II of Egypt and the king of the Hittites for the establishment of eternal peace and brotherhood.[51] Other points covered in that agreement signed, it would seem, at Kadesh, north of Damascus, included respect for each other's territorial integrity, the termination of a state of aggression and the setting up of a form of defensive alliance.

Since that date many agreements between the rival Middle Eastern powers were concluded, usually aimed at embodying in a ritual form a state of subservience between the parties or attempting to create a political alliance to contain the influence of an over-powerful empire.[52]

---

[49] See D. J. Bederman, *International Law in Antiquity*, Cambridge, 2001.

[50] Nussbaum, *Law of Nations*, pp. 1–2. Note the discovery in the excavated city of Ebla, the capital of a civilisation at least 4,500 years old, of a copy of a political treaty between Ebla and the city of Abarsal: see *Times Higher Education Supplement*, 19 May 1995, p. 20. See also R. Cohen, *On Diplomacy in the Ancient Near East: The Amarna Letters*, Discussion Paper of the Centre for the Study of Diplomacy, University of Leicester, 1995; O. Butkevych, 'History of Ancient International Law: Challenges and Prospects', 5 *Journal of the History of International Law*, 2003, p. 189; A. Altman, 'Tracing the Earliest Recorded Concepts of International Law. The Early Dynastic Period in Southern Mesopotamia', 6 *Journal of the History of International Law*, 2004, p. 153, and 'Tracing the Earliest Recorded Concepts of International Law. (2) The Old Akkadian and Ur III Periods in Mesopotamia', 7 *Journal of the History of International Law*, 2005, p. 115.

[51] Nussbaum, *Law of Nations*, pp. 1–2.

[52] Preiser emphasises that the era between the seventeenth and fifteenth centuries BC witnessed something of a competing state system involving five independent (at various times) states: Bernhardt, *Encyclopedia*, vol. VII, pp. 133–4.

The role of ancient Israel must also be noted. A universal ethical stance coupled with rules relating to warfare were handed down to other peoples and religions and the demand for justice and a fair system of law founded upon strict morality permeated the thought and conduct of subsequent generations.[53] For example, the Prophet Isaiah declared that sworn agreements, even where made with the enemy, must be performed.[54] Peace and social justice were the keys to man's existence, not power.

After much neglect, there is now more consideration of the cultures and standards that evolved, before the birth of Christ, in the Far East, in the Indian[55] and Chinese[56] civilisations. Many of the Hindu rules displayed a growing sense of morality and generosity and the Chinese Empire devoted much thought to harmonious relations between its constituent parts. Regulations controlling violence and the behaviour of varying factions with regard to innocent civilians were introduced and ethical values instilled in the education of the ruling classes. In times of Chinese dominance, a regional tributary-states system operated which fragmented somewhat in times of weakness, but this remained culturally alive for many centuries.

However, the predominant approach of ancient civilisations was geographically and culturally restricted. There was no conception of an

---

[53] See P. Weil, 'Le Judaisme et le Développement du Droit International', 151 HR, 1976, p. 253, and S. Rosenne, 'The Influence of Judaism on International Law', *Nederlands Tijdschrift voor Internationaal Recht*, 1958, p. 119.

[54] See Nussbaum, *Law of Nations*, p. 3.

[55] *Ibid.* See also C. H. Alexandrowicz, *An Introduction to the History of the Law of Nations in the East Indies*, Leiden, 1967, and Alexandrowicz, 'The Afro-Asian World and the Law of Nations (Historical Aspects)', 123 HR, 1967, p. 117; L. Chatterjee, *International Law and Inter-State Relations in Ancient India*, 1958; Nagendra Singh, 'The Distinguishing Characteristics of the Concept of the Law of Nations as it Developed in Ancient India', *Liber Amicorum for Lord Wilberforce* (eds. A. Bos and I. Brownlie), Oxford, 1987, p. 91; R. P. Anand, *International Law and the Developing Countries*, The Hague, 1987; *International Law and Practice in Ancient India* (ed. H. S. Bhatia), New Delhi, 1977; Nagendra Singh, *India and International Law*, New Delhi, 1969, and P. Bandyopadhyay, *International Law and Custom in Ancient India*, New Delhi, 1982.

[56] Nussbaum, *Law of Nations*, p. 4; Liu Tchoan Pas, *Le Droit des Gens et de la Chine Antique*, Paris, 2 vols., 1926; P. Gong, *The Standard of 'Civilisation' in International Society*, 1984, pp. 130–63; pp. 164–200 with regard to Japan; pp. 201–37 with regard to Siam; I. C. Y. Hsu, *China's Entrance into the Family of Nations*, Harvard, 1960; K. Iriye, 'The Principles of International Law in the Light of Confucian Doctrine', 120 HR, 1967, p. 1, and Wang Tieya, 'International Law in China', 221 HR, 1990 II, p. 195. See also C. F. Amerasinghe, 'South Asian Antecedents of International Law' in *International Law – Theory and Practice* (ed. K. Wellens), The Hague, 1998, p. 3, and E. Y.-J. Lee, 'Early Development of Modern International Law in East Asia – With Special Reference to China, Japan and Korea', 4 *Journal of the History of International Law*, 2002, p. 42.

international community of states co-existing within a defined frame-work. The scope for any 'international law' of states was extremely limited and all that one can point to is the existence of certain ideals, such as the sanctity of treaties, which have continued to this day as important ele-ments in society. But the notion of a universal community with its ideal of world order was not in evidence.

The era of classical Greece, from about the sixth century BC and on-wards for a couple of hundred years, has, one must note, been of over-whelming significance for European thought. Its critical and rational turn of mind, its constant questioning and analysis of man and nature and its love of argument and debate were spread throughout Europe and the Mediterranean world by the Roman Empire which adopted Hellenic cul-ture wholesale, and penetrated Western consciousness with the Renais-sance. However, Greek awareness was limited to their own competitive city-states and colonies. Those of different origin were barbarians not deemed worthy of association.

The value of Greece in a study of international law lies partly in the philosophical, scientific and political analyses bequeathed to mankind and partly in the fascinating state of inter-relationship built up within the Hellenistic world.[57] Numerous treaties linked the city-states together in a network of commercial and political associations. Rights were often granted to the citizens of the states in each other's territories and rules regarding the sanctity and protection of diplomatic envoys developed. Certain practices were essential before the declaration of war, and the horrors of war were somewhat ameliorated by the exercise, for example, of religious customs regarding sanctuaries. But no overall moral approach similar to those emerging from Jewish and Hindu thought, particularly, evolved. No sense of a world community can be traced to Greek ideology in spite of the growth of Greek colonies throughout the Mediterranean area. This was left to the able administrators of the Roman Empire.[58]

The Romans had a profound respect for organisation and the law.[59] The law knitted together their empire and constituted a vital source of

---

[57] Nussbaum, *Law of Nations*, pp. 5–9, and A. Lanni, 'The Laws of War in Ancient Greece', *Harvard Law School Public Law Research Paper No. 07-24*, 2007. See also G. Ténékidès, 'Droit International et Communautés Fédérales dans la Grèce des Cités', 90 HR, 1956, p. 469; S. L. Ager, *Interstate Arbitrations in the Greek World, 337-90 BC*, Berkeley, 1996, and Bernhardt, *Encyclopedia*, vol. VII, pp. 154–6.

[58] Bernhardt, *Encyclopedia*, vol. VII, pp. 136–9, and Nussbaum, *Law of Nations*, pp. 10–16.

[59] See e.g. A. Jolowicz, *Historical Introduction to Roman Law*, 3rd edn, London, 1972. See also A. Watson, *International Law in Archaic Rome*, Baltimore, 1993.

reference for every inhabitant of the far-flung domain. The early Roman law (the *jus civile*) applied only to Roman citizens. It was formalistic and hard and reflected the status of a small, unsophisticated society rooted in the soil.

It was totally unable to provide a relevant background for an expanding, developing nation. This need was served by the creation and progressive augmentation of the *jus gentium*. This provided simplified rules to govern the relations between foreigners, and between foreigners and citizens. The instrument through which this particular system evolved was the official known as the Praetor Peregrinus, whose function it was to oversee all legal relationships, including bureaucratic and commercial matters, within the empire.

The progressive rules of the *jus gentium* gradually overrode the narrow *jus civile* until the latter system ceased to exist. Thus, the *jus gentium* became the common law of the Roman Empire and was deemed to be of universal application.

It is this all-embracing factor which so strongly distinguishes the Roman from the Greek experience, although, of course, there was no question of the acceptance of other nations on a basis of equality and the *jus gentium* remained a 'national law' for the Roman Empire.

One of the most influential of Greek concepts taken up by the Romans was the idea of Natural Law.[60] This was formulated by the Stoic philosophers of the third century BC and their theory was that it constituted a body of rules of universal relevance. Such rules were rational and logical, and because the ideas and precepts of the 'law of nature' were rooted in human intelligence, it followed that such rules could not be restricted to any nation or any group but were of worldwide relevance. This element of universality is basic to modern doctrines of international law and the Stoic elevation of human powers of logical deduction to the supreme pinnacle of 'discovering' the law foreshadows the rational philosophies of the West. In addition to being a fundamental concept in legal theory, Natural Law is vital to an understanding of international law, as well as being an indispensable precursor to contemporary concern with human rights.

Certain Roman philosophers incorporated those Greek ideas of Natural Law into their own legal theories, often as a kind of ultimate justification

---

[60] See e.g. Lloyd, *Introduction to Jurisprudence*, pp. 79–169.

of the *jus gentium*, which was deemed to enshrine rational principles common to all civilised nations.

However, the law of nature was held to have an existence over and above that of the *jus gentium*. This led to much confusion over the exact relationship between the two ideas and different Roman lawyers came to different conclusions as to their identity and characteristics. The important factors though that need to be noted are the theories of the universality of law and the rational origins of legal rules that were founded, theoretically at least, not on superior force but on superior reason.

The classical rules of Roman law were collated in the *Corpus Juris Civilis*, a compilation of legal material by a series of Byzantine philosophers completed in AD 534.[61] Such a collection was to be invaluable when the darkness of the early Middle Ages, following the Roman collapse, began gradually to evaporate. For here was a body of developed laws ready made and awaiting transference to an awakening Europe.

At this stage reference must be made to the growth of Islam.[62] Its approach to international relations and law was predicated upon a state of hostility towards the non-Moslem world and the concept of unity, Dar al-Islam, as between Moslem countries. Generally speaking, humane rules of warfare were developed and the 'peoples of the book' (Jews and Christians) were treated better than non-believers, although in an inferior position to Moslems. Once the period of conquest was over and power was consolidated, norms governing conduct with non-Moslem states began to develop. The law dealing with diplomats was founded upon notions of hospitality and safety (*aman*), while rules governing international agreements grew out of the concept of respecting promises made.[63]

---

[61] See generally with regard to Byzantium, M. De Taube, 'L'Apport de Byzance au Développement du Droit International Occidental', 67 HR, 1939, p. 233, and S. Verosta, 'International Law in Europe and Western Asia between 100–650 AD', 113 HR, 1964, p. 489.

[62] See e.g. M. Al Ghunaimi, *The Muslim Conception of International Law and the Western Approach*, The Hague, 1968; A. Draz, 'Le Droit International Public et l'Islam', 5 *Revue Égyptienne de Droit International*, p. 17; C. Stumpf, 'Christian and Islamic Traditions of Public International Law', 7 *Journal of the History of International Law*, 2005, p. 69; H. Khadduri, 'Islam and the Modern Law of Nations', 50 AJIL, 1956, p. 358, and Khadduri, *War and Peace in the Law of Islam*, 2nd edn, Baltimore, 1962, and S. Mahmassani, 'The Principles of International Law in the Light of Islamic Doctrine', 117 HR, 1966, p. 205. See also 'L'Asile et les Refugiés dans la Tradition Musulmane', Report of the Sixty-Ninth Conference, International Law Association, London, 2000, p. 305, and Y. Ben Achour Yadh, 'La Civilisation Islamique et le Droit International', RGDIP, 2006, p. 19.

[63] See Bernhardt, *Encyclopedia*, vol. VII, pp. 141–2, and Nussbaum, *Law of Nations*, pp. 51–4.

The Middle Ages and the Renaissance

The Middle Ages were characterised by the authority of the organised Church and the comprehensive structure of power that it commanded.[64] All Europe was of one religion, and the ecclesiastical law applied to all, notwithstanding tribal or regional affiliations. For much of the period, there were struggles between the religious authorities and the rulers of the Holy Roman Empire.

These conflicts were eventually resolved in favour of the Papacy, but the victory over secularism proved of relatively short duration. Religion and a common legacy derived from the Roman Empire were strongly unifying influences, while political and regional rivalries were not. But before a recognised system of international law could be created, social changes were essential.

Of particular importance during this era were the authority of the Holy Roman Empire and the supranational character of canon law.[65] Nevertheless, commercial and maritime law developed apace. English law established the *Law Merchant*, a code of rules covering foreign traders, and this was declared to be of universal application.[66]

Throughout Europe, mercantile courts were set up to settle disputes between tradesmen at the various fairs, and while it is not possible to state that a Continental *Law Merchant* came into being, a network of common regulations and practices weaved its way across the commercial fabric of Europe and constituted an embryonic international trade law.[67]

Similarly, maritime customs began to be accepted throughout the Continent. Founded upon the Rhodian Sea Law, a Byzantine work, many of whose rules were enshrined in the Rolls of Oleron in the twelfth century, and other maritime textbooks, a series of commonly applied customs relating to the sea permeated the naval powers of the Atlantic and Mediterranean coasts.[68]

[64] Nussbaum, *Law of Nations*, pp. 17–23, and Bernhardt, *Encyclopedia*, vol. VII, pp. 143–9.

[65] Note in particular the influence of the Church on the rules governing warfare and the binding nature of agreements: see Nussbaum, *Law of Nations*, pp. 17–18, and Bernhardt *Encyclopedia*, vol. VII, pp. 146–7. See also M. Keen, *The Laws of War in the Late Middle Ages*, London, 1965.

[66] See G. Holdsworth, *A History of English Law*, London, 1924, vol. 5, pp. 60–3.

[67] *Ibid.*, pp. 63–129.

[68] Nussbaum, *Law of Nations*, pp. 29–31. Note also the influence of the Consolato del Mare, composed in Barcelona in the mid-fourteenth century, and the Maritime Code of Wisby (*c.* 1407) followed by the Hanseatic League.

Such commercial and maritime codes, while at this stage merely expressions of national legal systems, were amongst the forerunners of international law because they were created and nurtured against a backcloth of cross-national contacts and reflected the need for rules that would cover international situations.

Such rules, growing out of the early Middle Ages, constituted the seeds of international law, but before they could flourish, European thought had first to be developed by that intellectual explosion known as the Renaissance.

This complex of ideas changed the face of European society and ushered in the modern era of scientific, humanistic and individualistic thought.[69]

The collapse of the Byzantine Empire centred on Constantinople before the Turkish armies in 1453 drove many Greek scholars to seek sanctuary in Italy and enliven Western Europe's cultural life. The introduction of printing during the fifteenth century provided the means to disseminate knowledge, and the undermining of feudalism in the wake of economic growth and the rise of the merchant classes provided the background to the new inquiring attitudes taking shape.

Europe's developing self-confidence manifested itself in a sustained drive overseas for wealth and luxury items. By the end of the fifteenth century, the Arabs had been ousted from the Iberian peninsula and the Americas reached.

The rise of the nation-states of England, France and Spain in particular characterised the process of the creation of territorially consolidated independent units, in theory and doctrine, as well as in fact. This led to a higher degree of interaction between sovereign entities and thus the need to regulate such activities in a generally acceptable fashion. The pursuit of political power and supremacy became overt and recognised, as Machiavelli's *The Prince* (1513) demonstrated.

The city-states of Italy struggled for supremacy and the Papacy too became a secular power. From these hectic struggles emerged many of the staples of modern international life: diplomacy, statesmanship, the theory of the balance of power and the idea of a community of states.[70]

Notions such as these are immediately appreciable and one can identify with the various manoeuvres for political supremacy. Alliances, betrayals, manipulations of state institutions and the drive for power are not unknown to us. We recognise the roots of our society.

---

[69] See e.g. Friedmann, *Changing Structure*, pp. 114–16.
[70] See e.g. G. Mattingley, *Renaissance Diplomacy*, London, 1955.

It was the evolution of the concept of an international community of separate, sovereign, if competing, states, that marks the beginning of what is understood by international law. The Renaissance bequeathed the prerequisites of independent, critical thought and a humanistic, secular approach to life as well as the political framework for the future. But it is the latter factor which is vital to the subsequent growth of international law. The Reformation and the European religious wars that followed emphasised this, as did the growing power of the nations. In many ways these wars marked the decline of a continental system founded on religion and the birth of a continental system founded on the supremacy of the state.

Throughout these countries the necessity was felt for a new conception of human as well as state relationships. This search was precipitated, as has been intimated, by the decline of the Church and the rise of what might be termed 'free-thinking'. The theory of international law was naturally deeply involved in this reappraisal of political life and it was tremendously influenced by the rediscovery of Greco-Roman ideas. The Renaissance stimulated a rebirth of Hellenic studies and ideas of Natural Law, in particular, became popular.

Thus, a distinct value-system to underpin international relations was brought into being and the law of nations was heralded as part of the universal law of nature.

With the rise of the modern state and the emancipation of international relations, the doctrine of sovereignty emerged. This concept, first analysed systematically in 1576 in the *Six Livres de la République* by Jean Bodin, was intended to deal with the structure of authority within the modern state. Bodin, who based his study upon his perception of the politics of Europe rather than on a theoretical discussion of absolute principles, emphasised the necessity for a sovereign power within the state that would make the laws. While such a sovereign could not be bound by the laws he himself instituted, he was subject to the laws of God and of nature.[71]

The idea of the sovereign as supreme legislator was in the course of time transmuted into the principle which gave the state supreme power vis-à-vis other states. The state was regarded as being above the law. Such

---

[71] See A. Gardot, 'Jean Bodin – Sa Place Parmi les Fondateurs du Droit International', 50 HR, 1934, p. 549. See also, for a discussion of sovereignty and the treaty-making power in the late middle ages, T. Meron, 'The Authority to Make Treaties in the Late Middle Ages', 89 AJIL, 1995, p. 1.

notions as these formed the intellectual basis of the line of thought known as positivism which will be discussed later.[72]

The early theorists of international law were deeply involved with the ideas of Natural Law and used them as the basis of their philosophies. Included within that complex of Natural Law principles from which they constructed their theories was the significant merging of Christian and Natural Law ideas that occurred in the philosophy of St Thomas Aquinas.[73] He maintained that Natural Law formed part of the law of God, and was the participation by rational creatures in the Eternal Law. It complemented that part of the Eternal Law which had been divinely revealed. Reason, declared Aquinas, was the essence of man and thus must be involved in the ordering of life according to the divine will. Natural Law was the fount of moral behaviour as well as of social and political institutions, and it led to a theory of conditional acceptance of authority with unjust laws being unacceptable. Aquinas' views of the late thirteenth century can be regarded as basic to an understanding of present Catholic attitudes, but should not be confused with the later interpretation of Natural Law which stressed the concepts of natural rights.

It is with such an intellectual background that Renaissance scholars approached the question of the basis and justification of a system of international law. Maine, a British historical lawyer, wrote that the birth of modern international law was the grandest function of the law of nature and while that is arguable, the point must be taken.[74] International law began to emerge as a separate topic to be studied within itself, although derived from the principles of Natural Law.

The founders of modern international law

The essence of the new approach to international law can be traced back to the Spanish philosophers of that country's Golden Age.[75] The leading figure of this school was Francisco Vitoria, Professor of Theology at the University of Salamanca (1480–1546). His lectures were preserved by his students and published posthumously. He demonstrated a remarkably progressive attitude for his time towards the Spanish conquest of the

---

[72] Below, p. 49.   [73] *Summa Theologia*, English edn, 1927.

[74] H. Maine, *Ancient Law*, London, 1861, pp. 56 and 64–6.

[75] Note Preiser's view that '[t]here was hardly a single important problem of international law until the middle of the 17th century which was not principally a problem of Spain and the allied Habsburg countries': Bernhardt, *Encyclopedia*, vol. VII, p. 150. See also Nussbaum, *Law of Nations*, pp. 79–93.

South American Indians and, contrary to the views prevalent until then, maintained that the Indian peoples should be regarded as nations with their own legitimate interests. War against them could only be justified on the grounds of a just cause. International law was founded on the universal law of nature and this meant that non-Europeans must be included within its ambit. However, Vitoria by no means advocated the recognition of the Indian nations as equal to the Christian states of Europe. For him, opposing the work of the missionaries in the territories was a just reason for war, and he adopted a rather extensive view as to the rights of the Spaniards in South America. Vitoria was no liberal and indeed acted on behalf of the Spanish Inquisition, but his lectures did mark a step forward in the right direction.[76]

Suárez (1548–1617) was a Jesuit and Professor of Theology who was deeply immersed in medieval culture. He noted that the obligatory character of international law was based upon Natural Law, while its substance derived from the Natural Law rule of carrying out agreements entered into.[77]

From a totally different background but equally, if not more, influential was Alberico Gentili (1552–1608). He was born in Northern Italy and fled to England to avoid persecution, having converted to Protestantism. In 1598 his *De Jure Belli* was published.[78] It is a comprehensive discussion of the law of war and contains a valuable section on the law of treaties. Gentili, who became a professor at Oxford, has been called the originator of the secular school of thought in international law and he minimised the hitherto significant theological theses.

It is, however, Hugo Grotius, a Dutch scholar, who towers over this period and has been celebrated, if a little exaggeratedly, as the father of international law. He was born in 1583 and was the supreme Renaissance man. A scholar of tremendous learning, he mastered history, theology, mathematics and the law.[79] His primary work was the *De Jure Belli ac Pacis*,

---

[76] Nussbaum, *Law of Nations*, pp. 79–84, and Bernhardt, *Encyclopedia*, vol. VII, pp. 151–2. See also F. Vitoria, *De Indis et de Jure Belli Relectiones*, Classics of International Law, Washington, DC, 1917, and J. B. Scott, *The Spanish Origin of International Law, Francisco de Vitoria and his Law of Nations*, Washington, DC, 1934.

[77] Nussbaum, *Law of Nations*, pp. 84–91. See also *ibid.*, pp. 92–3 regarding the work of Ayala (1548–84).

[78] *Ibid.*, pp. 94–101. See also A. Van der Molen, *Alberico Gentili and the Development of International Law*, 2nd edn, London, 1968.

[79] Nussbaum, *Law of Nations*, pp. 102–14. See also W. S. M. Knight, *The Life and Works of Hugo Grotius*, London, 1925, and 'Commemoration of the Fourth Century of the Birth of Grotius' (various articles), 182 HR, 1984, pp. 371–470.

written during 1623 and 1624. It is an extensive work and includes rather more devotion to the exposition of private law notions than would seem appropriate today. He refers both to Vitoria and Gentili, the latter being of special influence with regard to many matters, particularly organisation of material.

Grotius finally excised theology from international law and emphasised the irrelevance in such a study of any conception of a divine law. He remarked that the law of nature would be valid even if there were no God: a statement which, although suitably clothed in religious protestation, was extremely daring. The law of nature now reverted to being founded exclusively on reason. Justice was part of man's social make-up and thus not only useful but essential. Grotius conceived of a comprehensive system of international law and his work rapidly became a university textbook. However, in many spheres he followed well-trodden paths. He retained the theological distinction between a just and an unjust war, a notion that was soon to disappear from treatises on international law, but which in some way underpins modern approaches to aggression, self-defence and liberation.

One of his most enduring opinions consists in his proclamation of the freedom of the seas. The Dutch scholar opposed the 'closed seas' concept of the Portuguese that was later elucidated by the English writer John Selden[80] and emphasised instead the principle that the nations could not appropriate to themselves the high seas. They belonged to all. It must, of course, be mentioned, parenthetically, that this theory happened to accord rather nicely with prevailing Dutch ideas as to free trade and the needs of an expanding commercial empire.

However, this merely points up what must not be disregarded, namely that concepts of law as of politics and other disciplines are firmly rooted in the world of reality, and reflect contemporary preoccupations. No theory develops in a vacuum, but is conceived and brought to fruition in a definite cultural and social environment. To ignore this is to distort the theory itself.

Positivism and naturalism

Following Grotius, but by no means divorced from the thought of previous scholars, a split can be detected and two different schools identified.

---

[80] In *Mare Clausum Sive de Dominio Maris*, 1635.

On the one hand there was the 'naturalist' school, exemplified by Samuel Pufendorf (1632–94),[81] who attempted to identify international law completely with the law of nature; and on the other hand there were the exponents of 'positivism', who distinguished between international law and Natural Law and emphasised practical problems and current state practices. Pufendorf regarded Natural Law as a moralistic system, and misunderstood the direction of modern international law by denying the validity of the rules about custom. He also refused to acknowledge treaties as in any way relevant to a discussion of the basis of international law. Other 'naturalists' echoed those sentiments in minimising or ignoring the actual practices of states in favour of a theoretical construction of absolute values that seemed slowly to drift away from the complexities of political reality.

One of the principal initiators of the positivist school was Richard Zouche (1590–1660), who lived at the same time as Pufendorf, but in England.[82] While completely dismissing Natural Law, he paid scant regard to the traditional doctrines. His concern was with specific situations and his book contains many examples from the recent past. He elevated the law of peace above a systematic consideration of the law of war and eschewed theoretical expositions.

In similar style Bynkershoek (1673–1743) stressed the importance of modern practice and virtually ignored Natural Law. He made great contributions to the developing theories of the rights and duties of neutrals in war, and after careful studies of the relevant facts decided in favour of the freedom of the seas.[83]

The positivist approach, like much of modern thought, was derived from the empirical method adopted by the Renaissance. It was concerned not with an edifice of theory structured upon deductions from absolute principles, but rather with viewing events as they occurred and discussing actual problems that had arisen. Empiricism as formulated by Locke and Hume[84] denied the existence of innate principles and postulated that ideas were derived from experience. The scientific method of experiment and verification of hypotheses emphasised this approach.

From this philosophical attitude, it was a short step to reinterpreting international law not in terms of concepts derived from reason but rather in terms of what actually happened between the competing states. What

---

[81] *On the Law of Nature and of Nations*, 1672. See also Nussbaum, *Law of Nations*, pp. 147–50.
[82] Nussbaum, *Law of Nations*, pp. 165–7.   [83] *Ibid.*, pp. 167–72.
[84] See Friedmann, *Legal Theory*, pp. 253–5.

states actually do was the key, not what states ought to do given basic rules of the law of nature. Agreements and customs recognised by the states were the essence of the law of nations.

Positivism developed as the modern nation-state system emerged, after the Peace of Westphalia in 1648, from the religious wars.[85] It coincided, too, with theories of sovereignty such as those propounded by Bodin and Hobbes,[86] which underlined the supreme power of the sovereign and led to notions of the sovereignty of states.

Elements of both positivism and naturalism appear in the works of Vattel (1714–67), a Swiss lawyer. His *Droit des Gens* was based on Natural Law principles yet was practically oriented. He introduced the doctrine of the equality of states into international law, declaring that a small republic was no less a sovereign than the most powerful kingdom, just as a dwarf was as much a man as a giant. By distinguishing between laws of conscience and laws of action and stating that only the latter were of practical concern, he minimised the importance of Natural Law.[87]

Ironically, at the same time that positivist thought appeared to demolish the philosophical basis of the law of nature and relegate that theory to history, it re-emerged in a modern guise replete with significance for the future. Natural Law gave way to the concept of natural rights.[88]

It was an individualistic assertion of political supremacy. The idea of the social contract, that an agreement between individuals pre-dated and justified civil society, emphasised the central role of the individual, and whether such a theory was interpreted pessimistically to demand an absolute sovereign as Hobbes declared, or optimistically to mean a conditional acceptance of authority as Locke maintained, it could not fail to be a revolutionary doctrine. The rights of man constitute the heart of the American[89] and French Revolutions and the essence of modern democratic society.

---

[85] See L. Gross, 'The Peace of Westphalia 1648–1948', 42 AJIL, 1948, p. 20; *Renegotiating Westphalia* (eds. C. Harding and C. L. Lim), The Hague, 1999, especially chapter 1, and S. Beaulac, 'The Westphalian Legal Orthodoxy – Myth or Reality?', 2 *Journal of the History of International Law*, 2000, p. 148.

[86] *Leviathan*, 1651.

[87] See Nussbaum, *Law of Nations*, pp. 156–64. See also N. Onuf, '*Civitas Maxima*: Wolff, Vattel and the Fate of Republicanism', 88 AJIL, 1994, p. 280.

[88] See e.g. J. Finnis, *Natural Law and Natural Rights*, Oxford, 1980, and R. Tuck, *Natural Rights Theories*, Cambridge, 1979.

[89] See e.g. N. Onuf and O. Onuf, *Federal Unions, Modern World*, Madison, 1994.

Yet, on the other hand, the doctrine of Natural Law has been employed to preserve the absoluteness of sovereignty and the sanctity of private possessions. The theory has a reactionary aspect because it could be argued that what was, ought to be, since it evolved from the social contract or was divinely ordained, depending upon how secular one construed the law of nature to be.

The nineteenth century

The eighteenth century was a ferment of intellectual ideas and ratio- nalist philosophies that contributed to the evolution of the doctrine of international law. The nineteenth century by contrast was a practical, ex- pansionist and positivist era. The Congress of Vienna, which marked the conclusion of the Napoleonic wars, enshrined the new international order which was to be based upon the European balance of power. International law became Eurocentric, the preserve of the civilised, Christian states, into which overseas and foreign nations could enter only with the consent of and on the conditions laid down by the Western powers. Paradoxically, whilst international law became geographically internationalised through the expansion of the European empires, it became less universalist in con- ception and more, theoretically as well as practically, a reflection of Eu- ropean values.[90] This theme, the relationship between universalism and particularism, appears time and again in international law. This century also saw the coming to independence of Latin America and the forging of a distinctive approach to certain elements of international law by the states of that region, especially with regard to, for example, diplomatic asylum and the treatment of foreign enterprises and nationals.[91]

There are many other features that mark the nineteenth century. Democracy and nationalism, both spurred on by the wars of the French revolution and empire, spread throughout the Continent and changed the essence of international relations.[92] No longer the exclusive concern

---

[90] See Nussbaum, *Law of Nations*, pp. 186–250, and, e.g., C. H. Alexandrowicz, *The European–African Confrontation*, Leiden, 1973. See also B. Bowden, 'The Colonial Origins of Interna- tional Law. European Expansion and the Classical Standard of Civilisation', 7 *Journal of the History of International Law*, 2005, p. 1, and C. Sylvest, 'International Law in Nineteenth- Century Britain', 75 BYIL, 2004, p. 9.

[91] See below, chapters 3 and 14 respectively. See also H. Gros Espiell, 'La Doctrine du Droit International en Amérique Latine avant la Première Conférence Panaméricaine', 3 *Journal of the History of International Law*, 2001, p. 1.

[92] See especially A. Cobban, *The Nation State and National Self-Determination*, London, 1969.

of aristocratic élites, foreign policy characterised both the positive and the negative faces of nationalism. Self-determination emerged to threaten the multinational empires of Central and Eastern Europe, while nationalism reached its peak in the unifications of Germany and Italy and began to exhibit features such as expansionism and doctrines of racial superiority. Democracy brought to the individual political influence and a say in government. It also brought home the realities of responsibility, for wars became the concern of all. Conscription was introduced throughout the Continent and large national armies replaced the small professional forces.[93] The Industrial Revolution mechanised Europe, created the economic dichotomy of capital and labour and propelled Western influence throughout the world. All these factors created an enormous increase in the number and variety of both public and private international institutions, and international law grew rapidly to accommodate them.[94] The development of trade and communications necessitated greater international co-operation as a matter of practical need. In 1815, the Final Act of the Congress of Vienna established the principle of freedom of navigation with regard to international waterways and set up a Central Commission of the Rhine to regulate its use. In 1856 a commission for the Danube was created and a number of other European rivers also became the subject of international agreements and arrangements. In 1865 the International Telegraphic Union was established and in 1874 the Universal Postal Union.[95]

European conferences proliferated and contributed greatly to the development of rules governing the waging of war. The International Committee of the Red Cross, founded in 1863, helped promote the series of Geneva Conventions beginning in 1864 dealing with the 'humanisation' of conflict, and the Hague Conferences of 1899 and 1907 established the Permanent Court of Arbitration and dealt with the treatment of prisoners and the control of warfare.[96] Numerous other conferences, conventions and congresses emphasised the expansion of the rules of international law and the close network of international relations. In addition, the academic study of international law within higher education developed with the appointment of professors of the subject and the appearance of specialist textbooks emphasising the practice of states.

---

[93] G. Best, *Humanity in Warfare*, London, 1980; Best, *War and Law Since 1945*, Oxford, 1994, and S. Bailey, *Prohibitions and Restraints in War*, Oxford, 1972.
[94] See e.g. *Bowett's Law of International Institutions*, and *The Evolution of International Organisations* (ed. E. Luard), Oxford, 1966.
[95] See further below, chapter 23.   [96] See further below, chapter 21.

Positivist theories dominate this century. The proliferation of the powers of states and the increasing sophistication of municipal legislation gave force to the idea that laws were basically commands issuing from a sovereign person or body. Any question of ethics or morality was irrelevant to a discussion of the validity of man-made laws. The approach was transferred onto the international scene and immediately came face to face with the reality of a lack of supreme authority.

Since law was ultimately dependent upon the will of the sovereign in national systems, it seemed to follow that international law depended upon the will of the sovereign states.

This implied a confusion of the supreme legislator within a state with the state itself and thus positivism had to accept the metaphysical identity of the state. The state had a life and will of its own and so was able to dominate international law. This stress on the abstract nature of the state did not appear in all positivist theories and was a late development.[97]

It was the German thinker Hegel who first analysed and proposed the doctrine of the will of the state. The individual was subordinate to the state, because the latter enshrined the 'wills' of all citizens and had evolved into a higher will, and on the external scene the state was sovereign and supreme.[98] Such philosophies led to disturbing results in the twentieth century and provoked a re-awakening of the law of nature, dormant throughout the nineteenth century.

The growth of international agreements, customs and regulations induced positivist theorists to tackle this problem of international law and the state; and as a result two schools of thought emerged.

The monists claimed that there was one fundamental principle which underlay both national and international law. This was variously posited as 'right' or social solidarity or the rule that agreements must be carried out (*pacta sunt servanda*). The dualists, more numerous and in a more truly positivist frame of mind, emphasised the element of consent.

For Triepel, another German theorist, international law and domestic (or municipal) law existed on separate planes, the former governing international relations, the latter relations between individuals and between the individual and the state. International law was based upon agreements between states (and such agreements included, according to Triepel, both

---

[97] See below, chapter 2.
[98] See e.g. S. Avineri, *Hegel's Theory of the Modern State*, London, 1972, and Friedmann, *Legal Theory*, pp. 164–76.

treaties and customs) and because it was dictated by the 'common will' of the states it could not be unilaterally altered.[99]

This led to a paradox. Could this common will bind individual states and, if so, why? It would appear to lead to the conclusion that the will of the sovereign state could give birth to a rule over which it had no control. The state will was not, therefore, supreme but inferior to a collection of states' wills. Triepel did not discuss these points, but left them open as depending upon legal matters. Thus did positivist theories weaken their own positivist outlook by regarding the essence of law as beyond juridical description. The nineteenth century also saw the publication of numerous works on international law, which emphasised state practice and the importance of the behaviour of countries to the development of rules of international law.[100]

The twentieth century

The First World War marked the close of a dynamic and optimistic century. European empires ruled the world and European ideologies reigned supreme, but the 1914–18 Great War undermined the foundations of European civilisation. Self-confidence faded, if slowly, the edifice weakened and the universally accepted assumptions of progress were increasingly doubted. Self-questioning was the order of the day and law as well as art reflected this.

The most important legacy of the 1919 Peace Treaty from the point of view of international relations was the creation of the League of Nations.[101] The old anarchic system had failed and it was felt that new institutions to preserve and secure peace were necessary. The League consisted of an Assembly and an executive Council, but was crippled from the start by the absence of the United States and the Soviet Union for most of its life and remained a basically European organisation.

While it did have certain minor successes with regard to the maintenance of international order, it failed when confronted with determined aggressors. Japan invaded China in 1931 and two years later withdrew from the League. Italy attacked Ethiopia, and Germany embarked unhindered

---

[99] Friedmann *Legal Theory*, pp. 576–7. See also below, chapter 4.
[100] See e.g. H. Wheaton, *Elements of International Law*, New York, 1836; W. E. Hall, *A Treatise on International Law*, Oxford, 1880; Von Martens, *Völkerrecht*, Berlin, 2 vols., 1883–6; Pradier-Fodéré, *Traité de Droit International Public*, Paris, 8 vols., 1855–1906; and Fiore, *Il Diritto Internazionale Codificato e la Sua Sanzione Giuridica*, 1890.
[101] See Nussbaum, *Law of Nations*, pp. 251–90, and below, chapter 22.

upon a series of internal and external aggressions. The Soviet Union, in a final gesture, was expelled from the organisation in 1939 following its invasion of Finland.

Nevertheless much useful groundwork was achieved by the League in its short existence and this helped to consolidate the United Nations later on.[102]

The Permanent Court of International Justice was set up in 1921 at The Hague and was succeeded in 1946 by the International Court of Justice.[103] The International Labour Organisation was established soon after the end of the First World War and still exists today, and many other international institutions were inaugurated or increased their work during this period.

Other ideas of international law that first appeared between the wars included the system of mandates, by which colonies of the defeated powers were administered by the Allies for the benefit of their inhabitants rather than being annexed outright, and the attempt was made to provide a form of minority protection guaranteed by the League. This latter creation was not a great success but it paved the way for later concern to secure human rights.[104]

After the trauma of the Second World War the League was succeeded in 1946 by the United Nations Organisation, which tried to remedy many of the defects of its predecessor. It established its site at New York, reflecting the realities of the shift of power away from Europe, and determined to become a truly universal institution. The advent of decolonisation fulfilled this expectation and the General Assembly of the United Nations currently has 192 member states.[105]

Many of the trends which first came to prominence in the nineteenth century have continued to this day. The vast increase in the number of international agreements and customs, the strengthening of the system of arbitration and the development of international organisations have established the essence of international law as it exists today.

Communist approaches to international law

Classic Marxist theory described law and politics as the means whereby the ruling classes maintained their domination of society. The essence of economic life was the ownership of the means of production, and all

---

[102] See also G. Scott, *The Rise and Fall of the League of Nations*, London, 1973.
[103] See below, chapter 19.   [104] See below, chapter 6.
[105] Following the admission of Montenegro on 28 June 2006.

power flowed from this control. Capital and labour were the opposing theses and their mutual antagonism would eventually lead to a revolution out of which a new, non-exploitive form of society would emerge.[106] National states were dominated by the capitalist class and would have to disappear in the re-organising process. Indeed, the theory was that law and the state would wither away once a new basis for society had been established[107] and, because classical international law was founded upon the state, it followed that it too would go.

However, the reality of power and the existence of the USSR surrounded by capitalist nations led to a modification in this approach. The international system of states could not be changed overnight into a socialist order, so a period of transition was inevitable. Nevertheless basic changes were seen as having been wrought.

Professor Tunkin, for example, emphasised that the Russian October revolution produced a new series of international legal ideas. These, it is noted, can be divided into three basic, interconnected groups: (a) principles of socialist internationalism in relations between socialist states, (b) principles of equality and self-determination of nations and peoples, primarily aimed against colonialism, and (c) principles of peaceful co-existence aimed at relations between states with different social systems.[108]

We shall briefly look at these concepts in this section, but first a historical overview is necessary.

During the immediate post-revolution period, it was postulated that a transitional phase had commenced. During this time, international law as a method of exploitation would be criticised by the socialist state, but it would still be recognised as a valid system. The two Soviet theorists Korovin and Pashukanis were the dominant influences in this phase. The transitional period demanded compromises in that, until the universal victory of the revolution, some forms of economic and technical

---

[106] See Lloyd, *Introduction to Jurisprudence*, chapter 10, and Friedmann, *Legal Theory*, chapter 29.

[107] Engels, *Anti-Duhring*, quoted in Lloyd, *Introduction to Jurisprudence*, pp. 773–4.

[108] *Theory of International Law*, London, 1974, p. 4, and *International Law* (ed. G. I. Tunkin), Moscow, 1986, chapter 3. See also B. S. Chimni, *International Law and World Order*, New Delhi, 1993, chapter 5; K. Grzybowski, *Soviet Public International Law*, Leiden, 1970, especially chapter 1, and generally H. Baade, *The Soviet Impact on International Law*, Leiden, 1964, and Friedmann, *Legal Theory*, pp. 327–40. See also R. St J. Macdonald, 'Rummaging in the Ruins, Soviet International Law and Policy in the Early Years: Is Anything Left?' in Wellens, *International Law*, p. 61.

co-operation would be required since they were fundamental for the existence of the international social order.[109] Pashukanis expressed the view that international law was an interclass law within which two antagonistic class systems would seek accommodation until the victory of the socialist system. Socialism and the Soviet Union could still use the legal institutions developed by and reflective of the capitalist system.[110] However, with the rise of Stalinism and the 'socialism in one country' call, the position hardened. Pashukanis altered his line and recanted. International law was not a form of temporary compromise between capitalist states and the USSR but rather a means of conducting the class war. The Soviet Union was bound only by those rules of international law which accorded with its purposes.[111]

The new approach in the late 1930s was reflected politically in Russia's successful attempt to join the League of Nations and its policy of wooing the Western powers, and legally by the ideas of Vyshinsky. He adopted a more legalistic view of international law and emphasised the Soviet acceptance of such principles as national self-determination, state sovereignty and the equality of states, but not others. The role of international law did not constitute a single international legal system binding all states. The Soviet Union would act in pursuance of Leninist–Stalinist foreign policy ideals and would not be bound by the rules to which it had not given express consent.[112]

The years that followed the Second World War saw a tightening up of Soviet doctrine as the Cold War gathered pace, but with the death of Stalin and the succession of Khrushchev a thaw set in. In theoretical terms the law of the transitional stage was replaced by the international law of peaceful co-existence. War was no longer regarded as inevitable between capitalist and socialist countries and a period of mutual tolerance and co-operation was inaugurated.[113]

Tunkin recognised that there was a single system of international law of universal scope rather than different branches covering socialist and capitalist countries, and that international law was founded upon agreements

[109] Tunkin, *Theory of International Law*, p. 5.
[110] *Ibid.*, pp. 5–6. See also H. Babb and J. Hazard, *Soviet Legal Philosophy*, Cambridge, MA, 1951.
[111] Grzybowski, *Soviet Public International Law*, pp. 6–9.   [112] *Ibid.*, p. 9.
[113] *Ibid.*, pp. 16–22. See also R. Higgins, *Conflict of Interests*, London, 1964, part III.

between states which are binding upon them. He defined contemporary general international law as:

> the aggregate of norms which are created by agreement between states of different social systems, reflect the concordant wills of states and have a generally democratic character, regulate relations between them in the process of struggle and co-operation in the direction of ensuring peace and peaceful co-existence and freedom and independence of peoples, and are secured when necessary by coercion effectuated by states individually or collectively.[114]

It is interesting to note the basic elements here, such as the stress on state sovereignty, the recognition of different social systems and the aim of peaceful co-existence. The role of sanctions in law is emphasised and reflects much of the positivist influence upon Soviet thought. Such pre-occupations were also reflected in the definition of international law contained in the leading Soviet textbook by Professor Kozhevnikov and others where it was stated that:

> international law can be defined as the aggregate of rules governing relations between states in the process of their conflict and co-operation, designed to safeguard their peaceful co-existence, expressing the will of the ruling classes of these states and defended in case of need by coercion applied by states individually or collectively.[115]

Originally, treaties alone were regarded as proper sources of international law but custom became accepted as a kind of tacit or implied agreement with great stress laid upon *opinio juris* or the legally binding element of custom. While state practice need not be general to create a custom, its recognition as a legal form must be.[116]

Peaceful co-existence itself rested upon certain basic concepts, for example non-intervention in the internal affairs of other states and the sovereignty of states. Any idea of a world authority was condemned as a violation of the latter principle. The doctrine of peaceful co-existence was also held to include such ideas as good neighbourliness, international co-operation and the observance in good faith of international obligations.

---

[114] *Theory of International Law*, p. 251. See also G. I. Tunkin, 'Co-existence and International Law', 95 HR, 1958, pp. 1, 51 ff., and E. McWhinney, 'Contemporary Soviet General Theory of International Law: Reflections on the Tunkin Era', 25 Canadian YIL, 1989, p. 187.

[115] *International Law*, Moscow, 1957, p. 7.

[116] *Theory of International Law*, p. 118. See also G. I. Tunkin, 'The Contemporary Soviet Theory of International Law', *Current Legal Problems*, London, 1978, p. 177.

The concept was regarded as based on specific trends of laws of societal development and as a specific form of class struggle between socialism and capitalism, one in which armed conflict is precluded.[117] It was an attempt, in essence, to reiterate the basic concepts of international law in a way that was taken to reflect an ideological trend. But it must be emphasised that the principles themselves have long been accepted by the international community.

While Tunkin at first attacked the development of regional systems of international law, he later came round to accepting a socialist law which reflected the special relationship between communist countries. The Soviet interventions in eastern Europe, particularly in Czechoslovakia in 1968, played a large part in augmenting such views.[118] In the Soviet view relations between socialist (communist) states represented a new, higher type of international relations and a socialist international law. Common socio-economic factors and a political community created an objective basis for lasting friendly relations whereas, by contrast, international capitalism involved the exploitation of the weak by the strong. The principles of socialist or proletarian internationalism constituted a unified system of international legal principles between countries of the socialist bloc arising by way of custom and treaty. Although the basic principles of respect for state sovereignty, non-interference in internal affairs and equality of states and peoples existed in general international law, the same principles in socialist international law were made more positive by the lack of economic rivalry and exploitation and by increased co-operation. Accordingly, these principles incorporated not only material obligations not to violate each other's rights, but also the duty to assist each other in enjoying and defending such rights against capitalist threats.[119]

The Soviet emphasis on territorial integrity and sovereignty, while designed in practice to protect the socialist states in a predominantly capitalist environment, proved of great attraction to the developing nations of the Third World, anxious too to establish their own national identities and counteract Western financial and cultural influences.

---

[117] Tunkin, 'Soviet Theory', pp. 35–48. See also F. Vallat, 'International Law – A Forward Look', 18 YBWA, 1964, p. 251; J. Hazard, 'Codifying Peaceful Co-existence', 55 AJIL, 1961, pp. 111–12; E. McWhinney, *Peaceful Co-existence and Soviet–Western International Law*, Leiden, 1964, and K. Grzybowski, 'Soviet Theory of International Law for the Seventies', 77 AJIL, 1983, p. 862.

[118] See Grzybowski, *Soviet Public International Law*, pp. 16–22.

[119] Tunkin, *Theory of International Law*, pp. 431–43.

With the decline of the Cold War and the onset of *perestroika* (re-structuring) in the Soviet Union, a process of re-evaluation in the field of international legal theory took place.[120] The concept of peaceful co-existence was modified and the notion of class warfare eliminated from the Soviet political lexicon. Global interdependence and the necessity for international co-operation were emphasised, as it was accepted that the tension between capitalism and socialism no longer constituted the major conflict in the contemporary world and that beneath the former dogmas lay many common interests.[121] The essence of new Soviet thinking was stated to lie in the priority of universal human values and the resolution of global problems, which is directly linked to the growing importance of international law in the world community. It was also pointed out that international law had to be universal and not artificially divided into capitalist, socialist and Third World 'international law' systems.[122]

Soviet writers and political leaders accepted that activities such as the interventions in Czechoslovakia in 1968 and Afghanistan in 1979 were contrary to international law, while the attempt to create a state based on the rule of law was seen as requiring the strengthening of the international legal system and the rule of law in international relations. In particular, a renewed emphasis upon the role of the United Nations became evident in Soviet policy.[123]

The dissolution of the Soviet Union in 1991 marked the end of the Cold War and the re-emergence of a system of international relations based upon multiple sources of power untrammelled by ideological de-terminacy. From that point,[124] Russia as the continuation of the former Soviet Union (albeit in different political and territorial terms) entered into the Western political system and defined its actions in terms of its own national interests free from principled hostility. The return to statehood of the Baltic states and the independence of the other former republics of the Soviet Union, coupled with the collapse of Yugoslavia, has constituted

---

[120] See, for example, *Perestroika and International Law* (eds. A. Carty and G. Danilenko), Edinburgh, 1990; R. Müllerson, 'Sources of International Law: New Tendencies in Soviet Thinking', 83 AJIL, 1989, p. 494; V. Vereshchetin and R. Müllerson, 'International Law in an Interdependent World', 28 *Columbia Journal of Transnational Law*, 1990, p. 291, and R. Quigley, '*Perestroika* and International Law', 82 AJIL, 1988, p. 788.

[121] Vereshchetin and Müllerson, 'International Law', p. 292.

[122] *Ibid.*   [123] See Quigley, '*Perestroika*', p. 794.

[124] See e.g. R. Müllerson, *International Law, Rights and Politics*, London, 1994. See also *The End of the Cold War* (eds. P. Allan and K. Goldmann), Dordrecht, 1992, and W. M. Reisman, 'International Law after the Cold War', 84 AJIL, 1990, p. 859.

a political upheaval of major significance. The Cold War had imposed a dualistic superstructure upon international relations that had had implications for virtually all serious international political disputes and had fettered the operations of the United Nations in particular. Although the Soviet regime had been changing its approach quite significantly, the formal demise both of the communist system and of the state itself altered the nature of the international system and this has inevitably had consequences for international law.[125] The ending of inexorable superpower confrontation has led to an increase in instability in Europe and emphasised paradoxically both the revitalisation and the limitations of the United Nations.

While relatively little has previously been known of Chinese attitudes, a few points can be made. Western concepts are regarded primarily as aimed at preserving the dominance of the bourgeois class on the international scene. Soviet views were partially accepted but since the late 1950s and the growing estrangement between the two major communist powers, the Chinese concluded that the Russians were interested chiefly in maintaining the status quo and Soviet–American superpower supremacy. The Soviet concept of peaceful co-existence as the mainstay of contemporary international law was treated with particular suspicion and disdain.[126]

The Chinese conception of law was, for historical and cultural reasons, very different from that developed in the West. 'Law' never attained the important place in Chinese society that it did in European civilisation.[127] A sophisticated bureaucracy laboured to attain harmony and equilibrium, and a system of legal rights to protect the individual in the Western sense did not really develop. It was believed that society would be best served by example and established morality, rather than by rules and sanctions. This Confucian philosophy was, however, swept aside after the successful

---

[125] See e.g. R. Bilder, 'International Law in the "New World Order": Some Preliminary Reflections', 1 *Florida State University Journal of Transnational Law and Policy*, 1992, p. 1.

[126] See H. Chiu, 'Communist China's Attitude towards International Law', 60 AJIL, 1966, p. 245; J. K. Fairbank, *The Chinese World Order*, Cambridge, 1968; J. Cohen, *China's Practice of International Law*, Princeton, 1972; Anglo-Chinese Educational Trust, *China's World View*, London, 1979; J. Cohen and H. Chiu, *People's China and International Law*, Princeton, 2 vols., 1974, and C. Kim, 'The People's Republic of China and the Charter-based International Legal Order', 72 AJIL, 1978, p. 317.

[127] See Lloyd, *Introduction to Jurisprudence*, pp. 760–3; S. Van der Sprenkel, *Legal Institutions in Northern China*, New York, 1962, and R. Unger, *Law in Modern Society*, New York, 1976, pp. 86–109.

communist revolution, to be replaced by strict Marxism–Leninism, with
its emphasis on class warfare.[128]

The Chinese seem to have recognised several systems of international
law, for example, Western, socialist and revisionist (Soviet Union), and
to have implied that only with the ultimate spread of socialism would
a universal system be possible.[129] International agreements are regarded
as the primary source of international law and China has entered into
many treaties and conventions and carried them out as well as other
nations.[130] One exception, of course, is China's disavowal of the so-called
'unequal treaties' whereby Chinese territory was annexed by other powers,
in particular the Tsarist Empire, in the nineteenth century.[131]

On the whole, international law has been treated as part of international
politics and subject to considerations of power and expediency, as well as
ideology. Where international rules conform with Chinese policies and
interests, then they will be observed. Where they do not, they will be
ignored.

However, now that the isolationist phase of its history is over, relations
with other nations established and its entry into the United Nations secured, China has adopted a more active role in international relations,
an approach more in keeping with its rapidly growing economic power.
China has now become fully engaged in world politics and this has led to
a legalisation of its view of international law, as indeed occurred with the
Soviet Union.

The Third World

In the evolution of international affairs since the Second World War one
of the most decisive events has been the disintegration of the colonial
empires and the birth of scores of new states in the so-called Third World.
This has thrust onto the scene states which carry with them a legacy of
bitterness over their past status as well as a host of problems relating to

---

Lloyd, *Introduction to Jurisprudence*, and H. Li, 'The Role of Law in Communist China',
   China Quarterly, 1970, p. 66, cited in Lloyd, *Introduction to Jurisprudence*, pp. 801–8.

129 See e.g. Cohen and Chiu, *People's China*, pp. 62–4.

130 *Ibid.*, pp. 77–82, and part VIII generally.

131 See e.g. I. Detter, 'The Problem of Unequal Treaties', 15 ICLQ, 1966, p. 1069; F. Nozari,
   Unequal Treaties in International Law, Stockholm, 1971; Chiu, 'Communist China's Attitude', pp. 239–67, and L.-F. Chen, *State Succession Relating to Unequal Treaties*, Hamden,
   1974.

their social, economic and political development.[132] In such circumstances it was only natural that the structure and doctrines of international law would come under attack. The nineteenth century development of the law of nations founded upon Eurocentrism and imbued with the values of Christian, urbanised and expanding Europe[133] did not, understandably enough, reflect the needs and interests of the newly independent states of the mid- and late twentieth century. It was felt that such rules had encouraged and then reflected their subjugation, and that changes were required.[134]

It is basically those ideas of international law that came to fruition in the nineteenth century that have been so clearly rejected, that is, those principles that enshrined the power and domination of the West.[135] The underlying concepts of international law have not been discarded. On the contrary. The new nations have eagerly embraced the ideas of the sovereignty and equality of states and the principles of non-aggression and non-intervention, in their search for security within the bounds of a commonly accepted legal framework.

While this new internationalisation of international law that has occurred in the last fifty years has destroyed its European-based homogeneity, it has emphasised its universalist scope.[136] The composition of, for example, both the International Court of Justice and the Security Council of the United Nations mirrors such developments. Article 9 of the Statute of the International Court of Justice points out that the main forms of civilisation and the principal legal systems of the world must be represented within the Court, and there is an arrangement that of the ten non-permanent seats in the Security Council five should go to Afro-Asian

---

[132] See e.g. R. P. Anand, 'Attitude of the Afro-Asian States Towards Certain Problems of International Law', 15 ICLQ, 1966, p. 35; T. O. Elias, *New Horizons in International Law*, Leiden, 1980, and Higgins, *Conflict of Interests*, part II. See also Hague Academy of International Law, Colloque, *The Future of International Law in a Multicultural World*, especially pp. 117–42, and Henkin, *How Nations Behave*, pp. 121–7.

[133] See e.g. Verzijl, *International Law in Historical Perspective*, vol. I, pp. 435–6. See also B. Roling, *International Law in an Expanded World*, Leiden, 1960, p. 10.

[134] The converse of this has been the view of some writers that the universalisation of international law has led to a dilution of its content: see e.g. Friedmann, *Changing Structure*, p. 6; J. Stone, *Quest for Survival: The Role of Law and Foreign Policy*, Sydney, 1961, p. 88, and J. Brierly, *The Law of Nations*, 6th edn, Oxford, p. 43.

[135] See e.g. Alexandrowicz, *European–African Confrontation*.

[136] See F. C. Okoye, *International Law and the New African States*, London, 1972; T. O. Elias, *Africa and the Development of International Law*, Leiden, 1972, and Bernhardt, *Encyclopedia*, vol. VII, pp. 205–51.

states and two to Latin American states (the others going to Europe and other states). The composition of the International Law Commission has also recently been increased and structured upon geographic lines.[137]

The influence of the new states has been felt most of all within the General Assembly, where they constitute a majority of the 192 member states.[138] The content and scope of the various resolutions and declarations emanating from the Assembly are proof of their impact and contain a record of their fears, hopes and concerns.

The Declaration on the Granting of Independence to Colonial Countries and Peoples of 1960, for example, enshrined the right of colonies to obtain their sovereignty with the least possible delay and called for the recognition of the principle of self-determination. This principle, which is discussed elsewhere in this book,[139] is regarded by most authorities as a settled rule of international law although with undetermined borders. Nevertheless, it symbolises the rise of the post-colonial states and the effect they are having upon the development of international law.

Their concern for the recognition of the sovereignty of states is complemented by their support of the United Nations and its Charter and supplemented by their desire for 'economic self-determination' or the right of permanent sovereignty over natural resources.[140] This expansion of international law into the field of economics was a major development of the twentieth century and is evidenced in myriad ways, for example, by the creation of the General Agreement on Tariffs and Trade, the United Nations Conference on Trade and Development, and the establishment of the International Monetary Fund and World Bank.

The interests of the new states of the Third World are often in conflict with those of the industrialised nations, witness disputes over nationalisations. But it has to be emphasised that, contrary to many fears expressed in the early years of the decolonisation saga, international law has not been discarded nor altered beyond recognition. Its framework has been retained as the new states, too, wish to obtain the benefits of rules such as those governing diplomatic relations and the controlled use of force, while campaigning against rules which run counter to their perceived interests.

While the new countries share a common history of foreign dominance and underdevelopment, compounded by an awakening of national

---

[137] By General Assembly resolution 36/39, twenty-one of the thirty-four members are to be nationals of Afro-Asian–Latin American states.

[138] See above, note 105.   [139] See below, chapter 5, p. 205.

[140] See below, chapter 14, p. 827.

identity, it has to be recognised that they are not a homogenous group. Widely differing cultural, social and economic attitudes and stages of development characterise them, and the rubric of the 'Third World' masks diverse political affiliations. On many issues the interests of the new states conflict with each other and this is reflected in the different positions adopted. The states possessing oil and other valuable natural resources are separated from those with few or none and the states bordering on oceans are to be distinguished from landlocked states. The list of diversity is endless and variety governs the make-up of the southern hemisphere to a far greater degree than in the north.

It is possible that in legal terms tangible differences in approach may emerge in the future as the passions of decolonisation die down and the Western supremacy over international law is further eroded. This trend will also permit a greater understanding of, and greater recourse to, historical traditions and conceptions that pre-date colonisation and an increasing awareness of their validity for the future development of international law.[141]

In the medium term, however, it has to be recognised that with the end of the Cold War and the rapid development of Soviet (then Russian)– American co-operation, the axis of dispute is turning from East–West to North–South. This is beginning to manifest itself in a variety of issues ranging from economic law to the law of the sea and human rights, while the impact of modern technology has hardly yet been appreciated.[142] Together with such factors, the development of globalisation has put additional stress upon the traditional tension between universalism and particularism.[143] Globalisation in the sense of interdependence of a high order of individuals, groups and corporations, both public and private, across national boundaries, might be seen as the universalisation of Western civilisation and thus the triumph of one special particularism.

---

[141] See e.g. H. Sarin, 'The Asian–African States and the Development of International Law', in Hague Academy Colloque, p. 117; Bernhardt, *Encyclopedia*, vol. VII, pp. 205–51, and R. Westbrook, 'Islamic International Law and Public International Law: Separate Expressions of World Order', 33 Va. JIL, 1993, p. 819. See also C. W. Jenks, *The Common Law of Mankind*, Oxford, 1958, p. 169. Note also the references by the Tribunal in the *Eritrea/Yemen* cases to historic title and regional legal traditions: see the judgment in Phase One: Territorial Sovereignty, 1998, 114 ILR, pp. 1, 37 ff. and Phase Two: Maritime Delimitation, 1999, 119 ILR, pp. 417, 448.

[142] See e.g. M. Lachs, 'Thoughts on Science, Technology and World Law', 86 AJIL, 1992, p. 673.

[143] See Koskenniemi, *Gentle Civilizer of Nations*. See also G. Simpson, *Great Powers and Outlaw States: Unequal Sovereigns in the International Legal Order*, Cambridge, 2004.

On the other hand, particularism (in the guise of cultural relativism) has sometimes been used as a justification for human rights abuses free from international supervision or criticism.

Suggestions for further reading

T. M. Franck, *The Power of Legitimacy Among Nations*, Oxford, 1990

L. Henkin, *International Law: Politics and Values*, Dordrecht, 1995

R. Higgins, *Problems and Process*, Oxford, 1994

A. Nussbaum, *A Concise History of the Law of Nations*, revised edition, New York, 1954

2

International law today

The expanding legal scope of international concern

International law since the middle of the last century has been developing in many directions, as the complexities of life in the modern era have multiplied. For, as already emphasised, law reflects the conditions and cultural traditions of the society within which it operates. The community evolves a certain specific set of values – social, economic and political – and this stamps its mark on the legal framework which orders life in that environment. Similarly, international law is a product of its environment. It has developed in accordance with the prevailing notions of international relations and to survive it must be in harmony with the realities of the age.

Nevertheless, there is a continuing tension between those rules already established and the constantly evolving forces that seek changes within the system. One of the major problems of international law is to determine when and how to incorporate new standards of behaviour and new realities of life into the already existing framework, so that, on the one hand, the law remains relevant and, on the other, the system itself is not too vigorously disrupted.

Changes that occur within the international community can be momentous and reverberate throughout the system. For example, the advent of nuclear arms created a status quo in Europe and a balance of terror throughout the world. It currently constitutes a factor of unease as certain states seek to acquire nuclear technology. Another example is the technological capacity to mine the oceans and the consequent questions as to the nature and beneficiaries of exploitation.[1] The rise of international terrorism has posited new challenges to the system as states and international organisations struggle to deal with this phenomenon while retaining

---

[1] See below, chapter 11.

respect for the sovereignty of states and for human rights.[2] There are several instances of how modern developments demand a constant reappraisal of the structure of international law and its rules.

The scope of international law today is immense. From the regulation of space expeditions to the question of the division of the ocean floor, and from the protection of human rights to the management of the international financial system, its involvement has spread out from the primary concern with the preservation of peace, to embrace all the interests of contemporary international life.

But the *raison d'être* of international law and the determining factor in its composition remains the needs and characteristics of the international political system. Where more than one entity exists within a system, there has to be some conception as to how to deal with other such entities, whether it be on the basis of co-existence or hostility. International law as it has developed since the seventeenth century has adopted the same approach and has in general (though with notable exceptions) eschewed the idea of permanent hostility and enmity. Because the state, while internally supreme, wishes to maintain its sovereignty externally and needs to cultivate other states in an increasingly interdependent world, it must acknowledge the rights of others. This acceptance of rights possessed by all states, something unavoidable in a world where none can stand alone, leads inevitably to a system to regulate and define such rights and, of course, obligations.

And so one arrives at some form of international legal order, no matter how unsophisticated and how occasionally positively disorderly.[3] The current system developed in the context of European civilisation as it progressed, but this has changed. The rise of the United States and the Soviet Union mirrored the decline of Europe, while the process of decolonisation also had a considerable impact. More recently, the collapse of the Soviet Empire and the Soviet Union, the rise of India and China as major powers and the phenomenon of globalisation are also impacting deeply upon the system. Faced with radical changes in the structure of power, international law needs to come to terms with new ideas and challenges.

---

[2] See below, chapter 20.

[3] For views as to the precise definition and characteristics of the international order or system or community, see G. Schwarzenberger and E. D. Brown, *A Manual of International Law*, 6th edn, London, 1976, pp. 9–12; H. Yalem, 'The Concept of World Order', 29 YBWA, 1975, and I. Pogany, 'The Legal Foundations of World Order', 37 YBWA, 1983, p. 277.

The Eurocentric character of international law has been gravely weakened in the last sixty years or so and the opinions, hopes and needs of other cultures and civilisations are now playing an increasing role in the evolution of world juridical thought.[4]

International law reflects first and foremost the basic state-oriented character of world politics and this essentially because the state became over time the primary repository of the organised hopes of peoples, whether for protection or for more expansive aims. Units of formal independence benefiting from equal sovereignty in law and equal possession of the basic attributes of statehood[5] have succeeded in creating a system enshrining such values. Examples that could be noted here include non-intervention in internal affairs, territorial integrity, non-use of force and equality of voting in the United Nations General Assembly. However, in addition to this, many factors cut across state borders and create a tension in world politics, such as inadequate economic relationships, international concern for human rights and the rise in new technological forces.[6] State policies and balances of power, both international and regional, are a necessary framework within which international law operates, as indeed are domestic political conditions and tensions. Law mirrors the concern of forces within states and between states.

It is also important to realise that states need law in order to seek and attain certain goals, whether these be economic well-being, survival and security or ideological advancement. The system therefore has to be certain enough for such goals to be ascertainable, and flexible enough to permit change when this becomes necessary due to the confluence of forces demanding it.[7]

International law, however, has not just expanded horizontally to embrace the new states which have been established since the end of the Second World War; it has extended itself to include individuals, groups and international organisations, both private and public, within its scope. It has also moved into new fields covering such issues as international trade, problems of environmental protection, human rights and outer space exploration.

[4] See e.g. L. C. Green, 'Is There a Universal International Law Today?', 23 Canadian YIL, 1985, p. 3.
[5] See below, chapter 5, p. 211.
[6] For examples of this in the context of the law relating to territory, see M. N. Shaw, *Title to Territory in Africa: International Legal Issues*, Oxford, 1986, pp. 1–11.
[7] See S. Hoffman, 'International Systems and International Law', 14 *World Politics*, 1961–2, p. 205.

The growth of positivism in the nineteenth century had the effect of focusing the concerns of international law upon sovereign states. They alone were the 'subjects' of international law and were to be contrasted with the status of non-independent states and individuals as 'objects' of international law. They alone created the law and restrictions upon their independence could not be presumed.[8] But the gradual sophistication of positivist doctrine, combined with the advent of new approaches to the whole system of international relations, has broken down this exclusive emphasis and extended the roles played by non-state entities, such as individuals, multinational firms and international institutions.[9] It was, of course, long recognised that individuals were entitled to the benefits of international law, but it is only recently that they have been able to act directly rather than rely upon their national states.

The Nuremberg and Tokyo Tribunals set up by the victorious Allies after the close of the Second World War were a vital part of this process. Many of those accused were found guilty of crimes against humanity and against peace and were punished accordingly. It was a recognition of individual responsibility under international law without the usual interposition of the state and has been reinforced with the establishment of the Yugoslav and Rwanda War Crimes Tribunals in the mid-1990s and the International Criminal Court in 1998.[10] Similarly the 1948 Genocide Convention provided for the punishment of offenders after conviction by national courts or by an international criminal tribunal.[11] The developing concern with human rights is another aspect of this move towards increasing the role of the individual in international law. The Universal Declaration of Human Rights adopted by the United Nations in 1948 lists a series of political and social rights, although it is only a guideline and not legally binding as such. The European Convention for the Protection of Human Rights and Fundamental Freedoms signed in 1950 and the International Covenants on Human Rights of 1966 are of a different nature and binding upon the signatories. In an effort to function satisfactorily various bodies of a supervisory and implementational nature were established. Within the European Union, individuals and corporations have certain rights of direct appeal to the European Court of Justice against decisions of the various Union institutions. In addition, individuals may appear before certain international tribunals. Nevertheless, the whole subject has been highly controversial, with some writers (for example Soviet theorists prior

---

[8] See the *Lotus* case, PCIJ, Series A, No. 10, p. 18.   [9] See further below, chapter 5.
[10] See below, chapter 8.   [11] *Ibid.*

to *perestroika*) denying that individuals may have rights as distinct from duties under international law, but it is indicative of the trend away from the exclusivity of the state.[12]

Together with the evolution of individual human rights, the rise of international organisations marks perhaps the key distinguishing feature of modern international law. In fact, international law cannot in the contemporary era be understood without reference to the growth in number and influence of such intergovernmental institutions, and of these the most important by far is the United Nations.[13] The UN comprises the vast majority of states (there are currently 192 member states) and that alone constitutes a political factor of high importance in the process of diplomatic relations and negotiations and indeed facilitates international co-operation and norm creation. Further, of course, the existence of the Security Council as an executive organ with powers to adopt resolutions in certain circumstances that are binding upon all member states is unique in the history of international relations.

International organisations have now been accepted as possessing rights and duties of their own and a distinctive legal personality. The International Court of Justice in 1949 delivered an Advisory Opinion[14] in which it stated that the United Nations was a subject of international law and could enforce its rights by bringing international claims, in this case against Israel following the assassination of Count Bernadotte, a United Nations official. Such a ruling can be applied to embrace other international institutions, like the International Labour Organisation and the Food and Agriculture Organisation, which each have a judicial character of their own. Thus, while states remain the primary subjects of international law, they are now joined by other non-state entities, whose importance is likely to grow even further in the future.

The growth of regional organisations should also be noted at this stage. Many of these were created for reasons of military security, for example NATO and the opposing Warsaw Pact organisations, others as an expression of regional and cultural identity such as the Organisation of African Unity (now the African Union) and the Organisation of American States. In a class of its own is the European Union which has gone far down the road of economic co-ordination and standardisation and has a range of

---

[12] See further below, chapters 6 and 7.   [13] See further below, chapter 22.
[14] *Reparation for Injuries Suffered in the Service of the United Nations*, ICJ Reports, 1949, p. 174; 16 AD, p. 318.

common institutions serviced by a growing bureaucracy stationed primarily at Brussels.

Such regional organisations have added to the developing sophistication of international law by the insertion of 'regional–international law sub-systems' within the universal framework and the consequent evolution of rules that bind only member states.[15]

The range of topics covered by international law has expanded hand in hand with the upsurge in difficulties faced and the proliferation in the number of participants within the system. It is no longer exclusively concerned with issues relating to the territory or jurisdiction of states narrowly understood, but is beginning to take into account the specialised problems of contemporary society. Many of these have already been referred to, such as the vital field of human rights, the growth of an international economic law covering financial and development matters, concern with environmental despoliation, the space exploration effort and the exploitation of the resources of the oceans and deep seabed. One can mention also provisions relating to the bureaucracy of international institutions (international administrative law), international labour standards, health regulations and communications controls. Many of these trends may be seen as falling within, or rather reflecting, the phenomenon of globalisation, a term which encompasses the inexorable movement to greater interdependence founded upon economic, communications and cultural bases and operating quite independently of national regulation.[16] This in

---

[15] See generally below, chapter 23.

[16] See e.g. A. Giddens, *The Consequences of Modernity*, Stanford, 1990; S. Sur, 'The State Between Fragmentation and Globalisation', 8 EJIL, 1997, p. 421; B. Simma and A. Paulus, 'The "International Community": Facing the Challenge of Globalisation. General Conclusions', 9 EJIL, 1998, p. 266, and P. M. Dupuy, 'International Law: Torn Between Coexistence, Co-operation and Globalisation. General Conclusions', 9 EJIL, 1998, p. 278. See also the Declaration of Judge Bedjaoui in the Advisory Opinion on *The Legality of the Threat or Use of Nuclear Weapons*, ICJ Reports, 1996, pp. 226, 270–1. Note that Philip Bobbitt has described five developments challenging the nation-state system, and thus in essence characterising the globalisation challenge, as follows: the recognition of human rights as norms requiring adherence within all states regardless of internal laws; the widespread deployment of weapons of mass destruction rendering the defence of state borders ineffectual for the protection of the society within; the proliferation of global and transnational threats transcending state boundaries such as those that damage the environment or threaten states through migration, population expansion, disease or famine; the growth of a world economic regime that ignores borders in the movement of capital investment to a degree that effectively curtails states in the management of their economic affairs; and the creation of a global communications network that penetrates borders electronically and threatens national languages, customs and cultures, *The Shield of Achilles*, London, 2002, p. xxii.

turn stimulates disputes of an almost ideological nature concerning, for example, the relationship between free trade and environmental protection.[17] To this may be added the pressures of democracy and human rights, both operating to some extent as countervailing influences to the classical emphasis upon the territorial sovereignty and jurisdiction of states.

Modern theories and interpretations

At this point some modern theories as to the nature and role of international law will be briefly noted.

Positive Law and Natural Law

Throughout the history of thought there has been a complex relationship between idealism and realism, between the way things ought to be and the way things are, and the debate as to whether legal philosophy should incorporate ethical standards or confine itself to an analysis of the law as it stands is a vital one that continues today.[18]

The positivist school, which developed so rapidly in the pragmatic, optimistic world of the nineteenth century, declared that law as it exists should be analysed empirically, shorn of all ethical elements. Moral aspirations were all well and good but had no part in legal science. Man-made law must be examined as such and the metaphysical speculations of Natural Law rejected because what counted were the practical realities, not general principles which were imprecise and vague, not to say ambiguous.[19]

This kind of approach to law in society reached its climax with Kelsen's 'Pure Theory of Law'. Kelsen defined law solely in terms of itself and eschewed any element of justice, which was rather to be considered within the discipline of political science. Politics, sociology and history were all

[17] See e.g. *Myers* v. *Canada* 121 ILR, pp. 72, 110.

[18] See e.g. D. Lyons, *Ethics and the Rule of Law*, London, 1984; R. Dworkin, *Taking Rights Seriously*, London, 1977; H. L. A. Hart, *The Concept of Law*, Oxford, 1961, and P. Stein and J. Shand, *Legal Values in Western Society*, Edinburgh, 1974. See also R. Dias, *Jurisprudence*, 5th edn, London, 1985.

[19] See Hart, *Concept of Law*, and Hart, 'Positivism and the Separation of Law and Morals', 71 *Harvard Law Review*, 1958, p. 593. Cf. L. Fuller, 'Positivism and Fidelity to Law – A Reply to Professor Hart', 71 *Harvard Law Review*, 1958, p. 630. See also D. Anzilotti, *Cours de Droit International*, Paris, 1929, and B. Kingsbury, 'Legal Positivism as Normative Politics: International Society, Balance of Power and Lassa Oppenheim's Positive International Law', 13 EJIL, 2002, p. 401.

excised from the pure theory which sought to construct a logical unified structure based on a formal appraisal.[20]

Law was to be regarded as a normative science, that is, consisting of rules which lay down patterns of behaviour. Such rules, or norms, depend for their legal validity on a prior norm and this process continues until one reaches what is termed the basic norm of the whole system. This basic norm is the foundation of the legal edifice, because rules which can be related back to it therefore become *legal* rules. To give a simple example, a court order empowering an official to enforce a fine is valid if the court had that power which depends upon an Act of Parliament establishing the court. A rule becomes a legal rule if it is in accordance with a previous (and higher) legal rule and so on. Layer builds upon layer and the foundation of it all is the basic norm.[21]

The weakness of Kelsen's 'pure' system lies primarily in the concept of the basic norm for it relies for its existence upon non-legal issues. In fact, it is a political concept, and in the United Kingdom it would probably be the principle of the supremacy of Parliament.[22]

This logical, structured system of validity founded upon an extra-legal concept encounters difficulties when related to international law. For Kelsen international law is a primitive legal order because of its lack of strong legislative, judicial and enforcement organs and its consequent resemblance to a pre-state society. It is accordingly characterised by the use of self-help.[23] The principles of international law are valid if they can be traced back to the basic norm of the system, which is hierarchical in the same sense as a national legal system. For Kelsen, the basic norm is the rule that identifies custom as the source of law, or stipulates that 'the states ought to behave as they customarily behaved'.[24] One of the prime rules of this category is *pacta sunt servanda* declaring that agreements must be carried out in good faith and upon that rule is founded the second stage within the international legal order. This second stage consists of the network of norms created by international treaties and conventions

---

[20] 'The Pure Theory of Law', 50 LQR, 1934, pp. 474, 477–85 and 51 LQR, 1935, pp. 517–22. See also the articles collected in 'The European Tradition in International Law: Hans Kelsen', 9 EJIL, 1998, pp. 287 ff.

[21] Kelsen, *Pure Theory*.

[22] See J. Stone, 'Mystery and Mystique in the Basic Norm', 26 MLR, 1963, p. 34, and J. Raz, *Practical Reason and Norms*, Oxford, 1975, pp. 129–31.

[23] *General Theory of Law and State*, Cambridge, 1946, pp. 328 ff. See also J. Lador-Lederer, 'Some Observations on the "Vienna School" in International Law', 17 NILR, 1970, p. 126.

[24] Kelsen, *General Theory of Law and State*, pp. 369–70.

and leads on to the third stage which includes those rules established by organs which have been set up by international treaties, for instance, decisions of the International Court of Justice.[25]

The problem with Kelsen's formulation of the basic norm of international law is that it appears to be tautological: it merely repeats that states which obey rules ought to obey those rules.[26] It seems to leave no room for the progressive development of international law by new practices accepted as law for that involves states behaving differently from the way they have been behaving. Above all, it fails to answer the question as to why custom is binding.

Nevertheless, it is a model of great logical consistency which helps explain, particularly with regard to national legal systems, the proliferation of rules and the importance of validity which gives as it were a mystical seal of approval to the whole structured process. It helps illustrate how rule leads to rule as stage succeeds stage in a progression of norms forming a legal order.

Another important element in Kelsen's interpretation of law is his extreme 'monist' stance. International law and municipal law are not two separate systems but one interlocking structure and the former is supreme. Municipal law finds its ultimate justification in the rules of international law by a process of delegation within one universal normative system.[27]

Kelsen's pure theory seemed to mark the end of that particular road, and positivism was analysed in more sociological terms by Hart in his book *The Concept of Law* in 1961.

Hart comprehends law as a system of rules, based upon the interaction of primary and secondary rules. The former, basically, specify standards of behaviour while the latter provide the means for identifying and developing them and thus specify the constitutional procedures for change. Primitive societies would possess only the primary rules and so would be characterised by uncertainty, inefficiency and stagnation, but with increasing sophistication the secondary rules would develop and identify authority and enable the rules to be adapted to changing circumstances in a regular and accepted manner.[28]

---

[25] *Ibid.*   [26] Hart terms this 'mere useless reduplication': *Concept of Law*, p. 230.

[27] *General Theory of Law and State*, pp. 366–8. See further below, chapter 4.

[28] *Concept of Law*, chapter 5. See also e.g. Dworkin, *Taking Rights Seriously*; Raz, *Practical Reason*, and N. MacCormick, *Legal Reasoning and Legal Theory*, Oxford, 1978.

The international legal order is a prime example of a simple form of social structure which consists only of the primary rules, because of its lack of a centralised legislature, network of recognised courts with compulsory jurisdiction and organised means of enforcement. Accordingly, it has no need of, or rather has not yet evolved, a basic norm or in Hart's terminology a rule of recognition, by reference to which the validity of all the rules may be tested. Following this train of thought, Hart concludes that the rules of international law do not as yet constitute a 'system' but are merely a 'set of rules'. Of course, future developments may see one particular principle, such as *pacta sunt servanda*, elevated to the state of a validating norm but in the present situation this has not yet occurred.[29]

This approach can be criticised for its over-concentration upon rules to the exclusion of other important elements in a legal system such as principles and policies,[30] and more especially as regards international law, for failing to recognise the sophistication or vitality of the system. In particular, the distinction between a system and a set of rules in the context of international law is a complex issue and one which is difficult to delineate.

The strength of the positivist movement waned in the last century as the old certainties disintegrated and social unrest grew. Law, as always, began to reflect the dominant pressures of the age, and new theories as to the role of law in society developed. Writers started examining the effects of sociological phenomena upon the legal order and the nature of the legal process itself, with analyses of judicial behaviour and the means whereby rules were applied in actual practice. This was typified by Roscoe Pound's view of the law as a form of social engineering, balancing the various interests within the society in the most efficacious way.[31] Law was regarded as a method of social control and conceptual approaches were rejected in favour of functional analyses. What actually happened within the legal system, what claims were being brought and how they were satisfied: these were the watchwords of the sociological school.[32]

It was in one sense a move away from the ivory tower and into the courtroom. Empirical investigations proliferated, particularly in the United States, and the sciences of psychology and anthropology as well

---

[29] *Concept of Law*, pp. 228–31.   [30] See Dworkin, *Taking Rights Seriously*.

[31] See e.g. *Philosophy of Law*, New Haven, 1954, pp. 42–7. See also M. D. A. Freeman, *The Legal Structure*, London, 1974, chapter 4.

[32] *Outlines of Jurisprudence*, 5th edn, Cambridge, 1943, pp. 116–19.

as sociology became allied to jurisprudence. Such concern with the wider social context led to the theories of Realism, which treated law as an institution functioning within a particular community with a series of jobs to do. A study of legal norms within a closed logical system in the Kelsenite vein was regarded as unable to reveal very much of the actual operation of law in society. For this an understanding of the behaviour of courts and the various legal officials was required. Historical and ethical factors were relegated to a minor role within the realist–sociological tradition, with its concentration upon field studies and 'technical' dissections. Legal rules were no longer to be accepted as the heart of the legal system.[33]

Before one looks at contemporary developments of this approach and how they have affected interpretations of international law, the revival of Natural Law has first to be considered.

In the search for meaning in life and an ethical basis to law, Natural Law has adopted a variety of different approaches. One of them has been a refurbishment of the principles enumerated by Aquinas and adopted by the Catholic Church, emphasising the dignity of man and the supremacy of reason together with an affirmation of the immorality (though not necessarily the invalidity) of law contrary to right reason and the eternal law of God.[34] A more formalistic and logic-oriented trend has been exemplified by writers such as Stammler, who tried to erect a logical structure of law with an inbuilt concept of 'Natural Law with a changing content'. This involved contrasting the *concept* of law, which was intended to be an abstract, formal definition universally applicable, with the *idea* of law, which embodies the purposes and direction of the system. This latter precept varied, of necessity, in different social and cultural contexts.[35]

As distinct from this formal idealist school, there has arisen a sociologically inspired approach to the theme of Natural Law represented by Gény and Duguit. This particular trend rejected the emphasis upon form, and concentrated instead upon the definition of Natural Law in terms

---

[33] See e.g. K. Llewellyn, *The Common Law Tradition*, Boston, 1960, and *Jurisprudence*, Chicago, 1962. See also W. Twining, *Karl Llewellyn and the Realist Movement*, London, 1973, and L. Loevinger, 'Jurimetrics – The Next Step Forward', 33 *Minnesota Law Review*, 1949, p. 455.

[34] See e.g. J. Maritain, *Man and the State*, Paris, 1951, and J. Dabin, *General Theory of Law*, 2nd edn, 1950.

[35] See e.g. R. Stammler, *Theory of Justice*, New York, 1925, and G. Del Vecchio, *Formal Bases of Law*, Boston, 1921.

of universal factors, physical, psychological, social and historical, which dominate the framework of society within which the law operated.[36]

The discussion of Natural Law increased and gained in importance following the Nazi experience. It stimulated a German philosopher, Radbruch, to formulate a theory whereby unjust laws had to be opposed by virtue of a higher, Natural Law.[37]

As far as international law is concerned, the revival of Natural Law came at a time of increasing concern with international justice and the formation of international institutions. Many of the ideas and principles of international law today are rooted in the notion of Natural Law and the relevance of ethical standards to the legal order, such as the principles of non-aggression and human rights.[38]

New approaches[39]

Traditionally, international law has been understood in a historical manner and studied chronologically. This approach was especially marked in the nineteenth century as international relations multiplied and international conferences and agreements came with increasing profusion. Between the world wars, the opening of government archives released a wealth of material and further stimulated a study of diplomatic history,

[36] See e.g. F. Gény, *Méthode d'Interprétation et Sources en Droit Privé Positif*, Paris, 1899, and L. Duguit, *Law in the Modern State*, New York, 1919, and 'Objective Law', 20 *Columbia Law Review*, 1920, p. 817.

[37] *Introduction to Legal Philosophy*, 1947. See also Hart, 'Positivism'; Fuller, 'Positivism', and Fuller, 'The Legal Philosophy of Gustav Radbruch', 6 *Journal of Legal Education*, 1954, p. 481.

[38] See H. Lauterpacht, *International Law and Human Rights*, London, 1950. Note more generally the approach of J. Rawls, *A Theory of Justice*, Oxford, 1971, and A. D'Amato, 'International Law and Rawls' Theory of Justice', 5 *Denver Journal of International Law and Policy*, 1975, p. 525. See also J. Boyle, 'Ideals and Things: International Legal Scholarship and the Prison-house of Language', 26 *Harvard International Law Journal*, 1985, p. 327; A. D'Amato, 'Is International Law Part of Natural Law?', 9 *Vera Lex*, 1989, p. 8; E. Midgley, *The Natural Law Tradition and the Theory of International Relations*, London, 1975, and C. Dominicé, 'Le Grand Retour du Droit Naturel en Droit des Gens', *Mélanges Grossen*, 1992, p. 399.

[39] See e.g. B. S. Chimni, *International Law and World Order*, New Delhi, 1993; A. Cassese, *International Law*, 2nd edn, Oxford, 2005, chapter 1, and R. Müllerson, *Ordering Anarchy: International Law in International Society*, The Hague, 2000. See also D. J. Bederman, *The Spirit of International Law*, Athens, 2002; A. Buchanan, *Justice, Legitimacy and Self-Determination*, Oxford, 2004; *International Law and its Others* (ed. A. Orford), Cambridge, 2006; S. Rosenne, *The Perplexities of Modern International Law*, Leiden, 2004, and P. M. Dupuy, *L'Unité de l'Ordre Juridique International*, Leiden, 2003.

while the creation of such international institutions as the League of Nations and the Permanent Court of International Justice encouraged an appreciation of institutional processes.

However, after the Second World War a growing trend appeared intent upon the analysis of power politics and the comprehension of international relations in terms of the capacity to influence and dominate. The approach was a little more sophisticated than might appear at first glance, for it involved a consideration of social and economic as well as political data that had a bearing upon a state's ability to withstand as well as direct pressures.[40] Nevertheless, it was a pessimistic interpretation because of its centring upon power and its uses as the motive force of inter-state activity.

The next 'wave of advance', as it has been called, witnessed the successes of the behaviouralist movement. This particular train of thought introduced elements of psychology, anthropology and sociology into the study of international relations and paralleled similar developments within the realist school. It reflected the altering emphasis from analyses in terms of idealistic or cynical ('realistic') conceptions of the world political order, to a mechanistic discussion of the system as it operates today, by means of field studies and other tools of the social sciences. Indeed, it is more a method of approach to law and society than a theory in the traditional sense.[41]

One can trace the roots of this school of thought to the changing conceptions of the role of government in society. The nineteenth-century ethic of individualism and the restriction of state intervention to the very minimum has changed radically. The emphasis is now more upon the responsibility of the government towards its citizens, and the phenomenal growth in welfare legislation illustrates this. Rules and regulations controlling wide fields of human activity, something that would have been unheard of in the mid-nineteenth century, have proliferated throughout the nations of the developed world and theory has had to try and keep up with such re-orientations.

---

[40] See e.g. H. Morgenthau, *Politics Among Nations*, 4th edn, New York, 1967, and K. Thompson, *Political Realism and the Crisis of World Politics: An American Approach to Foreign Policy*, Princeton, 1960. See also A. Slaughter Burley, 'International Law and International Relations Theory: A Dual Agenda', 87 AJIL, 1993, p. 205, and A.-M. Slaughter, *A New World Order*, Princeton, 2004; R. Aron, *Paix et Guerre Entre des Nations*, Paris, 1984; M. Koskenniemi, *The Gentle Civilizer of Nations*, Cambridge, 2001, chapter 6.

[41] See e.g. *Contending Approaches to International Politics* (eds. K. Knorr and J. Rosenau), Princeton 1969, and W. Gould and M. Barkun, *International Law and the Social Sciences*, Princeton, 1970.

Since the law now plays a much deeper role in society with the increase in governmental intervention, impetus has been given to legal theories that reflect this growing involvement. Law, particularly in the United States, is seen as a tool to effect changes in society and realist doctrine underlines this. It emphasises that it is community values and policy decisions that determine the nature of the law and accordingly the role of the judge is that much more important. He is no longer an interpreter of a body of formal legal rules, but should be seen more as an active element in making decisions of public policy.

This means that to understand the operation of law, one has to consider the character of the particular society, its needs and values. Law thus becomes a dynamic process and has to be studied in the context of society and not merely as a collection of legal rules capable of being comprehended on their own. The social sciences have led the way in this reinterpretation of society and their influence has been very marked on the behavioural method of looking at the law, not only in terms of general outlook but also in providing the necessary tools to dissect society and discover the way it operates and the direction in which it is heading. The interdisciplinary nature of the studies in question was emphasised, utilising all the social sciences, including politics, economics and philosophy.[42] In particular the use of the scientific method, such as obtaining data and quantitative analysis, has been very much in evidence.

Behaviouralism has divided the field of international relations into basically two studies, the first being a consideration of foreign policy techniques and the reasons whereby one particular course of action is preferred to another, and the second constituting the international systems analysis approach.[43] This emphasises the interaction of the various players on the international stage and the effects of such mutual pressures upon both the system and the participants. More than that, it examines

---

[42] Note Barkun's comment that 'the past theoretical approaches of the legal profession have involved logical manipulations of a legal corpus more often than the empirical study of patterns of human behaviour', *Law Without Sanctions*, New Haven, 1968, p. 3. See also R. A. Falk, 'New Approaches to the Study of International Law', in *New Approaches to International Relations* (ed. M. A. Kaplan), New York, 1968, pp. 357–80, and J. Frankel, *Contemporary International Theory and the Behaviour of States*, London, 1973, pp. 21–2.

[43] See e.g. C. A. McClelland, *Theory and the International System*, New York, 1966; M. A. Kaplan, *System and Process in International Politics*, New York, 1964; M. A. Kaplan and N. Katzenbach, *The Political Foundations of International Law*, New York, 1961, and R. A. Falk and C. Black, *The Future of International Legal Order*, Princeton, 1969. See also A. Kiss and D. Shelton, 'Systems Analysis of International Law: A Methodological Inquiry', 17 Netherlands YIL, 1986, p. 45.

the various international orders that have existed throughout history in an attempt to show how the dynamics of each particular system have created their own rules and how they can be used as an explanation of both political activity and the nature of international law. In other words, the nature of the international system can be examined by the use of particular variables in order to explain and to predict the role of international law.

For example, the period between 1848 and 1914 can be treated as the era of the 'balance of power' system. This system depended upon a number of factors, such as a minimum number of participants (accepted as five), who would engage in a series of temporary alliances in an attempt to bolster the weak and restrict the strong, for example the coalitions Britain entered into to overawe France. It was basic to this system that no nation wished totally to destroy any other state, but merely to humble and weaken, and this contributed to the stability of the order.[44]

This system nurtured its own concepts of international law, especially that of sovereignty which was basic to the idea of free-floating alliances and the ability of states to leave the side of the strong to strengthen the weak. The balance of power collapsed with the First World War and, after a period of confusion, a discernible, loose 'bipolar' system emerged in the years following the Second World War.

This was predicated upon the polarisation of capitalism and communism and the consequent rigid alliances that were created. It included the existence of a Third World of basically non-aligned states, the objects of rivalry and of competition while not in themselves powerful enough to upset the bipolar system. This kind of order facilitated 'frontier' conflicts where the two powers collided, such as in Korea, Berlin and Vietnam, as well as modified the nature of sovereignty within the two alliances thus allowing such organisations as NATO and the European Community (subsequently European Union) on the one hand, and the Warsaw Pact and COMECON on the other, to develop. The other side of this coin has been the freedom felt by the superpowers to control wavering states within their respective spheres of influence, for example, the Soviet actions in Poland, Hungary and Czechoslovakia and those of the USA, particularly within Latin America.[45]

---

[44] See J. Frankel, *International Relations in a Changing World*, London, 1979, pp. 152–7, and Kaplan and Katzenbach, *Political Foundations*, pp. 62–70.

[45] Kaplan and Katzenbach, *Political Foundations*, pp. 50–5. As far as the systems approach is concerned, see also S. Hoffman, 'International Systems and International Law' in *The*

Behaviouralism has been enriched by the use of such techniques as games theory.[46] This is a mathematical method of studying decision-making in conflict situations where the parties react rationally in the struggle for benefits. It can be contrasted with the fight situation, where the essence is the actual defeat of the opponent (for example, the Israel–Arab conflict), and with the debate situation, which is an effort to convince the participants of the rightness of one's cause. Other factors which are taken into account include communications, integration, environment and capabilities. Thus the range and complexity of this approach far exceeds that of prior theories.

All this highlights the switch in emphasis that has taken place in the consideration of law in the world community. The traditional view was generally that international law constituted a series of rules restricting the actions of independent states and forming exceptions to state sovereignty. The new theories tend to look at the situation differently, more from the perspective of the international order expanding its horizons than the nation-state agreeing to accept certain defined limitations upon its behaviour.

The rise of quantitative research has facilitated the collation and ordering of vast quantities of data. It is primarily a methodological approach utilising political, economic and social data and statistics, and converting facts and information into a form suitable for scientific investigation. Such methods with their behavioural and quantitative aspects are beginning to impinge upon the field of international law. They enable a greater depth of knowledge and comprehension to be achieved and a wider appreciation of all the various processes at work.[47]

International System (eds. K. Knorr and S. Verba), Westport, 1961, p. 205; G. Clark and L. Sohn, *World Peace Through World Law*, 3rd edn, Boston, 1966, and *The Strategy of World Order* (eds. R. A. Falk and S. Mendlovitz), New York, 4 vols., 1966. See now Bobbitt, *Shield*, book II.

[46] See e.g. R. Lieber, *Theory and World Politics*, London, 1972, chapter 2; *Game Theory and Related Approaches to Social Behaviour* (ed. H. Shubik), London, 1964, and W. J. M. Mackenzie, *Politics and Social Sciences*, London, 1967.

[47] Note also the functionalist approach to international law. This orientation emphasises the practical benefits to states of co-operation in matters of mutual interest: see e.g. W. Friedmann, *An Introduction to World Politics*, 5th edn, London, 1965, p. 57; F. Haas, *Beyond the Nation State*, Stanford, 1964; D. Mitrany, *A Working Peace System*, London, 1946; C. W. Jenks, *Law, Freedom and Welfare*, London, 1964, and J. Stone, *Legal Controls of International Conflict*, London, 1959. See also D. Johnston, 'Functionalism in the Theory of International Law', 25 Canadian YIL, 1988, p. 3.

The behavioural approach to international relations has been translated into international law theory by a number of writers, in particular
Professor McDougal, with some important modifications. This 'policy-
orientated' movement regards law as a comprehensive process of decision-
making rather than as a defined set of rules and obligations. It is an active
all-embracing approach, seeing international law as a dynamic system operating within a particular type of world order.[48] It therefore minimises
the role played by rules, for such a traditional conception of international
law 'quite obviously offers but the faintest glimpse of the structures, procedures and types of decision that take place in the contemporary world
community'.[49] It has been emphasised that the law is a constantly evolving
process of decision-making and the way that it evolves will depend on the
knowledge and insight of the decision-maker.[50] In other words, it is the
social process of constant human interaction that is seen as critical and
in this process, claims are continually being made in an attempt to max-
imise values at the disposal of the participants. Eight value-institution
categories have been developed to analyse this process: power, wealth,
enlightenment, skill, well-being, affection, respect and rectitude. This list
may be further developed. It is not exhaustive. Law is to be regarded as
a product of such social processes.[51] International law is the whole process of authoritative decision-making involving crucially the concepts of
authority and control. The former is defined in terms of the structure
of expectation concerning the identity and competence of the decision-
maker, whilst the latter refers to the actual effectiveness of a decision,
whether or not authorised.[52]

---

[48] See e.g. M. S. McDougal, 'International Law, Power and Policy', 82 HR, 1952, p. 133; M. S.
McDougal, H. Lasswell and W. M. Reisman, 'Theories about International Law: Prologue
to a Configurative Jurisprudence', 8 Va. JIL, 1968, p. 188; M. S. McDougal, 'International
Law and the Future', 50 *Mississippi Law Journal*, 1979, p. 259, and H. Lasswell and M. S.
McDougal, *Jurisprudence for a Free Society*, Yale, 1992. See also G. Scelle, *Manuel de Droit
International*, Paris, 1948, and Chimni, *International Law*, chapter 3.

[49] M. S. McDougal and W. M. Reisman, *International Law in Contemporary Perspective*, New
Haven, 1980, p. 5.

[50] M. S. McDougal, 'The Policy-Oriented Approach to Law', 40 *Virginia Quarterly Review*,
1964, p. 626. See also E. Suzuki, 'The New Haven School of International Law: An Invitation
to a Policy-Oriented Jurisprudence', 1 *Yale Studies in World Public Order*, 1974, p. 1.

[51] Suzuki, 'Policy-Oriented Jurisprudence', pp. 22–3. See also M. S. McDougal, 'Some Basic
Theoretical Concepts about International Law: A Policy-Oriented Framework of Inquiry',
4 *Journal of Conflict Resolution*, 1960, pp. 337–54.

[52] M. S. McDougal and H. Lasswell, 'The Identification and Appraisal of Diverse Systems of
Public Order', 53 AJIL, 1959, pp. 1, 9.

McDougal's work and that of his followers emphasises the long list of values, interests and considerations that have to be taken into account within the international system by the persons actually faced with making the decisions. This stress upon the so-called 'authoritative decision-maker', whether he or she be in the United States Department of State, in the British Foreign Office or 'anyone whose choice about an event can have some international significance',[53] as the person who in effect has to choose between different options respecting international legal principles, emphasises the practical world of power and authority.

Such a decision-maker is subject to a whole series of pressures and influences, such as the values of the community in which that person operates, and the interests of the particular nation-state served. He or she will also have to consider the basic values of the world order, for instance human dignity. This approach involves a complex dissection of a wide-ranging series of factors and firmly fixes international law within the ambit of the social sciences, both with respect to the procedures adopted and the tools of analysis. International law is seen in the following terms, as

> a comprehensive process of authoritative decision in which rules are con-
> tinuously made and remade; that the function of the rules of international
> law is to communicate the perspectives (demands, identifications and ex-
> pectations) of the peoples of the world about this comprehensive process
> of decision; and that the national application of these rules in particular in-
> stances requires their interpretation, like that of any other communication,
> in terms of who is using them, with respect to whom, for what purposes
> (major and minor), and in what context.[54]

Legal rules articulate and seek to achieve certain goals and this value factor must not be ignored. The values emphasised by this school are basically those of human dignity, familiar from the concepts of Western democratic society.[55] Indeed, Reisman has emphasised the Natural Law origins of this approach as well as the need to clarify a jurisprudence for those persons whose activities have led to innovations in such fields of international law as human rights and the protection of the environment.[56]

---

[53] McDougal and Reisman, *International Law*, p. 2.
[54] M. S. McDougal, 'A Footnote', 57 AJIL, 1963, p. 383.
[55] See M. S. McDougal, H. Lasswell and L. C. Chen, *Human Rights and World Public Order*, New Haven, 1980. For a discussion of the tasks required for a realistic inquiry in the light of defined goals, see McDougal, 'International Law and the Future', pp. 259, 267.
[56] 'The View from the New Haven School of International Law', PASIL, 1992, p. 118.

The policy-oriented movement has been greatly criticised by traditional international lawyers for unduly minimising the legal content of the subject and for ignoring the fact that nations generally accept international law as it is and obey its dictates.[57] States rarely indulge in a vast behavioural analysis, studiously considering every relevant element in a particular case and having regard to fundamental objectives like human dignity and welfare. Indeed, so to do may weaken international law, it has been argued.[58] In addition, the insertion of such value-concepts as 'human dignity' raises difficulties of subjectivity that ill fit within a supposedly objective analytical structure. Koskenniemi, for example, has drawn attention to the predilection of the policy-oriented approach to support the dominant power.[59]

Other writers, such as Professor Falk, accept the basic comprehensive approach of the McDougal school, but point to its inconsistencies and overfulsome cataloguing of innumerable interests. They tend to adopt a global outlook based upon a deep concern for human welfare and morality, but with an emphasis upon the importance of legal rules and structure.[60]

Professor Franck, however, has sought to refocus the essential question of the existence and operation of the system of international law in terms of inquiring into why states obey international law despite the undeveloped condition of the international legal system's structures, processes and enforcement mechanisms.[61] The answer is seen to lie in the concept of legitimacy. States will obey the rules because they see such rules and

---

[57] See in particular P. Allott, 'Language, Method and the Nature of International Law', 45 BYIL, 1971, p. 79. Higgins has vividly drawn attention to the differences in approach to international law adopted by American and British writers: 'Policy Considerations and the International Judicial Process', 17 ICLQ, 1968, p. 58. See also T. Farer, 'Human Rights in Law's Empire: The Jurisprudence War', 85 AJIL, 1991, p. 117.

[58] Allott, 'Language', pp. 128 ff.   [59] See *Gentle Civilizer of Nations*, pp. 474 ff.

[60] See e.g. R. A. Falk, *Human Rights and State Sovereignty*, New York, 1981, and Falk, *On Human Governance*, Cambridge, 1995. See also *The United Nations and a Just World Order* (eds. R. Falk, S. Kim and S. Mendlovitz), Boulder, 1991, and Chimni, *International Law*, chapter 4. But note the approach of, e.g., J. S. Watson, 'A Realistic Jurisprudence of International Law', 34 YBWA, 1980, p. 265, and M. Lane, 'Demanding Human Rights: A Change in the World Legal Order', 6 *Hofstra Law Review*, 1978, p. 269. See also Boyle, 'Ideals and Things'.

[61] T. M. Franck, *The Power of Legitimacy Among Nations*, Oxford, 1990. See also Franck, 'Fairness in the International Legal and Institutional System', 240 HR, 1993 III, p. 13, chapter 2; Franck, *Fairness in International Law and Institutions*, Oxford, 1995, chapter 2, and Franck, 'The Power of Legitimacy and the Legitimacy of Power: International Law in an Age of Power Disequilibrium', 100 AJIL, 2006, p. 88.

their institutional framework as possessing a high degree of legitimacy. Legitimacy itself is defined as 'a property of a rule or rule-making institution which itself exerts a pull towards compliance on those addressed normatively because those addressed believe that the rule or institution has come into being and operates in accordance with generally accepted principles of right process'.[62] Legitimacy may be empirically demonstrated but compliance may be measured not only by observing states acting in accordance with the principle in question, but also by observing the degree to which a violator actually exhibits deference to that principle even while violating it.

Legitimacy will depend upon four specific properties, it is suggested: determinacy (or readily ascertainable normative content or 'transparency'); symbolic validation (or authority approval); coherence (or consistency or general application) and adherence (or falling within an organised hierarchy of rules). In other words, it is proposed that there exist objectively verifiable criteria which help us to ascertain why international rules are obeyed and thus why the system works. This approach is supplemented by the view that legitimacy and justice as morality are two aspects of the concept of fairness, which is seen by Franck as the most important question for international law.[63] Franck, however, has also drawn attention to the 'emerging right to individuality'[64] within the context of a 'global identity crisis'[65] in which the growth of supranational institutions and the collapse of a range of states combine to undermine traditional certainties of world order. He notes that persons are increasingly likely to identify themselves as autonomous individuals and that this is both reflected and manifested in the rise and expansion of international human rights law and in the construction of multi-layered and freely selected affinities.[66] While such personal rights are increasingly protected in both national and international law, the question as to the appropriate balancing of individual, group and state rights is posed in more urgent form.

However, legitimacy may also be understood in a broader way in referring to the relationship with the international political system as a whole and as forming the link between power and the legal system. It imbues the normative order with authority and acceptability, although not as such legality. Legitimacy links law and politics in its widest sense and will depend upon the context out of which it emerges. One writer has concluded

---

[62] Franck, *Legitimacy*, p. 24.   [63] Franck, 'Fairness', p. 26.
[64] T. M. Franck, *The Empowered Self*, Oxford, 1999, p. 1.
[65] *Ibid.*, p. 3.   [66] *Ibid.*, pp. 278–80.

that legitimacy 'is a matter of history and thus is subject to change as new events emerge from the future and new understandings reinterpret the past'.[67] Legitimacy is important in that it constitutes a standard for the testing in the wider political environment of the relevance and acceptability of legal norms and practices. A rule seen as legitimate will benefit from a double dose of approval. A rule, institution or practice seen as illegal and illegitimate will be doubly disapproved of. A rule, or entity, which is legal but not legitimate will, it is suggested, not be able to sustain its position over the long term. A practice seen as illegal but legitimate is likely to form the nucleus of a new rule.

The recurring themes of the relationship between sovereign states and international society and the search for a convincing explanation for the binding quality of international law in a state-dominated world appear also in very recent approaches to international law theory which fall within the general critical legal studies framework.[68] Such approaches have drawn attention to the many inconsistencies and incoherences that persist within the international legal system. The search for an all-embracing general theory of international law has been abandoned in mainstream thought as being founded upon unverifiable propositions, whether religiously or sociologically based, and attention has switched to the analysis of particular areas of international law and in particular procedures for the settlement of disputes. The critical legal studies movement notes that the traditional approach to international law has in essence involved the transposition of 'liberal' principles of domestic systems onto the international scene, but that this has led to further problems.[69] Specifically, liberalism tries constantly to balance individual freedom and social order and, it is argued, inevitably ends up siding with either one or other of those propositions.[70]

---

[67] Bobbitt, *Shield*, p. 17.

[68] See e.g. *The Structure and Processes of International Law* (eds. R. St J. Macdonald and D. Johnston), Dordrecht, 1983; Boyle, 'Ideals and Things'; A. Carty, *The Decay of International Law? A Reappraisal of the Limits of Legal Imagination in International Affairs*, Manchester, 1986; D. Kennedy, *International Legal Structure*, Boston, 1987; M. Koskenniemi, *From Apology to Utopia*, Helsinki, 1989; F. V. Kratochwil, *Rules, Norms and Decisions: On the Conditions of Practical and Legal Reasoning in International Relations and Domestic Affairs*, Cambridge, 1989; P. Allott, *Eunomia*, Oxford, 1990; Allott, *The Health of Nations*, Cambridge, 2002; *Theory and International Law: An Introduction* (ed. Allott), London, 1991, and *International Law* (ed. M. Koskenniemi), Aldershot, 1992. See also I. Scobbie, 'Towards the Elimination of International Law: Some Radical Scepticism about Sceptical Radicalism', 61 BYIL, 1990, p. 339, and S. Marks, *The Riddle of All Constitutions: International Law, Democracy and the Critique of Ideology*, Cambridge, 2000.

[69] See e.g. Koskenniemi, *International Law*, p. xvi.

[70] Koskenniemi, *From Apology to Utopia*, p. 52.

Additionally, there are only two possibilities with regard to justice itself, it is either simply subjective or it is imposed. In either case, liberalism is compromised as a system.

The critical legal studies approach (sometimes termed the 'New Approaches to International Law' or NAIL) notes the close relationship that exists between law and society, but emphasises that conceptual analysis is also crucial since such concepts are not in themselves independent entities but reflect particular power relationships. The point is made that the nexus between state power and international legal concepts needs to be taken into consideration as well as the way in which such concepts in themselves reflect political factors. As Koskenniemi writes, 'a post-realist theory . . . aims to answer questions regarding the relationship of law and society and the legitimacy of constraint in a world of sovereigns as aspects of one single problem: the problem of power in concepts'.[71] The problem posed by the growth in the world community and the need to consider the range of different cultures and traditions within that community leads, it is suggested, to the decline of universality as such and the need to focus upon the specific contexts of particular problems.

In a more recent work, Koskenniemi has drawn attention not only to the continuing tension between the universalist and particularist impulses in international law,[72] but also to the related distinction between formalism and dynamism, or the contrast between rule-oriented and policy-oriented approaches. It is his view in essence that the latter approach might too easily be utilised to support a dominant political position.[73] It is the typical lawyer's answer in any event to declare that all depends upon the particular circumstances of the case and this approach is generalised in order to deal with the question of which of several relevant international rules is to predominate. It is in fact a way of noting that superior operating principles are difficult to find or justify and thus concluding that the search for universal concepts or principles is of little value. In effect, it is proposed that no coherent international system as such actually exists and that one should rather concentrate upon ad hoc legal concepts as reflecting power considerations and within the confines of the specific contexts in which the particular questions or issues have arisen. Like the policy-oriented approach, the critical legal studies view is to accept that

---

[71] *Ibid.*, p. xxi.

[72] See also M. Eyskens, 'Particularism versus Universalism' in *International Law – Theory and Practice* (ed. K. Wellens), The Hague, 1998, p. 11.

[73] *Gentle Civilizer of Nations.*

international law is more than a set of rules, but it then proceeds to emphasise the indeterminacy as such of law rather than seeing law as a collection of competing norms between which choices must be made.[74] One particular area of study in recent years has been that concerned with the position of women within international law, both in terms of the structure of the system and the, for example, relative absence of females from the institutions and processes of international law and in terms of substantive law, which has until recently paid little attention to the needs and concerns of women.[75]

The fragmentation of international law?[76]

The tremendous expansion of both the rules and the institutions of international law, with the rise of more and more specialist areas, such as trade law, environmental law and human rights law, has led to arguments that international law as a holistic system is in the process of fragmentation. This has led to the fear that the centre will not be able to hold and that international law might dissolve into a series of discrete localised or limited systems with little or no interrelationship. In many ways it is the explosion

---

[74] See Higgins, *Problems and Process*, p. 9. See also J. A. Beckett, 'Countering Uncertainty and Ending Up/Down Arguments: Prolegomena to a Response to NAIL', 16 EJIL, 2005, p. 213.

[75] See e.g. H. Charlesworth and C. M. Chinkin, *The Boundaries of International Law: A Feminist Analysis*, Manchester, 2000; H. Charlesworth, C. M. Chinkin and S. Wright, 'Feminist Approaches to International Law', 85 AJIL, 1991, p. 613; F. Tesón, 'Feminism and International Law: A Reply', 33 Va. JIL, 1993, p. 647, and *International Law: Modern Feminist Approaches* (eds. D. Buss and A. Manji), Oxford, 2005. See also the 'Final Report on Women's Equality and Nationality in International Law' in *Report of the Sixty-Ninth Conference*, International Law Association, London, 2000, p. 248. Note that article 25(2) of the Rules of the European Court of Human Rights requires that the Sections of the Court be 'gender balanced', while article 36(8)a(iii) of the Statute of the International Criminal Court 1998 declares that the selection process for judges of the Court should include the need for a 'fair representation of female and male judges'. See also ICC-ASP/1/Res.- 2 (2002) on the procedure for nomination of judges which required a minimum number of female and male candidates.

[76] See e.g. 'Fragmentation of International Law: Difficulties Arising from the Diversification and Expansion of International Law', Report of the Study Group of the International Law Commission (finalised by M. Koskenniemi), A/CN.4/L.682, 2006; M. Koskenniemi and P. Leino, 'Fragmentation of International Law? Postmodern Anxieties', 15 *Leiden Journal of International Law*, 2002, p. 553; M. Prost and P. K. Clark, 'Unity, Diversity and the Fragmentation of International Law', 5 *Chinese Journal of International Law*, 2006, p. 341; B. Simma and D. Pulkowski, 'Of Planets and the Universe: Self-contained Regimes in International Law', 17 EJIL, 2006, p. 483, and E. Benvenisti and G. W. Downs, 'The Empire's New Clothes: Political Economy and the Fragmentation of International Law', 60 *Stanford Law Review*, 2007, p. 595.

of what is termed globalisation, with the consequential spread of practices and mechanisms across the world,[77] that has precipitated this problem of fragmentation, being defined in one view as the 'emergence of specialised and relatively autonomous spheres of social action and structure'.[78] This has led to a debate as to the relationship between self-contained regimes in international law and the system as a whole,[79] with the fear being expressed that the rise of specialised rules and mechanisms that have no clear authority relationship might lead to conflicts between local systems and, at the least, inconsistency in the interpretation and development of international law.[80] While to some extent the former is a real danger,[81] there is still a powerful centralising dynamic in international law and indeed a strong presumption against normative conflict:[82] for example, the principle that special law (*lex specialis*) derogates from general law (*lex generalis*), so that the more detailed and specific rule will have priority.[83] It is also true that international law, as a decentralised system, has long had to face the problem of relating together a variety of rules derived from general treaties, specific treaties and customary law, while it is indeed the case that even with the increase in specialist areas of international law, there is an increasing tendency to relate hitherto discrete spheres.[84] Further, while decisions of international courts and tribunals may not always be compatible, there is a hierarchy of authority with the International Court of Justice at the summit.[85] The International Law Commission's Report on Fragmentation reached two principal conclusions, first that 'the

---

[77] See e.g. P. S. Berman, *The Globalisation of International Law*, Aldershot, 2005.

[78] International Law Commission Report on Fragmentation, p. 11.

[79] See, for an early example, B. Simma, 'Self-Contained Regimes', 16 Netherlands YIL, 1985, p. 111.

[80] See e.g. *Unity and Diversity in International Law* (eds. A. Zimmermann and R. Hofmann), Berlin, 2006; K. Wellens, 'Fragmentation of International Law and Establishment of an Accountability Regime for International Organizations', 25 *Michigan Journal of International Law*, 2004, p. 1159, and *L'Influence des Sources sur l'Unité et la Fragmentation du Droit International* (eds. K. C. Wellens and R. H. Viraxia), Brussels, 2006.

[81] See e.g. A. Reinisch, 'Necessity in International Arbitration – An Unnecessary Split of Opinions in Recent ICSID Cases? Comments on CMS v. Argentina and LG&E v. Argentina', 8 *Journal of World Investment and Trade*, 2007, p. 191.

[82] International Law Commission Report on Fragmentation, p. 25.

[83] See further below, chapter 3, p. 124.

[84] See e.g. with regard to human rights law and humanitarian law (or the laws of war), A. E. Cassimitis, 'International Humanitarian Law, International Human Rights Law, and Fragmentation of International Law', 56 ICLQ, 2007, p. 623. See further below, chapter 21, p. 1180.

[85] See further below, chapter 19, p. 1115.

emergence of special treaty-regimes (which should not be called "self-contained") has not seriously undermined legal security, predictability or the equality of legal subjects' and second that 'increasing attention will have to be given to the collision of norms and regimes and the rules, methods and techniques for dealing with such collisions'.[86]

Conclusion

The range of theories and approaches to international law and not least the emphasis upon the close relationship between international law and international relations[87] testifies both to the importance of the subject and the inherent difficulties it faces.[88] International law is clearly much more that a simple set of rules. It is a culture in the broadest sense in that it constitutes a method of communicating claims, counter-claims, expectations and anticipations as well as providing a framework for assessing and prioritising such demands.

International law functions in a particular, concrete world system, involving a range of actors from states to international organisations, companies and individuals, and as such needs to be responsive to the needs and aspirations of such participants. The international system is composed increasingly of co-operative and competing elements participating in cross-boundary activities, but the essential normative and structural nature of international law remains. Law is not the only way in which issues transcending borders are negotiated and settled or indeed fought over. It is one of a number of methods for dealing with an existing complex and shifting system, but it is a way of some prestige and influence for it is

---

[86] At pp. 248–9.

[87] See e.g. A.-M. Slaughter, A. S. Tulumello and S. Wood, 'International Law and International Relations Theory: A New Generation of Interdisciplinary Scholarship', 92 AJIL, 1998, p. 367, and Slaughter, *A New World Order*. See also Bobbitt, *Shield*, who posits the dying of the nation-state and its replacement by the market-state, with consequential changes with regard to both international law and its institutions, e.g. pp. 353 ff. and 667 ff.

[88] Note relatively recent arguments based on a revived power realism approach, particularly made in the US, that international law is simply a part of a complex of factors which are relevant, and implicitly subservient, to diplomacy and the pursuit of national interests: see e.g. J. L. Goldsmith and E. A. Posner, *The Limits of International Law*, Oxford, 2005, and M. J. Glennon, *Limits of Law, Prerogatives of Power: Interventionism after Kosovo*, New York, 2001, but cf. Franck, *Power of Legitimacy*; A. Van Aaken, 'To Do Away with International Law? Some Limits to the "Limits of International Law"', 17 EJIL, 2006, p. 289, and G. Simpson, *Great Powers and Outlaw States: Unequal Sovereigns in the International Legal Order*, Cambridge, 2004.

of its very nature in the form of mutually accepted obligations.[89] Law and politics cannot be divorced. They are not identical, but they do interact on several levels. They are engaged in a crucial symbiotic relationship. It does neither discipline a service to minimise the significance of the other.

Suggestions for further reading

P. Bobbitt, *The Shield of Achilles*, London, 2002

H. Charlesworth and C. Chinkin, *The Boundaries of International Law: A Feminist Analysis*, Manchester, 2000

T. M. Franck, *Fairness in International Law and Institutions*, Oxford, 1995
The Empowered Self, Oxford, 1999

M. Koskenniemi, *The Gentle Civilizer of Nations*, Cambridge, 2001

S. Marks, *The Riddle of All Constitutions: International Law, Democracy and the Critique of Ideology*, Cambridge, 2000

R. Müllerson, *Ordering Anarchy: International Law in International Society*, The Hague, 2000

---

[89] Higgins has noted that 'international law has to be identified by reference to what the actors (most often states), often without benefit of pronouncement by the International Court of Justice, believe normative in their relations with each other', *Problems and Process*, p. 18.

3

Sources

Ascertainment of the law on any given point in domestic legal orders is not usually too difficult a process.[1] In the English legal system, for example, one looks to see whether the matter is covered by an Act of Parliament and, if it is, the law reports are consulted as to how it has been interpreted by the courts. If the particular point is not specifically referred to in a statute, court cases will be examined to elicit the required information. In other words, there is a definite method of discovering what the law is. In addition to verifying the contents of the rules, this method also demonstrates how the law is created, namely, by parliamentary legislation or judicial case-law. This gives a degree of certainty to the legal process because one is able to tell when a proposition has become law and the

---

[1] See generally C. Parry, *The Sources and Evidences of International Law*, Cambridge, 1965; M. Sørensen, *Les Sources de Droit International*, Paris, 1946; V. D. Degan, *Sources of International Law*, The Hague, 1997; *Oppenheim's International Law* (eds. R. Y. Jennings and A. D. Watts), 9th edn, London, 1992, p. 22; I. Brownlie, *Principles of Public International Law*, 6th edn, Oxford, 2003, chapter 1; Nguyen Quoc Dinh, P. Daillier and A. Pellet, *Droit International Public*, 7th edn, Paris, 2002, p. 111; A. Boyle and C. Chinkin, *The Making of International Law*, Oxford, 2007; G. M. Danilenko, *Law-Making in the International Community*, The Hague, 1993; G. I. Tunkin, *Theory of International Law*, London, 1974, pp. 89–203; J. W. Verzijl, *International Law in Historical Perspective*, Leiden, 1968, vol. I, p. 1; H. Lauterpacht, *International Law: Collected Papers*, Cambridge, 1970, vol. I, p. 58; *Change and Stability in International Law-Making* (eds. A. Cassese and J. Weiler), Leiden, 1988; A. Bos, *A Methodology of International Law*, Amsterdam, 1984; A. Cassese, *International Law*, 2nd edn, Oxford, 2005, chapters 8–10; A. Pellet, 'Article 38' in *The Statute of the International Court of Justice: A Commentary* (eds. A. Zimmermann, C. Tomuschat and K. Oellers-Frahm), Oxford, 2006, p. 677; M. Virally, 'The Sources of International Law' in *Manual of Public International Law* (ed. M. Sørensen), London, 1968, p. 116; C. Tomuschat, 'Obligations Arising for States Without or Against Their Will', 241 HR, 1993, p. 195; B. Simma, 'From Bilateralism to Community Interest in International Law', 250 HR, 1994, p. 219; M. Mendelson, 'The International Court of Justice and the Sources of International Law' in *Fifty Years of the International Court of Justice* (eds. A. V. Lowe and M. Fitzmaurice), Cambridge, 1996, p. 63; G. Abi-Saab, 'Les Sources du Droit International – Un Essai de Déconstruction' in *Le Droit International dans un Monde en Mutation*, Montevideo, 1994, p. 29, and O. Schachter, 'Recent Trends in International Law-Making', 12 Australian YIL, 1992.

necessary mechanism to resolve any disputes about the law is evident. It reflects the hierarchical character of a national legal order with its gradations of authority imparting to the law a large measure of stability and predictability.

The contrast is very striking when one considers the situation in international law. The lack of a legislature, executive and structure of courts within international law has been noted and the effects of this will become clearer as one proceeds. There is no single body able to create laws internationally binding upon everyone, nor a proper system of courts with comprehensive and compulsory jurisdiction to interpret and extend the law. One is therefore faced with the problem of discovering where the law is to be found and how one can tell whether a particular proposition amounts to a legal rule. This perplexity is reinforced because of the anarchic nature of world affairs and the clash of competing sovereignties. Nevertheless, international law does exist and is ascertainable. There are 'sources' available from which the rules may be extracted and analysed.

By 'sources' one means those provisions operating within the legal system on a technical level, and such ultimate sources as reason or morality are excluded, as are more functional sources such as libraries and journals. What is intended is a survey of the process whereby rules of international law emerge.[2]

Article 38(1) of the Statute of the International Court of Justice is widely recognised as the most authoritative and complete statement as to the sources of international law.[3] It provides that:

> the Court, whose function is to decide in accordance with international law
> such disputes as are submitted to it, shall apply: (a) international conven-
> tions, whether general or particular, establishing rules expressly recognised
> by the contesting states; (b) international custom, as evidence of a general
> practice accepted as law; (c) the general principles of law recognised by
> civilised nations; (d) subject to the provisions of Article 59, judicial deci-
> sions and the teachings of the most highly qualified publicists of the various
> nations, as subsidiary means for the determination of rules of law.

Although this formulation is technically limited to the sources of international law which the International Court must apply, in fact since

---

[2] See also, e.g., M. S. McDougal and W. M. Reisman, 'The Prescribing Function: How International Law is Made', 6 *Yale Studies in World Public Order*, 1980, p. 249.

[3] See e.g. Brownlie, *Principles*, p. 5; *Oppenheim's International Law*, p. 24, and M. O. Hudson, *The Permanent Court of International Justice*, New York, 1934, pp. 601 ff.

the function of the Court is to decide disputes submitted to it 'in accordance with international law' and since all member states of the United Nations are *ipso facto* parties to the Statute by virtue of article 93 of the United Nations Charter (states that are non-members of the UN can specifically become parties to the Statute of the Court: Switzerland was the most obvious example of this until it joined the UN in 2002), there is no serious contention that the provision expresses the universal perception as to the enumeration of sources of international law.

Some writers have sought to categorise the distinctions in this provision, so that international conventions, custom and the general principles of law are described as the three exclusive law-creating processes while judicial decisions and academic writings are regarded as law-determining agencies, dealing with the verification of alleged rules.[4] But in reality it is not always possible to make hard and fast divisions. The different functions overlap to a great extent so that in many cases treaties (or conventions) merely reiterate accepted rules of customary law, and judgments of the International Court of Justice may actually create law in the same way that municipal judges formulate new law in the process of interpreting existing law.[5]

A distinction has sometimes been made between formal and material sources.[6] The former, it is claimed, confer upon the rules an obligatory character, while the latter comprise the actual content of the rules. Thus the formal sources appear to embody the constitutional mechanism for identifying law while the material sources incorporate the essence or subject-matter of the regulations. This division has been criticised particularly in view of the peculiar constitutional set-up of international law, and it tends to distract attention from some of the more important problems by its attempt to establish a clear separation of substantive and procedural elements, something difficult to maintain in international law.

---

[4] See e.g. G. Schwarzenberger, *International Law*, 3rd edn, London, 1957, vol. I, pp. 26–7.

[5] There are a number of examples of this: see below, chapter 4, p. 138.

[6] See e.g. Brownlie, *Principles*, p. 1. See also Nguyen Quoc Dinh *et al.*, *Droit International Public*, pp. 111–12, where it is noted that 'les sources *formelles* du droit sont les *procédés* d'élaboration du droit, les diverses techniques qui autorisent à considérer qu'une règle appartient au droit positif. Les sources *matérielles* constituent les fondements sociologiques des normes internationales, leur base politique, morale ou économique plus ou moins explicitée par la doctrine ou les sujets du droit', and Pellet, 'Article 38' p. 714.

Custom[7]

Introduction

In any primitive society certain rules of behaviour emerge and prescribe what is permitted and what is not. Such rules develop almost subconsciously within the group and are maintained by the members of the group by social pressures and with the aid of various other more tangible implements. They are not, at least in the early stages, written down or codified, and survive ultimately because of what can be called an aura of historical legitimacy.[8] As the community develops it will modernise its

---

[7] See generally, A. D'Amato, *The Concept of Custom in International Law*, Cornell, 1971; M. Akehurst, 'Custom as a Source of International Law', 47 BYIL, 1974–5, p. 1; M. Mendelson, 'The Formation of Customary International Law', 272 HR, 1999, p. 159; B. Cheng, 'Custom: The Future of General State Practice in a Divided World' in *The Structure and Process of International Law* (eds. R. St J. Macdonald and D. Johnston), Dordrecht, 1983, p. 513; A. E. Roberts, 'Traditional and Modern Approaches to Customary International Law: A Reconciliation', 95 AJIL, 2001, p. 757; H. Thirlway, *International Customary Law and Codification*, Leiden, 1972; *Sources of State Practice in International Law* (eds. R. Gaebler and M. Smolka-Day), Ardley, 2002; K. Wolfke, *Custom in Present International Law*, 2nd edn, Dordrecht, 1993, and Wolfke, 'Some Persistent Controversies Regarding Customary International Law', Netherlands YIL, 1993, p. 1; L. Kopelmanas, 'Custom as a Means of the Creation of International Law', 18 BYIL, 1937, p. 127; H. Lauterpacht, *The Development of International Law by the International Court*, Cambridge, 1958, pp. 368–93; J. Kunz, 'The Nature of Customary International Law', 47 AJIL, 1953, p. 662; R. J. Dupuy, 'Coutume Sage et Coutume Sauvage', *Mélanges Rousseau*, Paris, 1974, p. 75; B. Stern, 'La Coutume au Coeur du Droit International', *Mélanges Reuter*, Paris, 1981, p. 479; R. Y. Jennings, 'Law-Making and Package Deal', *Mélanges Reuter*, p. 347; G. Danilenko, 'The Theory of International Customary Law', 31 German YIL, 1988, p. 9; Barberis, 'Réfléxions sur la Coutume Internationale', AFDI, 1990, p. 9; L. Condorelli, 'Custom' in *International Law: Achievements and Perspectives* (ed. M. Bedjaoui), Paris, 1991, p. 206; M. Byers, 'Custom, Power and the Power of Rules', 17 *Michigan Journal of International Law*, 1995, p. 109; H. Thirlway, 'The Law and Procedure of the International Court of Justice: 1960–89 (Part Two)', 61 BYIL, 1990, pp. 3, 31, and Thirlway, 'The Law and Procedure of the International Court of Justice: 1960–89: Supplement, 2005: Parts One and Two', 76 BYIL, 2006, pp. 1, 92; J. Kammerhofer, 'The Uncertainty in the Formal Sources of International Law: Customary International Law and Some of Its Problems', 15 EJIL, 2004, p. 523; P. M. Dupuy, 'Théorie des Sources et Coutume en Droit International Contemporain' in *Le Droit International dans un Monde en Mutation*, p. 51; D. P. Fidler, 'Challenging the Classic Conception of Custom', German YIL, 1997, p. 198; R. Müllerson, 'On the Nature and Scope of Customary International Law', *Austrian Review of International and European Law*, 1998, p. 1; M. Byers, *Custom, Power and the Power of Rules*, Cambridge, 1999, and A. Carty, *The Decay of International Law?*, Manchester, 1986, chapter 3. See also the 'Statement of Principles Applicable to the Formation of General Customary International Law' in *Report of the Sixty-Ninth Conference*, International Law Association, London, 2000, p. 713.

[8] See e.g. R. Unger, *Law in Modern Society*, London, 1976, who notes that customary law can be regarded as 'any recurring mode of interaction among individuals and groups,

code of behaviour by the creation of legal machinery, such as courts and legislature. Custom, for this is how the original process can be described, remains and may also continue to evolve.[9] It is regarded as an authentic expression of the needs and values of the community at any given time.

Custom within contemporary legal systems, particularly in the developed world, is relatively cumbersome and unimportant and often of only nostalgic value.[10] In international law on the other hand it is a dynamic source of law in the light of the nature of the international system and its lack of centralised government organs.

The existence of customary rules can be deduced from the practice and behaviour of states and this is where the problems begin. How can one tell when a particular line of action adopted by a state reflects a legal rule or is merely prompted by, for example, courtesy? Indeed, how can one discover what precisely a state is doing or why, since there is no living 'state' but rather thousands of officials in scores of departments exercising governmental functions? Other issues concern the speed of creation of new rules and the effect of protests.

There are disagreements as to the value of a customary system in international law. Some writers deny that custom can be significant today as a source of law, noting that it is too clumsy and slow-moving to accommodate the evolution of international law any more,[11] while others declare that it is a dynamic process of law creation and more important than treaties since it is of universal application.[12] Another view recognises that custom is of value since it is activated by spontaneous behaviour and thus mirrors the contemporary concerns of society. However, since international law now has to contend with a massive increase in the pace and variety of state activities as well as having to come to terms with many different cultural and political traditions, the role of custom is perceived to be much diminished.[13]

together with the more or less explicit acknowledgement by these groups and individuals that such patterns of interaction produce reciprocal expectations of conduct that ought to be satisfied', p. 49. See also R. Dias, *Jurisprudence*, 5th edn, London, 1985, chapter 9, and H. L. A. Hart, *The Concept of Law*, Oxford, 1961.

[9] See e.g. D. Lloyd, *Introduction to Jurisprudence*, 4th edn, London, 1979, p. 649, and H. Maine, *Ancient Law*, London, 1861.

[10] See e.g. Dias, *Jurisprudence*.

[11] See e.g. W. Friedmann, *The Changing Structure of International Law*, New York, 1964, pp. 121–3. See also I. De Lupis, *The Concept of International Law*, Aldershot, 1987, pp. 112–16.

[12] E.g. D'Amato, *Concept of Custom*, p. 12.

[13] C. De Visscher, *Theory and Reality in Public International Law*, 3rd edn, Princeton, 1960, pp. 161–2.

There are elements of truth in each of these approaches. Amidst a wide variety of conflicting behaviour, it is not easy to isolate the emergence of a new rule of customary law and there are immense problems involved in collating all the necessary information. It is not always the best instrument available for the regulation of complex issues that arise in world affairs, but in particular situations it may meet the contingencies of modern life. As will be seen, it is possible to point to something called 'instant' customary law in certain circumstances that can prescribe valid rules without having to undergo a long period of gestation, and custom can and often does dovetail neatly within the complicated mechanisms now operating for the identification and progressive development of the principles of international law.

More than that, custom does mirror the characteristics of the decentralised international system. It is democratic in that all states may share in the formulation of new rules, though the precept that some are more equal than others in this process is not without its grain of truth. If the international community is unhappy with a particular law it can be changed relatively quickly without the necessity of convening and successfully completing a world conference. It reflects the consensus approach to decision-making with the ability of the majority to create new law binding upon all, while the very participation of states encourages their compliance with customary rules. Its imprecision means flexibility as well as ambiguity. Indeed, the creation of the concept of the exclusive economic zone in the law of the sea may be cited as an example of this process. This is discussed further in chapter 11. The essence of custom according to article 38 is that it should constitute 'evidence of a general practice accepted as law'. Thus, it is possible to detect two basic elements in the make-up of a custom. These are the material facts, that is, the actual behaviour of states, and the psychological or subjective belief that such behaviour is 'law'. As the International Court noted in the *Libya/Malta* case, the substance of customary law must be 'looked for primarily in the actual practice and *opinio juris* of states'.[14]

It is understandable why the first requirement is mentioned, since customary law is founded upon the performance of state activities and the convergence of practices, in other words, what states actually do. It is the psychological factor (*opinio juris*) that needs some explanation. If one left the definition of custom as state practice then one would be faced with the

---

[14] ICJ Reports, 1985, pp. 13, 29; 81 ILR, p. 239. See also the Advisory Opinion on the *Legality of the Threat or Use of Nuclear Weapons*, ICJ Reports, 1996, pp. 226, 253; 110 ILR, p. 163.

problem of how to separate international law from principles of morality or social usage. This is because states do not restrict their behaviour to what is legally required. They may pursue a line of conduct purely through a feeling of goodwill and in the hope of reciprocal benefits. States do not have to allow tourists in or launch satellites. There is no law imposing upon them the strict duty to distribute economic aid to developing nations. The bare fact that such things are done does not mean that they have to be done.

The issue therefore is how to distinguish behaviour undertaken because of a law from behaviour undertaken because of a whole series of other reasons ranging from goodwill to pique, and from ideological support to political bribery. And if customary law is restricted to the overt acts of states, one cannot solve this problem.

Accordingly, the second element in the definition of custom has been elaborated. This is the psychological factor, the belief by a state that behaved in a certain way that it was under a legal obligation to act that way. It is known in legal terminology as *opinio juris sive necessitatis* and was first formulated by the French writer François Gény as an attempt to differentiate legal custom from mere social usage.[15]

However, the relative importance of the two factors, the overt action and the subjective conviction, is disputed by various writers.[16] Positivists, with their emphasis upon state sovereignty, stress the paramount importance of the psychological element. States are only bound by what they have consented to, so therefore the material element is minimised to the greater value of *opinio juris*. If states believe that a course of action is legal and perform it, even if only once, then it is to be inferred that they have tacitly consented to the rule involved. Following on from this line of analysis, various positivist thinkers have tended to minimise many of the requirements of the overt manifestation, for example, with regard to repetition and duration.[17] Other writers have taken precisely the opposite line and maintain that *opinio juris* is impossible to prove and therefore

---

[15] *Méthode d'Interprétation et Sources en Droit Privé Positif,* 1899, para. 110.

[16] See e.g. R. Müllerson, 'The Interplay of Objective and Subjective Elements in Customary Law' in *International Law – Theory and Practice* (ed. K. Wellens), The Hague, 1998, p. 161.

[17] See e.g. D. Anzilotti, *Corso di Diritto Internazionale,* 3rd edn, 1928, pp. 73–6; K. Strupp, 'Les Règles Générales du Droit International de la Paix', 47 HR, 1934, p. 263; Tunkin, *Theory of International Law,* pp. 113–33, and 'Remarks on the Juridical Nature of Customary Norms of International Law', 49 *California Law Review,* 1961, pp. 419–21, and B. Cheng, 'United Nations Resolutions on Outer Space: "Instant" International Customary Law?', 5 *Indian Journal of International Law,* 1965, p. 23.

of no tremendous consequence. Kelsen, for one, has written that it is the courts that have the discretion to decide whether any set of usages is such as to create a custom and that the subjective perception of the particular state or states is not called upon to give the final verdict as to its legality or not.[18]

The material fact

The actual practice engaged in by states constitutes the initial factor to be brought into account. There are a number of points to be considered concerning the nature of a particular practice by states, including its duration, consistency, repetition and generality. As far as the duration is concerned, most countries specify a recognised time-scale for the acceptance of a practice as a customary rule within their municipal systems. This can vary from 'time immemorial' in the English common law dating back to 1189, to figures from thirty or forty years on the Continent.

In international law there is no rigid time element and it will depend upon the circumstances of the case and the nature of the usage in question. In certain fields, such as air and space law, the rules have developed quickly; in others, the process is much slower. Duration is thus not the most important of the components of state practice.[19] The essence of custom is to be sought elsewhere.

The basic rule as regards continuity and repetition was laid down in the *Asylum* case decided by the International Court of Justice (ICJ) in 1950.[20] The Court declared that a customary rule must be 'in accordance with a constant and uniform usage practised by the States in question'.[21] The case concerned Haya de la Torre, a Peruvian, who was sought by his government after an unsuccessful revolt. He was granted asylum by Colombia in its embassy in Lima, but Peru refused to issue a safe conduct to permit Torre to leave the country. Colombia brought the matter before

---

[18] 'Théorie du Droit International Coutumier', 1 *Revue International de la Théorie du Droit*, 1939, pp. 253, 264–6. See also P. Guggenheim, *Traité de Droit International Public*, Paris, 1953, pp. 46–8; T. Gihl, 'The Legal Character of Sources of International Law', 1 *Scandinavian Studies in Law*, 1957, pp. 53, 84, and *Oppenheim's International Law*, pp. 27–31.

[19] See D'Amato, *Concept of Custom*, pp. 56–8, and Akehurst, 'Custom as a Source', pp. 15–16. Judge Negulesco in an unfortunate phrase emphasised that custom required immemorial usage: *European Commission of the Danube*, PCIJ, Series B, No. 14, 1927, p. 105; 4 AD, p. 126. See also Brownlie, *Principles*, p. 7, and the *North Sea Continental Shelf* cases, ICJ Reports, 1969, pp. 3, 43; 41 ILR, pp. 29, 72.

[20] ICJ Reports, 1950, p. 266; 17 ILR, p. 280.

[21] ICJ Reports, 1950, pp. 276–7; 17 ILR, p. 284.

the International Court of Justice and requested a decision recognising that it (Colombia) was competent to define Torre's offence, as to whether it was criminal as Peru maintained, or political, in which case asylum and a safe conduct could be allowed.

The Court, in characterising the nature of a customary rule, held that it had to constitute the expression of a right appertaining to one state (Colombia) and a duty incumbent upon another (Peru). However, the Court felt that in the *Asylum* litigation, state practices had been so uncertain and contradictory as not to amount to a 'constant and uniform usage' regarding the unilateral qualification of the offence in question.[22] The issue involved here dealt with a regional custom pertaining only to Latin America and it may be argued that the same approach need not necessarily be followed where a general custom is alleged and that in the latter instance a lower standard of proof would be upheld.[23]

The ICJ emphasised its view that some degree of uniformity amongst state practices was essential before a custom could come into existence in the *Anglo-Norwegian Fisheries* case.[24] The United Kingdom, in its arguments against the Norwegian method of measuring the breadth of the territorial sea, referred to an alleged rule of custom whereby a straight line may be drawn across bays of less than ten miles from one projection to the other, which could then be regarded as the baseline for the measurement of the territorial sea. The Court dismissed this by pointing out that the actual practice of states did not justify the creation of any such custom. In other words, there had been insufficient uniformity of behaviour.

In the *North Sea Continental Shelf* cases,[25] which involved a dispute between Germany on the one hand and Holland and Denmark on the other over the delimitation of the continental shelf, the ICJ remarked that state practice, 'including that of states whose interests are specially affected', had to be 'both extensive and virtually uniform in the sense of the provision invoked'. This was held to be indispensable to the formation of a new rule of customary international law.[26] However, the Court emphasised in the *Nicaragua* v. *United States* case[27] that it was not necessary that the

---

[22] *Ibid.*   [23] See further below, p. 92.

[24] ICJ Reports, 1951, pp. 116, 131 and 138; 18 ILR, p. 86.

[25] ICJ Reports, 1969, p. 3; 41 ILR, p. 29.

[26] ICJ Reports, 1969, p. 43; 41 ILR, p. 72. Note that the Court was dealing with the creation of a custom on the basis of what had been purely a treaty rule. See Akehurst, 'Custom as a Source', p. 21, especially footnote 5. See also the *Paquete Habana* case, 175 US 677 (1900) and the *Lotus* case, PCIJ, Series A, No. 10, 1927, p. 18; 4 AD, p. 153.

[27] ICJ Reports, 1986, p. 14; 76 ILR, p. 349.

practice in question had to be 'in absolutely rigorous conformity' with the purported customary rule. The Court continued:

> In order to deduce the existence of customary rules, the Court deems it sufficient that the conduct of states should, in general, be consistent with such rules, and that instances of state conduct inconsistent with a given rule should generally have been treated as breaches of that rule, not as indications of the recognition of a new rule.[28]

The threshold that needs to be attained before a legally binding custom can be created will depend both upon the nature of the alleged rule and the opposition it arouses. This partly relates to the problem of ambiguity where it is not possible to point to the alleged custom with any degree of clarity, as in the *Asylum* case where a variety of conflicting and contradictory evidence had been brought forward.

On the other hand, an unsubstantiated claim by a state cannot be accepted because it would amount to unilateral law-making and compromise a reasonably impartial system of international law. If a proposition meets with a great deal of opposition then it would be an undesirable fiction to ignore this and talk of an established rule. Another relevant factor is the strength of the prior rule which is purportedly overthrown.[29] For example, the customary law relating to a state's sovereignty over its airspace developed very quickly in the years immediately before and during the First World War. Similarly, the principle of non-sovereignty over the space route followed by artificial satellites came into being soon after the launching of the first sputniks. Bin Cheng has argued that in such circumstances repetition is not at all necessary provided the *opinio juris* could be clearly established. Thus, 'instant' customary law is possible.[30]

This contention that single acts may create custom has been criticised, particularly in view of the difficulties of proving customary rules any other way but through a series of usages.[31] Nevertheless, the conclusion must be that it is the international context which plays the vital part in the creation of custom. In a society constantly faced with new situations because of the dynamics of progress, there is a clear need for a reasonably speedy method of responding to such changes by a system of prompt rule-formation. In

---

[28] ICJ Reports, 1986, p. 98; 76 ILR, p. 432.
[29] See D'Amato, *Concept of Custom*, pp. 60–1, and Akehurst, 'Custom as a Source', p. 19. See also Judge Alvarez, the *Anglo-Norwegian Fisheries* case, ICJ Reports, 1951, pp. 116, 152; 18 ILR, pp. 86, 105, and Judge Loder, the *Lotus* case, PCIJ, Series A, No. 10, 1927, pp. 18, 34.
[30] Cheng, 'United Nations Resolutions'.
[31] See e.g. Nguyen Quoc Dinh *et al.*, *Droit International Public*, pp. 325–6.

new areas of law, customs can be quickly established by state practices by virtue of the newness of the situations involved, the lack of contrary rules to be surmounted and the overwhelming necessity to preserve a sense of regulation in international relations.

One particular analogy that has been used to illustrate the general nature of customary law was considered by de Visscher. He likened the growth of custom to the gradual formation of a road across vacant land. After an initial uncertainty as to direction, the majority of users begin to follow the same line which becomes a single path. Not long elapses before that path is transformed into a road accepted as the only regular way, even though it is not possible to state at which precise moment this latter change occurs. And so it is with the formation of a custom. De Visscher develops this idea by reflecting that just as some make heavier footprints than others due to their greater weight, the more influential states of the world mark the way with more vigour and tend to become the guarantors and defenders of the way forward.[32]

The reasons why a particular state acts in a certain way are varied but are closely allied to how it perceives its interests. This in turn depends upon the power and role of the state and its international standing. Accordingly, custom should to some extent mirror the perceptions of the majority of states, since it is based upon usages which are practised by nations as they express their power and their hopes and fears. But it is inescapable that some states are more influential and powerful than others and that their activities should be regarded as of greater significance. This is reflected in international law so that custom may be created by a few states, provided those states are intimately connected with the issue at hand, whether because of their wealth and power or because of their special relationship with the subject-matter of the practice, as for example maritime nations and sea law. Law cannot be divorced from politics or power and this is one instance of that proposition.[33]

The influence of the United Kingdom, for example, on the development of the law of the sea and prize law in the nineteenth century when it was at the height of its power, was predominant. A number of propositions later accepted as part of international customary law appeared this way.

---

[32] De Visscher, *Theory and Reality*, p. 149. See also Lauterpacht, *Development of International Law*, p. 368; P. Cobbett, *Leading Cases on International Law*, 4th edn, London, 1922, p. 5, and Akehurst, 'Custom as a Source', pp. 22–3.

[33] See e.g. the *North Sea Continental Shelf* cases, ICJ Reports, 1969, pp. 3, 42–3; 41 ILR, pp. 29, 71–3.

Among many instances of this, one can point to navigation procedures. Similarly, the impact of the Soviet Union (now Russia) and the United States on space law has been paramount.[34]

One can conclude by stating that for a custom to be accepted and recognised it must have the concurrence of the major powers in that particular field. A regulation regarding the breadth of the territorial sea is unlikely to be treated as law if the great maritime nations do not agree to or acquiesce in it, no matter how many landlocked states demand it. Other countries may propose ideas and institute pressure, but without the concurrence of those most interested, it cannot amount to a rule of customary law. This follows from the nature of the international system where all may participate but the views of those with greater power carry greater weight.

Accordingly, the duration and generality of a practice may take second place to the relative importance of the states precipitating the formation of a new customary rule in any given field. Universality is not required, but some correlation with power is. Some degree of continuity must be maintained but this again depends upon the context of operation and the nature of the usage.

Those elements reflect the external manifestations of a practice and establish that it is in existence and exhibited as such. That does not mean that it is law and this factor will be considered in the next subsection. But it does mean that all states who take the trouble can discover its existence. This factor of conspicuousness emphasises both the importance of the context within which the usage operates and the more significant elements of the overt act which affirms the existence of a custom.

The question is raised at this stage of how significant a failure to act is. Just how important is it when a state, or more particularly a major state, does not participate in a practice? Can it be construed as acquiescence in the performance of the usage? Or, on the other hand, does it denote indifference implying the inability of the practice to become a custom until a decision one way or the other has been made? Failures to act are in themselves just as much evidence of a state's attitudes as are actions. They similarly reflect the way in which a nation approaches its environment. Britain consistently fails to attack France, while Chad consistently fails to send a man to the moon. But does this mean that Britain recognises a

---

[34] See e.g. Cheng, 'United Nations Resolutions'; C. Christol, *The Modern International Law of Outer Space*, New York, 1982, and Christol, *Space Law: Past, Present and Future*, The Hague, 1991. See further below, chapter 10.

rule not to attack its neighbour and that Chad accepts a custom not to launch rockets to the moon? Of course, the answer is in the first instance yes, and in the second example no. Thus, a failure to act can arise from either a legal obligation not to act, or an incapacity or unwillingness in the particular circumstances to act. Indeed, it has been maintained that the continued habit of not taking actions in certain situations may lead to the formation of a legal rule.[35]

The danger of saying that a failure to act over a long period creates a negative custom, that is a rule actually not to do it, can be shown by remarking on the absurdity of the proposition that a continual failure to act until the late 1950s is evidence of a legal rule not to send artificial satellites or rockets into space. On the other hand, where a particular rule of behaviour is established it can be argued that abstention from protest by states may amount to agreement with that rule.

In the particular circumstances of the *Lotus* case[36] the Permanent Court of International Justice, the predecessor of the International Court of Justice, laid down a high standard by declaring that abstention could only give rise to the recognition of a custom if it was based on a conscious duty to abstain. In other words, states had actually to be aware that they were not acting a particular way because they were under a definite obligation not to act that way. The decision has been criticised and would appear to cover categories of non-acts based on legal obligations, but not to refer to instances where, by simply not acting as against a particular rule in existence, states are tacitly accepting the legality and relevance of that rule.

It should be mentioned, however, that acquiescence must be based upon full knowledge of the rule invoked. Where a failure to take a course of action is in some way connected or influenced or accompanied by a lack of knowledge of all the relevant circumstances, then it cannot be interpreted as acquiescence.

What is state practice?

Some of the ingredients of state activities have been surveyed and attempts made to place them in some kind of relevant context. But what is state practice? Does it cover every kind of behaviour initiated by the state, or

---

[35] See e.g. Tunkin, *Theory of International Law*, pp. 116–17. But cf. D'Amato, *Concept of Custom*, pp. 61–3 and 88–9.

[36] PCIJ, Series A, No. 10, 1927, p. 18; 4 AD, p. 153.

is it limited to actual, positive actions? To put it more simply, does it include such things as speeches, informal documents and governmental statements or is it restricted to what states actually do?

It is how states behave in practice that forms the basis of customary law, but evidence of what a state does can be obtained from numerous sources. Obvious examples include administrative acts, legislation, decisions of courts and activities on the international stage, for example treaty-making.[37] A state is not a living entity, but consists of governmental departments and thousands of officials, and state activity is spread throughout a whole range of national organs. There are the state's legal officers, legislative institutions, courts, diplomatic agents and political leaders. Each of these engages in activity which relates to the international field and therefore one has to examine all such material sources and more in order to discover evidence of what states do.[38]

The obvious way to find out how countries are behaving is to read the newspapers, consult historical records, listen to what governmental authorities are saying and peruse the many official publications. There are also memoirs of various past leaders, official manuals on legal questions, diplomatic interchanges and the opinions of national legal advisors. All these methods are valuable in seeking to determine actual state practice.

In addition, one may note resolutions in the General Assembly, comments made by governments on drafts produced by the International Law Commission, decisions of the international judicial institutions, decisions of national courts, treaties and the general practice of international organisations.[39]

---

[37] See e.g. Pellet, 'Article 38', p. 751, and *Congo* v. *Belgium*, ICJ Reports, 2002, pp. 3, 23–4; 128 ILR, pp. 60, 78–80.

[38] See e.g. *Yearbook of the ILC*, 1950, vol. II, pp. 368–72, and the *Interhandel* case, ICJ Reports, 1959, p. 27. Note also Brierly's comment that not all contentions put forward on behalf of a state represent that state's settled or impartial opinion, *The Law of Nations*, 6th edn, Oxford, 1963, p. 60. See also Brownlie, *Principles*, p. 6, and Akehurst, 'Custom as a Source', p. 2.

[39] The United States has produced an extensive series of publications covering its practice in international law. See the Digests of International Law produced by Wharton (1887), Moore (1906) and Whiteman (1963–70). From 1973 to 1980 an annual *Digest of US Practice in International Law* has been produced, while three composite volumes covering the years 1981–8 have appeared. The series resumed with effect from the year 2000. See also H. A. Smith, *Great Britain and the Law of Nations*, London, 2 vols., 1932–5; A. D. McNair, *International Law Opinions*, Cambridge, 3 vols., 1956; C. Parry, *British Digest of International Law*, London, 1965, and E. Lauterpacht, *British Practice in International Law*, London, 1963–7. Several yearbooks now produce sections devoted to national practice, e.g. *British Yearbook of International Law* and *Annuaire Français de Droit International*.

International organisations in fact may be instrumental in the creation of customary law. For example, the Advisory Opinion of the International Court of Justice declaring that the United Nations possessed international personality was partly based on the actual behaviour of the UN.[40] The International Law Commission has pointed out that 'records of the cumulative practice of international organisations may be regarded as evidence of customary international law with reference to states' relations to the organisations'.[41] The International Court has also noted that evidence of the existence of rules and principles may be found in resolutions adopted by the General Assembly and the Security Council of the United Nations.[42]

States' municipal laws may in certain circumstances form the basis of customary rules. In the *Scotia* case decided by the US Supreme Court in 1871,[43] a British ship had sunk an American vessel on the high seas. The Court held that British navigational procedures established by an Act of Parliament formed the basis of the relevant international custom since other states had legislated in virtually identical terms. Accordingly, the American vessel, in not displaying the correct lights, was at fault. The view has also been expressed that mere claims as distinct from actual physical acts cannot constitute state practice. This is based on the precept that 'until it [a state] takes enforcement action, the claim has little value as a prediction of what the state will actually do'.[44] But as has been demonstrated this is decidedly a minority view.[45] Claims and conventions of states in various contexts have been adduced as evidence of state practice and it is logical that this should be so,[46] though the weight to be attached to such claims, may, of course, vary according to the circumstances. This

---

[40] The *Reparation* case, ICJ Reports, 1949, p. 174; 16 AD, p. 318. See also the *Reservations to the Genocide Convention* case, ICJ Reports, 1951, pp. 15, 25; 18 ILR, p. 364.

[41] *Yearbook of the ILC*, 1950, vol. II, pp. 368–72. See also Akehurst, 'Custom as a Source', p. 12.

[42] See the Court's advisory opinion in the *Construction of a Wall* case, ICJ Reports, 2004, pp. 136, 171; 129 ILR, pp. 37, 89–90.

[43] 14 Wallace 170 (1871). See also the *Nottebohm* case, ICJ Reports, 1955, pp. 4, 22; 22 ILR, p. 349, and the *Paquete Habana* case, 175 US 677 (1900).

[44] D'Amato, *Concept of Custom*, pp. 88 and 50–1. See also Judge Read (dissenting), the *Anglo-Norwegian Fisheries* case, ICJ Reports, 1951, pp. 116, 191; 18 ILR, pp. 86, 132.

[45] Akehurst, 'Custom as a Source', pp. 2–3. See also Thirlway, *International Customary Law*, p. 58.

[46] E.g. the *Asylum* case, ICJ Reports, 1950, pp. 266, 277; 17 ILR, p. 280; the *Rights of US Nationals in Morocco* case, ICJ Reports, 1952, pp. 176, 200, 209; 19 ILR, p. 255, and the *North Sea Continental Shelf* cases, ICJ Reports, 1969, pp. 3, 32–3, 47 and 53; 41 ILR, p. 29. See also the *Fisheries Jurisdiction* cases, ICJ Reports, 1974, pp. 3, 47, 56–8, 81–8, 119–20, 135 and 161; 55 ILR, p. 238.

approach is clearly the correct one since the process of claims and counter-claims is one recognised method by which states communicate to each other their perceptions of the status of international rules and norms. In this sense they operate in the same way as physical acts. Whether *in abstracto* or with regard to a particular situation, they constitute the raw material out of which may be fashioned rules of international law.[47] It is suggested that the formulation that 'state practice covers any act or state-ments by a state from which views about customary law may be inferred',[48] is substantially correct. However, it should be noted that not all elements of practice are equal in their weight and the value to be given to state conduct will depend upon its nature and provenance.

Opinio juris[49]

Once one has established the existence of a specified usage, it becomes necessary to consider how the state views its own behaviour. Is it to be regarded as a moral or political or legal act or statement? The *opinio juris*, or belief that a state activity is legally obligatory, is the factor which turns the usage into a custom and renders it part of the rules of international law. To put it slightly differently, states will behave a certain way because they are convinced it is binding upon them to do so.

The Permanent Court of International Justice expressed this point of view when it dealt with the *Lotus* case.[50] The issue at hand concerned a collision on the high seas (where international law applies) between the *Lotus*, a French ship, and the *Boz-Kourt*, a Turkish ship. Several people aboard the latter ship were drowned and Turkey alleged negligence by the French officer of the watch. When the *Lotus* reached Istanbul, the French officer was arrested on a charge of manslaughter and the case turned on whether Turkey had jurisdiction to try him. Among the various

---

[47] But see Thirlway, *International Customary Law*, pp. 58–9.

[48] Akehurst, 'Custom as a Source', p. 10. This would also include omissions and silence by states: *ibid.*

[49] *Ibid.*, pp. 31–42, and D'Amato, *Concept of Custom*, pp. 66–72. See also Pellet, 'Article 38', p. 753; Mendelson, 'Formation', p. 245; Bos, *Methodology*, pp. 236 ff.; P. Haggenmacher, 'Des Deux Éléments du Droit Coutumier dans la Pratique de la Cour Internationale', 91 *Revue Générale de Droit International Public*, 1985, p. 5; O. Elias, 'The Nature of the Subjective Element in Customary International Law', 44 ICLQ, 1995, p. 501; I. M. Lobo de Souza, 'The Role of State Consent in the Customary Process', 44 ICLQ, 1995, p. 521, and B. Cheng, '*Opinio Juris:* A Key Concept in International Law that is Much Misunderstood' in *International Law in the Post-Cold War World* (eds. S. Yee and W. Tieya), London, 2001, p. 56.

[50] PCIJ, Series A, No. 10, 1927, p. 18; 4 AD, p. 153.

arguments adduced, the French maintained that there existed a rule of customary law to the effect that the flag state of the accused (France) had exclusive jurisdiction in such cases and that accordingly the national state of the victim (Turkey) was barred from trying him. To justify this, France referred to the absence of previous criminal prosecutions by such states in similar situations and from this deduced tacit consent in the practice which therefore became a legal custom.

The Court rejected this and declared that even if such a practice of abstention from instituting criminal proceedings could be proved in fact, it would not amount to a custom. It held that 'only if such abstention were based on their [the states] being conscious of a duty to abstain would it be possible to speak of an international custom'.[51] Thus the essential ingredient of obligation was lacking and the practice remained a practice, nothing more.

A similar approach occurred in the *North Sea Continental Shelf* cases.[52] In the general process of delimiting the continental shelf of the North Sea in pursuance of oil and gas exploration, lines were drawn dividing the whole area into national spheres. However, West Germany could not agree with either Holland or Denmark over the respective boundary lines and the matter came before the International Court of Justice.

Article 6 of the Geneva Convention on the Continental Shelf of 1958 provided that where agreement could not be reached, and unless special circumstances justified a different approach, the boundary line was to be determined in accordance with the principle of equidistance from the nearest points of the baselines from which the breadth of the territorial sea of each state is measured. This would mean a series of lines drawn at the point where Germany met Holland on the one side and Denmark on the other and projected outwards into the North Sea. However, because Germany's coastline is concave, such equidistant lines would converge and enclose a relatively small triangle of the North Sea. The Federal Republic had signed but not ratified the 1958 Geneva Convention and was therefore not bound by its terms. The question thus was whether a case could be made out that the 'equidistance–special circumstances principle' had been absorbed into customary law and was accordingly binding upon Germany.

The Court concluded in the negative and held that the provision in the Geneva Convention did not reflect an already existing custom. It was

---

[51] PCIJ, Series A, No. 10, 1927, p. 28; 4 AD, p. 159.
[52] ICJ Reports, 1969, p. 3; 41 ILR, p. 29.

emphasised that when the International Law Commission had considered this point in the draft treaty which formed the basis of discussion at Geneva, the principle of equidistance had been proposed with considerable hesitation, somewhat on an experimental basis and not at all as an emerging rule of customary international law.[53] The issue then turned on whether practice subsequent to the Convention had created a customary rule. The Court answered in the negative and declared that although time was not of itself a decisive factor (only three years had elapsed before the proceedings were brought):

> an indispensable requirement would be that within the period in question, short though it might be, state practice, including that of states whose interests are specially affected, should have been both extensive and virtually uniform in the sense of the provision invoked, and should moreover have occurred in such a way as to show a general recognition that a rule of law or legal obligation is involved.[54]

This approach was maintained by the Court in the *Nicaragua* case[55] and express reference was made to the *North Sea Continental Shelf* cases. The Court noted that:

> for a new customary rule to be formed, not only must the acts concerned 'amount to a settled practice', but they must be accompanied by the *opinio juris sive necessitatis*. Either the States taking such action or other States in a position to react to it, must have behaved so that their conduct is 'evidence of a belief that this practice is rendered obligatory by the existence of a rule of law requiring it. The need for such a belief, i.e. the existence of a subjective element, is implicit in the very notion of the *opinio juris sive necessitatis*.'[56]

It is thus clear that the Court has adopted and maintained a high threshold with regard to the overt proving of the subjective constituent of customary law formation.

The great problem connected with the *opinio juris* is that if it calls for behaviour in accordance with law, how can new customary rules be created since that obviously requires action different from or

---

[53] ICJ Reports, 1969, pp. 32–41.
[54] *Ibid.*, p. 43. See also e.g. the *Asylum* case, ICJ Reports, 1950, pp. 266, 277; 17 ILR, p. 280, and the *Right of Passage* case, ICJ Reports, 1960, pp. 6, 42–3; 31 ILR, pp. 23, 55.
[55] ICJ Reports, 1986, p. 14; 76 ILR, p. 349.
[56] ICJ Reports, 1986, pp. 108–9; 76 ILR, pp. 442–3, citing ICJ Reports, 1969, p. 44; 41 ILR, p. 73.

contrary to what until then is regarded as law? If a country claims a three-mile territorial sea in the belief that this is legal, how can the rule be changed in customary law to allow claims of, for example, twelve miles, since that cannot also be in accordance with prevailing law?[57] Obviously if one takes a restricted view of the psychological aspects, then logically the law will become stultified and this demonstrably has not happened.

Thus, one has to treat the matter in terms of a process whereby states behave in a certain way in the belief that such behaviour is law or is becoming law. It will then depend upon how other states react as to whether this process of legislation is accepted or rejected. It follows that rigid definitions as to legality have to be modified to see whether the legitimating stamp of state activity can be provided or not. If a state proclaims a twelve-mile limit to its territorial sea in the belief that although the three-mile limit has been accepted law, the circumstances are so altering that a twelve-mile limit might now be treated as becoming law, it is vindicated if other states follow suit and a new rule of customary law is established. If other states reject the proposition, then the projected rule withers away and the original rule stands, reinforced by state practice and common acceptance. As the Court itself noted in the *Nicaragua* case,[58] '[r]eliance by a State on a novel right or an unprecedented exception to the principle might, if shared in principle by other States, tend towards a modification of customary international law'. The difficulty in this kind of approach is that it is sometimes hard to pinpoint exactly when one rule supersedes another, but that is a complication inherent in the nature of custom. Change is rarely smooth but rather spasmodic.

This means taking a more flexible view of the *opinio juris* and tying it more firmly with the overt manifestations of a custom into the context of national and international behaviour. This should be done to accommodate the idea of an action which, while contrary to law, contains the germ of a new law and relates to the difficulty of actually proving that a state, in behaving a certain way, does so in the belief that it is in accordance with the law. An extreme expression of this approach is to infer or deduce the *opinio juris* from the material acts. Judge Tanaka, in his Dissenting Opinion in the *North Sea Continental Shelf* cases, remarked that there was:

---

[57] See Akehurst, 'Custom as a Source', pp. 32–4 for attempts made to deny or minimise the need for *opinio juris*.
[58] ICJ Reports, 1986, pp. 14, 109; 76 ILR, pp. 349, 443.

no other way than to ascertain the existence of *opinio juris* from the fact
of the external existence of a certain custom and its necessity felt in the
international community, rather than to seek evidence as to the subjective
motives for each example of State practice.[59]

However, states must be made aware that when one state takes a course
of action, it does so because it regards it as within the confines of international law, and not as, for example, purely a political or moral gesture.
There has to be an aspect of legality about the behaviour and the acting
state will have to confirm that this is so, so that the international community can easily distinguish legal from non-legal practices. This is essential
to the development and presentation of a legal framework amongst the
states.[60]

Faced with the difficulty in practice of proving the existence of the
opinio juris, increasing reference has been made to conduct within international organisations. This is so particularly with regard to the United
Nations. The International Court of Justice has in a number of cases
utilised General Assembly resolutions as confirming the existence of
the *opinio juris*, focusing on the content of the resolution or resolutions in question and the conditions of their adoption.[61] The key, however, is the attitude taken by the states concerned, whether as parties
to a particular treaty or as participants in the adoption of a UN resolution.[62] The Court has also referred to major codification conventions

---

[59] ICJ Reports, 1969, pp. 3, 176; 41 ILR, pp. 29, 171. Lauterpacht wrote that one should
regard all uniform conduct of governments as evidencing the *opinio juris*, except where
the conduct in question was not accompanied by such intention: *The Development of
International Law*, p. 580; but cf. Cheng, 'Custom: The Future', p. 36, and Cheng, 'United
Nations Resolutions', pp. 530–2.

[60] Note D'Amato's view that to become a custom, a practice has to be preceded or accompanied by the 'articulation' of a rule, which will put states on notice than an action etc.
will have legal implications: *Concept of Custom*, p. 75. Cf. Akehurst, 'Custom as a Source',
pp. 35–6, who also puts forward his view that 'the practice of states needs to be accompanied by *statements* that something is already law before it can become law': such statements
need not be beliefs as to the truths of the given situation, *ibid.*, p. 37. Akehurst also draws a
distinction between permissive rules, which do not require express statements as to *opinio
juris*, and duty-imposing rules, which do: *ibid.*, pp. 37–8.

[61] See e.g. the *Legality of the Threat or Use of Nuclear Weapons* case, ICJ Reports, 1996,
pp. 226, 254–5; 110 ILR, p. 163. See also the *Western Sahara* case, ICJ Reports, 1975,
pp. 31–3; the *East Timor* case, ICJ Reports, 1995, pp. 90, 102; 105 ILR, p. 226; the *Nicaragua*
case, ICJ Reports, 1986, pp. 14, 100, 101 and 106; 76 ILR, p. 349; and the *Construction of
a Wall* case, ICJ Reports, 2004, pp. 136, 171–2; 129 ILR, pp. 37, 89–90.

[62] See the *Nicaragua* case, ICJ Reports, 1986, pp. 14, 99–100.

for the same purpose,[63] and to the work of the International Law Commission.[64]

Protest, acquiescence and change in customary law[65]

Customary law is thus established by virtue of a pattern of claim, absence of protest by states particularly interested in the matter at hand and acquiescence by other states.[66] Together with related notions such as recognition, admissions and estoppel, such conduct or abstinence from conduct forms part of a complex framework within which legal principles are created and deemed applicable to states.[67]

The Chamber of the International Court in the *Gulf of Maine* case defined acquiescence as 'equivalent to tacit recognition manifested by unilateral conduct which the other party may interpret as consent' and as founded upon the principles of good faith and equity.[68] Generally, where states are seen to acquiesce[69] in the behaviour of other states without protesting against them, the assumption must be that such behaviour is accepted as legitimate.[70]

Some writers have maintained that acquiescence can amount to consent to a customary rule and that the absence of protest implies agreement.

[63] See e.g. the *North Sea Continental Shelf* cases, ICJ Reports, 1969, pp. 3, 28–32 with regard to the 1958 Continental Shelf Convention and e.g. among many cases, *Cameroon v. Nigeria*, ICJ Reports, 2002, pp. 303, 429–30 with regard to the Vienna Convention on the Law of Treaties, 1969.

[64] See e.g. the *Gabčíkovo–Nagymaros* case, ICJ Reports, 1997, pp. 7, 38–42 and 46; 116 ILR, pp. 1, 47–51 and 55.

[65] See H. Lauterpacht, 'Sovereignty over Submarine Areas', 27 BYIL, 1950, p. 376; I. MacGibbon, 'Some Observations on the Part of Protest in International Law', 29 BYIL, 1953, p. 293, and MacGibbon, 'Customary International Law and Acquiescence', 33 BYIL, 1957, p. 115; Wolfke, *Custom*, pp. 157–65, and I. Sinclair, 'Estoppel and Acquiescence' in *Fifty Years of the International Court of Justice* (eds. A. V. Lowe and M. Fitzmaurice), Cambridge, 1996, p. 104.

[66] See, for a good example, the decision of the International Court in the *El Salvador/Honduras* case, ICJ Reports, 1992, pp. 351, 601; 97 ILR, pp. 266, 517, with regard to the joint sovereignty over the historic waters of the Gulf of Fonseca beyond the territorial sea of the three coastal states.

[67] See e.g. Sinclair, 'Estoppel and Acquiescence', p. 104 and below, chapter 10, p. 515.

[68] ICJ Reports, 1984, pp. 246, 305; 71 ILR, p. 74.

[69] Note that the Court has stated that 'the idea of acquiescence ... presupposes freedom of will', *Burkina Faso/Mali*, ICJ Reports, 1986, pp. 554, 597; 80 ILR, p. 459.

[70] See e.g. *Grand-Duchy of Luxembourg v. Cie. Luxembourgeoise de Télédiffusion*, 91 ILR, pp. 281, 286.

In other words where a state or states take action which they declare to be legal, the silence of other states can be used as an expression of *opinio juris* or concurrence in the new legal rule. This means that actual protests are called for to break the legitimising process.[71]

In the *Lotus* case, the Court held that 'only if such abstention were based on their [the states] being conscious of having a duty to abstain would it be possible to speak of an international custom'.[72] Thus, one cannot infer a rule prohibiting certain action merely because states do not indulge in that activity. But the question of not reacting when a state behaves a certain way is a slightly different one. It would seem that where a new rule is created in new fields of international law, for example space law, acquiescence by other states is to be regarded as reinforcing the rule whether it stems from actual agreement or lack of interest depending always upon the particular circumstances of the case. Acquiescence in a new rule which deviates from an established custom is more problematic.

The decision in the *Anglo-Norwegian Fisheries* case[73] may appear to suggest that where a state acts contrary to an established customary rule and other states acquiesce in this, then that state is to be treated as not bound by the original rule. The Court noted that 'in any event the . . . rule would appear to be inapplicable as against Norway inasmuch as she had always opposed any attempt to apply it to the Norwegian coast'.[74] In other words, a state opposing the existence of a custom from its inception would not be bound by it, but the problem of one or more states seeking to dissent from recognised customs by adverse behaviour coupled with the acquiescence or non-reaction of other states remains unsettled.

States fail to protest for very many reasons. A state might not wish to give offence gratuitously or it might wish to reinforce political ties or other diplomatic and political considerations may be relevant. It could be that to protest over every single act with which a state does not agree would be an excessive requirement. It is, therefore, unrealistic to expect every state

---

[71] See e.g. MacGibbon, 'Customary International Law', p. 131, and H. S. McDougal *et al.*, *Studies in World Public Order*, New Haven, 1960, pp. 763–72.

[72] PCIJ, Series A, No. 10, 1927, p. 28; 4 ILR, p. 159.

[73] ICJ Reports, 1951, p. 116; 18 ILR, p. 86.

[74] ICJ Reports, 1951, p. 131; 18 ILR, p. 93. See also the *North Sea Continental Shelf* cases, ICJ Reports, 1969, pp. 3, 26–7; 41 ILR, pp. 29, 55–6, and the *Asylum* case, ICJ Reports, 1950, pp. 266, 277–8; 17 ILR, pp. 280, 285.

to react to every single act of every other state. If one accepted that a failure to protest validated a derogation from an established custom in every case then scores of special relationships would emerge between different states depending upon acquiescence and protest. In many cases a protest might be purely formal or part of diplomatic manoeuvring designed to exert pressure in a totally different field and thus not intended to alter legal relationships.

Where a new rule which contradicts a prior rule is maintained by a large number of states, the protests of a few states would not overrule it, and the abstention from reaction by other countries would merely reinforce it. Constant protest on the part of a particular state when reinforced by the acquiescence of other states might create a recognised exception to the rule, but it will depend to a great extent on the facts of the situation and the views of the international community. Behaviour contrary to a custom contains within itself the seeds of a new rule and if it is endorsed by other nations, the previous law will disappear and be replaced, or alternatively there could be a period of time during which the two customs co-exist until one of them is generally accepted,[75] as was the position for many years with regard to the limits of the territorial sea.[76] It follows from the above, therefore, that customary rules are binding upon all states except for such states as have dissented from the start of that custom.[77] This raises the question of new states and custom, for the logic of the traditional approach would be for such states to be bound by all existing customs as at the date of independence. The opposite view, based upon the consent theory of law, would permit such states to choose which customs to adhere to at that stage, irrespective of the attitude of other states.[78] However, since such an approach could prove highly disruptive, the proviso is often made that by entering into relations without reservation with other states, new states signify their acceptance of the totality of international law.[79]

---

[75] See also protests generally: Akehurst, 'Custom as a Source', pp. 38–42.
[76] See below, chapter 11, p. 568.
[77] See e.g. the *North Sea Continental Shelf* cases, ICJ Reports, 1969, pp. 3, 38, 130; 41 ILR, pp. 29, 67, 137, and *The Third US Restatement of Foreign Relations Law*, St Paul, 1987, vol. I, pp. 25–6. See also T. Stein, 'The Approach of the Different Drummer: The Principle of the Persistent Objector in International Law', 26 *Harvard International Law Journal*, 1985, p. 457, and J. Charney, 'The Persistent Objector Rule and the Development of Customary International Law', 56 BYIL, 1985, p. 1.
[78] See e.g. Tunkin, *Theory of International Law*, p. 129.   [79] *Ibid.*

Regional and local custom[80]

It is possible for rules to develop which will bind only a set group of states, such as those in Latin America,[81] or indeed just two states.[82] Such an approach may be seen as part of the need for 'respect for regional legal traditions'.[83]

In the *Asylum* case,[84] the International Court of Justice discussed the Colombian claim of a regional or local custom peculiar to the Latin American states, which would validate its position over the granting of asylum. The Court declared that the 'party which relies on a custom of this kind must prove that this custom is established in such a manner that it has become binding on the other party'.[85] It found that such a custom could not be proved because of uncertain and contradictory evidence.

In such cases, the standard of proof required, especially as regards the obligation accepted by the party against whom the local custom is maintained, is higher than in cases where an ordinary or general custom is alleged.

In the *Right of Passage over Indian Territory* case,[86] Portugal claimed that there existed a right of passage over Indian territory as between the Portuguese enclaves, and this was upheld by the International Court of Justice over India's objections that no local custom could be established between only two states. The Court declared that it was satisfied that there had in the past existed a constant and uniform practice allowing free passage and that the 'practice was accepted as law by the parties and has given rise to a right and a correlative obligation'.[87] More generally, the Court stated that 'Where therefore the Court finds a practice clearly established between two States which was accepted by the Parties as

---

[80] See Akehurst, 'Custom as a Source', pp. 29–31; Thirlway, 'Supplement', p. 105; Pellet, 'Article 38', p. 762; D'Amato, *Concept of Custom*, chapter 8; G. Cohen-Jonathan, 'La Coutume Locale', AFDI, 1961, p. 133, and Wolfke, *Custom*, pp. 88–90. Local custom is sometimes referred to as regional or special custom.

[81] See e.g. H. Gros Espiel, 'La Doctrine du Droit International en Amérique Latine avant la Première Conférence Panaméricaine', 3 *Journal of the History of International Law*, 2001, p. 1.

[82] Note the claim by Honduras in the *El Salvador/Honduras* case, ICJ Reports, 1992, pp. 351, 597; 97 ILR, pp. 266, 513 that a 'trilateral local custom of the nature of a convention' could establish a condominium arrangement.

[83] See the *Eritrea/Yemen (Maritime Delimitation)* case, 119 ILR, pp. 417, 448.

[84] ICJ Reports, 1950, p. 266; 17 ILR, p. 280.

[85] ICJ Reports, 1950, p. 276; 17 ILR, p. 284.   [86] ICJ Reports, 1960, p. 6; 31 ILR, p. 23.

[87] ICJ Reports, 1960, p. 40; 31 ILR, p. 53. See Wolfke, *Custom*, p. 90.

governing the relations between them, the Court must attribute decisive effect to that practice for the purpose of determining their specific rights and obligations. Such a particular practice must prevail over any general rules.'[88]

Such local customs therefore depend upon a particular activity by one state being accepted by the other state (or states) as an expression of a legal obligation or right. While in the case of a general customary rule the process of consensus is at work so that a majority or a substantial minority of interested states can be sufficient to create a new custom, a local custom needs the positive acceptance of both (or all) parties to the rule.[89] This is because local customs are an exception to the general nature of customary law, which involves a fairly flexible approach to law-making by all states, and instead constitutes a reminder of the former theory of consent whereby states are bound only by what they assent to. Exceptions may prove the rule, but they need greater proof than the rule to establish themselves.

Treaties[90]

In contrast with the process of creating law through custom, treaties (or international conventions) are a more modern and more deliberate method.[91] Article 38 refers to 'international conventions, whether general or particular, establishing rules expressly recognised by the contracting states'. Treaties will be considered in more detail in chapter 16 but in this survey of the sources of international law reference must be made to the role of international conventions.

Treaties are known by a variety of differing names, ranging from Conventions, International Agreements, Pacts, General Acts, Charters, through to Statutes, Declarations and Covenants.[92] All these terms refer to a similar transaction, the creation of written agreements whereby the states participating bind themselves legally to act in a particular way or to set up particular relations between themselves. A series of conditions and

---

[88] ICJ Reports, 1960, p. 44.   [89] See Cohen-Jonathan, 'La Coutume Locale'.

[90] See generally A. D. McNair, *The Law of Treaties*, Oxford, 1961; Pellet, 'Article 38', p. 736, and A. Aust, *Modern Treaty Law and Practice*, 2nd edn, Cambridge, 2007. See further below, chapter 16.

[91] *Oppenheim's International Law* emphasises that 'not only is custom the original source of international law, but treaties are a source the validity and modalities of which themselves derive from custom', p. 31.

[92] See e.g. UKMIL, 70 BYIL, 1999, p. 404.

arrangements are laid out which the parties oblige themselves to carry out.[93]

The obligatory nature of treaties is founded upon the customary international law principle that agreements are binding (*pacta sunt servanda*). Treaties may be divided into 'law-making' treaties, which are intended to have universal or general relevance, and 'treaty-contracts', which apply only as between two or a small number of states. Such a distinction is intended to reflect the general or local applicability of a particular treaty and the range of obligations imposed. It cannot be regarded as hard and fast and there are many grey areas of overlap and uncertainty.[94]

Treaties are express agreements and are a form of substitute legislation undertaken by states. They bear a close resemblance to contracts in a superficial sense in that the parties create binding obligations for themselves, but they have a nature of their own which reflects the character of the international system. The number of treaties entered into has expanded over the last century, witness the growing number of volumes of the United Nations Treaty Series or the United Kingdom Treaty Series. They fulfil a vital role in international relations.

As governmental controls increase and the technological and communications revolutions affect international life, the number of issues which require some form of inter-state regulation multiplies.

For many writers, treaties constitute the most important sources of international law as they require the express consent of the contracting parties. Treaties are thus seen as superior to custom, which is regarded in any event as a form of tacit agreement.[95] As examples of important treaties one may mention the Charter of the United Nations, the Geneva Conventions on the treatment of prisoners and the protection of civilians and the Vienna Convention on Diplomatic Relations. All kinds of agreements exist, ranging from the regulation of outer space exploration to the control of drugs and the creation of international financial and development institutions. It would be impossible to telephone abroad or post a

---

[93] See the Vienna Convention on the Law of Treaties, 1969. Article 2(1)a defines a treaty for the purposes of the Convention as 'an international agreement concluded between states in written form and governed by international law, whether embodied in a single instrument or in two or more related instruments and whatever its particular designation'. See further below, p. 117 with regard to non-binding international agreements.

[94] See Virally, 'Sources', p. 126; Sørensen, Les Sources, pp. 58 ff., and Tunkin, *Theory of International Law*, pp. 93–5.

[95] Tunkin, *Theory of International Law*, pp. 91–113. See also R. Müllerson, 'Sources of International Law: New Tendencies in Soviet Thinking', 83 AJIL, 1989, pp. 494, 501–9, and Danilenko, 'Theory', p. 9.

letter overseas or take an aeroplane to other countries without the various international agreements that have laid down the necessary, recognised conditions of operation.

It follows from the essence of an international treaty that, like a contract, it sets down a series of propositions which are then regarded as binding upon the parties. How then is it possible to treat conventions as sources of international law, over and above the obligations imposed upon the contracting parties? It is in this context that one can understand the term 'law-making treaties'. They are intended to have an effect *generally*, not restrictively, and they are to be contrasted with those treaties which merely regulate limited issues between a few states. Law-making treaties are those agreements whereby states elaborate their perception of international law upon any given topic or establish new rules which are to guide them for the future in their international conduct. Such law-making treaties, of necessity, require the participation of a large number of states to emphasise this effect, and may produce rules that will bind all.[96] They constitute normative treaties, agreements that prescribe rules of conduct to be followed. Examples of such treaties may include the Antarctic Treaty and the Genocide Convention. There are also many agreements which declare the existing law or codify existing customary rules, such as the Vienna Convention on Diplomatic Relations of 1961.

Parties that do not sign and ratify the particular treaty in question are not bound by its terms. This is a general rule and was illustrated in the *North Sea Continental Shelf* cases[97] where West Germany had not ratified the relevant Convention and was therefore under no obligation to heed its terms. However, where treaties reflect customary law then non-parties are bound, not because it is a treaty provision but because it reaffirms a rule or rules of customary international law. Similarly, non-parties may come to accept that provisions in a particular treaty can generate customary law, depending always upon the nature of the agreement, the number of participants and other relevant factors.

---

[96] But this may depend upon the attitude of other states. This does not constitute a form of international legislation: see e.g. *Oppenheim's International Law*, p. 32; the *Reparation* case, ICJ Reports, 1949, p. 185; 16 AD, p. 318, and the *Namibia* case, ICJ Reports, 1971, p. 56; 49 ILR, p. 2. See also Brownlie, *Principles*, pp. 12–14, and R. Baxter, 'Treaties and Custom', 129 HR, 1970, p. 27. See also O. Schachter, 'Entangled Treaty and Custom' in *International Law at a Time of Perplexity* (ed. Y. Dinstein), Dordrecht, 1989, p. 717, and Y. Dinstein, 'The Interaction Between Customary International Law and Treaties', 322 HR, 2006, p. 247.

[97] ICJ Reports, 1969, pp. 3, 25; 41 ILR, pp. 29, 54.

The possibility that a provision in a treaty may constitute the basis of a rule which, when coupled with the *opinio juris*, can lead to the creation of a binding custom governing all states, not just those party to the original treaty, was considered by the International Court of Justice in the *North Sea Continental Shelf* cases[98] and regarded as one of the recognised methods of formulating new rules of customary international law. The Court, however, declared that the particular provision had to be 'of a fundamentally norm-creating character',[99] that is, capable of forming the basis of a general rule of law. What exactly this amounts to will probably vary according to the time and place, but it does confirm that treaty provisions may lead to custom providing other states, parties and non-parties to the treaty fulfil the necessary conditions of compatible behaviour and *opinio juris*. It has been argued that this possibility may be extended so that generalisable treaty provisions may of themselves, without the requirement to demonstrate the *opinio juris* and with little passage of time, generate *ipso facto* customary rules.[100] This, while recognising the importance of treaties, particularly in the human rights field, containing potential norm-creating provisions, is clearly going too far. The danger would be of a small number of states legislating for all, unless dissenting states actually entered into contrary treaties.[101] This would constitute too radical a departure for the current process of law-formation within the international community.

It is now established that even where a treaty rule comes into being covering the same ground as a customary rule, the latter will not be simply absorbed within the former but will maintain its separate existence. The Court in the *Nicaragua* case[102] did not accept the argument of the US that the norms of customary international law concerned with self-defence had been 'subsumed' and 'supervened' by article 51 of the United Nations Charter. It was emphasised that 'even if a treaty norm and a customary norm relevant to the present dispute were to have exactly the

[98] ICJ Reports, 1969, p. 41; 41 ILR, p. 71. The Court stressed that this method of creating new customs was not to be lightly regarded as having been attained, *ibid.*

[99] But see the minority opinions, ICJ Reports, 1969, pp. 56, 156–8, 163, 169, 172–80, 197–200, 221–32 and 241–7; 41 ILR, p. 85. See also the *Gulf of Maine* case, ICJ Reports, 1984, pp. 246, 295; 71 ILR, pp. 74, 122, and the *Libya/Malta Continental Shelf* case, ICJ Reports, 1985, pp. 13, 29–34; 81 ILR, pp. 239, 261–6.

[100] See D'Amato, *Concept of Custom*, p. 104, and D'Amato, 'The Concept of Human Rights in International Law', 82 *Columbia Law Review*, 1982, pp. 1110, 1129–47. See also Akehurst, 'Custom as a Source', pp. 42–52.

[101] D'Amato, 'Concept of Human Rights', p. 1146.

[102] ICJ Reports, 1986, p. 14; 76 ILR, p. 349.

same content, this would not be a reason for the Court to hold that the incorporation of the customary norm into treaty law must deprive the customary norm of its applicability as distinct from the treaty norm'.[103] The Court concluded that 'it will therefore be clear that customary international law continues to exist and to apply separately from international treaty law, even where the two categories of law have an identical content'.[104] The effect of this in the instant case was that the Court was able to examine the rule as established under customary law, whereas due to an American reservation, it was unable to analyse the treaty-based obligation.

Of course, two rules with the same content may be subject to different principles with regard to their interpretation and application; thus the approach of the Court as well as being theoretically correct is of practical value also. In many cases, such dual source of existence of a rule may well suggest that the two versions are not in fact identical, as in the case of self-defence under customary law and article 51 of the Charter, but it will always depend upon the particular circumstances.[105]

Certain treaties attempt to establish a 'regime' which will, of necessity, also extend to non-parties.[106] The United Nations Charter, for example, in its creation of a definitive framework for the preservation of international peace and security, declares in article 2(6) that 'the organisation shall ensure that states which are not members of the United Nations act in accordance with these Principles [listed in article 2] so far as may be necessary for the maintenance of international peace and security'. One can also point to the 1947 General Agreement on Tariffs and Trade (GATT) which set up a common code of conduct in international trade and has had an important effect on non-party states as well, being now transmuted into the World Trade Organisation.

On the same theme, treaties may be constitutive in that they create international institutions and act as constitutions for them, outlining their proposed powers and duties.

'Treaty-contracts' on the other hand are not law-making instruments in themselves since they are between only small numbers of states and on a limited topic, but may provide evidence of customary rules. For example, a series of bilateral treaties containing a similar rule may be evidence of the existence of that rule in customary law, although this proposition needs to

---

[103] ICJ Reports, 1986, pp. 94–5; 76 ILR, pp. 428–9. See also W. Czaplinski, 'Sources of International Law in the *Nicaragua* Case', 38 ICLQ, 1989, p. 151.
[104] ICJ Reports, 1986, p. 96; 76 ILR, p. 430.   [105] See further below, chapter 20, p. 1131.
[106] See further below, chapter 16, p. 928.

be approached with some caution in view of the fact that bilateral treaties by their very nature often reflect discrete circumstances.[107]

General principles of law[108]

In any system of law, a situation may very well arise where the court in considering a case before it realises that there is no law covering exactly that point, neither parliamentary statute nor judicial precedent. In such instances the judge will proceed to deduce a rule that will be relevant, by analogy from already existing rules or directly from the general principles that guide the legal system, whether they be referred to as emanating from justice, equity or considerations of public policy. Such a situation is perhaps even more likely to arise in international law because of the relative underdevelopment of the system in relation to the needs with which it is faced.

There are fewer decided cases in international law than in a municipal system and no method of legislating to provide rules to govern new situations.[109] It is for such a reason that the provision of 'the general principles of law recognised by civilised nations'[110] was inserted into article 38 as a source of law, to close the gap that might be uncovered in international law and solve this problem which is known legally as *non liquet*.[111] The

---

[107] See further below, p. 686, with regard to extradition treaties and below, p. 837, with regard to bilateral investment treaties.

[108] See e.g. B. Cheng, *General Principles of Law as Applied by International Courts and Tribunals*, London, 1953; A. D. McNair, 'The General Principles of Law Recognised by Civilised Nations', 33 BYIL, 1957, p. 1; H. Lauterpacht, *Private Law Sources and Analogies of International Law*, London, 1927; G. Herczegh, *General Principles of Law and the International Legal Order*, Budapest, 1969; O. Schachter, *International Law in Theory and Practice*, Dordrecht, 1991, pp. 50–5; O. Corten, *L'Utilisation du 'Raisonnable' par le Juge International*, Brussels, 1997; B. Vitanyi, 'Les Positions Doctrinales Concernant le Sens de la Notion de "Principes Généraux de Droit Reconnus par les Nations Civilisées"', 86 *Revue Générale de Droit International Public*, 1982, p. 48; H. Waldock, 'General Course on Public International Law', 106 HR, 1962, p. 54; Pellet, 'Article 38', p. 764; Thirlway, 'Supplement', p. 108; M. Sørensen, 'Principes de Droit International', 101 HR, 1960, p. 16, and V. Degan, 'General Principles of Law', 3 Finnish YIL, 1992, p. 1.

[109] Note that the International Court has regarded the terms 'principles' and 'rules' as essentially the same within international law: the *Gulf of Maine* case, ICJ Reports, 1984, pp. 246, 288–90. Introducing the adjective 'general', however, shifts the meaning to a broader concept.

[110] The additional clause relating to recognition by 'civilised nations' is regarded today as redundant: see e.g. Pellet, 'Article 38', p. 769.

[111] See e.g. J. Stone, *Of Law and Nations*, London, 1974, chapter 3; H. Lauterpacht, 'Some Observations on the Prohibition of *Non Liquet* and the Completeness of the Legal Order',

question of gaps in the system is an important one. It is important to appreciate that while there may not always be an immediate and obvious rule applicable to every international situation, 'every international situation is capable of being determined *as a matter of law*'.[112]

There are various opinions as to what the general principles of law concept is intended to refer. Some writers regard it as an affirmation of Natural Law concepts, which are deemed to underlie the system of international law and constitute the method for testing the validity of the positive (i.e. man-made) rules.[113] Other writers, particularly positivists, treat it as a sub-heading under treaty and customary law and incapable of adding anything new to international law unless it reflects the consent of states. Soviet writers like Tunkin subscribed to this approach and regarded the 'general principles of law' as reiterating the fundamental precepts of international law, for example, the law of peaceful co-existence, which have already been set out in treaty and custom law.[114]

Between these two approaches, most writers are prepared to accept that the general principles do constitute a separate source of law but of fairly limited scope, and this is reflected in the decisions of the Permanent Court of International Justice and the International Court of Justice. It is not clear, however, in all cases, whether what is involved is a general principle of law appearing in municipal systems or a general principle of international law. But perhaps this is not a terribly serious problem since both municipal legal concepts and those derived from existing international practice can be defined as falling within the recognised catchment area.[115]

Symbolae Verzijl, 1958, p. 196; Pellet, 'Article 38', p. 704; H. Thirlway, 'The Law and Procedure of the International Court of Justice', BYIL, 1988, p. 76, and Thirlway, 'Supplement', p. 44, and P. Weil, 'The Court Cannot Conclude Definitively . . . ? *Non Liquet* Revisited', 36 *Columbia Journal of Transnational Law*, 1997, p. 109. See also the *North Sea Continental Shelf* cases, ICJ Reports, 1969, p. 46; 41 ILR, p. 29, and the *Nicaragua* case, ICJ Reports, 1986, p. 135; 76 ILR, p. 349.

[112] *Oppenheim's International Law*, p. 13. See, however, the conclusion of the International Court that it was unable to state whether there was a rule of international law prohibiting or permitting the threat or use of nuclear weapons by a state in self-defence where its very survival was at stake: the *Legality of the Threat or Use of Nuclear Weapons* case, ICJ Reports, 1996, pp. 226, 244; 110 ILR, pp. 163, 194. Cf. the Dissenting Opinion of Judge Higgins, *ibid.*; 110 ILR, pp. 532 ff. See also *Eritrea/Yemen* (First Phase), 114 ILR, pp. 1, 119 and 121–2.

[113] See e.g. Lauterpacht, *Private Law Sources*. See also Waldock, 'General Course', p. 54; C. W. Jenks, *The Common Law of Mankind*, London, 1958, p. 169, and Judge Tanaka (dissenting), *South-West Africa* case, (Second Phase), ICJ Reports, 1966, pp. 6, 294–9; 37 ILR, pp. 243, 455–9.

[114] Tunkin, *Theory of International Law*, chapter 7.

[115] See Brownlie, *Principles*, p. 16 , and Virally, 'Sources', pp. 144–8.

While the reservoir from which one can draw contains the legal operations of 190 or so states, it does not follow that judges have to be experts
in every legal system. There are certain common themes that run through
the many different orders. Anglo-American common law has influenced a
number of states throughout the world, as have the French and Germanic
systems. There are many common elements in the law in Latin America,
and most Afro-Asian states have borrowed heavily from the European
experience in their efforts to modernise the structure administering the
state and westernise economic and other enterprises.[116]

Reference will now be made to some of the leading cases in this field to
illustrate how this problem has been addressed.

In the *Chorzów Factory* case in 1928,[117] which followed the seizure
of a nitrate factory in Upper Silesia by Poland, the Permanent Court
of International Justice declared that 'it is a general conception of law
that every violation of an engagement involves an obligation to make
reparation'. The Court also regarded it as:

> a principle of international law that the reparation of a wrong may con-
> sist in an indemnity corresponding to the damage which the nationals of
> the injured state have suffered as a result of the act which is contrary to
> international law.

The most fertile fields, however, for the implementation of municipal
law analogies have been those of procedure, evidence and the machinery of the judicial process. In the *German Settlers in Poland* case,[118] the
Court, approaching the matter from the negative point of view,[119] declared that 'private rights acquired under existing law do not cease on a
change of sovereignty ... It can hardly be maintained that, although the
law survived, private rights acquired under it perished. Such a contention

---

[116] See generally, R. David and J. Brierley, *Major Legal Systems in the World Today*, 2nd
edn, London, 1978. Note that the Tribunal in *AMCO* v. *Republic of Indonesia* stated
that while a practice or legal provisions common to a number of nations would be an
important source of international law, the French concepts of administrative unilateral
acts or administrative contracts were not such practices or legal provisions: 89 ILR,
pp. 366, 461.

[117] PCIJ, Series A, No. 17, 1928, p. 29; 4 AD, p. 258. See also the Chile–United States
Commission decision with regard to the deaths of Letelier and Moffitt: 31 ILM, 1982,
pp. 1, 9; 88 ILR, p. 727.

[118] PCIJ, Series B, No. 6, p. 36.

[119] See also the *South-West Africa* cases, ICJ Reports, 1966, pp. 3, 47; 37 ILR, pp. 243, 280–1,
for a statement that the notion of *actio popularis* was not part of international law as such
nor able to be regarded as imported by the concept of general principles of law.

is based on no principle and would be contrary to an almost universal opinion and practice.'[120] The International Court of Justice in the *Corfu Channel* case,[121] when referring to circumstantial evidence, pointed out that 'this indirect evidence is admitted in all systems of law and its use is recognised by international decisions'. International judicial reference has also been made to the concept of *res judicata*, that is that the decision in the circumstances is final, binding and without appeal.[122]

In the *Administrative Tribunal* case,[123] the Court dealt with the problem of the dismissal of members of the United Nations Secretariat staff and whether the General Assembly had the right to refuse to give effect to awards to them made by the relevant Tribunal. In giving its negative reply, the Court emphasised that:

> according to a well-established and generally recognised principle of law, a judgment rendered by such a judicial body is *res judicata* and has binding force between the parties to the dispute.[124]

The question of *res judicata* was discussed in some detail in the *Genocide Convention (Bosnia and Herzegovina v. Serbia and Montenegro)* case,[125] where the issue focused on the meaning of the 1996 decision of the Court rejecting preliminary objections to jurisdiction.[126] The Court emphasised that the principle 'signifies that the decisions of the Court are not only binding on the parties, but are final, in the sense that they cannot be reopened by the parties as regards the issues that have been determined, save by procedures, of an exceptional nature, specially laid down for that purpose. That principle signifies that the decisions of the Court are not

---

[120] See also the *Certain German Interests in Polish Upper Silesia* case, PCIJ, Series A, No. 7, p. 42, and the *Free Zones of Upper Savoy and the District of Gex* case, PCIJ, Series A/B, No. 46, p. 167.

[121] ICJ Reports, 1949, pp. 4, 18; 16 AD, pp. 155, 157.

[122] The *Corfu Channel* case, ICJ Reports, 1949, p. 248.

[123] ICJ Reports, 1954, p. 47; 21 ILR, p. 310.

[124] ICJ Reports, 1954, p. 53; 21 ILR, p. 314, and the *Laguna del Desierto (Argentina/Chile)* case, 113 ILR, pp. 1, 43, where it was stated that 'A judgment having the authority of *res judicata* is judicially binding on the Parties to the dispute. This is a fundamental principle of the law of nations repeatedly invoked in the jurisprudence, which regards the authority of *res judicata* as a universal and absolute principle of international law.' See also *AMCO v. Republic of Indonesia*, 89 ILR, pp. 366, 558; Cheng, *General Principles*, chapter 17; S. Rosenne, *The Law and Practice of the International Court, 1920–2005*, 4th edn, Leiden, 2006, pp. 1598 ff.; M. Shahabuddeen, *Precedent in the International Court*, Cambridge, 1996, pp. 30 and 168, and I. Scobbie, '*Res Judicata*, Precedent and the International Court', 20 Australian YIL, 2000, p. 299.

[125] ICJ Reports, 2007, para. 113.   [126] ICJ Reports, 1996, p. 595; 115 ILR, p. 110.

only binding on the parties, but are final, in the sense that they cannot be reopened by the parties as regards the issues that have been determined, save by procedures, of an exceptional nature, specially laid down for that purpose.'[127] The Court noted that two purposes, one general and one specific, underpinned the principle of res judicata, internationally as well as nationally. The first referred to the stability of legal relations that requires that litigation come to an end. The second was that it is in the interest of each party that an issue which has already been adjudicated in favour of that party not be argued again. It was emphasised that depriving a litigant of the benefit of a judgment it had already obtained must in general be seen as a breach of the principles governing the legal settlement of disputes. The Court noted that the principle applied equally to preliminary objections judgments and merits judgments and that since jurisdiction had been established by virtue of the 1996 judgment, it was not open to a party to assert in current proceedings that, at the date the earlier judgment was given, the Court had no power to give it, because one of the parties could now be seen to have been unable to come before it. This would be to call in question the force as res judicata of the operative clause of the judgment.[128]

Further, the Court in the preliminary objections phase of the *Right of Passage* case[129] stated that:

> it is a rule of law generally accepted, as well as one acted upon in the past by the Court, that, once the Court has been validly seized of a dispute, unilateral action by the respondent state in terminating its Declaration [i.e. accepting the jurisdiction of the Court], in whole or in part, cannot divest the Court of jurisdiction.

The Court has also considered the principle of estoppel which provides that a party that has acquiesced in a particular situation cannot then proceed to challenge it. In the *Temple* case[130] the International Court of Justice applied the doctrine, but in the *Serbian Loans* case[131] in 1929, in which French bondholders were demanding payment in gold francs as against paper money upon a series of Serbian loans, the Court declared the principle inapplicable.

As the International Court noted in the *ELSI* case,[132] there were limitations upon the process of inferring an estoppel in all circumstances, since

---

[127] *Ibid.*, at para. 115.   [128] *Ibid.*, at paras. 116–23.
[129] ICJ Reports, 1957, pp. 125, 141–2; 24 ILR, pp. 840, 842–3.
[130] ICJ Reports, 1962, pp. 6, 23, 31 and 32; 33 ILR, pp. 48, 62, 69–70.
[131] PCIJ, Series A, No. 20; 5 AD, p. 466.
[132] ICJ Reports, 1989, pp. 15, 44; 84 ILR, pp. 311, 350.

'although it cannot be excluded that an estoppel could in certain circumstances arise from a silence when something ought to have been said, there are obvious difficulties in constructing an estoppel from a mere failure to mention a matter at a particular point in somewhat desultory diplomatic exchanges'.[133] The meaning of estoppel was confirmed in *Cameroon v. Nigeria*,[134] where the Court emphasised that 'An estoppel would only arise if by its acts or declarations Cameroon had consistently made it fully clear that it had agreed to settle the boundary dispute submitted to the Court by bilateral avenues alone. It would further be necessary that, by relying on such an attitude, Nigeria had changed position to its own detriment or had suffered some prejudice.'

Another example of a general principle was provided by the Arbitration Tribunal in the *AMCO* v. *Republic of Indonesia* case,[135] where it was stated that 'the full compensation of prejudice, by awarding to the injured party the *damnum emergens* and *lucrum cessans* is a principle common to the main systems of municipal law, and therefore, a general principle of law which may be considered as a source of international law'. Another principle would be that of respect for acquired rights.[136] One crucial general principle of international law is that of *pacta sunt servanda*, or the idea that international agreements are binding. The law of treaties rests inexorably upon this principle since the whole concept of binding international agreements can only rest upon the presupposition that such instruments are commonly accepted as possessing that quality.[137]

Perhaps the most important general principle, underpinning many international legal rules, is that of good faith.[138] This principle is enshrined

---

[133] See also the *Eastern Greenland* case, PCIJ, Series A/B, No. 53, pp. 52 ff.; 6 AD, pp. 95, 100–2; the decision of the Eritrea/Ethiopia Boundary Commission of 13 April 2002, 130 ILR, pp. 1, 35–6; and the *Saiga (No. 2)* case, 120 ILR, pp. 143, 230; Brownlie, *Principles*, p. 615, and H. Thirlway, 'The Law and Procedure of the International Court of Justice, 1960–89 (Part One)', 60 BYIL, 1989, pp. 4, 29. See also below, chapter 10, p. 515.

[134] ICJ Reports, 1998, pp. 275, 303.   [135] 89 ILR, pp. 366, 504.

[136] See, for example, the *German Interests in Polish Upper Silesia* case, PCIJ, Series A, No. 7, 1926, p. 22; *Starrett Housing Corporation* v. *Iran* 85 ILR p. 34; the *Shufeld* claim, 5 AD, p. 179, and *AMCO* v. *Republic of Indonesia* 89 ILR, pp. 366, 496. See further below, p. 830.

[137] See Brownlie, *Principles*, pp. 591–2, and McNair, *Law of Treaties*, vol. I, chapter 30. See also article 26 of the Vienna Convention on the Law of Treaties, 1969, and *AMCO* v. *Republic of Indonesia* 89 ILR, pp. 366, 495–7.

[138] *Oppenheim's International Law* notes that this is 'of overriding importance', p. 38. See E. Zoller, *Bonne Foi en Droit International Public*, Paris, 1977; R. Kolb, *La Bonne Foie en Droit International Public*, Paris, 2000; Thirlway, 'Law and Procedure of the ICJ (Part One)' pp. 3, 7 ff., and Thirlway, 'Supplement', p. 7; and G. Fitzmaurice, *The Law and Procedure of the International Court of Justice*, Cambridge, 1986, vol. I, p. 183 and vol. II, p. 609.

in the United Nations Charter, which provides in article 2(2) that 'all Members, in order to ensure to all of them the rights and benefits result- ing from membership, shall fulfil in good faith the obligations assumed by them in accordance with the present Charter', and the elaboration of this provision in the Declaration on Principles of International Law Concern- ing Friendly Relations and Co-operation among States adopted by the General Assembly in resolution 2625 (XXV), 1970, referred to the obli- gations upon states to fulfil in good faith their obligations resulting from international law generally, including treaties. It therefore constitutes an indispensable part of the rules of international law generally.[139]

The International Court declared in the *Nuclear Tests* cases[140] that:

> One of the basic principles governing the creation and performance of legal obligations, whatever their source, is the principle of good faith. Trust and confidence are inherent in international co-operation, in particular in an age when this co-operation in many fields is becoming increasingly essential. Just as the very rule of *pacta sunt servanda* in the law of treaties is based on good faith, so also is the binding character of an international obligation assumed by unilateral obligation.

Nevertheless, the Court has made the point that good faith as a concept is 'not in itself a source of obligation where none would otherwise exist'.[141] The principle of good faith, therefore, is a background principle informing and shaping the observance of existing rules of international law and in addition constraining the manner in which those rules may legitimately be exercised.[142] As the International Court has noted, the principle of good faith relates 'only to the fulfilment of existing obligations'.[143] A further principle to be noted is that of *ex injuria jus non oritur*, which

---

[139] See also Case T-115/94, *Opel Austria Gmbh* v. *Republic of Austria*, 22 January 1997.

[140] ICJ Reports, 1974, pp. 253, 267; 57 ILR, pp. 398, 412.

[141] The *Border and Transborder Armed Actions* case (*Nicaragua* v. *Honduras*), ICJ Reports, 1988, p. 105; 84 ILR, p. 218. See also Judge Ajibolo's Separate Opinion in the *Libya/Chad* case, ICJ Reports, 1994, pp. 6, 71–4; 100 ILR, pp. 1, 69–72, and the statement by the Inter-American Court of Human Rights in the *Re-introduction of the Death Penalty in Peru* case, 16 *Human Rights Law Journal*, 1995, pp. 9, 13.

[142] See also the *Fisheries Jurisdiction* cases, ICJ Reports, 1974, pp. 3, 33; 55 ILR, pp. 238, 268; the *North Sea Continental Shelf* cases, ICJ Reports, 1969, pp. 3, 46–7; 41 ILR, pp. 29, 76; the *Lac Lannoux* case, 24 ILR, p. 119, and the *Legality of the Threat or Use of Nuclear Weapons* case, ICJ Reports, 1996, pp. 264 ff.; 110 ILR, pp. 163, 214–15. Note also Principles 19 and 27 of the Rio Declaration on Environment and Development, 1992, 31 ILM, 1992, p. 876.

[143] *Cameroon* v. *Nigeria*, ICJ Reports, 1998, pp. 275, 304.

posits that facts flowing from wrongful conduct cannot determine the law.[144]

Thus it follows that it is the Court which has the discretion as to which principles of law to apply in the circumstances of the particular case under consideration, and it will do this upon the basis of the inability of customary and treaty law to provide the required solution. In this context, one must consider the *Barcelona Traction* case[145] between Belgium and Spain. The International Court of Justice relied heavily upon the municipal law concept of the limited liability company and emphasised that if the Court were to decide the case in disregard of the relevant institutions of municipal law it would, without justification, invite serious legal difficulties. It would lose touch with reality, for there are no corresponding institutions of international law to which the Court could resort.[146]

However, international law did not refer to the municipal law of a particular state, but rather to the rules generally accepted by municipal legal systems which, in this case, recognise the idea of the limited company.

Equity and international law[147]

Apart from the recourse to the procedures and institutions of municipal legal systems to reinforce international law, it is also possible to see in a

---

[144] See e.g. the *Gabčíkovo–Nagymaros Project* case, ICJ Reports, 1997, pp. 7, 76; 116 ILR, p. 1, and the *Brcko* case, 36 ILM, 1997, pp. 396, 422.

[145] ICJ Reports, 1970, p. 3; 46 ILR, p. 178.

[146] ICJ Reports, 1970, p. 37; 46 ILR, p. 211. See also generally the *Abu Dhabi* arbitration, 1 ICLQ, 1952, p. 247; 18 ILR, p. 44, and *Texaco* v. *Libya* 53 ILR, p. 389.

[147] See M. Akehurst, 'Equity and General Principles of Law', 25 ICLQ, 1976, p. 801; B. Cheng, 'Justice and Equity in International Law', 8 *Current Legal Problems*, 1955, p. 185; V. Degan, *L'Equité et le Droit International*, Paris, 1970; C. de Visscher, *De l'Equité dans le Réglement Arbitral ou Judiciaire des Litiges de Droit International Public*, Paris, 1972; E. Lauterpacht, 'Equity, Evasion, Equivocation and Evolution in International Law', *Proceedings of the American Branch of the ILA*, 1977–8, p. 33, and E. Lauterpacht, *Aspects of the Administration of International Justice*, Cambridge, 1991, pp. 117–52; R. Y. Jennings, 'Equity and Equitable Principles', *Annuaire Suisse de Droit International*, 1986, p. 38; *Oppenheim's International Law*, p. 43; R. Higgins, *Problems and Process*, Oxford, 1994, chapter 13; M. Miyoshi, *Considerations of Equity in the Settlement of Territorial and Boundary Disputes*, The Hague, 1993; S. Rosenne, 'Equitable Principles and the Compulsory Jurisdiction of International Tribunals', *Festschrift für Rudolf Bindschedler*, Berne, 1980, p. 410, and Rosenne, 'The Position of the International Court of Justice on the Foundations of the Principle of Equity in International Law' in *Forty Years International Court of Justice: Jurisdiction, Equality and Equity* (eds. A. Bloed and P. Van Dijk), Dordrecht, 1988, p. 108; Pirotte, 'La Notion d'Équité dans la Jurisprudence Récente de la CIJ', 77 *Revue Générale de Droit International Public*, 1973, p. 131; Chattopadhyay, 'Equity in International Law: Its Growth and Development',

number of cases references to equity[148] as a set of principles constituting the values of the system. The most famous decision on these lines was that of Judge Hudson in the *Diversion of Water from the Meuse* case[149] in 1937 regarding a dispute between Holland and Belgium. Hudson pointed out that what are regarded as principles of equity have long been treated as part of international law and applied by the courts. 'Under article 38 of the Statute', he declared, 'if not independently of that article, the Court has some freedom to consider principles of equity as part of the international law which it must apply.' However, one must be very cautious in interpreting this, although on the broadest level it is possible to see equity (on an analogy with domestic law) as constituting a creative charge in legal development, producing the dynamic changes in the system rendered inflexible by the strict application of rules.[150]

The concept of equity[151] has been referred to in several cases. In the *Rann of Kutch Arbitration* between India and Pakistan in 1968[152] the Tribunal agreed that equity formed part of international law and that accordingly the parties could rely on such principles in the presentation of their cases.[153] The International Court of Justice in the *North*

---

5 *Georgia Journal of International and Comparative Law*, 1975, p. 381; R. Lapidoth, 'Equity in International Law', 22 *Israel Law Review*, 1987, p. 161; Schachter, *International Law*, p. 49; A. V. Lowe, 'The Role of Equity in International Law', 12 Australian YIL, 1992, p. 54; P. Weil, 'L'Équité dans la Jurisprudence de la Cour International de Justice' in Lowe and Fitzmaurice, *Fifty Years of the International Court of Justice*, p. 121; Pellet, 'Article 38', p. 723; Thirlway, 'Law and Procedure of the ICJ (Part One)', p. 49, and Thirlway, 'Supplement', p. 26. Note especially Judge Weeramantry's study of equity in the *Jan Mayen (Denmark v. Norway)* case, ICJ Reports, 1993, pp. 38, 211; 99 ILR, pp. 395, 579.

[148] Equity generally may be understood in the contexts of adapting law to particular areas or choosing between several different interpretations of the law (equity *infra legem*), filling gaps in the law (equity *praetor legem*) and as a reason for not applying unjust laws (equity *contra legem*): see Akehurst, 'Equity', and Judge Weeramantry, the *Jan Mayen* case, ICJ Reports, 1993, pp. 38, 226–34; 99 ILR, pp. 395, 594–602. See also below, chapter 17, for the extensive use of equity in the context of state succession.

[149] PCIJ, Series A/B, No. 70, pp. 73, 77; 8 AD, pp. 444, 450.

[150] See e.g. Judge Weeramantry, the *Jan Mayen (Denmark v. Norway)* case, ICJ Reports, 1993, pp. 38, 217; 99 ILR, pp. 395, 585. Cf. Judge Schwebel's Separate Opinion, ICJ Reports, 1993, p. 118; 99 ILR, p. 486.

[151] Note that the International Court in the *Tunisia/Libya Continental Shelf* case, ICJ Reports, 1982, pp. 18, 60; 67 ILR, pp. 4, 53, declared that 'equity as a legal concept is a direct emanation of the idea of justice'. However, see G. Abi-Saab's reference to the International Court's 'flight into equity' in 'The ICJ as a World Court' in Lowe and Fitzmaurice, *Fifty Years of the International Court of Justice*, pp. 3, 11.

[152] 50 ILR, p. 2.

[153] *Ibid.*, p. 18. In deciding the course of the boundary in two deep inlets, the Tribunal had recourse to the concept of equity: *ibid.*, p. 520.

Sea Continental Shelf cases directed a final delimitation between the parties – West Germany, Holland and Denmark – 'in accordance with equitable principles'[154] and discussed the relevance to equity in its consideration of the *Barcelona Traction* case.[155] Judge Tanaka, however, has argued for a wider interpretation in his Dissenting Opinion in the Second Phase of the *South-West Africa* cases[156] and has treated the broad concept as a source of human rights ideas.[157]

However, what is really in question here is the use of equitable principles in the context of a rule requiring such an approach. The relevant courts are not applying principles of abstract justice to the cases,[158] but rather deriving equitable principles and solutions from the applicable law.[159] The Court declared in the *Libya/Malta* case[160] that 'the justice of which equity is an emanation, is not an abstract justice but justice according to the rule of law; which is to say that its application should display consistency and a degree of predictability; even though it also looks beyond it to principles of more general application'.

Equity has been used by the courts as a way of mitigating certain inequities, not as a method of refashioning nature to the detriment of legal rules.[161] Its existence, therefore, as a separate and distinct source of law is at best highly controversial. As the International Court noted in the *Tunisia/Libya Continental Shelf* case,[162]

---

[154] ICJ Reports, 1969, pp. 3, 53; 41 ILR, pp. 29, 83. Equity was used in the case in order to exclude the use of the equidistance method in the particular circumstances: *ibid.*, pp. 48–50; 41 ILR, pp. 78–80.

[155] ICJ Reports, 1970, p. 3; 46 ILR, p. 178. See also the *Burkina Faso v. Mali* case, ICJ Reports, 1986, pp. 554, 631–3; 80 ILR, pp. 459, 532–5.

[156] ICJ Reports, 1966, pp. 6, 294–9; 37 ILR, pp. 243, 455–9. See also the *Corfu Channel* case, ICJ Reports, 1949, pp. 4, 22; 16 AD, p. 155.

[157] See also *AMCO v. Republic of Indonesia* 89 ILR, pp. 366, 522–3.

[158] The International Court of Justice may under article 38(2) of its Statute decide a case *ex aequo et bono* if the parties agree, but it has never done so: see e.g. Pellet, 'Article 38', p. 730.

[159] See the *North Sea Continental Shelf* cases, ICJ Reports, 1969, pp. 3, 47; 41 ILR, pp. 29, 76, and the *Fisheries Jurisdiction* cases, ICJ Reports, 1974, pp. 3, 33; 55 ILR, pp. 238, 268. The Court reaffirmed in the *Libya/Malta* case, ICJ Reports, 1985, pp. 13, 40; 81 ILR, pp. 238, 272, 'the principle that there can be no question of distributive justice'.

[160] ICJ Reports, 1985, pp. 13, 39; 81 ILR, pp. 238, 271.

[161] See the *North Sea Continental Shelf* cases, ICJ Reports, 1969, pp. 3, 49–50; 41 ILR, pp. 29, 78–80, and the *Anglo-French Continental Shelf* case, Cmnd 7438, 1978, pp. 116–17; 54 ILR, pp. 6, 123–4. See also the *Tunisia/Libya Continental Shelf* case, ICJ Reports, 1982, pp. 18, 60; 67 ILR, pp. 4, 53, and the *Gulf of Maine* case, ICJ Reports, 1984, pp. 246, 313–14 and 325–30; 71 ILR, pp. 74, 140–1 and 152–7.

[162] ICJ Reports, 1982, pp. 18, 60; 67 ILR, pp. 4, 53.

it is bound to apply equitable principles as part of international law, and to balance up the various considerations which it regards as relevant in order to produce an equitable result. While it is clear that no rigid rules exist as to the exact weight to be attached to each element in the case, this is very far from being an exercise of discretion or conciliation; nor is it an operation of distributive justice.[163]

The use of equitable principles, however, has been particularly marked in the 1982 Law of the Sea Convention. Article 59, for example, provides that conflicts between coastal and other states regarding the exclusive economic zone are to be resolved 'on the basis of equity', while by article 74 delimitation of the zone between states with opposite or adjacent coasts is to be effected by agreement on the basis of international law in order to achieve an equitable solution. A similar provision applies by article 83 to the delimitation of the continental shelf.[164] These provisions possess flexibility, which is important, but are also somewhat uncertain. Precisely how any particular dispute may be resolved, and the way in which that is likely to happen and the principles to be used are far from clear and an element of unpredictability may have been introduced.[165] The Convention on the Law of the Non-Navigational Uses of International Watercourses, 1997,[166] also lays great emphasis upon the concept of equity. Article 5, for example, provides that watercourse states shall utilise an international watercourse in an equitable and reasonable manner both in their own territories and in participating generally in the use, development and protection of such a watercourse.

Equity may also be used in certain situations in the delimitation of non-maritime boundaries. Where there is no evidence as to where a boundary line lies, an international tribunal may resort to equity. In the case of *Burkina Faso/Republic of Mali*,[167] for example, the Court noted with regard

---

[163] See generally R. Y. Jennings, 'The Principles Governing Marine Boundaries' in *Festschrift für Karl Doehring*, Berlin, 1989, p. 408, and M. Bedjaoui, 'L"énigme" des "principes équitables" dans le Droit des Délimitations Maritimes', *Revista Español de Derecho Internacional*, 1990, p. 376.

[164] See also article 140 providing for the equitable sharing of financial and other benefits derived from activities in the deep sea-bed area.

[165] However, see *Cameroon v. Nigeria*, ICJ Reports, 2002, pp. 303, 443, where the Court declared that its jurisprudence showed that in maritime delimitation disputes, 'equity is not a method of delimitation, but solely an aim that should be borne in mind in effecting the delimitation'. See further below, chapter 11, p. 590.

[166] Based on the Draft Articles of the International Law Commission: see the Report of the International Law Commission on the Work of its Forty-Sixth Session, A/49/10, 1994, pp. 197, 218 ff.

[167] ICJ Reports, 1986, pp. 554, 633; 80 ILR, pp. 459, 535.

to the pool of Soum, that 'it must recognise that Soum is a frontier pool; and that in the absence of any precise indication in the texts of the position of the frontier line, the line should divide the pool of Soum in an equitable manner'. This would be done by dividing the pool equally. Although equity did not always mean equality, where there are no special circumstances the latter is generally the best expression of the former.[168] The Court also emphasised that 'to resort to the concept of equity in order to modify an established frontier would be quite unjustified'.[169]

Although generalised principles or concepts that may be termed community value-judgements inform and pervade the political and therefore the legal orders in the broadest sense, they do not themselves constitute as such binding legal norms. This can only happen if they have been accepted as legal norms by the international community through the mechanisms and techniques of international law creation. Nevertheless, 'elementary principles of humanity' may lie at the base of such norms and help justify their existence in the broadest sense, and may indeed perform a valuable role in endowing such norms with an additional force within the system. The International Court has, for example, emphasised in the *Legality of the Threat or Use of Nuclear Weapons* Advisory Opinion[170] that at the heart of the rules and principles concerning international humanitarian law lies the 'overriding consideration of humanity'.

Judicial decisions[171]

Although these are, in the words of article 38, to be utilised as a subsidiary means for the determination of rules of law rather than as an actual source of law, judicial decisions can be of immense importance. While by virtue of

---

[168] *Ibid.*

[169] *Ibid.* See also the *El Salvador/Honduras* case, ICJ Reports, 1992, pp. 351, 514–15, and the *Brcko* case, 36 ILM, 1997, pp. 396, 427 ff. However, note that in the latter case, the Arbitral Tribunal was expressly authorised to apply 'relevant legal and equitable principles': see article V of Annex 2 of the Dayton Accords, 1995, *ibid.*, p. 400. See also J. M. Sorel, 'L'Arbitrage sur la Zona de Brcko Tragi-comédie en Trois Actes et un Épilogue à Suivre', AFDI, 1997, p. 253.

[170] ICJ Reports, 1996, pp. 226, 257, 262–3; 110 ILR, pp. 163, 207, 212–13. See also the *Corfu Channel* case, ICJ Reports, 1949, pp. 4, 22; 16 AD, p. 155. See further below, chapter 21, p. 1187.

[171] See e.g. Lauterpacht, *Development of International Law*; Waldock, 'General Course', and Schwarzenberger, *International Law*, pp. 30 ff. See also Thirlway, 'Law and Procedure of the ICJ (Part Two)', pp. 3, 127, and Thirlway, 'Supplement', p. 114; Pellet, 'Article 38', p. 784, and P. Cahier, 'Le Rôle du Juge dans l'Élaboration du Droit International' in *Theory of International Law at the Threshold of the 21st Century* (ed. J. Makerczyk), The Hague, 1996, p. 353.

article 59 of the Statute of the International Court of Justice the decisions of the Court have no binding force except as between the parties and in respect of the case under consideration, the Court has striven to follow its previous judgments and insert a measure of certainty within the process: so that while the doctrine of precedent as it is known in the common law, whereby the rulings of certain courts must be followed by other courts, does not exist in international law, one still finds that states in disputes and textbook writers quote judgments of the Permanent Court and the International Court of Justice as authoritative decisions.

The International Court of Justice itself will closely examine its previous decisions and will carefully distinguish those cases which it feels should not be applied to the problem being studied.[172] But just as English judges, for example, create law in the process of interpreting it, so the judges of the International Court of Justice sometimes do a little more than merely 'determine' it. One of the most outstanding instances of this occurred in the *Anglo-Norwegian Fisheries* case,[173] with its statement of the criteria for the recognition of baselines from which to measure the territorial sea, which was later enshrined in the 1958 Geneva Convention on the Territorial Sea and Contiguous Zone.

Other examples include the *Reparation* case,[174] which recognised the legal personality of international institutions in certain cases, the *Genocide* case,[175] which dealt with reservations to treaties, the *Nottebohm* case,[176] which considered the role and characteristics of nationality and the range of cases concerning maritime delimitation.[177]

Of course, it does not follow that a decision of the Court will be invariably accepted in later discussions and formulations of the law. One example of this is part of the decision in the *Lotus* case,[178] which was criticised and later abandoned in the Geneva Conventions on the Law of the Sea. But this is comparatively unusual and the practice of the Court is to examine its own relevant case-law with considerable attention and to depart from it rarely.[179] At the very least, it will constitute the starting point of analysis, so that, for example, the Court noted in the *Cameroon*

---

[172] See further Shahabuddeen, *Precedent.*
[173] ICJ Reports, 1951, p. 116; 18 ILR, p. 86. See further below, chapter 11, p. 558.
[174] ICJ Reports, 1949, p. 174; 16 AD, p. 318. See further below, chapter 23, p. 1296.
[175] ICJ Reports, 1951, p. 15; 18 ILR, p. 364.   [176] ICJ Reports, 1955, p. 4; 22 ILR, p. 349.
[177] See e.g. Thirlway, 'Supplement', p. 116, and see below, chapter 11, p. 590.
[178] PCIJ, Series A, No. 10, 1927, p. 18; 4 AD, p. 5. See below, p. 618.
[179] See e.g. *Qatar* v. *Bahrain*, ICJ Reports, 2001, pp. 40, 93; *Liechtenstein* v. *Germany*, ICJ Reports, 2005, p. 6 and the *Construction of a Wall* advisory opinion, ICJ Reports, 2004, pp. 135, 154–6; 129 ILR, pp. 37, 71–4.

v. *Nigeria* case that 'the real question is whether, in this case, there is cause not to follow the reasoning and conclusion of earlier cases'.[180]

In addition to the Permanent Court and the International Court of Justice, the phrase 'judicial decisions' also encompasses international arbitral awards and the rulings of national courts. There have been many international arbitral tribunals, such as the Permanent Court of Arbitration created by the Hague Conferences of 1899 and 1907 and the various mixed-claims tribunals, including the Iran–US Claims Tribunal, and, although they differ from the international courts in some ways, many of their decisions have been extremely significant in the development of international law. This can be seen in the existence and number of the Reports of International Arbitral Awards published since 1948 by the United Nations.

One leading example is the *Alabama Claims* arbitration,[181] which marked the opening of a new era in the peaceful settlement of international disputes, in which increasing use was made of judicial and arbitration methods in resolving conflicts. This case involved a vessel built on Merseyside to the specifications of the Confederate States, which succeeded in capturing some seventy Federal ships during the American Civil War. The United States sought compensation after the war for the depredations of the *Alabama* and other ships and this was accepted by the Tribunal. Britain had infringed the rules of neutrality and was accordingly obliged to pay damages to the United States. Another illustration of the impact of arbitral awards is the *Island of Palmas* case[182] which has proved of immense significance to the subject of territorial sovereignty and will be discussed in chapter 10. In addition, the growing significance of the case-law of the International Criminal Tribunal for the Former Yugoslavia and the International Criminal Tribunal for Rwanda needs to be noted. As a consequence, it is not rare for international courts of one type or another to cite each other's decisions, sometimes as support[183] and sometimes to disagree.[184]

---

[180] ICJ Reports, 1998, pp. 275, 292.

[181] J. B. Moore, *International Arbitrations*, New York, 1898, vol. I, p. 653.

[182] 2 RIAA, p. 829; 4 AD, p. 3. See also the *Beagle Channel* award, HMSO, 1977; 52 ILR, p. 93, and the *Anglo-French Continental Shelf* case, Cmnd 7438, 1978; 54 ILR, p. 6.

[183] See e.g. the references in the *Saiga (No. 2)* case, International Tribunal for the Law of the Sea, judgment of 1 July 1999, paras. 133–4; 120 ILR, p. 143, to the *Gabčíkovo–Nagymaros* case, ICJ Reports, 1997, p. 7.

[184] For example, the views expressed in the International Criminal Tribunal for the Former Yugoslavia's decision in the *Tadić* case (IT-94-1-A, paras. 115 ff; 124 ILR, p. 61) disapproving of the approach adopted by the ICJ in the *Nicaragua* case, ICJ Reports, 1986,

As has already been seen, the decisions of municipal courts[185] may provide evidence of the existence of a customary rule. They may also constitute evidence of the actual practice of states which, while not a description of the law as it has been held to apply, nevertheless affords examples of how states actually behave, in other words the essence of the material act which is so necessary in establishing a rule of customary law.[186] British and American writers, in particular, tend to refer fairly extensively to decisions of national courts.

One may, finally, also point to decisions by the highest courts of federal states, like Switzerland and the United States, in their resolution of conflicts between the component units of such countries, as relevant to the development of international law rules in such fields as boundary disputes. A boundary disagreement between two US states which is settled by the Supreme Court is in many ways analogous to the International Court of Justice considering a frontier dispute between two independent states, and as such provides valuable material for international law.[187]

Writers[188]

Article 38 includes as a subsidiary means for the determination of rules of law, 'the teachings of the most highly qualified publicists of the various nations'.

Historically, of course, the influence of academic writers on the development of international law has been marked. In the heyday of Natural Law it was analyses and juristic opinions that were crucial, while the role of state practice and court decisions was of less value. Writers such as Gentili, Grotius, Pufendorf, Bynkershoek and Vattel were the supreme authorities of the sixteenth to eighteenth centuries and determined the scope, form and content of international law.[189]

---

p. 14, with regard to the test for state responsibility in respect of paramilitary units. The International Court indeed reaffirmed its approach in the *Genocide Convention (Bosnia v. Serbia)* case, ICJ Reports, 2007, paras. 402 ff.

[185] See e.g. *Thirty Hogsheads of Sugar, Bentzon v. Boyle* 9 Cranch 191 (1815); the *Paquete Habana* 175 US 677 (1900) and the *Scotia* 14 Wallace 170 (1871). See also the *Lotus* case, PCIJ, Series A, No. 10, 1927, p. 18; 4 AD, p. 153. For further examples in the fields of state and diplomatic immunities particularly, see below, chapter 13.

[186] See e.g. *Congo v. Belgium*, ICJ Reports, 2002, pp. 3, 24; 128 ILR, pp. 60, 80.

[187] See e.g. *Vermont v. New Hampshire* 289 US 593 (1933) and *Iowa v. Illinois* 147 US 1 (1893).

[188] See e.g. Parry, *British Digest*, pp. 103–5 and Lauterpacht, *Development of International Law*, pp. 23–5. See also R. Y. Jennings, 'International Lawyers and the Progressive Development of International Law' in Makerczyk, *Theory of International Law at the Threshold of the 21st Century*, 1996, p. 325, and Pellet, 'Article 38', p. 790.

[189] See above, chapter 1.

With the rise of positivism and the consequent emphasis upon state sovereignty, treaties and custom assumed the dominant position in the exposition of the rules of the international system, and the importance of legalistic writings began to decline. Thus, one finds that textbooks are used as a method of discovering what the law is on any particular point rather than as the fount or source of actual rules. There are still some writers who have had a formative impact upon the evolution of particular laws, for example Gidel on the law of the sea,[190] and others whose general works on international law tend to be referred to virtually as classics, for example Oppenheim and Rousseau, but the general influence of textbook writers has somewhat declined.

Nevertheless, books are important as a way of arranging and putting into focus the structure and form of international law and of elucidating the nature, history and practice of the rules of law. Academic writings also have a useful role to play in stimulating thought about the values and aims of international law as well as pointing out the defects that exist within the system, and making suggestions as to the future.

Because of the lack of supreme authorities and institutions in the international legal order, the responsibility is all the greater upon the publicists of the various nations to inject an element of coherence and order into the subject as well as to question the direction and purposes of the rules.

States in their presentation of claims, national law officials in their opinions to their governments, the various international judicial and arbitral bodies in considering their decisions, and the judges of municipal courts when the need arises, all consult and quote the writings of the leading juristic authorities.[191]

Of course, the claim can be made, and often is, that textbook writers merely reflect and reinforce national prejudices,[192] but it is an allegation which has been exaggerated. It should not lead us to dismiss the value of writers, but rather to assess correctly the writer within his particular environment.

Other possible sources of international law

In the discussion of the various sources of law prescribed by the Statute of the International Court of Justice, it might have been noted that there is a

---

[190] *Droit International Public de la Mer*, Chateauroux, 3 vols., 1932–4.
[191] See Brownlie, *Principles*, pp. 23–4.
[192] See e.g. Huber in the *Spanish Zone of Morocco* case, 2 RIAA, pp. 615, 640; 2 AD, pp. 157, 164 (note). See also Carty, *Decay of International Law?*, pp. 128–31.

distinction between, on the one hand, actual sources of rules, that is those devices capable of instituting new rules such as law-making treaties, customary law and many decisions of the International Court of Justice since they cannot be confined to the category of merely determining or elucidating the law, and on the other hand those practices and devices which afford evidence of the existence of rules, such as juristic writings, many treaty-contracts and some judicial decisions both at the international and municipal level. In fact, each source is capable, to some extent, of both developing new law and identifying existing law. This results partly from the disorganised state of international law and partly from the terms of article 38 itself.

A similar confusion between law-making, law-determining and law-evidencing can be discerned in the discussion of the various other methods of developing law that have emerged since the conclusion of the Second World War. Foremost among the issues that have arisen and one that reflects the growth in the importance of the Third World states and the gradual de-Europeanisation of the world order is the question of the standing of the resolutions and declarations of the General Assembly of the United Nations.[193]

Unlike the UN Security Council, which has the competence to adopt resolutions under articles 24 and 25 of the UN Charter binding on all member states of the organisation,[194] resolutions of the Assembly are generally not legally binding and are merely recommendatory, putting forward opinions on various issues with varying degrees of majority

[193] See e.g. O. Y. Asamoah, *The Legal Significance of the Declarations of the General Assembly of the United Nations*, The Hague, 1966; D. Johnson, 'The Effect of Resolutions of the General Assembly of the United Nations', 32 BYIL, 1955–6, p. 97; J. Castañeda, *Legal Effects of United Nations Resolutions*, New York, 1969, and R. A. Falk, 'On the Quasi-Legislative Competence of the General Assembly', 60 AJIL, 1966, p. 782. See also A. Cassese, *International Law in a Divided World*, London, 1986, pp. 192–5; M. Virally, 'La Valeur Juridique des Recommendations des Organisations Internationales', AFDI, 1956, p. 69; B. Sloan, 'The Binding Force of a Recommendation of the General Assembly of the United Nations', 25 BYIL, 1948, p. 1, and Sloan, 'General Assembly Resolutions Revisited (40 Years After)', 58 BYIL, 1987, p. 39; Thirlway, 'Law and Procedure of the ICJ (Part One)', p. 6; O. Schachter, 'United Nations Law', 88 AJIL, 1994, p. 1; A. Pellet, 'La Formation du Droit International dans le Cadre des Nations Unies', 6 EJIL, 1995, p. 401, and Pellet, 'Article 38', p. 711; and S. Schwebel, 'United Nations Resolutions, Recent Arbitral Awards and Customary International Law' in *Realism in Law-Making* (eds. M. Bos and H. Siblesz), Dordrecht, 1986, p. 203. See also Judge Weeramantry's Dissenting Opinion in the *East Timor* case, ICJ Reports, 1995, pp. 90, 185; 105 ILR, pp. 226, 326.

[194] See e.g. the *Namibia* case, ICJ Reports, 1971, pp. 16, 54; 49 ILR, p. 29 and the *Lockerbie* case, ICJ Reports, 1992, pp. 3, 15; 94 ILR, p. 478. See further below, chapter 22.

support.[195] This is the classic position and reflects the intention that the Assembly was to be basically a parliamentary advisory body with the binding decisions being taken by the Security Council.

Nowadays, the situation is somewhat more complex. The Assembly has produced a great number of highly important resolutions and declarations and it was inevitable that these should have some impact upon the direction adopted by modern international law. The way states vote in the General Assembly and the explanations given upon such occasions constitute evidence of state practice and state understanding as to the law. Where a particular country has consistently voted in favour of, for example, the abolition of apartheid, it could not afterwards deny the existence of a usage condemning racial discrimination and it may even be that that usage is for that state converted into a binding custom.

The Court in the *Nicaragua* case tentatively expressed the view that the *opinio juris* requirement could be derived from the circumstances surrounding the adoption and application of a General Assembly resolution. It noted that the relevant

> *opinio juris* may, though with all due caution, be deduced from, *inter alia*, the attitude of the Parties [i.e. the US and Nicaragua] and the attitude of States towards certain General Assembly resolutions, and particularly resolution 2625 (XXV) entitled 'Declaration on Principles of International Law concerning Friendly Relations and Co-operation among States in accordance with the Charter of the United Nations'.[196]

The effect of consent to resolutions such as this one 'may be understood as acceptance of the validity of the rule or set of rules declared by the resolution by themselves'.[197] This comment, however, may well have referred solely to the situation where the resolution in question defines or elucidates an existing treaty (i.e. Charter) commitment.

Where the vast majority of states consistently vote for resolutions and declarations on a topic, that amounts to a state practice and a binding rule may very well emerge provided that the requisite *opinio juris* can be proved. For example, the 1960 Declaration on the Granting of Independence to Colonial Countries and Peoples, which was adopted with no opposition and only nine abstentions and followed a series of resolutions

---

[195] Some resolutions of a more administrative nature are binding: see e.g. article 17 of the UN Charter.

[196] ICJ Reports, 1986, pp. 14, 99–100; 76 ILR, pp. 349, 433–4.

[197] ICJ Reports, 1986, p. 100; 76 ILR, p. 434.

in general and specific terms attacking colonialism and calling for the self-determination of the remaining colonies, has, it would seem, marked the transmutation of the concept of self-determination from a political and moral principle to a legal right and consequent obligation, particularly taken in conjunction with the 1970 Declaration on Principles of International Law.[198]

Declarations such as that on the Legal Principles Governing Activities of States in the Exploration and Use of Outer Space (1963) can also be regarded as examples of state practices which are leading to, or have led to, a binding rule of customary law. As well as constituting state practice, it may be possible to use such resolutions as evidence of the existence of or evolution towards an *opinio juris* without which a custom cannot arise. Apart from that, resolutions can be understood as authoritative interpretations by the Assembly of the various principles of the United Nations Charter depending on the circumstances.[199]

Accordingly, such resolutions are able to speed up the process of the legalisation of a state practice and thus enable a speedier adaptation of customary law to the conditions of modern life. The presence of representatives of virtually all of the states of the world in the General Assembly enormously enhances the value of that organ in general political terms and in terms of the generation of state practice that may or may not lead to binding custom. As the International Court noted, for example, in the *Nicaragua* case,[200] 'the wording of certain General Assembly declarations adopted by states demonstrates their recognition of the principle of the prohibition of force as definitely a matter of customary international law'. The Court put the issue the following way in the *Legality of the Threat or Use of Nuclear Weapons* Advisory Opinion:[201]

> The Court notes that General Assembly resolutions, even if they are not binding, may sometimes have normative value. They can, in certain circumstances, provide evidence important for establishing the existence of a rule or the emergence of an *opinio juris*. To establish whether this is true of a General Assembly resolution, it is necesary to look at its content and

---

[198] See further below, chapter 5, p. 251.
[199] See e.g. O. Schachter, 'Interpretation of the Charter in the Political Organs of the United Nations' in *Law, States and International Order*, 1964, p. 269; R. Higgins, *The Development of International Law Through the Political Organs of the United Nations*, Oxford, 1963, and M. N. Shaw, *Title to Territory in Africa: International Legal Issues*, Oxford, 1986, chapter 2.
[200] ICJ Reports, 1986, pp. 14, 102; 76 ILR, pp. 349, 436.
[201] ICJ Reports, 1996, pp. 226, 254–5; 110 ILR, pp. 163, 204–5.

the conditions of its adoption; it is also necessary to see whether an *opinio juris* exists as to its normative character. Or a series of resolutions may show the gradual evolution of the *opinio juris* required for the establishment of a new rule.

The Court in this case examined a series of General Assembly resolutions concerning the legality of nuclear weapons and noted that several of them had been adopted with substantial numbers of negative votes and abstentions. It was also pointed out that the focus of such resolutions had not always been constant. The Court therefore concluded that these resolutions fell short of establishing the existence of an *opinio juris* on the illegality of nuclear weapons.[202]

Nevertheless, one must be alive to the dangers in ascribing legal value to everything that emanates from the Assembly. Resolutions are often the results of political compromises and arrangements and, comprehended in that sense, never intended to constitute binding norms. Great care must be taken in moving from a plethora of practice to the identification of legal norms.

As far as the practice of other international organisations is concerned,[203] the same approach, but necessarily tempered with a little more caution, may be adopted. Resolutions may evidence an existing custom or constitute usage that may lead to the creation of a custom and the *opinio juris* requirement may similarly emerge from the surrounding circumstances, although care must be exercised here.[204]

It is sometimes argued more generally that particular non-binding instruments or documents or non-binding provisions in treaties form a special category that may be termed 'soft law'. This terminology is meant to indicate that the instrument or provision in question is not of itself 'law', but its importance within the general framework of international legal development is such that particular attention requires to be paid to it.[205] 'Soft law' is not law. That needs to be emphasised, but a document,

---

[202] *Ibid.*, p. 255; 110 ILR, p. 205. See as to other cases, above, p. 84.

[203] See generally, as to other international organisations in this context, A. J. P. Tammes, 'Decisions of International Organs as a Source of International Law', 94 HR, 1958, p. 265; Virally, 'La Valeur Juridique', p. 66, and H. Thierry, 'Les Résolutions des Organes Internationaux dans la Jurisprudence de la Cour Internationale de Justice', 167 HR, 1980, p. 385.

[204] See the *Nicaragua* case, ICJ Reports, 1986, pp. 14, 100–2; 76 ILR, pp. 349, 434–6.

[205] See e.g. Boyle and Chinkin, *The Making of International Law*, pp. 211 ff.; Pellet, 'Article 38', p. 712; H. Hillgenberg, 'A Fresh Look at Soft Law', 10 EJIL, 1999, p. 499; M. Bothe, 'Legal and Non-Legal Norms – A Meaningful Distinction in International Relations', 11

for example, does not need to constitute a binding treaty before it can exercise an influence in international politics. The Helsinki Final Act of 1975 is a prime example of this. This was not a binding agreement, but its influence in Central and Eastern Europe in emphasising the role and importance of international human rights proved incalculable.[206] Certain areas of international law have generated more 'soft law', in the sense of the production of important but non-binding instruments, than others. Here one may cite particularly international economic law[207] and international environmental law.[208] The use of such documents, whether termed, for example, recommendations, guidelines, codes of practice or standards, is significant in signalling the evolution and establishment of guidelines, which may ultimately be converted into legally binding rules. This may be accomplished either by formalisation into a binding treaty or by acceptance as a customary rule, provided that the necessary conditions have been fulfilled. The propositions of 'soft law' are important and influential, but do not in themselves constitute legal norms. In many cases, it may be advantageous for states to reach agreements with each other or through international organisations which are not intended to be binding and thus subject to formal legal implementation, but which reflect a political intention to act in a certain way. Such agreements may be more flexible, easier to conclude and easier to adhere to for domestic reasons.

A study by the US State Department concerning non-binding international agreements between states[209] noted that

Netherlands YIL, 1980, p. 65; I. Seidl-Hohenveldern, 'International Economic Soft Law', 163 HR, 1980, p. 164, and Seidl-Hohenveldern, *International Economic Law*, 2nd edn, Dordrecht, 1992, p. 42; J. Gold, 'Strengthening the Soft International Law of Exchange Arrangements', 77 AJIL, 1983, p. 443; PASIL, 1988, p. 371; G. J. H. Van Hoof, *Re-thinking the Sources of International Law*, Deventer, 1983, p. 187; C. M. Chinkin, 'The Challenge of Soft Law: Development and Change in International Law', 38 ICLQ, 1989, p. 850; L. Henkin, *International Law, Politics and Values*, Dordrecht, 1995, pp. 94 and 192; W. M. Reisman, 'The Concept and Functions of Soft Law in International Politics' in *Essays in Honour of Judge Taslim Olawale Elias* (eds. E. G. Bello and B. Ajibola), Dordrecht, 1992, vol. I, p. 135; A. E. Boyle, 'Some Reflections on the Relationship of Treaties and Soft Law', 48 ICLQ, 1999, p. 901; F. Francioni, 'International "Soft Law": A Contemporary Assessment' in Lowe and Fitzmaurice, *Fifty Years of the International Court of Justice*, p. 167, and *Commitment and Compliance: The Role of Non-Binding Norms in the International Legal System* (ed. D. Shelton), Oxford, 2000

206 See e.g. the reference to it in the *Nicaragua* case, ICJ Reports, 1986, pp. 3, 100; 76 ILR, pp. 349, 434.

207 See e.g. Seidl-Hohenveldern, *International Economic Law*, pp. 42 ff.

208 See e.g. P. Birnie and A. Boyle, *International Law and the Environment*, 2nd edn, Oxford, 2002, pp. 24 ff.

209 Memorandum of the Assistant Legal Adviser for Treaty Affairs, US State Department, quoted in 88 AJIL, 1994, pp. 515 ff. See also A. Aust, 'The Theory and Practice of Informal

it has long been recognised in international practice that governments may agree on joint statements of policy or intention that do not establish legal obligations. In recent decades, this has become a common means of announcing the results of diplomatic exchanges, stating common positions on policy issues, recording their intended course of action on matters of mutual concern, or making political commitments to one another. These documents are sometimes referred to as non-binding agreements, gentlemen's agreements, joint statements or declarations.

What is determinative as to status in such situations is not the title given to the document in question, but the intention of the parties as inferred from all the relevant circumstances as to whether they intended to create binding legal relationships between themselves on the matter in question.

The International Law Commission

The International Law Commission was established by the General Assembly in 1947 with the declared object of promoting the progressive development of international law and its codification.[210] It consists of thirty-four members from Africa, Asia, America and Europe, who remain in office for five years each and who are appointed from lists submitted by national governments. The Commission is aided in its deliberations by consultations with various outside bodies including the Asian–African Legal Consultative Committee, the European Commission on Legal Cooperation and the Inter-American Council of Jurists.[211]

International Instruments', 35 ICLQ, 1984, p. 787; O. Schachter, 'The Twilight Existence of Nonbinding International Agreements', 71 AJIL, 1977, p. 296; McNair, *The Law of Treaties*, p. 6, and A. T. Guzman, 'The Design of International Agreements', 16 EJIL, 2005, p. 579.

[210] See, as to the relationship between codification and progressive development, Judge ad hoc Sørensen's Dissenting Opinion in the *North Sea Continental Shelf* cases, ICJ Reports, 1969, pp. 3, 242–3; 41 ILR, pp. 29, 217–19.

[211] See articles 2, 3 and 8 of the Statute of the ILC. See also e.g. B. Ramcharan, *The International Law Commission*, Leiden, 1977; *The Work of the International Law Commission*, 4th edn, New York, 1988; I. Sinclair, *The International Law Commission*, Cambridge, 1987; *The International Law Commission and the Future of International Law* (eds. M. R. Anderson, A. E. Boyle, A. V. Lowe and C. Wickremasinghe), London, 1998; *International Law on the Eve of the Twenty-first Century: Views from the International Law Commission*, New York, 1997; S. Rosenne, 'The International Law Commission 1949–59', 36 BYIL, 1960, p. 104, and Rosenne, 'Relations Between Governments and the International Law Commission', 19 YBWA, 1965, p. 183; B. Graefrath, 'The International Law Commission Tomorrow: Improving its Organisation and Methods of Work', 85 AJIL, 1991, p. 597, and R. P. Dhokalia, *The Codification of Public International Law*, Manchester, 1970.

Many of the most important international conventions have grown out of the Commission's work. Having decided upon a topic, the International Law Commission will prepare a draft. This is submitted to the various states for their comments and is usually followed by an international conference convened by the United Nations. Eventually a treaty will emerge. This procedure was followed in such international conventions as those on the Law of the Sea in 1958, Diplomatic Relations in 1961, Consular Relations in 1963, Special Missions in 1969 and the Law of Treaties in 1969. Of course, this smooth operation does not invariably occur, witness the many conferences at Caracas in 1974, and Geneva and New York from 1975 to 1982, necessary to produce a new Convention on the Law of the Sea.

Apart from preparing such drafts, the International Law Commission also issues reports and studies, and has formulated such documents as the Draft Declaration on Rights and Duties of States of 1949 and the Principles of International Law recognised in the Charter of the Nuremberg Tribunal and in the Judgment of the Tribunal of 1950. The Commission produced a set of draft articles on the problems of jurisdictional immunities in 1991, a draft statute for an international criminal court in 1994 and a set of draft articles on state responsibility in 2001. The drafts of the ILC are often referred to in the judgments of the International Court of Justice. Indeed, in his speech to the UN General Assembly in 1997, President Schwebel noted in referring to the decision in the *Gabčíkovo–Nagymaros Project* case[212] that the judgment:

> is notable, moreover, because of the breadth and depth of the importance given in it to the work product of the International Law Commission. The Court's Judgment not only draws on treaties concluded pursuant to the Commission's proceedings: those on the law of treaties, of State succession in respect of treaties, and the law of international watercourses. It gives great weight to some of the Commission's *Draft* Articles on State Responsibility, as did both Hungary and Slovakia. This is not wholly exceptional; it rather illustrates the fact that just as the judgments and opinions of the Court have influenced the work of the International Law Commission, so the work of the Commission may influence that of the Court.[213]

Thus, one can see that the International Law Commission is involved in at least two of the major sources of law. Its drafts may form the bases of

---

[212] ICJ Reports, 1997, p. 7; 116 ILR, p. 1.
[213] See www.icj-cij.org/icjwww/ipresscom/SPEECHES/Ga1997e.htm.

international treaties which bind those states which have signed and ratified them and which may continue to form part of general international law, and its work is part of the whole range of state practice which can lead to new rules of customary law. Its drafts, indeed, may constitute evidence of custom, contribute to the corpus of usages which may create new law and evidence the *opinio juris*.[214] In addition, it is not to be overlooked that the International Law Commission is a body composed of eminently qualified publicists, including many governmental legal advisers, whose reports and studies may be used as a method of determining what the law actually is, in much the same way as books.

Other bodies

Although the International Law Commission is by far the most important of the organs for the study and development of the law, there do exist certain other bodies which are involved in the same mission. The United Nations Commission on International Trade Law (UNCITRAL) and the United Nations Conference on Trade and Development (UNCTAD), for example, are actively increasing the range of international law in the fields of economic, financial and development activities, while temporary organs such as the Committee on the Principles of International Law have been engaged in producing various declarations and statements. Nor can one overlook the tremendous work of the many specialised agencies like the International Labour Organisation and the United Nations Educational, Scientific and Cultural Organisation (UNESCO), which are constantly developing international law in their respective spheres.

There are also some independent bodies which are actively involved in the field. The International Law Association and the Institut de Droit International are the best known of such organisations which study and stimulate the law of the world community, while the various Harvard Research drafts produced before the Second World War are still of value today.

Unilateral acts

In certain situations, the unilateral acts of states, including statements made by relevant state officials, may give rise to international legal

---

[214] See above, p. 84.

obligations.[215] Such acts might include recognition and protests, which are intended to have legal consequences. Unilateral acts, while not sources of international law as understood in article 38(1) of the Statute of the ICJ, may constitute sources of obligation.[216] For this to happen, the intention to be bound of the state making the declaration in question is crucial, as will be the element of publicity or notoriety.[217] Such intention may be ascertained by way of interpretation of the act, and the principle of good faith plays a crucial role. The International Court has stressed that where states make statements by which their freedom of action is limited, a restrictive interpretation is required.[218] Recognition will be important here in so far as third states are concerned, in order for such an act or statement to be opposable to them. Beyond this, such unilateral statements may be used as evidence of a particular view taken by the state in question.[219]

[215] See Virally, 'Sources', pp. 154–6; Brownlie, *Principles*, pp. 612–15; W. Fiedler, 'Unilateral Acts in International Law' in *Encyclopedia of Public International Law* (ed. R. Bernhardt), Amsterdam, 2000, vol. IV, p. 1018; G. Venturini, 'La Portée et les Effets Juridiques des Attitudes et des Actes Unilatéraux des États', 112 HR, 1964, p. 363; J. Charpentier, 'Engagements Unilatéraux et Engagements Conventionnels' in *Theory of International Law at the Threshold of the 21st Century*, p. 367; A. P. Rubin, 'The International Legal Effects of Unilateral Declarations', 71 AJIL, 1977, p. 1; K. Zemanek, 'Unilateral Legal Acts Revisited' in Wellens, *International Law*, p. 209; E. Suy, *Les Actes Unilateraux en Droit International Public*, Paris, 1962, and J. Garner, 'The International Binding Force of Unilateral Oral Declarations', 27 AJIL, 1933, p. 493. The International Law Commission has been studying the question of the Unilateral Acts of States since 1996, see A/51/10, pp. 230 and 328–9. See also the Fifth Report, A/CN.4/525, 2002.

[216] See e.g. the Report of the International Law Commission, A/57/10, 2002, p. 215.

[217] The *Nuclear Tests* cases, ICJ Reports, 1974, pp. 253, 267; 57 ILR, pp. 398, 412. See also the *Request for an Examination of the Situation in Accordance with Paragraph 63 of the Court's Judgment of 20 December 1974 in the Nuclear Tests (New Zealand v. France) Case*, ICJ Reports, 1995, pp. 288, 305; 106 ILR, pp. 1, 27; the *Nova-Scotia/Newfoundland* (First Phase) case, 2001, para. 3.14; 128 ILR, pp. 425, 449; and the *Eritrea/Ethiopia* case, 2002, para. 4.70; 130 ILR, pp. 1, 69. Such a commitment may arise in oral pleadings before the Court itself: see *Cameroon v. Nigeria*, ICJ Reports, 2002, p. 452.

[218] *Nuclear Tests* cases, ICJ Reports, 1974, pp. 253, 267; 57 ILR, pp. 398, 412. See also the *Nicaragua* case, ICJ Reports, 1986, pp. 14, 132; 76 ILR, pp. 349, 466, and the *Burkina Faso v. Mali* case, ICJ Reports, 1986, pp. 554, 573–4; 80 ILR, pp. 459, 477–8. The Court in the *North Sea Continental Shelf* cases declared that the unilateral assumption of the obligations of a convention by a state not party to it was 'not lightly to be presumed', ICJ Reports, 1969, pp. 3, 25; 41 ILR, p. 29. The Court in the *Malaysia/Singapore* case, ICJ Reports, 2008, para. 229, noted that a denial could not be interpreted as a binding undertaking where not made in response to a claim by the other party or in the context of a dispute between them.

[219] See e.g. the references to a press release issued by the Ministry of Foreign Affairs of Norway and the wording of a communication of the text of an agreement to Parliament by the Norwegian Government in the *Jan Mayen* case, ICJ Reports, 1993, pp. 38, 51; 99 ILR,

Hierarchy of sources and *jus cogens*[220]

The question of the hierarchy of sources is more complex than appears at first sight. Although there does exist a presumption against normative conflict,[221] international law is not as clear as domestic law in listing the order of constitutional authority[222] and the situation is complicated by the proliferation of international courts and tribunals existing in a non-hierarchical fashion,[223] as well as the significant expansion of international law, both substantively and procedurally. Judicial decisions and writings clearly have a subordinate function within the hierarchy in view of their description as subsidiary means of law determination in article 38(1) of the statute of the ICJ, while the role of general principles of law as a way of complementing custom and treaty law places that category fairly firmly in third place.[224] The question of priority as between custom and treaty law is more complex.[225] As a general rule, that which is later in time will have priority. Treaties are usually formulated to replace or codify existing custom,[226] while treaties in turn may themselves fall out of use and be replaced by new customary rules. However, where the same rule appears

pp. 395, 419. See also Judge Ajibola's Separate Opinion in the *Libya/Chad* case, ICJ Reports, 1994, pp. 6, 58; 100 ILR, pp. 1, 56.

[220] See D. Shelton, 'Normative Hierarchy in International Law', 100 AJIL, 2006, p. 291; M. Koskenniemi, 'Hierarchy in International Law: A Sketch', 8 EJIL, 1997, p. 566; B. Simma and D. Pulkowski, 'Of Planets and the Universe: Self-contained Regimes in International Law', 17 EJIL, 2006, p. 483; P. Weil, 'Towards Relative Normativity in International Law?', 77 AJIL, 1983, p. 413, and 'Vers une Normativité Relative en Droit International?' 86 RGDIP, 1982, p. 5; M. Akehurst, 'The Hierarchy of the Sources of International Law', 47 BYIL, 1974–5, p. 273, and Virally, 'Sources', pp. 165–6. See also H. Mosler, *The International Society as a Legal Community*, Leiden, 1980, pp. 84–6; Thirlway, 'Law and Procedure of the ICJ (Part One)', p. 143, and Thirlway, 'Supplement', p. 52, and U. Fastenrath, 'Relative Normativity in International Law', 4 EJIL, 1993, p. 305.

[221] See e.g. 'Fragmentation of International Law: Difficulties Arising from the Diversification and Expansion of International Law', Report of the Study Group of the International Law Commission (finalised by M. Koskenniemi), A/CN.4/L.682, 2006, p. 25.

[222] Pellet, however, notes that while there is no formal hierarchy as between conventions, custom and general principles, the International Court uses them in successive order and 'has organized a kind of complementarity between them', 'Article 38', p. 773. Dupuy argues that there is no hierarchy of sources: see *Droit International Public*, 8th edn, Paris, 2006, pp. 370 ff. The ILC Study on Fragmentation, however, agrees with writers proclaiming that 'treaties generally enjoy priority over custom and particular treaties over general treaties', p. 47.

[223] See further below, chapter 19, p. 1115.   [224] Pellet, 'Article 38', p. 780.

[225] *Ibid.*, p. 778, and see H. Villager, *Customary International Law and Treaties*, Dordrecht, 1985.

[226] See R. Baxter, 'Multilateral Treaties as Evidence of Customary International Law', BYIL, 1965–6, p. 275.

in both a treaty and a custom, there is no presumption that the latter is subsumed by the former. The two may co-exist.[227] There is in addition a principle to the effect that a special rule prevails over a general rule (*lex specialis derogat legi generali*), so that, for example, treaty rules between states as *lex specialis* would have priority as against general rules of treaty or customary law between the same states,[228] although not if the general rule in question was one of *jus cogens*.[229]

The position is complicated by the existence of norms or obligations deemed to be of a different or higher status than others, whether derived from custom or treaty. These may be obligations *erga omnes* or rules of *jus cogens*. While there may be significant overlap between these two in terms of the content of rules to which they relate, there is a difference in nature. The former concept concerns the scope of application of the relevant rule, that is the extent to which states as a generality may be subject to the rule in question and may be seen as having a legal interest in the matter.[230] It has, therefore, primarily a procedural focus. Rules of *jus cogens*, on the other hand, are substantive rules recognised to be of a higher status as such. The International Court stated in the *Barcelona Traction* case[231] that there existed an essential distinction between the obligations of a state towards the international community as a whole and those arising vis-à-vis another state in the field of diplomatic protection. By their very nature the former concerned all states and 'all states can be held to have a legal interest in their protection; they are obligations *erga omnes*'. Examples of such obligations included the outlawing of aggression and of genocide and the protection from slavery and racial discrimination.[232] To this one may

---

[227] See the *Nicaragua* case, ICJ Reports, 1986, pp. 14, 95.

[228] See ILC Report on Fragmentation, pp. 30 ff., and *Oppenheim's International Law*, pp. 1270 and 1280. See also the *Gabčíkovo–Nagymaros* case, ICJ Reports, 1997, pp. 7, 76; 116 ILR, pp. 1, 85; the *Beagle Channel* case, 52 ILR, pp. 141–2; the *Right of Passage* case, ICJ Reports, 1960, pp. 6, 44; 31 ILR, pp. 23, 56; the *Legality of the Threat or Use of Nuclear Weapons* case, ICJ Reports, 1996, pp. 226, 240; 110 ILR, pp. 163, 190; the *Tunisia/Libya Continental Shelf* case, ICJ Reports, 1982, pp. 18, 38; 67 ILR, pp. 4, 31, and the *Nicaragua* case, ICJ Reports, 1986, pp. 3, 137; 76 ILR, pp. 349, 471.

[229] See e.g. the *OSPAR (Ireland v. UK)* case, 126 ILR, p. 364, para. 84, and further below, p. 623.

[230] See e.g. Article 48 of the ILC Draft Articles on State Responsibility and the commentary thereto, A/56/10, pp. 126 ff. See also the *Furundžija* case before the International Criminal Tribunal for the Former Yugoslavia, 121 ILR, pp. 213, 260.

[231] ICJ Reports, 1970, pp. 3, 32; 46 ILR, pp. 178, 206.

[232] See also the *Nicaragua* case, ICJ Reports, 1986, pp. 14, 100; 76 ILR, pp. 349, 468, and Judge Weeramantry's Dissenting Opinion in the *East Timor* case, ICJ Reports, 1995, pp. 90, 172 and 204; 105 ILR pp. 226; 313 and 345. See, in addition, Simma, 'Bilateralism',

add the prohibition of torture.[233] Further, the International Court in the *East Timor* case stressed that the right of peoples to self-determination 'has an *erga omnes* character',[234] while reiterating in the *Genocide Convention (Bosnia v. Serbia)* case that 'the rights and obligations enshrined in the Convention are rights and obligations *erga omnes*'.[235]

This easing of the traditional rules concerning *locus standi* in certain circumstances with regard to the pursuing of a legal remedy against the alleged offender state may be linked to the separate question of superior principles in international law. Article 53 of the Vienna Convention on the Law of Treaties, 1969, provides that a treaty will be void 'if, at the time of its conclusion, it conflicts with a peremptory norm of general international law'. Further, by article 64, if a new peremptory norm of general international law emerges, any existing treaty which is in conflict with that norm becomes void and terminates. This rule (*jus cogens*) will also apply in the context of customary rules so that no derogation would be permitted to such norms by way of local or special custom.

Such a peremptory norm is defined by the Convention as one 'accepted and recognised by the international community of states as a whole as a norm from which no derogation is permitted and which can be modified only by a subsequent norm of general international law having the same character'.[236] The concept of *jus cogens* is based upon an acceptance of fundamental and superior values within the system and in some respects is akin to the notion of public order or public policy in domestic legal orders.[237] It also reflects the influence of Natural

pp. 230 ff.; M. Ragazzi, *The Concept of International Obligations* Erga Omnes, Oxford, 1997, and J. Crawford, *The International Law Commission's Articles on State Responsibility*, Cambridge, 2002, pp. 242–4.

[233] See e.g. the *Furundžija* case, 121 ILR, pp. 213, 260.

[234] ICJ Reports, 1995, pp. 90, 102; 105 ILR, p. 226.

[235] ICJ Reports, 1996, pp. 595, 616; 115 ILR, p. 10.

[236] It was noted in *US v. Matta-Ballesteros* that: 'Jus cogens norms which are nonderogable and peremptory, enjoy the highest status within customary international law, are binding on all nations, and cannot be preempted by treaty', 71 F.3d 754, 764 n. 4 (9th circuit, 1995).

[237] See e.g. J. Sztucki, *Jus Cogens and the Vienna Convention on the Law of Treaties*, New York, 1974; I. Sinclair, *The Vienna Convention on the Law of Treaties*, 2nd edn, Manchester, 1984, p. 203; M. Virally, 'Réflexions sur le *Jus Cogens*', 12 AFDI, 1966, p. 1; Shelton, 'Normative Hierarchy', pp. 297 ff.; C. Rozakis, *The Concept of Jus Cogens in the Law of Treaties*, Amsterdam, 1976; Cassese, *International Law*, chapter 11; Gomez Robledo, 'Le *Jus Cogens* International', 172 HR, 1981 p. 17; G. Gaja, '*Jus Cogens* beyond the Vienna Conventions', 172 HR, 1981, p. 279; Crawford, *ILC's Articles*, pp. 187–8 and 243; J. Verhoeven, 'Jus Cogens and Reservations or "Counter-Reservations" to the Jurisdiction of the International Court

Law thinking. Rules of *jus cogens* are not new rules of international law as such. It is a question rather of a particular and superior quality that is recognised as adhering in existing rules of international law. Various examples of rules of *jus cogens* have been provided, particularly during the discussions on the topic in the International Law Commission, such as an unlawful use of force, genocide, slave trading and piracy.[238] However, no clear agreement has been manifested regarding other areas,[239] and even the examples given are by no means uncontroverted. Nevertheless, the rise of individual responsibility directly for international crimes marks a further step in the development of *jus cogens* rules. Of particular importance, however, is the identification of the mechanism by which rules of *jus cogens* may be created, since once created no derogation is permitted.

A two-stage approach is here involved in the light of article 53: first, the establishment of the proposition as a rule of general international law and, secondly, the acceptance of that rule as a peremptory norm by the international law community of states as a whole. It will be seen therefore that a stringent process is involved, and rightly so, for the establishment of a higher level of binding rules has serious implications for the international law community. The situation to be avoided is that of foisting peremptory norms upon a political or ideological minority, for that in the long run would devalue the concept. The appropriate test would thus require universal acceptance of the proposition as a legal rule by states and recognition of it as a rule of *jus cogens* by an overwhelming majority

---

of Justice' in Wellens, *International Law*, p. 195, and L. Hannikainen, *Peremptory Norms (Jus Cogens) in International Law*, Helsinki, 1988. See also article 26 of the ILC's Articles on State Responsibility, 2001, and below, chapter 16, p. 944.

[238] *Yearbook of the ILC*, 1966, vol. II, p. 248. See, as regards the prohibition of torture as a rule of *jus cogens*, the decision of the International Criminal Tribunal for the Former Yugoslavia in the *Furundžija* case, 121 ILR, pp. 257–8 and 260–2; *Siderman* v. *Argentina* 26 F.2d 699, 714–18; 103 ILR, p. 454; *Ex Parte Pinochet (No. 3)* [2000] 1 AC 147, 247 (Lord Hope), 253–4 (Lord Hutton) and 290 (Lord Phillips); 119 ILR, pp. 135, 200, 206–7 and 244, and the *Al-Adsani* case, European Court of Human Rights, Judgment of 21 November 2001, para. 61; 123 ILR, pp. 24, 41–2. See also, as regards the prohibition of extrajudicial killing, the decision of the US District Court in *Alejandre* v. *Cuba* 121 ILR, pp. 603, 616, and as regards non-discrimination, the decision of the Inter-American Court of Human Rights in its advisory opinion concerning the *Juridical Condition and Rights of the Undocumented Migrants*, OC-18/03, Series A, No. 18 (2003).

[239] See e.g. Lord Slynn in *Ex Parte Pinochet (No. 1)* who stated that 'Nor is there any jus cogens in respect of such breaches of international law [international crimes] which require that a claim of state or head of state immunity . . . should be overridden', [2000] 1 AC 61, 79; 119 ILR, pp. 50, 67.

of states, crossing ideological and political divides.[240] It is also clear that only rules based on custom or treaties may form the foundation of *jus cogens* norms. This is particularly so in view of the hostile attitude of many states to general principles as an independent source of international law and the universality requirement of *jus cogens* formation. As article 53 of the Vienna Convention notes, a treaty that is contrary to an existing rule of *jus cogens* is void *ab initio*,[241] whereas by virtue of article 64 an existing treaty that conflicts with an emergent rule of *jus cogens* terminates from the date of the emergence of the rule. It is not void *ab initio*, nor by article 71 is any right, obligation or legal situation created by the treaty prior to its termination affected, provided that its maintenance is not in itself contrary to the new peremptory norm. Article 41(2) of the ILC's Articles on State Responsibility, 2001, provides that no state shall recognise as lawful a 'serious breach' of a peremptory norm.[242] Reservations that offended a rule of *jus cogens* may well be unlawful,[243] while it has been suggested that state conduct violating a rule of *jus cogens* may not attract a claim of state immunity.[244] The relationship between the rules of *jus cogens* and article 103 of the United Nations Charter, which states that obligations under the Charter have precedence as against obligations under other international agreements, was discussed by Judge Lauterpacht in his Separate Opinion in the *Bosnia* case.[245] He noted in particular that 'the relief which article 103 of the Charter may give the Security Council in case of conflict between one of its decisions and an operative treaty obligation cannot – as a matter of simple hierarchy of norms – extend to a conflict between a Security Council resolution and *jus cogens*'.

---

[240] See e.g. Sinclair, *Vienna Convention*, pp. 218–24, and Akehurst, 'Hierarchy'.

[241] See *Yearbook of the ILC*, 1966, vol. II, pp. 91–2.

[242] One that involves a gross or systematic failure by the responsible state to fulfil the obligation, article 40(2). See also article 50(d).

[243] See e.g. Judges Padilla Nervo, Tanaka and Sørensen in the *North Sea Continental Shelf* cases, ICJ Reports, 1969, pp. 3, 97, 182 and 248; 41 ILR, p. 29. See also General Comment No. 24 (52) of the UN Human Rights Committee, CCPR/C/21/Rev.1/Add.6.

[244] See e.g. Cassese, *International Law*, pp. 105 ff, citing the Dissenting Opinion of Judge Wald in *Princz v. Federal Republic of Germany*, a decision of the US Court of Appeals, 1994, 103 ILR, p. 618, but see the *Al-Adsani* case, European Court of Human Rights, Judgment of 21 November 2001; 123 ILR, p. 24.

[245] ICJ Reports, 1993, pp. 325, 440; 95 ILR, pp. 43, 158. See also the decision of the House of Lords in the *Al-Jedda* case, [2007] UKHL 58 concerning the priority of article 103 obligations (here Security Council resolutions) over article 5 of the European Convention on Human Rights.

Suggestions for further reading

M. Akehurst, 'Custom as a Source of International Law', 47 BYIL, 1974–5, p. 1

A. Boyle and C. Chinkin, *The Making of International Law*, Oxford, 2007

B. Cheng, *General Principles of Law as Applied by International Courts and Tribunals*, London, 1953

C. Parry, *The Sources and Evidences of International Law*, Cambridge, 1965

A. Pellet, 'Article 38' in *The Statute of the International Court of Justice: A Commentary* (eds. A. Zimmermann, C. Tomuschat and K. Oellers-Frahm), Oxford, 2006, p. 677

P. Weil, 'Towards Relative Normativity in International Law?', 77 AJIL, 1983, p. 413

4

International law and municipal law

The role of the state in the modern world is a complex one. According to legal theory, each state is sovereign and equal.[1] In reality, with the phenomenal growth in communications and consciousness, and with the constant reminder of global rivalries, not even the most powerful of states can be entirely sovereign. Interdependence and the close-knit character of contemporary international commercial and political society ensures that virtually any action of a state could well have profound repercussions upon the system as a whole and the decisions under consideration by other states. This has led to an increasing interpenetration of

---

[1] See generally *Oppenheim's International Law* (eds. R. Y. Jennings and A. D. Watts), 9th edn, London, 1992, vol. I, p. 52; L. Reydams, *Universal Jurisdiction: International and Municipal Legal Perspectives*, Oxford, 2004; Y. Shany, *Regulating Jurisdictional Relations Between National and International Courts*, Oxford, 2007; J. W. Verzijl, *International Law in Historical Perspective*, Leiden, 1968, vol. I, p. 90; R. A. Falk, *The Role of Domestic Courts in the International Legal Order*, Princeton, 1964; H. Kelsen, *Principles of International Law*, 2nd edn, London, 1966, pp. 290–4 and 551–88; I. Brownlie, *Principles of Public International Law*, 6th edn, Oxford, 2003, chapter 2; H. Lauterpacht, *International Law: Collected Papers*, Cambridge, 1970, vol. I, pp. 151–77; A. Cassese, *International Law*, 2nd edn, Oxford, 2005, chapter 12, and Cassese, 'Modern Constitutions and International Law', 192 HR, 1985 III, p. 335; Nguyen Quoc Dinh, P. Daillier and A. Pellet, *Droit International Public*, 7th edn, Paris, 2002, p. 92; R. Higgins, *Problems and Process*, Oxford, 1994, chapter 12; K. Marek, 'Les Rapports entre le Droit International et le Droit Interne à la Lumière de la Jurisprudence de la CIJ', *Revue Générale de Droit International Public*, 1962, p. 260; L. Ferrari-Bravo, 'International Law and Municipal Law: The Complementarity of Legal Systems' in *The Structure and Process of International Law* (eds. R. St J. Macdonald and D. Johnston), Dordrecht, 1983, p. 715; F. Morgenstern, 'Judicial Practice and the Supremacy of International Law', 27 BYIL, 1950, p. 42; B. Conforti, *International Law and the Role of Domestic Legal Systems*, The Hague, 1993; J. G. Starke, 'Monism and Dualism in the Theory of International Law Considered from the Standpoint of the Rule of Law', 92 HR, 1957, pp. 5, 70–80; H. Thirlway, 'The Law and Procedure of the International Court of Justice, 1960–89 (Part One)', 60 BYIL, 1989, pp. 4, 114; Report of the Committee on International Law and Municipal Law, International Law Association: Report of the Sixty-Sixth Conference, 1994, p. 326; V. Erades, *Interactions Between International and Municipal Law – A Comparative Caselaw Study*, Leiden, 1993, and V. Heiskanen, *International Legal Topics*, Helsinki, 1992, chapter 1.

international law and domestic law across a number of fields, such as human rights, environmental and international investment law, where at the least the same topic is subject to regulation at both the domestic and the international level (and indeed the regional level in the case of the European Union). With the rise and extension of international law, questions begin to arise paralleling the role played by the state within the international system and concerned with the relationship between the internal legal order of a particular country and the rules and principles governing the international community as a whole. Municipal law governs the domestic aspects of government and deals with issues between individuals, and between individuals and the administrative apparatus, while international law focuses primarily upon the relations between states. That is now, however, an overly simplistic assertion. There are many instances where problems can emerge and lead to difficulties between the two systems. In a case before a municipal court a rule of international law may be brought forward as a defence to a charge, as for example in *R* v. *Jones*, where the defence of seeking to prevent a greater crime (essentially of international law) was claimed with regard to the alleged offence of criminal damage (in English law),[2] or where a vessel is being prosecuted for being in what, in domestic law, is regarded as territorial waters but in international law would be treated as part of the high seas. Further, there are cases where the same situation comes before both national and international courts, which may refer to each other's decisions in a complex process of interaction. For example, the failure of the US to allow imprisoned foreign nationals access to consular assistance in violation of the Vienna Convention on Consular Relations, 1963 was the subject of case-law before the International Court of Justice,[3] the Inter-American Court of Human Rights[4] and US courts,[5] while there is a growing tendency for domestic courts to be used to address violations of international law.[6]

---

[2] [2006] UKHL 16; 132 ILR, p. 668. See further below, p. 146.

[3] See e.g. the *LaGrand* case, ICJ Reports, 2001, p. 466; 134 ILR, p. 1, and the *Avena* case, ICJ Reports, 2004, p. 12; 134 ILR, p. 120.

[4] *The Right to Information on Consular Assistance in the Framework of the Guarantees of the Due Process of Law*, Inter-American Court of Human Rights, Series A, No. 16, 1999.

[5] See e.g. *Breard* v. *Greene* 523 US 371 (1998) and *Sanchez-Llamas* v. *Oregon* 126 S Ct 2669 (2006). See also *Medillin* v. *Texas* 522 US (2008) (Slip Opinion).

[6] See e.g. *R* v. *Jones* [2006] UKHL 16; 132 ILR, p. 668; *ex parte Abbasi* [2002] EWCA Civ 1598; 126 ILR, p. 685, and *R* (*Gentle*) v. *Prime Minister* [2006] EWCA Civ 1689; 132 ILR, p. 721.

The theories[7]

Positivism stresses the overwhelming importance of the state and tends to regard international law as founded upon the consent of states. It is actual practice, illustrated by custom and by treaty, that formulates the role of international law, and not formalistic structures, theoretical deductions or moral stipulations. Accordingly, when positivists such as Triepel[8] and Strupp[9] consider the relationship of international law to municipal law, they do so upon the basis of the supremacy of the state, and the existence of wide differences between the two functioning orders. This theory, known as *dualism*, stresses that the rules of the systems of international law and municipal law exist separately and cannot purport to have an effect on, or overrule, the other.

This is because of the fundamentally different nature of inter-state and intra-state relations and the different legal structure employed on the one hand by the state and on the other hand as between states. Where municipal legislation permits the exercise of international law rules, this is on sufferance as it were and is an example of the supreme authority of the state within its own domestic jurisdiction, rather than of any influence maintained by international law within the internal sphere.[10]

Those writers who disagree with this theory and who adopt the *monist* approach tend to fall into two distinct categories: those who, like Lauterpacht, uphold a strong ethical position with a deep concern for human rights, and others, like Kelsen, who maintain a monist position on formalistic logical grounds. The monists are united in accepting a unitary view of law as a whole and are opposed to the strict division posited by the positivists.

The 'naturalist' strand represented in England by Lauterpacht's works sees the primary function of all law as concerned with the well-being of individuals, and advocates the supremacy of international law as the

---

[7] See above, chapters 1 and 2. See also J. H. Jackson, 'Status of Treaties in Domestic Legal Systems: A Policy Analysis', 86 AJIL, 1992, p. 310; N. Valticos, 'Pluralité des Ordres Juridiques et Unité de Droit International Public' in *Theory of International Law at the Threshold of the 21st Century* (ed. J. Markarczyk), The Hague, 1996, p. 301, and J. Dhommeaux, 'Monismes et Dualismes en Droit International des Droits de l'Homme', AFDI, 1995, p. 447.

[8] H. Triepel, *Völkerrecht und Landesrecht*, Berlin, 1899.

[9] K. Strupp, 'Les Règles Générales du Droit International de la Paix', 47 HR, 1934, p. 389. See also D. Anzilotti, *Corso di Diritto Internazionale*, 3rd edn, Rome, 1928, vol. I, pp. 43 ff.

[10] See *Oppenheim's International Law*, p. 53.

best method available of attaining this. It is an approach characterised by deep suspicion of an international system based upon the sovereignty and absolute independence of states, and illuminated by faith in the capacity of the rules of international law to imbue the international order with a sense of moral purpose and justice founded upon respect for human rights and the welfare of individuals.[11]

The method by which Kelsen elucidates his theory of monism is markedly different and utilises the philosophy of Kant as its basis. Law is regarded as constituting an order which lays down patterns of behaviour that ought to be followed, coupled with provision for sanctions which are employed once an illegal act or course of conduct has occurred or been embarked upon. Since the same definition appertains within both the internal sphere and the international sphere, a logical unity is forged, and because states owe their legal relationship to one another to the rules of international law, such as the one positing equality, since states cannot be equal before the law without a rule to that effect, it follows that international law is superior to or more basic than municipal law.[12]

Reference has already been made to Kelsen's hierarchical system whereby the legality of a particular rule is affirmed once it conforms to an anterior rule. This process of referring back to previous or higher rules ends with the so-called basic norm of the legal order. However, this basic norm is basic only in a relative sense, since the legal character of states, such as their jurisdiction, sovereignty and equality, is fixed by international law. Thus, Kelsen emphasises the unity of the entire legal order upon the basis of the predominance of international law by declaring that it is the basic norm of the international legal order which is the ultimate reason of validity of the national legal orders too.[13]

A third approach, being somewhat a modification of the dualist position and formulated by Fitzmaurice and Rousseau amongst others, attempts to establish a recognised theoretical framework tied to reality. This approach begins by denying that any common field of operation exists as between international law and municipal law by which one system is superior or inferior to the other. Each order is supreme in its own sphere,

---

[11] Lauterpacht, *International Law*. See also Lauterpacht, *International Law and Human Rights*, London, 1950.

[12] Kelsen, *Principles*, pp. 557–9. See also Kelsen, *General Theory of Law and State*, Cambridge, 1945, pp. 363–80. Note that Scelle, for example, founds international legal monism upon an intersocial monism, essentially a sociological explanation: see Nguyen Quoc Dinh *et al.*, *Droit International Public*, p. 96.

[13] See further above, chapter 2, p. 50.

much as French law and English law are in France and England. And just as one cannot talk in terms of the supremacy of French law over English law, but only of two distinct legal systems each operating within its own field, so it is possible to treat international law and municipal law in the same way. They are both the legal element contained within the domestic and international systems respectively, and they exist within different juridical orders.

What may, and often does, happen is what is termed a conflict of obligations, that is the state within its own domestic sphere does not act in accordance with its obligations as laid down by international law. In such a case, the domestic position is unaffected (and is not overruled by the contrary rule of international law) but rather the state as it operates internationally has broken a rule of international law and the remedy will lie in the international field, whether by means of diplomatic protest or judicial action.

This method of solving the problem does not delve deeply into theoretical considerations, but aims at being practical and in accord with the majority of state practice and international judicial decisions.[14] In fact, the increasing scope of international law has prompted most states to accept something of an intermediate position, where the rules of international law are seen as part of a distinct system, but capable of being applied internally depending on circumstance, while domestic courts are increasingly being obliged to interpret rules of international law.[15]

The role of municipal rules in international law[16]

The general rule with regard to the position of municipal law within the international sphere is that a state which has broken a stipulation of international law cannot justify itself by referring to its domestic legal situation. It is no defence to a breach of an international obligation to

---

[14] G. Fitzmaurice, 'The General Principles of International Law Considered from the Standpoint of the Rule of Law', 92 HR, 1957 II, pp. 5, 70–80. See also C. Rousseau, *Droit International Public*, Paris, 1979, pp. 4–16; E. Borchard, 'The Relations between International Law and Municipal Law', 27 *Virginia Law Review*, 1940, p. 137; M. S. McDougal, 'The Impact of International Law upon National Law: A Policy-Orientated Perspective' in McDougal *et al.*, *Studies in World Public Order*, New Haven, 1960, p. 157.

[15] See further as to relevant theories, Shany, *Regulating Jurisdictional Relations*, pp. 92 ff.

[16] See e.g. C. W. Jenks, *The Prospects of International Adjudication*, London, 1964, chapter 9; H. Lauterpacht, *The Development of International Law by the International Court*, London, 1958, and Morgenstern, 'Judicial Practice', pp. 43 ff.

argue that the state acted in such a manner because it was following the dictates of its own municipal laws. The reasons for this inability to put forward internal rules as an excuse to evade international responsibility are obvious. Any other situation would permit international law to be evaded by the simple method of domestic legislation.

Accordingly, state practice and decided cases have established this provision and thereby prevented countries involved in international litigation from pleading municipal law as a method of circumventing international law. Article 27 of the Vienna Convention on the Law of Treaties, 1969 lays down that in so far as treaties are concerned, a party may not invoke the provisions of its internal law as justification for its failure to carry out an international agreement, while article 46(1) provides that a state may not invoke the fact that its consent to be bound by a treaty has been expressed in violation of a provision of its internal law regarding competence to conclude treaties as invalidating its consent.[17] This is so unless the violation of its internal law in question was 'manifest and concerned a rule of fundamental importance'. Article 46(2) states that such a violation is manifest where it would be objectively evident to any state conducting itself in the matter in accordance with normal practice and in good faith. The International Court considered this provision in *Cameroon* v. *Nigeria* in the context of Nigeria's argument that the Maroua Declaration of 1975 signed by the two heads of state was not valid as it had not been ratified.[18] It was noted that article 7(2) of the Vienna Convention provided that heads of state belonged to the group of persons who in virtue of their functions and without having to produce full powers are considered as representing their state. The Court also took the view that 'there is no general legal obligation for States to keep themselves informed of legislative and constitutional developments in other States which are or may become important for the international relations of these States'.[19]

---

[17] Note also article 13 of the Draft Declaration on the Rights and Duties of States, 1949, which provides that every state 'has the duty to carry out in good faith its obligations arising from treaties and other sources of international law, and it may not invoke provisions in its constitution or its laws as an excuse for failure to perform this duty', *Yearbook of the ILC*, 1949, pp. 286, 289.

[18] ICJ Reports, 2002, pp. 303, 430 ff.

[19] *Ibid.*, p. 430. But see the view of the Court in the *Anglo-Norwegian Fisheries* case that the UK as a coastal state greatly interested in North Sea fishing 'could not have been ignorant' of a relevant Norwegian decree, despite claiming that Norway's delimitation system was not known to it: ICJ Reports, 1951, p. 116; 18 ILR, pp. 86, 101.

Such provisions are reflected in the case-law. In the *Alabama Claims* arbitration of 1872, the United States objected strenuously when Britain allowed a Confederate ship to sail from Liverpool to prey upon American shipping. It was held that the absence of British legislation necessary to prevent the construction or departure of the vessel could not be brought forward as a defence, and Britain was accordingly liable to pay damages for the depredations caused by the warship in question.[20] In the *Polish Nationals in Danzig* case, the Court declared that 'a State cannot adduce as against another State its own constitution with a view to evading obligations incumbent upon it under international law or treaties in force'.[21]

The International Court, in the *Applicability of the Obligation to Arbitrate* case,[22] has underlined 'the fundamental principle of international law that international law prevails over domestic law', while Judge Shahabuddeen emphasised in the *Lockerbie* case[23] that inability under domestic law to act was no defence to non-compliance with an international obligation. This was reinforced in the *LaGrand* case,[24] where the Court noted that the effect of the US procedural default rule,[25] which was to prevent counsel for the LaGrand brothers from raising the violation by the US of its obligations under the Vienna Convention on Consular Relations, 1963 before the US federal courts system, had no impact upon the responsibility of the US for the breach of the convention.[26] The Court underlined this approach in the *Avena* case,[27] noting that 'The rights guaranteed under the Vienna Convention are treaty rights which the United States has undertaken to comply with in relation to the individual concerned, irrespective of the due process rights under the United States constitutional law.' The

---

[20] J. B. Moore, *International Arbitrations*, New York, 1898, vol. I, pp. 495, 653. See also e.g. the *Free Zones* case, PCIJ, Series A/B, No. 46, 1932, p. 167; 6 AD, p. 362; the *Greco-Bulgarian Communities* case, PCIJ, Series B, No. 17, 1930, p. 32; 5 AD, p. 4, and the *Nottebohm* case, ICJ Reports, 1955, pp. 4, 20–1; 22 ILR, pp. 349, 357–8.

[21] PCIJ, Series A/B, No. 44, pp. 21, 24; 6 AD, p. 209. See also the *Georges Pinson* case, 5 RIAA, p. 327; 4 AD, p. 9.

[22] ICJ Reports, 1988, pp. 12, 34; 82 ILR, pp. 225, 252.

[23] ICJ Reports, 1992, pp. 3, 32; 94 ILR, pp. 478, 515. See also *Westland Helicopters Ltd and AOI* 80 ILR, pp. 595, 616.

[24] ICJ Reports, 2001, pp. 466, 497–8; 134 ILR, pp. 1, 35–6.

[25] This US federal rule of criminal law essentially prevents a claim from being heard before a federal court if it has not been presented to a state court: see ICJ Reports, 2001, pp. 477–8.

[26] See also the Advisory Opinion of the Inter-American Court of Human Rights on the *Promulgation and Enforcement of Law in Violation of the Convention*, 116 ILR, pp. 320, 332–3.

[27] ICJ Reports, 2004, pp. 12, 65; 134 ILR, pp. 120, 168.

Court took a step further in that case, which also concerned the failure to allow foreign prisoners access to the consular officials of their state in breach of the Vienna Convention on Consular Relations, declaring that 'the remedy to make good these violations should consist in an obligation on the United States to permit review and reconsideration of these nationals' cases by the United States courts . . . with a view to ascertaining whether in each case the violation of Article 36 committed by the competent authorities caused actual prejudice to the defendant in the process of administration of criminal justice'.[28] By way of contrast, the International Court pointed out in the *Elettronica Sicula SpA (ELSI)* case[29] that the fact that an act of a public authority may have been unlawful in municipal law did not necessarily mean that the act in question was unlawful in international law.

However, such expressions of the supremacy of international law over municipal law in international tribunals do not mean that the provisions of domestic legislation are either irrelevant or unnecessary.[30] On the contrary, the role of internal legal rules is vital to the workings of the international legal machine. One of the ways that it is possible to understand and discover a state's legal position on a variety of topics important to international law is by examining municipal laws.[31] A country will express its opinion on such vital international matters as the extent of its territorial sea, or the jurisdiction it claims or the conditions for the acquisition of nationality through the medium of its domestic law-making. Thus, it is quite often that in the course of deciding a case before it, an international court will feel the necessity to make a study of relevant pieces of municipal legislation. Indeed, there have been instances, such as the *Serbian Loans* case of 1929,[32] when the crucial issues turned upon the interpretation of internal law, and the rules of international law in

---

[28] *Ibid.*, p. 60. President Bush then issued an order to the state courts to give effect to the decision of the International Court: see 44 ILM, p. 461 (28 February 2005). The US also withdrew its acceptance of the Optional Protocol to the Vienna Convention on Consular Relations, which had provided for the jurisdiction of the International Court in cases of dispute over the convention.

[29] ICJ Reports, 1989, pp. 15, 73–4; 84 ILR, pp. 311, 379–80. See also *Compañía de Aguas del Aconquija* v. *Argentina* 41 ILM, 2002, pp. 1135, 1154.

[30] See e.g. Jenks, *Prospects*, pp. 547–603, and K. Marek, *Droit International et Droit Interne*, Paris, 1961. See also Brownlie, *Principles*, pp. 36–40.

[31] See e.g. the *Anglo-Iranian Oil Co.* case, ICJ Reports, 1952, p. 93; 19 ILR, p. 507.

[32] PCIJ, Series A, No. 20; 5 AD, p. 466. See also the *Brazilian Loans* case, PCIJ, Series A, No. 21.

a strict sense were not at issue. Further, a court may turn to municipal law concepts where this is necessary in the circumstances.[33] However, it is clear that caution is necessary where an international court or tribunal is considering concepts of national law in the absence of an express or implied requirement so to do and no automatic transposition should occur.[34]

In addition to the role of municipal law in revealing the legal position of the state on topics of international importance, the rules of municipal law can be utilised as evidence of compliance or non-compliance with international obligations. This was emphasised in the *Certain German Interests in Polish Upper Silesia* case, where the Permanent Court of International Justice declared that:

> From the standpoint of International Law and of the Court, which is its organ, municipal laws are merely facts which express the will and constitute the activities of States, in the same manner as do legal decisions or administrative measures. The Court is certainly not called upon to interpret the Polish law as such; but there is nothing to prevent the Court's giving judgment on the question whether or not, in applying that law, Poland is acting in conformity with its obligations towards Germany under the Geneva Convention.[35]

Nevertheless, and despite the many functions that municipal law rules perform within the sphere of international law, the point must be emphasised that the presence or absence of a particular provision within the internal legal structure of a state, including its constitution if there is one, cannot be applied to evade an international obligation. Any other solution would render the operations of international law rather precarious.

---

[33] See e.g. the *Barcelona Traction* case concerning the nature of a limited liability company, ICJ Reports, 1970, p. 3; 46 ILR, p. 178.

[34] See e.g. the *Exchange of Greek and Turkish Populations* case, PCIJ, Series B, No. 10, pp. 19–21; 3 AD, p. 378. See also the Separate Opinion of Judge McNair in the *South West Africa* case, ICJ Reports, 1950, p. 148; 17 ILR, p. 47, noting that private law institutions could not be imported into international law 'lock, stock and barrel'; the Separate Opinion of Judge Fitzmaurice in the *Barcelona Traction* case, ICJ Reports, 1970, pp. 3, 66–7; 46 ILR, pp. 178, 240–1, and the Separate and Dissenting Opinion of President Cassese in the *Erdemović* case, 111 ILR, pp. 298, 387 ff.

[35] PCIJ, Series A, No. 7, p. 19; 3 AD, p. 5. See also the *Saiga (No. 2)* case before the International Tribunal for the Law of the Sea, 120 ILR, pp. 143, 188, and *Benin v. Niger*, ICJ Reports, 2005, pp. 90, 125 and 148. For criticism, see e.g. Brownlie, *Principles*, pp. 38–40.

International law before municipal courts[36]

The problem of the role of international law within the municipal law system is, however, rather more complicated than the position discussed above, and there have been a number of different approaches to it. States are, of course, under a general obligation to act in conformity with the rules of international law and will bear responsibility for breaches of it, whether committed by the legislative, executive or judicial organs and irrespective of domestic law.[37] Further, international treaties may impose requirements of domestic legislation upon states parties,[38] while binding Security Council resolutions may similarly require that states take particular action within their jurisdictions.[39] There is indeed a clear trend towards the increasing penetration of international legal rules within domestic systems coupled with the exercise of an ever-wider jurisdiction with regard to matters having an international dimension by domestic courts. This has led to a blurring of the distinction between the two previously maintained autonomous zones of international and domestic law, a re-evaluation of the role of international legal rules and a greater preparedness by domestic tribunals to analyse the actions of their governments in the light of international law.[40] Further, domestic courts may often have to determine the meaning of an international rule that is relevant for a case before them[41] or to seek to resolve conflicts between international rules,

---

[36] See e.g. Morgenstern, 'Judicial Practice', pp. 48–66, and Conforti, *International Law*. See also H. Mosler, 'L'Application du Droit International Public par les Tribunaux Nationaux', 91 HR, 1957 I, p. 619; W. Wenger, 'Réflexions sur l'Application du Droit International Public par les Tribunaux Internes', 72 *Revue Générale de Droit International Public*, 1968, p. 921; E. Benveniste, 'Judges and Foreign Affairs: A Comment on the Institut de Droit International's Resolution on "The Activities of National Courts and the International Relations of their State"', 5 EJIL, 1994, p. 423.

[37] See e.g. the *Exchange of Greek and Turkish Populations* case, PCIJ, Series B, No. 10, p. 20, and the *Finnish Ships Arbitration*, 3 RIAA, p. 1484. See further below, chapter 14.

[38] See e.g. as to requirements imposed by anti-terrorist conventions, below, chapter 12, p. 673. See also the decision of Trial Chamber II in the *Furundžija* case, 121 ILR, pp. 218, 248–9.

[39] See as to the effect of counter-terrorism and weapons of mass destruction proliferation measures taken by the Security Council, below chapter 22, pp. 1208, 1210 and 1240.

[40] See e.g. Shany, *Regulating Jurisdictional Relations*; A. Nollkaemper, 'Internationally Wrongful Acts in Domestic Courts', 101 AJIL, 2007, p. 760, and *New Perspectives on the Divide Between National and International Law* (eds. A. Nollkaemper and J. E. Nijman), Oxford, 2007. See also Conforti, *International Law*.

[41] For example, the concept of jurisdiction as laid down in the European Convention on Human Rights: see *Al-Skeini* v. *Secretary of State for Defence* [2007] UKHL 26; 133 ILR, p. 693.

such as that between state immunity and the prohibition of torture[42] and that between treaty rules of human rights and binding Security Council resolutions.[43]

In this section, the approach adopted by municipal courts will be noted. We shall look first at the attitudes adopted by the British courts, and then proceed to note the views taken by the United States and other countries.[44]

The United Kingdom[45]

It is part of the public policy of the UK that the courts should in principle give effect to clearly established rules of international law.[46] Various theories have been put forward to explain the applicability of international law rules within the jurisdiction. One expression of the positivist–dualist position has been the doctrine of *transformation*. This is based upon the perception of two quite distinct systems of law, operating separately, and maintains that before any rule or principle of international law can have any effect within the domestic jurisdiction, it must be expressly and specifically 'transformed' into municipal law by the use of the appropriate constitutional machinery, such as an Act of Parliament. This doctrine grew from the procedure whereby international agreements are rendered operative in municipal law by the device of ratification by the sovereign and the idea has developed from this that any rule of international law must be transformed, or specifically adopted, to be valid within the internal legal order.

---

[42] See e.g. *Jones* v. *Saudi Arabia* [2006] UKHL 26; 129 ILR, p. 713.

[43] See *Al-Jedda* v. *Secretary of State for Defence* [2007] UKHL 58.

[44] Note the view expressed in *Oppenheim's International Law*, p. 54, that 'states show considerable flexibility in the procedures whereby they give effect within their territories to the rules of international law . . . while the procedures vary, the result that effect is given within states to the requirements of international law is by and large achieved by all states'.

[45] See e.g. Morgenstern, 'Judicial Practice'; H. Lauterpacht, 'Is International Law a Part of the Law of England?', 25 *Transactions of the Grotius Society*, 1939, p. 51; J. E. S. Fawcett, *The British Commonwealth in International Law*, London, 1963, chapter 2; *Oppenheim's International Law*, pp. 39–41, and W. Holdsworth, *Essays in Law and History*, Oxford, 1946, p. 260. See also J. Collier, 'Is International Law Really Part of the Law of England?', 38 ICLQ, 1989, p. 924; Higgins, *Problems and Process*, chapter 12; R. O'Keefe, 'Customary International Crimes in English Courts', 72 BYIL, 2001, p. 293; K. Reece Thomas, 'The Changing Status of International Law in English Domestic Law', 53 NILR, 2006, p. 371; S. Fatima, *Using International Law in Domestic Courts*, Oxford, 2005, and D. Feldman, 'Monism, Dualism and Constitutional Legitimacy', 20 Australian YIL, 1999, p. 105.

[46] See e.g. Upjohn J in *In re Claim by Herbert Wragg & Co. Ltd* [1956] Ch. 323, 334, and Lord Cross in *Oppenheimer* v. *Cattermole* [1976] AC 249, 277; 72 ILR, p. 446.

Another approach, known as the doctrine of *incorporation*, holds that international law is part of the municipal law automatically without the necessity for the interposition of a constitutional ratification procedure. The best-known exponent of this theory is the eighteenth-century lawyer Blackstone, who declared in his Commentaries that:

> the law of nations, wherever any question arises which is properly the object of its jurisdiction, is here adopted in its full extent by the common law, and it is held to be a part of the law of the land.[47]

This doctrine refers to customary international law and different rules apply to treaties. However, the previously accepted dichotomy between the reception of custom and treaty if now maintained absolutely would distort the many developments currently taking place. As will be seen, English courts have had to deal with the effect of legal decisions emanating from the EU and its Court of Justice and the European Court of Human Rights,[48] as well as the other consequences resulting from membership of the EU and of the Council of Europe; have been concerned with the interpretation of an increasing number of rules of international law incorporated into English law through the ratification of international treaties (particularly the significant number dealing with terrorist issues) and subsequent domestic legislation that they have required;[49] have sought to tackle conflicts of international legal rules and have dealt with the changing configuration of the doctrine of non-justiciability of issues raising questions as to the executive's conduct of foreign policy. They have also had to concern themselves with the validity of foreign laws deemed to conflict with international law and the acceptability of evidence obtained abroad in circumstances that may have violated international law.[50] English courts take judicial notice of international law, so that formal proof of a proposition does not need to be demonstrated (unlike propositions of foreign law) and this itself has been a key factor in determining the relationship between international law and domestic law. Judges are deemed to know international law. In practice this means that judges and lawyers trained in domestic law have had to grapple with the

---

[47] *Commentaries*, IV, chapter 5.
[48] See section 3(1) of the European Communities Act 1972 and section 2 of the Human Rights Act 1998, incorporating into domestic law respectively the EU treaties and the European Convention on Human Rights. See also *Kay* v. *Lambeth Borough Council* [2006] UKHL 10.
[49] See below, chapter 12, p. 673.
[50] See below, p. 186. See also *A & Ors* v. *Secretary of State for the Home Department* [2005] UKHL 71.

different sources of international law and the difficulties of this task have percolated through the relationship.

Customary international law

It is in this sphere that the doctrine of incorporation has become the main British approach. It is an old-established theory dating back to the eighteenth century, owing its prominence at that stage to the considerable discussion then taking place as to the precise extent of diplomatic immunity. A few of the more important cases will be briefly surveyed. In *Buvot* v. *Barbuit*,[51] Lord Talbot declared unambiguously that 'the law of nations in its full extent was part of the law of England', so that a Prussian commercial agent could not be rendered liable for failing to perform a decree. This was followed twenty-seven years later by *Triquet* v. *Bath*,[52] where Lord Mansfield, discussing the issue as to whether a domestic servant of the Bavarian Minister to Britain could claim diplomatic immunity, upheld the earlier case and specifically referred to Talbot's statement.

This acceptance of customary international law rules as part and parcel of the common law of England, so vigorously stated in a series of eighteenth-century cases, was subject to the priority granted to Acts of Parliament and tempered by the principle of *stare decisis* or precedent, maintained by the British courts and ensuring that the judgments of the higher courts are binding upon the lower courts of the hierarchical system. Accordingly, a rule of international law would not be implemented if it ran counter to a statute or decision by a higher court.[53] It is also important to admit that during this period the rules of customary international law were relatively few in number so that few conflicts between the systems were to be envisaged.

In the nineteenth century, a series of cases occurred which led many writers to dispute the validity of the hitherto accepted incorporation doctrine and replace it with the theory of transformation, according to which the rules of customary international law only form part of English law if they have been specifically adopted, either by legislation or case-law. The turning point in this saga is marked by the case of *R* v. *Keyn*[54] which concerned a German ship, the *Franconia*, which collided with and sank a British vessel in the English Channel within three miles of the English

---

[51] (1737) Cases t. Talbot 281.   [52] (1764) 3 Burr. 1478.
[53] But see *Trendtex Trading Corporation* v. *Central Bank of Nigeria* [1977] 2 WLR 356; 64 ILR, p. 111; below, p. 144.
[54] (1876) 2 Ex.D. 63.

coast. The German captain was indicted for manslaughter following the death of a passenger from the British ship, and the question that came before the Court for Crown Cases Reserved was whether an English court did indeed have jurisdiction to try the offence in such circumstances.

The Court came to the conclusion that no British legislation existed which provided for jurisdiction over the three-mile territorial sea around the coasts. It was true that such a rule might be said to exist in international law, but it was one thing to say that the state had the right to legislate over a part of what had previously been the high seas, and quite another to conclude that the state's laws operate at once there, independently of any legislation. One thing did not follow from another, and it was imperative to keep distinct on the one hand the power of Parliament to make laws, and on the other the authority of the courts, without appropriate legislation, to apply the criminal law where it could not have been applied before. The question, as Lord Cockburn emphasised, was whether, acting judicially, the Court could treat the power of Parliament to legislate as making up for the absence of actual legislation. The answer came in the negative and the German captain was released.

This case was seen by some as marking a change to a transformation approach,[55] but the judgment was in many respects ambiguous, dealing primarily with the existence or not of any right of jurisdiction over the territorial sea.[56] In many respects the differences between the incorporation and transformation theories have revolved in practice more around evidential questions than any comprehensive theoretical revolution. In any event, any doubts as to the outcome of any further *Franconia* situations were put to rest by the Territorial Waters Jurisdiction Act 1878, which expressed British jurisdiction rights in similar circumstances.

The opinions put forward in the *West Rand Gold Mining Co.* case[57] showed a further blurring of the distinction between the incorporation and transformation theories. Lord Alverstone declared that whatever had received the common consent of civilised nations must also have received the assent of Great Britain and as such would be applied by the municipal tribunals. However, he went on to modify the impact of this by noting that any proposed rule of international law would have to be proved by satisfactory evidence to have been 'recognised and acted upon by our own

---

[55] See e.g. Holdsworth, *Essays*, pp. 263–6, and W. Halsbury, *Laws of England*, 3rd edn, London, 1968, vol. VII, p. 264.

[56] See e.g. Lauterpacht, 'Is International Law a Part?', pp. 60–1.   [57] [1905] 2 KB 391.

country' or else be of such a nature that it could hardly be supposed any civilised state would repudiate it. Lord Mansfield's view in *Triquet's* case could not be so interpreted as to include within the common law rules of international law which appear in the opinions of textbook writers and as to which there is no evidence that Britain ever assented.[58] This emphasis on assent, it must be noted, bears a close resemblance to the views put forward by the Court in *R* v. *Keyn* as to the necessity for conclusive evidence regarding the existence and scope of any particular rule of customary law. Indeed, the problem is often one of the uncertainty of existence and scope of customary law.

Not long after the *West Rand* case, another important dispute came before the courts. In *Mortensen* v. *Peters,*[59] a Danish captain was convicted by a Scottish court for contravening a fishing by-law regarding the Moray Firth. His ship had been operating within the Moray Firth and was within the area covered by the relevant by-law, but it was beyond the three-mile limit recognised by international law. The issue came to the Scottish Court of Justiciary, where Lord Dunedin, in discussing the captain's appeal, concentrated upon the correct construction to be made of the relevant legislation. He noted that an Act of Parliament duly passed and assented to was supreme and the Court had no option but to give effect to its provisions. In other words, statutes had predominance over customary law, and a British court would have to heed the terms of an Act of Parliament even if it involved the breach of a rule of international law. This is so even though there is a presumption in British law that the legislation is to be so construed as to avoid a conflict with international law. Where such a conflict does occur, the statute has priority and the state itself will have to deal with the problem of the breach of a customary rule.[60]

This modified incorporation doctrine was clearly defined by Lord Atkin in *Chung Chi Cheung* v. *R.*[61] He noted that:

> international law has no validity except in so far as its principles are accepted and adopted by our own domestic law ... The courts acknowledge the existence of a body of rules which nations accept among themselves. On any judicial issue they seek to ascertain what the relevant rule is, and having

[58] *Ibid.*, pp. 407–8.   [59] (1906) 8 F.(J.) 93.
[60] See also 170 HC Deb., col. 472, 4 March 1907 and the Trawling in Prohibited Areas Prevention Act 1909.
[61] [1939] AC 160; 9 AD, p. 264. See also *Commercial and Estates Co. of Egypt* v. *Board of Trade* [1925] 1 KB 271, 295; 2 AD, p. 423.

found it they will treat it as incorporated into the domestic law, so far as it
is not inconsistent with rules enacted by statutes or finally declared by their
tribunals.

It goes without saying, of course, that any alleged rule of customary
law must be proved to be a valid rule of international law, and not merely
an unsupported proposition.

One effect of the doctrines as enunciated by the courts in practice is
that international law is not treated as a foreign law but in an evidential
manner as part of the law of the land. This means that whereas any rule
of foreign law has to be proved as a fact by evidence, as occurs with other
facts, the courts take judicial notice of any rule of international law and
may refer, for example, to textbooks rather than require the presence and
testimony of expert opinion.[62]

In ascertaining the existence and nature of any particular rule, the
courts may have recourse to a wider range of authoritative material than
would normally be the case, such as 'international treaties and conventions, authoritative textbooks, practice and judicial decisions' of the courts
of other countries.[63]

The case of *Trendtex Trading Corporation* v. *Central Bank of Nigeria*
raised anew many of these issues. The case concerned a claim for sovereign
or state immunity by the Central Bank of Nigeria.[64] In *Trendtex* all three
judges of the Court of Appeal accepted the incorporation doctrine as
the correct one. Lord Denning, reversing his opinion in an earlier case,[65]
stressed that otherwise the courts could not recognise changes in the
norms of international law.[66] Stephenson LJ emphasised in an important
statement that:

> it is the nature of international law and the specific problems of ascertaining
> it which create the difficulty in the way of adopting or incorporating or
> recognising as already incorporated a new rule of international law.[67]

---

[62] *Lord Advocate's Reference No. 1 of 2000*, 2001, SLT 507, 512–13.

[63] Per Lord MacMillan, *The Cristina* [1938] AC 485, 497; 9 AD, p. 250. See *Re Piracy Jure
Gentium* [1934] AC 586, 588; 7 AD, p. 213, and Stephenson LJ, *Trendtex Trading Corporation*
v. *Central Bank of Nigeria* [1977] 2 WLR 356, 379; 64 ILR, pp. 111, 135. But see also
Lauterpacht, 'Is International Law a Part?', p. 87, note m.

[64] [1977] 2 WLR 356; 64 ILR, p. 111. See further below, chapter 13.

[65] *R* v. *Secretary of State for the Home Department, ex parte Thakrar* [1974] 2 WLR 593, 597;
59 ILR, p. 450.

[66] [1977] 2 WLR 356, 365; 64 ILR, pp. 111, 128. See also Shaw LJ, *ibid.*, 386 and Stephenson
LJ, *ibid.*, 378–81.

[67] [1977] 2 WLR 356, 379.

The issue of *stare decisis*, or precedent, and customary international law was also discussed in this case. It had previously been accepted that the doctrine of *stare decisis* would apply in cases involving customary international law principles as in all other cases before the courts, irrespective of any changes in the meantime in such law.[68] This approach was reaffirmed in *Thai-Europe Tapioca Service Ltd* v. *Government of Pakistan*.[69] However, in *Trendtex*, Lord Denning and Shaw LJ emphasised that international law did not know a rule of *stare decisis*.[70] Where international law had changed, the court could implement that change 'without waiting for the House of Lords to do it'.[71] The true principle, noted Shaw LJ, was that 'the English courts must at any given time discover what the prevailing international rule is and apply that rule'.[72] This marked a significant approach and one that in the future may have some interesting consequences, for example, in the human rights field.

The dominant incorporationist approach was clearly reaffirmed by the Court of Appeal in *Maclaine Watson* v. *Department of Trade and Industry*.[73] This case concerned the consequences of the demise of the International Tin Council and the attempts *inter alia* to render states that were members of the ITC liable for the debts incurred by that unfortunate organisation. Nourse LJ emphasised that the *Trendtex* case had resolved the rivalry between the incorporation and transformation doctrines in favour of the former.[74] One of the major points at issue in the *Tin Council* litigation was whether a rule existed in international law stipulating that the states members of an international organisation with separate personality could be rendered liable for the latter's debts.

If such a rule did exist, the question would then arise as to how that would be accepted or manifested in the context of municipal law. This, of course, would depend upon the precise content of such a claimed international rule and, as Kerr LJ noted, no such rule did exist in international law permitting action against member states 'in any national court'.[75] It was

---

[68] See e.g. *Chung Chi Cheung* v. *R* [1939] AC 160, 169; 9 AD, p. 264. But see Morgenstern, 'Judicial Practice', pp. 80–2.

[69] [1975] 3 All ER 961, 967, 969–70; 64 ILR, p. 81.

[70] [1977] 2 WLR 356, 365; 64 ILR, pp. 111, 128.

[71] Per Lord Denning, [1977] 2 WLR 356, 366.

[72] *Ibid.*, 388; 64 ILR, p. 152. But cf. Stephenson LJ, *ibid.*, 381. See also e.g. Goff J, *I° Congreso del Partido* [1977] 3 WLR 778, 795; 64 ILR, p. 154. This approach was supported by Lord Slynn in *Ex Parte Pinochet (No. 1)* [2000] 1 AC 61, 77; 119 ILR, pp. 50, 65.

[73] [1988] 3 WLR 1033; 80 ILR, p. 49.   [74] [1988] 3 WLR 1116; 80 ILR, p. 132.

[75] [1988] 3 WLR 1095; 80 ILR, p. 109.

also not possible for an English court to remedy the gap in international law by itself creating such a rule.[76] Nourse LJ, however, took a different position on this point, stating that 'where it is necessary for an English court to decide such a question [i.e. an uncertain question of international law], and whatever the doubts and difficulties, it can and must do so'.[77] This, with respect, is not and cannot be the case, not least because it strikes at the heart of the community-based system of international law creation.

Lord Oliver in the House of Lords judgment[78] clearly and correctly emphasised that

> It is certainly not for a domestic tribunal in effect to legislate a rule into existence for the purposes of domestic law and on the basis of material that is wholly indeterminate.[79]

Such approaches find support in the *Pinochet* decisions. Lord Lloyd, for example, in *Ex Parte Pinochet* (*No. 1*) referred to the 'well-established principles of customary international law, which principles form part of the common law of England',[80] while Lord Slynn took the view that the doctrine of precedent did not apply to the incorporation of rules of customary international law.[81] Lord Millett in *Ex Parte Pinochet* (*No. 3*) stressed that 'Customary international law is part of the common law.'[82] In *Lord Advocate's Reference No. 1 of 2000*, the High Court of Justiciary stated that 'A rule of customary international law is a rule of Scots law',[83] and the point was emphasised by the Arbitration Tribunal in *Sandline* v. *Papua New Guinea* that 'it is part of the public policy of England that its courts should give effect to clearly established rules of international law.'[84]

The doctrine that customary international law formed part of the law of England was discussed by the House of Lords in *R* v. *Jones*,[85] where the issue focused upon whether the customary international law rule prohibiting aggression had automatically entered into English criminal law. Lord Bingham, while noting that the general principle was not at issue

---

[76] *Ibid.*   [77] [1988] 3 WLR 1118; 80 ILR, p. 135.

[78] [1989] 3 All ER 523; 81 ILR, p. 671.   [79] [1989] 3 All ER 554; 81 ILR, p. 715.

[80] [2000] 1 AC 61, 98 and see also at 90; 119 ILR, pp. 50, 87.

[81] See *Ex Parte Pinochet* (*No. 1*) [2000] 1 AC 61, 77; 119 ILR, pp. 50, 65.

[82] [2000] 1 AC 147, 276; 119 ILR, pp. 135, 230. See also *Regina (European Roma Rights Centre)* v. *Immigration Officer at Prague Airport and Another* [2004] UKHL 55, paras. 22 ff. (per Lord Bingham); 131 ILR, pp. 652, 671 ff.

[83] 2001 SLT 507, 512. See also S. Neff, 'International Law and Nuclear Weapons in Scottish Courts', 51 ICLQ, 2002, p. 171.

[84] 117 ILR, pp. 552, 560.   [85] [2006] UKHL 16; 132 ILR, p. 668.

between the parties, commented that he 'would for my part hesitate, at any rate without much fuller argument, to accept this proposition in quite the unqualified terms in which it has often been stated'. Preference was expressed for the view maintained by Brierly that international law was not a part, but was rather one of the sources, of English law.[86]

More specifically, the House of Lords unanimously accepted that the incorporation doctrine did not apply to the customary international law offence of aggression. While it was accepted that a crime recognised in customary international law 'may' be assimilated into domestic criminal law without statutory provision, this was not automatic.[87] The English courts no longer had the power to create new criminal offences, which could only now be done by statute, and in practice when domestic effect was sought for customary international crimes this was achieved through legislation.[88] Further, a charge of aggression would involve a determination not only of the guilt of the accused, but also of the state itself and possibly of other states, should the state go to war with allies and this raised constitutional issues as to non-justiciability.[89]

Accordingly, a degree of caution may therefore now be necessary with regard to the traditionally and baldly expressed proposition that customary international law is part of English law. This will be subject not only, as in the past, to the rule that common law (including where incorporating an international customary rule) gives way to statute, but also to considerations of a constitutional nature. Courts will be obliged to

---

[86] *Ibid.*, para. 11; 132 ILR, p. 675, and see J. Brierly, 'International Law in England' 51 LQR, 1935, 24, 31.

[87] *R* v. *Jones*, para. 23; 132 ILR, p. 680, per Lord Bingham, who noted that 'customary international law is applicable in the English courts only where the constitution permits', quoting O'Keefe, 'Customary International Crimes in English Courts', p. 335, and that 'international law could not create a crime triable directly, without the intervention of Parliament, in an English court', quoting Sir Franklin Berman, 'Jurisdiction: The State' in *Asserting Jurisdiction: International and European Legal Perspectives* (P. Capps, M. Evans and S. Konstadinidis eds.), Oxford, 2003, pp. 3, 11.

[88] *R* v. *Jones*, para. 28; 132 ILR, p. 683. See also *Knuller (Publishing, Printing and Promotions) Ltd* v. *Director of Public Prosecutions* [1973] AC 435. Lord Hoffmann in *R* v. *Jones* noted that 'new domestic offences should in my opinion be debated in Parliament, defined in a statute and come into force on a prescribed date. They should not creep into existence as a result of an international consensus to which only the executive of this country is a party', para. 62; 132 ILR, pp. 694–5, and see Lord Mance at paras. 102–3; 132 ILR, pp. 705–6. See also *Sosa* v. *Alvarez-Machain* (2004) 159 L Ed 2d 718, 765; 127 ILR, pp. 769, 807 (per Scalia J) and the Federal Court of Australia decision in *Nulyarimma* v. *Thompson* (1999) 165 ALR 621, 630; 120 ILR, pp. 353, 364.

[89] *R* v. *Jones*, para. 30; 132 ILR, p. 684, and Lord Hoffmann, paras. 63–7; 132 ILR, pp. 695–6. See further as to non-justiciability, below, p. 179.

conduct an enquiry, as before, into whether a particular provision indeed constitutes a rule of custom, and additionally into whether there are any constitutional bars to incorporation.

Treaties[90]

As far as treaties are concerned, different rules apply as to their application within the domestic jurisdiction for very good historical and political reasons. While customary law develops through the evolution of state practice, international conventions are in the form of contracts binding upon the signatories. For a custom to emerge it is usual, though not always necessary, for several states to act in a certain manner believing it to be in conformity with the law. Therefore, in normal circumstances the influence of one particular state is not usually decisive. In the case of treaties, the states involved may create new law that would be binding upon them irrespective of previous practice or contemporary practice. In other words, the influence of the executive is generally of greater impact where treaty law is concerned than is the case with customary law and this is particularly so where, as in the UK, ratification of treaties is an executive act.

It follows from this that were treaties to be rendered applicable directly within the state without any intermediate stage after signature and ratification and before domestic operation, the executive would be able to legislate without the legislature. Because of this, any incorporation theory approach to treaty law has been rejected. Indeed, as far as this topic is concerned, it seems to turn more upon the particular relationship between the executive and legislative branches of government than upon any preconceived notions of international law.

One of the principal cases in English law illustrating this situation is the case of the *Parlement Belge*.[91] It involved a collision between this ship and a British tug, and the claim for damages brought by the latter vessel

---

[90] See generally A. D. McNair, *The Law of Treaties*, Oxford, 1961, pp. 81–97; A. Aust, *Modern Treaty Law and Practice*, 2nd edn, Cambridge, 2007, chapter 10; F. A. Mann, 'The Enforcement of Treaties by English Courts', 44 *Transactions of the Grotius Society*, 1958–9, p. 29; R. Higgins in *The Effect of Treaties in Domestic Law* (eds. F. Jacobs and S. Roberts), London, 1987, p. 123; D. Lasok, 'Les Traités Internationaux dans la Système Juridique Anglaise', 70 *Revue Générale de Droit International Public*, 1966, p. 961; I. Sinclair, 'The Principles of Treaty Interpretation and their Application by the English Courts', 12 ICLQ, 1963, p. 508; I. Sinclair and S. J. Dickson, 'National Treaty Law and Practice: United Kingdom' in *National Treaty Law and Practice* (eds. M. Leigh and M. R. Blakeslee), 1995, p. 223, and C. Warbrick, 'Treaties', 49 ICLQ, 2000, p. 944.

[91] (1879) 4 PD 129.

before the Probate, Divorce and Admiralty division of the High Court. The *Parlement Belge* belonged to the King of the Belgians and was used as a cargo boat. During the case, the Attorney General intervened to state that the Court had no jurisdiction over the vessel as it was the property of the Belgian monarch, and that further, by a political agreement of 1876 between Britain and Belgium, the same immunity from foreign legal process as applied to warships should apply also to this packet boat. In discussing the case, the Court concluded that only public ships of war were entitled to such immunity and that such immunity could not be extended to other categories by a treaty without parliamentary consent. Indeed, it was stated that this would be 'a use of the treaty-making prerogative of the Crown ... without precedent, and in principle contrary to the law of the constitution'.[92]

It is the Crown which in the UK possesses the constitutional authority to enter into treaties and this prerogative power cannot be impugned by the courts.[93] However, this power may be affected by legislation. Section 6 of the European Parliamentary Elections Act 1978 provided, for example, that no treaty providing for any increase in the powers of the European Parliament would be ratified by the UK without being first approved by Parliament.[94] Thus it is that treaties cannot operate of themselves within the state, but require the passing of an enabling statute. The Crown in the UK retains the right to sign and ratify international agreements, but is unable to legislate directly. Before a treaty can become part of English law, an Act of Parliament is essential. This fundamental proposition was clearly spelt out by Lord Oliver in the House of Lords decision in *Maclaine Watson* v. *Department of Trade and Industry*.[95] He noted that:

> as a matter of the constitutional law of the United Kingdom, the royal prerogative, whilst it embraces the making of treaties, does not extend to altering the law or conferring rights on individuals or depriving individuals of rights which they enjoy in domestic law without the intervention of Parliament. Treaties, as it is sometimes expressed, are not self-executing.

---

[92] *Ibid.*, p. 154.
[93] See e.g. *Council of Civil Service Unions* v. *Minister for the Civil Service* [1985] AC 374, 418. See also *Rustomjee* v. *R* (1876) 2 QBD 69 and *Lonrho Exports* v. *ECGD* [1996] 4 All ER 673; 108 ILR, pp. 596, 611.
[94] See *R* v. *Secretary of State for Foreign and Commonwealth Affairs, ex parte Rees-Mogg* [1994] 2 WLR 115.
[95] [1989] 3 All ER 523, 531; 81 ILR, pp. 671, 684. See also *Lonrho Exports* v. *ECGD* [1996] 4 All ER 673, 687; 108 ILR, pp. 596, 611.

> Quite simply, a treaty is not part of English law unless and until it has been incorporated into the law by legislation.[96]

It therefore followed that as far as individuals were concerned such treaties were *res inter alia acta* from which they could not derive rights and by which they could not be deprived of rights or subjected to obligations.[97] Lord Templeman emphasised that 'Except to the extent that a treaty becomes incorporated into the laws of the United Kingdom by statute, the courts of the United Kingdom have no power to enforce treaty rights and obligations at the behest of a sovereign government or at the behest of a private individual.'[98] This was reaffirmed by Lord Bingham in *A (FC) and Others (FC)* v. *Secretary of State for the Home Department*, noting that 'a treaty, even if ratified by the United Kingdom, has no binding force in the domestic law of this country unless it is given effect by statute or expresses principles of customary international law'.[99] The interpretation of treaties not incorporated by statute into municipal law, and the decision as to whether they have been complied with, are matters exclusively for the Crown as 'the court must speak with the same voice as the Executive'.[100] An exception is where reference to a treaty is needed in order to explain the relevant factual background,[101] for example where the terms of a treaty are incorporated into a contract.[102] Where the legislation in question refers expressly to a relevant but unincorporated treaty, it is

---

[96] [1989] 3 All ER 523, 544–5; 81 ILR, p. 701. See also *Littrell* v. *USA (No. 2)* [1995] 1 WLR 82. But see R. Y. Jennings, 'An International Lawyer Takes Stock', 39 ICLQ, 1990, pp. 513, 523–6.

[97] [1989] 3 All ER 523, 544–5; 81 ILR, p. 701. See further as to the non-justiciability of unincorporated treaties, below, p. 183.

[98] [1989] 3 All ER 523, 526; 81 ILR, p. 676. See also *Ex Parte Brind* [1991] 1 AC 696, 747–8; 85 ILR, p. 29, and *R* v. *Lyons* [2002] UKHL 44; 131 ILR, p. 538.

[99] [2005] UKHL 71, para. 27. Lord Bingham in *R* v. *Asfaw* [2008] UKHL 31, para. 29 stated that, 'While, therefore, one would expect any government intending to legislate inconsistently with an obligation binding on the UK to make its intention very clear, there can on well known authority be no ground in domestic law for failing to give effect to an enactment in terms unambiguously inconsistent with such an obligation.'

[100] *Lonrho Exports* v. *ECGD* [1996] 4 All ER 673, 688; 108 ILR, pp. 596, 613. See also *GUR Corporation* v. *Trust Bank of Africa Ltd* [1986] 3 All ER 449, 454, 459 and 466–7; 75 ILR, p. 675, and *Sierra Leone Telecommunications* v. *Barclays Bank* [1998] 2 All ER 821, 828; 114 ILR, p. 466.

[101] Lord Oliver in *Maclaine Watson* v. *Department of Trade and Industry* emphasised that the conclusion of an international treaty is a question of fact, thus a treaty may be referred to as part of the factual background against which a particular issue arises, [1989] 3 All ER 523, 545; 81 ILR, pp. 671, 702. See further below, pp. 183–5.

[102] *Lonrho Exports* v. *ECGD* [1996] 4 All ER 673, 688; 108 ILR, pp. 596, 613.

permissible to utilise the latter in order to constrain any discretion provided for in the former.[103] Further, it has been argued that ratification of an international treaty (where no incorporation has taken place) may give rise to legitimate expectations that the executive, in the absence of statutory or executive indications to the contrary, will act in conformity with the treaty.[104]

However, treaties relating to the conduct of war, cession of territory and the imposition of charges on the public purse[105] do not need an intervening act of legislation before they can be made binding upon the citizens of the country.[106] A similar situation exists also with regard to relatively unimportant administrative agreements which do not require ratification, providing of course they do not purport to alter municipal law. In certain cases, Parliament will give its approval generically in advance for the conclusion of treaties in certain fields within specified limits, subject to the terms negotiated for particular treaties being promulgated by statutory instrument (secondary legislation).[107] Such exceptions occur because it is felt that, having in mind the historical compromises upon which the British constitutional structure is founded, no significant legislative powers are being lost by Parliament. In all other cases where the rights and duties of British subjects are affected, an Act of Parliament is necessary to render the provisions of the particular treaty operative within Britain. In conclusion, it may be stated that parliamentary legislation will

---

[103] See e.g. *R* v. *Secretary of State, On the Application of the Channel Tunnel Group* 119 ILR, pp. 398, 407–8.

[104] See Lord Woolf MR in *Ex Parte Ahmed and Patel* [1998] INLR 570, 584, relying upon the approach of the High Court of Australia in *Minister of Immigration* v. *Teoh*, as to which see below, p. 167. Hobhouse LJ in *Ex Parte Ahmed and Patel* noted that where the Secretary of State had adopted a specific policy, it was not possible to derive a legitimate expectation from the treaty going beyond the scope of the policy: at 592. Note, as to the special position of human rights treaties as against other multilateral treaties, e.g. *Matthew* v. *Trinidad and Tobago State* [2004] UKPC 33; 134 ILR, p. 687.

[105] See the evidence presented by the Foreign and Commonwealth Office to the Royal Commission on the Reform of the House of Lords, UKMIL, 70 BYIL, 1999, p. 405.

[106] See e.g. S. de Smith and R. Brazier, *Constitutional and Administrative Law*, 6th edn, London, 1989, pp. 140–2, and W. Wade and O. H. Phillips, *Constitutional and Administrative Law*, 9th edn, London, 1977, pp. 303–6. See also *Attorney-General for Canada* v. *Attorney-General for Ontario* [1937] AC 326, 347; 8 AD, p. 41; *Walker* v. *Baird* [1892] AC 491; *Republic of Italy* v. *Hambro's Bank* [1950] 1 All ER 430; *Cheney* v. *Conn* [1968] 1 WLR 242; 41 ILR, p. 421; *Porter* v. *Freudenberg* [1915] 1 KB 857, 874–80, and McNair, *Law of Treaties*, pp. 89–91.

[107] See the evidence presented by the Foreign and Commonwealth Office to the Royal Commission on the Reform of the House of Lords, UKMIL, 70 BYIL, 1999, p. 405, citing the examples of extradition and double-taxation treaties.

be required where a treaty for its application in the UK requires a modification of, or addition to, existing common law or statute, affects private rights, creates financial obligations for the UK, provides for an increase in the powers of the European Parliament, involves the cession of British territory or increases the powers of the Crown.[108]

There is no rule specifying the precise legislative method of incorporation of a treaty[109] and a variety of means are available in practice.[110] For example, a treaty may be incorporated into domestic law by being given the force of law in a statute with or without being scheduled to the relevant act; by being referred to in a statute otherwise than in an incorporating statute; by tangential reference in a statute;[111] and by statutory referral to definitions contained in a treaty.[112]

It is the practice in the UK to lay before both Houses of Parliament all treaties which the UK has either signed or to which it intends to accede.[113] The text of any agreement requiring ratification, acceptance, approval or accession has to be laid before Parliament at least twenty-one sitting days before any of these actions is taken.[114] This is termed the 'Ponsonby Rule'.[115] All treaties signed after 1 January 1997 and laid before Parliament

---

[108] Sinclair and Dickson, 'National Treaty Law', p. 230.

[109] See *Regina (European Roma Rights Centre)* v. *Immigration Officer at Prague Airport and Another* [2004] UKHL 55, para. 42; 131 ILR, p. 683 (per Lord Steyn).

[110] See e.g. Fatima, *Using International Law*, pp. 57 ff.

[111] For example, section 2 of the Asylum and Immigration Appeals Act 1993 provides that nothing in the immigration rules within the Immigration Act 1971 shall lay down any practice contrary to the Refugee Convention.

[112] See e.g the International Criminal Court Act 2001.

[113] It is also the practice to put before Parliament Orders in Council made under the United Nations Act 1946 in order, for example, to implement United Nations sanctions internally: see s. 1(4) of the Act and H. Fox and C. Wickremasinghe, 'UK Implementation of UN Economic Sanctions', 42 ICLQ, 1993, pp. 945, 959. See also *R* v. *HM Treasury and the Bank of England, ex parte Centro-Com*, Times Law Report, 7 October 1993.

[114] Since 1998, it has been the FCO's practice to apply the Ponsonby Rule also to treaties subject simply to the mutual notification of the completion of constitutional or other internal procedures by each party: see the evidence presented by the Foreign and Commonwealth Office to the Royal Commission on the Reform of the House of Lords, UKMIL, 70 BYIL, 1999, p. 408.

[115] See 171 HC Deb., col. 2001, 1 April 1924. This is regarded not as a binding rule but as a constitutional usage: see Wade and Phillips, *Constitutional and Administrative Law*, p. 304. See also the Foreign and Commonwealth Office Nationality, Treaty and Claims Department's handbook entitled *International Agreements: Practice and Procedure – Guidance Notes*, 1992, quoted in UKMIL, 63 BYIL, 1992, p. 705, and *Erskine May's Treatise on the Law, Privileges, Proceedings and Usages of Parliament* (eds. D. Limon and W. R. McKay), 22nd edn, London, 1997. If primary or secondary legislation is required in order to ensure compliance with obligations arising under a treaty, the Government will not ratify a treaty

under this rule are accompanied by an Explanatory Memorandum.[116] The UK government, however, is currently reviewing issues of governance, including the prerogative powers, which include the making and ratification of treaties, the deployment and use of armed forces abroad, acquiring and ceding territory and the conduct of diplomacy.[117] It has been proposed that the Ponsonby rule be placed on a statutory footing.[118]

There is in English law a presumption that legislation is to be so construed as to avoid a conflict with international law.[119] This operates particularly where the Act of Parliament which is intended to bring the treaty into effect is itself ambiguous. Accordingly, where the provisions of a statute implementing a treaty are capable of more than one meaning, and one interpretation is compatible with the terms of the treaty while others are not, it is the former approach that will be adopted. For, as Lord Diplock pointed out: 'Parliament does not intend to act in breach of international law, including therein specific treaty obligations.'[120]

However, where the words of a statute are unambiguous the courts have no choice but to apply them irrespective of any conflict with international agreements.[121] Of course, any breach of an international

---

until such legislation has been implemented: see Parliamentary Under-Secretary of State, 220 HC Deb., WA, cols. 483–4, 9 March 1993, quoted in UKMIL, 64 BYIL, 1993, p. 629.

[116] UKMIL, 70 BYIL, 1999, p. 406. See also the Second Report of the House of Commons Select Committee on Procedure – Parliamentary Scrutiny of Treaties, 2000, HC 210 (www.parliament.the-stationery-office.co.uk/pa/cm199900/cmselect/cmproced/210/21003.htm). See also the Government Response, HC 990 (www.parliament.the-stationery-office.co.uk/pa/cm199900/cmselect/cmproced/210/21003.htm).

[117] See *The Governance of Britain*, Cm 7170, 2007. See also the Prime Minister's statement to the House of Commons, Hansard HC vol. 462 col. 815, 3 July 2007, and C. Warbrick, 'The Governance of Britain', 57 ICLQ, 2008, p. 209. See further *The Governance of Britain – War, Powers and Treaties: Limiting Executive Powers*, Cm 7239, 2007.

[118] *The Governance of Britain*, para. 33, and Warbrick, 'Governance', p. 216.

[119] See e.g. *Garland* v. *British Rail Engineering Ltd* [1983] 2 AC 751; 93 ILR, p. 622, and *Ex Parte Brind* [1991] 1 AC 696, 748; 85 ILR, p. 29, where this presumption is referred to as 'a mere canon of construction which involves no importation of international law into the domestic field'. See also *Maxwell on the Interpretation of Statutes*, 12th edn, London, 1969, p. 183; *A (FC) and Others (FC)* v. *Secretary of State for the Home Department* [2005] UKHL 71, para. 27, and *Al-Skeini* v. *Secretary of State for Defence* [2007] UKHL 26, para. 45; 133 ILR, pp. 715–16 (per Lord Rodger).

[120] *Salomon* v. *Commissioners of Customs and Excise* [1967] 2 QB 116, 143; *Post Office* v. *Estuary Radio Ltd* [1968] 2 QB 740 and *Brown* v. *Whimster* [1976] QB 297. See also *National Smokeless Fuels Ltd* v. *IRC*, *The Times*, 23 April 1986, p. 36, and Lord Oliver in *Maclaine Watson* v. *Department of Trade and Industry* [1989] 3 All ER 523, 545; 81 ILR, pp. 671, 702.

[121] *Ellerman Lines* v. *Murray* [1931] AC 126; 5 AD, p. 342 and *IRC* v. *Collco Dealings Ltd* [1962] AC 1; 33 ILR, p. 1. See Sinclair, 'Principles of Treaty Interpretation', and C. Schreuer, 'The

obligation will import the responsibility of the UK at the international level irrespective of domestic considerations.[122] Attempts have been made in the past to consider treaties in the context of domestic legislation not directly enacting them, or as indications of public policy, particularly with regard to human rights treaties,[123] and it seems that account may be taken of them in seeking to interpret ambiguous provisions.[124] However, ministers are under no obligation to do this in reaching decisions.[125]

One particular issue has arisen in the case of the implementation of international obligations and that relates to United Nations sanctions. In the UK, such sanctions are enforced as a consequence of the United Nations Act 1946 which enables the Crown to adopt Orders in Council so that effect can be given to sanctions.[126] Such secondary legislation tends to be detailed and thus the possibility of differential interpretations arises. It is to be noted that the relevance and application of rules of the European

Interpretation of Treaties by Domestic Courts', 45 BYIL, 1971, p. 255. See also F. A. Mann, *Foreign Affairs in English Courts*, Oxford, 1986, pp. 97–114; R. Gardiner, 'Treaty Interpretation in the English Courts since *Fothergill* v. *Monarch Airlines* (1980)', 44 ICLQ, 1995, p. 620, and Fatima, *Using International Law*, pp. 65 ff.

[122] See above, p. 133.   [123] See e.g. *Blathwayt* v. *Baron Cawley* [1976] AC 397.

[124] See e.g. in the context of the European Convention on Human Rights prior to its incorporation by the Human Rights Act 1998, *R* v. *Secretary of State for the Home Department, ex parte Bhajan Singh* [1975] 2 All ER 1081; 61 ILR, p. 260; *R* v. *Chief Immigration Officer, Heathrow Airport, ex parte Salamat Bibi* [1976] 3 All ER 843; 61 ILR, p. 267; *R* v. *Secretary of State for the Home Department, ex parte Phansopkar* [1976] QB 606; 61 ILR, p. 390; *Waddington* v. *Miah* [1974] 1 WLR 683; 57 ILR, p. 175; *Cassell* v. *Broome* [1972] AC 1027; *Malone* v. *MPC* [1979] Ch. 344; 74 ILR, p. 304; *R* v. *Secretary of State for the Home Department, ex parte Anderson* [1984] 1 All ER 920; *Trawnik* v. *Ministry of Defence* [1984] 2 All ER 791 and *Ex Parte Launder* [1997] 1 WLR 839. In *R* v. *Secretary of State for the Home Department, ex parte Brind* [1991] 1 AC 696, it was held that subordinate legislation and executive discretion did not fall into this category. See also *Derbyshire County Council* v. *Times Newspapers Ltd* [1993] AC 534 HL; *Rantzen* v. *Mirror Group Newspapers (1986) Ltd* [1993] 3 WLR 953 CA; *Attorney-General* v. *Associated Newspapers Ltd* [1993] 3 WLR 74; *R* v. *Secretary of State for the Home Department, ex parte Wynne* [1993] 1 WLR 115 and *R* v. *Brown* [1993] 2 WLR 556. See also A. Cunningham, 'The European Convention on Human Rights, Customary International Law and the Constitution', 43 ICLQ, 1994, p. 537.

[125] See e.g. *R* v. *Secretary of State for the Home Department, ex parte Fernandes* [1984] 2 All ER 390.

[126] See e.g. the Iraq and Kuwait (UN Sanctions) Order 1990, SI 1990 No. 1651; the Serbia and Montenegro (UN Sanctions) Orders 1992 and 1993, SI 1992 No. 1302 and SI 1993 No. 1188; the Libya (UN Sanctions) Orders 1992 and 1993, SI 1992 Nos. 973 and 975 and SI 1993 No. 2807; the Former Yugoslavia (UN Sanctions) Order 1994, SI 1994 No. 2673.

Union may also be in issue.[127] Further, one may note the obligation contained in article 29 of the Statute of the International Criminal Tribunal for the Former Yugoslavia, adopted by binding UN Security Council resolution 827 (1993), for all states to co-operate with the Tribunal and in particular to 'comply without undue delay with any request for assistance or an order issued by a Trial Chamber', including the arrest and detention of persons and their surrender or transfer to the Tribunal. This was implemented by secondary legislation adopted under the United Nations Act 1946.[128]

In the interpretation of international treaties incorporated by statute, the English courts have adopted a broader approach than is customary in statutory interpretation.[129] In particular, recourse to the relevant *travaux préparatoires* may be possible.[130] However, different approaches have been taken by the British courts as to how to deal with the question of interpretation in such circumstances. In *Sidhu* v. *British Airways*, Lord Hope, adopting the broad approach signalled in *Fothergill* v. *Monarch Airlines*, stated that it was 'well-established that a purposive approach should be taken to the interpretation of international conventions which have the force of law in this country'.[131] Lord Mustill in *Semco Salvage* v. *Lancer Navigation* took a more traditional approach founded upon the relevant articles of the Vienna Convention on the Law of Treaties, 1969,[132] in particular emphasising the significance of a textual interpretation of the words

---

[127] See e.g. *Ex Parte Centro-Com* [1994] 1 CMLR 109; [1997] ECR I-81, and [1997] 3 WLR 239; 117 ILR, p. 444. See also R. Pavoni, 'UN Sanctions in EU and National Law: The Centro-Com Case', 48 ICLQ, 1999, p. 582. See further below, p. 1251, note 237.

[128] The UN (International Tribunal) (Former Yugoslavia) Order 1996, SI 1996 No. 716. See for differing approaches to this procedure, C. Warbrick, 'Co-operation with the International Criminal Tribunal for Yugoslavia', 45 ICLQ, 1996, p. 947, and H. Fox, 'The Objections to Transfer of Criminal Jurisdiction to the Tribunal', 46 ICLQ, 1997, p. 434.

[129] Lord Slynn stated in *R (Al Fawwaz)* v. *Governor of Brixton Prison* that 'to apply to extradition treaties the strict canons appropriate to the construction of domestic statutes would often tend to defeat rather than to serve [their] purpose', [2001] UKHL 69, para. 39, citing Lord Bridge in *Ex Parte Postlethwaite* [1988] AC 924, 947.

[130] See *Buchanan* v. *Babco* [1978] AC 141 and *Fothergill* v. *Monarch Airlines* [1981] AC 251; 74 ILR, p. 648. Compare in the latter case the restrictive approach of Lord Wilberforce, [1981] AC 278; 74 ILR, p. 656 with that of Lord Diplock, [1981] AC 283; 74 ILR, pp. 661–2. See also *Goldman* v. *Thai Airways International Ltd* [1983] 3 All ER 693. Note also that in *Wahda Bank* v. *Arab Bank plc* Times Law Reports, 16 December 1992, Phillips J referred to UN sanctions resolutions in examining the question of the applicability of the Order in Council implementing the sanctions internally to the case in question. See further *Re H (Minors)* [1998] AC 72.

[131] [1997] 1 All ER 193, 202.   [132] See below, chapter 16, p. 932.

in question as understood in their ordinary meaning.[133] In a rather special position is the Human Rights Act 1998, which incorporated the European Convention on Human Rights. Section 3(1) provides that, 'So far as it is possible to do so, primary and subordinate legislation must be read and given effect in a way which is compatible with Convention rights', although this does not affect the validity, continuing operation or enforcement of any incompatible primary legislation.[134] The obligation imposed by s. 3 arises crucially in relation to both previous and subsequent enactments.[135] Where legislation cannot be rendered compatible with Convention rights, then a declaration of incompatibility can be made under s. 4 and Parliament may then modify the offending provisions under s. 10. The courts have also adopted a broader, purposive approach to interpretation of domestic legislation in order to ensure its compatibility with the Convention.[136] In the process of interpreting domestic legislation so as to render it compatible if possible with the Convention rights, the courts 'must take into account'[137] any relevant jurisprudence from the European Court of Human Rights, although this is not a provision imposing an obligation to follow such case-law.[138] Reference should also be made to the growing importance of entry into the European Communities in this context. The case-law of the Communities demonstrates that fundamental rights are an integral part of the general principles of law, the observance of which the European Court of Justice seeks to ensure. The system provides that Community law prevails over national law and that the decisions of the European Court are to be applied by the domestic courts of the member states. The potential for change through this route is, therefore, significant.[139] Further, in interpreting domestic legislation made pursuant to the European Communities Act 1972 where the former appears to conflict with the Treaty of Rome (establishing the European Community),

---

[133] [1997] 1 All ER 502, 512.

[134] Section 3(2)b. Nor that of incompatible subordinate legislation where primary legislation prevents removal of the incompatibility: section 3(2)c.

[135] Section 3(2)a. See further H. Fenwick, *Civil Liberties and Human Rights*, 3rd edn, London, 2002, p. 139, and R. Clayton and H. Tomlinson, *Human Rights Law*, London, 2000, chapter 4.

[136] See e.g. the decision of the House of Lords in *R* v. *A* [2001] 2 WLR 1546 and *R (on the application of Alconbury Ltd)* v. *Secretary of State for the Environment, Transport and the Regions* [2001] 2 All ER 929.

[137] Section 2 of the Human Rights Act.   [138] See further below, chapter 7, p. 351.

[139] See e.g. *Nold* v. *EC Commission* [1974] ECR 491, 508 and *Rutili* v. *Ministry of Interior of French Republic* [1975] ECR 1219.

the House of Lords has held that a purposive approach should be adopted.[140]

The United States[141]

As far as the American position on the relationship between municipal law and customary international law is concerned, it appears to be very similar to British practice, apart from the need to take the Constitution into account. The US Supreme Court in *Boos* v. *Barry* emphasised that, 'As a general proposition, it is of course correct that the United States has a vital national interest in complying with international law.' However, the rules of international law were subject to the Constitution.[142]

An early acceptance of the incorporation doctrine was later modified as in the UK. It was stated in the *Paquete Habana* case[143] that

> international law is part of our law and must be ascertained and administered by the courts of justice of appropriate jurisdiction as often as questions of right depending upon it are duly presented for their determination.[144]

---

[140] *Pickstone* v. *Freemans* [1988] 3 WLR 265. See also *Litster* v. *Forth Dry Dock Engineering* [1989] 1 All ER 1194.

[141] See e.g. J. F. Murphy, *The United States and the Rule of Law in International Affairs*, Cambridge, 2004, chapter 2; J. J. Paust, *International Law as Law of the United States*, Durham, NC, 1996, and Paust, 'International Law as Law of the United States: Trends and Prospects', 1 Chinese JIL, 2002, p. 615; Morgenstern, 'Judicial Practice'; I. Seidl-Hohenveldern, 'Transformation or Adoption of International Law into Municipal Law', 12 ICLQ, 1963, p. 88; *Oppenheim's International Law*, pp. 74 ff.; C. Dickinson, 'The Law of Nations as Part of the National Law of the United States', 101 *University of Pennsylvania Law Review*, 1953, p. 793; R. A. Falk, *The Role of Domestic Courts in the International Legal Order*, Princeton, 1964; R. B. Lillich, 'Domestic Institutions' in *The Future of the International Legal Order* (eds. C. Black and R. A. Falk), New York, 1972, vol. IV, p. 384; L. Henkin, *Foreign Affairs and the Constitution*, New York, 1972; L. Henkin, 'International Law: as Law in the United States', 82 *Michigan Law Review*, 1984, p. 1555; J. J. Paust, 'Customary International Law: Its Nature, Sources and Status as Law in the United States', 12 *Michigan Journal of International Law*, 1990, p. 59, and L. Henkin, R. C. Pugh, O. Schachter and H. Smit, *International Law: Cases and Materials*, 3rd edn, St Paul, 1993, chapter 3. See also *Treaties and Other International Agreements: A Study Prepared for the Committee on Foreign Relations*, US Senate, 2001.

[142] 99 L Ed 2d 333, 345–7 (1988); 121 ILR, p. 551.

[143] 175 US 677 (1900). See also *Respublica* v. *De Longchamps* 1 Dall. 111.

[144] 175 US 677, 700. See *Hilton* v. *Guyot* 159 US 113 and *United States* v. *Melekh* 190 F.Supp. 67 (1960), cf. *Pauling* v. *McElroy* 164 F.Supp. 390 (1958).

Similarly, the early pure incorporation cases gave way to a more cautious approach.[145]

The current accepted position is that customary international law in the US is federal law and that its determination by the federal courts is binding on the state courts.[146] The similarity of approach with the UK is not surprising in view of common historical and cultural traditions, and parallel restraints upon the theories are visible. US courts are bound by the doctrine of precedent and the necessity to proceed according to previously decided cases, and they too must apply statute as against any rules of customary international law that do not accord with it.[147] The Court of Appeals reaffirmed this position in the *Committee of United States Citizens Living in Nicaragua* v. *Reagan* case,[148] where it was noted that 'no enactment of Congress can be challenged on the ground that it violates customary international law'.[149]

It has been noted that the political and judicial organs of the United States have the power to ignore international law, where this occurs pursuant to a statute or 'controlling executive act'. This has occasioned much controversy,[150] as has the general relationship between custom and inconsistent pre-existing statutes.[151] However, it is now accepted that statutes supersede earlier treaties or customary rules of international law.[152] It has also been held that it would run counter to the Constitution for a court to decide that a decision of the International Court of Justice overrules a binding decision of the US Supreme Court and thus affords a judicial

---

[145] See e.g. *Cook* v. *United States* 288 US 102 (1933); 6 AD, p. 3 and *United States* v. *Claus* 63 F.Supp. 433 (1944).

[146] See *US* v. *Belmont* 301 US 324, 331, 57 S.Ct. 758, 761 (1937); 8 AD, p. 34 and *Third US Restatement of Foreign Relations Law*, St Paul, 1987, vol. I, pp. 48–52. See also *Kadić* v. *Karadžić* 70 F.3d 232, 246 (2d Cir. 1995); 104 ILR, pp. 149, 159; and *In Re Estate of Ferdinand E. Marcos Human Rights Litigation* 978 F.2d 493, 502 (9th Cir. 1992); 103 ILR, pp. 521, 529. However, see C. A. Bradley and J. L. Goldsmith, 'Customary International Law as Federal Common Law: A Critique of the Modern Position', 110 *Harvard Law Review*, 1997, p. 816, and J. Paust, 'Customary International Law in the United States: Clean and Dirty Laundry', 40 German YIL, 1997, p. 78.

[147] See e.g. *Schroeder* v. *Bissell* 5 F.2d 838, 842 (1925).   [148] 859 F.2d 929 (1988).

[149] *Ibid.*, at 939. See also *Tag* v. *Rogers* 267 F.2d 664, 666 (1959); 28 ILR, p. 467 and *US* v. *Yunis (No. 3)* 724 F.2d 1086, 1091 (1991); 88 ILR, pp. 176, 181.

[150] See *Brown* v. *United States* 12 US (8 Cranch) 110, 128 (1814) and *Whitney* v. *Robertson* 124 US 190, 194 (1888). See also Henkin, 'International Law', p. 1555. See also *Rodriguez-Fernandez* v. *Wilkinson* 654 F.2d 1382 (1981); 505 F.Supp. 787 (1980); *US* v. *PLO* 695 F.Supp. 1456 (1988) and *Klinghoffer* v. *SNC Achille Lauro* 739 F.Supp. 854 (1990).

[151] See *Third US Restatement of Foreign Relations Law*, pp. 63–9 (§115); the *Reagan* case, 859 F.2d 929, and Goldklang, 'Back on Board the *Paquete Habana*', 25 Va. JIL, 1984, p. 143.

[152] See previous footnote.

remedy to an individual for a violation of the Constitution.[153] However, the question of the impact of a ruling of the International Court upon US courts has been discussed in the light of decisions of the former[154] as to the violation of the Vienna Convention on Consular Relations, 1963 by the failure to permit access to consular officials by imprisoned foreigners.[155]

There does exist, as in English law, a presumption that legislation does not run counter to international law and, as it was stated by the Court in *Schroeder* v. *Bissell*,[156]

> unless it unmistakably appears that a congressional act was intended to be in disregard of a principle of international comity, the presumption is that it was intended to be in conformity with it.[157]

The relationship between US law and customary law has been the subject of re-examination in the context of certain human rights situations. In *Filartiga* v. *Pena-Irala*,[158] the US Court of Appeals for the Second Circuit dealt with an action brought by Paraguayans against a Paraguayan for the torture and death of the son of the plaintiff. The claim was based on the Alien Tort Claims Act of 1789[159] which provides that '[t]he district courts shall have original jurisdiction of any civil action by an alien for a tort only, committed in violation of the law of nations'. The Court of Appeals held that torture constituted a violation of international customary law and was thus actionable. The Court accordingly held against the

---

[153] *Valdez* v. *Oklahoma*, US Court of Criminal Appeals of Oklahoma, Case No. PCD-2001-1011, 2002.

[154] See the *LaGrand* case (*Germany* v. *United States of America*), ICJ Reports, 2001, p. 466; 134 ILR, p. 1, and the *Avena and Other Mexican Nationals* case (*Mexico* v. *United States of America*), ICJ Reports, 2004, p. 12; 134 ILR, p. 120.

[155] See e.g. *Torres* v. *State of Oklahoma* 43 ILM, 2004, p. 1227, and *Sanchez-Llamas* v. *Oregon* 126 S. Ct. 2669 (2006), holding that a violation of article 36 of the Vienna Convention on Consular Relations did not necessarily require reversal of a criminal conviction or sentence. As to civil remedies, see *United States* v. *Rodriguez* 162 Fed. Appx. 853, 857 (11th Cir. 2006), *Cornejo* v. *County of San Diego* 504 F.3d 853, 872 (9th Cir. 2007) and *Gandara* v. *Bennett*, Court of Appeals for the Eleventh Circuit, judgment of 22 May 2008, holding that the Vienna Convention did not create judicially enforceable individual rights. It was emphasised in *Cornejo* that '[f]or any treaty to be susceptible to judicial enforcement it must both confer individual rights and be self-executing', at p. 856.

[156] 5 F.2d 838 (1925).

[157] *Ibid.*, p. 842. See also *Macleod* v. *United States* 229 US 416 (1913) and *Littlejohn & Co.* v. *United States* 270 US 215 (1926); 3 AD, p. 483.

[158] 630 F.2d 876 (1980); 77 ILR, p. 169. See e.g. R. B. Lillich, *Invoking Human Rights Law in Domestic Courts*, Charlottesville, 1985, and Comment, 'Torture as a Tort in Violation of International Law', 33 *Stanford Law Review*, 1981, p. 353.

[159] 28 USC 1350 (1988).

defendant despite the fact that both parties were alien and all the operative acts occurred in Paraguay. The Court also noted that in ascertaining
the content of international law, the contemporary rules and principles
of international law were to be interpreted and not those as of the date
of the prescribing statute.[160] Other cases came before the courts in which
the incorporation of international customary law provisions concerning
human rights issues was argued with mixed success.[161] An attempt to
obtain a judgment in the US against the Republic of Argentina for tortur-
ing its own citizens, however, ultimately foundered upon the doctrine of
sovereign immunity,[162] while it has been held that acts of 'international
terrorism' are not actionable under the Alien Tort Claims Act.[163] In *Kadić
v. Karadžić*,[164] the US Court of Appeals for the Second Circuit held that
claims based on official torture and summary executions did not exhaust
the list of actions that may be covered by the Alien Tort Claims Act and that
allegations of genocide, war crimes and other violations of international
humanitarian law would also be covered.[165] However, in *Sosa v. Alvarez-
Machain*,[166] the Supreme Court held that the Alien Tort Claims Act was a
jurisdictional statute creating no new causes of action and enacted on the
understanding that the common law would provide a cause of action for

[160] 630 F.2d 876, 881 (1980); 77 ILR, pp. 169, 175. See also *Amerada Hess* v. *Argentine Republic*
830 F.2d 421; 79 ILR, p. 1. The norms of international law were to be found by 'consulting
the works of jurists, writing professedly on public law; or by the general usage and practice
of nations; or by judicial decisions recognising and enforcing that law', 630 F.2d 876, 880;
77 ILR, p. 174, quoting *United States* v. *Smith* 18 US (5 Wheat.), 153, 160–1. See also *Kadić
v. Karadžić* 34 ILM, 1995, p. 1592.

[161] See e.g. *Fernandez* v. *Wilkinson* 505 F.Supp. 787 (1980) and *In re Alien Children Education
Litigation* 501 F.Supp. 544 (1980).

[162] *Siderman* v. *Republic of Argentina*, No. CV 82-1772-RMT (MCx) and *International Practitioner's Notebook*, July 1985, p. 1. See also below, chapter 13.

[163] *Tel-Oren* v. *Libyan Arab Republic* 517 F.Supp. 542 (1981), aff'd per curiam, 726 F.2d 774
(1984), *cert. denied* 53 USLW 3612 (1985); 77 ILR, p. 192. See e.g. A. D'Amato, 'What
Does *Tel-Oren* Tell Lawyers?', 79 AJIL, 1985, p. 92. See also *De Sanchez* v. *Banco Central de
Nicaragua* 770 F.2d 1385, 1398 (1985); 88 ILR, pp. 75, 90 and *Linder* v. *Portocarrero* 747
F.Supp. 1452; 99 ILR, p. 55.

[164] 34 ILM, 1995, p. 1592.

[165] Note that the US Torture Victim Protection Act 1992 provides a cause of action for
official torture and extrajudicial killing where an individual, under actual or apparent
authority or colour of law of any foreign law subjects, engages in such activities. This is
not a jurisdictional statute, so that claims of official torture will be pursued under the
jurisdiction conferred by the Alien Tort Claims Act or under the general federal question
jurisdiction of section 1331: see e.g. *Xuncax* v. *Gramajo* 886 F.Supp. 162 (1995); 104 ILR,
p. 165. In addition, local remedies must have been exhausted.

[166] 542 US 692, 714 ff. (2004).

the modest number of international law violations thought to carry personal liability at the time, being offences against ambassadors, violation of safe conducts, and piracy. The federal courts, it was declared, should not recognise claims under federal common law for violations of any international law norm with less 'definite content and acceptance among civilized nations' than these particular offences deemed to exist at the date of the adoption of the act.[167] Accordingly, both 'a specificity comparable to the features of the 18th-century paradigms' and a foundation resting upon 'a norm of international character accepted by the civilized world' were required in order to form the basis of a claim under the statute.[168]

The relative convergence of practice between Britain and the United States with respect to the assimilation of customary law is not reflected as regards the treatment of international treaties.[169] In the United Kingdom, it is the executive branch which negotiates, signs and ratifies international agreements, with the proviso that parliamentary action is required prior to the provisions of the agreement being accepted as part of English law. In the United States, on the other hand, Article VI Section 2 of the Constitution provides that:

> all Treaties made or which shall be made with the authority of the United States, shall be the supreme law of the land and the Judges in every state shall be bound thereby, anything in the Constitution or Laws of any state to the contrary notwithstanding.[170]

There is also a difference in the method of approval of treaties, for Article II of the Constitution notes that while the President has the power to make international agreements, he may only ratify them if at least two-thirds of the Senate approve.

There is an exception and this is the institution of the executive agreements. These are usually made by the President on his own authority, but still constitute valid treaties within the framework of international law. As distinct from ordinary treaties, the creation of executive agreements

---

[167] Ibid., at 732.

[168] Ibid., at 725 and 738. See also Vietnam Association for Victims of Agent Orange v. Dow Chemical Company, US Court of Appeals for the Second Circuit, Docket No. 05-1953-cv, 22 February 2008.

[169] See e.g. Jackson, 'Status of Treaties', p. 310, and D. Vagts, 'The United States and its Treaties: Observance and Breach', 95 AJIL, 2001, p. 313.

[170] See e.g. Ware v. Hylton 3 US (3 Dall.) 199 (1796) and Foster v. Neilson 27 US (2 Pet.) 253 (1829). See also on treaty powers and the 'reserved powers' of the states the tenth amendment, Missouri v. Holland 252 US 416 (1920); 1 AD, p. 4 and United States v. Curtiss-Wright Export Corporation 299 US 304 (1936); 8 AD, p. 48.

is not expressly covered by the Constitution, but rather implied from its terms and subsequent practice, and they have been extensively used. The Supreme Court, in cases following the 1933 Litvinov Agreement, which established US recognition of the Soviet government and provided for the assignment to the US of particular debts owing to the USSR, emphasised that such executive agreements possessed the same status and dignity as treaties made by the President with the advice and consent of the Senate under Article II of the Constitution.[171]

American doctrines as to the understanding of treaty law are founded upon the distinction between 'self-executing' and 'non-self-executing' treaties.[172] The former are able to operate automatically within the domestic sphere, without the need for any municipal legislation, while the latter require enabling acts before they can function inside the country and bind the American courts. Self-executing treaties apply directly within the United States as part of the supreme law of the land, whereas those conventions deemed not self-executing are obliged to undergo a legislative transformation and, until they do so, they cannot be regarded as legally enforceable against American citizens or institutions.[173]

But how does one know when an international agreement falls into one category or the other? This matter has absorbed the courts of the United States for many years, and the distinction appears to have been made upon the basis of political content. In other words, where a treaty involves political questions of definition or exposition, then the issue should be left to the legislative organs of the nation, rather than automatic operation.[174] Examples of this would include the acquisition or loss of territory

---

[171] See e.g. *United States* v. *Pink* 315 US 203 (1942); 10 AD, p. 48. See, as regards the President's power to settle claims and create new rules of law applicable to pending legislation, *Dames & Moore* v. *Regan* 101 SC 2972 (1981); 72 ILR, p. 270.

[172] See e.g. Y. Iwasawa, 'The Doctrine of Self-Executing Treaties in the United States: A Critical Analysis', 26 Va. JIL, 1986, p. 635; J. Paust, 'Self-Executing Treaties', 82 AJIL, 1986, p. 760; T. Buergenthal, 'Self-Executing and Non-Self-Executing Treaties in National and International Law', 235 HR, 1992 IV, p. 303, and C. M. Vázquez, 'The Four Doctrines of Self-Executing Treaties', 89 AJIL, 1995, p. 695.

[173] See e.g. *Foster* v. *Neilson* 27 US (2 Pet.) 253, 311, 7 L.Ed. 415 (1829); *United States* v. *Percheman* 32 US (7 Pet.) 51 (1833); *United States* v. *Postal* 589 F.2d 862, 875 (5th Cir. 1979), *cert. denied*, 444 US 832 and *Linder* v. *Portocarrero* 747 F.Supp. 1452, 1463; 99 ILR, pp. 55, 67–8.

[174] See Chief Justice Marshall, *Foster* v. *Neilson* 27 US (2 Pet.) 253, 314 (1829). See also J. C. Yoo, 'Globalism and the Constitution: Treaties, Non-Self-Execution, and the Original Understanding', 99 *Columbia Law Review*, 1999, p. 1955, and Vagts, 'US and its Treaties', p. 321.

and financial arrangements. The Supreme Court in *Edye* v. *Robertson*[175] declared that treaties which

> contain provisions which are capable of enforcement as between private parties in the courts of the country... [are] in the same category as other laws of Congress.

This would seem to mean that an international convention would become a law of the land, where its terms determine the rights and duties of private citizens, and contrasts with the position where a political issue is involved and the treaty is thereby treated as non-self-executing.

Of course such generalisations as these are bound to lead to considerable ambiguity and doubt in the case of very many treaties; and the whole matter was examined again in 1952 before the Supreme Court of California in *Sei Fujii* v. *California*.[176] The plaintiff was a Japanese citizen who had purchased some land in 1948 in California. By legislation enacted in that state, aliens had no right to acquire land. To prevent the property from going to the state, the plaintiff argued that, amongst other things, such legislation was not consistent with the Charter of the United Nations, an international treaty which called for the promotion of human rights without racial distinction.

The issue raised was whether the UN Charter was a self-executing treaty and, by virtue of such, part of the law of the land, which would supersede inconsistent local statutes. The Court declared that, in making a decision as to whether a treaty was self-executing or not, it would have to consult the treaty itself to try to deduce the intentions of the signatories and examine all relevant circumstances. Following *Edye's* case it would have to see whether the provisions of the treaty laid down rules that were to be enforceable of themselves in the municipal courts.

The Court concluded after a comprehensive survey that the relevant provisions of the UN Charter were not intended to be self-executing. They laid down various principles and objectives of the United Nations Organisation, but 'do not purport to impose legal obligations on the individual member nations or to create rights in private persons'. The Court held that it was obvious that further legislative action by the signatories would be called for to turn the principles of the UN into domestic laws binding upon the individual citizens of states.[177] Accordingly, they could not be regarded as part of the law of the land and could not operate to deflect

---

[175] 112 US 580 (1884).   [176] 38 Cal (2d) 718 (1952).   [177] *Ibid.*, p. 721.

the Californian legislation in question. The case was decided in favour of the plaintiff, but on other grounds altogether.[178]

As is the case with the UK system, it is possible for the US legislature to take action which not only takes no account of international law rules but may be positively contrary to them, and in such an instance the legislation would be supreme within the American jurisdiction.

In *Diggs* v. *Schultz*,[179] for example, the Court had to consider the effect of the Byrd Amendment which legalised the importation into the USA of strategic materials, such as chrome from Rhodesia, a course of action which was expressly forbidden by a United Nations Security Council resolution which in the circumstances was binding. The Court noted that the Byrd Amendment was 'in blatant disregard of our treaty undertakings' but concluded that: 'under our constitutional scheme, Congress can denounce treaties if it sees fit to do so, and there is nothing the other branches of government can do about it.' Although in municipal terms the Amendment was unchallengeable, the United States was, of course, internationally liable for the breach of an international legal rule.[180]

However, there is a presumption that Congress will not legislate contrary to the international obligations of the state[181] and a principle of

---

[178] See e.g. *People of Saipan ex rel. Guerrero* v. *United States Department of Interior* 502 F.2d 90 (1974); 61 ILR, p. 113. See also *Camacho* v. *Rogers* 199 F.Supp. 155 (1961) and *Diggs* v. *Dent* 14 ILM, 1975, p. 797. Note also O. Schachter, 'The Charter and the Constitution', 4 *Vanderbilt Law Review*, 1951, p. 643. In *Medellin* v. *Texas* 128 S. Ct. 1346 (2008), the US Supreme Court held that the decision of the International Court of Justice in the *Avena (Mexico* v. *US)* case, ICJ Reports, 2004, p. 12, requiring the US to provide 'further review and reconsideration' of the convictions in question, did not constitute directly enforceable federal law as the relevant treaties (the UN Charter, the Statute of the International Court and the Optional Protocol to the Vienna Convention on Consular Relations) were non-self-executing. See further as to the *Avena* case, below, chapter 13, p. 773 and chapter 19, p. 1103, note 305. See also the similar conclusion adopted by the Supreme Court of the Netherlands in *Association of Lawyers for Peace and Four Other Organizations* v. *State of the Netherlands*, Nr C02/217HR; LJN: AN8071; NJ 2004/329.

[179] 470 F.2d 461, 466–7 (1972); 60 ILR, pp. 393, 397. See also *Breard* v. *Greene* 523 US 371, 376 (1998) and *Havana Club Holding, Inc.* v. *Galleon SA* 974 F.Supp. 302 (SDNY 1997), aff'd 203 F.3d (2d Cir. 2000).

[180] This, of course, reflects the general rule. See e.g. G. Hackworth, *Digest of International Law*, Washington, 1940–4, vol. V, pp. 185–6 and 324–5. See also *Third US Restatement of Foreign Relations Law*, 1987, para. 115(1)b.

[181] See e.g. Marshall CJ, *Murray* v. *Schooner Charming Betsy* 6 US (2 Cranch) 64; *Weinberger* v. *Rossi* 456 US 25 (1982) and *Cook* v. *United States* 288 US 102 (1933). See also R. Steinhardt, 'The Role of International Law as a Canon of Domestic Statutory Construction', 43 *Vanderbilt Law Review*, 1990, p. 1103, and C. A. Bradley, 'The *Charming Betsy* Canon and Separation of Powers', 86 *Georgia Law Journal*, 1998, p. 479.

interpretation that where an act and a treaty deal with the same subject, the courts will seek to construe them so as to give effect to both of them without acting contrary to the wording of either. Where the two are inconsistent, the general rule has been posited that the later in time will prevail, provided the treaty is self-executing.[182]

The question of a possible conflict between treaty obligations and domestic legislation was raised in *United States* v. *Palestine Liberation Organisation*.[183] The Anti-Terrorism Act of the previous year[184] provided for the closure of all PLO offices in the United States and this was construed by the Attorney-General to include the PLO mission to the United Nations, an action which would have breached the obligations of the US under the United Nations Headquarters Agreement. However, the District Court found that it could not be established that the legislation clearly and unequivocally intended that an obligation arising out of the Headquarters Agreement, a valid treaty, was to be violated.[185]

The issue of the relationship between international treaties and municipal law came before the US Supreme Court in *Breard* v. *Greene*.[186] The Court noted that 'respectful consideration' should be given to the interpretation of an international treaty by a relevant international court;[187] however, 'it has been recognised in international law that absent a clear and express statement to the contrary, the procedural rules of the forum State govern the implementation of the treaty in that State'.[188] Accordingly, the effect of resort to a domestic procedural rule might result in preventing the provision of an international treaty from being applied in any given case. The Supreme Court also affirmed that international treaties under the Constitution were recognised as the 'supreme law of the land', but so were the provisions of the Constitution. An Act of Congress was

---

[182] See the decision of the Supreme Court in *Whitney* v. *Robertson* 124 US 190 (1888). The *Third US Restatement of Foreign Relations Law*, pp. 63 ff. suggests that an Act of Congress will supersede an earlier rule of international law or a provision in an international agreement 'if the purpose of the act to supersede the earlier rule or provision is clear or if the act and the earlier rule or provision cannot be fairly reconciled'.

[183] 695 F.Supp. 1456 (1988).   [184] 22 USCA, paras. 5201–3.

[185] *Ibid.* See the Advisory Opinion of the International Court in the *Applicability of the Obligation to Arbitrate* case, ICJ Reports, 1988, p. 12; 82 ILR, p. 225. See also DUSPIL, 1981–8, part I, pp. 8 ff.

[186] 140 L.Ed. 2d 529 (1998); 118 ILR, p. 22.

[187] The issue concerned the Vienna Convention on Consular Relations, 1963, and the international court in question was the International Court of Justice in *Paraguay* v. *USA*, ICJ Reports, 1998, p. 248; 118 ILR, p. 1.

[188] 140 L.Ed.2d 529, 537 (1998); 118 ILR, p. 22.

'on full parity' with a treaty, so that a later statute would render an earlier treaty null to the extent of any conflict.[189]

Other countries

In other countries where the English common law was adopted, such as the majority of Commonwealth states and, for example, Israel,[190] it is possible to say that in general the same principles apply. Customary law is regarded on the whole as part of the law of the land.[191] Municipal laws are presumed not to be inconsistent with rules of international law, but in cases of conflict the former have precedence.

The Canadian Supreme Court in the *Reference Re Secession of Quebec* judgment[192] noted that it had been necessary for the Court in a number of cases to look to international law to determine the rights or obligations of some actor within the Canadian legal system.[193] As far as treaties are concerned, Lord Atkin expressed the general position in *Attorney-General for Canada* v. *Attorney-General for Ontario*,[194] in a case dealing with the respective legislative competences of the Dominion Parliament and the provincial legislatures. He noted that within the then British Empire it was well enshrined that the making of a treaty was an executive act, while the performance of its obligations, if they involved alteration of the existing

---

[189] *Ibid.* See above, note 178.

[190] See the *Eichmann* case, 36 ILR, p. 5; R. Lapidoth, *Les Rapports entre le Droit International Public et le Droit Interne en Israel*, Paris, 1959, and Lapidoth, 'International Law Within the Israel Legal System', 24 *Israel Law Review*, 1990, p. 251. See also the *Affo* case before the Israeli Supreme Court, 29 ILM, 1990, pp. 139, 156–7; 83 ILR, p. 121, and *The Public Committee against Torture in Israel et al.* v. *The Government of Israel et al.*, HCJ 769/02. See also *A & B* v. *State of Israel*, Israeli Supreme Court, 11 June 2008.

[191] But see as to doubts concerning the application of the automatic incorporation of customary international law into Australia, I. Shearer, 'The Internationalisation of Australian Law', 17 *Sydney Law Review*, 1995, pp. 121, 124. See also G. Triggs, 'Customary International Law and Australian Law' in *The Emergence of Australian Law* (eds. M. P. Ellinghaus, A. J. Bradbrook and A. J. Duggan), 1989, p. 376. Note that Brennan J in *Mabo* v. *Queensland* (1992) 175 CLR 1, 41–2, stated that 'international law is a legitimate and important influence on the development of the common law'.

[192] (1998) 161 DLR (4th) 385, 399; 115 ILR, p. 536. See also G. La Forest, 'The Expanding Role of the Supreme Court of Canada in International Law Issues', 34 Canadian YIL, 1996, p. 89.

[193] See also *Reference re Powers to Levy Rates on Foreign Legations and High Commissioners' Residences* [1943] SCR 208; *Reference re Ownership of Offshore Mineral Rights of British Columbia* [1967] SCR 792; 43 ILR, p. 93, and *Reference re Newfoundland Continental Shelf* [1984] 1 SCR 86; 86 ILR, p. 593.

[194] [1937] AC 326; 8 AD, p. 41.

domestic law, required legislative action. 'The question', remarked Lord Atkin,

> is not how is the obligation formed, that is the function of the executive, but how is the obligation to be performed, and that depends upon the authority of the competent legislature or legislatures.[195]

The doctrine that customary international law forms part of the domestic law of Canada has been reaffirmed in a number of cases.[196] This has also been accepted in New Zealand[197] and in Australia.[198] In *Horgan v. An Taoiseach*, it was affirmed that 'established principles of customary international law may be incorporated into Irish domestic law *providing* that they are not contrary to the provisions of the Constitution, statute law or common law'.[199] The relationship between treaties and domestic law was examined by the High Court of Australia in *Minister of State for Immigration and Ethnic Affairs v. Teoh*.[200] The Court upheld the traditional doctrine to the effect that the provisions of an international

---

[195] *Ibid.*, pp. 347–8; 8 AD, pp. 43–4. See also *Pfizer Inc. v. Canada* [1999] 4 CF 441 and *R v. Council of Canadians* 2003 CanLII 28426, paras. 35–7 (2005), affirmed 2006 CanLII 400222, 217 OAC 316.

[196] See e.g. *Reference re Exemption of US Forces from Canadian Criminal Law* [1943] 4 DLR 11, 41 and *Reference re Powers to Levy Rates on Foreign Legations and High Commissioners' Residences* [1943] SCR 208.

[197] See e.g. *Marine Steel Ltd v. Government of the Marshall Islands* [1981] 2 NZLR 1; 64 ILR, p. 539; and *Governor of Pitcairn and Associated Islands v. Sutton* [1995] 1 NZLR 426; 104 ILR, p. 508. The courts have also referred to a presumption of statutory interpretation that, so far as wording allows, legislation should be read in a way that is consistent with New Zealand's obligations: see e.g. *Rajan v. Minister of Immigration* [1996] 3 NZLR 543, 551 and *Wellington District Legal Services v. Tangiora* [1998] 1 NZLR 129, 137; 115 ILR, pp. 655, 663. See, as to the use of treaties in statutory interpretation, *Attorney-General v. Zaoui* [2005] NZSC 38, [2006] 1 NZLR 289, (2005) 7 HRNZ 860. See also *Nguyen Tuong Van v. Public Prosecutor* [2004] SGCA 47; 134 ILR, p. 660 with regard to Singapore.

[198] See e.g. *Potter v. BHP Co. Ltd* (1906) 3 CLR 479, 495, 506–7 and 510; *Wright v. Cantrell* (1943) 44 SR (NSW) 45; *Polites v. Commonwealth* (1945) 70 CLR 60 and *Chow Hung Ching v. R* (1948) 77 CLR 449. These cases are unclear as to whether the incorporationist or transformation approaches have been adopted as the appropriate theoretical basis. As to the view that international law is the 'source' of domestic law, see Dixon J in *Chow Hung Ching* and Merkel J in *Nulyarimma v. Thompson* (1999) 165 ALR 621, 653–5; 120 ILR, p. 353. See also *Public International Law: An Australian Perspective* (eds. S. Blay, R. Piotrowicz and B. M. Tsamenyi), Oxford, 1997, chapter 5, and H. Burmeister and S. Reye, 'The Place of Customary International Law in Australian Law: Unfinished Business', 21 Australian YIL, 2001, p. 39.

[199] 132 ILR, pp. 407, 442.

[200] (1995) 128 ALR 353; 104 ILR, p. 466. See also Blay *et al.*, *Public International Law: An Australian Perspective*.

treaty to which Australia is a party do not form part of Australian law, and do not give rise to rights, unless those provisions have been validly incorporated into municipal law by statute.[201] It was noted that this was because of the constitutional separation of functions whereby the executive made and ratified treaties, while the legislature made and altered laws.[202] The majority of the Court, however, went on to hold that the fact that a treaty had not been incorporated did not mean that its ratification by the executive held no significance for Australian law. Where a statute or subordinate legislation was ambiguous, the courts should favour that construction which accorded with Australia's obligations under the particular treaty,[203] while a statute generally had to be interpreted as far as its language permitted so that it was in conformity and not in conflict with the established rules of international law.[204] Indeed, the Court felt that a narrow conception of ambiguity in this context should be rejected.[205] Referring to *Ex Parte Brind*,[206] the Court stated that this principle was no more than a canon of construction and did not import the terms of the treaty into municipal law.[207] Moving beyond this approach which is generally consistent with common law doctrines, the majority of the Court took the view that ratification of a convention itself would constitute an adequate foundation for a legitimate expectation (unless there were statutory or executive indications to the contrary) that administrative decision-makers would act in conformity with the unincorporated but

---

[201] See e.g. judgment by Mason CJ and Deane J, (1995) 128 ALR 353, 361. See also *Dietrich v. The Queen* (1992) 177 CLR 292, 305 and *Coe v. Commonwealth of Australia* (1993) 118 ALR 193, 200–1; 118 ILR, p. 322. Reaffirmed by the High Court in *Kruger v. Commonwealth of Australia* (1997) 146 ALR 126, 161; 118 ILR, p. 371. See e.g. *Kenneth Good v. Attorney-General*, Court of Appeal Civil Appeal No. 028 of 2005 for the similar situation in Botswana and *Nallaratnam Singarasa v. Attorney General*, S.C. Spl (LA) No. 182/99 (2006) with regard to Sri Lanka.

[202] (1995) 128 ALR 353, 362 and see e.g. *Simsek v. Macphee* (1982) 148 CLR 636, 641–2.

[203] Judgment of Mason CJ and Deane J. See also *Chung Kheng Lin v. Minister for Immigration* (1992) 176 CLR 1, 38. In *Kruger v. Commonwealth of Australia*, Dawson J noted that such a construction was not required where the obligations arise only under a treaty and the legislation in question was enacted before the treaty, (1997) 146 ALR 126, 161; 118 ILR, p. 371.

[204] See also *Kartinyeri v. The Commonwealth* (1998) 195 CLR 337 at 384 and *Ahmed Ali Al-Kateb v. Goodwin* [2004] HCA 37. In the latter case, McHugh J criticised the rule, but concluded that it was too well established to be repealed by judicial decision, *ibid.* at para. 65.

[205] (1995) 128 ALR 353, 361. See also *Polites v. The Commonwealth* (1945) 70 CLR 60, 68–9, 77, 80–1.

[206] [1991] 1 AC 696 at 748; 85 ILR, p. 29.　　　[207] (1995) 128 ALR 353, 362.

ratified convention.[208] This particular proposition is controversial in legal doctrine, but is an interesting example of the fact that internal decision-makers may not always be expected to be immune from the influence of obligations undertaken by the state.[209]

There are further signs of an increasingly flexible approach. For example, in *Hosking & Hosking* v. *Runting and Pacific Magazines NZ Ltd,*[210] the New Zealand Court of Appeal referred to the 'increasing recognition of the need to develop the common law consistently with international treaties to which New Zealand is a party. That is an international trend. The historical approach to the State's international obligations as having no part in the domestic law unless incorporated by statute is now recognised as too rigid.' Further, the Canadian Supreme Court, in noting that genocide was a crime in both customary international law and treaty law, declared that international law was therefore called upon to play a crucial role as an aid in interpreting domestic law, particularly as regards the elements of the crime of incitement to genocide, and emphasised the importance of interpreting domestic law in a manner that accorded with the principles of customary international law and with Canada's treaty obligations.[211] This, however, would go further than most common law states would accept.

Although the basic approach adopted by the majority of common law states is clear, complications have arisen where the country in question has a written constitution, whether or not specific reference is made

---

[208] *Ibid.,* 365. See also the judgment of Toohey J, *ibid.* at 371–2, and the judgment of Gaudron J, *ibid.* at 375–6. Cf. the judgment of McHugh J, *ibid.* at 385–7.

[209] Note that after the decision in *Teoh,* the Minister for Foreign Affairs and the Attorney General issued a Joint Statement (10 May 1995) denying the existence of any such legitimate expectation upon the ratification of a treaty: see M. Allars, 'One Small Step for Legal Doctrine, One Giant Leap Towards Integrity in Government: *Teoh's* Case and the Internationalisation of Administrative Law', 17 *Sydney Law Review,* 1995, pp. 204, 237–41. The Government also introduced the Administrative Decisions (Effect of International Instruments) Bill 1995 into the Parliament with the specific purpose of denying that treaties or conventions give rise to a legitimate expectation of how a decision-maker will make a decision in an area affected by such international instruments. See also *Trick or Treaty? Commonwealth Power to Make and Implement Treaties,* a Report by the Senate Legal and Constitutional References Committee, November 1995. See now also *Minister for Immigration and Multicultural Affairs; Ex Parte Lam* [2003] HCA 6, which is critical of *Teoh.*

[210] [2004] NZCA 34, para. 6.

[211] *Mugesera* v. *Canada (Minister of Citizenship and Immigration)* [2005] 2 SCR 100, para. 82; 132 ILR, pp. 295–6. See also *Baker* v. *Canada (Minister of Citizenship and Immigration)* [1999] 2 SCR 817, paras. 69–71.

therein to the treatment of international agreements. The use of international law in interpreting the Constitution has occasioned much debate in Australia.[212] In *Ahmed Ali Al-Kateb* v. *Godwin*, for example, two judges of the High Court of Australia came to radically different conclusions. One judge regarded the view that the Constitution should be read consistently with the rules of international law as 'heretical',[213] while another declared that 'opinions that seek to cut off contemporary Australian law (including constitutional law) from the persuasive force of international law are doomed to fail'.[214] This debate reflects differing approaches to constitutional interpretation.[215]

The Indian Constitution refers only in the vaguest of terms to the provisions of international law,[216] whereas by contrast the Irish Constitution clearly states that the country will not be bound by any treaty involving a charge upon public funds unless the terms of the agreement have been approved by the Dáil.[217] Under article 169(3) of the Cyprus Constitution, treaties concluded in accordance with that provision have as from

---

[212] See e.g. D. Hovell and G. Williams, 'A Tale of Two Systems: The Use of International Law in Constitutional Interpretation in Australia and South Africa', 29 *Melbourne University Law Review*, 2005, p. 95; H. Charlesworth, M. Chiam, D. Hovell and G. Williams, 'Deep Anxieties: Australia and the International Legal Order', 25 *Sydney Law Review*, 2003, pp. 423, 446–63; *International Law in Australia* (ed. K. W. Ryan), Sydney, 1984; Blay *et al.*, *Public International Law: An Australian Perspective*; A. Byrnes and H. Charlesworth, 'Federalism and the International Legal Order: Recent Developments in Australia', 79 AJIL, 1985, p. 622, and *Koowarta* v. *Bjelke-Petersen*, High Court of Australia, 39 ALR 417 (11 May 1982); 68 ILR, p. 181; *Tabag* v. *Minister for Immigration and Ethnic Affairs*, Federal Court of Australia, 45 ALR 705 (23 December 1982); *Commonwealth of Australia* v. *State of Tasmania*, High Court of Australia, 46 ALR 625 (1 July 1983); 68 ILR, p. 266; *Polyukhovich* v. *Commonwealth* (1991) 172 CLR 501 and *Minister for Foreign Affairs* v. *Magno* (1992) 37 FCR 298.

[213] [2004] HCA 37, para. 63 (McHugh J).   [214] *Ibid.*, para. 190 (Kirby J).

[215] Simpson and Williams have concluded that '[j]udges will approach extrinsic materials, such as international law, differently depending on whether they favour rigidly applying the Constitution as originally drafted and intended or, at the other extreme, updating the instrument for societal change consistent with a vision of the Constitution as a "living force"', A. Simpson and G. Williams, 'International Law and Constitutional Interpretation', 11 *Public Law Review*, 2000, pp. 205, 226.

[216] See e.g. D. D. Basu, *Commentaries on the Constitution of India*, New Delhi, 1962, vol. II, and *Constitutions of the World* (ed. R. Peaslee), 3rd edn, New York, 1968, vol. II, p. 308. See also K. Thakore, 'National Treaty Law and Practice: India' in Leigh and Blakeslee, *National Treaty Law and Practice*, p. 79.

[217] Peaslee, *Constitutions*, vol. III, p. 463 (article 29(5)2). Article 29 also states that Ireland accepts the generally recognised principles of international law as its rule of conduct in its relations with other states. See e.g. *Re O'Laighléis* 24 ILR, p. 420 and *Re Woods* 53 ILR, p. 552. See also *Crotty* v. *An Taoiseach* 93 ILR, p. 480; *McGimpsey* v. *Ireland* [1988] IR 567, and *Kavanagh* v. *Governor of Mountjoy Prison* [2002] 3 IR 97, 125–6; 132 ILR, pp. 394, 401–2. Note also the decision of the Irish High Court in *Horgan* v. *An Taoiseach* on 28

publication in the Official Gazette of the Republic 'superior force to any municipal law on condition that such treaties, conventions and agreements are applied by the other party thereto'.[218] In such cases where there is a written constitution, serious questions of constitutional law may be involved, and one would have to consider the situation as it arises and within its own political context.[219] But in general common law states tend to adopt the British approach.

The practice of those states which possess the civil law system, based originally on Roman law, manifests certain differences.[220] The Basic Law of the Federal Republic of Germany,[221] for example, specifically states in article 25 that 'the general rules of public international law are an integral part of federal law. They shall take precedence over the laws and shall directly create rights and duties for the inhabitants of the federal territory'.[222] This provision, which not only treats international law as part of municipal law but regards it as superior to municipal legislation, has been the subject of a great deal of controversy as writers and lawyers have tried to establish whether international legal rules would invalidate any inconsistent municipal legislation and, indeed, whether international rules could override the constitution. Similarly, the phrase 'general rules of public international law' has led to problems over interpretation as it may refer to all aspects of international law, including customary and treaty rules, or merely general principles common to all, or perhaps only certain nations.[223]

April 2003 reaffirming that article 29 does not confer individual rights, 132 ILR, pp. 407, 446.

[218] See e.g. *Malachtou v. Armefti and Armefti* 88 ILR, p. 199.

[219] See e.g. *International Law Chiefly as Interpreted and Applied in Canada* (ed. H. Kindred), 6th edn, Toronto, 2000, chapter 4; *Re Newfoundland Continental Shelf* [1984] 1 SCR 86, and C. Okeke, *The Theory and Practice of International Law in Nigeria*, London, 1986.

[220] See e.g. L. Wildhaber and S. Breitenmoser, 'The Relationship Between Customary International Law and Municipal Law in Western European Countries', 48 ZaöRV, 1988, p. 163; *Oppenheim's International Law*, pp. 63 ff., and Henkin *et al.*, *International Law: Cases and Materials*, pp. 154 ff.

[221] See H. D. Treviranus and H. Beemelmans, 'National Treaty Law and Practice: Federal Republic of Germany' in Leigh and Blakeslee, *National Treaty Law and Practice*, p. 43.

[222] See e.g. the *Parking Privileges for Diplomats* case, 70 ILR, p. 396.

[223] See e.g. *German Consular Notification* case (*Individual Constitutional Complaint Procedure*), BVerfG, 2 BvR 2115/01, 19 September 2006, and *Görgülü* case (*Individual Constitutional Complaint*), BVerfG, 2 BvR 1481/04 of 14 October 2004, 111 *Entscheidungen des Bundesverfassungsgerichts* (BVerfGE), 307–32, [2004] *Neue Juristische Wochenschrift* (NJW) 3407–3412. See also D. P. O'Connell, *International Law*, 2nd edn, London, 1970, vol. I, pp. 71–6, and sources therein cited. See also generally A. Drzemczewski, *The European Human Rights Convention in Domestic Law*, Oxford, 1983, and Peaslee, *Constitutions*, vol. III, p. 361.

As far as treaties are concerned, the German federal courts will regard these as superior to domestic legislation, though they will not be allowed to operate so as to affect the constitution. Article 59 of the Basic Law declares that treaties which regulate the political relations of the federation or relate to matters of federal legislation shall require the consent or participation, in the form of a federal law, of the bodies competent in any specific case for such federal legislation. Thereafter such treaties will be treated as incorporated into German law, but with the status (no higher) of a federal law. Such laws may indeed be challenged before the German courts by means of a constitutional complaint if the treaty in question contains provisions directly encroaching upon the legal sphere of the individual.[224]

Article 91(1) of the Netherlands Constitution 1983 requires the prior approval of Parliament before treaties, or their denunciation, become binding, while article 91(3) provides that any provisions of a treaty that conflict with the Constitution or which lead to conflicts with it may be approved by the Chambers of the Parliament, provided that at least two-thirds of the votes cast are in favour. Article 93 states that provisions of treaties and of decisions by international organisations which may be binding by virtue of their contents are to become binding after they have been published, while article 94 provides that statutory regulations in force within the kingdom shall not be applicable if such application is in conflict with provisions of treaties that are binding on all persons or with resolutions by international institutions.[225] Customary international law is not referred to in the Constitution. It is deemed to apply internally, although it seems that statute will prevail in cases of conflict.[226] It is for the courts to establish whether the provisions of a treaty or decision by an

---

[224] See the *Unification Treaty Constitutionality* case, 94 ILR, pp. 2, 54. See also the *East Treaties Constitutionality* case, 73 ILR, p. 691 and *the Görgülü* case (*Individual Constitutional Complaint*), BVerfG, 2 BvR 1481/04 of 14 October 2004, 111 *Entscheidungen des Bundesverfassungsgerichts* (BVerfGE), 307–32, [2004] *Neue Juristische Wochenschrift* (NJW) 3407–12.

[225] See e.g. E. A. Alkema, 'Fundamental Human Rights and the Legal Order of the Netherlands' in *International Law in the Netherlands* (eds. H. Van Panhuys *et al.*), Dordrecht, 1980, vol. III, p. 109; Peaslee, *Constitutions*, vol. III, p. 652; *Oppenheim's International Law*, p. 69, and H. Schermers, *The Effect of Treaties in Domestic Law* (eds. F. Jacobs and S. Roberts), Leiden, 1987, p. 109. See also e.g. *Nordstern Allgemeine Versicherungs AG* v. *Vereinigte Stinees Rheinreedereien* 74 ILR, p. 2 and *Public Prosecutor* v. *JO* 74 ILR, p. 130. Note also J. Klabbers, 'The New Dutch Law on the Approval of Treaties', 44 ICLQ, 1995, p. 629.

[226] See e.g. H. F. van Panhuys, 'The Netherlands Constitution and International Law: A Decade of Experience', 58 AJIL, 1964, pp. 88–108. See also *Handelskwekerij GJ Bier BV* v. *Mines de Potasse d'Alsace SA* 11 Netherlands YIL, 1980, p. 326.

international organisation are binding on all persons within the meaning of articles 93 and 94 of the Constitution.[227]

In a provision contained in other constitutions, article 10 of the Italian Constitution of 1947 stipulates that the Italian legal order 'shall conform with the generally recognised rules of international law'. This is interpreted to indicate that international customary law will override inconsistent ordinary national legislation.[228] Article 8(1) of the Portuguese Constitution provides that the rules and principles of general or customary international law are an integral part of Portuguese law,[229] while under article 87 of Poland's Constitution of 1997, a ratified international treaty, equal to a statute, is one of the sources of law.[230] The Supreme Court of Belgium has taken the view that directly effective treaty provisions have superiority over the Constitution,[231] as well as over a conflicting legislative act.[232]

The French Constitution of 1958 declares that treaties duly ratified and published shall operate as laws within the domestic system.[233] However, the Constitution provides that, although in principle it is the President of the Republic who negotiates and ratifies treaties, with regard to important treaties such as commercial treaties which entail some form of financial outlay, treaties relating to international organisations, treaties modifying legislation and treaties affecting personal status, ratification takes place by Act of Parliament. Once the relevant legislation has been passed, the agreement is promulgated and becomes binding upon the courts.

---

[227] See *Reinier van Arkel Foundation and Others* v. *Minister for Transport, Public Works and Water Management*, Case Nr 200401178/1; LJN: AR2181; *AB* 2005/12.

[228] Cassese, *International Law*, p. 225, note 21. See also the decision of the Italian Court of Cassation in *Canada* v. *Cargnello* 114 ILR, p. 559, and, for a similar view in Latvia, *Judgment of the Constitutional Court of the Republic of Latvia on a Request for Constitutional Review*, No. 2004–01–06 of 7 July 2004, *Latvian Herald*, 9 July 2004, No. 108, 3056.

[229] See e.g. the decision of the Supreme Court of Portugal in the *Brazilian Embassy Employee* case, May 1984, 116 ILR, p. 625.

[230] See *Resolution of the Supreme Court of 19 February 2003*, I KZP 47/02.

[231] B.M., Cass. 16 November 2004, nr P.04.0644.N, *Pas.* 2004, I, 1795, *RCJB* 2007, 36, *RW* 2005–06, 387, *CDPK* 2005, 610, *RABG* 2005, 504, *T.Strafr.* 2005, 285. See also *Gruyez and Rolland* v. *Municipality of Sint–Genesius–Rode*, Court of Appeal of Brussels, 28 January 2003, AR nr 2002/KR/412.

[232] *Franco-Suisse Le Ski* (*Hof van Cassatie/Cour de Cassation*), 21 May 1971, *Pas.* 1971, I, 886.

[233] See Title VI of the Constitution. See also e.g. Nguyen Quoc Dinh *et al.*, *Droit International Public*, pp. 231 ff.; P. M. Dupuy, *Droit International Public*, 8th edn, Paris, 2006, pp. 422 ff.; D. Alland, 'Jamais, Parfois, Toujours. Réflexions sur la Compétence de la Cour de Cassation en Matière d'Interprétation des Conventions Internationales', *Revue Générale de Droit International Public*, 1996, p. 599; V. Kronenberger, 'A New Approach to the Interpretation of the French Constitution in Respect to International Conventions: From Hierarchy of Norms to Conflict of Competence', NILR, 2000, p. 323.

Article 55 of the Constitution provides that duly ratified or approved treaties or agreements shall upon publication override domestic laws, subject only to the application of the treaty or agreement by the other party or parties to the treaty.[234] It is also now accepted that the French courts may declare a statute inapplicable for conflicting with an earlier treaty.[235] However, the Cour de Cassation has held that the supremacy of international agreements in the domestic order does not extend to constitutional provisions.[236]

In 1993, South Africa adopted a new (interim) constitution.[237] Whereas the previous constitutions of 1910, 1961 and 1983 had been silent on the question of international law, the 1993 Constitution contained several relevant provisions. Section 231(4) states that 'the rules of customary international law binding on the Republic, shall, unless inconsistent with this Constitution or an Act of Parliament, form part of the law of the Republic'. This formulation confirms essentially the common law position and would also suggest that the principle of *stare decisis* is not applicable to customary international law. As far as treaties are concerned, the previous position whereby an Act of Parliament was required in order to incorporate an international agreement has been modified. While the negotiation and signature of treaties is a function of the President (section 82(1)i), ratification is now a function of the Parliament (section 231(2)).[238]

---

[234] See e.g. O'Connell, *International Law*, pp. 65–8; Rousseau, *Droit International Public*, and Peaslee, *Constitutions*, vol. III, p. 312. See also *SA Rothmans International France and SA Philip Morris France* 93 ILR, p. 308.

[235] See the *Cafés Jacques Vabre* case, 16 *Common Market Law Review*, 1975, p. 336 and *In re Nicolo* 84 AJIL, 1990, p. 765; 93 ILR, p. 286. Under article 54 of the Constitution, the Constitutional Council may declare a treaty to be contrary to the Constitution, so that the Constitution must first be amended before the treaty may be ratified or approved. See e.g. *Re Treaty on European Union* 93 ILR, p. 337. See also *Ligue Internationale Contre le Racisme et l'Antisémitisme*, AFDI, 1993, p. 963 and AFDI, 1994, pp. 963 ff.

[236] See *Pauline Fraisse*, 2 June 2000, *Bulletin de l'Assemblée Plénière*, No. 4, p. 7 and *Levacher*, RFDA, 2000, p. 79. The position with regard to customary law is unclear: see e.g. *Aquarone*, RGDIP, 1997–4, pp. 1053–4; *Barbie*, Cass. Crim., 6 October 1983, Bull., p. 610 and *Kadahfi*, RGDIP, 2001–2, pp. 474–6.

[237] See 33 ILM, 1994, p. 1043. This interim constitution came into force on 27 April 1994 and was intended to remain in force for five years to be replaced by a constitution adopted by a Constitutional Assembly consisting of the National Assembly and Senate of Parliament: see below. See J. Dugard, *International Law: A South African Perspective*, 2nd edn, Kenwyn, 2000, and Hovell and Williams, 'A Tale of Two Systems', pp. 113 ff.

[238] See Dugard, *International Law*. Note that this change means that treaties entered into before the Constitution came into force do not form part of municipal law unless expressly incorporated by legislation, while those treaties that postdate the new Constitution may.

Section 231(3) provides that 'such international agreement shall be binding on the Republic and shall form part of the law of the Republic, provided Parliament expressly so provides and such agreement is not inconsistent with this constitution'. Thus South Africa has moved from the British system to a position akin to the civil law tradition. It should also be noted that this interim constitution expressly provides that the National Defence Force shall 'not breach international customary law binding on the Republic relating to aggression', while in armed conflict, it would 'comply with its obligations under international customary law and treaties binding on the Republic' (section 227(2)).[239]

These provisions were considered and refined by the Constitutional Assembly, which on 8 May 1996 adopted a new constitution.[240] Section 231(1) of this constitution provides that the negotiating and signing of all international agreements is the responsibility of the national executive, while such an agreement would only bind the Republic after approval by resolution in both the National Assembly and the National Council of Provinces.[241] Any international agreement becomes domestic law when enacted into law by national legislation, although a self-executing provision of an agreement that has been approved by Parliament is law in the Republic unless it is inconsistent with the Constitution or an Act of Parliament.[242] Section 232 provides that customary international law is law in the Republic unless it is inconsistent with the Constitution or an Act of Parliament, while section 233 stipulates that when interpreting any legislation, every court must prefer any reasonable interpretation of the legislation which is consistent with international law over any alternative interpretation that is inconsistent with international law. It is also to be particularly noted that section 200(2) of the Constitution states that the primary object of the defence force is to defend and protect the Republic,

---

[239] Note that article 144 of the Namibian Constitution provides that 'unless otherwise provided by this Constitution or Act of Parliament, the general rules of public international law and international agreements binding upon Namibia under this Constitution shall form part of the law of Namibia': see B. Erasmus, 'The Namibian Constitution and the Application of International Law', 15 *South African Yearbook of International Law*, 1989– 90, p. 81.

[240] See 36 ILM, 1997, p. 744.

[241] Section 231(2). This is unless either such an agreement is of a 'technical, administrative or executive nature' or it is one not requiring ratification (or accession), in which case tabling in the Assembly and the Council within a reasonable time is required: section 231(3).

[242] Section 231(4).

its territorial integrity and its people, 'in accordance with the Constitution and the principles of international law regulating the use of force'.[243]

The Russian Federation adopted a new constitution in 1993.[244] Under article 86, the President negotiates and signs treaties and signs the ratification documents, while under article 106 the Federal Council (the upper chamber of the federal parliament) must consider those federal laws adopted by the State Duma (the lower chamber) that concern the ratification and denunciation of international agreements. The Constitutional Court may review the constitutionality of treaties not yet in force (article 125(2)) and treaties that conflict with the Constitution are not to be given effect (article 125(6)). Article 15(4) of the new constitution provides that 'the generally recognised principles and norms of international law and the international treaties of the Russian Federation shall constitute part of its legal system. If an international treaty of the Russian Federation establishes other rules than those stipulated by the law, the rules of the international treaty shall apply.' Thus both treaty law and customary law are incorporated into Russian law, while treaty rules have a higher status than domestic laws.[245] The Constitutional Court takes the view that customary international law and international treaties ratified by Russia are norms incorporated into Russian law.[246]

---

[243] Note that O'Regan J stated in *Kaunda v. President of the Republic of South Africa* that 'our Constitution recognises and asserts that, after decades of isolation, South Africa is now a member of the community of nations, and a bearer of obligations and responsibilities in terms of international law', CCT 23/04, [2004] ZACC 5, para. 222.

[244] See G. M. Danilenko, 'The New Russian Constitution and International Law', 88 AJIL, 1994, p. 451 and Danilenko, 'Implementation of International Law in CIS States: Theory and Practice', 10 EJIL, 1999, p. 51; V. S. Vereshchetin, 'New Constitutions and the Old Problem of the Relationship between International Law and National Law', 7 EJIL, 1996, p. 29, and S. Y. Marochkin, 'International Law in the Courts of the Russian Federation: Practice of Application', 6 Chinese JIL, 2007, p. 329. See, as regards the practice of the Soviet Union, K. Grzybowski, *Soviet Public International Law*, Leiden, 1970, pp. 30–2.

[245] See also article 5 of the Russian Federal Law on International Treaties adopted on 16 June 1995, 34 ILM, 1995, p. 1370. This repeats article 15(4) of the Constitution and also provides that 'the provisions of officially published international treaties of the Russian Federation which do not require the publication of intra-state acts for application shall operate in the Russian Federation directly. Respective legal acts shall be adopted in order to effectuate other provisions of international treaties of the Russian Federation.' See further W. E. Butler, *The Law of Treaties in Russia and the Commonwealth of Independent States*, Cambridge, 2002, who notes that the change brought about by article 15(4) 'is among the most momentous changes of the twentieth century in the development of Russian Law', at p. 36.

[246] Butler, *Law of Treaties in Russia*, p. 37. See also generally, *Constitutional Reform and International Law in Central and Eastern Europe* (eds. R. Müllerson, M. Fitzmaurice

Under article 73(3) of the Japanese Constitution of 1946,[247] the Cabinet has authority to conclude treaties with the prior or subsequent approval of the Diet, although executive agreements may be entered into without such approval, usually by simple exchange of notes. Promulgation of a treaty takes place by publication in the Official Gazette under the name of the Emperor once the Diet has approved and the Cabinet ratified the agreement (article 7). Article 98(2) provides that 'treaties concluded by Japan and established laws of nations shall be faithfully observed' and this provision is taken as incorporating international law, both relevant treaty and customary law, into Japan's legal system.[248] Japan has also experienced some difficulty[249] in the context of the relative definition of self-governing and non-self-governing treaties.[250]

This survey of the attitudes adopted by various countries of the common law and civil law traditions leads to a few concluding remarks. The first of these is that a strict adherence to either the monist or the dualist position will not suffice. Most countries accept the operation of customary rules within their own jurisdictions, providing there is no conflict with existing laws, and some will allow international law to prevail over municipal provisions. One can regard this as a significant element in extending the principles and protection of international law, whether or not it is held that the particular provision permitting this, whether by constitutional enactment or by case-law, illustrates the superiority of municipal law in so acting.

The situation as regards treaties is much more complex, as different attitudes are maintained by different states. In some countries, certain treaties will operate internally by themselves (self-executing) while others must undergo a process of domestic legalisation. There are countries where legislation is needed for virtually all international agreements: for example,

---

and M. Andenas), The Hague, 1998; T. Schweisfurth and R. Alleweldt, 'The Position of International Law in the Domestic Legal Orders of Central and Eastern European Countries', 40 German YIL, 1997, p. 164; I. Ziemele, 'The Application of International Law in the Baltic States', 40 German YIL, 1997, p. 243, and W. Czaplinski, 'International Law and Polish Municipal Law', 53 ZaöRV, 1993, p. 871.

[247] See generally S. Oda, The Practice of Japan in International Law 1961–1970, Leiden, 1982, and Y. Iwasawa, 'The Relationship Between International Law and National Law: Japanese Experiences', 64 BYIL, 1993, p. 333. See also H. Oda, Japanese Law, 2nd edn, Oxford, 1999, and Y. Iwasawa, International Law, Human Rights, and Japanese Law – The Impact of International Law on Japanese Law, Oxford, 1998.

[248] Iwasawa, 'Relationship', p. 345.   [249] Ibid., pp. 349 ff.

[250] See generally with regard to China, T. Wang, 'International Law in China', 221 HR, 1990, p. 195.

Belgium.[251] It is by no means settled as a general principle whether treaties prevail over domestic rules. Some countries allow treaties to supersede all municipal laws, whether made earlier or later than the agreement. Others, such as Norway, adopt the opposite stance. Where there are written constitutions, an additional complicating factor is introduced and some reasonably stable hierarchy incorporating ordinary laws, constitutional provisions and international law has to be maintained. This is particularly so where a federal system is in operation. It will be up to the individual country to adopt its own list of preferences.[252]

Of course, such diverse attitudes can lead to confusion, but in the light of the present state of international law, it is inevitable that its enforcement and sphere of activity will become entangled with the ideas and practices of municipal law. Indeed, it is precisely because of the inadequate enforcement facilities that lie at the disposal of international law that one must consider the relationship with municipal law as of more than marginal importance. This is because the extent to which domestic courts apply the rules of international law may well determine the effectiveness of international legislation and judicial decision-making.

However, to declare that international legal rules therefore prevail over all relevant domestic legislation at all times is incorrect in the vast majority of cases and would be to overlook the real in the face of the ideal. States jealously guard their prerogatives, and few are more meaningful than the ability to legislate free from outside control; and, of course, there are democratic implications. The consequent supremacy of municipal legal systems over international law in the domestic sphere is not exclusive, but it does exist as an undeniable general principle.

It is pertinent to refer here briefly to the impact of the European Union.[253] The European Court of Justice has held that Community law has supremacy over ordinary national law,[254] and indeed over domestic

---

[251] See article 68 of the Constitution, which deals basically with treaties of commerce and treaties which impose obligations on the state or on individuals.

[252] See generally Drzemczewski, *Domestic Law*, and Peaslee, *Constitutions*, vol. III, pp. 76 and 689. See also, as regards the Philippines, the decision of the Supreme Court (en banc) in *The Holy See* v. *Starbright Sales Enterprises Inc.* 102 ILR, p. 163, and, as regards Poland, W. Czaplinski, 'International Law and Polish Municipal Law – A Case Study', 8 *Hague Yearbook of International Law*, 1995, p. 31.

[253] See e.g. S. Weatherill and P. Beaumont, *EC Law*, 3rd edn, London, 1999; L. Collins, *European Community Law in the United Kingdom*, 4th edn, London, 1990, and H. Kovar, 'The Relationship between Community Law and National Law' in *Thirty Years of Community Law* (Commission of the European Communities), 1981, p. 109. See also above, p. 156.

[254] See *Costa* v. *ENEL*, Case 6/64 [1964] ECR 585; 93 ILR, p. 23.

constitutional law.[255] In addition to the treaties creating the EC,[256] there is a great deal of secondary legislation issuing forth from its institutions, which can apply to the member states. This takes the form of regulations, decisions or directives. Of these, the first two are directly applicable and enforceable within each of the countries concerned without the need for enabling legislation. While it is true that the legislation for this type of activity has been passed – for example section 2(1) of the European Communities Act 1972[257] in the UK, which permits in advance this form of indirect law-making, and is thus assimilated into municipal law – the fact remains that the member states have accepted an extraterritorial source of law, binding in certain circumstances upon them. The effect is thus that directly effective Community law has precedence over inconsistent UK legislation. This was confirmed by the House of Lords in *Factortame Ltd* v. *Secretary of State for Transport*.[258] It was further noted that one of the consequences of UK entry into the European Communities and the European Communities Act 1972 was that an interim injunction could be granted, the effect of which would be to suspend the operation of a statute on the grounds that the legislation in question allegedly infringed Community law. This is one illustration of the major effect which joining the Community has had in terms of the English legal system and previously accepted legal principles. The mistake, however, should not be made of generalising from this specific relationship to the sphere of international law as a whole.

Justiciability, act of state and related doctrines

An issue is justiciable basically if it can be tried according to law.[259] It would, therefore, follow that matters that fall within the competence of the executive branch of government are not justiciable before the courts. Accordingly, the test as to whether a matter is or is not justiciable involves

---

[255] See *Internationale Handelsgesellschaft* v. *Einfuhr- und Vorratsstelle für Getreide und Futtermittel* [1970] ECR 1125.

[256] Including the treaties of Maastricht (1992), Amsterdam (1997), Nice (2001) and Lisbon (2007, not in force).

[257] See also section 2(4).

[258] See [1990] 2 AC 85, 140 (per Lord Bridge); 93 ILR, p. 652. See also *Ex parte Factortame (No. 2)* [1991] 1 AC 603; 93 ILR, p. 731; *R* v. *Secretary of State for Transport, ex parte Factortame*, European Court of Justice case C-213/89, 93 ILR, p. 669 and Case C-221/89, 93 ILR, p. 731.

[259] See Mann, *Foreign Affairs*, chapter 4. See also L. Collins, 'Foreign Relations and the Judiciary', 51 ICLQ, 2002, p. 485.

an illumination of that grey area where the spheres of executive and judiciary merge and overlap. Recent years have seen a reduction in the sphere of exclusive competence of the executive free from judicial oversight and a number of important cases have sought to redraw the boundary. Justiciability as a concept includes the doctrine of act of state, which generally concerns the activities of the executive in relations with other states,[260] but in the context of international law and municipal courts it refers particularly to the doctrine that no state can exercise jurisdiction over another state.[261] As such it is based upon the principles of the sovereignty and equality of states.[262] Non-justiciability acts as an evidential bar, since an issue cannot be raised or proved, in contrast to sovereign immunity, which provides that the courts cannot exercise the jurisdiction that exists with regard to the matter in question due to the status of the entity or individual concerned, although it is open to the state concerned to waive its immunity and thus remove the jurisdictional bar.[263] Non-justiciability will usually concern a clear inter-state relationship or situation which is impleaded in a seemingly private action, while immunity issues will invariably arise out of a state–private party relationship not usually relating to inter-state activities as such.[264]

The concept of non-justiciability rests upon a number of pillars, ranging from prerogative of the executive in the areas of foreign policy and national defence,[265] where it is essentially a rule of law principle in a democratic system of government delineating the separation of powers,[266] to respect for the sovereignty and independence of foreign states.[267] Accordingly, both domestic and foreign executive acts are covered. With regard

---

[260] See e.g. Wade and Phillips, *Constitutional and Administrative Law*, pp. 299–303; J. B. Moore, *Acts of State in English Law*, New York, 1906; Mann, *Foreign Affairs*, chapter 9; Singer, 'The Act of State Doctrine of the UK', 75 AJIL, 1981, p. 283; M. Akehurst, 'Jurisdiction in International Law', 46 BYIL, 1972–3, pp. 145, 240, and M. Zander, 'The Act of State Doctrine', 53 AJIL, 1959, p. 826.

[261] See Lord Pearson, *Nissan* v. *Attorney-General* [1970] AC 179, 239; 44 ILR, pp. 359, 390.

[262] See *Oppenheim's International Law*, p. 365.

[263] See further as to sovereign or state immunity and diplomatic immunity, below, chapter 13.

[264] See e.g. *Amalgamated Metal Trading* v. *Department of Trade and Industry*, *The Times*, 21 March 1989, p. 40.

[265] In the UK, areas traditionally covered by the Crown prerogative: see above, p. 149.

[266] See e.g. Lord Hoffmann in *R* v. *Lyons* [2002] UKHL 44, para. 40; 131 ILR, p. 555; Lord Millett in *R* v. *Lyons*, para. 105; 131 ILR, p. 575, and Richards J in the *CND* case [2002] EWHC 2777 (Admin), para. 60.

[267] See *Underhill* v. *Hernandez* 168 US 250, 252.

to the former,[268] the courts will refuse, or at the least be extremely reluctant, to adjudicate upon an exercise of sovereign power, such as making war and peace, making international treaties or ceding territory.[269] This would include the definition of territories within the UK[270] as well as the conduct of foreign affairs.[271] Lord Hoffmann held in R v. Jones that 'the making of war and peace and the disposition of the armed forces has always been regarded as a discretionary power of the Crown into the exercise of which the courts will not enquire'.[272] As far as the latter instance is

---

[268] See Nissan v. Attorney-General [1970] AC 179 and Buron v. Denman (1848) 145 ER 450. See also S. de Smith and R. Brazier, Constitutional and Administrative Law, 6th edn, London, 1989, pp. 145–51, and Mann, Foreign Affairs, chapter 10.

[269] Not simply because they form part of the Crown's prerogative powers, but because such powers are discretionary: see Council of Civil Service Unions v. Minister for the Civil Service [1984] 3 All ER 935, 956 and Lord Hoffmann in R v. Jones [2006] UKHL 16, para. 65; 132 ILR, pp. 695–6. See also Lord Reid in Chandler v. DPP [1964] AC 763, 791; Simon Brown LJ, R v. Ministry of Defence, ex parte Smith [1996] QB 517, 539; Laws LJ, Marchiori v. The Environment Agency [2002] EWCA Civ 3, paras. 38 and 40; 127 ILR, pp. 642 and 643; CND v. Prime Minister [2002] EWHC 2759 at paras. 15 (Simon Brown LJ), 50 (Maurice Kay J) and 59 (Richards J); 126 ILR, pp. 735, 750 and 753; and R (on the application of Abbasi) v. Secretary of State for Foreign and Commonwealth Affairs [2002] EWCA Civ 1598, para. 106(iii); 126 ILR, p. 725.

[270] See The Fagernes [1927] P 311, 324 (per Atkin LJ). See also Christian v. The Queen [2006] UKPC 47, paras. 9–10 (Lord Hoffmann) and 33 (Lord Woolf); 130 ILR, pp. 699–700, 707.

[271] See e.g. R (Al-Rawi) v. Secretary of State for Foreign and Commonwealth Affairs [2006] EWCA Civ 1279, paras. 131 ff. (Laws LJ), and cases cited in footnote 266 above.

[272] [2006] UKHL 16, para. 65; 132 ILR, p. 696. He concluded that 'The decision to go to war [against Iraq], whether one thinks it was right or wrong, fell squarely within the discretionary powers of the Crown to defend the realm and conduct its foreign affairs . . . The discretionary nature or non-justiciability of the power to make war is in my opinion simply one of the reasons why aggression is not a crime in domestic law', paras. 66 and 67, ibid., and see also Lord Mance, para. 103; ibid., pp. 705–6. More cautiously, Lord Bingham noted that 'there are well established rules that the courts will be very slow to review the exercise of prerogative powers in relation to the conduct of foreign affairs and the deployment of the armed services', para. 30, ibid., p. 684. The Jones approach was applied by the Court of Appeal in R (Gentle) v. Prime Minister [2006] EWCA Civ 1689, para. 33 (Clarke MR); 132 ILR, p. 737, where it was held that the question whether the UK had acted unlawfully in sending troops to Iraq was non-justiciable for two reasons: first, because it would require consideration of at least two international instruments (Security Council resolutions 678 and 1441) and, secondly, because it would require detailed consideration of policy decisions in the fields of foreign affairs and defence 'which are the exclusive responsibility of the executive government'. In the House of Lords, [2008] UKHL 20, their Lordships essentially focused on the meaning of article 2 of the European Convention on Human Rights, but Lord Bingham referred to the 'restraint traditionally shown by the courts in ruling on what has been called high policy – peace and war, the making of treaties, the conduct of foreign relations', ibid., para. 2, while Lord Hope noted that, 'The issue of legality in this area of international law [the use of force by states] belongs

concerned, Lord Wilberforce declared in *Buttes Gas and Oil Co. v. Hammer (No. 3):*[273]

> there exists in English law a general principle that the courts will not adjudicate upon the transactions of foreign sovereign states ... it seems desirable to consider this principle ... not as a variety of 'act of state' but one for judicial restraint or abstention.[274]

Such a principle was not one of discretion, but inherent in the nature of the judicial process. Although that case concerned litigation in the areas of libel and conspiracy, the House of Lords felt that a determination of the issue would have involved the court in reviewing the transactions of four sovereign states and having to find that part of those transactions was contrary to international law. Quite apart from the possibility of embarrassment to the foreign relations of the executive, there were no judicial or manageable standards by which to judge such issues.[275] It has been held, for example, that judicial review would not be appropriate in a matter which would have serious international repercussions and which was more properly the sphere of diplomacy.[276] Although the Court of Appeal has noted that the keeping and disposal of foreign bank notes for commercial purposes in the UK could not be treated as sovereign acts so as to bring the activity within the protection of the *Buttes* non-justiciability doctrine, the acts in question had to be of a sovereign rather than of a commercial nature and performed within the territory of a foreign state.[277] Legislation can, of course, impinge upon the question as to whether an issue is or is not justiciable,[278] while the State Immunity Act 1978 removed sovereign immunity for commercial transactions.[279]

---

to the area of relations between states ... [and] ... is a matter of political judgment ... It is not part of domestic law reviewable here', *ibid.*, para. 24 (and see para. 26). See also Lady Hale, *ibid.*, para. 58.

[273] [1982] AC 888; 64 ILR, p. 331.

[274] [1982] AC 888, 931; 64 ILR, p. 344. See also *Duke of Brunswick* v. *King of Hanover* (1848) 1 HLC 1. See Fatima, *Using International Law*, pp. 385 ff. Note also *R* v. *Director of the Serious Fraud Office and BAE Systems* [2008] EWHC 714 (Admin), paras. 74 and 160.

[275] [1982] AC 888, 938; 64 ILR, p. 351.

[276] See e.g. *R* v. *Secretary of State for Foreign and Commonwealth Affairs, ex parte Pirbhai* 107 ILR, p. 462. But see the *Abbasi* case below, p. 188.

[277] *A Ltd* v. *B Bank* 111 ILR, pp. 590, 594–6.

[278] So that, for example, issues related to war crimes were justiciable in the light of the International Criminal Courts Act 2001: see *R* v. *Jones* [2006] UKHL 16, paras. 4 and 28; 132 ILR, pp. 672 and 683.

[279] See *Empresa Exportadora de Azucar* v. *Industria Azucarera Nacional SA* [1983] 2 LL. R 171, 194–5; 64 ILR, p. 368. See further below, chapter 13.

One of the questions that the Court of Appeal addressed in *Maclaine Watson* v. *International Tin Council*[280] was whether in such circumstances the doctrine of non-justiciability survived. It was emphasised that the two concepts of immunity and non-justiciability had to be kept separate and concern was expressed that the *Buttes* non-justiciability principle could be used to prevent proceedings being brought against states in commercial matters, contrary to the Act.[281]

The issue of justiciability was discussed in *Maclaine Watson* v. *Department of Trade and Industry* both by the Court of Appeal[282] and by the House of Lords[283] in the context of the creation of the collapsed International Tin Council by a group of states by a treaty which was unincorporated into English law. Kerr LJ emphasised that the doctrine in this context rested upon the principles that unincorporated treaties do not form part of the law of England and that such international agreements were not contracts which the courts could enforce.[284] However, this did not prevent reference to an unincorporated treaty where it was necessary or convenient, for example in order to assess the legal nature of the International Tin Council.[285] Lord Oliver in the House of Lords decision reaffirmed the essence of the doctrine of non-justiciability. He noted that it was

> axiomatic that municipal courts have not and cannot have the competence to adjudicate upon or to enforce the rights arising out of transactions entered into by independent sovereign states between themselves on the plane of international law.[286]

However, this did not mean that the court must never look at or construe a treaty. A treaty could be examined as a part of the factual background against which a particular issue has arisen.[287] It was pointed out that the creation of the Council by a group of states was a sovereign act and that the adjudication of the rights and obligations between the member states of the Council and the Council itself could only be undertaken on the international plane.[288] In other words, the

---

[280] [1988] 3 WLR 1169; 80 ILR, p. 191.

[281] [1988] 3 WLR 1169, 1188 per Kerr LJ; 80 ILR, p. 209.

[282] [1988] 3 WLR 1033; 80 ILR, p. 49.   [283] [1989] 3 All ER 523; 81 ILR, p. 671.

[284] [1988] 3 WLR 1033, 1075; 80 ILR, pp. 49, 86.

[285] [1988] 3 WLR 1033, 1075–6. See also Nourse LJ, *ibid.*, p. 1130; 80 ILR, p. 148.

[286] [1989] 3 All ER 523, 544; 81 ILR, pp. 671, 700. See also *R* v. *Director of the Serious Fraud Office and BAE Systems* [2008] EWHC 714 (Admin), para. 107.

[287] [1989] 3 All ER 523, 545; 81 ILR, p. 701.

[288] [1989] 3 All ER 523, 559; 81 ILR, p. 722. See also Ralph Gibson LJ in the Court of Appeal judgment, [1988] 3 WLR 1033, 1143–4; 80 ILR, pp. 49, 163.

situation appeared to involve not only the *Buttes* form of act of state non-justiciability, but also non-justiciability on the basis of an unincorporated treaty.[289]

Hoffmann LJ in *Littrell* v. *USA (No. 2)*[290] pointed out in the context of a status of forces agreement (providing for the placement of NATO troops in the UK) that the courts could look at such agreement to ensure that the foreign troops were here by invitation since the conclusion of a treaty was as much a fact as any other,[291] but this could not be taken to mean that the courts would actually enforce the terms of an unincorporated treaty. Additionally, it would not be open to the courts to determine whether a foreign sovereign state had broken a treaty.[292] The basic position is that: 'Ordinarily speaking, English courts will not rule upon the true meaning and effect of international instruments which apply only at the level of international law.'[293] Further, the English courts are likely to decline to seek to determine an issue where this could be 'damaging to the public interest in the field of international relations, national security or defence'.[294] Lord Bingham noted in *R* v. *Jones* that the courts would be 'very slow to adjudicate upon rights arising out of transactions entered into between

---

[289] But see *Re McKerr*, where Lord Steyn noted that faced with the narrowness of this decision, a critical re-examination of this area of the law might become necessary in the future in the light of the 'growing support for the view that human rights treaties enjoy a special status', [2004] UKHL 12, paras. 51–2.

[290] [1995] 1 WLR 82, 93.

[291] Similarly, Colman J in *Westland Helicopters Ltd* v. *Arab Organisation for Industrialisation* [1995] 2 WLR 126, 149, held that reference to the terms of the treaty establishing an international organisation and to the terms of the basic statute of that organisation in order to ascertain the governing law of that organisation and its precise nature did not transgress the boundary between what was justiciable and what was non-justiciable.

[292] See *British Airways Board* v. *Laker Airways Ltd* [1985] AC 58, 85–6; *Ex parte Molyneaux* [1986] 1 WLR 331; 87 ILR, p. 329 and *Westland Helicopters Ltd* v. *Arab Organisation for Industrialisation* [1995] 2 WLR 126, 136. See also *Minister for Arts Heritage and Environment* v. *Peko-Wallsend Ltd* (1987) 75 ALR 218, 250–4; 90 ILR, pp. 32, 51–5, where the Australian Federal Court held that a Cabinet decision involving Australia's international relations in implementing a treaty was not a justiciable matter, and *Arab Republic of Syria* v. *Arab Republic of Egypt* 91 ILR, pp. 288, 305–6, where the Supreme Court of Brazil held that the courts of a third state could not exercise jurisdiction in a matter essentially of state succession between two other states even where the property was within the jurisdiction.

[293] *CND* v. *Prime Minister of the UK and Others* [2002] EWHC 2777 (Admin), paras. 23, 36 and 47. See also *R* v. *Lyons* [2002] 3 WLR 1562; 131 ILR, p. 538.

[294] *CND* v. *Prime Minister of the UK*, para. 47, cited with approval by the Irish High Court in *Horgan* v. *An Taoiseach*, judgment of 28 April 2003, as emphasising 'the strictly circumspect role which the courts adopt when called upon to exercise jurisdiction in relation to the Executive's conduct of international relations generally', 132 ILR, pp. 407, 440.

sovereign states on the plane of international law'.[295] However, the rule is not absolute.[296] The courts are willing to look at the terms of an unincorporated treaty in specific situations: first, as noted above, in order to ascertain certain facts such as the existence and terms of, and the parties to, a treaty or where the treaty in question is incorporated into a contract or referred to in domestic legislation and is necessary to a particular decision, and secondly, where the national courts have to adjudicate upon the interpretation of a particular international treaty in order to determine private rights and obligations under domestic law.[297] The latter proposition would operate, for example, with regard to extradition and asylum cases where a view has to be taken with regard to the Geneva Convention Relating to the Status of Refugees, 1951 as a result of domestic legislation, the Asylum and Immigration Act 1996.[298] In *Republic of Ecuador* v. *Occidental Exploration and Production Co.*, the Court of Appeal, while affirming this principle, emphasised that context was always important, so that a treaty intended by its signatories to give rise to rights in favour of private investors capable of enforcement under the treaty in consensual arbitration against one or other of its signatory states in domestic proceedings would fall within this exception and thus be justiciable.[299] The exception to non-justiciability laid down in the *CND* and *Occidental* cases was reaffirmed in *In the Matter of AY Bank Ltd*,[300] where it was held that the right to prove in the liquidation of a joint venture bank in the UK (involving the National Bank of Yugoslavia), upon the dissolution of the Federal Republic of Yugoslavia and its National Bank and consequential apportionment among the successor states, arose in domestic law, so

---

[295] [2006] UKHL 16, para. 30; 132 ILR, p. 684. See also *R (Islamic Human Rights Commission)* v. *CAA* [2006] EWHC 2465; 132 ILR, p. 707, and *R (Gentle)* v. *Prime Minister* [2008] UKHL 20, above, p. 181, note 272.

[296] See Lord Oliver in *JH Rayner (Mincing Lane) Ltd* v. *Department of Trade and Industry* [1990] 2 AC 418, 500. Lord Steyn in *Kuwait Airways Corporation* v. *Iraqi Airways Co. (Nos. 4 and 5)* [2002] 2 AC 883, 1101 considered that the principle was not 'a categorical rule'. See also Fatima, *Using International Law*, pp. 273 ff.

[297] See e.g. *CND* v. *Prime Minister* [2002] EWHC 2777 (Admin), paras. 35–6 (Simon Brown LJ) and 61(iii) (Richards J).

[298] See e.g. *Ex parte Adan* [2000] UKHL 67.

[299] [2005] EWCA Cic 1116, paras. 31 and 37. Mance LJ went on to say that 'For the English Court to treat the extent of such rights as non-justiciable would appear to us to involve an extension, rather than an application, of existing doctrines developed in different contexts', *ibid.* See also paras. 39–42. Somewhat confusingly, Mance LJ concluded that the doctrine of non-justiciability could not be ousted by consent, *ibid.*, para. 57.

[300] [2006] EWHC 830 (Ch), paras. 51 ff. See also *R* v. *Director of the Serious Fraud Office and BAE Systems* [2008] EWHC 714 (Admin), paras. 118–20.

that the existence of the Agreement on Succession Issues, signed by the successor states formally apportioning the assets and debts of the Former Yugoslavia, did not render the question non-justiciable.

The principle of non-justiciability, which includes but goes beyond the concept of act of state,[301] must exist in an international system founded upon sovereign and formally equal states.[302] Having said that, there is no doubt that the extent of the doctrine is open to question. While the courts would regard a question concerning the constitutionality of a foreign government as non-justiciable[303] and would not as a general rule inquire into the validity of acts done in a sovereign capacity, such as the constitutionality of foreign laws,[304] the latter proposition may be subject to exceptions. The House of Lords addressed the question in *Kuwait Airways Corporation* v. *Iraqi Airways Company*.[305] Lord Nicholls noted that in appropriate circumstances it was legitimate for an English court to have regard to the content of international law in deciding whether to recognise a foreign law and it did not flow inevitably from the non-justiciability principle that the judiciary must ignore a breach of international law committed by one state against another 'where the breach is plain and, indeed, acknowledged'.[306] In such cases, the difficulty discussed by Lord Wilberforce in *Buttes Gas and Oil* concerning the lack of judicial or manageable standards by which to deal with a sovereignty dispute between two foreign states did not apply.[307] The acceptability of a provision of foreign law had to be judged by contemporary standards and the courts had to give effect to clearly established rules of international law.[308] Where foreign legislation

---

[301] A distinction has recently been drawn between a narrower doctrine of act of state, which concerns the recognition of acts of a foreign state within its own territory, and a broader principle of non-justiciability in respect of 'certain sovereign acts' of a foreign state: see Mance J in *Kuwait Airways Corporation* v. *Iraqi Airways Company* 116 ILR, pp. 534, 568, basing himself upon Lord Wilberforce in *Buttes Gas and Oil* v. *Hammer* [1982] AC 888, 930–2; 64 ILR, p. 331. Mance J's analysis was approved by Lord Lloyd in *Ex Parte Pinochet* (*No. 1*) [2000] 1 AC 61, 102; 119 ILR, pp. 51, 91.

[302] See e.g. the decision of the Belgian Conseil d'État in *T* v. *Belgium* on 9 April 1998 that the process of declaring a foreign diplomat persona non grata was not justiciable both because the request from the receiving state was a matter between states and because it was the sending state that had to recall the person in question or terminate his functions and the Conseil d'État had no jurisdiction over an act emanating from a foreign state: 115 ILR, p. 442.

[303] See e.g. *Ex parte Turkish Cypriot Association* 112 ILR, p. 735.

[304] See *Buck* v. *Attorney-General* [1965] 1 Ch. 745; 42 ILR, p. 11.

[305] Decision of 16 May 2002, [2002] UKHL 19; 125 ILR, p. 677.

[306] *Ibid.*, para. 26.   [307] See above, p. 182.

[308] [2002] UKHL 19, para. 28. See also *Blathwayt* v. *Baron Cawley* [1976] AC 397, 426 and *Oppenheimer* v. *Cattermole* [1976] AC 249, 278.

was adopted consequential upon a fundamental breach of international law (such as the Iraqi invasion of Kuwait in 1990 and seizure of its assets), enforcement or recognition of such law by the courts would be 'manifestly contrary to the public policy of English law'. Further, it was emphasised that international law recognised that a national court may decline to give effect to legislative and other acts of foreign states which are in violation of international law.[309] Lord Steyn noted that the extension of the public policy exception to recognition of foreign laws from human rights violations to 'flagrant breaches of international law' was correct. Reference was made to the UN Charter, binding Security Council resolutions and international opinion in general.[310] Lord Hope emphasised that 'very narrow limits must be placed on any exception to the act of state rule', but there was no need for restraint on grounds of public policy 'where it is plain beyond dispute that a clearly established norm of international law has been violated'.[311] He concluded that 'a legislative act by a foreign state which is in flagrant breach of clearly established rules of international law ought not to be recognised by the courts of this country as forming part of the lex situs of that state'.[312]

The courts may also not feel constrained in expressing their views as to foreign sovereign activities where a breach of international law, particularly human rights, is involved[313] and may not feel constrained from investigating, in a dispute involving private rights, the legal validity of an act done by a citizen purporting to act on behalf of the sovereign or sovereign state.[314] It is clear that the courts will regard as non-justiciable policy decisions by the government concerning relationships with friendly foreign states, on the basis that foreign policy is pre-eminently an area for the government and not the courts.[315] In particular, a number of cases have laid down the proposition that decisions taken by the executive in its dealings with foreign states regarding the protection of British citizens abroad are non-justiciable.[316]

---

[309] [2002] UKHL 19, para. 29. See also *Oppenheim's International Law*, pp. 371 ff.
[310] [2002] UKHL 19, para. 114.   [311] *Ibid.*, paras. 138–40.
[312] *Ibid.*, para. 148. See also Lord Scott, *ibid.*, para. 192.
[313] See e.g. *Abbasi v. Secretary of State for Foreign and Commonwealth Affairs* [2002] EWCA Civ. 1598, paras. 57 and 66 (per Lord Phillips MR); 126 ILR, pp. 710 and 713.
[314] See e.g. *Dubai Bank v. Galadari*, *The Times*, 14 July 1990.
[315] See *Ex parte Everett* [1989] 1 QB 811; 84 ILR, p. 713; *Ex parte Ferhut Butt* 116 ILR, pp. 607, 620–1, and *Foday Saybana Sankoh* 119 ILR, pp. 389, 396. See further above, p. 180.
[316] See e.g. *Council of Civil Service Unions v. Minister for the Civil Service* [1985] 1 AC 374, 411 (per Lord Diplock); *Ex parte Pirbhai* 107 ILR, pp. 462, 479; *Ex parte Ferhut Butt* 116 ILR, pp. 607, 615 and 622 and *R (Suresh and Manickavasagam) v. Secretary of State for the Home Department* [2001] EWHC Admin 1028, para. 19; 123 ILR, p. 598.

This approach, however, is subject to some qualification.[317] This concerns in particular the evolving law of judicial review[318] both with regard to its scope concerning the executive and in terms of 'legitimate expectation',[319] or a reasonable expectation that a regular practice will continue. Where diplomatic protection of a national abroad is concerned, the Court of Appeal has noted that 'The Secretary of State must be free to give full weight to foreign policy considerations, which are not justiciable. However, this does not mean the whole process is immune from judicial scrutiny. The citizen's legitimate expectation is that his request will be "considered", and that in that consideration all relevant factors will be thrown into the balance.'[320] Taylor LJ referred, for example, in *ex parte Everett* to the 'normal expectation of every citizen' that, if he were subjected abroad to a violation of a fundamental right, the British government would not simply wash their hands of the matter and abandon him to his fate.[321] The Court in *Abbasi* concluded that judicial review would lie where the Foreign and Commonwealth Office, contrary to its stated policy, refused even to consider whether to make diplomatic representations on behalf of a subject whose fundamental rights were being violated. However, beyond this, no general proposition could be stated, being dependent upon the precise circumstances. In particular, there was no enforceable duty to protect the citizen, only a discretion.[322] In *Al-Rawi v. Secretary of State for Foreign and Commonwealth Affairs*, the Court of Appeal denied that any such legitimate expectation as to the exercise of discretion would extend to the position of non-nationals.[323]

The approach in *Abbasi* was approved in *Kaunda v. The President of the Republic of South Africa* by the Constitutional Court of South Africa,

---

[317] See Lord Phillips MR in *Abbasi v. Secretary of State for Foreign and Commonwealth Affairs* [2002] EWCA Civ. 1598, paras. 80 ff; 126 ILR, p. 718.

[318] See e.g. S. A. De Smith, H. Woolf and J. Jowell, *Judicial Review*, 5th edn, London, 1998, pp. 419 ff.

[319] See *Secretary of State for the Foreign and Commonwealth Office v. The Queen (on the application of Bancoult)* [2007] EWCA Civ 498, paras. 72 ff.

[320] Per Lord Phillips MR in *Abassi v. Secretary of State for Foreign and Commonwealth Affairs* [2002] EWCA Civ. 1598, para. 99.

[321] [1989] 1 QB 811, paras. 96–8.

[322] [2002] EWCA Civ 1598, paras. 104–7. The court concluded that this discretion was a very wide one but there was no reason why the decision or inaction of the Foreign Office should not be reviewable if it can be shown that the same is irrational or contrary to legitimate expectation. However, the court could not enter into the forbidden areas, including decisions affecting foreign policy, *ibid.*, para. 106(iii). See also *R v. Director of the Serious Fraud Office and BAE Systems* [2008] EWHC 714 (Admin), para. 56.

[323] [2006] EWCA Civ 1279, para. 89.

which noted that 'A decision as to whether, and if so, what protection should be given, is an aspect of foreign policy which is essentially the function of the executive.'[324] This did not mean that the South African courts had no jurisdiction to deal with issues concerned with diplomatic protection. Since the exercise of all public power was subject to constitutional control, this would also apply to an allegation that the government has failed to respond appropriately to a request for diplomatic protection. If, for instance, the decision were to be irrational or made in bad faith, the court could intervene to require the government to deal with the matter properly.[325]

Australian courts also have emphasised the importance of separation of powers and the need for courts to exercise considerable caution with regard to foreign policy, expressly citing the *Buttes* case.[326] The question of justiciability was one for the federal judicial branch.[327] It has been noted, for example, that any question of a dispute as to the assessment made by the executive and legislative branches of government of the 'terrorist threat' to the safety of the public would not be justiciable, but that this situation would change upon the adoption of relevant legislation.[328]

The US courts have similarly recognised the existence of areas of non-justiciability for sensitive political reasons. This is usually referred to as the political question doctrine and operates to prevent the courts from considering issues of political delicacy in the field of foreign affairs.[329] In

---

[324] CCT 23/04, [2004] ZACC 5, para. 77 (per Chief Justice Chaskalson). See also *Swissborough Diamond Mines* v. *South Africa*, Supreme Court, Transvaal Provincial Division, 1997, 132 ILR, p. 454, and the decision of the German Federal Constitutional Court in *Hess*, where it was held that 'the Federal Government enjoys wide discretion in deciding the question of whether and in what manner to grant protection against foreign States', BVerfGE 55, 349; 90 ILR 386, 395.

[325] CCT 23/04, [2004] ZACC 5, paras. 78–80.

[326] See the decision of the High Court of Australia in *Thorpe* v. *Commonwealth of Australia (No. 3)* (1997) 144 ALR 677, 690–1; 118 ILR, p. 353; *Re Ditfort* (1988) 19 FCR 347, 369; 87 ILR, p. 170; *Petrotimor Companhia de Petroleos SARL* v. *Commonwealth of Australia* [2003] FCAFC 3, and *Victoria Leasing Ltd* v. *United States* (2005) 218 ALR 640. See also G. Lindell, 'The Justiciability of Political Questions: Recent Developments' in *Australian Constitutional Perspectives* (eds. H. P. Lee and G. Winterton), Sydney, 1992, p. 180, and R. Garnett, 'Foreign States in Australian Courts', *Melbourne University Law Review*, 2005, p. 704.

[327] *Wilson* v. *Minister for Aboriginal and Torres Strait Islander Affairs* [1996] HCA 18; (1996) 189 CLR 1 at 11.

[328] *Thomas* v. *Mowbray* [2007] HCA 33, para. 107.

[329] See e.g. *Underhill* v. *Hernandez* 168 US 250 (1897), *Baker* v. *Carr* 369 US 181 (1962) and *American Insurance Association* v. *Garamendi*, US Court of Appeals for the Ninth Circuit, 23 June 2003. See also Henkin *et al.*, *International Law: Cases and Materials*, p. 178;

the *Greenham Women against Cruise Missiles* v. *Reagan* case,[330] for example, the Court held that a suit to prevent the US deployment of cruise
missiles at an air force base in the UK constituted a non-justiciable political question, not appropriate for judicial resolution.[331] Similarly, issues
relating to rights of succession to the assets of a foreign state were non-
justiciable.[332] Much will depend upon the particular circumstances of the
case. In *Linder* v. *Portocarrero*,[333] for instance, concerning the murder of
a US citizen working for the Nicaraguan government by rebel forces (the
Contras), the US Court of Appeals for the Eleventh Circuit held that the
political question doctrine was not implicated since the complaint neither challenged the legitimacy of US policy on Nicaragua nor sought to
require the Court to decide who was right and who was wrong in the
civil war in that country. The complaint was rather narrowly focused on
the lawfulness of the conduct of the defendants in a single incident. In
Koohi v. *United States*,[334] the US Court of Appeals for the Ninth Circuit
held that the courts were not precluded from reviewing military decisions, whether taken during war or peacetime, which caused injury to
US or enemy civilians. The Court in *Baker* v. *Carr*,[335] the leading case on
the political question doctrine, while noting that not every case touching
foreign relations was non-justiciable, provided a list of six factors that
might render a case non-justiciable.[336] The Court of Appeals underlined

---

L. Henkin, 'Is There a "Political Question" Doctrine?', 85 *Yale Law Journal*, 1976, p. 597;
J. Charney, 'Judicial Deference in Foreign Relations', 83 AJIL, 1989, p. 805, and T. M.
Franck, *Political Questions/Judicial Answers: Does the Rule of Law Apply to Foreign Affairs?*,
Princeton, 1992.

[330] 591 F.Supp. 1332 (1984); 99 ILR, p. 44.

[331] But see *Japan Whaling Association* v. *American Cetacean Society* 478 US 221 (1986), where
the Supreme Court held that the judicial interpretation of a US statute, even if it involved
foreign relations, was not a political question precluding justiciability. See also *Dellums*
v. *Bush* 752 F.Supp. 1141 (1990).

[332] See e.g. *Can and Others* v. *United States* 14 F.3d 160 (1994); 107 ILR, p. 255.

[333] 963 F.2d 332, 337 (1992); 99 ILR, pp. 54, 79.

[334] 976 F.2d 1328, 1331–2 (1992); 99 ILR, pp. 80, 84–5.   [335] 369 US 186, 211 (1962).

[336] That there should be (1) a textually demonstrable constitutional commitment of the issue
to a co-ordinate political department; or (2) a lack of judicially discoverable and manageable standards for resolving it; or (3) the impossibility of deciding without an initial
policy determination of a kind clearly for non-judicial discretion; or (4) the impossibility
of a court's undertaking independent resolution without expressing lack of respect due
co-ordinate branches of government; or (5) an unusual need for unquestioning adherence to a political decision already made; or (6) the potentiality of embarrassment of
multifarious pronouncements by various departments on one question, *Baker*, 369 US at
217. See also *Schneider* v. *Kissinger* 412 F.3d 190 (DC Cir. 2005); *Bancoult* v. *McNamara*
445 F.3d 427 (DC Cir. 2006); *Gonzalez-Vera* v. *Kissinger* 449 F.3d 1260 (2006).

in *Kadić* v. *Karadžić*[337] that 'judges should not reflexively invoke these doctrines [political question and act of state doctrines] to avoid difficult and somewhat sensitive decisions in the context of human rights'. The fact that judicially discoverable and manageable standards exist would indicate that the issues involved were indeed justiciable.[338] In *Corrie* v. *Caterpillar*, the US Court of Appeals for the Ninth Circuit reaffirmed that the political question doctrine was a jurisdictional issue and that the *Baker* v. *Carr* factors precluded justiciability, noting in particular that the provision of military assistance by the US to foreign states constituted such a political question.[339]

Also relevant in the context of non-justiciability is the doctrine of act of state. The *Third US Restatement of Foreign Relations Law*[340] provides that 'in the absence of a treaty or other unambiguous agreements regarding controlling legal principles, courts in the United States will generally refrain from examining the validity of a taking by a foreign state of property within its own territory, or from sitting in judgment on other acts of a governmental character done by a foreign state within its own territory and applicable there'.[341] In *Banco Nacional de Cuba* v. *Sabbatino*,[342] the US Supreme Court held that the act of state concept was not a rule of public international law, but related instead to internal constitutional balances.[343] It was a rule of judicial self-restraint. The Court declared that the judicial branch would not examine the validity of a taking of property within its own territory by a foreign sovereign government,[344] irrespective of the legality in international law of that action.[345] This basic approach

---

[337] 1995 US App. LEXIS 28826.

[338] See e.g. *Klinghoffer* v. *SNC Achille Lauro* 937 F.2d 44 (1991); *Nixon* v. *United States* 122 L.Ed.2d 1 (1993); *Can* v. *United States* 14 F.3d 160 (1994); *Schneider* v. *Kissinger* 310 F.Supp. 2d 251, 257–64 (DDC 2004).

[339] 503 F.3d 974 CA 9 (Wash.), 2007.   [340] 1987, para. 443, pp. 366–7.

[341] This doctrine is subject to modification by act of Congress, *ibid.*, para. 444.

[342] 376 US 398 (1964); 35 ILR, p. 2.

[343] 376 US 398, 427–8 (1964); 35 ILR, p. 37. In *United States* v. *Noriega* 746 F.Supp. 1506, 1521–3 (1990); 99 ILR, pp. 143, 163–5, the US District Court noted that the act of state doctrine was a function of the separation of powers, since it precluded judicial examination of the acts of foreign governments which might otherwise hinder the executive's conduct of foreign relations.

[344] 376 US 398 (1964); 35 ILR, p. 2.

[345] This approach was reversed by Congress in the Hickenlooper Amendment to the Foreign Assistance Act of 1964, Pub. L No. 86–663, para. 301(d)(4), 78 Stat. 1013 (1964), 79 Stat. 653, 659, as amended 22 USC, para. 23470(e)(2), (1982). Note that in *Williams & Humbert Ltd* v. *W & H Trade Marks (Jersey) Ltd* [1986] 1 All ER 129; 75 ILR, p. 312, the House of Lords held that an English court would recognise a foreign law effecting

was supported in a subsequent case,[346] whereas in *Alfred Dunhill of London Inc.* v. *Republic of Cuba*[347] the Supreme Court employed sovereign immunity concepts as the reason for not recognising the repudiation of the commercial obligations of a state instrumentality as an act of state. However, it now appears that there is an exception to the strict act of state doctrine where a relevant treaty provision between the parties specifies the standard of compensation to be payable and thus provides 'controlling legal principles'.[348]

In an important case in 1990, the Supreme Court examined anew the extent of the act of state doctrine. *Kirkpatrick* v. *Environmental Tectonics*[349] concerned a claim brought by an unsuccessful bidder on a Nigerian government contract in circumstances where the successful rival had bribed Nigerian officials. The Court unanimously held that the act of state doctrine did not apply since the validity of a foreign sovereign act was not at issue. The Court also made the point that act of state issues only arose when a court '*must decide* – that is, when the outcome of the case turns upon – the effect of official action by a foreign sovereign'.[350] While the doctrine clearly meant that a US court had to accept that the acts of foreign sovereigns taken within their jurisdictions were to be deemed valid, this did not extend to cases and controversies that might embarrass foreign governments in situations falling outside this. Act of state was not to be extended.[351]

Executive certificates

There is an established practice adopted by the British courts of applying to the executive branch of government for the conclusive ascertainment

---

compulsory acquisition and any change of title to property which came under the control of the foreign state as a result and would accept and enforce the consequences of that compulsory acquisition without considering its merits.

[346] *First National City Bank* v. *Banco Nacional de Cuba* 406 US 759 (1972); 66 ILR, p. 102.

[347] 96 S. Ct. 1854 (1976); 66 ILR, p. 212. See also M. Halberstam, 'Sabbatino Resurrected', 79 AJIL, 1985, p. 68.

[348] See *Kalamazoo Spice Extraction Co.* v. *Provisional Military Government of Socialist Ethiopia* 729 F.2d 422 (1984). See also *AIG* v. *Iran* 493 F.Supp. 522 (1980) and Justice Harlan in the *Sabbatino* case, 376 US 398, 428 (1964); 35 ILR, pp. 25, 37.

[349] 110 S. Ct. 701 (1990); 88 ILR, p. 93.   [350] 110 S.Ct. 701, 705 (1990).

[351] See also *Third US Restatement of Foreign Relations Law*, pp. 366–89; *Bandes* v. *Harlow & Jones* 82 AJIL, 1988, p. 820, where the Court of Appeals held that the act of state doctrine was inapplicable to takings by a foreign state of property located outside its territory, and *First American Corp.* v. *Al-Nahyan* 948 F.Supp. 1107 (1996). Note that the party claiming the application of the doctrine bears the burden of proving its applicability: see *Daventree Ltd* v. *Republic of Azerbaijan* 349 F.Supp.2d 736, 754 (SDNY 2004).

of certain facts. Examples include the status of a foreign state or government, questions as to whether a state of war is in operation as regards a particular country or as between two foreign states, and whether or not a particular person is entitled to diplomatic status. This means that in such matters of state the courts will consult the government and regard the executive certificate (or Foreign Office certificate as it is sometimes called), which is issued following the request, as conclusive, irrespective of any relevant rules of international law.[352] This was firmly acknowledged in *Duff Development Co. Ltd* v. *Kelantan*,[353] which concerned the status of the state of Kelantan in the Malay Peninsula and whether it was able to claim immunity in the English courts. The government declared that it was regarded as an independent state and the House of Lords noted that 'where such a statement is forthcoming, no other evidence is admissible or needed', and that:

> it was not the business of the Court to inquire whether the Colonial Office rightly concluded that the Sultan [of Kelantan] was entitled to be recognised as a sovereign by international law.[354]

This basic position was reaffirmed in *R* v. *Secretary of State for Foreign and Commonwealth Affairs, ex parte Trawnik*,[355] in which it was held that certificates under section 40(3) of the Crown Proceedings Act 1947 and section 21 of the State Immunity Act 1978 were reviewable in the courts only if they constituted a nullity in that they were not genuine certificates or if, on their face, they had been issued outside the scope of the relevant statutory power. The contents of such certificates were conclusive of the matters contained therein and, in so far as they related to recognition of foreign states, were matters within the realm of the royal prerogative and not subject to judicial review.

Problems have arisen in the context of the decision of the UK announced in 1980 not to accord recognition to governments, but rather to treat the question of an unconstitutional change of regimes as one

---

[352] See e.g. *Oppenheim's International Law*, pp. 1046 ff.

[353] [1924] AC 797; 2 AD, p. 124. See also *The Fagernes* [1927] P. 311; 3 AD, p. 126 and *Post Office* v. *Estuary Radio Ltd* [1968] 2 QB 740; 43 ILR, p. 114. But cf. *Hesperides Hotels* v. *Aegean Turkish Holidays* [1978] 1 All ER 277; 73 ILR p. 9.

[354] Note that under s. 7, Diplomatic Privileges Act 1964 and s. 21, State Immunity Act 1978, such certificates are 'conclusive evidence' as to issues of diplomatic and state immunity. See also s. 8, International Organisations Act 1968, and see further below, chapter 13.

[355] *The Times*, 18 April 1985, p. 4. See also C. Warbrick, 'Executive Certificates in Foreign Affairs: Prospects for Review and Control', 35 ICLQ, 1986, p. 138, and E. Wilmshurst, 'Executive Certificates in Foreign Affairs: The United Kingdom', 35 ICLQ, 1986, p. 157.

relating to diplomatic relations.[356] In *Republic of Somalia v. Woodhouse Drake and Carey (Suisse) SA*,[357] the court was faced with a confused situation concerning whether the interim government of Somalia was actually in effective control and the extent to which other factions controlled different areas of the country. The court noted that in reaching its decision as to whether the interim government was or was not the valid successor to the former legitimate government in the light of the degree of actual control exercised over the country, letters from the Foreign and Commonwealth Office became part of the evidence in the case. In so far as the three letters concerned statements as to what was happening in the country, 'such letters may not be the best evidence', but in so far as they dealt with the question as to whether and to what extent the UK government had dealings with the foreign government, such letters 'will almost certainly be the best and only conclusive evidence of that fact'.[358]

The United States State Department similarly offers 'suggestions' on such matters, although they tend to be more extensive than their British counterparts, and include comments upon the issues and occasionally the views of the executive.[359]

Suggestions for further reading

A. Cassese, 'Modern Constitutions and International Law', 192 HR, 1985 III, p. 335

S. Fatima, *Using International Law in Domestic Courts*, Oxford, 2005

D. Feldman, 'Monism, Dualism and Constitutional Legitimacy', 20 Australian YIL, 1999, p. 105

J. F. Murphy, *The United States and the Rule of Law in International Affairs*, Cambridge, 2004

J. J. Paust, *International Law as Law of the United States*, Durham, NC, 1996

Y. Shany, *Regulating Jurisdictional Relations Between National and International Courts*, Oxford, 2007

---

[356] See further below, chapter 9, p. 454.

[357] [1993] QB 54, 64–8; 94 ILR, pp. 608, 618–23.

[358] [1993] QB 54, 65; 94 ILR, pp. 608, 619. See also *Sierra Leone Telecommunications Co. Ltd v. Barclays Bank* [1998] 2 All ER 821; 114 ILR, p. 466 and *North Cyprus Tourism Centre Ltd v. Transport for London* [2005] EWHC 1698 (Admin).

[359] O'Connell, *International Law*, pp. 119–22. See *The Pisaro* 255 US 216 (1921); *Anderson v. NV Transandine Handelmaatschappij* 289 NY 9 (1942); 10 AD, p. 10; *Mexico v. Hoffman* 324 US 30 (1945); 12 AD, p. 143, and the *Navemar* 303 US 68 (1938); 9 AD, p. 176. See also M. Chorazak, 'Clarity and Confusion: Did *Republic of Austria v. Altmann* Revive State Department Suggestions of Foreign Sovereign Immunity?', 55 *Duke Law Journal*, 2005, p. 373.

5

The subjects of international law

Legal personality – introduction

In any legal system, certain entities, whether they be individuals or companies, will be regarded as possessing rights and duties enforceable at law.[1] Thus an individual may prosecute or be prosecuted for assault and a company can sue for breach of contract. They are able to do this because the law recognises them as 'legal persons' possessing the capacity to have and to maintain certain rights, and being subject to perform specific duties. Just which persons will be entitled to what rights in what circumstances will depend upon the scope and character of the law. But it is the function of the law to apportion such rights and duties to such entities as it sees fit. Legal personality is crucial. Without it institutions and groups cannot operate, for they need to be able to maintain and enforce claims. In municipal law individuals, limited companies and public corporations are recognised as each possessing a distinct legal personality, the terms of which are circumscribed by the relevant legislation.[2] It is the law which

[1] See e.g. I. Brownlie, *Principles of Public International Law*, 6th edn, Oxford, 2003, part II; J. Crawford, *The Creation of States in International Law*, 2nd edn, Oxford, 2006; D. P. O'Connell, *International Law*, 2nd edn, London, 1970, vol. I; J. W. Verzijl, *International Law in Historical Perspective*, Leiden, 1969, vol. II; O. Lissitzyn, 'Territorial Entities other than Independent States in the Law of Treaties', 125 HR, 1968, p. 5; C. Berezowski, in *Mélanges Offerts à Juraj Andrassy* (ed. Ibler), 1968, p. 31; H. Lauterpacht, *International Law: Collected Papers*, Cambridge, 1975, vol. II, p. 487; C. Rousseau, *Droit International Public*, Paris, 1974, vol. II; N. Mugerwa, 'Subjects of International Law' in *Manual of Public International Law* (ed. M. Sørensen), London, 1968, p. 247; G. Schwarzenberger, *International Law*, 3rd edn, London, 1957, vol. I, p. 89; A. Cassese, *International Law in a Divided World*, Oxford, 1986, chapter 4, and Cassese, *International Law*, 2nd edn, Oxford, 2005, part II; *International Law: Achievements and Prospects* (ed. M. Bedjaoui), Paris, 1991, part 1, title 1; *Oppenheim's International Law* (eds. R. Y. Jennings and A. D. Watts), 9th edn, London, 1992, chapter 2; R. Higgins, *Problems and Process*, Oxford, 1994, chapter 3; L. Henkin, R. Pugh, O. Schachter and H. Smit, *International Law: Cases and Materials*, 3rd edn, St Paul, 1993, chapters 4 and 5, and S. Rosenne, 'The Perplexities of Modern International Law', 291 HR, 2001, chapter VII.

[2] R. Dias, *Jurisprudence*, 5th edn, London, 1985, chapter 12.

will determine the scope and nature of personality. Personality involves the examination of certain concepts within the law such as status, capacity, competence, as well as the nature and extent of particular rights and duties. The status of a particular entity may well be determinative of certain powers and obligations, while capacity will link together the status of a person with particular rights and duties. The whole process operates within the confines of the relevant legal system, which circumscribes personality, its nature and definition. This is especially true in international law. A particular view adopted of the system will invariably reflect upon the question of the identity and nature of international legal persons.[3]

Personality in international law necessitates the consideration of the interrelationship between rights and duties afforded under the international system and capacity to enforce claims. One needs to have close regard to the rules of international law in order to determine the precise nature of the capacity of the entity in question. Certain preliminary issues need to be faced. Does the personality of a particular claimant, for instance, depend upon its possession of the capacity to enforce rights? Indeed, is there any test of the nature of enforcement, or can even the most restrictive form of operation on the international scene be sufficient? One view suggests, for example, that while the quality of responsibility for violation of a rule usually co-exists with the quality of being able to enforce a complaint against a breach in any legal person, it would be useful to consider those possessing one of these qualities as indeed having juridical personality.[4] Other writers, on the other hand, emphasise the crucial role played by the element of enforceability of rights within the international system.[5]

However, a range of factors needs to be carefully examined before it can be determined whether an entity has international personality and, if so, what rights, duties and competences apply in the particular case. Personality is a relative phenomenon varying with the circumstances. One of the distinguishing characteristics of contemporary international law has been the wide range of participants. These include states, international organisations, regional organisations, non-governmental organisations, public companies, private companies and individuals. To these may be added groups engaging in international terrorism. Not all such entities

---

[3] See, for example, the Soviet view: G. I. Tunkin, *Theory of International Law*, London, 1974.

[4] See e.g. M. Sørensen, 'Principes de Droit International Public', 101 HR, 1960, pp. 5, 127. For a wider definition, see H. Mosler, *The International Society as a Legal Community*, Dordrecht, 1980, p. 32.

[5] See e.g. Verzijl, *International Law*, p. 3.

will constitute legal persons, although they may act with some degree of influence upon the international plane. International personality is participation plus some form of community acceptance. The latter element will be dependent upon many different factors, including the type of personality under question. It may be manifested in many forms and may in certain cases be inferred from practice. It will also reflect a need. Particular branches of international law here are playing a crucial role. Human rights law, the law relating to armed conflicts and international economic law are especially important in generating and reflecting increased participation and personality in international law.

States

Despite the increasing range of actors and participants in the international legal system, states remain by far the most important legal persons and despite the rise of globalisation and all that this entails, states retain their attraction as the primary focus for the social activity of humankind and thus for international law.

Lauterpacht observed that: 'the orthodox positivist doctrine has been explicit in the affirmation that only states are subjects of international law'.[6] However, it is less clear that in practice this position was maintained. The Holy See (particularly from 1871 to 1929), insurgents and belligerents, international organisations, chartered companies and various territorial entities such as the League of Cities were all at one time or another treated as possessing the capacity to become international persons.[7]

Creation of statehood[8]

The relationship in this area between factual and legal criteria is a crucial shifting one. Whether the birth of a new state is primarily a question of

---

[6] Lauterpacht, *International Law*, p. 489.

[7] See Verzijl, *International Law*, pp. 17–43, and Lauterpacht, *International Law*, pp. 494–500. See also the *Western Sahara* case, ICJ Reports, 1975, pp. 12, 39; 59 ILR, pp. 30, 56, and *Survey of International Law in Relation to the Work of Codification of the International Law Commission*, Memorandum of the Secretary-General, 1949, A/CN.4/1/Rev.1, p. 24.

[8] See in particular Crawford, *Creation of States*, chapter 2; R. Higgins, *The Development of International Law through the Political Organs of the United Nations*, Oxford, 1963, pp. 11–57; K. Marek, *Identity and Continuity of States in Public International Law*, 2nd edn, Leiden, 1968; M. Whiteman, *Digest of International Law*, Washington, 1963, vol. I, pp. 221–33, 283–476, and Nguyen Quoc Dinh, P. Daillier and A. Pellet, *Droit International Public*, 7th edn, Paris, 2002, p. 407. See also Société Française pour le Droit International, *L'État Souverain*, Paris, 1994; L. Henkin, *International Law: Politics and Values*, Dordrecht, 1995, chapter 1; R. H. Jackson, *Quasi-States: Sovereignty, International Relations and the*

fact or law and how the interaction between the criteria of effectiveness and other relevant legal principles may be reconciled are questions of considerable complexity and significance. Since *terrae nullius* are no longer apparent,[9] the creation of new states in the future, once the decolonisation process is at an end, can only be accomplished as a result of the diminution or disappearance of existing states, and the need for careful regulation thus arises. Recent events such as the break-up of the Soviet Union, the Socialist Federal Republic of Yugoslavia and Czechoslovakia underline this. In addition, the decolonisation movement has stimulated a re-examination of the traditional criteria. Article 1 of the Montevideo Convention on Rights and Duties of States, 1933[10] lays down the most widely accepted formulation of the criteria of statehood in international law. It notes that the state as an international person should possess the following qualifications: '(a) a permanent population; (b) a defined territory; (c) government; and (d) capacity to enter into relations with other states'.

The Arbitration Commission of the European Conference on Yugoslavia[11] in Opinion No. 1 declared that 'the state is commonly defined as a community which consists of a territory and a population subject to an organised political authority' and that 'such a state is characterised by sovereignty'. It was also noted that the form of internal political organisation and constitutional provisions constituted 'mere facts', although it was necessary to take them into account in order to determine the government's sway over the population and the territory.[12]

Such provisions are neither exhaustive nor immutable. As will be seen below, other factors may be relevant, including self-determination and recognition, while the relative weight given to such criteria in particular

---

Third World, Cambridge, 1990, and A. James, *Sovereign Statehood: The Basis of International Society*, London, 1986.

[9] See, as regards Antarctica, O'Connell, *International Law*, p. 451. See also below, chapter 10, p. 535.

[10] 165 LNTS 19. International law does not require the structure of a state to follow any particular pattern: *Western Sahara* case, ICJ Reports, 1975, pp. 12, 43–4; 59 ILR, pp. 30, 60–1.

[11] Established pursuant to the Declaration of 27 August 1991 of the European Community: see Bull. EC, 7/8 (1991). See generally, M. Craven, 'The EC Arbitration Commission on Yugoslavia', 65 BYIL, 1994, p. 333, and below, p. 210.

[12] 92 ILR, pp. 162, 165. Note that *Oppenheim's International Law*, p. 120, provides that 'a state proper is in existence when a people is settled in a territory under its own sovereign government'.

situations may very well vary. What is clear, however, is that the relevant framework revolves essentially around territorial effectiveness.

The existence of a permanent population[13] is naturally required and there is no specification of a minimum number of inhabitants, as examples such as Nauru and Tuvalu[14] demonstrate. However, one of the issues raised by the Falkland Islands conflict does relate to the question of an acceptable minimum with regard to self-determination issues,[15] and it may be that the matter needs further clarification as there exists a number of small islands awaiting decolonisation.[16]

The need for a defined territory focuses upon the requirement for a particular territorial base upon which to operate. However, there is no necessity in international law for defined and settled boundaries. A state may be recognised as a legal person even though it is involved in a dispute with its neighbours as to the precise demarcation of its frontiers, so long as there is a consistent band of territory which is undeniably controlled by the government of the alleged state. For this reason at least, therefore, the 'State of Palestine' declared in November 1988 at a conference in Algiers cannot be regarded as a valid state. The Palestinian organisations did not control any part of the territory they claim.[17]

Albania prior to the First World War was recognised by many countries even though its borders were in dispute.[18] More recently, Israel has been accepted by the majority of nations as well as the United Nations as a valid state despite the fact that its frontiers have not been finally settled

---

[13] A nomadic population might not thus count for the purposes of territorial sovereignty, although the International Court in the *Western Sahara* case, ICJ Reports, 1975, pp. 12, 63–5; 59 ILR, pp. 30, 80–2, held that nomadic peoples did have certain rights with regard to the land they traversed.

[14] Populations of some 12,000 and 10,000 respectively: see *Whitaker's Almanack*, London, 2003, pp. 1010 and 1089.

[15] See below, p. 251.

[16] But see, as regards artificial islands, *United States* v. *Ray* 51 ILR, p. 225; *Chierici and Rosa* v. *Ministry of the Merchant Navy and Harbour Office of Rimini* 71 ILR, p. 283, and *Re Duchy of Sealand* 80 ILR, p. 683.

[17] See *Keesing's Record of World Events*, p. 36438 (1989). See also General Assembly resolution 43/77; R. Lapidoth and K. Calvo-Goller, 'Les Éléments Constitutifs de l'État et la Déclaration du Conseil National Palestinien du 15 Novembre 1988', AFDI, 1992, p. 777; J. Crawford, 'The Creation of the State of Palestine: Too Much Too Soon?', 1 EJIL, 1990, p. 307, and Crawford, 'Israel (1948–1949) and Palestine (1998–1999): Two Studies in the Creation of States' in *The Reality of International Law* (eds. G. Goodwin-Gill and S. Talmon), Oxford, 1999, p. 95. See below, p. 246, with regard to the evolution of Palestinian autonomy in the light of the Israel–Palestine Liberation Organisation (PLO) Declaration on Principles.

[18] See e.g. the *North Sea Continental Shelf* cases, ICJ Reports, 1969, pp. 3, 32.

and despite its involvement in hostilities with its Arab neighbours over its existence and territorial delineation.[19] What matters is the presence of a stable community within a certain area, even though its frontiers may be uncertain. Indeed, it is possible for the territory of the state to be split into distinct parts, for example Pakistan prior to the Bangladesh secession of 1971 or present-day Azerbaijan.

For a political society to function reasonably effectively it needs some form of government or central control. However, this is not a pre-condition for recognition as an independent country.[20] It should be re-garded more as an indication of some sort of coherent political structure and society, than the necessity for a sophisticated apparatus of executive and legislative organs.[21] A relevant factor here might be the extent to which the area not under the control of the government is claimed by another state as a matter of international law as distinct from *de facto* control. The general requirement might be seen to relate to the nineteenth-century concern with 'civilisation' as an essential of independent statehood and ignores the modern tendency to regard sovereignty for non-independent peoples as the paramount consideration, irrespective of administrative conditions.[22]

As an example of the former tendency one may note the *Aaland Islands* case of 1920. The report of the International Committee of Jurists appointed to investigate the status of the islands remarked, with regard to the establishment of the Finnish Republic in the disordered days fol-lowing the Russian revolution, that it was extremely difficult to name the date that Finland became a sovereign state. It was noted that:

---

[19] Brownlie, *Principles*, p. 71. In fact most of the new states emerging after the First World War were recognised *de facto* or *de jure* before their frontiers were determined by treaty: H. Lauterpacht, *Recognition in International Law*, Cambridge, 1948, p. 30. See *Deutsche Continental Gas-Gesellschaft* v. *Polish State* (1929), 5 AD, pp. 11, 15; the *Mosul Boundary* case, PCIJ, Series B, No. 12, p. 21; the *North Sea Continental Shelf* cases, ICJ Reports, 1969, pp. 3, 32; 41 ILR, pp. 29, 62, and the *Libya/Chad* case, ICJ Reports, 1994, pp. 6, 22 and 26; 100 ILR, pp. 5, 21 and 25. See also Jessup speaking on behalf of the US regarding Israel's admission to the UN, SCOR, 3rd year, 383rd meeting, p. 41. The Minister of State of the Foreign and Commonwealth Office in a statement on 5 February 1991, UKMIL, 62 BYIL, 1991, p. 557, noted that the UK 'recognises many states whose borders are not fully agreed with their neighbours'. See as to the doctrine of *uti possidetis*, the presumption that on independence entitites will retain existing boundaries, below, chapter 10, p. 525.

[20] See e.g. the Congo case, Higgins, *Development*, pp. 162–4, and C. Hoskyns, *The Congo Since Independence*, Oxford, 1965. See also Higgins, *Problems and Process*, p. 40, and Nguyen Quoc Dinh *et al.*, *Droit International Public*, pp. 415 ff.

[21] See the *Western Sahara* case, ICJ Reports, 1975, pp. 12, 43–4; 59 ILR, pp. 30, 60–1.

[22] See below, p. 251, on the right to self-determination.

[t]his certainly did not take place until a stable political organisation had been created, and until the public authorities had become strong enough to assert themselves throughout the territories of the state without the assistance of the foreign troops.[23]

Recent practice with regard to the new states of Croatia and Bosnia and Herzegovina emerging out of the former Yugoslavia suggests the modification of the criterion of effective exercise of control by a government throughout its territory. Both Croatia and Bosnia and Herzegovina were recognised as independent states by European Community member states[24] and admitted to membership of the United Nations (which is limited to 'states' by article 4 of the UN Charter[25])[26] at a time when both states were faced with a situation where non-governmental forces controlled substantial areas of the territories in question in civil war conditions. More recently, Kosovo declared independence on 17 February 2008 with certain Serb-inhabited areas apparently not under the control of the central government.[27] In such situations, lack of effective central control might be balanced by significant international recognition, culminating in membership of the UN. Nevertheless, a foundation of effective control is required for statehood. Conversely, however, a comprehensive breakdown in order and the loss of control by the central authorities in an independent state will not obviate statehood. Whatever the consequences in terms of possible humanitarian involvement, whether by the UN or otherwise depending upon the circumstances, the collapse of governance within a state (sometimes referred to as a 'failed state') has no necessary effect upon the status of that state as a state. Indeed the very

---

[23] LNOJ Sp. Supp. No. 4 (1920), pp. 8–9. But cf. the view of the Commission of Rapporteurs in this case, LN Council Doc. B7 21/68/106 (1921), p. 22.

[24] On 15 January 1992 and 6 April 1992 respectively: see *Keesing's Record of World Events*, 1992, pp. 38703, 38704 and 38833. But see the Yugoslav Arbitration Commission's Opinion No. 5 of 11 January 1992 noting that Croatia had not met the requirements laid down in the Draft Convention on Yugoslavia of 4 November 1991 and in the Declaration on Yugoslavia and Guidelines on the Recognition of New States in Eastern Europe and in the Soviet Union of 16 December 1991: see 92 ILR, p. 178. Opinion No. 4 expressed reservations concerning the independence of Bosnia and Herzegovina pending the holding of a referendum. A referendum showing a majority for independence, however, was held prior to recognition by the EC member states and admission by the UN, *ibid.*, p. 173. See also below, p. 209.

[25] See e.g. V. Gowlland-Debbas, 'Collective Responses to the Unilateral Declarations of Independence of Southern Rhodesia and Palestine', 61 BYIL, 1990, p. 135.

[26] On 22 May 1992. See M. Weller, 'The International Response to the Dissolution of the Socialist Federal Republic of Yugoslavia', 86 AJIL, 1992, p. 569.

[27] See further below, p. 204.

designation of 'failed state' is controversial and, in terms of international law, misleading.[28]

The capacity to enter into relations with other states is an aspect of the existence of the entity in question as well as an indication of the importance attached to recognition by other countries. It is a capacity not limited to sovereign nations, since international organisations, non-independent states and other bodies can enter into legal relations with other entities under the rules of international law. But it is essential for a sovereign state to be able to create such legal relations with other units as it sees fit. Where this is not present, the entity cannot be an independent state. The concern here is not with political pressure by one country over another, but rather the lack of competence to enter into legal relations. The difference is the presence or absence of legal capacity, not the degree of influence that may affect decisions.

The essence of such capacity is independence. This is crucial to state-hood and amounts to a conclusion of law in the light of particular cir-cumstances. It is a formal statement that the state is subject to no other sovereignty and is unaffected either by factual dependence upon other states or by submission to the rules of international law.[29] It is arguable that a degree of actual as well as formal independence may also be nec-essary. This question was raised in relation to the grant of independence by South Africa to its Bantustans. In the case of the Transkei, for ex-ample, a considerable proportion, perhaps 90 per cent, of its budget at one time was contributed by South Africa, while Bophuthatswana was split into a series of areas divided by South African territory.[30] Both the Organisation of African Unity and the United Nations declared such 'in-dependence' invalid and called upon all states not to recognise the new en-tities. These entities were, apart from South Africa, totally unrecognised.[31]

---

[28] See e.g. Crawford, *Creation of States*, pp. 719–22; S. Ratner, 'The Cambodia Settlement Agreements', 87 AJIL, 1993, p. 1, and T. M. Franck, 'The Democratic Entitlement', 29 *University of Richmond Law Review*, 1994, p. 1.

[29] See *Austro-German Customs Union* case, (1931) PCIJ, Series A/B, No. 41, pp. 41 (Court's Opinion) and 57–8 (Separate Opinion of Judge Anzilotti); 6 AD, pp. 26, 28. See also Marek, *Identity*, pp. 166–80; Crawford, *Creation of States*, pp. 62 ff., and Rousseau, *Droit International Public*, vol. II, pp. 53, 93.

[30] This was cited as one of the reasons for UK non-recognition, by the Minister of State, FCO: see UKMIL, 57 BYIL, 1986, pp. 507–8.

[31] The 1993 South African Constitution provided for the repeal of all laws concerning apartheid, including the four Status Acts which purported to create the 'independent states' of the four Bantustans, thus effectively reincorporating these areas into South Africa: see J. Dugard, *International Law – A South African Perspective*, Kenwyn, 1994, p. 346.

However, many states are as dependent upon aid from other states, and economic success would not have altered the attitude of the international community. Since South Africa as a sovereign state was able to alienate parts of its own territory under international law, these entities would appear in the light of the formal criteria of statehood to have been formally independent. However, it is suggested that the answer as to their status lay elsewhere than in an elucidation of this category of the criteria of statehood. It lay rather in understanding that actions taken in order to pursue an illegal policy, such as apartheid, cannot be sustained.[32]

An example of the complexities that may attend such a process is provided by the unilateral declaration of independence by Lithuania, one of the Baltic states unlawfully annexed by the Soviet Union in 1940, on 11 March 1990.[33] The 1940 annexation was never recognised *de jure* by the Western states and thus the control exercised by the USSR was accepted only upon a *de facto* basis. The 1990 declaration of independence was politically very sensitive, coming at a time of increasing disintegration within the Soviet Union, but went unrecognised by any state. In view of the continuing constitutional crisis within the USSR and the possibility of a new confederal association freely accepted by the fifteen Soviet republics, it was at that time premature to talk of Lithuania as an independent state, not least because the Soviet authorities maintained substantial control within that territory.[34] The independence of Lithuania and the other Baltic States was recognised during 1991 by a wide variety of states, including crucially the Soviet Union.[35]

It is possible, however, for a state to be accepted as independent even though, exceptionally, certain functions of government are placed in the hands of an outside body. In the case of Bosnia and Herzegovina, for example, the Dayton Peace Agreement of 1995 provided for a High

---

[32] See M. N. Shaw, *Title to Territory in Africa: International Legal Issues*, Oxford, 1986, pp. 161–2. See also OAU Resolution CM.Res.493 (XXVII), General Assembly resolution 31/61A and Security Council statements on 21 September 1979 and 15 December 1981. Note that the Minister of State at the Foreign and Commonwealth Office declared that 'the very existence of Bophuthatswana is a consequence of apartheid and I think that that is the principal reason why recognition has not been forthcoming', 126, HC Deb., cols. 760–1, 3 February 1988.

[33] See *Keesing's Record of World Events*, p. 37299 (1990).

[34] See e.g. the view of the UK government, 166 HC Deb., col. 697, Written Answers, 5 February 1990.

[35] See e.g. R. Müllerson, *International Law, Rights and Politics*, London, 1994, pp. 119 ff.

Representative to be appointed as the 'final authority in theatre' with regard to the implementation of the agreement,[36] and the High Representative has, for example, removed a number of persons from public office. None of this has been understood by the international community to affect Bosnia's status as an independent state, but the arrangement did arise as an attempt to reach and implement a peace agreement in the context of a bitter civil war with third-party intervention. More controversially, after a period of international administration,[37] Kosovo declared its independence on 17 February 2008, noting specifically that it accepted the obligations for Kosovo under the Comprehensive Proposal for the Kosovo Status Settlement (the Ahtisaari Plan).[38] This Plan called for 'independence with international supervision' and the obligations for Kosovo included human rights and decentralisation guarantees together with an international presence to supervise implementation of the Settlement. The provisions of the Settlement were to take precedence over all other legal provisions in Kosovo. The international presence was to take the form of an International Civilian Representative (ICR), who would also be the European Union Special Representative, to be appointed by the International Steering Group.[39] The ICR would be the final authority in Kosovo regarding interpretation of the civilian aspects of the Settlement and, in particular, would have the ability to annul decisions or laws adopted by the Kosovo authorities and sanction and remove public officials whose actions were determined to be inconsistent with the Settlement terms.[40] In addition, an international military presence, led by NATO, would ensure a safe environment throughout Kosovo.[41]

---

[36] See Annex 10 of the Dayton Peace Agreement. See also R. Caplan, 'International Authority and State Building: The Case of Bosnia and Herzegovina', 10 *Global Governance*, 2004, p. 53, and International Crisis Group, *Bosnia: Reshaping the International Machinery*, November 2001. The High Representative is nominated by the Steering Board of the Peace Implementation Council, a group of fifty-five countries and international organisations that sponsor and direct the peace implementation process, and this nomination is then endorsed by the Security Council. See further below, p. 231.

[37] See, as to the international administration of Kosovo, below, p. 232 and, as to recognition, below, chapter 9, p. 452.

[38] See www.assembly-kosova.org/? krye=news&newsid=1635&lang=en.

[39] To consist of France, Germany, Italy, Russia, the UK, the US, the EU, the European Commission and NATO.

[40] See S/2007/168 and S/2007/168/Add.1. Annex IX of the latter document details the role of the ICR.

[41] See Annex XI. An EU Rule of Law Mission (EULEX) was established on 16 February 2008 to support the Kosovan authorities.

Self-determination and the criteria of statehood

It is the criterion of government which, as suggested above, has been most affected by the development of the legal right to self-determination. The traditional exposition of the criterion concentrated upon the stability and effectiveness needed for this factor to be satisfied,[42] while the representative and democratic nature of the government has also been put forward as a requirement. The evolution of self-determination has affected the standard necessary as far as the actual exercise of authority is concerned, so that it appears a lower level of effectiveness, at least in decolonisation situations, has been accepted.[43] This can be illustrated by reference to a couple of cases.

The former Belgian Congo became independent on 30 June 1960 in the midst of widespread tribal fighting which had spread to the capital. Within a few weeks the Force Publique had mutinied, Belgian troops had intervened and the province of Katanga announced its secession. Notwithstanding the virtual breakdown of government, the Congo was recognised by a large number of states after independence and was admitted to the UN as a member state without opposition. Indeed, at the time of the relevant General Assembly resolution in September 1960, two different factions of the Congo government sought to be accepted by the UN as the legitimate representatives of the state. In the event, the delegation authorised by the head of state was accepted and that of the Prime Minister rejected.[44] A rather different episode occurred with regard to the Portuguese colony of Guinea-Bissau. In 1972, a UN Special Mission was dispatched to the 'liberated areas' of the territory and concluded that the colonial power had lost effective administrative control of large areas of the territory. Foreign observers appeared to accept the claim of the PAIGC, the local liberation movement, to control between two-thirds and three-quarters of the area. The inhabitants of these areas, reported the Mission, supported the PAIGC which was exercising effective *de facto* administrative control.[45] On 24 September 1973, the PAIGC proclaimed the Republic of Guinea Bissau an independent state. The issue of the 'illegal occupation by Portuguese military forces of certain sections of the Republic of Guinea-Bissau' came before the General Assembly and a number of states

---

[42] See Lauterpacht, *Recognition*, p. 28.   [43] See e.g. Crawford, *Creation of States*, pp. 107 ff.
[44] *Keesing's Contemporary Archives*, pp. 17594–5 and 17639–40, and Hoskyns, *Congo*, pp. 96–9.
[45] *Yearbook of the UN*, 1971, pp. 566–7, and A/AC.109/L 804, p. 19. See also A/8723/Rev.1 and Assembly resolution 2918 (XXVII).

affirmed the validity of the independence of the new state in international law. Western states denied that the criteria of statehood had been fulfilled. However, ninety-three states voted in favour of Assembly resolution 3061 (XXVIII) which mentioned 'the recent accession to independence of the people of Guinea-Bissau thereby creating the sovereign state of the Republic of Guinea-Bissau'. Many states argued in favour of this approach on the basis that a large proportion of the territory was being effectively controlled by the PAIGC, though it controlled neither a majority of the population nor the major towns.[46]

In addition to modifying the traditional principle with regard to the effectiveness of government in certain circumstances, the principle of self-determination may also be relevant as an additional criterion of statehood. In the case of Rhodesia, UN resolutions denied the legal validity of the unilateral declaration of independence on 11 November 1965 and called upon member states not to recognise it.[47] No state did recognise Rhodesia and a civil war ultimately resulted in its transformation into the recognised state of Zimbabwe. Rhodesia might have been regarded as a state by virtue of its satisfaction of the factual requirements of statehood, but this is a dubious proposition. The evidence of complete non-recognition, the strenuous denunciations of its purported independence by the international community and the developing civil war militate strongly against this. It could be argued on the other hand that, in the absence of recognition, no entity could become a state, but this constitutive theory of recognition is not acceptable.[48] The best approach is to accept the development of self-determination as an additional criterion of statehood, denial of which would obviate statehood. This can only be acknowledged in relation to self-determination situations and would not operate in cases, for example, of secessions from existing states.[49] In other words, in the case of an entity seeking to become a state and accepted by the international community as being entitled to exercise the right of self-determination,

---

[46] See GAOR, 28th Session, General Committee, 213rd meeting, pp. 25–6, 28, 30 and 31; GAOR, 28th session, plenary, 2156th meeting, pp. 8, 12 and 16, and 2157th meeting, pp. 22–5 and 65–7. See also *Yearbook of the UN*, 1973, pp. 143–7, and CDDH/SR.4, pp. 33–7. See also the Western Sahara situation, below, p. 213, and the recognition of Angola in 1975 despite the continuing civil war between the three liberation movements nominally allied in a government of national unity: see Shaw, *Title*, pp. 155–6.

[47] E.g. General Assembly resolutions 2024 (XX) and 2151 (XXI) and Security Council resolutions 216 (1965) and 217 (1966). See R. Higgins, *The World Today*, 1967, p. 94, and Crawford, *Creation of States*, pp. 129 ff. See also Shaw, *Title*.

[48] Below, chapter 9, p. 445.   [49] See further below, pp. 237 and 257.

it may well be necessary to demonstrate that the internal requirements of the principle have not been offended. One cannot define this condition too rigorously in view of state practice to date, but it would appear to be a sound proposition that systematic and institutionalised discrimination might invalidate a claim to statehood.

In particular, one may point to the practice of the international community concerning the successor states to the former Yugoslavia. The European Community adopted Guidelines on Recognition of New States in Eastern Europe and the Soviet Union on 16 December 1991,[50] which constituted a common position on the process of recognition of such new states and referred specifically to the principle of self-determination. The Guidelines underlined the need to respect the rule of law, democracy and human rights and mentioned specifically the requirement for guarantees for the rights of minorities. Although these Guidelines deal with the issue of recognition and not as such the criteria for statehood, the two are interlinked and conditions required for recognition may in the circumstances, especially where expressed in general and not specific terms, often in practice be interpreted as additions to the criteria for statehood.

Recognition

Recognition is a method of accepting certain factual situations and endowing them with legal significance, but this relationship is a complicated one. In the context of the creation of statehood, recognition may be viewed as constitutive or declaratory, as will be noted in more detail in chapter 9. The former theory maintains that it is only through recognition that a state comes into being under international law, whereas the latter approach maintains that once the factual criteria of statehood have been satisfied, a new state exists as an international person, recognition becoming merely a political and not a legal act in this context. Various modifications have been made to these theories, but the role of recognition, at the least in providing strong evidential demonstration of satisfaction of the relevant criteria, must be acknowledged. In many situations, expressed requirements for recognition may be seen as impacting upon the question of statehood as the comments in the previous section on the EC Guidelines indicate. There is also an integral relationship between recognition and

---

[50] For the text see 31 ILM, 1992, pp. 1486–7 and 92 ILR, p. 173.

the criteria for statehood in the sense that the more overwhelming the scale of international recognition is in any given situation, the less may be demanded in terms of the objective demonstration of adherence to the criteria. Conversely, the more sparse international recognition is, the more attention will be focused upon proof of actual adherence to the criteria concerned.

Extinction of statehood[51]

Extinction of statehood may take place as a consequence of merger, absorption or, historically, annexation. It may also occur as a result of the dismemberment of an existing state.[52] In general, caution needs to be exercised before the dissolution of a state is internationally accepted.[53] While the disappearance, like the existence, of a state is a matter of fact,[54] it is a matter of fact that is legally conditioned in that it is international law that will apportion particular legal consequences to particular factual situations and the appreciation of these facts will take place within a certain legal framework.

While it is not unusual for governments to disappear, it is rather rarer for states to become extinct. This will not happen in international law as a result of the illegal use of force, as the Kuwait crisis of August 1990 and the consequent United Nations response clearly demonstrates,[55] nor as a consequence of internal upheavals within a state,[56] but it may occur by consent. Three recent examples may be noted. On 22 May 1990, North and South Yemen united, or merged, to form one state, the Republic of Yemen,[57] while on 3 October 1990, the two German states reunified as a result of the constitutional accession of the *Länder* of the German

---

[51] See e.g. Crawford, *Creation of States*, pp. 700 ff., and *Oppenheim's International Law*, p. 206. See also H. Ruiz-Fabri, 'Genèse et Disparition de l'État à l'Époque Contemporaine', AFDI, 1992, p. 153.

[52] *Oppenheim's International Law*, pp. 206–7. Extinction of statehood may also take place as a consequence of the geographical disappearance of the territory of the state: see e.g. with regard to the precarious situation of Tuvalu, *Guardian*, 29 October 2001, p. 17.

[53] See e.g. Yugoslav Arbitration Commission, Opinion No. 8, 92 ILR, pp. 199, 201.

[54] *Ibid.*   [55] See further below, chapter 22, p. 941.

[56] Such as Somalia since the early 1990s: see e.g. Security Council resolutions 751 (1992); 767 (1992); 794 (1992); 814 (1993); 837 (1993); 865 (1993); 885 (1993) and 886 (1993). See also Crawford, *Creation of States*, pp. 412 ff.

[57] See *Keesing's Record of World Events*, p. 37470 (1990). See also 30 ILM, 1991, p. 820, and R. Goy, 'La Réunification du Yémen', AFDI, 1990, p. 249.

Democratic Republic to the Federal Republic of Germany.[58] The dissolution of Czechoslovakia[59] on 1 January 1993 and the establishment of the two new states of the Czech Republic and Slovakia constitutes a further example of the dismemberment, or disappearance, of a state.[60]

During 1991, the process of disintegration of the Soviet Union gathered force as the Baltic states reasserted their independence[61] and the other Republics of the USSR stated their intention to become sovereign. In December of that year, the Commonwealth of Independent States was proclaimed, and it was stated in the Alma Ata Declaration[62] that, with the establishment of the CIS, 'the Union of Soviet Socialist Republics ceases to exist'. The states of the CIS agreed to support 'Russia's continuance of the membership of the Union of Soviet Socialist Republics in the United Nations, including permanent membership of the Security Council, and other international organisations'.[63] It has been commonly accepted that Russia constitutes a continuation of the USSR, with consequential adjustments to take account of the independence of the other former Republics of the Soviet Union.[64] It is therefore a case of dismemberment basically consisting of the transformation of an existing state. The disappearance of the USSR was accompanied by the claim, internationally accepted, of the Russian Federation to be the continuation of that state. While the element of continuity is crucial in the framework of the rules of state succession,[65] it does constitute a complication in the context of extinction of states.

By way of contrast, not all the relevant parties accepted that the process of dissolution of the former Socialist Federal Republic of Yugoslavia during 1991–2 resulted in the dissolution of that state.[66] The Federal Republic of Yugoslavia, comprising the former Republics of Serbia and Montenegro, saw itself as the continuation of the former state within reduced boundaries, while the other former Republics disputed this and maintained rather that the Federal Republic of Yugoslavia (Serbia and

---

[58] See below, p. 227. See also C. Schrike, 'L'Unification Allemande', AFDI, 1990, p. 47, and W. Czaplinski, 'Quelques Aspects sur la Réunification de l'Allemagne', AFDI, 1990, p. 89.

[59] Termed at that stage the Czech and Slovak Federal Republic.

[60] See e.g. J. Malenovsky, 'Problèmes Juridiques Liés à la Partition de la Tchécoslovaquie', AFDI, 1993, p. 305.

[61] See L. Kherad, 'La Reconnaissance Internationale des États Baltes', RGDIP, 1992, p. 843.

[62] See 31 ILM, 1992, pp. 148–9.   [63] *Ibid.*, p. 151.

[64] See further below, p. 960.   [65] See below, chapter 17.

[66] See also A. Pellet, 'La Commission d'Arbitrage de la Conférence Européenne pour la Paix en Yougaslavie', AFDI, 1991, p. 329; AFDI, 1992, p. 220, and AFDI, 1993, p. 286.

Montenegro) was a successor to the former Yugoslavia precisely on the same basis as the other former Republics such as Croatia, Slovenia and Bosnia and Herzegovina. The matter was discussed by the Yugoslav Arbitration Commission. In Opinion No. 1 of 29 November 1991, it was noted that at that stage the Socialist Federal Republic of Yugoslavia was 'in the process of dissolution'.[67] However, in Opinion No. 8, adopted on 4 July 1992, the Arbitration Commission stated that the process of dissolution had been completed and that the Socialist Federal Republic of Yugoslavia (SFRY) no longer existed. This conclusion was reached on the basis of the fact that Slovenia, Croatia and Bosnia and Herzegovina had been recognised as new states, the republics of Serbia and Montenegro had adopted a new constitution for the 'Federal Republic of Yugoslavia' and UN resolutions had been adopted referring to 'the former SFRY'.[68] The Commission also emphasised that the existence of federal states was seriously compromised when a majority of the constituent entities, embracing a majority of the territory and population of the federal state, constitute themselves as sovereign states with the result that federal authority could no longer be effectively exercised.[69] The UN Security Council in resolution 777 (1992) stated that 'the state formerly known as the Socialist Federal Republic of Yugoslavia has ceased to exist'. This was reiterated in resolution 1022 (1995) in which the Security Council, in welcoming the Dayton Peace Agreement (the General Framework Agreement for Peace in Bosnia and Herzegovina) between the states of the former Yugoslavia and suspending the application of sanctions, stated that the Socialist Federal Republic of Yugoslavia 'has ceased to exist'. On 1 November 2000, Yugoslavia was admitted to the UN as a new member,[70] following its request sent to the Security Council on 27 October 2000.[71]

---

[67] 92 ILR, pp. 164–5. One should note the importance of the federal structure of the state in determining the factual situation regarding dissolution. The Arbitration Commission pointed out that in such cases 'the existence of the state implies that the federal organs represent the components of the Federation and wield effective power', *ibid.*, p. 165.

[68] See e.g. Security Council resolutions 752 and 757 (1992). See also the resolution adopted by the European Community at the Lisbon Council on 27 June 1992, quoted in part in Opinion No. 9, 92 ILR, pp. 204–5.

[69] 92 ILR, p. 201. In Opinions Nos. 9 and 10, the Arbitration Commission noted that the Federal Republic of Yugoslavia (Serbia and Montenegro) could not consider itself as the continuation of the SFRY, but was instead one of the successors to that state on the same basis as the recognised new states, *ibid.*, pp. 205 and 208.

[70] General Assembly resolution 55/12.

[71] See the *Application for Revision of the Judgment of 11 July 1996 (Bosnia and Herzegovina v. Yugoslavia)*, ICJ Reports, 2003, p. 7.

The fundamental rights of states

The fundamental rights of states exist by virtue of the international legal order, which is able, as in the case of other legal orders, to define the characteristics of its subjects.[72]

Independence[73]

Perhaps the outstanding characteristic of a state is its independence, or sovereignty. This was defined in the Draft Declaration on the Rights and Duties of States prepared in 1949 by the International Law Commission as the capacity of a state to provide for its own well-being and development free from the domination of other states, providing it does not impair or violate their legitimate rights.[74] By independence, one is referring to a legal concept and it is no deviation from independence to be subject to the rules of international law. Any political or economic dependence that may in reality exist does not affect the legal independence of the state, unless that state is formally compelled to submit to the demands of a superior state, in which case dependent status is concerned.

A discussion on the meaning and nature of independence took place in the *Austro-German Customs Union* case before the Permanent Court of International Justice in 1931.[75] It concerned a proposal to create a free trade customs union between the two German-speaking states and whether this was incompatible with the 1919 Peace Treaties (coupled with a subsequent protocol of 1922) pledging Austria to take no action to compromise its independence. In the event, and in the circumstances of the case, the Court held that the proposed union would adversely affect Austria's sovereignty. Judge Anzilotti noted that restrictions upon a state's liberty, whether arising out of customary law or treaty obligations, do not as such affect its independence. As long as such restrictions do not place

---

[72] See e.g. A. Kiss, *Répertoire de la Pratique Française en Matière de Droit International Public*, Paris, 1966, vol. II, pp. 21–50, and *Survey of International Law*, prepared by the UN Secretary-General, A/CN.4/245.

[73] *Oppenheim's International Law*, p. 382. See also N. Schrijver, 'The Changing Nature of State Sovereignty', 70 BYIL, 1999, p. 65; C. Rousseau, 'L'Indépendance de l'État dans l'Ordre International', 73 HR, 1948 II, p. 171; H. G. Gelber, *Sovereignty Through Independence*, The Hague, 1997; Brownlie, *Principles*, pp. 287 ff., and Nguyen Quoc Dinh *et al.*, *Droit International Public*, p. 422.

[74] *Yearbook of the ILC*, 1949, p. 286. Judge Huber noted in the *Island of Palmas* case that 'independence in regard to a portion of the globe is the right to exercise therein, to the exclusion of any other state, the functions of a state', 2 RIAA, pp. 829, 838 (1928); 4 AD, p. 3.

[75] PCIJ, Series A/B, No. 41, 1931; 6 AD, p. 26.

the state under the legal authority of another state, the former maintains its status as an independent country.[76]

The Permanent Court emphasised in the *Lotus* case[77] that '[r]estrictions upon the independence of states cannot therefore be presumed'. A similar point in different circumstances was made by the International Court of Justice in the *Nicaragua* case,[78] where it was stated that 'in international law there are no rules, other than such rules as may be accepted by the state concerned, by treaty or otherwise, whereby the level of armaments of a sovereign state can be limited, and this principle is valid for all states without exception'. The Court also underlined in the *Legality of the Threat or Use of Nuclear Weapons*[79] that '[s]tate practice shows that the illegality of the use of certain weapons as such does not result from an absence of authorisation but, on the contrary, is formulated in terms of prohibition'. The starting point for the consideration of the rights and obligations of states within the international legal system remains that international law permits freedom of action for states, unless there is a rule constraining this. However, such freedom exists within and not outside the international legal system and it is therefore international law which dictates the scope and content of the independence of states and not the states themselves individually and unilaterally.

The notion of independence in international law implies a number of rights and duties: for example, the right of a state to exercise jurisdiction over its territory and permanent population, or the right to engage upon an act of self-defence in certain situations. It implies also the duty not to intervene in the internal affairs of other sovereign states. Precisely what constitutes the internal affairs of a state is open to dispute and is in any event a constantly changing standard. It was maintained by the Western powers for many years that any discussion or action by the United Nations[80] with regard to their colonial possessions was contrary to international law.

---

[76] PCIJ, Series A/B, No. 41, 1931, p. 77 (dissenting); 6 AD, p. 30 See also the *North Atlantic Coast Fisheries* case (1910), Scott, *Hague Court Reports*, p. 141 at p. 170, and the *Wimbledon* case, PCIJ, Series A, No.1, 1923, p. 25; 2 AD, p. 99.

[77] PCIJ, Series A, No. 10, 1927, p. 18; 4 AD, pp. 153, 155.

[78] ICJ Reports, 1986, pp. 14, 135; 76 ILR, pp. 349, 469. See also the *Legality of the Threat or Use of Nuclear Weapons*, ICJ Reports, 1996, pp. 226, 238–9; 110 ILR, p. 163.

[79] ICJ Reports, 1996, pp. 226, 247; 110 ILR, p. 163.

[80] Article 2(7) of the UN Charter provides that 'nothing in the present Charter shall authorise the United Nations to intervene in matters which are essentially within the domestic jurisdiction of any state'. On the relationship between this article and the general international law provision, see Brownlie, *Principles*, pp. 290 ff.

However, this argument by the European colonial powers did not succeed and the United Nations examined many colonial situations.[81] In addition, issues related to human rights and racial oppression do not now fall within the closed category of domestic jurisdiction. It was stated on behalf of the European Community, for example, that the 'protection of human rights and fundamental freedoms can in no way be considered an interference in a state's internal affairs'. Reference was also made to 'the moral right to intervene whenever human rights are violated'.[82]

This duty not to intervene in matters within the domestic jurisdiction of any state was included in the Declaration on Principles of International Law Concerning Friendly Relations and Co-operation among States adopted in October 1970 by the United Nations General Assembly. It was emphasised that

> [n]o state or group of states has the right to intervene, directly or indirectly, for any reason whatever, in the internal or external affairs of any other state. Consequently, armed intervention and all other forms of interference or attempted threats against the personality of the state or against its political, economic and cultural elements, are in violation of international law.

The prohibition also covers any assistance or aid to subversive elements aiming at the violent overthrow of the government of a state. In particular, the use of force to deprive peoples of their national identity amounts to a violation of this principle of non-intervention.[83]

The principles surrounding sovereignty, such as non-intervention, are essential in the maintenance of a reasonably stable system of competing states. Setting limits on the powers of states vis-à-vis other states contributes to some extent to a degree of stability within the legal order. As the International Court of Justice pointed out in the *Corfu Channel* case

---

[81] See Higgins, *Development*, pp. 58–130; M. Rajan, *United Nations and Domestic Jurisdiction*, 2nd edn, London, 1961, and H. Kelsen, *Principles of International Law*, 2nd edn, London, 1966.

[82] E/CN.4/1991/SR. 43, p. 8, quoted in UKMIL, 62 BYIL, 1991, p. 556. See also statement of the European Community in 1992 to the same effect, UKMIL, 63 BYIL, pp. 635–6. By way of contrast, the Iranian *fatwa* condemning the British writer Salman Rushdie to death was criticised by the UK government as calling into question Iran's commitment to honour its obligations not to interfere in the internal affairs of the UK, *ibid.*, p. 635. See also M. Reisman, 'Sovereignty and Human Rights in Contemporary International Law', 84 AJIL, 1990, p. 866.

[83] See also the use of force, below, chapter 20.

in 1949, 'between independent states, respect for territorial sovereignty is an essential foundation of international relations.'[84]

By a similar token a state cannot purport to enforce its laws in the territory of another state without the consent of the state concerned. However, international law would seem to permit in some circumstances the state to continue to exercise its jurisdiction, notwithstanding the illegality of the apprehension.[85] It also follows that the presence of foreign troops on the territory of a sovereign state requires the consent of that state.[86]

Equality[87]

One other crucial principle is the legal equality of states, that is equality of legal rights and duties. States, irrespective of size or power, have the same juridical capacities and functions, and are likewise entitled to one vote in the United Nations General Assembly. The doctrine of the legal equality of states is an umbrella category for it includes within its scope the recognised rights and obligations which fall upon all states.

This was recognised in the 1970 Declaration on Principles of International Law. This provides that:

> All states enjoy sovereign equality. They have equal rights and duties and are equal members of the international community, notwithstanding differences of an economic, social, political or other nature.
>
> In particular, sovereign equality includes the following elements:
>
> (a) States are juridically equal;
> (b) Each state enjoys the rights inherent in full sovereignty;
> (c) Each state has the duty to respect the personality of other states;
> (d) The territorial integrity and political independence of the state are inviolable;
> (e) Each state has the right freely to choose and develop its political, social, economic and cultural systems;
> (f) Each state has the duty to comply fully and in good faith with its international obligations and to live in peace with other states.[88]

---

[84] ICJ Reports, 1949, pp. 4, 35; 16 AD, pp. 155, 167. See below, p. 575.

[85] See e.g. the *Eichmann* case, 36 ILR, p. 5. But see further below, p. 680.

[86] See the statement made on behalf of the European Community on 25 November 1992 with regard to the presence of Russian troops in the Baltic states, UKMIL, 63 BYIL, 1992, p. 724.

[87] *Oppenheim's International Law*, p. 339, and Nguyen Quoc Dinh *et al.*, *Droit International Public*, p. 428.

[88] See also Final Act of the Conference on Security and Co-operation in Europe, Helsinki, 1975, Cmnd 6198, pp. 2–3. See also O'Connell, *International Law*, pp. 322–4; P. Kooijmans,

In many respects this doctrine owes its origins to Natural Law thinking. Just as equality was regarded as the essence of man and thus contributed philosophically to the foundation of the state, so naturalist scholars treated equality as the natural condition of states. With the rise in positivism, the emphasis altered and, rather than postulating a general rule applicable to all and from which a series of rights and duties may be deduced, international lawyers concentrated upon the sovereignty of each and every state, and the necessity that international law be founded upon the consent of states.

The notion of equality before the law is accepted by states in the sense of equality of legal personality and capacity. However, it would not be strictly accurate to talk in terms of the equality of states in creating law. The major states will always have an influence commensurate with their status, if only because their concerns are much wider, their interests much deeper and their power more effective.[89]

Within the General Assembly of the United Nations, the doctrine of equality is maintained by the rule of one state, one vote.[90] However, one should not overlook the existence of the veto possessed by the USA, Russia, China, France and the United Kingdom in the Security Council.[91]

Peaceful co-existence

This concept has been formulated in different ways and with different views as to its legal nature by the USSR, China and the Third World. It was elaborated in 1954 as the Five Principles of Peaceful Co-existence by India and China, which concerned mutual respect for each other's territorial integrity and sovereignty, mutual non-aggression, non-interference in each other's affairs and the principle of equality.[92]

The idea was expanded in a number of international documents such as the final communiqué of the Bandung Conference in 1955 and in various resolutions of the United Nations.[93] Its recognised constituents also appear

---

The Doctrine of the Legal Equality of States, Leiden, 1964, and Marshall CJ, *The Antelope*, 10 Wheat., 1825, pp. 66, 122.

[89] See Nguyen Quoc Dinh *et al.*, *Droit International Public*, pp. 1062–3.

[90] See e.g. L. Sohn, *Cases on UN Law*, 2nd edn, Brooklyn, 1967, pp. 232–90, and G. Clark and L. Sohn, *World Peace Through World Law*, 3rd edn, New York, 1966, pp. 399–402.

[91] The doctrine of equality of states is also influential in areas of international law such as jurisdictional immunities, below, chapter 13, and act of state, above, chapter 4, p. 179.

[92] See e.g. Tunkin, *Theory*, pp. 69–75. See also B. Ramondo, *Peaceful Co-existence*, Baltimore, 1967, and R. Higgins, *Conflict of Interests*, London, 1965, pp. 99–170.

[93] See e.g. General Assembly resolutions 1236 (XII) and 1301 (XIII). See also *Yearbook of the UN*, 1957, pp. 105–9; *ibid.*, 1961, p. 524 and *ibid.*, 1962, p. 488.

in the list of Principles of the Charter of the Organisation of African Unity. Among the points enumerated are the concepts of sovereign equality, non-interference in the internal affairs of states, respect for the sovereignty and territorial integrity of states, as well as a condemnation of subversive activities carried out from one state and aimed against another. Other concepts that have been included in this category comprise such principles as non-aggression and the execution of international obligations in good faith. The Soviet Union had also expressed the view that peaceful co-existence constituted the guiding principle in contemporary international law.[94]

Protectorates and protected states[95]

A distinction is sometimes made between a protectorate and a protected state. In the former case, in general, the entity concerned enters into an arrangement with a state under which, while separate legal personality may be involved, separate statehood is not. In the case of a protected state, the entity concerned retains its status as a separate state but enters into a valid treaty relationship with another state affording the latter certain extensive functions possibly internally and externally. However, precisely which type of arrangement is made and the nature of the status, rights and duties in question will depend upon the circumstances and, in particular, the terms of the relevant agreement and third-party attitudes.[96] In the case of Morocco, the Treaty of Fez of 1912 with France gave the latter the power to exercise certain sovereign powers on behalf of the former, including all of its international relations. Nevertheless, the ICJ emphasised that Morocco had in the circumstances of the case remained a sovereign state.[97]

In the case of sub-Saharan Africa in the colonial period, treaties of protection were entered into with tribal entities that were not states. Such institutions were termed 'colonial protectorates' and constituted internal

---

[94] Tunkin, *Theory*, pp. 35–48.

[95] See *Oppenheim's International Law*, p. 266; Crawford, *Creation of States*, pp. 286 ff.; O'Connell, *International Law*, pp. 341–4, and Verzijl, *International Law*, pp. 412–27.

[96] See the *Tunis and Morocco Nationality Decrees* case, (1923) PCIJ, Series B, No. 4, p. 27; 2 AD, p. 349. See also the question of the Ionian Islands, M. F. Lindley, *The Acquisition and Government of Backward Territory in International Law*, London, 1926, pp. 181–2.

[97] *Rights of Nationals of the United States of America in Morocco*, ICJ Reports, 1952, pp. 176, 188; 19 ILR, pp. 255, 263. See also to the same effect, *Benaïm c. Procureur de la République de Bordeaux*, AFDI, 1993, p. 971.

colonial arrangements. They did not constitute international treaties with internationally recognised states.[98]

The extent of powers delegated to the protecting state in such circumstances may vary, as may the manner of the termination of the arrangement. In these cases, formal sovereignty remains unaffected and the entity in question retains its status as a state, and may act as such in the various international fora, regard being had of course to the terms of the arrangement. The obligation may be merely to take note of the advice of the protecting state, or it may extend to a form of diplomatic delegation subject to instruction, as in the case of Liechtenstein. Liechtenstein was refused admission to the League of Nations since it was held unable to discharge all the international obligations imposed by the Covenant in the light of its delegation of sovereign powers, such as diplomatic representation, administration of post, telegraph and telephone services and final decisions in certain judicial cases.[99] Liechtenstein, however, has been a party to the Statute of the International Court of Justice and was a party to the *Nottebohm*[100] case before the Court, a facility only open to states. Liechtenstein joined the United Nations in 1990.

Federal states[101]

There are various forms of federation or confederation, according to the relative distribution of power between the central and local organs. In some states, the residue of power lies with the central government, in others with the local or provincial bodies. A confederation implies a more flexible arrangement, leaving a considerable degree of authority and competence with the component units to the detriment of the central organ.[102]

The Yugoslav Arbitration Commission noted in Opinion No. 1 that in the case of a federal state embracing communities possessing a degree of autonomy where such communities participate in the exercise of political

---

[98] See *Cameroon* v. *Nigeria*, ICJ Reports, 2002, pp. 303, 404–7. See also the *Island of Palmas* case, 2 RIAA, pp. 826, 858–9, and Shaw, *Title*, chapter 1.

[99] See Crawford, *Creation of States*, pp. 479 ff.; Report of the 5th Committee of the League, 6 December 1920, G. Hackworth, *Digest of International Law*, Washington, 1940, vol. I, pp. 48–9, and Higgins, *Development*, p. 34, note 30.

[100] ICJ Reports, 1955, p. 4; 22 ILR, p. 349.

[101] See *Oppenheim's International Law*, p. 245. See also I. Bernier, *International Legal Aspects of Federalism*, London, 1973, and 17 *Revue Belge de Droit International*, 1983, p. 1.

[102] See also below, p. 219.

power within the framework of institutions common to the federation, the 'existence of the state implies that the federal organs represent the components of the federation and wield effective power'.[103] In addition, the existence of such a federal state would be seriously compromised 'when a majority of these entities, embracing the greater part of the territory and population, constitute themselves as sovereign states with the result that federal authority may no longer be effectively exercised'.[104]

The division of powers inherent in such arrangements often raises important questions for international law, particularly in the areas of personality, responsibility and immunity. Whether the federation dissolves into two or more states also brings into focus the doctrine of self-determination in the form of secession. Such dissolution may be the result of an amicable and constitutional agreement or may occur pursuant to a forceful exercise of secession. In the latter case, international legal rules may be pleaded in aid, but the position would seem to be that (apart from recognised colonial situations) there is no right of self-determination applicable to independent states that would justify the resort to secession. There is, of course, no international legal duty to refrain from secession attempts: the situation remains subject to the domestic law. However, should such a secession prove successful in fact, then the concepts of recognition and the appropriate criteria of statehood would prove relevant and determinative as to the new situation.[105]

The federal state will itself, of course, have personality, but the question of the personality and capability of the component units of the federation on the international plane can really only be determined in the light of the constitution of the state concerned and state practice. For instance, the then Soviet Republics of Byelorussia and the Ukraine were admitted as members of the United Nations in 1945 and to that extent possessed international personality.[106] Component states of a federation that have been provided with a certain restricted international competence may thus be accepted as having a degree of international personality. The issue has arisen especially with regard to treaties. Lauterpacht, in his Report on the Law of Treaties, for example, noted that treaties concluded by component units of federal states 'are treaties in the meaning of international law',[107] although Fitzmaurice adopted a different approach in his Report on the

[103] 92 ILR, p. 165.   [104] Opinion No. 8, *ibid.*, p. 201.   [105] See below, p. 256.

[106] See e.g. Bernier, *Federalism*, pp. 64–6. These entities were also members of a number of international organisations and signed treaties.

[107] *Yearbook of the ILC*, 1953, vol. II, p. 139.

Law of Treaties by stating that such units act as agents for the federation which alone possesses international personality and which is the entity bound by the treaty and responsible for its implementation.[108] Article 5(2) of the International Law Commission's Draft Articles on the Law of Treaties provided that

> [s]tates members of a federal union may possess a capacity to conclude treaties if such capacity is admitted by the federal constitution and within the limits there laid down

but this was ultimately rejected at the Vienna Conference on the Law of Treaties,[109] partly on the grounds that the rule was beyond the scope of the Convention itself. The major reasons for the rejection, however, were that the provision would enable third states to intervene in the internal affairs of federal states by seeking to interpret the constitutions of the latter and that, from another perspective, it would unduly enhance the power of domestic law to determine questions of international personality to the detriment of international law. This perhaps would indeed have swung the balance too far away from the international sphere of operation.

Different federations have evolved different systems with regard to the allocation of treaty-making powers. In some cases, component units may enter into such arrangements subject to varying conditions. The Constitution of Switzerland, for example, enables the cantons to conclude treaties with foreign states on issues concerning public economy, frontier relations and the police, subject to the provision that the Federal Council acts as the intermediary.[110] In the case of the United States, responsibility for the conduct of foreign relations rests exclusively with the Federal Government,[111] although American states have entered into certain compacts with foreign states or component units (such as Manitoba and Quebec, provinces of Canada) dealing with the construction and maintenance of highways and international bridges, following upon consultations with the foreign state conducted by the federal authorities. In any event, it is

---

[108] *Yearbook of the ILC*, 1958, vol. II, p. 24. Cf. Waldock, *ibid.*, 1962, vol. II, p. 36.

[109] A/CONF.39/SR.8, 28 April 1969.

[110] See e.g. A. Looper, 'The Treaty Power in Switzerland', 7 *American Journal of Comparative Law*, 1958, p. 178.

[111] See e.g. Article I, Section 10 of the US Constitution; *US* v. *Curtiss-Wright Export Corp.* 299 US 304 (1936); 8 AD, p. 48, and *Zachevning* v. *Miller* 389 US 429 (1968). See also generally, Brownlie, *Principles*, pp. 58–9; Whiteman, *Digest*, vol. 14, pp. 13–17, and Rousseau, *Droit International Public*, pp. 138–213 and 264–8.

clear that the internal constitutional structure is crucial in endowing the unit concerned with capacity. What, however, turns this into international capacity is recognition.

An issue recently the subject of concern and discussion has been the question of the domestic implementation of treaty obligations in the case of federations, especially in the light of the fact that component units may possess legislative power relating to the subject-matter of the treaty concerned. Although this issue lies primarily within the field of domestic constitutional law, there are important implications for international law. In the US, for example, the approach adopted has been to insert 'federal' reservations to treaties in cases where the states of the Union have exercised jurisdiction over the subject-matter in question, providing that the Federal Government would take appropriate steps to enable the competent authorities of the component units to take appropriate measures to fulfil the obligations concerned.[112] In general, however, there have been few restrictions on entry into international agreements.[113]

The question as to divided competence in federations and international treaties has arisen in the past, particularly with regard to conventions of the International Labour Organisation, which typically encompass areas subject to the law-making competence of federal component units. In Canada, for example, early attempts by the central government to ratify ILO conventions were defeated by the decisions of the courts on constitutional grounds, supporting the views of the provinces,[114] while the US has a poor record of ratification of ILO conventions on similar grounds of local competence and federal treaty-making.[115] The issue that arises therefore is either the position of a state that refuses to ratify or sign a treaty on grounds of component unit competence in the area in question or alternatively the problem of implementation and thus responsibility where ratification does take place. In so far as the latter is concerned, the issue has been raised in the context of article 36 of the Vienna Convention on Consular Relations, 1963, to which the US is a party, and which requires, among other things, that states parties inform a foreigner under arrest of his or her right to communicate with the relevant consulate. The International Court of Justice has twice held the US in violation of this

---

[112] See e.g. the proposed reservations to four human rights treaties in 1978, *US Ratification of the Human Rights Treaties* (ed. R. B. Lillich), Charlottesville, 1981, pp. 83–103.

[113] See e.g. *Missouri* v. *Holland* 252 US 416 (1920); 1 AD, p. 4.

[114] See especially, *Attorney-General for Canada* v. *Attorney-General for Ontario* [1937] AC 326; 8 AD, p. 41.

[115] Bernier, *Federalism*, pp. 162–3, and A. Looper, 'Federal State Clauses in Multilateral Instruments', 32 BYIL, 1955–6, p. 162.

requirement, noting that the domestic doctrine known as the procedural default rule, preventing a claimant from raising an issue on appeal or on review if it had not been raised at trial, could not excuse or justify that violation.[116] The US Supreme Court has held that while the International Court's decisions were entitled to 'respectful consideration', they were not binding.[117] This was so even though the US President in a memorandum dated 28 February 2005 had declared that the US would fulfil its obligations under the Avena decision by having states' courts give effect to it.[118] The Texas Court of Criminal Appeals, however, held that neither the Avena decision of the ICJ nor the President's memorandum constituted binding federal law pre-empting Texas law, so that Medellin (the applicant) would not be provided with the review called for by the International Court and by the President.[119]

In Australia, the issue has turned on the interpretation of the constitutional grant of federal power to make laws 'with respect to ... external affairs'.[120] Two recent cases have analysed this, in the light particularly of the established principle that the Federal Government could under this provision legislate on matters, not otherwise explicitly assigned to it, which possessed an intrinsic international aspect.[121]

In *Koowarta* v. *Bjelke-Petersen*[122] in 1982, the Australian High Court, in dealing with an action against the Premier of Queensland for breach of the Racial Discrimination Act 1975 (which incorporated parts of the International Convention on the Elimination of All Forms of Racial

---

[116] The *LaGrand* case, ICJ Reports, 2001, p. 104 and the *Avena* case, ICJ Reports, 2004, p. 12; 134 ILR, p. 120.

[117] *Medellin* v. *Dretke* 118 S.Ct. 1352 (2005) and *Sanchez-Llamas* v. *Oregon* 126 S.Ct. 2669 (2006); 134 ILR, p. 719.

[118] 44 ILM, 2005, p. 964.

[119] *Medellin* v. *Dretke*, Application No. AP-75,207 (Tex. Crim. App. 15 November 2006). Note that the US Supreme Court held that a writ of certiorari to consider the effect of the International Court's decision had been 'improvidently granted' prior to the Texas appeal: see 44 ILM, 2005, p. 965. However, the Supreme Court did grant certiorari on 30 April 2007 (after the Texas decision) to consider two questions: '1. Did the President of the United States act within his constitutional and statutory foreign affairs authority when he determined that the states must comply with the United States' treaty obligation to give effect to the Avena judgment in the cases of the 51 Mexican nationals named in the judgment? [and] 2. Are state courts bound by the Constitution to honor the undisputed international obligation of the United States, under treaties duly ratified by the President with the advice and consent of the Senate, to give effect to the Avena judgment in the cases that the judgment addressed?' See now *Medellin* v. *Texas*, 128 S.Ct. 1346 and above, p. 164, note 178.

[120] See e.g. L. R. Zines, *The High Court and the Constitution*, Sydney, 1981, and A. Byrnes and H. Charlesworth, 'Federalism and the International Legal Order: Recent Developments in Australia', 79 AJIL, 1985, p. 622.

[121] *R* v. *Burgess, ex parte Henry* 55 CLR 608 (1936); 8 AD, p. 54.   [122] 68 ILR, p. 181.

Discrimination adopted in 1965), held that the relevant legislation was valid with respect to the 'external affairs' provision under section 51(29) of the Constitution. In other words, the 'external affairs' power extended to permit the implementation of an international agreement, despite the fact that the subject-matter concerned was otherwise outside federal power. It was felt that if Australia accepted a treaty obligation with respect to an aspect of its own internal legal order, the subject of the obligation thus became an 'external affair' and legislation dealing with this fell within section 51(29), and was thereby valid constitutionally.[123] It was not necessary that a treaty obligation be assumed: the fact that the norm of non-discrimination was established in customary international law was itself sufficient in the view of Stephen J to treat the issue of racial discrimination as part of external affairs.[124]

In *Commonwealth of Australia* v. *Tasmania*,[125] the issue concerned the construction of a dam in an area placed on the World Heritage List established under the 1972 UNESCO Convention for the Protection of the World Cultural and Natural Heritage, to which Australia was a party. The Federal Government in 1983 wished to stop the scheme by reference *inter alia* to the 'external affairs' power as interpreted in *Koowarta*, since it possessed no specific legislative power over the environment. The majority of the Court held that the 'external affairs' power extended to the implementation of treaty obligations. It was not necessary that the subject-matter of the treaty be inherently international.

The effect of these cases seen, of course, in the context of the Australian Constitution, is to reduce the problems faced by federal states of implementing international obligations in the face of local jurisdiction.

The difficulties faced by federal states have also become evident with regard to issues of state responsibility.[126] As a matter of international law, states are responsible for their actions, including those of subordinate organs irrespective of domestic constitutional arrangements.[127] The

---

[123] *Ibid.*, pp. 223–4 (Stephen J); p. 235 (Mason J) and p. 255 (Brennan J).

[124] *Ibid.*, pp. 223–4.

[125] *Ibid.*, p. 266. The case similarly came before the High Court.

[126] See e.g. R. Higgins, 'The Concept of "the State": Variable Geometry and Dualist Perceptions' in *The International Legal System in Quest of Equity and Universality* (eds. L. Boisson de Chazournes and V. Gowlland-Debas), The Hague, 2001, p. 547.

[127] Article 4(1) of the International Law Commission's Articles on State Responsibility, 2001, provides that: 'The conduct of any State organ shall be considered an act of that State under international law, whether the organ exercises legislative, executive, judicial or any other functions, whatever position it holds in the organisation of the State, and whatever its character as an organ of the central government or of a territorial unit of the State.'

International Court in the *Immunity from Legal Process of a Special Rapporteur* case stated that it was a well-established rule of customary international law that 'the conduct of any organ of a State must be regarded as an act of that State'[128] and this applies to component units of a federal state. As the Court noted in its Order of 3 March 1999 on provisional measures in the *LaGrand* case, 'the international responsibility of a State is engaged by the action of the competent organs and authorities acting in that State, whatever they may be'. In particular, the US was under an obligation to transmit the Order to the Governor of the State of Arizona, while the Governor was under an obligation to act in conformity with the international undertakings of the US.[129] Similarly, the Court noted in the *Immunity from Legal Process of a Special Rapporteur* case that the government of Malaysia was under an obligation to communicate the Court's Advisory Opinion to the Malaysian courts in order that Malaysia's international obligations be given effect.[130]

Thus, international responsibility of the state may co-exist with an internal lack of capacity to remedy the particular international wrong. In such circumstances, the central government is under a duty to seek to persuade the component unit to correct the violation of international law,[131] while the latter is, it seems, under an international obligation to act in accordance with the international obligations of the state.

Federal practice in regulating disputes between component units is often of considerable value in international law. This operates particularly in cases of boundary problems, where similar issues arise.[132] Conversely, international practice may often be relevant in the resolution of conflicts between component units.[133]

See also J. Crawford, *The International Law Commission's Articles on State Responsibility*, Cambridge, 2002, pp. 94 ff.

[128] ICJ Reports, 1999, pp. 62, 87; 121 ILR, p. 367.

[129] ICJ Reports, 1999, pp. 9, 16; 118 ILR, p. 37. See also e.g. the *Pellat* case, 5 RIAA, p. 534 (1929).

[130] ICJ Reports, 1999, pp. 62, 88; 121 ILR, p. 367.

[131] Such issues arise from time to time with regard to human rights matters before international or regional human rights bodies: see e.g. *Toonen* v. *Australia*, Human Rights Committee, Communication No. 488/1992, 112 ILR, p. 328, and *Tyrer* v. *UK*, 2 European Human Rights Reports 1. See also *Matthews* v. *UK*, 28 European Human Rights Reports 361, and *RMD* v. *Switzerland*, *ibid.*, 224.

[132] See e.g. E. Lauterpacht, 'River Boundaries: Legal Aspects of the Shatt-Al-Arab Frontier', 9 ICLQ, 1960, pp. 208, 216, and A. O. Cukwurah, *The Settlement of Boundary Disputes in International Law*, Manchester, 1967.

[133] See also below, chapters 13 and 14.

Sui generis territorial entities

Mandated and trust territories[134]

After the end of the First World War and the collapse of the Axis and Russian empires, the Allies established a system for dealing with the colonies of the defeated powers that did not involve annexation. These territories would be governed according to the principle that 'the well-being and development of such peoples form a sacred trust of civilisation'. The way in which this principle would be put into effect would be to entrust the tutelage of such people to 'advanced nations who by reason of their resources, their experience or their geographical position' could undertake the responsibility. The arrangement would be exercised by them as mandatories on behalf of the League.[135]

Upon the conclusion of the Second World War and the demise of the League, the mandate system was transmuted into the United Nations trusteeship system under Chapters XII and XIII of the UN Charter.[136] The strategic trust territory of the Pacific, taken from Japan, the mandatory power, was placed in a special category subject to Security Council rather than Trusteeship Council supervision for security reasons,[137] while South

---

[134] See generally H. Duncan Hall, *Mandates, Dependencies and Trusteeships*, London, 1948; Whiteman, *Digest*, vol. I, pp. 598–911 and vol. XIII, pp. 679 ff.; C. E. Toussaint, *The Trusteeship System of the United Nations*, New York, 1957; Verzijl, *International Law*, vol. II, pp. 545–73; Q. Wright, *Mandates Under the League of Nations*, New York, 1930; J. Dugard, *The South West Africa/Namibia Dispute*, Berkeley, 1973, and S. Slonim, *South West Africa and the United Nations*, Leiden, 1973. See also *Oppenheim's International Law*, pp. 295 and 308, and Crawford, *Creation of States*, pp. 565 ff.

[135] See article 22 of the Covenant of the League of Nations. See also the *International Status of South West Africa*, ICJ Reports, 1950, pp. 128, 132; 17 ILR, p. 47; the *Namibia* case, ICJ Reports, 1971, pp. 16, 28–9; 49 ILR, pp. 2, 18–19; *Certain Phosphate Lands in Nauru*, ICJ Reports, 1992, pp. 240, 256; 97 ILR, pp. 1, 23 and *Cameroon v. Nigeria*, ICJ Reports, 2002, para. 212.

[136] See e.g. *Certain Phosphate Lands in Nauru*, ICJ Reports, 1992, pp. 240, 257; 97 ILR, pp. 1, 24. See also the discussion by Judge Shahabuddeen in his Separate Opinion, ICJ Reports, 1992, pp. 276 ff.; 97 ILR, p. 43. Note that the Court in this case stated that the arrangements whereby Nauru was to be administered under the trusteeship agreement by the governments of the UK, Australia and New Zealand together as 'the administering authority' did not constitute that authority an international legal person separate from the three states so designated: ICJ Reports, 1992, p. 258; 97 ILR, p. 25. See also *Cameroon v. Nigeria*, ICJ Reports, 2002, para. 212.

[137] See O. McHenry, *Micronesia: Trust Betrayed*, New York, 1975; Whiteman, *Digest*, vol. I, pp. 769–839; S. A. de Smith, *Micro-States and Micronesia*, New York, 1970; DUSPIL, 1973, pp. 59–67; *ibid.*, 1974, pp. 54–64; *ibid.*, 1975, pp. 94–104; *ibid.*, 1976, pp. 56–61; *ibid.*, 1977, pp. 71–98 and *ibid.*, 1978, pp. 204–31.

Africa refused to place its mandated territory under the system. Quite who held sovereignty in such territories was the subject of extensive debates over many decades.[138]

As far as the trust territory of the Pacific was concerned, the US signed a Covenant with the Commonwealth of the Northern Mariana Islands and Compacts of Free Association with the Federated States of Micronesia and with the Republic of the Marshall Islands. Upon their entry into force in autumn 1986, it was determined that the trusteeship had been terminated. This procedure providing for political union with the US was accepted by the Trusteeship Council as a legitimate exercise of self-determination.[139] However, the proposed Compact of Free Association with the Republic of Palau (the final part of the former trust territory) did not enter into force as a result of disagreement over the transit of nuclear-powered or armed vessels and aircraft through Palauan waters and airspace and, therefore, the US continued to act as administering authority under the trusteeship agreement.[140] These difficulties were eventually resolved.[141]

South West Africa was administered after the end of the First World War as a mandate by South Africa, which refused after the Second World War to place the territory under the trusteeship system. Following this, the International Court of Justice in 1950 in its Advisory Opinion on the *International Status of South West Africa*[142] stated that, while there was no legal obligation imposed by the United Nations Charter to transfer a mandated territory into a trust territory, South Africa was still bound by the terms of the mandate agreement and the Covenant of the League of Nations, and the obligations that it had assumed at that time. The Court emphasised that South Africa alone did not have the capacity to modify the international status of the territory. This competence rested with South Africa acting with the consent of the United Nations, as successor to the League of Nations. Logically flowing from this decision was the ability of the United Nations to hear petitioners from the territory in consequence of South Africa's refusal to heed United Nations decisions and in pursuance of League of Nations practices.[143]

---

[138] See in particular Judge McNair, *International Status of South West Africa*, ICJ Reports, 1950, pp. 128, 150 and the Court's view, *ibid.*, p. 132; 17 ILR, pp. 47, 49.

[139] See Security Council resolution 683 (1990).

[140] See 'Contemporary Practice of the United States Relating to International Law', 81 AJIL, 1987, pp. 405–8. See also *Bank of Hawaii* v. *Balos* 701 F.Supp. 744 (1988).

[141] See Security Council resolution 956 (1994).

[142] ICJ Reports, 1950, pp. 128, 143–4; 17 ILR, pp. 47, 57–60.

[143] ICJ Reports, 1955, p. 68; 22 ILR, p. 651 and ICJ Reports, 1956, p. 23; 23 ILR, p. 38.

In 1962 the ICJ heard the case brought by Ethiopia and Liberia, the two African members of the League, that South Africa was in breach of the terms of the mandate and had thus violated international law. The Court initially affirmed that it had jurisdiction to hear the merits of the dispute.[144] However, by the Second Phase of the case, the Court (its composition having slightly altered in the meanwhile) decided that Ethiopia and Liberia did not have any legal interest in the subject-matter of the claim (the existence and supervision of the mandate over South West Africa) and accordingly their contentions were rejected.[145] Having thus declared on the lack of standing of the two African appellants, the Court did not discuss any of the substantive questions which stood before it.

This judgment aroused a great deal of feeling, particularly in the Third World, and occasioned a shift in emphasis in dealing with the problem of the territory in question.[146]

The General Assembly resolved in October 1966 that since South Africa had failed to fulfil its obligations, the mandate was therefore terminated. South West Africa (or Namibia as it was to be called) was to come under the direct responsibility of the United Nations.[147] Accordingly, a Council was established to oversee the territory and a High Commissioner appointed.[148] The Security Council in a number of resolutions upheld the action of the Assembly and called upon South Africa to withdraw its administration from the territory. It also requested other states to refrain from dealing with the South African government in so far as Namibia was concerned.[149]

The Security Council ultimately turned to the International Court and requested an Advisory Opinion as to the *Legal Consequences for States of the Continued Presence of South Africa in Namibia*.[150] The Court concluded that South Africa's presence in Namibia was indeed illegal in view of the series of events culminating in the United Nations resolutions on the grounds of a material breach of a treaty (the mandate agreement) by South Africa, and further that 'a binding determination made by a competent organ of the United Nations to the effect that a situation is illegal cannot remain without consequence'. South Africa was obligated to withdraw its

---

[144] ICJ Reports, 1962, pp. 141 and 143.   [145] ICJ Reports, 1966, p. 6; 37 ILR, p. 243.
[146] See e.g. Dugard, *South West Africa/Namibia*, p. 378.   [147] Resolution 2145 (XXI).
[148] See General Assembly resolutions 2145 (XXI) and 2248 (XXII).
[149] See e.g. Security Council resolutions 263 (1969), 269 (1969) and 276 (1970).
[150] ICJ Reports, 1971, p. 16; 49 ILR, p. 3.

administration from the territory, and other states members of the United Nations were obliged to recognise the illegality and the invalidity of its acts with regard to that territory and aid the United Nations in its efforts concerning the problem.[151]

The opinion was approved by the Security Council in resolution 301 (1971), which also reaffirmed the national unity and territorial integrity of Namibia. In 1978 South Africa announced its acceptance of proposals negotiated by the five Western contact powers (UK, USA, France, Canada and West Germany) for Namibian independence involving a UN supervised election and peace-keeping force.[152] After some difficulties,[153] Namibia finally obtained its independence on 23 April 1990.[154]

Germany 1945

With the defeat of Germany on 5 June 1945, the Allied Powers assumed 'supreme authority' with respect to that country, while expressly disclaiming any intention of annexation.[155] Germany was divided into four occupation zones with four-power control over Berlin. The Control Council established by the Allies acted on behalf of Germany and in such capacity entered into binding legal arrangements. The state of Germany continued, however, and the situation, as has been observed, was akin to legal representation or agency of necessity.[156] Under the 1952 Treaty between the three Western powers and the Federal Republic of Germany, full sovereign powers were granted to the latter subject to retained powers concerning the making of a peace treaty, and in 1972 the Federal Republic of Germany and the German Democratic Republic, established in 1954 by the Soviet Union in its zone, recognised each other as sovereign states.[157]

However, following a series of dramatic events during 1989 in Central and Eastern Europe, deriving in essence from the withdrawal of

---

[151] ICJ Reports, 1971, pp. 52–8.

[152] 17 ILM, 1978, pp. 762–9, and DUSPIL, 1978, pp. 38–54. See Security Council resolution 435 (1978). See also *Africa Research Bulletin*, April 1978, p. 4829 and July 1978, p. 4935.

[153] See S/14459; S/14460/Rev.1; S/14461 and S/14462. [154] See 28 ILM, 1989, p. 944.

[155] See Whiteman, *Digest*, vol. I, pp. 325–6, and R. W. Piotrowicz, 'The Status of Germany in International Law', 38 ICLQ, 1989, p. 609. See also Crawford, *Creation of States*, p. 523.

[156] Brownlie, *Principles*, p. 107. See also Whiteman, *Digest*, p. 333, and I. D. Hendry and M. C. Wood, *The Legal Status of Berlin*, Cambridge, 1987.

[157] 12 AD, p. 16. Note also *Kunstsammlungen zu Weimar v. Elicofon* 94 ILR, p. 135. Both states became members of the UN the following year. See Crawford, *Creation of States*, pp. 523–6, and F. A. Mann, *Studies in International Law*, Oxford, 1973, pp. 634–59 and 660–706.

Soviet control, the drive for a reunified Germany in 1990 became un-stoppable.[158] A State Treaty on German Economic, Monetary and Social Union was signed by the Finance Ministers of the two German states on 18 May and this took effect on 1 July.[159] A State Treaty on Unifica-tion was signed on 31 August, providing for unification on 3 October by the accession to the Federal Republic of Germany of the *Länder* of the German Democratic Republic under article 23 of the Basic Law of the Federal Republic, with Berlin as the capital.[160] The external obstacle to unity was removed by the signing on 12 September of the Treaty on the Final Settlement with Respect to Germany, between the two German states and the four wartime allies (UK, USA, USSR and France).[161] Under this treaty, a reunified Germany agreed to accept the current Oder–Neisse border with Poland and to limit its armed forces to 370,000 persons, while pledging not to acquire atomic, chemical or biological weapons. The Agreement on the Settlement of Certain Matters Relating to Berlin between the Federal Republic and the three Western powers on 25 Septem-ber 1990 provided for the relinquishment of Allied rights with regard to Berlin.[162]

Condominium

In this instance two or more states equally exercise sovereignty with re-spect to a territory and its inhabitants. There are arguments as to the relationship between the states concerned, the identity of the sovereign for the purposes of the territory and the nature of the competences in-volved.[163] In the case of the New Hebrides, a series of Anglo-French agree-ments established a region of joint influence, with each power retaining sovereignty over its nationals and neither exercising separate authority

---

[158] See e.g. J. Frowein, 'The Reunification of Germany', 86 AJIL, 1992, p. 152; Schrike, 'L'Unification Allemande', p. 47; Czaplinski, 'Quelques Aspects', p. 89, and R. W. Piotrowicz and S. Blay, *The Unification of Germany in International and Domestic Law*, Amsterdam, 1997.

[159] See *Keesing's Record of World Events*, p. 37466 (1990). See also 29 ILM, 1990, p. 1108.

[160] *Keesing's*, p. 37661. See also 30 ILM, 1991, pp. 457 and 498.

[161] See 29 ILM, 1990, p. 1186.

[162] See 30 ILM, 1991, p. 445. See also the Exchange of Notes of the same date concerning the presence of allied troops in Berlin, *ibid.*, p. 450.

[163] Brownlie, *Principles*, pp. 113–14. See also O'Connell, *International Law*, pp. 327–8; A. Coret, *Le Condominium*, Paris, 1960; *Oppenheim's International Law*, p. 565, and V. P. Bantz, 'The International Legal Status of Condominia', 12 *Florida Journal of International Law*, 1998, p. 77.

over the area.[164] A Protocol listed the functions of the condominial government and vested the power to issue joint regulations respecting them in a British and a French High Commissioner. This power was delegated to resident commissioners who dealt with their respective nationals. Three governmental systems accordingly co-existed, with something of a legal vacuum with regard to land tenure and the civil transactions of the indigenous population.[165] The process leading to the independence of the territory also reflected its unique status as a condominium.[166] It was noted that the usual independence Bill would not have been appropriate, since the New Hebrides was not a British colony. Its legal status as an Anglo-French condominium had been established by international agreement and could only be terminated in the same fashion. The nature of the condominium was such that it assumed that the two metropolitan powers would always act together and unilateral action was not provided for in the basic constitutional documents.[167] The territory became independent on 30 July 1980 as the state of Vanuatu. The entity involved prior to independence grew out of an international treaty and established an administrative entity arguably distinct from its metropolitan governments but more likely operating on the basis of a form of joint agency with a range of delegated powers.[168]

The Central American Court of Justice in 1917[169] held that a condominium existed with respect to the Gulf of Fonseca providing for rights of co-ownership of the three coastal states of Nicaragua, El Salvador and Honduras. The issue was raised in the *El Salvador/Honduras* case before

[164] See e.g. 99 BFSP, p. 229 and 114 BFSP, p. 212.

[165] O'Connell, *International Law*, p. 328.

[166] Lord Trefgarne, the government spokesman, moving the second reading of the New Hebrides Bill in the House of Lords, 404 HL Deb., cols. 1091–2, 4 February 1980.

[167] See Mr Luce, Foreign Office Minister, 980 HC Deb., col. 682, 8 March 1980 and 985 HC Deb., col. 1250, 3 June 1980. See also D. P. O'Connell, 'The Condominium of the New Hebrides', 43 BYIL, p. 71.

[168] See also the joint Saudi Arabian–Kuwaiti administered Neutral Zone based on the treaty of 2 December 1922, 133 BFSP, 1930 Part II, pp. 726–7. See e.g. *The Middle East* (ed. P. Mansfield), 4th edn, London, 1973, p. 187. Both states enjoyed an equal right of undivided sovereignty over the whole area. However, on 7 July 1965, both states signed an agreement to partition the neutral zone, although the territory apparently retained its condominium status for exploration of resources purposes: see 4 ILM, 1965, p. 1134, and H. M. Alba-harna, *The Legal Status of the Arabian Gulf States*, 2nd rev. edn, Beirut, 1975, pp. 264–77. See also F. Ali Taha, 'Some Legal Aspects of the Anglo-Egyptian Condominium over the Sudan: 1899–1954', 76 BYIL, 2005, p. 337.

[169] 11 AJIL, 1917, p. 674.

the International Court of Justice.[170] The Court noted that a condominium arrangement being 'a structured system for the joint exercise of sovereign governmental powers over a territory' was normally created by agreement between the states concerned, although it could be created as a juridical consequence of a succession of states (as in the Gulf of Fonseca situation itself), being one of the ways in which territorial sovereignty could pass from one state to another. The Court concluded that the waters of the Gulf of Fonseca beyond the three-mile territorial sea were historic waters and subject to a joint sovereignty of the three coastal states. It based its decision, apart from the 1917 judgment, upon the historic character of the Gulf waters, the consistent claims of the three coastal states and the absence of protest from other states.[171]

International administration of territories

In such cases a particular territory is placed under a form of international regime, but the conditions under which this has been done have varied widely, from autonomous areas within states to relatively independent entities.[172] The UN is able to assume the administration of territories in specific circumstances. The trusteeship system was founded upon the supervisory role of the UN,[173] while in the case of South West Africa, the General Assembly supported by the Security Council ended South Africa's mandate and asserted its competence to administer the territory pending independence.[174] Beyond this, UN organs exercising their powers may assume a variety of administrative functions over particular territories where issues of international concern have arisen. Attempts were made to create such a regime for Jerusalem under the General Assembly partition resolution for Palestine in 1947 as a 'corpus separatum under a special international regime ... administered by the United Nations', but this never materialised for a number of reasons.[175] Further, the Security Council

---

[170] ICJ Reports, 1992, pp. 351, 597 ff.; 97 ILR, pp. 266, 513 ff. El Salvador and Nicaragua were parties to the 1917 decision but differed over the condominium solution. Honduras was not a party to that case and opposed the condominium idea.

[171] ICJ Reports, 1992, p. 601; 97 ILR, p. 517.

[172] See e.g. R. Wilde, International Territorial Administration, Oxford, 2008; M. Ydit, Internationalised Territories, Leiden, 1961; Crawford, Creation of States, pp. 501 ff.; Brownlie, Principles, pp. 60 and 167, and Rousseau, Droit International Public, vol. II, pp. 413–48.

[173] See further above, p. 224.   [174] See above, p. 225.

[175] Resolution 18(II). See e.g. E. Lauterpacht, Jerusalem and the Holy Places, London, 1968, and Ydit, Internationalised Territories, pp. 273–314.

in 1947 adopted a Permanent Statute for the Free Territory of Trieste, under which the Council was designated as the supreme administrative and legislative authority of the territory.[176]

More recently, the UN has become more involved in important administrative functions, authority being derived from a mixture of international agreements, domestic consent and the powers of the Security Council under Chapter VII to adopt binding decisions concerning international peace and security, as the case may be. For example, the 1991 Paris Peace Agreements between the four Cambodian factions authorised the UN to establish civil administrative functions in that country pending elections and the adoption of a new constitution. This was accomplished through the UN Transitional Authority in Cambodia (UNTAC), to which were delegated 'all powers necessary to ensure the implementation' of the peace settlement and which also exercised competence in areas such as foreign affairs, defence, finance and so forth.[177]

Annex 10 of the General Framework Agreement for Peace in Bosnia and Herzegovina (the Dayton Agreement)[178] established the post of High Representative with extensive powers with regard to the civilian implementation of the peace agreement and with the final authority to interpret the civilian aspects of the settlement.[179] This was endorsed and confirmed by the Security Council in binding resolution 1031 (1995). The relatively modest powers of the High Representative under Annex 10 were subsequently enlarged in practice by the Peace Implementation Council, a body

---

[176] See Security Council resolution 16 (1947). Like the Jerusalem idea, this never came into being. See also the experiences of the League of Nations with regard to the Saar and Danzig, Ydit, *Internationalised Territories*, chapter 3.

[177] See Article 6 and Annex I of the Paris Peace Settlement. See also C. Stahn, 'International Territorial Administration in the Former Yugoslavia: Origins, Developments and Challenges Ahead', ZaöRV, 2001, p. 107. UNTAC lasted from March 1992 to September 1993 and involved some 22,000 military and civilian personnel: see www.un.org/Depts/dpko/dpko/co_mission/untac.htm. Note also e.g. the operations of the UN Transition Group in Namibia which, in the process leading to Namibian independence, exercised a degree of administrative power: see Report of the UN Secretary-General, A/45/1 (1991), and the UN Transitional Administration for Eastern Slavonia (UNTAES), which facilitated the transfer of the territory from Serb to Croat rule over a two-year period: see Security Council resolution 1037 (1996).

[178] Initialled at Dayton, Ohio, and signed in Paris, 1995.

[179] The final authority with regard to the military implementation of the agreement remains the commander of SFOR: see article 12 of the Agreement on the Military Aspects of the Dayton Peace Agreement. Note also the establishment of the Human Rights Chamber, the majority of whose members are from other states: see below, chapter 7, p. 379, and the Commission for Displaced Persons and Refugees: see Annexes 6 and 7 of the Peace Agreement.

with fifty-five members established to review progress regarding the peace settlement, in the decisions it took at the Bonn Summit of December 1997 (the Bonn Conclusions).[180] These provided, for example, for measures to be taken against persons found by the High Representative to be in violation of legal commitments made under the Peace Agreement. This has included removal from public office, the competence to impose interim legislation where Bosnia's institutions had failed to do so[181] and 'other measures to ensure implementation of the Peace Agreement throughout Bosnia and Herzegovina and its Entities, as well as the smooth running of the common institutions'.[182] The High Representative has taken a wide-ranging number of decisions, from imposing the Law on Citizenship of Bosnia and Herzegovina in December 1997[183] and imposing the Law on the Flag of Bosnia and Herzegovina in February 1998[184] to enacting the Law on Changes and Amendments to the Election Law in January 2006 to mark the ongoing process of transferring High Representative powers to the domestic authorities in the light of the improving situation.[185] This unusual structure with regard to an independent state arises, therefore, from a mix of the consent of the parties and binding Chapter VII activity by the Security Council.

In resolution 1244 (1999), the Security Council authorised the Secretary-General to establish an interim international civil presence in Kosovo (UNMIK),[186] following the withdrawal of Yugoslav forces from

---

[180] See e.g. the documentation available at www.ohr.int/pic/archive.asp?so=d&sa=on. See also Security Council resolutions 1144 (1997), 1256 (1999) and 1423 (2002).

[181] www.ohr.int/pic/default.asp?content_id=5182. The competence of the High Representative to adopt binding decisions with regard to interim measures when the parties are unable to reach agreement remains in force until the Presidency or Council of Ministers has adopted a decision consistent with the Peace Agreement on the issue concerned.

[182] Paragraph XI of the Bonn Conclusions. See also Security Council resolutions 1247 (1999), 1395 (2000), 1357 (2001), 1396 (2002) and 1491 (2003).

[183] www.ohr.int/statemattersdec/default.asp?content_id=343.

[184] www.ohr.int/statemattersdec/default.asp?content_id=344.

[185] www.ohr.int/statemattersdec/default.asp?content_id=36465.

[186] See Stahn, 'International Territorial Administration', p. 111; T. Garcia, 'La Mission d'Administration Intérimaire des Nations Unies au Kosovo', RGDIP, 2000, p. 61, and M. Ruffert, 'The Administration of Kosovo and East Timor by the International Community', 50 ICLQ, 2001, p. 613. See also Kosovo and the International Community: A Legal Assessment (ed. C. Tomuschat), The Hague, 2002; B. Knoll, 'From Benchmarking to Final Status? Kosovo and the Problem of an International Administration's Open-Ended Mandate', 16 European Journal of International Law, 2005, p. 637; Kosovo: KFOR and Reconstruction, House of Commons Research Paper 99/66, 1999; A. Yannis, 'The UN as Government in Kosovo', 10 Global Governance, 2004, p. 67; International Crisis Group (ICG), Kosovo: Towards Final Status, January 2005, ICG, Kosovo: The Challenge of Transition,

that part of the country consequent upon NATO action. Under this resolution, UNMIK performed a wide range of administrative functions, including health and education, banking and finance, post and telecommunications, and law and order. It was tasked *inter alia* to promote the establishment of substantial autonomy and self-government in Kosovo, to co-ordinate humanitarian and disaster relief, support the reconstruction of key infrastructure, maintain civil law and order, promote human rights and assure the return of refugees. Administrative structures were established and elections held. The first regulation adopted by the Special Representative of the UN Secretary-General appointed under resolution 1244 vested all legislative and executive authority in Kosovo in UNMIK as exercised by the Special Representative.[187] This regulation also established that the law in the territory was that in existence in so far as this did not conflict with the international standards referred to in section 2 of the regulation, the fulfilment of the mandate given to UNMIK under resolution 1244, or the present or any other regulation issued by UNMIK. A Constitutional Framework for Provisional Self-Government was promulgated by the Special Representative in May 2001.[188] This comprehensive administrative competence was founded upon the reaffirmation of Yugoslavia's sovereignty and territorial integrity (and thus continuing territorial title over the province) and the requirement for 'substantial autonomy and meaningful self-administration for Kosovo'.[189] Accordingly, this arrangement illustrated a complete division between title to the territory and the exercise of power and control over it. It flowed from a binding Security Council resolution, which referred to Yugoslavia's consent to the essential principles therein contained.[190]

The United Nations Transitional Administration in East Timor (UNTAET) was established by Security Council resolution 1272 (1999) acting under Chapter VII. It was 'endowed with overall responsibility for the administration of East Timor' and 'empowered to exercise all legislative and executive authority, including the administration of justice'.[191]

February 2006, ICG, *Kosovo: No Good Alternatives to the Ahtisaari Plan*, 14 May 2007, and ICG, *Kosovo Countdown: A Blueprint for Transition*, 6 December 2007. Resolution 1244 also authorised an international military presence.

[187] Regulation 1 (1999). This was backdated to the date of adoption of resolution 1244.

[188] See UNMIK Regulation 9 (2001).   [189] Resolution 1244 (1999).

[190] See S/1999/649 and Annex 2 to the resolution. Kosovo declared independence on 17 February 2008: see below, p. 452 and above, p. 201.

[191] East Timor, a Portuguese non-self-governing territory, was occupied by Indonesia in 1974. These two states agreed with the UN on 5 May 1999 to a process of popular consultation

Its widespread mandate included, in addition to public administration, humanitarian responsibilities and a military component and it was authorised to take all necessary measures to fulfil its mandate. UNTAET's mandate was extended to 20 May 2002, the date of East Timor's independence as the new state of Timor-Leste.[192] It was thereafter succeeded by the United Nations Mission of Support in East Timor (UNMISET).[193]

Taiwan[194]

This territory was ceded by China to Japan in 1895 by the treaty of Shimonoseki and remained in the latter's hands until 1945. Japan undertook on surrender not to retain sovereignty over Taiwan and this was reaffirmed under the Peace Treaty, 1951 between the Allied Powers (but not the USSR and China) and Japan, under which all rights to the island were renounced without specifying any recipient. After the Chinese Civil War, the Communist forces took over the mainland while the Nationalist regime installed itself on Taiwan (Formosa) and the Pescadores. Both the US and the UK took the view at that stage that sovereignty over Taiwan was uncertain or undetermined.[195] The key point affecting status has been that both governments have claimed to represent the whole of China. No claim of separate statehood for Taiwan has been made and in such a case it is difficult to maintain that such an unsought status exists. Total lack of recognition of Taiwan as a separate independent state merely reinforces this point. In 1979 the US recognised the People's Republic of China as the sole and legitimate government of China.[196] Accordingly, Taiwan would

---

in the territory over its future. The inhabitants expressed a clear wish for a transitional process of UN authority leading to independence. Following the outbreak of violence, a multinational force was sent to East Timor pursuant to resolution 1264 (1999): see also the Report of the Secretary-General, S/1999/1024; www.un.org/peace/etimor/etimor.htm.

[192] See resolutions 1388 (2001) and 1392 (2002).   [193] See resolution 1410 (2002).

[194] See e.g. Crawford, *Creation of States*, pp. 198 ff.; *China and the Question of Taiwan* (ed. H. Chiu), New York, 1979; W. M. Reisman, 'Who Owns Taiwan?', 81 *Yale Law Journal*, p. 599; F. P. Morello, *The International Legal Status of Formosa*, The Hague, 1966; V. H. Li, *De-Recognising Taiwan*, Washington, DC, 1977, and L. C. Chiu, 'The International Legal Status of the Republic of China', 8 *Chinese Yearbook of International Law and Affairs*, 1990, p. 1. See also *The International Status of Taiwan in the New World Order* (ed. J. M. Henckaerts), London, 1996; *Let Taiwan be Taiwan* (eds. M. J. Cohen and E. Teng), Washington, 1990, and J. I. Charney and J. R. V. Prescott, 'Resolving Cross-Strait Relations Between China and Taiwan', 94 AJIL, 2000, p. 453.

[195] See Whiteman, *Digest*, vol. III, pp. 538, 564 and 565.

[196] See Crawford, *Creation of States*, pp. 209 ff. Note that the 1972 USA–China communiqué accepted that Taiwan was part of China, 11 ILM, pp. 443, 445. As to the 1979 changes, see 73 AJIL, p. 227. See also 833 HC Deb., col. 32, 13 March 1972, for the new British

appear to be a non-state territorial entity which is capable of acting independently on the international scene, but is most probably *de jure* part of China. It is interesting to note that when in early 1990 Taiwan sought accession to the General Agreement on Tariffs and Trade (GATT), it did so by requesting entry for the 'customs territory' of 'Taiwan, Penghu, Kinmen and Matsu', thus avoiding an assertion of statehood.[197] The accession of 'Chinese Taipei' to the World Trade Organisation was approved by the Ministerial Conference in November 2001.[198]

The 'Turkish Republic of Northern Cyprus' (TRNC)[199]

In 1974, following a coup in Cyprus backed by the military regime in Greece, Turkish forces invaded the island. The Security Council in resolution 353 (1974) called upon all states to respect the sovereignty, independence and territorial integrity of Cyprus and demanded an immediate end to foreign military intervention in the island that was contrary to such respect. On 13 February 1975 the Turkish Federated State of Cyprus was proclaimed in the area occupied by Turkish forces. A resolution adopted at the same meeting of the Council of Ministers and the Legislative Assembly of the Autonomous Turkish Cypriot Administration at which the proclamation was made, emphasised the determination 'to oppose resolutely all attempts against the independence of Cyprus and its partition or union with any other state' and resolved to establish a separate administration until such time as the 1960 Cyprus Constitution was amended to provide for a federal republic.[200]

---

approach, i.e. that it recognised the Government of the People's Republic of China as the sole legal Government of China and acknowledged the position of that government that Taiwan was a province of China, and see e.g. UKMIL, 71 BYIL, 2000, p. 537. See also *Reel v. Holder* [1981] 1 WLR 1226.

[197] See *Keesing's Record of World Events*, p. 37671 (1990). This failed, however, to prevent a vigorous protest by China: *ibid.* Note also the Agreements Concerning Cross-Straits Activities between unofficial organisations established in China and Taiwan in order to reach functional, non-political agreements, 32 ILM, 1993, p. 1217. A degree of evolution in Taiwan's approach was evident in the Additional Articles of the Constitution adopted in 1997.

[198] See www.wto.org/english/news_e/pres01_e/pr253_e.htm. As to Rhodesia (1965–79) and the Bantustans, see above, pp. 206 and 202.

[199] See Z. M. Necatigil, *The Cyprus Question and the Turkish Position in International Law*, 2nd edn, Oxford 1993; G. White, *The World Today*, April 1981, p. 135, and Crawford, *Creation of States*, pp. 143 ff.

[200] Resolution No. 2 in Supplement IV, Official Gazette of the TFSC, cited in Nadjatigil, *Cyprus Conflict*, p. 123.

On 15 November 1983, the Turkish Cypriots proclaimed their independence as the 'Turkish Republic of Northern Cyprus'.[201] This was declared illegal by the Security Council in resolution 541 (1983) and its withdrawal called for. All states were requested not to recognise the 'purported state' or assist it in any way. This was reiterated in Security Council resolution 550 (1984). The Committee of Ministers of the Council of Europe decided that it continued to regard the government of the Republic of Cyprus as the sole legitimate government of Cyprus and called for respect for the independence and territorial integrity of Cyprus.[202] The European Court of Human Rights in its judgment of 10 May 2001 in *Cyprus* v. *Turkey* concluded that, 'it is evident from international practice . . . that the international community does not recognise the "TRNC" as a state under international law' and declared that 'the Republic of Cyprus has remained the sole legitimate government of Cyprus'.[203] In the light of this and the very heavy dependence of the territory upon Turkey, it cannot be regarded as a sovereign state, but remains as a *de facto* administered entity within the recognised confines of the Republic of Cyprus and dependent upon Turkish assistance.[204]

The Saharan Arab Democratic Republic[205]

In February 1976, the Polisario liberation movement conducting a war to free the Western Saharan territory from Moroccan control declared the independent sovereign Saharan Arab Democratic Republic (SADR).[206] Over the succeeding years, many states recognised the new entity, including a majority of Organisation of African Unity members. In February 1982, the OAU Secretary-General sought to seat a delegation from SADR on that basis, but this provoked a boycott by some nineteen states and a major crisis. However, in November 1984 the Assembly of Heads of State and Government of the OAU did agree to seat a delegation from SADR,

---

[201] See *The Times*, 16 November 1983, p. 12, and 21(4) *UN Chronicle*, 1984, p. 17.

[202] Resolution (83)13 adopted on 24 November 1983.

[203] Application No. 25781/94; 120 ILR, p. 10. See *Loizidou* v. *Turkey (Preliminary Objections)*, Series A, No. 310, 1995; 103 ILR, p. 622, and *Loizidou* v. *Turkey (Merits)*, Reports 1996-VI, p. 2216; 108 ILR, p. 443. See also to the same effect, *Autocephalous Church of Cyprus* v. *Goldberg* 917 F.2d 278 (1990); 108 ILR, p. 488, and *Caglar* v. *Billingham* [1996] STC (SCD) 150; 108 ILR, p. 510.

[204] See also Foreign Affairs Committee, Third Report, Session 1986–7, Cyprus: HCP 23 (1986–7).

[205] See Shaw, *Title*, chapter 3.

[206] *Africa Research Bulletin*, June 1976, p. 4047 and July 1976, pp. 4078 and 4081.

despite Morocco's threat of withdrawal from the organisation.[207] This, therefore, can be taken as OAU recognition of statehood and, as such, of evidential significance. However, although in view of the reduced importance of the effectiveness of control criterion in such self-determination situations a credible argument can now be made regarding SADR's statehood, the issue is still controversial in view of the continuing hostilities and what appears to be effective Moroccan control. It is to be noted that the legal counsel to the UN gave an opinion in 2002 to the effect that Western Sahara continued as a non-self-governing territory and that this status was unaffected by the transfer of administrative authority to Morocco and Mauritania in 1975. The view was also taken that exploration and exploitation activities undertaken in disregard of the interests and wishes of the people of Western Sahara would violate international law.[208]

Various secessionist claimants

A number of secessionist claims from recognised independent states exist. The former territory of British Somaliland, being the northern part of the new state of Somalia after its independence in 1960, asserted its own independence on 17 May 1991.[209] A constitution was adopted in 2001, but the Organisation of African Unity refused to support any action that would affect the unity and sovereignty of Somalia.[210] 'Somaliland' is unrecognised by any state or international organisation, although a number of dealings with the authorities of that entity have taken place.[211] Following an armed conflict between Armenia and Azerbaijan in the early 1990s, Armenian forces captured and occupied the area of Nagorno-Karabakh (and seven surrounding districts) from Azerbaijan. Nagorno-Karabakh, an area with

---

[207] See *Keesing's Contemporary Archives*, pp. 33324–45.

[208] S/2002/161. The UK has stated that it regards the 'the sovereignty of Western Sahara as undetermined pending United Nations efforts to find a solution to the dispute over the territory', UKMIL, 76 BYIL, 2005, p. 720.

[209] See e.g. Crawford, *Creation of States*, pp. 412 ff., and *Somalia: A Country Study* (ed. H. C. Metz), 4th edn, Washington, 1993. See generally P. Kolsto, 'The Sustainability and Future of Unrecognized Quasi-States', 43 *Journal of Peace Research*, 2006, p. 723.

[210] See Report of the UN Secretary-General on the Situation in Somalia, S/2001/963, paras. 16 ff. (2001).

[211] See e.g. the provision of assistance to the authorities of the area by the UK and the visit to the UK and meetings with UK government officials by the 'president of Somaliland' in July 2006: see FCO Press Release, 16 August 2006. See also UKMIL, 76 BYIL, 2005, p. 715.

a majority ethnic Armenian population, declared its independence from Azerbaijan. However, it has not been recognised by any state (including Armenia) and the UN Security Council adopted resolutions 822, 853, 874 and 884 reaffirming the sovereign and territorial integrity of Azerbaijan and calling for withdrawal from the occupied territories of Azerbaijan.[212] The former USSR republic of Moldova became independent on 23 June 1990 as the USSR dissolved. On 2 September 1990 the 'Moldavian Republic of Transdniestria' was proclaimed as an independent state in an area of Moldova bordering Ukraine. This entity has been able to maintain itself as a result of Russian assistance. However, it has not been recognised by any state.[213] Similarly, the areas of South Ossetia and Abkhazia in Georgia have sought to establish separate *de facto* governments and independence respectively with Russian support and have similarly not been recognised by any state.[214]

Associations of states

There are a number of ways in which states have become formally associated with one another. Such associations do not constitute states but have a certain effect upon international law. Confederations, for example, are probably the closest form of co-operation and they generally involve several countries acting together by virtue of an international agreement, with some kind of central institutions with limited functions.[215] This is to be contrasted with federations. A federal unit is a state with strong

---

[212] See e.g. the Reports of the International Crisis Group on Nagorno-Karabakh of 14 September 2005, 11 October 2005 and 14 November 2007. See also resolution 1416 of the Council of Europe Parliamentary Assembly, 2005.

[213] See the Reports of the International Crisis Group on Moldova of 12 August 2003, 17 June 2004 and 17 August 2006. See also *Ilascu* v. *Moldova and Russia*, European Court of Human Rights, judgment of 8 July 2004, pp. 8–40.

[214] See the Reports of the International Crisis Group on South Ossetia of 26 November 2004, 19 April 2005 and 7 June 2007, and the Reports on Abkhazia of 15 September 2006 and 18 January 2007.

[215] Note, for example, the Preliminary Agreement Concerning the Establishment of a Confederation between the Federation of Bosnia and Herzegovina and the Republic of Croatia, 1994, 33 ILM, 1994, p. 605. This Agreement 'anticipated' the creation of a Confederation, but provides that its 'establishment shall not change the international identity or legal personality of Croatia or of the Federation'. The Agreement provided for co-operation between the parties in a variety of areas and for Croatia to grant the Federation of Bosnia and Herzegovina free access to the Adriatic through its territory. This Confederation did not come about.

centralised organs and usually a fairly widespread bureaucracy with extensive powers over the citizens of the state, even though the powers of the state are divided between the different units.[216] However, a state may comprise component units with extensive powers.[217]

There are in addition certain 'associated states' which by virtue of their smallness and lack of development have a close relationship with another state. One instance is the connection between the Cook Islands and New Zealand, where internal self-government is allied to external dependence.[218] Another example was the group of islands which constituted the Associated States of the West Indies. These were tied to the United Kingdom by the terms of the West Indies Act 1967, which provided for the latter to exercise control with regard to foreign and defence issues. Nevertheless, such states were able to and did attain their independence.[219]

The status of such entities in an association relationship with a state will depend upon the constitutional nature of the arrangement and may in certain circumstances involve international personality distinct from the metropolitan state depending also upon international acceptance. It must, however, be noted that such status is one of the methods accepted by the UN of exercising the right to self-determination.[220] Provided that an acceptable level of powers, including those dealing with domestic affairs, remain with the associated state, and that the latter may without undue difficulty revoke the arrangement, some degree of personality would appear desirable and acceptable.

The Commonwealth of Nations (the former British Commonwealth) is perhaps the most well known of the loose associations which group together sovereign states on the basis usually of common interests and historical ties. Its members are all fully independent states who cooperate through the assistance of the Commonwealth Secretariat and periodic conferences of Heads of Government. Regular meetings of particular ministers also take place. The Commonwealth does not constitute

---

[216] See Crawford, *Creation of States*, pp. 479 ff., and above, p. 217. See also with regard to the proposed arrangement between Gambia and Senegal, 21 ILM, 1982, pp. 44–7.

[217] See e.g. the Dayton Peace Agreement 1995, Annex 4 laying down the constitution of Bosnia and Herzegovina as an independent state consisting of two Entities, the Federation of Bosnia and Herzegovina and the Republika Srpska. The boundary between the two Entities was laid down in Annex 2.

[218] Crawford, *Creation of States*, pp. 625 ff. See also as regards Puerto Rico and Niue, *ibid.*

[219] See e.g. J. E. S. Fawcett, *Annual Survey of Commonwealth Law*, London, 1967, pp. 709–11.

[220] See, with regard to the successors of the trust territory of the Pacific, above, p. 224.

a legally binding relationship, but operates as a useful forum for discussions. Relations between Commonwealth members display certain special characteristics, for example, ambassadors are usually referred to as High Commissioners. It would appear unlikely in the circumstances that it possesses separate international personality.[221] However, the more that the Commonwealth develops distinctive institutions and establishes common policies with the capacity to take binding decisions, the more the argument may be made for international legal personality.

Following the dissolution of the Soviet Union and the coming to independence of the constituent Republics, with the Russian Federation being deemed the continuation of the Soviet Union, it was decided to establish the Commonwealth of Independent States.[222] Originally formed by Russia, Belarus and Ukraine on 8 December 1991, it was enlarged on 21 December 1991 to include eleven former Republics of the USSR. Georgia joined the CIS on 8 October 1993. Thus all the former Soviet Republics, excluding the three Baltic states, are now members of that organisation.[223] The agreement establishing the CIS provided for respect for human rights and other principles and called for co-ordination between the member states. The Charter of the CIS was adopted on 22 June 1993 as a binding international treaty[224] and laid down a series of principles ranging from respect for the sovereignty and territorial integrity of states, self-determination of peoples, prohibition of the use or threat of force and settlement of disputes by peaceful means. It was noted that the CIS was neither a state nor 'supranational' (article 1) and a number of common co-ordinating institutions were established. In particular, the Council of Heads of State is the 'highest body of the Commonwealth' and it may 'take decisions on the principal issues relating to the activity of the member states in the field of their mutual interests' (article 21), while the Council of the Heads of Government has the function of co-ordinating co-operation among executive organs of member states (article 22). Both Councils may

---

[221] See J. E. S. Fawcett, *The British Commonwealth in International Law*, London, 1963; *Oppenheim's International Law*, p. 256; O'Connell, *International Law*, pp. 346–56; Whiteman, *Digest*, vol. I, pp. 476–544; Rousseau, *Droit International Public*, vol. II, pp. 214–64, and Sale, *The Modern Commonwealth*, 1983. See also, as regards the French Community, Whiteman, *Digest*, pp. 544–82, and O'Connell, *International Law*, pp. 356–9.

[222] See e.g. J. Lippott, 'The Commonwealth of Independent States as an Economic and Legal Community', 39 German YIL, 1996, p. 334.

[223] See 31 ILM, 1992, pp. 138 and 147, and 34 ILM, 1995, p. 1298.

[224] See 34 ILM, 1995, p. 1279.

take decisions on the basis of consensus (article 23). A Council of Foreign Ministers was also established together with a Co-ordination and Consultative Committee, as a permanent executive and co-ordinating body of the Commonwealth.[225] The CIS has adopted in addition a Treaty on Economic Union[226] and a Convention on Human Rights and Fundamental Freedoms.[227] The increasing development of the CIS as a directing international institution suggests its possession of international legal personality.

The European Union[228] is an association, of twenty-seven states, which has established a variety of common institutions and which has the competence to adopt not only legal acts binding upon member states but also acts having direct effect within domestic legal systems. The Union consists essentially of the European Community (itself an amalgam of the European Coal and Steel Community, EURATOM and the European Economic Community) and two additional pillars, viz. the Common Foreign and Security Policy, and Justice and Home Affairs. Only the European Coal and Steel Community Treaty provided explicitly for international legal personality (article 6), but the case-law of the European Court of Justice demonstrates its belief that the other two communities also possess such personality.[229] It is also established that Community law has superiority over domestic law. The European Court of Justice early in the history of the Community declared that the Community constituted 'a new legal order of international law'.[230] In the circumstances, it seems hard to deny that the Community possesses international legal personality, but

---

[225] Note also the creation of the Council of Defence Ministers, the Council of Frontier Troops Chief Commanders, an Economic Court, a Commission on Human Rights, an Organ of Branch Co-operation and an Interparliamentary Assembly (articles 30–5).

[226] 24 September 1993, 34 ILM, 1995, p. 1298.

[227] 26 May 1995, see Council of Europe Information Sheet No. 36, 1995, p. 195.

[228] Established as such by article A, Title I of the Treaty on European Union (Maastricht) signed in February 1992 and in force as from 1 January 1993. See also the Treaty of Amsterdam, 1997, the Treaty of Nice, 2001 and the Treaty of Lisbon, 2007.

[229] See e.g. *Costa* v. *ENEL* [1964] ECR 585, 593; *Commission* v. *Council* [1971] ECR 263, 274; *Kramer* [1976] ECR 1279, 1308 and *Protection of Nuclear Materials* [1978] ECR 2151, 2179; *The Oxford Encyclopaedia of European Community Law* (ed. A. Toth), Oxford, 1991, p. 351; D. Lasok and J. Bridge, *Law and Institutions of the European Union* (ed. P. Lasok), 6th edn, London, 1994, chapter 2, and S. Weatherill and P. Beaumont, *EU Law*, 3rd edn, London, 1999. See also A. Peters, 'The Position of International Law Within the European Community Legal Order', 40 German YIL, 1997, p. 9, and D. Chalmers and A. Tomkins, *European Union Public Law*, Cambridge, 2007.

[230] *Van Gend en Loos* v. *Nederlandse Administratie des Belastingen* [1963] ECR 1.

unlikely that the co-operative processes involved in the additional two pillars are so endowed.[231] The European Community has the power to conclude and negotiate agreements in line with its external powers, to become a member of an international organisation and to have delegations in non-member countries. However, the Treaty on European Union contained no provision on the legal personality of the Union. The Union does not have institutionalised treaty-making powers, but is able to conclude agreements through the Council of the European Union or by asserting its position on the international stage, especially in connection with the Common Foreign and Security Policy. However, article 55 of the Treaty of Lisbon, 2007 provides for the insertion into the Treaty on European Union of a new article 46A, which expressly asserts that the European Union has legal personality.[232]

Conclusions

Whether or not the entities discussed above constitute international persons or indeed states or merely part of some other international person is a matter for careful consideration in the light of the circumstances of the case, in particular the claims made by the entity in question, the facts on the ground, especially with regard to third-party control and the degree of administrative effectiveness manifested, and the reaction of other international persons. The importance here of recognition, acquiescence and estoppel is self-evident. Acceptance of some international personality need not be objective so as to bind non-consenting states nor unlimited as to time and content factors. These elements will be considered below. It should, however, be noted here that the international community itself also has needs and interests that bear upon this question as to international status. This is particularly so with regard to matters of responsibility and the protection of persons via the rules governing the recourse to and conduct of armed conflicts.[233]

---

[231] See e.g. the Second Legal Adviser of the Foreign and Commonwealth Office, UKMIL, 63 BYIL, 1992, p. 660. But see also *Oppenheim's International Law*, p. 20. Note also the European Court of Justice's *Opinion No. 1/94, Community Competence to Conclude Certain International Agreements* [1994] ECR I-5276; 108 ILR, p. 225.

[232] The Treaty of Lisbon, 2007 is not yet in force.

[233] As to the specific regime established in the Antarctica Treaty, 1959, see below, p. 535. See also below, p. 628, with regard to the International Seabed Authority under the Law of the Sea Convention, 1982.

Special cases

The Sovereign Order of Malta

This Order, established during the Crusades as a military and medical association, ruled Rhodes from 1309 to 1522 and was given Malta by treaty with Charles V in 1530 as a fief of the Kingdom of Sicily. This sovereignty was lost in 1798, and in 1834 the Order established its headquarters in Rome as a humanitarian organisation.[234] The Order already had international personality at the time of its taking control of Malta and even when it had to leave the island it continued to exchange diplomatic legations with most European countries. The Italian Court of Cassation in 1935 recognised the international personality of the Order, noting that 'the modern theory of the subjects of international law recognises a number of collective units whose composition is independent of the nationality of their constituent members and whose scope transcends by virtue of their universal character the territorial confines of any single state'.[235] This is predicated upon the functional needs of the entity as accepted by third parties. It is to be noted, for example, that the Order maintains diplomatic relations with or is recognised by over eighty states and has observer status in the UN General Assembly.[236] It is not a state and it is questionable whether it has general international personality beyond those states and organisations expressly recognising it.[237]

The Holy See and the Vatican City[238]

In 1870, the conquest of the Papal states by Italian forces ended their existence as sovereign states. The question therefore arose as to the status

---

[234] *Oppenheim's International Law*, p. 329, note 7; O'Connell, *International Law*, pp. 85–6, and Whiteman, *Digest*, vol. I, pp. 584–7. See also Crawford, *Creation of States*, pp. 231 ff., and B. J. Theutenberg, *The Holy See, the Order of Malta and International Law*, Skara, 2003.

[235] *Nanni v. Pace and the Sovereign Order of Malta* 8 AD, p. 2. See also *Scarfò v. Sovereign Order of Malta* 24 ILR, p. 1; *Sovereign Order of Malta v. Soc. An. Commerciale* 22 ILR, p. 1, and Cassese, *International Law*, pp. 132–3.

[236] Crawford, *Creation of States*, p. 231.   [237] *Ibid.*, p. 233.

[238] See *Oppenheim's International Law*, p. 325; Crawford, *Creation of States*, pp. 221 ff.; J. Duursma, *Fragmentation and the International Relations of Microstates: Self-determination and Statehood*, Cambridge, 1996, pp. 374 ff.; Rousseau, *Droit International Public*, vol. II, pp. 353–77; *Le Saint-Siège dans les Relations Internationales* (ed. J. P. D'Onorio), Aix-en-Provence, 1989, and R. Graham, *Vatican Diplomacy: A Study of Church and State on the International Plane*, Princeton, 1959. See also Nguyen Quoc Dinh *et al.*, *Droit International Public*, p. 455.

in international law of the Holy See, deprived, as it then was, of normal territorial sovereignty. In 1929 the Lateran Treaty was signed with Italy which recognised the state of the Vatican City and 'the sovereignty of the Holy See in the field of international relations as an attribute that pertains to the very nature of the Holy See, in conformity with its traditions and with the demands of its mission in the world'.[239] The question thus interrelates with the problem of the status today of the Vatican City. The latter has no permanent population apart from Church functionaries and exists only to support the work of the Holy See. Italy carries out a substantial number of administrative functions with regard to the City. Some writers accordingly have concluded that it cannot be regarded as a state.[240] Nevertheless, it is a party to many international treaties and is a member of the Universal Postal Union and the International Telecommunications Union. It would appear that by virtue of recognition and acquiescence in the context of its claims, it does exist as a state. The Vatican City is closely linked with the Holy See and they are essentially part of the same construct.

The Holy See, the central organisational authority of the Catholic Church, continued after 1870 to engage in diplomatic relations and enter into international agreements and concordats.[241] Accordingly its status as an international person was accepted by such partners. In its joint eleventh and twelfth report submitted to the UN Committee on the Elimination of Racial Discrimination in 1993,[242] the Holy See reminded the Committee of its 'exceptional nature within the community of nations; as a sovereign subject of international law, it has a mission of an essentially religious and moral order, universal in scope, which is based on minimal territorial dimensions guaranteeing a basis of autonomy for the pastoral ministry of the Sovereign Pontiff'.[243] Crawford has concluded that the Holy See is both an international legal person in its own right and the government of a state (the Vatican City).[244]

---

[239] 130 BFSP, p. 791. See also O'Connell, *International Law*, p. 289, and *Re Marcinkus, Mennini and De Strobel* 87 ILR, p. 48.

[240] See M. Mendelson, 'The Diminutive States in the United Nations', 21 ICLQ, 1972, p. 609. See also Brownlie, *Principles*, p. 64.

[241] See e.g. the Fundamental Agreement between the Holy See and the State of Israel of 30 December 1993, 33 ILM, 1994, p. 153.

[242] CERD/C/226/Add. 6 (15 February 1993).

[243] See also the decision of the Philippines Supreme Court (en banc) in *The Holy See* v. *Starbright Sales Enterprises Inc.* 102 ILR, p. 163.

[244] Crawford, *Creation of States*, p. 230. The International Committee of the Red Cross also appears on the basis of state practice, particularly its participation in international

Insurgents and belligerents

International law has recognised that such entities may in certain circumstances, primarily dependent upon the *de facto* administration of specific territory, enter into valid arrangements.[245] In addition they will be bound by the rules of international law with respect to the conduct of hostilities and may in due course be recognised as governments. The traditional law is in process of modification as a result of the right to self-determination, and other legal principles such as territorial integrity, sovereign equality and non-intervention in addition to recognition will need to be taken into account.[246]

National liberation movements (NLMs)

The question of whether or not NLMs constitute subjects of international law and, if so, to what extent, is bound up with the development of the law relating to non-self-governing territories and the principle of self-determination. What is noticeable is not only the increasing status of NLMs during the decolonisation period, but also the fact that in many cases the international community turned to bodies other than the NLMs in controversial situations.

The UN trusteeship system permitted the hearing of individual petitioners and this was extended to all colonial territories. In 1977, the General Assembly Fourth Committee voted to permit representatives of certain NLMs from Portugal's African territories to participate in its work dealing with such territories.[247] The General Assembly endorsed the concept of observer status for liberation movements recognised by the Organisation of African Unity in resolution 2918 (XVII). In resolution 3247 (XXIX), the Assembly accepted that NLMs recognised by the OAU or

---

agreements, to be an international legal person to a limited extent: see Cassese, *International Law*, pp. 133–4.

[245] See *Oppenheim's International Law*, p. 165; Lauterpacht, *Recognition*, pp. 494–5; Brownlie, *Principles*, p. 63, and T. C. Chen, *Recognition*, London, 1951. See also Cassese, *International Law*, pp. 124 ff.; S. C. Neff, 'The Prerogatives of Violence – In Search of the Conceptual Foundations of Belligerents' Rights', 38 German YIL, 1995, p. 41, and Neff, *The Rights and Duties of Neutrals*, Manchester, 2000, pp. 200 ff.

[246] See below, p. 251.

[247] See M. N. Shaw, 'The International Status of National Liberation Movements', 5 *Liverpool Law Review*, 1983, p. 19, and R. Ranjeva, 'Peoples and National Liberation Movements' in *International Law: Achievements and Prospects* (ed. M. Bedjaoui), Paris, 1991, p. 101. See also Cassese, *International Law*, pp. 140 ff., and H. Wilson, *International Law and the Use of Force by National Liberation Movements*, Oxford, 1988.

the Arab League could participate in Assembly sessions, in conferences arranged under the auspices of the Assembly and in meetings of the UN specialised agencies and the various Assembly organs.[248]

The inclusion of the regional recognition requirement was intended both to require a minimum level of effectiveness with regard to the organisation concerned before UN acceptance and to exclude in practice secessionist movements. The Economic and Social Committee of the UN has also adopted a similar approach and under its procedural rules it may invite any NLM recognised by or in accordance with General Assembly resolutions to take part in relevant debates without a vote.[249]

The UN Security Council also permitted the Palestine Liberation Organisation (PLO) to participate in its debates with the same rights of participation as conferred upon a member state not a member of the Security Council, although this did raise serious constitutional questions.[250] Thus the possibility of observer status in the UN and related organs for NLMs appears to have been affirmatively settled in international practice. The question of international personality, however, is more complex and more significant, and recourse must be made to state practice.[251] Whether extensive state recognition of a liberation movement is of itself sufficient to confer such status is still a controversial issue.

The position of the PLO, however, began to evolve considerably with the Israel–PLO Declaration of Principles on Interim Self-Government Arrangements signed in Washington on 13 September 1993.[252] By virtue of

---

[248] While the leader of the PAIGC was not permitted to speak at the Assembly in 1973, the leader of the PLO was able to address the body in 1974: see A/C.4/SR.1978 p. 23 and resolution 3237 (XXIX).

[249] ECOSOC resolution 1949 (LVII), 8 May 1975, rule 73. See also, as regards the Human Rights Commission, CHR/Res.19 (XXIX). The General Assembly and ECOSOC have also called upon the specialised agencies and other UN-related organisations to assist the peoples and NLMs of colonial territories: see e.g. Assembly resolutions 33/41 and 35/29.

[250] See *Yearbook of the UN*, 1972, p. 70 and 1978, p. 297; S/PV 1859 (1975); S/PV 1870 (1976); *UN Chronicle*, April 1982, p. 16, and DUSPIL, 1975, pp. 73–5. See also Shaw, 'International Status'.

[251] See the *UN Headquarters Agreement* case, ICJ Reports, 1988, p. 12; 82 ILR, p. 225.

[252] 32 ILM, 1993, p. 1525. Note that letters of mutual recognition and commitment to the peace process were exchanged between the Prime Minister of Israel and the Chairman of the PLO on 9 September 1993. See e.g. K. Calvo-Goller, 'L'Accord du 13 Séptembre 1993 entre L'Israël et l'OLP: Le Régime d'Autonomie Prévu par la Déclaration Israël/OLP', AFDI, 1993, p. 435. See also Crawford, *Creation of States*, pp. 442 ff.; *New Political Entities in Public and Private International Law* (eds. A. Shapira and M. Tabory), The Hague, 1999; E. Benvenisti, 'The Status of the Palestinian Authority' in *Arab–Israeli Accords: Legal Perspectives* (eds. E. Cotrain and C. Mallat), The Hague, 1996, p. 47, and Benvenisti,

this Declaration, the PLO team in the Jordanian–Palestinian delegation to the Middle East Peace Conference was accepted as representing the Palestinian people. It was agreed to establish a Palestinian Interim Self-Government Authority as an elected Council for the Palestinian people in the West Bank and Gaza (occupied by Israel since 1967) for a transitional period of up to five years leading to a permanent solution. Its jurisdiction was to cover the territory of the West Bank and Gaza, save for issues to be negotiated in the permanent status negotiations. Upon the entry into force of the Declaration, a transfer of authority was to commence from the Israel military government and its civil administration. The Cairo Agreement of 4 May 1994[253] provided for the immediate withdrawal of Israeli forces from Jericho and the Gaza Strip and transfer of authority to a separately established Palestinian Authority. This Authority, distinct from the PLO it should be emphasised, was to have certain specified legislative, executive and judicial powers. The process continued with a transfer of further powers and responsibilities in a Protocol of 27 August 1995 and with the Interim Agreement on the West Bank and Gaza of 28 September 1995, under which an additional range of powers and responsibilities was transferred to the Palestinian Authority pending the election of the Council and arrangements were made for Israeli withdrawal from a number of cities and villages on the West Bank.[254] An accord concerning Hebron followed in 1997[255] and the Wye River agreement in 1998, both marking further Israeli redeployments, while the Sharm el Sheikh memorandum and a later Protocol of 1999 concerned safe-passage arrangements between the Palestinian Authority areas in Gaza and the West Bank.[256] The increase in the territorial and jurisdictional competence of the Palestinian Authority established as a consequence of these arrangements raised the question of legal personality. While Palestinian statehood has clearly not been accepted by the international community, the Palestinian Authority can be regarded as possessing some form of limited international

---

'The Israeli–Palestinian Declaration of Principles: A Framework for Future Settlement', 4 EJIL, 1993, p. 542, and P. Malanczuk, 'Some Basic Aspects of the Agreements Between Israel and the PLO from the Perspective of International Law', 7 EJIL, 1996, p. 485.

[253] 33 ILM, 1994, p. 622.

[254] See e.g. M. Benchikh, 'L'Accord Intérimaire Israélo-Palestinien sur la Cisjordanie et la bande de Gaza du 28 September 1995', AFDI, 1995, p. 7, and *The Arab–Israeli Accords: Legal Perspectives* (eds. E. Cotran and C. Mallat), The Hague, 1996.

[255] See e.g. A. Bockel, 'L'Accord d'Hebron (17 janvier 1997) et la Tentative de Relance du Processus de Paix Israélo-Palestinien', AFDI, 1997, p. 184.

[256] See A. Bockel, 'L'Issue du Processus de Paix Israélo-Palestinien en Vue?', AFDI, 1999, p. 165.

personality.[257] Such personality, however, derives from the agreements between Israel and the PLO and exists separately from the personality of the PLO as an NLM, which relies upon the recognition of third parties.[258]

As far as Namibia was concerned, the territory was regarded as having an international status[259] and there existed an NLM recognised as the authentic representative of the people[260] but it was, theoretically, administered by the UN Council for Namibia. This body was established in 1967 by the General Assembly in order to administer the territory and to prepare it for independence; it was disbanded in 1990. There were thirty-one UN member states on the Council, which was responsible to the General Assembly.[261] The Council sought to represent Namibian interests in international organisations and in conferences, and issued travel and identity documents to Namibians which were recognised by most states.[262] In 1974, the Council issued Decree No. 1 which sought to forbid the exploitation under South African auspices of the territory's resources, but little was in practice achieved by this Decree, which was not drafted in the clearest possible manner.[263] The status of the Council was unclear, but it was clearly recognised as having a role within the UN context and may thus have possessed some form of qualified personality. It was, of course, distinct from SWAPO, the recognised NLM.

International public companies

This type of entity, which may be known by a variety of names, for example multinational public enterprises or international bodies

---

[257] See e.g. K. Reece Thomas, 'Non-Recognition, Personality and Capacity: The Palestine Liberation Organisation and the Palestinian Authority in English Law', 29 *Anglo-American Law Review*, 2000, p. 228; *New Political Entities in Public and Private International Law With Special Reference to the Palestinian Entity* (eds. A. Shapiro and M. Tabory), The Hague, 1999, and C. Wasserstein Fassberg, 'Israel and the Palestinian Authority', 28 *Israel Law Review*, 1994, p. 319.

[258] See e.g. M. Tabory, 'The Legal Personality of the Palestinian Autonomy' in Shapira and Tabory, *New Political Entities*, p. 139.

[259] The *Namibia* case, ICJ Reports, 1971, p. 16; 49 ILR, p. 3.

[260] Assembly resolution 3295 (XXIX), recognising the South-West Africa People's Organisation (SWAPO) as the authentic representative of the Namibian people.

[261] The UK did not recognise the Council: see 408 HL Deb., col. 758, 23 April 1980.

[262] See e.g. J. F. Engers, 'The UN Travel and Identity Documents for Namibia', 65 AJIL, 1971, p. 571.

[263] See *Decolonisation*, No. 9, December 1977.

corporate, is characterised in general by an international agreement providing for co-operation between governmental and private enterprises.[264] One writer, for example, defined such entities as corporations which

> have not been constituted by the exclusive application of one national law; whose members and directors represent several national sovereignties; whose legal personality is not based, or at any rate not entirely, on the decision of a national authority or the application of a national law; whose operations, finally, are governed, at least partially, by rules that do not stem from a single or even from several national laws.[265]

Such enterprises may vary widely in constitutional nature and in competences. Examples of such companies would include INTELSAT, established in 1973 as an intergovernmental structure for a global commercial telecommunications satellite system; Eurofima, established in 1955 by fourteen European states in order to lease equipment to the railway administrations of those states, and the Bank of International Settlement, created in 1930 by virtue of a treaty between five states, and the host country, Switzerland. The personality question will depend upon the differences between municipal and international personality. If the entity is given a range of powers and is distanced sufficiently from municipal law, an international person may be involved, but it will require careful consideration of the circumstances.

Transnational corporations

Another possible candidate for international personality is the transnational or multinational enterprise. Various definitions exist of this important phenomenon in international relations.[266] They in essence constitute

---

[264] See e.g. D. Fligler, *Multinational Public Corporations*, Washington, DC, 1967; Brownlie, *Principles*, pp. 65–6, and D. A. Ijalaye, *The Extension of Corporate Personality in International Law*, Leiden, 1978, pp. 57–146. See also P. Muchlinski, *Multinational Enterprises and the Law*, updated edn, Oxford, 1999.

[265] Cited in Ijalaye, *Corporate Personality*, p. 69.

[266] See e.g. C. W. Jenks, in *Transnational Law in a Changing Society* (eds. W. Friedman, L. Henkin and O. Lissitzyn), New York, 1972, p. 70; H. Baade, in *Legal Problems of a Code of Conduct for Multinational Enterprises* (ed. N. Horn), Boston, 1980; J. Charney, 'Transnational Corporations and Developing Public International Law', *Duke Law Journal*, 1983, p. 748; F. Rigaux, 'Transnational Corporations' in Bedjaoui, *International Law: Achievements and Prospects*, p. 121, and Henkin *et al.*, *International Law: Cases*

private business organisations comprising several legal entities linked together by parent corporations and are distinguished by size and multinational spread. In the years following the *Barcelona Traction* case,[267] an
increasing amount of practice has been evident on the international plane
dealing with such corporations. What has been sought is a set of guidelines
governing the major elements of the international conduct of these entities.[268] However, progress has been slow and several crucial issues remain
to be resolved, including the legal effect, if any, of such guidelines.[269] The
question of the international personality of transnational corporations
remains an open one.[270]

---

and Materials, p. 368. See also Muchlinski, *Multinational Enterprises*; C. M. Vazquez,
'Direct vs Indirect Obligations of Corporations under International Law', 43 *Columbia
Journal of Transnational Law*, 2005, p. 927; F. Johns, 'The Invisibility of the Transnational Corporation: An Analysis of International Law and Legal Theory', 19 *Melbourne
University Law Review*, 1993–4, p. 893; D. Eshanov, 'The Role of Multinational Corporations from the Neoinstitutionalist and International Law Perspectives', 16 *New York
University Environmental Law Journal*, 2008, p. 110, and S. R. Ratner, 'Corporations
and Human Rights: A Theory of Legal Responsibility', 111 *Yale Law Journal*, 2001,
p. 443.

[267] ICJ Reports, 1970, pp. 3, 46–7; 46 ILR, pp. 178, 220–1.

[268] See e.g. OECD Guidelines for Multinational Enterprises, 75 US Dept. State Bull., p. 83
(1976), and ILO Tripartite Declaration of Principles concerning Multinational Enterprises
and Social Policy, 17 ILM, pp. 423–30. See also Baade, *Legal Problems*, pp. 416–40. Note
the OECD Principles of Corporate Governance, 1998 and the ILO Tripartite Declaration
of Principles concerning Multinational Enterprises and Social Policy, 2000. See also the
Draft Norms on Responsibilities for Transnational Corporations and Other Business Enterprises with Regard to Human Rights produced by the UN Sub-Commission on the
Promotion and Protection of Human Rights' Sessional Working Group on the working methods and activities of transnational corporations, E/CN.4/Sub.2/2002/13, August
2002, and *Human Rights Standards and the Responsibilities of Transnational Corporations*
(ed. M. Addo), The Hague, 1999.

[269] See the Draft Code of Conduct produced by the UN Commission on Transnational Corporations, 22 ILM, pp. 177–206; 23 ILM, p. 627 and *ibid.*, p. 602 (Secretariat report on
outstanding issues); E/1990/94 (1990) and the World Bank Guidelines on the Treatment
of Foreign Direct Investment, 31 ILM, 1992, p. 1366. The Commission ceased work in
1993. The Sub-Commission on the Promotion and Protection of Human Rights adopted
'Norms on the Responsibilities of Transnational Corporations and Other Business Enterprises with Regard to Human Rights' in 2003: see E/CN.4/Sub.2/2003/12/Rev.2. Note the
Andean Group commission decision 292 on a uniform code on Andean multinational
enterprises, 30 ILM, 1991, p. 1295, and the Eastern and Southern African states charter
on a regime of multinational industrial enterprises, *ibid.*, p. 696. See also the previous
footnote.

[270] The *Third US Restatement of Foreign Relations Law*, St Paul, 1987, p. 126 notes that the
transnational corporation, while an established feature of international life, 'has not yet
achieved independent status in international law'.

The right of all peoples to self-determination[271]

The establishment of the legal right

This principle, which traces its origin to the concepts of nationality and democracy as evolved primarily in Europe, first appeared in major form after the First World War. Despite President Wilson's efforts, it was not included in the League of Nations Covenant and it was clearly not regarded as a legal principle.[272] However, its influence can be detected in the various provisions for minority protection[273] and in the establishment of the mandates system based as it was upon the sacred trust concept. In the ten years before the Second World War, there was relatively little practice regarding self-determination in international law. A number of treaties concluded by the USSR in this period noted the principle,[274] but in the *Aaland Islands* case it was clearly accepted by both the International Commission of Jurists and the Committee of Rapporteurs dealing with the situation that the principle of self-determination was not a legal rule of international law, but purely a political concept.[275] The situation,

---

[271] See in general e.g. A. Cassese, *Self-Determination of Peoples*, Cambridge, 1995; K. Knop, *Diversity and Self-Determination in International Law*, Cambridge, 2002; U. O. Umozurike, *Self-Determination in International Law*, Hamden, 1972; A. Rigo-Sureda, *The Evolution of the Right of Self-Determination*, Leiden, 1973; M. Pomerance, *Self-Determination in Law and Practice*, Leiden, 1982; Shaw, *Title to Territory*, pp. 59–144; A. E. Buchanan, *Justice, Legitimacy and Self-Determination*, Oxford, 2004; D. Raic, *Statehood and the Law of Self-Determination*, The Hague, 2002; Crawford, *Creation of States*, pp. 107 ff., and Crawford, 'The General Assembly, the International Court and Self-Determination' in *Fifty Years of the International Court of Justice* (eds. A. V. Lowe and M. Fitzmaurice), Cambridge, 1996, p. 585; Rousseau, *Droit International Public*, vol. II, pp. 17–35; Wilson, *International Law*; Tunkin, *Theory*, pp. 60–9; and Tomuschat, *Modern Law of Self-Determination*. See also M. Koskenniemi, 'National Self-Determination Today: Problems of Legal Theory and Practice', 43 ICLQ, 1994, p. 241; H. Quane, 'The UN and the Evolving Right to Self-Determination', 47 ICLQ, 1998, p. 537, and W. Ofuatey-Kodjoe, 'Self Determination' in *United Nations Legal Order* (eds. O. Schachter and C. Joyner), Cambridge, 1995, vol. I, p. 349.

[272] See A. Cobban, *The Nation-State and National Self-Determination*, London, 1969; D. H. Miller, *The Drafting of the Covenant*, New York, 1928, vol. II, pp. 12–13; S. Wambaugh, *Plebiscites since the World War*, Washington, 1933, vol. I, p. 42, and Pomerance, *Self-Determination*.

[273] See e.g. I. Claude, *National Minorities*, Cambridge, 1955, and J. Lador-Lederer, *International Group Protection*, Leiden, 1968.

[274] See e.g. the Baltic States' treaties, Martens, *Recueil Général de Traités*, 3rd Series, XI, pp. 864, 877 and 888, and Cobban, *Nation-State*, pp. 187–218. See also Whiteman, *Digest*, vol. IV, p. 56.

[275] LNOJ Supp. No. 3, 1920, pp. 5–6 and Doc. B7/21/68/106[VII], pp. 22–3. See also J. Barros, *The Aaland Islands Question*, New Haven, 1968, and Verzijl, *International Law*, pp. 328–32.

which concerned the Swedish inhabitants of an island alleged to be part of Finland, was resolved by the League's recognition of Finnish sovereignty coupled with minority guarantees.

The Second World War stimulated further consideration of the idea and the principle was included in the UN Charter. Article 1(2) noted as one of the organisation's purposes the development of friendly relations among nations based upon respect for the principle of equal rights and self-determination, and article 55 reiterated the phraseology. It is disputed whether the reference to the principle in these very general terms was sufficient to entail its recognition as a binding right, but the majority view is against this. Not every statement of a political aim in the Charter can be regarded as automatically creative of legal obligations. On the other hand, its inclusion in the Charter, particularly within the context of the statement of purposes of the UN, provided the opportunity for the subsequent interpretation of the principle both in terms of its legal effect and consequences and with regard to its definition. It is also to be noted that Chapters XI and XII of the Charter deal with non-self-governing and trust territories and may be seen as relevant within the context of the development and definition of the right to self-determination, although the term is not expressly used.[276]

Practice since 1945 within the UN, both generally as regards the elucidation and standing of the principle and more particularly as regards its perceived application in specific instances, can be seen as having ultimately established the legal standing of the right in international law. This may be achieved either by treaty or by custom or indeed, more controversially, by virtue of constituting a general principle of law. All these routes are relevant, as will be seen. The UN Charter is a multilateral treaty which can be interpreted by subsequent practice, while the range of state and organisation practice evident within the UN system can lead to the formation of customary law. The amount of material dealing with self-determination in the UN testifies to the importance of the concept and some of the more significant of this material will be briefly noted.

Resolution 1514 (XV), the Declaration on the Granting of Independence to Colonial Countries and Peoples, adopted in 1960 by eighty-nine votes to none, with nine abstentions, stressed that:

---

[276] See e.g. O'Connell, *International Law*, p. 312; N. Bentwich and A. Martin, *Commentary on the Charter of the UN*, New York, 1950, p. 7; D. Nincic, *The Problem of Sovereignty in the Charter and the Practice of States*, The Hague, 1970, p. 221; H. Kelsen, *Law of the United Nations*, London, 1950, pp. 51–3, and H. Lauterpacht, *International Law and Human Rights*, The Hague, 1950, pp. 147–9. See also Judge Tanaka, *South-West Africa* cases, ICJ Reports, 1966, pp. 288–9; 37 ILR, pp. 243, 451–2.

all peoples have the right to self-determination; by virtue of that right they freely determine their political status and freely pursue their economic, social and cultural development.

Inadequacy of political, social, economic or educational preparedness was not to serve as a protest for delaying independence, while attempts aimed at the partial or total disruption of the national unity and territorial integrity of a country were deemed incompatible with the UN Charter. The Colonial Declaration set the terms for the self-determination debate in its emphasis upon the colonial context and its opposition to secession, and has been regarded by some as constituting a binding interpretation of the Charter.[277] The Declaration was reinforced by the establishment of a Special Committee on Decolonisation, which now deals with all dependent territories and has proved extremely active, and by the fact that virtually all UN resolutions dealing with self-determination expressly refer to it. Indeed, the International Court has specifically referred to the Colonial Declaration as an 'important stage' in the development of international law regarding non-self-governing territories and as the 'basis for the process of decolonisation'.[278]

In 1966, the General Assembly adopted the International Covenants on Human Rights. Both these Covenants have an identical first article, declaring *inter alia* that '[a]ll peoples have the right to self-determination. By virtue of that right they freely determine their political status', while states parties to the instruments 'shall promote the realisation of the right of self-determination and shall respect that right in conformity with the provisions of the Charter of the United Nations'. The Covenants came into force in 1976 and thus constitute binding provisions as between the parties, but in addition they also may be regarded as authoritative interpretations of several human rights provisions in the Charter, including self-determination. The 1970 Declaration on Principles of International Law Concerning Friendly Relations can be regarded as constituting an authoritative interpretation of the seven Charter provisions it expounds. The Declaration states *inter alia* that 'by virtue of the principle of equal rights and self-determination of peoples enshrined in the Charter of the United Nations, all people have the right freely to determine ... their political status' while all states are under the duty to respect this right in accordance with the Charter. The Declaration was specifically intended

---

[277] See e.g. O. Asamoah, *The Legal Significance of the Declarations of the General Assembly of the United Nations*, The Hague, 1966, pp. 177–85, and Shaw, *Title*, chapter 2.
[278] The *Western Sahara* case, ICJ Reports, 1975, pp. 12, 31 and 32; 59 ILR, pp. 14, 49.

to act as an elucidation of certain important Charter provisions and was indeed adopted without opposition by the General Assembly.[279]

In addition to this general, abstract approach, the UN organs have dealt with self-determination in a series of specific resolutions with regard to particular situations and this practice may be adduced as reinforcing the conclusions that the principle has become a right in international law by virtue of a process of Charter interpretation. Numerous resolutions have been adopted in the General Assembly and also the Security Council.[280] It is also possible that a rule of customary law has been created since practice in the UN system is still state practice, but the identification of the *opinio juris* element is not easy and will depend upon careful assessment and judgment.

Judicial discussion of the principle of self-determination has been relatively rare and centres on the *Namibia*[281] and *Western Sahara*[282] advisory opinions by the International Court. In the former case, the Court emphasised that 'the subsequent development of international law in regard to non-self-governing territories as enshrined in the Charter of the United Nations made the principle of self-determination applicable to all of them'.[283] The *Western Sahara* case reaffirmed this point.[284] This case arose out of the decolonisation of that territory, controlled by Spain as the colonial power but subject to irredentist claims by Morocco and Mauritania. The Court was asked for an opinion with regard to the legal ties between the territory at that time and Morocco and the Mauritanian entity. The Court stressed that the request for an opinion arose out of the consideration by the General Assembly of the decolonisation of Western Sahara and that the right of the people of the territory to self-determination constituted a basic assumption of the questions put to the Court.[285] After

---

[279] Adopted in resolution 2625 (XXV) without a vote. See e.g. R. Rosenstock, 'The Declaration of Principles of International Law Concerning Friendly Relations', 65 AJIL, 1971, pp. 16, 111 and 115.

[280] See e.g. Assembly resolutions 1755 (XVII); 2138 (XXI); 2151 (XXI); 2379 (XXIII); 2383 (XXIII) and Security Council resolutions 183 (1963); 301 (1971); 377 (1975) and 384 (1975).

[281] ICJ Reports, 1971, p. 16; 49 ILR, p. 3.

[282] ICJ Reports, 1975, p. 12; 59 ILR, p. 30. See also M. N. Shaw, 'The Western Sahara Case', 49 BYIL, p. 119.

[283] ICJ Reports, 1971, pp. 16, 31; 49 ILR, pp. 3, 21.

[284] ICJ Reports, 1975, pp. 12, 31; 59 ILR, pp. 30, 48.

[285] ICJ Reports, 1975, p. 68; 59 ILR, p. 85. See in particular the views of Judge Dillard that 'a norm of international law has emerged applicable to the decolonisation of those non-self-governing territories which are under the aegis of the United Nations', ICJ Reports, 1975, pp. 121–2; 59 ILR, p. 138. See also Judge Petren, ICJ Reports, 1975, p. 110; 59 ILR, p. 127.

analysing the Charter provisions and Assembly resolutions noted above, the Court concluded that the ties which had existed between the claimants and the territory during the relevant period of the 1880s were not such as to affect the application of resolution 1514 (XV), the Colonial Declaration, in the decolonisation of the territory and in particular the right to self-determination. In other words, it is clear that the Court regarded the principle of self-determination as a legal one in the context of such territories.

The Court moved one step further in the *East Timor (Portugal v. Australia) case*[286] when it declared that 'Portugal's assertion that the right of peoples to self-determination, as it evolved from the Charter and from United Nations practice, has an *erga omnes* character, is irreproachable.' The Court emphasised that the right of peoples to self-determination was 'one of the essential principles of contemporary international law'.[287] However, in that case, the Court, while noting that for both Portugal and Australia, East Timor (under Indonesian military occupation since the invasion of 1975) constituted a non-self-governing territory and pointing out that the people of East Timor had the right to self-determination, held that the absence of Indonesia from the litigation meant that the Court was unable to exercise its jurisdiction.[288] These propositions were all reaffirmed by the International Court in the *Construction of a Wall* advisory opinion.[289]

The issue of self-determination came before the Supreme Court of Canada in *Reference Re Secession of Quebec* in 1998 in the form of three questions posed. The second question asked whether there existed in international law a right to self-determination which would give Quebec the right unilaterally to secede.[290] The Court declared that the principle of self-determination 'has acquired a status beyond "convention" and is considered a general principle of international law'.[291]

---

[286] ICJ Reports, 1995, pp. 90, 102; 105 ILR, p. 226.   [287] *Ibid.*

[288] ICJ Reports, 1995, pp. 105–6. The reason related to the principle that the Court is unable to exercise jurisdiction over a state without the consent of that state. The Court took the view that Portugal's claims against Australia could not be decided upon without an examination of the position of Indonesia, which had not consented to the jurisdiction of the Court. See further below, chapter 19, p. 1078.

[289] ICJ Reports, 2004, pp. 136, 171–2; 129 ILR, pp. 37, 89–91.

[290] (1998) 161 DLR (4th) 385; 115 ILR, p. 536. The first question concerned the existence or not in Canadian constitutional law of a right to secede, and the third question asked whether in the event of a conflict constitutional or international law would have priority. See further below, chapter 10, p. 522, on the question of secession and self-determination.

[291] (1998) 161 DLR (4th) 434–5.

The definition of self-determination

If the principle exists as a legal one, and it is believed that such is the case, the question arises then of its scope and application. As noted above, UN formulations of the principle from the 1960 Colonial Declaration to the 1970 Declaration on Principles of International Law and the 1966 International Covenants on Human Rights stress that it is the right of 'all peoples'. If this is so, then all peoples would become thereby to some extent subjects of international law as the direct repositories of international rights, and if the definition of 'people' used was the normal political–sociological one,[292] a major rearrangement of international law perceptions would have been created. In fact, that has not occurred and an international law concept of what constitutes a people for these purposes has been evolved, so that the 'self' in question must be determined within the accepted colonial territorial framework. Attempts to broaden this have not been successful and the UN has always strenuously opposed any attempt at the partial or total disruption of the national unity and territorial integrity of a country.[293] The UN has based its policy on the proposition that 'the territory of a colony or other non-self-governing territory has under the Charter a status separate and distinct from the territory of the state administering it' and that such status was to exist until the people of that territory had exercised the right to self-determination.[294] Self-determination has also been used in conjunction with the principle of territorial integrity so as to protect the territorial framework of the colonial period in the decolonisation process and to prevent a rule permitting secession from independent states from arising.[295] The Canadian Supreme Court noted in the *Quebec* case that 'international law expects that the right to self-determination will be exercised by peoples within the framework of existing sovereign states and consistently with the maintenance of the territorial integrity of

---

[292] See e.g. Cobban, *Nation-State*, p. 107, and K. Deutsche, *Nationalism and Social Communications*, New York, 1952. See also the *Greco-Bulgarian Communities* case, PCIJ, Series B, No. 17; 5 AD, p. 4.

[293] See e.g. the Colonial Declaration 1960; the 1970 Declaration on Principles and article III [3] of the OAU Charter.

[294] 1970 Declaration on Principles of International Law. Note also that resolution 1541 (XV) declared that there is an obligation to transmit information regarding a territory 'which is geographically separate and is distinct ethnically and/or culturally from the country administering it'.

[295] See e.g. T. M. Franck, *The Power of Legitimacy Among Nations*, Oxford, 1990, pp. 153 ff.; Franck, 'Fairness in the International Legal and Institutional System', 240 HR, 1993 III, pp. 13, 127–49; Higgins, *Problems and Process*, chapter 11, and Shaw, *Title*, chapters 3 and 4.

those states'.[296] Self-determination as a concept is capable of developing further so as to include the right to secession from existing states,[297] but that has not as yet convincingly happened.[298] It clearly applies within the context, however, of decolonisation of the European empires and thus provides the peoples of such territories with a degree of international personality.

The principle of self-determination provides that the people of the colonially defined territorial unit in question may freely determine their own political status. Such determination may result in independence, integration with a neighbouring state, free association with an independent state or any other political status freely decided upon by the people concerned.[299] Self-determination also has a role within the context of creation of statehood, preserving the sovereignty and independence of states, in providing criteria for the resolution of disputes, and in the area of the permanent sovereignty of states over natural resources.[300]

Individuals[301]

The question of the status in international law of individuals is closely bound up with the rise in the international protection of human rights.

---

[296] (1998) 161 DLR (4th) 385, 436; 115 ILR, p. 536.

[297] Note that the Canadian Supreme Court did refer to 'exceptional circumstances' in which a right of secession 'may' arise: see further below, chapter 10, p. 289.

[298] But see further below, chapter 6, p. 522, with regard to the evolution of self-determination as a principle of human rights operating within independent states.

[299] *Western Sahara* case, ICJ Reports, 1975, pp. 12, 33 and 68. See also Judge Dillard, *ibid.*, p. 122; 59 ILR, pp. 30, 50, 85, 138. See Assembly resolution 1541 (XV) and the 1970 Declaration on Principles of International Law.

[300] See the *East Timor* case, ICJ Reports, 1995, pp. 90, 102; 105 ILR, p. 226, where Portugal claimed *inter alia* that Australia's agreement with Indonesia dealing with the exploration and exploitation of the continental shelf in the 'Timor Gap' violated the right of the people of East Timor to self-determination.

[301] See e.g. *Oppenheim's International Law*, chapter 8; Higgins, *Problems and Process*, pp. 48–55; Brownlie, *Principles*, chapter 25; O'Connell, *International Law*, pp. 106–12; C. Norgaard, *Position of the Individual in International Law*, Leiden, 1962; Cassese, *International Law*, pp. 142 ff.; Nguyen Quoc Dinh *et al.*, *Droit International Public*, p. 643; R. Müllerson, 'Human Rights and the Individual as a Subject of International Law: A Soviet View', 1 EJIL, 1990, p. 33; P. M. Dupuy, 'L'individu et le Droit International', 32 *Archives de Philosophie du Droit*, 1987, p. 119; H. Lauterpacht, *Human Rights in International Law*, London, 1951, and *International Law: Collected Papers*, vol. II, p. 487, and *The Individual's Duties to the Community and the Limitations on Human Rights and Freedoms under Article 29 of the Universal Declaration of Human Rights*, study prepared by Daes, 1983, E/CN.4/Sub.2/432/Rev.2. See also below, chapter 6.

This section will be confined to some general comments about the former. The object theory in this regard maintains that individuals constitute only the subject-matter of intended legal regulation as such. Only states, and possibly international organisations, are subjects of the law.[302] This has been a theory of limited value. The essence of international law has always been its ultimate concern for the human being and this was clearly manifest in the Natural Law origins of classical international law.[303] The growth of positivist theories, particularly in the nineteenth century, obscured this and emphasised the centrality and even exclusivity of the state in this regard. Nevertheless, modern practice does demonstrate that individuals have become increasingly recognised as participants and subjects of international law. This has occurred primarily but not exclusively through human rights law.

The link between the state and the individual for international law purposes has historically been the concept of nationality. This was and remains crucial, particularly in the spheres of jurisdiction and the international protection of the individual by the state. It is often noted that the claim of an individual against a foreign state, for example, becomes subsumed under that of his national state.[304] Each state has the capacity to determine who are to be its nationals and this is to be recognised by other states in so far as it is consistent with international law, although in order for other states to accept this nationality there has to be a genuine connection between the state and the individual in question.[305]

Individuals as a general rule lack standing to assert violations of international treaties in the absence of a protest by the state of nationality,[306] although states may agree to confer particular rights on individuals which will be enforceable under international law, independently of municipal law. Under article 304(b) of the Treaty of Versailles, 1919, for example, nationals of the Allied and Associated Powers could bring cases against Germany before the Mixed Arbitral Tribunal in their own names for

---

[302] See e.g. O'Connell, *International Law*, pp. 106–7.

[303] See e.g. Grotius, *De Jure Praedae Commentarius*, 1604, cited in Daes, *Individual's Duties*, p. 44, and Lauterpacht, *Human Rights*, pp. 9, 70 and 74.

[304] See the *Panevezys–Saldutiskis* case, PCIJ, Series A/B, No. 76; 9 AD, p. 308. See also the *Mavrommatis Palestine Concessions* case (Jurisdiction), PCIJ, Series A, No. 2 (1924); 2 AD, p. 27. See also below, chapter 14, p. 808.

[305] See the *Nottebohm* case, ICJ Reports, 1955, pp. 4, 22–3; 22 ILR, p. 349, and below, chapter 14, p. 808.

[306] See e.g. *US v. Noriega* 746 F.Supp. 1506, 1533 (1990); 99 ILR, pp. 143, 175.

compensation, while the Treaty of 1907 between five Central American states establishing the Central American Court of Justice provided for individuals to bring cases directly before the Court.[307]

This proposition was reiterated in the *Danzig Railway Officials* case[308] by the Permanent Court of International Justice, which emphasised that under international law treaties did not as such create direct rights and obligations for private individuals, although particular treaties could provide for the adoption of individual rights and obligations enforceable by the national courts where this was the intention of the contracting parties. Under the provisions concerned with minority protection in the 1919 Peace Treaties, it was possible for individuals to apply directly to an international court in particular instances. Similarly the Tribunal created under the Upper Silesia Convention of 1922 decided that it was competent to hear cases by the nationals of a state against that state.[309]

Since then a wide range of other treaties have provided for individuals to have rights directly and have enabled individuals to have direct access to international courts and tribunals. One may mention as examples the European Convention on Human Rights, 1950; the European Communities treaties, 1957; the Inter-American Convention on Human Rights, 1969; the Optional Protocol to the International Covenant on Civil and Political Rights, 1966; the International Convention for the Elimination of All Forms of Racial Discrimination, 1965 and the Convention on the Settlement of Investment Disputes, 1965.

However, the question of the legal personality of individuals under international law extends to questions of direct criminal responsibility also. It is now established that international law proscribes certain heinous conduct in a manner that imports direct individual criminal responsibility. This is dealt with in chapter 8.

International organisations

International organisations have played a crucial role in the sphere of international personality. Since the nineteenth century a growing number of such organisations have appeared and thus raised the issue of international legal personality. In principle it is now well established that international organisations may indeed possess objective international legal

---

[307] See Whiteman, *Digest*, vol. I, p. 39.   [308] PCIJ, Series B, No. 15 (1928); 4 AD, p. 287.
[309] See e.g. *Steiner and Gross* v. *Polish State* 4 AD, p. 291.

personality.[310] Whether that will be so in any particular instance will depend upon the particular circumstances of that case. Whether an organisation possesses personality in international law will hinge upon its constitutional status, its actual powers and practice. Significant factors in this context will include the capacity to enter into relations with states and other organisations and conclude treaties with them, and the status it has been given under municipal law. Such elements are known in international law as the indicia of personality. International organisations will be dealt with in chapter 23.

The acquisition, nature and consequences of legal personality – some conclusions

The above survey of existing and possible subjects of international law demonstrates both the range of interaction upon the international scene by entities of all types and the pressures upon international law to come to terms with the contemporary structure of international relations. The International Court clearly recognised the multiplicity of models of personality in stressing that 'the subjects of law in any legal system are not necessarily identical in their nature or in the extent of their rights'.[311] There are, however, two basic categories – objective and qualified personality. In the former case, the entity is subject to a wide range of international rights and duties and it will be entitled to be accepted as an international person by any other international person with which it is conducting relations. In other words, it will operate *erga omnes*. The creation of objective international personality will of necessity be harder to achieve and will require the action in essence of the international community as a whole or a substantial element of it. The Court noted in the *Reparation* case that:

> fifty states, representing the vast majority of the members of the international community, have the power, in conformity with international law, to bring into being an entity possessing objective international personality and not merely personality recognised by them alone, together with capacity to bring international claims.[312]

---

[310] See the *Reparation for Injuries* case, ICJ Reports, 1949, p. 174; 16 AD, p. 318. See also the *Interpretation of the Agreement of 25 March 1951 between the WHO and Egypt* case, ICJ Reports, 1980, pp. 73, 89–90; 62 ILR, pp. 450, 473–4.

[311] ICJ Reports, 1949, p. 178; 16 AD, p. 321.

[312] ICJ Reports, 1949, p. 185; 16 AD, p. 330. H. Lauterpacht wrote that, '[I]n each particular case the question whether ... a body is a subject of international law must be answered in a pragmatic manner by reference to actual experience and to the reason of the law as

The attainment of qualified personality, on the other hand, binding only the consenting subject, may arise more easily and it is clear that in this respect at least theory ought to recognise existing practice. Any legal person may accept that another entity possesses personality in relation to itself and that determination will operate only *in personam*.

States are the original and major subjects of international law. Their personality derives from the very nature and structure of the international system. Statehood will arise as a result of the factual satisfaction of the stipulated legal criteria. The constitutive theory of recognition is not really acceptable, although recognition, of course, contributes valuable evidence of adherence to the required criteria. All states, by virtue of the principle of sovereign equality, will enjoy the same degree of international legal personality. It has been argued that some international organisations, rather than being derivative subjects of international law, will as sovereign or self-governing legal communities possess an inherent personality directly from the system and will thus constitute general and even objective subjects of international law. Non-sovereign persons, including non-governmental organisations and individuals, would be derived subjects possessing only such international powers as conferred exceptionally upon them by the necessary subjects of international law.[313] This view may be questioned, but it is true that the importance of practice via the larger international organisations cannot be underestimated.

Similarly the role of the Holy See (particularly prior to 1929) as well as the UN experience demonstrates that the derivative denomination is unsatisfactory. The significance of this relates to their ability to extend their international rights and duties on the basis of both constituent instruments and subsequent practice and to their capacity to affect the creation of further international persons and to play a role in the norm-creating process.

Recognition, acquiescence and estoppel are important principles in the context of international personality, not only with regard to states and international organisations but throughout the range of subjects. They will affect not only the creation of new subjects but also the definition of their nature and rights and duties.

Personality may be acquired by a combination of treaty provisions and recognition or acquiescence by other international persons. For

distinguished from a preconceived notion as to who can be subjects of international law', *International Law and Human Rights*, p. 12.

[313] See e.g. F. Seyersted, 'International Personality of Intergovernmental Organisations', 4 IJIL, 1964, p. 19.

instance, the International Committee of the Red Cross, a private non-governmental organisation subject to Swiss law, was granted special functions under the 1949 Geneva Red Cross Conventions and has been accepted as being able to enter into international agreements under international law with international persons, such as with the EEC under the World Food Programme.[314] Another possible method of acquiring international personality is by subjecting an agreement between a recognised international person and a private party directly to the rules of international law. This would have the effect of rendering the latter an international person in the context of the arrangement in question so as to enable it to invoke in the field of international law the rights it derives from that arrangement.[315] While this currently may not be entirely acceptable to Third World states, this is probably because of a perception of the relevant rules of international law which may very well alter.[316] Personality may also be acquired by virtue of being directly subjected to international duties. This would apply to individuals in specific cases such as war crimes, piracy and genocide, and might in the future constitute the method by which transnational corporations may be accepted as international persons.

Community needs with regard to the necessity to preserve international stability and life may well be of relevance in certain exceptional circumstances. In the case of non-state territorial entities that are not totally dominated by a state, there would appear to be a community need to ensure that at least the rules relating to the resort to force and the laws of war operate. Not to accept some form of qualified personality in this area might be to free such entities from having to comply with such rules and that clearly would affect community requirements.[317] The determining point here, it is suggested, must be the degree of effective control maintained by the entity in its territorial confines. However, even so, recognition may overcome this hurdle, as the recognition of Byelorussia

---

[314] See e.g. Whiteman, *Digest*, vol. I, p. 48, and *Yearbook of the ILC*, 1981, vol. II, p. 12.

[315] See in particular the *Texaco* v. *Libya* case, 53 ILR, pp. 389, 457–62.

[316] Note the intriguing suggestion raised in the study prepared for the Economic Commission for Asia and the Far East, that an agreement between autonomous public entities (not being subjects of international law) might create an international person: UNJYB, 1971, pp. 215–18. The study was very cautious about this possibility.

[317] See the *Namibia* case, ICJ Reports, 1971, pp. 16, 56, 134 and 149; 49 ILR, pp. 3, 46, 124, 139. See also Security Council resolutions 326 (1973), 328 (1973), 403 (1977), 406 (1977), 411 (1977) and 424 (1978) in which the Council condemned Rhodesian attacks against neighbouring states and recognised that the entity was subject to the norms relating to the use of force.

and the Ukraine as non-sovereign state entities prior to the demise of the Soviet Union and the emergence of these entities as the independent states of Belarus and Ukraine demonstrated.[318]

All these entities may be easily contained within the category of qualified personality, possessing a limited range of rights and duties valid as against those accepting their personality. There are no preset rules governing the extent of rights and duties of international persons. This will depend upon the type of entity concerned, its claims and expectations, functions and attitude adopted by the international community. The exception here would be states which enter upon life with an equal range of rights and obligations. Those entities with objective personality will, it is suggested, benefit from a more elastic perception of the extent of their rights and duties in the form of a wider interpretation of implied powers through practice. However, in the case of qualified subjects implied powers will be more difficult to demonstrate and accept and the range of their rights and duties will be much more limited. The presumption, thus, will operate the other way.

The precise catalogue of rights and duties is accordingly impossible to list in advance; it will vary from case to case. The capacity to function on the international scene in legal proceedings of some description will not be too uncommon, while the power to make treaties will be less widespread. As to this the International Law Commission noted that 'agreements concluded between entities other than states or than international organisations seem too heterogeneous a group to constitute a general category, and the relevant body of international practice is as yet too exiguous for the characteristics of such a general category to be inferred from it'.[319] The extent to which subjects may be internationally responsible is also unclear, although in general such an entity will possess responsibility to the extent of its rights and duties; but many problem areas remain. Similarly controversial is the norm-creating role of such diverse entities, but the practice of all international persons is certainly relevant material upon which to draw in an elucidation of the rules and principles of international law, particularly in the context of the entity in question.

International personality thus centres, not so much upon the capacity of the entity as such to possess international rights and duties, as upon

---

[318] See e.g. UKMIL, 49 BYIL, 1978, p. 340. Byelorussia and the Ukraine were separate members of the UN and parties to a number of conventions: *ibid.*

[319] *Yearbook of the ILC*, 1981, vol. II, pp. 125–6.

the actual attribution of rights and/or duties on the international plane as determined by a variety of factors ranging from claims made to prescribed functions. Procedural capacity with regard to enforcement is important but not essential,[320] but in the case of non-individual entities the claimant will have to be in 'such a position that it possesses, in regard to its members, rights which it is entitled to ask them to respect'.[321] This, noted the International Court, expressed 'the essential test where a group, whether composed of states, of tribes or of individuals, is claimed to be a legal entity distinct from its members'.[322]

A wide variety of non-subjects exist and contribute to the evolution of the international system. Participation and personality are two concepts, but the general role played in the development of international relations and international law by individuals and entities of various kinds that are not international legal subjects as such needs to be appreciated.

Suggestions for further reading

A. Cassese, *Self-Determination of Peoples*, Cambridge, 1995

J. Crawford, *The Creation of States in International Law*, 2nd edn, Oxford, 2006

R. Higgins, *Problems and Process*, Oxford, 1994

N. Schrijver, 'The Changing Nature of State Sovereignty', 70 BYIL, 1999, p. 65

---

[320] See e.g. Norgaard, *Position of the Individual*, p. 35. See also the *Peter Pázmány University* case, PCIJ, Series A/B, No. 61 (1933); 7 AD, p. 490.

[321] *Reparation for Injuries* case, ICJ Reports, 1949, pp. 174, 178; 16 AD, pp. 318, 321.

[322] *Western Sahara* case, ICJ Reports, 1975, pp. 12, 63; 59 ILR, pp. 14, 80.

6

The international protection of human rights

The nature of human rights[1]

The preamble to the Universal Declaration of Human Rights adopted on
10 December 1948 emphasises that 'recognition of the inherent dignity
and of the equal and inalienable rights of all members of the human family is the foundation of freedom, justice and peace in the world'. While
there is widespread acceptance of the importance of human rights in the
international structure, there is considerable confusion as to their precise
nature and role in international law.[2] The question of what is meant by a
'right' is itself controversial and the subject of intense jurisprudential debate.[3] Some 'rights', for example, are intended as immediately enforceable

---

[1] See e.g. H. Lauterpacht, *International Law and Human Rights*, London, 1950; D. Weissbrodt,
J. Fitzpatrick and F. Newman, *International Human Rights*, 3rd edn, Cincinnati, 2001; J.
Rehman, *International Human Rights Law*, London, 2002; Nguyen Quoc Dinh, P. Daillier
and A. Pellet, *Droit International Public*, 7th edn, Paris, 2002, p. 656; F. Sudre, *Droit In-
ternational et Européen des Droits de l'Homme*, 3rd edn, Paris, 1997; M. S. McDougal, H.
Lasswell and L. C. Chen, *Human Rights and World Public Order*, New Haven, 1980; L. Sohn
and T. Buergenthal, *International Protection of Human Rights*, Indianapolis, 1973; *Human
Rights in International Law* (ed. T. Meron), Oxford, 2 vols., 1984; A. H. Robertson and J.
Merrills, *Human Rights in the World*, 4th edn, Manchester, 1996; A. Cassese, *International
Law*, 2nd edn, Oxford, 2005, chapter 19; *Guide to International Human Rights Practice* (ed.
H. Hannum), 4th edn, Ardsley, 2004; J. Donnelly, *International Human Rights*, Boulder,
1993; D. R. Forsythe, *Human Rights in International Relations*, 2nd edn, Cambridge, 2006;
R. Higgins, *Problems and Process*, Oxford, 1994, chapter 6; *Human Rights: An Agenda for
the Next Century* (eds. L. Henkin and L. Hargrove), Washington, 1994; T. Meron, *The Humanization of International Law*, The Hague, 2006; C. Tomuschat, *Human Rights*, Oxford,
2003; R. K. M. Smith, *Text and Materials on International Human Rights*, London, 2007;
and H. Steiner, P. Alston and R. Goodman, *International Human Rights in Context*, 3rd edn,
Oxford, 2008.

[2] See e.g. M. Moskowitz, *The Policies and Dynamics of Human Rights*, London, 1968,
pp. 98–9, and McDougal *et al.*, *Human Rights*, pp. 63–8.

[3] See e.g. W. N. Hohfeld, 'Fundamental Legal Conceptions as Applied to Judicial Reasoning',
23 *Yale Law Journal*, 1913, p. 16, and R. Dworkin, *Taking Rights Seriously*, London, 1977.
See also J. Shestack, 'The Jurisprudence of Human Rights' in Meron, *Human Rights in
International Law*, vol. I, p. 69, and M. Cranston, *What Are Human Rights?*, London, 1973.

binding commitments, others merely as specifying a possible future pattern of behaviour.[4] The problem of enforcement and sanctions with regard to human rights in international law is another issue which can affect the characterisation of the phenomenon. There are writers who regard the high incidence of non-compliance with human rights norms as evidence of state practice that argues against the existence of a structure of human rights principles in international law.[5] Although sight must not be lost of violations of human rights laws, such an approach is not only academically incorrect but also profoundly negative.[6] The concept of human rights is closely allied with ethics and morality. Those rights that reflect the values of a community will be those with the most chance of successful implementation. Positive rights may be taken to include those rights enshrined within a legal system, whether or not reflective of moral considerations, whereas a moral right is not necessarily enforceable by law. One may easily discover positive rights. Deducing or inferring moral rights is another matter entirely and will depend upon the perception of the person seeking the existence of a particular right.[7]

Rights may be seen as emanating from various sources, whether religion or the nature of man or the nature of society. The Natural Law view, as expressed in the traditional formulations of that approach or by virtue of the natural rights movement, is that certain rights exist as a result of a higher law than positive or man-made law. Such a higher law constitutes a universal and absolute set of principles governing all human beings in time and space. The natural rights approach of the seventeenth century, associated primarily with John Locke, founded the existence of such inalienable rights as the rights to life, liberty and property upon a social contract marking the end of the difficult conditions of the state of nature. This theory enabled recourse to be had to a superior type of law and thus

---

[4] Compare, for example, article 2 of the International Covenant on Civil and Political Rights, 1966 with article 2 of the International Covenant on Economic, Social and Cultural Rights, 1966.

[5] See e.g. J. S. Watson, 'Legal Theory, Efficacy and Validity in the Development of Human Rights Norms in International Law', *University of Illinois Law Forum*, 1979, p. 609; Watson, 'Autointerpretation, Competence and the Continuing Validity of Article 2(7) of the UN Charter', 71 AJIL, 1977, p. 60, and Watson, *Theory and Reality in the International Protection of Human Rights*, Ardsley, 1999.

[6] See e.g. R. Higgins, 'Reality and Hope and International Human Rights: A Critique', 9 *Hofstra Law Review*, 1981, p. 1485.

[7] See M. Cranston, 'What are Human Rights?' in Laquer and Rubin, *Human Rights Reader*, pp. 17, 19.

was able to provide a powerful method of restraining arbitrary power.[8] Although this approach fell out of favour in the nineteenth century due to the problems of its non-empirical and diffuse methodology, it proved of immense value in the last century in the establishment of human rights within the international community as universal principles. Positivism as a theory emphasised the authority of the state and as such left little place for rights in the legal system other than specific rights emanating from the constitutional structure of that system,[9] while the Marxist doctrine, although based upon the existence of certain immutable historical laws governing the development of society, nevertheless denied the existence of rights outside the framework of the legal order.[10] Modern rights theories cover a wide range of approaches, and this clearly emphasises the need to come to terms with the requirements of an evolving legal system that cannot be totally comprehended in terms of that system itself.[11]

Of particular interest is the work of the policy-oriented movement that seeks to identify, characterise and order a wide variety of relevant factors in the process of human rights creation and equipment. Eight interdependent values are noted (viz. demands relating to respect, power, enlightenment, well-being, health, skill, affection and rectitude) and various environmental influences stressed. Human dignity is seen as the key concept in relation to these values and to the ultimate goal of a world community in which a democratic distribution of values is sought.[12]

All these theories emphasise the complexity of the nature of the concept of human rights in the context of general legal and political processes, but also the importance and centrality of such notions. The broad issues are similarly raised within the framework of international law.

---

[8] See e.g. Lauterpacht, *International Law*; R. Tuck, *Natural Rights Theories*, Cambridge, 1979; J. Finnis, *Natural Law and Natural Rights*, Oxford, 1980, and McDougal *et al.*, *Human Rights*, pp. 68–71. See also Tomuschat, *Human Rights*, chapter 2, and above, chapter 1.

[9] See e.g. D. Lloyd, *Introduction to Jurisprudence*, 4th edn, London, 1979, chapter 4. See also H. Hart, *The Concept of Law*, Oxford, 1961; McDougal *et al.*, *Human Rights*, pp. 73–5, and above, chapters 1 and 2.

[10] See e.g. Lloyd, *Jurisprudence*, chapter 10, and McDougal *et al.*, *Human Rights*, pp. 76–9. See also below, p. 268.

[11] See e.g. J. Rawls, *A Theory of Justice*, Oxford, 1971; E. Cahn, *The Sense of Injustice*, Bloomington, 1949; R. Nozick, *Anarchy, State and Utopia*, Oxford, 1974, and Dworkin, *Taking Rights Seriously*. See also S. Davidson, *Human Rights*, Buckingham, 1993, chapter 3.

[12] See McDougal *et al.*, *Human Rights*, especially pp. 82–93.

Ideological approaches to human rights in international law

The view adopted by the Western world with regard to international human rights law in general terms has tended to emphasise the basic civil and political rights of individuals, that is to say those rights that take the form of claims limiting the power of government over the governed. Such rights would include due process, freedom of expression, assembly and religion, and political participation in the process of government. The consent of the governed is seen as crucial in this process.[13] The approach of the Soviet Union was to note the importance of basic rights and freedoms for international peace and security, but to emphasise the role of the state. Indeed, the source of human rights principles was seen as the state. Tunkin wrote that the content of the principle of respect for human rights in international law may be expressed in three propositions:

> (1) all states have a duty to respect the fundamental rights and freedoms of all persons within their territories; (2) states have a duty not to permit discrimination by reason of sex, race, religion or language, and (3) states have a duty to promote universal respect for human rights and to co-operate with each other to achieve this objective.[14]

In other words, the focus was not upon the individual (as in Western conceptions of human rights) but solely upon the state. Human rights were not directly regulated by international law and individuals were not subjects of international law. Indeed, human rights were implemented by the state and matters basically and crucially within the domestic affairs of the state. As Tunkin emphasised, 'conventions on human rights do not grant rights directly to individuals'.[15] Having stressed the central function of the state, the point was also made that the context of the international human rights obligations themselves was defined solely by the state in the light of the socio-economic advancement of that state. Accordingly, the nature and context of those rights would vary from state to state, depending upon the social system of the state in question. It was the particular

[13] See e.g. R. Hauser, 'A First World View', in *Human Rights and American Foreign Policy* (eds. D. P. Kommers and G. Loescher), Notre Dame, 1979, p. 85.

[14] G. Tunkin, *Theory of International Law*, London, 1974, p. 81. See also K. Tedin, 'The Development of the Soviet Attitude Towards Implementing Human Rights under the UN Charter', 5 HRJ, 1972, p. 399; R. N. Dean, 'Beyond Helsinki: The Soviet View of Human Rights in International Law', 21 Va. JIL, 1980, p. 55; P. Reddaway, 'Theory and Practice of Human Rights in the Soviet Union' in Kommers and Loescher, *Human Rights and American Foreign Policy*, p. 115, and Tomuschat, *Human Rights*, chapter 3.

[15] Tunkin, *Theory*, p. 83.

socio-economic system of a state that would determine the concrete expression of an international human rights provision.[16] In other words, the Soviet Union was able and willing to enter into many international agreements on human rights, on the basis that only a state obligation was incurred, with no direct link to the individual, and that such an obligation was one that the country might interpret in the light of its own socio-economic system. The supremacy or centrality of the state was the key in this approach. As far as the different kinds of human rights were concerned, the Soviet approach was to stress those dealing with economic and social matters and thus to minimise the importance of the traditional civil and political rights. However, a new approach to the question of international human rights began to emerge by the end of the 1980s, reflecting the changes taking place politically.[17] In particular, the USSR began to take a different approach with regard to human rights treaties.[18]

The general approach of the Third World states has combined elements of both the previous perceptions.[19] Concern with the equality and sovereignty of states, together with a recognition of the importance of social and economic rights, has characterised the Third World view. Such countries, in fact constituting a wide range of nations with differing interests and needs, and at different stages of development, have been much influenced by decolonisation and the struggle to obtain it and by the phenomenon of apartheid in South Africa. In addition, economic problems have played a large role in focusing their attention upon general developmental issues. Accordingly, the traditional civil and political rights have tended to lose their priority in the concerns of Third World states.[20] Of particular interest is the tension between the universalism of human rights and the relativism of cultural traditions. This has led to arguments by

---

[16] *Ibid.*, pp. 82–3.

[17] See e.g. V. Vereshchetin and R. Müllerson, 'International Law in an Interdependent World', 28 *Columbia Journal of Transnational Law*, 1990, pp. 291, 300.

[18] *Ibid.* Note that on 10 February 1989, the USSR recognised the compulsory jurisdiction of the International Court of Justice with regard to six human rights treaties, including the Genocide Convention, 1948; the Racial Discrimination Convention, 1965; the Convention on Discrimination against Women, 1979, and the Torture Convention, 1984.

[19] See e.g. R. Emerson, 'The Fate of Human Rights in the Third World', 27 *World Politics*, 1975, p. 201; G. Mower, 'Human Rights in Black Africa', 9 HRJ, 1976, p. 33; R. Zvobgo, 'A Third World View' in Kommers and Loescher, *Human Rights and American Foreign Policy*, p. 90, and M. Nawaz, 'The Concept of Human Rights in Islamic Law' in Symposium on International Law of Human Rights, 11 *Howard Law Journal*, 1965, p. 257.

[20] See generally T. Van Boven, 'Some Remarks on Special Problems Relating to Human Rights in Developing Countries', 3 *Revue des Droits de l'Homme*, 1970, p. 383. See further below, p. 391, on the Banjul Charter on Human and Peoples' Rights.

some adherents of the latter tendency that human rights can only be approached within the context of particular cultural or religious traditions, thus criticising the view that human rights are universal or transcultural. The danger, of course, is that states violating human rights that they have accepted by becoming parties to human rights treaties, as well as being bound by relevant customary international law, might seek to justify their actions by pleading cultural differences.[21]

The development of international human rights law[22]

In the nineteenth century, the positivist doctrines of state sovereignty and domestic jurisdiction reigned supreme. Virtually all matters that today would be classified as human rights issues were at that stage universally regarded as within the internal sphere of national jurisdiction. The major exceptions to this were related to piracy *jure gentium* and slavery. In the latter case a number of treaties were entered into to bring about its abolition.[23] Concern also with the treatment of sick and wounded soldiers and with prisoners of war developed as from 1864 in terms of international instruments,[24] while states were required to observe certain minimum standards in the treatment of aliens.[25] In addition, certain agreements of a general welfare nature were beginning to be adopted by the turn of the century.[26] The nineteenth century also appeared to accept a right of humanitarian intervention, although its range and extent were unclear.[27]

An important change occurred with the establishment of the League of Nations in 1919.[28] Article 22 of the Covenant of the League set up

---

[21] See e.g. Steiner, Alston and Goodman, *International Human Rights*, pp. 517 ff.; E. Brems, *Human Rights: Universality and Diversity*, The Hague, 2001, and A. D. Renteln, *International Human Rights: Universalism versus Relativism*, Newbury Park, 1990.

[22] See e.g. *The International Protection of Human Rights* (ed. E. Luard), London, 1967; Sohn and Buergenthal, *International Protection*; Lauterpacht, *International Law*; M. Moscowitz, *International Concern with Human Rights*, London, 1968, and M. Ganji, *The International Protection of Human Rights*, London, 1962.

[23] See e.g. C. Greenidge, *Slavery*, London, 1958, and V. Nanda and M. C. Bassiouni, 'Slavery and the Slave Trade: Steps towards Eradication', 12 *Santa Clara Law Review*, 1972, p. 424. See also ST/SOA/4.

[24] See generally G. Best, *War and Law Since 1945*, Oxford, 1994, and *Studies and Essays on International Humanitarian Law and Red Cross Principles* (ed. C. Swinarski), The Hague, 1984.

[25] See below, chapter 14.

[26] E.g. regarding the Prohibition of Night Work for Women in Industrial Employment and regarding the Prohibition of the Use of White Phosphorus in the Manufacture of Matches.

[27] See below, chapter 20, p. 1155.   [28] See below, chapter 23.

the mandates system for peoples in ex-enemy colonies 'not yet able to stand by themselves in the strenuous conditions of the modern world'. The mandatory power was obliged to guarantee freedom of conscience and religion and a Permanent Mandates Commission was created to examine the reports the mandatory authorities had undertaken to make. The arrangement was termed 'a sacred trust of civilisation'. Article 23 of the Covenant provided for just treatment of the native populations of the territories in question.[29] The 1919 peace agreements with Eastern European and Balkan states included provisions relating to the protection of minorities,[30] providing essentially for equality of treatment and opportunities for collective activity.[31] These provisions were supervised by the League of Nations, to whom there was a right of petition.[32]

Part XIII of the Treaty of Versailles provided for the creation of the International Labour Organisation, among the purposes of which were the promotion of better standards of working conditions and support for the right of association.[33] The impact of the Second World War upon the development of human rights law was immense as the horrors of the war and the need for an adequate international system to maintain international peace and protect human rights became apparent to all. In addition, the rise of non-governmental organisations, particularly in the sphere of human rights, has had an immense effect.[34] While the post-Second World War world witnessed the rise of intergovernmental committees and organs and courts to deal with human rights violations, whether by public debate, states' reports, comments, inter-state or individual petition procedures, recent years have seen the interposition of domestic amnesty laws and this

---

[29] See above, chapter 5, p. 224.

[30] See generally P. Thornberry, 'Is There a Phoenix in the Ashes? – International Law and Minority Rights', 15 *Texas International Law Journal*, 1980, p. 421; C. A. Macartney, *National States and National Minorities*, London, 1934, and I. Claude, *National Minorities: An International Problem*, Cambridge, 1955. See also M. N. Shaw, 'The Definition of Minorities in International Law' in *Protection of Minorities and Human Rights* (eds. Y. Dinstein and M. Tabory), Dordrecht, 1992, p. 1.

[31] See e.g. the *Minority Schools in Albania* case, PCIJ, Series A/B, No. 64, 1935, p. 17.

[32] See Thornberry, 'Phoenix', pp. 433–54, and M. Jones, 'National Minorities: A Case Study in International Protection', 14 *Law and Contemporary Problems*, 1949, pp. 599, 610–24. See further below, p. 293.

[33] See further below, p. 338.

[34] See e.g. Steiner, Alston and Goodman, *International Human Rights*, pp. 1420 ff., and C. Chinkin, 'The Role of Non-Governmental Organisations in Standard Setting, Monitoring and Implementation of Human Rights' in *The Changing World of International Law in the 21st Century* (eds. J. J. Norton, M. Andendas and M. Footer), The Hague, 1998.

has given rise to the question of the acceptability of impunity.[35] Further developments have included the establishments of truth and reconciliation commissions[36] and various other alternative justice systems such as the Rwandan Gaccaca court system,[37] while the extent to which participants in the international legal system apart from states have become involved both in the process of formulating and seeking the implementation of human rights and in being the subjects of human rights concern and regulation is marked.[38]

Some basic principles

Domestic jurisdiction[39]

The basic rule of international law providing that states have no right to encroach upon the preserve of other states' internal affairs is a consequence of the equality and sovereignty of states and is mirrored in article 2(7) of the UN Charter. It has, however, been subject to a process of reinterpretation in the human rights field[40] as this and the two succeeding

---

[35] See e.g. J. Gavron, 'Amnesties in the Light of Developments in International Law and the Establishment of the International Criminal Court', 51 ICLQ, 2002, p. 91. See also C. Jenkins, 'Amnesty for Gross Violations of Human Rights: A Better Way of Dealing with the Past?' in *Comparative Law in a Global Perspective* (ed. I. Edge), London, 2000, p. 345, and J. Dugard, 'Dealing with Crimes of a Past Regime: Is Amnesty Still an Option?', 16 Leiden JIL, 2000, p. 1. Note the Final Report of the Special Rapporteur on the Right to Restitution, Compensation and Rehabilitation for Victims of Gross Violations of Human Rights, E/CN.4/2000/62, January 2000, and *Chumbipuma Aguirre* v. *Peru*, the *Barrios Altos* case, where the Inter-American Court of Human Rights held that Peruvian amnesty laws were incompatible with the Inter-American Convention and thus void of any legal effect, judgment of 14 March 2001, 41 ILM, 2002, p. 93. Peru accepted this and altered its legislation, *ibid.*

[36] See e.g. Steiner, Alston and Goodman, *International Human Rights*, pp. 1344 ff.; the Promotion of National Unity and Reconciliation Act of South Africa 1995; R. G. Teitel, *Transitional Justice*, Oxford, 2001, and J. Dugard, 'Possible Conflicts of Jurisdiction with Truth Commissions' in *The Rome Statute of the International Criminal Court: A Commentary* (eds. A. Cassese, P. Gaeta and J. R. W. D. Jones), Oxford, 2002.

[37] See e.g. Steiner, Alston and Goodman, *International Human Rights*, pp. 1319 ff. See also below, chapter 8, p. 407.

[38] See e.g. *Non-State Actors and Human Rights* (ed. Philip Alston), Oxford, 2005, and A. Clapham, *Human Rights Obligations of Non-State Actors*, Oxford, 2006.

[39] See e.g. R. Higgins, *The Development of International Law Through the Political Organs of the United Nations*, Oxford, 1963; M. Rajan, *United Nations and Domestic Jurisdiction*, 2nd edn, London, 1961, and A. Cançado Trindade, 'The Domestic Jurisprudence of States in the Practice of the United Nations and Regional Organisations', 25 ICLQ, 1976, p. 715.

[40] Note that the question of the extent and content of domestic jurisdiction is a matter for international law: see *Nationality Decrees in Tunis and Morocco* cases, PCIJ, Series B, No. 4, 1923; 2 AD, p. 349. See also below, chapter 12.

chapters will make apparent, so that states may no longer plead this rule as a bar to international concern and consideration of internal human rights situations.[41] It is, of course, obvious that where a state accepts the right of individual petition under an international procedure, it cannot thereafter claim that the exercise of such a right constitutes interference with its domestic affairs.[42]

The exhaustion of domestic or local remedies rule[43]

This rule flows from the above principle. It is a method of permitting states to solve their own internal problems in accordance with their own constitutional procedures before accepted international mechanisms can be invoked, and is well established in general international law.[44] However, where such internal remedies are non-existent or unduly and unreasonably prolonged or unlikely to bring effective relief, the resort to international measures will not be required.[45] The existence of such a remedy must be certain not only in theory but also in practice.[46] A provision regarding the need to exhaust domestic remedies before the various international mechanisms may be resorted to appears in all the international and regional human rights instruments[47] and has been the subject of much consideration by the Human Rights Committee under the Optional Protocol

---

[41] See also the resolution of the Institut de Droit International, 1989, H/Inf (90) 1, p. 131.

[42] See e.g. *Miha* v. *Equatorial Guinea*, CCPR/C/51/D/414/1990, 10 August 1994, Human Rights Committee, para. 63.

[43] See e.g. A. Cançado Trindade, *The Application of the Rule of Exhaustion of Local Remedies in International Law*, Cambridge, 1983; C. Law, *The Local Remedies Rule in International Law*, Geneva, 1961, and C. F. Amerasinghe, *Local Remedies in International Law*, 2nd edn, Cambridge, 2004. See also C. F. Amerasinghe, 'The Rule of Exhaustion of Local Remedies and the International Protection of Human Rights', 17 *Indian Yearbook of International Affairs*, 1974, p. 3. and below, chapter 14, p. 819.

[44] See e.g. the *Ambatielos* case, 23 ILR, p. 306; the *Finnish Ships* case, 3 RIAA, p. 1479; 7 AD, p. 231, and the *Interhandel* case, ICJ Reports, 1959, pp. 26–7; 27 ILR, pp. 475, 490.

[45] See e.g. the *Robert E. Brown* case, 6 RIAA, p. 120; 2 AD, p. 66. See also the *Salem* case, 2 RIAA, p. 1161; 6 AD, p. 188; the *Nielsen* case, 2 *Yearbook of the ECHR*, p. 413; 28 ILR, p. 210, and the *Second Cyprus* case (*Greece* v. *UK*), 2 *Yearbook of the ECHR*, p. 186. See also the cases cited in the succeeding footnotes.

[46] See e.g. *Johnston* v. *Ireland*, European Court of Human Rights, Series A, No. 112 (1986); 89 ILR, p. 154, and *Open Door and Dublin Well Woman* v. *Ireland*, European Court of Human Rights, Series A, No. 246 (1992).

[47] See e.g. article 41(c), Civil and Political Rights Covenant and article 2, Optional Protocol; article 11(3), Racial Discrimination Convention; article 26, European Convention; article 50, Inter-American Convention, and article 50, Banjul Charter. See also ECOSOC resolution 1503 and UNESCO decision 104 EX/3.3, 1978, para. 14(IX).

procedure of the International Covenant on Civil and Political Rights,[48] and within the European Convention[49] and Inter-American Convention human rights systems.[50]

Priorities of rights

Certain rights may not be derogated from in the various human rights instruments even in times of war or other public emergency threatening the nation. In the case of the European Convention[51] these are the rights to life (except in cases resulting from lawful acts of war), the prohibition on torture and slavery, and non-retroactivity of criminal offences.[52] In the case of the Inter-American Convention,[53] the following rights are non-derogable: the rights to juridical personality, life and humane treatment, freedom from slavery, freedom from *ex post facto* laws, freedom

---

[48] See e.g. S. Joseph, J. Schultz and M. Castan, *The International Covenant on Civil and Political Rights*, 2nd edn, Oxford, 2005, chapter 6; the *Weinberger* case, Reports of the Human Rights Committee, A/36/40, p. 114 and A/44/40, p. 142 and the *Sara* case, A/49/40, annex X, Section C, para. 8.3. States are required to provide evidence that there would be a reasonable prospect that available remedies would be effective, *Torres Ramírez* v. *Uruguay, Selected Decisions under the Optional Protocol*, CCPR/C/OP/1, 1985, p. 3. See also e.g. *Baboeram-Adhin* v. *Suriname*, A/40/40, p. 187; 94 ILR, p. 377; *Muhonen* v. *Finland*, A/40/40, p. 164; 94 ILR, p. 389; *Solórzano* v. *Venezuela*, A/41/40, p. 134; 94 ILR, p. 400; *Holland* v. *Ireland* 115 ILR, p. 277 and *Faurisson* v. *France* 115 ILR, p. 355. See also, with regard to the UN Convention against Torture, *AE* v. *Switzerland*, CAT/C/14/D/24/ 1995.

[49] See, as to the position under the European Convention on Human Rights, e.g. the *Nielsen* case, 2 *Yearbook of the ECHR*, p. 413; the *Second Cyprus* case (*Greece* v. *UK*), 2 *Yearbook of the ECHR*, p. 186; the *Donnelly* case, 16 *Yearbook of the ECHR*, p. 212; *Kjeldsen* v. *Denmark*, 15 *Yearbook of the ECHR*, p. 428; 58 ILR, p. 117; *Drozd and Janousek* v. *France and Spain* 64 DR 97 (1989) and *Akdivar* v. *Turkey* 23 EHRR, 1997, p. 143. See also D. J. Harris, M. O'Boyle and C. Warbrick, *Law of the European Convention on Human Rights*, London, 1995, p. 608, and *Jacobs and White: European Convention on Human Rights* (eds. C. Ovey and R. C. A. White), 4th edn, Oxford, 2006, p. 485. The rule of exhaustion of domestic remedies applies also in inter-state cases: see *Cyprus* v. *Turkey* 2 DR 125 at 137–8 (first and second applications) and 13 DR 85, 150–3 (third application), although not with regard to legislative measures nor with regard to administrative actions in certain circumstances: see e.g. the *Greek* case, 12 *European Yearbook of Human Rights*, p. 196.

[50] See e.g. article 46(1)a of the Inter-American Convention on Human Rights, 1969 and article 37 of the Regulations of the Inter-American Commission on Human Rights. See also *Exceptions to the Exhaustion of Domestic Remedies in Cases of Indigency*, Advisory Opinion of the Inter-American Court of Human Rights, 1990, 12 HRLJ, 1991, p. 20, and *Annual Report of the Inter-American Commission on Human Rights 1993*, Washington, 1994, pp. 148, 185 and 266.

[51] Article 15. See generally, R. Higgins, 'Derogations Under Human Rights Treaties', 48 BYIL, 1976–7, p. 281.

[52] Articles 2, 3, 4(1) and 7.   [53] Article 27.

of conscience and religion, rights of the family, to a name, of the child, nationality and participation in government.[54] By article 4 of the International Covenant on Civil and Political Rights, the rights to life and recognition as a person before the law, the freedoms of thought, conscience and religion and the prohibition on torture, slavery, retroactivity of criminal legislation and imprisonment on grounds solely of inability to fulfil a contractual obligation are non-derogable.[55]

Such non-derogable rights clearly are regarded as possessing a special place in the hierarchy of rights.[56] In addition, it must be noted, many rights are subject to a limitation or clawback clause, whereby the absolute right provided for will not operate in certain situations.[57] Those rights therefore that are not so limited may be regarded as of particular value.[58]

Customary international law and human rights

In addition to the many international and regional treaty provisions concerning human rights to be noted in this and the next two chapters,[59] certain human rights may now be regarded as having entered into the category of customary international law in the light of state practice. These would certainly include the prohibition of torture, genocide and slavery and the principle of non-discrimination.[60] In addition, human rights established under treaty may constitute obligations *erga omnes* for the states parties.[61]

---

[54] Articles 3, 4, 5, 6, 9, 12, 17, 18, 19, 20 and 23.
[55] Articles 6, 7, 8(1) and (2), 11, 15, 16 and 18. Note that the Banjul Charter contains no specific derogations clause.
[56] The fact that a right may not be derogated from may constitute evidence that the right concerned is part of *jus cogens*.
[57] See e.g. articles 8–11 of the European Convention, articles 12–14, 15–16 and 21–2 of the Inter-American Convention and articles 12, 18, 19, 21 and 22 of the Civil and Political Rights Covenant. See also Higgins, 'Derogations'.
[58] See e.g. the due process rights.
[59] Note that questions relating to the interpretation of and reservations to human rights treaties will be noted below in chapter 16, pp. 932 and 913, while the issue of succession to human rights treaties will be noted below in chapter 17, p. 981.
[60] See e.g. *Third US Restatement of Foreign Relations Law*, St Paul, 1987, vol. II, pp. 161 ff. and *Filartiga* v. *Pena-Irala* 630 F.2d 876; 77 ILR, p. 169. See also T. Meron, *Human Rights and Humanitarian Norms as Customary Law*, Oxford, 1989 and the articles published in the Special Issue on Customary International Human Rights Law, 25 *Georgia Journal of International and Comparative Law*, 1995–6.
[61] See below, chapter 14, p. 807.

Evolving principles

Certain areas of international human rights law are rapidly evolving. First, for example, the increasing extraterritoriality of human rights is becoming evident in the case-law of the European Convention on Human Rights,[62] the approach of the Human Rights Committee under the International Covenant on Civil and Political Rights[63] and the case-law of the International Court of Justice.[64] Secondly, the responsibility of states to prevent human rights abuses is beginning to be seriously considered, particularly with regard to genocide[65] and torture,[66] while more generally the obligation upon states and, for example, international organisations positively to protect human rights is becoming part of the agenda of international human rights law. Thirdly, increasing interest is being manifested in national human rights institutions.[67]

The United Nations system – general[68]

There are a number of human rights provisions in the Charter.[69] Article 1 includes in the purposes of the organisation the promotion and

---

[62] See below, chapter 7, p. 349.

[63] See *Extraterritorial Application of Human Rights Treaties* (eds. F. Coomans and M. Kamminga), Antwerp, 2004. See also below, p. 315.

[64] See the *Construction of a Wall* case, ICJ Reports, 2004, pp. 136, 177 ff; 129 ILR. pp. 37, 96 ff.; and the *Genocide Convention (Bosnia v. Serbia)* case, ICJ Reports, 2007, para. 183.

[65] See e.g. the *Genocide Convention (Bosnia v. Serbia)* case, ICJ Reports, 2007, paras. 428 ff.

[66] See articles 2 and 16 of the Convention against Torture: see further below, p. 326. See also the Convention on the Prevention and Punishment of Crimes against Internationally Protected Persons, 1973 (art. 4); the Convention on the Safety of United Nations and Associated Personnel, 1994 (art. 11), and the International Convention on the Suppression of Terrorist Bombings, 1997 (art. 15).

[67] See e.g. the Vienna Declaration on Human Rights adopted by the UN in 1993, para. 36; General Assembly resolution 48/134, adopting the Paris Principles Relating to the Status and Functioning of National Institutions for Protection and Promotion of Human Rights, 1993; General Comment No. 10 of the Committee on Economic, Social and Cultural Rights, E/C.12/1998/25, and the Optional Protocol to the UN Convention against Torture, 2002, article 3.

[68] See generally *Bowett's Law of International Institutions* (eds. P. Sands and P. Klein), 5th edn, Manchester, 2001; Lauterpacht, *International Law*, pp. 145–220; *UN Action in the Field of Human Rights*, New York, 1981, and *Human Rights: Thirty Years after the Universal Declaration* (ed. B. Ramcharan), Dordrecht, 1979.

[69] Largely as a result of lobbying by non-governmental organisations at the San Francisco Conference: see J. Humphrey, 'The United Nations Charter and the Universal Declaration of Human Rights' in Luard, *International Protection*, chapter 3.

encouragement of respect for human rights and fundamental freedoms for all without distinction as to race, sex, language or religion. Article 13(1) notes that the General Assembly shall initiate studies and make recommendations regarding the realisation of human rights for all, while article 55 provides that the United Nations shall promote universal respect for and observance of human rights. In a significant provision, article 56 states that:

> all members pledge themselves to take joint and separate action in co-operation with the organisation for the achievement of the purposes set forth in article 55.[70]

The mandate system was replaced by the trusteeship system, one of the basic objectives of which was, by article 76, the encouragement of respect for human rights, while, with regard to non-self-governing territories, the administering powers under article 73 of the Charter recognised the principle that the interests of the inhabitants were paramount, and accepted as a sacred trust the obligation to promote the well-being of the inhabitants. It can thus be seen that the Charter provisions on human rights were very general and vague. No enforcement procedures were laid down. Some have argued that the term 'pledge' in article 56 had the effect of converting the enumerated purposes of article 55 into legal obligations,[71] but this has been disputed.[72] Certainly, as of 1946, this would have been a difficult proposition to sustain, particularly in view of the hortatory language used in the provisions and the fact that the respect for human rights stipulation does not identify precise legal rights.[73] However, in the *Namibia* case of 1971, the Court noted that under the UN Charter:

> the former Mandatory had pledged itself to observe and respect, in a territory having international status, human rights and fundamental freedoms for all without distinction as to race. To establish instead and to enforce,

---

[70] Under article 62, the Economic and Social Council has the power to make recommendations for the purpose of promoting respect for and observance of human rights.

[71] See e.g. Lauterpacht, *International Law*, pp. 47–9; Q. Wright, 'National Courts and Human Rights – the *Fujii* case', 45 AJIL, 1951, p. 73, and B. Sloan, 'Human Rights, the United Nations and International Law', 20 *Nordisk Tidsskrift for International Ret*, 1950, pp. 30–1. See also Judge Tanaka, *South West Africa* cases, ICJ Reports, 1966, pp. 6, 288–9; 37 ILR, pp. 243, 451–2.

[72] See M. O. Hudson, 'Integrity of International Instruments', 42 AJIL, 1948, pp. 105–8 and *Yearbook of the ILC*, 1949, p. 178. See also H. Kelsen, *The Law of the United Nations*, London, 1950, p. 29.

[73] See D. Driscoll, 'The Development of Human Rights in International Law' in Laquer and Rubin, *Human Rights Reader*, pp. 41, 43.

distinctions, exclusions, restrictions and limitations, exclusively based on grounds of race, colour, descent or national or ethnic origin which constitute a denial of fundamental human rights is a flagrant violation of the purposes and principles of the Charter.[74]

It may be that this provision can only be understood in the light of the special, international status of that territory, but in the light of extensive practice since the 1940s in the general area of non-discrimination and human rights, the broader interpretation is to be preferred.

The Charter does contain a domestic jurisdiction provision. Article 2(7) provides that:

> nothing contained in the present Charter shall authorise the United Nations to intervene in matters which are essentially within the domestic jurisdiction of any state

but as noted later[75] this has over the years been flexibly interpreted, so that human rights issues are no longer recognised as being solely within the domestic jurisdiction of states.

The elucidation, development and protection of human rights through the UN has proved to be a seminal event. A range of declarations and treaties has emerged, coupled with the establishment of a variety of advisory services and implementation and enforcement mechanisms. Large numbers of studies and reports of various kinds have appeared, while the whole process has been accompanied by extensive debate and consideration in a variety of UN organs and committees. Notwithstanding a certain degree of cynicism, it can be concluded that the acceptance of the centrality of human rights concerns within the international community has been due in no small measure to the unceasing consideration of human rights issues within the framework of the United Nations.

The cornerstone of UN activity has been without doubt the Universal Declaration of Human Rights adopted by the UN General Assembly on 10 December 1948.[76] The Declaration was approved without a dissenting vote

---

[74] ICJ Reports, 1971, pp. 16, 57; 49 ILR, pp. 3, 47. See also I. Brownlie, *Principles of Public International Law*, 6th edn, Oxford, 2003, pp. 546 ff.; E. Schwelb, 'The International Court of Justice and the Human Rights Clauses of the Charter', 66 AJIL, 1972, p. 337, and O. Schachter, 'The Charter and the Constitution', 4 *Vanderbilt Law Review*, 1951, p. 443.

[75] See below, p. 647.

[76] See e.g. *Oppenheim's International Law* (eds. R. Y. Jennings and A. D. Watts), 9th edn, London, 1992, p. 1001; M. Whiteman, *Digest of International Law*, Washington, 1965, vol. V, p. 237; J. Humphrey, 'The Universal Declaration on Human Rights' in Ramcharan, *Human Rights*, p. 21; J. Kunz, 'The United Nations Declaration of Human Rights', 43

(the Byelorussian SSR, Czechoslovakia, Poland, Ukrainian SSR, USSR, Yugoslavia and Saudi Arabia abstained). It was intended not as a legally binding document as such but, as its preamble proclaims, 'a common standard of achievement for all peoples and nations'. Its thirty articles cover a wide range of rights, from liberty and security of the person (article 3), equality before the law (article 7), effective remedies (article 8), due process (articles 9 and 10), prohibitions on torture (article 5) and arbitrary interference with privacy (article 12) to rights protecting freedom of movement (article 13), asylum (article 14), expression (article 19), conscience and religion (article 18) and assembly (article 20). One should also note that included in the Declaration are social and economic rights such as the right to work and equal pay (article 23), the right to social security (article 25) and the right to education (article 26).

Although clearly not a legally enforceable instrument as such, the question arises as to whether the Declaration has subsequently become binding either by way of custom[77] or general principles of law, or indeed by virtue of interpretation of the UN Charter itself by subsequent practice.[78] The Declaration has had a marked influence upon the constitutions of many states and upon the formulation of subsequent human rights treaties and resolutions.[79] It is also to be noted that in 1968, the Proclamation of Tehran at the conclusion of the UN-sponsored International Conference on Human Rights stressed that the Declaration constituted 'an obligation for members of the international community'.[80] The Declaration has also

AJIL, 1949, p. 316; E. Schwelb, 'The Influence of the Universal Declaration of Human Rights on International and National Law', PASIL, 1959, p. 217; A. Verdoodt, *Naissance et Signification de la Déclaration Universelle de Droits de l'Homme*, Paris, 1964; *The Universal Declaration of Human Rights: A Commentary* (eds. A. Eide, G. Alfredsson, G. Melander, L. A. Rehof and A. Rosas), Dordrecht, 1992; *The Universal Declaration of Human Rights: A Common Standard of Achievement* (eds. G. Alfredsson and A. Eide), The Hague, 1999, and P. R. Ghandi, 'The Universal Declaration of Human Rights at 50 Years', 41 German YIL, 1998, p. 206.

[77] Note that the Foreign and Commonwealth Office in a document issued in January 1991 on 'Human Rights in Foreign Policy' took the view that, although the Declaration was 'not in itself legally binding, much of its content can now be said to form part of customary international law', UKMIL, 62 BYIL, 1991, p. 592.

[78] See e.g. *Oppenheim's International Law*, p. 1002.

[79] See e.g. Schwelb, 'Influence'; J. Humphrey, 'The International Bill of Rights: Scope and Implementation', 17 *William and Mary Law Review*, 1975, p. 527; *Oppenheim's International Law*, pp. 1002–5; Judge Tanaka, *South-West Africa* cases, ICJ Reports, 1966, pp. 6, 288 and 293; 37 ILR, pp. 243, 451, 454, and the European Convention on Human Rights, 1950, below, chapter 7, p. 347.

[80] 23 GAOR, A/Conf. 32/41. See also the non-governmental Montreal Statement, 9 *Review of the International Commission of Jurists*, 1968, p. 94.

been referred to in many cases,[81] and its importance within the context of United Nations human rights law should not be disregarded.[82] The intention had been that the Declaration would be followed immediately by a binding universal convention on human rights, but this process took considerably longer than anticipated. In the meantime, a number of important international conventions dealing with selective human rights issues were adopted, including the Genocide Convention[83] and the Convention on the Elimination of Racial Discrimination.[84]

The Vienna Declaration and Programme of Action, adopted in 1993, emphasised that all human rights were universal, indivisible and interdependent and interrelated. The protection of human rights was seen as a priority objective of the UN and the interrelationship of democracy, development and respect for human rights and fundamental freedoms underlined. Additional facilities for the UN Centre for Human Rights were called for as well as the establishment of a UN High Commissioner for Human Rights. The Declaration made particular reference *inter alia* to the problems of racial discrimination, minorities, indigenous peoples, migrant workers, the rights of women, the rights of the child, freedom from torture, the rights of disabled persons and human rights education.[85] The post of UN High Commissioner for Human Rights was indeed established several months later[86] and filled in April 1994. In General Assembly resolution 48/141, it is provided that the UN High Commissioner for Human Rights would be the UN official with principal responsibility for UN human rights activities. The High Commissioner is responsible

---

[81] See e.g. *In re Flesche* 16 AD, pp. 266, 269; *The State (Duggan)* v. *Tapley* 18 ILR, pp. 336, 342; *Robinson* v. *Secretary-General of the UN* 19 ILR, pp. 494, 496; *Extradition of Greek National* case, 22 ILR, pp. 520, 524 and *Beth El Mission* v. *Minister of Social Welfare* 47 ILR, pp. 205, 207. See also *Corfu Channel* case, ICJ Reports, 1949, pp. 4, 22; 16 AD, pp. 155, 158 and *Filartiga* v. *Pena-Irala* 630 F.2d 876 (1980).

[82] The Vienna Declaration and Programme of Action adopted on 25 June 1993 at the UN Conference on Human Rights referred to the Declaration as the 'source of inspiration' and the 'basis for the United Nations in making advances in standard setting as contained in the existing international human rights instruments', 32 ILM, 1993, pp. 1661, 1663. The private International Law Association adopted a resolution in 1994 in which it noted that 'the Universal Declaration of Human Rights is universally regarded as an authoritative elaboration of the human rights provisions of the United Nations Charter' and that 'many if not all of the rights elaborated in the Universal Declaration of Human Rights are widely recognised as constituting rules of customary international law', Report of the Sixty-sixth Conference, Buenos Aires, 1994, p. 29.

[83] See below, p. 282.   [84] See further below, p. 311.   [85] See 32 ILM, 1993, pp. 1661 ff.

[86] See General Assembly resolution 48/141, 20 December 1993. See also A. Clapham, 'Creating the High Commissioner for Human Rights: The Outside Story', 5 EJIL, 1994, p. 556.

for promoting and protecting the effective enjoyment by all of all civil, cultural, economic, political and social rights, providing through the UN Centre for Human Rights and other appropriate institutions, advisory services and other assistance including education and engaging in dialogue with all governments with a view to securing respect for human rights. The High Commissioner may also make recommendations to competent bodies of the UN system with a view to improving the promotion and protection of all human rights,[87] has engaged in a series of visits to member states of the UN and become involved in co-ordination activities.[88]

The protection of the collective rights of groups and individuals[89]

International law since 1945 has focused primarily upon the protection of individual human rights, as can be seen from the Universal Declaration of Human Rights. In recent years, however, more attention has been given to various expressions of the concept of collective rights, although it is often difficult to maintain a strict differentiation between individual and collective rights. Some rights are purely individual, such as the right to life or freedom of expression, others are individual rights that are necessarily expressed collectively, such as freedom of assembly or the right to manifest one's own religion. Some rights are purely collective, such as the right to self-determination or the physical protection of the group as such through the prohibition of genocide, others constitute collective manifestations of individual rights, such as the right of persons belonging to minorities to enjoy their own culture and practise their own religion or use their own language. In addition, the question of the balancing of the legitimate rights of the state, groups and individuals is in practice crucial and sometimes not sufficiently considered. States, groups and individuals have legitimate rights and interests that should not be ignored. All within a state have an interest in ensuring the efficient functioning of that state in a manner consistent with respect for the rights of groups and individuals, while the balancing of the rights of groups and individuals may itself prove difficult and complex.

---

[87] See the first Report of the United Nations High Commissioner for Human Rights, 1995, A/49/36, p. 2.

[88] *Ibid.*, pp. 3 ff. Further details as to activities may be found on the website, www.ohchr.org.

[89] See e.g. D. Sanders, 'Collective Rights', 13 HRQ, 1991, p. 368, and N. Lerner, *Group Rights and Discrimination in International Law*, 2nd edn, The Hague, 2003.

Prohibition of genocide

The physical protection of the group as a distinct identity is clearly the first and paramount factor. The Convention on the Prevention and Punishment of the Crime of Genocide signed in 1948[90] reaffirmed that genocide, whether committed in time of war or peace, was a crime under international law. Genocide was defined as any of the following acts committed 'with intent to destroy, in whole or in part, a national, ethnical, racial or religious group as such':

> (a) killing members of the group; (b) causing serious bodily or mental harm to members of the group; (c) deliberately inflicting on the group conditions of life calculated to bring about its physical destruction in whole or in part; (d) imposing measures intended to prevent births within the group; (e) forcibly transferring children of the group to another group.

The Convention, which does not have an implementational system,[91] provides that persons charged with genocide shall be tried by a competent tribunal of the state in the territory of which the act was committed or by an international penal tribunal. Several points should be noted. First, the question of intent is such that states may deny genocidal activity by noting that the relevant intent to destroy in whole or in part was in fact absent.[92] Secondly, the groups protected do not include political groups.[93]

---

[90] See e.g. W. Schabas, *Genocide in International Law*, Cambridge, 2000; N. Robinson, *The Genocide Convention*, London, 1960; R. Lemkin, *Axis Rule in Occupied Europe*, London, 1944; L. Kuper, *Genocide*, Harmondsworth, 1981, and *International Action Against Genocide*, Minority Rights Group Report No. 53, 1984; *Genocide and Human Rights* (ed. J. Porter), Washington 1982, and I. Horowitz, *Taking Lives: Genocide and State Power*, New Brunswick, 1980. See also N. Ruhashyankiko, *Study on the Question of the Prevention and Punishment of the Crime of Genocide*, 1978, E/CN.4/Sub.2/416; B. Whittaker, *Revised and Updated Report on the Question of the Prevention and Punishment of the Crime of Genocide*, 1985, E/CN.4/Sub.2/1985/6; 'Contemporary Practice of the United States Relating to International Law', 79 AJIL, 1985, pp. 116 ff.; M. Shaw, *War and Genocide*, Oxford, 2003; C. Fournet, *The Crime of Destruction and the Law of Genocide*, Ashgate, 2007; M. N. Shaw, 'Genocide and International Law' in *International Law at a Time of Perplexity* (ed. Y. Dinstein), Dordrecht, 1989, p. 797, and G. Verdirame, 'The Genocide Definition in the Jurisprudence of the *Ad Hoc* Tribunals', 49 ICLQ, 2000, p. 578.

[91] But see Sub-Commission resolution 1994/11.

[92] See Kuper, *Genocide*, pp. 32–5, and N. Lewis, 'The Camp at Cecilio Baez', in *Genocide in Paraguay* (ed. R. Arens), Philadelphia, 1976, p. 58. See also Ruhashyankiko, *Study*, p. 25.

[93] See e.g. Kuper, *Genocide*, pp. 25–30, and Ruhashyankiko, *Study*, p. 21. See also Robinson, *Genocide Convention*, p. 59.

Thirdly, the concept of cultural genocide is not included,[94] and fourthly there is virtually no mention of means to prevent the crime (although the obligation is stated).

In the 1990s, the issue of genocide unfortunately ceased to be an item of primarily historical concern. Events in the former Yugoslavia and in Rwanda stimulated increasing anxiety in this context. The Statutes of both the International Criminal Tribunal for the Former Yugoslavia and the International Criminal Tribunal for Rwanda provide for the prosecution of individuals for the crime of genocide and a significant case-law has now developed through these tribunals.[95] In addition, the question of state responsibility for the crime of genocide has been raised.[96] The International Court of Justice in the *Case Concerning Application of the Convention on the Prevention and Punishment of the Crime of Genocide (Bosnia and Herzegovina* v. *Yugoslavia (Serbia and Montenegro))* was faced with Bosnian claims that Yugoslavia had violated the Genocide Convention.[97] The Court in its Order of 8 April 1993 on the Request for the Indication of Provisional Measures[98] held that article IX of the Convention[99] provided a valid jurisdictional basis,[100] while reaffirming[101] the view expressed in the Advisory Opinion on *Reservations to the Genocide Convention* that the crime of genocide 'shocks the conscience of mankind, results in great losses to humanity . . . and is contrary to moral law and to the spirit and aims of the United Nations'.[102] The Court called upon both parties not to take any action that might aggravate or extend the dispute over the prevention or punishment of the crime of genocide. The government of

---

[94] See e.g. Kuper, *Genocide*, p. 31; Robinson, *Genocide Convention*, p. 64, and Ruhashyankiko, *Study*, pp. 21 ff.

[95] See further below, chapter 8, pp. 430 ff.   [96] See further generally below, chapter 14.

[97] ICJ Reports, 1993, pp. 3 and 325; 95 ILR, pp. 1 and 43.

[98] ICJ Reports, 1993, pp. 3, 16; 95 ILR, pp. 1, 31. See also R. Maison, 'Les Ordonnances de la CIJ dans l'Affaire Relative à l'Application de la Convention sur la Prévention et la Répression du Crime du Génocide', 5 EJIL, 1994, p. 381.

[99] This provides that 'disputes between the Contracting Parties relating to the interpretation, application or fulfilment of the present Convention, including those relating to the responsibility of a state for genocide or for any of the other acts enumerated in article III, shall be submitted to the International Court of Justice at the request of any of the parties to the dispute'.

[100] The Court dismissed other suggested grounds for its jurisdiction in the case, ICJ Reports, 1993, p. 18; 95 ILR, p. 33.

[101] ICJ Reports, 1993, p. 23; 95 ILR, p. 38.

[102] ICJ Reports, 1951, pp. 15, 23; 18 ILR, pp. 364, 370, quoting the terms of General Assembly resolution 96 (I) of 11 December 1946.

Yugoslavia (Serbia and Montenegro) was requested to take all measures within its power to prevent commission of the crime of genocide, and was specifically called upon to ensure that 'any military, paramilitary or irregular armed units which may be directed or supported by it, as well as any organisations and persons which may be subject to its control, direction or influence, do not commit any acts of genocide'.[103] These provisional measures were reaffirmed by the Court in its Order on Provisional Measures of 13 September 1993 as measures which should be 'immediately and effectively implemented'.[104]

On 11 July 1996, the Court rejected the Preliminary Objections raised by Yugoslavia.[105] In particular, the Court emphasised that it followed from the object and purpose of the Genocide Convention that the rights and obligations contained therein were rights and obligations *erga omnes* and that the obligation upon each state to prevent and punish the crime of genocide was not dependent upon the type of conflict involved in the particular situation (whether international or domestic) and was not territorially limited by the Convention.[106] The type of state responsibility envisaged under article IX of the Convention did not exclude any form of state responsibility.[107] In addition, the Court observed that the Convention did not contain any clause the object or effect of which was to limit the scope of its jurisdiction *ratione temporis* so as to exclude events prior to a particular date.[108] Yugoslavia subsequently withdrew the counterclaims it had introduced against Bosnia,[109] while introducing an application in April 2001 for revision of the 1996 judgment on the basis that a 'new fact' had appeared since that state had become a new member of the UN during 2000. This was rejected by the Court.[110] On 26 February 2007, the Court rendered its judgment on the merits. The Court affirmed that the effect of the categorisation of genocide as a 'crime under international law', coupled with the obligation to prevent genocide contained in the Genocide Convention, is to prohibit states from committing

---

[103] ICJ Reports, 1993, pp. 3, 24; 95 ILR, pp. 1, 39.

[104] ICJ Reports, 1993, pp. 325, 350; 95 ILR, pp. 43, 68. See also the Separate Opinion of Judge Lauterpacht, ICJ Reports, 1993, pp. 407, 431–2; 95 ILR, pp. 125, 149–50.

[105] Now so called, rather than the former Yugoslavia (Serbia and Montenegro), as from, and in consequence of, the Dayton Peace Agreement initialled at Dayton, USA, on 11 November 1995 and signed in Paris on 14 December 1995.

[106] ICJ Reports, 1996, pp. 595, 615; 115 ILR, p. 1.   [107] ICJ Reports, 1996, p. 616.

[108] *Ibid.*, p. 617. See also the *Legality of the Threat or Use of Nuclear Weapons*, ICJ Reports, 1996, pp. 226, 240; 110 ILR, p. 163.

[109] ICJ, Order of 10 September 2001.

[110] ICJ Reports, 2003, p. 7. See further below, chapter 19, p. 1106.

genocide through the actions of their organs or persons or groups whose acts are attributable to them.[111] The Court also held that state responsibility could arise under the Convention for genocide and complicity, without an individual being convicted of the crime or an associated one,[112] and that such responsibility for genocide applied to a state wherever it may be acting.[113] It was noted that the essence of the intent, at the heart of the definition of genocide, is to destroy the protected group, in whole or in part, as such. It is a group which must have particular positive characteristics – national, ethnical, racial or religious – and not the lack of them. The intent must also relate to the group 'as such'. That means that the crime requires an intent to destroy a collection of people who have a particular group identity[114] and such intent refers to the intent to destroy at least a substantial part of the particular group and this may apply to a geographically limited area (such as Srebrenica).[115] The Court emphasised that claims against a state involving charges of exceptional gravity, such as genocide, must be proved by evidence that is fully conclusive.[116] However, the Court emphasised that the Convention established a separate and distinct duty to prevent genocide, which was both 'normative and compelling'[117] and an obligation of conduct, not of result,[118] provided that the offence was actually committed.[119] Such obligation arose at the instant that the state learned of, or should normally have learned of, the existence of a serious risk that genocide would be committed.[120] It was also held that Serbia was in violation of its duty to punish genocide.[121]

---

[111] ICJ Reports, 2007, paras. 161–7. See also *Democratic Republic of the Congo* v. *Rwanda*, ICJ Reports, 2006, pp. 6, 31–2, where the Court noted that the rights and obligations in the Genocide Convention were rights and obligations *erga omnes* and stated that the prohibition of genocide was 'assuredly' a norm of *jus cogens*.

[112] ICJ Reports, 2007, para. 182.   [113] *Ibid.*, para. 183.   [114] *Ibid.*, para. 193.

[115] *Ibid.*, paras. 198–9.

[116] *Ibid.*, para. 209 and see also para. 319. The Court, however, was not convinced, on the basis of the evidence before it, that it had been conclusively established that the massive killings of members of the protected group were committed with the specific intent (*dolus specialis*) on the part of the perpetrators to destroy, in whole or in part, the group as such, *ibid.*, para. 277, nor that deportations and expulsions of the protected group amounted to genocide for the same reason, *ibid.*, para. 334, nor indeed the imposition of terrible conditions on camp detainees and other allegations, *ibid.*, paras. 354, 370 and 376. The exception to this was with regard to Srebrenica, where the Court found that the necessary intent had been established to the required standard of proof, paras. 278–97.

[117] *Ibid.*, para. 427.   [118] *Ibid.*, para. 430.   [119] *Ibid.*, para. 431.   [120] *Ibid.*

[121] *Ibid.*, para. 450.

Prohibition of discrimination

Apart from the overwhelming requirement of protection from physical attack upon their very existence as a group, groups need protection from discriminatory treatment as such.[122] The norm of non-discrimination thus constitutes a principle relevant both to groups and to individual members of groups.

The International Convention on the Elimination of All Forms of Racial Discrimination[123] was signed in 1965 and entered into force in 1969. It builds on the non-discrimination provisions in the UN Charter. Racial discrimination is defined as:

> any distinction, exclusion, restriction or preference based on race, colour, descent or national or ethnic origin which has the purpose or effect of nullifying or impairing the recognition, enjoyment or exercise, on an equal footing, of human rights and fundamental freedoms in the political, economic, social, cultural or any other field of public life.

States parties undertake to prohibit racial discrimination and guarantee equality for all in the enjoyment of a series of rights and to assure to all within their jurisdiction effective protection and remedies regarding such human rights.[124] It is also fair to conclude that in addition to the existence of this Convention, the prohibition of discrimination on racial grounds is contrary to customary international law.[125] This conclusion may be reached on the basis *inter alia* of articles 55 and 56 of the UN Charter, articles 2 and 7 of the Universal Declaration of Human Rights, the International Covenants on Human Rights,[126] regional instruments on human

---

[122] See e.g. Rehman, *International Human Rights Law*, chapter 10; W. Vandenhole, *Non-discrimination and Equality in the View of the UN Human Rights Treaty Bodies*, Antwerp, 2005; Joseph *et al.*, *International Covenant*, chapter 23; A. Bayefsky, 'The Principle of Equality or Non-discrimination in International Law', 11 HRLJ, 1990, p. 1; J. Greenberg, 'Race, Sex and Religious Discrimination' in Meron, *Human Rights in International Law*, p. 307; W. McKean, *Equality and Discrimination under International Law*, Oxford, 1983, and T. Meron, *Human Rights Law-Making in the United Nations*, Oxford, 1986, chapters 1–3.

[123] See e.g. N. Lerner, *The UN Convention on the Elimination of All Forms of Racial Discrimination*, 2nd edn, Dordrecht, 1980.

[124] See further below, p. 311, with regard to the establishment of the Committee on the Elimination of Racial Discrimination. Note also the Convention on the Suppression and Punishment of the Crime of Apartheid, 1973.

[125] See e.g. the Dissenting Opinion of Judge Tanaka in the *South-West Africa* cases, ICJ Reports, 1966, pp. 3, 293; 37 ILR, pp. 243, 455.

[126] See below, p. 314.

rights protection[127] and general state practice. Discrimination on other grounds, such as religion[128] and gender,[129] may also be contrary to customary international law. The International Covenant on Civil and Political Rights provides in article 2(1) that all states parties undertake to respect and ensure to all individuals within their territories and within their jurisdictions the rights recognised in the Covenant 'without distinction of any kind such as race, colour, sex, language, religion, political or other

---

[127] See below, pp. 347 ff.

[128] See e.g. the Declaration on the Elimination of All Forms of Intolerance and of Discrimination Based on Religion or Belief, 1981, General Assembly resolution 36/55 and the appointment of a Special Rapporteur to examine situations inconsistent with the Declaration by the UN Commission on Human Rights, resolution 1986/20 of 10 March 1986. See also Odio Benito, *Elimination of All Forms of Intolerance and Discrimination Based on Religion or Belief*, New York, 1989, and Report on the Implementation of the Declaration on the Elimination of All Forms of Intolerance and of Discrimination Based on Religion or Belief, E/CN.4/1995/91, 1994. In 2000, the Commission on Human Rights changed the mandate title to 'Special Rapporteur on freedom of religion or belief': see ECOSOC decision 2000/261 and General Assembly resolution 55/97. On 14 December 2007, the Human Rights Council extended the mandate of the Special Rapporteur for a further period of three years. The UN Human Rights Committee has produced a General Comment on article 18 concerning freedom of thought, conscience and religion: see General Comment 22, 1993, HRI/GEN/1/Rev.1, 1994, and Joseph *et al.*, *International Covenant*, chapter 17. Note also S. Neff, 'An Evolving International Legal Norm of Religious Freedom: Problems and Prospects', 7 *California Western International Law Journal*, 1975, p. 543; A. Krishnaswami, *Study of Discrimination in the Matter of Religious Rights and Practices*, New York, 1960, E/CN.4/Sub.2/200/Rev.1; N. Lerner, 'Towards a Draft Declaration against Religious Intolerance and Discrimination', 11 *Israel Yearbook on Human Rights*, 1981, p. 82; B. Tahzib, *Freedom of Religion or Belief: Ensuring Effective International Legal Protection*, Dordrecht, 1995, and B. Dickson, 'The United Nations and Freedom of Religion', 44 ICLQ, 1995, p. 327.

[129] See the Convention on the Elimination of All Forms of Discrimination Against Women 1979, below, p. 322. Article 1 of the Convention provides that discrimination against women means any distinction, exclusion or restriction made on the basis of sex which has the effect or purpose of impairing or nullifying the recognition, enjoyment or exercise by women, irrespective of their marital status, on a basis of equality with men and women, of human rights and fundamental freedoms in the political, economic, social, cultural, civil or any other field. See e.g. McKean, *Equality*, chapter 10; Bayefsky, 'Equality', and Meron, *Human Rights Law-Making*, chapter 2. See also J. Morsink, 'Women's Rights in the Universal Declaration', 13 HRQ, 1991, p. 229; R. Cook, 'Women's International Human Rights Law', 15 HRQ, 1993, p. 230; *Human Rights of Women* (ed. R. Cook), Philadelphia, 1994, and M. A. Freeman and A. S. Fraser, 'Women's Human Rights' in Herkin and Hargrove, *Human Rights: An Agenda for the Next Century*, p. 103. Note also the UN General Assembly Declaration on Elimination of Violence against Women, 33 ILM, 1994, p. 1049. See also the London Declaration of International Law Principles on Internally Displaced Persons adopted by the International Law Association, *Report of the Sixty-Ninth Conference*, London, 2000, p. 794.

opinion, national or social origin, property, birth or other status'.[130] Article 26 stipulates that all persons are equal before the law and thus, 'the law shall prohibit any discrimination and guarantee to all persons equal and effective protection against discrimination on any ground such as race, colour, sex, language, religion, political or other opinion, national or social origin, property, birth or other status'.[131] The UN Human Rights Committee established under this Covenant[132] has noted in its General Comment 18 on Non-Discrimination[133] that non-discrimination 'constitutes a basic and general principle relating to the protection of human rights'. The Committee, while adopting the definition of the term 'discrimination' as used in the Racial Discrimination and Women's Discrimination Conventions, concludes that it should be understood to imply any distinction, exclusion, restriction or preference which is based on any ground such as race, colour, sex, language, religion, political or other opinion, national or social origin, property, birth or other status and which has the purpose or effect of nullifying or impairing the recognition, enjoyment or exercise by all persons, on an equal footing, of all rights and freedoms.

The principle of non-discrimination requires the establishment of equality in fact as well as formal equality in law. As the Permanent Court of International Justice noted in the *Minority Schools in Albania* case,[134] 'equality in law precludes discrimination of any kind; whereas equality in fact may involve the necessity of different treatment in order to attain a result which establishes an equilibrium between different situations'.[135] The appropriate test of acceptable differentiation in such circumstances will centre upon what is just or reasonable[136] or objectively and reasonably justified.[137] The application of equality in fact may also require the

---

[130] See also, for example, articles 2(2) and 3 of the International Covenant on Economic, Social and Cultural Rights, 1966. See M. C. Craven, *The International Covenant on Economic, Social and Cultural Rights*, Oxford, 1995, chapter 4, and see further below, p. 308.

[131] Note that this provision constitutes an autonomous or free-standing principle, whereas article 2(1) of that Covenant and articles 2 of the Universal Declaration of Human Rights, 14 of the European Convention on Human Rights and 2(1) of the Convention on the Rights of the Child prohibit discrimination in the context of specific rights and freedoms laid down in the instrument in question: see Bayefsky, 'Equality', pp. 3–4, and the Human Rights Committee's General Comment on Non-Discrimination, paragraph 12.

[132] See further below, p. 314.   [133] Adopted on 9 November 1989, CCPR/C/Rev.1/Add.1.

[134] PCIJ, Series A/B, No. 64, p. 19 (1935); 8 AD, pp. 386, 389–90.

[135] See also the Human Rights Committee's General Comment on Non-Discrimination, paragraph 8.

[136] See Judge Tanaka's Dissenting Opinion in the *South-West Africa* cases, ICJ Reports, 1966, pp. 3, 306; 37 ILR, pp. 243, 464.

[137] See e.g. the *Belgian Linguistics* case, European Court of Human Rights, Series A, No. 6, 1986, para. 10; 45 ILR, pp. 114, 165. See also the *Amendments to the Naturalisation*

introduction of affirmative action measures in order to diminish or eliminate conditions perpetuating discrimination. Such measures would need to be specifically targeted and neither absolute nor of infinite duration.[138]

The principle of self-determination as a human right[139]

The right to self-determination has already been examined in so far as it relates to the context of decolonisation.[140] The question arises whether this right, which has been widely proclaimed, has an application beyond the colonial context. Article 1 of both International Covenants on Human Rights provides that 'all peoples have the right to self-determination. By virtue of that right they freely determine their political status and freely pursue their economic, social and cultural development', while the Helsinki Final Act of 1975[141] refers to 'the principle of equal rights and self-determination . . . all peoples have the right, in full freedom, to determine, when and as they wish, their internal and external political status, without external interference, and to pursue as they wish their

Provisions of the Constitution of Costa Rica case, Inter-American Court of Human Rights, 1984, para. 56; 5 HRLJ, 1984, p. 172, and the Human Rights Committee's General Comment on Non-Discrimination, paragraph 13, which notes that 'not every differentiation of treatment will constitute discrimination, if the criteria for such differentiation are reasonable and objective and if the aim is to achieve a purpose which is legitimate under the Covenant'.

[138] See the Human Rights Committee's General Comment on Non-Discrimination, paragraph 10. See also article 1(4) of the Racial Discrimination Convention, article 4(1) of the Women's Discrimination Convention and article 27 of the International Covenant on Civil and Political Rights.

[139] See e.g. A. Buchanan, *Justice, Legitimacy and Self-Determination*, Oxford, 2004; J. Summers, *Peoples and International Law*, The Hague, 2007; K. Knop, *Diversity and Self-Determination in International Law*, Cambridge, 2002; T. D. Musgrave, *Self-Determination and National Minorities*, Oxford, 1997; W. Ofuatey-Kodjoe, 'Self Determination' in *United Nations Legal Order* (eds. O. Schachter and C. C. Joyner), Cambridge, 1995, vol. I, p. 349; A. Cassese, *Self-Determination of Peoples*, Cambridge, 1995; *Modern Law of Self-Determination* (ed. C. Tomuschat), Dordrecht, 1993; Higgins, *Problems and Process*, chapter 7; T. Franck, *The Power of Legitimacy Among Nations*, Oxford, 1990, pp. 153 ff.; Franck, 'Fairness in the International and Institutional System', 240 HR, 1993 III, pp. 13, 125 ff.; *The Rights of Peoples* (ed. J. Crawford), Oxford, 1988; *Peoples and Minorities in International Law* (eds. C. Brölmann, R. Lefeber and M. Zieck), Dordrecht, 1993, and P. Thornberry, 'Self-Determination, Minorities, Human Rights: A Review of International Instruments', 38 ICLQ, 1989, p. 867. See also M. Koskenniemi, 'National Self-Determination Today: Problems of Legal Theory and Practice', 43 ICLQ, 1994, p. 241; G. Simpson, 'The Diffusion of Sovereignty: Self-Determination in the Post-Colonial Age', 32 *Stanford Journal of International Law*, 1996, p. 255, and R. McCorquodale, 'Self-Determination: A Human Rights Approach', 43 ICLQ, 1994, p. 857.

[140] See above, chapter 5, p. 251.   [141] See further below, p. 372.

political, economic, social and cultural development'. Article 20 of the African Charter on Human and Peoples' Rights, 1981[142] stipulates that 'all peoples shall have the right to existence. They shall have the unquestionable and inalienable right to self-determination. They shall freely determine their political status and shall pursue their economic and social development according to the policy they have chosen.' The 1970 Declaration on Principles of International Law Concerning Friendly Relations[143] referred to the colonial situation and noted that subjection of peoples to alien subjugation, domination and exploitation constituted a violation of the principle. A number of UN resolutions have discussed the relevance of self-determination also to situations of alien occupation where the use of force has been involved.[144] The International Law Commission in 1988 expressed its view that the principle of self-determination was of universal application,[145] while the practice of the UN Human Rights Committee has been of particular significance.

Before this is briefly noted, reference must be made to the crucial importance of the principle of territorial integrity.[146] This norm protects the territorial framework of independent states and is part of the overall concept of the sovereignty of states. In terms of the concept of the freezing of territorial boundaries as at the moment of independence (save by mutual consent), the norm is referred to as *uti possidetis juris*.[147] This posits that boundaries established and existing at the moment of independence cannot be altered unless the relevant parties consent to change. It is supported by international instruments[148] and by judicial pronouncement. In the *Burkina Faso/Mali* case,[149] the Chamber of the International Court of Justice emphasised that *uti possidetis* constituted a general principle, whose purpose was to prevent the independence and stability of

---

[142] See further below, p. 391.   [143] General Assembly resolution 2625 (XXV).

[144] See, for an examination of state practice, e.g. Cassese, *Self-Determination*, pp. 90–9.

[145] *Yearbook of the ILC*, 1988, vol. II, Part 2, p. 64.

[146] General Assembly resolution 1514 (XV) 1960 (the Colonial Declaration) underlines that 'any attempt at the partial or total disruption of the national unity and the territorial integrity of a country is incompatible with the purposes and principles of the Charter of the UN', while resolution 2625 (XXV) 1970 (the Declaration on Principles of International Law Concerning Friendly Relations) emphasises that 'nothing in the foregoing paragraphs shall be construed as authorising or encouraging any action which would dismember or impair, totally or in part, the territorial integrity or political unity of sovereign or independent states'. See further below, chapter 10, p. 522.

[147] See further below, chapter 10, p. 525.

[148] See e.g. General Assembly resolutions 1514 (XV) and 1541 (XV) and Organisation of African Unity resolution 16 (I) 1964.

[149] ICJ Reports, 1986, pp. 554, 566–7; 80 ILR, pp. 440, 470–1.

new states from being endangered by fratricidal struggles provoked by the challenging of frontiers. This essential requirement of stability had induced newly independent states to consent to the respecting of colonial borders 'and to take account of it in the interpretation of the principle of self-determination of peoples'. The Arbitration Commission of the European Conference on Yugoslavia emphasised in Opinion No. 2[150] that 'it is well established that, whatever the circumstances, the right to self-determination must not involve changes to existing frontiers at the time of independence (*uti possidetis juris*) except where the states concerned agree otherwise'.

The principle of self-determination, therefore, applies beyond the colonial context, within the territorial framework of independent states. It cannot be utilised as a legal tool for the dismantling of sovereign states.[151] Its use, however, as a crucial principle of collective human rights[152] has been analysed by the Human Rights Committee in interpreting article 1 of the Civil and Political Rights Covenant.[153] In its General Comment on

[150] 92 ILR, pp. 167, 168. See further above, chapter 5, p. 256.

[151] The clause in the 1970 Declaration on Principles of International Law Concerning Friendly Relations (repeated in the UN Vienna Declaration on Human Rights, 1993), stating that nothing in the section on self-determination shall be construed as authorising or encouraging the dismembering or impairing of the territorial integrity of states conducting themselves in compliance with the principle of self-determination 'as described above and thus possessed of a government representing the whole people belonging to the territory without distinction as to race, creed or colour', may be seen, first, as establishing the primacy of the principle of territorial integrity and, secondly, as indicating the content of self-determination within the territory. Whether it also can be seen as offering legitimacy to secession from an independent state in exceptional circumstances is the subject of much debate. Cassese, for example, concludes that 'a racial or religious group may attempt secession, a form of external self-determination, when it is apparent that internal self-determination is absolutely beyond reach. Extreme and unremitting persecution and the lack of any reasonable prospect for peaceful challenge may make secession legitimate', *Self-Determination*, p. 120. See also R. Rosenstock, 'The Declaration on Principles of International Law', 65 AJIL, 1971, pp. 713, 732, and J. Crawford, *The Creation of States in International Law*, 2nd edn, Oxford, 2006, pp. 118 ff. The Canadian Supreme Court in the *Quebec Secession* case discussed the question without reaching a conclusion, (1998) 161 DLR (4th) 385, 437 ff.; 115 ILR, pp. 536, 582–7. It would appear that practice demonstrating the successful application of even this modest proposition is lacking.

[152] Note Brownlie's view that the principle of self-determination has a core of reasonable certainty and this consists in 'the right of a community which has a distinct character to have this character reflected in the institutions of government under which it lives', 'The Rights of Peoples in International Law' in Crawford, *Rights of Peoples*, pp. 1, 5.

[153] See in particular D. McGoldrick, *The Human Rights Committee*, Oxford, 1994, chapter 5; Cassese, *Self-Determination*, pp. 59 ff., and M. Nowak, *UN Covenant on Civil and Political Rights, CCPR Commentary*, 2nd edn, Kehl, 2005, part 1.

Self-Determination adopted in 1984,[154] the Committee emphasised that the realisation of the right was 'an essential condition for the effective guarantee and observance of individual human rights'. Nevertheless, the principle is seen as a collective one and not one that individuals could seek to enforce through the individual petition procedures provided in the First Optional Protocol to the Covenant.[155] The Committee takes the view, as Professor Higgins[156] noted,[157] that 'external self-determination requires a state to take action in its foreign policy consistent with the attainment of self-determination in the remaining areas of colonial or racist occupation. But internal self-determination is directed to their own peoples.' In the context of the significance of the principle of self-determination within independent states, the Committee has encouraged states parties to provide in their reports details about participation in social and political structures,[158] and in engaging in dialogue with representatives of states parties, questions are regularly posed as to how political institutions operate and how the people of the state concerned participate in the governance of their state.[159] This necessarily links in with consideration of other articles of the Covenant concerning, for example, freedom of expression (article 19), freedom of assembly (article 21), freedom of association (article 22) and the right to take part in the conduct of public affairs and to vote

---

[154] General Comment 12: see HRI/GEN/1/Rev.1, p. 12, 1994.

[155] See the *Kitok* case, Report of the Human Rights Committee, A/43/40, pp. 221, 228; 96 ILR, pp. 637, 645; the *Lubicon Lake Band* case, A/45/40, vol. II, pp. 1, 27; 96 ILR, pp. 667, 702; *EP* v. *Colombia*, A/45/40, vol. II, pp. 184, 187, and *RL* v. *Canada*, A/47/40, pp. 358, 365; 96 ILR, p. 706. However, in *Mahuika et al.* v. *New Zealand*, the Committee took the view that the provisions of article 1 may be relevant in the interpretation of other rights protected by the Covenant, in particular article 27 on the rights of persons belonging to minorities, A/56/40, vol. II, annex X, A. See also *Diergaardt et al.* v. *Namibia*, A/55/40, vol. II, annex IX, sect. M, para. 10.3.

[156] A member of the Committee from 1985 to 1995.

[157] Higgins, 'Postmodern Tribalism and the Right to Secession' in Brölmann *et al.*, *Peoples and Minorities in International Law*, p. 31.

[158] See e.g. the report of Colombia, CCPR/C/64/Add.3, pp. 9 ff., 1991. In the third periodic report of Peru, it was noted that the first paragraph of article 1 of the Covenant 'lays down the right of every people to self-determination. Under that right any people is able to decide freely on its political and economic condition or regime and hence establish a form of government suitable for the purposes in view. To this effect Peru adopted as its form of government the republican system which was embodied in the constitution of 1979, which stated that Peru was a democratic and social independent and sovereign republic based on work with a unitary representative and decentralised government', CCPR/C/83/Add.1, 1995, p. 4.

[159] See e.g. with regard to Canada, A/46/40, p. 12. See also A/45/40, pp. 120–1, with regard to Zaire.

(article 25). The right of self-determination, therefore, provides the overall framework for the consideration of the principles relating to democratic governance.[160] The Committee on the Elimination of Racial Discrimination adopted General Recommendation 21 in 1996 in which it similarly divided self-determination into an external and an internal aspect and noted that the latter referred to the 'right of every citizen to take part in the conduct of public affairs at any level'.[161] The Canadian Supreme Court has noted that self-determination 'is normally fulfilled through *internal* self-determination – a people's pursuit of its political, economic, social and cultural development within the framework of an existing state'.[162]

The protection of minorities[163]

Various attempts were made in the post-First World War settlements, following the collapse of the German, Ottoman, Russian and Austro-Hungarian Empires and the rise of a number of independent nation-based states in Eastern and Central Europe, to protect those groups to whom sovereignty and statehood could not be granted.[164] Persons

---

[160] See T. Franck, 'The Emerging Right to Democratic Governance', 86 AJIL, 1992, p. 46. See also P. Thornberry, 'The Democratic or Internal Aspect of Self-Determination' in Tomuschat, *Modern Law of Self-Determination*, p. 101.

[161] A/51/18.

[162] The *Quebec Secession* case, (1998) 161 DLR (4th) 385, 437–8; 115 ILR, p. 536.

[163] See e.g. *Oppenheim's International Law*, pp. 972 ff.; Nowak, *UN Covenant*, pp. 480 ff.; M. Weller, *Universal Minority Rights: A Commentary on the Jurisprudence of International Courts and Treaty Bodies*, Oxford, 2007; R. Higgins, 'Minority Rights: Discrepancies and Divergencies Between the International Covenant and the Council of Europe System' in *Liber Amicorum for Henry Schermers*, Dordrecht, 1994, p. 193; Shaw, 'Definition of Minorities'; P. Thornberry, *International Law and Minorities*, Oxford, 1991, and Thornberry, 'Phoenix', and 'Self-Determination', p. 867; G. Alfredsson, 'Minority Rights and a New World Order' in *Broadening the Frontiers of Human Rights: Essays in Honour of A. Eide* (ed. D. Gomien), Oslo, 1993; G. Alfredsson and A. M. de Zayas, 'Minority Rights: Protection by the UN', 14 HRLJ, 1993, p. 1; Brölmann *et al.*, *Peoples and Minorities in International Law*; *The Protection of Ethnic and Linguistic Minorities in Europe* (eds. J. Packer and K. Myntti), Turku, 1993; *Documents on Autonomy and Minority Rights* (ed. H. Hannum), Dordrecht, 1993; N. Rodley, 'Conceptual Problems in the Protection of Minorities: International Legal Developments', 17 HRQ, 1995, p. 48; A. Fenet *et al.*, *Le Droit et les Minorités*, Brussels, 1995; J. Rehman, *The Weakness in the International Protection of Minority Rights*, The Hague, 2000, and *International Human Rights Law*, chapters 11 and 12; Musgrave, *Self-Determination*, and *Minority and Group Rights in the New Millennium* (eds. D. Fottrell and B. Bowring), The Hague, 1999. See also the Capotorti Study on the Rights of Persons Belonging to Ethnic, Religious and Linguistic Minorities, E/CN.4/Sub.2/384/Rev.1, 1979.

[164] The minorities regime of the League consisted of five special minorities treaties binding Poland, the Serbo-Croat-Slovene state, Romania, Greece and Czechoslovakia; special

belonging to racial, religious or linguistic minorities were to be given the same treatment and the same civil and political rights and security as other nationals in the state in question. Such provisions constituted obligations of international concern and could not be altered without the assent of a majority of the League of Nations Council. The Council was to take action in the event of any infraction of minorities' obligations. There also existed a petition procedure by minorities to the League, although they had no standing as such before the Council or the Permanent Court of International Justice.[165] However, the schemes of protection did not work well, ultimately for a variety of reasons ranging from the sensitivities of newly independent states to international supervision of minority issues to overt exploitation of minority issues by Nazi Germany in order to subvert neighbouring countries. After the Second World War, the focus shifted to the international protection of universal individual human rights, although several instruments dealing with specific situations incorporated provisions concerning the protection of minorities,[166] and in 1947 the Sub-Commission on the Prevention of Discrimination and the Protection of Minorities was established.[167] It was not, however, until the adoption of the International Covenant on Civil and Political Rights in 1966 that the question of minority rights came back onto the international agenda. Article 27 of this Covenant provides that 'in those states in which ethnic, religious or linguistic minorities exist, persons belonging to such minorities shall not be denied the right, in community with the other members of their group, to enjoy their own culture, to profess and practise their own religion, or to use their own language'.

This modest and rather negative provision as formulated centres upon 'persons belonging' to minorities rather than upon minorities as such

minorities clauses in the treaties of peace with Austria, Bulgaria, Hungary and Turkey; five general declarations made on admission to the League by Albania, Latvia, Lithuania, Estonia and Iraq; a special declaration by Finland regarding the Aaland Islands, and treaties relating to Danzig, Upper Silesia and Memel: see generally Thornberry, *International Law and Minorities*, pp. 38 ff.

[165] In the early 1930s several hundred petitions were received but this dropped to virtually nil by 1939: see Thornberry, *International Law and Minorities*, pp. 434–6, and the Capotorti Report on the *Rights of Persons belonging to Ethnic, Religious and Linguistic Minorities*, 1979, E/CN.4/Sub.2/384/Rev.1, pp. 20–2. See also Macartney, *National States*, pp. 370 ff.; J. Stone, *International Guarantees of Minority Rights*, London, 1932, and Richard, *Le Droit de Petition*, Paris, 1932.

[166] See e.g. Annex IV of the Treaty of Peace with Italy, 1947; the Indian–Pakistan Treaty, 1950, and article 7 of the Austrian State Treaty, 1955. See also the provisions in the documents concerning the independence of Cyprus, Cmnd 1093, 1960.

[167] See further below, p. 307.

and does not define the concept of minorities.[168] Nevertheless, the UN Human Rights Committee has taken the opportunity to consider the issue in discussing states' reports, individual petitions and in a General Comment. In commenting upon states' reports made pursuant to the International Covenant, the Committee has made clear, for example, that the rights under article 27 apply to all members of minorities within a state party's territory and not just nationals,[169] and it has expressed concern with regard to the treatment of minorities within particular states.[170]

In the *Lovelace* case,[171] the Committee decided that there had been a violation of article 27 with regard to an Indian woman who, by having married a non-Indian, had lost her rights by Canadian law to reside on the Tobique Reserve, something which she wished to do upon the collapse of her marriage. The Committee noted that statutory restrictions affecting the right to residence on a reserve of a person belonging to the minority concerned had to have both a reasonable and objective justification and be consistent with the other provisions of the Covenant read as a whole. This had not been the case. There was no place outside the reserve where her right to access to her native culture and language could be conducted in community with other members of the minority in question.

In the *Kitok* case,[172] the Committee took the view with regard to a petition by a member of the Sami community in Sweden that where the regulation of economic activity was an essential element in the culture

---

[168] Attempts to define minorities have invariably focused upon the numerically inferior numbers of minorities and their non-dominant position, the existence of certain objective features differentiating them from the majority population (e.g. ethnic, religious or linguistic) coupled with the subjective wish of the minority concerned to preserve those characteristics. See e.g. Shaw, 'Definition of Minorities', and the Capotorti Report, p. 96. See also Council of Europe Assembly Recommendation 1255 (1955), H/Inf (95) 3, p. 88. Note that the Human Rights Committee in the *Ballantyne* case held that English-speaking citizens in Quebec did not constitute a minority since the term 'minority' applied to the whole state and not a part of it, 14 HRLJ, 1993, pp. 171, 176.

[169] See e.g. comments upon Norway's third periodic report, A/49/40, p. 23 and Japan's third periodic report, *ibid.*, p. 25. See also Joseph *et al., International Covenant,* chapter 24.

[170] See e.g. with regard to the third periodic report of Romania, A/49/40, p. 29 and that of Mexico, *ibid.*, p. 35, and the fourth periodic report of Russia, CCPR/C/79/Add.54, p. 5 and that of Ukraine, CCPR/C/79/Add.52, p. 4. Note also the criticism of the Democratic Republic of the Congo for its marginalisation, discrimination and, at times, persecution of some of the country's minorities, including pygmies, see CCPR/C/SR.2358, 2006, and of the situation in Kosovo, CCPR/C/SR.2394, 2006.

[171] I *Selected Decisions of the Human Rights Committee*, 1985, p. 83; 68 ILR, p. 17.

[172] A/43/40, p. 221; 96 ILR, p. 637.

of an economic community, its application to an individual could fall within article 27. It was emphasised that a restriction upon an individual member of a minority must be shown to have a reasonable and objective justification and to be necessary for the continued viability and welfare of the minority as a whole.

In the *Lubicon Lake Band* case,[173] the Committee upheld the complaint that the Canadian Government, in allowing the Provincial Government of Alberta to expropriate the Band's territory for the benefit of private corporate interests, violated article 27. It was held that the rights protected under article 27 included the right of persons in community with others to engage in economic and social activities which were part of the culture of the community to which they belonged. However, measures with only a limited impact on the way of life and livelihood of persons belonging to a minority would not necessarily violate article 27.[174]

The Committee adopted a General Comment on article 27 in 1994 after much discussion and hesitation due to fears that such a comment might be perceived to constitute an encouragement to secession.[175] The General Comment pointed to the distinction between the rights of persons belonging to minorities on the one hand, and the right to self-determination and the right to equality and non-discrimination on the other. It was emphasised that the rights under article 27 did not prejudice the sovereignty and territorial integrity of states, although certain minority rights, in particular those pertaining to indigenous communities, might consist of a way of life closely associated with territory and the use of its resources, such as fishing, hunting and the right to live in reserves protected by law. The Committee, in an important part of the General Comment, underlined that persons belonging to a minority need not be nationals or permanent residents of the state concerned so that migrant workers or even visitors might be protected under article 27. Whether an ethnic, religious or linguistic minority exists was an objective question, not dependent upon a decision of the state party. Although article 27 is negatively formulated, the Committee pointed out that positive measures of protection were required not only against the acts of the state party itself, but also against the acts of other persons within the state party. Positive measures may also be necessary to protect the identity of the minority concerned and legitimate

[173] A/45/40, vol. II, p. 1; 96 ILR, p. 667.
[174] See the *Länsmann* cases against Finland, 511/92 and 671/95, 115 ILR, p. 300, and Report of the Human Rights Committee 2005, volume II, A/60/40, pp. 90 ff.
[175] General Comment No. 23, HRI/GEN/1/Rev.1, p. 38.

differentiation was permitted so long as it was based on reasonable and objective criteria.

The UN General Assembly adopted a Declaration on the Rights of Persons Belonging to National or Ethnic, Religious and Linguistic Minorities in December 1992.[176] Article 1 provides that states 'shall protect the existence and the national or ethnic, cultural, religious and linguistic identity of minorities within their respective territories' and shall adopt appropriate legislative and other measures to achieve these ends. The Declaration states that persons belonging to minorities have the right to enjoy their own culture, practise and profess their own religion and to use their own language in private and in public without hindrance. Such persons also have the right to participate effectively in cultural, social, economic and public life. The UN Sub-Commission has been considering the question of minorities for many years and in 1994 agreed to establish a five-person inter-sessional working group[177] to examine peaceful and constructive solutions to situations involving minorities and, in particular, to review the practical application of the Declaration, to provide recommendations to *inter alia* the Sub-Commission and the UN High Commissioner for Human Rights to protect minorities where there is a risk of violence and generally to promote dialogue between minority groups in society and between those groups and governments. In 2005, the Commission on Human Rights appointed an Independent Expert on Minorities with the mandate to promote the implementation of the Declaration; to identify best practices and possibilities for technical co-operation by the Office of the United Nations High Commissioner for Human Rights at the request of Governments; and to co-operate closely with existing relevant UN bodies, while taking into account the views of non-governmental organisations and applying a gender perspective.[178]

The issue of minority rights has also been taken up recently particularly by European states, primarily as a consequence of the demise of the Soviet Union and its empire in Eastern Europe and the reintegration of Eastern and Central European states within the political system of

---

[176] Resolution 47/135. See e.g. *The UN Minority Rights Declaration* (eds. A. Phillips and A. Rosas), London, 1993.

[177] E/CN.4/Sub.2/1994/56. This was authorised by the Commission on Human Rights on 3 March 1995: see resolution 1995/24. See also E/CN.4/Sub.2/1995/51.

[178] Resolution 2005/79. The Independent Expert has, for example, drawn attention to the rights of women facing multiple forms of discrimination, exclusion and violence, such as women from minority communities, Press Release of 7 March 2006, and to problems faced by the Roma in Hungary, Press Release of 4 July 2006.

Western Europe. The specific response to questions of minority rights within the Council of Europe and the Conference (as from 1995 Organisation) on Security and Co-operation in Europe are addressed below.[179]

As has been noted, the UN Human Rights Committee has pointed to the special position of indigenous peoples as minorities with a particular relationship to their traditional territory. It has been accepted that such communities form a specific category of minorities with special needs.[180] The International Labour Organisation adopted Convention No. 107 on Indigenous and Tribal Populations in 1957, an instrument with a predominantly assimilationist approach to the question of indigenous peoples. It was partially revised in Convention No. 169 on Indigenous and Tribal Peoples in Independent Countries, 1989. The change in terminology from 'populations' to 'peoples' is instructive[181] and the latter Convention focuses far more upon the protection of the social, cultural, religious and spiritual values and practices of indigenous peoples. Unlike the prevailing approach to the definition of minorities generally, which intermingles objective and subjective criteria, this Convention stipulates in article 1(2) that 'self-identification as indigenous or tribal shall be regarded as a fundamental criterion' for determining the groups to which the Convention applies. The Sub-Commission recommended that a study of discrimination against indigenous populations should be made and this was completed in 1984.[182] A definition of indigenous populations was suggested and

---

[179] See below, pp. 365 and 376.

[180] See e.g. P. Thornberry, *Indigenous Peoples and Human Rights*, Manchester, 2002; S. Marquardt, 'International Law and Indigenous Peoples', 3 *International Journal on Group Rights*, 1995, p. 47; J. Berger and P. Hunt, 'Towards the International Protection of Indigenous Peoples' Rights', 12 NQHR, 1994, p. 405; C. Tennant, 'Indigenous Peoples, International Institutions, and the International Legal Literature from 1945–1993', 16 HRQ, 1994, p. 1; E. Stamatopoulou, 'Indigenous Peoples and the United Nations: Human Rights as a Developing Dynamic', 16 HRQ, 1994, p. 58; Crawford, *Rights of Peoples*; R. Barsh, 'Indigenous Peoples: An Emerging Object of International Law', 80 AJIL, 1986, p. 369; J. Anaya, *Indigenous Peoples in International Law*, 2nd edn, Oxford, 2004, and G. Bennett, *Aboriginal Rights in International Law*, London, 1978. See also *Justice Pending: Indigenous Peoples and Other Good Causes* (eds. G. Alfredsson and M. Stavropoulou), The Hague, 2002. Note in particular the cases of *Delgamuukw* v. *British Columbia* (1998) 153 DLR (4th) 193; 115 ILR, p. 446, Canadian Supreme Court, and *Mabo* v. *State of Queensland (No. 1)* (1988) 83 ALR 14; 112 ILR, p. 412 and *(No. 2)* (1992) 107 ALR 1; 112 ILR, p. 457. See also *The Richtersveld Community* case, 24 March 2003, Supreme Court of South Africa, 127 ILR, p. 507.

[181] But note that the Convention provides that the use of the term 'peoples' is not to be construed as having any implication as regards the rights that may attach to the term under international law (article 1(3)).

[182] The Martinez Cobo Report, E/CN.4/Sub.2/1986/7 and Adds. 1–4.

various suggestions made as to future action. In 1982, the Sub-Commission established a Working Group on Indigenous Populations[183] and a Declaration on the Rights of Indigenous Peoples was finally adopted in 2007.[184] The Declaration notes that indigenous peoples have the right to the full enjoyment, as a collective or as individuals, of all human rights and fundamental freedoms as recognised in the Charter of the United Nations, the Universal Declaration of Human Rights and international human rights law (article 1). They have the right to self-determination (article 3) and, in exercising their right to self-determination, have the right to autonomy or self-government in matters relating to their internal and local affairs, as well as ways and means for financing their autonomous functions (article 4). They further have the right to maintain and strengthen their distinctive political, economic, social and cultural characteristics, as well as their legal systems, while retaining the right to participate fully in the life of the state (article 5), the right to a nationality (article 6) and the collective right to live in freedom and security as distinct peoples free from any act of genocide or violence (article 7(2)). They also have the right not to be subjected to forced assimilation or destruction of their culture, while states are to provide effective mechanisms for prevention of, and redress for, *inter alia* any action which has the aim or effect of depriving them of their integrity as distinct peoples, or of their cultural values or ethnic identities (article 8). The Declaration also lists their rights to practise their cultural traditions, and to education, access to media and health practices, together with a range of rights concerning their distinctive relationship to the land (articles 9–37). The United Nations, its bodies, including the Permanent Forum on Indigenous Issues, and specialised agencies, including at the country level, and states are called upon to promote respect for and full application of the Declaration (article 42). A special rapporteur on indigenous peoples was appointed in 2001 and a Voluntary Fund for Indigenous Populations established in 1985.[185] A Permanent Forum on Indigenous Issues was set up in 2000[186] and UN Development Group Guidelines on Indigenous

---

[183] See E/CN.4/Sub.2/1982/33.

[184] A Draft Declaration was adopted in 1994: see resolution 1994/45, E/CN.4/Sub.2/1994/56, p. 103. See also R. T. Coulter, 'The Draft UN Declaration on the Rights of Indigenous Peoples: What Is It? What Does It Mean?', 13 NQHR, 1995, p. 123.

[185] See General Assembly resolution 40/131.

[186] See ECOSOC resolution 2000/22. Note that 1993 was designated International Year of the World's Indigenous Peoples, see E/CN.4/1994/AC.4/TN.4/2, while the International Decade of the World's Indigenous Peoples was declared by the General Assembly on

Peoples' Issues were produced in 2008.[187] An expert mechanism, consisting of five independent experts, on the rights of indigenous peoples was called for in Human Rights Council resolution 6/36, 2007, in order to provide the Council with thematic expertise.

The question of an American Declaration on Indigenous Peoples has also been under discussion within the Organisation of American States.[188] The Inter-American Court of Human Rights discussed the issue of the rights of indigenous peoples to ancestral lands and resources in *The Mayagna (Sumo) Awas Tingni Community* v. *Nicaragua* in 2001.[189] The Court emphasised the communitarian tradition regarding a communal form of collective property of the land and consequential close ties of indigenous people with that land,[190] and noted that the customary law of such people had especially to be taken into account so that 'possession of the land should suffice for indigenous communities lacking real title'.[191] In *Sawhoyamaxa Indigenous Community* v. *Paraguay*, the Court emphasised that the close ties of members of the indigenous communities with their traditional lands and the natural resources associated with their culture had to be secured under article 21 of the Inter-American Convention on Human Rights concerning the right to the use and enjoyment of property. The Court, in interpreting this provision, also took account of Convention No. 169 of the ILO, which required *inter alia* respect for the special importance for the cultural and spiritual values of the communities concerned of their relationship with their lands. The collecture nature of property ownership was also noted. In addition, the Court found a violation of the right to recognition as a person before the law under article 3 of the Convention as there had been no registration or official documentation

10 December 1994. See also the Committee on the Elimination of Racial Discrimination's General Recommendation 23 on Indigenous Peoples, 1997, A/52/18, annex V.

[187] www.2.ohchr.org/english/issues/indigenous/docs/guidelines.pdf.

[188] See the Draft Declaration on the Rights of Indigenous Peoples adopted in 1995, OEA/Ser.L/V/II/90; Doc. 9, rev. 1. For further discussions on the Draft Declaration, see e.g. GT/DADIN/doc.1/99 rev.2, 2000; Report of the Rapporteur of the Working Group, GT/DADIN/doc.83/02, 2002 and OEA/Ser.K/XVI, GT/DADIN/doc.301/07, 2007. See also, for example, resolutions AG/RES.1780 (XXI-0/01), 2001 and AG/RES. 2073 (XXXV-0/05), 2007.

[189] Series C, No. 79.   [190] *Ibid.*, para. 149.

[191] *Ibid.*, para. 151. Nicaragua was held to be obliged to create 'an effective mechanism for delimitation, demarcation and titling of the property of indigenous communities, in accordance with their customary law, values, customs and mores', *ibid.*, para. 164. See also the cases of the *Moiwana Community* v. *Suriname*, Judgment of 15 June 2005, Series C, No. 124 and the *Indigenous Community Yakye Axa* v. *Paraguay*, Judgment of 17 June 2005, Series C, No. 125.

for the existence of several members of the indigenous community. The Court ordered the state to adopt all legislative, administrative and other measures to guarantee the members of the community ownership rights over their traditional lands.[192]

Other suggested collective rights

The subject of much concern in recent years has been the question of a right to development.[193] In 1986, the UN General Assembly adopted the Declaration on the Right to Development.[194] This instrument reaffirms the interdependence and indivisibility of all human rights and seeks to provide a framework for a range of issues (article 9). The right to development is deemed to be an inalienable human right of all human beings and peoples to participate in and enjoy economic, social, cultural and political development (article 1), while states have the primary responsibility to create conditions favourable to its realisation (article 3), including the duty to formulate international development policies (article 4). States are particularly called upon to ensure *inter alia* equal opportunity for all in their access to basic resources, education, health services, food, housing, employment and the fair distribution of income. Effective measures are to be undertaken to ensure that women participate in the development process and appropriate economic and social reforms are to be carried out with a view to eradicating all social injustices (article 8). The question of encouraging the implementation of this Declaration was the subject of continuing UN attention,[195] with the reaffirmation of the right to

---

[192] Judgment of 29 March 2006, Series C, No. 146, paras. 17 ff., 187 ff. and 210 ff.

[193] See e.g. *Le Droit au Développement au Plan International* (ed. R. J. Dupuy), Paris, 1980; A. Pellet, *Le Droit International du Développement*, 2nd edn, Paris, 1987; K. Mbaye, 'Le Droit du Developpement comme un Droit de l'Homme', 5 *Revue des Droits de l'Homme*, 1972, p. 503; *Report of the UN Secretary-General on the International Dimensions of the Right to Development as a Human Right*, E/CN.4/1334, 1979; O. Schachter, 'The Emerging International Law of Development', 15 *Columbia Journal of Transnational Law*, 1976, p. 1; R. Rich, 'The Right to Development as an Emerging Human Right', 23 Va. JIL, 1983, p. 287; K. de Vey Mestdagh, 'The Right to Development', 28 NILR, 1981, p. 31; I. Brownlie, *The Human Right to Development*, Commonwealth Secretariat Human Rights Unit Occasional Paper, 1989; C. Weeramantry, 'The Right to Development', 25 *IJIL*, 1985, p. 482; P. Alston, 'Revitalising United Nations Work on Human Rights and Development', 18 *Melbourne University Law Review*, 1991, p. 216, and T. Kunanayakam, *Historical Analysis of the Principles Contained in the Declaration on the Right to Development*, HR/RD/1990/CONF.1, 1990.

[194] General Assembly resolution 41/128.

[195] Note e.g. the Global Consultation carried out in 1990, E/CN.4/1990/9/Rev.1, 1990: see R. Barsh, 'The Right to Development as a Human Right: Results of the Global Consultation',

development by the UN Vienna Declaration and Programme of Action, 1993[196] and the establishment by the UN Commission on Human Rights of a Working Group on the Right to Development in the same year.[197] It should also be noted that Principle 3 of the Rio Declaration on Environment and Development, 1992 stipulated that 'the right to development must be fulfilled so as to equitably meet developmental and environmental needs of present and future generations'.[198] While the general issue of development is clearly on the international agenda in the context of economic issues and broad human rights concerns, it is premature to talk in terms of a legal right in international law of groups or peoples or states to development.[199] Other suggested collective rights have included the right to a healthy environment[200] and the right to peace.[201]

The United Nations system – implementation[202]

The United Nations system has successfully generated a wide-ranging series of international instruments dealing with the establishment of

13 HRQ, 1991, p. 322; the Report of the UN Secretary-General, E/CN.4/1992/10, 1991 and the Concrete Proposals of the UN Secretary-General, E/CN.4/1993/16, 1993.

[196] See 32 ILM, 1993, p. 1661.

[197] Resolution 1993/22. The first report of this Working Group was at the end of 1993, E/CN.4/1994/21. The most recent mechanism has been the creation of an open-ended Working Group on the Right to Development in 1998, resolution 1998/72. A high-level task force on the implementation of the right to development was established by the Working Group in 2004: see e.g. A/HRC/8/WG.2/TF/2, 2008.

[198] 31 ILM, 1992, p. 876. See also below, chapter 15.

[199] Note that the Committee on Economic, Social and Cultural Rights has adopted a General Comment in which it is stated that international co-operation for development and thus the realisation of economic, social and cultural rights is an obligation for all states, General Comment 3 (1991), HRI/GEN/1/Rev.1, pp. 48, 52.

[200] See e.g. S. Prakash, 'The Right to the Environment. Emerging Implications in Theory and Praxis', 13 NQHR, 1995, p. 403. See further below, chapter 15 on international environmental law.

[201] See e.g. General Assembly resolutions 33/73 and 39/11. See also R. Bilder, 'The Individual and the Right to Peace', 11 Bulletin of Peace Proposals, 1982, p. 387, and J. Fried, 'The United Nations' Report to Establish a Right of the Peoples to Peace', 2 Pace Yearbook of International Law, 1990, p. 21.

[202] See The Future of UN Human Rights Treaty Monitoring (eds. P. Alston and J. Crawford), Cambridge, 2000; Human Rights: International Protection, Monitoring and Enforcement (ed. J. Symonides), Aldershot, 2003; Steiner, Alston and Goodman, International Human Rights; Rehman, International Human Rights Law, chapters 2–5; Tomuschat, Human Rights, chapters 6–8; United Nations Action in the Field of Human Rights, New York, 1994; The United Nations and Human Rights (ed. P. Alston), Oxford, 1992; Guide to International Human Rights Practice (ed. H. Hannum), 4th edn, Ardsley, 2004; Ramcharan, Human Rights: Thirty Years After the Universal Declaration, and UN Law/Fundamental

standards and norms in the human rights field.[203] The question of implementation will now be addressed.

Political bodies – general

The General Assembly has power under article 13 of the Charter to initiate studies and make recommendations regarding *inter alia* human rights. Human rights items on its agenda may originate in Economic and Social Council (ECOSOC) reports or decisions taken by the Assembly at earlier sessions to consider particular matters, or are proposed for inclusion by the UN organs, the Secretary-General or member states. Most items on human rights go to the Assembly's Third Committee (Social, Humanitarian and Cultural Committee), but others may be referred to other committees such as the Sixth Committee (Legal) or the First Committee (Political and Security) or the Special Political Committee. The Assembly has also established subsidiary organs under Rule 161, several of which deal with human rights issues, such as the Special Committee on Decolonisation, the UN Council for Namibia, the Special Committee against Apartheid, the Special Committee to Investigate Israeli Practices in the Occupied Territories and the Committee on the Exercise of the Inalienable Rights of the Palestine People.[204] ECOSOC may, under article 62 of the Charter, make recommendations on human rights, draft conventions for the Assembly and call international conferences on human rights matters. It consists of fifty-four members of the UN elected by the General Assembly and hears annually the reports of a wide range of bodies including the UN High Commissioner for Refugees, the UN Children's Fund, the UN Conference on Trade and Development, the UN Environment Programme and the World Food Council. Of its subsidiary bodies, the Commission on

---

Rights (ed. A. Cassese), Alphen aan den Rijn, 1979. See also Lauterpacht, *International Law*, chapter 11; F. Ermacora, 'Procedure to Deal with Human Rights Violations', 7 *Revue des Droits de l'Homme*, 1974, p. 670; Robertson and Merrills, *Human Rights*, and A. A. Cançado Trindade, 'Co-existence and Co-ordination of Mechanisms of International Protection of Human Rights', 202 HR, 1987, p. 9.

[203] See also e.g. the Slavery Convention, 1926 and Protocol, 1953; the Supplementary Convention on the Abolition of Slavery, the Slave Trade and Institutions and Practices Similar to Slavery, 1956; the Convention for the Suppression of the Traffic in Persons and of the Exploitation of the Prostitution of Others, 1949; the Convention on the Status of Refugees, 1951 and Protocol, 1967; the Convention relating to the Status of Stateless Persons, 1954 and the Convention on the Reduction of Statelessness 1961.

[204] See *UN Action*, chapter 1. Note also the relevant roles of the other organs of the UN, the Security Council, Trusteeship Council, International Court and Secretariat, *ibid.*

Human Rights and the Commission on the Status of Women have the most direct connection with human rights issues.[205] The Commission on Human Rights was replaced by the Human Rights Council in 2006.

The Commission on Human Rights (1946–2006)[206]

This was established in 1946 as a subsidiary organ of ECOSOC with extensive terms of reference, including making studies, preparing recommendations and drafting international instruments on human rights. Originally consisting of forty-three representatives of member states of the UN selected by ECOSOC on the basis of equitable geographic distribution,[207] that number was increased to fifty-three by resolution 1990/48 in May 1990. For its first twenty years, it took the view that it had no power to take any action with regard to complaints concerning human rights violations, despite receiving many via the Secretary-General.[208] However, in 1967, ECOSOC resolution 1235 (XLII) authorised the Commission and its Sub-Commission on Prevention of Discrimination and Protection of Minorities to examine information relevant to gross violations of human rights contained in communications, and to study such situations as revealed a consistent pattern of violations with a view to making recommendations to ECOSOC.[209] This constituted the public debate function of the Commission relating to specific situations. The situations in question referred at first primarily to Southern Africa. In 1967, also, the Commission set up an ad hoc working group of experts on South Africa and has since established working groups on Chile; Situations revealing a Consistent Pattern of Gross Violations of Human Rights; Disappearances; the Right to Development and structural adjustment programmes and economic, social and cultural rights. Special rapporteurs were appointed by the Commission to deal with situations in specific countries, such as, for

---

[205] *Ibid.*, pp. 13 ff. See also Assembly resolutions 1991B (XVIII) and 2847 (XXVI).

[206] See e.g. N. Rodley and D. Weissbrodt, 'United Nations Non-Treaty Procedures for Dealing with Human Rights Violations' in Hannum, *Guide to International Human Rights Practice*, p. 65; Lauterpacht, *International Law*, chapter 11; Steiner, Alston and Goodman, *International Human Rights*, chapter 9, and T. Buergenthal and J. V. Torney, *International Human Rights and International Education*, Washington, DC, 1976, pp. 75 ff. See also *UN Action*, p. 20, and H. Tolley, 'The Concealed Crack in the Citadel', 6 HRQ, 1984, p. 420. A Commission on the Status of Women was also created: see *UN Action*, p. 15, and below, p. 322.

[207] See ECOSOC resolutions 6 (I), 1946; 9 (II), 1946; 845 (XXXII), 1961; 1147 (XLI), 1966 and 1979/36, 1979.

[208] See e.g. Report of the First Session of the Commission, E/259, para. 22.

[209] See Tolley, 'Concealed Crack', pp. 421 ff., and ECOSOC resolution 728F.

example, Afghanistan, Cuba, El Salvador, Equatorial Guinea, Guatemala, Iran, Sudan, the Democratic Republic of the Congo and Iraq. Special Rapporteurs were also appointed to deal with particular thematic concerns such as summary executions, torture, mercenaries, religious intolerance and the sale of children. In an attempt to provide some co-ordination, the first meeting of special rapporteurs and other mechanisms of the special procedures of the Commission took place in 1994.[210]

A series of informal working groups were created to prepare drafts of international instruments, such as the Declaration on Religious Intolerance, the Convention against Torture and instruments on minority rights and the rights of the child.[211] The Commission also established a Group of Three pursuant to article IX of the Apartheid Convention to consider states' reports under that Convention. In 1970 a new procedure for dealing with human rights complaints was introduced in ECOSOC resolution 1503 (XLVIII).[212] By virtue of this resolution as modified in 2000,[213] the Sub-Commission appointed annually a Working Group on Communications to meet to consider communications received and to pass on to the Sub-Commission those that appeared to reveal 'a consistent pattern of gross and reliably attested violations of human rights'. These were examined by the Working Group on Situations of the Sub-Commission which then determined whether or not to refer particular situations to the Commission.[214] Those so transmitted were examined in two separate closed meetings by the Commission, which then decided whether or not to take further action, such as appointing an independent expert or discussing the matter under the resolution 1235 public procedure. The procedure, which was confidential until the final stage, did not fulfil initial high expectations. The confidentiality requirement and the highly political nature of the Commission itself combined to frustrate hopes that had been raised.[215]

---

[210] See E/CN.4/1995/5. See also the report of the meeting of special rapporteurs/representatives/experts and chairpersons of working groups of the special procedures of the Commission on Human Rights and of the advisory services programme, May 1995, E/CN.4/1996/50.

[211] See e.g. UN Action, pp. 20–3.

[212] See e.g. P. Alston, 'The Commission on Human Rights' in Alston, United Nations and Human Rights, pp. 126, 145 ff., and M. Bossuyt, 'The Development of Special Procedures of the United Nations Commission on Human Rights', 6 HRLJ, 1985, p. 179.

[213] ECOSOC resolution 2000/3.   [214] See also Sub-Committee resolution 1 (XXIV), 1971.

[215] See e.g. T. Van Boven, 'Human Rights Fora at the United Nations' in International Human Rights Law and Practice (ed. J. C. Tuttle), Philadelphia, 1978, p. 83; H. Möller, 'Petitioning the United Nations', 1 Universal Human Rights, 1979, p. 57; N. Rodley, 'Monitoring

Despite good work in the field of standard-setting and in drawing attention to abuses of human rights, albeit on rather less than a universalist basis, the Commission began to attract an increasing level of criticism, mainly concerning political selectivity and the failure to review objectively the situation in particular countries.[216] The High Level Panel on Threats, Challenge and Change convened by the United Nations Secretary-General concluded in its Report of 2004 that, 'In recent years, the Commission's capacity to perform these tasks has been undermined by eroding credibility and professionalism.'[217] As a result, the Human Rights Council was created to replace the Commission by General Assembly resolution 60/251 on 3 April 2006.

The Human Rights Council

The Council was established with a higher status in the UN hierarchy as a subsidiary organ of the General Assembly with forty-seven members,[218] elected by a majority of members of the Assembly for three years for up to two consecutive terms. The Commission's special procedures function was retained, although all functions and responsibilities of the Commission assumed by the Council are subject to a review aimed at their rationalisation and improvement. A new universal periodic review mechanism by which the human rights record of all countries is to be examined was also established. This was intended as a partial response to the criticisms of

Human Rights by the UN System and Non-governmental Organisations' in Kommers and Loescher, *Human Rights and American Foreign Policy*, p. 157, and Tolley, 'Concealed Crack', pp. 429 ff. Note that the Commission chairman began the practice of announcing the names of the countries subject to complaints under resolution 1503, although no further details were disclosed: see e.g. E/CN.4/1984/77, p. 151, naming Albania, Argentina, Benin, Haiti, Indonesia, Malaysia, Pakistan, Paraguay, the Philippines, Turkey and Uruguay.

216 See e.g. the Amnesty International Report, 'Meeting the Challenge', AI Index, IOR 40/008/2005.

217 www.un.org/secureworld/report3.pdf, at para. 283. See also the Secretary-General's Report, 'In Larger Freedom: Towards Development, Security and Human Rights for All', A/59/2005, at para. 182. It was noted that the Commission had been 'undermined by the politicisation of its sessions and the selectivity of its work', A/59/2005/Add.1, para. 2. Note also, for example, the inability of the Commission in 1990 even to discuss draft resolutions relating to China and Iraq: E. Zoller, '46th Session of the United Nations Commission on Human Rights', 8(2) NQHR, 1990, pp. 140, 142. Note also the election of Libya to chair the Commission in 2003.

218 Distributed regionally with thirteen seats for the African group; thirteen seats for the Asian group; six seats for the Eastern European group; eight seats for the Latin American and Caribbean group and seven seats for the Western European and Other group.

the Commission's selectivity.[219] The Council adopted resolution 5/1 on 18 June 2007 entitled 'United Nations Human Rights Council: Institution-Building', which ranged over a wide area and established the details of the universal periodic review mechanism. The principles laid down for this mechanism include the universality of human rights, universal coverage and equal treatment of all states and the conduct of the review in an objective, transparent, non-selective, constructive, non-confrontational and non-politicised manner. This resolution also laid down details for the conduct and review of the special procedures, provided for the creation of the Human Rights Council Advisory Committee, composed of eighteen experts serving in their personal capacity, intended to function as a think-tank for the Council and work at its direction, and provided for the establishment of a confidential complaints procedure based upon the mechanism created by ECOSOC resolution 1503 (1970).[220]

Expert bodies established by UN organs

The Sub-Commission on the Promotion and Protection of Human Rights[221]

The Sub-Commission, initially entitled the Sub-Commission on Prevention of Discrimination and Protection of Minorities, was established by the Commission in 1947 with wide terms of reference.[222] It came to an end in 2006 as a consequence of General Assembly resolution 60/251, which established the Human Rights Council. The Sub-Commission was composed of twenty-six members elected by the Commission on the basis of nominations of experts made by the UN member states and it

---

[219] See e.g. F. J. Hampson, 'An Overview of the Reform of the UN Human Rights Machinery', 7 *Human Rights Law Review*, 2007, p. 7.

[220] The Council also adopted at its first session in June 2006 the International Convention for the Protection of All Persons from Enforced Disappearances and the UN Declaration on the Rights of Indigenous Peoples. A Code of Conduct for Special Procedures Mandate-holders was adopted at the fifth session of the Council.

[221] See e.g. A. Eide, 'The Sub-Commission on Prevention of Discrimination and Protection of Minorities' in Alston, *United Nations and Human Rights*, p. 211; Tolley, 'Concealed Crack', pp. 437 ff.; J. Gardeniers, H. Hannum and C. Kruger, 'The UN Sub-Committee on Prevention of Discrimination and Protection of Minorities: Recent Developments', 4 HRQ, 1982, p. 353, and L. Garber and C. O'Conner, 'The 1984 UN Sub-Commission on Prevention of Discrimination and Protection of Minorities', 79 AJIL, 1985, p. 168. See also *UN Action*, pp. 23–4.

[222] See e.g. *UN Action*, p. 23. See also resolutions E/259, 1947; E/1371, 1949, and 17 (XXXVII), 1981.

was renamed the Sub-Commission on the Promotion and Protection of Human Rights in 1999.[223] Members served in their individual capacity for four-year terms[224] and the composition reflected an agreed geographical pattern.[225] The Sub-Commission produced a variety of studies by rapporteurs[226] and established a number of subsidiary bodies. The Working Group on Communications functioned within the framework of the resolution 1503 procedure, while the Working Group on Contemporary Forms of Slavery[227] and the Working Group on the Rights of Indigenous Populations[228] prepared material within the areas of their concern.[229] The Sub-Commission from 1987 produced an annual report listing all states that had proclaimed, extended or ended a state of emergency.[230]

The International Covenant on Economic, Social and Cultural Rights[231]

The International Covenant on Economic, Social and Cultural Rights was adopted in 1966 and entered into force in 1976. Article 2 provides that each state party undertakes to take steps to the maximum of its available resources 'with a view to achieving progressively the full realisation of the rights recognised in the present Covenant'. In other words, an evolving programme is envisaged depending upon the goodwill and resources of states rather than an immediate binding legal obligation with regard to the rights in question. The rights included range from self-determination (article 1), the right to work (articles 6 and 7), the right to social security (article 9), adequate standard of living (article 11) and education

---

[223] See E/1999/INF/2/Add.2.

[224] See ECOSOC resolution 1986/35 with effect from 1988. Before this, the term was for three years and originally for two years.

[225] See ECOSOC resolution 1334 (XLIV), 1968, and decision 1978/21, 1978.

[226] See e.g. the Capotorti Study, above, footnote 165, and the Ruhashyankiko Study, above, footnote 90. See also the Daes Study on the *Individual's Duties to the Community*, E/CN.4/Sub.2/432/Rev.2, 1983 and the Questiaux Study on *States of Emergency*, E/CN.4/Sub.2/1982/15, 1982.

[227] Resolution 11 (XXVII), 1974, established the Working Group on Slavery. Its name was changed in 1988: see resolution 1988/42. See K. Zoglin, 'United Nations Action Against Slavery: A Critical Evaluation', 8 HRQ, 1986, p. 306.

[228] See resolution 2 (XXXIV), 1981. See also E/CN.4/Sub.2/1982/33, and above, p. 298.

[229] See e.g. the S. Chernichenko and W. Treat Study on *The Administration of Justice and the Human Rights of Detainees: The Right to a Fair Trial*, E/CN.4/Sub.2/1994/24, 1994.

[230] See e.g. E/CN.4/Sub.2/1987/19/Rev.1; E/CN.4/Sub.2/1991/28 and E/CN.4/Sub.2/1995/20 and Corr. 1.

[231] See e.g. Craven, *Covenant*.

(article 13) to the right to take part in cultural life and enjoy the benefits of scientific progress and its applications (article 15).

Under the Covenant itself, states parties were obliged to send periodic reports to ECOSOC.[232] In 1978, a Sessional Working Group was set up, consisting of fifteen members elected by ECOSOC from amongst states parties for three-year renewable terms. The Group met annually and reported to the Council. It was not a success, however, and in 1985 it was decided to establish a new committee of eighteen members, this time composed of independent experts.[233] Accordingly in 1987 the new Committee on Economic, Social and Cultural Rights commenced operation.[234] But it is to be especially noted that unlike, for example, the Racial Discrimination Committee, the Human Rights Committee and the Torture Committee, the Economic Committee is not autonomous and it is responsible not to the states parties but to a main organ of the United Nations. As will be seen by comparison with the other bodies, the Economic Committee has at its disposal only relatively weak means of implementation.

The implementation of this Covenant faces particular difficulties in view of the perceived vagueness of many of the principles contained therein, the relative lack of legal texts and judicial decisions, and the ambivalence of many states in dealing with economic, social and cultural rights. In addition, problems of obtaining relevant and precise information have loomed large, not least in the light of the fact that comparatively few non-governmental organisations focus upon this area.[235]

The Committee initially met annually in Geneva for three-week sessions, though it now meets twice per year. Its primary task lies in

---

[232] See articles 16–22 of the Covenant, and *UN Chronicle*, July 1982, pp. 68–70. See generally on implementation B. S. Ramcharan, 'Implementing the International Covenants on Human Rights' in Ramcharan, *Human Rights: Thirty Years After the Universal Declaration*, p. 159; P. Alston, 'Out of the Abyss: The Challenge Confronting the New UN Committee on Economic, Social and Cultural Rights', 9 HRQ, 1987, p. 332; P. Alston and G. Quinn, 'The Nature and Scope of States Parties' Obligations under the International Covenant on Economic, Social and Cultural Rights', 9 HRQ, 1987, p. 156; P. Alston, 'The Committee on Economic, Social and Cultural Rights' in Alston, *United Nations and Human Rights*, p. 473; B. Simma, 'The Implementation of the International Covenant on Economic, Social and Cultural Rights' in *The Implementation of Economic, Social and Cultural Rights* (ed. F. Matscher), Kehl am Rhein, 1991, p. 75, and S. Leckie, 'The Committee on Economic, Social and Cultural Rights' in Alston and Crawford, *Future*, chapter 6.

[233] See ECOSOC resolution 1985/17.

[234] See P. Alston and B. Simma, 'First Session of the UN Committee on Economic, Social and Cultural Rights', 81 AJIL, 1987, p. 747, and 'Second Session of the UN Committee on Economic, Social and Cultural Rights', 82 AJIL, 1988, p. 603.

[235] See Alston, 'The Economic Rights Committee', p. 474.

examining states' reports, drawing upon a list of questions prepared by its pre-sessional working group. The problem of overdue reports from states parties applies here as it does with regard to other human rights implementation committees. The Economic Rights Committee adopted a decision at its sixth session, whereby it established a procedure allowing for the consideration of the situation of particular states where those states had not produced reports for a long time, thus creating a rather valuable means of exerting pressure upon recalcitrant states parties.[236] Additional information may also be requested from states parties where this is felt necessary.[237] The Committee also prepares 'General Comments', the second of which on international technical assistance measures was adopted at its fourth session in 1990.[238] The third general comment, adopted in 1991, is of particular interest and underlines that although the Covenant itself appears promotional and aspirational, nevertheless certain obligations of immediate effect are imposed upon states parties. These include the non-discrimination provisions and the undertaking to take steps which should be taken within a reasonably short time after the Covenant has entered into force for the state concerned and which should be 'deliberate, concrete and targeted as clearly as possible towards meeting the obligations recognised in the Covenant'. The Committee also emphasised that international co-operation for development, and thus for the realisation of economic, social and cultural rights, was an obligation for all states.[239] General Comment 4, adopted in 1991, discussed the right to adequate housing,[240] while General Comment 5, adopted in 1994, dealt with the rights of persons with disabilities.[241] General Comment 6, adopted in 1995, concerned the economic, social and cultural rights of older persons,[242] General Comment 16, adopted in 2005, concerned the equal treatment of men and women with regard to the enjoyment of all economic, social and cultural rights,[243] while General Comments 18 and 19, adopted in 2005 and 2007 respectively, concerned the right to work and the right to social security. The Committee also holds general discussions on particular

---

[236] See e.g. E/C.12/1994/20, p. 18.   [237] *Ibid.*, pp. 16–18.
[238] See HRI/GEN/Rev.1, p. 45.   [239] *Ibid.*, p. 48.   [240] *Ibid.*, p. 53.
[241] E/1995/22, p. 99. On disabilities and human rights, see also the final report of Leandro Despouy, Special Rapporteur on Human Rights and Disability, of the Sub-Commission on Prevention of Discrimination and Protection of Minorities, E/CN.4/Sub.2/1991/31; General Assembly resolution 3447 (XXX) of 9 December 1975 adopting the Declaration of the Rights of Disabled Persons, and General Assembly resolution 37/52 of 3 December 1982 adopting the World Programme of Action concerning Disabled Persons, A/37/351/Add.1 and Corr. 1, chapter VIII.
[242] E/C.12/1995/16, adapted in 1995.   [243] E/C.12/2005/4.

rights in the form of a 'day of general discussion'.[244] It cannot hear individual petitions, nor has it an inter-state complaints competence.[245]

Expert bodies established under particular treaties[246]

A number of expert committees have been established under particular treaties. They are not subsidiary organs of the UN, but autonomous, although in practice they are closely connected with it, being serviced, for example, by the UN Secretariat through the UN Centre for Human Rights in Geneva.[247] These committees are termed 'UN Treaty Organs'.

The Committee on the Elimination of Racial Discrimination[248]

Under Part II of the Convention on the Elimination of All Forms of Racial Discrimination, 1965, a Committee of eighteen experts was established

---

[244] At the ninth session, for example, in the autumn of 1993, the Committee discussed the right to health, E/1994/23, p. 56, while at the tenth session in May 1994 the role of social safety-nets as a means of protecting economic, social and cultural rights was discussed: see E/1995/22, p. 70. See also generally C. Dommen, 'Building from a Solid Basis: The Fourth Session of the Committee on Economic, Social and Cultural Rights', 8 NQHR, 1990, p. 199, and C. Dommen and M. C. Craven, 'Making Way for Substance: The Fifth Session of the Committee on Economic, Social and Cultural Rights', 9 NQHR, 1991, p. 93.

[245] Note, however, that at its seventh session in 1992, the Committee formally proposed that an optional protocol providing for some kind of petition procedure be drafted and adopted: see E/1993/22, pp. 87 ff., and Craven, Covenant, pp. 98 ff. See also E/C.12/1994/12 and E/C.12/1995/SR.50, December 1995. A working group was established in 2003 to achieve this and the matter is still under consideration: see e.g. A/HRC/8/WG.4/3, 2008.

[246] See e.g. Alston and Crawford, Future, and S. Lewis-Anthony and M. Scheinin, 'Treaty-Based Procedures for Making Human Rights Complaints Within the UN System' in Hannum, Guide to International Human Rights Practice, p. 43. See also M. O'Flaherty, Human Rights and the UN: Practice Before the Treaty Bodies, 2nd edn, The Hague, 2002.

[247] This link with the Secretariat has been termed ambiguous, particularly in the light of the difficulties in performing the two functions carried out by the Secretariat (Charter-based political activities and expert activities): see e.g. T. Opsahl, 'The Human Rights Committee' in Alston, United Nations and Human Rights, pp. 367, 388.

[248] See e.g. M. Banton, 'Decision-Taking in the Committee on the Elimination of Racial Discrimination' in Alston and Crawford, Future, p. 55; K. J. Partsch, 'The Committee on the Elimination of Racial Discrimination' in Alston, United Nations and Human Rights, p. 339; T. Meron, Human Rights Law-Making in the United Nations, Oxford, 1986, chapter 1; K. Das, 'The International Convention on the Elimination of All Forms of Racial Discrimination' in The International Dimension of Human Rights (eds. K. Vasak and P. Alston), Paris, 1982, p. 307; Lerner, UN Convention and 'Curbing Racial Discrimination – Fifteen Years CERD', 13 Israel Yearbook on Human Rights, 1983, p. 170; M. R. Burrowes, 'Implementing the UN Racial Convention – Some Procedural Aspects', 7 Australian YIL, p. 236, and T. Buergenthal, 'Implementing the UN Racial Convention', 12 Texas International Law Journal, 1977, p. 187.

consisting of persons serving in their personal capacity and elected by the states parties to the Convention.[249] States parties undertook to submit reports every two years regarding measures adopted to give effect to the provisions of the Convention to the Committee, which itself would report annually through the UN Secretary-General to the General Assembly. The Committee may make suggestions and general recommendations based on the examination of the reports and information received from the states parties, which are reported to the General Assembly together with any comments from states parties.[250] The Committee is also able to operate early warning measures and urgent procedures. Early warning measures are directed at preventing existing problems from escalating into conflicts, while urgent procedures are to respond to problems requiring immediate attention to prevent or limit the scale or number of serious violations of the Convention. Decisions, statements or resolutions may be adopted. Such action has been taken in relation to more than twenty states parties. The Committee has, for example, conducted two field visits in connection with the procedure and has drawn the attention of the Secretary-General, the Security Council or other relevant bodies to issues in relation to six states parties. For example, in 1993, the Committee, concerned at events in the former Yugoslavia, sought additional information on the implementation of the Convention as a matter of urgency.[251] This information was provided during the autumn of 1994 and the spring of 1995.[252]

The Committee has also established a procedure to deal with states whose reports are most overdue. Under this procedure, the Committee proceeds to examine the situation in the state party concerned on the basis of the last report submitted.[253] At its forty-ninth session, the Committee further decided that states parties whose initial reports were excessively overdue by five years or more would also be scheduled for a review of implementation of the provisions of the Convention. In the absence of an initial report, the Committee considers all information submitted by the state party to other organs of the United Nations or, in the absence of such material, reports and information prepared by organs of the United

---

[249] Rules of Procedure have been adopted, see CERD/C/35/Rev. 3 (1986), and are revised from time to time: see, for example, A/48/18, p. 137.

[250] Articles 8 and 9 of the Convention.   [251] A/48/18, paras. 496–506.

[252] See e.g. CERD/C/248/Add.1 (Federal Republic of Yugoslavia); CERD/C/249/Add.1 (Croatia) and CERD/C/247/Add.1 (Bosnia and Herzegovina). See also CERD/C/65/DEC.1 (Darfur, 2004); CERD/C/66/DAR/Dec.2 (Darfur, 2005); CERD/C/DEC/1 (USA, 2006); and CERD/C/DEC/SUR/5 (Suriname, 2006).

[253] See e.g. A/48/18, p. 20.

Nations. In practice the Committee also considers relevant information from other sources, including from non-governmental organisations, whether it is an initial or a periodic report that is seriously overdue.[254]

Under article 11, one state party may bring a complaint against another state party and the Committee will seek to resolve the complaint. Should the matter not be so settled, either party may refer it back to the Committee and by article 12 an ad hoc Conciliation Commission may be established, which will report back to the Committee with any recommendation thought proper for the amicable solution of the dispute.[255] In addition to hearing states' reports and inter-state complaints, the Committee may also hear individual petitions under the article 14 procedure. This, however, is subject to the state complained of having made a declaration recognising the competence of the Committee to receive and consider such communications. If such a declaration has not been notified by a state, therefore, the Committee has no authority to hear a petition against the state.[256] Under this procedure, consideration of communications is confidential and the Committee may be assisted by a five-person working group making recommendations to the full Committee. The Committee began hearing individual communications in 1984 and a number of important cases have now been completed.[257]

The Committee regularly meets twice a year and has interpreted articles of the Convention, discussed reports submitted to it, adopted decisions[258] and general recommendations,[259] obtained further information from states parties and co-operated closely with the International Labour Organisation and UNESCO. Many states have enacted legislation as a consequence of the work of the Committee and its record of impartiality is very good.[260] The Committee also receives copies of petitions and

---

[254] See e.g. A/57/18, p. 99.   [255] Article 13.

[256] The provision entered into force on 31 December 1982 upon the tenth declaration.

[257] See e.g. the Report of the Committee for its forty-eighth session, A/48/18, 1994, pp. 105 and 130, and for the sixtieth and sixty-first sessions, A/57/18, p. 128. Note, for example, the case of *Durmic v. Serbia and Montenegro* concerning discrimination against Roma in Serbia, CERD/C/68/D/29/2003, 2006.

[258] For example, the decision adopted on 19 March 1993 requesting the governments of the Federal Republic of Yugoslavia (Serbia and Montenegro) and Croatia to submit further information concerning implementation of the Convention: see A/48/18, p. 112.

[259] See, for example, General Recommendation XII (42) encouraging successor states to declare that 'they continue to be bound' by the obligations of the Convention if predecessor states were parties to it; General Recommendation XIV (42) concerning non-discrimination, A/48/18, pp. 113 ff. and General Recommendation XXIX concerning discrimination based upon descent, A/57/18, p. 111.

[260] See e.g. Lerner, *UN Convention*.

reports sent to UN bodies dealing with trust and non-self-governing territories in the general area of Convention matters and may make comments upon them.[261] The general article 9 reporting system appears to work well, with large numbers of reports submitted and examined, but some states have proved tardy in fulfilling their obligations.[262] The Committee has published guidelines for states parties as to the structure of their reports.[263]

The Committee, in order to speed up consideration of states' reports, has instituted the practice of appointing country rapporteurs, whose function it is to prepare analyses of reports of states parties.[264] The Committee has also called for additional technical assistance to be provided by the UN to help in the reporting process, while it has expressed serious concern that financial difficulties are beginning to affect its functioning.[265]

The Human Rights Committee[266]

The International Covenant on Civil and Political Rights was adopted in 1966 and entered into force in 1976.[267] By article 2, all states parties undertake to respect and to ensure to all individuals within their territory and subject to their jurisdiction the rights recognised in the Covenant. These rights are clearly intended as binding obligations. They include the right of peoples to self-determination (article 1), the right to life (article 6),

---

[261] Article 15. See e.g. A/48/18, p. 107.

[262] See e.g. A/38/18, pp. 14–24. Note, for example, that by late 1983 fifteen reminders had been sent to Swaziland requesting it to submit its fourth, fifth, sixth and seventh overdue periodic reports, *ibid.*, p. 21. See also A/44/18, pp. 10–16.

[263] See CERD/C/70/Rev.1, 6 December 1983.

[264] See e.g. A/44/18, 1990, p. 7 and A/48/18, 1994, p. 149.   [265] A/44/18, p. 91.

[266] See e.g. Joseph *et al.*, *International Covenant*; Nowak, *UN Covenant*; Steiner, Alston and Goodman, *International Human Rights*, pp. 844 ff.; McGoldrick, *Human Rights Committee*; Opsahl, 'Human Rights Committee', p. 367; D. Fischer, 'Reporting under the Convention on Civil and Political Rights: The First Five Years of the Human Rights Committee', 76 AJIL, 1982, p. 142; Ramcharan, 'Implementing the International Covenants'; E. Schwelb, 'The International Measures of Implementation of the International Covenant on Civil and Political Rights and of the Optional Protocol', 12 *Texas International Law Review*, 1977, p. 141; M. Nowak, 'The Effectiveness of the International Covenant on Civil and Political Rights – Stock-taking after the First Eleven Sessions of the UN Human Rights Committee', 2 HRLJ, 1981, p. 168 and 5 HRLJ, 1984, p. 199. See also M. Bossuyt, *Guide to the Travaux Préparatoires of the International Covenant on Civil and Political Rights*, The Hague, 1987; F. Jhabvala, 'The Practice of the Covenant's Human Rights Committee, 1976–82: Review of State Party Reports', 6 HRQ, 1984, p. 81, and P. R. Ghandhi, 'The Human Rights Committee and the Right of Individual Communication', 57 BYIL, 1986, p. 201.

[267] See Rehman, *International Human Rights Law*, p. 83.

prohibitions on torture and slavery (articles 7 and 8), the right to liberty and security of the person (article 9), due process (article 14), freedom of thought, conscience and religion (article 18), freedom of association (article 22) and the rights of persons belonging to minorities to enjoy their own culture (article 27).

A Human Rights Committee was established under Part IV of the Covenant. It consists of eighteen independent and expert members, elected by the states parties to the Covenant for four-year terms, with consideration given to the need for equitable geographical distribution and representation of the different forms of civilisation and of the principal legal systems.[268] The Committee meets three times a year (in Geneva and New York) and operates by way of consensus.[269] The Covenant is primarily implemented by means of a reporting system, whereby states parties provide information on the measures adopted to give effect to the rights recognised in the Covenant. Initial reports are made within one year of the entry into force of the Covenant for the state in question and general guidelines have been issued.[270] The Committee has decided that subsequent reports would be required every five years,[271] and the first of the second periodic reports became due in 1983. The reports are discussed by the Committee with representatives of the state concerned (following upon the precedent established by the Committee on the Elimination of Racial Discrimination).[272] The practice used to be that Committee members would informally receive information from sources other than the reporting state provided the source is not publicly identified. This enabled the Committee to be more effective than would otherwise have been the case.[273] However, no doubt due to the ending of Soviet control in Eastern Europe and the demise of the Soviet Union, there appears to be no

---

[268] See articles 28–32 of the Covenant.

[269] See e.g. Nowak, 'Effectiveness', p. 169, 1981 3 HRLJ, 1982, p. 209 and 1984, p. 202. See also A/36/40, annex VII, Introduction; CCPR/C/21/Rev.1 and A/44/40, p. 173.

[270] See article 40 and CCPR/C/5. Supplementary reports may be requested: see Rule 70(2) of the provisional rules of procedure, CCPR/C/3/Rev.1. See now the Rules of Procedure 2001, CCPR/C/3/Rev.6 and the revised consolidated guidelines 2001, CCPR/C/66/GUI/Rev.2.

[271] See CCPR/C/18; CCPR/C/19 and CCPR/C/19/Rev.1. See also CCPR/C/20 regarding guidelines. Several states have been lax about producing reports, e.g. Zaire and the Dominican Republic, while the initial report of Guinea was so short as to be held by the Committee as not providing sufficient information: see Nowak, 'Effectiveness', 1984, p. 200.

[272] See Buergenthal, 'Implementing', pp. 199–201, and Fischer, 'Reporting', p. 145.

[273] Fischer, 'Reporting', pp. 146–7.

problem now about acknowledging publicly the receipt of information from named non-governmental organisations.[274] The Committee may also seek additional information from the state concerned. For example, in October 1992, the Committee adopted a decision requesting the governments of the Federal Republic of Yugoslavia (Serbia and Montenegro), Croatia and Bosnia-Herzegovina to submit a short report concerning measures to prevent *inter alia* ethnic cleansing and arbitrary killings.[275] Such reports were forthcoming and were discussed with the state representatives concerned and comments adopted. The Committee thereafter adopted an amendment to its rules of procedure permitting it to call for reports at any time deemed appropriate.[276] The Committee has also noted that the peoples within a territory of a former state party to the Covenant remain entitled to the guarantees of the Covenant.[277] Where states parties have failed to report over several reporting cycles, or request a postponement of their scheduled appearance before the Committee at short notice, the Committee may continue to examine the situation in the particular state on the basis of material available to it.[278]

Under article 40(4), the Committee is empowered to make such 'general comments as it may deem appropriate'. After some discussion, a consensus was adopted in 1980, which permitted such comments provided that they promoted co-operation between states in the implementation of the Covenant, summarised the experience of the Committee in examining states' reports and drew the attention of states parties to matters relating to the improvement of the reporting procedure and the implementation of the Covenant. The aim of the Committee was to engage in a constructive dialogue with each reporting state, and the comments would be non-country-specific.[279] However, in 1992, the Committee decided that at the end of the consideration of each state party's report, specific comments would be adopted referring to the country in question and such comments

---

[274] Such documents may now be officially distributed, rather than being informally made available to Committee members individually: see McGoldrick, *Human Rights Committee*, p. liii.

[275] CCPR/C/SR/1178/Add.1.

[276] New Rule 66(2), see CCPR/C/SR/1205/Add.1. See also S. Joseph, 'New Procedures Concerning the Human Rights Committee's Examination of State Reports', 13 NQHR, 1995, p. 5.

[277] See, with regard to former Yugoslavia, CCPR/C/SR.1178/Add.1, pp. 2–3 and CCPR/C/79/Add.14–16. See, with regard to the successor states of the USSR, CCPR/C/79/Add.38 (Azerbaijan). See also I. Boerefijn, 'Towards a Strong System of Supervision', 17 HRQ, 1995, p. 766.

[278] See e.g. A/56/40, vol. I, p. 25.   [279] CCPR/C/18.

would express both the satisfaction and the concerns of the Committee as appropriate.[280] These specific comments are in a common format and refer to 'positive aspects' of the report and 'principal subjects for concern', as well as 'suggestions and recommendations'.[281] The Committee has also adopted the practice, where a due report has not been forthcoming, of considering the measures taken by the state party in question to give effect to rights in the Covenant in the absence of a report but in the presence of representatives of the state and of adopting provisional concluding observations.[282]

The Committee has also adopted a variety of General Comments.[283] These comments are generally non-controversial. One interesting comment on article 6 (the right to life), however, emphasised the Committee's view that 'the designing, testing, manufacture, possession and development of nuclear weapons are among the greatest threats to the right to life', and that the 'production, testing, possession and deployment and use of nuclear weapons should be prohibited and recognised as crimes against humanity'.[284]

In April 1989, the Committee adopted a General Comment on the rights of the child, as the process of adopting the Convention on the Rights of the Child neared its climax. It noted the importance of economic, social and cultural measures, such as the need to reduce infant mortality and prevent exploitation. Freedom of expression was referred to, as was

---

[280] See A/47/40, p. 4.

[281] See, for example, the comments concerning Colombia in September 1992, CCPR/C/79/Add.2; Guinea in April 1993, CCPR/C/79/Add.20; Norway in November 1993, CCPR/C/79/Add.27; Morocco in November 1994, CCPR/C/79/Add.44; the Russian Federation in July 1995, CCPR/C/79/Add.54; Estonia in November 1995, CCPR/C/79/Add.59 and the United Kingdom in July 1995, CCPR/C/79/Add.55 and, relating to Hong Kong, in November 1995, CCPR/C/79/Add.57. Note that in September 1995, Mexico responded to the Committee's Concluding Comments upon its report by issuing Observations, CCPR/C/108.

[282] See Rule 70 of its Rules of Procedure 2005. The procedures are described, for example, in the 2005–6 Report of the Committee, A/61/40, paras. 49 ff. (2006)

[283] See e.g. T. Opsahl, 'The General Comments of the Human Rights Committee' in *Festschrift für Karl Josef Partsch zum 75*, Berlin, 1989, p. 273.

[284] CCPR/C/21/Add.4, 14 November 1984. Note that the International Court of Justice gave an Advisory Opinion on 8 July 1996 at the request of the General Assembly of the UN concerning the *Legality of the Threat or Use of Nuclear Weapons*, in which it was noted that the right not to be arbitrarily deprived of one's life applied also in hostilities. Whether a particular loss of life was arbitrary within the terms of article 6 would depend on the situation and would be decided by reference to the law applicable in armed conflict and not deduced from the terms of the Covenant itself, ICJ Reports, 1996, para. 25; 110 ILR, pp. 163, 190.

the requirement that children be protected against discrimination on grounds such as race, sex, religion, national or social origin, property or birth. Responsibility for guaranteeing the necessary protection lies, it was stressed, with the family, society and the state, although it is primarily incumbent upon the family. Special attention needed to be paid to the right of every child to acquire a nationality.[285]

In November 1989, an important General Comment was adopted on non-discrimination. Discrimination was to be understood to imply for the purposes of the Covenant:

> any distinction, exclusion, restriction or preference which is based on any ground such as race, colour, sex, language, religion, political or other opinion, national or social origin, property, birth or other status, and which has the purpose or effect of nullifying or impairing the recognition, enjoyment or exercise by all persons, on an equal footing, of all rights and freedoms.[286]

Identical treatment in every instance was not, however, demanded. The death sentence could not, under article 6(5) of the Covenant, be imposed on persons under the age of eighteen or upon pregnant women. It was also noted that the principle of equality sometimes requires states parties to take affirmative action in order to diminish or eliminate conditions which cause or help to perpetuate discrimination prohibited by the Covenant. In addition, it was pointed out that not every differentiation constituted discrimination, if the criteria for such differentiation were reasonable and objective and if the aim was to achieve a purpose which was legitimate under the Covenant.[287]

Important General Comments on Minorities[288] and Reservations[289] were adopted in 1994. In 1997, the Committee noted in General Comment 26 that the rights in the Covenant belonged to the people living in the territory of the state party concerned and that international law did not permit a state which had ratified or acceded or succeeded to the Covenant to denounce it or withdraw from it,[290] while in General Comment 28 the Committee pointed out that the rights which persons belonging to minorities enjoyed under article 27 of the Covenant in respect of their language, culture and religion did not authorise any state, group or person

---

[285] A/44/40, pp. 173–5.   [286] CCPR/C/21/Rev.1/Add.1, p. 3.
[287] *Ibid.*, p. 4. See also above, p. 286.
[288] HRI/GEN/1/Rev.1, 1995. See further above, p. 293
[289] CCPR/C/21/Rev.1/Add.6. See further below, p. 913.   [290] A/53/40, annex VII.

to violate the right to the equal enjoyment by women of any Covenant rights, including the right to equal protection of the law.[291]

Under article 41 of the Covenant, states parties may recognise the competence of the Committee to hear inter-state complaints. Both the complainant and the object state must have made such declarations. The Committee will seek to resolve the issue and, if it is not successful, it may under article 42 appoint, with the consent of the parties, an ad hoc Conciliation Commission.[292]

The powers of the Human Rights Committee were extended by Optional Protocol I to the Civil and Political Rights Covenant with regard to ratifying states to include the competence to receive and consider individual communications alleging violations of the Covenant by a state party to the Protocol.[293] The individual must have exhausted all available domestic remedies (unless unreasonably prolonged) and the same matter must not be in the process of examination under another international procedure.[294] The procedure under the Optional Protocol is divided into several stages. The gathering of basic information is done by the Secretary-General and laid before the Working Group on Communications of the Committee, which recommends whether, for example, further information is required from the applicant or the relevant state party and whether the communication should be declared inadmissible. The procedure before the Committee itself is divided into an admissibility and a merits stage. Interim decisions may be made by the Committee and ultimately a 'final view' communicated to the parties.[295]

---

[291] CCPR/C/21/Rev.1/Add.10, 2000. General Comment 29 adopted in 2001 dealt with the question of non-derogable provisions, see CCPR/C/21/Rev.1/Add.11. Note also General Comment 32 concerning the right to equality before courts and tribunals and to a fair trial, CCPR/C/GC/32, 2007.

[292] The inter-state procedure has not been used to date.

[293] Signed in 1966 and in force as from 23 March 1976. See e.g. H. Steiner, 'Individual Claims in a World of Massive Violations: What Role for the Human Rights Committee?' in Alston and Crawford, *Future*, p. 15; P. R. Ghandi, *The Human Rights Committee and the Right of Individual Communication: Law and Practice*, Aldershot, 1998; A. de Zayas, H. Möller and T. Opsahl, 'Application of the International Covenant on Civil and Political Rights under the Optional Protocol by the Human Rights Committee', 28 German YIL, 1985, p. 9, and *Selected Decisions of the Human Rights Committee under the Optional Protocol*, New York, vol. I, 1985 and vol. II, 1990. Two states (Jamaica and Trinidad and Tobago) have denounced the Protocol.

[294] Article 5, Optional Protocol.

[295] See Nowak, 'Effectiveness', 1980, pp. 153 ff., and 1981 Report of Human Rights Committee, A/36/40, pp. 85–91.

An increasing workload, however, began to cause difficulties as the number of parties to the Optional Protocol increased. By mid-2006, 1,490 communications had been registered. Of these, 547 had been the subject of a final view (of which 429 concluded that a violation had occurred), 449 were declared inadmissible and 218 were discontinued or withdrawn, leaving 276 yet to be concluded.[296] In order to deal with the growth in applications, the Committee decided at its thirty-fifth session to appoint a Special Rapporteur to process new communications as they were received (i.e. between sessions of the Committee), and this included requesting the state or individual concerned to provide additional written information or observations relevant to the question of the admissibility of the communication.[297] The Committee has also authorised its five-member Working Group on Communications to adopt a decision declaring a communication admissible, providing there is unanimity.[298] The Committee may also adopt interim measures of protection under Rule 92 of its Rules of Procedure 2005. This has been used primarily in connection with cases submitted by or on behalf of persons sentenced to death and awaiting execution.[299] Such a request was made, for example, to Trinidad and Tobago in the *Ashby* case pending examination of the communication, but to no avail. After the individual was executed, the Committee adopted a decision expressing its indignation at the failure of the state party to comply with the request for interim measures and deciding to continue consideration of the case.[300] Where the state concerned has disregarded the Committee's decisions under Rule 92, the Committee has found that the state party has violated its obligations under the Optional Protocol.[301]

The Committee, however, is not a court with the power of binding decision on the merits of cases. Indeed, in instances of non-compliance with its final views, the Optional Protocol does not provide for an enforcement mechanism, nor indeed for sanctions, although follow-up techniques are being developed in order to address such problems.[302]

---

[296] Report of the Committee for 2005–6, A/61/40, para. 89 (2006).
[297] A/44/40, pp. 139–40. See also Rule 91 of the amended Rules of Procedure, *ibid.*, p. 180.
[298] *Ibid.*, p. 140.
[299] See, in particular, *Canepa* v. *Canada*, A/52/40, vol. II, annex VI, sect. K. See also *Ruzmetov* v. *Uzbekistan*, A/61/40, vol. II, p. 31 (2006) and *Boucherf* v. *Algeria, ibid.*, p. 312.
[300] A/49/40, pp. 70–1.   [301] See *Piandiong et al.* v. *The Philippines*, A/54/40, para. 420(b).
[302] Note that in October 1990, the Committee appointed a Special Rapporteur to follow up cases, CCPR/C/SR.1002, p. 8. See Rule 101 of the Rules of Procedure 2005. In 1994, the Committee decided that every form of publicity would be given to follow-up activities, including separate sections in annual reports, the issuing of annual press communiqués and the institution of such practices in a new rule of procedure (Rule 99)

A variety of interesting decisions have so far been rendered. The first group of cases concerned complaints against Uruguay, in which the Committee found violations by that state of rights recognised in the Covenant.[303] In the *Lovelace* case,[304] the Committee found Canada in breach of article 27 of the Covenant protecting the rights of minorities since its law provided that an Indian woman, whose marriage to a non-Indian had broken down, was not permitted to return to her home on an Indian reservation. In the *Mauritian Women* case[305] a breach of Covenant rights was upheld where the foreign husbands of Mauritian women were liable to deportation whereas the foreign wives of Mauritian men would not have been.

The Committee has also held that the Covenant's obligations cover the decisions of diplomatic authorities of a state party regarding citizens living abroad.[306] In the *Robinson* case,[307] the Committee considered whether a state was under an obligation itself to make provision for effective representation by counsel in a case concerning a capital offence, in circumstances where the counsel appointed by the author of the communication declines to appear. The Committee emphasised that it was axiomatic that legal assistance be available in capital cases and decided that the absence of counsel constituted unfair trial.

The Committee has dealt with the death penalty issue in several cases[308] and has noted, for example, that such a sentence may only be imposed in accordance with due process rights.[309] The Committee has also taken the view that where the extradition of a person facing the death penalty may expose the person to violation of due process rights in the receiving state, the extraditing state may be in violation of the Covenant.[310]

---

emphasising that follow-up activities were not confidential, A/49/40, pp. 84–6. See also A/56/40, vol. I, p. 131.

[303] These cases are reported in 1 HRLJ, 1980, pp. 209 ff. See, for other cases, 2 HRLJ, 1981, pp. 130 ff.; *ibid.*, pp. 340 ff.; 3 HRLJ, 1982, p. 188; 4 HRLJ, 1983, pp. 185 ff. and 5 HRLJ, 1984, pp. 191 ff. See also Annual Reports of the Human Rights Committee, 1981 to date.

[304] 1981 Report of the Human Rights Committee, A/36/40, p. 166.

[305] *Ibid.*, p. 134.

[306] See e.g. the *Waksman* case, 1 HRLJ, 1980, p. 220 and the *Lichtensztejn* case, 5 HRLJ, 1984, p. 207.

[307] A/44/40, p. 241 (1989).

[308] See e.g. *Thompson* v. *St Vincent and the Grenadines*, A/56/40, vol. II, annex X, sect. H, para. 8.2.

[309] See e.g. the *Berry, Hamilton, Grant, Currie* and *Champagnie* cases against Jamaica, A/49/40, vol. II, pp. 20, 37, 50, 73 and 136.

[310] See the *Ng* case, concerning extradition from Canada to the US. The Committee found that there was no evidence of such a risk, A/49/40, vol. II, p. 189.

The Committee has also noted that execution by gas asphyxiation would violate the prohibition in article 7 of cruel and inhuman treatment.[311] The issue faced in the *Vuolanne* case[312] was whether the procedural safeguards in article 9(4) of the Covenant on Civil and Political Rights, whereby a person deprived of his liberty is to be allowed recourse to the courts, applied to military disciplinary detention. The Committee was very clear that it did. One issue of growing importance concerns the question of the extraterritorial application of human rights treaties, that is whether a state party to a particular human rights treaty is obliged to apply it outside of its own territory where it is acting abroad either by way of its state agents or organs or because it is in control of an area beyond its border. The Committee has consistently taken the view that the Covenant does apply in such circumstances, whether it be with regard to state agents acting abroad[313] or with regard to the obligations of Israel within the occupied territories.[314]

It is already apparent that the Committee has proved a success and is performing a very important role in the field of human rights protection.[315]

The Committee on the Elimination of Discrimination Against Women

The Commission on the Status of Women was established in 1946 as one of the functional commissions of ECOSOC and has played a role both in standard-setting and in the elaboration of further relevant instruments.[316] The Committee on the Elimination of All Forms of

---

[311] *Ibid.*   [312] *Ibid.*, p. 249.

[313] See e.g. *López Burgos v. Uruguay*, case no. 52/79, 68 ILR, p. 29, or *Lilian Celiberti de Casariego v. Uruguay*, case no. 56/79, 68 ILR, p. 41, concerning the activities of Uruguayan agents in Brazil and Argentina respectively.

[314] See e.g. CCPR/C/79/Add.93, para. 10 and CCPR/CO/78/ISR, para. 11 (concluding observations on Israel's reports). This approach was affirmed by the International Court of Justice in the *Construction of a Wall* case, ICJ Reports, 2004, pp. 136, 178–9; 129, ILR, pp. 37, 97–8.

[315] The second optional protocol aimed at the abolition of the death penalty was adopted in 1990, while the desirability of a third optional protocol to the Covenant, concerning the right to a fair trial and a remedy, has been considered by the Commission on Human Rights: see E/CN.4/Sub.2.1994/24, Sub-Commission resolution 1994/35 and Commission resolution 1994/107.

[316] See ECOSOC resolutions 1/5 (1946), 2/11 (1946) and 48 (IV) (1947). See also L. Reanda, 'The Commission on the Status of Women' in Alston, *United Nations and Human Rights*, p. 265. The mandate of the Commission was revised by ECOSOC resolutions 1987/22 and

Discrimination Against Women was established under article 22 of the 1979 Convention on the Elimination of all Forms of Discrimination Against Women.[317] This Convention is implemented by means of states' reports. It is composed of twenty-three experts serving in individual capacities for four-year terms. It held its first regular session in October 1982 and at its second session examined the reports of seven states parties regarding measures taken to comply with the terms of the Convention. It reports annually to the UN General Assembly through ECOSOC.[318] The Committee has provided guidelines to states parties on reporting, whereby initial reports are intended to be detailed and comprehensive with subsequent reports being of an updating nature.[319] Since 1990, subsequent reports are examined first by a pre-sessional working group. Following discussion of a report, the Committee provides concluding comments. The Committee, in addition to hearing states' reports, may make suggestions and general recommendations, which are included in the report.[320] Since 1997 the process of adopting a general recommendation is preceded by an open dialogue between the Committee, non-governmental organisations and others regarding the topic of the general recommendation

1996/6. There is also an individual petition procedure by which complaints are considered by a Working Group on Communications which then reports to the Commission. The Commission in turn reports to ECOSOC.

[317] This came into force in 1981. See R. Jacobson, 'The Committee on the Elimination of Discrimination against Women' in Alston, *United Nations and Human Rights*, p. 444; A. Byrnes, 'The "Other" Human Rights Body: The Work of the Committee on the Elimination of Discrimination Against Women', 14 *Yale Journal of International Law*, 1989, p. 1; M. Galey, 'International Enforcement of Women's Rights', 6 HRQ, 1984, p. 463, and M. Wadstein, 'Implementation of the UN Convention on the Elimination of All Forms of Discrimination against Women', 6 NQHR, 1988, p. 5. See also R. Cook, 'Women's International Human Rights Law', 15 HRQ, 1993, p. 230; *Human Rights of Women* (ed. R. Cook), Philadelphia, 1994; M. Freeman and A. Fraser, 'Women's Human Rights' in Herlin and Hargrove, *Human Rights: An Agenda for the Next Century*, p. 103; Rehman, *International Human Rights Law*, chapter 13; Steiner, Alston and Goodman, *International Human Rights*, pp. 175 and 541; J. Morsink, 'Women's Rights in the Universal Declaration', 13 HRQ, 1991, p. 229; H. Charlesworth and C. Chinkin, *The Boundaries of International Law: A Feminist Analysis*, Manchester, 2000, and M. Bustelo, 'The Committee on the Elimination of Discrimination against Women at the Crossroads' in Alston and Crawford, *Future*, p. 79.

[318] See articles 17–21 of the Convention and the first Report of the Committee, A/38/45, and *UN Chronicle*, November 1983, pp. 65–86.

[319] See CEDAW/C/7Rev.3 and with regard to reports submitted from 1 January 2003, www.un.org/womenwatch/daw/cedaw/guidelines.PDF.

[320] Article 21.

and a discussion of a draft prepared by a Committee member. General Recommendation No. 5 called upon states parties to make more use of 'temporary special measures such as positive action, preferential treatment or quota systems to advance women's integration into education, the economy, politics and employment', while General Recommendation No. 8 provided that states parties should take further measures to ensure to women, on equal terms with men and without discrimination, the opportunity to represent their government at the international level.[321] General Recommendation No. 12 called upon states parties to include in their reports information on measures taken to deal with violence against women, while General Recommendation No. 14 called for measures to be taken to eradicate the practice of female circumcision. General Recommendation No. 19 (1992) dealt at some length with the problem of violence against women in general and specific terms, and General Recommendation No. 21 is concerned with equality in marriage and family relations.[322] In 1999, the Committee adopted a General Recommendation No. 24 on women and health. General Recommendation No. 25 was adopted in 2004 and concerned temporary special measures.[323]

The Committee, however, met only for one session of two weeks a year, which was clearly inadequate. This was increased to two sessions a year from 1997.[324] An Optional Protocol adopted in 1999 and in force as from December 2000 allows for the right of individual petition provided a number of conditions are met, including the requirement for the exhaustion of domestic remedies. In addition, the Protocol creates an inquiry procedure enabling the Committee to initiate inquiries into situations of grave or systematic violations of women's rights where it has received reliable information of grave or systematic violations by a state party of rights established in the Convention.[325] In recent years, the importance of women's rights has received greater recognition. The Vienna Declaration and Programme of Action adopted in 1993 emphasised that the human rights of women should be brought into the

---

[321] A/43/38 (1988).   [322] HRI/GEN/1/Rev.1, 1994, pp. 72 ff.

[323] HRI/GEN/1/Rev.7, 2004, p. 282.

[324] Although the Committee met exceptionally for three sessions during 2002 to deal with backlog reports. However, see General Assembly resolution 60/230 concering the extension of meeting time in 2005 and 2006.

[325] See, for example, for an earlier view, R. Cook, 'The Elimination of Sexual Apartheid: Prospects for the Fourth World Conference on Women', *ASIL Issue Papers on World Conferences*, Washington, 1995, pp. 48 ff.

mainstream of UN system-wide activity and that women's rights should be regularly and systematically addressed throughout the UN bodies and mechanisms.[326] In the light of this, the fifth meeting of Chairpersons of Human Rights Treaty Bodies in 1994 agreed that the enjoyment of the human rights of women by each treaty body within the competence of its mandate should be closely monitored. Each of the treaty bodies took steps to examine its guidelines with this in mind.[327] It should also be noted, for example, that the Special Rapporteur on Torture was called upon by the Commission on Human Rights in 1994 to examine questions concerning torture directed disproportionately or primarily against women.[328] In addition, the General Assembly adopted a Declaration on the Elimination of Violence Against Women in February 1994,[329] and a Special Rapporteur on Violence against Women, its Causes and Consequences was appointed in 1994.[330] The International Labour Organisation established the promotion of equality of opportunity and treatment of men and women in employment as a priority item in its programme and budget for 1994/5.[331] The Committee on the Rights of the Child has also discussed the issue of the 'girl-child' and the question of child prostitution.[332]

---

[326] See Part II, Section 3, 32 ILM, 1993, p. 1678. See also the Beijing Conference 1995, Cook, 'Elimination of Sexual Apartheid'; the Beijing plus 5 process, see General Assembly resolution 55/71. In 2000, the General Assembly adopted resolution S-23/3 containing a Political Declaration and a statement on further actions and initiatives to implement the Beijing Declaration and Platform for Action.

[327] See HRI/MC/1995/2. See also the Report of the Expert Group Meeting on the Development of Guidelines for the Integration of Gender Perspectives into Human Rights Activities and Programmes, E/CN.4/1996/105, 1995. This called *inter alia* for the use of gender-inclusive language in human rights instruments and standards, the identification, collection and use of gender-disaggregated data, gender-sensitive interpretation of human rights mechanisms and education and the promotion of a system-wide co-ordination and collaboration on the human rights of women within the UN.

[328] See resolution 1994/37. See also the Report of the Special Rapporteur of January 1995, E/CN.4/1995/34, p. 8.

[329] Resolution 48/104, see 33 ILM, 1994, p. 1049. Note also the adoption of the Inter-American Convention on the Prevention, Punishment and Eradication of Violence Against Women in June 1994, *ibid.*, p. 1534 and the March 2002 Joint Declaration by the Special Rapporteur on women's rights of the Inter-American Commission on Human Rights, the Special Rapporteur on Violence Against Women, its Causes and its Consequences of the UN Commission on Human Rights, and the Special Rapporteur on the Rights of Women in Africa of the African Commission on Human and Peoples' Rights which called for the elimination of violence and discrimination against women: see www.cidh.org/declaration.women.htm.

[330] See E/CN.4/2003/75.   [331] E/CN.4/Sub.2/1994/5, p. 6.

[332] See further below, p. 331.

The Committee Against Torture[333]

The prohibition of torture is contained in a wide variety of human rights[334] and humanitarian law treaties,[335] and has become part of customary international law. Indeed it is now established as a norm of *jus cogens*.[336] Issues concerning torture have come before a number of human rights organs, such as the Human Rights Committee,[337] the European Court of Human Rights[338] and the International Criminal Tribunal on the Former Yugoslavia.[339]

The Convention against Torture and Other Cruel, Inhuman or Degrading Treatment or Punishment was signed on 10 December 1984 and entered into force in 1987. It built particularly upon the

---

[333] See e.g. M. Nowak and E. McArther, *The UN Convention Against Torture: A Commentary*, Oxford, 2008; A. Byrnes, 'The Committee Against Torture' in Alston, *United Nations and Human Rights*, p. 509; R. Bank, 'Country-Oriented Procedures under the Convention against Torture: Towards a New Dynamism' in Alston and Crawford, *Future*, p. 145; Rehman, *International Human Rights Law*, chapter 15; N. Rodley, *The Treatment of Prisoners under International Law*, 2nd edn, Oxford, 1999; A. Boulesbaa, *The UN Convention on Torture and Prospects for Enforcement*, The Hague, 1999; M. Evans, 'Getting to Grips with Torture', 51 ICLQ, 2002, p. 365; J. Burgers and H. Danelius, *The United Nations Convention against Torture*, Boston, 1988; Meron, *Human Rights in International Law*, pp. 126–30, 165–6, 511–15; S. Ackerman, 'Torture and Other Forms of Cruel and Unusual Punishment in International Law', 11 *Vanderbilt Journal of Transnational Law*, 1978, p. 653; Amnesty International, *Torture in the Eighties*, London, 1984; A. Dormenval, 'UN Committee Against Torture: Practice and Perspectives', 8 NQHR, 1990, p. 26; Z. Haquani, 'La Convention des Nations Unies Contre la Torture', 90 RGDIP, 1986, p. 127; N. Lerner, 'The UN Convention on Torture', 16 *Israel Yearbook on Human Rights*, 1986, p. 126, and R. St J. Macdonald, 'International Prohibitions against Torture and other Forms of Similar Treatment or Punishment' in *International Law at a Time of Perplexity* (ed. Y. Dinstein), Dordrecht, 1987, p. 385.

[334] See e.g. article 5 of the Universal Declaration; article 7 of the Civil and Political Rights Covenant; article 3 of the European Convention on Human Rights; article 5 of the Inter-American Convention on Human Rights; article 5 of the African Charter on Human and Peoples' Rights; the UN Convention against Torture, 1984; the European Convention on the Prevention of Torture, 1987 and the Inter-American Convention to Prevent and Punish Torture, 1985.

[335] See e.g. the four Geneva Red Cross Conventions, 1949 and the two Additional Protocols of 1977.

[336] See e.g. *Ex parte Pinochet (No. 3)* [2000] 1 AC 147, 198; 119 ILR, p. 135 and the *Furundžija* case, 121 ILR, pp. 213, 260–2. See also *Al-Adsani* v. *UK*, European Court of Human Rights, Judgment of 21 November 2001, para. 61; 123 ILR, pp. 24, 41–2.

[337] See e.g. *Vuolanne* v. *Finland*, 265/87, 96 ILR, p. 649, and generally Joseph *et al.*, *International Covenant*, chapter 9.

[338] See e.g. *Selmouni* v. *France*, Judgment of 28 July 1999.

[339] See e.g. the *Delalić* case, IT-96-21, Judgment of 16 November 1998.

Declaration on the Protection of All Persons from being subjected to Torture and Other Cruel, Inhuman and Degrading Treatment or Punishment adopted by the General Assembly in 1975.[340] Other relevant instruments preceding the Convention were the Standard Minimum Rules for the Treatment of Prisoners, 1955, the Code of Conduct for Law Enforcement Officers, 1979 (article 5) and the Principles of Medical Ethics, 1982 (Principles 1 and 2).[341]

Torture is defined in article 1 of the Convention against Torture to mean:

> [a]ny act by which severe pain or suffering, whether physical or mental, is intentionally inflicted on a person for such purposes as obtaining from him or a third person information or a confession, punishing him for an act he or a third person has committed or is suspected of having committed, or intimidating or coercing him or a third person, or for any reason based on discrimination of any kind, when such pain or suffering is inflicted by or at the instigation of or with the consent or the acquiescence of a public official or other person acting in an official capacity. It does not include pain or suffering arising only from, inherent in or incidental to lawful sanctions.

The states parties to the Convention are under duties *inter alia* to take measures to prevent such activities in territories under their jurisdiction (article 2), not to return a person to a country where he may be subjected to torture (article 3), to make torture a criminal offence and establish jurisdiction over it (articles 4 and 5),[342] to prosecute or extradite persons charged with torture (article 7) and to provide a remedy for persons tortured (article 14).

The Committee against Torture was established under Part II of the Convention against Torture, 1984 and commenced work in 1987. It consists of ten independent experts. In an interesting comment on the proliferation of international human rights committees and the dangers of inconsistencies developing, article 17(2) provides that in nominating experts, states parties should 'bear in mind the usefulness of nominating persons who are also members of the Human Rights Committee'.

---

[340] General Assembly resolution 3452 (XXX).

[341] Note also the Principles on the Protection of Persons under Detention or Imprisonment adopted by the General Assembly in 1989. See generally *Human Rights: A Compilation of International Instruments*, United Nations, New York, vol. I (First Part), 1993, Section H.

[342] See, as far as the UK is concerned, sections 134 and 135 of the Criminal Justice Act 1988.

The Committee receives states' reports (article 19), has an inter-state complaint competence (article 21) and may hear individual communications (article 22). In both the latter cases, it is necessary that the state or states concerned should have made a declaration accepting the competence of the Committee.[343] Article 20 of the Convention provides that if the Committee receives 'reliable evidence' that torture is being systematically practised in the territory of a state party, it may invite the state in question to co-operate in examining the evidence. The Committee may designate one or more of its members to make a confidential inquiry. In doing so, it shall seek the co-operation of the state concerned and, with the latter's agreement, such an inquiry may include a visit to its territory. The Committee will transmit the findings of the inquiry to the state, together with appropriate comments or suggestions. The proceedings up to this point are to be confidential, but the Committee may, after consulting the state, decide to include a summary account of the results in its annual report. This additional, if cautiously phrased, power may provide the Committee with a significant role.[344] It should be noted that states parties have the ability to 'opt out' of this procedure if they so wish at the time of signature or ratification, or accession.[345]

The conduct of the reporting procedure bears much resemblance to the practice of the UN Human Rights Committee.[346] Guidelines have been issued for states parties and the discussions with state representatives are held with a view to establishing a constructive dialogue. Many problems facing other treaty bodies also appear with regard to the Committee against Torture, for example, overdue reports and problems relating to implementation of the Convention generally. The Committee may also make comments on states' reports in the form of concluding observations[347] and may issue general comments.[348] Interim measures of protection may also

---

[343] See e.g. the Committee's report of Spring 2002, A/57/44, p. 82.

[344] Note e.g. the report of the Committee on Sri Lanka in this context, A/57/44, p. 59 (2002). See also E. Zoller, 'Second Session of the UN Commission against Torture', 7 NQHR, 1989, p. 250.

[345] Article 28(1). See e.g. A/57/44, p. 81.

[346] As at May 2006, the Committee had received a total of 194 reports, with 192 overdue: see A/61/44, p. 5 (2006).

[347] See e.g. A/61/44, pp. 6 ff. (2006).

[348] To date only one has been issued on the implementation of article 3 concerning deportation to states where there is substantial reason to fear torture: see A/53/44, annex IX.

be granted under Rule 108(1) and this is monitored by the rapporteurs for new complaints and interim measures.[349]

The first three cases before the Committee under article 22 were admissibility decisions concerning Argentinian legislation exempting junior military officers from liability for acts of torture committed during the 1976–83 period and its compatibility with the Torture Convention.[350] The Committee noted that there existed a general rule of international law obliging all states to take effective measures to prevent and punish acts of torture. However, the Convention took effect only from its date of entry (26 June 1987) and could not be applied retroactively to cover the enactment of legislation prior to that date. Therefore, the communications were inadmissible. However, the Committee did criticise the Argentinian legislation and stated that Argentina was morally bound to provide a remedy to the victims of torture.[351] In May 2002, the Committee revised its rules of procedure and established the function of a Rapporteur for follow-up of decisions on complaints submitted under article 22.[352] The Committee has held that where substantial grounds exist for believing that the applicant would be in danger of being subjected to torture, the expulsion or return of the applicant by the state party concerned to the state in which he might be tortured would constitute a violation of article 3 of the Convention.[353] The Committee has also emphasised that the risk of torture must be assessed on grounds that go beyond mere theory or suspicion. The risk need not be highly probable, but it must be personal and present. While the Committee does give considerable weight to findings of fact made by the organs of the state party concerned, it is not bound by these and has the power of free assessment of the facts arising in the circumstances of each case. It has been particularly underlined that the prohibition enshrined in article 3 of the Convention was an absolute one.[354] It has also been noted that where complaints of torture are made during court

---

[349] *Ibid.*, pp. 82–3. See also A/57/44, p. 219.

[350] *OR, MM and MS v. Argentina*, communications nos. 1–3/1988. Decisions of 23 November 1989. See 5 *Interights Bulletin*, 1990, p. 12.

[351] The Committee has, however, held that where the effect of the violations continues after the date that the Convention comes into force for the state concerned and where those effects constitute a breach of the Convention, then the matter can be considered: see e.g. *AA v. Azerbaijan*, A/61/44, pp. 255, 259 (2006).

[352] See e.g. A/61/44, p. 86 (2006).   [353] *Khan* v. *Canada*, CAT/C/13/D/15/1994.

[354] See *Dadar* v. *Canada*, A/61/44, pp. 233 ff. (2006).

proceedings, it is desirable that they be elucidated by means of independent proceedings.[355] A complaint must be submitted by the alleged
victim, or by a close relative or a duly authorised representative, and
must first be declared admissible. Requirements include that the matter must not be before another tribunal, that domestic remedies have
been exhausted and that the complaint must reach a 'basic level of
substantiation'.[356]

An Optional Protocol to the Convention to enable the Committee
through a new Subcommittee on Prevention to conduct regular visits
to places of detention and make recommendations to states parties was
adopted by the General Assembly in December 2002 and came into force
in 2006. Under the Protocol, states parties must establish a 'national preventive mechanism' for the prevention of torture at the domestic level.
Visits by the Subcommittee and the national preventive mechanism to
any place under the state party's jurisdiction and control where persons
are, or may be, deprived of their liberty must be permitted by the state
concerned.[357]

In 1985, the United Nations Commission on Human Rights appointed
a Special Rapporteur on Torture to examine questions relevant to torture
and to seek and receive credible and reliable information on such questions and to respond to that information without delay.[358] The work of
the rapporteur includes the sending of urgent appeals and an increasing
number of country visits. He is directed to co-operate closely with the
Committee against Torture.[359] The rapporteur also works with other UN
officials. In 1994, for example, the rapporteur accompanied the Special
Rapporteur on Rwanda on a visit to that country, while later that year the
rapporteur accompanied the Special Rapporteur on Extrajudicial, Summary or Arbitrary Executions on a visit to Colombia.[360] The rapporteur
produces an annual report.[361]

---

[355] *Parot* v. *Spain*, CAT/C/14/D/6/1990.
[356] *RT* v. *Switzerland*, A/61/44, pp. 249, 253 (2006). See also article 22 of the Convention and
Rule 107(b) of the Rules of Procedure.
[357] See General Assembly resolution 57/199.   [358] Resolution 1985/33.
[359] See e.g. E. Zoller, '46th Session of the United Nations Commission on Human Rights',
8(2) NQHR, 1990, pp. 140, 166.
[360] See E/CN.4/1995/34, pp. 6–7. See also the European Convention on the Prevention of Torture, below, p. 362, and the African guidelines on torture
adopted in 2002, www.achpr.org/english/communiques/communique32_en.html and
www.apt.ch/africa/rig/Robben20Island%20Guidelines.pdf.
[361] See e.g. A/62/221 (2007).

The Committee on the Rights of the Child[362]

The Convention on the Rights of the Child was adopted by the General Assembly on 20 November 1989.[363] It provides that in all actions concerning children, the best interests of the child shall be a primary consideration. A variety of rights are stipulated, including the inherent right to life (article 6); the right to a name and to acquire a nationality (article 7); the right to freedom of expression (article 13); the right to freedom of thought, conscience and religion (article 14); the right not to be subjected to arbitrary or unlawful interference with privacy, family, home or correspondence and the right to the enjoyment of the highest attainable standard of health (article 24).

States parties agree to take all appropriate measures to protect the child from all forms of physical and mental violence (article 19) and from economic exploitation (article 32) and the illicit use of drugs (article 33), and there are specific provisions relating to refugees and disabled children. In addition, states parties agree to respect the rules of international humanitarian law applicable to armed conflicts relevant to children (article 38). This provision was one response to the use of children in the Iran–Iraq war.

Article 43 of the Convention on the Rights of the Child provides for the establishment of a Committee. This Committee, which was elected in 1991, was originally composed of ten independent experts[364] and has the competence to hear states' reports (article 44). The Committee itself submits reports every two years to the General Assembly through ECOSOC. The Committee can recommend to the General Assembly that the Secretary-General be requested to undertake on its behalf studies on

---

[362] See e.g. T. Buck, *International Child Law*, London, 2005; G. Lansdown, 'The Reporting Procedures under the Convention on the Rights of the Child' in Alston and Crawford, *Future*, p. 113; Rehman, *International Human Rights Law*, chapter 14; *Revisiting Children's Rights: 10 Years of the UN Convention on the Rights of the Child* (ed. D. Fottrell), The Hague, 2000; D. McGoldrick, 'The UN Convention on the Rights of the Child', 5 *International Journal of Law and the Family*, 1991, p. 132; M. Santos Pais, 'The Convention on the Rights of the Child and the Work of the Committee', 26 *Israel Law Review*, 1992, p. 16, and Santos Pais, 'Rights of Children and the Family' in Herkin and Hargrove, *Human Rights: An Agenda for the Next Century*, p. 183. See also G. Van Bueren, *The International Law on the Rights of the Child*, Dordrecht, 1995, and *The United Nations Convention on the Rights of the Child* (ed. S. Detrick), Dordrecht, 1992.

[363] The Convention came into force on 2 September 1990. Note also the Declaration on the Rights of the Child adopted by the General Assembly in resolution 1386 (XIV), 1959 and the proclamation of 1979 as the International Year of the Child in resolution 31/169.

[364] The membership has increased to eighteen.

specific issues relating to the rights of the child, an innovation in the functions of such treaty bodies, and it can make suggestions and general recommendations (article 45). The Committee (like the Committee on Economic, Social and Cultural Rights) sets aside time for general discussions on particular topics in accordance with Rule 75 of its provisional rules of procedure. For example, at its second session in 1992, the Committee discussed the question of children in armed conflicts,[365] while at its fourth session, the problem of the economic exploitation of children was discussed.[366] A general discussion on the 'girl-child' was held at the eighth session of the Committee in 1995,[367] and one on the administration of juvenile justice at the ninth session.[368]

As part of the general reporting process, the Committee adopted an urgent action procedure at its second session. Provided that the state concerned has ratified the Convention, that the situation is serious and there is a risk of further violations, the Committee may send a communication to the state 'in a spirit of dialogue' and may request the provision of additional information or suggest a visit.[369] At its fourth session, the Committee established a working group to study ways and means whereby the urgent action procedure could be pursued effectively.[370] The Committee has produced a set of guidelines concerning states' reports[371] and a presessional working group considers these reports and draws up a list of issues needing further clarification which is sent to the state concerned.[372] As is the case with other reporting mechanisms, the state whose report is being considered by the Committee is invited to send representatives to the appropriate meetings. After the process is completed, the Committee issues Concluding Observations in which both the positive aspects of the report considered and the problems identified are noted, together

---

[365] A/49/41, pp. 94 ff. This led to a recommendation to the General Assembly to request the Secretary-General to undertake a special study on the means to protect children in armed conflicts: see CRC/C/SR.72, p. 2 and resolution 48/157. This led to the adoption of the Optional Protocol on the Involvement of Children in Armed Conflict, General Assembly resolution 54/263, 25 May 2000, which entered into force on 12 February 2002. Note that the question of the protection of children in armed conflicts was referred to in the Vienna Declaration and Programme of Action, 1993, Part II, B, 4: see 32 ILM, 1993, p. 1680. See also G. Van Bueren, 'The International Legal Protection of Children in Armed Conflicts', 43 ICLQ, 1994, p. 809, and M. Happold, *Child Soldiers in International Law*, Manchester, 2005.

[366] A/49/41, pp. 99 ff.

[367] See CRC/C/38, p. 47. This led to the adoption of the Optional Protocol on the Question of the Sale of Children, Child Prostitution and Child Pornography: see General Assembly resolution 54/263 of 25 May 2000 which entered into force on 18 January 2002.

[368] See CRC/C/43, p. 64.   [369] See CRC/C/SR.42, p. 2 and A/49/41, pp. 69–71.

[370] *Ibid.*   [371] See CRC/C/5.   [372] See e.g. CRC/C/121, 2002.

with suggestions and recommendations.[373] Various follow-up measures to the consideration of reports exist, but usually they consist of the request for the provision of further information.[374] The Committee also holds 'days of discussion' to examine relevant issues[375] and issues General Comments.[376]

The Committee on the Protection of Migrant Workers[377]

The International Convention on the Protection of the Rights of All Migrant Workers and Members of Their Families was adopted by the General Assembly and opened for signature in December 1990.[378] The Convention defines a migrant worker as 'a person who is to be engaged, is engaged, or has been engaged in a remunerated activity in a state of which he or she is not a national' (article 2). This includes, for example, frontier and seasonal workers, workers on offshore installations and specified-employment workers, but excludes employees of international organisations or official state employees abroad, refugees, stateless persons, students and workers on offshore installations who have not been admitted to take up residence and engage in a remunerated activity in the state of employment (article 3).

Migrant workers are entitled to equality of treatment with nationals in areas such as matters before courts and tribunals (article 18), terms of employment (article 25), freedom to join trades unions (article 26), medical treatment (article 28), access to education for their children (article 30) and respect for cultural identity (article 31). Migrant workers are protected from collective expulsion (article 22). Further provisions deal with additional rights for migrant workers and members of their families in a documented or regular situation (Part IV).

---

[373] See e.g. A/49/41, pp. 20 ff.; CRC/C/38, pp. 10 ff. and CRC/C/43, pp. 10 ff. See also CRC/C/121, 2002, pp. 8 ff.

[374] See e.g. CRC/C/27/Rev.3, 1995 detailing such measures up to mid-1995.

[375] See e.g. the day of discussion on 'The private sector as service provider and its role in implementing child rights' held in September 2002, CRC/C/121, p. 145.

[376] *Ibid.*, p. 159 (on 'The role of national human rights institutions in promoting and protecting children's rights'). In 2007, the Committee adopted General Comment No. 10 on the rights of children in juvenile justice.

[377] See e.g. K. Samson, 'Human Rights Co-ordination within the UN System' in Alston, *United Nations and Human Rights*, pp. 620, 641 ff.; S. Hune and J. Niessen, 'Ratifying the UN Migrant Workers Convention: Current Difficulties and Prospects', 12 NQHR, 1994, p. 393, and S. Hune and J. Niessen, 'The First UN Convention on Migrant Workers', 9 NQHR, 1991, p. 133.

[378] The necessary twenty ratifications were achieved on 10 December 2002. The Convention came into force on 1 April 2003.

The Convention provided for the creation of a Committee of fourteen independent experts (Part VII). States parties are required to provide reports on measures taken to give effect to the provisions of the Convention (article 73). An inter-state complaints procedure is provided for in article 76, on the condition that the states concerned have made a declaration expressly recognising the competence of the Committee to hear such complaints, while under article 77 an individual complaints procedure can be used with regard to states that have made a declaration recognising the competence of the Committee in this regard.[379]

The Committee on the Rights of Persons with Disabilities

The Convention on the Rights of Persons with Disabilities was adopted in December 2006 and is not yet in force. The Convention provides for the prohibition of discrimination against persons with disability and for equality of opportunity and accessibility. States parties are to undertake immediate, effective and appropriate measures to raise awareness and combat prejudices and harmful practices (articles 5–9). A twelve-person Committee is provided for to examine states' reports on measures taken to give effect to the obligations under the Convention (articles 34–6). States parties to the Optional Protocol recognise the competence of the Committee to hear individual communications alleging a violation of the Convention against them. Further, where the Committee receives reliable information indicating grave or systematic violations by a state party of Convention rights, the Committee may invite the state to co-operate in the examination of the information and submit observations. The Committee may proceed to conduct an inquiry confidentially. A state party may, however, on signature or ratification of the Optional Protocol, declare that it does not accept the inquiry competence of the Committee.

The Committee on Enforced Disappearances

The Convention for the Protection of All Persons from Enforced Disappearance was adopted in December 2006 and is not yet in force. It requires states parties to make enforced disappearance, defined as the deprivation of liberty by agents of the state or persons acting with the support or acquisition of the state coupled with the refusal to acknowledge the deprivation of liberty or concealment of the fate of the person in question (article 2), a criminal law offence (article 4). It is stated to be a crime against humanity (article 5). A ten-person Committee on Enforced Disappearances is

---

[379] See the Report of the Committee for 2006–7, A/62/48 (2007).

provided for to examine states' reports on measures taken to give effect to the obligations under the Convention (article 29), to hear inter-state complaints (article 32) and to hear individual communications (article 31). The Committee may also, upon receiving a request for urgent action, transmit a request to the state party concerned to take interim measures to locate and protect the person in question (article 30). Where the Committee receives reliable information indicating a serious violation, it may seek, in consultation with the state party concerned, to organise a visit (article 33). Further, where the Committee receives information appearing to contain well-founded indications that enforced disappearance is being practised on a widespread or systematic basis in the territory under the jurisdiction of a state party, it may, after seeking information from the state, urgently bring the matter to the attention of the General Assembly through the Secretary-General (article 34).

Conclusions

Most international human rights conventions obligate states parties to take certain measures with regard to the provisions contained therein, whether by domestic legislation or otherwise.[380] In addition, all nine of the treaty bodies discussed above require states parties to make periodic reports.[381] Seven have the competence to consider individual communications,[382] five may consider inter-state complaints,[383] while three may inquire into allegations of grave or systematic violations.[384]

---

[380] See e.g. article 2 of the Civil and Political Rights Covenant, 1966; article 1 of the European Convention on Human Rights, 1950; articles 1 and 2 of the American Convention on Human Rights, 1969; article 5 of the Genocide Convention, 1948; article 4 of the Convention on the Suppression and Punishment of the Crime of Apartheid, 1973 and article 3 of the Slavery Convention, 1926.

[381] Note that the Convention on the Rights of Persons with Disabilities and the Convention on Enforced Disappearance are not yet in force. See also article 7 of the Apartheid Convention, 1973. Several conventions provide for the communication of information to the UN Secretary-General: see e.g. article 33 of the Convention Relating to the Status of Stateless Persons, 1954 and articles 35 and 36 of the Convention Relating to the Status of Refugees, 1951.

[382] The Economic and Social Committee and the Committee on the Rights of the Child do not.

[383] The Human Rights Committee, the Committee on the Elimination of Racial Discrimination, the Committee on Migrant Workers, the Committee against Torture and the Committee on Enforced Disappearances.

[384] The Committee against Torture, the Committee on the Elimination of Discrimination against Women and the Committee on the Rights of Persons with Disabilities. Note the competence to visit under the Convention on Enforced Disappearance.

The proliferation of committees raises problems concerned both with resources and with consistency.[385] The question of resources is a serious and ongoing difficulty. The Vienna Declaration and Programme of Action, 1993 emphasised the necessity for a substantial increase in the resources for the human rights programme of the UN and particularly called for sufficient funding to be made available to the UN Centre for Human Rights, which *inter alia* provides the administrative support for the human rights organs and committees discussed in this chapter.[386] The various human rights committees themselves have pointed to the resource problem.[387] The Committee on the Elimination of Racial Discrimination and the Committee against Torture changed their financing system so that, since January 1994, they have been financed under the regular budget of the United Nations.[388] The Committee on Economic, Social and Cultural Rights sought additional resources from the Economic and Social Council.[389] Nevertheless, the fact remains that human rights activity within the UN system is seriously underfunded.

The question of consistency in view of the increasing number of human rights bodies within the UN system has been partially addressed by the establishment of an annual system of meetings between the chairpersons of the treaty bodies.[390] Issues of concern have been discussed, ranging from the need to encourage states to ratify all human rights treaties, concern about reservations made to human rights treaties,[391] attempts to establish that successor states are automatically bound by obligations under

[385] See e.g. E. Tistounet, 'The Problem of Overlapping among Different Treaty Bodies' in Alston and Crawford, *Future*, p. 383.

[386] See Part II, Section A of the Vienna Declaration and Programme of Action, 32 ILM, 1993, pp. 1674–5.

[387] See e.g. the Human Rights Committee, A/49/44, and the Committee Against Torture, A/50/44. See also the Report of the Secretary-General to the sixth meeting of chairpersons of treaty bodies, HRI/MC/1995/2, p. 13.

[388] See General Assembly resolution 47/111 and HRI/MC/1995/2, p. 14.

[389] *Ibid.*, p. 15.

[390] See General Assembly resolution 49/178, 1994, which endorsed the recommendation of the chairpersons that the meetings be held annually. The first meeting of the chairpersons of treaty bodies was held in 1984, A/39/484 and the second in 1988, A/44/98. See also e.g. A/62/224 (2007). A working group on the harmonisation of working methods of the treaty bodies has been established, see e.g. HRI/MC/2006/3 and HRI/MC/2007/2. Note also that the first inter-committee meeting of the human rights treaty bodies took place in September 2002, HRI/ICM/2002/3.

[391] See further below, chapter 16, p. 912.

international human rights treaties from the date of independence irrespective of confirmation,[392] the formulation of new norms and instruments and the promotion of human rights education, to consideration of the continuing problem of overdue reports[393] and the role of non-governmental organisations.[394] The development of early warning and preventive procedures by the committees is to be particularly noted.[395] The Committee on the Elimination of Racial Discrimination, for example, under its urgent procedures may, since 1994, review the human rights situation in states parties that give rise for especial concern,[396] while the Human Rights Committee is able to request states parties to submit special urgent reports.[397]

The UN Secretary-General in his report entitled 'In Larger Freedom' emphasised the need for streamlining procedures and called for the implementation of harmonised guidelines on reporting.[398] The UN High Commissioner for Human Rights, noting that the treaty bodies system had developed ad hoc and does not function as an integrated and indivisible framework for human rights protection, has called for a unified standing treaty body and proposed a series of models.[399] While greater harmonisation and integration is to be encouraged, as is increased training and logistical assistance for states, there may be disadvantages in one human rights body, not only in terms of locating the necessary expertise, but also in political terms by having such authority concentrated in one organ and thus being particularly susceptible to political pressure.

---

[392] See further below, chapter 17, p. 981.

[393] For example, the Committee on the Elimination of Racial Discrimination and the Committee on Economic, Social and Cultural Rights have established procedures enabling them to examine the situation in the state concerned: see above, pp. 311 and 308. Other Committees have sought to hold meetings with the officials of the states concerned in order to encourage submission of overdue reports, HRI/MC/1995/2, p. 7.

[394] See e.g. HRI/MC/1995.

[395] The role of the treaty bodies in seeking to prevent human rights violations has been emphasised: see e.g. A/47/628, para. 44.

[396] See above, p. 311.

[397] See above, p. 314. See also above, p. 331, with regard to the procedures of the Committee on the Rights of the Child.

[398] A/59/2005 and A/59/2005/Add.3.

[399] Concept Paper on the Proposal for a Unified Standing Treaty Body, HRI/MC/2006/2, 2006.

The specialised agencies

The International Labour Organisation[400]

The ILO was created in 1919 and expanded in 1946.[401] The Declaration of Philadelphia of 1944 (which was incorporated in the ILO constitution in 1946) reaffirmed the basic principles of the organisation. These are (a) that labour is not a commodity, (b) that freedom of expression and of association are essential to sustained progress and (c) that poverty anywhere constitutes a danger to prosperity everywhere. The ILO is composed of a unique tripartite structure involving governments, workers and employers and consists of three organs: a General Conference of representatives of member states (the International Labour Conference), the Governing Body and the International Labour Office.[402] The ILO constitution enables the organisation to examine and elaborate international labour standards, whether Conventions or Recommendations. The former are the more

---

[400] See e.g. Weissbrodt, Fitzpatrick and Newman, *International Human Rights*, chapter 16; L. Betten, 'At its 75th Anniversary, the International Labour Organisation Prepares Itself for an Active Future', 12 NQHR, 1994, p. 425; L. Swepston, 'Human Rights Complaints Procedures of the International Labour Organisation' in Hannum, *Guide to International Human Rights Practice*, p. 89; V. Leary, 'Lessons from the Experience of the International Labour Organisation' in Alston, *United Nations and Human Rights*, p. 580; C. W. Jenks, 'Human Rights, Social Justice and Peace' in *The International Protection of Human Rights* (eds. A. Schou and A. Eide), Stockholm, 1968, p. 227, and *Social Justice in the Law of Nations*, Oxford, 1970; E. A. Landy, *The Effectiveness of International Supervision: Thirty Years of ILO Experience*, New York, 1966, and 'The Implementation Procedures of the International Labour Organisation', 20 *Santa Clara Law Review*, 1980, p. 633; N. Valticos, 'The Role of the ILO: Present Action and Future Perspectives' in Ramcharan, *Human Rights: Thirty Years After the Universal Declaration*, p. 211, *Le Droit International du Travail*, Paris, 1980, and 'The International Labour Organisation' in *The International Dimensions of Human Rights* (eds. K. Vasak and P. Alston), Paris, 1982, vol. I, p. 363; F. Wolf, 'ILO Experience in Implementation of Human Rights', 10 *Journal of International Law and Economics*, 1975, p. 599; J. M. Servais, 'ILO Standards on Freedom of Association and Their Implementation', 123 *International Labour Review*, 1984, p. 765, and Robertson and Merrills, *Human Rights*, p. 282. See also H. K. Nielsen, 'The Concept of Discrimination in ILO Convention No. 111', 43 ICLQ, 1994, p. 827.

[401] An agreement bringing the ILO into relationship with the UN as a specialised agency under article 63 of the UN Charter came into force on 14 December 1946: see General Assembly resolution 50 (I).

[402] See *UN Action*, p. 28. The tripartite structure means that the delegation of each member state to the International Labour Conference includes two representatives of the government, one representative of workers and one representative of the employers. There are fifty-six members of the Governing Body, with twenty-eight government representatives and fourteen each from employers' and workers' organisations.

formal method of dealing with important matters, while the latter consist basically of guidelines for legislation. Between 1919 and 1994, 175 Conventions and 182 Recommendations were adopted by the ILO, all dealing basically with issues of social justice.[403] Under article 19 of the ILO constitution, all members must submit Conventions and Recommendations to their competent national authorities within twelve to eighteen months of adoption. Under article 22, states which have ratified Conventions are obligated to make annual reports on measures taken to give effect to them to the International Labour Office.[404] Under article 19, members must also submit reports regarding both unratified Conventions and Recommendations to the Director-General of the International Labour Office at appropriate intervals as requested by the Governing Body, concerning the position of their law and practice in regard to the matters dealt with in the Convention or Recommendation and showing the extent to which effect has been given or is proposed to be given to the provisions of the Convention or Recommendation, including a statement of the difficulties which prevent or delay ratification of the Convention concerned.[405] In 1926–7, a Committee of Experts on the Application of Conventions and Recommendations was established to consider reports submitted by member states. The comments of the twenty-member Committee, appointed by the Governing Body on the suggestion of the Director-General of the International Labour Office, on ratified Conventions take the form of 'observations' included in the printed report of the Committee in the case of more important issues, or 'requests' to the government concerned for information, which are not published in the report of the Committee. In the case of unratified Conventions and Recommendations, a 'general survey' of the application of the particular instrument in question is carried out.[406] A Committee on the Application of Conventions and Recommendations of the International Labour Conference is appointed at each of

---

[403] See Valticos, 'International Labour Organisation', p. 365, and Swepston, 'Human Rights Complaints Procedures of the International Labour Organisation', p. 100. See also E/CN.4/Sub.2/1994/5, p. 3.

[404] However, in practice the annual rule is relaxed: see Valticos, 'International Labour Organisation', p. 368. Governments are obliged by article 23(2) to communicate copies of the reports to employers' and workers' organisations.

[405] The latter provision does not, of course, apply in the case of Recommendations.

[406] Valticos, 'International Labour Organisation', pp. 369–70, and Wolf, 'ILO Experience', pp. 608–10. See e.g. *Freedom of Association and Collective Bargaining: General Survey*, Geneva, 1983.

its annual sessions, composed of tripartite representatives to discuss relevant issues based primarily upon the general report of the Committee of Experts.[407] It may also draw up a 'Special List' of cases to be drawn to the attention of the Conference.

Two types of procedure exist. Under articles 24 and 25, a representation may be made by employers' or workers' organisations to the Office to the effect that any of the members have failed to secure the effective observation of any Convention to which it is a party. If deemed receivable by the Governing Body, the matter is examined first by a committee of three of the Governing Body then by the Governing Body itself. States are invited to reply and both the original representation and the reply (if any) may be publicised by the Governing Body. There have not been many representations of this kind.[408] Under articles 26–9 and 31–3 any member may file a complaint against another member state that the effective observance of a ratified Convention has not been secured. The Governing Body may call for a reply by the object state or establish a commission of inquiry. Such a commission is normally composed of three experts and the procedure adopted is of a judicial nature. Recourse may be had by the parties to the International Court of Justice. Ultimately the Governing Body may recommend to the Conference such action as it considers wise and expedient. The complaints procedure was first used by Ghana against Portugal regarding the Abolition of Forced Labour Convention, 1957 in its African territories.[409]

A special procedure regarding freedom of association was established in 1951, with a Committee on Freedom of Association which examines a wide range of complaints. It consists of nine members (three from each of the tripartite elements in the ILO). The Committee submits detailed reports to the Governing Body with proposed conclusions and suggested recommendations to be made to the state concerned, and a considerable case-law has been built up.[410] A Fact-finding and

---

[407] The Committee usually consists of 200 members.

[408] But see e.g. Official Bulletin of the ILO, 1956, p. 120 (Netherlands Antilles); *ibid.*, 1967, p. 267 (Brazil) and *ibid.*, 1972, p. 125 (Italy). See also *ibid.*, 1978 (Czechoslovakia).

[409] See Official Bulletin of the ILO, 1962; *ibid.*, 1963 (Liberia) and *ibid.*, 1971 (Greece).

[410] See e.g. G. Von Potobsky, 'Protection of Trade Union Rights: Twenty Years Work of the Committee on Freedom of Association', 105 *International Labour Review*, 1972, p. 69. See also Servais, 'ILO Standards', and *Freedom of Association: Digest of Decisions of the Freedom of Association Committee of the Governing Body of the ILO*, 3rd edn, Geneva, 1985. By the end of 1991, over 1,600 cases had been considered by the Committee: see Swepston, 'Human Rights Complaints Procedures of the International Labour Organisation', p. 109.

Conciliation Commission has been created for more serious and politically delicate cases which operates with the consent of the state concerned. Accordingly, few questions have been dealt with,[411] although in 1992 a visit was made to South Africa and recommendations made to the ILO and ECOSOC. The government of that country sent a response to the Director-General of the ILO and, at the request of ECOSOC, the ILO Committee on Freedom of Association examined South Africa's report in 1994. The Committee's report, noting changes taking place in that country, was approved by the Governing Body and transmitted to ECOSOC.[412] In addition, a system of 'direct contacts' has been instituted, consisting of personal visits by ILO officials, or independent persons named by the Director-General, in order to assist in overcoming particular difficulties. These have included, for example, questions regarding freedom of association in Argentina in 1990 and the situation of Haitian workers on sugar plantations in the Dominican Republic in 1991.[413]

The United Nations Educational, Scientific and Cultural Organisation[414]

UNESCO came into being in November 1946 and was brought into relationship with the UN on 14 December that year.[415] The aim of the organisation, proclaimed in article 1 of its constitution, is to contribute to peace and security by promoting collaboration through education, science and culture 'in order to further universal respect for justice, for the rule of law and for the human rights and fundamental freedoms which are affirmed for the peoples of the world'. The organisation consists of a General

---

[411] See Valticos, 'International Labour Organisation', pp. 384 ff. See also Official Bulletin of the ILO, 1966 (Japan), and N. Valticos, 'Un Double Type d'Enquête de l'OIT au Chili', AFDI, 1975, p. 483.

[412] E/CN.4/Sub.2/1994/5, p. 4.

[413] See N. Valticos, 'Une Nouvelle Forme d'Action Internationale: Les "Contacts Directs"', 27 AFDI, 1981, p. 481, and V. Leary, 'Lessons from the Experience of the International Labour Organisation' in Alston, United Nations and Human Rights, p. 611.

[414] See e.g. S. Marks, 'The Complaints Procedure of the United Nations Educational, Scientific and Cultural Organisation' in Hannum, Guide to International Human Rights Practice, p. 107; D. Weissbrodt and R. Farley, 'The UNESCO Human Rights Procedure: An Evaluation', 16 HRQ, 1994, p. 391; P. Alston, 'UNESCO's Procedures for Dealing with Human Rights Violations', 20 Santa Clara Law Review, 1980, p. 665; H. S. Saba, 'UNESCO and Human Rights' in Vasak and Alston, International Dimensions of Human Rights, vol. II, p. 401; Robertson and Merrills, Human Rights, p. 288, and UN Action, pp. 308 and 321.

[415] See General Assembly resolution 50 (I).

Conference which meets every two years and in which all member states are represented, an Executive Board, elected by the conference, and a secretariat headed by a Director-General. Under article 4(4), member states undertake to submit Conventions and Resolutions to the competent national authorities within a year of adoption and may be required to submit reports on action taken.[416] Unlike the ILO, UNESCO has no constitution provision for reviewing complaints concerning the implementation of conventions procedure. However, in 1962 a Protocol instituting a Conciliation and Good Offices Commission was adopted to help resolve disputes arising between states parties to the 1960 Convention against Discrimination in Education. It entered into force in 1968 and the first meeting of the eleven-member Commission was in 1971. It aims to make available its good offices in order to reach a friendly settlement between the states parties to the convention in question. In 1978 the Executive Board of UNESCO adopted decision 104 EX/3.3, by which it established a procedure to handle individual communications alleging violations of human rights. Ten conditions for admissibility are laid down, including the requirement that the human rights violated must fall within UNESCO's competence in the fields of education, science, culture and information, and the need for the communication to be compatible with international human rights interests. The condition with regard to domestic remedies is rather different than is the case with other human rights organs, in that all the communication needs to do is to 'indicate whether an attempt has been made to exhaust domestic remedies . . . and the result of such an attempt, if any'. The investigating body is the Executive Board's Committee on Conventions and Recommendations, which is composed of twenty-four members and normally meets twice a year in private session.[417] The examination of communications is confidential. The Committee decides whether a communication is admissible and then makes a decision on the merits. The task of the Committee is to reach a 'friendly solution designed to advance the promotion of the human rights falling within UNESCO's fields of competence'.[418] Confidential reports are submitted to the Executive Board each session, which contain appropriate information

---

[416] See, for example, the obligation to submit reports under article 7 of the 1960 Convention against Discrimination in Education. See also *UN Action*, p. 163.

[417] Formerly the Committee on Conventions and Recommendations in Education, *ibid.*, pp. 321–2. See also A/CONF.157/PC/61/Add.6, 1993.

[418] Decision 104.EX/3.3, para. 14(k).

plus recommendations.[419] It is also to be noted that under this procedure the Director-General generally has a role in seeking to strengthen the action of UNESCO in promoting human rights and initiating consultations in confidence to help reach solutions to particular human rights problems.[420] UNESCO published a report in 1993 concerning the operations of the procedure, noting that the Committee had examined 414 cases between 1978 and 1993, of which it settled 241 individual cases.[421] It is unclear how successful the procedure has been, in view of the strict confidentiality which binds it,[422] the length of time taken to produce results and the high proportion of cases declared inadmissible.[423]

A special procedure to deal with disappeared persons has been established by the Committee. Communications dealing with such persons are placed on a Special List, if insufficient information is forthcoming from the government in question, and examined by the Committee.[424] In addition to *cases* concerning violations of human rights which are individual and specific, UNESCO may also examine *questions* of massive, systematic or flagrant violations of human rights resulting either from a policy contrary to human rights applied by a state or from an accumulation of individual cases forming a consistent pattern.[425] In the instance of such *questions*, the issue is to be discussed by the Executive Board of the General Conference in public.[426]

---

[419] In the April 1980 session, for example, forty-five communications were examined as to admissibility, of which five were declared inadmissible, thirteen admissible, twenty suspended and seven deleted from the agenda. Ten communications were examined on the merits, UNESCO Doc. 21 C/13, para. 65. Between 1978 and September 2003 508 communications were examined: see Marks, 'UNESCO Complaints Procedure', p. 120.

[420] *Ibid.*, paras. 8 and 9.

[421] See UNESCO Doc. 141/EX/6 and Weissbrodt and Farley, 'UNESCO Human Rights Procedure', p. 391. It was noted that during this period, 129 individuals were either released or acquitted, 20 authorised to leave and 34 to return to the state concerned, 24 were able to resume banned employment or activity, and 11 were able to resume a banned publication or broadcast, *ibid.*

[422] See G. H. Dumont, 'UNESCO's Practical Action on Human Rights', 122 *International Social Sciences Journal*, 1989, p. 585, and K. Partsch, 'La Mise en Oeuvre des Droit de l'Homme par l'UNESCO', 36 AFDI, 1990, p. 482.

[423] Weissbrodt and Farley note that of sixty-four cases studied only five were declared admissible, 'UNESCO Human Rights Procedure', p. 399. Of these, three concerned one particular country in Latin America. One case was considered over a nine-and-a-half-year period and another was considered over eight-and-a-half years.

[424] UNESCO Doc. 108 EX/CR/HR/PROC/2 Rev. (1979).

[425] Decision 104. EX/3.3, para. 10.   [426] *Ibid.*, para. 18.

Suggestions for further reading

The Future of UN Human Rights Treaty Monitoring (eds. P. Alston and J. Crawford), Cambridge, 2000

Guide to International Human Rights Practice (ed. H. Hannum), 4th edn, Ardsley, 2004

T. Meron, *The Humanization of International Law*, The Hague, 2006

J. Rehman, *International Human Rights Law*, London, 2002

A. H. Robertson and J. Merrills, *Human Rights in the World*, 4th edn, Manchester, 1996

H. Steiner, P. Alston and R. Goodman, *International Human Rights in Context*, 3rd edn, Oxford, 2008

C. Tomuschat, *Human Rights*, Oxford, 2003

The regional protection of human rights

Europe[1]

The Council of Europe

The Council of Europe was founded in 1949 as a European organisation for encouraging and developing intergovernmental and interparliamentary co-operation. Its aim as laid down in article 1 of the Statute is to achieve a greater unity between member states for the purpose of safeguarding and realising the ideals and principles which are their common heritage and facilitating their economic and social progress. The principles of the Council of Europe as established in article 3 of the Statute include pluralist democracy, respect for human rights and the rule of law. A Committee of Ministers, consisting of the Foreign Ministers of member states, and a Parliamentary Assembly, consisting of delegations of members of national parliaments, constitute the principal organs of the Council of Europe, together with a Secretary-General and supporting secretariat. There also exists a Standing Conference of Local and Regional Authorities of Europe, consisting of national delegations of local and regional elected representatives. The Council of Europe also maintains a number of support and assistance programmes.[2]

The demise of the Soviet Empire in Eastern and Central Europe has been the primary reason for the great increase in member states over the last few years.[3] The process of joining the Council of Europe has provided the Council with some influence over prospective members and this has led both to expert advice and assistance being proffered and to commitments being entered into in the field of human rights by applicants. For

---

[1] See generally *Monitoring Human Rights in Europe* (eds. A. Bloed, L. Leicht, M. Nowak and A. Rosas), Dordrecht, 1993.
[2] See e.g. A/CONF.157/PC/66/Add.2, 1993.
[3] With the entry of Montenegro in May 2007, the number of member states reached forty-seven.

example, Parliamentary Assembly Opinion No. 191 on the Application for Membership by the Former Yugoslav Republic of Macedonia[4] notes that the applicant entered into commitments relating to revision and establishment of new laws (for example, with respect to the organisation and functioning of the criminal justice system), amendment of the constitution in order to include the right to a fair trial, and agreement to sign a variety of international instruments including the European Convention on Human Rights, the European Convention on the Prevention of Torture and the Framework Convention for the Protection of National Minorities. In addition, the applicant agreed to co-operate fully in the monitoring process for implementation of Assembly Order No. 508 (1995) on the honouring of obligations and commitments by member states of the Council of Europe as well as in monitoring processes established by virtue of the Committee of Ministers Declaration of 10 November 1994. The Council of Europe has also moved beyond agreeing or noting commitments made at the time of application for membership and approval thereof to consideration of how those commitments have been honoured once an applicant has become a member state. The Committee of Ministers Declaration of 10 November 1994 provides a mechanism for examining state practice in this area and one may expect further developments in this context.[5] In 1999, the Council of Europe established the office of the Commissioner for Human Rights within the General Secretariat to promote education and awareness in the field of human rights.[6] The

---

[4] 16 HRLJ, 1995, p. 372. See also Parliamentary Assembly Opinion No. 190 on the Application of Ukraine for Membership, *ibid.*, p. 373, and Opinion Nos. 183 (1995) on the Application of Latvia for Membership, 188 (1995) on the Application of Moldova for Membership and 189 (1995) on the Application of Albania for Membership, H/INF (95) 3 pp. 77 ff. Note that under Recommendation 1055 (1995), the Assembly decided to suspend the procedure concerning its statutory opinion on Russia's request for membership in the light of the situation in Chechnya. However, Russia joined the Council of Europe in early 1996.

[5] See further below, p. 359. Note also Assembly Order 508 (1995). The Committee on the Honouring of Obligations and Commitments by Member States of the Council of Europe (known as the Monitoring Committee) commenced operations in April 1997 under the authorisation of Assembly resolution 1115 (1997). This Committee is responsible for verifying the fulfilment of the obligations assumed by the member states under the terms of the Council of Europe Statute, the European Convention on Human Rights and all other Council of Europe conventions to which they are parties, as well as the honouring of the commitments entered into by the authorities of member states upon their accession to the Council of Europe. It reports directly to the Assembly.

[6] Committee of Ministers resolution (99) 50. The Commissioner cannot consider individual petitions and exercises functions other than those of the supervisory bodies of Council of Europe human rights instruments. No general reporting system exists in this framework.

Commissioner may also issue opinions[7] and make recommendations[8] and undertake visits.[9]

Although a large number of treaties between member states have been signed under the auspices of the Council of Europe, undoubtedly the most important has been the European Convention on Human Rights.

The European Convention on Human Rights[10]

The Convention was signed on 4 November 1950 and entered into force in September 1953.[11] Together with thirteen Protocols, it covers a wide variety of primarily civil and political rights.[12] The preamble notes that the European states are like-minded and have a common heritage of political tradition, ideals, freedoms and the rule of law. The rights covered

---

[7] See e.g. CommDH(2002)7, Opinion 1/2002 on certain aspects of the United Kingdom 2001 derogation from article 5(1) of the European Convention on Human Rights.

[8] See e.g. Recommendations CommDH/Rec(2001)1 concerning the rights of aliens wishing to enter a Council of Europe member state and the enforcement of expulsion orders, and CommDH/Rec(2002)1 concerning certain rights that must be guaranteed during the arrest and detention of persons following 'cleansing' operations in the Chechen Republic of the Russian Federation.

[9] See e.g. the visit to Russia including Chechnya, Press Release 072a (2003).

[10] See e.g. *Jacobs and White: The European Convention on Human Rights* (eds. C. Ovey and R. C. A. White), 4th edn, Oxford, 2006; D. J. Harris, M. O'Boyle and C. Warbrick, *Law of the European Convention on Human Rights*, London, 1995; M. W. Janis, R. S. Kay and A. W. Bradley, *European Human Rights Law: Text and Materials*, 3rd edn, Oxford, 2008; S. Greer, *The European Convention on Human Rights: Achievements, Problems and Prospects*, Cambridge, 2006; G. Letsas, *A Theory of Interpretation of the European Convention on Human Rights*, Oxford, 2007; *La Convention Européenne des Droits de l'Homme* (eds. P. Imbert and L. Pettiti), Paris, 1995; L. J. Clements, N. Mole and A. Simmons, *European Human Rights: Taking a Case under the Convention*, 2nd edn, London, 1999; *The European System for the Protection of Human Rights* (eds. R. St J. Macdonald, F. Matscher and H. Petzold), Dordrecht, 1993; A. H. Robertson and J. G. Merrills, *Human Rights in Europe*, 4th edn, Manchester, 2001; P. Van Dijk, G. J. H. Van Hoof, A. Van Rijn and L. Zwaak, *Theory and Practice of the European Convention on Human Rights*, 4th edn, Antwerp, 2006; P. J. Velu and R. Ergel, *La Convention Européenne des Droits de l'Homme*, Brussels, 1990; G. Cohen-Jonathan, *La Convention Européenne des Droits de l'Homme*, Paris, 1989; E. Lambert, *Les Effets des Arrêts de la Cour Européenne des Droits de l'Homme*, Brussels, 1999, and K. Starmer, *European Human Rights Law*, London, 1999. See also L. G. Loucaides, *Essays on the Developing Law of Human Rights*, Dordrecht, 1995; J. G. Merrills, *The Development of International Law by the European Court of Human Rights*, 2nd edn, Manchester, 1993, and A. Drzemczewski, *The European Human Rights Convention in Domestic Law*, Oxford, 1983.

[11] All forty-seven member states of the Council of Europe have ratified the Convention.

[12] Protocol No. 14, dealing with procedural issues, is not yet in force: see below, p. 360. Economic and social rights are covered in the European Social Charter, 1961. See below, p. 360.

in the Convention itself include the right to life (article 2), prohibition of torture and slavery (articles 3 and 4), right to liberty and security of person (article 5), right to a fair and public hearing within a reasonable time by an independent and impartial tribunal established by law (article 6), prohibition of retroactive criminal legislation (article 7), right to respect for private and family life (article 8), freedom of thought, conscience and religion (article 9), freedom of expression (article 10), freedom of assembly and association (article 11), the right to marry and found a family (article 12), the right to an effective remedy before a national authority if one of the Convention rights or freedoms is violated (article 13) and a non-discrimination provision regarding the enjoyment of rights and freedoms under the Convention (article 14). In addition, several protocols have been added to the substantive rights protected under the Convention. Protocol No. 1 protects the rights of property, education and free elections by secret ballots, Protocol No. 4 prohibits imprisonment for civil debt and protects *inter alia* the rights of free movement and choice of residence and the right to enter one's own country, Protocol No. 6 provides for the abolition of the death penalty, while Protocol No. 7 provides *inter alia* that an alien lawfully resident in a state shall not be expelled therefrom except in pursuance of a decision reached in accordance with the law, that a person convicted of a criminal offence shall have the right to have that conviction or sentence reviewed by a higher tribunal and that no one may be tried or punished again in criminal proceedings for an offence for which he has already been finally acquitted or convicted. Protocol No. 12 prohibits discrimination, while Protocol No. 13 abolishes the death penalty. Like other international treaties, the European Convention imposes obligations upon states parties to respect a variety of provisions. In this instance the Convention has also been incorporated into the domestic legislation of all current states parties[13] although the Convention does not provide as to how exactly the states parties are to implement internally the relevant obligations.[14] It has been emphasised that:

> unlike international treaties of the classic kind, the Convention comprises more than mere reciprocal engagements between contracting states. It

---

[13] The UK incorporated the Convention in the Human Rights Act 1998. See e.g. J. Polakiewicz and V. Jacob-Foltzer, 'The European Human Rights Convention in Domestic Law', 12 HRLJ, 1991, pp. 65 and 125, and Harris *et al.*, *Law of the European Convention*, p. 24, note 2.

[14] See e.g. the *Swedish Engine Drivers' Union* case, Series A, vol. 20, 1976, p. 18; 58 ILR, pp. 19, 36. See also the *Belgian Linguistics* case, Series A, vol. 6, 1968, p. 35; 45 ILR, pp. 136, 165.

creates, over and above a network of mutual and bilateral undertakings, objective obligations, which in the words of the preamble, benefit from a 'collective enforcement'.[15]

In addition, a more teleological and flexible approach to the interpretation of the Convention has been adopted.[16] The European Court of Human Rights has emphasised that the Convention is a living instrument to be interpreted in the light of present-day conditions and this approach applies not only to the substantive rights protected under the Convention, but also to those provisions which govern the operation of the Convention's enforcement machinery.[17] In addition, the Court has noted that the object and purpose of the Convention as an instrument for the protection of individuals requires that its provisions be interpreted and applied so as to make its safeguards practical and effective.[18] The Convention should also be interpreted as far as possible in harmony with other principles of international law.[19] It has been emphasised that the Convention constitutes a 'constitutional instrument of European public order ("ordre public")'.[20] The Convention applies, of course, within the territory of contracting states, but the issue of its extraterritorial application has been addressed. The Court has interpreted the concept of 'jurisdiction' under article 1 to include the possibility of application to extradition or expulsion of a person by a contracting state to the territory of a non-contracting state[21] and the situation where acts of the authorities of contracting states, whether performed within or outside national boundaries, produce effects outside their own territory.[22] Further, in a significant move, the Court in *Loizidou* v. *Turkey* emphasised that the responsibility of a contracting state may also arise when it exercises effective control or 'effective overall control'

---

[15] See article 1 and *Ireland* v. *UK*, Series A, vol. 25, 1978, pp. 90–1; 58 ILR, pp. 188, 290–1. See also *Loizidou* v. *Turkey*, Series A, vol. 310, 1995, pp. 22–3; 103 ILR, p. 622.

[16] See e.g. the *Tyrer* case, Series A, vol. 26, 1978; 58 ILR, p. 339, and see also the *Marckx* case, Series A, vol. 31, 1979; 58 ILR, p. 561, although not to the extent of adding new rights or new jurisdictions thereby, see *Johnston* v. *Ireland*, Judgment of 18 December 1986 and *Banković* v. *Belgium*, Judgment of 12 December 2001, 123 ILR, p. 94. See also below, chapter 16, p. 937.

[17] See *Loizidou* v. *Turkey*, Series A, vol. 310, 1995, p. 23; 103 ILR, p. 622.

[18] See *Soering* v. *UK*, Series A, vol. 161, 1989, p. 34; 98 ILR, p. 270; *Artico* v. *Italy*, Series A, vol. 37, p. 16 and *Loizidou* v. *Turkey*, Series A, vol. 310, p. 23; 103 ILR, p. 622.

[19] See *Al-Adsani* v. *UK*, Judgment of 21 November 2001, para. 60; 123 ILR, p. 41.

[20] *Loizidou* v. *Turkey*, Series A, vol. 310, pp. 24 and 27; 103 ILR, p. 622.

[21] See e.g. *Soering* v. *UK*, Series A, vol. 161, 1989, pp. 35–6.

[22] See e.g. *Drozd and Janousek* v. *France and Spain*, Series A, vol. 240, 1992, p. 29. See also *Issa* v. *Turkey*, Judgment of 30 May 2000, and *Öcalan* v. *Turkey*, Judgment of 14 December 2000.

of an area outside its national territory, irrespective of the lawfulness of such control, whether by the state's own agents and officials or by the acts of a subordinate local administration.[23] Despite this, the Court has stated that its recognition of the exercise of extraterritorial jurisdiction by a contracting state is exceptional and that the Convention's notion of jurisdiction is essentially territorial.[24] These principles were reaffirmed in *Ilaşcu v. Moldova and Russia*, where the Court, while emphasising that jurisdiction was primarily territorial, noted that in exceptional circumstances the state might not be responsible for Convention violations where it was prevented from exercising its authority in a part of its territory, whether as a result of military occupation by the armed forces of another state which effectively controls the territory concerned, acts of war or rebellion, or the acts of a foreign state supporting the installation of a separatist state within the territory of the state concerned.[25] Further, a state's responsibility will be engaged where, as a consequence of military action, whether lawful or unlawful, it exercises in practice effective control of an area situated outside its national territory. Overall control of an area would suffice and the responsibility of the state would extent not only to the acts of its own soldiers and officials, but also to acts of the local administration which survives there by virtue of its military and other support.[26]

Linked with the territorial jurisdictional issue is the question whether the Court has jurisdiction over the states in question (or jurisdiction *ratione personae*). In *Behrami v. France*, the Court, in an application against a number of states with regard to activities undertaken as part of the international presence in Kosovo (whether military, KFOR, or civil, UNMIK), had to decide whether the acts in question were attributable or imputable to the states concerned such as to found jurisdiction or whether the acts were imputable rather to the UN. The Court concluded that KFOR was exercising lawfully delegated Chapter VII powers of the UN Security Council

---

[23] Series A, vol. 310, p. 20; 103 ILR, p. 622. See also *Cyprus v. Turkey*, European Court of Human Rights, Judgment of 10 May 2001, paras. 75 ff.; 120 ILR, p. 10.

[24] See *Banković v. Belgium*, Judgment of 12 December 2001, paras. 63, 67 and 71; 123 ILR, pp. 110, 111 and 113. The Court noted that 'the Convention is a multi-lateral treaty operating · · · in an essentially regional context and notably in the legal space (*espace juridique*) of the contracting states', *ibid.*, para. 80. See also *Issa v. Turkey*, Judgment of 16 November 2004, paras. 65 ff., where the Court held that the degree of control exercised by Turkish troops during a large-scale incursion into northern Iraq did not amount to overall control, and *Assanidze v. Georgia*, Judgment of 8 April 2004.

[25] Judgment of 8 July 2004 at paras. 312–13.   [26] *Ibid.*, paras. 314–19.

so that the impugned action was, in principle, 'attributable' to the UN and thus not to the states brought before the Court.[27]

The convention system

With the coming into force of Protocol 11 on 1 November 1998, a single permanent and full-time Court was established, so that the former Court and Commission ceased to exist. The new Court consists of a number of judges equal to that of the contracting parties to the Convention. Judges are elected by the Parliamentary Assembly of the Council of Europe for six-year terms.[28] To consider cases before it, the Court may sit in Committees of three judges, in Chambers of seven judges and in a Grand Chamber of seventeen judges.[29] The Rules of Court provide for the establishment of at least four Sections, the compositions of which are to be geographically and gender-balanced and reflective of the different legal systems among the contracting states.[30] The Chambers of seven judges provided for in the amended Convention are constituted from the Sections, as are the Committees of three judges.[31] The plenary Court is responsible for the election of the President and Vice-Presidents of the Court, the appointment of the Presidents of the Chambers, constituting Chambers and adopting rules of procedure.[32]

In ascertaining whether an application is admissible, the President of the Chamber to which it has been assigned will appoint a judge as Judge Rapporteur to examine the application and decide whether it should be considered by a Committee of three or a Chamber.[33] A Committee, acting unanimously, may decide to declare the application inadmissible or strike it out of the list.[34] That decision is final. In other cases, the application will be considered by a Chamber on the basis of the Judge Rapporteur's report.

---

[27] Judgment of 2 May 2007, paras. 141 ff.; similarly with regard to those activitites falling within the framework of the UNMIK, deemed to be a subsidiary organ of the Security Council, para. 143. But see *Bosphorus Airways* v. *Ireland*, Judgment of 30 June 2005. See, as to the situation in Kosovo, above, chapter 5, pp. 204 and 232.

[28] Articles 22 and 23. Note that there will no longer be a prohibition on two judges having the same nationality. The terms of office of the judges will end at the age of seventy.

[29] Article 27.   [30] Rule 25. There are now five Sections.   [31] Rules 26 and 27.

[32] Article 26.   [33] Rule 49.

[34] *Ibid.* and article 28. In so doing, the Committee will take into account the report of the Judge Rapporteur, Rule 53. Note that the Court has the right to strike out an application at any stage of the proceedings where it concludes that the applicant does not intend to pursue his application or the matter has been resolved or, for any other reason established by the Court, it is no longer justified to continue the examination of the application. However, the Court shall continue the examination of an application if respect for human rights as defined in the Convention and the Protocols thereto so requires: see article 37.

The Chamber may hold oral hearings. The question of admissibility will then be decided. Once an application is declared admissible, the Chamber may invite the parties to submit further evidence and written observations and a hearing on the merits may be held if the Chamber decides or one of the parties so requests.[35] At this point the respondent government is usually contacted for written observations.[36] Where a serious question affecting the interpretation of the Convention or its Protocols is raised in a case, or where the resolution of a question might lead to a result inconsistent with earlier case-law, the Chamber may, unless one of the parties to the case objects, relinquish jurisdiction in favour of the Grand Chamber.[37]

The Court may give advisory opinions, although in very restrictive circumstances.[38] In all cases before a Chamber or the Grand Chamber, a

---

[35] Rule 59.

[36] In the case of inter-state cases, the respondent government will be automatically contacted: see Rule 51.

[37] Article 30. While there is no specific power in the Convention under which the Court may order interim measures of protection with binding effect, Rule 39 of the Rules of Court provides that the Chamber or, where appropriate, its President may, at the request of a party or of any other person concerned, or of its own motion, indicate to the parties any interim measure which it considers should be adopted in the interests of the parties or of the proper conduct of the proceedings before it. The Court in *Mamatkulov and Abdurasulovic* v. *Turkey*, Judgment of 6 February 2003, referring to the practice of other international organs including the International Court of Justice and the Inter-American Court and Commission of Human Rights, held that article 34 of the Convention requires that applicants are entitled to exercise their right to individual application effectively, while article 3, relevant in the context of expulsion, also necessitated an effective examination of the issues in question. The Court noting that Rule 39 indications 'permit it to carry out an effective examination of the application and to ensure that the protection afforded by the Convention is effective', concluded that 'any state party to the Convention to which interim measures have been indicated in order to avoid irreparable harm being caused to the victim of an alleged violation must comply with those measures and refrain from any act or omission that will undermine the authority and effectiveness of the final judgment', paras. 107–10.

[38] Article 47. Only the Committee of Ministers can make such a request and advisory opinions cannot deal with any question relating to the content or scope of the rights and freedoms laid down in Section 1 of the Convention and its Protocols or with any question which the Court or Committee of Ministers might have to consider during proceedings instituted in accordance with the Convention. The first request for an advisory opinion concerned the co-existence of the Convention on Human Rights of the Commonwealth of Independent States and the European Convention on Human Rights, but on 2 June 2004 the Court concluded unanimously that the request did not come within its advisory competence. The first advisory opinion was given on 12 February 2008, where the Court unanimously concluded that it was not compatible with the European Convention on Human Rights for a list of candidates for election to the post of judge at the Court to be rejected on the sole

contracting party, one of whose nationals is an applicant, shall have the right to submit written comments and to take part in hearings, while the President of the Court may, in the interest of the proper administration of justice, invite any contracting party which is not a party to the proceedings, or any person concerned who is not the applicant to submit written comments or take part in hearings.[39] Once an application has been declared admissible, the Court will pursue the examination of the case and place itself at the disposal of the parties with a view to securing a friendly settlement.[40] If a friendly settlement is reached, the Court will strike the case out of its list.[41] Hearings before the Court will be in public unless the Court in exceptional circumstances decides otherwise. The Court will be able to afford just satisfaction to the injured party if necessary, where a violation is found and the domestic law of the contracting party concerned allows only partial reparation to be made.[42] Under article 43, within a period of three months from the date of the judgment of the Chamber, any party to the case may, in exceptional cases, request that the case be referred to the Grand Chamber. A panel of five judges of the Grand Chamber will accept this request if the case raises a serious question affecting the interpretation or application of the Convention or Protocols, or a serious issue of general importance. If the panel does accept the request, the Grand Chamber will decide the case by means of a judgment. Judgments of the Grand Chamber will be final, as will those of a Chamber where the parties declare that they will not request that the case be referred to the Grand Chamber, or three months after the date of judgment if reference to the Grand Chamber has not been requested, or when the panel of the Grand Chamber rejects the request to refer. The final judgment will be published[43] and is binding upon the parties,[44] and it will be transmitted to the Committee of Ministers, which shall supervise its execution.[45]

A number of crucial changes took place as a result of the reform of the system under Protocol 11. The right of individual petition became automatic rather than dependent upon the acceptance of the state complained against,[46] the new Court became full-time, the function of the Committee of Ministers was limited to the supervision of the execution of the judgments of the Court rather than including a decision-making

---

ground that there was no woman included in the proposed list and called for exceptions to the principle that lists must contain a candidate of the under-represented sex to be defined as soon as possible.

[39] Article 36.   [40] Article 38. Proceedings in the latter case will be confidential.
[41] Article 39.   [42] Article 41.   [43] Article 44.   [44] Article 46(1).
[45] Article 46(2).   [46] Compare former article 25 with current article 34.

function in the absence of referral of a Commission report to the Court,[47] the number of judges in a Chamber was reduced from nine to seven, the right of third-party intervention became part of the Convention itself rather than a Rule of Court and hearings became public apart from the friendly settlement process. However, under article 30, the parties to a case are able to prevent the relinquishment of jurisdiction by a Chamber in favour of the Grand Chamber. In addition, where a case is referred to the Grand Chamber under article 43, the Grand Chamber will include the President of the Chamber and the judge who sat in respect of the state party concerned, who will thus be involved in a rehearing of a case that they have already heard. This unusual procedure remains a source of some disquiet.

The Convention provides for the right of both inter-state and individual application. Under article 33, any contracting state may institute a case against another contracting state. To date applications have been lodged with the Commission by states involving seven situations.[48] The first inter-state application to reach the Court was *Ireland* v. *UK*.[49] Such applications are a means of bringing to the fore an alleged breach of the European public order, so that, for example, it is irrelevant whether the applicant state has been recognised by the respondent state.[50] Article 34 provides for the right of individual petition to the Commission and this has proved to be a crucial provision.[51] This right is now automatic.[52] The

---

[47] See former article 32 and e.g. P. Leuprecht, 'The Protection of Human Rights by Political Bodies: The Example of the Committee of Ministers of the Council of Europe' in *Progress in the Spirit of Human Rights: Festschrift für Felix Ermacora* (eds. M. Nowak, D. Steurer and H. Tretter), Kehl, 1988, p. 95.

[48] *Cyprus case (Greece v. UK)*, 1956 and 1957, two applications; *Austria v. Italy*, 1960; five applications against Greece, 1967–70; *Ireland v. UK*, 1971; *Cyprus v. Turkey*, 1974–94, four applications, and five applications against Turkey, 1982. See also the application brought by Georgia against Russia, 2007.

[49] Series A, vol. 25, 1978; 58 ILR, p. 188. Note also the Court's decision in *Cyprus v. Turkey*, Judgment of 10 May 2001; 120 ILR, p. 10.

[50] *Cyprus v. Turkey (Third Application)* 13 DR 85 (1978).

[51] The total number of new applications in 2007 was estimated at 54,000, of which 41,700 were allocated to a decision body. As at 31 December 2007, there were a total of 103,850 applications pending, of which some 79,000 were pending before a decision body: see Annual Report for 2007 (2008), p. 134.

[52] Note that the issue of reservations to former articles 25 and 46 (concerning the jurisdiction of the Court prior to Protocol XI) was discussed in the case-law. The Court noted that while temporal reservations could be valid, reservations beyond this were not: see *Loizidou v. Turkey (Preliminary Objections)*, Series A, vol. 310, 1995; 103 ILR, p. 622. The Court, in dismissing the territorial limitations upon the Turkish declarations under articles 25 and 46, held that such declarations therefore took effect as valid declarations without such

Convention system does not contemplate an *actio popularis*.[53] Individuals cannot raise abstract issues, but must be able to claim to be the victim of a violation of one or more of the Convention rights.[54] However, the Court has emphasised that:

> an individual may, under certain conditions, claim to be the victim of a violation occasioned by the mere existence of secret measures or of legislation permitting secret measures, without having to allege that such measures were in fact applied to him.[55]

A near relative of the victim, for example, could also raise an issue where the violation alleged was personally prejudicial or where there existed a valid personal interest.[56]

The Court may only deal with a matter once all domestic remedies have been exhausted according to the generally accepted rules of international law and within a period of six months from the date on which the final decision was taken.[57] Such remedies must be effective. Where there are no domestic remedies to exhaust, the act or decision complained against will itself normally be taken as the 'final decision' for the purposes of article 26.[58] The need to exhaust domestic remedies applies also in the

limitations, Series A, vol. 310 pp. 27–9. Turkey had argued that if the limitations were not upheld, the declarations themselves would fall. Not to adopt this approach would, the Court noted, have entailed a weakening of the Convention system for the protection of human rights, which constituted a European constitutional public order, and would run counter to the aim of greater unity in the maintenance and further realisation of human rights, *ibid*. See also the Commission Report in *Chrysostomos* v. *Turkey* 68 DR 216.

[53] See e.g. *X* v. *Austria* 7 DR 87 (1976) concerning legislation on abortion.

[54] See e.g. *Pine Valley* v. *Ireland*, Series A, vol. 222, 1991; *Johnston* v. *Ireland*, Series A, vol. 112, 1986; *Marckx* v. *Belgium*, Series A, vol. 31, 1979; *Campbell and Cosans* v. *UK*, Series A, vol. 48, 1982; *Eckle* v. *Federal Republic of Germany*, Series A, vol. 51, 1982 and *Vijayanathan and Pusparajah* v. *France*, Series A, vol. 241-B, 1992.

[55] The *Klass* case, Series A, vol. 28, 1979, pp. 17–18; 58 ILR, pp. 423, 442. See also e.g. the *Marckx* case, Series A, vol. 31, 1979, pp. 12–14; 58 ILR, pp. 561, 576; the *Dudgeon* case, Series A, vol. 45, 1982, p. 18; 67 ILR, pp. 395, 410; the *Belgian Linguistics* case, Series A, vol. 6, 1968; 45 ILR, p. 136 and *Norris* v. *Ireland*, Series A, No. 142, 1988; 89 ILR, p. 243.

[56] See e.g. Application 100/55, *X* v. *FRG*, 1 *Yearbook of the ECHR*, 1955–7, p. 162 and Application 1478/62, *Y* v. *Belgium*, *Yearbook of the ECHR*, 1963, p. 590. See also *Cyprus* v. *Turkey*, Judgment of 10 May 2001; 120 ILR, p. 10.

[57] Article 35. See *Akdivar* v. *Turkey*, Judgment of 16 September 1996. As to the meaning of domestic or local remedies in international law, see below, p. 819.

[58] See e.g. *X* v. *UK*, 8 DR, pp. 211, 212–13 and *Cyprus* v. *Turkey*, *Yearbook of the European Convention on Human Rights*, 1978, pp. 240–2. Where, however, there is a permanent state of affairs which is still continuing, the question of the six-month rule can only arise after the state of affairs has ceased to exist: see e.g. *De Becker* v. *Belgium*, 2 *Yearbook of the*

case of inter-state cases as does the six-month rule.[59] In addition, no petition may be dealt with which is anonymous or substantially the same as a matter already examined, and any petition which is incompatible with the Convention, manifestly ill-founded[60] or an abuse of the right of petition is to be rendered inadmissible.[61]

The Court, in an ever-increasing number of judgments,[62] has developed a jurisprudence of considerable importance.[63] It has operated on the basis of a number of evolving principles. In particular, the Court will allow states a degree of leeway in a system composed of obligations of contracting states and a European-level supervisory mechanism. The doctrine of 'the margin of appreciation' means that the Court will not interfere in certain domestic spheres while retaining a general overall supervision. For example, in *Brannigan and McBride* v. *UK*, the Court held that states benefit from a 'wide margin of appreciation' with regard to the process of determining the existence and scope of a public emergency permitting derogation from certain provisions of the Convention under article 15.[64] This margin of appreciation will vary depending upon the content of the rights in question in substantive proceedings or on the balancing of rights in contention. It will be wider with regard to issues of personal morality,[65] but narrower in other cases.[66] The essential point is, as the Court noted in *Z* v. *UK*, that: 'It is fundamental to the machinery of protection established by the Convention that the national systems themselves provide redress for breaches of its provision, the Court exercising its supervisory role subject to the principle of

---

European Convention on Human Rights, 1958, pp. 214, 244. The rule is strict and cannot be waived by the state concerned: see *Walker* v. *UK*, Judgment of 25 January 2000.

[59] See *Cyprus* v. *Turkey*, Judgment of 10 May 2001, paras. 82 ff. Note that the Court suggested that the remedies provided by the 'Turkish Republic of Northern Cyprus' had to be taken into account in this situation, *ibid*. See above, chapter 5, p. 235.

[60] See e.g. *Boyle and Rice* v. *UK*, Series A, vol. 131, 1988. This does not apply to inter-state cases.

[61] Article 35. See Harris *et al.*, *Law of the European Convention*, pp. 608 ff.; *Jacobs and White*, chapter 24 and e.g. the *Vagrancy* case, Series A, vol. 12, 1971; 56 ILR, p. 351.

[62] One judgment was delivered in its first year of operation in 1960; 6 in 1976; 17 in 1986; 25 in 1989; 126 in 1996; 695 in 2000; 844 in 2002 and 1,503 in 2007: see *Survey of Activities 2007* (2008).

[63] See e.g. P. Mahoney, 'Judicial Activism and Judicial Self-Restraint in the European Court of Human Rights: Two Sides of the Same Coin', 11 HRLJ, 1990, p. 57.

[64] Series A, No. 258-B, 1994, para. 43.

[65] See e.g. *Handyside* v. *UK*, Series A, vol. 24, 1981; 58 ILR, p. 150.

[66] E.g. fair trial and due process questions: see e.g. *The Sunday Times* v. *UK*, Series A, vol. 30, 1979; 58 ILR, p. 491.

subsidiarity.'[67] This also means that the Court is wary of undertaking fact-finding[68] and similarly cautious about indicating which measures a state should take in order to comply with its obligations under the Convention.[69]

The Court has dealt with a number of critical issues. In *Ireland* v. *UK*,[70] for example, the Court found that the five interrogation techniques used by the UK Forces in Northern Ireland amounted to a practice of inhuman and degrading treatment, contrary to article 3.[71] In *McCann* v. *UK*,[72] the Court narrowly held that the killing by members of the security forces of three members of an IRA unit suspected of involvement in a bombing mission in Gibraltar violated the right to life under article 2. In *Golder* v. *UK*,[73] the Court inferred from article 6(1) a fundamental right of access to the courts, and the Court has emphasised the importance of fair trial mechanisms such as the principle of contempt of court.[74] The Court has also developed a considerable jurisprudence in the field of due process[75] that is having a significant impact upon domestic law, not least in the UK. A brief reference to some further examples will suffice. In the *Marckx* case,[76] the Court emphasised that Belgian legislation discriminating against illegitimate children violated the Convention, while in the *Young, James and Webster* case[77] it was held that railway workers dismissed for refusing to join a trade union in the UK were entitled to compensation. In the *Brogan* case,[78] the Court felt that periods of detention under anti-terrorist legislation in the UK before appearance before a judge or other judicial officer of at least four days violated the Convention. This

[67] Judgment of 10 May 2001, para. 103.
[68] See e.g. the *Tanli* case, Judgment of 10 April 2001.
[69] The *Vgt Verein gegen Tierfabriken* case, Judgment of 28 June 2001, para. 78.
[70] Series A, vol. 25, 1978; 58 ILR, p. 188.
[71] See also *Cyprus* v. *Turkey*, where the Court held that the discriminatory treatment of the Greek Cypriots in the Turkish occupied north of Cyprus amounted to degrading treatment, Judgment of 10 May 2001, paras. 302–11; 120 ILR, p. 10.
[72] Series A, vol. 324, 1995.   [73] Series A, vol. 18, 1975; 57 ILR, p. 200.
[74] See e.g. *Handyside* v. *UK*, Series A, vol. 24, 1981; 58 ILR, p. 150; the *Dudgeon* case, Series A, vol. 45, 1982; 67 ILR, p. 395 and the *Sunday Times* case, Series A, vol. 30, 1979; 58 ILR, p. 491.
[75] See e.g. S. Trechsel, 'Liberty and Security of Person' in Macdonald *et al.*, *European System*, p. 277; P. Van Dijk, 'Access to Court', *ibid.*, p. 345; O. Jacot-Guillarmod, 'Rights Related to Good Administration (Article 6)', *ibid.*, p. 381; Harris *et al.*, *Law of the European Convention*, chapter 6; and *Digest of Strasbourg Case-law relating to the European Convention on Human Rights*, Strasbourg, 1984, vol. II (article 6).
[76] Series A, vol. 31, 1979; 58 ILR, p. 561.   [77] Series A, vol. 44, 1981; 62 ILR, p. 359.
[78] Series A, vol. 145, 1988.

decision, however, prompted a notice of derogation under article 15 of the Convention by the UK government.[79]

In the important *Soering* case,[80] the Court unanimously held that the extradition of a German national from the UK to the United States, where the applicant feared he would be sentenced to death on a charge of capital murder and be subjected to the 'death row' phenomenon, would constitute a breach of article 3 of the Convention prohibiting torture and inhuman and degrading treatment and punishment. Further, the Court has held that the deportation to Iran of a woman who in the circumstances would have been at risk of punishment by stoning would violate article 3.[81] The Court has also emphasised that national security considerations had no application where article 3 violations were in question.[82]

The Court has approached its task in a generally evolving way. For example, it has deduced from a number of substantive provisions that circumstances may arise in which a state would have a positive obligation to conduct an inquiry or effective official investigation. This would arise, for instance, where individuals have been killed as a result of the use of force by agents of the state,[83] or while in custody,[84] or 'upon proof of an arguable claim that an individual, who was last seen in the custody of agents of the state, subsequently disappeared in a context which may be considered life-threatening'.[85] Similarly, the Court has held that the right to life under article 2 entails also the obligation upon states to take appropriate steps for the safeguarding of life within the jurisdiction.[86] Linked with these provisions is article 13 which requires the state party to provide a remedy, effective in law and in practice, which is able both to deal with the substance of the applicant's complaint and to provide an appropriate legal redress.[87] The jurisprudence of the Court with regard to Article 13 demonstrates that in an increasing number of cases that provision is

---

[79] For the text, see e.g. 7 NQHR, 1989, p. 255. See also *Brannigan and McBride v. UK*, Series A, vol. 258-B, 1993.

[80] Series A, vol. 161, 1989. See also *Mamatkulov and Abdurasulovic v. Turkey*, European Court of Human Rights, Judgment of 6 February 2003, paras. 66 ff.

[81] *Jabari v. Turkey*, Judgment of 11 July 2000.

[82] *Chahal v. UK*, Judgment of 15 November 1996.

[83] See e.g. *McCann v. UK*, Series A, vol. 324, 1996.

[84] E.g. *Tanli*, Judgment of 10 April 2001, para. 152.

[85] *Cyprus v. Turkey*, Judgment of 10 May 2001, para. 132; 120 ILR, p. 10.

[86] *LCB v. UK*, Judgment of 9 June 1998.

[87] *Soering v. UK*, Judgment of 7 July 1989, at para. 120. See also *Aksoy v. Turkey*, Judgment of 18 December 1996, at para. 95 and *Akdeniz v. Turkey*, Judgment of 31 May 2005, at para. 138.

understood as requiring states to undertake an effective investigation into arguable claims of the violation of Convention rights. This has included claims of violations of Articles 2, 3, 5 and 6.[88]

Execution of Court decisions is the responsibility of the Committee of Ministers.[89] This is a political body, the executive organ of the Council of Europe,[90] and consists of the Foreign Ministers, or their deputies, of all the member states.[91] Under article 15 of the Statute of the Council of Europe, the Committee of Ministers, acting on the recommendation of the Parliamentary Assembly or on its own initiative, considers the action required to further the aims of the Council of Europe, including the conclusion of conventions or agreements, and the adoption by governments of a common policy with regard to particular matters. Under article 16 of the Statute, it decides with binding effect all matters relating to the internal organisation and arrangements of the Council of Europe. Resolutions and recommendations on a wide variety of issues are regularly adopted.[92] The Committee of Ministers performs a variety of functions with regard to the protection of human rights. For example, in its Declaration on Compliance with Commitments Accepted by Member States of the Council of Europe, adopted on 10 November 1994, the Committee decided that it would consider the question of implementation of commitments concerning the situation of democracy, human rights and the rule of law in any member state which may be referred to it by member states, the Secretary-General or on the basis of a recommendation of the Parliamentary Assembly.

Where the Court has found a violation, the matter will be placed on the agenda of the Committee of Ministers and will stay there until the respondent government has confirmed that any sum awarded in just satisfaction under article 41 has been paid and/or any required individual measure has been taken and/or any general measures have been adopted

---

[88] E.g. *Kaya* v. *Turkey*, Judgment of 19 February 1998, at para. 107; *Ilhan* v. *Turkey*, Judgment of 27 June 2000, at para. 97; *Kurt* v. *Turkey*, Judgment of 25 May 1998, at para. 140 and *Kudla* v. *Poland*, Judgment of 26 October 2000, at paras. 146–9. The Court has noted that 'the requirements of Article 13 are broader than a Contracting State's obligation under Article 2 to conduct an effective investigation into the disappearance of a person last seen in the hands of the authorities', *Akdeniz* v. *Turkey*, Judgment of 31 May 2005, at para. 139 and *Estamirov and Others* v. *Russia*, Judgment of 12 October 2006, at para. 118.
[89] Article 46(2).   [90] Article 13 of the Statute of the Council of Europe.
[91] Article 14 of the Statute of the Council of Europe.
[92] These are non-binding. Resolutions relate to the general work of the Council as such, while recommendations concern action which it is suggested should be taken by the governments of member states.

preventing new similar violations or putting an end to continuing violation.[93] Information so provided by states is to be accessible to the public,
unless the Committee decides otherwise in order to protect legitimate
public or private interests.[94]

Despite the reform of the Convention system by Protocol No. 11, difficulties remain. Applications continue to increase inexorably.[95] As a consequence, Protocol No. 14 provides that a single judge will be able to
declare an application inadmissible and a committee of three judges will
be able to rule on repetitive cases where the underlying matter is already
the subject of well-established case-law. In addition, a new admissibility
requirement will be added to article 35 so that an application may be
declared inadmissible where the applicant has not suffered a significant
disadvantage and where an examination on the merits by the Court is not
seen as necessary in terms of respect for human rights, provided that the
matter has been examined by a domestic tribunal. Judges will be elected
for non-renewable periods of nine years.[96]

The European Social Charter[97]

The wide social and economic differences between the European states,
coupled with the fact that economic and social rights often depend for
their realisation upon economic resources, has meant that this area of

---

[93] Rules 3 and 4. Very occasionally there have been difficulties. For example, the decision
of the Court in *Loizidou* v. *Turkey* awarding the applicant compensation for deprivation
of property rights remains to be implemented: see e.g. *Jacobs and White*, pp. 502 ff. See
also e.g. interim Committee resolutions DH (2000) 105 and DH (2001) 80. Note that
where the Court finds a systemic defect in the national legal order, which has or is likely to
produce a large number of applications, a remedy may be required of the state that would
apply to the class of individuals in the same category: see *Broniowski* v. *Poland*, Judgment
of 22 June 2004. See also V. Colandrea, 'On the Power of the European Court of Human
Rights to Order Specific Non-monetary Measures', 7 *Human Rights Law Review*, 2007,
p. 396.

[94] Rule 5.   [95] See above, p. 354.

[96] The Protocol was opened for signature on 30 May 2004. In order to come into force it
requires all contracting states to ratify it. To date, only Russia has failed to ratify. See
L. Caflisch, 'The Reform of the European Court of Human Rights: Protocol No. 14 and
Beyond', 6 *Human Rights Law Review*, 2006, p. 403, and A. Mowbray, 'Faltering Steps on
the Path to Reform of the Strasbourg Enforcement System', 7 *Human Rights Law Review*,
2007, p. 609. Note the Interim and Final Reports of the Group of Wise Persons to the
Committee of Ministers in May and November 2006, CM (2006) 88 and CM (2006) 203.

[97] See e.g. D. J. Harris, *The European Social Charter*, 2nd edn, Charlottesville, 2000, 'A Fresh
Impetus for the European Charter', 41 ICLQ, 1992, p. 659, and 'The System of Supervision
of the European Social Charter – Problems and Options for the Future' in *The Future*

concern has lagged far behind that of civil and political rights. Seven years of negotiations were necessary before the Charter was signed in 1961.[98]

The Charter consists of a statement of long-term objectives coupled with a list of more restricted rights. The Charter covers labour rights and trade union rights,[99] the protection of specific groups such as children, women, disabled persons and migrant workers,[100] social security rights,[101] and protection of the family.[102] In an attempt to deal with economic disparities within Europe, the Charter provides for a system whereby only ten of the forty-five paragraphs (including five 'key articles'[103]) need to be accepted upon ratification. The Charter[104] is implemented by the European Committee of Social Rights, consisting of fifteen independent experts elected for a six-year period, renewable once. States parties submit annual reports on some of the provisions of the Charter. These provisions have been divided since 2007 into four thematic groups, each group being the subject of an annual review.[105] These reports are examined by the

---

of European Social Policy (ed. L. Betten), 2nd edn, Deventer, 1991, p. 1; 25 Years of the European Social Charter (eds. A. P. C. M. Jaspers and L. Betten), 1988; H. Wiebringhaus, 'La Charte Sociale Européenne: 20 Ans Après la Conclusion du Traité', AFDI, 1982, p. 934; O. Kahn-Freund, 'The European Social Charter' in European Law and the Individual (ed. F. G. Jacobs), London, 1976, and 'La Charte Sociale Européenne et la Convention Européenne des Droits de l'Homme', 8 HRJ, 1975, p. 527; F. M. Van Asbeck, 'La Charte Sociale Européenne' in Mélanges Rolin, Paris, 1964, p. 427, and T. Novitz, 'Remedies for Violation of Social Rights Within the Council of Europe' in The Future of Remedies in Europe (eds. C. Kilpatrick, T. Novitz and P. Skidmore), London, 2000, p. 230.

[98] As at April 2008, there were thirty-nine states parties to the Charter.

[99] Articles 1–6, 9–10.   [100] Articles 7–8, 15, 18–19.   [101] Articles 11–14.

[102] Articles 16–17. An Additional Protocol was signed in 1988 which added four more economic and social rights, guaranteeing the rights to equal opportunities in employment without discrimination based on sex; information and consultation of workers within the undertaking; participation in the determination and improvement of working conditions, and social protection of elderly persons. The Protocol entered into force on 4 September 1992.

[103] Out of the following seven rights: the right to work, organise, bargain collectively, social security, social and medical assistance, and the rights of the family to special protection and of migrant workers and their families to protection and assistance: see article 20.

[104] As amended by the Turin Protocol 1991 and as revised in 1996. The revised Charter came into force in 1999 and gathered together the rights contained in the 1961 instrument as amended and the 1988 Protocol and added new rights, such as the right to protection against poverty and social exclusion, the right to housing, the right to protection in cases of termination of employment and the right to protection against sexual harassment in the workplace.

[105] These groups are employment, training and equal opportunities; health, social security and social protection; labour rights; and children, families and migrants respectively.

Committee and its conclusions published. If a state does not implement a Committee decision, the Committee of Ministers addresses a recommendation to the state to the same effect. A system of Collective Complaints was established by an Additional Protocol adopted in 1995. This provides that international organisations of employers and trade unions, other international non-governmental organisations with consultative status with the Council of Europe placed on a list for this purpose by the Governmental Committee, and representative national organisations of employers and trade unions within the jurisdiction of the contracting party against which they have lodged a complaint may submit complaints alleging unsatisfactory application of the Charter.[106] Contracting parties may also make a declaration recognising the right of any other representative national non-governmental organisation within their jurisdiction which has particular competence in the matters governed by the Charter to lodge complaints against them.[107] Such complaints are lodged with the European Committee of Social Rights, which makes a decision on both admissibility and on the merits. Its decision is sent to the parties concerned and to the Committee of Ministers, which adopts a resolution on the matter.

The European Convention for the Prevention of Torture and Inhuman and Degrading Treatment or Punishment[108]

This innovative Convention was signed in 1987 and came into force on 1 February 1989.[109] The purpose of the Convention is to enable the supervision of persons deprived of their liberty and, in particular, to prevent

---

[106] Article 1.   [107] Article 2.

[108] See e.g. M. Evans and R. Morgan, *Combating Torture in Europe – The Work and Standards of the European Committee for the Prevention of Torture*, Strasbourg, 2001; J. Murdoch, 'The Work of the Council of Europe's Torture Committee', 5 EJIL, 1994, p. 220; M. Evans and R. Morgan, 'The European Torture Committee: Membership Issues', 5 EJIL, 1994, p. 249; A. Cassese, 'A New Approach to Human Rights: The European Convention for the Prevention of Torture', 83 AJIL, 1989, p. 128, and Cassese, 'Une Nouvelle Approche des Droits de l'Homme: La Convention Européenne pour la Prévention de la Torture', 93 RGDIP, 1989, p. 6; M. Evans and R. Morgan, 'The European Convention on the Prevention of Torture: Operational Practice', 41 ICLQ, 1992, p. 590, and C. Jenkins, 'An Appraisal of the Role and Work of the European Committee for the Prevention of Torture and Inhuman or Degrading Treatment or Punishment', SOAS Working Paper No. 11, 1996.

[109] All forty-seven members of the Council of Europe are parties. By Protocol No. 1 non-member states of the Council of Europe are allowed to accede to the Convention at the invitation of the Committee of Ministers, CPT/Inf (93) 17. This came into force in March 2002.

the torture or other ill-treatment of such persons.[110] The Committee for the Prevention of Torture was established under the Convention,[111] placing, as it has noted, a 'proactive non-judicial mechanism alongside the existing reactive judicial mechanisms of the European Commission and European Court of Human Rights'.[112] The Committee is given a fact-finding and reporting function. The Committee is empowered to carry out both visits of a periodic nature and ad hoc visits to places of detention in order to examine the treatment of persons deprived of their liberty with a view to strengthening, if necessary, the protection of such persons from torture and from inhuman or degrading treatment or punishment. Periodic visits are carried out to all contracting parties on a regular basis, while ad hoc visits are organised when they appear to the Committee to be required in the circumstances.[113] Thus periodic visits are planned in advance.[114] The real innovation of the Convention, however, lies in the competence of the Committee to visit places of detention when the situation so warrants.[115] When the Committee is not in session, the Bureau (i.e. the President and Vice-President of the Committee)[116] may in cases of urgency decide, on the Committee's behalf, on the carrying out of such an ad hoc visit.[117] States parties agree to permit visits to any place within their jurisdiction where persons are deprived of their liberty by a public

[110] The Committee established under the Convention described its function in terms of strengthening 'the *cordon sanitaire* that separates acceptable and unacceptable treatment or behaviour': see First General Report, CPT (91) 3, para. 3.

[111] See Resolution DH (89) 26 of the Committee of Ministers adopted on 19 September 1989 for the election of the members of the Committee. Note that under Protocol No. 2 to the Convention, the members of the Committee may be re-elected twice (rather than once as specified in article 5). The Protocol came into force in March 2002.

[112] See Fifth General Report, CPT/Inf (95) 10, 1995, p. 3.

[113] See articles 1 and 7. See also the Rules of Procedure of the Committee, 1989, CPT/Inf (89) 2, especially Rules 29–35. The Rules have been amended on a number of occasions, the most recent being 12 March 1997. See also Seventeenth General Report, 2007, CPT/Inf (2007) 39, p. 14.

[114] Note that in 2001, 17 visits took place, CPT/Inf (2002) 15. By January 2003, 146 visits had taken place, 98 periodic and 48 ad hoc: see www.cpt.coe.int/en/about.htm. In the period August 2006 to July 2007, the Committee made periodic visits to ten states and ad hoc visits to six states: see Seventeenth General Report, 2007, CPT/Inf (2007) 39, pp. 20 ff.

[115] A significant number of ad hoc visits have been made, e.g. to Turkey and Northern Ireland in the early years of operation of the Committee: see Murdoch, 'Work of the Council of Europe's Torture Committee', p. 227. In 2001, for example, ad hoc visits were made to Albania, Spain, Russia, Romania, Macedonia and Turkey, CPT/Inf (2002) 15, while in 2006–7 ad hoc visits were made to Greece, Hungary, Russia, Serbia (Kosovo), Spain and Turkey.

[116] Rule 10 of the Rules of Procedure.   [117] Rule 31 of the Rules of Procedure.

authority,[118] although in exceptional circumstances, the competent authorities of the state concerned may make representations to the Committee against a visit at the time or place proposed on grounds of national defence, public safety, serious disorder, the medical condition of a person or because an urgent interrogation relating to a serious crime is in progress.[119] The Committee may interview in private persons deprived of their liberty and may communicate freely with any person whom it believes can supply relevant information.[120]

After each visit, the Committee draws up a report for transmission to the party concerned. That report will remain confidential[121] unless and until the state party concerned decides to make it public.[122] Where a state refuses to co-operate or to improve matters in the light of recommendations made, the Committee may decide, after the state has had an opportunity to make known its views, by a two-thirds majority to issue a public statement.[123] The Committee makes an annual general report on its activities to the Committee of Ministers, which is transmitted to the Parliamentary Assembly and made public.[124] The relationship between the approach taken by the Committee as revealed in its published reports and the practice under the European Human Rights Convention is

[118] Article 2.   [119] Article 9(1).   [120] Article 8.

[121] As does the information gathered by the Committee in relation to a visit and its consultations with the contracting state concerned, article 11(1).

[122] See Rules 40–2. Most reports have been published together with the comments of contracting states upon them: see e.g. Report to the Government of Liechtenstein, CPT/Inf (95) 7 and the Interim Report of the Government of Liechtenstein, CPT/Inf (95) 8; Report to the Government of Italy, CPT/Inf (95) 1 and the Response of the Government of Italy, CPT/Inf (95) 2; Report to the Government of the UK, CPT/Inf (94) 17 and the Response of the Government of the UK, CPT/Inf (94) 18; Report to the Government of Greece, CPT/Inf (94) 20 and the Response of the Government of Greece, CPT/Inf (94) 21. The Fifth General Report of the Committee revealed that twenty-one of the thirty-seven visit reports had been published and that there was good reason to believe that most of the remaining sixteen would be published soon, CPT/Inf (95) 10, p. 6. According to its 12th Report covering 2001, 91 of the 129 visit reports so far drawn up had been placed in the public domain. On 6 February 2002, the Committee of Ministers of the Council of Europe 'encourage[d] all Parties to the Convention to authorise publication, at the earliest opportunity, of all CPT visit reports and of their responses', CPT/Inf (2002) 15. See also CPT/Inf (2007), Appendix 4.

[123] Article 10(2). See e.g. the public statements concerning police detention conditions in Turkey, CPT/Inf (93) 1, paras. 21 and 37. The situation concerning Chechnya, Russia, has also led to public statements being made in 2001, 2003 and 2007: see e.g. CPT/Inf (2002) 15, Appendix 6 and CPT/Inf (2007), Appendix 9.

[124] Article 12. This is subject to the rules of confidentiality in article 11. Note that the Committee reports also include general substantive sections for the general guidance of states: see, for a collection of these, The CPT Standards, CPT/Inf/E (2002) 1.

particularly interesting and appears to demonstrate that the Committee has adopted a more flexible attitude to issues relating to detention and ill-treatment.[125]

The Council of Europe Framework Convention for the Protection of National Minorities[126]

The question of minorities is addressed in the European Convention on Human Rights only in terms of one possible ground of prohibited discrimination stipulated in article 14. However, the Council of Europe has been dealing with the issue of minorities in a more vigorous manner in more recent years. Resolution 192 (1988) of the Standing Conference of Local and Regional Authorities of Europe proposed the text of a European Charter for Regional or Minority Languages, while Recommendation 1134 (1990) of the Parliamentary Assembly on the Rights of Minorities called for either a protocol to the European Convention or a special convention on this topic.[127] The Committee of Ministers adopted on 22 June 1992 the European Charter for Regional or Minority Languages.[128] Under this Charter, a variety of measures to promote the use of regional or minority languages is suggested, for example, in the fields of education, court proceedings, public services, media, cultural facilities, economic and social life and transfrontier exchanges. Implementation is by periodic reports to the Secretary-General of the Council of Europe in a form prescribed by the Committee of Ministers.[129] Such reports are examined by a committee of experts,[130] composed of one member per contracting party, nominated by the party concerned, appointed for a period of six years and eligible for re-appointment.[131] Bodies or associations legally established in a party may draw the attention of the committee of experts to matters relating to the undertakings entered into by that party and, on the basis of states' reports, the committee will itself report to the Committee of Ministers. The committee of experts' report may be accompanied by the comments which the parties have been requested to make and may also contain the proposals of the committee of experts to the Committee of Ministers for

---

[125] See e.g. Murdoch, 'Work of the Council of Europe's Torture Committee', pp. 238 ff.
[126] See generally, P. Thornberry and M. Estebanez, *The Council of Europe and Minorities*, Strasbourg, 1994, and G. Pentasugglia, *Minorities in International Law*, Strasbourg, 2002.
[127] See also Recommendations 1177 (1992) and 1201 (1993).
[128] It came into force in March 1998.
[129] Article 15. See e.g. the reports by Germany, MIN-LANG/PR (2000) 1 and by the UK, MIN-LANG/PR (2002) 5.
[130] Article 16. See e.g. the report on Germany, ECRML (2002) 1.   [131] Article 17.

the preparation of such recommendations of the latter body to one or more of the parties as may be required.[132] The Secretary-General also makes a two-yearly detailed report to the Parliamentary Assembly on the application of the Charter.[133] The Committee of Ministers may invite any non-member state of the Council of Europe to accede to the Charter.[134]

At the Vienna Meeting of Heads of State and Government of the Council of Europe in October 1993, it was decided that a legal instrument would be drafted with regard to the protection of national minorities, and appendix II of the Vienna Declaration instructed the Committee of Ministers to work upon both a framework convention on national minorities and a draft protocol on cultural rights complementing the European Convention on Human Rights.[135] The Framework Convention for the Protection of National Minorities was adopted by the Committee of Ministers on 10 November 1994 and opened for signature on 1 February 1995.[136] The Framework Convention underlines the right to equality before the law of persons belonging to national minorities and prohibits discrimination based on belonging to a national minority. Contracting parties to the Framework Convention undertake to adopt, where necessary, adequate measures to promote in all areas of economic, social, political and cultural life, full and effective equality between persons belonging to a national minority and to the majority.[137] The parties agree to promote the conditions necessary for persons belonging to minorities to develop their culture and to preserve the essential elements of their identity, namely their religion, language, traditions and cultural heritage.[138] The collective expression of individual human rights of persons belonging to national minorities is to be respected,[139] while in areas inhabited by such persons traditionally

---

[132] See e.g. the Committee of Ministers Recommendations to the Netherlands, RecChL (2001) 1 and to Germany, RecChL (2002) 1.

[133] Article 16. See the first biennial report in 2000, Doc. 8879, and the second in 2002, Doc. 9540.

[134] Article 20.

[135] See 14 HRLJ, 1993, pp. 373 ff. See also the Explanatory Report to the Framework Convention for the Protection of National Minorities, 1995. An ad hoc Committee for the Protection of National Minorities (CAHMIN) was established. Note that in January 1996, it was decided to suspend the work of the Committee on the drafting of an Additional Protocol: see CAHMIN (95) 22 Addendum, 1996.

[136] The Convention came into force on 1 February 1998.   [137] Article 4.

[138] Article 5. The parties also agree to refrain from assimilation policies and practices where this is against the will of persons belonging to national minorities.

[139] E.g. the freedoms of peaceful assembly, association, expression and thought, conscience and religion, article 7. See also articles 8 and 9.

or in substantial numbers, the parties shall endeavour to ensure as far as possible the condition which would make it possible to use the minority languages in relations between those persons and the administrative authorities.[140] By article 15, the parties agree to refrain from measures which alter the geographic proportions of the population in areas inhabited by persons belonging to national minorities.

The implementation of this Framework Convention is monitored by the Committee of Ministers of the Council of Europe[141] with the assistance of an advisory committee of experts[142] and on the basis of periodic reports from contracting states.[143] The Committee of Ministers adopted rules on monitoring arrangements in 1997[144] and the Advisory Committee started operating in June 1998. The Committee examines state reports,[145] which are made public by the Council of Europe upon receipt from the state party, and prepares an opinion on the measures taken by that party.[146] The Committee may request additional information from a state party or other sources, including individuals and NGOs, but cannot deal with individual complaints. It may hold meetings with governments, and has to do so if the government concerned so requests, and may hold meetings with others than the governments concerned, during the course of country visits. Having received the opinion of the Advisory Committee, the Committee of Ministers will take the final decisions (called conclusions) concerning the adequacy of the measures taken by the state party. Where appropriate, it may also adopt recommendations in respect of the state party concerned. The conclusions and recommendations of the Committee of Ministers shall be made public upon their adoption, together with

---

[140] Upon request and where such a request corresponds to a real need, article 10(2). Similarly with regard to the display of traditional local names, street names and other topographical indications intended for the public in the minority language, article 11(3), and with regard to adequate opportunities for being taught the minority language or for receiving instruction in that language, article 14(2).

[141] Article 24. Note that parties which are not members of the Council of Europe shall participate in the implementation mechanism according to modalities to be determined. Accordingly, the Federal Republic of Yugoslavia became a party to the Convention on 11 May 2001 and its first report became due on 1 September 2002.

[142] Article 26.   [143] Article 25. The first reports became due on 1 February 1999.

[144] Resolution (97) 10 and see H(1998)005 rev.11.

[145] Guidelines for such reports have been issued by the Committee: see e.g. ACFC/INF(2003)001 and ACFC/INF(1998)001.

[146] See, for a list of opinions delivered as of January 2003, ACFC(2002)Opinions bil. See also the Collection of Resolutions and Recommendations Referred to by the Advisory Committee in its Opinions, 2007 and the Activities of the Council of Europe in the Field of the Protection of National Minorities, DH-MIN (2005) 003.

any comments the state party may have submitted in respect of the opinion delivered by the Advisory Committee. The opinion of the Advisory Committee is as a rule made public together with the conclusions of the Committee of Ministers. A first cycle of monitoring began in 1998 with thirty-four opinions adopted by the Advisory Committee and twenty-nine resolutions adopted by the Committee of Ministers. A second cycle of monitoring began in February 2004.

While the range of rights accorded to members of minorities is clearly greater than that envisaged in UN instruments,[147] its ambit is narrower in being confined to 'national minorities'. The Framework Convention itself provides no definition of that term since no consensus existed as to its meaning,[148] although Recommendation 1201 (1993) adopted by the Parliamentary Assembly and reaffirmed in Recommendation 1255 (1995) suggests that it refers to persons who reside on the territory of the state concerned and are citizens of it; maintain longstanding, firm and lasting ties with that state; display distinctive ethnic, cultural, religious or linguistic characteristics; are sufficiently representative, although smaller in numbers than the rest of the population of that state or of a region of that state; and are motivated by a concern to preserve together that which constitutes their common identity, including their culture, their traditions, their religion or their language. The narrowing of regard to persons belonging to national minorities who are citizens of the state concerned is perhaps a matter of concern.[149] The issue of the protection of minority rights is the subject of continuing discussion as to both their nature and scope.[150]

The Council of Europe has adopted measures with regard to other areas of human rights activities of some relevance to the above issues.[151]

---

[147] See above, p. 293.

[148] See the Explanatory Report to the Convention, which states that, 'It was decided to adopt a pragmatic approach, based on the recognition that at this stage, it is impossible to arrive at a definition capable of mustering general support of all Council of Europe member States', H(1995)010, para. 12. The European Court of Human Rights has also referred to the problem of defining national minorities: see *Gorzelik* v. *Poland*, Judgment of 20 December 2001, para. 62.

[149] See e.g. R. Higgins, 'Minority Rights Discrepancies and Divergencies Between the International Covenant and the Council of Europe System' in *Liber Amicorum for Henry Schermers*, The Hague, 1994.

[150] See e.g. Parliamentary Assembly Recommendation Rec 1492 (2001) and the response of the Advisory Committee dated 14 September 2001.

[151] See e.g. the European Charter of Local Self-Government, 1985; the European Convention on the Participation of Foreigners in Public Life at Local Level, 1992; the European Outline Convention on Transfrontier Co-operation between Territorial Communities or

The European Union[152]

The Treaty of Rome, 1957 established the European Economic Community and is not of itself a human rights treaty. However, the European Court of Justice has held that subsumed within Community law are certain relevant unwritten general principles of law, emanating from several sources.[153] The Court noted in the *Internationale Handelsgesellschaft* case[154] that 'respect for fundamental rights forms an integral part of the general principles of law protected by the Court of Justice',[155] while in *Nold* v. *Commission*,[156] the Court emphasised that measures incompatible with fundamental rights recognised and protected by the constitutions of member states could not be upheld. It was also held that international treaties for the protection of human rights on which member states have collaborated, or of which they are signatories, could supply guidelines which should be followed within the framework of Community law.[157] The European Convention on Human Rights is clearly the prime example of this and it has been referred to on several occasions by

Authorities, 1980; the European Convention on the Legal Status of Migrant Workers, 1977 and the European Convention on the Exercise of Children's Rights, 1995.

[152] See e.g. D. Chalmers and A. Tomkins, *European Union Public Law*, Cambridge, 2007; *European Fundamental Rights and Freedoms* (ed. D. Ehlers), Berlin, 2007; *The European Union and Human Rights* (eds. N. Neuwahl and A. Rosas), Dordrecht, 1995; *The EU and Human Rights* (ed. P. Alston), Oxford, 1999; L. Betten and N. Grief, *EU Law and Human Rights*, London, 1998; S. Weatherill and P. Beaumont, *EU Law*, 3rd edn, London, 1999; T. C. Hartley, *The Foundations of European Community Law*, 6th edn, Oxford, 2007; L. N. Brown and T. Kennedy, *The Court of Justice of the European Communities*, 4th edn, London, 1994, chapter 15; M. Mendelson, 'The European Court of Justice and Human Rights', 1 *Yearbook of European Law*, 1981, p. 126, and H. Schermers, 'The European Communities Bound by Fundamental Human Rights', 27 *Common Market Law Review*, 1990, p. 249.

[153] See e.g. *Stauder* v. *City of Ulm* [1969] ECR 419; *Internationale Handelsgesellschaft* [1970] ECR 1125; *Nold* v. *EC Commission* [1974] ECR 491; *Kirk* [1984] ECR 2689 and *Johnston* v. *Chief Constable of the RUC* [1986] 3 CMLR 240. See also the Joint Declaration by the European Parliament, the Council and the Commission of 5 April 1979, *Official Journal*, 1977, C103/1; the Joint Declaration Against Racism and Xenophobia, 11 June 1986, *Official Journal*, 1986, C158/1 and the European Parliament's Declaration of Fundamental Rights and Freedoms, 1989, *EC Bulletin*, 4/1989.

[154] [1970] ECR 1125, 1134.

[155] See also *Re Accession of the European Community to the Convention for the Protection of Human Rights and Fundamental Freedoms* 108 ILR, p. 225 and *Kremzow* v. *Austria* [1997] ECR I-2629; 113 ILR, p. 264.

[156] [1974] ECR 491, 507.

[157] See e.g. *Hauer* v. *Land Rheinland-Pfaltz* [1979] ECR 3727 and *SPUC* v. *Grogan* [1991] ECR I-4685.

the Court.[158] Indeed the question has also been raised and considered without resolution as to whether the Community should itself accede to the European Convention on Human Rights.[159]

The Treaty on European Union (the Maastricht Treaty), 1992 amended the Treaty of Rome and established the European Union, founded on the European Communities supplemented by the policies and forms of co-operation established under the 1992 Treaty. Article F(2) of Title I noted that the Union 'shall respect fundamental rights', as guaranteed by the European Convention on Human Rights and as they result from common constitutional traditions, 'as general principles of Community law'. Under article K.1 of Title VI, the member states agreed that asylum, immigration, drug, fraud, civil and criminal judicial co-operation, customs co-operation and certain forms of police co-operation would be regarded as 'matters of common interest', which under article K.2 would be dealt with in compliance with the European Convention on Human Rights and the Convention relating to the Status of Refugees, 1951. The provisions under Title V on the Common Foreign and Security Policy may also impact upon human rights, so that, for instance, the European Union sent its own human rights observers to Rwanda within this framework.[160] From the early 1990s, the European Communities began to include human rights references in its trade and aid policies, formalised in article 177(2), and from the mid-1990s, all trade and co-operation agreements contained provisions concerning respect for human rights.[161]

The Treaty of Amsterdam, which came into force on 1 May 1999, inserted a new article 6 into the Treaty on European Union, which stated that the European Union 'is founded on the principles of liberty, democracy,

---

[158] See e.g. *Rutili* [1975] ECR 1219; *Valsabbia* v. *Commission* [1980] ECR 907; *Kirk* [1984] ECR 2689; *Dow Chemical Ibérica* v. *Commission* [1989] ECR 3165; *ERT* [1991] ECR I-2925 and *X* v. *Commission* [1992] ECR II-2195 and 16 HRLJ, 1995, p. 54. Note also the Joint Declaration on Human Rights, 1977, by which the three EC institutions undertook to respect the European Convention on Human Rights, OJ 1977 C103/1.

[159] See e.g. 'Accession of the Communities to the European Convention on Human Rights', *EC Bulletin*, Suppl. 2/79. Note that the President of the European Court of Human Rights suggested in January 2003 that the EU should accede to the Convention: see www.echr.coe.int/eng/Edocs/SpeechWildhaber.htm.

[160] See J. Van Der Kaauw, 'European Union', 13 NQHR, 1995, p. 173. Note, however, that the European Court of Justice held in Opinion 2/94 that the EC had no competence to accede to the European Convention as it did not have any general human rights competence, [1996] ECR I-1759.

[161] See e.g. E. Riedel and M. Will, 'Human Rights Clauses in External Agreements' in Alston, *The EU and Human Rights*, p. 723.

respect for human rights and fundamental freedoms, and the rule of law, principles which are common to the Member States', and provided that the Union 'shall respect fundamental rights as guaranteed by' the European Convention on Human Rights.[162] Member states violating these principles in a 'serious and persistent' manner risk the suspension of certain of their rights deriving from the application of the Union Treaty.[163] In addition, candidate countries have to respect these principles to join the Union.[164] The European Union adopted the Charter of Fundamental Rights in December 2000. This instrument, for example, notes the principle of the equality before the law of all people,[165] prohibits discrimination on any ground,[166] provides for a number of workers' rights and citizens' rights, and requests the Union to protect cultural, religious and linguistic diversity. Quite what the legal status of this Charter was[167] and how it related to the Strasbourg system were open questions.[168] However, Advocates-General of the European Court of Justice have been referring to the Charter with great frequency as part of a shared set of values within the Union,[169] as has the Court of First Instance[170] and more recently the European Court of Justice.[171] Further, the Lisbon Treaty, 2007 (which is not as yet in force) provides for article 6 to be revised so that the Charter would have legally binding force[172] and

---

[162] See the discussion by the European Court of Justice of these principles in the context of the European Arrest Warrant, C-303/05, *Advocaten voor de Wereld*, Judgment of 3 May 2007. See A. Hinarejos, 'Recent Human Rights Developments in the EU Courts', 7 *Human Rights Law Review*, 2007, p. 793.

[163] Article 7. See also the amendments introduced by the Nice Treaty, 2001.

[164] Article 49. See also the Copenhagen Criteria 1993, including stable institutions guaranteeing democracy, the rule of law, human rights and the protection of minorities, EC Bulletin 6-1993, I.13.

[165] Article 20.   [166] Article 21.

[167] Note the official UK view that it is a political declaration and not legally binding, 365 HC Deb., col. 614W, 27 March 2001; UKMIL, 72 BYIL, 2001, p. 564.

[168] However, article 52(3) of the Charter specifies that any rights that 'correspond' to those already articulated by the Human Rights Convention shall have the same meaning and scope.

[169] See e.g. *BECTU* [2001] ECR I-4881 and *Netherlands* v. *Parliament and Council* [2001] ECR I-7079.

[170] See e.g. *Jégo-Quéré* v. *Commission* [2002] ECR II-2365.

[171] See e.g. *European Parliament* v. *Council* [2006] ECR I-5769 and C-411/04 P, *Salzgitter Mannesmann* v. *Commission*, Judgment of 25 January 2007.

[172] Although a Protocol to the treaty provides that the Charter does not extend the ability of the Court of Justice to find the law or practices of the UK and Poland to be inconsistent with the Charter and that no new justiciable rights applicable to these states have been created, and that a provision of the Charter referring to national laws and practices shall

opens the way for the accession of the EU to the European Convention on Human Rights.

The Union, more generally, seeks in some measure to pay regard to human rights as internationally defined, in its activities.[173] As noted above, there appears now to be a formal policy, for example, to include a human rights clause in co-operation agreements with third countries, which incorporates a provision for the suspension of the agreement in case of a breach of the essential elements of the agreement in question, including respect for human rights.[174] The European Parliament is also active in consideration of human rights issues.[175]

The OSCE (Organisation for Security and Co-operation in Europe)[176]

What was initially termed the 'Helsinki process', and which more formally was referred to as the Conference on Security and Co-operation in Europe, developed out of the Final Act of the Helsinki meeting, which was signed on 1 August 1975 after two years of discussions by the representatives of the then thirty-five participating states.[177] The Final Act[178] dealt primarily with questions of international security and state relations, and was seen

only apply to the UK and Poland to the extent that the rights or principles in the Charter are recognised in the laws and practices of these two states.

[173] See e.g. the Commission Report on the Implementation of Actions to Promote Human Rights and Democracy, 1994, COM 9(5) 191, 1995.

[174] See e.g. 13 NQHR, 1995, pp. 276 and 460.

[175] See e.g. the Annual Reports of the Parliament on Respect for Human Rights in the European Community, www.europarl.europa.eu/comparl/afet/droi/annual_reports.htm.

[176] See, for example, A. Bloed, 'Monitoring the CSCE Human Dimension: In Search of its Effectiveness' in Monitoring Human Rights in Europe (eds. Bloed et al.), Dordrecht, 1993, p. 45; The CSCE (ed. A. Bloed), Dordrecht, 1993; Human Rights, International Law and the Helsinki Accord (ed. T. Buergenthal), Montclair, NJ, 1977; J. Maresca, To Helsinki – The CSCE 1973–75, Durham, 1987; T. Buergenthal, 'The Helsinki Process: Birth of a Human Rights System' in Human Rights in the World Community (eds. R. Claude and B. Weston), 2nd edn, Philadelphia, 1992, p. 256; Essays on Human Rights in the Helsinki Process (eds. A. Bloed and P. Van Dijk), Dordrecht, 1985; A. Bloed and P. Van Dijk, The Human Dimension of the Helsinki Process, Dordrecht, 1991; D. McGoldrick, 'Human Rights Developments in the Helsinki Process', 39 ICLQ, 1990, p. 923, and McGoldrick, 'The Development of the Conference on Security and Co-operation in Europe – From Process to Institution' in Legal Visions of the New Europe (eds. B. S. Jackson and D. McGoldrick), London, 1993, p. 135. See also the OSCE Handbook published regularly and available at www.osce.org/publications/handbook/files/handbook.pdf.

[177] I.e. all the states of Western and Eastern Europe, except Albania, plus the United States and Canada.

[178] For the text, see, for example, 14 ILM, 1975, p. 1292.

as the method by which the post-war European territorial settlement would be finally accepted. In the Western view, the Final Act constituted a political statement and accordingly could not be regarded as a binding treaty. Nonetheless, the impact of the Final Act on developments in Europe has far exceeded the impact of most legally binding treaties.

The Final Act set out in 'Basket I' a list of ten fundamental principles dealing with relations between participating states, principle 7 of which refers to 'respect for human rights and fundamental freedoms, including freedom of thought, conscience, religion and belief'. 'Basket III' dealt with Co-operation in Humanitarian and Other Fields and covered family reunification, free flow of information and cultural and educational co-operation.[179]

At the third 'follow-up' meeting at Vienna in January 1989, great progress regarding human rights occurred,[180] primarily as a result of the changed attitudes in the then USSR and in Eastern Europe, especially as regards the extent of the detailed provisions and the recognition of concrete rights and duties. The part entitled 'Questions Relating to Security in Europe' contained a Principles section, in which *inter alia* the parties confirmed their respect for human rights and their determination to guarantee their effective exercise. Paragraphs 13–27 contain in a detailed and concrete manner a list of human rights principles to be respected, ranging from due process rights to equality and non-discrimination and the rights of religious communities, and from the rights of minorities to the rights of refugees. The provision in which states agree to respect the right of their citizens to contribute actively, either individually or collectively, to the promotion and protection of human rights, constitutes an important innovation of great practical significance, as does the comment that states will respect the right of persons to observe and promote the implementation of CSCE provisions.

The part entitled 'Co-operation in Humanitarian and Other Fields' included an important section on Human Contacts in which the right to leave one's country and return thereto was reaffirmed. It was decided that all outstanding human contacts applications would be resolved within six months and that thereafter there would be a series of regular reviews. Family reunion issues were to be dealt with in as short a time as possible and in normal practice within one month. The parties committed

---

[179] 'Basket II' covered co-operation in the fields of economics, science, technology and the environment.
[180] See the text of the Concluding Document in 10 HRLJ, 1989, p. 270.

themselves to publishing all laws and statutory regulations concerning movement by individuals within their territory and travel between states, an issue that had caused a great deal of controversy, while the right of members of religions to establish and maintain personal contacts with each other in their own and other countries, *inter alia* through travel and participation in religious events, was proclaimed.[181]

In a further significant development, the Vienna Concluding Document contained a part entitled 'Human Dimension of the CSCE' in which some implementation measures were provided for. The participating states decided to exchange information and to respond to requests for information and to representations made to them by other participating states on questions relating to the human dimension of the CSCE. Bilateral meetings would be held with other participating states that so request, in order to examine such questions, while such questions could be brought to the attention of other participating states through diplomatic channels or raised at further 'follow-up' meetings or at meetings of the Conference on the Human Dimension. The procedure is confidential.[182]

The Concluding Document of the Copenhagen meeting in 1990[183] constituted a further crucial stage in the development of the process. The participating states proclaimed support for the principles of the rule of law, free and fair elections, democracy, pluralism and due process rights. Paragraph 1 of Chapter 1 emphasised that the protection and promotion of human rights was one of the basic purposes of government. A variety of specific rights, including the freedoms of expression, assembly, association, thought, conscience and religion, and the rights to leave one's own country and return and to receive legal assistance, the rights of the child, the rights of national minorities and the prohibition of torture are proclaimed. Time-limits were imposed with regard to the Vienna Human Dimension mechanism.

---

[181] Paragraphs 18 and 32.

[182] The mechanism was used over 100 times between 1989 and 1992: see Bloed and Van Dijk, *Human Dimension*, p. 79, and McGoldrick, 'Development of the CSCE', p. 139. See also H. Tretter, 'Human Rights in the Concluding Document of the Vienna Follow-up Meeting of the Conference on Security and Co-operation in Europe of January 15, 1989', 10 HRLJ, 1989, p. 257; R. Brett, *The Development of the Human Dimension Machinery*, Essex University, 1992, and A. Bloed and P. Van Dijk, 'Supervisory Mechanisms for the Human Dimension of the CSCE: Its Setting-up in Vienna, its Present Functioning and its Possible Development towards a General Procedure for the Peaceful Settlement of Disputes' in Bloed and Van Dijk, *Human Dimension*, p. 74.

[183] See 8 NQHR, 1990, p. 302 and Cm 1324 (1990).

The Charter of Paris, adopted at the Summit of Heads of State and of Government in 1990,[184] called for more regular consultations at ministerial and senior official level and marked an important stage in the institutionalisation of the process, with a Council of Foreign Ministers, a Committee of Senior Officials and a secretariat being established. The section on Human Rights, Democracy and Rule of Law consisted of a list of human rights, including the right to effective remedies, full respect for which constituted 'the bedrock' for the construction of 'the new Europe'. The Moscow Human Dimension meeting of 1991[185] described the Human Dimension mechanism as an essential achievement of the CSCE process and it was strengthened. The time-limits provided for at Copenhagen were reduced[186] and a resource list of experts was to be established,[187] with three experts being appointed by each participating state in order to allow for CSCE missions to be created to assist states requesting such help in facilitating the resolution of a particular question or problem related to the human dimension of the CSCE. The observations of the missions of experts together with the comments of the state concerned were to be forwarded to CSCE states within three weeks of the submission of the observations to the state concerned and might be discussed by the Committee of Senior Officials, who could consider follow-up measures.[188]

By the time of the Helsinki Conference in 1992, the number of participating states had risen to fifty-two,[189] the political climate in Europe having changed dramatically after the establishment of democratic regimes in Eastern Europe, the ending of the Soviet Union and the rise of tensions in Yugoslavia and other parts of Eastern Europe. The participating states strongly reaffirmed that Human Dimension commitments were matters of direct and legitimate concern to all participating states and did not belong exclusively to the internal affairs of the states concerned, while

---

[184] See 30 ILM, 1991, p. 190.   [185] See 30 ILM, 1991, p. 1670 and Cm 1771 (1991).

[186] So that, for example, the written responses to requests for information were to occur within ten days, and the bilateral meetings were to take place as a rule within one week of the date of request, Section I(1).

[187] The Council of Ministers of the CSCE subsequently decided that the Office of Democratic Institutions and Human Rights (formerly the Office for Free Elections) would be the appropriate institution establishing the resource list.

[188] A variety of missions have now been employed in, for example, Nagorno-Karabakh, Georgia, Chechnya, Moldova and Croatia. See generally OSCE Handbook, Vienna, 2007.

[189] There are currently fifty-six participating states. Note also the report entitled 'Common Purposes: Towards a More Effective OSCE' produced by a Panel of Eminent Persons in 2005 and the new OSCE Rules of Procedure adopted in 2006: see OSCE Handbook.

gross violations of such commitments posed a special threat to stability. This reference of the link between human rights and international stability was to increase in the following years. At Helsinki, the CSCE was declared to be a regional arrangement in the sense of Chapter VIII of the UN Charter.[190] The post of High Commissioner on National Minorities was established in order to provide early warning and early action where appropriate, concerning tensions relating to national minority issues that have the potential to develop into a conflict within the CSCE area affecting peace, stability or relations between participating states.[191] The High Commissioner, who acts in confidence, was also mandated to collect relevant information and make visits. Where the High Commissioner concludes that there is a *prima facie* risk of potential conflict in such situations, an early warning is to be issued, which will be promptly conveyed by the Chairman-in-Office of the CSCE to the Committee of Senior Officials. The High Commissioner is able to make recommendations to participating states regarding the treatment of national minorities.[192] In addition, a number of general recommendations have been made with regard to Roma[193] and other matters.[194]

As far as the Human Dimension mechanism was concerned, the Conference decided to permit any participating state to provide information on situations and cases that are the subject of requests for information, and it was also decided that in years in which a review conference was not being held, a three-week meeting at expert level of participating states would be organised in order to review implementation of the CSCE Human

---

[190] See further below, p. 1273.
[191] See Section II of the Helsinki Decisions. Note that the High Commissioner deals with situations and not with individual complaints. See also *Quiet Diplomacy in Action: The OSCE High Commissioner on National Minorities* (ed. W. A. Kemp), The Hague, 2001; K. Drzewicki, 'The OSCE High Commissioner on National Minorities – Confronting Traditional and Emerging Challenges' in *OSCE and Minorities. Assessment and Priorities* (ed. S. Parzymies), Warsaw, 2007, and J. Packer, 'The OSCE High Commissioner on National Minorities: Pyrometer, Prophylactic, Pyrosvestis' in *Minorities, Peoples and Self-Determination* (eds. N. Ghanea and A. Xanthaki), Leiden, 2005, p. 249.
[192] See generally www.osce.org/hcnm/documents.html.
[193] See www.osce.org/documents/hcnm/2000/03/241_en.pdf.
[194] See e.g. the Hague Recommendation on Education Rights of National Minorities, 1996; the Oslo Recommendations on Linguistic Rights of National Minorities, 1998; the Lund Recommendations on Effective Participation of National Minorities in Public Life, 1999; the Guidelines on the Use of Minority Languages in the Broadcast Media, 2003, and the Recommendations on Policing in Multi-Ethnic Societies, 2006: see www.osce.org/hcnm/documents.html.

Dimension commitments. In addition, it was provided that the Office of Democratic Institutions and Human Rights would begin organising Human Dimension seminars.[195]

The next major step in the process took place at Budapest at the end of 1994.[196] The CSCE, in recognition of the institutional changes underway in recent years, changed its name to the OSCE (the Organisation for Security and Co-operation in Europe) and took a number of steps in the field of security and conflict management. The Conference emphasised that human rights, the rule of law and democratic institutions represented a crucial contribution to conflict prevention and that the protection of human rights constituted an 'essential foundation of democratic civil society',[197] and it was decided that Human Dimension issues would be regularly dealt with by the Permanent Council,[198] with the Office of Democratic Institutions and Human Rights (based in Warsaw) acting as the main institution of the Human Dimension in an advisory capacity to the organisation, with enhanced roles in election monitoring and the dispatch of missions.[199] States were encouraged to use the Human Dimension mechanism (now termed the Moscow Mechanism) and the Chairman-in-Office was encouraged to inform the Permanent Council of serious cases of alleged non-implementation of Human Dimension commitments. Further, an OSCE Representative on Freedom of the Media was appointed in 1997 and the role increased in 2004 to include the task of combating the misuse of hate speech regulations in order to silence legitimate dissent and alternative opinion.[200] Thus, step by step over recent years, the Helsinki process has transformed itself into an institutional structure with a particular interest in describing and requiring the implementation of human rights.[201]

---

[195] Section VI of the Helsinki Decisions and www.osce.org/odihr/.
[196] See 5 HRLJ, 1994, p. 449. [197] Section VIII of the Budapest Decisions.
[198] This group is responsible for the day-to-day operations of the OSCE and its members are the permanent representatives of the member states meeting weekly. It is based in Vienna.
[199] Note also that the Monitoring Section within the ODIHR analyses human rights developments and compliance with Human Dimension commitments by participating states and alerts the Chairman-in-Office to serious deteriorations in respect for human rights.
[200] See *OSCE Handbook*, p. 34 and the Sofia Decision 12, para. 16, 2004.
[201] An OSCE Advisory Panel for the Prevention of Torture was established in 1998: see e.g. the Final Report of the Supplementary Human Dimension Meeting on Human Rights and Inhuman Treatment and Punishment 2000, www.osce.org/documents/odihr/2000/03/1787_en.pdf, and a restructured Advisory Panel of Experts on Freedom of Religion or Belief was established in 2000. Note that as a consequence of the Dayton Peace Agreement on Bosnia, 1995, it was agreed that the OSCE would supervise elections in that country and would closely monitor human rights throughout Bosnia and would

The OSCE has also established a number of missions in order to help mitigate conflicts[202] and adopted a Treaty on Open Skies and a Convention on Conciliation and Arbitration within the OSCE in 1992. Although some overlay with the Council of Europe system does exist, the fact that a large proportion of participating states are now members of the Council of Europe obviates the most acute dangers inherent in differing human rights systems. Nevertheless, as the Council of Europe system moves beyond the strictly legal enforcement stage and as the OSCE develops and strengthens its institutional mechanisms, some overlapping is inevitable. However, in general terms, the OSCE system remains politically based and expressed, while the essence of the Council of Europe system remains juridically focused.

The CIS Convention on Human Rights and Fundamental Freedoms[203]

The Commonwealth of Independent States, which links together the former Republics of the Soviet Union (with the exception of the three Baltic states), adopted a Convention on Human Rights in May 1995. Under this Convention, a standard range of rights is included, ranging from the right to life, liberty and security of person, equality before the judicial system, respect for private and family life, to freedom of religion, expression, assembly and the right to marry. The right to work is included (article 14) as is the right to social security, the right to education and the right of every minor child to special protective measures (article 17). The right of persons belonging to national minorities to express and develop their ethnic, linguistic, religious and cultural identity is protected (article 21), while everyone has the right to take part in public affairs, including voting (article 29). It is intended that the implementation of the Convention be monitored by the Human Rights Commission of the CIS (article 34). Under Section II of the Regulations of the Human Rights Commission, adopted in September 1993, states parties may raise human rights matters falling within the

---

appoint an international human rights Ombudsman: see MC (5) Dec/1, 1995. The OSCE also has a role in Kosovo: see *OSCE Handbook*, p. 46.

202 See OSCE Handbook, pp. 39 ff. Of particular importance, perhaps, is the Minsk Process, dealing with the Nagorno-Karabakh conflict, *ibid.*, p. 76.

203 See H/INF (95) 3, pp. 195 ff. See also the essays contained in 17 HRLJ, 1996 concerning the CIS and human rights.

Convention with other states parties and, if no satisfactory response is received within six months, the matter may be referred to the Commission. Domestic remedies need to be exhausted. Under Section III of the Regulations, the Commission may examine individual and collective applications submitted by any person or non-governmental organisation. The Convention entered into force on 11 August 1998 upon the third ratification.

Concerned with the level of protection afforded under this Convention (in particular the facts that the members of the Commission are appointed representatives of member states and the Commission implements the instrument by means of recommendations) and the problems of co-existence with the Council of Europe human rights system, the Parliamentary Assembly of the Council of Europe adopted a resolution in 2001 calling upon member or applicant states which are also members of the CIS not to sign or ratify the CIS Convention. In addition, it recommended that those that already had should issue a legally binding declaration stating that the European Convention procedures would not be replaced or weakened through recourse to the CIS Convention procedures.[204]

The Human Rights Chamber of Bosnia and Herzegovina

The Chamber was established under Annex 6 of the Dayton Peace Agreement, 1995.[205] It consisted of fourteen members, eight of whom (not to be citizens of Bosnia or of any neighbouring state) were appointed by the Committee of Ministers of the Council of Europe.[206] The Chamber considered alleged or apparent violations of human rights as provided in the European Convention on Human Rights, as well as alleged or apparent discrimination on any ground. Applications could be submitted by all persons or groups of persons, including by way of referral from the Ombudsman, claiming to be a victim of a violation or acting on behalf

---

[204] Resolution 1249 (2001). See also recommendation 1519 (2001) stating that recourse to the CIS Commission should not be regarded as another procedure of international settlement within the meaning of article 35(2)b of the European Convention.

[205] As part of the Commission on Human Rights, the other part being the Ombudsman: see article II of Annex 6 of the Dayton Agreement.

[206] See resolutions (93)6 and (96)8. It should be noted that, at the time, Bosnia was not a member of the Council of Europe.

of victims who were deceased or missing.[207] There were a number of admissibility requirements similar to those of international human rights bodies, including the exhaustion of effective remedies and the submission of the application within six months of the date of any final decision. The Chamber normally sat in panels[208] of seven, four of whom were not to be citizens of Bosnia or a neighbouring state. In such cases, the decision could be reviewed by the full Chamber.[209] The President could refer to the plenary Chamber any application not yet placed before a panel where a serious question was raised as to the interpretation of the Agreement or any other international agreement therein referred to or it appeared that a final decision should be taken without delay or there appeared to be any other justified reason.[210] Decisions were final and binding.[211] The work of the Chamber, primarily concerning housing-related issues[212] and property rights,[213] steadily increased.[214] According to the Agreement Pursuant to Article XIV of Annex 6 of the Dayton Agreement, 2003, the mandate of the Human Rights Chamber expired on 31 December 2003. This Agreement established a five-member Human Rights Commission to operate during 2004 within the framework of the Constitutional Court of Bosnia and Herzegovina. After 1 January 2004, new cases alleging human rights violations were decided by the Constitutional Court.

---

[207] Article VIII.

[208] Two panels were set up under Rule 26 of the Rules of Procedure 1996, as amended in 1998 and 2001.

[209] Article X.   [210] Rule 29.

[211] Article XI. The Chamber could also order provisional measures: see article X. These were made particularly in housing-related cases where eviction was threatened: see *Annual Report 2000*, p. 6.

[212] For example, the question of refugees seeking to regain possession of properties from which they had fled and which were being used to house other persons: see e.g. *Bašić et al. v. Republika Srpska*, Cases Nos. CH/98/752 et al., *Decisions of the Human Rights Chamber August–December 1999*, 2000, pp. 149 ff.

[213] For example, the question of restriction on withdrawal of foreign currency from bank accounts: see e.g. *Poropat* v. *Bosnia*, Cases Nos. CH/97/42, 52, 105 and 108, and the question of pensions from the Yugoslav army, *Šećerbegović* v. *Bosnia*, Cases Nos. CH/98/706, 740 and 776. Note in particular, however, the case of *Boudellaa et al.* v. *Bosnia and Herzegovina and the Federation of Bosnia and Herzegovina*, Judgment of 11 October 2002, where in a case involving expulsion of Bosnian citizens of Algerian origin into the custody of the US on terrorism charges, the chamber found that the respondents had violated relevant human rights provisions.

[214] In 1996, 31 applications were received; 83 in 1997; 3,226 in 2000. By the end of 2000, a total of 6,675 applications had been registered and a total of 669 separate decisions reached: see *Annual Report 2000*, p. 3.

The Inter-American Convention on Human Rights[215]

The Inter-American Convention, which came into force in 1978, contains a range of rights to be protected by the states parties.[216] The rights are fundamentally those protected by the European Convention, but with some interesting differences.[217] For example, under article 4 the right to life is deemed to start in general as from conception,[218] while the prohibition on torture and inhuman or degrading treatment is more extensively expressed and is in the context of the right to have one's physical, mental and moral integrity respected (article 5). In addition, articles 18 and 19 of the Inter-American Convention protect the right to a name and the specific rights of the child, article 23 provides for a general right to participation in the context of public affairs and article 26 provides for the progressive achievement of the economic, social and cultural rights contained in the Charter of the Organisation of American States, 1948, as amended by the Protocol of Buenos Aires, 1967.[219]

The Inter-American Commission on Human Rights was created in 1959 and its first Statute approved by the OAS Council in 1960. In 1971, it was recognised as one of the principal organs of the OAS.[220] Under its

---

[215] See generally J. M. Pasqualucci, *The Practice and Procedure of the Inter-American Court of Human Rights*, Cambridge, 2003; H. J. Steiner, P. Alston and R. Goodman, *International Human Rights in Context*, 3rd edn, Oxford, 2008, pp. 1020 ff.; *The Inter-American System of Human Rights* (eds. D. J. Harris and S. Livingstone), Oxford, 1998; T. Buergenthal and D. Shelton, *Protecting Human Rights in the Americas*, 4th edn, Strasbourg, 1995; D. Shelton, 'The Inter-American Human Rights System' in *Guide to International Human Rights Practice* (ed. H. Hannum), 4th edn, Ardsley, 2004, p. 127, and T. Buergenthal and R. Norris, *The Inter-American System*, Dobbs Ferry, 5 vols., 1983–4. See also J. Rehman, *International Human Rights Law*, London, 2003, chapter 8; A. H. Robertson and J. G. Merrills, *Human Rights in the World*, 4th edn, London, 1996, chapter 6; S. Davidson, *The Inter-American Court of Human Rights*, Aldershot, 1992; S. Davidson, 'Remedies for Violations of the American Convention on Human Rights', 44 ICLQ, 1995, p. 405, and C. Grossman, 'Proposals to Strengthen the Inter-American System of Protection of Human Rights', 32 German YIL, 1990, p. 264.

[216] The Convention currently has twenty-four parties: see *Annual Report of the Inter-American Commission on Human Rights 2006*, Washington, 2007.

[217] See e.g. J. Frowein, 'The European and the American Conventions on Human Rights – A Comparison', 1 HRLJ, 1980, p. 44. See also the American Declaration of the Rights and Duties of Man, 1948.

[218] See e.g. 10 DR, 1977, p. 100.

[219] The Charter of the OAS has also been amended by the Protocols of Cartagena de Indias, 1985; Washington, 1992 and Managua, 1993.

[220] See e.g. C. Medina, 'The Inter-American Commission on Human Rights and the Inter-American Court of Human Rights: Reflections on a Joint Venture', 12 HRQ, 1990, p. 439.

original Statute, it had wide powers to promote the awareness and study of human rights in America and to make recommendations to member states. In 1965, the Statute was revised and the Commission's powers expanded to include *inter alia* the examination of communications. With the entry into force of the 1969 Convention in 1978, the Commission's position was further strengthened. The Commission has powers regarding all member states of the OAS, not just those that have ratified the Convention, and its Statute emphasises that the human rights protected include those enumerated in both the Convention and the American Declaration of the Rights and Duties of Man.[221] Article 44 of the Convention provides that any person or group of persons or any non-governmental entity legally recognised in one or more of the OAS states may lodge petitions with the Commission alleging a violation of the Convention by a state party.[222] Contrary to the European Convention prior to its reform in Protocol 11, this right is automatic, whereas the right of inter-state complaint, again contrary to the European Convention, is under article 45 subject to a prior declaration recognising the competence of the Commission in this regard. The admissibility requirements in articles 46 and 47 are very broadly similar to those in the European Convention, as is the procedure laid down in article 48 and the drawing-up of a report in cases in which a friendly settlement has been achieved.[223] The Commission has dealt with a number of issues in the individual application procedure. During 1994, for example, just under 300 cases were opened and the total number of cases being processed by early 1995 was 641.[224] In 2006, 1,325 complaints were received.[225]

The Commission has a wide-ranging competence to publicise human rights matters by way of reports, studies, lectures and so forth. It may also make recommendations to states on the adoption of progressive measures in favour of human rights and conduct on-site investigations with

---

[221] See generally the *Basic Documents Pertaining to Human Rights in the Inter-American System*, Washington, 1992. The competence of the Commission to hear petitions relates to the rights in the Convention for states parties and to rights in the American Declaration for states not parties to the Convention.

[222] Note that this is far broader than the equivalent article 34 of the European Convention, which requires that the applicant be a victim.

[223] Articles 49–51. The Secretary-General of the OAS has played the role assigned in the European Convention to the Committee of Ministers.

[224] See *Annual Report 1994*, p. 39.   [225] *Annual Report 2006*, chapter III.

the consent of the state in question.[226] It provides states generally with advisory services in the human rights field and submits an annual report to the OAS General Assembly. Many special reports have been published dealing with human rights in particular states, e.g. Argentina, Bolivia, Chile, Colombia, Cuba, Dominican Republic, El Salvador, Guatemala, Haiti, Nicaragua, Paraguay, Suriname and Uruguay.[227] The Commission has also devoted attention to certain themes, such as disappearances, torture, refugees and economic and social rights.[228] Special Rapporteurs have been appointed, for example, on the rights of indigenous peoples, the rights of women and the rights of the child.[229] The Inter-American Court of Human Rights has declared that the Commission also has the authority to determine that any domestic law of a state party has violated the obligations assumed in ratifying or acceding to the Convention[230] and that the Commission may consequentially recommend that states repeal or amend the law that is in violation of the Convention. For the Commission to be able to do this, the law may have come to its attention by any means, regardless of whether or not that law is applied in any specific case before the Commission.[231] In the light of this, the Commission in 1994, for example, made a thorough study of the contempt laws (*leyes de desacato*), and concluded that many of these do not meet international human rights standards. The Commission recommended that all member states of the OAS that have such laws should repeal or amend them to bring them into line with international instruments, and with the obligations acquired

---

[226] In 1994, for example, with regard to Guatemala, Haiti, the Bahamas, Ecuador and Jamaica, see *Annual Report 1994*, pp. 21 ff., while in 2006 on-site visits were made to Haiti, Colombia, Bolivia, Dominican Republic, Brazil, Argentina and Peru, *Annual Report 2006*, chapter II C, paras. 34 ff.

[227] See *Annual Report 1994*, chapter IV, with regard to Colombia, Cuba, El Salvador and Guatemala, and *Annual Report 2006*, chapter IV, with regard to Colombia, Cuba, Haiti and Venezuela.

[228] See e.g. *Annual Report 1992–3*, pp. 539 ff. See also e.g. AG/Res.443, 1979, AG/Res.666, 1983, AG/Res.547, 1981, AG/Res.624, 1982 and AG/Res.644, 1983 (torture). In its *Annual Report 2000*, the Commission reported on migrant workers and made recommendations with regard to asylum and international crimes, and the promotion and protection of the mentally ill, chapter VI.

[229] *Annual Report 2006*, chapter II D, paras. 49 ff. See as to the Special Rapporteur for Freedom of Expression, *Annual Report 2006*, vol. II.

[230] *Some Powers of the Inter-American Commission on Human Rights*, Advisory Opinion OC-13/93 of 16 July 1993, Series A, No. 13, para. 26.

[231] *International Responsibility for Issuing and Applying Laws in Violation of the Convention*, Advisory Opinion OC-14/94 of 9 December 1994, Series A, No. 14, para. 39.

under those instruments, so as to harmonise their laws with human rights treaties.[232]

In 1985, the OAS General Assembly adopted the Inter-American Convention to Prevent and Punish Torture,[233] while in 1988 an Additional Protocol on Economic, Social and Cultural Rights was signed.[234] Under article 19 of this instrument, states parties agreed to provide periodic reports on the progressive measures undertaken to ensure respect for the rights set forth therein. Such reports go to the Secretary-General of the OAS, who sends them to the Inter-American Economic and Social Council and the Inter-American Council for Education, Science and Culture, with a copy to both the Inter-American Commission on Human Rights and the specialised agencies of the inter-American system. Violations by a state party of the rights to organise and join trades unions (article 8(a)) and to education (article 13) 'may give rise' to application of the system of individual or inter-state petition under the Inter-American Convention on Human Rights.

A Protocol on the Abolition of the Death Penalty was adopted on 8 June 1990[235] and a Convention on Forced Disappearances of Persons was adopted on 9 June 1994.[236] Under article 13 of this Convention, states parties agree that the processing of petitions or communications presented to the Inter-American Commission alleging the forced disappearance of persons will be subject to the procedures established under the Inter-American Convention on Human Rights, the Statute and Regulations of the Commission and the Statute and Rules of the Court. Particular reference is made to precautionary measures.[237] Under article 14, when

---

[232] *Annual Report 1994*, pp. 199 ff.

[233] This entered into force in February 1987. Under the Convention, states parties agree to inform the Inter-American Commission of measures taken in application of the Convention, and the Commission 'will endeavour in its annual report to analyse the existing situation in the member states of the Organisation of American States in regard to the prevention and elimination of torture', article 17.

[234] This came into force in November 1999. Eleven states parties were required for the Additional Protocol to come into force. See also L. Le Blanc, 'The Economic, Social and Cultural Rights Protocol to the American Convention and its Background', 10 NQHR, 1992, 130.

[235] This entered into force the following year. It currently has eight parties. See e.g. C. Cerna, 'US Death Penalty Tested Before the Inter-American Commission on Human Rights', 10 NQHR, 1992, p. 155.

[236] This entered into force in March 1996.

[237] Article 63(2) of the Convention states that in cases of extreme gravity and urgency, and when necessary to avoid irreparable damage to persons, the Court shall adopt such provisional measures as it deems pertinent in matters it has under consideration. With

the Commission receives a petition or communication alleging forced disappearance, its Executive Secretariat shall urgently and confidentially address the respective government and shall request that government to provide as soon as possible information as to the whereabouts of the allegedly disappeared person. The OAS also adopted the Inter-American Convention on the Prevention, Punishment and Eradication of Violence Against Women in 1994, which entered into force in March the following year. Article 10 provides that states parties are to include in their national reports to the Inter-American Commission of Women information on measures taken in this area, while under article 11, both states parties and the Commission of Women may request of the Inter-American Court advisory opinions on the interpretations of this Convention. Article 12 provides a procedure whereby any person, group of persons or any non-governmental entity legally recognised in one or more member states of the OAS may lodge petitions with the Inter-American Commission on Human Rights alleging violations of the duties of states under article 7 to pursue without delay and by all appropriate means policies to prevent, punish and eradicate violence against women.[238] The question of indigenous peoples has also been addressed and on 18 September 1995, the Inter-American Commission adopted a Draft Declaration on the Rights of Indigenous Peoples.[239]

The Commission itself consists of seven members elected in a personal capacity by the OAS General Assembly for four-year terms.[240] The Commission may indicate precautionary measures as provided for in article

---

respect to a case not yet submitted to the Court, it may act at the request of the Commission. Article 19(c) of the Statute of the Commission provides that the Commission has the power to request the Court to take such provisional measures as it considers appropriate in serious and urgent cases which have not yet been submitted to it for consideration, whenever this becomes necessary to prevent irreparable injury to persons. Under article 29 of the Regulations of the Commission, the Commission may on its own initiative or at the request of a party take any action it considers necessary for the discharge of its functions. In particular, in urgent cases, when it becomes necessary to avoid irreparable damage to persons, the Commission may request that provisional measures be taken to avoid irreparable damage in cases where the denounced facts are true. Article 24 of the Rules of Procedure of the Inter-American Court provides that at any stage of the proceeding involving cases of extreme gravity and urgency and when necessary to avoid irreparable damage to persons, the Court may, at the request of a party or on its own motion, order whatever provisional measures it deems appropriate, pursuant to article 63(2) of the Convention.

[238] Note also the Inter-American Convention on the Elimination of All Forms of Discrimination against Persons with Disabilities, 1999. This came into force in September 2001.

[239] See above, chapter 6, p. 298.   [240] See articles 34–8 of the Convention.

25 of the Commission's Rules of Procedure. This grants the Commission the power in serious and urgent cases, and whenever necessary according to the information available, either on its own initiative or upon request by a party, to request that the state concerned adopt precautionary measures to prevent irreparable harm to persons. The Commission may also request information from the interested parties related to any aspect of the adoption and observance of the precautionary measures.[241] Of particular interest has been the granting of precautionary measures in favour of individuals captured in connection with the US-led military operation against the former Taliban regime in Afghanistan and the Al-Qaida organisation and their detention at the US naval base at Guantanamo Bay, Cuba. Such measures were first granted on 12 March 2002 and requested that the United States take the 'urgent measures necessary to have the legal status of the detainees at Guantanamo determined by a competent tribunal'. The Commission considered that, without this determination, the fundamental and non-derogable rights of the detainees might not be recognised and guaranteed by the United States. Such measures were repeated on four separate occasions and amplified in response to information indicating the possible torture or other cruel, inhuman or degrading treatment or punishment of detainees at Guantanamo Bay or the possible removal of detainees to jurisdictions where they could be subjected to torture. As these measures were not complied with – the US arguing that the Commission lacked jurisdiction – the Commission adopted resolution no. 2/06 on 28 July 2006, noting that the failure of the United States to give effect to the Commission's precautionary measures had resulted in irreparable prejudice to the fundamental rights of the detainees at Guantanamo Bay, including their rights to liberty and to humane treatment, and urging the US to close the Guantanamo Bay facility without delay; to remove the detainees from Guantanamo Bay through a process undertaken in full accordance with applicable forms of international human rights and humanitarian law; to ensure that detainees who may face a risk of torture elsewhere are provided with a fair and independent examination of their circumstances and to ensure that any instances of torture at Guantanamo Bay are investigated, prosecuted and punished.[242]

---

[241] See, for recent examples, *Annual Report 2001*, chapter III C. I and *Annual Report 2006*, chapter III C I.

[242] See *Annual Report 2006*, chapter III E and see also 45 ILM, 2006, pp. 669 ff.

Where in the case of petitions received, a friendly settlement has not been achieved,[243] then under article 50 a report will be drawn up, together with such proposals and recommendations as are seen fit, and transmitted to the parties. The Commission may, under article 46 of the Rules of Procedure, adopt the follow-up measures it deems appropriate, such as requesting information from the parties and holding hearings in order to verify compliance with friendly settlement agreements and its recommendations and report thereon. It also publishes a table indicating whether its recommendations have achieved total or partial compliance from the state concerned or whether compliance is pending.[244]

After its report, a three-month period is then available during which the Commission or the state concerned (but not the individual concerned) may go to the Inter-American Court of Human Rights.[245] The Court consists of seven judges serving in an individual capacity and elected by an absolute majority of the states parties to the Convention in the OAS General Assembly for six-year terms.[246] The jurisdiction of the Court is subject to a prior declaration under article 62. Article 63(2) of the Convention provides that, in cases of extreme gravity and urgency, and when necessary to avoid irreparable damage to persons, the Court, in matters not yet submitted to it, may adopt such provisional measures as it deems pertinent in matters under its consideration. Where a case has not yet been submitted to it, the Court may act at the request of the Commission. This power has been used on a number of occasions.[247]

---

[243] See, for examples of friendly settlement procedures, *Annual Report 2001*, chapter III C. 4.

[244] See *Annual Report 2006*, chapter III D.

[245] Article 51. If this does not happen and the matter is not settled with the state concerned, the Commission by a majority vote may set forth its own opinion and conclusions on the matter, which may be published. See, for example, *Annual Report 1983–4*, pp. 23–75.

[246] Articles 52–4. See also Davidson, *Inter-American Court*; C. Cerna, 'The Structure and Functioning of the Inter-American Court of Human Rights (1979–1992)', 63 BYIL, 1992, p. 135, and L. E. Frost, 'The Evolution of the Inter-American Court of Human Rights', 14 HRQ, 1992, p. 171.

[247] The first time was in January 1988, against Honduras, following the killing of a person due to testify before it and concerns expressed about the safety of other witnesses, H/Inf. (88) 1, p. 64. See also the provisional measures adopted by the Court against Peru, in similar circumstances, in August 1990, 11 HRLJ, 1990, p. 257, and the *Alemán Lacayo* v. *Nicaragua* case, Series E, Order of 2 February 1996; the *Álvarez et al.* v. *Colombia* case, Series E, Order of 22 July 1997, and the *Constitutional Court* case, Series E, Order of 14 August 2000. See also *Hilaire and Others* v. *Trinidad and Tobago*, Judgment of 21 June 2002. The Court also granted provisional measures, for example, to protect the lives and personal integrity of witnesses in the *Mapiripán Massacre* case against Colombia, see

Under article 64, the Court also possesses an advisory jurisdiction with regard to the interpretation of the Inter-American Convention and other conventions concerning the protection of human rights in the American states at the request of any member state of the OAS. The Court has dealt with a variety of important issues by way of advisory opinions.[248] In *Definition of Other Treaties Subject to the Interpretation of the Inter-American Court*,[249] the Court took the view that the object of the Convention was to integrate the regional and universal systems of human rights protection and that, therefore, any human rights treaty to which American states were parties could be the subject of an advisory opinion. In *The Effect of Reservations*,[250] the Court stressed that human rights treaties involve the establishment of legal orders within which obligations are created towards all individuals within their jurisdiction and concluded that an instrument of ratification of adherence containing a reservation compatible with the object and purpose of the Convention does not require acceptance by the other states parties and the instrument thus enters into force as of the moment of deposit.[251] In a manner reminiscent of and clearly influenced by the European Court of Human Rights, the Inter-American Court stated that human rights treaties were different in nature from traditional multilateral treaties, since they focused not upon the reciprocal exchange of rights for the mutual benefit of the contracting states, but rather upon the protection of the basic rights of individuals. The obligations were *erga omnes*, rather than with regard to particular other states.[252]

In an important discussion of freedom of expression in the *Licensing of Journalists* case,[253] the Court advised that the compulsory licensing of journalists was incompatible with article 13, the freedom of expression provision in the Convention, if it denied any person access to the full use of the media as a means of expressing opinions. The Court emphasised that freedom of expression could only be restricted on the basis of 'compelling governmental interest' and that the restriction must be 'closely tailored

---

Annual Report of the Inter-American Court of Human Rights 2005, p. 39, and in the case of the *Children and Adolescents Deprived of Liberty in the 'Complexo do Tatuapé' of FEBEM* against Brazil, *ibid.*, p. 41.

[248] Of the nineteen advisory opinions issued between 1959 and 2005, twelve concerned the interpretation of the Convention, four concerned the interpretation of other treaties and three concerned the compatibility between domestic laws and international instruments: see *Annual Report 2005*, p. 60.

[249] 22 ILM, 1983, p. 51; 67 ILR, p. 594.   [250] 22 ILM, 1983, p.33; 67 ILR, p. 559.

[251] Para. 37. See article 74 of the Convention.   [252] *Ibid.*, para. 29. See also below, p. 937.

[253] 7 HRLJ, 1986, p. 74; 75 ILR, p. 31.

to the accomplishment of the legitimate governmental objective neces-sitating it'.[254] In the *Habeas Corpus* case,[255] the Court declared that the writ of habeas corpus was a non-suspendable 'judicial guarantee' for the protection of rights from which no derogation was permitted under the Convention under article 27. Reference was made to the 'insep-arable bond between the principle of legality, democratic institutions and the rule of law'. The Court also emphasised that only democratic govern-ments could avail themselves of the right to declare a state of emergency and then only under closely circumscribed conditions. The Court has also addressed the issue of the relationship between itself and the American Declaration of the Rights and Duties of Man, 1948 in the *Interpretation of the American Declaration* case.[256] In an opinion likely to be of signif-icance in view of the fact that, for example, the USA is not a party to the Convention but, as a member of the OAS, has signed the Declara-tion, the Court stressed that in interpreting the Declaration regard had to be had to the current state of the Inter-American system and that, by a process of authoritative interpretation, the member states of the OAS have agreed that the Declaration contains and defines the human rights norms referred to in the OAS Charter.[257] Since the Charter was a treaty, the Court could, therefore, interpret the Declaration under article 64.[258] This rather ingenious argument is likely to open the door to a variety of advisory opinions on a range of important issues.

In the *Right to Information on Consular Assistance* opinion requested by Mexico,[259] the Court declared that article 36 of the Vienna Convention on Consular Relations, 1963, providing for the right to consular assistance of detained foreign nationals,[260] was part of international human rights law and that the state must comply with its duty to inform the detainee of the rights that the article confers upon him at the time of his arrest or at least before he makes his first statement before the authorities. Further, it was held that the enforceability of the right was not subject to the protests of the sending state and that the failure to observe a detained foreign national's right to information, recognised in article 36(1)(b) of

---

[254] *Ibid.*, para. 45. See also the *Sunday Times* case, European Court of Human Rights, Series A, vol. 30, 1979.

[255] 9 HRLJ, 1988, p. 94; 96 ILR, p. 392.   [256] 28 ILM, 1989, p. 378; 96 ILR, p. 416.

[257] *Ibid.*, pp. 388–9. See also T. Buergenthal, 'The Revised OAS Charter and the Protection of Human Rights', 69 AJIL, 1975, p. 828.

[258] The problem was that the Declaration clearly was not a treaty and article 64 provides for advisory opinions regarding the Convention itself and 'other treaties'.

[259] Series A 16, OC-16/99, 1999.   [260] See further below, chapter 13, p. 773.

the Vienna Convention, was prejudicial to the due process of law. In such circumstances, imposition of the death penalty constituted a violation of the right not to be deprived of life 'arbitrarily', as stipulated in the relevant provisions of the human rights treaties,[261] involving therefore the international responsibility of the state and the duty to make reparation.

The exercise of the Court's contentious jurisdiction was, however, less immediately successful. In the *Gallardo* case,[262] the Court remitted the claim to the Commission declaring it inadmissible, noting that a state could not dispense with the processing of the case by the Commission, while in the *Velásquez Rodríguez*[263] and *Godínez Cruz*[264] cases the Court in 'disappearance' situations found that Honduras had violated the Convention.[265] In the former case, it was emphasised that states had a legal responsibility to prevent human rights violations and to use the means at their disposal to investigate and punish such violations. Where this did not happen, the state concerned had failed in its duty to ensure the full and free exercise of these rights within the jurisdiction.[266] In *Loayza Tamayo* v. *Peru*, the Court held Peru responsible for a number of breaches of the Convention concerned with the detention and torture of the applicant and for the absence of a fair trial.[267] In *Chumbipuma Aguirre* v. *Peru*, the *Barrios Altos* case, the Court tackled the issue of domestic amnesty laws and held that the Peruvian amnesty laws in question were incompatible with the Inter-American Convention and thus void of any legal effect.[268] The Court has also addressed the question of indigenous peoples in several cases, in which it has emphasised the close ties of such peoples with their traditional lands and the natural resources associated with their culture in the context particularly of the right to the use and enjoyment of property in article 21 of the Convention. It has concluded that the traditional possession of their lands by indigenous peoples has equivalent effects to those of a state-granted full property title; that traditional possession entitles indigenous peoples to demand official recognition and registration

---

[261] I.e. article 4 of the Inter-American Convention on Human Rights and article 6 of the International Covenant on Civil and Political Rights.

[262] 20 ILM, 1981, p. 1424; 67 ILR, p. 578.   [263] 9 HRLJ, 1988, p. 212; 95 ILR, p. 232.

[264] H/Inf (90) 1, p. 80; 95 ILR, p. 320 (note).

[265] Note also the award of compensation to the victims in both of these cases, *ibid.*, pp. 80–1.

[266] At paras. 174–6. See also *Castillo Páez* v. *Peru*, Series C, No. 34, 1997; 116 ILR, p. 451.

[267] Series C, No. 33, 1997; 116 ILR, p. 338.

[268] Judgment of 14 March 2001, 41 ILM, 2002, p. 93. See also generally C. Martin, 'Catching Up with the Past: Recent Decisions of the Inter-American Court of Human Rights Addressing Gross Human Rights Violations Perpetrated During the 1970–1980s', 7 *Human Rights Law Review*, 2007, p. 774.

of property titles; that members of such peoples who have been obliged to leave their traditional lands maintain property rights thereto even though they lack legal title, unless the lands have been lawfully transferred to innocent third parties; and that in the latter instance, such members are entitled to restitution thereof or to obtain other lands of equal extension and quality.[269] In the period between 1959 and 2005, the Court issued 62 orders of provisional measures, 19 advisory opinions and 139 judgments.[270]

The Banjul Charter on Human and Peoples' Rights[271]

This Charter was adopted by the Organisation of African Unity in 1981 and came into force in 1986. Currently all fifty-three members of the African Union (as the OAU was renamed in 2000) are parties.[272] The Charter contains a wide range of rights, including in addition to the traditional civil and political rights, economic, social and cultural rights and

---

[269] See e.g. *Sawhoyamaxa Indigenous Community* v. *Paraguay*, Judgment of 29 March 2006. See further above, chapter 6, p. 293.

[270] See *Annual Report 2005*, p. 57.

[271] See e.g. U. O. Umozurike, *The African Charter on Human and Peoples' Rights*, The Hague, 1997; R. Murray, *The African Commission on Human and Peoples' Rights*, London, 2000; *The African Charter on Human and Peoples' Rights* (eds. M. Evans and R. Murray), Cambridge, 2002; Rehman, *International Human Rights Law*, chapter 9; Steiner, Alston and Goodman, *International Human Rights*, p. 1062; E. Ankumah, *The African Commission on Human and Peoples' Rights*, Dordrecht, 1996; R. Gittleman, 'The African Charter on Human and Peoples' Rights: A Legal Analysis', 22 Va. JIL, 1981, p. 667; Robertson and Merrills, *Human Rights in the World*, p. 242; U. O. Umozurike, 'The Protection of Human Rights under the Banjul (African) Charter on Human and Peoples' Rights', 1 *African Journal of International Law*, 1988, p. 65; A. Bello, 'The African Charter on Human and Peoples' Rights', 194 HR, 1985, p. 5; S. Neff, 'Human Rights in Africa', 33 ICLQ, 1984, p. 331; U. O. Umozurike, 'The African Charter on Human and Peoples' Rights', 77 AJIL, 1983, p. 902; B. Ramcharan, 'The Travaux Préparatoires of the African Commission on Human Rights', HRLJ, 1992, p. 307; W. Benedek, 'The African Charter and Commission on Human and Peoples' Rights: How to Make It More Effective', 14 NQHR, 1993, p. 25; C. Flinterman and E. Ankumeh, 'The African Charter on Human and Peoples' Rights' in Hannum, *Guide to International Human Rights Practice*, p. 171; M. A. Baderin, 'Recent Developments in the African Regional Human Rights System', 5 *Human Rights Law Review*, 2005, p. 117, and C. Beyani, 'Recent Developments in the African Human Rights System 2004–2006', 7 *Human Rights Law Review*, 2007, p. 582. See also F. Ouguergouz, 'La Commission Africaine des Droits de l'Homme et des Peuples', AFDI, 1989, p. 557; K. Mbaye, *Les Droits de l'Homme en Afrique*, Paris, 1992, and M. Hamalengwa, C. Flinterman and E. Dankwa, *The International Law of Human Rights in Africa – Basic Documents and Annotated Bibliography*, Dordrecht, 1988.

[272] See www.achpr.org/english/ratifications/ratification_african%20charter.pdf.

various peoples' rights. In this latter category are specifically mentioned the rights to self-determination, development and a generally satisfactory environment.[273] The reference to the latter two concepts is unusual in human rights instruments and it remains to be seen both how they will be interpreted and how they will be implemented.

One question that is immediately posed with respect to the notion of 'peoples' rights' is to ascertain the definition of a people. If experience with the definition of self-determination in the context of the United Nations is any guide,[274] and bearing in mind the extreme sensitivity which African states have manifested with regard to the stability of the existing colonial borders,[275] then the principle is likely to be interpreted in the sense of independent states. This was confirmed in the *Katangese Peoples' Congress* v. *Zaire*,[276] where the Commission declared that Katanga was obliged to exercise a variant of self-determination that was compatible with the sovereignty and territorial integrity of Zaire.

The African Charter is the first human rights convention that details the duties of the individual to the state, society and family.[277] Included are the duties to avoid compromising the security of the state and to preserve and strengthen social and national solidarity and independence. It remains to be seen whether this distinctive approach brings with it more problems than advantages.

The Charter set up the African Commission on Human and Peoples' Rights, consisting of eleven persons appointed by the Conference of the Heads of State and Government of the OAU for six-year renewable terms, to implement the Charter. The Secretary to the Commission is appointed by the Secretary-General of the Organisation of African Unity. The Commission has important educational and promotional responsibilities,[278] including undertaking studies, organising conferences, disseminating information and making recommendations to governments. This is quite unlike the European Commission as it used to be prior to Protocol 11, but rather more similar to the Inter-American Commission. The African Commission has developed a range of special mechanisms, including the appointment of Special Rapporteurs (not being independent experts but

---

[273] See articles 19–22.   [274] See above, chapter 5, p. 256.
[275] See e.g. M. N. Shaw, *Title to Territory in Africa*, Oxford, 1986.
[276] Case No. 75/92: see 13 NQHR, 1995, p. 478.   [277] See articles 27–9.
[278] See article 45 and Rule 87 of the Rules of Procedure 1995. See also A. Bello, 'The Mandate of the African Commission on Human and Peoples' Rights', 1 *African Journal of International Law*, 1988, p. 31.

Commission members)[279] and working groups;[280] and the adoption of country and thematic resolutions.[281]

The Commission may hear as of right inter-state complaints.[282] The first such complaint was brought in 1999 by the Democratic Republic of the Congo alleging *inter alia* that it had been the victim of aggression perpetrated by Burundi, Rwanda and Uganda. The Commission held that the respondent states had contravened the principle of the peaceful settlement of disputes and had violated article 23 of the African Charter concerning the right to peace. It concluded that the three states concerned had occupied parts of the Congo in violation of the Charter and had committed a series of human rights violations as a consequence.[283]

Other, non-state, communications may also be sent to the Commission and the terminology used is far more flexible than is the case in the other regional human rights systems.[284] Where it appears that one or more communications apparently relates to special cases which reveal the existence of a series of serious or massive violations of rights, the Commission will draw the attention of the Assembly of Heads of State and Government to these special cases. The Commission may then be asked to conduct an in-depth study of these cases and make a factual report, accompanied by its finding and recommendations.[285] The Commission

---

[279] Covering topics such as the rights of women, refugees, asylum seekers and internally displaced persons in Africa; freedom of expression; human rights defenders in Africa, and prisons and conditions of detention in Africa: see e.g. Beyani, 'Recent Developments', p. 588.

[280] Covering issues such as economic, social and cultural rights; indigenous populations and communities; and the death penalty: e.g. *ibid.*, p. 589.

[281] Such as the resolutions expressing deep concern about the violation of human rights and international humanitarian law in Darfur, e.g. ACHPR/Res.74(XXXVII)05, 2005 and about the continued attacks on the independence of the judiciary by the government of Zimbabwe, e.g. resolution adopted by the Executive Council of the African Commission on Human and Peoples' Rights, 9th Ordinary Session, June 2006, Ex. CL/279 (ix), Annex III, p. 99. See also Beyani, 'Recent Developments', pp. 592 ff., and the resolution concerning the protection of human rights defenders in Africa, ACHPR/Res.69(XXXV)04, 2004.

[282] Articles 47–54. See also Rules 88 ff. of the Rules of Procedure.

[283] Communication 227/99, African Commission, *Twentieth Activity Report*, EX.CL/279 (IX), Annex IV, pp. 111 ff. See also Beyani, 'Recent Developments', pp. 598 ff.

[284] See article 55. There are a number of admissibility requirements: see article 56. For recent decisions on communications, see African Commission, *Twentieth Activity Report*.

[285] Article 58(1) and (2). Further, a case of emergency duly noted by the Commission shall be submitted to the Chairman of the Assembly of Heads of State and Government who may request an in-depth study, article 58(3).

is able to suggest provisional measures where appropriate.[286] The Commission adopted Rules of Procedure in 1988, which were amended in 1995.[287] A number of important individual communications have been dealt with.[288] In addition, there is an obligation upon states parties to produce reports every two years upon the measures taken to implement the rights under the Charter.[289] The Commission was given authority by the OAU to study the reports and make observations upon them and has indeed adopted guidelines. However, to date, it is fair to conclude that the reporting procedure has encountered serious problems, not least in that many states have failed to submit reports or adequate reports,[290] while the financial resources difficulties faced by the Commission have been significant. No provision was made for a Court in the Charter, but a Protocol on the Establishment of an African Court of Human and Peoples' Rights was signed in 1998.[291] Under this Protocol, the Court has advisory, conciliatory and contentious jurisdiction. The African Commission, states parties and African intergovernmental organisations have automatic access to the Court,[292] but not individuals or non-governmental organisations, whose access depends upon the state concerned having made

---

[286] Rule 111. See e.g. G. J. Naldi, 'Interim Measures of Protection in the African System for the Protection of Human and Peoples' Rights', 2 *African Human Rights Law Journal*, 2002, p. 1. The Commission has taken the view that the adoption of interim measures is binding on the parties: see e.g. *Saro-Wiwa* v. *Nigeria*, 7 *International Human Rights Reports*, 2000, p. 274.

[287] See 40 *The Review, International Commission of Jurists*, 1988, p. 26.

[288] See e.g. *Lawyers for Human Rights* v. *Swaziland*, Communication 251/2002, 13 *International Human Rights Reports*, 2006, p. 887, concerning the overthrow of constitutional democracy and the banning of political parties. See also *Zimbabwe Human Rights NGO Forum* v. *Zimbabwe*, African Commission, *Twenty-First Activity Report*, Annex III, pp. 54 ff. See S. Gumedz, 'Bringing Communications Before the African Commission on Human and Peoples' Rights', 3 *African Human Rights Law Journal*, 2003, p. 118.

[289] Article 62. See also Rules 81–6.

[290] See e.g. G. Oberleitner and C. Welch, 'Africa: 15th Session African Commission on Human and Peoples' Rights', 12 NQHR, 1994, p. 333; Rehman, *International Human Rights Law*, p. 255, and M. Vans, T. Ige and R. Murray, 'The Reporting Mechanism of the African Charter on Human and Peoples' Rights' in *The African Charter on Human and Peoples' Rights* (eds. M. Evans and R. Murray), Cambridge, 2002, p. 36.

[291] This came into force on 25 January 2004. Judges were elected in 2006. See e.g. D. Padilla, 'An African Human Rights Court: Reflections from the Perspective of the Inter-American System', 2 *African Human Rights Law Journal*, 2002, p. 185; R. W. Eno, 'The Jurisdiction of the African Court on Human and Peoples' Rights', 2 *African Human Rights Law Journal*, 2002, p. 223, and R. Murray, 'A Comparison Between the African and European Courts of Human Rights', 2 *African Human Rights Law Journal*, 2002, p. 195.

[292] Article 5.

a declaration accepting the jurisdiction of the Court to hear relevant applications.[293]

The Arab Charter on Human Rights[294]

An Arab Charter on Human Rights was adopted by the Council of the League of Arab States on 15 September 1994 and a revised version was adopted by the League of Arab States in May 2004. It affirms the principles contained in the UN Charter, the Universal Declaration of Human Rights, the International Covenants on Human Rights and the Cairo Declaration on Human Rights in Islam.[295] Reference is made to the national identity of the Arab states and the right to self-determination is affirmed. A number of traditional human rights are also provided for, including the right to liberty and security of persons, equality of persons before the law, fair trial, protection of persons from torture, the right to own private property, freedom to practise religious observance and freedom of peaceful assembly and association.[296] The Charter also provides for the election of a seven-person Arab Human Rights Committee to consider states' reports.[297] The Charter came into force on 24 January 2008 upon the seventh ratification.[298]

---

[293] Article 34(6).

[294] See e.g. M. Rishmawi, 'The Revised Arab Charter on Human Rights: A Step Forward?', 5 *Human Rights Law Review*, 2005, p. 361, and R. K. M. Smith, *Textbook on International Human Rights*, Oxford, 2002, p. 87. See also Robertson and Merrills, *Human Rights in the World*, p. 238, and A. A. A. Naim, 'Human Rights in the Arab World: A Legal Perspective', 23 HRQ, 2001, p. 70.

[295] Adopted in 1990 by the Nineteenth Islamic Conference of Foreign Ministers. This Declaration emphasises that all rights and freedoms provided for are subject to Islamic Shari'ah (article 24), which is also 'the only source of reference for the explanation or clarification of any of the articles in the Declaration' (article 25).

[296] Articles 8, 11, 12, 13, 14, 30, 31 and 35. The right to development is proclaimed as a fundamental human right, see article 37.

[297] Articles 45 and 48.

[298] Note, however, the statement by the UN High Commissioner for Human Rights expressing concern with regard to the incompatibility of some of the provisions of the Arab Charter with international norms and standards. These concerns included the approach to the death penalty for children and the rights of women and non-citizens. The High Commissioner also noted that in equating Zionism with racism, the Arab Charter was 'not in conformity with General Assembly resolution 46/86, which rejects that Zionism is a form of racism and racial discrimination': see statement of 30 January 2008, www.unhchr.ch/huricane/huricane.nsf/0/6C211162E43235FAC12573E00056E19D? opendocument.

Suggestions for further reading

The *African Charter on Human and Peoples' Rights* (eds. M. Evans and R. Murray), Cambridge, 2002

Guide to International Human Rights Practice (ed. H. Hannum), 4th edn, Ardsley, 2004

Jacobs and White: The European Convention on Human Rights (eds. C. Ovey and R. C. A. White), 4th edn, Oxford, 2006

J. M. Pasqualucci, *The Practice and Procedure of the Inter-American Court of Human Rights*, Cambridge, 2003

H. J. Steiner, P. Alston and R. Goodman, *International Human Rights in Context*, 3rd edn, Oxford, 2008

P. Van Dijk, G. J. H. Van Hoof, A. Van Rijn and L. Zwaak, *Theory and Practice of the European Convention on Human Rights*, 4th edn, Antwerp, 2006

8

Individual criminal responsibility in international law[1]

The rise of individual criminal responsibility directly under international law marks the coming together of elements of traditional international law with more modern approaches to human rights law and humanitarian law, and involves consideration of domestic as well as international enforcement mechanisms. Although the rights of individuals in international law have evolved significantly in the post-1945 era, the placing of obligations directly upon persons as opposed to states has a distinct, if narrow, pedigree.[2] Those committing piracy or slave trading[3] have long been regarded as guilty of crimes against international society bearing direct responsibility, for which they may be punished by international tribunals or by any state at all. Jurisdiction to hear the offence is not confined to, for example, the state on whose territory the act took place, or the national state of the offender or the victim. This universal jurisdiction over piracy constitutes a long-established principle of the world community.[4]

---

[1] See e.g. A. Cassese, *International Criminal Law*, 2nd edn, Oxford, 2008; W. Schabas, *An Introduction to the International Criminal Court*, 3rd edn, Cambridge, 2007; R. Cryer, H. Friman, D. Robinson and E. Wilmshurst, *An Introduction to International Criminal Law and Procedure*, Cambridge, 2007; I. Bantekas and S. Nash, *International Criminal Law*, 2nd edn, London, 2003; G. Werle, *Principles of International Criminal Law*, The Hague, 2005; C. de Than and E. Shorts, *International Criminal Law and Human Rights*, London, 2003; S. R. Ratner and J. Abrams, *Accountability for Human Rights Atrocities in International Law: Beyond the Nuremberg Legacy*, 2nd edn, Oxford, 2001; K. Kittichaisaree, *International Criminal Law*, Oxford, 2001, and *Justice for Crimes Against Humanity* (eds. M. Lattimer and P. Sands), Oxford, 2003.

[2] See e.g. M. C. Bassiouni, *Crimes Against Humanity in International Criminal Law*, 2nd edn, The Hague, 1999. As to state responsibility for international offences, see below, chapter 14.

[3] See as to slave trading, article 99 of the Law of the Sea Convention, 1982 and below, chapter 11, p. 616.

[4] See e.g. *In re Piracy Jure Gentium* [1934] AC 586; 7 AD, p. 213. See also D. H. Johnson, 'Piracy in Modern International Law', 43 *Transactions of the Grotius Society*, 1957, p. 63, and G. E. White, 'The Marshall Court and International Law: The Piracy Cases', 83 AJIL, 1989, p. 727. See also the Separate Opinion of Judge Guillaume in *Congo* v. *Belgium*, ICJ

All states may both arrest and punish pirates, provided of course that they have been apprehended on the high seas[5] or within the territory of the state concerned. The punishment of the offenders takes place whatever their nationality and wherever they happened to carry out their criminal activities.

Piracy under international law (or piracy *jure gentium*) must be distinguished from piracy under municipal law. Offences that may be characterised as piratical under municipal laws do not necessarily fall within the definition of piracy in international law, and thus are not susceptible to universal jurisdiction (depending of course upon the content and form of international conventions). Piracy *jure gentium* was defined in article 15 of the High Seas Convention, 1958 (and reaffirmed in article 101 of the 1982 Convention on the Law of the Sea) as illegal acts of violence, detention or depredation committed for private ends by the crew or passengers of a private ship or private aircraft and directed against another ship or aircraft (or persons or property therein) on the high seas or *terra nullius*.[6] Attempts to commit such acts are sufficient to constitute piracy and it is not essential for the attempt to have been successful.[7]

However, the range of offences under international law for which individuals bore international responsibility was narrow indeed.[8] It is doubtful whether it had extended beyond piracy and slave trading by the turn of the twentieth century. Even then, jurisdiction was exercisable in practice only by domestic courts. It is a modern phenomenon to establish international courts or tribunals to exercise jurisdiction directly over individuals with regard to specified crimes. As will be seen in chapter 12, domestic courts are indeed exercising a greater jurisdiction with regard to offences with international elements, for example, with regard to torture or war crimes committed outside of the territory of the state concerned provided that the alleged offender is within the territory of the state, but this is only where an international treaty authorises states to exercise such

---

Reports, 2002, pp. 3, 37–8; 128 ILR, pp. 60, 92–4, and *R* v. *Jones* [2006] UKHL 16; 132 ILR, p. 668.

[5] Article 105 of the Law of the Sea Convention, 1982 (reproducing article 19 of the Geneva Convention on the High Seas, 1958).

[6] See further below, chapter 11, p. 615.

[7] *In re Piracy Jure Gentium* [1934] AC 586; 7 AD, p. 213.

[8] See the advisory opinion of the Inter-American Court of Human Rights in the *Re-Introduction of the Death Penalty in the Peruvian Constitution* case, 16 HRLJ, 1995, pp. 9, 14, noting that individual responsibility may only be invoked for violations that are defined in international instruments as crimes under international law.

jurisdiction and this has been brought into effect internally.[9] However, the focus of this chapter is upon courts established internationally or with an international element in order to prosecute individuals directly accused of international offences.

International criminal courts and tribunals

After the conclusion of the First World War, a commission set up by the Allied Powers recommended that as the defeated powers had violated the laws of war, high officials, including the Kaiser, be prosecuted for ordering such crimes and on the basis of command responsibility. It was also suggested that an Allied High Tribunal be established to try violations of the laws and customs of war and the laws of humanity.[10] Accordingly, the Treaty of Versailles, 1919 noted that the German government recognised the right of the Allied and Associated Powers to bring individuals accused of crimes against the laws and customs of war before military tribunals (article 228) and established the individual responsibility of the Kaiser (article 227). In the event, the Netherlands refused to hand over the Kaiser and only a few trials were held before German courts in Leipzig with, at best, mixed results.[11]

The Charter annexed to the Agreement for the Prosecution and Punishment of the Major War Criminals, 1945 provided specifically for individual responsibility for crimes against peace, war crimes and crimes against humanity. There was also a conspiracy charge.[12] The Nuremberg Tribunal, composed of four principal judges (from the US, UK, USSR and France) and four alternates, was the first international criminal

---

[9] See below, p. 673.

[10] See the Report of the Commission to the Preliminary Peace Conference, 14 AJIL, 1920, p. 95. See also Cryer *et al.*, *Introduction to International Criminal Law*, pp. 91–2, and T. Meron, 'Reflections on the Prosecution of War Crimes by International Tribunals', 100 AJIL, 2006, p. 551.

[11] See C. Mullins, *The Leipzig Trials*, London, 1921. See also e.g. the International Convention for the Protection of Submarine Telegraph Cables, 1884; the Agreement for the Suppression of the Circulation of Obscene Publications, 1910; the International Convention for the Suppression of the Circulation of and Traffic in Obscene Publications 1924; the Agreement Concerning the Suppression of Opium-Smoking, 1931; the Convention for the Suppression of the Illicit Traffic in Dangerous Drugs, 1936, and the International Convention for the Suppression of Counterfeiting Currency, 1929 with regard to the establishment of individual responsibility in the case of specific issues.

[12] See article 6, 39 AJIL, 1945, Supp., p. 259. See also H. Lauterpacht, *International Law and Human Rights*, London, 1950, p. 6, and Cryer *et al.*, *Introduction to International Criminal Law*, pp. 92 ff.

tribunal and marks the true starting-point for international criminal law. It affirmed in ringing and lasting terms that 'international law imposes duties and liabilities upon individuals as well as upon states' as 'crimes against international law are committed by men, not by abstract entities, and only by punishing individuals who commit such crimes can the provisions of international law be enforced'. Included in the relevant category for which individual responsibility was posited were crimes against peace, war crimes and crimes against humanity.[13] In addition, a number of war crimes trials were instituted within Allied-occupied Germany under the authority of Control Council Law No. 10.[14] The International Military Tribunal for the Far East was established in January 1946 to deal with Japanese war crimes.[15] This Tribunal was composed of judges from eleven states[16] and it essentially reaffirmed the Nuremberg Tribunal's legal findings as to, for example, the criminality of aggressive war and the rejection of the absolute defence of superior orders.[17] The Charter of the Tribunal also provided for individual responsibility with regard to certain crimes.[18]

The provisions of the Nuremberg Charter can now be regarded as part of international law, particularly since the General Assembly in 1946 affirmed the principles of this Charter and the decision of the Tribunal.[19] The Assembly also stated that genocide was a crime under international

---

[13] See 41 AJIL, 1947, p. 220. See also I. Brownlie, *International Law and the Use of Force by States*, Oxford, 1963, p. 167; T. Taylor, *An Anatomy of the Nuremberg Trial*, London, 1993, and A. Tusa and J. Tusa, *The Nuremberg Trial*, London, 1983.

[14] 36 ILR, p. 31. Twelve major US trials took place in Nuremberg, see H. Levie, *Terrorism in War: The Law of War Crimes*, New York, 1992, pp. 72 ff., while trials took place in the British occupied sector of Germany under the Royal Warrant of 1946, see A. P. V. Rogers, 'War Crimes Trials under the Royal Warrant, British Practice 1945–1949', 39 ICLQ, 1990, p. 780, and see also *R v. Jones* [2006] UKHL 16, para. 22 (Lord Bingham); 132 ILR, p. 679, and *Re Sandrock and Others* 13 ILR, p. 297.

[15] Established by a proclamation by General MacArthur of 19 January 1946, so authorised by the Allied Powers in order to implement the Potsdam Declaration: see *Hirota v. MacArthur* 335 US 876 and TIAS, 1946, No. 1589, p. 3; 15 AD, p. 485.

[16] US, UK, USSR, Australia, Canada, China, France, India, the Netherlands, New Zealand and the Philippines.

[17] See e.g. B. V. A. Röling and A. Cassese, *The Tokyo Trial and Beyond*, Cambridge, 1992, and S. Horowitz, *The Tokyo Trial*, International Conciliation No. 465 (1950). But see as to criticisms of the process, R. Minear, *Victor's Justice: The Tokyo War Crimes Trial*, Princeton, 1971.

[18] Article 5.

[19] Resolution 95(I). See also the International Law Commission's Report on Principles of the Nuremberg Tribunal, *Yearbook of the ILC*, 1950, vol. II, p. 195, and the Convention on the Non-Applicability of Statutory Limitations to War Crimes and Crimes Against Humanity, 1968.

law bearing individual responsibility.[20] This was reaffirmed in the Genocide Convention of 1948, which also called for prosecutions by either domestic courts or 'an international penal tribunal'.[21] The International Law Commission produced a Draft Code of Offences against the Peace and Security of Mankind in 1954, article 1 of which provided that 'offences against the peace and security of mankind, as defined in this Code, are crimes under international law, for which the responsible individuals shall be punishable'.[22]

Individual responsibility has also been confirmed with regard to grave breaches of the four 1949 Geneva Red Cross Conventions and 1977 Additional Protocols I and II dealing with armed conflicts. It is provided specifically that the High Contracting Parties undertake to enact any legislation necessary to provide effective penal sanctions for persons committing or ordering to be committed any of a series of grave breaches.[23] Such grave breaches include wilful killing, torture or inhuman treatment, extensive destruction and appropriation of property not justified by military necessity and carried out unlawfully and wantonly, unlawful deportation or transfer of protected persons and the taking of hostages.[24] Protocol I of 1977 extends the list to include, for example, making the civilian population the object of attack and launching an attack against works or installations containing dangerous forces in the knowledge that such attack will cause excessive loss of life or damage to civilians or their property when committed wilfully and causing death or serious injury; other activities such as transferring civilian population from the territory of an occupying power to that of an occupied area or deporting from an occupied area, apartheid and racial discrimination and attacking clearly recognised historic monuments, works of art or places of worship, may also constitute grave breaches when committed wilfully.[25]

---

[20] Resolution 96(1).

[21] Note that the International Convention on the Suppression and Punishment of the Crime of Apartheid of 1973 declared apartheid to be an international crime involving direct individual criminal responsibility.

[22] A/2693, and 45 AJIL, 1954, Supp., p. 123.

[23] See article 49 of the First Geneva Convention, article 50 of the Second Geneva Convention, article 129 of the Third Geneva Convention and article 146 of the Fourth Geneva Convention. See further below, chapter 21, p. 1199.

[24] See e.g. article 50 of the First Geneva Convention, article 51 of the Second Geneva Convention, article 130 of the Third Geneva Convention and article 147 of the Fourth Geneva Convention. See also L. C. Green, *The Contemporary Law of Armed Conflict*, 2nd edn, Manchester, 2000, chapter 18.

[25] See article 85 of Protocol I.

Any individual, regardless of rank or governmental status, would be personally liable for any war crimes or grave breaches committed, while the principle of command (or superior) responsibility means that any person in a position of authority ordering the commission of a war crime or grave breach would be as accountable as the subordinate committing it.[26] The International Law Commission in 1991 provisionally adopted a Draft Code of Crimes Against the Peace and Security of Mankind,[27] which was revised in 1996.[28] The 1996 Draft Code provides for individual criminal responsibility[29] with regard to aggression,[30] genocide,[31] a crime against humanity,[32] a crime against United Nations and associated personnel[33] and war crimes.[34] The fact that an individual may be responsible for the crimes in question is deemed not to affect the issue of state responsibility.[35] The Security Council in two resolutions on the Somali situation in the early 1990s unanimously condemned breaches of humanitarian law and stated that the authors of such breaches or those who had ordered their commission would be held 'individually responsible' for them,[36] while Security Council resolution 674 (1990) concerning Iraq's occupation of Kuwait, reaffirming Iraq's liability under the Fourth Geneva Convention, 1949 dealing with civilian populations of occupied areas, noted that such responsibility for grave breaches extended to 'individuals who commit or order the commission of grave breaches'.[37]

The International Criminal Tribunal for the Former Yugoslavia (ICTY)[38]

It was, however, the events in the former Yugoslavia that impelled a renewal of interest in the establishment of an international criminal court, which had long been under consideration, but in a desultory fashion.[39]

---

[26] See further below, pp. 404 and 408.   [27] A/46/10 and 30 ILM, 1991, p. 1584.
[28] A/51/10, p. 9.   [29] See article 2.   [30] See article 16.   [31] Article 17.
[32] Article 18.   [33] Article 19.   [34] Article 20.   [35] Article 4.
[36] Resolutions 794 (1992) and 814 (1993).
[37] See also e.g. the Special Section on Iraqi War Crimes, 31 Va. JIL, 1991, p. 351.
[38] See e.g. W. Schabas, *The UN International Criminal Tribunals: The Former Yugoslavia, Rwanda and Sierra Leone*, Cambridge, 2006; V. Morris and M. P. Scharf, *An Insider's Guide to the International Criminal Tribunal for Former Yugoslavia*, New York, 1995; R. Kerr, *The International Criminal Tribunal for Former Yugoslavia: An Exercise in Law, Politics and Diplomacy*, Oxford, 2004; the series of articles on the ICTY published in 2 *Journal of International Criminal Justice*, 2004, pp. 353 ff. and 37 *New England Law Review*, 2002–3, pp. 865 ff.
[39] See e.g. B. Ferencz, 'An International Criminal Code and Court: Where They Stand and Where They're Going', 30 *Columbia Journal of Transnational Law*, 1992, p. 375.

The Yugoslav experience, and the Rwanda massacres of 1994, led to the establishment of two specific war crimes tribunals by the use of the authority of the UN Security Council to adopt decisions binding upon all member states of the organisation under Chapter VII of the Charter, rather than by an international conference as was to be the case with the International Criminal Court. This method was used in order both to enable the tribunal in question to come into operation as quickly as possible and to ensure that the parties most closely associated with the subject-matter of the war crimes alleged should be bound in a manner not dependent upon their consent (as would be necessary in the case of a court established by international agreement). The establishment of the Tribunal was preceded by a series of steps. In Security Council resolutions 764 (1992), 771 (1992) and 820 (1993) grave concern was expressed with regard to breaches of international humanitarian law and the responsibilities of the parties were reaffirmed. In particular, individual responsibility for the commission of grave breaches of the 1949 Conventions was emphasised. Under resolution 780 (1992), the Security Council established an impartial Commission of Experts to examine and analyse information concerning evidence of grave breaches of the Geneva Conventions and other violations of international humanitarian law committed in the territory of the former Yugoslavia. The Commission produced a report in early 1993 in which it concluded that grave breaches and other violations of international humanitarian law had been committed in the territory of the former Yugoslavia, including wilful killing, 'ethnic cleansing', mass killings, torture, rape, pillage and destruction of civilian property, the destruction of cultural and religious property and arbitrary arrests.[40]

The Security Council then adopted resolution 808 (1993) calling for the establishment of an international tribunal to prosecute 'persons responsible for serious violations of international humanitarian law committed in the territory of the former Yugoslavia since 1991'. The Secretary-General of the UN produced a report incorporating a draft statute and commentary,[41] which was adopted by the Security Council in resolution 827 (1993) acting under Chapter VII of the UN Charter.[42]

---

[40] See S/25274. See also M.C. Bassiouni, 'The United Nations Commission of Experts Established Pursuant to Security Council Resolution 780 (1992)', 88 AJIL, 1994, p. 784.
[41] S/25704 (1993).
[42] The Statute has been subsequently amended: see Security Council resolutions 1166 (1998), 1329 (2000), 1411 (2002), 1431 (2002), 1481 (2003), 1597 (2005) and 1660 (2006).

The Tribunal has the power to prosecute persons responsible for serious violations of international humanitarian law committed in the territory of the former Yugoslavia since 1991 (articles 1 and 8 of the Statute). The absence of a closing date meant that the later conflict in Kosovo could be the subject of prosecutions.[43] The Tribunal consists of three main organs: the Registry, the office of the Prosecutor and the Chambers.[44] The Registry is the administrative body,[45] while the Office of the Prosecutor is responsible for investigations, issuing of indictments and bringing matters to trial. There are currently three Trial Chambers, each consisting of a presiding judge and two other judges, and an Appeals Chamber, consisting of seven members but sitting in a panel of five, headed by a President. Of the seven, five come from the ICTY and two from the International Criminal Tribunal for Rwanda.[46] The Chambers have a maximum of sixteen permanent judges and a maximum of twelve *ad litem* judges drawn from a pool of twenty-seven such judges elected by the General Assembly for four-year renewable terms.[47]

Articles 2 to 5 of the Statute lay down the crimes with regard to which the Tribunal can exercise jurisdiction. These are: grave breaches of the Geneva Conventions of 1949, violation of the laws or customs of war, genocide and crimes against humanity.[48]

Article 7 establishes that persons who 'planned, instigated, ordered, committed or otherwise aided and abetted in the planning, preparation or execution' of crimes listed in articles 2 to 5 shall be individually responsible for the crime. This article also provides that the official position of any accused person is not to relieve a person of criminal responsibility nor mitigate punishment, while the fact that a subordinate committed the crime is not to relieve a superior of responsibility if the latter knew or had reason to know that the subordinate was about to or had committed the crime and the superior failed to take the necessary and reasonable measures to prevent the acts or to punish the perpetrators thereof. It is also stipulated that the fact that an accused person acted pursuant to an order of a government or of a superior will not relieve him of criminal responsibility, although this may constitute a mitigating factor if the Tribunal determines that justice so requires. The Appeals Chamber of the Tribunal

---

[43] See Security Council resolution 1160 (1998) and *Milutinović*, ICTY, A. Ch. 8 June 2004. See also as to events in the Former Yugoslav Republic of Macedonia, *In re: The Republic of Macedonia I*, ICTY, T. Ch. 4 October 2002.
[44] Article 11.   [45] Article 17.   [46] Article 14.
[47] Articles 12 and 13.   [48] See further below, p. 430.

in the *Tadić* case confirmed that customary international law had imposed criminal responsibility for serious violations of humanitarian law governing internal as well as international armed conflicts.[49]

The Tribunal and national courts have concurrent jurisdiction with regard to the prosecution of relevant accused persons, but the Tribunal has primacy over national courts, so that the former may request the latter to defer to its competence.[50] States are obliged to co-operate with the International Tribunal in the investigation and prosecution of persons accused of committing serious violations of international humanitarian law and must comply without undue delay with any request for assistance or an order issued by a Trial Chamber, including the identification and location of persons; the taking of testimony and the production of evidence; the arrest or detention of persons; and the surrender or the transfer of the accused to the International Tribunal.[51] No person may be tried by a national court for acts constituting serious violations of international humanitarian law under the Statute, for which he or she has already been tried by the International Tribunal, but the Tribunal may try a person for relevant acts after trial by a national court where the act for which he or she was tried was characterised as an ordinary crime; or where the national court proceedings were not impartial or independent, were designed to shield the accused from international criminal responsibility, or the case was not diligently prosecuted.[52]

Investigations into alleged offences under the Statute are initiated by the Prosecutor either *ex officio* or on the basis of information obtained from any source, particularly from governments, United Nations organs, intergovernmental and non-governmental organisations. Information received is assessed by the Prosecutor, who then decides whether there is a sufficient basis to proceed. The Prosecutor may question suspects, victims and witnesses, collect evidence and conduct on-site investigations.

---

[49] See IT-94-1-AR72, 2 October 1995, p. 70; 105 ILR, p. 419. See further below, chapter 21, p. 1194.

[50] Article 9. Under Rule 9 of the Rules of Procedure and Evidence as amended, deferral of national proceedings may be requested where the act being investigated or which is the subject of those proceedings is characterised as an ordinary crime; or there is a lack of impartiality or independence, or the investigations or proceedings are designed to shield the accused from international criminal responsibility, or the case is not diligently prosecuted; or what is in issue is closely related to, or otherwise involves, significant factual or legal questions which may have implications for investigations or prosecutions before the Tribunal. See as to the different situation with regard to the International Criminal Court, below, p. 410.

[51] Article 29.   [52] Article 10.

Where it is determined that a *prima facie* case exists, the Prosecutor shall prepare an indictment containing a concise statement of the facts and the crime or crimes with which the accused is charged, and this indictment is then transmitted to a judge of the Trial Chamber, who will review it. If satisfied that a *prima facie* case has been established by the Prosecutor, the judge will confirm the indictment. If not so satisfied, the indictment shall be dismissed. Upon confirmation of an indictment, the judge may, at the request of the Prosecutor, issue such orders and warrants for the arrest, detention, surrender or transfer of persons, and any other orders as may be required for the conduct of the trial. It will then be for the Trial Chambers to ensure that the trial is fair and expeditious and that proceedings are conducted in accordance with the rules of procedure and evidence, with full respect for the rights of the accused and due regard for the protection of victims and witnesses.[53] Judgment will then be reached by the Trial Chamber concerned and punishment, limited to imprisonment, imposed upon conviction.[54] Appeal is to the Appeals Chamber on the grounds either of an error of law invalidating the decision or of an error of fact occasioning a miscarriage of justice. The Appeals Chamber may affirm, reverse or revise the decisions taken by the Trial Chambers.[55]

The Tribunal has dealt with a number of significant issues.[56] In an early case, the Appeal Chamber held that it had the power to review the question of the legality of the establishment of the Tribunal and noted that the Security Council had adopted a decision under Chapter VII of the UN Charter binding on all member states to create the Tribunal in the framework of the restoration of international peace and security.[57]

As of early March 2008, the Tribunal had issued 161 indictments; 111 proceedings had been concluded, with regard to which 53 individuals had been sentenced, 9 acquitted and 36 indictments withdrawn (including where the accused had died). Four persons indicted were still at large, including Radovan Karadžić and Ratko Mladić, the leaders of the Bosnian Serbs during the war.[58] However, the UN Security Council has

---

[53] Articles 18–20.   [54] Article 24.   [55] Article 25.   [56] See further below, pp. 435 ff.

[57] *Tadić*, IT-94-1-AR72, 2 October 1995, p. 70, paras. 30 ff.; 105 ILR, p. 419. After this decision, the Dayton Peace Agreement was signed, which includes the obligation placed upon all states of the former Yugoslavia to co-operate with the Tribunal: see Article X, Annex 1-A.

[58] See www.un.org/icty/glance-e/index.htm. Note the death in custody of the Yugoslav President Slobodan Milošević on 11 March 2006 during his trial on sixty-six counts of violations of the Statute including genocide: see ICTY Annual Report 2006, A/61/271 – S/2006/666, para. 55. After the text above was written, Radovan Karadžić was arrested in Belgrade and sent to the Tribunal, who assigned his case to a Trial Chamber: see IT-95-5/18-I, 22 July 2008.

confirmed a completion strategy which is intended to ensure a phased and co-ordinated completion of the Tribunal's mission by the end of 2010.[59] Under this strategy, the ICTY has concentrated on the prosecution and trial of the most senior leaders while referring other cases involving intermediate and lower-rank accused to national courts. Two main categories of cases have been referred to national courts in the region of the former Yugoslavia, being those cases that were investigated to different levels by the Tribunal's Prosecution which did not result in the issuance of an indictment by the ICTY and the small number of cases that were investigated by the Tribunal's Prosecution and that resulted in the confirmation of indictments by the Tribunal and the transfer of accused persons to the Tribunal's custody. Cases began to be transferred to the national courts of successor states to the former Yugoslavia, particularly Bosnia and Croatia, in 2005.[60] By mid-2007, thirteen 'lower to mid-level accused' had been transferred to local courts.[61]

The International Criminal Tribunal for Rwanda (ICTR)[62]

Following events in Rwanda during 1994 and the mass slaughter that took place, the Security Council decided in resolution 955 (1994) to establish an International Criminal Tribunal for Rwanda, with the power to prosecute persons responsible for serious violations of international humanitarian law. The Statute of this Tribunal was annexed to the body of the Security Council resolution and bears many similarities to the Statute of the Yugoslav Tribunal.

---

[59] See resolutions 1503 (2003) and 1534 (2004). Under the resolutions the Trial Chambers were required to complete their business by 2008 and the Appeals Chamber by 2010. See also D. Raab, 'Evaluating the ICTY and Its Completion Strategy', 3 *Journal of International Criminal Justice*, 2005, p. 82.

[60] See M. Bohlander, 'Referring an Indictment from the ICTY and ICTR to Another Court – Rule 11 *bis* and the Consequences for the Law of Extradition', 55 ICLQ, 2006, p. 219. See also below, pp. 409 ff.

[61] See ICTY Annual Report 2007, A/62/172 – S/2007/469, para. 10.

[62] See e.g. UN Secretary-General Reports S/1994/879 and S/1994/906 and the Report of the Special Rapporteur for Rwanda of the UN Commission on Human Rights, S/1994/1157, annex I and annex II, and the Report of the Commission of Experts, S/1994/1125. See also V. Morris and M. P. Scharf, *The International Criminal Tribunal for Rwanda*, New York, 1998; L. J. van den Herik, *The Contribution of the Rwanda Tribunal to the Development of International Law*, The Hague, 2005; L. Sunga, 'The Commission of Experts on Rwanda and the Creation of the International Criminal Tribunal for Rwanda', 16 HRLJ, 1995, p. 121, and R. S. Lee, 'The Rwanda Tribunal', 9 *Leiden Journal of International Law*, 1996, p. 37.

The Rwanda Tribunal consists of three Trial Chambers, an Office of the Prosecutor and a Registry with the same functions as those of the Yugoslav Tribunal.[63] The Chambers are composed of sixteen permanent independent judges, no two of whom may be nationals of the same state, and a maximum at any one time of nine *ad litem* independent judges. The ICTR and the ICTY share a joint Appeals Chamber, two members of whom are members of the Rwanda Tribunal.[64]

Articles 2 to 4 stipulate the crimes over which the Tribunal has jurisdiction. Article 2 deals with genocide; article 3 with crimes against humanity, being the crimes of (a) murder; (b) extermination; (c) enslavement; (d) deportation; (e) imprisonment; (f) torture; (g) rape; (h) persecutions on political, racial and religious grounds; and (i) other inhumane acts, when committed as part of a widespread or systematic attack against any civilian population on national, political, ethnic, racial or religious grounds; and article 4 deals with violations of article 3 common to the Geneva Conventions and of Additional Protocol II.[65] Article 6 provides for individual criminal responsibility with regard to persons planning, ordering, committing or aiding the crimes listed, while provisions similar to the Statute of the Yugoslav Tribunal with regard to the absence of immunity for persons holding official positions, command responsibility and superior orders apply.

The Tribunal has jurisdiction with regard to serious violations of international humanitarian law committed in the territory of Rwanda and Rwandan citizens responsible for such violations committed in the territory of neighbouring states between 1 January 1994 and 31 December 1994.[66] As is the case with the ICTY, the ICTR has concurrent jurisdiction with national courts and has primacy over national courts of all states, while at any stage of the procedure, the Tribunal may formally request national courts to defer to its competence.[67] Similarly, no person may be tried before a national court for acts constituting serious violations of international humanitarian law under the present Statute, for which he or she has already been tried by the International Criminal Tribunal for Rwanda, while a person who has been tried before a national court for acts constituting serious violations of international humanitarian law may be subsequently tried by the Tribunal only if either the act for which

---

[63] Article 10.
[64] See Security Council resolution 1329 (2000). The two Tribunals shared a Prosecutor until a separate Prosecutor was appointed to the ICTR in 2003; see Security Council resolution 1503 (2003).
[65] See below, chapter 21, p. 1194.   [66] Article 7.   [67] Article 8.

he or she was tried was characterised as an ordinary crime; or the national court proceedings were not impartial or independent, were designed to shield the accused from international criminal responsibility, or the case was not diligently prosecuted.[68]

After several difficult early years, during which problems of misman-agement with regard to the Office of the Prosecutor and the Registry predominated,[69] the Tribunal began to produce some significant deci-sions. These commenced with the *Kambanda* case,[70] which was the first time that a former head of government was convicted for the crime of genocide (after having pleaded guilty), and the *Akayesu* case,[71] in which for the first time an international tribunal was called upon to interpret the definition of genocide in the Genocide Convention, 1948 and to define the crime of rape in international law. However, the rate of progress has been disappointing and tensions with Rwanda have surfaced from time to time.[72]

As in the case of the ICTY, the Rwanda Tribunal has formulated a completion strategy, which has been affirmed by Security Council reso-lutions 1503 (2003) and 1534 (2004), although it had in 2002 adopted Rule 11 *bis* of the Rules of Procedure permitting the transfer of cases to national jurisdictions. The Security Council, as with the ICTY, increased the number of *ad litem* judges and various other management decisions were taken. A separate Prosecutor for the ICTR was appointed in 2003. Attention was focused upon the prosecution of individuals who allegedly were in positions of leadership, and those who allegedly bore the greatest responsibility for the genocide, while the Prosecutor is continuously re-viewing his files to determine which cases may be suitable for referral to national jurisdictions for trial. Such decision is for judicial determination. The Prosecutor also holds discussions with states, including Rwanda, re-garding the referral of cases to national jurisdictions for trial, in particular with respect to accused persons who were investigated but not indicted by his office. Considerations of fair trial in the state concerned are also a relevant factor, as well as the alleged status and extent of participation of the individual during the genocide, the alleged connection that the individual may have had with other cases, the need to cover the major geographical areas of Rwanda, the availability of evidence with regard to

---

[68] Article 9.

[69] See e.g. Report of the Secretary-General on the Activities of the Office of Internal Oversight Services, A/51/789 and ICTR Annual Report 1997, A/52/582 – S/1997/868.

[70] ICTR T. Ch. 4 September 1998.   [71] ICTR T. Ch. 1 2 September 1998.

[72] As of May 2007, twenty-seven judgments, involving thirty-three accused, had been ren-dered: see ICTR Annual Report 2007, A/62/284 – S/007/502.

the individual concerned and the availability of investigative material for transmission to a state for national prosecution.[73]

The International Criminal Court (ICC)[74]

Article VI of the Genocide Convention, 1948 provided for persons charged with genocide to be tried either by a court in the territory where the act had been committed or by an 'international penal tribunal' to be established. The International Law Commission was asked to study the possibility of the establishment of such an international court and a report was produced.[75] The matter was then transmitted to the General Assembly which produced a draft statute.[76] However, the question was postponed until a definition of aggression had been achieved and the draft Code of Offences completed. Due primarily to political reasons, no further progress was made until Trinidad and Tobago proposed the creation of a permanent international criminal court to deal with drug trafficking in 1989. Given additional urgency by the developing Yugoslav situation in the early 1990s, the International Law Commission adopted a Draft Statute for an International Criminal Court in 1994.[77] This draft statute proposed that an international criminal court be established with jurisdiction not only over genocide, war crimes, crimes against humanity and aggression, but also over certain 'treaty crimes' such as terrorism and drugs offences found in UN conventions. The draft statute was also less expansive than the International Criminal Court Statute proved to be in a number of ways, including not providing for the Prosecutor to initiate investigations on his or her own authority. However, the ILC draft proved very

[73] See Report on the Completion Strategy of the ICTR 2007, S/2007/676, paras. 32 ff. Of the fourteen indicted persons still at large, five have been earmarked for trial at the Tribunal on the basis of the leadership roles they played during the 1994 genocide, *ibid.*, para. 38.

[74] See e.g. Schabas, *International Criminal Court*; *The Permanent International Criminal Court: Legal and Policy Issues* (eds. D. McGoldrick, P. Rowe and E. Donelly), Oxford, 2004; *The Rome Statute of the International Criminal Court* (eds. A. Cassese, P. Gaeta and J. R. W. D. Jones), Oxford, 2002; M. C. Bassiouni, 'The Permanent International Criminal Court' in Lattimer and Sands, *Justice for Crimes Against Humanity*, p. 173; B. Broomhall, *International Justice and the International Criminal Court: Between Sovereignty and the Rule of Law*, Oxford, 2003, and *The International Criminal Court: The Making of the Rome Statute* (ed. R. Lee), The Hague, 1999.

[75] See General Assembly resolution 260 (III) B and A/CN.4/15 and A/CN.4/20 (1950).

[76] UNGAOR A/2645.

[77] See Report of the ILC on the Work of its 46th Session, A/49/10, pp. 43 ff. See in particular J. Crawford, 'The ILC's Draft Statute for an International Criminal Court', 88 AJIL, 1994, p. 140, and Crawford, 'The Making of the Rome Statute' in *From Nuremberg to The Hague: The Future of International Criminal Justice* (ed. P. Sands), Cambridge, 2003, p. 109.

influential and a Preparatory Committee was convened in December 1995.[78] The work of this Committee[79] led to the Rome Conference in 1998, which produced after some effort the Rome Statute on the International Criminal Court on 17 July 1998.[80] Sixty states were needed to ratify the Rome Statute in order for it to come into force and this duly happened on 1 July 2002. Unlike the two international criminal tribunals (for the former Yugoslavia and for Rwanda), the ICC is the product not of a binding Security Council resolution, but of an international treaty. This was essentially because states, while being prepared to accept the creation of geographically limited and temporally constrained (in Rwanda's case) tribunals by Security Council action, were not willing to be so bound by the establishment of a permanent international criminal court with much more extensive jurisdiction without express consent. Secondly, it is to be noted that the range and content of the Rome Statute is far greater than those of the two international criminal tribunals. The Rome Statute contains 128 articles, while the ICTY Statute contains 34 articles and the ICTR Statute 32 articles

The Statute provides that the jurisdiction of the International Criminal Court is limited to the 'most serious crimes of concern to the international community as a whole', being genocide, crimes against humanity, war crimes and aggression,[81] and that a person who commits a crime within the jurisdiction of the Court 'shall be individually responsible and liable for punishment' in accordance with the Statute.[82] The ICC only has jurisdiction with respect to crimes committed after the Statute came into force and with respect to states which have become parties to the Statute.[83]

---

[78] General Assembly resolution 50/46. See also resolutions 51/207 and 52/160.

[79] See A/51/22 and A/CONF.183/13 (III), p. 5.

[80] See Schabas, *International Criminal Court*, pp. 18 ff.

[81] Article 5. These provisions are further defined in detail in articles 6–8 and see below, p. 430. In addition, article 9 provides for the preparation of Elements of Crimes to assist the Court in the interpretation and application of articles 6, 7 and 8. This was adopted on 9 September 2002 by the Assembly of States Parties, together with the Rules of Procedure and Evidence. However, jurisdiction cannot be exercised with regard to the crime of aggression until the Statute has been amended by its definition and the acceptance of conditions for jurisdiction. A review conference is due to take place in 2009 during which the issue is to be discussed.

[82] Article 25.

[83] Article 11. Note, however, that a state may make a declaration under article 12(3) to permit the Court to exercise jurisdiction in the particular case as from 1 July 2002. Note also that under article 124, a state may, upon ratification, decide not to accept the jurisdiction of the ICC over war crimes with regard to its nationals or to crimes committed on its territory for a period of seven years. In fact, only France and Colombia have taken advantage of this provision.

Further, jurisdiction may only be exercised provided either the state on the territory of which the conduct in question occurred (or if the crime was committed on board a vessel or aircraft, the state of registration of that vessel or aircraft) or the state of which the person accused of the crime is a national is a party to the Statute.[84] This means that the jurisdiction of the ICC is not universal, but territorial or personal in nature. It also means that the national of a state which is not a party to the Statute may be prosecuted where the crime is committed in the territory of a state which is a party. However, the Court may also have jurisdiction where a situation has been referred to the Prosecutor by the Security Council acting under Chapter VII of the Charter, which is thereby binding and in which case it is unnecessary that a relevant state be a party to the Statute.[85] This has happened with regard to the situation in Darfur, Sudan, which was referred to the Prosecutor on 31 March 2005 by the Security Council in resolution 1593. After a preliminary examination of the situation, an investigation was opened on 1 June 2005 and after a twenty-month investigation into crimes allegedly committed in Darfur since 1 July 2002, the Prosecutor presented evidence to the judges and a summons to two named Sudanese individuals, one being a government minister and the other a military officer, to appear was issued with regard to charges alleging the commission of war crimes and crimes against humanity.[86] Warrants of arrest were issued on 27 April 2007 against the two individuals by Pre-Trial Chamber I.[87]

In addition to the Security Council referral, the ICC is also able to exercise its jurisdiction with regard to one or more of the crimes in question where the situation in which one or more of these crimes appears to have been committed has been referred to the Prosecutor by a state party to the Statute,[88] or the where Prosecutor has himself or herself initiated an investigation.[89] In the latter case, where the Prosecutor concludes, after having analysed the seriousness of the information received, that there is a reasonable basis to proceed to an investigation, a request for authorisation of an investigation, together with any supporting material collected, will be submitted to the Pre-Trial Chamber. Victims may also make representations to the Pre-Trial Chamber, in accordance with the

---

[84] Article 12(2).   [85] Article 13(b).

[86] See www.icc-cpi.int/library/organs/otp/ICC-OTP_Fact-Sheet-Darfur-20070227_en.pdf.

[87] See ICC-02/05-01/07-2 01-05-2007 1/16 CB PT and ICC-02/05-01/07-3 01-05-2007 1/17 CB PT. See also Schabas, *International Criminal Court*, pp. 47 ff. The Prosecutor applied for a warrant of arrest against the President of Sudan on 14 July 2008 alleging genocide, war crimes and crimes against humanity, ICC-OTP-20080714-PR341-ENG.

[88] Articles 13(a) and 14.   [89] Article 13(c).

Rules of Procedure and Evidence. Where the Pre-Trial Chamber, upon examination of the request and the supporting material, considers that there is a reasonable basis to proceed with an investigation, and that the case appears to fall within the jurisdiction of the Court, it shall authorise the commencement of the investigation, without prejudice to subsequent determinations by the Court with regard to the jurisdiction and admissibility of a case.[90]

There have been three examples to date of referral by a state party. In December 2003, Uganda referred to the Prosecutor the situation with regard to the Lord's Resistance Army;[91] in April 2004, the Democratic Republic of the Congo referred to the Prosecutor the situation of crimes committed in its territory;[92] and in December 2004, the Central African Republic referred the situation in its country during the armed conflict of 2002–3 to the Prosecutor.[93]

However, in a concession to obtain the support of states to the ICC, article 16 provides that no investigation or prosecution may be commenced

---

[90] Article 15. The refusal of the Pre-Trial Chamber to authorise the investigation will not preclude the presentation of a subsequent request by the Prosecutor based on new facts or evidence regarding the same situation. If, after the preliminary examination referred to in paragraphs 1 and 2, the Prosecutor concludes that the information provided does not constitute a reasonable basis for an investigation, he or she shall inform those who provided the information. This shall not preclude the Prosecutor from considering further information submitted to him or her regarding the same situation in the light of new facts or evidence.

[91] In July 2004, an investigation was opened by the Prosecutor, and on 8 July 2005, warrants of arrest for crimes against humanity and war crimes against five senior commanders of the Lord's Resistance Army were issued under seal by Pre-Trial Chamber II. These warrants were made public on 13 October 2005: see www.icc-cpi.int/library/cases/ICC_20051410-056-1_English.pdf and Schabas, *International Criminal Court*, pp. 36 ff.

[92] See ICC-OTP-20040419-50-En. An investigation was opened in June 2004, the first such investigation by the Prosecutor: see ICC-OTP-20040623-59-En. An arrest warrant was issued in early 2006 against Thomas Lubanga Dyilo, who was charged on various counts concerning the recruitment and use of child soldiers: see *ICC Newsletter*, No. 10, November 2006. However, a stay on proceedings was ordered and the accused released due to fair trial considerations. An appeal is pending, ICC-01/04-01/06, 2 July 2008. An arrest warrant was issued against Germain Katanga on 2 July 2007 and he was transferred to the custody of the Court in October that year: see www.icc-cpi.int/library/cases/DRC-18-10-07_En.pdf. An arrest warrant was issued against Mathieu Ngudjolo Chui on 7 July 2007 and he was transferred to the custody of the Court in February 2008: see www.icc-cpi.int/pressrelease_details&id=329.html. Both the latter individuals are also charged with regard to the situation in the Congo. See also Schabas, *International Criminal Court*, pp. 42 ff.

[93] An investigation was opened by the Prosecutor in May 2007: see www.icc-cpi.int/library/press/pressreleases/ICC-OTP-BN-20070522-220_A_EN.pdf and Schabas, *International Criminal Court*, pp. 51–2.

or proceeded with for a period of twelve months after the Security Council, in a resolution adopted under Chapter VII of the Charter, has so requested the Court. Such request may be renewed by the Council under the same conditions.[94] Article 98(2) provides that the Court may not proceed with a request for surrender which would require the requested state to act inconsistently with its obligations under international agreements pursuant to which the consent of a sending state is required to surrender a person of that state to the Court, unless the Court can first obtain the co-operation of the sending state for the giving of consent for the surrender. The provision, which was intended to deal with conflicting obligations, such as the position of soldiers stationed overseas under Status of Forces agreements which allow the sending state to exercise elements of criminal jurisdiction with regard to its soldiers, has been used by the US for a much broader purpose. The US has signed a number of bilateral agreements with states, some parties to the Rome Statute and some not, which provide that no nationals, current or former officials, or military personnel of either party may be surrendered or transferred by the other state to the ICC for any purpose. This tactic has been widely criticised and is highly controversial.[95]

A key feature of the ICC, and one that distinguished it from the two international criminal tribunals, is that it is founded upon the concept of complementarity, which means essentially that the national courts have priority. A case will be inadmissible and the Court will be unable to exercise jurisdiction in a number of situations.[96] These are, first, where the case is being investigated or prosecuted by a state which has jurisdiction over it, unless the state is unwilling or unable genuinely to carry out the

---

[94] See Security Council resolution 1422 (2002) calling for the ICC to defer any exercise of jurisdiction for twelve months if a case arises involving current or former officials or personnel from a contributing state not a party to the Rome Statute over acts or omissions relating to a UN established or authorised operation. This was renewed for a further twelve months in resolution 1487 (2003), but not subsequently: see e.g. D. McGoldrick, 'Political and Legal Responses to the ICC' in McGoldrick *et al. The Permanent International Criminal Court*, p. 415. However, resolutions 1497 (2003) and 1593 (2005) provide that personnel from a state not a party to the Rome Statute will be subject to the exclusive jurisdiction of that state for all acts related to the multinational force or UN force in Liberia and Darfur respectively: see Cryer *et al., Introduction to International Criminal Law*, pp. 142 ff.

[95] See e.g. Cryer *et al., Introduction to International Criminal Law*, pp. 144–5; M. Benzing, 'US Bilateral Non-Surrender Agreements and Article 98 of the Statute of the International Criminal Court', 8 *Max Planck Yearbook of United Nations Law*, 2004, p. 182, and Schabas, *International Criminal Court*, pp. 29 ff.

[96] Article 17. See also the *Thomas Lubanga Dyilo* case, ICC-01/04-01/06, Decision on the Prosecutor's Application for a Warrant of Arrest, 10 February 2006.

investigation or prosecution; secondly, where the case is being investigated or prosecuted by a state which has jurisdiction over it and the state has decided not to prosecute the person concerned, unless the decision resulted from the unwillingness[97] or inability[98] of the state genuinely to prosecute; and thirdly, where the person concerned has already been tried for conduct which is the subject of the complaint, unless the proceedings before the court other than the ICC were for the purpose of shielding the person concerned from criminal responsibility for crimes within the jurisdiction of the ICC or where those proceedings were not conducted independently or impartially.[99]

The Court consists of four organs. These are respectively the Presidency; an Appeals Division, a Trial Division and a Pre-Trial Division; the Office of the Prosecutor; and the Registry.[100] The eighteen judges elected must be independent and serve on a full-time basis,[101] have competence in criminal law or in relevant areas of international law and must represent the principal legal systems in the world, as well as reflect equitable geographical representation and the need for a fair representation of male and female judges. The judges are elected by the Assembly of States Parties using rather complicated voting rules.[102] The Presidency, consisting of the President and the First and Second Vice-Presidents, is responsible for the proper administration of the Court (apart from the Office of the Prosecutor),[103] while the Registry is responsible for the non-judicial aspects of the administration and servicing of the Court.[104] The Office of the Prosecutor acts independently as a separate organ of the Court. It is responsible for receiving referrals and any substantiated information on crimes within the jurisdiction of the Court, for examining them and for conducting investigations and prosecutions before the Court.[105] The Office is headed by the Prosecutor who is elected by secret ballot by members of the Assembly of States Parties and assisted by one or more Deputy Prosecutors.[106]

---

[97] In order to determine this, the Court must consider whether the proceedings were being undertaken or the decision made in order to shield the person concerned from criminal responsibility for crimes within the jurisdiction of the ICC; whether there has been an unjustified delay in the proceedings, and whether the proceedings have been conducted independently or impartially, article 17(2)a–c.

[98] In order to determine this, the Court must consider whether, due to a total or substantial collapse or unavailability of its national judicial system, the state is unable to obtain the accused or the necessary evidence and testimony or is otherwise unable to carry out its proceedings, article 17(3).

[99] Article 20(3).   [100] Article 34.   [101] Article 40.   [102] Article 36.
[103] Article 38.   [104] Article 43.   [105] See further articles 53–5.   [106] Article 42.

The Pre-Trial Division is composed of judges with predominantly criminal trial experience, who serve in the Division for a period of three years. The Pre-Trial Chamber is composed either of a single judge or of a bench of three judges[107] and confirms or rejects the authorisation to commence an investigation and makes a preliminary determination that the case falls within the jurisdiction of the Court, without prejudice to subsequent determinations by the Court with regard to the jurisdiction and admissibility of a case. The Pre-Trial Chamber may also review a decision of the Prosecutor not to proceed with an investigation either on its own initiative, or at the request of the state making a referral under article 14, or the United Nations Security Council under article 13(b),[108] and can issue warrants of arrests and summons to appear before the Court at the request of the Prosecutor, issue orders to grant the rights of the parties in the proceeding, and, where necessary, provide for the protection and privacy of victims and witnesses, the preservation of evidence, the protection of persons who have been arrested or appeared in response to a summons, and the protection of national security information. Within a reasonable time after the person's surrender or voluntary appearance before the Court, the Pre-Trial Chamber holds a hearing in the presence of the Prosecutor, the person charged and his/her counsel to confirm or reject the charges. Once the Pre-Trial Chamber has confirmed the charges and committed the person for trial by the Trial Chamber, the Presidency will establish a Trial Chamber to conduct subsequent proceedings.

The Trial Division is also predominantly composed of judges with criminal trial experience who serve for a period of three years. Three judges of the Division carry out the judicial functions of the Trial Chamber.[109] The primary function of the Trial Chamber is to ensure that a trial is fair and expeditious, and is conducted with full respect for the rights of the accused with regard for the protection of victims and witnesses.[110] The Trial Chamber will determine whether the accused is innocent or guilty. In the latter case, imprisonment for a specified number of years, which may not exceed a maximum of thirty years or a term of life imprisonment, may be imposed. Financial penalties may also be imposed[111] and the Trial Chamber can also order a convicted person to pay money for compensation, restitution or rehabilitation for victims.[112] The trial must be held in public unless special circumstances require that certain proceedings be in

---

[107] Article 39(2)(b)(iii). [108] Article 53. [109] Article 39(2)(b)(ii).
[110] Article 64. [111] Article 77. [112] Article 75(2).

closed session to protect confidential or sensitive information to be given in evidence, or to protect victims and witnesses.[113]

The Appeals Division is composed of judges with established competence in relevant areas of international law and the Appeals Chamber is composed of all the judges assigned to the Appeals Division.[114] The Prosecutor or the convicted person can appeal against the decisions of the Pre-Trial and Trial Chambers to the Appeals Chamber. A sentence may be appealed on the ground of procedural error, error of fact, error of law, or any other ground that affects the fairness or reliability of the proceedings or decision. Further, a sentence may be appealed on the ground of disproportion between the crime and the sentence.[115] The Appeals Chamber may decide to reverse or amend the decision, judgment or sentence, or order a new trial before a different Trial Chamber.[116]

Hybrid courts and other internationalised domestic courts and tribunals[117]

In addition to the temporary and geographically limited international criminal tribunals and the permanent International Criminal Court, a new style of judicial institution has made an appearance recently in which both international and national elements co-exist in varying combinations. Such institutions, which may for convenience be termed hybrid courts, exist primarily to enhance legitimacy and increase acceptability both locally and internationally, invariably in difficult post-conflict situations where reliance upon purely domestic mechanisms carries significant political risks or costs. However, as will be seen, there are a number of models adopted which differ as to formal legal origin, constitutional status, applicable law and structure. Some of these mechanisms may more

---

[113] Article 68.   [114] Article 39(2)(b)(i).

[115] Article 81. Either party may appeal against decisions as to, for example, jurisdiction or admissibility; decisions as to the grant or denial of the release of the person being investigated or prosecuted; and decisions of the Pre-Trial Chamber to act on its own initiative under article 56(3): see article 82.

[116] Article 83. The revision of the sentence can be requested if new evidence has been discovered which was not available at the time of the trial and is sufficiently important or decisive for the Appeals Chamber to revise or amend the sentence: see article 84.

[117] See e.g. *Internationalized Criminal Courts* (eds. C. P. R. Romano, A. Nollkaemper and J. K. Kleffner), Oxford, 2004; Cryer *et al.*, *Introduction to International Criminal Law*, chapter 9; Schabas, *The UN International Criminal Tribunals*; and L. A. Dickinson, 'The Promise of Hybrid Courts', 97 AJIL, 2003, p. 295.

correctly be termed internationalised courts or tribunals[118] as the balance between the international and the domestic tips far to the latter. They are essentially domestic courts applying domestic law, but with a heightened international element in terms, for example, of their function or origins, the basis of their applicable law or the use of international experts. Some courts are difficult to place along the spectrum, but together this category marks an extension of international concern and involvement in issues focusing upon individual criminal responsibility for what are international crimes, even if subsequently incorporated into domestic law.

The Special Court for Sierra Leone

The Special Court for Sierra Leone was established, following a particularly violent civil war, by virtue of an agreement between the UN and Sierra Leone dated 16 January 2002, pursuant to Security Council resolution 1315 (2000), in order to prosecute persons bearing 'the greatest responsibility for serious violations of international humanitarian law and Sierra Leonean law committed in the territory of Sierra Leone since 30 November 1996' on the basis of individual criminal responsibility.[119] However, it is stipulated that any transgressions by peacekeepers and related personnel present in the country by virtue of agreements with the UN or other governments or regional organisations or otherwise with the consent of the Sierra Leonean government are within the 'primary jurisdiction' of the sending state.[120]

The Special Court consists of the Chambers (two Trial Chambers and an Appeals Chamber), the Prosecutor and the Registry. Three judges serve

---

[118] See for this terminology, M. P. Scharf, 'The Iraqi High Tribunal', 5 *Journal of International Criminal Justice*, 2007, pp. 258, 259.

[119] Article 1 of the Agreement contained in S/2002/246, Appendix II, and articles 1 and 6 of the Statute of the Special Court, contained in S/2002/246, Appendix III, and see Security Council resolution 1436 (2002) affirming 'strong support' for the Court, and the Report on the Special Court by Professor A. Cassese, the independent expert commissioned by the UN Secretary-General to review the work of the Special Court, December 2006, www. sc-sl.org/documents/independentexpertreport.pdf. See also R. Cryer, 'A "Special Court" for Sierra Leone', 50 ICLQ, 2001, p. 435; Schabas, *The UN International Criminal Tribunals*; A. Smith, 'Sierra Leone: The Intersection of Law, Policy and Practice', P. Mochochoko and G. Tortora, 'The Management Committee for the Special Court for Sierra Leone', and W. A. Schabas, 'Internationalized Courts and their Relationship with Alternative Accountability Mechanisms' in Romano *et al.*, *Internationalized Criminal Courts*, at pp. 125, 141 and 157 respectively.

[120] Article 1(2) of the Statute of the Special Court for Sierra Leone.

in each Trial Chamber, of whom one is appointed by the Sierra Leonean government and two are appointed by the UN Secretary-General. Five judges sit in the Appeals Chamber, of whom two are appointed by the government and three by the UN Secretary-General.[121] The Appeals Chamber hears appeals from persons convicted by the Trial Chamber or from the Prosecutor on the grounds of procedural error, an error on a question of law invalidating the decision or an error of fact which has occasioned a miscarriage of justice. The Appeals Chamber may affirm, reverse or revise the decisions taken by the Trial Chamber. In so acting, the judges of the Appeals Chamber of the Special Court are to be guided by the decisions of the Appeals Chamber of the International Tribunals for the former Yugoslavia and for Rwanda. In the interpretation and application of the laws of Sierra Leone, they are to be guided by the decisions of the Supreme Court of Sierra Leone.[122]

The Prosecutor, who is appointed by the UN Secretary-General for a three-year term and acts independently as a separate organ of the Special Court, is responsible for the investigation and prosecution of persons who bear the greatest responsibility for serious violations of international humanitarian law and crimes under Sierra Leonean law committed in the territory of Sierra Leone since 30 November 1996. The Office of the Prosecutor has the power to question suspects, victims and witnesses, to collect evidence and to conduct on-site investigations. The Prosecutor is assisted by a Sierra Leonean Deputy Prosecutor, and by a mixture of Sierra Leonean and international staff.[123] The Registry is responsible for the administration and servicing of the Special Court and is appointed by the UN Secretary-General after consultation with the President of the Special Court.[124]

The jurisdiction of the Special Court mirrors the hybrid nature of its creation and staffing. The Court has jurisdiction with regard to crimes against humanity; violations of article 3 common to the Geneva Conventions and of Additional Protocol II; other serious violations of

---

[121] Article 12(1). Eight judges were appointed in July 2002: see UN Press Release SG/A/813. There are currently eleven judges and one alternate judge.

[122] Article 20. Under article 21, the convicted person or the Prosecutor may apply to the Appeals Chamber for review where a new fact has been discovered which was not known at the time of the proceedings before the Trial Chamber or Appeals Chamber and which could have been a decisive factor in reaching the decision. The Appeals Chamber may reject the application, reconvene the Trial Chamber or retain jurisdiction over the matter.

[123] Article 15. [124] Article 16.

international humanitarian law[125] and certain crimes under Sierra Leonean law.[126] Article 8 of the Statute provides that the Special Court and the national courts of Sierra Leone have concurrent jurisdiction, but that the Special Court has primacy over the national courts and that at any stage of the procedure it may formally request a national court to defer to its competence. The Annual Report of the Special Court for 2006–7 notes that thirteen persons were indicted, all between March and September 2003. Of these, nine were in custody, one dead, one still at large, while two indictments were withdrawn. Trials of the nine in custody began in 2004 and 2005 in three joint trials. Of particular interest is the Charles Taylor case. He was the former President of Liberia. His claim to immunity was rejected by the Appeals Chamber in May 2004[127] and he is currently standing trial in The Hague at the premises of the ICC.[128] Judgment in the *AFRC* trial was handed down on 20 June 2007 and the three accused convicted of offences. Sentencing took place on 19 July 2007 and the appeal against sentencing was dismissed on 22 February 2008.[129] On 2 August 2007, Trial Chamber I reached a decision in the trial of three persons accused of being leaders of the so-called 'Civil Defence Forces', of whom one died prior to pronouncement of judgment, in which the two remaining accused were convicted.[130] The Special Court adopted a completion strategy under which proceedings were due to be completed in 2007.[131] However, this date was not able to be met.

---

125 Articles 2–4 of the Statute.
126 Article 5 of the Statute. These crimes relate to offences relating to the abuse of girls under the Prevention of Cruelty to Children Act 1926 and offences relating to the wanton destruction of property under the Malicious Damages Act 1861. However, the Special Court has no jurisdiction with regard to any person under the age of fifteen at the time of the alleged commission of the crime. No person may be tried before a national court of Sierra Leone for acts for which he or she has already been tried by the Special Court. But a person who has been tried by a national court for the acts referred to in articles 2 to 4 of the Statute may be subsequently tried by the Special Court if either the act for which he or she was tried was characterised as an ordinary crime; or the national court proceedings were not impartial or independent, or were designed to shield the accused from international criminal responsibility or the case was not diligently prosecuted: see article 9.
127 See www.sc-sl.org/Documents/Taylor/SCSL-03-01-I-059.pdf.
128 See Annual Report 2006–7, p. 5.   129 See www.sc-sl.org/AFRC.html.
130 See www.sc-sl.org/documents/CDF/SCSL-04-14-T-785A.pdf. See also S. M. Meisenberg, 'Legality of Amnesties in International Humanitarian Law – The Lomé Decision of the Special Court for Sierra Leone', 86 *International Review of the Red Cross*, 2004, p. 837.
131 See A/59/816 – S/2005/350.

The Extraordinary Chambers of Cambodia

The Khmer Rouge regime under Pol Pot took power in Cambodia in 1975 following a civil war and proceeded to commit widescale atrocities which are believed to have resulted in the death of well over 1 million people. The regime was ousted by a Vietnamese invasion in 1979. In 1997, the Cambodian government requested the United Nations (UN) to assist in establishing a trial process in order to prosecute the senior leaders of the Khmer Rouge. In 2001, the Cambodian National Assembly passed a law to create a court to try serious crimes committed during the Khmer Rouge regime. On 13 May 2003, after a long period of negotiation, the UN General Assembly approved a Draft Agreement between the UN and Cambodia providing for Extraordinary Chambers in the courts of Cambodia, with the aim of bringing to trial senior leaders of Democratic Kampuchea and those who were most responsible for the crimes and serious violations of Cambodian penal law, international humanitarian law and custom, and international conventions recognised by Cambodia, that were committed during the period from 17 April 1975 to 6 January 1979.[132] The Agreement was ratified by Cambodia on 19 October 2004.

Article 2 of the Agreement provided that the Extraordinary Chambers were to have subject-matter jurisdiction consistent with that laid down in the Cambodian Law (of 2001) and that the Agreement was to be implemented via that law. However, it is provided also that the Vienna Convention on the Law of Treaties, 1969 is to apply to the Agreement. Accordingly, the Agreement must be seen as an international treaty, although one closely linked with the relevant domestic law. The Chambers are composed of a Trial Chamber, consisting of three Cambodian judges and two international judges, and a Supreme Court Chamber, serving as both appellate chamber and final instance and consisting of four Cambodian judges and three international judges. The UN Secretary-General was to nominate seven judges and the Cambodian Supreme

---

[132] See General Assembly resolutions 57/228A and 57/228B and A/57/806. See also R. Williams, 'The Cambodian Extraordinary Chambers – A Dangerous Precedent for International Justice?', 53 ICLQ, 2004, p. 227; G. Acquaviva, 'New Paths in International Criminal Justice? The Internal Rules of the Cambodian Extraordinary Chambers', 6 *Journal of International Criminal Justice*, 2008, p. 129; C. Etcheson, 'The Politics of Genocide Justice in Cambodia' and E. E. Meijer, 'The Extraordinary Chambers in the Courts of Cambodia for Prosecuting Crimes Committed by the Khmer Rouge: Jurisdiction, Organization and Procedure of an Internationalized Tribunal' in Romano *et al.*, *Internationalized Criminal Courts*, at pp. 181 and 207 respectively.

Council of Magistracy, the highest domestic judicial body, was to choose five of these to serve in the Chambers.[133] The Agreement also provided for independent co-investigation judges, one Cambodian and one international, who are responsible for the conduct of investigations,[134] and two independent co-prosecutors, one Cambodian and one international, competent to appear in both Chambers, who are responsible for the conduct of the prosecutions.[135]

The jurisdiction of the Extraordinary Chambers covers the crime of genocide as defined in the Genocide Convention, 1948, crimes against humanity as defined in the 1998 Rome Statute of the International Criminal Court and grave breaches of the 1949 Geneva Conventions and such other crimes as are defined in Chapter II of the Cambodian Law of 2001.[136] The procedure of the Chambers is to be in accordance with Cambodian law, but where Cambodian law does not deal with a particular matter, or where there is uncertainty regarding the interpretation or application of a relevant rule of Cambodian law, or where there is a question regarding the consistency of such a rule with international standards, guidance may also be sought in procedural rules established at the international level. It is also provided that the Extraordinary Chambers are to exercise their jurisdiction in accordance with international standards of justice, fairness and due process of law, as set out in Articles 14 and 15 of the 1966 International Covenant on Civil and Political Rights, to which Cambodia is a party.[137]

A list of five suspects was submitted by the prosecutors on 19 July 2007 to the Chambers with a request that they be indicted and, on 31 July 2007, the first suspect (Khang Khek Ieu, known as 'Duch') was indicted.[138] To

---

[133] Article 3 of the Agreement. The Secretary-General nominated seven judges in March 2006 and the Supreme Council of Magistracy approved a list of thirty Cambodian and international judges in May that year to be followed by appointment by Royal Decree. The judges were duly sworn in in July 2006 and Internal Rules were adopted in June 2007 and revised in February 2008.

[134] Article 5.

[135] Article 6. In the case of both the co-investigating judges and co-prosecutors, the UN Secretary-General was to make two nominations out of which the Supreme Council of Magistracy was to choose one international investigating judge and one international prosecutor. Any differences between the two co-investigating judges and the two co-prosecutors are to be settled by a Pre-Trial Chamber of five judges, three appointed by the Supreme Council of the Magistracy, with one as President, and two appointed by the Supreme Council of the Magistracy upon nomination by the Secretary-General: see article 7.

[136] Article 9.   [137] Article 12.

[138] Case file No. 001/18-07-2007-ECCC/OCIJ. See also Annual Report 2007, p. 11.

date, five suspects are before the Chambers[139] and two appeal proceedings have taken place.[140]

Kosovo Regulation 64 panels[141]

Following the conflict between the Federal Republic of Yugoslavia (as it then was, today Serbia) and NATO in 1999, the Security Council adopted resolution 1244, which *inter alia* called for the establishment of an 'international civil presence' in Kosovo. The international civil presence was granted responsibilities, including promoting 'the establishment, pending a final settlement, of substantial autonomy and self-government'; performing basic civilian administrative functions; organising the development of provisional institutions for democratic and autonomous self-government pending a political settlement; and protecting and promoting human rights.[142] The competence of the international civil presence carried out by the UN Interim Administration Mission in Kosovo (UNMIK) was extensive. Section 1.1 of the first regulation issued by UNMIK in 1999 stated that: 'All legislative and executive authority with respect to Kosovo, including the administration of the judiciary, is vested in UNMIK and is exercised by the Special Representative of the Secretary General',[143] while section 1.2 provided that the Special Representative could appoint any person to perform functions in the civil administration in Kosovo, including the judiciary, or remove such person in accordance with the applicable law.[144]

Following a series of disturbances in 2000, UNMIK Regulation 2000/6 was adopted, providing for the appointment of international judges and prosecutors,[145] and UNMIK Regulation 2000/64 was adopted, providing for UNMIK to create panels (known as Regulation 64 panels) of three judges, including at least two international judges, at the request

---

[139] Annual Report 2007, pp. 9 ff   [140] Annual Report 2007, pp. 13–14.

[141] See e.g. J. Cerone and C. Baldwin, 'Explaining and Evaluating the UNMIK Court System' and J. C. Cady and N. Booth, 'Internationalized Courts in Kosovo: An UNMIK Perspective' in Romano *et al.*, *Internationalized Criminal Courts*, at pp. 41 and 59 respectively. See also S. de Bertodano, 'Current Developments in Internationalized Courts', 1 *Journal of International Criminal Justice*, 2003, pp. 226, 239 ff., and *Finding the Balance: The Scales of Justice in Kosovo*, International Crisis Group, 2002.

[142] Paragraphs 10 and 11.   [143] UNMIK/REG/1991/1, S/1999/987, p. 14.

[144] As amended in UNMIK/REG/2000/54.

[145] Initially in Mitrovica and then in all domestic courts and the Supreme Court: see UNMIK Regulation 2000/34. Note that attempts to establish a Kosovo War and Ethnic Crimes Court were abandoned in September 2000: see Cady and Booth, 'Internationalized Courts in Kosovo', p. 60.

of the accused, defence counsel or prosecutor. Such international judges functioned as regular court judges in Kosovo with powers derived from domestic legislation, but their involvement in a case was under either their own control or at the behest of the UN Secretary-General's Special Representative in Kosovo. The applicable law was stated to be regulations promulgated by the Special Representative and subsidiary instruments issued thereunder and the law in force in Kosovo on 22 March 1989.[146] However, problems surfaced, particularly with regard to the high rate of national judge convictions overturned by retrials by international judges and lack of systematic publication of case decisions and brevity of such decisions.[147] Kosovo declared independence in early 2008.[148]

East Timor Special Panels for Serious Crimes[149]

Following a period of violence in East Timor instigated by pro-Indonesian militia after the ending of the long Indonesian occupation, the Security Council established the UN Transitional Administration in East Timor (UNTAET) with a wide-ranging mandate to administer the territory.[150] By Regulation No. 1 adopted on 27 November 1999, all legislative and executive authority with respect to East Timor, including the administration of the judiciary, was vested in UNTAET and exercised by the Transitional Administrator. This administrator was given the competence further to appoint any person to perform functions in the civil administration in the territory, including the judiciary, or remove such person and to issue regulations and directives. UNTAET created a new courts

---

[146] See UNMIK/REG/1999/24 and UNMIK/REG/2000/59. Section 1.3 provided that all persons exercising public functions were to observe internationally recognised human rights standards as reflected in particular in the Universal Declaration of Human Rights, the International Covenants on Human Rights, the European Convention on Human Rights, the Racial Discrimination Convention, the Women's Discrimination Convention, the Torture Convention and the Rights of the Child Convention.

[147] See e.g. de Bertodano, 'Current Developments in Internationalized Courts', pp. 239 ff.

[148] See above, chapter 5, p. 201.

[149] See e.g. S. de Bertodano, 'East Timor: Trials and Tribulations' in Romano *et al.*, *Internationalized Criminal Courts*, p. 79; S. Linton, 'Prosecuting Atrocities at the District Court of Dili', 2 *Melbourne Journal of International Law*, 2001, p. 414, and S. Linton and C. Reiger, 'The Evolving Jurisprudence and Practice of East Timor's Special Panels for Serious Crimes on Admission of Guilt, Duress and Superior Orders', 4 *Yearbook of International Humanitarian Law*, 2001, p. 1. See also the report produced by the Judicial System Monitoring Programme in April 2007, www.jsmp.minihub.org/Reports/2007/SPSC/SERIOUS%20CRIMES%20DIGEST%20(Megan)%20250407.pdf.

[150] Resolution 1272 (1999). See also resolution 1264 (1999) and S/1999/24.

system,[151] including the establishment of special panels to deal with serious crimes within the District Court of Dili and in the Court of Appeal.[152] These serious crimes were defined as genocide, war crimes, crimes against humanity, murder, sexual offences and torture,[153] for which there was individual criminal responsibility.[154] The applicable law was the law of East Timor as promulgated by sections 2 and 3 of UNTAET Regulation No. 1999/1 and any subsequent UNTAET regulations and directives; and, where appropriate, applicable treaties and recognised principles and norms of international law, including the established principles of the international law of armed conflict.

The Panels in the District Court of Dili were to be composed of two international judges and one East Timorese judge, as were the Panels in the Court of Appeal in Dili. In cases of special importance or gravity, a panel of five judges composed of three international and two East Timorese judges could be established.[155] However, the system had barely started before 2003 and in the *Armando Dos Santos* case, the Court of Appeal held, in a decision much criticised,[156] that since the Indonesian occupation was illegal, Indonesian law was never validly in force so that domestic law was Portuguese law and, further, Regulation 2000/15 could not be applied retroactively so that only Portuguese law could be applied to crimes committed before 6 June 2000.[157] On 20 May 2002, the UN handed over its authority to the new institutions of East Timor and UNTAET was replaced by the UN Mission of Support in East Timor (UNMISET), although UNTAET regulations continued in force. In May 2005, UNMISET came to an end and the Serious Crimes Unit closed. Partly no doubt as a consequence, the Special Panels suspended operations indefinitely. By this time, fifty-five trials, most involving relatively low-level defendants, had taken place, eighty-four individuals had been convicted and three acquitted.[158]

---

[151] UNTAET Regulations 2000/11 and 2000/14.

[152] Regulation 2000/15.   [153] Defined in sections 4–10 of Regulation 2000/15.

[154] Section 14.   [155] Section 22.

[156] See de Bertodano, 'East Timor', pp. 90 ff., and de Bertodano, 'Current Developments in Internationalized Courts: East Timor – Justice Denied', 2 *Journal of International Criminal Justice*, 2004, p. 910.

[157] Case No. 16/201: see www.jsmp.minihub.org/Judgements/courtofappeal/Ct_of_App-dos_Santos_English22703.pdf.

[158] See the digest of cases before the Special Panels, produced in 2007, www.jsmp.minihub.org/Reports/2007/SPSC/SERIOUS%20CRIMES%20DIGEST%20(Megan)%20250407.pdf.

The Bosnia War Crimes Chamber[159]

In January 2003, the Office of the High Representative in Bosnia[160] and the International Criminal Tribunal for the Former Yugoslavia issued a set of joint conclusions recommending the creation of a specialised chamber within the State Court of Bosnia and Herzegovina to try war crimes cases.[161] This was supported by the UN Security Council.[162] The Chamber came into being in 2005 with jurisdiction concerning cases referred to it by the ICTY pursuant to Rule 11 *bis* of the ICTY Rules of Procedure and Evidence with regard to lower- to mid-level accused persons. As such, this procedure forms part of the completion strategy of the ICTY.[163] In addition, the Chamber has jurisdiction with regard to cases submitted to it by the Office of the Prosecutor of the ICTY where investigations have not been completed, and the first case was referred to the Chamber on 1 September 2005.[164] Further, the Chamber also has jurisdiction over what have been termed 'Rules of the Road' cases. The 'Rules of the Road' procedure was first established in response to the widespread fear of arbitrary arrest and detention immediately after the conflict in Bosnia. Originally, the Bosnian authorities were obliged to submit every war crimes case proposed for prosecution in Bosnia to the Office of the Prosecutor of the ICTY to determine whether the evidence was sufficient by international standards before proceeding to arrest. This review function was subsequently assumed by the Special Department for War Crimes within the Office of the Prosecutor of the State Court of Bosnia in October 2004. Where the case has not yet led to a confirmed indictment and where the prosecutor determines that the case is 'highly sensitive', it will be passed to the Chamber, otherwise it will be tried before the relevant cantonal or district court. If, however, the indictment has been confirmed, the case will remain with the relevant cantonal or district court.

The Chamber has both trial and appeals chambers and there are currently five judicial panels, each comprising two international judges and one local judge, the latter of whom is the presiding judge of the

---

[159] See Cryer *et al.*, *Introduction to International Criminal Law*, pp. 159 ff.; Bohlander, 'Referring an Indictment from the ICTY and the ICTR to Another Court', p. 219; *Looking for Justice – The War Crimes Chamber in Bosnia and Herzegovina*, Human Rights Watch, 2006, and *Narrowing the Impunity Gap – Trials Before Bosnia's War Crimes Chamber*, Human Rights Watch, 2007.

[160] As to the High Representative, see above, chapter 5, p. 231.

[161] See www.un.org/icty/pressreal/2003/p723-e.htm.

[162] See resolution 1503 (2003).   [163] See above, p. 407.

[164] *Prosecutor v. Radovan Stanković*, ICTY, Case No. IT-96-23/2-AR11 bis.1, Decision on Rule 11 *bis* Referral (Appeals Chamber), 1 September 2005, para. 30.

panel. The Office of the Prosecutor of the State Court includes a Special Department for War Crimes and there are five international prosecutors and one international acting prosecutor, as well as eight local prosecutors, including the deputy prosecutor.[165] The Registry manages the process of appointing and engaging international judges and prosecutors. The international judges are appointed by the High Representative after a joint recommendation of the President of the State Court and the President of the High Judicial and Prosecutorial Council, while the international prosecutors are appointed by the High Representative following a joint recommendation from the Bosnian Chief Prosecutor, the President of the High Judicial and Prosecutorial Council and the Registry.[166]

As of October 2006, the Chamber had confirmed a total of eighteen indictments involving thirty-two defendants. In addition to cases initiated locally, the Chamber had received five Rule 11 *bis* referrals, involving nine accused, from the ICTY.[167] The applicable law is that of Bosnia, including criminal and criminal procedure codes introduced by the High Representative in 2003.

The Special Tribunal for Lebanon[168]

Following the assassination of Rafiq Hariri, the former Prime Minister of Lebanon, in February 2005, the Security Council established an International Independent Investigation Commission to aid the Lebanese authorities in their investigation. As a result of its report and the request of the Lebanese government to establish 'a tribunal of an international character' to try those persons accused of the assassination,[169] the Security Council adopted resolution 1664 (2006) calling upon the UN Secretary-General to negotiate an agreement with the government of Lebanon aimed at establishing a tribunal of an international character based on the highest international standards of criminal justice. The Secretary-General's report[170] was accepted by the Council in resolution 1757 (2007). Acting

---

[165] See Human Rights Watch, *Looking for Justice*, pp. 4 ff.

[166] The appointments by the High Representative are made under the powers vested in him by article 5, annex 10, of the Dayton Peace Accord.

[167] See Human Rights Watch, *Narrowing the Impunity Gap*, p. 5.

[168] See e.g. Cryer *et al.*, *Introduction to International Criminal Law*, p. 155; B. Fassbender, 'Reflections on the International Legality of the Special Tribunal for Lebanon', C. Aptel, 'Some Innovations in the Statute of the Special Tribunal for Lebanon', and N. N. Jurdi, 'The Subject-Matter Jurisdiction of the Special Tribunal for Lebanon', 5 *Journal of International Criminal Justice*, 2007, pp. 1091, 1107 and 1125 respectively.

[169] See Security Council resolutions 1595 (2005), 1636 (2005) and 1644 (2005). See also S/2005/783 and S/2006/375.

[170] S/2006/893 and S/2007/150. See resolutions 1686 (2006) and 1748 (2007) calling for the work of the Commission to continue.

under Chapter VII of the Charter, the Council established the Special Tribunal for Lebanon by virtue of an agreement with the government of Lebanon, annexed to the resolution. The Statute of the Tribunal is attached to the agreement.

The Tribunal has jurisdiction not only with regard to those responsible for the assassination of Rafiq Hariri but also with regard to those responsible for other attacks that occurred in Lebanon between 1 October 2004 and 12 December 2005, or any later date decided by the parties and with the consent of the Security Council, that are seen as connected in accordance with the principles of criminal justice and are of a nature and gravity similar to the attack of 14 February 2005.[171] The Tribunal is to be composed of the Chambers, the Prosecutor, the Registry and the Defence Office. The Chambers, to be composed of between eleven and fourteen independent judges, are to consist of a Pre-Trial Judge, a Trial Chamber and an Appeals Chamber. A single international judge is to serve as Pre-Trial Judge, while three judges are to serve in the Trial Chamber, being one Lebanese judge and two international judges. Five judges are to serve in the Appeals Chamber, of whom two are to be Lebanese and three international judges.[172] The Prosecutor and the Registrar are to be appointed by the UN Secretary-General after consultation with the Lebanese government, while the Head of the Defence Office is to be appointed by the Secretary-General after consultation with the President of the Tribunal.[173] The applicable law is Lebanese criminal law and the Tribunal is to have concurrent jurisdiction with Lebanese courts and have primacy over them.[174]

The Iraqi High Tribunal[175]

The Governing Council of Iraq was authorised by the Coalition Provisional Authority on 10 December 2003 to establish the Iraqi Special

---

[171] Article 1 of the Statute.   [172] Articles 7 and 8 of the Statute.

[173] Articles 11, 12 and 13 of the Statute. The Registrar was appointed on 11 March 2008: see www.un.org/apps/news/story.asp?NewsID=25925&Cr=Leban&Cr1.

[174] Articles 2 and 4 of the Statute.

[175] See e.g. Scharf, 'The Iraqi High Tribunal', Cryer et al., Introduction to International Criminal Law, p. 160; I. Bantekas, 'The Iraqi Special Tribunal for Crimes against Humanity', 54 ICLQ, 2004, p. 237; M. C. Bassiouni, 'Post-Conflict Justice in Iraq: An Appraisal of the Iraq Special Tribunal', 38 Cornell International Law Journal, 2005, p. 327; M. Sissons and A. S. Bassin, 'Was the Dujail Trial Fair?', 5 Journal of International Criminal Justice, 2007, p. 272; G. Mettraux, 'The 2005 Revision of the Statute of the Iraqi Special Tribunal', 5 Journal of International Criminal Justice, 2007, p. 287; S. de Bertodano, 'Were There More Acceptable Alternatives to the Iraqi High Tribunal?', 5 Journal of International Criminal Justice, 2007, p. 294.

Tribunal to hear crimes alleged against the former regime of Saddam Hussein.[176] A revised Statute was enacted in 2005 and the tribunal renamed the Iraqi High Tribunal. The Tribunal has jurisdiction over genocide, crimes against humanity and war crimes, the definitions of which are based upon the provisions of the Rome Statute and newly incorporated into Iraqi law, committed between 16 July 1968 and 1 May 2003[177] by Iraqi nationals or residents.[178] Persons accused of committing crimes within the jurisdiction of the Tribunal bear individual criminal responsibility.[179] The Tribunal has concurrent jurisdiction with national courts but primacy over them. Article 6(b) of the Statute provides that the President of the Tribunal shall be required to appoint non-Iraqi nationals to act in advisory capacities or as observers to the Trial Chambers and to the Appeals Chamber. The role of the non-Iraqi nationals is stated to be to provide assistance to the judges with respect to international law and the experience of similar tribunals (whether international or otherwise), and to monitor the protection by the Tribunal of general due process of law standards. In appointing such non-Iraqi experts, the President of the Tribunal is entitled to request assistance from the international community, including the United Nations. However, the judges and prosecutors of the Tribunal are all Iraqi nationals. Criticisms have been made of the Tribunal, including the fact that it can impose the death penalty, as for example with regard to Saddam Hussein upon his conviction in the *Dujail* case.[180]

The Serbian War Crimes Chamber

On 1 July 2003, the Serbian National Assembly adopted a law establishing a specialised War Crimes Chamber within the Belgrade District Court to prosecute and investigate crimes against humanity and serious violations of international humanitarian law as defined in Serbian law. A War Crimes Prosecutor's Office was established in Belgrade. The Chamber consists of two panels of three judges each selected from the Belgrade District Court

---

[176] Order No. 48.

[177] The dates reflect the commencement of the Ba'ath party control of Iraq and the end of the Saddam Hussein regime.

[178] Articles 1 and 11–14 of the Statute of the Tribunal.   [179] Article 15.

[180] See e.g. N. Bhuta, 'Fatal Errors: The Trial and Appeal Judgments in the *Dujail* Case', 6 *Journal of International Criminal Justice*, 2008, p. 39; M. P. Scharf and M. A. Newton, 'The Iraq High Tribunal's *Dujail* Trial Opinion', *ASIL Insight*, 18 December 2006, www.asil.org/insights/2006/12/insights061218.html, and Human Rights Watch report on the *Dujail* trial, http://hrw.org/english/docs/2007/06/22/iraq16230.htm.

or seconded from other courts, and two investigative judges. It is, however, essentially a national court.[181]

International crimes

A brief survey of some of the main features of international crimes for which individual criminal responsibility now exists will follow, noting that issues concerning the jurisdiction of purely domestic courts for those international crimes that have been incorporated into domestic legislation are covered in chapter 12, while state responsibility for such offences is covered in chapter 14.

Genocide[182]

Article 4 of the Statute of the ICTY, by way of example, provides that:

> 2. Genocide means any of the following acts committed with intent to destroy, in whole or in part, a national, ethnical, racial or religious group, as such: (a) killing members of the group; (b) causing serious bodily or mental harm to members of the group; (c) deliberately inflicting on the group conditions of life calculated to bring about its physical destruction in whole or in part; (d) imposing measures intended to prevent births within the group; (e) forcibly transferring children of the group to another group

and that the following acts shall be punishable:

> (a) genocide; (b) conspiracy to commit genocide; (c) direct and public incitement to commit genocide; (d) attempt to commit genocide; (e) complicity in genocide.[183]

---

[181] The War Crimes Chamber's first trial, the *Ovcara* case, began on 9 March 2004. As of 2006, three trials had been completed and three others were ongoing: see *Unfinished Business – Serbia's War Crimes Chamber*, Human Rights Watch, 2007, pp. 1 ff. See also M. Ellis, 'Coming to Terms with its Past: Serbia's New Court for the Prosecution of War Crimes', 22 *Berkeley Journal of International Law*, 2004, p. 165. The ICTY has referred some cases to this Chamber: see e.g. *Vladimir Kovačević*, ICTY Referral Bench, 2006.

[182] See e.g. Cryer *et al.*, *Introduction to International Criminal Law*, chapter 10; Werle, *Principles of International Criminal Law*, part 3; and Cassese, *International Criminal Law*, chapter 6. This section should also be read with the relevant section in chapter 6 above: see p. 282.

[183] See also article IV of the Genocide Convention, 1948, article 2 of the Statute of the ICTR and article 6 of the Statute of the ICC.

Genocide has been regarded as an international crime since the Second World War and the Genocide Convention, 1948 was a critical step in that process. The crime of genocide has also been included in the operative provisions of the statutes of most of the courts and tribunals discussed in the previous section. Case-law before the two international criminal tribunals (ICTY and ICTR) has, however, helped clarify many of the relevant principles. For example, perhaps the distinctive feature of the crime is the importance of establishing the specific intent to destroy the group in question in whole or in part, for genocide is more than the act of killing. This was emphasised by the ICTY in the *Jelisić* case, which noted that 'it is in fact the *mens rea* [i.e. the intention as distinct from the actual act] which gives genocide its speciality and distinguishes it from an ordinary crime and other crimes against international humanitarian law'.[184] This was reaffirmed by the ICTR in the *Akayesu* case,[185] which defined the specific intent necessary as 'the specific intention, required as a constitutive element of the crime, which demands that the perpetrator clearly seeks to produce the act charged'. The Trial Chamber underlined the difficulties in establishing the critical intent requirement and held that recourse may be had in the absence of confessions to inferences from facts.[186] In the *Ruggiu* case, the ICTR held that a person who incites others to commit genocide must himself have a specific intent to commit genocide.[187] However, in the *Jelisić* case, the ICTY pointed to the difficulty in practice of proving the genocidal intention of an individual if the crimes committed were not widespread or backed up by an organisation or a system.[188] This may be distinguished from the *Ruggiu* case, where a systematic scheme to destroy the Tutsis was not in doubt.

The element of intention was further discussed by the ICTY in the *Krstić* case, where it was noted that the intent to eradicate a group within a limited geographical area, such as a region of a country or even a municipality, could be characterised as genocide,[189] while 'the intent to destroy a group, even if only in part, means seeking to destroy a distinct part of the group as opposed to an accumulation of isolated individuals within it'. The part of the group sought to be destroyed had to constitute a distinct element.[190] In the decision of the Appeal Chamber in this case, it was emphasised that it was well established that

---

[184] IT-95-10, para. 66.   [185] ICTR-96-4-T, 1998, para. 498.

[186] *Ibid.*, para. 523. See also the cases of *Kayishema and Ruzindana*, ICTR-95-1-T, 1999, paras. 87 ff. and *Musema*, ICTR-96-13-T, 2000, paras. 884 ff.

[187] ICTR-97-32-I, 2000, para. 14.   [188] IT-95-10, paras. 100–1.

[189] IT-98-33-T, 2001, para. 589.   [190] *Ibid.*, para. 590.

where a conviction for genocide relies on the intent to destroy a protected group 'in part', the part must be a substantial part of that group. The aim of the Genocide Convention is to prevent the intentional destruction of entire human groups, and the part targeted must be significant enough to have an impact on the group as a whole.[191]

It was concluded that the intent requirement of genocide under article 4 of the Statute was satisfied where evidence shows that the alleged perpetrator

intended to destroy at least a substantial part of the protected group. The determination of when the targeted part is substantial enough to meet this requirement may involve a number of considerations. The numeric size of the targeted part of the group is the necessary and important starting point, though not in all cases the ending point of the inquiry. The number of individuals targeted should be evaluated not only in absolute terms, but also in relation to the overall size of the entire group. In addition to the numeric size of the targeted portion, its prominence within the group can be a useful consideration. If a specific part of the group is emblematic of the overall group, or is essential to its survival, that may support a finding that the part qualifies as substantial within the meaning of Article 4.[192]

It was also emphasised that each perpetrator must possess the necessary specific intent.[193]

The intention to 'destroy' means the physical or biological destruction of all or part of the group and not, for example, attacks upon the cultural or sociological characteristics of a group in order to remove its separate identity.[194] The sometimes difficult question of the definition of membership of the groups specifically referred to in the relevant instruments has also been analysed. In *Akayesu*,[195] the Trial Chamber of the Rwanda Tribunal leaned towards the objective definition of membership of groups,[196] but this has been mitigated by other cases emphasising the importance of subjective elements as part of the relevant framework.[197]

---

[191] IT-98-33-A, 2004, para. 8.   [192] *Ibid.*, para. 12.   [193] *Ibid.*, para. 134.
[194] *Ibid.*, para. 25.   [195] ICTR-96-4-T, 1998, paras. 511 ff.
[196] In *Kayishema and Ruzindana*, ICTR-95-1-T, 1999, paras. 522 ff., the Trial Chamber emphasised the importance of the designation contained in identity cards.
[197] See *Rutaganda*, ICTR-96-3-T, 1999, paras. 55 ff. See also *Bagilishima*, ICTR-95-1A-T, 2001, para. 65, where the Trial Chamber concluded that 'if a victim was perceived by a perpetrator as belonging to a protected group, the victim could be considered by the Chamber as a member of the protected group, for the purposes of genocide'. See also the Report of the UN Commission of Inquiry on Darfur, S/2005/60, paras. 500 ff.

In so far as the material elements of the crime are concerned, killing is clearly the key conduct involved and it has been held that the act in question must be intentional if not necessarily premeditated.[198] Forced migration (or 'ethnic cleansing') as such does not constitute genocide,[199] but may amount to a pattern of conduct demonstrating genocidal intent.[200] The *Akayesu* case has also been important in emphasising that rape and sexual violence may amount to genocide when committed with the necessary specific intent to commit genocide. The Trial Chamber concluded that 'Sexual violence was an integral part of the process of destruction, specifically targeting Tutsi women and specifically contributing to their destruction and to the destruction of the Tutsi group as a whole.'[201] Further, where it is intended to prevent births within the group whether by impelling the child born of rape to be part of another group or where the woman raped refuses subsequently to procreate, this may amount to genocide.[202] The Rwanda Tribunal has also held that genocide may be committed by omission as well as by acts.[203]

War Crimes[204]

War crimes are essentially serious violations of the rules of customary and treaty law concerning international humanitarian law, otherwise known as the law governing armed conflicts.[205] Article 2 of the Statute of the ICTY, by way of example, provides for jurisdiction with regard to:

---

[198] See e.g. *Stakić*, IT-97-24-T, 2003, para. 515.

[199] See e.g. the *Eichmann* case, 36 ILR, p. 5 and the *Brdjanin* case, IT-99-36-T, 2004, para. 118. See also the *Blagojević* case, where, in addition, the Appeals Chamber of the ICTY held that awareness of facts related to the forcible transfer operation was insufficient to prove complicity in genocide in the absence of knowledge of mass killings at Srebrenica, IT-02-60-A, 2007, paras. 119 ff.

[200] See e.g. the *Review of the Indictments Concerning Karadžić and Mladić Pursuant to Rule 61 of the Rules of Procedure and Evidence*, ICTY, IT-95-5-R61 and IT-95-18-R61, 11 July 1996, para. 94, 108 ILR, pp. 134–5. See also ad hoc Judge Lauterpacht's Separate Opinion in the *Genocide Convention (Bosnia and Herzegovina v. Yugoslavia)* case, ICJ Reports, 1993, pp. 325, 431–2, and the ICC Elements of Crimes, article 6(c), footnote 4, UN Doc. PCNICC/2000/1/Add.2 (2000).

[201] ICTR-96-4-T, para. 731.   [202] *Ibid.*, paras. 507–8.

[203] *Kambanda*, ICTR-97-23-S, 1998, paras. 39–40.

[204] See e.g. Cryer *et al.*, *Introduction to International Criminal Law*, chapter 12; Werle, *Principles of International Criminal Law*, part 5; and Cassese, *International Criminal Law*, chapter 4.

[205] See further as to international humanitarian law, below, chapter 21.

grave breaches of the Geneva Conventions of 12 August 1949, namely the
following acts against persons or property protected under the provisions
of the relevant Geneva Convention: (a) wilful killing; (b) torture or inhuman treatment, including biological experiments; (c) wilfully causing great
suffering or serious injury to body or health; (d) extensive destruction and
appropriation of property, not justified by military necessity and carried
out unlawfully and wantonly; (e) compelling a prisoner of war or a civilian
to serve in the forces of a hostile power; (f) wilfully depriving a prisoner of
war or a civilian of the rights of fair and regular trial; (g) unlawful deportation or transfer or unlawful confinement of a civilian; (h) taking civilians
as hostages.

Article 3 provides for jurisdiction for violation of the laws or customs
of war. Such violations include, but are not be limited to:

(a) employment of poisonous weapons or other weapons calculated to cause
unnecessary suffering; (b) wanton destruction of cities, towns or villages, or
devastation not justified by military necessity; (c) attack, or bombardment,
by whatever means, of undefended towns, villages, dwellings, or buildings;
(d) seizure of, destruction or wilful damage done to institutions dedicated to
religion, charity and education, the arts and sciences, historic monuments
and works of art and science; (e) plunder of public or private property.[206]

Accordingly, war crimes are a discrete part of the principles of international humanitarian law, being those which have become accepted as
criminal offences for which there is individual responsibility (in addition
to state responsibility). Essentially, war crimes law applies to individuals
and international humanitarian law to states. There is a long history of
provision for individual responsibility for war crimes,[207] and article 6(b) of
the Nuremberg Charter included war crimes within the jurisdiction of the
Tribunal, while the concept of grave breaches of the Geneva Conventions

---

[206] See article 8 of the Statute of the ICC, which is exhaustive rather than illustrative in
its exposition of fifty offences and is divided into sections dealing with: grave breaches
of the Geneva Conventions of 12 August 1949; other serious violations of the laws and
customs applicable in international armed conflict, within the established framework
of international law; in the case of an armed conflict not of an international character,
serious violations of article 3 common to the four Geneva Conventions of 12 August 1949
and other serious violations of the laws and customs applicable in armed conflicts not
of an international character, within the established framework of international law. See
also article 4 of the Statute of the ICTR concerning violations of article 3 common to the
Geneva Conventions and of Additional Protocol II of 1977; article 3 of the Statute of the
Special Court for Sierra Leone and article 14 of the Statute of the Iraqi High Tribunal.
[207] See e.g. the US Army Lieber Code, April 1864.

of 1949 recognised certain violations as crimes subject to universal jurisdiction. Traditionally, international humanitarian law has distinguished
between international and non-international armed conflicts, with legal provision being relatively modest with regard to the latter. However,
common article 3 to the Geneva Conventions laid down certain minimum
standards which were elaborated in Additional Protocol II of 1977.[208] In
addition, since the conflict in Rwanda was clearly an internal one, the
ICTR Statute necessarily provided for individual responsibility for violations of the principles concerning non-international armed conflicts,
in effect recognising that common article 3 and Additional Protocol II
formed the basis of criminal liability.

The key modern decision has been the *Tadić* case before the ICTY.
The Appeals Chamber in the jurisdictional phase of the case noted that
an armed conflict existed whenever there was a resort to armed force
between states or protracted armed violence between governmental authorities and organised armed groups or between such groups within a
state. International humanitarian law applied from the initiation of such
armed conflicts and extended beyond the cessation of hostilities until a
general conclusion of peace was reached; or, in the case of internal conflicts, a peaceful settlement achieved. Until that moment, international
humanitarian law continued to apply in the whole territory of the warring
states or, in the case of internal conflicts, the whole territory under the
control of a party, whether or not actual combat takes place there.[209] The
distinction between international and non-international armed conflicts
was thus minimised. Although it was noted that international law did not
regulate internal conflict in all aspects, it was held to 'cover such areas
as protection of civilians from hostilities, in particular from indiscriminate attacks, protection of civilian objects, in particular cultural property,
protection of all those who do not (or no longer) take active part in hostilities, as well as prohibition of means of warfare proscribed in international
armed conflicts and ban of certain methods of conducting hostilities'.[210]
Further, it was held that individual criminal responsibility existed with
regard to violations laid down in customary and treaty law, irrespective
of whether the conflict was an international or an internal one.[211] It was
concluded that in order for article 3 of the ICTY Statute to be applicable,
the violation had to be 'serious', which meant that it had to constitute a

---

[208] See below, chapter 21, p. 1194.
[209] IT-94-1-T, Decision of 2 October 1995, para. 70, 105 ILR, pp. 453, 486.
[210] *Ibid.*, para. 127.   [211] *Ibid.*, para. 129.

breach of a rule protecting important values, and the breach must involve grave consequences for the victim. In addition, the violation of the rule must entail, under customary or conventional law, the individual criminal responsibility of the person breaching the rule.[212]

This *Tadić* judgment can now be taken as reflecting international law and it is to be noted that a significant number of provisions dealing with international conflicts now apply to internal conflicts as laid down in the Statute of the International Criminal Court.[213]

Crimes against humanity[214]

Article 6(c) of the Nuremberg Charter included 'crimes against humanity' within the jurisdiction of the Tribunal and these were defined as 'murder, extermination, enslavement, deportation and other inhumane acts committed against any civilian population, before or during the war, or persecutions on political, racial or religious grounds in execution of or in connection with any crime within the jurisdiction of the Tribunal, whether or not in violation of the law of the country where perpetrated.'[215]

Article 5 of the Statute of the ICTY provided for jurisdiction with regard to the following crimes when committed in armed conflict, whether international or internal in character, and directed against any civilian population: '(a) murder; (b) extermination; (c) enslavement; (d) deportation; (e) imprisonment; (f) torture; (g) rape; (h) persecutions on political, racial and religious grounds; (i) other inhumane acts'. Article 3 of the Statute of the ICTR is in similar form, other than that it is specified that the crimes in question (which are the same as those specified in the ICTY Statute) must have been committed as part of a widespread or systematic attack against any civilian population on national, political, ethnic, racial or religious grounds. Article 7 of the Statute of the ICC notes that the crimes in question (enforced disappearance and apartheid are added to the list appearing in

---

[212] *Ibid.*, para. 94. See also e.g. the *Galić* case, IT-98-29-T, 2003, para. 11 and the *Kanyabashi* decision on jurisdiction, ICTR-96-15-T, 1997, para. 8.

[213] See article 8(2)(c) and (e) of the Statute.

[214] See e.g. Cryer *et al.*, *Introduction to International Criminal Law*, chapter 11; Werle, *Principles of International Criminal Law*, part 4; and Cassese, *International Criminal Law*, chapter 5. See also Bassiouni, *Crimes Against Humanity in International Criminal Law*.

[215] The Tokyo Charter was in similar terms, as was Allied Control Council Law No. 10 save that it added rape, imprisonment and torture to the list of inhumane acts and did not require a connection to war crimes or aggression: see Cryer *et al.*, *Introduction to International Criminal Law*, pp. 188 ff.

the Statutes of the two international criminal tribunals) have to be committed as part of a widespread or systematic attack directed against any civilian population, with knowledge of the attack.

Although article 5 of the ICTY Statute did not specifically refer, unlike the other instruments, to the necessity of a widespread or systematic attack as the required framework for the commission of acts amounting to crimes against humanity, this was incorporated into the jurisprudence through the *Tadić* trial decision of 7 May 1997. This interpreted the phrase 'directed against any civilian population' as meaning 'that the acts must occur on a widespread or systematic basis, that there must be some form of a governmental, organizational or group policy to commit these acts and that the perpetrator must know of the context within which his actions are taken'.[216]

The requirement of 'widespread or systematic' was examined in *Akayesu*, where the Trial Chamber declared that the concept of widespread could be defined as 'massive, frequent, large scale action, carried out collectively with considerable seriousness and directed against a multiplicity of victims', while 'systematic' could be defined as 'thoroughly organised and following a regular pattern on the basis of a common policy involving substantial public or private resources'. It was noted that there was no requirement that this policy must be adopted formally as the policy of a state, although there had to be some kind of preconceived plan or policy.[217] In *Blaškić*, the ICTY Trial Chamber defined 'systematic' in terms of

> the existence of a political objective, a plan pursuant to which the attack is perpetrated or an ideology, in the broad sense of the word, that is, to destroy, persecute or weaken a community; the perpetration of a criminal act on a very large scale against a group of civilians or the repeated and continuous commission of inhumane acts linked to one another; the preparation and use of significant public or private resources, whether military or other, and the implication of high-level political and/or military authorities in the definition and establishment of the methodical plan. The plan, however, need not necessarily be declared expressly or even stated clearly and precisely. It may be surmised from the occurrence of a series of events.[218]

In *Kunarac*, the ICTY Appeals Chamber held that while proof that the attack was directed against a civilian population and proof that it was

---

[216] IT-94-1-T, para. 644, 112 ILR, pp. 1, 214. See also paras. 645 ff. This was reaffirmed in the decision of the Appeals Chamber of 15 July 1999, para. 248, 124 ILR, pp. 61, 164.

[217] ICTR-96-4-T, 1998, para. 580.   [218] IT-95-14-T, 2000, paras. 203–4, 122 ILR, pp. 1, 78

widespread or systematic were legal elements of the crime, it was not necessary to show that they were the result of the existence of a policy or plan. The existence of a policy or plan could be evidentially relevant, but it was not a legal element of the crime.[219]

Many of the same acts may constitute both war crimes and crimes against humanity, but what is distinctive about the latter is that they do not need to take place during an armed conflict. However, to constitute crimes against humanity the acts in question have to be committed as part of a widespread or systematic activity, and to be committed against any civilian population, thus any reference to nationality is irrelevant. However, it is important to maintain a clear distinction between civilian and non-civilian in this context. The Trial Chamber in the *Martić* case noted that one could not allow the term 'civilian' for the purposes of a crime against humanity to include all persons who were not actively participating in combat, including those who were *hors de combat*, at the time of the crimes, as this would blur the necessary distinction between combatants and non-combatants.[220]

Of course, any act of genocide by definition will constitute also a crime against humanity, although the reverse is clearly not the case. What is required for crimes against humanity is an 'attack' and this has been broadly defined. In the *Akayesu* case, for example, this term was defined as an

> unlawful act of the kind enumerated in Article 3(a) to (i) of the Statute, like murder, extermination, enslavement etc. An attack may also be non-violent in nature, like imposing a system of apartheid, which is declared a crime against humanity in Article 1 of the Apartheid Convention of 1973, or exerting pressure on the population to act in a particular manner, may come under the purview of an attack, if orchestrated on a massive scale or in a systematic manner.[221]

It is also necessary for the alleged perpetrator to be aware that his act was part of a broader attack. The Appeals Chamber in its jurisdiction decision in *Tadić* concluded that to convict an accused of crimes against humanity, it had to be proved that the crimes were related to the attack on a civilian population and that the accused knew that his crimes were so related.[222] This is so even if he does not identify with the aims of the attack and his act was committed for personal reasons.[223]

---

[219] IT-96-23&23/1, 2002, para. 98.
[220] IT-95-11-T, 2007, paras. 55–6.   [221] ICTR-96-4-T, 1998, para. 581.
[222] IT-94-1-A, 1999, para. 271, 124 ILR, pp. 61, 173.   [223] *Ibid.*, paras. 255 ff.

Aggression[224]

Aggression is recognised as a crime in customary international law. Article 6 of the Nuremberg Charter defined its jurisdiction as including '(a) Crimes against peace. Namely, planning, preparation, initiation, or waging of a war of aggression or a war in violation of international treaties, agreements or assurances, or participation in a common plan or conspiracy for the accomplishment of any of the foregoing' and a number of defendants were convicted of offences under this head. General Assembly resolution 95(1) affirmed the principles recognised by the Nuremberg Charter and its judgment. Aggression was termed the 'supreme international crime' in one of the judgments.[225] The Tokyo Charter included the same principle as did Allied Control Council Law No. 10. General Assembly resolution 3314 (XXIX) of 14 December 1974 contained a definition of aggression in contravention of the Charter.[226] The crime of aggression is referred to in article 5 of the Statute of the ICC, but in no other such instrument. Indeed, article 5(2) provides that the Court cannot exercise jurisdiction over the crime of aggression until a provision is adopted defining the crime and setting out the conditions under which the Court may exercise jurisdiction with respect to it. The delay in achieving this has been caused by several problems. The first is that, unlike the other substantive international crimes, aggression is a crime of 'leadership' and necessarily requires that it be determined as an initial point that the state, of whom the accused is a 'leader' in some capacity, has committed aggression. This is a wholly different proposition from asserting the responsibility of individuals for genocide, war crimes or crimes against humanity. It is also unclear what differences may exist between the state's act of aggression and the individual's crime of aggression. Secondly, article 5(2) of the ICC Statute provides that the conditions for the exercise of the Court's jurisdiction must be consistent with the relevant provisions of the UN Charter. The Security Council has the competence under Chapter VII of the Charter

---

[224] See e.g. Cryer et al., *Introduction to International Criminal Law*, chapter 13; and Werle, *Principles of International Criminal Law*, part 6. See also Y. Dinstein, *War, Aggression and Self-Defence*, 4th edn, Cambridge, 2005, and see further below, chapter 22, p. 1240.

[225] See Judgment 186, 41 AJIL, 1947, p. 172.

[226] See also the General Treaty for the Renunciation of War (the 'Kellogg–Briand Pact'), 1928, which condemned recourse to war as an instrument of international policy; article 1 of the International Law Commission's Draft Code of Offences against Peace and Security, 1954, and article 1(2) of the revised Draft Code adopted in 1996. Article 16 of the latter instrument provides that a leader who as leader or organiser actively participates in or orders the planning, preparation, initiation or waging of aggression committed by a state shall be responsible for a crime of aggression.

to determine whether an act of aggression has taken place and it has been argued that a prior determination by the Council is necessary before the Court may exercise jurisdiction with regard to individual responsibility for aggression. This has been contested.[227] However, the question of the relationship between the competences of the Council and Court respectively is unsettled. These matters are currently being negotiated by the Assembly of States Parties to the Rome Statute.[228]

Conclusion – fair trial provisions

Part of the rapidly developing international law concerning individual responsibility for international crimes relates to the protection of the human rights of the accused. The following provisions constitute the essence of the requirements of fair trial. Article 21 of the ICTY Statute, for example, provides that:

> 1. All persons shall be equal before the International Tribunal.
>
> 2. In the determination of charges against him, the accused shall be entitled to a fair and public hearing, subject to article 22 of the Statute [which concerns the protection of victims and witnesses].
>
> 3. The accused shall be presumed innocent until proved guilty according to the provisions of the present Statute.
>
> 4. In the determination of any charge against the accused pursuant to the present Statute, the accused shall be entitled to the following minimum guarantees, in full equality:
>
> > (a) to be informed promptly and in detail in a language which he understands of the nature and cause of the charge against him;
> >
> > (b) to have adequate time and facilities for the preparation of his defence and to communicate with counsel of his own choosing;
> >
> > (c) to be tried without undue delay;
> >
> > (d) to be tried in his presence, and to defend himself in person or through legal assistance of his own choosing; to be informed, if he does not have legal assistance, of this right; and to have legal assistance assigned to

---

[227] See e.g. Cryer *et al.*, *Introduction to International Criminal Law*, pp. 276 ff. See also A. Carpenter, 'The International Criminal Court and the Crime of Aggression', 64 *Nordic Journal of International Law*, 1995, p. 223; A. Zimmermann, 'The Creation of a Permanent International Criminal Court', 25 *Suffolk Transnational Law Review*, 2005, p. 1, and C. Kress, 'Versailles–Nuremberg–The Hague: Germany and the International Criminal Law', 40 *International Lawyer*, 2006, p. 15.

[228] See e.g. the Fifth Session of the Assembly of States Parties, February 2007, ICC-ASP/5/35, Annex II and the Report of the Special Working Group on the Crime of Aggression, 13 December 2007, www.icc-cpi.int/library/asp/ICC-ASP-6-SWGCA-1_English.pdf.

him, in any case where the interests of justice so require, and without payment by him in any such case if he does not have sufficient means to pay for it;

(e) to examine, or have examined, the witnesses against him and to obtain the attendance and examination of witnesses on his behalf under the same conditions as witnesses against him;

(f) to have the free assistance of an interpreter if he cannot understand or speak the language used in the International Tribunal;

(g) not to be compelled to testify against himself or to confess guilt.

This formulation is essentially repeated in article 20 of the ICTR Statute. Article 55 of the ICC Statute provides that:

1. In respect of an investigation under this Statute, a person:

(a) Shall not be compelled to incriminate himself or herself or to confess guilt;

(b) Shall not be subjected to any form of coercion, duress or threat, to torture or to any other form of cruel, inhuman or degrading treatment or punishment;

(c) Shall, if questioned in a language other than a language the person fully understands and speaks, have, free of any cost, the assistance of a competent interpreter and such translations as are necessary to meet the requirements of fairness; and

(d) Shall not be subjected to arbitrary arrest or detention, and shall not be deprived of his or her liberty except on such grounds and in accordance with such procedures as are established in this Statute.

2. Where there are grounds to believe that a person has committed a crime within the jurisdiction of the Court and that person is about to be questioned either by the Prosecutor, or by national authorities pursuant to a request made under Part 9, that person shall also have the following rights of which he or she shall be informed prior to being questioned:

(a) To be informed, prior to being questioned, that there are grounds to believe that he or she has committed a crime within the jurisdiction of the Court;

(b) To remain silent, without such silence being a consideration in the determination of guilt or innocence;

(c) To have legal assistance of the person's choosing, or, if the person does not have legal assistance, to have legal assistance assigned to him or her, in any case where the interests of justice so require, and without payment by the person in any such case if the person does not have sufficient means to pay for it; and

(d) To be questioned in the presence of counsel unless the person has voluntarily waived his or her right to counsel.

In addition, article 66 provides for the presumption of innocence and for the fact that it is for the Prosecutor to prove the guilt of the accused beyond reasonable doubt. Article 67 lays down that:

1. In the determination of any charge, the accused shall be entitled to a public hearing, having regard to the provisions of this Statute, to a fair hearing conducted impartially, and to the following minimum guarantees, in full equality:

(a) To be informed promptly and in detail of the nature, cause and content of the charge, in a language which the accused fully understands and speaks;

(b) To have adequate time and facilities for the preparation of the defence and to communicate freely with counsel of the accused's choosing in confidence;

(c) To be tried without undue delay;

(d) Subject to article 63, paragraph 2, to be present at the trial, to conduct the defence in person or through legal assistance of the accused's choosing, to be informed, if the accused does not have legal assistance, of this right and to have legal assistance assigned by the Court in any case where the interests of justice so require, and without payment if the accused lacks sufficient means to pay for it;

(e) To examine, or have examined, the witnesses against him or her and to obtain the attendance and examination of witnesses on his or her behalf under the same conditions as witnesses against him or her. The accused shall also be entitled to raise defences and to present other evidence admissible under this Statute;

(f) To have, free of any cost, the assistance of a competent interpreter and such translations as are necessary to meet the requirements of fairness, if any of the proceedings of or documents presented to the Court are not in a language which the accused fully understands and speaks;

(g) Not to be compelled to testify or to confess guilt and to remain silent, without such silence being a consideration in the determination of guilt or innocence;

(h) To make an unsworn oral or written statement in his or her defence; and

(i) Not to have imposed on him or her any reversal of the burden of proof or any onus of rebuttal.

2. In addition to any other disclosure provided for in this Statute, the Prosecutor shall, as soon as practicable, disclose to the defence evidence in

the Prosecutor's possession or control which he or she believes shows or tends to show the innocence of the accused, or to mitigate the guilt of the accused, or which may affect the credibility of prosecution evidence. In case of doubt as to the application of this paragraph, the Court shall decide.[229]

Suggestions for further reading

A. Cassese, *International Criminal Law*, 2nd edn, Oxford, 2008

R. Cryer, H. Friman, D. Robinson and E. Wilmshurst, *An Introduction to International Criminal Law and Procedure*, Cambridge, 2007

W. Schabas, *An Introduction to the International Criminal Court*, 3rd edn, Cambridge, 2007

The UN International Criminal Tribunals: The Former Yugoslavia, Rwanda and Sierra Leone, Cambridge 2006

---

[229] Note among other relevant issues, the principle of command responsibility, whereby a superior is criminally responsible for acts committed by subordinates that he knew or had reason to know had been or were about to be committed and no action was taken: see e.g. Green, *Armed Conflict*, pp. 303–4; I. Bantekas, 'The Contemporary Law of Superior Responsibility', 93 AJIL, 1999, p. 573, and Kittichaisaree, *International Criminal Law*, p. 251. See also article 87 of Additional Protocol I, 1977; article 7(3) of the Statute of the International Criminal Tribunal for the Former Yugoslavia, 1993; article 6(3) of the Statute of the International Criminal Tribunal for Rwanda, 1994 and article 28 of the Statute of the International Criminal Court, 1998. Note the *Čelebići* case, IT-96-21, 16 November 1998, paras. 370 ff.; the *Krnojela* case, IT-97-25-A, 17 September 2003 and the *Blagojević* case, IT-02-60-A, 2007. Further, military necessity may not be pleaded as a defence, see e.g. *In re Lewinski (called von Manstein)*, 16 AD, p. 509, and the claim of superior orders will not provide a defence, although it may be taken in mitigation depending upon the circumstances: see e.g. Green, *Armed Conflict*, pp. 305–7; Green, *Superior Orders in National and International Law*, Leiden, 1976; Kittichaisaree, *International Criminal Law*, p. 266, and Y. Dinstein, *The Defence of 'Obedience to Superior Orders' in International Law*, Leiden, 1965. See also article 8 of the Nuremberg Charter, 39 AJIL, 1945, Supp., p. 259; Principle IV of the International Law Commission's Report on the Principles of the Nuremberg Tribunal 1950, *Yearbook of the ILC*, 1950, vol. II, p. 195; article 7(4) of the Statute of the International Criminal Tribunal for the Former Yugoslavia, 1993; article 6(4) of the Statute of the International Criminal Tribunal for Rwanda, 1994 and article 33 of the Statute of the International Criminal Court, 1998.

9

Recognition

International society is not an unchanging entity, but is subject to the ebb and flow of political life.[1] New states are created and old units fall away. New governments come into being within states in a manner contrary to declared constitutions whether or not accompanied by force. Insurgencies occur and belligerent administrations are established in areas of territory hitherto controlled by the legitimate government. Each of these events creates new facts and the question that recognition is concerned with revolves around the extent to which legal effects should flow from such occurrences. Each state will have to decide whether or not to recognise the particular eventuality and the kind of legal entity it should be accepted as.

Recognition involves consequences both on the international plane and within municipal law. If an entity is recognised as a state in, for example, the United Kingdom, it will entail the consideration of rights and duties that would not otherwise be relevant. There are privileges permitted to

---

[1] See generally e.g. J. Crawford, *The Creation of States in International Law*, 2nd edn, Oxford, 2006; *Oppenheim's International Law* (eds. R. Y. Jennings and A. D. Watts), 9th edn, London, 1992; H. Lauterpacht, *Recognition in International Law*, Cambridge, 1947; T. C. Chen, *The International Law of Recognition*, London, 1951; J. Charpentier, *La Reconnaissance Internationale et l'Évolution du Droit des Gens*, Paris, 1956; T. L. Galloway, *Recognising Foreign Governments*, Washington, 1978; J. Verhoeven, *La Reconnaissance Internationale dans la Pratique Contemporaine*, Paris, 1975 and Verhoeven, 'La Reconnaissance Internationale, Déclin ou Renouveau?', AFDI, 1993, p. 7; J. Dugard, *Recognition and the United Nations*, Cambridge, 1987; H. Blix, 'Contemporary Aspects of Recognition', 130 HR, 1970-II, p. 587; J. Salmon, 'Reconnaissance d'État', 25 *Revue Belge de Droit International*, 1992, p. 226; S. Talmon, *Recognition in International Law: A Bibliography*, The Hague, 2000; T. D. Grant, *The Recognition of States: Law and Practice in Debate and Evolution*, London, 1999, and *Third US Restatement on Foreign Relations Law*, Washington, 1987, vol. I, pp. 77 ff. See also Nguyen Quoc Dinh, P. Daillier and A. Pellet, *Droit International Public*, 7th edn, Paris, 2002, pp. 556 ff.; P. M. Dupuy, *Droit International Public*, 8th edn, Paris, 2006, p. 95, and L. Henkin, R. C. Pugh, O. Schachter and H. Smit, *International Law: Cases and Materials*, 3rd edn, St Paul, 1993, pp. 244 ff.

a foreign state before the municipal courts that would not be allowed to other institutions or persons.

It is stating the obvious to point to the very strong political influences that bear upon this topic.[2] In more cases than not the decision whether or not to recognise will depend more upon political considerations than exclusively legal factors. Recognition is not merely applying the relevant legal consequences to a factual situation, for sometimes a state will not want such consequences to follow, either internationally or domestically.

To give one example, the United States refused for many years to recognise either the People's Republic of China or North Korea, not because it did not accept the obvious fact that these authorities exercised effective control over their respective territories, but rather because it did not wish the legal effects of recognition to come into operation.[3] It is purely a political judgment, although it has been clothed in legal terminology. In addition, there are a variety of options open as to what an entity may be recognised as. Such an entity may, for example, be recognised as a full sovereign state, or as the effective authority within a specific area or as a subordinate authority to another state.[4] Recognition is a statement by an international legal person as to the status in international law of another real or alleged international legal person or of the validity of a particular factual situation. Once recognition has occurred, the new situation is deemed opposable to the recognising state, that is the pertinent legal consequences will flow. As such, recognition constitutes participation in the international legal process generally while also being important within the context of bilateral relations and, of course, domestically.

Recognition of states

There are basically two theories as to the nature of recognition. The constitutive theory maintains that it is the act of recognition by other states that creates a new state and endows it with legal personality and not the process by which it actually obtained independence. Thus, new states are

---

[2] See e.g. H. A. Smith, *Great Britain and the Law of Nations*, London, 1932, vol. I, pp. 77–80.

[3] See e.g. M. Kaplan and N. Katzenbach, *The Political Foundations of International Law*, New York, 1961, p. 109.

[4] See e.g. *Carl Zeiss Stiftung* v. *Rayner and Keeler* [1967] AC 853; 43 ILR, p. 23, where the Court took the view that the German Democratic Republic was a subordinate agency of the USSR, and the recognition of the Ciskei as a subordinate body of South Africa, *Gur Corporation* v. *Trust Bank of Africa Ltd* [1986] 3 All ER 449; 75 ILR, p. 675.

established in the international community as fully fledged subjects of international law by virtue of the will and consent of already existing states.[5] The disadvantage of this approach is that an unrecognised 'state' may not be subject to the obligations imposed by international law and may accordingly be free from such restraints as, for instance, the prohibition on aggression. A further complication would arise if a 'state' were recognised by some but not other states. Could one talk then of, for example, partial personality?

The second theory, the declaratory theory, adopts the opposite approach and is a little more in accord with practical realities.[6] It maintains that recognition is merely an acceptance by states of an already existing situation. A new state will acquire capacity in international law not by virtue of the consent of others but by virtue of a particular factual situation. It will be legally constituted by its own efforts and circumstances and will not have to await the procedure of recognition by other states. This doctrine owes a lot to traditional positivist thought on the supremacy of the state and the concomitant weakness or non-existence of any central guidance in the international community.

For the constitutive theorist, the heart of the matter is that fundamentally an unrecognised 'state' can have no rights or obligations in international law. The opposite stance is adopted by the declaratory approach that emphasises the factual situation and minimises the power of states to confer legal personality.

Actual practice leads to a middle position between these two perceptions. The act of recognition by one state of another indicates that the former regards the latter as having conformed with the basic requirements of international law as to the creation of a state. Of course, recognition is highly political and is given in a number of cases for purely political reasons. This point of view was emphasised by the American representative on the Security Council during discussions on the Middle East in May 1948. He said that it would be:

---

[5] See e.g. Crawford, *Creation of States*, pp. 19 ff. and J. Salmon, *La Reconnaissance d'État*, Paris, 1971. See also R. Rich and D. Turk, 'Symposium: Recent Developments in the Practice of State Recognition', 4 EJIL, 1993, p. 36.

[6] See e.g. J. L. Brierly, *The Law of Nations*, 6th edn, Oxford, 1963, p. 138; I. Brownlie, *Principles of Public International Law*, 6th edn, Oxford, 2003, p. 87; D. P. O'Connell, *International Law*, 2nd edn, London, 1970, vol. I, pp. 128 ff.; S. Talmon, 'The Constitutive Versus the Declaratory Theory of Recognition: Tertium Non Datur?', 75 BYIL, 2004, p. 101, and Crawford, *Creation of States*, pp. 22 ff. See also the *Tinoco* arbitration, 1 RIAA, p. 369; 2 AD, p. 34 and *Wulfsohn* v. *Russian Republic* 138 NE 24; 2 AD, p. 39.

highly improper for one to admit that any country on earth can question the sovereignty of the United States of America in the exercise of the high political act of recognition of the *de facto* status of a state.

Indeed, he added that there was no authority that could determine the legality or validity of that act of the United States.[7] This American view that recognition is to be used as a kind of mark of approval was in evidence with regard to the attitude adopted towards Communist China for a generation.[8]

The United Kingdom, on the other hand, has often tended to extend recognition once it is satisfied that the authorities of the state in question have complied with the minimum requirements of international law, and have effective control which seems likely to continue over the country.[9] Recognition is constitutive in a political sense, for it marks the new entity out as a state within the international community and is evidence of acceptance of its new political status by the society of nations. This does not imply that the act of recognition is legally constitutive, because rights and duties do not arise as a result of the recognition.

Practice over the last century or so is not unambiguous but does point to the declaratory approach as the better of the two theories. States which for particular reasons have refused to recognise other states, such as in the Arab world and Israel and the USA and certain communist nations,[10] rarely contend that the other party is devoid of powers and obligations before international law and exists in a legal vacuum. The stance is rather that rights and duties are binding upon them, and that recognition has not been accorded for primarily political reasons. If the constitutive theory were accepted it would mean, for example, in the context of the former Arab non-recognition of Israel, that the latter was not bound by international law rules of non-aggression and non-intervention. This has not been adopted in any of the stances of non-recognition of 'states'.[11]

---

[7] See M. Whiteman, *Digest of International Law*, Washington, 1968, vol. II, p. 10.

[8] See generally D. Young, 'American Dealings with Peking', 45 *Foreign Affairs*, 1966, p. 77, and Whiteman, *Digest*, vol. II, pp. 551 ff. See also A/CN.4/2, p. 53.

[9] See Lauterpacht, *Recognition*, p. 6.

[10] See 39 *Bulletin of the US Department of State*, 1958, p. 385.

[11] See e.g. the *Pueblo* incident, 62 AJIL, 1968, p. 756 and *Keesing's Contemporary Archives*, p. 23129; Whiteman, *Digest*, vol. II, pp. 604 ff. and 651; 'Contemporary Practice of the UK in International Law', 6 ICLQ, 1957, p. 507, and *British Practice in International Law* (ed. E. Lauterpacht), London, 1963, vol. II, p. 90. See also N. Mugerwa, 'Subjects of International Law' in *Manual of International Law* (ed. M. Sørensen), London, 1968, pp. 247, 269.

Of course, if an entity, while meeting the conditions of international law as to statehood, went totally unrecognised, this would undoubtedly hamper the exercise of its rights and duties, especially in view of the absence of diplomatic relations, but it would not seem in law to amount to a decisive argument against statehood itself.[12] For example, the Charter of the Organisation of American States adopted at Bogotá in 1948 notes in its survey of the fundamental rights and duties of states that:

> the political existence of the state is independent of recognition by other states. Even before being recognised the state has the right to defend its integrity and independence.[13]

And the Institut de Droit International emphasised in its resolution on recognition of new states and governments in 1936 that the

> existence of the new state with all the legal effects connected with that existence is not affected by the refusal of one or more states to recognise.[14]

In the period following the end of the First World War, the courts of the new states of Eastern and Central Europe regarded their states as coming into being upon the actual declaration of independence and not simply as a result of the Peace Treaties. The tribunal in one case pointed out that the recognition of Poland in the Treaty of Versailles was only declaratory of the state which existed 'par lui-même'.[15] In addition, the Arbitration Commission established by the International Conference on Yugoslavia in 1991 stated in its Opinion No. 1 that 'the existence or disappearance of the state is a question of fact' and that 'the effects of recognition by other states are purely declaratory'.[16]

On the other hand, the constitutive theory is not totally devoid of all support in state practice. In some cases, the creation of a new state, or the establishment of a new government by unconstitutional means, or the occupation of a territory that is legally claimed will proceed uneventfully and be clearly accomplished for all to see and with little significant opposition.

---

[12] See above, chapter 5.

[13] Article 9. This became article 12 of the Charter as amended in 1967. See also the Montevideo Convention on Rights and Duties of States, 1933, article 3.

[14] 39 *Annuaire de L'Institut de Droit International*, 1936, p. 300. See also *Third US Restatement*, pp. 77–8.

[15] *Deutsche Continental Gas-Gesellschaft* v. *Polish State* 5 AD, p. 11.

[16] 92 ILR, pp. 162, 165. See also the decision of the European Court of Human Rights in *Loizidou* v. *Turkey (Preliminary Objections)*, Series A, No. 310, 1995, at p. 14; 103 ILR, p. 621, and *Chuan Pu Andrew Wang and Others* v. *Office of the Federal Prosecutor*, Swiss Supreme Court, First Public Law Chamber, decision of 3 May 2004, No. 1A.3/2004; partly published as BGE 130 II 217, para. 5.3.

However, in many instances, the new entity or government will be inse-
cure and it is in this context that recognition plays a vital role. In any
event, and particularly where the facts are unclear and open to different
interpretations, recognition by a state will amount to a declaration by that
state of how it understands the situation, and such an evaluation will be
binding upon it. It will not be able to deny later the factual position it has
recognised, unless, of course, circumstances radically alter in the meantime. In this sense, recognition can be constitutive. Indeed, the Yugoslav
Arbitration Commission noted in Opinion No. 8 that 'while recognition
of a state by other states has only declarative value, such recognition,
along with membership of international organisations, bears witness to
these states' conviction that the political entity so recognised is a reality
and confers on it certain rights and obligations under international law'.[17]
By way of contrast, the fact of non-recognition of a 'new state' by a vast
majority of existing states will constitute tangible evidence for the view
that such an entity has not established its conformity with the required
criteria of statehood.[18]

Another factor which leans towards the constitutive interpretation of
recognition is the practice in many states whereby an unrecognised state
or government cannot claim the rights available to a recognised state
or government before the municipal courts. This means that the act of
recognition itself entails a distinct legal effect and that after recognition
a state or government would have enforceable rights within the domestic
jurisdiction that it would not have had prior to the recognition.[19]

This theoretical controversy is of value in that it reveals the functions of
recognition and emphasises the impact of states upon the development of
international law. It points to the essential character of international law,
poised as it is between the state and the international community. The
declaratory theory veers towards the former and the constitutive doctrine
towards the latter.

There have been a number of attempts to adapt the constitutive theory.[20]
Lauterpacht maintained, for example, that once the conditions prescribed
by international law for statehood have been complied with, there is a duty

---

[17] 92 ILR, pp. 199, 201.
[18] See *Democratic Republic of East Timor* v. *State of the Netherlands* 87 ILR, pp. 73, 74.
[19] See below, p. 471.
[20] Note the reference to the 'relativism inherent in the constitutive theory of recognition' with
regard to the situation where some states recognised the Federal Republic of Yugoslavia as
the continuator of the Federal Republic of Yugoslavia and others did not: see the *Genocide
Convention (Bosnia* v. *Serbia)* case, ICJ Reports, 2007, Dissenting Opinion of Judge Al-
Khasawneh, para. 8.

on the part of existing states to grant recognition. This is because, in the absence of a central authority in international law to assess and accord legal personality, it is the states that have to perform this function on behalf, as it were, of the international community and international law.[21]

This operation is both declaratory, in that it is based upon certain definite facts (i.e. the entity fulfils the requirements of statehood) and constitutive in that it is the acceptance by the recognising state of the particular community as an entity possessing all the rights and obligations that are inherent in statehood. Before the act of recognition, the community that is hoping to be admitted as a state will only have such rights and duties as have been expressly permitted to it, if any.

The Lauterpacht doctrine is an ingenious bid to reconcile the legal elements in a coherent theory. It accepts the realities of new creations of states and governments by practical (and occasionally illegal) means, and attempts to assimilate this to the supremacy of international law as Lauterpacht saw it. However, in so doing it ignores the political aspects and functions of recognition, that is, its use as a method of demonstrating or withholding support from a particular government or new community. The reality is that in many cases recognition is applied to demonstrate political approval or disapproval. Indeed, if there is a duty to grant recognition, would the entity involved have a right to demand this where a particular state (or states) is proving recalcitrant? If this were so, one would appear to be faced with the possibility of a non-state with as yet no rights or duties enforcing rights against non-recognising states.

Nevertheless, state practice reveals that Lauterpacht's theory has not been adopted.[22] The fact is that few states accept that they are obliged in every instance to accord recognition. In most cases they will grant recognition, but that does not mean that they have to, as history with regard to some Communist nations and with respect to Israel illustrates. This position was supported in Opinion No. 10 of the Yugoslav Arbitration Commission in July 1992, which emphasised that recognition was 'a discretionary act that other states may perform when they choose and in a manner of their own choosing, subject only to compliance with the imperatives of general international law'.[23]

The approach of the United States was emphasised in 1976. The Department of State noted that:

---

[21] *Recognition*, pp. 24, 55, 76–7.

[22] See e.g. H. Waldock, 'General Course on Public International Law', 106 HR, 1962, p. 154. See also Mugerwa, 'Subjects', pp. 266–90.

[23] 92 ILR, pp. 206, 208.

[i]n the view of the United States, international law does not require a state to recognise another entity as a state; it is a matter for the judgment of each state whether an entity merits recognition as a state. In reaching this judgment, the United States has traditionally looked to the establishment of certain facts. These facts include effective control over a clearly defined territory and population; an organised governmental administration of that territory and a capacity to act effectively to conduct foreign relations and to fulfil international obligations. The United States has also taken into account whether the entity in question has attracted the recognition of the international community of states.[24]

The view of the UK government was expressed as follows:

The normal criteria which the government apply for recognition as a state are that it should have, and seem likely to continue to have, a clearly defined territory with a population, a government who are able of themselves to exercise effective control of that territory, and independence in their external relations. Other factors, including some United Nations resolutions, may also be relevant.[25]

Recent practice suggests that 'other factors' may, in the light of the particular circumstances, include human rights and other matters. The European Community adopted a Declaration on 16 December 1991 entitled 'Guidelines on the Recognition of New States in Eastern Europe and in the Soviet Union' in which a common position on the process of recognition of the new states was adopted. It was noted in particular that recognition required:

- respect for the provisions of the Charter of the United Nations and the commitments subscribed to in the Final Act of Helsinki and in the Charter of Paris,[26] especially with regard to the rule of law, democracy and human rights;
- guarantees for the rights of ethnic and national groups and minorities in accordance with the commitments subscribed to in the framework of the CSCE;[27]
- respect for the inviolability of all frontiers which can only be changed by peaceful means and by common agreement;

---

[24] DUSPIL, 1976, pp. 19–20.
[25] 102 HC Deb., col. 977, Written Answer, 23 October 1986. See also 169 HC Deb., cols. 449–50, Written Answer, 19 March 1990. As to French practice, see e.g. Journal Officiel, Débats Parl., AN, 1988, p. 2324.
[26] See above, chapter 7, p. 372.   [27] See above, chapter 7, p. 376.

- acceptance of all relevant commitments with regard to disarmament and nuclear non-proliferation as well as to security and regional stability;
- commitment to settle by agreement, including where appropriate by recourse to arbitration, all questions concerning state succession and regional disputes.[28]

On the same day that the Guidelines were adopted, the European Community also adopted a Declaration on Yugoslavia,[29] in which the Community and its member states agreed to recognise the Yugoslav republics fulfilling certain conditions. These were that such republics wished to be recognised as independent; that the commitments in the Guidelines were accepted; that provisions laid down in a draft convention under consideration by the Conference on Yugoslavia were accepted, particularly those dealing with human rights and the rights of national or ethnic groups; and that support would be given to the efforts of the Secretary-General of the UN and the Security Council and the Conference on Yugoslavia. The Community and its member states also required that the particular Yugoslav republic seeking recognition would commit itself prior to recognition to adopting constitutional and political guarantees ensuring that it had no territorial claims towards a neighbouring Community state. The United States took a rather less robust position, but still noted the relevance of commitments and assurances given by the new states of Eastern Europe and the former USSR with regard to nuclear safety, democracy and free markets within the process of both recognition and the establishment of diplomatic relations.[30]

Following a period of UN administration authorised by Security Council resolution 1244 (1999),[31] the Yugoslav (later Serbian) province of Kosovo declared independence on 17 February 2008. This was preceded by

---

[28] UKMIL, 62 BYIL, 1991, pp. 559–60. On 31 December 1991, the European Community issued a statement noting that Armenia, Azerbaijan, Belarus, Kazakhstan, Moldova, Turkmenistan, Ukraine and Uzbekistan had given assurances that the requirements in the Guidelines would be fulfilled. Accordingly, the member states of the Community declared that they were willing to proceed with the recognition of these states, *ibid.*, p. 561. On 15 January 1992, a statement was issued noting that Kyrghyzstan and Tadzhikistan had accepted the requirements in the Guidelines and that they too would be recognised, UKMIL, 63 BYIL, 1992, p. 637.

[29] UKMIL, 62 BYIL, 1991, pp. 560–1.

[30] See the announcement by President Bush on 25 December 1991, 2(4 & 5) *Foreign Policy Bulletin*, 1992, p. 12, as cited in Henkin *et al.*, *International Law*, pp. 252–3. See also, as to the importance of democratic considerations, S. D. Murphy, 'Democratic Legitimacy and the Recognition of States and Governments', 48 ICLQ, 1999, p. 545.

[31] See above, chapter 5, p. 204.

the Comprehensive Proposal for the Kosovo Status Settlement formulated by Martti Ahtisaari which had in March 2007 called for independence for Kosovo with international supervision.[32] This was rejected by Serbia. The international community was divided as to the question of recognition of Kosovo's independence. It was recognised swiftly by the US, the UK, Germany and the majority of EU states, Japan and others. Russia and Serbia, on the other hand, made it clear that they opposed recognition, as did Spain and Greece. Accordingly, in the current circumstances, while many countries recognise Kosovo, many do not and entry into the UN is not possible until, for example, Russia is prepared to lift its opposition in view of its veto power.[33] For those states that have recognised Kosovo, the latter will be entitled to all the privileges and responsibilities of statehood in the international community and within the legal systems of the recognising states. However, for those that have not, the state and diplomatic agents of Kosovo will not be entitled to, for example, diplomatic and state immunities, while the international status of Kosovo will be controversial and disputed. While recognition may cure difficulties in complying with the criteria of statehood, a situation where the international community is divided upon recognition will, especially in the absence of UN membership, ensure the continuation of uncertainty.

There are many different ways in which recognition can occur and it may apply in more than one kind of situation. It is not a single, constant idea but a category comprising a number of factors. There are indeed different entities which may be recognised, ranging from new states, to new governments, belligerent rights possessed by a particular group and territorial changes. Not only are there various objects of the process of recognition, but recognition may itself be *de facto* or *de jure* and it may arise in a variety of manners.

Recognition is an active process and should be distinguished from cognition, or the mere possession of knowledge, for example, that the entity involved complies with the basic international legal stipulations as to statehood. Recognition implies both cognition of the necessary facts and an intention that, so far as the acting state is concerned, it is willing that the legal consequences attendant upon recognition should operate.

---

[32] See S/2007/168 and S/2007/168/Add.1.

[33] One month after the declaration of independence, twenty-eight states had recognised the independence of Kosovo, including sixteen of the twenty-seven EU member states and six of the UN Security Council's fifteen members: see 'Kosovo's First Month', International Crisis Group Europe Briefing No. 47, 18 March 2008, p. 3.

For example, the rules as to diplomatic and sovereign immunities should apply as far as the envoys of the entity to be recognised are concerned. It is not enough for the recognising state simply to be aware of the facts, it must desire the coming into effect of the legal and political results of recognition. This is inevitable by virtue of the discretionary nature of the act of recognition, and is illustrated in practice by the lapse in time that often takes place between the events establishing a new state or government and the actual recognition by other states. Once given, courts have generally regarded recognition as retroactive so that the statehood of the entity recognised is accepted as of the date of statehood (which is a question of fact), not from the date of recognition.[34]

Recognition of governments[35]

The recognition of a new government is quite different from the recognition of a new state. As far as statehood is concerned, the factual situation will be examined in terms of the accepted criteria.[36] Different considerations apply where it is the government which changes. Recognition will only really be relevant where the change in government is unconstitutional. In addition, recognition of governments as a category tends to minimise the fact that the precise capacity or status of the entity so recognised may be characterised in different ways. Recognition may be of a *de facto*[37] government or administration or of a government or administration in effective control of only part of the territory of the state in question. Recognition constitutes acceptance of a particular situation

---

[34] See e.g. Chen, *Recognition*, pp. 172 ff. See also the views of the Yugoslav Arbitration Commission as to the date of succession of the former Yugoslav republics, Opinion No. 11, 96 ILR, p. 719. Note that retroactivity of recognition is regarded by Oppenheim as a rule of convenience rather than of principle: see *Oppenheim's International Law*, p. 161.

[35] See e.g. I. Brownlie, 'Recognition in Theory and Practice', 53 BYIL, 1982, p. 197; C. Warbrick, 'The New British Policy on Recognition of Governments', 30 ICLQ, 1981, p. 568; M. J. Peterson, 'Recognition of Governments Should Not Be Abolished', 77 AJIL, 1983, p. 31, and Peterson, *Recognition of Governments: Legal Doctrine and State Practice*, London, 1997; N. Ando, 'The Recognition of Governments Reconsidered', 28 *Japanese Annual of International Law*, 1985, p. 29; C. Symmons, 'United Kingdom Abolition of the Doctrine of Recognition: A Rose by Another Name', *Public Law*, 1981, p. 248; S. Talmon, 'Recognition of Governments: An Analysis of the New British Policy and Practice', 63 BYIL, 1992, p. 231, and Talmon, *Recognition of Governments in International Law*, Oxford, 1998; B. R. Roth, *Governmental Illegitimacy in International Law*, Oxford, 1999; *Oppenheim's International Law*, p. 150; Nguyen Quoc Dinh *et al.*, *Droit International Public*, p. 415, and Galloway, *Recognising Foreign Governments*.

[36] See above, chapter 5, p. 197.   [37] See further below, p. 459.

by the recognising state both in terms of the relevant factual criteria and in terms of the consequential legal repercussions, so that, for example, recognition of an entity as the government of a state implies not only that this government is deemed to have satisfied the required conditions, but also that the recognising state will deal with the government as the governing authority of the state and accept the usual legal consequences of such status in terms of privileges and immunities within the domestic legal order.

Political considerations have usually played a large role in the decision whether or not to grant recognition. However, certain criteria have emerged to cover recognition of illegal changes in government. Such criteria amounted to an acceptance of the realities of the transfer of power and suggested that once a new government effectively controlled the country and that this seemed likely to continue, recognition should not be withheld. The United Kingdom on a number of occasions adopted this approach.[38] It was declared by the Under-Secretary of State for Foreign Affairs in 1970 that the test employed was whether or not the new government enjoyed, 'with a reasonable prospect of permanence, the obedience of the mass of the population . . . effective control of much of the greater part of the territory of the state concerned'.[39]

It is this attitude which prompted such policies as the recognition of the communist government of China and the Russian-installed government of Hungary in 1956 after the failure of the uprising. However, this general approach cannot be regarded as an absolute principle in view of the British refusal over many years to recognise as states North Vietnam, North Korea and the German Democratic Republic.[40] The effective control of a new government over the territory of the state is thus an important guideline to the problem of whether to extend recognition or not, providing such control appears well established and likely to continue. But it was no more than that and in many cases appeared to yield to political considerations.

The *Tinoco* arbitration[41] constitutes an interesting example of the 'effective control' concept. In 1919, the government of Tinoco in Costa Rica was overthrown and the new authorities repudiated certain

---

[38] See the Morrison statement, 485 HC Deb., cols. 2410–11, 21 March 1951.
[39] 799 HC Deb., col. 23, 6 April 1970. See also Foreign Office statements, 204 HL Deb., col. 755, 4 July 1957 and 742 HC Deb., cols. 6–7, Written Answer, 27 February 1967.
[40] See e.g. D. Greig, 'The Carl-Zeiss Case and the Position of an Unrecognised Government in English Law', 83 LQR, 1967, pp. 96, 128–30 and *Re Al-Fin Corporation's Patent* [1970] Ch. 160; 52 ILR, p. 68.
[41] 1 RIAA, p. 369 (1923); 2 AD, p. 34.

obligations entered into by Tinoco with regard to British nationals. Chief Justice Taft, the sole arbitrator, referred to the problems of recognition or non-recognition as relating to the Tinoco administration. He decided that since the administration was in effective control of the country, it was the valid government irrespective of the fact that a number of states, including the United Kingdom, had not recognised it. This was so despite his opinion that:

> the non-recognition by other nations of a government claiming to be a national personality, is usually appropriate evidence that it has not attained the independence and control entitling it by international law to be classed as such.[42]

Where recognition has been refused because of the illegitimacy or irregularity of origin of the government in question, rather than because of the lack of effectiveness of its control in the country, such non-recognition loses some of its evidential weight. In other words, where the degree of authority asserted by the new administration is uncertain, recognition by other states will be a vital factor. But where the new government is firmly established, non-recognition will not affect the legal character of the new government. The doctrine of effective control is an indication of the importance of the factual nature of any situation. But in those cases where recognition is refused upon the basis of the improper origins of the new government, it will have less of an impact than if recognition is refused because of the absence of effective control. Taft's view of the nature of recognition is an interesting amalgam of the declaratory and constitutive theories, in that recognition can become constitutive where the factual conditions (i.e. the presence or absence of effective control) are in dispute, but otherwise is purely declaratory or evidential.

A change in government, however accomplished, does not affect the identity of the state itself. The state does not cease to be an international legal person because its government is overthrown. That is not at issue. The recognition or non-recognition of a new administration is irrelevant to the legal character of the country. Accordingly one can see that two separate recognitions are involved and they must not be confused. Recognition of a state will affect its legal personality, whether by creating or acknowledging it, while recognition of a government affects the status of the administrative authority, not the state.

It is possible, however, for recognition of state and government to occur together in certain circumstances. This can take place upon the creation

---

[42] 1 RIAA, p. 380; 2 AD, p. 37.

of a new state. Israel, to take one example, was recognised by the United States and the United Kingdom by the expedient of having its government recognised *de facto*.[43] Recognition of the government implies recognition of the state, but it does not work the other way.

It should be noted that recognition of a government has no relevance to the establishment of new persons in international law. Where it is significant is in the realm of diplomatic relations. If a government is unrecognised, there is no exchange of diplomatic envoys and thus problems can arise as to the enforcement of international rights and obligations.

Although the effective control doctrine is probably accepted as the most reliable guide to recognition of governments, there have been other theories put forward, the most prominent amongst them being the Tobar doctrine or the so-called doctrine of legitimacy. This suggested that governments which came into power by extra-constitutional means should not be recognised, at least until the change had been accepted by the people.[44] This policy was applied particularly by the United States in relation to Central America and was designed to protect stability in that delicate area adjacent to the Panama Canal. Logically, of course, the concept amounts to the promotion of non-recognition in all revolutionary situations and it is, and was, difficult to reconcile with reality and political consideration. In American eyes it became transmuted into the Wilson policy of democratic legitimacy. Where the revolution was supported by the people, it would be recognised. Where it was not, there would be no grant of recognition. It was elaborated with respect to the Soviet Union until 1933, but gradually declined until it can now be properly accepted merely as a political qualification for recognition to be considered by the recognising state.[45]

A doctrine advocating the exact opposite, the automatic recognition of governments in all circumstances, was put forward by Estrada, the Mexican Secretary of Foreign Relations.[46] But this suffers from the same disadvantage as the legitimacy doctrine. It attempts to lay down a clear test for recognition in all instances excluding political considerations and

---

[43] See e.g. Whiteman, *Digest*, vol. II, p. 168.

[44] See e.g. Mugerwa, 'Subjects', p. 271, and 2 AJIL, 1908, Supp., p. 229.

[45] See e.g. G. H. Hackworth, *Digest of International Law*, Washington, DC, 1940, vol. I, pp. 181 ff. See also 17 AJIL, 1923, Supp., p. 118; O'Connell, *International Law*, pp. 137–9, and Whiteman, *Digest*, vol. II, p. 69.

[46] See e.g. 25 AJIL, 1931, Supp., p. 203; P. Jessup, 'The Estrada Doctrine', 25 AJIL, 1931, p. 719, and Whiteman, *Digest*, vol. II, p. 85. See also Talmon, 'Recognition of Governments', p. 263; Chen, *Recognition*, p. 116; O'Connell, *International Law*, pp. 134–5, and C. Rousseau, *Droit International Public*, Paris, 1977, vol. III, p. 555.

exigencies of state and is thus unrealistic, particularly where there are competing governments.[47] It has also been criticised as minimising the distinction between recognition and maintenance of diplomatic relations.[48]

The problem, of course, was that recognition of a new government that has come to power in a non-constitutional fashion was taken to imply approval. Allied with the other factors sometimes taken into account in such recognition situations,[49] an unnecessarily complicated process had resulted. Accordingly, in 1977 the United States declared that:

> US practice has been to de-emphasise and avoid the use of recognition in cases of changes of governments and to concern ourselves with the question of whether we wish to have diplomatic relations with the new governments... The Administration's policy is that establishment of relations does not involve approval or disapproval but merely demonstrates a willingness on our part to conduct our affairs with other governments directly.[50]

In 1980, the UK government announced that it would no longer accord recognition to governments as distinct from states.[51] This was stated to be primarily due to the perception that recognition meant approval, a perception that was often embarrassing, for example, in the case of regimes violating human rights. There were, therefore, practical advantages in not according recognition as such to governments. This change to a policy of not formally recognising governments had in fact taken place in certain

---

[47] See e.g. Peterson, 'Recognition', p. 42, and C. Rousseau, 'Chroniques des Faits Internationaux', 93 RGDIP, 1989, p. 923.

[48] Warbrick, 'New British Policy', p. 584.

[49] For example, the democratic requirement noted by President Wilson, President Rutherford Hayes' popular support condition and Secretary of State Seward's criterion of ability to honour international obligations: see statement by US Department of State, DUSPIL, 1977, pp. 19, 20. See also *Third US Restatement*, para. 203, note 1. The Organisation of American States adopted a resolution in 1965 recommending that states contemplating recognition of a new government should take into account whether that government proposes to hold elections within a reasonable time, 5 ILM, 1966, p. 155.

[50] DUSPIL, 1977, p. 20. See also DUSPIL, 1981–8, vol. I, 1993, p. 295. Note that Deputy Secretary of State Christopher stated in 1977 that unscheduled changes of government were not uncommon in this day and age and that 'withholding diplomatic relations from these regimes after they have obtained effective control penalises us', *ibid.*, p. 18. See also, as regards Afghanistan and the continuation of diplomatic relations, 72 AJIL, 1978, p. 879. Cf. the special circumstances of the recognition of the government of China, DUSPIL, 1978, pp. 71–3 and *ibid.*, 1979, pp. 142 ff. But cf. Petersen, 'Recognition'.

[51] See 408 HL Deb., cols. 1121–2, 28 April 1980. See also Symmons, 'United Kingdom Abolition', p. 249.

civil law countries rather earlier. Belgium[52] and France[53] appear, for example, to have adopted this approach in 1965. By the late 1980s, this approach was also adopted by both Australia[54] and Canada,[55] and indeed by other countries.[56]

The change, however, did not remove all problems, but rather shifted the focus from formal recognition to informal 'dealings'. The UK announced that it would continue to decide the nature of dealings with unconstitutional regimes:

> in the light of [an] assessment of whether they are able of themselves to exercise effective control of the territory of the state concerned, and seem likely to continue to do so.[57]

The change, therefore, is that recognition of governments is abolished but that the criterion for dealing with such regimes is essentially the same as the former test for the recognition of governments.[58] In that context, regard should also be had to the phrase 'of themselves'.[59]

De facto and de jure recognition[60]

In addition to the fact that there are different entities to be recognised, recognition itself may take different forms. It may be either de facto or de

---

[52] See 11 *Revue Belge de Droit International*, 1973, p. 351.

[53] See 69 RGDIP, 1965, p. 1089. See also 83 RGDIP, 1979, p. 808; G. Charpentier, 'Pratique Française du Droit International', AFDI, 1981, p. 911, and Rousseau, *Droit International Public*, p. 555.

[54] See J. G. Starke, 'The New Australian Policy of Recognition of Foreign Governments', 62 *Australian Law Journal*, 1988, p. 390.

[55] See 27 Canadian YIL, 1989, p. 387. See also *Re Chateau-Gai Wines Ltd and Attorney-General for Canada* [1970] Ex CR 366; 55 ILR, p. 38.

[56] See e.g. the Netherlands, 22 Netherlands YIL, 1991, p. 237, and New Zealand, *Attorney-General for Fiji* v. *Robt Jones House Ltd* [1989] 2 NZLR 69 at 70–1; 80 ILR, p. 1. The European Union has stated that 'it does not recognise governments, and even less political personalities, but states, according to the most common international practice', *Bulletin of the European Union*, 1999–7/8, p. 60 and UKMIL, 70 BYIL, 1999, p. 424.

[57] 408 HL Deb., cols. 1121–2, 28 April 1980. This has been reaffirmed on a number of occasions: see e.g. UKMIL, 69 BYIL, 1998, p. 477 and UKMIL, 72 BYIL, 2001, p. 577.

[58] See *Gur Corporation* v. *Trust Bank of Africa* [1987] 1 QB 599; 75 ILR, p. 675.

[59] See, as regards the different approaches adopted to the Cambodian and Ugandan experiences, Symmons, 'United Kingdom Abolition', p. 250, and UKMIL, 50 BYIL, 1979, p. 296. See also above, chapter 4, p. 192. See, as to recognition of belligerency and insurgency, e.g. O'Connell, *International Law*, pp. 148–53; Lauterpacht, *Recognition*, p. 270, and *Oppenheim's International Law*, pp. 161 ff.

[60] See e.g. *Oppenheim's International Law*, p. 154.

jure. A more correct way of putting this might be to say that a government (or other entity or situation) may be recognised *de facto* or *de jure*.

Recognition *de facto* implies that there is some doubt as to the long-term viability of the government in question. Recognition *de jure* usually follows where the recognising state accepts that the effective control displayed by the government is permanent and firmly rooted and that there are no legal reasons detracting from this, such as constitutional subservience to a foreign power. *De facto* recognition involves a hesitant assessment of the situation, an attitude of wait and see, to be succeeded by *de jure* recognition when the doubts are sufficiently overcome to extend formal acceptance. To take one instance, the United Kingdom recognised the Soviet government *de facto* in 1921 and *de jure* in 1924.[61] A slightly different approach is adopted in cases of civil war where the distinction between *de jure* and *de facto* recognition is sometimes used to illustrate the variance between legal and factual sovereignty. For example, during the 1936–9 Spanish Civil War, the United Kingdom, while recognising the Republican government as the *de jure* government, extended *de facto* recognition to the forces under General Franco as they gradually took over the country. Similarly, the government of the Italian conquering forces in Ethiopia was recognised *de facto* by the UK in 1936, and *de jure* two years later.[62]

By this method a recognising state could act in accordance with political reality and its own interests while reserving judgment on the permanence of the change in government or its desirability or legality. It is able to safeguard the affairs of its citizens and institutions by this, because certain legal consequences will flow in municipal law from the recognition.[63]

There are in reality few meaningful distinctions between a *de facto* and a *de jure* recognition, although only a government recognised *de jure* may enter a claim to property located in the recognising state.[64] Additionally, it is generally accepted that *de facto* recognition does not of itself include the exchange of diplomatic relations.

Premature recognition[65]

There is often a difficult and unclear dividing line between the acceptable recognition of a new state, particularly one that has emerged or is emerging

---

[61] See e.g. O'Connell, *International Law*, p. 161. See also the Morrison statement, above, note 38.

[62] See below, pp. 473 and 474.   [63] See below, p. 471.

[64] See e.g. *Haile Selassie* v. *Cable and Wireless Ltd (No. 2)* [1939] 1 Ch. 182; 9 AD, p. 94.

[65] See e.g. *Oppenheim's International Law*, pp. 143 ff. and Nguyen Quoc Dinh *et al.*, *Droit International Public*, p. 558.

as a result of secession, and intervention in the domestic affairs of another state by way of premature or precipitate recognition, such as, for example, the view taken by the Nigerian federal government with respect to the recognition of 'Biafra' by five states.[66] In each case, the state seeking to recognise will need to consider carefully the factual situation and the degree to which the criteria of statehood (or other relevant criteria with regard to other types of entity with regard to which recognition is sought) have been fulfilled. It is therefore a process founded upon a perception of fact. In the case of Croatia, it could be argued that the recognition of that state by the European Community and its member states (together with Austria and Switzerland) on 15 January 1992 was premature.[67] Croatia at that time, and for several years thereafter, did not effectively control some one-third of its territory. In addition, the Yugoslav Arbitration Commission had taken the view in Opinion No. 5 on 11 January 1992 that Croatia did not meet fully the conditions for recognition laid down in the European Community Guidelines of 16 December 1991,[68] since the Constitutional Act adopted by Croatia did not fully incorporate the required guarantees relating to human rights and minority rights.[69] It could also be argued that the recognition of Bosnia-Herzegovina on 6 April 1992 by the European Community and member states and on 7 April 1992 by the USA was premature, particularly since the government of that state effectively controlled less than one-half of its territory, a situation that continued until the Dayton Peace Agreement of November 1995.[70] On the other hand, it could be argued that in the special

---

[66] See e.g. J. Stremlau, *The International Politics of the Nigerian Civil War, 1967–70*, Princeton, 1977, pp. 127–9, and D. Ijalaye, 'Was "Biafra" at Any Time a State in International Law?', 65 AJIL, 1971, p. 51. See also Lauterpacht, *Recognition*, pp. 7–8.

[67] See e.g. R. Müllerson, *International Law, Rights and Politics*, London, 1994, p. 130, and R. Rich, 'Recognition of States: The Collapse of Yugoslavia and the Soviet Union', 4 EJIL, 1993, p. 36.

[68] See above, p. 451.

[69] 92 ILR, pp. 179, 181. Note that the President of Croatia on 15 January 1992 announced that Croatia would abide by the necessary conditions and on 8 May 1992 its Constitution was amended. The amended Constitution was considered by the Arbitration Commission on 4 July 1992, which concluded that the requirements of general international law with regard to the protection of minorities had been satisfied, *ibid.*, p. 209. Note, however, the critical views of the UN Human Rights Committee with regard to the distinctions made in the Croatian Constitution between ethnic Croats and other citizens: see CCPR/C/79/Add.15, p. 3. Croatia became a member of the UN on 22 May 1992. See also M. Weller, 'The International Response to the Dissolution of the Socialist Federal Republic of Yugoslavia', 86 AJIL, 1992, p. 569.

[70] See e.g. Weller, 'International Response'. Cf. the views of the UK Minister of State at the Foreign Office, UKMIL, 63 BYIL, 1992, p. 645. Note that Bosnia became a member of the UN on 22 May 1992.

circumstances of Former Yugoslavia, the international community (particularly by means of membership of the UN which is restricted to states) was prepared to accept a loosening of the traditional criteria of statehood, so that essentially international recognition compensated for lack of effectivity.

Recognition may also be overdue, in the sense that it occurs long after it is clear as a matter of fact that the criteria of statehood have been satisfied, but in such cases, different considerations apply since recognition is not compulsory and remains a political decision by states.[71]

Implied recognition[72]

Recognition itself need not be express, that is in the form of an open, unambiguous and formal communication, but may be implied in certain circumstances.[73] This is due to the fact that recognition is founded upon the will and intent of the state that is extending the recognition. Accordingly, there are conditions in which it might be possible to declare that in acting in a certain manner, one state has by implication recognised another state or government. Because this facility of indirect or implied recognition is available, states may make an express declaration to the effect that a particular action involving another party is by no means to be interpreted as comprehending any recognition. This attitude was maintained by Arab countries with regard to Israel, and in certain other cases.[74] It automatically excludes any possibility of implied recognition but

---

[71] See e.g. with regard to the delays in recognising Macedonia, Henkin et al., *International Law*, p. 253, and Nguyen Quoc Dinh et al., *Droit International Public*, p. 565. Israel, of course, remained unrecognised by its Arab neighbours until long after its establishment in 1948. It was recognised in 1979 by Egypt and in 1995 by Jordan.

[72] See e.g. *Oppenheim's International Law*, p. 169; Lauterpacht, *Recognition*, pp. 369–408, and Chen, *Recognition*, pp. 201–16. See also Talmon, 'Recognition of Governments', pp. 255 ff., and M. Lachs, 'Recognition and Modern Methods of International Co-operation', 35 BYIL, 1959, p. 252.

[73] Note that article 7 of the Montevideo Convention on Rights and Duties of States, 1933 provides that 'the recognition of a state may be express or tacit. The latter results from any act which implies the intention of recognising the new state.' See also R. Higgins, *The Development of International Law by the Political Organs of the United Nations*, Oxford, 1963, pp. 140 ff.

[74] See e.g. UK and North Vietnam, Cmd 9763, p. 3, note 1, and Israel and Arab countries, International Convention on the Elimination of all Forms of Racial Discrimination, 1965: see *Human Rights International Instruments*, UN, ST/HR/4/rev.4, 1982. Note that Egypt withdrew its declarations regarding non-recognition of Israel with regard to this Convention on 18 January 1980, *ibid.*, p. 86.

does suggest that without a definite and clear waiver, the result of some international actions may be recognition of a hitherto unrecognised entity in certain circumstances.

The point can best be explained by mentioning the kind of conditions which may give rise to the possibility of a recognition where no express or formal statement has been made. A message of congratulations to a new state upon attaining sovereignty will imply recognition of that state, as will the formal establishment of diplomatic relations,[75] but the maintenance of informal and unofficial contacts (such as those between the United States and Communist China during the 1960s and early 1970s in Warsaw) will not.[76] The issuing of a consular *exequatur*, the accepted authorisation permitting the performance of consular functions, to a representative of an unrecognised state will usually amount to a recognition of that state, though not in all cases.[77] A British Consul has operated in Taiwan, but the UK does not recognise the Taiwan government.[78] It is possible that the conclusion of a bilateral treaty between the recognising and unrecognised state, as distinct from a temporary agreement, might imply recognition, but the matter is open to doubt since there are a number of such agreements between parties not recognising each other. One would have to study the circumstances of the particular case to clarify the issue.[79]

---

[75] See O'Connell, *International Law*, pp. 154–5. Note that the UK stated that in the case of Namibia 'there was no formal recognition of statehood, but it was implicit in the establishment of diplomatic relations in March 1990', UKMIL, 63 BYIL, 1992, p. 642. Instructing an ambassador to make suitable, friendly contact with the new administration in question might also suffice: see UKMIL, 50 BYIL, 1979, p. 294.

[76] See e.g. *Pan American World Airways Inc. v. Aetna Casualty and Surety Co.* 13 ILM, 1974, pp. 1376, 1397.

[77] See *Oppenheim's International Law*, p. 171, note 9.

[78] Discussions with an unrecognised entity conducted by consular officers will not of itself imply recognition: see e.g. H. de Smith, *Great Britain and the Law of Nations*, London, 1932, vol. I, p. 79, and *Civil Air Transport Inc. v. Central Air Transport Corporation* [1953] AC 70, 88–9. The establishment of an office in the UK, for example, of an unrecognised entity is not as such prohibited nor does it constitute recognition: see e.g. with regard to the PLO, 483 HL Deb., cols. 1248–52, 27 January 1987 and UKMIL, 58 BYIL, 1987, p. 531. Note that under section 1 of the Diplomatic and Consular Premises Act 1987, the permission of the Foreign Secretary is required if the premises in question are to be regarded as diplomatic or consular.

[79] See e.g. *Republic of China v. Merchants' Fire Assurance Corporation of New York* 30 F.2d 278 (1929); 5 AD, p. 42 and *Clerget v. Banque Commerciale pour l'Europe du Nord* 52 ILR, p. 310. See, with regard to the special position as between the German Federal Republic and the German Democratic Republic, *Re Treaty on the Basis of Relations Between the Federal Republic of Germany and the German Democratic Republic* 78 ILR, p. 150. See also Whiteman, *Digest*, vol. II, pp. 567 ff.

The making of claims by a state against an entity will not necessarily imply recognition.[80]

Recognition is not normally to be inferred from the fact that both states have taken part in negotiations and signed a multilateral treaty,[81] for example the United Nations Charter. Practice shows that many of the member states or their governments are not recognised by other member states.[82] Although Israel and many Arab countries are UN members, this did not affect Arab non-recognition of the Israeli state.[83] However, where the state concerned has voted in favour of membership in the UN of the entity in question, it is a natural inference that recognition has occurred. The UK, for example, regarded its vote in favour of UN membership for the former Yugoslav republic of Macedonia as amounting to recognition of that entity as a state.[84] Indeed, irrespective of recognition by individual states, there is no doubt that membership of the UN is powerful evidence of statehood since being a state is a necessary precondition to UN membership by virtue of article 4 of the UN Charter.[85]

In the case of common participation in an international conference, similar considerations apply, although the element of doubt has often stimulated non-recognising states to declare expressly that their presence and joint signature on any agreement issuing forth from the meeting is in no way to be understood as implying recognition. Such has been the case particularly with the Arab states over the years with regard to Israel.

State practice has restricted the possible scope of operation of this concept of implied recognition to a few instances only and all the relevant surrounding circumstances will have to be carefully evaluated before one can deduce from conduct the intention to extend recognition. States like to retain their control of such an important political instrument as recognition and are usually not keen to allow this to be inferred from the

---

[80] See e.g. with regard to Formosa/Taiwan, 6 ICLQ, 1957, p. 507 and with regard to Turkish-occupied northern Cyprus, 957 HC Deb., col. 247, Written Answer, 8 November 1978.

[81] See e.g. UKMIL, 49 BYIL, 1978, p. 339 and Whiteman, *Digest*, vol. II, pp. 563 ff. See also *Civil Aeronautics Administration* v. *Singapore Airlines Ltd* [2004] 1 SLR 570; [2004] SGCA 3, para. 35; 133 ILR, pp. 371, 383.

[82] See the Memorandum on the Legal Aspects of the Problem of Representation in the United Nations, S/1466, 1950 and 4 *International Organisation*, 1950, pp. 356, 359.

[83] See e.g. Q. Wright, 'Some Thoughts about Recognition', 44 AJIL, 1950, p. 548. See also, with regard to the Ukraine and Byelorussia, members of the UN prior to the demise of the USSR of which they were constituent republics, UKMIL, 55 BYIL, 1978, p. 339.

[84] See 223 HC Deb., col. 241, Written Answer, 22 April 1993 and UKMIL, 64 BYIL, 1993, p. 601. Note that a similar view was taken with regard to the Democratic People's Republic of Korea, 62 BYIL, 1991, p. 559.

[85] See the *Conditions of Membership of the United Nations* case, ICJ Reports, 1948, pp. 57 ff.; 15 AD, p. 333.

way they behave. They prefer recognition to be, in general, a formal act accorded after due thought.

Conditional recognition

The political nature of recognition has been especially marked with reference to what has been termed conditional recognition. This refers to the practice of making the recognition subject to fulfilment of certain conditions, for example, the good treatment of religious minorities as occurred with regard to the independence of some Balkan countries in the late nineteenth century, or the granting of most-favoured-nation status to the recognised state. One well-known instance of this approach was the Litvinov Agreement of 1933 whereby the United States recognised the Soviet government upon the latter undertaking to avoid acts prejudicial to the internal security of the USA, and to come to a settlement of various financial claims.[86]

However, breach of the particular condition does not invalidate the recognition. It may give rise to a breach of international law and political repercussions but the law appears not to accept the notion of a conditional recognition as such. The status of any conditions will depend upon agreements specifically made by the particular parties.[87] It is, however, important to distinguish conditional recognition in this sense from the evolution of criteria for recognition generally, although the two categories may in practice overlap.[88]

Collective recognition[89]

The expediency of collective recognition has often been noted. This would amount to recognition by means of an international decision, whether

---

[86] See e.g. *United States* v. *Pink* 315 US 203, 229 (1942), Whiteman, *Digest,* vol. II, pp. 120 ff.; 10 AD, p. 48, and A. Kiss, *Répertoire de la Pratique Française en Matière de Droit International Public,* Paris, 1962–72, vol. III, pp. 40 ff.

[87] See e.g. Lauterpacht, *Recognition,* chapter 19. See also the Treaty of Berlin, 1878 concerning Bulgaria, Montenegro, Serbia and Romania and the provisions dealing with freedom of religion, articles V, XXVII, XXXV and XLIII.

[88] See further above, p. 451, with regard to the approach of the European Community to the emergence of new states in Eastern Europe and out of the former USSR and Yugoslavia. This constituted a co-ordinated stand with regard to criteria for recognition by the Community and its member states rather than collective recognition as such.

[89] See e.g. Higgins, *Development of International Law;* Dugard, *Recognition;* Lauterpacht, *Recognition,* p. 400; Chen, *Recognition,* p. 211, and *Oppenheim's International Law,* pp. 177 ff.

by an international organisation or not. It would, of course, signify the importance of the international community in its collective assertion of control over membership and because of this it has not been warmly welcomed, nor can one foresee its general application for some time to come. The idea has been discussed particularly since the foundation of the League of Nations and was re-emphasised with the establishment of the United Nations. However, it rapidly became clear that member states reserved the right to extend recognition to their own executive authorities and did not wish to delegate it to any international institution. The most that could be said is that membership of the United Nations constitutes powerful evidence of statehood. But that, of course, is not binding upon other member states who are free to refuse to recognise any other member state or government of the UN.[90]

Withdrawal of recognition[91]

Recognition once given may in certain circumstances be withdrawn. This is more easily achieved with respect to *de facto* recognition, as that is by its nature a cautious and temporary assessment of a particular situation. Where a *de facto* government loses the effective control it once exercised, the reason for recognition disappears and it may be revoked. It is in general a preliminary acceptance of political realities and may be withdrawn in accordance with a change in political factors.[92] *De jure* recognition, on the other hand, is intended to be more of a definitive step and is more difficult to withdraw.

Of course, where a government recognised *de jure* has been overthrown a new situation arises and the question of a new government will have to be faced, but in such instances withdrawal of recognition of the previous administration is assumed and does not have to be expressly stated, providing always that the former government is not still in existence and carrying on the fight in some way. Withdrawal of recognition of one government without recognising a successor is a possibility and indeed was the approach adopted by the UK and France, for example, with regard to Cambodia in 1979.[93] However, with the adoption of the new British

---

[90] See further above, p. 445.   [91] See Lauterpacht, *Recognition*, p. 349.

[92] Withdrawal of *de facto* recognition does not always entail withdrawal of *de jure* recognition: see, with regard to Latvia, *Re Feivel Pikelny's Estate*, 32 BYIL, 1955–6, p. 288.

[93] See 975 HC Deb., col. 723, 6 December 1979, and C. Warbrick, 'Kampuchea: Representation and Recognition', 30 ICLQ, 1981, p. 234. See also AFDI, 1980, p. 888.

policy on recognition with regard to governments,[94] the position is now that the UK government will neither recognise nor withdraw recognition of regimes.[95]

Withdrawal of recognition in other circumstances is not a very general occurrence but in exceptional conditions it remains a possibility. The United Kingdom recognised the Italian conquest of Ethiopia *de facto* in 1936 and *de jure* two years later. However, it withdrew recognition in 1940, with the intensification of fighting and the dispatch of military aid.[96] Recognition of belligerency will naturally terminate with the defeat of either party, while the loss of one of the required criteria of statehood would affect recognition. It is to be noted that the 1979 recognition of the People's Republic of China as the sole legal government of China entailed the withdrawal of recognition or 'derecognition' of the Republic of China (Taiwan). This was explained to mean that, 'so far as the formal foreign relations of the United States are concerned, a government does *not* exist in Taiwan any longer'.[97]

Nevertheless, this was not to affect the application of the laws of the United States with respect to Taiwan in the context of US domestic law.[98] To some extent in this instance the usual consequences of non-recognition have not flowed, but this has taken place upon the background of a formal and deliberate act of policy.[99] It does show how complex the topic of recognition has become.

The usual method of expressing disapproval with the actions of a particular government is to break diplomatic relations. This will adequately demonstrate aversion as did, for example, the rupture in diplomatic relations between the UK and the USSR in 1927, and between some Arab countries and the United States in 1967, without entailing the legal consequences and problems that a withdrawal of recognition would initiate. But one must not confuse the ending of diplomatic relations with a withdrawal of recognition.

---

[94] See above, p. 458.   [95] 424 HL Deb., col. 551, 15 October 1981.

[96] See *Azazh Kebbeda* v. *Italian Government* 9 AD, p. 93.

[97] US reply brief in the Court of Appeals in *Goldwater* v. *Carter* 444 US 996 (1979), quoted in DUSPIL, 1979, pp. 143–4.

[98] Taiwan Relations Act, Pub. L. 96–8 Stat. 22 USC 3301–3316, s. 4.

[99] Also of interest is the UK attitude to the 'republic of Somaliland'. This territory is part of Somalia but proclaimed independence in 1991. It is totally unrecognised by any state, but the UK maintains 'continuing contacts' with it and works 'very closely' with it: see HL Deb., vol. 677, col. 418, 16 January 2006 and HL Deb., vol. 683, col. 212, 14 June 2006. See also M. Schoiswohl, *Status and (Human Rights) Obligations of Non-Recognized De Facto Regimes in International Law: The Case of 'Somaliland'*, Leiden, 2004.

Since recognition is ultimately a political issue, no matter how circumscribed or conditioned by the law, it logically follows that, should a state perceive any particular situation as justifying a withdrawal of recognition, it will take such action as it regards as according with its political interests.

Non-recognition[100]

There has been developing since the 1930s a doctrine of non-recognition where, under certain conditions, a factual situation will not be recognised because of strong reservations as to the morality or legality of the actions that have been adopted in order to bring about the factual situation. It is a doctrine that has also been reinforced by the principle that legal rights cannot derive from an illegal situation (*ex injuria jus non oritur*).[101]

This approach was particularly stimulated by the Japanese invasion of Manchuria in 1931. The US Secretary of State declared in 1932 that the illegal invasion would not be recognised as it was contrary to the 1928 Pact of Paris (the Kellogg–Briand Pact) which had outlawed war as an instrument of national policy. The doctrine of not recognising any situation, treaty or agreement brought about by non-legal means was named the Stimson doctrine after the American Secretary of State who put it forward. It was reinforced not long afterwards by a resolution of the Assembly of the League of Nations stressing that League members should not recognise any situation, treaty or agreement brought about by means contrary to the League's Covenant or the Pact of Paris.[102]

However, state practice until the Second World War was not encouraging. The Italian conquest of the Empire of Ethiopia was recognised and the German takeover of Czechoslovakia accepted. The Soviet Union made a series of territorial acquisitions in 1940, ranging from areas of Finland to the Baltic States (of Lithuania, Estonia and Latvia) and Bessarabia. These

---

[100] See e.g. Lauterpacht, *Recognition*, pp. 416–20, and *Oppenheim's International Law*, pp. 183 ff. See also R. Langer, *Seizure of Territory*, Princeton, 1947; Hackworth, *Digest*, vol. I, p. 334; I. Brownlie, *International Law and the Use of Force by States*, Oxford, 1963, chapter 25; Dugard, *Recognition*, pp. 24 ff. and 81 ff., and Crawford, *Creation of States*, pp. 120 ff. See also S. Talmon *La Non Reconnaissance Collective des États Illégaux*, Paris, 2007.

[101] See e.g. *Oppenheim's International Law*, pp. 183–4, and the *Namibia* case, ICJ Reports, 1971, pp. 16, 46–7; 49 ILR, pp. 2, 36–7.

[102] LNOJ, Sp. Supp. no. 101, p. 8. This principle was reiterated in a number of declarations subsequently: see e.g. 34 AJIL, 1940, Supp., p. 197. See also O'Connell, *International Law*, pp. 143–6.

were recognised *de facto* over the years by Western powers (though not by the United States).[103]

The doctrine was examined anew after 1945. Article 2(4) of the UN Charter prohibits the threat or use of force *inter alia* against the territorial integrity of states, while the draft Declaration on the Rights and Duties of States, 1949, emphasised that territorial acquisitions by states were not to be recognised by other states where achieved by means of the threat or use of force or in any other manner inconsistent with international law and order. The Declaration on Principles of International Law, 1970, also included a provision to the effect that no territorial acquisition resulting from the threat or use of force shall be recognised as legal,[104] and Security Council resolution 242 (1967) on the solution to the Middle East conflict emphasised 'the inadmissibility of the acquisition of territory by war'.[105]

Rhodesia unilaterally proclaimed its independence in November 1965 and in the years of its existence did not receive official recognition from any state at all, although it did maintain diplomatic relations with South Africa and Portugal prior to the revolution of 1974. The day following the Rhodesian declaration of independence, the Security Council passed a resolution calling upon all states not to accord it recognition and to refrain from assisting it.[106] The Council imposed selective mandatory economic sanctions on Rhodesia and these were later made comprehensive.[107] Similar action was also taken with regard to the Bantustans, territories of South Africa declared by that state to be independent.[108] The Security Council also adopted resolution 541 in 1983, which deplored the purported

---

[103] O'Connell, *International Law*, pp. 143–6.

[104] See also article 11 of the Montevideo Convention on the Rights and Duties of States, 1933; article 17 of the Bogotá Charter of the OAS, 1948, and article 52 of the Vienna Convention on the Law of Treaties, 1969. Note also article 5(3) of the Consensus Definition of Aggression, 1974, adopted by the General Assembly in resolution 3314 (XXIX).

[105] See also Security Council resolutions 476 (1980) and 478 (1980) declaring purported changes in the status of Jerusalem by Israel to be null and void, and resolution 491 (1981) stating that Israel's extension of its laws, jurisdiction and administration to the Golan Heights was without international legal effect.

[106] Security Council resolution 216 (1965). See also Security Council resolutions 217 (1965), 277 (1970) and 288 (1970).

[107] See e.g. Security Council resolutions 221 (1961), 232 (1966) and 253 (1968). See also M. N. Shaw, *Title to Territory in Africa*, Oxford, 1986, p. 160; R. Zacklin, *The United Nations and Rhodesia*, Oxford, 1974, and J. Nkala, *The United Nations, International Law and the Rhodesian Crisis*, Oxford, 1985.

[108] See e.g. General Assembly resolution 31/6A and the Security Council statements of 21 September 1979 and 15 December 1981, Shaw, *Title to Territory*, p. 149. See also J. Dugard, *International Law, A South African Perspective*, Kenwyn, 1994, chapter 5.

secession of part of Cyprus occupied by Turkey in 1974 and termed the proposed Turkish Cypriot state 'legally invalid'.[109] In 1990, the Security Council adopted resolution 662, which declared the Iraqi annexation of Kuwait 'null and void' and called on all states and institutions not to recognise the annexation.[110] The principle of non-recognition of title to territory acquired through aggression in violation of international law was also reaffirmed in the *Brcko Inter-Entity Boundary* award with regard to aggression in Bosnia.[111]

The role of non-recognition as an instrument of sanction as well as a means of pressure and a method of protecting the wronged inhabitants of a territory was discussed more fully in the Advisory Opinion of the International Court of Justice in the *Namibia* case, 1971, dealing with South Africa's presence in that territory. The Court held that since the continued South African occupancy was illegal, member states of the United Nations were obliged to recognise that illegality and the invalidity of South Africa's acts concerning Namibia and were under a duty to refrain from any actions implying recognition of the legality of, or lending support or assistance to, the South African presence and administration.[112]

The legal effects of recognition

In this section some of the legal results that flow from the recognition or non-recognition of an entity, both in the international sphere and within the municipal law of particular states, will be noted. Although recognition may legitimately be regarded as a political tool, it is one that nevertheless entails important consequences in the legal field.

Internationally

In the majority of cases, it can be accepted that recognition of a state or government is a legal acknowledgement of a factual state of affairs. Nevertheless, it should not be assumed that non-recognition of, for example,

---

[109] See above, chapter 5, p. 235. See also *Cyprus* v. *Turkey*, European Court of Human Rights, Judgment of 10 May 2001, paras. 60–1; 120 ILR, p. 10.

[110] See below, chapter 22, p. 1253.   [111] 36 ILM, 1997, pp. 396, 422.

[112] ICJ Reports, 1971, pp. 16, 54, 56; 49 ILR, pp. 2, 44, 46. Non-member states of the UN were similarly obliged, *ibid*. The non-recognition obligation did not extend, however, to certain acts of a humanitarian nature the effect of which could only be ignored to the detriment of the inhabitants of the territory, *ibid.*, p. 56 and *Cyprus* v. *Turkey*, European Court of Human Rights, Judgment of 10 May 2001, paras. 90–8; 120 ILR, p. 10. See also above, chapter 5, p. 225.

a state will deprive that entity of rights and duties before international law, excepting, of course, those situations where it may be possible to say that recognition is constitutive of the legal entity.

In general, the political existence of a state is independent of recognition by other states, and thus an unrecognised state must be deemed subject to the rules of international law. It cannot consider itself free from restraints as to aggressive behaviour, nor can its territory be regarded as *terra nullius*. States which have signed international agreements are entitled to assume that states which they have not recognised but which have similarly signed the agreement are bound by that agreement. For example, the United Kingdom treated the German Democratic Republic as bound by its signature of the 1963 Nuclear Test Ban Treaty even when the state was not recognised by the UK.

Non-recognition, with its consequent absence of diplomatic relations, may affect the unrecognised state in asserting its rights or other states in asserting its duties under international law, but will not affect the existence of such rights and duties. The position is, however, different under municipal law.

Internally

Because recognition is fundamentally a political act, it is reserved to the executive branch of government. This means that the judiciary must as a general principle accept the discretion of the executive and give effect to its decisions. The courts cannot recognise a state or government. They can only accept and enforce the legal consequences which flow from the executive's political decision, although this situation has become more complex with the change in policy from express recognition of governments to acceptance of dealings with such entities.

To this extent, recognition is constitutive, because the act of recognition itself creates legal results within the domestic jurisdiction. In the United Kingdom and the United States particularly, the courts feel themselves obliged to accept the verdict of the executive branch of government as to whether a particular entity should be regarded as recognised or not. If the administration has recognised a state or government and so informs the judiciary by means of a certificate, the position of that state or government within the municipal structure is totally transformed.

It may sue in the domestic courts and be granted immunity from suit in certain instances. Its own legislative and executive acts will be given effect to in the courts of the recognising state and its own diplomatic representatives will be able to claim the various immunities accorded to the official envoys of a recognised state. In addition, it will be entitled to possession in the recognising state of property belonging to its predecessor.

The UK[113]

The English courts have adopted the attitude over many years that an entity unrecognised by the Foreign Office would be treated before the courts as if it did not exist and accordingly it would not be able to claim immunity before the courts.[114] This meant in one case that ships of the unrecognised 'Provisional Government of Northern Russia' would not be protected by the courts from claims affecting them.[115] Similarly an unrecognised state or government is unable to appear before the courts as a plaintiff in an action. This particular principle prevented the revolutionary government of Berne in 1804 from taking action to restrain the Bank of England from dealing with funds belonging to the previous administration of the city.[116]

The leading case in English law on the issue of effects of recognition of an entity within the domestic sphere is *Luther* v. *Sagor*.[117] This concerned the operations and produce of a timber factory in Russia owned by the plaintiffs, which had been nationalised in 1919 by the Soviet government. In 1920 the defendant company purchased a quantity of wood from the USSR and this was claimed in England by the plaintiffs as their property since it had come from what had been their factory. It was argued by them that the 1919 Soviet decree should be ignored before the English courts since the United Kingdom had not recognised the Soviet government. The lower court agreed with this contention and the matter then came to the Court of Appeal.[118]

In the meantime the UK recognised the Soviet government *de facto* and the Foreign Office informed the Court of Appeal of this in writing. The result was that the higher court was bound to take note of the Soviet decree and accordingly the plaintiffs lost their case, since a court must give effect to the legislation of a recognised state or government. The Court also held that the fact that the Soviet government was recognised

---

[113] See e.g. Talmon, 'Recognition of Governments', pp. 275 ff.; Greig, 'Carl-Zeiss Case', and J. G. Merrills, 'Recognition and Construction', 20 ICLQ, 1971, p. 476.

[114] See e.g. *Halsbury's Laws of England*, 4th edn, London, 1977, vol. XVIII, p. 735.

[115] *The Annette* [1919] P. 105; 1 AD, p. 43.

[116] *The City of Berne* v. *The Bank of England* (1804) 9 Ves. Jun. 347.

[117] [1921] 1 KB 456; 1 AD, p. 47.   [118] [1921] 3 KB 532; 1 AD, p. 49.

de facto and not *de jure* did not affect the issue. Another interesting point is that since the Foreign Office certificate included a statement that the former Provisional Government of Russia recognised by the UK had been dispersed during December 1917, the Court inferred the commencement of the Soviet government from that date.

The essence of the matter was that the Soviet government was now accepted as the sovereign government of the USSR as from December 1917. And since recognition once given is retroactive and relates back to the date that the authority of the government was accepted as being established, and not the date on which recognition is granted, the Soviet decree of 1919 was deemed to be a legitimate act of a recognised government. This was so even though at that date the Soviet government was not recognised by the United Kingdom.

The purpose of the retroactivity provision[119] is to avoid possible influence in the internal affairs of the entity recognised, since otherwise legislation made prior to recognition might be rejected. However, this will depend always upon the terms of the executive certificate by which the state informs its courts of the recognition. Should the Foreign Office insist that the state or government in question is to be recognised as a sovereign state or government as of the date of the action, the courts would be bound by this.

As is the case with legislation, contracts made by an unrecognised government will not be enforced in English courts. Without the required action by the political authorities, an unrecognised entity does not exist as a legal person before the municipal courts. The case of *Luther* v. *Sagor* suggested that in general the legal consequences of a *de facto* recognition would be the same as a *de jure* one. This was emphasised in *Haile Selassie* v. *Cable and Wireless Ltd (No. 2)*,[120] but regarded as restricted to acts in relation to persons or property in the territory which the *de facto* government has been recognised as effectively controlling.

In other words, a different situation would ensue with regard to persons or property situated outside the territory of the state or government. In the *Haile Selassie* case, the Emperor of Ethiopia was suing a British company for money owing to him under an agreement. The problem was that when the action was brought, the UK had recognised the Italian forces as the *de facto* authority in Ethiopia while Haile Selassie was still recognised as the *de jure* sovereign. The Court held that since the case concerned a debt

---

[119] See e.g. *Oppenheim's International Law*, p. 161, and Whiteman, *Digest*, vol. II, pp. 728–45.
[120] [1939] 1 Ch. 182; 9 AD, p. 94.

recoverable in England and not the validity of acts with regard to persons or property in Ethiopia, the *de jure* authority, Emperor Haile Selassie, was entitled to the sum due from the company, and the *de facto* control of the Italians did not affect this.

However, before the defendant's appeal was heard, the United Kingdom extended *de jure* recognition to the Italian authorities in Ethiopia. The Court of Appeal accepted that this related back to, and was deemed to operate as from the date of, the *de facto* recognition. Since this had occurred prior to the case starting, it meant that the Italian government was now to be recognised as the *de jure* government of Ethiopia, before and during the time of the hearing of the action. Accordingly, Haile Selassie was divested of any right whatsoever to sue for the recovery of the money owing.

This problem of the relationship between a *de facto* government and a *de jure* government as far as English courts were concerned, manifested itself again during the Spanish Civil War. The case of the *Arantzazu Mendi*[121] concerned a private steamship registered in Bilbao in the Basque province of Spain. In June 1937, following the capture of that region by the forces of General Franco, the opposing Republican government issued a decree requisitioning all ships registered in Bilbao. Nine months later the Nationalist government of Franco also passed a decree taking control over all Bilbao vessels. In the meantime, the *Arantzazu Mendi* itself was in London when the Republican government issued a writ to obtain possession of the ship. The owners opposed this while accepting the Nationalists' requisition order.

It was accepted rule of international law that a recognised state cannot be sued or otherwise brought before the courts of another state. Accordingly, the Nationalists argued that since their authority had been recognised *de facto* by the UK government over the areas they actually controlled, their decree was valid and could not be challenged in the English courts. Therefore, the action by the Republican government must be dismissed.

The case came before the House of Lords, where it was decided that the Nationalist government, as the *de facto* authority of much of Spain including the region of Bilbao, was entitled to be regarded as a sovereign state and was able to benefit from the normal immunities which follow therefrom. Thus, the action by the Republican government failed.

---

[121] [1939] AC 256; 9 AD, p. 60.

The House of Lords pointed out that it did not matter that the territory over which the *de facto* authority was exercising sovereign powers was from time to time increased or diminished.[122] This case marks the high-point in the attribution of characteristics to a *de facto* authority and can be criticised for its over-generous assessment of the status of such an entity.[123]

The problems faced by the English court when the rights and obligations of a *de jure* government and a *de facto* government, claiming the same territory, appear to be in conflict have been briefly noted. Basically, the actions of a *de facto* authority with regard to people and property within this sphere of control will be recognised in an English court, but where property is situated and recoverable in England, the *de jure* sovereign will have precedence. A similarly complicated situation arises where the interests of two recognised *de jure* governments of the same state are involved, as one supersedes the other. Problems can arise concerning the issue of retroactivity, that is, how far the court will relate back actions of a *de jure* government, since recognition is normally retroactive to the moment of inception of the particular state or government.

The matter was discussed in the *Gdynia Ameryka Linie* v. *Boguslawski* case.[124] During the Second World War the Polish government-in-exile stationed in London was recognised by the UK as the *de jure* government of Poland. However, on 28 June 1945 the communist provisional government was established with effective control of the country and at midnight on 5 July the UK recognised that government as the *de jure* government of Poland. A couple of days prior to this recognition, the Polish government-in-exile made an offer to Polish seamen of compensation in the event of leaving the merchant navy service. The money was to be paid by the particular employers to seamen not wanting to work for the communist provisional government. In the *Boguslawski* case the employers refused to pay the compensation to seamen requesting it, and argued that the UK recognition *de jure* of the provisional government was retroactive to 28 June, this being the date that the government effectively took control of the country. If this was the case, then acts of the government-in-exile after 28 June ceased to be of effect and thus the offers of compensation could not be enforced in the English courts.

The House of Lords emphasised the general proposition that recognition operates retroactively. However, they modified the statement by

---

[122] See e.g. Lord Atkin, [1939] AC 256, 264–5.
[123] See e.g. Lauterpacht, *Recognition*, pp. 288–94.   [124] [1953] AC 11; 19 ILR, p. 72.

declaring that the courts had to give effect not only to acts done by the new government after recognition, but also to acts done before the recognition 'in so far as those acts related to matters under its control at the time when the acts were done'.[125] It was stated that while the recognition of the new government had certain retroactive effects, the recognition of the old government remained effective down to the date when it was in fact withdrawn. Problems might have arisen had the old government, before withdrawal of recognition, attempted to take action with respect to issues under the control of the new government. However, that was not involved in this case.

In other words, and in the circumstances of the case, the principle of retroactivity of recognition was regarded as restricted to matters within the effective control of the new government. Where something outside the effective control of the new government is involved, it would appear that the recognition does not operate retroactively and that prior to the actual date of recognition one would have to accept and put into effect the acts of the previous *de jure* government.

This could lead to many complicated situations, especially where a court is faced with conflicting courses of action, something which is not hard to envisage when one *de jure* government has been superseded by another. It could permit abuses of government such as where a government, knowing itself to be about to lose recognition, awards its supporters financial or other awards in decrees that may be enforced in English courts. What would happen if the new government issued contrary orders in an attempt to nullify the effect of the old government's decrees is something that was not examined in the *Boguslawski* case.

Another case which came before the courts in the same year was *Civil Air Transport Inc.* v. *Central Air Transport Corporation*,[126] and it similarly failed to answer the question mentioned above. It involved the sale of aircraft belonging to the nationalist government of China, which had been flown to the British Crown Colony of Hong Kong. Such aircraft were sold to an American company after the communist government established effective control over the country but before it had been recognised by the UK. The Court accepted that the nationalist government had been entitled to the aircraft and pointed out that:

---

[125] Lord Reid, [1953] AC 11, 44–5; 19 ILR, pp. 81, 83.
[126] [1953] AC 70; 19 ILR, pp. 85, 93, 110. See also F. A. Mann, 'Recognition of Sovereignty', 16 MLR, 1953, p. 226.

retroactivity of recognition operates to validate acts of a *de facto* Government which has subsequently become the new *de jure* Government, and not to invalidate acts of the previous *de jure* Government.[127]

It is to be noted that the communist government did not attempt to nullify the sale to the American company. Had it done so, a new situation would have been created, but it is as yet uncertain whether that would have materially altered the legal result.

The general doctrine adhered to by the UK with regard to recognition (and now diplomatic dealings) is that it will be accorded upon the evidence of effective control. It is used to acknowledge factual situations and not as a method of exhibiting approval or otherwise. However, this is not so in all cases and there are a number of governments in effective control of their countries and unrecognised by the UK. One major example was the former German Democratic Republic. Since the prime consequence of non-recognition is that the English courts will not give effect to any laws of an unrecognised entity, problems are thus likely to arise in ordinary international political and commercial life.

The issue came before the courts in the *Carl Zeiss Stiftung* v. *Rayner and Keeler Ltd (No. 2)* case.[128] It concerned the Carl Zeiss foundation which was run by a special board, reconstituted in 1952 as the Council of Gera. The problem was that it was situated in the German Democratic Republic (GDR) and the establishment of the Council of Gera as the governing body of the Carl Zeiss foundation was effected by a reorganisation of local government in the GDR. When Carl Zeiss brought a claim before the English courts, the issue was at once raised as to whether, in view of the UK non-recognition of the GDR, the governing body of the foundation could be accepted by the courts. The Court of Appeal decided that since the Foreign Office certified that the UK recognised 'the State and Government of the Union of Soviet Socialist Republics as *de jure* entitled to exercise governing authority in respect of that zone'[129] (i.e. the GDR, being the former Soviet zone of occupation), it was not possible to give effect to any rules or regulations laid down by the GDR. The House of Lords, however, extricated the English courts system from a rather difficult position by means of an elaborate fiction.

It stated that as a Foreign Office certificate is binding on the courts as to the facts it contains, it logically followed that the courts must recognise

---

[127] [1953] AC 70, 90; 19 ILR, pp. 110, 113.
[128] [1967] AC 853; 43 ILR, p. 42. See also Greig, 'Carl-Zeiss Case'.
[129] [1966] 1 Ch. 596; 43 ILR, p. 25.

the USSR as the *de jure* governing authority of East Germany, irrespective of the creation of the GDR. The courts were not entitled to enter into a political examination of the actual situation but were obliged to accept and give effect to the facts set out in the Foreign Office certificate. Thus, the Soviet Union was the *de jure* sovereign and the GDR government must be accepted as a subordinate and dependent body.

Accordingly, the Court could recognise the existence of the Carl Zeiss Stiftung by virtue of the UK recognition of the *de jure* status of the Soviet Union, the GDR as an administrative body being relevant only as a legal creature of the USSR.

The problem brought out in the *Carl Zeiss* case and sidestepped there was raised again in a series of cases concerning Rhodesia, following the unilateral declaration of independence by the Smith regime in 1965. Basically, if a government or state which exercises effective control over its own territory is unrecognised by the UK a strict enforcement of the 'no recognition, no existence' rule could lead to much hardship and inconvenience. Accordingly, in *Adams* v. *Adams*[130] a Rhodesian divorce decree was not recognised in an English court. However, in *Hesperides Hotels Ltd* v. *Aegean Turkish Holidays*,[131] concerning an action in trespass with respect to hotels owned by Greek Cypriots but run by Turkish Cypriots following the Turkish invasion of 1974, Lord Denning stated *obiter* that he believed that the courts could recognise the laws and acts of an unrecognised body in effective control of territory, at least with regard to laws regulating the day-to-day affairs of the people.[132] It is certainly an attractive approach, provided it is carefully handled and strictly limited to determinations of a humanitarian and non-sovereign nature.[133] In *Caglar* v. *Bellingham*, it was noted that while the existence of a foreign unrecognised government could be acknowledged in matters relating to commercial obligations or matters of private law between individuals or matters of routine administration such as registration of births, marriages and deaths, the courts would not acknowledge the existence of an unrecognised state if to do so would involve them in acting inconsistently with the foreign

---

[130] [1971] P. 188; 52 ILR, p. 15.
[131] [1978] QB 205; 73 ILR, p. 9. See also M. N. Shaw, 'Legal Acts of an Unrecognised Entity', 94 LQR, 1978, p. 500.
[132] [1978] QB 205, 218; 73 ILR, pp. 9, 15. See also Steyn J, *Gur Corporation* v. *Trust Bank of Africa Ltd* [1986] 3 WLR 583, 589, 592; 75 ILR, p. 675.
[133] See further the *Namibia* case, ICJ Reports, 1971, pp. 16, 56; 49 ILR, pp. 2, 46, and *Cyprus* v. *Turkey*, European Court of Human Rights, Judgment of 10 May 2001, paras. 90–8; 120 ILR, p. 10.

policy or diplomatic stance of the UK.[134] In *Emin* v. *Yeldag*, the Court held that private acts taking place within an unrecognised state could be regarded as valid within the English legal system provided that there was no statutory prohibition[135] and that such acceptance did not compromise the UK government in the conduct of foreign relations.[136] Indeed, where the issue concerns the lawful acts of a person recognised as existing in English law, they will be justiciable before the English courts and will not be tainted by illegality because the unrecognised state can be associated with the actions.[137]

In many cases, however, the problems with regard to whether an entity is or is not a 'state' arise in connection with the interpretation of a particular statutory provision. The approach of the courts has been to focus upon the construction of the relevant instrument rather than upon the Foreign Office certificate or upon any definition in international law of statehood.[138]

Some of the consequential problems of non-recognition were addressed in the Foreign Corporations Act 1991. This provides that a corporation incorporated in a territory not recognised by the UK government as a state would be regarded as having legal personality within the UK where the laws of that territory were applied by a settled court system. In other words, the territory would be treated for this purpose as if it were a recognised state, thereby enabling its legislation to be applied in this circumstance on the normal conflict of rules basis. The point should, however, be stressed that the legislation was not intended at all to impact upon recognition issues as such.[139]

---

[134] 108 ILR, p. 510, at 534.

[135] Such as in *Adams* v. *Adams* [1970] 3 All ER 572 in view of the relationship between the UK and Southern Rhodesia.

[136] [2002] 1 FLR 956. This contradicted the earlier case of *B* v. *B* [2000] FLR 707, where a divorce obtained in the unrecognised 'Turkish Republic of Northern Cyprus' was not recognised. See also *Parent and Others* v. *Singapore Airlines Ltd and Civil Aeronautics Administration* 133 ILR, p. 264.

[137] See *North Cyprus Tourism Centre Ltd* v. *Transport for London* [2005] EWHC 1698 (Admin), para. 50.

[138] See e.g. *Re Al-Fin Corporation's Patent* [1970] Ch. 160; 52 ILR, p. 68; *Reel* v. *Holder* [1981] 1 WLR 1226; 74 ILR, p. 105 and *Caglar* v. *Bellingham* 108 ILR, p. 510 at 528, 530 and 539, where the statutory term 'foreign state' was held to mean a state recognised by the UK.

[139] This legislation was adopted essentially to deal with the situation following *Arab Monetary Fund* v. *Hashim (No. 3)* [1991] 2 WLR, whereby the legal personality of a company not incorporated in a territory recognised as a state would not be recognised in English law. See UKMIL, 62 BYIL, 1991, pp. 565–8. See also the decision of the Special Commissioners in *Caglar* v. *Bellingham*, 108 ILR, p. 510 at 530, where it was emphasised that the intention of

Since the UK decision to abandon recognition of governments in 1980, the question arises as to the attitude of the courts on this matter. In particular, it appears that they may be called upon to examine the nature of the UK government's dealings with a new regime in order to determine its status for municipal law purposes.[140]

In *Gur Corporation* v. *Trust Bank of Africa*[141] the Court was in fact called upon to decide the status of Ciskei. This territory, part of South Africa, was one of the Bantustans granted 'independence' by South Africa. This was accomplished by virtue of the Status of Ciskei Act 1981. The preliminary issue that came before the Court in a commercial dispute was whether Ciskei had *locus standi* to sue or be sued in England. The Foreign and Commonwealth Office certified that Ciskei was not recognised as an independent sovereign state either *de facto* or *de jure* and that representations were made to South Africa in relation to matters occurring in Ciskei. The Court of Appeal held that it was able to take account of such declarations and legislation as were not in conflict with the certificates.

The effect of that, noted Lord Donaldson, was that the Status of Ciskei Act 1981 could be taken into account, except for those provisions declaring the territory independent and relinquishing South African sovereignty. This led to the conclusion that the Ciskei legislature was in fact exercising power by virtue of delegation from the South African authorities.[142] Accordingly, the government of Ciskei could sue or be sued in the English courts 'as being a subordinate body set up by the Republic of South Africa to act on its behalf'.[143] Clearly the Court felt that the situation was analogous to the *Carl Zeiss* case. Whether this was in fact so is an open question. It is certainly open to doubt whether the terms of the certificates in the cases were on all fours. In the *Gur* case, the executive was far more cautious and non-committal. Indeed, one of the certificates actually stated that the UK government did not have a formal position regarding the exercise of governing authority over the territory of Ciskei,[144] whereas in *Carl Zeiss* the certificate noted expressly that the USSR was recognised as *de jure* entitled to exercise governing authority in respect

the legislation was not to affect at all the government's policy on recognition, but to sever the connection with public international law and deal with issues of private international law.

140 See 409 HL Deb., cols. 1097–8 and Symmons, 'United Kingdom Abolition', pp. 254–60.
141 [1987] 1 QB 599; 75 ILR, p. 675.   142 [1987] 1 QB 599, 623; 75 ILR, p. 696.
143 [1987] 1 QB 599, 624. See also Nourse LJ, *ibid.*, pp. 624–66; 75 ILR, pp. 696–9.
144 [1987] 1 QB 599, 618–19; 75 ILR, p. 690.

of the territory (the GDR).[145] The gap was bridged by construction and inference.

More widely, it is unclear to what extent the change in policy on recognition of governments has actually led to a change in attitude by the courts. There is no doubt that the attitude adopted by the government in certifying whether or not diplomatic dealings were in existence with regard to the entity in question is crucial. An assertion of such dealing would, it appears, be determinative.[146] The problem arises where the Foreign Office statement is more ambiguous than the mere assertion of dealings with the entity. The consequence is that a greater burden is imposed on the courts as an answer as to status is sought. On the one hand, the *Gur* case suggests that the courts are not willing to examine for themselves the realities of any given situation, but would seek to infer from the terms of any certificate what the answer ought to be.[147] On the other hand, Hobhouse J in the High Court in *Republic of Somalia* v. *Woodhouse Drake and Carey (Suisse) SA*[148] took the wider view that in deciding whether a regime was the government of a state, the court would have to take into account the following factors: (a) whether it is the constitutional government of the state; (b) the degree, nature and stability of administrative control, if any, that it of itself exercises over the territory of the state; (c) whether the UK government has any dealings with it, and if so the nature of those dealings; and (d) in marginal cases, the extent of international recognition that it has as the government of the state.[149] Part of the answer as to why a different emphasis is evident is no doubt due to the fact that in the latter case, there were competing bodies claiming to be the government of Somalia and the situation on the ground as a matter of fact was deeply confused. It should also be noted that in the *Republic of Somalia* case, the court took the view that Foreign Office statements were no more than part of the evidence in the case, although likely to be the best evidence as to whether the government had dealings with the entity in question.[150]

---

[145] [1966] 1 Ch. 596; 43 ILR, p. 25.

[146] See e.g. the *Arantzazu Mendi* [1939] AC 256, 264; 9 AD, p. 60, and *Gur Corporation* v. *Trust Bank of Africa* [1987] 1 QB 599, 625; 75 ILR, p. 675. See also *Republic of Somalia* v. *Woodhouse Drake and Carey (Suisse) SA* [1993] QB 54, 65–6; 94 ILR, p. 620.

[147] See e.g. F. A. Mann, 'The Judicial Recognition of an Unrecognised State', 36 ICLQ, 1987, p. 349, and Beck, 'A South African Homeland Appears in the English Court: Legitimation of the Illegitimate?', 36 ICLQ, 1987, p. 350.

[148] [1993] QB 54; 94 ILR, p. 608.   [149] [1993] QB 54, 68; 94 ILR, p. 622.

[150] [1993] QB 54, 65; 94 ILR, p. 619. This was reaffirmed in *Sierra Leone Telecommunications Co. Ltd* v. *Barclays Bank* [1998] 2 All ER 821; 114 ILR, p. 466. See also K. Reece Thomas,

The USA

The situation in the United States with regard to the recognition or non-recognition of foreign entities is similar to that pertaining in the UK, with some important differences. Only a recognised state or government can in principle sue in the US courts.[151] This applies irrespective of the state of diplomatic relations, providing there is no war between the two.[152] However, an unrecognised state or government may in certain circumstances be permitted access before the American courts. This would appear to depend on the facts of each case and a practical appreciation of the entity in question.[153] For example, in *Transportes Aeros de Angola* v. *Ronair*,[154] it was held that in the particular circumstances where the US State Department had clearly stated that allowing the plaintiff (a corporation owned by the unrecognised government of Angola) access to the Court would be consistent with the foreign policy interests of the United States, the jurisdictional bar placed upon the Court would be deemed to have been lifted.

As in the UK, a declaration by the executive will be treated as binding the courts, but in the USA the courts appear to have a greater latitude. In the absence of the 'suggestion' clarifying how far the process of non-recognition is to be applied, the courts are more willing than their UK counterparts to give effect to particular acts of an unrecognised body. Indeed, in the *Carl Zeiss* case Lords Reid and Wilberforce referred in approving terms to the trend evident in decisions of US courts to give recognition to the 'actual facts or realities found to exist in the territory in question', in the interests of justice and common sense. Such recognition did not apply to every act, but in Lord Wilberforce's words, it did apply to 'private rights, or acts of everyday occurrence, or perfunctory acts of administration'.[155] How far this extends, however, has never been precisely defined.

It was the difficulties engendered by the American Civil War that first stimulated a reappraisal of the 'no recognition, no existence' doctrine. It

---

'Non-recognition, Personality and Capacity: The Palestine Liberation Organisation and the Palestine Authority in English Law', 29 *Anglo-American Law Review*, 2000, p. 228.

[151] See e.g. *Republic of Vietnam* v. *Pfizer* 556 F.2d 892 (1977); 94 ILR, p. 199.

[152] See *Banco Nacional de Cuba* v. *Sabbatino* 376 US 398, 412; 35 ILR, p. 2 and *National Oil Corporation* v. *Libyan Sun Oil Co.* 733 F.Supp. 800 (1990); 94 ILR, p. 209.

[153] See above, p. 234, regarding Taiwan after 1 January 1979. See also *Wulfsohn* v. *Russian Republic* 234 NY 372 (1924); 2 AD, p. 39.

[154] 544 F.Supp. 858, 863–4 (1982); 94 ILR, pp. 202, 208–9.

[155] [1967] AC 853, 954; 43 ILR, pp. 23, 66.

was not possible to ignore every act of the Confederate authorities and so the idea developed that such rules adopted by the Confederate states as were not hostile to the Union or the authority of the Central Government, or did not conflict with the terms of the US Constitution, would be treated as valid and enforceable in the courts system.[156] The doctrine was developed in a case before the New York Court of Appeals, when, discussing the status of the unrecognised Soviet government, Judge Cardozo noted that an unrecognised entity which had maintained control over its territory, 'may gain for its acts and decrees a validity quasi-governmental, if violence to fundamental principles of justice or to our public policy might otherwise be done'.[157]

This thesis progressed rapidly in the period immediately preceding the American recognition of the USSR and led in *Salimoff v. Standard Oil Co. of New York*[158] to the enforcement of a Soviet oil nationalisation decree, with the comment that: 'to refuse to recognise that Soviet Russia is a government regulating the internal affairs of the country, is to give to fictions an air of reality which they do not deserve'.

This decision, diametrically opposed to the *Luther v. Sagor* approach,[159] constituted a step towards the abolition of differences between the judicial treatment of the acts of recognised and unrecognised governments.

However, the limits of this broad doctrine were more carefully defined in *The Maret*,[160] where the Court refused to give effect to the nationalisation of an Estonian ship by the government of the unrecognised Soviet Republic of Estonia. However, the ship in dispute was located in an American port at the date of the nationalisation order, and there appears to be a difference in treatment in some cases depending upon whether the property was situated inside or outside the country concerned.

One can mention, in contrast to *The Maret*, the case of *Upright v. Mercury Business Machines*,[161] in which the non-recognition of the German Democratic Republic was discussed in relation to the assignment of a bill to the plaintiff by a state-controlled company of the GDR. The judge of the New York Supreme Court declared, in upholding the plaintiff's claim, that a foreign government, although unrecognised by the executive:

---

[156] See e.g. *Texas v. White* 74 US 700 (1868).
[157] *Sokoloff v. National City Bank of New York* 239 NY 158 (1924); 2 AD, p. 44.
[158] 262 NY 220 (1933); 7 AD, pp. 22, 26.   [159] [1921] 1 KB 456; 1 AD, p. 47; above, p. 472.
[160] 145 F.2d 431 (1944); 12 AD, p. 29.   [161] 213 NYS (2d) 417 (1961); 32 ILR, p. 65.

may nevertheless have *de facto* existence which is judicially cognisable. The acts of such a *de facto* government may affect private rights and obligations arising either as a result of activity in, or with persons or corporations within, the territory controlled by such *de facto* government.

However, the creation of judicial entities by unrecognised states will not be allowed to circumvent executive policy. In *Kunstsammlungen zu Weimar* v. *Elicofon*,[162] the KZW was an East German governmental agency until 1969, when it was transformed into a separate juristic person in order to avoid the problems relating to unrecognised states in the above litigation. This concerned the recovery of pictures stolen from a museum during the American occupation of Germany.

As a branch of an unrecognised state, the KZW could not of course be permitted to sue in an American court, but the change of status in 1969 was designed to circumvent this. The Court, however, refused to accept this and emphasised that to allow the KZW to intervene in the case 'would render our government's non-recognition of the German Democratic Republic a meaningless gesture'.[163] Further, in *Autocephalous Church of Cyprus* v. *Goldberg*, the Court of Appeals held that it would not give effect to confiscatory decrees adopted by the unrecognised 'Turkish Federated State of Cyprus', later called the 'Turkish Republic of Northern Cyprus'.[164]

In *Ministry of Defense of the Islamic Republic of Iran* v. *Gould*,[165] the Court was faced with an action in which the unrecognised Iranian government sought to enforce an award. However, the US intervened and filed a statement of interest supporting Iran's argument and this proved of significant influence. This general approach was reinforced in *National Petrochemical* v. *The M/T Stolt Sheaf*,[166] where the Court stressed that the executive must have the power to deal with unrecognised governments and that therefore the absence of formal recognition did not necessarily result in a foreign government being barred from access to US courts.[167] However, where the executive has issued a non-recognition certificate and makes known its view that in the instant case the unrecognised party

---

[162] 358 F.Supp. 747 (1972); 61 ILR, p. 143.
[163] 358 F.Supp. 747, 757; 61 ILR, p. 154. See also *Federal Republic of Germany* v. *Elicofon*, 14 ILM, 1976, p. 806, following the US recognition of the GDR in which KZW was permitted to intervene in the litigation in progress. See also *Transportes Aereos de Angola* v. *Ronair* 544 F.Supp. 858.
[164] 917 F.2d 278 (1990); 108 ILR, p. 488.
[165] 1988 *Iranian Assets Litig. Rep.* 15, 313. See also 82 AJIL, 1988, p. 591.
[166] 860 F.2d 551 (1988); 87 ILR, p. 583.   [167] 860 F.2d 551, 554.

should not be permitted access to the courts, the courts appear very willing to comply.[168]

It is somewhat difficult to reconcile the various American cases or to determine the extent to which the acts of an unrecognised state or government may be enforced in the courts system of the United States. But two factors should be particularly noted. First of all, the declaration of the executive is binding. If that intimates that no effect is to be given to acts of the unrecognised entity, the courts will be obliged to respect this. It may also be the case that the State Department 'suggestions' will include some kind of hint or indication which, while not clearly expressed, may lead the courts to feel that the executive is leaning more one way than another in the matter of the government's status, and this may influence the courts. For example, in the *Salimoff*[169] case the terms of the certificate tended to encourage the court to regard the Soviet government as a recognised government, whereas in the case of *The Maret*[170] the tone of the executive's statement on the Soviet Republic of Estonia was decidedly hostile to any notion of recognition or enforcement of its decrees.

The second point is the location of the property in question. There is a tendency to avoid the enforcement of acts and decrees affecting property situated outside the unrecognised state or government and in any event the location of the property often introduces additional complications as regards municipal law provision.[171]

There is some uncertainty in the United States as to the operation of the retroactivity doctrine, particularly as it affects events occurring outside the country. There is a line of cases suggesting that only those acts of the unrecognised government performed in its own territory could be validated by the retroactive operation of recognition[172] while, on the other hand, there are cases illustrating the opposite proposition decided by the Supreme Court.[173]

---

[168] See e.g. *Republic of Panama* v. *Republic National Bank of New York* 681 F.Supp. 1066 (1988); 86 ILR, p. 1 and *Republic of Panama* v. *Citizens & Southern International Bank* 682 F.Supp. 1144 (1988); 86 ILR, p. 10. See also T. Fountain, 'Out From the Precarious Orbit of Politics: Reconsidering Recognition and the Standing of Foreign Governments to Sue in US Courts', 29 Va. JIL, 1989, p. 473.

[169] 262 NY 220 (1933); 7 AD, p. 22.   [170] 145 F.2d 431 (1944); 12 AD, p. 29.

[171] See e.g. *Civil Air Transport Inc.* v. *Central Air Transport Corporation* [1953] AC 70; 19 ILR, p. 85.

[172] See e.g. *Lehigh Valley Railroad Co.* v. *Russia* 21 F.2d 396 (1927); 4 AD, p. 58.

[173] See e.g. *US* v. *Pink* 315 US 203 (1942); 10 AD, p. 48, and *US* v. *Belmont* 301 US 324 (1937); 8 AD, p. 34.

Suggestions for further reading

J. Crawford, *The Creation of States in International Law*, 2nd edn, Oxford, 2006

J. Dugard, *Recognition and the United Nations*, Cambridge, 1987

H. Lauterpacht, *Recognition in International Law*, Cambridge, 1947

S. Talmon, *Recognition of Governments in International Law*, Oxford, 1998

10

Territory

The concept of territory in international law

International law is based on the concept of the state. The state in its turn lies upon the foundation of sovereignty, which expresses internally the supremacy of the governmental institutions and externally the supremacy of the state as a legal person.[1]

But sovereignty itself, with its retinue of legal rights and duties, is founded upon the fact of territory. Without territory a legal person cannot be a state.[2] It is undoubtedly the basic characteristic of a state and the one most widely accepted and understood. There are currently some 200 distinct territorial units, each one subject to a different territorial sovereignty and jurisdiction.

Since such fundamental legal concepts as sovereignty and jurisdiction can only be comprehended in relation to territory, it follows that the legal nature of territory becomes a vital part in any study of international law. Indeed, the principle whereby a state is deemed to exercise exclusive power over its territory can be regarded as a fundamental axiom of

---

[1] See e.g. *Oppenheim's International Law* (eds. R. Y. Jennings and A. D. Watts), 9th edn, London, 1992, chapter 5; J. Castellino and S. Allen, *Title to Territory in International Law: A Temporal Analysis*, Aldershot, 2002; G. Distefano, *L'Ordre International entre Légalité et Effectivité: Le Titre Juridique dans le Contentieux Territorial*, Paris, 2002; R. Y. Jennings, *The Acquisition of Territory in International Law*, Manchester, 1963; J. H. W. Verzijl, *International Law in Historical Perspective*, Leiden, 1970, vol. III, pp. 297 ff.; Nguyen Quoc Dinh, P. Daillier and A. Pellet, *Droit International Public*, 7th edn, Paris, 2002, pp. 464 ff. and pp. 529 ff.; M. N. Shaw, 'Territory in International Law', 13 Netherlands YIL, 1982, p. 61; N. Hill, *Claims to Territory in International Law and Relations*, London, 1945; J. Gottman, *The Significance of Territory*, Charlottesville, 1973; S. Akweenda, *International Law and the Protection of Namibia's Territorial Integrity*, The Hague, 1997; S. P. Sharma, *Territorial Acquisition, Disputes and International Law*, The Hague, 1997; W. Schoenborn, 'La Nature Juridique du Territoire', 30 HR, 1929, p. 85, and K. H. Kaikobad, *Interpretation and Revision of International Boundary Decisions*, Cambridge, 2007.

[2] See *Oppenheim's International Law*, p. 563.

classical international law.[3] The development of international law upon the basis of the exclusive authority of the state within an accepted territorial framework meant that territory became 'perhaps the fundamental concept of international law'.[4] Most nations indeed developed through a close relationship with the land they inhabited.[5]

The central role of territory in the scheme of international law may be seen by noting the development of legal rules protecting its inviolability. The principle of respect for the territorial integrity of states is well founded as one of the linchpins of the international system, as is the norm prohibiting interference in the internal affairs of other states.[6] A number of factors, however, have tended to reduce the territorial exclusivity of the state in international law. Technological and economic changes have had an impact as interdependence becomes more evident and the rise of such transnational concerns as human rights and self-determination have tended to impinge upon this exclusivity.[7] The growth of international organisations is another relevant factor, as is the development of the 'common heritage' concept in the context of the law of the sea and air law.[8] Nevertheless, one should not exaggerate the effects upon international law doctrine today of such trends.[9] Territorial sovereignty remains as a key concept in international law.

Since the law reflects political conditions and evolves, in most cases, in harmony with reality, international law has had to develop a series of rules governing the transfer and control of territory. Such rules, by the

---

[3] See L. Delbez, 'Du Territoire dans ses Rapports avec l'État', 39 *Revue Générale de Droit International Public*, 1932, p. 46. See also Hill, *Claims to Territory*, p. 3.

[4] D. P. O'Connell, *International Law*, 2nd edn, London, 1970, vol. I, p. 403. See also Jennings, *Acquisition*, p. 87, and Judge Huber, *The Island of Palmas* case, 2 RIAA, pp. 829, 838 (1928).

[5] See generally, Gottman, *Significance*.

[6] See e.g. articles 2(4) and 2(7) of the UN Charter; the 1970 Declaration on Principles of International Law adopted by the UN General Assembly, resolution 2625 (XXV), and article 1 of the 1974 Consensus Definition of Aggression adopted by the General Assembly, resolution 3314 (XXIX).

[7] See e.g. R. Falk, 'A New Paradigm for International Legal Studies: Prospects and Proposals', 84 *Yale Law Journal*, 1975, pp. 969, 973, 1020. See also H. Lauterpacht, *International Law and Human Rights*, London, 1950, and C. W. Jenks, *The Common Law of Mankind*, London, 1958.

[8] See e.g. the Treaty on Outer Space, 1967 and the Convention on the Law of the Sea, 1982. See also Shaw, 'Territory', pp. 65–6; and below, p. 541.

[9] See e.g. the *Asylum* case, ICJ Reports, 1950, pp. 266, 275; 17 ILR, pp. 280, 283. The International Court emphasised in the *Malaysia/Singapore* case, ICJ Reports, 2008, para. 122, the 'central importance in international law and relations of state sovereignty over territory and of the stability and certainty of that sovereignty'.

very nature of international society, have often (although not always) had the effect of legitimising the results of the exercise of power. The lack of a strong, central authority in international law has emphasised, even more than municipal legal structures, the way that law must come to terms with power and force.

The rules laid down by municipal legislation and judicial decisions regarding the transfer and control of land within a particular state are usually highly detailed, for they deal with one of the basic resources and wealth-creating factors of the nation. Land law has often reflected the power balance within a society, with feudal arrangements being succeeded by free market contracts and latterly the introduction of comprehensive provisions elaborating the rights and duties of landlords and their tenants, and the development of more sophisticated conveyancing techniques. A number of legal interests are capable of existing over land and the possibility exists of dividing ownership into different segments.[10] The treatment of territory in international law has not reached this sophisticated stage for a number of reasons, in particular the horizontal system of territorial sovereignty that subsists internationally as distinct from the vertical order of land law that persists in most municipal systems. There is thus a critical difference in the consequences that result from a change in the legal ownership of land in international law and in municipal law.

In international law a change in ownership of a particular territory involves also a change in sovereignty, in the legal authority governing the area. This means that the nationality of the inhabitants is altered, as is the legal system under which they live, work and conduct their relations, whereas in municipal law no such changes are involved in an alteration of legal ownership. Accordingly international law must deal also with all the various effects of a change in territorial sovereignty and not confine its attentions to the mere mechanism of acquisition or loss of territory.[11]

Territorial sovereignty

Judge Huber noted in the *Island of Palmas* case[12] that:

> sovereignty in relation to a portion of the surface of the globe is the legal condition necessary for the inclusion of such portion in the territory of any particular state.

[10] See e.g. R. Megarry and H. W. R. Wade, *The Law of Real Property*, 5th edn, London, 1984.

[11] See below, chapter 17, dealing with the problems of state succession.

[12] 2 RIAA, pp. 829, 838 (1928); 4 AD, pp. 103, 104. See also the Report of the Commission of Jurists in the *Aaland Islands* case, LNOJ, Supp. no. 3, p. 6.

Brierly defined territorial sovereignty in terms of the existence of rights over territory rather than the independence of the state itself or the relation of persons to persons. It was a way of contrasting 'the fullest rights over territory known to the law' with certain minor territorial rights, such as leases and servitudes.[13] Territorial sovereignty has a positive and a negative aspect. The former relates to the exclusivity of the competence of the state regarding its own territory,[14] while the latter refers to the obligation to protect the rights of other states.[15]

The international rules regarding territorial sovereignty are rooted in the Roman law provisions governing ownership and possession, and the classification of the different methods of acquiring territory is a direct descendant of the Roman rules dealing with property.[16] This has resulted in some confusion. Law, being so attached to contemporary life, cannot be easily transposed into a different cultural milieu.[17] And, as shall be noted, the Roman method of categorising the different methods of acquiring territory faces difficulties when applied in international law.

The essence of territorial sovereignty is contained in the notion of title. This term relates to both the factual and legal conditions under which territory is deemed to belong to one particular authority or another. In other words, it refers to the existence of those facts required under international law to entail the legal consequences of a change in the juridical status of a particular territory.[18] As the International Court noted in the *Burkina Faso/Mali* case,[19] the word 'title' comprehends both any evidence which may establish the existence of a right and the actual source of that right.[20]

One interesting characteristic that should be noted and which again points to the difference between the treatment of territory under

---

[13] *The Law of Nations*, 6th edn, Oxford, 1963, p. 162.

[14] See Judge Huber, *Island of Palmas* case, 2 RIAA, pp. 829, 838 (1928); 4 AD, pp. 103, 104.

[15] 2 RIAA, p. 839. See also Shaw, 'Territory', pp. 73 ff., and S. Bastid, 'Les Problèmes Territoriaux dans la Jurisprudence de la Cour Internationale', 107 HR, 1962, pp. 360, 367.

[16] See e.g. Schoenborn, 'Nature Juridique', p. 96. See also O'Connell, *International Law*, pp. 403–4. Note in particular the Roman law distinction between *imperium* and *dominium*: Shaw, 'Territory', p. 74.

[17] See, as regards the theories concerning the relationship between states and territory, Shaw, 'Territory', pp. 75–9.

[18] See e.g. Jennings, *Acquisition*, p. 4. See also I. Brownlie, *Principles of Public International Law*, 6th edn, Oxford, 2003, p. 119.

[19] ICJ Reports, 1986, pp. 554, 564; 80 ILR, pp. 440, 459.

[20] This was reaffirmed in the *Land, Island and Maritime Frontier (El Salvador/Honduras)* case, ICJ Reports, 1992, pp. 351, 388; 97 ILR, pp. 266, 301.

international law and municipal law is that title to territory in international law is more often than not relative rather than absolute.[21] Thus, a court, in deciding to which of contending states a parcel of land legally belongs, will consider all the relevant arguments and will award the land to the state which relatively speaking puts forward the better (or best) legal case.[22] Title to land in municipal law is much more often the case of deciding in uncertain or contentious circumstances which party complies with the legal requirements as to ownership and possession, and in that sense title is absolute. It is not normally a question of examining the facts to see which claimant can under the law put forward a better claim to title. Further, not all rights or links will amount to territorial sovereignty. Personal ties of allegiance may exist but these may not necessarily lead to a finding of sovereignty.[23] The special characteristics of the territory need to be taken into account, as does the particular structure of the sovereignty in question.[24]

Disputes as to territory in international law may be divided into different categories. The contention may be over the status of the country itself, that is, all the territory comprised in a particular state, as for example Arab claims against Israel at one time and claims formerly pursued by Morocco against Mauritania.[25] Or the dispute may refer to a certain area on the borders of two or more states, as for example Somali claims against the north-east of Kenya and south-east of Ethiopia.[26] Similarly, claims to territory may be based on a number of different grounds, ranging from the traditional method of occupation or prescription to the newer concepts such as self-determination, with various political and legal factors, for example, geographical contiguity, historical demands and economic

---

[21] See e.g. the *Eastern Greenland* case, PCIJ, Series A/B, No. 53, 1933, p. 46; 6 AD, p. 95.

[22] See the *Minquiers and Ecrehos* case, ICJ Reports, 1953, pp. 47, 52; 20 ILR, p. 94. The Court noted in the *Malaysia/Singapore* case, ICJ Reports, 2008, para. 120, that the passing of sovereignty may be by way of agreement between states, either in the form of a treaty or tacitly arising from the conduct of the parties. The emphasis was to be placed on the intention of the parties.

[23] *Western Sahara* case, ICJ Reports, 1975, pp. 12, 48, 64 and 68; 59 ILR, p. 14. See also *Qatar* v. *Bahrain*, ICJ Reports, 2001, para. 86. But see as to the confirmatory value of such ties, the *Malaysia/Singapore* case, ICJ Reports, 2008, paras. 74–5. Note that there is a critical difference between territorial sovereignty on the one hand and the regular rights of property on the other, *ibid.*, paras. 138–9 and 222.

[24] See e.g. the *Western Sahara* case, ICJ Reports, 1975, pp. 12, 41–3; 59 ILR, p. 14; the *Rann of Kutch* case, 50 ILR, p. 2; the *Dubai/Sharjah* award, 91 ILR, pp. 543, 587 and the *Eritrea/ Yemen* case, 114 ILR, pp. 1, 116.

[25] See below, p. 524.   [26] See below, p. 525.

elements, possibly being relevant. These issues will be noted during the course of this chapter.

Apart from territory actually under the sovereignty of a state, international law also recognises territory over which there is no sovereign. Such territory is known as *terra nullius*. In addition, there is a category of territory called *res communis* which is (in contrast to *terra nullius*) generally not capable of being reduced to sovereign control. The prime instance of this is the high seas, which belong to no-one and may be used by all. Another example would be outer space. The concept of common heritage of mankind has also been raised and will be examined in this chapter.

New states and title to territory[27]

The problem of how a state actually acquires its own territory in international law is a difficult one and one that may ultimately only be explained in legal–political terms. While with long-established states one may dismiss the question on the basis of recognition and acceptance, new states pose a different problem since, under classical international law, until a new state is created, there is no legal person in existence competent to hold title. None of the traditional modes of acquisition of territorial title satisfactorily resolves the dilemma, which has manifested itself particularly in the post-Second World War period with the onset of decolonisation. The international community has traditionally approached the problem of new states in terms of recognition, rather than in terms of acquisition of title to territory. This means that states have examined the relevant situation and upon ascertainment of the factual conditions have accorded recognition to the new entity as a subject of international law. There has been relatively little discussion of the method by which the new entity itself acquires the legal rights to its lands. The stress has instead been on compliance with factual requirements as to statehood coupled with the acceptance of this by other states.[28]

One approach to this problem has been to note that it is recognition that constitutes the state, and that the territory of the state is, upon recognition, accepted as the territory of a valid subject of international law irrespective

---

[27] See Jennings, *Acquisition*, pp. 36 ff.; J. G. Starke, 'The Acquisition of Title to Territory by Newly Emerged States', 41 BYIL, 1965–6, p. 411; J. Crawford, *The Creation of States in International Law*, 2nd edn, Oxford, 2006, and M. N. Shaw, *Title to Territory in Africa*, Oxford, 1986, pp. 168–73.

[28] See e.g. *Oppenheim's International Law*, p. 677.

of how it may have been acquired.[29] While this theory is not universally or widely accepted,[30] it does nevertheless underline how the emphasis has been upon recognition of a situation and not upon the method of obtaining the rights in law to the particular territory.[31]

One major factor that is relevant is the crucial importance of the doctrine of domestic jurisdiction. This constitutes the legal prohibition on interference within the internal mechanisms of an entity and emphasises the supremacy of a state within its own frontiers. Many of the factual and legal processes leading up to the emergence of a new state are therefore barred from international legal scrutiny and this has proved a deterrent to the search for the precise method by which a new entity obtains title to the territory in question.[32]

In recent years, however, the scope of the domestic jurisdiction rule has been altered. Discussions in international conferences and institutions, such as the United Nations, have actively concerned themselves with conditions in non-independent countries and it has been accepted that territorial sovereignty in the ordinary sense of the words does not really exist over mandate or trust territories.[33] This is beginning to encourage a re-examination of the procedures of acquiring title. However, the plea of domestic jurisdiction does at least illustrate the fact that not only international law but also municipal law is involved in the process of gaining independence.

There are basically two methods by which a new entity may gain its independence as a new state: by constitutional means, that is by agreement with the former controlling administration in an orderly devolution of power, or by non-constitutional means, usually by force, against the will of the previous sovereign.

The granting of independence according to the constitutional provisions of the former power may be achieved either by agreement between the former power and the accepted authorities of the emerging state, or by a purely internal piece of legislation by the previous sovereign. In many cases a combination of both procedures is adopted. For example, the independence of Burma was preceded by a Burmese–United Kingdom

---

[29] *Ibid.*   [30] See above, chapter 9.

[31] See e.g. Jennings, *Acquisition*, p. 37, and Starke, 'Acquisition of Title', p. 413.

[32] See Shaw, *Title to Territory*, pp. 168–9.

[33] See e.g. *International Status of South-West Africa*, ICJ Reports, 1950, p. 128; 17 ILR, p. 47; the *South West Africa* cases, ICJ Reports, 1966, p. 6; 37 ILR, p. 243; the *Namibia* case, ICJ Reports, 1971, p. 16; 49 ILR, p. 2, and the *Western Sahara* case, ICJ Reports, 1975, p. 12; 59 ILR, p. 14. See further above, chapter 5, p. 224.

agreement and treaty (June and October, 1947) and by the Burma Independence Act of 1947 passed by the British legislature, providing for
Burmese independence to take effect on 4 January 1948. In such cases
what appears to be involved is a devolution or transfer of sovereignty
from one power to another and the title to the territory will accordingly
pass from the previous sovereign to the new administration in a conscious
act of transference.

However, a different situation arises where the new entity gains its
independence contrary to the wishes of the previous authority, whether
by secession or revolution. It may be that the dispossessed sovereign may
ultimately make an agreement with the new state recognising its new
status, but in the meantime the new state might well be regarded by other
states as a valid state under international law.[34]

The principle of self-determination is also very relevant here. Where a
state gains its sovereignty in opposition to the former power, new facts are
created and the entity may well comply with the international requirements as to statehood, such as population, territory and government.
Other states will then have to make a decision as to whether or not to
recognise the new state and accept the legal consequences of this new
status. But at this point a serious problem emerges.

For a unit to be regarded as a state under international law it must
conform with the legal conditions as to settled population, a definable
area of land and the capacity to enter into legal relations. However, under
traditional international law, until one has a state one cannot talk in
terms of title to the territory, because there does not exist any legal person
capable of holding the legal title. So to discover the process of acquisition
of title to territory, one has first to point to an established state. A few
ideas have been put forward to explain this. One theory is to concentrate
upon the factual emergence of the new state and to accept that since a
new state is in existence upon a certain parcel of land, international law
should look no further but accept the reality of possession at the moment
of independence as denoting ownership, that is, legal title.[35] While in most
cases this would prove adequate as far as other states are concerned, it can
lead to problems where ownership is claimed of an area not in possession
and it does little to answer the questions as to the international legal
explanation of territorial sovereignty. Another approach is to turn to the

---

[34] Shaw, *Title to Territory*. See also D. Greig, *International Law*, 2nd edn, London, 1976,
p. 156.
[35] See e.g. *Oppenheim's International Law*, p. 677, and Starke, 'Acquisition of Title', p. 413.

constitutive theory of recognition, and declare that by recognition not only is a new state in the international community created, but its title to the territory upon which it is based is conclusively determined.[36] The disadvantage of this attitude is that it presupposes the acceptance of the constitutive theory by states in such circumstances, something which is controversial.[37]

One possibility that could be put forward here involves the abandonment of the classical rule that only states can acquire territorial sovereignty, and the substitution of a provision permitting a people to acquire sovereignty over the territory pending the establishment of the particular state. By this method the complicated theoretical issues related to recognition are avoided. Some support for this view can be found in the provision in the 1970 Declaration on Principles of International Law that the territory of a colony or other non-self-governing entity possesses, under the United Nations Charter, a status separate and distinct from that of the administering power, which exists until the people have exercised the right of self-determination.[38] However, the proposition is a controversial one and must remain tentative.[39]

The acquisition of additional territory

The classical technique of categorising the various modes of acquisition of territory is based on Roman law and is not adequate.[40] Many of the leading cases do not specify a particular category or mode but tend to adopt an overall approach. Five modes of acquisition are usually detailed: occupation of *terra nullius*, prescription, cession, accretion and subjugation (or conquest); and these are further divided into original and derivative modes.[41]

Boundary treaties and boundary awards

Boundary treaties, whereby either additional territory is acquired or lost or uncertain boundaries are clarified by agreement between the states concerned, constitute a root of title in themselves. They constitute a special

---

[36] Starke, 'Acquisition of Title', p. 413. See also Jennings, *Acquisition*, p. 37.
[37] See above, chapter 9, p. 445.
[38] See the *Namibia* case, ICJ Reports, 1971, pp. 16, 31; 49 ILR, pp. 2, 21.
[39] See Shaw, *Title to Territory*, pp. 171–3.   [40] See O'Connell, *International Law*, p. 405.
[41] See *Oppenheim's International Law*, p. 677, and Brownlie, *Principles*, pp. 127 ff.

kind of treaty in that they establish an objective territorial regime valid *erga omnes*.[42] Such a regime will not only create rights binding also upon third states, but will exist outside of the particular boundary treaty and thus will continue even if the treaty in question itself ceases to apply.[43] The reason for this exceptional approach is to be found in the need for the stability of boundaries.[44] Further, the establishment or confirmation of a particular boundary line by way of referring in a treaty to an earlier document (which may or may not be binding of itself) laying down a line is also possible and as such invests the line in question with undoubted validity.[45] Indeed, this earlier document may also be a map upon which a line has been drawn.

Accordingly, many boundary disputes in fact revolve around the question of treaty interpretation. It is accepted that a treaty should be interpreted in the light of Articles 31 and 32 of the Vienna Convention on the Law of Treaties, 1969, 'in good faith, in accordance with the ordinary meaning to be given to its terms in their context and in the light of its object and purpose'.[46] Essentially the aim is to find the 'common will' of the parties, a concept which includes consideration of the subsequent conduct of the parties.[47] Since many of the boundary treaties that need to be interpreted long pre-date the coming into force of the Vienna Convention,[48] the problem of the applicability of its provisions has arisen. Courts have taken the view that the Convention in this respect at least represents customary international law, thus apparently obviating the problem.[49]

More generally, the difficulty in seeking to interpret both general concepts and geographical locations used in early treaties in the

---

[42] See *Eritrea/Yemen* 114 ILR, p. 48.

[43] See *Libya/Chad*, ICJ Reports, 1994, pp. 6, 37; 100 ILR, p. 1.

[44] *Ibid.* and the *Temple* case, ICJ Reports, 1962, pp. 6, 34; 33 ILR, p. 48.

[45] See *Libya/Chad*, ICJ Reports, 1994, pp. 6, 23; 33 ILR, p. 48. See also *Cameroon* v. *Nigeria*, ICJ Reports, 2002, paras. 50–1.

[46] *Libya/Chad*, pp. 21–2.

[47] See the *Argentina/Chile Frontier Award (La Palena)* 38 ILR, pp. 10, 89 and the *Eritrea/Ethiopia* case, decision of 13 April 2002, 130 ILR, pp. 1, 34. See also, with regard to acquiescence, below, p. 515.

[48] See article 4 providing that the Convention applies only to treaties concluded after the coming into force of the Convention itself (27 January 1980).

[49] See e.g. *Libya/Chad*, ICJ Reports, 1994, pp. 6, 21–2; the *Beagle Channel* case, 52 ILR, pp. 93, 124 and the *Botswana/Namibia* case, ICJ Reports, 1999, pp. 1045, 1059–60. But cf. the Separate Opinion of Judge Oda, *ibid.*, p. 1118. See also D. W. Greig, *Intertemporality and the Law of Treaties*, British Institute of International and Comparative Law, 2001, pp. 108 ff.

light of modern scientific knowledge has posed difficulties. In the *Botswana/Namibia* case, the Court, faced with the problem of identifying the 'main channel' of the River Chobe in the light of an 1890 treaty, emphasised that 'the present-day state of scientific knowledge' could be used in order to illuminate terms of that treaty.[50] In the *Eritrea/Ethiopia* case, the Boundary Commission referred to the principle of contemporaneity, by which it meant that a treaty should be interpreted by reference to the circumstances prevailing when the treaty was concluded. In particular, the determination of a geographical name (whether of a place or of a river) depended upon the contemporary understanding of the location to which that name related at the time of the treaty. However, in seeking to understand what that was, reference to subsequent practice and to the objects of the treaty was often required.[51] In interpreting a boundary treaty, in particular in seeking to resolve ambiguities, the subsequent practice of the parties will be relevant. Even where such subsequent practice cannot in the circumstances constitute an authoritative interpretation of the treaty, it may be deemed to 'be useful' in the process of specifying the frontier in question.[52] However, where the boundary line as specified in the pertinent instrument is clear, it cannot be changed by a court in the process of interpreting delimitation provisions.[53]

Like boundary treaties, boundary awards may also constitute roots or sources of legal title to territory.[54] A decision by the International Court or arbitral tribunal allocating title to a particular territory or determining the boundary line as between two states will constitute establishment or confirmation of title that will be binding upon the parties themselves and for all practical purposes upon all states in the absence of maintained protest.[55] It is also possible that boundary allocation decisions that do not constitute international judicial or arbitral awards may be binding,

---

[50] ICJ Reports, 1999, pp. 1045, 1060. But see here the Declaration of Judge Higgins noting that the task of the Court was to 'decide what general idea the parties had in mind, and then make reality of that general idea through the use of contemporary knowledge' rather than to decide *in abstracto* 'by a mechanistic appreciation of relevant indicia', *ibid.*, p. 1114. See also the *Argentina/Chile Award (La Laguna del Desierto)* 113 ILR, pp. 1, 76. In the *Cameroon* v. *Nigeria* case, the Court, in seeking to determine the location of the mouth of the River Ebeji, emphasised that 'the Court must seek to ascertain the intention of the parties at the time', ICJ Reports, 2002, pp. 303, 346.

[51] Decision of 13 April 2002, 130 ILR, pp. 1, 34.

[52] *Cameroon* v. *Nigeria*, ICJ Reports, 2002, pp. 303, 345. [53] *Ibid.*, p. 370.

[54] See e.g. Brownlie, *Principles*, p. 132.

[55] See e.g. the *Land, Island and Maritime Frontier Dispute (El Salvador/Honduras)*, ICJ Reports, 1992, pp. 351, 401; 97 ILR, p. 112.

providing that it can be shown that the parties consented to the initial decision.[56]

Accretion[57]

This describes the geographical process by which new land is formed and becomes attached to existing land, as for example the creation of islands in a river mouth or the change in direction of a boundary river leaving dry land where it had formerly flowed. Where new land comes into being within the territory of a state, it forms part of the territory of the state and there is no problem. When, for example, an island emerged in the Pacific after an under-sea volcano erupted in January 1986, the UK government noted that: 'We understand the island emerged within the territorial sea of the Japanese island of Iwo Jima. We take it therefore to be Japanese territory.'[58]

As regards a change in the course of a river forming a boundary, a different situation is created depending whether it is imperceptible and slight or a violent shift (*avulsion*). In the latter case, the general rule is that the boundary stays at the same point along the original river bed.[59] However, where a gradual move has taken place the boundary may be shifted.[60] If the river is navigable, the boundary will be the middle of the navigable channel, whatever slight alterations have occurred, while if the river is not navigable the boundary will continue to be the middle of the river itself. This aspect of acquiring territory is relatively unimportant in international law but these rules have been applied in a number of cases involving disputes between particular states of the United States of America.[61]

---

[56] See e.g. the *Dubai/Sharjah* case, 91 ILR, pp. 543, 577 (where the Court of Arbitration termed such procedures 'administrative decisions', *ibid.*) and *Qatar/Bahrain*, ICJ Reports, 2001, paras. 110 ff.

[57] See e.g. C. C. Hyde, *International Law*, 2nd edn, Boston, 1947, vol. I, pp. 355–6; O'Connell, *International Law*, pp. 428–30, and *Oppenheim's International Law*, pp. 696–8.

[58] 478 HL Deb., col. 1005, Written Answer, 17 July 1986. See also A. J. Day, *Border and Territorial Disputes*, 2nd edn, London, 1987, p. 277, regarding a new island appearing after a cyclone in 1970 on a river boundary between India and Bangladesh. Title is disputed. See also *Georgia* v. *South Carolina* 111 L.Ed.2d 309; 91 ILR, p. 439.

[59] See e.g. *Georgia* v. *South Carolina* 111 L.Ed.2d 309, 334; 91 ILR, pp. 439, 458. See also the *Land, Island and Maritime Frontier Dispute (El Salvador/Honduras)*, ICJ Reports, 1992, pp. 351, 546.

[60] ICJ Reports, 1992, pp. 351, 546.

[61] See e.g. *The Anna* 5 C.Rob. 373 (1805); *Arkansas* v. *Tennessee* 246 US 158 (1918); *Louisiana* v. *Mississippi* 282 US 458 (1940); *Georgia* v. *South Carolina* 111 L.Ed.2d 309; 91 ILR,

Cession[62]

This involves the peaceful transfer of territory from one sovereign to another (with the intention that sovereignty should pass) and has often taken place within the framework of a peace treaty following a war. Indeed the orderly transference of sovereignty by agreement from a colonial or administering power to representatives of the indigenous population could be seen as a form of cession.

Because cession has the effect of replacing one sovereign by another[63] over a particular piece of territory, the acquiring state cannot possess more rights over the land than its predecessor had. This is an important point, so that where a third state has certain rights, for example, of passage over the territory, the new sovereign must respect them. It is expressed in the land law phrase that the burden of obligations runs with the land, not the owner. In other words, the rights of the territorial sovereign are derived from a previous sovereign, who could not, therefore, dispose of more than he had.

This contrasts with, for example, accretion which is treated as an original title, there having been no previous legal sovereign over the land.

The *Island of Palmas* case[64] emphasised this point. It concerned a dispute between the United States and the Netherlands. The claims of the United States were based on an 1898 treaty with Spain, which involved the cession of the island. It was emphasised by the arbitrator and accepted by the parties that Spain could not thereby convey to the Americans greater rights than it itself possessed.

The basis of cession lies in the intention of the relevant parties to transfer sovereignty over the territory in question.[65] Without this it cannot legally operate. Whether an actual delivery of the property is also required for

---

p. 439, and the *Chamizal* arbitration, 5 AJIL, 1911, p. 782. See also E. Lauterpacht, 'River Boundaries: Legal Aspects of the Shatt-Al-Arab Frontier', 9 ICLQ, 1960, pp. 208, 216; L. J. Bouchez, 'The Fixing of Boundaries in International Boundary Rivers', 12 ICLQ, 1963, p. 789; S. McCaffrey, *The Law of International Watercourses*, 2nd edn, Oxford, 2007, and the *Botswana/Namibia* case, ICJ Reports, 1999, p. 1045.

[62] See e.g. *Oppenheim's International Law*, pp. 679–86, and O'Connell, *International Law*, pp. 436–40.

[63] See *Christian* v. *The Queen* [2006] UKPC 47, para. 11, 130 ILR 696, 700, 711, where the Privy Council noted that cession 'contemplates a transfer of sovereignty by one sovereign power to another'.

[64] 2 RIAA, p. 829 (1928); 4 AD, p. 103.

[65] Sovereignty over the territorial sea contiguous to and the airspace above the territory concerned would pass with the land territory: see the *Grisbadarna* case, 11 RIAA, p. 147 (1909) and the *Beagle Channel* case, HMSO, 1977; 52 ILR, p. 93. This suggests the corollary

a valid cession is less certain. It will depend on the circumstances of the case. For example, Austria ceded Venice to France in 1866, and that state within a few weeks ceded the territory to Italy. The cession to the Italian state through France was nonetheless valid.[66] In the *Iloilo* case,[67] it was held that the cession of the Philippines to the United States took place, on the facts of the case, upon the ratification of the Treaty of Paris of 1898, even though American troops had taken possession of the town of Iloilo two months prior to this.

Although instances of cession usually occur in an agreement following the conclusion of hostilities,[68] it can be accomplished in other circumstances, such as the purchase of Alaska by the United States in 1867 from Russia or the sale by Denmark of territories in the West Indies in 1916 to the United States. It may also appear in exchanges of territories or pure gifts of territory.[69]

Conquest and the use of force

How far a title based on force can be regarded as a valid, legal right recognisable by other states and enforceable within the international system is a crucial question. Ethical considerations are relevant and the principle that an illegal act cannot give birth to a right in law is well established in municipal law and is an essential component of an orderly society.

However, international law has sometimes to modify its reactions to the consequences of successful violations of its rules to take into account the exigencies of reality. The international community has accepted the results of illegal aggression in many cases by virtue of recognition.

Conquest, the act of defeating an opponent and occupying all or part of its territory, does not of itself constitute a basis of title to the land.[70] It

---

that a cession of the territorial sea or airspace would include the relevant land territory: see *Oppenheim's International Law*, p. 680. But see Brownlie, *Principles*, pp. 117–18.

[66] See *Oppenheim's International Law*, p. 681. Note also that in 1859 Austria ceded Lombardy to France, which then ceded it to Sardinia without having taken possession: see O'Connell, *International Law*, p. 438. Cf. *The Fama* 5 C.Rob. 106, 115 (1804).

[67] 4 RIAA, p. 158 (1925); 3 AD, p. 336.

[68] Note now that article 52 of the Vienna Convention on the Law of Treaties, 1969 provides that a treaty is void if its conclusion has been procured by the threat or use of force in violation of the principles of international law embodied in the Charter of the United Nations. However, prior treaties of cession are subject to the rule of intertemporal law: see below, p. 508.

[69] See, for further examples, *Oppenheim's International Law*, pp. 681–2.

[70] *Ibid.*, p. 699. See also S. Korman, *The Right of Conquest*, Oxford, 1996.

does give the victor certain rights under international law as regards the territory, the rights of belligerent occupation,[71] but the territory remains subject to the legal title of the ousted sovereign.[72] Sovereignty as such does not merely pass by conquest to the occupying forces, although complex situations may arise where the legal status of the territory occupied is, in fact, in dispute prior to the conquest.[73]

Conquest, of course, may result from a legal or an illegal use of force. By the Kellogg–Briand Pact of 1928, war was outlawed as an instrument of national policy, and by article 2(4) of the United Nations Charter all member states must refrain from the threat or use of force against the territorial integrity or political independence of any state. However, force will be legitimate when exercised in self-defence.[74] Whatever the circumstances, it is not the successful use of violence that in international law constituted the valid method of acquiring territory. Under the classical rules, formal annexation of territory following upon an act of conquest would operate to pass title. It was a legal fiction employed to mask the conquest and transform it into a valid method of obtaining land under international law.[75] However, it is doubtful whether an annexation proclaimed while war is still in progress would have operated to pass a good title to territory. Only after a war is concluded could the juridical status of the disputed territory be finally determined. This follows from the rule that has developed to the effect that the control over the relevant territory by the state purporting to annex must be effective and that there must be no reasonable chance of the former sovereign regaining the land.

These points were emphasised by the Nuremberg War Crimes Tribunal after the Second World War, in discussing the various purported German annexations of 1939 and 1940. The Tribunal firmly declared that annexations taking place before the conclusion of a war were ineffective and invalid in international law.[76] Intention to annex was a crucial aspect

---

[71] See e.g. M. S. McDougal and F. P. Feliciano, *Law and Minimum World Public Order*, New Haven, 1961, pp. 733–6 and 739–44, and J. Stone, *Legal Controls of International Conflict*, London, 1959, pp. 744–51. See also E. Benveniste, *The International Law of Occupation*, Princeton, 1993.

[72] See generally *The Arab–Israeli Conflict* (ed. J. N. Moore), Princeton, 4 vols., 1974–89.

[73] But cf. Y. Blum, 'The Missing Reversioner', in *ibid.*, vol. II, p. 287.

[74] See article 51 of the UN Charter and below, chapter 20.

[75] See e.g. *Oppenheim's International Law*, p. 699. See also O'Connell, *International Law*, pp. 431–6.

[76] O'Connell, *International Law*, p. 436. See also e.g. *Re Goering* 13 AD, p. 203 (1946).

of the equation so that, for example, the conquest of Germany by the Allies in 1945 did not give rise to an implied annexation by virtue of the legislative control actually exercised (as it could have done) because the Allies had specifically ruled out such a course in a joint declaration.[77] It is, however, clear today that the acquisition of territory by force alone is illegal under international law. This may be stated in view of article 2(4) of the UN Charter and other practice. Security Council resolution 242, for example, emphasised the 'inadmissibility of the acquisition of territory by war', while the 1970 Declaration of Principles of International Law adopted by the UN General Assembly provides that:

> the territory of a state shall not be the object of acquisition by another state resulting from the threat or use of force. No territorial acquisition resulting from the threat or use of force shall be recognised as legal.[78]

In Security Council resolution 662 (1990), adopted unanimously, the Council decided that the declared Iraqi annexation of Kuwait 'under any form and whatever pretext has no legal validity and is considered null and void'. All states and institutions were called upon not to recognise the annexation and to refrain from actions which might be interpreted as indirect recognition.[79]

Acquisition of territory following an armed conflict would require further action of an international nature in addition to domestic legislation to annex. Such further necessary action would be in the form either of a treaty of cession by the former sovereign or of international recognition.[80]

The exercise of effective control

It is customary in the literature to treat the modes of occupation and prescription as separate categories. However, there are several crucial factors

---

[77] Cmd 6648 (1945). See also *Oppenheim's International Law*, pp. 699–700.

[78] See also article 5(3) of the Consensus Definition of Aggression adopted in 1974 by the UN General Assembly. Similarly, by article 52 of the Vienna Convention on the Law of Treaties, 1969, a treaty providing for the transfer of territory may be void for duress.

[79] See *The Kuwait Crisis – Basic Documents* (eds. E. Lauterpacht, C. Greenwood, M. Weller and D. Bethlehem), Cambridge, 1991, p. 90.

[80] See, for example, Security Council resolution 497 (1981), condemning Israel's decision to extend its laws, jurisdiction and administration to the occupied Golan Heights. The UN has also condemned Israel's policy of establishing settlements in the occupied territories: see e.g. Security Council resolution 465 (1980). See further below, chapter 20, with regard to self-determination and the use of force.

that link the concepts, so that the acquisition of territory by virtue of these methods, based as they are upon the exercise of effective control, is best examined within the same broad framework. The traditional definition of these two modes will be noted first.

Occupation is a method of acquiring territory which belongs to no one (*terra nullius*) and which may be acquired by a state in certain situations. The occupation must be by a state and not by private individuals, it must be effective and it must be intended as a claim of sovereignty over the area. The high seas cannot be occupied in this manner for they are *res communis*, but vacant land may be subjected to the sovereignty of a claimant state. It relates primarily to uninhabited territories and islands, but may also apply to certain inhabited lands.

The issue was raised in the *Western Sahara* case before the International Court of Justice.[81] The question was asked as to whether the territory in question had been *terra nullius* at the time of colonisation. It was emphasised by the Court that the concept of *terra nullius* was a legal term of art used in connection with the mode of acquisition of territory known as 'occupation'.[82] The latter mode was defined legally as an original means of peaceably acquiring sovereignty over territory otherwise than by cession or succession.[83] In an important statement, the Court unambiguously asserted that the state practice of the relevant period (i.e. the period of colonisation) indicated that territories inhabited by tribes or peoples having a social and political organisation were not regarded as *terrae nullius*.[84] Further, international case-law has recognised that sovereign title may be suspended for a period of time in circumstances that do not lead to the status of *terra nullius*. Such indeterminacy could be resolved by the relevant parties at a relevant time.[85]

In fact the majority of territories brought under European control were regarded as acquired by means of cessions, especially in Asia and

---

[81] ICJ Reports, 1975, p. 12; 59 ILR, p. 14. See also M. N. Shaw, 'The *Western Sahara* case', 49 BYIL, 1978, pp. 119, 127–34.

[82] ICJ Reports, 1975, pp. 12, 39; 59 ILR, pp. 14, 56.   [83] *Ibid.*

[84] *Ibid.* This ran counter to some writers of the period: see e.g. M. F. Lindley, *The Acquisition and Government of Backward Territory in International Law*, London, 1926, pp. 11–20; J. Westlake, *Chapters on the Principles of International Law*, London, 1894, pp. 141–2; Jennings, *Acquisition*, p. 20, and *Oppenheim's International Law*, p. 687, footnote 4.

[85] See *Eritrea/Yemen*, 114 ILR, pp. 1, 51. See also N. S. M. Antunes, 'The *Eritrea–Yemen* Arbitration: First Stage – The Law of Title to Territory Re-averred', 48 ICLQ, 1999, p. 362, and A. Yannis, 'The Concept of Suspended Sovereignty in International Law and Its Implications in International Politics', 13 EJIL, 2002, p. 1037.

Africa.[86] However, there were instances of title by occupation, for example Australia, and many sparsely inhabited islands.

Occupation, both in the normal sense of the word and in its legal meaning, was often preceded by discovery, that is the realisation of the existence of a particular piece of land.[87] But mere realisation or sighting was never considered (except for periods in the fifteenth and sixteenth centuries and this is not undisputed) as sufficient to constitute title to territory. Something more was required and this took the form of a symbolic act of taking possession, whether it be by the raising of flags or by solemn proclamations or by more sophisticated ritual expressions. As time passed, the conditions changed and the arbitrator in the *Island of Palmas* case pointed to the modern effect of discovery as merely giving an inchoate title which had to be completed within a reasonable time by the effective occupation of the relevant region. Discovery only put other states on notice that the claimant state had a prior interest in the territory which, to become legally meaningful, had to be supplemented by effective occupation within a certain period.[88]

Prescription[89] is a mode of establishing title to territory which is not *terra nullius* and which has been obtained either unlawfully or in circumstances wherein the legality of the acquisition cannot be demonstrated. It is the legitimisation of a doubtful title by the passage of time and the presumed acquiescence of the former sovereign, and it reflects the need for stability felt within the international system by recognising that territory in the possession of a state for a long period of time and uncontested cannot be taken away from that state without serious consequences for the international order. It is the legitimisation of a fact. If it were not for some such doctrine, the title of many states to their territory would be jeopardised.[90] The International Court in the *Botswana/Namibia* case,

---

[86] See Shaw, *Title to Territory*, chapter 1, and C. H. Alexandrowicz, *The European–African Confrontation*, Leiden, 1973.

[87] See e.g. *Oppenheim's International Law*, pp. 689–90, and F. A. F. Von der Heydte, 'Discovery, Symbolic Annexation and Virtual Effectiveness in International Law', 29 AJIL, 1935, p. 448. See also A. S. Keller, O. J. Lissitzyn and F. J. Mann, *Creation of Rights of Sovereignty Through Symbolic Acts, 1400–1800*, New York, 1938.

[88] 2 RIAA, pp. 829, 846 (1928); 4 AD, pp. 103, 108.

[89] See generally e.g. D. H. Johnson, 'Acquisitive Prescription in International Law', 27 BYIL, 1950, p. 332, and H. Post, 'International Law Between Dominium and Imperium' in *Reflections on Principles and Practice of International Law* (eds. T. D. Gill and W. P. Heere), The Hague, 2000, p. 147.

[90] As noted in the *Grisbadarna* case, 'it is a settled principle of the law of nations that a state of things which actually exists and has existed for a long time should be changed as little as possible', J. B. Scott, *Hague Court Reports*, New York, 1916, vol. I, pp. 121, 130.

while making no determination of its own, noted that the two parties were agreed that acquisitive prescription was recognised in international law and further agreed on the criteria to be satisfied for the establishment of such a title, viz. the possession must be *à titre de souverain*, peaceful and uninterrupted, public and endure for a certain length of time. The Court did not contradict this position.[91]

Prescription differs from occupation in that it relates to territory which has previously been under the sovereignty of a state. In spite of this, both concepts are similar in that they may require evidence of sovereign acts by a state over a period of time. And although distinct in theory, in practice these concepts are often indistinct since sovereignty over an area may lapse and give rise to doubts whether an abandonment has taken place,[92] rendering the territory *terra nullius*.

In fact, most cases do not fall into such clear theoretical categories as occupation or prescription. Particular modes of acquisition that can be unambiguously related to the classic definitions tend not to be specified. Most cases involve contesting claims by states, where both (or possibly all) the parties have performed some sovereign acts. As in the instance of occupation, so prescription too requires that the possession forming the basis of the title must be by virtue of the authority of the state or *à titre de souverain*, and not a manifestation of purely individual effort unrelated to the state's sovereign claims. And this possession must be public so that all interested states can be made aware of it.

This latter requirement also flows logically from the necessity for the possession to be peaceful and uninterrupted, and reflects the vital point that prescription rests upon the implied consent of the former sovereign to the new state of affairs. This means that protests by the dispossessed sovereign may completely block any prescriptive claim.[93]

In the *Chamizal* arbitration[94] between the United States and Mexico, the Rio Grande River forming the border between the parties changed course and the United States claimed the ground between the old and the new river beds partly on the basis of peaceful and uninterrupted possession. This claim was dismissed in view of the constant protests by Mexico and

---

[91] ICJ Reports, 1999, pp. 1045, 1101 ff.

[92] For abandonment of territory, the fact of the loss plus the intention to abandon is required. This is very rare: see e.g. the *Delagoa Bay* case, C. Parry, *British Digest of International Law*, Cambridge, 1965, vol. V, p. 535, and the *Frontier Land* case, ICJ Reports, 1959, p. 209; 27 ILR, p. 62. See also Brownlie, *Principles*, pp. 138–9.

[93] See Johnson, 'Acquisitive Prescription', pp. 343–8.

[94] 5 AJIL 1911, p. 782. See also the *Minquiers and Ecrehos* case, ICJ Reports, 1953, pp. 47, 106–8; 20 ILR, pp. 94, 142–4.

in the light of a Convention signed by both parties that there existed a dispute as to the boundary which had to be resolved. The fact that Mexico did not go to war over the issue was not of itself sufficient to make the possession of the tract of land by the United States peaceful.

Thus acquiescence in the case of prescription, whether express or implied from all the relevant circumstances, is essential, whereas in the case of occupation it is merely an evidential point reinforcing the existence of an effective occupation, but not constituting the essence of the legal claim.

Precisely what form the protest is to take is open to question but resort to force is not acceptable in modern international law, especially since the 1928 Kellogg–Briand Pact and article 2(4) of the United Nations Charter.[95] The bringing of a matter before the United Nations or the International Court of Justice will be conclusive as to the existence of the dispute and thus of the reality of the protests, but diplomatic protests will probably be sufficient. This, however, is not accepted by all academic writers, and it may well be that in serious disputes further steps should be taken such as severing diplomatic relations or proposing arbitration or judicial settlement.[96] What is clear is that anything less than sustained and credible protests may well risk the title of the dispossessed party.

The requirement of a 'reasonable period' of possession is similarly imprecise and it is not possible to point to any defined length of time.[97] It will depend, as so much else, upon all the circumstances of the case, including the nature of the territory and the absence or presence of any competing claims.

In the *Minquiers and Ecrehos* case,[98] concerning disputed sovereignty over a group of islets and rocks in the English Channel, claimed by both France and the United Kingdom, the International Court of Justice exhaustively examined the history of the region since 1066. However, its decision was based primarily on relatively recent acts relating to the exercise of jurisdiction and local administration as well as the nature of

---

[95] See above, p. 500, and below, chapter 20.

[96] See e.g. Johnson, 'Acquisitive Prescription', pp. 353–4, and I. MacGibbon, 'Some Observations on the Part of Protest in International Law', 30 BYIL, 1953, p. 293. Cf. Brownlie, *Principles*, p. 149, who notes that 'if acquiescence is the crux of the matter (and it is believed that it is) one cannot dictate what its content is to be'.

[97] In the *British Guiana and Venezuela Boundary* case, the parties agreed to adopt a fifty-year adverse holding rule, 89 BFSP, 1896, p. 57.

[98] ICJ Reports, 1953, p. 47; 20 ILR, p. 94.

legislative enactments referable to the territory in question. And upon these grounds, British sovereignty was upheld. The sovereign acts of the United Kingdom relating to the islets far outweighed any such activities by the French authorities and accordingly the claims of the latter were dismissed.

As in other cases, judgment was given not on the basis of clearly defined categories of occupation or prescription, but rather in the light of the balance of competing state activities.

De Visscher has attempted to render the theoretical classifications more consonant with the practical realities by the introduction of the concept of historical consolidation.[99] This idea is founded on proven long use, which reflects a complex of interests and relations resulting in the acquisition of territory (including parts of the sea). Such a grouping of interests and relations is considered by the courts in reaching a decision as of more importance than the mere passage of time, and historical consolidation may apply to *terra nullius* as well as to territories previously occupied. Thus it can be distinguished from prescription. It differs from occupation in that the concept has relevance to the acquisition of parts of the sea, as well as of land. And it may be brought into existence not only by acquiescence and consent, but also by the absence of protest over a reasonable period by relevant states.[100]

However, de Visscher's discussion, based on the *Anglo-Norwegian Fisheries* case,[101] does fail to note the important distinction between the acquisition of territory in accordance with the rules of international law, and the acquisition of territory as a permitted exception to the generally accepted legal principles. The passage in the *Anglo-Norwegian Fisheries* case relied upon[102] is really concerned with general acquiescence with regard to a maritime area, while the criticism has been made[103] that de Visscher has over-emphasised the aspect of 'complex of interests and relations which *in themselves* have the effect of attaching a territory or an expanse of sea to a given state'.[104] Effectiveness, therefore, rather than consolidation would be the appropriate term. Both occupation and prescription rely primarily upon effective possession and control. The element of time is here also relevant as it affects the effectiveness of control.

---

[99] *Theory and Reality in Public International Law*, 1968, p. 209. See below, p. 520.
[100] *Ibid.* [101] ICJ Reports, 1951, pp. 116, 138; 18 ILR, pp. 86, 100. [102] *Ibid.*
[103] See Jennings, *Acquisition*, pp. 25–6. See also D. H. Johnson, 'Consolidation as a Root of Title in International Law', *Cambridge Law Journal*, 1955, pp. 215, 223.
[104] De Visscher, *Theory and Reality*, p. 209, emphasis added. See further below, p. 515.

Intertemporal law[105]

One question that arises is the problem of changing conditions related to particular principles of international law, in other words the relevant time period at which to ascertain the legal rights and obligations in question. This can cause considerable difficulties since a territorial title may be valid under, for example, sixteenth-century legal doctrines but ineffective under nineteenth-century developments. The general rule in such circumstances is that in a dispute the claim or situation in question (or relevant treaty, for example)[106] has to be examined according to the conditions and rules in existence at the time it was made and not at a later date. This meant, for example, that in the *Island of Palmas* case,[107] the Spanish claim to title by discovery, which the United States declared it had inherited, had to be tested in the light of international legal principles in the sixteenth century when the discovery was made. This aspect of the principle is predicated upon a presumption of, and need for, stability.[108]

But it was also noted in this case that while the creation of particular rights was dependent upon the international law of the time, the continued existence of such rights depended upon their according with the evolving conditions of a developing legal system, although this stringent test would not be utilised in the case of territories with an 'established order of things'.[109] This proviso has in practice been carefully and flexibly interpreted within the context of all the relevant rules relating to the acquisition of territory, including recognition and acquiescence.[110] However,

---

[105] See e.g. the *Western Sahara* case, ICJ Reports, 1975, pp. 12, 38–9; 59 ILR, pp. 14, 55. See also Shaw, 'Western Sahara Case', pp. 152–3; Jennings, *Acquisition*, pp. 28–31; T. O. Elias, 'The Doctrine of Intertemporal Law', 74 AJIL, 1980, p. 285; Brownlie, *Principles*, pp. 124–5; *Oppenheim's International Law*, pp. 1281–2; G. Fitzmaurice, *The Law and Procedure of the International Court of Justice*, Cambridge, 1986, vol. I, p. 135, and H. Thirlway, 'The Law and Procedure of the International Court of Justice 1960–1989 (Part One)', 60 BYIL, 1989, pp. 4, 128. See also R. Higgins, 'Time and the Law: International Perspectives on an Old Problem', 46 ICLQ, 1997, p. 501, and Greig, *Intertemporality*.

[106] See e.g. the *Right of Passage* case, ICJ Reports, 1960, pp. 6, 37; 31 ILR, pp. 23, 50.

[107] 2 RIAA, pp. 829, 845 (1928); 4 AD, p. 103.

[108] See e.g. *Eritrea/Yemen*, 114 ILR, pp. 1, 46 and 115; *Eritrea/Ethiopia* case, 2002, 130 ILR, pp. 1, 34 and *Cameroon v. Nigeria*, ICJ Reports, 2002, pp. 303, 404–5.

[109] 2 RIAA, pp. 839–45. See P. Jessup, 'The Palmas Island Arbitration', 22 AJIL, 1928, p. 735. See also M. Sørensen, 'Le Problème Dit du Droit Intertemporal dans l'Ordre International', *Annuaire de l'Institut de Droit International*, Basle, 1973, pp. 4 ff., and subsequent discussions, *ibid.*, at pp. 50 ff., and the Resolution adopted by the Institut de Droit International, *Annuaire de l'Institut de Droit International*, 1975, pp. 536 ff.

[110] Note that the 1970 Declaration on Principles of International Law provides that the concept of non-acquisition of territory by force was not to be affected *inter alia* by any international agreement made prior to the Charter and valid under international law.

the Court in the *Aegean Sea Continental Shelf* case[111] declared that the phrase 'disputes relating to the territorial status of Greece' contained in a Greek reservation to the 1928 Kellogg–Briand Pact had to be interpreted 'in accordance with the rules of international law as they exist today, and not as they existed in 1931'. The evolution of international law concerning the continental shelf, therefore, had to be considered, so that the territorial status of Greece was taken to include its continental shelf, although that concept was completely unknown in the 1920s. How far this aspect of the principle of international law may be extended is highly controversial. The better view is to see it as one element in the bundle of factors relevant to the determination of effective control, but one that must be applied with care.[112]

Critical date

In certain situations there may exist a determining moment at which it might be inferred that the rights of the parties have crystallised so that acts after that date cannot alter the legal position.[113] Such a moment might be the date of a particular treaty where its provisions are at issue[114] or the date of occupation of territory.[115] It is not correct that there will or should always be such a critical date in territorial disputes, but where there is, acts undertaken after that date will not be taken into consideration, unless such acts are a normal continuation of prior acts and are not undertaken for the purpose of improving the legal position of the party relying on them.[116]

The concept of a critical date is of especial relevance with regard to the doctrine of *uti possidetis*, which posits that a new state has the boundaries of the predecessor entity, so that the moment of independence itself is

---

[111] ICJ Reports, 1978, pp. 3, 33–4; 60 ILR, pp. 562, 592. See Elias, 'Intertemporal Law', pp. 296 ff. See also the Indian argument regarding the invalidity of Portugal's title to Goa, SCOR, S/PV-987, 11, 18 December 1961.

[112] See, as to time and the interpretation of treaties, above, p. 496.

[113] L. F. E. Goldie, 'The Critical Date', 12 ICLQ, 1963, p. 1251. See also G. Fitzmaurice, 'The Law and Procedure of the International Court of Justice, 1951–4: Points of Substance, Part II', 32 BYIL, 1955–6, p. 20; Y. Blum, *Historic Titles in International Law*, The Hague, 1965, pp. 208–22, and Brownlie, *Principles*, p. 125. See also M. N. Shaw, 'The Heritage of States: The Principle of *Uti Possidetis Juris* Today', 67 BYIL, 1996, pp. 75, 130, and Shaw, 'Title, Control and Closure? The Experience of the Eritrea–Ethiopia Boundary Commission', 56 ICLQ, 2007, pp. 755, 760 ff.

[114] See e.g. the *Island of Palmas* case, 2 RIAA, p. 845.

[115] See e.g. the *Eastern Greenland* case, PCIJ, Series A/B, No. 53, p. 45.

[116] See the *Indonesia/Malaysia* case, ICJ Reports, 2002, pp. 625, 682. See also *Argentina/Chile* 38 ILR, pp. 10, 79–80 and *Nicaragua* v. *Honduras*, ICJ Reports, 2007, para. 117. Note also the *Malaysia/Singapore* case, ICJ Reports, 2008, paras. 32–6.

invariably the critical date.[117] This does not preclude the possibility that the relevant territorial situation or rights had crystallised at an earlier time, in the sense of having become established and not altered subsequently.[118] Where there is more than one state involved, then the date of later independence[119] or possibly the dates of the independence of the respective states,[120] may be taken depending on the circumstances.[121] Further, it is possible for there to be different critical dates for different circumstances (for example, land and maritime disputes within the same case).[122] However, the date of independence may simply mark the date of succession to boundaries which have been established with binding force by earlier instruments.[123]

The moment of independence may not be 'critical' for these purposes for several possible reasons. There may be a dispute between the parties as to whether the date of independence or the date of the last exercise of jurisdiction for administrative organisational purposes by the former sovereign is the more appropriate date[124] or the *uti possidetis* line may in some circumstances only be determined upon a consideration of materials appearing later than the date of independence,[125] or such a 'critical date' may have been moved to a later date than that of independence by a subsequent treaty[126] or by an adjudication award.[127] The importance of the critical date concept, thus, is relative and depends entirely upon the circumstances of the case.[128]

---

[117] The *Burkina Faso/Mali* case, ICJ Reports, 1986, p. 568; 80 ILR, p. 440. This may be reinforced by the terms of the *compromis* itself. For example, in the *Eritrea/Ethiopia* case, the parties referred specifically to the principle of respect for borders existing at the moment of independence, 130 ILR, pp. 1, 43 and see further below, p. 525.

[118] *Eritrea/Ethiopia* case, 130 ILR, pp. 1, 102–3.   [119] *Ibid.*, p. 43.

[120] See the *Benin/Niger* case, ICJ Reports, 2005, pp. 90, 120. See also the views of the Arbitration Commission of the Conference on Yugoslavia in Opinion No. 11 as to the varying dates of succession (and independence) of the successor states of the Former Yugoslavia: see 96 ILR, pp. 719, 722.

[121] See the *Burkino Faso/Mali* case, ICJ Reports, 1986, p. 570; 80 ILR, p. 440, and the *Dubai/Sharjah* case, 91 ILR, pp. 590–4 for examples where the concept was held to be of little or no practical value.

[122] See e.g. *Nicaragua* v. *Honduras*, ICJ Reports, 2007, para. 123.

[123] As in the *Libya/Chad* case, ICJ Reports, 1994, p. 6; 100 ILR, p. 1.

[124] See the *Burkina Faso/Mali* case, ICJ Reports, 1986, p. 570; 80 ILR, p. 440.

[125] See the *El Salvador/Honduras* case, ICJ Reports, 1992, pp. 56 ff.; 97 ILR, p. 112.

[126] See the *Beagle Channel* case, 21 RIAA, pp. 55, 82–3; 52 ILR, p. 93.

[127] The *El Salvador/Honduras* case, ICJ Reports, 1992, p. 401; 97 ILR, p. 112. See also the *Burkina Faso/Mali* case, ICJ Reports, 1986, p. 570; 80 ILR, p. 440, and the Separate Opinion of Judge Ajibola, the *Libya/Chad* case, ICJ Reports, 1994, p. 91; 100 ILR, p. 1.

[128] See e.g. the *Burkino Faso/Mali* case, ICJ Reports, 1986, p. 570; 80 ILR, p. 440, for an example where the concept was held to be of little or no practical value. A similar view

Sovereign activities (*effectivités*)

The exercise of effective authority, therefore, is the crucial element. As Huber argued, 'the actual continuous and peaceful display of state functions is in case of dispute the sound and natural criterion of territorial sovereignty'.[129]

However, control, although needing to be effective, does not necessarily have to amount to possession and settlement of all of the territory claimed. Precisely what acts of sovereignty are necessary to found title will depend in each instance upon all the relevant circumstances of the case, including the nature of the territory involved, the amount of opposition (if any) that such acts on the part of the claimant state have aroused, and international reaction.

Indeed in international law many titles will be deemed to exist not as absolute but as relative concepts. The state succeeding in its claim for sovereignty over *terra nullius* over the claims of other states will in most cases have proved not an absolute title, but one relatively better than that maintained by competing states and one that may take into account issues such as geography and international responses.[130] The Court noted in the *Eastern Greenland* case that 'It is impossible to read the records of the decisions in cases as to territorial sovereignty without observing that in many cases the tribunal has been satisfied with very little in the way of the actual exercise of sovereign rights, provided that the other state could not make out a superior claim. This is particularly true in the case of claims to sovereignty over areas in thinly populated or unsettled countries.'[131] However, the arbitral tribunal in *Eritrea/Yemen* emphasised that the issue did not turn solely upon relativity since 'there must be some absolute minimum requirement' for the acquisition of territorial sovereignty.[132]

---

was taken in the *Dubai/Sharjah* case, 91 ILR, pp. 590–4 and the *Eritrea/Yemen Arbitration*, 114 ILR, pp. 1, 32.

[129] 2 RIAA, pp. 829, 840 (1928). The Tribunal in *Eritrea/Yemen* noted that 'The modern international law of the acquisition (or attribution) of territory generally requires that there be: an intentional display of power and authority over the territory, by the exercise of jurisdiction and state functions, on a continuous and peaceful basis', 114 ILR, pp. 1, 69.

[130] See the *Island of Palmas* case, 2 RIAA, pp. 829, 840 (1928); 4 AD, p. 103. See also the *Eastern Greenland* case, PCIJ, Series A/B, No. 53, 1933, p. 46; 6 AD, p. 95; the *Clipperton Island* case, 26 AJIL, 1932, p. 390; 6 AD, p. 105, and the *Minquiers and Ecrehos* case, ICJ Reports, 1953, p. 47; 20 ILR, p. 94.

[131] PCIJ, Series A/B, No. 53, pp. 45–6. See also *Qatar v. Bahrain*, ICJ Reports, 2001, para. 198, and *Indonesia/Malaysia*, ICJ Reports, 2002, pp. 625, 682. Note also the *Malaysia/Singapore* case, ICJ Reports, 2008, paras. 62–7.

[132] 114 ILR, pp. 1, 118. Other obvious factors in such situations would include consideration of the geographical position, *ibid.*, p. 119.

In the *Island of Palmas* arbitration[133] the dispute concerned sovereignty over a particular island in the Pacific. The United States declared that, since by a treaty of 1898 Spain had ceded to it all Spanish rights possessed in that region and since that included the island discovered by Spain, the United States of America therefore had a good title. The Netherlands, on the other hand, claimed the territory on the basis of the exercise of various rights of sovereignty over it since the seventeenth century. The arbitrator, Max Huber, in a judgment which discussed the whole nature of territorial sovereignty, dismissed the American claims derived from the Spanish discovery as not effective to found title.[134] Huber declared that the Netherlands possessed sovereignty on the basis of 'the actual continuous and peaceful display of state functions' evidenced by various administrative acts performed over the centuries.[135] It was also emphasised that manifestations of territorial sovereignty may assume different forms, according to conditions of time and place. Indeed, 'the intermittence and discontinuity compatible with the maintenance of the right necessarily differ according as inhabited or uninhabited regions are involved'. Additionally, geographical factors were relevant.[136]

The *Clipperton Island* arbitration[137] concerned a dispute between France and Mexico over an uninhabited island. The arbitrator emphasised that the actual, and not the nominal, taking of possession was a necessary condition of occupation, but noted that such taking of possession may be undertaken in different ways depending upon the nature of the territory concerned. In this case, a proclamation of sovereignty by a French naval officer later published in Honolulu was deemed sufficient to create a valid title. Relevant to this decision was the weakness of the Mexican claims to the guano-rich island, as well as the uninhabited and inhospitable nature of the territory.

These two cases, together with the *Eastern Greenland* case,[138] reveal that the effectiveness of the occupation may indeed be relative and may in certain rare circumstances be little more than symbolic. In the *Eastern Greenland* case before the Permanent Court of International Justice, both Norway and Denmark claimed sovereignty over Eastern Greenland.

---

[133] 2 RIAA, p. 829 (1928).   [134] *Ibid.*, p. 846.   [135] *Ibid.*, pp. 867–71.

[136] *Ibid.*, p. 840. See also, in this context, the American claim to the Howland, Baker and Jarvis Islands in the Pacific Ocean, where it was argued that the administration of the islands as part of the US Wildlife Refuge System constituted sufficient occupation, DUSPIL, 1975, pp. 92–4.

[137] 26 AJIL, 1932, p. 390; 6 AD, p. 105.

[138] PCIJ, Series A/B, No. 53, 1933, p. 46; 6 AD, p. 95.

Denmark had colonies in other parts of Greenland and had granted concessions in the uninhabited Eastern sector. In addition, it proclaimed that all treaties and legislation regarding Greenland covered the territory as a whole, as for example its establishment of the width of the territorial sea, and it sought to have its title to all of the territory recognised by other states. The Court felt that these acts were sufficient upon which to base a good title and were superior to various Norwegian actions such as the wintering of expeditions and the erection of a wireless station in Eastern Greenland, against which Denmark had protested. It is also to be noted that it was not until 1931 that Norway actually claimed the territory.

Such activity in establishing a claim to territory must be performed by the state in the exercise of sovereign powers (*à titre de souverain*)[139] or by individuals whose actions are subsequently ratified by their state,[140] or by corporations or companies permitted by the state to engage in such operations and thus performed on behalf of the sovereign.[141] Otherwise, any acts undertaken are of no legal consequence.[142] Another relevant factor, although one of uncertain strength, is the requirement of the intention by the state in performing various activities to assert claim in its sovereign capacity. In other words the facts are created pursuant to the will of the state to acquire sovereignty. This point was stressed in the *Eastern Greenland* case,[143] but appears not to have been considered as of first importance in the *Island of Palmas* case[144] or in the *Minquiers and Ecrehos* case,[145] where concern centred upon the nature and extent of the actual actions carried out by the contending states. Whatever the precise role of this subjective element, some connection between the actions undertaken and the assertion of sovereignty is necessary.

Account will also be taken of the nature of the exercise of the sovereignty in question, so that in the *Rann of Kutch* case, it was noted that:

---

[139] That is, those made as a 'public claim of right or assertion of sovereignty ... as well as legislative acts', *Eritrea/Yemen*, 114 ILR, pp. 1, 69. See also the *Minquiers and Ecrehos* case, ICJ Reports, 1953, pp. 47, 65 and 69; 20 ILR, p. 94. Such acts need to relate clearly to the territory in question,*Indonesia/Malaysia*, ICJ Reports, 2002, pp. 625, 682–3.

[140] The Court has emphasised that 'activities by private persons cannot be seen as *effectivités* if they do not take place on the basis of official regulations or under governmental authority', *Indonesia/Malaysia*, ICJ Reports, 2002, pp. 625, 683.

[141] *Botswana/Namibia*, ICJ Reports, 1999, pp. 1045, 1105.

[142] See Judge McNair, the *Anglo-Norwegian Fisheries* case, ICJ Reports, 1951, pp. 116, 184; 18 ILR, pp. 86, 113, and McNair, *International Law Opinions*, Cambridge, 1956, vol. I, p. 21. See also O'Connell, *International Law*, pp. 417–19.

[143] PCIJ, Series A/B, No. 53, 1933, p. 46; 6 AD, p. 95.

[144] 2 RIAA, p. 829 (1928); 4 AD, p. 103.   [145] ICJ Reports, 1953, p. 47; 20 ILR, p. 94.

the rights and duties which by law and custom are inherent in and characteristic of sovereignty present considerable variations in different circumstances according to time and place, and in the context of various political
systems.[146]

Similarly, the Court was willing to take into account the special characteristics of the Moroccan state at the relevant time in the *Western Sahara*
case[147] in the context of the display of sovereign authority, but it was the
exercise of sovereignty which constituted the crucial factor. While international law does appear to accept a notion of geographical or natural
unity of particular areas, whereby sovereignty exercised over a certain
area will raise the presumption of title with regard to an outlying portion
of the territory comprised within the claimed unity,[148] it is important not
to overstate this. It operates to raise a presumption and no more and
that within the wider concept of display of effective sovereignty which
need not apply equally to all parts of the territory.[149] Neither geographical
unity nor contiguity are as such sources of title with regard to all areas
contained within the area in question, nor is the proximity of islands
to the mainland determinative as such of the question of legal title.[150]
The Tribunal in the *Eritrea/Yemen* case felt able to consider separately
the legal situation with regard to sub-groups existing within such natural unities,[151] as did the Boundary Commission in the *Eritrea/Ethiopia*
case.[152] However, the significance in law of state activities or *effectivités*
will depend upon the existence or not of a legal title to the territory.
Where there is such a valid legal title, this will have pre-eminence and
effectivités may play a confirmatory role. However, where the *effectivités*
are in contradiction to the title, the latter will have pre-eminence. In the
absence of any legal title, then *effectivités* must invariably be taken into
consideration, while where the legal title is not capable of exactly defining the relevant territorial limits, *effectivités* then play an essential role in
showing how the title is interpreted in practice.[153] Accordingly, examples

[146] Annex I, 7 ILM, 1968, pp. 633, 674; 50 ILR, p. 2.
[147] ICJ Reports, 1975, pp. 12, 43–4; 59 ILR, pp. 14, 60. See also the *Dubai/Sharjah Border Arbitration*, 91 ILR, pp. 543, 585–90.
[148] *Eritrea/Yemen*, 114 ILR, pp. 1, 120 ff., and see Fitzmaurice, *Law and Procedure*, vol. I, pp. 312 ff.
[149] See the *Island of Palmas* case, 2 RIAA, p. 840.
[150] See *Nicaragua v. Honduras*, ICJ Reports, 2007, para. 161.
[151] 114 ILR, pp. 1, 120 ff.   [152] *Eritrea/Ethiopia* 130 ILR, pp. 1, 84 ff.
[153] *Burkina Faso/Mali*, ICJ Reports, 1986, pp. 554, 586–7; 80 ILR, p. 440, and the *El Salvador/Honduras* case where the Chamber also noted that these principles applied to both

of state practice may confirm or complete but not contradict legal title established, for example, by boundary treaties.[154] In the absence of any clear legal title to any area, state practice comes into its own as a law-establishing mechanism. But its importance is always contextual in that it relates to the nature of the territory and the nature of competing state claims.[155]

The role of subsequent conduct: recognition, acquiescence and estoppel

Subsequent conduct may be relevant in a number of ways: first, as a method of determining the true interpretation of the relevant boundary instrument in the sense of the intention of the parties;[156] secondly, as a method of resolving an uncertain disposition or situation, for example, whether a particular area did or did not fall within the colonial territory in question for purposes of determining the *uti possidetis* line[157] or thirdly, as a method of modifying such an instrument or pre-existing arrangement. The *Eritrea/Ethiopia* Boundary Commission explained the general principle that 'the effect of subsequent conduct may be so clear in relation to matters that appear to be the subject of a given treaty that the application of an otherwise pertinent treaty provision may be varied, or may even cease to control the situation, regardless of its original meaning'.[158] The various manifestations of the subsequent conduct of relevant parties have a common foundation in that they all rest to a stronger or weaker extent upon the notion of consent.[159] They reflect expressly or impliedly the presumed will of a state, which in turn may in some situations prove of great importance in the acquisition of title to territory. However, there are significant theoretical differences between the three concepts (recognition, acquiescence and estoppel), even if in practice the dividing lines are often blurred. In any event, they flow to some extent from the fundamental principles of good faith and equity.

---

colonial and post-colonial *effectivités*, ICJ Reports, 1992, pp. 351, 398; 97 ILR, p. 266. See also *Benin/Niger*, ICJ Reports, 2005, pp. 120, 127 and 149.

[154] See also *Cameroon* v. *Nigeria*, ICJ Reports, 2002, pp. 353–5.

[155] See also the general statement of principle in *Eritrea/Ethiopia* 130 ILR, pp. 1, 42. As to the role of equity in territorial disputes, see above, chapter 3, p. 108.

[156] See Article 31(3)(b) of the Vienna Convention on the Law of Treaties, 1969. See also the *Argentina/Chile* case, 38 ILR, pp. 10, 89.

[157] See the *El Salvador/Honduras* case, ICJ Reports, 1992, pp. 351, 401, 558 ff.

[158] *Eritrea/Ethiopia*, 130 ILR, p. 35. See also Shaw, 'Title, Control and Closure?', pp. 776 ff.

[159] Consent, of course, is the basis of cession: see above, p. 499.

Recognition is a positive act by a state accepting a particular situation and, even though it may be implied from all the relevant circumstances, it is nevertheless an affirmation of the existence of a specific factual state of affairs,[160] even if that accepted situation is inconsistent with the term in a treaty.[161] Acquiescence, on the other hand, occurs in circumstances where a protest is called for and does not happen[162] or does not happen in time in the circumstances.[163] In other words, a situation arises which would seem to require a response denoting disagreement and, since this does not transpire, the state making no objection is understood to have accepted the new situation.[164] The idea of estoppel in general is that a party which has made or consented to a particular statement upon which another party relies in subsequent activity to its detriment or the other's benefit cannot thereupon change its position.[165] This rests also upon the notion of preclusion.[166]

While, of course, the consent of a ceding state to the cession is essential, the attitude adopted by other states is purely peripheral and will not affect the legality of the transaction. Similarly, in cases of the acquisition of title over *terra nullius*, the acquiescence of other states is not strictly relevant although of useful evidential effect.[167] However, where two or more states have asserted competing claims, the role of consent by third parties is

---

[160] See e.g. the *Eastern Greenland* case, PCIJ, Series A/B, No. 53, 1933, pp. 46, 51–2; 6 AD, pp. 95, 100, and the *Western Sahara* case, ICJ Reports, 1975, pp. 12, 49–57; 59 ILR, pp. 14, 66. See also G. Schwarzenberger, 'Title to Territory: Response to a Challenge', 51 AJIL, 1957, p. 308.

[161] See e.g. the *Taba* case, 80 ILR, pp. 224, 297–8 and 306.

[162] See Brownlie, *Principles*, p. 151, and I. MacGibbon, 'The Scope of Acquiescence in International Law', 31 BYIL, 1954, p. 143.

[163] See the *Land, Island and Maritime Frontier (El Salvador/Honduras)* case, ICJ Reports, 1992, pp. 351, 577; 97 ILR, pp. 266, 493, and *Eritrea/Yemen*, 114 ILR, pp. 1, 84.

[164] See e.g. the *Libya/Chad* case, ICJ Reports, 1994, pp. 6, 35; 100 ILR, pp. 1, 34, where the Court noted that 'If a serious dispute had indeed existed regarding frontiers, eleven years after the conclusion of the 1955 Treaty, one would expect it to have been reflected in the 1966 Treaty.' See also the *Malaysia/Singapore* case, ICJ Reports, 2008, paras. 231 ff.

[165] See the *Temple* case, ICJ Reports, 1962, pp. 6, 29 ff.; 33 ILR, p. 48; the *Cameroon v. Nigeria (Preliminary Objections)* case, ICJ Reports, 1998, pp. 275, 303, and the *Eritrea/Ethiopia* case, 130 ILR, p. 68 ff.

[166] See e.g. the *Gulf of Maine* case, ICJ Reports, 1984, p. 305; 71 ILR, p. 74. The Court in the *Malaysia/Singapore* case, ICJ Reports, 2008, para. 228, emphasised that a party relying on an estoppel must show among other things that, 'it has taken distinct acts in reliance on the other party's statement'.

[167] Note that the Tribunal in *Eritrea/Yemen* emphasised that 'Repute is also an important ingredient for the consolidation of title', 114 ILR, pp. 1, 136.

much enhanced. In the *Eastern Greenland* case,[168] the Court noted that Denmark was entitled to rely upon treaties made with other states (apart from Norway) in so far as these were evidence of recognition of Danish sovereignty over all of Greenland.

Recognition and acquiescence are also important in cases of acquisition of control contrary to the will of the former sovereign. Where the possession of the territory is accompanied by emphatic protests on the part of the former sovereign, no title by prescription can arise, for such title is founded upon the acquiescence of the dispossessed state, and in such circumstances consent by third states is of little consequence. However, over a period of time recognition may ultimately validate a defective title, although much will depend upon the circumstances, including the attitude of the former sovereign. Where the territory involved is part of the high seas (i.e. *res communis*), acquiescence by the generality of states may affect the subjection of any part of it to another's sovereignty, particularly by raising an estoppel.[169]

Acquiescence and recognition[170] are also relevant where the prescriptive title is based on what is called immemorial possession, that is, the origin of the particular situation is shrouded in doubt and may have been lawful or unlawful but is deemed to be lawful in the light of general acquiescence by the international community or particular acquiescence by a relevant other state. Accordingly, acquiescence may constitute evidence reinforcing a title based upon effective possession and control, rendering it definitive.[171]

Estoppel is a legal technique whereby states deemed to have consented to a state of affairs cannot afterwards alter their position.[172] Although

---

[168] PCIJ, Series A/B, No. 53, 1933, pp. 46, 51–2; 6 AD, pp. 95, 100.

[169] See the *Anglo-Norwegian Fisheries* case, ICJ Reports, 1951, p. 116; 18 ILR, p. 86.

[170] Note also the role of recognition in the context of new states and territory, above, p. 445.

[171] See the *Land, Island and Maritime Frontier (El Salvador/Honduras)* case, ICJ Reports, 1992, pp. 351, 579; 97 ILR, pp. 266, 495. The Court, for example, in the *Indonesia/Malaysia* case felt that it 'cannot disregard' the failure of Indonesia or its predecessor, the Netherlands, to protest at the construction of lighthouses and other administrative activities on territory claimed to be Indonesian and noted that 'such behaviour is unusual', ICJ Reports, 2002, pp. 625, 685.

[172] See e.g. D. W. Bowett, 'Estoppel before International Tribunals and its Relation to Acquiescence', 33 BYIL, 1957, p. 176; Thirlway, 'Law and Procedure', p. 29; A. Martin, *L'Estoppel en Droit International Public*, Paris, 1979; C. Dominicé, 'A Propos du Principe de l'Estoppel en Droit des Gens' in *Recueil d'Études de Droit International en Hommage à Paul Guggenheim*, Geneva, 1968, p. 327, and I. Sinclair, 'Estoppel and Acquiescence' in *Fifty Years of the International Court of Justice* (eds. A. V. Lowe and M. Fitzmaurice), Cambridge, 1996, p. 104.

it cannot found title by itself, it is of evidential and often of practical importance. Estoppel may arise either by means of a prior recognition or acquiescence, but the nature of the consenting state's interest is vital. Where, for example, two states put forward conflicting claims to territory, any acceptance by one of the other's position will serve as a bar to a renewal of contradictory assertions. This was illustrated in the *Eastern Greenland* case,[173] where the Court regarded the Norwegian acceptance of treaties with Denmark, which incorporated Danish claims to all of Greenland, as preventing Norway from contesting Danish sovereignty over the area.

The leading case on estoppel is the *Temple of Preah Vihear*[174] which concerned a border dispute between Cambodia and Thailand. The frontier was the subject of a treaty in 1904 between Thailand and France (as sovereign over French Indo-China which included Cambodia) which provided for a delimitation commission. The border was duly surveyed but was ambiguous as to the siting of the Preah Vihear temple area. Thailand called for a map from the French authorities and this placed the area within Cambodia. The Thai government accepted the map and asked for further copies.[175] A number of other incidents took place, including a visit by a Thai prince to the temple area for an official reception with the French flag clearly flying there, which convinced the International Court that Thailand had tacitly accepted French sovereignty over the disputed area.[176] In other words, Thailand was estopped by its conduct from claiming that it contested the frontier in the temple area. However, it is to be noted that estoppel in that case was one element in a complexity of relevant principles which included prescription and treaty interpretation. The case also seemed to show that in situations of uncertainty and ambiguity, the doctrines of acquiescence and estoppel come into their own,[177] but it would not appear correct to refer to estoppel as a rule of substantive law.[178] The extent to which silence as such may create an estoppel is unclear and much will depend upon the surrounding circumstances, in particular the notoriety of the situation, the length of silence maintained in the light of that notoriety and the type of conduct that would be seen as reasonable

---

[173] PCIJ, Series A/B, No. 53, 1933, pp. 46, 68; 6 AD, pp. 95, 102.

[174] ICJ Reports, 1962, p. 6; 33 ILR, p. 48. See D. H. Johnson, 'The Case Concerning the Temple of Preah Vihear', 11 ICLQ, 1962, p. 1183, and J. P. Cot, 'Cour Internationale de Justice: Affaire du Temple de Préah Vihéar', AFDI, 1962, p. 217.

[175] ICJ Reports, 1962, pp. 6, 23; 33 ILR, pp. 48, 62.

[176] ICJ Reports, 1962, pp. 30–2; 33 ILR, p. 68.

[177] See also the *Award of the King of Spain* case, ICJ Reports, 1960, p. 192; 30 ILR, p. 457.

[178] See e.g. Jennings, *Acquisition*, pp. 47–51.

in the international community in order to safeguard a legal interest.[179] The existence of an estoppel should not, however, be lightly assumed.[180]

Subsequent conduct itself would in the material sense include the examples of the exercise of sovereign activity, various diplomatic and similar exchanges and records, and maps. So far as the status of maps is concerned, this will depend upon the facts of their production as an item of evidence. It was noted in the *Burkina Faso/Mali* case that 'maps are only extrinsic evidence of varying reliability or unreliability which may be used, along with other evidence of a circumstantial kind, to establish or reconstitute the real facts'.[181] In such circumstances, courts have often exhibited a degree of caution, taking into account, for example, that some maps may be politically self-serving and that topographic knowledge at the time the map is made may be unreliable.[182] However, maps annexed to treaties illustrating the boundary so delimited will be accepted as authoritative.[183] Where there is a conflict between the text of an instrument and an annexed map, all the relevant circumstances will need to be considered in order to arrive at a correct understanding of the intentions of the authors of the relevant delimitation instrument.[184] Beyond this, it is possible that cartographic material, prepared in order to help draft a delimitation instrument, may itself be used as assistance in seeking to determine the intentions of the parties where the text itself is ambiguous, while more generally the effect of a map will in other circumstances vary according to

---

[179] See e.g. the *Anglo-Norwegian Fisheries* case, ICJ Reports, 1951, pp. 116, 139; 18 ILR, pp. 86, 101, the *North Sea Continental Shelf* cases, ICJ Reports, 1969, pp. 3, 26; 41 ILR, pp. 29, 55, the *Gulf of Maine* case, ICJ Reports, 1984, pp. 246, 308; 71 ILR, pp. 74, 135, and the *ELSI* case, ICJ Reports, 1989, pp. 15, 44; 84 ILR, pp. 311, 350. See also M. Koskenniemi, 'L'Affaire du Passage par le Great Belt', AFDI, 1992, p. 905.

[180] In *Cameroon* v. *Nigeria (Preliminary Objections)*, the Court emphasised that, 'An estoppel would only arise if by its acts or declarations Cameroon had consistently made it fully clear that it had agreed to settle the boundary dispute submitted to the Court by bilateral avenues alone. It would further be necessary that, by relying on such an attitude, Nigeria had changed its position to its own detriment or had suffered some prejudice', ICJ Reports, 1998, pp. 275, 303.

[181] ICJ Reports, 1986, pp. 554, 582; 80 ILR, p. 440. Note that the Court in the *Malaysia/Singapore* case, ICJ Reports, 2008, paras. 267–72, noted that a map may give a good indication of the official position of the party concerned, particularly where it is an admission against interest.

[182] See the *Eritrea/Ethiopia* case, 130 ILR, pp. 38 ff. See also the *Eritrea/Yemen* case, 114 ILR, pp. 1, 94 ff.

[183] 114 ILR, pp. 1, 94 ff., and *Eritrea/Ethiopia*, 130 ILR, pp. 39 and 45 ff. Note that a treaty provision may provide for an avowedly incorrect geographical feature on an annexed map as part of the boundary line: see *Cameroon* v. *Nigeria*, ICJ Reports, 2002, p. 372.

[184] ICJ Reports, 2002, pp. 383–4. See also p. 385.

a number of factors ranging from its provenance and cartographic quality to its consistency with other maps and the use made of it by the parties.[185]

One argument has been that peaceful possession coupled with acts of administration may in the absence of protest found the basis of title by way of 'historical consolidation'.[186] However, the International Court has emphasised that this doctrine is 'highly controversial and cannot replace the established modes of acquisition of title under international law'. It was also noted that a period of such activity of some twenty years was 'far too short, even according to the theory relied on it'.[187]

Conclusions

It will be clear from the above that apart from the modes of acquisition that rely purely on the consent of the state and the consequences of sovereignty (cession or accretion), the method of acquiring additional territory is by the sovereign exercise of effective control. Both occupation and prescription are primarily based upon effective possession and, although the time element is a factor in prescription, this in fact is really concerned with the effectiveness of control.

The principle of effective control applies in different ways to different situations, but its essence is that 'the continuous and peaceful display of territorial sovereignty ... is as good as title'.[188] Such control has to be deliberate sovereign action, but what will amount to effectiveness is relative and will depend upon, for example, the geographical nature of the region, the existence or not of competing claims and other relevant factors, such as international reaction.[189] It will not be necessary for such control to be equally effective throughout the region.[190] The doctrine of effectiveness has displaced earlier doctrines relating to discovery and symbolic annexation as in themselves sufficient to generate title.[191] Effectiveness has also a temporal as well as a spatial dimension as the doctrine of intertemporal

---

[185] *Ibid.*, pp. 366 ff. See also the *Eritrea/Ethiopia* case, 130 ILR, pp. 39 ff.
[186] See e.g. the *Anglo-Norwegian Fisheries* case, ICJ Reports, 1951, pp. 116, 138, and De Visscher, *Theory and Reality*, p. 209.
[187] *Cameroon v. Nigeria*, ICJ Reports, 2002, p. 352. See above, p. 507.
[188] Judge Huber, *Island of Palmas* case, 2 RIAA, pp. 829, 839 (1928); 4 AD, p. 103.
[189] See further above, p. 511.   [190] See above, p. 512.
[191] See in this context article 35 of the General Act of the Congress of Berlin, 1885, in which the parties recognised the obligation to 'ensure the establishment of authority in the regions occupied by them on the coast of the African continent'.

law has emphasised, while clearly the public or open nature of the control is essential. The acquiescence of a party directly involved is also a very important factor in providing evidence of the effectiveness of control. Where a dispossessed sovereign disputes the control exercised by a new sovereign, title can hardly pass. Effectiveness is related to the international system as a whole, so that mere possession by force is not the sole determinant of title. This factor also emphasises and justifies the role played by recognition.

Bilateral recognition is important as evidence of effective control and should be regarded as part of that principle. International recognition, however, involves not only a means of creating rules of international law in terms of practice and consent of states, but may validate situations of dubious origin. A series of recognitions may possibly validate an unlawful acquisition of territory and could similarly prevent effective control from ever hardening into title.[192] The significance of UN recognition is self-evident, so that the UN Security Council itself could adopt a binding resolution ending a territorial dispute by determining the boundary in question.[193]

Sovereign territory may not only be acquired, it may also be lost in ways that essentially mirror the modes of acquisition. Territory may be lost by express declaration or conduct such as a treaty of cession or acceptance of secession; by loss of territory by erosion or natural geographic activity or by acquiescence through prescription. Further, territory may be abandoned, but in order for this to operate both the physical act of abandonment and the intention to surrender title are required.[194]

---

[192] See e.g. Security Council resolution 216 (1965) concerning Rhodesia; General Assembly resolution 31/6A and Security Council Statements of 21 September 1979 and 15 December 1981 concerning the South African Bantustans; Security Council resolution 541 (1983) with regard to the 'Turkish Republic of Northern Cyprus' and Security Council resolution 662 (1990) concerning the Iraqi annexation of Kuwait.

[193] See particularly Security Council resolution 687 (1991) in which the international boundary between Kuwait and Iraq was deemed to be that agreed by both parties in 'Minutes' agreed in 1963. This boundary was then formally guaranteed by the Council in Section A, paragraph 4 of this resolution. See e.g. M. H. Mendelson and S. C. Hulton, 'The Iraq–Kuwait Boundary', 64 BYIL, 1993, p. 135. See also Security Council resolution 833 (1993) and S/26006.

[194] See e.g. Brownlie, *Principles*, p. 138; *Oppenheim's International Law*, pp. 716–18, and G. Marston, 'The British Acquisition of the Nicobar Islands, 1869', 69 BYIL, 1998, p. 245. See also e.g. the *Eastern Greenland* case, PCIJ, Series A/B, No. 53, 1933, p. 47; 6 AD, p. 95 and the *Malaysia/Singapore* case, ICJ Reports, 2008, paras. 117, 196, 223, 230 and 275.

Territorial integrity, self-determination and sundry claims

There are a number of other concepts which may be of some relevance in territorial situations ranging from self-determination to historical and geographical claims. These may not necessarily be legal principles as such but rather purely political or moral expressions. Although they may be extremely persuasive within the international political order, they would not necessarily be juridically effective. One of the core principles of the international system is the need for stability and finality in boundary questions and much flows from this.[195] Case-law has long maintained this principle.[196] Reflective of this concept is the principle of territorial integrity.

The principle of the territorial integrity of states is well established and is protected by a series of consequential rules prohibiting interference within the domestic jurisdiction of states as, for example, article 2(7) of the United Nations Charter, and forbidding the threat or use of force against the territorial integrity and political independence of states, particularly article 2(4) of the United Nations Charter. This principle has been particularly emphasised by Third World states and also by other regions.[197]

However, it does not apply where the territorial dispute centres upon uncertain frontier demarcations. In addition, the principle appears to conflict on the face of it with another principle of international law, that of the self-determination of peoples.[198]

This principle, noted in the United Nations Charter and emphasised in the 1960 Colonial Declaration, the 1966 International Covenants on Human Rights and the 1970 Declaration on Principles of International Law, can be regarded as a rule of international law in the light of, *inter alia*, the number and character of United Nations declarations and resolutions and actual state practice in the process of decolonisation. However, it has been interpreted as referring only to the inhabitants of non-independent

---

[195] See K. H. Kaikobad, 'Some Observations on the Doctrine of the Continuity and Finality of Boundaries', 54 BYIL, 1983, p. 119, and Shaw, 'Heritage of States', pp. 75, 81.

[196] See e.g. the *Temple* case, ICJ Reports, 1962, pp. 6, 34; 33 ILR, p. 48; the *Libya/Chad* case, ICJ Reports, 1994, pp. 6, 37; 100 ILR, p. 1; the *Beagle Channel* case, 21 RIAA, pp. 55, 88; 52 ILR, p. 93, and the *Dubai/Sharjah* case, 91 ILR, pp. 543, 578.

[197] See generally, Shaw, *Title to Territory*, chapter 5. But see, as regards Europe, Principle III of the Helsinki Final Act, 14 ILM, 1975, p. 1292 and the Guidelines on Recognition of New States in Eastern Europe and the Soviet Union adopted by the European Community and its member states on 16 December 1991, 92 ILR, p. 173.

[198] See *Burkina Faso/Mali*, ICJ Reports, 1986, pp. 554, 565; 80 ILR, p. 469.

territories.[199] Practice has not supported its application as a principle conferring the right to secede upon identifiable groups within already independent states.[200] The Canadian Supreme Court in the *Reference Re Secession of Quebec* case declared that 'international law expects that the right to self-determination will be exercised by peoples within the framework of existing sovereign states and consistently with the maintenance of the territorial integrity of those states',[201] and that the right to unilateral secession 'arises only in the most extreme of cases and, even then, under carefully defined circumstances'.[202] The only arguable exception to this rule that the right to external self-determination applies only to colonial situations (and arguably situations of occupation) might be where the group in question is subject to 'extreme and unremitting persecution' coupled with the 'lack of any reasonable prospect for reasonable challenge',[203] but even this is controversial not least in view of definitional difficulties.[204] The situation of secession is probably best dealt with in international law within the framework of a process of claim, effective control and international recognition.

Accordingly the principle of self-determination as generally accepted fits in with the concept of territorial integrity,[205] as it cannot apply once a colony or trust territory attains sovereignty and independence, except, arguably, in extreme circumstances. Probably the most prominent exponent of the relevance of self-determination to post-independence situations has

---

[199] As to the application of the principle to Gibraltar, see UKMIL, 70 BYIL, 1999, p. 443.

[200] See J. Crawford, 'State Practice and International Law in Relation to Secession', 69 BYIL, 1998, p. 85; Nguyen Quoc Dinh *et al.*, *Droit International Public*, p. 525, and *Self-Determination in International Law: Quebec and Lessons Learned* (ed. A. Bayefsky), The Hague, 2000. See also above, chapter 5, p. 256. Self-determination does have a continuing application in terms of human rights situations within the territorial framework of independent states (i.e. internal self-determination), *ibid.*

[201] (1998) 161 DLR (4th) 385, 436; 115 ILR, p. 536.

[202] (1998) 161 DLR (4th) 385, 438.

[203] A. Cassese, *Self-Determination of Peoples*, Cambridge, 1995, p. 120. See also T. Musgrave, *Self-Determination and National Minorities*, Oxford, 1997, pp. 188 ff.; J. Castellino, *International Law and Self-Determination*, The Hague, 2000, and K. Knop, *Diversity and Self-Determination in International Law*, Cambridge, 2002, pp. 65 ff. See also Judge Wildhaber's Concurring Opinion (joined by Judge Ryssdal) in *Loizidou* v. *Turkey*, Judgment of 18 December 1996, 108 ILR, pp. 443, 470–3. See also *Secession: International Law Perspectives* (ed. M. G. Kohen), Cambridge, 2006.

[204] The Court in the *Quebec* case, citing Cassese, *Self-Determination*, suggested that the right to external self-determination (i.e. secession) might apply to cases of foreign occupation and as a last resort where a people's right to internal self-determination (i.e. right to public participation, etc.) was blocked, *ibid*, pp. 438 ff.

[205] This analysis is supported by *Burkina Faso/Mali*, ICJ Reports, 1986, p. 554; 80 ILR, p. 459.

been Somalia with its claims to those parts of Ethiopia and Kenya populated by Somali tribes, but that country received very little support for its
demands.[206]

Self-determination cannot be used to further larger territorial claims
in defiance of internationally accepted boundaries of sovereign states, but
it may be of some use in resolving cases of disputed frontier lines on the
basis of the wishes of the inhabitants. In addition, one may point to the
need to take account of the interests of the local population where the
determination of the boundary has resulted in a shift in the line, at least
in the view of one of the parties.[207] Geographical claims have been raised
throughout history.[208] France for long maintained that its natural frontier
in the east was the west bank of the Rhine, and the European powers
in establishing their presence upon African coastal areas often claimed
extensive hinterland territories. Much utilised also was the doctrine of
contiguity, whereby areas were claimed on the basis of the occupation of
territories of which they formed a geographical continuation. However,
such claims, although relevant in discussing the effectivity and limits of
occupation, are not able in themselves to found title, and whether or not
such claims will be taken into account at all will depend upon the nature
of the territory and the strength of competing claims.[209] A rather special
case is that of islands close to the coast of the mainland. The Tribunal
in *Eritrea/Yemen* stated that: 'There is a strong presumption that islands
within the twelve-mile coastal belt will belong to the coastal state', to be
rebutted only by evidence of a superior title.[210]

---

[206] Shaw, *Title to Territory*, chapter 5. See also the Moroccan approach, *ibid.*

[207] See, with regard to the preservation of acquired rights, *El Salvador/Honduras*, ICJ Reports, 1992, pp. 351, 400; 97 ILR, p. 112. See also *Cameroon* v. *Nigeria*, ICJ Reports, 2002, pp. 370 and 373–4. In particular, the Court stated in relation to the Bakassi peninsula and Lake Chad regions which contain Nigerian populations, that 'the implementation of the present judgment will afford the parties a beneficial opportunity to co-operate in the interests of the population concerned, in order notably to enable it to continue to have access to educational and health services comparable to those it currently enjoys', *ibid.*, p. 452. The Court also referred to the commitment of the Cameroon Agent made during the Oral Pleadings to protect Nigerians living in the areas recognised as belonging to Cameroon, *ibid.*, p. 452 and para. V(C) of the Dispositif.

[208] Shaw, *Title to Territory*, p. 195; Jennings, *Acquisition*, p. 74, and Hill, *Claims to Territory*, pp. 77–80.

[209] See the *Eastern Greenland* case, PCIJ, Series A/B, No. 53, 1933, p. 46; 6 AD, p. 95, and the *Western Sahara* case, ICJ Reports, 1975, pp. 12, 42–3; 59 ILR, pp. 14, 59. See generally, B. Feinstein, 'Boundaries and Security in International Law and Practice', 3 Finnish YIL, 1992, p. 135.

[210] 114 ILR, pp. 1, 124 and 125. But see *Nicaragua* v. *Honduras*, ICJ Reports, 2007, para. 161, where the Court noted that 'proximity [of islands to the mainland] as such is not necessarily determinative of legal title'.

Of some similarity are claims based upon historical grounds.[211] This was one of the grounds upon which Iraq sought to justify its invasion and annexation of the neighbouring state of Kuwait in August 1990,[212] although the response of the United Nations demonstrated that such arguments were unacceptable to the world community as a whole.[213] Morocco too has made extensive claims to Mauritania, Western Sahara and parts of Algeria as territories historically belonging to the old Moroccan empire.[214] But such arguments are essentially political and are of but little legal relevance. The International Court of Justice in the *Western Sahara* case[215] of 1975 accepted the existence of historical legal ties between the tribes of that area and Morocco and Mauritania, but declared that they were not of such a nature as to override the right of the inhabitants of the colony to self-determination and independence.[216]

The doctrine of uti possidetis[217]

The influence of the principle of territorial integrity may be seen in the Latin American idea of *uti possidetis*, whereby the administrative divisions

---

[211] See e.g. Shaw, *Title to Territory*, pp. 193–4; Jennings, *Acquisition*, pp. 76–8, and Hill, *Claims to Territory*, pp. 81–91.

[212] See *Keesing's Record of World Events*, p. 37635, 1990. Note that Iraq made a similar claim to Kuwait in the early 1960s, although not then taking military action: see Jennings, *Acquisition*, p. 77, note 2.

[213] See e.g. Security Council resolution 662 (1990); Lauterpacht *et al.*, *The Kuwait Crisis: Basic Documents*, p. 90.

[214] Shaw, *Title to Territory*, pp. 193–4. Note also the claims advanced by Indonesia to West Irian, *ibid.*, p. 22.

[215] ICJ Reports, 1975, p. 12; 59 ILR, p. 14.

[216] See also *Eritrea/Yemen*, 114 ILR, pp. 1, 37 ff. The Tribunal also discounted the notion of reversion of title, *ibid.*, pp. 40 and 115.

[217] See e.g. H. Ghebrewebet, *Identifying Units of Statehood and Determining International Boundaries*, Frankfurt am Main, 2006; A. O. Cukwurah, *The Settlement of Boundary Disputes in International Law*, Manchester, 1967, p. 114; P. De La Pradelle, *La Frontière*, Paris, 1928, pp. 86–7; D. Bardonnet, 'Les Frontières Terrestres et la Relativité de leur Tracé', 153 HR, 1976 V, p. 9; Shaw, 'Heritage of States', p. 75; M. Kohen, *Possession Contestée et Souveraineté Territoriale*, Geneva, 1997, chapter 6, and *ibid.*, '*Uti Possidetis*, Prescription et Pratique Subséquent à un Traité dans l'Affaire de l'*Ile de Kasikili/Sedudu* devant la Cour Internationale de Justice', 43 German YIL, 2000, p. 253; G. Nesi, *L'Uti Possidetis Iuris nel Diritto Internazionale*, Padua, 1996; S. Lalonde, *Determining Boundaries in a Conflicted World*, Ithaca, 2002; Luis Sánchez Rodríguez, 'L'*Uti Possidetis* et les Effectivités dans les Contentieux Territoriaux et Frontaliers', 263 HR, 1997, p. 149; J. M. Sorel and R. Mehdi, 'L'*Uti Possidetis* Entre la Consécration Juridique et la Pratique: Essai de Réactualisation', AFDI, 1994, p. 11; *Oppenheim's International Law*, pp. 669–70; T. Bartoš, '*Uti Possidetis. Quo Vadis?*', 18 Australian YIL, 1997, p. 37; 'L'Applicabilité de l'*Uti Possidetis Juris* dans les Situations de Sécession ou de Dissolution d'États', Colloque, RBDI, 1998, p. 5, and *Démembrements d'États et Délimitations Territoriales* (ed. O. Corten), Brussels, 1999.

of the Spanish empire in South America were deemed to constitute the boundaries for the newly independent successor states, thus theoretically excluding any gaps in sovereignty which might precipitate hostilities and encourage foreign intervention.[218] It is more accurately reflected in the practice of African states, explicitly stated in a resolution of the Organisation of African Unity in 1964, which declared that colonial frontiers existing as at the date of independence constituted a tangible reality and that all member states pledged themselves to respect such borders.[219]

Practice in Africa has reinforced the approach of emphasising the territorial integrity of the colonially defined territory, witness the widespread disapproval of the attempted creation of secessionist states whether in the former Belgian Congo, Nigeria or Sudan. Efforts to prevent the partition of the South African controlled territory of Namibia into separate Bantustans as a possible prelude to a dissolution of the unity of the territory are a further manifestation of this.[220]

The question of *uti possidetis* was discussed by a Chamber of the International Court in *Burkina Faso* v. *Republic of Mali*,[221] where the *compromis* (or special agreement) by which the parties submitted the case to the Court specified that the settlement of the dispute should be based upon respect for the principle of the 'intangibility of frontiers inherited from colonisation'.[222] It was noted, however, that the principle had in fact developed into a general concept of contemporary customary international law and was unaffected by the emergence of the right of peoples to self-determination.[223] In the African context particularly, the obvious purpose of the principle was 'to prevent the independence

---

[218] See the *Colombia–Venezuela* arbitral award, 1 RIAA, pp. 223, 228 (1922); 1 AD, p. 84; the *Beagle Channel* case, HMSO, 1977; 52 ILR, p. 93, and *Land, Island and Maritime Frontier Dispute (El Salvador/Honduras)*, ICJ Reports, 1992, pp. 351, 544; 97 ILR, pp. 266, 299–300.

[219] AHG/Res.16(1). See Security Council resolution 1234 (1999) which refers directly to OAU resolution 16(1) and see also article 4(i) of the Protocol Relating to the Establishment of the Peace and Security Council of the African Union, 2002, and the preamble to the Protocol on Politics, Defence and Security Cooperation adopted by the Southern African Development Community in 2001: see further below, chapter 18, p. 1026. See Shaw, *Title to Territory*, pp. 185–7. See also the Separate Opinion by Judge Ajibola in the *Libya/Chad* case, ICJ Reports, pp. 6, 83 ff.; 100 ILR, pp. 1, 81 ff.

[220] Shaw, *Title to Territory*, chapter 5. The principle has also been noted in Asian practice: see e.g. the *Temple of Preah Vihear* case, ICJ Reports, 1962, p. 6; 33 ILR, p. 48, and the *Rann of Kutch* case, 7 ILM, 1968, p. 633; 50 ILR, p. 2.

[221] ICJ Reports, 1986, p. 554; 80 ILR, p. 459.   [222] ICJ Reports, 1986, p. 557; 80 ILR, p. 462.

[223] ICJ Reports, 1986, p. 565; 80 ILR, p. 469.

and stability of new states being endangered by fratricidal struggles provoked by the challenging of frontiers following the withdrawal of the
administering power'.[224] The application of the principle has the effect
of freezing the territorial title existing at the moment of independence
to produce what the Chamber described as the 'photograph of the territory' at the critical date.[225] The Chamber, however, went further than
emphasising the application of the principle to Africa. It declared that
the principle applied generally and was logically connected with the phenomenon of independence wherever it occurred in order to protect the
independence and stability of new states.[226] *Uti possidetis* was defined as
follows:

> The essence of the principle lies in its primary aim of securing respect for the
> territorial boundaries at the moment when independence is achieved. Such
> territorial boundaries might be no more than delimitations between differ-
> ent administrative divisions or colonies all subject to the same sovereign.
> In that case, the application of the principle of *uti possidetis* resulted in
> administrative boundaries being transformed into international frontiers
> in the full sense of the term.[227]

The application of this principle beyond the purely colonial context was
underlined particularly with regard to the former USSR[228] and the former
Yugoslavia. In the latter case, the Yugoslav Arbitration Commission established by the European Community and accepted by the states of the
former Yugoslavia made several relevant comments. In Opinion No. 2,
the Arbitration Commission declared that 'whatever the circumstances,
the right to self-determination must not involve changes to existing

---

[224] *Ibid.*

[225] ICJ Reports, 1986, p. 568; 80 ILR, p. 473. See, as to the notion of critical date, above,
p. 509.

[226] ICJ Reports, 1986, p. 565; 80 ILR, p. 470.

[227] ICJ Reports, 1986, p. 566; 80 ILR, p. 459. This was reaffirmed by the Court in the
Land, Island and Maritime Frontier Dispute (El Salvador/Honduras) case, ICJ Reports,
1992, pp. 351, 386–7; 97 ILR, pp. 266, 299–300. The Court in the latter case went on to
note that '*uti possidetis juris* is essentially a retrospective principle, investing as international boundaries administrative limits intended originally for quite other purposes', *ibid.*,
p. 388; 79 ILR, p. 301. See M. N. Shaw, 'Case Concerning the Land, Island and Maritime
Frontier Dispute', 42 ICLQ, 1993, p. 929. See also *Nicaragua v. Honduras*, ICJ Reports,
2007, paras. 151 ff.

[228] See e.g. R. Yakemtchouk, 'Les Conflits de Territoires and de Frontières dans les États de
l'Ex-URSS', AFDI, 1993, p. 401. See also, with regard to the application of *uti possidetis*
to the dissolution of the Czech and Slovak Federal Republic, J. Malenovsky, 'Problèmes
Juridiques Liés à la Partition de la Tchécoslovaquie', *ibid.*, p. 328.

frontiers at the time of independence (*uti possidetis juris*) except where the states concerned agree otherwise'.[229] In Opinion No. 3, the Arbitration Commission emphasised that, except where otherwise agreed, the former boundaries[230] became frontiers protected by international law. This conclusion, it was stated, derived from the principle of respect for the territorial status quo and from the principle of *uti possidetis*.[231] It is thus arguable that, at the least, a presumption exists that, in the absence of evidence to the contrary, internally defined units within a pre-existing sovereign state will come to independence within the spatial framework of that territorially defined unit.[232]

Beyond uti possidetis

The principle of *uti possidetis* is not able to resolve all territorial or boundary problems.[233] Where there is a relevant applicable treaty, then this will

---

[229] 92 ILR, p. 168. See also A. Pellet, 'Note sur la Commission d'Arbitrage de la Conférence Européenne pour la Paix en Yugoslavie', AFDI, 1991, p. 329, and Pellet, 'Activité de la Commission d'Arbitrage de la Conférence Européenne pour la Paix en Yugoslavie', AFDI, 1992, p. 220.

[230] The Arbitration Commission was here dealing specifically with the internal boundaries between Serbia and Croatia and Serbia and Bosnia-Herzegovina.

[231] 92 ILR, p. 171. The Arbitration Commission specifically cited here the views of the International Court in the *Burkina Faso/Mali* case: see above, p. 526. Note also that the Under-Secretary of State of the Foreign and Commonwealth Office stated in January 1992 that 'the borders of Croatia will become the frontiers of independent Croatia, so there is no doubt about that particular issue. That has been agreed amongst the Twelve, that will be our attitude towards those borders. They will just be changed from being republican borders to international frontiers', UKMIL, 63 BYIL, 1992, p. 719.

[232] See e.g. M. N. Shaw, 'Peoples, Territorialism and Boundaries', 3 EJIL, 1997, pp. 477, 504, but cf. S. Ratner, 'Drawing a Better Line: *Uti Possidetis* and the Borders of New States', 90 AJIL, 1996, pp. 590, 613 ff. and M. Craven, 'The European Community Arbitration Commission on Yugoslavia', 65 BYIL, 1995, pp. 333, 385 ff.

[233] See generally K. H. Kaikobad, *Interpretation and Revision of International Boundary Decisions*, Cambridge, 2007; M. Kohen, 'La Relation Titres/Effectivités dans le Contentieux Territorial à la Lumière de la Jurisprudence Récente', 108 RGDIP, 2004, p. 561; M. Mendelson, 'The Cameroon–Nigeria Case in the International Court of Justice: Some Territorial Sovereignty and Boundary Delimitation Issues', 75 BYIL, 2004, p. 223; B. H. Oxman, 'The Territorial Temptation: A Siren Song at Sea', 100 AJIL, 2006, p. 830, and S. R. Ratner, 'Land Feuds and Their Solutions: Finding International Law Beyond the Tribunal Chamber', 100 AJIL, 2006, p. 808. Note that the International Court has emphasised that the principle of *uti possidetis* applies to territorial as well as boundary problems: see the *Land, Island and Maritime Frontier Dispute (El Salvador/Honduras)* case, ICJ Reports, 1992, pp. 351, 387; 97 ILR, pp. 266, 300.

dispose of the matter completely.[234] Indeed, once defined in a treaty, an international frontier achieves permanence so that even if the treaty itself were to cease to be in force, the continuance of the boundary would be unaffected and may only be changed with the consent of the states directly concerned.[235] On the other hand, where the line which is being transformed into an international boundary by virtue of the principle cannot be conclusively identified by recourse to authoritative material, then the principle of *uti possidetis* must allow for the application of other principles and rules. Essentially these other principles focus upon the notion of *effectivités* or effective control.

The issue was extensively analysed by the International Court in the *Burkina Faso/Mali* case[236] and later in the *Land, Island and Maritime Frontier Dispute (El Salvador/Honduras; Nicaragua Intervening)* case.[237] The Court noted the possible relevance of colonial *effectivités*, immediate post-colonial *effectivités* and more recent *effectivités*. Each of these might be relevant in the context of seeking to determine the *uti possidetis* pre-independence line. In the case of colonial *effectivités*, i.e. the conduct of the colonial administrators as proof of the effective exercise of territorial jurisdiction in the area during the colonial period, the Court in the former case distinguished between certain situations. Where the act concerned corresponded to the title comprised in the *uti possidetis juris*, then the *effectivités* simply confirmed the exercise of the right derived from a legal title. Where the act did not correspond with the law as described, i.e. the territory subject to the dispute was effectively administered by a state other than the one possessing the legal title, preference would be given to the holder of the title. In other words, where there was a clear *uti possidetis* line, this would prevail over inconsistent practice. Where, however, there was no clear legal title, then the *effectivités* 'play an essential role in showing how the title is interpreted in practice'.[238] It would then

---

[234] See the *Libya/Chad* case, ICJ Reports, 1994, pp. 6, 38–40; 100 ILR, pp. 1, 37–9. See also *Oppenheim's International Law*, p. 663. Note that by virtue of article 11 of the Convention on Succession of States in Respect of Treaties, 1978, a succession of states does not as such affect a boundary established by a treaty or obligations or rights established by a treaty and relating to the regime of a boundary. Article 62 of the Vienna Convention on the Law of Treaties, 1969 provides that the doctrine of *rebus sic stantibus* does not apply to boundary treaties: see below, chapter 16, p. 950.

[235] ICJ Reports, 1994, p. 37; 100 ILR, p. 36.   [236] ICJ Reports, 1986, p. 554; 80 ILR, p. 440.

[237] ICJ Reports, 1992, p. 351; 97 ILR, p. 266. See also Shaw, 'Land, Island and Maritime Frontier Dispute'.

[238] ICJ Reports, 1986, pp. 554, 586–7; 80 ILR, pp. 440, 490–1.

become a matter for evaluation by the Court with regard to each piece of practice adduced. This approach was reaffirmed in the *Land, Island and Maritime Frontier Dispute* case with regard to the grant of particular lands to individuals or to Indian communities or records of such grants.[239] Where the colonial *effectivités* were insufficient to establish the position of the relevant administrative line, the principle of *uti possidetis* could not operate.[240] The Court also noted in the *Land, Island and Maritime Frontier Dispute* case that it could have regard in certain instances to documentary evidence of post-independence *effectivités* when it considered that they afforded indications with respect to the *uti possidetis* line, provided that there was a relationship between the *effectivités* concerned and the determination of the boundary in question.[241] Such post-independence practice could be examined not only in relation to the identification of the *uti possidetis* line but also in the context of seeking to establish whether any acquiescence could be demonstrated both as to where the line was and as to whether any changes in that line could be proved to have taken place.[242] This post-independence practice could even be very recent practice and was not confined to immediate post-independence practice.

Where the *uti possidetis* line could be determined neither by authoritative decisions by the appropriate authorities at the relevant time nor by subsequent practice with regard to a particular area, recourse to equity[243] might be necessary. What this might involve would depend upon the circumstances. In the *Burkina Faso/Mali* case, it meant that a particular frontier pool would be equally divided between the parties;[244] in the *Land, Island and Maritime Frontier Dispute* case, it meant that resort could be had to an unratified delimitation of 1869.[245] It was also noted that the suitability of topographical features in providing an identifiable and convenient boundary was a material aspect.[246]

---

[239] ICJ Reports, 1992, pp. 351, 389; 97 ILR, pp. 266, 302.

[240] See e.g. *Nicaragua v. Honduras*, ICJ Reports, 2007, para. 167.

[241] ICJ Reports, 1992, p. 399; 97 ILR, p. 266.

[242] See e.g. ICJ Reports, 1992, pp. 408, 485, 514, 525, 563 and 565; 97 ILR, pp. 321, 401, 430, 441, 479 and 481. See also *Nicaragua v. Honduras*, ICJ Reports, 2007, paras. 168 ff. Such post-colonial *effectivités* could show whether either of the contending states had displayed sufficient evidence of sovereign authority in order to establish legal title, *ibid.*

[243] I.e. equity *infra legem* or within the context of existing legal principles.

[244] ICJ Reports, 1986, pp. 554, 633; 80 ILR, pp. 440, 535.

[245] ICJ Reports, 1992, pp. 351, 514–15; 97 ILR, pp. 266, 430–1.

[246] ICJ Reports, 1992, p. 396; 97 ILR, p. 309.

International boundary rivers[247]

Special rules have evolved in international law with regard to boundary rivers. In general, where there is a navigable channel, the boundary will follow the middle line of that channel (the *thalweg* principle).[248] Where there is no such channel, the boundary line will, in general, be the middle line of the river itself or of its principal arm.[249] These respective boundary lines would continue as median lines (and so would shift also) if the river itself changed course as a result of gradual accretion on one bank or degradation of the other bank. Where, however, the river changed course suddenly and left its original bed for a new channel, the international boundary would continue to be the middle of the deserted river bed.[250] It is possible for the boundary to follow one of the banks of the river, thus putting it entirely within the territory of one of the states concerned where this has been expressly agreed, but this is unusual.[251]

---

[247] See e.g. *Oppenheim's International Law*, pp. 664–6; S. W. Boggs, *International Boundaries*, New York, 1940; L. J. Bouchez, 'International Boundary Rivers', 12 ICLQ, 1963, p. 789; A. Patry, 'Le Régime des Cours d'Eau Internationaux', 1 Canadian YIL, 1963, p. 172; R. Baxter, *The Law of International Waterways*, Harvard, 1964; Verzijl, *International Law*, vol. III, pp. 537 ff.; H. Dipla, 'Les Règles de Droit International en Matière de Délimitation Fluviale: Remise en Question?', 89 RGDIP, 1985, p. 589; H. Ruiz Fabri, 'Règles Coutumières Générales et Droit International Fluvial', AFDI, 1990, p. 818; F. Schroeter, 'Les Systèmes de Délimitation dans les Fleuves Internationaux', AFDI, 1992, p. 948, and L. Caflisch, 'Règles Générales du Droit des Cours d'Eaux Internationaux', 219 HR, 1989, p. 75.

[248] See e.g. the *Botswana/Namibia* case, ICJ Reports, 1999, p. 1062 and the *Benin/Niger* case, ICJ Reports, 2005, p. 149. See also *State of New Jersey* v. *State of Delaware* 291 US 361 (1934) and the *Laguna (Argentina/Chile)* case, 113 ILR, pp. 1, 209. See, as to the use of the thalweg principle with regard to wadis (dried river beds), Mendelson and Hutton, 'Iraq–Kuwait Boundary', pp. 160 ff.

[249] See e.g. the *Argentine–Chile Frontier* case, 38 ILR, pp. 10, 93. See also article 2A(1) of Annex I(a) of the Israel–Jordan Treaty of Peace, 1994.

[250] See e.g. the *Chamizal* case, 11 RIAA, p. 320.

[251] See e.g. the Iran–Iraq agreements of 1937 and 1975. See E. Lauterpacht, 'River Boundaries: Legal Aspects of the Shatt-al-Arab Frontier', 9 ICLQ, 1960, p. 208; K. H. Kaikobad, *The Shatt-al-Arab Boundary Question*, Oxford, 1980, and Kaikobad, 'The Shatt-al-Arab River Boundary: A Legal Reappraisal', 56 BYIL, 1985, p. 49. See, as to the question of equitable sharing of international watercourses, McCaffrey, *The Law of International Watercourses*; Brownlie, *Principles*, p. 259; the *Gabčíkovo–Nagymaros* case, ICJ Reports, 1997, pp. 7, 54; 116 ILR, p. 1; the Convention on the Law of the Non-Navigational Uses of International Watercourses, 1997, and the Separate Opinion of Judge Kooijmans, *Botswana/Namibia*, ICJ Reports, 1999, pp. 1045, 1148 ff. See also P. Wouters, 'The Legal Response to International Water Conflicts: The UN Watercourses Convention and Beyond', 42 German YIL, 1999, p. 293. Note that in March 2003, the establishment of a Water Cooperation Facility

The Falkland Islands[252]

The long dispute between the UK and Argentina over the Falkland Islands (or Las Malvinas) well illustrates the complex factors involved in resolving issues as to title to territory. The islands were apparently discovered by a British sea captain in 1592, but it is only in 1764 that competing acts of sovereignty commenced. In that year the French established a settlement on East Falklands and in 1765 the British established one on West Falklands. In 1767 the French sold their settlement to Spain. The British settlement was conquered by the Spaniards in 1770 but returned the following year. In 1774 the British settlement was abandoned for economic reasons, but a plaque asserting sovereignty was left behind. The Spaniards left in 1811. In 1816, the United Provinces of the River Plate (Argentina) declared their independence from Spain and four years later took formal possession of the islands. In 1829 the British protested and two years later an American warship evicted Argentinian settlers from the islands, following action by the Argentinian Governor of the territory against American rebels. In 1833 the British captured the islands and have remained there ever since. The question has arisen therefore as to the basis of British title. It was originally argued that this lay in a combination of discovery and occupation, but this would be questionable in the circumstances.[253] It would perhaps have been preferable to rely on conquest and subsequent annexation for, in the 1830s, this was perfectly legal as a method of acquiring territory,[254] but for political reasons this was not claimed. By the 1930s the UK approach had shifted to prescription as the basis of title,[255] but of course this was problematic in the light of Argentinian protests made intermittently throughout the period since 1833.

---

to mediate in disputes between countries sharing a single river basis was announced: see http://news.bbc.co.uk/1/hi/sci/tech/2872427.stm.

[252] See e.g. J. Goebel, *The Struggle for the Falklands*, New Haven, 1927; F. L. Hoffmann and O. M. Hoffmann, *Sovereignty in Dispute*, Boulder, CO, 1984; The Falkland Islands Review, Cmnd 8787 (1983); Chatham House, *The Falkland Islands Dispute – International Dimensions*, London, 1982; W. M. Reisman, 'The Struggle for the Falklands', 93 *Yale Law Journal*, 1983, p. 287, and M. Hassan, 'The Sovereignty Dispute over the Falkland Islands', 23 Va. JIL, 1982, p. 53. See also House of Commons Foreign Affairs Committee, Session 1983/4, 5th Report, 2681, and Cmnd 9447 (1985), and Foreign and Commonwealth Office statement to the House of Commons Foreign Affairs Committee on 5 June 2006, UKMIL, 77 BYIL, 2006, pp. 760 ff.

[253] See A. D. McNair, *International Law Opinions*, Cambridge, 1956, vol. I, pp. 299–300.

[254] See e.g. Lindley, *Acquisition*, pp. 160–5 and above, p. 500.

[255] See e.g. P. Beck, *Guardian*, 26 July 1982, p. 7.

The principle of self-determination as applicable to a recognised British non-self-governing territory has recently been much relied upon by the UK government,[256] but something of a problem is posed by the very small size of the territory's population (some 1,800) although this may not be decisive.

It would appear that conquest formed the original basis of title, irrespective of the British employment of other principles. This, coupled with the widespread recognition by the international community, including the United Nations, of the status of the territory as a British Colony would appear to resolve the legal issues, although the matter is not uncontroversial.

'The common heritage of mankind'

The proclamation of certain areas as the common heritage of mankind has raised the question as to whether a new form of territorial regime has been, or is, in process of being created.[257] In 1970, the UN General Assembly adopted a Declaration of Principles Governing the Seabed and Ocean Floor in which it was noted that the area in question and its resources were the common heritage of mankind. This was reiterated in articles 136 and 137 of the 1982 Convention on the Law of the Sea, in which it was provided that no sovereign or other rights would be recognised with regard to the area (except in the case of minerals recovered in accordance with the Convention) and that exploitation could only take place in accordance with the rules and structures established by the Convention.[258] Article XI of the 1979 Moon Treaty emphasises that the moon and its natural resources are the common heritage of mankind, and thus incapable of national appropriation and subject to a particular regime of exploitation.[259] As is noted in the next section, attempts were being made to establish a common heritage regime over the Antarctic. There are certain common characteristics relating to the concept. Like *res communis*,

---

[256] See e.g. the Prime Minister, HC Deb., col. 946, 13 May 1982.

[257] See e.g. K. Baslar, *The Concept of the Common Heritage of Mankind in International Law*, The Hague, 1998; Brownlie, *Principles*, chapter 12; A. Cassese, *International Law*, 2nd edn, Oxford, 2005, pp. 92 ff.; B. Larschan and B. C. Brennan, 'The Common Heritage of Mankind Principle in International Law', 21 *Columbia Journal of International Law*, 1983, p. 305; R. Wolfrum, 'The Principle of the Common Heritage of Mankind', 43 ZaöRV, 1983, p. 312; S. Gorove, 'The Concept of "Common Heritage of Mankind"', 9 *San Diego Law Review*, 1972, p. 390, and C. Joyner, 'Legal Implications of the Common Heritage of Mankind', 35 ICLQ, 1986, p. 190.

[258] See further below, chapter 11, p. 628.   [259] See further below, p. 548.

the areas in question are incapable of national appropriation. Sovereignty is not an applicable principle and the areas in question would not be 'owned', nor would any jurisdictional rights exist outside the framework of the appropriate common heritage regime institutional arrangements. However, while a *res communis* regime permits freedom of access, exploration and exploitation, a common heritage regime as envisaged in the examples noted above would strictly regulate exploration and exploitation, would establish management mechanisms and would employ the criterion of equity in distributing the benefits of such activity.

It is too early to predict the success or failure of this concept. The 1982 Law of the Sea Convention entered into force in 1994, while the Moon Treaty has the bare minimum number of ratifications and its exploitation provisions are not yet operative. As a legal concept within the framework of the specific treaties concerned, it provides an interesting contrast to traditional *jus communis* rules, although the extent of the management structures required to operate the regime may pose considerable problems.[260]

The polar regions[261]

The Arctic region is of some strategic importance, constituting as it does a vast expanse of inhospitable territory between North America and Russia.

---

[260] Questions have arisen as to whether the global climate could be regarded as part of the common heritage of mankind. However, international environmental treaties have not used such terminology, but have rather used the phrase 'common concern of mankind', which is weaker and more ambiguous: see e.g. the Convention on Biological Diversity, 1992. See A. Boyle, 'International Law and the Protection of the Global Atmosphere' in *International Law and Global Climate Change* (eds. D. Freestone and R. Churchill), London, 1991, chapter 1, and P. Birnie and A. Boyle, *International Law and the Environment*, 2nd edn, Oxford, 2002, p. 143. See also below, chapter 15.

[261] See e.g. D. R. Rothwell, *The Polar Regions and the Development of International Law*, Cambridge, 1996; O'Connell, *International Law*, pp. 448–50; T. W. Balch, 'The Arctic and Antarctic Regions and the Law of Nations', 4 AJIL, 1910, p. 265; G. Triggs, *International Law and Australian Sovereignty in Antarctica*, Sydney, 1986; R. D. Hayton, 'Polar Problems and International Law', 52 AJIL, 1958, p. 746, and M. Whiteman, *Digest of International Law*, Washington, 1962, vol. II, pp. 1051–61. See also W. Lakhtine, 'Rights over the Arctic', 24 AJIL, 1930, p. 703; Mouton, 'The International Regime of the Polar Regions', 101 HR, 1960, p. 169; F. Auburn, *Antarctic Law and Politics*, Bloomington, 1982; *International Law for Antarctica* (eds. F. Francioni and T. Scovazzi), 2nd edn, The Hague, 1997; A. D. Watts, *International Law and the Antarctic Treaty System*, Cambridge, 1992; E. J. Sahurie, *The International Law of Antarctica*, 1992; C. Joyner, *Antarctica and the Law of the Sea*, The Hague, 1992; *The Antarctic Legal Regime* (eds. C. Joyner and S. Chopra), Dordrecht, 1988; *The Antarctic Environment and International Law* (eds. P. Sands, J. Verhoeven and M. Bruce), London, 1992, and E. Franckx, *Maritime Claims in the Arctic*, The Hague, 1993.

It consists to a large extent of ice packs beneath which submarines may operate.

Denmark possesses Greenland and its associated islands within the region,[262] while Norway has asserted sovereign rights over Spitzbergen and other islands. The Norwegian title is based on occupation and long exploitation of mineral resources and its sovereignty was recognised by nine nations in 1920, although the Soviet Union had protested.[263]

More controversial are the respective claims made by Canada[264] and the former USSR.[265] Use has been made of the concept of contiguity to assert claims over areas forming geographical units with those already occupied, in the form of the so-called sector principle. This is based on meridians of longitude as they converge at the North Pole and as they are placed on the coastlines of the particular nations, thus producing a series of triangular sectors with the coasts of the Arctic states as their baselines.

The other Arctic states of Norway, Finland, Denmark and the United States have abstained from such assertions. Accordingly, it is exceedingly doubtful whether the sector principle can be regarded as other than a political proposition.[266] Part of the problem is that such a large part of this region consists of moving packs of ice. The former USSR made some claims to relatively immovable ice formations as being subject to its national sovereignty,[267] but the overall opinion remains that these are to be treated as part of the high seas open to all.[268]

Occupation of the land areas of the Arctic region may be effected by states by relatively little activity in view of the decision in the *Eastern Greenland* case[269] and the nature of the territory involved.

Claims have been made by seven nations (Argentina, Australia, Chile, France, New Zealand, Norway and the United Kingdom) to the Antarctic

---

[262] See G. H. Hackworth, *Digest of International Law*, Washington, DC, 1940, vol. I.

[263] *Ibid.*, pp. 465 ff. See also O'Connell, *International Law*, p. 499.

[264] Hackworth, *Digest*, vol. I, p. 463. But note Canadian government statements denying that the sector principle applies to the ice: see e.g. 9 ILM, 1970, pp. 607, 613. See also I. Head, 'Canadian Claims to Territorial Sovereignty in the Arctic Regions', 9 *McGill Law Journal*, 1962–3, p. 200.

[265] Hackworth, *Digest*, vol. I, p. 461. Such claims have been maintained by Russia: see e.g. http://news.nationalgeographic.com/news/2007/09/070921-arctic-russia.html and see below, chapter 11, p. 588.

[266] See e.g. *Oppenheim's International Law*, p. 693.

[267] See e.g. Lakhtine, 'Rights over the Arctic', p. 461.

[268] See e.g. Balch, 'Arctic and Antarctic Regions', pp. 265–6.

[269] PCIJ, Series A/B, No. 53, 1933, p. 46; 6 AD, p. 95.

region, which is an ice-covered landmass in the form of an island.[270]
Such claims have been based on a variety of grounds, ranging from mere
discovery to the sector principle employed by the South American states,
and most of these are of rather dubious quality. Significantly, the United
States of America has refused to recognise any claims at all to Antarctica,
and although the American Admiral Byrd discovered and claimed Marie
Byrd Land for his country, the United States refrained from adopting
the claim.[271] Several states have recognised the territorial aspirations of
each other in the area, but one should note that the British, Chilean and
Argentinian claims overlap.[272]

However, in 1959 the Antarctic Treaty was signed by all states concerned with territorial claims or scientific exploration in the region.[273] Its
major effect, apart from the demilitarisation of Antarctica, is to suspend,
although not to eliminate, territorial claims during the life of the treaty.
Article IV(2) declares that:

> no acts or activities taking place while the present treaty is in force shall
> constitute a basis for asserting, supporting or denying a claim to territorial
> sovereignty in Antarctica or create any rights of sovereignty in Antarctica.
> No new claim or enlargement of an existing claim to territorial sovereignty
> in Antarctica shall be asserted while the present treaty is in force.

Since the treaty does not provide for termination, an ongoing regime
has been created which, because of its inclusion of all interested parties, appears to have established an international regime binding on
all.[274] Subsequent meetings of the parties have resulted in a number of recommendations, including proposals for the protection of

---

[270] See e.g. O'Connell, *International Law*, pp. 450–3; Mouton, 'International Regime', and G.
Triggs, 'Australian Sovereignty in Antarctica – Part I', 13 *Melbourne University Law Review*,
1981, p. 123, and Triggs, *International Law and Australian Sovereignty in Antarctica*. See
also UKMIL, 54 BYIL, 1983, pp. 488 ff.

[271] See Hackworth, *Digest*, vol. I, p. 457. See also DUSPIL, 1975, pp. 107–11, and Whiteman,
Digest, vol. II, pp. 250–4, 1254–6 and 1262.

[272] See e.g. Cmd 5900.

[273] See *Handbook of the Antarctic Treaty System*, US Department of State, 9th edn, 2002, also
available at www.state.gov/g/oes/rls/rpts/ant/.

[274] Note that the Federal Fiscal Court of Germany stated in the *Antarctica Legal Status*
case that Antarctica was not part of the sovereign territory of any state, 108 ILR, p.
654. See, as to the UK view that the British Antarctic Territory is the oldest territorial claim to a part of the continent, although most of it was counter-claimed by either
Chile or Argentina, UKMIL, 71 BYIL, 2000, p. 603. Nevertheless, it was accepted that
the effect of the Antarctic Treaty was to set aside disputes over territorial sovereignty,
ibid.

flora and fauna in the region, and other environmental preservation measures.[275]

Of the current forty-three parties to the treaty, twenty-eight have consultative status. Full participation in the work of the consultative meetings of the parties is reserved to the original parties to the treaty and those contracting parties which demonstrate substantial scientific research activity in the area. Antarctic treaty consultative meetings take place annually.[276]

The issue of a mineral resources regime has been under discussion since 1979 by the consultative parties and a series of special meetings on the subject held.[277] This resulted in the signing in June 1988 of the Convention on the Regulation of Antarctic Minerals Resource Activities.[278] The Convention provided for three stages of mineral activity, being defined as prospecting, exploration and development. Four institutions were to be established, once the treaty came into force (following sixteen ratifications or accessions, including the US, the former USSR and claimant states). The Commission was to consist of the consultative parties, any other party to the Convention engaged in substantive and relevant research in the area and any other party sponsoring mineral resource activity. A Scientific, Technical and Environmental Advisory Committee consisting of all parties to the Convention was to be established, as were Regulatory Committees, in order to regulate exploration and development activity in a specific area. Such committees would consist of ten members of the Commission, including the relevant claimant and additional claimants up to a maximum of four, the US, the former USSR and representation of developing countries. A system for Special Meetings of Parties, consisting of all parties to the Convention, was also provided for. Several countries signed the Convention.[279] However, opposition to the Convention began to grow. The signing of the 1988 Convention on mineral resource activities stimulated opposition and in resolution 43/83, adopted by the General Assembly that year, 'deep regret' was expressed that such a convention should have been signed despite earlier resolutions calling for a

---

[275] See e.g. the 1980 Convention on the Conservation of Antarctic Marine Living Resources. See also M. Howard, 'The Convention on the Conservation of Antarctic Marine Living Resources: A Five Year Review', 38 ICLQ, 1989, p. 104.

[276] The most recent being in New Delhi in 2007 and Kiev in 2008: see e.g. www.scar.org/Treaty/ATCM%20meeting%20list.

[277] See e.g. Keesing's Contemporary Archives, p. 32834 and 21(9) UN Chronicle, 1984, p. 45.

[278] See e.g. C. Joyner, 'The Antarctic Minerals Negotiating Process', 81 AJIL, 1987, p. 888.

[279] See e.g. the Antarctic Minerals Act 1989, which provided for a UK licensing system for exploration and exploitation activities in Antarctica.

moratorium on negotiations to create a minerals regime in the Antarctic. France and Australia proposed at the October 1989 meeting of the signatories of the Antarctic Treaty that all mining be banned in the area, which should be designated a global 'wilderness reserve'.[280]

At a meeting of the consultative parties to the Antarctic Treaty in April 1991 the Protocol on Environmental Protection to the Antarctic Treaty was adopted, article 7 of which prohibited any activity relating to mineral resources other than scientific research. This prohibition is to continue unless there is in force a binding legal regime on Antarctic mineral resource activities that includes an agreed means of determining whether and, if so, under which conditions any such activities would be acceptable. A review conference with regard to the operation of the Protocol may be held after it has been in force for fifty years if so requested.[281] In addition, a Committee for Environmental Protection was established.[282] This effectively marked the end of the limited mining approach, which had led to the signing of the Convention on the Regulation of Antarctic Mineral Resource Activities. The Protocol came into force in 1998 and may be seen as establishing a comprehensive integrated environmental regime for the area.[283]

Leases and servitudes[284]

Various legal rights exercisable by states over the territory of other states, which fall short of absolute sovereignty, may exist. Such rights are attached to the land and so may be enforced even though the ownership of the particular territory subject to the rights has passed to another sovereign. They are in legal terminology formulated as rights *in rem*.

---

[280] See *Keesing's Record of World Events*, p. 36989, 1989.   [281] Article 25.

[282] *Guardian*, 30 April 1991, p. 20. See also C. Redgwell, 'Environmental Protection in Antarctica: The 1991 Protocol', 43 ICLQ, 1994, p. 599.

[283] See e.g. D. R. Rothwell, 'Polar Environmental Protection and International Law: The 1991 Antarctic Protocol', 11 EJIL, 2000, p. 591. Four of the annexes (on environmental impact assessment, conservation of flora and fauna, waste disposal and marine pollution) to the Protocol came into force in 1998 and the fifth (on the Antarctic protected area system) in 2002. A Malaysian initiative at the UN to consider making Antarctica a 'common heritage of mankind' appears to have foundered: see e.g. Redgwell, 'Environmental Protection', and General Assembly resolutions 38/77 and 39/152, and A/39/583.

[284] See e.g. *Oppenheim's International Law*, pp. 670 ff.; H. Reid, *International Servitudes*, Chicago, 1932, and F. A. Vali, *Servitudes in International Law*, 2nd edn, London, 1958. See also Parry, *Digest*, vol. IIB, 1967, pp. 373 ff., and article 12, Vienna Convention on Succession of States in Respect of Treaties, 1978.

Leases of land rose into prominence in the nineteenth century as a way of obtaining control of usually strategic points without the necessity of actually annexing the territory. Leases were used extensively in the Far East, as for example Britain's rights over the New Territories amalgamated with Hong Kong,[285] and sovereignty was regarded as having passed to the lessee for the duration of the lease, upon which event it would revert to the original sovereign who made the grant.

An exception to this usual construction of a lease in international law as limited to a defined period occurred with regard to the Panama Canal, with the strip of land through which it was constructed being leased to the United States in 1903 'in perpetuity'. However, by the 1977 Panama Canal Treaty, sovereignty over the Canal Zone was transferred to Panama. The United States had certain operating and defensive rights until the treaty ended in 1999.[286]

A servitude exists where the territory of one state is under a partic-ular restriction in the interests of the territory of another state. Such limitations are bound to the land as rights *in rem* and thus restrict the sovereignty of the state concerned, even if there is a change in control of the relevant territory, for instance upon merger with another state or upon decolonisation.[287]

Examples of servitudes would include the right to use ports or rivers in, or a right of way across, the territory so bound, or alternatively an obligation not to fortify particular towns or areas in the territory.[288]

Servitudes may exist for the benefit of the international community or a large number of states. To give an example, in the *Aaland Islands* case in 1920, a Commission of Jurists appointed by the Council of the League of Nations declared that Finland since its independence in 1918 had succeeded to Russia's obligations under the 1856 treaty not to fortify the islands. And since Sweden was an interested state in that the islands are situated near Stockholm, it could enforce the obligation although not a party to the 1856 treaty. This was because the treaty provisions had established a special international regime with obligations enforceable

---

[285] See 50 BFSP, 1860, p. 10 and 90 BFSP, 1898, p. 17. See now 23 ILM, 1984, pp. 1366 ff. for the UK–China agreement on Hong Kong. See also Cmnd 9543 (1985) and the 1985 Hong Kong Act, providing for the termination of British sovereignty and jurisdiction over the territory as from 1 July 1997.

[286] See e.g. 72 AJIL, 1978, p. 225. This superseded treaties of 1901, 1903, 1936 and 1955 governing the Canal. See also A. Rubin, 'The Panama Canal Treaties', YBWA, 1981, p. 181.

[287] See the *Right of Passage* case, ICJ Reports, 1960, p. 6; 31 ILR, p. 23.

[288] See e.g. J. B. Brierly, *The Law of Nations*, 6th edn, Oxford, 1963, p. 191.

by interested states and binding upon any state in possession of the islands.[289] Further, the Tribunal in *Eritrea/Yemen* noted that the traditional open fishing regime in the southern Red Sea together with the common use of the islands in the area by the populations of both coasts was capable of creating historic rights accruing to the two states in dispute in the form of an international servitude.[290] The award in this case emphasised that the findings of sovereignty over various islands in the Red Sea entailed 'the perpetuation of the traditional fishing regime in the region'.[291]

The situation of the creation of an international status by treaty, which is to be binding upon all and not merely upon the parties to the treaty, is a complex one and it is not always clear when it is to be presumed. However, rights attached to territory for the benefit of the world community were created with respect to the Suez and Panama Canals. Article 1 of the Constantinople Convention of 1888[292] declared that 'the Suez Maritime Canal shall always be free and open in time of war as in time of peace, to every vessel of commerce or of war without distinction of flag' and this international status was in no way affected by the Egyptian nationalisation of the Canal Company in 1956. Egypt stressed in 1957 that it was willing to respect and implement the terms of the Convention, although in fact it consistently denied use of the canal to Israeli ships and vessels bound for its shores or carrying its goods.[293] The canal was reopened in 1975 following the disengagement agreement with Israel, after a gap of eight years.[294] Under article V of the 1979 Peace Treaty between Israel and Egypt, it was provided that ships of Israel and cargoes destined for or coming from Israel were to enjoy 'the right of free passage through the Suez Canal...on the basis of the Constantinople Convention of 1888, applying to all nations'.

In the *Wimbledon* case,[295] the Permanent Court of International Justice declared that the effect of article 380 of the Treaty of Versailles, 1919 maintaining that the Kiel Canal was to be open to all the ships of all countries at peace with Germany was to convert the canal from an internal to an international waterway 'intended to provide under treaty guarantee easier access to the Baltic for the benefit of all nations of the world'.

---

[289] LNOJ, Sp. Supp. no. 3, 1920, pp. 3, 16–19.   [290] 114 ILR, pp. 1, 40–1.

[291] *Ibid.*, p. 137.   [292] See e.g. O'Connell, *International Law*, pp. 582–7.

[293] See Security Council Doc. S/3818, 51 AJIL, 1957, p. 673.

[294] See DUSPIL, 1974, pp. 352–4 and 760.

[295] PCIJ, Series A, No. 1, 1923, p. 24; 2 AD, p. 99. See generally Baxter, *Law of International Waterways*.

Some of the problems relating to the existence of servitudes have arisen by virtue of the *North Atlantic Fisheries* arbitration.[296] This followed a treaty signed in 1818 between the United Kingdom and the United States, awarding the inhabitants of the latter country 'forever ... the liberty to take fish of every kind' from the southern coast of Newfoundland. The argument arose as to Britain's capacity under the treaty to issue fishing regulations binding American nationals. The arbitration tribunal decided that the relevant provision of the treaty did not create a servitude, partly because such a concept was unknown by American and British statesmen at the relevant time (i.e. 1818). However, the terms of the award do leave open the possibility of the existence of servitudes, especially since the tribunal did draw a distinction between economic rights (as in the case) and a grant of sovereign rights which could amount to a servitude in international law.[297]

The law of outer space[298]

There were a variety of theories prior to the First World War with regard to the status of the airspace above states and territorial waters[299] but the outbreak of that conflict, with its recognition of the security implications

---

[296] 11 RIAA, p. 167 (1910). [297] See, as to landlocked states, below, chapter 11, p. 607.

[298] See e.g. C. Q. Christol, *The Modern International Law of Outer Space*, New York, 1982, and Christol, *Space Law*, Deventer, 1991; *Space Law* (ed. P. S. Dempsey), Oxford, 2004; F. Lyall and P. B. Larsen, *Space Law*, Aldershot, 2007; J. E. S. Fawcett, *Outer Space*, Oxford, 1984; S. Gorove, 'International Space Law in Perspective', 181 HR, 1983, p. 349, and Gorove, *Developments in Space Law*, Dordrecht, 1991; M. Marcoff, *Traité de Droit International Public de l'Espace*, Fribourg, 1973, and Marcoff, 'Sources du Droit International de l'Espace', 168 HR, p. 9; N. Matte, *Aerospace Law*, Montreal, 1969; *Le Droit de l'Espace* (ed. J. Dutheil de la Rochère), Paris, 1988; P. M. Martin, *Droit International des Activités Spatiales*, Masson, 1992; B. Cheng, 'The 1967 Space Treaty', *Journal de Droit International*, 1968, p. 532, Cheng, 'The Moon Treaty', 33 *Current Legal Problems*, 1980, p. 213, Cheng, 'The Legal Status of Outer Space', *Journal of Space Law*, 1983, p. 89, Cheng, 'The UN and the Development of International Law Relating to Outer Space', 16 *Thesaurus Acroasium*, Thessaloniki, 1990, p. 49, and Cheng, *Studies in International Space Law*, Oxford, 1997. See also *Oppenheim's International Law*, chapter 7; Nguyen Quoc Dinh *et al.*, *Droit International Public*, p. 1254; R. G. Steinhardt, 'Outer Space' in *United Nations Legal Order* (eds. O. Schachter and C. C. Joyner), Cambridge, 1995, vol. II, p. 753; *Manual on Space Law* (eds. N. Jasentulajana and R. Lee), New York, 4 vols., 1979; *Space Law – Basic Documents* (eds. K. H. Böckstiegel and M. Berkö), Dordrecht, 1991; *Outlook on Space Law* (eds. S. G. Lafferanderie and D. Crowther), The Hague, 1997; G. H. Reynolds and R. P. Merges, *Outer Space*, 2nd edn, Boulder, CO, 1997.

[299] See e.g. *Oppenheim's International Law*, pp. 650–1, and N. Matte, *Treatise on Air–Aeronautical Law*, Montreal, 1981, chapters 4 and 5.

of use of the air, changed this and the approach that then prevailed, with little dissension, was based upon the extension of state sovereignty upwards into airspace. This was acceptable both from the defence point of view and in the light of evolving state practice regulating flights over national territory.[300] It was reflected in the 1919 Paris Convention for the Regulation of Aerial Navigation, which recognised the full sovereignty of states over the airspace above their land and territorial sea.[301] Accordingly, the international law rules protecting sovereignty of states apply to the airspace as they do to the land below. As the International Court noted in the *Nicaragua* case, 'The principle of respect for territorial sovereignty is also directly infringed by the unauthorised overflight of a state's territory by aircraft belonging to or under the control of the government of another state.'[302] The Court noted in the *Benin/Niger* case that 'a boundary represents the line of separation between areas of state sovereignty, not only on the earth's surface but also in the subsoil and in the superjacent column of air'.[303]

There is no right of innocent passage through the airspace of a state.[304] Aircraft may only traverse the airspace of states with the agreement of those states, and where that has not been obtained an illegal intrusion will be involved which will justify interception, though not (save in very exceptional cases) actual attack.[305] However, the principle of the complete sovereignty of the subjacent state is qualified not only by the various multilateral and bilateral conventions which permit airliners to cross and land in the territories of the contracting states under recognised conditions

---

[300] Matte, *Treatise*, pp. 91–6.

[301] Article 1. Each party also undertook to accord in peacetime freedom of innocent passage to the private aircraft of other parties so long as they complied with the rules made by or under the authority of the Convention. Articles 5–10 provided that the nationality of aircraft would be based upon registration and that registration would take place in the state of which their owners were nationals. An International Commission for Air Navigation was established. See also the 1928 American Convention on Commercial Aviation.

[302] ICJ Reports, 1986, pp. 14, 128; 76 ILR, p. 1.   [303] ICJ Reports, 2005, p. 142.

[304] See e.g. *Oppenheim's International Law*, p. 652. It should, however, be noted that articles 38 and 39 of the Convention on the Law of the Sea, 1982 provide for a right of transit passage through straits used for international navigation between one part of the high seas or an exclusive economic zone and another part of the high seas or an exclusive economic zone for aircraft as well as ships. Note also that under article 53 of this Convention, aircraft have a right of overflight with regard to designated air routes above archipelagic waters.

[305] See also *Pan Am Airways* v. *The Queen* (1981) 2 SCR 565; 90 ILR, p. 213, with regard to the exercise of sovereignty over the airspace above the high seas.

and in the light of the accepted regulations, but also by the development of the law of outer space.

Ever since the USSR launched the first earth satellite in 1957, space exploration has developed at an ever-increasing rate.[306] Satellites now control communications and observation networks, while landings have been made on the moon and information-seeking space probes dispatched to survey planets like Venus and Saturn. The research material gathered upon such diverse matters as earth resources, ionospheric activities, solar radiation, cosmic rays and the general structure of space and planet formations has stimulated further efforts to understand the nature of space and the cosmos.[307] This immense increase in available information has also led to the development of the law of outer space, formulating generally accepted principles to regulate the interests of the various states involved as well as taking into account the concern of the international community as a whole.

The definition and delimitation of outer space

It soon became apparent that the *usque ad coelum* rule, providing for state sovereignty over territorial airspace to an unrestricted extent, was not viable where space exploration was concerned. To obtain the individual consents of countries to the passage of satellites and other vehicles orbiting more than 100 miles above their surface would prove cumbersome in the extreme and in practice states have acquiesced in such traversing. This means that the sovereignty of states over their airspace is limited in height at most to the point where the airspace meets space itself. Precisely where this boundary lies is difficult to say and will depend upon technological and other factors, but figures between 50 and 100 miles have been put forward.[308]

As conventional aircraft are developed to attain greater heights, so states will wish to see their sovereignty extend to those heights and, as well as genuine uncertainty, this fear of surrendering what may prove to be in

---

[306] Note the role played by the UN Committee on the Peaceful Uses of Outer Space established in 1958 and consisting currently of sixty-nine states. The Committee has a Legal Sub-Committee and a Scientific and Technical Sub-Committee: see, in particular, Christol, *Modern International Law*, pp. 13–20, and www.unoosa.org/oosa/COPUOS/copuos.html.

[307] See e.g. Fawcett, *Outer Space*, chapter 7.

[308] The UK has noted, for example, that, 'for practical purposes the limit [between airspace and outer space] is considered to be as high as any aircraft can fly', 70 BYIL, 1999, p. 520.

the future valuable sovereign rights has prevented any agreement on the delimitation of this particular frontier.[309]

The regime of outer space

Beyond the point separating air from space, states have agreed to apply the international law principles of *res communis*, so that no portion of outer space may be appropriated to the sovereignty of individual states. This was made clear in a number of General Assembly resolutions following the advent of the satellite era in the late 1950s. For instance, UN General Assembly resolution 1962 (XVII), adopted in 1963 and entitled the Declaration of Legal Principles Governing the Activities of States in the Exploration and Use of Outer Space, lays down a series of applicable legal principles which include the provisions that outer space and celestial bodies were free for exploration and use by all states on a basis of equality and in accordance with international law, and that outer space and celestial bodies were not subject to national appropriation by any means.[310] In addition, the Declaration on International Co-operation in the Exploration and Use of Outer Space adopted in resolution 51/126, 1996, called for further international co-operation, with particular attention being given to the benefit for and the interests of developing countries and countries with incipient space programmes stemming from such international co-operation conducted with countries with more advanced space capabilities.[311] Such resolutions constituted in many cases and in the circumstances expressions of state practice and *opinio juris* and were thus part of customary law.[312]

---

[309] See generally Christol, *Modern International Law*, chapter 10, and see also e.g. UKMIL, 64 BYIL, 1993, p. 689. A variety of suggestions have been put forward regarding the method of delimitation, ranging from the properties of the atmosphere to the lowest possible orbit of satellites. They appear to fall within either a spatial or a functional category: see *ibid.*, and UN Doc. A/AC.105/C.2/7/Add.1, 21 January 1977. Some states have argued for a 110 km boundary: see e.g. USSR, 21(4) *UN Chronicle*, 1984, p. 37; others feel it is premature to establish such a fixed delimitation, e.g. USA and UK, *ibid.* See also 216 HL Deb., col. 975, 1958–9, and D. Goedhuis, 'The Problems of the Frontiers of Outer Space and Airspace', 174 HR, 1982, p. 367.

[310] See also General Assembly resolutions 1721 (XVI) and 1884 (XVIII).

[311] See also 'The Space Millennium: The Vienna Declaration on Space and Human Development' adopted by the Third United Nations Conference on the Exploration and Peaceful Uses of Outer Space (UNISPACE III), Vienna, 1999: see www.oosa.unvienna.org/unisp-3/.

[312] See above, chapter 3, and B. Cheng, 'United Nations Resolutions on Outer Space: "Instant" International Customary Law?', 5 IJIL, 1965, p. 23.

The legal regime of outer space was clarified by the signature in 1967 of the Treaty on Principles Governing the Activities of States in the Exploration and Use of Outer Space, including the Moon and Other Celestial Bodies. This reiterates that outer space, including the moon and other celestial bodies, is not subject to national appropriation by any means and emphasises that the exploration and use of outer space must be carried out for the benefit of all countries. The Treaty does not establish as such a precise boundary between airspace and outer space but it provides the framework for the international law of outer space.[313] Article 4 provides that states parties to the Treaty agree:

> not to place in orbit around the earth any objects carrying nuclear weapons or any other kinds of weapons of mass destruction, install such weapons on celestial bodies, or station such weapons in outer space in any other manner.

There are, however, disagreements as to the meaning of this provision.[314] The article bans only nuclear weapons and weapons of mass destruction from outer space, the celestial bodies and from orbit around the earth, but article 1 does emphasise that the exploration and use of outer space 'shall be carried out for the benefit and in the interests of all countries' and it has been argued that this can be interpreted to mean that any military activity in space contravenes the Treaty.[315]

Under article 4, only the moon and other celestial bodies must be used exclusively for peaceful purposes, although the use of military personnel for scientific and other peaceful purposes is not prohibited. There are minimalist and maximalist interpretations as to how these provisions are to be understood. The former, for example, would argue that only aggressive military activity is banned, while the latter would prohibit all military behaviour.[316] Article 6 provides for international responsibility

---

[313] See e.g. Christol, *Modern International Law*, chapter 2. See also *Oppenheim's International Law*, p. 828.

[314] The issue became particularly controversial in the light of the US Strategic Defence Initiative ('Star Wars'), which aimed to develop a range of anti-satellite and anti-missile weapons based in space. The UN Committee on the Peaceful Uses of Outer Space considered the issue, although without the participation of the US, which objected to the matter being considered: see e.g. 21(6) *UN Chronicle*, 1984, p. 18.

[315] See e.g. Marcoff, *Traité*, pp. 361 ff.

[316] See e.g. Christol, *Modern International Law*, pp. 25–6. See also Goedhuis, 'Legal Issues Involved in the Potential Military Uses of Space Stations' in *Liber Amicorum for Rt Hon. Richard Wilberforce* (eds. M. Bos and I. Brownlie), Oxford, 1987, p. 23, and Gorove, *Developments*, part VI.

for national activities in outer space, including the moon and other celestial bodies, whether such activities are carried on by governmental agencies or by non-governmental entities, and for assuring that national activities are carried out in conformity with the Treaty. The activities of non-governmental entities in outer space, including the moon and other celestial bodies, require authorisation and continuing supervision by the appropriate state party to the Treaty. When activities are carried on in outer space, including the moon and other celestial bodies, by an international organisation, responsibility for compliance with the Treaty is to be borne both by the international organisation and by the states parties to the Treaty participating in such organisation.[317]

Under article 8, states retain jurisdiction and control over personnel and vehicles launched by them into space and under article 7 they remain responsible for any damage caused to other parties to the Treaty by their space objects.[318]

This aspect of space law was further developed by the Convention on International Liability for Damage Caused by Space Objects signed in 1972, article XII of which provides for the payment of compensation in accordance with international law and the principles of justice and equity for any damage caused by space objects. Article II provides for absolute liability to pay such compensation for damage caused by a space object on the surface of the earth or to aircraft in flight, whereas article III provides for fault liability for damage caused elsewhere or to persons or property on board a space object.[319] This Convention was invoked by Canada in 1979 following the damage allegedly caused by Soviet Cosmos 954.[320] As

---

[317] See e.g. B. Cheng, 'Article VI of the 1967 Treaty Revisited', 1 *Journal of Space Law*, 1998, p. 7.

[318] See further Cheng, *Studies in Space Law*, chapters 17 and 18.

[319] See e.g. the Exchange of Notes between the UK and Chinese governments with regard to liability for damages arising during the launch phase of the Asiasat Satellite in 1990 in accordance with *inter alia* the 1967 and 1972 Conventions, UKMIL, 64 BYIL, 1993, p. 689.

[320] The claim was for $6,401,174.70. See 18 ILM, 1979, pp. 899 ff. See also Christol, *Modern International Law*, pp. 59 ff., and Christol, 'International Liability for Damage Caused by Space Objects', 74 AJIL, 1980, p. 346. B. Cheng has drawn attention to difficulties concerning the notion of damage here as including environmental damage: see International Law Association, Report of the Sixty-ninth Conference, London, 2000, p. 581. Note also that under article 3 of the 1967 Treaty, all states parties to the Treaty agree to carry on activities 'in accordance with international law', which clearly includes rules relating to state responsibility. See also Gorove, *Developments*, part V, and B. Hurwitz, *State Liability for Outer Space Activities in Accordance with the 1972 Convention on International Liability for Damage Caused by Space Objects*, Dordrecht, 1992.

a reinforcement to this evolving system of state responsibility, the Convention on the Registration of Objects Launched into Outer Space was opened for signature in 1975, coming into force in 1976. This laid down a series of stipulations for the registration of information regarding space objects, such as, for example, their purpose, location and parameters, with the United Nations Secretary-General.[321] In 1993, the UN General Assembly adopted Principles Relevant to the Use of Nuclear Power Sources in Outer Space.[322] Under these Principles, the launching state is, prior to the launch, to ensure that a thorough and comprehensive safety assessment is conducted and made publicly available. Where a space object appears to malfunction with a risk of re-entry of radioactive materials to the earth, the launching state is to inform states concerned and the UN Secretary-General and respond promptly to requests for further information or consultations sought by other states. Principle 8 provides that states shall bear international responsibility for national activities involving the use of nuclear power sources in outer space, whether such activities are carried out by governmental agencies or by non-governmental agencies. Principle 9 provides that each state which launches or procures the launching of a space object and each state from whose territory or facility a space object is launched shall be internationally liable for damage caused by such space object or its component parts.

The Agreement on the Rescue of Astronauts, the Return of Astronauts and the Return of Objects Launched into Outer Space was signed in 1968 and sets out the legal framework for the provision of emergency assistance to astronauts. It provides for immediate notification of the launching authority or, if that is not immediately possible, a public announcement regarding space personnel in distress as well as the immediate provision of assistance. It also covers search and rescue operations as well as a guarantee of prompt return. The Convention also provides for recovery of space objects.[323]

---

[321] The International Law Association adopted in 1994 the 'Buenos Aires International Instrument on the Protection of the Environment from Damage Caused by Space Debris'. This provides that each state or international organisation party to the Instrument that launches or procures the launching of a space object is internationally liable for damage arising therefrom to another state, persons or objects, or international organisation party to the Instrument as a consequence of space debris produced by any such object: see Report of the Sixty-sixth Conference at Buenos Aires, London, 1994, p. 7.

[322] Resolution 47/68.

[323] The UK Outer Space Act 1986, for example, provides a framework for private sector space enterprises by creating a licensing system for outer space activities and by establishing a system for indemnification for damage suffered by third parties or elsewhere. The Act also

In 1979, the Agreement Governing the Activities of States on the Moon and other Celestial Bodies was adopted.[324] This provides for the demilitarisation of the moon and other celestial bodies, although military personnel may be used for peaceful purposes, and reiterates the principle established in the 1967 Outer Space Treaty. Under article IV, the exploration and the use of the moon shall be the province of all mankind and should be carried out for the benefit of all. Article XI emphasises that the moon and its natural resources are the common heritage of mankind and are not subject to national appropriation by any means. That important article emphasises that no private rights of ownership over the moon or any part of it or its natural resources in place may be created, although all states parties have the right to exploration and use of the moon. The states parties also agreed under article XI(5) and (7) to establish an international regime to govern the exploitation of the resources of the moon, when this becomes feasible.[325] The main purposes of the international regime to be established are to include:

a. the orderly and safe development of the natural resources of the moon;
b. the rational management of those resources;
c. the expansion of opportunities in the use of those resources; and
d. an equitable sharing by all states parties in the benefits derived from those resources, whereby the interests and needs of the developing countries, as well as the efforts of those countries which have

establishes a statutory register of the launch of space objects. Note also that the US has signed a number of agreements with other states providing for assistance abroad in the event of an emergency landing of the space shuttle. These agreements also provide for US liability to compensate for damage and loss caused as a result of an emergency landing, in accordance with the 1972 Treaty: see Cumulative DUSPIL 1981–8, vol. II, p. 2269. In 1988 an Agreement on Space Stations was signed between the US, the governments of the member states of the European Space Agency, Japan and Canada. This provides *inter alia* for registration of flight elements as space objects under the Registration Convention of 1975, each state retaining jurisdiction over the elements it so registers and personnel in or on the space station who are its nationals. There is also an interesting provision (article 22) permitting the US to exercise criminal jurisdiction over misconduct committed by a non-US national in or on a non-US element of the manned base or attached to the manned base, which endangers the safety of the manned base or the crew members thereon. Before proceeding to trial with such a prosecution, the US shall consult with the partner state whose nationality the alleged perpetrator holds, and shall either have received the agreement of that partner to the prosecution or failed to have received an assurance that the partner state intends to prosecute.

324 This came into force in July 1984: see C. Q. Christol, 'The Moon Treaty Enters into Force', 79 AJIL, 1985, p. 163.
325 See e.g. Cheng, 'Moon Treaty', pp. 231–2, and Christol, *Modern International Law*, chapters 7 and 8.

contributed either directly or indirectly to the exploration of the moon, shall be given special consideration.

Several points are worth noting. First, the proposed international regime is only to be established when exploitation becomes feasible. Secondly, it appears that until the regime is set up, there is a moratorium on exploitation, although not on 'exploration and use', as recognised by articles XI(4) and VI(2). This would permit the collection of samples and their removal from the moon for scientific purposes. Thirdly, it is to be noted that private ownership rights of minerals or natural resources not in place are permissible under the Treaty.[326]

Telecommunications[327]

Arguably the most useful application of space exploitation techniques has been the creation of telecommunications networks. This has revolutionised communications and has an enormous educational as well as entertainment potential.[328]

The legal framework for the use of space in the field of telecommunications is provided by the various INTELSAT (international telecommunications satellites) agreements which enable the member states of the International Telecommunications Union to help develop and establish the system, although much of the work is in fact carried out by American corporations, particularly COMSAT. In 1971 the communist countries established their own network of telecommunications satellites, called INTER-SPUTNIK. The international regime for the exploitation of the orbit/spectrum resource[329] has built upon the 1967 Treaty, the 1973 Telecommunications Convention and Protocol and various International Telecommunication Union Radio Regulations. Regulation of the radio spectrum is undertaken at the World Administrative Radio Conferences and by the principal organs of the ITU.

---

[326] See below, chapter 11, p. 628, regarding the 'common heritage' regime envisaged for the deep seabed under the 1982 Convention on the Law of the Sea.

[327] See e.g. A. Matteesco-Matté, *Les Télécommunications par Satellites*, Paris, 1982; M. L. Smith, *International Regulation of Satellite Communications*, Dordrecht, 1990, and J. M. Smits, *Legal Aspects of Implementing International Telecommunications Links*, Dordrecht, 1992.

[328] See e.g. the use by India of US satellites to beam educational television programmes to many thousands of isolated settlements that would otherwise not have been reached, DUSPIL, 1976, pp. 427–8.

[329] See Christol, *Space Law*, chapter 11.

However, there are a number of problems associated with these ventures, ranging from the allocation of radio wave frequencies to the dangers inherent in direct broadcasting via satellites to willing and unwilling states alike. Questions about the control of material broadcast by such satellites and the protection of minority cultures from 'swamping' have yet to be answered, but are being discussed in various UN organs, for instance UNESCO and the Committee on the Peaceful Uses of Outer Space.[330]

Two principles are relevant in this context: freedom of information, which is a right enshrined in many international instruments,[331] and state sovereignty. A number of attempts have been made to reconcile the two.

In 1972, UNESCO adopted a Declaration of Guiding Principles on the Use of Satellite Broadcasting, in which it was provided that all states had the right to decide on the content of educational programmes broadcast to their own peoples, while article IX declared that prior agreement was required for direct satellite broadcasting to the population of countries other than the country of origin of the transmission. Within the UN support for the consent principle was clear, but there were calls for a proper regulatory regime, in addition.[332]

In 1983, the General Assembly adopted resolution 37/92 entitled 'Principles Governing the Use by States of Artificial Earth Satellites for International Direct Television Broadcasting'. This provides that a state intending to establish or authorise the establishment of a direct television broadcasting satellite service must first notify the proposed receiving state or states and then consult with them. A service may only be established after this and on the basis of agreements and/or arrangements in conformity with the relevant instruments of the International Telecommunications Union. However, the value of these principles is significantly reduced in the light of the fact that nearly all the Western states voted against the resolution.[333]

ITU regulations call for technical co-ordination between the sending and receiving states as to frequency and orbital positioning before any

---

[330] See Christol, *Modern International Law*, chapter 12, and N. Matte, 'Aerospace Law: Telecommunications Satellites', 166 HR, 1980, p. 119. See also the study requested by the 1982 Conference, A/AC.107/341, and the European Convention on Transfrontier Television, 1988 and EEC Directive 89/552 on the Pursuit of Television Broadcasting Activities. See also Gorove, *Developments*, part II, chapter 5.

[331] See e.g. article 19, International Covenant on Civil and Political Rights, 1966; article 10, Universal Declaration of Human Rights, 1948, and article 10, European Convention on Human Rights, 1950.

[332] See e.g. N. M. Matte, *Space Activities and Emerging International Law*, London, 1985, p. 438. See also A/8771 (1972).

[333] These included France, West Germany, the UK, USA and Japan.

direct broadcasting by satellite can be carried out and thus do not affect regulation of the conduct of the broadcast activity as such, although the two elements are clearly connected.[334]

The question of remote sensing has also been under consideration for many years by several bodies, including the UN Committee on the Peaceful Uses of Outer Space. Remote sensing refers to the detection and analysis of the earth's resources by sensors carried in aircraft and spacecraft and covers, for example, meteorological sensing, ocean observation, military surveillance and land observation. It clearly has tremendous potential, but the question of the uses of the information received is highly controversial.[335] In 1986, the General Assembly adopted fifteen principles relating to remote sensing.[336] These range from the statement that such activity is to be carried out for the benefit and in the interests of all countries, taking into particular account the needs of developing countries, to the provision that sensing states should promote international co-operation and environmental protection on earth. There is, however, no requirement of prior consent from states that are being sensed,[337] although consultations in order to enhance participation are called for there. One key issue relates to control over the dissemination of information gathered by satellite. Some have called for the creation of an equitable regime for the sharing of information[338] and there is concern over the question of access to data about states by those, and other, states. The USSR and France, for example, jointly proposed the concept of the inalienable right of states to dispose of their natural resources and of information concerning those resources,[339] while the US in particular pointed to the practical problems this would cause and the possible infringement of freedom of information. The UN Committee on the Peaceful Uses of Outer Space

---

[334] See Matte, *Space Activities and Emerging International Law*, pp. 453 ff. See also J. Chapman and G. I. Warren, 'Direct Broadcasting Satellites: The ITU, UN and the Real World', 4 *Annals of Air and Space Law*, 1979, p. 413.

[335] See e.g. Christol, *Modern International Law*, chapter 13, and 21(4) *UN Chronicle*, 1984, p. 32. See also the Study on Remote Sensing, A/AC.105/339 and Add.1, 1985, and Gorove, *Developments*, part VII.

[336] General Assembly resolution 41/65.

[337] Note that the 1967 Outer Space Treaty provides for freedom of exploration and use, although arguments based *inter alia* on permanent sovereignty over natural resources and exclusive sovereignty over airspace have been put forward: see e.g. A/AC.105/171, Annex IV (1976) and A/AC.105/C.2/SR.220 (1984).

[338] See e.g. A. E. Gotlieb, 'The Impact of Technology on the Development of Contemporary International Law', 170 HR, p. 115.

[339] A/AC.105/C.2/L.99 (1974).

has been considering the problem for many years and general agreement has proved elusive.[340] The Principles on Remote Sensing provide that the sensed state shall have access to the primary and processed data produced upon a non-discriminatory basis and on reasonable cost terms. States conducting such remote sensing are to bear international responsibility for their activities.

The increase in the use of satellites for all of the above purposes has put pressure upon the geostationary orbit. This is the orbit 22,300 miles directly above the equator, where satellites circle at the same speed as the earth rotates. It is the only orbit capable of providing continuous contact with ground stations via a single satellite. The orbit is thus a finite resource.[341] However, in 1976, Brazil, Colombia, the Congo, Ecuador, Indonesia, Kenya, Uganda and Zaire signed the Bogotá Declaration under which they stated that 'the segments of geostationary synchronous orbit are part of the territory over which equatorial states exercise their sovereignty'.[342]

Other states have vigorously protested against this and it therefore cannot be taken as other than an assertion and a bargaining counter.[343] Nevertheless, the increase in satellite launches and the limited nature of the geostationary orbit facility call for urgent action to produce an acceptable series of principles governing its use.[344]

Suggestions for further reading

A. Cassese, *Self-Determination of Peoples*, Cambridge, 1995

B. Cheng, *Studies in International Space Law*, Oxford, 1997

J. Crawford, *The Creation of States in International Law*, 2nd edn, Oxford, 2006

J. Crawford, 'State Practice and International Law in Relation to Secession', 69 BYIL, 1998, p. 85

R. Y. Jennings, *The Acquisition of Territory in International Law*, Manchester, 1963

F. Lyall and P. B. Larsen, *Space Law*, Aldershot, 2007

M. N. Shaw, *Title to Territory in Africa*, Oxford, 1986

---

[340] See e.g. A/AC.105/320, Annex IV (1983).

[341] See e.g. article 33 of the 1973 International Telecommunications Convention, and Christol, *Modern International Law*, pp. 451 ff. See also the Study on the Feasibility of Closer Spacing of Satellites in the Geostationary Orbit, A/AC.105/340 (1985) and A/AC105/404 (1988). See also Gorove, *Developments*, part II, chapters 3 and 4.

[342] Gorove, *Developments*, pp. 891–5. See also ITU Doc. WARC-155 (1977) 81-E.

[343] See e.g. DUSPIL, 1979, pp. 1187–8.

[344] Note also the Convention on International Interests in Mobile Equipment, 2001 and the draft protocol on matters specific to space property.

11

The law of the sea

The seas have historically performed two important functions: first, as a medium of communication, and secondly as a vast reservoir of resources, both living and non-living. Both of these functions have stimulated the development of legal rules.[1] The fundamental principle governing the law of the sea is that 'the land dominates the sea' so that the land territorial situation constitutes the starting point for the determination of the maritime rights of a coastal state.[2]

The seas were at one time thought capable of subjection to national sovereignties. The Portuguese in particular in the seventeenth century proclaimed huge tracts of the high seas as part of their territorial domain, but these claims stimulated a response by Grotius who elaborated the doctrine of the open seas, whereby the oceans as *res communis*

---

[1] See e.g. *UN Convention on the Law of the Sea 1982* (eds. M. Nordquist *et al.*), The Hague, 6 vols., 1985–2003; D. Anderson, *Modern Law of the Sea: Selected Essays*, The Hague, 2007; *Law of the Sea, Environmental Law and Settlement of Disputes* (eds. T. M. Ndiaye and R. Wolfrum), The Hague, 2007; *Law of the Sea: Progress and Prospects* (eds. D. Freestone, R. Barnes and D. Ong), Oxford, 2006; L. B. Sohn and J. E. Noyes, *Cases and Materials on the Law of the Sea*, Ardsley, 2004; E. D. Brown, *The International Law of the Sea*, Aldershot, 2 vols., 1994; *Oppenheim's International Law* (eds. R. Y. Jennings and A. D. Watts), 9th edn, London, 1992, chapter 6; Nguyen Quoc Dinh, P. Daillier and A. Pellet, *Droit International Public*, 7th edn, Paris, 2002, p. 1139; T. Treves, 'Codification du Droit International et Pratique des États dans le Droit de la Mer', 223 HR, 1990 IV, p. 9; R. R. Churchill and A. V. Lowe, *The Law of the Sea*, 3rd edn, Manchester, 1999; R. J. Dupuy and D. Vignes, *Traité du Nouveau Droit de la Mer*, Brussels, 1985; *Le Nouveau Droit International de la Mer* (eds. D. Bardonnet and M. Virally), Paris, 1983; D. P. O'Connell, *The International Law of the Sea*, Oxford, 2 vols., 1982–4; *New Directions in the Law of the Sea*, Dobbs Ferry, vols. I–VI (eds. R. Churchill, M. Nordquist and S. H. Lay), 1973–7; *ibid.*, VII–XI (eds. M. Nordquist and K. Simmons), 1980–1, and S. Oda, *The Law of the Sea in Our Time*, Leiden, 2 vols., 1977. See also the series *Limits in the Seas*, published by the Geographer of the US State Department.

[2] See e.g. *Qatar v. Bahrain*, ICJ Reports, 2001, pp. 40, 97; *North Sea Continental Shelf* cases, ICJ Reports, 1969, pp. 3, 51 and *Nicaragua v. Honduras*, ICJ Reports, 2007, paras. 113 and 126.

were to be accessible to all nations but incapable of appropriation.[3] This view prevailed, partly because it accorded with the interests of the North European states, which demanded freedom of the seas for the purposes of exploration and expanding commercial intercourse with the East.

The freedom of the high seas rapidly became a basic principle of international law, but not all the seas were so characterised. It was permissible for a coastal state to appropriate a maritime belt around its coastline as territorial waters, or territorial sea, and treat it as an indivisible part of its domain. Much of the history of the law of the sea has centred on the extent of the territorial sea or the precise location of the dividing line between it and the high seas and other recognised zones. The original stipulation linked the width of the territorial sea to the ability of the coastal state to dominate it by military means from the confines of its own shore. But the present century has witnessed continual pressure by states to enlarge the maritime belt and thus subject more of the oceans to their exclusive jurisdiction.

Beyond the territorial sea, other jurisdictional zones have been in process of development. Coastal states may now exercise particular jurisdictional functions in the contiguous zone, and the trend of international law today is moving rapidly in favour of even larger zones in which the coastal state may enjoy certain rights to the exclusion of other nations, such as fishery zones, continental shelves and, more recently, exclusive economic zones. However, in each case whether a state is entitled to a territorial sea, continental shelf or exclusive economic zone is a question to be decided by the law of the sea.[4]

This gradual shift in the law of the sea towards the enlargement of the territorial sea (the accepted maximum limit is now a width of 12 nautical miles in contrast to 3 nautical miles some forty years ago), coupled with the continual assertion of jurisdictional rights over portions of what were regarded as high seas, reflects a basic change in emphasis in the attitude of states to the sea.

The predominance of the concept of the freedom of the high seas has been modified by the realisation of resources present in the seas and seabed beyond the territorial seas. Parallel with the developing tendency to assert ever greater claims over the high seas, however, has been the move towards

---

[3] *Mare Liberum*, 1609. See also O'Connell, *International Law of the Sea*, vol. I, pp. 9 ff. The closed seas approach was put by e.g. J. Selden, *Mare Clausum*, 1635.

[4] *El Salvador/Honduras (Nicaragua Intervening)*, ICJ Reports, 1990, pp. 92, 126; 97 ILR, p. 214.

proclaiming a 'common heritage of mankind' regime over the seabed of the high seas. The law relating to the seas, therefore, has been in a state of flux for several decades as the conflicting principles have manifested themselves.

A series of conferences have been held, which led to the four 1958 Conventions on the Law of the Sea and then to the 1982 Convention on the Law of the Sea.[5] The 1958 Convention on the High Seas was stated in its preamble to be 'generally declaratory of established principles of international law', while the other three 1958 instruments can be generally accepted as containing both reiterations of existing rules and new rules.

The pressures leading to the Law of the Sea Conference, which lasted between 1974 and 1982 and involved a very wide range of states and international organisations, included a variety of economic, political and strategic factors. Many Third World states wished to develop the exclusive economic zone idea, by which coastal states would have extensive rights over a 200-mile zone beyond the territorial sea, and were keen to establish international control over the deep seabed, so as to prevent the technologically advanced states from being able to extract minerals from this vital and vast source freely and without political constraint. Western states were desirous of protecting their navigation routes by opposing any weakening of the freedom of passage through international straits particularly, and wished to protect their economic interests through free exploitation of the resources of the high seas and the deep seabed. Other states and groups of states sought protection of their particular interests.[6] Examples here would include the landlocked and geographically disadvantaged states, archipelagic states and coastal states. The effect of this kaleidoscopic range of interests was very marked and led to the 'package deal' concept of the final draft. According to this approach, for example, the Third World accepted passage through straits and enhanced continental shelf rights beyond the 200-mile limit from the coasts in return for the internationalisation of deep sea mining.[7]

The 1982 Convention contains 320 articles and 9 Annexes. It was adopted by 130 votes to 4, with 17 abstentions. The Convention entered

---

[5] The 1958 Convention on the Territorial Sea and the Contiguous Zone came into force in 1964; the 1958 Convention on the High Seas came into force in 1962; the 1958 Convention on Fishing and Conservation of Living Resources came into force in 1966 and the 1958 Convention on the Continental Shelf came into force in 1964.

[6] See Churchill and Lowe, *Law of the Sea*, pp. 15 ff.

[7] See e.g. H. Caminos and M. R. Molitor, 'Progressive Development of International Law and the Package Deal', 79 AJIL, 1985, p. 871.

into force on 16 November 1994, twelve months after the required 60 ratifications. In order primarily to meet Western concerns with regard to the International Seabed Area (Part XI of the Convention), an Agreement relating to the Implementation of Part XI of the 1982 Convention was adopted on 29 July 1994.[8]

Many of the provisions in the 1982 Convention repeat principles enshrined in the earlier instruments and others have since become customary rules, but many new rules were proposed. Accordingly, a complicated series of relationships between the various states exists in this field, based on customary rules and treaty rules.[9] All states are *prima facie* bound by the accepted customary rules, while only the parties to the five treaties involved will be bound by the new rules contained therein, and since one must envisage some states not adhering to the 1982 Conventions, the 1958 rules will continue to be of importance.[10] During the twelve-year period between the signing of the Convention and its coming into force, the influence of its provisions was clear in the process of law creation by state practice.[11]

The territorial sea

Internal waters[12]

Internal waters are deemed to be such parts of the seas as are not either the high seas or relevant zones or the territorial sea, and are accordingly classed as appertaining to the land territory of the coastal state. Internal waters, whether harbours, lakes or rivers, are such waters as are to be found on the landward side of the baselines from which the width of the territorial and other zones is measured,[13] and are assimilated with the territory of

---

[8] See further below, p. 632.

[9] See the *North Sea Continental Shelf* cases, ICJ Reports, 1969, pp. 3, 39; 41 ILR, pp. 29, 68; the *Fisheries Jurisdiction (UK v. Iceland)* case, ICJ Reports, 1974, p. 1; 55 ILR, p. 238 and the *Anglo-French Continental Shelf* case, Cmnd 7438, 1978; 54 ILR, p. 6. See also above, chapter 3, p. 77.

[10] Note that by article 311(1) of the 1982 Convention, the provisions of this Convention will prevail as between the states parties over the 1958 Conventions.

[11] See e.g. J. R. Stevenson and B. H. Oxman, 'The Future of the UN Convention on the Law of the Sea', 88 AJIL, 1994, p. 488.

[12] See e.g. Brown, *International Law of the Sea*, vol. I, chapter 5; O'Connell, *International Law of the Sea*, vol. I, chapter 9; V. D. Degan, 'Internal Waters', Netherlands YIL, 1986, p. 1 and Churchill and Lowe, *Law of the Sea*, chapter 3.

[13] Article 5(1) of the 1958 Convention on the Territorial Sea and article 8(1) of the 1982 Convention. Note the exception in the latter provision with regard to archipelagic states, below, p. 565. See also *Regina v. Farnquist* (1981) 54 CCC (2d) 417; 94 ILR, p. 238.

the state. They differ from the territorial sea primarily in that there does not exist any right of innocent passage from which the shipping of other states may benefit. There is an exception to this rule where the straight baselines enclose as internal waters what had been territorial waters.[14]

In general, a coastal state may exercise its jurisdiction over foreign ships within its internal waters to enforce its laws, although the judicial authorities of the flag state (i.e. the state whose flag the particular ship flies) may also act where crimes have occurred on board ship. This concurrent jurisdiction may be seen in two cases.

In *R v. Anderson*,[15] in 1868, the Court of Criminal Appeal in the UK declared that an American national who had committed manslaughter on board a British vessel in French internal waters was subject to the jurisdiction of the British courts, even though he was also within the sovereignty of French justice (and American justice by reason of his nationality), and thus could be correctly convicted under English law. The US Supreme Court held in *Wildenhus'* case[16] that the American courts had jurisdiction to try a crew member of a Belgian vessel for the murder of another Belgian national when the ship was docked in the port of Jersey City in New York.[17]

A merchant ship in a foreign port or in foreign internal waters is automatically subject to the local jurisdiction (unless there is an express agreement to the contrary), although where purely disciplinarian issues related to the ship's crew are involved, which do not concern the maintenance of peace within the territory of the coastal state, then such matters would by courtesy be left to the authorities of the flag state to regulate.[18] Although some writers have pointed to theoretical differences between the common law and French approaches, in practice the same fundamental proposition applies.[19]

---

[14] Article 5(2) of the 1958 Convention on the Territorial Sea and article 8(2) of the 1982 Convention. See below, p. 559.

[15] 1 Cox's Criminal Cases 198.

[16] 120 US 1 (1887). See also *Armament Dieppe SA v. US* 399 F.2d 794 (1968).

[17] See the Madrid incident, where US officials asserted the right to interview a potential defector from a Soviet ship in New Orleans, 80 AJIL, 1986, p. 622.

[18] See e.g. *NNB v. Ocean Trade Company* 87 ILR, p. 96, where the Court of Appeal of The Hague held that a coastal state had jurisdiction over a foreign vessel where the vessel was within the territory of the coastal state and a dispute arose affecting not only the internal order of the ship but also the legal order of the coastal state concerned. The dispute concerned a strike on board ship taken on the advice of the International Transport Workers' Federation.

[19] See e.g. Churchill and Lowe, *Law of the Sea*, pp. 65 ff. See also J. L. Lenoir, 'Criminal Jurisdiction over Foreign Merchant Ships', 10 *Tulane Law Review*, 1935, p. 13. See, with regard to the right of access to ports and other internal waters, A. V. Lowe, 'The Right of

However, a completely different situation operates where the foreign vessel involved is a warship. In such cases, the authorisation of the captain or of the flag state is necessary before the coastal state may exercise its jurisdiction over the ship and its crew. This is due to the status of the warship as a direct arm of the sovereign of the flag state.[20]

Baselines[21]

The width of the territorial sea is defined from the low-water mark around the coasts of the state. This is the traditional principle under customary international law and was reiterated in article 3 of the Geneva Convention on the Territorial Sea and the Contiguous Zone in 1958 and article 5 of the 1982 Convention, and the low-water line along the coast is defined 'as marked on large-scale charts officially recognised by the coastal state'.[22]

In the majority of cases, it will not be very difficult to locate the low-water line which is to act as the baseline for measuring the width of the territorial sea.[23] By virtue of the 1958 Convention on the Territorial Sea and the 1982 Law of the Sea Convention, the low-water line of a low-tide elevation[24] may now be used as a baseline for measuring the breadth of the territorial sea if it is situated wholly or partly within the the territorial sea

Entry into Maritime Ports in International Law', 14 *San Diego Law Review*, 1977, p. 597, and O'Connell, *International Law of the Sea*, vol. II, chapter 22. See also the Dangerous Vessels Act 1985.

20 See *The Schooner Exchange* v. *McFaddon* 7 Cranch 116 (1812). See also 930 HC Deb., col. 450, Written Answers, 29 April 1977.

21 See e.g. W. M. Reisman and G. S. Westerman, *Straight Baselines in International Maritime Boundary Delimitation*, New York, 1992; J. A. Roach and R. W. Smith, *United States Responses to Excessive Maritime Claims*, 2nd edn, The Hague, 1996, and L. Sohn, 'Baseline Considerations' in *International Maritime Boundaries* (eds. J. I. Charney and L. M. Alexander), Dordrecht, 1993, vol. I, p. 153.

22 See *Qatar* v. *Bahrain*, ICJ Reports, 2001, pp. 40, 97 and *Eritrea/Yemen (Phase Two: Maritime Delimitation)*, 119 ILR, pp. 417, 458. See also Churchill and Lowe, *Law of the Sea*, chapter 2; O'Connell, *International Law of the Sea*, vol. I, chapter 5; *Oppenheim's International Law*, p. 607, and M. Mendelson, 'The Curious Case of *Qatar* v. *Bahrain* in the International Court of Justice', 72 BYIL, 2001, p. 183.

23 See the *Dubai/Sharjah Border Award* 91 ILR, pp. 543, 660–3, where the Arbitral Tribunal took into account the outermost permanent harbour works of the two states as part of the coast for the purpose of drawing the baselines.

24 See article 11(1), Convention on the Territorial Sea, 1958 and article 13(1), Law of the Sea Convention, 1982. A low-tide elevation is a naturally formed area of land which is surrounded by and above water at low tide, but submerged at high tide. See e.g. G. Marston, 'Low-Tide Elevations and Straight Baselines', 46 BYIL, 1972–3, p. 405, and D. Bowett, 'Islands, Rocks, Reefs and Low-Tide Elevations in Maritime Boundary Delimitations' in Charney and Alexander, *International Maritime Boundaries*, vol. I, p. 131.

measured from the mainland or an island. However, a low-tide elevation wholly situated beyond the territorial sea will generate no territorial sea of its own.[25] When a low-tide elevation is situated in the overlapping area of the territorial sea of two states, both are in principle entitled to use this as part of the relevant low-water line in measuring their respective territorial sea.[26] However, the International Court has taken the view that low-tide elevations may not be regarded as part of the territory of the state concerned and thus cannot be fully assimilated with islands.[27] A low-tide elevation with a lighthouse or similar installation built upon it may be used for the purpose of drawing a straight baseline.[28]

Sometimes, however, the geography of the state's coasts will be such as to cause certain problems: for instance, where the coastline is deeply indented or there are numerous islands running parallel to the coasts, or where there exist bays cutting into the coastlines. Special rules have evolved to deal with this issue, which is of importance to coastal states, particularly where foreign vessels regularly fish close to the limits of the territorial sea. A more rational method of drawing baselines might have the effect of enclosing larger areas of the sea within the state's internal waters, and thus extend the boundaries of the territorial sea further than the traditional method might envisage.

This point was raised in the *Anglo-Norwegian Fisheries* case,[29] before the International Court of Justice. The case concerned a Norwegian decree delimiting its territorial sea along some 1,000 miles of its coastline. However, instead of measuring the territorial sea from the low-water line, the Norwegians constructed a series of straight baselines linking the outermost parts of the land running along the skjaergaard (or fringe of islands and rocks) which parallels the Norwegian coastline. This had the effect of enclosing within its territorial limits parts of what would normally have been the high seas if the traditional method had been utilised. As a result, certain disputes involving British fishing boats arose, and the United

---

[25] Article 13(2) of the Law of the Sea Convention, 1982. Further, low-tide elevations situated within 12 miles of another such elevation but beyond the territorial sea of the state may not themselves be used for the determination of the breadth of the territorial sea, the so-called 'leap-frogging method', *Qatar* v. *Bahrain*, ICJ Reports, 2001, pp. 40, 102. See also *Nicaragua* v. *Honduras*, ICJ Reports, 2007, para. 141, but see *Eritrea/Yemen*, 114 ILR, pp. 1, 138.

[26] *Qatar* v. *Bahrain*, ICJ Reports, 2001, pp. 40, 101.

[27] *Ibid.*, pp. 40, 102 and *Nicaragua* v. *Honduras*, ICJ Reports, 2007, para. 141.

[28] See article 7(4) of the Law of the Sea Convention, 1982. See also article 47(4) with regard to archipelagic baselines.

[29] ICJ Reports, 1951, p. 116; 18 ILR, p. 86.

Kingdom challenged the legality of the Norwegian method of baselines under international law. The Court held that it was the outer line of the skjaergaard that was relevant in establishing the baselines, and not the low-water line of the mainland. This was dictated by geographic realities. The Court noted that the normal method of drawing baselines that are parallel to the coast (the *tracé parallèle*) was not applicable in this case because it would necessitate complex geometrical constructions in view of the extreme indentations of the coastline and the existence of the series of islands fringing the coasts.[30]

Since the usual methods did not apply, and taking into account the principle that the territorial sea must follow the general direction of the coasts, the concept of straight baselines drawn from the outer rocks could be considered.[31] The Court also made the point that the Norwegian system had been applied consistently over many years and had met no objections from other states, and that the UK had not protested until many years after it had first been introduced.[32] In other words, the method of straight baselines operated by Norway:

> had been consolidated by a constant and sufficiently long practice, in the face of which the attitude of governments bears witness to the fact that they did not consider it to be contrary to international law.[33]

Thus, although noting that Norwegian rights had been established through actual practice coupled with acquiescence, the Court regarded the straight baseline system itself as a valid principle of international law in view of the special geographic conditions of the area. The Court provided criteria for determining the acceptability of any such delimitations. The drawing of the baselines had not to depart from the general direction of the coast, in view of the close dependence of the territorial sea upon the land domain; the baselines had to be drawn so that the sea area lying within them had to be sufficiently closely linked to the land domain to be subject to the regime of internal waters, and it was permissible to consider

---

[30] ICJ Reports, 1951, p. 128; 18 ILR, p. 91. Note also the Court's mention of the *courbe tangente* method of drawing arcs of circles from points along the low-water line, *ibid.*

[31] ICJ Reports, 1951, p. 129; 18 ILR, p. 92. Other states had already used such a system: see e.g. H. Waldock, 'The Anglo-Norwegian Fisheries Case', 28 BYIL, 1951, pp. 114, 148. See also I. Brownlie, *Principles of Public International Law*, 6th edn, Oxford, 2003, pp. 176 ff.

[32] ICJ Reports, 1951, p. 138; 18 ILR, p. 101. Cf. Judge McNair, ICJ Reports, 1951, pp. 171–80; 18 ILR, p. 123.

[33] ICJ Reports, 1951, p. 139; 18 ILR, p. 102.

in the process 'certain economic interests peculiar to a region, the reality and importance of which are evidenced by long usage'.[34]

These principles emerging from the *Fisheries* case were accepted by states as part of international law within a comparatively short period.

Article 4 of the Geneva Convention on the Territorial Sea, 1958 declared that the straight baseline system could be used in cases of indented coastlines or where there existed a skjaergaard, provided that the general direction of the coast was followed and that there were sufficiently close links between the sea areas within the lines and the land domain to be subject to the regime of internal waters. In addition, particular regional economic interests of long standing may be considered where necessary.[35]

A number of states now use the system, including, it should be mentioned, the United Kingdom as regards areas on the west coast of Scotland.[36] However, there is evidence that, perhaps in view of the broad criteria laid down, many states have used this system in circumstances that are not strictly justifiable in law.[37] However, the Court made it clear in *Qatar* v. *Bahrain* that

> the method of straight baselines, which is an exception to the normal rules for the determination of baselines, may only be applied if a number of conditions are met. This method must be applied restrictively. Such conditions are primarily that either the coastline is deeply indented and cut into, or that there is a fringe of islands along the coast in its immediate vicinity.[38]

Further, the Court emphasised that the fact that a state considers itself a multiple-island state or a *de facto* archipelago does not allow it to

---

[34] ICJ Reports, 1951, p. 133; 18 ILR, p. 95.

[35] See also article 7 of the 1982 Convention. Note that straight baselines may not be drawn to and from low-tide elevations, unless lighthouses or similar installations which are permanently above sea level have been built on them: see article 4(3), 1958 Convention on the Territorial Sea and article 7(4), 1982 Convention on the Law of the Sea. See also *Qatar* v. *Bahrain*, ICJ Reports, 2001, pp. 40, 100–1 and 102.

[36] Territorial Waters Order in Council, 1964, article 3, s. 1, 1965, Part III, s. 2, p. 6452A. See also the Territorial Sea (Limits) Order 1989 regarding the Straits of Dover. See generally, as regards state practice, Churchill and Lowe, *Law of the Sea*, pp. 38–41, who note that some fifty-five to sixty-five states have used straight baselines, and M. Whiteman, *Digest of International Law*, Washington, vol. IV, pp. 21–35.

[37] See Churchill and Lowe, *Law of the Sea*, p. 39. See also the objection of the European Union to the use by Iran and Thailand of straight baselines along practically their entire coastlines, UKMIL, 69 BYIL, 1998, pp. 540–2, and US objections to the use of straight baselines by Thailand, DUSPIL, 2000, p. 703.

[38] ICJ Reports, 2001, pp. 40, 103.

deviate from the normal rules for the determination of baselines unless the relevant conditions are met.[39]

Where the result of the straight baseline method is to enclose as internal waters areas previously regarded as part of the territorial sea or high seas, a right of innocent passage shall be deemed to exist in such waters by virtue of article 5(2) of the 1958 Convention.[40]

Bays[41]

Problems also arise as to the approach to be adopted with regard to bays, in particular whether the waters of wide-mouthed bays ought to be treated as other areas of the sea adjacent to the coast, so that the baseline of the territorial sea would be measured from the low-water mark of the coast of the bay, or whether the device of the straight baseline could be used to 'close off' the mouth of the bay of any width and the territorial limit measured from that line.

It was long accepted that a straight closing line could be used across the mouths of bays, but there was considerable disagreement as to the permitted width of the bay beyond which this would not operate.[42] The point was settled in article 7 of the 1958 Convention on the Territorial Sea. This declared that:

> if the distance between the low-water marks of the natural entrance points of a bay does not exceed twenty-four miles, a closing line may be drawn between these two low-water marks, and the waters enclosed thereby shall be considered as internal waters,

otherwise a straight baseline of 24 miles may be drawn.[43]

This provision, however, does not apply to historic bays. These are bays the waters of which are treated by the coastal state as internal in view of historic rights supported by general acquiescence rather than any specific

---

[39] *Ibid.* The Court rejected Bahrain's claim that certain maritime features east of its main islands constituted a fringe of islands: *ibid.*

[40] See also article 8(2) of the 1982 Convention.

[41] See e.g. Brown, *International Law of the Sea*, vol. I, p. 28; Churchill and Lowe, *Law of the Sea*, pp. 41 ff., and O'Connell, *International Law of the Sea*, vol. I, p. 209. See also G. Westerman, *The Juridical Bay*, Oxford, 1987.

[42] See e.g. the *North Atlantic Coast Fisheries* case, 11 RIAA, p. 167 (1910) and the *Anglo-Norwegian Fisheries* case, ICJ Reports, 1951, p. 116; 18 ILR, p. 86, to the effect that no general rules of international law had been uniformly accepted.

[43] See also article 10 of the 1982 Convention.

principle of international law.[44] A number of states have claimed historic bays: for example, Canada with respect to Hudson Bay (although the US has opposed this)[45] and certain American states as regards the Gulf of Fonseca.[46] The question of this Gulf came before the International Court in the *Land, Island and Maritime Frontier Dispute (El Salvador/Honduras; Nicaragua intervening)*.[47] The Court noted that the states concerned and commentators were agreed that the Gulf was a historic bay, but this was defined in terms of the particular historical situation of that Gulf, especially as it constituted a pluri-state bay, for which there were no agreed and codified general rules of the kind well established for single-state bays.[48] In the light of the particular historical circumstances and taking particular note of the 1917 decision, the Court found that the Gulf, beyond a long-accepted 3-mile maritime belt for the coastal states, constituted historic waters subject to the co-ownership or a condominium of the three coastal states.[49] The Court continued by noting that the vessels of other states would enjoy a right of innocent passage in the waters beyond the coastal belt in order to ensure access to any one of the three coastal states.[50] Having decided that the three states enjoyed a condominium within the Gulf, the Court concluded that there was a tripartite presence at the closing line of the Gulf.[51]

The United States Supreme Court has taken the view that where waters are outside the statutory limits for inland waters, the exercise of sovereignty required to establish title to a historic bay amounted to the exclusion of all foreign vessels and navigation from the area claimed. The continuous authority exercised in this fashion had to be coupled with the acquiescence of states. This was the approach in the *US* v. *State*

---

[44] See the *Tunisia/Libya Continental Shelf* case, ICJ Reports, 1982, pp. 18, 74; 67 ILR, pp. 4, 67.

[45] See Whiteman, *Digest*, vol. IV, pp. 250–7.

[46] See *El Salvador* v. *Nicaragua* 11 AJIL, 1917, p. 674.

[47] ICJ Reports, 1992, p. 351; 97 ILR, p. 266.

[48] ICJ Reports, 1992, p. 589; 97 ILR, p. 505. But cf. the Dissenting Opinion of Judge Oda, ICJ Reports, 1992, p. 745; 97 ILR, p. 661.

[49] ICJ Reports, 1992, p. 601; 97 ILR, p. 517. See also generally C. Symmons, *Historic Waters in the Law of the Sea: A Modern Re-appraisal*, The Hague, 2007.

[50] ICJ Reports, 1992, p. 605; 97 ILR, p. 521.

[51] ICJ Reports, 1992, pp. 608–9; 97 ILR, pp. 524–5. See also M. N. Shaw, 'Case Concerning the Land, Island and Maritime Frontier Dispute (*El Salvador/Honduras: Nicaragua Intervening*), Judgment of 11 September 1992', 42 ICLQ, 1993, p. 929, and A. Gioia, 'The Law of Multinational Bays and the Case of the Gulf of Fonseca', Netherlands YIL, 1993, p. 81.

of Alaska case[52] concerning the waters of Cook Inlet. The Supreme Court held that Alaska had not satisfied the terms and that the Inlet had not been regarded as a historic bay under Soviet, American or Alaskan sovereignty. Accordingly, it was the federal state and not Alaska which was entitled to the subsurface of Cook Inlet.[53]

In response to the Libyan claim to the Gulf of Sirte (Sidra) as a historic bay and the consequent drawing of a closing line of nearly 300 miles in length in 1973, several states immediately protested, including the US and the states of the European Community.[54] The US in a note to Libya in 1974 referred to 'the international law standards of past open, notorious and effective exercise of authority, and the acquiescence of foreign nations'[55] and has on several occasions sent naval and air forces into the Gulf in order to maintain its opposition to the Libyan claim and to assert that the waters of the Gulf constitute high seas.[56] Little evidence appears, in fact, to support the Libyan contention.

Islands[57]

As far as islands are concerned, the general provisions noted above regarding the measurement of the territorial sea apply. Islands are defined in the 1958 Convention on the Territorial Sea as consisting of 'a naturally-formed area of land, surrounded by water, which is above water at high tide',[58] and they can generate a territorial sea, contiguous zone, exclusive

---

[52] 422 US 184 (1975). See also L. J. Bouchez, *The Regime of Bays in International Law*, Leiden, 1963, and the *Tunisia–Libya Continental Shelf* case, ICJ Reports, 1982, pp. 18, 74; 67 ILR, pp. 4, 67.

[53] See also *United States* v. *California* 381 US 139 (1965); *United States* v. *Louisiana* (*Louisiana Boundary Case*) 394 US 11 (1969); *United States* v. *Maine* (*Rhode Island and New York Boundary Case*) 471 US 375 (1985) and *Alabama and Mississippi Boundary Case, United States* v. *Louisiana* 470 US 93 (1985).

[54] See Churchill and Lowe, *Law of the Sea*, p. 45, and UKMIL, 57 BYIL, 1986, pp. 579–80. See also F. Francioni, 'The Gulf of Sidra Incident (*United States* v. *Libya*) and International Law', 5 *Italian Yearbook of International Law*, 1980–1, p. 85.

[55] See 68 AJIL, 1974, p. 510. See also Cumulative DUSPIL 1981–8, Washington, 1994, vol. II, p. 1810.

[56] See e.g. UKMIL, 57 BYIL, 1986, pp. 581–2.

[57] See e.g. H. W. Jayewardene, *The Regime of Islands in International Law*, Dordrecht, 1990; D. W. Bowett, *The Legal Regime of Islands in International Law*, New York, 1979; C. Symmons, *The Maritime Zone of Islands in International Law*, The Hague, 1979; J. Simonides, 'The Legal Status of Islands in the New Law of the Sea', 65 *Revue de Droit International*, 1987, p. 161, and R. O'Keefe, 'Palm-Fringed Benefits: Island Dependencies in the New Law of the Sea', 45 ICLQ, 1996, p. 408.

[58] Article 10(1). See also article 121(1) of the 1982 Convention.

economic zone and continental shelf where relevant.[59] Where there exists a chain of islands which are less than 24 miles apart, a continuous band of territorial sea may be generated.[60] However, article 121(3) of the 1982 Convention provides that 'rocks which cannot sustain human habitation or economic life of their own shall have no exclusive economic zone or continental shelf'.[61] Article 121(3) begs a series of questions, such as the precise dividing line between rocks and islands and as to the actual meaning of an 'economic life of their own', and a number of states have made controversial claims.[62] Whether this provision over and above its appearance in the Law of the Sea Convention is a rule of customary law is unclear.[63]

Archipelagic states[64]

Problems have arisen as a result of efforts by states comprising a number of islands to draw straight baselines around the outer limits of their islands,

---

[59] Article 121(2) of the 1982 Convention. See also the *Jan Mayen (Denmark v. Norway)* case, ICJ Reports, 1993, pp. 37, 64–5; 99 ILR, pp. 395, 432–3. Article 10(2) of the 1958 Convention on the Territorial Sea referred only to the territorial sea of islands.

[60] See *Eritrea/Yemen (Phase Two: Maritime Delimitation)*, 119 ILR, pp. 417, 463.

[61] See the *Jan Mayen* report, 20 ILM, 1981, pp. 797, 803; 62 ILR, pp. 108, 114, and the Declaration by Judge Evensen in the *Jan Mayen (Denmark v. Norway)* case, ICJ Reports, 1993, pp. 37, 84–5; 99 ILR, pp. 395, 452–3. Note, as regards Rockall and the conflicting UK, Irish, Danish and Icelandic views, Symmons, *Maritime Zone*, pp. 117–18, 126; E. D. Brown, 'Rockall and the Limits of National Jurisdiction of the United Kingdom', 2 *Marine Policy*, 1978, pp. 181–211 and 275–303, and O'Keefe, 'Palm-Fringed Benefits'. See also 878 HC Deb., col. 82, Written Answers, and *The Times*, 8 May 1985, p. 6 (Danish claims) and the *Guardian*, 1 May 1985, p. 30 (Icelandic claims). UK sovereignty over the uninhabited island of Rockall was proclaimed in 1955 and confirmed by the Island of Rockall Act 1972, UKMIL, 68 BYIL, 1997, p. 589. The UK Minister of State declared that the 12-mile territorial sea around Rockall was consistent with the terms of the 1982 Convention and that there was no reason to believe that this was not accepted by the international community, apart from the Republic of Ireland, UKMIL, 60 BYIL, 1989, p. 666. The UK claim to a 200-mile fishing zone around Rockall made in the Fishery Limits Act 1976 was withdrawn in 1997 consequent upon accession to the Law of the Sea Convention, 1982 and the 12-mile territorial sea confirmed: see UKMIL, 68 BYIL, 1997, pp. 599–600 and UKMIL, 71 BYIL, 2000, p. 601.

[62] See e.g. Churchill and Lowe, *Law of the Sea*, pp. 163–4, and J. I. Charney, 'Rocks that Cannot Sustain Human Habitation', 93 AJIL, 1999, p. 873.

[63] Churchill and Lowe, *Law of the Sea*, p. 164.

[64] See e.g. Brown, *International Law of the Sea*, vol. I, chapter 8; Churchill and Lowe, *Law of the Sea*, chapter 6; O'Connell, *International Law of the Sea*, vol. I, chapter 6; Bowett, *Legal Regime*, chapter 4; C. F. Amerasinghe, 'The Problem of Archipelagos in the International Law of the Sea', 23 ICLQ, 1974, p. 539, and D. P. O'Connell, 'Mid-Ocean Archipelagos in International Law', 45 BYIL, 1971, p. 1.

thus 'boxing in' the whole territory. Indonesia in particular has resorted to this method, against the protests of a number of states since it tends to reduce previously considered areas of the high seas extensively used as shipping lanes to the sovereignty of the archipelago state concerned.[65]

There has been a great deal of controversy as to which international law principles apply in the case of archipelagos and the subject was not expressly dealt with in the 1958 Geneva Convention.[66] Article 46(a) defines an archipelagic state as 'a state constituted wholly by one or more archipelagos and may include other islands', while article 46(b) defines archipelagos as 'a group of islands, including parts of islands, interconnecting waters and other natural features which are so closely interrelated that such islands, waters and other natural features form an intrinsic geographical, economic and political entity, or which historically have been regarded as such'. This raises questions as to whether states that objectively fall within the definition are therefore automatically to be regarded as archipelagic states. The list of states that have not declared that they constitute archipelagic states, although they would appear to conform with the definition, would include the UK and Japan.[67] Bahrain contended in *Qatar v. Bahrain* that it constituted a '*de facto* archipelago or multiple island state' and that it could declare itself an archipelagic state under the Law of the Sea Convention, 1982, enabling it to take advantage of the straight baselines rule contained in article 47. The Court, however, noted that such a claim did not fall within Bahrain's formal submissions and thus it did not need to take a position on the issue.[68] Article 47 provides that an archipelagic state may draw straight archipelagic baselines joining the outermost points of the outermost islands and drying reefs of the archipelago, which would then serve as the relevant baselines for other purposes. There are a number of conditions before this may be done, however, and article 47 provides as follows:

---

[65] O'Connell, 'Mid-Ocean Archipelagos', pp. 23–4, 45–7 and 51, and Whiteman, *Digest*, vol. IV, p. 284. See also the Indonesian Act No. 4 of 18 February 1960 Concerning Indonesian Waters, extracted in Brown, *International Law of the Sea*, vol. II, p. 98; the Philippines Act to Define the Baselines of the Territorial Sea of the Philippines, Act No. 3046 of 17 June 1961, and the Philippines Declaration with respect to the 1982 Convention, *ibid.*, pp. 100–1 (with objections from the USSR and Australia, *ibid.*, pp. 101–2). See, as to the US objection to the Philippines Declaration, Cumulative DUSPIL 1981–8, vol. II, p. 1066, and to claims relating to the Faroes, Galapagos, Portugal and Sudan, Roach and Smith, *United States Responses*, pp. 112 ff.

[66] But see, as regards 'coastal archipelagos', article 4 of the 1958 Convention on the Territorial Sea.

[67] See e.g. Churchill and Lowe, *Law of the Sea*, p. 121.

[68] ICJ Reports, 2001, paras. 181–3.

1. An archipelagic state may draw straight archipelagic baselines joining the outermost points of the outermost islands and drying reefs of the archipelago provided that within such baselines are included the main islands and in areas in which the ratio of the area of the water to the area of the land, including atolls, is between 1 to 1 and 9 to 1.

2. The length of such baselines shall not exceed 100 nautical miles, except that up to 3 per cent of the total number of baselines enclosing any archipelago may exceed that length, up to a maximum length of 125 nautical miles.

3. The drawing of such baselines shall not depart to any appreciable extent from the general configuration of the archipelago.

4. Such baselines shall not be drawn from low-tide elevations, unless lighthouses or similar installations which are permanently above sea level have been built on them or where a low-tide elevation is situated wholly or partly at a distance not exceeding the breadth of the territorial sea from the nearest island.

5. The system of such baselines shall not be applied by an archipelagic state in such a manner as to cut off from the high seas or the exclusive economic zone the territorial sea of another state.

6. If a part of the archipelagic waters of an archipelagic state lies between two parts of an immediately adjacent neighbouring state, existing rights and all other legitimate interests which the latter state has traditionally exercised in such waters and all rights stipulated by agreement between those states shall continue and be respected.

7. For the purpose of computing the ratio of water to land under paragraph 1, land areas may include waters lying within the fringing reefs of islands and atolls, including that part of a steep-sided oceanic plateau which is enclosed or nearly enclosed by a chain of limestone islands and drying reefs lying on the perimeter of the plateau.

8. The baselines drawn in accordance with this article shall be shown on charts of a scale or scales adequate for ascertaining their position. Alternatively, lists of geographic co-ordinates of points, specifying the geodetic datum, may be substituted.

9. The archipelagic states shall give due publicity to such charts or lists of geographical co-ordinates and shall deposit a copy of each such chart or list with the Secretary-General of the United Nations.

All the waters within such baselines are archipelagic waters[69] over which the state has sovereignty,[70] but existing agreements, traditional fishing

---

[69] Article 50 provides that within its archipelagic waters, the archipelagic state may draw closing lines for the delimitation of internal waters.

[70] Article 49.

rights and existing submarine cables must be respected.[71] In addition, ships of all states shall enjoy the rights of innocent passage through archipelagic waters[72] and all the ships and aircraft are to enjoy a right of archipelagic sea lanes passage through such lanes and air routes designated by the archipelagic state for 'continuous and expeditious passage'.[73]

In response to a reported closure in 1988 of the Straits of Sunda and Lombok by Indonesia, the US stressed that the archipelagic provisions of the 1982 Convention reflected customary international law and that those straits were subject to the regime of archipelagic sea lanes passage. Accordingly, it was pointed out that any interference with such passage would violate international law.[74]

The width of the territorial sea[75]

There has historically been considerable disagreement as to how far the territorial sea may extend from the baselines. Originally, the 'cannon-shot' rule defined the width required in terms of the range of shore-based artillery, but at the turn of the nineteenth century, this was transmuted into the 3-mile rule. This was especially supported by the United States and the United Kingdom, and any detraction had to be justified by virtue of historic rights and general acquiescence as, for example, the Scandinavian claim to 4 miles.[76]

However, the issue was much confused by the claims of many coastal states to exercise certain jurisdictional rights for particular purposes: for example, fisheries, customs and immigration controls. It was not until after the First World War that a clear distinction was made between claims to enlarge the width of the territorial sea and claims over particular zones.

Recently the 3-mile rule has been discarded as a rule of general application to be superseded by contending assertions. The 1958 Geneva Convention on the Territorial Sea did not include an article on the subject because of disagreements among the states, while the 1960 Geneva Conference failed to accept a United States–Canadian proposal for a

---

[71] Article 51.   [72] Article 52.

[73] Article 53. For recent state practice, see Churchill and Lowe, *Law of the Sea*, pp. 125 ff.

[74] 83 AJIL, 1989, pp. 559–61. See also Cumulative DUSPIL 1981–8, vol. II, p. 2060.

[75] See e.g. Brown, *International Law of the Sea*, vol. I, p. 43; Churchill and Lowe, *Law of the Sea*, pp. 71 ff., and O'Connell, *International Law of the Sea*, vol. I, chapter 4. See also *Oppenheim's International Law*, p. 611.

[76] See e.g. H. S. K. Kent, 'Historical Origins of the Three-mile Limit', 48 AJIL, 1954, p. 537, and *The Anna* (1805) 165 ER 809. See also *US* v. *Kessler* 1 Baldwin's C C Rep. 15 (1829).

6-mile territorial sea coupled with an exclusive fisheries zone for a further 6 miles by only one vote.[77]

Article 3 of the 1982 Convention, however, notes that all states have the right to establish the breadth of the territorial sea up to a limit not exceeding 12 nautical miles from the baselines. This clearly accords with the evolving practice of states.[78] The UK adopted a 12-mile limit in the Territorial Sea Act 1987, for instance, as did the US by virtue of Proclamation No. 5928 in December 1988.[79]

The juridical nature of the territorial sea[80]

The territorial sea appertains to the territorial sovereignty of the coastal state and thus belongs to it automatically. For example, all newly independent states (with a coast) come to independence with an entitlement to a territorial sea.[81] There have been a number of theories as to the precise legal character of the territorial sea of the coastal state, ranging from treating the territorial sea as part of the *res communis*, but subject to certain rights exercisable by the coastal state, to regarding the territorial sea as part of the coastal state's territorial domain subject to a right of innocent passage by foreign vessels.[82] Nevertheless, it cannot be disputed that the coastal state enjoys sovereign rights over its maritime belt and extensive jurisdictional control, having regard to the relevant rules of international law. The fundamental restriction upon the sovereignty of the coastal state is the right of other nations to innocent passage through the territorial sea, and this distinguishes the territorial sea from the internal waters of the state, which are fully within the unrestricted jurisdiction of the coastal nation.

---

[77] See O'Connell, *International Law of the Sea*, vol. I, pp. 163–4.

[78] The notice issued by the Hydrographic Department of the Royal Navy on 1 January 2008 shows that 156 states or territories claim a 12-mile territorial sea, with 16 states or territories claiming less than this and only 7 states claiming more than 12 miles: see www.ukho.gov.uk/content/amdAttachments/2008/annual_nms/12.pdf. A table of National Maritime Claims issued by the UN shows that, as of 24 October 2007, 141 states claimed a territorial sea of 12 miles or under, with 8 states claiming a larger territorial sea: see A/56/58 and www.un.org/Depts/los/LEGISLATIONANDTREATIES/PDFFILES/.

[79] As to delimitation of the territorial sea, see below, p. 591.

[80] See Brown, *International Law of the Sea*, vol. I, chapter 6; O'Connell, *International Law of the Sea*, vol. I, chapter 3. See also Brownlie, *Principles*, pp. 186 ff., and Churchill and Lowe, *Law of the Sea*, chapter 4.

[81] *Nicaragua v. Honduras*, ICJ Reports, 2007, para. 234.

[82] O'Connell, *International Law of the Sea*, vol. I, pp. 60–7.

Articles 1 and 2 of the Convention on the Territorial Sea, 1958[83] provide that the coastal state's sovereignty extends over its territorial sea and to the airspace and seabed and subsoil thereof, subject to the provisions of the Convention and of international law. The territorial sea forms an undeniable part of the land territory to which it is bound, so that a cession of land will automatically include any band of territorial waters.[84]

The coastal state may, if it so desires, exclude foreign nationals and vessels from fishing within its territorial sea and (subject to agreements to the contrary) from coastal trading (known as cabotage), and reserve these activities for its own citizens.

Similarly the coastal state has extensive powers of control relating to, amongst others, security and customs matters. It should be noted, however, that how far a state chooses to exercise the jurisdiction and sovereignty to which it may lay claim under the principles of international law will depend upon the terms of its own municipal legislation, and some states will not wish to take advantage of the full extent of the powers permitted them within the international legal system.[85]

The right of innocent passage

The right of foreign merchant ships (as distinct from warships) to pass unhindered through the territorial sea of a coast has long been an accepted principle in customary international law, the sovereignty of the coast state notwithstanding. However, the precise extent of the doctrine is blurred and open to contrary interpretation, particularly with respect to the requirement that the passage must be 'innocent'.[86] Article 17 of the 1982 Convention lays down the following principle: 'ships of all states, whether coastal or land-locked, enjoy the right of innocent passage through the territorial sea'.

The doctrine was elaborated in article 14 of the Convention on the Territorial Sea, 1958, which emphasised that the coastal state must not

---

[83] See also article 2 of the 1982 Convention.

[84] See the *Grisbadarna* case, 11 RIAA, p. 147 (1909) and the *Beagle Channel* case, HMSO, 1977; 52 ILR, p. 93. See also Judge McNair, *Anglo-Norwegian Fisheries* case, ICJ Reports, 1951, pp. 116, 160; 18 ILR, pp. 86, 113.

[85] See also *R* v. *Keyn* (1876) 2 Ex.D. 63 and the consequential Territorial Waters Jurisdiction Act 1878.

[86] See Brown, *International Law of the Sea*, vol. I, pp. 53 ff.; Churchill and Lowe, *Law of the Sea*, pp. 82 ff., and O'Connell, *International Law of the Sea*, vol. I, chapter 7. See also *Oppenheim's International Law*, p. 615.

hamper innocent passage and must publicise any dangers to navigation in the territorial sea of which it is aware. Passage is defined as navigation through the territorial sea for the purpose of crossing that sea without entering internal waters or of proceeding to or from that sea without entering internal waters or of proceeding to or from internal waters. It may include temporary stoppages, but only if they are incidental to ordinary navigation or necessitated by distress or *force majeure*.[87]

The coastal state may not impose charges for such passage unless they are in payment for specific services,[88] and ships engaged in passage are required to comply with the coastal state's regulations covering, for example, navigation in so far as they are consistent with international law.[89]

Passage ceases to be innocent under article 14(4) of the 1958 Convention where it is 'prejudicial to the peace, good order or security of the coastal state' and in the case of foreign fishing vessels when they do not observe such laws and regulations as the coastal state may make and publish to prevent these ships from fishing in the territorial sea. In addition, submarines must navigate on the surface and show their flag.

Where passage is not innocent, the coastal state may take steps to prevent it in its territorial sea and, where ships are proceeding to internal waters, it may act to forestall any breach of the conditions to which admission of such ships to internal waters is subject. Coastal states have the power temporarily to suspend innocent passage of foreign vessels where it is essential for security reasons, provided such suspension has been published and provided it does not cover international straits.

Article 19(2) of the 1982 Convention has developed the notion of innocent passage contained in article 14(4) of the 1958 Convention by the provision of examples of prejudicial passage such as the threat or use of force; weapons practice; spying; propaganda; breach of customs, fiscal, immigration or sanitary regulations; wilful and serious pollution; fishing; research or survey activities and interference with coastal communications or other facilities. In addition, a wide-ranging clause includes 'any activity not having a direct bearing on passage'. This would appear to have altered the burden of proof from the coastal state to the other party with regard to innocent passage, as well as being somewhat difficult to define. By virtue of article 24 of the 1982 Convention, coastal states must not hamper the

---

[87] See article 18 of the 1982 Convention. Passage includes crossing the territorial sea in order to call at roadsteads or port facilities outside internal waters: article 18(1) and see the *Nicaragua* case, ICJ Reports, 1986, pp. 12, 111; 76 ILR, p. 1.

[88] Article 26 of the 1982 Convention.   [89] See article 21(4) of the 1982 Convention.

innocent passage of foreign ships, either by imposing requirements upon them which would have the practical effect of denying or impairing the right or by discrimination. Article 17 of the Geneva Convention on the Territorial Sea, 1958 provided that foreign ships exercising the right of innocent passage were to comply with the laws and regulations enacted by the coastal state, in particular those relating to transport and navigation. This was developed in article 21(1) of the 1982 Convention, which expressly provided that the coastal state could adopt laws and regulations concerning innocent passage with regard to:

(a) the safety of navigation and the regulation of maritime traffic;
(b) the protection of navigational aids and facilities and other facilities or installations;
(c) the protection of cables and pipelines;
(d) the conservation of the living resources of the sea;
(e) the prevention of infringement of the fisheries laws and regulations of the coastal state;
(f) the preservation of the environment of the coastal state and the prevention, reduction and control of pollution thereof;
(g) marine scientific research and hydrographic surveys;
(h) the prevention of infringement of the customs, fiscal, immigration or sanitary laws and regulations of the coastal state.

Breach of such laws and regulations will render the offender liable to prosecution, but will not make the passage non-innocent as such, unless article 19 has been infringed.[90]

One major controversy of considerable importance revolves around the issue of whether the passage of warships in peacetime is or is not innocent.[91] The question was further complicated by the omission of an article on the problem in the 1958 Convention on the Territorial Sea, and the discussion of innocent passage in a series of articles headed 'Rules applicable to all ships'. This has led some writers to assert that this includes warships by inference, but other authorities maintain that such an important issue could not be resolved purely by omission and inference, especially in view of the reservations by many states to the Convention rejecting the principle of innocent passage for warships and in the light

---

[90] Under article 22 of the 1982 Convention, the coastal state may establish designated sea lanes and traffic separation schemes in its territorial sea. See UKMIL, 64 BYIL, 1993, p. 688 for details of traffic separation schemes around the UK.

[91] See e.g. O'Connell, *International Law of the Sea*, vol. I, pp. 274–97. See also *Oppenheim's International Law*, p. 618.

of comments in the various preparatory materials to the 1958 Geneva Convention.[92]

It was primarily the Western states, with their preponderant naval power, that historically maintained the existence of a right of innocent passage for warships, to the opposition of the then communist and Third World nations. However, having regard to the rapid growth in their naval capacity and the ending of the Cold War, Soviet attitudes underwent a change.[93]

In September 1989, the US and the USSR issued a joint 'Uniform Interpretation of the Rules of International Law Governing Innocent Passage'.[94] This reaffirmed that the relevant rules of international law were stated in the 1982 Convention. It then provided that:

> [a]ll ships, including warships, regardless of cargo, armament or means of propulsion, enjoy the right of innocent passage through the territorial sea in accordance with international law, for which neither prior notification nor authorisation is required.

The statement noted that where a ship in passage through the territorial sea was not engaged in any of the activities laid down in article 19(2), it was 'in innocent passage' since that provision was exhaustive. Ships in passage were under an obligation to comply with the laws and regulations of the coastal state adopted in conformity with articles 21, 22, 23 and 25 of the 1982 Convention, provided such laws and regulations did not have the effect of denying or impairing the exercise of the right of innocent passage.

This important statement underlines the view that the list of activities laid down in article 19(2) is exhaustive so that a ship passing through the territorial sea not engaging in any of these activities is in innocent passage. It also lends considerable weight to the view that warships have indeed

---

[92] O'Connell, *International Law of the Sea*, vol. I, pp. 290–2. See also Brownlie, *Principles*, pp. 188–9.

[93] See also Churchill and Lowe, *Law of the Sea*, pp. 54–6. The issue was left open at the Third UN Conference on the Law of the Sea and does not therefore appear in the 1982 Convention. Note, however, that Western and communist states both proposed including a reference to warships in early sessions of the Conference: see UNCLOS III, Official Records, vol. III, pp. 183, 203, 192 and 196. See also article 29(2) of the 1975 Informal Single Negotiating Text. The right of warships to innocent passage was maintained by the US following an incident during which four US warships sailed through Soviet territorial waters off the Crimean coast: see *The Times*, 19 March 1986, p. 5.

[94] See 84 AJIL, 1990, p. 239.

a right of innocent passage through the territorial sea and one that does not necessitate prior notification or authorisation.[95]

Jurisdiction over foreign ships [96]

Where foreign ships are in passage through the territorial sea, the coastal state may only exercise its criminal jurisdiction as regards the arrest of any person or the investigation of any matter connected with a crime committed on board ship in defined situations. These are enumerated in article 27(1) of the 1982 Convention, reaffirming article 19(1) of the 1958 Convention on the Territorial Sea, as follows:

> (a) if the consequences of the crime extend to the coastal state; or (b) if the crime is of a kind likely to disturb the peace of the country or the good order of the territorial sea; or (c) if the assistance of the local authorities has been requested by the master of the ship or by a diplomatic agent or consular officer of the country of the flag state; or (d) if such measures are necessary for the suppression of illicit traffic in narcotic drugs or pyschotropic substances.[97]

However, if the ship is passing through the territorial sea having left the internal waters of the coastal state, then the coastal state may act in any manner prescribed by its laws as regards arrest or investigation on board ship and is not restricted by the terms of article 27(1). But the authorities of the coastal state cannot act where the crime was committed before the ship entered the territorial sea, providing the ship is not entering or has not entered internal waters.

Under article 28 of the 1982 Convention, the coastal state should not stop or divert a foreign ship passing through its territorial sea for the purpose of exercising civil jurisdiction in relation to a person on board ship, nor levy execution against or arrest the ship, unless obligations are involved which were assumed by the ship itself in the course of, or for the

---

[95] See also Cumulative DUSPIL 1981–8, vol. II, pp. 1844 ff., and UKMIL, 65 BYIL, 1994, pp. 642–7. See also Cumulative DUSPIL 1981–8, vol. II, p. 1854 with regard to the claim by some states that the passage of nuclear-powered ships or ships carrying nuclear substances through territorial waters requires prior authorisation or prior consent. See also UKMIL, 62 BYIL, 1991, pp. 632–3 with regard to UK views on claims concerning prior authorisation or consent with regard to the passage of ships carrying hazardous wastes.

[96] See e.g. O'Connell, *International Law of the Sea*, vol. I, chapters 23 and 24. See also *Oppenheim's International Law*, p. 620, and Brown, *International Law of the Sea*, vol. I, p. 62. Note that these rules are applicable to foreign ships and government commercial ships.

[97] The latter phrase was added by article 27(1) of the 1982 Convention.

purpose of, its voyage through waters of the coastal state, or unless the ship is passing through the territorial sea on its way from internal waters. The above rules do not, however, prejudice the right of a state to levy execution against or to arrest, for the purpose of any civil proceedings, a foreign ship lying in the territorial sea or passing through the territorial sea after leaving internal waters.[98]

Warships and other government ships operated for non-commercial purposes are immune from the jurisdiction of the coastal state, although they may be required to leave the territorial sea immediately for breach of rules governing passage and the flag state will bear international responsibility in cases of loss or damage suffered as a result.[99]

International straits[100]

Article 16(4) of the 1958 Convention on the Territorial Sea declares that:

> there shall be no suspension of the innocent passage of foreign ships through straits which are used for international navigation between one part of the high seas and another part of the high seas or the territorial sea of a foreign state.

This provision should be read in conjunction with the decision in the *Corfu Channel* case.[101] In this case, British warships passing through the straits were fired upon by Albanian guns. Several months later, an augmented force of cruisers and destroyers sailed through the North Corfu Channel and two of them were badly damaged after striking mines. This impelled the British authorities to sweep the Channel three weeks later,

---

[98] See also article 20 of the 1958 Convention on the Territorial Sea and the Contiguous Zone.

[99] Articles 29–32 of the 1982 Convention. See also articles 21–3 of the 1958 Convention on the Territorial Sea and the Contiguous Zone.

[100] See e.g. Brown, *International Law of the Sea*, vol. I, chapter 7; Churchill and Lowe, *Law of the Sea*, chapter 5; O'Connell, *International Law of the Sea*, vol. I, chapter 8; R. Lapidoth, *Les Détroits en Droit International*, Paris, 1972; T. L. Koh, *Straits in International Navigation*, London, 1982; J. N. Moore, 'The Regime of Straits and the Third United Nations Conference on the Law of the Sea', 74 AJIL, 1980, p. 77; W. M. Reisman, 'The Regime of Straits and National Security', *ibid.*, p. 48; H. Caminos, 'Le Régime des Détroits dans la Convention des Nations Unies de 1982 sur le Droit de la Mer', 205 HR, 1987 V, p. 9; S. N. Nandan and D. H. Anderson, 'Straits Used for International Navigation: A Commentary on Part III of the UN Convention on the Law of the Sea 1982', 60 BYIL, 1989, p. 159; *Oppenheim's International Law*, p. 633; Nguyen Quoc Dinh *et al.*, *Droit International Public*, p. 1168, and B. B. Jia, *The Regime of Straits in International Law*, Oxford, 1998.

[101] ICJ Reports, 1949, p. 4; 16 AD, p. 155.

and to clear it of some twenty mines of German manufacture. The Court, in a much-quoted passage, emphasised that:

> states in time of peace have a right to send their warships through straits used for international navigation between two parts of the high seas without the previous authorisation of a coastal state, provided that the passage is innocent.[102]

It was also noted that the minesweeping operation was in no way 'innocent' and was indeed a violation of Albania's sovereignty, although the earlier passages by British naval vessels were legal.[103]

The 1982 Convention established a new regime for straits used for international navigation. The principle is reaffirmed that the legal status of the waters of the straits in question is unaffected by the provisions dealing with passage.[104]

A new right of transit passage is posited with respect to straits used for international navigation between one part of the high seas or an exclusive economic zone and another part of the high seas or an exclusive economic zone.[105] It involves the exercise of the freedom of navigation and overflight solely for the purpose of continuous and expeditious transit of the strait and does not preclude passage through the strait to enter or leave a state bordering that strait.[106] States bordering the straits in question are not to hamper or suspend transit passage.[107]

There are three exceptions to the right: under article 36 where a route exists through the strait through the high seas or economic zone of similar navigational convenience; under article 38(1) in the case of a strait formed by an island of a state bordering the strait and its mainland, where there exists seaward of the island a route through the high seas or economic zone of similar navigational convenience; and under article 45 where straits connect an area of the high seas or economic zone with the territorial

---

[102] *Ibid.*, p. 28; 16 AD, p. 161. The Court emphasised that the decisive criterion regarding the definition of 'strait' was the geographical situation of the strait as connecting two parts of the high seas, coupled with the fact that it was actually used for international navigation, *ibid.* Note that article 16(4) added to the customary rights the right of innocent passage from the high seas to the territorial sea of a state. This was of particular importance to the question of access through the straits of Tiran to the Israeli port of Eilat: see further below, note 115.

[103] *Ibid.*, pp. 30–1, 33; 16 AD, pp. 163, 166. Note the final settlement of the case, UKMIL, 63 BYIL, 1992, p. 781.

[104] Articles 34 and 35.

[105] Article 37. See also R. P. Anand, 'Transit Passage and Overflight in International Straits', 26 IJIL, 1986, p. 72, and *Oppenheim's International Law*, p. 636.

[106] Article 38.   [107] Article 44.

sea of a third state. Ships and aircraft in transit must observe the relevant international regulations and refrain from all activities other than those incidental to their normal modes of continuous and expeditious transit, unless rendered necessary by *force majeure* or by distress.[108] Thus, although there is no formal requirement for 'innocent' transit passage, the effect of articles 38 and 39 would appear to be to render transit passage subject to the same constraints. Under article 45, the regime of innocent passage will apply with regard to straits used for international navigation excluded from the transit passage provisions by article 38(1) and to international straits between a part of the high seas or economic zone and the territorial sea of a foreign state. In such cases, there shall be no suspension of the right to innocent passage.[109] The regime of transit passage specifically allows for the passage of aircraft and probably for underwater submarines, while there are fewer constraints on conduct during passage and less power for the coastal state to control passage than in the case of innocent passage.[110] Transit passage cannot be suspended for security or indeed any other reasons.[111]

It is unclear whether the right of transit passage has passed into customary law. Practice is as yet ambiguous.[112] Some states have provided explicitly for rights of passage through international straits. When the UK extended its territorial sea in 1987 to 12 miles, one of the consequences was that the high sea corridor through the Straits of Dover disappeared. The following year an agreement was signed with France which related to the delimitation of the territorial sea in the Straits of Dover and a joint declaration was issued in which both governments recognised:

> rights of unimpeded transit passage for merchant vessels, state vessels and, in particular, warships following their normal mode of navigation, as well as the right of overflight for aircraft, in the Straits of Dover. It is understood that, in accordance with the principles governing this regime under the rules of international law, such passage will be exercised in a continuous and expeditious manner.[113]

---

[108] Article 39. Under articles 41 and 42, the coastal state may designate sea lanes and traffic separation schemes through international straits.

[109] Article 45(2).

[110] See articles 38–42. See also, as to the differences between the regimes of innocent passage through the territorial sea, transit passage and archipelagic sea lanes passage, Nandan and Anderson, 'Straits', p. 169.

[111] Article 44.

[112] See Churchill and Lowe, *Law of the Sea*, p. 113, but cf. O. Schachter, 'International Law in Theory and Practice', 178 HR, 1982, pp. 9, 281.

[113] Cmnd 557. See also 38 ICLQ, 1989, pp. 416–17 and AFDI, 1988, p. 727.

A number of straits are subject to special regimes, which are unaffected by the above provisions.[114] One important example is the Montreux Convention of 1936 governing the Bosphorus and Dardanelles Straits. This provides for complete freedom of transit or navigation for merchant vessels during peacetime and for freedom of transit during daylight hours for some warships giving prior notification to Turkey.[115]

The contiguous zone[116]

Historically some states have claimed to exercise certain rights over particular zones of the high seas. This has involved some diminution of the principle of the freedom of the high seas as the jurisdiction of the coastal state has been extended into areas of the high seas contiguous to the territorial sea, albeit for defined purposes only. Such restricted jurisdiction zones have been established or asserted for a number of reasons: for instance, to prevent infringement of customs, immigration or sanitary laws of the coastal state, or to conserve fishing stocks in a particular area, or to enable the coastal state to have exclusive or principal rights to the resources of the proclaimed zone.

In each case they enable the coastal state to protect what it regards as its vital or important interests without having to extend the boundaries of its territorial sea further into the high seas. It is thus a compromise between the interests of the coastal state and the interests of other maritime nations

---

[114] Article 35(c).

[115] See e.g. Churchill and Lowe, *Law of the Sea*, pp. 114 ff. See also UKMIL, 57 BYIL, 1986, p. 581, and F. A. Vali, *The Turkish Straits and NATO*, Stanford, 1972. Note that the dispute as to the status of the Strait of Tiran and the Gulf of Aqaba between Israel and its Arab neighbours was specifically dealt with in the treaties of peace. Article 5(2) of the Israel–Egypt Treaty of Peace, 1979 and article 14(3) of the Israel–Jordan Treaty of Peace, 1994 both affirm that the Strait and Gulf are international waterways open to all nations for unimpeded and non-suspendable freedom of navigation and overflight. As to the US–USSR Agreement on the Bering Straits Region, see 28 ILM, 1989, p. 1429. See also, as to the Great Belt dispute between Finland and Denmark, M. Koskenniemi, 'L'Affaire du Passage par le Grand-Belt', AFDI, 1992, p. 905. See, as to other particular straits, e.g. S. C. Truver, *Gibraltar and the Mediterranean*, Alphen, 1982; M. A. Morris, *The Strait of Magellan*, Dordrecht, 1989; G. Alexander, *The Baltic Straits*, Alphen, 1982, and M. Leiffer, *Malacca, Singapore and Indonesia*, Alphen, 1978.

[116] See A. V. Lowe, 'The Development of the Concept of the Contiguous Zone', 52 BYIL, 1981, p. 109; Brown, *International Law of the Sea*, vol. I, chapter 9; Churchill and Lowe, *Law of the Sea*, chapter 7, and O'Connell, *International Law of the Sea*, vol. II, chapter 27. See also S. Oda, 'The Concept of the Contiguous Zone', ICLQ, 1962, p. 131; *Oppenheim's International Law*, p. 625, and Nguyen Quoc Dinh *et al.*, *Droit International Public*, p. 1174.

seeking to maintain the status of the high seas, and it marks a balance of competing claims. The extension of rights beyond the territorial sea has, however, been seen not only in the context of preventing the infringement of particular domestic laws, but also increasingly as a method of maintaining and developing the economic interests of the coastal state regarding maritime resources. The idea of a contiguous zone (i.e. a zone bordering upon the territorial sea) was virtually formulated as an authoritative and consistent doctrine in the 1930s by the French writer Gidel,[117] and it appeared in the Convention on the Territorial Sea. Article 24 declared that:

> In a zone of the high seas contiguous to its territorial sea, the coastal state may exercise the control necessary to:
>
> (a) Prevent infringement of its customs, fiscal, immigration or sanitary regulations within its territory or territorial sea;
> (b) Punish infringement of the above regulations committed within its territory or territorial sea.

Thus, such contiguous zones were clearly differentiated from claims to full sovereignty as parts of the territorial sea, by being referred to as part of the high seas over which the coastal state may exercise particular rights. Unlike the territorial sea, which is automatically attached to the land territory of the state, contiguous zones have to be specifically claimed.

While sanitary and immigration laws are relatively recent additions to the rights enforceable over zones of the high seas and may be regarded as stemming by analogy from customs regulations, in practice they are really only justifiable since the 1958 Convention. On the other hand, customs zones have a long history and are recognised in customary international law as well. Many states, including the UK and the USA, have enacted legislation to enforce customs regulations over many years, outside their territorial waters and within certain areas, in order to suppress smuggling which appeared to thrive when faced only with territorial limits of 3 or 4 miles.[118]

Contiguous zones, however, were limited to a maximum of 12 miles from the baselines from which the territorial sea is measured. So if the

---

[117] A. Gidel, 'La Mer Territoriale et la Zone Contigue', 48 HR, 1934, pp. 137, 241.
[118] E.g. the British Hovering Acts of the eighteenth and nineteenth centuries. See O'Connell, *International Law of the Sea*, vol. II, pp. 1034–8, and the similar US legislation, *ibid.*, pp. 1038 ff.

coastal state already claimed a territorial sea of 12 miles, the question of contiguous zones would not arise.

This limitation, plus the restriction of jurisdiction to customs, sanitary and immigration matters, is the reason for the decline in the relevance of contiguous zones in international affairs in recent years. Under article 33 of the 1982 Convention, however, a coastal state may claim a contiguous zone (for the same purpose as the 1958 provisions) up to 24 nautical miles from the baselines. In view of the accepted 12 miles territorial sea limit, such an extension was required in order to preserve the concept. One crucial difference is that while under the 1958 system the contiguous zone was part of the high seas, under the 1982 Convention it would form part of the exclusive economic zone complex.[119] This will clearly have an impact upon the nature of the zone.

The exclusive economic zone[120]

This zone has developed out of earlier, more tentative claims, particularly relating to fishing zones,[121] and as a result of developments in the negotiating processes leading to the 1982 Convention.[122] It marks a compromise between those states seeking a 200-mile territorial sea and those wishing a more restricted system of coastal state power.

One of the major reasons for the call for a 200-mile exclusive economic zone has been the controversy over fishing zones. The 1958 Geneva Convention on the Territorial Sea did not reach agreement on the creation of fishing zones and article 24 of the Convention does not give exclusive

---

[119] See article 55, which states that the exclusive economic zone is 'an area beyond and adjacent to the territorial seas'. The notice issued by the Hydrographic Department of the Royal Navy on 1 January 2008 shows that eighty-one states or territories claim a contiguous zone: see www.ukho.gov.uk/content/amdAttachments/2008/annual_nms/12.pdf.

[120] See e.g. *The Exclusive Economic Zone and the United Nations Law of the Sea Convention, 1982–2000* (eds. E. Franckx and P. Gautier), Brussels, 2003; Brown, *International Law of the Sea*, vol. I, chapters 10 and 11; Churchill and Lowe, *Law of the Sea*, chapter 9; D. J. Attard, *The Exclusive Economic Zone in International Law*, Oxford, 1986; O'Connell, *International Law of the Sea*, vol. I, chapter 15; *Oppenheim's International Law*, p. 782, and Nguyen Quoc Dinh *et al.*, *Droit International Public*, p. 1175. See also F. Orrego Vicuña, 'La Zone Économique Exclusive', 199 HR, 1986 IV, p. 9; Orrego Vicuña, *The Exclusive Economic Zone, Regime and Legal Nature under International Law*, Cambridge, 1989; B. Kwiatowska, *The 200 Mile Exclusive Economic Zone in the New Law of the Sea*, Dordrecht, 1989; R. W. Smith, *Exclusive Economic Zone Claims. An Analysis and Primary Documents*, Dordrecht, 1986, and F. Rigaldies, 'La Zone Économique Exclusive dans la Pratique des États', Canadian YIL, 1997, p. 3.

[121] O'Connell, *International Law of the Sea*, vol. I, chapter 14.   [122] *Ibid.*, pp. 559 ff.

fishing rights in the contiguous zone. However, increasing numbers of states have claimed fishing zones of widely varying widths. The European Fisheries Convention, 1964, which was implemented in the UK by the Fishing Limits Act 1964, provided that the coastal state has the exclusive right to fish and exclusive jurisdiction in matters of fisheries in a 6-mile belt from the baseline of the territorial sea; while within the belt between 6 and 12 miles from the baseline, other parties to the Convention have the right to fish, provided they had habitually fished in that belt between January 1953 and December 1962. This was an attempt to reconcile the interests of the coastal state with those of other states who could prove customary fishing operations in the relevant area. In view of the practice of many states in accepting at one time or another a 12-mile exclusive fishing zone, either for themselves or for some other states, it seems clear that there has already emerged an international rule to that effect. Indeed, the International Court in the *Fisheries Jurisdiction* cases[123] stated that the concept of the fishing zone, the area in which a state may claim exclusive jurisdiction independently of its territorial sea for this purpose, had crystallised as customary law in recent years and especially since the 1960 Geneva Conference, and that 'the extension of that fishing zone up to a twelve mile limit from the baselines appears now to be generally accepted'. That much is clear, but the question was whether international law recognised such a zone in excess of 12 miles.

In 1972, concerned at the proposals regarding the long-term effects of the depletion of fishing stocks around her coasts, Iceland proclaimed unilaterally a 50-mile exclusive fishing zone. The UK and the Federal Republic of Germany referred the issue to the ICJ and specifically requested the Court to decide whether or not Iceland's claim was contrary to international law.

The Court did not answer that question, but rather held that Iceland's fishing regulations extending the zone were not binding upon the UK and West Germany, since they had in no way acquiesced in them. However, by implication the ICJ based its judgment on the fact that there did not exist any rule of international law permitting the establishment of a 50-mile fishing zone. Similarly, it appeared that there was no rule prohibiting claims beyond 12 miles and that the validity of such claims would depend upon all relevant facts of the case and the degree of recognition by other states.

---

[123] ICJ Reports, 1974, pp. 8, 175; 55 ILR, p. 238.

The Court emphasised instead the notion of preferential rights, which it regarded as a principle of customary international law. Such rights arose where the coastal state was 'in a situation of special dependence on coastal fisheries'.[124] However, this concept was overtaken by developments at the UN Conference and the 1982 Convention. Article 55 of the 1982 Convention provides that the exclusive economic zone is an area beyond and adjacent to the territorial sea, subject to the specific legal regime established under the Convention.

Under article 56, the coastal state in the economic zone has *inter alia*:

(a) sovereign rights for the purpose of exploring and exploiting, conserving and managing the natural resources, whether living[125] or non-living, of the waters superjacent to the seabed and of the seabed and its subsoil and with regard to other activities for the economic exploitation and exploration of the zone, such as the production of energy from the water, currents and winds;

(b) jurisdiction with regard to (i) the architecture and use of artificial islands, installations and structures;[126] (ii) marine scientific research;[127] (iii) the protection and preservation of the marine environment.[128]

Article 55 provides that the zone starts from the outer limit of the territorial sea, but by article 57 shall not extend beyond 200 nautical miles from the baselines from which the breadth of the territorial sea is measured. Accordingly, in reality, the zone itself would be no more than 188 nautical miles where the territorial sea was 12 nautical miles, but rather more where the territorial sea of the coastal state was less than 12 miles. Where the relevant waters between neighbouring states are less than 400 miles, delimitation becomes necessary.[129] Islands generate economic zones, unless they consist of no more than rocks which cannot sustain human habitation.[130]

Article 58 lays down the rights and duties of other states in the exclusive economic zone. These are basically the high seas freedom of navigation, overflight and laying of submarine cables and pipelines. It is also provided that in exercising their rights and performing their duties, states should have due regard to the rights, duties and laws of the coastal state.

124 ICJ Reports, 1974, pp. 23–9; 55 ILR, p. 258.
125 See also articles 61–9.   126 See also article 60.
127 See further Part XIII of the Convention and see Churchill and Lowe, *Law of the Sea*, chapter 15.
128 See further Part XII of the Convention and see Churchill and Lowe, *Law of the Sea*, chapter 14.
129 See further below, p. 590.
130 Article 121(3). See also *Qatar v. Bahrain*, ICJ Reports, 2001, pp. 40, 97 and above, p. 565.

In cases of conflict over the attribution of rights and jurisdiction in the zone, the resolution is to be on the basis of equity and in the light of all the relevant circumstances.[131] Article 60(2) provides that in the exclusive economic zone, the coastal state has jurisdiction to apply customs laws and regulations in respect of artificial islands, installations and structures. The International Tribunal for the Law of the Sea took the view in *M/V Saiga (No. 2) (Admissibility and Merits)* that a coastal state was not competent to apply its customs laws in respect of other parts of the economic zone.[132] Accordingly, by applying its customs laws to a customs radius which included parts of the economic zone, Guinea had acted contrary to the Law of the Sea Convention.[133]

A wide variety of states have in the last two decades claimed exclusive economic zones of 200 miles.[134] A number of states that have not made such a claim have proclaimed fishing zones.[135] It would appear that such is the number and distribution of states claiming economic zones, that the existence of the exclusive economic zone as a rule of customary law is firmly established. This is underlined by the comment of the International Court of Justice in the *Libya/Malta Continental Shelf* case[136] that 'the institution of the exclusive economic zone . . . is shown by the practice of states to have become a part of customary law'.[137]

In addition to such zones, some other zones have been announced by states over areas of the seas. Canada has, for example, claimed a 100-mile-wide zone along her Arctic coastline as a special, pollution-free zone.[138]

---

[131] Article 59. [132] 120 ILR, pp. 143, 190. [133] *Ibid.*, p. 192.

[134] The Hydrographic Department of the Royal Navy noted that as of 1 January 2008, 126 states and territories had proclaimed 200-mile economic zones: see www.ukho.gov.uk/content/amdAttachments/2008/annual_nms/12.pdf. No state has appeared to claim an economic zone of a different width. See also the US Declaration of an exclusive economic zone in March 1983, which did not, however, assert a right of jurisdiction over marine scientific research over the zone, 22 ILM, 1983, pp. 461 ff. On 22 September 1992, eight North Sea littoral states and the European Commission adopted a Ministerial Declaration on the Coordinated Extension of Jurisdiction in the North Sea in which it was agreed that these states would establish exclusive economic zones if they had not already done so, UKMIL, 63 BYIL, 1992, p. 755.

[135] The Hydrographic Department of the Royal Navy noted that as of 1 January 2008, forty-five states and territories had proclaimed fishery zones of varying breadths up to 200 miles: see www.ukho.gov.uk/content/amdAttachments/2008/annual_nms/12.pdf.

[136] ICJ Reports, 1985, p. 13; 81 ILR, p. 238.

[137] ICJ Reports, 1985, p. 33; 81 ILR, p. 265. See also the *Tunisia/Libya* case, ICJ Reports, 1982, pp. 18, 74; 67 ILR, pp. 4, 67.

[138] See O'Connell, *International Law of the Sea*, vol. II, pp. 1022–5. See also the Canadian Arctic Water Pollution Prevention Act 1970. The US has objected to this jurisdiction: see e.g. *Keesing's Contemporary Archives*, pp. 23961 and 24129. The Canadian claim was reiterated in September 1985, *ibid.*, p. 33984.

Certain states have also asserted rights over what have been termed security or neutrality zones,[139] but these have never been particularly well received and are rare.

In an unusual arrangement, pursuant to a US–USSR Maritime Boundary Agreement of 1 June 1990, it was provided that each party would exercise sovereign rights and jurisdiction derived from the exclusive economic zone jurisdiction of the other party in a 'special area' on the other party's side of the maritime boundary in order to ensure that all areas within 200 miles of either party's coast would fall within the resource jurisdiction of one party or the other. It would appear that jurisdiction over three special areas within the USSR's 200-mile economic zone and one special area within the US's 200-mile economic zone were so transferred.[140]

The continental shelf[141]

The continental shelf is a geological expression referring to the ledges that project from the continental landmass into the seas and which are covered with only a relatively shallow layer of water (some 150–200 metres) and which eventually fall away into the ocean depths (some thousands of metres deep). These ledges or shelves take up some 7 to 8 per cent of the total area of ocean and their extent varies considerably from place to place. Off the western coast of the United States, for instance, it is less than 5 miles wide, while, on the other hand, the whole of the underwater area of the North Sea and Persian Gulf consists of shelf.

The vital fact about the continental shelves is that they are rich in oil and gas resources and quite often are host to extensive fishing grounds.

---

[139] O'Connell, *International Law of the Sea*, vol. I, p. 578, note 95 regarding North Korea's proclamation of a 50-mile security zone in 1977. See also Cumulative DUSPIL 1981–8, vol. II, pp. 1750 ff. detailing US practice objecting to peacetime security or military zones. Note also the establishment of the 'exclusion zone' around the Falkland Islands in 1982: see 22 HC Deb., cols. 296–7, 28 April 1982. See e.g. R. P. Barston and P. W. Birnie, 'The Falkland Islands/Islas Malvinas Conflict. A Question of Zones', 7 *Marine Policy*, 1983, p. 14.

[140] 84 AJIL, 1990, pp. 885–7.

[141] See e.g. Brown, *International Law of the Sea*, vol. I, chapters 10 and 11; O'Connell, *International Law of the Sea*, vol. I, chapter 13; Churchill and Lowe, *Law of the Sea*, chapter 8; Z. J. Slouka, *International Custom and the Continental Shelf*, The Hague, 1968; C. Vallée, *Le Plateau Continental dans le Droit International Positif*, Paris, 1971; V. Marotta Rangel, 'Le Plateau Continental dans la Convention de 1982 sur le Droit de la Mer', 194 HR, 1985 V, p. 269, and H. Lauterpacht, 'Sovereignty over Submarine Areas', 27 BYIL, 1950, p. 376. See also *Oppenheim's International Law*, p. 764, and Nguyen Quoc Dinh *et al.*, *Droit International Public*, p. 1183.

This stimulated a round of appropriations by coastal states in the years following the Second World War, which gradually altered the legal status of the continental shelf from being part of the high seas and available for exploitation by all states until its current recognition as exclusive to the coastal state.

The first move in this direction, and the one that led to a series of similar and more extensive claims, was the Truman Proclamation of 1945.[142] This pointed to the technological capacity to exploit the riches of the shelf and the need to establish a recognised jurisdiction over such resources, and declared that the coastal state was entitled to such jurisdiction for a number of reasons: first, because utilisation or conservation of the resources of the subsoil and seabed of the continental shelf depended upon co-operation from the shore; secondly, because the shelf itself could be regarded as an extension of the land mass of the coastal state, and its resources were often merely an extension into the sea of deposits lying within the territory; and finally, because the coastal state, for reasons of security, was profoundly interested in activities off its shores which would be necessary to utilise the resources of the shelf.

Accordingly, the US government proclaimed that it regarded the 'natural resources of the subsoil and seabed of the continental shelf beneath the high seas but contiguous to the coasts of the United States as appertaining to the United States, subject to its jurisdiction and control'. However, this would in no way affect the status of the waters above the continental shelf as high seas.

This proclamation precipitated a whole series of claims by states to their continental shelves, some in similar terms to the US assertions, and others in substantially wider terms. Argentina and El Salvador, for example, claimed not only the shelf but also the waters above and the airspace. Chile and Peru, having no continental shelf to speak of, claimed sovereignty over the seabed, subsoil and waters around their coasts to a limit of 200 miles, although this occasioned vigorous protests by many states.[143] The problems were discussed over many years, leading to the 1958 Geneva Convention on the Continental Shelf.[144]

---

[142] Whiteman, *Digest*, vol. IV, p. 756.

[143] *Ibid.*, pp. 794–9 and see also *Oppenheim's International Law*, pp. 768–9.

[144] Note that in the *Abu Dhabi* case, the arbitrator declared that the doctrine of the continental shelf in 1951 was not yet a rule of international law, 18 ILR, p. 144. See also to the same effect (with regard to 1949), *Reference Re: The Seabed and Subsoil of the Continental Shelf Offshore Newfoundland*, 5 DLR (46), p. 385; 86 ILR, p. 593 *per* Supreme Court of Canada (1984).

In the *North Sea Continental Shelf* cases,[145] the Court noted that:

> the rights of the coastal state in respect of the area of continental shelf that
> constitutes a natural prolongation of its land territory into and under the
> sea exist *ipso facto* and *ab initio*, by virtue of its sovereignty over the land,
> and as an extension of it in an exercise of sovereign rights for the purpose
> of exploring the seabed and exploiting its natural resources. In short there
> is here an inherent right.

The development of the concept of the exclusive economic zone has to
some extent confused the issue, since under article 56 of the 1982 Convention the coastal state has sovereign rights over all the natural resources
of its exclusive economic zone, including the seabed resources.[146] Accordingly, states possess two sources of rights with regard to the seabed,[147]
although claims with regard to the economic zone, in contrast to the continental shelf, need to be specifically made. It is also possible, as will be
seen, that the geographical extent of the shelf may be different from that
of the 200-mile economic zone.

Definition

Article 1 of the 1958 Convention on the Continental Shelf defined the
shelf in terms of its exploitability rather than relying upon the accepted
geological definition, noting that the expression referred to the seabed
and subsoil of the submarine areas adjacent to the coast but outside the
territorial sea to a depth of 200 metres or 'beyond that limit to where the
depth of the superjacent waters admits of the exploitation of the natural
resources of the said areas'.

This provision caused problems, since developing technology rapidly
reached a position to extract resources to a much greater depth than 200
metres, and this meant that the outer limits of the shelf, subject to the
jurisdiction of the coastal state, were consequently very unclear. Article
1 was, however, regarded as reflecting customary law by the Court in
the *North Sea Continental Shelf* case.[148] It is also important to note that
the basis of title to continental shelf is now accepted as the geographical

---

[145] ICJ Reports, 1969, pp. 3, 22; 41 ILR, pp. 29, 51.   [146] See above, p. 582.
[147] Note that the International Court in the *Libya/Malta Continental Shelf* case, ICJ Reports,
1985, pp. 13, 33; 81 ILR, pp. 238, 265, stated that the two concepts were 'linked together
in modern law'.
[148] ICJ Reports, 1969, pp. 3, 39; 41 ILR, pp. 29, 68.

criterion, and not reliance upon, for example, occupation or effective control. The Court emphasised this and declared that:

> The submarine areas concerned may be deemed to be actually part of the territory over which the coastal state already has dominion in the sense that although covered with water, they are a prolongation or continuation of that territory, an extension of it under the sea.[149]

This approach has, however, been somewhat modified. Article 76(1) of the 1982 Convention provides as to the outer limit of the continental shelf that:

> [t]he continental shelf of a coastal state comprises the seabed and subsoil of the submarine areas that extend beyond its territorial sea throughout the natural prolongation of its land territory to the outer edge of the continental margin, or to a distance of 200 nautical miles from the baselines from which the breadth of the territorial sea is measured where the outer edge of continental margin does not extend up to that distance.[150]

Thus, an arbitrary, legal and non-geographical definition is provided. Where the continental margin actually extends beyond 200 miles, geographical factors are to be taken into account in establishing the limit, which in any event shall not exceed either 350 miles from the baselines or 100 miles from the 2,500-metre isobath.[151] Where the shelf does not extend as far as 200 miles from the coast, natural prolongation is complemented as a guiding principle by that of distance.[152] Not surprisingly, this complex formulation has caused difficulty[153] and, in an attempt to provide a mechanism to resolve problems, the Convention established a Commission on the Limits of the Continental Shelf, consisting of

---

[149] ICJ Reports, 1969, p. 31; 41 ILR, p. 60.

[150] See article 76(3) for a definition of the continental margin. See also D. N. Hutchinson, 'The Seaward Limit to Continental Shelf', 56 BYIL, 1985, p. 133, and Brown, *International Law of the Sea*, vol. I, p. 140.

[151] Article 76(4), (5), (6), (7), (8) and (9). See also Annex II to the Final Act concerning the special situation for a state where the average distance at which the 200-metre isobath occurs is not more than 20 nautical miles and the greater proportion of the sedimentary rock of the continental margin lies beneath the rise.

[152] See the *Libya/Malta Continental Shelf* case, ICJ Reports, 1985, pp. 13, 33–4; 81 ILR, pp. 238, 265–6. See also the *Tunisia/Libya* case, ICJ Reports, 1982, pp. 18, 61; 67 ILR, pp. 4, 54 and the *Gulf of Maine* case, ICJ Reports, 1984, pp. 246, 277; 71 ILR, pp. 57, 104.

[153] See e.g. Churchill and Lowe, *Law of the Sea*, p. 149, and Nguyen Quoc Dinh *et al.*, *Droit International Public*, p. 1187. There are particular problems, for instance, with regard to the meaning of the terms 'oceanic ridges', 'submarine ridges' and 'submarine elevations' appearing in article 76(3) and (6).

twenty-one experts elected by the states parties. Article 4 of Annex II to the Convention provides that a coastal state intending to establish the outer limits to its continental shelf beyond 200 nautical miles is obliged to submit particulars of such limits to the Commission along with support- ing scientific and technical data as soon as possible but in any case within ten years of the entry into force of the Convention for that state. The limits of the shelf established by a coastal state on the basis of these recommen- dations are final and binding.[154] The first submission to the Commission was made by the Russian Federation on 21 December 2001.[155] In support of this claim, Russian explorers planted the national flag on the seabed below the North Pole on 2 August 2007, arguing that parts of underwater mountains underneath the Pole were extensions of the Eurasian conti- nent.[156] A joint submission in respect of the area of the Celtic Sea and the Bay of Biscay was made by France, Ireland, Spain and the UK on 19 May 2006,[157] while on 21 April 2008, the Commission confirmed Australia's continental shelf claim made in 2004.[158]

Islands generate continental shelves, unless they consist of no more than rocks which cannot sustain human habitation.[159]

The rights and duties of the coastal state[160]

The coastal state may exercise 'sovereign rights' over the continental shelf for the purposes of exploring it and exploiting its natural resources under article 77 of the 1982 Convention. Such rights are exclusive in that no other state may undertake such activities without the express consent of the coastal state. These sovereign rights (and thus not territorial title as such since the Convention does not talk in terms of 'sovereignty') do not depend upon occupation or express proclamation.[161] The Truman concept of resources, which referred only to mineral resources, has been extended

---

[154] Article 76(8). See also www.un.org/Depts/los/clcs_new/clcs_home.htm.
[155] See UN Press Release, SEA/1729, 21 December 2001.
[156] See ASIL Insight, vol. 11, issue 27, 8 November 2007.
[157] See e.g. UKMIL, 77 BYIL, 2006, pp. 767–8, and H. Llewellyn, 'The Commission on the Limits of the Continental Shelf: Joint Submission by France, Ireland, Spain, and the United Kingdom', 56 ICLQ, 2007, p. 677.
[158] See UN Press Release, SEA/1899, 21 April 2008.
[159] Article 121(3). See also *Qatar* v. *Bahrain*, ICJ Reports, 2001, pp. 40, 97, and above, p. 565.
[160] See *Oppenheim's International Law*, p. 773 and Churchill and Lowe, *Law of the Sea*, p. 151.
[161] See also article 2 of the Continental Shelf Convention, 1958.

to include organisms belonging to the sedentary species.[162] However, this vague description did lead to disputes between France and Brazil over lobster, and between the USA and Japan over the Alaskan King Crab in the early 1960s.[163] The sovereign rights recognised as part of the continental shelf regime specifically relate to natural resources, so that, for example, wrecks lying on the shelf are not included.[164] The Convention expressly states that the rights of the coastal state do not affect the status of the superjacent waters as high seas, or that of the airspace above the waters.[165] This is stressed in succeeding articles which note that, subject to its right to take reasonable measures for exploration and exploitation of the continental shelf, the coastal state may not impede the laying or maintenance of cables or pipelines on the shelf. In addition, such exploration and exploitation must not result in any unjustifiable interference with navigation, fishing or the conservation of the living resources of the sea.[166]

The coastal state may, under article 80 of the 1982 Convention,[167] construct and maintain installations and other devices necessary for exploration on the continental shelf and is entitled to establish safety zones around such installations to a limit of 500 metres, which must be respected by ships of all nationalities. Within such zones, the state may take such measures as are necessary for their protection. But although under the jurisdiction of the coastal state, these installations are not to be considered as islands. This means that they have no territorial sea of their own and their presence in no way affects the delimitation of the territorial waters of the coastal state. Such provisions are, of course, extremely

---

[162] See article 77(4) of the 1982 Convention and article 2(4) of the 1958 Continental Shelf Convention.

[163] See e.g. O'Connell, *International Law of the Sea*, vol. I, pp. 501–2.

[164] See e.g. Churchill and Lowe, *Law of the Sea*, p. 152; E. Boesten, *Archaeological and/or Historical Valuable Shipwrecks in International Waters*, The Hague, 2002, and C. Forrest, 'An International Perspective on Sunken State Vessels as Underwater Cultural Heritage', 34 *Ocean Development and International Law*, 2003, p. 41. See also articles 149 (protection of cultural objects found in the International Seabed Area) and 303 (wrecks and the rights of coastal states in the contiguous zone).

[165] Article 78 of the 1982 Convention and article 3 of the 1958 Continental Shelf Convention. Note that the reference to 'high seas' in the latter is omitted in the former for reasons related to the new concept of the exclusive economic zone.

[166] Articles 78 and 79 of the 1982 Convention and articles 4 and 5 of the 1958 Continental Shelf Convention.

[167] Applying *mutatis mutandis* article 60, which deals with the construction of artificial islands, installations and structures in the exclusive economic zone. See also article 5 of the 1958 Continental Shelf Convention.

important when considering the status of oil rigs situated, for example, in the North Sea. To treat them as islands for legal purposes would cause difficulties.[168]

Where the continental shelf of a state extends beyond 200 miles, article 82 of the 1982 Convention provides that the coastal state must make payments or contributions in kind in respect of the exploitation of the non-living resources of the continental shelf beyond the 200-mile limit. The payments are to be made annually after the first five years of production at the site in question on a sliding scale up to the twelfth year, after which they are to remain at 7 per cent. These payments and contributions are to be made to the International Seabed Authority, which shall distribute them amongst state parties on the basis of 'equitable sharing criteria, taking into account the interests and needs of developing states particularly the least developed and the landlocked among them'.[169]

Maritime delimitation[170]

While delimitation is in principle an aspect of territorial sovereignty, where other states are involved, agreement is required. However valid in domestic law, unilateral delimitations will not be binding upon third

---

[168] See also N. Papadakis, *The International Legal Regime of Artificial Islands*, Leiden, 1977.

[169] Note also that by article 82(3) a developing state which is a net importer of the mineral resource in question is exempt from such payments and contributions.

[170] See e.g. *UN Handbook on the Delimitation of Maritime Boundaries*, New York, 2000; N. Antunes, *Towards the Conceptualisation of Maritime Delimitation*, The Hague, 2003; Churchill and Lowe, *Law of the Sea*, chapter 10; E. D. Brown, *Sea-Bed Energy and Mineral Resources and the Law of the Sea*, London, 1984–6, vols. I and III; M. D. Evans, *Relevant Circumstances and Maritime Delimitation*, Oxford, 1989, and P. Weil, *The Law of Maritime Delimitation – Reflections*, Cambridge, 1989. See also *International Maritime Boundaries* (eds. J. I. Charney and L. M. Alexander), Washington, vols. I–III, 1993–8, and *ibid.* (eds. J. I. Charney and R. W. Smith), vol. IV, 2002 and *ibid.* (eds. D. A. Colson and R. W. Smith), vol. V, 2005, The Hague; M. Kamga, *Délimitation Maritime sur la Côte Atlantique Africaine*, Brussels, 2006; *Maritime Delimitation* (eds. R. Lagoni and D. Vignes), Leiden, 2006; Y. Tanaka, *Predictability and Flexibility in the Law of Maritime Delimitation*, Oxford, 2006; D. A. Colson, 'The Delimitation of the Outer Continental Shelf between Neighbouring States', 97 AJIL, 2003, p. 91; V. D. Degan, 'Consolidation of Legal Principles on Maritime Delimitation', 6 Chinese YIL, 2007, p. 601; L. D. M. Nelson, 'The Roles of Equity in the Delimitation of Maritime Boundaries', 84 AJIL, 1990, p. 837; J. I. Charney, 'Progress in International Maritime Boundary Delimitation Law', 88 AJIL, 1994, p. 227, and Charney, 'Central East Asian Maritime Boundaries and the Law of the Sea', 89 AJIL, 1995, p. 724; *Oppenheim's International Law*, p. 776, and Nguyen Quoc Dinh *et al.*, *Droit International Public*, pp. 1178 and 1187 ff.

states.[171] The International Court noted in *Nicaragua* v. *Honduras* that the establishment of a permanent maritime boundary was 'a matter of grave importance and agreement is not easily to be presumed'.[172] It was also pointed out that the principle of *uti possidetis* applied in principle to maritime spaces.[173]

In so far as the delimitation of the territorial sea between states with opposite or adjacent coasts is concerned,[174] article 15 of the 1982 Convention, following basically article 12 of the Geneva Convention on the Territorial Sea, 1958, provides that where no agreement has been reached, neither state may extend its territorial sea beyond the median line every point of which is equidistant from the nearest point on the baselines from which the territorial sea is measured.[175] However, particular geographical circumstances may make it difficult to establish clear baselines and this may make it therefore impossible to draw an equidistance line.[176] In such an exceptional case, the Court would consider alternative lines drawn by the states, for example bisector lines.[177]

The provision as to the median line, however, does not apply where it is necessary by reason of historic title or other special circumstances to delimit the territorial sea of the two states in a different way. The Court in *Qatar* v. *Bahrain* noted that article 15 was to be regarded as having a customary law character[178] and may be referred to as the 'equidistance/special circumstances' principle. The Court went on to declare that, 'The most logical and widely practised approach is first to draw provisionally an

---

[171] See the *Anglo-Norwegian Fisheries* case, ICJ Reports, 1951, p. 132. The International Court noted in the *Gulf of Maine* case, ICJ Reports, 1984, pp. 246, 299; 77 ILR, pp. 57, 126, that 'no maritime delimitation between states with opposite or adjacent coasts may be effected unilaterally by one of those states. Such delimitation must be sought and effected by means of an agreement, following negotiations conducted in good faith and with the genuine intention of achieving a positive result. Where, however, such agreement cannot be achieved, delimitation should be effected by recourse to a third party possessing the necessary competence.'

[172] ICJ Reports, 2007, para. 253.   [173] *Ibid.*, para. 156 and see above, p. 525.

[174] See Churchill and Lowe, *Law of the Sea*, pp. 182 ff.

[175] See also *Qatar* v. *Bahrain*, ICJ Reports, 2001, pp. 40, 94. The International Court in *Nicaragua* v. *Honduras*, ICJ Reports, 2007, para. 269, noted that 'the methods governing territorial sea delimitations have needed to be, and are, more clearly articulated in international law than those used for the other, more functional maritime areas'.

[176] See *Nicaragua* v. *Honduras*, ICJ Reports, 2007, paras. 277 ff. The Court in *Qatar* v. *Bahrain* noted that an equidistance line could only be drawn where the baselines were known, ICJ Reports, 2001, pp. 40, 94.

[177] *Nicaragua* v. *Honduras*, ICJ Reports, 2007, para. 287.

[178] See also e.g. the *Dubai/Sharjah* case, 91 ILR, pp. 543, 663.

equidistance line and then to consider whether that line must be adjusted in the light of the existence of special circumstances.'[179]

This was underlined in the arbitration award in *Guyana* v. *Suriname*, which emphasised that article 15 placed 'primacy on the median line as the delimitation line between the territorial seas of opposite or adjacent states'.[180] The tribunal noted that international courts were not constrained by a finite list of special circumstances, but needed to assess on a case-by-case basis with reference to international case-law and state practice.[181] Navigational interests, for example, could constitute such special circumstances.[182] The tribunal also held that a 3-mile territorial sea delimitation line did not automatically extend outwards in situations where the territorial sea was extended to 12 miles, but rather that a principled method had to be found that took into account any special circumstances, including historical arrangements made.[183]

Separate from the question of the delimitation of the territorial sea, but increasingly convergent with it, is the question of the delimitation of the continental shelf and of the exclusive economic zone between opposite or adjacent states. The starting point of any delimitation of these areas is the entitlement of the state to a given maritime area. Such entitlement in the case of the continental shelf was originally founded upon the concept of natural prolongation of the land territory into the sea,[184] but with the emergence of the exclusive economic zone a new approach was introduced based upon distance from the coast.[185] The two concepts in fact became close.

Article 6 of the Continental Shelf Convention, 1958 declared that in the absence of agreement and unless another boundary line was justified by special circumstances, the continental shelf boundary should be determined 'by application of the principle of equidistance from the nearest points of the baselines from which the breadth of the territorial sea of each state is measured', that is to say by the introduction of the equidistance or median line which would operate in relation to the sinuosities of the particular coastlines.

---

[179] ICJ Reports, 2001, pp. 40, 94. See also *Nicaragua* v. *Honduras*, ICJ Reports, 2007, para. 268.

[180] Award of 17 September 2007, para. 296. See also UKMIL, 77 BYIL, 2006, p. 764.

[181] Award of 17 September 2007, paras. 302–3. See also the *Jan Mayen* case, ICJ Reports, 1993, pp. 38, 61–4.

[182] Award of 17 September 2007, para. 306.   [183] *Ibid.*, paras. 311 ff.

[184] The *North Sea Continental Shelf* cases, ICJ Reports, 1969, pp. 3, 22.

[185] See *Barbados* v. *Trinidad and Tobago*, Award of 11 April 2006, para. 224.

This provision was considered in the *North Sea Continental Shelf* cases[186] between the Federal Republic of Germany on the one side and Holland and Denmark on the other. The problem was that the application of the equidistance principle of article 6 would give Germany only a small share of the North Sea continental shelf, in view of its concave northern shoreline between Holland and Denmark. The question arose as to whether the article was binding upon the Federal Republic of Germany at all, since it had not ratified the 1958 Continental Shelf Convention.

The Court held that the principles enumerated in article 6 did not constitute rules of international customary law and therefore Germany was not bound by them.[187] The Court declared that the relevant rule was that:

> delimitation is to be effected by agreement in accordance with equitable principles, and taking account of all the relevant circumstances, in such a way as to leave as much as possible to each party all those parts of the continental shelf that constitute a natural prolongation of its land territory into and under the sea, without encroachment on the natural prolongation of the land territory of the others.[188]

The Court, therefore, took the view that delimitation was based upon a consideration and weighing of relevant factors in order to produce an equitable result. Included amongst the range of factors was the element of a reasonable degree of proportionality between the lengths of the coastline and the extent of the continental shelf.[189] In the *Anglo-French Continental Shelf* case,[190] both states were parties to the 1958 Convention, so that article 6 applied.[191] It was held that article 6 contained one overall rule, 'a combined equidistance–special circumstances rule', which in effect:

> gives particular expression to a general norm that, failing agreement, the boundary between states abutting on the same continental shelf is to be determined on equitable principles.[192]

---

[186] ICJ Reports, 1969, p. 3; 41 ILR, p. 29.   [187] See above, chapter 3, p. 85.

[188] ICJ Reports, 1969, pp. 3, 53; 41 ILR, pp. 29, 83.

[189] ICJ Reports, 1969, pp. 3, 52; 41 ILR, pp. 29, 82.

[190] Cmnd 7438 (1978); 54 ILR, p. 6. See also D. W. Bowett, 'The Arbitration between the United Kingdom and France Concerning the Continental Shelf Boundary in the English Channel of South-Western Approaches', 49 BYIL, 1978, p. 1.

[191] Although subject to a French reservation regarding the Bay of Granville to which the UK had objected, Cmnd 7438, p. 50; 54 ILR, p. 57.

[192] Cmnd 7438, p. 48; 54 ILR, p. 55.

The choice of method of delimitation, whether equidistance or any other method, depended upon the pertinent circumstances of the case. The fundamental norm under both customary law and the 1958 Convention was that the delimitation had to be in accordance with equitable principles.[193] The Court took into account 'special circumstances' in relation to the situation of the Channel Islands which justified a delimitation other than the median line proposed by the UK.[194] In addition, the situation of the Scilly Isles was considered and they were given only 'half-effect' in the delimitation in the Atlantic area since

> what equity calls for is an appropriate abatement of the disproportionate effects of a considerable projection on the Atlantic continental shelf of a somewhat attenuated projection of the coast of the United Kingdom.[195]

In the *Tunisia/Libya Continental Shelf* case,[196] the Court, deciding on the basis of custom as neither state was a party to the 1958 Convention, emphasised that 'the satisfaction of equitable principles is, in the delimitation process, of cardinal importance'. The concept of natural prolongation was of some importance depending upon the circumstances, but not on the same plane as the satisfaction of equitable principles.[197] The Court also employed the 'half-effect' principle for the Kerkennah Islands,[198] and emphasised that each continental shelf dispute had to be considered on its own merits having regard to its peculiar circumstances, while no attempt should be made to 'overconceptualise the application of the principles and rules relating to the continental shelf'.[199] The view of the Court that 'the principles are subordinate to the goal' and that '[t]he principles to be indicated . . . have to be selected according to their appropriateness for reaching an equitable result'[200] led to criticism that the carefully drawn restriction on equity in the *North Sea Continental Shelf* cases[201] had been

---

[193] Cmnd 7438, pp. 59–60; 54 ILR, p. 66.

[194] Cmnd 7438, p. 94; 54 ILR, p. 101. This arose because of the presence of the British islands close to the French coast, which if given full effect would substantially reduce the French continental shelf. This was *prima facie* a circumstance creative of inequity, *ibid.*

[195] Cmnd 7438, pp. 116–17; 54 ILR, p. 123.

[196] ICJ Reports, 1982, p. 18; 67 ILR, p. 4. See also L. L. Herman, 'The Court Giveth and the Court Taketh Away', 33 ICLQ, 1984, p. 825.

[197] ICJ Reports, 1982, p. 47; 67 ILR, p. 40. See also ICJ Reports, 1982, p. 60; 67 ILR, p. 53.

[198] ICJ Reports, 1982, p. 89; 67 ILR, p. 82. This was specified in far less constrained terms than in the *Anglo-French Continental Shelf* case, Cmnd 7438, pp. 116–17; 54 ILR, p. 123. See e.g. Judge Gros' Dissenting Opinion, ICJ Reports, 1982, pp. 18, 150; 67 ILR, p. 143.

[199] ICJ Reports, 1982, p. 92; 67 ILR, p. 85.   [200] ICJ Reports, 1982, p. 59; 67 ILR, p. 52.

[201] ICJ Reports, 1969, pp. 3, 49–50; 41 ILR, pp. 29, 79.

overturned and the element of predictability minimised. The dangers of an equitable solution based upon subjective assessments of the facts, regardless of the law of delimitation, were pointed out by Judge Gros in his Dissenting Opinion.[202]

The Court in the *North Sea Continental Shelf* cases[203] in general discussed the relevance of the use of equitable principles in the context of the difficulty of applying the equidistance rule in specific geographical situations where inequity might result. In such a case, recourse may be had to equitable principles, provided a reasonable result was reached.

In the *Anglo-French Continental Shelf* case,[204] it was emphasised that:

> the appropriateness of the equidistance method or any other method for the purpose of effecting an equitable delimitation is a function or reflection of the geographical and other relevant circumstances of each particular case.

The methodological aspect here is particularly important, based as it is upon the requisite geographical framework.

Article 83 of the 1982 Convention provides simply that delimitation 'shall be effected by agreement on the basis of international law . . . in order to achieve an equitable solution'. This was emphasised by the Court in *Tunisia/Libya*, where it was stated that the 'principles and rules applicable to the delimitation of the continental shelf areas are those which are appropriate to bring about an equitable result'.[205] In the *Gulf of Maine* case,[206] which dealt with the delimitation of both the continental shelf and fisheries zones of Canada and the United States,[207] the Chamber of the ICJ produced two principles reflecting what general international law prescribes in every maritime delimitation. First, there could be no unilateral delimitations. Delimitations had to be sought and effected by agreement between the parties or, if necessary, with the aid of third parties. Secondly, it held that 'delimitation is to be effected by the application of equitable criteria and by the use of practical methods capable of ensuring, with regard to the geographic configuration of the area and other relevant

---

[202] ICJ Reports, 1982, pp. 18, 153; 67 ILR, pp. 4, 146.

[203] ICJ Reports, 1969, pp. 3, 35–6; 41 ILR, pp. 29, 64.

[204] Cmnd 7438, p. 59; 54 ILR, p. 66.   [205] ICJ Reports, 1982, pp. 18, 49.

[206] ICJ Reports, 1984, p. 246; 71 ILR, p. 74. See also J. Schneider, 'The Gulf of Maine Case: The Nature of an Equitable Result', 79 AJIL, 1985, p. 539.

[207] A 'single maritime boundary' was requested by the parties, ICJ Reports, 1984, pp. 246, 253; 71 ILR, p. 80.

circumstances, an equitable result'.[208] The Court took as its starting point the criterion of the equal division of the areas of convergence and overlapping of the maritime projections of the coastlines of the states concerned, a criterion regarded as intrinsically equitable. This, however, had to be combined with the appropriate auxiliary criteria in the light of the relevant circumstances of the area itself. As regards the practical methods necessary to give effect to the above criteria, like the criteria themselves these had to be based upon geography and the suitability for the delimitation of both the seabed and the superjacent waters. Thus, it was concluded, geometrical methods would serve.[209] It will be noted that the basic rule for delimitation of the continental shelf is the same as that for the exclusive economic zone,[210] but the same boundary need not necessarily result.[211] The Chamber in the *Gulf of Maine* case indeed strongly emphasised 'the unprecedented aspect of the case which lends it its special character', in that a single line delimiting both the shelf and fisheries zone was called for by the parties.

Criteria found equitable with regard to a continental shelf delimitation need not necessarily possess the same properties with regard to a dual delimitation.[212] The above principles were reflected in the arbitral award in the *Guinea/Guinea-Bissau Maritime Delimitation* case in 1985.[213] The Tribunal emphasised that the aim of any delimitation process was to achieve an equitable solution having regard to the relevant circumstances.[214] In the instant case, the concepts of natural prolongation and economic factors were in the circumstances of little assistance.[215] In the *Libya/Malta Continental Shelf* case,[216] the International Court, in deciding the case according to customary law since Libya was not a party to the 1958

---

[208] ICJ Reports, 1984, pp. 299–300; 71 ILR, pp. 126–7. This was regarded as the fundamental norm of customary international law governing maritime delimitation, ICJ Reports, 1984, p. 300.

[209] ICJ Reports, 1984, pp. 328–9; 71 ILR, p. 155. Note that the Chamber gave 'half-effect' to Seal Island for reasons of equity, ICJ Reports, 1984, p. 337; 71 ILR, p. 164.

[210] Article 74 of the 1982 Convention.

[211] See e.g. the Australia–Papua New Guinea Maritime Boundaries Treaty of 1978, cited in Churchill and Lowe, *Law of the Sea*, p. 160.

[212] ICJ Reports, 1984, pp. 246, 326; 71 ILR, p. 153.

[213] See 25 ILM, 1986, p. 251; 77 ILR, p. 636. The tribunal consisted of Judge Lachs, President, and Judges Mbaye and Bedjaoui.

[214] 25 ILM, 1986, p. 289; 77 ILR, pp. 675–6.

[215] 25 ILM, 1986, pp. 300–2; 77 ILR, p. 686. It should be noted that the delimitation concerned a single line delimiting the territorial waters, continental shelves and economic zones of the respective countries.

[216] ICJ Reports, 1985, p. 13; 81 ILR, p. 239.

Convention on the Continental Shelf, emphasised the distance criterion. This arose because of the relevance of the economic zone concept, which was now held to be part of customary law, and the fact that an economic zone could not exist without rights over the seabed and subsoil similar to those enjoyed over a continental shelf. Thus the 200-mile limit of the zone had to be taken into account with regard to the delimitation of the continental shelf.[217] The fact that the law now permitted a state to claim a shelf of up to 200 miles from its coast, irrespective of geological characteristics, also meant that there was no reason to ascribe any role to geological or geographical factors within that distance.[218]

Since the basis of title to the shelf up to the 200-mile limit is recognised as the distance criterion, the Court felt that the drawing of a median line between opposite states was the most judicious manner of proceeding with a view to the eventual achievement of an equitable result. This provisional step had to be tested in the light of equitable principles in the context of the relevant circumstances.[219] The Court also followed the example of the *Tunisia/Libya* case[220] in examining the role of proportionality and in treating it as a test of the equitableness of any line.

However, the Court did consider the comparability of coastal lengths in the case as part of the process of reaching an equitable boundary, and used the disparity of coastal lengths of the parties as a reason for adjusting the median line so as to attribute a larger shelf area to Libya.[221] The general geographical context in which the islands of Malta exist as a relatively small feature in a semi-enclosed sea was also taken into account in this context.[222]

The Court in its analysis also referred to a variety of well-known examples of equitable principles, including abstention from refashioning nature, non-encroachment by one party on areas appertaining to the other, respect due to all relevant circumstances and the notions that equity did not necessarily mean equality and that there could be no question of distributive justice.[223] The Court, however, rejected Libya's argument that a state with a greater landmass would have a greater claim to the shelf

---

[217] The Court emphasised that this did not mean that the concept of the continental shelf had been absorbed by that of the economic zone, but that greater importance had to be attributed to elements, such as distance from the coast, which are common to both, ICJ Reports, 1985, p. 33; 81 ILR, p. 265.

[218] *Ibid.*   [219] ICJ Reports, 1985, p. 47; 81 ILR, p. 279.

[220] See above, p. 595.   [221] ICJ Reports, 1985, pp. 48–50; 81 ILR, p. 280.

[222] ICJ Reports, 1985, p. 52; 81 ILR, p. 284.

[223] ICJ Reports, 1985, pp. 39–40; 81 ILR, p. 271.

and dismissed Malta's view that the relative economic position of the two states was of relevance.[224]

In conclusion, the Court reiterated in the operative provisions of its judgment, the following circumstances and factors that needed to be taken into account in the case:

(1) the general configuration of the coasts to the parties, their oppositeness, and their relationship to each other within the general context;

(2) the disparity in the lengths of the relevant coasts of the parties and the distance between them;

(3) the need to avoid in the delimitation any excessive disproportion between the extent of the continental shelf areas appertaining to the coastal state and the length of the relevant part of its coast, measured in the general direction of the coastlines.[225]

In the *St Pierre and Miquelon* case,[226] the Court of Arbitration emphasised that the delimitation process commenced with the identification of the geographical context of the dispute in question and indeed pointed out that geographical features were at the heart of delimitation.[227] The identification of the relevant coastlines in each particular case, however, generates specific problems. Accordingly, the way in which the geographical situation is described may suggest particular solutions, so that the seemingly objective process of geographical identification may indeed constitute a crucial element in the adoption of any particular juridical answer. In the *St Pierre and Miquelon* case, the Court divided the area into two zones, the southern and western zones. In the latter case, any seaward extension of the islands beyond their territorial sea would cause some degree of encroachment and cut-off to the seaward projection towards the south from points located on the southern shore of Newfoundland. The Court felt here that any enclaving of the islands within their territorial sea would be inequitable and the solution proposed was to grant the islands an additional 12 miles from the limits of the territorial sea as an exclusive economic zone.[228] In the case of the southern zone, where the islands had a coastal opening seawards unobstructed by any opposite or

---

[224] ICJ Reports, 1985, pp. 40–1; 81 ILR, p. 272. The Court also noted that an equitable boundary between the parties had in the light of the general geographical situation to be south of a notional median line between Libya and Sicily, ICJ Reports, 1985, p. 51; 81 ILR, p. 283.

[225] ICJ Reports, 1985, pp. 56–8; 81 ILR, p. 288.   [226] 31 ILM, 1992, p. 1145; 95 ILR, p. 645.

[227] 31 ILM, 1992, pp. 1160–1; 95 ILR, pp. 660–3.

[228] 31 ILM, 1992, pp. 1169–70; 95 ILR, p. 671.

laterally aligned Canadian coast, the Court held that France was entitled to an outer limit of 200 nautical miles, provided that such a projection was not allowed to encroach upon or cut off a parallel frontal projection of the adjacent segments of the Newfoundland southern coast. In order to achieve this, the Court emphasised the importance of the breadth of the coastal opening of the islands towards the south, thus resulting in a 200-mile, but narrow, corridor southwards from the islands as their economic zone.[229] Having decided upon the basis of geographical considerations, the Court felt it necessary to assure itself that the delimitation proposed was not 'radically inequitable'.[230] This it was able to do on the basis of facts submitted by the parties. The Court also considered the criterion of proportionality and satisfied itself that there was no disproportion in the areas appertaining to each of the parties.[231]

In the *Jan Mayen (Denmark v. Norway)* case,[232] the question of the de-limitation of the continental shelf between the islands of Greenland and Jan Mayen was governed in the circumstances by article 6 of the 1958 Convention, accepted as substantially identical to customary law in requiring an equitable delimitation.[233] The International Court noted that since a delimitation between opposite coasts was in question, one needed to begin by taking provisionally the median line and then enquiring whether 'special circumstances'[234] required another boundary line.[235] In particular, one needed to take into account the disparity between the respective coastal lengths of the relevant area and, since in this case that of Greenland was more than nine times that of Jan Mayen, an unqualified use of equidistance would produce a manifestly disproportionate result.[236] In addition,

---

[229] 31 ILM, 1992, pp. 1170–1; 95 ILR, pp. 671–3.

[230] 31 ILM, 1992, p. 1173; 95 ILR, p. 675. The phrase comes from the *Gulf of Maine* case, ICJ Reports, 1984, pp. 246, 342; 71 ILR, pp. 74, 169, where it was defined as 'likely to entail catastrophic repercussions for the livelihood and economic well-being of the population of the parties concerned'.

[231] 31 ILM, 1992, p. 1176; 95 ILR, p. 678.   [232] ICJ Reports, 1993, p. 37; 99 ILR, p. 395.

[233] ICJ Reports, 1993, p. 58; 99 ILR, p. 426. But see the Separate Opinion of Judge Oda, ICJ Reports, 1993, pp. 102–14; 99 ILR, pp. 470–82.

[234] The Court noted that the category of 'special circumstances' incorporated in article 6 was essentially the same as the category of 'relevant circumstances' developed in customary international law since both were designed to achieve an equitable solution, ICJ Reports, 1993, p. 62; 99 ILR, p. 430. Special circumstances were deemed to be those that 'might modify the result produced by an unqualified application of the equidistance principle', while relevant circumstances could be described as 'a fact necessary to be taken into account in the delimitation process', *ibid.*

[235] ICJ Reports, 1993, pp. 59–61; 99 ILR, pp. 427–9.

[236] ICJ Reports, 1993, pp. 65–9; 99 ILR, pp. 433–7.

the question of equitable access to fish stocks for vulnerable fishing communities needed to be considered. Since the principal resource in the area
was capelin, which was centred on the southern part of the area of overlapping claims, the adoption of a median line would mean that Denmark
could not be assured of equitable access to the capelin. This was a further
reason for adjusting the median line towards the Norwegian island of Jan
Mayen.[237] However, there was no need to consider the presence of ice as
this did not materially affect access to fishery resources,[238] nor the limited
population of Jan Mayen, socio-economic factors or security matters in
the circumstances.[239]

   In discussing the variety of applicable principles, a distinction has traditionally been drawn between opposite and adjacent states for the purposes of delimitation. In the former case, the Court has noted that there
is less difficulty in applying the equidistance method than in the latter,
since the distorting effect of an individual geographical feature in the case
of adjacent states is more likely to result in an inequitable delimitation.
Accordingly, greater weight is to be placed upon equidistance in a delimitation of the shelf between opposite states in the context of equitable
considerations,[240] than in the case of adjacent states where the range of
applicable equitable principles may be more extensive and the relative
importance of each particular principle less clear. Article 83 of the 1982
Convention, however, makes no distinction between delimitations on the
basis of whether the states are in an opposite or adjacent relationship. The
same need to achieve an equitable solution on the basis of international
law is all that is apparent and recent moves to a presumption in favour of
equidistance in the case of opposite coasts may well apply also to adjacent
states.

---

[237] ICJ Reports, 1993, pp. 70–2; 99 ILR, pp. 438–40. But see the Separate Opinion of Judge
   Schwebel, ICJ Reports, 1993, pp. 118–20; 99 ILR, pp. 486–8.
[238] ICJ Reports, 1993, pp. 72–3; 99 ILR, pp. 440–1.
[239] ICJ Reports, 1993, pp. 73–5; 99 ILR, pp. 441–3. But see the Separate Opinion of Judge
   Oda, ICJ Reports, 1993, pp. 114–17; 99 ILR, pp. 482–5. Note also the discussion of equity
   in such situations in the Separate Opinion of Judge Weeramantry, ICJ Reports, 1993, pp.
   211 ff.; 99 ILR, p. 579 ff.
[240] See *North Sea Continental Shelf* cases, ICJ Reports, 1969, pp. 3, 36–7; 41 ILR, pp. 29, 65;
   the *Anglo-French Continental Shelf* case, Cmnd 7438, pp. 58–9; 54 ILR, p. 65; the *Tunisia–
   Libya Continental Shelf* case, ICJ Reports, 1982, pp. 18, 88; 67 ILR, pp. 4, 81; the *Gulf of
   Maine* case, ICJ Reports, 1984, pp. 246, 325; 71 ILR, p. 74, and the *Jan Mayen* case, ICJ
   Reports, 1993, p. 37; 99 ILR, p. 395. See also article 6 of the Continental Shelf Convention,
   1958.

The weight to be given to the criterion of proportionality between the length of the coastline and the area of continental shelf has also been the subject of some consideration and opinions have varied. It is a factor that must be cautiously applied.[241]

Article 74 of the 1982 Convention provides that delimitation of the exclusive economic zone between states with opposite or adjacent coasts is to be effected by agreement on the basis of international law,[242] 'in order to achieve an equitable solution'. Since this phrase is identical to the provision on delimitation of the continental shelf,[243] it is not surprising that cases have arisen in which states have sought a single maritime boundary, applying both to the continental shelf and the economic zone.

In the *Gulf of Maine* case,[244] the Chamber of the International Court took the view that the criteria for a single maritime boundary[245] were those that would apply to both the continental shelf and economic zones (in this case a fisheries zone) and not criteria that relate to only one of these areas.[246] Nevertheless, the overall requirement for the establishment of

---

[241] The Court in the *North Sea Continental Shelf* cases, in discussing this issue, called for a reasonable degree of proportionality, ICJ Reports, 1969, pp. 3, 52; 41 ILR, pp. 29, 82, while in the *Anglo-French Continental Shelf* case the Tribunal emphasised that it was disproportion rather than proportionality that was relevant in the context of the equities, Cmnd 7438, pp. 60–1; 54 ILR, pp. 6, 67. But cf. the *Tunisia/Libya Continental Shelf* case, ICJ Reports, 1982, pp. 18, 75; 67 ILR, pp. 4, 75. See also the *Libya/Malta Continental Shelf* case, ICJ Reports, 1985, pp. 48–50; 81 ILR, p. 280.

[242] As referred to in article 38 of the Statute of the ICJ.

[243] Article 83. Note that the International Court declared that 'the identity of the language which is employed, even though limited of course to the determination of the relevant principles and rules of international law, is particularly significant', the *Gulf of Maine* case, ICJ Reports, 1984, pp. 246, 295; 71 ILR, pp. 74, 122. The Court declared in the *Jan Mayen Maritime Delimitation (Denmark v. Norway)* case, ICJ Reports, 1993, pp. 37, 59; 99 ILR, pp. 395, 427, that the statement in article 74(1) and the corresponding provision in article 83(1) with regard to the aim of any delimitation process being an equitable solution, 'reflects the requirements of customary law as regards the delimitation both of continental shelf and of exclusive economic zones'. The Tribunal in *Eritrea/Yemen (Phase Two: Maritime Delimitation)* stated in relation to articles 74 and 83 that these provisions resulted from a last-minute endeavour at the conference to get agreement on a very controversial matter and so 'were consciously designed to decide as little as possible', 119 ILR, pp. 417, 454.

[244] ICJ Reports, 1984, p. 246; 71 ILR, p. 74.

[245] The Court has emphasised that the notion of a single maritime line stems from state practice and not from treaty law, thus underlining its position in customary law: see *Qatar v. Bahrain*, ICJ Reports, 2001, pp. 40, 93; *Cameroon v. Nigeria*, ICJ Reports, 2002, pp. 303, 440–1; *Barbados v. Trinidad and Tobago*, Award of 11 April 2006, para. 235 and *Guyana v. Suriname*, Award of 17 September 2007, para. 334.

[246] *Gulf of Maine* case, ICJ Reports, 1984, p. 326; 71 ILR, p. 153.

such a boundary is the need to achieve an equitable solution and this brings into consideration a range of factors that may or may not be deemed relevant or decisive by the Court. It is in the elucidation of such factors that difficulties have been encountered and it would be over-optimistic to assert that the situation is clear, although very recent cases have moved towards a degree of predictability. In the *Gulf of Maine* case, the Court emphasised that the relevant criteria had to be essentially determined 'in relation to what may be properly called the geographical features of the area', but what these are is subject to some controversy and did not appear to cover scientific and other facts relating to fish stocks, oil exploration, scientific research or common defence arrangements.[247] In the *Guinea/Guinea-Bissau Maritime Delimitation* case,[248] the Tribunal was called upon to draw a single line dividing the territorial sea, economic zone and continental shelf of the two states concerned. In the case of the latter two zones, the Tribunal noted that the use of the equidistance method was unsatisfactory since it exaggerated the importance of insignificant coastal features. Rather one had to consider the whole coastline of West Africa.[249] The Tribunal also considered that the evidence with regard to the geological and geomorphological features of the continental shelf was unsatisfactory,[250] while general economic factors were rejected as being unjust and inequitable, since they were based upon an evaluation of data that was constantly changing.[251] The question of a single maritime boundary arose again in the *St Pierre and Miquelon (Canada/France)* case,[252] where the Tribunal was asked to establish a single delimitation as between the parties governing all rights and jurisdiction that the parties may exercise under international law in these maritime areas. In such cases, the Tribunal, following the *Gulf of Maine* decision, took the view that in a single or all-purpose delimitation, article 6 of the Geneva Convention on the Continental Shelf, 1958, which governed the delimitation of the continental shelf, did not have mandatory force as regards the establishment of that single maritime line.[253]

---

[247] ICJ Reports, 1984, p. 278; 71 ILR, p. 105.   [248] 77 ILR, p. 635.
[249] *Ibid.*, pp. 679–81.   [250] *Ibid.*, pp. 685–7.   [251] *Ibid.*, pp. 688–9.
[252] 31 ILM, 1992, p. 1145; 95 ILR, p. 645. See also M. D. Evans, 'Less Than an Ocean Apart: The St Pierre and Miquelon and Jan Mayen Islands and the Delimitation of Maritime Zones', 43 ICLQ, 1994, p. 678; K. Highet, 'Delimitation of the Maritime Areas Between Canada and France', 87 AJIL, 1993, p. 452, and H. Ruiz Fabri, 'Sur la Délimitation des Espaces Maritimes entre le Canada et la France', 97 RGDIP, 1993, p. 67.
[253] 31 ILM, 1992, p. 1163; 95 ILR, p. 663.

However, where there did not exist a special agreement between the parties asking the Court to determine a single maritime boundary applicable both to the continental shelf and the economic zone, the Court declared in the *Jan Mayen Maritime Delimitation (Denmark* v. *Norway)* case[254] that the two strands of the applicable law had to be examined separately. These strands related to the effect of article 6 of the Geneva Convention on the Continental Shelf, 1958 upon the continental shelf and the rules of customary international law with regard to the fishery zone.[255]

Recent cases have seen further moves towards clarity and simplicity. In *Eritrea/Yemen (Phase Two: Maritime Delimitation)*, the Tribunal noted that it was a generally accepted view that between coasts that are opposite to each other, the median or equidistance line normally provided an equitable boundary in accordance with the requirements of the 1982 Convention.[256] It also reaffirmed earlier case-law to the effect that proportionality was not an independent mode or principle of delimitation, but a test of the equitableness of a delimitation arrived at by other means.[257] The Tribunal also considered the role of mid-sea islands in a delimitation between opposite states and noted that to give them full effect would produce a disproportionate effect.[258] Indeed, no effect was given to some of the islands in question.[259]

In *Qatar* v. *Bahrain*, the Court emphasised the close relationship between continental shelf and economic zone delimitations[260] and held that the appropriate methodology was first to provisionally draw an equidistance line and then to consider whether circumstances existed which must lead to an adjustment of that line.[261] Further, it was noted that 'the equidistance/special circumstances' rule, applicable to territorial sea

---

[254] ICJ Reports, 1993, p. 37; 99 ILR, p. 395. See also M. D. Evans, 'Case Concerning Maritime Delimitation in the Area Between Greenland and Jan Mayen (*Denmark* v. *Norway*)', 43 ICLQ, 1994, p. 697.

[255] But see the Separate Opinion of Judge Oda, who took the view that the regime of the continental shelf was independent of the concept of the exclusive economic zone and that the request to draw a single maritime boundary was misconceived, ICJ Reports, 1993, pp. 96–7; 99 ILR, pp. 464–5.

[256] 119 ILR, pp. 417, 457.

[257] *Ibid.*, p. 465. See also the *North Sea Continental Shelf* cases, ICJ Reports, 1969, pp. 3, 52; 41 ILR, p. 29 and the *Anglo-French Continental Shelf* case, Cmnd 7438; 54 ILR, p. 6.

[258] 119 ILR, p. 454.

[259] *Ibid.*, p. 461. Note that the Tribunal rejected the enclaving of some islands as had occurred in the *Anglo-French Continental Shelf* case, *ibid.*, p. 463.

[260] ICJ Reports, 2001, pp. 40, 110.   [261] *Ibid.*, p. 111.

delimitation, and the 'equidistance/relevant circumstances' rule as developed since 1958 in case-law and practice regarding the delimitation of the continental shelf and the exclusive economic zone were 'closely related'.[262] The Court did not consider the existence of pearling banks to be a circumstance justifying a shift in the equidistance line[263] nor was the disparity in length of the coastal fronts of the states.[264] It was also considered that for reasons of equity in order to avoid disproportion, no effect could be given to Fasht al Jarim, a remote projection of Bahrain's coastline in the Gulf area, which constituted a maritime feature located well out to sea and most of which was below water at high tide.[265]

This approach was reaffirmed by the Court in *Cameroon v. Nigeria*, where it was noted that 'the applicable criteria, principles and rules of delimitation' concerning a line 'covering several zones of coincident jurisdiction' could be expressed in 'the so-called equitable principles/relevant circumstances method'. This method, 'which is very similar to the equidistance/special circumstances method' concerning territorial sea delimitation, 'involves first drawing an equidistance line, then considering whether there are factors calling for the adjustment or shifting of that line in order to achieve an "equitable result"'.[266] Such a line had to be constructed on the basis of the relevant coastlines of the states in question and excluded taking into account the coastlines of third states and the coastlines of the parties not facing each other.[267] Further, the Court emphasised that 'equity is not a method of delimitation, but solely an aim that should be borne in mind in effecting the delimitation',[268] thus putting an end to a certain trend in previous decades to put the whole emphasis in delimitation upon an equitable solution, leaving substantially open the question of what factors to take into account and how to rank them. The geographical configuration of the maritime area in question was an important element in this case and the Court stressed that while certain geographical peculiarities of maritime areas could be taken into account, this would be solely as relevant circumstances for the purpose, if necessary, of shifting the provisional delimitation line. In the present case, the Court did not consider the configuration of the coastline a relevant circumstance justifying altering the equidistance line.[269] Similarly the Court did not feel it necessary to take

---

[262] *Ibid.*, p. 111.   [263] *Ibid.*, p. 112.
[264] *Ibid.*, p. 114. This was in view of the recognition that Bahrain had sovereignty over the Hawar Islands, a factor which mitigated any serious disparity.
[265] *Ibid.*, p. 115.   [266] ICJ Reports, 2002, pp. 303, 441.   [267] *Ibid.*, p. 442.
[268] *Ibid.*, p. 443.   [269] *Ibid.*, pp. 443–5.

into account the existence of Bioko, an island off the coast of Cameroon but belonging to a third state, Equatorial Guinea, nor was it concluded that there existed 'a substantial difference in the lengths of the parties' respective coastlines' so as to make it a factor to be considered in order to adjust the provisional delimitation line.[270]

In the *Barbados* v. *Trinidad and Tobago* arbitration award of 11 April 2006, it was noted that equitable considerations *per se* constituted an imprecise concept in the light of the need for stability and certainty in the outcome of the legal process and it was emphasised that the search for predictable, objectively determined criteria for delimitation underlined that the role of equity lies within and not beyond the law.[271] The process of achieving an equitable result was constrained by legal principle, as both equity and stability were integral parts of the delimitation process.[272] The tribunal concluded that the determination of the line of delimitation followed a two-step approach. First, a provisional line of equidistance is constructed and this constitutes the practical starting point. Secondly, this line is examined in the light of relevant circumstances, which are case specific, so as to determine whether it is necessary to adjust the provisional equidistance line in order to achieve an equitable result. This approach was termed the 'equidistance/relevant circumstances' principle so that certainty would thus be combined with the need for an equitable result.[273]

Conclusion

Accordingly, there is now a substantial convergence of applicable principles concerning maritime delimitation, whether derived from customary law or treaty. In all cases, whether the delimitation is of the territorial sea, continental shelf or economic zone (or of the latter two together), the appropriate methodology to be applied is to draw a provisional equidistance line as the starting position and then see whether any relevant or special circumstances exist which may warrant a change in that line in order to

---

[270] *Ibid.*, p. 446. See also, as to the relevance of oil practice by the parties, *ibid.*, pp. 447–8, and *Eritrea/Yemen (Phase Two: Maritime Delimitation)*, 119 ILR, pp. 417, 443 ff.

[271] Award of 11 April 2006, para. 230. See also B. Kwiatkowska, 'The 2006 Barbados/Trinidad and Tobago Maritime Delimitation (Jurisdiction and Merits) Award', in Ndiaye and Wolfrum, *Law of the Sea, Environmental Law and Settlement of Disputes*, p. 917.

[272] Award of 11 April 2006, paras. 243 and 244.

[273] *Ibid.*, para. 242. See also para. 317. This approach was approved in *Guyana* v. *Suriname*, Award of 17 September 2007, paras. 340–1.

achieve an equitable result. The presumption in favour of that line is to be welcomed as a principle of value and clarity.

As to the meaning of special or relevant circumstances, or the criteria that need to be taken into account, case-law provides a range of clear indications. Equity is not a method of delimitation and nature cannot be totally refashioned, but some modification of the provisional equidistance line may be justified for the purpose of, for example, 'abating the effects of an incidental special feature from which an unjustifiable difference of treatment could result'.[274] The following principles may be noted. First, the delimitation should avoid the encroachment by one party on the natural prolongation of the other or its equivalent in respect of the economic zone and should avoid to the extent possible the interruption of the maritime projection of the relevant coastlines.[275] Secondly, the configuration of the coast may be relevant where the drawing of an equidistance line may unduly prejudice a state whose coast is particularly concave or convex within the relevant area of the delimitation when compared with that of its neighbours. But the threshold for this is relatively high.[276] Thirdly, a 'substantial difference in the lengths of the parties' respective coastlines may be a factor to be taken into consideration' in mitigation of an equidistance line so as to avoid a disproportionate and inequitable result.[277] Fourthly, the presence of islands or other similar maritime features may be relevant to the equities of the situation and may justify a modification of the provisional equidistance line.[278] Fifthly, security considerations may be taken into account, but the precise effects of this are unclear. Sixthly, resource-related criteria, such as the distribution of fish stocks, have been treated cautiously and have not generally been accepted as a relevant circumstance.[279] Finally, the prior conduct of the parties may be relevant, for example, where there is sufficient practice to show that a provisional boundary has been agreed. In the *Tunisia/Libya* case, the Court held that a line close to the coast which neither party had crossed when granting offshore oil and gas concessions and which thus constituted a *modus*

---

[274] The *North Sea Continental Shelf* cases, ICJ Reports, 1969, pp. 3, 50.
[275] *Barbados* v. *Trinidad and Tobago*, Award of 11 April 2006, para. 232.
[276] *Cameroon* v. *Nigeria*, ICJ Reports, 2002, pp. 303, 445–6.
[277] See e.g. *Cameroon* v. *Nigeria*, ICJ Reports, 2002, pp. 303, 446–7 and *Barbados* v. *Trinidad and Tobago*, Award of 11 April 2006, para. 240.
[278] See e.g. the *Anglo-French Continental Shelf* case, 54 ILR, p. 6 and *Qatar* v. *Bahrain*, ICJ Reports, 2001, pp. 40, 114 ff.
[279] *Gulf of Maine*, ICJ Reports, 1984, pp. 246, 342 and *Barbados* v. *Trinidad and Tobago*, Award of 11 April 2006, paras. 228 and 241.

vivendi was highly relevant,[280] although in *Cameroon* v. *Nigeria*, the Court emphasised that only if such concessions were based on express or tacit agreement between the parties could they be taken into account for the purposes of a delimitation.[281]

Landlocked states[282]

Article 3 of the Geneva Convention on the High Seas, 1958 provided that 'in order to enjoy freedom of the seas on equal terms with coastal states, states having no sea coast should have free access to the sea'.[283] Article 125 of the 1982 Convention on the Law of the Sea is formulated as follows:

> 1. Land-locked states shall have the right of access to and from the sea for the purpose of exercising the rights provided for in this Convention including those relating to the freedom of the high seas and the common heritage of mankind. To this end, land-locked states shall enjoy freedom of transit through the territory of transit states by all means of transport.
>
> 2. The terms and modalities for exercising freedom of transit shall be agreed between the land-locked states and the transit state concerned through bilateral, subregional or regional agreements.
>
> 3. Transit states, in the exercise of their full sovereignty over their territory, shall have the right to take all measures necessary to ensure that the rights and facilities provided for in this Part for land-locked states shall in no way infringe their legitimate interests.

It will thus be seen that there is no absolute right of transit, but rather that transit depends upon arrangements to be made between the landlocked and transit states. Nevertheless, the affirmation of a right of access to the sea coast is an important step in assisting landlocked states. Articles 127 to 130 of the 1982 Convention set out a variety of terms for the

---

[280] ICJ Reports, 1982, pp. 18, 71, 84 and 80–6.

[281] ICJ Reports, 2002, pp. 303, 447–8. See also *Guyana* v. *Suriname*, Award of 17 September 2007, paras. 378 ff.

[282] See e.g. S. C. Vasciannie, *Land-Locked and Geographically Disadvantaged States in the International Law of the Sea*, Oxford, 1990; J. Symonides, 'Geographically Disadvantaged States in the 1982 Convention on the Law of the Sea', 208 HR, 1988, p. 283; M. I. Glassner, *Bibliography on Land-Locked States*, 4th edn, The Hague, 1995; L. Caflisch, 'Land-locked States and their Access to and from the Sea', 49 BYIL, 1978, p. 71, and I. Delupis, 'Land-locked States and the Law of the Sea', 19 *Scandinavian Studies in Law*, 1975, p. 101. See also Churchill and Lowe, *Law of the Sea*, chapter 18.

[283] See also the Convention on Transit Trade of Land-Locked States, 1965.

operation of transit arrangements, while article 131 provides that ships flying the flag of landlocked states shall enjoy treatment equal to that accorded to other foreign ships in maritime ports. Ships of all states, whether coastal states or landlocked states, have the right of innocent passage in the territorial sea and freedom of navigation in the waters beyond the territorial sea.[284]

It is also to be noted that landlocked states have the right to participate upon an equitable basis in the exploitation of an appropriate part of the surplus of the living resources of the economic zones of coastal states of the same subregion or region, taking into account relevant economic and geographical factors.[285] Geographically disadvantaged states have the same right.[286] The terms and modalities of such participation are to be established by the states concerned through bilateral, subregional or regional agreements, taking into account a range of factors, including the need to avoid effects detrimental to fishing communities or fishing industries of the coastal state and the nutritional needs of the respective states.[287]

With regard to provisions concerning the international seabed regime, article 148 of the 1982 Convention provides that the effective participation of developing states in the International Seabed Area shall be promoted, having due regard to their special interests and needs, and in particular to the special need of the landlocked and geographically disadvantaged among them to overcome obstacles arising from their disadvantaged location, including remoteness from the Area and difficulty of access to and from it.[288]

---

[284] See e.g. article 14(1) of the Geneva Convention on the Territorial Sea, 1958; articles 2(1) and 4 of the Geneva Convention on the High Seas, 1958 and articles 17, 38(1), 52(1), 53(2), 58(1), 87 and 90 of the 1982 Convention.

[285] Article 69(1) of the 1982 Convention.

[286] Article 70(1). Geographically disadvantaged states are defined in article 70(2) as 'coastal states, including states bordering enclosed or semi-enclosed seas, whose geographical situation makes them dependent upon the exploitation of the living resources of the exclusive economic zones of other states in the subregion or region for adequate supplies of fish for the nutritional purposes of their populations or parts thereof, and coastal states which can claim no exclusive economic zone of their own'.

[287] See articles 69(2) and 70(2). Note also articles 69(4) and 70(5) restricting such rights of participation of developed landlocked states to developed coastal states of the same subregion or region. By article 71, the provisions of articles 69 and 70 do not apply in the case of a coastal state whose economy is overwhelmingly dependent on the exploitation of the living resources of its exclusive economic zone.

[288] See also articles 152, 160 and 161.

The high seas[289]

The closed seas concept proclaimed by Spain and Portugal in the fifteenth and sixteenth centuries, and supported by the Papal Bulls of 1493 and 1506 dividing the seas of the world between the two powers, was replaced by the notion of the open seas and the concomitant freedom of the high seas during the eighteenth century.

The essence of the freedom of the high seas is that no state may acquire sovereignty over parts of them.[290] This is the general rule, but it is subject to the operation of the doctrines of recognition, acquiescence and prescription, where, by long usage accepted by other nations, certain areas of the high seas bounding on the territorial waters of coastal states may be rendered subject to that state's sovereignty. This was emphasised in the *Anglo-Norwegian Fisheries* case.[291]

The high seas were defined in Article 1 of the Geneva Convention on the High Seas, 1958 as all parts of the sea that were not included in the territorial sea or in the internal waters of a state. This reflected customary international law, although as a result of developments the definition in article 86 of the 1982 Convention includes: all parts of the sea that are not included in the exclusive economic zone, in the territorial sea or in the internal waters of a state, or in the archipelagic waters of an archipelagic state.

Article 87 of the 1982 Convention (developing article 2 of the 1958 Geneva Convention on the High Seas) provides that the high seas are open to all states and that the freedom of the high seas is exercised under the conditions laid down in the Convention and by other rules of international law. It includes *inter alia* the freedoms of navigation, overflight, the laying of submarine cables and pipelines,[292] the construction of artificial islands and other installations permitted under international law,[293] fishing, and the conduct of scientific research.[294] Such freedoms are to be exercised with due regard for the interests of other states in their exercise of the

---

[289] See e.g. Brown, *International Law of the Sea*, vol. I, chapter 14; O'Connell, *International Law of the Sea*, vol. II, chapter 21, and Churchill and Lowe, *Law of the Sea*, chapter 11. See also *Oppenheim's International Law*, pp. 710 ff. and Nguyen Quoc Dinh *et al.*, *Droit International Public*, p. 1194.

[290] See article 2 of the 1958 High Seas Convention and article 89 of the 1982 Convention.

[291] ICJ Reports, 1951, p. 116; 18 ILR, p. 86. See above, p. 559.

[292] Subject to Part VI of the Convention, dealing with the continental shelf.

[293] Subject to Part VI of the Convention, dealing with the continental shelf.

[294] Subject to Part VI of the Convention, dealing with the continental shelf, and Part XIII, dealing with marine scientific research.

freedom of the high seas, and also with due regard for the rights under the Convention regarding activities in the International Seabed Area.[295]

Australia and New Zealand alleged before the ICJ, in the *Nuclear Tests* case,[296] that French nuclear testing in the Pacific infringed the principle of the freedom of the seas, but this point was not decided by the Court. The 1963 Nuclear Test Ban Treaty prohibited the testing of nuclear weapons on the high seas as well as on land, but France was not a party to the treaty, and it appears not to constitute a customary rule binding all states, irrespective of the treaty.[297] Nevertheless, article 88 of the 1982 Convention provides that the high seas shall be reserved for peaceful purposes.

Principles that are generally acknowledged to come within article 2 include the freedom to conduct naval exercises on the high seas and the freedom to carry out research studies.

The freedom of navigation[298] is a traditional and well-recognised facet of the doctrine of the high seas, as is the freedom of fishing.[299] This was reinforced by the declaration by the Court in the *Fisheries Jurisdiction* cases[300] that Iceland's unilateral extension of its fishing zones from 12 to 50 miles constituted a violation of article 2 of the High Seas Convention, which is, as the preamble states, 'generally declaratory of established principles of international law'. The freedom of the high seas applies not only to coastal states but also to states that are landlocked.[301]

The question of freedom of navigation on the high seas in times of armed conflict was raised during the Iran–Iraq war, which during its

---

[295] See below, p. 628.

[296] ICJ Reports, 1974, pp. 253 and 457; 57 ILR, pp. 350, 605. See also the Order of the International Court of Justice of 22 September 1995 in the *Request for an Examination of the Situation in Accordance with Paragraph 63 of the Court's Judgment of 20 December 1974 in the Nuclear Tests (New Zealand v. France)* case, ICJ Reports, 1995, p. 288, where the Court refused to accede to a request by New Zealand to re-examine the 1974 judgment in view of the resumption by France of underground nuclear testing in the South Pacific.

[297] Note, however, the development of regional agreements prohibiting nuclear weapons: see the Treaty of Tlatelolco for the Prohibition of Nuclear Weapons in Latin America, 1967, which extends the nuclear weapons ban to the territorial sea, airspace and any other space over which a state party exercises sovereignty in accordance with its own legislation; the Treaty of Rarotonga establishing a South Pacific Nuclear-Free Zone, 1985; the African Nuclear Weapon-Free Treaty, 1996 and the Treaty on the Southeast Asia Nuclear Weapon-Free Zone, 1995.

[298] See the *Corfu Channel* case, ICJ Reports, 1949, pp. 4, 22; 16 AD, p. 155, and *Nicaragua v. United States*, ICJ Reports, 1986, pp. 14, 111–12; 76 ILR, pp. 349, 445.

[299] See the *Anglo-Norwegian Fisheries* case, ICJ Reports, 1951, pp. 116, 183; 18 ILR, pp. 86, 131. See also below, p. 623.

[300] ICJ Reports, 1974, p. 3.   [301] See above, p. 607.

latter stages involved attacks upon civilian shipping by both belligerents. Rather than rely on the classical and somewhat out-of-date rules of the laws of war at sea,[302] the UK in particular analysed the issue in terms of the UN Charter. The following statement was made:[303]

> The UK upholds the principle of freedom of navigation on the high seas and condemns all violations of the law of armed conflicts including attacks on merchant shipping. Under article 51 of the UN Charter, a state actively engaged in armed conflict (as in the case of Iran and Iraq) is entitled in exercise of its inherent right of self-defence to stop and search a foreign merchant ship on the high seas if there is reasonable ground for suspecting that the ship is taking arms to the other side for use in the conflict. This is an exceptional right: if the suspicion proves to be unfounded and if the ship has not committed acts calculated to give rise to suspicion, then the ship's owners have a good claim for compensation for loss caused by the delay. This right would not, however, extend to the imposition of a maritime blockade or other forms of economic warfare.

Jurisdiction on the high seas[304]

The foundation of the maintenance of order on the high seas has rested upon the concept of the nationality of the ship, and the consequent jurisdiction of the flag state over the ship. It is, basically, the flag state that will enforce the rules and regulations not only of its own municipal law but of international law as well. A ship without a flag will be deprived of many of the benefits and rights available under the legal regime of the high seas.

Each state is required to elaborate the conditions necessary for the grant of its nationality to ships, for the registration of ships in its territory and for the right to fly its flag.[305] The nationality of the ship will depend upon the flag it flies, but article 91 of the 1982 Convention also stipulates that there must be a 'genuine link' between the state and the ship.[306] This

---

[302] See e.g. Churchill and Lowe, *Law of the Sea*, chapter 17, and C. J. Colombos, *International Law of the Sea*, 6th edn, London, 1967, part II.

[303] *Parliamentary Papers*, 1987–8, HC, Paper 179–II, p. 120 and UKMIL, 59 BYIL, 1988, p. 581.

[304] See e.g. *Oppenheim's International Law*, p. 731.

[305] Article 5 of the 1958 High Seas Convention and article 91 of the 1982 Convention.

[306] Article 5 of the High Seas Convention, 1958 had added to this the requirement that 'in particular the state must effectively exercise its jurisdiction and control in administrative, technical and social matters over ships flying its flag'. This requirement appears in article 94 of the 1982 Convention.

provision, which reflects 'a well-established rule of general international law',[307] was intended to check the use of flags of convenience operated by states such as Liberia and Panama which would grant their nationality to ships requesting such because of low taxation and the lack of application of most wage and social security agreements. This enabled the ships to operate at very low costs indeed. However, what precisely the 'genuine link' consists of and how one may regulate any abuse of the provisions of article 5 are unresolved questions. Some countries, for example the United States, maintain that the requirement of a 'genuine link' really only amounts to a duty to exercise jurisdiction over the ship in an efficacious manner, and is not a pre-condition for the grant, or the acceptance by other states of the grant, of nationality.[308]

An opportunity did arise in 1960 to discuss the meaning of the provision in the *IMCO* case.[309] The International Court was called upon to define the 'largest ship-owning nations' for the purposes of the constitution of a committee of the Inter-Governmental Maritime Consultative Organisation. It was held that the term referred only to registered tonnage so as to enable Liberia and Panama to be elected to the committee. Unfortunately, the opportunity was not taken of considering the problems of flags of convenience or the meaning of the 'genuine link' in the light of the true ownership of the ships involved, and so the doubts and ambiguities remain.

The UN Conference on Conditions of Registration of Ships, held under the auspices of the UN Conference on Trade and Development, convened in July 1984 and an agreement was signed in 1986. It attempts to deal with the flags of convenience issue, bearing in mind that nearly one-third of the world's merchant fleet by early 1985 flew such flags. It specifies that flag states should provide in their laws and regulations for the ownership of ships flying their flags and that those should include appropriate provision for participation by nationals as owners of such ships, and that such provisions should be sufficient to permit the flag state to exercise effectively its jurisdiction and control over ships flying its flag.[310]

The issue of the genuine link arose in the context of the Iran–Iraq war and in particular Iranian attacks upon Kuwaiti shipping. This prompted

---

[307] See the 1999 decision of the International Tribunal for the Law of the Sea in *M/V Saiga (No. 2)*, 120 ILR, pp. 143, 175.
[308] See Churchill and Lowe, *Law of the Sea*, pp. 213 ff.
[309] ICJ Reports, 1960, p. 150; 30 ILR, p. 426.
[310] *Keesing's Contemporary Archives*, p. 33952.

Kuwait to ask the UK and the USA to reflag Kuwaiti tankers. The USA agreed in early 1987 to reflag eleven such tankers under the US flag and to protect them as it did other US-flagged ships in the Gulf.[311] The UK also agreed to reflag some Kuwaiti tankers, arguing that only satisfaction of Department of Trade and Industry requirements was necessary.[312] Both states argued that the genuine link requirement was satisfied and, in view of the ambiguity of state practice as to the definition of genuine link in such instances, it is hard to argue that the US and UK acted unlawfully. The International Tribunal for the Law of the Sea in *M/V Saiga (No. 2)* has underlined that determination of the criteria and establishment of the procedures for granting and withdrawing nationality to ships are matters within the exclusive jurisdiction of the flag state, although disputes concerning such matters may be subject to the dispute settlement procedures of the 1982 Convention. The question of the nationality of a ship was a question of fact to be determined on the basis of evidence adduced by the parties.[313] The conduct of the flag state, 'at all times material to the dispute', was an important consideration in determining the nationality or registration of a ship.[314] The Tribunal has also confirmed that the requirement of a genuine link was in order to secure effective implementation of the duties of the flag state and not to establish criteria by reference to which the validity of the registration of ships in a flag state may be challenged by other states.[315]

Ships are required to sail under the flag of one state only and are subject to its exclusive jurisdiction (save in exceptional cases). Where a ship does sail under the flags of more than one state, according to convenience, it may be treated as a ship without nationality and will not be able to claim any of the nationalities concerned.[316] A ship that is stateless, and does not fly a flag, may be boarded and seized on the high seas. This point was accepted by the Privy Council in the case of *Naim Molvan* v.

---

[311] See 26 ILM, 1987, pp. 1429–30, 1435–40 and 1450–2. See also 37 ICLQ, 1988, pp. 424–45, and M. H. Nordquist and M. G. Wachenfeld, 'Legal Aspects of Reflagging Kuwaiti Tankers and Laying of Mines in the Persian Gulf', 31 German YIL, 1988, p. 138.

[312] See e.g. 119 HC Deb., col. 645, 17 July 1987.

[313] 120 ILR, pp. 143, 175–6. See also the decision by the International Tribunal for the Law of the Sea in the *Grand Prince* case, 2001, paras. 81 ff., 125 ILR, pp. 272, 297 ff. See www.itlos.org/start2_en.html.

[314] *M/V Saiga*, 120 ILR, pp. 143, 176 and the *Grand Prince* case, 2001, para. 89, 125 ILR, pp. 272, 299.

[315] *M/V Saiga*, 120 ILR, pp. 143, 179.

[316] Article 6 of the 1958 Convention and article 92 of the 1982 Convention.

Attorney-General for Palestine,[317] which concerned the seizure by the British navy of a stateless ship attempting to convey immigrants into Palestine.

The basic principle relating to jurisdiction on the high seas is that the flag state alone may exercise such rights over the ship.[318] This was elaborated in the *Lotus* case,[319] where it was held that 'vessels on the high seas are subject to no authority except that of the state whose flag they fly'.[320] This exclusivity is without exception regarding warships and ships owned or operated by a state where they are used only on governmental non-commercial service. Such ships have, according to articles 95 and 96 of the 1982 Convention, 'complete immunity from the jurisdiction of any state other than the flag state'.[321]

Exceptions to the exclusivity of flag-state jurisdiction

However, this basic principle is subject to exceptions regarding other vessels, and the concept of the freedom of the high seas is similarly limited by the existence of a series of exceptions.

Right of visit

Since the law of the sea depends to such an extent upon the nationality of the ship, it is well recognised in customary international law that warships have a right of approach to ascertain the nationality of ships. However, this right of approach to identify vessels does not incorporate the right to board or visit ships. This may only be undertaken, in the absence of hostilities between the flag states of the warship and a merchant vessel and in the absence of special treaty provisions to the contrary, where the ship is engaged in piracy or the slave trade, or, though flying a foreign flag or no flag at all, is in reality of the same nationality as the warship or of no nationality. But the warship has to operate carefully in such circumstances,

---

[317] [1948] AC 351; 13 AD, p. 51. See also e.g. *US* v. *Dominguez* 604 F.2d 304 (1979); *US* v. *Cortes* 588 F.2d 106 (1979); *US* v. *Monroy* 614 F.2d 61 (1980) and *US* v. *Marino-Garcia* 679 F.2d 1373 (1982). In the latter case, the Court referred to stateless vessels as 'international pariahs', *ibid.*, p. 1383.

[318] See article 6 of the 1958 Convention and article 92 of the 1982 Convention.

[319] PCIJ, Series A, No. 10, 1927, p. 25; 4 AD, p. 153. See also *Sellers* v. *Maritime Safety Inspector* [1999] 2 NZLR 44, 46–8; 120 ILR, p. 585.

[320] Note that duties of the flag state are laid down in articles 94, 97, 98, 99, 113 and 115 of the 1982 Convention.

[321] See articles 8 and 9 of the High Seas Convention, 1958.

since it may be liable to pay compensation for any loss or damage sustained if its suspicions are unfounded and the ship boarded has not committed any act justifying them. Thus, international law has settled for a narrow exposition of the right of approach, in spite of earlier tendencies to expand this right, and the above provisions were incorporated into article 22 of the High Seas Convention. Article 110 of the 1982 Convention added to this list a right of visit where the ship is engaged in unauthorised broadcasting and the flag state of the warship has under article 109 of the Convention jurisdiction to prosecute the offender.

Piracy [322]

The most formidable of the exceptions to the exclusive jurisdiction of the flag state and to the principle of the freedom of the high seas is the concept of piracy. Piracy is strictly defined in international law and was declared in article 101 of the 1982 Convention to consist of any of the following acts:

> (a) Any illegal acts of violence, detention or any act of depredation, committed for private ends by the crew or the passengers of a private ship or private aircraft and directed: (i) on the high seas, against another ship or aircraft, or against persons or property on board such ship or aircraft; (ii) against a ship, aircraft, persons or property in a place outside the jurisdiction of any state; (b) Any act of voluntary participation in the operation of a ship or of an aircraft with knowledge of facts making it a pirate ship or aircraft; (c) Any act of inciting or of intentionally facilitating an act described in subparagraph (a) or (b). [323]

The essence of piracy under international law is that it must be committed for private ends. In other words, any hijacking or takeover for political reasons is automatically excluded from the definition of piracy. Similarly, any acts committed on the ship by the crew and aimed at the ship itself or property or persons on the ship do not fall within this category.

Any and every state may seize a pirate ship or aircraft whether on the high seas or on *terra nullius* and arrest the persons and seize the property on board. In addition, the courts of the state carrying out the seizure

---

[322] See e.g. Brown, *International Law of the Sea*, vol. I, p. 299; *Oppenheim's International Law*, p. 746, and B. H. Dubner, *The Law of International Sea Piracy*, The Hague, 1979.

[323] See also article 15 of the High Seas Convention, 1958. Note that article 105 of the 1982 Convention deals with the seizure of pirate boats or aircraft, while article 106 provides for compensation in the case of seizure without adequate grounds. See also *Athens Maritime Enterprises Corporation v. Hellenic Mutual War Risks Association* [1983] 1 All ER 590; 78 ILR, p. 563.

have jurisdiction to impose penalties, and may decide what action to take regarding the ship or aircraft and property, subject to the rights of third parties that have acted in good faith.[324] The fact that every state may arrest and try persons accused of piracy makes that crime quite exceptional in international law, where so much emphasis is placed upon the sovereignty and jurisdiction of each particular state within its own territory. The first multilateral treaty concerning the regional implementation of the Convention's provisions on piracy was the Regional Cooperation Agreement on Combating Piracy and Armed Robbery against Ships in Asia in 2005, which calls for the establishment of an information-sharing centre in Singapore and extends the regulation of piracy beyond the high seas to events taking place in internal waters, territorial seas and archipelagic waters.[325]

The slave trade[326]

Although piracy may be suppressed by all states, most offences on the high seas can only be punished in accordance with regulations prescribed by the municipal legislation of states, even where international law requires such rules to be established. Article 99 of the 1982 Convention provides that every state shall take effective measures to prevent and punish the transport of slaves in ships authorised to fly its flag and to prevent the unlawful use of its flag for that purpose. Any slave taking refuge on board any ship, whatever its flag, shall *ipso facto* be free.[327] Under article 110, warships may board foreign merchant ships where they are reasonably suspected of engaging in the slave trade; offenders must be handed over to the flag state for trial.[328]

---

[324] See article 19 of the 1958 Convention and article 105 of the 1982 Convention. See also the Convention for the Suppression of Unlawful Acts Against the Safety of Maritime Navigation, 1988 and Protocol, 1989. Note that on 18 April 2008, a French court charged six Somalis with piracy following the release of hostages taken from a French yacht that they had allegedly seized in the Gulf of Aden. The Somalis were apprehended by French forces and removed to France with the permission of the President of Somalia: see www.news.bbc.co.uk/1/hi/world/Europe/7355598.stm.

[325] See 44 ILM, 2005, p. 829.

[326] See e.g. Brown, *International Law of the Sea*, vol. I, p. 309.

[327] See also article 13 of the High Seas Convention, 1958.

[328] See also article 22 of the High Seas Convention, 1958. Several international treaties exist with the aim of suppressing the slave trade and some provide for reciprocal rights of visits and search on the high seas: see e.g. Churchill and Lowe, *Law of the Sea*, pp. 171–2. Note also that under article 108 of the 1982 Convention all states are to co-operate in the suppression of the illicit drug trade.

Unauthorised broadcasting[329]

Under article 109 of the 1982 Convention, all states are to co-operate in the suppression of unauthorised broadcasting from the high seas. This is defined to mean transmission of sound or TV from a ship or installation on the high seas intended for reception by the general public, contrary to international regulations but excluding the transmission of distress calls. Any person engaged in such broadcasting may be prosecuted by the flag state of the ship, the state of registry of the installation, the state of which the person is a national, any state where the transmission can be received or any state where authorised radio communication is suffering interference.

Any of the above states having jurisdiction may arrest any person or ship engaging in unauthorised broadcasting on the high seas and seize the broadcasting apparatus.[330]

Hot pursuit[331]

The right of hot pursuit of a foreign ship is a principle designed to ensure that a vessel which has infringed the rules of a coastal state cannot escape punishment by fleeing to the high seas. In reality it means that in certain defined circumstances a coastal state may extend its jurisdiction onto the high seas in order to pursue and seize a ship which is suspected of infringing its laws. The right, which has been developing in one form or another since the nineteenth century,[332] was comprehensively elaborated in article 111 of the 1982 Convention, building upon article 23 of the High Seas Convention, 1958.

It notes that such pursuit may commence when the authorities of the coastal state have good reason to believe that the foreign ship has violated its laws. The pursuit must start while the ship, or one of its boats, is within the internal waters, territorial sea or contiguous zone of the coastal state and may only continue outside the territorial sea or contiguous zone if it is uninterrupted. However, if the pursuit commences while the foreign

---

[329] See e.g. J. C. Woodliffe, 'The Demise of Unauthorised Broadcasting from Ships in International Waters', 1 *Journal of Estuarine and Coastal Law*, 1986, p. 402, and Brown, *International Law of the Sea*, vol. I, p. 312.

[330] See also article 110 of the 1982 Convention. In addition, see the European Agreement for the Prevention of Broadcasting transmitted from Stations outside National Territories.

[331] See e.g. N. Poulantzas, *The Right of Hot Pursuit in International Law*, 2nd edn, The Hague, 2002, and *Oppenheim's International Law*, p. 739. See also W. C. Gilmore, 'Hot Pursuit: The Case of R v. Mills and Others', 44 ICLQ, 1995, p. 949.

[332] See e.g. the *I'm Alone* case, 3 RIAA, p. 1609 (1935); 7 AD, p. 203.

ship is in the contiguous zone, then it may only be undertaken if there has been a violation of the rights for the protection of which the zone was established. The right may similarly commence from the archipelagic waters. In addition, the right will apply *mutatis mutandis* to violations in the exclusive economic zone or on the continental shelf (including safety zones around continental shelf installations) of the relevant rules and regulations applicable to such areas.

Hot pursuit only begins when the pursuing ship has satisfied itself that the ship pursued or one of its boats is within the limits of the territorial sea or, as the case may be, in the contiguous zone or economic zone or on the continental shelf. It is essential that prior to the chase a visual or auditory signal to stop has been given at a distance enabling it to be seen or heard by the foreign ship and pursuit may only be exercised by warships or military aircraft or by specially authorised government ships or planes. The right of hot pursuit ceases as soon as the ship pursued has entered the territorial waters of its own or a third state. The International Tribunal for the Law of the Sea has emphasised that the conditions laid down in article 111 are cumulative, each one of them having to be satisfied in order for the pursuit to be lawful.[333] In stopping and arresting a ship in such circumstances, the use of force must be avoided if at all possible and, where it is unavoidable, it must not go beyond what is reasonable and necessary in the circumstances.[334]

Collisions

Where ships are involved in collisions on the high seas, article 11 of the High Seas Convention declares, overruling the decision in the *Lotus* case,[335] that penal or disciplinary proceedings may only be taken against the master or other persons in the service of the ship by the authorities of either the flag state or the state of which the particular person is a national. It also provides that no arrest or detention of the ship, even for investigation purposes, can be ordered by other than the authorities of the flag state. This was reaffirmed in article 97 of the 1982 Convention.

---

[333] *M/V Saiga*, 120 ILR, pp. 143, 194.

[334] *Ibid.*, p. 196. See also the *I'm Alone* case, 3 RIAA, p. 1609 (1935); 7 AD, p. 203, and the *Red Crusader* case, 35 ILR, p. 485. Note that article 22(1)f of the Straddling Stocks Convention, 1995 provides that an inspecting state shall avoid the use of force except when and to the degree necessary to ensure the safety of the inspectors and where the inspectors are obstructed in the execution of their duties. In addition, the force used must not exceed that reasonably required in the circumstances.

[335] PCIJ, Series A, No. 10, 1927, p. 25; 4 AD, p. 153.

Treaty rights and agreements[336]

In many cases, states may by treaty permit each other's warships to exercise certain powers of visit and search as regards vessels flying the flags of the signatories to the treaty.[337] For example, most of the agreements in the nineteenth century relating to the suppression of the slave trade provided that warships of the parties to the agreements could search and sometimes detain vessels suspected of being involved in the trade, where such vessels were flying the flags of the treaty states. The Convention for the Protection of Submarine Cables of 1884 gave the warships of contracting states the right to stop and ascertain the nationality of merchant ships that were suspected of infringing the terms of the Convention, and other agreements dealing with matters as diverse as arms trading and liquor smuggling contained like powers. Until recently, the primary focus of such activities in fact concerned drug trafficking.[338] However, the question of the proliferation of weapons of mass destruction (WMD) is today of great importance.[339] This issue has been tackled by a mix of international treaties, bilateral treaties, international co-operation and Security Council action. Building on the Security Council statement in 1992 identifying the proliferation of WMD as a threat to international peace and security,[340] the US announced the Proliferation Security Initiative in May 2003. A statement of Interdiction Principles agreed by participants in the initiative in September 2003 provided for the undertaking of effective measures to interdict the transfer or transport of WMD, their delivery systems and related materials to and from states and non-state actors of proliferation concern. Such measures were to include the boarding and

---

[336] See e.g. Churchill and Lowe, *Law of the Sea*, pp. 218 ff.

[337] This falls within article 110, which notes that 'Except where acts of interference derive from powers conferred by treaty…'.

[338] See the UK–US Agreement on Vessels Trafficking in Drugs, 1981 and *US v. Biermann*, 83 AJIL, 1989, p. 99; 84 ILR, p. 206. See also e.g. the Vienna Convention Against Illicit Traffic in Narcotic Drugs and Psychotropic Substances, 1988 and the Council of Europe Agreement on Illicit Traffic by Sea, 1995. But see as to enforcement of the Straddling Stocks Convention, below, p. 623.

[339] See e.g. M. Byers, 'Policing the High Seas: The Proliferation Security Initiative', 98 AJIL, 2004, p. 526; D. Joyner, 'The Proliferation Security Initiative: Nonproliferation, Counter-proliferation and International Law', 30 Yale JIL, 2005, p. 507; D. Guilfoyle, 'Interdicting Vessels to Enforce the Common Interest: Maritime Countermeasures and the Use of Force', 56 ICLQ, 2007, p. 69, and Guilfoyle, 'Maritime Interdiction of Weapons of Mass Destruction', 12 *Journal of Conflict and Security Law*, 2007, p. 1. See also the statement of the UK Foreign Office Minister of 25 April 2006, UKMIL, 77 BYIL, 2006, pp. 773–4.

[340] S/23500, 31 January 1992.

search of any vessel flying the flag of one of the participants, with their consent, in internal waters, territorial seas or beyond the territorial seas, where such vessel is reasonably suspected of carrying WMD materials to or from states or non-state actors of proliferation concern.[341] In addition, the US has signed a number of bilateral WMD interdiction agreements, providing for consensual boarding of vessels.[342]

In a further development, Security Council resolution 1540 (2004) required all states *inter alia* to prohibit and criminalise the transfer of WMD and delivery systems to non-state actors, although there is no direct reference to interdiction.[343] In addition, a Protocol adopted in 2005 to the Convention on the Suppression of Unlawful Acts against the Safety of Maritime Navigation provides essentially for the criminalisation of knowingly transporting WMD and related materials by sea and provides for enforcement by interdiction on the high seas.[344]

Pollution[345]

Article 24 of the 1958 Convention on the High Seas called on states to draw up regulations to prevent the pollution of the seas by the discharge of oil or the dumping of radioactive waste, while article 1 of the Convention on the Fishing and Conservation of the Living Resources of the High Seas, of the same year, declared that all states had the duty to adopt, or co-operate with other states in adopting, such measures as may be necessary for the conservation of the living resources of the high seas. Although these provisions have not proved an unqualified success, they have been reinforced by an interlocking series of additional agreements covering the environmental protection of the seas.

The International Convention relating to Intervention on the High Seas in Cases of Oil Pollution Casualties, signed in 1969 and in force as of June 1975, provides that the parties to the Convention may take such measures on the high seas:

---

[341] Participants include the US, UK, Australia, Canada, France, Germany, Italy, Japan, the Netherlands, New Zealand, Norway, Poland, Portugal, Singapore, Spain and Turkey: see Guilfoyle, 'Maritime Interdiction', p. 12.

[342] Including with Liberia, Panama, Croatia, Cyprus and Belize: see Guilfoyle, 'Maritime Interdiction', p. 22.

[343] See below, chapter 22, pp. 1208 and 1240.

[344] Guilfoyle, 'Maritime Interdiction', pp. 28 ff.

[345] See Brown, *International Law of the Sea*, vol. I, chapter 15; Churchill and Lowe, *Law of the Sea*, chapter 15, and O'Connell, *International Law of the Sea*, vol. II, chapter 25. See also below, chapter 15.

as may be necessary to prevent, mitigate or eliminate grave and imminent danger to their coastline or related interests from pollution or threat of pollution of the sea by oil, following upon a maritime casualty or acts related to such a casualty, which may reasonably be expected to result in major harmful consequences.

This provision came as a result of the *Torrey Canyon* incident in 1967[346] in which a Liberian tanker foundered off the Cornish coast, spilling massive quantities of oil and polluting large stretches of the UK and French coastlines. As a last resort to prevent further pollution, British aircraft bombed the tanker and set it ablaze. The Convention on Intervention on the High Seas provided for action to be taken to end threats to the coasts of states, while the Convention on Civil Liability for Oil Pollution Damage, also signed in 1969 and which came into effect in June 1975, stipulated that the owners of ships causing oil pollution damage were to be liable to pay compensation.

The latter agreement was supplemented in 1971 by the Convention on the Establishment of an International Fund for Compensation for Oil Pollution Damage which sought to provide for compensation in circumstances not covered by the 1969 Convention and aid shipowners in their additional financial obligations.

These agreements are only a small part of the web of treaties covering the preservation of the sea environment. Other examples include the 1954 Convention for the Prevention of Pollution of the Seas by Oil, with its series of amendments designed to ban offensive discharges; the 1972 Oslo Convention for the Prevention of Marine Pollution by Dumping from Ships and Aircraft and the subsequent London Convention on the Dumping of Wastes at Sea later the same year; the 1973 Convention for the Prevention of Pollution from Ships; and the 1974 Paris Convention for the Prevention of Marine Pollution from Land-Based Sources.[347]

Under the 1982 Convention nearly fifty articles are devoted to the protection of the marine environment. Flag states still retain the competence to legislate for their ships, but certain minimum standards are imposed

---

[346] 6 ILM, 1967, p. 480. See also the *Amoco Cadiz* incident in 1978, e.g. Churchill and Lowe, *Law of the Sea*, p. 241, and the *Aegean Sea* and *Braer* incidents in 1992–3, e.g. G. Plant, '"Safer Ships, Cleaner Seas": Lord Donaldson's Inquiry, UK Government's Response and International Law', 44 ICLQ, 1995, p. 939.

[347] Also a variety of regional and bilateral agreements have been signed, Churchill and Lowe, *Law of the Sea*, pp. 263–4.

upon them.[348] It is also provided that states are responsible for the fulfilment of their international obligations concerning the protection and preservation of the marine environment and are liable in accordance with international law. States must also ensure that recourse is available in accordance with their legal systems for prompt and adequate compensation or other relief regarding damage caused by pollution of the marine environment by persons under their jurisdiction.[349]

States are under a basic obligation to protect and preserve the marine environment.[350] Article 194 of the 1982 Convention also provides that:

> 1. States shall take, individually or jointly as appropriate, all measures consistent with this Convention that are necessary to prevent, reduce and control pollution of the marine environment from any source, using for this purpose the best practicable means at their disposal and in accordance with their capabilities, and they shall endeavour to harmonise their policies in this connection.
>
> 2. States shall take all measures necessary to ensure that activities under their jurisdiction or control are so conducted as not to cause damage by pollution to other States and their environment, and that pollution arising from incidents or activities under their jurisdiction or control does not spread beyond the areas where they exercise sovereign rights in accordance with this Convention.
>
> 3. The measures taken pursuant to this Part shall deal with all sources of pollution of the marine environment. These measures shall include, *inter alia*, those designed to minimise to the fullest possible extent:
>
> (a) the release of toxic, harmful, or noxious substances, especially those which are persistent, from land-based sources, from or through the atmosphere or by dumping;
>
> (b) pollution from vessels, in particular measures for preventing accidents and dealing with emergencies, ensuring the safety of operations at sea, preventing intentional and unintentional discharges, and regulating the design, construction, equipment, operation and manning of vessels;
>
> (c) pollution from installations and devices used in exploitation of the natural resources of the seabed and subsoil, in particular measures for preventing accidents and dealing with emergencies, ensuring the safety of operations at sea, and regulating the design, construction, equipment, operation and manning of such installations or devices;

---

[348] See article 211. See also generally articles 192–237, covering *inter alia* global and regional co-operation, technical assistance, monitory and environmental assessment, and the development of the enforcement of international and domestic law preventing pollution.
[349] Article 235.　　　[350] Article 192.

(d) pollution from other installations and devices operating in the marine environment, in particular for preventing accidents and dealing with emergencies, ensuring the safety of operations at sea, and regulating the design, construction, equipment, operation and manning of such installations or devices.

4. In taking measures to prevent, reduce or control pollution of the marine environment, states shall refrain from unjustifiable interference with activities carried out by other states in the exercise of their rights and in pursuance of their duties in conformity with this Convention.[351]

Straddling stocks[352]

The freedom to fish on the high seas is one of the fundamental freedoms of the high seas, but it is not total or absolute.[353] The development of

---

[351] See also the Mox case, the International Tribunal for the Law of the Sea, Provisional Measures Order of 3 December 2001, www.itlos.org/start2_en.html; the OSPAR award of 2 July 2003, see www.pca-cpa.org/upload/files/OSPAR%20Award.pdf; the arbitral tribunal's suspension of proceedings, Order No. 3 of 24 June 2003 and Order No. 4 of 14 November 2003, see www.pca-cpa.org/upload/files/MOX%20Order%20no3.pdf and www.pca-cpa.org/upload/files/MOX%20Order%20No4.pdf and 126 ILR, pp. 257 ff. and 310 ff. See also the decision of the European Court of Justice of 30 May 2006, Case C-459/03, *Commission v. Ireland*, 45 ILM, 2006, p. 1074, where the Court found that by instituting proceedings against the UK under the Law of the Sea Convention dispute settlement mechanisms, Ireland had breached its obligations under articles 10 and 292 of the European Community Treaty and articles 192 and 193 of the European Atomic Energy Treaty.

[352] See e.g. Brown, *International Law of the Sea*, vol. I, p. 226; Churchill and Lowe, *Law of the Sea*, p. 305; F. Orrego Vicuña, *The Changing International Law of High Seas Fisheries*, Cambridge, 1999; W. T. Burke, *The New International Law of Fisheries*, Oxford, 1994; H. Gherari, 'L'Accord de 4 août 1995 sur les Stocks Chevauchants et les Stocks de Poisson Grands Migrateurs', 100 RGDIP, 1996, p. 367; B. Kwiatowska, 'Creeping Jurisdiction beyond 200 Miles in the Light of the 1982 Law of the Sea Convention and State Practice', 22 *Ocean Development and International Law*, 1991, p. 167; E. Miles and W. T. Burke, 'Pressures on the UN Convention on the Law of the Sea 1982 Arising from New Fisheries Conflicts: The Problem of Straddling Stocks', 20 *Ocean Development and International Law*, 1989, p. 352; E. Meltzer, 'Global Overview of Straddling and Highly Migratory Fish Stocks: The Nonsustainable Nature of High Seas Fisheries', 25 *Ocean Development and International Law*, 1994, p. 256; P. G. G. Davies and C. Redgwell, 'The International Legal Regulation of Straddling Fish Stocks', 67 BYIL, 1996, p. 199; D. H. Anderson, 'The Straddling Stocks Agreement of 1995 – An Initial Assessment', 45 ICLQ, 1996, p. 463, and D. Freestone and Z. Makuch, 'The New International Environmental Law of Fisheries: The 1995 United Nations Straddling Stocks Agreement', 7 *Yearbook of International Environmental Law*, 1996, p. 3.

[353] See article 2 of the High Seas Convention, 1958 and articles 1 and 6 of the Geneva Convention on Fishing and Conservation of the Living Resources of the High Seas, 1958, and article 116 of the 1982 Convention. In particular, the freedom to fish is subject to a state's treaty obligations, to the interests and rights of coastal states and to the requirements of

exclusive economic zones has meant that the area of high seas has shrunk appreciably, so that the bulk of fish stocks are now to be found within the economic zones of coastal states. In addition, the interests of such coastal states have extended to impinge more clearly upon the regulation of the high seas.

Article 56(1) of the 1982 Convention provides that coastal states have sovereign rights over their economic zones for the purpose of exploring and exploiting, conserving and managing the fish stocks of the zones concerned. Such rights are accompanied by duties as to conservation and management measures in order to ensure that the fish stocks in exclusive economic zones are not endangered by over-exploitation and that such stocks are maintained at, or restored to, levels which can produce the maximum sustainable yield.[354] Where the same stock or stocks of associated species occur within the exclusive economic zones of two or more coastal states, these states shall seek either directly or through appropriate subregional or regional organisations to agree upon the measures necessary to co-ordinate and ensure the conservation and development of such stocks.[355] Article 116(b) of the 1982 Convention states that the freedom to fish on the high seas is subject to the rights and duties as well as the interests of coastal states as detailed above, while the 1982 Convention lays down a general obligation upon states to co-operate in taking such measures for their respective nationals as may be necessary for the conservation of the living resources of the high seas and a variety of criteria are laid down for the purpose of determining the allowable catch and establishing other conservation measures.[356]

A particular problem is raised with regard to straddling stocks, that is stocks of fish that straddle both exclusive economic zones and high seas, for if the latter were not in some way regulated, fishery stocks regularly present in the exclusive economic zone could be depleted by virtue of unrestricted

---

conservation. See generally on international fisheries law, www.oceanlaw.net/ and above, p. 581, with regard to the *Fisheries Jurisdiction* case.

[354] Article 61. See also article 62.

[355] Article 63(1). This is without prejudice to the other provisions of this Part of the 1982 Convention.

[356] See articles 117–20. A series of provisions in the 1982 Convention apply with regard to particular species, e.g. article 64 concerning highly migratory species (such as tuna); article 65 concerning marine mammals (such as whales, for which see also the work of the International Whaling Commission); article 66 concerning anadromous species (such as salmon); article 67 concerning catadromous species (such as eels) and article 68 concerning sedentary species (which are regarded as part of the natural resources of a coastal state's continental shelf: see article 77(4)).

fishing of those stocks while they were present on the high seas. Article 63(2) of the 1982 Convention stipulates that where the same stock or stocks of associated species occur both within the exclusive economic zone and in an area beyond and adjacent to the zone (i.e. the high seas), the coastal state and the states fishing for such stocks in the adjacent area shall seek, either directly or through appropriate subregional or regional organisations, to agree upon the measures necessary for the conservation of these stocks in the adjacent area.

The provisions in the 1982 Convention, however, were not deemed to be fully comprehensive[357] and, as problems of straddling stocks grew more apparent,[358] a Straddling Stocks Conference was set up in 1993 and produced an agreement two years later. The Agreement emphasises the need to conserve and manage straddling fish stocks and highly migratory species and calls in particular for the application of the precautionary approach.[359] Coastal states and states fishing on the high seas shall pursue co-operation in relation to straddling and highly migratory fish stocks either directly or through appropriate subregional or regional organisations and shall enter into consultations in good faith and without delay at the request of any interested state with a view to establishing appropriate arrangements to ensure conservation and management of the stocks.[360] Much emphasis is placed upon subregional and regional organisations and article 10 provides that in fulfilling their obligation to co-operate through such organisations or arrangements, states shall *inter alia* agree on measures to ensure the long-term sustainability of straddling and highly migratory fish stocks and agree as appropriate upon participatory rights such as allocations of allowable catch or levels of fishing effort. In particular, the establishment of co-operative mechanisms for effective

---

[357] See e.g. Burke, *New International Law of Fisheries*, pp. 348 ff., and B. Kwiatowska, 'The High Seas Fisheries Regime: At a Point of No Return?', 8 *International Journal of Marine and Coastal Law*, 1993, p. 327.

[358] E.g. with regard to the Grand Banks of Newfoundland, the Bering Sea, the Barents Sea, the Sea of Okhotsk and off Patagonia and the Falklands, see Anderson, 'Straddling Stocks Agreement', p. 463.

[359] See articles 5 and 6 of the Straddling Stocks Agreement. See also, with regard to this approach, below, chapter 15, p. 868. See generally on the agreement which came into force on 11 December 2001, www.un.org/Depts/los/convention_agreements/ convention_overview_fish_stocks.htm.

[360] Article 8. Note that by article 1(3) the agreement 'applies *mutatis mutandis* to other fishing entities whose vessels fish on the high seas'. This was intended to refer to Taiwan: see e.g. Orrego Vicuña, *High Seas Fisheries*, p. 139, and Anderson, 'Straddling Stocks Agreement', p. 468.

monitoring, control, surveillance and enforcement, decision-making procedures facilitating the adoption of such measures of conservation and management, and the promotion of the peaceful settlement of disputes are called for. The focus in terms of implementation is upon the flag state. Article 18 provides that flag states shall take such measures as may be necessary to ensure that their vessels comply with subregional and regional conservation and management measures, while article 19 provides that flag states must enforce such measures irrespective of where violations occur and investigate immediately any alleged violation. Article 21 deals specifically with subregional and regional co-operation in enforcement and provides that in any area of the high seas covered by such an organisation or arrangement, a state party which is also a member or participant in such an organisation or arrangement may board and inspect fishing vessels flying the flag of another state party to the Agreement. This applies whether that state party is or is not a member of or a participant in such a subregional or regional organisation or arrangement. The boarding and visiting powers are for the purpose of ensuring compliance with the conservation and management measures established by the organisation or arrangement. Where, following a boarding and inspection, there are clear grounds for believing that a vessel has engaged in activities contrary to the relevant conservation and management measures, the inspecting state shall secure evidence and promptly notify the flag state. The flag state must respond within three working days and either fulfil its investigation and enforcement obligations under article 19 or authorise the inspecting state to investigate. In the latter case, the flag state must then take enforcement action or authorise the inspecting state to take such action. Where there are clear grounds for believing that the vessel has committed a serious violation and the flag state has failed to respond or take action as required, the inspectors may remain on board and secure evidence and may require the master to bring the vessel into the nearest appropriate port.[361] Article 23 provides that a port state has the right and duty to take measures in accordance with international law to promote the effectiveness of subregional, regional and global conservation and management measures.[362]

One of the major regional organisations existing in this area is the North Atlantic Fisheries Organisation (NAFO), which came into being

---

[361] See also article 22.
[362] Note that by article 17(3) the fishing entities referred to in article 1(3) may be requested to co-operate with the organisations or arrangements in question.

following the Northwest Atlantic Fisheries Convention, 1978. The organisation has established a Fisheries Commission with responsibility for conservation measures in the area covered by this Convention. The European Community is a party to the Convention, although it has objected on occasions to NAFO's total catch quotas and the share-out of such quotas among state parties. In particular, a dispute developed with regard to the share-out of Greenland halibut, following upon a decision by NAFO to reduce the EC share of this fishery in 1995.[363] The EC formally objected to this decision using NAFO procedures and established its own halibut quota, which was in excess of the NAFO quota. In May 1994, Canada had amended its Coastal Fisheries Protection Act 1985 in order to enable it to take action to prevent further destruction of straddling stocks and by virtue of which any vessel from any nation fishing at variance with good conservation rules could be rendered subject to Canadian action. In early 1995, regulations were issued in order to protect Greenland halibut outside Canada's 200-mile limit from overfishing. On 9 March 1995, Canadian officers boarded a Spanish vessel fishing on the high seas on the Grand Banks some 245 miles off the Canadian coast. The captain was arrested and the vessel seized and towed to a Canadian harbour. Spain commenced an application before the International Court, but this failed on jurisdictional grounds.[364] In April 1995, an agreement between the EC and Canada was reached, under which the EC obtained an increased quota for Greenland halibut and Canada stayed charges against the vessel and agreed to repeal the provisions of the regulation banning Spanish and Portuguese vessels from fishing in the NAFO regulatory area. Improved control and enforcement procedures were also agreed.[365] Problems have also arisen in other areas: for example, the 'Donut Hole', a part of the high seas in the Bering Sea surrounded by the exclusive economic zones of Russia and the US,[366] and the 'Peanut Hole', a part of the high seas in the Sea of Okhotsk surrounded by Russia's economic zone. In 2001, the Convention on the Conservation and Management of Highly Migratory Fish Stocks in the Western and Central Pacific Ocean was signed. This agreement establishes a Commission to determine *inter alia* the

---

[363] See e.g. P. G. G. Davies, 'The EC/Canadian Fisheries Dispute in the Northwest Atlantic', 44 ICLQ, 1995, p. 927.

[364] ICJ Reports, 1998, p. 432.

[365] See European Commission Press Release, WE/15/95, 20 April 1995.

[366] See the Convention on the Conservation and Management of Pollock Resources in the Central Bering Sea, 1994.

total allowable catch within the area and to adopt standards for fishing operations.[367]

The international seabed[368]

Introduction

In recent years the degree of wealth contained beneath the high seas has become more and more apparent. It is estimated that some 175 billion dry tonnes of mineable manganese nodules are in existence, scattered over some 15 per cent of the seabed. This far exceeds the land-based reserves of the metals involved (primarily manganese, nickel, copper and cobalt).[369] While this source of mineral wealth is of great potential importance to the developed nations possessing or soon to possess the technical capacity to mine such nodules, it poses severe problems for developing states, particularly those who are dependent upon the export earnings of a few categories of minerals. Zaire, for example, accounts for over one third of total cobalt production, while Gabon and India each account for around 8 per cent of total manganese production.[370] By the early 1990s, there appeared to be six major deep sea mining consortia with the participation of numerous American, Japanese, Canadian, British, Belgian, German, Dutch and French companies.[371] The technology to mine is at an advanced stage and some basic investment has been made, although it is unlikely that there will be considerable mining activity for several years to come.

---

[367] Note also the existence of other agreements with regard to specific species of fish, e.g. the International Convention for the Conservation of Atlantic Tuna, 1966; the Convention for the Conservation of Southern Bluefin Tuna, 1993 and the Indian Ocean Tuna Commission Agreement, 1993.

[368] See e.g. Brown, *International Law of the Sea*, vol. I, chapter 17; O'Connell, *International Law of the Sea*, vol. I, chapter 12; Churchill and Lowe, *Law of the Sea*, chapter 12; E. Luard, *The Control of the Seabed*, Oxford, 1974; B. Buzan, *Seabed Politics*, New York, 1976; T. G. Kronmiller, *The Lawfulness of Deep Seabed Mining*, New York, 2 vols., 1980; E. D. Brown, *Sea-Bed Energy and Mineral Resources and the Law of the Sea*, London, 3 vols., 1986; A. M. Post, *Deepsea Mining and the Law of the Sea*, The Hague, 1983; A. D. Henchoz, *Règlementations Nationales et Internationales de l'Exploration et de l'Exploitation des Grans Fonds Marins*, Zurich, 1992; *Oppenheim's International Law*, p. 812, and Nguyen Quoc Dinh *et al.*, *Droit International Public*, p. 1210.

[369] See e.g. *Seabed Mineral Resource Development*, UN Dept. of International Economic and Social Affairs, 1980, ST/ESA/107, pp. 1–2.

[370] *Ibid.*, p. 3. Zaire is now called the Democratic Republic of the Congo.

[371] *Ibid.*, pp. 10–12.

In 1969, the UN General Assembly adopted resolution 2574 (XXIV) calling for a moratorium on deep seabed activities and a year later a Declaration of Principles Governing the Seabed and Ocean Floor and the Subsoil Thereof, beyond the Limits of National Jurisdiction ('the Area') was adopted. This provided that the Area and its resources were the 'common heritage of mankind' and could not be appropriated, and that no rights at all could be acquired over it except in conformity with an international regime to be established to govern its exploration and exploitation.

The 1982 Law of the Sea Convention (Part XI)

Under the Convention, the Area[372] and its resources are deemed to be the common heritage of mankind and no sovereign or other rights may be recognised. Minerals recovered from the Area in accordance with the Convention are alienable, however.[373] Activities in the Area are to be carried out for the benefit of mankind as a whole by or on behalf of the International Seabed Authority (the Authority) established under the Convention.[374] The Authority is to provide for the equitable sharing of such benefits.[375] Activities in the Area are to be carried out under article 153 by the Enterprise (i.e. the organ of the Authority established as its operating arm) and by states parties or state enterprises, or persons possessing the nationality of state parties or effectively controlled by them, acting in association with the Authority. The latter 'qualified applicants' will be required to submit formal written plans of work to be approved by the Council after review by the Legal and Technical Commission.[376]

This plan of work is to specify two sites of equal estimated commercial value. The Authority may then approve a plan of work relating to one of these sites and designate the other as a 'reserved site' which may only

---

[372] Defined in article 1 as the 'seabed and ocean floor and subsoil thereof beyond national jurisdiction'. This would start at the outer edge of the continental margin or at least at a distance of 200 nautical miles from the baselines.

[373] Articles 136 and 137.

[374] See below, p. 633. Note that certain activities in the Area do not need the consent of the Authority, e.g. pipeline and cable laying and scientific research not concerning seabed resources: see articles 112, 143 and 256.

[375] Article 140. See also article 150.

[376] See also Annex III, articles 3 and 4. Highly controversial requirements for transfer of technology are also included, ibid., article 5.

be exploited by the Authority, via the Enterprise or in association with developing states.[377]

Resolution I of the Conference established a Preparatory Commission to make arrangements for the operation of the Authority and the International Tribunal for the Law of the Sea. [378]

Resolution II of the Conference made special provision for eight 'pioneer investors', four from France, Japan, India and the USSR and four from Belgium, Canada, the Federal Republic of Germany, Italy, Japan, the Netherlands, the UK and the USA, and possibly others from developing states, to be given pioneer status. Each investor must have invested at least $30 million in preparation for seabed mining, at least 10 per cent of which must be invested in a specific site. Sponsoring states must provide certification that this has happened.[379] Such pioneer investors are to be able to carry out exploration activities pending entry into force of the Convention with priority over the other applicants (apart from the Enterprise) in the allocation of exploitation contracts.[380] India, France, Japan and the USSR were registered as pioneer investors in 1987 on behalf of various consortia.[381] China was registered as a pioneer investor in March 1991,[382] while the multinational Interoceanmetal Joint Organisation was registered as a pioneer investor in August that year.[383] Several sites have

---

[377] Ibid., articles 8 and 9. The production policies of the Authority are detailed in article 151 of the Convention.

[378] 21(4) UN Chronicle, 1984, pp. 44 ff. See also 25 ILM, 1986, p. 1329 and 26 ILM, 1987, p. 1725.

[379] See Churchill and Lowe, Law of the Sea, p. 230.

[380] See 21(4) UN Chronicle, 1984, pp. 45–7.

[381] See LOS/PCN/97–99 (1987). See also the Understanding of 5 September 1986 making various changes to the rules regarding pioneer operations, including extending the deadline by which the $30 million investment had to be made and establishing a Group of Technical Experts, LOS/PCN/L.41/Rev.1. See also Brown, International Law of the Sea, vol. I, pp. 448–54. An Understanding of 30 August 1990 dealt with training costs, transfer of technology, expenditure on exploration and the development of a mine site for the Authority, ibid., pp. 454–5, while an Understanding of 22 February 1991 dealt with the avoidance of overlapping claims signed by China on the one hand and seven potential pioneer investor states on the other (Belgium, Canada, Italy, the Netherlands, Germany, the UK and the US), ibid., p. 455.

[382] Brown, International Law of the Sea, vol. I, p. 455.

[383] Ibid., p. 456. This organisation consisted of Bulgaria, Czechoslovakia, Poland, the Russian Federation and Cuba. See, for the full list of registered pioneer investors, www.isa.org.jm/en/default.htm. The first fifteen-year contracts for exploration for polymetallic nodules in the deep seabed were signed at the headquarters of the International Seabed Authority in Jamaica in March 2001, ibid.

been earmarked for the Authority, all on the Clarion–Clipperton Ridge in the North-Eastern Equatorial Pacific.

The regime for the deep seabed, however, was opposed by the United States in particular and, as a consequence, it voted against the adoption of the 1982 Convention. The UK also declared that it would not sign the Convention until a satisfactory regime for deep seabed mining was established.[384] Concern was particularly expressed regarding the failure to provide assured access to seabed minerals, lack of a proportionate voice in decision-making for countries most affected, and the problems that would be caused by not permitting the free play of market forces in the development of seabed resources.[385]

The Reciprocating States Regime

As a result of developments in the Conference on the Law of the Sea, many states began to enact domestic legislation with the aim of establishing an interim framework for exploration and exploitation of the seabed pending an acceptable international solution. The UK Deep Sea Mining (Temporary Provisions) Act 1981, for example, provided for the granting of exploration licences (but not in respect of a period before 1 July 1981) and exploitation licences (but not for a period before 1 January 1988).[386]

A 1982 Agreement[387] called for consultations to avoid overlapping claims under national legislation and for arbitration to resolve any dispute.[388] The Preparatory Commission, however, adopted a declaration in 1985 stating that any claim, agreement or action regarding the Area and its resources undertaken outside the Commission itself, which was

---

[384] See e.g. *The Times*, 16 February 1984, p. 4, and 33 HC Deb., col. 404, 2 December 1982.

[385] See e.g. the US delegate, *UN Chronicle*, June 1982, p. 16.

[386] The Act also provided for a Deep Sea Mining Levy to be paid by the holder of an exploitation licence into a Deep Sea Mining Fund and for mutual recognition of licences. A number of countries adopted similar, unilateral legislation, e.g. the US in 1980, 19 ILM, 1980, p. 1003; 20 ILM, 1981, p. 1228 and 21 ILM, 1982, p. 867; West Germany, 20 ILM, 1981, p. 393 and 21 ILM, 1982, p. 832; the USSR, 21 ILM, 1982, p. 551; France, 21 ILM, 1982, p. 808, and Japan, 22 ILM, 1983, p. 102: see Brown, *International Law of the Sea*, vol. I, pp. 456 ff.

[387] The 1982 Agreement Concerning Interim Arrangements Relating to Polymetallic Nodules of the Deep Seabed (France, Federal Republic of Germany, UK, US), 21 ILM, 1982, p. 950.

[388] See also the Provisional Understanding Regarding Deep Seabed Mining (Belgium, France, Federal Republic of Germany, Italy, Japan, Netherlands, UK, US), 23 ILM, 1984, p. 1354.

incompatible with the 1982 Convention and its related resolutions, 'shall not be recognised'.[389]

The 1994 Agreement on Implementation of the Seabed Provisions of the Convention on the Law of the Sea [390]

Attempts to ensure the universality of the 1982 Convention system and thus prevent the development of conflicting deep seabed regimes began in earnest in 1990 in consultations sponsored by the UN Secretary-General, with more flexibility being shown by states.[391] Eventually, the 1994 Agreement emerged. The states parties undertake in article 1 to implement Part XI of the 1982 Convention in accordance with the Agreement. By article 2, the Agreement and Part XI are to be interpreted and applied together as a single instrument and, in the event of any inconsistency, the provisions in the former document are to prevail. States can only express their consent to become bound by the Agreement if they at the same time or previously express their consent to be bound by the Convention. Thus, conflicting systems operating with regard to the seabed became impossible. The Agreement also provides in article 7 for provisional application if it had not come into force on 16 November 1994 (the date on which the Convention came into force).[392] The Agreement was thus able to be provisionally applied by states that had consented to its adoption in the General Assembly, unless they had otherwise notified the depositary (the UN Secretary-General) in writing; by states and entities signing the agreement, unless they had otherwise notified the depositary in writing; by states and entities which had consented to its provisional application

---

[389] See *Law of the Sea Bulletin*, no. 6, October 1985, p. 85. But see the 1987 Agreement on the Resolution of Practical Problems, 26 ILM, 1987, p. 1502. This was an attempt by the states involved to prevent overlapping claims.

[390] 33 ILM, 1994, p. 1309. See also B. H. Oxman, 'The 1994 Agreement and the Convention', 88 AJIL, 1994, p. 687; L. B. Sohn, 'International Law Implications of the 1994 Agreement', *ibid.*, p. 696; J. I. Charney, 'US Provisional Application of the 1994 Deep Seabed Agreement', *ibid.*, p. 705; D. H. Anderson, 'Further Efforts to Ensure Universal Participation in the United Nations Convention on the Law of the Sea', 43 ICLQ, 1994, p. 886, and Report of the UN Secretary-General, A/50/713, 1 November 1995.

[391] See e.g. D. H. Anderson, 'Efforts to Ensure Universal Participation in the United Nations Convention on the Law of the Sea', 42 ICLQ, 1993, p. 654, and Brown, *International Law of the Sea*, vol. I, p. 462.

[392] The Agreement came into force on 28 July 1996, being thirty days after the date on which forty states had established their consent to be bound under procedures detailed in articles 4 and 5.

by so notifying the depositary in writing; and by states which had acceded to the Agreement.

The Annex to the Agreement addresses a number of issues raised by developed states. In particular, it is provided that all organs and bodies established under the Convention and Agreement are to be cost-effective and based upon an evolutionary approach taking into account the functional needs of such organs or bodies; a variety of institutional arrangements are detailed with regard to the work of the International Seabed Authority (section 1); the work of the Enterprise is to be carried out initially by the Secretariat of the Authority and the Enterprise shall conduct its initial deep seabed mining operations through joint ventures that accord with sound commercial principles (section 2); decision-making in the Assembly and Council of the Authority is to comply with a series of specific rules[393] (section 3); the Assembly upon the recommendation of the Council may conduct a review at any time of matters referred to in article 155(1) of the Convention, notwithstanding the provisions of that article as a whole (section 4); and transfer of technology to the Enterprise and developing states is to be sought on fair and reasonable commercial terms on the open market or through joint-venture arrangements (section 5).[394]

The International Seabed Authority [395]

The Authority is the autonomous organisation which the states parties to the 1982 Convention have agreed is to organise and control activities in the Area, particularly with a view to administering its resources.[396] It became fully operational in June 1996. The principal organs of the Authority are the Assembly, the Council and the Secretariat. Also to be noted are the Legal and Technical Commission and the Finance Committee. The

---

[393] Note especially the increase in the role of the Council vis-à-vis the Assembly with regard to general policy matters. Note also that the Agreement guarantees a seat on the Council for the state 'on the date of entry into force of the Convention having the largest economy in terms of gross domestic product', i.e. the US (section 3, para. 15a), and establishes groups of states on the Council of states with particular interests (section 3, paras. 10 and 15).

[394] Thus, the provisions in the Convention on the mandatory transfer of technology are not to apply (section 5, para. 2). Note also that provisions in the Convention regarding production ceilings and limitations, participation in commodity agreements, etc. are not to apply (section 6, para. 7).

[395] Details of the Authority may be found at www.isa.org.jm/en/default.htm.

[396] Article 157.

Assembly is composed of all members of the Authority, i.e. all states parties to the Convention, and at July 2007 there were 155.[397] The Assembly is the supreme organ of the Authority with powers to elect *inter alia* the Council, Secretary-General and the members of the Governing Boards of the Enterprise and its Director-General, to establish subsidiary organs and to assess the contributions of members to the administrative budget. It has the power to establish the general policy of the Authority.[398] The Council consists of thirty-six members elected by the Assembly in accordance with certain criteria.[399] The Council is the executive organ of the Authority and has the power to establish the specific policies to be pursued by the Authority.[400] The Council has two organs, an Economic Planning Commission and a Legal and Technical Commission.[401] The

---

[397] See www.isa.org.jm/en/about/members/states. See also article 159(1).

[398] Article 160. However, the effect of the 1994 Agreement on Implementation has been to reduce the power of the Assembly in favour of the Council by providing in Annex, section 3 that decisions of the Assembly in areas for which the Council also has competence or on any administrative, budgetary or financial matter be based upon the recommendations of the Council, and if these recommendations are not accepted, the matter has to be returned to the Council. Further, this section also provides that, as a general rule, decision-making in the organs of the Authority should be by consensus.

[399] Article 161(1) provides for members to be elected in the following order: (a) four members from among those states parties which, during the last five years for which statistics are available, have either consumed more than 2 per cent of total world consumption or have had net imports of more than 2 per cent of total world imports of the commodities produced from the categories of minerals to be derived from the Area, and in any case one state from the Eastern European (Socialist) region, as well as the largest consumer; (b) four members from among the eight states parties which have the largest investments in preparation for and in the conduct of activities in the Area, either directly or through their nationals, including at least one state from the Eastern European (Socialist) region; (c) four members from among states parties which, on the basis of production in areas under their jurisdiction, are major net exporters of the categories of minerals to be derived from the Area, including at least two developing states whose exports of such minerals have a substantial bearing upon their economies; (d) six members from among developing states parties, representing special interests. The special interests to be represented shall include those of states with large populations, states which are landlocked or geographically disadvantaged, states which are major importers of the categories of minerals to be derived from the Area, states which are potential producers of such minerals, and least developed states; (e) eighteen members elected according to the principle of ensuring an equitable geographical distribution of seats in the Council as a whole, provided that each geographical region shall have at least one member elected under this subparagraph. For this purpose, the geographical regions shall be Africa, Asia, Eastern European (Socialist), Latin America and Western European and Others.

[400] Article 162. In some cases, Council decisions have to be adopted by consensus and in others by two-thirds majority vote: see article 161.

[401] Articles 163–5. As to the secretariat, see articles 166–9.

organ of the Authority actually carrying out activities in the Area is the Enterprise.[402]

Settlement of disputes[403]

The 1982 Convention contains detailed and complex provisions regarding the resolution of law of the sea disputes. Part XV, section 1 lays down the general provisions. Article 279 expresses the fundamental obligation to settle disputes peacefully in accordance with article 2(3) of the UN Charter and using the means indicated in article 33,[404] but the parties are able to choose methods other than those specified in the Convention.[405] States of the European Union, for example, have agreed to submit fisheries disputes amongst member states to the European Court of Justice under the EC Treaty.

Article 283 of the Convention provides that where a dispute arises, the parties are to proceed 'expeditiously to an exchange of views regarding its settlement by negotiation or other peaceful means' and article 284 states that the parties may resort if they wish to conciliation procedures, in which case a conciliation commission will be established, whose report will be non-binding.[406] Where no settlement is reached by means freely chosen by the parties, the compulsory procedures laid down in Part XV, section 2 become operative.[407] Upon signing, ratifying or acceding to the Convention, or at any time thereafter, a state may choose one of the following means of dispute settlement: the International Tribunal for the Law of the Sea,[408] the International Court of Justice,[409] an arbitral tribunal

---

[402] See article 170 and Annex IV.

[403] See e.g. N. Klein, *Dispute Settlement in the UN Convention on the Law of the Sea*, Cambridge, 2005; J. G. Merrills, *International Dispute Settlement*, 4th edn, Cambridge, 2005, chapter 8; Churchill and Lowe, *Law of the Sea*, chapter 19; J. Collier and A. V. Lowe, *The Settlement of Disputes in International Law*, Oxford, 1999, chapter 5; A. E. Boyle, 'Dispute Settlement and the Law of the Sea Convention: Problems of Fragmentation and Jurisdiction', 46 ICLQ, 1997, p. 37; R. Ranjeva, 'Le Règlement des Différends' in *Traité du Nouveau Droit de la Mer* (eds. R. J. Dupuy and D. Vignes), Paris, 1985, p. 1105; J. P. Quéneudec, 'Le Choix des Procédures de Règlement des Différends selon la Convention des NU sur le Droit de la Mer' in *Mélanges Virally*, Paris, 1991, p. 383, and A. O. Adede, *The System for the Settlement of Disputes under the United Nations Convention on the Law of the Sea*, Dordrecht, 1987.

[404] See further below, chapter 18.   [405] Article 280.

[406] See Annex V, Section 1.   [407] See articles 286 and 287.

[408] Annex VI.   [409] See below, chapter 19.

under Annex VII[410] or a special arbitral tribunal under Annex VIII for specific disputes.[411]

There are some exceptions to the obligation to submit a dispute to one of these mechanisms in the absence of a freely chosen resolution process by the parties. Article 297(1) provides that disputes concerning the exercise by a coastal state of its sovereign rights or jurisdiction in the exclusive economic zone may only be subject to the compulsory settlement procedure in particular cases.[412] Article 297(2) provides that while disputes concerning marine scientific research shall be settled in accordance with section 2 of the Convention, the coastal state is not obliged to accept the submission to such compulsory settlement of any dispute arising out of the exercise by the coastal state of a right or discretion to regulate, authorise and conduct marine scientific research in its economic zone or on its continental shelf or a decision to order suspension or cessation of such research.[413] Article 297(3) provides similarly that while generally disputes with regard to fisheries shall be settled in accordance with section 2, the coastal state shall not be obliged to accept the submission to compulsory settlement of any dispute relating to its sovereign rights with respect to the

---

[410] This procedure covers both disputes concerning states and those concerning international organisations, such as the European Union. A five-person tribunal is chosen by the parties from a panel to which each state party may make up to four nominations. Annex VII arbitrations have included *Australia and New Zealand* v. *Japan (Southern Bluefin Tuna)*, Award of 4 August 2000, 119 ILR, p. 508; *Ireland* v. *UK (Mox)* 126 ILR, pp. 257 ff. and 310 ff.; *Barbados* v. *Trinidad and Tobago*, Award of 11 April 2006 and *Guyana* v. *Suriname*, Award of 17 September 2007. The latter cases may be found on the Permanent Court of Arbitration website, www.pca-cpa.org.

[411] I.e. relating to fisheries, protection and preservation of the marine environment, marine scientific research, or navigation, including pollution from vessels and by dumping: see article 1, Annex VIII. The nomination process is slightly different from Annex VII situations.

[412] That is, with regard to an allegation that a coastal state has acted in contravention of the provisions of the Convention in regard to the freedoms and rights of navigation, overflight or the laying of submarine cables and pipelines, or in regard to other internationally lawful uses of the sea specified in article 58; or when it is alleged that a state in exercising these freedoms, rights or uses has acted in contravention of the Convention or of laws or regulations adopted by the coastal state in conformity with the Convention and other rules of international law not incompatible with the Convention; or when it is alleged that a coastal state has acted in contravention of specified international rules and standards for the protection and preservation of the marine environment which are applicable to the coastal state and which have been established by the Convention or through a competent international organisation or diplomatic conference in accordance with the Convention.

[413] In such a case, the dispute is to be submitted to the compulsory conciliation provisions under Annex V, section 2, provided that the conciliation commission shall not call in question the exercise by the coastal state of its discretion to designate specific areas as referred to in article 246, paragraph 6, or of its discretion to withhold consent in accordance with article 246, paragraph 5.

living resources in the exclusive economic zone or their exercise, including its discretionary powers for determining the allowable catch, its harvesting capacity, the allocation of surpluses to other states and the terms and conditions established in its conservation and management laws and regulations.[414] There are also three situations with regard to which states may opt out of the compulsory settlement procedures.[415]

The Convention also provides for a Seabed Disputes Chamber of the International Tribunal for the Law of the Sea,[416] which under article 187 shall have jurisdiction with regard to matters concerning the Deep Seabed and the International Seabed Authority. By article 188, inter-state disputes concerning the exploitation of the international seabed are to be submitted only to the Seabed Disputes Chamber.

One problem that has arisen has been where a dispute arises under one or more conventions including the 1982 Law of the Sea Convention, and the impact that this may have upon dispute settlement. In the *Southern Bluefin Tuna* case between Australia and New Zealand on the one hand and Japan on the other,[417] the arbitration tribunal had to consider the effect of the 1993 Convention for the Conservation of Southern Bluefin Tuna, the binding settlement procedures of which require the consent of all parties to the dispute. However, these states were also parties to the 1982 Convention, the provisions of which concerning highly migratory fish stocks (which included the southern bluefin tuna) referred to compulsory arbitration.[418] The parties were unable to agree within the Commission established by the 1993 Convention and the applicants invoked the compulsory arbitration provisions of the 1982 Convention. The International Tribunal for the Law of the Sea indicated provisional measures[419] and the matter went to arbitration. Japan argued that the dispute was one under the 1993 Convention so that its consensual settlement procedures were applicable[420] and not the compulsory procedures under the 1982 Convention. The tribunal held that the dispute was one common to both Conventions and that there was only one dispute. Article 281(1) of the 1982 Convention provides essentially for the priority of procedures agreed to by the parties, so that the 1982 Convention's provisions would

---

[414] In such a case, the dispute in certain cases is to be submitted to the compulsory conciliation provisions under Annex V, section 2: see further article 297(3)(b).

[415] Disputes concerning delimitation and claims to historic waters; disputes concerning military and law enforcement activities, and disputes in respect of which the Security Council is exercising its functions: see article 298(1).

[416] See Annex VI, section 4.   [417] 119 ILR, p. 508.   [418] See Part XV and Annex VII.

[419] 117 ILR, p. 148. The International Tribunal called for arbitration and stated that the latter tribunal would *prima facie* have jurisdiction.

[420] See article 16 of the 1993 Convention.

only apply where no settlement had been reached using the other means agreed by the parties and the agreement between the parties does not exclude any further procedure. Since article 16 of the 1993 Convention fell within the category of procedures agreed by the parties and thus within article 281(1), the intent and thus the consequence of article 16 was to remove proceedings under that provision from the reach of the compulsory procedures of the 1982 Convention.[421] Accordingly, the extent to which the compulsory procedures of the 1982 Convention apply depends on the circumstances and, in particular, the existence and nature of any other agreement between the parties relating to peaceful settlement.[422]

Outside the framework of the 1982 Convention, states may adopt a variety of means of resolving disputes, ranging from negotiations, inquiries,[423] conciliation[424] and arbitration[425] to submission to the International Court of Justice.[426]

The International Tribunal for the Law of the Sea [427]

The Tribunal was established as one of the dispute settlement mechanisms under Part XV of the Law of the Sea Convention. The Statute of the

---

[421] See 119 ILR, pp. 549–52.

[422] See also B. Oxman, 'Complementary Agreements and Compulsory Jurisdiction', 95 AJIL, 2001, p. 277. Note that the Arbitral Tribunal established under Annex VII of the Convention in the *Mox* case, between Ireland and the UK, suspended hearings on 13 June 2003 due to uncertainty as to whether relevant provisions of the Convention fell within the competence of the European Community or member states: see Order No. 3 of 24 June 2003 and Order No. 4 of 14 November 2003, 126 ILR, pp. 257 ff. and 310 ff. See also the decision of the European Court of Justice of 30 May 2006, Case C-459/03, *Commission* v. *Ireland*.

[423] E.g. the *Red Crusader* incident, 35 ILR, p. 485. See further on these mechanisms, below, chapters 18 and 19.

[424] E.g. the *Jan Mayen Island Continental Shelf* dispute, 20 ILM, 1981, p. 797; 62 ILR, p. 108.

[425] E.g. the *Anglo-French Continental Shelf* case, Cmnd 7438; 54 ILR, p. 6.

[426] E.g. the *Anglo-Norwegian Fisheries* case, ICJ Reports, 1951, p. 116; 18 ILR, p. 84; the *North Sea Continental Shelf* cases, ICJ Reports, 1969, p. 16; 41 ILR, p. 29 and others referred to in this chapter.

[427] See e.g. P. C. Rao and R. Khan, *The International Tribunal for the Law of the Sea: Law and Practice*, The Hague, 2001; P. C. Rao and P. Gautier, *Rules of the International Tribunal for the Law of the Sea: A Commentary*, The Hague, 2006; M. M. Marsit, *Le Tribunal du Droit de la Mer*, Paris, 1999; A. E. Boyle, 'The International Tribunal for the Law of the Sea and the Settlement of Disputes' in *The Changing World of International Law in the 21st Century* (eds. J. Norton, M. Andenas and M. Footer), The Hague, 1998; D. Anderson, 'The International Tribunal for the Law of the Sea', in *Remedies in International Law* (eds. M. D. Evans and S. V. Konstanidis), Oxford, 1998, p. 71; J. Collier and V. Lowe, *The Settlement of Disputes in International Law*, Oxford, 1999, chapter 5; Churchill and Lowe, *Law of the Sea*, chapter 19; Merrills, *International Dispute Settlement*, chapter 8; Nguyen Quoc Dinh et al., *Droit International Public*, p. 912, and G. Eiriksson, *The International Tribunal for the Law of the Sea*, The Hague, 2000. See also www.itlos.org.

Tribunal[428] provides that it shall be composed of twenty-one independent members enjoying the highest reputation for fairness and integrity and of recognised competence in the field of the law of the sea, while the representation of the principal legal systems of the world and equitable geographical distribution are to be assured.[429] Judges are elected for nine-year terms by the states parties to the Convention.[430] The Statute also allows for the appointment of ad hoc judges. Article 17 provides that where the Tribunal includes a member of the nationality of one of the parties to the dispute, any other party may choose a person to participate as a member of the Tribunal. Where in a dispute neither or none of the parties have a judge of the same nationality, they may choose a person to participate as a member of the Tribunal.[431] The Tribunal may also, at the request of a party or of its own motion, decide to select no fewer than two scientific or technical experts to sit with it, but without the right to vote.[432]

The Tribunal, based in Hamburg, is open to states parties to the Convention[433] and to entities other than states parties in accordance with Part XI of the Convention, concerning the International Seabed Area, thereby including the International Seabed Authority, state enterprises and natural and juridical persons in certain circumstances,[434] or in any case submitted pursuant to any other agreement conferring jurisdiction on the Tribunal which is accepted by all the parties to that case.[435] The jurisdiction of the Tribunal comprises all disputes and all applications submitted to it in accordance with the Convention and all matters specifically provided for in any other agreement which confers jurisdiction on the Tribunal.[436] The provisions of the Convention and other rules of international law not

---

[428] Annex VI of the Convention.

[429] Article 2 of the Statute. A quorum of eleven judges is required to constitute the Tribunal, article 13.

[430] Article 5.

[431] See also articles 8, 9 and 18–22 of the Rules of the Tribunal 1997 (as amended in March and September 2001). Note, in particular, that under article 22 of the Rules, a non-state entity may choose an ad hoc judge in certain circumstances.

[432] Article 289 of the Convention and article 15 of the Rules.

[433] Article 292(1) of the Convention and article 20(1) of the Statute. This would include the European Community (now Union): see article 1(2) of the Convention.

[434] See in particular articles 153 and 187 of the Convention. See also A. Serdy, 'Bringing Taiwan into the International Fisheries Fold: The Legal Personality of a Fishing Entity', 75 BYIL, 2004, p. 183.

[435] Article 20(2) of the Statute.

[436] Article 21. Where the parties to a treaty in force covering law of the sea matters so agree, any disputes concerning the interpretation or application of such treaty may be submitted to the Tribunal, article 22.

incompatible with the Convention constitute the applicable law of the Tribunal.[437]

Pursuant to Part XI, section 5 of the Convention and article 14 of the Statute, a Seabed Disputes Chamber of the Tribunal has been formed with jurisdiction to hear disputes regarding activities in the international seabed area. The Chamber is composed of eleven judges representing the principal legal systems of the world and with equitable geographical distribution.[438] Ad hoc chambers consisting of three judges may be established if a party to a dispute so requests. The composition is determined by the Seabed Disputes Chamber with the approval of the parties to the dispute.[439] The Chamber shall apply the provisions of the Convention and other rules of international law not incompatible with the Convention,[440] together with the rules, regulation and procedures of the International Seabed Authority adopted in accordance with the Convention and the terms of contracts concerning activities in the International Seabed Area in matters relating to those contracts.[441] The Seabed Disputes Chamber has jurisdiction to give advisory opinions at the request of the Assembly or the Council of the International Seabed Authority on legal questions arising within the scope of their activities and such opinions shall be given as a matter of urgency.[442] In addition, the Tribunal may create such chambers of three or more persons as it considers necessary[443] and a five-person Chamber of Summary Procedure.[444]

---

[437] Article 293 of the Convention and article 23 of the Statute.

[438] See article 35. The Chamber shall be open to the states parties, the International Seabed Authority and the other entities referred to in Part XI, section 5 of the Convention. Ad hoc judges may be chosen: see articles 23–5 of the Rules.

[439] Articles 187 and 188 of the Convention and article 36 of the Statute. See also article 27 of the Rules.

[440] Article 293 of the Convention.

[441] Article 38 of the Statute. The decisions of the Seabed Chamber shall be enforceable in the territories of the states parties in the same manner as judgments or orders of the highest court of the state party in whose territory the enforcement is sought, article 39. Articles 115–23 of the Rules deal with procedural issues in contentious cases before the Chamber.

[442] See articles 159(10) and 191. See also articles 130–7 of the Rules.

[443] See article 15(1). A Chamber for Fisheries Disputes (1997), a Chamber for Marine Environment Disputes (1997) and a Chamber for Maritime Delimitation Disputes (2007) have been formed under this provision. Under article 15(2), the Tribunal may form a chamber for dealing with a specific dispute if the parties so wish and a Chamber was formed in December 2000 to deal with the *Swordfish Stocks* dispute between Chile and the European Community. See also articles 29 and 30 and 107–9 of the Rules.

[444] Article 15(3). This may hear cases on an accelerated procedure basis and provisional measures applications when the full Tribunal is not sitting: see article 25(2). See also article 28 of the Rules.

The Tribunal[445] and the Seabed Disputes Chamber have the power to prescribe provisional measures in accordance with article 290 of the Convention.[446] Article 290 provides *inter alia* that if a dispute has been duly submitted to the Tribunal, which considers that *prima facie* it has jurisdiction, any provisional measures considered appropriate under the circumstances to preserve the respective rights of the parties to the dispute or to prevent serious harm to the marine environment pending the final decision may be prescribed. Such provisional measures may be modified or revoked as soon as the circumstances justifying them have changed or ceased to exist. Further, the Tribunal or, with respect to activities in the International Seabed Area, the Seabed Disputes Chamber, may prescribe, modify or revoke provisional measures if it considers that *prima facie* the tribunal which is to be constituted would have jurisdiction and that the urgency of the situation so requires. Once constituted, the tribunal to which the dispute has been submitted may modify, revoke or affirm those provisional measures. The Convention also makes it clear that provisional measures are binding, requiring the parties to the dispute to comply promptly with any provisional measures prescribed under article 290.[447]

Where a party does not appear before the Tribunal, the other party may request that the Tribunal continue the hearings and reach a decision.[448] Before so doing, the Tribunal must satisfy itself not only that it has jurisdiction, but also that the claim is well founded in fact and law.[449] A party may present a counter-claim in its counter-memorial, provided that it is directly concerned with the subject-matter of the claim of the other party and that it comes within the jurisdiction of the Tribunal.[450] The Statute provides also for third-party intervention, where a state party considers that it has an interest of a legal nature which may be affected by the decision in any dispute. It is for the Tribunal to decide on this request and, if

---

[445] See also the Resolution on Internal Judicial Practice, 31 October 1997, and articles 40–2 of the Rules.

[446] Article 25(1) of the Statute. See also articles 89–95 of the Rules. See e.g. S. Rosenne, *Provisional Measures in International Law: The International Court of Justice and the International Tribunal for the Law of the Sea*, The Hague, 2004.

[447] See article 290(6) of the Convention. Article 95(1) of the Rules declares that each party is required to submit to the Tribunal a report and information on compliance with any provisional measures prescribed.

[448] See generally Part III of the Rules concerning the procedure of the Tribunal. As to preliminary proceedings and preliminary objections, see article 294 of the Convention and articles 96 and 97 of the Rules.

[449] Article 28.   [450] See article 98 of the Rules.

such a request is granted, the decision of the Tribunal in the dispute shall be binding upon the intervening state party in so far as it relates to matters in respect of which that state party intervened.[451] This is different from the equivalent provision relating to the International Court of Justice and thus should avoid the anomalous position of the non-party intervener.[452] There is, however, a right to intervene in cases where the interpretation or application of the Convention is in question.[453] Decisions of the Tribunal are final and binding as between the parties to the dispute.[454]

The Tribunal also has jurisdiction to give advisory opinions on a legal question if an international agreement related to the purposes of the Convention specifically provides for the submission to the Tribunal of a request for such an opinion.[455]

The Tribunal has heard a number of cases since its first case in 1997. Most of these cases have concerned article 292 of the Convention which provides that where a state party has detained a vessel flying the flag of another state party and has not complied with the prompt release requirement upon payment of a reasonable bond or other financial security, the question of release from detention may be submitted to the Tribunal.[456] In the *Camouco* case,[457] for example, the Tribunal discussed the scope of the article and held that it would not be logical to read into it the requirement of exhaustion of local remedies. Article 292 provided for an independent remedy and no limitation should be read into it that would have the effect of defeating its very object and purpose.[458] The Tribunal found a violation of article 292 in the case of the *Volga*, where it was held that the bond set for the release of the vessel in question, while reasonable in terms of the financial condition, was not reasonable in that the non-financial conditions set down by the Respondent with regard to the vessel carrying a vessel monitoring system (VMS) and the submission of information about the owner of the ship could not be considered as

---

[451] Article 31. See also articles 99–104 of the Rules. [452] See below, chapter 19, p. 1097.

[453] Article 32.

[454] Article 33. In the case of a dispute as to the meaning or scope of the decision, the Tribunal shall construe it upon the request of any party. See also articles 126–9 of the Rules.

[455] Article 138 of the Rules. In such cases, articles 130–7 of the Rules concerning the giving of advisory opinions by the Seabed Disputes Chamber shall apply *mutatis mutandis*.

[456] See e.g. Y. Tanaka, 'Prompt Release in the United Nations Convention on the Law of the Sea: Some Reflections on the Itlos Jurisprudence', 51 NILR, 2004, p. 237, and D. R. Rothwell and T. Stephens, 'Illegal Southern Ocean Fishing and Prompt Release: Balancing Coastal and Flag State Rights and Interests', 53 ICLQ, 2004, p. 171.

[457] Case No. 5, judgment of 7 February 2000. See 125 ILR, p. 164.

[458] *Ibid.*, paras. 57 and 58.

components of the bond or other financial security for the purposes of article 292 of the Convention. It was also held that the circumstances of the seizure of the vessel were not relevant to a consideration of a breach of article 292, while the proceeds of the catch were irrelevant to the bond issue.[459] In the *Hoshinmaru (Japan* v. *Russia)* case, the Tribunal held that it was not reasonable that a bond should be set on the basis of the maximum penalties applicable to the owner and the Master, nor was it reasonable that the bond should be calculated on the basis of the confiscation of the vessel, given the circumstances of the case. In setting a reasonable bond for the release of the vessel the Tribunal stated that the amount of the bond should be proportionate to the gravity of the alleged offences.[460]

The *Mox* case[461] was a case where the parties (Ireland and the UK) appeared before the Tribunal at the provisional measures stage under article 290(5), while later moving to an arbitral tribunal for the merits. The Tribunal prescribed provisional measures requiring the parties to exchange information regarding the possible consequences for the Irish Sea arising out of the commissioning of the Mox nuclear plant, to monitor the risks or the effects of the operation of the plant and to devise, as appropriate, measures to prevent any pollution of the marine environment which might result from the operation of the plant. In so doing, the Tribunal specifically mentioned statements made by the UK concerning *inter alia* transportation of radioactive material, which the Tribunal characterised as 'assurances' and which it placed 'on record'.[462]

The *Saiga (No. 2) (Saint Vincent and the Grenadines* v. *Guinea)* case[463] has been one of the most important decisions to date made by the Tribunal.[464] Issues addressed included the impermissibility of extending customs jurisdiction into the exclusive economic zone, the failure to comply with the rules underpinning the right of hot pursuit under article 111 of the Law of the Sea Convention, the use of force and admissibility issues such as the registration of the vessel and the need for a 'genuine link'.[465]

---

[459] 126 ILR, p. 433. See also as to prompt release issues, the *Juno Trader* 128 ILR, p. 267.

[460] See www.itlos.org/start2_en.html (6 August 2007).

[461] Case No. 10, Order of 3 December 2001. See 126 ILR, pp. 257 ff. and 310 ff.

[462] *Ibid.*, paras. 78–80. See also as to provisional measures, the *Land Reclamation (Malaysia* v. *Singapore)* case, 126 ILR, p. 487.

[463] Case No. 2, judgment of 1 July 1999. See 120 ILR, p. 143.

[464] See e.g. B. H. Oxman and V. Bantz, 'The *M/V "Saiga" (No. 2) (St Vincent and the Grenadines* v. *Guinea)*', 94 AJIL, 2000, p. 40, and L. de la Fayette, 'The *M/V Saiga (No. 2)* Case', 49 ICLQ, 2000, p. 467.

[465] See above, p. 611.

The Tribunal's part in the *Southern Bluefin Tuna* case[466] was limited to the grant of provisional measures.[467] Thereafter the matter went to arbitration.[468] As far as the Tribunal was concerned, this was the first case applying article 290(5) of the Law of the Sea Convention regarding the grant of provisional measures pending the constitution of an arbitral tribunal to which the dispute had been submitted. The Tribunal thus had to satisfy itself that *prima facie* the arbitral tribunal would have jurisdiction.[469] This the Tribunal was able to do and the measures it prescribed included setting limits on the annual catches of the fish in question. The Tribunal's judgment in the application for prompt release in the *Grand Prince* case[470] focused on jurisdiction and, in particular, whether the requirements under article 91 of the Law of the Sea Convention regarding nationality of ships had been fulfilled.[471] The Tribunal emphasised that, like the International Court, it had to satisfy itself that it had jurisdiction to hear the application and thus possessed the right to deal with all aspects of jurisdiction, whether or not they had been expressly raised by the parties.[472] The Tribunal concluded that the documentary evidence submitted by the applicant failed to establish that it was the flag state of the vessel when the application was made, so that the Tribunal did not have jurisdiction to hear the case.[473]

Suggestions for further reading

D. Anderson, *Modern Law of the Sea: Selected Essays*, The Hague, 2007

R. Churchill and A. V. Lowe, *The Law of the Sea*, 3rd edn, Manchester, 1999

International Maritime Boundaries (eds. J. I. Charney and L. M. Alexander), Washington, vols. I–III, 1993–8, *ibid.* (eds. J. I. Charney and R. W. Smith), vol. IV, 2002 and *ibid.* (eds. D. A. Colson and R. W. Smith), vol. V, 2005, The Hague

Law of the Sea: Progress and Prospects (eds. D. Freestone, R. Barnes and D. Ong), Oxford, 2006

---

[466] Case Nos. 3 and 4, Order of 27 August 1999. See 117 ILR, p. 148.

[467] See e.g. R. Churchill, 'The Southern Bluefin Tuna Cases', 49 ICLQ, 2000, p. 979, and B. Kwiatkowska, 'The Southern Bluefin Tuna Cases', 15 *International Journal of Marine and Coastal Law*, 2000, p. 1 and 94 AJIL, 2000, p. 150.

[468] 119 ILR, p. 508. See e.g. A. E. Boyle, 'The *Southern Bluefin Tuna* Arbitration', 50 ICLQ, 2001, p. 447.

[469] See the Order, paras. 40 ff.; 117 ILR, pp. 148, 160. See also above, p. 637.

[470] Case No. 8, judgment of 20 April 2001. See 125 ILR, p. 272.

[471] *Ibid.*, paras. 62 ff.   [472] *Ibid.*, para. 79.   [473] *Ibid.*, para. 93.

12

Jurisdiction

Jurisdiction concerns the power of the state under international law to regulate or otherwise impact upon people, property and circumstances and reflects the basic principles of state sovereignty, equality of states and non-interference in domestic affairs.[1] Jurisdiction is a vital and indeed central feature of state sovereignty, for it is an exercise of authority which may alter or create or terminate legal relationships and obligations. It may be achieved by means of legislative, executive or judicial action. In each case, the recognised authorities of the state as determined by the legal system of that state perform certain functions permitted them which affect the life around them in various ways. In the UK, Parliament passes binding statutes, the courts make binding decisions and the administrative machinery of government has the power and jurisdiction (or legal authority) to enforce the rules of law. It is particularly necessary to distinguish between the capacity to make law, whether by legislative or executive or judicial action (prescriptive jurisdiction or the jurisdiction to prescribe) and the capacity to ensure compliance with such law whether by executive

---

[1] See e.g. C. E. Amerasinghe, *Jurisdiction of International Tribunals*, The Hague, 2003; *Universal Jurisdiction: National Courts and the Prosecution of Serious Crimes under International Law* (ed. S. Macedo), Philadelphia, 2004; L. Reydams, *Universal Jurisdiction: International and Municipal Legal Perspectives*, Oxford, 2002; *La Saisine des Jurisdictions Internationales* (eds. H. Ruiz Fabri and J.-M. Sorel), Paris, 2006; Y. Shany, *The Competing Jurisdictions of International Courts and Tribunals*, Oxford, 2003; M. Hirst, *Jurisdiction and the Ambit of the Criminal Law*, Oxford, 2003; M. Akehurst, 'Jurisdiction in International Law', 46 BYIL, 1972–3, p. 145; F. A. Mann, 'The Doctrine of Jurisdiction in International Law', 111 HR, 1964, p. 1, and Mann, 'The Doctrine of Jurisdiction in International Law Revisited After Twenty Years', 186 HR, 1984, p. 9; D. W. Bowett, 'Jurisdiction: Changing Problems of Authority over Activities and Resources', 53 BYIL, 1982, p. 1; R. Y. Jennings, 'Extraterritorial Jurisdiction and the United States Antitrust Laws', 33 BYIL, 1957, p. 146; *Oppenheim's International Law* (eds. R. Y. Jennings and A. D. Watts), 9th edn, London, 1992, pp. 456 ff.; I. Brownlie, Principles of Public International Law, 6th edn, Oxford, 2003, chapters 14 and 15; O. Schachter, *International Law in Theory and Practice*, Dordrecht, 1991, chapter 12, and R. Higgins, *Problems and Process*, Oxford, 1994, chapter 4. See also *Third US Restatement of Foreign Relations Law*, 1987, vol. I, part IV.

action or through the courts (enforcement jurisdiction or the jurisdiction to enforce). Jurisdiction, although primarily territorial, may be based on other grounds, for example nationality, while enforcement is restricted by territorial factors.

To give an instance, if a man kills somebody in Britain and then manages to reach the Netherlands, the British courts have jurisdiction to try him, but they cannot enforce it by sending officers to the Netherlands to apprehend him. They must apply to the Dutch authorities for his arrest and dispatch to Britain. If, on the other hand, the murderer remains in Britain then he may be arrested and tried there, even if it becomes apparent that he is a German national. Thus, while prescriptive jurisdiction (or the competence to make law) may be exercised as regards events happening within the territorial limits irrespective of whether or not the actors are nationals, and may be founded on nationality as in the case of a British subject suspected of murder committed abroad who may be tried for the offence in the UK (if he is found in the UK, of course), enforcement jurisdiction is another matter entirely and is essentially restricted to the presence of the suspect in the territorial limits.[2]

However, there are circumstances in which it may be possible to apprehend a suspected murderer, but the jurisdictional basis is lacking. For example, if a Frenchman has committed a murder in Germany he cannot be tried for it in Britain, notwithstanding his presence in the country, although, of course, both France and Germany may apply for his extradition and return to their respective countries from Britain.

Thus, while jurisdiction is closely linked with territory it is not exclusively so tied. Many states have jurisdiction to try offences that have taken place outside their territory, and in addition certain persons, property and situations are immune from the territorial jurisdiction in spite of being situated or taking place there. Diplomats, for example, have extensive immunity from the laws of the country in which they are working[3] and various sovereign acts by states may not be questioned or overturned in the courts of a foreign country.[4]

The whole question of jurisdiction is complex, not least because of the relevance also of constitutional issues and conflict of laws rules. International law tries to set down rules dealing with the limits of a state's exercise

---

[2] Reference has also been made to the jurisdiction to adjudicate, whereby persons or things are rendered subject to the process of a state's court system: see *Third US Restatement of Foreign Relations Law*, p. 232.
[3] See below, chapter 13, p. 750.   [4] *Ibid.*, p. 697.

of governmental functions while conflict of laws (or private international law) will attempt to regulate in a case involving a foreign element whether the particular country has jurisdiction to determine the question, and secondly, if it has, then the rules of which country will be applied in resolving the dispute.

The grounds for the exercise of jurisdiction are not identical in the cases of international law and conflict of laws rules. In the latter case, specific subjects may well be regulated in terms of domicile or residence (for instance as regards the recognition of foreign marriages or divorces) but such grounds would not found jurisdiction where international law matters were concerned.[5] Although it is by no means impossible or in all cases difficult to keep apart the categories of international law and conflict of laws, nevertheless the often different definitions of jurisdiction involved are a confusing factor.

One should also be aware of the existence of disputes as to jurisdictional competence within the area of constitutional matters. These problems arise in federal court structures, as in the United States, where conflicts as to the extent of authority of particular courts may arise.

While the relative exercise of powers by the legislative, executive and judicial organs of government is a matter for the municipal legal and political system, the extraterritorial application of jurisdiction will depend upon the rules of international law, and in this chapter we shall examine briefly the most important of these rules.

The principle of domestic jurisdiction[6]

It follows from the nature of the sovereignty of states that while a state is supreme internally, that is within its own territorial frontiers, it must not intervene in the domestic affairs of another nation. This duty of non-intervention within the domestic jurisdiction of states provides for the shielding of certain state activities from the regulation of international law. State functions which are regarded as beyond the reach of international legal control and within the exclusive sphere of state management include the setting of conditions for the grant of nationality

---

[5] See generally, G. C. Cheshire and P. M. North, *Private International Law*, 13th edn, London, 1999. Questions may also arise as to the conditions required for leave for service abroad: see e.g. *Al-Adsani* v. *Government of Kuwait and Others* 100 ILR, p. 465.

[6] See e.g. Brownlie, *Principles*, pp. 290 ff., and M. S. Rajan, *United Nations and Domestic Jurisdiction*, 2nd edn, London, 1961. See further above, chapter 4.

and the elaboration of the circumstances in which aliens may enter the country.

However, the influence of international law is beginning to make itself felt in areas hitherto regarded as subject to the state's exclusive jurisdiction. For example, the treatment by a country of its own nationals is now viewed in the context of international human rights regulations, although in practice the effect of this has often been disappointing.[7]

Domestic jurisdiction is a relative concept, in that changing principles of international law have had the effect of limiting and reducing its extent[8] and in that matters of internal regulation may well have international repercussions and thus fall within the ambit of international law. This latter point has been emphasised by the International Court of Justice. In the *Anglo-Norwegian Fisheries* case[9] it was stressed that:

> [a]lthough it is true that the act of delimitation [of territorial waters] is necessarily a unilateral act, because only the coastal state is competent to undertake it, the validity of the delimitation with regard to other states depends upon international law.[10]

The principle was also noted in the *Nottebohm* case,[11] where the Court remarked that while a state may formulate such rules as it wished regarding the acquisition of nationality, the exercise of diplomatic protection upon the basis of nationality was within the purview of international law. In addition, no state may plead its municipal laws as a justification for the breach of an obligation of international law.[12]

Accordingly, the dividing line between issues firmly within domestic jurisdiction on the one hand, and issues susceptible to international legal regulation on the other, is by no means as inflexible as at first may appear.

Article 2(7) of the UN Charter declares that:

> [n]othing contained in the present Charter shall authorise the United Nations to intervene in matters which are essentially within the domestic jurisdiction of any state or shall require the members to submit such matters to settlement under the present Charter.

---

[7] See above, chapters 6 and 7.

[8] Whether a matter is or is not within the domestic jurisdiction of states is itself a question for international law: see *Nationality Decrees in Tunis and Morocco* case, PCIJ, Series B, No. 4, 1923, pp. 7, 23–4; 2 AD, pp. 349, 352.

[9] ICJ Reports, 1951, p. 116; 18 ILR, p. 86.   [10] ICJ Reports, 1951, p. 132; 18 ILR, p. 95.

[11] ICJ Reports, 1955, pp. 4, 20–1; 22 ILR, pp. 349, 357.   [12] See above, chapter 4, p. 133.

This paragraph, intended as a practical restatement and reinforcement of domestic jurisdiction, has constantly been reinterpreted in the decades since it was first enunciated. It has certainly not prevented the United Nations from discussing or adopting resolutions relating to the internal policies of member states and the result of over fifty years of practice has been the further restriction and erosion of domestic jurisdiction.

In the late 1940s and 1950s, the European colonial powers fought a losing battle against the United Nations debate and adoption of resolutions concerning the issues of self-determination and independence for their colonies. The involvement of the United Nations in human rights matters is constantly deepening and, until their disappearance, South Africa's domestic policies of apartheid were continually criticised and condemned. The expanding scope of United Nations concern has succeeded in further limiting the extent of the doctrine of domestic jurisdiction.[13] Nevertheless, the concept does retain validity in recognising the basic fact that state sovereignty within its own territorial limits is the undeniable foundation of international law as it has evolved, and of the world political and legal system.[14]

Legislative, executive and judicial jurisdiction

Legislative jurisdiction[15] refers to the supremacy of the constitutionally recognised organs of the state to make binding laws within its territory. Such acts of legislation may extend abroad in certain circumstances.[16] The state has legislative exclusivity in many areas. For example, a state lays down the procedural techniques to be adopted by its various organs, such as courts, but can in no way seek to alter the way in which foreign courts operate. This is so even though an English court might refuse to recognise a judgment of a foreign court on the grounds of manifest bias. An English law cannot then be passed purporting to alter the procedural conditions under which the foreign courts operate.

---

[13] See e.g. R. Higgins, *The Development of International Law Through the Political Organs of the United Nations*, Oxford, 1963. See also the view of the British Foreign Secretary on 27 January 1993 that article 2(7) was 'increasingly eroded as humanitarian concerns prevail over the respect for each nation's right to manage or mis-manage its affairs and its subjects', UKMIL, 64 BYIL, 1993, p. 599.

[14] Note also the importance of the doctrine of the exhaustion of domestic remedies: see above, chapter 6, p. 273.

[15] See e.g. Akehurst, 'Jurisdiction', pp. 179 ff.   [16] See further below, p. 688.

International law accepts that a state may levy taxes against persons not within the territory of that state, so long as there is some kind of real link between the state and the proposed taxpayer, whether it be, for example, nationality or domicile.[17] A state may nationalise foreign-owned property situated within its borders,[18] but it cannot purport to take over foreign-owned property situated abroad. It will be obvious that such a regulation could not be enforced abroad, but the reference here is to the prescriptive jurisdiction, or capacity to pass valid laws.

The question of how far a court will enforce foreign legislation is a complicated one within, basically, the field of conflict of laws, but in practice it is rare for one state to enforce the penal or tax laws of another state.[19]

Although legislative supremacy within a state cannot be denied, it may be challenged. A state that adopts laws that are contrary to the provisions of international law, for example as regards the treatment of aliens or foreign property within the country, will render itself liable for a breach of international law on the international scene, and will no doubt find itself faced with protests and other action by the foreign state concerned. It is also possible that a state which abuses the rights it possesses to legislate for its nationals abroad may be guilty of a breach of international law. For example, if France were to order its citizens living abroad to drive only French cars, this would most certainly infringe the sovereignty and independence of the states in which such citizens were residing and would constitute an illegitimate exercise of French legislative jurisdiction.[20]

Executive jurisdiction relates to the capacity of the state to act within the borders of another state.[21] Since states are independent of each other and possess territorial sovereignty,[22] it follows that generally state

---

[17] Akehurst, 'Jurisdiction', pp. 179–80.   [18] See below, chapter 14, p. 827.

[19] See e.g. Cheshire and North, *Private International Law*, chapter 8. English courts in general will not enforce the penal laws of foreign states. It will be for the court to decide what a foreign penal law is. See also *Huntington* v. *Attrill* [1893] AC 150, and Marshall CJ, *The Antelope* 10 Wheat 123 (1825). As far as tax laws are concerned, see *Government of India* v. *Taylor* [1955] AC 491; 22 ILR, p. 286. See in addition *Attorney-General of New Zealand* v. *Ortiz* [1982] 3 All ER 432; 78 ILR, p. 608, particularly Lord Denning, and *ibid.* [1983] 3 All ER 93 (House of Lords); 78 ILR, p. 631. See also *Williams & Humbert* v. *W & H Trade Marks* [1985] 2 All ER 619 and [1986] 1 All ER 129 (House of Lords); 75 ILR, p. 269, and *Re State of Norway's Application* [1986] 3 WLR 452 and [1989] 1 All ER 745, 760–2 (House of Lords). See also above, p. 186.

[20] See Mann, 'Doctrine of Jurisdiction', pp. 36–62.   [21] See Akehurst, 'Jurisdiction', p. 147.

[22] See e.g. *Lotus* case, PCIJ, Series A, No. 10, 1927, p. 18; 4 AD, p. 153, and the *Island of Palmas* case, 2 RIAA, pp. 829, 838 (1928); 4 AD, p. 103.

officials may not carry out their functions on foreign soil (in the absence of express consent by the host state)[23] and may not enforce the laws of their state upon foreign territory. It is also contrary to international law for state agents to apprehend persons or property abroad. The seizure of the Nazi criminal Eichmann by Israeli agents in Argentina in 1960 was a clear breach of Argentina's territorial sovereignty and an illegal exercise of Israeli jurisdiction.[24] Similarly, the unauthorised entry into a state of military forces of another state is clearly an offence under international law.

Judicial jurisdiction[25] concerns the power of the courts of a particular country to try cases in which a foreign factor is present. There are a number of grounds upon which the courts of a state may claim to exercise such jurisdiction. In criminal matters these range from the territorial principle to the universality principle and in civil matters from the mere presence of the defendant in the country to the nationality and domicile principles. It is judicial jurisdiction which forms the most discussed aspect of jurisdiction and criminal questions are the most important manifestation of this.

Civil jurisdiction[26]

Although jurisdiction in civil matters is enforced in the last resort by the application of the sanctions of criminal law, there are a number of differences between civil and criminal issues in this context.

In general it is fair to say that the exercise of civil jurisdiction has been claimed by states upon far wider grounds than has been the case in criminal matters, and the resultant reaction by other states much more muted.[27] This is partly due to the fact that public opinion is far more easily roused where a person is tried abroad for criminal offences than if a person is involved in a civil case.

In common law countries, such as the United States and Britain, the usual basis for jurisdiction in civil cases remains service of a writ upon the defendant within the country, even if the presence of the defendant

---

[23] This cannot, of course, be taken too far. An official would still be entitled, for example, to sign a contract: see Akehurst, 'Jurisdiction', p. 147.

[24] See further below, p. 680.   [25] See e.g. Akehurst, 'Jurisdiction', pp. 152 ff.

[26] *Ibid.*, pp. 170 ff.; Mann, 'Doctrine of Jurisdiction', pp. 49–51, and Brownlie, *Principles*, p. 298. See also Bowett, 'Jurisdiction', pp. 1–4.

[27] See e.g. Akehurst, 'Jurisdiction', pp. 152 ff.

is purely temporary and coincidental.[28] In continental European countries on the other hand, the usual ground for jurisdiction is the habitual
residence of the defendant in the particular state.

Many countries, for instance the Netherlands, Denmark and Sweden,
will allow their courts to exercise jurisdiction where the defendant in
any action possesses assets in the state, while in matrimonial cases the
commonly accepted ground for the exercise of jurisdiction is the domicile
or residence of the party bringing the action.[29]

In view of, for example, the rarity of diplomatic protests and the relative
absence of state discussions, some writers have concluded that customary
international law does not prescribe any particular regulations as regards
the restriction of courts' jurisdiction in civil matters.[30]

Criminal jurisdiction[31]

International law permits states to exercise jurisdiction (whether by way of
legislation, judicial activity or enforcement) upon a number of grounds.[32]
There is no obligation to exercise jurisdiction on all, or any particular
one, of these grounds. This would be a matter for the domestic system to
decide. The importance of these jurisdictional principles is that they are
accepted by all states and the international community as being consistent
with international law. Conversely, attempts to exercise jurisdiction upon
another ground would run the risk of not being accepted by another state.

The territorial principle

The territorial basis for the exercise of jurisdiction reflects one aspect
of the sovereignty exercisable by a state in its territorial home, and is
the indispensable foundation for the application of the series of legal

---

[28] See e.g. *Maharanee of Baroda* v. *Wildenstein* [1972] 2 All ER 689. See also the Civil Jurisdiction and Judgments Act 1982.

[29] See, for example, the 1970 Hague Convention on the Recognition of Divorces and Legal
Separations.

[30] See e.g. Akehurst, 'Jurisdiction', p. 177. Cf. Mann, 'Doctrine of Jurisdiction', pp. 49–51,
and see also Brownlie, *Principles*, p. 298, and Bowett, 'Jurisdiction', pp. 3–4.

[31] See e.g. Akehurst, 'Jurisdiction', pp. 152 ff.; Mann, 'Doctrine of Jurisdiction', pp. 82 ff., and
D. P. O'Connell, *International Law*, 2nd edn, London, 1970, vol. II, pp. 823–31.

[32] It was noted in the *Wood Pulp* case that 'the two undisputed bases on which state jurisdiction
is founded in international law are territoriality and nationality', [1998] 4 CMLR 901 at
920; 96 ILR, p. 148.

rights that a state possesses.[33] That a country should be able to legislate with regard to activities within its territory and to prosecute for offences committed upon its soil is a logical manifestation of a world order of independent states and is entirely understandable since the authorities of a state are responsible for the conduct of law and the maintenance of good order within that state. It is also highly convenient since in practice the witnesses to the crime will be situated in the country and more often than not the alleged offender will be there too.[34]

Thus, all crimes committed (or alleged to have been committed) within the territorial jurisdiction of a state may come before the municipal courts and the accused if convicted may be sentenced. This is so even where the offenders are foreign citizens.[35] The converse of the concept of territorial jurisdiction is that the courts of one country do not, as a general principle, have jurisdiction with regard to events that have occurred or are occurring in the territory of another state.[36] Further, there is a presumption that legislation applies within the territory of the state concerned and not outside.[37] One state cannot lay down criminal laws for another in

---

[33] See Lord Macmillan, *Compañía Naviera Vascongado* v. *Cristina SS* [1938] AC 485, 496–7; 9 AD, pp. 250, 259. Note also Bowett's view that the 'dynamism and adaptability of the principle in recent years has been quite remarkable', 'Jurisdiction', p. 5, and Marshall CJ in *The Schooner Exchange* v. *McFaddon* 7 Cranch 116, 136 (1812) to the effect that '[t]he jurisdiction of the nation within its own territory is necessarily exclusive and absolute'. Donaldson LJ also pointed to the general presumption in favour of the territoriality of jurisdiction, *R* v. *West Yorkshire Coroner, ex parte Smith* [1983] QB 335, 358; 78 ILR, p. 550. See also, for the view that the concept of jurisdiction is essentially territorial, *Banković* v. *Belgium*, European Court of Human Rights, Judgment of 12 December 2001, paras. 63, 67 and 71; 123 ILR, pp. 110, 111 and 113, and *Al-Skeini* v. *Secretary of State for Defence* [2007] UKHL 26, para. 109, per Lord Brown; 133 ILR, p. 736.

[34] See e.g. the Separate Opinion of Judge Guillaume in *Congo* v. *Belgium*, ICJ Reports, 2002, pp. 3, 36; 128 ILR, pp. 60, 92.

[35] See e.g. *Holmes* v. *Bangladesh Binani Corporation* [1989] 1 AC 1112, 1137; 87 ILR, pp. 365, 380–1, per Lord Griffiths and Lord Browne-Wilkinson in *Ex parte Pinochet (No. 3)* [2000] 1 AC 147, 188; 119 ILR, p. 139.

[36] See e.g. *Kaunda* v. *President of South Africa* (CCT 23/04) [2004] ZACC 5 (4 August 2004) and *R* v. *Cooke* [1998] 2 SCR 597.

[37] See as to the UK, e.g. F. Bennion, *Statutory Interpretation*, 4th London, edn, 2002, p. 282. See also *Clark (Inspector of Taxes)* v. *Oceanic Contractors Inc.* [1983] 2 AC 130, 145, per Lord Scarman; *Al Sabah* v. *Grupo Torras SA* [2005] UKPC 1, [2005] 2 AC 333, para. 13, per Lord Walker of Gestingthorpe for the Privy Council; *Lawson* v. *Serco Limited* [2006] UKHL 3, [2006] ICR 250, para. 6, per Lord Hoffmann; *Agassi* v. *Robinson (Inspector of Taxes)* [2006] UKHL 23, [2006] 1 WLR 1380, paras. 16, 20, per Lord Scott of Foscote and Lord Walker of Gestingthorpe, and *Al-Skeini* v. *Secretary of State for Defence* [2007] UKHL 26, paras. 11 ff. per Lord Bingham. But note that in *Masri* v. *Consolidated Contractors* [2008] EWCA Civ 303 at para. 31, it was said that, 'nowadays the presumption has little

the absence of consent, nor may it enforce its criminal legislation in the territory of another state in the absence of consent.[38]

The principal ground for the exercise of criminal jurisdiction is, therefore, territoriality,[39] although it is not the only one. There are others, such as nationality, but the majority of criminal prosecutions take place in the territory where the crime has been committed. However, the territorial concept is more extensive than at first appears since it encompasses not only crimes committed wholly on the territory of a state but also crimes in which only part of the offence has occurred in the state: one example being where a person fires a weapon across a frontier killing somebody in the neighbouring state. Both the state where the gun was fired and the state where the injury actually took place have jurisdiction to try the offender, the former under the subjective territorial principle of territoriality and the latter under the objective territorial principle. Of course, which of the states will in the event exercise its jurisdiction will depend upon where the offender is situated, but the point remains that both the state where the offence was commenced and the state where the offence was concluded may validly try the offender.[40] For example, the Scottish Solicitor General made it clear that Scottish courts had jurisdiction with regard to the alleged bombers of the airplane which exploded over the Scottish town of Lockerbie as the locus of the

---

force and it is simply a matter of construction'. See also *Société Eram Shipping Co. Ltd* v. *Cie Internationale de Navigation* [2004] 1AC 260, para. 54 (per Lord Hoffmann) and *Office of Fair Trading* v. *Lloyds TSB Bank plc* [2007] UKHL 48.

[38] See e.g. the Separate Opinion of Judge Guillaume, *Congo* v. *Belgium*, ICJ Reports, 2002, pp. 3, 36; 128 ILR, pp. 60, 92. However, in a situation of belligerent occupation, the occupier may exercise certain criminal enforcement powers with regard to the local population: see the Fourth Geneva Convention on the Protection of Civilian Persons, articles 64–78.

[39] See the statement by a Home Office Minister, noting that 'As a general rule, our courts have jurisdiction to try offences that are committed within this country's territory only. This is because generally speaking the Government believes that trials are best conducted in the jurisdiction in which they occurred not least because there are very real difficulties associated with the obtaining of evidence necessary to effectively prosecute here offences that are committed in foreign jurisdictions. The Government have no plans to depart from this general rule', HC Deb., vol. 445 col. 1419, Written Answer, 2 May 2006, UKMIL, 77 BYIL, 2006, p. 756.

[40] See e.g. the *Lotus* case, PCIJ, Series A, No. 10, 1927, pp. 23, 30; 4 AD, pp. 153, 159, and Judge Moore, *ibid.*, p. 73; the Harvard Research Draft Convention on Jurisdiction with Respect to Crime, 29 AJIL, 1935, Supp., p. 480 (article 3), and Akehurst, 'Jurisdiction', pp. 152–3. See Lord Wilberforce, *DPP* v. *Doot* [1973] AC 807, 817; 57 ILR, pp. 117, 119 and *R* v. *Berry* [1984] 3 All ER 1008. See also *Strassheim* v. *Dailey* 221 US 280 (1911); *US* v. *Columba-Colella* 604 F.2d 356 and *US* v. *Perez-Herrera* 610 F.2d 289.

offences.[41] Such a situation would also apply in cases of offences against immigration regulations and in cases of conspiracy where activities have occurred in each of two, or more, countries.[42] Accordingly, courts are likely to look at all the circumstances in order to determine in which jurisdiction the substantial or more significant part of the crime in question was committed.[43]

The nature of territorial sovereignty in relation to criminal acts was examined in the *Lotus* case.[44] The relevant facts may be summarised as follows. The French steamer, the *Lotus*, was involved in a collision on the high seas with the *Boz-Kourt*, a Turkish collier. The latter vessel sank and eight sailors and passengers died as a result. Because of this the Turkish authorities arrested the French officer of the watch (at the time of the incident) when the *Lotus* reached a Turkish port. The French officer was charged with manslaughter and France protested strongly against this action, alleging that Turkey did not have the jurisdiction to try the offence. The case came before the Permanent Court of International Justice, which was called upon to decide whether there existed an international rule prohibiting the Turkish exercise of jurisdiction.

Because the basis of international law is the existence of sovereign states, the Court regarded it as axiomatic that restrictions upon the

---

[41] Before the International Court in oral pleadings at the provisional measures phase of the *Lockerbie* case, CR 92/3, pp. 11–12, UKMIL, 63 BYIL, 1992, p. 722. The trial of the two accused took place in the Netherlands, but in a facility that was deemed to be a Scottish court, with Scottish judges and lawyers and under Scots law: see e.g. A. Aust, 'Lockerbie: The Other Case', 49 ICLQ, 2000, p. 278, and for the verdict, see 94 AJIL, 2000, p. 405.

[42] See e.g. *Board of Trade* v. *Owen* [1957] AC 602, 634 and *DPP* v. *Stonehouse* [1977] 2 All ER 909, 916; 73 ILR, p. 252. In *R* v. *Abu Hamza*, *The Times*, 30 November 2006, the Court of Appeal (Criminal Division) held that it was an offence for a person to incite a foreign national in England and Wales to commit murder abroad. See also the Home Secretary speaking as to the Criminal Justice Bill on 14 April 1993, and noting that the effect of the proposed legislation would be to ensure that where a fraud had a significant connection with the UK, British courts would have jurisdiction, whether or not the final element of the crime occurred within the country, UKMIL, 64 BYIL, 1993, pp. 646–7. See G. Gilbert, 'Crimes Sans Frontières: Jurisdictional Problems in English Law', 63 BYIL, 1992, pp. 415, 430 ff. Note also Akehurst, who would restrict the operation of the doctrine so that jurisdiction could only be claimed by the state where the primary effect is felt, 'Jurisdiction', p. 154.

[43] See e.g. La Forest J in *Libman* v. *The Queen* (1985) 21 CCC (3d) 206 and Lord Griffiths in *Somchai Liangsiriprasert* v. *The United States* [1991] 1 AC 225; 85 ILR, p. 109.

[44] PCIJ, Series A, No. 10, 1927; 4 AD, p. 153. See e.g. Mann, 'Doctrine of Jurisdiction', pp. 33–6, 39, 92–3; J. W. Verzijl, *The Jurisprudence of the World Court*, Leiden, vol. I, 1965, pp. 73–98, and Schachter, 'International Law', p. 250. See also *Oppenheim's International Law*, p. 478.

independence of states could not be presumed.[45] However, a state was not able to exercise its power outside its frontiers in the absence of a permissive rule of international law. But, continued the Court, this did not mean that 'international law prohibits a state from exercising jurisdiction in its own territory, in respect of any case which relates to acts which have taken place abroad and in which it cannot rely on some permissive rule of international law'. In this respect, states had a wide measure of discretion limited only in certain instances by prohibitive rules.[46] Because of this, countries had adopted a number of different rules extending their jurisdiction beyond the territorial limits so that 'the territoriality of criminal law, therefore, is not an absolute principle of international law and by no means coincides with territorial sovereignty'.[47] The Court rejected the French claim that the flag state had exclusive jurisdiction over the ship on the high seas, saying that no rule to that effect had emerged in international law, and stated that the damage to the Turkish vessel was equivalent to affecting Turkish territory so as to enable that country to exercise jurisdiction on the objective territorial principle, unrestricted by any rule of international law prohibiting this.[48]

The general pronouncements by the Court leading to the dismissal of the French contentions have been criticised by writers for a number of years, particularly with respect to its philosophical approach in treating states as possessing very wide powers of jurisdiction which could only be restricted by proof of a rule of international law prohibiting the action concerned.[49] It is widely accepted today that the emphasis lies the other way around.[50] It should also be noted that the *Lotus* principle as regards collisions at sea has been overturned by article 11(1) of the High Seas Convention, 1958, which emphasised that only the flag state or the state of which the alleged offender was a national has jurisdiction over sailors regarding incidents occurring on the high seas. The territorial principle covers crimes committed not only upon the land territory of the state but also upon the territorial sea and in certain cases upon the contiguous and

---

[45] PCIJ, Series A, No. 10, 1927, pp. 18–19; 4 AD, p. 155.

[46] PCIJ, Series A, No. 10, 1927, p. 19; 4 AD, p. 156.

[47] PCIJ, Series A, No. 10, 1927, p. 20.   [48] *Ibid.*, p. 24; 4 AD, p. 158.

[49] See e.g. G. Fitzmaurice, 'The General Principles of International Law Considered from the Standpoint of the Rule of Law', 92 HR, 1957, pp. 1, 56–7, and H. Lauterpacht, *International Law: Collected Papers*, Cambridge, 1970, vol. I, pp. 488–9.

[50] See e.g. the *Anglo-Norwegian Fisheries* case, ICJ Reports, 1951, p. 116; 18 ILR, p. 86 and the *Nottebohm* case, ICJ Reports, 1955, p. 4; 22 ILR, p. 349.

other zones and on the high seas where the state is the flag state of the vessel.[51]

As modern communications develop, so states evolve new methods of dealing with new problems. In the case of the Channel Tunnel, for example, providing a land link between the UK and France, these countries entered into an agreement whereby each state was permitted to exercise jurisdiction within the territory of the other. The Protocol concerning Frontier Controls and Policing, Co-operation in Criminal Justice, Public Safety and Mutual Assistance relating to the Channel Fixed Link was signed on 25 November 1991.[52] Under this Protocol, French and UK frontier control officers are empowered to work in specified parts of one another's territory. These areas are termed 'control zones' and are located at Cheriton, Coquelles, on board through trains and at international railway stations. The frontier control laws and regulations of one state thus apply and may be enforced in the other. In particular, the officers of the adjoining state shall in their exercise of national powers be permitted in the control zone in the host state to detain or arrest persons in accordance with the frontier control laws and regulations of the adjoining state. Article 38(2) of the Protocol provides that within the Fixed Link (i.e. the Tunnel), each state shall have jurisdiction and shall apply their own law when it cannot be ascertained with certainty where an offence has been committed or when an offence committed in the territory of one state is related to an offence committed on the territory of the other state or when an offence has begun in or has been continued in its own territory.[53] However, it is also provided that the state which first receives the person suspected of having committed such an offence shall have priority in exercising jurisdiction.

Another example of such cross-state territorial jurisdictional arrangements may be found in the Israel–Jordan Treaty of Peace, 1994. Annex I(b) and (c) of the Treaty, relating to the Naharayim/Baqura Area and the Zofar/Al-Ghamr Area respectively, provides for a special regime on a temporary basis. Although each area itself is recognised as under Jordan's sovereignty, with Israeli private land ownership rights and property

---

[51] See above, chapter 11.

[52] The Protocol was brought into force in the UK by the Channel Tunnel (International Arrangements) Order 1993: see e.g. UKMIL, 64 BYIL, 1993, p. 647. See also the Protocol of 29 May 2000, UKMIL, 71 BYIL, 2000, p. 589, and the *Eurotunnel* case, partial award of 30 January 2007, 132 ILR, p. 1.

[53] This is in addition to the normal territorial jurisdiction of the states within their own territory up to the frontier in the Tunnel under the sea, article 38(1).

interests, Jordan undertakes to grant unimpeded entry to, exit from, land usage and movement within the area to landowners and to their invitees or employees and not to apply its customs or immigration legislation to such persons. In particular, Jordan undertakes to permit with minimum formality the entry of uniformed Israeli police officers for the purpose of investigating crime or dealing with other incidents solely involving the landowners, their invitees or employees. Jordan undertakes also not to apply its criminal laws to activities in the area involving only Israeli nationals, while Israeli laws applying to the extraterritorial activities of Israelis may be applied to Israelis and their activities in the area. Israel could also take measures in the area to enforce such laws.[54]

Thus although jurisdiction is primarily and predominantly territorial, it is not inevitably and exclusively so and states are free to consent to arrangements whereby jurisdiction is exercised outside the national territory and whereby jurisdiction by other states is exercised within the national territory.[55]

A rather more unusual situation developed with regard to persons detained by the US in Guantanamo Bay Naval Base, situated in a part of the island of Cuba leased to the US pursuant to agreements made in 1903 and 1934. Following the conflict in Afghanistan in 2001 and thereafter, persons were taken to and held in Guantanamo Bay, which the US initially argued lay outside federal jurisdiction, being under US control but not sovereignty.[56] The Supreme Court, however, in *Rasul* v. *Bush* held that District Courts did have jurisdiction to hear petitions challenging the legality of detention of foreign nationals who had been detained abroad in connection with an armed conflict and held at Guantanamo Bay.[57]

---

[54] See also e.g. the treaties of 1903 and 1977 between the US and Panama concerning jurisdictional rights over the Panama Canal Zone and the NATO Status of Forces Agreement, 1951 regulating the exercise of jurisdiction of NATO forces based in other NATO states. The Boundary Commission in *Eritrea/Ethiopia* noted that it was not unknown for states to locate a checkpoint or customs post in the territory of a neighbouring state, Decision of 13 April 2002, 130 ILR, pp. 1, 112.

[55] Jurisdiction, and its concomitant international responsibility for acts done in the exercise of that jurisdiction, may also exist on the basis of the acts of officials committed abroad and on the basis of actual control of the territory in question in specific contexts. See e.g. *Loizidou* v. *Turkey* (*Preliminary Objections*), European Court of Human Rights, Series A, No. 310, 1995, p. 20; 103 ILR, p. 621. For the European Convention on Human Rights, see above, chapter 7 and for international responsibility, see below, chapter 14.

[56] Relying upon *Johnson* v. *Eisenträger* 339 US 763 (1950).

[57] 542 US 466 (2004). Congress then passed the Detainee Treatment Act of 2005, which denied jurisdiction concerning an application for habeas corpus with regard to an alien detainee at Guantanamo Bay. In *Hamdan* v. *Rumsfeld* 548 US 557, 576–7, the Court

The nationality principle[58]

Since every state possesses sovereignty and jurisdictional powers and since every state must consist of a collection of individual human beings, it is essential that a link between the two be legally established. That link connecting the state and the people it includes in its territory is provided by the concept of nationality.[59]

By virtue of nationality, a person becomes entitled to a series of rights ranging from obtaining a valid passport enabling travel abroad to being able to vote. In addition, nationals may be able to undertake various jobs (for example in the diplomatic service) that a non-national may be barred from. Nationals are also entitled to the protection of their state and to various benefits prescribed under international law. On the other hand, states may not mistreat the nationals of other states nor, ordinarily, conscript them into their armed forces, nor prosecute them for crimes committed outside the territory of the particular state.

held this provision inapplicable to pending cases. The Military Commissions Act of 2006 subsequently provided for denial of jurisdiction with regard to detained aliens determined to be an enemy combatant with effect from 11 September 2001, i.e. including applications pending at the time of the adoption of this Act. However, in *Boumediene* v. *Bush* 553 US – (2008), US Supreme Court, 12 June 2008, Slip Opinion, it was held that the doctrine of habeas corpus did apply, thus permitting applications by detained enemy combatants to the federal courts challenging their detention. Justice Kennedy, writing for the majority, while noting that, 'In considering both the procedural and substantive standards used to impose detention to prevent acts of terrorism, proper deference must be accorded to the political branches', declared that, 'The laws and Constitution are designed to survive, and remain in force, in extraordinary times.' *Ibid.*, pp. 67 and 70.

[58] Akehurst, 'Jurisdiction', pp. 156–7; Harvard Research Draft Convention on Jurisdiction with Respect to Crime, 29 AJIL, 1935, Supp., pp. 519 ff.; M. Whiteman, *Digest of International Law*, Washington, DC, 1967, vol. VIII, pp. 1–22, 64–101, 105–13, 119–87; R. Donner, *The Regulation of Nationality in International Law*, 2nd edn, New York, 1995; D. Campbell and J. Fisher, *International Immigration and Nationality Law*, The Hague, 1993; M. J. Verwilghen, 'Conflits de Nationalité, Plurinationalité et Apatridie', 277 HR, 1999, p. 9; J. F. Rezek, 'Le Droit International de la Nationalité', 198 HR, 1986 III, p. 333; H. Silving, 'Nationality in Comparative Law', 5 *American Journal of Comparative Law*, 1956, p. 410, and Brownlie, *Principles*, p. 301 and chapter 19. See also Nguyen Quoc Dinh, P. Daillier and A. Pellet, *Droit International Public*, 7th edn, Paris, 2002, pp. 492 ff., and below, chapter 14, p. 808.

[59] Note that several instruments provide for a right to a nationality: see e.g. the Universal Declaration on Human Rights, 1948; the International Covenant on Civil and Political Rights, 1966; the Convention on the Rights of the Child, 1989 and the European Convention on Nationality, 1997. See also A. Grossman, 'Nationality and the Unrecognised State', 50 ICLQ, 2001, p. 849.

The concept of nationality is important since it determines the benefits to which persons may be entitled and the obligations (such as conscription) which they must perform. The problem is that there is no coherent, accepted definition of nationality in international law and only conflicting descriptions under the different municipal laws of states. Not only that, but the rights and duties attendant upon nationality vary from state to state.

Generally, international law leaves the conditions for the grant of nationality to the domestic jurisdiction of states.

This was the central point in the *Nationality Decrees in Tunis and Morocco* case.[60] This concerned a dispute between Britain and France over French nationality decrees which had the effect of giving French nationality to the children of certain British subjects. The Court, which had been requested to give an advisory opinion by the Council of the League of Nations, declared that:

> [t]he question of whether a certain matter is or is not solely within the jurisdiction of a state is an essentially relative question, it depends upon the development of international relations. Thus, in the present state of international law, questions of nationality are, in the opinion of this court, in principle within this reserved domain.[61]

However, although states may prescribe the conditions for the grant of nationality, international law is relevant, especially where other states are involved. As was emphasised in article 1 of the 1930 Hague Convention on the Conflict of Nationality Laws:

> it is for each state to determine under its own law who are its nationals. This law shall be recognised by other states in so far as it is consistent with international conventions, international custom and the principles of law generally recognised with regard to nationality.

The International Court of Justice noted in the *Nottebohm* case[62] that, according to state practice, nationality was:

> a legal bond having as its basis a social fact of attachment, a genuine connection of existence, interests and sentiments, together with the existence of reciprocal rights and duties.

---

[60] PCIJ, Series B, No. 4, 1923; 2 AD, p. 349.
[61] PCIJ, Series B, No. 4, 1923, p. 24.
[62] ICJ Reports, 1955, pp. 4, 23; 22 ILR, pp. 349, 360. See also below, p. 813.

It was a legal manifestation of the link between the person and the state granting nationality and a recognition that the person was more closely connected with that state than with any other.[63]

Since the concept of nationality provides the link between the individual and the benefits of international law, it is worth pointing to some of the basic ideas associated with the concept, particularly with regard to its acquisition.[64]

In general, the two most important principles upon which nationality is founded in states are first by descent from parents who are nationals (*jus sanguinis*) and second by virtue of being born within the territory of the state (*jus soli*).

It is commonly accepted that a child born of nationals of a particular state should be granted the nationality of that state by reason of descent. This idea is particularly utilised in continental European countries, for example, France, Germany and Switzerland, where the child will receive the nationality of his father, although many municipal systems do provide that an illegitimate child will take the nationality of his mother. On the other hand, in common law countries such as Britain and the US the doctrine of the *jus sanguinis* is more restricted, so that where a father has become a national by descent it does not always follow that that fact alone will be sufficient to make the child a national.

The common law countries have tended to adopt the *jus soli* rule, whereby any child born within the territorial limits of the state automatically becomes a national thereof.[65] The British Nationality Act of 1948, for example, declared that 'every person born within the United Kingdom and Colonies · · · shall be a citizen of the United Kingdom and Colonies by birth'.[66] There is an exception to this, however, which applies to virtually every country applying the *jus soli* rule, and that is with regard to persons entitled to immunity from the jurisdiction of the state. In other words, the children of diplomatic personnel born within the country do

---

[63] See below, chapter 14, p. 815, as to dual nationality and state responsibility for injuries to aliens.

[64] See e.g. Brownlie, *Principles*, p. 378; P. Weiss, *Nationality and Statelessness in International Law*, 2nd edn, Germantown, 1979, and H. F. Van Panhuys, *The Role of Nationality in International Law*, Leiden, 1959.

[65] See e.g. *United States v. Wong Kim Ark* 169 US 649 (1898).

[66] But see now the British Nationality Act of 1981.

not automatically acquire its nationality.[67] Precisely how far this exception extends varies from state to state. Some countries provide that this rule applies also to the children of enemy alien fathers[68] born in areas under enemy occupation.[69]

Nationality may also be acquired by the wives of nationals, although here again the position varies from state to state. Some states provide for the automatic acquisition of the husband's nationality, others for the conditional acquisition of nationality and others merely state that the marriage has no effect as regards nationality. Problems were also caused in the past by the fact that many countries stipulated that a woman marrying a foreigner would thereby lose her nationality.

The Convention of 1957 on the Nationality of Married Women provides that contracting states accept that the marriage of one of their nationals to an alien shall not automatically affect the wife's nationality, although a wife may acquire her husband's nationality by special procedures should she so wish.

It should be noted also that article 9 of the Convention on the Elimination of All Forms of Discrimination against Women, 1979 provides that states parties shall grant women equal rights with men to acquire, change or retain their nationality and that in particular neither marriage to an alien nor change of nationality by the husband during marriage shall automatically change the nationality of the wife, render her stateless or force upon her the nationality of the husband. It is also provided that women shall have equal rights with men with respect to the nationality of their children. As far as children themselves are concerned, article 24(3) of the International Covenant on Civil and Political Rights, 1966 stipulated that every child has the right to acquire a nationality, while this is reaffirmed in article 7 of the Convention on the Rights of the Child, 1989.

Nationality may be obtained by an alien by virtue of a naturalisation process usually involving a minimum period of residence, but the conditions under which this takes place vary considerably from country to country.[70]

---

[67] See e.g. *In re Thenault* 47 F.Supp. 952 (1942) and article 12, Convention on Conflict of Nationality Law, 1930. See also article II, Optional Protocol on Acquisition of Nationality (UN Conference on Diplomatic Law), 1961.

[68] But see *Inglis v. Sailor's Snug Harbour* 3 Peters 99 (1830), US Supreme Court.

[69] Note the various problems associated with possible extensions of the *jus soli* rule, e.g. regarding births on ships: see Brownlie, *Principles*, pp. 379 ff. See also *Lam Mow v. Nagle* 24 F.2d 316 (1928); 4 AD, pp. 295, 296.

[70] See e.g. Weiss, *Nationality*, p. 101.

Civil jurisdiction, especially as regards matters of personal status, in a number of countries depends upon the nationality of the parties involved. So that, for example, the appropriate matrimonial law in any dispute for a Frenchman anywhere would be French law. However, common law countries tend to base the choice of law in such circumstances upon the law of the state where the individual involved has his permanent home (domicile).

Many countries, particularly those with a legal system based upon the continental European model, claim jurisdiction over crimes committed by their nationals, notwithstanding that the offence may have occurred in the territory of another state.[71] Common law countries tend, however, to restrict the crimes over which they will exercise jurisdiction over their nationals abroad to very serious ones.[72] In the UK this is generally limited to treason, murder and bigamy committed by British nationals abroad.[73] Under section 21 of the Antarctic Act 1994, when a British national does or omits to do anything in Antarctica which would have constituted an offence if committed in the UK, then such person will be deemed to have committed an offence and be liable to be prosecuted and punished if convicted. In addition, the War Crimes Act 1991 provides for

---

[71] See e.g. Gilbert, 'Crimes', p. 417. See also *Re Gutierrez* 24 ILR, p. 265, *Public Prosecutor v. Antoni* 32 ILR, p. 140 and *Serre et Régnier, Recueil Dalloz Sirey (jurisprudence)*, 1991, p. 395.

[72] See the statement by a Home Office Minister, noting that 'We have exceptionally, however, assumed extra-territorial jurisdiction over some serious crime, such as murder, where the factors in favour of the ability to prosecute here outweigh those against', HC Deb., vol. 445, col. 1419, Written Answer, 2 May 2006, UKMIL, 77 BYIL, 2006, p. 756. Note, however, the comment by Lord Rodger that 'there can be no objection in principle to Parliament legislating for British citizens outside the United Kingdom, provided that the particular legislation does not offend against the sovereignty of other states', *Al-Skeini* v. *Secretary of State for Defence* [2007] UKHL 26, para. 46; 133 ILR, p. 716.

[73] See e.g. the Official Secrets Acts 1911 (s. 10), 1970 (s. 8) and 1989 (s. 15); the Offences Against the Person Act 1861 ss. 9 and 57; the Merchant Shipping Act 1894 s. 686(1) and *R* v. *Kelly* [1982] AC 665; 77 ILR, p. 284 and the Suppression of Terrorism Act 1978 s. 4. See P. Arnell, 'The Case for Nationality-Based Jurisdiction', 50 ICLQ, 2001, p. 955. This has now been extended to cover various sexual offences committed abroad: see the Sexual Offences (Conspiracy and Incitement) Act 1996; the Sex Offenders Act 1997 and the Sexual Offences Act 2003 s. 72, and certain offences of bribery and corruption committed overseas by UK companies or nationals: see the Anti-Terrorism Crime and Security Act 2001, Part 12. Note that in *Skiriotes* v. *Florida* 313 US 69, 73 (1941); 10 AD, pp. 258, 260, Hughes CJ declared that 'the United States is not debarred by any rule of international law from governing the conduct of its own citizens upon the high seas or even in foreign countries when the rights of other nations or their nationals are not infringed'. See also DUSPIL, 1976, pp. 449–57, regarding legislation to subject US nationals and citizens to US district court jurisdiction for crimes committed outside the US, particularly regarding Antarctica.

jurisdiction against a person who was on 8 March 1990 or subsequently
became a British citizen or resident in the UK. Proceedings for murder,
manslaughter or culpable homicide may be brought against that person
in the UK, irrespective of his nationality at the time of the alleged offence,
if the offence was committed during the Second World War in a place
that was part of Germany or under German occupation and constituted
a violation of the laws and customs of war.[74] Further, the common law
countries have never protested against the extensive use of the nationality
principle to found jurisdiction in criminal matters by other states.

It should be finally noted that by virtue of article 91 of the 1982 Convention on the Law of the Sea, ships have the nationality of the state whose
flag they are entitled to fly. Each state is entitled to fix the conditions for
the grant of its nationality to ships, for the registration of ships in its territory and for the right to fly its flag. However, there must be a genuine link
between the state and the ship.[75] By article 17 of the Chicago Convention
on International Civil Aviation, 1944, aircraft have the nationality of the
state in which they are registered, although the conditions for registration
are a matter for domestic law.[76]

The passive personality principle [77]

Under this principle, a state may claim jurisdiction to try an individual
for offences committed abroad which have affected or will affect nationals
of the state.

The leading case on this particular principle is the *Cutting* case in 1886[78]
which concerned the publication in Texas of a statement defamatory of
a Mexican by an American citizen. Cutting was arrested while in Mexico
and convicted of the offence (a crime under Mexican law) with Mexico
maintaining its right to jurisdiction upon the basis of the passive personality principle. The United States strongly protested against this, but there

---

[74] See also, with regard to the nationality of ships and aircraft, above, chapter 11, p. 611,
and below, p. 677, and as to the nationality of corporations, below, chapter 14, p. 815. See
further, as to the nationality of claims, below, chapter 14, p. 808.

[75] See also article 5 of the Geneva Convention on the High Seas, 1958.

[76] See article 19.

[77] See e.g. Akehurst, 'Jurisdiction', pp. 162–6; Mann, 'Doctrine of Jurisdiction', pp. 40–1;
E. Beckett, 'The Exercise of Criminal Jurisdiction over Foreigners', 6 BYIL, 1925, p. 44
and Beckett, 'Criminal Jurisdiction over Foreigners', 8 BYIL, 1927, p. 108; W. W. Bishop,
'General Course of Public International Law, 1965', 115 HR, 1965, pp. 151, 324, and
Higgins, *Problems and Process*, p. 65. See also the *Eichmann* case, 36 ILR, pp. 5, 49–57, 304.

[78] J. B. Moore, *Digest of International Law*, Washington, 1906, vol. II, p. 228.

was an inconclusive end to the incident, the charges being withdrawn by the injured party.[79]

A strong attack on this principle was made by Judge Moore, in a Dissenting Opinion in the *Lotus* case,[80] since the Turkish criminal code provided for jurisdiction where harm resulted to a Turkish national. However, the Court did not resolve the issue and concentrated upon the objective territorial jurisdiction principle.[81]

The overall opinion has been that the passive personality principle is rather a dubious ground upon which to base claims to jurisdiction under international law and it has been strenuously opposed by the US[82] and the UK, although a number of states apply it.

However, article 9 of the International Convention against the Taking of Hostages, 1979, in detailing the jurisdictional bases that could be established with regard to the offence, included the national state of a hostage 'if that state considers it appropriate'.[83] The possibility of using the passive personality concept was taken up by the US in 1984 in the Comprehensive Crime Control Act[84] *inter alia* implementing the Convention and in the provision extending the special maritime and territorial jurisdiction of the US to include '[a]ny place outside the jurisdiction of any nation with respect to an offence by or against a national of the United States'.[85] In 1986, following the *Achille Lauro* incident,[86] the US adopted the Omnibus Diplomatic Security and Anti-Terrorism Act,[87] inserting into the criminal

---

[79] See *US Foreign Relations*, 1886, p. viii; 1887, p. 757; and 1888, vol. II, p. 1114.

[80] PCIJ, Series A, No. 10, 1927, p. 92; 4 AD, p. 153.

[81] PCIJ, Series A, No. 10, 1927, pp. 22–3. See also O'Connell, *International Law*, vol. II, pp. 901–2, and Higgins, *Problems and Process*, pp. 65–6.

[82] See, for example, US protests to Greece, concerning the service of summonses by Greek Consuls in the US on US nationals involved in accidents with Greek nationals occurring in the United States, DUSPIL, 1973, pp. 197–8 and DUSPIL, 1975, pp. 339–40.

[83] See *Rees v. Secretary of State for the Home Department* [1986] 2 All ER 321. See generally, J. J. Lambert, *Terrorism and Hostages in International Law*, Cambridge, 1990. See also article 3(1)c of the Convention on the Prevention and Punishment of Crimes against Internationally Protected Persons, 1973 and article 5(1)c of the Convention against Torture, 1984.

[84] See new section 1203 of the Criminal Code, 18 USC para. 1203, Pub. L. No. 98-473, ch. 19, para. 2002(a), 98 Stat. 1976, 2186.

[85] Pub. L. No. 98-473, para. 1210, 98 Stat. at 2164. Note also article 689(1) of the French Code of Criminal Procedure adopted in 1975.

[86] See below, p. 679.

[87] Pub. L. No. 99-399, tit. XII, para. 1202(a), 100 Stat. 853, 896. See e.g. C. Blakesley, 'Jurisdictional Issues and Conflicts of Jurisdiction' in *Legal Responses to International Terrorism* (ed. M. C. Bassiouni), Charlottesville, 1988. See also article 689 of the French Code of Criminal Procedure 1975.

code a new section which provided for US jurisdiction over homicide and physical violence outside the US where a national of the US is the victim. The section is less sweeping than it appears, since the written certification of the Attorney General is required, before a prosecution may commence by the US, to the effect that the offence was intended to coerce, intimidate or retaliate against a government or a civilian population.

In *US* v. *Yunis (No. 2)*[88] the issue concerned the apprehension of a Lebanese citizen by US agents in international waters and his prosecution in the US for alleged involvement in the hijacking of a Jordanian airliner. The only connection between the hijacking and the US was the fact that several American nationals were on that flight. The Court accepted that both the universality principle[89] and the passive personality principle provided an appropriate basis for jurisdiction in the case. It was stated that although the latter principle was the most controversial of the jurisdictional principles in international law, 'the international community recognises its legitimacy'.[90] It was pointed out that although the US had historically opposed the passive personality principle, it had been accepted by the US and the international community in recent years in the sphere of terrorist and other internationally condemned crimes.[91] Judges Higgins, Kooijmans and Buergenthal in their Joint Separate Opinion in the *Congo* v. *Belgium (Arrest Warrant)* case noted that in this particular context, the passive personality principle 'today meets with relatively little opposition'.[92]

The protective principle[93]

This principle provides that states may exercise jurisdiction over aliens who have committed an act abroad which is deemed prejudicial to the

---

[88] 681 F.Supp. 896 (1988); 82 ILR, p. 344. See also *US* v. *Yunis (No. 3)* 924 F.2d 1086, 1091; 88 ILR, pp. 176, 181.

[89] See below, p. 668.   [90] 681 F.Supp. 896, 901; 82 ILR, p. 349.

[91] 681 F.Supp. 896, 902; 82 ILR, p. 350. Note that a comment to paragraph 402 of the *Third US Restatement of Foreign Relations Law*, vol. I, p. 240, states that the passive personality principle 'is increasingly accepted as applied to terrorist and other organised attacks on a state's nationals by reason of their nationality, or to assassinations of a state's diplomatic representatives or other officials'. See also *US* v. *Benitez* 741 F.2d 1312, 1316 (1984), cert. denied, 471 US 1137, 105 S. Ct. 2679 (1985).

[92] ICJ Reports, 2002, pp. 3, 63, 76–7; 128 ILR, pp. 60, 118, 132.

[93] See e.g. Akehurst, 'Jurisdiction', pp. 157–9; Harvard Research, pp. 543–63, and M. Sahovic and W. W. Bishop, 'The Authority of the State: Its Range with Respect to Persons and Places' in *Manual of Public International Law* (ed. M. Sørensen), London, 1968, pp. 311, 362–5. See also M. S. McDougal, H. Lasswell and V. Vlasic, *Law and Public Order in Space*, New Haven, 1963, pp. 699–701.

security of the particular state concerned. It is a well-established concept, although there are uncertainties as to how far it extends in practice and particularly which acts are included within its net.[94]

The principle is justifiable on the basis of protection of a state's vital interests, since the alien might not be committing an offence under the law of the country where he is residing and extradition might be refused if it encompassed political offences. However, it is clear that it is a principle that can easily be abused, although usually centred upon immigration and various economic offences, since far from protecting important state functions it could easily be manipulated to subvert foreign governments. Nevertheless, it exists partly in view of the insufficiency of most municipal laws as far as offences against the security and integrity of foreign states are concerned.[95]

This doctrine seems to have been applied in the British case of *Joyce* v. *Director of Public Prosecutions*,[96] involving the infamous pro-Nazi propagandist 'Lord Haw-Haw'. Joyce was born in America, but in 1933 fraudulently acquired a British passport by declaring that he had been born in Ireland. In 1939, he left Britain and started working for German radio. The following year, he claimed to have acquired German nationality. The case turned on whether the British court had jurisdiction to try him after the war, on a charge of treason. The House of Lords decided that jurisdiction did exist in this case. Joyce had held himself out to be a British subject and had availed himself of the protection (albeit fraudulently) of a British passport. Accordingly he could be deemed to owe allegiance to the Crown, and be liable for a breach of that duty. The fact that the treason occurred outside the territory of the UK was of no consequence since states were not obliged to ignore the crime of treason committed against them outside their territory. Joyce was convicted and suffered the penalty for his actions.[97]

---

[94] See e.g. *In re Urios* 1 AD, p. 107 and article 694(1) of the French Code of Criminal Procedure.

[95] See e.g. *Rocha* v. *US* 288 F.2d 545 (1961); 32 ILR, p. 112; *US* v. *Pizzarusso* 388 F. 2d 8 (1968), and *US* v. *Rodriguez* 182 F.Supp. 479 (1960). See also the *Italian South Tyrol Terrorism* case, 71 ILR, p. 242.

[96] [1946] AC 347; 15 AD, p. 91.

[97] See, with regard to US practice, *Rocha* v. *US* 288 F.2d 545 (1961); *US* v. *Pizzarusso* 388 F.2d 8 (1968) and *US* v. *Layton* 509 F.Supp. 212 (1981). See also *Third US Restatement of Foreign Relations Law*, vol. I, pp. 237 ff. and the Omnibus Diplomatic Security and Anti-Terrorism Act 1986. The US has also asserted jurisdiction on the basis of the protective principle over aliens on the high seas: see the Maritime Drug Law Enforcement Act 1986 and *US* v. *Gonzalez* 776 F.2d 931 (1985) and see also S. Murphy, 'Extraterritorial Application of US Laws to Crimes on Foreign Vessels', 97 AJIL, 2003, p. 183.

The protective principle is often used in treaties providing for multiple jurisdictional grounds with regard to specific offences.[98]

The universality principle [99]

Under this principle, each and every state has jurisdiction to try particular offences. The basis for this is that the crimes involved are regarded as particularly offensive to the international community as a whole. There are two categories that clearly belong to the sphere of universal jurisdiction, which has been defined as the competence of the state to prosecute alleged offenders and to punish them if convicted, irrespective of the place of commission of the crime and regardless of any link of active or passive nationality or other grounds of jurisdiction recognised by international law.[100] These are piracy[101] and war crimes. However, there are a growing number of other offences which by international treaty may be subject to the jurisdiction of contracting parties and which form a distinct category closely allied to the concept of universal jurisdiction.

War crimes, crimes against peace and crimes against humanity

In addition to piracy, war crimes are now accepted by most authorities as subject to universal jurisdiction, though of course the issues

---

[98] See e.g. the Hostages Convention, 1979; the aircraft hijacking conventions and the Safety of United Nations and Associated Personnel Convention, 1994: see below, pp. 676 ff.

[99] See e.g. Akehurst, 'Jurisdiction', pp. 160–6; Bowett, 'Jurisdiction', pp. 11–14; Harvard Research, pp. 563–92; Jennings, 'Extraterritorial Jurisdiction', p. 156; Gilbert, 'Crimes', p. 423; K. C. Randall, 'Universal Jurisdiction under International Law', 66 *Texas Law Review*, 1988, p. 785; M. C. Bassiouni, *Crimes Against Humanity in International Criminal Law*, Dordrecht, 1992; L. Reydams, *Universal Jurisdiction*, Oxford, 2003; Redress Report on Legal Redress for Victims of International Crimes, March 2004; M. Inazumi, *Universal Jurisdiction in Modern International Law for Prosecuting Serious Crimes under International Law*, Antwerp, 2005; R. O'Keefe, 'Universal Jurisdiction: Clarifying the Basic Concept', 2 *Journal of International Criminal Justice*, 2004, p. 735; A. H. Butler, 'The Doctrine of Universal Jurisdiction: A Review of the Literature,' 11 *Criminal Law Forum*, 2001, p. 353; M. Henzelin, *Le Principe de l'Universalité en Droit Pénal International*, Brussels, 2000, and L. Benvenides, 'The Universal Jurisdiction Principle: Nature and Scope', 1 *Annuario Mexicano de Derecho Internacional*, 2001, p. 58. See also the *Princeton Principles on Universal Jurisdiction*, Princeton, 2001 and the Cairo Arusha Principles on Universal Jurisdiction in Respect of Gross Human Rights Violations, Inazumi, *Universal Jurisdiction*, p. 5. Note also H. Kissinger, 'The Pitfalls of Universal Jurisdiction', *Foreign Affairs*, July/August 2001.

[100] See the resolution adopted by the Institut de Droit International on 26 August 2005, para. 1.

[101] As to piracy, see above, chapter 8, p. 398 and chapter 11, p. 615

involved are extremely sensitive and highly political.[102] While there is little doubt about the legality and principles of the war crimes decisions emerging after the Second World War, a great deal of controversy arose over suggestions of war crimes with regard to American personnel connected with the Vietnam war,[103] Pakistani soldiers involved in the Bangladesh war of 1971 and persons concerned with subsequent conflicts.

Article 6 of the Charter of the International Military Tribunal of 1945 referred to crimes against peace, violations of the law and customs of war and crimes against humanity as offences within the jurisdiction of the Tribunal for which there was to be individual responsibility.[104] This article can now be regarded as part of international law. In a resolution unanimously approved by the General Assembly of the United Nations in 1946, the principles of international law recognised by the Charter of the Nuremberg Tribunal and the judgment of the Tribunal were expressly confirmed.[105] The General Assembly in 1968 adopted a Convention on the Non-Applicability of Statutory Limitations to War Crimes and Crimes Against Humanity, reinforcing the general conviction that war crimes form a distinct category under international law, susceptible to universal jurisdiction,[106] while the four Geneva 'Red Cross' Conventions of 1949 also contain provisions for universal jurisdiction over grave breaches.[107] Such grave breaches include wilful killing, torture or inhuman treatment, unlawful deportation of protected

---

[102] See e.g. Akehurst, 'Jurisdiction', p. 160; A. Cowles, 'Universality of Jurisdiction over War Crimes', 33 *California Law Review*, 1945, p. 177; Brownlie, *Principles*, pp. 303–5; Bowett, 'Jurisdiction', p. 12; Higgins, *Problems and Process*, p. 56; Mann, 'Doctrine of Jurisdiction', p. 93, and Bassiouni, *Crimes against Humanity*, p. 510. See also the *Eichmann* case, 36 ILR, pp. 5 and 277 and the UN War Crimes Commission, 15 *Law Reports of Trials of War Criminals*, 1949, p. 26. However, cf. the Separate Opinion of Judge Guillaume in *Congo v. Belgium*, ICJ Reports, 2002, pp. 3, 42; 128 ILR, p. 98 (restricting universal jurisdiction to piracy) and the Joint Separate Opinion, *ibid.*, pp. 3, 78; 128 ILR, p. 134 (universal jurisdiction may possibly exist with regard to the Geneva Conventions of 1949 on war crimes, etc.). See further above, chapter 8.

[103] See e.g. *Calley* v. *Calloway* 382 F.Supp. 650 (1974), rev'd 519 F.2d 184 (1975), cert. denied 425 US 911 (1976).

[104] See also article 228 of the Treaty of Versailles, 1919.

[105] Resolution 95 (I). See also *Yearbook of the ILC*, 1950, vol. II, p. 195; 253 HL Deb., col. 831, 2 December 1963; the *British Manual of Military Law*, Part III, 1958, para. 637; Brownlie, *Principles*, pp. 561 ff., and P. Weiss, 'Time Limits for the Prosecution of Crimes against International Law', 53 BYIL, 1982, pp. 163, 188 ff.

[106] See e.g. Weiss, 'Time Limits'.

[107] See article 49 of the First Geneva Convention; article 50 of the Second Geneva Convention; article 129 of the Third Geneva Convention and article 146 of the Fourth Geneva

persons and the taking of hostages. The list was extended in Protocol I of 1977 to the 1949 Conventions to include, for example, attacking civilian populations.[108]

Nuremberg practice demonstrates that crimes against peace consist of the commission by the authorities of a state of acts of aggression. In theory this is not controversial, but in practice serious problems are likely to arise within the framework of universal jurisdiction.[109] However, whether this category can be expanded to include support for international terrorism is open to question. Crimes against humanity clearly cover genocide and related activities. They differ from war crimes in applying beyond the context of an international armed conflict, but cover essentially the same substantive offences.[110] The UN Secretary-General's Report on the Establishment of an International Tribunal for the Former Yugoslavia[111] noted in the commentary to article 5 of what became the Statute of the Tribunal[112] that 'crimes against humanity are aimed at any civilian population and are prohibited regardless of whether they are committed in an armed conflict, international or internal in character' and that 'crimes against humanity refer to inhumane acts of a very serious nature, such as wilful killing, torture or rape, committed as part of a widespread or systematic attack against any civilian population on national, political, ethnic, racial or religous grounds'.[113] The 1998 Rome Statute for the International Criminal Court provides that jurisdiction is limited to the 'most serious crimes of concern to the international community as a whole' being genocide, crimes against humanity, war crimes and aggression,[114] and that a person who commits a crime within the jurisdiction of the Court 'shall be individually responsible and liable for punishment' in accordance with the Statute.[115]

Convention. See also e.g. G. I. A. D. Draper, *The Red Cross Conventions*, London, 1958, p. 105. Cf. Bowett, 'Jurisdiction', p. 12.

[108] See further above, chapter 8, and below, chapter 21.

[109] See e.g. *R* v. *Jones* [2006] UKHL 16; 132 ILR, p. 668, and see above, chapter 4, p. 146.

[110] See e.g. Brownlie, *Principles*, p. 562; L. C. Green, *The Contemporary Law of Armed Conflict*, 2nd edn, Manchester, 2000, chapter 18; E. Schwelb, 'Crimes Against Humanity', 23 BYIL, 1946, p. 178. See also the Commentary to article 20 of the Draft Statute for an International Criminal Court which refers to the concept as a term of art, Report of the International Law Commission, A/49/10, 1994, p. 75.

[111] S/25704, 1993, at paragraphs 47–8.   [112] Security Council resolution 827 (1993).

[113] See article 3 of the Statute of the International Criminal Tribunal for Rwanda, 1994, Security Council resolution 955 (1994). See also the *Barbie* case, 100 ILR, p. 330 and the *Touvier* case, *ibid.*, p. 337.

[114] Article 5.   [115] Article 25.

The International Law Commission adopted a Draft Code of Crimes against the Peace and Security of Mankind in 1996.[116] Article 8 provides that each state party shall take such measures as may be necessary to establish its jurisdiction over the crimes laid down in the Draft, while article 9 provides that a state in whose territory an individual alleged to have committed a crime against the peace and security of mankind is present shall either extradite or prosecute that individual. The Commentary to this article declares that the national courts of states parties would be entitled to exercise the 'broadest possible jurisdiction' over the crimes 'under the principle of universal jurisdiction'.[117] The Crimes against the Peace and Security of Mankind, for which there is individual responsibility, comprise aggression (article 16);[118] genocide (article 17); crimes against humanity (article 18); crimes against UN and associated personnel (article 19); and war crimes (article 20).[119]

The fact that a particular activity may be seen as an international crime does not of itself establish universal jurisdiction and state practice does not appear to have moved beyond war crimes, crimes against peace and crimes against humanity in terms of permitting the exercise of such jurisdiction. In particular, references made to, for example, apartheid, mercenaries and environmental offences in the 1991 Draft but omitted in the Draft Code adopted in 1996 must be taken as *de lege ferenda*.

In so far as universal jurisdiction as manifested in domestic courts is concerned, the starting point is the *Eichmann* case[120] decided by the District Court of Jerusalem and the Supreme Court of Israel in 1961. Eichmann was prosecuted and convicted under an Israeli law of 1951 for

---

[116] Report of the International Law Commission, A/51/10, 1996, p. 9. This had been under consideration since 1982: see General Assembly resolution 36/106 of 10 December 1981. A Draft Code was formulated in 1954 by the ILC and submitted to the UN General Assembly: see *Yearbook of the ILC*, 1954, vol. II, p. 150. The General Assembly postponed consideration of it until a definition of aggression had been formulated, resolution 897 (IX). This was achieved in 1974: see resolution 3314 (XXIX). A Draft Code was provisionally adopted in 1991: see A/46/10 and 30 ILM, 1991, p. 1584.

[117] Report of the International Law Commission, A/51/10, 1996, p. 51. This does not apply to the crime of aggression.

[118] Article 8 provides that jurisdiction concerning individuals will rest with an international criminal court.

[119] Additional crimes referred to in the 1991 Draft also included recruitment, use, financing and training of mercenaries; international terrorism; illicit traffic in narcotic drugs and wilful and severe damage to the environment.

[120] 36 ILR, pp. 5 and 277. See also the *Barbie* cases, 78 ILR, pp. 78, 125, 136 and *Demjanjuk v. Petrovsky* 776 F.2d 571 (1985); 79 ILR, p. 534. See also *Keesing's Record of World Events*, p. 36189 regarding the *Demjanjuk* case in Israel.

war crimes, crimes against the Jewish people and crimes against humanity. The District Court declared that far from limiting states' jurisdiction with regard to such crimes, international law was actually in need of the legislative and judicial organs of every state giving effect to its criminal interdictions and bringing the criminals to trial. The fact that the crimes were committed prior to the establishment of the state of Israel did not prevent the correct application of its powers pursuant to universal jurisdiction under international law. Israel's municipal law merely reflected the offences existing under international law.

It is a matter for domestic law whether the presence of the accused is required for the exercise of the jurisdiction of the particular domestic court. Different states adopt different approaches. The Belgian Court of Cassation took the view in its decision of 12 February 2003 in *HSA et al.* v. *SA et al.* that the presence of the accused was not necessary.[121] But this was in the context of the Belgian Statute of 1993, as amended in 1999, which provided for a wide jurisdiction in the case of genocide, crimes against humanity and war crimes. This Statute was amended on 23 April 2003 to provide that the alleged serious violation of international law in question shall be one committed against a person who at the time of the commission of the acts is a Belgian national or legally resident in Belgium for at least three years and that any prosecution, including a preliminary investigation phase, may only be undertaken at the request of the Federal Prosecutor. In addition, the Federal Prosecutor may decide not to proceed where it appears that in the interests of the proper administration of justice and in compliance with Belgium's international obligations, the case would be better placed before an international court or the court of the place where the acts were committed or the courts of the state of nationality of the alleged offender or the courts of the place where he may be found.[122] The Statute was further amended on 5 August 2003, requiring a foreigner wishing to submit an application to be resident in Belgium for a minimum of three years.[123] It appears that Belgium has in effect ceased to permit prosecutions under the universal jurisdiction model in the absence of the accused.[124] This is consistent with the approach of the Institut de Droit International which has stated that 'the exercise of

---

[121] Relating to the indictment of defendants Ariel Sharon, Amos Yaron and others concerning events in the Shabra and Shatilla camps in Lebanon in 1982, No. P. 02.1139. F/1.

[122] See article 16(2), 42 ILM, 2003, pp. 1258 ff.

[123] *Moniteur Belge*, 7 August 2003, pp. 40506–15.

[124] See e.g. Inazumi, *Universal Jurisdiction*, p. 97. See also S. Ratner, 'Belgium's War Crimes Statute: A Postmortem', 97 AJIL, 2003, p. 888.

universal jurisdiction requires the presence of the alleged offender in the territory of the prosecuting state or on board a vessel flying its flag or an aircraft which is registered under its laws or other lawful forms of control over the alleged offender'.[125]

The Supreme Court of Spain decided on 25 February 2003 in the *Guatemalan Genocide* case that jurisdiction would cover only acts of genocide in which Spanish nationals were victims.[126] However, this decision was overturned on 26 September 2005 by the Constitutional Court which decided that the domestic jurisdiction provision with regard to crimes against humanity was not limited to cases involving Spanish nationals who were victims of genocide and that no tie to Spain was needed in order to initiate a complaint.[127]

Treaties providing for jurisdiction

In addition to the accepted universal jurisdiction to apprehend and try pirates and war criminals, there are a number of treaties which provide for the suppression by the international community of various activities, ranging from the destruction of submarine cables to drug trafficking and slavery.[128] These treaties provide for the exercise of state jurisdiction but not for universal jurisdiction. Some conventions establish what might be termed a quasi-universal jurisdiction in providing for the exercise of jurisdiction upon a variety of bases by as wide a group of states parties as possible coupled with an obligation for states parties to establish such jurisdiction in domestic law. In many instances the offence involved will constitute *jus cogens*. The view is sometimes put forward that where a norm of *jus cogens* exists, particularly where the offence is regarded as especially serious, universal jurisdiction as such may be created.[129] More correct is the approach that in such circumstances international law recognises that domestic legal orders may validly establish and exercise jurisdiction over the alleged offenders. Such circumstances thus include the presence of

---

[125] Resolution adopted on 26 August 2005, para. 3(b).

[126] Judgment No. 327/2003. See also the same court's decision a few months later in the *Peruvian Genocide* case, where it was held that Spanish courts could not exercise universal jurisdiction over claims of genocide and other serious crimes alleged to have been committed by Peruvian officials from 1986, Judgment No. 712/2003.

[127] Judgment No. 237/2005. See e.g. N. Roht-Arriaza, '*Guatemala Genocide* Case. Judgment no. STC 237/2005', 100 AJIL, 2006, p. 207.

[128] See e.g. Akehurst, 'Jurisdiction', pp. 160–1.

[129] See e.g. Millett LJ in *Ex parte Pinochet* (*No. 3*) [2000] 1 AC 147, 275; 119 ILR, p. 229. See also R. Van Alebeek, 'The *Pinochet* Case: International Human Rights Law on Trial', 71 BYIL, 2000, p. 29.

the accused in the state concerned and in this way may be differentiated from universal jurisdiction as such, where, for example, a pirate may be apprehended on the high seas and then prosecuted in the state. Therefore, the type of jurisdiction at issue in such circumstances cannot truly be described as universal, but rather as quasi-universal.[130] Judges Higgins, Kooijmans and Buergenthal in their Joint Separate Opinion in *Congo* v. *Belgium* referred to this situation rather as an 'obligatory territorial jurisdiction over persons' or 'the jurisdiction to establish a territorial jurisdiction over persons for extraterritorial events' rather than as true universal jurisdiction.[131]

There are a number of treaties that follow the quasi-universal model, that is providing for certain defined offences to be made criminal offences within the domestic orders of states parties; accepting an obligation to arrest alleged offenders found on the national territory and then prosecuting those persons on the basis of a number of stated jurisdictional grounds, ranging from territoriality to nationality and passive personality grounds. Such treaties normally also provide for mutual assistance and for the offences in question to be deemed to be included as extraditable offences in any extradition treaty concluded between states parties. The agreements in question include, for example, the UN Torture Convention, 1984[132] and treaties relating to hostage-taking, currency counterfeiting, hijacking and drug trafficking. Such treaties are then normally implemented nationally.[133]

It is interesting to note that the International Law Commission's Draft Statute for an International Criminal Court proposed that the court would have jurisdiction in certain conditions with regard to a range of 'treaty crimes',[134] but this suggestion was not found acceptable in later discussions

---

[130] The phrase 'conditional universal jurisdiction' has also been suggested: see A. Cassese, 'When may Senior State Officials be Tried for International Crimes?', 13 EJIL, 2002, pp. 853, 856.

[131] ICJ Reports, 2002, pp. 3, 74–5; 128 ILR, pp. 60, 130–1. See also the Separate Opinion of Judge Guillaume, who uses the term 'subsidiary universal jurisdiction' to refer to the international conventions in question providing for the trial of offenders arrested on national territory and not extradited: *ibid.*, p. 40; 128 ILR, p. 96.

[132] See further above, chapter 6, p. 326.

[133] See e.g. the UK Taking of Hostages Act 1982.

[134] That is those arising out of the Geneva Conventions of 1949 and Protocol I thereto; the Hague Convention, 1970; the Montreal Convention, 1971; the Apartheid Convention, 1973; the Internationally Protected Persons Convention, 1973; the Hostages Convention, 1979; the Torture Convention, 1984; the Safety of Maritime Navigation Convention and Protocol, 1988 and the Convention against Illicit Traffic in Narcotic Drugs and

and does not appear in the 1998 Rome Statute. It is helpful to look at some of these treaties. The Convention against Torture, 1984 provides that each state party shall ensure that all acts of torture are offences under domestic criminal law[135] and shall take such measures as may be necessary to establish its jurisdiction over torture offences where committed in any territory under its jurisdiction or on board a ship or aircraft registered in the state concerned or when the alleged offender is a national or when the victim is a national if that state considers it appropriate.[136] Further, each state party agrees to either extradite or prosecute alleged offenders,[137] while agreeing that the offences constitute extraditable offences within the context of extradition agreements concluded between states parties.[138] This Convention was the subject of consideration in *Ex parte Pinochet (No. 3)*, where the majority of the House of Lords held that torture committed outside the UK was not a crime punishable under UK law until the provisions of the Convention against Torture were implemented by s. 134 of the Criminal Justice Act 1988.[139] Lord Millett, however, took the view that torture was a crime under customary international law with universal jurisdiction and that since customary international law was part of the common law,[140] English courts 'have and always have had extraterritorial criminal jurisdiction in respect of universal jurisdiction under customary international law'.[141] The Convention on the Prevention and Punishment of Crimes against Internationally Protected Persons, including Diplomatic Agents, was adopted in 1973 by the General Assembly of the United Nations and came into force in 1977. This stipulates that contracting states should make acts such as assaults upon the person, premises and transport of such persons a crime under their domestic law.[142] This, of course, would require little if any revision of existing penal statutes. Each state is to establish its jurisdiction over these crimes when committed in its territory or on board ships or aircraft registered in its territory, or when the alleged offender is a national or when the crimes have been committed against an internationally protected person functioning on behalf of that state.[143] A person is regarded as internationally protected where he is a head of

---

Psychotropic Substances, 1988: see Report of the International Law Commission, A/49/10, 1994, pp. 141 ff.

[135] Article 4.   [136] Article 5.   [137] Article 7.   [138] Article 8.

[139] [2000] 1 AC 147, 148, 159–60, 188–90, 202, 218–19 and 233; 119 ILR, p. 135.

[140] See above, chapter 4, p. 141.

[141] [2000] 1 AC 147, 276; 119 ILR, p. 135. See also e.g. R. O'Keefe, 'Customary International Crimes in English Courts', 72 BYIL, 2001, p. 293.

[142] Article 2. See e.g. the UK Internationally Protected Persons Act 1978.   [143] Article 3.

state or government, or foreign minister abroad, or state representative or official of an international organisation.[144]

The International Convention against the Taking of Hostages, 1979 came into force in 1983 and, like the Internationally Protected Persons Treaty, requires each state party to make the offence punishable under national law,[145] and provides that states parties must either extradite or prosecute an alleged offender found on their territory and incorporate the offence of hostage-taking into existing and future extradition treaties. The grounds upon which a state party may exercise jurisdiction are laid down in article 5 and cover offences committed in its territory or on board a ship or aircraft registered in that state; by any of its nationals, or if that state considers it appropriate, by stateless persons having their habitual residence in its territory; in order to compel that state to do or abstain from doing any act; or with respect to a hostage who is a national of that state, if that state considers it appropriate.

The Convention on the Safety of United Nations and Associated Personnel, 1994 provides that attacks upon UN or associated personnel or property be made a crime under national law by each state party[146] and that jurisdiction should be established with regard to such offences when the crime is committed in the territory of that state or on board a ship or aircraft registered in that state or when the alleged offender is a national of that state. States parties may also establish their jurisdiction over any such crimes when committed by a stateless person whose habitual residence is in the state concerned, or with regard to a national of that state, or in an attempt to compel that state to do or to abstain from doing any act.[147] In addition, the state in whose territory the alleged offender is present shall either prosecute or extradite such person.[148]

As far as the hijacking of and other unlawful acts connected with aircraft is concerned, the leading treaties are the Tokyo Convention on Offences and Certain Other Acts Committed on Board Aircraft, 1963, the Hague Convention for the Suppression of Unlawful Seizure of Aircraft, 1970 and the Montreal Convention for the Suppression of Unlawful Acts against the Safety of Civil Aviation, 1971. The latter two instruments arose as a result of the wave of aircraft hijacking and attacks upon civilian planes that took place in the late 1960s, and tried to deal with the problem of how to apprehend and punish the perpetrators of such deeds.

---

[144] Article 1.   [145] See e.g. the UK Taking of Hostages Act 1982.
[146] Article 9.   [147] Article 10.   [148] Article 14.

The Tokyo Convention applies to both general offences and acts which, whether or not they are offences, may or do jeopardise the safety of the aircraft or of persons or property therein or which jeopardise good order and discipline on board. It provides for the jurisdiction of the contracting state over aircraft registered therein while the aircraft is in flight, or on the surface of the high seas or on any other area outside the territory of any state. Contracting states are called upon to take the necessary measures to establish jurisdiction by municipal law over such aircraft in such circumstances. In addition, the Convention permits interference with an aircraft in flight in order to establish criminal jurisdiction over an offence committed on board in certain specific circumstances by contracting states not being the state of registration. The circumstances specified are where the offence has effect on the territory of such state; has been committed by or against a national or permanent resident of such state; is against the security of such state; consists of a breach of any rules or regulations relating to the flight or manoeuvre of aircraft in force in such state or where the exercise of jurisdiction is necessary to ensure the observance of any obligation of such state under a multilateral international agreement.[149] No obligation to extradite is provided for.

The Hague Convention provides that any person who, on board an aircraft in flight, is involved in the unlawful seizure of that aircraft (or attempts the same), commits an offence which contracting states undertake to make punishable by severe penalties. Each contracting state is to take such measures as may be necessary to establish its jurisdiction over the offence or related acts of violence when the offence is committed on board an aircraft registered in that state, when the aircraft in question lands in its territory with the alleged offender still on board or when the offence is committed on board an aircraft leased without a crew to a lessee who has his principal place of business, or if the lessee has no such place of business, his permanent residence, in that state. The Convention also provides that contracting states in the territory of which an alleged offender is found must either extradite or prosecute him.

The Montreal Convention contains similar rules as to jurisdiction and extradition as the Hague Convention but is aimed at controlling and punishing attacks and sabotage against civil aircraft in flight and on the ground

---

[149] Article 4. See S. Shuber, *Jurisdiction over Crimes on Board Aircraft*, The Hague, 1973; N. D. Joyner, *Aerial Hijacking as an International Crime*, Dobbs Ferry, 1974, and E. McWhinney, *Aerial Piracy and International Terrorism*, 2nd edn, Dordrecht, 1987. See also the US Anti-Hijacking Act of 1974.

rather than dealing with hijacking directly.[150] A Protocol to the Montreal Convention was signed in 1988. This provides for the suppression of unlawful acts of violence at airports serving international civil aviation which cause or are likely to cause serious injury, and acts of violence which destroy or seriously damage the facilities of an airport serving international civil aviation or aircraft not in service located thereon or disrupt the service of the airport.[151]

The wide range of jurisdictional bases is to be noted, although universality as such is not included. Nevertheless, condemnation of this form of activity is widespread and it is likely that hijacking has become an international crime of virtually universal jurisdiction in practice.[152] Further, it is possible that international terrorism may in time be regarded as a crime of universal jurisdiction.[153]

Of course questions as to enforcement will arise where states fail either to respect their obligations under the above Conventions or, if they are not parties to them, to respect customary law on the reasonable assumption that state practice now recognises hijacking as an unlawful act.[154] A number of possibilities exist, in addition to recourse to the United Nations

[150] Note that neither the Tokyo nor the Hague Conventions apply to aircraft used in military, customs or police services: see articles 1(4) and 3(2) respectively.

[151] Note the Hindawi episode, where the European Community imposed sanctions upon Syria in a situation where it emerged during a court case in the UK that an attempt to smuggle a bomb onto an Israeli airliner in 1986 in London had been supported by Syrian intelligence: see *Keesing's Contemporary Archives*, pp. 34771–2 and 34883–4.

[152] See *US* v. *Yunis (No. 2)* 681 F.Supp. 896, 900–1 (1988); 82 ILR, pp. 344, 348. See also *US* v. *Yunis (No. 3)* 924 F.2d 1086, 1091 (1991); 88 ILR, pp. 176, 181.

[153] Note that in *Flatow* v. *Islamic Republic of Iran*, the US District Court stated that 'international terrorism is subject to universal jurisdiction', 999 F.Supp. 1, 14 (1998); 121 ILR, p. 618. See also the Convention on the Protection of All Persons from Enforced Disappearance, 2006, which requires all states parties to make enforced disappearance a criminal offence and further defines the widespread or systematic practice of enforced disappearance as a crime against humanity. States parties must take the necessary measures to establish jurisdiction on the basis of territoriality, nationality or, where the state deems it appropriate, the passive personality principle and must then either prosecute or extradite. The offence of enforced disappearance is deemed to be included as an extraditable offence in any extradition treaty existing between states parties before the entry into force of the Convention and states parties undertake to include it as an extraditable offence in future treaties, while the offence is not to be regarded as a political offence or as an offence connected with a political offence or as an offence inspired by political motives. Accordingly, a request for extradition based on such an offence may not be refused on these grounds alone. Further, no person may be sent to a state where there are substantial grounds for believing that he or she may be the subject of an enforced disappearance.

[154] See e.g. General Assembly resolution 2645 (XXV) and Security Council resolution 286 (1970).

and the relevant international air organisations.[155] Like-minded states may seek to impose sanctions upon errant states. The 1978 Bonn Declaration, for example, agreed that 'in cases where a country refuses the extradition or prosecution of, those who have hijacked an aircraft and/or does not return such aircraft' action would be taken to cease all flights to and from that country and its airlines.[156] Bilateral arrangements may also be made, which provide for the return of, or prosecution of, hijackers.[157] States may also, of course, adopt legislation which enables them to prosecute alleged hijackers found in their territory,[158] or more generally seeks to combat terrorism. The 1984 US Act to Combat International Terrorism, for example, provides for rewards for information concerning a wide range of terrorist acts primarily (although not exclusively) within the territorial jurisdiction of the US.[159]

Other acts of general self-help have also been resorted to. In 1973, for example, Israeli warplanes intercepted a civil aircraft in Lebanese airspace in an unsuccessful attempt to apprehend a guerrilla leader held responsible for the killing of civilians aboard hijacked aircraft. Israel was condemned for this by the UN Security Council[160] and the International Civil Aviation Organisation.[161]

On the night of 10–11 October 1985, an Egyptian civil aircraft carrying the hijackers of the Italian cruise ship *Achille Lauro* was intercepted over the Mediterranean Sea by US Navy fighters and compelled to land in Sicily. The US justified its action generally by reference to the need to combat international terrorism, while the UK Foreign Secretary noted it was relevant to take into account the international agreements on hijacking and hostage-taking.[162] However, nothing in these Conventions, it is suggested, would appear to justify an interception of a civilian aircraft over the high

---

[155] See above, chapter 10, p. 542.

[156] See UKMIL, 49 BYIL, 1978, p. 423. The states making the Declaration were the UK, France, US, Canada, West Germany, Italy and Japan.

[157] See e.g. the US–Cuban Memorandum of Understanding on Hijacking of Aircraft and Vessels and Other Offences, 1973.

[158] See e.g. the US Anti-Hijacking Act of 1974 and the UK Civil Aviation Act 1982 s. 92 and the Aviation Security Act 1982.

[159] See further, as to international terrorism, below, chapter 20, p. 1159.

[160] Resolution 337 (1973).   [161] ICAO Doc. 9050-LC/169-1, at p. 196 (1973).

[162] See *Keesing's Contemporary Archives*, p. 34078 and *The Times*, 6 February 1986, p. 4. In this context, one should also note the hijack of a TWA airliner in June 1985, the murder of a passenger and the prolonged detention in the Lebanon of the remaining passengers and the crew: see *Keesing's Contemporary Archives*, p. 34130. See also A. Cassese, *Violence and Law in the Modern Age*, Cambridge, 1988, chapter 4.

seas or over any area other than the territory of the intercepting state and for specified reasons. The apprehension of terrorists is to be encouraged, but the means must be legitimate. On 4 February 1986, the Israeli Air Force intercepted a Libyan civil aircraft en route from Libya to Syria in an attempt to capture terrorists, arguing that the aircraft in question was part of a terrorist operation.[163]

Nevertheless, there may be circumstances where an action taken by a state as a consequence of hostile hijacking or terrorist operations would be justifiable in the context of self-defence.[164]

Illegal apprehension of suspects and the exercise of jurisdiction[165]

It would appear that unlawful apprehension of a suspect by state agents acting in the territory of another state is not a bar to the exercise of jurisdiction. Such apprehension would, of course, constitute a breach of international law and the norm of non-intervention involving state responsibility,[166] unless the circumstances were such that the right of self-defence could be pleaded.[167] It could be argued that the seizure, being a violation of international law, would only be compounded by permitting the abducting state to exercise jurisdiction,[168] but international practice on the whole demonstrates otherwise.[169] In most cases a distinction is clearly drawn between the apprehension and jurisdiction to prosecute and one should also distinguish situations where the apprehension has

---

[163] See *The Times*, 5 February 1986, p. 1.

[164] See e.g. as to the 1976 Entebbe incident, below, chapter 20, p. 1143.

[165] See e.g. F. Morgenstern, 'Jurisdiction in Seizures Effected in Violation of International Law', 29 BYIL, 1952, p. 256; P. O'Higgins, 'Unlawful Seizure and Irregular Extradition', 36 BYIL, 1960, p. 279; A. Lowenfeld, 'US Law Enforcement Abroad: The Constitution and International Law', 83 AJIL, 1989, p. 880, Lowenfeld, 'US Law Enforcement Abroad: The Constitution and International Law, Continued', 84 AJIL, 1990, p. 444, Lowenfeld, 'Kidnapping by Government Order: A Follow-Up', 84 AJIL, 1990, p. 712, and Lowenfeld, 'Still More on Kidnapping', 85 AJIL, 1991, p. 655. See also F. A. Mann, 'Reflections on the Prosecution of Persons Abducted in Breach of International Law' in *International Law at a Time of Perplexity* (ed. Y. Dinstein), Dordrecht, 1989, p. 407, and Higgins, *Problems and Process*, p. 69.

[166] See e.g. article 2(4) of the United Nations Charter and *Nicaragua* v. *US*, ICJ Reports, 1986, p. 110; 76 ILR, p. 349. See further below, chapter 20.

[167] Note, in particular, the view of the Legal Adviser of the US Department of State to the effect that '[w]hile international law therefore permits extraterritorial "arrests" in situations which permit a valid claim of self-defence, decisions about any extraterritorial arrest entail grave potential implications for US personnel, for the United States, and for our relations with other states', 84 AJIL, 1990, pp. 725, 727.

[168] See Mann, 'Jurisdiction', p. 415.

[169] See e.g. the *Eichmann* case, 36 ILR, pp. 5 and 277.

taken place on or over the high seas from cases where it has occurred without consent on the territory of another state. A further distinction that has been made relates to situations where the abduction has taken place from a state with which the apprehending state has an extradition treaty which governs the conditions under which movement of alleged offenders occurs between the two. A final distinction may be drawn as between cases depending upon the type of offences with which the offender is charged, so that the problem of the apprehension interfering with the prosecution may be seen as less crucial in cases where recognised international crimes are alleged.[170] Of course, any such apprehension would constitute a violation of the human rights of the person concerned, but whether that would impact upon the exercise of jurisdiction as such is the key issue here.

Variations in approaches are evident between states. The US Court of Appeals in *US* v. *Toscanino*[171] held that the rule that jurisdiction was unaffected by an illegal apprehension[172] should not be applied where the presence of the defendant has been secured by force or fraud, but this approach has, it seems, been to a large extent eroded. In *US ex rel. Lujan* v. *Gengler*[173] it was noted that the rule in *Toscanino* was limited to cases of 'torture, brutality and similar outrageous conduct'.[174] The issue came before the US Supreme Court in *Sosa* v. *Alvarez-Machain*,[175] in which the view was taken that the issue essentially revolved around a strict interpretation of the relevant extradition treaty between Mexico and the US. The Court noted that where the terms of an extradition treaty in force between the states concerned prohibited abduction then jurisdiction could not be exercised. Otherwise the rule in *Ker* would apply and the prosecution would proceed. This applied even though there were some differences between the cases, in that, unlike the situation in *Ker*, the US government had been involved in the abduction

---

[170] See Higgins, *Problems and Process*, p. 69.   [171] 500 F.2d 267 (1974); 61 ILR, p. 190.

[172] See, in particular, *Ker* v. *Illinois* 119 US 436 (1886) and *Frisbie* v. *Collins* 342 US 519 (1952). These cases have given rise to the reference to the Ker–Frisbie doctrine.

[173] 510 F.2d 62 (1975); 61 ILR, p. 206. See also *US* v. *Lira* 515 F.2d 68 (1975); Lowenfeld, 'Kidnapping', p. 712; *Afouneh* v. *Attorney-General* 10 AD, p. 327, and *Re Argoud* 45 ILR, p. 90.

[174] This approach was reaffirmed in *US* v. *Yunis* both by the District Court, 681 F.Supp. 909, 918–21 (1988) and by the Court of Appeals, 30 ILM, 1991, pp. 403, 408–9.

[175] 119 L Ed 2d 441 (1992); 95 ILR, p. 355. See also M. Halberstam, 'In Defence of the Supreme Court Decision in *Alvarez-Machain*', 86 AJIL, 1992, p. 736, and M. J. Glennon, 'State-Sponsored Abduction: A Comment on *United States* v. *Alvarez-Machain*', *ibid.*, p. 746.

and the state from whose territory the apprehension took place had protested.[176]

In the UK, the approach has appeared to alter somewhat. In *R* v. *Plymouth Justices, ex parte Driver*,[177] it was noted that once a person was in lawful custody within the jurisdiction, the court had no power to inquire into the circumstances in which he had been brought into the jurisdiction. However, in *R* v. *Horseferry Road Magistrates' Court, ex parte Bennett*,[178] the House of Lords declared that where an extradition treaty existed with the relevant country under which the accused could have been returned, 'our courts will refuse to try him if he has been forcibly brought within our jurisdiction in disregard of those procedures by a process to which our own police, prosecuting or other executive authorities have been a knowing party'.[179] The approach in this case was extended in *R* v. *Latif* to cover entrapment.[180] However, where an accused was taking legal action to quash a decision to proceed with an extradition request, the fact that he had been lured into the jurisdiction was not sufficient to vitiate the proceedings since safeguards as to due process existed in the light of the Home Secretary's discretion and under the law of the state to whom he was to be extradited.[181] Further, in *Ex parte Westfallen*, the High Court took the view that where there had been no illegality, abuse of power or

---

[176] 119 L Ed 2d 451; 95 ILR, p. 363. See also the Dissenting Opinion, which took the view that the abduction had in fact violated both international law and the extradition treaty, 119 L Ed 2d 456–79; 95 ILR, pp. 369–79. The accused was eventually acquitted and returned to Mexico: see *Alvarez-Machain* v. *United States* 107 F.3d 696, 699 (9th Cir. 1996). He also commenced an action for compensation. In that action the US Court of Appeals for the Ninth Circuit stated that his abduction was a violation of the law of nations in that international human rights law had been breached: see *Alvarez-Machain* v. *United States* 41 ILM, 2002, pp. 130, 133.

[177] [1986] 1 QB 95; 77 ILR, p. 351. See also *Ex parte Susannah Scott* (1829) 9 B & C 446; *Sinclair* v. *HM Advocate* (1890) 17 R (J) 38 and *R* v. *Officer Commanding Depot Battalion RASC Colchester, ex parte Elliott* [1949] 1 All ER 373. Cf. *R* v. *Bow Street Magistrates, ex parte Mackerson* (1981) 75 Cr App R 24.

[178] [1993] 3 WLR 90; 95 ILR, p. 380.

[179] [1993] 3 WLR 105; 95 ILR, p. 393, per Lord Griffiths. See also Lord Bridge, [1993] 3 WLR 110; 95 ILR, p. 399 and Lord Slynn, [1993] 3 WLR 125; 95 ILR, p. 416. The House of Lords was also influenced by the decision of the South Africa Supreme Court in *State* v. *Ebrahim*, 95 ILR, p. 417, where the conviction and sentence before a South African court of a person were set aside as a consequence of his illegal abduction by state officials from Swaziland. This view was based both on Roman-Dutch and South African common law and on international law.

[180] [1996] 1 WLR 104, see Lord Steyn, at 112–13. See also *R* v. *Mullen* [1999] 2 Cr App R 143.

[181] See *In re Schmidt* [1995] 1 AC 339; 111 ILR, p. 548 (House of Lords).

violation of international law or of the domestic law of the foreign states involved, the decisions under challenge could not be impugned nor the subsequent criminal proceedings be vitiated.[182]

The US Alien Tort Claims Act[183]

Under this Act, the First Congress established original district court jurisdiction over all causes where an alien sues for a tort 'committed in violation of the law of nations or a treaty of the United States'.[184] In *Filartiga* v. *Pena-Irala*,[185] the US Court of Appeals for the Second Circuit interpreted this provision to permit jurisdiction over a private tort action by a Paraguayan national against a Paraguayan police official for acts of torture perpetrated in that state, it being held that torture by a state official constituted a violation of international law. This amounted to an important move in the attempt to exercise jurisdiction in the realm of international human rights violations, although one clearly based upon a domestic statute permitting such court competence. The relevant issues in such actions would thus depend upon the definition of the 'law of nations' in particular cases.[186]

In *Tel-Oren* v. *Libyan Arab Republic*,[187] however, the Court dismissed an action under the same statute brought by survivors and representatives of persons murdered in an armed attack on an Israeli bus in 1978 for lack of subject-matter jurisdiction. The three judges differed in their reasoning. Judge Edwards held that the law of nations did not impose liability on non-state entities like the PLO. Judge Bork, in a departure from the *Filartiga* principles, declared that 'an explicit grant of a cause of action [had to exist] before a private individual [will] be allowed to enforce principles of international law in a federal tribunal',[188] while Senior Judge Robb held that the case was rendered non-justiciable by the political question doctrine.

---

[182] [1998] 1 WLR 652, 665–7. See also C. Warbrick, 'Judicial Jurisdiction and Abuse of Process', 49 ICLQ, 2000, p. 489.

[183] 28 USC, para. 1350 (1982), originally enacted as part of the Judiciary Act of 1789. See also 28 USC, para. 1331, and above, chapter 4, p. 159.

[184] Cassese notes that the extensive civil jurisdiction claimed under this Act has not been challenged by other states, 'When may Senior State Officials', p. 859.

[185] 630 F.2d 876 (2d Cir. 1980); 77 ILR, p. 169. See also 577 F.Supp. 860 (1984); 77 ILR, p. 185, awarding punitive damages.

[186] In establishing the content of the 'law of nations', the courts must interpret international law as it exists today, 630 F.2d 876, 881 (1980); 77 ILR, pp. 169, 175.

[187] 726 F.2d 774 (1984); 77 ILR, p. 204. See also 'Agora', 79 AJIL, 1985, pp. 92 ff. for a discussion of the case.

[188] 726 F.2d 801; 77 ILR, p. 230.

Further restrictions upon the *Filartiga* doctrine have also been manifested. It has, for example, been held that the Alien Tort Claims Act does not constitute an exception to the principle of sovereign immunity so that a foreign state could not be sued,[189] while it has also been held that US citizens could not sue for violations of the law of nations under the Act.[190]

In *Sanchez-Espinoza* v. *Reagan*,[191] suit was brought against a variety of present and former US executive officials for violation *inter alia* of domestic and international law with regard to the US support of the 'Contra' guerrillas fighting against the Nicaraguan government. The Alien Tort Claims Act was cited, but the Court of Appeals noted that the statute arguably only covered private, non-governmental acts that violated a treaty or customary international law and, relying on *Tel-Oren*, pointed out that customary international law did not cover private conduct 'of this sort'.[192] Thus the claim for damages could only be sustained to the extent that the defendants acted in an official capacity and, even if the Alien Tort Claims Act applied to official state acts, the doctrine of domestic sovereign immunity precluded the claim. In *Kadić* v. *Karadžić*,[193] the US Court of Appeals emphasised the 'liability of private persons for certain violations of customary international law and the availability of the Alien Tort Act to remedy such violations'.[194] In particular, it was noted that the proscription of genocide and war crimes and other violations of international humanitarian law applied to both state and non-state actors, although torture and summary execution (when not perpetrated in the course of genocide or war crimes) were proscribed by international law only when committed by state officials or under colour of law.[195] Even in this case, it may be that all that was required was 'the semblance of official authority' rather than establishing statehood under the formal criteria of international law.[196] The Court also held that the Torture Victim Protection Act 1992, which provides a cause of action for torture and extrajudicial killing by an individual 'under actual or apparent authority, or colour of law, of any foreign nation', was not itself a jurisdictional statute and depended upon the establishment of jurisdiction under either

---

[189] *Siderman* v. *Republic of Argentina* 965 F.2d 699 (1992).
[190] *Handel* v. *Artukovic* 601 F.Supp. 1421 (1985); 79 ILR, p. 397.
[191] 770 F.2d 202 (1985); 80 ILR, p. 586.   [192] 770 F.2d 206–7; 80 ILR, pp. 590–1.
[193] 34 ILM, 1995, p. 1592.   [194] *Ibid.*, p. 1600.   [195] *Ibid.*, pp. 1602–6.
[196] *Ibid.*, p. 1607.

the Alien Tort Act or under the general federal question jurisdiction of section 1331.[197]

The Alien Tort Act was relied upon again in the *Amerada Hess* case which concerned the bombing of a ship in international waters by Argentina during the Falklands war and where it was claimed that the federal courts had jurisdiction under the Act. A divided Court of Appeals[198] held that the Act provided, and the Foreign Sovereign Immunities Act did not preclude,[199] federal subject-matter jurisdiction over suits in tort by aliens against foreign sovereigns for violations of international law. However, the Supreme Court unanimously disagreed.[200] It was noted that the Act did not expressly authorise suits against foreign states and that at the time the Foreign Sovereign Immunities Act was enacted, the 1789 Act had never provided the jurisdictional basis for a suit against a foreign state.[201] Since the Congress had decided to deal comprehensively with sovereign immunity in the Foreign Sovereign Immunities Act, it appeared to follow that this Act alone provided the basis for federal jurisdiction over foreign states. This basis was thus exclusive. The Court did note, however, that the Alien Tort Claims Act was unaffected by the Foreign Sovereign Immunities Act in so far as non-state defendants were concerned.[202] In *Alvarez-Machain* v. *United States*, the accused in the case noted above[203] commenced an action for compensation under the Act following his acquittal. The Court of Appeals for the Ninth Circuit rejected the claim that the Act required that the international law principle violated should also constitute a norm of *jus cogens*. The Court also rejected the contention that the applicant could sue for the violation of Mexican sovereignty implicit in his abduction. However, it affirmed that the applicant's rights to freedom of movement, to remain in his country and to security of his person (which are part of the 'law of nations') were violated, while his detention was arbitrary since

---

[197] *Ibid.*, pp. 1607–8. Note, however, that since the Antiterrorism and Effective Death Penalty Act 1996 amending the Foreign Sovereign Immunities Act, an exception to immunity is created with regard to states, designated by the Department of State as terrorist states, which committed a terrorist act, or provided material support and resources to an individual or entity which committed such an act, which resulted in the death or personal injury of a US citizen.
[198] *Amerada Hess Shipping Corp.* v. *Argentine Republic* 830 F.2d 421 (1987); 79 ILR, p. 8.
[199] See below, chapter 13, p. 707.
[200] *Argentine Republic* v. *Amerada Hess Shipping Corp.* 109 S. Ct. 683 (1989); 81 ILR, p. 658.
[201] 109 S. Ct. 689; 81 ILR, pp. 664–5.
[202] 109 S. Ct. 690. See also *Smith* v. *Libya* 101 F.3d 239 (1996); 113 ILR, p. 534.
[203] See above, p. 681.

not pursuant to a Mexican warrant. Accordingly, compensation under the Act could be claimed.[204]

The Alien Tort Claims Act was further discussed by the Supreme Court in *Sosa* v. *Alvarez-Machain*, where it was held that the Alien Tort Claims Act was a jurisdictional statute creating no new causes of action and enacted on the understanding that the common law would provide a cause of action for the modest number of international law violations thought to carry personal liability at the time, being offences against ambassadors, violation of safe conducts and piracy.[205]

Extradition[206]

The practice of extradition enables one state to hand over to another state suspected or convicted criminals who have fled to the territory of the former. It is based upon bilateral treaty law and does not exist as an obligation upon states in customary law.[207] It is usual to derive from existing treaties on the subject certain general principles, for example that of double criminality, i.e. that the crime involved should be a crime in both states concerned,[208] and that of specialty, i.e. a person surrendered may be tried and punished only for the offence for which extradition had been sought and granted.[209] In general, offences of a political

---

[204] 41 ILM, 2002, p. 130. See also the decision of 3 June 2003.

[205] 542 US 692, 714 ff. (2004) and see above, chapter 4, p. 160. Note that in *Rasul* v. *Bush*, the Supreme Court held that it was immaterial that the petitioners invoking the Alien Tort statute were being held in military custody in Guantanamo Bay, 542 US 466 (2004).

[206] See e.g. I. A. Shearer, *Extradition in International Law*, Leiden, 1971; M. C. Bassiouni, *International Extradition and World Public Order*, Leiden, 1974; C. Nicholls, C. Montgomery and J. B. Knowles, *The Law of Extradition and Mutual Assistance*, 2nd edn, Oxford, 2007; I. Stanbrook and C. Stanbrook, *The Law and Practice of Extradition*, 2nd edn, Oxford, 2000; M. Forde, *The Law of Extradition in the UK*, London, 1995; A. Jones and A. Doobay, *Jones and Doobay on Extradition and Mutual Assistance*, London, 2004; G. Gilbert, *Aspects of Extradition Law*, Dordrecht, 1991, and Gilbert, *Transnational Fugitive Offenders in International Law: Extradition and Other Mechanisms*, The Hague, 1998; L. Henkin, R. C. Pugh, O. Schachter and H. Smit, *International Law: Cases and Materials*, 3rd edn, St Paul, 1993, p. 1111 and *Oppenheim's International Law*, p. 958. See also Study of the Secretariat on Succession of States in Respect of Bilateral Treaties, *Yearbook of the ILC*, 1970, vol. II, pp. 102, 105.

[207] See e.g. the Joint Declaration of Judges Evensen, Tarassov, Guillaume and Aguilar Maudsley, the *Lockerbie* case, ICJ Reports, 1992, pp. 3, 24; 94 ILR, pp. 478, 507 and the Dissenting Opinion of Judge Bedjaoui, ICJ Reports, 1992, p. 38; 94 ILR, p. 521.

[208] But see now the House of Lords decisions in *Government of Denmark* v. *Nielsen* [1984] 2 All ER 81; 74 ILR, p. 458 and *United States Government* v. *McCaffery* [1984] 2 All ER 570.

[209] See e.g. *Oppenheim's International Law*, p. 961.

character have been excluded,[210] but this would not cover terrorist activities.[211] As noted above, it is common for many treaties laying down multiple bases for the exercise of jurisdiction to insist that states parties in whose territory the alleged offender is present either prosecute or extradite such person.[212] In addition, many treaties provide for the automatic inclusion within existing bilateral extradition treaties between states parties to such treaties of the offence concerned.[213] Many states will not allow the extradition of nationals to another state,[214] but this is usually in circumstances where the state concerned has wide powers to prosecute nationals for offences committed abroad. Further, the relevance of human rights law to the process should be noted in that extradition to a state that may torture or inhumanely treat the person concerned would, for example, violate the European Convention on Human Rights.[215]

---

[210] *Ibid.*, p. 962.

[211] See e.g. the European Convention on the Suppression of Terrorism, 1977, article 1 of which provides a list of offences which are not to be regarded as political offences or inspired by political motives, an approach which is also adopted in article 11 of the Convention for the Suppression of Terrorist Bombing, 1997. See also the *McMullen* case, 74 AJIL, 1980, p. 434; the *Eain* case, *ibid.*, p. 435; *Re Piperno, ibid.*, p. 683 and *US* v. *Mackin* 668 F.2d 122 (1981); 79 ILR, p. 459. A revised directive on international extradition was issued by the US Department of State in 1981: see 76 AJIL, 1982, pp. 154–9. Note also the view of the British Home Secretary, *The Times*, 25 June 1985, p. 1, that the political offences 'loophole' as it applied to violent offences was not suitable to extradition arrangements between the democratic countries 'sharing the same high regard for the fundamental principles of justice and operating similar independent judicial systems'. The UK law relating to extradition was consolidated in the Extradition Act 1989. Note in addition the Extradition Act 2003, providing *inter alia* for fast-track extradition procedures within the European Union, extended by the UK in the Extradition Act 2003 (Designation of Part 2 Territories) Order 2003 to the US despite an assymetrical arrangement with the US under the UK–US Extradition Treaty, 2003: see e.g. Nicholls *et al.*, *Law of Extradition*, pp. 10 ff. and *Norris* v. *Secretary of State for the Home Department* [2006] UWHC 280 (Admin) and *Norris* v. *USA* [2008] UKHL 16. See also *Government of Belgium* v. *Postlethwaite* [1987] 2 All ER 985 and *R* v. *Chief Metropolitan Magistrate, ex parte Secretary of State for the Home Department* [1988] 1 WLR 1204.

[212] See above, p. 673.

[213] See e.g. article 8 of the Hague Convention for the Suppression of the Unlawful Seizure of Aircraft, 1970, article 8 of the Montreal Convention for the Suppression of Unlawful Acts against the Safety of Civil Aviation, 1971, article 8 of the Internationally Protected Persons Convention, 1973 and article 4 of the European Convention for the Suppression of Terrorism, 1977.

[214] See e.g. article 3(1) of the French Extradition Law of 1927, and article 16 of the Basic Law of the Federal Republic of Germany.

[215] See e.g. the *Soering* case, European Court of Human Rights, 1989, Series A, No. 161; 98 ILR, p. 270 and *Saadi* v. *Italy*, European Court of Human Rights, judgment of 28 February 2008.

Extraterritorial jurisdiction[216]

Claims have arisen in the context of economic issues whereby some states, particularly the United States, seek to apply their laws outside their territory[217] in a manner which may precipitate conflicts with other states.[218] Where the claims are founded upon the territorial and nationality theories of jurisdiction, problems do not often arise, but claims made upon the basis of the so-called 'effects' doctrine have provoked considerable controversy. This goes beyond the objective territorial principle to a situation where the state assumes jurisdiction on the grounds that the behaviour of a party is producing 'effects' within its territory. This is so even though all the conduct complained of takes place in another state.[219] The effects doctrine has been energetically maintained particularly by the US in the area of antitrust regulation.[220] The classic statement of the American

---

[216] See e.g. *Extraterritorial Jurisdiction* (ed. A. V. Lowe), London, 1983; D. Rosenthal and W. Knighton, *National Laws and International Commerce*, London, 1982; K. M. Meessen, 'Antitrust Jurisdiction under Customary International Law', 78 AJIL, 1984, p. 783; A. V. Lowe, 'Blocking Extraterritorial Jurisdiction: The British Protection of Trading Interests Act 1980', 75 AJIL, 1981, p. 257; Akehurst, 'Jurisdiction', pp. 190 ff.; *Extraterritorial Application of Law and Responses Thereto* (ed. C. Olmstead), Oxford, 1984; B. Stern, 'L'Extra-territorialité "Revisitée": Où Il est Question des Affaires Alvarez-Machain, Pâte de Bois et de Quelques Autres', AFDI, 1992, p. 239; Higgins, *Problems and Process*, p. 73, and *Oppenheim's International Law*, p. 466. See also P. Torremans, 'Extraterritorial Application of EC and US Competition Law', 21 *European Law Review*, 1996, p. 280.

[217] Note that there is a general presumption against the extraterritorial application of legislation: see e.g. the House of Lords decision in *Holmes* v. *Bangladesh Biman Corporation* [1989] 1 AC 1112, 1126; 87 ILR, pp. 365, 369, per Lord Bridge, and *Air India* v. *Wiggins* [1980] 1 WLR 815, 819; 77 ILR, pp. 276, 279, per Lord Bridge, and the US Supreme Court decision in *EEOC* v. *Arabian American Oil Company and Aramco Services* 113 L Ed 2d 274, 282 (1991); 90 ILR, pp. 617, 622.

[218] The UK government has stated that it opposes all assertions of extraterritorial jurisdiction by other states on UK individuals and/or companies: see Ministerial Statement, HL Deb., vol. 673, cWA277–8, 21 July 2005, UKMIL, 76 BYIL, 2006, p. 850.

[219] The true 'effects' doctrine approach should be distinguished from other heads of jurisdiction such as the objective territorial principle, where part of the offence takes place within the jurisdiction: see e.g. *US* v. *Noriega* 808 F.Supp. 791 (1992); 99 ILR, p. 143. In many cases the disputes have centred upon nationality questions, the US regarding subsidiaries of US companies abroad as of US nationality even where such companies have been incorporated abroad, while the state of incorporation has regarded them as of its nationality and thus subject not to US law but to its law: see e.g. Higgins, *Problems and Process*, p. 73.

[220] See e.g. the US Sherman Antitrust Act 1896, 15 USC, paras. 1 ff. See also the controversies engendered by the US freezing of Iranian assets in 1979 and the embargo imposed under the Export Administration Act in 1981 and 1982 on equipment intended for use on the Siberian gas pipeline, R. Edwards, 'Extraterritorial Application of the US Iranian Assets Control Regulations', 75 AJIL, 1981, p. 870; J. Bridge, 'The Law and Politics of United

doctrine was made in *US* v. *Aluminum Co. of America*,[221] in which the Court declared that:

> any state may impose liabilities, even upon persons not within its allegiance, for conduct outside its borders that has consequences within its borders which the state reprehends.[222]

The doctrine was to some extent modified by the requirement of intention and the view that the effect should be substantial, but the wide-ranging nature of the concept aroused considerable opposition outside the US, as did American attempts to take evidence abroad under very broad pre-trial discovery provisions in US law[223] and the possibility of treble damage awards.[224] The US courts, perhaps in view of the growing opposition of foreign states, modified their approach in the *Timberlane Lumber Co.* v. *Bank of America*[225] and *Mannington Mills* v. *Congoleum Corporation*[226] cases. It was stated that in addition to the effects test, of the earlier cases, the courts had to take into account a balancing test, 'a jurisdictional rule of reason', involving a consideration of other nations' interests and the full nature of the relationship between the actors concerned and the US.[227] A series of factors that needed to be considered in the process of balancing was put forward in the latter case.[228] The view taken by the

States Foreign Policy Export Controls', 4 *Legal Studies*, 1984, p. 2, and A. V. Lowe, 'Public International Law and the Conflict of Laws', 33 ICLQ, 1984, p. 575.

[221] 148 F.2d 416 (1945).

[222] *Ibid.*, p. 443. This approach was reaffirmed in a series of later cases: see e.g. *US* v. *Timken Roller Bearing Co.* 83 F.Supp. 284 (1949), affirmed 341 US 593 (1951); *US* v. *The Watchmakers of Switzerland Information Center, Inc.* cases, 133 F.Supp. 40 and 134 F.Supp. 710 (1963); 22 ILR, p. 168, and *US* v. *General Electric Co.* 82 F.Supp. 753 (1949) and 115 F.Supp. 835 (1953). See also *Hazeltine Research Inc.* v. *Zenith Radio Corporation* 239 F.Supp. 51 (1965), affirmed 395 US 100 (1969).

[223] See e.g. the statement of the UK Attorney General that 'the wide investigating procedures under the United States antitrust legislation against persons outside the United States who are not United States citizens constitute an "extraterritorial" infringement of the proper jurisdiction and sovereignty of the United Kingdom', *Rio Tinto Zinc* v. *Westinghouse Electric Corporation* [1978] 2 WLR 81; 73 ILR, p. 296. See also Lowe, *Extraterritorial Jurisdiction*, pp. 159–60 and 165–71. But see *Société Internationale* v. *Rogers* 357 US 197 (1958); 26 ILR, p. 123; *US* v. *First National City Bank* 396 F.2d 897 (1968); 38 ILR, p. 112; *In re Westinghouse Electric Corporation* 563 F.2d 992 (1977) and *In re Uranium Antitrust Litigation* 480 F.Supp. 1138 (1979).

[224] See e.g. Meessen, 'Antitrust Jurisdiction', p. 794.

[225] 549 F.2d 597 (1976); 66 ILR, p. 270.   [226] 595 F.2d 1287 (1979); 66 ILR, p. 487.

[227] See particularly K. Brewster, *Antitrust and American Business Abroad*, New York, 1958.

[228] 595 F.2d 1287, 1297 (1979); 66 ILR, pp. 487, 496. See also the *Timberlane* case, 549 F.2d 597, 614 (1976); 66 ILR, pp. 270, 285. The need for judicial restraint in applying the effects doctrine in the light of comity was emphasised by the State Department: see 74 AJIL,

Third Restatement of Foreign Relations Law,[229] it should be noted, is that a state may exercise jurisdiction based on effects in the state, when the effect or intended effect is substantial and the exercise of jurisdiction is reasonable. It is noted that the principle of reasonableness calls for limiting the exercise of jurisdiction so as to minimise conflict with the jurisdiction of other states, particularly the state where the act takes place.[230] However, the assumption by the courts of a basically diplomatic function, that is, weighing and considering the interests of foreign states, stimulated criticism.[231]

The US courts modified their approach. In *Laker Airways* v. *Sabena*,[232] the Court held *inter alia* that once US antitrust law was declared applicable, it could not be qualified or ignored by virtue of comity. The judicial interest balancing under the *Timberlane* precedent should not be engaged in since the courts on both sides of the Atlantic were obliged to follow the directions of the executive. Accordingly, the reconciliation of conflicting interests was to be undertaken only by diplomatic negotiations. Quite how such basic and crucial differences of opinion over the effects doctrine can be resolved is open to question and international fora have been suggested as the most appropriate way forward.[233]

In the *Hartford Fire Insurance Co.* v. *California* case before the US Supreme Court,[234] Judge Souter writing for the majority stated that it

---

1980, pp. 179–83. See also the US Foreign Trade Antitrust Improvements Act 1982, where jurisdiction was said to be dependent on 'direct, substantial and reasonably foreseeable effect'.

[229] Para. 402, p. 239 and para. 403, p. 250.

[230] See also the US Department of Justice, *Antitrust Enforcement Guidelines for International Operations*, 1988, pp. 31–2. But see now the Supreme Court's decision in *Hartford Fire Insurance Co.* v. *California* 113 S. Ct. 2891 (1993), discussed below.

[231] See e.g. H. Maier, 'Interest Balancing and Extraterritorial Jurisdiction', 31 *American Journal of Comparative Law*, 1983, p. 579, and Maier, 'Resolving Extraterritorial Conflicts or There and Back Again', 25 Va. JIL, 1984, p. 7; W. Fugate, 'Antitrust Aspect of the Revised Restatement of Foreign Relations Law', *ibid.*, p. 49, and Bowett, 'Jurisdiction', pp. 21–2. See also Lowe, *Extraterritorial Jurisdiction*, pp. 58–62.

[232] 731 F.2d 909 (1984). However, cf. the continuation of the *Timberlane* litigation, 749 F.2d 1378 (1984), which reaffirms the approach of the first *Timberlane* case.

[233] See e.g. Bowett, 'Jurisdiction', pp. 24–6 and Meessen, 'Antitrust Jurisdiction', pp. 808–10. See also Lowe, *Extraterritorial Jurisdiction*, part 3.

[234] 113 S. Ct. 2891 (1993). See e.g. A. F. Lowenfeld, 'Conflict, Balancing of Interest, and the Exercise of Jurisdiction to Prescribe: Reflections of the *Insurance Antitrust Case*', 89 AJIL, 1995, p. 42; P. R. Trimble, 'The Supreme Court and International Law: The Demise of *Restatement* Section 403', *ibid.*, p. 53, and L. Kramer, 'Extraterritorial Application of American Law after the *Insurance Antitrust Case*: A Reply to Professors Lowenfeld and Trimble', *ibid.*, p. 750.

was well established that the relevant US legislation (the Sherman Act) 'applies to foreign conduct that was meant to produce and did in fact produce some substantial effect in the United States'.[235] It was felt that a person subject to regulation by two states (here the UK with regard to the London reinsurance market and the US) could comply with the laws of both and there was no need in this case to address other considerations concerning international comity.[236] The Dissenting Opinion in this case took the view that such exercise of extraterritorial jurisdiction was subject to the test of reasonableness,[237] a view that the majority did not embrace.

Foreign states had started reacting to the effects doctrine by the end of the 1970s and early 1980s by enacting blocking legislation. Under the UK Protection of Trading Interests Act 1980, for example, the Secretary of State in dealing with extraterritorial actions by a foreign state may prohibit the production of documents or information to the latter's courts or authorities. In addition, a UK national or resident may sue in an English court for recovery of multiple damages paid under the judgment of a foreign court.[238]

The Protection of Trading Interests Act was used in connection with the action by the liquidator of Laker Airways to sue various major airlines, the Midland Bank and McDonnell Douglas in the US for conspiracy to violate the antitrust laws of the United States. Two of the airlines, British Airways and British Caledonian, sought to prevent this suit in the US by bringing an action to restrain the liquidator in the UK. Thus, the effects doctrine was not actually in issue in the case, which centred upon the application of the US antitrust law in connection with alleged conspiratorial activities in the US. The UK government, holding the view that the Bermuda II agreement regulating transatlantic airline activity[239] prohibited antitrust actions against UK airlines, issued instructions under the 1980 Act forbidding compliance with any requirement imposed

---

[235] 113 S. Ct. 2891, at 2909.   [236] *Ibid.*, at 2911.   [237] *Ibid.*, at 2921.

[238] See Lowe, 'Conflict of Law', pp. 257–82; 50 BYIL, 1979, pp. 357–62 and 21 ILM, 1982, pp. 840–50. See also the Australian Foreign Proceedings (Prohibition of Certain Evidence) Act 1976, the Danish Limitation of Danish Shipowners' Freedom to Give Information to Authorities of Foreign Countries 1967 and the Finnish Law Prohibiting a Shipowner in Certain Cases to Produce Documents 1968. In some cases, courts have applied aspects of domestic law to achieve the same aim: see e.g. the *Fruehauf* case, 5 ILM, 1966, p. 476. Several states have made diplomatic protests at extraterritorial jurisdictional claims: see e.g. *Report of the 51st Session of the International Law Association*, 1964, pp. 565 ff.

[239] See *The Use of Airspace and Outer Space* (ed. Chia-Jui Cheng), The Hague, 1993, pp. 25 ff.

pursuant to US antitrust measures, including the provision of informa-tion.[240] The Court of Appeal felt that the order and directions required them in essence to prevent the *Laker* action in the US,[241] but the House of Lords disagreed.[242] It was held that the order and directions did not affect the appellant's right to pursue the claim in the US because the 1980 Act was concerned with 'requirements' and 'prohibitions' imposed by a foreign court,[243] so that the respondents would not be prohibited by the direction from paying damages on a 'judgment' given against them in the US.[244] In fact the Court refused to restrain the US action.

The Court also refused to grant judicial review of the order and direc-tions, since the appellant had failed to show that no reasonable minister would have issued such order and directions, this being the requisite test in ministerial decisions concerning international relations.[245] The case, however, did not really turn on the 1980 Act, but it was the first time the issue had come before the courts.[246]

The dispute over extraterritoriality between the US and many other states has been apparent across a range of situations since the freezing of Iranian assets and the Siberian pipeline episode. The operation of the Western supervision of technological exports to the communist bloc through COCOM was also affected, while that system still existed, since the US sought to exercise jurisdiction with respect to exports from third states to communist states.[247] The adoption of legislation in the US im-posing sanctions on Cuba, Iran and Libya has also stimulated opposition in view of the extraterritorial reach of such measures. The extension of

---

[240] The Protection of Trading Interests (US Anti-trust Measures) Order 1983. Two directions were issued as well.

[241] *British Airways Board* v. *Laker Airways Ltd* [1983] 3 All ER 375; 74 ILR, p. 36.

[242] [1984] 3 All ER 39; 74 ILR, p. 65. But see also *Midland Bank plc* v. *Laker Airways Ltd* [1986] 2 WLR 707; 118 ILR, p. 540.

[243] S. 1(3).   [244] [1984] 3 All ER 39, 55–6; 74 ILR, p. 84.

[245] [1984] 3 All ER 39, 54–5; 74 ILR, p. 83. See also *Associated Provincial Picture Houses Ltd* v. *Wednesbury Corp.* [1947] 2 All ER 680.

[246] See also the statement by the Minister of State, Department of Trade and Industry, listing the statutory instruments, orders and directions made under the Protection of Trading Interests Act, 220 HC Deb., cols. 768–70, Written Answers, 12 March 1993; UKMIL, 64 BYIL, 1993, pp. 644–6.

[247] See the US and UK agreement in 1984 to consult should problems appear to arise with regard to the application of US export controls to individuals or businesses in the UK, or if the UK were contemplating resorting to the Protection of Trading Interests Act in relation to such controls, 68 HC Deb., col. 332, Written Answer, 23 November 1984, and 88 HC Deb., col. 373, Written Answer, 6 December 1985. See also Current Legal Developments, 36 ICLQ, 1987, p. 398.

sanctions against Cuba in the Cuban Democracy Act of 1992, for example, prohibited the granting of licences under the US Cuban Assets Control Regulations for certain transactions between US-owned or controlled firms in the UK and Cuba, and this led to the adoption of an order under the Protection of Trading Interests Act 1980 by the UK government.[248] The adoption of the Helms-Burton legislation in March 1996, amending the 1992 Act by further tightening sanctions against Cuba, provided *inter alia* for the institution of legal proceedings before the US courts against foreign persons or companies deemed to be 'trafficking' in property expropriated by Cuba from American nationals.[249] In addition, the legislation enables the US to deny entry into the country of senior executives (and their spouses and minors) of companies deemed by the US State Department to be so 'trafficking'. This legislation, together with the adoption of the D'Amato Act in mid-1996,[250] led to protests from many states, including the UK and Canada.[251] The Inter-American Juridical Committee of the Organisation of American States, 'directed' by the OAS General Assembly 'to examine and decide upon the validity under international law' of the Helms-Burton legislation,[252] unanimously concluded that:

> the exercise of such jurisdiction over acts of 'trafficking in confiscated prop-
> erty' does not conform with the norms established by international law for
> the exercise of jurisdiction in each of the following respects:
>   a) A prescribing state does not have the rights to exercise jurisdiction
> over acts of 'trafficking' abroad by aliens unless specific conditions are
> fulfilled which do not appear to be satisfied in this situation.

---

[248] See UKMIL, 64 BYIL, 1993, p. 643. The proposed adoption of this legislation led to UK protests as well: see UKMIL, 63 BYIL, 1992, pp. 726 ff.

[249] This part of the legislation was suspended by the President for six months as from July 1996: see, as to the legislation, 35 ILM, 1996, p. 357.

[250] Intended to impose sanctions on persons or entities participating in the development of the petroleum resources of Iran or Libya. As to the legislation concerning Iran and Libya, see 35 ILM, 1996, p. 1273.

[251] Canada also announced that legislation would be introduced under the Foreign Extraterritorial Measures Act 1985 to help protect Canadian companies against the US Act: see Canadian Foreign Affairs Ministry Press Release No. 115, 17 June 1996. Note that the UN General Assembly, in resolution 50/10 (1995), called upon the US to end its embargo against Cuba. See also A. F. Lowenfeld, 'Congress and Cuba: The Helms-Burton Act', 90 AJIL, 1996, p. 419; B. M. Clagett, 'Title III of the Helms-Burton Act is Consistent with International Law', *ibid.*, p. 434; S. K. Alexander, 'Trafficking in Confiscated Cuban Property', 16 *Dickinson Journal of International Law*, 1998, p. 523, and A. V. Lowe, 'US Extraterritorial Jurisdiction: The Helms-Burton and D'Amato Acts', 46 ICLQ, 1997, p. 378.

[252] OAS Doc. OEA/SER.P AG/doc.3375/96, 4 June 1996.

> b) A prescribing state does not have the rights to exercise jurisdiction over acts of 'trafficking' abroad by aliens under circumstances where neither the alien nor the conduct in question has any connnection with its territory and where no apparent connection exists between such acts and the protection of its essential sovereign interests.[253]

The European Community, in particular, took a strong stance on the US approach. It declared in a letter to the Congressional Committee considering changes in the US export control legislation in March 1984 that:

> US claims to jurisdiction over European subsidiaries of US companies and over goods and technology of US origin located outside the US are contrary to the principles of international law and can only lead to clashes of both a political and legal nature. These subsidiaries, goods and technology must be subject to the laws of the country where they are located.[254]

There was an attempt to solve such extraterritoriality conflicts in the Agreement Regarding the Application of Competition Laws signed by the European Commission on 23 September 1991 with the US.[255] This called *inter alia* for notification and co-ordination of such activities, with emphasis placed upon the application of comity. However, the European Court of Justice held that the Commission had acted *ultra vires* in concluding such an agreement.[256] The Agreement was re-introduced in the Decision of the Council and the Commission of 10 April 1995, which rectified certain competence problems arising as a result of the decision.[257] Nevertheless, it remains of uncertain value, not least because the question of private law suits in the US is not dealt with. The root problems of conflict have not been eradicated at all.

The adoption in 1992 of US legislation amending the Cuban Assets Control Regime stimulated a *démarche* from the European Community protesting against the extraterritorial application of US law,[258] as did the adoption of the Helms-Burton Act of 1996.[259] However, the EU–US

---

253 CJI/SO/II/doc.67/96 rev. 5, para. 9, 23 August 1996; 35 ILM, 1996, pp. 1329, 1334. It should be noted that under article 98 of the Charter of the OAS, Opinions of the Committee have no binding effect.

254 Cited in Current Legal Developments, 36 ICLQ, 1987, p. 399. See also UKMIL, 56 BYIL, 1985, pp. 480–1.

255 See 30 ILM, 1991, p. 1487. See also Torremans, 'Extraterritorial', pp. 289 ff.

256 Case C-327/91, *French Republic v. Commission of the European Communities* [1994] ECR I-3641.

257 [1995] OJ L 95/45.   258 See UKMIL, 63 BYIL, 1992, p. 725.

259 See e.g. European Commission Press Release WE 27/96, 18 July 1996 and 35 ILM, 1996, p. 397. See also Council Regulation No. 2271/96, 36 ILM, 1997, p. 127, and the Canadian

Memorandum of Understanding of 1997 provided for the continued suspension by the US of Title III so long as the EU continued efforts to promote democracy in Cuba.[260]

However, the European Community itself has wrestled with the question of exercising jurisdiction over corporations not based in the Community in the field of competition law.[261] In *ICI* v. *Commission*,[262] the European Court of Justice established jurisdiction with regard to a series of restrictive agreements to fix the price of dyestuffs on the ground that the defendant undertakings had corporate subsidiaries that were based within the Community, and declined to follow the Advocate General's suggestion[263] that jurisdiction should be founded upon direct and immediate, reasonably foreseeable and substantial effect.

The *Wood Pulp* case[264] concerned a number of non-EC companies and an association of US companies alleged to have entered into a price-fixing arrangement. The European Commission had levied fines on the jurisdictional basis that the effects of the price agreements and practices were direct, substantial and intended within the EC.[265] An action was then commenced before the European Court of Justice for annulment of the Commission's decision under article 173 of the EEC Treaty. Advocate General Darmon argued that international law permitted a state (and therefore the EC) to apply its competition laws to acts done by foreigners abroad if those acts had direct, substantial and foreseeable effects within the state concerned.[266]

The Court, however, took the view that the companies concerned had acted within the EC and were therefore subject to Community law. It was noted that where producers from third states sell directly to purchasers within the Community and engage in price competition in order to win orders from those customers, that constitutes competition within

Foreign Extraterritorial Measures Act 1996 (countering the Helms-Burton Act), *ibid.*, p. 111.

[260] 36 ILM, 1997, p. 529. On 18 May 1998, the Understanding with Respect to Disciplines for the Strengthening of Investment Protection was reached whereby the EU agreed to suspend action in the World Trade Organisation against the extraterritorial aspects of Helms-Burton in exchange for an EU-wide exemption by the US from the extraterritorial elements of the Act: see UKMIL, 76 BYIL, 2006, pp. 850–1.

[261] But not the UK: see e.g. *Attorney General's Reference (No. 1 of 1982)* [1983] 3 WLR 72, where the Court of Appeal refused to extend the scope of local jurisdiction over foreign conspiracies based on the effects principle.

[262] [1972] ECR 619; 48 ILR, p. 106.   [263] [1972] ECR 619, 693–4.

[264] A. *Ahlstrom Oy* v. *Commission* [1988] 4 CMLR 901.   [265] *Ibid.*, p. 916.

[266] *Ibid.*, p. 932.

the Community, and, where such producers sell at prices that are actually co-ordinated, that restricts competition within the Community within the meaning of article 85 of the EEC Treaty. It was stressed that the decisive factor was the place where the price-fixing agreement was actually implemented, not where the agreement was formulated.[267] In other words, the Court founded its jurisdiction upon an interpretation of the territoriality principle, if somewhat stretched. It did not take the opportunity presented to it by the opinion of the Advocate General of accepting the effects principle of jurisdiction. Nevertheless, the case does appear to suggest that price-fixing arrangements intended to have an effect within the Community that are implemented there would be subject to the jurisdiction of the Community, irrespective of the nationality of the companies concerned and of the place where the agreement was reached.[268]

Suggestions for further reading

M. Akehurst, 'Jurisdiction in International Law', 46 BYIL, 1972–3, p. 145

R. Donner, *The Regulation of Nationality in International Law*, 2nd edn, New York, 1995

F. A. Mann, 'The Doctrine of Jurisdiction in International Law Revisited After Twenty Years', 186 HR, 1984, p. 9

L. Reydams, *Universal Jurisdiction: International and Municipal Legal Perspectives*, Oxford, 2002

---

[267] *Ibid.*, pp. 940–1. Note that the Court held that the association of US companies (KEA) was not subject to Community jurisdiction on the ground that it had not played a separate role in the implementation within the Community of the arrangements in dispute, *ibid.*, pp. 942–3.

[268] See e.g. D. Lange and J. B. Sandage, 'The *Wood Pulp* Decision and its Implications for the Scope of EC Competition Law', 26 *Common Market Law Review*, 1989, p. 137, and L. Collins, *European Community Law in the United Kingdom*, 4th edn, London, 1990, p. 7. See also S. Weatherill and P. Beaumont, *EU Law*, 3rd edn, London, 1999, chapter 22.

13

Immunities from jurisdiction

In the previous chapter, the circumstances in which a state may seek
to exercise its jurisdiction in relation to civil and criminal matters were
considered. In this chapter the reverse side of this phenomenon will be
examined, that is those cases in which jurisdiction cannot be exercised as
it normally would because of special factors. In other words, the concern
is with immunity from jurisdiction and those instances where there exist
express exceptions to the usual application of a state's legal powers.

The concept of jurisdiction revolves around the principles of state
sovereignty, equality and non-interference. Domestic jurisdiction as a
notion attempts to define an area in which the actions of the organs of
government and administration are supreme, free from international legal
principles and interference. Indeed, most of the grounds for jurisdiction
can be related to the requirement under international law to respect the
territorial integrity and political independence of other states.

Immunity from jurisdiction, whether as regards the state itself or as
regards its diplomatic representatives, is grounded in this requirement.
Although constituting a derogation from the host state's jurisdiction, in
that, for example, the UK cannot exercise jurisdiction over foreign ambassadors
within its territory, it is to be construed nevertheless as an essential
part of the recognition of the sovereignty of foreign states, as well as an
aspect of the legal equality of all states.

Sovereign immunity[1]

Sovereignty until comparatively recently was regarded as appertaining to
a particular individual in a state and not as an abstract manifestation

[1] See generally e.g. H. Fox, *The Law of State Immunity*, Oxford, 2002; A. Dickinson, R.
Lindsay and J. P. Loonam, *State Immunity: Selected Materials and Commentary*, Oxford,
2004; I. Pingel-Lenuzza, *Les Immunités des États en Droit International*, Brussels, 1998; J.
Bröhmer, *State Immunity and the Violation of Human Rights*, The Hague, 1997; G. M. Badr,

of the existence and power of the state.[2] The sovereign was a definable
person, to whom allegiance was due. As an integral part of this mystique, the sovereign could not be made subject to the judicial processes
of his country. Accordingly, it was only fitting that he could not be sued
in foreign courts. The idea of the personal sovereign would undoubtedly
have been undermined had courts been able to exercise jurisdiction over
foreign sovereigns. This personalisation was gradually replaced by the abstract concept of state sovereignty, but the basic mystique remained. In
addition, the independence and equality of states made it philosophically
as well as practically difficult to permit municipal courts of one country to manifest their power over foreign sovereign states, without their
consent.[3] Until recently, the international law relating to sovereign (or
state) immunity relied virtually exclusively upon domestic case-law and
latterly legislation, although the European Convention on State Immunity, 1972 was a notable exception. However, in 2004 the UN adopted the
Convention on Jurisdictional Immunities of States and Their Property.[4]

State Immunity, The Hague, 1984; S. Sucharitkul, State Immunities and Trading Activities
in International Law, Leiden, 1959, and Sucharitkul, 'Immunities of Foreign States before
National Authorities', 149 HR, 1976, p. 87; I. Sinclair, 'The Law of Sovereign Immunity:
Recent Developments', 167 HR, 1980, p. 113; A. Aust, 'The Law of State Immunity', 53
ICLQ, 2004, p. 255; UN Legislative Series, Materials on Jurisdictional Immunities of States
and Their Property, New York, 1982; 10 Netherlands YIL, 1979; J. Candrian, L'Immunité
des États face aux Droits de l'Homme et à la Protection des Biens Culturels, Zurich, 2005;
Droit des Immunités et Exigencies du Procès Équitable (ed. I. Pingel), Paris, 2004; H. Lauter-
pacht, 'The Problem of Jurisdictional Immunities of Foreign States', 28 BYIL, 1951, p. 220;
R. Higgins, 'Certain Unresolved Aspects of the Law of State Immunity', 29 NILR, 1982,
p. 265; J. Crawford, 'International Law of Foreign Sovereigns: Distinguishing Immune
Transactions', 54 BYIL, 1983, p. 75; C. J. Lewis, State and Diplomatic Immunity, 3rd edn,
London, 1990; C. H. Schreuer, State Immunity: Some Recent Developments, Cambridge,
1988; Nguyen Quoc Dinh, P. Daillier and A. Pellet, Droit International Public, 7th edn,
Paris, 2002, p. 450, and Oppenheim's International Law (eds. R. Y. Jennings and A. D.
Watts), 9th edn, London, 1992, p. 341. See also the cases on sovereign immunity collected
in ILR, volumes 63–5; ILA, Report of the Sixtieth Conference, 1982, p. 325 and Report of
the Sixty-sixth Conference, 1994, p. 452; Annuaire de l'Institut de Droit International, vol.
64 I, 1991, p. 84, and Report of the International Law Commission, 1991, A/46/10, p. 8.
[2] See A. Watts, 'The Legal Position in International Law of Heads of State, Heads of Governments and Foreign Ministers', 247 HR, 1994 III, p. 13.
[3] See also Ex parte Pinochet (No. 3) [2000] 1 AC 147, 201 (per Lord Browne-Wilkinson) and
268–9 (per Lord Millett); 119 ILR, pp. 152, 221–3.
[4] See e.g. E. Denza, 'The 2005 UN Convention on State Immunity in Perspective', 55 ICLQ,
2006, p. 395; R. Gardiner, 'UN Convention on State Immunity: Form and Function', 55
ICLQ, 2006, p. 407; G. Hafner and L. Lange, 'La Convention des Nations Unies sur les
Immunités Jurisdictionnelles des États et de Leurs Biens', 50 AFDI, 2004, p. 45, and H. Fox,
'In Defence of State Immunity: Why the UN Convention on State Immunity is Important',
55 ICLQ, 2006, p. 399.

The classic case illustrating the relationship between territorial juris-diction and sovereign immunity is *The Schooner Exchange* v. *McFaddon*,[5] decided by the US Supreme Court. Chief Justice Marshall declared that the jurisdiction of a state within its own territory was exclusive and absolute, but it did not encompass foreign sovereigns. He noted that the:

> perfect equality and absolute independence of sovereigns . . . have given rise to a class of cases in which every sovereign is understood to waive the exercise of a part of that complete exclusive territorial jurisdiction, which has been stated to be the attribute of every nation.[6]

Lord Browne-Wilkinson stated in *Ex parte Pinochet* (*No. 3*) that,

> It is a basic principle of international law that one sovereign state (the forum state) does not adjudicate on the conduct of a foreign state. The foreign state is entitled to procedural immunity from the processes of the forum state. This immunity extends to both criminal and civil liability.[7]

Lord Millett in *Holland* v. *Lampen-Wolfe* put the point as follows:

> State immunity . . . is a creature of customary international law and derives from the equality of sovereign states. It is not a self-imposed restriction on the jurisdiction of its courts which the United Kingdom has chosen to adopt. It is a limitation imposed from without upon the sovereignty of the United Kingdom itself.[8]

Sovereign immunity is closely related to two other legal doctrines, non-justiciability and act of state. Reference has been made earlier to the inter-action between the various principles,[9] but it is worth noting here that the concepts of non-justiciability and act of state posit an area of international activity of states that is simply beyond the competence of the domestic tribunal in its assertion of jurisdiction, for example, that the courts would not adjudicate upon the transactions of foreign sovereign states.[10] On the

---

[5] 7 Cranch 116 (1812).

[6] *Ibid.*, p. 137. It therefore followed that, 'national ships of war entering the port of a friendly power open for their reception, are to be considered as exempted by the consent of that power from its jurisdiction'. Such rules would not apply to private ships which are susceptible to foreign jurisdiction abroad. See also *Republic of the Philippines* v. *Pimentel* 553 US_(2008), US Supreme Court, 12 June 2008, Slip Opinion, pp. 11–12.

[7] [2000] 1 AC 147, 201; 119 ILR, p. 152.   [8] [2000] 1 WLR 1573, 1588; 119 ILR, p. 367.

[9] See above, chapter 4, p. 179.

[10] See e.g. *Buttes Gas and Oil Co.* v. *Hammer (No. 3)* [1982] AC 888; 64 ILR, p. 332; *Buck* v. *Attorney-General* [1965] 1 Ch. 745; 42 ILR, p. 11 and Goff J, *I° Congreso del Partido* [1978] 1 QB 500, 527–8; 64 ILR, pp. 154, 178–9. See also Sinclair, 'Sovereign Immunity', p. 198.

other hand, the principle of jurisdictional immunity asserts that in particular situations a court is prevented from exercising the jurisdiction that it possesses. Thus, immunity from jurisdiction does not mean exemption from the legal system of the territorial state in question. The two concepts are distinct. In *International Association of Machinists & Aerospace Workers v. OPEC*,[11] it was declared that the two concepts were similar in that they reflect the need to respect the sovereignty of foreign states, but that they differed in that the former went to the jurisdiction of the court and was a principle of international law, whereas the latter constituted a prudential doctrine of domestic law having internal constitutional roots. Accordingly, the question of sovereign immunity is a procedural one and one to be taken as a preliminary issue,[12] logically preceding the issue of act of state.[13]

In practice, however, the distinction is not always so evident and arguments presented before the court founded both upon non-justiciability and sovereign immunity are to be expected. It is also an interesting point to consider the extent to which the demise of the absolute immunity approach has affected the doctrine of non-justiciability.

As far as the act of state doctrine is concerned in particular in this context, some disquiet has been expressed by courts that the application of that principle may in certain circumstances have the effect of reintroducing the absolute theory of sovereign immunity. In *Letelier v. Republic of Chile*,[14] for example, Chile argued that even if its officials had ordered

---

See further above, p. 182. Note also that 'a claim to state immunity is essentially a public claim that demands open litigation', *Harb v. King Fahd* [2005] EWCA Civ 632, para. 28, per Thorpe LJ.

[11] 649 F.2d 1354, 1359; 66 ILR, pp. 413, 418. Reaffirmed in *Asociacion de Reclamantes v. The United Mexican States* 22 ILM, 1983, pp. 625, 641–2. See also *Ramirez v. Weinberger* 23 ILM, 1984, p. 1274; *Goldwater v. Carter* 444 US 996 (1979) and *Empresa Exportadora de Azucar v. Industria Azucarera Nacional SA* [1983] 2 LL. R 171; 64 ILR, p. 368.

[12] This has been reaffirmed by the International Court of Justice in its Advisory Opinion in the *Difference Relating to Immunity from Legal Process* case, ICJ Reports, 1999, pp. 62, 88; 121 ILR, pp. 405, 432–3. Mance LJ stated in the Court of Appeal decision in *Jones v. Saudi Arabia* that 'claims to state immunity should be resolved at an early stage in the proceedings', [2004] EWCA Civ 1394, para. 10; 129 ILR, p. 653. See also *Republic of the Philippines v. Pimentel* 553 US-(2008), US Supreme Court, 12 June 2008, Slip Opinion, p. 11, holding that consideration of the merits of the case where sovereign immunity was pleaded would itself constitute an infringement of sovereign immunity.

[13] See e.g. *Siderman v. Republic of Argentina* 965 F.2d 699 (1992); 103 ILR, p. 454.

[14] 488 F.Supp. 665 (1980); 63 ILR, p. 378. Note that the US Court of Appeals has held that the Foreign Sovereign Immunities Act 1976 does not supersede the act of state doctrine: see *Helen Liu v. Republic of China* 29 ILM, 1990, p. 192.

the assassination of Letelier in the US, such acts could not be the subject of discussion in the US courts as the orders had been given in Chile. This was not accepted by the Court since to do otherwise would mean emasculating the Foreign Sovereign Immunities Act by permitting a state to bring back the absolute immunity approach 'under the guise of the act of state doctrine'.[15] In somewhat different circumstances, Kerr LJ signalled his concern in *Maclaine Watson* v. *The International Tin Council*[16] that the doctrine of non-justiciability might be utilised to bypass the absence of sovereign immunity with regard to a state's commercial activities.

Of course, once a court has determined that the relevant sovereign immunity legislation permits it to hear the case, it may still face the act of state argument. Such legislation implementing the restrictive immunity approach does not supplant the doctrine of act of state or non-justiciability,[17] although by accepting that the situation is such that immunity does not apply the scope for the non-justiciability plea is clearly much reduced.[18]

The absolute immunity approach

The relatively uncomplicated role of the sovereign and of government in the eighteenth and nineteenth centuries logically gave rise to the concept of absolute immunity, whereby the sovereign was completely immune from foreign jurisdiction in all cases regardless of circumstances. However, the unparalleled growth in the activities of the state, especially with regard to commercial matters, has led to problems and in most countries to a modification of the above rule. The number of governmental agencies and public corporations, nationalised industries and other state organs created a reaction against the concept of absolute immunity, partly because it would enable state enterprises to have an advantage over private companies. Accordingly many states began to adhere to the doctrine of restrictive immunity, under which immunity was available as regards governmental activity, but not where the state was engaging in commercial activity. Governmental acts with regard to which immunity would be granted are termed acts *jure imperii*, while those relating to private or trade activity are termed acts *jure gestionis*.

---

[15] 488 F.Supp. 665, 674.   [16] [1988] 3 WLR 1169, 1188; 80 ILR, pp. 191, 209.

[17] See *International Association of Machinists & Aerospace Workers* v. *OPEC* 649 F.2d 1354, 1359–60; 66 ILR, pp. 413, 418. See also *Liu* v. *Republic of China* 29 ILM, 1990, pp. 192, 205.

[18] See the interesting discussion of the relationship between non-justiciability and immunity by Evans J in *Australia and New Zealand Banking Group* v. *Commonwealth of Australia*, 1989, transcript, pp. 59–60.

The leading practitioner of the absolute immunity approach has been the United Kingdom, and this position was established in a number of important cases.[19]

In the *Parlement Belge* case,[20] the Court of Appeal emphasised that the principle to be deduced from all the relevant preceding cases was that every state

> declines to exercise by means of its courts any of its territorial jurisdiction over the person of any sovereign or ambassador of any other state, or over the public property of any state which is destined to public use... though such sovereign, ambassador or property be within its jurisdiction.[21]

The wide principle expressed in this case gave rise to the question as to what kind of legal interest it was necessary for the foreign sovereign to have in property so as to render it immune from the jurisdiction of the British courts.

Commonly regarded as the most extreme expression of the absolute immunity doctrine is the case of the *Porto Alexandre*.[22] This concerned a Portuguese requisitioned vessel against which a writ was issued in an English court for non-payment of dues for services rendered by tugs near Liverpool. The vessel was exclusively engaged in private trading operations, but the Court felt itself constrained by the terms of the *Parlement Belge* principle to dismiss the case in view of the Portuguese government interest.

Differences of opinion as to the application of the immunity rules were revealed in the House of Lords in the *Cristina* case.[23] This followed a Spanish Republican government decree requisitioning ships registered in Bilbao which was issued while the *Cristina* was on the high seas. On its arrival in Cardiff the Republican authorities took possession of the ship, whereupon its owners proceeded to issue a writ claiming possession. The case turned on the argument to dismiss the case, by the Republican government, in view of its sovereign immunity. The majority of the House

---

[19] But note a series of early cases which are not nearly so clear in their adoption of a broad absolute immunity doctrine: see e.g. *The Prins Frederik* (1820) 2 Dod. 451; *Duke of Brunswick* v. *King of Hanover* (1848) 2 HLC 1 and *De Haber* v. *Queen of Portugal* (1851) 17 QB 171. See also Phillimore J in *The Charkieh* (1873) LR 4A and E 59.

[20] (1880) 5 PD 197.

[21] Brett LJ, *ibid.*, pp. 214–15. Note, of course, that the principle relates to public property destined for public, not private, use.

[22] [1920] P. 30; 1 AD, p. 146. See e.g. Sinclair, 'Sovereign Immunity', p. 126. See also *The Jupiter* [1924] P. 236, 3 AD, p. 136.

[23] [1938] AC 485; 9 AD, p. 250.

of Lords accepted this in view of the requisition decree taking over the ship.

However, two of the Lords criticised the *Porto Alexandre* decision and doubted whether immunity covered state trading vessels,[24] while Lord Atkin took more of a fundamentalist absolute approach.[25]

In *Krajina* v. *Tass Agency*[26] the Court of Appeal held that the Agency was a state organ of the USSR and was thus entitled to immunity from local jurisdiction. This was followed in *Baccus SRL* v. *Servicio Nacional del Trigo*,[27] where the Court felt that the defendants, although a separate legal person under Spanish law, were in effect a department of state of the Spanish government. How the entity was actually constituted was regarded as an internal matter, and it was held entitled to immunity from suit.

A different view from the majority was taken by Lord Justice Singleton who, in a Dissenting Opinion, condemned what he regarded as the extension of the doctrine of sovereign immunity to separate legal entities.[28]

There is some limitation to the absolute immunity rule to the extent that a mere claim by a foreign sovereign to have an interest in the contested property would have to be substantiated before the English court would grant immunity. Since this involves some submission by the foreign sovereign to the local jurisdiction, immunity is not unqualifiedly absolute. Once the court is clear that the claim by the sovereign is not merely illusory or founded on a manifestly defective title, it will dismiss the case. This was brought out in *Juan Ysmael* v. *Republic of Indonesia*[29] in which the asserted interest in a vessel by the Indonesian government was regarded as manifestly defective so that the case was not dismissed on the ground of sovereign immunity.[30]

American cases, however, have shown a rather different approach, one that distinguishes between ownership on the one hand and possession and control on the other. In two cases particularly, immunity was refused

---

[24] See e.g. Lord Macmillan, [1938] AC 485, 498; 9 AD, p. 260.

[25] [1938] AC 485, p. 490. See also *Berizzi Bros. C.* v. *SS Pesaro* 271 US 562 (1926); 3 AD, p. 186 and *The Navemar* 303 US 68 (1938); 9 AD, p. 176.

[26] [1949] 2 All ER 274; 16 AD, p. 129. See also Cohen LJ, [1949] 2 All ER 274, 281.

[27] [1957] 1 QB 438; 23 ILR, p. 160.   [28] [1957] 1 QB 438, 461; 23 ILR, p. 169.

[29] [1955] AC 72; 21 ILR, p. 95. See also *USA and France* v. *Dollfus Mieg et Compagnie* [1952] AC 582; 19 ILR, p. 163.

[30] See Higgins, 'Unresolved Aspects', p. 273, who raises the question as to whether this test would be rigorous in an era of restrictive immunity. See also R. Higgins, *Problems and Process*, Oxford, 1994, chapter 5.

where the vessels concerned, although owned by the states claiming immunity, were held subject to the jurisdiction since at the relevant time they were not in the possession or control of these states.[31]

Since the courts will not try a case in which a foreign state is the defendant, it is necessary to decide what a foreign state is in each instance. Where doubts are raised as to the status of a foreign entity and whether or not it is to be regarded as a state for the purposes of the municipal courts, the executive certificate issued by the UK government will be decisive.

The case of *Duff Development Company v. Kelantan*[32] is a good example of this point. Kelantan was a Malay state under British protection. Both its internal and external policies were subject to British direction and it could in no way be described as politically independent. However, the UK government had issued an executive certificate to the effect that Kelantan was an independent state and that the Crown neither exercised nor claimed any rights of sovereignty or jurisdiction over it. The House of Lords, to whom the case had come, declared that once the Crown recognised a foreign ruler as sovereign, this bound the courts and no other evidence was admissible or needed. Accordingly, Kelantan was entitled to sovereign immunity from the jurisdiction of the English courts.

The restrictive approach

A number of states in fact started adopting the restrictive approach to immunity, permitting the exercise of jurisdiction over non-sovereign acts, at a relatively early stage.[33] The Supreme Court of Austria in 1950, in a comprehensive survey of practice, concluded that in the light of the increased activity of states in the commercial field the classic doctrine of absolute immunity had lost its meaning and was no longer a rule of international

---

[31] *The Navemar* 303 US 68 (1938); 9 AD, p. 176 and *Republic of Mexico v. Hoffman* 324 US 30 (1945); 12 AD, p. 143.

[32] [1924] AC 797; 2 AD, p. 124. By s. 21 of the State Immunity Act 1978, an executive certificate is deemed to be conclusive as to, for example, statehood in this context. See also *Trawnik v. Gordon Lennox* [1985] 2 All ER 368 as to the issue of a certificate under s. 21 on the status of the Commander of UK Forces in Berlin.

[33] See e.g. Belgium and Italy, Lauterpacht, 'Problem'; Badr, *State Immunity*, chapter 2; Sinclair, 'Sovereign Immunity' and I. Brownlie, *Principles of Public International Law*, 6th edn, Oxford, 2003, pp. 323 ff. See also the Brussels Convention on the Immunity of State-owned Ships, 1926, which assimilated the position of such ships engaged in trade to that of private ships regarding submission to the jurisdiction, and the 1958 Conventions on the Territorial Sea and on the High Seas. See now articles 31, 32, 95 and 96 of the 1982 Convention on the Law of the Sea.

law.[34] In 1952, in the Tate letter, the United States Department of State declared that the increasing involvement of governments in commercial activities coupled with the changing views of foreign states to absolute immunity rendered a change necessary and that thereafter 'the Department [will] follow the restrictive theory of sovereign immunity'.[35] This approach was also adopted by the courts, most particularly in *Victory Transport Inc.* v. *Comisaria General de Abasteciementos y Transportes*.[36] In this case, the Court, in the absence of a State Department 'suggestion' as to the immunity of the defendants, a branch of the Spanish Ministry of Commerce, affirmed jurisdiction since the chartering of a ship to transport wheat was not strictly a political or public act. The restrictive theory approach was endorsed by four Supreme Court Justices in *Alfred Dunhill of London Inc.* v. *Republic of Cuba*.[37]

As far as the UK was concerned, the adoption of the restrictive approach occurred rather later.[38]

In the *Philippine Admiral* case,[39] the vessel, which was owned by the Philippine government, had writs issued against it in Hong Kong by two shipping corporations. The Privy Council, hearing the case on appeal from the Supreme Court of Hong Kong, reviewed previous decisions on sovereign immunity and concluded that it would not follow the *Porto Alexandre* case.[40] Lord Cross gave four reasons for not following the earlier case. First, that the Court of Appeal wrongly felt that they were bound by the *Parlement Belge*[41] decision. Secondly, that the House of Lords in *The Cristina*[42] had been divided on the issue of immunity for state-owned vessels engaged in commerce. Thirdly, that the trend of opinion was against the absolute immunity doctrine; and fourthly that it was 'wrong' to apply the doctrine since states could in the Western world be sued in their

---

[34] *Dralle* v. *Republic of Czechoslovakia* 17 ILR, p. 155. This case was cited with approval by the West German Supreme Constitutional Court in *The Empire of Iran* 45 ILR, p. 57 and by the US Court of Appeals in *Victory Transport Inc.* v. *Comisaria General de Abasteciementos y Transportes* 35 ILR, p. 110.

[35] *26 Department of State Bulletin*, 984 (1952).

[36] 35 ILR, p. 110. See also e.g. *National City Bank of New York* v. *Republic of China* 22 ILR, p. 210 and *Rich* v. *Naviera Vacuba* 32 ILR, p. 127.

[37] 15 ILM, 1976, pp. 735, 744, 746–7; 66 ILR, pp. 212, 221, 224.

[38] See, for some early reconsiderations, Lord Denning in *Rahimtoola* v. *Nizam of Hyderabad* [1958] AC 379, 422; 24 ILR, pp. 175, 190.

[39] [1976] 2 WLR 214; 64 ILR, p. 90. Sinclair describes this as a 'historic landmark', 'Sovereign Immunity', p. 154. See also R. Higgins, 'Recent Developments in the Law of Sovereign Immunity in the United Kingdom', 71 AJIL, 1977, pp. 423, 424.

[40] [1920] P. 30; 1 AD, p. 146.   [41] (1880) 5 PD 197.   [42] [1938] AC 485; 9 AD, p. 250.

own courts on commercial contracts and there was no reason why foreign states should not be equally liable to be sued.[43] Thus, the Privy Council held that in cases where a state-owned merchant ship involved in ordinary trade was the object of a writ, it would not be entitled to sovereign immunity and the litigation would proceed.

In the case of *Thai-Europe Tapioca Service Ltd* v. *Government of Pakistan*,[44] a German-owned ship on charter to carry goods from Poland to Pakistan had been bombed in Karachi by Indian planes during the 1971 war. Since the agreement provided for disputes to be settled by arbitration in England, the matter came eventually before the English courts. The cargo had previously been consigned to a Pakistani corporation, and that corporation had been taken over by the Pakistani government. The shipowners sued the government for the sixty-seven-day delay in unloading that had resulted from the bombing. The government pleaded sovereign immunity and sought to have the action dismissed.

The Court of Appeal decided that since all the relevant events had taken place outside the jurisdiction and in view of the action being *in personam* against the foreign government rather than against the ship itself, the general principle of sovereign immunity would have to stand.

Lord Denning declared in this case that there were certain exceptions to the doctrine of sovereign immunity. It did not apply where the action concerned land situated in the UK or trust funds lodged in the UK or debts incurred in the jurisdiction for services rendered to property in the UK, nor was there any immunity when a commercial transaction was entered into with a trader in the UK 'and a dispute arises which is properly within the territorial jurisdiction of our courts'.[45]

This unfortunate split approach, absolute immunity for actions *in personam* and restrictive immunity for actions *in rem* did not, however, last long. In *Trendtex Trading Corporation Ltd* v. *Central Bank of Nigeria*,[46] all three judges of the Court of Appeal accepted the validity of the restrictive approach as being consonant with justice, comity and international practice.[47] The problem of precedent was resolved for two of the judges by declaring that international law knew no doctrine of *stare decisis*.[48] The

---

[43] [1976] 2 WLR 214, 232; 64 ILR, pp. 90, 108. Note that Lord Cross believed that the absolute theory still obtained with regard to actions *in personam*, [1976] 2 WLR 214, 233.

[44] [1975] 1 WLR 1485; 64 ILR, p. 81.   [45] [1975] 1 WLR 1485, 1490–1; 64 ILR, p. 84.

[46] [1977] 2 WLR 356; 64 ILR, p. 122.

[47] [1977] 2 WLR 356, 366–7 (Denning MR), 380 (Stephenson LJ) and 385–6 (Shaw LJ).

[48] *Ibid.*, pp. 365–6 and 380. But cf. Stephenson LJ, *ibid.*, p. 381. See further above, chapter 4, p. 145.

clear acceptance of the restrictive theory of immunity in *Trendtex* was reaffirmed in later cases,[49] particularly by the House of Lords in the *I° Congreso del Partido* case[50] and in *Alcom Ltd* v. *Republic of Colombia*.[51] The majority of states now have tended to accept the restrictive immunity doctrine[52] and this has been reflected in domestic legislation.[53] In particular, the US Foreign Sovereign Immunities Act 1976,[54] provides in section 1605 for the grounds upon which a state may be subject to the jurisdiction (as general exceptions to the jurisdictional immunity of a foreign state), while the UK State Immunity Act 1978[55] similarly provides for a general rule of immunity from the jurisdiction of the courts with a range of exceptions thereto.[56]

---

[49] See e.g. *Hispano Americana Mercantil SA* v. *Central Bank of Nigeria* [1979] 2 LL. R 277; 64 ILR, p. 221.

[50] [1981] 2 All ER 1064; 64 ILR, p. 307, a case concerned with the pre-1978 Act common law. See also *Planmount Ltd* v. *Republic of Zaire* [1981] 1 All ER 1110; 64 ILR, p. 268.

[51] [1984] 2 All ER 6; 74 ILR, p. 179. See also *Jones* v. *Saudi Arabia* [2006] UKHL 26, para. 8 (per Lord Bingham); 129 ILR, pp. 716.

[52] See e.g. the *Administration des Chemins de Fer du Gouvernement Iranien* case, 52 ILR, p. 315 and the *Empire of Iran* case, 45 ILR, p. 57; see also Sinclair, 'Sovereign Immunity'; Badr, *State Immunity*; and UN, *Materials*. Note also *Abbott* v. *Republic of South Africa* before the Spanish Constitutional Court, 86 ILR, p. 512; *Manauta* v. *Embassy of Russian Federation* 113 ILR, p. 429 (Argentinian Supreme Court); *US* v. *Friedland* 182 DLR (4th) 614; 120 ILR, p. 417 and *CGM Industrial* v. *KPMG* 1998 (3) SA 738; 121 ILR, p. 472.

[53] See e.g. the Singapore State Immunity Act 1979; the Pakistan State Immunity Ordinance 1981; the South African Foreign States Immunities Act 1981; the Canadian State Immunity Act 1982 and the Australian Foreign States Immunities Act 1985. See also article 5 of the UN Convention on Jurisdictional Immunities of States and Their Property, 2004. Note that this Convention, which is not in force as at the date of writing, does not apply to criminal proceedings.

[54] See e.g. G. Delaume, 'Public Debt and Sovereign Immunity: The Foreign Sovereign Immunities Act of 1976', 71 AJIL, 1977, p. 399; Sinclair, 'Sovereign Immunity', pp. 243 ff., and D. Weber, 'The Foreign Sovereign Immunities Act of 1976', 3 *Yale Studies in World Public Order*, 1976, p. 1. Note that in *Republic of Austria* v. *Altmann*, the US Supreme Court held that the Foreign Sovereign Immunities Act applied to acts which occurred prior to its enactment and even prior to the adoption by the US of the restrictive immunity approach in 1952, 541 US 677 (2004).

[55] See e.g. D. W. Bowett, 'The State Immunity Act 1978', 37 *Cambridge Law Journal*, 1978, p. 193; R. C. A. White, 'The State Immunity Act 1978', 42 MLR, 1979, p. 72; Sinclair, 'Sovereign Immunity', pp. 257 ff., and M. N. Shaw, 'The State Immunity Act 1978', *New Law Journal*, 23 November 1978, p. 1136.

[56] See also the 1972 European Convention on State Immunity. The Additional Protocol to the European Convention, which establishes a European Tribunal in matters of State Immunity to determine disputes under the Convention, came into force on 22 May 1985, to be composed initially of the same members as the European Court of Human Rights: see Council of Europe Press Release, C(85)39. See generally UN, *Materials*, Part I 'National Legislation', and Badr, *State Immunity*, chapter 3. See also the Inter-American

The former Soviet Union and some other countries generally adhered to the absolute immunity theory, although in practice entered into many bilateral agreements permitting the exercise of jurisdiction in cases where a commercial contract had been signed on the territory of the other state party.[57]

Sovereign and non-sovereign acts

With the acceptance of the restrictive theory, it becomes crucial to analyse the distinction between those acts that will benefit from immunity and those that will not. In the *Victory Transport* case,[58] the Court declared that it would (in the absence of a State Department suggestion)[59] refuse to grant immunity, unless the activity in question fell within one of the categories of strictly political or public acts: viz. internal administrative acts, legislative acts, acts concerning the armed forces or diplomatic activity and public loans.

However, the basic approach of recent legislation[60] has been to proclaim a rule of immunity and then list the exceptions, so that the onus of proof falls on the other side of the line.[61] This approach is mirrored in article 5

Draft Convention on Jurisdictional Immunity of States, 22 ILM, 1983, p. 292. Note that the large number of cases precipitated by the 1979 Iran Hostages Crisis and the US freezing of assets were argued on the basis of the restrictive theory, before being terminated: see e.g. R. Edwards, 'Extraterritorial Application of the US Iranian Assets Control Regulations', 75 AJIL, 1981, p. 870. See also *Dames and Moore* v. *Regan* 101 S. Ct. 1972 (1981); 72 ILR, p. 270.

57 See, for a number of examples, UN, *Materials*, pp. 134–50. See also M. M. Boguslavsky, 'Foreign State Immunity: Soviet Doctrine and Practice', 10 Netherlands YIL, 1979, p. 167. See, as to Philippines practice, *US* v. *Ruiz and De Guzman* 102 ILR, p. 122; *US* v. *Guinto, Valencia and Others, ibid.*, p. 132 and *The Holy See* v. *Starbright Sales Enterprises, ibid.*, p. 163.

58 336 F.2d 354 (1964); 35 ILR, p. 110. See also P. Lalive, 'L'Immunité de Juridiction des États et des Organisations Internationales', 84 HR, 1953, p. 205, and Lauterpacht, 'Problem', pp. 237–9.

59 Note that since the 1976 Foreign Sovereign Immunities Act, the determination of such status is a judicial, not executive, act.

60 See e.g. s. 1 of the State Immunity Act 1978; s. 1604 of the US Foreign Sovereign Immunities Act 1976 and s. 9 of the Australian Foreign States Immunities Act 1985. See also *Saudi Arabia* v. *Nelson* 123 L Ed 2d 47 (1993); 100 ILR, p. 544.

61 See also article 15 of the European Convention on State Immunity, 1972. Article II of the Revised Draft Articles for a Convention on State Immunity adopted by the International Law Association in 1994, Report of the Sixty-sixth Conference, 1994, p. 22, provides that: 'In principle, a foreign state shall be immune from the adjudicatory jurisdiction of a forum state for acts performed by it in the exercise of its sovereign authority, i.e. *jure imperii*. It shall not be immune in the circumstances provided in article III.'

of the UN Convention on Jurisdictional Immunities of States and Their Property, 2004, which notes that:[62]

> A state enjoys immunity in respect of itself and its property, from the jurisdiction of the courts of another state subject to the provisions of the present Convention.

In such circumstances, the way in which the 'state' is defined for sovereign immunity purposes becomes important. Article 2(1)b of the Convention declares that 'state' means: (i) the state and its various organs of government; (ii) constituent units of a federal state or political subdivisions of the state, which are entitled to perform acts in the exercise of sovereign authority, and are acting in that capacity; (iii) agencies or instrumentalities of the state or other entities, to the extent that they are entitled to perform and are actually performing acts in the exercise of sovereign authority of the state; and (iv) representatives of the state acting in that capacity.[63]

With the adoption of the restrictive theory of immunity, the appropriate test becomes whether the activity in question is of itself sovereign (*jure imperii*) or non-sovereign (*jure gestionis*). In determining this, the predominant approach has been to focus upon the nature of the transaction rather than its purpose.[64]

However, it should be noted that article 2(2) of the Convention provides that:

---

[62] There is extensive state practice on whether immunity should be seen as a derogation from territorial sovereignty and thus to be justified in each particular case, or as a rule of international law as such, thus not requiring substantiation in each and every case: see *Yearbook of the ILC*, 1980, vol. II, part 2, pp. 142 ff.

[63] Note that the provision in point (iv) is somewhat confusing in the light of article 3 which states that the Convention is without prejudice to the privileges and immunities of diplomatic and consular missions, special missions and missions to international organisations, and the immunities granted to heads of state.

[64] See e.g. s. 1603(d) of the US Foreign Sovereign Immunities Act of 1976. The section-by-section analysis of the Act emphasises that 'the fact that goods or services to be procured through a contract are to be used for a public purpose is irrelevant; it is the initially commercial nature of an activity or transaction that is critical', reproduced in UN, *Materials*, pp. 103, 107. See also the *Empire of Iran* case, 45 ILR, pp. 57, 80–1; *Trendtex Trading Corporation Ltd* v. *Central Bank of Nigeria* [1977] 2 WLR 356; 64 ILR, p. 122; *Non-resident Petitioner* v. *Central Bank of Nigeria* 16 ILM, 1977, p. 501 (a German case); *Planmount Ltd* v. *Republic of Zaire* [1981] 1 All ER 1110; 64 ILR, p. 268 and *Saudi Arabia* v. *Nelson* 123 L Ed 2d 47 (1993); 100 ILR, p. 544 (US Supreme Court). See also article I of the Revised Draft Articles for a Convention on State Immunity adopted by the International Law Association in 1994, Report of the Sixty-sixth Conference, 1994, p. 23.

> In determining whether a contract or transaction is a 'commercial transaction'... reference should be made primarily to the nature of the contract or transaction, but its purpose should also be taken into account if the parties to the contract or transaction have so agreed, or if, in the practice of the state of the forum, that purpose is relevant to determining the non-commercial character of the contract or transaction.

The reason for the modified 'nature' test was in order to provide an adequate safeguard and protection for developing countries, particularly as they attempt to promote national economic development. The ILC Commentary notes that a two-stage approach is posited, to be applied successively. First, reference should be made primarily to the nature of the contract or transaction and, if it is established that it is non-commercial or governmental in nature, no further enquiry would be needed. If, however, the contract or transaction appeared to be commercial, then reference to its purpose should be made in order to determine whether the contract or transaction was truly sovereign or not. States should be given an opportunity to maintain that in their practice a particular contract or transaction should be treated as non-commercial since its purpose is clearly public and supported by reasons of state. Examples given include the procurement of medicaments to fight a spreading epidemic, and food supplies.[65] This approach, a modification of earlier drafts,[66] is not uncontroversial and some care is required. It would, for example, be unhelpful if the purpose criterion were to be adopted in a manner which would permit it to be used to effect a considerable retreat from the restrictive immunity approach. This is not to say, however, that no consideration whatsoever of the purpose of the transaction in question should be undertaken.

Lord Wilberforce in *I° Congreso del Partido*[67] emphasised that in considering whether immunity should be recognised one had to consider the whole context in which the claim is made in order to identify the 'relevant act' which formed the basis of that claim. In particular, was it an act *jure gestionis*, or in other words 'an act of a private law character such as a private citizen might have entered into'?[68] This use of the private law/public law dichotomy, familiar to civil law systems, was particularly noticeable, although different states draw the distinction at

---

[65] Report of the International Law Commission, 1991, pp. 29–30.
[66] *Yearbook of the ILC*, 1983, vol. II, part 2.   [67] [1983] AC 244, 267; 64 ILR, pp. 307, 318.
[68] [1983] AC 244, 262; 64 ILR, p. 314.

different points.[69] It should also be noted, however, that this distinction is less familiar to common law systems. In addition, the issues ascribed to the governmental sphere as distinct from the private area rest upon the particular political concept proclaimed by the state in question, so that a clear and comprehensive international consensus regarding the line of distinction is unlikely.[70] The characterisation of an act as *jure gestionis* or *jure imperii* will also depend upon the perception of the issue at hand by the courts. Lord Wilberforce also noted that while the existence of a governmental purpose or motive could not convert what would otherwise be an act *jure gestionis* or an act of private law into one done *jure imperii*,[71] purpose may be relevant if throwing some light upon the nature of what was done.[72]

The importance of the contextual approach at least as the starting point of the investigation was also emphasised by the Canadian Supreme Court in *United States of America* v. *The Public Service Alliance of Canada and Others (Re Canada Labour Code).*[73] It was noted that the contextual approach was the only reasonable basis for applying the restrictive immunity doctrine for the alternative was to attempt the impossible, 'an antiseptic distillation of a "once-and-for-all" characterisation of the activity in question, entirely divorced from its purpose'.[74] The issue was also considered by the Supreme Court of Victoria, Australia, in *Reid* v. *Republic of Nauru*,[75] which stated that in some situations the separation of act, motive and purpose might not be possible. The motive or purpose underlying particular conduct may constitute part of the definition of the act itself in some cases, while in others the nature or quality of the act performed might not be ascertainable without reference to the context within which it is carried out. The Court also made the point that a relevant factor was the perception held or policy adopted in each particular country as to the attributes of sovereignty itself.[76] The point that 'unless we can inquire into the purpose of such acts, we cannot determine their nature' was also made by the US Court of Appeals in *De Sanchez* v. *Banco Central de Nicaragua and Others.*[77]

---

[69] See e.g. Sinclair, 'Sovereign Immunity', pp. 210–13, and the *Empire of Iran* case, 45 ILR, pp. 57, 80. See also article 7 of the European Convention on State Immunity, 1972.
[70] See e.g. Crawford, 'International Law', p. 88, and Lauterpacht, 'Problem', pp. 220, 224–6.
[71] [1983] AC 244, 267; 64 ILR, p. 318.   [72] [1983] AC 244, 272; 64 ILR, p. 323.
[73] (1992) 91 DLR (4th) 449; 94 ILR, p. 264.   [74] [1992] 91 DLR (4th) 463; 94 ILR, p. 278.
[75] [1993] 1 VR 251; 101 ILR, p. 193.   [76] [1993] 1 VR 253; 101 ILR, pp. 195–6.
[77] 770 F.2d 1385, 1393 (1985); 88 ILR, pp. 75, 85.

The particular issue raised in the *Congreso* case was whether immunity could be granted where, while the initial transaction was clearly commercial, the cause of the breach of the contract in question appeared to be an exercise of sovereign authority. In that case, two vessels operated by a Cuban state-owned shipping enterprise and delivering sugar to a Chilean company were ordered by the Cuban government to stay away from Chile after the Allende regime had been overthrown. The Cuban government pleaded sovereign immunity on the grounds that the breach of the contract was occasioned as a result of a foreign policy decision. The House of Lords did not accept this and argued that once a state had entered the trading field, it would require a high standard of proof of a sovereign act for immunity to be introduced. Lord Wilberforce emphasised that:

> in order to withdraw its action from the sphere of acts done *jure gestionis*, a state must be able to point to some act clearly done *jure imperii*[78]

and that the appropriate test was to be expressed as follows:

> it is not just that the purpose or motive of the act is to serve the purposes of the state, but that the act is of its own character a governmental act, as opposed to an act which any private citizen can perform.[79]

In the circumstances of the case, that test had not been satisfied. One of the two ships, the *Playa Larga*, had been owned at all relevant times by the Cuban government, but the second ship, the *Marble Islands*, was owned by a trading enterprise not entitled to immunity. When this ship was on the high seas, it was taken over by the Cuban government and ordered to proceed to North Vietnam, where its cargo was eventually donated to the people of that country. The Court was unanimous in rejecting the plea of immunity with regard to the *Playa Larga*, but was split over the second ship.

Two members of the House of Lords, Lord Wilberforce and Lord Edmund-Davies, felt that the key element with regard to the *Marble Islands*, as distinct from the *Playa Larga*, where the government had acted as owner of the ship and not as governmental authority, was that the Republic of Cuba directed the disposal of the cargo in North Vietnam. This was not part of any commercial arrangement which was conducted by the demise charterer, who was thus responsible for the civil wrongs

---

[78] [1981] 2 All ER 1064, 1075; 64 ILR, p. 320.
[79] *Ibid.*, quoting the judge at first instance, [1978] 1 All ER 1169, 1192; 64 ILR, p. 179.

committed. The acts of the government were outside this framework and accordingly purely governmental.[80]

However, the majority held that the Cuban government had acted in the context of a private owner in discharging and disposing of the cargo in North Vietnam and had not regarded itself as acting in the exercise of sovereign powers. Everything had been done in purported reliance upon private law rights in that the demise charterers had sold the cargo to another Cuban state enterprise by ordinary private law sale and in purported reliance upon the bill of lading which permitted the sale in particular instances. It was the purchaser that donated the cargo to the Vietnamese people.[81]

In many respects, nevertheless, the minority view is the more acceptable one, in that in reality it was the Cuban government's taking control of the ship and direction of it and its cargo that determined the issue and this was done as a deliberate matter of state policy. The fact that it was accomplished by the private law route rather than, for example, by direct governmental decree should not settle the issue conclusively. In fact, one thing that the case does show is how difficult it is in reality to distinguish public from private acts.[82]

In *Littrell v. United States of America (No. 2)*,[83] Hoffman LJ in the Court of Appeal emphasised that it would be facile in the case, which concerned medical treatment for a US serviceman on an American base in the UK, to regard the general military context as such as determinative. One needed to examine carefully all the relevant circumstances in order to decide whether a sovereign or a non-sovereign activity had been involved. Important factors to be considered included where the activity actually took place, whom it involved and what kind of act itself was involved.[84] In *Holland v. Lampen-Wolfe*, the House of Lords dealt with a case concerning

---

[80] [1981] 2 All ER 1064, 1077 and 1081; 64 ILR, pp. 321, 327.

[81] [1981] 2 All ER 1079–80, 1082 and 1083; 64 ILR, pp. 325, 328, 329.

[82] Note that if the State Immunity Act 1978 had been in force when the cause of action arose in this case, it is likely that the claim of immunity would have completely failed: see s. 10. See also *Kuwait Airways Corporation v. Iraqi Airways Co.* [1995] 1 WLR 1147, where the House of Lords separated out a series of events and held that an initial sovereign act did not characterise the situation as a whole: see below, p. 714.

[83] [1995] 1 WLR 82, 95; 100 ILR, p. 438. Note that the case, as it concerned foreign armed forces in the UK, fell outside the State Immunity Act 1978 and was dealt with under common law.

[84] See also *Hicks v. US* 120 ILR, p. 606, where the Employment Appeal Tribunal held that the primary purpose of recreation facilities at an airbase was to increase the effectiveness of the central military activity of that base which was clearly a sovereign activity.

the activities of a US citizen and civilian teaching at a US military base in the UK who argued that a memorandum written by the defendant was libellous.[85] Relying upon Hoffman LJ's approach, the House of Lords emphasised that the context in which the act concerned took place was the provision of education within a military base, an activity designed 'as part of the process of maintaining forces and associated civilians on the base by US personnel to serve the needs of the US military authorities'.[86] Accordingly, the defendant was entitled to immunity.

The problem of sovereign immunity with regard to foreign bases was also addressed by the Canadian Supreme Court in *United States of America v. The Public Service Alliance of Canada (Re Canada Labour Code)*.[87] The Court emphasised that employment at the base was a multifaceted activity and could neither be labelled as such as sovereign or commercial in nature. One had to determine which aspects of the activity were relevant to the proceedings at hand and then to assess the impact of the proceedings on these attributes as a whole.[88] The closer the activity in question was to undisputable sovereign acts, such as managing and operating an offshore military base, the more likely it would be that immunity would be recognised. In *Kuwait Airways Corporation v. Iraqi Airways Co.*,[89] Lord Goff, giving the leading judgment in the House of Lords, adopted Lord Wilberforce's statement of principle in *Congreso* and held that 'the ultimate test of what constitutes an act *jure imperii* is whether the act in question is of its own character a governmental act, as opposed to an act which any private citizen can perform'.[90] Further, the Court held that the fact that an initial act was an act *jure imperii* did not determine as such the characterisation of subsequent acts.[91]

---

[85] Similarly a US citizen and civilian.

[86] [2000] 1 WLR 1573, 1577 (per Lord Hope, who stated that 'the context is all important', *ibid.*).

[87] (1992) 91 DLR (4th) 449; 94 ILR, p. 264.   [88] (1992) 91 DLR (4th) 466; 94 ILR, p. 281.

[89] [1995] 1 WLR 1147, 1160; 103 ILR, p. 340. For later proceedings in this case, see 116 ILR, p. 534 (High Court); [2000] 2 All ER (Comm.) 360; [2001] 2 WLR 1117 (Court of Appeal) and [2002] UKHL 19 (House of Lords).

[90] Note that in *Sengupta v. Republic of India* 65 ILR, pp. 325, 360, it was emphasised that in deciding whether immunity applied, one had to consider whether it was the kind of contract an individual might make, whether it involved the participation of both parties in the public functions of the state, the nature of the alleged breach and whether the investigation of the claim would involve an investigation into the public or sovereign acts of the foreign state.

[91] [1995] 1 WLR 1147, 1162–3. See further below, p. 731.

State immunity and violations of human rights [92]

With the increasing attention devoted to the relationship between international human rights law and domestic systems, the question has arisen as to whether the application of sovereign immunity in civil suits against foreign states for violations of human rights law has been affected. To date state practice suggests that the answer to this is negative. In *Saudi Arabia v. Nelson*, the US Supreme Court noted that the only basis for jurisdiction over a foreign state was the Foreign Sovereign Immunities Act 1976 and, unless a matter fell within one of the exceptions, the plea of immunity would succeed.[93] It was held that although the alleged wrongful arrest, imprisonment and torture by the Saudi government of Nelson would amount to abuse of the power of its police by that government, 'a foreign state's exercise of the power of its police has long been understood for the purposes of the restrictive theory as peculiarly sovereign'.[94] However, the US Foreign Sovereign Immunities Act was amended in 1996 by the Antiterrorism and Effective Death Penalty Act which created an exception to immunity with regard to states, designated by the Department of State as terrorist states, which committed a terrorist act, including hostage-taking, or provided material support and resources to an individual or entity which committed such an act which resulted in the death or personal injury of a US citizen.[95] In *Simpson v. Libya*, the US Court of Appeals held that the hostage exception to immunity applied where three conditions had been met: where the state in question had been designated as a 'state sponsor of terrorism'; where it had been provided with a reasonable

---

[92] See e.g. Bröhmer, *State Immunity*; S. Marks, 'Torture and the Jurisdictional Immunity of Foreign States', 1997 CLJ, p. 8; R. van Alebeek, 'The *Pinochet* Case', 71 BYIL, 2000, pp. 49 ff., and van Alebeek, *Immunities of States and Their Officials in International Criminal Law and International Human Rights Law*, Oxford, 2008; K. Reece Thomas and J. Small, 'Human Rights and State Immunity: Is There Immunity From Civil Liability for Torture?', 50 NILR, 2003, p. 1; K. Parlett, 'Immunity in Civil Proceedings for Torture: The Emerging Exception', 2 *European Human Rights Law Review*, 2006, p. 49; H. Fox, 'State Immunity and the International Crime of Torture', 2 *European Human Rights Law Review*, 2006, p. 142; Redress, *Immunity v Accountability*, London, 2005, and L. Caplan, 'State Immunity, Human Rights and *Jus Cogens*: A Critique of the Normative Hierarchy Theory', 97 AJIL, 2003, p. 741.

[93] 123 L Ed 2d 47, 61 (1993); 100 ILR, pp. 544, 553.

[94] 123 L Ed 2d 47, 57. See also e.g. *Controller and Auditor General* v. *Sir Ronald Davidson* [1996] 2 NZLR 278 and *Princz* v. *Federal Republic of Germany* 26 F.3d 1166 (DC Cir. 1994).

[95] This provision is retroactive. See *Flatow* v. *Islamic Republic of Iran* 999 F.Supp. 1 (1998); 121 ILR, p. 618 and *Alejandre* v. *Republic of Cuba* 996 F.Supp. 1239 (1997); 121 ILR, p. 603.

opportunity to arbitrate the claim; and where the claimant or victim was a citizen of the US. The Court found it unnecessary for the plaintiff to have to show that the hostage-taker had issued a demand showing his intended purposes to a third party, since the definition of hostage-taking focused on the state of mind of the hostage-taker himself. Accordingly, third-party awareness of a hostage-taker's intent was not a required element.[96]

In *Bouzari* v. *Iran*, the Superior Court of Justice of Ontario, Canada, noted, in the light of the Canadian State Immunity Act 1982, that 'regardless of the state's ultimate purpose, exercises of police, law enforcement and security powers are inherently exercises of governmental authority and sovereignty'[97] and concluded that an international custom existed to the effect that there was an ongoing rule providing state immunity for acts of torture committed outside the forum state.[98] The English Court of Appeal in *Al-Adsani* v. *Government of Kuwait*[99] held that the State Immunity Act provided for immunity for states apart from specific listed express exceptions, and there was no room for implied exceptions to the general rule even where the violation of a norm of *jus cogens* (such as the prohibition of torture) was involved. The Court rejected an argument that the term 'immunity' in domestic legislation meant immunity from sovereign acts that were in accordance with international law, thus excluding torture for which immunity could not be claimed. In *Holland* v. *Lampen-Wolfe*, the House of Lords held that recognition of sovereign immunity did not involve a violation of the rights of due process contained in article 6 of the European Convention on Human Rights since it was argued that immunity derives from customary international law while the obligations under article 6 derived from a treaty freely entered into by the UK. Accordingly, 'The United Kingdom cannot, by its own act of acceding to the Convention and without the consent of the United States, obtain a power of adjudication over the United States which international law denies it.'[100] The European Court of Human Rights in *Al-Adsani* v. *UK*

---

[96] 470 F.3d 356 (2006).   [97] 124 ILR, pp. 427, 435.

[98] *Ibid.*, p. 443. The Court dismissed arguments that either the Convention against Torture or the International Covenant on Civil and Political Rights imposed an obligation on states to create a civil remedy with regard to acts of torture committed abroad, or that such an obligation existed as a rule of *jus cogens*: see at pp. 441 and 443.

[99] (1996) 1 LL. R 104; 107 ILR, p. 536. But see Evans LJ in *Al-Adsani* v. *Government of Kuwait* 100 ILR, p. 465, which concerned leave to serve proceedings upon the government of Kuwait and in which it had been held that there was a good arguable case that, under the State Immunity Act, there was no immunity for a state in respect of alleged acts of torture.

[100] [2000] 1 WLR 1573, 1588 (per Lord Millett); 119 ILR, p. 384.

analysed this issue, that is whether state immunity could exist with regard to civil proceedings for torture in the light of article 6 of the European Convention.[101] The Court noted that the grant of sovereign immunity to a state in civil proceedings pursued the legitimate aim of complying with international law to promote comity and good relations between states through the respect of another state's sovereignty and that the European Convention on Human Rights should be interpreted in harmony with other rules of international law, including that relating to the grant of state immunity.[102] The Court concluded that it could not discern in the relevant materials before it, 'any firm basis for concluding that, as a matter of international law, a state no longer enjoys immunity from civil suit in the courts of another state where acts of torture are alleged'[103] and held that immunity thus still applied in such cases.[104]

In *Jones* v. *Saudi Arabia*, the House of Lords, faced with claims that individuals had been systematically tortured while in official custody in Saudi Arabia, held that under Part 1 of the State Immunity Act 1978, an approach reflecting that adopted in international law (particularly in the UN Convention on Jurisdictional Immunities), a foreign state was immune unless one of the exceptions provided for in the legislation applied. None of the exceptions mentioned injuries caused by torture abroad.[105] Further, the fact that torture was prohibited by a *jus cogens* rule of international law did not suffice to remove the immunity granted by international law to a state nor to confer jurisdiction to hear civil claims in respect of torture committed outside of the state where it was sought to exercise jurisdiction.[106] Particular emphasis was placed on the distinction between the prohibition of torture as a substantive rule of law and the existence of the rule of immunity which constitutes a procedural bar to the exercise of jurisdiction and does not contradict the prohibition.[107] Lord Hoffmann underlined that as a matter of international practice, no procedural rule of international law had developed enabling states to

---

[101] Judgment of 21 November 2001; 123 ILR, p. 24.

[102] *Ibid.*, paras. 54 and 55.   [103] *Ibid.*, para. 61.

[104] *Ibid.*, para. 66. This decision was later affirmed in *Kalogeropoulou* v. *Greece and Germany*, European Court of Human Rights, judgment of 12 December 2002; 129 ILR, p. 537.

[105] [2006] UKHL 26, para. 9 (per Lord Bingham); 129 ILR, p. 717.

[106] *Ibid.*, paras. 24–8; 129 ILR, pp. 726–8.

[107] See e.g. para. 24 (Lord Bingham) and para. 44 (Lord Hoffmann), 129 ILR, pp. 726 and 732, both citing Fox, *State Immunity*, p. 525 to this effect, who further noted that the existence of immunity merely diverted any breach of the prohibition 'to a different method of settlement'.

assume civil jurisdiction over other states in cases in which torture was alleged.[108]

In the case of criminal proceedings, the situation is rather different. Part I of the State Immunity Act (the substantive part) does not apply to criminal proceedings, although Part III (concerning certain status issues) does. In *Ex parte Pinochet (No. 3)*,[109] the House of Lords held by six votes to one that General Pinochet was not entitled to immunity in extradition proceedings (which are criminal proceedings) with regard to charges of torture and conspiracy to torture where the alleged acts took place after the relevant states (Chile, Spain and the UK) had become parties to the Convention against Torture, although the decision focused on head of state immunity and the terms of the Convention.[110]

Commercial acts

Of all state activities for which immunity is no longer to be obtained, that of commercial transactions is the primary example and the definition of such activity is crucial.[111]

Section 3(3) of the State Immunity Act 1978 defines the term 'commercial transaction' to mean:

(a) any contract for the supply of goods or services;

(b) any loan or other transaction for the provision of finance and any guarantee or indemnity in respect of any such transaction or of any other financial obligation; and

(c) any other transaction or activity (whether of a commercial, industrial, financial, professional or other similar character) into which a state enters or in which it engages otherwise than in the exercise of sovereign authority.

---

[108] *Ibid.*, paras. 45 ff.; 129 ILR, pp. 732 ff. Note that the controversial case of *Ferrini* v. *Federal Republic of Germany* before the Italian Court of Cassation is to contrary effect, (2004) Cass sez un 5044/04: see P. De Sena and F. De Vittor, 'State Immunity and Human Rights: The Italian Supreme Court Decision on the *Ferrini* Case', 16 EJIL, 2005, p. 89; Fox, 'State Immunity and the Crime of Torture', and Lords Bingham and Hoffmann in *Jones* v. *Saudi Arabia* at paras. 22 and 63 respectively.

[109] [2000] 1 AC 147; 119 ILR, p. 135.

[110] See further below, p. 735. Note, however, that Lords Hope, Millett and Phillips held that there was no immunity for widespread and systematic acts of official torture, [2000] 1 AC 147, 246–8, 275–7, 288–92; 119 ILR, pp. 198–201, 228–31, 242–7.

[111] In his discussion of the development of the restrictive theory of sovereign or state immunity in *Alcom* v. *Republic of Colombia* [1984] 2 All ER 6, 9; 74 ILR, pp. 180, 181, Lord Diplock noted that the critical distinction was between what a state did in the exercise of its sovereign authority and what it did in the course of commercial activities. The former enjoyed immunity, the latter did not. See also Schreuer, *State Immunity*, chapter 2.

Thus a wide range of transactions are covered[112] and, as Lord Diplock pointed out,[113] the 1978 Act does not adopt the straightforward dichotomy between acts *jure imperii* and those *jure gestionis*. Any contract falling within section 3 would be subject to the exercise of jurisdiction and the distinction between sovereign and non-sovereign acts in this context would not be relevant, except in so far as transactions falling within section 3(3)c were concerned, in the light of the use of the term 'sovereign authority'. The Act contains no reference to the public/private question, but the *Congreso* case (dealing with the pre-Act law) would seem to permit examples from foreign jurisdictions to be drawn upon in order to determine the nature of 'the exercise of sovereign authority'.

Section 3(1) of the State Immunity Act provides that a state is not immune as respects proceedings relating to:

(a) a commercial transaction entered into by the state; or
(b) an obligation of the state which by virtue of a contract (whether a commercial transaction or not) falls to be performed wholly or partly in the United Kingdom.[114]

The scope of section 3(1)a was discussed by the Court in *Australia and New Zealand Banking Group* v. *Commonwealth of Australia*.[115] This case arose out of the collapse of the International Tin Council in 1985. The ensuing litigation sought, by various routes, to ascertain whether the member states of the ITC (which was itself an international organisation with separate personality) could be held liable themselves for the debts of that organisation – a prospect vigorously opposed by the states concerned. The case in question concerned an attempt by the brokers and banks to hold the member states of the ITC liable in tort for losses caused by misrepresentation and fraudulent trading.

It was argued by the defendants that as far as section 3(1) was concerned, the activity in question had to be not only commercial within the Act's definition but also undertaken 'otherwise than in the exercise of sovereign authority'. Evans J saw little difference in practice between the two terms in the context.[116] The defendants also argued that the term

---

[112] Thus, for example, the defence of sovereign immunity was not available in an action relating to a contract for the repair of an ambassador's residence, *Planmount Ltd* v. *Republic of Zaire* [1981] 1 All ER 1110; 64 ILR, p. 268.

[113] *Alcom* v. *Republic of Colombia* [1984] 2 All ER 6, 10; 74 ILR, p. 183.

[114] Note that by s. 3(3), s. 3(1) does not apply to a contract of employment between a state and an individual.

[115] 1989, transcript, pp. 52 ff.   [116] *Ibid.*, p. 54.

'activity' meant something more than a single act or sequence of acts. Evans J did not accept this, but did emphasise that the activity in question had to be examined in context. It was held that both the trading and loan contracts under discussion in the case were commercial and that, if it could be demonstrated that the member states of the ITC had authorised them, such authorisation would amount to commercial activity within the meaning of section 3.[117] However, in practice the distinction between commercial activities undertaken by a state and activities undertaken under the colour of sovereign authority may be a difficult one to draw. In *AIC Ltd* v. *Nigeria*, the High Court decided that proceedings to register a foreign judgment were not proceedings relating to a commercial transaction even if the foreign judgment concerned proceedings relating to such a transaction, so that the exception to immunity did not apply.[118] In *KJ International* v. *MV Oscar Jupiter*, the Supreme Court of South Africa held that a commercial transaction was not necessarily a transaction with a commercial purpose and that where a ship had been transferred by the Romanian government to one company which had then transferred it to another, the activities of the latter could not be seen as commercial transactions of the government. Accordingly, no loss of immunity would take place for this reason. However, the transfer of the ship by the Romanian government to the Moldovan government to be operated by the latter for profit did constitute a commercial transaction, so that immunity was lost.[119] In *Svenska Petroleum* v. *Lithuania*, the Court of Appeal emphasised that the distinction between a commercial transaction and a transaction entered into by a state in the exercise of its sovereign authority drawn in s. 3 of the State Immunity Act, which was virtually identical to article 2(1)c of the UN Convention on Jurisdictional Immunities which was accepted as reflecting the current international thinking on the topic,[120] was not an easy matter to determine.[121] It was held that s. 3 was one of a group of sections dealing with the courts' adjudicative jurisdiction and that it was therefore natural to interpret the phrase in that context as being directed to the subject-matter of the proceedings themselves rather than the source of the legal relationship which had given rise to them.[122] Accordingly, the

---

[117] *Ibid.*, pp. 56–7.

[118] [2003] EWHC 1357; 129 ILR, p. 571. This was approved by the Court of Appeal in *Svenska Petroleum* v. *Lithuania* [2006] EWCA Civ 1529, para. 137.

[119] 131 ILR, p. 529.

[120] Citing Lord Bingham in *Jones* v. *Saudi Arabia* [2006] UKHL 26, para. 8, and see below, p. 725.

[121] [2006] EWCA Civ 1529, paras. 132–3.   [122] *Ibid.*, para. 137.

government of Lithuania was not immune from proceedings to enforce an arbitration award.

The scope of section 3(1)b was discussed by the Court of Appeal in *Maclaine Watson* v. *Department of Trade and Industry*,[123] which concerned the direct action by the brokers and banks against the member states of the ITC in respect of liability for the debts of the organisation on a contractual basis. It was held that the 'contract' referred to need not have been entered into by the state as such. That particular phrase was absent from section 3(1)b. Accordingly, the member states would not have been able to benefit from immunity in the kind of secondary liability of a guarantee nature that the plaintiffs were *inter alia* basing their case upon.[124] This view was adopted in the tort action against the member states[125] in the more difficult context where the obligation in question was a tortious obligation on the part of the member states, that is the authorisation or procuring of a misrepresentation inducing the creditors concerned to make a contract with another party (the ITC).[126]

Section 1603(d) of the US Foreign Sovereign Immunities Act 1976 defines 'commercial activity' as 'a regular course of commercial conduct or a particular commercial transaction or act'. It is also noted that the commercial character of an activity is to be determined by reference to the nature of the activity rather than its purpose. The courts have held that the purchases of food were commercial activities[127] as were purchases of cement,[128] the sending by a government ministry of artists to perform in the US under a US impresario[129] and activities by state airlines.[130]

The issuance of foreign governmental Treasury notes has also been held to constitute a commercial activity, but one which once validly statute-barred by passage of time cannot be revived or altered.[131]

---

[123] [1988] 3 WLR 1033; 80 ILR, p. 49.

[124] [1988] 3 WLR 1104–5 (Kerr LJ) and 1130 (Nourse LJ); 80 ILR, pp. 119, 148.

[125] *Australia and New Zealand Banking Group* v. *Commonwealth of Australia*, 1989, transcript, pp. 57–9.

[126] It should be noted that Evans J reached his decision on this point only with considerable hesitation and reluctance, *ibid.*, p. 59.

[127] See e.g. *Gemini Shipping* v. *Foreign Trade Organisation for Chemicals and Foodstuffs* 63 ILR, p. 569 and *ADM Milling Co.* v. *Republic of Bolivia* 63 ILR, p. 56.

[128] *NAC* v. *Federal Republic of Nigeria* 63 ILR, p. 137.

[129] *United Euram Co.* v. *USSR* 63 ILR, p. 228.   [130] *Argentine Airlines* v. *Ross* 63 ILR, p. 195.

[131] *Schmidt* v. *Polish People's Republic* 742 F.2d 67 (1984). See also *Jackson* v. *People's Republic of China* 596 F.Supp. 386 (1984); *Amoco Overseas Oil Co.* v. *Compagnie Nationale Algérienne* 605 F.2d 648 (1979); 63 ILR, p. 252 and *Corporacion Venezolana de Fomenta* v. *Vintero Sales* 629 F.2d 786 (1980); 63 ILR, p. 477.

In *Callejo v. Bancomer*,[132] a case in which a Mexican bank refused to redeem a certificate of deposit, the District Court dismissed the action on the ground that the bank was an instrumentality of the Mexican government and thus benefited from sovereign immunity, although the Court of Appeals decided the issue on the basis that the act of state doctrine applied since an investigation of a sovereign act performed wholly within the foreign government's territory would otherwise be required. In other cases, US courts have dealt with the actions of Mexican banks consequent upon Mexican exchange control regulations on the basis of sovereign immunity.[133] However, the Supreme Court in *Republic of Argentina v. Weltover Inc.*[134] held that the act of issuing government bonds was a commercial activity and the unilateral rescheduling of payment of these bonds also constituted a commercial activity. The Court, noting that the term 'commercial' was largely undefined in the legislation, took the view that its definition related to the meaning it had under the restrictive theory of sovereign immunity and particularly as discussed in *Alfred Dunhill v. Republic of Cuba*.[135] Accordingly, 'when a foreign government acts, not as regulator of a market, but in the manner of a private player within it, the foreign sovereign's actions are "commercial" within the meaning of the FSIA . . . the issue is whether the particular actions that the foreign state performs (whatever the motives behind them) are the *type* of actions by which a private party engages in "trade or traffic or commerce"'. In this case, the bonds in question were debt instruments that could be held by

---

[132] 764 F.2d 1101 (1985). See also *Chisholm v. Bank of Jamaica* 643 F.Supp. 1393 (1986); 121 ILR, p. 487. Note that in *Dole Food Co. v. Patrickson*, the US Supreme Court, in its decision of 22 April 2003, held that in order to constitute an instrumentality under the Foreign Sovereign Immunities Act, the foreign state concerned must itself own a majority of a corporation's shares. Indirect subsidiaries would not benefit from immunity since such companies cannot come within the statutory language granting instrumentality status to an entity a 'majority of whose shares or other ownership interest is owned by a foreign state or political subdivision thereof': see s. 1603(b)(2). Only direct ownership would satisfy the statutory requirement. The statutory reference to ownership of 'shares' showed that Congress intended coverage to turn on formal corporate ownership and a corporation and its shareholders were distinct entities. Further, instrumentality status was to be determined as at the time of the filing of the complaint: see Case No. 01–593, pp. 4–8.

[133] See e.g. *Braka v. Nacional Financiera*, No. 83-4161 (SDNY 9 July 1984) and *Frankel v. Banco Nacional de Mexico*, No. 82-6457 (SDNY 31 May 1983), cited in 80 AJIL, 1986, p. 172, note 5.

[134] 119 L Ed 2d 394 (1992); 100 ILR, p. 509.

[135] 425 US 682 (1976); 66 ILR, p. 212. Here, the plurality stated that a foreign state engaging in commercial activities was exercising only those powers that can be exercised by private citizens, 425 US 704.

private persons and were negotiable and could be traded on the international market.[136] This approach was followed in *Guevera* v. *Peru* by the Court of Appeals for the Eleventh Circuit, which held that a foreign state's offer of a reward in exchange for information concerning a fugitive fell within the 'commercial activity' exception to immunity.[137]

The purchase of military equipment by Haiti for use by its army[138] and a military training agreement whereby a foreign soldier was in the US were held not to be commercial activities.[139] It has also been decided that Somalia's participation in an Agency for International Development programme constituted a public or governmental act,[140] while the publication of a libel in a journal distributed in the US was not a commercial activity where the journal concerned constituted an official commentary of the Soviet government.[141] Section 1604(a)4 also provides for an exception to immunity where 'rights in immovable property situated in the United States are in issue' and the Supreme Court in *Permanent Mission of India to the US* v. *City of New York* held that this provided jurisdiction over a suit brought by New York City to establish tax liens on real property owned by the governments of India and Mongolia.[142]

Many cases before the US courts have, however, centred upon the jurisdictional requirements of section 1605(a), which states that a foreign state is not immune in any case in which the action is based upon a commercial activity carried on in the US by a foreign state; or upon an act performed in the US in connection with a foreign state's commercial activity elsewhere; or upon an act outside the territory of the US in connection with a foreign state's commercial activity elsewhere, when that act causes a direct effect in the US.[143]

---

[136] 119 L Ed 2d 394, 405; 100 ILR, p. 515. Reaffirmed in *Saudi Arabia* v. *Nelson* 123 L Ed 2d 47, 61 (1993); 100 ILR, pp. 545, 553.

[137] DC Docket No. 04-23223-CV-MGC, 1 November 2006.

[138] *Aerotrade Inc.* v. *Republic of Haiti* 63 ILR, p. 41.

[139] *Castro* v. *Saudi Arabia* 63 ILR, p. 419.

[140] *Transamerican Steamship Corp.* v. *Somali Democratic Republic* 590 F.Supp. 968 (1984) and 767 F.2d 998. This is based upon the legislative history of the 1976 Act: see the HR Rep. No. 1487, 94th Cong., 2d Sess. 16 (1976).

[141] *Yessenin-Volpin* v. *Novosti Press Agency* 443 F.Supp. 849 (1978); 63 ILR, p. 127. See also Schreuer, *State Immunity*, pp. 42–3, providing a list of criteria with respect to identifying commercial transactions.

[142] 127 S. Ct. 2352 (2007).

[143] See e.g. *International Shoe Co.* v. *Washington* 326 US 310 (1945); *McGee* v. *International Life Insurance Co.* 355 US 220 (1957); *Libyan-American Oil Co.* v. *Libya* 482 F.Supp. 1175 (1980); 62 ILR, p. 220; *Perez et al.* v. *The Bahamas* 482 F.Supp. 1208 (1980); 63 ILR,

In *Zedan* v. *Kingdom of Saudi Arabia*,[144] for example, the US Court of Appeals in discussing the scope of section 1605(a)(2) emphasised that the commercial activity in question taking place in the US had to be substantial, so that a telephone call in the US which initiated a sequence of events which resulted in the plaintiff working in Saudi Arabia was not sufficient. Additionally, where an act is performed in the US in connection with a commercial activity of a foreign state elsewhere, this act must in itself be sufficient to form the basis of a cause of action,[145] while the direct effect in the US provision of an act abroad in connection with a foreign state's commercial activity elsewhere was subject to a high threshold. As the Court noted,[146] in cases where this clause was held to have been satisfied, 'something legally significant actually happened in the United States'.[147] However, in *Republic of Argentina* v. *Weltover Inc.*,[148] the Court rejected the suggestion that section 1605(a)(2) contained any unexpressed requirement as to substantiality or foreseeability and supported the Court of Appeals' view that an effect was direct if it followed as an immediate consequence of the defendant's activity.[149] In the case, it was sufficient that the respondents had designated their accounts in New York as the place of payment and Argentina had made some interest payments into them prior to the rescheduling decision.

Article 10 of the UN Convention on Jurisdictional Immunities provides that there is no immunity where a state engages in a 'commercial transaction' with a foreign natural or juridical person (but not another state) in a situation where by virtue of the rules of private international law a dispute comes before the courts of another state, unless the parties to the commercial transaction otherwise expressly agree. However, the

---

p. 350 and *Thos. P. Gonzalez Corp* v. *Consejo Nacional de Produccion de Costa Rica* 614 F.2d 1247 (1980); 63 ILR, p. 370, aff'd 652 F.2d 186 (1982).

[144] 849 F.2d 1511 (1988).

[145] *Ibid.* Note that the Supreme Court in *Saudi Arabia* v. *Nelson* 123 L Ed 2d 47, 58–9; 100 ILR, pp. 545, 550–1, held that the phrase 'based on' appearing in the section, meant 'those elements of a claim that, if proven, would entitle a plaintiff to relief under his theory of the case'.

[146] 849 F.2d 1515.

[147] Referring to the cases of *Transamerican Steamship Corp.* v. *Somali Democratic Republic* 767 F.2d 998, 1004, where demand for payment in the US by an agency of the Somali government and actual bank transfers were held to be sufficient, and *Texas Trading & Milling Corp.* v. *Federal Republic of Nigeria* 647 F.2d 300, 312; 63 ILR, pp. 552, 563, where refusal to pay letters of credit issued by a US bank and payable in the US to financially injured claimants was held to suffice.

[148] 119 L Ed 2d 394 (1992); 100 ILR, p. 509.

[149] 119 L Ed 2d 407; 100 ILR, p. 517, citing 941 F.2d at 152.

immunity of a state is unaffected where a state enterprise or other entity established by a state which has an independent legal personality and is capable of suing or being sued and acquiring, owning or possessing and disposing of property, including property which that state has authorised it to operate or manage, is involved in a proceeding which relates to a commercial transaction in which that entity is engaged.

Article 2(1)c of the Convention provides that the term 'commercial transaction' means:

(i) any commercial contract or transaction for the sale of goods or the supply of services;

(ii) any contract for a loan or other transaction of a financial nature, including any obligation of guarantee or of indemnity in respect of any such loan or transaction;

(iii) any other contract or transaction of a commercial, industrial, trading or professional nature, but not including a contract of employment of persons.[150]

Contracts of employment

Section 4(1) of the State Immunity Act 1978 provides that a state is not immune as respects proceedings relating to a contract of employment between the state and an individual where the contract was made in the UK or where the work is to be performed wholly or in part there.[151] The section does not apply if at the time of the proceedings the individual is a national of the state concerned[152] or at the time the contract was made the individual was neither a national nor habitual resident of the UK or the parties to the contract have otherwise agreed in writing. However, these provisions do not apply with regard to members of a diplomatic mission or consular post,[153] a fact that has rendered section 4(1) significantly weaker.[154] There have been a number of cases concerning immunity and contracts of employment, particularly with regard to employment at foreign embassies. In *Sengupta* v. *Republic of India*, for example, a broad

---

[150] See as to earlier drafts of this provision, Report of the International Law Commission, 1991, pp. 13 and 69, and *Yearbook of the ILC*, 1986, vol. II, part 2, p. 8.

[151] See e.g. H. Fox, 'Employment Contracts as an Exception to State Immunity: Is All Public Service Immune?', 66 BYIL, 1995, p. 97, and R. Garnett, 'State Immunity in Employment Matters', 46 ICLQ, 1997, p. 81.

[152] See e.g. *Arab Republic of Egypt* v. *Gamal Eldin* [1996] 2 All ER 237.

[153] S. 16(1)a.

[154] See e.g. *Saudi Arabia* v. *Ahmed* [1996] 2 All ER 248; 104 ILR, p. 629.

decision prior to the 1978 Act, the Employment Appeal Tribunal held on the basis of customary law that immunity existed with regard to a contract of employment dispute since the workings of the mission in question constituted a form of sovereign activity.[155]

The position in other countries is varied. In *United States of America v. The Public Service Alliance of Canada (Re Canada Labour Code)*, for example, it was held that the conduct of labour relations at a foreign military base was not a commercial activity so that the US was entitled to sovereign immunity in proceedings before a labour tribunal,[156] while in *Norwegian Embassy* v. *Quattri*, for example, the Italian Court of Cassation referred to an international trend of restricting immunity with regard to employment contracts. The Court held that under customary international law immunity was available, but this was restricted to acts carried out in the exercise of the foreign state's public law functions. Accordingly, no immunity existed with regard to acts carried out by the foreign state in the capacity of a private individual under the internal law of the receiving state. An example of this would be employment disputes where the employees' duties were of a merely auxiliary nature and not intrinsic to the foreign public law entity.[157] In *Barrandon* v. *USA*, the French Court of Cassation (1992) and subsequently the Court of Appeal of Versailles (1995) held that immunity was a privilege not guaranteed by an international treaty to which France was a party and could only be invoked by a state which believed it was entitled to rely upon it. Immunity from jurisdiction was limited to acts of sovereign power (*puissance publique*) or acts performed in the interest of a public service. In the instant case, the plaintiff, a nurse and medical secretary at the US embassy, had performed functions clearly in the interest of a public service of the respondent state and immunity was therefore applicable.[158] However, on appeal the Court of Cassation (1998) reversed this decision and held that her tasks did not give her any special responsibility for the performance of the public

---

[155] 65 ILR, p. 325. See also *Military Affairs Office of the Embassy of the State of Kuwait* v. *Caramba-Coker*, EAT 1054/02/RN, Employment Appeals Tribunal (2003) and *Aziz* v. *Republic of Yemen* [2005] EWCA Civ 745.

[156] (1992) 91 DLR (4th) 449; 94 ILR, p. 264.

[157] 114 ILR, p. 525. See also *Canada* v. *Cargnello* 114 ILR, p. 559. See also a number of German cases also holding that employment functions forming part of the core sphere of sovereign activity of the foreign states would attract immunity, otherwise not, *X* v. *Argentina* 114 ILR, p. 502; the *French Consulate Disabled Employee* case, 114 ILR, p. 508 and *Muller* v. *USA* 114 ILR, p. 513.

[158] 113 ILR, p. 464.

service of the embassy, so that her dismissal was an ordinary act of administration so that immunity was not applicable.[159] Practice is far from consistent. Courts in a number of states have accepted immunity claims in such state immunity/employment situations,[160] while courts in others have rejected such claims.[161]

Other non-immunity areas

Domestic and international instruments prohibit sovereign immunity in cases of tortious activity.[162] Article 11 of the European Convention on State Immunity, 1972, for example, refers to 'redress for injury to the person or damage to tangible property, if the facts which occasioned the injury or damage occurred in the territory of the state of the forum, and if the author of the injury or damage was present in that territory at the time when those facts occurred'.

Section 5 of the UK State Immunity Act provides that a state is not immune as respects proceedings in respect of death or personal injury, or damage to or loss of tangible property, caused by an act or omission in the UK,[163] while section 1605(a)(5) of the US Foreign Sovereign Immunities Act 1976, although basically similar, does include exceptions relating to the exercise of the state's discretionary functions and to claims arising out of malicious prosecution, abuse of process, libel, slander, misrepresentation, deceit or interference with contractual rights. In *Letelier* v. *Chile*,[164] the Court rejected a claim that the torts exception in this

---

[159] 116 ILR, p. 622. The case was remitted to the Court of Appeal for decision.

[160] See e.g. the *Brazilian Embassy Employee* case, 116 ILR, p. 625 (Portuguese Supreme Court) and *Ramos* v. *USA* 116 ILR, p. 634 (High Court of Lisbon).

[161] See e.g. *Landano* v. *USA* 116 ILR, p. 636 (Labour Court of Geneva); *Nicoud* v. *USA* 116 ILR, p. 650 (Labour Court of Geneva); *M* v. *Arab Republic of Egypt* 116 ILR, p. 656 (Swiss Federal Tribunal); *R* v. *Republic of Iraq* 116 ILR, p. 664 (Swiss Federal Tribunal); *François* v. *State of Canada* 115 ILR, p. 418 (Labour Court of Brussels); *Kingdom of Morocco* v. *DR* 115 ILR, p. 421 (Labour Court of Brussels); *De Queiroz* v. *State of Portugal* 115 ILR, p. 430 (Labour Court of Brussels); *Zambian Embassy* v. *Sendanayake* 114 ILR, p. 532 (Italian Court of Cassation), and *Carbonar* v. *Magurno* 114 ILR, p. 534 (Italian Court of Cassation).

[162] See e.g. Schreuer, *State Immunity*, chapter 3.

[163] See also s. 6 of the Canadian State Immunity Act 1982; s. 6 of the South African Foreign Sovereign Immunity Act 1981; s. 7 of the Singapore State Immunity Act 1979; and s. 13 of the Australian Foreign States Immunities Act 1985. See also article 12 of the UN Convention on Jurisdictional Immunities.

[164] 488 F.Supp. 665 (1980); 63 ILR, p. 378.

legislation referred only to private acts and held that it could apply to political assassinations.[165]

Sections 6-11 of the UK Act detail the remainder of the wide-ranging non-immunity areas and include proceedings relating to immovable property (section 6)[166] except with regard to proceedings concerning a state's title to or right to possession of property used for the purposes of a diplomatic mission;[167] patents, trademarks, designs, plant breeders' rights or copyrights (section 7); proceedings relating to a state's membership of a body corporate, an unincorporated body or partnership, with members other than states which is incorporated or constituted under UK law or is controlled from or has its principal place of business in the UK (section 8); where a state has agreed in writing to submit to arbitration and with respect to proceedings in the UK courts relating to that arbitration (section 9); Admiralty proceedings with regard to state-owned ships used or intended for use for commercial purposes (section 10); and proceedings relating to liability for various taxes, such as VAT (section 11). This, together with generally similar provisions in the legislation of other states,[168] demonstrates how restricted the concept of sovereign acts is now becoming in practice in the context of sovereign immunity, although definitional problems remain.

The personality issue – instrumentalities and parts of the state[169]

Whether the absolute or restrictive theory is applied, the crucial factor is to determine the entity entitled to immunity. If the entity, in very general terms, is not part of the apparatus of state, then no immunity can arise. Shaw LJ in *Trendtex Trading Corporation Ltd* v. *Central Bank of*

---

[165] Note that the Greek Special Supreme Court in *Margellos* v. *Federal Republic of Germany* held that in customary international law a foreign state continued to enjoy immunity in respect of a tort committed in another state in which its armed forces had participated, 129 ILR, p. 526. See also article 31 of the European Convention on State Immunity. See also the *Distomo Massacre* case, 129 ILR, p. 556.

[166] The winding-up of a company is not protected by immunity where the state is not directly impleaded: see s. 6(3) and *Re Rafidain* [1992] BCLC 301; 101 ILR, p. 332.

[167] S. 16(1)b.

[168] See e.g. s. 1605 of the US Foreign Sovereign Immunities Act 1976 and ss. 10–21 of the Australian Foreign States Immunities Act 1985. Note in particular the inclusion in the US legislation of an exception to immunity with regard to rights in property taken in violation of international law, s. 1605(a)(3), which does not appear in other domestic legislation.

[169] See e.g. Schreuer, *State Immunity*, chapter 5.

Nigeria[170] cautioned against too facile an attribution of immunity particularly in the light of the growth of governmental functions, since its acceptance resulted in a significant disadvantage to the other party.

A department of government would, however, be entitled to immunity, even if it had a separate legal personality under its own law.[171] The issue was discussed in detail in the *Trendtex* case. It was emphasised that recourse should be had to all the circumstances of the case. The fact of incorporation as a separate legal identity was noted in *Baccus SRL v. Servicio Nacional del Trigo*[172] and both Donaldson J at first instance and Denning MR emphasised this.[173] The question arises in analysing whether a body is a corporation or not, and indeed whether it is or is not an arm of government, as to which law is relevant. Each country may have its own rules governing incorporation, and similarly with regard to government departments. Should English law therefore merely accept the conclusions of the foreign law? The majority of the Court in *Baccus* was of the view that foreign law was decisive in questions relating to incorporation and whether corporateness was consistent with the recognition of immunity, and to a certain extent this was accepted in *Trendtex*. Shaw LJ declared that 'the constitution and powers of Nigerian corporation must be viewed in the light of the domestic law of Nigeria'.[174] However, the status on the international scene of the entity in question must be decided, it was held, by the law of the country in which the issue as to its status has been raised. The Court had to determine whether the Nigerian Bank could constitute a government department as understood in English law.[175] It was also noted that where a material difference existed between English law and the foreign law, this would be taken into account, but the Court was satisfied that this was not the case in *Trendtex*.

This position of pre-eminence for English law must not be understood to imply the application of decisions of English courts relating to immunities granted internally. These could be at best only rough guides to be utilised depending on the circumstances of each case. If the view taken by the foreign law was not conclusive, neither was the attitude adopted by the foreign government. It was a factor to be considered, again, but no more than that. In this, the Court followed *Krajina v. Tass Agency*.[176] The point

---

[170] [1977] 2 WLR 356, 383; 64 ILR, pp. 122, 147.
[171] *Baccus SRL v. Servicio Nacional del Trigo* [1957] 1 QB 438; 23 ILR, p. 160.
[172] [1957] 1 QB 438, 467.   [173] [1977] 2 WLR 356, 370; 64 ILR, p. 133.
[174] [1977] 2 WLR 356, 385; 64 ILR, p. 149.   [175] [1977] 2 WLR 356, 385; 64 ILR, p. 175.
[176] [1949] 2 All ER 274.

was also made that the evidence provided by Nigerian officials, including the High Commissioner, that the Bank was a government organ, was not conclusive. This was because the officials might very well be applying a test of governmental control which would not be decisive for the courts of this country.[177]

Of more importance was the legislative intention of the government in creating and regulating the entity and the degree of its control. Stephenson LJ in fact based his decision upon this point. An express provision in the creative legislation to the effect that the Bank was an arm of government was not necessary, but the Bank had to prove that the intention to make it an organ of the Nigerian state was of necessity to be implied from the enabling Central Bank of Nigeria Act 1958 and subsequent decrees. This the Bank had failed to do and Stephenson LJ accordingly allowed the appeal.[178] It could be argued that the judge was placing too much stress upon this aspect, particularly in the light of the overall approach of the Court in applying the functional rather than the personality test. In many ways, Stephenson LJ was also looking at the attributes of the Bank but from a slightly different perspective. He examined the powers and duties of the entity and denied it immunity since the intention of the government to establish the Bank as an arm of itself could not be clearly demonstrated. The other judges were concerned with the functions of the Bank as implying governmental status *per se*.

The Court clearly accepted the functional test as the crucial guide to the determination of sovereign immunity. In this it was following the modern approach which has precipitated the change in emphasis from the personality of the entity for which immunity is claimed to the nature of the subject matter. This functional test looks to the powers, duties and control of the entity within the framework of its constitution and activities.

In such difficult borderline decisions, the proposition put forward by Shaw LJ is to be welcomed. He noted that:

> where the issue of status trembles on a fine edge, the absence of any positive indication that the body in question was intended to possess sovereign status and its attendant privileges must perforce militate against the view that it enjoys that status or is entitled to those privileges.[179]

---

177 [1977] 2 WLR 356, 370 and 374; 64 ILR, p. 137, 139.
178 [1977] 2 WLR 356, 374–6. See also Shaw LJ, *ibid.*, p. 384; 64 ILR, p. 149.
179 *Ibid.*

In *Czarnikow Ltd v. Rolimpex*,[180] the House of Lords accepted as correct the findings of the arbitrators that although Rolimpex had been established by the Polish government and was controlled by it, it was not so closely connected with the government as to be an organ or department of the state. It had separate legal personality and had considerable freedom in day-to-day commercial activities.

Under section 14(1) of the State Immunity Act of 1978, a state is deemed to include the sovereign or other head of state in his public capacity,[181] the government and any department of that government, but not any entity 'which is distinct from the executive organs of the government of the state and capable of suing or being sued'. This modifies the *Baccus* and *Trendtex* approaches to some extent. Such a separate entity would only be immune if the proceedings related to acts done 'in the exercise of sovereign authority' and the circumstances are such that a state would have been so immune.[182] In determining such a situation, all the relevant circumstances should be taken into consideration.[183] In *Kuwait Airways Corporation v. Iraqi Airways Co.*, the House of Lords, in discussing the position of the Iraqi Airways Company (IAC), analysed the relevant transactions as a whole but felt able to separate out differing elements and treat them discretely. In brief, aircraft of the plaintiffs (KAC) had been seized by IAC consequent upon the Iraqi invasion of Kuwait in 1990 and pursuant to orders from the Iraqi government. Revolutionary Command Council[184] resolution 369 purported to dissolve KAC and transfer all of its assets to IAC. From that point on, IAC treated the aircraft in question as part of its own fleet. The issue was whether the fact that the initial appropriation was by governmental action meant that the plea of immunity continued to be available to IAC. The House of Lords held that it was not. Once resolution 369 came into effect the situation changed and immunity was no longer applicable since the retention and use of the aircraft were not acts done in the exercise of sovereign authority. A characterisation of the appropriation of the property as a sovereign act could not be determinative of the characterisation of its subsequent retention and use.[185]

The US Foreign Sovereign Immunities Act of 1976 provides in section 1603 that 'foreign state' includes a political subdivision of such a state

---

[180] [1979] AC 351, 364 (Lord Wilberforce) and 367 (Viscount Dilhorne).
[181] See further below, p. 735.   [182] S. 14(2).
[183] See e.g. *Holland* v. *Lampen-Wolfe* [2000] 1 WLR 1573.
[184] Essentially the Iraqi government.
[185] [1995] 1 WLR 1147, 1163 (per Lord Goff). Cf. Lord Mustill at 1174 who argued that the context should be taken as a whole so that immunity continued.

and its agencies or instrumentalities. This is defined to mean any entity which is a separate legal person and which is an organ of a foreign state or political subdivision thereof or a majority of whose shares or other ownership interest is owned by a foreign state or political subdivision thereof and which is neither a citizen of a state of the United States nor created under the laws of any third country.[186] This issue of personality has occasioned problems and some complex decisions.[187]

In *First National City Bank* v. *Banco Para el Comercio Exterior de Cuba (Bancec),*[188] for example, the Supreme Court suggested a presumption of separateness for state entities, under which their separate legal personalities were to be recognised unless applicable equitable principles mandated otherwise or the parent entity so completely dominated the subsidiary as to render it an agent of the parent.[189]

The meaning of the term 'government' as it appears in section 14(1) of the State Immunity Act was discussed in *Propend Finance* v. *Sing.* The Court of Appeal held that it must be given a broad meaning and, in particular, that it should be construed in the light of the concept of sovereign authority. Accordingly, 'government' meant more than it would in other contexts in English law where it would mean simply the government of the United Kingdom. In particular it would include the performance of police functions as part of governmental activity. Further, individual employees or officers of a foreign state were entitled to the same protection as that which envelops the state itself. The Court thus concluded that both the Australian Federal Police superintendent and Commissioner, the defendants in the case, were covered by state immunity.[190] The view that the agent of a foreign state would enjoy immunity in respect of his acts of a sovereign or governmental nature was reaffirmed in *Re P (No. 2)*. The Court accepted that the removal from the country of the family of a diplomat based in the UK and their return to the US at the end of his mission was in compliance with a direct order from his government. This

---

[186] See e.g. *Gittler* v. *German Information Centre* 408 NYS 2d 600 (1978); 63 ILR, p. 170; *Carey* v. *National Oil Co.* 453 F.Supp. 1097 (1978); 63 ILR, p. 164 and *Yessenin-Volpin* v. *Novosti Press Agency* 443 F.Supp. 849 (1978); 63 ILR, p. 127. See also Sinclair, 'Sovereign Immunity', pp. 248–9 and 258–9. Note, in addition, articles 6 and 7 of the European Convention on State Immunity, 1972.

[187] See also article 2(1)b of the UN Convention on Jurisdictional Immunities: see above, p. 725.

[188] 462 US 611 (1983); 80 ILR, p. 566.

[189] See also *Foremost-McKesson Inc.* v. *Islamic Republic of Iran* 905 F.2d 438 (1990).

[190] 111 ILR, pp. 611, 667–71.

was held to constitute an act of a governmental nature and thus subject to state immunity.[191] In *Jones* v. *Saudi Arabia*, the House of Lords, overturning the Court of Appeal decision to the contrary on this point, held that there was 'a wealth of authority to show that ... the foreign state is entitled to claim immunity for its servants as it could if sued itself. The foreign state's right to immunity cannot be circumvented by suing its servants or agents.'[192]

One particular issue that has caused controversy in the past relates to the status of component units of federal states.[193] There have been cases asserting immunity[194] and denying immunity[195] in such circumstances. In *Mellenger* v. *New Brunswick Development Corporation*,[196] Lord Denning emphasised that since under the Canadian Constitution

> Each provincial government, within its own sphere, retained its independence and autonomy directly under the Crown ... It follows that the Province of New Brunswick is a sovereign state in its own right and entitled if it so wishes to claim sovereign immunity.

However, article 28 of the European Convention on State Immunity, 1972 provides that constituent states of a federal state do not enjoy immunity, although this general principle is subject to the proviso that federal state parties may declare by notification that their constituent states may invoke the benefits and carry out the obligations of the Convention.[197]

The State Immunity Act follows this pattern in that component units of a federation are not entitled to immunity. However, section 14(5) provides that the Act may be made applicable to the 'constituent territories of a

---

[191] [1998] 1 FLR 1027, 1034–5; 114 ILR, p. 485. See also J. C. Barker, 'State Immunity, Diplomatic Immunity and Act of State: A Triple Protection Against Legal Action?', 47 ICLQ, 1998, p. 950.

[192] [2006] UKHL 26, para. 10 (per Lord Bingham); 129 ILR, p. 717. This applied to acts done to such persons as servants or agents, officials or functionaries of the state, *ibid.*

[193] See e.g. I. Bernier, *International Legal Aspects of Federalism*, London, 1973, pp. 121 ff. and Sucharitkul, *State Immunities*, p. 106.

[194] See e.g. *Feldman* c. *État de Bahia*, Pasicrisie Belge, 208, II, 55; *État de Céara* c. *Dorr et autres* 4 AD, p. 39; *État de Céara* c. *D'Archer de Montgascon*, 6 AD, p. 162 and *Dumont* c. *État d'Amazonas* 15 AD, p. 140. See also *État de Hesse* c. *Jean Neger* 74 Revue Générale de Droit International Public, 1970, p. 1108.

[195] See e.g. *Sullivan* v. *State of Sao Paulo* 122 F.2d 355 (1941); 10 AD, p. 178.

[196] [1971] 2 All ER 593, 595; 52 ILR, pp. 322, 324. See also *Swiss-Israel Trade Bank* v. *Salta* 55 ILR, p. 411.

[197] See e.g. I. Sinclair, 'The European Convention on State Immunity', 22 ICLQ, 1973, pp. 254, 279–80.

federal state by specific Order in Council'.[198] Where no such order is made, any such 'constituent territory' would be entitled to immunity only if it conformed with section 14(2), being a separate entity acting in the exercise of sovereign authority and in circumstances in which the state would be immune.[199] While the matter is thus determined in so far as the Act operates in the particular circumstances, s. 16(4) states that Part I of the Act does not apply to criminal proceedings. In the case of *Alamieyeseigha* v. *CPS*, the Court did not accept that the state of Bayelsa, a constituent unit of the Nigerian Federation, and its Governor were entitled to state immunity with regard to criminal proceedings, a claim made on the basis of *Mellenger*.[200] Key to the decision was the fact that Bayelsa state had no legal powers to conduct foreign relations on its own behalf, external affairs being exclusively reserved to the federal government under the Nigerian Constitution. As further and decisive evidence, the Court referred to the certificate from the UK Foreign Office to the effect that Bayelsa was a constituent territory of the Federal Republic of Nigeria.[201]

Article 2(1)b of the UN Convention on Jurisdictional Immunities, it should be noted, includes within its definition of state, 'constituent units of a federal state'.[202] The issue of the status of the European Community in this context was raised in the course of the ITC litigation as the EEC was a party to the sixth International Tin Agreement, 1982 under which the ITC was constituted. The Court of Appeal in *Maclaine Watson* v. *Department of Trade and Industry*[203] held that the EEC's claim to sovereign immunity was untenable. It had been conceded that the EEC was not a state and thus could not rely on the State Immunity Act 1978, but it was argued that the Community was entitled to immunity analogous to sovereign immunity under the rules of common law. This approach was held by Kerr

---

[198] An Order in Council has been made with respect to the constituent territories of Austria, SI 1979 no. 457, and Germany, SI 1993 no. 2809. The Act may also be extended to dependent territories: see e.g. the State Immunity (Overseas Territories) Order 1979, SI 1979 no. 458 and the State Immunity (Jersey) Order 1985, SI 1985 no. 1642.

[199] See e.g. *BCCI* v. *Price Waterhouse* [1997] 4 All ER 108; 111 ILR, p. 604.

[200] [2005] EWHC 2704.   [201] *Ibid.*, paras. 38 ff.

[202] See also the Report of the International Law Commission, 1991, p. 13. Note that article I of the Revised Draft Articles for a Convention on State Immunity adopted by the International Law Association in 1994 defines the term 'foreign state' to include the government of the state, any other state organs and agencies and instrumentalities of the state not possessing legal personality distinct from the state. No specific reference to units of federal states is made.

[203] [1988] 3 WLR 1033; 80 ILR, p. 49.

LJ to be 'entirely misconceived'.[204] Although the EEC had personality in international law and was able to exercise powers and functions analogous to those of sovereign states, this did not lead on to immunity as such. This was because sovereign immunity was 'a derogation from the normal exercise of jurisdiction by the courts and should be accorded only in clear cases',[205] while the concept itself was based upon the equality of states. The EEC Treaty, 1957 and the Merger Treaty, 1965 themselves made no claim for general immunity and nothing else existed upon which such a claim could be based.[206]

The personality issue – immunity for government figures[207]

The question of immunity *ratione personae* arises particularly and most strongly in the case of heads of state. Such immunity issues may come into play either with regard to international tribunals or within domestic orders. Taking the first, it is clear that serving heads of state, and other governmental officials, may be rendered susceptible to the jurisdiction of international tribunals, depending, of course, upon the terms of the constitutions of such tribunals. The provisions of, for example, the Versailles Treaty, 1919 (article 227); the Charter of the International Military Tribunal at Nuremberg, 1945 (article 7); the Statutes of the Yugoslav and Rwanda International Criminal Tribunals (articles 7 and 6 respectively); the Rome Statute of the International Criminal Court, 1998 (article 27) and the Statute for the Special Court for Sierra Leone, 2002 (article 6(2)) all expressly state that individual criminal responsibility will exist irrespective of any official status, including that of head of state. This was reaffirmed by the Special Court for Sierra Leone in its decision concerning the claim for immunity made by Charles Taylor.[208]

---

[204] [1988] 3 WLR 1107; 80 ILR, p. 122.

[205] *Victory Transport* v. *Comisaria General de Abastecimientos y Transportes* 336 F.2d 354 (1964), cited with approval by Ackner LJ in *Empresa Exportadora de Azucar* v. *Industria Azucarera Nacional* [1983] 2 LL. R 171, 193 and Lord Edmund-Davies in *I° Congreso del Partido* [1983] 1 AC 244, 276.

[206] [1988] 3 WLR 1033, 1108–12; 80 ILR, pp. 49, 123. Nourse and Ralph Gibson LLJ agreed with Kerr LJ completely on this issue, *ibid.*, pp. 1131 and 1158; 80 ILR, pp. 150, 180.

[207] See e.g. Y. Simbeye, *Immunity and International Criminal Law*, Aldershot, 2004, and A. Borghi, *L'Immunité des Dirigeants Politiques en Droit International*, Geneva, 2003.

[208] Case No. SCSL-2003-01-I, Decision on Immunity from Jurisdiction, 31 May 2004, 128 ILR, p. 239.

The situation of immunity before domestic courts is more complex.[209] First, the question of the determination of the status of head of state before domestic courts is primarily a matter for the domestic order of the individual concerned. In *Republic of the Philippines* v. *Marcos (No. 1)*,[210] for example, the US Court of Appeals for the Second Circuit held that the Marcoses, the deposed leader of the Philippines and his wife, were not entitled to claim sovereign immunity. In a further decision, the Court of Appeals for the Fourth Circuit held in *In re Grand Jury Proceedings, Doe No. 770*[211] that head of state immunity was primarily an attribute of state sovereignty, not an individual right, and that accordingly full effect should be given to the revocation by the Philippines government of the immunity of the Marcoses.[212] Also relevant would be the attitude adopted by the executive in the state in which the case is being brought. In *US* v. *Noriega*,[213] the District Court noted that head of state immunity was grounded in customary international law, but in order to assert such immunity, a government official must be recognised as head of state and this had not happened with regard to General Noriega.[214] This was confirmed by the Court of Appeals for the Eleventh Circuit, who noted that the judiciary deferred to the executive in matters concerning jurisdiction over foreign sovereigns and their instrumentalities, and, in the Noriega situation, the executive had demonstrated the view that he should not be granted head of state status. This was coupled with the fact that he had never served as constitutional ruler of Panama and that state had not sought immunity for him; further the charges related to his private enrichment.[215] In *First American Corporation* v. *Al-Nahyan*, the District Court noted that the Foreign Sovereign Immunities Act did not affect the right of the US government to file a Suggestion of Immunity asserting

---

[209] See e.g. the observations submitted by the UK government to the European Court of Human Rights concerning *Association SOS Attentats* v. *France*, regarding the immunity of President Gaddafi of Libya in criminal and civil proceedings in France, UKMIL, 77 BYIL, 2006, pp. 735 ff.

[210] 806 F.2d 344 (1986); 81 ILR, p. 581. See also e.g. *Re Honecker* 80 ILR, p. 365.

[211] 817 F.2d 1108 (1987); 81 ILR, p. 599.

[212] See also *Doe* v. *United States of America* 860 F.2d 40 (1988); 121 ILR, p. 567.

[213] 746 F.Supp. 1506, 1519 (1990); 99 ILR, pp. 143, 161.

[214] See also Watts, 'Legal Position', pp. 52 ff. See also H. Fox, 'The Resolution of the Institute of International Law on the Immunities of Heads of State and Government', 51 ICLQ, 2002, p. 119.

[215] 117 F.3d 1206 (1997); 121 ILR, p. 591. See also *Flatow* v. *Islamic Republic of Iran* 999 F.Supp. 1 (1998); 121 ILR, p. 618.

immunity with regard to a head of state and this would be binding on the courts.[216]

Secondly, international law has traditionally made a distinction between the official and private acts of a head of state.[217] In the case of civil proceedings, this means that a head of state may be susceptible to the jurisdiction where the question concerns purely private acts as distinct from acts undertaken in exercise or ostensible exercise of public authority.[218]

Thirdly, serving heads of state benefit from absolute immunity from the exercise of the jurisdiction of a foreign domestic court.[219] This was reaffirmed in *Ex parte Pinochet (No. 3)*. Lord Browne-Wilkinson, for example, noted that, 'This immunity enjoyed by a head of state in power and an ambassador in post is a complete immunity attaching to the person of the head of state or ambassador and rendering him immune from all actions or prosecutions whether or not they relate to matters done for the benefit of the state.'[220] Lord Hope referred to the '*jus cogens* character of the immunity enjoyed by serving heads of state *ratione personae*'.[221] This approach affirming the immunity of a serving head of state is endorsed by the decision of the French Cour de Cassation in the *Ghaddafi* case.[222] In *Tachiona* v. *USA*, the Court of Appeals for the Second Circuit, although deciding the issue as to the immunity of President Mugabe of Zimbabwe on the basis of diplomatic immunity, expressly doubted that the Foreign Sovereign Immunities Act was meant to change the common

---

[216] 948 F.Supp. 1107 (1996); 121 ILR, p. 577.

[217] See e.g. Draft Articles with Commentary on Jurisdictional Immunities, ILC Report, 1991, A/46/10, pp. 12, 15, 18 and 22.

[218] See e.g. *Republic of the Philippines* v. *Marcos (No. 1)*, 806 F.2d 344 (1986); 81 ILR, p. 581; *Jimenez* v. *Aristeguieta* 33 ILR, p. 353; *Lafontant* v. *Aristide* 103 ILR, pp. 581, 585 and *Mobutu and Republic of Zaire* v. *Société Logrine* 113 ILR, p. 481. See also Watts, 'Legal Position', pp. 54 ff.

[219] See e.g. Watts, 'Legal Position', p. 54. See also *Djibouti* v. *France*, ICJ Reports, 2008, paras. 170 ff.

[220] [2000] 1 AC 147, 201–2; 119 ILR, p. 135.

[221] [2000] 1 AC 244. See also Lord Goff at 210; Lord Saville at 265 and Lord Millett at 269. See also the decision of 12 February 2003 of the Belgian Court of Cassation in *HSA et al.* v. *SA et al.*, No. P. 02.1139. F/1, affirming the immunity of Prime Minister Sharon of Israel.

[222] Arrêt no. 1414, 14 March 2001, Cass. Crim. 1. See e.g. S. Zappalà, 'Do Heads of State in Office Enjoy Immunity from Jurisdiction for International Crimes? The *Ghaddafi* Case Before the French Cour de Cassation', 12 EJIL, 2001, p. 595. See also *Tatchell* v. *Mugabe*, unreported decision of the Bow Street Magistrates' Court, 14 January 2004, affirming the absolute immunity of President Mugabe, the Head of State of Zimbabwe.

law of head of state immunity,[223] a proposition affirmed in earlier case-law.[224]

Fourthly, the immunity of a former head of state differs in that it may be seen as moving from a status immunity (*ratione personae*) to a functional immunity (*ratione materiae*), so that immunity will only exist for official acts done while in office. The definition of official acts is somewhat unclear, but it is suggested that this would exclude acts done in clear violation of international law. It may be concluded at the least from the judgment in *Ex parte Pinochet (No. 3)* that the existence of the offence in question as a crime under international law by convention will, when coupled in some way by a universal or extraterritorial mechanism of enforcement, operate to exclude a plea of immunity *ratione materiae* at least in so far as states parties to the relevant treaty are concerned.[225] This may be a cautious reading and the law in this area is likely to evolve further.

The question as to whether immunities *ratione personae* apply to other governmental persons has been controversial.[226] The International Law Commission, for example, in its commentary on the Draft Articles on Jurisdictional Immunities (which led to the UN Convention on Jurisdictional Immunities) distinguished between the special position as regards immunities *ratione personae* of personal sovereigns (which would include heads of state) and diplomatic agents and that of other representatives of the government who would have only immunities *ratione materiae*.[227]

---

[223] 386 F.3d 205 (2004).

[224] See *Wei Ye v. Jiang Zemin* 383 F.3d 620 (2004), noting also that the State Department's suggestion as to immunity was conclusive.

[225] [2000] 1 AC 147 at e.g. 204–5 (Lord Browne-Wilkinson); 246 (Lord Hope); 262 (Lord Hutton); 266–7 (Lord Saville); 277 (Lord Millett); 290 (Lord Phillips); 119 ILR, p. 135. Note that by virtue of s. 20 of the State Immunity Act cross-referring to the Diplomatic Privileges Act 1964 incorporating the Vienna Convention on Diplomatic Relations, 1961, the immunities of a head of state were assimilated to those of the head of a diplomatic mission. Article 39(2) of the Vienna Convention provides that once a diplomat's functions have come to an end, immunity will only exist as regards acts performed 'in the exercise of his functions'.

[226] Note that as far as UK law is concerned, the provisions of s. 20(1) of the State Immunity Act do not apply so that the analogy with diplomatic agents is not relevant: see previous footnote.

[227] See the Report of the International Law Commission, 1991, pp. 24–7. See also Watts, 'Legal Position', pp. 53 and 102, who adopts a similar position. Lord Millett in *Ex parte Pinochet (No. 3)* took the view that immunity *ratione personae* was 'only narrowly available. It is confined to serving heads of state and heads of diplomatic missions, their families and servants. It is not available to serving heads of government who are not also heads of state...', [2000] 1 AC 147 at 268; 119 ILR, p. 135.

However, in its judgment in the *Congo* v. *Belgium* case, the International Court of Justice stated that, 'in international law it is firmly established that... certain holders of high-ranking office in a state, such as the head of state, head of government and minister for foreign affairs, enjoy immunities from jurisdiction in other states, both civil and criminal'.[228] The Court took the view that serving Foreign Ministers would benefit from immunity *ratione personae* on the basis that such immunities were in order to ensure the effective performance of their functions on behalf of their states.[229] The extent of such immunities would be dependent upon the functions exercised, but they were such that 'throughout the duration of his or her office, he or she when abroad enjoys full immunity from criminal jurisdiction and inviolability',[230] irrespective of whether the acts in question have been performed in an official or a private capacity.[231] This absolute immunity from the jurisdiction of foreign courts would also apply with regard to war crimes or crimes against humanity.[232] Immunities derived from customary international law would remain opposable to national courts even where such courts exercised jurisdiction under various international conventions requiring states parties to extend their criminal jurisdiction to cover the offences in question.[233] The Court concluded by noting that after a person ceased to hold the office of Foreign Minister, the

---

[228] ICJ Reports, 2002, pp. 3, 20; 128 ILR, p. 76. See also A. Cassese, 'When May Senior State Officials Be Tried for International Crimes?', 13 EJIL, 2002, p. 853. See also *Djibouti* v. *France*, ICJ Reports, 2008, paras. 181 ff.

[229] ICJ Reports, 2002, pp. 3, 21–2.   [230] *Ibid.*, p. 22.   [231] *Ibid.*   [232] *Ibid.*, p. 24.

[233] *Ibid.*, pp. 24–5. See, as to such conventions, above, chapter 12, p. 673. See also the application brought by the Government of the Republic of the Congo against France on 9 December 2002. France consented to the Court's jurisdiction on 11 April 2003. In its Application, the Republic of the Congo seeks the annulment of the investigation and prosecution measures taken by the French judicial authorities further to a complaint for crimes against humanity and torture filed by various associations against *inter alia* the President of the Republic of the Congo, Mr Denis Sassou Nguesso, and the Congolese Minister of the Interior, Mr Pierre Oba, together with other individuals including General Norbert Dabira, Inspector-General of the Congolese Armies. The Application further states that, in connection with these proceedings, an investigating judge of the Meaux *tribunal de grande instance* issued a warrant for the President of the Republic of the Congo to be examined as a witness. The Republic of the Congo declares this to be a violation of international law. See also the order of the ICJ of 17 June 2003 refusing an indication of provisional measures in this case. Rwanda introduced an application against France on 18 April 2007 concerning international arrest warrants issued by the latter's judicial authorities against three Rwandan officials on 20 November 2006 and a request sent to the United Nations Secretary-General that President Paul Kagame of Rwanda should stand trial at the International Criminal Tribunal for Rwanda (ICTR). France has to date not given its consent to this application and there is no other jurisdictional basis.

courts of other countries may prosecute with regard to acts committed before or after the period of office and also 'in respect of acts committed during that period of office in a private capacity'.[234] This appears to leave open the question of prosecution for acts performed in violation of international law (such as, for example, torture), unless these are deemed to fall within the category of private acts.

It is also uncertain as to how far the term used by the Court, 'holders of high-ranking office in a state', might extend and practice is unclear.[235]

Waiver of immunity

It is possible for a state to waive its immunity from the jurisdiction of the court. Express waiver of immunity from jurisdiction, however, which must be granted by an authorised representative of the state,[236] does not of itself mean waiver of immunity from execution.[237] In the case of implied waiver, some care is required. Section 2 of the State Immunity Act provides for loss of immunity upon submission to the jurisdiction, either by a prior written agreement[238] or after the particular dispute has arisen. A state is deemed to have submitted to the jurisdiction where the state has instituted proceedings or has intervened or taken any step in the

---

[234] ICJ Reports, 2002, pp. 25–6. But see the Dissenting Opinion of Judge Al-Khasawneh.

[235] See above, note 228. See also *Application for Arrest Warrant Against General Shaul Mofaz*, decision of the Bow Street Magistrates' Court, 12 February 2004, where it was held that a serving Defence Minister of another state would benefit from immunities before the English court, 128 ILR, p. 709.

[236] See e.g. *R* v. *Madan* [1961] QB 1, 7. Although this was a case on diplomatic immunity which preceded the 1964 Diplomatic Privileges Act incorporating the Vienna Convention on Diplomatic Relations, 1961, the Court of Appeal in *Aziz* v. *Republic of Yemen* [2005] EWCA Civ 745, para. 48, held the statement to be of general application, including with regard to a consideration of waiver of state immunity under the 1978 Act.

[237] See e.g. article 20 of the UN Convention on Jurisdictional Immunities. Note, however, that the issue will turn upon the interpretation of the terms of the waiver: see *A Company* v. *Republic of X* [1990] 2 LL. R 520; 87 ILR, p. 412. However, it is suggested that the principle that waiver of immunity from jurisdiction does not of itself constitute a waiver of immunity from the grant of relief by the courts is of the nature of a presumption, thus placing the burden of proof to the contrary upon the private party and having implications with regard to the standard of proof required. See also *Sabah Shipyard* v. *Pakistan* [2002] EWCA Civ. 1643 at paras. 18 ff.

[238] Overruling *Kahan* v. *Pakistan Federation* [1951] 2 KB 1003; 18 ILR, p. 210. Submission to the jurisdiction by means of a provision in a contract must be in clear, express language. The choice of UK law as the governing law of the contract did not amount to such a submission: see *Mills* v. *USA* 120 ILR, p. 612.

proceedings.[239] Article 8 of the UN Convention on Jurisdictional Immunities is essentially to the same effect.[240]

If a state submits to proceedings, it is deemed to have submitted to any counter-claim arising out of the same legal relationship or facts as the claim.[241] A provision in an agreement that it is to be governed by the law of the UK is not to be taken as a submission. By section 9 of the State Immunity Act, a state which has agreed in writing to submit a dispute to arbitration is not immune from proceedings in the courts which relate to the arbitration.[242] In *Svenska Petroleum* v. *Lithuania*, the Court of Appeal held that a failure to challenge an award made without jurisdiction did not of itself amount to an agreement in writing on Lithuania's part to submit the dispute to arbitration.[243] However, the Court noted that there was no basis for construing section 9 of the State Immunity Act (particularly when viewed in the context of the provisions of section 13 dealing with execution) as excluding proceedings relating to the enforcement of a foreign arbitral award. It was emphasised that arbitration was a consensual procedure and the principle underlying section 9 was that, if a state had

---

[239] But not where the intervention or step taken is only for the purpose of claiming immunity, or where the step taken by the state is in ignorance of facts entitling it to immunity if those facts could not reasonably have been ascertained and immunity is claimed as soon as reasonably practicable, s. 2(5). See also article 1 of the European Convention on State Immunity, 1972.

[240] This provides that: '1. A state cannot invoke immunity from jurisdiction in a proceeding before a court of another state if it has: (a) itself instituted the proceeding; or (b) intervened in the proceeding or taken any other step relating to the merits. However, if the state satisfies the court that it could not have acquired knowledge of facts on which a claim to immunity can be based until after it took such a step, it can claim immunity based on those facts, provided it does so at the earliest possible moment. 2. A state shall not be considered to have consented to the exercise of jurisdiction by a court of another state if it intervenes in a proceeding or takes any other step for the sole purpose of: (a) invoking immunity; or (b) asserting a right or interest in property at issue in the proceeding. 3. The appearance of a representative of a state before a court of another state as a witness shall not be interpreted as consent by the former state to the exercise of jurisdiction by the court. 4. Failure on the part of a state to enter an appearance in a proceeding before a court of another state shall not be interpreted as consent by the former state to the exercise of jurisdiction by the court'.

[241] See also article 1 of the European Convention on State Immunity, 1972 and article 9 of the UN Convention on Jurisdictional Immunities.

[242] See also article 12 of the European Convention on State Immunity, 1972 and article 17 of the UN Convention on Jurisdictional Immunities.

[243] [2006] EWCA Civ 1529, para. 113. See also *Donegal* v. *Zambia* [2007] EWHC 197 (Comm), holding that written submissions to the jurisdiction with regard to a compromise agreement amounted to a waiver of immunity.

agreed to submit to arbitration, it had thus rendered itself amenable to such process as might be necessary to render the arbitration effective.[244]

The issue of waiver is also a key factor in many US cases. Section 1605(a)(1) of the Foreign Sovereign Immunities Act 1976 provides that a foreign state is not immune where it has waived its immunity either expressly or by implication, notwithstanding any withdrawal of the waiver which the foreign state may purport to effect, except in accordance with the terms of the waiver.[245] The Court of Appeals has held, however, that the implied waiver provision did not extend to conduct constituting a violation of *jus cogens*.[246]

Pre-judgment attachment [247]

Section 1610(d) of the US Foreign Sovereign Immunities Act 1976 prohibits the attachment of the property of a foreign state before judgment unless that state has explicitly waived its immunity from attachment prior to judgment and the purpose of the attachment is to secure satisfaction of a judgment that has been or may be entered against the foreign state. A variety of cases in the US has arisen over whether general waivers contained in treaty provisions may be interpreted as permitting pre-judgment attachment, in order to prevent the defendant from removing his assets from the jurisdiction. The courts generally require clear evidence of the intention to waive pre-judgment attachment, although that actual phrase need not necessarily be used.[248]

---

[244] [2006] EWCA Civ 1529, paras. 117 and 123. See also *The Akademik Fyodorov* 131 ILR, p. 460.

[245] See e.g. *Siderman* v. *Republic of Argentina* 965 F.2d 699 (1992); 103 ILR, p. 454. It should also be noted that a substantial number of bilateral treaties expressly waive immunity from jurisdiction. This is particularly the case where the states maintaining the absolute immunity approach are concerned: see e.g. UN, *Materials*, part III. See also *USA* v. *Friedland* (1998) 40 OR (3d) 747; 120 ILR, p. 418.

[246] *Smith* v. *Libya* 101 F.3d 239 (1996); 113 ILR, p. 534. See also *Hirsch* v. *State of Israel* 962 F.Supp. 377 (1997); 113 ILR, p. 543.

[247] See e.g. J. Crawford, 'Execution of Judgments and Foreign Sovereign Immunity', 75 AJIL, 1981, pp. 820, 867 ff., and Schreuer, *State Immunity*, p. 162.

[248] See e.g. *Behring International Inc.* v. *Imperial Iranian Air Force* 475 F.Supp. 383 (1979); 63 ILR, p. 261; *Reading & Bates Corp.* v. *National Iranian Oil Company* 478 F.Supp. 724 (1979); 63 ILR, p. 305; *New England Merchants National Bank* v. *Iran Power Generation and Transmission Company* 19 ILM, 1980, p. 1298; 63 ILR, p. 408; *Security Pacific National Bank* v. *Government of Iran* 513 F.Supp. 864 (1981); *Libra Bank Ltd* v. *Banco Nacional de Costa Rica* 676 F.2d 47 (1982); 72 ILR, p. 119; *S & S Machinery Co.* v. *Masinexportimport* 706 F.2d 411 (1981); 107 ILR, p. 239, and *O'Connell Machinery* v. *MV Americana* 734 F.2d 115 (1984); 81 ILR, p. 539. See also article 23 of the European Convention on State

Under the UK State Immunity Act 1978, no relief may be given against a state by way of injunction or order for specific performance, recovery of land or recovery of any property without the written consent of that state.[249] The question has therefore arisen as to whether a *Mareva* injunction,[250] ordering that assets remain within the jurisdiction pending the outcome of the case, may be obtained, particularly since this type of injunction is interlocutory and obtained without notice (*ex parte*). It is suggested that an application for a *Mareva* injunction may indeed be made without notice since immunity may not apply in the circumstances of the case. In applying for such an injunction, a plaintiff is under a duty to make full and frank disclosure and the standard of proof is that of a 'good and arguable case', explaining, for example, why it is contended that immunity would not be applicable. It is then for the defendant to seek to discharge the injunction by arguing that these criteria have not been met. The issue as to how the court should deal with such a situation was discussed in *A Company* v. *Republic of X*.[251] Saville J noted that the issue of immunity had to be finally settled at the outset so that when a state sought to discharge a *Mareva* injunction on the grounds of immunity, the court could not allow the injunction to continue on the basis that the plaintiff has a good arguable case that immunity does not exist, for if immunity did exist 'then the court simply has no power to continue the injunction'. Accordingly, a delay between the granting of the injunction *ex parte* and the final determination by the court of the issue was probably unavoidable.[252] The situation is generally the same in other countries.[253]

Immunity prohibiting such action. Article 18 of the UN Convention on Jurisdictional Immunities provides that 'no pre-judgment measures of constraint, such as attachment or arrest, against property of a state may be taken in connection with a proceeding before a court of another state unless and except to the extent that: (a) the state has expressly consented to the taking of such measures as indicated: (i) by international agreement; (ii) by an arbitration agreement or in a written contract; or (iii) by a declaration before the court or by a written communication after a dispute between the parties has arisen; or (b) the state has allocated or earmarked property for the satisfaction of the claim which is the object of that proceeding'.

[249] S. 13(2).

[250] See *Mareva Compania Naviera* v. *International Bulkcarriers* [1975] 2 LL. R 509. See also S. Gee, *Mareva Injunctions & Anton Piller Relief*, 2nd edn, London, 1990, especially at p. 22.

[251] [1990] 2 LL. R 520; 87 ILR, p. 412.

[252] [1990] 2 LL. R 525; 87 ILR, p. 417, citing *Maclaine Watson* v. *Department of Trade and Industry* [1988] 3 WLR 1033 at 1103–4 and 1157–8.

[253] But see the case of *Condor and Filvem* v. *Minister of Justice* 101 ILR, p. 394 before the Italian Constitutional Court in 1992.

Immunity from execution[254]

Immunity from execution is to be distinguished from immunity from jurisdiction, particularly since it involves the question of the actual seizure of assets appertaining to a foreign state. As such it poses a considerable challenge to relations between states and accordingly states have proved unwilling to restrict immunity from enforcement judgment in contradistinction to the situation concerning jurisdictional immunity. Consent to the exercise of jurisdiction does not imply consent to the execution or enforcement of any judgment obtained.[255]

Article 23 of the European Convention on State Immunity, 1972 prohibits any measures of execution or preventive measures against the property of a contracting state in the absence of written consent in any particular case. However, the European Convention provides for a system of mutual enforcement of final judgments rendered in accordance with its provisions[256] and an Additional Protocol provides for proceedings to be taken before the European Tribunal of State Immunity, consisting basically of members of the European Court of Human Rights. Article 19 of the UN Convention on Jurisdictional Immunities provides that no post-judgment measures of constraint, such as attachment, arrest or execution, against property of a state may be taken in connection with a proceeding before a court of another state unless, and except to the extent that, the state has expressly consented to the taking of such measures as indicated by international agreement; an arbitration agreement or in a written contract; or by a declaration before the court or by a written communication after a dispute between the parties has arisen; or where the state has allocated or earmarked property for the satisfaction of the claim which is the object of that proceeding; or where it has been established that the property is specifically in use or intended for use by the state for other than government non-commercial purposes and is in the territory of the state of the forum, provided that post-judgment measures of constraint may only be taken against property

---

[254] See e.g. Schreuer, *State Immunity*, chapter 6; Sinclair, 'Sovereign Immunity', chapter 4; Nguyen Quoc Dinh *et al.*, *Droit International Public*, p. 453; Crawford, 'Execution of Judgments'; A. Reinisch, 'European Court Practice Concerning State Immunity from Enforcement Measures', 17 EJIL, 2006, p. 803; H. Fox, 'Enforcement Jurisdiction, Foreign State Property and Diplomatic Immunity', 34 ICLQ, 1985, p. 115, and various articles in 10 Netherlands YIL, 1979.

[255] See e.g. article 20 of the UN Convention on Jurisdictional Immunities.

[256] Article 20 of the European Convention on State Immunity.

that has a connection with the entity against which the proceeding was directed.

Section 13(2)b of the UK State Immunity Act provides, for instance, that 'the property of a state shall not be subject to any process for the enforcement of a judgment or arbitration award or, in an action *in rem*, for its arrest, detention or sale'. Such immunity may be waived by written consent but not by merely submitting to the jurisdiction of the courts,[257] while there is no immunity from execution in respect of property which is for the time being in use or intended for use for commercial purposes.[258] It is particularly to be noted that this latter stipulation is not to apply to a state's central bank or other monetary authority.[259] Thus, a *Trendtex* type of situation could not arise again in the same form. It was emphasised in *AIC Ltd* v. *Federal Government of Nigeria* that this absolute immunity accorded to the property of a foreign state's central bank applied irrespective of the source of the funds in the account or the purpose for which the account was maintained,[260] while in *AIG Capital Partners Inc.* v. *Republic of Kazakhstan*, it was noted that the term 'property' in the Act had to be given a broad meaning and included all real and personal property, including any right or interest, whether legal, equitable or contractual. The property in question appertained to the central bank if held in its name, irrespective of the capacity in which the bank held it or the purpose for which it was held.[261]

It is also interesting that the corresponding provision in the US Foreign Sovereign Immunities Act of 1976 is more restrictive with regard to immunity from execution.[262] The principle that existence of immunity from

---

[257] S. 13(3). See also s. 14 of the South African Foreign Sovereign Immunity Act 1981; s. 14 of the Pakistan State Immunity Ordinance 1981; s. 15 of the Singapore State Immunity Act 1979 and s. 31 of the Australian Foreign States Immunities Act 1985.

[258] S. 13(4).

[259] S. 14(4), which provides that, 'Property of a state's central bank or other monetary authority shall not be regarded for the purposes of subsection (4) of section 13 above as in use or intended for use for commercial purposes; and where any such bank or authority is a separate entity subsections (1) to (3) of that section shall apply to it as if references to a state were references to the bank or authority.' See also Fox, *State Immunity*, p. 393, and W. Blair, 'The Legal Status of Central Bank Investments under English Law' [1998] CLJ, pp. 374, 380–1.

[260] [2003] EWHC 1357, paras. 46 ff.; 129 ILR, p. 571.

[261] [2005] EWHC 2239 (Comm), paras. 33 ff.; 129 ILR, p. 589.

[262] S. 1610. Thus, for example, there would be no immunity with regard to property taken in violation of international law. See also *First National City Bank* v. *Banco Para El Comercio Exterior de Cuba* 462 US 611 (1983); 80 ILR, p. 566; *Letelier* v. *Republic of Chile* 748 F.2d 790 (1984) and *Foxworth* v. *Permanent Mission of the Republic of Uganda to the United*

jurisdiction does not automatically entail immunity from execution has been reaffirmed in the case-law on a number of occasions.[263]

In 1977, the West German Federal Constitutional Court in the *Philippine Embassy* case[264] declared that:

> forced execution of judgment by the state of the forum under a writ of execution against a foreign state which has been issued in respect of non-sovereign acts ... of that state, or property of that state which is present or situated in the territory of the state of the forum, is inadmissible without the consent of the foreign state if ... such property serves sovereign purposes of the foreign state.

In particular it was noted that:

> claims against a general current bank account of the embassy of a foreign state which exists in the state of the forum and the purpose of which is to cover the embassy's costs and expenses are not subject to forced execution by the state of the forum.[265]

This was referred to approvingly by Lord Diplock in *Alcom Ltd* v. *Republic of Colombia*,[266] a case which similarly involved the attachment of a bank account of a diplomatic mission. The House of Lords unanimously accepted that the general rule in international law was not overturned in the State Immunity Act. In *Alcom*, described as involving a question of law of 'outstanding international importance',[267] it was held that such a bank account would not fall within the section 13(4) exception relating to commercial purposes, unless it could be shown by the person seeking to attach the balance that 'the bank account was earmarked by the foreign state solely ... for being drawn on to settle liabilities incurred in

---

Nations 796 F.Supp. 761 (1992); 99 ILR, p. 138. See also G. R. Delaume, 'The Foreign Sovereign Immunities Act and Public Debt Litigation: Some Fifteen Years Later', 88 AJIL, 1994, pp. 257, 266. Note that in 1988, the legislation was amended to include a provision that, with regard to measures of execution following confirmation of an arbitral award, all the commercial property of the award debtor was open to execution: new s. 1610(a)(6), *ibid.*

[263] See e.g. *Abbott* v. *South Africa* 113 ILR, p. 411 (Spanish Constitutional Court); *Centre for Industrial Development* v. *Naidu* 115 ILR, p. 424 and *Flatow* v. *Islamic Republic of Iran* 999 F.Supp. 1 (1998); 121 ILR, p. 618. See also *The Akademik Fyodorov*, 131 ILR, pp. 460, 485–6.

[264] See UN, *Materials*, p. 297; 65 ILR, pp. 146, 150.

[265] UN, *Materials*, pp. 300–1; 65 ILR, p. 164.

[266] [1984] 2 All ER 6; 74 ILR, p. 180, overturning the Court of Appeal Decision, [1984] 1 All ER 1; 74 ILR, p. 170.

[267] [1984] 2 All ER 14; 74 ILR, p. 189.

commercial transactions'.[268] The onus of proof lies upon the applicant. It is also to be noted that under section 13(5) of the Act, a certificate by a head of mission to the effect that property was not in use for commercial purposes was sufficient evidence of that fact, unless the contrary was proven.[269] The question of determining property used for commercial purposes is a significant and complex one that will invariably depend upon an analysis of various factors, as seen in the light of the law of the forum state,[270] for example the present and future use of the funds and their origin.[271]

In *Banamar* v. *Embassy of the Democratic and Popular Republic of Algeria*,[272] the Italian Supreme Court reaffirmed the rule that customary international law forbids measures of execution against the property of foreign states located in the territory of the state seeking to exercise jurisdiction and used for sovereign purposes, and held that it lacked jurisdiction to enforce a judgment against a foreign state by ordering execution against bank accounts standing in the name of that state's embassy. This approach appears to have been modified in *Condor and Filvem* v. *Minister of Justice*[273] before the Italian Constitutional Court in 1992. The Court held that it could no longer be affirmed that there existed an international customary rule forbidding absolutely coercive measures against the property of foreign states. In order for immunity against execution not to apply, it is necessary not only to demonstrate that the activity or transaction concerned was *jure gestionis*, but also to show that the property to which the request for execution refers is not destined to accomplish public functions (*jure imperii*) of the foreign state.[274]

However, the Spanish Constitutional Court in *Abbott* v. *South Africa* held that bank accounts held by foreign states used for the purposes of ordinary diplomatic or consular activity were immune from attachment or execution even where the funds were also used for commercial

---

[268] [1984] 2 All ER 13; 74 ILR, p. 187. But cf. *Birch Shipping Corporation* v. *Embassy of the United Republic of Tanzania* 507 F.Supp. 311 (1980); 63 ILR, p. 524. But see the decision of the Swiss Federal Tribunal in 1990 in *Z* v. *Geneva Supervisory Authority for the Enforcement of Debts and Bankruptcy*, 102 ILR, p. 205, holding that funds allocated for the diplomatic service of a foreign state were immune from attachment.

[269] Such certificate had been issued by the Colombian Ambassador. See below, p. 750, with regard to diplomatic immunities.

[270] See the West German Federal Constitutional Court decision in the *National Iranian Oil Co.* case, 22 ILM, 1983, p. 1279.

[271] See e.g. *Eurodif Corporation* v. *Islamic Republic of Iran* 23 ILM, 1984, p. 1062.

[272] 84 AJIL, 1990, p. 573; 87 ILR, p. 56. See also *Libya* v. *Rossbeton SRL*, 87 ILR, p. 63.

[273] 101 ILR, p. 394.   [274] *Ibid.*, pp. 401–2.

purposes,[275] while the Austrian Supreme Court held in *Leasing West GmbH v. Algeria* that a general bank account of a foreign embassy allocated partly but not exclusively for diplomatic purposes was immune from enforcement proceedings without the consent of the state concerned. Attachment could only take place if the account could be shown to be used exclusively for private purposes.[276]

The burden and standard of proof

Since section 1 of the State Immunity Act stipulates that a state is immune from the jurisdiction of the courts of the UK except as provided in the following sections, it is clear that the burden of proof lies upon the plaintiff to establish that an exception to immunity applies.[277] However, the court is under a duty to ensure that effect is given to the immunity conferred by the State Immunity Act 1978 and of its own motion if necessary.[278]

As far as the standard of proof is concerned, the Court of Appeal in *Maclaine Watson v. Department of Trade and Industry*[279] held that whenever a claim of immunity is made, the court must deal with it as a preliminary issue and on the normal test of balance of probabilities.[280] It would be insufficient to apply the 'good arguable case' test usual in Order 11[281] cases with regard to leave to serve.[282] To have decided otherwise would have meant that the state might have lost its claim for immunity upon the more impressionistic 'good arguable case' basis, which in practice is decided upon affidavit evidence only, and would have been precluded from pursuing its claim at a later stage since that could well be construed

---

[275] 113 ILR, pp. 411, 423–4.   [276] 116 ILR, p. 526.

[277] See also Staughton J in *Rayner* v. *Department of Trade and Industry* [1987] BCLC 667; *Donegal* v. *Zambia* [2007] EWHC 197 (Comm), para. 428, and Fox, *State Immunity*, p. 177.

[278] Mummery J stated that, 'The overriding duty of the court, of its own motion, is to satisfy itself that effect has been given to the immunity conferred by the State Immunity Act 1978. That duty binds all tribunals and courts, not just the court or tribunal which heard the original proceedings. If the tribunal in the original proceedings has not given effect to the immunity conferred by the Act, then it must be the duty of the appeal tribunal to give effect to it by correcting the error': see *United Arab Emirates* v. *Abdelghafar* [1995] ICR 65, 73–4; 104 ILR, pp. 647, 654–5. See also *Military Affairs Office of the Embassy of Kuwait* v. *Caramba-Coker*, Appeal No. EAT/1054/02/RN, Employment Appeal Tribunal (2003).

[279] [1988] 3 WLR 1033, 1103 and 1157; 80 ILR, pp. 49, 118, 179.

[280] This would be done procedurally under Order 12, Rule 8 of the Rules of the Supreme Court, 1991. See also *A Company* v. *Republic of X* 87 ILR, pp. 412, 417.

[281] Rules of the Supreme Court, 1991.

[282] See e.g. *Vitkovice Horni* v. *Korner* [1951] AC 869.

as submission to the jurisdiction under section 2(3) of the State Immunity Act.

The question of service of process upon a foreign state arose in *Westminster City Council* v. *Government of the Islamic Republic of Iran*,[283] where Peter Gibson J held that without prior service upon the Iranian government, the court was unable to deal with the substantive issue before it which concerned the attempt by the Westminster City Council to recover from the Iranian government charges incurred by it in rendering the Iranian embassy safe after it had been stormed in the famous 1980 siege. In the absence of diplomatic relations between the UK and Iran at that time and in the absence of Iranian consent, there appeared to be no way to satisfy the requirement in section 12 of the State Immunity Act that 'any writ or other document required to be served for instituting proceedings against a state shall be served by being transmitted through the Foreign and Commonwealth Office to the Ministry of Foreign Affairs of the state'. The question also arose in *Kuwait Airways Corporation* v. *Iraqi Airways*.[284] Since at the relevant time there was no British diplomatic presence in Baghdad, the necessary documents were lodged pursuant to Order 11, Rule 7 at the Central Office, whence they were sent to the Foreign and Commonwealth Office and thence to the Iraqi Embassy in London with a request for transmission to Baghdad. The House of Lords held that since the writ was not forwarded to the Iraqi Ministry of Foreign Affairs in Baghdad, the writ was not served as required under section 12(1) of the 1978 Act.[285]

Conclusion

Although sovereign immunity is in various domestic statutes proclaimed as a general principle, subject to wide-ranging exceptions, it is, of course, itself an exception to the general rule of territorial jurisdiction. The enumeration of non-immunity situations is so long, that the true situation of a rapidly diminishing exception to jurisdiction should be appreciated. In many instances, it has only been with practice that it has become apparent how much more extensive the submission to jurisdiction has become under domestic legislation. In *Letelier* v. *Republic of Chile*,[286] for example, section 1605(a)5 providing for foreign state liability for injury,

---

[283] [1986] 3 All ER 284; 108 ILR, p. 557.   [284] [1995] 1 WLR 1147; 103 ILR, p. 340.
[285] [1995] 1 WLR 1156 (per Lord Goff). See also *AN International Bank Plc* v. *Zambia* 118 ILR, p. 602.
[286] 488 F.Supp. 665 (1980); 63 ILR, p. 378.

death and loss of property occurring in the US was used to indict the
secret service of Chile with regard to the murder of a former Chilean
Foreign Minister in Washington. Similarly in *Verlinden* v. *Central Bank
of Nigeria*,[287] the Supreme Court permitted a Dutch company to sue the
Central Bank of Nigeria in the US,[288] although the *Tel-Oren*[289] case may
mark a modification of this approach. The amendment to the Act providing for jurisdiction in cases of state-sponsored terrorism has also been
a significant development.[290]

The principle of diplomatic immunity may often be relevant in a
sovereign immunity case. This is considered in the next section.

Diplomatic law [291]

Rules regulating the various aspects of diplomatic relations constitute one
of the earliest expressions of international law. Whenever in history there

[287] 22 ILM, 1983, p. 647; 79 ILR, p. 548.
[288] Nevertheless, it would appear that the Foreign Sovereign Immunities Act of 1976 does
require some minimum jurisdictional links: see generally *International Shoe Co.* v. *Washington* 326 US 310 (1945) and *Perez* v. *The Bahamas* 482 F.Supp. 1208 (1980); 63 ILR,
p. 350, cf. State Immunity Act of 1978.
[289] 726 F.2d 774 (1984); 77 ILR, p. 193. See further above, p. 683.
[290] See above, p. 715.
[291] See e.g. E. Denza, *Diplomatic Law*, 3rd edn, Oxford, 2008; P. Cahier, *Le Droit Diplomatique Contemporain*, Geneva, 1962; M. Hardy, *Modern Diplomatic Law*, Manchester, 1968;
Do Naslimento e Silva, *Diplomacy in International Law*, Leiden, 1973; L. S. Frey and M.
L. Frey, *The History of Diplomatic Immunity*, Ohio, 1999; *Satow's Guide to Diplomatic
Practice* (ed. P. Gore-Booth), 5th edn, London, 1979; B. Sen, *A Diplomat's Handbook of
International Law and Practice*, 3rd edn, The Hague, 1988; J. Brown, 'Diplomatic Im-
munity: State Practice under the Vienna Convention on Diplomatic Relations', 37 ICLQ,
1988, p. 53; Société Français de Droit International, *Aspects Récents du Droit des Relations
Diplomatiques*, Paris, 1989; G. V. McClanahan, *Diplomatic Immunity*, London, 1989; B. S.
Murty, *The International Law of Diplomacy*, Dordrecht, 1989; L. Dembinski, *The Modern
Law of Diplomacy*, Dordrecht, 1990; J. Salmon, *Manuel de Droit Diplomatique*, Brussels,
1994, and Salmon, 'Immunités et Actes de la Fonction', AFDI, 1992, p. 313; J. C. Barker,
The Abuse of Diplomatic Privileges and Immunities, Aldershot, 1996, and Barker, *The Pro-
tection of Diplomatic Personnel*, Aldershot, 2006; C. E. Wilson, *Diplomatic Privileges and
Immunities*, Tucson, 1967; M. Whiteman, *Digest of International Law*, Washington, 1970,
vol. VII; *Third US Restatement of Foreign Relations Law*, St Paul, 1987, pp. 455 ff.; House of
Commons Foreign Affairs Committee, *The Abuse of Diplomatic Immunities and Privileges*,
1984 and the UK Government Response to the *Report*, Cmnd 9497, and *Memorandum
on Diplomatic Privileges and Immunities in the United Kingdom*, UKMIL, 63 BYIL, 1992,
p. 688. See also R. Higgins, 'The Abuse of Diplomatic Privileges and Immunities: Recent
United Kingdom Experience', 79 AJIL, 1985, p. 641, and Higgins, *Problems and Process*,
Oxford, 1994, p. 86; A. James, 'Diplomatic Relations and Contacts', 62 BYIL, 1991, p. 347;
Nguyen Quoc Dinh *et al.*, *Droit International Public*, p. 739, and *Oppenheim's International
Law*, chapters 10 and 11.

has been a group of independent states co-existing, special customs have developed on how the ambassadors and other special representatives of other states were to be treated.[292]

Diplomacy as a method of communication between various parties, including negotiations between recognised agents, is an ancient institution and international legal provisions governing its manifestations are the result of centuries of state practice. The special privileges and immunities related to diplomatic personnel of various kinds grew up partly as a consequence of sovereign immunity and the independence and equality of states, and partly as an essential requirement of an international system. States must negotiate and consult with each other and with international organisations and in order to do so need diplomatic staffs. Since these persons represent their states in various ways, they thus benefit from the legal principle of state sovereignty. This is also an issue of practical convenience.

Diplomatic relations have traditionally been conducted through the medium of ambassadors[293] and their staffs, but with the growth of trade and commercial intercourse the office of consul was established and expanded. The development of speedy communications stimulated the creation of special missions designed to be sent to particular areas for specific purposes, often with the head of state or government in charge. To some extent, however, the establishment of telephone, telegraph, telex and fax services has lessened the importance of the traditional diplomatic personnel by strengthening the centralising process. Nevertheless, diplomats and consuls do retain some useful functions in the collection of information and pursuit of friendly relations, as well as providing a permanent presence in foreign states, with all that that implies for commercial and economic activities.[294]

The field of diplomatic immunities is one of the most accepted and uncontroversial of international law topics, as it is in the interest of all states ultimately to preserve an even tenor of diplomatic relations, although not all states act in accordance with this. As the International Court noted in the *US Diplomatic and Consular Staff in Tehran* case:[295]

---

[292] See e.g. G. Mattingley, *Renaissance Diplomacy*, London, 1955, and D. Elgavish, 'Did Diplomatic Immunity Exist in the Ancient Near East?', 2 *Journal of the History of International Law*, 2000, p. 73. See also Watts, 'Legal Position'.

[293] See, as to the powers of ambassadors, *First Fidelity Bank NA* v. *Government of Antigua and Barbuda Permanent Mission* 877 F.2d 189 (1989); 99 ILR, p. 125.

[294] See generally *Satow's Guide*, chapter 1.   [295] ICJ Reports, 1980, p. 3; 61 ILR, p. 504.

the rules of diplomatic law, in short, constitute a self-contained regime, which on the one hand, lays down the receiving state's obligations regarding the facilities, privileges and immunities to be accorded to diplomatic missions and, on the other, foresees their possible abuse by members of the mission and specifies the means at the disposal of the receiving state to counter any such abuse.[296]

The Vienna Convention on Diplomatic Relations, 1961

This treaty, which came into force in 1964,[297] emphasises the functional necessity of diplomatic privileges and immunities for the efficient conduct of international relations[298] as well as pointing to the character of the diplomatic mission as representing its state.[299] It both codified existing laws and established others.[300] Questions not expressly regulated by the Convention continue to be governed by the rules of customary international law.[301] The International Court has recently emphasised that the Convention continues to apply notwithstanding the existence of a state of armed conflict between the states concerned.[302]

There is no right as such under international law to diplomatic relations, and they exist by virtue of mutual consent.[303] If one state does not

---

[296] ICJ Reports, 1980, p. 40; 61 ILR, p. 566. See also, affirming that the rules of diplomatic law constitute a self-contained regime, the decision of the German Federal Constitutional Court of 10 June 1997, *Former Syrian Ambassador to the German Democratic Republic* 115 ILR, p. 597.

[297] The importance of the Convention was stressed in the *Iranian Hostages* case, ICJ Reports, 1980, pp. 330–430; 61 ILR, p. 556. Many of its provisions are incorporated into English law by the Diplomatic Privileges Act 1964.

[298] See also *767 Third Avenue Associates* v. *Permanent Mission of the Republic of Zaire to the United Nations* 988 F.2d 295 (1993); 99 ILR, p. 194.

[299] See *Yearbook of the ILC*, 1958, vol. II, pp. 94–5. The extraterritorial theory of diplomatic law, according to which missions constituted an extension of the territory of the sending state, was of some historic interest but not of practical use, *ibid.* See also *Radwan* v. *Radwan* [1973] Fam. 24; 55 ILR, p. 579 and *McKeel* v. *Islamic Republic of Iran* 722 F.2d 582 (1983); 81 ILR, p. 543. Note that in *US* v. *Kostadinov* 734 F.2d 906, 908 (1984); 99 ILR, pp. 103, 107, the term 'mission' in the Convention was defined not as the premises occupied by diplomats, but as a group of people sent by one state to another.

[300] See e.g. the *Iranian Hostages* case, ICJ Reports, 1980, pp. 3, 24; 61 ILR, p. 550.

[301] Preamble to the Convention.

[302] *Democratic Republic of the Congo* v. *Uganda*, ICJ Reports, 2005, pp. 168, 274. See also the *Iranian Hostages* case, ICJ Reports, 1980, pp. 3, 40; and the decisions of the Eritrea–Ethiopia Claims Commission on 19 December 2005, in the Partial Award, Diplomatic Claim, Ethiopia's Claim 8, para. 24 and the Partial Award, Diplomatic Claim, Eritrea's Claim 20, para. 20.

[303] Article 2.

wish to enter into diplomatic relations, it is not legally compelled so to do. Accordingly, the Convention specifies in article 4 that the sending state must ensure that the consent (or *agrément*) of the receiving state has been given for the proposed head of its mission, and reasons for any refusal of consent do not have to be given. Similarly, by article 9 the receiving state may at any time declare any member of the diplomatic mission *persona non grata* without having to explain its decision, and thus obtain the removal of that person.[304] However, the principle of consent as the basis of diplomatic relations may be affected by other rules of international law. For example, the Security Council in resolution 748 (1992), which imposed sanctions upon Libya, decided that 'all states shall: (a) significantly reduce the number and level of the staff at Libyan diplomatic missions and consular posts and restrict or control the movement within their territory of all such staff who remain . . .'.

The main functions of a diplomatic mission are specified in article 3 and revolve around the representation and protection of the interests and nationals of the sending state, as well as the promotion of information and friendly relations. Article 41(1) also emphasises the duty of all persons enjoying privileges and immunities to respect the laws and regulations of the receiving state and the duty not to interfere in the internal affairs of that state.

Article 13 provides that the head of the mission is deemed to have taken up his functions in the receiving state upon presentation of credentials. Heads of mission are divided into three classes by article 14, viz. ambassadors or nuncios accredited to heads of state and other heads of mission of equivalent rank; envoys, ministers and internuncios accredited to heads of state; and chargés d'affaires accredited to ministers of foreign affairs.[305] It is customary for a named individual to be in charge of a diplomatic mission. When, in 1979, Libya designated its embassies as 'People's Bureaux' to be run by revolutionary committees, the UK insisted upon and obtained the nomination of a named person as the head of the mission.[306]

---

[304] See e.g. the Ethiopian demand that Eritrea reduce its diplomatic staff at the commencement of the armed conflict between the states: see Eritrea–Ethiopia Claims Commission, decision of 19 December 2005, Partial Award, Eritrea's Claim 20, paras. 40 ff.

[305] The rules as to heads of missions are a modern restatement of the rules established in 1815 by the European powers: see Denza, *Diplomatic Law*, p. 110.

[306] Comment by Sir Antony Acland, Minutes of Evidence Taken Before the Foreign Affairs Committee, *Report*, p. 20. See also DUSPIL, 1979, pp. 571–3.

The inviolability of the premises of the mission

In order to facilitate the operations of normal diplomatic activities, article 22 of the Convention specifically declares that the premises of the mission are inviolable and that agents of the receiving state are not to enter them without the consent of the mission. This appears to be an absolute rule[307] and in the Sun Yat Sen incident in 1896, the Court refused to issue a writ of habeas corpus with regard to a Chinese refugee held against his will in the Chinese legation in London.[308] Precisely what the legal position would be in the event of entry without express consent because, for example, of fire-fighting requirements or of danger to persons within that area, is rather uncertain under customary law, but under the Convention any justification pleaded by virtue of implied consent would be regarded as at best highly controversial.[309] The receiving state is under a special duty to protect the mission premises from intrusion or damage or 'impairment of its dignity'.[310] The US Supreme Court, for example, while making specific reference to article 22 of the Vienna Convention, emphasised in *Boos* v. *Barry* that, 'The need to protect diplomats is grounded in our Nation's important interest in international relations . . . Diplomatic personnel are essential to conduct the international affairs so crucial to the well-being of this Nation.'[311] It was also noted that protecting foreign diplomats in the US ensures that similar protection would be afforded to US diplomats abroad.[312] The Supreme Court upheld a District of Columbia statute which made it unlawful to congregate within 500 feet of diplomatic premises and refuse to disperse after having been so ordered by the police, and stated that, 'the "prohibited quantum of disturbance" is whether normal

---

[307] See e.g. *767 Third Avenue Associates* v. *Permanent Mission of the Republic of Zaire to the United Nations* 988 F.2d 295 (1993); 99 ILR, p. 194.

[308] A. D. McNair, *International Law Opinions*, Oxford, 1956, vol. I, p. 85. The issue was resolved by diplomatic means.

[309] The original draft of the article would have permitted such emergency entry, but this was rejected: see Denza, *Diplomatic Law*, pp. 144 ff. In 1973 an armed search of the Iraqi Embassy in Pakistan took place and considerable quantities of arms were found. As a result the Iraqi ambassador and an attaché were declared *personae non grata*, ibid., p. 149. As to further examples, see *ibid.*, pp. 149–50. A search by US troops of the residence of the Nicaraguan ambassador in Panama in 1989 was condemned in a draft Security Council resolution by a large majority, but was vetoed by the US, *ibid*. Nevertheless, Denza concludes that, 'In the last resort, however, it cannot be excluded that entry without the consent of the sending State may be justified in international law by the need to protect human life', *ibid.*, p. 150.

[310] See e.g. the statement of US President Johnson after a series of demonstrations against the US Embassy in Moscow in 1964–5, 4 ILM, 1965, p. 698.

[311] 99 L.Ed.2d 333, 345–6 (1988); 121 ILR, p. 551.   [312] *Ibid.*

embassy activities have been or are about to be disrupted'.[313] By the same token, the premises of a mission must not be used in a way which is incompatible with the functions of the mission.[314]

In 1979, the US Embassy in Tehran, Iran was taken over by several hundred demonstrators. Archives and documents were seized and fifty diplomatic and consular staff were held hostage. In 1980, the International Court declared that, under the 1961 Convention (and the 1963 Convention on Consular Relations):

> Iran was placed under the most categorical obligations, as a receiving state, to take appropriate steps to ensure the protection of the United States Embassy and Consulates, their staffs, their archives, their means of communication and the free movement of the members of their staffs.[315]

These were also obligations under general international law.[316] The Court in particular stressed the seriousness of Iran's behaviour and the conflict between its conduct and its obligations under 'the whole corpus of the international rules of which diplomatic and consular law is comprised, rules the fundamental character of which the Court must here again strongly affirm'.[317] In *Congo* v. *Uganda*, the International Court held that attacks on the Ugandan Embassy in Kinshasa, the capital of Congo, and attacks on persons on the premises by Congolese armed forces constituted a violation of article 22.[318] In addition, the Court emphasised that the Vienna

---

[313] 99 L.Ed.2d 351. See also *Minister for Foreign Affairs and Trade* v. *Magno* 112 ALR 529 (1992–3); 101 ILR, p. 202.

[314] Article 41(3) of the Vienna Convention. Note that in *Canada* v. *Edelson*, 131 ILR, p. 279, the Israeli Supreme Court held that a dispute over a lease granted to Canada, as represented by the Canadian Ambassador, raised issues of state immunity rather than diplomatic immunity. It was further held that there was no state immunity with regard to the lease of buildings for a residence for the Ambassador as leasing was a private law act.

[315] The *Iranian Hostages* case, ICJ Reports, 1980, pp. 3, 30–1; 61 ILR, p. 556. This the Iranians failed to do, ICJ Reports, 1980, pp. 31–2. The Court emphasised that such obligations concerning the inviolability of the members of a diplomatic mission and of the premises, property and archives of the mission continued even in cases of armed conflict or breach of diplomatic relations, *ibid.*, p. 40. See also DUSPIL, 1979, pp. 577 ff.; K. Gryzbowski, 'The Regime of Diplomacy and the Tehran Hostages', 30 ICLQ, 1981, p. 42, and L. Gross, 'The Case Concerning United States Diplomatic and Consular Staff in Tehran: Phase of Provisional Measures', 74 AJIL, 1980, p. 395.

[316] See e.g. *Belgium* v. *Nicod and Another* 82 ILR, p. 124.

[317] The *Iranian Hostages* case, ICJ Reports, 1980, p. 42; 61 ILR, p. 568. The Court particularly instanced articles 22, 25, 26 and 27 and analogous provisions in the 1963 Consular Relations Convention, *ibid.*

[318] ICJ Reports, 2005, paras. 337–8 and 340.

Convention not only prohibits any infringements of the inviolability of the mission by the receiving state itself but also puts the receiving state under an obligation to prevent others, such as armed militia groups, from doing so.[319]

On 8 May 1999, during the Kosovo campaign, the Chinese Embassy in Belgrade was bombed by the US. The US declared that it had been a mistake and apologised. In December 1999, the US and China signed an Agreement providing for compensation to be paid by the former to the latter of $28m. At the same time, China agreed to pay $2.87m to the US to settle claims arising out of rioting and attacks on the US Embassy in Beijing, the residence of the US consulate in Chengdu and the consulate in Guangzhu.[320]

On 17 April 1984, a peaceful demonstration took place outside the Libyan Embassy in London. Shots from the Embassy were fired that resulted in the death of a policewoman. After a siege, the Libyans inside left and the building was searched in the presence of a Saudi Arabian diplomat. Weapons and other relevant forensic evidence were found.[321] The issue raised here, in the light of article 45(a) which provides that after a break in diplomatic relations, 'the receiving state must . . . respect and protect the premises of the mission', is whether that search was permissible. The UK view is that article 45(a) does not mean that the premises continue to be inviolable[322] and this would clearly appear to be correct. There is a distinction between inviolability under article 22 and respect and protection under article 45(a).

The suggestion has also been raised that the right of self-defence may also be applicable in this context. It was used to justify the search of personnel leaving the Libyan Embassy[323] and the possibility was noted

---

[319] *Ibid.*, para. 342, citing the *Iranian Hostages* case, ICJ Reports, 1980, pp. 30–2. See also the condemnation by the Eritrea–Ethiopia Claims Commission of the entry, ransacking and seizure by Ethiopian security agents of the Eritrean Embassy residence, as well as vehicles and other property, without Eritrea's consent, Partial Award, Diplomatic Claim, Eritrea's Claim 20, para. 46.

[320] See DUSPIL, 2000, pp. 421–8. In addition, the US had earlier made a number of *ex gratia* payments to the individuals injured and to the families of those killed in the Embassy bombing, *ibid.*, p. 428. See also Denza, *Diplomatic Law*, p. 166.

[321] See Foreign Affairs Committee, *Report*, p. xxvi.

[322] Memorandum by the Foreign and Commonwealth Office, Foreign Affairs Committee, *Report*, p. 5.

[323] *Ibid.*, p. 9. Such a search was declared essential for the protection of the police, *ibid.* Note the reference to self-defence is both to domestic and international law, *ibid.*

that in certain limited circumstances it may be used to justify entry into an embassy.[324]

A rather different issue arises where mission premises have been abandoned. The UK enacted the Diplomatic and Consular Premises Act in 1987, under which states wishing to use land as diplomatic or consular premises are required to obtain the consent of the Secretary of State. Once such consent has been obtained (although this is not necessary in the case of land which had this status prior to the coming into force of the Act), it could be subsequently withdrawn. The Secretary of State has the power to require that the title to such land be vested in him where that land has been lying empty, or without diplomatic occupants, and could cause damage to pedestrians or neighbouring buildings because of neglect, providing that he is satisfied that to do so is permissible under international law (section 2). By section 3 of the Act, the Secretary of State is able to sell the premises, deduct certain expenses and transfer the residue to the person divested of his interest.

This situation occurred with respect to the Cambodian Embassy in London, whose personnel closed the building after the Pol Pot takeover of Cambodia in 1975, handing the keys over to the Foreign Office.[325] In 1979, the UK withdrew its recognition of the Cambodian government after the Vietnamese invasion and since that date had had no dealings with any authority as the government of that country. Squatters moved in shortly thereafter. These premises were made subject to section 2 of the Diplomatic and Consular Premises Act in 1988[326] and the Secretary of State vested the land in himself. This was challenged by the squatters and in *R v. Secretary of State for Foreign and Commonwealth Affairs, ex parte Samuel*,[327] Henry J held that the Secretary of State had acted correctly and in accordance with the duty imposed under article 45 of the Vienna Convention. The Court of Appeal dismissed an appeal,[328] holding that the

---

[324] See the comments of the Legal Adviser to the FCO, Minutes of Evidence, Foreign Affairs Committee, *Report*, p. 28. Of course, entry can be made into the building with the consent of the receiving state, as for example when Iran requested the UK to eject militants who had taken over their London embassy in 1980.

[325] See C. Warbrick, 'Current Developments', 38 ICLQ, 1989, p. 965.

[326] See s. 2 of the Diplomatic and Consular Premises (Cambodia) Order, SI 1988 no. 30.

[327] *The Times*, 10 September 1988.

[328] *The Times*, 17 August 1989; 83 ILR, p. 232. Note that in *Secretary of State for Foreign and Commonwealth Affairs v. Tomlin, The Times*, 4 December 1990; [1990] 1 All ER 920, the Court of Appeal held that in this situation, the extended limitation period of thirty years under s. 15(1) of and Schedule 1 to the Limitation Act 1980 was applicable and the squatters could not rely on twelve years' adverse possession.

relevant section merely required that the Secretary of State be satisfied that international law permitted such action.[329]

In *Westminster City Council* v. *Government of the Islamic Republic of Iran*,[330] the issue concerned the payment of expenses arising out of repairs to the damaged and abandoned Iranian Embassy in London in 1980. The council sought to register a land charge, but the question of the immunity of the premises under article 22 of the Vienna Convention was raised. Although the Court felt that procedurally it was unable to proceed,[331] reference was made to the substantive issue and it was noted that the premises had ceased to be diplomatic premises in the circumstances and thus the premises were not 'used' for the purpose of the mission as required by article 22, since that phrase connoted the present tense. The inviolability of diplomatic premises, however, must not be confused with extraterritoriality. Such premises do not constitute part of the territory of the sending state.[332]

Whether a right of diplomatic asylum exists within general international law is doubtful and in principle refugees are to be returned to the authorities of the receiving state in the absence of treaty or customary rules to the contrary. The International Court in the *Asylum* case between Colombia and Peru[333] emphasised that a decision to grant asylum involves a derogation from the sovereignty of the receiving state 'and constitutes an intervention in matters which are exclusively within the competence of that state. Such a derogation from territorial sovereignty cannot be recognised unless its legal basis is established in each particular case.' Where treaties exist regarding the grant of asylum, the question will arise as to the respective competences of the sending and receiving state or the state granting asylum and the territorial state. While the diplomats of the sending state may provisionally determine whether a refugee meets any condition laid down for the grant of asylum under an applicable treaty this would not bind the receiving state, for 'the principles of international law do not recognise any rule of unilateral and definitive qualification by

---

[329] Note that in the US, embassies temporarily abandoned due to broken relations may be sequestered and turned to other uses pending resumption of relations. This has been the case with regard to Iranian, Cambodian and Vietnamese properties that have been in the custody of the Office of Foreign Missions: see McClanahan, *Diplomatic Immunity*, pp. 53 and 110. See also the US Foreign Missions Act 1982.

[330] [1986] 3 All ER 284; 108 ILR, p. 557.   [331] See above, p. 748.

[332] See e.g. *Persinger* v. *Islamic Republic of Iran* 729 F.2d 835 (1984). See also *Swiss Federal Prosecutor* v. *Kruszyk* 102 ILR, p. 176.

[333] ICJ Reports, 1950, pp. 266, 274–5.

the state granting asylum'.[334] It may be that in law a right of asylum will arise for 'urgent and compelling reasons of humanity',[335] but the nature and scope of this is unclear.

The diplomatic bag

Article 27 provides that the receiving state shall permit and protect free communication on behalf of the mission for all official purposes. Such official communication is inviolable and may include the use of diplomatic couriers and messages in code and in cipher, although the consent of the receiving state is required for a wireless transmitter.[336]

Article 27(3) and (4) deals with the diplomatic bag,[337] and provides that it shall not be opened or detained[338] and that the packages constituting the diplomatic bag 'must bear visible external marks of their character and may contain only diplomatic documents or articles intended for official use'.[339] The need for a balance in this area is manifest. On the one hand, missions require a confidential means of communication, while on the other the need to guard against abuse is clear. Article 27, however, lays the emphasis upon the former.[340] This is provided that article 27(4) is complied with. In the Dikko incident on 5 July 1984, a former Nigerian minister was kidnapped in London and placed in a crate to be flown to Nigeria. The crate was opened at Stansted Airport, although accompanied by a person claiming diplomatic status. The crate[341] did not contain an official seal and was thus clearly not a diplomatic bag.[342] When, in March

---

[334] *Ibid.*, p. 274.   [335] *Oppenheim's International Law*, p. 1084.

[336] There was a division of opinion at the Vienna Conference between the developed and developing states over this issue. The former felt that the right to instal and use a wireless did not require consent: see Denza, *Diplomatic Law*, pp. 214 ff.

[337] Defined in article 3(2) of the Draft Articles on the Diplomatic Courier and the Diplomatic Bag adopted by the International Law Commission in 1989 as 'the packages containing official correspondence, and documents or articles intended exclusively for official use, whether accompanied by diplomatic courier or not, which are used for the official communication referred to in article 1 and which bear visible external marks of their character' as a diplomatic bag: see *Yearbook of the ILC*, 1989, vol. II, part 2, p. 15.

[338] Article 27(3).   [339] Article 27(4).

[340] This marked a shift from earlier practice: see *Yearbook of the ILC*, 1989, vol. II, part 2, p. 15.

[341] An accompanying crate contained persons allegedly part of the kidnapping operation.

[342] See Foreign Affairs Committee, *Report*, pp. xxxiii–xxxiv. Note also the incident in 1964 when an Israeli was found bound and drugged in a crate marked 'diplomatic mail' at Rome Airport. As a result, the Italians declared one Egyptian official at the Embassy *persona non grata* and expelled two others, *Keesing's Contemporary Archives*, p. 20580. In 1980, a crate bound for the Moroccan Embassy in London split open at Harwich to reveal $500,000 worth of drugs, *The Times*, 13 June 1980. In July 1984, a lorry belonging to the

2000, diplomatic baggage destined for the British High Commission in Harare was detained and opened by the Zimbabwe authorities, the UK government protested vigorously and announced the withdrawal of its High Commissioner for consultations.[343]

In view of suspicions of abuse, the question has arisen as to whether electronic screening, not involving opening or detention, of the diplomatic bag is legitimate. The UK appears to take the view that electronic screening of this kind would be permissible, although it claims not to have carried out such activities, but other states do not accept this.[344] It is to be noted that after the Libyan Embassy siege in April 1984, the diplomatic bags leaving the building were not searched.[345] However, Libya had entered a reservation to the Vienna Convention, reserving its right to open a diplomatic bag in the presence of an official representative of the diplomatic mission concerned. In the absence of permission by the authorities of the sending state, the diplomatic bag was to be returned to its place of origin. Kuwait and Saudi Arabia made similar reservations which were not objected to.[346] This is to be contrasted with a Bahraini reservation to article 27(3) which would have permitted the opening of diplomatic bags in certain circumstances.[347] The Libyan reservation could have been relied upon by the UK in these conditions.

It is also interesting to note that after the Dikko incident, the UK Foreign Minister stated that the crates concerned were opened because of the suspicion of human contents. Whether the crates constituted diplomatic bags or not was a relevant consideration with regard to a right to search, but:

> the advice given and the advice which would have been given had the crate constituted a diplomatic bag took fully into account the overriding duty to preserve and protect human life.[348]

USSR was opened for inspection by West German authorities on the grounds that a lorry itself could not be a bag. The crates inside the lorry were accepted as diplomatic bags and not opened, Foreign Affairs Committee, *Report*, p. xiii, note 48.

[343] See UKMIL, 71 BYIL, 2000, pp. 586–7.

[344] See the Legal Adviser, FCO, Foreign Affairs Committee, *Report*, p. 23. See also 985 HC Deb., col. 1219, 2 June 1980, and Cmnd 9497. See further *Yearbook of the ILC*, 1988, vol. II, part 1, p. 157, and Denza, *Diplomatic Law*, pp. 238 ff.

[345] Foreign Affairs Committee, *Report*, p. xxx.

[346] See Denza, *Diplomatic Law*, pp. 229 ff. The UK did not object and regarded the reservations in fact as reflective of customary law prior to the Convention, Memorandum of the FCO, Foreign Affairs Committee, *Report*, p. 4.

[347] This was objected to, Foreign Affairs Committee, *Report*, p. 4, and see Denza, *Diplomatic Law*, pp. 230–1.

[348] See Foreign Affairs Committee, *Report*, p. 50.

This appears to point to an implied exception to article 27(3) in the interests of humanity. It is to be welcomed, provided, of course, it is applied solely and strictly in these terms.

The issue of the diplomatic bag has been considered by the International Law Commission, in the context of article 27 and analogous provisions in the 1963 Consular Relations Convention, the 1969 Convention on Special Missions and the 1975 Convention on the Representation of States in their Relations with International Organisations. Article 28 of the Draft Articles on the Diplomatic Courier and the Diplomatic Bag, as finally adopted by the International Law Commission in 1989, provides that the diplomatic bag shall be inviolable wherever it may be. It is not to be opened or detained and 'shall be exempt from examination directly or through electronic or other technical device'. However, in the case of the consular bag, it is noted that if the competent authorities of the receiving or transit state have serious reason to believe that the bag contains something other than official correspondence and documents or articles intended exclusively for official use, they may request that the bag be opened in their presence by an authorised representative of the sending state. If this request is refused by the authorities of the sending state, the bag is to be returned to its place of origin.[349] It was thought that this preserved existing law. Certainly, in so far as the consular bag is concerned, the provisions of article 35(3) of the Vienna Convention on Consular Relations are reproduced, but the stipulation of exemption from electronic or other technical examination does not appear in the Vienna Convention on Diplomatic Relations and the view of the Commission that this is mere clarification[350] is controversial.[351]

As far as the diplomatic courier is concerned, that is, a person accompanying a diplomatic bag, the Draft Articles provide for a regime of privileges, immunities and inviolability that is akin to that governing diplomats. He is to enjoy personal inviolability and is not liable to any form of arrest or detention (draft article 10), his temporary accommodation is inviolable (draft article 17), and he will benefit from immunity from the criminal and civil jurisdiction of the receiving or transit state in

---

[349] Draft article 28(2). See *Yearbook of the ILC*, 1989, vol. II, part 2, pp. 42–3. See also S. McCaffrey, 'The Forty-First Session of the International Law Commission', 83 AJIL, 1989, p. 937.

[350] *Yearbook of the ILC*, 1989, vol. II, part 2, p. 43.

[351] See e.g. *Yearbook of the ILC*, 1980, vol. II, pp. 231 ff.; *ibid.*, 1981, vol. II, pp. 151 ff. and *ibid.*, 1985, vol. II, part 2, pp. 30 ff. See also A/38/10 (1983) and the Memorandum by Sir Ian Sinclair, member of the ILC, dealing with the 1984 session on this issue, Foreign Affairs Committee, *Report*, pp. 79 ff.

respect of all acts performed in the exercise of his functions (draft article 18). In general, his privileges and immunities last from the moment he enters the territory of the receiving or transit state until he leaves such state (draft article 21).[352]

Diplomatic immunities – property

Under article 22 of the Vienna Convention, the premises of the mission are inviolable[353] and, together with their furnishings and other property thereon and the means of transport, are immune from search, requisition, attachment or execution. By article 23, a general exception from taxation in respect of the mission premises is posited. The Court in the *Philippine Embassy* case explained that, in the light of customary and treaty law, 'property used by the sending state for the performance of its diplomatic functions in any event enjoys immunity even if it does not fall within the material or spatial scope' of article 22.[354] It should also be noted that the House of Lords in *Alcom Ltd* v. *Republic of Colombia*[355] held that under the State Immunity Act 1978 a current account at a commercial bank in the name of a diplomatic mission would be immune unless the plaintiff could show that it had been earmarked by the foreign state solely for the settlement of liabilities incurred in commercial transactions. An account used to meet the day-to-day running expenses of a diplomatic mission would therefore be immune. This approach was also based upon the obligation contained in article 25 of the Vienna Convention on Diplomatic Relations, which provided that the receiving state 'shall accord full facilities for the performance of the functions of the mission'. The House of Lords noted that the negative formulation of this principle meant that neither the executive nor the legal branch of government in the receiving state must act in such manner as to obstruct the mission in carrying out its functions.[356]

Section 16(1)b of the State Immunity Act provides, however, that the exemption from immunity in article 6 relating to proceedings involving immovable property in the UK did not extend to proceedings concerning 'a state's title to or its possession of property used for the purposes of a

---

[352] See e.g. McClanahan, *Diplomatic Immunity*, p. 64, and *Yearbook of the ILC*, 1985, vol. II, part 2, pp. 36 ff.
[353] By article 30(1) of the Convention, the private residence of a diplomatic agent shall enjoy the same inviolability and protection as the premises of the mission.
[354] See UN, *Materials*, pp. 297, 317; 65 ILR, pp. 146, 187.
[355] [1984] 2 All ER 6; 74 ILR, p. 180.
[356] [1984] 2 All ER 9; 74 ILR, p. 182. See also Denza, *Diplomatic Law*, pp. 156–9 and 202.

diplomatic mission'. It was held in *Intpro Properties (UK) Ltd* v. *Sauvel*[357] by the Court of Appeal that the private residence of a diplomatic agent, even where used for embassy social functions from time to time, did not constitute use for the purposes of a diplomatic mission and that in any event the proceedings did not concern the French government's title to or possession of the premises, but were merely for damages for breach of a covenant in a lease. Accordingly, there was no immunity under section 16.

It is to be noted that by article 24 of the Vienna Convention, the archives and documents of the mission are inviolable at any time and wherever they may be.[358] Although 'archives and documents' are not defined in the Convention, article 1(1)k of the Vienna Convention on Consular Relations provides that the term 'consular archives' includes 'all the papers, documents, correspondence, books, films, tapes and registers of the consular post together with the ciphers and codes, the card-indexes and any article of furniture intended for their protection or safekeeping'. The term as used in the Diplomatic Relations Convention cannot be less than this.[359]

The question of the scope of article 24 was discussed by the House of Lords in *Shearson Lehman* v. *Maclaine Watson (No. 2)*,[360] which concerned the intervention by the International Tin Council in a case on the grounds that certain documents it was proposed to adduce in evidence were inadmissible. This argument was made in the context of article 7 of the International Tin Council (Immunities and Privileges) Order 1972 which stipulates that the ITC should have the 'like inviolability of official archives as . . . is accorded in respect of the official archives of a diplomatic mission'. Lord Bridge interpreted the phrase 'archives and documents of the mission' in article 24 as referring to the archives and documents 'belonging to or held by the mission'.[361] Such protection was not confined to executive or judicial action by the host state, but would cover, for example, the situation where documents were put into circulation by virtue of theft or other improper means.[362]

---

[357] [1983] 2 All ER 495; 64 ILR, p. 384.
[358] This goes beyond previous customary law: see e.g. *Rose* v. *R* [1947] 3 DLR 618. See also *Renchard* v. *Humphreys & Harding Inc.* 381 F.Supp. 382 (1974); the *Iranian Hostages* case, ICJ Reports, 1980, pp. 3, 36, and Denza, *Diplomatic Law*, pp. 189 ff.
[359] See e.g. Denza, *Diplomatic Law*, p. 195.   [360] [1988] 1 WLR 16; 77 ILR, p. 145.
[361] [1988] 1 WLR 24; 77 ILR, p. 150.
[362] [1988] 1 WLR 27; 77 ILR, p. 154. See also *Fayed* v. *Al-Tajir* [1987] 2 All ER 396; 86 ILR, p. 131.

Diplomatic immunities – personal

The person of a diplomatic agent[363] is inviolable under article 29 of the Vienna Convention and he may not be detained or arrested.[364] This principle is the most fundamental rule of diplomatic law and is the oldest established rule of diplomatic law.[365] In resolution 53/97 of January 1999, for example, the UN General Assembly strongly condemned acts of violence against diplomatic and consular missions and representatives,[366] while the Security Council issued a presidential statement, condemning the murder of nine Iranian diplomats in Afghanistan.[367] States recognise that the protection of diplomats is a mutual interest founded on functional requirements and reciprocity.[368] The receiving state is under an obligation to 'take all appropriate steps' to prevent any attack on the person, freedom or dignity of diplomatic agents.[369]

After a period of kidnappings of diplomats, the UN Convention on the Prevention and Punishment of Crimes against Internationally Protected Persons, Including Diplomatic Agents was adopted in 1973. This provides that states parties must make attacks upon such persons a crime in internal law with appropriate penalties and take such measures as may be necessary to establish jurisdiction over these crimes. States parties are obliged

[363] Defined in article 1(e) as the head of the mission or a member of the diplomatic staff of the mission. See above, p. 735, with regard to head of state immunities. See also e.g. *US v. Noriega* 746 F.Supp. 1506, 1523–5; 99 ILR, pp. 145, 165–7.

[364] Note that by article 26 the receiving state is to ensure to all members of the mission freedom of movement and travel in its territory, subject to laws and regulations concerning prohibited zones or zones regulated for reasons of national security.

[365] See Denza, *Diplomatic Law*, pp. 256 ff.

[366] See also resolution 42/154 and Secretary-General's Reports A/INF/52/6 and Add.1 and A/53/276 and Corr.1.

[367] SC/6573 (15 September 1998). See also the statement of the UN Secretary-General, SG/SM/6704 (14 September 1998).

[368] See e.g. the US Supreme Court in *Boos* v. *Barry* 99 L Ed 2d 333, 346 (1988); 121 ILR, pp. 499, 556.

[369] Note that in *Harb* v. *King Fahd* [2005] EWCA Civ 632, para. 40, the Court of Appeal held that article 29 was not breached by the court hearing an issue relating to sovereign immunity in open court where the sovereign in question wished a challenge to an application for maintenance to be held in private. In *Mariam Aziz* v. *Aziz and Sultan of Brunei* [2007] EWCA Civ 712, paras. 88 ff., it was held by the Court of Appeal that while under international law a state is obliged to take steps to prevent physical attacks on, or physical interference with, a foreign head of state in the jurisdiction, it was doubted whether the rule extended to preventing conduct by individuals which was simply offensive or insulting to a foreign head of state abroad.

to extradite or prosecute offenders.[370] The most blatant example of the breach of the obligation to protect diplomats was the holding of the US diplomats as hostages in Iran in 1979–80, where the International Court held that the inaction of the Iranian government faced with the detention of US diplomatic and consular staff over an extended period constituted a 'clear and serious violation' of article 29.[371] In *Congo* v. *Uganda*, the International Court held that the maltreatment by Congo forces of persons within the Ugandan Embassy constituted a violation of article 29 in so far as such persons were diplomats, while the maltreatment of Ugandan diplomats at the airport similarly breached the obligations laid down in article 29.[372]

However, in exceptional cases, a diplomat may be arrested or detained on the basis of self-defence or in the interests of protecting human life.[373]

Article 30(1) provides for the inviolability of the private residence[374] of a diplomatic agent, while article 30(2) provides that his papers, correspondence and property[375] are inviolable. Section 4 of the Diplomatic Privileges Act 1964 stipulates that where a question arises as to whether a person is or is not entitled to any privilege or immunity under the Act, which incorporates many of the provisions of the Vienna Convention, a certificate issued by or under the authority of the Secretary of State stating any fact relating to that question shall be conclusive evidence of that fact.

---

[370] See articles 2, 3, 6 and 7. Such crimes are by article 8 deemed to be extraditable offences in any extradition treaty between states parties. See *Duff* v. *R* [1979] 28 ALR 663; 73 ILR, p. 678.

[371] ICJ Reports, 1980, pp. 3, 32, 35–7; 61 ILR, p. 530.

[372] ICJ Reports, 2005, paras. 338–40. See also the decision of the Eritrea–Ethiopia Claims Commission on 19 December 2005 in Partial Award, Diplomatic Claim, Ethiopia's Claim 8, that Eritrea was liable for violating article 29 by arresting and briefly detaining the Ethiopian Chargé d'Affaires in September 1998 and October 1999 without regard to his diplomatic immunity.

[373] ICJ Reports, 1980, p. 40. See also Denza, *Diplomatic Law*, p. 267.

[374] As distinct from the premises of the mission. Such residence might be private leased or leased by the sending state for use as such residential premises and may indeed be temporary only. Temporary absence would not lead to a loss of immunity, but permanent absence would: see e.g. *Agbor* v. *Metropolitan Police Commissioner* [1969] 2 All ER 707 and Denza, *Diplomatic Law*, pp. 270 ff. S. 9 of the Criminal Law Act 1977 makes it a criminal offence knowingly to trespass on any premises which are the private residence of a diplomatic agent.

[375] Except that this is limited by article 31(3): see below, p. 767. Possession alone of property would be sufficient, it appears, to attract inviolability: see Denza, *Diplomatic Law*, p. 277.

As far as criminal jurisdiction is concerned, diplomatic agents enjoy complete immunity from the legal system of the receiving state,[376] although there is no immunity from the jurisdiction of the sending state.[377] This provision noted in article 31(1) reflects the accepted position under customary law. The only remedy the host state has in the face of offences alleged to have been committed by a diplomat is to declare him *persona non grata* under article 9.[378] Specific problems have arisen with regard to motoring offences.[379]

Article 31(1) also specifies that diplomats[380] are immune from the civil and administrative jurisdiction of the state in which they are serving, except in three cases:[381] first, where the action relates to private immovable property situated within the host state (unless held for mission purposes);[382] secondly, in litigation relating to succession matters in which

---

[376] See e.g. *Dickinson* v. *Del Solar* [1930] 1 KB 376; 5 AD, p. 299; the *Iranian Hostages* case, ICJ Reports, 1980, pp. 3, 37; 61 ILR, p. 530 and *Skeen* v. *Federative Republic of Brazil* 566 F.Supp. 1414 (1983); 121 ILR, p. 481. See also Denza, *Diplomatic Law*, pp. 280 ff.

[377] Article 31(4).

[378] See e.g. the incident in Washington DC in 1999, when an attaché of the Russian Embassy was declared *persona non grata* for suspected 'bugging' of the State Department, 94 AJIL, 2000, p. 534.

[379] However, the US has tackled the problem of unpaid parking fines by adopting s. 574 of the Foreign Operations, Export Financing and Related Programs Appropriations Act 1994, under which 110 per cent of unpaid parking fines and penalties must be withheld from that state's foreign aid. In addition, the State Department announced in December 1993 that registration renewal of vehicles with unpaid or unadjudicated parking tickets more than one year old would be withheld, thus rendering the use of such vehicles illegal in the US: see 'Contemporary Practice of the United States Relating to International Law', 88 AJIL, 1994, p. 312. It is also required under the US Diplomatic Relations Act 1978 that diplomatic missions, their members and families hold liability insurance and civil suits against insurers are permitted. Note that the UK has stated that persistent failure by diplomats to respect parking regulations and to pay fixed penalty parking notices 'will call into question their continued acceptability as members of diplomatic missions in London', UKMIL, 63 BYIL, 1992, p. 700. See also Denza, *Diplomatic Law*, pp. 288–9 and UKMIL, 77 BYIL, 2006, pp. 741 ff.

[380] Note that a diplomat who is a national or permanent resident of the receiving state will only enjoy immunity from jurisdiction and inviolability in respect of official acts performed in the exercise of his functions, article 38.

[381] Article 31(1)a, b and c. Note that there is no immunity from the jurisdiction of the sending state, article 31(4).

[382] See *Intpro Properties (UK) Ltd* v. *Sauvel* [1983] 2 All ER 495; 64 ILR, p. 384. In the *Deputy Registrar* case, 94 ILR, pp. 308, 311, it was held that article 31(1)a was declaratory of customary international law. In *Hildebrand* v. *Champagne* 82 ILR, p. 121, it was held that this provision did not cover the situation where a claim was made for payment for charges under a lease. See also *Largueche* v. *Tancredi Feni* 101 ILR, p. 377 and *De Andrade* v. *De Andrade* 118 ILR, pp. 299, 306–7. Article 13 of the UN Convention on Jurisdictional

the diplomat is involved as a private person (for example as an executor or heir); and, finally, with respect to unofficial professional or commercial activity engaged in by the agent.[383] In a document issued by the Foreign Office in 1987, entitled *Memorandum on Diplomatic Privileges and Immunities in the United Kingdom*,[384] it was noted that a serious view was taken of any reliance on diplomatic immunity from civil jurisdiction to evade a legal obligation and that such conduct could call into question the continued acceptability in the UK of a particular diplomat.[385] By article 31(2), a diplomat cannot be obliged to give evidence as a witness, while by article 31(3), no measures of execution may be taken against such a person except in the cases referred to in article 31(1)a, b and c and provided that the measures concerned can be taken without infringing the inviolability of his person or of his residence. Diplomatic agents are generally exempt from the social security provisions in force in the receiving state,[386] from all dues and taxes, personal or real, regional or municipal except for indirect taxes,[387] from personal and public services[388] and from customs duties and inspection.[389] The personal baggage of a diplomat is exempt from inspection unless there are serious grounds for presuming that it contains articles not covered by the specified exemptions in article 36(1). Inspections can only take place in the presence of the diplomat or his authorised representative.[390]

Article 37 provides that the members of the family of a diplomatic agent forming part of his household[391] shall enjoy the privileges and immunities specified in articles 29 to 36 if not nationals of the receiving state.[392] In UK practice, members of the family include spouses and minor children

---

Immunities provides for an exception to state immunity for proceedings which relate to the determination of any right or interest of the state in, or its possession or use of, or any obligation of the state arising out of its interest in, or its possession or use of, immovable property situation in the forum state.

[383] See *Portugal* v. *Goncalves* 82 ILR, p. 115. This exception does not include ordinary contracts incidental to life in the receiving state, such as a contract for domestic services: see *Tabion* v. *Mufti* 73 F.3d 535 and Denza, *Diplomatic Law*, pp. 301 ff. See also *De Andrade* v. *De Andrade* 118 ILR, pp. 299, 306–7, noting that the purchase by a diplomat of the home unit as an investment was not a commercial activity within the meaning of the provision.

[384] See UKMIL, 58 BYIL, 1987, p. 549.

[385] Annex F, reproducing a memorandum dated February 1985, *ibid.*, p. 558. See Annex F of the 1992 Memorandum, UKMIL, 63 BYIL, 1992, p. 698.

[386] Article 33.   [387] Article 34 and see subsections b to g for certain other exceptions.

[388] Article 35.   [389] Article 36(1).   [390] Article 36(2).

[391] See Brown, 'Diplomatic Immunity', pp. 63–6 and Denza, *Diplomatic Law*, pp. 391 ff.

[392] The rationale behind this is to ensure the diplomat's independence and ability to function free from harassment: see Denza, *Diplomatic Law*, pp. 393–4.

(i.e. under the age of eighteen); children over eighteen not in permanent paid employment (such as students); persons fulfilling the social duties of hostess to the diplomatic agent; and the parent of a diplomat living with him and not engaged in paid permanent employment.[393]

Members of the administrative and technical staff (and their households), if not nationals or permanent residents of the receiving state, may similarly benefit from articles 29–35,[394] except that the article 31(1) immunities do not extend beyond acts performed in the course of their duties, while members of the service staff, who are not nationals or permanent residents of the receiving state, benefit from immunity regarding acts performed in the course of official duties.[395]

Immunities and privileges start from the moment the person enters the territory of the receiving state on proceeding to take up his post or, if already in the territory, from the moment of official notification under article 39.[396] In *R* v. *Governor of Pentonville Prison, ex parte Teja*,[397] Lord Parker noted that it was fundamental to the claiming of diplomatic immunity that the diplomatic agent 'should have been in some form accepted or received by this country'.[398] This view was carefully interpreted by the Court of Appeal in *R* v. *Secretary of State for the Home Department, ex parte Bagga*[399] in the light of the facts of the former case so that, as Parker LJ held, if a person already in the country is employed as a secretary, for example, at an embassy, nothing more than notification is required before that person would be entitled to immunities. While it had been held in

---

[393] *Ibid.*, pp. 394–5. Since the Civil Partnership Act 2004, household would include same sex partners. See, for the slightly different US practice, *ibid.*, pp. 395–6. The term 'spouse' may be interpreted to include more than one wife in a polygamous marriage forming part of the household of the diplomat and may include a partner not being married to the diplomat, *ibid.*, pp. 394–6.

[394] The privileges specified in article 36(1) in relation to exemption from customs duties and taxes apply only to articles imported at the time of first installation.

[395] Customary law prior to the Vienna Convention was most unclear on immunities of such junior diplomatic personnel and it was recognised that these provisions in article 37 constituted a development in such rules: see e.g. Denza, *Diplomatic Law*, pp. 401 ff. and *Yearbook of the ILC*, 1958, vol. II, pp. 101–2. See also S v. *India* 82 ILR, p. 13.

[396] See also article 10, which provides that the Ministry of Foreign Affairs of the receiving state shall be notified of the appointment of members of the mission, their arrival and their final departure or the termination of their functions with the mission. There are similar requirements with regard to family members and private servants. See also *Lutgarda Jimenez* v. *Commissioners of Inland Revenue* [2004] UK SPC 00419 (23 June 2004), and Denza, *Diplomatic Law*, pp. 88 ff.

[397] [1971] 2 QB 274; 52 ILR, p. 368.   [398] [1971] 2 QB 282; 52 ILR, p. 373.

[399] [1991] 1 QB 485; 88 ILR, p. 404.

R v. *Lambeth Justices, ex parte Yusufu*[400] that article 39, in the words of Watkins LJ, provided 'at most some temporary immunity between entry and notification to a person who is without a diplomat', the court in *Bagga* disagreed strongly.[401] Immunity clearly did not depend upon notification and acceptance,[402] but under article 39 commenced upon entry. Article 40 provides for immunity where the person is in the territory in transit between his home state and a third state to which he has been posted.[403] Where, however, a diplomat is in a state which is neither the receiving state nor a state of transit between his state and the receiving state, there will be no immunity.[404] Immunities and privileges normally cease when the person leaves the country or on expiry of a reasonable period in which to do so.[405] However, by article 39(2) there would be continuing immunity with regard to those acts that were performed in the exercise of his functions as a member of the mission. It follows from this formulation that immunity would not continue for a person leaving the receiving state for any act which was performed outside the exercise of his functions as a member of a diplomatic mission even though he was immune from prosecution at the time. This was the view taken by the US Department of State with regard to an incident where the ambassador of Papua New Guinea was responsible for a serious automobile accident involving damage to five cars and injuries to two persons.[406] The ambassador was withdrawn from the US and assurances sought by Papua New Guinea that any criminal investigation of the incident or indictment of the former ambassador under US domestic law would be quashed were rejected. The US refused to accept the view that international law precluded the prosecution of the former diplomat for non-official acts committed during his period of accreditation.[407] In *Propend Finance* v. *Sing*, the Court took a broad view

---

[400] [1985] Crim. LR 510; 88 ILR, p. 323.

[401] [1991] 1 QB 485, 498; 88 ILR, pp. 404, 412.

[402] [1991] 1 QB 499; 88 ILR, p. 413, 'save possibly in the case of a head of mission or other person of diplomatic rank', *ibid.* See also *Lutgarda Jimenez* v. *Commissioners of Inland Revenue* [2004] UK SPC 00419 (23 June 2004), and Denza, *Diplomatic Law*, p. 431.

[403] See Brown, 'Diplomatic Immunity', p. 59, and *Bergman* v. *de Sieyès* 170 F.2d 360 (1948). See also *R* v. *Governor of Pentonville Prison, ex parte Teja* [1971] 2 QB 274; 52 ILR, p. 368. Note that such immunity only applies to members of his family if they were accompanying him or travelling separately to join him or return to their country, *Vafadar* 82 ILR, p. 97.

[404] See e.g. *Public Prosecutor* v. *JBC* 94 ILR, p. 339.

[405] Article 39, and see *Shaw* v. *Shaw* [1979] 3 All ER 1; 78 ILR, p. 483.

[406] See 81 AJIL, 1987, p. 937.

[407] See the *Tabatabai* case, 80 ILR, p. 388; *US* v. *Guinand* 688 F.Supp. 774 (1988); 99 ILR, p. 117; *Empson* v. *Smith* [1965] 2 All ER 881; 41 ILR, p. 407 and *Shaw* v. *Shaw* [1979] 3

of diplomatic functions, including within this term police liaison functions so that immunity continued under article 39(2).[408]

In the *Former Syrian Ambassador to the GDR* case, the German Federal Constitutional Court held that article 39(2) covered the situation where the ambassador in question was accused of complicity in murder by allowing explosives to be transferred from his embassy to a terrorist group. He was held to have acted in the exercise of his official functions. It was argued that diplomatic immunity from criminal proceedings knew of no exception for particularly serious crimes, the only resort being to declare him *persona non grata*.[409] The Court, in perhaps a controversial statement, noted that article 39(2), while binding on the receiving state, was not binding on third states.[410] Accordingly the continuing immunity of the former ambassador to the German Democratic Republic under article 39(2) was not binding upon the Federal Republic of Germany.

Although a state under section 4 of the State Immunity Act of 1978 is subject to the local jurisdiction with respect to contracts of employment made or wholly or partly to be performed in the UK, section 16(1)a provides that this is not to apply to proceedings concerning the employment of the members of a mission within the meaning of the Vienna Convention[411] and this was reaffirmed in *Sengupta* v. *Republic of India*,[412] a case concerning a clerk employed at the Indian High Commission in London.[413]

All ER 1; 78 ILR, p. 483. See also Y. Dinstein, 'Diplomatic Immunity from Jurisdiction *Ratione Materiae*', 15 ICLQ, 1966, p. 76.

[408] 111 ILR, pp. 611, 659–61. See also *Re P (No. 2)* [1998] 1 FLR 1027; 114 ILR, p. 485.

[409] 121 ILR, pp. 595, 607–8.

[410] *Ibid.*, pp. 610–12. See B. Fassbender, 'S v. Berlin Court of Appeal and District Court of Berlin-Tiergarten', 92 AJIL, 1998, pp. 74, 78.

[411] Or to members of a consular post within the meaning of the 1963 Consular Relations Convention enacted by the Consular Relations Act of 1968.

[412] 64 ILR, p. 352. See further above, p. 725.

[413] Diplomatic agents are also granted exemptions from certain taxes and customs duties. However, this does not apply to indirect taxes normally incorporated in the price paid; taxes on private immovable property in the receiving state unless held on behalf of the sending state for purposes of the mission; various estate, succession or inheritance duties; taxes on private income having its source in the receiving state; charges for specific services, and various registration, court and record fees with regard to immovable property other than mission premises: see article 34 of the Vienna Convention. See also *UK Memorandum*, p. 693.

Waiver of immunity

By article 32 of the 1961 Vienna Convention, the sending state may waive the immunity from jurisdiction of diplomatic agents and others possessing immunity under the Convention.[414] Such waiver must be express.[415] Where a person with immunity initiates proceedings, he cannot claim immunity in respect of any counter-claim directly connected with the principal claim.[416] Waiver of immunity from jurisdiction in respect of civil or administrative proceedings is not to be taken to imply waiver from immunity in respect of the execution of the judgment, for which a separate waiver is necessary.

In general, waiver of immunity has been unusual, especially in criminal cases.[417] In a memorandum entitled *Department of State Guidance for Law Enforcement Officers With Regard to Personal Rights and Immunities of Foreign Diplomatic and Consular Personnel*[418] the point is made that waiver of immunity does not 'belong' to the individual concerned, but is for the benefit of the sending state. While waiver of immunity in the face of criminal charges is not common, 'it is routinely sought and occasionally granted'. However, Zambia speedily waived the immunity of an official at its London embassy suspected of drugs offences in 1985.[419]

In *Fayed* v. *Al-Tajir*,[420] the Court of Appeal referred to an apparent waiver of immunity by an ambassador made in pleadings by way of defence. Kerr LJ correctly noted that both under international and English law, immunity was the right of the sending state and that therefore 'only the sovereign can waive the immunity of its diplomatic representatives. They cannot do so themselves.'[421] It was also pointed out that the defendant's defence filed in the proceedings brought against him was not an appropriate vehicle for waiver of immunity by a state.[422] In *A Company* v. *Republic of X*,[423] Saville J noted that whether or not there was a

---

[414] See Denza, *Diplomatic Law*, pp. 330 ff.
[415] See e.g. *Public Prosecutor* v. *Orhan Olmez* 87 ILR, p. 212.
[416] See e.g. *High Commissioner for India* v. *Ghosh* [1960] 1 QB 134; 28 ILR, p. 150.
[417] See McClanahan, *Diplomatic Immunity*, p. 137, citing in addition an incident where the husband of an official of the US Embassy in London was suspected of gross indecency with a minor, where immunity was not waived, but the person concerned was returned to the US. But see Denza, *Diplomatic Law*, pp. 345 ff., noting the examples of waivers of immunity.
[418] Reproduced in 27 ILM, 1988, pp. 1617, 1633.
[419] McClanahan, *Diplomatic Immunity*, pp. 156–7.   [420] [1987] 2 All ER 396.
[421] *Ibid.*, p. 411.   [422] *Ibid.*, pp. 408 (Mustill LJ) and 411–12 (Kerr LJ).
[423] [1990] 2 LL. R 520, 524; 87 ILR, pp. 412, 416, citing *Kahan* v. *Pakistan Federation* [1951] 2 KB 1003; 18 ILR, p. 210.

power to waive article 22 immunities (and he was unconvinced that there existed such a power), no mere *inter partes* agreement could bind the state to such a waiver, but only an undertaking or consent given to the Court itself at the time when the Court is asked to exercise jurisdiction over or in respect of the subject matter of the immunities. In view of the principle that immunities adhere to the state and not the individual concerned, such waiver must be express and performed clearly by the state as such.

Consular privileges and immunities: the Vienna Convention on Consular Relations, 1963 [424]

Consuls represent their state in many administrative ways, for instance, by issuing visas and passports and generally promoting the commercial interests of their state. They have a particular role in assisting nationals in distress with regard to, for example, finding lawyers, visiting prisons and contacting local authorities, but they are unable to intervene in the judicial process or internal affairs of the receiving state or give legal advice or investigate a crime.[425] They are based not only in the capitals of receiving states, but also in the more important provincial cities. However, their political functions are few and they are accordingly not permitted the same degree of immunity from jurisdiction as diplomatic agents.[426] Consuls must possess a commission from the sending state and the authorisation (*exequatur*) of a receiving state.[427] They are entitled to the same exemption from taxes and customs duties as diplomats.

Article 31 emphasises that consular premises are inviolable and may not be entered by the authorities of the receiving state without consent. Like diplomatic premises, they must be protected against intrusion or

---

[424] See e.g. L. T. Lee, *Consular Law and Practice*, 2nd edn, Durham, 1991, and Lee, *Vienna Convention on Consular Relations*, Durham, 1966; M. A. Ahmad, *L'Institution Consulaire et le Droit International*, Paris, 1973, and *Satow's Guide*, book III. See also Nguyen Quoc Dinh *et al.*, *Droit International Public*, p. 757; *Oppenheim's International Law*, pp. 1142 ff., and *Third US Restatement of Foreign Relations Law*, pp. 474 ff. The International Court in the *Iranian Hostages* case stated that this Convention codified the law on consular relations, ICJ Reports, 1980, pp. 3, 24; 61 ILR, pp. 504, 550. See also the Consular Relations Act 1968.

[425] See e.g. the UK Foreign Office leaflet entitled 'British Consular Services Abroad' quoted in UKMIL, 70 BYIL, 1999, p. 530, and see also *Ex parte Ferhut Butt* 116 ILR, pp. 607, 618.

[426] See further above, p. 725, with regard to employment and sovereign immunity disputes, a number of which concerned consular activities.

[427] Articles 10, 11 and 12.

impairment of dignity,[428] and similar immunities exist with regard to archives and documents[429] and exemptions from taxes.[430] Article 35 provides for freedom of communication, emphasising the inviolability of the official correspondence of the consular post and establishing that the consular bag should be neither opened nor detained. However, in contrast to the situation with regard to the diplomatic bag,[431] where the authorities of the receiving state have serious reason to believe that the bag contains other than official correspondence, documents or articles, they may request that the bag be opened and, if this is refused, the bag shall be returned to its place of origin.

Article 36(1) constitutes a critical provision and, as the International Court emphasised in the *LaGrand (Germany* v. *USA)* case, it 'establishes an interrelated regime designed to facilitate the implementation of the system of consular protection'.[432] Article 36(1)a provides that consular officers shall be free to communicate with nationals of the sending state and to have access to them, while nationals shall have the same freedom of communication with and access to consular officers. In particular, article 36(1)b provides that if the national so requests, the authorities of the receiving state shall without delay inform the consular post of the sending state of any arrest or detention. The authorities in question shall inform the national of the sending state without delay of his or her rights. Similarly, any communication from the detained national to the consular post must be forwarded without delay. The International Court held that article 36(1) created individual rights for the persons concerned which could be invoked by the state, which, by virtue of the Optional Protocol on Compulsory Settlement of Disputes attached to the Convention, may be brought before the Court.[433] The International Court has subsequently underlined that violations of individual rights under this provision may also violate the rights of the state itself, while such violations could also constitute violations of the individual.[434]

The Court held that the US had breached its obligations under article 36(1)[435] by not informing the LaGrand brothers of their rights under

---

[428] But note Security Council resolution 1193 (1998) condemning the Taliban authorities in Afghanistan for the capture of the Iranian consulate-general. See also *R (B)* v. *Secretary of State for Foreign and Commonwealth Affairs* [2004] EWCA Civ 1344; 131 ILR, p. 616.

[429] Article 33.   [430] Article 32.   [431] See above, p. 759.

[432] ICJ Reports, 2001, pp. 466, 492; 134 ILR, pp. 1, 31. See also the *Avena (Mexico* v. *USA)* case, ICJ Reports, 2004, pp. 12, 39; 134 ILR, pp. 120, 142.

[433] ICJ Reports, 2001, p. 494; 134 ILR, p. 33.

[434] The *Avena (Mexico* v. *USA)* case, ICJ Reports, 2004, pp. 12, 36; 134 ILR, pp. 120, 139.

[435] ICJ Reports, 2001, p. 514; 134 ILR, p. 52. In an Advisory Opinion of 1 October 1999, the Inter-American Court of Human Rights concluded that the duty to notify detained

that provision 'without delay'.[436] The International Court reaffirmed its approach in the *Avena* case, brought by Mexico against the US on substantially similar grounds to the *LaGrand* case.[437]

Article 41 provides that consular officers may not be arrested or detained except in the case of a grave crime and following a decision by the competent judicial authority. If, however, criminal proceedings are instituted against a consul, he must appear before the competent authorities. The proceedings are to be conducted in a manner that respects his official position and minimises the inconvenience to the exercise of consular functions. Under article 43 their immunity from jurisdiction is restricted in both criminal and civil matters to acts done in the official exercise of consular functions.[438] In *Koeppel and Koeppel* v. *Federal Republic of Nigeria*,[439] for example, it was held that the provision of refuge by the Nigerian Consul-General to a Nigerian national was an act performed in the exercise of a consular function within the meaning of article 43 and thus attracted consular immunity.

The Convention on Special Missions, 1969 [440]

In many cases, states will send out special or ad hoc missions to particular countries to deal with some defined issue in addition to relying upon the permanent staffs of the diplomatic and consular missions. In such circumstances, these missions, whether purely technical or politically

---

foreign nationals of the right to seek consular assistance under article 36(1) constituted part of the corpus of human rights, Series A 16, OC-16/99, 1999 and 94 AJIL, 2000, p. 555. See above, chapter 7, p. 389. Note that the International Court in the *LaGrand* case felt it unnecessary to deal with this argument, ICJ Reports, 2001, pp. 466, 494–5. As to the right of access to nationals, see also the Yugoslav incident of summer 2000, where the UK protested at the absence of information with regard to the arrest by Yugoslavia of British citizens seconded to the UN Mission in Kosovo: see UKMIL, 71 BYIL, 2000, p. 608.

[436] The Court has noted that the obligation on the detaining authorities to provide the necessary information under article 36(1)b arises once it is realised that the detainee is a foreign national or when there are grounds to think that the person is probably a foreign national, the *Avena* case, ICJ Reports, 2004, pp. 12, 43 and 49; 134 ILR, pp. 120, 146 and 153.

[437] ICJ Reports, 2004, p. 12. See as to the obligations of the US in the two cases as found by the International Court, below, chapter 19, p. 1103. See also as to the response of the US courts to these cases, above, chapter 4, pp. 135 and 164, note 178.

[438] See e.g. *Princess Zizianoff* v. *Kahn and Bigelow* 4 AD, p. 384. See generally, as to consular functions, DUSPIL, 1979, pp. 655 ff. Note that waiver of consular immunities under article 45, in addition to being express, must also be in writing.

[439] 704 F.Supp. 521 (1989); 99 ILR, p. 121.

[440] See e.g. Hardy, *Modern Diplomatic Law*, p. 89, and *Oppenheim's International Law*, pp. 1125 ff. The Convention came into force in June 1985.

important, may rely on certain immunities which are basically derived from the Vienna Conventions by analogy with appropriate modifications. By article 8, the sending state must let the host state know of the size and composition of the mission, while according to article 17 the mission must be sited in a place agreed by the states concerned or in the Foreign Ministry of the receiving state.

By article 31 members of special missions have no immunity with respect to claims arising from an accident caused by a vehicle, used outside the official functions of the person involved, and by article 27 only such freedom of movement and travel as is necessary for the performance of the functions of the special mission is permitted.

The question of special missions was discussed in the *Tabatabai* case before a series of German courts.[441] The Federal Supreme Court noted that the Convention had not yet come into force and that there were conflicting views as to the extent to which it reflected existing customary law. However, it was clear that there was a customary rule of international law which provided that an ad hoc envoy, charged with a special political mission by the sending state, may be granted immunity by individual agreement with the host state for that mission and its associated status and that therefore such envoys could be placed on a par with members of the permanent missions of states.[442] The concept of immunity protected not the diplomat as a person, but rather the mission to be carried out by that person on behalf of the sending state. The question thus turned on whether there had been a sufficiently specific special mission agreed upon by the states concerned, which the Court found in the circumstances.[443] In *US* v. *Sissoko*, the District Court held that the Convention on Special Missions, to which the US was not a party, did not constitute customary international law and was thus not binding upon the Court.[444]

The Vienna Convention on the Representation of States in their Relations with International Organisations of a Universal Character, 1975 [445]

This treaty applies with respect to the representation of states in any international organisation of a universal character, irrespective of whether

---

[441] See 80 ILR, p. 388. See also Böckslaff and Koch, 'The Tabatabai Case: The Immunity of Special Envoys and the Limits of Judicial Review', 25 German YIL, 1982, p. 539.

[442] 80 ILR, pp. 388, 419.   [443] *Ibid.*, p. 420.

[444] 999 F.Supp. 1469 (1997); 121 ILR, p. 600. See also *Re Bo Xilai* 76 BYIL, 2005, p. 601.

[445] See e.g. J. G. Fennessy, 'The 1975 Vienna Convention on the Representation of States in their Relations with International Organisations of a Universal Character', 70 AJIL, 1976, p. 62.

or not there are diplomatic relations between the sending and the host states.

There are many similarities between this Convention and the 1961 Vienna Convention. By article 30, for example, diplomatic staff enjoy complete immunity from criminal jurisdiction, and immunity from civil and administrative jurisdiction in all cases, save for the same exceptions noted in article 31 of the 1961 Convention. Administrative, technical and service staff are in the same position as under the latter treaty (article 36).

The mission premises are inviolable and exempt from taxation by the host state, while its archives, documents and correspondence are equally inviolable.

The Convention has received an unenthusiastic welcome, primarily because of the high level of immunities it provides for on the basis of a controversial analogy with diplomatic agents of missions.[446] The range of immunities contrasts with the general situation under existing conventions such as the Convention on the Privileges and Immunities of the United Nations, 1946.[447]

The immunities of international organisations

As far as customary rules are concerned, the position is far from clear and it is usually dealt with by means of a treaty, providing such immunities to the international institution sited on the territory of the host state as are regarded as functionally necessary for the fulfilment of its objectives.

Probably the most important example is the General Convention on the Privileges and Immunities of the United Nations of 1946, which sets out the immunities of the United Nations and its personnel and emphasises the inviolability of its premises, archives and documents.[448]

---

[446] It should be noted that among those states abstaining in the vote adopting the Convention were France, the US, Switzerland, Austria, Canada and the UK, all states that host the headquarters of important international organisations: see Fennessy, '1975 Vienna Convention', p. 62.

[447] See in particular article IV. See also, for a similar approach in the Convention on the Privileges and Immunities of the Specialised Agencies, 1947, article V.

[448] See further below, chapter 23, p. 1318. See, as to the privileges and immunities of foreign armed forces, including the NATO Status of Forces Agreement, 1951, which provides for a system of concurrent jurisdiction, S. Lazareff, *Status of Military Forces under Current International Law*, Leiden, 1971; Brownlie, *Principles*, pp. 362 ff., and J. Woodliffe, *The Peacetime Use of Foreign Military Installations under Modern International Law*, Dordrecht, 1992.

Suggestions for further reading

E. Denza, *Diplomatic Law*, 3rd edn, Oxford, 2008

A. Dickinson, R. Lindsay and J. P. Loonam, *State Immunity: Selected Materials and Commentary*, Oxford, 2004

H. Fox, *The Law of State Immunity*, Oxford, 2002

C. H. Schreuer, *State Immunity: Some Recent Developments*, Cambridge, 1988

I. Sinclair, 'The Law of Sovereign Immunity: Recent Developments', 167 HR, 1980, p. 113

A. Watts, 'The Legal Position in International Law of Heads of State, Heads of Governments and Foreign Ministers', 247 HR, 1994 III, p. 13

14

State responsibility

State responsibility is a fundamental principle of international law, arising out of the nature of the international legal system and the doctrines of state sovereignty and equality of states. It provides that whenever one state commits an internationally unlawful act against another state, international responsibility is established between the two. A breach of an international obligation gives rise to a requirement for reparation.[1]

Accordingly, the focus is upon principles concerned with second-order issues, in other words the procedural and other consequences flowing from a breach of a substantive rule of international law.[2] This has led to a number of issues concerning the relationship between the rules of

---

[1] See generally J. Crawford, *The International Law Commission's Articles on State Responsibility*, Cambridge, 2002; *Obligations Multilatérales, Droit Impératif et Responsabilité Internationale des États* (ed. P. M. Dupuy), Paris, 2003; *Issues of State Responsibility before International Judicial Institutions* (eds. M. Fitzmaurice and D. Sarooshi), Oxford, 2003; M. Forteau, *Droit de la Sécurité Collective et Droit de la Responsabilité Internationale de l'État*, Paris, 2006; N. H. B. Jørgensen, *The Responsibility of States for International Crimes*, Oxford, 2003; *International Responsibility Today: Essays in Memory of Oscar Schachter* (ed. M. Ragazzi), The Hague, 2005; S. Villalpando, *L'Émergence de la Communauté Internationale dans la Responsabilité des États*, Paris, 2005; C. Eagleton, *The Responsibility of States in International Law*, New York, 1928; *International Law of State Responsibility for Injuries to Aliens* (ed. R. B. Lillich), Charlottesville, 1983; R. B. Lillich, 'Duties of States Regarding the Civil Rights of Aliens', 161 HR, 1978, p. 329, and Lillich, *The Human Rights of Aliens in Contemporary International Law*, Charlottesville, 1984; I. Brownlie, *System of the Law of Nations: State Responsibility, Part I*, Oxford, 1983; Bin Cheng, *General Principles of Law as Applied by International Courts and Tribunals*, London, 1953; *United Nations Codification of State Responsibility* (eds. M. Spinedi and B. Simma), New York, 1987; Société Français de Droit International, *La Responsabilité dans le Système International*, Paris, 1991; B. Stern, 'La Responsabilité Internationale Aujourd'hui ... Demain ... ' in *Mélanges Apollis*, Paris, 1992; Nguyen Quoc Dinh, P. Daillier and A. Pellet, *Droit International Public*, 7th edn, Paris, 2002, p. 729, and *Oppenheim's International Law* (eds. R. Y. Jennings and A. D. Watts), 9th edn, London, 1992, chapter 4. See also the Secretary-General's Compilation of Decisions of International Courts, Tribunals and Other Bodies, A/62/62, 1 February 2007, as supplemented by A/62/62/Add.1, 17 April 2007.

[2] See *Yearbook of the ILC*, 1973, vol. II, pp. 169–70. The issue of state responsibility for injuries caused by lawful activities will be noted in chapter 15.

state responsibility and those relating to other areas of international law. The question as to the relationship between the rules of state responsibility and those relating to the law of treaties arose, for example, in the *Rainbow Warrior* Arbitration between France and New Zealand in 1990.[3] The arbitration followed the incident in 1985 in which French agents destroyed the vessel *Rainbow Warrior* in harbour in New Zealand. The UN Secretary-General was asked to mediate and his ruling in 1986[4] provided *inter alia* for French payment to New Zealand and for the transference of two French agents to a French base in the Pacific, where they were to stay for three years and not to leave without the mutual consent of both states.[5] However, both the agents were repatriated to France before the expiry of the three years for various reasons, without the consent of New Zealand. The 1986 Agreement contained an arbitration clause and this was invoked by New Zealand. The argument put forward by New Zealand centred upon the breach of a treaty obligation by France, whereas that state argued that only the law of state responsibility was relevant and that concepts of *force majeure* and distress exonerated it from liability.

The arbitral tribunal decided that the law relating to treaties was relevant, but that the legal consequences of a breach of a treaty, including the determination of the circumstances that may exclude wrongfulness (and render the breach only apparent) and the appropriate remedies for breach, are subjects that belong to the customary law of state responsibility.[6]

It was noted that international law did not distinguish between contractual and tortious responsibility, so that any violation by a state of any obligation of whatever origin gives rise to state responsibility and consequently to the duty of reparation.[7] In the *Gabčíkovo–Nagymaros Project* case, the International Court reaffirmed the point that

> A determination of whether a convention is or is not in force, and whether it has or has not been properly suspended or denounced, is to be made pursuant to the law of treaties. On the other hand, an evaluation of the extent to which the suspension or denunciation of a convention, seen as incompatible with the law of treaties, involves the responsibility of the state which proceeded to it, is to be made under the law of state responsibility.[8]

The Arbitration Commission on Yugoslavia also addressed the issue of the relationship between state responsibility and other branches of

---

[3] 82 ILR, p. 499.   [4] See 81 AJIL, 1987, p. 325 and 74 ILR, p. 256.
[5] See also the Agreement between France and New Zealand of 9 July 1986, 74 ILR, p. 274.
[6] 82 ILR, pp. 499, 551.   [7] *Ibid*. See further below, p. 801.
[8] ICJ Reports, 1997, pp. 7, 38; 116 ILR, p. 1.

international law in Opinion No. 13, when asked a question as to whether any amounts due in respect of war damage might affect the distribution of assets and debts in the succession process affecting the successor states of the Former Yugoslavia. The Commission, in producing a negative answer, emphasised that the question of war damage was one that fell within the sphere of state responsibility, while the rules relating to state succession fell into a separate area of international law. Accordingly, the two issues had to be separately decided.[9]

Matters regarding the responsibility of states are necessarily serious and it is well established that a party asserting a fact must prove it.[10] The Eritrea–Ethiopia Claims Commission has taken the position that 'clear and convincing evidence' would be required in order to support findings as to state responsibility,[11] while the International Court has held that claims against a state involving 'charges of exceptional gravity' must be proved by evidence that is 'fully conclusive'.[12]

In addition to the wide range of state practice in this area, the International Law Commission worked extensively on this topic. In 1975 it took a decision for the draft articles on state responsibility to be divided into three parts: part I to deal with the origin of international responsibility, part II to deal with the content, forms and degrees of international responsibility and part III to deal with the settlement of disputes and the implementation of international responsibility.[13] Part I was provisionally adopted by the Commission in 1980[14] and the Draft Articles were finally adopted on 9 August 2001.[15] General Assembly resolution 56/83 of

[9] 96 ILR, pp. 726, 728.
[10] See e.g. *Genocide Convention (Bosnia* v. *Serbia)* case, ICJ Reports, 2007, para. 204.
[11] See e.g. Partial Award, Prisoners of War, Eritrea's Claim 17, 1 July 2003, paras. 46 and 49, and Partial Award, Civilian Claims, Ethiopia's Claim 5, 17 December 2004, para. 35.
[12] *Genocide Convention (Bosnia* v. *Serbia)* case, ICJ Reports, 2007, para. 209. See as to evidence and the International Court, below, chapter 19, p. 1088.
[13] *Yearbook of the ILC*, 1975, vol. II, pp. 55–9. See also P. Allott, 'State Responsibility and the Unmaking of International Law', 29 *Harvard International Law Journal*, 1988, p. 1; S. Rosenne, *The ILC's Draft Articles on State Responsibility*, Dordrecht, 1991; 'Symposium: The ILC's State Responsibility Articles', 96 AJIL, 2002, p. 773; 'Symposium: Assessing the Work of the International Law Commission on State Responsibility', 13 EJIL, 2002, p. 1053, and P. M. Dupuy, 'Quarante Ans de Codification de Droit de la Responsabilité Internationale des États: Un Bilan', 107 RGDIP, 2003, p. 305.
[14] *Yearbook of the ILC*, 1980, vol. II, part 2, pp. 30 ff.
[15] ILC Commentary 2001, A/56/10, 2001. This Report contains the Commentary of the ILC to the Articles, which will be discussed in the chapter. The Commentary may also be found in Crawford, *Articles*. Note that the ILC Articles do not address issues of either the responsibility of international organisations or the responsibility of individuals: see articles 57 and 58.

12 December 2001 annexed the text of the articles and commended them to governments, an unusual procedure which must be seen as giving particular weight to the status of the articles.[16]

The nature of state responsibility

The essential characteristics of responsibility hinge upon certain basic factors: first, the existence of an international legal obligation in force as between two particular states; secondly, that there has occurred an act or omission which violates that obligation and which is imputable to the state responsible, and finally, that loss or damage has resulted from the unlawful act or omission.[17]

These requirements have been made clear in a number of leading cases. In the *Spanish Zone of Morocco* claims,[18] Judge Huber emphasised that:

> responsibility is the necessary corollary of a right. All rights of an international character involve international responsibility. Responsibility results in the duty to make reparation if the obligation in question is not met.[19]

and in the *Chorzów Factory* case,[20] the Permanent Court of International Justice said that:

> it is a principle of international law, and even a greater conception of law, that any breach of an engagement involves an obligation to make reparation.

Article 1 of the International Law Commission's Articles on State Responsibility reiterates the general rule, widely supported by practice,[21] that every internationally wrongful act of a state entails responsibility.

---

[16] See also General Assembly resolution 59/35. Assembly resolution 62/61 of 8 January 2008 further commended the Articles on State Responsibility to states and decided to examine the question of a convention on the topic. See also S. Rosenne, 'State Responsibility: *Festina Lente*', 75 BYIL, 2004, p. 363, and J. Crawford and S. Olleson, 'The Continuing Debate on a UN Convention on State Responsibility', 54 ICLQ, 2005, p. 959.

[17] See e.g. H. Mosler, *The International Society as a Legal Community*, Dordrecht, 1980, p. 157, and E. Jiménez de Aréchaga, 'International Responsibility' in *Manual of Public International Law* (ed. M. Sørensen), London, 1968, pp. 531, 534.

[18] 2 RIAA, p. 615 (1923); 2 AD, p. 157.   [19] 2 RIAA, p. 641.

[20] PCIJ, Series A, No. 17, 1928, p. 29; 4 AD, p. 258. See also the *Corfu Channel* case, ICJ Reports, pp. 4, 23; 16 AD, p. 155; the *Spanish Zone of Morocco* case, 2 RIAA, pp. 615, 641 and the *Mayagna (Sumo) Indigenous Community of Awas Tingni* v. *Nicaragua*, Inter-American Court of Human Rights, Judgment of 31 August 2001 (Ser. C) No. 79, para. 163.

[21] See e.g. ILC Commentary 2001, p. 63.

Article 2 provides that there is an internationally wrongful act of a state when conduct consisting of an action or omission is attributable to the state under international law and constitutes a breach of an international obligation of the state.[22] This principle has been affirmed in the case-law.[23] It is international law that determines what constitutes an internationally unlawful act, irrespective of any provisions of municipal law.[24] Article 12 stipulates that there is a breach of an international obligation[25] when an act of that state is not in conformity with what is required of it by that obligation, regardless of its origin or character.[26] A breach that is of a continuing nature extends over the entire period during which the act continues and remains not in conformity with the international obligation in question,[27] while a breach that consists of a composite act will also extend over the entire period during which the act or omission continues and remains not in conformity with the international obligation.[28] A state assisting another state[29] to commit an internationally wrongful act will also be responsible if it so acted with knowledge of the circumstances and where it would be wrongful if committed by that state.[30] State responsibility may co-exist with individual responsibility. The two are not mutually exclusive.[31]

---

[22] See *Yearbook of the ILC*, 1976, vol. II, pp. 75 ff. and ILC Commentary 2001, p. 68.

[23] See e.g. *Chorzów Factory* case, PCIJ, Series A, No. 9, p. 21 and the *Rainbow Warrior* case, 82 ILR, p. 499.

[24] Article 3. See generally *Yearbook of the ILC*, 1979, vol. II, pp. 90 ff.; *ibid.*, 1980, vol. II, pp. 14 ff. and ILC Commentary 2001, p. 74. See also *Noble Ventures* v. *Romania*, ICSID award of 12 October 2005, para. 53 and above, chapter 4, pp. 133 ff.

[25] By which the state is bound at the time the act occurs, Article 13 and ILC Commentary 2001, p. 133. This principle reflects the general principle of intertemporal law: see e.g. the *Island of Palmas* case, 2 RIAA, pp. 829, 845 and above, chapter 9, p. 508.

[26] See the *Gabčíkovo–Nagymaros (Hungary* v. *Slovakia) Project* case, ICJ Reports, 1997, pp. 7, 38; 116 ILR, p. 1 and ILC Commentary 2001, p. 124.

[27] See article 14. See also e.g. the *Rainbow Warrior* case, 82 ILR, p. 499; the *Gabčíkovo–Nagymaros (Hungary* v. *Slovakia) Project* case, ICJ Reports, 1997, pp. 7, 54; *Genocide Convention (Bosnia* v. *Serbia)* case, ICJ Reports, 2007, para. 431; *Loizidou* v. *Turkey*, Merits, European Court of Human Rights, Judgment of 18 December 1996, paras. 41–7 and 63–4; 108 ILR, p. 443 and *Cyprus* v. *Turkey*, European Court of Human Rights, Judgment of 10 May 2001, paras. 136, 150, 158, 175, 189 and 269; 120 ILR, p. 10.

[28] Article 15.

[29] Or directing or controlling it, see article 17; or coercing it, see article 18.

[30] Article 16. See also the *Genocide Convention (Bosnia* v. *Serbia)* case, ICJ Reports, 2007, para. 420.

[31] See article 58. See also the *Genocide Convention (Bosnia* v. *Serbia)* case, ICJ Reports, 2007, para. 173, and A. Nollkaemper, 'Concurrence between Individual Responsibility and State Responsibility in International Law', 52 ICLQ, 2003, p. 615.

The question of fault [32]

There are contending theories as to whether responsibility of the state for unlawful acts or omissions is strict or whether it is necessary to show some fault or intention on the part of the officials concerned. The principle of objective responsibility (the so-called 'risk' theory) maintains that the liability of the state is strict. Once an unlawful act has taken place, which has caused injury and which has been committed by an agent of the state, that state will be responsible in international law to the state suffering the damage irrespective of good or bad faith. To be contrasted with this approach is the subjective responsibility concept (the 'fault' theory) which emphasises that an element of intentional (*dolus*) or negligent (*culpa*) conduct on the part of the person concerned is necessary before his state can be rendered liable for any injury caused.

The relevant cases and academic opinions are divided on this question, although the majority tends towards the strict liability, objective theory of responsibility.

In the *Neer* claim[33] in 1926, an American superintendent of a Mexican mine was shot. The USA, on behalf of his widow and daughter, claimed damages because of the lackadaisical manner in which the Mexican authorities pursued their investigations. The General Claims Commission dealing with the matter disallowed the claim, in applying the objective test.

In the *Caire* claim,[34] the French–Mexican Claims Commission had to consider the case of a French citizen shot by Mexican soldiers for failing to supply them with 5,000 Mexican dollars. Verzijl, the presiding commissioner, held that Mexico was responsible for the injury caused in accordance with the objective responsibility doctrine, that is 'the responsibility for the acts of the officials or organs of a state, which may devolve upon it even in the absence of any "fault" of its own'.[35]

A leading case adopting the subjective approach is the *Home Missionary Society* claim[36] in 1920 between Britain and the United States. In this

---

[32] See e.g. Crawford, *Articles*, p. 12; H. Lauterpacht, *Private Law Sources and Analogies of International Law*, Cambridge, 1927, pp. 135–43; Nguyen Quoc Dinh *et al.*, *Droit International Public*, p. 766; Brownlie, *Principles of Public International Law*, 6th edn, Oxford, 2003, pp. 425 ff. and Brownlie, *System*, pp. 38–46, and Aréchaga, 'International Responsibility', pp. 534–40. See also J. G. Starke, 'Imputability in International Delinquencies', 19 BYIL, 1938, p. 104, and Cheng, *General Principles*, pp. 218–32.

[33] 4 RIAA, p. 60 (1926); 3 AD, p. 213.   [34] 5 RIAA, p. 516 (1929); 5 AD, p. 146.

[35] 5 RIAA, pp. 529–31. See also *The Jessie*, 6 RIAA, p. 57 (1921); 1 AD, p. 175.

[36] 6 RIAA, p. 42 (1920); 1 AD, p. 173.

case, the imposition of a 'hut tax' in the protectorate of Sierra Leone triggered off a local uprising in which Society property was damaged and missionaries killed. The tribunal dismissed the claim of the Society (presented by the US) and noted that it was established in international law that no government was responsible for the acts of rebels where it itself was guilty of no breach of good faith or negligence in suppressing the revolt. It should, therefore, be noted that the view expressed in this case is concerned with a specific area of the law, viz. the question of state responsibility for the acts of rebels. Whether one can analogise from this generally is open to doubt.

In the *Corfu Channel* case,[37] the International Court appeared to lean towards the fault theory[38] by saying that:

> it cannot be concluded from the mere fact of the control exercised by a state over its territory and waters that that state necessarily knew, or ought to have known, of any unlawful act perpetrated therein, nor yet that it necessarily knew, or should have known, the authors. This fact, by itself and apart from other circumstances, neither involves *prima facie* responsibility nor shifts the burden of proof.[39]

On the other hand, the Court emphasised that the fact of exclusive territorial control had a bearing upon the methods of proof available to establish the knowledge of that state as to the events in question. Because of the difficulties of presenting direct proof of facts giving rise to responsibility, the victim state should be allowed a more liberal recourse to inferences of fact and circumstantial evidence.[40]

However, it must be pointed out that the Court was concerned with Albania's knowledge of the laying of mines,[41] and the question of *prima facie* responsibility for *any* unlawful act committed within the territory of the state concerned, irrespective of attribution, raises different issues. It cannot be taken as proof of the acceptance of the fault theory. It may be concluded that doctrine and practice support the objective theory and that this is right, particularly in view of the proliferation of state organs

---

[37] ICJ Reports, 1949, p. 4; 16 AD, p. 155.

[38] See e.g. *Oppenheim's International Law*, p. 509.

[39] ICJ Reports, 1949, pp. 4, 18; 16 AD, p. 157. Cf. Judges Krylov and Ecer, *ibid.*, pp. 71–2 and 127–8. See also Judge Azevedo, *ibid.*, p. 85.

[40] ICJ Reports, 1949, pp. 4, 18.   [41] See Brownlie, *Principles*, pp. 427–9.

and agencies.[42] The Commentary to the ILC Articles emphasised that the Articles did not take a definitive position on this controversy, but noted that standards as to objective or subjective approaches, fault, negligence or want of due diligence would vary from one context to another depending upon the terms of the primary obligation in question.[43]

Imputability [44]

Imposing upon the state absolute liability wherever an official is involved encourages that state to exercise greater control over its various departments and representatives. It also stimulates moves towards complying with objective standards of conduct in international relations.

State responsibility covers many fields. It includes unlawful acts or omissions directly committed by the state and directly affecting other states: for instance, the breach of a treaty, the violation of the territory of another state, or damage to state property. An example of the latter heading is provided by the incident in 1955 when Bulgarian fighter planes shot down an Israeli civil aircraft of its state airline, El Al.[45] Another example of state responsibility is illustrated by the *Nicaragua* case,[46] where the International Court of Justice found that acts imputable to the US included the laying of mines in Nicaraguan internal or territorial waters and certain attacks on Nicaraguan ports, oil installations and a naval base by its agents.[47] In the *Corfu Channel* case,[48] Albania was held responsible for the consequences of mine-laying in its territorial waters on the basis

---

[42] The question of intention is to be distinguished from the problem of causality, i.e. whether the act or omission in question actually caused the particular loss or damage: see e.g. the *Lighthouses* case, 23 ILR, p. 352.

[43] ILC Commentary 2001, pp. 69–70.

[44] See e.g. *Yearbook of the ILC*, 1973, vol. II, p. 189. See also Brownlie, *System*, pp. 36–7 and chapter 7; Nguyen Quoc Dinh *et al.*, *Droit International Public*, p. 773; L. Condorelli, 'L'Imputation à l'État d'un Fait Internationallement Illicite', 188 HR, 1984, p. 9, and R. Higgins, 'The Concept of "the State": A Variable Geometry and Dualist Perceptions' in *Mélanges Abi-Saab*, The Hague, 2001, p. 547.

[45] See the *Aerial Incident* case, ICJ Reports, 1955, pp. 127, 130. See also the incident where a Soviet fighter plane crashed in Belgium. The USSR accepted responsibility for the loss of life and damage that resulted and compensation was paid: see 91 ILR, p. 287, and J. Salmon, 'Chute sur le Territoire Belge d'un Avion Militaire Sovietique de 4 Juillet 1989, Problèmes de Responsabilité', *Revue Belge de Droit International*, 1990, p. 510.

[46] *Nicaragua* v. *United States*, ICJ Reports, 1986, p. 14; 76 ILR, p. 349.

[47] ICJ Reports, 1986, pp. 48–51 and 146–9; 76 ILR, pp. 382, 480.

[48] ICJ Reports, 1949, p. 4; 16 AD, p. 155.

of knowledge possessed by that state as to the presence of such mines, even though there was no finding as to who had actually laid the mines. In the *Rainbow Warrior* incident,[49] the UN Secretary-General mediated a settlement in which New Zealand received *inter alia* a sum of $7 million for the violation of its sovereignty which occurred when that vessel was destroyed by French agents in New Zealand.[50] The state may also incur responsibility with regard to the activity of its officials in injuring a national of another state, and this activity need not be one authorised by the authorities of the state.

The doctrine depends on the link that exists between the state and the person or persons actually committing the unlawful act or omission. The state as an abstract legal entity cannot, of course, in reality 'act' itself. It can only do so through authorised officials and representatives. The state is not responsible under international law for all acts performed by its nationals. Since the state is responsible only for acts of its servants that are imputable or attributable to it, it becomes necessary to examine the concept of imputability (also termed attribution). Imputability is the legal fiction which assimilates the actions or omissions of state officials to the state itself and which renders the state liable for damage resulting to the property or person of an alien.

Article 4 of the ILC Articles provides that the conduct of any state organ (including any person or entity having that status in accordance with the internal law of the state) shall be considered as an act of the state concerned under international law where the organ exercises legislative, executive, judicial or any other function, whatever position it holds in the organisation of the state and whatever its character as an organ of the central government or of a territorial unit of the state. This approach reflects customary law. As the International Court noted in *Difference Relating to Immunity from Legal Process of a Special Rapporteur*, 'According to a well-established rule of international law, the conduct of any organ of a state must be regarded as an act of that state.'[51] The International Court

---

[49] See 81 AJIL, 1987, p. 325 and 74 ILR, pp. 241 ff. See also above, p. 778.

[50] Note also the *USS Stark* incident, in which a US guided missile frigate on station in the Persian Gulf was attacked by Iraqi aircraft in May 1987. The Iraqi government agreed to pay compensation of $27 million: see 83 AJIL, 1989, pp. 561–4.

[51] ICJ Reports, 1999, pp. 62, 87; 121 ILR, pp. 405, 432. See also e.g. the *OSPAR (Ireland v. UK)* case, Final Award, 2 July 2003, para. 144; 126 ILR, 334, 379, the *Massey* case, 4 RIAA, p. 155 (1927); 4 AD, p. 250 and the *Salvador Commercial Company* case, 15 RIAA, p. 477 (1902). As an example of the state organ concerned being from the judiciary, see the *Sunday Times* case, European Court of Human Rights, Series A, vol. 30, 1979; 58 ILR,

in the *Genocide Convention (Bosnia* v. *Serbia)* case regarded it as 'one of the cornerstones of the law of state responsibility, that the conduct of any state organ is to be considered an act of the state under international law, and therefore gives rise to the responsibility of the state if it constitutes a breach of an obligatrion of the state'. It was a rule of customary international law.[52] It would clearly cover units and sub-units within a state.[53]

Article 5, in reaction to the proliferation of government agencies and parastatal entities, notes that the conduct of a person or of an entity not an organ of the state under article 4 but which is empowered by the law of that state to exercise elements of governmental authority shall be considered an act of the state under international law, provided the person or entity is acting in that capacity in the particular instance. This provision is intended *inter alia* to cover the situation of privatised corporations which retain certain public or regulatory functions. Examples of the application of this article might include the conduct of private security firms authorised to act as prison guards or where private or state-owned airlines exercise certain immigration controls[54] or with regard to a railway company to which certain police powers have been granted.[55]

Article 5 issues may also arise where an organ or an agent of a state are placed at the disposal of another international legal entity in a situation where both the state and the entity exercise elements of control over the organ or agent in question. This occurs most clearly where a military contingent is placed by a state at the disposal of the UN for peace-keeping purposes. Both the state and the UN will exercise a certain jurisdiction over the contingent. The question arose in *Behrami* v. *France* before the European Court of Justice as to whether troops from certain NATO states forming part of KFOR and concerned in the particular instance with demining operations in the province of Kosovo could fall under the jurisdiction of the Court or whether the appropriate responsible organ was KFOR operating under the authority of the United Nations, a body not susceptible

---

p. 491, and from the legislature, see e.g. the *Young, James and Webster* case, European Court of Human Rights, Series A, vol. 44, 1981; 62 ILR, p. 359.

[52] ICJ Reports, 2007, para. 385.

[53] Thus, not only would communes, provinces and regions of a unitary state be concerned, see e.g. the *Heirs of the Duc de Guise* case, 13 RIAA, p. 161 (1951); 18 ILR, p. 423, but also the component states of a federal state, see e.g. the *LaGrand (Provisional Measures)* case, ICJ Reports, 1999, pp. 9, 16; 118 ILR, pp. 39, 46, the *Davy* case, 9 RIAA, p. 468 (1903); the *Janes* case, 4 RIAA, p. 86 (1925); 3 AD, p. 218 and the *Pellat* case, 5 AD, p. 145. See also *Yearbook of the ILC*, 1971, vol. II, part I, pp. 257 ff. and ILC Commentary 2001, pp. 84 ff.

[54] ILC Commentary 2001, p. 92.   [55] *Yearbook of the ILC*, 1974, vol. II, pp. 281–2.

to the jurisdiction of the Court. The Court held that the key question was whether the UN Security Council retained ultimate authority and control so that operational command only was delegated and that this was so in the light of resolution 1244. Accordingly, responsibility for the impugned action was attributable to the UN, so that jurisdiction did not exist with regard to the states concerned for the European Court.[56]

Article 6 provides that the conduct of an organ placed at the disposal of a state by another state shall be considered as an act of the former state under international law, if that organ was acting in the exercise of elements of the governmental authority of the former state. This would, for example, cover the UK Privy Council acting as the highest judicial body for certain Commonwealth countries.[57]

Ultra vires acts

An unlawful act may be imputed to the state even where it was beyond the legal capacity of the official involved, providing, as Verzijl noted in the *Caire* case,[58] that the officials 'have acted at least to all appearances as competent officials or organs or they must have used powers or methods appropriate to their official capacity'.

This was reaffirmed in the *Mossé* case,[59] where it was noted that:

> Even if it were admitted that... officials... had acted... outside the statutory limits of the competence of their service, it should not be deduced, without further ado, that the claim is not well founded. It would still be necessary to consider a question of law... namely whether in the international order the state should be acknowledged responsible for acts performed by officials within the apparent limits of their functions, in accordance with a line of conduct which was not entirely contrary to the instructions received.

In *Youman's* claim,[60] militia ordered to protect threatened American citizens in a Mexican town instead joined the riot, during which the Americans were killed. These unlawful acts by the militia were imputed to the state of Mexico, which was found responsible by the General Claims Commission. In the *Union Bridge Company* case,[61] a British official of the Cape

---

[56] Judgment of 2 May 2007, paras. 134 ff. See also *Bosphorus Airways v. Ireland*, European Court of Human Rights, judgment of 30 June 2005. As to the Kosovo situation, see above, chapter 9, p. 452.

[57] *Yearbook of the ILC*, 1974, vol. II, p. 288 and ILC Commentary 2001, p. 98.

[58] 5 RIAA, pp. 516, 530 (1929); 5 AD, pp. 146, 148.

[59] 13 RIAA, p. 494 (1953); 20 ILR, p. 217. [60] 4 RIAA, p. 110 (1926); 3 AD, p. 223.

[61] 6 RIAA, p. 138 (1924); 2 AD, p. 170.

Government Railway mistakenly appropriated neutral property during the Boer War. It was held that there was still liability despite the honest mistake and the lack of intention on the part of the authorities to appropriate the material in question. The key was that the action was within the general scope of duty of the official. In the *Sandline* case, the Tribunal emphasised that, 'It is a clearly established principle of international law that acts of a state will be regarded as such even if they are *ultra vires* or unlawful under the internal law of the state . . . their [institutions, officials or employees of the state] acts or omissions when they purport to act in their capacity as organs of the state are regarded internationally as those of the state even though they contravene the internal law of the state.'[62]

Article 7 of the ILC Articles provides that the conduct of an organ or of a person or entity empowered to exercise elements of governmental authority shall be considered an act of the state under international law if acting in that capacity, even if it exceeds its authority or contravenes instructions.[63] This article appears to lay down an absolute rule of liability, one not limited by reference to the apparent exercise of authority and, in the context of the general acceptance of the objective theory of responsibility, is probably the correct approach.[64]

Although private individuals are not regarded as state officials so that the state is not liable for their acts, the state may be responsible for failing to exercise the control necessary to prevent such acts. This was emphasised in the *Zafiro* case[65] between Britain and America in 1925. The Tribunal held the latter responsible for the damage caused by the civilian crew of a naval ship in the Philippines, since the naval officers had not adopted effective preventative measures.

State control and responsibility

Article 8 of the ILC Articles provides that the conduct of a person or group of persons shall be considered as an act of state under international

---

[62] 117 ILR, pp. 552, 561. See also *Azinian* v. *United Mexican States* 121 ILR, pp. 1, 23; *SPP(ME) Ltd* v. *Egypt* 106 ILR, p. 501 and *Metalclad Corporation* v. *United Mexican States* 119 ILR, pp. 615, 634.

[63] See ILC Commentary 2001, p. 99 and see also *Yearbook of the ILC*, 1975, vol. II, p. 67.

[64] See e.g. the *Caire* case, 5 RIAA, p. 516 (1929); 5 AD, p. 146; the *Velásquez Rodríguez* case, Inter-American Court of Human Rights, Series C, No. 4, 1989, para. 170; 95 ILR, pp. 259, 296 and *Ilaşcu* v. *Moldova and Russia*, European Court of Human Rights, judgment of 8 July 2004, para. 319. See also T. Meron, 'International Responsibility of States for Unauthorised Acts of Their Officials', 33 BYIL, 1957, p. 851.

[65] 6 RIAA, p. 160 (1925); 3 AD, p. 221. See also *Re Gill* 5 RIAA, p. 157 (1931); 6 AD, p. 203.

law if the person or group of persons is in fact acting on the instructions of, or under the direction or control of, that state in carrying out the conduct. The first proposition is uncontroversial, but difficulties have arisen in seeking to define the necessary direction or control required for the second proposition. The Commentary to the article emphasises that, 'Such conduct will be attributable to the state only if it directed or controlled the specific operation and the conduct complained of was an integral part of the operation.'[66] Recent case-law has addressed the issue.

In the *Nicaragua* case, the International Court declared that in order for the conduct of the *contra* guerrillas to have been attributable to the US, who financed and equipped the force, 'it would in principle have to be proved that that state had effective control of the military or paramilitary operation in the course of which the alleged violations were committed'.[67] In other words, general overall control would have been insufficient to ground responsibility. However, in the *Tadić* case, the International Criminal Tribunal for the Former Yugoslavia adopted a more flexible approach, noting that the degree of control might vary according to the circumstances and a high threshold might not always be required.[68] In this case, of course, the issue was of individual criminal responsibility. Further, the situation might be different where the state deemed responsible was in clear and uncontested effective control of the territory where the violation occurred. The International Court of Justice in the *Namibia* case stated that, 'Physical control of a territory and not sovereignty or legitimacy of title, is the basis of state liability for acts affecting other states.'[69] This was reaffirmed in *Loizidou* v. *Turkey*, where the European Court of Human Rights noted that, bearing in mind the object and purpose of the European Convention on Human Rights,

> the responsibility of a contracting party may also arise when as a consequence of military action – whether lawful or unlawful – it exercises effective control of an area outside its national territory. The obligation to secure, in such an area, the rights and freedoms set out in the Convention, derives from the fact of such control whether it be exercised directly, through its armed forces, or through a subordinate local administration.[70]

---

[66] ILC Commentary 2001, p. 104.   [67] ICJ Reports, 1986, pp. 14, 64–5; 76 ILR, p. 349.
[68] 38 ILM, 1999, pp. 1518, 1541.   [69] ICJ Reports, 1971, pp. 17, 54; 42 ILR, p. 2.
[70] Preliminary Objections, European Court of Human Rights, Series A, No. 310, 1995, pp. 20, 24; 103 ILR, p. 621, and the merits judgment, European Court of Human Rights, Judgment of 18 December 1996, para. 52; 108 ILR, p. 443. See also *Cyprus* v. *Turkey*, European Court of Human Rights, Judgment of 10 May 2001, para. 76; 120 ILR, p. 10.

The International Court returned to the issue in the *Genocide Convention (Bosnia v. Serbia)* case and reaffirmed its approach in the *Nicaragua* case. It noted that the Appeal Chamber's judgment in *Tadić* did not concern issues of state responsibility nor a question that was indispensable for the exercise of its jurisdiction. It held that the 'overall control' test was not appropriate for state responsibility and that the test under customary law was that reflected in article 8 whereby the state would be responsible for the acts of persons or groups (neither state organs nor equated with such organs) where an organ of the state gave the instructions or provided the direction pursuant to which the perpetrators of the wrongful act acted or where it exercised effective control over the action during which the wrong was committed.[71]

Article 9 of the ILC Articles provides that the conduct of a person or a group of persons shall be considered as an act of the state under international law if the person or group was in fact exercising elements of the governmental authority in the absence or default of the official authorities and in circumstances such as to call for the exercise of those elements of authority.[72]

Mob violence, insurrections and civil wars

Where the governmental authorities have acted in good faith and without negligence, the general principle is one of non-liability for the actions of rioters or rebels causing loss or damage.[73] The state, however, is under a duty to show due diligence. Quite what is meant by this is difficult to quantify and more easily defined in the negative.[74] It should also be noted that special provisions apply to diplomatic and consular personnel.[75]

Article 10 of the ILC Articles provides that where an insurrectional movement is successful either in becoming the new government of a state or in establishing a new state in part of the territory of the pre-existing

---

[71] ICJ Reports, 2007, paras. 403–6.

[72] See e.g. the *Yeager* case, 17 Iran–US CTR, 1987, pp. 92, 104.

[73] See e.g. the *Home Missionary Society* case, 6 RIAA, pp. 42, 44 (1920); 1 AD, p. 173; the *Youmans* case, 4 RIAA, p. 110 (1926); 3 AD, p. 223 and the *Herd* case, 4 RIAA, p. 653 (1930). See also P. Dumberry, 'New State Responsibility for Internationally Wrongful Acts by an Insurrectional Movement', 17 EJIL, 2006, p. 605.

[74] E.g. Judge Huber, the *Spanish Zone of Morocco* claims, 2 RIAA, pp. 617, 642 (1925); 2 AD, p. 157. See Brownlie, *Principles*, pp. 436 ff. and the *Sambaggio* case, 10 RIAA, p. 499 (1903). See also *Yearbook of the ILC*, 1957, vol. II, pp. 121–3, and G. Schwarzenberger, *International Law*, 3rd edn, London, 1957, pp. 653 ff.

[75] See above, chapter 13, pp. 764 ff.

state, it will be held responsible for its activities prior to its assumption of authority.[76]

The issue of the responsibility of the authorities of a state for activities that occurred prior to its coming to power was raised before the Iran–US Claims Tribunal. In *Short v. The Islamic Republic of Iran*,[77] the Tribunal noted that the international responsibility of a state can be engaged where the circumstances or events causing the departure of an alien are attributable to it, but that not all departures of aliens from a country in a period of political turmoil would as such be attributable to that state.[78] In the instant case, it was emphasised that at the relevant time the revolutionary movement had not yet been able to establish control over any part of Iranian territory and the government had demonstrated its loss of control. Additionally, the acts of supporters of a revolution cannot be attributed to the government following the success of the revolution, just as acts of supporters of an existing government are not attributable to the government. Accordingly, and since the claimant was unable to identify any agent of the revolutionary movement the actions of whom forced him to leave Iran, the claim for compensation failed.[79] In *Yeager v. The Islamic Republic of Iran*,[80] the Tribunal awarded compensation for expulsion, but in this case it was held that the expulsion was carried out by the Revolutionary Guards after the success of the revolution. Although the Revolutionary Guards were not at the time an official organ of the Iranian state, it was determined that they were exercising governmental authority with the knowledge and acquiescence of the revolutionary state, making Iran liable for their acts.[81]

Falling somewhat between these two cases is *Rankin v. The Islamic Republic of Iran*,[82] where the Tribunal held that the claimant had not proved that he had left Iran after the revolution as a result of action by the Iranian government and the Revolutionary Guards as distinct from leaving because of the general difficulties of life in that state during the revolutionary period. Thus Iranian responsibility was not engaged.

Where a state subsequently acknowledges and adopts conduct as its own, then it will be considered as an act of state under international law entailing responsibility, even though such conduct was not attributable

---

[76] See E. M. Borchard, *The Diplomatic Protection of Citizens Abroad*, New York, 1927, p. 241 and the *Bolivian Railway Company* case, 9 RIAA, p. 445 (1903). See also the ILC Commentary 2001, p. 112.

[77] 16 Iran–US CTR, p. 76; 82 ILR, p. 148.   [78] 16 Iran–US CTR, p. 83; 82 ILR, pp. 159–60.

[79] 16 Iran–US CTR, p. 85; 82 ILR, p. 161.   [80] 17 Iran–US CTR, p. 92; 82 ILR, p. 178.

[81] 17 Iran–US CTR, p. 104; 82 ILR, p. 194.   [82] 17 Iran–US CTR, p. 135; 82 ILR, p. 204.

to the state beforehand.[83] In the *Iranian Hostages* case, for example, the International Court noted that the initial attack on the US Embassy by militants could not be imputable to Iran since they were clearly not agents or organs of the state. However, the subsequent approval of the Ayatollah Khomeini and other organs of Iran to the attack and the decision to maintain the occupation of the Embassy translated that action into a state act. The militants thus became agents of the Iranian state for whose acts the state bore international responsibility.[84]

Circumstances precluding wrongfulness [85]

Where a state consents to an act by another state which would otherwise constitute an unlawful act, wrongfulness is precluded provided that the act is within the limits of the consent given.[86] The most common example of this kind of situation is where troops from one state are sent to another at the request of the latter.[87] Wrongfulness is also precluded where the act constitutes a lawful measure of self-defence taken in conformity with the Charter of the UN.[88] This would also cover force used in self-defence as defined in the customary right as well as under article 51 of the Charter, since that article refers in terms to the 'inherent right' of individual and collective self-defence.[89] Further, the ILC Commentary makes it clear that the fact that an act is taken in self-defence does not necessarily mean that all wrongfulness is precluded, since the principles relating to human rights and humanitarian law have to be respected. The International Court, in particular, noted in its advisory opinion in the *Legality of the Threat or Use of Nuclear Weapons* that, 'Respect for the environment is one of the elements that go to assessing whether an action is in conformity with the principles of necessity and proportionality' and thus in accordance with the right to self-defence.[90]

---

[83] Article 11 and see ILC Commentary 2001, p. 118.

[84] ICJ Reports, 1980, pp. 3, 34–5; 61 ILR, pp. 530, 560. See also above, chapter 13, p. 755.

[85] See e.g. M. Whiteman, *Digest of International Law*, Washington, 1970, vol. VII, pp. 837 ff.; *Yearbook of the ILC*, 1979, vol. II, part 1, pp. 21 ff.; *ibid.*, 1980, vol. II, pp. 26 ff. and ILC Commentary 2001, p. 169. See also Nguyen Quoc Dinh *et al.*, *Droit International Public*, p. 782, and A. V. Lowe, 'Precluding Wrongfulness or Responsibility: A Plea for Excuses', 10 EJIL, 1999, p. 405.

[86] See article 20 of the ILC Articles. See further ILC Commentary 2001, p. 173.

[87] See e.g. the dispatch of UK troops to Muscat and Oman in 1957, 574 HC Deb., col. 872, 29 July 1957, and to Jordan in 1958, SCOR, 13th Sess., 831st meeting, para. 28.

[88] Article 21 and see also ILC Commentary 2001, p. 177.

[89] See further below, chapter 20, p. 1131.

[90] ICJ Reports, 1996, pp. 226, 242; 110 ILR, p. 163.

Article 22 of the ILC Articles provides that the wrongfulness of an act is precluded if and to the extent that the act constitutes a countermeasure.[91] International law originally referred in this context to reprisals, whereby an otherwise unlawful act is rendered legitimate by the prior application of unlawful force.[92] The term 'countermeasures' is now the preferred term for reprisals not involving the use of force.[93] Countermeasures may be contrasted with the provisions laid down in article 60 of the Vienna Convention on the Law of Treaties, 1969, which deals with the consequences of a material breach of a treaty in terms of the competence of the other parties to the treaty to terminate or suspend it.[94] While countermeasures do not as such affect the legal validity of the obligation which has been breached by way of reprisal for a prior breach, termination of a treaty under article 60 would under article 70 free the other parties to it from any further obligations under that treaty.

The International Court stated in the *Gabčíkovo–Nagymaros Project* case that,

> In order to be justifiable, a countermeasure must meet certain conditions... In the first place it must be taken in response to a previous international wrongful act of another state and must be directed against that state... Secondly, the injured state must have called upon the state committing the wrongful act to discontinue its wrongful conduct or to make reparation for it... In the view of the Court, an important consideration is that the effects of a countermeasure must be commensurate with the injury suffered, taking account of the rights in question... [and] its purpose must be to induce the wrongdoing state to comply with its obligations under international law, and... the measure must therefore be reversible.[95]

---

[91] See ILC Commentary 2001, p. 180. See also Crawford, *Articles*, pp. 47 ff.

[92] See e.g. the *Naulilaa* case, 2 RIAA, p. 1025 (1928); 4 AD, p. 466 and the *Cysne* case, 2 RIAA, p. 1056; 5 AD, p. 150.

[93] See e.g. the *US–France Air Services Agreement* case, 54 ILR, pp. 306, 337. See also Report of the International Law Commission, 1989, A/44/10 and *ibid.*, 1992, A/47/10, pp. 39 ff. See also C. Annacker, 'Part Two of the International Law Commission's Draft Articles on State Responsibility', 37 German YIL, 1994, pp. 206, 234 ff.; M. Dawidowicz, 'Public Law Enforcement Without Public Law Safeguards? An Analysis of State Practice on Third-Party Countermeasures and Their Relationship to the UN Security Council', 77 BYIL, 2006, p. 333; E. Zoller, *Peacetime Unilateral Remedies: An Analysis of Countermeasures*, New York, 1984, and O. Y. Elagab, *The Legality of Non-Forcible Counter-Measures in International Law*, Oxford, 1988.

[94] See further below, chapter 16, p. 948.

[95] ICJ Reports, 1997, pp. 7, 55–7; 116 ILR, p. 1. Note that the ILC took the view that the duty to choose measures that are reversible is not absolute, ILC Commentary 2001, p. 332. See also the *Nicaragua* case, ICJ Reports, 1986, pp. 14, 102; 76 ILR, p. 1.

In other words, lawful countermeasures must be in response to a prior wrongful act and taken in the light of a refusal to remedy it, directed against the state committing the wrongful act and proportionate. Further, there is no requirement that the countermeasures taken should be with regard to the same obligation breached by the state acting wrongfully. Thus, the response to a breach of one treaty may be action taken with regard to another treaty, provided that the requirements of necessity and proportionality are respected.[96]

The ILC Articles deal further with countermeasures in Chapter II. Article 49 provides that an injured state[97] may only take countermeasures against a state responsible for the wrongful act in order to induce the latter to comply with the obligations consequent upon the wrongful act.[98] Countermeasures are limited to the non-performance for the time being of international obligations of the state taking the measures and shall, as far as possible, be taken in such a way as to permit the resumption of performance of the obligation in question.[99] Article 50 makes it clear that countermeasures shall not affect the obligation to refrain from the threat or use of force as embodied by the UN Charter, obligations for the protection of human rights, obligations of a humanitarian character prohibiting reprisals and other obligations of *jus cogens*.[100] By the same token, obligations under any applicable dispute settlement procedure between the two states continue,[101] while the state taking countermeasures must respect the inviolability of diplomatic or consular agents, premises, archives and documents.[102] Article 51 emphasises the requirement for proportionality, noting that countermeasures must be commensurate with the injury suffered, taking into account the gravity of the internationally wrongful act and the rights in question.[103] Article 52 provides that before taking countermeasures, the injured state must call upon the responsible

---

[96] See ILC Commentary 2001, pp. 326–7.   [97] See further below, p. 796.
[98] See further below, p. 800.   [99] See ILC Commentary 2001, p. 328.
[100] See Eritrea–Ethiopia Claims Commission, Partial Award, Prisoners of War, Eritrea's Claim 17, 1 July 2003, para. 159, noting that Ethiopia's suspension of prisoner of war exchanges could not be justified as a countermeasure as it affected obligations of a human rights or humanitarian nature.
[101] See e.g. 'Symposium on Counter-Measures and Dispute Settlement,' 5 EJIL, 1994, p. 20, and Report of the International Law Commission, 1995, A/50/10, pp. 173 ff. See also Annacker, 'Part Two', pp. 242 ff.
[102] See further ILC Commentary 2001, p. 333.
[103] See the *US–France Air Services Agreement Arbitration* 54 ILR, pp. 303, 337. See also the ILC Commentary 2001, p. 341 and the Report of the ILC on its 44th Session, 1992, A/47/10, p. 70.

state to fulfil its obligations and notify that state of any decision to take countermeasures while offering to negotiate. However, the injured state may take such countermeasures as are necessary to preserve its rights. Where the wrongful acts have ceased or the matter is pending before a court or tribunal with powers to take binding decisions, then countermeasures should cease (or where relevant, not be taken).[104] Countermeasures shall be terminated as soon as the responsible state has complied with its obligations.[105]

Force majeure has long been accepted as precluding wrongfulness,[106] although the standard of proof is high. In the *Serbian Loans* case,[107] for example, the Court declined to accept the claim that the First World War had made it impossible for Serbia to repay a loan. In 1946, following a number of unauthorised flights of US aircraft over Yugoslavia, both states agreed that only in cases of emergency could such entry be justified in the absence of consent.[108] Article 23 of the ILC Articles provides for the preclusion of wrongfulness where the act was due to the occurrence of an irresistible force or of an unforeseen event beyond the control of the state, making it materially impossible in the circumstances to perform obligation.[109] In the *Gill* case,[110] for example, a British national residing in Mexico had his house destroyed as a result of sudden and unforeseen action by opponents of the Mexican government. The Commission held that failure to prevent the act was due not to negligence but to genuine inability to take action in the face of a sudden situation.

The emphasis, therefore, is upon the happening of an event that takes place without the state being able to do anything to rectify the event or avert its consequences. There had to be a constraint which the state was

---

104 See ILC Commentary 2001, p. 345.   105 *Ibid.*, p. 349.
106 See e.g. *Yearbook of the ILC*, 1961, vol. II, p. 46 and ILC Commentary 2001, p. 183.
107 PCIJ, Series A, No. 20, 1929, p. 39. See also the *Brazilian Loans* case, PCIJ, Series A, No. 20, 1929, p. 120; 5 AD, p. 466.
108 *Yearbook of the ILC*, 1979, vol. II, p. 60 and ILC Commentary 2001, pp. 189–90. This example would cover both *force majeure* and distress (discussed below). Note also that article 18(2) provides that stopping and anchoring by ships during their passage through the territorial sea of another state is permissible where rendered necessary by distress or *force majeure*. See also article 14(3) of the Convention on the Territorial Sea and Contiguous Zone, 1958.
109 However, this principle does not apply if the situation of *force majeure* is due wholly or partly to the conduct of the state invoking it or the state has assumed the risk of that situation occurring, article 23(2). See also *Libyan Arab Foreign Investment Company* v. *Republic of Burundi* 96 ILR, pp. 279, 318.
110 5 RIAA, p. 159 (1931); 6 AD, p. 203.

unable to avoid or to oppose by its own power.[111] In other words, the conduct of the state is involuntary or at least involves no element of free choice.[112]

The issue of *force majeure* was raised by France in the *Rainbow Warrior* arbitration in 1990.[113] It was argued that one of the French agents repatriated to France without the consent of New Zealand had to be so moved as a result of medical factors which amounted to *force majeure*. The Tribunal, however, stressed that the test of applicability of this doctrine was one of 'absolute and material impossibility' and a circumstance rendering performance of an obligation more difficult or burdensome did not constitute a case of *force majeure*.[114]

Article 24 provides that wrongfulness is precluded if the author of the conduct concerned had no other reasonable way in a situation of distress of saving the author's life or the lives of other persons entrusted to his care.[115] This would cover, for example, the agreement in the 1946 US–Yugoslav correspondence that only in an emergency would unauthorised entry into foreign airspace be justified,[116] or the seeking of refuge in a foreign port without authorisation by a ship's captain in storm conditions.[117]

The difference between distress and *force majeure* is that in the former case there is an element of choice. This is often illusory since in both cases extreme peril exists and whether or not the situation provides an opportunity for real choice is a matter of some difficulty.[118] The Tribunal in the *Rainbow Warrior* arbitration[119] noted that three conditions were required to be satisfied in order for this defence to be applicable to the French action in repatriating its two agents: first, the existence of exceptional circumstances of extreme urgency involving medical and other considerations of an elementary nature, provided always that a prompt recognition of the existence of those exceptional circumstances is subsequently obtained from the other interested party or is clearly demonstrated; secondly, the re-establishment of the original situation as soon as the reasons of emergency invoked to justify the breach of the obligation (i.e. the repatriation) had disappeared; thirdly, the existence of a good faith effort to try to

---

[111] *Yearbook of the ILC*, 1979, vol. II, p. 133.   [112] ILC Commentary 2001, p. 183.

[113] 82 ILR, pp. 499, 551.   [114] *Ibid.*, p. 553.

[115] ILC Commentary 2001, p. 189. This would not apply if the situation of distress is due wholly or partly to the conduct of the state invoking it or the act in question is likely to create a comparable or greater peril, article 24(2).

[116] See above, p. 541.

[117] *Yearbook of the ILC*, 1979, vol. II, p. 134 and ILC Commentary 2001, pp. 189–90.

[118] *Yearbook of the ILC*, 1979, vol. II, pp. 133–5.   [119] 82 ILR, pp. 499, 555.

obtain the consent of New Zealand according to the terms of the 1986 Agreement.[120] It was concluded that France had failed to observe these conditions (except as far as the removal of one of the agents on medical grounds was concerned).

Article 25 provides that necessity may not be invoked unless the act was the only means for the state to safeguard an essential interest against a 'grave and imminent peril' and the act does not seriously impair an essential interest of the other state or states or of the international community as a whole. Further, necessity may not be invoked if the international obligation in question excludes the possibility or the state has itself contributed to the situation of necessity.[121] An example of this kind of situation is provided by the *Torrey Canyon*,[122] where a Liberian oil tanker went aground off the UK coast but outside territorial waters, spilling large quantities of oil. After salvage attempts, the UK bombed the ship. The ILC took the view that this action was legitimate in the circumstances because of a state of necessity.[123] It was only after the incident that international agreements were concluded dealing with this kind of situation.[124]

The Tribunal in the *Rainbow Warrior* case took the view that the defence of state necessity was 'controversial'.[125] However, the International Court in the *Gabčíkovo–Nagymaros Project* case considered that it was 'a ground recognised in customary international law for precluding the wrongfulness of an act not in conformity with an international obligation', although it could only be accepted 'on an exceptional basis'.[126] The Court referred to the conditions laid down in an earlier version of, and essentially reproduced in, article 25 and stated that such conditions must be cumulatively satisfied.[127] In *M/V Saiga* (*No. 2*), the International

---

[120] See above, p. 779.   [121] See ILC Commentary 2001, p. 194.

[122] Cmnd 3246, 1967. See also below, chapter 15, p. 900, note 322.

[123] *Yearbook of the ILC*, 1980, vol. II, p. 39. See also the *Company General of the Orinoco* case, 10 RIAA, p. 280.

[124] See e.g. the International Convention Relating to Intervention on the High Seas in Cases of Oil Pollution Casualties, 1969.

[125] 82 ILR, pp. 499, 554–5. The doctrine has also been controversial in academic writings: see *Yearbook of the ILC*, 1980, vol. II, part 1, pp. 47–9. See also J. Barboza, 'Necessity (Revisited) in International Law' in *Essays in Honour of Judge Manfred Lachs* (ed. J. Makarczyk), The Hague, 1984, p. 27, and R. Boed, 'State of Necessity as a Justification for Internationally Wrongful Conduct', 3 *Yale Human Rights and Development Journal*, 2000, p. 1.

[126] ICJ Reports, 1997, pp. 7, 40; 116 ILR, p. 1. See also *R v. Director of the Serious Fraud Office and BAE Systems* [2008] EWHC 714 (Admin), paras. 143 ff.

[127] ICJ Reports, 1997, p. 41. In addition, the state could not be the sole judge of whether these strictly defined conditions had been met. See also the *Construction of a Wall* advisory opinion, ICJ Reports, 2004, pp. 136, 194–5; 129 ILR, pp. 37, 113–15.

Tribunal for the Law of the Sea discussed the doctrine on the basis of the ILC draft as approved by the International Court, but found that it did not apply as no evidence had been produced by Guinea to show that its essential interests were in grave and imminent peril and, in any event, Guinea's interests in maximising its tax revenue from the sale of gas oil to fishing vessels could be safeguarded by means other than extending its customs law to parts of the exclusive economic zone.[128]

Invocation of state responsibility[129]

Article 42 of the ILC Articles stipulates that a state is entitled as an injured state[130] to invoke[131] the responsibility of another state if the obligation breached is owed to that state individually or to a group of states, including that state or the international community as a whole, and the breach of the obligation specially affects that state or is of such a character as radically to change the position of all the other states to which the obligation is owed with respect to the further performance of the obligation. Responsibility may not be invoked if the injured state has validly waived the claim or is to be considered as having, by reason of its conduct, validly acquiesced in the lapse of the claim.[132] Any waiver would need to be clear and unequivocal,[133] while the question of acquiescence would have to be judged carefully in the light of the particular circumstances.[134] Where several states are injured by the same wrongful act, each state may separately invoke responsibility,[135] and where several states are responsible, the responsibility of each may be invoked.[136]

---

[128] 120 ILR, pp. 143, 191–2.

[129] See e.g. Annacker, 'Part Two', pp. 214 ff. See also ILC Commentary 2001, p. 294.

[130] The provisions concerning the injured state were particularly complex in earlier formulations: see e.g. article 40 of Part II of the ILC Draft Articles of 1996. See also Crawford, *Articles*, pp. 23 ff.

[131] I.e. taking measures of a formal kind, such as presenting a claim against another state or commencing proceedings before an international court or tribunal but not simply protesting: see ILC Commentary 2001, p. 294.

[132] Article 45. See also ILC Commentary 2001, p. 307.

[133] See the *Nauru (Preliminary Objection)* case, ICJ Reports, 1992, pp. 240, 247; 97 ILR, p. 1.

[134] ICJ Reports, 1992, pp. 253–4.

[135] Article 46. See also ILC Commentary 2001, p. 311.

[136] Article 47. See also ILC Commentary 2001, p. 313, noting that the general rule in international law is that of separate responsibility of a state for its own wrongful acts. There is neither a rule of joint and separate responsibility nor a prohibition of this. It will depend on the circumstances. See the *Eurotunnel* case, 132 ILR, pp. 1, 59–60. Note that the UK has taken the position that with regard to combined operations in Iraq, 'each nation

In the *Barcelona Traction* case, the International Court referred to the obligations of a state towards the international community as a whole as distinct from those owed to another state.[137] Article 48 builds upon this principle and provides that a state other than an injured state may invoke the responsibility of another state if either the obligation is owed to a group of states including that state, and is established for the protection of a collective interest of the group, or the obligation breached is owed to the international community as a whole. In such cases, cessation of the wrongful act and assurances and guarantees of non-repetition may be claimed,[138] as well as reparation.[139]

The consequences of internationally wrongful acts

Cessation

The state responsible for the internationally wrongful act is under an obligation to cease that act, if it is continuing, and to offer appropriate assurances and guarantees of non-repetition if circumstances so require.[140] The Tribunal in the *Rainbow Warrior* case held that in order for cessation to arise, the wrongful act had to have a continuing character and the violated rule must still be in force at the date the order is given.[141] The obligation to offer assurances of non-repetition was raised by Germany and discussed by the Court in the *LaGrand* case.[142] The Court held that a US commitment to ensure implementation of specific measures was sufficient to meet Germany's request for a general assurance of non-repetition,[143] while with regard to Germany's request for specific assurances, the Court noted that should the US fail in its obligation of consular notification, it would then be incumbent upon that state to allow the review and reconsideration of any conviction and sentence of a German

would be directly liable for the consequences of actions taken by its own forces', HC Deb., vol. 436, col. 862W, 12 July 2005, UKMIL, 76 BYIL, 2005, p. 875.

[137] ICJ Reports, 1970, pp. 3, 32; 46 ILR, p. 178.

[138] As per article 30.   [139] See ILC Commentary 2001, p. 318.

[140] Article 30 and see ILC Commentary 2001, p. 216. See also C. Derman, 'La Cessation de l'Acte Illicite', *Revue Belge de Droit International Public*, 1990 I, p. 477.

[141] 82 ILR, pp. 499, 573.

[142] ICJ Reports, 2001, p. 466; 134 ILR, p. 1. Cf. the *Avena (Mexico v. USA)* case, ICJ Reports, 2004, pp. 12, 68; 134 ILR, pp. 120, 171.

[143] ICJ Reports, 2001, pp. 466, 512–13, 134 ILR, pp. 1, 50–1. This was reaffirmed in the *Avena (Mexico v. USA)* case, ICJ Reports, 2004, pp. 12, 69; 134 ILR, pp. 120, 172.

national taking place in these circumstances by taking account of the violation of the rights contained in the Vienna Convention on Consular Relations.[144]

Reparation[145]

The basic principle with regard to reparation, or the remedying of a breach of an international obligation for which the state concerned is responsible,[146] was laid down in the *Chorzów Factory* case, where the Permanent Court of International Justice emphasised that,

> The essential principle contained in the actual notion of an illegal act is that reparation must, as far as possible, wipe out all the consequences of the illegal act and re-establish the situation which would, in all probability, have existed if that act had not been committed.[147]

This principle was reaffirmed in a number of cases, including, for example, by the International Court in the *Gabčíkovo–Nagymaros Project* case[148] and in the *Genocide Convention (Bosnia v. Serbia)* case,[149] and by the International Tribunal for the Law of the Sea in *M/V Saiga (No. 2).*[150]

---

[144] ICJ Reports, 2001, pp. 466, 513–41; 134 ILR, pp. 1, 51–2. See, as to consular notification, above, chapter 13, p. 773.

[145] See e.g. M. Whiteman, *Damages in International Law*, Washington, 3 vols., 1937–43; F. A. Mann, 'The Consequences of an International Wrong in International and National Law', 48 BYIL, 1978, p. 1; de Aréchaga, 'International Responsibility', pp. 564 ff., and de Aréchaga,'International Law in the Past Third of the Century', 159 HR, 1978, pp. 1, 285–7. See also Cheng, *General Principles*, pp. 233 ff.; Brownlie, *System*, part VIII, and C. Gray, *Judicial Remedies in International Law*, Oxford, 1987.

[146] See e.g. C. Dominicé, 'Observations sur les Droits de l'État Victime d'un Fiat Internationalement Illicite' in *Droit International* (ed. P. Weil), Paris, 1982, vol. I, p. 25, and B. Graefrath, 'Responsibility and Damage Caused: Relationship between Responsibility and Damage', HR, 1984 II, pp. 19, 73 ff.

[147] PCIJ, Series A, No. 17, 1928, pp. 47–8. In an earlier phase of the case, the Court stated that, 'It is a principle of international law that the breach of an engagement involves an obligation to make reparation in an adequate form. Reparation therefore is the indispensable complement of a failure to apply a convention', PCIJ, Series A, No. 9, 1927, p. 21. See also the *Iranian Hostages* case, ICJ Reports, 1980, pp. 3, 45; 61 ILR, pp. 530, 571, where the Court held that Iran was under a duty to make reparation to the US.

[148] ICJ Reports, 1997, pp. 7, 80; 116 ILR, p. 1.

[149] ICJ Reports, 2007, para. 460. See also the *Construction of a Wall* advisory opinion, ICJ Reports, 2004, pp. 136, 198; 129 ILR, pp. 37, 117–18 and *Democratic Republic of the Congo v. Uganda*, ICJ Reports, 2005, pp. 168, 257.

[150] 120 ILR, pp. 143, 199. See also *S.D. Myers v. Canada* 121 ILR, pp. 72, 127–8; *Aloeboetoe v. Suriname*, Inter-American Court of Human Rights, 1993, Series C, No. 15 at para. 43; 116 ILR, p. 260; *Loayza Tamayo v. Peru (Reparations)*, Inter-American Court of Human

Article 31 of the Articles on State Responsibility provides that the responsible state is under an obligation to make full reparation for the injury caused by the internationally wrongful act and that injury includes any damage, whether material or moral, caused by the internationally wrongful act of a state. The obligation to make reparation is governed in all its aspects by international law, irrespective of domestic law provisions.[151] Article 34 provides that full reparation for the injury caused by the internationally wrongful act shall take the form of restitution, compensation and satisfaction, either singly or in combination.[152]

Restitution in kind is the obvious method of performing the reparation, since it aims to re-establish the situation which existed before the wrongful act was committed.[153] While restitution has occurred in the past,[154] it is more rare today, if only because the nature of such disputes has changed. A large number of cases now involve expropriation disputes, where it is politically difficult for the state concerned to return expropriated property to multinational companies.[155] Recognising some of these problems, article 35 provides for restitution as long as and to the extent that it is not

Rights, 1998, Series C, No. 42 at para. 84; 116 ILR, p. 388, and *Suarez-Rosero v. Ecuador (Reparations)*, Inter-American Court of Human Rights, 1999, Series C, No. 44 at para. 39; 118 ILR, p. 92, regarding this as 'one of the fundamental principles of general international law, repeatedly elaborated upon by the jurisprudence'. See also the decision of 14 March 2003 of an UNCITRAL Arbitral Tribunal in *CME Czech Republic BV* v. *The Czech Republic*, Final Award.

[151] See e.g. *Suarez-Rosero v. Ecuador (Reparations)*, Inter-American Court of Human Rights, 1999, Series C, No. 44 at para. 42; 118 ILR, p. 92. See also article 32 of the ILC Articles.

[152] See also ILC Commentary 2001, p. 235 and *Suarez-Rosero v. Ecuador (Reparations)*, Inter-American Court of Human Rights, 1999, Series C, No. 44 at para. 42; 118 ILR, p. 92. Note further that interest is payable on any principal sum payable when necessary to achieve full reparation and will run from the date the principal sum should have been paid until the date it is paid, article 38 and see ILC Commentary 2001, p. 268. Article 39 provides that in the determination of reparation, account shall be taken of the contribution to the injury by wilful or negligent action or omission of the injured state or any person or entity in relation to whom reparation is sought: see also ILC Commentary 2001, p. 275 and the *LaGrand* case, ICJ Reports, 2001, pp. 466, 487 and 508; 134 ILR, pp. 1, 26 and 46.

[153] See e.g. Annacker, 'Part Two', pp. 221 ff.

[154] See e.g. the post-1945 Peace Treaties with Hungary, Romania and Italy. See also the *Spanish Zone of Morocco* case, 2 RIAA, p. 617 (1925); 2 AD, p. 157; the *Martini* case, 2 RIAA, p. 977 (1930); 5 AD, p. 153; the *Palmagero Gold Fields* case, 5 RIAA, p. 298 (1931) and the *Russian Indemnity* case, 11 RIAA, p. 431 (1912). Brownlie notes that in certain cases, such as the illegal possession of territory or acquisition of objects of special cultural, historical or religious significance, restitution may be the only legal remedy, *System*, p. 210, and the *Temple* case, ICJ Reports, 1962, pp. 6, 36–7; 33 ILR, pp. 48, 73.

[155] See e.g. the *Aminoil* case, 66 ILR, pp. 529, 533.

materially impossible and does not involve a burden out of all proportion to the benefit deriving from restitution instead of compensation.[156] In the *Rainbow Warrior* arbitration,[157] New Zealand sought *inter alia* an Order that the French Government return its agents from France to their previous place of confinement in the Pacific as required by the original agreement of 9 July 1986. New Zealand termed this request '*restitutio in integrum*'. France argued that 'cessation' of the denounced behaviour was the appropriate terminology and remedy, although in the circumstances barred by time.[158] The Tribunal pointed to the debate in the International Law Commission on the differences between the two concepts[159] and held that the French approach was correct.[160] The obligation to end an illegal situation was not reparation but a return to the original obligation, that is cessation of the illegal conduct. However, it was held that since the primary obligation was no longer in force (in the sense that the obligation to keep the agents in the Pacific island concerned expired under the initial agreement on 22 July 1989), an order for cessation of the illegal conduct could serve no purpose.[161]

The question of the appropriate reparation for expropriation was discussed in several cases. In the *BP* case,[162] the tribunal emphasised that there was

> no explicit support for the proposition that specific performance, and even less so *restitutio in integrum*, are remedies of public international law available at the option of a party suffering a wrongful breach by a co-contracting party... the responsibility incurred by the defaulting party for breach of an obligation to perform a contractual undertaking is a duty to pay damages... the concept of *restitutio in integrum* has been employed merely as a vehicle for establishing the amount of damages.[163]

However, in the *Texaco* case,[164] which similarly involved Libyan nationalisation of oil concessions, the arbitrator held that restitution in kind under international law (and indeed under Libyan law) constituted

---

[156] See also ILC Commentary 2001, p. 237.

[157] 82 ILR, p. 499. [158] *Ibid.*, p. 571.

[159] See e.g. *Yearbook of the ILC*, 1981, vol. II, part 1, pp. 79 ff. [160] 82 ILR, p. 572.

[161] *Ibid.*, p. 573. Note that article 30 of the ILC Articles provides that the injured state is entitled, where appropriate, to obtain assurances or guarantees of non-repetition of the wrongful act.

[162] 53 ILR, p. 297. This concerned the expropriation by Libya of BP oil concessions.

[163] *Ibid.*, p. 347. [164] 17 ILM, 1978, p. 1; 53 ILR, p. 389.

the normal sanction for non-performance of contractual obligations and
that it is inapplicable only to the extent that restoration of the *status quo
ante* is impossible.[165]

This is an approach that in political terms, particularly in international
contract cases, is unlikely to prove acceptable to states since it appears a
violation of sovereignty. The problems, indeed, of enforcing such restitution awards against a recalcitrant state may be imagined.[166]

The International Court noted in the *Gabčíkovo–Nagymaros Project
(Hungary/Slovakia)* case that it was a 'well-established rule of international law that an injured state is entitled to obtain compensation from
the state which has committed an internationally wrongful act for the
damage caused by it'.[167] Article 36(1) provides that in so far as damage
caused by an internationally wrongful act is not made good by restitution, the state responsible is under an obligation to give compensation.[168]
Article 36(2) states that the compensation to be provided shall cover
any financially assessable damage including loss of profits in so far as
this is established.[169] The aim is to deal with economic losses actually
caused. Punitive or exemplary damages go beyond the concept of reparation as such[170] and were indeed held in *Velásquez Rodríguez* v. *Honduras*

---

[165] 17 ILM, 1978, p. 36; 53 ILR, pp. 507–8. In fact the parties settled the dispute by Libya
supplying $152 million worth of crude oil, 17 ILM, 1998, p. 2.

[166] These points were explained by the arbitrator in the *Liamco* case, 20 ILM, 1981, pp. 1,
63–4; 62 ILR, pp. 141, 198. See also the *Aminoil* case, 21 ILM, 1982, p. 976; 66 ILR, p. 519.
See further e.g. A. Fatouros, 'International Law and the International Contract', 74 AJIL,
1980, p. 134. The issue of compensation for expropriated property is discussed further
below, p. 827.

[167] ICJ Reports, 1997, pp. 7, 81; 116 ILR, p. 1. See also the *Construction of a Wall* case, ICJ
Reports, 2004, pp. 136, 198; 129 ILR, pp. 37, 117–18, and the *Genocide Convention (Bosnia
v. Serbia)* case, ICJ Reports, 2007, para. 460. In the latter case, the Court referred to article
36.

[168] In the *Gabčíkovo–Nagymaros Project* case, ICJ Reports, 1997, pp. 7, 81; 116 ILR, p. 1, the
Court held that both states were entitled to claim and obliged to provide compensation.
Accordingly, the parties were called upon to renounce or cancel all financial claims and
counter-claims. See more generally D. Shelton, *Remedies in International Human Rights
Law*, 2nd edn, Oxford, 2005, and C. N. Brower and J. D. Brueschke, *The Iran–United
States Claims Tribunal*, The Hague, 1998, chapters 14–18.

[169] See ILC Commentary 2001, p. 243. See also the Report of the International Law Commission on the Work of its Forty-Fifth Session, A/48/10, p. 185.

[170] See generally Whiteman, *Damages*, and Aréchaga, 'International Responsibility', p. 571.
See also N. Jorgensen, 'A Reappraisal of Punitive Damages in International Law', 68 BYIL,
1997, p. 247; *Yearbook of the ILC*, 1956, vol. II, pp. 211–12, and Annacker, 'Part Two',
pp. 225 ff.

(*Compensation*) to be a principle 'not applicable in international law at this time'.[171]

Compensation is usually assessed on the basis of the 'fair market value' of the property lost, although the method used to calculate this may depend upon the type of property involved.[172] Loss of profits may also be claimed where, for example, there has been interference with use and enjoyment or unlawful taking of income-producing property or in some cases with regard to loss of future income.[173]

Damage includes both material and non-material (or moral) damage.[174] Monetary compensation may thus be paid for individual pain and suffering and insults. In the *I'm Alone*[175] case, for example, a sum of $25,000 was suggested as recompense for the indignity suffered by Canada, in having a ship registered in Montreal unlawfully sunk. A further example of this is provided by the France–New Zealand Agreement of 9 July 1986, concerning the sinking of the vessel *Rainbow Warrior* by French agents in New Zealand, the second paragraph of which provided for France to pay the sum of $7 million as compensation to New Zealand for 'all the damage which it has suffered'.[176] It is clear from the context that it covered more than material damage.[177] In the subsequent arbitration in 1990, the Tribunal declared that

> an order for the payment of monetary compensation can be made in respect of the breach of international obligations involving . . . serious moral and legal damage, even though there is no material damage.[178]

However, the Tribunal declined to make an order for monetary compensation, primarily since New Zealand was seeking alternative remedies.[179]

Satisfaction constitutes a third form of reparation. This relates to non-monetary compensation and would include official apologies, the punishment of guilty minor officials or the formal acknowledgement of the unlawful character of an act.[180] The Tribunal in the *Rainbow Warrior*

---

[171] Inter-American Court of Human Rights, 1989, Series C, No. 7, pp. 34, 52; 95 ILR, p. 306.

[172] See on this the analysis in the ILC Commentary 2001, pp. 255 ff. See also the UNCITRAL Arbitral Tribunal decision of 14 March 2003 in *CME Czech Republic BV* v. *The Czech Republic*, Final Award.

[173] *Ibid.*, pp. 260 ff. [174] See article 31(2).

[175] 3 RIAA, p. 1609 (1935); 7 AD, p. 203. [176] 74 ILR, pp. 241, 274.

[177] See the Arbitral Tribunal in the *Rainbow Warrior* case, 82 ILR, pp. 499, 574.

[178] 82 ILR, pp. 499, 575. [179] *Ibid.*

[180] See Annacker, 'Part Two', pp. 230 ff.; C. Barthe, 'Réflexions sur la Satisfaction en Droit International', 49 AFDI, 2003, p. 105; de Aréchaga, 'International Responsibility', p. 572;

arbitration[181] pointed to the long-established practice of states and international courts of using satisfaction as a remedy for the breach of an international obligation, particularly where moral or legal damage had been done directly to the state. In the circumstances of the case, it concluded that the public condemnation of France for its breaches of treaty obligations to New Zealand made by the Tribunal constituted 'appropriate satisfaction'.[182] The Tribunal also made an interesting 'Recommendation' that the two states concerned establish a fund to promote close relations between their respective citizens and additionally recommended that the French government 'make an initial contribution equivalent to $2 million to that fund'.[183]

In some cases, a party to a dispute will simply seek a declaration that the activity complained of is illegal.[184] In territorial disputes, for example, such declarations may be of particular significance. The International Court, however, adopted a narrow view of the Australian submissions in the *Nuclear Tests* case,[185] an approach that was the subject of a vigorous dissenting opinion.[186] Article 37 of the ILC Articles provides that a state responsible for a wrongful act is obliged to give satisfaction for the injury thereby caused in so far as it cannot be made good by restitution or compensation. Satisfaction may consist of an acknowledgement of the breach, an expression of regret, a formal apology or another appropriate modality.[187] An example of such another modality might be an assurance or guarantee of non-repetition.[188]

D. W. Bowett, 'Treaties and State Responsibility' in *Mélanges Virally*, Paris, 1991, pp. 137, 144; and Schwarzenberger, *International Law*, p. 653. See also the *I'm Alone* case, 3 RIAA, pp. 1609, 1618 (1935); 7 AD, p. 206 and the *Corfu Channel* case, ICJ Reports, 1949, pp. 4, 35; 16 AD, pp. 155, 167.

[181] 82 ILR, p. 499.   [182] 82 ILR, p. 577.

[183] *Ibid.*, p. 578. See also the *Genocide Convention (Bosnia v. Serbia)*, ICJ Reports, 2007, para. 463.

[184] See e.g. *Certain German Interests in Polish Upper Silesia*, PCIJ, Series A, No. 7, p. 18 (1926) and the *Corfu Channel* case, ICJ Reports, 1949, pp. 4, 35; 16 AD, p. 155. Note also that under article 41 of the European Convention on Human Rights, 1950, the European Court of Human Rights may award 'just satisfaction', which often takes the form of a declaration by the Court that a violation of the Convention has taken place: see e.g. the *Neumeister* case, European Court of Human Rights, Series A, No. 17 (1974); 41 ILR, p. 316. See also the *Pauwels* case, *ibid.*, No. 135 (1989); the *Lamy* case, *ibid.*, No. 151 (1989) and the *Huber* case, *ibid.*, No. 188 (1990).

[185] ICJ Reports, 1974, p. 253; 57 ILR, p. 398.

[186] ICJ Reports, 1974, pp. 312–19; 57 ILR, p. 457.

[187] See ILC Commentary 2001, p. 263. Satisfaction is not to be disproportionate to the injury and not in a form which is humiliating to the responsible state, article 37(3).

[188] See above, p. 800.

Serious breaches of peremptory norms (jus cogens)

One of the major debates taking place with regard to state responsibility concerns the question of international crimes. A distinction was drawn in article 19 of the ILC Draft Articles 1996 between international crimes and international delicts within the context of internationally unlawful acts. It was provided that an internationally wrongful act which results from the breach by a state of an international obligation so essential for the protection of fundamental interests of the international community that its breach was recognised as a crime by that community as a whole constitutes an international crime. All other internationally wrongful acts were termed international delicts.[189] Examples of such international crimes provided were aggression, the establishment or maintenance by force of colonial domination, slavery, genocide, apartheid and massive pollution of the atmosphere or of the seas. However, the question as to whether states can be criminally responsible has been highly controversial.[190] Some have argued that the concept is of no legal value and cannot be justified in principle, not least because the problem of exacting penal sanctions from states, while in principle possible, could only be creative of instability.[191] Others argued that, particularly since 1945, the attitude towards certain crimes by states has altered so as to bring them within the realm of international law.[192] The Rapporteur in his commentary to draft article 19 pointed to three specific changes since 1945 in this context to justify its inclusion: first, the development of the concept of *jus cogens* as a set of principles from which no derogation is permitted;[193] secondly, the rise of individual criminal responsibility directly under international law; and thirdly, the UN Charter and its provision for enforcement action against a state in the event of threats to or breaches of the peace or acts of

---

[189] See M. Mohr, 'The ILC's Distinction between "International Crimes" and "International Delicts" and Its Implications' in Spinedi and Simma, *UN Codification*, p. 115, and K. Marek, 'Criminalising State Responsibility', 14 *Revue Belge de Droit International*, 1978–9, p. 460.

[190] See e.g. *Oppenheim's International Law*, pp. 533 ff. See also G. Gilbert, 'The Criminal Responsibility of States', 39 ICLQ, 1990, p. 345, and N. Jorgensen, *The Responsibility of States for International Crimes*, Oxford, 2000. As to individual criminal responsibility, see above, chapter 8.

[191] See e.g. I. Brownlie, *International Law and the Use of Force by States*, Oxford, 1963, pp. 150–4.

[192] See e.g. de Aréchaga, 'International Law'.

[193] See e.g. article 53 of the Vienna Convention on the Law of Treaties, 1969 and below, p. 944.

aggression.[194] However, the ILC changed its approach[195] in the light of the controversial nature of the suggestion and the Articles as finally approved in 2001 omit any mention of international crimes of states, but rather seek to focus upon the particular consequences flowing from a breach of obligations *erga omnes* and of peremptory norms (*jus cogens*).[196]

Article 41 provides that states are under a duty to co-operate to bring to an end, through lawful means, any serious breach[197] by a state of an obligation arising under a peremptory norm of international law[198] and not to recognise as lawful any such situation.[199]

Diplomatic protection and nationality of claims[200]

The doctrine of state responsibility with regard to injuries to nationals rests upon twin pillars, the attribution to one state of the unlawful acts and omissions of its officials and its organs (legislative, judicial and executive) and the capacity of the other state to adopt the claim of the injured party. Indeed article 44 of the ILC Articles provides that the responsibility of a state may not be invoked if the claim is not brought in accordance with any applicable rule relating to nationality of claims.[201]

Nationality is the link between the individual and his or her state as regards particular benefits and obligations. It is also the vital link between the

---

[194] *Yearbook of the ILC*, 1976, vol. II, pp. 102–5. Note also the Report of the International Law Commission, 1994, A/49/10, pp. 329 ff. and *ibid.*, 1995, A/50/10, pp. 93 ff.

[195] See Crawford, *Articles*, pp. 17 ff. for a critical analysis of draft article 19 and a discussion of subsequent developments.

[196] See above, chapter 3, p. 123.

[197] Article 40(2) describes a breach as serious if it involves a gross or systematic failure by the responsible state to fulfil the obligation.

[198] Examples given of peremptory norms are the prohibitions of aggression, slavery and the slave trade, genocide, racial discrimination and apartheid, and torture, and the principle of self-determination: see ILC Commentary 2001, pp. 283–4.

[199] See, as to examples of non-recognition, above, chapter 9, p. 468. Article 41(3) is in the form of a saving clause, providing that the article is without prejudice to other consequences referred to in Part Two of the Articles and to such further consequences that such a breach may have under international law.

[200] See e.g. *Oppenheim's International Law*, p. 511; Nguyen Quoc Dinh *et al.*, *Droit International Public*, p. 808; Brownlie, *Principles*, pp. 459 ff., and A. Vermeer-Künzli, 'A Matter of Interest: Diplomatic Protection and State Responsibility *Erga Omnes*', 56 ICLQ, 2007, p. 553. See also F. Orrego Vicuña, 'Interim Report on the Changing Law of Nationality of Claims', International Law Association, Report of the Sixty-Ninth Conference, London, 2000, p. 631.

[201] See ILC Commentary 2001, p. 304.

individual and the benefits of international law. Although international law is now moving to a stage whereby individuals may acquire rights free from the interposition of the state, the basic proposition remains that in a state-oriented world system, it is only through the medium of the state that the individual may obtain the full range of benefits available under international law, and nationality is the key.[202]

The principle of diplomatic protection originally developed in the context of the treatment by a state of foreign nationals. However, the International Court has pointed out that, 'Owing to the substantive development of international law over recent decades in respect of the rights it accords to individuals, the scope *ratione materiae* of diplomatic protection, originally limited to alleged violations of the minimum standard of treatment of aliens, has subsequently widened to include, *inter alia*, internationally guaranteed human rights'.[203]

The International Law Commission adopted Draft Articles on Diplomatic Protection in 2006.[204] Article 1 provides that, for the purposes of the draft articles,

> diplomatic protection consists of the invocation by a state, through diplomatic action or other means of peaceful settlement, of the responsibility of another state for an injury caused by an internationally wrongful act of that state to a natural or legal person that is a national of the former state with a view to the implementation of such responsibility.[205]

A state is under a duty to protect its nationals and it may take up their claims against other states. Diplomatic protection includes, in a broad sense, consular action, negotiation, mediation, judicial and arbitral proceedings, reprisals, a retort, severance of diplomatic relations, and economic pressures.[206] There is under international law, however, no obligation for states to provide diplomatic protection for their nationals

---

[202] See further on nationality, above, chapter 12, p. 659. Note also the claim for reparations made by Croatia in its application of 2 July 1999 to the International Court against Yugoslavia in the *Application of the Genocide Convention* case both on behalf of the state and 'as *parens patriae* for its citizens', Application, pp. 20–1.

[203] *Diallo (Guinea v. Democratic Republic of the Congo)*, ICJ Reports, 2007, para. 39.

[204] See Report of the ILC on its 58th Session, A/61/10, 2006, p. 13.

[205] See the *Diallo (Guinea v. Democratic Republic of the Congo)* case, ICJ Reports, 2007, para. 39, where the Court noted that article 1 reflected customary law.

[206] *Kaunda v. President of South Africa* CCT 23/04, [2004] ZACC 5, paras. 26–7 and *Van Zyl v. Government of RSA* [2007] SCA 109 (RSA), para. 1.

abroad,[207] although it can be said that nationals have a right to request their government to consider diplomatic protection and that government is under a duty to consider that request rationally.[208]

In addition, once a state does this, the claim then becomes that of the state. This is a result of the historical reluctance to permit individuals the right in international law to prosecute claims against foreign countries, for reasons relating to state sovereignty and non-interference in internal affairs.

This basic principle was elaborated in the *Mavrommatis Palestine Concessions* case.[209] The Permanent Court of International Justice pointed out that:

> By taking up the case of one of its subjects and by resorting to diplomatic action or international judicial proceedings on his behalf, a state is in reality asserting its own rights, its right to ensure, in the person of its subjects, respect for the rules of international law . . .

Once a state has taken up a case on behalf of one of its subjects before an international tribunal, in the eyes of the latter the state is sole claimant.[210] It follows that the exercise of diplomatic protection cannot be regarded as intervention contrary to international law by the state concerned. Coupled with this right of the state is the constraint that a state may in principle adopt the claims only of its own nationals. Diplomatic protection may not extend to the adoption of claims of foreign subjects,[211] although it has been suggested 'as an exercise in progressive development of the law' that a state

---

[207] See e.g. *HMHK* v. *Netherlands* 94 ILR, p. 342 and *Comercial F SA* v. *Council of Ministers* 88 ILR, p. 691. See also *Kaunda* v. *President of South Africa* CCT 23/04, [2004] ZACC 5, paras. 29 and 34, noting that diplomatic protection is not recognised in international law as a human right, but a prerogative of the state to be exercised at its discretion (per Chief Justice Chaskalson).

[208] See *Van Zyl* v. *Government of RSA* [2007] SCA 109 (RSA), para. 6.

[209] PCIJ, Series A, No. 2, 1924, p. 12. See the *Panevezys–Saldutiskis* case, PCIJ, Series A/B, No. 76; 9 AD, p. 308. See also Vattel, who noted that 'whoever ill-treats a citizen indirectly injures the state, which must protect that citizen', *The Law of Nations*, 1916 trans., p. 136.

[210] See e.g. *Lonrho Exports Ltd* v. *ECGD* [1996] 4 All ER 673, 687; 108 ILR, p. 596.

[211] However, note article 20 of the European Community Treaty, under which every person holding the nationality of a member state (and thus a citizen of the European Union under article 17) is entitled to receive diplomatic protection by the diplomatic or consular authority of any member state on the same conditions as nationals of that state when in the territory of a third state where the country of his or her nationality is not represented.

may adopt the claim of a stateless person or refugee who at the dates of the injury and presentation of the claim is lawfully and habitually resident in that state.[212] Such diplomatic protection is not a right of the national concerned, but a right of the state which it may or may not choose to exercise.[213] It is not a duty incumbent upon the state under international law. As the Court noted in the *Barcelona Traction* case,

> within the limits prescribed by international law, a state may exercise diplomatic protection by whatever means and to whatever extent it thinks fit, for it is its own right that the state is asserting. Should the natural or legal person on whose behalf it is acting consider that their rights are not adequately protected, they have no remedy in international law.[214]

The UK takes the view that the taking up of a claim against a foreign state is a matter within the prerogative of the Crown, but various principles are outlined in its publication, 'Rules regarding the Taking up of International Claims by Her Majesty's Government', stated to be based on international law.[215] This distinguishes between formal claims and informal representations. In the former case, Rule VIII provides that, 'If, in exhausting any municipal remedies, the claimant has met with prejudice or obstruction, which are a denial of justice, HMG [Her Majesty's Government] may intervene on his behalf in order to secure justice.' In the latter case, the UK will consider making representations if, when all legal remedies have been exhausted, the British national has evidence of a miscarriage or denial of justice. This may apply to cases where fundamental violations of the national's human rights had demonstrably altered the course of justice. The UK has also stated that it would consider making

---

[212] See article 8 of the Draft Articles on Diplomatic Protection. In *R v. Al-Rawi* [2006] EWCA Civ 1279, para. 89, the Court of Appeal held that there was no basis for accepting that non-British nationals enjoyed an *Abbasi* expectation that the UK government would consider making representations to a foreign state on their behalf. Article 8 was not regarded as part of customary international law, *ibid.*, paras. 118–20. Note the special position of a national working for an international organisation, where there may be a danger to the independence of the official where diplomatic protection is exercised: see e.g. the *Reparation* case, ICJ Reports, 1949, pp. 174, 183.

[213] See e.g. the *Interhandel* case, ICJ Reports, 1957, pp. 6, 27; *Administrative Decision No. V* 7 RIAA, p. 119; 2 AD, pp. 185, 191 and *US v. Dulles* 222 F.2d 390. See also DUSPIL, 1973, pp. 332–4.

[214] ICJ Reports, 1970, pp. 3, 44; 46 ILR, p. 178.

[215] See 37 ICLQ, 1988, p. 1006 and UKMIL, 70 BYIL, 1999, p. 526.

direct representations to third governments where it is believed that they were in breach of their international obligations.[216]

The issue was discussed by the Court of Appeal in *Abbasi v. Secretary of State*.[217] It was noted that there was no authority which supported the imposition of an enforceable duty on the UK authorities to protect its citizens; however, the Foreign Office had a discretion whether to exercise the right it had to protect British citizens and had indicated what a citizen may expect of it through, for example, the Rules regarding the Taking up of International Claims. The Court concluded that, in view of the Rules and official statements made,[218] there was a 'clear acceptance by the government of a role in relation to protecting the rights of British citizens abroad, where there is evidence of miscarriage or denial of justice'.[219] While the expectations raised by such Rules and statements were limited and the discretion wide, there was no reason why any decision or inaction by the government should not be judicially reviewable under English law, if it could be shown that such decision or inaction were irrational or contrary to legitimate expectation. It might thus be said that there existed an obligation to consider the position of any particular British citizen and consider the extent to which some action might be taken on his behalf.[220] This legitimate expectation of the citizen was that his or her request would be 'considered', and that in that consideration 'all relevant factors will be thrown into the balance'.[221] The Court held that the 'extreme case' where judicial review would lie in relation to diplomatic protection would be if the Foreign and Commonwealth Office were, contrary to its stated practice, to refuse even to consider whether to make diplomatic representations on behalf of a subject whose fundamental rights were being violated.[222]

The scope of a state to extend its nationality[223] to whomsoever it wishes is unlimited, except perhaps in so far as it affects other states. Article 1 of the Hague Convention on Certain Questions Relating to the Conflict of Nationality Laws, 1930, for example, provides that,

---

[216] UKMIL, 70 BYIL, 1999, pp. 528–9.   [217] [2002] EWCA Civ. 1598; 126 ILR, p. 685.
[218] See UKMIL, 70 BYIL, 1999, pp. 528–9.   [219] [2002] EWCA Civ. 1598, para. 92.
[220] *Ibid.*, para. 106.   [221] *Ibid.*, paras. 98–9.
[222] *Ibid.*, para. 104. The Court noted that, 'In such, unlikely, circumstances we consider that it would be appropriate for the court to make a mandatory order to the Foreign Secretary to give due consideration to the applicant's case', *ibid.*
[223] Whether acquired by birth, descent, succession of states, naturalisation, or in another manner not inconsistent with international law: see article 4 of the ILC Draft Articles on Diplomatic Protection.

It is for each state to determine under its own law who are its nationals. This law shall be recognised by other states in so far as it is consistent with international conventions, international custom, and the principles of law generally recognised with regard to nationality...[224]

In the *Nottebohm* case,[225] the International Court of Justice decided that only where there existed a genuine link between the claimant state and its national could the right of diplomatic protection arise. However, the facts of that case are critical to understanding the pertinent legal proposition. The Government of Liechtenstein instituted proceedings claiming restitution and compensation for Nottebohm against Guatemala for acts of the latter which were alleged to be contrary to international law. Guatemala replied that Nottebohm's right to Liechtenstein nationality and thus its diplomatic protection was questionable. The person in question was born in Germany in 1881 and, still a German national, applied for naturalisation in Liechtenstein in 1939. The point was, however, that since 1905 (and until 1943 when he was deported as a result of war measures) Nottebohm had been permanently resident in Guatemala and had carried on his business from there. The Court noted that Liechtenstein was entirely free, as was every state, to establish the rules necessary for the acquisition of its nationality, but the crux of the matter was whether Guatemala was obliged to recognise the grant of Liechtenstein nationality. The exercise of diplomatic protection by a state regarding one of its nationals brought the whole issue of nationality out of the sphere of domestic jurisdiction and onto the plane of international law.[226] The Court emphasised that, according to state practice, nationality was a legal manifestation of the link between the person and the state granting nationality and the recognition

---

[224] See *Nationality Decrees in Tunis and Morocco*, PCIJ Reports, 1923, Series B, No. 4, p. 24. See also article 3(2) of the European Convention on Nationality, 1997. This would include the rules of international human rights law: see e.g. *Proposed Amendments to the Naturalisation Provision of the Political Constitution of Costa Rica*, Inter-American Court of Human Rights, 1984, Series A, No. 4, para. 38; 79 ILR, p. 282.

[225] ICJ Reports, 1955, p. 4; 22 ILR, p. 349. The Court emphasised that to exercise protection, e.g. by applying to the Court, was to place oneself on the plane of international law, *ibid.*, p. 16. See the *Nationality Decrees in Tunis and Morocco* case, PCIJ, Series B, No. 4, 1923, pp. 7, 21; 2 AD, p. 349, where it was noted that while questions of nationality were in principle within the domestic jurisdiction of states, the right of a state to use its discretion was limited by obligations undertaken towards other states. See also the *Flegenheimer* claim, 14 RIAA, p. 327 (1958); 25 ILR, p. 91, and article 1 of the 1930 Hague Convention on Nationality. See further on nationality and international law, above, chapter 12, p. 659.

[226] ICJ Reports, 1955, pp. 20–1; 22 ILR, p. 357.

that the person was more closely connected with that state than with any other.[227]

Having brought out these concepts, the Court emphasised the tenuous nature of Nottebohm's links with Liechtenstein and the strength of his connection with Guatemala. Nottebohm had spent only a very short period of time in Liechtenstein and one of his brothers lived in Vaduz. Beyond that and the formal naturalisation process, there were no other links with that state. On the other hand, he had lived in Guatemala for some thirty years and had returned there upon obtaining his papers from Vaduz. Since the Liechtenstein nationality 'was granted without regard to the concept . . . adopted in international relations' in the absence of any genuine connection, the Court held that Liechtenstein was not able to extend its diplomatic protection to Nottebohm as regards Guatemala.[228] The case has been subject to criticism relating to the use of the doctrine of 'genuine connection' by the Court. The doctrine had until then been utilised with regard to the problems of dual nationality, so as to enable a decision to be made on whether one national state may sue the other on behalf of the particular national. Its extension to the issue of diplomatic protection appeared to be a new move altogether.[229]

The ILC in its Draft Articles on Diplomatic Protection adopted in 2006 did not require establishment of a genuine link as a requirement of nationality[230] and the Commentary argues that the *Nottebohm* case should be limited to its facts alone.[231]

The nationality must exist at the date of the injury, and should continue until at least the date of the formal presentation of the claim, although this latter point may depend upon a variety of other facts, for example any agreement between the contending states as regards the claim.[232]

---

[227] ICJ Reports, 1955, p. 23; 22 ILR, p. 359.

[228] ICJ Reports, 1955, pp. 25–6; 22 ILR, p. 362.

[229] See generally, Brownlie, *Principles*, chapter 19, and R. Y. Jennings, 'General Course on Principles of International Law', 121 HR, 1967, pp. 323, 459.

[230] Article 4 provides that a state of nationality means a state whose nationality that person has acquired, in accordance with the law of that state, by birth, descent, naturalisation, succession of states or in any other manner, not inconsistent with international law.

[231] Report of the ILC on its 58th Session, A/61/10, 2006, pp. 32–3. See also the *Flegenheimer* claim, 14 RIAA, p. 327 (1958); 25 ILR, p. 91.

[232] See e.g. Borchard, *Diplomatic Protection*, pp. 660 ff.; Whiteman, *Digest*, vol. VIII, 1967, pp. 1243–7, and the *Nottebohm* case, ICJ Reports, 1955, p. 4; 22 ILR, p. 349. See also the view of the US State Department that it has consistently declined to espouse claims which have not been continuously owned by US nationals: see 76 AJIL, 1982, pp. 836–9, and the Rules regarding International Claims issued by the UK Foreign and Commonwealth Office, 1985, to the same effect: see 37 ICLQ, 1988, p. 1006. See also I. Sinclair, 'Nationality

Where an individual possesses dual or multiple nationality, any state of which he is a national may adopt a claim of his against a third state[233] and there appears no need to establish a genuine link between the state of nationality and the dual or multiple national.[234] In the case of more than one state of nationality, the rule appears to be that the state with which he has the more effective connection may be able to espouse his claim as against the other state. In the *Mergé* case,[235] it was emphasised that the principle based on the sovereign equality of states, which excludes diplomatic protection in the case of dual nationality, must yield before the principle of effective nationality whenever such nationality is that of the claimant state. However, where such predominance is not proved, there would be no such yielding. In other words, the test for permitting protection by a state of a national against another state of which he is also a national is the test of effectiveness. This approach was reaffirmed by the Iran–US Claims Tribunal, where the Full Tribunal held that it had jurisdiction over claims against Iran by a dual national when the 'dominant and effective nationality' at the relevant time was American.[236] Article 7 of the ILC Draft Articles on Diplomatic Protection provides that a state of nationality may not exercise diplomatic protection in respect of a person against a state of which the person is also a national unless the nationality of the former state is predominant, both at the time of the injury and at the date of the official presentation of the claim.

As far as a corporation is concerned, it appears that there must be some tangible link between it and the state seeking to espouse its claim. Different

---

of Claims: British Practice', 27 BYIL, 1950, p. 125. Note that article 5(2) of the ILC Draft Articles provides that protection may be offered even where the person was not a national at the date of the injury, provided that the person had the nationality of a predecessor state or lost his or her previous nationality and acquired, for a reason unrelated to the bringing of the claim, the nationality of the former state in a manner not inconsistent with international law.

[233] 14 RIAA, p. 236 (1955); 22 ILR, p. 443. See also the *Canevaro* case, 11 RIAA, p. 397 (1912). See article 6(1) of the ILC Draft Articles on Diplomatic Protection. See also article 3 of the Hague Convention on Certain Questions Relating to the Conflict of Nationality Laws, 1930.

[234] See e.g. the *Salem* case, 2 RIAA, p. 1161 (1932); 6 AD, p. 188; the *Mergé* claim, 14 RIAA, p. 236 (1955); 22 ILR, p. 443 and *Dallal* v. *Iran* 3 Iran–US CTR, 1983, p. 23.

[235] 14 RIAA, p. 236 (1955); 22 ILR, p. 443. See also the *Canevaro* case, 11 RIAA, p. 397 (1912). Cf. the *Salem* case, 2 RIAA, p. 1161 (1932); 6 AD, p. 188.

[236] *Islamic Republic of Iran* v. *USA*, Case No. A/18, 5 Iran–US CTR, p. 251; 75 ILR, p. 176; *Esphahanian* v. *Bank Tejarat* 2 Iran–US CTR, p. 157; 72 ILR, p. 478, and *Malek* v. *Islamic Republic of Iran* 19 Iran–US CTR, p. 48. See also *Saghi* v. *Islamic Republic of Iran* 87 AJIL, 1993, p. 447 and the decision of the Canadian Supreme Court in *Schavernoch* v. *Foreign Claims Commission* 1 SCR 1092 (1982); 90 ILR, p. 220.

cases have pointed to various factors, ranging from incorporation of the company in the particular state to the maintenance of the administrative centre of the company in the state and the existence of substantial holdings by nationals in the company.[237]

The Court in the *Barcelona Traction* case[238] remarked that the traditional rule gave the right of diplomatic protection of a corporation to the state under the laws of which it is incorporated and in whose territory it has its registered office. Any application of the *Nottebohm* doctrine of the 'genuine connection' was rejected as having no general acceptance. Nevertheless, it remains true that some meaningful link must bind the state to the company which seeks its protection. The position as regards the shareholders in a company was discussed in that case. It concerned a dispute between Belgium and Spain relating to a company established in 1911 in Canada, which was involved in the production of electricity in Spain and the majority of whose shares were owned by Belgian nationals. After the Second World War, the Spanish authorities took a number of financial measures which resulted in harm to the company, and in 1948 it was declared bankrupt. The case concerned a Belgian claim in respect of injury to the shareholders, who were Belgian nationals, because of the steps that Spain had adopted. Spain replied by denying that Belgium had any standing in the case since the injury had been suffered by the company and not the shareholders.

The Court rejected the Belgian claim on the grounds that it did not have a legal interest in the matter. Although shareholders may suffer if wrong is done to a company, it is only the rights of the latter that have been infringed and thus entitle it to institute action. If, on the other hand (as did not happen here), the direct rights of the shareholders were affected, for example as regards dividends, then they would have an independent right of action; but otherwise, only if the company legally ceased to exist. The Court emphasised that the general rule of international law stated that where an unlawful act was committed against a company representing foreign capital, only the national state of the company could sue. In this case Canada had chosen not to intervene in the dispute. To accept the idea of the diplomatic protection of shareholders would, in the opinion of the International Court of Justice, result in the creation of an atmosphere of confusion and insecurity in economic relations especially since the shares

---

[237] See e.g. Brownlie, *Principles*, pp. 463 ff., and Schwarzenberger, *International Law*, pp. 387–412. See also *Sola Tiles Inc.* v. *Islamic Republic of Iran* 83 ILR, p. 460.

[238] ICJ Reports, 1970, pp. 3, 42; 46 ILR, pp. 178, 216.

of international companies are 'widely scattered and frequently change hands'.[239]

Article 9 of the ILC Draft Articles on Diplomatic Protection provides that the nationality of a corporation is the state where it was incorporated, although when the corporation is controlled by nationals of another state or states and has no substantial business activities in the state of incorporation, and the seat of management and the financial control of the corporation are both located in another state, that state shall be regarded as the state of nationality. Article 11 provides that the state of nationality of shareholders shall not be entitled to provide diplomatic protection to shareholders where the injury is to the corporation, unless the corporation has ceased to exist according to the law of the state of incorporation for a reason unrelated to the injury; or the corporation had, at the date of injury, the nationality of the state alleged to be responsible for causing the injury, and incorporation in that state was required by it as a precondition for doing business there.[240]

The International Court returned to the question of corporations in the *Diallo* case,[241] noting that,

> What matters, from the point of view of international law, is to determine whether or not these have a legal personality independent of their members. Conferring independent corporate personality on a company implies granting it rights over its own property, rights which it alone is capable of protecting. As a result, only the state of nationality may exercise diplomatic protection on behalf of the company when its rights are injured by a wrongful act of another state. In determining whether a company possesses independent and distinct legal personality, international law looks to the rules of the relevant domestic law.[242]

In so far as the shareholders of such corporations in the context of diplomatic protection were concerned, the Court emphasised that,

> The exercise by a state of diplomatic protection on behalf of a natural or legal person, who is *associé* or shareholder, having its nationality, seeks to engage the responsibility of another state for an injury caused to that person by an internationally wrongful act committed by that state. Ultimately, this is no

---

[239] ICJ Reports, 1970, p. 49; 46 ILR, p. 223. See also the Separate Opinion of Judge Oda, the *Elettronica Sicula (US v. Italy)* case, ICJ Reports, 1989, pp. 15, 84; 84 ILR, pp. 311, 390.

[240] However, where the injury is a direct one to shareholders as distinct from the corporation, their state of nationality is entitled to exercise diplomatic protection in respect of them: see article 12.

[241] ICJ Reports, 2007, paras. 60 ff.   [242] *Ibid.*, para. 61.

more than the diplomatic protection of a natural or legal person as defined by Article 1 of the ILC draft Articles; what amounts to the internationally wrongful act, in the case of *associés* or shareholders, is the violation by the respondent state of their direct rights in relation to a legal person, direct rights that are defined by the domestic law of that state, as accepted by both Parties, moreover. On this basis, diplomatic protection of the direct rights of *associés* of a SPRL or shareholders of a public limited company is not to be regarded as an exception to the general legal régime of diplomatic protection for natural or legal persons, as derived from customary international law.[243]

The United Kingdom, according to the set of Rules regarding the Taking up of International Claims produced by the Foreign Office in 1985,[244] may intervene in *Barcelona Traction* situations where a national has an interest as a shareholder or otherwise, and the company is defunct, although this is regarded as an exceptional instance. The United Kingdom may also intervene where it is the national state of the company that actively wrongs the company in which a United Kingdom national has an interest as a shareholder or in some other respect; otherwise the UK would normally take up such a claim only in concert with the government of the state of incorporation of the company.[245] Further, practice varies as between states[246] and under different treaty regimes.[247]

---

[243] *Ibid.*, para. 64. The Court also examined whether the general rule that where an unlawful act was committed against a foreign company only the national state of the company could sue still remained and concluded that it did, *ibid.*, paras. 87 ff.

[244] See above, p. 811. The increase in the number of bilateral investment treaties in the 1970s may be partly explained as the response to the post-*Barcelona Traction* need to protect shareholders. See e.g. M. Sornarajah, 'State Responsibility and Bilateral Investment Treaties', 20 *Journal of World Trade Law*, 1986, pp. 79, 87. Note that in the *Diallo* case, ICJ Reports, 2007, para. 88, the Court noted that questions as to the rights of companies and their shareholders were in contemporary international law more a matter for bilateral and multilateral treaties for the protection of foreign investments and that the role of diplomatic protection 'had somewhat faded'.

[245] See also the position adopted by the UK in the *III Finance Ltd* v. *Aegis Consumer Finance Inc.* litigation before the US courts to the effect that entities incorporated in any territory for which the UK is internationally responsible are the UK citizens for the purposes of the US federal alienage jurisdiction statute in question, UKMIL, 71 BYIL, 2000, pp. 552 ff., and similarly in the *Chase Manhattan Bank* v. *Traffic Stream (BVI) Infrastructure Ltd* litigation, UKMIL, 72 BYIL, 2001, p. 603.

[246] See e.g. W. K. Geck, 'Diplomatic Protection' in *Encyclopedia of Public International Law* (ed. R. Bernhardt), Amsterdam, 1992, vol. X, p. 1053.

[247] See e.g. the Algiers Declaration concerning the settlement of US–Iranian claims, 20 ILR, 1981, p. 230; the Convention on the Settlement of Investment Disputes, 1965, article 25 and *Third US Restatement of Foreign Relations Law*, Washington, 1987, vol. I, pp. 127–8.

The position with regard to ships is rather different. The International Tribunal for the Law of the Sea in *M/V Saiga (No. 2)* emphasised that under the Law of the Sea Convention, 1982 it is the flag state that bears the rights and obligations with regard to the ship itself so that 'the ship, every thing on it and every person involved or interested in its obligations are treated as an entity linked to the flag state. The nationalities of these persons are not relevant.'[248]

The exhaustion of local remedies[249]

Customary international law provides that before international proceedings are instituted or claims or representations made, the remedies provided by the local state should have been exhausted.[250] There is a theoretical dispute as to whether the principle of exhaustion of local remedies is a substantive or procedural rule or some form of hybrid concept,[251] but the purpose of the rule is both to enable the state to have an opportunity to redress the wrong that has occurred within its own legal order and to reduce the number of international claims that might be brought. Another factor, of course, is the respect that is to be accorded to the sovereignty and jurisdiction of foreign states by not pre-empting the operation of their legal systems. Article 44 of the ILC Articles on State Responsibility provides that the responsibility of a state may not be

---

[248] 120 ILR, pp. 143, 184–5 and see e.g. article 292 of the Law of the Sea Convention, 1982. See also the *Grand Prince (Belize v. France)* case, ITLOS, judgment of 20 April 2001, 125 ILR, p. 272.

[249] See further above, chapter 6, p. 273. See also the *Panevezys Railway* case, PCIJ, Series A/B, No. 76 (1939); 9 AD, p. 308; Whiteman, *Digest*, vol. III, p. 1558; Borchard, *Diplomatic Protection*, pp. 817–18; A. A. Cançado Trindade, *The Application of the Rule of Exhaustion of Local Remedies in International Law*, Cambridge, 1983; C. Law, *The Local Remedies Rule in International Law*, Geneva, 1961; C. F. Amerasinghe, *Local Remedies in International Law*, Cambridge, 2nd edn, 2004, and J. Kokott, 'Interim Report on the Exhaustion of Local Remedies', International Law Association, Report of the Sixty-Ninth Conference, London, 2000, p. 606.

[250] See e.g. the *Interhandel (Switzerland v. USA)* case, ICJ Reports, 1959, pp. 6, 27 and the *Diallo (Guinea v. Democratic Republic of Congo)* case, ICJ Reports, 2007, paras. 42 and 44. See also *Ex parte Ferhut Butt* 116 ILR, pp. 607, 614–15 (High Court) and 619 (Court of Appeal). The requirement also arises in a number of treaties: see e.g. article 35, European Convention on Human Rights; article 46, Inter-American Convention on Human Rights; article 5, Optional Protocol I, International Covenant on Civil and Political Rights; and article 295 of the Law of the Sea Convention.

[251] See e.g. the discussions in *Yearbook of the* ILC, 1977, vol. II, part 2, pp. 30 ff. and Report of the ILC on its 54th Session, 2002, pp. 131 ff. See also Kokott, 'Interim Report', pp. 612 ff.

invoked if the claim is one to which the rule of exhaustion of local remedies applies and any available and effective local remedy has not been
exhausted.[252]

Article 14 of the ILC Draft Articles on Diplomatic Protection reiterates
the customary rule, noting that no international claim in respect of an
injury to a national may be presented before that national has exhausted
local remedies, which are defined as legal remedies open to an injured
person before the judicial or administrative courts or bodies, whether
ordinary or special, of the state alleged to be responsible for causing the
injury. Article 15 provides that local remedies do not need to be exhausted
where there are no reasonably available local remedies to provide effective
redress, or the local remedies provide no reasonable possibility of such
redress; there is undue delay in the remedial process which is attributable
to the state alleged to be responsible; there was no relevant connection
between the injured person and the state alleged to be responsible at the
date of injury; the injured person is manifestly precluded from pursuing local remedies; or the state alleged to be responsible has waived the
requirement that local remedies be exhausted.[253]

The general rule was well illustrated in the *Ambatielos* arbitration[254]
between Greece and Britain. The former brought proceedings arising
out of a contract signed by Ambatielos, which were rejected by the tribunal since the remedies available under English law had not been fully
utilised. In particular, he had failed to call a vital witness and he had
not appealed to the House of Lords from the decision of the Court of
Appeal.

The requirement to exhaust local[255] remedies applies only to available
effective remedies. It will not be sufficient to dismiss a claim merely because the person claiming had not taken the matter to appeal, where
the appeal would not have affected the basic outcome of the case. This
was stressed in the *Finnish Ships* arbitration[256] where shipowners brought

---

[252] ILC Commentary 2001, p. 305.
[253] The International Court noted in the *Diallo* case, ICJ Reports, 2007, para. 47, that administrative remedies can only be taken into consideration for purposes of the local
remedies rule if they are aimed at vindicating a right and not at obtaining a favour, unless
they constitute an essential prerequisite for the admissibility of subsequent contentious
proceedings.
[254] 12 RIAA, p. 83 (1956); 23 ILR, p. 306.
[255] The terms domestic or municipal remedies are also used.
[256] 2 RIAA, p. 1479 (1934); 7 AD, p. 231.

a claim before the Admiralty Transport Arbitration Board, but did not appeal against the unfavourable decision. It was held that since the appeal could only be on points of law, which could not overturn the vital finding of fact that there had been a British requisition of ships involved, any appeal would have been ineffective. Accordingly the claims of the shipowners would not be dismissed for non-exhaustion of local remedies.

In the *Interhandel* case,[257] the United States seized the American assets of a company owned by the Swiss firm Interhandel, in 1942, which was suspected of being under the control of a German enterprise. In 1958, after nine years of litigation in the US courts regarding the unblocking of the Swiss assets in America, Switzerland took the matter to the International Court of Justice. However, before a decision was reached, the US Supreme Court readmitted Interhandel into the legal proceedings, thus disposing of Switzerland's argument that the company's suit had been finally rejected. The Court dismissed the Swiss government's claim since the local remedies available had not been exhausted. Criticism has been levelled against this judgment on the ground that litigation extending over practically ten years could hardly be described as constituting an 'effective' remedy. However, the fact remains that the legal system operating in the United States had still something to offer the Swiss company even after that time.

The local remedies rule does not apply where one state has been guilty of a direct breach of international law causing immediate injury to another state, as for instance where its diplomatic agents are assaulted. But it does apply where the state is complaining of injury to its nationals.[258] The local remedies rule may be waived by treaty stipulation, as for example in Article V of the US–Mexico General Claims Convention of 1923 and Article XI of the Convention on International Liability for Damage caused by Space Objects, 1972.

The issue of local remedies was clarified in the *Elettronica Sicula SpA* (*ELSI*) case,[259] which referred to the concept as 'an important principle

[257] ICJ Reports, 1959, p. 6; 27 ILR, p. 475. The Court declared that the 'rule that local remedies must be exhausted before international proceedings may be instituted is a well-established principle of customary international law', ICJ Reports, 1959, p. 27; 27 ILR, p. 490. See also Rules VII and VIII of the International Claims Rules of the FCO, above, p. 811; Pleadings, *Israel* v. *Bulgaria*, ICJ Reports, 1959, pp. 531–2, and T. Meron, 'The Incidence of the Rule of Exhaustion of Local Remedies', 25 BYIL, 1959, p. 95. Note, in addition, the *North American Dredging Co.* claim, 4 RIAA, p. 26 (1926); 3 AD, p. 4.

[258] See e.g. the *Heathrow Airport User Charges Arbitration*, 102 ILR, pp. 215, 277 ff.

[259] ICJ Reports, 1989, p. 15; 84 ILR, p. 311.

of customary international law'.[260] The case concerned an action brought by the US against Italy alleging injuries to the Italian interests of two US corporations. Italy claimed that local remedies had not been exhausted, while the US argued that the doctrine did not apply since the case was brought under the Treaty of Friendship, Commerce and Navigation, 1948 between the two states which provided for the submission of disputes relating to the treaty to the International Court, with no mention of local remedies. The Chamber of the Court, however, firmly held that while the parties to an agreement could if they so chose dispense with the local remedies requirement in express terms, it 'finds itself unable to accept that an important principle of customary international law should be held to have been tacitly dispensed with'.[261] In other words, the presumption that local remedies need to be exhausted can only be rebutted by express provision to the contrary.

The Chamber also dealt with a claim by the US that the doctrine did not apply to a request for a declaratory judgment finding that the treaty in question had been violated. This claim in effect was based on the view that the doctrine would not apply in cases of direct injury to a state. The Chamber felt unable to find in the case a dispute over alleged violation of the treaty resulting in direct injury to the US that was both distinct from and independent of the dispute with regard to the two US corporations.[262] It was stressed that the matter 'which colours and pervades the US claim as a whole' was the alleged damage to the two US corporations.[263] In the light of this stringent test, it therefore seems that in such mixed claims involving the interests both of nationals and of the state itself one must assume that the local remedies rule applies.

The claim that local remedies had not in fact been exhausted in the case because the two US corporations had not raised the treaty issue before the Italian courts was rejected. It was held that it was sufficient if the essence of the claim had been brought before the competent tribunals. Accordingly, identity of claims as distinct from identity of issues is not required. The Chamber was not convinced that there clearly remained some remedy which the corporations, independently of their Italian subsidiary (ELSI), ought to have pursued and exhausted.[264]

---

[260] ICJ Reports, 1989, p. 42; 84 ILR, p. 348.   [261] *Ibid.*
[262] ICJ Reports, 1989, pp. 42–4; 84 ILR, pp. 348–50.
[263] ICJ Reports, 1989, p. 43; 84 ILR, p. 349.
[264] ICJ Reports, 1989, pp. 46–8; 84 ILR, pp. 352–4. See e.g. M. H. Adler, 'The Exhaustion of the Local Remedies Rule After the International Court of Justice's Decision in *ELSI*', 39 ICLQ, 1990, p. 641, and F. A. Mann, 'Foreign Investment in the International Court of

The treatment of aliens[265]

The question of the protection of foreign nationals is one of those issues in international law most closely connected with the different approaches adopted to international relations by the Western and Third World nations. Developing countries, as well as communist countries formerly, have long been eager to reduce what they regard as the privileges accorded to capitalist states by international law. They lay great emphasis upon the sovereignty and independence of states and resent the economic influence of the West. The Western nations, on the other hand, have wished to protect their investments and nationals abroad and provide for the security of their property.

The diplomatic protection of nationals abroad developed as the number of nationals overseas grew as a consequence of increasing trading activities and thus the relevant state practice multiplied. In addition, since the US–UK Jay Treaty of 1794 numerous mixed claims commissions were established to resolve problems of injury to aliens,[266] while a variety of national claims commissions were created to distribute lump sums received from foreign states in settlement of claims.[267] Such international and national claims procedures together with diplomatic protection therefore enabled nationals abroad to be aided in cases of loss or injury in state responsibility situations.[268]

Justice: The *ELSI Case*', 86 AJIL, 1992, pp. 92, 101–2. See also the *M/V Saiga (No. 2)* case, 120 ILR, pp. 143, 182–4 and the *LaGrand* case, ICJ Reports, 2001, pp. 466, 487–8; 134 ILR, pp. 1, 26–7.

[265] See references in footnote 1. See also Guha Roy, 'Is the Law of Responsibility of States for Injury to Aliens a Part of Universal International Law?', 55 AJIL, 1961, p. 863; A. Fatouros, 'International Law and the Third World', 50 *Virginia Law Review*, 1964, p. 783; I. Shihata, *Legal Treatment of Foreign Investment*, Dordrecht, 1993; *Oppenheim's International Law*, p. 903, and *Third US Restatement of Foreign Relations Law*, Washington, 1987, vol. II, p. 184. See also the Principles Concerning Admission and Treatment of Aliens adopted by the Asian–African Legal Consultative Committee at its fourth session: www.aalco.org/Principle%20Concerning%20admission%20and%20Treatment%20of%20aliens.htm.

[266] See e.g. A. M. Stuyt, *Survey of International Arbitrations, 1794–1889*, 3rd edn, Dordrecht, 1990.

[267] See e.g. *International Claims* (eds. R. B. Lillich and B. Weston), Charlottesville, 1982, and R. B. Lillich and B. Weston, *International Claims: Their Settlements by Lump-Sum Agreements*, Charlottesville, 2 vols., 1975. See also the US–People's Republic of China Claims Settlement Agreement of 1979, DUSPIL, 1979, pp. 1213–15, and Whiteman, *Digest*, vol. VIII, pp. 933–69.

[268] Note the establishment of the UN Compensation Commission following the ending of the Gulf War in 1991 to enable the settlement of claims arising out of that conflict: see below, chapter 22, p. 1249.

The relevant standard of treatment

The developed states of the West have argued historically that there exists an 'international minimum standard' for the protection of foreign nationals that must be upheld irrespective of how the state treats its own nationals, whereas other states maintained that all the state need do is treat the alien as it does its own nationals (the 'national treatment standard'). The reason for the evolution of the latter approach is to be found in the increasing resentment of Western economic domination rather than in the necessary neglect of basic standards of justice. The Latin American states felt, in particular, that the international minimum standard concept had been used as a means of interference in internal affairs.[269] Accordingly, the Calvo doctrine was formulated. This involved a reaffirmation of the principle of non-intervention coupled with the assertion that aliens were entitled only to such rights as were accorded nationals and thus had to seek redress for grievances exclusively in the domestic arena.[270] It was intended as a shield against external interference. The international standard concept itself developed during the nineteenth century and received extensive support in case-law.

In the *Neer* case,[271] for example, where the American superintendent of a mine in Mexico had been killed, the Commission held 'that the propriety of governmental acts should be put to the test of international standards', while in the *Certain German Interests in Polish Upper Silesia* case,[272] the Court recognised the existence of a common or generally accepted international law respecting the treatment of aliens, which is applicable to them despite municipal legislation. In the *Garcia* case,[273] the US–Mexican Claims Commission emphasised that there existed an international standard concerning the taking of human life, and in the *Roberts* claim,[274] reference was made to the test as to whether aliens were treated in accordance with ordinary standards of civilisation. If the principle is clear, the contents or definition of that principle are far from clear. In the *Neer* claim,[275] the Commission stated that the treatment of an alien, in order to constitute an international delinquency,

---

[269] See e.g. Guha Roy, 'Law of Responsibility'; J. Castañeda, 'The Underdeveloped Nations and the Development of International Law', 15 *International Organisation*, 1961, p. 38, and R. P. Anand, *New States and International Law*, Delhi, 1972.

[270] See e.g. Lillich, 'Duties', p. 349.   [271] 4 RIAA, p. 60 (1926); 3 AD, p. 213.

[272] PCIJ, Series A, No. 7, 1926; 3 AD, p. 429.

[273] 4 RIAA, p. 119 (1926). See also the *Chattin* case, 4 RIAA, p. 282 (1927); 4 AD, p. 248.

[274] 4 RIAA, p. 77 (1926); 3 AD, p. 227.

[275] 4 RIAA, pp. 60, 61–2 (1926); 3 AD, p. 213. See similarly the *Chattin* case, 4 RIAA, p. 282 (1927); 4 AD, p. 248.

should amount to an outrage, to bad faith, to wilful neglect of duty, or to an insufficiency of governmental action so far short of international standards that every reasonable and impartial man would readily recognise its insufficiency.

In other words, a fairly high threshold is specified before the minimum standard applies. Some indeed have argued that the concept never involved a definite standard with a fixed content, but rather a 'process of decision',[276] a process which would involve an examination of the responsibility of the state for the injury to the alien in the light of all the circumstances of the particular case.[277] The issue of the content of such a standard has often been described in terms of the concept of denial of justice.[278] In effect, that concept refers to the improper administration of civil and criminal justice as regards an alien.[279] It would include the failure to apprehend and prosecute those wrongfully causing injury to an alien, as in the *Janes* claim,[280] where an American citizen was killed in Mexico. The identity of the murderer was known, but no action had been taken for eight years. The widow was awarded $12,000 in compensation for the non-apprehension and non-punishment of the murderer. It would also include unreasonably long detention and harsh and unlawful treatment in prison.[281]

A progressive attempt to resolve the divide between the national and international standard proponents was put forward by Garcia-Amador in a report on international responsibility to the International Law Commission in 1956. He argued that the two approaches were now synthesised in the concept of the international recognition of the essential rights of man.[282] He formulated two principles: first, that aliens had to enjoy the same rights and guarantees as enjoyed by nationals, which should not in any case be less than the fundamental human rights recognised and defined in international instruments; secondly, international responsibility would only be engaged if internationally recognised fundamental human rights were affected.[283] This approach did not prove attractive to the ILC at that time in the light of a number of problems. However, human rights

---

[276] M. S. McDougal et al., Studies in World Public Order, New Haven, 1960, p. 869.

[277] See Lillich, 'Duties', p. 350.

[278] See e.g. A. V. Freeman, The International Responsibility of States for Denial of Justice, London, 1938.

[279] See AMCO v. Indonesia (Merits) 89 ILR, pp. 405, 451.

[280] 4 RIAA, p. 82 (1926); 3 AD, p. 218.

[281] See e.g. the Roberts claim, 4 RIAA, p. 77 (1926); 3 AD, p. 227 and the Quintanilla claim, 4 RIAA, p. 101 (1926); 3 AD, p. 224.

[282] Yearbook of the ILC, 1956, vol. II, pp. 173, 199–203.

[283] Yearbook of the ILC, 1957, vol. II, pp. 104, 112–13.

law has developed considerably in recent years[284] and can now be regarded as establishing certain minimum standards of state behaviour with regard to civil and political rights. It is noticeable, for example, that the relevant instruments do not refer to nationals and aliens specifically, but to all individuals within the territory and subject to the jurisdiction of the state without discrimination.[285] One should also note the special efforts being made to deal with non-nationals, in particular the UN Declaration on the Human Rights of Individuals who are not Nationals of the Country in which they Live,[286] and the continuing concern with regard to migrant workers.[287]

Some differences as regards the relative rights and obligations of nationals and aliens are, of course, inevitable. Non-nationals do not have political rights and may be banned from employment in certain areas (e.g. the diplomatic corps), although they remain subject to the local law. It is also unquestioned that a state may legitimately refuse to admit aliens, or may accept them subject to certain conditions being fulfilled. Whether a state may expel aliens with equal facility is more open to doubt.

A number of cases assert that states must give convincing reasons for expelling an alien. In, for example, the *Boffolo* case,[288] which concerned an Italian expelled from Venezuela, it was held that states possess a general right of expulsion, but it could only be resorted to in extreme circumstances and accomplished in a manner least injurious to the person affected. In addition, the reasons for the expulsion must be stated before an international tribunal when the occasion demanded. Many municipal systems provide that the authorities of a country may deport aliens without reasons having to be stated. The position under customary international law is therefore somewhat confused. As far as treaty law is concerned, article 13 of the International Covenant on Civil and Political Rights stipulates that an alien lawfully in the territory of a state party to the Convention

---

[284] See above, chapters 6 and 7.

[285] See e.g. article 2 of the International Covenant on Civil and Political Rights, 1966 and article 1 of the European Convention on Human Rights, 1950.

[286] General Assembly resolution 40/144. See also E/CN.4/Sub.2/392 (1977) and R. B. Lillich and S. Neff, 'The Treatment of Aliens and International Human Rights Norms', 21 German YIL, 1978, p. 97.

[287] See further above, chapter 6, p. 333.

[288] 10 RIAA, p. 528 (1903). See also *Dr Breger's* case, Whiteman, *Digest*, vol. VIII, p. 861; R. Plender, *International Migration Law*, 2nd edn, Dordrecht, 1988, and G. Goodwin-Gill, *International Law and the Movement of Persons Between States*, Oxford, 1978.

may be expelled therefrom only in pursuance of a decision reached in accordance with law and shall, except where compelling reasons of national security otherwise require, be allowed to submit the reasons against his expulsion and to have his case reviewed by and be represented for the purpose before, the competent authority.

Article 3 of the European Convention on Establishment, 1956, provides that nationals of other contracting states lawfully residing in the territory may be expelled only if they endanger national security or offend against public order or morality, and Article 4 of the Fourth Protocol (1963) of the European Convention on Human Rights declares that 'collective expulsion of aliens is prohibited'.[289] The burden of proving the wrongfulness of the expelling state's action falls upon the claimant alleging expulsion and the relevant rules would also apply where, even though there is no direct law or regulation forcing the alien to leave, his continued presence in that state is made impossible because of conditions generated by wrongful acts of the state or attributable to it.[290] Where states have expelled aliens, international law requires their national state to admit them.[291]

The expropriation of foreign property[292]

The expansion of the Western economies since the nineteenth century in particular stimulated an outflow of capital and consequent heavy

---

[289] Note also article 1 of Protocol 7 (1984) of the European Convention on Human Rights to the same general effect as article 13. See, as regards refugees, the 1951 Convention Relating to the Status of Refugees and the 1967 Protocol, and G. Goodwin-Gill, *The Refugee in International Law*, 2nd edn, Oxford, 1996.

[290] See *Rankin* v. *The Islamic Republic of Iran* 17 Iran–US CTR, pp. 135, 142; 82 ILR, pp. 204, 214. See also Goodwin-Gill, *International Law and the Movement of Persons*; Brownlie, *Principles*, pp. 498 ff., and M. Pellonpaa, *Expulsion in International Law*, Helsinki, 1984.

[291] This is a general principle, but cf. Lord Denning in the *Thakrar* case, [1974] QB 684; 59 ILR, p. 450. Note that the Lord Chancellor, in dealing with the expulsion of British aliens from East Africa, accepted that in international law a state was under a duty as between other states to accept expelled nationals: see 335 HL Deb., col. 497, 14 September 1972. See also *Van Duyn* v. *Home Office* [1974] ECR 1337; 60 ILR, p. 247.

[292] See e.g. G. White, *Nationalisation of Foreign Property*, London, 1961; B. Wortley, *Expropriation of Public International Law*, 1959; A. F. Lowenfeld, *International Economic Law*, 2nd edn, Oxford, 2008, part VI; M. Sornarajah, *The International Law on Foreign Investment*, 2nd edn, Cambridge, 2004, and Sornarajah, *The Settlement of Foreign Investment Disputes*, The Hague, 2000; I. Brownlie, 'Legal Status of Natural Resources', 162 HR, 1979, p. 245; R. Higgins, 'The Taking of Property by the State: Recent Developments in International Law', 176 HR, 1982, p. 267, and *The Valuation of Nationalised Property in International Law* (ed. R. B. Lillich), Charlottesville, 3 vols., 1972–5. See also *Oppenheim's International Law*, pp. 911 ff.; P. Muchlinski, *Multinational Enterprises and the Law*, 2nd edn, Oxford,

investment in the developing areas of the world. This resulted in substantial areas of local economies falling within the ownership and control
of Western corporations. However, with the granting of independence
to the various Third World countries and in view of the nationalisation
measures taken by the Soviet Union after the success of the communist
revolution, such properties and influence began to come under pressure.

In assessing the state of international law with regard to the expropriation of the property of aliens, one is immediately confronted with two
opposing objectives, although they need not be irreconcilable in all cases.
On the one hand, the capital-exporting countries require some measure
of protection and security before they will invest abroad and, on the other
hand, the capital-importing countries are wary of the power of foreign investments and the drain of currency that occurs, and are often stimulated
to take over such enterprises. Nationalisation for one reason or another is
now a common feature not only in communist and Afro-Asian states, but
also in Western Europe. The need to acquire control of some key privately
owned property is felt by many states to be an essential requirement in
the interests of economic and social reform. Indeed it is true to say that
extensive sectors of the economies of most West European states were at
some stages under national control after having been taken into public
ownership.

Since it can hardly be denied that nationalisation is a perfectly legitimate measure for a state to adopt and clearly not illegal as such under
international law,[293] the problem arises where foreign property is involved.
Not to expropriate such property in a general policy of nationalisation
might be seen as equivalent to proposing a privileged status within the
country for foreign property, as well as limiting the power of the state
within its own jurisdiction. There is no doubt that under international
law, expropriation of alien property is legitimate.[294] This is not disputed.
However, certain conditions must be fulfilled.[295]

1999, pp. 491 ff.; A. Mouri, *The International Law of Expropriation as Reflected in the Work
of the Iran–US Claims Tribunal*, Dordrecht, 1994; P. M. Norton, 'A Law of the Future or a
Law of the Past? Modern Tribunals and the International Law of Expropriation', 85 AJIL,
1991, p. 474; N. Schrijver, *Sovereignty over Natural Resources*, Cambridge, 1997, and F.
Beveridge, *The Treatment and Taxation of Foreign Investment under International Law*,
Manchester, 2000.

293 See e.g. *De Sanchez v. Banco Central de Nicaragua and Others* 770 F.2d 1385, 1397; 88 ILR,
pp. 75, 89.

294 See e.g. *AMCO v. Indonesia (Merits)* 89 ILR, pp. 405, 466.

295 See e.g. the World Bank Guidelines on the Treatment of Foreign Direct Investment, 31
ILM, 1992, p. 1363.

The question, of course, arises as to the stage at which international law in fact becomes involved in such a situation. Apart from the relevance of the general rules relating to the treatment of aliens noted in the preceding section, the issue will usually arise out of a contract between a state and a foreign private enterprise. In such a situation, several possibilities exist. It could be argued that the contract itself by its very nature becomes 'internationalised' and thus subject to international law rather than (or possibly in addition to) the law of the contracting state. The consequences of this would include the operation of the principle of international law that agreements are to be honoured (*pacta sunt servanda*) which would constrain the otherwise wide competence of a state party to alter unilaterally the terms of a relevant agreement. This proposition was adopted by the Arbitrator in the *Texaco* v. *Libya* case in 1977,[296] where it was noted that this may be achieved in various ways: for example, by stating that the law governing the contract referred to 'general principles of law', which was taken to incorporate international law; by including an international arbitration clause for the settlement of disputes; and by including a stabilisation clause in an international development agreement, preventing unilateral variation of the terms of the agreement.[297] However, this approach is controversial and case-law is by no means consistent.[298] International law will clearly be engaged where the expropriation is unlawful, either because of, for example, the discriminatory manner in which it is carried out or the offering of inadequate or no compensation.[299]

---

[296] 53 ILR, p. 389.

[297] See e.g. C. Greenwood, 'State Contracts in International Law – The Libyan Oil Arbitrations', 53 BYIL, 1982, pp. 27, 41 ff. See also A. Fatouros, 'International Law and the Internationalised Contract', 74 AJIL, 1980, p. 134.

[298] See e.g. J. Paulsson, 'The ICSID *Klöckner* v. *Cameroon* Award: The Duties of Partners in North–South Economic Development Agreements', 1 *Journal of International Arbitration*, 1984, p. 145; the *Aminoil* case, 21 ILM, 1982, p. 976; 66 ILR, p. 519, and D. W. Bowett, 'State Contracts with Aliens: Contemporary Developments on Compensation for Termination or Breach', 59 BYIL, 1988, p. 49.

[299] See in particular article 1 of Protocol I of the European Convention on Human Rights, 1950 as regards the protection of the right to property and the prohibition of deprivation of possessions 'except in the public interest and subject to the conditions provided for by law and by the general principles of international law'. See e.g. the following cases: *Marckx*, European Court of Human Rights, Series A, No. 31; 58 ILR, p. 561; *Sporrong and Lönnroth*, ECHR, Series A, No. 52; 68 ILR, p. 86; *Loizidou* v. *Turkey*, Judgment of 18 December 1996; 108 ILR, p. 444. See also e.g. *Jacobs and White European Convention on Human Rights* (eds. C. Ovey and R. C. A. White), 4th edn, Oxford, 2006, chapter 15. However, it has been held that the reference to international law did not apply to the taking

The property question

Higgins has pointed to 'the almost total absence of any analysis of conceptual aspects of property'.[300] Property would clearly include physical objects and certain abstract entities, for example, shares in companies, debts and intellectual property. The 1961 Harvard Draft Convention on the International Responsibility of States for Injuries to Aliens[301] discusses the concept of property in the light of 'all movable and immovable property, whether tangible or intangible, including industrial, literary and artistic property as well as rights and interests in property'. In the *Liamco* case the arbitration specifically mentioned concession rights as forming part of incorporeal property,[302] a crucial matter as many expropriation cases in fact involve a wide variety of contractual rights.[303]

The nature of expropriation[304]

Expropriation involves a taking of property,[305] but actions short of direct possession of the assets in question may also fall within the category. The 1961 Harvard Draft would include, for example, 'any such unreasonable interference with the use, enjoyment or disposal of property as to justify an inference that the owner thereof will not be able to use, enjoy or dispose of the property within a reasonable period of time after the inception of such interference'.[306] In 1965, for example, after a series of Indonesian decrees, the UK government stated that:

by a state of the property of its own nationals: see *Lithgow*, European Court of Human Rights, Series A, No. 102; 75 ILR, p. 438; *James*, ECHR, Series A, No. 98; 75 ILR, p. 397 and *Mellacher*, ECHR, Series A, No. 169. See also Brock, 'The Protection of Property Rights Under the European Convention on Human Rights', *Legal Issues of European Integration*, 1986, p. 52.

[300] Higgins, 'Taking of Property', p. 268.   [301] 55 AJIL, 1961, p. 548 (article 10(7)).

[302] 20 ILM, 1981, pp. 1, 53; 62 ILR, pp. 141, 189. See also the *Shufeldt* case, 2 RIAA, pp. 1083, 1097 (1930); 5 AD, p. 179.

[303] See also below, p. 839, concerning the definition of 'investments' in bilateral investment treaties. See also article 1(6) of the European Energy Charter Treaty, 1994.

[304] See e.g. R. Dolzer and C. Schreuer, *Principles of International Investment Law*, Oxford, 2008, chapter 6.

[305] The North American Free Trade Agreement (NAFTA) Arbitration Tribunal noted that the term 'expropriation', 'carries with it the connotation of a "taking" by a government-type authority of a person's "property" with a view to transferring ownership of that property to another person, usually the authority that exercised its *de jure* or *de facto* power to do the "taking"', *S.D. Myers* v. *Canada* 121 ILR, pp. 72, 122.

[306] 55 AJIL, 1961, pp. 553–4 (article 10(3)a).

in view of the complete inability of British enterprises and plantations to exercise and enjoy any of their rights of ownership in relation to their properties in Indonesia, Her Majesty's Government has concluded that the Indonesian Government has expropriated this property.[307]

In *Starrett Housing Corporation* v. *Government of the Islamic Republic of Iran* before the Iran–US Claims Tribunal,[308] it was emphasised by the Tribunal that:

> measures taken by a state can interfere with property rights to such an extent that these rights are rendered so useless that they must be deemed to have been expropriated, even though the state does not purport to have expropriated them and the legal title to the property formally remains with the original owner.

In that case, it was held that a taking had occurred by the end of January 1980 upon the appointment by the Iranian Housing Ministry of a temporary manager of the enterprise concerned, thus depriving the claimants of the right to manage and of effective control and use.[309] However, a series of events prior to that date, including armed incursions and detention of personnel, intimidation and interference with supplies and needed facilities, did not amount to a taking of the property, since investors in foreign countries assume certain risks with regard to disturbances and even revolution. The fact that the risks materialise, held the Tribunal, did not mean that property rights affected by the events could be deemed to have been taken.[310] There is clearly an important, but indistinct, dividing line here.

It has also been held that the seizure of a controlling stock interest in a foreign corporation is a taking of control of the assets and profits of the enterprise in question.[311] In *Biloune* v. *Ghana Investment Centre*, an

---

[307] BPIL, 1964, p. 200. See also 4 ILM, 1965, pp. 440–7. Note also *Shanghai Power Co.* v. *US* 4 Cl. Ct. 237 (1983), where it was held that the settlement of the plaintiff's claim by the US government in an agreement with China for less than its worth did not constitute a taking for which compensation was required in the context of the Fifth Amendment.

[308] Interlocutory Award, 4 Iran–US CTR, p. 122; 85 ILR, p. 349.

[309] 4 Iran–US CTR, p. 154; 85 ILR, p. 390. See also *Harza Engineering Co.* v. *The Islamic Republic of Iran* 1 Iran–US CTR, p. 499; 70 ILR, p. 117, and *AIG* v. *The Islamic Republic of Iran* 4 Iran–US CTR, p. 96. See also *SEDCO* v. *NIOC* 84 ILR, p. 483.

[310] 4 Iran–US CTR, p. 156; 85 ILR, p. 392. Cf. the Concurring Opinion by Judge Holtzmann on this issue, 4 Iran–US CTR, pp. 159, 178; 85 ILR, p. 414.

[311] *Kalamazoo Spice Extraction Company* v. *The Provisional Military Government of Socialist Ethiopia* 86 ILR, p. 45 and 90 ILR, p. 596. See also *Agip SpA* v. *The Government of the Popular Republic of the Congo* 67 ILR, p. 319 and *Benvenuti and Bonfant* v. *The Government of the Popular Republic of the Congo, ibid.*, p. 345.

investor began construction work relying upon government representations although without building permits; a stop order was then issued based upon the absence of such permit. The Tribunal held that an indirect expropriation had taken place because the totality of the circumstances had the effect of causing the irreparable cessation of work on the project.[312]

Where the taking constitutes a process rather than one clear act, there will be a problem of determining when the process has reached the point at which an expropriation in fact has occurred.[313] This issue may be important, for example, in determining the valuation date for compensation purposes. In *Santa Elena* v. *Costa Rica*, the Tribunal stated that 'a property has been expropriated when the effect of the measures taken by the state has been to deprive the owner of title, possession or access to the benefit and economic use of his property... This is a matter of fact for the Tribunal to assess in the light of the circumstances of the case.'[314]

The expropriation of a given property may also include a taking of closely connected ancillary rights, such as patents and contracts, which had not been directly nationalised.[315]

---

[312] 95 ILR, pp. 183, 207–10. See also *Metalclad Corporation* v. *United Mexican States* 119 ILR, pp. 615, 639–40, a case under the North American Free Trade Agreement (NAFTA), article 1110 of which prohibits direct and indirect expropriation, where the Tribunal noted that expropriation included 'covert or incidental interference with the use of property which has the effect of depriving the owner, in whole or in significant part, of the use of reasonably to be expected economic benefit of property even if not necessarily to the obvious benefit of the host state', para. 108. See also *CME* v. *Czech Republic* 9 ICSID Reports, p. 121 and *Middle East Cement Shipping* v. *Egypt* 7 ICSID Reports, p. 178.

[313] See e.g. *Generation Ukraine* v. *Ukraine* 44 ILM 2005, p. 404, paras. 20.22 and 20.26, noting that the plea of 'creeping expropriation' proceeded on the basis of an investment existing at a particular time that was eroded by a series of acts attributable to the state to the extent that it is violative of the relevant international standard of protection against expropriation. See also *Siemens* v. *Argentina*, Award of 6 February 2007, and W. M. Reisman and R. D. Sloane, 'Indirect Expropriation and Its Valuation in the BIT Generation', 74 BYIL, 2003, p. 115.

[314] 39 ILM, 2000, pp. 1317, 1329.

[315] PCIJ, Series A, No. 7, 1926. See also the *Norwegian Shipowners' Claims* case, 1 RIAA, p. 307 (1922) and the *Sporrong and Lönnroth* case before the European Court of Human Rights, Series A, No. 52 (1982); 68 ILR, p. 86. See also *Papamichalopoulos* v. *Greece*, European Court of Human Rights, Series A, No. 260 (1993), p. 15. Note in addition *Revere Copper* v. *Opic* 56 ILR, p. 258. See G. C. Christie, 'What Constitutes a Taking of Property under International Law?', 38 BYIL, 1962, p. 307; DUSPIL, 1976, p. 444; Brownlie, *System and State Responsibility*, pp. 24–5; Whiteman, *Digest*, vol. VIII, pp. 1006 ff., and *Third US Restatement on Foreign Relations Law*, vol. II, pp. 200–1.

Public purposes

The Permanent Court in the *Certain German Interests in Polish Upper Silesia* case noted that expropriation must be for 'reasons of public utility, judicial liquidation and similar measures'.[316] How far this extends is open to dispute, although it will cover wartime measures.

The issue was raised in the *BP* case,[317] where the reason for the expropriation of the BP property was the Libyan belief that the UK had encouraged Iran to occupy certain Persian Gulf Islands. The arbitrator explained that the taking violated international law, 'as it was made for purely extraneous political reasons and was arbitrary and discriminatory in character'.[318] This is ambiguous as to the public purpose issue, and in the *Liamco* case[319] it was held that 'the public utility principle is not a necessary requisite for the legality of a nationalisation'.[320] It is to be noted, however, that the 1962 General Assembly Resolution on Permanent Sovereignty over Natural Resources mentions this requirement,[321] although the 1974 Charter of Economic Rights and Duties of States does not.[322] The question may thus still be an open one,[323] although later practice suggests that general measures taken on a non-discriminatory basis for the public good would not constitute unlawful expropriation. The

---

[316] PCIJ, Series A, No. 7, 1926, p. 22.   [317] 53 ILR, p. 297.   [318] *Ibid.*, p. 329.
[319] 20 ILM, 1981, p. 1; 62 ILR, p. 141.   [320] 20 ILM, 1981, pp. 58–9; 62 ILR, p. 194.
[321] Paragraph 4 of the 1962 Resolution provides that '[n]ationalization, expropriation or requisitioning shall be based on grounds or reasons of public utility, security or the national interest which are recognized as overriding purely individual or private interests, both domestic and foreign. In such cases the owner shall be paid appropriate compensation in accordance with the rules in force in the state taking such measures in the exercise of its sovereignty and in accordance with international law. In any case where the question of compensation gives rise to a controversy, the national jurisdiction of the state taking such measures shall be exhausted. However, upon agreement by sovereign states and other parties concerned, settlement of the dispute should be made through arbitration or international adjudication.'
[322] Article 2(2)c of the 1974 Charter provides that every state has the right to 'nationalise, expropriate or transfer ownership of foreign property in which case appropriate compensation should be paid by the state adopting such measures, taking into account its relevant laws and regulations and all circumstances that the state considers pertinent. In any case where the question of compensation gives rise to a controversy, it shall be settled under the domestic law of the nationalising state and by its tribunals, unless it is freely and mutually agreed by all states concerned that other peaceful means be sought on the basis of the sovereign equality of states and in accordance with the principle of free choice of means.'
[323] See also *Agip SpA v. The Government of the Popular Republic of the Congo* 67 ILR, pp. 319, 336–9.

Tribunal in *Santa Elena* v. *Costa Rica* took the view that international law permitted expropriation of foreign-owned property *inter alia* for a public purpose and noted that this might include a taking for environmental reasons.[324]

Compensation

The requirement often stipulated is for prompt, adequate and effective compensation, the formula used by US Secretary of State Hull on the occasion of Mexican expropriations.[325] It is the standard maintained in particular by the United States[326] and found in an increasing number of bilateral investment treaties.[327] However, case-law has been less clear. Early cases did not use the Hull formulation[328] and the 1962 Permanent Sovereignty Resolution referred to 'appropriate compensation', a phrase cited with approval by the arbitrator in the *Texaco* case[329] as a rule of customary law in view of the support it achieved. This was underlined in the *Aminoil* case,[330] where the tribunal said that the standard of 'appropriate compensation' in the 1962 resolution 'codifies positive principles'.[331] It was stated that the determination of 'appropriate compensation' was better accomplished by an inquiry into all the circumstances relevant to the particular concrete case than through abstract theoretical discussion.[332] However, while the 'appropriate compensation' formula of the 1962 resolution is linked to both national and international law, the 1974 Charter of Economic Rights and Duties of States links the formula to domestic law and considerations only. The former instrument is accepted as a reflection

---

[324] 39 ILM, 2000, pp. 1317, 1329. The fact that the taking was for a laudable environmental reason did not affect the duty to pay compensation, *ibid.* See also *Too* v. *Greater Modesto Insurance Associates* 23 Iran–US CTR, p. 378; *Methanex* v. *USA* 44 ILM, 2005, p. 1345 and *Saluka* v. *Czech Republic*, Partial Award, 17 March 2006.

[325] Hackworth, *Digest*, vol. III, 1940–4, p. 662. See also Muchlinski, *Multinational Enterprises*, pp. 496 ff., and E. Lauterpacht, 'Issues of Compensation and Nationality in the Taking of Energy Investments', 8 *Journal of Energy and Natural Resources Law*, 1990, p. 241.

[326] See e.g. DUSPIL, 1976, p. 444, and D. Robinson, 'Expropriation in the Restatement (Revised)', 78 AJIL, 1984, p. 176.

[327] Robinson, 'Expropriation', p. 178. See further below, p. 837.

[328] See e.g. the *Chorzów Factory* case, PCIJ, Series A, No. 17, 1928, p. 46; 4 AD, p. 268 and the *Norwegian Shipowners' Claims* case, 1 RIAA, pp. 307, 339–41 (1922). See also O. Schachter, 'Compensation for Expropriation', 78 AJIL, 1984, p. 121.

[329] 17 ILM, 1978, pp. 3, 29; 53 ILR, pp. 389, 489. See also *Banco Nacional de Cuba* v. *Chase Manhattan Bank* 658 F.2d 875 (1981); 66 ILR, p. 421.

[330] 21 ILM, 1982, p. 976; 66 ILR, p. 519. [331] 21 ILM, 1982, p. 1032; 66 ILR, p. 601.

[332] 21 ILM, 1982, p. 1033.

of custom, while the latter is not.[333] But in any event, it is unclear whether in practice there would be a substantial difference in result.[334]

It should also be noted that section IV(1) of the World Bank Guidelines on the Treatment of Foreign Direct Investment provides that a state may not expropriate foreign private investment except where this is done in accordance with applicable legal procedures, in pursuance in good faith of a public purpose, without discrimination on the basis of nationality and against the payment of appropriate compensation. Section IV(2) notes that compensation will be deemed to be appropriate where it is adequate, prompt and effective.[335] Article 13 of the European Energy Charter Treaty, 1994 provides that expropriation must be for a purpose which is in the public interest, not discriminatory, carried out under due process of law and accompanied by the payment of prompt, adequate and effective compensation.[336]

In the sensitive process of assessing the extent of compensation, several distinct categories should be noted. There is generally little dispute about according compensation for the physical assets and other assets of the enterprise such as debts or monies due. Although there are differing methods as to how to value such assets in particular cases,[337] the essential

---

[333] See e.g. the *Texaco* case, 17 ILM, 1978, pp. 1, 29–31; 53 ILR, p. 489. Note that the *Third US Restatement of Foreign Relations Law*, p. 196 (para. 712), refers to the requirement of 'just compensation' and not the Hull formula. This is defined as 'an amount equivalent to the value of the property taken and to be paid at the time of taking or within a reasonable time thereafter with interest from the date of taking and in a form economically usable by the foreign national', *ibid.*, p. 197. See also Schachter, 'Compensation', p. 121.

[334] See generally also R. Dolzer, 'New Foundation of the Law of Expropriation of Alien Property', 75 AJIL, 1981, p. 533, and M. Sornarajah, 'Compensation for Expropriation', 13 *Journal of World Trade Law*, 1979, p. 108, and Sornarajah, *International Law on Foreign Investment*.

[335] 31 ILM, 1992, p. 1382. Note also that article 1110 of the North American Free Trade Agreement, 1992 (NAFTA) provides that no party shall directly or indirectly nationalise or expropriate an investment of an investor of another party in its territory or take a measure tantamount to nationalisation or expropriation except where it is for a public purpose, on a non-discriminatory basis, in accordance with due process of law and upon payment of compensation. The payment of compensation is to be the fair market value of the expropriated investment immediately before the expropriation took place and should not reflect any change in value occurring because the intended expropriation had become known earlier. Valuation criteria shall include going concern value, asset value (including declared tax value of tangible property) and other criteria, as appropriate to determine fair market value. In addition, compensation shall be paid with interest, without delay and be fully realisable. See 32 ILM, 1993, p. 605.

[336] 34 ILM, 1995, p. 391.

[337] See e.g. the *Aminoil* case, 21 ILM, 1982, pp. 976, 1038; 66 ILR, pp. 519, 608–9.

principle is that of fair market value.[338] Interest on the value of such assets will also normally be paid.[339] There is, however, disagreement with regard to the award of compensation for the loss of future profits. In *AMCO* v. *Indonesia*,[340] the Arbitral Tribunal held that:

> the full compensation of prejudice, by awarding to the injured party, the *damnum emergens* [loss suffered] and the *lucrum cessans* [expected profits] is a principle common to the main systems of municipal law, and therefore, a general principle of law which may be considered as a source of international law,

although the compensation that could be awarded would cover only direct and foreseeable prejudice and not more remote damage.[341]

In *Metalclad Corporation* v. *United Mexican States*, the Tribunal noted that normally the fair market value of a going concern which has a history of profitable operation may be based on an estimate of future profits subject to a discounted cash flow analysis,[342] but where the enterprise has not operated for a sufficiently long time to establish a performance record or where it has failed to make a profit, future profits cannot be used so that to determine the fair market value, reference instead to the actual investment made may be appropriate.[343]

However, it has been argued that one may need to take into account whether the expropriation itself was lawful or unlawful. In *INA Corporation* v. *The Islamic Republic of Iran*,[344] the Tribunal suggested that in the case of a large-scale, lawful nationalisation, 'international law has undergone

---

[338] Fair market value means essentially the amount that a willing buyer would pay a willing seller for the shares of a going concern, ignoring the expropriation situation completely: see e.g. *INA Corporation* v. *The Islamic Republic of Iran* 8 Iran–US CTR, pp. 373, 380; 75 ILR, p. 603.

[339] See the Memorandum of the Foreign and Commonwealth Office on the Practice of International Tribunals in Awarding Interest, UKMIL, 63 BYIL, 1992, p. 768.

[340] 24 ILM, 1985, pp. 1022, 1036–7; 89 ILR, pp. 405, 504. See also the *Chorzów Factory* case, PCIJ, Series A, No. 17, 1928; 4 AD, p. 268; the *Sapphire* case, 35 ILR, p. 136; the *Norwegian Shipowners' Claims* case, 1 RIAA, p. 307 (1922); the *Lighthouses Arbitration* 23 ILR, p. 299, and *Benvenuti and Bonfant* v. *The Government of the Popular Republic of the Congo* 67 ILR pp. 345, 375–9.

[341] 24 ILM, 1985, pp. 1022, 1037; 89 ILR, p. 505. See also *Sola Tiles Inc.* v. *Islamic Republic of Iran* 83 ILR, p. 460.

[342] 119 ILR, pp. 615, 641. See also *Benvenuti and Bonfant* v. *The Government of the Popular Republic of the Congo* 67 ILR, p. 345 and *AGIP SPA* v. *The Government of the Popular Republic of the Congo* 67 ILR, p. 318.

[343] 119 ILR, pp. 641–2. See also *Phelps Dodge Corporation* v. *Iran* 10 Iran–US CTR, 1986, pp. 121, 132–3 and *Biloune* v. *Ghana Investment Centre* 95 ILR, pp. 183, 228–9.

[344] 8 Iran–US CTR, p. 373; 75 ILR, p. 595.

a gradual reappraisal, the effect of which may be to undermine the doctrinal value of any "full" or "adequate" (when used as identical to "full") compensation standard'. However, in a situation involving an investment of a small amount shortly before the nationalisation, international law did allow for compensation in an amount equal to the fair market value of the investment.[345] However, Judge Lagergren noted that the 'fair market value' standard would normally be discounted in cases of lawful large-scale nationalisations in taking account of 'all circumstances'.[346]

In *Amoco International Finance Corporation* v. *The Islamic Republic of Iran*,[347] Chamber Three of the Iran–US Claims Tribunal held that the property in question had been lawfully expropriated and that 'a clear distinction must be made between lawful and unlawful expropriations, since the rules applicable to the compensation to be paid by the expropriating state differ according to the legal characterisation of the taking'.[348] In the case of an unlawful taking, full restitution in kind or its monetary equivalent was required in order to re-establish the situation which would in all probability have existed if the expropriation had not occurred,[349] while in the case of lawful taking, the standard was the payment of the full value of the undertaking at the moment of dispossession. The difference was interpreted by the Tribunal to mean that compensation for lost profits was only available in cases of wrongful expropriation. As far as the actual method of valuation was concerned, the Tribunal rejected the 'discounted cash flow' method, which would involve the estimation of the likely future earnings of the company at the valuation date and discounting such earnings to take account of reasonably foreseeable risks, since it was likely to amount to restitution as well as being too speculative.[350]

Bilateral investment treaties

In practice, many of the situations involving commercial relations between states and private parties fall within the framework of bilateral

---

[345] 8 Iran–US CTR, p. 378; 75 ILR, p. 602. [346] 8 Iran–US CTR, p. 390; 75 ILR, p. 614.

[347] 15 Iran–US CTR, pp. 189, 246–52; 83 ILR, p. 500.

[348] 15 Iran–US CTR, p. 246; 83 ILR, p. 565.

[349] See also Judge Lagergren's Separate Opinion in *INA Corporation* v. *The Islamic Republic of Iran* 8 Iran–US CTR, p. 385; 75 ILR, p. 609.

[350] But see e.g. *AIG* v. *The Islamic Republic of Iran* 4 Iran–US CTR, pp. 96, 109–10, where in a case of lawful expropriation lost profits were awarded. See also Brownlie, *Principles*, pp. 508 ff.; Section IV of the World Bank Guidelines, and article 13 of the European Energy Charter Treaty, 1994.

agreements.[351] These arrangements are intended to encourage investment in a way that protects the basic interests of both the capital-exporting and capital-importing states. Indeed, there has been a remarkable expansion in the number of such bilateral investment treaties.[352] The British government, for example, has stated that it is policy to conclude as many such agreements as possible in order to stimulate investment flows. It has also been noted that they are designed to set standards applicable in international law.[353] The provisions of such agreements indeed are remarkably uniform and constitute valuable state practice.[354] While normally great care has to be taken in inferring the existence of a rule of customary international law from a range of bilateral treaties, the very number and uniformity of such agreements make them significant exemplars.

Some of these common features of such treaties may be noted. First, the concept of an investment is invariably broadly defined. In article 1(a) of the important UK–USSR bilateral investment treaty, 1989,[355] for example, it is provided that:

[351] See e.g. Lowenfeld, *International Economic Law*, pp. 554 ff.; E. Denza and D. Brooks, 'Investment Protection Treaties: United Kingdom Experience', 36 ICLQ, 1987, p. 908; A. Akinsanya, 'International Protection of Direct Foreign Investments in the Third World', 36 ICLQ, 1987, p. 58; F. A. Mann, 'British Treaties for the Promotion and Protection of Investments', 52 BYIL, 1981, p. 241; D. Vagts, 'Foreign Investment Risk Reconsidered: The View From the 1980s', 2 *ICSID Review – Foreign Investment Law Journal*, 1987, p. 1; P. B. Gann, 'The US Bilateral Investment Treaties Program', 21 *Stanford Journal of International Law*, 1986, p. 373, and I. Pogany, 'The Regulation of Foreign Investment in Hungary', 4 *ICSID Review – Foreign Investment Law Journal*, 1989, p. 39. See also J. Kokott, 'Interim Report on the Role of Diplomatic Protection in the Field of the Protection of Foreign Investment', International Law Association, Report of the Seventieth Conference, New Delhi, 2002, p. 259, and C. McLachlan, 'Investment Treaties and General International Law', 57 ICLQ, 2008, p. 361.

[352] Kokott estimates that close to 2,000 are in existence, 'Interim Report', p. 263. See, for earlier figures, 35 ILM, 1996, p. 1130; Denza and Brooks, 'Investment Protection Treaties', p. 913, and UKMIL, 58 BYIL, 1987, p. 621. Lowenfeld estimates that as of 2006, some 2,400 to 2,600 bilateral investment treaties were in effect, *International Economic Law*, p. 554.

[353] See the text of the Foreign Office statement in UKMIL, 58 BYIL, 1987, p. 620. Such agreements are in UK practice usually termed investment promotion and protection agreements (IPPAs). In March 2000, it was stated that the UK had entered into ninety-three such treaties, UKMIL, 71 BYIL, 2000, p. 606.

[354] See Kokott, 'Interim Report', p. 263. See also R. Dolzer, 'New Foundations of the Law of Expropriation of Alien Property', 75 AJIL, 1981, pp. 553, 565–6, and B. Kishoiyian, 'The Utility of Bilateral Investment Treaties in the Formulation of Customary International Law', 14 *Netherlands Journal of International Law and Business*, 1994, p. 327.

[355] Text reproduced in 29 ILM, 1989, p. 366.

the term 'investment' means every kind of asset and in particular, though not exclusively, includes:

(i) movable and immovable property and any other related property rights such as mortgages;

(ii) shares in, and stocks, bonds and debentures of, and any other form of participation in, a company or business enterprise;

(iii) claims to money, and claims to performance under contract having a financial value;

(iv) intellectual property rights, technical processes, know-how and any other benefit or advantage attached to a business;

(v) rights conferred by law or under contract to undertake any commercial activity, including the search for, or the cultivation, extraction or exploitation of natural resources.[356]

Secondly, both parties undertake to encourage and create favourable conditions for investment, to accord such investments 'fair and equitable treatment' and to refrain from impairing by unreasonable or discriminatory measures the management, maintenance, use, enjoyment or disposal of investments in its territory.[357] Thirdly, investments by the contracting parties are not to be treated less favourably than those of other states.[358] As far as expropriation is concerned, article 5 of the UK–USSR agreement, by way of example, provides that investments of the contracting parties are not to be expropriated:

> except for a purpose which is in the public interest and is not discriminatory and against the payment, without delay, of prompt and effective compensation. Such compensation shall amount to the real value of the investment expropriated immediately before the expropriation or before the impending expropriation became public knowledge, whichever is the earlier, shall be made within two months of the date of expropriation, after which interest at a normal commercial rate shall accrue until the date of payment and shall be effectively realisable and be freely transferable. The investor affected shall have a right under the law of the contracting state making the expropriation, to prompt review, by a judicial or other independent authority of that party, of his or its case and of the valuation of his or its investment in accordance with the principles set out in this paragraph.

---

[356] See also, for example, the similar provisions in the UK–Philippines Investment Agreement, 1981 and the UK–Hungary Investment Agreement, 1987. See also article 1(6) of the European Energy Charter Treaty, 1994.

[357] See e.g. article 2 of the UK–USSR agreement.

[358] See e.g. article 3 of the UK–USSR agreement.

Such practice confirms the traditional principles dealing with the conditions of a lawful expropriation and compensation, noting also the acceptance of the jurisdiction of the expropriating state over the issues of the legality of the expropriation and the valuation of the property expropriated.[359] An attempt to produce a Multilateral Agreement on Investment commenced in 1995 within the framework of the Organisation of Economic Co-operation and Development, but foundered in 1998.[360]

Lump-sum agreements

Many disputes over expropriation of foreign property have in fact been resolved directly by the states concerned on the basis of lump-sum settlements, usually after protracted negotiations and invariably at valuation below the current value of the assets concerned.[361] For example, the UK–USSR Agreement on the Settlement of Mutual Financial and Property Claims, 1986[362] dealt with UK government claims of the order of £500 million in respect of Russian war debt and private claims of British nationals amounting to some £400 million.[363] In the event, a sum in the region of £45 million was made available to satisfy these claims.[364] The

---

[359] Note that provisions for compensation for expropriation may also be contained in Treaties of Friendship, Commerce and Navigation as part of a framework arrangement dealing with foreign trade and investment: see e.g. article IV(3) of the Convention of Establishment, 1959 between the US and France, 11 UST 2398.

[360] See e.g. S. J. Canner, 'The Multilateral Agreement on Investment', 31 *Cornell International Law Journal*, 1998, p. 657; A. Böhmer, 'The Struggle for a Multilateral Agreement on Investment – An Assessment of the Negotiation Process in the OECD', 41 German YIL, 1998, p. 267, and T. Waelde, 'Multilateral Investment Agreements (MITs) in the Year 2000' in *Mélanges Philippe Kahn*, Paris, 2000, p. 389. See also www.oecd.org/EN/document/0,,EN-document-92-3-no-6-27308-92,00.html. Discussions on investment continue within the framework of the World Trade Organisation: see www.wto.org/english/tratop_e/invest_e/invest_e.htm.

[361] See e.g. Lillich and Weston, *International Claims: Their Settlement by Lump-Sum Agreements*, and Lillich and Weston, 'Lump-Sum Agreements: Their Continuing Contribution to the Law of International Claims', 82 AJIL, 1988, p. 69. See also D. J. Bederman, 'Interim Report on Lump Sum Agreements and Diplomatic Protection', International Law Association, Report of the Seventieth Conference, New Delhi, 2002, p. 230.

[362] Cm 30. Note that this agreement dealt with claims arising before 1939.

[363] As against these claims, the USSR had made extensive claims in the region of £2 billion in respect of alleged losses caused by British intervention in the USSR between 1918 and 1921: see UKMIL, 57 BYIL, 1986, p. 606.

[364] The British government waived its entitlement to a share in the settlement in respect of its own claims, *ibid.*, p. 608.

Agreement also provided that money held in diplomatic bank accounts in the UK belonging to the pre-revolutionary Russian Embassy, amounting to some £2.65 million, was released to the Soviet authorities. As is usual in such agreements, each government was solely responsible for settling the claims of its nationals.[365] This was accomplished in the UK through the medium of the Foreign Compensation Commission, which acts to distribute settlement sums 'as may seem just and equitable to them having regard to all the circumstances'. A distinction was made as between bond and property claims and principles enunciated with regard to exchange rates at the relevant time.[366]

The question arises thus as to whether such agreements constitute state practice in the context of international customary rules concerning the level of compensation required upon an expropriation of foreign property. A Chamber of the Iran–US Claims Tribunal in *SEDCO* v. *National Iranian Oil Co.*[367] noted that deriving general principles of law from the conduct of states in lump-sum or negotiated settlements in other expropriation cases was difficult because of the 'questionable evidentiary value... of much of the practice available'. This was because such settlements were often motivated primarily by non-juridical considerations. The Chamber also held incidentally that bilateral investment treaties were also unreliable evidence of international customary standards of compensation. Views differ as to the value to be attributed to such practice,[368] but caution is required before accepting bilateral investment treaties and lump-sum agreements as evidence of customary law. This is particularly so with regard to the latter since they deal with specific situations rather than laying down a framework for future activity.[369] Nevertheless, it would be equally unwise to disregard them entirely. As with all examples of state practice and behaviour, careful attention must be paid to all the relevant circumstances both of the practice maintained and the principle under consideration.

---

[365] See also the UK–China Agreement on the Settlement of Property Claims 1987, UKMIL, 58 BYIL, 1987, p. 626.

[366] See, with respect to the UK–USSR agreement, the Foreign Compensation (USSR) (Registration and Determination of Claims) Order 1986, SI 1986/2222 and the Foreign Compensation (USSR) (Distribution) Order 1987.

[367] 10 Iran–US CTR, pp. 180, 185; 80 AJIL, 1986, p. 969.

[368] See e.g. Bowett, 'State Contracts with Aliens', pp. 65–6.

[369] Note the view of the International Court in the *Barcelona Traction* case that such settlements were *sui generis* and provided no guide as to general international practice, ICJ Reports, 1969, pp. 4, 40.

Non-discrimination

It has been argued that non-discrimination is a requirement for a valid and lawful expropriation.[370] Although it is not mentioned in the 1962 resolution, the arbitrator in the *Liamco*[371] case strongly argued that a discriminatory nationalisation would be unlawful.[372] Nevertheless, in that case, it was held that Libya's action against certain oil companies was aimed at preserving its ownership of the oil and was non-discriminatory. Indeed, the arbitrator noted that the political motive itself was not the predominant motive for nationalisation and would not *per se* constitute sufficient proof of a purely discriminatory measure.[373] While the discrimination factor would certainly be a relevant factor to be considered, it would in practice often be extremely difficult to prove in concrete cases.

The Multilateral Investment Guarantee Agency [374]

One approach to the question of foreign investment and the balancing of the interests of the states concerned is provided by the Convention Establishing the Multilateral Investment Guarantee Agency, 1985, which came into force in 1988.[375] This Agency is part of the World Bank group and offers political risk insurance (guarantees) to investors and lenders. Membership is open to all members of the World Bank. Article 2 provides that the purpose of the Agency, which is an affiliate of the World Bank, is to encourage the flow of investment for productive purposes among member countries and, in particular, to developing countries. This is to be achieved in essence by the provision of insurance cover 'against non-commercial risks', such as restrictions on the transfer of currency, measures of expropriation, breaches of government contracts and losses resulting from war or civil disturbances.[376]

---

[370] See e.g. White, *Nationalisation*, pp. 119 ff. See also A. Maniruzzaman, 'Expropriation of Alien Property and the Principle of Non-Discrimination in the International Law of Foreign Investment', 8 *Journal of Transnational Law and Policy*, 1999, p. 141.

[371] 20 ILM, 1981, p. 1; 62 ILR, p. 141.   [372] 20 ILM, 1981, pp. 58–9; 62 ILR, p. 194.

[373] 20 ILM, 1981, p. 60. See also Section IV of the World Bank Guidelines on the Treatment of Foreign Direct Investment, and article 13 of the European Energy Charter Treaty, 1994.

[374] See e.g. S. K. Chatterjee, 'The Convention Establishing the Multilateral Investment Guarantee Agency', 36 ICLQ, 1987, p. 76, and I. Shihata, *The Multilateral Investment Guarantee Agency and Foreign Investment*, Dordrecht, 1987. The Convention came into force on 12 April 1988: see 28 ILM, 1989, p. 1233 and see also www.miga.org/.

[375] See e.g. the UK Multilateral Investment Guarantee Agency Act 1988.

[376] Article 11.

It is also intended that the Agency would positively encourage investment by means of research and the dissemination of information on investment opportunities. It may very well be that this initiative could in the long term reduce the sensitive nature of the expropriation mechanism.

Suggestions for further reading

I. Brownlie, *System of the Law of Nations: State Responsibility, Part I*, Oxford, 1983

J. Crawford, *The International Law Commission's Articles on State Responsibility*, Cambridge, 2002

W. K. Geck, 'Diplomatic Protection' in *Encyclopedia of Public International Law* (ed. R. Bernhardt), Amsterdam, 1992, vol. X, p. 1053

C. Gray, *Judicial Remedies in International Law*, Oxford, 1987

International Responsibility Today: Essays in Memory of Oscar Schachter (ed. M. Ragazzi), The Hague, 2005

'Symposium: The ILC's State Responsibility Articles', 96 AJIL, 2002, p. 773

15

International environmental law

Recent years have seen an appreciable growth in the level of understanding of the dangers facing the international environment[1] and an extensive range of environmental problems is now the subject of serious international concern.[2] These include atmospheric pollution, marine pollution,

[1] See generally P. Birnie and A. Boyle, *International Law and the Environment*, 2nd edn, Oxford, 2002; C. Redgwell, *Intergenerational Trusts and Environmental Protection*, Manchester, 1999; P. Sands, *Principles of International Environmental Law*, Manchester, 2nd edn, 2003; E. Benvenisti, *Sharing Transboundary Resources*, Cambridge, 2002; M. Bothe and P. Sand, *La Politique de l'Environnement: De la Réglementation aux Instruments Économique*, The Hague, 2003; *The Oxford Handbook of International Environmental Law* (eds. D. Bodansky, J. Brunee and E. Hay), Oxford, 2007; R. Romi, *Droit International et Européen de l'Environnement*, Paris, 2005; R. Wolfrum and N. Matz, *Conflicts in International Environmental Law*, Berlin, 2003; A. Kiss and J.-P. Beurier, *Droit International de l'Environnement*, 3rd edn, Paris, 2004; A. Kiss and D. Shelton, *A Guide to International Environmental Law*, The Hague, 2007, and Kiss, 'International Protection of the Environment' in *The Structure and Process of International Law* (eds. R. St J. Macdonald and D. Johnston), The Hague, 1983, p. 1069; J. Barros and D. M. Johnston, *The International Law of Pollution*, New York, 1974; *International Environmental Law* (eds. L. Teclaff and A. Utton), New York, 1974; *Trends in Environmental Policy and Law* (ed. M. Bothe), Gland, 1980; Hague Academy of International Law Colloque 1973, *The Protection of the Environment and International Law* (ed. A. Kiss); *ibid.*, Colloque 1984, *The Future of the International Law of the Environment* (ed. R. J. Dupuy); J. Schneider, *World Public Order of the Environment*, Toronto, 1979; *International Environmental Law* (eds. C. D. Gurumatry, G. W. R. Palmer and B. Weston), St Paul, 1994; E. Brown Weiss, *In Fairness to Future Generations: International Law, Common Patrimony and Intergenerational Equity*, Dobbs Ferry, 1989; A. Boyle, 'Nuclear Energy and International Law: An Environmental Perspective', 60 BYIL, 1989, p. 257, and Nguyen Quoc Dinh, P. Daillier and A. Pellet, *Droit International Public*, 7th edn, Paris, 2002, p. 1269. See also *Selected Multilateral Treaties in the Field of the Environment*, Cambridge, 2 vols., 1991; A. O. Adede, *International Environmental Law Digest*, Amsterdam, 1993, and P. Sands and P. Galizzi, *Documents in International Environmental Law*, Manchester, 2nd edn, 2003.

[2] This may be measured by the fact that in July 1993, the International Court of Justice established a special Chamber to deal with environmental questions. It has as yet heard no cases. See R. Ranjeva, 'L'Environnement, La Cour Internationale de Justice et sa Chambre Spéciale pour les Questions d'Environnement', AFDI, 1994, p. 433. Note also the Environmental Annex (Annex IV) to the Israel–Jordan Peace Treaty, 1995 and article 18 of the Treaty, 34 ILM, 1995, p. 43. See also Annex II on Water Related Matters.

global warming and ozone depletion, the dangers of nuclear and other extra-hazardous substances and threatened wildlife species.[3] Such problems have an international dimension in two obvious respects. First, pollution generated from within a particular state often has a serious impact upon other countries. The prime example would be acid rain, whereby chemicals emitted from factories rise in the atmosphere and react with water and sunlight to form acids. These are carried in the wind and fall eventually to earth in the rain, often thousands of miles away from the initial polluting event. Secondly, it is now apparent that environmental problems cannot be resolved by states acting individually. Accordingly, co-operation between the polluting and the polluted state is necessitated. However, the issue becomes more complicated in those cases where it is quite impossible to determine from which country a particular form of environmental pollution has emanated. This would be the case, for example, with ozone depletion. In other words, the international nature of pollution, both with regard to its creation and the damage caused, is now accepted as requiring an international response.

The initial conceptual problem posed for international law lies in the state-oriented nature of the discipline. Traditionally, a state would only be responsible in the international legal sense for damage caused where it could be clearly demonstrated that this resulted from its own unlawful activity.[4] This has proved to be an inadequate framework for dealing with environmental issues for a variety of reasons, ranging from difficulties of proof to liability for lawful activities and the particular question of responsibility of non-state offenders. Accordingly, the international community has slowly been moving away from the classic state responsibility approach to damage caused towards a regime of international co-operation.

A broad range of international participants are concerned with developments in this field. States, of course, as the dominant subjects of the international legal system are deeply involved, as are an increasing number of international organisations, whether at the global, regional or bilateral level. The United Nations General Assembly has adopted a

---

[3] See, as to endangered species, e.g. M. Carwardine, *The WWF Environment Handbook*, London, 1990, and S. Lyster, *International Wildlife Law*, Cambridge, 1985. See also the Convention on International Trade in Endangered Species, 1973 covering animals and plants, and the Convention on Biological Diversity, 1992, which *inter alia* calls upon parties to promote priority access on a fair and equitable basis by all parties, especially developing countries, to the results and benefits arising from biotechnologies based upon genetic resources provided by contracting parties.
[4] See further above, chapter 14.

number of resolutions concerning the environment,[5] and the UN Environment Programme was established after the Stockholm Conference of 1972. This has proved a particularly important organisation in the evolution of conventions and instruments in the field of environmental protection. It is based in Nairobi and consists of a Governing Council of fifty-eight members elected by the General Assembly. UNEP has been responsible for the development of a number of initiatives, including the 1985 Vienna Convention for the Protection of the Ozone Layer and the 1987 Montreal Protocol and the 1992 Convention on Biodiversity.[6] An Inter-Agency Committee on Sustainable Development was set up in 1992 to improve co-operation between the various UN bodies concerned with this topic. In the same year, the UN Commission on Sustainable Development was established by the General Assembly and the Economic and Social Council of the UN (ECOSOC). It consists of fifty-three states elected by ECOSOC for three-year terms and it exists in order to follow up the UN Conference on Environment and Development 1992.[7] The techniques of supervision utilised in international bodies include reporting,[8] inspection[9] and standard-setting through the adoption of conventions, regulations, guidelines and so forth. In 1994 it was agreed to transform the Global Environment Facility from a three-year pilot programme[10] into a permanent financial mechanism to award grants and concessional funds to developing countries for global environmental protection projects.[11] The Facility focuses upon climate change, the destruction of biological diversity, the pollution of international waters and ozone depletion. Issues of land-degradation[12] also fall within this framework.[13] In addition, a wide range of non-governmental organisations are also concerned with environmental issues.

---

[5] See e.g. resolutions 2398 (XXII); 2997 (XXVII); 34/188; 35/8; 37/137; 37/250; 42/187; 44/244; 44/228; 45/212 and 47/188.

[6] See generally www.unep.org/.

[7] See generally www.un.org/esa/sustdev/csd.htm.

[8] As e.g. under the Prevention of Marine Pollution from Land-Based Sources Convention, 1974 and the Basle Convention on the Control of Transboundary Movements of Hazardous Wastes, 1989.

[9] See e.g. the Antarctic Treaty, 1959 and the Protocol on Environmental Protection, 1991. See, with regard to the International Whaling Commission, P. Birnie, *International Regulation of Whaling*, New York, 1985, p. 199.

[10] See 30 ILM, 1991, p. 1735.   [11] See 33 ILM, 1994, p. 1273.

[12] See also the UN Convention to Combat Desertification, 1994, *ibid.*, p. 1328.

[13] See generally www.gefweb.org/.

It has been argued that there now exists an international human right to a clean environment.[14] There are, of course, a range of general human rights provisions that may have a relevance in the field of environmental protection, such as the right to life, right to an adequate standard of living, right to health, right to food and so forth, but specific references to a human right to a clean environment have tended to be few and ambiguous. The preamble to the seminal Stockholm Declaration of the UN Conference on the Human Environment 1972 noted that the environment was 'essential to ... the enjoyment of basic human rights – even the right to life itself', while Principle 1 stated that 'Man has the fundamental right to freedom, equality and adequate conditions of life, in an environment of a quality that permits a life of dignity and well-being.' Article 24 of the African Charter of Human and Peoples' Rights, 1981 provided that 'all people shall have the right to a general satisfactory environment favourable to their development', while article 11 of the Additional Protocol to the American Convention on Human Rights, 1988 declared that 'everyone shall have the right to live in a healthy environment' and that 'the states parties shall promote the protection, preservation and improvement of the environment'. Article 29 of the Convention on the Rights of the Child, 1989 explicitly referred to the need for the education of the child to be directed *inter alia* to 'the development of respect for the natural environment'.

The final text of the Conference on Security and Co-operation in Europe (CSCE) meeting on the environment in Sofia in 1989 reaffirmed respect for the right of individuals, groups and organisations concerned with the environment to express freely their views, to associate with others and assemble peacefully, to obtain and distribute relevant information and to participate in public debates on environmental issues.[15] It should also be noted that the Convention on Environmental Impact Assessment in a Transboundary Context, 1991 calls for the 'establishment

---

[14] See, for example, M. Pallemaerts, 'International Environmental Law from Stockholm to Rio: Back to the Future?' in *Greening International Law* (ed. P. Sands), London, 1993, pp. 1, 8; *Environnement et Droits de l'Homme* (ed. P. Kromarek), Paris, 1987; G. Alfredsson and A. Ovsiouk, 'Human Rights and the Environment', 60 *Nordic Journal of International Law*, 1991, p. 19; W. P. Gormley, *Human Rights and Environment*, Leiden, 1976; *Human Rights and Environmental Protection* (ed. A. Cançado Trindade), 1992; D. Shelton, 'Whatever Happened in Rio to Human Rights?', 3 *Yearbook of International Environmental Law*, 1992, p. 75; Birnie and Boyle, *International Law and the Environment*, pp. 252 ff., and *Human Rights Approaches to Environmental Protection* (eds. M. Anderson and A. E. Boyle), Oxford, 1996. See also M. Déjeant-Pons and M. Pallemaerts, *Human Rights and the Environment*, Council of Europe, 2002.

[15] CSCE/SEM.36. See also EC Directive 90/313, 1990.

of an environmental impact assessment procedure that permits public participation' in certain circumstances.

However, the references to human rights in the Rio Declaration on Environment and Development adopted at the UN Conference on Environment and Development in 1992[16] are rather sparse. Principle 1 declares that human beings are 'at the centre of concerns for sustainable development. They are entitled to a healthy and productive life in harmony with nature.' Beyond this tangential reference, human rights concerns were not, it is fair to say, at the centre of the documentation produced by the 1992 conference. In fact, it is fair to say that the focus of the conference was rather upon states and their sovereign rights than upon individuals and their rights.

Nevertheless, moves to associate the two areas of international law are progressing cautiously. In 1994, the final report on Human Rights and the Environment was delivered to the UN Sub-Commission on Prevention of Discrimination and Protection of Minorities (as it was then called).[17] The Report contains a set of Draft Principles on Human Rights and the Environment, which includes the notion that 'human rights, an ecologically sound environment, sustainable development and peace are interdependent and indivisible' and that 'all persons have the right to a secure, healthy and ecologically sound environment. This right and other human rights, including civil, cultural, economic, political and social rights, are universal, interdependent and indivisible.' It remains to be seen whether this initiative will bear fruit.[18] The Institut de Droit International, a private but influential association, adopted a resolution on the environment at its Strasbourg Session in September 1997. Article 2 of this noted that 'Every human being has the right to live in a healthy environment'.[19]

An important stage has been reached with the adoption of the Aarhus Convention on Access to Information, Public Participation in Decision-Making and Access to Justice in Environmental Matters, 1998,[20] which

[16] See generally, as to the Rio Conference, S. Johnson, *The Earth Summit*, Dordrecht, 1993.
[17] E/CN.4/Sub.2/1994/9.
[18] Note also the European Charter on Environment and Health, 1989 and the Dublin Declaration on the Environmental Imperative adopted by the European Council, 1990.
[19] See also L. Loucaides, 'Environmental Protection through the Jurisprudence of the European Convention on Human Rights', 75 BYIL, 2004, p. 249.
[20] Adopted through the United Nations Economic Commission for Europe. The Convention came into force on 30 October 2001, see generally www.unece.org/env/pp/, and the first meeting of states parties took place in October 2002. Note that governments accepted in January 2003 a Protocol which obliges companies to register annually their releases into

explicitly links human rights and the environment and recognises that 'adequate protection of the environment is essential to human well-being and the enjoyment of basic human rights, including the right to life itself'. Article 1 provides that each contracting party 'shall guarantee the rights of access to information, public participation in decision-making and access to justice in environmental matters' and thereby marks the acceptance by parties of obligations towards their own citizens. Article 9 stipulates that parties should establish a review procedure before a court of law or other independent and impartial body for any persons who consider that their request for information has not been properly addressed, and article 15 provides that 'optional arrangements of a non-confrontational, non-judicial and consultative status' should be established for reviewing compliance with the Convention. Such arrangements are to allow for appropriate public involvement 'and may include the option of considering communications from members of the public on matters relating to this Convention'. Decision 1/7 adopted on 30 October 2002 set up an eight-member Compliance Committee to consider submissions made with regard to allegations of non-compliance with the Convention by one party against another or by members of the public against any contracting party unless that party has opted out of the procedure within one year of becoming a party. The Committee may also prepare a report on compliance with or implementation of the provisions of the Convention and monitor, assess and facilitate the implementation of and compliance with the reporting requirements made under article 10, paragraph 2, of the Convention and specified in Decision 1/8.[21]

The question of the relationship between the protection of the environment and the need for economic development is another factor underpinning the evolution of environmental law. States that are currently attempting to industrialise face the problem that to do so in an environmentally safe way is very expensive and the resources that can be devoted to this are extremely limited. The Stockholm Declaration of the United Nations Conference on the Human Environment 1972 emphasised in Principle 8 that 'economic and social development is essential for ensuring a favourable living and working environment for man and for creating

---

the environment and transfer to other companies of certain pollutants. This information will then appear in the Pollutant Release and Transfer Register.

[21] See generally R. R. Churchill and G. Uffstein, 'Autonomous Institutional Arrangements in Multilateral Environmental Agreements: A Little-Noticed Phenomenon in International Law', 94 AJIL, 2000, p. 623.

conditions on earth that are necessary for the improvement of the quality of life', while the sovereign right of states to exploit their own resources was also stressed.[22] Principle 2 of the Rio Declaration, adopted at the United Nations Conference on Environment and Development 1992, noted that states have 'the sovereign right to exploit their own resources pursuant to their own environmental and developmental policies', while Principle 3 stated that 'the right to development must be fulfilled so as to equitably meet developmental and environmental needs of present and future generations'. The correct balance between development and environmental protection is now one of the main challenges facing the international community and reflects the competing interests posed by the principle of state sovereignty on the one hand and the need for international co-operation on the other. It also raises the issue as to how far one takes into account the legacy for future generations of activities conducted at the present time or currently planned. Many developmental activities, such as the creation of nuclear power plants for example, may have significant repercussions for many generations to come.[23] The Energy Charter Treaty[24] signed at Lisbon in 1994 by OECD and Eastern European and CIS states refers to environmental issues in the context of energy concerns in a rather less than robust fashion. Article 19 notes that contracting parties 'shall strive to minimise in an economically efficient manner harmful environmental impacts'. In so doing, parties are to act 'in a cost-effective manner'. Parties are to 'strive to take precautionary measures to prevent or minimise environmental degradation' and agree that the polluter should 'in principle, bear the cost of pollution, including transboundary pollution, with due regard to the public interest and without distorting investment in the energy cycle or international trade'.

---

[22] Principle 21. See also S. P. Subedi, 'Balancing International Trade with Environmental Protection', 25 Brooklyn Journal of International Law, 1999, p. 373; T. Schoenbaum, 'International Trade and Protection of the Environment', 91 AJIL, 1997, p. 268, and N. Bernasconi-Osterwalder, D. Magraw, M. J. Oliva, M. Orellana and E. Tuerk, Environment and Trade: A Guide to WTO Jurisprudence, London, 2006. Note the OECD Declaration on Integrating Climate Change Adaptation into Development Cooperation, 2006.

[23] See e.g. A. D'Amato, 'Do We Owe a Duty to Future Generations to Preserve the Global Environment?', 84 AJIL, 1990, p. 190; Sands, Principles, p. 199; E. Weiss, 'Our Rights and Obligations to Future Generations for the Environment', 84 AJIL, 1990, p. 198, and Weiss, Intergenerational Equity. See also Minors Oposa v. Secretary of the Department of Environment and Natural Resources, Supreme Court of the Philippines, 33 ILM, 1994, pp. 173, 185, and Judge Weeramantry's Dissenting Opinion in the Request for an Examination of the Situation in Accordance with Paragraph 63 of the Nuclear Tests Case, ICJ Reports, 1995, pp. 288, 341; 106 ILR, pp. 1, 63.

[24] 33 ILM, 1995, p. 360.

One potentially innovative method for linking economic underdevelopment and protection of the environment is the 'debt for nature swaps' arrangement, whereby debts owed abroad may be converted into an obligation upon the debtor state to spend the amount of the debt upon local environment projects.[25]

State responsibility and the environment[26]

The basic duty of states

The principles of state responsibility[27] dictate that states are accountable for breaches of international law. Such breaches of treaty or customary international law enable the injured state to maintain a claim against the violating state, whether by way of diplomatic action or by way of recourse to international mechanisms where such are in place with regard to the subject matter at issue. Recourse to international arbitration or to the International Court of Justice is also possible provided the necessary jurisdictional basis has been established. Customary international law imposes several important fundamental obligations upon states in the area of environmental protection. The view that international law supports an approach predicated upon absolute territorial sovereignty, so that a state could do as it liked irrespective of the consequences upon other states, has long been discredited. The basic duty upon states is not so to act as to injure the rights of other states.[28] This duty has evolved partly out of the regime concerned with international waterways. In the *International Commission on the River Oder* case,[29] for example, the Permanent Court of International Justice noted that 'this community of interest in a navigable river becomes the basis of a common legal right, the essential features of which are the perfect equality of all riparian states in the use of the whole course of the river and the exclusion of any preferential privileges

[25] See e.g. F. G. Minujin, 'Debt-for-Nature Swops: A Financial Mechanism to Reduce Debt and Preserve the Environment', 21 *Environmental Policy and Law*, 1991, p. 146, and S. George, *The Debt Boomerang*, London, 1992, pp. 30–1.

[26] See e.g. B. D. Smith, *State Responsibility and the Marine Environment*, Oxford, 1988. See also R. Lefeber, *Transboundary Environmental Interference and the Origin of State Liability*, Dordrecht, 1996.

[27] See further above, chapter 14.

[28] See the doctrine expressed by Judson Harmon, Attorney-General of the United States in 1895, 21 *Op. Att'y. Gen.* 274, 283 (1895), cited in V. P. Nanda, *International Environmental Law and Policy*, New York, 1995, pp. 155–6.

[29] PCIJ, Series A, No. 23 (1929); 5 AD, p. 83.

of any riparian state in relation to others'.[30] But the principle is of far wider application. It was held in the *Island of Palmas* case[31] that the concept of territorial sovereignty incorporated an obligation to protect within the territory the rights of other states.

In the *Trail Smelter* arbitration,[32] the Tribunal was concerned with a dispute between Canada and the United States over sulphur dioxide pollution from a Canadian smelter, built in a valley shared by British Columbia and the state of Washington, which damaged trees and crops on the American side of the border. The Tribunal noted that:

> under principles of international law, as well as the law of the United States, no state has the right to use or permit the use of territory in such a manner as to cause injury by fumes in or to the territory of another or the properties or persons therein, when the case is of serious consequence and the injury is established by clear and convincing evidence.[33]

The International Court reinforced this approach, by emphasising in the *Corfu Channel* case[34] that it was the obligation of every state 'not to allow knowingly its territory to be used for acts contrary to the rights of other states'.[35] The Court also noted in the *Request for an Examination of the Situation in Accordance with Paragraph 63 of the Nuclear Tests Case 1974* case in 1995, that its conclusion with regard to French nuclear testing in the Pacific was 'without prejudice to the obligations of states to respect and protect the environment'.[36] In addition, in its Advisory Opinion to the UN General Assembly on the *Legality of the Threat or Use of Nuclear Weapons*, the Court declared that 'the existence of the general obligation of states to ensure that activities within their jurisdiction and control respect

---

[30] PCIJ, Series A, No. 23 (1929), p. 27; 5 AD, p. 84. See also the case concerning the *Auditing of Accounts between the Netherlands and France*, arbitral award of 12 March 2004, para. 97.

[31] 2 RIAA, pp. 829, 839 (1928).

[32] See 33 AJIL, 1939, p. 182 and 35 AJIL, 1941, p. 684; 9 AD, p. 315. See also J. E. Read, 'The Trail Smelter Arbitration', 1 Canadian YIL, 1963, p. 213; R. Kirgis, 'Technological Challenge of the Shared Environment: US Practice', 66 AJIL, 1974, p. 291, and L. Goldie, 'A General View of International Environmental Law – A Survey of Capabilities, Trends and Limits' in *Hague Colloque 1973*, pp. 26, 66–9.

[33] 35 AJIL, 1941, p. 716; 9 AD, p. 317. Canada invoked the *Trail Smelter* principle against the United States when an oil spill at Cherry Point, Washington, resulted in contamination of beaches in British Columbia: see 11 Canadian YIL, 1973, p. 333.

[34] ICJ Reports, 1949, pp. 4, 22; 16 AD, pp. 155, 158.

[35] See also the Dissenting Opinion of Judge de Castro in the *Nuclear Tests* case, ICJ Reports, 1974, pp. 253, 388; 57 ILR, pp. 350, 533, and the *Lac Lanoux* case, 24 ILR, p. 101.

[36] ICJ Reports, 1995, pp. 288, 306; 106 ILR, pp. 1, 28.

the environment of other states or of areas beyond national control is now part of the corpus of international law relating to the environment.[37]

This judicial approach has now been widely reaffirmed in international instruments. Article 192 of the Law of the Sea Convention, 1982 provides that 'states have the obligation to protect and preserve the marine environment', while article 194 notes that 'states shall take all measures necessary to ensure that activities under their jurisdiction and control are so conducted as not to cause damage by pollution to other states and their environment'.[38] The shift of focus from the state alone to a wider perspective including the high seas, deep seabed and outer space is a noticeable development.[39]

It is, however, Principle 21 of the Stockholm Declaration of 1972 that is of especial significance. It stipulates that, in addition to the sovereign right to exploit their own resources pursuant to their own environmental policies, states have 'the responsibility to ensure that activities within their jurisdiction or control do not cause damage to the environment of other states or of areas beyond the limits of national jurisdiction'. Although a relatively modest formulation repeated in Principle 2 of the Rio Declaration 1992 (with the addition of a reference to developmental policies), it has been seen as an important turning-point in the development of international environmental law.[40] Several issues of importance are raised in the formulation contained in Principle 21 and to those we now turn.

The appropriate standard

It is sometimes argued that the appropriate standard for the conduct of states in this field is that of strict liability. In other words, states are under an absolute obligation to prevent pollution and are thus liable for its effects irrespective of fault.[41] While the advantage of this is the increased

---

[37] ICJ Reports, 1996, para. 29; 35 ILM, 1996, pp. 809, 821. See also the *Gabčíkovo–Nagymaros Project* case, ICJ Reports, 1997, pp. 6, 67; 116 ILR, p. 1.

[38] See also Principle 3 of the UN Environment Programme Principles of Conduct in the Field of the Environment concerning Resources Shared by Two or More States, 1978; the Charter of Economic Rights and Duties of States adopted in General Assembly resolution 1974 3281 (XXIX) and General Assembly resolution 34/186 (1979).

[39] See Boyle, 'Nuclear Energy', p. 271.

[40] See e.g. Sands, *Principles*, pp. 235–6, terming it the 'cornerstone of international environmental law'. See also the preamble to the Convention on Long-Range Transboundary Air Pollution, 1979 and the *Legality of the Threat or Use of Nuclear Weapons* advisory opinion, ICJ Reports, 1996, pp. 226, 241; 110 ILR, pp. 163, 191.

[41] See e.g. Goldie, 'General View', pp. 73–85, and Schneider, *World Public Order*, chapter 6. See also G. Handl, 'State Liability for Accidental Transnational Environmental Damage

responsibility placed upon the state, it is doubtful whether international law has in fact accepted such a general principle.[42] The leading cases are inconclusive. In the *Trail Smelter* case[43] Canada's responsibility was accepted from the start, the case focusing upon the compensation due and the terms of the future operation of the smelter,[44] while the strict theory was not apparently accepted in the *Corfu Channel* case.[45] In the *Nuclear Tests* case[46] the Court did not discuss the substance of the claims concerning nuclear testing in view of France's decision to end its programme.

It is also worth considering the *Gut Dam* arbitration between the US and Canada.[47] This concerned the construction of a dam by the Canadian authorities, with US approval, straddling the territory of the two states, in order to facilitate navigation in the St Lawrence River, prior to the existence of the Seaway. The dam affected the flow of water in the river basin and caused an increase in the level of water in the river and in Lake Ontario. This, together with the incidence of severe storms, resulted in heavy flooding on the shores of the river and lake and the US government claimed damages. The tribunal awarded a lump sum payment to the US, without considering whether Canada had been in any way negligent or at fault with regard to the construction of the dam. However, one must be cautious in regarding this case as an example of a strict liability approach, since the US gave its approval to the construction of the dam on the condition that US citizens be indemnified for any damage or detriment incurred as a result of the construction or operation of the dam in question.[48]

Treaty practice is variable. The Convention on International Liability for Damage Caused by Space Objects, 1972 provides for absolute liability for damage caused by space objects on the surface of the earth or to aircraft in flight (article II), but for fault liability for damage caused elsewhere or to persons or property on board a space object (article III).[49] Most treaties, however, take the form of requiring the exercise of diligent

by Private Persons', 74 AJIL, 1980, p. 525; Birnie and Boyle, *International Law and the Environment*, pp. 182 ff., and Sands, *Principles*, pp. 881 ff.

[42] See e.g. Boyle, 'Nuclear Energy', pp. 289–97, and Handl, 'State Liability', pp. 535–53.

[43] 33 AJIL, 1939, p. 182 and 35 AJIL, 1941, p. 681; 9 AD, p. 315.

[44] See Boyle, 'Nuclear Energy', p. 292, and G. Handl, 'Balancing of Interests and International Liability for the Pollution of International Watercourses: Customary Principles of Law Revisited', 13 Canadian YIL, 1975, pp. 156, 167–8.

[45] ICJ Reports, 1949, pp. 4, 22–3; 16 AD, pp. 155, 158.

[46] ICJ Reports, 1974, p. 253; 57 ILR, p. 350.   [47] 8 ILM, 1969, p. 118.

[48] See Schneider, *World Public Order*, p. 165. Cf. Handl, 'State Liability', pp. 525, 538 ff.

[49] See e.g. the Canadian claim in the Cosmos 954 incident, 18 ILM, 1992, p. 907.

control of sources of harm, so that responsibility is engaged for breaches of obligations specified in the particular instruments.[50]

The test of due diligence is in fact the standard that is accepted generally as the most appropriate one.[51] Article 194 of the Convention on the Law of the Sea, 1982, for example, provides that states are to take 'all measures ... that are necessary to prevent, reduce and control pollution of the marine environment from any source, using for this purpose the best practicable means at their disposal and in accordance with their capabilities'. Accordingly, states in general are not automatically liable for damage caused irrespective of all other factors. However, it is rather less clear what is actually meant by due diligence. In specific cases, such as the Convention on the Law of the Sea, 1982, for example, particular measures are specified and references made to other relevant treaties. In other cases, the issue remains rather more ambiguous.[52] The test of due diligence undoubtedly imports an element of flexibility into the equation and must be tested in the light of the circumstances of the case in question. States will be required, for example, to take all necessary steps to prevent substantial pollution and to demonstrate the kind of behaviour expected of 'good government',[53] while such behaviour would probably require the establishment of systems of consultation and notification.[54] It is also important to note that elements of remoteness and foreseeability are part of the framework of the liability of states. The damage that occurs must have been caused by the pollution under consideration. The tribunal in

---

[50] See e.g. article 1 of the London Convention on the Prevention of Marine Pollution by Dumping of Wastes, 1972; article 2 of the Convention on Long-Range Transboundary Air Pollution, 1979; article 2 of the Vienna Convention for the Protection of the Ozone Layer, 1985 and articles 139, 194 and 235 of the Convention on the Law of the Sea, 1982; articles 7 and 8 of the Convention for the Regulation of Antarctic Mineral Resources Activities, 1988 and article 2 of the Convention on the Protection and Use of Transboundary Watercourses and International Lakes, 1992. See also the Commentary by the International Law Commission to article 7 of the Draft Articles on the Law of the Non-Navigational Uses of International Watercourses, Report of the International Law Commission, 46th Session, 1994, pp. 236 ff.

[51] This is the view taken by the ILC in its Commentary on the Draft Articles on Prevention of Transboundary Harm from Hazardous Activities, 2001, Report of the ILC on its 53rd Session, A/56/10, p. 392. See also e.g. Handl, 'State Liability', pp. 539–40; Boyle, 'Nuclear Energy', p. 272, and Birnie and Boyle, International Law and the Environment, pp. 112 ff.

[52] See e.g. the Long-Range Transboundary Air Pollution Convention, 1979.

[53] I.e. the standard of conduct expected from a government mindful of its international obligations: see R. J. Dupuy, 'International Liability for Transfrontier Pollution', in Bothe, Trends in Environmental Policy and Law, pp. 363, 369.

[54] See Responsibility and Liability of States in Relation to Transfrontier Pollution, an OECD Report by the Environment Committee, 1984, p. 4.

the *Trail Smelter* case[55] emphasised the need to establish the injury 'by clear and convincing evidence'.

Damage caused

The first issue is whether indeed any damage must actually have been caused before international responsibility becomes relevant. Can there be liability for risk of damage? It appears that at this stage international law in general does not recognise such a liability,[56] certainly outside of the category of ultra-hazardous activities.[57] This is for reasons both of state reluctance in general and with regard to practical difficulties in particular. It would be difficult, although not impossible, both to assess the risk involved and to determine the compensation that might be due.

However, it should be noted that article 1(4) of the Convention on the Law of the Sea, 1982 defines pollution of the marine environment as 'the introduction by man, directly or indirectly, of substances or energy into the marine environment ... which results or is likely to result in ... deleterious effects'. In other words, actual damage is not necessary in this context. It is indeed possible that customary international law may develop in this direction, but it is too early to conclude that this has already occurred. Most general definitions of pollution rely upon damage or harm having been caused before liability is engaged.[58]

The next issue is to determine whether a certain threshold of damage must have been caused. In the *Trail Smelter* case,[59] the Tribunal focused on the need to show that the matter was of 'serious consequence', while article 1 of the Convention on Long-Range Transboundary Air Pollution, 1979 provides that the pollution concerned must result 'in deleterious effects of such a nature as to endanger human health, harm living resources and ecosystems and material property and impair or interfere with amenities and other legitimate uses of the environment'.[60] Article 3 of the ILA

---

[55] 35 AJIL, 1941, p. 716; 9 AD, p. 317.

[56] See e.g. Kiss, 'International Protection', p. 1076.   [57] See below, p. 887.

[58] See also the commentary to the Montreal Rules adopted by the ILA in 1982, Report of the Sixtieth Conference, p. 159. Note, however, that the International Law Commission's Draft Articles on Prevention of Transboundary Harm from Hazardous Activities, adopted in 2001, concern activities not prohibited by international law which involve a 'risk of causing significant transboundary harm', Report of the ILC on its 53rd Session, p. 380.

[59] 35 AJIL, 1941, p. 716; 9 AD, p. 317.

[60] Note also that General Assembly resolution 2995 (XXVII) refers to 'significant harmful results'. See also article 1 of the ILC's Draft Articles on Prevention of Transboundary Harm from Hazardous Activities, Report of the ILC on its 53rd Session, p. 380.

Montreal Rules 1982 stipulates that states are under an obligation to prevent, abate and control transfrontier pollution to such an extent that no substantial injury is caused in the territory of another state.[61] Such formulations do present definitional problems and the qualification as to the threshold of injury required is by no means present in all relevant instruments.[62] The issue of relativity and the importance of the circumstances of the particular case remain significant factors, but less support can be detected at this stage for linkage to a concept of reasonable and equitable use of its territory by a state occasioning liability for use beyond this.[63]

As far as the range of interests injured by pollution is concerned, the *Trail Smelter* case[64] focused upon loss of property. Later definitions of pollution in international instruments have broadened the range to include harm to living resources or ecosystems, interference with amenities and other legitimate uses of the environment or the sea. Article 1(4) of the Convention on the Law of the Sea, 1982, for example, includes impairment of quality for use of sea water and reduction of amenities. Article 1(2) of the Vienna Convention on the Ozone Layer, 1985 defines adverse effects upon the ozone layer as changes in the physical environment including climatic changes 'which have significant deleterious effects on human health or on the composition, resilience and productivity of natural and managed ecosystems or on materials useful to mankind',[65] while the Climate Change Convention, 1992 defines adverse effects of climate change as 'changes in the physical environment or biota resulting from climate change which have significant deleterious effects on the composition, resilience or productivity of natural and managed ecosystems or on the operation of socio-economic systems or on human health and welfare'.[66]

---

[61] Note the formulation by L. Oppenheim, *International Law*, 8th edn, London, 1955, vol. I, p. 291, that the interference complained of must be 'unduly injurious to the inhabitants of the neighbouring state'.

[62] See e.g. Principle 21 of the Stockholm Declaration and article 194 of the Convention on the Law of the Sea, 1982.

[63] See the views of e.g. R. Quentin-Baxter, *Yearbook of the ILC*, 1981, vol. II, part 1, pp. 112–19, and S. McCaffrey, *ibid.*, 1986, vol. II, part 1, pp. 133–4. See also Boyle, 'Nuclear Energy', p. 275, and 'Chernobyl and the Development of International Environmental Law' in *Perestroika and International Law* (ed. W. Butler), London, 1990, pp. 203, 206.

[64] 35 AJIL, 1941, p. 684; 9 AD, p. 315. See also A. Rubin, 'Pollution by Analogy: The Trail Smelter Arbitration', 50 *Oregon Law Review*, 1971, p. 259.

[65] See also the OECD Recommendation of Equal Right of Access in Relation to Transfrontier Pollution, 1977 and article 1(15) of the Convention on the Regulation of Antarctic Mineral Resource Activities, 1988.

[66] Article 1(1).

The Convention on Regulation of Antarctic Mineral Resources, 1988[67] defines damage to the environment and ecosystem of that polar region as 'any impact on the living or non-living components of that environment or those ecosystems, including harm to atmospheric, marine or terrestrial life, beyond that which is negligible or which has been assessed and judged to be acceptable pursuant to [the] Convention'.[68] The Convention on the Protection and Use of Transboundary Watercourses and International Lakes, 1992 defines 'transboundary impact', which is the subject of provision, in terms of 'any significant adverse effect on the environment resulting from a change in the conditions of transboundary waters caused by a human activity'.[69] The Council of Europe's Convention on Civil Liability for Environmental Damage, 1993 defines damage to include loss or damage by 'impairment of the environment',[70] while the environment itself is taken to include natural resources both abiotic and biotic, property forming part of the cultural heritage and 'the characteristic aspects of the landscape'.[71] The type of harm that is relevant clearly now extends beyond damage to property,[72] but problems do remain with regard to general environmental injury that cannot be defined in material form.[73]

Liability for damage caused by private persons

A particular problem relates to the situation where the environmental injury is caused not by the state itself but by a private party.[74] A state is,

---

[67] See generally on Antarctica, C. Redgwell, 'Environmental Protection in Antarctica: The 1991 Protocol', 43 ICLQ, 1994, p. 599, and above, chapter 10, p. 534. Note Annex VI to the Protocol on Environmental Protection to the Antarctic Treaty, Liability Arising from Environmental Emergencies, 2005. See also, with regard to the Arctic, D. R. Rothwell, 'International Law and the Protection of the Arctic Environment', 44 ICLQ, 1995, p. 280.

[68] Article 1(15). See also article 2 of the Convention on Environmental Impact Assessment in a Transboundary Context, 1991 and article 1 of the Code of Conduct on Accidental Pollution of Transboundary Inland Waters, 1990.

[69] Article 1(2).   [70] Article 2(7)c.

[71] Article 2(10). See also article 1 of the ILC's Draft Principles on the Allocation of Loss in the Case of Transboundary Harm Arising out of Hazardous Activities, 2006, A/61/10, pp. 110, 121.

[72] Note that the Canadian claim for clean-up costs consequential upon the crash of a Soviet nuclear-powered satellite was settled: see 18 ILM, 1979, p. 902.

[73] Note that Security Council resolution 687 (1991) declared that Iraq was liable under international law inter alia 'for any direct loss, damage, including environmental damage and the depletion of natural resources' occurring as a result of the unlawful invasion and occupation of Kuwait.

[74] See e.g. Handl, 'State Liability', and G. Doeker and T. Gehring, 'Private or International Liability for Transnational Environmental Damage – The Precedent of Conventional Liability Regimes', 2 Journal of Environmental Law, 1990, p. 1.

of course, responsible for unlawful acts of its officials causing injury to nationals of foreign states[75] and retains a general territorial competence under international law. In general, states must ensure that their international obligations are respected on their territory. Many treaties require states parties to legislate with regard to particular issues, in order to ensure the implementation of specific obligations. Where an international agreement requires, for example, that certain limits be placed upon emissions of a particular substance, the state would be responsible for any activity that exceeded the limit, even if it were carried out by a private party, since the state had undertaken a binding commitment.[76] Similarly where the state has undertaken to impose a prior authorisation procedure upon a particular activity, a failure so to act which resulted in pollution violating international law would occasion the responsibility of the state.

In some cases, an international agreement might specifically provide for the liability of the state for the acts of non-state entities. Article 6 of the Outer Space Treaty, 1967, for example, stipulates that states parties bear international responsibility for 'national activities in outer space . . . whether such activities are carried out by governmental agencies or by non-governmental agencies'.[77]

Prevention of transboundary harm from hazardous activities[78]

The International Law Commission started considering in 1978 the topic of 'International Liability for the Injurious Consequences of Acts Not Prohibited by International Law'[79] and the main focus of the work of

---

[75] See above, chapter 14.   [76] See below, p. 873.

[77] See also article I of the Convention on International Liability for Damage Caused by Space Objects, 1972 and article XIV of the Moon Treaty, 1979. See further below, p. 893, with regard to civil liability schemes.

[78] See e.g. J. Barboza, 'International Liability for the Injurious Consequences of Acts not Prohibited by International Law and Protection of the Environment', 247 HR, 1994 III, p. 291; A. Boyle, 'State Responsibility and International Liability for Injurious Consequences of Acts not Prohibited by International Law: A Necessary Distinction?', 39 ICLQ, 1990, p. 1; M. Akehurst, 'International Liability for Injurious Consequences Arising out of Acts not Prohibited by International Law', 16 Netherlands YIL, 1985, p. 3; D. B. Magraw, 'Transboundary Harm: The International Law Commission's Study of International Liability', 80 AJIL, 1986, p. 305, and C. Tomuschat, 'International Liability for Injurious Consequences Arising out of Acts not Prohibited by International Law: The Work of the International Law Commission' in *International Responsibility for Environmental Harm* (eds. F. Francioni and T. Scovazzi), London, 1991, p. 37. See also Birnie and Boyle, *International Law and the Environment*, p. 105, and Sands, *Principles*, pp. 901 ff.

[79] See *Yearbook of the ILC*, 1978, vol. II, part 2, p. 149.

the Commission was on environmental harm.[80] It was argued that international liability differed from state responsibility in that the latter is dependent upon a prior breach of international law,[81] while the former constitutes an attempt to develop a branch of law in which a state may be liable internationally with regard to the harmful consequences of an activity which is in itself not contrary to international law. This was a controversial approach. The theoretical basis and separation from state responsibility were questioned.[82] The ILC revised its work and eventually adopted Draft Articles on Prevention of Transboundary Harm from Hazardous Activities in 2001.[83]

Article 1 of the Draft provides that the articles are to apply to activities not prohibited by international law which involve a 'risk of causing significant transboundary harm through their physical consequences'. The Commentary to the Draft Articles specifies that the notion of risk is to be taken objectively 'as denoting an appreciation of possible harm resulting from an activity which a properly informed observer had or ought to have had'.[84] Members of the Commission had in the past been divided as to whether the focus of the topic should be upon risk or upon harm;[85] this now appears settled. Article 2 of the Draft provides that 'risk of causing significant transboundary harm' is to be defined as including 'a high probability of causing significant transboundary harm and a low probability of causing disastrous transboundary harm'.[86] In other words, the relevant threshold is established by a combination of risk and harm and this threshold must reach a level deemed 'significant'.[87] The International Law Commission has taken the view that this term, while factually based, means something more than 'detectable', but need not reach the level of 'serious' or 'substantial'.[88] The state of origin (i.e. where the activities are taking place or are to take place) 'shall take all appropriate measures to

---

[80] See e.g. Quentin-Baxter's preliminary report, *Yearbook of the ILC*, 1980, vol. II, part 1, p. 24.

[81] See above, chapter 14.

[82] See e.g. Boyle, 'State Responsibility', p. 3, and I. Brownlie, *System of the Law of Nations: State Responsibility, Part I*, Oxford, 1983, p. 50.

[83] Report of the ILC on its 53rd Session, p. 379.   [84] *Ibid.*, p. 385.

[85] See e.g. S. McCaffrey, 'The Fortieth Session of the International Law Commission', 83 AJIL, 1989, pp. 153, 170, and McCaffrey, 'The Forty-First Session of the International Law Commission', 83 AJIL, 1989, pp. 937, 944.

[86] Report of the ILC on its 53rd Session, p. 386.

[87] *Ibid.*, p. 387. See also article 1 of the Code of Conduct on Accidental Pollution of Transboundary Inland Waters adopted by the Economic Commission for Europe in 1990.

[88] Report of ILC on its 53rd Session, p. 388.

prevent significant transboundary harm or at any event to minimise the risk thereof'.[89] The relevant test is that of due diligence, this being that which is generally considered to be appropriate and proportional to the degree of risk of transboundary harm in the particular instance and this test requires the state to keep up to date with technological and scientific developments.[90]

States are to co-operate in good faith in trying to prevent such activities from causing significant transboundary injury and in minimising the effects of the risk, and they are to seek the assistance as necessary of competent international organisations.[91] The state is to take legislative, administrative and other action, including the establishment of suitable monitoring mechanisms to implement the provisions in the draft articles,[92] and is to require prior authorisation for any activities within the scope of the article.[93] In deciding upon such authorisation, the state must base its answer on an assessment of the possible transboundary harm, including any environmental impact assessment.[94] If a risk is indeed indicated by such an assessment, timely notification must be made to the state likely to be affected[95] and information provided,[96] while the states concerned are to enter into consultation with a view to achieving acceptable solutions regarding measures to be adopted in order to prevent or minimise the risk of causing significant transboundary harm or to minimise the risk thereof. Such solutions must be based on an equitable balance of interests.[97]

Article 10 of the Draft lays down a series of relevant factors and circumstances in achieving this 'equitable balance of interests'. These include the degree of risk of significant transboundary harm and the availability of means of preventing or minimising such risk or of repairing the harm; the importance of the activity, taking into account its overall advantages of a social, economic and technical character for the state of origin in relation to the potential harm for the states likely to be affected; the risk of significant harm to the environment and the availability of means of preventing or minimising such risk or restoring the environment; the economic viability of the activity in relation to the costs of prevention demanded by the states likely to be affected and to the possibility of carrying out the activity elsewhere or by other means or replacing it with an alternative activity; the degree to which the states likely to be affected

---

[89] Article 3.   [90] Report of the ILC on its 53rd Session, p. 394.
[91] Article 4.   [92] Article 5.   [93] Article 6.   [94] Article 7.
[95] Articles 8 and 17.   [96] Article 8. See also articles 12, 13 and 14.   [97] Article 9.

are prepared to contribute to the costs of prevention; and the standards
of protection which the states likely to be affected apply to the same or
comparable activities and the standards applied in comparable regional
or international practice.[98]

In 2006, the ILC adopted the Draft Principles on the Allocation of Loss
in the Case of Transboundary Harm Arising out of Hazardous Activities,[99]
the purpose of which is to ensure prompt and adequate compensation to
victims of transboundary damage and to preserve and protect the environment. States are to take all necessary measures to ensure such compensation is available, including the imposition of liability upon operators
without requiring proof of fault.[100]

The problems of the state responsibility approach

The application of the classical international law approach, founded upon
state responsibility for breaches of international obligations and the requirement to make reparation for such breaches, to environmental problems is particularly problematic. The need to demonstrate that particular damage has been caused to one state by the actions of another state
means that this model can only with difficulty be applied to more than
a small proportion of environmental problems. In many cases it is simply impossible to prove that particular damage has been caused by one
particular source, while this bilateral focus cannot really come to terms
with the fact that the protection of the environment of the earth is truly
a global problem requiring a global or pan-state response and one that
cannot be successfully tackled in such an arbitrary and piecemeal fashion. Accordingly, the approach to dealing with environmental matters has
shifted from the bilateral state responsibility paradigm to establishment
and strengthening of international co-operation.

International co-operation

A developing theme of international environmental law, founded upon
general principles, relates to the requirement for states to co-operate in
dealing with transboundary pollution issues. Principle 24 of the Stockholm Declaration 1972 noted that 'international matters concerning the

---

[98] This article draws upon article 6 of the Convention on the Law of the Non-Navigational
Uses of International Watercourses, 1997.
[99] A/61/10, p. 110.   [100] Principles 3 and 4.

protection and improvement of the environment should be handled in a co-operative spirit', while Principle 7 of the Rio Declaration 1992 emphasised that 'states shall co-operate in a spirit of global partnership to conserve, protect and restore the health and integrity of the Earth's ecosystem'. Principle 13 of the Rio Declaration refers both to national and international activities in this field by stating that:

> states shall develop national law regarding liability and compensation for the victims of pollution and other environmental damage. States shall also co-operate in an expeditious and more determined manner to develop further international law regarding liability and compensation for adverse effects of environmental damage caused by activities within their jurisdiction or control to areas beyond their jurisdiction.[101]

The *Corfu Channel* case[102] established the principle that states are not knowingly to allow their territory to be used for acts contrary to the rights of other states and from this can be deduced a duty to inform other states of known environmental hazards. A large number of international agreements reflect this proposition. Article 198 of the Convention on the Law of the Sea, 1982, for example, provides that 'when a state becomes aware of cases in which the marine environment is in imminent danger of being damaged or had been damaged by pollution, it shall immediately notify other states it deems likely to be affected by such damage, as well as the competent international authorities'.[103] Article 13 of the Basle Convention on the Control of Transboundary Movement of Hazardous Wastes, 1989 provides that states parties shall, whenever it comes to their knowledge, ensure that in the case of an accident occurring during the transboundary movement of hazardous wastes which are likely to present risks to human health and the environment in other states, those states are immediately informed.[104]

It is also to be noted that in 1974 the OECD (the Organisation for Economic Co-operation and Development) adopted a Recommendation that prior to the initiation of works or undertakings that might create a risk of significant transfrontier pollution, early information should be

---

[101] See also Principle 27.   [102] ICJ Reports, 1949, pp. 4, 22; 16 AD, pp. 155, 158.
[103] See also article 211(7).
[104] See also e.g. article 8 of the International Convention for the Prevention of Pollution from Ships, 1973; Annex 6 of the Helsinki Convention on the Protection of the Marine Environment of the Baltic Sea, 1974 and article 9 of the Barcelona Convention for the Protection of the Mediterranean Sea, Protocol of Co-operation in Case of Emergency, 1976.

provided to states that are or may be affected.[105] In 1988, the OECD adopted a Council Decision in which it is provided that states must provide information for the prevention of and the response to accidents at hazardous installations and transmit to exposed countries the results of their studies on proposed installations. A duty to exchange emergency plans is stipulated, as well as a duty to transmit immediate warning to exposed countries where an accident is an imminent threat.[106] The point is also emphasised in the Rio Declaration of 1992. Principle 18 provides that states shall immediately notify other states of any natural disasters or other emergencies that are likely to produce sudden harmful effects on the environment of those states, while Principle 19 stipulates that states shall provide prior and timely notification and relevant information to potentially affected states on activities that may have a significant adverse transboundary environmental effect and shall consult with those states at an early stage and in good faith.[107]

One may also point to a requirement of prior consultation. Article 5 of the ILA Montreal Rules provides that states planning to carry out activities which might entail a significant risk of transfrontier pollution shall give early notice to states likely to be affected. This provision builds upon, for example, the *Lac Lanoux* arbitration between France and Spain,[108] which concerned the proposed diversion of a shared watercourse. The arbitral tribunal noted in particular the obligation to negotiate in such circumstances.[109] Some treaties establish a duty of prior notification, one early example being the Nordic Convention on the Protection of the Environment, 1974. Article 5 of the Long-Range Transboundary Air Pollution Convention, 1979 provides that consultations shall be held, upon request, at an early stage between the state within whose jurisdiction the activity is to be conducted and states which are actually affected by or exposed to a significant risk of long-range transboundary air pollution.[110] The

---

[105] Title E, para. 6. See also the OECD Recommendation for the Implementation of a Regime of Equal Right of Access and Non-Discrimination in Relation to Transfrontier Pollution, 1977, Title C, para. 8.

[106] C(88)84.

[107] See also article 3 of the Convention on Environmental Impact Assessment in a Transboundary Context, 1991 and Principle 5 of the ILC Draft Principles on the Allocation of Loss, 2006, A/61/10, p. 166.

[108] 24 ILR, p. 101.

[109] *Ibid.*, p. 119. See also the *North Sea Continental Shelf* cases, ICJ Reports, 1969, pp. 3, 46–7; 41 ILR, pp. 29, 76.

[110] Note also that article 8(b) calls for the exchange of information *inter alia* on major changes in national policies and in general industrial development and on their potential

increasing range of state practice[111] has led the International Law Association to conclude that 'a rule of international customary law has emerged that in principle a state is obliged to render information on new or increasing pollution to a potential victim state'.[112] Article 8 of the ILC's Draft Articles on Prevention of Transboundary Harm from Hazardous Activities 2001 provides that where an assessment indicates a risk of causing significant transboundary harm, the state of origin is to inform the state likely to be affected with timely notification and information and may not take any decision on authorisation within six months of the response of the state likely to be affected.[113]

The evolution of a duty to inform states that might be affected by the creation of a source of new or increasing pollution has been accompanied by consideration of an obligation to make environmental impact assessments.[114] This requirement is included in several treaties.[115] Article 204 of the Convention on the Law of the Sea, 1982 provides that states should 'observe, measure, evaluate and analyse by recognised scientific methods, the risks or effects of pollution on the marine environment' and in particular 'shall keep under surveillance the effects of any activities which they permit or in which they engage in order to determine whether these activities are likely to pollute the marine environment'. Reports are to be published, while under article 206, when states have reasonable grounds for believing that planned activities under their jurisdiction or control may cause substantial pollution of, or significant and harmful changes

---

impact, which would be likely to cause significant changes in long-range transboundary air pollution.

[111] See ILA, Report of the Sixtieth Conference, 1982, pp. 172–3.

[112] *Ibid.*, p. 173. See also Institut de Droit International, Resolution on Transboundary Air Pollution, 1987, but cf. Sands, *Principles*, pp. 321–2. Note also e.g. the UNEP Recommendation concerning the Environment Related to Offshore Drilling and Mining within the Limits of National Jurisdiction, 1981 and the Canada–Denmark Agreement for Co-operation Relating to the Marine Environment, 1983.

[113] Report of the ILC on its 53rd Session, p. 406. See also Principle 19 of the Rio Declaration, article 3 of the Convention on Environmental Impact Assessment in a Transboundary Context, 1991 and the Convention on the Law of the Non-Navigational Uses of International Watercourses, 1997, below, p. 883.

[114] See e.g. the UNEP Principles of Environmental Impact Assessment, 1987. See also Sands, *Principles*, pp. 799 ff.

[115] See e.g. the Kuwait Regional Convention for Co-operation on the Protection of the Marine Environment from Pollution, 1978, article XI; the Nordic Environmental Protection Convention, 1974, article 6, and the Protocol on Environmental Protection to the Antarctica Treaty, 1991, article 8. See also article 7 of the Draft Articles on Prevention of Transboundary Harm from Hazardous Activities 2001, Report of the ILC on its 53rd Session, p. 402.

to, the marine environment, 'they shall, as far as practicable, assess the potential effects of such activities on the marine environment and shall communicate reports of such assessments'.[116]

The EEC Council Directive 85/337 provides that member states shall adopt all necessary measures to ensure that, before consent is given, projects likely to have significant effects on the environment are made subject to an assessment with regard to their effects,[117] while the issue was taken further in the Convention on Environmental Impact Assessment in a Transboundary Context, 1991. Under this Convention, states parties are to take the necessary legal, administrative and other measures to ensure that prior to a decision to authorise or undertake a proposed activity listed in Appendix I[118] that is likely to cause a significant adverse transboundary impact, an environmental impact assessment is carried out. The party of origin must notify any party which may be affected of the proposed activity, providing full information. Once the affected party decides to participate in the environmental impact assessment procedure under the provisions of the Convention, it must supply information to the party of origin of the proposed activity at its request relating to the potentially affected environment under its jurisdiction.[119] The documentation to be submitted to the competent authority of the party of origin is detailed in Appendix III and it is comprehensive. Consultations must take place between the party of origin and the affected parties concerning the potential transboundary impact and the measures to reduce or eliminate the impact,[120] and in taking the final decision on the proposed activity the parties

---

[116] A similar process is underway with regard to the siting of nuclear power installations: see e.g. the agreements between Spain and Portugal, 1980; the Netherlands and the Federal Republic of Germany, 1977; Belgium and France, 1966; and Switzerland and the Federal Republic of Germany, 1982. See also Boyle, 'Chernobyl', at p. 212.

[117] See also Directive 2004/35/EC, 21 April 2004, of the European Parliament and of the Council on environmental liability with regard to the prevention and remedying of environmental damage, as amended by Directive 2006/21/EC.

[118] These activities include crude oil and certain other refineries; thermal power stations and other combustion installations with a certain minimum power output and nuclear installations; nuclear facilities; major cast iron and steel installations; asbestos plants; integrated chemical installations; construction of motorways, long-distance railway lines and long airport runways; pipelines; large trading ports; toxic and dangerous waste installations; large dams and reservoirs; major mining; offshore hydrocarbon production; major oil and chemical storage facilities; deforestation of large areas.

[119] If it decides not so to participate, the environmental impact assessment procedure will continue or not according to the domestic law and practice of the state of origin, article 3(4).

[120] Article 5.

shall ensure that due account is taken of the outcome of the environmental impact assessment and consultations held.[121] Post-project analyses may also be carried out under article 7.[122] Other instruments provide for such environmental impact assessments[123] and some international organisations have developed their own assessment requirements.[124] The question of environmental impact assessments was raised by Judge Weeramantry in his Dissenting Opinion in the *Request for an Examination of the Situation in Accordance with Paragraph 63 of the Court's Judgment in the 1974 Nuclear Tests Case*.[125] It was noted that the magnitude of the issue brought by New Zealand before the Court (the underground testing by France in the South Pacific of nuclear devices) was such as to make the principle of environmental impact assessments applicable. The Judge declared that 'when a matter is brought before it which raises serious environmental issues of global importance, and a prima facie case is made out of the possibility of environmental damage, the Court is entitled to take into account the Environmental Impact Assessment principle in determining its preliminary approach'.[126]

Other principles of international co-operation in the field of environmental protection are beginning to emerge and inform the development of legal norms. Principle 15 of the Rio Declaration states that 'in order to protect the environment, the precautionary approach shall be widely applied by states according to their capabilities. Where there are threats of serious or irreversible damage, lack of full scientific certainty shall not be used as a reason for postponing cost-effective measures to prevent environmental degradation.' This marks a step away from the traditional approach, which required states to act on the basis of scientific knowledge and constitutes a recognition that in certain circumstances to await formal scientific proof may prevent urgent action being taken in time. The Vienna Convention for the Protection of the Ozone Layer, 1985 and the 1987 Montreal Protocol to that Convention both referred in their respective preambles to 'precautionary measures',[127] while the Bergen Ministerial Declaration on Sustainable Development, 1990 noted that in order to

---

[121] Article 6(1). Account must also be taken of concerns expressed by the public of the affected party in the areas likely to be affected under article 3(8).
[122] See also Appendix V.
[123] See e.g. the Antarctic Environment Protocol, 1991.
[124] See e.g. the World Bank under its Operational Directive 4.00 of 1989.
[125] ICJ Reports, 1995, pp. 288, 344; 106 ILR, p. 1.   [126] ICJ Reports, 1995, p. 345.
[127] See also the preamble to the 1994 Oslo Protocol to the 1979 Long-Range Transboundary Air Pollution Convention and EC Regulation 178/2002 (with regard to food).

achieve sustainable development, policies must be based on the precautionary principle. It was emphasised that 'environmental measures must anticipate, prevent and attack the causes of environmental degradation' and part of Principle 15 of the Rio Declaration was repeated. The Convention on the Protection and Use of Transboundary Watercourses and International Lakes, 1992 provides in article 2(5)a that the parties would be guided by 'the precautionary principle, by virtue of which action to avoid the potential transboundary impact of the release of hazardous substances shall not be postponed on the ground that scientific research has not fully proved a causal link between these substances, on the one hand and the potential transboundary impact, on the other'. References to the precautionary principle appear also in the Convention on Biodiversity, 1992[128] and in the Convention on Climate Change, 1992.[129] The principle was described by Judge Weeramantry as one gaining increasing support as part of the international law of the environment.[130]

Recognition has also emerged of the special responsibility of developed states in the process of environmental protection.[131] Principle 7 of the Rio Declaration stipulates that 'states have common but differentiated responsibilities'. In particular, it is emphasised that 'the developed

---

[128] Although the reference in the Preamble does not expressly invoke the term. See generally *International Law and the Conservation of Biological Diversity* (eds. M. Bowman and C. Redgwell), Dordrecht, 1995.

[129] Article 3(3). See also article 174 (ex article 130r(2)) of the EC Treaty and article 4(3) of the OAU Bamako Convention on the Ban of the Import into Africa and the Control of Transboundary Movement and Management of Hazardous Wastes within Africa, 1991. Note also articles 5 and 6 of the Straddling Fish Stocks and Highly Migratory Fish Stocks Agreement, 1995.

[130] In his Dissenting Opinion in the *Request for an Examination of the Situation in Accordance with Paragraph 63 of the Court's Judgment in the 1974 Nuclear Tests Case*, ICJ Reports, 1995, pp. 288, 342; 106 ILR, pp. 1, 64. See *The Precautionary Principle and International Law* (eds. D. Freestone and E. Hey), Dordrecht, 1996; P. Martin-Bidou, 'Le Principe de Précaution en Droit International de l'Environnement', 103 RGDIP, 1999, p. 631, and *Le Principe de Précaution, Signification et Conséquences* (eds. E. Zaccai and J. N. Missa), Brussels, 2000; Birnie and Boyle, *International Law and the Environment*, pp. 115 ff.; Sands, *Principles*, pp. 266 ff.; *Le Principe de Précaution: Aspects de Droit International et Communautaire* (ed. C. Leben), Paris, 2002, and A. Trouwborst, *Evolution and Status of the Precautionary Principle in International Law*, The Hague, 2002. See also the Commentary to the ILC Draft Articles on Prevention of Transboundary Harm from Hazardous Activities, 2001, Report of the ILC on its 53rd Session, p. 414 and the Guidelines for Applying the Precautionary Principle to Biodiversity Conservation and Natural Resource Management adopted by the International Union for the Conservation of Nature in May 2007.

[131] See e.g. D. French, 'Developing States and International Environmental Law: The Importance of Differentiated Responsibilities', 49 ICLQ, 2000, p. 35.

countries acknowledge the responsibility that they bear in the international pursuit of sustainable development in view of the pressures their societies place on the global environment and of the technologies and financial resources they command'. Article 3(1) of the Convention on Climate Change provides that the parties should act to protect the climate system 'on the basis of equity and in accordance with their common but differentiated responsibilities and respective capabilities' so that the developed countries would take the lead in combating climate change.[132]

In addition, the concept of sustainable development has been evolving in a way that circumscribes the competence of states to direct their own development.[133] The International Court in the *Gabčíkovo–Nagymaros Project* case referred specifically to the concept of sustainable development,[134] while Principle 3 of the Rio Declaration notes that the right to development must be fulfilled so as to 'equitably meet developmental and environmental needs of present and future generations'[135] and Principle 4 states that in order to achieve sustainable development, environmental protection shall constitute an integral part of the development process.[136] Principle 27 called for co-operation in the further development of

---

[132] See also articles 4 and 12. Note that the 1990 amendment to the 1987 Montreal Protocol on the Ozone Depleting Substances provides that the capacity of developing countries to comply with their substantive obligations will depend upon the implementation by the developed countries of their financial obligations.

[133] See e.g. *Sustainable Development and International Law* (ed. W. Lang), Dordrecht, 1995; *Sustainable Development and Good Governance* (eds. K. Ginther, E. Denters and P. de Waart), Dordrecht, 1995; Sands, *Principles*, pp. 252 ff., and Sands, 'International Law in the Field of Sustainable Development', 65 BYIL, 1994, p. 303; M.-C. Cordonier Segger and C. G. Weeramantry, *Sustainable Justice: Reconciling Economic, Social and Environmental Law*, Leiden, 2005; P. S. Elder, 'Sustainability', 36 *McGill Law Journal*, 1991, p. 832; D. McGoldrick, 'Sustainable Development and Human Rights: An Integrated Conception', 45 ICLQ, 1996, p. 796; *International Law and Sustainable Development* (eds. A. Boyle and D. Freestone), Oxford, 1999; *Environmental Law, the Economy and Sustainable Development* (eds. R. Revesz, P. Sands and R. Stewart), Cambridge, 2000; Birnie and Boyle, *International Law and the Environment*, p. 84, and X. Fuentes, 'Sustainable Development and the Equitable Utilisation of International Watercourses', 69 BYIL, 1998, p. 119. See also the Report of the ILA Committee on Legal Aspects of Sustainable Development, ILA, Report of the Sixty-sixth Conference, 1994, p. 111 and Report of the Seventieth Conference, 2002, p. 308.

[134] ICJ Reports, 1997, pp. 7, 78; 116 ILR, p. 1. See also the *Shrimp/Turtle* case, WTO Appellate Body, 38 ILM, 1999, p. 121, para. 129.

[135] See also Principle 1 of the Stockholm Declaration 1972.

[136] Note that article 2(1)vii of the Agreement Establishing the European Bank for Reconstruction and Development, 1990 calls upon the Bank to promote 'environmentally sound and sustainable development'.

international law in the field of sustainable development.[137] The Climate Change Convention declares in article 3(4) that 'the parties have a right to, and should, promote sustainable development', while the Biodiversity Convention refers on several occasions to the notion of 'sustainable use'.[138] Quite what is meant by sustainable development is somewhat unclear and it may refer to a range of economic, environmental and social factors.[139] Clearly, however, some form of balance between these factors will be necessitated.[140]

Another emerging principle, more widely accepted in some countries and regions than others, is the notion that the costs of pollution should be paid by the polluter.[141] Principle 16 of the Rio Declaration notes that 'the polluter should, in principle, bear the costs of pollution, with due regard to the public interests and without distorting international trade and investment'. The principle has been particularly applied with regard to civil liability for damage resulting from hazardous activities[142] and has particularly been adopted by the Organisation for Economic Co-operation and Development[143] and the European Community.[144] The polluter-pays principle has been referred to both in the International Convention on Oil Pollution Preparedness, Response and Co-operation, 1990 and in the Convention on the Transboundary Effects of Industrial Accidents, 1992

---

[137] See also Agenda 21, adopted at the Rio Conference on Environment and Development, 1992, paras. 8 and 39.

[138] See e.g. the Preamble and articles 1, 8, 11, 12, 16, 17 and 18. See also the Statement of Principles for a Global Consensus on the Management, Conservation and Sustainable Development of All Types of Forests, adopted at the Rio Conference, 1992.

[139] See e.g. M. Redclift, 'Reflections on the "Sustainable Development" Debate', 1 *International Journal of Sustainable Development and World Ecology*, 1994, p. 3. Note that the Report of the GATT Panel on the United States Restrictions on the Import of Tuna declares that the objective of sustainable development, which includes the protection and preservation of the environment, has been widely recognised by the contracting parties to the General Agreement on Tariffs and Trade, 33 ILM, 1994, p. 839.

[140] Note that the General Assembly established the Commission on Sustainable Development in resolution 47/191 in order to ensure an effective follow-up to the 1992 Conference on Environment and Development as well as generally to work for the integration of environment and development issues and to examine the progress of the implementation of Agenda 21 (the programme of action adopted by the Conference) in order to achieve sustainable development.

[141] See e.g. Sands, *Principles*, pp. 279 ff., and A. Boyle, 'Making the Polluter Pay? Alternatives to State Responsibility in the Allocation of Transboundary Environmental Costs' in Francioni and Scovazzi, *International Responsibility for Environmental Harm*, p. 363.

[142] See further below, p. 893.

[143] See e.g. the OECD Council Recommendations C(74)223 (1974) and C(89)88 (1989).

[144] See Article 174 of the EC Treaty.

as 'a general principle of international environmental law'.[145] Again, quite how far this principle actually applies is uncertain. It is, in particular, unclear whether all the costs of an environmental clean-up would be covered. State practice appears to demonstrate that such costs should be apportioned between the parties.[146]

Atmospheric pollution[147]

Perhaps the earliest perceived form of pollution relates to the pollution of the air. The burning of fossil fuels releases into the atmosphere sulphur dioxide and nitrogen oxides which change into acids and are carried by natural elements and fall as rain or snow or solid particles. Such acids have the effect of killing living creatures in lakes and streams and of damaging soils and forests.[148] While the airspace above the territorial domain of a state forms part of that state,[149] the imprecise notion of the atmosphere would combine elements of this territorial sovereignty with areas not so defined. The legal characterisation of the atmosphere, therefore, is confused and uncertain, but one attractive possibility is to refer to it as a shared resource or area of common concern.[150]

The question of how one defines the term 'pollution' has been addressed in several international instruments. In a Recommendation adopted in 1974 by the Organisation for Economic Co-operation and Development,[151] pollution is broadly defined as 'the introduction by man, directly or indirectly, of substances or energy into the environment resulting in deleterious effects of such a nature as to endanger human health, harm living resources and ecosystems, and impair or interfere with amenities and other legitimate uses of the environment'.[152] This definition was substantially reproduced in the Geneva Convention on Long-Range

---

[145] See also article 2(5)b of the Convention on the Protection and Use of Transboundary Watercourses and International Lakes, 1992 and Principle 4 of the ILC Draft Principles on the Allocation of Loss, 2006, A/61/10, p. 151.

[146] See e.g. Boyle, 'Making the Polluter Pay?', p. 365, and Birnie and Boyle, *International Law and the Environment*, p. 92.

[147] See Sands, *Principles*, pp. 317 ff., and Birnie and Boyle, *International Law and the Environment*, chapter 10.

[148] See *Keesing's Record of World Events*, pp. 36782 ff. (1989).

[149] See above, chapter 10, p. 541.

[150] See e.g. Birnie and Boyle, *International Law and the Environment*, p. 503.

[151] OECD Doc.C(74)224, cited in P. Sands, *Chernobyl: Law and Communication*, Cambridge, 1988, p. 150.

[152] *Ibid.*, Title A.

Transboundary Air Pollution, 1979[153] and in the Montreal Rules of International Law Applicable to Transfrontier Pollution adopted by the International Law Association in 1982.[154] Several points ought to be noted at this stage. First, actual damage must have been caused. Pollution likely to result as a consequence of certain activities is not included. Secondly, the harm caused must be of a certain level of intensity, and thirdly, the question of interference with legitimate uses of the environment requires further investigation.

The core obligation in customary international law with regard to atmospheric pollution was laid down in the *Trail Smelter* case,[155] which provided that no state had the right to use or permit the use of its territory in such a manner as to cause injury by fumes in or to the territory of another state or to persons or property therein, where the case was of serious consequence and the injury established by clear and convincing evidence.[156]

In 1979, on the initiative of the Scandinavian countries and under the auspices of the UN Economic Commission for Europe, the Geneva Convention on Long-Range Transboundary Air Pollution was signed.[157] The definition of pollution is reasonably broad,[158] while article 1(b) defines long-range transboundary air pollution as air pollution whose physical origin is situated wholly or in part within the area under the national jurisdiction of one state and which has adverse effects in the area under

---

[153] The major difference being the substitution of 'air' for 'environment' in view of the focus of the Convention.

[154] Note that the term 'air' was replaced by 'environment'. See also article 1 of the Paris Convention for the Prevention of Marine Pollution from Land-Based Sources, 1974 and article 2 of the Barcelona Convention for the Protection of the Mediterranean Sea against Pollution, 1976. The Institut de Droit International, in a draft resolution accompanying its final report on Air Pollution Across National Frontiers, defines pollution as 'any physical, chemical or biological alteration in the composition or quality of the atmosphere which results directly or indirectly from human action or omission and produces injurious or deleterious effects across national frontiers', 62 I *Annuaire de l'Institut de Droit International*, 1987, p. 266.

[155] 35 AJIL, 1941, p. 716; 9 AD, p. 317.

[156] Note also the adoption in 1963 of the Treaty Banning Nuclear Weapon Tests in the Atmosphere, Outer Space and Under Water.

[157] See e.g. A. Rosencranz, 'The ECE Convention of 1979 on Long-Range Transboundary Air Pollution', 75 AJIL, 1981, p. 975; L. Tollan, 'The Convention on Long-Range Transboundary Air Pollution', 19 *Journal of World Trade Law*, 1985, p. 615, and A. Kiss, 'La Convention sur la Pollution Atmosphérique Transfrontière à Longue Distance', *Revue Juridique de l'Environnement*, 1981, p. 30. See also P. Okowa, *State Responsibility for Transboundary Air Pollution*, Oxford, 2000. See generally www.unece.org/env/lrtap/.

[158] See above, p. 871.

the jurisdiction of another state at such a distance that it is not generally possible to distinguish the contribution of individual emission sources or groups of sources.

The obligations undertaken under the Convention, however, are modest. States 'shall endeavour to limit and, as far as possible, gradually reduce and prevent air pollution, including long-range transboundary air pollution'.[159] The question of state liability for damage resulting from such pollution is not addressed. The Convention provides that states are to develop policies and strategies by means of exchanges of information and consultation[160] and to exchange information to combat generally the discharge of air pollutants.[161] Consultations are to be held upon request at an early stage between contracting parties actually affected by or exposed to a significant risk of long-range transboundary air pollution and contracting parties within which and subject to whose jurisdiction a significant contribution to such pollution originates or could originate, in connection with activities carried on or contemplated therein.[162]

The parties also undertook to develop the existing 'Co-operative programme for the monitoring and evaluation of the long-range transmission of air pollutants in Europe' (EMEP) and in 1984 a Protocol was adopted dealing with the long-term financing of the project. Further Protocols to the Convention have been adopted. In 1985, the Helsinki Protocol was signed, dealing with the reduction of sulphur emissions or their transboundary fluxes by at least 30 per cent as soon as possible and at the latest by 1993, using 1980 levels as the basis for the calculation of reductions. This Protocol requires parties to report annually to the Executive Body of the Convention.[163] The Sophia Protocol was adopted in 1988 and concerned the control of emissions of nitrogen oxides or their transboundary fluxes. Under this Protocol the contracting parties undertook to reduce their national annual emissions of nitrogen oxides or their transboundary fluxes so that by the end of 1994 these would not exceed those of 1987. Negotiations for further reductions in national annual emissions were provided for, as was the exchange of technology in relevant areas and of information. In 1991, the Protocol concerning the control of emissions of volatile organic compounds and their transboundary fluxes was adopted.

---

[159] Article 2.

[160] Article 3. Note that under article 6, states undertake to develop the best policies and strategies using the 'best available technology which is economically feasible'.

[161] Article 4. See also article 8.   [162] Article 5. See also article 8(b).

[163] As to EU obligations concerning the curbing of emissions of sulphur dioxide and nitrogen dioxide, see e.g. Directive 99/30/EC and Sands, *Principles*, pp. 761 ff.

Specific targets and timetables are established. However, the Protocol provides for a choice of at least three ways to meet the requirements, to be determined by the parties upon signature and dependent upon the level of volatile organic compounds emissions. In 1994, the Oslo Protocol on Further Reduction of Sulphur Emissions was adopted,[164] specifying sulphur emission ceilings for parties for the years 2000, 2005 and 2010, and accompanied by a reporting requirement to the Executive Body on a periodic basis.[165] An Implementation Committee was provided for in order to review the implementation of the Protocol and compliance by the parties with their obligations.[166] In 1998 two further protocols were concluded, one on persistent organic pollutants and the other on heavy metals. A Protocol of 1999 is intended to abate acidification, eutrophication and ground-level ozone. In 1997 a revised Implementation Committee was established and this has the responsibility to review compliance with all the Protocols of the Convention under a common procedure. It considers questions of non-compliance with a view to finding a 'constructive solution' and reports to the Executive Board.[167]

In 2001, the Stockholm Convention on Persistent Organic Pollutants was signed. The Convention provides for the control of the production, trade in, disposal and use of twelve named persistent organic pollutants (although there is a health exception temporarily for DDT). There is a procedure to add other such pollutants to the list and an interim financial mechanism with the Global Environmental Facility (GEF)[168] was established as the principal entity to help developing countries.[169] In May 2005, a conference of states parties established a subsidiary body, the Persistent Organic Pollutants Review Committee,[170] in order to assist in implementation activities.

---

[164] See 33 ILM, 1994, p. 1540.   [165] Article 5.   [166] Article 7.

[167] See Executive Board Decision 1997/2, annex, as amended in 2001, ECE/EB.AIR/75, annex V. The Executive Board may take decisions concerning the compliance of parties: see e.g. Decision 2002/8 criticising Spain. See, for the Board's decisions, www.unece.org/env/lrtap/conv/report/eb_decis.htm, and see the Committee's Ninth Report, 2006, ECE/EB.AIR/2006/3 and Adds. 1 and 2.

[168] The Global Environmental Facility was itself set up in 1991 to aid developing countries to fund projects and programmes protecting the global environment. In particular, the Facility supports projects related to biodiversity, climate change, international waters, land degradation, the ozone layer and persistent organic pollutants: see www.gefweb.org/interior.aspx?id=50. See also the Beijing Declaration of the Second Global Environmental Facility 2003, 44 ILM, 2005, p. 1004.

[169] See the Convention website, www.pops.int/.

[170] www.pops.int/documents/meetings/poprc/meeting_docs/reports/report_E.pdf.

In 1986 a Protocol to the Paris Convention for the Prevention of Marine Pollution from Land-Based Sources[171] extended that agreement to atmospheric emissions of pollutants.[172] Article 212 of the Law of the Sea Convention, 1982 requires states to adopt laws and regulations to prevent, reduce and control atmospheric pollution of the marine environment, although no specific standards are set.[173]

Ozone depletion and global warming[174]

The problem of global warming and the expected increase in the temperature of the earth in the decades to come has focused attention on the issues particularly of the consumption of fossil fuels and deforestation. In addition, the depletion of the stratospheric ozone layer, which has the effect of letting excessive ultraviolet radiation through to the surface of the earth, is a source of considerable concern. The problem of the legal characterisation of the ozone layer is a significant one. Article 1(1) of the Vienna Convention for the Protection of the Ozone Layer, 1985 defines this area as 'the layer of atmospheric ozone above the planetary boundary layer'. This area would thus appear, particularly in the light of the global challenge posed by ozone depletion and climate change, to constitute a distinct unit with an identity of its own irrespective of national sovereignty or shared resources claims. UN General Assembly resolution

---

[171] See below, p. 898.

[172] Note also that in 1987 the Second International Conference on the Protection of the North Sea urged states to ratify the Protocol: see 27 ILM, 1988, p. 835; while in 1990 North Sea states agreed to achieve by 1999 a reduction of 50 per cent or more in atmospheric and river-borne emissions of hazardous substances, provided that best available technology permitted this: see IMO Doc. MEPC 29/INF.26.

[173] Note that the Canada–United States Air Quality Agreement, 1991 required the reduction of sulphur dioxide and nitrogen oxide emissions from the two states to agreed levels by the year 2000. Compliance monitoring by continuous emission monitoring systems was provided for.

[174] See e.g. *International Law and Global Climate Change* (eds. R. Churchill and D. Freestone), Dordrecht, 1991; *Implementing the Climate Regime. International Compliance* (eds. O. S. Stokke, J. Hovi and G. Ulfstein), London, 2005; P. Lawrence, 'International Legal Regulation for Protection of the Ozone Layer: Some Problems of Implementation', 2 *Journal of Environmental Law*, 1990, p. 17; T. Stoel, 'Fluorocarbon: Mobilising Concern and Action' in *Environmental Protection, The International Dimension* (eds. D. A. Kay and H. K. Jacobson), 1983, p. 45; Engelmann, 'A Look at Some Issues Before an Ozone Convention', 8 *Environmental Policy and Law*, 1982, p. 49; Heimsoeth, 'The Protection of the Ozone Layer', 10 *Environmental Policy and Law*, 1983, p. 34, and Birnie and Boyle, *International Law and the Environment*, p. 516. See also www.unep.org/ozone/index-en.shtml.

43/53, for example, states that global climate change is 'the common concern of mankind'.[175] Whatever the precise legal status of this area, what is important is the growing recognition that the scale of the challenge posed can only really be tackled upon a truly international or global basis.

In the first serious effort to tackle the problem of ozone depletion, the Vienna Convention for the Protection of the Ozone Layer was adopted in 1985, entering into force three years later. This Convention is a framework agreement, providing the institutional structure for the elaboration of Protocols laying down specific standards concerning the production of chlorofluorocarbons (CFCs), the agents which cause the destruction of the ozone layer. Under the Convention, contracting parties agree to take appropriate measures to protect human health and the environment against adverse effects resulting or likely to result from human activities which modify or are likely to modify the ozone layer.[176] The parties also agree to co-operate in the collection of relevant material and in the formulation of agreed measures, and to take appropriate legislative or administrative action to control, limit, reduce or prevent human activities under their jurisdiction or control 'should it be found that these activities have or are likely to have adverse effects resulting from modification or likely modification of the ozone layer'.[177] A secretariat and disputes settlement mechanism were established.[178] However, overall the Convention is little more than a framework within which further action could be taken.

In 1987 the Montreal Protocol on Substances that Deplete the Ozone Layer was adopted and this called for a phased reduction of CFCs and a freeze on the use of halons.[179] The control measures of the Protocol are

---

[175] See also the Noordwijk Declaration of the Conference on Atmospheric Pollution and Climate Change, 1989. See e.g. C. A. Fleischer, 'The International Concern for the Environment: The Concept of Common Heritage' in Bothe, *Trends in Environmental Law and Policy*, p. 321.

[176] Article 2(1). 'Adverse effects' is defined in article 1(2) to mean 'changes in the physical environment or biota, including changes in climate, which have significant deleterious effects on human health or on the composition, resilience and productivity of natural and managed ecosystems or on materials useful to mankind'.

[177] Article 2.

[178] Articles 7 and 11. See also the UN Environment Programme, *Handbook for the Vienna Convention for the Protection of the Ozone Layer*, 7th edn, Nairobi, 2006.

[179] See 26 ILM, 1987, p. 1541 and 28 ILM, 1989, p. 1301. See also R. Benedick, *Ozone Diplomacy*, Cambridge, MA, 1991, and A. C. Aman, 'The Montreal Protocol on Substances that Deplete the Ozone Layer: Providing Prospective Remedial Relief for Potential Damage to the Environmental Commons' in Francioni and Scovazzi, *International Responsibility for Environmental Harm*, p. 185. See also UN Environment Programme, *Handbook for the Montreal Protocol on Substances that Deplete the Ozone Layer*, 7th edn, Nairobi, 2006.

based on the regulation of the production of 'controlled substances'[180] by the freezing of their consumption[181] at 1986 levels followed by a progressive reduction, so that by mid-1998 consumption was to be reduced by 20 per cent in comparison with the 1986 figure. From mid-1998 onwards consumption was to be reduced to 50 per cent of the 1986 level.[182] However, this was subsequently felt to have been insufficient and, in 1989, the parties to the Convention and Protocol adopted the Helsinki Declaration on the Protection of the Ozone Layer in which the parties agreed to phase out the production and consumption of CFCs controlled by the Protocol as soon as possible, but not later than the year 2000, and to phase out halons and control and reduce other substances which contribute significantly to ozone depletion as soon as feasible. An Implementation Committee was established under the Montreal Protocol together with a non-compliance procedure, whereby a party querying the carrying out of obligations by another party can submit its concerns in writing to the secretariat. The secretariat with the party complained against will examine the complaint and the matter will then be passed to the Implementation Committee, which will try and secure a friendly settlement and make a report to the meeting of the parties, which can take further measures to ensure compliance with the Protocol.

The parties to the Protocol made a series of Adjustments and Amendments to the Protocol in June 1990,[183] the main ones being that 1992 consumption and production levels were not to exceed 1986 levels, while 1995 levels were not to exceed 50 per cent with 10 per cent exception to satisfy basic domestic needs; 1997 levels were not to exceed 15 per cent, with 10 per cent exception permitted, and 2000 levels were not to exceed 0 per cent with 15 per cent exception permitted. Broadly similar consumption and production targets have also been laid down with regard to halons. The 1990 Amendments made specific reference to the requirement to take into account the developmental needs of developing countries and the need for the transfer of alternative technologies, and a Multilateral Fund was established. Further Adjustments were made in Copenhagen

---

[180] I.e. ozone-depleting substances listed in Annex A.

[181] This is defined to constitute production plus imports minus exports of controlled substances: see articles 1(5) and (6) and 3.

[182] There are two exceptions, however, first for the purposes of 'industrial rationalisation between parties' and secondly with regard to certain developing countries: see article 5.

[183] See 30 ILM, 1991, p. 537.

in 1992,[184] introducing changes to the timetable for the phasing out of various substances, listing new controlled substances and adopting new reporting requirements. The Implementation Committee was enlarged and the Multilateral Fund adopted on a permanent basis.[185]

Action with regard to the phenomenon of global warming has been a lot slower. General Assembly resolutions 43/53 (1988) and 44/207 (1989) recognised that climate change was a common concern of mankind and determined that necessary and timely action should be taken to deal with this issue. The General Assembly also called for the convening of a conference on world climate change, as did the UNEP Governing Council Decision on Global Climate Change of 25 May 1989. In addition, the Hague Declaration on the Environment 1989, signed by twenty-four states, called for the establishment of new institutional authority under the auspices of the UN to combat any further global warming and for the negotiation of the necessary legal instruments. The UN Framework Convention on Climate Change was adopted in 1992.[186]

The objective of the Convention is to achieve stabilisation of greenhouse gases in the atmosphere at a level that would prevent dangerous anthropogenic interference with the climate system and such level should be achieved within a time-frame sufficient to allow ecosystems to adapt naturally to climate change, to ensure food production is not threatened and to enable economic development to proceed in a sustainable manner.[187] The states parties undertake *inter alia* to develop, update and publish national inventories of anthropogenic emissions by sources and removals by sinks[188] of all greenhouse gases not covered by the Montreal Protocol; to formulate, implement and update national and, where appropriate, regional programmes containing measures to mitigate climate

---

[184] See 32 ILM, 1993, p. 874. Further amendments were made in Montreal, 1997, and Beijing, 1999, increasing the substances covered: see www.unep.ch/ozone/treaties.shtml. See also the Montreal Adjustment on the Production and Consumption of HCFCs 2007.

[185] See also EC Regulation 91/594 of 4 March 1991, providing that after 30 June 1997 there should be no production of CFCs unless the European Commission had determined that such production was essential.

[186] 31 ILM, 1992, p. 849. See e.g. J. Werksman, 'Designing a Compliance System for the UN Framework Convention on Climate Change' in *Improving Compliance with International Environmental Agreements* (eds. J. Cameron, J. Werksman, P. Rodinck *et al.*), London, 1996, p. 85. See also Birnie and Boyle, *International Law and the Environment*, p. 523, and Sands, *Principles*, pp. 357 ff. See also http://unfccc.int/.

[187] Article 2.

[188] Defined as any process, activity or mechanism which removes a greenhouse gas, an aerosol or a precursor of a greenhouse gas from the atmosphere, article 1(8).

changes; to promote and co-operate in the development, application and transfer of technologies and processes to control, reduce or prevent such anthropogenic emissions; to promote sustainable management and conservation of sinks and reservoirs of all greenhouse gases not controlled by the Montreal Protocol; to take climate change considerations into account to the extent feasible in their relevant social, economic and environmental policies; and to promote and co-operate in research, exchange of information and education in the field of climate change.[189] Developed country parties, and certain other parties listed in Annex I,[190] commit themselves to take the lead in modifying longer-term trends in anthropogenic emissions and particularly to adopt national policies and take corresponding measures on the mitigation of climate change by limiting anthropogenic emissions of greenhouse gases and protecting and enhancing greenhouse gas sinks and reservoirs.[191] Developed country and other Annex I parties must submit within six months of the Convention coming into force and periodically thereafter, detailed information on such matters with the aim of returning anthropogenic emissions to their 1990 levels. This information provided is to be reviewed by the Conference of the parties on a periodic basis.[192] In addition, developed country parties and other developed parties included in Annex II[193] are to provide the financial resources to enable the developing country parties to meet their obligations under the Convention and generally to assist them in coping with the adverse effects of climate change. The parties agree to give full consideration to actions necessary to assist developing country parties that may be, for example, small island countries, countries with low-lying coastal areas, countries prone to natural disasters, drought and desertification and landlocked and transit states.[194]

The Conference of the parties is established as the supreme body of the Convention and has the function *inter alia* to review the implementation of the Convention, periodically examine the obligations of the parties and the institutional arrangements established, promote the exchange of information, facilitate at the request of two or more parties the co-ordination of measures taken to address climate change, promote and

---

[189] Article 4(1).
[190] For example, former European Soviet Republics such as Belarus, the Ukraine and the Baltic states.
[191] Article 4(2)a.   [192] Article 4(2)b.
[193] Essentially European Union countries, the US, Australia, Canada, New Zealand, Iceland, Japan, Switzerland and Turkey.
[194] Article 4(8).

guide the development of comparable methodologies for the preparation of inventories, assess the implementation of the Convention by the parties, consider and adopt regular reports on implementation and make recommendations on any matters necessary for the implementation of the Convention.[195] In addition, the Convention provides for a secretariat to be established, together with a subsidiary body for scientific and technological advice and a subsidiary body for implementation.[196] The Convention as a whole is a complex document and the range of commitments entered into, particularly by developed country parties, is not wholly clear.

The Convention entered into force in 1994 and the following year the first session of the Conference was held in Berlin.[197] It was agreed that the pledges by the developed country parties to reduce emissions by 2000 to 1990 levels were not adequate and preparations were commenced to draft a further legal instrument by 1997. It was also agreed not to establish new commitments for developing country parties, but rather to assist the implementation of existing commitments. The parties decided to initiate a pilot phase for joint implementation projects, providing for investment from one party in greenhouse gas emissions reduction opportunities in another party. In addition, it was decided to establish a permanent secretariat in Bonn and two subsidiary advisory bodies.

The 1997 Kyoto Protocol[198] commits developed country parties to individual, legally binding targets to limit or reduce their greenhouse gas emissions, adding up to a total cut of at least 5 per cent from 1990 levels in the 'commitment period' of 2008–2012. Developing countries are obliged simply to meet existing commitments. Certain activities since 1990 which have the effect of removing greenhouse gases, such as forestry schemes (so-called 'carbon sinks'), may be offset against emission targets. The Protocol also allows states to aggregate their emissions, thus allowing, for example, European Union members if they wish to be counted together permitting less developed members to increase emissions on the account of other members. In addition, states may receive credits for supporting emission-reducing projects in other developed states ('joint implementation') and in certain circumstances in developing states ('the clean development mechanism'), and the possibility has been provided for trading emission permits, so that some countries

---

[195] Article 7.   [196] Articles 8–10.   [197] See 34 ILM, 1995, p. 1671.
[198] This came into force on 16 February 2005. See D. Freestone and C. Streck, *Legal Aspects of Implementing the Kyoto Protocol Mechanisms: Making Kyoto Work*, Oxford, 2005.

may purchase the unused emission quotas of other countries ('emissions trading').[199]

The Conference of the Parties meets regularly to review the Convention and Protocol. There are two supplementary bodies, one on scientific and technological advice and one on implementation. The financial mechanism of the Convention is operated by the Global Environment Facility, established by the World Bank, UN Environment Programme and UN Development Programme in 1991, while advice is received from the Intergovernmental Panel on Climate Change, established by the World Meteorological Organisation and the UN Environmental Programme.[200] Annex 1 countries (essentially the developed states) must provide annual inventory reports on greenhouse gas emissions to the secretariat, which are subject to in-depth and technical review.[201] Developing countries are subject to weaker reporting requirements. There is a Compliance Committee with facilitative and enforcement branches for parties to the Kyoto Protocol (as amended by the Marrakesh Accords 2001).[202]

Outer space[203]

The Outer Space Treaty, 1967 provides that the exploration and use of outer space is to be carried out for the benefit and in the interests of all states.[204] The harmful contamination of space or celestial bodies is to be avoided, as are adverse changes in the environment of the earth resulting from the introduction of extraterrestrial matter.[205] Nuclear weapons and other weapons of mass destruction are not to be placed in orbit around the earth, installed on celestial bodies or stationed in outer space, and the moon and other celestial bodies are to be used exclusively for peaceful purposes.[206] The Agreement Governing the Activities of States on the

---

[199] Further advances were made at meetings in Buenos Aires 1998, Bonn 2001 and Marrakesh 2001: see unfccc.int/issues/mechanisms.html.

[200] See www.ipcc.ch/.

[201] The requirements are more stringent with regard to the Kyoto Protocol parties.

[202] Note the Fourth Assessment Report of the Intergovernmental Panel on Climate Change, 2007, which analysed the dangers of human-induced climate change. It was endorsed by governments by consensus: see www.ipcc.ch.

[203] See further above, chapter 10, p. 541. See also Birnie and Boyle, *International Law and the Enviroment*, p. 534, and Sands, *Principles*, pp. 382 ff.

[204] Article 1.   [205] Article 9.

[206] Article 4. See also the Principles Relevant to the Use of Nuclear Power Sources in Outer Space, adopted by the UN General Assembly in resolution 47/68 (1992). Goals for radioactive protection and safety are stipulated.

Moon and Other Celestial Bodies, 1979 provides that the moon and its natural resources are the 'common heritage of mankind' and are to be used exclusively for peaceful purposes.[207] Article VII stipulates that in exploring and using the moon, states parties are to take measures to prevent the disruption of the existing balance of its environment whether by introducing adverse changes in that environment or by its harmful contamination through the introduction of extra-environmental matter or otherwise.

There is, in particular, a growing problem with regard to debris located in outer space. Such debris, consisting of millions of objects of varying size in space,[208] constitutes a major hazard to spacecraft. While liability for damage caused by objects launched into space is absolute,[209] the specific problem of space debris has been addressed in the Buenos Aires International Instrument on the Protection of the Environment from Damage Caused by Space Debris, adopted by the International Law Association at its 1994 Conference.[210] The draft emphasises the obligations to co-operate in the prevention of damage to the environment, in promoting the development and exchange of technology to prevent, reduce and control space debris and in the flow and exchange of information, and to hold consultations when there is reason to believe that activities may produce space debris likely to cause damage to the environment or to persons or objects or significant risks thereto. The principle proclaimed by the draft is that each state or international organisation party to the instrument that launches or procures the launching of a space object is internationally liable for damage arising therefrom to another party to the instrument as a consequence of space debris produced by any such object.[211]

---

[207] See articles III and XI.

[208] Such debris may result from pollution from spacecraft, abandoned satellites, orbital explosions and satellite break-ups or hardware released during space launches and other normal manoeuvres. See e.g. L. Roberts, 'Addressing the Problem of Orbital Space Debris: Combining International Regulatory and Liability Regimes', 15 *Boston College International and Comparative Law Review*, 1992, p. 53. See also S. Gorove, 'Towards a Clarification of the Term "Space Objects" – An International Legal and Policy Imperative?', 21 *Journal of Space Law*, 1993, p. 10.

[209] See e.g. B. Hurwitz, *Space Liability for Outer Space Activities*, Dordrecht, 1992, and see further above, chapter 10, p. 546.

[210] Report of the Sixty-sixth Conference, Buenos Aires, 1994, pp. 317 ff. This, of course, is not a binding treaty, but a suggested draft from an influential private organisation.

[211] Article 8 of the draft.

International watercourses[212]

International watercourses are systems of surface waters and ground waters which are situated in more than one state.[213] Such watercourses form a unitary whole and normally flow into a common terminus. While there has historically been some disagreement as to the extent of the watercourse system covered, particularly whether it includes the complete river basin with all associated tributaries and groundwater systems, a broader definition is the approach adopted in recent years. Customary law has developed rules with regard to equal riparian rights to international rivers,[214] but these were not extensive.[215] The International Law Association, a

---

[212] See e.g. Sands, *Principles*, chapter 10, and Birnie and Boyle, *International Law and the Environment*, chapter 6. See also S. McCaffrey, *The Law of International Watercourses*, 2nd edn, Oxford, 2007; O. McIntyre, *Environmental Protection of International Watercourses in International Law*, Aldershot, 2007; A. Rieu-Clarke, *A Fresh Approach to International Law in the Field of Sustainable Development: Lessons from the Law of International Watercourses*, London, 2007; R. Baxter, *The Law of International Waterways*, Cambridge, MA, 1964; C. Bourne, 'International Law and Pollution of International Rivers and Lakes', 21 *University of Toronto Law Journal*, 1971, p. 193; F. Florio, 'Water Pollution and Related Principles of International Law', 17 Canadian YIL, 1979, p. 134; J. Lammers, *Pollution of International Watercourses: A Search for Substantive Rules and Principles*, The Hague, 1984; S. McCaffrey, 'The Law of International Watercourses: Some Recent Developments and Unanswered Questions', 17 *Denver Journal of International Law and Policy*, 1989, p. 505; J. G. Polakiewicz, 'La Responsabilité de l'État en Matière de Pollution des Eaux Fluviales ou Souterraines Internationales', *Journal de Droit International*, 1991, p. 283; H. Ruiz Fabri, 'Règles Coutumières Générales et Droit International Fluvial', AFDI, 1990, p. 818; J. Sette-Camara, 'Pollution of International Rivers', 186 HR, 1984, p. 117, and P. Wouters, 'The Legal Response to Water Conflicts: The UN Watercourses Convention and Beyond', 42 German YIL, 1999, p. 293.

[213] See e.g. article 1(1) of the UN Convention on the Protection and Use of Transboundary Watercourses and International Lakes, 1992 and article 2 of the Convention on the Law of the Non-Navigational Uses of International Watercourses, 1997. See also Report of the International Law Commission on its 46th Session, 1994, p. 197.

[214] See the *Territorial Jurisdiction of the International Commission of the Oder* case, PCIJ, Series A, No. 23, p. 27; 5 AD, p. 83. The Permanent Court noted here that, 'the community of interest in a navigable river becomes the basis of a common legal right, the essential features of which are the perfect equality of all riparian states in the user of the whole course of the river and the exclusion of any preferential privilege of any one riparian state in relation to the others'. This was reaffirmed in the case concerning the *Auditing of Accounts between the Netherlands and France*, arbitral award of 12 March 2004, para. 97. The International Court has noted that, 'Modern development of international law has strengthened this principle for non-navigational uses of international watercourses', the *Gabčíkovo–Nagymaros Project* case, ICJ Reports, 1997, pp. 7, 56; 116 ILR, p. 1.

[215] See the *Lac Lanoux* case, 24 ILR, p. 101. The tribunal noted, for example, that while the interests of riparian states had to be taken into account by a riparian state proposing changes to the river system, there was no rule precluding the use of hydraulic power of

private organisation of international lawyers, proposed the Helsinki Rules on the Uses of the Waters of International Rivers in 1966,[216] in which it was noted that each basin state was entitled to a reasonable and equitable share in the beneficial use of the waters and that all states were obliged to prevent new forms of water pollution that would cause substantial injury in the territory of other basin states.[217]

In 1992, the Convention on the Protection and Use of Transboundary Watercourses and International Lakes was adopted in Helsinki within the framework of the UN Economic Commission for Europe.[218] Under this Convention, all parties must take all appropriate measures to prevent, control and reduce any significant adverse effect on the environment resulting from a change in the conditions of transboundary waters caused by a human activity. Such effects on the environment include effects on human health and safety, flora, fauna, soil, air, water, climate, landscape and also effects on the cultural heritage.[219] In taking such measures, states parties are to be guided by the precautionary principle[220] and by the polluter-pays principle, by which the costs of pollution prevention, control and reduction measures are to be borne by the polluter.[221] Each party undertakes to set emission limits for discharges from point sources into surface waters based on best available technology[222] and to define, where appropriate, water-quality objectives and adopt water-quality criteria[223] for the purpose of preventing, controlling and reducing transboundary impact. The measures to be taken must ensure, for example, the application of low- and non-waste technology; the prior licensing of waste-water discharge; the application of biological or equivalent processes to municipal waste water; the use of environmental impact assessments and sustainable water-resources management.[224]

The Convention also calls for the parties to establish monitoring programmes, to co-operate in research and development projects and to

---

international watercourses without a prior agreement between the interested states, *ibid.*, p. 130.
[216] Report of the Fifty-second Conference, 1966, p. 484.
[217] See also the Rules on Water Pollution in an International Drainage Basin adopted by the ILA in 1982, Report of the Sixtieth Conference, 1982, p. 535, and the Rules on International Groundwaters adopted in 1986, Report of the Sixty-second Conference, 1986. See also the work of the Institut de Droit International, *Annuaire de l'Institut de Droit International*, 1979, p. 193.
[218] See also the Protocol on Civil Liability and Compensation for Damage Caused by the Transboundary Effects of Industrial Accidents on Transboundary Waters, 2003.
[219] Articles 1(2) and 2(1).   [220] See above, p. 867.   [221] See above, p. 870.
[222] This is defined in Annex I.   [223] See Annex III.   [224] Article 3.

exchange relevant information as early as possible.[225] Riparian parties are to enter into bilateral or multilateral agreements or arrangements in order to co-ordinate their activities and to consult together at the request of any one riparian party.[226] Article 7 provides that the parties 'shall support appropriate international efforts to elaborate rules, criteria and procedures in the field of responsibility and liability'.

The Convention on the Law of the Non-Navigational Uses of International Watercourses, 1997 provides that watercourse states shall in their respective territories utilise an international watercourse in an 'equitable and reasonable manner'. In particular, optimal utilisation must be consistent with adequate protection of the watercourse.[227] Factors relevant to equitable and reasonable utilisation include, in addition to physical factors of a natural character and the social and economic needs of the watercourse states concerned, the 'conservation, protection, development and economy of use of the water resources of the watercourse and the costs of measures taken to that effect'.[228] Article 7 provides that watercourse states shall take all appropriate measures to prevent the causing of significant harm to other watercourse states. Where such harm is caused, consultations are to take place in order to eliminate or mitigate such harm and with regard to compensation where appropriate. Articles 9 and 11 provide for regular exchanges of data and information, while watercourse states are to exchange information and consult in particular on the possible effects of planned measures on the condition of an international watercourse. Before a watercourse state implements or permits the implementation of planned measures which may have a significant adverse effect upon other watercourse states, it is to provide such states with timely notification and sufficient technical data and information for the evaluation of the possible effects of the planned measures.[229] Unless otherwise agreed, the notified states have a period of six months for such evaluation during which exchanges of data and information are to take place and the planned measures are not to be implemented without the consent of the notified states. If no reply to the notification is received, the notifying state may

---

[225] Articles 4–6 and 11–13. Provisions regarding notification about critical situations and mutual asssistance appear in articles 14 and 15.

[226] Articles 9 and 10.

[227] Article 5. This provision was expressly referred to by the International Court in the *Gabčíkovo–Nagymaros Project* case, ICJ Reports, 1997, pp. 7, 80; 116 ILR, p. 1. See also article 8 which emphasises that watercourse states shall co-operate in order to attain optimal utilisation and adequate protection of an international watercourse.

[228] Article 6.   [229] Article 12.

proceed to implement the planned measures. If a reply is received, the states are to consult and negotiate with a view to arriving at an equitable resolution of the situation.[230] Where a watercourse state has serious reason to believe that measures that may have a significant adverse impact are being planned, it may itself set in motion the above procedures.[231]

Article 20 stipulates that watercourse states shall protect and preserve the ecosystems of international watercourses[232] and shall act to prevent, reduce and control pollution[233] of an international watercourse that may cause significant harm to other watercourse states or to their environment. Watercourse states are to take all necessary measures to prevent the introduction of species, alien or new, into an international watercourse which may have effects detrimental to the ecosystem of the watercourse resulting in significant harm to other watercourse states.[234]

It is thus clear that the international community is coming to terms with the need to protect the environment of international watercourses.[235] How evolving international environmental rules relate to the more traditional principles of international law was one of the issues before the International Court in the *Gabčíkovo–Nagymaros Project* case.[236] Hungary and Czechoslovakia entered into a treaty in 1977 by which there would be created on the Danube between the two states a barrage system, a dam, a reservoir, hydro-electric power stations and a 25-kilometre canal for diverting the Danube from its original course through a system of locks. A dispute developed in the light of Hungary's growing environmental concerns. Hungary suspended work on the project in 1989, while Czechoslovakia (now the Czech and Slovak Federal Republic) proceeded with a 'provisional solution' as from 1991, which involved damming the

---

[230] Articles 11–17.

[231] Article 18. Article 19 provides for an expedited procedure where there is the utmost urgency in the implementation of planned measures.

[232] See also article 23 with regard to measures necessary to protect and preserve the marine environment.

[233] Pollution is here defined as 'any detrimental alteration in the composition or quality of the waters of an international watercourse which results directly or indirectly from human conduct', article 21(1).

[234] Article 22.

[235] Note that a variety of regional and bilateral agreements and arrangements exist with regard to international watercourses: see e.g. the agreements concerning the International Commission of the Rhine, the US–Canadian International Joint Commission and provisions concerning the Zambezi River System and the Niger Basin. See Sands, *Principles*, pp. 459 ff., and Birnie and Boyle, *International Law and the Environment*, pp. 323 ff.

[236] ICJ Reports, 1997, p. 7; 116 ILR, p. 1.

Danube at a point on Czechoslovakian territory. In 1992, Hungary announced the termination of the treaty of 1977 and related instruments. The case came before the International Court ultimately by way of a Special Agreement in 1993 between Hungary and Slovakia (the successor to the former Czech and Slovak Federal Republic in so far as the project was concerned). The case essentially revolved around the relationship between the treaty and subsequent environmental concerns. The Court emphasised that newly developed norms of environmental law were relevant for the implementation of the treaty,[237] while 'The awareness of the vulnerability of the environment and the recognition that environmental risks have to be assessed on a continuous basis have become much stronger in the years since the treaty's conclusion.'[238] However, the Court found that the treaty was still in force and Hungary was not entitled to terminate it.[239]

Ultra-hazardous activities[240]

It has been argued that ultra-hazardous activities form a distinct category in the field of international environmental law and one in which the principle of strict or absolute liability operates. The definition of what constitutes such activity, of course, is somewhat uncertain, but the characterisation can be taken to revolve around the serious consequences that are likely to flow from any damage that results, rather than upon the likelihood of pollution occurring from the activity in question. The focus therefore is upon the significant or exceptional risk of severe transnational damage.[241] The effect of categorising a particular activity as ultra-hazardous would, it appears, be to accept the strict liability principle rather than the due diligence standard commonly regarded as the general rule in pollution

---

[237] ICJ Reports, 1997, p. 67.   [238] Ibid., p. 68.

[239] Ibid., pp. 76 and 82. Note that in March 2003, the establishment of a Water Co-operation Facility to mediate in disputes between countries sharing a single river basin was announced: see http://news.bbc.co.uk/1/hi/sci/tech/2872427.stm.

[240] See e.g. Sands, Principles, chapter 12, and Birnie and Boyle, International Law and the Environment, chapters 8 and 9. See also D. A. Bagwell, 'Hazardous and Noxious Substances', 62 Tulane Law Review, 1988, p. 433; L. F. Goldie, 'Concepts of Strict and Absolute Liability and the Ranking of Liability in Terms of Relative Exposure to Risk', 16 Netherlands YIL, 1985, p. 247; Barboza, 'International Liability', pp. 331 ff.; W. Jenks, 'The Scope and Nature of Ultra-Hazardous Liability in International Law', 117 HR, 1966, p. 99; Handl, 'State Liability', pp. 553 ff., and R. J. Dupuy, La Responsabilité des États pour les Dommages d'Origine Technologique et Industrielle, Paris, 1976, pp. 206–9.

[241] Handl, 'State Liability', p. 554.

situations.[242] In other words, the state under whose territory or jurisdiction the activity took place would be liable irrespective of fault. This
exception to the general principle can be justified as a method of moving
the burden of proof and shifting the loss clearly from the victim to the
state. It would also operate as a further incentive to states to take action
in areas of exceptional potential harm.

In determining what areas of activity could be characterised as ultra-
hazardous, some caution needs to be exercised. There can be little doubt
that nuclear activities fall within this category as a general rule, but beyond
this there appears to be no agreement. The Convention on International
Liability for Damage caused by Space Objects, 1972 specifically provides
that a launching state shall be absolutely liable to pay compensation for
damage caused by its space objects on the surface of the earth,[243] but this
is the only clear example of its kind.

Nuclear activities [244]

The use of nuclear technology brings with it risks as well as benefits and
the accident at the Chernobyl nuclear reactor in 1986[245] brought home to
international opinion just how devastating the consequences of a nuclear
mishap could be. Concern in this area had hitherto focused upon the
issue of nuclear weapons. In 1963 the Treaty Banning Nuclear Weapons
Testing in the Atmosphere, Outer Space and Under Water was signed.[246]
However, France and China did not become parties to this treaty and continued atmospheric nuclear testing. Australia and New Zealand sought
a declaration from the International Court that French atmospheric nuclear testing was contrary to international law, but the Court decided the
case on the basis that a subsequent French decision to end such testing was

---

[242] See above, p. 853.   [243] See above, p. 546.

[244] See e.g. Sands, *Chernobyl: Law and Communication*; Boyle, 'Nuclear Energy' and 'Chernobyl'; J. C. Woodliffe, 'Tackling Transboundary Environmental Hazards in Cases of
Emergency: The Emerging Legal Framework' in *Current Issues in European and International Law* (eds. R. White and B. Smythe), London, 1990, and Woodliffe, 'Chernobyl:
Four Years On', 39 ICLQ, 1990, p. 461.

[245] See Sands, *Chernobyl: Law and Communication*, pp. 1–2. See also IAEA, *Summary Report
on the Post Accident Review Meeting on the Chernobyl Accident*, Vienna, 1986.

[246] See also the Treaty on the Prohibition of the Emplacement of Nuclear Weapons and other
Weapons of Mass Destruction on the Sea-Bed, 1971; the Treaty for the Prohibition of
Nuclear Weapons in Latin America, 1967 and the South Pacific Nuclear Free Zone Treaty,
1985.

binding and thus the issue was moot.[247] In response to renewed French nuclear testing in the South Pacific in 1995, albeit underground rather than atmospheric, New Zealand asked the International Court to review the situation pursuant to the 1974 judgment and declare that France was acting illegally as being likely to cause the introduction into the marine environment of radioactive material and in failing to conduct an environmental impact assessment. While the Court referred to 'the obligations of states to respect and protect the natural environment', it declared that the request had to be dismissed as not falling within the relevant paragraph of the 1974 judgment permitting a re-examination of the situation since the latter judgment had concerned atmospheric tests alone.[248] Measures to prevent the spread of nuclear weapons were adopted in the Nuclear Non-Proliferation Treaty of 1968, although the possession itself of nuclear weapons does not contravene international law.[249]

A variety of international organisations are now involved to some extent in the process of developing rules and principles concerning nuclear activities and environmental protection. The International Atomic Energy Agency, to take the prime example, was established in 1956 in order to encourage the development of nuclear power, but particularly since the Chernobyl accident its nuclear safety role has been emphasised. The Convention on Assistance in Cases of Nuclear Emergency, 1986, for example, gave it a co-ordinating function and an obligation to provide appropriate resources where so requested.[250] The IAEA has established a series of standards and guidelines including, for example, in the context of the design, construction and operation of nuclear power plants, although such standards do not have the force of law.[251] Other international organisations also have a role to play in the sphere of nuclear activities.[252]

---

[247] See the *Nuclear Tests* cases, ICJ Reports, 1974, p. 253; 57 ILR, p. 398.

[248] *Request for an Examination of the Situation in Accordance with Paragraph 63 of the Court's Judgment of 1974 in the Nuclear Tests Case*, ICJ Reports, 1995, pp. 288, 305–6; 106 ILR, pp. 1, 27–8.

[249] See e.g. M. N. Shaw, 'Nuclear Weapons and International Law' in *Nuclear Weapons and International Law* (ed. I. Pogany), London, 1987, p. 1. See also below, chapter 21, p. 1187.

[250] See further below, p. 891.

[251] Note, however, that under the Geneva Convention on the High Seas, 1958, states are to take account of IAEA standards in preventing pollution of the seas from the dumping of nuclear waste.

[252] E.g. EURATOM (established in 1957), the Nuclear Energy Agency of the OECD (established in 1957) and the ILO (International Labour Organisation). See Boyle, 'Nuclear Energy', pp. 266–8.

The provision of information

There appears to be a general principle requiring that information be provided in certain situations[253] and several bilateral agreements have expressed this in the context of nuclear accidents.[254] In general, such agreements provide that each state is to inform the other without delay of any emergency resulting from civil nuclear activities and any other incident that could have radiological consequences for the second state. Reciprocal information systems are set up and warning notification centres established. Such agreements, however, do not cover exchange of military information.[255]

Following the Chernobyl accident and the failure of the USSR to provide immediate information, the Vienna Convention on Early Notification of a Nuclear Accident, 1986 was rapidly adopted, under the auspices of the IAEA. This provides that in the event of a nuclear accident, the relevant state shall 'forthwith notify, directly or through the International Atomic Energy Agency... those states which are or may be physically affected... of the nuclear accident, its nature, the time of its occurrence and its exact location'. Additionally, such states must be promptly provided with information relevant to minimising the radiological consequences.[256] States are to respond promptly to a request for further information or consultations sought by an affected state.[257]

It is also to be noted that although the Convention does not apply to military nuclear accidents, the five nuclear weapons states made Statements of Voluntary Application indicating that they would apply the Convention to all nuclear accidents, including those not specified in that agreement.[258]

Since this Convention was adopted, a variety of bilateral agreements have been signed which have been more wide-ranging than those signed beforehand and which in some cases have gone beyond the provisions specified in the Notification Convention. The agreements signed by the

---

[253] See above, p. 865. See also Principle 20 of the Stockholm Declaration and Principle 9 of the Rio Declaration.

[254] The first was concluded between France and Belgium in 1966 concerning the Ardennes Nuclear Power Station. Other examples include Switzerland–Federal Republic of Germany, 1978 and France–UK, 1983. The latter agreement was supplemented by a formal arrangement between the UK Nuclear Installations Inspectorate and the French equivalent for the continuous exchange of information on safety issues.

[255] See Woodliffe, 'Tackling Transboundary Environmental Hazards', at pp. 117–20.

[256] Article 2. See also article 5.   [257] Article 6.

[258] See text in 25 ILM, 1986, p. 1394.

UK with Norway, the Netherlands and Denmark during 1987–8, for example, specify that there is an obligation to notify the other parties if there is an accident or activity in the territory of the notifying state from which a transboundary effect of radiological safety significance is likely and additionally where abnormal levels of radiation are registered that are not caused by release from facilities or activities in the notifying state's territory. Extensive provisions dealing with exchanges of information are also included.[259]

The provision of assistance[260]

The earliest treaty providing for assistance in the event of radiation accidents was the Nordic Mutual Assistance Agreement, 1963. This dealt with the general terms of assistance, the advisory and co-ordinating role of the IAEA, financing, liability and privileges and immunities. The United Nations established the UN Disaster Relief Office (UNDRO) in 1972[261] and this provides assistance in pre-disaster planning. In 1977 the IAEA concluded an agreement with UNDRO with the purpose of co-ordinating their assistance activities in the nuclear accident field and in 1984 published a series of guidelines[262] setting out the mechanics of co-operation between states, including references to the problems of costs, liability, privileges and immunities.

In 1986, following the Chernobyl accident and at the same time as the Notification Convention, the Vienna Convention on Assistance in the Case of a Nuclear Accident or Radiological Emergency was adopted. This provides that a state in need of assistance in the event of a nuclear accident or radiological emergency may call for such assistance from any other state party either directly or through the IAEA.[263] This applies whether or not

---

[259] See e.g. Woodliffe, 'Chernobyl', p. 464. See the European Community Council Directive 87/600 of December 1987, which provides for the early exchange of information in the event of a radiological emergency. See also the EC Environmental Information Directive 1990 providing for a right of access to environmental information; article 9 of the Convention for the Protection of the Marine Environment of the North-East Atlantic, 1992 and Chapter III of the Convention on Civil Liability for Damage Resulting from Activities Dangerous to the Environment, 1993.

[260] See e.g. A. O. Adede, *The IAEA Notification and Assistance Conventions in Case of a Nuclear Accident: Landmarks in the History of Multilateral Treaty-Making*, London, 1987.

[261] A Disaster Relief Coordinator was provided for in General Assembly resolution 2816 (XXVI). See Sands, *Chernobyl: Law and Communication*, p. 45.

[262] Guidelines for Mutual Emergency Assistance Arrangements in Connection with a Nuclear Accident or Radiological Emergency, Sands, *Chernobyl: Law and Communication*, p. 199.

[263] Article 2(1).

such accident or emergency originated within its territory, jurisdiction or control. States requesting assistance (which may include medical assistance and help with regard to the temporary relocation of displaced persons[264]) must provide details of the type of assistance required and other necessary information.[265] The IAEA must respond to a request for assistance by making available appropriate resources allocated for this purpose and by transmitting promptly the request to other states and international organisations possessing the necessary resources. In addition, if requested by the state seeking assistance, the IAEA will co-ordinate the assistance at the international level. The IAEA is also required to collect and disseminate to the states parties information concerning the availability of experts, equipment and materials and with regard to methodologies, techniques and available research data relating to the response to such situations.[266] The general range of assistance that can be provided by the Agency is laid down in some detail.[267]

In general terms, the Assistance Convention seeks to balance considerations relating to the sovereignty of the requesting state,[268] the legitimate rights of the assisting state or states[269] and the interests of the international community in rendering rapid assistance to affected states. Whether the balance achieved is a fair one is open to discussion.[270]

Nuclear safety

The Convention on Nuclear Safety was adopted by the IAEA in 1994. This emphasises that responsibility for nuclear safety rests with the state having jurisdiction over a nuclear installation[271] and obliges states parties to take legislative and administrative measures to implement Convention obligations[272] via a regulatory body[273] and to submit reports to periodic

---

[264] Article 2(5).   [265] Article 2(2).   [266] Article 5.   [267] *Ibid.*

[268] Under article 3(a), and unless otherwise agreed, the requesting state has the overall direction, control, co-ordination and supervision of the assistance within its territory.

[269] Under article 7, the assisting state is entitled, unless it offers its assistance without costs, to be reimbursed for all the costs incurred by it, which are to be provided promptly, and under article 10(2), unless otherwise agreed, a requesting state is liable to compensate the assisting state for all loss of or damage to equipment or materials and for the death of or injury to personnel of the assisting party or persons acting on its behalf. There is no provision dealing with liability for damage caused by the assisting state. See also article 8 dealing with privileges and immunities.

[270] See e.g. Sands, *Chernobyl: Law and Communication*, p. 47, and Woodliffe, 'Tackling Transboundary Environmental Hazards', p. 127.

[271] Defined as 'a land-based civil nuclear power plant', article 2(1).

[272] Articles 4 and 7.   [273] Article 8.

review meetings of all parties.[274] The Convention provides that operators of nuclear installations must be licensed[275] and it is the operators that remain primarily responsible for the safety of the installations.[276] The Convention specifies a number of safety considerations, but these are not in the form of binding obligations upon the parties.[277]

Civil liability[278]

In addition to the issue of the responsibility or liability of the state for the activity under consideration, the question of the proceedings that may be taken by the individual victims is also raised. One possible approach is to permit the victim to have access to the legal system of the foreign polluter and thus to all remedies available on a non-discriminatory basis. This would have the effect of transforming the transboundary pollution into a national matter.[279] This approach is evident in some treaties.[280] The problem is that while placing the foreign victim on a par with nationals within the domestic legal system of the offender, it depends for its value upon the legal system possessing internal legislation of appropriate substantive content. This is not always the case. There are, however, several international agreements dealing specifically with the question of civil liability in the sphere of nuclear activities which operate on the basis of certain common general principles.

The OECD Paris Convention on Third Party Liability in the Field of Nuclear Energy, 1960[281] provides that the operator of a nuclear installation shall be liable for damage to or loss of life of any person and damage to or loss of any property (other than the nuclear installation and associated property or means of transport). The IAEA Vienna Convention on Civil Liability for Nuclear Damage, 1963 has similar provisions, but is aimed at

---

[274] Articles 5 and 20–5. The IAEA is to provide the secretariat for the meetings of the parties, article 28.

[275] Article 7(2)ii.   [276] Article 9.

[277] Articles 10–19. See also the Joint Convention on the Safety of Spent Fuel and Radioactive Waste Management, 1997, which is based upon the IAEA's Principles of Radioactive Waste Management, 1995 and the Code of Practice on the International Transboundary Movement of Radioactive Waste, 1990. Its main provisions are similar to those of the Nuclear Safety Convention.

[278] See e.g. Birnie and Boyle, *International Law and the Environment*, pp. 476 ff., and Sands, *Principles*, pp. 904 ff.

[279] See e.g. Boyle, 'Nuclear Energy', pp. 297–8.

[280] See e.g. the Nordic Convention on the Protection of the Environment, 1974. See also OECD Recommendations C(74)224, C(76)55 and C(77)28.

[281] Together with Protocols of 1964 and 1982.

global participation. However, both the Paris Convention and the Vienna Convention systems have suffered from relatively limited participation and a Joint Protocol was adopted in 1988 linking the Paris and Vienna Convention regimes, so that parties under each of these conventions may benefit from both of them. In 1997 a Protocol to Amend the 1963 Vienna Convention and a Convention on Supplementary Compensation for Nuclear Damage were adopted by over eighty states. These instruments increased the scope of liability of operators to a limit of not less than 300 million Special Drawing Rights (approx 400 million US dollars) and the geographical scope of the Convention. In addition, an improved definition of nuclear damage, to include, for example, environmental damage, was provided.[282]

These conventions operate upon similar principles. It is the actual operator of the nuclear installation or ship that is to bear the loss[283] and this is on the basis of absolute or strict liability. Accordingly, no proof of fault or negligence is required. The conventions require operators to possess appropriate liability insurance or other financial security under the conditions laid down by the competent public authorities, unless the operator is itself a state,[284] and the relevant states are to ensure that claims up to the liability limits are met.[285] This recognition of the residual responsibility of the state is unique.[286] The amount of liability of the operator may, however, be limited.[287] The relevant conventions also determine

---

[282] See e.g. 36 ILM, 1997, p. 1454, and *ibid.*, p. 1473. See also www.iaea.or.at/worldatom/Documents/Legal/protamend.shtm and www.iaea.or.at/worldatom/Documents/Legal/supcomp.shtml. Note also the Brussels Convention on the Liability of Operators of Nuclear Ships, 1962, which provides that the operator of a nuclear ship shall be absolutely liable for any nuclear damage upon proof that such damage has been caused by a nuclear incident involving the nuclear fuel of, or radioactive products or waste produced in, such ship, and the Convention Relating to Civil Liability in the Field of Maritime Carriage of Nuclear Material, 1971, which provides that a person held liable for damage caused by a nuclear incident shall be exonerated from such liability if the operator of a nuclear installation is liable for such damage under either the Paris or Vienna Conventions.

[283] A carrier or handler of nuclear material may be regarded as such an operator where the latter consents and the necessary legislative framework so provides: see e.g. article 4(d) of the Paris Convention.

[284] See e.g. article 10 of the Paris Convention, article VII of the Vienna Convention and article III of the Brussels Convention on Nuclear Ships.

[285] *Ibid.*

[286] Cf. the Convention on Civil Liability for Oil Pollution Damage, 1969.

[287] See articles V and VI of the Vienna Convention as amended in 1997, articles 7 and 8 of the Paris Convention and articles III and V of the Brussels Convention on Nuclear Ships.

which state has jurisdiction over claims against operators or their insurers. In general, jurisdiction lies with the state where the nuclear incident occurred, although where a nuclear incident takes place outside the territory of a contracting party or where the place of the nuclear incident cannot be determined with certainty, jurisdiction will lie with the courts of the contracting party in whose territory the nuclear installation of the operator liable is situated.[288] Judgments given by the competent courts are enforceable in the territory of any contracting party.

The issue of inter-state claims is more difficult, as was demonstrated by the aftermath of the Chernobyl accident. Many states have paid compensation to persons affected within their jurisdiction by the fallout from that accident, but while positions have been reserved with regard to claims directly against the former USSR, it seems that problems relating to the obligations actually owed by states and the doubt over the requisite standard of care have prevented such claims from actually being made.[289]

Hazardous wastes[290]

The increasing problem of the disposal of toxic and hazardous wastes and the practice of dumping in the Third World, with its attendant severe health risks, has prompted international action.[291] The Oslo Convention for the Prevention of Marine Pollution by Dumping from Ships and Aircraft, 1972[292] provides for a ban on the dumping of certain substances[293] and for controls to be placed on the dumping of others.[294] The London Convention on the Prevention of Marine Pollution by Dumping of Wastes and Other Matter, 1972[295] prohibits the dumping of wastes except as provided in the Convention itself, and this is strictly controlled.

---

[288] Article 13 of the Paris Convention, article XI of the Vienna Convention and article X of the Brussels Convention on Nuclear Ships.

[289] See e.g. Sands, *Chernobyl: Law and Communication*, pp. 26–8.

[290] See e.g. Sands, *Principles*, chapter 12, and Birnie and Boyle, *International Law and the Environment*, chapter 8.

[291] See *Keesing's Record of World Events*, pp. 36788–9 (1989). See also Principle 6 of the Stockholm Declaration 1972 and Principle 14 of the Rio Declaration 1992.

[292] This is limited essentially to the North-East Atlantic area.

[293] Listed in Annex I.   [294] Listed in Annex II.   [295] This is a global instrument.

In 1988, the Organisation of African Unity adopted a resolution proclaiming the dumping of nuclear and industrial wastes in Africa to be a crime against Africa and its people. In 1991, the OAU adopted the Bamako Convention on the Ban of the Import into Africa and the Control of Transboundary Movement and Management of Hazardous Wastes within Africa,[296] under which parties are to prohibit the import of all hazardous wastes for any reason into Africa by non-parties and to prohibit the dumping at sea of such wastes. The OECD has adopted a number of Decisions and Recommendations concerning the transfrontier movements and exports of hazardous wastes.[297] In 1989 the OECD adopted a Recommendation[298] noting that the polluter-pays principle should apply to accidents involving hazardous substances. The Basle Convention on the Control of Transboundary Movements of Hazardous Wastes and Their Disposal, 1989 provides that parties shall prohibit the export of hazardous and other wastes to parties which have prohibited the import of such wastes and have so informed the other parties. In the absence of prohibition by the importing state, export to that state of such wastes is only permissible where consent in writing to the specific import is obtained.[299] The Convention also provides that any proposed transboundary movement of hazardous wastes must be notified to the competent authorities of the states concerned by the state of export. The latter shall not allow the generator or exporter of hazardous wastes to commence the transboundary movement without the written consent of the state of import and any state of transit.[300]

In 1990, the IAEA adopted a Code of Practice on the International Transboundary Movement of Radioactive Waste,[301] emphasising that every state should ensure that such movements take place only with the prior notification and consent of the sending, receiving and transit states in accordance with their respective laws and regulations. Appropriate regulatory authorities were called for, as well as the necessary administrative

---

[296] 30 ILM, 1991, p. 773.
[297] See e.g. 23 ILM, 1984, p. 214; 25 ILM, 1986, p. 1010 and 28 ILM, 1989, pp. 277 and 259.
[298] C(89)88.
[299] Article 4. Note also the Convention on the Prior Informed Consent Procedure for Certain Hazardous Chemicals and Pesticides in International Trade, 1998.
[300] Article 6.   [301] 30 ILM, 1991, p. 556.

and technical capacity to manage and dispose of such waste in a manner consistent with international safety standards.[302]

The Convention on the Transboundary Effects of Industrial Accidents adopted in 1992 applies to industrial accidents in an installation or during transportation resulting from activities involving hazardous substances (identified in Annex I). It does not apply to nuclear accidents, accidents at military installations, dam failures, land-based transport accidents, accidental release of genetically modified organisms, accidents caused by activities in the marine environment or spills of oil or other harmful substances at sea.[303] The Convention provides that parties of origin[304] should identify hazardous activities within the jurisdiction and ensure that affected parties are notified of any such proposed or existing activity. Consultations are to take place on the identification of those hazardous activities that may have transboundary effects.[305] A variety of preventive measures are posited.[306] In particular, the party of origin shall require the operator in charge of such hazardous activity to demonstrate the safe performance of that activity by the provision of information.[307] Parties are to develop policies on the siting of new hazardous activities and on significant modifications to existing hazardous activities, while adequate emergency preparedness to respond to industrial accidents is to be established and maintained.[308] An industrial accident notification system is established,[309] while by article 13 the parties 'shall support appropriate international efforts to elaborate rules, criteria and procedures in the field of responsibility and liability'.[310]

---

[302] See now also the Principles of Radioactive Waste Management, 1995 and the Joint Convention on the Safety of Spent Fuel and Radioactive Waste Management, 1997.

[303] Article 2(2).

[304] I.e. parties under whose jurisdiction an industrial accident occurs or is capable of occurring, article 1(g).

[305] Article 4. See also Annexes II and III.   [306] See article 6 and Annex IV.

[307] Article 6(2) and Annex V.   [308] Articles 7 and 8 and Annex V.

[309] Article 10 and Annex IX.

[310] See also the Memorandum of Understanding Concerning Establishment of the Inter-Organisation Programme for the Sound Management of Chemicals, 1995 signed by the Food and Agriculture Organisation, the International Labour Organisation, the Organisation for Economic Co-operation and Development, the UN Industrial Development Programme, the UN Environment Programme and the World Health Organisation. The areas for co-ordination include the international assessment of chemical risks, information exchange and the prevention of illegal international traffic in toxic and dangerous products: see 34 ILM, 1995, p. 1311.

Marine pollution[311]

Marine pollution can arise from a variety of sources, including the operation of shipping, dumping at sea,[312] activities on the seabed[313] and the effects of pollution originating on the land and entering the seas.[314] There are a large number of treaties, bilateral, regional and multilateral, dealing with such issues and some of the more significant of them in the field of pollution from ships will be briefly noted.

Pollution from ships

The International Convention for the Prevention of Pollution of the Sea by Oil, 1954 basically prohibits the discharge of oil within 50 miles of land and has been essentially superseded by the International Convention for

---

[311] See e.g. Sands, *Principles*, chapter 9; Birnie and Boyle, *International Law and the Environment*, chapter 7; R. Churchill and A. V. Lowe, *The Law of the Sea*, 3rd edn, Manchester, 1999, chapter 15; A. E. Boyle, 'Marine Pollution under the Law of the Sea Convention', 79 AJIL, 1985, p. 347; L. Caflisch, 'International Law and Ocean Pollution: The Present and the Future', 8 *Revue Belge de Droit International*, 1972, p. 7, and O. Schachter, 'The Value of the 1982 UN Convention on the Law of the Sea: Preserving our Freedoms and Protecting the Environment', 23 *Ocean Development and International Law*, 1992, p. 55.

[312] See above, p. 620, and Churchill and Lowe, *Law of the Sea*, p. 363. See also D. Bodansky, 'Protecting the Marine Environment from Vessel-Source Pollution: UNCLOS III and Beyond', 18 *Ecology Law Quarterly*, 1991, p. 719, and Y. Sasamura, 'Prevention and Control of Marine Pollution from Ships', 25 *Law of the Sea Institute Proceedings*, 1993, p. 306.

[313] See Churchill and Lowe, *Law of the Sea*, p. 370.

[314] Articles 194 and 207 of the Convention on the Law of the Sea, 1982 provide in general terms for states to reduce marine pollution from land-based sources. Note that the Montreal Guidelines on the Protection of the Environment Against Pollution from Land-Based Sources, 1985 built upon article 207. A number of regional conventions (many of them UN Environment Programme Regional Seas Conventions) lay down specific rules dealing with the control of particular substances: see e.g. the Barcelona Convention for the Protection of the Mediterranean Sea Against Pollution, 1976 and its two Protocols of 1980 and 1982; the Kuwait Regional Convention for Co-operation on Protection of the Marine Environment from Pollution, 1978 and Protocols of 1978, 1989 and 1990; the Abidjan Convention for Co-operation in the Protection and Development of the Marine and Coastal Environment of the West and Central Africa Region, 1981 and Protocol of 1981; the Lima Convention for the Protection of the Marine Environment and Coastal Areas of the South-East Pacific, 1981 and Protocols; the Cartagena Convention for the Protection and Development of the Marine Environment of the Wider Caribbean Region, 1983 and two Protocols of 1983 and 1990; the Convention on the Protection of the Black Sea Against Pollution, 1992; the Convention for the Protection of the Marine Environment of the North-East Atlantic, 1992 and the Convention on the Protection of the Marine Environment of the Baltic Sea Area, 1992.

the Prevention of Pollution from Ships, 1973,[315] which is concerned with all forms of non-accidental pollution from ships apart from dumping. In Annexes and other amendments and Protocols to the Convention,[316] detailed standards are laid down covering oil, noxious liquid substances in bulk, harmful substances carried by sea in packaged form, sewage and garbage. The Convention covers ships flying the flag of, or operated under the authority of, a state party, but does not apply to warships or state-owned ships used only on governmental non-commercial service.

Article 211(2) of the Convention on the Law of the Sea, 1982 provides that states are to legislate for the prevention, reduction and control of pollution of the marine environment from vessels flying their flag or of their registry. Such rules are to have the same effect at least as that of generally accepted international rules and standards established through the competent international organisation[317] or general diplomatic conference. States are also to ensure that the ships of their nationality or of their registry comply with 'applicable international rules and standards' and with domestic rules governing the prevention, reduction and control of pollution.[318] In addition, coastal states have jurisdiction physically to inspect, and, where the evidence so warrants, commence proceedings against ships in their territorial waters, where there are clear grounds for believing that the ship concerned has violated domestic or international pollution regulations.[319] It should also be noted that a state in whose port a vessel is may take legal proceedings against that vessel not only where it is alleged to have violated that state's pollution laws or applicable international rules in its territorial sea or economic zone,[320] but also in respect of any discharge outside its internal waters, territorial sea or exclusive economic zone in violation of applicable international rules and standards.[321]

---

[315] Known as the MARPOL Convention. This was modified by Protocols of 1978 and 1997 and has been further amended: see www.imo.org/Conventions/contents.asp?doc_id=678&topic_id=258.

[316] Note e.g. that Annexes I and II are fully binding, while Annexes III, IV and V are options which a state may declare it does not accept when first becoming a party to the Convention, article 14.

[317] The International Maritime Organisation: see www.imo.org.

[318] Article 217.   [319] Article 220(2).   [320] Article 220(1).

[321] Article 218, a provision characterised as 'truly innovatory' by Churchill and Lowe, Law of the Sea, p. 350.

Where an accident takes place, the Convention Relating to Intervention on the High Seas in Cases of Oil Pollution Casualties, 1969[322] permits states parties to take such measures on the high seas as may be necessary to prevent, mitigate or eliminate grave and imminent danger to their coastline or related interests from pollution or threat of pollution of the sea by oil.[323] An International Convention on Oil Pollution Preparedness, Response and Co-operation was signed in London in November 1990, with the purpose of ensuring prompt and effective action in the event of a pollution incident. It requires ships to carry detailed plans for dealing with pollution emergencies. Pollution incidents must be reported without delay and, in the event of a serious incident, other states likely to be affected must be informed and details given to the International Maritime Organisation. National and regional systems for dealing with such incidents are encouraged and the contracting parties agree to co-operate and provide advisory services, technical support and equipment at the request of other parties.[324]

As far as liability is concerned, the Convention on Civil Liability for Oil Pollution Damage, 1969 provides that where oil escaping from a ship causes damage on the territory or territorial sea of a contracting party, the shipowner is strictly liable for such damage, which includes the costs of both preventive measures and further loss or damage caused by such measures.[325] This liability is limited, however, unless the pollution is the

---

[322] The adoption of this Convention followed the *Torrey Canyon* incident in 1967 in which a ship aground, although on the high seas, was bombed in order to reduce the risk of oil pollution: see Churchill and Lowe, *Law of the Sea*, p. 354. See also the Report of the Home Office, Cmnd 3246 (1967).

[323] This was extended by a Protocol of 1973 to cover pollution from substances other than oil. Note that the International Convention on Salvage, 1989 seeks to integrate environmental factors into the salvage rewards system.

[324] See e.g. the Bonn Agreement for Co-operation in Dealing with Pollution of the North Sea by Oil, 1969 and the Agreement for Co-operation in Dealing with Pollution of the North Sea by Oil and Other Harmful Substances, 1983. Many of the UN Environment Programme Regional Seas Conventions have Protocols dealing with emergency situations: see e.g. Sands, *Principles*, pp. 399 ff.

[325] Except where the damage results from war or acts of God; is wholly caused by an act or omission done by a third party with intent to cause damage; or where the damage is wholly caused by the negligent or other wrongful act of any government or other authority responsible for the maintenance of navigational aids: see articles II and III. See also the Convention on Civil Liability for Oil Pollution Damage Resulting from Exploration and Exploitation of Seabed Mineral Resources, 1977, which establishes the liability of the operator of an installation under the jurisdiction of a party for pollution damage resulting from incidents taking place beyond the coastal low-water line.

result of the fault of the shipowner.[326] The shipowner must maintain insurance or other financial security to cover its liability. Claims may be brought in the courts of the party in which loss or damage has occurred or preventive measures taken and the judgments of such courts are generally recognisable and enforceable in the courts of all parties. The 1969 Convention was amended by the Protocol on Liability, 1992,[327] which includes in the definition of damage compensation for impairment of the environment provided that this is limited to costs of reasonable measures of reinstatement actually undertaken or to be undertaken.[328] The Convention on the Establishment of an International Fund for Compensation for Oil Pollution Damage was adopted in 1971 and enables compensation to be paid in certain cases not covered by the Civil Liability Convention. The Convention and Protocols of 1976 and 1984 were superseded by a Protocol of 1992 and the Convention ceased to be in force as from 24 May 2002. The 1992 Protocol established a separate, 1992 International Oil Pollution Compensation Fund, known as the 1992 Fund.[329]

Suggestions for further reading

P. Birnie and A. Boyle, *International Law and the Environment*, 2nd edn, Oxford, 2002

R. Churchill and A. V. Lowe, *The Law of the Sea*, 3rd edn, Manchester, 1999

P. Okowa, *State Responsibility for Transboundary Air Pollution*, Oxford, 2000

The Oxford Handbook of International Environmental Law (eds. D. Bodansky, J. Brunee and E. Hay), Oxford, 2007

P. Sands, *Principles of International Environmental Law*, 2nd edn, Manchester, 2003

---

[326] Article V.

[327] When this entered into force on 30 May 1996, the 1969 Convention became known as the International Convention on Civil Liability for Oil Pollution Damage, 1992.

[328] Article 2(3).

[329] Amendments adopted in 2000 raised the amounts of compensation: see generally Sands, *Principles*, pp. 912 ff. See also www.imo.org/Conventions/contents.asp?topic_id=256&doc_id=661.

16

The law of treaties

Compared with municipal law the various methods by which rights and duties may be created in international law are relatively unsophisticated.[1] Within a state, legal interests may be established by contracts between two or more persons, or by agreements under seal, or under the developed system for transferring property, or indeed by virtue of legislation or judicial decisions. International law is more limited as far as the mechanisms for the creation of new rules are concerned. Custom relies upon a measure of state practice supported by *opinio juris* and is usually, although not invariably, an evolving and timely process. Treaties, on the other hand, are a more direct and formal method of international law creation.

States transact a vast amount of work by using the device of the treaty, in circumstances which underline the paucity of international law procedures when compared with the many ways in which a person within a state's internal order may set up binding rights and obligations. For instance, wars will be terminated, disputes settled, territory acquired,

[1] See generally A. D. McNair, *The Law of Treaties*, Oxford, 1961; J. Klabbers, *The Concept of Treaty in International Law*, Dordrecht, 1996; A. Aust, *Modern Treaty Law and Practice*, 2nd edn, Cambridge, 2007; M. Fitzmaurice and O. Elias, *Contemporary Issues in the Law of Treaties*, Utrecht, 2005; *Les Conventions de Vienne de 1969 et de 1986 sur le Droit des Traités: Commentaire Article par Article* (eds. O. Corten and P. Klein), Brussels, 3 vols., 2006; *Developments of International Law in Treaty Making* (eds. R. Wolfrum and V. Röben), Berlin, 2005; *Multilateral Treaty Calendar* (ed. C. Wiktor), The Hague, 1998; *Multilateral Treaty-Making* (ed. V. Gowlland-Debas), The Hague, 2000; I. Detter, *Essays on the Law of Treaties*, Stockholm, 1967; T. O. Elias, *The Modern Law of Treaties*, London, 1974; D. P. O'Connell, *International Law*, 2nd edn, London, 1970, vol. I, pp. 195 ff.; I. Sinclair, *The Vienna Convention on the Law of Treaties*, 2nd edn, Manchester, 1984; P. Reuter, *Introduction to the Law of Treaties*, 2nd edn, Geneva, 1995; S. Bastid, *Les Traités dans la Vie Internationale*, Paris, 1985, and S. Rosenne, *Developments in the Law of Treaties 1945–1986*, Cambridge, 1989. See also *Oppenheim's International Law* (eds. R. Y. Jennings and A. D. Watts), 9th edn, London, 1992, p. 1197; Nguyen Quoc Dinh, P. Daillier and A. Pellet, *Droit International Public*, 7th edn, Paris, 2002, p. 117; I. Brownlie, *Principles of Public International Law*, 6th edn, Oxford, 2003, chapter 27, and M. Fitzmaurice, 'Actors and Factors in the Evolution of Treaty Norms (An Empirical Study)', 4 *Austrian Review of International and European Law*, 1999, p. 1.

special interests determined, alliances established and international organisations created, all by means of treaties. No simpler method of reflecting the agreed objectives of states really exists and the international convention has to suffice both for straightforward bilateral agreements and complicated multilateral expressions of opinions. Thus, the concept of the treaty and how it operates becomes of paramount importance to the evolution of international law.

A treaty is basically an agreement between parties on the international scene. Although treaties may be concluded, or made, between states and international organisations, they are primarily concerned with relations between states. An International Convention on the Law of Treaties was signed in 1969 and came into force in 1980, while a Convention on Treaties between States and International Organisations was signed in 1986.[2] The emphasis, however, will be on the appropriate rules which have emerged as between states. The 1969 Vienna Convention on the Law of Treaties partly reflects customary law[3] and constitutes the basic framework for any discussion of the nature and characteristics of treaties. Certain provisions of the Convention may be regarded as reflective of customary international law, such as the rules on interpretation,[4] material breach[5] and fundamental change of circumstances.[6] Others may not be so regarded, and constitute principles binding only upon state parties.

The fundamental principle of treaty law is undoubtedly the proposition that treaties are binding upon the parties to them and must be performed in good faith.[7] This rule is termed *pacta sunt servanda* and is arguably

---

[2] This was based upon the International Law Commission's Draft Articles on the Law of Treaties between States and International Organisations or between International Organisations, *Yearbook of the ILC*, 1982, vol. II, part 2, pp. 9 ff. These articles were approved by the General Assembly and governmental views solicited and received. A plenipotentiary conference was held between 18 February and 21 March 1986 to produce a Convention based on those draft articles. See Assembly resolutions 37/112, 38/139 and 39/86.

[3] See e.g. the *Namibia* case, ICJ Reports, 1971, pp. 16, 47; 49 ILR, pp. 2, 37 and the *Fisheries Jurisdiction* case, ICJ Reports, 1973, pp. 3, 18; 55 ILR, pp. 183, 198. See also Rosenne, *Developments*, p. 121.

[4] See e.g. the *Beagle Channel* case, HMSO, 1977, p. 7; 52 ILR, p. 93; the *La Bretagne* case, 82 ILR, pp. 590, 612; the *Golder* case, European Court of Human Rights, Series A, No. 18, p. 14; 57 ILR, pp. 201, 213–14 and the *Lithgow* case, European Court of Human Rights, Series A, No. 102, para. 114; 75 ILR, pp. 438, 482–3.

[5] See e.g. the *Namibia* case, ICJ Reports, 1971, pp. 16, 47; 49 ILR, pp. 2, 37.

[6] See e.g. the *Fisheries Jurisdiction* cases (jurisdictional phase), ICJ Reports, 1973, pp. 3, 21; 55 ILR, pp. 183, 201.

[7] Note also the references to good faith in articles 31, 46 and 69 of the 1969 Convention. See the *Nuclear Tests* cases, ICJ Reports, 1974, pp. 253, 268; 57 ILR, pp. 398, 413; the *Nicaragua*

the oldest principle of international law. It was reaffirmed in article 26 of the 1969 Convention,[8] and underlies every international agreement for, in the absence of a certain minimum belief that states will perform their treaty obligations in good faith, there is no reason for countries to enter into such obligations with each other.

The term 'treaty' itself is the one most used in the context of international agreements but there are a variety of names which can be, and sometimes are, used to express the same concept, such as protocol, act, charter, covenant, pact and concordat. They each refer to the same basic activity and the use of one term rather than another often signifies little more than a desire for variety of expression.

A treaty is defined, for the purposes of the Convention, in article 2 as:

> an international agreement concluded between states in written form and governed by international law, whether embodied in a single instrument or in two or more related instruments and whatever its particular designation.[9]

In addition to excluding agreements involving international organisations, the Convention does not cover agreements between states which are to be governed by municipal law, such as a large number of commercial accords. This does not mean that such arrangements cannot be characterised as international agreements, or that they are invalid, merely that they are not within the purview of the 1969 Convention. Indeed, article 3 stresses that international agreements between states and other subjects of international law or between two or more subjects of international law, or oral agreements, do not lose their validity by being excluded from the framework of the Convention.

---

case, ICJ Reports, 1986, pp. 392, 418; 76 ILR, pp. 104, 129 and the *Legality of the Threat or Use of Nuclear Weapons* case, ICJ Reports, 1996, para. 102; 110 ILR, pp. 163, 214. See also J. F. O'Connor, *Good Faith in International Law*, Aldershot, 1991; E. Zoller, *La Bonne Foi en Droit International Public*, Paris, 1977, and H. Thirlway, 'The Law and Procedure of the International Court of Justice, 1960–89 (Part One)', 60 BYIL, 1989, pp. 4, 7.

[8] See e.g. the *Gabčíkovo–Nagymaros Project* case, ICJ Reports, 1997, pp. 7, 78–9; 116 ILR, p. 1.

[9] The same definition is given (substituting states and international organisations for states alone) in the 1986 Convention on Treaties between States and International Organisations and in draft article 2(1) of the ILC Draft Articles on the Effects of Armed Conflicts on Treaties, A/CN.4/178, 2007, p. 5. See also H. Thirlway, 'The Law and Procedure of the International Court of Justice 1960–1989: Supplement, 2006, Part Three', 77 BYIL, 2006, pp. 1, 3; M. Fitzmaurice, 'The Identification and Character of Treaties and Treaty Obligations between States in International Law', 73 BYIL, 2002, p. 141, and P. Gautier, 'Article 2' in Corten and Klein, *Conventions de Vienne*, p. 45.

There are no specific requirements of form in international law for the existence of a treaty,[10] although it is essential that the parties intend to create legal relations as between themselves by means of their agreement.[11] This is logical since many agreements between states are merely statements of commonly held principles or objectives and are not intended to establish binding obligations. For instance, a declaration by a number of states in support of a particular political aim may in many cases be without legal (though not political) significance, as the states may regard it as a policy matter and not as setting up juridical relations between themselves. To see whether a particular agreement is intended to create legal relations, all the facts of the situation have to be examined carefully.[12] Examples of non-binding international agreements would include the Final Act of the Conference on Security and Co-operation in Europe, 1975.[13]

The International Court regarded a mandate agreement as having the character of a treaty,[14] while in the *Anglo-Iranian Oil Co.* case[15] doubts were expressed about whether a concession agreement between a private company and a state constituted an international agreement in the sense of a treaty.[16] Optional declarations with regard to the compulsory jurisdiction of the International Court itself under article 36(2) of the Statute of the Court have been regarded as treaty provisions,[17] while declarations made by way of unilateral acts concerning legal or factual situations may have the effect of creating legal obligations.[18] In the latter instance, of course, a treaty as such is not involved.

Where the parties to an agreement do not intend to create legal relations or binding obligations or rights thereby under international law,

---

[10] See e.g. the *Newfoundland/Nova Scotia* arbitration, 2001, para. 3.15. See also the *Aegean Sea Continental Shelf* case, ICJ Reports, 1978, pp. 3, 39; 60 ILR, p. 511. See K. Raustiala, 'Form and Substance in International Agreements', 99 AJIL, 2005, p. 581.

[11] See e.g. *Third US Restatement of Foreign Relations Law*, Washington, 1987, vol. I, p. 149.

[12] Registration of the agreement with the United Nations under article 102 of the UN Charter is one useful indication. However, as the International Court pointed out in the *Qatar v. Bahrain* case, non-registration does not affect the actual validity of an international agreement nor its binding quality, ICJ Reports, 1994, pp. 115, 121; 102 ILR, pp. 1, 18.

[13] See further above, chapter 7, p. 372.

[14] *South-West Africa* cases, ICJ Reports, 1962, pp. 319, 330; 37 ILR, pp. 3, 12.

[15] ICJ Reports, 1952, pp. 93, 112; 19 ILR, pp. 507, 517.

[16] But see *Texaco v. Libya*, 53 ILR, p. 389.

[17] The *Fisheries Jurisdiction* cases, ICJ Reports, 1973, pp. 3, 16; 55 ILR, pp. 183, 196.

[18] The *Nuclear Tests* case, ICJ Reports, 1974, pp. 253, 267; 57 ILR, pp. 398, 412. See also the Ihlen Declaration, held to constitute a binding statement, in the *Eastern Greenland* case, PCIJ, Series A/B, No. 53, 1933; 6 AD, p. 95 and *Burkina Faso v. Mali*, ICJ Reports, 1986, pp. 554, 573–4; 80 ILR, pp. 459, 477. See further above, chapter 3, p. 121.

the agreement will not be a treaty, although, of course, its political effect may still be considerable.[19] Of particular interest are memoranda of understanding, which are not as such legally binding,[20] but may be of legal consequence.[21] In fact a large role is played in the normal course of interstate dealings by informal non-treaty instruments precisely because they are intended to be non-binding and are thus flexible, confidential and relatively speedy in comparison with treaties.[22] They may be amended with ease and without delay and may be terminated by reasonable notice (subject to provision to the contrary). It is this intention not to create a binding arrangement governed by international law which marks the difference between treaties and informal international instruments.[23] The

---

[19] The test will focus upon the intent of the parties as seen in the language and context of the document concerned, the circumstances of its conclusion and the explanations given by the parties: see the view of the US Assistant Legal Adviser for Treaty Affairs, 88 AJIL, 1994, p. 515. See also O. Schachter, 'The Twilight Existence of Nonbinding International Agreements', 71 AJIL, 1977, p. 296, and Rosenne, *Developments*, p. 91. See e.g. the Helsinki Final Act of 1975, which was understood to be non-binding and thus not a treaty by the parties involved, DUSPIL, 1975, pp. 326–7.

[20] The UK Foreign Office has noted that a memorandum of understanding is 'a form frequently used to record informal arrangements between states on matters which are inappropriate for inclusion in treaties or where the form is more convenient than a treaty (e.g. for confidentiality). They may be drawn up as a single document using non-treaty terms, signed on behalf of two or more governments, or consist of an exchange of notes or letters recording an understanding between two governments', UKMIL, 71 BYIL, 2000, p. 534, and see FCO, *Treaties and MOUs: Guidance on Practice and Procedures*, 2nd edn, 2004, www.fco.gov.uk/resources/en/pdf/pdf8/fco_pdf_treatymous. See also Aust, *Modern Treaty Law*, chapter 3.

[21] See e.g. the dispute between the USA and the UK as to the legal status of a memorandum of understanding relating to the US–UK Air Services Agreement, 1977 (Bermuda II) in the context of *Heathrow Airport User Charges* Arbitration, UKMIL, 63 BYIL, 1992, pp. 712 ff. and 88 AJIL, 1994, pp. 738 ff. The Tribunal noted that the memorandum of understanding was not a source of independent legal rights and duties but 'consensual subsequent practice of the parties' and an aid to the interpretation of the Bermuda II Agreement, 102 ILR, pp. 215, 353. In the *Iron Rhine (Belgium/Netherlands)* case, arbitral award of 24 May 2005, paras. 156 ff., the Tribunal noted that the memorandum in question, while not as such binding, in the circumstances of the case was not legally irrelevant.

[22] See e.g. Rosenne, *Developments*, pp. 107 ff.; A. Aust, 'The Theory and Practice of Informal International Instruments', 35 ICLQ, 1986, p. 787; R. Baxter, 'International Law in "Her Infinite Variety"', 29 ICLQ, 1980, p. 549, and Roessler, 'Law, *De Facto* Agreements and Declarations of Principles in International Economic Relations', 21 German YIL, 1978, p. 41.

[23] Aust provides as examples the UK memoranda of understanding on deportations with Jordan, Libya and Lebanon in 2005, *Modern Treaty Law*, p. 21. See also *AS & DD (Libya)* v. *Secretary of State for the Home Department* [2008] EWCA Civ 289 and *Othman (Jordan)* v. *Secretary of State for the Home Department* [2008] EWCA Civ 290.

International Court addressed this issue in the *Qatar* v. *Bahrain* case,[24] with regard to Minutes dated 25 December 1990 signed by the parties and Saudi Arabia. The Court emphasised that whether an agreement constituted a binding agreement would depend upon 'all its actual terms' and the circumstances in which it had been drawn up,[25] and in the situation involved in the case, the Minutes were to be construed as an international agreement creating rights and obligations for the parties since on the facts they enumerated the commitments to which the parties had consented.[26] In addition, a treaty may contain a variety of provisions, not all of which constitute legal obligations.[27]

The 1969 Convention also concerns treaties which are the constituent instruments of international organisations, such as the United Nations Charter, and internal treaties adopted within international organisations.[28]

The making of treaties[29]

Formalities

Treaties may be made or concluded by the parties in virtually any manner they wish. There is no prescribed form or procedure, and how a treaty is formulated and by whom it is actually signed will depend upon the intention and agreement of the states concerned. Treaties may be drafted as between states, or governments, or heads of states, or governmental departments, whichever appears the most expedient. For instance, many

---

[24] ICJ Reports, 1994, p. 112; 102 ILR, p. 1.

[25] ICJ Reports, 1994, p. 121; 102 ILR, p. 18, citing the *Aegean Sea Continental Shelf* case, ICJ Reports, 1978, p. 39; 60 ILR, p. 511.

[26] ICJ Reports, 1994, pp. 121–2; 102 ILR, pp. 18–19. See also K. Widdows, 'What is an International Agreement in International Law?', 50 BYIL, 1979, p. 117, and J. A. Barberis, 'Le Concept de "Traité International" et ses Limites', AFDI, 1984, p. 239.

[27] See the *Oil Platforms (Preliminary Objections)* case, ICJ Reports, 1996, pp. 803, 820; 130 ILR, pp. 174, 201. Note that the use of the word 'treaty' may not necessarily be determinative of its legal status, for example 'treaties' signed with representatives of indigenous peoples during the colonial period giving protectorate or territorial or sovereignty rights to the colonial power: see *Cameroon* v. *Nigeria*, ICJ Reports, 2002, pp. 303, 404 ff. and the *Island of Palmas* case, UNRIAA, vol. II, pp. 858–9. See also I. Brownlie, *Treaties with Indigenous Peoples*, Oxford, 1992.

[28] Article 5. See further Rosenne, *Developments*, chapter 4.

[29] See e.g. H. Blix, *Treaty-Making Power*, New York, 1960, and E. W. Vierdag, 'The Time of the Conclusion of a Multilateral Treaty: Article 30 of the Vienna Convention on the Law of Treaties and Related Provisions', 59 BYIL, 1988, p. 75. See also *Oppenheim's International Law*, p. 1222, and Nguyen Quoc Dinh *et al.*, *Droit International Public*, p. 125.

of the most important treaties are concluded as between heads of state, and many of the more mundane agreements are expressed to be as between government departments, such as minor trading arrangements.

Where precisely in the domestic constitutional establishment the power to make treaties is to be found depends upon each country's municipal regulations and varies from state to state. In the United Kingdom, the treaty-making power is within the prerogative of the Crown,[30] whereas in the United States it resides with the President 'with the advice and consent of the Senate' and the concurrence of two-thirds of the Senators.[31] International law leaves such matters to domestic law.[32]

Nevertheless, there are certain rules that apply in the formation of international conventions. In international law, states have the capacity to make agreements, but since states are not identifiable human persons, particular principles have evolved to ensure that persons representing states indeed have the power so to do for the purpose of concluding the treaty in question. Such persons must produce what is termed 'full powers' according to article 7 of the Convention, before being accepted as capable of representing their countries.[33] 'Full powers' refers to documents certifying status from the competent authorities of the state in question. This provision provides security to the other parties to the treaty that they are making agreements with persons competent to do so.[34] However, certain persons do not need to produce such full powers, by virtue of their position and functions. This exception refers to heads of state and government, and foreign ministers for the purpose of performing all acts relating to the conclusion of the treaty; heads of diplomatic missions for the purpose of adopting the text of the treaty between their country and the country to which they are accredited; and representatives accredited to international conferences or organisations for the purpose of adopting the text of the treaty in that particular conference or organisation. The International Court noted in the preliminary objections to jurisdiction phase of the *Genocide*

---

[30] See e.g. S. de Smith and R. Brazier, *Constitutional and Administrative Law*, 6th edn, London, 1989, p. 140.

[31] See e.g. *Third US Restatement of Foreign Relations Law*, p. 159. See, with regard to the Presidential power to terminate a treaty, DUSPIL, 1979, pp. 724 ff., and *Goldwater v. Carter* 617 F.2d 697 and 100 S. Ct. 533 (1979). See also L. Henkin, 'Restatement of the Foreign Relations Law of the United States (Revised)', 74 AJIL, 1980, p. 954.

[32] See e.g. *Cameroon v. Nigeria*, ICJ Reports, 2002, pp. 303, 429.

[33] See Sinclair, *Vienna Convention*, pp. 29 ff.; Aust, *Modern Treaty Law*, chapter 5, and M. Jones, *Full Powers and Ratification*, Cambridge, 1946.

[34] See *Yearbook of the ILC*, 1966, vol. II, p. 193.

Convention (Bosnia v. Serbia) case that, 'According to international law, there is no doubt that every head of state is presumed to be able to act on behalf of the state in its international relations.'[35]

Sinclair notes that UK practice distinguishes between 'general full powers' held by the Secretary of State for Foreign and Commonwealth Affairs, Ministers of State and Parliamentary Under-Secretaries in the Foreign and Commonwealth Office and UK Permanent Representatives to the UN, European Communities and General Agreement on Tariffs and Trade, which enable any treaty to be negotiated and signed, and 'special full powers' granted to a particular person to negotiate and sign a specific treaty.[36]

Any act relating to the making of a treaty by a person not authorised as required will be without any legal effect, unless the state involved afterwards confirms the act.[37] One example of this kind of situation arose in 1951 with regard to a convention relating to the naming of cheeses. It was signed by a delegate on behalf of both Sweden and Norway, but it appeared that he had authority only from Norway. However, the agreement was subsequently ratified by both parties and entered into effect.[38]

Consent

Once a treaty has been drafted and agreed by authorised representatives, a number of stages are then necessary before it becomes a binding legal obligation upon the parties involved. The text of the agreement drawn up by the negotiators of the parties has to be adopted and article 9 provides that adoption in international conferences takes place by the vote of two-thirds of the states present and voting, unless by the same majority it is decided to apply a different rule. This procedure follows basically the practices recognised in the United Nations General Assembly[39] and carried out in the majority of contemporary conferences. An increasing number of conventions are now adopted and opened for signature by means of UN General Assembly resolutions, such as the 1966 International Covenants on Human Rights and the 1984 Convention against Torture, using normal Assembly voting procedures. Another significant point is the tendency in

---

[35] ICJ Reports, 1996, pp. 595, 622; 115 ILR, p. 1 and see also *Cameroon v. Nigeria*, ICJ Reports, 2002, pp. 303, 430.
[36] Sinclair, *Vienna Convention*, p. 32. See also *Satow's Guide to Diplomatic Practice*, 5th edn, London, 1979, p. 62.
[37] Article 8. [38] See *Yearbook of the ILC*, 1966, vol. II, p. 195.
[39] See article 18 of the UN Charter.

recent conferences to operate by way of consensus so that there would be no voting until all efforts to reach agreement by consensus have been exhausted.[40] In cases other than international conferences, adoption will take place by the consent of all the states involved in drawing up the text of the agreement.[41]

The consent of the states parties to the treaty in question is a vital factor, since states may (in the absence of a rule being also one of customary law) be bound only by their consent. Treaties are in this sense contracts between states and if they do not receive the consent of the various states, their provisions will not be binding upon them. There are, however, a number of ways in which a state may express its consent to an international agreement. It may be signalled, according to article 11, by signature, exchange of instruments constituting a treaty, ratification, acceptance, approval or accession. In addition, it may be accomplished by any other means, if so agreed.

Consent by signature[42]

A state may regard itself as having given its consent to the text of the treaty by signature in defined circumstances noted by article 12, that is, where the treaty provides that signature shall have that effect, or where it is otherwise established that the negotiating states were agreed that signature should have that effect, or where the intention of the state to give that effect to the signature appears from the full powers of its representative or was expressed during the negotiations.

Although consent by ratification is probably the most popular of the methods adopted in practice, consent by signature does retain some significance, especially in light of the fact that to insist upon ratification in each case before a treaty becomes binding is likely to burden the administrative machinery of government and result in long delays. Accordingly, provision is made for consent to be expressed by signature.[43] This would be appropriate for the more routine and less politicised of treaties. The

---

[40] See e.g. the Third UN Conference on the Law of the Sea, Sinclair, *Vienna Convention*, pp. 37–9. See also the UN *Juridical Yearbook*, 1974, pp. 163–4, where the Director of the General Legal Division, Office of Legal Affairs, declared that the term 'consensus' in UN organs, 'was used to describe a practice under which every effort is made to achieve unanimous agreement; and if that could not be done, those dissenting from the general trend were prepared simply to make their position and reservations known and placed on the record'. See also Aust, *Modern Treaty Law*, pp. 86 ff.

[41] Article 9(1). This reflects the classic rule, Sinclair, *Vienna Convention*, p. 33.

[42] See *Yearbook of the ILC*, 1966, vol. II, p. 196.

[43] See, for example, the Maroua Declaration, *Cameroon v. Nigeria*, ICJ Reports, 2002, pp. 303, 429–30.

act of signature is usually a formal affair. Often in the more important treaties, the head of state will formally add his signature in an elaborate ceremony. In multilateral conventions, a special closing session will be held at which authorised representatives will sign the treaty. However, where the convention is subject to acceptance, approval or ratification, signature will in principle be a formality and will mean no more than that state representatives have agreed upon an acceptable text, which will be forwarded to their particular governments for the necessary decision as to acceptance or rejection.[44] However, signature has additional meaning in that in such cases and pending ratification, acceptance or approval, a state must refrain from acts which would defeat the object and purpose of the treaty until such time as its intentions with regard to the treaty have been made clear.[45]

Consent by exchange of instruments

Article 13 provides that the consent of states to be bound by a treaty constituted by instruments exchanged between them may be expressed by that exchange when the instruments declare that their exchange shall have that effect or it is otherwise established that those states had agreed that the exchange of instruments should have that effect.

Consent by ratification[46]

The device of ratification by the competent authorities of the state is historically well established and was originally devised to ensure that the representative did not exceed his powers or instructions with regard to the making of a particular agreement. Although ratification (or approval) was originally a function of the sovereign, it has in modern times been made subject to constitutional control.

---

[44] The International Court has stated that, 'signed but unratified treaties may constitute an accurate expression of the understanding of the parties at the time of signature', *Qatar v. Bahrain*, ICJ Reports, 2001, pp. 40, 68.

[45] Article 18. See Sinclair, *Vienna Convention*, pp. 42–4, and *Certain German Interests in Polish Upper Silesia*, PCIJ, Series A, No. 7, 1926, p. 30. See also H. Thirlway, 'The Law and Procedure of the International Court of Justice 1960–1989 (Part Four)', 63 BYIL, 1992, pp. 1, 48 ff., and J. Klabbers, 'How to Defeat a Treaty's Object and Purpose Pending Entry into Force: Towards Manifest Intent', 34 *Vanderbilt Journal of Transnational Law*, 2001, p. 283. Note that having signed the Rome Statute for the International Criminal Court in December 2000, the US withdrew its signature in May 2002: see www.state.gov/r/pa/prs/ps/2002/9968.htm.

[46] Defined in article 2(1)b as 'the international act...whereby a state establishes on the international plane its consent to be bound by a treaty'. It is thus to be distinguished as a concept from ratification in the internal constitutional sense, although clearly there is an important link: see *Yearbook of the ILC*, 1966, vol. II, pp. 197–8. See also Brownlie, *Principles*, pp. 582–3.

The advantages of waiting until a state ratifies a treaty before it becomes a binding document are basically twofold, internal and external. In the latter case, the delay between signature and ratification may often be advantageous in allowing extra time for consideration, once the negotiating process has been completed. But it is the internal aspects that are the most important, for they reflect the change in political atmosphere that has occurred in the last 150 years and has led to a much greater participation by a state's population in public affairs. By providing for ratification, the feelings of public opinion have an opportunity to be expressed with the possibility that a strong negative reaction may result in the state deciding not to ratify the treaty under consideration.

The rules relating to ratification vary from country to country. In the United Kingdom, although the power of ratification comes within the prerogative of the Crown, it has become accepted that treaties involving any change in municipal law, or adding to the financial burdens of the government or having an impact upon the private rights of British subjects will be first submitted to Parliament and subsequently ratified. There is, in fact, a procedure known as the Ponsonby Rule which provides that all treaties subject to ratification are laid before Parliament at least twenty-one days before the actual ratification takes place.[47] Different considerations apply in the case of the United States.[48] However, the question of how a state effects ratification is a matter for internal law alone and outside international law.

Article 14 of the 1969 Vienna Convention notes that ratification will express a state's consent to be bound by a treaty where the treaty so provides; it is otherwise established that the negotiating states were agreed that ratification should be required; the representative of the state has signed the treaty subject to ratification or the intention of the state to sign the treaty subject to ratification appears from the full powers of its representative or was expressed during negotiations.

Within this framework, there is a controversy as to which treaties need to be ratified. Some writers maintain that ratification is only necessary if it is clearly contemplated by the parties to the treaty,[49] and this approach has been adopted by the United Kingdom.[50] On the other hand, it has been suggested that ratification should be required unless the treaty clearly

---

[47] See above, chapter 4, p. 152.   [48] Ibid., p. 161.

[49] See e.g. G. Fitzmaurice, 'Do Treaties Need Ratification?', 15 BYIL, 1934, p. 129, and O'Connell, International Law, p. 222. See also H. Blix, 'The Requirement of Ratification', 30 BYIL, 1953, p. 380.

[50] See e.g. Sinclair, Vienna Convention, p. 40, and O'Connell, International Law, p. 222.

reveals a contrary intention.[51] The United States, in general, will dispense with ratification only in the case of executive agreements.[52] Ratification in the case of bilateral treaties is usually accomplished by exchanging the requisite instruments, but in the case of multilateral treaties the usual procedure is for one party to collect the ratifications of all states, keeping all parties informed of the situation. It is becoming more accepted that in such instances, the Secretary-General of the United Nations will act as the depositary for ratifications.[53] In some cases, signatures to treaties may be declared subject to 'acceptance' or 'approval'. The terms, as noted in articles 11 and 14(2), are very similar to ratification and similar provisions apply. Such variation in terminology is not of any real significance and only refers to a somewhat simpler form of ratification.

Consent by accession[54]

This is the normal method by which a state becomes a party to a treaty it has not signed either because the treaty provides that signature is limited to certain states, and it is not such a state, or because a particular deadline for signature has passed. Article 15 notes that consent by accession is possible where the treaty so provides, or the negotiating states were agreed or subsequently agree that consent by accession could occur in the case of the state in question. Important multilateral treaties often declare that states or, in certain situations, other specific entities may accede to the treaty at a later date, that is after the date after which it is possible to signify acceptance by signature.[55]

Reservations to treaties[56]

A reservation is defined in article 2 of the Convention as:

> a unilateral statement, however phrased or named, made by a state, when signing, ratifying, accepting, approving or acceding to a treaty, whereby it

---

[51] See e.g. McNair, *Law of Treaties*, p. 133.

[52] O'Connell, *International Law*, p. 222. See also DUSPIL, 1974, pp. 216–17 and *ibid.*, 1979, pp. 678 ff.

[53] See P. T. B. Kohona, 'Some Notable Developments in the Practice of the UN Secretary-General as a Depositary of Multilateral Treaties: Reservations and Declarations', 99 AJIL, 2005, p. 433.

[54] See *Yearbook of the ILC*, 1966, vol. II, p. 199.

[55] See e.g. articles 26 and 28 of the Convention on the Territorial Sea and the Contiguous Zone.

[56] See e.g. Aust, *Modern Treaty Law*, chapter 8; A. Pellet, 'Article 19' in Corten and Klein, *Conventions de Vienne*, p. 641; C. Redgwell, 'Universality or Integrity? Some Reflections on Reservations to General Multilateral Treaties', 64 BYIL, 1993, p. 245; G. Gaja, 'Unruly

purports to exclude or to modify the legal effect of certain provisions of the treaty in their application to that state.[57]

Where a state is satisfied with most of the terms of a treaty, but is unhappy about particular provisions, it may, in certain circumstances, wish to refuse to accept or be bound by such provisions, while consenting to the rest of the agreement. By the device of excluding certain provisions, states may agree to be bound by a treaty which otherwise they might reject entirely. This may have beneficial results in the cases of multilateral conventions, by inducing as many states as possible to adhere to the proposed treaty. To some extent it is a means of encouraging harmony amongst states of widely differing social, economic and political systems, by concentrating upon agreed, basic issues and accepting disagreement on certain other matters.

The capacity of a state to make reservations to an international treaty illustrates the principle of sovereignty of states, whereby a state may refuse its consent to particular provisions so that they do not become binding upon it. On the other hand, of course, to permit a treaty to become honeycombed with reservations by a series of countries could well jeopardise the

---

Treaty Reservations', *Le Droit International à l'Heure de sa Codifications*, Milan, 1987, p. 313; J. K. Gamble, 'Reservations to Multilateral Treaties: A Macroscopic View of State Practice', 74 AJIL, 1980, p. 372; G. Fitzmaurice, 'Reservations to Multilateral Treaties', 2 ICLQ, 1953, p. 1; D. W. Bowett, 'Reservations to Non-restricted Multilateral Treaties', 48 BYIL, 1976–7, p. 67; P. H. Imbert, *Les Réserves aux Traités Multilatéraux*, Paris, 1979; Sinclair, *Vienna Convention*, chapter 3; D. W. Greig, 'Reservations: Equity as a Balancing Force?', 16 Australian YIL, 1995, p. 21; O'Connell, *International Law*, pp. 229 ff.; J. M. Ruda, 'Reservations to Treaties', 146 HR, 1975, p. 95; G. Horn, *Reservations and Interpretative Declarations to Multilateral Treaties*, Leiden, 1988; *Oppenheim's International Law*, p. 1241, and Nguyen Quoc Dinh *et al.*, *Droit International Public*, p. 178. See also A. Pellet, Reports on the Law and Practice Relating to Reservations to Treaties, e.g. Report of the International Law Commission, 2007, A/62/10, pp. 15 ff. The intention is to draw up a Guide to Practice consisting of guidelines which, while not binding in themselves, might guide the practice of states and international organisations with regard to reservations and interpretative declarations on the basis of the Commission's fundamental decision not to call into question the work of the Vienna Conventions. The Draft Guidelines adopted to date may be found at A/62/10, pp. 46 ff.

57 Article 2(1)d of the Vienna Convention on the Law of Treaties between States and International Organisations, 1986 provides that a reservation means 'a unilateral statement, however phrased or named, made by a state or by an international organisation when signing, ratifying, formally confirming, accepting, approving or acceding to a treaty, whereby it purports to exclude or to modify the legal effect of certain provisions of the treaty in their application to that state or to that organisation'. See also the definition contained in draft guideline 1.1 of the ILC Guide to Practice, Report of the ILC on its 54th Session, 2002, p. 50.

whole exercise. It could seriously dislocate the whole purpose of the agreement and lead to some complicated inter-relationships amongst states. This problem does not arise in the case of bilateral treaties, since a reservation by one party to a proposed term of the agreement would necessitate a renegotiation.[58] An agreement between two parties cannot exist where one party refuses to accept some of the provisions of the treaty.[59] This is not the case with respect to multilateral treaties, and here it is possible for individual states to dissent from particular provisions, by announcing their intention either to omit them altogether, or understand them in a certain way. Accordingly, the effect of a reservation is simply to exclude the treaty provision to which the reservation has been made from the terms of the treaty in force between the parties.[60]

Reservations must be distinguished from other statements made with regard to a treaty that are not intended to have the legal effect of a reservation, such as understandings, political statements or interpretative declarations. In the latter instance, no binding consequence is intended with regard to the treaty in question. What is involved is a political manifestation for primarily internal effect that is not binding upon the other parties.[61] A distinction has been drawn between 'mere' interpretative declarations and 'qualified' interpretative declarations,[62] with the latter category

---

[58] See the statement of British practice to this effect, UKMIL, 68 BYIL, 1997, p. 482.

[59] See *Yearbook of the ILC*, 1966, vol. II, p. 203. See also draft guideline 1.5.1 of the ILC Guide to Practice, Report of the ILC on its 54th Session, 2002, p. 55.

[60] See e.g. *Legality of the Use of Force* (*Yugoslavia v. USA*), Provisional Measures Order, ICJ Reports, 1999, pp. 916, 924 and the *Fisheries Jurisdiction* (*Spain v. Canada*) case, ICJ Reports, 1998, p. 432.

[61] See e.g. the *Temeltasch* case, 5 *European Human Rights Reports*, 1983, p. 417 on the difference between reservations and interpretative declarations generally and in the context of the European Human Rights Convention. Cf. the *Ette* case, European Court of Human Rights, Series A, No. 117. See, for examples of UK practice, UKMIL, 68 BYIL, 1997, p. 483. See also L. D. M. Nelson, 'Declarations, Statements and "Disguised Reservations" with respect to the Convention on the Law of the Sea', 50 ICLQ, 2001, p. 767; R. Sapienza, 'Les Déclarations Interprétatives Unilatérales et l'Interprétation des Traités', 103 RGDIP, 1999, p. 601, and P. H. Imbert, 'Reservations to the European Convention on Human Rights before the Strasbourg Commission', 33 ICLQ, 1984, p. 558 and *UN Juridical Yearbook*, 1976, pp. 220–1. Draft guideline 1.2 of the ILC Guide to Practice provides that an interpretative declaration means 'a unilateral statement, however phrased or named, made by a state or an international organisation whereby that state or international organisation purports to specify or clarify the meaning or scope attributed by the declarant to a treaty or to certain of its provisions', Report of the ILC on its 54th Session, 2002, p. 52.

[62] See D. McRae, 'The Legal Effect of Interpretative Declarations', 49 BYIL, 1978, p. 155. See also the *Temeltasch* case, pp. 432–3 and the First Pellet Report, pp. 58 ff.

capable in certain circumstances of constituting reservations.[63] Another way of describing this is to draw a distinction between 'simple interpretative declarations' and 'conditional interpretative declarations'.[64] The latter is described in the ILC Guide to Practice as referring to a situation where the state subjects its consent to be bound by the treaty to a specific interpretation of the treaty, or specific provisions of it.[65]

In the *Anglo-French Continental Shelf* case,[66] the Arbitral Tribunal emphasised that French reservations to article 6 of the Geneva Convention on the Continental Shelf, 1958, challenged by the UK, had to be construed in accordance with the natural meaning of their terms.[67] The UK contended that the third French reservation to article 6 (which concerned the non-applicability of the principle of equidistance in areas of 'special circumstances' as defined by the French government, naming specifically *inter alia* the Bay of Granville) was in reality only an interpretative declaration. The Tribunal, however, held that although this reservation contained elements of interpretation, it also constituted a specific condition imposed by France on its acceptance of the article 6 delimitation regime. This went beyond mere interpretation as it made the application of that regime dependent upon acceptance by other states of France's designation of the named areas as involving 'special circumstances'. It therefore had the purpose of seeking to exclude or modify the legal effect of certain treaty provisions with regard to their application by the reserving state and thus constituted a reservation.[68]

In the *Belilos* case[69] in 1988, the European Court of Human Rights considered the effect of one particular interpretative declaration made by Switzerland upon ratification.[70] The Court held that one had to look

---

[63] Quite what the effect might be of the former is unclear: see e.g. the First Pellet Report, p. 60.

[64] See e.g. Nelson, 'Declarations', p. 776.

[65] Draft guideline 1.2.1, Report of the ILC on its 54th Session, 2002, p. 52.

[66] Cmnd 7438 (1979); 54 ILR, p. 6.

[67] Cmnd 7438, pp. 41–2; 54 ILR, pp. 48–9. It was also stressed that reservations have to be appreciated in the light of the law in force at the time that the reservations (and any objections to them) are made, Cmnd 7438, p. 35; 54 ILR, p. 42.

[68] Cmnd 7438, p. 43; 54 ILR, p. 50.

[69] European Court of Human Rights, Series A, No. 132. See also S. Marks, 'Reservations Unhinged: The *Belilos* Case Before the European Court of Human Rights', 39 ICLQ, 1990, p. 300.

[70] Switzerland made in total two interpretative declarations and two reservations upon ratification of the European Convention on Human Rights. The declaration in question concerned article 6, paragraph 1 of the Convention dealing with the right to fair trial and

behind the title given to the declaration in question and to seek to determine its substantive content. It was necessary to ascertain the original intention of those drafting the declaration and thus recourse to the *travaux préparatoires* was required. In the light of these, the Court felt that Switzerland had indeed intended to 'avoid the consequences which a broad view of the right of access to the courts...would have for the system of public administration and of justice in the cantons and consequently ...put forward the declaration as qualifying [its] consent to be bound by the Convention'.[71] Having so decided, the Court held that the declaration in question, taking effect as a reservation, did not in fact comply with article 64 of the Convention, which prohibited reservations of a general character[72] and required a brief statement of the law in force necessitating the reservation.[73] Accordingly, the declaration was invalid. It is hard to escape the conclusion that the Court has accepted a test favourable to states as to the situations under which a declaration may be regarded as a reservation, only to emphasise the requirements of article 64 concerning the validity of reservations to the European Convention. One should therefore be rather cautious before applying the easier test regarding interpretative declarations generally. Nevertheless, there remains a problem of states making interpretative declarations that seek to act as reservations to treaties that prohibit reservations. In such situations, it is likely that the effect of such declarations would be ineffective as against other parties who would therefore be entitled to regard the treaty as in force fully between all the parties, taking no account of the declaration.[74]

In order to determine whether a unilateral statement made constitutes a reservation or an interpretative declaration, the statement will have to be interpreted in good faith in accordance with the ordinary meaning to be given to its terms and within the context of the treaty in question. The intention of the state making the statement at that time will also need to

provided that Switzerland considered that that right was intended solely to ensure ultimate control by the judiciary over the acts or decisions of the public authorities. The issue concerned the right of appeal from the Lausanne Police Board to the Criminal Cassation Division of the Vaud Cantonal Court, which could not in fact hear fresh argument, receive witnesses or give a new ruling on the merits, and whether the declaration prevented the applicant from relying on article 6 in the circumstances.

[71] At pp. 18–19.   [72] *Ibid.*, pp. 20–1.   [73] *Ibid.*, pp. 21–2.
[74] See e.g. Nelson, 'Declarations', p. 781. See also below, p. 920.

be considered.[75] In the special case of a bilateral treaty, an interpretative declaration made by one party which is accepted by the other party will constitute an authoritative interpretation of that treaty.[76]

The general rule that became established was that reservations could only be made with the consent of all the other states involved in the process. This was to preserve as much unity of approach as possible to ensure the success of an international agreement and to minimise deviations from the text of the treaty. This reflected the contractual view of the nature of a treaty,[77] and the League of Nations supported this concept.[78] The effect of this was that a state wishing to make a reservation had to obtain the consent of all the other parties to the treaty. If this was not possible, that state could either become a party to the original treaty (minus the reservation, of course) or not become a party at all. However, this restrictive approach to reservations was not accepted by the International Court of Justice in the *Reservations to the Genocide Convention* case.[79] This was an advisory opinion by the Court, requested by the General Assembly after some states had made reservations to the 1948 Genocide Convention, which contained no clause permitting such reservations, and a number of objections were made.

The Court held that:

> a state which has made and maintained a reservation which has been objected to by one or more parties to the Convention but not by others, can be regarded as being a party to the Convention if the reservation is compatible with the object and purpose of the Convention.

Compatibility, in the Court's opinion, could be decided by states individually since it was noted that:

> if a party to the Convention objects to a reservation which it considers incompatible with the object and purpose of the Convention, it can ... consider that the reserving state is not a party to the Convention.[80]

---

[75] See draft guideline 1.3.1 of the ILC Guide to Practice, Report of the ILC on its 54th Session, 2002, p. 53. Draft guideline 1.3.2 also states that the phrasing or name used provides an indication of the purported legal effect, *ibid.*

[76] *Ibid.*, p. 56.

[77] See Sinclair, *Vienna Convention*, pp. 54–5, and Ruda, 'Reservations', p. 112. See also Redgwell, 'Universality or Integrity', p. 246.

[78] Report of the Committee of Experts for the Progressive Codification of International Law, 8 LNOJ, pp. 880–1 (1927).

[79] ICJ Reports, 1951, p. 15; 18 ILR, p. 364.   [80] ICJ Reports, 1951, pp. 29–30.

The Court did emphasise the principle of the integrity of a convention, but pointed to a variety of special circumstances with regard to the Genocide Convention in question, which called for a more flexible interpretation of the principle. These circumstances included the universal character of the UN under whose auspices the Convention had been concluded; the extensive participation envisaged under the Convention; the fact that the Convention had been the product of a series of majority votes; the fact that the principles underlying the Convention were general principles already binding upon states; that the Convention was clearly intended by the UN and the parties to be definitely universal in scope and that it had been adopted for a purely humanitarian purpose so that state parties did not have interests of their own but a common interest. All these factors militated for a flexible approach in this case.

The Court's approach, although having some potential disadvantages,[81] was in keeping with the move to increase the acceptability and scope of treaties and with the trend in international organisations away from the unanimity rule in decision-making and towards majority voting.[82] The 1969 Convention on the Law of Treaties accepted the Court's views.[83]

By article 19, reservations may be made when signing, ratifying, accepting, approving or acceding to a treaty, but they cannot be made where the reservation is prohibited by the treaty, or where the treaty provides that only specified reservations may be made and these do not include the reservation in question, or where the reservation is not compatible with the object and purpose of the treaty.[84]

In the instances where a reservation is possible, the traditional rule requiring acceptance by all parties will apply where, by article 20(2), 'it appears from the limited number of the negotiating states and the object and purpose of a treaty that the application of the treaty in its entirety between all the parties is an essential condition of the consent of each one to be bound by the treaty'.

---

[81] See e.g. Fitzmaurice, 'Reservations'.

[82] Although the International Law Commission was initially critical, it later changed its mind: see *Yearbook of the ILC*, 1951, vol. II, pp. 130–1, cf. *ibid.*, 1962, vol. II, pp. 62–5 and 178–9. Note also that the UN General Assembly in 1959 resolved that the Secretary-General as a depositary was to apply the Court's approach to all conventions concluded under UN auspices unless they contained provisions to the contrary.

[83] See Redgwell, 'Universality or Integrity', pp. 253 ff.

[84] See also draft guideline 1.3.1 of the ILC Guide to Practice, A/61/10, 2006, pp. 327 ff.

Article 20(4) then outlines the general rules to be followed with regard to treaties not within article 20(2) and not constituent instruments of international organisations. These are that:

(a) acceptance by another contracting state of a reservation constitutes the reserving state a party to the treaty in relation to that other state if or when the treaty is in force for those states;

(b) an objection by another contracting state to a reservation does not preclude the entry into force of the treaty as between the objecting and reserving states unless a contrary intention is definitely expressed by the objecting state;

(c) an act expressing a state's consent to be bound by the treaty and containing a reservation is effective as soon as at least one other contracting state has accepted the reservation.

The effect of reservations is outlined in article 21. This declares that a reservation established with regard to another party modifies, for the reserving state in its relations with the other party, the provisions of the treaty to which the reservation relates, to the extent of the reservation. The other party is similarly affected in its relations with the reserving state. An example of this was provided by the Libyan reservation to the 1961 Vienna Convention on Diplomatic Relations with regard to the diplomatic bag, permitting Libya to search the bag with the consent of the state whose bag it was, and insist that it be returned to its state of origin. Since the UK did not object to the reservation, it could have acted similarly with regard to Libya's diplomatic bags.[85] However, the reservation does not modify the provisions of the treaty for the other parties to the treaty as between themselves.

Article 21(3) provides that where a state objects to a reservation, but not to the entry into force of the treaty between itself and the reserving state, then 'the provisions to which the reservation relates do not apply as between the two states to the extent of the reservation'. This provision was applied by the arbitration tribunal in the *Anglo-French Continental Shelf* case, where it was noted that:

> the combined effect of the French reservations and their rejection by the United Kingdom is neither to render article 6 [of the Geneva Convention on the Continental Shelf, 1958] inapplicable *in toto*, as the French Republic contends, nor to render it applicable *in toto*, as the United Kingdom

---

[85] See Foreign Affairs Committee, *Report on the Abuse of Diplomatic Immunities and Privileges*, 1984, pp. 23–4, and above, chapter 13, p. 760.

primarily contends. It is to render the article inapplicable as between the two countries to the extent of the reservations.[86]

A number of important issues, however, remain unresolved. In particular, it is unclear what effect an impermissible reservation has.[87] One school of thought takes the view that such reservations are invalid,[88] another that the validity of any reservation is dependent upon acceptance by other states.[89] While there is a presumption in favour of the permissibility of reservations, this may be displaced if the reservation is prohibited explicitly or implicitly by the treaty or it is contrary to the object and purpose of the treaty.[90] A further problem is to determine when these conditions under which reservations may be deemed to be impermissible have been met. This is especially difficult where it is contended that the object and purpose of a treaty have been offended. The meaning of the term is not free from uncertainty,[91] although it has been accepted that a reservation to a particular method of dispute settlement laid down in a treaty would not normally be seen as contrary to the object and purpose of a treaty.[92]

---

[86] Cmnd 7438 (1979), p. 45; 54 ILR, p. 52. See also A. E. Boyle, 'The Law of Treaties and the Anglo-French Continental Shelf Arbitration', 29 ICLQ, 1980, p. 498, and Sinclair, *Vienna Convention*, pp. 70–6.

[87] See e.g. J. K. Koh, 'Reservations to Multilateral Treaties: How International Legal Doctrine Reflects World Vision', 23 *Harvard International Law Journal*, 1982, p. 71, and Redgwell, 'Universality or Integrity', p. 263. See also above, p. 915, concerning interpretative declarations being used as 'disguised' reservations where no reservations are permitted under the treaty in question.

[88] See e.g. Bowett, 'Reservations', pp. 77 and 84. Impermissible reservations are divided into those that may be severed from ratification of or accession to the convention in question and those that are contrary to the object and purpose of the treaty. In the latter case, both the reservation and the whole acceptance of the treaty by the reserving state are to be regarded as nullities. This question of permissibility is the preliminary issue; the question of opposability, or the reaction of other states, is a secondary issue, presupposing the permissibility of the reservation, *ibid.*, p. 88. See also *Oppenheim's International Law*, p. 1247, note 1.

[89] See e.g. Ruda, 'Reservations', p. 190.   [90] See the First Pellet Report, p. 50.

[91] Note that draft guideline 3.1.5 of the ILC Guide to Practice provides that, 'A reservation is incompatible with the object and purpose of the treaty if it affects an essential element of the treaty that is necessary to its general thrust, in such a way that the reservation impairs the *raison d'être* of the treaty': see A/62/10, 2007, pp. 66 ff. Draft guideline 3.1.6 states that, 'The object and purpose of the treaty is to be determined in good faith, taking account of the terms of the treaty in their context. Recourse may also be had in particular to the title of the treaty, the preparatory work of the treaty and the circumstances of its conclusion and, where appropriate, the subsequent practice agreed upon by the parties', *ibid.*, pp. 77 ff.

[92] See e.g. *Yugoslavia v. Spain*, ICJ Reports, 1999, pp. 761, 772; *Yugoslavia v. USA*, ICJ Reports, 1999, pp. 916, 924 and *Democratic Republic of the Congo v. Rwanda*, ICJ Reports,

The question is also raised as to the authority able to make such a determination. At the moment, unless the particular treaty otherwise provides,[93] whether a reservation is impermissible is a determination to be made by states parties to the treaty themselves. In other words, it is a subjective application of objective criteria.[94] Once the impermissibility of a reservation has been demonstrated, there are two fundamental possibilities. Either the treaty provision to which the reservation has been attached applies in full to the state that made the impermissible reservation or the consent of the state to the treaty as a whole is vitiated so that the state is no longer a party to the treaty. A further question is whether the other parties to the treaty may accept and thus legitimate an impermissible reservation or whether a determination of impermissibility is conclusive. All that can be said is that state practice on the whole is somewhat inconclusive.

There is a trend with regard to human rights treaties to regard impermissible reservations as severing that reservation so that the provision in question applies in full to the reserving state.[95] In the *Belilos* case,[96] the European Court of Human Rights laid particular emphasis upon Switzerland's commitment to the European Convention on Human Rights,[97] so that the effect of defining the Swiss declaration as a reservation which was then held to be invalid was that Switzerland was bound by the provision (article 6) in full. This view was reaffirmed in the *Loizidou (Preliminary Objections)* case.[98] The Court analysed the validity of the territorial restrictions attached to Turkey's declarations under former articles 25 and

---

2006, pp. 6, 32. In a joint separate opinion, five judges suggested that the principle is not necessarily absolute in scope, ICJ Reports, 2006, pp. 6, 70 ff. See also draft guideline 3.1.13 of the ILC Guide to Practice, A/62/10, 2007, pp. 116 ff.

[93] Note e.g. that article 20(2) of the International Convention on the Elimination of All Forms of Racial Discrimination, 1965 provides that a reservation will be regarded as contrary to the object and purpose of the treaty if at least two-thirds of the states parties to the convention object to the reservation.

[94] See e.g. Ago, *Yearbook of the ILC*, 1965, vol. I, p. 161.

[95] See e.g. Y. Tyagi, 'The Conflict of Law and Policy on Reservations to Human Rights Treaties', 71 BYIL, 2000, p. 181; Aust, *Modern Treaty Law*, pp. 146 ff.; *Human Rights as General Norms and a State's Right to Opt Out: Reservations and Objections to Human Rights Conventions* (ed. J. P. Gardner), London, 1997, and K. Korkelia, 'New Challenges to the Regime of Reservations under the International Covenant on Civil and Political Rights', 13 EJIL, 2002, p. 437. See also the Second Pellet Report, 1996, A/CN.4/4777.Add.1.

[96] European Court of Human Rights, Series A, No. 132. See also above, p. 916.

[97] The Court noted that 'it is beyond doubt that Switzerland is, and regards itself as, bound by the Convention irrespective of the validity of the declaration', *ibid.*, p. 22.

[98] European Court of Human Rights, Series A, No. 310 (1995); 103 ILR, p. 621.

46 recognising the competence of the Commission and the Court[99] and held that they were impermissible under the terms of the Convention. The Court then concluded that the effect of this in the light of the special nature of the Convention as a human rights treaty was that the reservations were severable so that Turkey's acceptance of the jurisdiction of the Commission and the Court remained in place, unrestricted by the terms of the invalid limitations attached to the declarations.[100]

The UN Human Rights Committee in its controversial General Comment 24/52 of 2 November 1994[101] emphasised the special nature of human rights treaties and expressed its belief that the provisions of the Vienna Convention on the Law of Treaties were 'inappropriate to address the problems of reservations to human rights treaties'. The Committee took the view that provisions contained in the International Covenant on Civil and Political Rights, 1966, which represented customary international law could not be the subject of reservations, while in the case of reservations to non-derogable provisions not falling into this category, states had 'a heavy onus' to justify such reservations. The Committee also emphasised that the effect of an unacceptable reservation would normally be that the provision operated in full with regard to the party making such a reservation and not that the Covenant would not be in force at all for such a state party. The Committee also regarded itself as the only body able to determine whether a specific reservation was or was not compatible with the object and purpose of the Covenant.[102]

The controversy with regard to this included the issue as to the powers of the Committee and other such monitoring organs as distinct from courts which under their constituent treaties had the competence to

---

[99] These were held to constitute 'a disguised reservation', ECHR, Series A, No. 310, p. 22.

[100] Ibid., pp. 22–9.

[101] CCPR/C/21/Rev.1/Add. 6. See also 15 Human Rights Law Journal, 1994, p. 464, and M. Nowak, 'The Activities of the UN Human Rights Committee: Developments from 1 August 1992 to 31 July 1995', 16 Human Rights Law Journal, 1995, pp. 377, 380.

[102] See the critical observations made by the governments of the US and the UK with regard to this General Comment, 16 Human Rights Law Journal, 1995, pp. 422 ff. Note in particular the US view that 'reservations contained in the United States instruments of ratification are integral parts of its consent to be bound by the Covenant and are not severable. If it were to be determined that any one or more of them were ineffective, the ratification as a whole could thereby be nullified', ibid., p. 423. The UK government took the view that while 'severability of a kind may well offer a solution in appropriate cases', severability would involve excising both the reservation and the parts of the treaty to which it related, ibid., p. 426. It was noted that a state which sought to ratify a human rights treaty subject to a reservation 'which is fundamentally incompatible with participation in the treaty regime' could not be regarded as a party to that treaty, ibid.

interpret the same in a binding manner.[103] The International Law Commission adopted Preliminary Conclusions on Reservations to Normative Multilateral Treaties Including Human Rights Treaties in 1997, in which it reaffirmed the applicability of the Vienna Convention on the Law of Treaties reservations regime to all treaties, including human rights treaties. The ILC accepted that human rights monitoring bodies were competent to comment and express recommendations upon *inter alia* the admissibility of reservations, but declared that this did not affect 'the traditional modalities of control' by contracting parties in accordance with the two Vienna Conventions of 1969 and 1986, nor did it mean that such bodies could exceed the powers given to them for the performance of their general monitoring role. It was particularly emphasised that 'it is the reserving state that has the responsibility of taking action' in the event of inadmissibility and such state could modify or withdraw the reservation or withdraw from the treaty.[104]

There is, however, apart from this controversy, the question as to the large number of reservations to human rights treaties, many of which have been criticised as being contrary to the object and purpose of the treaties.[105]

In general, reservations are deemed to have been accepted by states that have raised no objections to them at the end of a period of twelve months

---

[103] See also e.g. C. Redgwell, 'Reservations to Treaties and Human Rights General Comment No. 24 (52)', 46 ICLQ, 1997, p. 390.

[104] Report of the ILC on its 49th Session, A/52/10, pp. 126–7. See also the working group on reservations established by the UN human rights treaty organs, A/60/278; HRI/MC/2005/5/Add.1; and HRI/MC/2006/5. Draft guideline 3.1.12 of the ILC Guide to Practice notes that, 'To assess the compatibility of a reservation with the object and purpose of a general treaty for the protection of human rights, account shall be taken of the indivisibility, interdependence and interrelatedness of the rights set out in the treaty as well as the importance that the right or provision which is the subject of the reservation has within the general thrust of the treaty, and the gravity of the impact the reservation has upon it': see A/62/10, 2007, pp. 113 ff.

[105] See e.g. the Convention on the Elimination of Discrimination Against Women, 1979, General Recommendations No. 4 (1987), No. 20 (1992) and No. 21 (1994) of the Committee on the Elimination of Discrimination Against Women. See generally B. Clark, 'The Vienna Conventions Reservations Regime and the Convention on Discrimination against Women', 85 AJIL, 1991, p. 281, and R. J. Cook, 'Reservations to the Convention on the Elimination of All Forms of Discrimination against Women', 30 Va. JIL, 1990, p. 643. See also Council of Europe Parliamentary Assembly Recommendation 1223 (1993) on Reservations Made by Member States to Council of Europe Conventions; W. A. Schabas, 'Reservations to Human Rights Treaties: Time for Innovation and Reform', 32 Canadian YIL, 1994, p. 39, and I. Ziemele, *Reservations to Human Rights Treaties and the Vienna Convention Regime: Conflict, Harmony or Reconciliation*, Leiden, 2004.

after notification of the reservation, or by the date on which consent to be bound by the treaty was expressed, whichever is the later.[106] Reservations must be in writing and communicated to the contracting states and other states entitled to become parties to the treaty, as must acceptances of, and objections to, reservations.

Most multilateral conventions today will in fact specifically declare their position as regards reservations. Some, however, for example the Geneva Convention on the High Seas, 1958, make no mention at all of reservations, while others may specify that reservations are possible with regard to certain provisions only.[107] Still others may prohibit altogether any reservations.[108]

Reservations to a multilateral treaty may be withdrawn, subject to agreement to the contrary, only when the other states to the treaty have received notification of that withdrawal.[109]

Entry into force of treaties

Basically treaties will become operative when and how the negotiating states decide, but in the absence of any provision or agreement regarding this, a treaty will enter into force as soon as consent to be bound by the treaty has been established for all the negotiating states.[110] In many cases, treaties will specify that they will come into effect upon a certain date or after a determined period following the last ratification. It is usual where multilateral conventions are involved to provide for entry into force upon ratification by a fixed number of states, since otherwise large multilateral treaties may be prejudiced. The Geneva Convention on the High Seas, 1958, for example, provides for entry into force on the thirtieth day following the deposit of the twenty-second instrument of ratification with the United Nations Secretary-General, while the Convention on the

---

[106] Article 20(5) of the Vienna Convention on the Law of Treaties. See the Inter-American Court of Human Rights, Advisory Opinion on *The Effect of Reservations on the Entry into Force of the American Convention on Human Rights*, 22 ILM, 1983, p. 37; 67 ILR, p. 559.

[107] E.g. the 1958 Geneva Convention on the Continental Shelf, article 12(1). See also above, p. 917, regarding article 64 of the European Convention on Human Rights, 1950.

[108] See e.g. article 37 of the Convention on Damage Caused by Foreign Aircraft to Third Parties on the Surface, 1952.

[109] See article 22(3)a of the Vienna Convention on the Law of Treaties and *Democratic Republic of the Congo* v. *Rwanda*, ICJ Reports, 2006, paras. 41–2. See also draft guideline 2.5.2 and 2.5.8 of the ILC Guide, A/58/10, 2003, pp. 201 ff. and 231 ff.

[110] Article 24. See Sinclair, *Vienna Convention*, pp. 44–7. See also Thirlway, 'Law and Procedure (Part four)', pp. 32 ff., and Aust, *Modern Treaty Law*, chapter 9.

Law of Treaties, 1969 itself came into effect thirty days after the deposit of the thirty-fifth ratification and the Rome Statute for the International Criminal Court required sixty ratifications. Of course, even though the necessary number of ratifications has been received for the treaty to come into operation, only those states that have actually ratified the treaty will be bound. It will not bind those that have merely signed it, unless of course, signature is in the particular circumstances regarded as sufficient to express the consent of the state to be bound.

Article 80 of the 1969 Convention (following article 102 of the United Nations Charter) provides that after their entry into force, treaties should be transmitted to the United Nations Secretariat for registration and publication. These provisions are intended to end the practice of secret treaties, which was regarded as contributing to the outbreak of the First World War, as well as enabling the United Nations Treaty Series, which contains all registered treaties, to be as comprehensive as possible.[111]

The application of treaties[112]

Once treaties enter into force, a number of questions can arise as to the way in which they apply in particular situations. In the absence of contrary intention, the treaty will not operate retroactively so that its provisions will not bind a party as regards any facts, acts or situations prior to that state's acceptance of the treaty.[113] Unless a different intention appears from the treaty or is otherwise established, article 29 provides that a treaty is binding upon each party in respect of its entire territory. This is the general rule, but it is possible for a state to stipulate that an international agreement will apply only to part of its territory. In the past, so-called 'colonial application clauses' were included in some treaties by the European colonial powers, which declared whether or not the terms of the particular agreement would extend to the various colonies.[114]

---

[111] Article 102 of the UN Charter also provides that states may not invoke an unregistered treaty before any UN organ. See also above, p. 905, and http://untreaty.un.org/.

[112] See e.g. Nguyen Quoc Dinh et al., Droit International Public, p. 217, and Oppenheim's International Law, p. 1248.

[113] Article 28. See Yearbook of the ILC, 1966, vol. II, pp. 212–13 and the Mavrommatis Palestine Concessions case, PCIJ, Series A, No. 2, 1924. Note article 4 of the Convention, which provides that, without prejudice to the application of customary law, the Convention will apply only to treaties concluded by states after the entry into force of the Convention with regard to such states.

[114] See Sinclair, Vienna Convention, pp. 87–92. See also e.g. article 63 of the European Convention on Human Rights, 1950. Practice would appear to suggest that, in the absence of

With regard to the problem of successive treaties on the same subject matter, article 30 provides that:

1. Subject to article 103 of the Charter of the United Nations,[115] the rights and obligations of states parties to successive treaties relating to the same subject-matter shall be determined in accordance with the following paragraphs.

2. When a treaty specifies that it is subject to, or that it is not to be considered as incompatible with, an earlier or later treaty, the provisions of that other treaty prevail.

3. When all the parties to the earlier treaty are parties also to the later treaty but the earlier treaty is not terminated or suspended in operation under article 59,[116] the earlier treaty applies only to the extent that its provisions are compatible with those of the later treaty.

4. When the parties to the later treaty do not include all the parties to the earlier one:
   (a) as between states parties to both treaties the same rule applies as in paragraph 3;
   (b) as between a state party to both treaties and a state party to only one of the treaties, the treaty to which both states are parties governs their mutual rights and obligations.

5. Paragraph 4 is without prejudice to article 41,[117] or to any question of the termination or suspension of the operation of a treaty under article 60[118] or to any question of responsibility which may arise for a state from the conclusion or application of a treaty, the provisions of which are incompatible with its obligations towards another state under another treaty.

The problem raised by successive treaties is becoming a serious one with the growth in the number of states and the increasing number of treaties entered into, and the added complication of enhanced activity at the

---

evidence to the contrary, a treaty would under customary law apply to all the territory of a party, including colonies: see e.g. McNair, *Law of Treaties*, pp. 116–17.

[115] This stipulates that in the event of a conflict between the obligations of a member state of the UN under the Charter and their obligations under any other international agreement, the former shall prevail. See also the *Lockerbie (Libya v. UK; Libya v. US)* case, ICJ Reports, 1992, pp. 3, 15; 94 ILR, pp. 478, 498.

[116] This deals with termination or suspension of a treaty by a later treaty: see further below, p. 947.

[117] This deals with agreements to modify multilateral treaties between certain of the parties only: see further below, p. 931.

[118] This deals with material breach of a treaty: see further below, p. 947.

regional level.[119] The rules laid down in article 30 provide a general guide and in many cases the problem will be resolved by the parties themselves expressly.

Third states

A point of considerable interest with regard to the creation of binding rules of law for the international community centres on the application and effects of treaties upon third states, i.e. states which are not parties to the treaty in question.[120] The general rule is that international agreements bind only the parties to them. The reasons for this rule can be found in the fundamental principles of the sovereignty and independence of states, which posit that states must consent to rules before they can be bound by them. This, of course, is a general proposition and is not necessarily true in all cases. However, it does remain as a basic line of approach in international law. Article 34 of the Convention echoes the general rule in specifying that 'a treaty does not create either obligations or rights for a third state without its consent'.[121]

It is quite clear that a treaty cannot impose obligations upon third states and this was emphasised by the International Law Commission during its deliberations prior to the Vienna Conferences and Convention.[122] There is, however, one major exception to this and that is where the provisions of the treaty in question have entered into customary law.[123] In such a case, all states would be bound, regardless of whether they had been parties to the original treaty or not. One example of this would be the laws relating to warfare adopted by the Hague Conventions earlier this century and now regarded as part of customary international law.[124]

This point arises with regard to article 2(6) of the United Nations Charter which states that:

---

[119] See Sinclair, *Vienna Convention*, pp. 93–8, and Aust, *Modern Treaty Law*, chapter 12. See also McNair, *Law of Treaties*, pp. 219 ff.

[120] See e.g. Sinclair, *Vienna Convention*, pp. 98–106; Aust, *Modern Treaty Law*, chapter 14, and *Oppenheim's International Law*, p. 1260. The rule is sometimes referred to by the maxim *pacta tertiis nec nocent nec prosunt*. See also Thirlway, 'Law and Procedure (Part One)', p. 63.

[121] See also below, chapter 17, p. 970, on succession of states in respect of treaties.

[122] *Yearbook of the ILC*, 1966, vol. II, p. 227.

[123] Article 38. See above, chapter 3, p. 95 and the *North Sea Continental Shelf* cases, ICJ Reports, 1969, p. 3; 41 ILR, p. 29. See also *Yearbook of the ILC*, 1966, vol. II, p. 230.

[124] See below, chapter 21, p. 1168.

the organisation shall ensure that states which are not members of the United Nations act in accordance with these principles so far as may be necessary for the maintenance of international peace and security.

It is sometimes maintained that this provision creates binding obligations rather than being merely a statement of attitude with regard to non-members of the United Nations.[125] This may be the correct approach since the principles enumerated in article 2 of the Charter can be regarded as part of customary international law, and in view of the fact that an agreement may legitimately provide for enforcement sanctions to be implemented against a state guilty of aggression. Article 75 of the Convention provides:

> the provisions of the Convention are without prejudice to any obligation in relation to a treaty which may arise for an aggressor state in consequence of measures taken in conformity with the Charter of the United Nations with reference to that state's aggression.

Article 35 notes that an obligation may arise for a third state from a term of a treaty if the parties to the treaty so intend and if the third state expressly accepts that obligation in writing.[126]

As far as rights allocated to third states by a treaty are concerned, the matter is a little different. The Permanent Court of International Justice declared in the *Free Zones* case[127] that:

> the question of the existence of a right acquired under an instrument drawn between other states is . . . one to be decided in each particular case: it must be ascertained whether the states which have stipulated in favour of a third state meant to create for that state an actual right which the latter has accepted as such.

Article 36 of the Vienna Convention provides that:

> a right arises for a third state from a provision of a treaty if the parties to the treaty intend the provision to accord that right either to the third state, or to a group of states to which it belongs, or to all states, and the third state assents thereto. Its assent shall be presumed so long as the contrary is not indicated, unless the treaty otherwise provides.

[125] See e.g. H. Kelsen, *The Law of the United Nations*, London, 1950, pp. 106–10. See also McNair, *Law of Treaties*, pp. 216–18.

[126] See, as to the creation here of a collateral agreement forming the basis of the obligation, *Yearbook of the ILC*, 1966, vol. II, p. 227.

[127] PCIJ, Series A/B, No. 46, 1932, pp. 147–8; 6 AD, pp. 362, 364.

Further, particular kinds of treaties may create obligations or rights *erga omnes* and in such cases, all states would presumptively be bound by them and would also benefit. Examples might include multilateral treaties establishing a particular territorial regime, such as the Suez and Kiel Canals or the Black Sea Straits.[128] In the *Wimbledon* case,[129] the Permanent Court noted that 'an international waterway ... for the benefit of all nations of the world' had been established. In other words, for an obligation to be imposed by a treaty upon a third state, the express agreement of that state in writing is required, whereas in the case of benefits granted to third states, their assent is presumed in the absence of contrary intention. This is because the general tenor of customary international law has leaned in favour of the validity of rights granted to third states, but against that of obligations imposed upon them, in the light of basic principles relating to state sovereignty, equality and non-interference.

The amendment and modification of treaties

Although the two processes of amending and modifying international agreements share a common aim in that they both involve the revision of treaties, they are separate activities and may be accomplished in different manners. Amendments refer to the formal alteration of treaty provisions, affecting all the parties to the particular agreement, while modifications relate to variations of certain treaty terms as between particular parties only. Where it is deemed desirable, a treaty may be amended by agreement between the parties, but in such a case all the formalities as to the conclusion and coming into effect of treaties as described so far in this chapter will have to be observed except in so far as the treaty may otherwise provide.[130] It is understandable that as conditions change, the need may arise to alter some of the provisions stipulated in the international agreement in question. There is nothing unusual in this and it is a normal facet of international relations. The fact that such alterations must be effected with

---

[128] See e.g. Aust, *Modern Treaty Law*, pp. 258–9; Nguyen Quoc Dinh *et al.*, *Droit International Public*, p. 248, and N. Ragazzi, *The Concept of International Obligations Erga Omnes*, Oxford, 1997. See further, as to *erga omnes* obligations, above, chapter 14, p. 807.

[129] PCIJ, Series A, No. 1, 1923, p. 22; 2 AD, p. 99. See also *Yearbook of the ILC*, 1966, vol. II, pp. 228–9, and E. Jiménez de Aréchaga, 'International Law in the Past Third of a Century', 159 HR, 1978, pp. 1, 54, and de Aréchaga, 'Treaty Stipulations in Favour of Third States', 50 AJIL, 1956, pp. 338, 355–6.

[130] Article 39. See also Sinclair, *Vienna Convention*, pp. 106–9; Aust, *Modern Treaty Law*, chapter 15, and *Yearbook of the ILC*, 1966, vol. II, p. 232.

the same formalities that attended the original formation of the treaty is only logical since legal rights and obligations may be involved and any variation of them involves considerations of state sovereignty and consent which necessitate careful interpretation and attention. It is possible, however, for oral or tacit agreement to amend, providing it is unambiguous and clearly evidenced. Many multilateral treaties lay down specific conditions as regards amendment. For example, the United Nations Charter in article 108 provides that amendments will come into force for all member states upon adoption and ratification by two-thirds of the members of the organisation, including all the permanent members of the Security Council.

Problems can occur where, in the absence of specific amendment processes, some of the parties oppose the amendments proposed by others. Article 40 of the Vienna Convention specifies the procedure to be adopted in amending multilateral treaties, in the absence of contrary provisions in the treaty itself. Any proposed amendment has to be notified to all contracting states, each one of which is entitled to participate in the decision as to action to be taken and in the negotiation and conclusion of any agreements. Every state which has the right to be a party to the treaty possesses also the right to become a party to the amendment, but such amendments will not bind any state which is a party to the original agreement and which does not become a party to the amended agreement,[131] subject to any provisions to the contrary in the treaty itself.

The situation can become a little more complex where a state becomes a party to the treaty after the amendments have come into effect. That state will be a party to the amended agreement, except as regards parties to the treaty that are not bound by the amendments. In this case the state will be considered as a party to the unamended treaty in relation to those states.

Two or more parties to a multilateral treaty may decide to change that agreement as between themselves in certain ways, quite irrespective of any amendment by all the parties. This technique, known as modification, is possible provided it has not been prohibited by the treaty in question and provided it does not affect the rights or obligations of the other parties. Modification, however, is not possible where the provision it is intended to alter is one 'derogation from which is incompatible with the effective execution of the object and purpose of the treaty as a whole'.[132] A treaty

---

[131] See article 30(4)b.   [132] Article 41.

may also be modified by the terms of another later agreement[133] or by the establishment subsequently of a rule of *jus cogens*.[134]

Treaty interpretation[135]

One of the enduring problems facing courts and tribunals and lawyers, both in the municipal and international law spheres, relates to the question of interpretation.[136] Accordingly, rules and techniques have been put forward to aid judicial bodies in resolving such problems.[137] As far as international law is concerned, there are three basic approaches to treaty interpretation.[138] The first centres on the actual text of the agreement and emphasises the analysis of the words used.[139] The second looks to the intention of the parties adopting the agreement as the solution to ambiguous provisions and can be termed the subjective approach in contradistinction to the objective approach of the previous school.[140] The third approach adopts a wider perspective than the other two and emphasises the object and purpose of the treaty as the most important backcloth against which

---

[133] See article 30, and above, p. 927.

[134] See above, chapter 3, p. 123, and below, p. 944.

[135] See e.g. Sinclair, *Vienna Convention*, chapter 5; J. M. Sorel, 'Article 31' in Corten and Klein, *Conventions de Vienne*, p. 1289; Y. Le Bouthillier, 'Article 32' in *ibid.*, p. 1339; A. Papaux, 'Article 33' in *ibid.*, p. 1373; G. Fitzmaurice, 'The Law and Procedure of the International Court of Justice, 1951–4', 33 BYIL, 1957, p. 203 and 28 BYIL, 1951, p. 1; H. Lauterpacht, 'Restrictive Interpretation and the Principle of Effectiveness in the Interpretation of Treaties', 26 BYIL, 1949, p. 48; M. S. McDougal, H. Lasswell and J. C. Miller, *The Interpretation of Agreements and World Public Order*, Yale, 1967; E. Gordon, 'The World Court and the Interpretation of Constitutive Treaties', 59 AJIL, 1965, p. 794; O'Connell, *International Law*, pp. 251 ff., and Brownlie, *Principles*, pp. 602 ff. See also S. Sur, *L'Interprétation en Droit International Public*, Paris, 1974; M. K. Yasseen, 'L'Interprétation des Traités d'après la Convention de Vienne', 151 HR, 1976 III, p. 1; H. Thirlway, 'The Law and Practice of the International Court of Justice 1960–1989 (Part Three)', 62 BYIL, 1991, pp. 2, 16 ff. and '(Part Four)', 62 BYIL, 1992, p. 3, and Thirlway, 'The Law and Procedure of the International Court of Justice 1960–1989; Supplement, 2006: Part Three', 77 BYIL, 2006, p. 1; Aust, *Modern Treaty Law*, chapter 13; Nguyen Quoc Dinh *et al.*, *Droit International Public*, p. 252, and *Oppenheim's International Law*, p. 1266.

[136] Note that a unilateral interpretation of a treaty by the organs of one state would not be binding upon the other parties: see McNair, *Law of Treaties*, pp. 345–50, and the *David J. Adams* claim, 6 RIAA, p. 85 (1921); 1 AD, p. 331.

[137] But see J. Stone, 'Fictional Elements in Treaty Interpretation', 1 *Sydney Law Review*, 1955, p. 344.

[138] See Sinclair, *Vienna Convention*, pp. 114–15, and Fitzmaurice, 'Reservations'.

[139] See Fitzmaurice, 'Law and Procedure', pp. 204–7.

[140] See e.g. H. Lauterpacht, 'De l'Interprétation des Traités: Rapport et Projet de Résolutions', 43 *Annuaire de l'Institut de Droit International*, 1950, p. 366.

the meaning of any particular treaty provision should be measured.[141] This teleological school of thought has the effect of underlining the role of the judge or arbitrator, since he will be called upon to define the object and purpose of the treaty, and it has been criticised for encouraging judicial law-making. Nevertheless, any true interpretation of a treaty in international law will have to take into account all aspects of the agreement, from the words employed to the intention of the parties and the aims of the particular document. It is not possible to exclude completely any one of these components.

Articles 31 to 33 of the Vienna Convention comprise in some measure aspects of all three doctrines. Article 31 lays down the fundamental rules of interpretation and can be taken as reflecting customary international law.[142] Article 31(1) declares that a treaty shall be interpreted 'in good faith in accordance with the ordinary meaning to be given to the terms of the treaty in their context and in the light of its object and purpose'.[143] The International Court noted in the *Competence of the General Assembly for the Admission of a State to the United Nations* case[144] that 'the first duty of a tribunal which is called upon to interpret and apply the provisions of a treaty is to endeavour to give effect to them in their natural and ordinary meaning in the context in which they occur'.[145] On the basis of this provision, for example, the European Court of Human Rights held in the *Lithgow* case[146] that the use of the phrase 'subject to the conditions provided for . . . by the general principles of international law' in article 1 of

---

[141] See e.g. Fitzmaurice, 'Reservations', pp. 7–8 and 13–14, and 'Law and Procedure', pp. 207–9.

[142] The International Court has on a number of occasions reaffirmed that articles 31 and 32 of the Vienna Convention reflect customary law: see e.g. the *Genocide Convention (Bosnia v. Serbia)* case, ICJ Reports, 2007, paras. 160 ff.; *Indonesia/Malaysia* case, ICJ Reports, 2002, pp. 625, 645–6; the *Botswana/Namibia* case, ICJ Reports, 1999, p. 1045; the *Libya/Chad* case, ICJ Reports, 1994, pp. 6, 21–2; 100 ILR, pp. 1, 20–1, and the *Qatar v. Bahrain* case, ICJ Reports, 1995, pp. 6, 18; 102 ILR, pp. 47, 59. Other courts and tribunals have done likewise: see e.g. the GATT Dispute Settlement Panel Report on United States Restrictions on Imports of Tuna in 1994, 33 ILM, 1994, pp. 839, 892; the case concerning the *Auditing of Accounts between the Netherlands and France*, arbitral award of 12 March 2004, para. 59 and the *Iron Rhine (Belgium/Netherlands)*, arbitral award of 24 May 2005, para. 45. See also *Oppenheim's International Law*, p. 1271.

[143] See e.g. the *German External Debts* arbitration, 19 ILM, 1980, pp. 1357, 1377. See also Judge Ajibola's Separate Opinion in the *Libya/Chad* case, ICJ Reports, 1994, pp. 6, 71; 100 ILR, pp. 1, 69. As to 'object and purpose', see e.g. the *LaGrand* case, ICJ Reports, 2001, para. 102; 134 ILR, p. 41.

[144] ICJ Reports, 1950, pp. 4, 8; 17 ILR, pp. 326, 328.

[145] See also the *La Bretagne* arbitration (*Canada v. France*), 82 ILR, pp. 590, 620.

[146] European Court of Human Rights, Series A, No. 102, para. 114; 75 ILR, pp. 438, 482.

Protocol I of the European Convention in the context of compensation for interference with property rights, could not be interpreted as extending the general principles of international law in this field to establish standards of compensation for the nationalisation of property of nationals (as distinct from aliens).[147] The word 'context' is held to include the preamble and annexes of the treaty as well as any agreement or instrument made by the parties in connection with the conclusion of the treaty.[148]

The Eritrea–Ethiopia Boundary Commission in its boundary delimitation decision emphasised that the elements contained in article 31(1) were guides to establishing what the parties actually intended or their 'common will'[149] and in this process the principle of 'contemporaneity' is relevant. This means that a treaty should be interpreted by reference to the circumstances prevailing when the treaty was concluded,[150] so that, for instance, expressions and geographical names used in the instrument should be given the meaning that they would have possessed at that time.[151] However, as the International Court has noted, this does not prevent it from taking into account in interpreting a treaty, 'the present-day state of scientific knowledge, as reflected in the documentary material submitted to it by the parties'.[152]

It has also been noted that the process of interpretation 'is a judicial function, whose purpose is to determine the precise meaning of a provision, but which cannot change it'.[153]

In addition, any subsequent agreement or practice relating to the treaty must be considered together with the context.[154] Subsequent practice may indeed have a dual role: it may act as an instrument of interpretation and

---

[147] See also the *James* case, European Court of Human Rights, Series A, No. 98, para. 61; 75 ILR, pp. 397, 423, and the Advisory Opinions of the Inter-American Court of Human Rights in the *Enforceability of the Right to Reply* case, 79 ILR, pp. 335, 343, and the *Meaning of the Word 'Laws'* case, 79 ILR, pp. 325, 329.

[148] Article 31(2). See also the *US Nationals in Morocco* case, ICJ Reports, 1952, pp. 176, 196; 19 ILR, pp. 255, 272; the *Beagle Channel* case, HMSO, 1977, p. 12; 52 ILR, p. 93, and the *Young Loan* arbitration, 59 ILR, pp. 495, 530.

[149] 130 ILR, pp. 1, 34. See also Lord McNair in the *Argentina/Chile Frontier* case, 38 ILR, pp. 10, 89.

[150] See *Cameroon* v. *Nigeria*, ICJ Reports, 2002, pp. 303, 346. See also D. W. Greig, *Intertemporality and the Law of Treaties*, London, 2001, and, as to the doctrine of intertemporal law, above, chapter 10, p. 508.

[151] *Eritrea–Ethiopia*, 130 ILR, pp. 1, 34–5.

[152] *Botswana/Namibia*, ICJ Reports, 1999, pp. 1045, 1060.

[153] See e.g. the *Laguna del Desierto* case, 113 ILR, pp. 1, 44.

[154] Article 31(3)a and b.

it may also mark an alteration in the legal relations between the parties established by the treaty in question.[155]

The provision whereby any relevant rules of international law applicable in the relations between the parties shall be taken into account in interpreting a treaty[156] was used somewhat controversially in the *Oil Platforms (Iran v. USA)* case to justify recourse to the rules concerning the use of force in the context of the Treaty of Amity, Economic Relations and Consular Rights, 1955.[157]

Where the interpretation according to the provisions of article 31 needs confirmation, or determination since the meaning is ambiguous or obscure, or leads to a manifestly absurd or unreasonable result, recourse may be had to supplementary means of interpretation under article 32. These means include the preparatory works (*travaux préparatoires*) of the treaty and the circumstances of its conclusion and may be employed in the above circumstances to aid the process of interpreting the treaty in question.[158] Nevertheless, the International Court has

---

[155] As to the latter, see e.g. the *Temple* case, ICJ Reports, 1962, p. 6; 33 ILR, p. 48, the *Namibia* case, ICJ Reports, 1971, pp. 16, 22; 49 ILR, p. 2, the *Taba* case, 80 ILR, p. 226 and *Eritrea–Ethiopia*, 130 ILR, pp. 1, 34 ff.

[156] Article 31(3)c.

[157] ICJ Reports, 2003, pp. 161, 182; 130 ILR, pp. 323, 341–2. Judge Higgins in her Separate Opinion noted that, 'The Court reads this provision as incorporating the totality of the substantive international law (which in paragraph 42 of the Judgment is defined as comprising Charter law) on the use of force. But this is to ignore that Article 31, paragraph 3, requires "the context" to be taken into account: and "the context" is clearly that of an economic and commercial treaty', *ibid.*, pp. 225, 237; 130 ILR, pp. 383, 395. See also *Iran v. USA*, Case No. A/18, 5 Iran–US CTR, p. 251; 75 ILR, pp. 175, 188, where the Full Tribunal held, citing article 31(3)c, that jurisdiction existed over claims against Iran by dual Iran–US nationals when the dominant and effective nationality of the claimant at the relevant period was that of the US, and *Loizidou v. Turkey (Preliminary Objections)*, European Court of Human Rights, Series A, No. 310, p. 25; 103 ILR, p. 621.

[158] See *Yearbook of the ILC*, 1966, vol. II, p. 223, doubting the rule in the *River Oder* case, PCIJ, Series A, No. 23, 1929; 5 AD, pp. 381, 383, that the *travaux préparatoires* of certain provisions of the Treaty of Versailles could not be taken into account since three of the states before the Court had not participated in the preparatory conference. See also the *Young Loan* case, 59 ILR, pp. 495, 544–5; Sinclair, *Vienna Convention*, pp. 141–7, and the *Lithgow* case, European Court of Human Rights, Series A, No. 102, para. 117; 75 ILR, pp. 438, 484. Note that in both the *Libya/Chad* case, ICJ Reports, 1994, pp. 6, 27; 100 ILR, pp. 1, 26, and *Qatar v. Bahrain* case, ICJ Reports, 1995, pp. 6, 21; 102 ILR, pp. 47, 62, the International Court held that while it was not necessary to have recourse to the *travaux préparatoires* to elucidate the content of the instruments in question, it could turn to them to confirm its reading of the text. See also the *Construction of a Wall* advisory opinion, ICJ Reports, 2004, pp. 136, 174 ff.; 129 ILR, pp. 37, 92 ff.

underlined that 'interpretation must be based above all upon the text of the treaty'.[159]

Case-law provides some interesting guidelines to the above-stated rules. In the *Interpretation of Peace Treaties* case,[160] the Court was asked whether the UN Secretary-General could appoint the third member of a Treaty Commission upon the request of one side to the dispute where the other side (Bulgaria, Hungary and Romania) refused to appoint its own representative. It was emphasised that the natural and ordinary meaning of the terms of the Peace Treaties with the three states concerned envisaged the appointment of the third member after the other two had been nominated. The breach of a treaty obligation could not be remedied by creating a Commission which was not the kind of Commission envisaged by the Treaties. The principle of effectiveness could not be used by the Court to attribute to the provisions for the settlement of disputes in the Peace Treaties a meaning which would be contrary to their letter and spirit. The Court also stressed the nature of the disputes clause as being one that had to be strictly construed. Thus, the character of the provisions to be interpreted is significant in the context of utilising the relevant rules of interpretation. The principle of effectiveness[161] will be used, however, in order to give effect to provisions in accordance with the intentions of the parties[162] and in accordance with the rules of international law.[163]

In two areas, it should be noted, the principle of effectiveness allied with the broader purposes approach has been used in an especially dynamic manner. In the case of treaties that also operate as the constitutional documents of an international organisation, a more flexible method of interpretation would seem to be justified, since one is dealing with an instrument that is being used in order to accomplish the stated aims

---

[159] The *Libya/Chad* case, ICJ Reports, 1994, pp. 6, 22; 100 ILR, pp. 1, 21.

[160] ICJ Reports, 1950, pp. 221, 226–30; 17 ILR, pp. 318, 320–2. See also *Yearbook of the ILC*, 1966, vol. II, p. 220.

[161] The International Court in the *Fisheries Jurisdiction (Spain v. Canada)* case declared that the principle of effectiveness 'has an important role in the law of treaties', ICJ Reports, 1999, pp. 432, 455.

[162] See e.g. the *Ambatielos* case, ICJ Reports, 1952, p. 28; 19 ILR, p. 416. See also the *Corfu Channel* case, ICJ Reports, 1949, pp. 4, 24; 16 AD, pp. 155, 169 and *Yearbook of the ILC*, 1966, vol. II, p. 219.

[163] See e.g. the *Fisheries Jurisdiction (Spain v. Canada)* case, ICJ Reports, 1999, pp. 432, 455, the *Right of Passage (Preliminary Objections)* case, ICJ Reports, 1957, p. 142 and the *Laguna del Desierto* case, 113 ILR, pp. 1, 45.

of that organisation. In addition, of course, the concept and nature of subsequent practice possesses in such cases an added relevance.[164] This approach has been used as a way of inferring powers, not expressly provided for in the relevant instruments, which are deemed necessary in the context of the purposes of the organisation.[165] This programmatic interpretation doctrine in such cases is now well established and especially relevant to the United Nations, where over sixty years of practice related to the principles of the organisation by over 190 states is manifest.

The more dynamic approach to interpretation is also evident in the context of human rights treaties, such as the European Convention on Human Rights, which created a system of implementation.[166] It has been held that a particular legal order was thereby established involving objective obligations to protect human rights rather than subjective, reciprocal rights.[167] Accordingly, a more flexible and programmatic or

---

[164] Note that by article 5, the Vienna Convention is deemed to apply to any treaty which is the constituent instrument of an international organisation. See also C. F. Amerasinghe, *Principles of the Institutional Law of International Organisations*, Cambridge, 1996, chapter 2, and Amerasinghe, 'Interpretation of Texts in Open International Organisations', 65 BYIL, 1994, p. 175; M. N. Shaw, *Title to Territory in Africa: International Legal Issues*, Oxford, 1986, pp. 64–73; S. Rosenne, 'Is the Constitution of an International Organisation an International Treaty?', 12 *Communicazioni e Studi*, 1966, p. 21, and G. Distefano, 'La Pratique Subséquente des Etats Parties à un Traité', AFDI, 1994, p. 41.

[165] See e.g. the *Reparations* case, ICJ Reports, 1949, p. 174; 16 AD, p. 318; the *Certain Expenses of the UN* case, ICJ Reports, 1962, p. 151; 34 ILR, p. 281; the *Competence of the General Assembly for the Admission of a State* case, ICJ Reports, 1950, p. 4; 17 ILR, p. 326, and the *Namibia* case, ICJ Reports, 1971, p. 16; 49 ILR, p. 2. See also Shaw, *Title to Territory*; R. Higgins, 'The Development of International Law by the Political Organs of the United Nations', PASIL, 1965, p. 119, and H. G. Schermers and N. M. Blokker, *International Institutional Law*, 3rd edn, The Hague, 1995, chapter 9. See further below, chapter 23, pp. 1305 ff.

[166] See further above, chapter 7, p. 347. See also J. G. Merrills, *The Development of International Law by the European Court of Human Rights*, 2nd edn, Manchester, 1993, chapter 4. Note that the European Court of Human Rights in *Loizidou* v. *Turkey (Preliminary Objections)*, Series A, No. 310, p. 26 (1995); 103 ILR, p. 621, emphasised the fundamental differences as between the role and purposes of the International Court of Justice and the European Court. See also the *Genocide Convention (Bosnia* v. *Serbia)* case, ICJ Reports, 2007, paras. 403 ff.

[167] See e.g. *Austria* v. *Italy*, 4 *European Yearbook of Human Rights*, 1960, pp. 116, 140 and *Ireland* v. *UK*, Series A, No. 25, p. 90 (1978). See also the Advisory Opinion of the Inter-American Court of Human Rights on the *Effect of Reservations on the Entry into Force of the American Convention on Human Rights*, 22 ILM, 1983, pp. 37, 47; 67 ILR, pp. 559, 568, which adopted a similar approach.

purpose-oriented method of interpretation was adopted, emphasising that the Convention constituted a living instrument that had to be interpreted 'in the light of present-day conditions'.[168] In addition, the object and purpose of the Convention requires that its provisions be interpreted so as to make its safeguards practical and effective.[169]

Indeed, in this context, it was noted in the *Licensing of Journalists* case[170] that while it was useful to compare the Inter-American Convention on Human Rights with other relevant international instruments, this approach could not be utilised to read into the Convention restrictions existing in other treaties. In this situation, 'the rule most favourable to the individual must prevail'.

Article 31(4) provides that a special meaning shall be given to a term if it is established that the parties so intended. It would appear that the standard of proof is fairly high, since a derogation from the ordinary meaning of the term is involved. It is not enough that one party only uses the particular term in a particular way.[171]

Where a treaty is authenticated in more than one language, as often happens with multilateral agreements, article 33 provides that, in the absence of agreement, in the event of a difference of meaning that the normal processes of interpretation cannot resolve, the meaning which best reconciles the texts, having regard to the object and purpose of the treaty, shall be adopted.[172]

---

[168] See e.g. the *Tyrer* case, European Court of Human Rights, Series A, No. 26, at p. 15 (1978); 58 ILR, pp. 339, 553; the *Marckx* case, ECHR, Series A, No. 32, at p. 14 (1979); 58 ILR, pp. 561, 583; the *Wemhoff* case, ECHR, Series A, No. 7 (1968); 41 ILR, p. 281, and the *Loizidou* case, ECHR, Series A, No. 310, p. 23; 103 ILR, p. 621. See also H. Waldock, 'The Evolution of Human Rights Concepts and the Application of the European Convention on Human Rights' in *Mélanges Offerts à Paul Reuter*, Paris, 1981, p. 535. Note also the approach taken by the UN Human Rights Committee in its General Comment 24/52 of 2 November 1994 on Reservations: see 15 *Human Rights Law Journal*, 1994, p. 464, and above, p. 923.

[169] See e.g. *Soering* v. *UK*, European Court of Human Rights, Series A, No. 161, p. 34 (1989); 98 ILR, p. 270; *Artico* v. *Italy*, ECHR, Series A, No. 37 (1980) and *Loizidou* v. *Turkey*, ECHR, Series A, No. 310, p. 23 (1995); 103 ILR, p. 621.

[170] Advisory Opinion of the Inter-American Court of Human Rights, 1985, 75 ILR, pp. 30, 47–8.

[171] See the *Eastern Greenland* case, PCIJ, Series A/B, No. 53, 1933, p. 49; 6 AD, p. 95, and the *Anglo-French Continental Shelf* case, Cmnd 7438, p. 50; 54 ILR, p. 6.

[172] See the *LaGrand* case, ICJ Reports, 2001, para. 101; 134 ILR, pp. 1, 40–1, the *Mavrommatis Palestine Concessions* case, PCIJ, Series A, No. 2, p. 19; 2 AD, p. 27, which called for the more restrictive interpretation in such cases, and the *Young Loan* case, 59 ILR, p. 495. See also Aust, *Modern Treaty Law*, pp. 250 ff.

Invalidity, termination and suspension of the operation of treaties[173]

General provisions

Article 42 states that the validity and continuance in force of a treaty may only be questioned on the basis of the provisions in the Vienna Convention. Article 44 provides that a state may only withdraw from or suspend the operation of a treaty in respect of the treaty as a whole and not particular parts of it, unless the treaty otherwise stipulates or the parties otherwise agree. If the appropriate ground for invalidating, terminating, withdrawing from or suspending the operation of a treaty relates solely to particular clauses, it may only be invoked in relation to those clauses where:

(a) the said clauses are separable from the remainder of the treaty with regard to their application;

(b) it appears from the treaty or is otherwise established that acceptance of those clauses was not an essential basis of consent of the other party or parties to be bound by the treaty as a whole; and

(c) continued performance of the remainder of the treaty would not be unjust.

Thus the Convention adopts a cautious approach to the general issue of separability of treaty provisions in this context.[174]

Article 45 in essence provides that a ground for invalidity, termination, withdrawal or suspension may no longer be invoked by the state where, after becoming aware of the facts, it expressly agreed that the treaty is valid or remains in force or by reason of its conduct may be deemed to have acquiesced in the validity of the treaty or its continuance in force.[175]

---

[173] Nguyen Quoc Dinh et al., Droit International Public, p. 302, and Oppenheim's International Law, p. 1284. See also N. Kontou, The Termination and Revision of Treaties in the Light of New Customary International Law, Oxford, 1995, and Aust, Modern Treaty Law, chapters 16 and 17.

[174] See Judge Lauterpacht, the Norwegian Loans case, ICJ Reports, 1957, pp. 9, 55–9; 24 ILR, pp. 782, 809, and Sinclair, Vienna Convention, pp. 165–7.

[175] See e.g. the Arbitral Award by the King of Spain case, ICJ Reports, 1960, pp. 192, 213–14; 30 ILR, pp. 457, 473, and the Temple case, ICJ Reports, 1962, pp. 6, 23–32; 33 ILR, pp. 48, 62. See also the Argentina–Chile case, 38 ILR, p. 10 and above, chapter 10.

Invalidity of treaties

Municipal law

A state cannot plead a breach of its constitutional provisions as to the making of treaties as a valid excuse for condemning an agreement. There has been for some years disagreement amongst international lawyers as to whether the failure to abide by a domestic legal limitation by, for example, a head of state in entering into a treaty, will result in rendering the agreement invalid or not.[176] The Convention took the view that in general it would not, but that it could in certain circumstances.

Article 46(1) provides that:

> state may not invoke the fact that its consent to be bound by a treaty has been expressed in violation of a provision of its internal law regarding competence to conclude treaties as invalidating its consent unless that violation was manifest and concerned a rule of its internal law of fundamental importance.

Violation will be regarded as manifest if it would be 'objectively evident' to any state conducting itself in the matter in accordance with normal practice, and in good faith.[177] For example, where the representative of the state has had his authority to consent on behalf of the state made subject to a specific restriction which is ignored, the state will still be bound by that consent save where the other negotiating states were aware of the restriction placed upon his authority to consent prior to the expression of that consent.[178] This particular provision applies as regards a person authorised to represent a state and such persons are defined in article 7 to include heads of state and government and foreign ministers in addition to persons possessing full powers.[179]

The International Court dealt with this question in *Cameroon* v. *Nigeria*, where it had been argued by Nigeria that the Maroua Declaration of 1975 between the two states was not valid as its constitutional rules had not been complied with. The Court noted that the Nigerian head of state had signed the Declaration and that a limitation of his

---

[176] See Sinclair, *Vienna Convention*, pp. 169–71, distinguishing between the constitutionalist and internationalist schools, and K. Holloway, *Modern Trends in Treaty Law*, London, 1967, pp. 123–33. See also *Yearbook of the ILC*, 1966, vol. II, pp. 240–1.

[177] Article 46(2).

[178] Article 47. See e.g. the *Eastern Greenland* case, PCIJ, Series A/B, No. 53, 1933; 6 AD, p. 95, and *Qatar* v. *Bahrain*, ICJ Reports, 1994, pp. 112, 121–2; 102 ILR, pp. 1, 18–19.

[179] See above, p. 908.

capacity would not be 'manifest' unless at least properly publicised. This was especially so since heads of state are deemed to represent their states for the purpose of performing acts relating to the conclusion of treaties.[180] The Court also noted that 'there is no general legal obligation for states to keep themselves informed of legislative and constitutional developments in other states which are or may become important for the international relations of these states'.[181]

It should, of course, also be noted that a state may not invoke a provision of its internal law as a justification for its failure to carry out an international obligation. This is a general principle of international law[182] and finds its application in the law of treaties by virtue of article 27 of the 1969 Vienna Convention.

Error

Unlike the role of mistake in municipal laws of contract, the scope in international law of error as invalidating a state's consent is rather limited. In view of the character of states and the multiplicity of persons actually dealing with the negotiation and conclusion of treaties, errors are not very likely to happen, whether they be unilateral or mutual.

Article 48 declares that a state may only invoke an error in a treaty as invalidating its consent to be bound by the treaty, if the error relates to a fact or situation which was assumed by that state to exist at the time when the treaty was concluded and formed an essential basis of its consent to be bound by the treaty. But if the state knew or ought to have known of the error, or if it contributed to that error, then it cannot afterwards free itself from the obligation of observing the treaty by pointing to that error.

This restrictive approach is in harmony with the comments made in a number of cases, including the *Temple* case,[183] where the International Court of Justice rejected Thailand's argument that a particular map contained a basic error and therefore it was not bound to observe it, since 'the plea of error cannot be allowed as an element vitiating consent if the party advancing it contributed by its own conduct to the error, or could have avoided it, or if the circumstances were such as to put that party on

---

[180] ICJ Reports, 2002, pp. 303, 430.   [181] *Ibid.*, pp. 430–1.

[182] See e.g. the *Alabama Claims* arbitration, J. B. Moore, *International Arbitrations*, New York, 1898, vol. I, p. 495, and the *Greco-Bulgarian Communities* case, PCIJ, Series B, No. 17, p. 32; 5 AD, p. 4. See also the *Applicability of the Obligation to Arbitrate under Section 21 of the United Nations Headquarters Agreement* case, ICJ Reports, 1988, pp. 12, 34–5; 82 ILR, pp. 225, 252.

[183] ICJ Reports, 1960, p. 6; 33 ILR, p. 48.

notice of a possible error'.[184] The Court felt that in view of the character and qualifications of the persons who were involved on the Thai side in examining the map, Thailand could not put forward a claim of error.

Fraud and corruption

Where a state consents to be bound by a treaty as a result of the fraudulent conduct of another negotiating state, that state may under article 49 invoke the fraud as invalidating its consent to be bound. Where a negotiating state directly or indirectly corrupts the representative of another state in order to obtain the consent of the latter to the treaty, that corruption may under article 50 be invoked as invalidating the consent to be bound.[185]

Coercion

Of more importance than error, fraud or corruption in the law of treaties is the issue of coercion as invalidating consent. Where consent has been obtained by coercing the representative of a state, whether by acts or threats directed against him, it shall, according to article 51 of the Convention, be without any legal effect.[186]

The problem of consent obtained by the application of coercion against the state itself is a slightly different one. Prior to the League of Nations, it was clear that international law did not provide for the invalidation of treaties on the grounds of the use or threat of force by one party against the other and this was a consequence of the lack of rules in customary law prohibiting recourse to war. With the signing of the Covenant of the League in 1919, and the Kellogg–Briand Pact in 1928 forbidding the resort to war to resolve international disputes, a new approach began to be taken with regard to the illegality of the use of force in international relations.

With the elucidation of the Nuremberg principles and the coming into effect of the Charter of the United Nations after the Second World War, it became clear that international law condemned coercive activities by states.

Article 2(4) of the United Nations Charter provides that:

> [a]ll members shall refrain in their international relations from the threat or use of force against the territorial integrity or political independence of any state, or in any other measure inconsistent with the purposes of the United Nations.

---

[184] ICJ Reports, 1960, p. 26; 33 ILR, p. 65.

[185] Such instances are very rare in practice: see *Yearbook of the ILC*, 1966, vol. II, pp. 244–5 and Sinclair, *Vienna Convention*, pp. 173–6.

[186] See e.g. *First Fidelity Bank NA* v. *Government of Antigua and Barbuda Permanent Mission* 877 F. 2d 189, 192 (1989); 99 ILR, pp. 126, 130.

It followed that treaties based on coercion of a state should be regarded as invalid.[187]

Accordingly, article 52 of the Convention provides that '[a] treaty is void if its conclusion has been procured by the threat or use of force in violation of the principles of international law embodied in the Charter of the United Nations'. This article was the subject of much debate in the Vienna Conference preceding the adoption of the Convention. Communist and certain Third World countries argued that coercion comprised not only the threat or use of force but also economic and political pressures.[188] The International Law Commission did not take a firm stand on the issue, but noted that the precise scope of the acts covered by the definition should be left to be determined in practice by interpretation of the relevant Charter provisions.[189]

The Vienna Conference, however, issued a Declaration on the Prohibition of Military, Political or Economic Coercion in the Conclusion of Treaties, which condemned the exercise of such coercion to procure the formation of a treaty. These points were not included in the Convention itself, which leaves one to conclude that the application of political or economic pressure to secure the consent of a state to a treaty may not be contrary to international law, but clearly a lot will depend upon the relevant circumstances.

In international relations, the variety of influences which may be brought to bear by a powerful state against a weaker one to induce it to adopt a particular line of policy is wide-ranging and may cover not only coercive threats but also subtle expressions of displeasure. The precise nuances of any particular situation will depend on a number of factors, and it will be misleading to suggest that all forms of pressure are as such violations of international law.

The problem was noted by Judge Padilla Nervo in the International Court in the *Fisheries Jurisdiction* case[190] when he stated that:

> there are moral and political pressures which cannot be proved by the so-called documentary evidence, but which are in fact indisputably real and which have, in history, given rise to treaties and conventions claimed to be freely concluded and subjected to the principle of *pacta sunt servanda.*[191]

---

[187] See *Yearbook of the ILC*, 1966, vol. II, pp. 246–7. See also the *Fisheries Jurisdiction* case, ICJ Reports, 1973, pp. 3, 14; 55 ILR, pp. 183, 194.

[188] See Sinclair, *Vienna Convention*, pp. 177–9.

[189] *Yearbook of the ILC*, 1966, vol. II, pp. 246–7.

[190] ICJ Reports, 1973, p. 3; 55 ILR, p. 183.

[191] ICJ Reports, 1973, p. 47; 55 ILR, p. 227.

It should also be noted that the phrase 'in violation of the principles of international law embodied in the Charter' was used so that article 52 should by no means be construed as applying solely to members of the United Nations but should be treated as a universal rule.

Jus cogens[192]

Article 53 of the Convention provides that:

> [a] treaty is void if, at the time of its conclusion, it conflicts with a peremptory norm of general international law. For the purposes of the present Convention, a peremptory norm of general international law is a norm accepted and recognised by the international community of states as a whole as a norm from which no derogation is permitted, and which can be modified only by a subsequent norm of general international law having the same character.

Article 64 declares that '[i]f a new peremptory norm of general international law emerges, any existing treaty which is in conflict with that norm becomes void and terminates'.[193]

As noted in chapter 3,[194] the concept of *jus cogens*, of fundamental and entrenched rules of international law, is well established in doctrine now, but controversial as to content and method of creation. The insertion of articles dealing with *jus cogens* in the 1969 Convention underlines the basic principles with regard to treaties.

Consequences of invalidity

Article 69 provides that an invalid treaty is void and without legal force. If acts have nevertheless been performed in reliance on such a treaty, each party may require any other party to establish as far as possible in their

---

[192] See e.g. J. Sztucki, *Jus Cogens and the Vienna Convention on the Law of Treaties*, New York, 1974; C. Rozakis, *The Concept of Jus Cogens in the Law of Treaties*, Leiden, 1976; L. Hannikainen, *Peremptory Norms (Jus Cogens) in International Law*, Helsinki, 1988; E. Suy, 'Article 53' in Corten and Klein, *Conventions de Vienne*, p. 1905; A. Gomez Robledo, 'Le *Jus Cogens* International: Sa Genèse, Sa Nature, Ses Fonctions', 172 HR, 1981, p. 9; L. Alexidze, 'Legal Nature of *Jus Cogens* in Contemporary International Law', 172 HR, p. 219; G. Gaja, '*Jus Cogens* Beyond the Vienna Convention', 172 HR, 1981, p. 271; Nguyen Quoc Dinh *et al.*, *Droit International Public*, p. 202, and *Oppenheim's International Law*, p. 1292. See also *Yearbook of the ILC*, 1966, vol. II, pp. 247–8, and Sinclair, *Vienna Convention*, chapter 7.

[193] See also article 71 and below, p. 945. See also A. Lagerwall, 'Article 64' in Corten and Klein, *Conventions de Vienne*, p. 2299.

[194] See above, p. 123.

mutual relations the position that would have existed if the acts had not been performed. Acts performed in good faith before the invalidity was invoked are not rendered unlawful by reason only of the invalidity of the treaty.

Where a treaty is void under article 53, article 71 provides that the parties are to eliminate as far as possible the consequences of any act performed in reliance on any provision which conflicts with *jus cogens* and bring their mutual relations into conformity with the peremptory norm. Where a treaty terminates under article 64, the parties are released from any obligation further to perform the treaty, but this does not affect any right, obligation or legal situation of the parties created through the execution of the treaty prior to its termination, provided that the rights, obligations or situations may be maintained thereafter in conformity with the new peremptory norm.

The termination of treaties[195]

There are a number of methods available by which treaties may be terminated or suspended.

Termination by treaty provision or consent

A treaty may be terminated or suspended in accordance with a specific provision in that treaty, or otherwise at any time by consent of all the parties after consultation.[196] Where, however, a treaty contains no provision regarding termination and does not provide for denunciation or withdrawal specifically, a state may only denounce or withdraw from that treaty where the parties intended to admit such a possibility or where the right may be implied by the nature of the treaty.[197] In General Comment No. 26 of 1997, the UN Human Rights Committee, noting that the International Covenant on Civil and Political Rights had no provision for termination or denunciation, concluded on the basis of the Vienna Convention provisions, that the parties had not intended to admit of such

---

[195] See e.g. E. David, *The Strategy of Treaty Termination*, New Haven, 1975; A. Vamvoukis, *Termination of Treaties in International Law*, Oxford, 1985, and R. Plender, 'The Role of Consent in the Termination of Treaties', 57 BYIL, 1986, p. 133. See also Thirlway, 'Law and Procedure (Part Four)', pp. 63 ff., and Aust, *Modern Treaty Law*, chapter 16.

[196] Articles 54 and 57.

[197] Article 56. Examples given by J. Brierly, *The Law of Nations*, 6th edn, Oxford, 1963, p. 331, include treaties of alliance and commerce. See also *Nicaragua v. US*, ICJ Reports, 1984, pp. 392, 420; 76 ILR, pp. 1, 131.

a possibility. The Committee based itself on the fact that states parties were able to withdraw their acceptance of the right of inter-state complaint, while the First Optional Protocol, concerning the right of individual communication, provided in terms for denunciation. The Committee also emphasised that the Covenant, as an instrument codifying universal human rights, was not the type of treaty which, by its nature, implies a right of denunciation.[198]

A treaty may, of course, come to an end if its purposes and objects have been fulfilled or if it is clear from its provisions that it is limited in time and the requisite period has elapsed. The Tribunal in the *Rainbow Warrior* case[199] held that the breach of the New Zealand–France Agreement, 1986, concerning the two captured French agents that had sunk the vessel in question,[200] had commenced on 22 July 1986 and had run continuously for the three years' period of confinement of the agents stipulated in the agreement. Accordingly, the period concerned had expired on 22 July 1989, so that France could not be said to be in breach of its international obligations after that date. However, this did not exempt France from responsibility for its previous breaches of its obligations, committed while these obligations were in force. Claims arising out of a previous infringement of a treaty which has since expired acquire an existence independent of that treaty.[201] The termination of a treaty does not affect any right, obligation or legal situation of the parties created through the execution of the treaty prior to its termination.[202]

Just as two or more parties to a multilateral treaty may modify as between themselves particular provisions of the agreement,[203] so they may under article 58 agree to suspend the operation of treaty provisions

---

[198] A/53/40, annex VII.　　　[199] 82 ILR, pp. 499, 567–8.　　　[200] See above, p. 779.

[201] See the Dissenting Opinion of Judge McNair in the *Ambatielos* case, ICJ Reports, 1952, pp. 28, 63; 19 ILR, pp. 416, 433.

[202] Article 70(1)b of the 1969 Vienna Convention. See below, p. 952. Note that in draft article 3 of the ILC Draft Articles on the Effects of Armed Conflicts on Treaties, A/CN.4/178, 2007, p. 7, it is provided that the outbreak of an armed conflict does not necessarily terminate or suspend the operation of treaties as (a) between the parties to the armed conflict and (b) between one or more parties to the armed conflict and a third state. Draft article 10 provides that a state exercising its rights of individual or collective self-defence in accordance with the Charter of the United Nations is entitled to suspend in whole or in part the operation of a treaty incompatible with the exercise of that right, subject to any consequences resulting from a later determination by the Security Council of that state as an aggressor. This formulation is based upon article 7 of the resolution on the effects of armed conflicts on treaties adopted by the Institut de Droit International in 1985, *ibid.*, p. 18.

[203] Article 41 and above, p. 931.

temporarily and as between themselves alone if such a possibility is provided for by the treaty. Such suspension may also be possible under that article, where not prohibited by the treaty in question, provided it does not affect the rights or obligations of the other parties under the particular agreement and provided it is not incompatible with the object and purpose of the treaty.

Where all the parties to a treaty later conclude another agreement relating to the same subject matter, the earlier treaty will be regarded as terminated where it appears that the matter is to be governed by the later agreement or where the provisions of the later treaty are so incompatible with those of the earlier one that the two treaties are not capable of being applied at the same time.[204]

Material breach[205]

There are two approaches to be considered. First, if one state violates an important provision in an agreement, it is not unnatural for the other states concerned to regard that agreement as ended by it. It is in effect a reprisal or countermeasure,[206] a rather unsubtle but effective means of ensuring the enforcement of a treaty. The fact that an agreement may be terminated where it is breached by one party may act as a discouragement to any party that might contemplate a breach of one provision but would be unwilling to forgo the benefits prescribed in others. On the other hand, to render treaties revocable because one party has acted contrary to what might very well be only a minor provision in the agreement taken as a whole, would be to place the states participating in a treaty in rather a vulnerable position. There is a need for flexibility as well as certainty in such situations. Customary law supports the view that something more than a mere breach itself of a term in an agreement would be necessary to give the other party or parties the right to abrogate that agreement. In the *Tacna-Arica* arbitration,[207] between Chile and Peru, the arbitrator noted, in referring to an agreement about a plebiscite in former Peruvian territory occupied by Chile, that:

---

[204] Article 59.

[205] See e.g. S. Rosenne, *Breach of Treaty*, Cambridge, 1985. See also D. N. Hutchinson, 'Solidarity and Breaches of Multilateral Treaties', 59 BYIL, 1988, p. 151, and M. M. Gomaa, *Suspension or Termination of Treaties on Grounds of Breach*, The Hague, 1996.

[206] See above, chapter 14, p. 794.

[207] 2 RIAA, p. 921 (1925).

[i]t is manifest that if abuses of administration could have the effect of terminating such an agreement, it would be necessary to establish such serious conditions as the consequence of administrative wrongs as would operate to frustrate the purpose of the agreement.[208]

The relevant provision of the Vienna Convention is contained in article 60, which codifies existing customary law.[209] Article 60(3) declares that a material breach of a treaty consists in either a repudiation of the treaty not permitted by the Vienna Convention or the violation of a provision essential to the accomplishment of the object or purpose of the treaty.[210] The second part of article 60(3) was applied in the *Rainbow Warrior* case,[211] where the obligation to confine the two French agents in question on a Pacific Island for a minimum period of three years was held to have constituted the object or purpose of the New Zealand–France Agreement, 1986 so that France committed a material breach of this treaty by permitting the agents to leave the island before the expiry of the three-year period.

Where such a breach occurs in a bilateral treaty, then under article 60(1) the innocent party may invoke that breach as a ground for terminating the treaty or suspending its operation in whole or in part. The International Court has made clear that it is only a material breach of the treaty itself, by a state party to it, which entitles the other party to rely on it for grounds of termination.[212] Further, termination on the basis of a breach which has not yet occurred, such as Hungary's purported termination of a bilateral treaty on the basis of works done by Czechoslovakia which had not at the time resulted in a diversion of the Danube River, would be deemed premature and would not be lawful.[213]

There is a rather different situation in the case of a multilateral treaty since a number of innocent parties are involved that might not wish the treaty to be denounced by one of them because of a breach by another state. To cover such situations, article 60(2) prescribes that a material breach of a multilateral treaty by one of the parties entitles:

---

[208] *Ibid.*, pp. 943–4.
[209] See the *Gabčíkovo–Nagymaros Project* case, ICJ Reports, 1997, pp. 7, 38; 116 ILR, p. 1. See also B. Simma and C. J. Tams, 'Article 60' in Corten and Klein, *Conventions de Vienne*, p. 2131.
[210] See the *Namibia* case, ICJ Reports, 1971, pp. 16, 46–7; 49 ILR, pp. 2, 37.
[211] 82 ILR, pp. 499, 564–6.
[212] The *Gabčíkovo–Nagymaros Project* case, ICJ Reports, 1997, pp. 7, 65; 116 ILR, p. 1.
[213] ICJ Reports, 1997, p. 66.

(a) the other parties by unanimous agreement to suspend the operation of the treaty in whole or in part or to terminate it either:
  (i) in the relations between themselves and the defaulting state, or
  (ii) as between all the parties;
(b) a party specially affected by the breach to invoke it as a ground for suspending the operation of the treaty in whole or in part in the relations between itself and the defaulting state;
(c) any party other than the defaulting state to invoke the breach as a ground for suspending the operation of the treaty in whole or in part with respect to itself if the treaty is of such a character that a material breach of its provisions by one party radically changes the position of every party with respect to the further performance of its obligations under the treaty.[214]

It is interesting to note that the provisions of article 60 regarding the definition and consequences of a material breach do not apply, by article 60(5), to provisions relating to the 'protection of the human person contained in treaties of a humanitarian character, in particular to provisions prohibiting any form of reprisals against persons protected by such treaties'. This is because objective and absolute principles are involved and not just reciprocal rights and duties.[215]

Supervening impossibility of performance[216]

Article 61 of the Convention[217] is intended to cover such situations as the submergence of an island, or the drying up of a river where the consequence of such events is to render the performance of the treaty impossible. Where the carrying out of the terms of the agreement becomes impossible because of the 'permanent disappearance or destruction of an object indispensable for the execution of the treaty', a party may validly terminate or withdraw from it. However, where the impossibility is only temporary, it may be invoked solely to suspend the operation of the treaty. Impossibility cannot be used in this way where it arises from the breach

---

[214] See *Yearbook of the ILC*, 1966, vol. II, pp. 253–5. See also the *Namibia* case, ICJ Reports, 1971, pp. 16, 47; 49 ILR, p. 37, and the *US–France Air Services Agreement* case, 54 ILR, pp. 304, 331.

[215] See e.g. G. Fitzmaurice, 'General Principles of International Law Considered from the Standpoint of the Rule of Law', 92 HR, 1957, pp. 1, 125–6, and above, chapter 7, p. 348.

[216] See e.g. McNair, *Law of Treaties*, pp. 685–8, and Sinclair, *Vienna Convention*, pp. 190–2.

[217] This is also a codification of customary law: see the *Gabčíkovo–Nagymaros Project* case, ICJ Reports, 1997, pp. 7, 38; 116 ILR, p. 1.

by the party attempting to terminate or suspend the agreement of a treaty or other international obligation owed to any other party to the treaty.[218]

Fundamental change of circumstances[219]

The doctrine of *rebus sic stantibus* is a principle in customary international law providing that where there has been a fundamental change of circumstances since an agreement was concluded, a party to that agreement may withdraw from or terminate it. It is justified by the fact that some treaties may remain in force for long periods of time, during which fundamental changes might have occurred. Such changes might encourage one of the parties to adopt drastic measures in the face of a general refusal to accept an alteration in the terms of the treaty. However, this doctrine has been criticised on the grounds that, having regard to the absence of any system for compulsory jurisdiction in the international order, it could operate as a disrupting influence upon the binding force of obligations undertaken by states. It might be used to justify withdrawal from treaties on rather tenuous grounds.[220]

The modern approach is to admit the existence of the doctrine, but severely restrict its scope.[221] The International Court in the *Fisheries Jurisdiction* case declared that:

> [i]nternational law admits that a fundamental change in the circumstances which determined the parties to accept a treaty, if it has resulted in a radical transformation of the extent of the obligations imposed by it, may, under

---

[218] See *Yearbook of the ILC*, 1966, vol. II, p. 256. See also the *Gabčíkovo–Nagymaros Project* case, ICJ Reports, 1997, pp. 7, 63–4; 116 ILR, p. 1.

[219] See e.g. M. N. Shaw and C. Fournet, 'Article 62' in Corten and Klein, *Conventions de Vienne*, p. 2229; D. F. Vagts, '*Rebus* Revisited: Changed Circumstances in Treaty Law', 43 *Columbia Journal of Transnational Law*, 2004–5, p. 459; M. Bennett and N. Roughan, '*Rebus Sic Stantibus* and the Treaty of Waitangi', 37 *Victoria University Wellington Law Review* 2006, 505; C. Hill, *The Doctrine of Rebus Sic Stantibus in International Law*, Leiden, 1934; O. Lissitzyn, 'Treaties and Changed Circumstances (*Rebus Sic Stantibus*)', 61 AJIL, 1967, p. 895; P. Cahier, 'Le Changement Fondamental de Circonstances et la Convention de Vienne de 1969 sur le Droit des Traités' in *Mélanges Ago*, Milan, 1987, vol. I, p. 163, and Vamvoukis, *Termination*, part 1. See also *Yearbook of the ILC*, 1966, vol. II, pp. 257 ff. Note the decision in *TWA Inc.* v. *Franklin Mint Corporation* 23 ILM, 1984, pp. 814, 820, that a private person could not plead the *rebus* rule.

[220] This was apparently occurring in the immediate pre-1914 period: see J. Garner, 'The Doctrine of *Rebus Sic Stantibus* and the Termination of Treaties', 21 AJIL, 1927, p. 409, and Sinclair, *Vienna Convention*, p. 193. See also G. Harastzi, 'Treaties and the Fundamental Change of Circumstances', 146 HR, 1975, p. 1.

[221] See e.g. the *Free Zones* case, PCIJ, Series A/B, No. 46, pp. 156–8; 6 AD, pp. 362, 365.

certain conditions, afford the party affected a ground for invoking the termination or suspension of the treaty.[222]

Before the doctrine may be applied, the Court continued, it is necessary that such changes 'must have increased the burden of the obligations to be executed to the extent of rendering the performance something essentially different from that originally undertaken'.[223]

Article 62 of the Vienna Convention, which the International Court of Justice regarded in many respects as a codification of existing customary law,[224] declares that:

1. A fundamental change of circumstances which has occurred with regard to those existing at the time of the conclusion of a treaty, and which was not foreseen by the parties, may not be invoked as a ground for terminating or withdrawing from the treaty unless:
   (a) the existence of those circumstances constituted an essential basis of the consent of the parties to be bound by the treaty; and
   (b) the effect of the change is radically to transform the extent of obligations still to be performed under the treaty.
2. A fundamental change of circumstances may not be invoked as a ground for terminating or withdrawing from a treaty:
   (a) if the treaty establishes a boundary; or
   (b) if the fundamental change is the result of a breach by the party invoking it either of an obligation under the treaty or of any other international obligation owed to any other party to the treaty.

The article also notes that instead of terminating or withdrawing from a treaty in the above circumstances, a party might suspend the operation of the treaty.

The doctrine was examined in the *Gabčíkovo–Nagymaros Project* case, where the International Court concluded that:

The changed circumstances advanced by Hungary are, in the Court's view, not of such a nature, either individually or collectively, that their effect would radically transform the extent of the obligations still to be performed in order to accomplish the Project. A fundamental change of circumstances must have been unforeseen; the existence of the circumstances at the time of the Treaty's conclusion must have constituted an essential basis of the consent of the parties to be bound by the Treaty. The negative and conditional

---

[222] ICJ Reports, 1973, pp. 3, 20–1; 55 ILR, p. 183.   [223] *Ibid.*

[224] ICJ Reports, 1973, p. 18. See also the *Gabčíkovo–Nagymaros Project* case, ICJ Reports, 1997, pp. 7, 38; 116 ILR, p. 1.

wording of article 62 of the Vienna Convention on the Law of Treaties is a clear indication moreover that the stability of treaty relations requires that the plea of fundamental change of circumstances should be applied only in exceptional cases.[225]

Consequences of the termination or suspension of a treaty

Article 70 provides that:

1. Unless the treaty otherwise provides or the parties otherwise agree, the termination of a treaty under its provisions or in accordance with the present Convention:
   (a) releases the parties from any obligation further to perform the treaty;
   (b) does not affect any right, obligation or legal situation of the parties created through the execution of the treaty prior to its termination.
2. If a state denounces or withdraws from a multilateral treaty, paragraph 1 applies in the relations between that state and each of the other parties to the treaty from the date when such denunciation or withdrawal takes effect.

Article 72 provides that:

1. Unless the treaty otherwise provides or the parties otherwise agree, the suspension of the operation of a treaty under its provisions or in accordance with the present Convention:
   (a) releases the parties between which the operation of the treaty is suspended from the obligation to perform the treaty in their mutual relations during the period of the suspension;
   (b) does not otherwise affect the legal relations between the parties established by the treaty.
2. During the period of the suspension the parties shall refrain from acts tending to obstruct the resumption of the operation of the treaty.[226]

Dispute settlement[227]

Article 66 provides that if a dispute has not been resolved within twelve months by the means specified in article 33 of the UN Charter then further

---

[225] ICJ Reports, 1997, p. 65. This was followed by the European Court of Justice in *Racke* v. *Hauptzollamt Mainz* [1998] ECR I-3655, 3705–7. Draft article 3 of the ILC Draft Articles on the Effects of Armed Conflicts on Treaties, A/CN.4/178, 2007, p. 7, provides that the outbreak of an armed conflict does not necessarily terminate or suspend the operation of treaties as (a) between the parties to the armed conflict and (b) between one or more parties to the armed conflict and a third state.

[226] See also article 65 with regard to the relevant procedures to be followed.

[227] See e.g. Aust, *Modern Treaty Law*, chapter 20; H. Ruiz Fabri, 'Article 66' in Corten and Klein, *Conventions de Vienne*, p. 2391, and J. G. Merrills, *International Dispute Settlement*, 4th edn, Cambridge, 2004. See also below, chapter 18.

procedures will be followed. If the dispute concerns article 53 or 64 (*jus cogens*), any one of the parties may by a written application submit it to the International Court of Justice for a decision unless the parties by common consent agree to submit the dispute to arbitration. If the dispute concerns other issues in the Convention, any one of the parties may by request to the UN Secretary-General set in motion the conciliation procedure laid down in the Annex to the Convention.

Treaties between states and international organisations[228]

The International Law Commission completed Draft Articles on the Law of Treaties between States and International Organisations or between International Organisations in 1982 and the Vienna Convention on the Law of Treaties between States and International Organisations was adopted in 1986.[229] Its provisions closely follow the provisions of the 1969 Vienna Convention *mutatis mutandis*. However, article 73 of the 1986 Convention notes that 'as between states parties to the Vienna Convention on the Law of Treaties of 1969, the relations of those states under a treaty between two or more states and one or more international organisations shall be governed by that Convention'. Whether this provision affirming the superiority of the 1969 Convention for states will in practice prejudice the interests of international organisations is an open question. In any event, there is no doubt that the strong wish of the Conference adopting the 1986 Convention was for uniformity, despite arguments that the position of international organisations in certain areas of treaty law was difficult to assimilate to that of states.[230]

Special concern in the International Law Commission focused on the effects that a treaty concluded by an international organisation has upon the member states of the organisation. Article 36 *bis* of the ILC Draft[231] provided that:

> Obligations and rights arise for states members of an international organization from the provisions of a treaty to which that organization is a party when the parties to the treaty intend those provisions to be the means of

---

[228] See e.g. G. Gaja, 'A "New" Vienna Convention on Treaties Between States and International Organisations or Between International Organisations: A Critical Commentary', 58 BYIL, 1987, p. 253, and F. Morgenstern, 'The Convention on the Law of Treaties Between States and International Organisations or Between International Organisations' in *International Law at a Time of Perplexity* (ed. Y. Dinstein), Dordrecht, 1989, p. 435.

[229] See above, footnote 2.   [230] See Morgenstern, 'Convention', pp. 438–41.

[231] Described in the ILC Commentary as the article arousing the most controversy, *Yearbook of the ILC*, 1982, vol. II, part 2, p. 43.

establishing such obligations and according such rights and have defined their conditions and effects in the treaty or have otherwise agreed thereon, and if:

(a) the states members of the organization, by virtue of the constituent instrument of that organization or otherwise, have unanimously agreed to be bound by the said provisions of the treaty; and

(b) the assent of the states members of the organization to be bound by the relevant provisions of the treaty has been duly brought to the knowledge of the negotiating states and negotiating organizations.

Such a situation would arise, for example, in the case of a customs union, which was an international organisation, normally concluding tariff agreements to which its members are not parties. Such agreements would be of little value if they were not to be immediately binding on member states.[232]

However, despite the fact that the European Community was particularly interested in the adoption of this draft article, it was rejected at the Conference.[233] It was replaced by article 74(3) of the Convention, which provides:

> The provisions of the present Convention shall not prejudge any question that may arise in regard to the establishment of obligations and rights for states members of an international organisation under a treaty to which that organisation is a party.

Accordingly, the situation in question would fall to be resolved on the basis of the consent of the states concerned in the specific circumstances and on a case-by-case basis.

The other area of difference between the 1986 and 1969 Conventions concerns the provisions for dispute settlement. Since international organisations cannot be parties to contentious proceedings before the International Court, draft article 66 provided for the compulsory arbitration of disputes concerning issues relating to the principles of *jus cogens*, with the details of the proposed arbitral tribunal contained in the Annex. The provisions of the 1969 Convention relating to the compulsory conciliation of disputes concerning the other articles were incorporated in the draft with little change. The 1986 Convention itself, however, adopted a different approach. Under article 66(2), where an international organisation authorised under article 96 of the UN Charter to request advisory

---

[232] *Ibid.*, pp. 43–4.   [233] See e.g. Gaja, '"New" Vienna Convention', p. 264.

opinions is a party to a dispute concerning *jus cogens*, it may apply for an advisory opinion to the International Court, which 'shall be accepted as decisive by all the parties to the dispute concerned'. If the organisation is not so authorised under article 96, it may follow the same procedure acting through a member state. If no advisory opinion is requested or the Court itself does not comply with the request, then compulsory arbitration is provided for.[234]

Suggestions for further reading

A. Aust, *Modern Treaty Law and Practice*, 2nd edn, Cambridge, 2007

M. Fitzmaurice and O. Elias, *Contemporary Issues in the Law of Treaties*, Utrecht, 2005

I. Sinclair, *The Vienna Convention on the Law of Treaties*, 2nd edn, Manchester, 1984

---

[234] See also above, chapter 14, p. 778, regarding the relationship between treaties and state responsibility. The issue of state succession to treaties is covered in chapter 17, p. 966.

17

State succession

Political entities are not immutable. They are subject to change. New states appear and old states disappear.[1] Federations, mergers, dissolutions and secessions take place. International law has to incorporate such events into its general framework with the minimum of disruption and instability. Such changes have come to the fore since the end of the Second World War and the establishment of over 100 new, independent countries.

Difficulties may result from the change in the political sovereignty over a particular territorial entity for the purposes of international law and the world community. For instance, how far is a new state bound by

---

[1] See generally D. P. O'Connell, *State Succession in Municipal Law and International Law*, Cambridge, 2 vols., 1967; O'Connell, 'Recent Problems of State Succession in Relation to New States', 130 HR, 1970, p. 95; K. Zemanek, 'State Succession after Decolonisation', 116 HR, 1965, p. 180; O. Udokang, *Succession of New States to International Treaties*, New York, 1972; J. H. W. Verzijl, *International Law in Historical Perspective*, Leiden, 1974, vol. VII; I. Brownlie, *Principles of Public International Law*, 6th edn, Oxford, 2003, chapter 29; UN, *Materials on Succession of States*, New York, 1967 and supplement A/CN.4/263, 1972, and UN, *Materials on Succession of States in Matters Other than Treaties*, New York, 1978; International Law Association, *The Effect of Independence on Treaties*, London, 1965; Z. Mériboute, *La Codification de la Succession d'États aux Traités*, Paris, 1984; S. Torres Bernardez, 'Succession of States' in *International Law: Achievements and Prospects* (ed. M. Bedjaoui), Paris, 1991, p. 381; D. Bardonnet, *La Succession d'États à Madagascar*, Paris, 1970; R. Müllerson, 'The Continuity and Succession of States by Reference to the Former USSR and Yugoslavia', 42 ICLQ, 1993, p. 473; M. Koskenniemi and M. Lehto, 'La Succession d'États dans l'ex-URSS', AFDI, 1992, p. 179; M. Bedjaoui, 'Problèmes Récents de Succession d'États dans les États Nouveaux', 130 HR, 1970, p. 455; *Oppenheim's International Law* (eds. R. Y. Jennings and A. D. Watts), 9th edn, London, 1992, p. 208; J. Crawford, *The Creation of States in International Law*, 2nd edn, Oxford, 2006; P. Radan, *The Break-up of Yugoslavia and International Law*, London, 2002; Nguyen Quoc Dinh, P. Daillier and A. Pellet, *Droit International Public*, 7th edn, Paris, 2002, p. 538; M. N. Shaw, 'State Succession Revisited', 5 Finnish YIL, 1994, p. 34; *Succession of States* (ed. M. Mrak), The Hague, 1999; B. Stern, 'La Succession d'États', 262 HR, 1996, p. 9; *State Succession: Codification Tested against Facts* (eds. P. M. Eisemann and M. Koskenniemi), Dordrecht, 2000, and *State Practice Regarding State Succession and Issues of Recognition* (eds. J. Klabbers *et al.*), The Hague, 1999.

the treaties and contracts entered into by the previous sovereign of the territory? Does nationality automatically devolve upon the inhabitants to replace that of the predecessor? What happens to the public property of the previous sovereign, and to what extent is the new authority liable for the debts of the old?

State succession in international law cannot be confused with succession in municipal law and the transmission of property and so forth to the relevant heir. Other interests and concerns are involved and the principles of state sovereignty, equality of states and non-interference prevent a universal succession principle similar to domestic law from being adopted. Despite attempts to assimilate Roman law views regarding the continuity of the legal personality in the estate which falls by inheritance,[2] this approach could not be sustained in the light of state interests and practice. The opposing doctrine, which basically denied any transmission of rights, obligations and property interests between the predecessor and successor sovereigns, arose in the heyday of positivism in the nineteenth century. It manifested itself again with the rise of the decolonisation process in the form of the 'clean slate' principle, under which new states acquired sovereignty free from encumbrances created by the predecessor sovereign.

The issue of state succession can arise in a number of defined circumstances, which mirror the ways in which political sovereignty may be acquired by, for example, decolonisation of all or part of an existing territorial unit, dismemberment of an existing state, secession, annexation and merger. In each of these cases a once-recognised entity disappears in whole or in part to be succeeded by some other authority, thus precipitating problems of transmission of rights and obligations. However, the question of state succession does not infringe upon the normal rights and duties of states under international law. These exist by virtue of the fundamental principles of international law and as a consequence of sovereignty and not as a result of transference from the previous sovereign. The issue of state succession should also be distinguished from questions of succession of governments, particularly revolutionary succession, and consequential patterns of recognition and responsibility.[3]

In many cases, such problems will be dealt with by treaties, whether multilateral treaties dealing with primarily territorial dispositions as, for example, the Treaty of St Germain, 1919, which resolved some succession questions relating to the dissolution of the Austro-Hungarian

---

[2] See O'Connell, *State Succession*, vol. I, pp. 9 ff.   [3] See above, chapters 9 and 14.

Empire,[4] or bilateral agreements as between, for instance, colonial power and new state, which, however, would not bind third states. The system of devolution agreements signed by the colonial power with the successor, newly decolonised state, was used by, for example, the UK, France and the Netherlands. Such agreements provided in general that all the rights and benefits, obligations and responsibilities devolving upon the colonial power in respect of the territory in question arising from valid international instruments, would therefore devolve upon the new state.[5] This system, however, was not seen as satisfactory by many new states and several of them resorted to unilateral declarations, providing for a transitional period during which treaties entered into by the predecessor state would continue in force and be subject to review as to which should be accepted and which rejected.[6] In the case of bilateral treaties, those not surviving under customary law would be regarded as having terminated at the end of the period.

However, the issue of state succession in international law is particularly complex. Many of the rules have developed in specific response to particular political changes and such changes have not always been treated in a consistent manner by the international community.[7] The Arbitration Commission established by the Conference on Yugoslavia, for instance, emphasised that 'there are few well-established principles of international law that apply to state succession. Application of these principles is largely to be determined case by case, though the 1978 and 1983 Vienna Conventions do offer some guidance',[8] while the German Federal Supreme Court noted in the *Espionage Prosecution* case that 'the problem of state succession is one of the most disputed areas of

---

[4] See O'Connell, *State Succession*, vol. II, pp. 178–82. This treaty provided for the responsibility of the successor states of the Austro-Hungarian Empire for the latter's public debts. See also the Italian Peace Treaty, 1947.

[5] See e.g. the UK–Burma Agreement of 1947. See also N. Mugerwa, 'Subjects of International Law' in *Manual of Public International Law* (ed. M. Sørensen), London, 1968, pp. 247, 300–1, and *Yearbook of the ILC*, 1974, vol. II, p. 186. See also O'Connell, *State Succession*, vol. II, pp. 352–73, and Brownlie, *Principles*, p. 633.

[6] See e.g. the Tanganyika statement of December 1961, quoted in Mugerwa, 'Subjects', p. 302, subsequently followed by similar declarations by, for example, Uganda, Kenya and Burundi. See also *Yearbook of the ILC*, 1974, vol. II, p. 192. In Zambia's case, it was stated that the question would be governed by customary international law: see O'Connell, *State Succession*, vol. II, p. 115.

[7] See Shaw, 'State Succession Revisited'.

[8] Opinion No. 13, 96 ILR, pp. 726, 728. See also *Oppenheim's International Law*, p. 236, and *Third US Restatement of Foreign Relations Law*, Washington, 1987, p. 100.

international law.[9] The international aspects of succession are governed through the rules of customary international law. There are two relevant Conventions, the Vienna Convention on Succession of States in Respect of Treaties, 1978, which entered into force in 1996, and the Vienna Convention on Succession of States in Respect of State Property, Archives and Debts, 1983, which is not yet in force. However, many of the provisions contained in these Conventions reflect existing international law.

State succession itself may be briefly defined as the replacement of one state by another in the responsibility for the international relations of territory.[10] However, this formulation conceals a host of problems since there is a complex range of situations that stretches from continuity of statehood through succession to non-succession. State succession is essentially an umbrella term for a phenomenon occurring upon a factual change in sovereign authority over a particular territory. In many circumstances it is unclear as to which rights and duties will flow from one authority to the other and upon which precise basis. Much will depend upon the circumstances of the particular case, for example whether what has occurred is a merger of two states to form a new state; the absorption of one state into another, continuing state; a cession of territory from one state to another; secession of part of a state to form a new state; the dissolution or dismemberment of a state to form two or more states, or the establishment of a new state as a result of decolonisation. The role of recognition and acquiescence in this process is especially important.

The relevant date of succession is the date at which the successor state replaces the predecessor state in the responsibility for the international relations of the territory to which the succession relates.[11] This is invariably the date of independence. However, problems may arise where successive dates of independence arise with regard to a state that is slowly disintegrating, such as Yugoslavia. The Yugoslav Arbitration Commission noted

---

[9] Case No. 2 BGz 38/91, 94 ILR, pp. 68, 77–8.

[10] See article 2 of the Vienna Conventions of both 1978 and 1983 and Opinion No. 1 of the Yugoslav Arbitration Commission, 92 ILR, pp. 162, 165. See also *Guinea-Bissau* v. *Senegal*, 83 ILR, pp. 1, 22 and the *El Salvador/Honduras* case, ICJ Reports, 1992, pp. 351, 598; 97 ILR, pp. 266, 514.

[11] See article 2(1)e of the Vienna Convention on Succession of States to Treaties, 1978 and article 11 of the Vienna Convention on Succession of States in respect of State Property, Archives and Debts, 1983. See also Opinion No. 11 of the Yugoslav Arbitration Commission, 96 ILR, p. 719.

that the date of succession was a question of fact to be assessed in the light of all the relevant circumstances.[12]

Continuity and succession

Questions relating to continuity and succession may be particularly difficult.[13] Where a new entity emerges, one has to decide whether it is a totally separate creature from its predecessor, or whether it is a continuation of it in a slightly different form. For example, it seems to be accepted that India is the same legal entity as British India and Pakistan is a totally new state.[14] Yugoslavia was generally regarded as the successor state to Serbia,[15] and Israel as a completely different being from British mandated Palestine.[16] Cession or secession of territory from an existing state will not affect the continuity of the latter state, even though its territorial dimensions and population have been diminished. Pakistan after the independence of Bangladesh is a good example of this. In such a case, the existing state remains in being, complete with the rights and duties incumbent upon it, save for those specifically tied to the ceded or seceded territory. Where, however, a state is dismembered so that all of its territory falls within the territory of two or more states, these rights and duties will be allocated as between the successor states. In deciding whether continuity or succession has occurred with regard to one of the parties to the process, one has to consider the classical criteria of the creation of statehood,[17] together with assertions as to status made by the parties directly concerned and the attitudes adopted by third states and international organisations.

This issue has arisen recently with regard to events concerning the Soviet Union and Yugoslavia. In the former case, upon the demise of the USSR, the Russian Federation took the position that it was the continuation of that state.[18] This was asserted particularly with regard to membership of the UN.[19] Of great importance was the Decision of the Council of Heads of State of the Commonwealth of Independent States

---

[12] See Opinion No. 11, 96 ILR, p. 719. However, see also the Yugoslav Agreement on Succession Issues of June 2001, 41 ILM, 2002, p. 3. See further below, p. 989.

[13] See e.g. M. Craven, 'The Problem of State Succession and the Identity of States under International Law', 9 EJIL, 1998, p. 142.

[14] See e.g. *Yearbook of the ILC*, 1962, vol. II, pp. 101–3.

[15] See e.g. O'Connell, *State Succession*, vol. II, pp. 378–9. See also *Artukovic* v. *Rison* 784 F.2d 1354 (1986).

[16] O'Connell, *State Succession*, vol. II, pp. 155–7.   [17] See above, chapter 5, p. 197.

[18] See e.g. R. Müllerson, *International Law, Rights and Politics*, London, 1994, pp. 140–5, and Y. Blum, 'Russia Takes over the Soviet Union's Seat at the United Nations', 3 EJIL, 1992, p. 354.

[19] See 31 ILM, 1992, p. 138.

on 21 December 1991 supporting Russia's continuance of the membership of the USSR in the UN, including permanent membership of the
Security Council, and other international organisations.[20] Although not
all of the instruments produced by the Commonwealth of Independent
States at the end of 1991 were strictly consistent with the continuity principle,[21] it is clear that Russia's claim to be the continuation of the USSR
(albeit within different borders of course) was supported by the other
former Republics and was accepted by international practice.[22] A rather
special situation arose with respect to the Baltic states (Estonia, Latvia
and Lithuania), which became independent after the First World War,
but were annexed by the Soviet Union in 1940. This annexation had
been refused recognition by some states[23] and accepted *de facto* but not
de jure by some others.[24] The Baltic states declared their independence
in August 1991.[25] The European Community adopted a Declaration on
27 August 1991 welcoming 'the restoration of the sovereignty and independence of the Baltic states which they lost in 1941'.[26] The United States
recognised the restoration of the independence of the Baltic states on
4 September 1991.[27] The implication of this internationally accepted
restoration of independence would appear to be that these states do not
constitute successor states to the former USSR and would therefore be

---

[20] *Ibid.*, p. 151.

[21] For example, the Minsk Agreement signed by Russia, Belarus and Ukraine stated that the
USSR 'as a subject of international law no longer existed', while the Alma Ata Declaration,
signed by all of the former Soviet Republics except for Georgia (which acceded in 1993) and
the Baltic states, stated that 'with the establishment of the Commonwealth of Independent
States, the Union of Soviet Socialist Republics ceases to exist', *ibid.*, pp. 147–9.

[22] See e.g. the views expressed by the Secretary of State for Foreign and Commonwealth
Affairs, UKMIL, 63 BYIL, 1992, pp. 639 and 652–5, and the comments by an official of
the FCO submitted to the Outer House of the Court of Session in Scotland in *Coreck
Maritime GmbH* v. *Sevrybokholodflot*, UKMIL, 64 BYIL, 1993, p. 636. As to French practice recognising Russia as the continuation of the USSR, see AFDI, 1993, p. 1038. See
also L. Henkin, R. C. Pugh, O. Schachter and H. Smit, *International Law: Cases and
Materials*, 3rd edn, St Paul, 1993, p. 539. Note that there is a distinction between the
issue of continuity or succession to membership of international organisations and continuity or succession generally. However, the nature and importance of the UN is such
that the question of membership of that organisation is strong evidence of continuity
generally.

[23] For example the USA: see *Oppenheim's International Law*, p. 193. As to French practice,
see AFDI, 1993, p. 1038 and *Gerbaud* v. *Meden* 18 ILR, p. 288.

[24] See, for example, the UK: see *A/S Tallinna Laevauhisus* v. *Tallinna Shipping Co. (The
Vapper)* (1946) 79 LL. R 245 and the statement of the Secretary of State for the Foreign
and Commonwealth Office on 16 January 1991, 183 HC Deb., col. 853.

[25] See Müllerson, *International Law*, pp. 119–20.

[26] See UKMIL, 62 BYIL, 1991, p. 558.   [27] See Müllerson, *International Law*, p. 121.

free of such rights and obligations as would be consequential upon such succession.[28]

In contrast to this situation, the issue of Yugoslavia has been more complicated and tragic. The collapse of the Socialist Federal Republic of Yugoslavia (the SFRY) took place over several months[29] as the various constituent republics proclaimed independence.[30] The process was regarded as having been completed in the view of the Arbitration Commission on Yugoslavia[31] by the time of its Opinion No. 8 issued on 4 July 1992.[32] The Commission noted that a referendum had been held in Bosnia and Herzegovina in February and March 1992 producing a majority in favour of independence, while Serbia and Montenegro had a established 'a new state, the "Federal Republic of Yugoslavia"' on 27 April 1992. The Commission noted that the common federal bodies of the SFRY had ceased to function, while Slovenia, Croatia and Bosnia had been recognised by the member states of the European Community and other states and had been admitted to membership of the UN.[33] The conclusion was that the former SFRY had ceased to exist.[34] This was particularly reaffirmed in Opinion No. 10.[35]

Nevertheless, the Federal Republic of Yugoslavia (Serbia and Montenegro) continued to maintain that it constituted not a new state, but the continuation of the former SFRY. This claim was opposed by the other former republics of the SFRY[36] and by the international community.[37]

---

[28] See Shaw, 'State Succession Revisited', pp. 56 ff.

[29] See generally M. Weller, 'The International Response to the Dissolution of the Socialist Federal Republic of Yugoslavia', 86 AJIL, 1992, p. 569; Y. Blum, 'UN Membership of the "New" Yugoslavia: Continuity or Break ?', 86 AJIL, 1992, p. 830, and Müllerson, *International Law*, pp. 125 ff.

[30] Slovenia and Croatia on 25 June 1991 (postponed for three months) and Macedonia on 17 September 1991. Bosnia and Herzegovina adopted a resolution on sovereignty on 14 October 1991. The view taken at this point by Opinion No. 1 issued by the Arbitration Commission, established by the Conference on Yugoslavia convened by the European Community on 17 August 1991, was that 'the Socialist Federal Republic of Yugoslavia was in process of dissolution', 92 ILR, p. 166. See also M. Craven, 'The EC Arbitration Commission on Yugoslavia', 66 BYIL, 1995, p. 333.

[31] Which consisted of five of the Presidents of Constitutional Courts in EC countries, chaired by M. Badinter.

[32] 92 ILR, p. 199.

[33] On 22 May 1992: see General Assembly resolutions, 46/236; 46/237 and 46/238. Note that the 'Former Yugoslav Republic of Macedonia' was admitted to the UN on 8 April 1993: see Security Council resolution 817 (1993).

[34] 92 ILR, p. 202. See also Opinion No. 9, *ibid.*, p. 203.   [35] *Ibid.*, p. 206.

[36] See e.g. E/CN.4/1995/121 and E/CN.4/1995/122.

[37] Note, for example, that both the International Monetary Fund (on 15 December 1992) and the World Bank (on 25 February 1993) found that the former Yugoslavia had ceased

The Security Council, for example, in resolution 777 (1992) declared that 'the state formerly known as the Socialist Federal Republic of Yugoslavia has ceased to exist' and that 'the Federal Republic of Yugoslavia (Serbia and Montenegro) cannot continue automatically the membership of the former Socialist Federal Republic of Yugoslavia in the United Nations'.[38] However, the Yugoslav position changed in 2000 and it requested admission to the UN as a new member.[39] The question as to the legal status of Yugoslavia as between 1992 and 2000 remained a source of some controversy, since its admission to the UN in 2000 could not operate retroactively. The International Court in 2003 described this situation as *sui generis* and fraught with legal difficulties,[40] but in its judgment in the series of cases brought by Yugoslavia against NATO members following the Kosovo conflict in 1999, the Court concluded that Yugoslavia had been a a member of the UN (and thus a party to the Statute of the Court) from 1 November 2000 and that the *sui generis* status of that state could not have amounted to membership of the UN.[41] Accordingly, while in 1996 the Court decided that Yugoslavia could appear before it in the *Genocide Convention (Bosnia v. Serbia)* case, it held in 2003 that the situation as to Yugoslavia's status was *sui generis* and not without legal difficulty but finally decided in 2004 that Yugoslavia could not bring an action against NATO states as it had not been a member of the UN and thus a party to the Statute in 1999.[42] In its decision on the merits in the *Genocide Convention* case in 2007, the Court noted that its decision of 1996 constituted *res judicata* and could not be re-opened in the light of its subsequent rulings.[43]

State succession also covers the situation of unification. One method of unification is by the creation of a totally new state, such as the merger of the Yemen Arab Republic and the People's Democratic Republic of

---

to exist: see P. R. Williams, 'State Succession and the International Financial Institutions', 43 ICLQ, 1994, pp. 776, 802–3.

[38] See also Security Council resolution 757 (1992) and General Assembly resolution 47/1. See also the letter dated 29 September 1992 from the UN Legal Counsel carefully analysing the legal situation in terms of representation, A/47/485, Annex and the *Genocide Convention* case, ICJ Reports, 1993, pp. 3, 13–14; 95 ILR, pp. 1, 28–9.

[39] It was so admitted on 1 November 2000: see General Assembly resolution 55/12. On 4 February 2003, the name of the country was officially changed from the Federal Republic of Yugoslavia to Serbia and Montenegro and thence to Serbia upon the secession of Montenegro on 28 June 2006: see General Assembly resolution 60/264. See also Crawford, *Creation of States*, pp. 707 ff.

[40] See *Application for Revision of the Judgment of 11 July 1996*, ICJ Reports, 2003, pp. 7, 31.

[41] *Serbia and Montenegro* v. *UK*, ICJ Reports, 2004, pp. 1307, 1335 ff.

[42] See the critical comments on this 'change of position' by the Court by seven judges in their joint declaration, *ibid*, pp. 1353, 1355–7.

[43] ICJ Reports, 2007, paras. 105 ff.

Yemen. Under the agreement between the two states of 22 April 1990 the establishment of the Republic of Yemen was accomplished by way of a merger of the two existing states into a new entity with a new name.[44] Unification may also be achieved by the absorption of one state by another in circumstances where the former simply disappears and the latter continues, albeit with increased territory and population. Such was the case with Germany.

Following the conclusion of the Second World War, Germany was divided into the US, USSR, UK and French zones of occupation and a special Berlin area not forming part of any zone.[45] Supreme authority was exercised initially by the Commanders-in-Chief of the Armed Forces of the Four Allied Powers[46] and subsequently by the three Allied High Commissioners in Bonn, with parallel developments occurring in the Soviet zone. The Convention on Relations between the Three Powers and the Federal Republic of Germany (FRG), which came into force in 1955, terminated the occupation regime and abolished the Allied High Commission. The Three Allied Powers retained, however, their rights and obligations with regard to Berlin[47] and relating to 'Germany as a whole, including the reunification of Germany and a peace settlement'.[48] Recognition of the German Democratic Republic (GDR) was on the same basis, i.e. as a sovereign state having full authority over internal and external affairs subject to the rights and responsibilities of the Four Powers in respect of Berlin and Germany as a whole.[49] Accordingly, it was accepted that in some sense Germany as a whole continued to exist as a state in international law.[50] The question of the relationship of the two German states to each other and with respect to the pre-1945 German state has occasioned considerable interest

---

[44] Article 1 of the Agreement declared that 'there shall be established between the State of the Yemen Arab Republic and the State of the People's Democratic Republic of Yemen . . . a full and complete union, based on a merger, in which the international personality of each of them shall be integrated in a single international person called "the Republic of Yemen"': see 30 ILM, 1991, p. 820.

[45] See e.g. the *Fourth Report of the Foreign Affairs Committee, Session 1989–90*, June 1990. Note that part of the Soviet zone was placed under Soviet administration (the city of Königsberg, now Kaliningrad and the surrounding area) and the territory of Germany east of the Oder–Neisse line was placed under Polish administration.

[46] Article 2 of the Agreement on Control Machinery in Germany of 14 November 1944, as amended by the Agreement of 1 May 1945.

[47] See, in particular, I. Hendry and M. Wood, *The Legal Status of Berlin*, Cambridge, 1987. See also Cmd 8571, 1952 and the Quadripartite Agreement on Berlin, Cmnd 5135, 1971.

[48] Article 2 of the Relations Convention. Parallel developments took place in the Soviet zone. Note the USSR–German Democratic Republic Treaty of 1955.

[49] See the Fourth Report, p. 2.   [50] *Ibid.*, p. 3.

and generated no little complexity, not least because the Federal German Republic always claimed to be the successor of the pre-1945 Germany.[51]

On 18 May 1990 a treaty between the two German states was signed establishing a Monetary, Economic and Social Union. In essence this integrated the GDR into the FRG economic system, with the Deutsche Mark becoming legal tender in the GDR and with the Bundesbank becoming the central bank for the GDR as well as for the FRG.[52] On 31 August 1990, a second treaty was signed between the two German states which provided for unification on 3 October 1990 by the accession of the GDR under article 23 of the Basic Law of the Federal Republic. On 12 September 1990 the Treaty on the Final Settlement With Respect to Germany was signed by the two German states and the Four Allied Powers.[53] This latter agreement settled definitively matters arising out of the Second World War. It confirmed the borders of unified Germany as those of the FRG and the GDR (i.e. the post-war Oder–Neisse frontier with Poland), provided for a reduction in the armed forces of Germany and for the withdrawal of Soviet forces from the territory of the GDR. The Four Allied Powers terminated their rights and responsibilities regarding Berlin and Germany as a whole so that the united Germany has full sovereignty over its internal and external affairs.[54]

The Treaty between the Federal Republic of Germany and the German Democratic Republic of 31 August 1990 clearly provided that the latter was simply assimilated into the former. Article 1 of the Treaty stipulated that, 'upon the accession of the German Democratic Republic to the Federal Republic of Germany in accordance with article 23 of the Basic Law[55] taking effect on 3 October 1990, the Länder of Brandenburg, Mecklenburg-Western Pomerania, Saxony, Saxony-Anhalt and Thuringia[56] shall become Länder of the Federal Republic of Germany'. This approach, whereby

---

[51] See e.g. Brownlie, *Principles*, pp. 78–9; M. Whiteman, *Digest of International Law*, Washington, 1963, vol. I, pp. 332–8, and F. A. Mann, 'Germany's Present Legal Status Revisited', 16 ICLQ, 1967, p. 760. See also the decision of the Federal Constitutional Court of the Federal Republic of Germany in *Re Treaty on the Basis of Relations Between the Federal Republic of Germany and the German Democratic Republic 1972*, 78 ILR, p. 149.

[52] See 29 ILM, 1990, p. 1108.   [53] See 29 ILM, 1990, p. 1186.

[54] Note that by the Declaration of 1 October 1990, the Allied Powers suspended all rights and responsibilities relating to Berlin and to Germany as a whole upon the unification of Germany, pending the entry into force of the Treaty on the Final Settlement: see Annex 2 of the Observations by the Government to the Fourth Report, October 1990, Cm 1246.

[55] This provided that the Basic Law was to apply in Greater Berlin and specified *Länder* (forming the Federal Republic of Germany), while 'in other parts of Germany it shall be put into force on their accession'. This method had been used to achieve the accession of the Saarland in 1956.

[56] I.e. the constituent provinces of the German Democratic Republic.

unified Germany came about by a process of absorption of the constituent provinces of the former German Democratic Republic into the existing Federal Republic of Germany by way of the extension of the constitution of the latter, is reinforced by other provisions in the Unification Treaty. Article 7, for example, provided that the financial system of the FRG 'shall be extended to the territory specified in article 3' (i.e. the *Länder* of the former GDR), while article 8 declared that 'upon the accession taking effect, federal law shall enter into force in the territory specified in article 3'.[57] International practice also demonstrates acceptance of this approach.[58] No state objected to this characterisation of the process.[59] In other words, the view taken by the parties directly concerned and accepted by the international community demonstrates acceptance of the unification as one of the continuity of the Federal Republic of Germany and the disappearance or extinction of the German Democratic Republic.

Succession to treaties[60]

The importance of treaties within the international legal system requires no repetition.[61] They constitute the means by which a variety of legal obligations are imposed or rights conferred upon states in a wide range of matters from the significant to the mundane. Treaties are founded upon the pre-existing and indispensable norm of *pacta sunt servanda* or the

---

[57] Note also that under article 11, treaties entered into by the Federal Republic of Germany would continue and extend to the *Länder* of the former German Democratic Republic, while under article 12, the question of the continuation, amendment or expiry of treaties entered into by the former German Democratic Republic was to be discussed individually with contracting parties: see below, p. 971.

[58] Such as the European Community. See, for example, GATT document L/6759 of 31 October 1990 in which the Commission of the European Community stated that Germany had become united by way of the accession of the GDR to the FRG. See generally T. Oeter, 'German Unification and State Succession', 51 ZaöRV, 1991, p. 349; J. Frowein, 'Germany Reunited', *ibid.*, p. 333, and R. W. Piotrowicz and S. K. N. Blay, *The Unification of Germany in International and Domestic Law*, Amsterdam, 1997. See also UK Foreign Office affidavit, UKMIL, 68 BYIL, 1997, p. 520.

[59] See also *Oppenheim's International Law*, p. 210.

[60] Note particularly the work of the International Law Commission on this topic: see *Yearbook of the International Law Commission*, 1974, vol. II, part 1, pp. 157 ff., and the five Reports of Sir Humphrey Waldock (*ibid.*, 1968, vol. II, p. 88; 1969, vol. II, p. 45; 1970, vol. II, p. 25; 1971, vol. II, part 1, p. 143 and 1972, vol. II, p. 1) and the Report of Sir Francis Vallat (*ibid.*, 1974, vol. II, part 1, p. 1). See also the International Law Association, *The Effect of Independence on Treaties*, London, 1965; A. Aust, *Modern Treaty Law and Practice*, 2nd edn, Cambridge, 2007, chapter 21, and M. Craven, *The Decolonisation of International Law: State Succession and the Law of Treaties*, Oxford, 2007.

[61] See above, chapter 16.

acceptance of treaty commitments as binding. Treaties may fall within the following categories: multilateral treaties, including the specific category of treaties concerning international human rights; treaties concerned with territorial definition and regimes; bilateral treaties; and treaties that are treated as 'political' in the circumstances.

The rules concerning succession to treaties are those of customary international law together with the Vienna Convention on Succession of States in Respect of Treaties, 1978, which came into force in 1996 and which applies with regard to a succession taking place after that date.[62]

As far as devolution agreements are concerned, article 8 of the Convention provides that such agreements of themselves cannot affect third states and this reaffirms an accepted principle, while article 9, dealing with unilateral declarations, emphasises that such a declaration by the successor state alone cannot of itself affect the rights and obligations of the state and third states. In other words, it would appear, the consent of the other parties to the treaties in question or an agreement with the predecessor state with regard to bilateral issues is required.

Categories of treaties: territorial, political and other treaties

Treaties may for succession purposes be generally divided into three categories. The first relates to territorially grounded treaties, under which rights or obligations are imposed directly upon identifiable territorial units. The prime example of these are agreements relating to territorial definition. Waldock, in his first Report on Succession of States and Governments in Respect of Treaties in 1968, declared that 'the weight both of opinion and practice seems clearly to be in favour of the view that boundaries established by treaties remain untouched by the mere fact of a succession. The opinion of jurists seems, indeed, to be unanimous on the point... [and] State practice in favour of the continuance in force of boundaries established by treaty appears to be such as to justify the conclusion that a general rule of international law exists to that effect',[63] while Bedjaoui has noted that 'in principle the territory devolves upon the successor State on the basis of the pre-existing boundaries'.[64]

For reasons relating to the maintenance of international stability, this approach has been clearly supported by state practice. The Latin American concept of *uti possidetis juris*, whereby the administrative divisions of the

---

[62] See article 7. [63] *Yearbook of the International Law Commission*, 1968, vol. II, pp. 92–3.
[64] *Ibid.*, p. 112.

former Spanish empire were to constitute the boundaries of the newly independent states in South America in the first third of the nineteenth century was the first internationally accepted expression of this approach.[65]
It was echoed in US practice[66] and explicitly laid down in resolution 16
of the meeting of Heads of State and Government of the Organisation
of African Unity in 1964, by which all member states pledged themselves
to respect colonial borders.[67] The principle of succession to colonial borders was underlined by the International Court in the *Burkina Faso/Mali*
case.[68] The extension of the principle of *uti possidetis* from decolonisation to the creation of new states out of existing independent states is
supported by international practice, taking effect as the transformation
of administrative boundaries into international boundaries generally.[69]
Of course, much will depend upon the particular situation, including the
claims of the states concerned and the attitude adopted by third states and
international organisations, particularly the United Nations. This principle regarding the continuity of borders in the absence of consent to the
contrary is reinforced by other principles of international law, such as the
provision enshrined in article 62(2) of the Vienna Convention on the Law

---

[65] See, for example, the *Colombia–Venezuela* arbitral award, 1 RIAA, pp. 223, 228 and the
Beagle Channel award, 52 ILR, p. 93. See also A. O. Cukwurah, *The Settlement of Boundary
Disputes in International Law*, Manchester, 1967, p. 114; O'Connell, *State Succession*, vol.
II, pp. 273 ff., and P. De La Pradelle, *La Frontière*, Paris, 1928, pp. 86–7.

[66] See the view of the US Secretary of State in 1856 that the US regarded it 'as an established
principle of the public law and of international right that when a European colony in
America becomes independent it succeeds to the territorial limits of the colony as it stood
in the hands of the present country', Manning's *Diplomatic Correspondence*, vol. III (Great
Britain), doc. 2767, cited in Cukwurah, *Settlement*, p. 106.

[67] See, for example, M. N. Shaw, *Title to Territory in Africa: International Legal Issues*, Oxford,
1986, pp. 185–7, and other works cited in chapter 10, p. 525.

[68] ICJ Reports, 1986, pp. 554, 565; 80 ILR, pp. 440, 469–70. See also the Arbitration Commission on Yugoslavia, which noted in Opinion No. 3 with respect to the status of the
former internal boundaries between Serbia on the one hand and Croatia and Bosnia and
Herzegovina on the other, that 'except where otherwise agreed, the former boundaries
become frontiers protected by international law. This conclusion follows from the principle of respect for the territorial status quo and in particular, from the principle of *uti
possidetis. Uti possidetis* ... is today recognised as a general principle', 92 ILR, pp. 170, 171.

[69] See also article 5 of the Minsk Agreement establishing the Commonwealth of Independent
States of 8 December 1991 and the Alma Ata Declaration of 21 December 1991, which
reaffirmed the territorial integrity of the former Republics of the USSR. Note also that under
the Treaty on the General Delimitation of the Common State Frontiers of 29 October
1992, the boundary between the two new states of the Czech Republic and Slovakia,
emerging out of Czechoslovakia on 1 January 1993, was to be that of the administrative
border existing between the Czech and Slovak parts of the former state. See further above,
chapter 10, p. 528.

of Treaties, which stipulates that a fundamental change in circumstances may not be invoked as a ground for terminating or withdrawing from a treaty that establishes a boundary.[70] In addition, article 11 of the Vienna Convention on Succession to Treaties, although in terminology which is cautious and negative, specifies that

> A succession of States does not as such affect:
>
> (a) a boundary established by treaty; or
> (b) obligations and rights established by a treaty and relating to the regime of a boundary.

The International Court dealt with succession to boundary treaties generally in the *Libya/Chad* case, where it was declared that 'once agreed, the boundary stands, for any other approach would vitiate the fundamental principle of the stability of boundaries, the importance of which has been repeatedly emphasised by the Court'.[71] More particularly, the Court emphasised that 'a boundary established by treaty thus achieves a permanence which the treaty itself does not necessarily enjoy. The treaty can cease to be in force without in any way affecting the continuance of the boundary... when a boundary has been the subject of agreement, the continued existence of that boundary is not dependent upon the continuing life of the treaty under which the boundary is agreed'.[72] It is particularly important to underline that the succession takes place, therefore, not as such to the boundary treaty but rather to the boundary as established by the treaty. The Tribunal in the *Eritrea/Yemen* case emphasised that boundary and territorial treaties made between two parties constituted a special category of treaties representing a 'legal reality which necessarily impinges upon third states, because they have effect *erga omnes*'.[73]

Territorially grounded treaties extend somewhat beyond the establishment of boundaries into the more controversial area of agreements creating other territorial regimes, such agreements being termed 'localised' or 'real' or 'dispositive'.[74] Examples of such arrangements might include demilitarised zones, rights of transit, port facilities and other servitudes generally.[75] Despite some reservations by members of the

---

[70] See above, chapter 16, p. 950. [71] ICJ Reports, 1994, pp. 6, 37; 100 ILR, pp. 1, 36.
[72] *Ibid.* [73] 114 ILR, pp. 1, 48.
[74] See O'Connell, *State Succession*, vol. II, pp. 231 ff. See also Udokang, *Succession*, pp. 327 ff.
[75] See Shaw, *Title to Territory*, pp. 244–8. See also the *Free Zones* case, PCIJ, Series A/B, No. 46, 1932, p. 145; 6 AD, pp. 362, 364 and the *Aaland Islands* case, LNOJ, Sp. Supp. No. 3, 1920, p. 18. See above, chapter 10, p. 538, and *Yearbook of the ILC*, 1974, vol. II, pp. 157 and 196 ff. Note that, by article 12(3), the provisions of article 12 do not apply to treaties

International Law Commission[76] and governments,[77] article 12 of the Vienna Convention provides that a succession of states does not as such affect obligations or rights relating to the use of any territory or to restrictions upon its use established by a treaty for the benefit of any foreign state, group of states or all states and considered as attaching to the territory in question. The International Court declared that article 12 reflected a rule of customary law in addressing the issue of territorial regimes in the *Gabčíkovo–Nagymaros Project* case and confirmed that treaties concerning water rights or navigation on rivers constituted territorial treaties.[78] It also noted that since the 1977 treaty in question in that case between Hungary and Czechoslovakia established *inter alia* the navigational regime for an important section of an international waterway, a territorial regime within the meaning of article 12 was created.[79]

Political or 'personal' treaties establish rights or obligations deemed to be particularly linked to the regime in power in the territory in question and to its political orientation. Examples of such treaties would include treaties of alliance or friendship or neutrality.[80] Such treaties do not bind successor states for they are seen as exceptionally closely tied to the nature of the state which has ceased to exist. However, it is not at all clear what the outer limits are to the concept of political treaties and difficulties over definitional problems do exist. Apart from the categories of territorial and political treaties, where succession rules in general are clear, other treaties cannot be so easily defined or categorised for succession purposes and must be analysed separately.

Succession to treaties generally

Practice seems to suggest 'a tendency'[81] or 'a general inclination'[82] to succession to 'some categories of multilateral treaties'[83] or to 'certain

---

providing for the establishment of foreign military bases on the territory concerned. See further Brownlie, *Principles*, pp. 633 ff., and O'Connell, *State Succession*, vol. II, pp. 12–23 and 231 ff.

[76] See, for example, *Yearbook of the ILC*, 1974, vol. I, pp. 206–7.

[77] See, for example, *UN Conference on Succession of States in Respect of Treaties*, 1977, Comments of Governments (A/Conf.80/5), pp. 145, 153, 161, 167, 170, 171 and 173.

[78] ICJ Reports, 1997, pp. 7, 72; 116 ILR, p. 1.

[79] *Ibid.*, pp. 71–2. See also J. Klabbers, 'Cat on a Hot Tin Roof: The World Court, State Succession and the *Gabčíkovo–Nagymaros* case', 11 *Leiden Journal of International Law*, 1998, p. 345.

[80] See, for example, O'Connell, *State Succession*, vol. II, pp. 2, 80 and 136, and *Oppenheim's International Law*, p. 211.

[81] O'Connell, *State Succession*, vol. II, p. 212.   [82] Udokang, *Succession*, p. 225.

[83] O'Connell, *State Succession*, vol. II, p. 213.

multilateral conventions'.[84] However, this 'modern-classical' approach is difficult to sustain as a general rule of comprehensive applicability.[85] One simply has to examine particular factual situations, take note of the claims made by the relevant states and mark the reactions of third states. In the case of bilateral treaties, the starting-point is from a rather different perspective. In such cases, the importance of the individual contractual party is more evident, since only two states are involved and the treaty is thus more clearly reciprocal in nature. Accordingly, the presumption is one of non-succession, depending upon all the particular circumstances of the case. Practice with regard to the US, Panama, Belgium and Finland supports the 'clean slate' approach.[86]

Absorption and merger

Where one state is absorbed by another and no new state is created (such as the 1990 accession to the Federal Republic of Germany of the *Länder* of the German Democratic Republic), the former becomes extinct whereas the latter simply continues albeit in an enlarged form. The basic situation is that the treaties of the former, certainly in so far as they may be deemed 'political',[87] die with the state concerned,[88] although territorial treaties defining the boundaries of the entity absorbed will continue to define such boundaries. Other treaties are also likely to be regarded as at an end.[89] However, treaties of the absorbing state continue and will extend to the territory of the extinguished state. These principles are, of course, subject to contrary intention expressed by the parties in question. For example, in the case of German unification, article 11 coupled with Annex I of the Unification Treaty, 1990 excluded from the extension of treaties of the Federal Republic of Germany to the territory of the former German Democratic Republic a series of treaties dealing primarily with NATO matters.

Article 31(1) of the Vienna Convention on Succession to Treaties provides that where two or more states unite and form one successor state, treaties continue in force unless the successor state and the other state party or states parties otherwise agree or it appears that this would be incompatible with the object and purpose of the treaty or would radically

---

[84] Udokang, *Succession*, p. 225.
[85] But see Jenks' view that multilateral law-making treaties devolve upon successor states, 'State Succession in Respect of Law-making Treaties', 29 BYIL, 1952, pp. 105, 108–10.
[86] See, for example, Udokang, *Succession*, pp. 412–15.
[87] See here, for example, *Oppenheim's International Law*, p. 211; Oeter, 'German Unification', p. 363, and Koskenniemi and Lehto, 'La Succession', p. 203.
[88] *Oppenheim's International Law*, p. 211.   [89] *Ibid.*, pp. 212–13.

change the conditions for its operation. Article 31(2) provides that such treaties would apply only in respect of the part of the territory of the successor state in respect of which the treaty was in force at the date of the succession of states. This is so unless the successor state makes a notification that the multilateral treaty in question shall apply in respect of its entire territory[90] or, if the multilateral treaty in question is one in which by virtue either of its terms or by reason of the limited number of participants and its object and purpose the participation of any other state must be considered as requiring the consent of all the parties,[91] the successor state and the other states parties otherwise agree. This general principle would apply also in the case of a bilateral treaty, unless the successor state and the other state party otherwise agree.[92]

While these provisions bear some logic with regard to the situation where two states unite to form a new third state,[93] they do not really take into account the special circumstances of unification where one state simply takes over another state in circumstances where the latter is extinguished. In these situations, the model provided by German unification appears to be fully consistent with international law and of value as a precedent. Article 11 of the Unification Treaty of 31 August 1990 provided that all international treaties and agreements to which the FRG was a contracting party were to retain their validity and that the rights and obligations arising therefrom would apply also to the territory of the GDR.[94] Article 12 provided that international treaties of the GDR were to be discussed with the parties concerned with a view to regulating or confirming their continued application, adjustment or expiry, taking into account protection of confidence, the interests of the state concerned, the

---

[90] Unless it appears from the treaty or is otherwise established that the application of the treaty in respect of the entire territory of the successor state would be incompatible with the object and purpose of the treaty or would radically change the conditions for its operation (article 31(3)).

[91] Article 17(3).

[92] See the examples of the union of Egypt and Syria to form the United Arab Republic between 1958 and 1961 and the union of Tanganyika and Zanzibar in 1964, where the treaties of the component territories continued in force within those territorial limits: see O'Connell, *State Succession*, vol. II, pp. 71–8. The article 31 situation has to be distinguished from the situation involving a 'newly independent state', see article 29 and below, p. 977, and from the article 15 situation, where part of the territory of one state is transferred to another state, below, p. 973.

[93] But see above, pp. 967 ff., with regard to boundary treaties and below, p. 981, regarding human rights treaties.

[94] However, as noted, Annex I to the Treaty provided that certain listed treaties are not to apply to the territory of the former GDR. These treaties relate in essence to NATO activities.

treaty obligations of the FRG as well as the principles of a free, democratic order governed by the rule of law, and respecting the competence of the European Communities. The united Germany would then determine its position after such consultations. It was also stipulated that should the united Germany intend to accede to international organisations or other multilateral treaties of which the GDR, but not the FRG, was a member, agreement was to be reached with the respective contracting parties and the European Communities, where the competence of the latter was affected. The situation thus differs from the scenario envisaged in article 31 of the 1978 treaty.[95]

In the case of mergers to form a new third state, the formulation in article 31 is more relevant and acceptable. Practice appears to support that approach. For example, in the cases of both the Egypt–Syria merger to form the United Arab Republic in 1958[96] and the union of Tanganyika and Zanzibar to form Tanzania in 1964,[97] the continuation of treaties in the territories to which they had applied before the respective mergers was stipulated.[98]

Cession of territory from one state to another

When part of the territory of one state becomes part of the territory of another state, the general rule is that the treaties of the former cease to apply to the territory while the treaties of the latter extend to the territory. Article 15 of the Vienna Convention on Succession of States to Treaties, dealing with this 'moving-frontiers' rule,[99] provides for this, with the proviso that where it appears from the treaty concerned or is otherwise established that the application of the treaty to the territory would be incompatible with the object and purpose of the treaty or would radically change the condition for its operation, this extension should not happen. This is basically consistent with state practice. When, for example, the US annexed Hawaii in 1898, its treaties were extended to the islands and

---

[95] It should also be noted that the *Third US Restatement of Foreign Relations Law*, Washington, 1987, p. 108, provides that 'when a state is absorbed by another state, the international agreements of the absorbed state are terminated and the international agreements of the absorbing state become applicable to the territory of the absorbed state'.

[96] See O'Connell, *State Succession*, vol. II, pp. 71 ff., and D. Cottran, 'Some Legal Aspects of the Formation of the United Arab Republic and the United Arab States', 8 ICLQ, 1959, p. 346.

[97] See O'Connell, *State Succession*, vol. II, pp. 77 ff.

[98] See also *Ltd Partnership Z v. High Court (Obergericht) of the Canton of Thurgau*, Federal Supreme Court, Insolvency Chamber, 15 June 2005, partly published as BGE 131 III 448.

[99] *Yearbook of the ILC*, 1974, vol. II, p. 208.

Belgium was informed that US–Belgium commercial agreements were thenceforth to be applied to Hawaii also.[100] Similarly it was held that after 1919, German treaties would not apply to Alsace-Lorraine, while French treaties would thereafter be extended to that territory.[101] Article 15 would therefore seem to reiterate existing custom,[102] although there have been indications to the contrary in the past.[103]

Secession from an existing state to form a new state or states

The factual situations out of which a separation or dismemberment takes place are many and varied. They range from a break-up of a previously created entity into its previous constituent elements, as in the 1961 dissolution of the United Arab Republic into the pre-1958 states of Egypt and Syria or the dissolution of the Federation of Mali, to the complete fragmenting of a state into a variety of successors not being co-terminous with previous territorial units, such as the demise of Austria-Hungary in 1919.[104] Where there is a separation or secession from an independent state which continues, in order to create a new state, the former continues as a state, albeit territorially reduced, with its international rights and obligations intact.[105] With regard to the seceding territory itself, the leading view appears to be that the newly created state will commence international life free from the treaty rights and obligations applicable to its former sovereign.[106] Reasons for this include the important point that it is difficult to maintain as a rule of general application that states that have not signed particular treaties are bound by them.

State practice has essentially reinforced the basic proposition. When Belgium seceded from the Netherlands in 1830, it was deemed to start

---

[100] See e.g. O'Connell, *State Succession*, vol. II, pp. 377–8.   [101] *Ibid.*, p. 379.
[102] The exception to the 'moving treaty-frontiers' rule reflects the concept that 'political treaties' would not pass, *ibid.*, p. 25. See further above, p. 964, with regard to the re-unification of Germany in 1990. See also article IX of Annex 1 of the Anglo-Chinese Agreement, 1984 on Hong Kong, below, p. 1008.
[103] See, for example, O'Connell, *State Succession*, vol. II, pp. 374 ff.
[104] *Ibid.*, chapter 10.
[105] Save, of course, with regard to those that relate solely to the seceding territory.
[106] See O'Connell, *State Succession*, vol. II, pp. 88 ff., and *Oppenheim's International Law*, p. 222. See also the *Third US Restatement of Foreign Relations Law*, p. 108, which provides that 'When part of a state becomes a new state, the new state does not succeed to the international agreements to which the predecessor state was party, unless, expressly or by implication, it accepts such agreements and the other party or parties thereto agree or acquiesce.'

international life with 'a clean slate' and the same approach was adopted with regard to the secession of Cuba from Spain in 1898 and that of Panama from Colombia in 1903. Similarly, when Finland seceded from the Russian Empire after the First World War, the view taken by the UK and the US was that Finland was not bound by the existing Russian treaties dealing with the territory.[107]

While essentially this is the position taken by the Vienna Convention on Succession to Treaties with regard to decolonised territories (discussed in the following subsection), article 34 provides that 'any treaty in force at the date of the succession of states in respect of the entire territory of the predecessor state continues in force in respect of each successor state so formed'. Any treaty which applied only to part of the territory of the predecessor state which has become a successor state will continue in force in respect of the latter only. These provisions will not apply if the states concerned otherwise agree or if it appears from the treaty or is otherwise established that the application of the treaty in respect of the successor state would be incompatible with the object and purpose of the treaty or would radically change the conditions for its operation.[108]

As far as the predecessor state is concerned in such a situation (assuming the predecessor state remains in existence), article 35 provides that existing treaties remain in force after the succession in respect of the remaining territory, unless the parties otherwise agree or it is established that the treaty related only to the territory which has separated from the predecessor state or it appears from the treaty or is otherwise established that the application of the treaty in respect of the predecessor state would be incompatible with the object and purpose of the treaty or would radically change the conditions for its operation.

The approach in the Vienna Convention was adopted on the basis of the International Law Commission draft which had taken the position that 'in modern international law having regard to the need for the maintenance of the system of multilateral treaties and of the stability of treaty relationships, as a general rule the principle of *de jure* continuity should apply'.[109] This may have been an attempt to distinguish decolonised territories (termed 'newly independent states' in the Convention) from other

---

[107] *Yearbook of the International Law Commission*, 1974, vol. II, part 1, p. 263. See also O'Connell, *State Succession*, vol. II, pp. 96–100, and *Oppenheim's International Law*, p. 222. See also *Yearbook of the ILC*, 1974, vol. II, part 1, pp. 265–6.

[108] See *Yearbook of the ILC*, 1974, vol. II, pp. 260 ff.

[109] *Yearbook of the ILC*, 1974, vol. II, part 1, p. 169. See also UKMIL, 69 BYIL, 1998, p. 482.

examples of independence, but it constitutes a rather different approach from the traditional one and the formulation in article 34 cannot be taken as necessarily reflective of customary law. Much will depend upon the views of the states concerned.

What can be said is that the requirements of international stability in certain areas in particular will stimulate states generally to encourage an approach of succession to multilateral obligations by the newly independent secessionist states. The Guidelines on Recognition of New States in Eastern Europe and the Soviet Union adopted by the European Community on 16 December 1991 certainly noted that the common position of EC member states on recognition required *inter alia* 'acceptance of all relevant commitments with regard to disarmament and nuclear non-proliferation as well as to security and regional stability'.[110] But, of course, conditions attached to the essentially political process of recognition are not the same as accepting consequences arising out of succession itself. However, there were certainly indications that the United States was taking the position that Russia and the non-Baltic successor states to the USSR should be regarded as bound by some at least of the Soviet treaties.[111] This approach was clearly developed in view of the political need to ensure continuity with regard to arms control agreements and mechanisms.[112] Of course, the impact of Russia constituting the continuance of the Soviet Union is to maintain in force for the former the obligations of the latter, but there was concern about the control of the nuclear and other weapons subject to treaty regulation which were now situated in the successor states to the USSR. The signing of agreements with the major successor states appears to have mitigated the strength of this particular approach. Indeed, it should be noted that separate agreements with the nuclear successor states of Ukraine, Belarus and Kazakhstan were apparently required in order to ensure the compliance of those states with regard to the arms control treaties binding upon the Soviet Union,[113] although these states

---

[110] See 92 ILR, pp. 173–4.

[111] See Müllerson, 'Continuity'. See also T. Love, 'International Agreement Obligations after the Soviet Union's Break-up: Current United States Practice and its Consistency with International Law', 26 *Vanderbilt Journal of Transnational Law*, 1993, pp. 373, 396, who notes that the US practice of arguing that treaties are binding upon the republics (apart from the special case of Russia) is inconsistent with the views expressed in the US Restatement, *ibid.*, p. 410. The views of the US Restatement are referred to above, p. 974, note 106.

[112] Müllerson, 'Continuity', at pp. 398–401.

[113] See 'US–CIS Protocol to START Treaty', 86 AJIL, 1992, p. 799. See also the Agreement on Joint Measures with Respect to Nuclear Weapons, 31 ILM, 1992, p. 152, and Müllerson, *International Law*, pp. 150–2.

had agreed generally to be bound by international obligations deriving from treaties signed by the USSR.[114] The US and Ukraine agreed by an exchange of notes on 10 May 1995 that in so far as bilateral treaties between them were concerned, article 34 of the Convention would be taken as 'a point of departure'. A treaty-by-treaty review by the two states was conducted, as a result of which it was decided that some treaties had become obsolete, others would not be applied and others, specifically listed in the Annex to the note, were to be regarded as still in force.[115]

Whether in view of the greatly increased network of multilateral treaties and the vastly enhanced interdependence of states founded and manifested upon such agreement, it is possible to say that the international community is moving towards a position of a presumption of continuity, is in reality difficult to establish. Certainly the potentially disruptive effect of the creation of new states needs to be minimised, but it is far too early to be able to declare that continuity or a presumption of continuity is now the established norm.

'Newly independent states'

The post-Second World War period saw the dismantling of the overseas European empires. Based in international legal terms upon the principle of self-determination, which was founded upon a distinction between such territories and the metropolitan authority, decolonisation produced a number of changes in the international legal system.[116] The Vienna Convention on Succession to Treaties sought to establish a special category relating to decolonised territories. These were termed 'newly independent states' and defined in article 2(1)f as successor states 'the territory of which immediately before the date of the succession of states was a dependent territory for the international relations of which the predecessor state was responsible'.[117] Article 16 laid down the general rule that such states were not bound to maintain in force or to become a party to any treaty by reason only of the fact that the treaty had been in force regarding the territory in question at the date of succession. This approach was deemed to build upon the traditional 'clean slate' principle applying to new states

---

[114] Alma Ata Declaration, 21 December 1991, 21 ILM, 1992, pp. 148, 149.

[115] See 89 AJIL, 1995, p. 761. The note specifically excluded matters concerning succession to USA–USSR bilateral arms limitation and related agreements, with regard to which special mechanisms had been established.

[116] See above, chapter 5, p. 251.

[117] See also the Vienna Convention on Succession to State Property, Archives and Debt, 1983, article 2(1)e.

created out of existing states, such as the United States and the Spanish American Republics when they had obtained independence.[118] This was also consistent with the view taken by the UN Secretariat in 1947 when discussing Pakistan's position in relation to the organisation, where it was noted that 'the territory which breaks off, Pakistan, will be a new state; it will not have the treaty rights and obligations of the old state'.[119]

It should be noted that the provision dealing with bilateral treaties was more vigorously worded, no doubt because the personal and reciprocal nature of such treaties is that more obvious, or in the words of the International Law Commission 'dominant', and also because, unlike the case of multilateral treaties, there is no question of the treaty coming into force between the new state and the predecessor state.[120] While state practice demonstrates some continuity in areas such as air services agreements and trade agreements, the Commission felt that this did not reflect a customary rule, as distinct from the will of the states concerned, and that the fundamental rule with regard to bilateral treaties was that their continuance in force after independence was a matter for agreement, express or tacit, between the newly independent state and the other state party which had contracted with the predecessor state.[121] Article 24 notes that a bilateral treaty in force for the territory in question is considered to be in force for the newly independent state and the other state party where they expressly so agree or by reason of their conduct they are to be considered as having so agreed.[122]

There is, of course, a distinction between a new state being obliged to become a party to a treaty binding the predecessor state and having the facility or perhaps even the right to become a party to that treaty. Practice shows that new states may benefit from a 'fast track' method of participating in treaties. For example, new states are not required to adhere to the formal mechanism of accession as if they were existing

---

[118] See *Yearbook of the ILC*, 1974, vol. II, part 1, p. 211. See also, as to the theoretical basis of the 'clean slate' principle, the Separate Opinion of Judge Weeramantry, *Application of the Genocide Convention (Bosnia and Herzegovina v. Yugoslavia)*, ICJ Reports, 1996, pp. 595, 644; 115 ILR, p. 10.

[119] *Yearbook of the ILC*, 1974, vol. II, part 1, p. 211.

[120] *Ibid.*, p. 237.   [121] *Ibid.*, pp. 237–9.

[122] The above rules also apply to newly independent states (as defined in the Convention) formed from two or more territories: see article 30 (referring to articles 16–29). Where a treaty affects one or more but not all of the territories in question, there is a presumption that on succession it will apply to the newly independent state, *ibid*. See also *Re Bottali* 78 ILR, p. 105 and *M v. Federal Department of Justice and Police* 75 ILR, p. 107.

non-party states[123] and article 17 of the Vienna Convention provides that a 'newly independent state' may by a notification of succession establish its status as a party to a multilateral treaty which at the date of succession was in force in respect of the territory to which the succession relates, unless it appears from the treaty or is otherwise established that the application of the treaty in respect of the newly independent state would be incompatible with the object and purpose of the treaty or would radically change the conditions of its operation. In addition, where it appears from the nature of the treaty itself that the participation of any other state would require the consent of all the parties, such consent must be forthcoming for the new state to participate.[124]

The 'clean slate' principle has also in practice been mitigated by the terms of the process by which many colonies achieved independence. A number of colonial powers, particularly the United Kingdom, adopted the practice of concluding devolution agreements by which certain treaties signed on behalf of the territory becoming independent continued to apply to the newly independent state.[125] While such agreements would be considered *res inter alios* with regard to third states, they were of value in establishing the appropriate framework for relations between the former colonial power and the new state. Other newly independent states adopted the practice of making unilateral declarations by which they made known their views as to treaty succession. Such unilateral declarations often took the form of specifying that treaties would continue in force for an interim period during which time they would be reviewed,[126] but they could not in themselves, of course, alter treaty relationships with third states.[127] Devices such as devolution agreements and unilateral declarations were of value, however, in mitigating the effects that an absolute 'clean slate' approach might otherwise have had.

Dissolution of states

Where an existing state comes to an end as an international person and is replaced by two or more other states, it is accepted that political treaties will not continue but that territorially grounded treaties will continue to attach

---

[123] See *Oppenheim's International Law*, p. 229.   [124] Article 17(3). See also article 27(2).

[125] See, for example, O'Connell, *State Succession*, vol. II, pp. 352 ff., and *Yearbook of the ILC*, 1974, vol. II, part 1, pp. 182–7. See also article 8 of the Vienna Convention.

[126] See, for a survey of practice, *Yearbook of the ILC*, 1974, vol. II, part 1, pp. 187–93.

[127] See article 9 of the Vienna Convention.

to the territories in question now subject to new sovereign arrangements. The situation with regard to other treaties is more uncertain.[128]

State practice concerning dissolution has centred to all intents and purposes upon the dismemberment of 'unions of state', that is the ending of what had originally been a union of two international persons. Examples would include Colombia in 1829–31; Norway/Sweden in 1905; the United Arab Republic in 1960; the Mali Federation in 1960; the Federation of Rhodesia and Nyasaland in 1963[129] and the Czech and Slovak Federal Republic in 1992.[130] It is difficult to deduce clear rules of state succession from these episodes since much depended upon the expressed intentions of the states concerned. Perhaps a presumption in favour of continuity of treaties with regard to each component part may be suggested, but this is subject to expressed intention to the contrary.[131]

Article 34 of the Vienna Convention provides for treaties in force for all or part of the predecessor state to continue in force with regard to the specific territory unless the states concerned otherwise agree or it appears from the treaty or is otherwise established that the application of the treaty would be incompatible with the object and purpose of the treaty or would radically change the conditions of its operation. Whether this constitutes a rule of customary law also is unclear, but in the vast majority of situations the matter is likely to be regulated by specific agreements. Upon the dissolution of the Czech and Slovak Federal Republic, for example, on 1 January 1993, the UK took the position that, as appropriate, treaties and agreements in force to which the UK and that state were parties remained

---

[128] See, for example, O'Connell, *State Succession*, vol. II, pp. 219–20.

[129] See *Yearbook of the ILC*, 1974, vol. II, part 1, pp. 260–3, and O'Connell, *State Succession*, vol. II, pp. 164 ff.

[130] This state consisted of two distinct units, the Czech Republic and the Slovak Republic, each with their own parliament. The Constitutional Law on the Dissolution of the Czech and Slovak Republic of 25 November 1992 provided for the dissolution of that state and for the establishment of the successor states of the Czech Republic and Slovakia. At the same time, the two republics issued a joint declaration informing the international community that the two successor states would succeed to all international treaties to which the predecessor state had been a party and that where necessary negotiations would take place, particularly where the impact upon the two republics differed: see J. Malenovsky, 'Problèmes Juridiques Liées à la Partition de la Tchécoslovaquie, y compris Tracé de la Frontière', AFDI, 1993, p. 305.

[131] The case of the dissolution of the Austro-Hungarian Empire in 1918 was a special case, since it could be regarded as a dissolution of the union of Austria and Hungary (where the latter, unlike the former, asserted continuity) coupled with the secession of territories that either joined other states, such as Romania, or were merged into new states, such as Poland or Czechoslovakia.

in force as between the UK and the successor states.[132] The question of Yugoslavia was more complicated in that until 2000, the Federal Republic of Yugoslavia maintained that it was a continuation of the former Socialist Federal Republic of Yugoslavia, while the other former republics maintained that the former SFRY had come to an end to be replaced by a series of new states.

The issue of article 34 and automatic succession arose in the *Application of the Genocide Convention (Bosnia and Herzegovina v. Yugoslavia)* case, where Bosnia argued that the rule applied with regard to the Genocide Convention and Yugoslavia denied this. The Court, however, did not make a determination on this point.[133] The issue arose again in the *Gabčíkovo–Nagymaros Project* case, where the parties argued as to whether the rule of automatic succession applied or not. The Court similarly declined to make a determination and focused instead on the significance of article 12.[134]

International human rights treaties

A territorial treaty binds successor states by virtue of attaching to the territory itself and establishing a particular regime that transcends the treaty. Can it be maintained that international human rights treaties are analogous and thus 'attach' to the inhabitants concerned within the territory of the predecessor state and thus continue to bind successor states? There is no doubt that human rights treaties constitute a rather specific category of treaties. They establish that obligations are owed directly to individuals and often provide for direct access for individuals to international mechanisms.[135] The very nature of international human rights treaties varies somewhat from that of traditional international agreements. The International Court in the *Reservations to the Genocide Convention* case emphasised that 'in such a Convention the contracting states do not have any interests of their own; they merely have, one and all, a common interest, namely, the accomplishment of those high purposes which are

---

[132] See the letters sent by the UK Prime Minister to the Prime Ministers of the Czech Republic and Slovakia on 1 January 1993, UKMIL, 65 BYIL, 1994, pp. 586 ff.

[133] ICJ Reports, 1996, pp. 595, 611–12; 115 ILR, p. 1. See also M. Craven, 'The *Genocide* Case, the Law of Treaties and State Succession', 68 BYIL, 1997, p. 127.

[134] ICJ Reports, 1997, pp. 7, 71; 116 ILR, p. 1. As to article 12, see above, p. 970.

[135] See R. Higgins, *Problems and Process*, Oxford, 1994, p. 95.

the *raison d'être* of the Convention'.[136] In the *Barcelona Traction* case,[137] the Court differentiated between obligations of a state towards the international community as a whole and those arising vis-à-vis another state. The former are obligations that derive 'from the outlawing of aggression and of genocide, as also from the principles and rules concerning the basic rights of the human person, including protection from slavery and racial discrimination'. In view of the importance of such rights, 'all States can be held to have a legal interest in their protection; they are obligations *erga omnes*'. It is also the case that the process of interpretation of international human rights treaties is more dynamic than is the case with regard to other international agreements. Human rights treaties create not merely subjective, reciprocal rights but rather particular legal orders involving objective obligations to protect human rights.[138]

Where a state party to human rights treaties either disintegrates completely or from which another state or states are created, and the classical rules of succession were followed, there is a danger that this might result in a situation where people formerly protected by such treaties are deprived of such protection as a consequence or by-product of state succession.[139] The practice of the UN Human Rights Committee[140] with regard to the Yugoslav tragedy is particularly interesting here. After the conclusion of its 45th session, the UN Human Rights Committee requested special reports with regard to specific issues (for example, the policy of 'ethnic cleansing', arbitrary detention, torture and advocacy of hatred) from Bosnia and Herzegovina, Croatia and the Federal Republic of Yugoslavia (Serbia and Montenegro), noting 'that all the peoples within the territory of the former Yugoslavia are entitled to the guarantees of the Covenant'.[141] Representatives of all three states appeared before the Committee to discuss the relevant issues, no objection being made to the competence of the Committee, even though only Croatia had actually notified the Secretary-General of

---

[136] ICJ Reports, 1951, pp. 15, 23; 18 ILR, p. 364.

[137] ICJ Reports, 1970, pp. 4, 32; 46 ILR, pp. 178, 206.

[138] See, for example, *Austria* v. *Italy*, 4 European Yearbook of Human Rights, 1960, pp. 116, 140; *Ireland* v. *UK*, European Court of Human Rights, Series A, vol. 20, 1978, pp. 90–1, and *Effect of Reservations on the Entry into Force of the American Convention on Human Rights*, 67 ILR, pp. 559, 568. See also above, chapter 16, p. 937.

[139] Note that the editors of *Oppenheim's International Law* take the view that in cases of the separation resulting in the creation of a new state, the latter 'is bound by – or at least entitled to accede to – general treaties of a "law-making" nature, especially those of a humanitarian character, previously binding on it as part of the state from which it has separated', p. 222.

[140] See above, chapter 6, p. 314.   [141] CCPR/C/SR.1178/Add.1, pp. 2–3.

its succession to the human rights treaties of the former Yugoslavia.[142] In the formal Comments of the Human Rights Committee upon the initial short reports submitted by the three states,[143] the Committee emphasised clearly and unambiguously that 'all the peoples within the territory of the former Yugoslavia are entitled to the guarantees of the Covenant'.[144] In its General Comment No. 26 of October 1997, the Committee took the view that 'once the people are accorded the protection of the rights under the Covenant, such protection devolves with territory and continues to belong to them, notwithstanding change in government . . . or State succession'.[145]

The Commission on Human Rights adopted resolution 1994/16 on 25 February 1994 in which it 'reiterates its call to successor states which have not yet done so to confirm to appropriate depositories that they continue to be bound by obligations under international human rights treaties' and 'emphasises the special nature of the human rights treaties aimed at the protection of human rights and fundamental freedoms'. In addition, the Commission requested the human rights treaty bodies to continue further the 'continuing applicability of the respective international human rights treaties to successor states' and the Secretary-General 'to encourage successor states to confirm their obligations under the international human

---

[142] See Müllerson, *International Law*, p. 157. In the ensuing discussion in the Committee, Müllerson (at the time a member) noted that human rights treaties besides being inter-state instruments also conferred rights upon individuals 'who could not be deprived of those rights in the event of state succession', while Serrano Caldera emphasised that 'state succession should be viewed as a matter of the acquired rights of the population of the state that had ratified the Covenant, which were not diluted when a state was divided'. CCPR/C/SR.1178/Add.1, pp. 2, 4 and 9.

[143] These reports were supplemented by Special Reports from each of the three states in April 1993: see that of Croatia, CCPR/C/87; that of the Federal Republic of Yugoslavia (Serbia and Montenegro), CCPR/C/88, and that of Bosnia and Herzegovina, CCPR/C/89.

[144] See CCPR/C/79/Add. 14–16, 28 December 1992. Note that at its 49th session, the UN Commission on Human Rights adopted resolution 1993/23 of 5 March 1993 in which it encouraged successor states to confirm to appropriate depositaries that they continued to be bound by obligations under relevant international human rights treaties. See also the Report of the UN Secretary-General, E/CN.4/1994/68. On 25 May 1994, the Committee on the Elimination of Racial Discrimination sent a communication to those successor states of the USSR that had not yet declared their adherence or succession to the Convention, inviting them to confirm the applicability of compliance with the Convention's provisions: see E/CN.4/1995/80, p. 3.

[145] A/53/40, annex VII. Cf. Aust, *Modern Treaty Law*, pp. 371–2. See also M. Kamminga, 'State Succession in respect of Human Rights Treaties', 6 EJIL, 1995, p. 469, and A. Rasulov, 'Revisiting State Succession to Humanitarian Treaties: Is There a Case for Automaticity?', 14 EJIL, 2003, p. 141.

rights treaties to which their predecessors were a party as from the date of their independence'.[146] In addition, the fifth meeting of persons chairing the human rights treaty bodies in September 1994 took the view that successor states were automatically bound by obligations under international human rights instruments from the respective date of independence and that observance of the obligations should not depend on a declaration of confirmation made by the government of the successor state.[147]

The issue of succession to the Genocide Convention in the Yugoslav situation was raised before the International Court specifically in the Preliminary Objections phase of the *Application of the Genocide Convention (Bosnia-Herzegovina* v. *Yugoslavia)* case. The Court held that it was unnecessary to determine this question in the circumstances since both Bosnia and Yugoslavia were clearly parties to the Convention by one means or another by the date of the filing of the Application.[148] The issue was, however, addressed particularly in two Separate Opinions. Judge Shahabuddeen declared that 'to effectuate its object and purpose, the [Genocide] Convention would fall to be construed as implying the expression of a unilateral undertaking by each party to the Convention to treat successor states as continuing as from independence any status which the predecessor state had as a party to the Convention'. It was suggested that it might be possible to extend this object and purpose argument to human rights treaties generally.[149] Judge Weeramantry in his Separate Opinion undertook a close analysis of the underlying principles and concluded by pointing to 'a principle of contemporary international law that there is automatic state succession to so vital a human rights convention as the Genocide Convention'.[150] One of the main reasons for this was the danger of gaps appearing in the system of human rights protection as between the dissolution of the predecessor state and the acceptance of human rights treaty obligations by the successor state or states.

Accordingly, the question of continued application of human rights treaties within the territory of a predecessor state irrespective of a succession is clearly under consideration. Whether such a principle has been clearly established is at the present moment unclear. However, with regard to those human rights which are established as a matter of customary international law, the new state will be bound by these as such.

---

[146] See also Commission on Human Rights Resolution 1995/18 adopted on 24 February 1995.
[147] E/CN.4/1995/80, pp. 3–4.   [148] ICJ Reports, 1996, pp. 595, 612.
[149] *Ibid.*, p. 636.   [150] *Ibid.*, pp. 645 ff.

Succession with respect to matters other than treaties

Membership of international organisations[151]

Succession to membership of international organisations will proceed (depending upon the terms of the organisation's constitution) according to whether a new state is formed or an old state continues in a slightly different form. In the case of the partition of British India in 1947, India was considered by the UN General Assembly as a continuation of the previous entity, while Pakistan was regarded as a new state, which had then to apply for admission to the organisation.[152] Upon the merger of Egypt and Syria in 1958 to form the United Arab Republic, the latter was treated as a single member of the United Nations, while upon the dissolution of the merger in 1961, Syria simply resumed its separate membership of the organisation.[153] In the case of the merger of North and South Yemen in 1990, the new state simply replaced the predecessor states as a member of the relevant international organisations. Where the predecessor state is dissolved and new states are created, such states will have to apply anew for membership to international organisations. For example, the new states of the Czech Republic and Slovakia were admitted as new members of the UN on 19 January 1993.[154]

The Sixth (Legal) Committee of the General Assembly considered the situation of new states being formed through division of a member state and the membership problem and produced the following principles:[155]

> 1. That, as a general rule, it is in conformity with legal principles to presume that a state which is a member of the Organization of the United Nations does not cease to be a member simply because its Constitution or frontier

---

[151] See O'Connell, *State Succession*, vol. II, pp. 183 ff., and H. G. Schermers and N. M. Blokker, *International Institutional Law*, 3rd edn, The Hague, 1995, pp. 73 ff.

[152] This issue, of a separation of part of an existing state to form a new state, was considered by the UN to be on a par with the separation from the UK of the Irish Free State and from the Netherlands of Belgium, where the remaining portions continued as existing states: see O'Connell, *State Succession*, vol. I, pp. 184–7.

[153] *Ibid.*, pp. 197–8. This situation, which differed from the India–Pakistan precedent of 1947, has been criticised: see e.g. C. Rousseau, 'Sécession de la Syrie et de la RUA', 66 RGDIP, 1962, p. 413. See also E. Cotran, 'Some Legal Aspects of the Formation of the United Arab Republic and the United Arab States', 8 ICLQ, 1959, p. 346.

[154] See Schermers and Blokker, *International Institutional Law*, pp. 73 and 77. See above, p. 960, with regard to the position of the Russian Federation and the Federal Republic of Yugoslavia and membership of the UN.

[155] A/CN.4/149, p. 8, quoted in O'Connell, *State Succession*, vol. I, p. 187.

has been subjected to changes, and that the extinction of the state as a legal personality recognised in the international order must be shown before its rights and obligations can be considered thereby to have ceased to exist.

2. That when a new state is created, whatever may be the territory and the populations which it comprises and whether or not they formed part of a state member of the United Nations, it cannot under the system of the Charter claim the status of a member of the United Nations unless it has been formally admitted as such in conformity with the provisions of the Charter.

3. Beyond that, each case must be judged according to its merits.

Succession to assets and debts[156]

The relevant international law in this area is based upon customary law. The Vienna Convention on Succession to State Property, Archives and Debts, 1983 is not currently in force, although most of its provisions (apart from those concerning 'newly independent states') are reflective of custom. The primary rule with regard to the allocation of assets (including archives) and debts in succession situations is that the relevant parties should settle such issues by agreement. Virtually all of the rules that are formulated, for example in the Vienna Convention, 1983, are deemed to operate only where such agreement has not taken place.[157] In addition, the Arbitration Commission on Yugoslavia declared in Opinion No. 9 that 'the successor states to the SFRY must together settle all aspects of the succession by agreement'[158] and reinforced this approach in Opinion No. 14, declaring that 'the first principle applicable to state succession is that

---

[156] See generally, O'Connell, *State Succession*, vol. I, pp. 199 ff.; E. H. Feilchenfeld, *Public Debts and State Succession*, New York, 1931; UN, *Materials on Succession of States in Matters Other than Treaties*, New York, 1978; International Law Association Reports on Aspects of the Law of State Succession 2004 (preliminary) and 2006 (final); A. Stanič, 'Financial Aspects of State Succession: The Case of Yugoslavia', 12 EJIL, 2001, p. 751; C. Rousseau, *Droit International Public*, Paris, 1977, vol. III, p. 374; M. Streinz, 'Succession of States in Assets and Liabilities – A New Regime?', 26 German YIL, 1983, p. 198; P. Monnier, 'La Convention de Vienne sur la Succession d'États en Matière de Biens, Archives et Dettes d'État', AFDI, 1984, p. 221; V. D. Degan, 'State Succession Especially in Respect of State Property and Debts', 4 Finnish YIL, 1993, p. 130; Mrak, *Succession of States*, and E. Nathan, 'The Vienna Convention on Succession of States in Respect of State Property, Archives and Debts' in *International Law at a Time of Perplexity* (ed. Y. Dinstein), Dordrecht, 1989, p. 489. See also *Yearbook of the ILC*, 1981, vol. II, part 2.

[157] See, for example, articles 14, 17, 18, 22, 23, 27, 28, 30, 31, 37, 38, 40 and 41.

[158] 92 ILR, p. 205.

the successor states should consult with each other and agree a settlement of all questions relating to the succession'.[159]

State property[160]

The classic rule postulates that only the public property of the predecessor state passes automatically to the successor state,[161] but this, of course, raises the question of the definition of public property. The distinction between public and private property is to some extent based upon the conceptual differences between public and private law, a distinction unknown to common law countries. Although in many cases there will be a relevant agreement to define what is meant by public property in this context,[162] this does not always occur and recourse to municipal law is often required. This indeed may be necessitated to a large extent also because international law itself simply does not provide many of the required definitions with regard to, for example, public companies or public utility undertakings.[163]

The relevant municipal law for such purposes is that of the predecessor state. It is that law which will define the nature of the property in question and thus in essence decide its destination in the event of a succession.[164] Article 8 of the Vienna Convention, 1983 provides that state property for the purposes of the Convention means 'property, rights and interests which, at the date of the succession of states, were, according to the internal law of the predecessor state owned by that state'[165] and this can be taken as reflective of customary law. The Arbitration Commission on Yugoslavia reiterated this position by declaring that 'to determine whether the property, debts and archives belonged to the SFRY, reference should

---

[159] 96 ILR, p. 731.

[160] Note that private rights are unaffected as such by a succession: see, for example, *Oppenheim's International Law*, p. 216, and below, p. 1001.

[161] See, for example, the United Nations Tribunal for Libya, 22 ILR, p. 103. See also International Law Association, *Final Report*, p. 1.

[162] See, for example, the treaties concerned with the establishment of Cyprus in 1960, 382 UNTS, pp. 3 ff., and the Treaty of Peace with Italy, 1947, 49 UNTS, annex XIV, p. 225.

[163] For an example, see the dispute concerning property belonging to the Order of St Mauritz and St Lazarus, AFDI, 1965, p. 323. See also Stern, 'Succession', p. 329.

[164] See the *Chorzów Factory* case, PCIJ, Series A, No. 7, p. 30 and the *German Settlers in Upper Silesia* case, PCIJ, Series B, No. 6, p. 6, but cf. the *Peter Pazmany University* case, PCIJ, Series A/B, No. 61, p. 236.

[165] See also *Yearbook of the ILC*, 1970, vol. II, pp. 136–43 and *ibid.*, 1981, vol. II, p. 23; cf. O'Connell, *State Succession*, vol. I, pp. 202–3.

be had to the domestic law of the SFRY in operation at the date of succession'.[166] The relevant date for the passing of the property is the date of succession[167] and this is the date of independence, although difficulties may arise in the context of the allocation of assets and debts where different dates of succession occur for different successor states.[168] Such problems would need to be resolved on the basis of agreement between the relevant parties.[169]

The Arbitration Commission was faced with two particular problems. First, the 1974 SFRY Constitution had transferred to the constituent republics ownership of many items of property. This, held the Commission, led to the conclusion that such property could not be held to have belonged to the SFRY whatever their origin or initial financing.[170] Secondly, the Commission was faced with the concept of 'social ownership', a concept regarded as particularly highly developed in the SFRY. In the event, the Commission resolved the dilemma by adopting a mixture of the territorial principle and a functional approach. It was noted that 'social ownership' was 'held for the most part by "associated labour organisations" – bodies with their own legal personality, operating in a single republic and coming within its exclusive jurisdiction. Their property, debts and archives are not to be divided for purposes of state succession: each successor state exercises its sovereign powers in respect of them.'[171] However, where other organisations operated 'social ownership' either at the federal level or in two or more republics, 'their property, debts and archives should be divided between the successor states in question if they exercised public prerogatives on behalf of the SFRY of individual republics'. Where such public prerogatives were not being exercised, the organisations should be

---

[166] Opinion No. 14, 96 ILR, p. 732.
[167] Note that article 10 of the Vienna Convention, 1983 provides that the date of the passing of state property of the predecessor state is that of the date of succession of states 'unless otherwise agreed by the states concerned or decided by an appropriate international body'. Article 21 repeats this principle in the context of state archives and article 35 with regard to state debts.
[168] See e.g. Arbitration Commission Opinion No. 11, 96 ILR, p. 719. Cf. the Yugoslav Agreement on Succession Issues of June 2001, 41 ILM, 2002, p. 3. See also *AY Bank Ltd* v. *Bosnia and Herzegovina and Others* [2006] EWHC 830 (Ch) and C. Stahn, 'The Agreement on Succession Issues of the Former Socialist Federal Republic of Yugoslavia', 96 AJIL, 2002, p. 379.
[169] See the Yugoslav Agreement on Succession Issues, 2001, articles 3 and 7 of Annex A and article 4(3) of Annex B.
[170] Opinion No. 14, 96 ILR, p. 732.   [171] *Ibid.*

regarded as private-sector enterprises to which state succession does not apply.[172]

The Yugoslav Agreement on Succession Issues, 2001, however, provides that, 'It shall be for the successor state on whose territory immovable and tangible movable property is situated to determine, for the purposes of this Annex, whether that property was state property of the SFRY in accordance with international law.'[173]

It is a recognised principle of customary international law that the public property of a predecessor state with respect to the territory in question passes to the successor state.[174] Thus, as a general rule, the test of succession of public, or state, property as so characterised under the laws of the predecessor state is a territorial one.

However, one needs to distinguish here between immovable and movable property. State immovable property situated in the territory to which the succession relates passes to the successor state.[175] This is provided for in the Vienna Convention, 1983.[176] It is also evident in state practice,[177] most recently being reaffirmed by the Arbitration Commission on Yugoslavia[178] and in the Yugoslav Agreement on Succession Issues, 2001.[179]

In the case of immovable property situated outside the successor state or states, traditional state practice posits that where the predecessor state continues in existence this property should remain with the predecessor state (subject to agreement to the contrary by the states concerned, of

---

[172] *Ibid.*

[173] Article 6 of Annex A. This is to be contrasted with the more usual reference to domestic law at the relevant time.

[174] See, for example, the *Third US Restatement of Foreign Relations Law*, pp. 102 ff.; Brownlie, *Principles*, pp. 624–5, and O'Connell, *State Succession*, vol. I, pp. 199–200. See also the *Peter Pazmany University* case, PCIJ, Series A/B, No. 61, 1933, p. 237 and *Haile Selassie v. Cable and Wireless Ltd (No. 2)* [1939] Ch. 182; 9 AD, p. 94. See also *Kunstsammlungen zu Weimar v. Elicofon* 536 F.Supp. 829, 855 (1981); 94 ILR, pp. 133, 180. Note that under article 11, which basically reflects practice, no compensation is payable for the passing of state property unless otherwise agreed, and article 12 provides that third states' property in the territory of the predecessor state remains unaffected by the succession.

[175] E.g. fixed military installations, prisons, airports, government offices, state hospitals and universities: see *Yearbook of the ILC*, 1981, vol. II, part 2, p. 33.

[176] In article 14 (with regard to the transfer of part of a state to another state); article 15(i)a (with regard to 'newly independent states'); article 16 (upon a uniting of states to form one successor state); article 17 (with regard to separation of part of a state to form a new state) and article 18 (with regard to the dissolution of a state).

[177] See, for example, O'Connell, *State Succession*, vol. I, pp. 220–1. See also *Yearbook of the ILC*, 1981, vol. II, part 2, p. 29.

[178] Opinion No. 14, 96 ILR, p. 731.   [179] Article 2(1) of Annex A.

course). Only special circumstances might modify this principle.[180] Where the predecessor state ceases to exist, it would appear that its property abroad should be divided proportionately between the successor states.[181]

Article 15(1)b of the Convention makes out a special, and highly controversial, case for 'newly independent states'. This provides that 'immovable property, having belonged to the territory to which the succession of states relates, situated outside it and having become state property of the predecessor state during the period of dependence, shall pass to the successor state', while other immovable state property situated outside the territory 'shall pass to the successor state in proportion to the contribution of the dependent territory'. Neither of these propositions can be regarded as part of customary international law and their force would thus be dependent upon the coming into effect of the Convention, should this happen.[182]

As far as movable property connected with the territory in question is concerned,[183] the territorial principle continues to predominate. O'Connell notes that 'such property as is destined specifically for local use is acquired by the successor state',[184] while the formulation in the Vienna Convention, 1983 is more flexible. This provides that 'movable state property of the predecessor state connected with the activity of the

---

[180] See, for example, *Oppenheim's International Law*, p. 223, note 6.

[181] *Ibid.*, at p. 221. Article 18(1)b of the Vienna Convention, 1983 provides that 'immovable state property of the predecessor state situated outside its territory shall pass to the successor states in equitable proportions'. Note that the Yugoslav Agreement on Succession Issues, 2001 deals specifically with the allocation of diplomatic and consular premises: see Annex B.

[182] It is to be noted that article 15 does not, unlike other succession situations, refer to agreements between the predecessor and successor states. This was deliberate as the International Law Commission, which drafted the articles upon which the Convention is based, felt that this was required as a recognition of the special circumstances of decolonisation and the fact that many such agreements are unfavourable to the newly independent state: see *Yearbook of the ILC*, 1981, vol. II, part 2, p. 38. The article is also unusual in that it provides that immovable state property situated outside the territory and movable state property other than that already covered in the article 'to the creation of which the dependent territory has contributed' shall pass to the successor state in proportion to the contribution of the dependent territory. This was intended to introduce the application of equity to the situation and was designed to preserve *inter alia*, 'the patrimony and the historical and cultural heritage of the people inhabiting the dependent territory concerned', *ibid.* It is unclear how far this extends. It may cover contributions to international institutions made where the territory is a dependent territory, but beyond this one can only speculate.

[183] E.g. currency and state public funds, *Yearbook of the ILC*, 1981, vol. II, part 2, pp. 35–6.

[184] O'Connell, *State Succession*, vol. I, p. 204.

predecessor state in respect of the territory to which the succession of states applies shall pass to the successor state'.[185] There are, however, likely to be difficulties of precision in specific cases with regard to borderline instances of what may be accepted as either property 'destined specifically for local use' or property 'connected with the activity of the predecessor State in . . . the territory'. The view taken by the Arbitration Commission in Opinion No. 14 appears to be even more flexible for it simply notes that 'public property passes to the successor state on whose territory it is situated'.[186] However, particular kinds of property may be dealt with differently. For example, the Yugoslav Agreement on Succession Issues provides that the rule is not to apply to tangible state property of great importance to the cultural heritage of one of the successor states and which originated there, even though situated elsewhere at the date of independence. Such property is to go to the state whose cultural heritage it is.[187] Secondly, military property is to be made the subject of special arrangements.[188]

The situation with regard to movable property outside of the territory in question is more complicated. Article 17(1)c of the Vienna Convention, 1983 provides that such property (in the case of separation of part of a state) 'shall pass to the successor state in an equitable proportion'. This must be regarded as a controversial proposition since it appears to modify the dominant territorial approach to the succession of state property.[189] However, in the case of the dissolution of the predecessor state, the argument in favour of an equitable division of movable property not linked to the territory in respect of which the succession occurs is much stronger.[190] The Arbitration Commission on Yugoslavia limited itself to noting the general principle that state property, debts and archives of the SFRY (other than immovable property within each of the successor states) should be divided between the successor states[191] and that while each category of

---

[185] Article 17. See also articles 14(2)b, 15(1)d and 18(1)c.

[186] 96 ILR, p. 731. See also article 3(1) of Annex A of the Yugoslav Agreement on Succession Issues, 2001.

[187] Article 3(2) of Annex A.   [188] Article 4(1).

[189] See O'Connell, *State Succession*, vol. I, p. 204. Cf. *Yearbook of the ILC*, 1981, vol. II, part 1, pp. 46–7.

[190] See article 18(1)d of the Vienna Convention, 1983. See also the decision of the Austrian Supreme Court in *Republic of Croatia et al.* v. *Girocredit Bank AG der Sparkassen* 36 ILM, 1997, p. 1520.

[191] Opinion No. 14, 96 ILR, pp. 731–2. See now the Yugoslav Agreement on Succession Issues, 2001 as discussed.

assets and liabilities need not be divided equitably, the overall outcome had to be an equitable division.[192]

The state succession situation which in general poses the least problem is that of absorption or merger, since the absorbing or newly created state respectively will simply take over the assets and debts of the extinguished state. The issues were, however, discussed in detail in the context of German unification. Article 21 of the Unification Treaty provides that the assets of the German Democratic Republic which served directly specified administrative tasks were to become Federal assets[193] and were to be used to discharge public tasks in the territory of the former GDR. Article 22 dealt with public assets of legal entities in that territory, including the land and assets in the agricultural sectors which did not serve directly specified administrative tasks.[194] Such financial assets were to be administered in trust by the Federal Government and be appointed by federal law equally between the Federal Government on the one hand and the *Länder* of the former GDR on the other, with the local authorities receiving an appropriate share of the *Länder* allocation. The Federal Government was to use its share to discharge public tasks in the territory of the former GDR, while the distribution of the *Länder* share to the individual *Länder* was to take place upon the basis of population ratio. Publicly owned assets used for the housing supply became the property of the local authorities together with the assumption by the latter of a proportionate share of the debts, with the ultimate aim of privatisation.

In fact, state practice demonstrates that with the exception of some clear and basic rules, all will depend upon the particular agreement reached in the particular circumstances. In the case of the former Czech and Slovak Federal Republic, the two successor states agreed to divide the assets

---

[192] Opinion No. 13, *ibid.*, p. 728. The Yugoslav Agreement on Succession Issues, 2001 provides that where the allocation of property results in a 'significantly unequal distribution' of SFRY state property, then the matter may be raised with the Joint Committee established under article 5 of the Annex.

[193] Unless they were earmarked on 1 October 1989 predominantly for administrative tasks which under the Basic Law of the FRG are to be discharged by the *Länder*, local authorities or other public administrative bodies, in which case they will accrue to the appropriate institution of public administration. Administrative assets used predominantly for tasks of the former Ministry of State Security/Office for National Security are to accrue to the Trust Agency established under the Law on the Privatisation and Reorganisation of Publicly Owned Assets (Trust Law) of 17 June 1990 for the purpose of privatising former publicly owned companies.

[194] These were termed 'financial assets' and deliberately exclude social insurance assets.

and liabilities of the predecessor state[195] in the ratio of two to one (the approximate population ratio of the two new states).[196] In the case of the former Soviet Union, Russia and the successor states signed agreements in 1991 and 1992 apportioning assets and liabilities of the predecessor state with the share of Russia being 61.34 per cent and the Ukraine being 16.37 per cent.[197] In the case of the former Yugoslavia, the Agreement on Succession Issues of 2001, in addition to the provisions referred to above,[198] provided for the distribution of assets on the basis of agreed proportions.[199] Financial assets in the International Monetary Fund (IMF) and World Bank were distributed on a slightly different proportional basis (that became known as the IMF key).[200] The IMF key was also used with regard to the distribution of assets in the Bank of International Settlements in an arrangement dated 10 April 2001.[201]

State archives

Archives are state property with special characteristics. Many are difficult by their nature to divide up, but they may be relatively easily reproduced

---

[195] Apart from immovable property located within each republic which went to the republic concerned in accordance with the territorial principle.

[196] See, for example, Degan, 'State Succession', p. 144.

[197] See Müllerson, *International Law*, p. 144, and Stern, 'Succession', pp. 379 ff. The proportions were reached using four criteria: the participation of the republics concerned in the imports and exports respectively of the former USSR, the proportion of GNP, and the proportion of populations: see W. Czaplinski, 'Equity and Equitable Principles in the Law of State Succession' in Mark, *Succession of States*, pp. 61, 71. However, several successor states refused to accept this and the arrangement never came into being, and in 1993 Russia claimed all of the assets and liabilities of the former USSR, see Stern, 'Succession', p. 405, and a number of bilateral agreements were signed to reflect this, see International Law Association, *Final Report*, pp. 7 ff. A special agreement was reached in 1997 with regard to the division of the Black Sea fleet based in the Crimea in Ukraine, following a number of unsuccessful efforts: Stern 'Succession', p. 386.

[198] See above, pp. 989–91.

[199] These were Bosnia and Herzegovina 15.5 per cent; Croatia 23 per cent; Macedonia 7.5 per cent: Slovenia 16 per cent and Yugoslavia 38 per cent: see article 4 of Annex C. This proportion was also used for all other rights and interests of the SFRY not otherwise covered in the Agreements (such as patents, trade marks, copyrights and royalties), Annex F.

[200] This was as follows: Bosnia and Herzegovina 13.20 per cent; Croatia 28.49 per cent; Macedonia 5.40 per cent; Slovenia 16.39 per cent and FRY 36.52 per cent: see IMF Press Release No. 92/92, 15 December 1992. See also P. Williams, 'State Succession and the International Financial Institutions', 43 ICLQ, 1994, pp. 776, 802, n. 168, and I. Shihata, 'Matters of State Succession in the World Bank's Practice' in Mark, *Succession of States*, pp. 75, 87.

[201] See Appendix to the Yugoslav Agreement on Succession Issues, 2001.

and duplicated. Archives are a crucial part of the heritage of a community and may consist of documents, numismatic collections, iconographic documents, photographs and films. The issue has been of great concern to UNESCO, which has called for the restitution of archives as part of the reconstitution and protection of the national cultural heritage and has appealed for the return of an irreplaceable cultural heritage to those that created it.[202] In this general context, one should also note articles 149 and 303 of the 1982 Convention on the Law of the Sea. The former provides that all objects of an archaeological and historical nature found in the International Seabed Area are to be preserved or disposed of for the benefit of mankind as a whole, 'particular regard being paid to the preferential rights of the state or country of origin, or the state of historical and archaeological origin', while the latter stipulates that states have the duty to protect objects of an archaeological and historical nature found at sea and shall co-operate for this purpose.

In general, treaties between European states dealing with cessions of territory included archival clauses providing for the treatment of archives, while such clauses are very rare in cases of decolonisation.[203]

Article 20 of the 1983 Vienna Convention provides that state archives in the present context means:

> all documents of whatever date and kind, produced or received by the predecessor state in the exercise of its functions which, at the date of the succession of states, belonged to the predecessor state according to its internal law and were preserved by it directly or under its control as archives for whatever purpose.

Generally, such archives will pass as at the date of succession and without compensation, without as such affecting archives in the territory owned by a third state.[204]

Where part of the territory of a state is transferred by that state to another state, in the absence of agreement, the part of the state archives of the predecessor state which, for normal administration of the territory

---

[202] UNESCO, Records of the General Conference, 18th Session, Resolutions, 1974, pp. 68 ff., 20 C/102, 1978, paras. 18–19; and UNESCO Records of the General Conference, 20th Session, Resolutions, 1978, pp. 92–3. See also *Yearbook of the ILC*, 1979, vol. II, part 1, pp. 78–80. Note in addition the call for a New International Cultural Order: see e.g. M. Bedjaoui, *Towards a New International Economic Order*, Paris, 1979, pp. 75 ff. and 245 ff., and General Assembly Resolutions 3026A (XXVII); 3148 (XXVIII); 3187 (XXVIII); 3391 (XXX) and 31/40.

[203] *Yearbook of the ILC*, 1979, vol. II, part 1, p. 93.   [204] Articles 21–4.

concerned, should be at the disposal of the state to which the territory is transferred, shall pass to the successor state, as shall any part of the state archives that relates exclusively or principally to the territory.[205] In the case of 'newly independent states', the same general provisions apply,[206] but with some alterations. Archives having belonged to the territory in question and having become state archives of the predecessor state during the period of dependence are to pass to the successor state. The reference here to archives that became state archives is to pre-colonial material, whether kept by central government, local governments or tribes, religious ministers, private enterprises or individuals.[207] One may mention here the Treaty of Peace with Italy of 1947, which provided that Italy was to restore all archives and objects of historical value belonging to Ethiopia or its natives and removed from Ethiopia to Italy since October 1935.[208] In the case of Vietnam, the 1950 Franco-Vietnamese agreement provided for the return as of right of all historical archives,[209] while a dispute between France and Algeria has been in existence since the latter's independence over pre-colonial material removed to France.[210]

Article 28(2) provides that the passing or the appropriate reproduction of parts of the state archives of the predecessor state (other than those already discussed above) of interest to the territory concerned is to be determined by agreement, 'in such a manner that each of these states [i.e. predecessor and successor] can benefit as widely and equitably as possible from those parts of the state archives of the predecessor state'. The reference here is primarily to material relating to colonisation and the colonial period, and in an arrangement of 1975, the French specifically noted the practice of microfilming in the context of France's acquisition of Algeria.[211] Article 28(3) emphasises that the predecessor state is to provide the newly independent state with the best available evidence from its state archives relating to territorial title and boundary issues. This is important as many post-colonial territorial disputes will invariably revolve around the interpretation of colonial treaties delimiting frontiers and colonial administrative practice concerning the area in contention.[212]

---

[205] Article 27.   [206] Article 28(1)b and c.
[207] *Yearbook of the ILC*, 1981, vol. II, part 2, p. 62.   [208] 49 UNTS, p. 142.
[209] See *Yearbook of the ILC*, 1979, vol. II, part 1, p. 113.   [210] *Ibid.*, pp. 113–14.
[211] *Yearbook of the ILC*, 1981, vol. II, part 2, p. 64.
[212] See, for example, the Mali–Upper Volta (Burkina Faso) border dispute, Shaw, *Title to Territory*, pp. 257–8, and the *Burkina Faso/Mali* case, ICJ Reports, 1986, p. 554; 80 ILR, p. 459.

Where two or more states unite to form one successor state, the state archives of the former will pass to the latter.[213] Where part of a state secedes to form another state, unless the states otherwise agree the part of the state archives of the predecessor state, which for normal administration of the territory concerned should be in that territory, will pass, as will those parts of the state archives that relate directly to the territory that is the subject of the succession.[214]

The same provisions apply in the case of a dissolution of a state, which is replaced by two or more successor states, in the absence of agreement, with the addition that other state archives are to pass to the successor states in an equitable manner, taking into account all relevant circumstances.[215] These principles were confirmed in the Yugoslav Agreement on Succession Issues, 2001,[216] while it was additionally provided that archives other than those falling within these categories are to be the subject of an agreement between the successor states as to their equitable distribution.[217]

Articles 28, 30 and 31 also contain a paragraph explaining that the relevant agreements over state archives 'shall not infringe the right of the peoples of those states to development, to information about their history and to their cultural heritage'. Despite the controversy over whether such a right does indeed exist in law as a right and precisely how such a provision might be interpreted in practice in concrete situations, the general concept of encouraging awareness and knowledge of a people's heritage is to be supported.[218]

Public debt[219]

This is an area of particular uncertainty and doubt has been expressed as to whether there is a rule of succession in such circumstances.[220] As in other parts of state succession, political and economic imperatives play

---

[213] Article 29.   [214] Article 30.

[215] Article 31. Note in particular the dispute between Denmark and Iceland, after the dissolution of their Union, over valuable parchments: see Verzijl, *International Law*, vol. VII, 1974, p. 153, and *Yearbook of the ILC*, 1981, vol. II, part 1, pp. 68–9, and the Treaty of St Germain of 1919 with Austria which contained provisions relating to the succession to archives of various new or reconstituted states.

[216] See Annex D.   [217] *Ibid.*, article 6.

[218] See further, with regard to article 3(2) of Annex A of the Yugoslav Agreement on Succession Issues, 2001, above, p. 991.

[219] See generally, O'Connell, *State Succession*, vol. I, chapters 15–17; *Yearbook of the ILC*, 1977, vol. II, part 1, pp. 49 ff., and Zemanek, 'State Succession'.

[220] See e.g. Brownlie, *Principles*, pp. 625–6.

a large role and much practice centres upon agreements made between relevant parties.

The public debt (or national debt) is that debt assumed by the central government in the interests of the state as a whole. It constitutes a particularly sensitive issue since third parties are involved who are often reluctant to accept a change in the identity of the debtor. This encourages an approach based on the continuing liability for the debt in question and in situations where a division of debt has taken place for that situation to continue with the successor state being responsible to the predecessor state (where this continues, of course) for its share rather than to the creditor directly. And as article 36 of the Vienna Convention, 1983 notes, a succession of states does not as such affect the rights and obligations of creditors.[221]

Public debts[222] may be divided into national debts, being debts owned by the state as a whole; local debts, being debts contracted by a sub-governmental territorial unit or other form of local authority, and localised debts, being debts incurred by the central government for the purpose of local projects or areas.[223]

Local debts clearly pass under customary international law to the successor state, since they constitute arrangements entered into by sub-governmental territorial authorities now transferred to the jurisdiction of the successor state and a succession does not directly affect them. In effect, they continue to constitute debts borne by the specific territory in question.[224] Similarly, localised debts, being closely attached to the territory to which the succession relates, also pass to the successor state in conformity with the same territorial principle.[225]

There appears to be no definitive answer to the question as to the allocation of the national debt as such. In the case of absorption or merger, the expanding or newly created state respectively will simply take over

---

[221] Note that the Convention does not deal with private creditors, a point which is criticised in the *Third US Restatement on Foreign Relations Law*, p. 106, but article 6 of the Convention constitutes in effect a savings clause here.

[222] Note that the Convention is concerned with state debts which are defined in article 33 as 'any financial obligation of a predecessor state arising in conformity with international law with another state, an international organisation or any other subject of international law'.

[223] See O'Connell, *State Succession*, vol. I, chapters 15–17, and *Yearbook of the ILC*, 1981, vol. II, part 1, p. 76. A variety of other distinctions have also been drawn, *ibid.*

[224] See, for example, O'Connell, *State Succession*, vol. I, pp. 416 ff.

[225] *Ibid.* See also *Yearbook of the ILC*, 1981, vol. II, part 1, p. 90, and the *Ottoman Public Debt* case, 1 RIAA, p. 529 (1925).

the national debt of the extinguished state.[226] The German unification example is instructive. Article 23 of the Unification Treaty provided that the total national budget debt of the German Democratic Republic was to be assumed by a special Federal fund administered by the Federal Minister of Finance. The Federal Government was to be liable for the obligations of the special fund which was to service the debt and might raise loans *inter alia* to redeem debts and to cover interest and borrowing costs. Until 31 December 1993, the Federal Government and the Trust Agency were each to reimburse one half of the interest payments made by the special fund. As from 1 January 1994, the Federal Government, the Trust Agency and the *Länder* of the former GDR assumed the total debt accrued at that date by the special fund, which was dissolved. The sureties, warranties and guarantees assumed by the GDR were taken over by the Federal Republic, while the interests of the GDR in the Berlin State Bank were transferred to the *Länder* of the former GDR. The liabilities arising from the GDR's responsibility for the Berlin State Bank were assumed by the Federal Government.

In the case of secession or separation where the predecessor state continues to exist, it would appear that the presumption is that the responsibility for the general public debt of the predecessor state remains with the predecessor state after the succession.[227] This would certainly appear to be the case where part of a state is transferred to another state.[228] Generally the paucity of practice leads one to be reluctant to claim that a new rule of international law has been established with regard to such situations, so that the general principle of non-division of the public debt is not displaced. However, successor states may be keen to establish their international creditworthiness by becoming involved in a debt allocation arrangement in circumstances where in strict international law this may not be necessary.[229] Further, the increasing pertinence of the notion of equitable distribution might have an impact upon this question.

A brief review of some practice may serve to illustrate the complexity of the area. When Texas seceded from Mexico in 1840, for example, it denied any liability for the latter's debts, although an *ex gratia* payment was in the circumstances made. However, no part of Colombia's debt was assumed

---

[226] Article 39 of the Convention provides that where two or more states unite to form a successor state, the state debts of the former states will pass to the successor state.

[227] See the *Ottoman Public Debt* case, 1 RIAA, p. 529.

[228] See *Yearbook of the ILC*, 1977, vol. II, part 1, p. 81.

[229] See Williams, 'State Succession', pp. 786 and 802–3.

by Panama upon its independence in 1903. The arrangements made in the peace treaties of 1919 and 1923 were complex, but it can be noted that while no division of the public debt occurred with regard to some territories emerging from the collapsed empires, in most cases there was a negotiated and invariably complicated settlement. The successor states of the Austro-Hungarian Empire, for example, assumed responsibility for such portions of the pre-war bonded debt as were determined by the Reparations Committee, while Turkey took over a share of the Ottoman public debt on a revenue proportionality basis.[230] When in 1921, the Irish Free State separated from the United Kingdom, it was provided that the public debt of the UK would be apportioned 'as may be fair and equitable', having regard to any claims by way of set-off or counter-claim.

The agreement between India (the continuation of British India) and Pakistan (the new state) provided for the responsibility of the former with regard to all the financial obligations, including loans and guarantees, of British India. India thus remained as the sole debtor of the national debt, while Pakistan's share of this, as established upon the basis of proportionality relating to its share of the assets of British India that it received, became a debt to India.[231]

With regard to secured debts, the general view appears to be that debts secured by mortgage of assets located in the territory in question survive the transfer of that territory. The Treaties of St Germain and Trianon in 1919, for example (articles 203 and 186 respectively), provided that assets thus pledged would remain so pledged with regard to that part of the national debt that it had been agreed would pass to the particular successor state. Such debts had to be specifically secured and the securities had to be 'railways, salt mines or other property'.[232] However, where debts have been charged to local revenue, the presumption lies the other way.

Much will depend upon the circumstances and it may well be that where the seceding territory constituted a substantial or meaningful part of the predecessor state, considerations of equity would suggest some form of apportionment of the national debt. It was with this in mind, together with the example of the UK–Irish Free State Treaty of 1921, that led the International Law Commission to propose the draft that led to article 40 of the Vienna Convention, 1983.

---

[230] See, for example, O'Connell, *State Succession*, vol. I, pp. 397–401, and Feilchenfeld, *Public Debts*, pp. 431 ff.

[231] O'Connell, *State Succession*, vol. I, pp. 404–6.   [232] *Ibid.*, p. 411.

Article 40 provides that where part of a state separates to form another state, unless otherwise agreed, the state debt of the predecessor state passes to the successor state 'in an equitable proportion' taking into account in particular the property, rights and interests which pass to the successor state in relation to that debt.[233] It is doubtful that this proposition constitutes a codification of customary law as such in view of the confused and disparate practice of states to date, but it does reflect a viable approach.

However, in the case of separation where the predecessor state ceases to exist, some form of apportionment of the public debt is required and the provision in article 41 for an equitable division taking into account in particular the property, rights and interests which pass to the successor states in relation to that debt, is reasonable and can be taken to reflect international practice.[234] The basis for any equitable apportionment of debts would clearly depend upon the parties concerned and would have to be regulated by agreement. A variety of possibilities exists, including taxation ratio, extent of territory, population, nationality of creditors, taxable value as distinct from actual revenue contributions, value of assets and contributions of the territory in question to the central administration.[235] The Yugoslav Agreement on Succession Issues, 2001 provides that 'allocated debts', that is external debts where the final beneficiary of the debt is located on the territory of a specific successor state or group of successor states, are to be accepted by the successor state on the territory of which the final beneficiary is located.[236]

In common with the other parts of the 1983 Convention, a specific article is devoted to the situation of the 'newly independent state'. Article 38 provides that 'no state debt of the predecessor state shall pass to the newly independent state' in the absence of an agreement between the

---

[233] The same rule applies in the case of the transfer of part of a state to another state: see article 37.

[234] See, for example, *Oppenheim's International Law*, p. 221.

[235] In the 1919 peace treaties, the principle of distribution proportional to the future paying capacity of the ceded territories was utilised, measured by reference to revenues contributed in the pre-war years, while in the Treaty of Lausanne, 1923, concerning the consequences of the demise of the Ottoman Empire, the principle considered was that of proportional distribution based solely upon actual past contributions to the amortisation of debts: see O'Connell, *State Succession*, vol. I, pp. 454–6. Cf. *Yearbook of the ILC*, 1981, vol. II, part 2, p. 113. The phrase ultimately adopted in the Vienna Convention was: 'taking into account, in particular, the property, rights and interests which pass to the successor state in relation to that state debt'. In other words, stress was laid upon the factor of proportionality of assets to debts.

[236] Article 2(1)b of Annex C.

parties providing otherwise, 'in view of the link between the state debt of the predecessor state connected with its activity in the territory to which the succession of states relates and the property, rights and interests which pass to the newly independent state'. State practice generally in the decolonisation process dating back to the independence of the United States appears to show that there would be no succession to part of the general state debt of the predecessor state, but that this would differ where the debt related specifically to the territory in question.[237] It is unlikely that this provision reflects customary law.

Private rights

The question also arises as to how far a succession of states will affect, if at all, private rights. Principles of state sovereignty and respect for acquired or subsisting rights are relevant here and often questions of expropriation provide the context. As far as those inhabitants who become nationals of the successor state are concerned, they are fully subject to its laws and regulations, and apart from the application of international human rights rules, they have little direct recourse to international law in these circumstances. Accordingly what does become open to discussion is the protection afforded to aliens by international provisions relating to the succession of rights and duties upon a change of sovereignty.

It is within this context that the doctrine of acquired rights[238] has been formulated. This relates to rights obtained by foreign nationals and has been held by some to include virtually all types of legal interests. Its import is that such rights continue after the succession and can be enforced against the new sovereign. Some writers declare this proposition to be a fundamental principle of international law,[239] while others describe it merely as a source of confusion.[240] There is a certain amount of disagreement as to its extent. On the one hand, it has been held to mean that the passing of sovereignty has no effect upon such rights, and on the other that

---

[237] See *Yearbook of the ILC*, 1981, vol. II, part 1, pp. 91–105 and *ibid.*, 1977, vol. II, part 1, pp. 86–107. Note the varied practice of succession to public debts in the colonisation process, *ibid.*, pp. 87–8, and with regard to annexations, *ibid.*, pp. 93–4. See also *West Rand Gold Mining Co. v. R* [1905] 2 KB 391, and O'Connell, *State Succession*, vol. I, pp. 373–83.

[238] See, in particular, O'Connell, *State Succession*, chapter 10; *Oppenheim's International Law*, pp. 215 ff., and Brownlie, *Principles*, pp. 626 ff. See also T. H. Cheng, *State Succession and Commercial Obligations*, New York, 2006.

[239] See e.g. O'Connell, *State Succession*, vol. I, pp. 239–40.

[240] See e.g. Brownlie, *Principles*, p. 627.

it implies no more than that aliens should be, as far as possible, insulated from the changes consequent upon succession.

The principle of acquired rights was discussed in a number of cases that came before the Permanent Court of International Justice between the two world wars, dealing with the creation of an independent Poland out of the former German, Russian and Austrian Empires. Problems arose specifically with regard to rights obtained under German rule, which were challenged by the new Polish authorities. In the *German Settlers'* case,[241] Poland had attempted to evict German settlers from its lands, arguing that since many of them had not taken transfer of title before the Armistice they could be legitimately ejected. According to the German system, such settlers could acquire title either by means of leases, or by means of an arrangement whereby they paid parts of the purchase price at regular intervals and upon payment of the final instalment the land would become theirs. The Court held that German law would apply in the circumstances until the final transfer of the territory and that the titles to land acquired in this fashion would be protected under the terms of the 1919 Minorities Treaty. More importantly, the Court declared that even in the absence of such a treaty:

> private rights acquired under existing law do not cease on a change of sovereignty . . . even those who contest the existence in international law of a general principle of state succession do not go so far as to maintain that private rights, including those acquired from the state as the owner of the property, are invalid as against a successor in sovereignty.[242]

The fact that there was a political purpose behind the colonisation scheme would not affect the private rights thus secured, which could be enforced against the new sovereign. It is very doubtful that this would be accepted today. The principles emerging from such inter-war cases affirming the continuation of acquired rights have modified the views expressed in the *West Rand Central Gold Mining Company* case[243] to the

---

[241] PCIJ, Series B, No. 6, 1923; 2 AD, p. 71. The proposition was reaffirmed in the *Certain German Interests in Polish Upper Silesia* case, PCIJ, Series A, No. 7, 1926; 3 AD, p. 429 and the *Chorzów Factory* case, PCIJ, Series A, No. 17, 1928; 4 AD, p. 268. See also the *Mavrommatis Palestine Concessions* case, PCIJ, Series A, No. 5, 1924 and *US* v. *Percheman* 7 Pet. 51 (1830).

[242] See also *El Salvador/Honduras*, ICJ Reports, 1992, pp. 351, 400, referring to 'full respect for acquired rights', the *German–Poland Border Treaty Constitutionality* case, 108 ILR, p. 656, and cf. *Gosalia* v. *Agarwal* 118 ILR, p. 429.

[243] [1905] 2 KB 391.

effect that, upon annexation, the new sovereign may choose which of the contractual rights and duties adopted by the previous sovereign it wishes to respect.

The inter-war cases mark the high-water mark of the concept of the continuation of private rights upon succession, but they should not be interpreted to mean that the new sovereign cannot alter such rights. The expropriation of alien property is possible under international law subject to certain conditions.[244] What the doctrine does indicate is that there is a presumption of the continuation of foreign acquired rights, though the matter is best regulated by treaty. Only private rights that have become vested or acquired would be covered by the doctrine. Thus, where rights are to come into operation in the future, they will not be binding upon the new sovereign. Similarly, claims to unliquidated damages will not continue beyond the succession. Claims to unliquidated damages occur where the matter in dispute has not come before the judicial authorities and the issue of compensation has yet to be determined by a competent court or tribunal. In the *Robert E. Brown* claim,[245] an American citizen's prospecting licence had been unjustifiably cancelled by the Boer republic of South Africa in the 1890s and Brown's claim had been dismissed in the Boer courts. In 1900 the United Kingdom annexed the republic and Brown sought (through the US government) to hold it responsible. This contention was rejected by the arbitration tribunal, which said that Brown's claim did not represent an acquired right since the denial of justice that had taken place by the Boer court's wrongful rejection of his case had prevented the claim from becoming liquidated. The tribunal also noted that liability for a wrongful act committed by a state did not pass to the new sovereign after succession.

The fact that the disappearance of the former sovereign automatically ends liability for any wrong it may have committed is recognised as a rule of international law, although where the new state adopts the illegal actions of the predecessor, it may inherit liability since it itself is in effect committing a wrong. This was brought out in the *Lighthouses* arbitration[246] in 1956 between France and Greece, which concerned the latter's liability to respect concessions granted by Turkey to a French company

---

[244] See above, chapter 14, p. 827.

[245] 6 RIAA, p. 120 (1923); 2 AD, p. 66. See also the *Hawaiian Claims* case, 6 RIAA, p. 157 (1925); 3 AD, p. 80.

[246] 12 RIAA, p. 155 (1956); 23 ILR, p. 659. Cf. the decision of the Namibian Supreme Court in *Minister of Defence, Namibia* v. *Mwandinghi* 91 ILR, p. 341, taking into account the provisions of the Namibian Constitution.

regarding territory subsequently acquired by Greece. The problem of the survival of foreign nationals' rights upon succession is inevitably closely bound up with ideological differences and economic pressures.[247]

State succession and nationality[248]

The issue of state succession and nationality links together not only those two distinct areas, but also the question of human rights. The terms under which a state may award nationality are solely within its control[249] but problems may arise in the context of a succession. In principle, the issue of nationality will depend upon the municipal regulations of the predecessor and successor states. The laws of the former will determine the extent to which the inhabitants of an area to be ceded to another authority will retain their nationality after the change in sovereignty, while the laws of the successor state will prescribe the conditions under which the new nationality will be granted. The general rule would appear to be that nationality will change with sovereignty, although it will be incumbent upon the new sovereign to declare the pertinent rules with regard to people born in the territory or resident there, or born abroad of parents who are nationals of the former regime. Similarly, the ceding state may well provide for its former citizens in the territory in question to retain

---

[247] As to state succession to wrongful acts, see e.g. P. Dumberry, *State Succession to International Responsibility*, The Hague, 2007; W. Czaplinski, 'State Succession and State Responsibility', 28 Canadian YIL, 1990, p. 339 and M. J. Volkovitsch, 'Righting Wrongs: Towards a New Theory of State Succession to Responsibility for International Delicts', 92 *Columbia Law Review*, 1992, p. 2162. See also *Minister of Defence* v. *Mwandinghi* (SA 5/91) [1991] NASC 5; 1992 (2) SA 355 (NmS) (25 October 1991).

[248] See O'Connell, *State Succession*, vol. I, chapters 20 and 21; P. Weis, *Nationality and Statelessness in International Law*, 2nd edn, Alphen aan den Rijn, 1979; I. Ziemele, *State Continuity and Nationality: Past, Present and Future as Defined by International Law*, The Hague, 2005; P. Dumberry, 'Obsolete and Unjust: The Rule of Continuous Nationality in the Context of State Succession', 76 *Nordic Journal of International Law*, 2007, p. 153; C. Economidès, 'Les Effets de la Succession d'États sur la Nationalité', 103 RGDIP, 1999, p. 577; *Nationalité, Minorités et Succession d'États en Europe de l'Est* (eds. E. Decaux and A. Pellet), Paris, 1996; European Commission for Democracy Through Law, *Citizenship and State Succession*, Strasbourg, 1997; *Oppenheim's International Law*, p. 218, and Reports of the International Law Commission, A/50/10, 1995, p. 68; A/51/10, 1996, p. 171; A/52/10, 1997, p. 11; A/53/10, 1998, p. 189 and A/54/10, 1999, p. 12. See also above, chapters 12, p. 659, and 14, p. 808.

[249] See e.g. article 1 of the Hague Convention on Certain Questions relating to the Conflict of Nationality Laws, 1930, the *Nationality Decrees in Tunis and Morocco* case, PCIJ, Series B, No. 4, p. 24 (1923); 2 AD, p. 349, the *Acquisition of Polish Nationality* case, PCIJ, Series B, No. 7, p. 16; 2 AD, p. 292, and the *Nottebohm* case, ICJ Reports, 1955, p. 23; 22 ILR, p. 349.

their nationality, thus creating a situation of dual nationality. This would not arise, of course, where the former state completely disappears.

Some states acquiring territory may provide for the inhabitants to obtain the new nationality automatically while others may give the inhabitants an option to depart and retain their original nationality. Actual practice is varied and much depends on the circumstances, but it should be noted that the 1961 Convention on the Reduction of Statelessness provides that states involved in the cession of territory should ensure that no person becomes stateless as a result of the particular change in sovereignty. There may indeed be a principle in international law to the effect that the successor state should provide for the possibility of nationals of the predecessor state living in or having a substantial connection with the territory taken over by the successor state.[250] It may indeed be, on the other hand, that such nationals have the right to choose their nationality in such situations, although this is unclear. The Arbitration Commission on Yugoslavia referred in this context to the principle of self-determination as proclaimed in article 1 of the two International Covenants on Human Rights, 1966. The Commission stated that, 'by virtue of that right every individual may choose to belong to whatever ethnic, religious or language community he wishes'. Further, it was noted that:

> In the Commission's view one possible consequence of this principle might be for the members of the Serbian population in Bosnia and Herzegovina and Croatia to be recognised under agreements between the Republics as having the nationality of their choice, with all the rights and obligations which that entails with respect to the states concerned.[251]

In 1997 the European Convention on Nationality was adopted.[252] Article 19 provides that states parties should seek to resolve issues

---

[250] See *Oppenheim's International Law*, p. 219.

[251] Opinion No. 2, 92 ILR, pp. 167, 168–9. The Commission concluded by stating that the Republics 'must afford the members of those minorities and ethnic groups [i.e. the Serbian population in Bosnia-Herzegovina and Croatia] all the human rights and fundamental freedoms recognised in international law, including, where appropriate, the right to choose their nationality', *ibid.*, p. 169.

[252] See also the Declaration on the Consequences of State Succession for the Nationality of Natural Persons, European Commission for Democracy Through Law, 1996, CDL-NAT (1996)007e-rev-restr. and the Council of Europe Convention on the Avoidance of Statelessness in Relation to State Succession, 2006, which provides that any person with the nationality of the predecessor state who has or would become stateless as a result of state succession has the right to nationality of a state concerned in accordance with the Convention.

concerning nationality and state succession by agreement between themselves. Article 18 stipulates that in deciding on the granting or the retention of nationality in cases of state succession, each state party concerned shall take account, in particular, of the genuine and effective link of the person concerned with the state; the habitual residence of the person concerned at the time of state succession; the will of the person concerned and the territorial origin of the person concerned. In the case of non-nationals, article 20 provides for respect for the principle that nationals of a predecessor state habitually resident in the territory over which sovereignty is transferred to a successor state and who have not acquired its nationality shall have the right to remain in that state.

In 1999, the International Law Commission adopted Draft Articles on Nationality of Natural Persons in Relation to a Succession of States.[253] Article 1 (defined as the 'very foundation' of the draft articles[254]), reaffirming the right to a nationality, provides that individuals who on the date of succession had the nationality of the predecessor state, irrespective of the mode of acquisition of that nationality, have the right to the nationality of at least one of the states concerned. States are to take all appropriate measures to prevent persons who had the nationality of the predecessor state on the date of succession from becoming stateless as a result of the succession,[255] while persons having their habitual residence in the territory concerned are presumed to acquire the nationality of the successor state.[256] The intention of the latter provision is to avoid a gap arising between the date of succession and the date of any agreement or legislation granting nationality.[257] Article 11 stipulates that each state concerned shall grant a right to opt for its nationality to persons concerned who have appropriate connection with that state if those persons would otherwise become stateless as a result of the succession of states, and that when this right has been exercised, the state whose nationality they have opted for shall attribute its nationality to such persons. Conversely, the state whose nationality they have renounced shall withdraw its nationality from such persons, unless they would thereby become stateless.

---

[253] See Report of the International Law Commission on its 51st Session, A/54/10, 1999, p. 12.

[254] *Ibid.*, p. 29.

[255] Article 4. Article 16 provides that persons concerned shall not be arbitrarily deprived of the nationality of the predecessor state nor arbitrarily denied the right to acquire the nationality of the successor state.

[256] Article 5. Article 12 states that the status of persons concerned as habitual residents shall not be affected by the succession of states.

[257] Report of the International Law Commission on its 51st Session, p. 40.

Article 12 provides that where the acquisition or loss of nationality in relation to the succession of states would impair the unity of a family, the states concerned shall take all appropriate measures to allow that family to remain together or to be reunited.[258]

The second part of the set of draft articles concerns specific succession situations and their implications for nationality. Article 20 concerns the situation where one state transfers part of its territory to another state. Here the successor state shall attribute its nationality to the persons concerned who have their habitual residence in the transferred territory and the predecessor state shall withdraw its nationality from such persons, unless otherwise indicated by the exercise of the right of option which such persons shall be granted. The predecessor state shall not, however, withdraw its nationality before such persons acquire the nationality of the successor state. Where two or more states unite to form one successor state, the successor state shall attribute its nationality to all persons who on the date of succession held the nationality of the predecessor state.[259]

In the case both of the dissolution of the predecessor state to form two or more successor states and the separation of parts of a territory to form one or more successor states while the predecessor state continues to exist, the same fundamental rules apply. Articles 22 and 24 respectively provide that each successor state shall, unless otherwise indicated by the exercise of a right of option,[260] attribute its nationality to (a) persons concerned having their habitual residence in its territory; and (b) other persons concerned having an appropriate legal connection with a constituent unit of the predecessor state that has become part of that successor state; and to (c) persons not otherwise entitled to a nationality of any state concerned having their habitual residence in a third state, who were born in or, before leaving the predecessor state, had their last habitual residence in what has become the territory of that successor state or having any other

---

[258] A child born after the date of succession who has not acquired any nationality has the right to the nationality of the state concerned on whose territory he/she was born, article 13.

[259] Article 21. This the Commission concluded was a rule of customary law: see Report of the International Law Commission on its 51st Session, p. 80.

[260] Article 23 provides that successor states shall grant a right of option to persons concerned covered by the provisions of article 22 who are qualified to acquire the nationality of two or more successor states, while each successor state shall grant a right to opt for its nationality to persons concerned who are not covered by the provisions of article 22. Where the predecessor state continues, article 26 provides that both the predecessor and successor states shall grant a right of option to all persons concerned who are qualified to have the nationality of both the predecessor and successor states or of two or more successor states.

appropriate connection with that successor state.[261] These provisions are meant to prevent a situation, such as occurred with regard to some successor states of the former Yugoslavia and Czechoslovakia, where the test of nationality of the successor state centred upon the possession of the citizenship of the former constituent republics rather than upon habitual residence, thus having the effect of depriving certain persons of the nationality of the successor state.[262]

Hong Kong[263]

Of particular interest in the context of state succession and the decolonisation process has been the situation with regard to Hong Kong. While Hong Kong island and the southern tip of the Kowloon peninsula (with Stonecutters island) were ceded to Britain in perpetuity,[264] the New Territories (comprising some 92 per cent of the total land area of the territory) were leased to Britain for ninety-nine years commencing 1 July 1898.[265] Accordingly, the British and Chinese governments opened negotiations and in 1984 reached an agreement. This Agreement took the form of a Joint Declaration and Three Annexes[266] and lays down the system under which Hong Kong has been governed as from 1 July 1997. A Hong Kong

---

[261] In the case of categories (b) and (c), the provision does not apply to persons who have their habitual residence in a third state and also have the nationality of that other or any other state: see article 8.

[262] See Report of the International Law Commission on its 51st Session, pp. 83–5, and J. F. Rezek, 'Le Droit International de la Nationalité', 198 HR, 1986, pp. 342–3. Article 25 provides that in the case where the predecessor state continues, then it shall withdraw its nationality from persons concerned who are qualified to acquire the nationality of the successor state in accordance with article 24. It shall not, however, withdraw its nationality before such persons acquire the nationality of the successor state. Unless otherwise indicated by the exercise of a right of option, the predecessor state shall not, however, withdraw its nationality from such persons who: (a) have their habitual residence in its territory; (b) are not covered by subparagraph (a) and have an appropriate legal connection with a constituent unit of the predecessor state that has remained part of the predecessor state; (c) have their habitual residence in a third state, and were born in or, before leaving the predecessor state, had their last habitual residence in what has remained part of the territory of the predecessor state or have any other appropriate connection with that state.

[263] See e.g. R. Mushkat, *One Country, Two International Legal Personalities*, Hong Kong, 1997, and Mushkat, 'Hong Kong and Succession of Treaties', 46 ICLQ, 1997, p. 181.

[264] See the Treaty of Nanking, 1842, 30 BFSP, p. 389 and the Convention of Peking, 1860, 50 BFSP, p. 10.

[265] 90 BFSP, p. 17. All three treaties were denounced by China as 'unequal treaties'.

[266] See 23 ILM, 1984, p. 1366.

Special Administrative Region (SAR) was established, which enjoys a high degree of autonomy, except in foreign and defence affairs. It is vested with executive, legislative and independent judicial power, including that of final adjudication. The laws of Hong Kong remain basically unaffected. The government of the SAR is composed of local inhabitants and the current social and economic systems continue unchanged. The SAR retains the status of a free port and a separate customs territory and remains an international financial centre with a freely convertible currency. Using the name of 'Hong Kong, China', the SAR may on its own maintain and develop economic and cultural relations and conclude relevant agreements with states, regions and relevant international organisations. Existing systems of shipping management continue and shipping certificates relating to the shipping register are issued under the name of 'Hong Kong, China'.

These policies are enshrined in a Basic Law of the SAR to remain unchanged for fifty years. Annex I of the Agreement also provides that public servants in Hong Kong, including members of the police and judiciary, will remain in employment and upon retirement will receive their pension and other benefits due to them on terms no less favourable than before and irrespective of their nationality or place of residence. Airlines incorporated and having their principal place of business in Hong Kong continue to operate and the system of civil aviation management continues. The SAR has extensive authority to conclude agreements in this field. Rights and freedoms in Hong Kong are maintained, including freedoms of the person, of speech, of the press, of assembly, of belief, of movement, to strike and to form and join trade unions. In an important provision, article XIII of Annex I stipulates that the provisions of the International Covenants on Human Rights, 1966 are to continue in force. Accordingly, a high level of succession is provided for, but it is as well to recognise that the Hong Kong situation is unusual.

Suggestions for further reading

M. Craven, 'The Problem of State Succession and the Identity of States under International Law', 9 EJIL, 1998, p. 142

D. P. O'Connell, *State Succession in Municipal Law and International Law*, Cambridge, 2 vols., 1967

M. N. Shaw, 'State Succession Revisited', 5 Finnish YIL, 1994, p. 34

Succession of States (ed. M. Mrak), The Hague, 1999

18

The settlement of disputes by peaceful means

It is fair to say that international law has always considered its fundamental purpose to be the maintenance of peace.[1] Although ethical preoccupations stimulated its development and inform its growth, international law has historically been regarded by the international community primarily as a means to ensure the establishment and preservation of world peace and security. This chapter is concerned with the procedures available within the international order for the peaceful resolution of disputes and conflicts, except for judicial procedures covered elsewhere.[2]

---

[1] See generally J. G. Merrills, *International Dispute Settlement*, 4th edn, Cambridge, 2005, and Merrills, 'The Mosaic of International Dispute Settlement Procedures: Complementary or Contradictory?', 54 NILR, 2007, p. 361; F. Orrego Vicuña, *International Dispute Settlement in an Evolving Global Society: Constitutionalization, Accessibility, Privatization*, Cambridge, 2004; J. Collier and V. Lowe, *The Settlement of Disputes in International Law*, Cambridge, 1999; United Nations, *Handbook on the Peaceful Settlement of Disputes Between States*, New York, 1992; L. Henkin, R. C. Pugh, O. Schachter and H. Smit, *International Law: Cases and Materials*, 3rd edn, St Paul, 1993, chapter 10; David Davies Memorial Institute, *International Disputes: The Legal Aspects*, London, 1972; K. V. Raman, *Dispute Settlement Through the UN*, Dobbs Ferry, 1977; O. R. Young, *The Intermediaries*, Princeton, 1967; D. W. Bowett, 'Contemporary Developments in Legal Techniques in the Settlement of Disputes', 180 HR, 1983, p. 171, and B. S. Murty, 'Settlement of Disputes' in *Manual of Public International Law* (ed. M. Sørensen), London, 1968, p. 673. See also Nguyen Quoc Dinh, P. Daillier and A. Pellet, *Droit International Public*, 7th edn, Paris, 2002, p. 821; K. Oellers-Frahm and A. Zimmermann, *Dispute Settlement in Public International Law*, Berlin, 2001; C. P. Economides, 'L'Obligation de Règlement Pacifique des Différends Internationaux' in *Mélanges Boutros-Ghali*, Brussels, 1999, p. 405; A. Peters, 'International Dispute Settlement: A Network of Cooperational Duties', 14 EJIL, 2003, p. 1; P. Pazartzis, *Les Engagements Internationaux en Matière de Règlement Pacifique des Différends entre États*, Paris, 1992, and *The UN Decade of International Law: Reflections on International Dispute Settlement* (eds. M. Brus, S. Muller and S. Wiemers), Dordrecht, 1991.

[2] See above, chapter 6 with regard to regional human rights courts; chapter 8 with regard to international criminal courts and tribunals; chapter 11 with regard to dispute settlement under the Convention on the Law of the Sea and chapter 19 with regard to the International Court of Justice.

Basically the techniques of conflict management fall into two categories: diplomatic procedures and adjudication. The former involves an attempt to resolve differences either by the contending parties themselves or with the aid of other entities by the use of the discussion and fact-finding methods. Adjudication procedures involve the determination by a disinterested third party of the legal and factual issues involved, either by arbitration or by the decision of judicial organs.

The political approach to conflict settlement is divided into two sections, with the measures applicable by the United Nations being separately examined (in chapter 22) as they possess a distinctive character. Although for the sake of convenience each method of dispute settlement is separately examined, it should be noted that in any given situation a range of mechanisms may well be utilised. A good example of this is afforded by the successful settlement of the Chad–Libya boundary dispute. Following a long period of conflict and armed hostilities since the dispute erupted in 1973, the two states signed a Framework Agreement on the Peaceful Settlement of the Territorial Dispute on 31 August 1989 in which they undertook to seek a peaceful solution within one year. In the absence of a political settlement, the parties undertook to take the matter to the International Court.[3] After inconclusive negotiations, the dispute was submitted to the International Court by notification of the Framework Agreement by the two parties.[4] The decision of the Court was delivered on 3 February 1994. The Court accepted the argument of Chad that the boundary between the two states was defined by the Franco-Libyan Treaty of 10 August 1955.[5] Following this decision, the two states concluded an agreement providing for Libyan withdrawal from the Aouzou Strip by 30 May 1994. The agreement provided for monitoring of this withdrawal by United Nations observers.[6] The two parties also agreed to establish a joint team of experts to undertake the delimitation of the common frontier in accordance with the decision of the International Court.[7] On 4 May 1994, the Security Council adopted resolution 915 (1994) establishing

---

[3] See Report of the UN Secretary-General, S/1994/512, 27 April 1994, 33 ILM, 1994, p. 786, and generally M. M. Ricciardi, 'Title to the Aouzou Strip: A Legal and Historical Analysis', 17 *Yale Journal of International Law*, 1992, p. 301.

[4] Libya on 31 August 1990 and Chad on 3 September 1990: see the *Libya/Chad* case, ICJ Reports, 1994, pp. 6, 14; 100 ILR, pp. 1, 13.

[5] ICJ Reports, 1994, p. 40; 100 ILR, p. 39.

[6] 100 ILR, p. 102, article 1. See also 33 ILM, 1994, p. 619.

[7] 100 ILR, p. 103, article 6. See also the letter of the UN Secretary-General to the Security Council, S/1994/432, 13 April 1994, *ibid.*, pp. 103–4.

the UN Aouzou Strip Observer Group (UNASOG) and authorising the deployment of observers and support staff for a period up to forty days.[8] On 30 May, Libya and Chad signed a Joint Declaration stating that the withdrawal of the Libyan administration and forces had been effected as of that date to the satisfaction of both parties as monitored by UNASOG.[9] The Security Council terminated the mandate of UNASOG upon the successful conclusion of the mission by resolution 926 (1994) on 13 June that year.[10]

However, states are not obliged to resolve their differences at all, and this applies in the case of serious legal conflicts as well as peripheral political disagreements. All the methods available to settle disputes are operative only upon the consent of the particular states.[11] This, of course, can be contrasted with the situation within municipal systems. It is reflected in the different functions performed by the courts in the international and domestic legal orders respectively, and it is one aspect of the absence of a stable, central focus within the world community.

The mechanisms dealing with the peaceful settlement of disputes require in the first instance the existence of a dispute. The definition of a dispute has been the subject of some consideration by the International Court,[12] but the reference by the Permanent Court in the *Mavrommatis Palestine Concessions (Jurisdiction)* case[13] to 'a disagreement over a point of law or fact, a conflict of legal views or of interests between two persons' constitutes an authoritative indication. A distinction is sometimes made between legal and political disputes, or justiciable and non-justiciable disputes.[14] Although maintained in some international treaties, it is to some extent unsound, in view of the fact that any dispute will involve some political considerations and many overtly political disagreements may be resolved by judicial means. Whether any dispute is to be termed legal or political may well hinge upon the particular circumstances of

---

[8] Note that on 14 April, the Security Council adopted resolution 910 (1994) by which the initial UN reconnaissance team was exempted from sanctions operating against Libya by virtue of resolution 748 (1992). The observer group received a similar exemption by virtue of resolution 915 B.

[9] See Report of the UN Secretary-General, S/1994/672, 6 June 1994, 100 ILR, pp. 111 ff. The Joint Declaration was countersigned by the Chief Military Observer of UNASOG as a witness.

[10] *Ibid.*, p. 114.

[11] With the exception of binding Security Council resolutions: see further below, chapter 22, p. 1241.

[12] See further below, chapter 19, p. 1067.   [13] PCIJ, Series A, No. 2, 1924, p. 11.

[14] See H. Lauterpacht, *The Function of Law in the International Community*, London, 1933, especially pp. 19–20.

the case, the views adopted by the relevant parties and the way in which they choose to characterise their differences. It is in reality extremely difficult to point to objective general criteria clearly differentiating the two.[15] This does not, however, imply that there are not significant differences between the legal and political procedures available for resolving problems. For one thing, the strictly legal approach is dependent upon the provisions of the law as they stand at that point, irrespective of any reforming tendencies the particular court may have, while the political techniques of settlement are not so restricted. It is also not unusual for political and legal organs to deal with aspects of the same basic situation.[16]

The role of political influences and considerations in inter-state disputes is obviously a vital one, and many settlements can only be properly understood within the wider international political context. In addition, how a state proceeds in a dispute will be conditioned by political factors. If the dispute is perceived to be one affecting vital interests, for example, the state would be less willing to submit the matter to binding third party settlement than if it were a more technical issue, while the existence of regional mechanisms will often be of political significance.

Article 2(3) of the United Nations Charter provides that:

[a]ll members shall settle their international disputes by peaceful means in such a manner that international peace and security and justice are not endangered.

The 1970 Declaration on Principles of International Law Concerning Friendly Relations and Co-operation among States[17] develops this principle and notes that:

states shall accordingly seek early and just settlement of their international disputes by negotiation, inquiry, mediation, conciliation, arbitration, judicial settlement, resort to regional agencies or arrangements or other peaceful means of their choice.

The same methods of dispute settlement are stipulated in article 33(1) of the UN Charter, although in the context of disputes the continuance of

---

[15] See further below, p. 1067.

[16] See the *Iranian Hostages* case, ICJ Reports, 1980, pp. 3, 22–3; 61 ILR, pp. 530, 548–9 and the *Nicaragua* case, ICJ Reports, 1984, pp. 392, 435–6; 76 ILR, pp. 104, 146–7.

[17] General Assembly resolution 2625 (XXV). See also the Manila Declaration on the Peaceful Settlement of International Disputes, General Assembly resolution 37/590; resolutions 2627 (XXV); 2734 (XXV); 40/9; the Declaration on the Prevention and Removal of Disputes and Situations which may Threaten International Peace and Security, resolution 43/51 and the Declaration on Fact-finding, resolution 46/59.

which are likely to endanger international peace and security. The 1970 Declaration, which is not so limited, asserts that in seeking an early and just settlement, the parties are to agree upon such peaceful means as they see appropriate to the circumstances and nature of the dispute.

There would appear, therefore, to be no inherent hierarchy with respect to the methods specified and no specific method required in any given situation. States have a free choice as to the mechanisms adopted for settling their disputes.[18] This approach is also taken in a number of regional instruments, including the American Treaty on Pacific Settlement (the Pact of Bogotá), 1948 of the Organisation of American States, the European Convention for the Peaceful Settlement of Disputes, 1957 and the Helsinki Final Act of the Conference on Security and Co-operation in Europe, 1975. In addition, it is to be noted that the parties to a dispute have the duty to continue to seek a settlement by other peaceful means agreed by them, in the event of the failure of one particular method. Should the means elaborated fail to resolve a dispute, the continuance of which is likely to endanger the maintenance of international peace and security, the parties under article 37(1) of the Charter, 'shall refer it to the Security Council'.[19]

Diplomatic methods of dispute settlement

Negotiation[20]

Of all the procedures used to resolve differences, the simplest and most utilised form is understandably negotiation. It consists basically of discussions between the interested parties with a view to reconciling divergent

---

[18] See article 33(1) of the UN Charter and section I(3) and (10) of the Manila Declaration.

[19] Emphasis added.

[20] See UN Handbook, chapter II; Collier and Lowe, *Settlement*, chapter 2; Merrills, *International Dispute Settlement*, chapter 1, and Merrills, 'Mosaic'; and H. Lachs, 'The Law and Settlement of International Disputes' in Brus *et al.*, *Dispute Settlement*, pp. 287–9. See also Murty, 'Settlement', pp. 678–9; A. Watson, *Diplomacy*, London, 1982; F. Kirgis, *Prior Consultation in International Law*, Charlottesville, 1983; P. J. De Waart, *The Element of Negotiation in the Pacific Settlement of Disputes between States*, The Hague, 1973; A. Lall, *Modern International Negotiation*, New York, 1966; G. Geamanu, 'Théorie et Pratique des Négociations en Droit International', 166 HR, 1980 I, p. 365; B. Y. Diallo, *Introduction à l'Étude et à la Pratique de la Négociation*, Paris, 1998; N. E. Ghozali, 'La Négociation Diplomatique dans la Jurisprudence Internationale', *Revue Belge de Droit International*, 1992, p. 323, and D. Anderson, 'Negotiations and Dispute Settlement' in *Remedies in International Law* (ed. M. Evans), Oxford, 1998, p. 111. Note also that operative paragraph 10 of the Manila Declaration emphasises that direct negotiations are a 'flexible and effective means of peaceful settlement'.

opinions, or at least understanding the different positions maintained. It does not involve any third party, at least at that stage, and so differs from the other forms of dispute management. In addition to being an extremely active method of settlement itself, negotiation is normally the precursor to other settlement procedures as the parties decide amongst themselves how best to resolve their differences.[21] It is eminently suited to the clarification, if not always resolution, of complicated disagreements. It is by mutual discussions that the essence of the differences will be revealed and the opposing contentions elucidated. Negotiations are the most satisfactory means to resolve disputes since the parties are so directly engaged. Negotiations, of course, do not always succeed, since they do depend on a certain degree of mutual goodwill, flexibility and sensitivity. Hostile public opinion in one state may prevent the concession of certain points and mutual distrust may fatally complicate the process, while opposing political attitudes may be such as to preclude any acceptable negotiated agreement.[22]

In certain circumstances there may exist a duty to enter into negotiations arising out of particular bilateral or multilateral agreements.[23] Article 283(1) of the Convention on the Law of the Sea, 1982 provides, for example, that when a dispute arises between states parties concerning the interpretation or application of the Convention, 'the parties to the dispute shall proceed expeditiously to an exchange of views regarding its settlement by negotiation or other peaceful means'.[24] Other treaties may

---

[21] See Judge Nervo, *Fisheries Jurisdiction* case, ICJ Reports, 1973, pp. 3, 45; 55 ILR, pp. 183, 225. See also the *Mavrommatis Palestine Concessions* case, PCIJ, Series A, No. 2, 1924, p. 15, noting that 'Before a dispute can be made the subject of an action at law, its subject matter should have been clearly defined by diplomatic negotiations', and the *Right of Passage* (*Preliminary Objections*) case, ICJ Reports, 1957, pp. 105, 148; 24 ILR, pp. 840, 848–9. The Court noted in the *Free Zones of Upper Savoy and the District of Gex* case, PCIJ, Series A, No. 22, p. 13; 5 AD, pp. 461, 463, that the judicial settlement of disputes was 'simply an alternative to the direct and friendly settlement of such disputes between the parties'.

[22] Note that certain treaties provide for consultations in certain circumstances: see article 84 of the Vienna Convention on the Representation of States in their Relations with International Organisations, 1975; article 41 of the Convention on Succession of States in Respect of Treaties, 1978 and article 42 of the Convention on Succession of States in Respect of Property, Archives and Debts, 1983.

[23] See the *Fisheries Jurisdiction* case, ICJ Reports, 1974, p. 3; 55 ILR, p. 238. See also article 8(2) of the Antarctic Treaty, 1959; article 15 of the Moon Treaty, 1979; article 41 of the Vienna Convention on Succession of States in Respect of Treaties, 1978; article 84 of the Vienna Convention on the Representation of States in their Relations with International Organisations, 1975 and article 283 of the Convention on the Law of the Sea, 1982.

[24] This provision has been discussed by the International Tribunal for the Law of the Sea. See e.g. the *Southern Bluefin Tuna* cases, 28 ILM, 1999, p. 1624 and the *Mox* case, 41 ILM, 2002,

predicate resort to third-party mechanisms upon the failure of negotiations.[25] In addition, although it has been emphasised that: 'Neither in the Charter or otherwise in international law is any general rule to be found to the effect that the exhaustion of diplomatic negotiations constitutes a precondition for a matter to be referred to the Court',[26] it is possible that tribunals may direct the parties to engage in negotiations in good faith and may indicate the factors to be taken into account in the course of negotiations between the parties.[27] Where there is an obligation to negotiate, this would imply also an obligation to pursue such negotiations as far as possible with a view to concluding agreements.[28] The Court held in the *North Sea Continental Shelf* cases that:

> the parties are under an obligation to enter into negotiations with a view to arriving at an agreement, and not merely to go through a formal process of negotiation as a sort of prior condition . . . they are under an obligation so to conduct themselves that the negotiations are meaningful, which will not be the case when either of them insists upon its own position without contemplating any modification of it.[29]

p. 405. In the *Land Reclamation* case, 126 ILR, p. 487, it was held that there was no need to continue the exchange of views where it was clear that the exchange could yield no positive result, *ibid.*, para. 48. In *Barbados v. Trinidad and Tobago*, arbitral award of 11 April 2006, paras. 201–3, it was held that article 283(1) could not reasonably be interpreted to require that, when several years of negotiations had already failed to resolve the dispute, further and separate exchanges of views would be required. It was noted that the requirement of article 283(1) for settlement by negotiation is in relation to the obligation to agree upon a delimitation under articles 74 and 83, subsumed within the negotiations which those articles require already to have taken place.

[25] See e.g. the Revised General Act for the Settlement of Disputes 1949; the International Maritime Organisation Treaty, 1948 and the Convention on the Law of the Sea, 1982.

[26] *Cameroon v. Nigeria (Preliminary Objections)*, ICJ Reports, 1998, pp. 275, 303.

[27] See the *North Sea Continental Shelf* cases, ICJ Reports, 1969, pp. 3, 53–4; 41 ILR, pp. 29, 83. See also the *Fisheries Jurisdiction* case, ICJ Reports, 1974, pp. 3, 32; 55 ILR, pp. 238, 267.

[28] See the *Railway Traffic between Lithuania and Poland* case, PCIJ, Series A/B, No. 42, p. 116; 6 AD, pp. 403, 405. Section I, paragraph 10 of the Manila Declaration declares that when states resort to negotiations, they should 'negotiate meaningfully, in order to arrive at an early settlement acceptable to the parties'. Article 4(e) of the International Law Association's draft International Instrument on the Protection of the Environment from Damage Caused by Space Debris provides that 'to negotiate in good faith . . . means *inter alia* not only to hold consultations or talks but also to pursue them with a view of reaching a solution': see Report of the Sixty-sixth Conference, Buenos Aires, 1994, p. 319.

[29] ICJ Reports, 1969, pp. 3, 47; 41 ILR, pp. 29, 76. The Court has noted that, 'like all similar obligations to negotiate in international law, the negotiations have to be conducted in good faith', *Cameroon v. Nigeria*, ICJ Reports, 2002, pp. 303, 423. Questions as to the meaning

The Court in the *German External Debts* case emphasised that although an agreement to negotiate did not necessarily imply an obligation to reach an agreement, 'it does imply that serious efforts towards that end will be made'.[30] In the *Lac Lanoux* arbitration, it was stated that 'consultations and negotiations between the two states must be genuine, must comply with the rules of good faith and must not be mere formalities'.[31] Examples of infringement of the rules of good faith were held to include the unjustified breaking off of conversations, unusual delays and systematic refusal to give consideration to proposals or adverse interests.[32]

The point was also emphasised by the International Court in the *Legality of the Threat or Use of Nuclear Weapons*, where it noted the reference in article VI of the Treaty on the Non-Proliferation of Nuclear Weapons to 'pursue negotiations in good faith on effective measures relating to cessation of the nuclear arms race at an early date and to nuclear disarmament, and on a treaty on general and complete disarmament under strict and effective international control'. The Court then declared that:

> The legal import of that obligation goes beyond that of a mere obligation of conduct: the obligation involved here is an obligation to achieve a precise result – nuclear disarmament in all it aspects – by adopting a particular course of conduct, namely, the pursuit of negotiations on the matter in good faith.[33]

Where disputes are by their continuance likely to endanger the maintenance of international peace and security, article 33 of the UN Charter provides that the parties to such disputes shall first of all seek a solution by negotiation, inquiry or mediation, and then resort, if the efforts have not borne fruit, to more complex forms of resolution.[34]

---

of 'negotiations' arose in both *Nicaragua* v. *Honduras*, ICJ Reports, 1988, pp. 69, 99 and *Democratic Republic of the Congo* v. *Rwanda*, ICJ Reports, 2006, pp. 6, 46 ff.

[30] 47 ILR, pp. 418, 454.   [31] 24 ILR, pp. 101, 119.

[32] *Ibid.*, p. 128. See also the *Tacna–Arica Arbitration*, 2 RIAA, pp. 921 ff.

[33] ICJ Reports, 1996, pp. 226, 263–4; 110 ILR, pp. 163, 213–14. The Court usually urges the parties to negotiate when making an order granting (or indeed declining) provisional measures: see e.g. the *Great Belt* case, ICJ Reports, 1991, p. 12 and the *Pulp Mills on the River Uruguay* orders of 13 July 2006 and 23 January 2007. See further as to provisional measures, below, chapter 19, p. 1093.

[34] See the *North Sea Continental Shelf* cases, ICJ Reports, 1969, pp. 3, 47; 41 ILR, pp. 29, 77 and the *Fisheries Jurisdiction* cases, ICJ Reports, 1974, pp. 3, 32; 55 ILR, p. 267.

Good offices and mediation[35]

The employment of the procedures of good offices and mediation involves the use of a third party, whether an individual or individuals, a state or group of states or an international organisation, to encourage the contending parties to come to a settlement. Unlike the techniques of arbitration and adjudication, the process aims at persuading the parties to a dispute to reach satisfactory terms for its termination by themselves. Provisions for settling the dispute are not prescribed.

Technically, good offices are involved where a third party attempts to influence the opposing sides to enter into negotiations, whereas mediation implies the active participation in the negotiating process of the third party itself. In fact, the dividing line between the two approaches is often difficult to maintain as they tend to merge into one another, depending upon the circumstances. One example of the good offices method is the role played by the US President in 1906 in concluding the Russian–Japanese War,[36] or the function performed by the USSR in assisting in the peaceful settlement of the India–Pakistan dispute in 1965.[37] Another might be the part played by France in encouraging US–North Vietnamese negotiations to begin in Paris in the early 1970s.[38] A mediator, such as the US Secretary of State in the Middle East in 1973–4,[39] has an active and vital function to perform in seeking to cajole the disputing parties into accepting what are often his own proposals. It is his responsibility to reconcile the different claims and improve the atmosphere pervading the discussions. The UN Secretary-General can sometimes play an important role

---

[35] See UN Handbook, p. 33; Collier and Lowe, *Settlement*, p. 27; Merrills, *International Dispute Settlement*, chapter 2; R. R. Probst, *'Good Offices' In the Light of Swiss International Practice and Experience*, Dordrecht, 1989; *New Approaches to International Mediation* (eds. C. R. Mitchell and K. Webb), New York, 1988; J. Brierly, *The Law of Nations*, 6th edn, Oxford, 1963, pp. 373–6, and Murty, 'Settlement', pp. 680–1. See also *International Mediation in Theory and Practice* (eds. S. Touval and I. W. Zartman), Boulder, 1985, and *Mediation in International Relations* (eds. J. Bercovitch and J. Z. Rubin), London, 1992.

[36] Murty, 'Settlement', p. 681. Note also the exercise of US good offices in relation to a territorial dispute between France in regard to its protectorate of Cambodia and Thailand, SCOR, First Year, 81st meeting, pp. 505–7.

[37] See GAOR, 21st session, supp. no. 2, part I, chapter III.

[38] See AFDI, 1972, pp. 995–6. Note also the role played by Cardinal Samoré, a Papal mediator in the Beagle Channel dispute between Argentina and Chile, between 1978 and 1985: see Merrills, *International Dispute Settlement*, p. 30, and 24 ILM, 1985, pp. 1 ff. See also below, p. 1054.

[39] See DUSPIL, 1974, pp. 656–8 and *ibid.*, pp. 759–62.

by the exercise of his good offices.[40] An example of this was provided in the situation relating to Afghanistan in 1988. The Geneva Agreements of that year specifically noted that a representative of the Secretary-General would lend his good offices to the parties.[41] Good offices may also be undertaken by the Secretary-General jointly with office-holders of regional organisations.[42]

The Hague Conventions of 1899 and 1907 laid down many of the rules governing these two processes. It was stipulated that the signatories to the treaties had a right to offer good offices or mediation, even during hostilities, and that the exercise of the right was never to be regarded by either of the contending sides as an unfriendly act.[43] It was also explained that such procedures were not binding. The Conventions laid a duty upon the parties to a serious dispute or conflict to resort to good offices or mediation as far as circumstances allow, before having recourse to arms.[44] This, of course, has to be seen in the light of the relevant Charter provisions regarding the use of force, but it does point to the part that should be played by these diplomatic procedures.

Inquiry[45]

Where differences of opinion on factual matters underlie a dispute between parties, the logical solution is often to institute a commission of

---

[40] See Security Council resolution 367 (1975) requesting the UN Secretary-General to undertake a good offices mission to Cyprus. See the statement by the Secretary-General of the functions of good offices cited in UN Handbook, pp. 35–6. See also B. G. Ramcharan, 'The Good Offices of the United Nations Secretary-General in the Field of Human Rights', 76 AJIL, 1982, p. 130. Note also paragraph 12 of the Declaration on the Prevention and Removal of Disputes and Situations Which May Threaten International Peace and Security, 1988, General Assembly resolution 43/51. See also below, chapter 22, p. 1222.

[41] S/19835, annex. See also Security Council resolution 622 (1988).

[42] For example with the Chairman of the Organisation of African Unity with regard to the Western Sahara and Mayotte situations, UN Handbook, p. 39, and with the Secretary-General of the Organisation of American States with regard to Central America, ibid.

[43] Article 3 of Hague Convention No. I, 1899 and Convention No. I, 1907.

[44] Ibid., article 2.

[45] See Collier and Lowe, Settlement, p. 24; Merrills, International Dispute Settlement, chapter 3, and N. Bar-Yaacov, The Handling of International Disputes by Means of Inquiry, London, 1974. See also UN Handbook, pp. 24 ff.; T. Bensalah, L'Enquête Internationale dans le Règlement des Conflits, Paris, 1976; P. Ruegger, 'Quelques Réflexions sur le Rôle Actuel et Futur des Commissions Internationales d'Enquête' in Mélanges Bindschedler, Paris, 1980, p. 427, and Ruegger, 'Nouvelles Réflexions sur le Rôle des Procédures Internationales d'Enquête dans la Solution des Conflits Internationaux' in Études en l'Honneur de Robert Ago, Milan, 1987, p. 327.

inquiry to be conducted by reputable observers to ascertain precisely the facts in contention.[46] Provisions for such inquiries were first elaborated in the 1899 Hague Conference as a possible alternative to the use of arbitration.[47] However, the technique is limited in that it can only have relevance in the case of international disputes, involving neither the honour nor the vital interests of the parties, where the conflict centres around a genuine disagreement as to particular facts which can be resolved by recourse to an impartial and conscientious investigation.[48]

Inquiry was most successfully used in the Dogger Bank incident of 1904 where Russian naval ships fired on British fishing boats in the belief that they were hostile Japanese torpedo craft.[49] The Hague provisions were put into effect[50] and the report of the international inquiry commission contributed to a peaceful settlement of the issue.[51] This encouraged an elaboration of the technique by the 1907 Hague Conference,[52] and a wave of support for the procedure.[53] The United States, for instance, concluded forty-eight bilateral treaties between 1913 and 1940 with provisions in each one of them for the creation of a permanent inquiry commission. These agreements were known as the 'Bryan treaties'.[54]

---

[46] Inquiry as a specific procedure under consideration here is to be distinguished from the general process of inquiry or fact-finding as part of other mechanisms for dispute settlement, such as through the UN or other institutions. See *Fact-Finding Before International Tribunals* (ed. R. B. Lillich), Charlottesville, 1992.

[47] See Bar-Yaacov, *International Disputes*, chapter 2. The incident of the destruction of the US battleship *Maine* in 1898, which precipitated the American–Spanish War, was particularly noted as an impetus to the evolution of inquiry as an important 'safety valve' mechanism, *ibid.*, pp. 33–4. This was particularly in the light of the rival national inquiries that came to opposing conclusions in that episode: see the inquiry commission in that case, *Annual Register*, 1898, p. 362.

[48] Article 9, 1899 Hague Convention for the Pacific Settlement of International Disputes.

[49] Bar-Yaacov, *International Disputes*, chapter 3. See also Merrills, *International Dispute Settlement*, pp. 47 ff., and J. B. Scott, *The Hague Court Reports*, New York, 1916, p. 403.

[50] The Commission of Inquiry consisted of four naval officers of the UK, Russian, French and American fleets, plus a fifth member chosen by the other four (in the event an Austro-Hungarian). It was required to examine all the circumstances, particularly with regard to responsibility and blame.

[51] It was found that there was no justification for the Russian attack. In the event, both sides accepted the report and the sum of £65,000 was paid by Russia to the UK, Bar-Yaacov, *International Disputes*, p. 70.

[52] *Ibid.*, chapter 4. Note also the *Tavignano* inquiry, Scott, *Hague Court Reports*, New York, 1916, p. 413; the *Tiger* inquiry, Bar-Yaacov, *International Disputes*, p. 156, and the *Tubantia* inquiry, Scott, *Hague Court Reports*, New York, 1932, p. 135. See also Merrills, *International Dispute Settlement*, pp. 49 ff., and Bar-Yaacov, *International Disputes*, pp. 141–79.

[53] Bar-Yaacov, *International Disputes*, chapter 5.

[54] These were prefigured by the Taft or Knox Treaties of 1911 (which did not come into operation), *ibid.*, pp. 113–17. The USSR also signed a number of treaties which provide for joint inquiries with regard to frontier incidents, *ibid.*, pp. 117–19.

However, the use of commissions of inquiry in accordance with the Hague Convention of 1907 proved in practice to be extremely rare. The *Red Crusader* inquiry of 1962[55] followed an interval of some forty years since the previous inquiry. This concerned an incident between a British trawler and a Danish fisheries protection vessel, which subsequently involved a British frigate. Although instituted as a fact-finding exercise, it did incorporate judicial aspects. A majority of the Commission were lawyers and the procedures followed a judicial pattern. In addition, aspects of the report reflected legal findings, such as the declaration that the firing on the trawler by the Danish vessel in an attempt to stop it escaping arrest for alleged illegal fishing, 'exceeded legitimate use of armed force'.[56] In the *Letelier and Moffitt* case, the only decision to date under one of the Bryan treaties, a US–Chile Commission was established in order to determine the amount of compensation that would be paid by Chile to the US in respect of an assassination alleged to have been carried out by it in Washington DC.[57] As in the *Red Crusader* inquiry, the Commission in its decision in January 1992 made a number of judicial determinations and the proceedings were conducted less as a fact-finding inquiry and more as an arbitration.[58]

The value of inquiry within specified institutional frameworks, nevertheless, has been evident. Its use has increased within the United Nations generally[59] and in the specialised agencies.[60] Inquiry is also part of other

---

[55] *Ibid.*, pp. 179–95, and Merrills, *International Dispute Settlement*, pp. 53 ff. See also 35 ILR, p. 485; Cmnd 776, and E. Lauterpacht, *The Contemporary Practice of the UK in the Field of International Law*, London, 1962, vol. I, pp. 50–3.

[56] Lauterpacht, *Contemporary Practice*, p. 53; Merrills, *International Dispute Settlement*, p. 55, and Bar-Yaacov, *International Disputes*, p. 192.

[57] Chile denied liability but agreed to make an *ex gratia* payment equal to the amount of compensation that would be payable upon a finding of liability, such amount to be determined by the Commission.

[58] 88 ILR, p. 727, and see Merrills, *International Dispute Settlement*, pp. 56 ff.

[59] See the announcement by the UN Secretary-General of a mission in 1988 to Iran and Iraq to investigate the situation of prisoners of war at the request of those states, S/20147. See also Security Council resolution 384 (1975) concerning East Timor. The General Assembly adopted a Declaration on Fact-Finding in resolution 46/59 (1991). See also the operation of the UN Compensation Commission established to resolve claims against Iraq resulting from its invasion of Kuwait in 1990 and described by the UN Secretary-General as performing an 'essentially fact-finding function', S/2259, 1991, para. 20: see Collier and Lowe, *Settlement*, p. 42, and Merrills, *International Dispute Settlement*, p. 61, and the work of the World Bank Inspection Panel. See further below, pp. 1040 and 1042.

[60] See article 26 of the Constitution of the International Labour Organisation. See also the inquiry by the International Civil Aviation Organisation in 1983 into the shooting down of a Korean airliner, Collier and Lowe, *Settlement*, p. 26.

processes of dispute settlement in the context of general fact-finding.[61] But inquiry as a separate mechanism in accordance with the Hague Convention of 1907 has fallen out of favour.[62] In many disputes, of course, the determination of the relevant circumstances would simply not aid a settlement, whilst its nature as a third-party involvement in a situation would discourage some states.

Conciliation[63]

The process of conciliation involves a third-party investigation of the basis of the dispute and the submission of a report embodying suggestions for a settlement. As such it involves elements of both inquiry and mediation, and in fact the process of conciliation emerged from treaties providing for permanent inquiry commissions.[64] Conciliation reports are only proposals and as such do not constitute binding decisions.[65] They are thus different from arbitration awards. The period between the world wars was the heyday for conciliation commissions and many treaties made provision for them as a method for resolving disputes. But the process

[61] Note, for example, article 90 of Protocol I to the Geneva Red Cross Conventions, 1949 providing for the establishment of an International Fact-Finding Commission, and Security Council resolution 780 (1992) establishing a Commission of Experts to investigate violations of international humanitarian law in the Former Yugoslavia: see M. C. Bassiouni, 'The United Nations Commission of Experts Established Pursuant to Security Council Resolution 780 (1992)', 88 AJIL, 1994, p. 784.

[62] Note, however, the Permanent Court of Arbitration's Optional Rules for Fact-Finding Commissions of Inquiry, effective December 1997: see http://pca-cpa.org/ENGLISH/BD/inquiryenglish.htm.

[63] See UN Handbook, pp. 45 ff.; Lauterpacht, Function of Law, pp. 260–9; Merrills, International Dispute Settlement, chapter 4; Collier and Lowe, Settlement, p. 29; Murty, 'Settlement', pp. 682–3; H. Fox, 'Conciliation' in David Davies Memorial Institute, International Disputes, p. 93; J. P. Cot, La Conciliation Internationale, Paris, 1968; Bowett, 'Contemporary Developments', chapter 2; V. Degan, 'International Conciliation: Its Past and Future', Völkerrecht und Rechtsphilosophie, 1980, p. 261; and R. Donner, 'The Procedure of International Conciliation: Some Historical Aspects', 1 Journal of the History of International Law, 1999, p. 103.

[64] See Murty, 'Settlement'. Merrills notes that by 1940, nearly 200 conciliation treaties had been concluded, International Dispute Settlement, p. 66.

[65] See paragraph 6 of the annex to the Vienna Convention on the Law of Treaties, 1969. The Vienna Convention for the Protection of the Ozone Layer, 1985 provides that conciliation awards should be considered in good faith, while article 85(7) of the Vienna Convention on the Representation of States in their Relations with International Organisations provides that any party to the dispute may declare unilaterally that it will abide by the recommendations in the report as far as it is concerned. Note that article 14(3) of the Treaty Establishing the Organisation of Eastern Caribbean States, 1981 stipulates that member states undertake to accept the conciliation procedure as compulsory.

has not been widely employed and certainly has not justified the faith evinced in it by states between 1920 and 1938.[66]

Nevertheless, conciliation processes do have a role to play. They are extremely flexible and by clarifying the facts and discussing proposals may stimulate negotiations between the parties. The rules dealing with conciliation were elaborated in the 1928 General Act on the Pacific Settlement of International Disputes (revised in 1949). The function of the commissions was defined to include inquiries and mediation techniques. Such commissions were to be composed of five persons, one appointed by each opposing side and the other three to be appointed by agreement from amongst the citizens of third states. The proceedings were to be concluded within six months and were not to be held in public. The conciliation procedure was intended to deal with mixed legal–factual situations and to operate quickly and informally.[67]

There have of late been a number of proposals to reactivate the conciliation technique, but how far they will succeed in their aim remains to be seen.[68] A number of multilateral treaties do, however, provide for conciliation as a means of resolving disputes. The 1948 American Treaty of Pacific Settlement; 1957 European Convention for the Peaceful Settlement of Disputes; the 1964 Protocol on the Commission of Mediation, Conciliation and Arbitration to the Charter of the Organisation of African Unity (now the African Union); the 1969 Vienna Convention on the Law of Treaties; the 1981 Treaty Establishing the Organisation of Eastern Caribbean States; the 1975 Convention on the Representation of States in their Relations with International Organisations; the 1978 Vienna

---

[66] But note the Chaco Commission, 1929, the Franco-Siamese Conciliation Commission, 1947 and the Franco-Swiss Commission, 1955: see Merrills, *International Dispute Settlement*, pp. 67 ff. See also Bar-Yaacov, *International Disputes*, chapter 7.

[67] Article 15(1) of the Geneva General Act as amended provides that 'The task of the Conciliation Commission shall be to elucidate the questions in dispute, to collect with that object all necessary information by means of enquiry or otherwise, and to endeavour to bring the parties to an agreement. It may, after the case has been examined, inform the parties of the terms of settlement which seem suitable to it, and lay down the period within which they are to make their decision.'

[68] See the Regulations on the Procedure of Conciliation adopted by the Institut de Droit International, *Annuaire de l'Institut de Droit International*, 1961, pp. 374 ff. See also the UN Model Rules for the Conciliation of Disputes Between States, 1995, General Assembly resolution 50/50, and the Optional Conciliation Rules adopted by the Permanent Court of Arbitration in 1996: see *Basic Documents: Conventions, Rules, Model Clauses and Guidelines*, The Hague, 1998. Note also the Optional Rules for Conciliation of Disputes Relating to Natural Resources and the Environment adopted by the Permanent Court of Arbitration in April 2002.

Convention on Succession of States in respect of Treaties; the 1982 Convention on the Law of the Sea and the 1985 Vienna Convention on the Protection of the Ozone Layer, for example, all contain provisions concerning conciliation.

The conciliation procedure was used in the Iceland–Norway dispute over the continental shelf delimitation between Iceland and Jan Mayen island.[69] The agreement establishing the Conciliation Commission stressed that the question was the subject of continuing negotiations and that the Commission report would not be binding, both elements characteristic of the conciliation method. The Commission had also to take into account Iceland's strong economic interests in the area as well as other factors. The role of the concept of natural prolongation within continental shelf delimitation was examined as well as the legal status of islands and relevant state practice and court decisions. The solution proposed by the Commission was for a joint development zone, an idea that would have been unlikely to come from a judicial body reaching a decision solely on the basis of the legal rights of the parties. In other words, the flexibility of the conciliation process seen in the context of continued negotiations between the parties was demonstrated.[70]

Such commissions have also been established outside the framework of specific treaties, for example by the United Nations. Instances would include the Conciliation Commission for Palestine under General Assembly resolution 194 (III), 1948, and the Conciliation Commission for the Congo under resolution 1474 (ES-IV) of 1960.

International institutions and dispute settlement[71]

Regional organisations[72]

Article 52(1) of Chapter VIII of the UN Charter provides that nothing in the Charter precludes the existence of regional arrangements or agencies

---

[69] 20 ILM, 1981, p. 797; 62 ILR, p. 108. The Commission Report was accepted by the parties, 21 ILM, 1982, p. 1222.

[70] See also the 1929 Chaco Conciliation Commission; the 1947 Franco-Siamese Commission; the 1952 Belgian–Danish Commission; the 1954–5 Franco-Swiss Commission and the 1958 Franco-Mexican Commission. See UN Handbook, p. 48 and Nguyen Quoc Dinh et al., Droit International Public, p. 838.

[71] See below, chapter 22 for peaceful settlement of disputes through the United Nations and chapter 23 generally with regard to international institutions.

[72] See Bowett's Law of International Institutions (eds. P. Sands and P. Klein), 5th edn, London, 2001; Merrills, International Dispute Settlement, chapter 11; Murty, 'Settlement', pp. 725–8; K. Oellers-Frahm and N. Wühler, Dispute Settlement in Public International Law, New York, 1984, pp. 92 ff., and Nguyen Quoc Dinh et al., Droit International Public, pp. 838 ff.

for dealing with such matters relating to the maintenance of international peace and security as are appropriate for regional action, provided that such arrangements or agencies and their activities are consistent with the purposes and principles of the UN.[73] Article 52(2) stipulates that members of the UN entering into such arrangements or agencies are to make every effort to settle local disputes peacefully through such regional arrangements or by such regional agencies before referring them to the Security Council, and that the Security Council encourages the development of the peaceful settlement of local disputes through such regional arrangements. That having been said, article 52(4) stresses that the application of articles 34 and 35 of the UN Charter relating to the roles of the Security Council and General Assembly remains unaffected.[74] The supremacy of the Security Council is reinforced by article 53(1) which provides that while the Council may, where appropriate, utilise such regional arrangements or agencies for enforcement action under its authority, 'no enforcement action shall be taken under regional arrangements or by regional agencies without the authorisation of the Security Council'. It should also be noted that by article 24 the Security Council possesses 'primary responsibility for the maintenance of international peace and security', while article 103 of the Charter emphasises that, in the event of a conflict between the obligations of a UN member under the Charter and obligations under any other international agreement, the former are to prevail.[75] In addition, under article 36, the Security Council may 'at any stage of a dispute . . . recommend appropriate procedures or methods of adjustment',[76] while article 37 provides that should the parties to a dispute fail to settle it, they 'shall refer it to the Security Council'. Furthermore, should the Council itself deem that the continuance of a dispute is likely to endanger the maintenance of international peace and security, 'it shall decide whether to take action under article 36 or to recommend such terms of settlement as it may consider appropriate'.[77] Thus, although reference where appropriate to regional organisations or arrangements should take place, this

---

[73] See *The Charter of the United Nations* (ed. B. Simma), 2nd edn, Oxford, 2002, pp. 807 ff. See also H. Saba, 'Les Accords Régionaux dans la Charte des Nations Unies', 80 HR, 1952 I, p. 635; D. E. Acevedo, 'Disputes under Consideration by the UN Security Council or Regional Bodies' in *The International Court of Justice at a Crossroads* (ed. L. F. Damrosch), Dobbs Ferry, 1987; B. Andemicael, *Regionalism and the United Nations*, Dobbs Ferry, 1979; J. M. Yepes, 'Les Accords Régionaux et le Droit International', 71 HR, 1947 II, p. 235.

[74] See further below, chapter 22, p. 1273.

[75] See the *Nicaragua* case, ICJ Reports, 1984, pp. 392, 440; 76 ILR, pp. 104, 151.

[76] This refers to disputes the continuance of which is likely to endanger the maintenance of international peace and security, article 33.

[77] Article 37(2).

does not affect the comprehensive role of the UN through the Security Council or General Assembly in dealing in various ways with disputes between states.[78] While provisions contained in regional instruments may prevent or restrict resort to mechanisms outside those instruments,[79] this does not constrain in any way the authority or competence of the UN.[80] In many cases, a matter may be simultaneously before both the UN and a regional organisation and such concurrent jurisdiction does not constitute a jurisdictional problem for the UN.[81] In practice and in relation to the adoption of active measures, the UN is likely to defer to appropriate regional mechanisms while realistic chances exist for a regional settlement.[82]

Various regional organisations have created machinery for the settlement of disputes.

The African Union (Organisation of African Unity)[83]

The Organisation of African Unity was established in 1963. Article XIX of its Charter referred to the principle of 'the peaceful settlement of disputes

---

[78] Note that section I, paragraph 6 of the Manila Declaration on the Pacific Settlement of International Disputes adopted in General Assembly resolution 37/10, 1982, provides that states parties to relevant regional arrangements or agencies shall make every effort to settle disputes through such mechanisms, but that this 'does not preclude states from bringing any dispute to the attention of the Security Council or of the General Assembly in accordance with the Charter of the United Nations'.

[79] See below, p. 1273.

[80] See M. Bartos, 'L'ONU et la Co-opération Régionale', 27 RGDIP, 1956, p. 7.

[81] The International Court noted in the *Nicaragua* case, ICJ Reports, 1984, pp. 392, 440; 76 ILR, pp. 104, 151, in the context of contended regional discussions, that 'even the existence of active negotiations in which both parties might be involved should not prevent both the Security Council and the Court from exercising their separate functions under the Charter and the Statute of the Court'.

[82] In such cases, the Security Council is likely to inscribe the dispute on its agenda and, providing the dispute is not one actually endangering international peace and security, refer the matter to the appropriate regional agency under article 52(2) and (3), keeping it under review on the agenda: see UN Handbook, p. 96.

[83] See e.g. K. D. Magliveras and G. J. Naldi, *The African Union and the Predecessor Organisation of African Unity*, The Hague, 2004. The Organisation of African Unity was established in 1963 and replaced by the African Union with the coming into force of the Constitutive Act in May 2001. As to the OAU, see generally T. Maluwa, 'The Peaceful Settlement of Disputes among African States, 1963–1983: Some Conceptual Issues and Practical Trends', 38 ICLQ, 1989, p. 299; S. G. Amoo and I. W. Zartman, 'Mediation by Regional Organisations: The Organisation of African Unity (OAU) in Chad' in Bercovitch and Rubin, *Mediation in International Relations*, p. 131; B. Boutros Ghali, *L'Organisation de l'Unité Africaine*, Paris, 1968; M. Bedjaoui, 'Le Règlement Pacifique des Différends Africains', AFDI, 1972, p. 85; B. Andemicael, *Le Règlement Pacifique des Différends Survenant entre États Africains*, New York, 1973; E. Jouve, *L'Organisation de l'Unité Africaine*, Paris, 1984; T. O. Elias,

by negotiation, mediation, conciliation or arbitration' and to assist in achieving this a Commission of Mediation, Conciliation and Arbitration was established by the Protocol of 21 July 1964.[84] The jurisdiction of the Commission was not, however, compulsory and it was not utilised. African states were historically unwilling to resort to judicial or arbitral methods of dispute settlement and in general preferred informal third-party involvement through the medium of the OAU. In the Algeria–Morocco boundary dispute,[85] for example, the OAU established an ad hoc commission consisting of the representatives of seven African states to seek to achieve a settlement of issues arising out of the 1963 clashes.[86] Similarly in the Somali–Ethiopian conflict,[87] a commission was set up by the OAU in an attempt to mediate.[88] This commission failed to resolve the dispute, although it did reaffirm the principle of the inviolability of frontiers of member states as attained at the time of independence.[89] In a third case, the Western Sahara dispute,[90] an OAU committee was established in July 1978, which sought unsuccessfully to reach a settlement in the conflict,[91] while the OAU also established committees to try to mediate in the Chad civil war, again with little success.[92] Despite mixed success, it became fairly established practice that in a dispute involving African states, initial recourse will be made to OAU mechanisms, primarily ad hoc commissions or committees.

In an attempt to improve the mechanisms available, the OAU approved a Mechanism for Conflict Prevention, Management and Resolution in 1993 (termed the Cairo Declaration).[93] It was intended to anticipate and

---

Africa and the Development of International Law, Leiden, 1972; Z. Cervenka, *The Organisation of African Unity and its Charter*, London, 1968, and M. N. Shaw, 'Dispute Settlement in Africa', 37 YBWA, 1983, p. 149.

[84] Elias, *Africa*, chapter 9.

[85] See I. Brownlie, *African Boundaries*, London, 1979, p. 55, and M. N. Shaw, *Title to Territory in Africa: International Legal Issues*, Oxford, 1986, pp. 196–7.

[86] See *Keesing's Contemporary Archives*, pp. 19939–40, and Shaw, 'Dispute Settlement', p. 153.

[87] See Brownlie, *African Boundaries*, p. 826. See also Shaw, *Title to Territory*, pp. 197–201.

[88] *Africa Research Bulletin*, May 1973, p. 2845 and *ibid.*, June 1973, pp. 2883–4 and 2850.

[89] *Ibid.*, August 1980, pp. 5763–4. This is the principle of *uti possidetis*: see further above, chapter 10, p. 525.

[90] See Shaw, *Title to Territory*, pp. 123 ff.

[91] *Ibid.*, and Shaw, 'Dispute Settlement', pp. 160–2.

[92] Shaw, 'Dispute Settlement', pp. 158–60.

[93] AHG/Dec. 1 (XXVIII) and see the Report of the OAU Secretary-General, Doc. CM/1747 (LVIII) and AHG/Dec. 3 (XXIX), 1993. See also M. C. Djiena-Wembon, 'A Propos du Nouveau Mécanisme de l'OUA sur les Conflits', 98 RGDIP, 1994, p. 377, and R. Ranjeva, 'Reflections on the Proposals for the Establishment of a Pan-African Mechanism for the Prevention and Settlement of Conflicts' in *Towards More Effective Supervision by International Organisations* (eds. N. Blokker and S. Muller), Dordrecht, 1994, vol. I, p. 93.

prevent situations of potential conflict from developing further; however, it was not successful and in 2001 the OAU Assembly decided to incorporate the Central Organ of the Mechanism as one of the organs of the African Union (which had come into force in May that year).[94] The Protocol Relating to the Establishment of the Peace and Security Council of the African Union was adopted by the First Ordinary Session of the Assembly of the African Union on 9 July 2002.[95] This instrument creates the Peace and Security Council as a 'standing decision-making organ for the prevention, management and resolution of conflicts', to be supported by the Commission of the African Union,[96] a Panel of the Wise,[97] a Continental Early Warning System,[98] an African Standby Force[99] and a Special Fund.[100] A series of guiding principles are laid down, including early response to crises, respect for the rule of law and human rights, respect for the sovereignty and territorial integrity of member states and respect for borders inherited on the achievement of independence.[101] The Council is composed of fifteen members based on equitable regional representation and rotation[102] and its functions include the promotion of peace, security and stability in Africa; early warning and preventive diplomacy; peacemaking including the use of good offices, mediation, conciliation and inquiry; peace-support operations and intervention; peace-building; and humanitarian action.[103] Article 9 provides that the Council 'shall take initiatives and action it deems appropriate' with regard to situations of potential and full-blown conflicts and shall use its discretion to effect

[94] See e.g. C. A. A. Packer and D. Rukare, 'The New African Union and its Constitutive Act', 96 AJIL, 2002, p. 365.

[95] This is stated to replace the Cairo Declaration 1993 and to supersede the resolution and decisions of the OAU relating to the Mechanism for Conflict Prevention, Management and Resolution in Africa which are in conflict with the Protocol: see article 22(1) and (2).

[96] See further article 10.

[97] This is to be composed of five highly respected African personalities selected by the chairperson of the Commission after consultation with the member states concerned and shall undertake such action at the request of the Council or chairperson of the Commission or at its own initiative as deemed appropriate for the prevention of conflicts: see article 11.

[98] This is to include an observation and monitoring centre to be known as 'the situation room' located at the Conflict Management Directorate of the African Union, together with observation and monitoring units of the Regional Mechanisms: see article 12.

[99] This is to consist of standby multidisciplinary contingents and shall perform functions such as observation missions, peace support missions, interventions, preventive deployment, peace-building and humanitarian assistance: see articles 13–15.

[100] Article 2.   [101] Article 4.   [102] Article 5.

[103] Article 6. See also the list of powers in article 7.

entry, whether through the collective intervention of the Council itself
or through its chairperson and/or the chairperson of the Commission,
the Panel of the Wise, and/or in collaboration with the regional mechanisms.[104] The Protocol came into force on 26 December 2003.

There are in addition a number of subregional organisations in Africa
which are playing an increasing role in conflict resolution. First and foremost is the Economic Community of West African States (ECOWAS) created in 1975. The constituent instrument was revised in 1993[105] and article
58 of the revised treaty refers to the responsibility of ECOWAS to prevent
and settle regional conflicts, with the ECOWAS Cease-fire Monitoring
Group (ECOMOG) as the adopted regional intervention force. The mission of ECOWAS is to promote economic integration and its institutions
include the Authority of Heads of State and Government; the Council of
Ministers; the Community Parliament; the Economic and Social Council; the Community Court of Justice; a secretariat and a co-operation
fund. ECOWAS intervened in the Liberian civil war in 1990 via a Cease-
Fire Monitoring Group (ECOMOG)[106] and has been concerned with the
conflicts in Sierra Leone and Guinea-Bissau.[107] An ECOWAS Mechanism
for Conflict Prevention, Management and Resolution, Peacekeeping and
Security was established in 1999 and a Protocol on Democracy and Good
Governance adopted in 2001.[108]

The Southern African Development Community (SADC) was established in 1992.[109] In 1996 it decided to establish an Organ on Politics,
Defence and Security Co-operation and in 2001 it adopted a Protocol
on Politics, Defence and Security Co-operation.[110] Under this Protocol,

---

[104] See further article 16.
[105] There was a further revision in the Protocol of 2001 adopted at Dakar.
[106] See e.g. *Regional Peace-Keeping and International Enforcement: The Liberian Crisis* (ed. M. Weller), Cambridge, 1994, and see further below, chapter 22, p. 1276.
[107] See e.g. Security Council resolutions 1132 (1997) and 1233 (1999).
[108] The Mechanism's highest decision-making body is the Authority, consisting of the heads of state, with powers to act on all matters concerning conflict prevention, management and resolution, peace-keeping, security, humanitarian support, peace-building, control of cross-border crime and proliferation of small arms, see article 6, while a nine-person Mediation and Security Council is mandated to take appropriate decisions under the Protocol on behalf of the Authority, see articles 7–10. See also Security Council resolution 1197 (1998).
[109] See e.g. B. Chigora, 'The SAD Community', 11 *African Journal of International and Comparative Law*, 2000, p. 522. It evolved out of the Southern African Development Co-ordination Conference established in 1979.
[110] See www.sadc.int/index.php?lang=english&path=legal/protocols/&page=p_politics_defence_and_security_co-operation.

the objective of the Organ is to promote peace and security in the region and in particular to 'consider enforcement action in accordance with international law and as a matter of last resort where peaceful means have failed'.[111] A number of structures of the Organ were set up,[112] including a chairperson,[113] the troika (the chairperson together with the incoming and outgoing chairpersons), a ministerial committee,[114] an Inter-State Politics and Diplomacy Committee[115] and an Inter-State Defence and Security Committee.[116] The Organ has jurisdiction to seek to resolve any 'significant inter-state conflict'[117] or any 'significant intra-state conflict'.[118] It may employ a variety of peaceful means, including diplomacy, negotiations, mediation, arbitration and adjudication by an international tribunal and shall establish an early warning system to prevent the outbreak or escalation of a conflict. Where peaceful means fail, the chairperson acting on the advice of the Ministerial Committee may recommend to the Summit of the Community that enforcement action be taken, but such action may only be taken as a matter of last resort and only with the authorisation of the UN Security Council.[119]

The Organisation of American States[120]

Article 23 of the Charter of the OAS, signed at Bogotá in 1948 and as amended by the Protocol of Cartagena de Indias, 1985, provides that international disputes between member states must be submitted to the Organisation for peaceful settlement, although this is not to be interpreted as an impairment of the rights and obligations of member states under

---

[111] Article 2(f).   [112] Article 3.   [113] See further article 4.   [114] See further article 5.
[115] See further article 6.   [116] See further article 7.
[117] I.e. one concerning territorial boundaries or natural resources or in which aggression or military force has occurred or where peace and security of the region or of another state party who is not a party to the conflict is threatened: see article 11(2)a.
[118] I.e. one involving large-scale violence, including genocide and gross violation of human rights or a military coup or a civil war or a conflict threatening the peace and security of the region or of another state party, article 11(2)b.
[119] Article 11(3).
[120] See Merrills, *International Dispute Settlement*, pp. 282 ff., and Bowett's *International Institutions*, pp. 205 ff. See also E. Jiménez de Aréchaga, 'La Co-ordination des Systèmes de l'ONU et de l'Organisation des États Américains pour le Règlement Pacifique des Différends et la Sécurité Collective', 111 HR, 1964 I, p. 423, and A. Cançado Trindade, 'Mécanismes de Règlement Pacifiques des Différends en Amérique Centrale: De Contadora à Esquipulas II', AFDI, 1987, p. 798.

articles 34 and 35 of the UN Charter.[121] The 1948 American Treaty of Pacific Settlement (the Pact of Bogotá, to be distinguished from the Charter) sets out the procedures in detail, ranging from good offices, mediation and conciliation to arbitration and judicial settlement by the International Court of Justice. This treaty, however, has not been successful[122] and in practice the OAS has utilised the Inter-American Peace Committee created in 1940 for peaceful resolution of disputes. This was replaced in 1970 by the Inter-American Committee on Peaceful Settlement, a subsidiary organ of the Council. Since the late 1950s the Permanent Council of the OAS, a plenary body at ambassadorial level, has played an increasingly important role.[123] One example concerned the frontier incidents that took place on the border between Costa Rica and Nicaragua in 1985. The Council set up a fact-finding committee and, after hearing its report, adopted a resolution calling for talks to take place within the Contadora negotiating process.[124] The Esquipulas II agreement of 14 November 1987 established an International Verification and Follow-up Commission to be composed of the Foreign Ministers of the Contadora and Support Group States together with the secretaries-general of the UN and OAS.[125]

The Arab League[126]

The Arab League, established in 1945, aims at increasing co-operation between the Arab states. Its facilities for peaceful settlement of disputes amongst its members are not, however, very well developed, and in

---

[121] Note that as originally drafted in the 1948 Charter, article 20 (as it then was) provided that submission to the OAS procedures had to occur prior to referral to the Security Council of the UN.

[122] Although note the *Nicaragua* v. *Honduras* case, ICJ Reports, 1988, pp. 69, 88; 84 ILR, pp. 218, 243, where the Court held that it had jurisdiction by virtue of article XXXI of the Pact of Bogotá.

[123] See articles 82–90 of the OAS Charter.

[124] OAS Permanent Council resolutions CP/Res. 427 (618/85); CP/doc. 1592/85 and A/40/737-S/17549, annex IV.

[125] The countries involved in the Contadora negotiating process were Colombia, Mexico, Panama and Venezuela, while the Support Group consisted of Argentina, Brazil, Peru and Uruguay. See A/43/729-S/20234.

[126] See H. A. Hassouna, *The League of Arab States and Regional Disputes*, Leiden, 1975; Bowett, 'Contemporary Development', p. 229; M. Abdennabi, *La Ligue des États Arabes et les Conflits Inter-Arabes (1962–1980)*, 1985; B. Boutros Ghali, 'The Arab League 1945–1970', 25 *Revue Égyptienne de Droit International*, 1969, p. 67; and S. Al-Kadhem, 'The Role of the League of Arab States in Settling Inter-Arab Disputes', 32 *Revue Égyptienne de Droit International*, 1976, p. 1. See also www.al-bab.com/arab/docs/league.htm.

practice consist primarily of informal conciliation attempts. One notable exception was the creation in 1961 of an Inter-Arab Force to keep the peace between Iraq and Kuwait.[127] An Arab Security Force was sent to Lebanon in 1976 to be succeeded by the Arab Deterrent Force between 1976 and 1983. The Arab League was not able to play a significant part in either the Kuwait crisis of 1990–1 or the Iraq crisis of 2002–3.

Europe[128]

The European Convention for the Peaceful Settlement of Disputes adopted by the Council of Europe in 1957 provides that legal disputes (as defined in article 36(2) of the Statute of the International Court of Justice) are to be sent to the International Court, although conciliation may be tried before this step is taken.[129] Other disputes are to go to arbitration, unless the parties have agreed to accept conciliation.

Within the NATO alliance,[130] there exist good offices facilities, and inquiry, mediation, conciliation and arbitration procedures may be instituted. In fact, the Organisation proved of some use, for instance in the longstanding 'cod war' between Britain and Iceland, two NATO partners.[131] The Organisation on Security and Co-operation in Europe (OSCE) has gradually been establishing dispute resolution mechanisms.[132] Under the key documents of this organisation,[133] the participating states are to endeavour in good faith to reach a rapid and equitable solution of their disputes by using a variety of means. Under the Valletta Report 1991, as amended by the Stockholm Decision of 1992, any party to a dispute may request the establishment of a Dispute Settlement Mechanism, which

---

[127] Note also the pan-Arab 'peacekeeping force' in the Lebanon between 1976 and 1982: see *Keesing's Contemporary Archives*, pp. 28117 ff. See also I. Pogany, *The Arab League and Peacekeeping in Lebanon*, London, 1987. The Council also appointed committees to deal with the 1963 Algerian–Moroccan and Democratic People's Republic of Yemen–Yemen Arab Republic boundary disputes, H. A. Hassouna, 'The League of Arab States and the United Nations: Relations in the Peaceful Settlement of Disputes', New York, 1979, p. 312. See also Simma, *Charter of the United Nations*, p. 852.

[128] See L. Caflisch, 'Vers des Mécanismes Pan-Européennes de Règlement Pacifique des Différends', 97 *Revue Générale de Droit International Public*, 1993, p. 1.

[129] Note that some states have entered reservations to this provision.

[130] See *Bowett's International Institutions*, p. 191, and Merrills, *International Dispute Settlement*, p. 280. See also www.nato.int/.

[131] Merrills, *International Dispute Settlement*, p. 287. Such procedures were also proposed following the Suez crisis in 1956 and with regard to the Cyprus crisis in 1963: see Nguyen Quoc Dinh *et al.*, *Droit International Public*, pp. 855–6.

[132] See generally above, chapter 7, p. 372, and below, chapter 23, p. 1289.

[133] See the Helsinki Final Act 1975; the Charter of Paris 1990 and the Valletta Report of the Meeting of Experts on Peaceful Settlement of Disputes 1991.

once established may offer comments or advice with regard to negotiations between the parties in dispute, or any other appropriate dispute settlement process, and may engage in fact-finding and other conciliation functions. The Convention on Conciliation and Arbitration was signed in 1992 and came into force two years later. Under this Convention, a Court of Conciliation and Arbitration[134] has been established in Geneva. Conciliation may be undertaken by a Conciliation Commission constituted for each dispute and drawn from a list established under the Convention.[135] The Commission will draw up a report containing its proposals for the peaceful settlement of the dispute and the parties will then have a period of thirty days during which to examine the proposals. If the parties do not accept the proposed settlement, the report will be forwarded to the OSCE Council through the Senior Council (formerly the Committee of Senior Officials).[136] The Convention also provided for the establishment of Arbitral Tribunals, similarly constituted for each dispute and drawn from a list.[137] Such a tribunal would be set up by express agreement between the parties in dispute[138] or where the state brought to arbitration has agreed in advance to accept the jurisdiction of the Tribunal.[139] The award of the Tribunal would be final and binding as between the parties.[140]

In addition, the OSCE is able to send Missions to various participating states, with their consent, as part of its early warning, conflict prevention and crisis management responsibilities. Such Missions have been sent to Yugoslavia to promote dialogue between the populations of Kosovo, Sanjak and Vojvodina and the authorities of the state; to the Former Yugoslav Republic of Macedonia; to Georgia; Moldova; Tajikistan; Estonia; Ukraine and Chechnya. Additional Missions have operated in Albania and Kosovo,[141] Moldova and Georgia.[142] Under the General Framework

---

[134] This consists of the conciliators and arbitrators appointed under articles 3 and 4.

[135] See articles 1 and 2. Each state party is to appoint two conciliators, article 3.

[136] Article 25.

[137] Articles 2 and 4. Each state party is to appoint one arbitrator and one alternate.

[138] Either between two or more states parties to the Convention or between one or more states parties to the Convention and one or more OSCE participating states, article 26(1).

[139] Article 26.

[140] Article 31. See also UN Handbook, p. 87, and OSCE Handbook 2000, Vienna, p. 37 and see www.osce.org/publications/handbook/.

[141] See OSCE Handbook 1996, pp. 16 ff., and Annual Report for 2001. A series of Sanctions Assistance Missions, operating under the guidance of the OSCE/EU Sanctions Co-ordinator, was sent to various countries in order to assist them in maintaining sanctions imposed by the Security Council in the Yugoslav crisis, ibid., p. 36.

[142] See Annual Report for 2007, pp. 54 and 60. Note also the Minsk Process established by the OSCE in 1995 in order to resolve the dispute between Armenia and Azerbaijan concerning Nagorno-Karabakh: see www.osce.org/item/21979.html.

Agreement for Peace in Bosnia and Herzegovina, initialled at Dayton on 21 November 1995 and signed in Paris on 14 December 1995, the OSCE was made responsible for the supervision of elections,[143] for providing the framework for the conduct of discussions between the Bosnian parties on confidence and security-building measures and for measures of subregional arms control,[144] and for assisting in the creation of a Bosnian Commission on Human Rights.[145]

International organisations and facilities of limited competence[146]

The various specialised agencies[147] which encourage international co-operation in functional spheres have their own procedures for settling disputes between their members relating to the interpretation of their constitutional instruments. Such procedures vary from organisation to organisation, although the general pattern involves recourse to one of the main organs of the institution upon the failure of negotiations. If this fails to result in a settlement, the matter may be referred to the International Court of Justice or to arbitration unless otherwise agreed.[148] In such cases, recourse to the Court is by way of a request for an Advisory Opinion, although by virtue of constitutional provisions, the judgment of the Court would be accepted as binding and not as advisory.[149] In other cases, the

---

[143] See Annex 3 of the Agreement.

[144] Annex 1-B of the Agreement. The subregional arms control involves Yugoslavia, Croatia and Bosnia.

[145] Annex 6 of the Agreement. See also article 22 of the ASEAN Charter, 2007, which calls for the maintenance and establishment of dispute settlement mechanisms to resolve disputes between ASEAN members: see below, chapter 23, p. 1294.

[146] See generally C. A. Colliard, 'Le Règlement des Différends dans les Organisations Intergou-vernementales de Caractère Non Politique' in *Mélanges Basdevant*, Paris, 1960, p. 152, and G. Malinverni, *Le Règlement des Différends dans les Organisations Internationales Économiques*, Leiden, 1974. It should also be noted that several international treaties ex-pressly provide mechanisms and methods for the peaceful resolution of disputes arising therefrom: see e.g. with regard to the Convention on the Law of the Sea, above, chap-ter 11, p. 635, and with regard to the Convention on the Law of Treaties, above, chapter 16, p. 952.

[147] See Murty, 'Settlement', pp. 729–32. See further below, chapter 23, p. 1285.

[148] See article 37 of the International Labour Organisation Constitution; article 14(2) of the UNESCO Constitution; article 75 of the World Health Organisation Constitution; article 17 of the Constitution of the Food and Agriculture Organisation; article XVII of the International Atomic Energy Agency Statute and articles 50 and 82 of the Convention of the International Telecommunications Union.

[149] See C. F. Amerasinghe, *Principles of the Institutional Law of International Organisations*, 2nd edn, Cambridge, 2005, pp. 199 ff.

opinions to be given by the International Court or by an arbitral tribunal are to be non-binding.[150] A number of organisations provide for other mechanisms of inquiry and dispute settlement.[151]

There are a number of procedures and mechanisms which seek to resolve disputes in particular areas, usually economic and involving mixed disputes, that is between states and non-state entities. These processes are becoming of considerable significance and many of them are having a meaningful impact upon general international law. This section will briefly survey some of these.

The dispute settlement procedures established under the General Agreement on Tariffs and Trade[152] commenced with bilateral consultations under article XXII.[153] From this point, article XXIII provided for a party to refer a dispute for conciliation[154] where it was felt that 'any benefit accruing to it directly or indirectly' under GATT was being 'nullified or impaired'. A Panel, composed of experts chosen by the Director-General of GATT, then would seek to ascertain the relevant facts and reach a settlement.[155] The approach was pragmatic and focused on achieving a settlement between the parties. The report of the Panel would be sent to the GATT Council, which would usually adopt it by consensus. Where the disputing parties had not implemented the recommendations within a reasonable time, the complaining party was able to take retaliatory action with the authorisation of the Council. Such instances were in fact very rare.[156] In 1989, a series of improvements was adopted pending the conclusion of the Uruguay Round of negotiations. These

---

[150] See article 22(1) of the UN Industrial Development Organisation (UNIDO) Constitution and article 65 of the International Maritime Organisation Constitution.

[151] See the 1962 Special Protocol to the UNESCO Convention against Discrimination in Education which provides for a Conciliation and Good Offices Commission and the 1962 Special Protocol to the ILO Convention against Discrimination in Education which provides for a Conciliation and Good Offices Commission: see Murty, 'Settlement', pp. 729–30, and Bowett's International Institutions, chapter 3. See also the World Intellectual Property Organisation Mediation, Arbitration and Expedited Arbitration Rules 1994, 34 ILM, 1995, p. 559.

[152] See further below, chapter 23, p. 1286.

[153] See UN Handbook, pp. 136 ff.; J. H. Jackson, The World Trading System, 2nd edn, Cambridge, MA, 1997, chapter 4, and T. Flory, 'Les Accords du Tokyo Round du GATT et la Réforme des Procédures de Règlement des Différends dans la Système Commercial Interétatique', 86 RGDIP, 1982, p. 235.

[154] Before this stage, a party could seek the good offices of the Director-General of GATT to facilitate a confidential conciliation: see the 1982 GATT Ministerial Declaration.

[155] See in particular the 1979 Understanding on Dispute Settlement.

[156] See Henkin et al., International Law: Cases and Materials, p. 1414.

improvements included the provision that the Council would normally accept the report of the Panel within fifteen months of the complaint and provisions relating to mediation, conciliation and arbitration were added.[157]

The GATT process was absorbed within the World Trade Organisation, which came into being on 1 January 1995. Annex 2 of the Marrakesh Agreement Establishing the World Trade Organisation, 1994 is entitled 'Understanding on Rules and Procedures Governing the Settlement of Disputes'.[158] Under the WTO scheme, disputes arising out of the agreements contained in the Final Act of the Uruguay Round are dealt with by the WTO General Council acting as the Dispute Settlement Body. Where a member state considers that a measure adopted by another member state has deprived it of a benefit accruing to it directly or indirectly under the GATT or other covered agreements, it may call for consultations with the other party and the latter must reply within ten days and enter into consultations within thirty days of receiving the request. If bilateral consultations have failed to resolve the dispute, the parties may agree to bring the dispute to the WTO Director-General, who may offer good offices, conciliation or mediation assistance. Where consultations fail to produce a settlement after sixty days, the complaining state may turn to the Dispute Settlement Body. This Body may establish a three-member panel, whose report should be produced within six months. Detailed procedures are laid down in the Understanding. The panel report is adopted by the

---

[157] See E. Canal-Forgues and R. Ostrihansky, 'New Developments in GATT Dispute Settlement Procedures', 24 *Journal of World Trade*, 1990, and J.-G. Castel, 'The Uruguay Round and the Improvements to the GATT Dispute Settlement Rules and Procedures', 38 ICLQ, 1989, p. 834.

[158] See e.g. A. F. Lowenfeld, *International Economic Law*, 2nd edn, Oxford, 2008, part III; J. H. Jackson, *Sovereignty, the WTO, and Changing Fundamentals of International Law*, Cambridge, 2006, chapter 5; *Dispute Settlement in the WTO* (eds. J. Cameron and K. Campbell), London, 1998; Collier and Lowe, *Settlement*, p. 99; R. Yerxa and B. Wilson, *Key Issues in WTO Dispute Settlement – The First Ten Years*, Cambridge, 2005; M. Matsushita, T. J. Schoenbaum and P. C. Mavroidis, *The World Trade Organization: Law, Practice, and Policy*, 2nd edn, Oxford, 2006; T. Broude, *International Governance in the WTO: Judicial Boundaries and Political Capitulation*, London, 2004; D. Z. Cass, *The Constitutionalization of the World Trade Organization: Legitimacy, Democracy, and Community in the International Trading System*, Oxford, 2005; *Bowett's International Institutions*, p. 379; A. H. Qureshi, *International Economic Law*, London, 1999, p. 287; J. Pauwelyn, 'Enforcement and Countermeasures in the WTO', 94 AJIL, 2000, p. 335, and J. Cameron and K. R. Gray, 'Principles of International Law in the WTO Dispute Settlement Body', 50 ICLQ, 2001, p. 248. See also WTO Secretariat, *The WTO Dispute Settlement Procedures*, 2nd edn, Cambridge, 2001 and www.wto.org/english/tratop_e/dispu_e/dispu_e.htm.

Dispute Settlement Body within sixty days, unless there is a consensus against adoption or one of the parties notifies an intention to appeal on grounds of law. The standing Appellate Body established by the Dispute Settlement Body consists of seven experts, three of whom may sit to hear appeals at any one time. Appeal proceedings generally are to last no more than sixty (or at most ninety) days. Unless there is a consensus against adoption within thirty days, the Dispute Settlement Body will accept the Appellate Body report.

Within thirty days of the adoption of the report, the parties must agree to comply with the recommendations and if this does not happen within a reasonable period, the party concerned must offer mutually acceptable compensation. If after twenty days, no satisfactory compensation is agreed, the complaining state may request authorisation from the Dispute Settlement Body to suspend concessions or obligations against the other party and this should be granted within thirty days of the end of the reasonable period. In any event, the Dispute Settlement Body will monitor the implementation of rulings or recommendations.[159]

There are two particular points to make. First, there have been a significant number of cases initiated before the Dispute Settlement Body[160] and, secondly, the establishment of an Appellate Body, composed of trade law experts, is having an important impact upon the development of international trade law.[161] As a reflection of the latter, a number of issues of general international law interest have been dealt with, ranging from consideration of the Vienna Convention on the Law of Treaties and treaty

---

[159] Rules of Conduct were adopted in December 1996: see WT/DSB/RC/1 and www. wto.org/english/tratop_e/dispu_e/rc_e.htm. See also the Working Procedures for Appellate Review, WT/AB/WP/4 and www.wto.org/english/tratop_e/dispu_e/ab_e.htm. The Doha Ministerial Declaration of November 2001 stated that negotiations on improvements and clarifications of the Dispute Settlement Understanding would take place with a view to agreement by May 2003. However, negotiations are continuing: see e.g. Hong Kong Ministerial Declaration of December 2005, WT/MIN(05)/DEC.

[160] Over 200 by mid-2000: see Cameron and Gray, 'WTO Dispute Settlement', p. 250, and 373 by early March 2008: see www.wto.org/english/tratop_e/dispu_e/dispu_status_e.htm.

[161] See e.g. D. M. McRae, 'The Emerging Appellate Jurisdiction in International Trade Law' in Campbell and Cameron, *Dispute Settlement*, p. 1, and Jackson, *Sovereignty, the WTO*, pp. 163 ff. There have been eighty-six notices of appeal as of the end of 2007: see Annual Report of the Appellate Body, 2007, Annex III. Lowenfeld, *International Economic Law*, p. 211, concludes that the WTO Dispute Settlement Mechanism 'is a great success – more so than any other arrangement for resolving international legal disputes at government level'.

interpretation¹⁶² to questions relating to procedural issues such as burden of proof.¹⁶³

A number of regional dispute mechanisms concerning economic questions have been established. The most developed is the European Union, which has a fully functioning judicial system with the Court of Justice in Luxembourg with wide-ranging jurisdiction.¹⁶⁴ Other relevant, but modest regional economic mechanisms include Mercosur (Argentina, Brazil, Paraguay and Uruguay),¹⁶⁵ Comesa¹⁶⁶ and ECOWAS.¹⁶⁷

The North American Free Trade Agreement (NAFTA), 1992, linking the US, Mexico and Canada, aims at the free movement and liberalisation of goods, services, people and investment, and also contains dispute settlement provisions.¹⁶⁸ The principal mechanisms are contained in Chapters 11, 14, 19 and 20 of the Agreement. Under Chapter 11¹⁶⁹ investment disputes may be raised by individual investors of one state party against another state party and, if not resolved by negotiations, may be submitted to arbitration either under the World Bank's International Centre for the Settlement of Investment Disputes (ICSID) or the ICSID Additional Facility or the rules of the United Nations Commission for International

¹⁶² See e.g. the *Standards for Reformulated and Conventional Gasoline* case, 1996, WT/DS2/AB/R and the *Import Prohibition of Certain Shrimp and Shrimp Products* case, 1998, WT/DS58/AB/R. See also D. Palmeter and P. C. Mavroidis, 'The WTO Legal System: Sources of Law', 92 AJIL, 1998, p. 398, and Jackson, *Sovereignty, the WTO*, pp. 182 ff.
¹⁶³ See e.g. *Imports of Agricultural, Textile and Industrial Products*, 1999, WT/DS90/AB/R.
¹⁶⁴ As to which see e.g. D. Chalmers, C. Hadjiemmanuil, G. Monti and A. Tomkins, *European Union Law: Text and Materials*, Cambridge, 2006; S. Weatherill and P. Beaumont, *EU Law*, 3rd edn, London, 1999, and Weatherill, *Cases and Materials on EU Law*, 8th edn, Oxford, 2007; and A. Arnull, *The European Court of Justice*, 2nd edn, Oxford, 2006.
¹⁶⁵ See the Mercosur Treaty, 1991. The Protocol of Brasilia, 1991 (complemented by Decision 17 1998) establishes a rudimentary dispute settlement system for states parties based upon diplomatic negotiations with arbitration as a last resort. Arbitration was not used until 1999 and the first arbitral award was the *Siscomex* case: see D. Ventura, 'First Arbitration Award in Mercosur – A Community Law in Evolution?', 14 *Leiden Journal of International Law*, 2000, p. 447. See also www.mercosur.int/msweb/.
¹⁶⁶ See the Treaty Establishing the Common Market for Eastern and Southern Africa, 1993.
¹⁶⁷ The Economic Community of West African States: see the treaty of 1975 and revisions of 1993 and 2001 and Protocol 1 on the Community Court of Justice, 1999.
¹⁶⁸ See 32 ILM, 1993, pp. 682 ff. See also *Bowett's International Institutions*, p. 222; D. S. Huntington, 'Settling Disputes under the North American Free Trade Agreement', 34 *Harvard International Law Journal*, 1993, p. 407; Collier and Lowe, *Settlement*, p. 111; N. Kinnear, A. Bjorkland and J. Hannaford, *Investment Disputes under NAFTA*, The Hague, 2006, and *NAFTA Investment Law and Arbitration: Past Issues, Current Practice, Future Prospects* (ed. T. Weiler), Ardsley, 2004. See also www.nafta-sec-alena.org/DefaultSite/index_e.aspx.
¹⁶⁹ Articles 1101–14 of the Agreement.

Trade Law (UNCITRAL).[170] Tribunals established under NAFTA must apply both the NAFTA Treaty and applicable rules of international law.[171] Interim measures of protection may be ordered and the award of the tribunal is final and binding.[172] Questions relating to interpretation of the Treaty must be remitted to the Free Trade Commission,[173] whose interpretations are binding.[174] Chapter 19 provides for bi-national panel reviews of anti-dumping, countervailing duty and injury final determinations. These panels may also review amendments made by any of the state parties to their anti-dumping or countervailing duty law.[175]

The dispute settlement provisions of Chapter 20 are applicable primarily to inter-state disputes concerning the interpretation or application of the NAFTA, including disputes relating to the financial services provisions of Chapter 14. Should attempts to resolve the particular dispute by consultation within certain time limits, and good offices, mediation and conciliation by the Free Trade Commission within certain time limits fail, the parties may request that the Commission establish a five-person Arbitral Panel.[176]

A neutral chairperson is chosen within fifteen days by the parties in dispute (or by one of the parties chosen by lot if there is no agreement) and within a further fifteen days, two panellists of the nationality of the opposing party are chosen by each party.[177] The panel may obtain expert advice and a Scientific Review Board may be created to provide assistance on technical factual questions raised by the parties. The panel provides an Initial Report, within ninety days of the appointment of the last panellist, as to its findings and recommendations. Comments may then be received from the parties and the panel may reconsider its report. Within thirty days of the Initial Report, the panel will send its Final Report to the

---

[170] See below, p. 1043.   [171] See article 1131.   [172] Articles 1134 and 1136.

[173] Established under article 2001 of Chapter 20 and consisting of cabinet-level representation of the states parties with a general remit to supervise implementation of the agreement and to resolve disputes concerning its interpretation and application. The Commission also established and oversees the NAFTA secretariat comprising national sections, article 2002.

[174] See articles 1131 and 1132. See also e.g. with regard to the terms 'fair and equitable treatment' and 'full protection and security' under article 1105, *Mondev International Ltd v. USA* 6 ICSID Reports, 2002, p. 192, paras. 100 ff.; *United Parcel Service of America v. Canada* 7 ICSID Reports, 2002, p. 288, para. 97; *Loewen Group v. USA* 7 ICSID Reports, 2003, p. 442, paras. 124 ff. and *Methanex v. USA*, award of 3 August 2005, Part II, Chapter H, para. 23.

[175] See articles 1903–5.   [176] See articles 2003–8.   [177] See article 2011.

Commission.[178] The parties must then agree to a settlement of the dispute in the light of the panel's recommendations within thirty days.[179] If this does not happen, the complaining party may suspend the application to the party complained against of benefits of equivalent effect until such time as they have reached agreement on a resolution of the dispute.[180]

The World Bank (i.e. the International Bank for Reconstruction and Development and the International Development Association) established in 1993 an Inspection Panel system providing an independent forum for private citizens who believe that their interests have been or may be harmed by a project financed by the World Bank.[181] Upon receipt of a request by such private persons, the three-person Panel decides whether it is within its mandate and, if so, sends it to Bank Management who prepare a response for the Panel. A preliminary review is undertaken by the Panel that includes an independent assessment of the merits of Bank Management's response. A recommendation is then submitted to the Board of the Bank as to whether the claims should be investigated. If the Board approves a recommendation to investigate, the Panel proceeds with the investigation and its findings are then sent to the Board and to Bank Management. The management must then within six weeks submit its recommendations to the Board on what actions the Bank should take in response to the Panel's findings. The Board will then make a final decision as to future action based upon the Panel's findings and the recommendations of Bank Management.[182]

The International Centre for Settlement of Investment Disputes was established under the auspices of the World Bank by the Convention on the Settlement of Investment Disputes Between States and the Nationals of Other States, 1965 and administers ad hoc arbitrations.[183] It constitutes

---

[178] See articles 2014–17.   [179] Article 2018.   [180] Article 2019.

[181] See e.g. I. Shihata, *The World Bank Inspection Panel*, Oxford, 1994; D. L. Clark, *A Citizen's Guide to the World Bank Inspection Panel*, 2nd edn, Washington, 1999; D. Clark, *Demanding Accountability: Civil Society and the World Bank Inspection Panel*, Lanham, 2003; G. Alfredsson, R. Ring and G. Melander, *The Inspection Panel of the World Bank: A Different Complaints Procedure*, The Hague, 2001; 'Conclusions of the Second Review of the World Bank Inspection Panel', 39 ILM, 2000, p. 243, and A. Gowlland Gualtieri, 'The Environmental Accountability of the World Bank to Non-State Actors', 72 BYIL, 2002, p. 213. See also the Inspection Panel's Annual Report, 2006/7.

[182] As of June 2007, forty-six requests had been sent to the Panel, of these thirty-five resulted in Board approval of the Panel's recommendations: see http://siteresources. worldbank.org/EXTINSPECTIONPANEL/Resources/Summary_of_Inpection_Panel_ Cases_%5updated%5D.pdf.

[183] See Lowenfeld, *International Economic Law*, pp. 536 ff.; R. Dolzer and C. Schreuer, *Principles of International Investment Law*, Oxford, 2008, pp. 222 ff.; C. Schreuer, *The ICSID*

a framework within which conciliation and arbitration takes place and provides an autonomous system free from municipal law in which states and non-state investors (from member states) may settle disputes. States parties to the Convention[184] undertake to recognise awards made by arbitration tribunals acting under the auspices of the Centre as final and binding in their territories and to enforce them as if they were final judgments of national courts.[185] The jurisdiction of the Centre extends to 'any legal dispute arising directly out of an investment, between a contracting state . . . and a national of another contracting state, which the parties to the dispute consent in writing to submit to the Centre'.[186] Accordingly, states must not only become parties to the Convention, but also agree in writing to the submission of the particular dispute to the settlement procedure, although this may be achieved in a concession agreement between the investor and the state concerned. In fact, bilateral investment treaties between states parties to the Convention frequently provide for recourse to arbitration under the auspices of the Centre in the event of an investment dispute.[187] Further, a number of multilateral treaties now provide for the submission to ICSID of disputes arising.[188] In 1978, the Centre introduced the ICSID Additional Facility which extends its jurisdiction to include disputes where only one of the parties is a contracting state or a national of a contracting state and disputes not arising directly out of an investment, provided the dispute relates to a transaction which has 'features that distinguish it from an ordinary commercial transaction' and further provides for fact-finding proceedings.

Convention: A Commentary, Cambridge, 2001; Broches, 'The Convention on the Settlement of Investment Disputes', 3 *Columbia Journal of Transnational Law*, 1966, p. 263, and Broches, 'The Convention on the Settlement of Investment Disputes Between States and Nationals of Other States', 136 HR, 1972, p. 350; D. O'Keefe, 'The International Centre for the Settlement of Investment Disputes', 34 YBWA, 1980, p. 286; *The International Arbitral Process: Public and Private* (ed. J. G. Wetter), Dobbs Ferry, 1979, vol. II, p. 139; Collier and Lowe, *Settlement*, p. 59, and P. Muchlinski, *Multinational Enterprises and the Law*, Oxford, 1995, pp. 540 ff. See also www.worldbank.org/icsid/.

[184] In becoming parties, states may expressly include or exclude certain kinds of disputes: see article 25(4). As of 2007, there were 144 contracting states (Bolivia denounced the convention in that year), Annual Report, 2007: see www.worldbank.org/icsid.

[185] Wetter, *Arbitral Process*, vol. II, p. 139.   [186] Article 25(1) of the Convention.

[187] See I. Pogany, 'The Regulation of Foreign Investment in Hungary', 4 *ICSID Review – Foreign Investment Law Journal*, 1989, pp. 39, 51. See also the case of *Asian Agricultural Products* v. *Sri Lanka* 30 ILM, 1991, p. 577.

[188] See e.g. article 1120 of the NAFTA Treaty, 1992 and *Metalclad Corporation* v. *United Mexican States* 119 ILR, p. 615. See also article 26(4) of the European Energy Charter, 1995.

The Convention requires individuals to be nationals of a state other than the one complained against and article 25(2) specifically excludes dual nationals. Nationality is determined according to the rules of the state of nationality claimed and must exist both at the date on which the parties consented to submit such dispute to conciliation or arbitration as well as on the date on which the request was registered. The same principles apply to companies, except that article 25(2)b includes also juridical persons which had the nationality of the contracting state party to the dispute on the date on which consent to submission of the dispute occurred and which 'because of foreign control, the parties agreed should be treated as a national of another contracting state for the purposes of this Convention'. This may be achieved in a bilateral investment treaty and may be implied in the circumstances.[189]

Disputes are referred to conciliation commissions or arbitral tribunals constituted under ICSID's auspices. Conciliation has been rare, but arbitration more frequent.[190] The Secretary-General may be asked to establish an Arbitral Tribunal by either party to a dispute that falls within the jurisdiction of ICSID. The parties nominate an uneven number of arbitrators with the chosen arbitrators deciding upon a neutral president of the tribunal. The applicable law is as agreed by the parties and otherwise the law of the contracting state party to the dispute together with such rules of international law as may be applicable.[191] Awards are binding and not subject to any appeal or other remedy other than those provided within the Convention system itself.[192] Each contracting state is obliged to recognise ICSID awards and enforce pecuniary obligations imposed as if they were final judgments in its own courts.[193] A number of significant awards have now been made.[194]

---

[189] See e.g. *AMCO* v. *Indonesia* 1 ICSID Reports, p. 377.

[190] As of May 2008, 139 cases had been concluded with 125 pending: see www.worldbank.org/icsid/cases/cases.htm.

[191] See Chapter IV of the Convention.   [192] Article 53.

[193] Article 54. However, this is subject to domestic legislation as regards sovereign immunity: see article 55.

[194] See P. Lalive, 'The First "World Bank" Arbitration (*Holiday Inns* v. *Morocco*) – Some Legal Problems', 51 BYIL, 1980, p. 123. See also *AGIP Spa* v. *Government of the Popular Republic of the Congo* 67 ILR, p. 318; *Benvenuti and Bonfant* v. *Government of the Popular Republic of the Congo, ibid.*, p. 345, dealing with questions of state responsibility and damages, and *LETCO* v. *Government of Liberia* 89 ILR, p. 313 and *Tradex Hellas SA* v. *Albania*, 1999, ARB/94/2 concerning expropriation. See also *Metalclad Corporation* v. *United Mexican States* 119 ILR, p. 615, concerning state responsibility, expropriation and compensation

Another procedure of growing importance is the Court of Arbitration of the International Chamber of Commerce.[195] A number of agreements provide for the settlement of disputes by arbitration under the Rules of the International Chamber of Commerce and several cases have been heard.[196] Also to be noted is the set of rules adopted by the UN Commission on International Trade Law (UNCITRAL) in 1966.[197]

An institution which constitutes a mixed model, combining elements of inter-state arbitration with elements of state–individual arbitration is the Iran–United States Claims Tribunal which was established in The Hague by the Claims Settlement Declaration in 1981.[198] The Tribunal is an international arbitral body set up to adjudicate claims of US nationals against Iran and of Iranian nationals against the United States arising out of alleged violations of property rights as a result of the circumstances surrounding the hostage crisis. The Tribunal also has jurisdiction to hear certain official claims between the US and Iran arising out of contractual arrangements for the purchase and sale of goods and services, and disputes relating to the interpretation and implementation of the Claims Settlement Agreement itself. As another indication of its mixed character, article V of the Claims Settlement Declaration provides that the Tribunal shall apply 'such choice of law rules and principles of commercial and

and *SGS Société de Surveillance SA v. Pakistan* 129 ILR, p. 360, concerning e.g. relations between domestic courts and ICSID tribunals and the definition of investment.

[195] See Wetter, *Arbitral Process*, vol. II, p. 145. See also www.iccwbo.org/index_court.asp.

[196] See *Dalmia Cement v. National Bank of Pakistan* 67 ILR, p. 611 and the *Westland Helicopters* case, 80 ILR, p. 595.

[197] See e.g. I. Dore, *The UNCITRAL Framework for Arbitration in Contemporary Perspective*, London, 1993, and www.uncitral.org/en-index.htm.

[198] See 1 Iran–US CTR, pp. 3–56; 20 ILM, 1981, pp. 223 ff. See also *The Jurisprudence of the Iran–United States Claims Tribunal* (ed. G. H. Aldrich), Oxford, 1996; Lowenfeld, *International Economic Law*, pp. 541 ff.; Stewart and Sherman, 'Development at the Iran–United States Claims Tribunal: 1981–1983', 24 Va. JIL, 1983, p. 1; D. Lloyd Jones, 'The Iran–United States Claims Tribunal: Private Rights and State Responsibility', 24 Va. JIL, 1984, p. 259; *The Iran–US Claims Tribunal 1981–83* (ed. R. Lillich), Charlottesville, 1984; *The Iran–United States Claims Tribunal: Its Contribution to the Law of State Responsibility* (eds. R. Lillich and D. B. Magraw), New York, 1998; S. J. Toope, *Mixed International Arbitration*, Cambridge, 1990, chapter 9; D. D. Caron, 'The Nature of the Iran–United States Claims Tribunal and the Evolving Structure of International Dispute Resolution', 84 AJIL, 1990, p. 104; A. Avanessian, *Iran–United States Claims Tribunal in Action*, The Hague, 1993; R. Khan, *The Iran–United States Claims Tribunal*, Dordrecht, 1990; W. Mapp, *The Iran–United States Claims Tribunal: The First Ten Years 1981–1991*, Manchester, 1993, and the *Iran–United States Claims Tribunal Reports*, 1981 to date. See also www.iusct.org/index-english.html.

international law as the Tribunal determines to be applicable, taking into account relevant usages of the trade, contract provisions and changed circumstances'.

In order to ensure payment of awards to US nationals, a Security Account was established with one billion dollars capital from Iranian assets frozen in the US as a result of the hostages crisis. Once the sum falls below $500 million, Iran is under an obligation to replenish the Account.[199] Under the terms of the Agreement, all claims had to be filed by 19 January 1982.[200] The Tribunal has nine judges, three each chosen by Iran and the US and three by the remaining six. It sits in three chambers of three persons each and in important cases in plenary session. It operates under UNCITRAL Rules, save as modified by the parties or the Tribunal.[201] Awards are final and binding and enforceable in any foreign court in accordance with domestic law.[202]

A variety of important issues have been addressed by the Tribunal, including the treatment of dual nationality in claims[203] and in particular issues relating to expropriation.[204] Although claims of under $250,000 are to be represented by the government of the national concerned, claims in excess of this are presented by the individual claimants themselves, while the agents of the two states are present during the hearing with the right of audience.[205] Nevertheless, the Tribunal has emphasised on several occasions that the claim remains that of the individual and is not that of the state, as would be normal in classical state responsibility situations.[206]

Whether this model will be used in other similar situations is an open question, particularly since the trend in the post-war era has tended towards the lump-sum settlement of such disputes.[207] But the value of

---

[199] By early 1989, this had taken place on twenty-six occasions: see 83 AJIL, 1989, p. 915.

[200] Approximately 1,000 claims for amounts of $250,000 or more, and 2,800 claims for amounts of less than $250,000 were filed within the time limit, which does not apply to disputes between the two Governments concerning the interpretation of the Algiers Declarations. By the end of March 2008, there had been 600 awards and 83 interim and interlocutory awards filed and 133 decisions filed. Altogether 3,936 cases had been finalised by award, decision or order: see Communiqué of 25 April 2008.

[201] Article III of the Claims Settlement Declaration.

[202] Article IV of the Claims Settlement Declaration.

[203] See above, chapter 14, p. 815.   [204] See above, chapter 14, p. 827.

[205] See H. Fox, 'States and the Undertaking to Arbitrate', 37 ICLQ, 1988, pp. 1, 21.

[206] See State Party Responsibility for Awards Rendered Against Its Nationals, Case A/21, 14 Iran–US CTR, pp. 324, 330.

[207] See above, chapter 14, p. 840.

the Tribunal in general terms in resolving the large number of claims in question and in addressing significant issues of international law cannot be denied.

The establishment of the UN Compensation Commission constitutes an interesting and significant development.[208] It was created by Security Council resolution 692 (1991) to process claims for compensation for 'any direct loss, damage, including environmental damage and the depletion of natural resources, or injury to foreign Governments, nationals and corporations, as a result of Iraq's unlawful invasion and occupation of Kuwait'.[209] It constitutes a subsidiary organ of the Security Council and comprises a Governing Council (being the fifteen members at any given time of the Security Council), a secretariat and Commissioners appointed to review and resolve claims.[210] In resolution 705 (1991), the Security Council, acting under Chapter VII, decided that compensation to be paid by Iraq should not exceed 30 per cent of the annual value of the exports of petroleum and petroleum products from Iraq.[211] In resolution 706 (1991), the Council authorised states to import a certain amount of Iraqi petroleum and petroleum products in order to pay for essential food and humanitarian purchases by Iraq and provide payments for the UN Compensation Commission via the Compensation Fund.[212]

---

[208] See e.g. D. Campanelli, 'The United Nations Compensation Commission (UNCC): Reflections on its Judicial Character', 4 *The Law and Practice of International Courts and Tribunals*, 2005, p. 107; V. Heiskanen, 'The United Nations Compensation Commission', 296 HR, 2002, p. 314; Collier and Lowe, *Settlement*, p. 41; *The United Nations Compensation Commission: A Handbook* (eds. M. Frigessi di Ratalma and T. Treves), The Hague, 1999; A. Kolliopoulos, *La Commission d'Indemnisation des Nations Unies et le Droit de la Responsabilité Internationale*, Paris, 2001; A. Grattini, 'The UN Compensation Commission: Old Rules, New Procedures on War Reparations', 13 EJIL, 2002, p. 161; D. Caron and B. Morris, 'The United Nations Compensation Commission: Practical Justice, Not Retribution', 13 EJIL, 2002, p. 183, and M. B. Fox, 'Imposing Liability for Losses from Aggressive War: An Economic Analysis of the UN Compensation Commission', 13 EJIL, 2002, p. 201.

[209] Paragraph 16 of resolution 687 (1991) established that 'Iraq ... is liable under international law for any direct loss, damage, including environmental damage and the depletion of natural resources, or injury to foreign Governments, nationals and corporations, as a result of Iraq's unlawful invasion and occupation of Kuwait' and paragraph 18 of the resolution established a fund to pay compensation for such claims together with a Commission to administer it.

[210] See Report of the Secretary-General of 2 May 1991, S/22559.

[211] See also Report of the Secretary-General, S/22661, May 1991.

[212] See also the Report of the Secretary-General, S/23006, 1991 and Security Council resolution 712 (1991).

Iraq at first refused to co-operate,[213] but in 1996, the 'oil for food' scheme put forward in resolution 986 (1995) began to function. This resolution provided also that 30 per cent of the proceeds of such oil sales were to be allocated to the Compensation Fund. This percentage was reduced to 25 per cent in resolution 1330 (2000). The Compensation Commission has received an overwhelming number of claims. Some 2.6 million claims from around 100 states were received.[214] The claims were divided into six categories.[215] The deadline of 1 January 1995 was set for the filing of category A to D claims; 1 January 1996 for the filing of category E and F claims and 1 February 1997 for category F environmental claims. Provisional Rules were adopted by the Commission in 1992.[216] Claims are subject to a preliminary assessment by the secretariat and then sent to panels of commissioners sitting in private. Recommendations are then sent to the Governing Council for decision from which there is no appeal. The first compensation awards were made in spring 1995.[217] By March 2003, 2,597,527 claims had been resolved and $16,708,302,236 compensation paid.[218] The Commission has awarded compensation with regard

---

[213] In resolution 778 (1992) the Council called upon states which held frozen assets representing the proceeds of sales of Iraqi petroleum to transfer these to a special escrow account, from which 30 per cent would be transferred to the Compensation Fund.

[214] See 35 ILM, 1996, p. 942, and Collier and Lowe, *Settlement*, p. 43 (the claims included those from some 1 million Egyptian workers). See also www.unog.ch/uncc/theclaims.htm. The claims amounted to over $300 billion.

[215] Category 'A' claims cover claims of individuals arising from their departure from Iraq or Kuwait between the date of Iraq's invasion of Kuwait on 2 August 1990 and the date of the ceasefire, 2 March 1991, with compensation for successful claims being set by the Governing Council at the fixed sum of US $2,500 for individual claimants and US $5,000 for families. Category 'B' claims cover individual claims for serious personal injury or death of spouse, children or parents, with compensation set at US $2,500 for individual claimants and up to US $10,000 for families. Category 'C' claims cover individual claims for damages up to $100,000. Category 'D' claims cover individual claims for damages above $100,000. Category 'E' claims cover claims of corporations, other private legal entities and public sector enterprises. Category 'F' claims cover claims made by governments and international organisations for various losses. See e.g. Decision 1, S/22885, annex II, paras. 14–16 and S/23765, annex. In Decision 11, it was decided that members of the Allied Coalition Forces were not eligible for compensation unless in accordance with the adopted criteria, the claimants were prisoners-of-war and the loss or injury arose from mistreatment in violation of international humanitarian law, S/24363, annex II, *ibid*. See also A/AC.26/1994/2, reproduced in 34 ILM, 1995, p. 307.

[216] See S/AC.26/1992/10 and 31 ILM, 1992, p. 1053.

[217] S/AC.26/1995/2–5. See also 35 ILM, 1996, p. 956. For examples of claims, see e.g. 109 ILR, p. 1 and the *Egyptian Workers' Claims* 117 ILR, p. 195.

[218] See www.unog.ch/uncc/status.htm.

to damage caused within Saudi Arabia, Israel, Jordan and Gulf states by Iraqi Scud missiles fired during the conflict.[219]

The Commission constitutes an interesting hybrid between a fact-finding political organ and a quasi-judicial mechanism.[220] It has been noted that panels are required, in the absence of specific guidance by the Security Council or the Governing Council, to apply international law.[221] It has had to deal with a remarkable number of claims with great success and has proceeded upon an expedited basis by relying upon computerised handling of smaller claims and without a judicial hearing stage.[222]

Binding methods of dispute settlement

As has been seen, there is a considerable variety of means, mechanisms and institutions established to resolve disputes in the field of international law. However, a special place is accorded to the creation of judicial bodies. Such courts and tribunals may be purely inter-state or permit individuals to appear as applicants or respondents.[223] They may be permanent or temporary, being established to resolve one particular dispute. In resolving disputes, a variety of techniques is likely to be used and references to judicial bodies should be seen as part of a larger process of peaceful settlement. As Jennings has written, 'the adjudicative process can serve, not only to resolve classical legal disputes, but it can also serve as an important tool of preventive diplomacy in more complex situations'.[224] The following section will deal with arbitration and the following chapter with the International Court of Justice.

---

[219] See the Report and Recommendations Concerning the Third Instalment of 'E2' Claims, S/AC.26/1999/R.40, para. 77.

[220] See the Report of the UN Secretary-General of 2 May 1991, S/22559. This Report in particular emphasised that the Compensation Commission was neither a Court nor an Arbitral Tribunal, but 'a political organ that performs an essentially fact-finding function of examining the claims, verifying their validity, evaluating losses, assessing payments and resolving disputed claims'. It was recognised, however, that 'some elements of due process should be built into the procedure', ibid., para. 20: see Collier and Lowe, Settlement, p. 42, and Merrills, International Dispute Settlement, p. 61. See also the Guidelines adopted by the Governing Council on 2 August 1991, S/22885. Both documents are reproduced in 30 ILM, 1991, pp. 1703 ff. Note that Collier and Lowe refer to the UNCC as prominent amongst 'the most notable recent innovations', Settlement, p. 41.

[221] See article 31 of the Rules and the Egyptian Workers' Claims 117 ILR, pp. 195, 247.

[222] See Collier and Lowe, Settlement, p. 43.   [223] See above, note 2.

[224] R. Y. Jennings, 'Presentation' in Increasing the Effectiveness of the International Court of Justice (eds. C. Peck and R. S. Lee), The Hague, 1997, p. 79.

Arbitration[225]

In determining whether a body established by states to settle a dispute is of a judicial, administrative or political nature, the Tribunal in the *Laguna del Desierto* case emphasised that 'the practice of international law is to look at the nature of the procedure followed by those states before the body in question'.[226]

The procedure of arbitration grew to some extent out of the processes of diplomatic settlement and represented an advance towards a developed international legal system. In its modern form, it emerged with the Jay Treaty of 1794 between Britain and America, which provided for the establishment of mixed commissions to solve legal disputes between the parties.[227] The procedure was successfully used in the *Alabama Claims* arbitration[228] of 1872 between the two countries, which resulted in the UK having to pay compensation for the damage caused by a Confederate warship built in the UK. This success stimulated further arbitrations, for example the *Behring Sea*[229] and *British Guiana and Venezuela Boundary*[230] arbitrations at the close of the nineteenth century.[231]

The 1899 Hague Convention for the Pacific Settlement of Disputes included a number of provisions on international arbitration, the object of

---

[225] See e.g. Merrills, *International Dispute Settlement*, chapter 5; Wetter, *Arbitral Process*; L. Simpson and H. Fox, *International Arbitration*, London, 1959; L. Malintoppi, 'Methods of Dispute Resolution in Inter-State Litigation: When States Go To Arbitration Rather Than Adjudication', 5 *The Law and Practice of International Courts and Tribunals*, 2006, p. 133; L. Caflisch, 'L'Avenir de l'Arbitrage Interétatique', AFDI, 1979, p. 9; B. S. Murty, 'Settlement'. See also Nguyen Quoc Dinh *et al.*, *Droit International Public*, p. 866; Oellers-Frahm and Zimmermann, *Dispute Settlement*; Economides, 'L'Obligation de Règlement Pacifique'; S. Schwebel, *International Arbitration: Three Salient Problems*, Cambridge, 1987; A. M. Stuyt, *Survey of International Arbitrations (1794–1984)*, Dordrecht, 1990; V. Coussirat-Coustere and P. M. Eisemann, *Repertory of International Arbitral Jurisprudence*, Dordrecht, 4 vols., 1989–91; C. Gray and B. Kingsbury, 'Developments in Dispute Settlement: International Arbitration since 1945', 63 BYIL, 1992, p. 97; L. Sohn, 'International Arbitration Today', 108 HR, 1976, p. 1; *International Arbitration* (ed. F. Soons), Dordrecht, 1990, and H. Fox, 'States and the Undertaking to Arbitrate', 37 ICLQ, 1988, p. 1.

[226] 113 ILR, pp. 1, 42.

[227] See Simpson and Fox, *International Arbitration*, pp. 1–4, and R. C. Morris, *International Arbitration and Procedure*, New Haven, 1911. Note also the Treaty of Ghent, 1814, which incorporated the concept of a neutral element within the commission, *ibid.* See also G. Schwarzenberger, 'Present-Day Relevance of the Jay Treaty Arbitrations', 53 *Notre Dame Lawyer*, 1978, p. 715.

[228] J. B. Moore, *International Arbitrations*, Washington, DC, 1898, vol. I, p. 495.

[229] *Ibid.*, p. 755.   [230] 92 BFSP, p. 970.

[231] See also 'Projet de Règlement pour la Procédure Arbitrale Internationale', *Annuaire de l'Institut de Droit International*, 1877, p. 126.

which was deemed to be under article 15, 'the settlement of differences between states by judges of their own choice and on the basis of respect for law'. This became the accepted definition of arbitration in international law. It was repeated in article 37 of the 1907 Hague Conventions and adopted by the Permanent Court of International Justice in the case concerning the *Interpretation of Article 3, paragraph 2, of the Treaty of Lausanne*[232] and by the International Court.[233]

International arbitration was held to be the most effective and equitable manner of dispute settlement, where diplomacy had failed. An agreement to arbitrate under article 18 implied the legal obligation to accept the terms of the award. In addition, a Permanent Court of Arbitration was established.[234] It is not really a court since it is not composed of a fixed body of judges. It consists of a panel of persons, nominated by the contracting states[235] (each one nominating a maximum of four), comprising individuals 'of known competency in questions of international law, of the highest moral reputation and disposed to accept the duties of an arbitrator'.[236] Where contracting states wish to go to arbitration, they are entitled to choose the members of the tribunal from the panel. Thus, it is in essence machinery facilitating the establishment of arbitral tribunals. The PCA also consists of an International Bureau, which acts as the registry of the Court and keeps its records, and a Permanent Administrative Council, exercising administrative control over the Bureau. Administrative support was provided in this context by the Bureau in the *Heathrow Airport User Charges* arbitration.[237] The PCA has been used in a variety of cases from an early date.[238]

---

[232] PCIJ, Series B, No. 12, p. 26.

[233] See *Qatar* v. *Bahrain*, ICJ Reports, 2001, para. 113. See also the *Dubai/Sharjah Border Arbitration* 91 ILR, pp. 543, 574 and 575.

[234] See Murty, 'Settlement', p. 685; M. Hudson, *The Permanent Court of International Justice 1920–1942*, New York, 1943, p. 11; *The Permanent Court of Arbitration: International Arbitration and Dispute Settlement* (eds. P. Hamilton, H. C. Requena, L. van Scheltinga and B. Shifman), The Hague, 1999; J. Allain, *A Century of International Adjudication: The Rule of Law and its Limits*, The Hague, 2000, chapter 1, and J. Jonkman, 'The Role of the Permanent Court of Arbitration in International Dispute Resolution', 279 HR, 1999, p. 9. See also www.pca-cpa.org/.

[235] There are currently 107.   [236] Article 44 of the Convention as revised in 1907.

[237] See 88 AJIL, 1994, p. 739, note 4.

[238] See e.g. the UK–France Agreement of 1903, providing for referral of differences of a legal nature to the Permanent Court of Arbitration, so long as the 'vital interests' of the parties were not involved, Cd 1837.

Between 1900 and 1932 some twenty disputes went through the PCA procedure, but from that point the numbers began to fall drastically. However, more recently the PCA has started to play an increasingly important role, so much so that an element of 'institutionalisation' of arbitration has been detected by some writers.[239] It has served as the registry in, for example, the two phases of the *Eritrea–Yemen* arbitration[240] and for the *Eritrea–Ethiopia* Boundary Commission[241] and Claims Commission[242] and in the *Larsen* v. *Hawaiian Kingdom* arbitration.[243] It also provided facilities in cases such as the *Mox* arbitration between the UK and Ireland[244] and *Saluka Investments* v. *Czech Republic*.[245] The PCA has also adopted, for example, Optional Rules for Arbitrating Disputes between Two States,[246] Optional Rules for Arbitrating Disputes between Two Parties of Which Only One is a State,[247] Optional Rules of Arbitration Involving International Organisations and States,[248] and Optional Rules for Arbitration of Disputes Relating to Natural Resources and/or the Environment in 2001.[249] The International Law Commission itself formulated a set of Model Rules on Arbitral Procedure, which was adopted by the General Assembly in 1958.[250]

Arbitration tribunals may be composed in different ways.[251] There may be a single arbitrator or a collegiate body. In the latter case, each party will appoint an equal number of arbitrators with the chairman or umpire

---

[239] See Malintoppi, 'Methods of Dispute Resolution', p. 135. See generally H. Von Mangoldt, 'Arbitration and Conciliation' in Wetter, *Arbitral Process*, vol. V, pp. 243 ff., and D. Johnson, 'International Arbitration Back in Favour?', 34 YBWA, 1980, p. 305.

[240] See 114 ILR, p. 1 (Phase One: Territorial Sovereignty) and 119 ILR, p. 417 (Phase Two: Maritime Delimitation).

[241] Decision of 13 April 2002: see 129 ILR, p. 1.

[242] See S/2001/608. As to some Eritrea–Ethiopia Claims Commission decisions, see above, chapter 13, p. 756, note 319.

[243] See 119 ILR, p. 566.   [244] See 126 ILR, p. 310.   [245] Partial Award of 17 March 2006.

[246] In 1992: see 32 ILM, 1993, p. 572. These are based upon the UNCITRAL (United Nations Commission on International Trade Law) Arbitration Rules, adopted by the UN General Assembly on 15 December 1976 in resolution 31/98.

[247] With effect from 1993: see http://pca-cpa.org/ENGLISH/BD/1stateeng.htm.

[248] With effect from 1996: see http://pca-cpa.org/ENGLISH/BD/2igoenglish.htm.

[249] See www.pca-cpa.org/ENGLISH/EDR/ENRrules.htm.

[250] Resolution 1262 (XI). These are, however, merely optional. See also Report of the ILC, 1958, A/3859. Note also the 1928 General Act, the 1929 General Treaty of Inter-American Arbitration and the 1949 Revised General Act. See also *Yearbook of the ILC*, 1953, vol. II, p. 208.

[251] See e.g. Merrills, *International Dispute Settlement*, pp. 95 ff. It is, of course, an issue for the parties to decide.

being appointed by either the parties or the arbitrators already nominated. In many cases, a head of state will be suggested as a single arbitrator and he will then nominate an expert or experts in the field of international law or other relevant disciplines to act for him.[252] Under the PCA system, and in the absence of agreement to the contrary, each party selects two arbitrators from the panel, only one of whom may be a national of the state. These arbitrators then choose an umpire, but if they fail to do so, this task will be left to a third party, nominated by agreement. If this also fails to produce a result, a complicated process then ensues culminating in the drawing of lots.

States are not obliged to submit a dispute to the procedure of arbitration, in the absence of their consent.[253] This consent may be expressed in arbitration treaties, in which the contracting states agree to submit certain kinds of disputes that may arise between them to arbitration, or in specific provisions of general treaties, which provide for disputes with regard to the treaty itself to be submitted to arbitration,[254] although the number of treaties dealing primarily with the peaceful settlement of disputes has declined since 1945.[255] Consent to the reference of a dispute to arbitration with regard to matters that have already arisen is usually expressed by means of a *compromis*, or special agreement, and the terms in which it is couched are of extreme importance. This is because the jurisdiction of the tribunal is defined in relation to the provisions of the treaty or *compromis*, whichever happens to be the relevant document in the particular case. However, in general, the tribunal may determine its competence in interpreting the *compromis* and other documents concerned in the case.[256]

---

[252] E.g. the *Argentina–Chile* case, 38 ILR, p. 10 and the *Beagle Channel* case, HMSO, 1977; 52 ILR, p. 93. Note also the *Interpretation of Peace Treaties* case, ICJ Reports, 1950, p. 221; 17 ILR, p. 318.

[253] See e.g. the *Eastern Carelia* case, PCIJ, Series B, No. 5, 1923, p. 27; 2 AD, p. 394 and the *Ambatielos* case, ICJ Reports, 1953, p. 19; 20 ILR, p. 547.

[254] See *Arbitration and Security: The Systematic Survey of the Arbitration Conventions and Treaties of Mutual Security Deposited with the League of Nations*, Geneva, 1927, and *Systematic Survey of Treaties for the Pacific Settlement of International Disputes 1928–1948*, New York, 1949.

[255] See L. Sohn, 'Report on the Changing Role of Arbitration in the Settlement of International Disputes', International Law Association, 1966, pp. 325, 334.

[256] In the absence of agreement to the contrary. See e.g. the *Nottebohm* case, ICJ Reports, 1953, pp. 111, 119; 20 ILR, pp. 567, 572. See also article 48 of the Hague Convention, 1899, and article 73 of the Hague Convention, 1907.

The law to be applied in arbitration proceedings is international law,[257] but the parties may agree upon certain principles to be taken into account by the tribunal and specify this in the *compromis*. In this case, the tribunal must apply the rules specified. For example, in the *British Guiana and Venezuela Boundary* dispute,[258] it was stated that occupation for fifty years should be accepted as constituting a prescriptive title to territory. And in the *Trail Smelter* case,[259] the law to be applied was declared to be US law and practice with regard to such questions as well as international law.[260]

Agreements sometimes specify that the decisions should be reached in accordance with 'law and equity' and this means that the general principles of justice common to legal systems should be taken into account as well as the provisions of international law. Such general principles may also be considered where there are no specific rules covering the situation under discussion.[261] The rules of procedure of the tribunal are often specified in the *compromis* and decided by the parties by agreement as the process commences. Hague Convention I of 1899 as revised in 1907 contains agreed procedure principles, which would apply in the absence of express stipulation. It is characteristic of arbitration that the tribunal is competent to determine its own jurisdiction and therefore interpret the relevant

---

[257] See e.g. the *Norwegian Shipowners' Claims* case, 1 RIAA, 1921, p. 309 and the *Dubai/Sharjah* case, 91 ILR, pp. 543, 585–8. Note that article 28 of the 1928 General Act for the Pacific Settlement of International Disputes, as revised in 1949, provides that where nothing is laid down in the arbitration agreement as to the law applicable to the merits of the case, the tribunal should apply the substantive rules as laid down in article 38 of the Statute of the International Court of Justice (i.e. international treaties, custom and general principles of law). See further above, chapter 3, p. 70.

[258] 92 BFSP, p. 970.   [259] 3 RIAA, 1938, p. 1908; 9 AD, p. 315.

[260] Note that in international commercial arbitrations, the reference often incorporates municipal law: see e.g. the *BP* case, 53 ILR, p. 297, where the basic reference was to 'the principles of the Law of Libya common to the principles of international law'. See also the wide reference to the Iran–United States Claims Tribunal to decide all cases 'on the basis of respect for law, applying such choice of law rules and principles of commercial and international law as the Tribunal determines to be applicable, taking into account relevant usages of the trade, contract provisions and changed circumstances', above, p. 1043. By way of contrast, the tribunal in the *OSPAR (Ireland v. UK)* case, operating on the basis of article 32 of the OSPAR Convention, held that the only applicable law was the Convention itself, 126 ILR, p. 334.

[261] See e.g. *Re Competence of the Conciliation Commission* 22 ILR, p. 867 and above, chapter 3, p. 98. See also article 28 of the 1928 General Act as revised in 1949, article 10 of the ILC Model Articles and articles 26 and 28 of the European Convention for the Peaceful Settlement of Disputes. Note in addition the *Rann of Kutch* case, 50 ILR, p. 520.

instruments determining that jurisdiction.[262] Once an arbitral award has been made, it is final and binding upon the parties,[263] but in certain circumstances the award itself may be regarded as a nullity.[264] There is disagreement amongst lawyers as to the grounds on which such a decision may be taken. It is, however, fairly generally accepted that where a tribunal exceeds its powers under the *compromis*, its award may be treated as a nullity, although this is not a common occurrence. Such excess of power (*excès de pouvoir*) may be involved where the tribunal decides a question not submitted to it, or applies rules it is not authorised to apply. The main example of the former is the *North-Eastern Boundary* case[265] between Canada and the United States, where the arbitrator, after being asked to decide which of two lines constituted the frontier, in fact chose a third line.

It is sometimes argued that invalidity of the *compromis* is a ground of nullity,[266] while the corruption of a member of the tribunal or a serious departure from a fundamental rule of procedure are further possibilities as grounds of nullity.[267] Article 35 of the Model Rules on Arbitral Procedure drawn up by the International Law Commission, for example, provides for a successful plea of nullity in three cases: excess of power, corruption of a tribunal member or serious departure from a fundamental rule of procedure, including failure to state the reasons for the award.[268] 'Essential

---

[262] See the *Nottebohm* (*Preliminary Objections*) case, ICJ Reports, 1953, pp. 111, 119; 20 ILR, pp. 567, 571–3. See also Arbitration Commission on Yugoslavia, Interlocutory Decision of 4 July 1992, 92 ILR, pp. 194, 197.

[263] Articles 81 and 84, Hague Convention I, 1907. The principle of *res judicata* also applies to arbitration awards: see e.g. the *Trail Smelter* case, 3 RIAA, 1938, p. 1905; 9 AD, p. 324 and the *Orinoco Steamship Co.* case, 11 RIAA, 1910, p. 227.

[264] See e.g. W. M. Reisman, *Nullity and Revision*, New Haven, 1971; E. K. Nantwi, *The Enforcement of International Judicial Decisions and Arbitral Awards in Public International Law*, Leiden, 1967, and O. Schachter, 'The Enforcement of International Judicial and Arbitral Decisions', 54 AJIL, 1960, p. 1.

[265] See C. C. Hyde, *International Law*, 2nd edn, Boston, 1945, vol. III, p. 1636. See also the *Pelletier* case, *ibid.*, p. 1640; the *Panama–Costa Rica Boundary* case, 11 RIAA, 1900, p. 519 and *US Foreign Relations*, 1914, p. 994; the *Chamizal* case, 11 RIAA, p. 309, and the *Cerruti* arbitrations, 6 AJIL, 1912, p. 965.

[266] See e.g. Murty, 'Settlement', pp. 693–4, and A. D. McNair, *The Law of Treaties*, Oxford, 1961, pp. 66–77.

[267] See Schachter, 'Enforcement', p. 3. See also, as regards corruption, Moore, *International Arbitrations*, vol. II, pp. 1660–4, and the *Buraimi* arbitration, Wetter, *Arbitral Process*, vol. III, p. 357 and 545 HC Deb., col. 199, 1955.

[268] See the *British Guiana and Venezuela Boundary* case, 92 BFSP, p. 160, and Wetter, *Arbitral Process*, vol. III, pp. 81 ff. See also the *Arbitral Award by the King of Spain* case, ICJ Reports, 1960, pp. 188, 216; 30 ILR, pp. 457, 476.

error' has also been suggested as a ground of nullity, but the definition of this is far from unambiguous.[269] It would appear not to cover the evaluation of documents and evidence,[270] but may cover manifest errors[271] such as not taking into account a relevant treaty or a clear mistake as to the appropriate municipal law.[272] Of course, once a party recognises the award as valid and binding, it will not be able to challenge the validity of the award at a later stage.[273] In certain circumstances, it may be open to a party to request a revision or re-opening of the award in order to provide for rectification of an error or consideration of a fact unknown at the time to the tribunal and the requesting party which is of such a nature as to have a decisive influence on the award.[274]

Arbitration as a method of settling disputes combines elements of both diplomatic and judicial procedures. It depends for its success on a certain amount of goodwill between the parties in drawing up the *compromis* and constituting the tribunal, as well as actually enforcing the award subsequently made. A large part depends upon negotiating processes. On the other hand, arbitration is an adjudicative technique in that the award is final and binding and the arbitrators are required to base their decision on law.[275] It will be seen in the following section just how close arbitration is to judicial settlement of disputes by the International Court of Justice, and it is no coincidence that the procedure of arbitration through the PCA began to decline with the establishment and consolidation of the Permanent Court of International Justice in the 1920s.

In recent years, there has been a rise in the number of inter-state arbitrations. The *Rann of Kutch* case,[276] the *Anglo-French Continental Shelf* case,[277] the *Beagle Channel* case[278] and the *Taba* case[279] were all the subject of

---

[269] See e.g. Murty, 'Settlement', p. 696, and Merrills, *International Dispute Settlement*, pp. 113 ff.

[270] *Arbitral Award by the King of Spain*, ICJ Reports, 1960, pp. 188, 215–16; 30 ILR, pp. 457, 475. See also, as regards the Argentinian claim of nullity of the *Beagle Channel* award, 17 ILM, 1978, p. 738; 52 ILR, pp. 267–85.

[271] See the *Trail Smelter* case, 3 RIAA, 1938, pp. 1905, 1957; 9 AD, p. 331.

[272] See e.g. the *Schreck* case, Moore, *International Arbitrations*, vol. II, p. 1357.

[273] *Arbitral Award by the King of Spain*, ICJ Reports, 1960, pp. 188, 213; 30 ILR, p. 473.

[274] See e.g. Wetter, *Arbitral Process*, vol. II, pp. 539 ff. See also article 29 of the ILC Model Rules.

[275] See the definition of arbitration in *Yearbook of the ILC*, 1953, vol. II, p. 202.

[276] 50 ILR, p. 2. See also J. G. Wetter, 'The Rann of Kutch Arbitration', 65 AJIL, 1971, p. 346.

[277] Cmnd 7438, 1978; 54 ILR, p. 6. See further above, chapter 11, p. 593.

[278] HMSO, 1977; 52 ILR, p. 93. See M. N. Shaw, 'The Beagle Channel Arbitration Award', 6 *International Relations*, 1978, p. 415.

[279] 80 ILR, p. 244. See also D. W. Bowett, 'The Taba Award of 29 September 1988', 23 *Israel Law Review*, 1989, p. 429; G. Lagergren, 'The Taba Tribunal 1986–89', 1 *African Journal*

arbitral awards, usually successfully.[280] More recent examples include the *Eritrea–Yemen* arbitration,[281] the *Eritrea–Ethiopia* boundary delimitation case[282] and the *Barbados* v. *Trinidad and Tobago* maritime delimitation case.[283] It may be that further such issues may be resolved in this fashion, although a lot depends on the evaluation of the parties as to the most satisfactory method of dispute settlement in the light of their own particular interests and requirements.

Arbitration is an extremely useful process where some technical expertise is required, or where greater flexibility and speed than is available before the International Court is desired.[284] The states themselves choose the arbitrators, lay down the applicable law and rules of procedure, as well as set the timetable. In addition, the states involved may wish for the proceedings to be confidential, something which is not achievable in the International Court with its public oral hearings and publication of written proceedings. However, the parties pay all the costs of the arbitration, including the fees due to the registrar and arbitrators, while in the International Court, the judges and members of the registry are paid by the UN.[285]

Arbitration may be the appropriate mechanism to utilise as between states and international institutions, since only states may appear before the ICJ in contentious proceedings. The establishment of arbitral tribunals

---

of *International and Comparative Law*, 1989, p. 525, and P. Weil, 'Some Observations on the Arbitral Award in the Taba Case', 23 *Israel Law Review*, 1989, p. 1.

[280] Argentina initially rejected the award in the *Beagle Channel* case, but later mediation and negotiations resolved the issue: see 17 ILM, 1978, p. 738 and 24 ILM, 1985, p. 1.

[281] 114 ILR, p. 1 and 119 ILR, p. 417.

[282] See 129 ILR, p. 1. See also M. N. Shaw, 'Title, Control and Closure? The Experience of the Eritrea–Ethiopia Boundary Commission', 56 ICLQ, 2007, p. 755.

[283] Award of 11 April 2006. See also the *Guyana* v. *Suriname* maritime delimitation case, award of 17 September 2007, see further on maritime delimitations, above, chapter 11, p. 590.

[284] For example in the *Argentina–Chile* case of 1966, the tribunal consisted of a lawyer and two geographical experts, 38 ILR, p. 10. See Malintoppi, 'Methods of Dispute Resolution', and R. Y. Jennings, 'The Differences Between Conducting a Case in the ICJ and in an *Ad Hoc* Tribunal – An Insider's View', *Liber Amicorum Judge Shigeru Oda* (eds. N. Ando, E. McWhinney and R. Wolfrum), The Hague, 2002, p. 893.

[285] Note that article 287 of the Convention on the Law of the Sea, 1982 provides that where a state has not chosen by a written declaration one of the dispute settlement methods laid down, it will be deemed to have opted for arbitration under Annex VII of the Convention. In the case of such arbitrations, the parties nominate one each of the five-member tribunal, with the remaining members being chosen by agreement. In the absence of such agreement, the President of the International Tribunal for the Law of the Sea will make the necessary appointments: see e.g. the *Barbados* v. *Trinidad and Tobago* arbitration of 11 April 2006 and the *Guyana* v. *Suriname* arbitration of 17 September 2007.

has often been undertaken in order to deal relatively quietly and cheaply with a series of problems within certain categories, for example, the mixed tribunals established after the First World War to settle territorial questions, or the Mexican Claims commissions which handled various claims against Mexico.[286] An attempt was made to tackle issues raised by the situation in the Former Yugoslavia by the establishment of an Arbitration Commission.[287] However, the Commission, while issuing a number of Opinions on issues concerning, for example, statehood, recognition, human rights and boundary matters, was not able to act as an arbitration tribunal as between the parties to the conflict.

Like arbitration, judicial settlement is a binding method of dispute settlement, but by means of an established and permanent body. There are a number of international and regional courts deciding disputes between subjects of international law, in accordance with the rules and principles of international law.[288] However, by far the most important, both by prestige and jurisdiction, is the International Court of Justice, and this is the subject of the following chapter.

Suggestions for further reading

J. Collier and V. Lowe, *The Settlement of Disputes in International Law*, Cambridge, 1999

J. G. Merrills, *International Dispute Settlement*, 4th edn, Cambridge, 2005

F. Orrego Vicuña, *International Dispute Settlement in an Evolving Global Society: Constitutionalization, Accessibility, Privatization*, Cambridge, 2004

United Nations, *Handbook on the Peaceful Settlement of Disputes Between States*, New York, 1992

---

[286] See e.g. A. H. Feller, *Mexican Claims Commissions 1923–1934*, New York, 1935.

[287] Established pursuant to the Declaration of 27 August 1991 of the European Community: see Bull. EC, 7/8 (1991). See generally, M. Craven, 'The EC Arbitration Commission on Yugoslavia', 66 BYIL, 1995, p. 333.

[288] See above, note 2.

19

The International Court of Justice[1]

The impetus to create a world court for the international community developed as a result of the atmosphere engendered by the Hague Conferences of 1897 and 1907. The establishment of the Permanent Court of Arbitration, although neither permanent nor, in fact, a court, marked

---

[1] See e.g. S. Rosenne, *The Law and Practice of the International Court, 1920–2005*, 4th edn, Leiden, 4 vols., 2006, and Rosenne, *The World Court*, 6th edn, Dordrecht, 2005; *The Statute of the International Court of Justice: A Commentary* (eds. A. Zimmermann, C. Tomuschat and K. Oellers-Frahm), Oxford, 2006; M. S. M. Amr, *The Role of the International Court of Justice as the Principal Judicial Organ of the United Nations*, The Hague, 2003; G. Guillaume, *La Cour Internationale de Justice à l'Aube du XXIe Siècle: Le Regard d'un Juge*, Paris, 2003; *Fifty Years of the International Court of Justice* (eds. A. V. Lowe and M. Fitzmaurice), Cambridge, 1996; G. G. Fitzmaurice, *The Law and Procedure of the International Court of Justice*, Cambridge, 2 vols., 1986; H. Thirlway, 'The Law and Procedure of the International Court of Justice (1960–1989)' series of articles in the *British Year Book of International Law* from volume 60, 1989 to volume 70, 2003, and Thirlway, 'The Law and Procedure of the International Court of Justice 1960–1989, Supplement 2005: Parts One and Two', 76 BYIL, 2005, p. 1, and Thirlway, 'The Law and Procedure of the International Court of Justice 1960–1989, Supplement 2006: Part Three', 77 BYIL, 2006, p. 1; R. Y. Jennings, 'The International Court of Justice after Fifty Years', 89 AJIL, 1995, p. 493, and Jennings, 'The Role of the International Court of Justice', 68 BYIL, 1997, p. 1; G. Guyomar, *Commentaire du Règlement de la CIJ*, Paris, 1983; E. McWhinney, *The World Court and the Contemporary Law-Making Process*, Alphen aan den Rijn, 1979; T. O. Elias, *The International Court of Justice and Some Contemporary Problems*, Alphen aan den Rijn, 1983; J. G. Merrills, *International Dispute Settlement*, Cambridge, 4th edn, 2005, chapters 6 and 7; *The Future of the International Court of Justice* (ed. L. Gross), Dobbs Ferry, 2 vols., 1976; *The International Court of Justice at a Crossroads* (ed. L. Damrosch), Dobbs Ferry, 1987; E. Lauterpacht, *Aspects of the Administration of International Justice*, Cambridge, 1991; T. M. Franck, 'Fairness in the International Legal and Institutional System', 240 HR, 1993 III, pp. 13, 302; R. Higgins, *Problems and Process*, Oxford, 1994, chapter 11; *Increasing the Effectiveness of the International Court of Justice* (eds. C. Peck and R. S. Lee), The Hague, 1997; *The International Court of Justice: Its Future Role after Fifty Years* (eds. A. S. Muller, D. Raič and J. M. Thuránszky), The Hague, 1997; Nguyen Quoc Dinh, P. Daillier and A. Pellet, *Droit International Public*, 7th edn, Paris, 2002, p. 889; B. S. Murty, 'Settlement of Disputes' in *Manual of Public International Law* (ed. M. Sørensen), London, 1968, p. 673; K. H. Kaikobad, *The International Court of Justice and Judicial Review*, The Hague, 2000, and E. McWhinney, *Judicial Settlement of International Disputes*, Alphen aan den Rijn, 1991.

an important step forward in the consolidation of an international legal system.[2] However, no lasting concrete steps were taken until after the conclusion of the First World War. The Covenant of the League of Nations called for the formulation of proposals for the creation of a world court and in 1920 the Permanent Court of International Justice (PCIJ) was created. It stimulated efforts to develop international arbitral mechanisms. Together with arbitration, the Permanent Court was intended to provide a reasonably comprehensive system serving the international community. It was intended as a way to prevent outbreaks of violence by enabling easily accessible methods of dispute settlement in the context of a legal and organisational framework to be made available.[3]

The PCIJ was superseded after the Second World War by the International Court of Justice (ICJ), described in article 92 of the Charter as the 'principal judicial organ' of the United Nations. In essence, it is a continuation of the Permanent Court, with virtually the same statute and jurisdiction, and with a continuing line of cases, no distinction being made between those decided by the PCIJ and those by the ICJ.[4]

The organisation of the Court [5]

The ICJ is composed of fifteen members:

> elected regardless of their nationality, from among persons of high moral character, who possess the qualifications required in their respective countries for appointment to the highest judicial offices, or are jurisconsults of recognised competence in international law.[6]

The procedure for the appointment of judges is interesting in that it combines both legal and political elements, while seeking to exclude as far as possible the influence of national states over them. The system established by the Root–Phillimore plan in 1920 is in essence followed. This plan played a large part in the actual creation of the PCIJ and

---

[2] See above, chapter 18, p. 1049.
[3] For an assessment of its work, see e.g. Rosenne, *Law and Practice*, vol. I, pp. 16 ff.
[4] See e.g. M. Shahabuddeen, *Precedent in the World Court*, Cambridge, 1996, pp. 22 ff.
[5] See e.g. Rosenne, *Law and Practice*, vol. I, chapter 6 and vol. III, chapter 17. See also H. Thirlway, 'Procedural Law and the International Court of Justice' in Lowe and Fitzmaurice, *Fifty Years of the International Court of Justice*, p. 389.
[6] Article 2, Statute of the ICJ.

succeeded in allaying many suspicions regarding the composition of the proposed Court.[7]

The members of the Court are elected by the General Assembly and Security Council (voting separately) from a list of qualified persons drawn up by the national groups of the Permanent Court of Arbitration, or by specially appointed national groups in the case of UN members that are not represented in the PCA.[8] This provision was inserted to restrict political pressures in the selection of judges. The elections are staggered and take place once every three years, with respect to five judges each time. In this way some element of continuity amongst the Court is maintained.

In practice, there is close co-ordination between the Assembly and Security Council in electing judges and political factors do obtrude, especially in view of the requirement contained in article 9 of the Statute that the

> electors should bear in mind not only that the persons to be elected should individually possess the qualifications required, but also that in the body as a whole the representation of the main forms of civilisation and of the principal legal systems of the world should be assured.

This process has attracted much criticism on the grounds of attendant politicisation but in the circumstances it is difficult to see a way to avoid this completely.[9] The opinions of individual judges can be crucial, particularly in sensitive cases, and the alteration in the stance adopted by the Court with regard to the *Namibia* case between 1966[10] and 1971[11] can be attributed in large measure to changes in the composition of the Court that took place in the intervening period. Candidates must obtain an absolute majority of votes in both the Assembly and the Council,[12] and no two successful applicants may be of the same nationality.[13]

The members of the Court are elected for nine years and may be re-elected.[14] They enjoy diplomatic privileges and immunities when on

---

[7] See e.g. Murty, 'Settlement', p. 700. See also L. Lloyd, *Peace Through Law*, London, 1997.

[8] Articles 4 and 5 of the ICJ Statute. In practice, governments exercise a major influence upon the nominations process of the national groups: see Merrills, *International Dispute Settlement*, pp. 147 ff.

[9] See e.g. Rosenne, *Law and Practice*, vol. I, pp. 382 ff., and Rosenne, 'The Composition of the Court' in Gross, *Future of the International Court of Justice*, vol. I, pp. 377, 381–6. See also G. Abi-Saab, 'The International Court as a World Court' in Lowe and Fitzmaurice, *Fifty Years of the International Court of Justice*, p. 3.

[10] ICJ Reports, 1966, p. 6; 37 ILR, p. 243.

[11] ICJ Reports, 1971, p. 16; 49 ILR, p. 2.   [12] Article 10, Statute of the ICJ.

[13] Article 3, Statute of the ICJ.   [14] Article 13, Statute of the ICJ.

official business,[15] and a judge cannot be dismissed unless it is the unanimous opinion of the other members of the Court that he or she has ceased to fulfil the required conditions.[16] These include the requirement that no member may exercise any political or administrative function or engage in any other professional occupation. No member may act as agent, advocate, or counsel in any case and no member may participate in the decision of any case in which he has previously taken part as agent, advocate or counsel for one of the parties, or as a member of a national or international court, or of a commission of inquiry, or in any other capacity.[17] The Court elects a president and vice-president for a three-year term which can be renewed,[18] and it is situated at The Hague.[19]

Since the aim of the election procedures relating to the composition of the Court is to produce a judicial body of independent members rather than state representatives, the Statute provides in article 31 that judges of the nationality of each of the parties in a case before the Court shall retain their right to sit in that case. However, the effect of this is somewhat reduced by the provision in that article that the parties to a dispute before the ICJ are entitled to choose a person to sit as judge for the duration of that case, where they do not have a judge of their nationality there

---

[15] Article 19, Statute of the ICJ.   [16] Article 18, Statute of the ICJ.

[17] Articles 16 and 17, Statute of the ICJ. Note the problem raised particularly in the *Namibia* case, ICJ Reports, 1971, pp. 3, 6 and 9, of judges who had previously been involved in the dispute albeit in another capacity. The Court did not accept the need to remove the judges in question. Practice, however, has been variable and, for example, Judges Fleischhauer (former UN Legal Counsel) and Higgins (former member of the Human Rights Committee) felt unable to take part in the *Application of the Genocide Convention* case: see CR 96/5, 29 April 1996, p. 6. In the *Construction of a Wall* case, ICJ Reports, 2004, pp. 136, 142; 129 ILR, pp. 37, 58–9, and the Court's Order of 30 January 2004, objections made to the participation of Judge Elaraby for playing a 'leading role in recent years in the very Emergency Special Session from which the advisory opinion request has now emerged' and other diplomatic and political involvement in the Middle East question prior to election to the Court were dismissed by the Court, citing the *Namibia* opinion. See also Rosenne, 'Composition', pp. 388–90, and *Law and Practice*, vol. I, pp. 400 ff. and vol. III, pp. 1056 ff.; P. Couvreur, 'Article 17' in Zimmermann *et al.*, *Statute of the International Court*, p. 337; H. Thirlway, 'The Law and Procedure of the International Court of Justice 1960–1989', 72 BYIL, 2001, p. 38, and M. N. Shaw, 'The International Court of Justice: A Practical Perspective', 46 ICLQ, 1997, pp. 831, 845–6.

[18] Article 21, Statute of the ICJ.

[19] Article 22, Statute of the ICJ. Note that article 31(5) of the Statute provides that where there are several parties 'in the same interest' they shall be treated *inter alia* for the purposes of appointing ad hoc judges as one party only: see Rosenne, *Law and Practice*, vol. III, p. 1093, and *Serbia and Montenegro* v. *Belgium*, ICJ Reports, 2004, pp. 279, 287.

already.[20] This procedure of appointing ad hoc judges may be criticised as possibly adversely affecting the character of the Court as an independent organ of legal experts.[21] The reason for the establishment and maintenance of the provision may be found within the realm of international politics and the need for political legitimacy and can only be understood as such.[22] Nevertheless, it may be argued that the procedure increases the judicial resources available to the Court in enabling the appointing state's arguments to be fully appreciated.[23] Judge ad hoc Lauterpacht in the *Application of the Genocide (Provisional Measures)* case in a discussion of the nature of the ad hoc judge, declared that together with the duty of impartiality, the ad hoc judge has the special obligation to ensure that so far as is reasonable, every relevant argument in favour of the party appointing him has been fully appreciated in the course of collegial reflection.[24] In practice the institution has not resulted in any disruption of the functioning of the ICJ.[25] While it is overwhelmingly the case that ad hoc judges

---

[20] It is possible for states in this position not to appoint ad hoc judges: see e.g. the *Temple of Preah Vihear* case, ICJ Reports, 1962, p. 6; 33 ILR, p. 48. Note that in *Djibouti v. France*, ICJ Reports, 2008, para. 6, an ad hoc judge was appointed for France as the French judge on the Court recused himself.

[21] See e.g. H. Lauterpacht, *The Function of Law in the International Community*, Oxford, 1933, pp. 215 ff. This provision should be distinguished from article 27(2) of the European Convention on Human Rights, which similarly provides for the appointment of an ad hoc judge to the Court. In this case, the Court deals with the provisions of municipal law of the member states of the Council of Europe and measures their conformity with the Convention. It is thus necessary to retain some expertise as to the domestic system in the case in question. Note that it is possible for an ad hoc judge to be of the same nationality as that of one of the permanent judges: see e.g. *Liechtenstein v. Germany*, ICJ Reports, 2005, p. 6, and Rosenne, *Law and Practice*, vol. III, p. 1092, note 68.

[22] See e.g. S. Schwebel, 'National Judges and Judges Ad Hoc of the International Court of Justice', 48 ICLQ, 1998, p. 889; N. Valticos, 'L'Évolution de la Notion de Judge *Ad Hoc*', 50 *Revue Hellénique de Droit International*, 1997, pp. 11–12; H. Thierry, 'Au Sujet du Juge *Ad Hoc*', in *Liber Amicorum Judge Ruda* (eds. C. A. Armas Barea *et al.*), The Hague, 2000, p. 285; P. Kooijmans, 'Article 31' in Zimmermann *et al.*, *Statute of the International Court*, p. 495; Rosenne, *Law and Practice*, vol. III, pp. 1085 ff., and L. V. Prott, *The Latent Power of Culture and the International Judge*, Abingdon, 1979.

[23] See Franck, 'Fairness', p. 312. See also N. Singh, *The Role and Record of the International Court of Justice*, Dordrecht, 1989, pp. 193–4.

[24] ICJ Reports, 1993, pp. 325, 408–9; 95 ILR, pp. 43, 126–7, and see also at the Counter-Claims Order phase of the case, ICJ Reports, 1997, pp. 243, 278; 115 ILR, p. 206. Judge Lauterpacht's views were cited with approval by Judge ad hoc Franck in his Dissenting Opinion in *Indonesia/Malaysia*, ICJ Reports, 2002, pp. 625, 693.

[25] Note that Practice Direction VII of the Court now requires that 'parties, when choosing a judge *ad hoc* pursuant to Article 31 of the Statute and Article 35 of the Rules of Court, should refrain from nominating persons who are acting as agent, counsel or advocate in another case before the Court or have acted in that capacity in the three years preceding

support the state that has so nominated them, this is not invariably so.[26] The Court has also permitted the use of ad hoc judges in advisory proceedings, although only where it has found that an opinion is requested 'upon a legal question' actually pending between two or more states.[27]

Article 29 of the Statute of the ICJ provides for the establishment of a Chamber of Summary Procedure for the speedy dispatch of business by five judges. It has not as yet been called upon. More controversially, a seven-member Chamber for Environmental Matters was established in July 1993.[28] Article 26 permits the creation of Chambers composed of three or more members as the Court may determine for dealing with particular categories of cases[29] or to deal with a particular case. This procedure was revised in the 1978 Rules of Court[30] and used for the first time in the *Gulf of Maine* case.[31] The question of the composition of the Chamber is decided by the Court after the parties have been consulted, and in such cases the identity of the judges to comprise the Chamber is clearly of critical value. In the *Gulf of Maine* case it was alleged that Canada and the US threatened to withdraw the case if their wishes as to composition were not carried out.[32] Judge Oda has underlined that 'in practical terms, therefore, it is inevitable, if a chamber is to be viable, that its composition must result from a consensus between the parties and the Court', although the

the date of the nomination. Furthermore, parties should likewise refrain from designating as agent, counsel or advocate in a case before the Court a person who sits as judge *ad hoc* in another case before the Court.' Practice Direction VIII provides in addition that 'parties should refrain from designating as agent, counsel or advocate in a case before the Court a person who in the three years preceding the date of the designation was a Member of the Court, judge *ad hoc*, Registrar, Deputy-Registrar or higher official of the Court'.

[26] See e.g. the *Application for Revision and Interpretation of the Judgment* made in the *Tunisia/Libya* case, ICJ Reports, 1985, p. 192; 81 ILR, p. 419, and the *Great Belt* (*Finland* v. *Denmark*) case, ICJ Reports, 1991, p. 12; 94 ILR, p. 446.

[27] See article 102(3) of the Rules of Court 1978. See the *Western Sahara* case, ICJ Reports, 1975, p. 12; 59 ILR, p. 30. Cf. the *Namibia* case, ICJ Reports, 1971, p. 16; 49 ILR, p. 2. See also L. Gross, 'The International Court of Justice: Consideration of Requirements for Enhancing its Roles in the International Legal Order' in Gross, *Future of the International Court of Justice*, vol. I, p. 61.

[28] See International Court of Justice, *Yearbook 1993–1994*, The Hague, 1994, p. 18. It has not yet been called upon, no doubt partly because whether or not an issue is an environmental one may indeed be very much in dispute between the parties: see R. Higgins, 'Respecting Sovereign States and Running a Tight Ship', 50 ICLQ, 2001, pp. 121, 122.

[29] Labour cases and cases relating to transit and communications are specifically mentioned.

[30] See articles 15–18 and 90–3 of the Rules of Court.

[31] ICJ Reports, 1982, p. 3 and *ibid.*, 1984, p. 246; 71 ILR, p. 58. The Chamber consisted of Judge Ago (President) and Judges Gros, Mosler and Schwebel and Judge ad hoc Cohen.

[32] See e.g. Merrills, *International Dispute Settlement*, p. 150, and Brauer, 'International Conflict Resolution: The ICJ Chambers and the Gulf of Maine Dispute', 23 Va. JIL, 1982–3, p. 463. See also Singh, *Role and Record*, p. 110.

Chamber is a component of the Court and 'the process of election whereby it comes into being should be as judicially impartial as its subsequent functioning'.[33]

Recourse to a Chamber provides the parties with flexibility in the choice of judges to hear the case and to that extent parallels arbitration.[34] Of the first two matters before Chambers of the Court, perhaps the more interesting from the perspective of the future development of the ICJ was the *Burkina Faso–Mali* case,[35] since African states had hitherto been most reluctant in permitting third-party binding settlement of their disputes. Chambers of the Court have also been utilised in the *Elettronica Sicula* case,[36] the *Land, Island and Maritime Frontier Dispute* between El Salvador and Honduras (Nicaragua intervening),[37] the *Application for Revision of the Judgment in El Salvador/Honduras (Nicaragua intervening)*[38] and *Benin/Niger*.[39]

The Rules of the Court, which govern its procedure and operations, were adopted in 1946 and revised in 1972 and 1978.[40] Articles 79 and 80 of the 1978 Rules were amended in 2000 and 2005.[41] The internal judicial practice of the Court has been the source of discussion in recent years[42] and some changes have taken place.[43] The Court, for example,

---

[33] ICJ Reports, 1987, pp. 10, 13; 97 ILR, pp. 139, 142.

[34] Although concern was expressed about the unity of the jurisprudence of the Court by frequent use of ad hoc Chambers: see H. Mosler, 'The *Ad Hoc* Chambers of the International Court of Justice' in *International Law at a Time of Perplexity* (ed. Y. Dinstein), Dordrecht, 1989, p. 449. See also S. Schwebel, 'Chambers of the International Court of Justice formed for Particular Cases', *ibid.*, p. 739; E. Valencia-Ospina, 'The Use of Chambers of the International Court of Justice' in Lowe and Fitzmaurice, *Fifty Years of the International Court of Justice*, p. 503; Rosenne, *Law and Practice*, vol. III, pp. 1068 ff.; P. Palchetti, 'Article 26' in Zimmermann *et al.*, *Statute of the International Court*, p. 439, and Franck, 'Fairness', pp. 314 ff. As to the precedential value of decisions of Chambers, see Shahabuddeen, *Precedent*, pp. 171 ff. See also Thirlway, 'Law and Procedure', 2001, pp. 38, 46.

[35] See 22 ILM, 1983, p. 1252 and Communiqué of the ICJ No. 85/8, 1 May 1985. The Chamber consisted of Judge Bedjaoui (President) and Judges Lachs and Ruda, with Judges ad hoc Luchaire and Abi-Saab: see ICJ Reports, 1986, p. 554; 80 ILR, p. 441.

[36] ICJ Reports, 1989, p. 15; 84 ILR, p. 311.

[37] See ICJ Reports, 1987, p. 10; 97 ILR, pp. 112 and 139 and ICJ Reports, 1992, p. 351.

[38] ICJ Reports, 2003, p. 392; 129 ILR, p. 1   [39] ICJ Reports, 2005, p. 90.

[40] See Rosenne, *Law and Practice*, vol. III, p. 1074.   [41] See below, pp. 1074 and 1096.

[42] See e.g. D. Bowett *et al.*, *The International Court of Justice: Process, Practice and Procedures*, London, 1997. See also e.g. Jennings, 'Role', pp. 8 ff.; M. Bedjaoui, 'La "Fabrication" des Arrêts de la Cour Internationale de Justice' in *Mélanges Virally*, Paris, 1991, p. 87, and S. Oda, 'The International Court of Justice Viewed from the Bench', 244 HR, 1993 VII, p. 13. See also Shaw, 'International Court', pp. 862 ff.

[43] See the 1976 Resolution on Practice, International Court of Justice, *Acts and Documents Concerning the Organisation of the Court*, The Hague, 1989, p. 165. See also Higgins, 'Respecting Sovereign States'.

now adopts Practice Directions.[44] The Court has the power to regulate its own procedure.[45] Written pleadings are governed by articles 44 to 53 of the Rules of Court, which in fact allow the parties considerable latitude. While it is for the Court itself to determine the number, order and timing of filings of pleadings, this is done in consultation with the parties and the Court is ready to allow parties to extend time limits or determine whether, for example, there should be further rounds of pleadings.[46]

The jurisdiction of the Court[47]

General

The International Court is a judicial institution that decides cases on the basis of international law as it exists at the date of the decision. It cannot formally create law as it is not a legislative organ.[48] The Court has emphasised that, 'it states the existing law and does not legislate. This is so even if, in stating and applying the law, the Court necessarily

---

[44] There are currently twelve, the majority seeking essentially to ensure that the parties keep strictly to the Rules concerning pleadings and to restrict the tendency to produce large numbers of annexes. Practice Direction XII provides that written statements and documents submitted by international non-governmental organisations in advisory proceedings shall not be considered as part of the case file, but rather as publications in the public domain and available for consultation.

[45] See e.g. Judge Weeramantry's Dissenting Opinion in the *Request for an Examination of the Situation in Accordance with Paragraph 63 of the Nuclear Tests Case*, ICJ Reports, 1995, pp. 288, 320; 106 ILR, pp. 1, 42, where he noted that this power enabled it to devise a procedure *sui generis*.

[46] The memorial is to contain a statement of relevant facts, a statement of law and the submissions. The counter-memorial is to contain an admission or denial of the facts stated in the memorial, any additional facts if necessary, observations upon the statement of law in the memorial and a statement of law in answer thereto and the submissions: see articles 49(1) and (2) of the Rules. The reply and rejoinder, if authorised by the Court, are to be directed at bringing out the issues still dividing the parties, article 49(3).

[47] See e.g. Rosenne, *Law and Practice*, vol. II, and C. Tomuschat, 'Article 36' in Zimmermann et al., *Statute of the International Court*, p. 589. See also M. N. Shaw, 'The Security Council and the International Court of Justice: Judicial Drift and Judicial Function' in Muller et al., *International Court of Justice: Future Role*, p. 219; W. M. Reisman, 'The Supervisory Jurisdiction of the International Court of Justice: International Arbitration and International Adjudication', 258 HR, 1996, p. 9, and S. A. Alexander, 'Accepting the Compulsory Jurisdiction of the International Court of Justice with Reservations', 14 *Leiden Journal of International Law*, 2001, p. 89. See also the series of articles by Thirlway on 'The Law and Procedure of the International Court of Justice' in the *British Year Book of International Law* from 1989 to date.

[48] See the *Fisheries Jurisdiction* case, ICJ Reports, 1974, pp. 3, 19; 55 ILR, pp. 238, 254.

has to specify its scope and sometimes note its general trend.[49] Its views as to what the law is are of the highest authority. However, the matters that come before it are invariably intertwined with political factors. On occasions, such matters are also the subject of consideration before the political organs of the UN or other international organisations or indeed the subject of bilateral negotiations between the parties. This raises issues as to the proper function and role of the Court. The International Court of Justice is by virtue of article 92 of the Charter the 'principal judicial organ of the United Nations'. It is also, as Judge Lachs put it, 'the guardian of legality for the international community as a whole, both within and without the United Nations'.[50] It has been emphasised that the 'function of the Court is to state the law'[51] and it can only decide on the basis of law.[52] The issue of judicial function was examined in an important joint declaration by seven judges in *Serbia and Montenegro* v. *UK*,[53] one of the cases brought by what was originally the Federal Republic of Yugoslavia against NATO countries arising out of the Kosovo conflict in 1999. It was noted that when choosing between various grounds upon which to accept or reject jurisdiction, there were three criteria to guide the Court. These were, first, consistency with previous case-law in order to provide predictability as 'consistency is the essence of judicial reasoning'; secondly, certitude, whereby the Court should choose the ground most secure in law, and, thirdly, as the principal judicial organ of the United Nations, the Court should be 'mindful of the possible implications and consequences for the other pending cases'.[54]

Nevertheless, political factors cannot but be entwined with questions of law. The Court has noted that while political aspects may be present in any legal dispute brought before it, the Court was only concerned to establish that the dispute in question was a legal dispute 'in the sense of a dispute capable of being settled by the application of principles and rules of international law'.[55] The fact that other elements are present cannot detract

---

[49] *Legality of the Threat or Use of Nuclear Weapons*, ICJ Reports, 1996, pp. 226, 237.
[50] The *Lockerbie* case, ICJ Reports, 1992, pp. 3, 26; 94 ILR, pp. 478, 509.
[51] The *Northern Cameroons* case, ICJ Reports, 1963, pp. 15, 33; 35 ILR, pp. 353, 369.
[52] See the *Haya de la Torre* case, ICJ Reports, 1951, pp. 71, 79; 18 ILR, p. 349. See also Judge Weeramantry's Dissenting Opinion in the *Lockerbie* case, ICJ Reports, 1992, pp. 3, 56; 94 ILR, pp. 478, 539.
[53] ICJ Reports, 2004, p. 1307.   [54] *Ibid.*, pp. 1353–4.
[55] The *Armed Actions (Nicaragua* v. *Honduras)* case, ICJ Reports, 1988, pp. 16, 91; 84 ILR, pp. 218, 246. See also the *Certain Expenses of the United Nations* case, ICJ Reports, 1962, pp. 151, 155; 34 ILR, pp. 281, 285, and the *Tadić* case before the Appeals Chamber of the International Criminal Tribunal for the Former Yugoslavia, IT-94-1-AR72, p. 11. See also

from the characterisation of a dispute as a legal dispute.[56] The Court has also referred to the assessment of the legality of the possible conduct of states with regard to international legal obligations as an 'essentially judicial task'.[57] Accordingly, 'the task of the Court must be to respond, on the basis of international law, to the particular legal dispute brought before it. As it interprets and applies the law, it will be mindful of context, but its task cannot go beyond that.'[58]

The fact that the same general political situation may come before different organs of the UN has raised the problem of concurrent jurisdiction. The Court, however, has been consistently clear that the fact that the issue before the Court is also the subject of active negotiations between the parties,[59] or the subject of good offices activity by the UN Secretary-General[60] or the subject of consideration by the Security Council[61] or regional organisations,[62] will not detract from the competence of the Court or the exercise of its judicial function. The Court has noted that the Security Council has functions of a political nature, while the Court itself has functions of a legal nature, and that therefore both organs could perform their separate but complementary functions with respect to the same events.[63] The Court may also indicate provisional measures of protection at the same time as the UN Secretary-General is organising a fact-finding mission to investigate the same events.[64] The Court's

---

R. Higgins, 'Policy Considerations and the International Judicial Process', 17 ICLQ, 1968, pp. 58, 74.

[56] ICJ Reports, 1988, p. 92; 84 ILR, p. 247. See also the *Iranian Hostages* case, ICJ Reports, 1980, pp. 7, 19–20; 61 ILR, pp. 530, 545–6 and *Legality of the Threat or Use of Nuclear Weapons*, ICJ Reports, 1996, pp. 226, 234; 110 ILR, pp. 163, 184. See, for the view that rather than concentrate upon definitions of legal and political questions, one should focus upon the distinctions between political and legal methods of dispute settlement, R. Y. Jennings, 'Gerald Gray Fitzmaurice', 55 BYIL, 1984, pp. 1, 18, and R. Higgins, 'Policy Considerations', p. 74.

[57] See the Advisory Opinion on the *Legality of the Use by a State of Nuclear Weapons in Armed Conflict*, ICJ Reports, 1996, pp. 66, 73; 110 ILR pp. 1, 13. See also e.g. the *Certain Expenses* case, ICJ Reports, 1962, pp. 151, 155; 34 ILR, pp. 281, 284–5.

[58] *Democratic Republic of the Congo v. Uganda*, ICJ Reports, 2005, pp. 168, 190. See also the Separate Opinion of Judge Simma, *ibid.*, p. 335.

[59] See the *Aegean Sea Continental Shelf* case, ICJ Reports, 1976, pp. 3, 12; 60 ILR, pp. 562, 571.

[60] See the *Iranian Hostages* case, ICJ Reports, 1980, pp. 7, 21–2; 61 ILR, pp. 530, 547–8.

[61] See the *Nicaragua* case, ICJ Reports, 1984, pp. 392, 431–4; 76 ILR, pp. 104, 142–5.

[62] ICJ Reports, 1984, p. 440 and *Cameroon v. Nigeria (Preliminary Objections)*, ICJ Reports, 1998, pp. 275, 307.

[63] ICJ Reports, 1984, p. 435; 76 ILR, p. 146.

[64] *Cameroon v. Nigeria (Provisional Measures)*, ICJ Reports, 1996, pp. 13, 22.

essential function is to resolve in accordance with international law disputes placed before it[65] and to refrain from deciding points not included in the final submissions of the parties.[66] The provision as to international law relates to the sources of law available for application by the Court and is considered subsequently.[67] The obligation to decide was referred to by the Court in the *Libya/Malta* (*Application for Permission to Intervene*) case,[68] where it was noted that it was the duty of the Court 'to give the fullest decision it may in the circumstances of each case'.[69] However, this obligation is subject, for example, to jurisdictional limitations (for example, with regard to the rights of third states)[70] and questions related to judicial propriety.[71]

The nature of a legal dispute

Article 36(2) of the Statute of the Court requires that a matter brought before it should be a legal dispute.[72] Although it is not possible to point to a specific definition, the approach adopted by the Permanent Court in the *Mavrommatis Palestine Concessions* (*Jurisdiction*) case[73] constitutes

---

[65] See e.g. *Democratic Republic of the Congo v. Uganda*, ICJ Reports, 2005, pp. 168, 190. See also Judge Weeramantry's Dissenting Opinion in the *Lockerbie* case, ICJ Reports, 1992, pp. 3, 56; 94 ILR, pp. 478, 539.

[66] This rule (known as the *non ultra petita* rule) has been termed by Judge Buergenthal in his Separate Opinion in the *Oil Platforms* (*Iran* v. *USA*) case, ICJ Reports, 2003, pp. 161, 271; 130 ILR, pp. 323, 426, 'a cardinal rule which does not allow the Court to deal with a subject in the *dispositif* [operative paragraphs] of its judgment that the parties to the case have not, in their final submissions, asked it to adjudicate'. See the *Request for the Interpretation of the Judgment in the Asylum Case*, ICJ Reports, 1950, pp. 395, 402; the *Qatar* v. *Bahrain* case, ICJ Reports, 2001, pp. 40, 96–7 and the *Democratic Republic of the Congo v. Belgium* case, ICJ Reports, 2002, pp. 3, 18–19; 128 ILR, pp. 60, 73–5. See also Rosenne, *Law and Practice*, vol. II, p. 576.

[67] See below, p. 1086.   [68] ICJ Reports, 1984, pp. 3, 25; 70 ILR, pp. 527, 554.

[69] See also Judge Weeramantry's Dissenting Opinion in the *East Timor* case, ICJ Reports, 1995, pp. 90, 158; 105 ILR, pp. 226, 299. See also generally M. Bedjaoui, 'Expediency in the Decisions of the International Court of Justice', 71 BYIL, 2000, p. 1.

[70] See e.g. the *Monetary Gold* case, ICJ Reports, 1954, p. 32; 21 ILR, p. 399, and the *East Timor* case, ICJ Reports, 1995, pp. 90, 105; 105 ILR, pp. 226, 246.

[71] See further below, p. 1086.

[72] The Court noted in the *Nuclear Tests* case, ICJ Reports, 1974, pp. 253, 270–1; 57 ILR, pp. 398, 415–16, that 'the existence of a dispute is the primary condition for the Court to exercise its judicial function'. It is also a question which is 'essentially preliminary', ICJ Reports, 1974, p. 260; 57 ILR, p. 405.

[73] PCIJ, Series A, No. 2, 1924, p. 11. See also the *South-West Africa* cases, ICJ Reports, 1962, pp. 319, 328; 37 ILR, pp. 3, 10; the *Nuclear Tests* case, ICJ Reports, 1974, p. 253; 57 ILR, p. 398; *Liechtenstein* v. *Germany*, ICJ Reports, 2005, pp. 6, 18 and *Democratic Republic of the Congo* v. *Rwanda*, ICJ Reports, 2006, pp. 6, 40.

the appropriate starting point. The Court declared that a dispute could be regarded as 'a disagreement over a point of law or fact, a conflict of legal views or of interests between two persons'. It is to be distinguished from a situation which might lead to international friction or give rise to a dispute. This is a subtle but important difference since, for the process of settlement to operate successfully, there has to be a specific issue or issues readily identifiable to be resolved.

In the *Interpretation of Peace Treaties* case[74] the Court noted that 'whether there exists an international dispute is a matter for objective determination' and pointed out that in the instant case 'the two sides hold clearly opposite views concerning the question of the performance or the non-performance of certain treaty obligations' so that 'international disputes have arisen'. A mere assertion is not sufficient; it must be shown that the claim of one party is positively opposed by the other.[75] This approach was reaffirmed in the *Applicability of the Obligation to Arbitrate under Section 21 of the United Nations Headquarters Agreement* case,[76] where the Court in an advisory opinion noted that the consistent challenge by the UN Secretary-General to the decisions contemplated and then taken by the US Congress and Administration with regard to the closing of the PLO offices in the US (which of necessity included the PLO Mission to the United Nations in New York) demonstrated the existence of a dispute between the US and the UN relating to the Headquarters Agreement. In the *East Timor* case[77] the Court again reaffirmed its earlier case-law and went on to note that 'Portugal has rightly or wrongly, formulated complaints of fact and law against Australia, which the latter has denied. By virtue of this denial, there is a legal dispute.' This acceptance of a relatively low threshold was underlined in the *Application of the Genocide Convention (Bosnia*

---

[74] ICJ Reports, 1950, pp. 65, 74; 17 ILR, pp. 331, 336.

[75] *South-West Africa* cases, ICJ Reports, 1962, pp. 319, 328; 37 ILR, pp. 3, 10 and the *Nicaragua* case, ICJ Reports, 1984, pp. 392, 429–41; 76 ILR, pp. 104, 140. See also *Larsen* v. *Hawaiian Kingdom* 119 ILR, pp. 566, 587. Note also that Kelsen wrote that 'a dispute is a legal dispute if it is to be settled by the application of legal norms, that is to say, by the application of existing law', *Principles of International Law* (ed. R. W. Tucker), 2nd edn, New York, 1966, p. 526. See also Rosenne, *Law and Practice*, vol. II, pp. 517 ff. Higgins has made the point that generally the Court has taken a robust attitude as to what is a 'legal' matter, *Problems and Process*, p. 195. See also V. Gowlland-Debbas, 'The Relationship between the International Court of Justice and the Security Council in the Light of the *Lockerbie* Case', 88 AJIL, 1994, p. 643.

[76] ICJ Reports, 1988, pp. 12, 30; 82 ILR, pp. 225, 248.   [77] ICJ Reports, 1995, pp. 90, 99–100.

and Herzegovina v. *Yugoslavia)* case,[78] where the Court stated that 'by reason of the rejection by Yugoslavia of the complaints formulated against it by Bosnia-Herzegovina, "there is a legal dispute" between them'. Such denial of the allegations made against Yugoslavia had occurred 'whether at the stage of proceedings relating to the requests for the indication of provisional measures, or at the stage of the present proceedings relating to those objections'.[79] In other words, in order for a matter to constitute a legal dispute, it is sufficient for the respondent to an application before the Court merely to deny the allegations made even if the jurisdiction of the Court is challenged.[80]

While it is for the parties to put forward their views, and particularly for the applicant, in its application, to present to the Court the dispute with which it wishes to seize the Court,[81] it is for the Court itself to determine the subject-matter of the dispute before it.[82] This will be done by taking into account not only the submission but the application as a whole, the arguments of the applicant before the Court and other documents referred to, including the public statements of the applicant.[83] Should the Court conclude that the dispute in question has disappeared by the time the Court makes its decision, because, for example, the object of the claim has been achieved by other means, then the 'necessary consequences' will be drawn and no decision may be given.[84] In all events, the determination on an objective basis of the existence of a dispute is for the Court itself.[85]

---

[78] ICJ Reports, 1996, pp. 595, 615. See also *Liechtenstein* v. *Germany*, ICJ Reports, 2005, pp. 6, 19.

[79] ICJ Reports, 1996, pp. 595, 614.

[80] See also *El Salvador/Honduras*, ICJ Reports, 1992, pp. 351, 555; 97 ILR, p. 112.

[81] Note that article 40(1) of the Statute requires that the application indicate the subject of the dispute and that article 38(2) of the Rules requires that the 'precise nature of the claim' be specified in the application.

[82] See e.g. *Spain* v. *Canada*, ICJ Reports, 1998, pp. 432, 449; 123 ILR, pp. 189, 209–10 and *Nicaragua* v. *Colombia*, ICJ Reports, 2007, para. 38.

[83] The *Nuclear Tests* case, ICJ Reports, 1974, pp. 253, 263; 57 ILR, pp. 398, 408. Note that new claims formulated during the course of proceedings will be declared inadmissible where such claims would, if admitted, transform the subject of the dispute originally brought before the Court in the application: see e.g. *Nicaragua* v. *Honduras*, ICJ Reports, 2007, para. 108.

[84] The *Nuclear Tests* case, ICJ Reports, 1974, pp. 253, 271; 57 ILR, p. 416. See also the *Northern Cameroons* case, ICJ Reports, 1963, pp. 15, 38; 35 ILR, p. 353 and *Democratic Republic of the Congo* v. *Belgium*, ICJ Reports, 2002, pp. 3, 14–15; 128 ILR, pp. 60, 69–71.

[85] *Spain* v. *Canada*, ICJ Reports, 1998, pp. 432, 448; 123 ILR, pp. 189, 208–9.

It is also clear that the exhaustion of diplomatic negotiations is not a prerequisite to going to the Court.[86]

Contentious jurisdiction[87]

The jurisdiction of the International Court falls into two distinct parts: its capacity to decide disputes between states, and its capacity to give advisory opinions when requested so to do by particular qualified entities. The latter will be noted in the following section.

The Court has underlined that the question as to the establishment of jurisdiction is a matter for the Court itself. Although a party seeking to assert a fact must prove it, the issue of jurisdiction is a question of law to be resolved by the Court in the light of the relevant facts.[88] Further, jurisdiction must be determined at the time that the act instituting proceedings was filed, so that if the Court had jurisdiction at that date, it will continue to have jurisdiction irrespective of subsequent events.[89] Subsequent events may lead to a finding that an application has become moot, but cannot deprive the Court of jurisdiction.[90] It should also be noted that in dealing with issues of jurisdiction, the Court will not attach as much importance to matters of form as would be the case in domestic law.[91] The Court possesses an inherent jurisdiction to take such action as may be required in order to ensure that the exercise of its jurisdiction over

---

[86] *Cameroon* v. *Nigeria* (*Preliminary Objections*), ICJ Reports, 1998, pp. 275, 303. The question of non-exhaustion of domestic remedies is an admissibility issue: see below, p. 1071.

[87] See e.g. Rosenne, *Law and Practice*, vol. II, and R. Szafarz, *The Compulsory Jurisdiction of the International Court of Justice*, Dordrecht, 1993.

[88] See the *Fisheries Jurisdiction* (*Spain* v. *Canada*) case, ICJ Reports, 1998, pp. 432, 450; 123 ILR, pp. 189, 210–11. See also the *Armed Actions* (*Nicaragua* v. *Honduras*) case, ICJ Reports, 1988, p. 76; 84 ILR, p. 231 and *Serbia and Montenegro* v. *UK*, ICJ Reports, 2004, pp. 1307, 1322.

[89] See e.g. *Democratic Republic of the Congo* v. *Rwanda*, ICJ Reports, 2006, pp. 6, 29. However, the Court has held that it would not penalise a defect in procedure which the applicant could easily remedy, *ibid.*

[90] *Democratic Republic of the Congo* v. *Belgium*, ICJ Reports, 2002, pp. 3, 12–13; 128 ILR, pp. 60, 67–8.

[91] See the *Application of the Genocide Convention* (*Preliminary Objections*) case, ICJ Reports, 1996, pp. 595, 613; 115 ILR, pp. 10, 26. See also the *Mavrommatis Palestine Concessions* case, PCIJ, Series A, No. 2, p. 34; 2 AD, p. 27, and the *Northern Cameroons* case, ICJ Reports, 1963, pp. 15, 28; 35 ILR, pp. 353, 363. The Court in *Cameroon* v. *Nigeria* (*Provisional Measures*), ICJ Reports, 1994, p. 105; 106 ILR, p. 144, in fixing relevant time limits for the parties, noted that Cameroon had submitted an additional application after its original application, by which it sought to extend the object of the dispute. It was intended as an amendment to the first application. There is no provision in the Statute and Rules of the

the merits, once established, is not frustrated, and to ensure the orderly settlement of all matters in dispute, to ensure the 'inherent limitations on the exercise of the judicial function' of the Court and to 'maintain its judicial character'.[92] The Court has also held that where jurisdiction exists over a dispute on a particular matter, no separate basis for jurisdiction is required in order to consider the question of remedies.[93]

It has been emphasised that the function of a decision on jurisdiction is solely to determine whether the case on the merits may proceed 'and not to engage in a clarification of a controverted issue of a general nature', while a case will not be declined simply on the basis of the alleged motives of one of the parties or because the judgment may have implications in another case.[94] The Court has freedom to select the ground upon which it will base its judgment and when its jurisdiction is challenged on diverse grounds, it is free to base its decision on one or more grounds of its own choosing, in particular 'the ground which in its judgment is more direct and conclusive'.[95] Once the Court has reached a decision on jurisdiction, that decision assumes the character of *res judicata*,[96] that is it becomes final and binding upon the parties. Subject only to the possibility of revision under article 61 of the Statute,[97] the findings of a judgment are, for the purposes of the case and between the parties, to be taken as correct, and may not be reopened on the basis of claims that doubt has been thrown on them by subsequent events.[98]

As well as the question of the jurisdiction of the Court, which essentially concerns issues as to the consent of the parties, it is necessary that the application be admissible.[99] Admissibility refers to the application of relevant general rules of international law, such as exhaustion of local remedies in cases concerning diplomatic protection.[100] Objections to

---

Court for amendment of applications as such, although in this case Nigeria consented to the request and the Court accepted it.

[92] The *Nuclear Tests* case, ICJ Reports, 1974, pp. 253, 259; 57 ILR, pp. 398, 404, citing the *Northern Cameroons* case, ICJ Reports, 1963, pp. 15, 29; 35 ILR, pp. 353, 365. See also below, p. 1074.

[93] The *LaGrand* case, ICJ Reports, 2001, pp. 466, 485; 134 ILR, pp. 1, 24.

[94] *Serbia and Montenegro* v. *UK*, ICJ Reports, 2004, pp. 1307, 1323.   [95] *Ibid.*, p. 1325.

[96] See the *Genocide Convention (Bosnia* v. *Serbia)* case, ICJ Reports, 2007, paras. 117 ff. See further as to *res judicata*, above, chapter 3, p. 101.

[97] See below, p. 1105.

[98] The *Genocide Convention (Bosnia* v. *Serbia)* case, ICJ Reports, 2007, para. 120.

[99] See e.g. *Serbia and Montenegro* v. *UK*, ICJ Reports, 2004, pp. 1307, 1322.

[100] See e.g. *Democratic Republic of the Congo* v. *Uganda*, ICJ Reports, 2005, pp. 168, 276 and the *Diallo (Guinea* v. *Democratic Republic of the Congo)* case, ICJ Reports, 2007, paras.

admissibility normally take the form of an assertion that, even if the Court has jurisdiction and the facts stated by the applicant state are assumed to be correct, nonetheless there are reasons why the Court should not proceed to an examination of the merits.[101] Together they form the necessary prerequisite to the Court proceeding to address the merits of a case. Also of relevance in the pre-merits consideration of an application to the Court is the question of standing or jurisdiction *ratione personae*, a matter which logically arises before a consideration of jurisdiction and admissibility. It refers to the question of the receivability of the request, sometimes termed the process of seisin, which constitutes 'a procedural step independent of the basis of jurisdiction invoked', although the question as to whether the Court has been validly seized is a question of jurisdiction.[102]

Article 34 of the Statute of the Court declares that only states may be parties in cases before the Court. This is of far-reaching importance since it prohibits recourse to the Court by private persons and international organisations, save in so far as some of the latter may be able to obtain advisory opinions. The Court is open to all states that are parties to the Statute. Article 93 of the UN Charter provides that all UN members are *ipso facto* parties to the Statute of the ICJ, and that non-members of the UN may become a party to the Statute on conditions determined by the General Assembly upon the recommendation of the Security Council. In the case of Switzerland, for example, the Assembly and Security Council declared that it could become a party to the Statute of the ICJ provided it accepted the provisions of that Statute, accepted all the obligations of a UN member under Article 94 of the Charter (i.e. undertaking to comply with the decision of the Court), and agreed to pay a certain amount towards the expenses of the Court.[103] The Security Council has in fact resolved that access to the ICJ for a state not party to the Statute is possible provided that such state has previously deposited with the registrar of the Court a declaration (either general or particular) accepting the jurisdiction of the Court and undertaking to comply in good faith with the decision or decisions of

33 ff. See also Rosenne, *Law and Practice*, vol. II, pp. 817 ff.; Tomuschat, 'Article 36', p. 646 and article 79 of the Rules of Court.

[101] See the *Oil Platforms (Iran v. USA)* case, ICJ Reports, 2003, pp. 161, 177; 130 ILR, pp. 323, 337.

[102] *Qatar/Bahrain*, ICJ Reports, 1995, pp. 6, 23–4: 102 ILR, pp. 1, 64–5.

[103] General Assembly resolution 91 (I). Switzerland became a member of the UN in September 2002. See also Rosenne, *Law and Practice*, vol. II, p. 598. Japan, Liechtenstein, Nauru and San Marino were also in the same position until 1956, 1990, 1999 and 1992 respectively.

the Court.[104] West Germany filed a general declaration with the ICJ on this basis before it joined the UN,[105] while Albania[106] and Italy[107] filed particular declarations with respect to cases with which they were involved.

Article 35(2) of the Statute further provides that the conditions under which the Court shall be open to states other than those parties to the Statute shall be laid down by the Security Council[108] 'subject to the special provisions contained in treaties in force'. The Court has rather restrictively interpreted this condition to refer to treaties in force as at the date of the entry into force of the Statute and providing for the jurisdiction of what was then the new Court.[109] Although only states may be parties before the Court, the Court may request information relevant to cases before it from public international organisations and may receive information presented by these organisations on their own initiative.[110]

The question as to whether a party has the right to appear before the Court under the Statute is not dependent upon consent and is an issue which the Court itself must enquire into and determine prior to considering any objections to jurisdiction and admissibility.[111] Article 35(1) of the Statute provides that the Court shall be open to the states parties to the Statute, or as the Court itself has stated, 'The Court can exercise its judicial function only in respect of those states which have access to it under article 35.' Only states which have access to the Court, therefore, are in a position to confer jurisdiction upon it.[112] In *Serbia and Montenegro v. UK*,[113] the Court concluded that Serbia and Montenegro

---

[104] Security Council resolution 9 (1946).

[105] The *North Sea Continental Shelf* case, ICJ Reports, Pleadings, vol. I, pp. 6, 8.

[106] The *Corfu Channel* case, ICJ Reports, 1949, p. 4; 16 AD, p. 155.

[107] The *Monetary Gold* case, ICJ Reports, 1954, p. 19; 21 ILR, p. 399.

[108] Such conditions were laid down in Security Council resolution 9 (1946).

[109] ICJ Reports, 2004, pp. 1307, 1350. The Court accepted that no such prior treaties referring to the jurisdiction of the Court had been brought to its attention, *ibid.*

[110] Article 34(2), Statute of the ICJ. See also Rosenne, *Law and Practice*, vol. II, pp. 620 ff. Individuals, groups and corporations have no right of access to the Court: see here also H. Lauterpacht, *International Law and Human Rights*, London, 1950, p. 48. Note that Judge Higgins has written that, 'There is some flexibility I think for possible *amicus* briefs by NGOs in advisory opinion cases, and I think that a useful possibility for the Court to explore', 'Respecting Sovereign States', p. 123. See now Practice Direction XII with regard to the provision of written information by international non-governmental organisations in advisory proceedings.

[111] *Serbia and Montenegro v. UK*, ICJ Reports, 2004, pp. 1307, 1322 and 1326.

[112] *Ibid.*, p. 1326.

[113] ICJ Reports, 2004, p. 1307. This was one of a series of cases brought by the Federal Republic of Yugoslavia (the precursor to Serbia and Montenegro) against NATO countries in 1999, so that the point in question applied to other respondent states.

could not be regarded as a party to the Statute at the time of the application.[114]

The Court has certain inherent powers flowing from its role as a judicial organ.[115] These would include in certain circumstances the right of its own motion to put an end to proceedings in a case.[116] However, this would appear to be restricted to two circumstances: first, in cases before the adoption of article 38(5) of the Rules, where an application is made without a basis of jurisdiction in the hope that the other state would accept it,[117] and, secondly, where the Court accedes to the request of respondent states to remove cases from the list on the grounds of being manifestly lacking in jurisdiction.[118] This approach by the Court in the *Serbia and Montenegro* v. *UK* case was criticised by Judge Kooijmans[119] and by Judge Higgins, who noted that there was nothing in the case-law to suggest that the exercise of the Court's inherent powers in the absence of discontinuance was limited to the two circumstances referred to by the Court.[120] Judge Higgins emphasised that, 'The Court's inherent jurisdiction derives from its judicial character and the need for powers to regulate matters connected with the administration of justice, not every aspect of which may have been foreseen in the Rules.' The 'very occasional need' to exercise such inherent powers might arise at any stage, from summary dismissal of a case to jurisdictional questions to merits issues.[121]

Under article 79(9) of the Rules, there are three ways in which the Court may dispose of a preliminary objection to jurisdiction. It may uphold the challenge, reject the challenge or declare that the objection does not possess, in the circumstances of the case, an exclusively preliminary character, in which case the matter will be dealt with together with a

---

[114] *Ibid.*, pp. 1336–7. As to the relevant details of the case, see above, chapter 17, p. 963.

[115] See e.g. C. Brown, 'The Inherent Powers of International Courts and Tribunals', 76 BYIL, 2005, p. 195.

[116] *Serbia and Montenegro* v. *UK*, ICJ Reports, 2004, pp. 1307, 1321. The Rules do not provide for such a procedure.

[117] See below, p. 1076, note 131.

[118] See e.g. *Yugoslavia* v. *Spain*, ICJ Reports, 1999, pp. 761, 773–4 and *Yugoslavia* v. *USA*, ICJ Reports, 1999, pp. 916, 925–6.

[119] ICJ Reports, 2004, pp. 1307, 1370 ff.   [120] *Ibid.*, p. 1361.

[121] *Ibid.*, pp. 1361–2. The question, therefore, that Judge Higgins believed that the Court should have addressed was whether it was possible to say that in the case, 'the circumstances are such that it is reasonable, necessary and appropriate for the Court to strike the case off the List as an exercise of inherent power to protect the integrity of the judicial process', *ibid.*, p. 1362.

consideration of the merits.[122] The Court has stated that in principle, a party raising preliminary objections to its jurisdiction is entitled to have those objections answered in the preliminary stage of the proceedings, unless the Court does not have before it all facts necessary to decide the question raised or if answering the preliminary objection would determine the dispute, or some elements thereof, on the merits.[123]

Article 36(1)

The Court has jurisdiction under article 36(1) of its Statute in all cases referred to it by parties, and regarding all matters specially provided for in the UN Charter or in treaties or conventions in force.[124] As in the case of arbitration, parties may refer a particular dispute to the ICJ by means of a special agreement, or *compromis*, which will specify the terms of the dispute and the framework within which the Court is to operate.[125] This method was used in the *Minquiers and Ecrehos* case,[126] and in a number of others.[127]

The jurisdiction of the Court is founded upon the consent of the parties,[128] which need not be in any particular form and in certain

---

[122] See e.g. *Nicaragua* v. *Colombia*, ICJ Reports, 2007, para. 48. See also the preliminary objections judgment in *Cameroon* v. *Nigeria*, ICJ Reports, 1998, p. 275.

[123] *Nicaragua* v. *Columbia*, ICJ Reports, 2007, para. 51. It is possible, however, for the determination by the Court of its jurisdiction to 'touch upon certain aspects of the merits of the case', *ibid*.

[124] See also article 40 of the ICJ Statute and article 39 of the Rules of Court.

[125] See e.g. L. C. Marion, 'La Saisine de la CIJ par Voie de Compromis', 99 RGDIP, 1995, p. 258.

[126] ICJ Reports, 1953, p. 47; 20 ILR, p. 94.

[127] See e.g. the *Belgium/Netherlands Frontier Land* case, ICJ Reports, 1959, p. 209; 27 ILR, p. 62, the *Tunisia/Libya Continental Shelf* case, ICJ Reports, 1982, p. 18; 67 ILR, p. 4 and the *Libya/Chad* case, ICJ Reports, 1974, p. 6; 100 ILR, p. 1.

[128] See the *Nicaragua* case, ICJ Reports, 1986, pp. 3, 32; 76 ILR, pp. 349, 366. The Court noted in the *Application for the Interpretation and Revision of the Judgment in the Tunisia/Libya Case*, ICJ Reports, 1985, pp. 192, 216; 81 ILR, pp. 419, 449, that it was 'a fundamental principle' that 'the consent of states parties to a dispute, is the basis of the Court's jurisdiction in contentious cases', citing here the *Interpretation of Peace Treaties* case, ICJ Reports, 1950, p. 71; 17 ILR, pp. 331, 335. See also *Cameroon* v. *Nigeria*, ICJ Reports, 2002, pp. 303, 421 and *Democratic Republic of the Congo* v. Rwanda, ICJ Reports, 2006, pp. 6, 18. The Court further noted that, 'its jurisdiction is based on the consent of the parties and is confined to the extent accepted by them' and that 'the conditions to which such consent is subject must be regarded as constituting the limits thereon . . . The examination of such conditions relates to its jurisdiction and not to the admissibility of the application', *ibid.*, p. 39. See also *Djibouti* v. *France*, ICL Reports, 2008, para. 48.

circumstances the Court will infer it from the conduct of the parties. In the *Corfu Channel (Preliminary Objections)* case,[129] the Court inferred consent from the unilateral application of the plaintiff state (the United Kingdom) coupled with subsequent letters from the other party involved (Albania) intimating acceptance of the Court's jurisdiction. The idea whereby the consent of a state to the Court's jurisdiction may be established by means of acts subsequent to the initiation of proceedings is referred to as the doctrine of *forum prorogatum*.[130] It will usually arise where one party files an application with the Court unilaterally inviting another state to accept jurisdiction with regard to the particular dispute where jurisdiction would not otherwise exist with regard to the matter at issue. If the other state accedes to this, then the Court will have jurisdiction.[131]

The doctrine has been carefully interpreted to avoid giving the impression of a creeping extension by the Court of its own jurisdiction by means of fictions. Consent has to be clearly present, if sometimes inferred, and not merely a technical creation.[132] The Court has emphasised that such consent has to be 'voluntary and indisputable'.[133] In the

---

[129] ICJ Reports, 1948, p. 15; 15 AD, p. 349.

[130] See e.g. Rosenne, *Law and Practice*, vol. II, pp. 672 ff., and S. Yee, 'Forum Prorogatum in the International Court', 42 German YIL, 1999, p. 147.

[131] See article 38(5) of the Rules. The Republic of the Congo filed an application against France on 9 December 2002 with regard to which the former gave its consent on 11 April 2003: see ICJ Press Release 2003/14 and the Court's Order of 17 June 2003, while France consented to jurisdiction with regard to an application dated 9 January 2006 brought by Djibouti: see the Court's judgment of 4 June 2008, noting that, 'For the Court to exercise jurisdiction on the basis of *forum prorogatum*, the element of consent must be either explicit or clearly to be deduced from the relevant conduct of a State' (para. 62) and that the extent of consent (and thus the jurisdiction of the Court) depended upon the matching of the application made with the expression by the other party of its consent, para. 65. It was emphasised that, 'Where jurisdiction is based on *forum prorogatum*, great care must be taken regarding the scope of the consent as circumscribed by the respondent State', para. 87. On 18 April 2007, Rwanda filed an application against France, but as of the date of writing, France has not given its consent to jurisdiction: see ICJ Press Release 2007/11.

[132] See e.g. the *Monetary Gold* case, ICJ Reports, 1954, pp. 19, 31; 21 ILR, pp. 399, 406. But cf. the *Treatment in Hungary of Aircraft of the USA* case, ICJ Reports, 1964, pp. 99, 103; the *Aerial Incident (USA v. USSR)* case, ICJ Reports, 1956, pp. 6, 9, 12, 15 and the two *Antarctic* cases, ICJ Reports, 1958, p. 158 and *ibid.*, 1959, p. 276. Note that article 38(2) of the 1978 Rules of the Court stipulates that the application shall specify as far as possible the legal grounds upon which the jurisdiction of the Court is said to be based. See also *Djibouti v. France*, ICJ Reports, 2008, para. 163.

[133] *Corfu Channel (Preliminary Objection)*, ICJ Reports, 1948, p. 27. See also *Application of the Genocide Convention*, ICJ Reports, 1996, pp. 595, 621.

Corfu Channel case the UK sought to found the Court's jurisdiction *inter alia* on the recommendation of the Security Council that the dispute be referred to the Court, which it was agreed was a 'decision' binding upon member states of the UN in accordance with article 25 of the Charter.[134] Accordingly it was maintained by the UK that Albania was obliged to accept the Court's jurisdiction irrespective of its consent. The ICJ did not deal with this point, since it actually inferred consent, but in a joint separate opinion, seven judges of the Court rejected the argument, which was regarded as an attempt to introduce a new meaning of compulsory jurisdiction.[135] A particularly difficult case with regard to the question as to whether relevant events demonstrated an agreement between the parties to submit a case to the Court is that of *Qatar v. Bahrain*.[136] The issue centred upon minutes of a meeting signed by the Foreign Ministers of both states (the Doha Minutes) in December 1990. The status of such Minutes was controverted,[137] but the Court held that they constituted an agreement under international law.[138] There was also disagreement over the substance of the Minutes and thus the subject matter of the dispute to be placed before the Court. Bahrain defined the issue as including the question of 'sovereignty' over Zubarah, while Qatar merely accepted that that was how Bahrain characterised the issue.[139] The Court concluded that this was sufficient to lay the whole dispute, including this element, before it.[140] Questions do therefore remain with regard to the extent of the consensual principle after this decision.[141]

---

[134] Although not a member of the UN, Albania had agreed to assume the obligations of a member with regard to the dispute. This application was on the basis of that part of article 36(1) which specifies that the Court's jurisdiction also comprised 'all matters specifically provided for in the Charter' of the UN.

[135] ICJ Reports, 1948, pp. 15, 31–2; 15 AD, pp. 349, 354.

[136] ICJ Reports, 1994, p. 112 and ICJ Reports, 1995, p. 6; 102 ILR, pp. 1 and 47. See M. Evans, 'Case Concerning Maritime Delimitation and Territorial Questions Between Qatar and Bahrain (*Qatar v. Bahrain*), Jurisdiction and Admissibility', 44 ICLQ, 1995, p. 691.

[137] The argument revolving around whether any application to the Court had to be by both parties or whether unilateral application was provided for.

[138] ICJ Reports, 1994, p. 121; 102 ILR, p. 18.

[139] ICJ Reports, 1995, pp. 9–11; 102 ILR, pp. 50–2.

[140] ICJ Reports, 1995, pp. 17 and 25; 102 ILR, pp. 58 and 66. This was disputed by four of the five dissenting judges, who argued that the Zubarah sovereignty issue had not been properly laid before it, ICJ Reports, 1995, pp. 49, 55 ff., 72 and 74–5; 102 ILR, pp. 90, 96 ff., 113 and 115–16.

[141] See also E. Lauterpacht, '"Partial" Judgements and the Inherent Jurisdiction of the International Court of Justice' in Lowe and Fitzmaurice, *Fifty Years of the International Court of Justice*, p. 465.

It is a well-established principle that the Court will only exercise jurisdiction over a state with its consent[142] and it 'cannot therefore decide upon legal rights of third states not parties to the proceedings'.[143] As a consequence of this principle, the Court will not entertain actions between states that in reality implead a third state without its consent. This rule was underlined in the *Monetary Gold* case,[144] where it was noted that where the legal interests of the third party 'would form the very subject-matter of the decision', the Court could not entertain proceedings in the absence of that state. In the *Nicaragua* case, the Court noted that the circumstances of the *Monetary Gold* case 'probably represent the limit of the power of the Court to refuse to exercise its jurisdiction'.[145] This approach was underlined in the *Nauru* case, where the Court emphasised that the absence of a request from a third party to intervene 'in no way precludes the Court from adjudicating upon claims submitted to it, provided that the legal interests of the third state which may possibly be affected do not form the very subject-matter of the decision that is applied for'.[146] The test referred to was whether the determination of the third state's responsibility was a pre-requisite for the claims raised before the Court by one party against the other.[147] In the *East Timor* case,[148] the Court held that it could not rule on the lawfulness of the conduct of another state which was not a party to the case, whatever the nature of the obligations in question (i.e. even if they were *erga omnes* obligations as was the case with regard to the right to self-determination).[149] It was felt that in view of the situation, the Court would have to rule on the lawfulness of Indonesia's conduct with regard to East Timor as a pre-requisite for deciding upon Portugal's claims against Australia[150] and that such a determination would constitute

---

[142] See e.g. the *Libya/Malta* case, ICJ Reports, 1984, pp. 3, 24; 70 ILR, pp. 527, 553, the *Nicaragua* case, ICJ Reports, 1984, pp. 392, 431; 76 ILR, pp. 104, 142, the *El Salvador/Honduras* case, ICJ Reports, 1990, pp. 92, 114–16; 97 ILR, pp. 214, 235–7, and the *Nauru* case, ICJ Reports, 1992, pp. 240, 259–62; 97 ILR, pp. 1, 26–9.

[143] *Cameroon* v. *Nigeria*, ICJ Reports, 2002, pp. 303, 421.

[144] ICJ Reports, 1954, pp. 19, 54; 21 ILR, pp. 399, 406. In this case, Italy asked that the governments of the UK, US and France should deliver to it any share of the monetary gold that might be due to Albania under Part III of the Paris Act of 14 January 1946, as satisfaction for alleged damage to Italy by Albania. Albania chose not to intervene in the case.

[145] ICJ Reports, 1984, pp. 392, 431; 76 ILR, pp. 104, 142.

[146] ICJ Reports, 1992, pp. 240, 261; 97 ILR, p. 28.

[147] *Ibid.* See also *Democratic Republic of the Congo* v. *Uganda*, ICJ Reports, 2005, pp. 168, 237–8.

[148] ICJ Reports, 1995, pp. 90, 101 ff.   [149] *Ibid.*, p. 102.   [150] *Ibid.*, p. 104.

the very subject matter of the judgment requested and thus infringe the *Monetary Gold* principle.[151]

Apart from those instances where states specifically refer a dispute to it, the Court may also be granted jurisdiction over disputes arising from international treaties where such treaties contain a 'compromissory clause' providing for this.[152] In fact, quite a large number of international treaties, both bilateral and multilateral, do include a clause awarding the ICJ jurisdiction with respect to questions that might arise from the interpretation and application of the agreements.[153] Examples of the more important of such conventions include the 1948 Genocide Convention, 1965 Convention on Investment Disputes, the 1965 International Convention on the Elimination of all Forms of Racial Discrimination and the 1970 Hague Convention on Hijacking. In the *Application of the Genocide Convention (Bosnia v. Yugoslavia)* case,[154] the Court founded its jurisdiction upon article IX of the Genocide Convention. In the *US Diplomatic and Consular Staff in Tehran* case (the *Iranian Hostages* case),[155] the Court founded jurisdiction upon article 1 of the Optional Protocols concerning the Compulsory Settlement of Disputes (to which both Iran and the US were parties), which accompany both the Vienna Convention on Diplomatic Relations, 1961 and the Vienna Convention on Consular Relations, 1963. Common article 1 of the Protocol provides that disputes arising out of the interpretation or application of the Conventions lie within the compulsory jurisdiction of the International Court of Justice. The Court also founded jurisdiction in the *Nicaragua*[156] case *inter alia* upon a treaty provision, article XXIV(2) of the 1956 US–Nicaragua Treaty of Friendship, Commerce and Navigation providing for submission of disputes over the interpretation or application of the treaty to the ICJ unless the parties agree to settlement by some other specific means.

---

[151] *Ibid.*, p. 105. See also *Larsen v. Hawaiian Kingdom* 119 ILR, pp. 566, 588–92.

[152] See also article 40 of the ICJ Statute and article 38 of the Court's Rules.

[153] See Rosenne, *Law and Practice*, vol. II, chapter 11. There are almost 300 such treaties, bilateral and multilateral, currently listed on the Court's website: see www.icj-cij.org/icjwww/ibasicdocuments/ibasictext/ibasictreatiesandotherdocs.htm. To these need to be added treaties giving such jurisdiction to the Permanent Court of International Justice: see article 37 of the Court's Statute. See also J. Charney, 'Compromisory Clauses and the Jurisdiction of the International Court of Justice', 81 AJIL, 1989, p. 85.

[154] ICJ Reports, 1996, pp. 595, 615–17 on preliminary objections. See also ICJ Reports, 1993, pp. 3 and 325; 95 ILR, pp. 18 and 43 (the two Orders on Provisional Measures).

[155] ICJ Reports, 1980, pp. 3, 24; 61 ILR, pp. 530, 550.

[156] ICJ Reports, 1984, pp. 392, 426–9; 76 ILR, pp. 104, 137. See Briggs, '*Nicaragua v. United States*: Jurisdiction and Admissibility', 79 AJIL, 1985, p. 373.

In its judgment on jurisdiction and admissibility in the *Case Concerning Border and Transborder Armed Actions (Nicaragua v. Honduras)*,[157] the International Court emphasised that the existence of jurisdiction was a question of law and dependent upon the intention of the parties. The issue of jurisdiction in the case centred, in the view of the Court, upon article 31 of the Pact of Bogotá, 1948, which declared that the parties '[i]n conformity with article 36(2) of the Statute of the International Court of Justice . . . recognise, in relation to any other American state, the jurisdiction of the Court as compulsory *ipso facto* . . . in all disputes of a juridical nature that arise among them' concerning the interpretation of a treaty, any question of international law, the existence of a fact which if established would constitute the breach of an international obligation or the nature or extent of the reparation to be made for the breach of an international obligation. Objections to jurisdiction put forward by Honduras on the grounds that article 31 was not intended to have independent force, and was merely an encouragement to the parties to deposit unilateral declarations of acceptance of the Court's compulsory jurisdiction, and that article 31 would only operate after the exhaustion of conciliation procedures referred to in article 32, were rejected on the basis of interpretation.[158]

Article 31 nowhere envisaged that the undertaking contained therein might be amended subsequently by unilateral declaration and the reference to article 36(2) of the Statute was insufficient to have that effect,[159] while the reference in article 32 of the Pact to a right of recourse to the International Court upon the failure of conciliation provided a second basis for the jurisdiction of the Court and not a limitation upon the first.[160] In other words, the commitment contained in article 31 of the Pact was sufficient to enable the Court to exercise jurisdiction.[161]

Where a treaty in force provides for reference of a matter to the PCIJ or to a tribunal established by the League of Nations, article 37 of the Statute declares that such matter shall be referred to the ICJ, provided the parties

---

[157] ICJ Reports, 1988, pp. 69, 76; 84 ILR, pp. 218, 231.

[158] ICJ Reports, 1988, pp. 78–90. The decision to affirm jurisdiction and admissibility was unanimous.

[159] *Ibid.*, pp. 85–8.   [160] *Ibid.*, pp. 88–90.

[161] By article 6 of the Pact, article 31 would not apply to matters already settled by arrangement between the parties, or by arbitral award or by decision of an international court, or which are governed by agreements or treaties in force on the date of the conclusion of the Pact. See *Nicaragua v. Colombia*, ICJ Reports, 2007, paras. 53 ff. and 120, where the Court rejected Colombia's objection to jurisdiction on the basis of article 31.

to the dispute are parties to the Statute. It is basically a bridging provision and provides some measure of continuity between the old Permanent Court and the new International Court.[162] Under article 36(6) of the Statute, the Court has the competence to decide its own jurisdiction in the event of a dispute.[163]

Article 36(2)[164]

This article has been of great importance in extending the jurisdiction of the International Court. Article 36(2), the so-called 'optional clause', stipulates that:

> The states parties to the present Statute may at any time declare that they recognise as compulsory *ipso facto* and without special agreement, in relation to any other state accepting the same obligation, the jurisdiction of the Court in all legal disputes concerning:
>
> (a) the interpretation of a treaty;
> (b) any question of international law;
> (c) the existence of any fact which, if established, would constitute a breach of an international obligation;
> (d) the nature or extent of the reparation to be made for the breach of an international obligation.

This provision was intended to operate as a method of increasing the Court's jurisdiction, by the gradual increase in its acceptance by more and more states. By the end of 1984, forty-seven declarations were in force and

---

[162] See e.g. the *Ambatielos* case (Preliminary Objections), ICJ Reports, 1952, p. 28; 19 ILR, p. 416 and the *Barcelona Traction* case (Preliminary Objections), ICJ Reports, 1964, p. 6; 46 ILR, p. 18. Cf. the *Aerial Incident* case, ICJ Reports, 1959, p. 127; 27 ILR, p. 557.

[163] See I. Shihata, *The Power of the International Court to Determine Its Own Jurisdiction*, The Hague, 1965. This is a characteristic of the judicial function generally: see e.g. the *Effect of Awards* case, ICJ Reports, 1954, pp. 47, 51–2; 21 ILR, pp. 310, 312, and the *Nottebohm* case, ICJ Reports, 1953, pp. 111, 119; 20 ILR, pp. 567, 572. See also the *Tadić* case before the Appeals Chamber of the International Criminal Tribunal for the Former Yugoslavia, IT-94-1-AR72, pp. 7–9.

[164] See e.g. Rosenne, *Law and Practice*, vol. II, chapter 12. See also J. G. Merrills, 'The Optional Clause Today', 50 BYIL, 1979, p. 87, and Merrills, 'The Optional Clause Revisited', 64 BYIL, 1993, p. 197; L. Gross, 'Compulsory Jurisdiction under the Optional Protocol: History and Practice' in Damrosch, *International Court of Justice at a Crossroads*, p. 19; E. Gordon, '"Legal Disputes" Under Article 36(2) of the Statute', *ibid.*, p. 183; M. Vogiatzi, 'The Historical Evolution of the Optional Clause', 2 *Non-State Actors and International Law*, 2002, p. 41, and M. Fitzmaurice, 'The Optional Clause System and the Law of Treaties', 20 Australian YIL, 2000, p. 127.

deposited with the UN Secretary-General, comprising less than one-third of the parties to the ICJ Statute. By 15 May 2008, this number had risen to sixty-five.[165]

The Court discussed the nature of such declarations in the *Cameroon* v. *Nigeria* (*Preliminary Objections*) case and stated that,

> Any state party to the Statute, in adhering to the jurisdiction of the Court in accordance with article 36, paragraph 2, accepts jurisdiction in its relations with states previously having adhered to that clause. At the same time, it makes a standing offer to the other states parties to the Statute which have not yet deposited a declaration of acceptance. The day one of those states accepts that offer by depositing in its turn its declaration of acceptance, the consensual bond is established and no further condition needs to be met.[166]

Declarations pursuant to article 36(2) are in the majority of cases conditional and, as noted, are dependent upon reciprocity for operation. This means that the Court will only have jurisdiction under article 36(2) to the extent that both the declarations of the two parties in dispute cover the same issue or issues. The doctrine of the lowest common denominator thus operates since the acceptance, by means of the optional clause, by one state of the jurisdiction of the Court is in relation to any other state accepting the same obligation. It is not that declarations in identical terms from the parties are necessary, but both declarations must grant jurisdiction to the Court regarding the dispute in question.

In practice, this can lead to the situation where one party may rely on a condition, or reservation, expressed in the declaration of the other party. This occurred in the *Norwegian Loans* case,[167] between France and Norway. The Court noted that:

> since two unilateral declarations are involved, such jurisdiction is conferred upon the Court only to the extent to which the declarations coincide in conferring it. A comparison between the two declarations shows that the French declaration accepts the Court's jurisdiction within narrower limits than the Norwegian declaration; consequently, the common will of the parties, which is the basis of the Court's jurisdiction, exists within these narrower limits indicated by the French reservation.[168]

---

[165] See www.icj-cij.org/icjwww/ibasicdocuments/ibasictext/ibasicdeclarations.htm.

[166] ICJ Reports, 1998, pp. 275, 291.   [167] ICJ Reports, 1957, p. 9; 24 ILR, p. 782.

[168] ICJ Reports, 1957, p. 23; 24 ILR, p. 786. But note Judge Lauterpacht's individual opinion, ICJ Reports, 1957, p. 34; 24 ILR, p. 793. See also the *Right of Passage* case, ICJ Reports,

Accordingly, Norway was entitled to invoke the French reservation to defeat the jurisdiction of the Court. However, much will depend upon the precise terms of the declarations. Declarations made under the optional clause in the Statute of the PCIJ and still in force are deemed to continue with respect to the ICJ,[169] but in the *Aerial Incident* case[170] between Israel and Bulgaria, the Court declared that this in fact only applied to states signing the ICJ Statute in 1945 and did not relate to states, like Bulgaria, which became a party to the Statute many years later as a result of admission to the United Nations.

The issue also arose in the jurisdictional phase of the *Nicaragua* case.[171] Nicaragua had declared that it would accept the compulsory jurisdiction of the Permanent Court in 1929 but had not ratified this. The US argued that accordingly Nicaragua never became a party to the Statute of the Permanent Court and could not therefore rely on article 36(5). The Court, in an interesting judgment, noted that the Nicaraguan declaration, unconditional and unlimited as to time, had 'a certain potential effect' and that the phrase in article 36(5) 'still in force' could be so interpreted as to cover declarations which had only potential and not binding effect. Ratification of the Statute of the ICJ in 1945 by Nicaragua had the effect, argued the Court, of transforming this potential commitment into an effective one.[172] Since this was so, Nicaragua could rely on the US declaration of 1946 accepting the Court's compulsory jurisdiction as the necessary reciprocal element.[173]

The reservations that have been made in declarations by states under the optional clause, restricting the jurisdiction of the ICJ, vary a great deal from state to state, and are usually an attempt to prevent the Court becoming involved in a dispute which is felt to concern vital interests. One condition made by a number of states, particularly the United States

---

1957, pp. 125, 145; 24 ILR, pp. 840, 845 and the *Interhandel* case, ICJ Reports, 1959, pp. 6, 23; 27 ILR, pp. 475, 487.

[169] Article 36(5), Statute of the ICJ.   [170] ICJ Reports, 1959, p. 127; 27 ILR, p. 557.

[171] ICJ Reports, 1984, pp. 392, 403–12; 76 ILR, pp. 104, 114.

[172] The Court also noted that since Court publications had placed Nicaragua on the list of states accepting the compulsory jurisdiction of the ICJ by virtue of article 36(5) and that no states had objected, one could conclude that the above interpretation had been confirmed, *ibid.* The Court also regarded the conduct of the parties as reflecting acquiescence in Nicaragua's obligations when article 36(5) was argued, ICJ Reports, 1984, pp. 411–15; 76 ILR, p. 122.

[173] But see the Separate Opinions of Judges Mosler, ICJ Reports, 1984, pp. 461–3; Oda, *ibid.*, pp. 473–89; Ago, *ibid.*, pp. 517–27 and Jennings, *ibid.*, pp. 533–45, and the Dissenting Opinion of Judge Schwebel, *ibid.*, pp. 562–600; 76 ILR, pp. 172, 184, 228, 244 and 273.

of America, stipulates that matters within the domestic jurisdiction 'as determined by' that particular state are automatically excluded from the purview of the Court.[174] The validity of this type of reservation (known as the 'Connally amendment' from the American initiator of the relevant legislation) has been widely questioned,[175] particularly since it appears to contradict the power of the Court under article 36(6) to determine its own jurisdiction, and in reality it withdraws from the Court the jurisdiction conferred under the declaration itself. Indeed, it is a well-established principle of international law that the definition of domestic jurisdiction is an issue of international and not domestic law.[176]

Many reservations relate to requirements of time (*ratione temporis*),[177] according to which acceptances of jurisdiction are deemed to expire automatically after a certain period or within a particular time after notice of termination has been given to the UN Secretary-General. Some states exclude the jurisdiction of the ICJ with respect to disputes arising before or after a certain date in their declarations.[178] Reservations *ratione personae* may also be made, for example the UK reservation concerning disputes between member states of the British Commonwealth.[179] Reservations may also be made *ratione materiae*, excluding disputes where other means of dispute settlement have been agreed.[180] Other restrictive grounds exist.[181] However, once the Court is dealing with a dispute, any subsequent

---

[174] See Rosenne, *Law and Practice*, vol. II, pp. 748 ff.

[175] See e.g. L. Henkin, 'The Connally Reservation Revisited and, Hopefully, Contained', 65 AJIL, 1971, p. 374, and Preuss, 'The International Court of Justice, the Senate and Matters of Domestic Jurisdiction', 40 AJIL, 1946, p. 720. See also Judge Lauterpacht, *Norwegian Loans* case, ICJ Reports, 1957, pp. 9, 43–66; 24 ILR, pp. 782, 800; the *Interhandel* case, ICJ Reports, 1959, pp. 6, 77–8 and 93; 27 ILR, pp. 475, 524, 534, and A. D'Amato, 'Modifying US Acceptance of the Compulsory Jurisdiction of the World Court', 79 AJIL, 1985, p. 385.

[176] See above, chapter 12, p. 647.

[177] See Rosenne, *Law and Practice*, vol. II, pp. 751 ff., and Merrills, 'Revisited', pp. 213 ff.

[178] Rosenne, *Law and Practice*, vol. II, pp. 753 ff. The UK, for example, excluded disputes arising out of events occurring between 3 September 1939 and 2 September 1945 in its 1963 declaration, Cmnd 2248. This was altered in the 1969 declaration, which is expressed to apply only to disputes arising after 24 October 1945, Cmnd 3872.

[179] See Merrills, 'Revisited', pp. 219 ff.

[180] *Ibid.*, pp. 224 ff. See the *Nauru* case, ICJ Reports, 1992, pp. 240, 245–7; 97 ILR, pp. 1, 12–14. The Court emphasised that declarations made under article 36(2) related only to disputes between states and did not therefore cover disputes arising out of a trusteeship agreement between the Administering Authority and the indigenous population, *ibid.* See also the *Guinea-Bissau/Senegal* case, ICJ Reports, 1990, p. 64 and *ibid.*, 1991, p. 54; 92 ILR, pp. 1 and 30.

[181] See e.g. reservations relating to territorial matters, Merrills, 'Revisited', pp. 234 ff.

expiry or termination of a party's declaration will not modify the jurisdiction of the case.[182]

A state may withdraw or modify its declaration.[183] The US declaration
of 1946 provided for termination after a six-month period of notice.
What the Court in the jurisdictional phase of the *Nicaragua* case[184] had to
decide was whether a modifying notification[185] expressly deemed to apply
immediately could have effect over the original declaration. It decided
that the six-month notice provision remained valid and could be invoked
by Nicaragua against the US, since it was an undertaking that constituted
an integral part of the instrument that contained it.

Article 36(2) declarations constitute unilateral acts and the Court will
interpret them in order to establish whether or not mutual consent has
been given to its jurisdiction and 'in a natural and reasonable way, having
due regard to the intention of the state concerned at the time when it
accepted the compulsory jurisdiction of the Court'.[186]

The Court has emphasised that there is a 'fundamental distinction
between the existence of the Court's jurisdiction over a dispute, and the
compatibility with international law of the particular acts which are the
subject of the dispute'.[187] This is so even with regard to rights and obligations *erga omnes* or peremptory norms of general international law
(*jus cogens*). The mere fact that a principle has this elevated character in
the international legal system is not enough of itself to confer jurisdiction, for this is dependent upon the consent of the parties.[188] However,
the Court has also emphasised that whether or not it finds that it has

---

[182] See e.g. the *Nottebohm* case, ICJ Reports, 1953, p. 111; 20 ILR, p. 567. See also Judge
Shahabuddeen's Separate Opinion, the *Request for an Examination of the Situation in the
Nuclear Tests Case*, ICJ Reports, 1995, pp. 288, 315.

[183] See e.g. Rosenne, *Law and Practice*, vol. II, pp. 783 ff. A state may waive its jurisdictional
reservation, but this must be done unequivocally, *Application for Revision and Interpretation of the Judgment in the Tunisia/Libya Case*, ICJ Reports, 1985, pp. 192, 216; 81 ILR,
pp. 419, 449, and the *Nicaragua* case, ICJ Reports, 1986, pp. 14, 33; 76 ILR, pp. 349, 367.

[184] ICJ Reports, 1984, pp. 392, 415–21; 76 ILR, p. 126.

[185] Excluding disputes related to Central America for a two-year period. See e.g. A. Chayes,
'Nicaragua, the United States and the World Court', 85 *Columbia Law Review*, 1985,
p. 1445; K. Highet, 'Litigation Implications of the US Withdrawal from the *Nicaragua*
case', 79 AJIL, 1985, p. 992, and US Department of State Statement on the US Withdrawal
from the Proceedings Initiated by Nicaragua in the International Court of Justice, 22 ILM,
1985, p. 246.

[186] *Spain v. Canada*, ICJ Reports, 1998, pp. 432, 454; 123 ILR, pp. 189, 214.

[187] *Serbia and Montenegro v. UK*, ICJ Reports, 2004, pp. 1307, 1351.

[188] *Democratic Republic of the Congo v. Rwanda*, ICJ Reports, 2006, pp. 6, 32 and 52. As to
obligations *erga omnes* and *jus cogens*, see above, chapter 3, p. 123.

jurisdiction with regard to a particular dispute, the parties 'remain in all cases responsible for acts attributable to them that violate the rights of other states'.[189]

Once the Court has established jurisdiction, its treatment of the substance of the dispute will be framed by the terms of the jurisdiction it has found exists, for the Court as a matter of principle cannot deal with issues that lie outside of the consensual ambit it has determined subsists with regard to the dispute in question.[190] However, the Court has the competence to determine the meaning of its own jurisdiction and may interpret the terms of the relevant *compromis*, or treaty or declaration as it deems appropriate in the circumstances.[191] In the *Oil Platforms (Iran v. USA)* case, for example, the Court founded its jurisdiction upon article XXI(2) of the 1955 US–Iran Treaty of Amity, Economic Relations and Consular Rights concerning disputes as to the interpretation or application of that treaty. Article XX(1)d of that treaty provided that the treaty 'shall not preclude the application of measures ... necessary to fulfil the obligations of a High Contracting Party for the maintenance or restoration of international peace and security, or necessary to protect its essential security interests'. The Court noted, in what may be seen as an expansive approach, that 'the interpretation and application of that article will necessarily entail an assessment of the conditions of legitimate self-defence under international law' and further held that the question of the application of that article 'involves the principle of the prohibition in international law of the use of force, and the qualification to it constituted by the right of self-defence'.[192]

Sources of law, propriety and legal interest

In its deliberations, the Court will apply the rules of international law as laid down in article 38 (treaties, custom, general principles of law).[193]

---

[189] *Serbia and Montenegro v. UK*, ICJ Reports, 2004, pp. 1307, 1351.

[190] See e.g. the *Oil Platforms (Iran v. USA)* case, ICJ Reports, 2003, pp. 161, 183; 130 ILR, pp. 323, 342.

[191] See article 36(6) of the Statute and Rosenne, *Law and Practice*, vol. II, pp. 812 ff.

[192] ICJ Reports, 2003, pp. 161, 182–3. Note that at the preliminary objections to jurisdiction phase, the Court regarded that provision as 'confined to affording the Parties a possible defence on the merits to be used should the occasion arise', ICJ Reports, 1996, pp. 803, 811.

[193] See further above, chapter 3. Note that the Court may be specifically requested by the parties to consider particular factors. In the *Tunisia/Libya* case, ICJ Reports, 1982, pp. 18,

However, the Court may decide a case *ex aequo et bono*, i.e. on the basis of justice and equity untrammelled by technical legal rules where the parties agree.[194] This has not yet occurred, although it should not be confused with the ability of the ICJ to apply certain equitable considerations in a case within the framework of international law.[195] The question of gaps in international law in addressing a case arose in the Advisory Opinion concerning *The Legality of the Threat or Use of Nuclear Weapons*.[196] Although not a contentious case and therefore not as such binding, the fact that the Court was unable to give its view on a crucial issue in international law may have ramifications. The Court took the view that it could not 'conclude definitively whether the threat or use of nuclear weapons would be lawful or unlawful in an extreme circumstance of self-defence, in which the very survival of a state would be at stake'.[197] This appearance of a *non-liquet* is of some concern as a matter of principle, unconnected with the substance of the legal principle in question.[198]

Before dealing with the merits of a case, the Court may have to deal with preliminary objections as to its jurisdiction or as to the admissibility of the application.[199] Preliminary objections must be made within three months after the delivery of the Memorial of the applicant state.[200] The Court has emphasised that objections to jurisdiction require decision at the preliminary stage of the proceedings.[201] A decision on preliminary objections to jurisdiction cannot determine merits issues, even where dealt with in connection with preliminary objections. Such reference can only

---

21; 67 ILR, pp. 3, 14, the *compromis* specifically asked the Court to take into account 'the recent trends admitted at the Third Conference on the Law of the Sea'.

[194] Article 38(2) of the Statute. See also A. Pellet, 'Article 38' in Zimmermann *et al.*, *Statute of the International Court*, p. 677 and see above, chapter 3, p. 105.

[195] See e.g. above, chapter 11, p. 590.   [196] ICJ Reports, 1966, p. 226; 110 ILR, 163.

[197] ICJ Reports, 1966, pp. 226, 263 and 266. This is the subject of a strong rebuttal by Judge Higgins in her Dissenting Opinion, *ibid.*, pp. 583, 584 ff.

[198] See above, chapter 3, p. 98.

[199] 'Or other objection', with regard to which a decision is requested before consideration of the merits: see article 79 of the Rules of Court 1978 and the previous sections of this chapter.

[200] Prior to the amendment of article 79 adopted in December 2000, such objections could have been made within the time limit fixed for the delivery of the Counter-Memorial (usually six or nine months). See e.g. *Cameroon v. Nigeria (Preliminary Objections)*, ICJ Reports, 1998, p. 275. See also S. Rosenne, 'The International Court of Justice: Revision of Articles 79 and 80 of the Rules of Court', 14 *Leiden Journal of International Law*, 2001, p. 77.

[201] The *Nicaragua* case, ICJ Reports, 1986, pp. 3, 30–1; 76 ILR, pp. 349, 364–5.

be provisional.[202] Where it has established its right to exercise jurisdiction, the Court may well decline to exercise that right on grounds of propriety. In the *Northern Cameroons* case,[203] the Court declared that:

> it may pronounce judgment only in connection with concrete cases where there exists, at the time of adjudication, an actual controversy involving a conflict of legal interests between the parties. The Court's judgment must have some practical consequence in the sense that it can affect existing legal rights or obligations of the parties, thus removing uncertainty from their legal relations.

Further, events subsequent to the filing of the application may render the application without object, so that the Court is not required to give a decision.[204]

In addition, and following the *South-West Africa* cases (Second Phase) in 1966,[205] it may be necessary for the Court to establish that the claimant state has a legal interest in the subject matter of the dispute. The fact that political considerations may have motivated the application is not relevant, so long as a legal dispute is in evidence. Similarly, the fact that a particular dispute has other important aspects is not of itself sufficient to render the application inadmissible.[206]

Evidence

Unlike domestic courts, the International Court is flexible with regard to the introduction of evidence.[207] Strict rules of admissibility common

---

[202] See the *South-West Africa* cases, ICJ Reports, 1966, pp. 3, 37; 37 ILR, pp. 243, 270. It is to be noted that admissibility issues may be discussed at the merits stage: see e.g. the *East Timor* case, ICJ Reports, 1995, p. 90; 105 ILR, p. 226. See also C. M. Chinkin, 'East Timor Moves into the World Court', 4 EJIL, 1993, p. 206.

[203] ICJ Reports, 1963, pp. 15, 33–4; 35 ILR, pp. 353, 369.

[204] See e.g. the *Armed Actions (Nicaragua v. Honduras)* case, ICJ Reports, 1988, pp. 69, 95; 84 ILR, p. 218; the *Nuclear Tests* case, ICJ Reports, 1974, pp. 253, 272; 57 ILR, p. 348; the *Lockerbie (Preliminary Objections)* case, ICJ Reports, 1998, pp. 9, 26; 117 ILR, pp. 1, 24; and *Democratic Republic of the Congo v. Belgium*, ICJ Reports, 2002, pp. 3, 14–15; 128 ILR, pp. 60, 69–70.

[205] ICJ Reports, 1966, p. 6; 37 ILR, p. 243.   [206] See above, p. 1065.

[207] See e.g. K. Highet, 'Evidence and Proof of Facts' in Damrosch, *International Court of Justice at a Crossroads*, pp. 355, 357, and C. F. Amerasinghe, 'Presumptions and Inferences in Evidence in International Litigation', 3 *The Law and Practice of International Courts and Tribunals*, 2004, p. 394. See also D. V. Sandifer, *Evidence before International Tribunals*, Charlottesville, 1975; S. Schwebel, *Justice in International Law*, Cambridge, 1994, p. 125; K. Highet, 'Evidence, the Court and the *Nicaragua* Case', 81 AJIL, 1987, p. 1;

in domestic legal systems do not exist here.[208] The Court has the competence *inter alia* to determine the existence of any fact which if established would constitute a breach of an international obligation.[209] It may make all arrangements with regard to the taking of evidence,[210] call upon the agents to produce any document or to supply any explanations as may be required,[211] or at any time establish an inquiry mechanism or obtain expert opinion.[212] The Court may indeed make on-site visits.[213] However, it has no power to compel production of evidence generally, nor may witnesses be subpoenaed, nor is there is any equivalent to proceedings for contempt of court.[214] The use of experts has been comparatively rare[215] as has been recourse to witnesses.[216] Agents are rarely asked to produce documents or supply explanations and there have been only two on-site visits to date.[217] This has meant that the Court has sought to evaluate claims primarily upon an assessment of the documentary evidence provided, utilising also legal techniques such as inferences and admissions against interest.[218]

The Court will make its own determination of the facts and then apply the relevant rules of international law to those facts it has found to exist and which are necessary in order to respond to the submissions of the

M. Kazazi, *Burden of Proof and Related Issues*, The Hague, 1996, and T. M. Franck, *Fairness in International Law and Institutions*, Oxford, 1995, pp. 335 ff.

[208] President Schwebel in his address to the UN General Assembly on 27 October 1997 noted that the Court's 'attitude to evidence is demonstrably flexible': see www.icj-cij.org/icjwww/ipresscom/SPEECHES/Ga1997e.htm. See e.g. the introduction of illegally obtained evidence in the *Corfu Channel* case, ICJ Reports, 1949, pp. 4, 32–6; 16 AD, p. 155.

[209] Article 36 of the Statute.   [210] Article 48 of the Statute.   [211] Article 49 of the Statute.

[212] Article 50 of the Statute. By article 43(5), the Court may hear witnesses and experts, as well as agents, counsel and advocates.

[213] Article 44(2) of the Statute and article 66 of the Rules of Court.

[214] See K. Highet, 'Evidence, the Court and the *Nicaragua* Case', p. 10.

[215] But see the *Corfu Channel* case, ICJ Reports, 1949, p. 4; 16 AD, p. 155.

[216] But see *ibid.*, and the *Tunisia/Libya* case, ICJ Reports, 1989, p. 18; 67 ILR, p. 4; the *Libya/Malta* case, ICJ Reports, 1985, p. 13; 81 ILR, p. 238, and the *Nicaragua* case, ICJ Reports, 1986, p. 14; 76 ILR, p. 349.

[217] First, in the *Diversion of the River Meuse* case, PCIJ, Series A/B, No. 70, and secondly in the *Gabčíkovo–Nagymaros Project* case, ICJ Communiqué No. 97/3, 17 February 1997 and see ICJ Reports, 1997, pp. 7, 14; 116 ILR, p. 1.

[218] See e.g. the *Iranian Hostages* case, ICJ Reports, 1980, pp. 3, 9; 61 ILR, pp. 530, 535. See also F. A. Mann, 'Foreign Investment in the International Court of Justice: The *ELSI* Case', 86 AJIL, 1992, pp. 92, 94–5, and the *El Salvador/Honduras* case, ICJ Reports, 1992, pp. 351, 574; 97 ILR, pp. 112, 490. Note in particular the *Nicaragua* case, ICJ Reports, 1986, p. 14; 76 ILR, p. 349. The difficulties of proving facts in this case were exacerbated by the absence of the respondent state during the proceedings on the merits.

parties, including defences and counter-claims. These findings of facts require an assessment of the evidence, which necessitates the Court deciding which of the material before it is relevant and of probative value with regard to the alleged facts. In so doing, the Court will make its own assessment of the weight, reliability and value of the evidence produced by the parties.[219] The Court has noted that it will treat with caution evidentiary materials specially prepared for the case in question[220] and also materials emanating from a single source, but would give particular attention to reliable evidence acknowledging facts or conduct unfavourable to the state represented by the person making them.[221] Weight would also be given to evidence that has not been challenged by impartial persons for the correctness of what it contains and special attention given to evidence obtained by skilled judicial examination and cross-examination of persons directly involved.[222] However, the evidence of government and military figures of a state involved in litigation before the Court would be treated with 'great reserve'.[223] The Court has also noted that witness statements produced in the form of affidavits should be treated with caution and in assessing such affidavits, a number of factors would have to be taken into account, including whether they had been made by state officials or private persons not interested in the outcome of the proceedings and whether a particular affidavit attests to the existence of facts or represents only an opinion with regard to certain events. Evidence which is contemporaneous with the period concerned may, however, be of special value. Further, a statement by a competent governmental official with regard to boundary lines is likely to have greater weight than sworn statements of a private person.[224]

---

[219] *Democratic Republic of the Congo* v. *Uganda*, ICJ Reports, 2005, pp. 168, 200.

[220] However, the Court has noted that affidavits prepared for litigation purposes may be received if they attest to personal knowledge of facts by a particular individual, *Nicaragua* v. *Honduras*, ICJ Reports, 2007, para. 244.

[221] *Democratic Republic of the Congo* v. *Uganda*, ICJ Reports, 2005, pp. 168, 200 and 206. See also *Nicaragua* v. *USA*, ICJ Reports, 1986, pp. 14, 41; 76 ILR, p. 349.

[222] *Democratic Republic of the Congo* v. *Uganda*, ICJ Reports, 2005, pp. 168, 201. See also the *Genocide Convention (Bosnia* v. *Serbia)* case, ICJ Reports, 2007, para. 213, where it was held that in principle the Court would accept as highly persuasive relevant findings of fact made by the International Criminal Tribunal for the Former Yugoslavia at trial, unless they had been upset on appeal. In addition, any evaluation by the Tribunal based on the facts was entitled to due weight. However, the procedural stages prior to a decision, which did not involve definitive rulings, should not be given weight, *ibid.*, paras. 216 ff.

[223] *Democratic Republic of the Congo* v. *Uganda*, ICJ Reports, 2005, pp. 168, 203.

[224] *Nicaragua* v. *Honduras*, ICJ Reports, 2007, para. 244.

The Court may also take judicial notice of facts which are public knowledge, primarily through media dissemination, provided that caution was shown and that the reports do not emanate from a single source.[225] In *Democratic Republic of the Congo* v. *Uganda*, the Court noted the particular importance of consistency and concordance in evaluating press information.[226]

The burden of proof lies upon the party seeking to assert a particular fact or facts,[227] although the Court has also stated that there was no burden of proof to be discharged in the matter of jurisdiction.[228] On the other hand, the burden of proof, and a relatively high one, lies upon the applicant state who wishes to intervene. Such state 'must demonstrate convincingly what it asserts, and thus . . . bear the burden of proof', although it need only show that its interest may be affected, not that it will or must be so affected. It must identify the interest of a legal nature in question and show how that interest may be affected.[229] The actual standard of proof required will vary with the character of the particular issue of fact.[230] In the *Genocide Convention (Bosnia* v. *Serbia)* case, the Court emphasised that it had long recognised that 'claims against a state involving charges of exceptional gravity must be proved by evidence that is fully conclusive'.

---

[225] See the *Nicaragua* case, ICJ Reports, 1986, pp. 14, 41; 76 ILR, p. 349.

[226] ICJ Reports, 2005, pp. 168, 204. As to the value of maps as evidence, see *ibid.*, p. 206 and above, chapter 10, p. 519.

[227] See e.g. the *Nicaragua (Jurisdiction and Admissibility)* case, ICJ Reports, 1984, pp. 392, 437; 76 ILR, p. 1; the *Fisheries Jurisdiction (Spain* v. *Canada)* case, ICJ Reports, 1998, pp. 432, 450; the *Avena (Mexico* v. *USA)* case, ICJ Reports, 2004, pp. 12, 41; 134 ILR, pp. 120, 144, and the *Genocide Convention (Bosnia* v. *Serbia)* case, ICJ Reports, 2007, para. 204. Note also the view taken by the Arbitral Tribunal for Dispute over Inter-Entity Boundary in Brcko Area in its Award of 14 February 1997. The Appendix to the Order lays down the Principles Applicable to the Admissibility of Evidence and notes *inter alia* that each party bears the burden of proving its own case and, in particular, facts alleged by it. The party having the burden of proof must not only bring evidence in support of its allegations, but must also convince the Tribunal of their truth. The Tribunal is not bound to adhere to strict judicial rules of evidence, the probative force of evidence being for the Tribunal to determine. Where proof of a fact presents extreme difficulty, the Tribunal may be satisfied with less conclusive, i.e. *prima facie*, evidence: see 36 ILM, 1997, pp. 396, 402–3.

[228] See the *Fisheries Jurisdiction (Spain* v. *Canada)* case, ICJ Reports, 1998, pp. 432, 450.

[229] *El Salvador/Honduras (Intervention)*, ICJ Reports, 1990, pp. 92, 117–18; 97 ILR, pp. 112, 238–9 and *Indonesia/Malaysia (Intervention)*, ICJ Reports, 2001, para. 29. As to third-party intervention, see below, p. 1097.

[230] Judge Higgins in her Separate Opinion in the *Oil Platforms (Iran* v. *USA)* case, ICJ Reports, 2003, pp. 161, 233; 130 ILR, pp. 323, 392, noted that 'the Court's prime objective appears to have been to retain a freedom in evaluating the evidence, relying on the facts and circumstances of each case'. See also Judge Shahabuddeen's Dissenting Opinion in the *Qatar* v. *Bahrain* case, ICJ Reports, 1995, pp. 6, 63; 102 ILR, pp. 1, 104.

The Court would need to 'be fully convinced that allegations made in the proceedings, that the crime of genocide or the other acts enumerated in Article III [of the Genocide Convention] have been committed, have been clearly established' and it has noted that the same standard of proof would apply to the proof of attribution for such acts.[231]

Evidence which has been illegally or improperly acquired may also be taken into account, although no doubt where this happens its probative value would be adjusted accordingly.[232] In the second provisional measures order in the *Application of the Genocide Convention (Bosnia v. Yugoslavia)* case, for example, the Court was prepared to admit a series of documents even though submitted on the eve of and during the oral hearings despite being 'difficult to reconcile with an orderly progress of the procedure before the Court, and with respect for the principle of equality of the parties'.[233] In dealing with questions of evidence, the Court proceeds upon the basis that its decision will be based upon the facts occurring up to the close of the oral proceedings on the merits of the case.[234]

In so far as the scope of the Court's decision is concerned, it was noted in the *Nicaragua* case that the Court 'is bound to confine its decision to those points of law which are essential to the settlement of the dispute before it'.[235] In so doing, the Court will seek to ascertain 'the true subject of the dispute' taking into consideration the submissions, the applications, oral arguments and other documents placed before it.[236]

---

[231] ICJ Reports, 2007, para. 209. See also *Corfu Channel (United Kingdom v. Albania)*, ICJ Reports, 1949, p. 17. Judge Higgins in her Separate Opinion in the *Oil Platforms (Iran v. USA)* case, ICJ Reports, 2003, pp. 161, 234, noted that 'the graver the charge the more confidence there must be in the evidence relied on'.

[232] See e.g. the *Corfu Channel* case, ICJ Reports, 1949, pp. 4, 32–6; 16 AD, p. 155. See also H. Thirlway, 'Dilemma or Chimera? Admissibility of Illegally Obtained Evidence in International Adjudication', 78 AJIL, 1984, p. 622, and G. Marston, 'Falsification of Documentary Evidence Before International Tribunals: An Aspect of the *Behring Sea* Arbitration, 1892–3', 71 BYIL, 2000, p. 357. See also the difficulties in the *Qatar v. Bahrain* case, International Court of Justice, Order of 17 February 1999.

[233] ICJ Reports, 1993, pp. 325, 336–7. Article 56 of the Rules provides that after the closure of written proceedings, no further documents may be submitted to the Court by either party except with the consent of the other party or, in the absence of consent, where the Court, after hearing the parties, authorises production where it is felt that the documents are necessary.

[234] The *Nicaragua* case, ICJ Reports, 1986, pp. 3, 39; 76 ILR, pp. 349, 373. Although note that in the *Lockerbie* case, ICJ Reports, 1992, pp. 3, 13; 94 ILR, pp. 478, 496, the Court referred in detail to Security Council resolution 748 (1992) adopted three days after the close of the oral hearings.

[235] ICJ Reports, 1986, pp. 3, 110; 76 ILR, pp. 349, 444.

[236] The *Nuclear Tests* case, ICJ Reports, 1974, pp. 466–7.

Provisional measures [237]

Under article 41 of the Statute, the Court has the power to indicate, if it considers that circumstances so require, any provisional (or interim) measures which ought to be taken to preserve the respective rights of either party. In deciding upon a request for provisional measures, the Court need not finally satisfy itself that it has jurisdiction on the merits of the case, although it has held that it ought not to indicate such measures unless the provisions invoked by the applicant appear *prima facie* to afford a basis upon which the jurisdiction of the Court might be founded,[238] whether the request for the indication of provisional measures is made by the applicant or by the respondent in the proceedings on the merits.[239] In establishing the Court's *prima facie* jurisdiction to deal with the merits of the case, the question of the nature and extent of the rights for which

---

[237] See e.g. Rosenne, *Law and Practice*, vol. III, chapter 24, and Rosenne, *Provisional Measures in International Law: The International Court of Justice and the Tribunal for the Law of the Sea*, Oxford, 2005; K. Oellers-Frahm, 'Article 41' in Zimmermann *et al.*, *Statute of the International Court*, p. 923; S. Oda, 'Provisional Measures' in Lowe and Fitzmaurice, *Fifty Years of the International Court of Justice*, p. 541; B. Oxman, 'Jurisdiction and the Power to Indicate Provisional Measures' in Damrosch, *International Court of Justice at a Crossroads*, p. 323; C. Gray, *Judicial Remedies in International Law*, Oxford, 1987, pp. 69–74; Elias, *International Court*, chapter 3; J. G. Merrills, 'Interim Measures of Protection and the Substantive Jurisdiction of the International Court', 36 *Cambridge Law Journal*, 1977, p. 86, and Merrills, 'Reflections on the Incidental Jurisdiction of the International Court of Justice' in *Remedies in International Law* (eds. M. Evans and S. V. Konstanidis), Oxford, 1998, p. 51; L. Gross, 'The Case Concerning United States Diplomatic and Consular Staff in Tehran: Phase of Provisional Measures', 74 AJIL, 1980, p. 395, and M. Mendelson, 'Interim Measures of Protection in Cases of Contested Jurisdiction', 46 BYIL, 1972–3, p. 259. See also articles 73–8 of the Rules of Court 1978.

[238] See e.g. the *Avena (Mexico v. USA)* case, ICJ Reports, 2003, pp. 77, 87; 134 ILR, pp. 104, 113; *Democratic Republic of the Congo v. Rwanda*, ICJ Reports, 2002, p. 241 and the two *Pulp Mills (Argentina v. Uruguay)* applications for provisional measures, ICJ Reports, 2006, pp. 113, 128–9 and ICJ Reports, 2007, para. 24. See also the request for the indication of provisional measures in the *Legality of the Use of Force (Yugoslavia v. Belgium)* case, ICJ Reports, 1999, pp. 124, 132; the *Arbitral Award of 31 July 1989 (Guinea-Bissau v. Senegal)* case, ICJ Reports, 1990, pp. 64, 68; 92 ILR, pp. 9, 13, the *Great Belt* case, ICJ Reports, 1991, pp. 12, 15; 94 ILR, pp. 446, 453, where jurisdiction was not at issue, and *Cameroon v. Nigeria*, ICJ Reports, 1996, pp. 13, 21, where it was. The Court in *Application of the Genocide Convention (Bosnia v. Yugoslavia)*, ICJ Reports, 1993, pp. 3, 12; 95 ILR, pp. 1, 27, declared that jurisdiction included both jurisdiction *ratione personae* and jurisdiction *ratione materiae*. Note that Jiménez de Aréchaga, a former President of the Court, has written that 'interim measures will not be granted unless a majority of judges believes at the time that there will be jurisdiction over the merits', 'International Law in the Past Third of a Century', 159 HR, 1978 I, pp. 1, 161.

[239] The *Pulp Mills (Argentina v. Uruguay)* case, Provisional Measures, Order of 23 January 2007, ICJ Reports, 2007, para. 24.

protection is being sought in the request for the indication of provisional measures has no bearing, this being addressed once the Court's *prima facie* jurisdiction over the merits of the case has been established.[240]

The Court, when considering a request for the indication of provisional measures, 'must be concerned to preserve ... the rights which may subsequently be adjudged by the Court to belong either to the Applicant or to the Respondent',[241] without being obliged at that stage of the proceedings to rule on those rights.[242] Thus, the purpose of exercising the power is to protect 'rights which are the subject of dispute in judicial proceedings'[243] and thus the measures must be such that once the dispute over those rights has been resolved by the Court's judgment on the merits, they would no longer be required.[244] These are awarded to assist the Court to ensure the integrity of the proceedings. Such interim measures were granted by the Court in the *Fisheries Jurisdiction* case,[245] to protect British fishing rights in Icelandic-claimed waters, and again in the *Nuclear Tests* case.[246] In the *Fisheries Jurisdiction* case, the Court emphasised that article 41 presupposes 'that irreparable prejudice should not be caused to rights which are the subject of dispute in judicial proceedings'.[247] However, it was noted in the *Lockerbie* case[248] that the measures requested by Libya 'would be likely to impair the rights which appear *prima facie* to be enjoyed by the United Kingdom by virtue of Security Council resolution 748 (1992)'. The Court has also stated that its power to indicate provisional measures can

---

[240] *Ibid.*, para. 25.

[241] *Cameroon v. Nigeria*, Provisional Measures, Order of 15 March 1996, ICJ Reports, 1996 (I), p. 22, para. 35.

[242] The *Avena (Mexico v. USA)* case, Provisional Measures, Order of 5 February 2003, ICJ Reports, 2003, pp. 77, 89; 134 ILR, pp. 104, 115.

[243] The *Aegean Sea Continental Shelf* case, ICJ Reports, 1976, pp. 3, 9; 60 ILR, pp. 524, 530 and the *Iranian Hostages* case, ICJ Reports, 1979, pp. 7, 19; 61 ILR, pp. 513, 525. See also the *Arbitral Award of 31 July 1989* case, ICJ Reports, 1990, pp. 64, 69; 92 ILR, pp. 9, 14.

[244] *Arbitral Award of 31 July 1989* case, ICJ Reports, 1990, p. 69; 92 ILR, pp. 9, 14.

[245] ICJ Reports, 1972, p. 12; 55 ILR, p. 160. See also the *Anglo-Iranian Oil Co.* case, ICJ Reports, 1951, p. 89; 19 ILR, p. 501.

[246] ICJ Reports, 1973, p. 99; 57 ILR, p. 360. They were also granted in the *Iranian Hostages* case, ICJ Reports, 1979, pp. 7, 19; 61 ILR, pp. 513, 525 and in the *Nicaragua* case, ICJ Reports, 1980, p. 169; 76 ILR, p. 35. See also the *Great Belt* case, ICJ Reports, 1991, p. 12; 94 ILR, p. 446, *Application of the Genocide Convention (Bosnia v. Yugoslavia)*, ICJ Reports, 1993, pp. 3 and 325; 95 ILR, p. 1, and the *Cameroon v. Nigeria* case, ICJ Reports, 1996, p. 13. See also the *LaGrand* case, ICJ Reports, 1999, p. 9; 118 ILR, p. 37.

[247] ICJ Reports, 1972, pp. 12, 16, 30, 34; 55 ILR, pp. 160, 164; 56 ILR, pp. 76, 80. See also the *Iranian Hostages* case, ICJ Reports, 1979, pp. 7, 19; 61 ILR, p. 525, *Application of the Genocide Convention (Bosnia v. Yugoslavia)*, ICJ Reports, 1993, pp. 3, 19; 95 ILR, pp. 1, 34 and *Cameroon v. Nigeria*, ICJ Reports, 1996, pp. 13, 21–2.

[248] ICJ Reports, 1992, pp. 3, 15; 95 ILR, pp. 478, 498.

be exercised only if there is an 'urgent necessity to prevent irreparable prejudice to such rights, before the Court has given its final decision'[249] and that 'the sound administration of justice requires that a request for the indication of provisional measures founded on Article 73 of the Rules of Court be submitted in good time'.[250]

Provisional measures or recommendations or statements as to relevant international obligations may also be indicated or made by the Court, independently of requests by the parties, with a view to preventing 'the aggravation or extension of the dispute whenever it considers that circumstances so require'.[251] In *Cameroon v. Nigeria*, the Court referred explicitly not only to the rights of each party, but also by calling on the parties to observe an agreement reached for cessation of hostilities, to take all necessary steps to preserve relevant evidence in the disputed area and to co-operate with a proposed UN fact-finding mission.[252] The Court also took care to link with the rights of the parties that were being protected the danger to persons within the disputed area.[253]

The question of the legal effects of orders indicating provisional measures was discussed and decided by the Court for the first time in the *LaGrand* case. The Court addressed the issue in the light of the object and purpose of the Statute[254] which was to enable it to fulfil its functions and in particular to reach binding decisions. The Court declared that:

> The context in which article 41 has to be seen within the Statute is to prevent the Court from being hampered in the exercise of its functions because the respective rights of the parties to a dispute before the Court

---

[249] See e.g. the*Great Belt (Finland v. Denmark)* case, Provisional Measures, Order of 29 July 1991, ICJ Reports 1991, pp. 12, 17; *Republic of the Congo v. France*, Provisional Measures, Order of 17 June 2003, ICJ Reports 2003, p. 107, para. 22 and the *Pulp Mills (Argentina v. Uruguay)* case, Provisional Measures, Order of 23 January 2007, ICJ Reports, 2007, para. 32. See also *Cameroon v. Nigeria*, ICJ Reports, 1996, pp. 13, 22 and the *Avena (Mexico v. USA)* case, ICJ Reports, 2003, pp. 77, 90; 134 ILR, pp. 104, 116.

[250] The *LaGrand (Germany v. USA)* case, Provisional Measures, Order of 3 March 1999, ICJ Reports, 1999 (I), p. 14, para. 19; 118 ILR, p. 44.

[251] *Cameroon v. Nigeria*, ICJ Reports, 1996, pp. 13, 23. See also the *Burkina Faso/Mali* case, ICJ Reports, 1986, pp. 3, 9; 80 ILR, pp. 440, 456 and the *Pulp Mills (Argentina v. Uruguay)* case, Provisional Measures, Order of 23 January 2007, ICJ Reports, 2007, paras. 49 and 53.

[252] See the *dispositif*, ICJ Reports, 1996, pp. 13, 24–5.

[253] *Ibid.*, p. 23. See also J. D'Aspremont, 'The Recommendations Made by the International Court of Justice', 56 ICLQ, 2007, p. 185. Note that the Court may make such recommendations even where it refuses to grant an order for provisional measures.

[254] Referring to article 33(4) of the Vienna Convention on the Law of Treaties, 1969, which the Court noted reflected customary law, ICJ Reports, 2001, pp. 466, 506.

are not preserved. It follows from the object and purpose of the Statute, as well as from the terms of article 41 when read in this context, that the power to indicate provisional measures entails that such measures should be binding, inasmuch as the power in question is based on the necessity, when the circumstances call for it, to safeguard, and to avoid prejudice to, the right of the parties as determined by the final judgment of the Court. The contention that provisional measures indicated under article 41 might not be binding would be contrary to the object and purpose of that article.[255]

This clear and unanimous decision that provisional measures orders are binding until judgment on the merits is likely to have a significant impact.[256]

Counter-claims [257]

Article 80 of the Rules of Court provides that the Court may entertain a counter-claim only if it comes within the jurisdiction of the Court and 'is directly connected with the subject-matter of the claim of the other party'.[258] A counter-claim constitutes a separate claim, or 'autonomous legal act', while requiring to be linked to the principal claim.[259] It goes beyond a mere defence on the merits to the principal claim, but cannot be used as a means of referring to a court claims which exceed the limits of its jurisdiction as recognised by the parties.[260] The Rule does not define what is meant by direct connection and this is a matter for the discretion of the

---

[255] *Ibid.*, pp. 502–3. The Court also referred to a related reason, the principle that parties to a case must abstain from any measure capable of exercising a prejudicial effect regarding the execution of the decision to be given and not to allow any step to be taken which might aggravate or extend the dispute, citing the *Electricity Company of Sofia and Bulgaria*, PCIJ, Series A/B, No. 79, p. 199, *ibid.*, p. 503. The Court also noted that the preparatory work leading to the adoption of article 41 did not preclude the conclusion that orders under that article have binding force, *ibid.*, pp. 503 ff.

[256] See *Democratic Republic of the Congo* v. *Uganda*, ICJ Reports, 2005, pp. 168, 258 and the *Genocide Convention (Bosnia* v. *Serbia)* case, ICJ Reports, 2007, paras. 452 and 468.

[257] See e.g. Rosenne, *Law and Practice*, vol. III, p. 1232, and Rosenne, 'Counter-Claims in the International Court of Justice Revisited' in *Liber Amicorum Judge Ruda* (eds. C. A. Armas *et al.*), The Hague, 2000, p. 457.

[258] As revised in 2000. One major difference from the text of the previous Rule 80 is to emphasise the role of the Court. See Rosenne, 'Revision', p. 83. The Rule also provides that 'a counter-claim shall be made in the Counter-Memorial and shall appear as part of the submissions contained therein. The right of the other party to present its views in writing on the counter-claim, in an additional pleading, shall be preserved, irrespective of any decision of the Court, in accordance with Article 45, paragraph 2, of these Rules, concerning the filing of further written pleadings.'

[259] *Application of the Genocide Convention (Counter-Claims)*, ICJ Reports, 1997, pp. 243, 256.

[260] *Ibid.*, p. 257.

Court, which has noted that 'the degree of connection between the claims must be assessed both in fact and in law'.[261] The direct connection of facts has been referred to in terms of 'facts of the same nature . . . [that] form part of the same factual complex'[262] while in the *Application of the Genocide Convention* case the direct connection of law appeared in that both parties sought the same legal aim, being the establishment of legal responsibility for violations of the Genocide Convention.[263] In the *Oil Platforms (Iran v. USA)* case, the Court held that it was open to the parties to challenge the admissibility of counter-claims in general at the merits stage of the proceedings, even though the counter-claims had previously been found admissible. That was because the earlier incidental proceedings were concerned only with the question of whether the requirements of article 80 of the Rules had been complied with, i.e. that the counter-claim is directly connected with the subject-matter of the principal claim. A more general challenge, going beyond the terms of article 80, was therefore possible at the merits stage.[264]

Third-party intervention [265]

There is no general right of intervention in cases before the Court by third parties as such, nor any procedure for joinder of new parties by the

---

[261] *Ibid.*, p. 258. See also the *Oil Platforms (Iran v. USA) (Counter-Claims)*, case, ICJ Reports, 1998, pp. 190, 204–5. The Court has also noted that counter-claims do not have to rely on identical instruments to meet the 'connection' test of article 80: see *Democratic Republic of the Congo v. Uganda*, ICJ Reports, 2005, pp. 168, 275.

[262] See *Application of the Genocide Convention (Counter-Claims)*, ICJ Reports, 1997, pp. 243, 258 and *Cameroon v. Nigeria*, International Court of Justice, Order of 30 June 1999. See also the *Oil Platforms (Iran v. USA) (Counter-Claims)* case, ICJ Reports, 1998, pp. 190, 205; *Democratic Republic of the Congo v. Uganda (Counter-Claims)*, Order of 29 November 2001, ICJ Reports, 2001, p. 664 and *Democratic Republic of the Congo v. Uganda*, ICJ Reports, 2005, pp. 168, 259 ff.

[263] *Application of the Genocide Convention (Counter-Claims)*, ICJ Reports, 1997, pp. 243, 258. In *Cameroon v. Nigeria*, the 'same legal aim' was the establishment of legal responsibility for frontier incidents, International Court of Justice, Order of 30 June 1999. See also the *Oil Platforms (Iran v. USA) (Counter-Claims)* case, ICJ Reports, 1998, pp. 190, 205.

[264] ICJ Reports, 2003, pp. 161, 210. See also *Democratic Republic of the Congo v. Uganda*, ICJ Reports, 2005, pp. 168, 261.

[265] See e.g. Rosenne, *Law and Practice*, vol. III, chapter 26, and Rosenne, *Intervention in the International Court of Justice*, Dordrecht, 1993; J. M. Ruda, 'Intervention Before the International Court of Justice' in Lowe and Fitzmaurice, *Fifty Years of the International Court of Justice*, p. 487; C. M. Chinkin, 'Third Party Intervention Before the International Court of Justice', 80 AJIL, 1986, p. 495; Elias, *International Court*, chapter 4, and P. Jessup, 'Intervention in the International Court', 75 AJIL, 1981, p. 903. See also articles 81–6 of the Rules of Court 1978.

Court itself, nor any power by which the Court can direct that third states be made a party to proceedings.[266] However, under article 62 of the Statute of the ICJ, any state which considers that it has an interest of a legal nature which may be affected by the decision in a case, may submit a request to be permitted to intervene,[267] while under article 63, where the construction of a convention to which states other than those concerned in the case are parties is in question,[268] the Registrar of the Court shall notify all such states forthwith. Every state so notified has the right to intervene in the proceedings.[269]

Essentially, the Court may permit an intervention by a third party even though it be opposed by one or both of the parties to the case. The purpose of such intervention is carefully circumscribed and closely defined in terms of the protection of a state's interest of a legal nature which may be affected by a decision in an existing case, and accordingly intervention cannot be used as a substitute for contentious proceedings, which are based upon consent. Thus the intervener does not as such become a party to the case.[270]

The Court appeared to have set a fairly high threshold of permitted intervention. In the *Nuclear Tests* case,[271] Fiji sought to intervene in the dispute between France on the one hand and New Zealand and Australia on the other, but the Court postponed consideration of this and, after its judgment that the issue was moot, it was clearly unnecessary to take any further steps regarding Fiji. Malta sought to intervene in the *Tunisia/Libya Continental Shelf* case[272] in the light of its shelf delimitation dispute with Libya in order to submit its views to the Court. The Court felt that the real purpose of Malta's intervention was unclear and

---

[266] See the *Libya/Malta* case, ICJ Reports, 1984, p. 25; 70 ILR, p. 527, and the *Nicaragua* case, ICJ Reports, 1984, p. 431; 76 ILR, p. 104.

[267] See C. Chinkin, 'Article 62' in Zimmermann *et al.*, *Statute of the International Court*, p. 1331. See also article 81 of the Rules of Court. It is for the Court itself to decide upon any request for permission to intervene: see the *Tunisia/Libya (Intervention)* case, ICJ Reports, 1981, pp. 3, 12; 62 ILR, p. 608.

[268] See here the *SS Wimbledon* case, PCIJ, Series A, No. 1 (1923); 2 AD, p. 4; the *Haya de la Torre* case, ICJ Reports, 1951, pp. 71, 76–7; 18 ILR, pp. 349, 356–7, and the *Nicaragua* case, ICJ Reports, 1984, pp. 215–16; 76 ILR, pp. 74–5. See also C. Chinkin, 'Article 63' in Zimmermann *et al.*, *Statute of the International Court*, p. 1369.

[269] See the *Wimbledon* case, PCIJ, Series A, No. 1 (1923), pp. 9–13, and the *Haya de la Torre* case, ICJ Reports, 1951, p. 71; 18 ILR, p. 349.

[270] *El Salvador/Honduras (Intervention)*, ICJ Reports, 1990, pp. 92, 134–5; 97 ILR, p. 112. See also E. Lauterpacht, *Aspects*, pp. 26 ff.

[271] ICJ Reports, 1974, p. 253; 57 ILR, p. 398.   [272] ICJ Reports, 1982, p. 18; 67 ILR, p. 4.

did not relate to any legal interest of its own directly in issue as between Tunisia and Libya in the proceedings or as between itself and either one of those countries.[273] While Malta did have an interest similar to other states in the area in the case in question, the Court said[274] that in order to intervene under article 62 it had to have an interest of a legal nature which might be affected by the Court's decision in the instant case.

However, the Court granted permission for the very first time in the history of both the ICJ and its predecessor to a third state intervening under article 62 of the Statute to Nicaragua in the case concerning the *Land, Island and Maritime Frontier Dispute (El Salvador/Honduras)*. The Court held unanimously that Nicaragua had demonstrated that it had an interest of a legal nature which might be affected by part[275] of the judgment of the Chamber on the merits of the case.[276] The intervening state does not need to demonstrate a basis of jurisdiction, since the competence of the Court is here not founded upon the consent of the parties as such but is rather derived from the consent given by the parties in becoming parties to the Court's Statute to the Court's exercise of its powers conferred by the Statute.[277] The purpose of intervention, it was emphasised, was to protect a state's 'interest of a legal nature' that might be affected by a decision in an existing case already established between other states, the parties to the case, and not to enable a third state to 'tack on a new case'.[278]

---

[273] ICJ Reports, 1981, pp. 3, 12; 62 ILR, pp. 612, 621.

[274] ICJ Reports, 1981, p. 19; 62 ILR, p. 628. The Court also refused Italy permission to intervene under article 62 in the *Libya/Malta* case: see ICJ Reports, 1984, p. 3; 70 ILR, p. 527. The Court also refused permission to El Salvador to intervene in the *Nicaragua* case under article 63: see ICJ Reports, 1984, p. 215; 76 ILR, p. 74, inasmuch as it related to the current phase of the proceedings. The Court here more controversially also refused to hold a hearing on the issue, *ibid.*, but see Separate Opinion of five of the judges, ICJ Reports, 1984, p. 219; 76 ILR, p. 78.

[275] I.e. concerning the legal regime of the waters within the Gulf of Fonseca only and not the other issues in dispute, such as maritime delimitations and delimitation of the land frontier between El Salvador and Honduras.

[276] ICJ Reports, 1990, p. 92; 97 ILR, p. 112.

[277] ICJ Reports, 1990, p. 133; 97 ILR, p. 254. The Court noted that 'the procedure of intervention is to ensure that a state with possibly affected interests may be permitted to intervene even though there is no jurisdictional link and it therefore cannot become a party', ICJ Reports, 1990, p. 135, 97 ILR, p. 256. In the earlier cases it was not felt necessary to decide this issue: see e.g. the *Tunisia/Libya* case, ICJ Reports, 1981, pp. 3, 20; 62 ILR, pp. 612, 629, and the *Libya/Malta* case, ICJ Reports, 1984, pp. 3, 28; 70 ILR, pp. 527, 557.

[278] ICJ Reports, 1990, pp. 133–4.

The Court in *Cameroon* v. *Nigeria*, repeating the formulation adopted in *El Salvador/Honduras*,[279] stated that it followed from the juridical nature and purpose of intervention that the existence of a valid link of jurisdiction between the intended intervener and the parties was not a requirement for the success of the application. Indeed, 'the procedure of intervention is to ensure that a state with possibly affected interests may be permitted to intervene even though there is no jurisdictional link and it therefore cannot become a party'.[280] A jurisdictional link between the intervening state and the parties to the case is, accordingly, only necessary where the former wishes actually to become a party to the case.[281]

In *Indonesia/Malaysia (Philippines Intervening)*, the Court addressed the meaning of 'interest of a legal nature' and concluded that it referred not only to the *dispositif*, or the operative paragraphs, of the judgment but also to the reasons constituting the necessary steps to it.[282] In deciding whether to permit an intervention, the Court had to decide in relation to all the circumstances of the case, whether the legal claims which the proposed intervening state has outlined might indeed be affected by the decision in the case between the parties. The state seeking to intervene had to 'demonstrate convincingly what it asserts'[283] and where the state relies on an interest of a legal nature other than in the subject matter of the case itself, it 'necessarily bears the burden of showing with a particular clarity the existence of the interest of a legal nature which it claims to have'.[284]

The Court in the merits stage of the *El Salvador/Honduras* case,[285] noting that Nicaragua as the intervening state could not thereby as such become a party to the proceedings, concluded that that state could not therefore

[279] *Ibid.*, p. 135.   [280] ICJ Reports, 1999, pp. 1034–5.

[281] *El Salvador/Honduras (Intervention)*, ICJ Reports, 1990, pp. 92, 135; 97 ILR, p. 112.

[282] ICJ Reports, 2001, pp. 575, 596.

[283] *El Salvador/Honduras (Intervention)*, ICJ Reports, 1990, pp. 92, 117–18; 97 ILR, p. 112. And, on the basis of documentary evidence, see *Indonesia/Malaysia (Philippines Intervening)*, ICJ Reports, 2001, pp. 575, 603. As to the burden and scope of proof generally, see above, p. 1088.

[284] *Indonesia/Malaysia (Philippines Intervening)*, ICJ Reports, 2001, pp. 575, 598. The Court concluded that the Philippines had shown in the instruments it had invoked 'no legal interest on its part that might be affected by reasoning or interpretations of the Court in the main proceedings, either because they form no part of the arguments of Indonesia and Malaysia or because their respective reliance on them does not bear on the issue of retention of sovereignty by the Sultanate of Sulu as described by the Philippines in respect of its claim in North Borneo', *ibid.*, pp. 603–4.

[285] ICJ Reports, 1992, pp. 351, 609; 97 ILR, pp. 266, 525.

become bound by the judgment.[286] The intervener upon obtaining permission from the Court to intervene acquires the right to be heard, but not the obligation of being bound by the decision.[287] Since neither of the parties had given any indication of consent to Nicaragua being recognised to have any status which would enable it to rely on the judgment,[288] it followed that the decision of the Court could not bind Nicaragua and thus was not *res judicata* for it.[289]

Applications to intervene have to be filed 'as soon as possible, and not later than the closure of the written proceedings'.[290]

Remedies [291]

There has been relatively little analysis of the full range of the remedial powers of the Court.[292] In the main, an applicant state will seek a declaratory judgment that the respondent has breached international law. Such declarations may extend to provision for future conduct as well as characterisation of past conduct. Requests for declaratory judgments may also be coupled with a request for reparation for losses suffered as a consequence of the illegal activities or damages for injury of various kinds, including non-material damage.[293] Such requests for damages may include not only direct injury to the state in question but also with regard to its citizens or their property.[294] The Court may also interpret a relevant international

---

[286] This was partly because article 59 of the Statute of the Court refers to the binding effect of a judgment as between the parties only, ICJ Reports, 1992, p. 609; 97 ILR, p. 525.

[287] ICJ Reports, 1992, p. 610; 97 ILR, p. 526.

[288] Since the consent of the existing parties is required for an intervener to become itself a party to the case, *ibid.*

[289] *Ibid.*

[290] Rule 81(1). See also *Indonesia/Malaysia (Philippines Intervening)*, ICJ Reports, 2001, pp. 575, 584 ff.

[291] See also above, chapter 14, p. 800.

[292] But see e.g. Gray, *Judicial Remedies*, and I. Brownlie, 'Remedies in the International Court of Justice' in Lowe and Fitzmaurice, *Fifty Years of the International Court of Justice*, p. 557. Note that the Court has stated that where jurisdiction exists over a dispute on a particular matter, no separate basis for jurisdiction is required by the Court to consider the remedies a party has requested for the breach of the obligation: see the *LaGrand (Germany v. USA)* case, ICJ Reports, 2001, pp. 466, 485; 134 ILR, pp. 1, 24, and the *Avena (Mexico v. USA)* case, ICJ Reports, 2004, pp. 12, 33; 134 ILR, pp. 120, 136–7.

[293] See e.g. the *I'm Alone* case, 3 RIAA, 1935, p. 1609 and the *Rainbow Warrior* case, 74 ILR, pp. 241, 274 and 82 ILR, pp. 499, 575. See also *Democratic Republic of the Congo v. Uganda*, ICJ Reports, 2005, pp. 168, 279.

[294] Note that the Bosnian application to the Court in the *Application of the Genocide Convention (Bosnia v. Yugoslavia)* case included a claim 'to pay Bosnia and Herzegovina, in

legal provision so that individual rights as well as state rights are recognised in a particular case, thus opening the door to a claim for damages on behalf of the former by the national state where there has been a breach of such rights.[295] Reparation may conceivably extend to full restitution, or *restitutio in integrum*.[296] The Court in the *Great Belt* case allowed for the possibility of an order for the modification or dismantling of disputed works.[297] The question of restitution also arose in the *Democratic Republic of the Congo* v. *Belgium* case, where the Court concluded that Belgium was under an obligation to cancel the arrest warrant concerned on the basis of the need for restitution.[298]

The issue of reparation was also raised in the *Gabčíkovo–Nagymaros Project* case,[299] where the Court concluded that both parties had committed internationally wrongful acts and that therefore both parties were entitled both to receive and to pay compensation. In the light of such 'intersecting wrongs', the Court declared that the issue of compensation could be satisfactorily resolved in the framework of an overall settlement by the mutual renunciation or cancellation of all financial claims and counter-claims.[300] The parties may also request the Court's assistance with regard to matters yet to be decided between the parties. Accordingly, in the *Gabčíkovo–Nagymaros Project* case, the Court, having reached its decision on the past conduct of the parties, proceeded in its judgment to exercise its prescriptive competence, that is 'to determine what the future conduct of the Parties should be'.[301]

---

its own right and as *parens patriae* for its citizens, reparations for damages to persons and property as well as to the Bosnian economy and environment caused by the foregoing violations of international law in a sum to be determined by the Court', ICJ Reports, 1993, pp. 3, 7; 95 ILR, p. 1.

[295] See the *LaGrand* case, ICJ Reports, 2001, pp. 466, 514 ff.; 134 ILR, pp. 1, 53, paras. 3 and 4 of the *dispositif* contained in paragraph 128 of the judgment.

[296] See the *Chorzów Factory* case, PCIJ, Series A, No. 13, and the *Iranian Hostages* case, ICJ Reports, 1980, p. 4; 61 ILR, p. 502, for possible authority for such a power. See also Gray, *Remedies*, pp. 95–6.

[297] ICJ Reports, 1991, pp. 12, 19; 94 ILR, p. 446.

[298] ICJ Reports, 2002, pp. 3, 31–2; 128 ILR, pp. 60, 87–8. But see the Joint Separate Opinion of Judges Higgins, Kooijmans and Buergenthal, which expressed the view that 'As soon as he ceased to be Minister for Foreign Affairs, the illegal consequences attaching to the warrant also ceased', *ibid.*, pp. 89–90. See also the Dissenting Opinion of Judge Van den Wyngaert, *ibid.*, p. 183.

[299] ICJ Reports, 1997, pp. 7, 81 ff.; 116 ILR, p. 1.   [300] *Ibid.*, pp. 7, 80–1

[301] *Ibid.*, pp. 75–6. The Court concluded that, 'It is for the Parties themselves to find an agreed solution that takes account of the objectives of the Treaty, which must be pursued in a joint and integrated way, as well as the norms of international environmental law and the principles of the law of international watercourses', *ibid.*, p. 78.

The Court may also refer to, and thus incorporate in its judgment, a statement of one of the parties, and in effect treat it as a binding unilateral statement. In the *LaGrand* case, the Court noted the 'substantial activities' that the US declared that it was carrying out in order to comply with the Convention in question and concluded that such behaviour 'expresses a commitment to follow through with the efforts in this regard' and must be regarded as meeting Germany's request for a general assurance of non-repetition.[302] In *Cameroon* v. *Nigeria*, the Court referred, both in the text of its judgment and in the *dispositif*, to a statement of the Cameroonian Agent as to the treatment of Nigerians living in his country and stated that it took note with satisfaction of the 'commitment thus undertaken'.[303]

The Court took a further step when, in the *LaGrand* case, it referred to the 'obligation . . . to review' of the US in cases of conviction and death sentence imposed upon a foreign national whose rights under the Vienna Convention on Consular Relations had not been respected,[304] while in operative paragraph (7) of the *dispositif*, the Court, by a majority of fourteen votes to one, concluded that in such situations, 'the United States of America, by means of its own choosing, shall allow the review and reconsideration of the conviction and sentence by taking account of the violation of the rights set forth in that Convention'.[305]

Where the Court reserves the question of reparation to a later stage of proceedings, neither party may call in question such findings of the Court in the earlier judgment as have become *res judicata* and seek to re-litigate these findings. Where the parties seek to negotiate a resolution by direct negotiations, the Court has emphasised that such negotiations have to be

---

[302] ICJ Reports, 2001, pp. 466, 512–13 and 513–14; 134 ILR, pp. 1, 50–1 and 51–2. See also the *Avena (Mexico* v. *USA)* case, ICJ Reports, 2004, pp. 12, 69; 134 ILR, pp. 120, 172.

[303] ICJ Reports, 2002, pp. 303, 452 and 457, para. V(C) of the *dispositif.*

[304] ICJ Reports, 2001, pp. 466, 514; 134 ILR, pp. 1, 51–2. See also above, chapter 13, p. 773.

[305] ICJ Reports, 2001, pp. 466, 514 ff.; 134 ILR, pp. 1, 51 ff. But see R. Y. Jennings, 'The *LaGrand* Case', 1 *The Law and Practice of International Courts and Tribunals*, 2002, pp. 1, 40. See also the *Avena (Mexico* v. *USA)* case, ICJ Reports, 2004, pp. 12, 69–70, where the Court emphasised as an 'important point' that it had been addressing issues of principle with regard to the Vienna Convention on Consular Relations and that its comments with regard to Mexican nationals, the subject of the application, could not be taken to mean that the principles did not apply to all foreign nationals in the US in a similar position. The Court also concluded that it was for the United States to find an appropriate remedy with regard to the individuals in question having the nature of review and reconsideration according to the criteria indicated in the judgment, *ibid.*, p. 70. See as to the response of the US and relevant US case-law, above, chapter 4, p. 164, n. 178. See also the Request for the Interpretation of the *Avena* judgment, Provisional Measures, ICJ Reports, Order of 16 July 2008.

conducted in good faith and in order to find an agreed solution based on the findings of the judgment of the Court in question.[306]

Enforcement

Once given, the judgment of the Court under article 60 is final and without appeal. Although it has no binding force except between the parties and in respect of the particular case under article 59, such decisions are often very influential in the evolution of new rules of international law.[307] The Court itself is not concerned with compliance and takes the view that 'once the Court has found that a state has entered into a commitment concerning its future conduct it is not the Court's function to contemplate that it will not comply with it'.[308]

Under article 94 of the UN Charter, each member state undertakes to comply with the decision of the Court in any case to which it is a party and if this does not occur, the other party may have recourse to the Security Council which may make recommendations or take binding decisions. Examples of non-compliance would include Albania in the *Corfu Channel* case,[309] Iceland in the *Fisheries Jurisdiction* case[310] and Iran in the *Iranian Hostages* case.[311] However, since the 1990s the record of compliance has been generally good. For example, despite initial reservations, both Libya[312] and Nigeria[313] accepted the judgments of the Court in favour of their opponents in the litigation in question. The political costs of non-compliance have to be taken into account by potentially recalcitrant states.[314]

---

[306] *Democratic Republic of the Congo* v. *Uganda*, ICJ Reports, 2005, pp. 168, 257.

[307] See generally Shahabuddeen, *Precedent*.

[308] The *Nuclear Tests* case, ICJ Reports, 1974, p. 477.

[309] ICJ Reports, 1949, p. 4; 16 AD, p. 155.   [310] ICJ Reports, 1974, p. 3; 55 ILR, p. 238.

[311] ICJ Reports, 1980, p. 3; 61 ILR, p. 530. During the 1970s and part of the 1980s there was reluctance by some respondent states to appear before the Court at all: see e.g. the *Fisheries Jurisdiction* case, ICJ Reports, 1974, p. 3; 55 ILR, p. 238; the *Nuclear Tests* case, ICJ Reports, 1974, p. 253; 57 ILR, p. 350; the *Iranian Hostages* case, ICJ Reports, 1980, p. 3; 61 ILR, p. 530 and the *Nicaragua* case, ICJ Reports, 1986, p. 14. See also article 53 of the Statute and H. Thirlway, *Non-Appearance before the International Court of Justice*, Cambridge, 1985; G. G. Fitzmaurice, 'The Problem of the "Non-appearing" Defendant Government', 51 BYIL, 1980, p. 89, and J. Elkind, *Non-Appearance before the ICJ, Functional and Comparative Analysis*, Dordrecht, 1984.

[312] See the *Libya/ Chad* case, ICJ Reports, 1994, p. 40. See also above, chapter 18, p. 1011.

[313] *Cameroon* v. *Nigeria*, ICJ Reports, 2002, p. 303.

[314] See e.g. C. Paulson, 'Compliance with Final Judgments of the International Court of Justice since 1987', 98 AJIL, 2004, p. 434, and A. P. Llamzon, 'Jurisdiction and Compliance in Recent Decisions of the International Court of Justice', 18 EJIL, 2007, p. 815.

Application for interpretation of a judgment[315]

Article 60 of the Statute provides that, 'The judgment is final and without appeal. In the event of dispute as to the meaning or scope of the judgment, the Court shall construe it upon the request of any party.' Rule 98(1) states that in the event of dispute as to the meaning or scope of a judgment any party may make a request for its interpretation. The object of the request must be solely to obtain clarification of the meaning and the scope of what the Court has decided with binding force and not to obtain an answer to questions not so decided.[316] Accordingly, a request for interpretation must relate to the operative part of the judgment and not the reasons for the judgment, unless these are inseparable from the operative part.[317] The need to avoid impairing the finality, and delaying the implementation, of judgments means that the question of the admissibility of the request needs 'particular attention'.[318]

In addition, it is necessary that there should exist a dispute as to the meaning or scope of the judgment as to which see the Request for the Interpretation of the *Avena* judgment, Provisional Measures, order of 16 July 2008, paras. 44 ff.).

Application for revision of a judgment[319]

Under article 61 of the Statute, an application for revision of a judgment may only be made when based upon the discovery of some fact of such a nature as to be a decisive factor, which fact was, when the judgment was given, unknown to the Court and also to the party claiming revision,

---

[315] See e.g. Rosenne, *Law and Practice*, vol. III, pp. 1616 ff., and Rosenne, *Interpretation, Revision and Other Recourse from International Judgments and Awards*, Leiden, 2007, and K. H. Kaikobad, *Interpretation and Revision of International Boundary Decisions*, Cambridge, 2007, part III. See also A. Zimmermann and T. Thienel, 'Article 60' in Zimmermann *et al.*, *Statute of the International Court*, p. 1275.

[316] See *Request for Interpretation of the Judgment of 20 November 1950 in the Asylum* case, ICJ Reports, 1950, p. 402; 17 ILR, p. 339 and *Application for Revision and Interpretation of the Judgment of 24 February 1982 in the Case Concerning the Continental Shelf (Tunisia/Libya)*, ICJ Reports, 1985, pp. 191, 214–20; 81 ILR, pp. 420, 447.

[317] See *Request for Interpretation of the Judgment of 11 June 1998 (Cameroon v. Nigeria)*, ICJ Reports, 1999, pp. 31, 35.

[318] *Ibid.*, p. 36. The Court noted that, 'The language and structure of article 60 of the Statute reflect the primacy of the principle of *res judicata*. That principle must be maintained', *ibid.* As to *res judicata*, see above, p. 101.

[319] See e.g. Rosenne, *Law and Practice*, vol. III, pp. 1623 ff., and Rosenne, *Interpretation*, chapter 6, and Kaikobad, *Interpretation and Revision*, part IV. See also A. Zimmermann and R. Geiss, 'Article 61' in Zimmermann *et al.*, *Statute of the International Court*, p. 1299.

provided that such ignorance was not due to negligence. The application must be made within six months of the discovery of the new fact and within ten years of the date of the judgment. In the *Application for Revision and Interpretation of the Judgment of 24 February 1982 in the Case Concerning the Continental Shelf (Tunisia/Libya)*,[320] the Court decided that the 'new fact' in question, namely the text of a resolution of the Libyan Council of Ministers of 28 March 1968 setting out the western boundary of the Libyan oil concessions in the first sector of the delimitation, was a fact that could have been discovered through the application of normal diligence. If Tunisia was ignorant of the facts, it was due to its own negligence.[321] In addition, it could not be said that the new facts alleged were of such a nature as to be a decisive factor as required by article 61.[322] In the *Application for Revision of the Judgment of 11 July 1996 Concerning Application of the Genocide Convention (Preliminary Objections)*, the Court noted that the first stage of the procedure was to examine the question of admissibility of the request.[323] The Court emphasised that article 61 required that the application for revision be based upon the discovery of some fact which was unknown when the judgment was given. Thus the fact must have been in existence at the date of the judgment and discovered subsequently. A fact occurring several years after the judgment would not be regarded as 'new'.[324] Drawing legal consequences from post-judgment facts or reinterpreting a legal situation *ex post facto* would not fall within the terms of article 61. In the *Application for Revision of the Judgment of 11 September 1992 Concerning the El Salvador/Honduras (Nicaragua Intervening) Case*,[325] El Salvador sought revision of one sector of the land boundary between it and Honduras that had been determined by the Court in the earlier judgment. The Court detailed the requirements of article 61,[326]

---

[320] ICJ Reports, 1985, pp. 191, 198–214; 81 ILR, p. 431.

[321] ICJ Reports, 1985, pp. 206–7; 81 ILR, p. 439.

[322] ICJ Reports, 1985, pp. 213–14; 81 ILR, p. 446.

[323] ICJ Reports, 2003, pp. 7, 11. See also the *Application for Revision of the Judgment of 11 September 1992 Concerning the El Salvador/Honduras (Nicaragua Intervening) Case*, ICJ Reports, 2003, pp. 392, 398. The latter case is the first article 61 judgment by a chamber. See e.g. M. N. Shaw, 'Application for Revision of the Judgment of 11 September 1992', 54 ICLQ, 2005, p. 999.

[324] ICJ Reports, 2003, pp. 7, 30.   [325] ICJ Reports, 2003, pp. 392, 398–9.

[326] The application should be based upon the 'discovery' of a 'fact'; the fact the discovery of which is relied on must be 'of such a nature as to be a decisive factor'; the fact should have been 'unknown' to the Court and to the party claiming revision when the judgment was given; ignorance of this fact must not be 'due to negligence'; and the application for revision must be 'made at latest within six months of the discovery of the new fact' and before ten years have elapsed from the date of the judgment.

and held that each of the conditions laid down in the provision had to be fulfilled, otherwise the application would be dismissed.[327]

Examination of a situation after the judgment

The Court may have the competence to re-examine a situation dealt with by a previous decision where the terms of that decision so provide. This is likely to be rare for it runs the risk of allowing the parties to re-litigate an issue already decided simply because some of the circumstances have changed. In the *Request for an Examination of the Situation in Accordance with Paragraph 63 of the Court's Judgment of 20 December 1974 in the Nuclear Tests (New Zealand v. France) Case*,[328] the Court was asked to act in accordance with paragraph 63 of its 1974 decision in the light of further proposed French nuclear tests in the South Pacific. Paragraph 63 had noted that 'if the basis of this Judgment were to be affected, the Applicant could request an examination of the situation in accordance with the provisions of the Statute'.[329] The 1974 judgment had concluded that there was no need for a decision on New Zealand's claims with regard to French nuclear testing as France had undertaken not to carry out any further atmospheric nuclear testing.

The Court implicitly accepted that 'a special procedure' in the sense of a re-examination of a situation in the light of changed circumstances could be established as a result of the terms of the original decision which did not amount to either an interpretation of the judgment under article 60 or a revision of the judgment under article 61.[330] Such a procedure would in fact have the aim not of seeking changes in the original judgment, but rather of preserving it intact faced with an apparent challenge to it by one of the parties at a later date. As Judge Weeramantry noted, '[t]he Court used its undoubted powers of regulating its own procedure to devise a procedure *sui generis*'.[331] However, in the instant case, the Court found that the basis of its 1974 judgment was a French undertaking not to conduct any further atmospheric nuclear tests and that therefore it was only a resumption of nuclear testing in the atmosphere that would affect the

---

[327] ICJ Reports, 2003, pp. 392, 399 and 404.
[328] ICJ Reports, 1995, p. 288; 106 ILR, p. 1.   [329] ICJ Reports, 1974, p. 477.
[330] *Ibid.*, pp. 303–4. Judge Weeramantry noted that the request for an examination of the situation was 'probably without precedent in the annals of the Court' and one that did not fit in with any of the standard applications recognised by the Rules of the Court for revision or interpretation of a judgment, *ibid.*, p. 320.
[331] *Ibid.*, p. 320.

basis of that judgment and that had not occurred.[332] Accordingly, New Zealand's request for an examination of the situation was rejected.

The advisory jurisdiction of the Court [333]

In addition to having the capacity to decide disputes between states, the ICJ may give advisory opinions. Article 65 of the Statute declares that 'the Court may give an advisory opinion on any legal question at the request of whatever body may be authorised by or in accordance with the Charter of the United Nations to make such a request', while article 96 of the Charter notes that as well as the General Assembly and Security Council, other organs of the UN and specialised agencies where so authorised by the Assembly may request such opinions on legal questions arising within the scope of their activities.[334]

Unlike contentious cases, the purpose of the Court's advisory jurisdiction is not to settle, at least directly or as such, inter-state disputes, but rather to 'offer legal advice to the organs and institutions requesting the opinion'.[335] Accordingly, the fact that the question put to the Court does not relate to a specific dispute does not affect the competence of the

---

[332] *Ibid.*, pp. 305–6. France was proposing to undertake a series of underground nuclear tests. This it eventually did.

[333] See e.g. Rosenne, *Law and Practice*, vol. III, chapter 30; D. Negulesco, 'L'Évolution de la Procédure des Avis Consultatif de la Cour Permanente de Justice Internationale', 57 HR, 1936, p. 1; K. Keith, *The Extent of the Advisory Jurisdiction of the International Court of Justice*, Leiden, 1971; M. Pomerance, *The Advisory Jurisdiction of the International Court in the League and UN Eras*, Baltimore, 1973; D. Pratap, *The Advisory Jurisdiction of the International Court*, Oxford, 1972; D. Greig, 'The Advisory Jurisdiction of the International Court and the Settlement of Disputes Between States', 15 ICLQ, 1966, p. 325; R. Higgins, 'A Comment on the Current Health of Advisory Opinions' in Lowe and Fitzmaurice, *Fifty Years of the International Court of Justice*, p. 567; G. Abi-Saab, 'On Discretion: Reflections on the Nature of the Consultative Function of the International Court of Justice' in *International Law, the International Court of Justice and Nuclear Weapons* (eds. L. Boisson de Chazournes and P. Sands), Cambridge, 1999, p. 36, and Nguyen Quoc Dinh *et al.*, *Droit International Public*, p. 907.

[334] See J. Frowein and K. Oellers-Frahm, 'Article 65' in Zimmermann *et al.*, *Statute of the International Court*, p. 1401, and K. Oellers-Frahm, 'Article 96 UN Charter', *ibid.*, p. 181. See further as to advisory opinions which are to be recognised as binding, below, chapter 23, p. 1304.

[335] The *Legality of the Threat or Use of Nuclear Weapons* case, ICJ Reports, 1996, pp. 226, 236; 110 ILR, p. 163. In the *Construction of a Wall* case, ICJ Reports, 2004, pp. 136, 162–3; 129 ILR, pp. 37, 80, the Court noted that 'advisory opinions have the purpose of furnishing to the requesting organs the elements of law necessary for them in their action'. It was then for the requesting organ to draw conclusions from the Court's findings.

Court, nor does it matter that the question posed is abstract in nature.[336] Similarly, the fact that a legal question also has political aspects will not deprive the Court of its jurisdiction, nor of its function, which is to assess the legality of the possible conduct of states with regard to obligations imposed upon them by international law.[337] In addressing the question put to the Court by a political organ of the UN, the Court will not have regard to the origins or the political history of the request nor to the distribution of votes with regard to the relevant resolution. The fact that any answer given by the Court might become a factor in relation to the subject matter of the request in other fora is also irrelevant in determining the appropriate response of the Court to the request for the advisory opinion.[338] Further, the lack of clarity in the drafting of the question would not deprive the Court of jurisdiction. Such uncertainty could be clarified by the Court as a matter of interpretation. Indeed, the Court may 'broaden, interpret and even reformulate the questions put', seeing its role essentially as identifying the relevant principles and rules, interpreting them and applying them, 'thus offering a reply to the question posed based on law'.[339]

Originally, the Court took the broad view that it would not exercise its advisory jurisdiction in respect of a central issue in a dispute between the parties where one of these parties refused to take part in the proceedings.[340] However, the scope of this principle, which was intended to reflect the sovereignty and independence of states, has been reduced in a number of subsequent cases before the Court, so that the presumption is that the Court, subject to jurisdictional issues, would answer a request for an advisory opinion. In the *Interpretation of Peace Treaties* case,[341] for example, which concerned the interpretation of the 1947 peace agreements with

---

[336] The *Legality of the Threat or Use of Nuclear Weapons* case, ICJ Reports, 1996, pp. 226, 236; 110 ILR, p. 163. See also the *Construction of a Wall* case, ICJ Reports, 2004, pp. 136, 154; 129 ILR, p. 37.

[337] The *Legality of the Threat or Use of Nuclear Weapons* case, ICJ Reports, 1996, pp. 226, 234 and the *Construction of a Wall* case, ICJ Reports, 2004, pp. 136, 155 and 159–60.

[338] The *Legality of the Threat or Use of Nuclear Weapons* case, ICJ Reports, 1996, pp. 226, 236.

[339] The *Construction of a Wall* case, ICJ Reports, 2004, pp. 136, 153–4 and 160. See also the *Legality of the Threat or Use of Nuclear Weapons* case, ICJ Reports, 1996, pp. 226, 234.

[340] See the *Eastern Carelia* case, PCIJ, Series B, No. 5, 1923; 2 AD, p. 394. Note that the Court dealt with the consent of an interested party as a matter not of the competence or jurisdiction of the Court, but of the judicial propriety of giving an opinion: see the *Western Sahara* case, ICJ Reports, 1975, p. 25 and the *Construction of a Wall* case, ICJ Reports, 2004, pp. 136, 157–8.

[341] ICJ Reports, 1950, pp. 65, 71; 17 ILR, pp. 331, 335.

Bulgaria, Hungary and Romania, it was stressed that whereas the basis of the Court's jurisdiction in contentious proceedings rested upon the consent of the parties to the dispute, the same did not apply with respect to advisory opinions. Such opinions were not binding upon anyone and were given not to the particular states but to the organs which requested them. The Court declared that 'the reply of the Court, itself an "organ of the United Nations", represents its participation in the activities of the organisation, and in principle should not be refused'. Similarly, the Court emphasised in the *Reservations to the Genocide Convention* case, that the object of advisory opinions was 'to guide the United Nations in respect of its own action'. Thus, the Court would lean towards exercising its jurisdiction, despite the objections of a concerned party, where it would be providing guidance for an international body with respect to the application of an international treaty. In fact, the Court has said that only 'compelling reasons' should lead the Court to refuse to give an opinion on grounds of propriety as distinct from grounds of lack of jurisdiction.[342]

In the *Western Sahara* case,[343] the ICJ gave an advisory opinion as regards the nature of the territory and the legal ties therewith of Morocco and Mauritania at the time of colonisation, notwithstanding the objections of Spain, the administering power. The Court distinguished the case from the *Eastern Carelia* dispute on a number of grounds, the most important being that the dispute in the *Western Sahara* case had arisen within the framework of the General Assembly's decolonisation proceedings and the object of the request for the advisory opinion (by the Assembly) was to obtain from the Court an opinion which would aid the Assembly in the decolonisation of the territory.[344] Accordingly, the matter fell within the *Peace Treaties/Reservations* cases category of opinions to guide the UN.[345] The Court noted that it was the fact that inadequate material was available

---

[342] See e.g. the *Legality of the Threat or Use of Nuclear Weapons* case, ICJ Reports, 1996, pp. 226, 235 and the *Construction of a Wall* case, ICJ Reports, 2004, pp. 136, 156 and 164.

[343] ICJ Reports, 1975, p. 12; 59 ILR, p. 14.

[344] ICJ Reports, 1975, pp. 24–5; 59 ILR, p. 42. It was also noted that in the *Eastern Carelia* case, Russia had objected to the Court's jurisdiction and was neither a member of the League (at that time) nor a party to the Statute of the PCIJ, whereas in the *Western Sahara* case, Spain was a UN member and thus a party to the Statute of the ICJ. It had therefore given its consent in general to the exercise by the Court of its advisory jurisdiction. Further, Spain's objection was to the restriction of the reference to the Court to the historical aspects of the Sahara question, *ibid.*

[345] The Court emphasised that the central core of the issue was not a dispute between Spain and Morocco, but rather the nature of Moroccan (and Mauritanian) rights at the time of colonisation, ICJ Reports, 1975, p. 27; 59 ILR, p. 44.

for an opinion that impelled the PCIJ to refuse to consider the *Eastern Carelia* issue, notwithstanding that this arose because of a refusal of one of the parties to participate in the proceedings. In the *Western Sahara* case, an abundance of documentary material was available to the Court.[346] It is therefore evident that the general rule expressed in the *Eastern Carelia* case has been to a very large extent weakened.[347] However, it would not be correct to say that it has been entirely eroded. There may indeed be circumstances where the lack of consent of an interested party may render the giving of an advisory opinion incompatible with the judicial character of the Court.[348] Further, the need to have 'sufficient information and evidence' to enable the Court to reach a judicial conclusion still remains.[349] However, the primary criterion appears to be whether the request for an advisory opinion is made with the aim of obtaining assistance in the proper exercise of the functions of the requesting organ. This poses the question as to the proper exercise of functions.[350]

In examining the question posed by the requesting organ, the Court will operate on the same basis as in contentious cases with regard to the nature of evidence, as well as the burden and standard of proof,[351] regard being had to the different purposes of contentious and advisory proceedings. In addition, the Court has a certain latitude in advisory proceedings as distinct from contentious proceedings, since it is not as such determining the rights and duties of the parties to the case but providing advice to the requesting organ as to the legal issues comprised in the question asked. That would seem to import a responsibility to provide 'a balanced opinion', taking account of the relevant context, particularly

---

[346] ICJ Reports, 1975, pp. 28–9; 59 ILR, p. 45. See also the *Construction of a Wall* case, ICJ Reports, 2004, pp. 136, 161–2, where the Court noted the detailed information available to it from UN and other sources.

[347] See also the *Difference Relating to Immunity from Legal Process* case, ICJ Reports, 1999, pp. 62, 78–9; 121 ILR, p. 405 and the *Construction of a Wall* case, ICJ Reports, 2004, pp. 136, 156–7, where the Court concluded that it had a duty to satisfy itself each time it was asked to give an advisory opinion as to the propriety of the exercise of its judicial function, by reference to the criterion of 'compelling reasons', *ibid.*, p. 157.

[348] See the *Western Sahara* case, ICJ Reports, 1975, pp. 12, 25. See also e.g. the Separate Opinion of Judge Higgins in the *Construction of a Wall* case, ICJ Reports, 2004, pp. 136, 209–10.

[349] See the *Western Sahara* case, ICJ Reports, 1975, pp. 12, 28–9.   [350] *Ibid.*, p. 210.

[351] See above, p. 1088. Note that in her Separate Opinion in the *Construction of a Wall* case, ICJ Reports, 2004, pp. 136, 211, 213 and 214, Judge Higgins declared *inter alia* that she found the history of the Arab–Israeli dispute as recounted by the Court 'neither balanced nor satisfactory'. See also the Separate Opinion of Judge Kooijmans, *ibid.*, p. 220.

where a dispute between states is apparent in the situation in the sense of referring to all relevant legal issues.[352]

With regard to the jurisdiction of the Court to given an opinion, article 96(2) of the Charter provides that, in addition to the Security Council and the General Assembly:

> [o]ther organs of the United Nations and specialised agencies which may at any time be so authorised by the General Assembly, may also request advisory opinions of the Court on legal questions arising within the scope of their activities.

The Court in the request for an advisory opinion by the World Health Organisation on the *Legality of the Use by a State of Nuclear Weapons in Armed Conflict*[353] found that three conditions were required in order to found the jurisdiction of the Court in such circumstances: first, that the specialised agency in question must be duly authorised by the General Assembly to request opinions from the Court; secondly, that the opinion requested was on a legal question, and thirdly, that the question must be one arising within the scope of activities of the requesting agency.[354] The Court examined the functions of the WHO in the light of its Constitution[355] and subsequent practice, and concluded that the organisation was authorised to deal with the effects on health of the use of nuclear weapons and of other hazardous activities and to take preventive measures with the aim of protecting the health of populations in the event of such weapons being used or such activities engaged in. However, the question put to the Court, it was emphasised, concerned not the effects of the use of nuclear weapons on health, but the legality of the use of such weapons in view of their health and environmental effects. Accordingly, the Court held that the question posed in the request for the advisory opinion did not arise within the scope of activities of the organisation as defined in its Constitution.[356]

---

[352] ICJ Reports, 2004, p. 136. See also the Separate Opinion of Judge Kooijmans, *ibid.*, p. 223 and the Separate Opinion of Judge Owada, *ibid.*, pp. 267 ff. See generally *Agora*, 99 AJIL, 2005, p. 1.

[353] ICJ Reports, 1996, p. 66.

[354] *Ibid.*, pp. 71–2. See also the *Application for Review of Judgment No. 273 (Mortished)* case, ICJ Reports, 1982, pp. 325, 333–4; 69 ILR, pp. 330, 344–5.

[355] See article 2(a) to (v) of the WHO Constitution adopted on 22 July 1946 and amended in 1960, 1975, 1977, 1984 and 1994.

[356] ICJ Reports, 1996, pp. 66, 75 ff.; 110 ILR, p. 1.

The advisory opinion in the *Difference Relating to Immunity from Legal Process* case was the first time the Court had received a request under article VIII, section 30, of the General Convention on the Privileges and Immunities of the UN, 1946, which allowed for recourse to the Court for an advisory opinion where a difference has arisen between the UN and a member state. The particular interest in this provision is that it stipulates that the opinion given by the Court 'shall be accepted as decisive by the parties'. The importance of advisory opinions delivered by the Court is therefore not to be underestimated.[357]

The role of the Court

There are a variety of other issues currently facing the Court. As far as access to it is concerned, it has, for example, been suggested that the power to request advisory opinions should be given to the UN Secretary-General[358] and to states and national courts,[359] while the possibility of permitting international organisations to become parties to contentious proceedings has been raised.[360] Perhaps more centrally, the issue of the relationship between the Court and the political organs of the UN, particularly the Security Council, has been raised anew as a consequence of the revitalisation of the latter in recent years and its increasing activity.[361] The Court possesses no express power of judicial review of UN activities, although it is the principal judicial organ of the organisation and has in that capacity dealt on a number of occasions with the meaning of UN

---

[357] Among other influential Advisory Opinions delivered by the Court are the *Reparations* case, ICJ Reports, 1949, p. 174; 16 AD, p. 318; the *Admissions* case, ICJ Reports, 1948, p. 57; 15 AD, p. 333, and the *Certain Expenses* case, ICJ Reports, 1962, p. 151; 34 ILR, p. 281. See also the *WHO–Egypt* case, ICJ Reports, 1980, p. 73; 62 ILR, p. 451; the *Administrative Tribunal* cases, ICJ Reports, 1973, p. 166; 54 ILR, p. 381; ICJ Reports, 1982, p. 325; 69 ILR, p. 330; ICJ Reports, 1987, p. 18; 83 ILR, p. 296 and the *Applicability of the Obligation to Arbitrate* case, ICJ Reports, 1988, p. 12; 82 ILR, p. 225.

[358] See e.g. Higgins, 'Current Health', p. 569, and S. Schwebel, 'Authorising the Secretary-General of the United Nations to Request Advisory Opinions', 78 AJIL, 1984, p. 4. See also UN Secretary-General, *Agenda for Peace*, New York, 1992, A/47/277, para. 38.

[359] See e.g. S. Schwebel, 'Preliminary Rulings by the International Court of Justice at the Instance of National Courts', 28 Va. JIL, 1988, p. 495, and S. Rosenne, 'Preliminary Rulings by the International Court of Justice at the Instance of National Courts: A Reply', 29 Va. JIL, 1989, p. 40.

[360] See e.g. D. Bowett *et al.*, *The International Court of Justice: Process, Practice and Procedures*, London, 1997.

[361] See e.g. M. Bedjaoui, *The New World Order and the Security Council*, Dordrecht, 1994. See also below, chapter 22, p. 1268.

resolutions and organs.[362] In the *Lockerbie* case,[363] the Court was faced with a new issue, that of examining the relative status of treaty obligations and binding decisions adopted by the Security Council. In its decision on provisional measures, the Court accepted that by virtue of article 103 of the UN Charter obligations under the Charter (including decisions of the Security Council imposing sanctions) prevailed over obligations contained in other international agreements.[364]

The decisions and advisory opinions of the ICJ (and PCIJ before it) have played a vital part in the evolution of international law.[365] Further, the increasing number of applications in recent years have emphasised that the Court is now playing a more central role within the international legal system than thought possible two decades ago.[366] Of course, many of the most serious of international conflicts may never come before the Court, due to a large extent to the unwillingness of states to place their vital interests in the hands of binding third-party decision-making, while the growth of other means of regional and global resolution of disputes cannot be ignored.

[362] See e.g. the *Reparation* case, ICJ Reports, 1949, p. 174; 16 AD, p. 318, concerning the legal personality of the UN, the *Certain Expenses* case, ICJ Reports, 1962, p. 151; 34 ILR, p. 281, by virtue of which the UN was able to take action which did not amount to enforcement action outside of the framework of the Security Council, thus enabling the creation of peacekeeping missions, and the *Namibia* case, ICJ Reports, 1971, p. 56; 94 ILR, p. 2, recognising the succession of the UN to the League of Nations with regard to mandated territories and enshrining the principle of self-determination within international law. See also the *East Timor* case, ICJ Reports, 1995, pp. 90, 103–4; 105 ILR, p. 226.

[363] ICJ Reports, 1992, p. 3; 94 ILR, p. 478.

[364] ICJ Reports, 1992, p. 15; 94 ILR, p. 498.

[365] Indeed the importance of the pleadings in the evolution of international law has been noted: see e.g. P. Sands, 'Pleadings and the Pursuit of International Law' in *Legal Visions of the 21st Century* (eds. A. Anghie and G. Sturges), The Hague, 1998, while dissenting opinions may also be significant: see e.g. the Dissenting Opinion of Judge Franck in the *Indonesia/Malaysia* case, ICJ Reports, 2002, p. 3. See also, as to the international bar, Shaw, 'A Practical Look at the International Court of Justice' in Evans, *Remedies*, pp. 11, 12 ff.; A. Watts, 'Enhancing the Effectiveness of Procedures of International Dispute Settlement', 5 *Max Planck Yearbook of United Nations Law*, 2001, pp. 21, 24 ff., and the Declaration of Judge Ad Hoc Cot in the '*Grand Prince*' case, International Tribunal for the Law of the Sea, 2001, p. 3; 125 ILR, p. 272.

[366] See e.g. K. Highet, 'The Peace Palace Hots Up: The World Court in Business Again?', 85 AJIL, 1991, p. 646. See also e.g. A. Pellet, 'Strengthening the Role of the International Court of Justice as the Principal Judicial Organ of the United Nations', 3 *The Law and Practice of International Courts and Tribunals*, 2004, p. 159; P. Kooijmans, 'The ICJ in the 21st Century: Judicial Restraint, Judicial Activism, or Proactive Judicial Policy', 56 ICLQ, 2007, p. 741, and R. Higgins, 'A Babel of Judicial Voices? Ruminations from the Bench', 55 ICLQ, 2006, p. 791.

Proliferation of courts and tribunals

The proliferation of judicial organs on the international and regional level has been one characteristic of recent decades.[367] It has reflected the increasing scope and utilisation of international law on the one hand and an increasing sense of the value of resolving disputes by impartial third-party mechanisms on the other. It is now possible to identify an accepted international practice of turning to such mechanisms as a reasonably effective way of settling differences in a manner that is reflective of the rule of law and the growth of international co-operation. The importance of this practice to the evolution of international law is self-evident, as the development of legal rules and the creation of legal institutions with accompanying compulsory adjudication go hand in hand.

The European Court of Justice, the European Court of Human Rights, the new African Court of Human Rights and the Inter-American Court of Human Rights have been joined by the two Tribunals examining war crimes in Bosnia and Rwanda and by the new International Criminal Court.[368] In addition, the International Tribunal for the Law of the Sea is in operation[369] and a variety of other relevant mechanisms have arisen, ranging from the World Trade Organisation's Dispute Settlement provisions creating an Appellate Body[370] to administrative tribunals and economic courts.[371] Again, the work of arbitration tribunals, whether established to hear one case or a series of similar cases, is of direct relevance.

It is unclear how this may impinge upon the work of the International Court in the long run. Some take the view that proliferation will lead to inconsistency and confusion, others that it underlines the vigour and

---

[367] See e.g. S. Rosenne, 'The Perplexities of Modern International Law', 291 HR, 2002, pp. 13, 125; J. I. Charney, 'The Implications of Expanding International Dispute Settlement Systems: The 1982 Convention on the Law of the Sea', 90 AJIL, 1996, p. 69, and Charney, 'The Multiplicity of International Tribunals and Universality of International Law', 271 HR, 1998, p. 101; Oda, 'The International Court of Justice from the Bench', 244 HR, 1993 VII, pp. 9, 139 ff.

[368] See further above, chapters 6, 7 and 8. See also with regard to the fragmentation of international law generally, above, chapter 2, p. 65.

[369] See above, chapter 11, p. 638.   [370] See above, chapter 18, p. 1036.

[371] See e.g. the Court of Justice of the European Communities, the Economic Court of the Commonwealth of Independent States, the Court of Justice of the Common Market of Eastern and Southern Africa, and the Court of Justice of the African Union: see Y. Shany, The Competing Jurisdictions of International Courts and Tribunals, Oxford, 2003, p. 5. See further as to economic courts and tribunals, above, chapter 18, p. 1034, and as to non-compliance mechanisms in the field of environmental law, above, chapter 15.

relevance of international law in an era of globalisation.[372] Evidence to date
suggests the latter rather than the former. Inconsistency may sometimes
flow from the subject matter of the dispute or the different functions
of the courts in question, but it is not necessarily fatal to the development of international law. Of particular note, and only partly because it is
somewhat exceptional, has been the difference of view between the International Court on the one hand and the International Criminal Tribunal
for the Former Yugoslavia and the European Court of Human Rights on
the other as to the test of control for the responsibility of a state with
regard to the activities of non-state organs over which influence is exercised.[373] The courts and tribunals are now regularly referring to each
other's decisions,[374] and some issues of international law, such as treaty
interpretation principles, are regularly discussed in a range of courts and
tribunals.[375] It is also true that the same situation may arise before two or
more dispute settlement mechanisms.[376]

---

[372] See e.g. G. Guillaume, 'The Future of International Judicial Institutions', 44 ICLQ,
1995, p. 848; S. Rosenne, 'Establishing the International Tribunal for the Law of the
Sea', 89 AJIL, 1995, p. 806; T. Buergenthal, 'Proliferation of International Courts and
Tribunals: Is it Good or Bad?', 14 *Leiden Journal of International Law*, 2001, p. 267;
R. Higgins, 'The ICJ, ECJ, and the Integrity of International Law', 52 ICLQ, 2003,
pp. 1, 12 ff., and Higgins, 'A Babel of Judicial Voices?'; Shany, *Competing Jurisdictions*;
F. K. Tiba, 'What Caused the Multiplicity of International Courts and Tribunals?', 10
Gonzaga Journal of International Law, 2006, p. 202; B. Kingsbury, 'Is the Proliferation
of International Courts and Tribunals a Systemic Problem?', 31 *New York University
Journal of International Law and Politics*, 1999, p. 679; P. M. Dupuy, 'The Danger of
Fragmentation or Unification of the International Legal System and the ICJ', 31 *New
York University Journal of International Law and Politics*, 1999, p. 791, and J. Charney,
'Is International Law Threatened by Multiple International Tribunals?', 271 HR, 1998,
p. 101. See also the speeches on proliferation, of ICJ Presidents Schwebel (1999), www.icj-
cij.org/court/index.php?pr=87&pt=3&p1=1&p2=3&p3=1; Guillaume (2001), www.icj-
cij.org/court/index.php?pr=82&pt=3&p1=1&p2=3&p3=1; and Higgins (2007), www.icj-
cij.org/presscom/files/7/14097pdf.

[373] See above, chapter 14, p. 789.

[374] See e.g. the reference to the International Court's judgment in *Democratic Republic of the
Congo v. Uganda* in the International Criminal Court's confirmation of charges in the
Thomas Lubanga Dyilo case, ICC-01/04-01/06, 29 January 2007, paras. 212 ff., and
the reference in *Nicaragua v. Honduras*, ICJ Reports, 2007, paras. 68 ff., to a decision
of the Central American Court of Justice. See also the discussion by the International
Court of judgments of the International Criminal Tribunal for the Former Yugoslavia,
the *Genocide Convention (Bosnia v. Serbia)* case, ICJ Reports, 2007, e.g. at paras. 195 ff.
The European and Inter-American Courts of Human Rights have long referred to each
other's judgments: see generally above, chapter 7.

[375] See generally above, chapter 16.

[376] E.g. the *Mox* case: see Shany, *Competing Jurisdictions*, p. 9, and see above, chapter 11,
p. 643.

Of course, many of the other tribunals concern disputes between individuals and states rather than inter-state disputes and those in specialist areas, such as human rights, investment problems or employment issues. The International Tribunal for the Law of the Sea is beginning to deal with questions that have been before the International Court, such as jurisdiction and nationality and provisional measures issues, but it is also concerned with specific and limited matters, particularly the prompt release of arrested foreign vessels, and non-state parties may become parties to cases before it.[377] Nevertheless, all of these courts and tribunals and other organs relate in some way to international law and thus may contribute to its development and increasing scope. Together with a realisation of this increasing spread of institutions must come a developing sense of interest in and knowledge of the work of such courts and tribunals. The special position of the International Court as the principal judicial organ of the UN and as the pre-eminent inter-state forum has led some to suggest a referral or consultative role for it, enabling it to advise other courts and tribunals. While it is difficult to see this as a realistic or practical project, increasing co-operation between the International Court and other judicial bodies is taking place and all the relevant courts and tribunals are well aware of each other's work.[378]

Suggestions for further reading

D. Bowett *et al.*, *The International Court of Justice: Process, Practice and Procedures*, London, 1997

R. Y. Jennings, 'The Role of the International Court of Justice', 68 BYIL, 1997, p. 1

J. G. Merrills, *International Dispute Settlement*, 4th edn, Cambridge, 2005

S. Rosenne, *The Law and Practice of the International Court, 1920–2005*, 4th edn, Leiden, 4 vols., 2006

---

[377] See generally above, chapter 11.

[378] See the speech by President Higgins to the Legal Advisers of the Ministries of Foreign Affairs, 29 October 2007, www.icj-cij.org/pressscom/files/7/14097.pdf.

20

International law and the use of force by states

The rules governing resort to force form a central element within international law, and together with other principles such as territorial sovereignty and the independence and equality of states provide the framework for international order.[1] While domestic systems have, on the whole, managed to prescribe a virtual monopoly on the use of force for the governmental institutions, reinforcing the hierarchical structure of authority and control, international law is in a different situation. It must seek to minimise and regulate the resort to force by states, without itself being able to enforce its will. Reliance has to be placed on consent, consensus, reciprocity and good faith. The role and manifestation of force in the world community is, of course, dependent upon political and other non-legal factors as well as upon the current state of the law, but the law must seek to provide mechanisms to restrain and punish the resort to violence.

---

[1] See e.g. Y. Dinstein, *War, Aggression and Self-Defence*, 4th edn, Cambridge, 2005; C. Gray, *International Law and the Use of Force*, 2nd edn, Oxford, 2004; S. Neff, *War and the Law of Nations: A General History*, Cambridge, 2005; O. Corten, *Le Droit Contre La Guerre*, Paris, 2008; M. Byers, *War Law*, London, 2005; D. Kennedy, *Of Law and War*, Princeton, 2006; T. M. Franck, *Recourse to Force*, Cambridge, 2002; D. W. Bowett, *Self-Defence in International Law*, Manchester, 1958; I. Brownlie, *International Law and the Use of Force by States*, Oxford, 1963; J. Stone, *Aggression and World Order*, Berkeley, 1958; J. Stone, *Legal Controls of International Conflict*, 2nd edn, Berkeley, 1959, and Stone, *Conflict Through Consensus*, Berkeley, 1977; M. S. McDougal and F. Feliciano, *Law and Minimum World Public Order*, New Haven, 1961, and McDougal and Feliciano, *The International Law of War*, New Haven, 1994; H. Waldock, 'The Regulation of the Use of Force by Individual States in International Law', 81 HR, 1982, p. 415; J. Murphy, *The United Nations and the Control of International Violence*, Totowa, 1982; R. A. Falk, *Legal Order in a Violent World*, Princeton, 1968; A. Cassese, *Violence and Law in the Modern Age*, Cambridge, 1988; *Law and Force in the New International Order* (eds. L. Damrosch and D. J. Scheffer), Boulder, 1991, and Nguyen Quoc Dinh, P. Daillier and A. Pellet, *Droit International Public*, 7th edn, Paris, 2002, p. 933.

Law and force from the 'just war' to the United Nations[2]

The doctrine of the just war arose as a consequence of the Christianisation of the Roman Empire and the ensuing abandonment by Christians of pacificism. Force could be used provided it complied with the divine will. The concept of the just war embodied elements of Greek and Roman philosophy and was employed as the ultimate sanction for the maintenance of an ordered society. St Augustine (354–430)[3] defined the just war in terms of avenging of injuries suffered where the guilty party has refused to make amends. War was to be embarked upon to punish wrongs and restore the peaceful status quo but no further. Aggression was unjust and the recourse to violence had to be strictly controlled. St Thomas Aquinas[4] in the thirteenth century took the definition of the just war a stage further by declaring that it was the subjective guilt of the wrongdoer that had to be punished rather than the objectively wrong activity. He wrote that war could be justified provided it was waged by the sovereign authority, it was accompanied by a just cause (i.e. the punishment of wrongdoers) and it was supported by the right intentions on the part of the belligerents.

With the rise of the European nation-states, the doctrine began to change.[5] It became linked with the sovereignty of states and faced the paradox of wars between Christian states, each side being convinced of the justice of its cause. This situation tended to modify the approach to the just war. The requirement that serious attempts at a peaceful resolution of the dispute were necessary before turning to force began to appear. This reflected the new state of international affairs, since there now existed a series of independent states, uneasily co-existing in Europe in a primitive balance of power system. The use of force against other states, far from

---

[2] See e.g. L. C. Green, *The Contemporary Law of Armed Conflict*, 2nd edn, Manchester, 2000; G. Best, *War and Law Since 1945*, Oxford, 1994; S. Bailey, *Prohibitions and Restraints in War*, Oxford, 1972; M. Walzer, *Just and Unjust Wars*, 2nd edn, New York, 1977, and T. M. Franck, *Fairness in International Law and Institutions*, Oxford, 1995, chapter 8. See also Brownlie, *Use of Force*, pp. 5 ff.; Dinstein, *War*, chapter 3, and C. Greenwood, 'The Concept of War in Modern International Law', 36 ICLQ, 1987, p. 283.

[3] See J. Eppstein, *The Catholic Tradition of the Law of Nations*, 1935, pp. 65 ff.; Bailey, *Prohibitions*, pp. 6–9, and Brownlie, *Use of Force*, p. 5.

[4] *Summa Theologica*, II, ii, 40. See Bailey, *Prohibitions*, p. 9. See also Von Elbe, 'The Evolution of the Concept of the Just War in International Law', 33 AJIL, 1939, p. 669, and C. Parry, 'The Function of Law in the International Community' in *Manual of Public International Law* (ed. M. Sørensen), London, 1968, pp. 1, 27.

[5] Brownlie, *Use of Force*, pp. 7 ff.

strengthening the order, posed serious challenges to it and threatened to undermine it. Thus the emphasis in legal doctrine moved from the application of force to suppress wrongdoers to a concern (if hardly apparent at times) to maintain the order by peaceful means. The great Spanish writer of the sixteenth century, Vitoria,[6] emphasised that 'not every kind and degree of wrong can suffice for commencing war', while Suarez[7] noted that states were obliged to call the attention of the opposing side to the existence of a just cause and request reparation before action was taken. The just war was also implied in immunity of innocent persons from direct attack and the proportionate use of force to overcome the opposition.[8]

Gradually it began to be accepted that a certain degree of right might exist on both sides, although the situation was confused by references to subjective and objective justice. Ultimately, the legality of the recourse to war was seen to depend upon the formal processes of law. This approach presaged the rise of positivism with its concentration upon the sovereign state, which could only be bound by what it had consented to. Grotius,[9] in his systematising fashion, tried to exclude ideological considerations as the basis of a just war, in the light of the destructive seventeenth-century religious conflicts, and attempted to redefine the just war in terms of self-defence, the protection of property and the punishment for wrongs suffered by the citizens of the particular state.

But with positivism and the definitive establishment of the European balance of power system after the Peace of Westphalia, 1648, the concept of the just war disappeared from international law as such.[10] States were sovereign and equal, and therefore no one state could presume to judge whether another's cause was just or not. States were bound to honour agreements and respect the independence and integrity of other countries, and had to try and resolve differences by peaceful methods.

But where war did occur, it entailed a series of legal consequences. The laws of neutrality and war began to operate as between the parties and third states and a variety of legal situations at once arose. The fact that the war may have been regarded as unjust by any ethical standards

---

[6] *De Indis et de Jure Belli Relectiones*, ss. 14, 20–3, 29 and 60, cited in Bailey, *Prohibitions*, p. 11.

[7] See *ibid.*, pp. 11–12. Suarez felt that the only just cause was a grave injustice that could not be avenged or repaired in any other way, *ibid.*

[8] *Ibid.*, pp. 12–15.

[9] *Ibid.*, chapter 2, and Brownlie, *Use of Force*, p. 13. See *De Jure Belli ac Pacis*, 1625.

[10] See e.g. Brownlie, *Use of Force*, pp. 14 ff. See also L. Gross, 'The Peace of Westphalia, 1648–1948', 42 AJIL, 1948, p. 20.

did not in any way affect the legality of force as an instrument of the sovereign state nor alter in any way the various rules of war and neutrality that sprang into operation once the war commenced. Whether the cause was just or not became irrelevant in any legal way to the international community (though, of course, important in political terms) and the basic issue revolved around whether in fact a state of war existed.[11] The doctrine of the just war arose with the increasing power of Christianity and declined with the outbreak of the inter-Christian religious wars and the establishment of an order of secular sovereign states. Although war became a legal state of affairs which permitted force to be used and in which a series of regulatory conditions were recognised, there existed various other methods of employing force that fell short of war with all the legal consequences as regards neutrals and conduct that that entailed. Reprisals and pacific blockades[12] were examples of the use of force as 'hostile measures short of war'.

These activities were undertaken in order to assert or enforce rights or to punish wrongdoers. There were many instances in the nineteenth century in particular of force being used in this manner against the weaker states of Latin America and Asia.[13] There did exist limitations under international law of the right to resort to such measures but they are probably best understood in the context of the balance of power mechanism of international relations that to a large extent did help minimise the resort to force in the nineteenth century, or at least restrict its application.

The First World War marked the end of the balance of power system and raised anew the question of unjust war. It also resulted in efforts to rebuild international affairs upon the basis of a general international institution which would oversee the conduct of the world community to ensure that aggression could not happen again. The creation of the League of Nations reflected a completely different attitude to the problems of force in the international order.[14]

The Covenant of the League declared that members should submit disputes likely to lead to a rupture to arbitration or judicial settlement or inquiry by the Council of the League. In no circumstances were members to resort to war until three months after the arbitral award or judicial decision or report by the Council. This was intended to provide a

---

[11] Brownlie, *Use of Force*, pp. 26–8.   [12] *Ibid.*   [13] *Ibid.*, pp. 28 ff.
[14] *Ibid.*, chapter 3. But note Hague Convention II of 1907, which provided that the parties would not have recourse to armed forces for the recovery of contract debts claimed from the government of one country by the government of another as being due to its nationals.

cooling-off period for passions to subside and reflected the view that such a delay might well have broken the seemingly irreversible chain of tragedy that linked the assassination of the Austrian Archduke in Sarajevo with the outbreak of general war in Europe. League members agreed not to go to war with members complying with such an arbitral award or judicial decision or unanimous report by the Council.[15]

The League system did not, it should be noted, prohibit war or the use of force, but it did set up a procedure designed to restrict it to tolerable levels. It was a constant challenge of the inter-war years to close the gaps in the Covenant in an effort to achieve the total prohibition of war in international law and this resulted ultimately in the signing in 1928 of the General Treaty for the Renunciation of War (the Kellogg–Briand Pact).[16] The parties to this treaty condemned recourse to war and agreed to renounce it as an instrument of national policy in their relations with one another.[17]

In view of the fact that this treaty has never been terminated and in the light of its widespread acceptance,[18] it is clear that prohibition of the resort to war is now a valid principle of international law. It is no longer possible to set up the legal relationship of war in international society. Thus, for example, it is unnecessary to declare war in order to engage legitimately in armed conflict.[19]

However, the prohibition on the resort to war does not mean that the use of force in all circumstances is illegal. Reservations to the treaty by some states made it apparent that the right to resort to force in self-defence was still a recognised principle in international law.[20] Whether in fact measures short of war such as reprisals were also prohibited or were left untouched by the treaty's ban on war was unclear and subject to conflicting interpretations.[21]

---

[15] Brownlie, *Use of Force*, chapter 4. See especially articles 10–16 of the Covenant.

[16] See e.g. Dinstein, *War*, chapter 4; A. K. Skubiszewski, 'The Use of Force by States' in Sørensen, *Manual of Public International Law*, pp. 739, 742–4, and Brownlie, *Use of Force*, pp. 74–92.

[17] Article I.

[18] It came into force on 24 July 1929 and is still in effect. Many inter-war treaties reaffirmed the obligations imposed by the Pact: see e.g. Brownlie, *Use of Force*, pp. 75–6.

[19] See e.g. *Yossi Beilin v. The Prime Minister of Israel* HCJ 6204/06, 2006. See also C. Greenwood, 'Scope of Application of Humanitarian Law' in *Handbook of Humanitarian Law in Armed Conflicts* (ed. D. Fleck), Oxford, 1999, p. 43, and I. Detter, *The Law of War*, 2nd edn, Cambridge, 2004, pp. 9 ff.

[20] See e.g. Cmd 3153, p. 10.

[21] See Brownlie, *Use of Force*, p. 87. Cf. Bowett, *Self-Defence*, p. 136.

The UN Charter[22]

Article 2(4) of the Charter declares that:

> [a]ll members shall refrain in their international relations from the threat or use of force against the territorial integrity or political independence of any state, or in any other manner inconsistent with the purposes of the United Nations.

This provision is regarded now as a principle of customary international law and as such is binding upon all states in the world community.[23] The reference to 'force' rather than war is beneficial and thus covers situations in which violence is employed which fall short of the technical requirements of the state of war.

Article 2(4) was elaborated as a principle of international law in the 1970 Declaration on Principles of International Law and analysed systematically. First, wars of aggression constitute a crime against peace for which there is responsibility under international law. Secondly, states must not threaten or use force to violate existing international frontiers (including demarcation or armistice lines) or to solve international disputes. Thirdly, states are under a duty to refrain from acts of reprisal involving the use of force. Fourthly, states must not use force to deprive peoples of their right to self-determination and independence. And fifthly, states must refrain from organising, instigating, assisting or participating in acts of civil strife or terrorist acts in another state and must not encourage the formation of armed bands for incursion into another state's territory. Many of these items are crucial, but ambiguous. Although the Declaration is not of itself a binding legal document, it is important as an interpretation of the relevant Charter provisions.[24] Important exceptions to article 2(4) exist in relation to collective measures taken by the United

---

[22] See J. P. Cot, A. Pellet and M. Forteau, *La Charte des Nations Unies: Commentaire Article par Article*, 3rd edn, Paris, 2005, and *The Charter of the United Nations* (ed. B. Simma), 2nd edn, Oxford, 2002.

[23] See e.g. Skubiszewski, 'Use of Force', p. 745, and L. Henkin, R. C. Pugh, O. Schachter and H. Smit, *International Law: Cases and Materials*, 3rd edn, St Paul, 1993, p. 893. See also the *Third US Restatement of Foreign Relations Law*, St Paul, 1987, p. 27; Cot *et al.*, *Charte*, p. 437 (N. Schrijver), and Simma, *Charter*, p. 112.

[24] See e.g. G. Arangio-Ruiz, *The UN Declaration on Friendly Relations and the System of Sources of International Law*, Alphen aan den Rijn, 1979, and R. Rosenstock, 'The Declaration on Principles of International Law Concerning Friendly Relations', 65 AJIL, 1971, p. 713. See also General Assembly resolution 42/22, the Declaration on the Enhancement of the Effectiveness of the Principle of Refraining from the Threat or Use of Force in International Relations, 1987.

Nations[25] and with regard to the right of self-defence.[26] Whether such an exception exists with regard to humanitarian intervention is the subject of some controversy.[27]

Article 2(6) of the Charter provides that the UN 'shall ensure that states which are not members of the United Nations act in accordance with these Principles so far as may be necessary for the maintenance of international peace and security'. In fact, many of the resolutions adopted by the UN are addressed simply to 'all states'. In particular, for example, Security Council resolution 757 (1992) adopted under Chapter VII of the Charter, and therefore binding upon all member states, imposed comprehensive sanctions upon the Federal Republic of Yugoslavia (Serbia and Montenegro). However, the invocation in that decision was to 'all states' and not to 'member states'.

'Force'

One point that was considered in the past[28] and is now being reconsidered is whether the term 'force' in article 2(4) includes not only armed force[29] but, for example, economic force.[30] Does the imposition of boycotts or embargoes against particular states or groups of states come within article 2(4), so rendering them illegal?[31] Although that provision is not modified in any way, the preamble to the Charter does refer to the need to ensure that 'armed force' should not be used except in the common interest, while article 51, dealing with the right to self-defence, specifically refers to armed force, although that is not of itself conclusive as to the permissibility of other forms of coercion.

The 1970 Declaration on Principles of International Law recalled the 'duty of states to refrain ... from military, political, economic or any other form of coercion aimed against the political independence or territorial integrity of any state' and the International Covenants on Human Rights

---

[25] See below, chapter 22, p. 1235.   [26] See below, p. 1131.   [27] See below, p. 1155.

[28] An attempt by Brazil to prohibit 'economic measures' in article 2(4) itself was rejected, 6 UNCIO, Documents, p. 335. See also L. M. Goodrich, E. Hambro and A. P. Simons, *Charter of the United Nations*, 3rd edn, New York, 1969, p. 49.

[29] See e.g. the mining of Nicaraguan harbours by the US, the *Nicaragua* case, ICJ Reports, 1986, pp. 14, 128; 76 ILR, p. 349.

[30] See Simma, *Charter*, p. 118.

[31] See e.g. *Economic Coercion and the New International Economic Order* (ed. R. B. Lillich), Charlottesville, 1976, and *The Arab Oil Weapon* (eds. J. Paust and A. Blaustein), Dobbs Ferry, 1977.

adopted in 1966 emphasised the right of all peoples freely to pursue their economic, social and cultural development. This approach was under-lined in the Charter of Economic Rights and Duties of States, approved by the General Assembly in 1974, which particularly specified that 'no state may use or encourage the use of economic, political or any other type of measures to coerce another state in order to obtain from it the subordination of the exercise of its sovereign rights'. The question of the legality of the open use of economic pressures to induce a change of pol-icy by states was examined with renewed interest in the light of the Arab oil weapon used in 1973–4 against states deemed favourable to Israel.[32] It does seem that there is at least a case to be made out in support of the view that such actions are contrary to the United Nations Charter, as interpreted in numerous resolutions and declarations. But whether such action constitutes a violation of article 2(4) is dubious.[33]

It is to be noted that article 2(4) covers threats of force as well as use of force.[34] This issue was addressed by the International Court in its Advisory Opinion to the General Assembly on the *Legality of the Threat or Use of Nuclear Weapons*. The Court stated that a 'signalled intention to use force if certain events occur' could constitute a threat under article 2(4) where the envisaged use of force would itself be unlawful. Examples given included threats to secure territory from another state or causing it to 'follow or not follow certain political or economic paths'.[35] The Court appeared to accept that the mere possession of nuclear weapons did not of itself constitute a threat. However, noting that the policy of nuclear deterrence functioned on the basis of the credibility of the possibility of resorting to those weapons in certain circumstances, it was stated that whether this amounted to a threat would depend upon whether the particular use of force envisaged would be directed against the territorial integrity or political independence of a state or against the purposes of the UN. If

---

[32] Paust and Blaustein, *Arab Oil Weapon*.   [33] See e.g. Dinstein, *War*, p. 86.

[34] Brownlie, *Use of Force*, p. 364, notes that a threat of force consists 'in an express or implied promise by a government of a resort to force conditional on non-acceptance of certain demands of that government'. See also N. Stürchler, *The Threat of Force in International Law*, Cambridge, 2007; M. Roscini, 'Threats of Armed Force and Contemporary International Law', 54 NILR, 2007, p. 229; R. Sadurska, 'Threats of Force', 82 AJIL, 1988, p. 239, and N. White and R. Cryer, 'Unilateral Enforcement of Resolution 687: A Threat Too Far?', 29 *California Western International Law Journal*, 1999, p. 243.

[35] This was cited with approval by the arbitral tribunal in *Guyana* v. *Suriname*, award of 17 September 2007, paras. 439 and 445, where an order by Surinamese naval vessels to an oil rig to leave the area within twelve hours or face the consequences was deemed to constitute such a threat.

the projected use of the weapons was intended as a means of defence and there would be a consequential and necessary breach of the principles of necessity and proportionality, this would suggest that a threat contrary to article 2(4) existed.[36] One key point here would be the definition of proportionality, in particular would it relate to the damage that might be caused or rather to the scope of the threat to which the response in self-defence is proposed? If the latter is the case, and logic suggests this, then the threat to use nuclear weapons in response to the prior use of nuclear or possibly chemical or bacteriological weapons becomes less problematic.[37]

The provisions governing the resort to force internationally do not affect the right of a state to take measures to maintain order within its jurisdiction. Accordingly, such a state may forcibly quell riots, suppress insurrections and punish rebels without contravening article 2(4). In the event of injury to alien persons or property, the state may be required to make reparation to the state of the alien concerned,[38] but apart from this the prohibition on force in international law is not in general applicable within domestic jurisdictions.[39] Accordingly, international law posits a general prohibition on the use of force. In order for force to be legitimate, it must fall within one of the accepted exceptions. These are essentially the right to self-defence[40] and enforcement action mandated by the United Nations Security Council.[41] Whether force may also be used in cases of extreme humanitarian need is discussed below.[42]

'Against the territorial integrity or political independence of any state'

Article 2(4) of the Charter prohibits the use of force 'against the territorial integrity or political independence of any state, or in any other manner

---

[36] ICJ Reports, 1996, pp. 226, 246–7; 110 ILR, p. 163.

[37] Note that article 2(b) of the Draft Articles on the Effects of Armed Conflicts on Treaties defines 'armed conflict' as 'a state of war or a conflict which involves armed operations which by their nature or extent are likely to affect the operation of treaties between States parties to the armed conflict or between State parties to the armed conflict and third States, regardless of a formal declaration of war or other declaration by any or all of the parties to the armed conflict': see I. Brownlie's Third Report on the Effects of Armed Conflicts on Treaties, A/CN.4/578, 2007, p. 5.

[38] See above, chapter 14, p. 823.

[39] But see below, p. 1148, regarding self-determination, and p. 1148, regarding civil wars, and see with regard to non-international armed conflicts, below, chapter 21, p. 1194.

[40] See below, p. 1131.   [41] See below, chapter 22, p. 1251.   [42] Below, p. 1155.

inconsistent with the purposes of the United Nations'.[43] There is a debate as to whether these words should be interpreted restrictively,[44] so as to permit force that would not contravene the clause, or as reinforcing the primary prohibition,[45] but the weight of opinion probably suggests the latter position. The 1965 Declaration on the Inadmissibility of Intervention in the Domestic Affairs of States[46] emphasised that:

> [n]o state has the right to intervene, directly or indirectly, for any reason whatsoever, in the internal or external affairs of any other state. Consequently, armed intervention and all other forms of interference or attempted threats against the personality of the state or against its political, economic and cultural elements, are condemned.

This was reaffirmed in the 1970 Declaration on Principles in International Law,[47] with the proviso that not only were such manifestations condemned, but they were held to be in violation of international law. The International Court of Justice in the *Corfu Channel* case[48] declared specifically, in response to a British claim to be acting in accordance with a right of intervention in minesweeping the channel to secure evidence for judicial proceedings, that:

> the alleged right of intervention [was] the manifestation of a policy of force, such as has, in the past, given rise to most serious abuses and such as cannot . . . find a place in international law.

The Court noted that to allow such a right in the present case as a derogation from Albania's territorial sovereignty would be even less admissible:

> for, from the nature of things it would be reserved for the most powerful states, and might easily lead to perverting the administration of international justice itself.

---

[43] The International Court has described the prohibition against the use of force as a 'cornerstone of the United Nations Charter', *Democratic Republic of the Congo* v. *Uganda*, ICJ Reports, 2005, pp. 168, 223.

[44] See e.g. Bowett, *Self-Defence*, p. 152.

[45] See Brownlie, *Use of Force*, p. 268. See also Skubiszewski, 'Use of Force', pp. 745–6.

[46] General Assembly resolution 2131 (XX).   [47] General Assembly resolution 2625 (XXV).

[48] ICJ Reports, 1949, pp. 4, 35; 16 AD, pp. 155, 167. See also Brownlie, *Use of Force*, pp. 283–9, and H. Lauterpacht, *The Development of International Law by the International Court*, London, 1958, p. 90.

The essence of international relations, concluded the Court, lay in the respect by independent states of each other's territorial sovereignty.[49] In addition, the Eritrea–Ethiopia Claims Commission took the position that recourse to force would violate international law even where some of the territory concerned was territory to which the state resorting to force had a valid claim. It noted that 'border disputes between states are so frequent that any exception to the threat or use of force for territory that is allegedly occupied unlawfully would create a large and dangerous hole in a fundamental rule of international law'.[50]

Categories of force

Various measures of self-help ranging from economic retaliation to the use of violence pursuant to the right of self-defence have historically been used. Since the establishment of the Charter regime there are basically three categories of compulsion open to states under international law. These are retorsion, reprisal and self-defence.[51]

Retorsion[52]

Retorsion is the adoption by one state of an unfriendly and harmful act, which is nevertheless lawful, as a method of retaliation against the injurious legal activities of another state. Examples include the severance of diplomatic relations and the expulsion or restrictive control of aliens, as well as various economic and travel restrictions. Retorsion is a legitimate method of showing displeasure in a way that hurts the other state while remaining within the bounds of legality. The Hickenlooper Amendments to the American Foreign Assistance Act are often quoted as an instance of

---

[49] See the *Nicaragua* case, ICJ Reports, 1986, pp. 14, 109–10; 76 ILR, pp. 349, 443–4, and see further below, p. 1131.

[50] Partial Award, *Jus Ad Bellum*, Ethiopia's Claims 1–8, 2005, para. 10: see 45 ILM, 2006, pp. 430, 433. This statement was cited by the arbitral tribunal in *Guyana* v. *Suriname*, award of 17 September 2007, para. 423. See also C. Gray, 'The Eritrea/Ethiopia Claims Commission Oversteps Its Boundaries: A Partial Award?', 17 EJIL, 2006, p. 699.

[51] As to the use of force by the UN, see below, chapter 22, p. 1251.

[52] See e.g. Nguyen Quoc Dinh *et al.*, *Droit International Public*, p. 957; Skubiszewski, 'Use of Force', p. 753, and G. von Glahn, *Law Among Nations*, 7th edn, Boston, 1996, pp. 533 ff.

retorsion since they required the United States President to suspend foreign aid to any country nationalising American property without proper compensation. This procedure was applied only once, as against Ceylon (now Sri Lanka) in 1963, and has now been effectively repealed by the American Foreign Assistance Act of 1973.[53] Retorsion would also appear to cover the instance of a lawful act committed in retaliation to a prior unlawful activity.[54]

Reprisals[55]

Reprisals are acts which are in themselves illegal and have been adopted by one state in retaliation for the commission of an earlier illegal act by another state. They are thus distinguishable from acts of retorsion, which are in themselves lawful acts. The classic case dealing with the law of reprisals is the *Naulilaa* dispute[56] between Portugal and Germany in 1928. This concerned a German military raid on the colony of Angola, which destroyed property, in retaliation for the mistaken killing of three Germans lawfully in the Portuguese territory.

The tribunal, in discussing the Portuguese claim for compensation, emphasised that before reprisals could be undertaken, there had to be sufficient justification in the form of a previous act contrary to international law. If that was established, reprisals had to be preceded by an unsatisfied demand for reparation and accompanied by a sense of proportion between the offence and the reprisal. In fact, the German claim that it had acted lawfully was rejected on all three grounds. Those general rules are still applicable but have now to be interpreted in the light of the prohibition on the use of force posited by article 2(4) of the United Nations Charter. Thus, reprisals short of force (now usually termed countermeasures)[57] may still be undertaken legitimately, while reprisals involving armed force may be lawful where resorted to in conformity with the right

---

[53] See e.g. R. B. Lillich, 'Requiem for Hickenlooper', 69 AJIL, 1975, p. 97, and C. F. Amerasinghe, 'The Ceylon Oil Expropriations', 58 AJIL, 1964, p. 445.

[54] See also, with regard to countermeasures, above, chapter 14, p. 794.

[55] See e.g. Skubiszewski, 'Use of Force', pp. 753–5; Brownlie, *Use of Force*, pp. 219–23 and 281–2; D. W. Bowett, 'Reprisals Including Recourse to Armed Force', 66 AJIL, 1972, p. 1, and R. W. Tucker, 'Reprisals and Self-Defence: The Customary Law', 66 AJIL, 1972, p. 581.

[56] 2 RIAA, p. 1011 (1928); 4 AD, p. 526. See also G. Hackworth, *Digest of International Law*, Washington, 1943, vol. VI, p. 154.

[57] See above, chapter 14, p. 794.

of self-defence.[58] Reprisals as such undertaken during peacetime are thus unlawful, unless they fall within the framework of the principle of self-defence.[59] Sometimes regarded as an aspect of reprisal is the institution of pacific blockade.[60] This developed during the nineteenth century and was extensively used as a forceful application of pressure against weaker states. In the absence of war or armed hostilities, the vessels of third states were probably exempt from such blockade, although this was disputed by some writers.

Pacific blockades may be instituted by the United Nations Security Council,[61] but cannot now be resorted to by states since the coming into force of the Charter of the United Nations. The legality of the so-called 'quarantine' imposed by the United States upon Cuba in October 1962 to prevent certain weapons reaching the island appears questionable and should not be relied upon as an extension of the doctrine of pacific blockades.[62]

---

[58] See Dinstein, *War*, p. 222. But see Bowett, 'Reprisals'. See also SCOR, 19th Year, 111th meeting, 8 April 1964, in which the Security Council condemned reprisals as contrary to the UN Charter and deplored the UK bombing of Fort Harib, and R. B. Lillich, 'Forcible Self-Help under International Law', 62 *US Naval War College International Law Studies*, 1980, p. 129. Note that the US State Department has declared that, 'it is clear that the United States has taken the categorical position that reprisals involving the use of force are illegal under international law', 'Memorandum on US Practice with Respect to Reprisals', 73 AJIL, 1979, p. 489. As for episodes that appear to be on the borderline between self-defence and reprisals, see e.g. R. A. Falk, 'The Beirut Raid and the International Law of Retaliation', 63 AJIL, 1969, p. 415, and Y. Blum, 'The Beirut Raid and the International Double Standard', 64 AJIL, 1970, p. 73.

[59] The International Court declared in the *Legality of the Threat or Use of Nuclear Weapons* that, 'armed reprisals in time of peace . . . are considered to be unlawful . . . any right to [belligerent] reprisals would, like self-defence, be governed *inter alia* by the principle of proportionality', ICJ Reports, 1996, pp. 226, 246; 110 ILR, p. 163. Note that reprisals taking place within an armed conflict (belligerent reprisals) are permitted in response to prior violation of the laws of armed conflict by the opposing side: see Y. Dinstein, *The Conduct of Hostilities under the Law of International Armed Conflict*, Cambridge, 2004, pp. 220 ff., and C. Greenwood, 'The Twilight of the Law of Belligerent Reprisals', 20 Netherlands YIL, 1989, pp. 35, 38.

[60] See e.g. Skubiszewski, 'Use of Force', pp. 755–7, and Brownlie, *Use of Force*, pp. 223–4.

[61] See below, chapter 22, p. 1241.

[62] See e.g. Q. Wright, 'The Cuban Quarantine', 57 AJIL, 1963, p. 546, and M. S. McDougal, 'The Soviet–Cuban Quarantine and Self-Defence', *ibid.*, p. 597. See also A. Chayes, *The Cuban Missile Crisis*, Oxford, 1974. But note the rather different declaration by the UK of a Total Exclusion Zone during the Falklands conflict, above, chapter 11, p. 584, note 139.

The right of self-defence[63]

The traditional definition of the right of self-defence in customary international law arose out of the *Caroline* case.[64] This dispute revolved around an incident in 1837 in which British subjects seized and destroyed a vessel in an American port. This had taken place because the *Caroline* had been supplying groups of American nationals, who had been conducting raids into Canadian territory. In the correspondence with the British authorities which followed the incident, the US Secretary of State laid down the essentials of self-defence. There had to exist 'a necessity of self-defence, instant, overwhelming, leaving no choice of means, and no moment for deliberation'. Not only were such conditions necessary before self-defence became legitimate, but the action taken in pursuance of it must not be unreasonable or excessive, 'since the act, justified by the necessity of self-defence, must be limited by that necessity, and kept clearly within it'. These principles were accepted by the British government at that time and are accepted as part of customary international law.[65]

Article 51 of the Charter provides that:

> Nothing in the present Charter shall impair the inherent right of individual or collective self-defence if an armed attack occurs against a member of the United Nations, until the Security Council has taken the measures necessary to maintain international peace and security. Measures taken by members in the exercise of this right of self-defence shall be immediately reported

[63] See Bowett, *Self-Defence*, and Brownlie, *Use of Force*, chapter 13. See also I. Brownlie, 'The Use of Force in Self-Defence', 37 BYIL, 1961, p. 183; Dinstein, *War*, chapters 7 and 8; Gray, *Use of Force*, chapter 4; Franck, *Recourse*, chapters 3–7; S. Alexandrov, *Self-defence against the Use of Force in International Law*, The Hague, 1996; J. Delivanis, *La Légitime Défense en Droit International*, Paris, 1971; Byers, *War Law*, Part Two; S. Schwebel, 'Aggression, Intervention and Self-Defence in Modern International Law', 136 HR, 1972, p. 411; O. Schachter, 'The Right of States to Use Armed Force', 82 *Michigan Law Review*, 1984, p. 1620, Schachter, 'Self-Defence and the Rule of Law', 83 AJIL, 1989, p. 259, and Schachter, *International Law in Theory and Practice*, Dordrecht, 1991, chapter 8; N. Ochoa-Ruiz and E. Salamanca-Aguado, 'Exploring the Limits of International Law relating to the Use of Force in Self-defence', 16 EJIL, 2005, p. 499; Cot *et al.*, *Charte*, p. 506 (A. Cassese); Nguyen Quoc Dinh *et al.*, *Droit International Public*, p. 941, and Simma, *Charter*, p. 788.

[64] 29 BFSP, p. 1137 and 30 BFSP, p. 195. See also R. Y. Jennings, 'The Caroline and McLeod Cases', 32 AJIL, 1938, p. 82.

[65] See e.g. the Legal Adviser to the US Department of State, who noted that 'the exercise of the inherent right of self-defence depends upon a prior delict, an illegal act that presents an immediate, overwhelming danger to an actual and essential right of the state. When these conditions are present, the means used must then be proportionate to the gravity of the threat or danger', DUSPIL, 1975, p. 17.

to the Security Council and shall not in any way affect the authority and responsibility of the Security Council under the present Charter to take at any time such action as it deems necessary in order to maintain or restore international peace and security.

There has been extensive controversy as to the precise extent of the right of self-defence[66] in the light of article 51, with some writers arguing that article 51 in conjunction with article 2(4) was exhaustive[67] and others maintaining that the opening phrase in article 51 specifying that 'nothing in the present Charter shall impair the inherent right of . . . self-defence' meant that there existed in customary international law a right of self-defence over and above the specific provisions of article 51, which referred only to the situation where an armed attack had occurred.[68]

The International Court of Justice in the *Nicaragua* case,[69] however, clearly established that the right of self-defence existed as an inherent right under customary international law as well as under the UN Charter. It was stressed that:

> Article 51 of the Charter is only meaningful on the basis that there is a 'natural' or 'inherent' right of self-defence and it is hard to see how this can be other than of a customary nature, even if its present content has been confirmed and influenced by the Charter . . . It cannot, therefore, be held that article 51 is a provision which 'subsumes and supervenes' customary international law.

Accordingly, customary law continued to exist alongside treaty law (i.e. the UN Charter) in this field. There was not an exact overlap and the rules did not have the same content. The Court also discussed the notion of an 'armed attack' and noted that this included not only action by regular

---

66 Note that article 21 of the International Law Commission's Articles on State Responsibility, 2001, provides that, 'The wrongfulness of an act of a State is precluded if the act constitutes a lawful measure of self-defence taken in conformity with the Charter of the United Nations.'

67 See e.g. Brownlie, *Use of Force*, pp. 112–13 and 264 ff., and E. Jiménez de Aréchaga, 'International Law in the Past Third of the Century', 159 HR, 1978, pp. 1, 87–98. See also Skubiszewski, 'Use of Force', pp. 765–8, and H. Kelsen, *The Law of the United Nations*, London, 1950, p. 914.

68 See e.g. Bowett, *Self Defence*, pp. 185–6; Stone, *Aggression and World Order*, pp. 43, 95–6. See also H. Waldock, 'General Course on Public International Law', 166 HR, 1980, pp. 6, 231–7; Simma, *Charter*, pp. 790 ff.; Gray, *Use of Force*, pp. 98 ff.; J. Brierly, *The Law of Nations*, 6th edn, Oxford, 1963, pp. 417–18, and D. P. O'Connell, *International Law*, 2nd edn, London, 1970, vol. I, p. 317. See also e.g. 6 UNCIO, Documents, where it is noted that 'the use of arms in legitimate self-defence remains admitted and unimpaired'.

69 ICJ Reports, 1986, pp. 14, 94; 76 ILR, pp. 349, 428.

armed forces across an international border, but additionally the sending by or on behalf of a state of armed bands or groups which carry out acts of armed force of such gravity as to amount to an actual armed attack conducted by regular armed forces or its substantial involvement therein.[70] In this situation, the focus would then shift to a consideration of the involvement of the state in question so as to render it liable and to legitimate action in self-defence against it.[71]

In order to be able to resort to force in self-defence, a state has to be able to demonstrate that it has been the victim of an armed attack and it bears the burden of proof.[72] The Court has noted that it is possible that the mining of a single military vessel might suffice,[73] but an attack on a ship owned, but not flagged, by a state will not be equated with an attack on that state.[74] However, it is necessary to show that the state seeking to resort to force in self-defence has itself been intentionally attacked. In a series of incidents discussed by the Court in the *Oil Platforms* case, it was noted that none of them appeared to have been aimed specifically and deliberately at the US.[75] In seeking to determine how serious an attack must be in order to validate a self-defence response, the Court in the *Nicaragua* case[76] distinguished 'the most grave forms of the use of force (those constituting an armed attack) from other less grave forms' and this was reaffirmed in the *Oil Platforms* case.[77] It is, nevertheless, extremely difficult to define this more closely.

In many cases, however, it might be difficult to determine the moment when an armed attack had commenced in order to comply with the requirements of article 51 and the resort to force in self-defence. For example, it has been argued that with regard to actions against aircraft,

---

[70] The Court noted that this provision, contained in article 3(g) of the Definition of Aggression annexed to General Assembly resolution 3314 (XXIX) of 1974, reflected customary international law, ICJ Reports, 1986, p. 103; 76 ILR, p. 437.

[71] See e.g. Gray, *Use of Force*, pp. 108 ff.

[72] The *Oil Platforms (Iran v. US)* case, ICJ Reports, 2003, pp. 161, 189 and 190; 130 ILR, pp. 323, 348–50.

[73] *Ibid.*, p. 195.   [74] *Ibid.*, p. 191.

[75] *Ibid.* The incidents included missile attack from a distance that meant it could not have been aimed at a particular vessel (the US *Sea Isle City*) as distinct from 'some target in Kuwaiti waters'; an attack on a non-US flagged vessel; the alleged firing on US helicopters from Iranian gunboats that the Court found unproven; and mine-laying that could not be shown to have been aimed at the US, *ibid.*, pp. 191–2. However, this requirement for a deliberate and intentional attack on the target state, rather than merely an indiscriminate attack, is controversial and open to question.

[76] ICJ Reports, 1986, pp. 14, 101.

[77] ICJ Reports, 2003, pp. 161, 187; 130 ILR, pp. 323, 346.

an armed attack begins at the moment that the radar guiding the anti-aircraft missile has 'locked on'.[78] Further, one argument that has been made with regard to Israel's first strike in June 1967 is that the circumstances were such that an armed attack could be deemed to have commenced against it.[79]

Another aspect of the problem as to what constitutes an armed attack is the difficulty of categorising particular uses of force for these purposes. For example, would an attack upon an embassy or diplomats abroad constitute an armed attack legitimating action in self-defence? On 7 August 1998, the US embassies in Kenya and Tanzania were bombed, causing the loss of over 250 lives and appreciable damage to property. On 20 August, the US launched a series of cruise missile attacks upon installations in Afghanistan and Sudan associated with the organisation of Bin Laden deemed responsible for the attacks. In so doing, the US declared itself to be acting in accordance with article 51 of the Charter and in exercise of its right of self-defence.[80]

While it is clear that the right of self-defence applies to armed attacks by other states, the question has been raised whether the right of self-defence applies in response to attacks by non-state entities.[81] Where it is the state itself which has dispatched armed bands to carry out acts of armed force of such gravity as to amount to an actual armed attack conducted by regular armed forces, then force in self-defence can legitimately be used. The difficulties arise in more ambiguous circumstances. In the *Nicaragua* case, the Court did not accept that the right of self-defence extended to situations where a third state had provided assistance to rebels in the form of the provision of weapons or logistical or other support, although this form of assistance could constitute a threat or use of force, or amount to intervention in the internal or external affairs of the state.[82] This lays open the problem that in certain circumstances a state under attack from groups supported by another state may not be able under this definition to respond militarily if the support given by that other state does not reach the threshold laid down. Judge Jennings referred to this issue in his Dissenting Opinion, noting that, 'it seems dangerous to define unnecessarily strictly the conditions for lawful self-defence, so as to leave a large area where

---

[78] See Gray, *Use of Force*, p. 108, footnote 48.   [79] See below, p. 1138.

[80] See 'Contemporary Practice of the United States', 93 AJIL, 1999, p. 161. The US stated that the missile strikes 'were a necessary and proportionate response to the imminent threat of further terrorist attacks against US personnel and facilities', *ibid.*, p. 162 and S/1998/780.

[81] See e.g. Dinstein, *War*, pp. 204 ff.   [82] ICJ Reports, 1986, pp. 103–4; 76 ILR, pp. 437–8.

both a forcible response to force is forbidden, and yet the United Nations employment of force, which was intended to fill that gap, is absent'.[83]

The line between assistance from a third state to groups (whether characterised as terrorists or rebels or freedom fighters) which would give rise to the legitimate use of force in self-defence against such state and assistance which fell below this is difficult to specify in practice. The International Court in its advisory opinion in the *Construction of a Wall* case[84] appeared to adopt what at first sight is a very restrictive approach by noting that article 51 recognised 'the existence of an inherent right of self-defence in the case of armed attack by one state against another state' and declaring that the provision did not apply with regard to Israel's actions since these were taken with regard to threats originating from within the occupied territories and not imputable to another state. However, this cannot be read to mean that self-defence does not exist with regard to an attack by a non-state entity emanating from a territory outside of the control of the target state. Further, the legal source of Israeli actions in the occupied territories, whether or not they legitimated the construction of the wall or security barrier in whole or in part, would appear to lie rather in the laws of armed conflict (international humanitarian law) and the competence of an occupying state to take action to maintain public order and protect its own forces.[85]

The Court failed to take the opportunity to revisit the ambiguities of the *Nicaragua* decision in *Democratic Republic of the Congo* v. *Uganda*.[86] In this case, the Court found that there was no satisfactory proof of involvement in attacks, direct or indirect, on Uganda by the Congo government and that such attacks did not emanate from armed bands or irregulars sent by or on behalf of the Congo. Such attacks were non-attributable, therefore, on the evidence to the Congo. Since the Court concluded that the legal and factual circumstances for the exercise of a right of self-defence by Uganda against the Congo were not present, 'accordingly' there was no need to address the issue as to whether and under which conditions contemporary international law provides for a right of self-defence against large-scale

---

[83] ICJ Reports, 1986, pp. 543–4; 76 ILR, p. 877. Franck suggests that Security Council practice following the 11 September 2001 attack on the World Trade Center has followed Judge Jennings' approach: see *Recourse*, p. 63, and below, p. 1159.

[84] ICJ Reports, 2004, pp. 136, 194. Cf. the Separate Opinions of Judge Higgins, *ibid.*, p. 215 and Judge Kooijmans, *ibid.*, p. 230.

[85] See article 43 of the Hague Regulations 1907. See further below, chapter 21, p. 1181.

[86] ICJ Reports, 2005, p. 168.

attacks by irregular forces.[87] Since the Court addressed itself only to actions that Uganda might or might not take against the Congo as such, it did not deal with the increasingly important question as to whether action might be taken in self-defence against an armed attack by a non-state actor as distinct from another state.[88]

This is perhaps surprising in view of evolving state practice with regard to international terrorism and, in particular, whether terrorist acts could constitute an 'armed attack' within the meaning of the Charter or indeed customary law.[89] The day after the 11 September 2001 attacks upon the World Trade Center in New York, the Security Council adopted resolution 1368 in which it specifically referred to 'the inherent right of individual or collective self-defence in accordance with the Charter'. Resolution 1373 (2001) reaffirmed this and, acting under Chapter VII, adopted a series of binding decisions, including a provision that all states shall 'take the necessary steps to prevent the commission of terrorist acts'. Such binding Security Council resolutions declaring international terrorism to be a threat to international peace and security with regard to which the right of self-defence is operative as such lead to the conclusion that large-scale attacks by non-state entities might amount to 'armed attacks' within the meaning of article 51 without the necessity to attribute them to another state and thus justify the use of force in self-defence by those states so attacked.[90]

Further recognition that particular hostile actions by non-state entities could amount to 'attacks' may be found in Security Council resolution 1701 (2006), in which both the 'attacks' by Hizbollah, an armed militia controlling parts of Lebanon, upon Israel (which precipitated the summer 2006 armed conflict) and Israeli 'offensive military operations' were condemned.

On 7 October 2001, the US notified the Security Council that it was exercising its right of self-defence in taking action in Afghanistan against the Al-Qaeda organisation deemed responsible for the 11 September attacks

---

[87] *Ibid.*, pp. 222–3.
[88] See the Separate Opinions of Judge Kooijmans, *ibid.*, p. 314 and Judge Simma, *ibid.*, pp. 336 ff.
[89] See e.g. Dinstein, *War*, pp. 201 ff.; Franck, *Recourse*, chapter 4, and Gray, *Use of Force*, pp. 165 ff. See also M. Byers, 'Terrorism, the Use of Force and International Law after 11 September', 51 ICLQ, 2002, p. 401, and L. Condorelli, 'Les Attentats du 11 Septembre et Leur Suite', 105 RGDIP, 2001, p. 829. As to terrorism, see further below, p. 1159.
[90] See the Separate Opinions of Judge Kooijmans and Judge Simma in *Democratic Republic of the Congo* v. *Uganda*, ICJ Reports, 2005, pp. 168, 314 and 337 respectively.

and the Taliban regime in that country which was accused of providing bases for the organisation.[91] The members of the NATO alliance invoked article 5 of the NATO Treaty[92] and the parties to the Inter-American Treaty of Reciprocal Assistance, 1947 invoked a comparable provision.[93] Both provisions refer specifically both to an 'armed attack' and to article 51 of the Charter. Accordingly, the members of both these alliances accepted that what had happened on 11 September constituted an armed attack within the meaning of article 51 of the Charter. In fact, neither treaty was activated as the US acted on its own initiative with specific allies (notably the UK), relying on the right of self-defence with the support or acquiescence of the international community.[94]

A further issue is whether a right to anticipatory or pre-emptive self-defence exists. This would appear unlikely if one adopted the notion that self-defence is restricted to responses to actual armed attacks. The concept

---

[91] See S/2001/946. See also 'Contemporary Practice of the United States', 96 AJIL, 2002, p. 237.

[92] See www.nato.int/terrorism/factsheet.htm. Article 5 provides that: 'The Parties agree that an armed attack against one or more of them in Europe or North America shall be considered an attack against them all and consequently they agree that, if such an armed attack occurs, each of them, in exercise of the right of individual or collective self-defence recognised by article 51 of the Charter of the United Nations, will assist the Party or Parties so attacked by taking forthwith, individually and in concert with the other Parties, such action as it deems necessary, including the use of armed force, to restore and maintain the security of the North Atlantic area.'

[93] Article 3(1) provides that, 'The High Contracting Parties agree that an armed attack by any State against an American State shall be considered as an attack against all the American States and, consequently, each one of the said Contracting Parties undertakes to assist in meeting the attack in the exercise of the inherent right of individual or collective self-defense recognized by Article 51 of the Charter of the United Nations.'

[94] See e.g. Byers, 'Terrorism', pp. 409–10; E. Cannizzaro, 'Entités Non-étatique et Régime Internationale de l'Emploi de la Force – une Étude sur le Cas de la Réaction Israélienne au Liban', 111 Revue Générale de Droit International Public, 2007, p. 333, and K. N. Trapp, 'Back to Basics: Necessity, Proportionality, and the Right of Self-Defence against Non-State Terrorist Actors', 56 ICLQ, 2007, p. 141. The resolution of the Institut de Droit International adopted on 27 October 2007 states in para. 10 that, 'In the event of an armed attack against a state by non-state actors, article 51 of the Charter as supplemented by customary international law applies as a matter of principle.' Note that the Chatham House Principles on International Law on the Use of Force in Self-Defence, 55 ICLQ, 2006, pp. 963, 969, provide that the right to self-defence may apply to attacks by non-state actors where the attack is large-scale; if the right to self-defence is exercised in the territory of another state, then that state is unable or unwilling to deal itself with the non-state actors and that it is necessary to use force from outside to deal with the threat in circumstances where the consent of the territorial state cannot be obtained; and the force used in self-defence may only be directed against the government of the state where the attacker is found in so far as is necessary to avert or end the attack.

of anticipatory self-defence is of particular relevance in the light of modern weaponry that can launch an attack with tremendous speed, which may allow the target state little time to react to the armed assault before its successful conclusion, particularly if that state is geographically small.[95] States have employed pre-emptive strikes in self-defence. Israel, in 1967, launched a strike upon its Arab neighbours, following the blocking of its southern port of Eilat and the conclusion of a military pact between Jordan and Egypt. This completed a chain of events precipitated by the mobilisation of Egyptian forces on Israel's border and the eviction of the United Nations peacekeeping forces from the area by the Egyptian President.[96] It could, of course, also be argued that the Egyptian blockade itself constituted the use of force, thus legitimising Israeli actions without the need for 'anticipatory' conceptions of self-defence, especially when taken together with the other events.[97] It is noteworthy that the United Nations in its debates in the summer of 1967 apportioned no blame for the outbreak of fighting and did not condemn the exercise of self-defence by Israel.

The International Court in the *Nicaragua* case[98] expressed no view on the issue of the lawfulness of a response to an imminent threat of an armed attack since, on the facts of the case, that problem was not raised. The trouble, of course, with the concept of anticipatory self-defence is that it involves fine calculations of the various moves by the other party. A pre-emptive strike embarked upon too early might constitute an aggression. There is a difficult line to be drawn. The problem is that the nature of the international system is such as to leave such determinations to be made by the states themselves, and in the absence of an acceptable, institutional

---

[95] Contrast Bowett, *Use of Force*, pp. 118–92, who emphasises that 'no state can be expected to await an initial attack which, in the present state of armaments, may well destroy the state's capacity for further resistance and so jeopardise its very existence', and Franck, *Fairness*, p. 267, who notes that in such circumstances 'the notion of anticipatory self-defence is both rational and attractive', with Brownlie, *Use of Force*, p. 275, and L. Henkin, *How Nations Behave*, 2nd edn, New York, 1979, pp. 141–5. See also R. Higgins, *The Development of International Law Through the Political Organs of the United Nations*, Oxford, 1963, pp. 216–21; Franck, *Recourse*, chapter 7, and I. Brownlie, *Principles of Public International Law*, 6th edn, Oxford, 2003, pp. 701 ff.

[96] See generally, *The Arab–Israeli Conflict* (ed. J. N. Moore), Princeton, 3 vols., 1974.

[97] Note that Gray writes that Israel did not argue that it acted in anticipatory self-defence but rather in self-defence following the start of the conflict, *Use of Force*, pp. 130–1. See also Dinstein, *War*, p. 192.

[98] ICJ Reports, 1986, pp. 14, 103; 76 ILR, p. 437. See also *Democratic Republic of the Congo v. Uganda*, ICJ Reports, 2005, pp. 168, 222.

alternative, it is difficult to foresee a modification of this. States generally are not at ease with the concept of anticipatory self-defence, however,[99] and one possibility would be to concentrate upon the notion of 'armed attack' so that this may be interpreted in a relatively flexible manner.[100] One suggestion has been to distinguish anticipatory self-defence, where an armed attack is foreseeable, from interceptive self-defence, where an armed attack is imminent and unavoidable so that the evidential problems and temptations of the former concept are avoided without dooming threatened states to making the choice between violating international law and suffering the actual assault.[101] According to this approach, self-defence is legitimate both under customary law and under article 51 of the Charter where an armed attack is imminent. It would then be a question of evidence as to whether that were an accurate assessment of the situation in the light of the information available at the relevant time. This would be rather easier to demonstrate than the looser concept of anticipatory self-defence and it has the merit of being consistent with the view that the right to self-defence in customary law exists as expounded in the *Caroline* case.[102] In any event, much will depend upon the characterisation of the threat and the nature of the response, for this has to be proportionate.[103]

---

[99] See e.g. the Security Council debate on, and condemnation of, Israel's bombing of the Iraqi nuclear reactor in 1981 on the basis of anticipatory self-defence, 20 ILM, 1981, pp. 965–7. See also A. Cassese, *International Law in a Divided World*, Oxford, 1986, pp. 230 ff., who concludes that a consensus is growing to the effect that anticipatory self-defence is allowed but under strict conditions relating to proof of the imminence of an armed attack that would jeopardise the life of the target state and the absence of peaceful means to prevent the attack, *ibid.*, p. 233. However, in *International Law*, 2nd edn, Oxford, 2005, p. 362, Cassese states that, 'it is more judicious to consider such action [anticipatory self-defence] *as legally prohibited*, while admittedly knowing that there may be cases where breaches of the prohibition may be justified on moral and political grounds and the community will eventually condone them or mete out lenient condemnation' (emphasis in original).

[100] See e.g. the Dissenting Opinion of Judge Schwebel, *Nicaragua* case, ICJ Reports, 1986, pp. 14, 347–8; 76 ILR, pp. 349, 681. But see Dinstein, *War*, pp. 187 ff. Note also the suggestion that attacks on computer networks may also fall within the definition of armed attack if fatalities are caused, e.g. where the computer-controlled systems regulating waterworks and dams are disabled: see Y. Dinstein, 'Computer Network Attacks and Self-Defence', 76 *International Law Studies, US Naval War College*, 2001, p. 99.

[101] See Dinstein, *War*, pp. 191–2. [102] See above, p. 1131.

[103] However, note that the Report of the UN High Level Panel on Threats, Challenges and Change, A/59/565, 2004, at para. 188, declared that 'a threatened state, according to long established international law, can take military action as long as the threatened attack is *imminent*, no other means would deflect it and the action is proportionate' (emphasis in original). The response of the UN Secretary-General, *In Larger Freedom*, A/59/2005, para. 124, also stated that imminent threats were covered by the right to self-defence. The

Nevertheless, it is safe to conclude that the concept of self-defence extends to a response to an attack that is reasonably and evidentially perceived to be imminent, however that is semantically achieved. The *Caroline* criteria remain critical.[104]

There have, however, been suggestions that the notion of anticipatory self-defence, controversial though that is, could be expanded to a right of 'pre-emptive self-defence' (sometimes termed 'preventive self-defence') that goes beyond the *Caroline* limits enabling the use of force in order to defend against, or prevent, possible attacks. The US note to the UN on 7 October 2001, concerning action in Afghanistan, included the sentence that, 'We may find that our self-defence requires further actions with respect to other organisations and other states.'[105] This approach was formally laid down in the 2002 National Security Strategy of the US[106] and reaffirmed in the 2006 National Security Strategy, which emphasised the role of pre-emption in national security strategy.[107] In so far as it goes beyond the *Caroline* criteria, this doctrine of pre-emption must be seen as going beyond what is currently acceptable in international law.[108]

The concepts of necessity and proportionality are at the heart of self-defence in international law.[109] The Court in the *Nicaragua* case stated that there was a 'specific rule whereby self-defence would warrant only

resolution adopted by the Institut de Droit International on 27 October 2007, para. 3, notes that the right to self-defence arises 'in the case of an actual or manifestly imminent armed attack' and that it may be exercised 'only when there is no lawful alternative in practice in order to forestall, stop or repel the armed attack'.

[104] See also the Chatham House Principles on International Law on the Use of Force in Self-Defence, 55 ICLQ, 2006, pp. 963, 964–5.

[105] S/2001/946. See also Byers, 'Terrorism', p. 411.

[106] 41 ILM, 2002, p. 1478. See also M. E. O'Connell, 'The Myth of Preemptive Self-Defence', ASIL, Task Force on Terrorism, 2002, www.asil.org/taskforce/oconnell.pdf; M. Bothe, 'Terrorism and the Legality of Pre-emptive Force', 14 EJIL, 2003, p. 227, and W. M. Reisman and A. Armstrong, 'Past and Future of the Claim of Preemptive Self-Defense', 100 AJIL, 2006, p. 525.

[107] See C. Gray, 'The Bush Doctrine Revisited: The 2006 National Security Strategy of the USA', 5 *Chinese Journal of International Law*, 2006, p. 555.

[108] See e.g. the Report of the UN High Level Panel on Threats, Challenges and Change, A/59/565, 2004, at paras. 189 ff. and the UN Secretary-General's Report, *In Larger Freedom*, A/59/2005, para. 125, both essentially saying that where a threat is less than imminent, resort should be had to the Security Council. The resolution adopted by the Institut de Droit International on 27 October 2007 notes in para. 6 that, 'There is no basis in international law for the doctrine of "preventive" self-defence in the absence of an actual or manifestly imminent armed attack.' See also the Chatham House Principles on International Law on the Use of Force in Self-Defence, 55 ICLQ, 2006, pp. 963, 968.

[109] See e.g. Brownlie, *Use of Force*, p. 279, footnote 2; J. Graham, *Necessity, Proportionality and the Use of Force by States*, Cambridge, 2004; Gray, *Use of Force*, pp. 120 ff., and Dinstein, *War*, pp. 237 ff.

measures which are proportional to the armed attack and necessary to respond to it, a rule well established in customary international law',[110] and in the Advisory Opinion it gave to the General Assembly on the *Legality of the Threat or Use of Nuclear Weapons* it was emphasised that '[t]he submission of the exercise of the right of self-defence to the conditions of necessity and proportionality is a rule of customary international law'.[111] Quite what will be necessary[112] and proportionate[113] will depend on the circumstances of the case.[114] The necessity criterion raises important evidential as well as substantive issues. It is essential to demonstrate that, as a reasonable conclusion on the basis of facts reasonably known at the time, the armed attack that has occurred or is reasonably believed to be imminent requires the response that is proposed. In the *Oil Platforms* case,[115] the Court held that it was not satisfied that the US attacks on the oil platforms in question were necessary in order to respond to the attack on the *Sea Isle City* and the mining of the USS *Samuel B Roberts*, noting in particular that there was no evidence that the US had complained to Iran of the military activities of the platforms (contrary to its conduct with regard to other events such as minelaying and attacks on neutral shipping). Further, the US had admitted that one attack on an oil platform had been a 'target of opportunity'. It has been argued that, 'Necessity is a threshold, and the criterion of imminence can be seen to be an aspect of it, inasmuch as it requires that there be no time to pursue non-forcible measures with a reasonable chance of averting or stopping the attack.'[116]

---

[110] ICJ Reports, 1986, pp. 14, 94 and 103; 76 ILR, pp. 349, 428 and 437.

[111] ICJ Reports, 1996, pp. 226, 245; 110 ILR, p. 163. The Court affirmed that this 'dual condition' also applied to article 51, whatever the means of force used, *ibid.*

[112] See Judge Ago's Eighth Report on State Responsibility to the International Law Commission, where it was noted that the concept of necessity centred upon the availability of other means to halt the attack so that 'the state attacked . . . must not, in the particular circumstances, have had any means of halting the attack other than recourse to armed force', *Yearbook of the ILC*, 1980, vol. II, part 1, p. 69.

[113] Judge Ago noted that the correct relationship for proportionality was not between the conduct constituting the armed attack and the opposing conduct, but rather between the action taken in self-defence and the purpose of halting and repelling the armed attack, so that '[t]he action needed to halt and repulse the attack may well have to assume dimensions disproportionate to those of the attack suffered', *ibid.*, p. 69. See also J. G. Gardam, 'Proportionality and Force in International Law', 87 AJIL, 1993, p. 391.

[114] Note that the UK declared that Turkish operations in northern Iraq in 1998 'must be proportionate to the threat', UKMIL, 69 BYIL, 1998, p. 586.

[115] ICJ Reports, 2003, pp. 161, 198.

[116] The Chatham House Principles on International Law on the Use of Force in Self-Defence, 55 ICLQ, 2006, pp. 963, 967.

Quite what response would be regarded as proportionate is sometimes difficult to quantify. It raises the issue as to what exactly is the response to be proportionate to. Is it the actual attack or the threat or likelihood of further attacks? And what if the attack in question is but part of a continuing series of such attacks to which response has thus far been muted or nonexistent? In the *Oil Platforms* case, the Court felt it necessary to consider the scale of the whole operation that constituted the US response, which included *inter alia* the destruction of two Iranian frigates and a number of other naval vessels and aircraft, to the mining by an unidentified agency of a single warship without loss of life.[117] In *Democratic Republic of the Congo v. Uganda*,[118] the Court, while finding that the preconditions for the exercise of self-defence did not exist in the circumstances, stated that 'the taking of airports and towns [by Ugandan forces] many hundreds of kilometers from Uganda's border would not seem proportionate to the series of transborder attacks it claimed had given rise to the right of self-defence, nor to be necessary to that end'.

Proportionality as a criterion of self-defence may also require consideration of the type of weaponry to be used, an investigation that necessitates an analysis of the principles of international humanitarian law. The International Court in the *Legality of the Threat or Use of Nuclear Weapons* case took the view that the proportionality principle may 'not in itself exclude the use of nuclear weapons in self-defence in all circumstances', but that 'a use of force that is proportionate under the law of self-defence, must, in order to be lawful, also meet the requirements of the law applicable in armed conflict'. In particular, the nature of such weapons and the profound risks associated with them would be a relevant consideration for states 'believing they can exercise a nuclear response in self-defence in accordance with the requirements of proportionality'.[119] One especial difficulty relates to whether in formulating the level of response a series of activities may be taken into account, rather than just the attack immediately preceding the act of self-defence. The more likely answer is that where such activities clearly form part of a sequence or chain of events, then the test of proportionality will be so interpreted as to incorporate this. It also appears inevitable that it will be the state contemplating such action that will first have to make that determination,[120] although

---

[117] ICJ Reports, 2003, pp. 161, 198; 130 ILR, pp. 323, 357–8.

[118] ICJ Reports, 2005, pp. 168, 223.

[119] ICJ Reports, 1996, pp. 226, 245; 110 ILR, p. 163. See further below, p. 1187.

[120] See e.g. H. Lauterpacht, *The Function of Law in the International Community*, London, 1933, p. 179.

it will be subject to consideration by the international community as a whole and more specifically by the Security Council under the terms of article 51.[121]

It is also important to emphasise that article 51 requires that states report 'immediately' to the Security Council on measures taken in the exercise of their right to self-defence and that action so taken may continue 'until the Security Council has taken the measures necessary to maintain international peace and security'.[122]

The protection of nationals abroad[123]

In the nineteenth century, it was clearly regarded as lawful to use force to protect nationals and property situated abroad and many incidents occurred to demonstrate the acceptance of this position.[124] Since the adoption of the UN Charter, however, it has become rather more controversial since of necessity the 'territorial integrity and political independence' of the target state is infringed,[125] while one interpretation of article 51 would deny that 'an armed attack' could occur against individuals abroad within

---

[121] See e.g. D. Grieg, 'Self-Defence and the Security Council: What Does Article 51 Require?', 40 ICLQ, 1991, p. 366.

[122] Note that the Court pointed out in *Democratic Republic of the Congo* v. *Uganda*, ICJ Reports, 2005, pp. 168, 222, that Uganda did not report to the Security Council events that it had regarded as requiring it to act in self-defence. See Dinstein, *War*, p. 218, who argues that failure to report measures taken in the exercise of the right of self-defence 'should not be fatal, provided that the substantive conditions for the exercise of this right are met'.

[123] See e.g. M. B. Akehurst, 'The Use of Force to Protect Nationals Abroad', 5 *International Relations*, 1977, p. 3, and Akehurst, 'Humanitarian Intervention' in *Intervention in World Politics* (ed. H. Bull), Oxford, 1984, p. 95; Dinstein, *War*, pp. 231 ff.; Gray, *Use of Force*, pp. 126 ff.; Franck, *Recourse*, chapter 6; Waldock, 'General Course', p. 467; L. C. Green, 'Rescue at Entebbe – Legal Aspects', 6 *Israel Yearbook on Human Rights*, 1976, p. 312, and M. N. Shaw, 'Some Legal Aspects of the Entebbe Incident', 1 *Jewish Law Annual*, 1978, p. 232. See also T. Schweisfurth, 'Operations to Rescue Nationals in Third States Involving the Use of Force in Relation to the Protection of Human Rights', German YIL, 1980, p. 159; J. R. d'Angelo, 'Resort to Force to Protect Nationals', 21 Va. JIL, 1981, p. 485; J. Paust, 'The Seizure and Recovery of the *Mayaguez*', 85 *Yale Law Journal*, 1976, p. 774; D. W. Bowett, 'The Use of Force for the Protection of Nationals Abroad' in *The Current Legal Regulation of the Use of Force* (ed. A. Cassese), Oxford, 1986, p. 39, and N. Ronzitti, *Rescuing Nationals Abroad Through Military Coercion and Intervention on Grounds of Humanity*, Oxford, 1985.

[124] See e.g. Brownlie, *Use of Force*, pp. 289 ff.

[125] There is, of course, a different situation where the state concerned has consented to the action or where nationals are evacuated from a state where law and order has broken down: see Gray, *Use of Force*, p. 129.

the meaning of that provision since it is the state itself that must be under attack, not specific persons outside the jurisdiction.[126]

The issue has been raised in recent years in several cases. In 1964, Belgium and the United States sent forces to the Congo to rescue hostages (including nationals of the states in question) from the hands of rebels, with the permission of the Congolese government,[127] while in 1975 the US used force to rescue an American cargo boat and its crew captured by Cambodia.[128] The most famous incident, however, was the rescue by Israel of hostages held by Palestinian and other terrorists at Entebbe, following the hijack of an Air France airliner.[129] The Security Council debate in that case was inconclusive. Some states supported Israel's view that it was acting lawfully in protecting its nationals abroad, where the local state concerned was aiding the hijackers,[130] others adopted the approach that Israel had committed aggression against Uganda or used excessive force.[131]

The United States has in recent years justified armed action in other states on the grounds partly of the protection of American citizens abroad. It was one of the three grounds announced for the invasion of Grenada in 1984[132] and one of the four grounds put forward for the intervention in Panama in December 1989.[133] However, in both cases the level of threat against the US citizens was such as to raise serious questions concerning the satisfaction of the requirement of proportionality.[134] The US conducted a bombing raid on Libya on 15 April 1986 as a consequence of alleged Libyan involvement in an attack on US servicemen in West Berlin.

---

[126] See e.g. Brownlie, *Use of Force*, pp. 289 ff.

[127] See M. Whiteman, *Digest of International Law*, Washington, 1968, vol. V, p. 475. See also R. B. Lillich, 'Forcible Self-Help to Protect Human Rights', 53 *Iowa Law Review*, 1967, p. 325.

[128] Paust, 'Seizure and Recovery'. See also DUSPIL, 1975, pp. 777–83.

[129] See e.g. Akehurst, 'Use of Force'; Green, 'Rescue at Entebbe', and Shaw, 'Legal Aspects'.

[130] See e.g. S/PV.1939, pp. 51–5; S/PV.1940, p. 48 and S/PV.1941, p. 31.

[131] See e.g. S/PV.1943, pp. 47–50 and S/PV.1941, pp. 4–10, 57–61 and 67–72. Note that Egypt attempted without success a similar operation in Cyprus in 1978: see *Keesing's Contemporary Archives*, p. 29305. In 1980, the US attempted to rescue its nationals held hostage in Iran but failed: see S/13908 and the *Iranian Hostages* case, ICJ Reports, 1980, pp. 3, 43; 61 ILR, pp. 530, 569.

[132] See the statement of Deputy Secretary of State Dam, 78 AJIL, 1984, p. 200. See also W. Gilmore, *The Grenada Intervention*, London, 1984, and below, p. 1151.

[133] See the statements by the US President and the Department of State, 84 AJIL, 1990, p. 545.

[134] In the case of Grenada, it was alleged that some American students were under threat: see Gilmore, *Grenada*, pp. 55–64. In the Panama episode one American had been killed and several harassed: see V. Nanda, 'The Validity of United States Intervention in Panama Under International Law', 84 AJIL, 1990, pp. 494, 497.

This was justified by the US as an act of self-defence.[135] On 26 June 1993, the US launched missiles at the headquarters of the Iraqi military intelligence in Baghdad as a consequence of an alleged Iraqi plot to assassinate former US President Bush in Kuwait. It was argued that the resort to force was justified as a means of protecting US nationals in the future.[136] It is difficult to extract from the contradictory views expressed in these incidents the apposite legal principles. While some states affirm the existence of a rule permitting the use of force in self-defence to protect nationals abroad, others deny that such a principle operates in international law. There are states whose views are not fully formed or coherent on this issue. The UK Foreign Minister concluded on 28 June 1993 that:[137]

> Force may be used in self-defence against threats to one's nationals if: (a) there is good evidence that the target attacked would otherwise continue to be used by the other state in support of terrorist attacks against one's nationals; (b) there is, effectively, no other way to forestall imminent further attacks on one's nationals; (c) the force employed is proportionate to the threat.

On balance, and considering the opposing principles of saving the threatened lives of nationals and the preservation of the territorial integrity of states, it would seem preferable to accept the validity of the rule in carefully restricted situations consistent with the conditions laid down in the *Caroline* case.[138] Whether force may be used to protect property abroad is less controversial. It is universally accepted today that it is not lawful to have resort to force merely to save material possessions abroad.

Conclusions

Despite controversy and disagreement over the scope of the right of self-defence, there is an indisputable core and that is the competence of states

---

[135] See President Reagan's statement, *The Times*, 16 April 1986, p. 6. The UK government supported this: see *The Times*, 17 April 1986, p. 4. However, there are problems with regard to proportionality in view of the injuries and damage apparently caused in the air raid. One US serviceman was killed in the West Berlin action. The role of the UK in consenting to the use of British bases for the purposes of the raid is also raised. See also UKMIL, 57 BYIL, 1986, pp. 639–42 and 80 AJIL, 1986, pp. 632–6, and C. J. Greenwood, 'International Law and the United States' Air Operation Against Libya', 89 *West Virginia Law Review*, 1987, p. 933.

[136] See Security Council Debates S/PV. 3245, 1993, and UKMIL, 64 BYIL, 1993, pp. 731 ff. See also D. Kritsiotis, 'The Legality of the 1993 US Missile Strike on Iraq and the Right of Self-Defence in International Law', 45 ICLQ, 1996, p. 162.

[137] 227 HC Deb., col. 658; 64 BYIL, 1993, p. 732.   [138] See above, p. 1131.

to resort to force in order to repel an attack. A clear example of this was provided in the Falklands conflict. Whatever doubts may be entertained about the precise roots of British title to the islands, it is very clear that after the Argentinian invasion of the territory, the UK possessed in law the right to act to restore the *status quo ante* and remove the Argentinian troops.[139] Security Council resolution 502 (1982), in calling for an immediate withdrawal of Argentinian forces and determining that a breach of the peace existed, reinforced this. It should also be noted that it is accepted that a state is entitled to rely upon the right of self-defence even while its possession of the territory in question is the subject of controversy.[140]

Collective self-defence[141]

Historically the right of states to take up arms to defend themselves from external force is well established as a rule of customary international law. Article 51, however, also refers to 'the inherent right of... collective self-defence' and the question therefore arises as to how far one state may resort to force in the defence of another. The idea of collective self-defence, however, is rather ambiguous. It may be regarded merely as a pooling of a number of individual rights of self-defence within the framework of a particular treaty or institution, as some writers have suggested,[142] or it may form the basis of comprehensive regional security systems. If the former were the case, it might lead to legal difficulties should Iceland resort to force in defence of Turkish interests, since actions against Turkey would in no way justify an armed reaction by Iceland pursuant to its individual right of self-defence.

In fact, state practice has adopted the second approach. Organisations such as NATO and the Warsaw Pact were established after the Second World War, specifically based upon the right of collective self-defence under article 51. By such agreements, an attack upon one party is treated as an attack upon all,[143] thus necessitating the conclusion that collective

---

[139] See above, chapter 10, p. 532.
[140] See e.g. Brownlie, *Use of Force*, pp. 382–3. See also above, p. 1128.
[141] See e.g. Dinstein, *War*, chapter 9, and Gray, *Use of Force*, chapter 5.
[142] See e.g. Bowett, *Self-Defence*, p. 245, cf. Goodrich, Hambro and Simons, *Charter*, p. 348. See also Brownlie, *Use of Force*, pp. 328–9.
[143] See e.g. article 5 of the NATO Treaty, 1949.

self-defence is something more than a collection of individual rights of self-defence, but another creature altogether.[144]

This approach finds support in the *Nicaragua* case.[145] The Court stressed that the right to collective self-defence was established in customary law but added that the exercise of that right depended upon both a prior declaration by the state concerned that it was the victim of an armed attack and a request by the victim state for assistance. In addition, the Court emphasised that 'for one state to use force against another, on the ground that that state has committed a wrongful act of force against a third state, is regarded as lawful, by way of exception, only when the wrongful act provoking the response was an armed attack'.[146]

The invasion of Kuwait by Iraq on 2 August 1990 raised the issue of collective self-defence in the context of the response of the states allied in the coalition to end that conquest and occupation. The Kuwaiti government in exile appealed for assistance from other states.[147] Although the armed action from 16 January 1991 was taken pursuant to UN Security Council resolutions,[148] it is indeed arguable that the right to collective self-defence is also relevant in this context.[149]

Intervention[150]

The principle of non-intervention is part of customary international law and founded upon the concept of respect for the territorial sovereignty

---

[144] Note article 52 of the UN Charter, which recognises the existence of regional arrangements and agencies, dealing with such matters relating to international peace and security as are appropriate for regional action, provided they are consistent with the purposes and principles of the UN: see further below, chapter 22, p. 1273.

[145] ICJ Reports, 1986, pp. 14, 103–5; 76 ILR, pp. 349, 437.

[146] ICJ Reports, 1986, p. 110. See also *ibid.*, p. 127; 76 ILR, pp. 444 and 461. This was reaffirmed in the *Oil Platforms (Iran* v. *USA)* case, ICJ Reports, 2003, pp. 161, 186; 130 ILR, pp. 323, 346.

[147] See *Keesing's Record of World Events*, pp. 37631 ff. (1990).

[148] See below, chapter 22, p. 1253.

[149] Note that Security Council resolution 661 (1990) specifically referred in its preamble to 'the inherent right of individual or collective self-defence, in response to the armed attack by Iraq against Kuwait'. See also the *Barcelona Traction* case, ICJ Reports, 1970, pp. 3, 32; 46 ILR, pp. 178, 206.

[150] See e.g. Gray, *Use of Force*, chapter 3; Nguyen Quoc Dinh *et al.*, *Droit International Public*, p. 947; T. Komarknicki, 'L'Intervention en Droit International Moderne', 62 RGDIP, 1956, p. 521; T. Farer, 'The Regulation of Foreign Armed Intervention in Civil Armed Conflict', 142 HR, 1974 II, p. 291, and J. E. S. Fawcett, 'Intervention in International Law', 103 HR, 1961 II, p. 347.

of states.[151] Intervention is prohibited where it bears upon matters in which each state is permitted to decide freely by virtue of the principle of state sovereignty. This includes, as the International Court of Justice noted in the *Nicaragua* case,[152] the choice of political, economic, social and cultural systems and the formulation of foreign policy. Intervention becomes wrongful when it uses methods of coercion in regard to such choices, which must be free ones.[153] There was 'no general right of intervention in support of an opposition within another state' in international law. In addition, acts constituting a breach of the customary principle of non-intervention will also, if they directly or indirectly involve the use of force, constitute a breach of the principle of the non-use of force in international relations.[154] The principle of respect for the sovereignty of states was another principle closely allied to the principles of the prohibition of the use of force and of non-intervention.[155]

Civil wars[156]

International law treats civil wars as purely internal matters, with the possible exception of self-determination conflicts.[157] Article 2(4) of the UN

---

[151] See the *Corfu Channel* case, ICJ Reports, 1949, pp. 4, 35; 16 AD, pp. 155, 167 and the *Nicaragua* case, ICJ Reports, 1986, pp. 14, 106; 76 ILR, pp. 349, 440. See also the Declaration on the Inadmissibility of Intervention in the Domestic Affairs of States, 1965 and the Declaration on the Principles of International Law, 1970, above, p. 1127.

[152] ICJ Reports, 1986, pp. 14, 108; 76 ILR, p. 442. See also S. McCaffrey, 'The Forty-First Session of the International Law Commission', 83 AJIL, 1989, p. 937.

[153] ICJ Reports, 1986, p. 108.   [154] ICJ Reports, 1986, pp. 109–10; 76 ILR, p. 443.

[155] ICJ Reports, 1986, p. 111; 76 ILR, p. 445.

[156] See e.g. Gray, *Use of Force*, pp. 60 ff.; *Law and Civil War in the Modern World* (ed. J. N. Moore), Princeton, 1974; *The International Regulation of Civil Wars* (ed. E. Luard), Oxford, 1972; *The International Law of Civil Wars* (ed. R. A. Falk), Princeton, 1971; T. Fraser, 'The Regulation of Foreign Intervention in Civil Armed Conflict', 142 HR, 1974, p. 291, and W. Friedmann, 'Intervention, Civil War and the Rule of International Law', PASIL, 1965, p. 67. See also R. Higgins, 'Intervention and International Law' in Bull, *Intervention in World Politics*, p. 29; C. C. Joyner and B. Grimaldi, 'The United States and Nicaragua: Reflections on the Lawfulness of Contemporary Intervention', 25 Va. JIL, 1985, p. 621, and Schachter, *International Law*, pp. 158 ff.

[157] Note that the Declaration on Principles of International Law concerning Friendly Relations, 1970 emphasised that all states were under a duty to refrain from any forcible action which deprives people of their right to self-determination and that 'in their actions against, and resistance to, such forcible action' such peoples could receive support in accordance with the purpose and principles of the UN Charter. Article 7 of the Consensus Definition of Aggression in 1974 referred ambiguously to the right of peoples entitled to but forcibly deprived of the right to self-determination, 'to struggle to that end and to seek and receive support, in accordance with the principles of the Charter and in conformity' with the 1970

Charter prohibits the threat or use of force in international relations, not in domestic situations. There is no rule against rebellion in international law. It is within the domestic jurisdiction of states and is left to be dealt with by internal law. Should the rebellion succeed, the resulting situation would be dealt with primarily in the context of recognition. As far as third parties are concerned, traditional international law developed the categories of rebellion, insurgency and belligerency.

Once a state has defined its attitude and characterised the situation, different international legal provisions would apply. If the rebels are regarded as criminals, the matter is purely within the hands of the authorities of the country concerned and no other state may legitimately interfere. If the rebels are treated as insurgents, then other states may or may not agree to grant them certain rights. It is at the discretion of the other states concerned, since an intermediate status is involved. The rebels are not mere criminals, but they are not recognised belligerents. Accordingly, the other states are at liberty to define their legal relationship with them. Insurgency is a purely provisional classification and would arise, for example, where a state needed to protect nationals or property in an area under the *de facto* control of the rebels.[158] On the other hand, belligerency is a formal status involving rights and duties. In the eyes of classical international law, other states may accord recognition of belligerency to rebels when certain conditions have been fulfilled. These were defined as the existence of an armed conflict of a general nature within a state, the occupation by the rebels of a substantial portion of the national territory, the conduct of hostilities in accordance with the rules of war and by organised groups operating under a responsible authority and the existence of circumstances rendering it necessary for the states contemplating recognition to define their attitude

Declaration. Article 1(4) of Additional Protocol I to the Geneva 'Red Cross' Conventions of 1949, adopted in 1977, provided that international armed conflict situations 'include armed conflicts in which peoples are fighting against colonial domination and alien occupation and against racist regimes in the exercise of their right to self-determination' as enshrined in the Charter of the UN and the 1970 Declaration. Whether this means that articles 2(4) and 51 of the Charter now apply to self-determination conflicts so that the peoples in question have a valid right to use force in self-defence is controversial and difficult to maintain. However, the use of force to suppress self-determination is now clearly unacceptable, as is help by third parties given to that end, but the provision of armed assistance to peoples seeking self-determination would appear to remain unlawful: see Gray, *Use of Force*, pp. 52 ff.; A. Cassese, *Self-Determination of Peoples*, Cambridge, 1995, p. 193; and H. Wilson, *International Law and the Use of Force by National Liberation Movements*, Oxford, 1988. See as to the principle of self-determination, above, chapter 5, p. 251.

[158] See e.g. H. Lauterpacht, *Recognition in International Law*, Cambridge, 1947, pp. 275 ff.

to the situation.[159] This would arise, for example, where the parties to the conflict are exercising belligerent rights on the high seas. Other maritime countries would feel compelled to decide upon the respective status of the warring sides, since the recognition of belligerency entails certain international legal consequences. Once the rebels have been accepted by other states as belligerents they become subjects of international law and responsible in international law for all their acts. In addition, the rules governing the conduct of hostilities become applicable to both sides, so that, for example, the recognising states must then adopt a position of neutrality.

However, these concepts of insurgency and belligerency are lacking in clarity and are extremely subjective. The absence of clear criteria, particularly with regard to the concept of insurgency, has led to a great deal of confusion. The issue is of importance since the majority of conflicts in the years since the conclusion of the Second World War have been in essence civil wars. The reasons for this are many and complex and ideological rivalry and decolonisation within colonially imposed boundaries are amongst them.[160] Intervention may be justified on a number of grounds, including response to earlier involvement by a third party. For instance, the USSR and Cuba justified their activities in the Angolan civil war of 1975–6 by reference to the prior South African intervention,[161] while the United States argued that its aid to South Vietnam grew in proportion to the involvement of North Vietnamese forces in the conflict.[162]

The international law rules dealing with civil wars depend upon the categorisation by third states of the relative status of the two sides to the conflict. In traditional terms, an insurgency means that the recognising state may, if it wishes, create legal rights and duties as between itself and the insurgents, while recognition of belligerency involves an acceptance of a position of neutrality (although there are some exceptions to this rule) by the recognising states. But in practice, states very rarely make an express acknowledgement as to the status of the parties to the conflict, precisely in order to retain as wide a room for manoeuvre as possible. This means that the relevant legal rules cannot really operate as intended

---

[159] See e.g. N. Mugerwa, 'Subjects of International Law' in Sørensen, *Manual of Public International Law*, pp. 247, 286–8. See also R. Higgins, 'International Law and Civil Conflict' in Luard, *International Regulation of Civil Wars*, pp. 169, 170–1.

[160] See e.g. M. N. Shaw, *Title to Territory in Africa: International Legal Issues*, Oxford, 1986.

[161] See e.g. C. Legum and T. Hodges, *After Angola*, London, 1976.

[162] See e.g. *Law and the Indo-China War* (ed. J. N. Moore), Charlottesville, 1972. See also *The Vietnam War and International Law* (ed. R. A. Falk), Princeton, 4 vols., 1968–76.

in classical law and that it becomes extremely difficult to decide whether a particular intervention is justified or not.[163]

Aid to the authorities of a state[164]

It would appear that in general outside aid to the government authorities to repress a revolt[165] is perfectly legitimate,[166] provided, of course, it was requested by the government. The problem of defining the governmental authority entitled to request assistance was raised in the Grenada episode. In that situation, the appeal for the US intervention was allegedly made by the Governor-General of the island,[167] but controversy exists as to whether this in fact did take place prior to the invasion and whether the Governor-General was the requisite authority to issue such an appeal.[168] The issue resurfaced in a rather different form regarding the Panama invasion of December 1989. One of the legal principles identified by the US Department of State as the basis for the US action was that of assistance to the 'lawful and democratically elected government in Panama'.[169] The problem with this was that this particular government had been prevented by General Noriega from actually taking office and the issue raised was therefore whether an elected head of state who is prevented from ever acting as such may be regarded as a governmental authority capable of requesting assistance including armed force from another state. This in fact runs counter to the test of acceptance in international law of governmental authority, which is firmly based upon effective control rather than upon the nature of the regime, whether democratic, socialist or otherwise.[170]

---

[163] But see below, chapter 22, p. 1257, with regard to the increasing involvement of the UN in internal conflicts and the increasing tendency to classify such conflicts as possessing an international dimension.

[164] See e.g. L. Doswald-Beck, 'The Legal Validity of Military Intervention by Invitation of the Government', 56 BYIL, 1985, p. 189, and Gray, *Use of Force*, pp. 68 ff.

[165] See *Nicaragua* v. *USA*, ICJ Reports, 1986, pp. 14, 126, where the Court noted that intervention is 'already allowable at the request of the government of a state'; however, apparently not where the recipient state is forcibly suppressing the right to self-determination of a people entitled to such rights: see above, p. 1148, note 157.

[166] Until a recognition of belligerency, of course, although this has been unknown in modern times: see e.g. Lauterpacht, *Recognition*, pp. 230–3.

[167] See the statement by Deputy Secretary of State Dam, 78 AJIL, 1984, p. 200.

[168] See e.g. J. N. Moore, *Law and the Grenada Mission*, Charlottesville, 1984, and Gilmore, *Grenada*. See also Higgins, *Development of International Law*, pp. 162–4 regarding the Congo crisis of 1960, where that state's President and Prime Minister sought to dismiss each other.

[169] 84 AJIL, 1990, p. 547.   [170] See above, chapter 9, p. 454.

The general proposition, however, that aid to recognised governmental authorities is legitimate,[171] would be further reinforced where it could be shown that other states were encouraging or directing the subversive operations of the rebels. In such cases, it appears that the doctrine of collective self-defence would allow other states to intervene openly and lawfully on the side of the government authorities.[172] Some writers have suggested that the traditional rule of permitting third-party assistance to governments would not extend to aid where the outcome of the struggle has become uncertain or where the rebellion has become widespread and seriously aimed at overthrowing the government.[173] While this may be politically desirable for the third state, it may put at serious risk entirely deserving governments.[174] Practice, however, does suggest that many forms of aid, such as economic, technical and arms provision arrangements, to existing governments faced with civil strife, are acceptable.[175] There is an argument, on the other hand, for suggesting that substantial assistance to a government clearly in the throes of collapse might be questionable as intervention in a domestic situation that is on the point of resolution, but there are considerable definitional problems here.

Aid to rebels[176]

The reverse side of the proposition is that aid to rebels is contrary to international law. The 1970 Declaration on Principles of International Law emphasised that:

[171] Note that article 20 of the International Law Commission's Articles on State Responsibility, 2001, provides that 'Valid consent by a State to the commission of a given act by another State precludes the wrongfulness of that act in relation to the former State to the extent that the act remains within the limits of that consent.'

[172] But in the light of the principles propounded in the *Nicaragua* case, ICJ Reports, 1986, pp. 104, 120–3; 76 ILR, pp. 349, 438, 454–7.

[173] See e.g. Q. Wright, 'US Intervention in the Lebanon', 53 AJIL, 1959, pp. 112, 122. See also R. A. Falk, *Legal Order in a Violent World*, Princeton, 1968, pp. 227–8 and 273, and Doswald-Beck, 'Legal Validity', p. 251.

[174] However, where consent to the presence of foreign troops has been withdrawn by the government of the state concerned, the continuing presence of those troops may constitute (in the absence of any legitimate exercise of the right of self-defence) an unlawful use of force: see e.g. *Democratic Republic of the Congo* v. *Uganda*, ICJ Reports, 2005, pp. 168, 213 and 224. See also article 3(e) of the Consensus Definition of Aggression, 1974.

[175] See, with regard to the UK continuance of arms sales to Nigeria during its civil war, Higgins, 'International Law and Civil Conflict', p. 173. Note also the US policy of distinguishing between traditional suppliers of arms and non-traditional suppliers of arms in such circumstances. It would support aid provided by the former (as the UK in Nigeria), but not the latter: see DUSPIL, 1976, p. 7.

[176] See e.g. Gray, *Use of Force*, pp. 87 ff.

[n]o state shall organise, assist, foment, finance, incite or tolerate subversive, terrorist or armed activities directed towards the violent overthrow of the regime of another state, or interfere in civil strife in another state.[177]

The Declaration also provided that:

[e]very state shall refrain from any action aimed at the partial or total disruption of the national unity and territorial integrity of any other state or country.

In the *Nicaragua* case,[178] the Court declared that the principle of non-intervention prohibits a state 'to intervene, directly or indirectly, with or without armed force, in support of an internal opposition in another state' and went on to say that acts which breach the principle of non-intervention 'will also, if they directly or indirectly involve the use of force, constitute a breach of the principle of the non-use of force in international relations'. Further, the Court emphasised in *Democratic Republic of the Congo v. Uganda*[179] that where such an unlawful military intervention reaches a certain magnitude and duration, it would amount to 'a grave violation of the prohibition on the use of force expressed in article 2, paragraph 4, of the Charter'.

In reality, state practice is far from clear.[180] Where a prior, illegal intervention on the government side has occurred, it may be argued that aid to the rebels is acceptable. This was argued by a number of states with regard to the Afghanistan situation, where it was argued that the Soviet intervention in that state amounted to an invasion.[181]

---

[177] See also in similar terms the Declaration on the Inadmissibility of Intervention in the Domestic Affairs of States, 1965, above, p. 1126. Article 3(g) of the General Assembly's Consensus Definition of Aggression, 1974, characterises as an act of aggression 'the sending by or on behalf of a state of armed bands, groups, irregulars or mercenaries, which carry out acts of armed force against another state'. See also, with regard to US aid to the Nicaraguan 'Contras', Chayes, *Cuban Missile Crisis*, and the *Nicaragua* case, ICJ Reports, 1986, p. 14; 76 ILR, p. 349.

[178] ICJ Reports, 1986, pp. 14, 108 and 109–10. These propositions were reaffirmed by the Court in *Democratic Republic of the Congo v. Uganda*, ICJ Reports, 2005, pp. 168, 227.

[179] ICJ Reports, 2005, p. 168.

[180] See e.g. Syrian intervention in the Jordanian civil war of 1970 and in the Lebanon in 1976 and see Gray, *Use of Force*, pp. 85 ff.

[181] See e.g. *Keesing's Contemporary Archives*, pp. 30339, 30364 and 30385. See also General Assembly resolutions ES–62; 35/37; 36/34; 37/37 and 38/29 condemning the USSR for its armed intervention in Afghanistan. See also Doswald-Beck, 'Legal Validity', pp. 230 ff.

The situation in the Democratic Republic of the Congo

The situation in the Democratic Republic of the Congo in 1999 and after, with intervention against the government by Uganda and Rwanda (seeking initially to act against rebel movements operating against them from Congolese territory and then assisting rebels against the Congo government) and on behalf of the government by a number of states, including Zimbabwe, Angola and Namibia, is instructive.[182] In resolution 1234 (1999), the Security Council recalled the inherent right of individual and collective self-defence in accordance with article 51 and reaffirmed the need for all states to refrain from interfering in the internal affairs of other states. It called upon states to bring to an end the presence of uninvited forces of foreign states.[183] The Council in resolution 1291 (1999) called for the orderly withdrawal of all foreign forces from the Congo in accordance with the Lusaka Ceasefire Agreement.[184] Security Council resolution 1304 (2000) went further and, acting under Chapter VII, demanded that 'Uganda and Rwanda, which have violated the sovereignty and territorial integrity of the Democratic Republic of the Congo, withdraw all their forces from the territory of the Democratic Republic of the Congo without delay'. An end to all other foreign military presence and activity was also called for in conformity with the provisions of the Lusaka Agreement.[185] The UN also established a mission in the Congo (MONUC) in 1999, whose mandate was subsequently extended.[186] The situation demonstrates the UN approach, reflecting international law, to the effect that while aid by foreign states to the government was acceptable,[187] aid to rebels by foreign states was not. Side by side with this, the UN did recognise the problem posed by foreign militias based in the eastern region of the Democratic Republic of the Congo (particularly the Rwanda

---

[182] See Gray, *Use of Force*, pp. 60–4, 70–1, 247–50 and 258–9. See also P. N. Okowa, 'Congo's War: The Legal Dimension of a Protracted Conflict', 77 BYIL, 2006, p. 203.

[183] Gray, *Use of Force*, pp. 61–2, noting that the Security Council took a clear position that aid to the government was permissible, while intervention or force to overthrow the government was not. The Democratic Republic of the Congo had written to the Security Council accusing Rwanda and Uganda of aggression and justifying its invitation to Angola, Namibia and Zimbabwe as a response to foreign intervention: see *UN Yearbook*, 1998, pp. 82–8 and S/1998/827.

[184] See S/1999/815.

[185] See also Security Council resolutions 1341 (2001) and 1355 (2001). Security Council resolution 1376 (2001) welcomed the withdrawal of some forces, including the full Namibian contingent, from the Congo. See also resolutions 1417 (2002), 1457 (2003) and 1468 (2003). Essentially condemnation was reserved by name for Rwanda and Uganda.

[186] See further below, chapter 22, p. 1264.   [187] See Okowa, 'Congo', p. 224.

Interahamwe who had been involved in the 1994 genocide and the Ugandan Lord's Resistance Army) and called for them to be disarmed.[188]

Humanitarian intervention[189]

This section concerns the question as to whether there can be said to be a right of humanitarian intervention by individual states. The issue of intervention by the UN in situations of humanitarian need and as a consequence of Security Council action is covered in the next chapter.

It has sometimes been argued that intervention in order to protect the lives of persons situated within a particular state and not necessarily nationals of the intervening state is permissible in strictly defined situations. This has some support in pre-Charter law and it may very well have been the case that in the nineteenth century such intervention was accepted under international law.[190] However, it is difficult to reconcile today with article 2(4) of the Charter[191] unless one either adopts a rather artificial

---

[188] See e.g. Security Council resolutions 1756 (2007) and 1794 (2007).

[189] See e.g. Gray, *Use of Force*, pp. 31 ff.; Dinstein, *War*, pp. 70 ff.; Franck, *Recourse*, chapter 9; Byers, *War Law*, Part Three; N. J. Wheeler, *Saving Strangers: Humanitarian Intervention in International Society*, Oxford, 2002; R. Goodman, 'Humanitarian Intervention and Pretexts for War', 100 AJIL, 2006, p. 107; D. Kennedy, *The Dark Sides of Virtue*, Princeton, 2004; *Humanitarian Intervention* (eds. J. L. Holzgrefe and R. O. Keohane), Cambridge, 2003; S. Chesterman, *Just War or Just Peace: Humanitarian Intervention and International Law*, Oxford, 2001; *Humanitarian Intervention and the United Nations* (ed. R. B. Lillich), Charlottesville, 1973; R. B. Lillich, 'Forcible Self-Help by States to Protect Human Rights', 53 *Iowa Law Review*, 1967, p. 325, and Lillich, 'Intervention to Protect Human Rights', 15 *McGill Law Journal*, 1969, p. 205, and Lillich, 'Humanitarian Intervention Through the United Nations: Towards the Development of Criteria', 53 ZaöRV, 1993, p. 557; T. M. Franck and N. S. Rodley, 'After Bangladesh: The Law of Humanitarian Intervention by Military Force', 67 AJIL, 1973, p. 275; J. P. Fonteyne, 'The Customary International Law Doctrine of Humanitarian Intervention', 4 *California Western International Law Journal*, 1974, p. 203; Chilstrom, 'Humanitarian Intervention under Contemporary International Law', 1 *Yale Studies in World Public Order*, 1974, p. 93; N. D. Arnison, 'The Law of Humanitarian Intervention' in *Refugees in the 1990s: New Strategies for a Restless World* (ed. H. Cleveland), 1993, p. 37; D. J. Scheffer, 'Towards a Modern Doctrine of Humanitarian Intervention', 23 *University of Toledo Law Review*, 1992, p. 253; D. Kritsiotis, 'Reappraising Policy Objections to Humanitarian Intervention', 19 *Michigan Journal of International Law*, 1998, p. 1005; N. Tsagourias, *The Theory and Praxis of Humanitarian Intervention*, Manchester, 1999, and F. Tesón, *Humanitarian Intervention: An Inquiry into Law and Morality*, 2nd edn, New York, 1997.

[190] See e.g. H. Ganji, *International Protection of Human Rights*, New York, 1962, chapter 1 and references cited in previous footnote.

[191] See, in particular, I. Brownlie, 'Humanitarian Intervention', in Moore, *Law and Civil War*, p. 217.

definition of the 'territorial integrity' criterion in order to permit temporary violations or posits the establishment of the right in customary law.
Practice has also been in general unfavourable to the concept, primarily
because it might be used to justify interventions by more forceful states
into the territories of weaker states.[192] Nevertheless, it is not inconceivable
that in some situations the international community might refrain from
adopting a condemnatory stand where large numbers of lives have been
saved in circumstances of gross oppression by a state of its citizens due to
an outside intervention. In addition, it is possible that such a right might
evolve in cases of extreme humanitarian need. One argument used to justify the use of Western troops to secure a safe haven in northern Iraq after
the Gulf War was that it was taken in pursuance of the customary international law principle of humanitarian intervention in an extreme situation. Security Council resolution 688 (1991) condemned the widespread
repression by Iraq of its Kurd and Shia populations and, citing this, the
US, UK and France proclaimed 'no-fly zones' in the north and south of
the country.[193] There was no express authorisation from the UN. It was
argued by the UK that the no-fly zones were 'justified under international
law in response to a situation of overwhelming humanitarian necessity'.[194]

The Kosovo crisis of 1999 raised squarely the issue of humanitarian intervention.[195] The justification for the NATO bombing campaign, acting
out of area and without UN authorisation, in support of the repressed
ethnic Albanian population of that province of Yugoslavia, was that of
humanitarian necessity. The UK Secretary of State for Defence stated that,

---

[192] See e.g. M. B. Akehurst, 'Humanitarian Intervention' in Bull, *Intervention in World Politics*,
p. 95.

[193] See the views expressed by a Foreign Office legal advisor to the House of Commons
Foreign Affairs Committee, UKMIL, 63 BYIL, 1992, pp. 827–8. This is to be compared
with the views of the Foreign Office several years earlier where it was stated that the best
case that could be made was that it was not 'unambiguously illegal': see UKMIL, 57 BYIL,
1986, p. 619. See also Gray, *Use of Force*, pp. 33 ff., and below, chapter 22, p. 1254.

[194] UKMIL, 70 BYIL, 1999, p. 590. See also UKMIL, 75 BYIL, 2004, p. 857.

[195] See e.g. Gray, *Use of Force*, pp. 37 ff.; N. S. Rodley and B. Çali, 'Kosovo Revisited: Hu-
manitarian Intervention on the Fault Lines of International Law', 7 *Human Rights Law
Review*, 2007, p. 275; B. Simma, 'NATO, the UN and the Use of Force: Legal Aspects', 10
EJIL, 1999, p. 1; Kofi A. Annan, *The Question of Intervention: Statements by the Secretary-
General*, New York, 1999; 'NATO's Kosovo Intervention', various writers, 93 AJIL, 1999,
pp. 824–62; D. Kritsiotis, 'The Kosovo Crisis and NATO's Application of Armed Force
Against the Federal Republic of Yugoslavia', 49 ICLQ, 2000, p. 330; P. Hilpod, 'Humani-
tarian Intervention: Is There a Need for a Legal Reappraisal?', 12 EJIL, 2001, p. 437, and
'Kosovo: House of Commons Foreign Affairs Committee 4th Report, June 2000', various
memoranda, 49 ICLQ, 2000, pp. 876–943.

'In international law, in exceptional circumstances and to avoid a human-itarian catastrophe, military action can be taken and it is on that legal basis that military action was taken.'[196] The Security Council by twelve votes to three rejected a resolution condemning NATO's use of force.[197] After the conflict, and after an agreement had been reached between NATO and Yugoslavia,[198] the Council adopted resolution 1244 (1999) which wel-comed the withdrawal of Yugoslav forces from the territory and decided upon the deployment under UN auspices of international civil and mil-itary presences. Member states and international organisations were, in particular, authorised to establish the international security presence and the resolution laid down the main responsibilities of the civil presence. There was no formal endorsement of the NATO action, but no condem-nation.[199] It can be concluded that the doctrine of humanitarian interven-tion in a crisis situation was invoked and not condemned by the UN, but it received meagre support.[200] It is not possible to characterise the legal situation as going beyond this.[201]

---

[196] UKMIL, 70 BYIL, 1999, p. 586. A Foreign Office Minister wrote that, 'a limited use of force was justifiable in support of the purposes laid down by the Security Council but without the Council's express authorisation when that was the only means to avert an immediate and overwhelming humanitarian catastrophe', ibid., p. 587 and see also ibid., p. 598. The UK Prime Minister wrote to Parliament in 2004 stating that force may be used by states 'In exceptional circumstances, when it is the only way to avert an overwhelming humanitarian catastrophe, as in Kosovo in 1999', HC Deb., 22 March 2004, vol. 419, col. 561W–562W, UKMIL, 75 BYIL, 2004, p. 853.

[197] SCOR, 3989th meeting, 26 March 1999.   [198] See 38 ILM, 1999, p. 1217.

[199] Note that Yugoslavia made an application in April 1999 to the International Court against ten of the nineteen NATO states, alleging that these states, by participating in the use of force, had violated international law. The Court rejected the application made for provisional measures in all ten cases: see e.g. Yugoslavia v. Belgium, ICJ Reports, 1999, p. 124, and upheld preliminary objections as to jurisdiction and admissibility: see e.g. Serbia and Montenegro v. UK, ICJ Reports, 2004, p. 1307.

[200] See also the Nicaragua case, ICJ Reports, 1986, pp. 14, 134–5; 76 ILR, p. 349, where the Court stated that the use of force could not be the appropriate method to monitor or ensure respect for human rights in Nicaragua.

[201] Note that the UK produced a set of Policy Guidelines on Humanitarian Crises in 2001. This provided inter alia that the Security Council should authorise action to halt or avert massive violations of humanitarian law and that, in response to such crises, force may be used in the face of overwhelming and immediate humanitarian catastrophe when the government cannot or will not avert it, when all non-violent methods have been exhausted, the scale of real or potential suffering justifies the risks of military action, if there is a clear objective to avert or end the catastrophe, there is clear evidence that such action would be welcomed by the people at risk and that the consequences for suffering of non-action would be worse than those of intervention. Further, the use of force should be collective, limited in scope and proportionate to achieving the humanitarian objective and consistent with international humanitarian law, UKMIL, 72 BYIL, 2001, p. 696.

One variant of the principle of humanitarian intervention is the contention that intervention in order to restore democracy is permitted as such under international law.[202] One of the grounds given for the US intervention in Panama in December 1989 was the restoration of democracy,[203] but apart from the problems of defining democracy, such a proposition is not acceptable in international law in view of the clear provisions of the UN Charter. Nor is there anything to suggest that even if the principle of self-determination could be interpreted as applying beyond the strict colonial context[204] to cover 'democracy', it could constitute a norm superior to that of non-intervention.

More recently, there has been extensive consideration of the 'responsibility to protect' as a composite concept comprising the responsibilities to prevent catastrophic situations, to react immediately when they do occur and to rebuild afterwards.[205] Such an approach may be seen as an effort to redefine the principle of humanitarian intervention in a way that seeks to minimise the motives of the intervening powers and there is no doubt that it reflects an important trend in international society and one that is influential, particularly in the context of UN action. Such responsibilities are deemed to fall both upon states and the international community and notably include the commitment to reconstruction after intervention or initial involvement. As they have been broadly and flexibily proposed, emphasising, for example, the obligation of states to protect human rights on their territory and the primary focus upon the UN with regard to any military action, the sharp edges of the humanitarian intervention doctrine have been blunted, but it remains to be seen how influential this approach may be.[206]

---

[202] See e.g. J. Crawford, 'Democracy and International Law', 44 BYIL, 1993, p. 113; B. R. Roth, *Governmental Illegitimacy in International Law*, Oxford, 1999; Franck, *Fairness*, chapter 4, and Franck, *The Empowered Self*, Oxford, 1999; Gray, *Use of Force*, pp. 49 ff., and O. Schachter, 'The Legality of Pro-Democratic Invasion', 78 AJIL, 1984, p. 645.

[203] See e.g. *Keesing's Record of World Events*, p. 37112 (1989). See also Nanda, 'Validity', p. 498.

[204] See above, chapter 6, p. 289.

[205] See e.g. International Commission on Intervention and State Sovereignty, *The Responsibility to Protect*, Ottawa, 2001; Report of the UN High Level Panel on Threats, Challenges and Change, A/59/565, 2004, at paras. 201–3; UN Secretary-General, *In Larger Freedom*, A/59/2005, paras. 16–22; World Summit Outcome, General Assembly resolution 60/1, 2005, paras. 138–9, and C. Stahn, 'Responsibility to Protect: Political Rhetoric or Emerging Legal Norm?', 101 AJIL, 2007, p. 99.

[206] It should also be emphasised that the documents cited in the previous footnote are ambiguous as to the right of individual states to intervene by force in the territory of other states.

Terrorism and international law[207]

The use of terror as a means to achieve political ends is not a new phenomenon, but it has recently acquired a new intensity. In many cases, terrorists deliberately choose targets in uninvolved third states as a means of pressurising the government of the state against which it is in conflict or its real or potential or assumed allies.[208] As far as international law is concerned, there are a number of problems that can be identified. The first major concern is that of definition.[209] For example, how widely should the offence be defined, for instance should attacks against property as well as attacks upon persons be covered? And to what extent should one take into account the motives and intentions of the perpetrators? Secondly, the relationship between terrorism and the use of force by states in response is posed.[210] Thirdly, the relationship between terrorism and human rights needs to be taken into account.

Despite political difficulties, increasing progress at an international and regional level has been made to establish rules of international law with regard to terrorism. A twin-track approach has been adopted, dealing both with particular manifestations of terrorist activity and with a general condemnation of the phenomenon.[211] In so far as the first is concerned, the UN has currently adopted thirteen international conventions concerning

---

[207] See e.g. Gray, *Use of Force*, pp. 135 ff.; T. Becker, *Terrorism and the State*, Oxford, 2006; *Legal Aspects of International Terrorism* (eds. A. E. Evans and J. Murphy), Lexington, 1978; R. Friedlander, *Terrorism*, Dobbs Ferry, 1979; R. B. Lillich and T. Paxman, 'State Responsibility for Injuries to Aliens Caused by Terrorist Activity', 26 *American Law Review*, 1977, p. 217; *International Terrorism and Political Crimes* (ed. M. C. Bassiouni), 1975; E. McWhinney, *Aerial Piracy and International Terrorism*, 2nd edn, Dordrecht, 1987; A. Cassese, *Terrorism, Politics and Law*, Cambridge, 1989; V. Lowe, '"Clear and Present Danger": Responses to Terrorism', 54 ICLQ, 2005, p. 185; G. Guillaume, 'Terrorism and International Law', 53 ICLQ, 2004, p. 537; J. Pejic, 'Terrorist Acts and Groups: A Role for International Law', 75 BYIL, 2004, p. 71; J. Delbrück, 'The Fight Against Global Terrorism', German YIL, 2001, p. 9, and A. Cassese, 'Terrorism is Also Disrupting Some Crucial Legal Categories of International Law', 95 AJIL, 2001, p. 993. See also the UN website on terrorism, www.un.org/terrorism/.

[208] The hijack of TWA Flight 847 on 14 June 1985 by Lebanese Shi'ites is one example of this phenomenon: see e.g. *The Economist*, 22 June 1985, p. 34.

[209] See e.g. B. Saul, *Defining Terrorism in International Law*, Oxford, 2006 and articles on the Quest for a Legal Definition, 4 *Journal of International Criminal Justice*, 2006, pp. 894 ff.

[210] See above, p. 1134.

[211] See, with regard to the failed attempt by the League of Nations in the 1937 Convention for the Prevention and Punishment of Terrorism to establish a comprehensive code, e.g. Murphy, *United Nations*, p. 179. See also T. M. Franck and B. Lockwood, 'Preliminary Thoughts Towards an International Convention on Terrorism', 68 AJIL, 1974, p. 69.

terrorism, dealing with issues such as hijacking, hostages and terrorist bombings.[212] Many of these conventions operate on a common model, establishing the basis of quasi-universal jurisdiction with an interlocking network of international obligations. The model comprises a definition of the offence in question and the automatic incorporation of such offences within all extradition agreements between states parties coupled with obligations on states parties to make this offence an offence in domestic law, to establish jurisdiction over this offence (usually where committed in the territory of the state or on board a ship or aircraft registered there, or by a national of that state or on a discretionary basis in some conventions where nationals of that state have been victims) and, where the alleged offender is present in the territory, either to prosecute or to extradite to another state that will.[213]

In addition, the UN has sought to tackle the question of terrorism in a comprehensive fashion. In December 1972, the General Assembly set up an ad hoc committee on terrorism[214] and in 1994 a Declaration on Measures to Eliminate International Terrorism was adopted.[215] This condemned 'all acts, methods and practices of terrorism, as criminal and unjustifiable, wherever and by whomever committed', noting that 'criminal acts intended or calculated to provoke a state of terror in the general public, a group or person or persons or particular persons for political purposes are in any circumstance unjustifiable, whatever the considerations of a political, philosophical, ideological, racial, ethnic, religious or any other nature that may be invoked to justify them'. States are also obliged to refrain from organising, instigating, facilitating, financing or tolerating terrorist activities and to take practical measures to ensure that their territories are not used for terrorist installations, training camps or for the

---

[212] See the Conventions on Offences Committed on Board Aircraft, 1963; for the Suppression of Unlawful Seizure of Aircraft, 1970; for the Suppression of Unlawful Acts against the Safety of Civil Aviation, 1971; on the Prevention and Punishment of Crimes against Internationally Protected Persons including Diplomatic Agents, 1973; against the Taking of Hostages, 1979; on the Physical Protection of Nuclear Material, 1980; for the Suppression of Unlawful Acts of Violence at Airports, Protocol 1988; for the Suppression of Unlawful Acts against the Safety of Maritime Navigation, 1988; for the Suppression of Unlawful Acts against the Safety of Fixed Platforms on the Continental Shelf, Protocol 1988; on the Marking of Plastic Explosives for the Purpose of Identification, 1991; for the Suppression of Terrorist Bombing, 1997; for the Suppression of the Financing of Terrorism, 1999 and for the Suppression of Acts of Nuclear Terrorism, 2005.

[213] See further above, chapter 12, p. 673.

[214] See General Assembly resolution 3034 (XXVII).

[215] General Assembly resolution 49/60.

preparation of terrorist acts against other states. States are further obliged to apprehend and prosecute or extradite perpetrators of terrorist acts and to co-operate with other states in exchanging information and combating terrorism.[216] The Assembly has also adopted a number of resolutions calling for ratification of the various conventions and for improvement in co-operation between states in this area.[217] In September 2006, the General Assembly adopted 'The United Nations Global Counter-Terrorism Strategy',[218] comprising a Plan of Action, including condemnation of terrorism in all its forms and manifestations as it constitutes 'one of the most serious threats to international peace and security'; international co-operation; addressing the conditions conducive to the spread of terrorism; adoption of a variety of measures to prevent and combat terrorism; adoption of measures to build states' capacity to prevent and combat terrorism; and, finally, measures to ensure respect for human rights for all and the rule of law as the fundamental basis of the fight against terrorism.

An Ad Hoc Committee was established in 1996[219] to elaborate international conventions on terrorism. The Conventions for the Suppression of Terrorist Bombing, 1997 and of the Financing of Terrorism, 1999 resulted, as did a Convention for the Suppression of Acts of Nuclear Terrorism, 2005. The Committee is currently working on drafting a comprehensive convention on international terrorism.[220]

The Security Council has also been active in dealing with the terrorism threat.[221] In particular, it has characterised international terrorism as a

---

[216] A supplementary declaration was adopted in 1996, which emphasised in addition that acts of terrorism and assisting them are contrary to the purposes and principles of the UN. The question of asylum-seekers who had committed terrorist acts was also addressed, General Assembly resolution 51/210. See also resolution 55/158, 2001 and the 2005 World Summit Outcome, resolution 60/1.

[217] See e.g. resolutions 34/145, 35/168 and 36/33.   [218] Resolution 60/288.

[219] General Assembly resolution 51/210.

[220] See e.g. A/59/37, 2004; A/60/37, 2005; A/61/37, 2006; A/62/37, 2007, and A/63/37, 2008 and General Assembly resolutions 57/27, 2003 and 62/71, 2008. See also M. Hmoud, 'Negotiating the Draft Comprehensive Convention on International Terrorism', 4 *Journal of International Criminal Justice*, 2006, p. 1031. Major areas of contention have focused on the definition of terrorism, the scope of the proposed convention and the relationship between the proposed convention and the conventions dealing with specific terrorist crimes, *ibid.*

[221] For example, in resolution 579 (1985), it condemned unequivocally all acts of hostage-taking and abduction, and see also the statement made by the President of the Security Council on behalf of members condemning the hijacking of the *Achille Lauro* and generally 'terrorism in all its forms, whenever and by whomever committed', 9 October 1985, S/17554, 24 ILM, 1985, p. 1656.

threat to international peace and security. This approach has evolved. In resolution 731 (1992), the Security Council, in the context of criticism of Libya for not complying with requests for the extradition of suspected bombers of an airplane, referred to 'acts of international terrorism that constitute threats to international peace and security', and in resolution 1070 (1996) adopted with regard to Sudan it reaffirmed that 'the suppression of acts of international terrorism, including those in which states are involved, is essential for the maintenance of international peace and security'.[222]

It was, however, the 11 September 2001 attack upon the World Trade Center that moved this process onto a higher level. In resolution 1368 (2001) adopted the following day, the Council, noting that it was '*Determined* to combat by all means threats to international peace and security caused by terrorist attack', unequivocally condemned the attack and declared that it regarded such attacks 'like any act of international terrorism, as a threat to international peace and security'.[223] Resolution 1373 (2001) reaffirmed this proposition and the need to combat by all means in accordance with the Charter, threats to international peace and security caused by terrorist acts.[224] Acting under Chapter VII, the Council made a series of binding decisions demanding *inter alia* the prevention and suppression of the financing of terrorist acts, the criminalisation of wilful provision or collection of funds for such purposes and the freezing of financial assets and economic resources of persons and entities involved in terrorism. Further, states were called upon to refrain from any support to those involved in terrorism and take action against such persons, and to co-operate with other states in preventing and suppressing terrorist acts and acting against the perpetrators. The Council also declared that acts, methods and practices of terrorism were contrary to the purposes and principles of the UN and that knowingly financing, planning and inciting terrorist acts were also contrary to the purposes and principles of the UN. Crucially, the Council established a Counter-Terrorism Committee

---

[222] See also resolution 1189 (1998), concerning the bombings of the US Embassies in East Africa, and resolution 1269 (1999), which reaffirms many of the points made in the 1994 General Assembly Declaration.

[223] See further above, p. 1134, with regard to recognition of the right to self-defence in this context.

[224] Note also the condemnation of the terrorist bombing in Bali in October 2002: see resolution 1438 (2002); of the taking of hostages in Moscow in October 2002 referred to as a terrorist act: see resolution 1440 (2002); and of the terrorist attacks in Kenya in November 2002: see resolution 1450 (2002).

to monitor implementation of the resolution. States were called upon to report to the Committee on measures they had taken to implement the resolution. The Committee was also mandated to maintain a dialogue with states on the implemention of resolution 1624 (2005) on prohibiting incitement to commit terrorist acts and promoting dialogue and understanding among civilisations.

In resolution 1377 (2001), the Council, in addition to reaffirming earlier propositions, declared that acts of international terrorism 'constitute one of the most serious threats to international peace and security in the twenty-first century' and requested the Counter-Terrorism Committee to assist in the promotion of best-practice in the areas covered by resolution 1373, including the preparation of model laws as appropriate, and to examine the availability of various technical, financial, legislative and other programmes to facilitate the implementation of resolution 1373.[225] The Counter-Terrorism Committee was strengthened in 2004 by the establishment of the Executive Directorate, comprising a number of experts and administrative and support staff.[226] A further committee was established by resolution 1540 (2004) to examine the implementation of the resolution, which requires all states to establish domestic controls to prevent access by non-state actors to nuclear, chemical and biological weapons, and their means of delivery, and to take effective measures to prevent proliferation of such items and establish appropriate controls over related materials.[227]

The Counter-Terrorism Committee has now received a large number of reports, and has reviewed and responded to many of them. The Committee has since 2005 been conducting visits to member states.[228]

---

[225] See also resolution 1456 (2003), which *inter alia* called upon the Counter-Terrorism Committee to intensify its work through reviewing states' reports and facilitating international assistance and co-operation. Note the establishment of a Security Council committee (the 1267 committee) to oversee sanctions imposed upon Al-Qaida and the Taliban and associated individuals and entities, resolution 1267 (1999). In resolution 1566 (2004), the Security Council established a working group to recommend practical measures against individuals and groups engaged in terrorist activities not subject to the 1267 committee's review. See also resolution 1822 (2008).

[226] See resolution 1535 (2004). The mandate of the Executive Directorate has been extended to the end of 2010: see resolution 1805 (2008).

[227] See also resolutions 1673 (2006) and 1810 (2008), extending the mandate of the committee to April 2011.

[228] See the website of the Committee, www.un.org/sc/ctc. Note also the case of *Boudellaa et al.* v. *Bosnia and Herzegovina and the Federation of Bosnia and Herzegovina*, Judgment of 11 October 2002, Human Rights Chamber of Bosnia and Herzegovina, paras. 93–8. See further above, chapter 7, p. 379.

In addition to UN activities, a number of regional instruments condemning terrorism have been adopted. These include the European Convention on the Suppression of Terrorism, 1977;[229] the Council of Europe Convention on the Prevention of Terrorism, 2005; the European Union Framework Decision on Terrorism, 2002, the South Asian Association for Regional Co-operation Regional Convention on Suppression of Terrorism, 1987 and Additional Protocol of 2005; the Arab Convention for the Suppression of Terrorism, 1998; the Convention of the Organisation of the Islamic Conference on Combating International Terrorism, 1999; the Commonwealth of Independent States Treaty on Co-operation in Combating Terrorism, 1999; the African Union Convention on the Prevention and Combating of Terrorism, 1999 and Protocol of 2005; the ASEAN Convention on Counter Terrorism, 2007, and the Organisation of American States Inter-American Convention against Terrorism, 2002.[230] In addition, the Organisation on Security and Co-operation in Europe adopted a Ministerial Declaration and Plan of Action on Combating Terrorism in 2001.[231]

Coupled with the increase in international action to suppress international terrorism has been a concern that this should be accomplished in conformity with the principles of international human rights law and international humanitarian law.[232] This has been expressed by the UN Secretary-General[233] and UN human rights organs.[234] In 2005, the UN

---

[229] Note that a Protocol amending the Convention was adopted by the Committee of Ministers of the Council of Europe in February 2003. This incorporates new offences into the Convention, being those referred to in the international conventions adopted after 1977.

[230] Note also the establishment of the Inter-American Committee Against Terrorism in 1999, AF/Res. 1650 (XXIX-0/99).

[231] See www.osce.org/docs/english/1990–1999/mcs/9buch01e.htm.

[232] See e.g. H. J. Steiner, P. Alston and R. Goodman, *International Human Rights in Context*, 3rd edn, Oxford, 2008, chapter 5, and D. Pokempner, 'Terrorism and Human Rights: The Legal Framework', in *Terrorism and International Law* (eds. M. Schmitt and G. L. Beruto), San Remo, 2003, p. 39.

[233] See Report of the Secretary-General on the Work of the Organisation, A/57/1, 2002, p. 1, where the Secretary-General stated that, 'I firmly believe that the terrorist menace must be suppressed, but states must ensure that counter-terrorist measures do not violate human rights.'

[234] See e.g. the statement of the Committee on the Elimination of Racial Discrimination of 8 March 2002, A/57/18, pp. 106–7, and the statement by the Committee against Torture of 22 November 2001, CAT/C/XXVII/Misc.7. Note also that on 27 March 2003, the legal expert of the Counter-Terrorism Committee briefed the UN Human Rights Committee: see UN Press Release of that date. See also the report on Terrorism and Human Rights by Special Rapporteur K. K. Koufa to the UN Sub-Commission on the Promotion and Protection of Human Rights, 2004, E/CN.4/Sub.2/2004/40. Note that the Security

Commission on Human Rights, for example, appointed a Special Rapporteur on the 'promotion and protection of human rights and fundamental freedoms while countering terrorism'.[235] Particular concerns have focused on 'shoot to kill' policies in the context of combating suicide bombings reportedly adopted by some states[236] and the practice of secret detention and illegal transfer of detainees across international boundaries ('extraordinary rendition').[237] The situation of detainees in the US military base in Guantanamo Bay, Cuba, has been a matter of particular concern.[238] All of these issues have demonstrated the tension between

Council's Counter-Terrorism Committee has emphasised that states in adopting measures to counter terrorism must comply with all their international law obligations, including those relating to human rights law, refugee law and humanitarian law, and issued policy guidance to the Executive Directorate noting that human rights should be incorporated into its communications strategy: see S/AC.40/2006/PG.2.

[235] See resolution 2005/80. This mandate was assumed by the Human Rights Council: see General Assembly resolution 60/251 and see Council resolution 6/28. See further on the Human Rights Council, above, chapter 6, p. 306. The Special Rapporteur produced a report on terrorist-profiling practices and human rights in 2007: see A/HRC/4/26.

[236] See e.g. A/HRC/4/26, pp. 21 ff. and the report of the Special Rapporteur on extrajudicial, summary or arbitrary executions, A/CN.4/2006/53, paras. 44 ff. In particular, the need for resort to force as a last resort and the requirement of proportionality were emphasised: see also the Code of Conduct for Law Enforcement Officers, General Assembly resolution 34/169.

[237] See e.g. L. N. Sadat, 'Ghost Prisoners and Black Sites: Extraordinary Rendition under International Law', 37 *Case Western Reserve Journal of International Law*, 2005–6, p. 309, and J. T. Parry, 'The Shape of Modern Torture: Extraordinary Rendition and Ghost Detainees', 6 *Melbourne Journal of International Law*, 2005, p. 516.

[238] See e.g. Lord Steyn, 'Guantanamo Bay: The Legal Black Hole', 53 ICLQ, 2004, p. 1; F. Johns, 'Guantanamo Bay and the Annihilation of the Exception', 16 EJIL, 2005, p. 613, and T. Gill and E. van Sliedregt, 'Guantanamo Bay: A Reflection on the Legal Status and Rights of "Unlawful Enemy Combatants"', 1 *Utrecht Law Review*, 2005, p. 28. Note in particular the joint report by the five UN Special Rapporteurs respectively on arbitrary detention, on the independence of judges and lawyers, on torture, on freedom of religion or belief and on the right of everyone to physical and mental health, 16 February 2006, and the reports by the Council of Europe's Committee on Legal Affairs and Human Rights on secret detentions and illegal transfer of detainees involving Council of Europe members of 22 January 2006, AS/Jur (2006) 03 rev. and of 7 June 2007, AS/Jur (2007) 36. The Inter-American Commission on Human Rights granted precautionary measures in favour of detainees in Guantanamo Bay requesting the US to take 'urgent measures necessary to have the legal status of the detainees at Guantanamo Bay determined by a competent tribunal': see Annual Report of the IACHR, 2002, chapter III(C)(1), para. 80, first precautionary measures reiterated and amplified in 2003, 2004 and 2005: see B. D. Tittemore, 'Guantanamo Bay and the Precautionary Measures of the Inter-American Commission on Human Rights: A Case for International Oversight in the Struggle Against Terrorism', 6 *Human Rights Law Review*, 2006, p. 378. See also with regard to US courts and Guantanamo Bay, above, chapter 4, p. 164, note 178.

combating international terrorism and respecting human rights and the need to accomplish the former without jettisoning the latter.

Regional organisations have also been concerned by this dilemma. The Council of Europe adopted international guidelines on human rights and anti-terrorism measures in July 2002,[239] seeking to integrate condemnation of terrorism and efficient combating of the phenomenon with the need to respect human rights. In particular, guideline XVI provides that in the fight against terrorism, states may never act in breach of peremptory norms of international law (*jus cogens*) nor in breach of international humanitarian law. The Inter-American Commission on Human Rights adopted a Report on Terrorism and Human Rights in October 2002.[240]

Suggestions for further reading

I. Brownlie, *International Law and the Use of Force by States*, Oxford, 1963
Y. Dinstein, *War, Aggression and Self-Defence*, 4th edn, Cambridge, 2005
T. M. Franck, *Recourse to Force*, Cambridge, 2002
C. Gray, *International Law and the Use of Force*, 2nd edn, Oxford, 2004

---

[239] Supplemented in March 2005 by guidelines concerning the protection of victims of terrorist acts.
[240] OEA/Ser.L/V/II.116, Doc. 5 rev. 1 corr.

21

International humanitarian law

In addition to prescribing laws governing resort to force (*jus ad bellum*), international law also seeks to regulate the conduct of hostilities (*jus in bello*). These principles cover, for example, the treatment of prisoners of war, civilians in occupied territory, sick and wounded personnel, prohibited methods of warfare and human rights in situations of conflict.[1] This subject was originally termed the laws of war and then the laws of armed conflict. More recently, it has been called international humanitarian law. Although international humanitarian law is primarily derived from a number of international conventions, some of these represent in whole or in part rules of customary international law, and it is possible to say that a number of customary international law principles exist over and above conventional rules,[2] although international humanitarian law

---

[1] See e.g. Y. Dinstein, *The Conduct of Hostilities under the Law of International Armed Conflict*, Cambridge, 2004; *Les Nouvelles Frontières du Droit International Humanitaire* (ed. J.-F. Flauss), Brussels, 2003; T. Meron, *The Humanization of International Law*, The Hague, 2006; UK Ministry of Defence, *Manual on the Law of Armed Conflict*, Oxford, 2004; L. Green, *The Contemporary Law of Armed Conflict*, 2nd edn, Manchester, 2000; I. Detter, *The Law of War*, 2nd edn, Cambridge, 2000; G. Best, *Humanity in Warfare*, London, 1980, and Best, *War and Law Since 1945*, Oxford, 1994; A. P. V. Rogers, *Law on the Battlefield*, Manchester, 1996; *Handbook of Humanitarian Law in Armed Conflict* (ed. D. Fleck), Oxford, 1995; *Studies and Essays on International Humanitarian Law and Red Cross Principles* (ed. C. Swinarski), Dordrecht, 1984; *The New Humanitarian Law of Armed Conflict* (ed. A. Cassese), Naples, 1979; G. I. A. D. Draper, 'The Geneva Conventions of 1949', 114 HR, p. 59, and Draper 'Implementation and Enforcement of the Geneva Conventions and of the two Additional Protocols', 164 HR, 1979, p. 1; F. Kalshoven, *The Law of Warfare*, Leiden, 1973; M. Bothe, K. Partsch and W. Solf, *New Rules for Victims of Armed Conflict*, The Hague, 1982, and J. Pictet, *Humanitarian Law and the Protection of War Victims*, Dordrecht, 1982. See also *Documents on the Laws of War* (ed. A. Roberts and R. Guelff), 3rd edn, Oxford, 2000; Nguyen Quoc Dinh, P. Daillier and A. Pellet, *Droit International Public*, 7th edn, Paris, 2002, p. 962; T. Meron, 'The Humanisation of Humanitarian Law', 94 AJIL, 2000, p. 239, and C. Rousseau, *Le Droit des Conflits Armés*, Paris, 1983.

[2] See e.g. T. Meron, 'Revival of Customary Humanitarian Law', 99 AJIL, 2005, p. 817, and *Customary International Humanitarian Law* (eds. J.-M. Henckaerts and L. Doswald-Beck), Cambridge, 2005. See also G. H. Aldrich, 'Customary International Humanitarian

is one of the most highly codified parts of international law. Reliance upon relevant customary international law rules is particularly important where one or more of the states involved in a particular conflict is not a party to a pertinent convention. A good example of this relates to the work of the Eritrea–Ethiopia Claims Commission, which noted that since Eritrea did not become a party to the four Geneva Conventions of 1949 until 14 August 2000, the applicable law before that date for relevant claims was customary international humanitarian law.[3] On the other hand, treaty provisions that cannot be said to be part of customary international law[4] will bind only those states that are parties to them. This is particularly important with regard to some provisions deemed controversial by some states contained in Additional Protocols I and II to the Geneva Conventions, 1949. One additional factor that has emerged recently has been the growing convergence between international humanitarian law and international human rights law. This is discussed below.[5]

Development

The law in this area developed from the middle of the nineteenth century. In 1864, as a result of the pioneering work of Henry Dunant,[6] who had been appalled by the brutality of the battle of Solferino five years earlier, the Geneva Convention for the Amelioration of the Condition of the Wounded in Armies in the Field was adopted. This brief instrument was revised in 1906. In 1868 the Declaration of St Petersburg prohibited the use of small explosive or incendiary projectiles. The laws of war were codified at the Hague Conferences of 1899 and 1907.[7]

Law – An Interpretation on Behalf of the International Committee of the Red Cross', 76 BYIL, 2005, p. 503, and J. M. Henckaerts, 'Customary International Humanitarian Law – A Rejoinder to Judge Aldrich', *ibid.*, p. 525.

[3] See e.g. Eritrea–Ethiopia Claims Commission, Partial Award, Prisoners of War, Eritrea's Claim 17, 1 July 2003, paras. 38 ff. It was, however, accepted that the Conventions 'have largely become expressions of customary international law', *ibid.*, para. 40. See also Eritrea–Ethiopia Claims Commission, Partial Award, Civilian Claims, Eritrea's Claims 15, 16, 23 and 27–32, 17 December 2004, para. 28.

[4] As to which, see above, chapter 3, p. 93.   [5] See below, p. 1180.

[6] See e.g. C. Moorehead, *Dunant's Dream*, London, 1998.

[7] See e.g. Green, *Contemporary Law*, chapter 2, and *The Centennial of the First International Peace Conference* (ed. F. Kalshoven), The Hague, 2000. See also Symposium on the Hague Peace Conferences, 94 AJIL, 2000, p. 1. The Nuremberg Tribunal regarded Hague Convention IV and Regulations on the Laws and Customs of War on Land, 1907 as declaratory of customary law: see 41 AJIL, 1947, pp. 172, 248–9. See also the Report of the UN Secretary-General on the Statute for the International Criminal Tribunal for the Former Yugoslavia,

A series of conventions were adopted at these conferences concerning land and naval warfare, which still form the basis of the existing rules. It was emphasised that belligerents remained subject to the law of nations and the use of force against undefended villages and towns was forbidden. It defined those entitled to belligerent status and dealt with the measures to be taken as regards occupied territory. There were also provisions concerning the rights and duties of neutral states and persons in case of war,[8] and an emphatic prohibition on the employment of 'arms, projectiles or material calculated to cause unnecessary suffering'. However, there were inadequate means to implement and enforce such rules with the result that much appeared to depend on reciprocal behaviour, public opinion and the exigencies of morale.[9] A number of conventions in the inter-war period dealt with rules concerning the wounded and sick in armies in the field and prisoners of war.[10] Such agreements were replaced by the Four Geneva 'Red Cross' Conventions of 1949 which dealt respectively with the amelioration of the condition of the wounded and sick in armed forces in the field, the amelioration of the condition of wounded, sick and shipwrecked members of the armed forces at sea, the treatment of prisoners of war and the protection of civilian persons in time of war.[11] The Fourth Convention was an innovation and a significant attempt to protect civilians who, as a result of armed hostilities or occupation, were in the power of a state of which they were not nationals.

The foundation of the Geneva Conventions system is the principle that persons not actively engaged in warfare should be treated humanely.[12] A number of practices ranging from the taking of hostages to torture, illegal

---

Security Council resolutions 808 (1993) and 823 (1993), S/25704 and 32 ILM, 1993, pp. 1159, 1170, and the Advisory Opinion of the International Court of Justice in *Legality of the Threat or Use of Nuclear Weapons*, ICJ Reports, 1996, pp. 226, 258; 110 ILR, p. 163.

[8] See S. C. Neff, *The Rights and Duties of Neutrals*, Manchester, 2000.

[9] Note, however, the Martens Clause in the Preamble to the Hague Convention concerning the Laws and Customs of War on Land, which provided that 'in cases not included in the Regulations . . . the inhabitants and the belligerents remain under the protection and the rule of the principles of the law of nations, as they result from the usages established among civilised peoples from the laws of humanity and the dictates of the public conscience'.

[10] See e.g. the 1929 Conventions, one revising the 1864 and 1906 instruments on wounded and sick soldiers, the other on the treatment of prisoners of war.

[11] Note that as of May 2008, 194 states are parties to the Geneva Conventions.

[12] See, for example, article 1(2) of Additional Protocol I, 1977, which provides that, 'In case not covered by this Protocol or by other international agreements, civilians and combatants remain under the protection and authority of the principles of international law derived from established custom, from the principles of humanity and from the dictates of public conscience.'

executions and reprisals against persons protected by the Conventions are prohibited, while a series of provisions relate to more detailed points, such as the standard of care of prisoners of war and the prohibition of deportations and indiscriminate destruction of property in occupied territory. In 1977, two Additional Protocols to the 1949 Conventions were adopted.[13] These built upon and developed the earlier Conventions. While many provisions may be seen as reflecting customary law, others do not and thus cannot constitute obligations upon states that are not parties to either or both of the Protocols.[14] Protocol III was adopted in 2005 and introduced a third emblem to the two previously recognised ones (the Red Cross and the Red Crescent) in the form of a red diamond within which either a Red Cross or Red Crescent, or another emblem which has been in effective use by a High Contracting Party and was the subject of a communication to the other High Contracting Parties and the International Committee of the Red Cross through the depositary prior to the adoption of this Protocol, may be inserted. This allows in particular for the use of the Israeli Red Magen David (Shield of David) symbol.[15]

The International Court of Justice has noted that the 'Law of the Hague', dealing primarily with inter-state rules governing the use of force or the 'laws and customs of war' as they were traditionally termed, and the 'Law of Geneva', concerning the protection of persons from the effects of armed conflicts, 'have become so closely interrelated that they are considered to have gradually formed one single complex system, known today as international humanitarian law'.[16]

The scope of protection under international humanitarian law

The rules of international humanitarian law seek to extend protection to a wide range of persons, but the basic distinction drawn has been between combatants and those who are not involved in actual hostilities. Common

---

[13] See e.g. Swinarski, *Studies and Essays*, part B, and Draper, 'Implementation and Enforcement'. See also B. Wortley, 'Observations on the Revision of the 1949 Geneva "Red Cross" Conventions', 54 BYIL, 1983, p. 143, and G. Aldrich, 'Prospects for US Ratification of Additional Protocol I to the 1949 Geneva Conventions', 85 AJIL, 1991, p. 1.

[14] For example, article 44 of Protocol I: see below, p. 1173.

[15] The Red Lion and Sun that used to be used by Iran was also included as a Geneva Convention emblem: see e.g. Detter, *Law of War*, p. 293.

[16] See the Advisory Opinion on the *Legality of the Threat or Use of Nuclear Weapons*, ICJ Reports, 1996, pp. 226, 256; 110 ILR, p. 163. The Court also noted that '[t]he provisions of the Additional Protocols of 1977 give expression and attest to the unity and complexity of that law', *ibid*.

article 2 of the Geneva Conventions provides that the Conventions 'shall apply to all cases of declared war or of any other armed conflict which may arise between two or more of the High Contracting Parties even if the state of war is not recognised by them . . . [and] to all cases of partial or total occupation of the territory of a High Contracting Party, even if the said occupation meets with no armed resistance'. The rules contained in these Conventions cannot be renounced by those intended to benefit from them, thus precluding the possibility that the power which has control over them may seek to influence the persons concerned to agree to a mitigation of protection.[17]

The wounded and sick

The First Geneva Convention concerns the Wounded and Sick on Land and emphasises that members of the armed forces and organised militias, including those accompanying them where duly authorised,[18] 'shall be respected and protected in all circumstances'. They are to be treated humanely by the party to the conflict into whose power they have fallen on a non-discriminatory basis and any attempts upon their lives or violence to their person is strictly prohibited. Torture or biological experimentation is forbidden, nor are such persons to be wilfully left without medical assistance and care.[19] The wounded and sick of a belligerent who fall into enemy hands are also to be treated as prisoners of war.[20] Further, the parties to a conflict shall take all possible measures to protect the wounded and sick and ensure their adequate care and to 'search for the dead and prevent their being despoiled'.[21] The parties to the conflict are to record as soon as possible the details of any wounded, sick or dead persons of the adversary party and to transmit them to the other side through particular means.[22] This Convention also includes provisions as to medical units and establishments, noting in particular that these should not be

---

[17] See article 7 of the first three Conventions and article 8 of the fourth. Note that Security Council resolution 1472, adopted under Chapter VII on 28 March 2003, called on 'all parties concerned' to the Iraq conflict of March–April 2003 to abide strictly by their obligations under international law and particularly the Geneva Conventions and the Hague Regulations, 'including those relating to the essential civilian needs of the people of Iraq'.

[18] See article 13. See also UK, *Manual*, chapter 7.

[19] Article 12. See also Green, *Armed Conflict*, chapter 11.

[20] Article 14. Thus the provisions of the Third Geneva Convention will apply to them: see below, p. 1172.

[21] Article 15.   [22] Article 16 and see article 122 of the Third Geneva Convention.

attacked,[23] and deals with the recognised emblems (i.e. the Red Cross, the Red Crescent and, after Protocol III, the Red Diamond).[24]

The Second Geneva Convention concerns the Condition of Wounded, Sick and Shipwrecked Members of Armed Forces at Sea and is very similar to the First Convention, for instance in its provisions that members of the armed forces and organised militias, including those accompanying them where duly authorised, and who are sick, wounded or shipwrecked are to be treated humanely and cared for on a non-discriminatory basis, and that attempts upon their lives and violence and torture are prohibited.[25] The Convention also provides that hospital ships may in no circumstances be attacked or captured but respected and protected.[26] The provisions in these Conventions were reaffirmed in and supplemented by Protocol I, 1977, Parts I and II. Article 1(4), for example, supplements common article 2 contained in the Conventions and provides that the Protocol is to apply in armed conflicts in which peoples are fighting against colonial domination and alien occupation and against racist regimes as enshrined in the UN Charter and the Declaration on Principles of International Law, 1970.

Prisoners of war[27]

The Third Geneva Convention of 1949 is concerned with prisoners of war, and consists of a comprehensive code centred upon the requirement of humane treatment in all circumstances.[28] The definition of prisoners of war in article 4, however, is of particular importance since it has been regarded as the elaboration of combatant status. It covers members of the armed forces of a party to the conflict (as well as members of militias and other volunteer corps forming part of such armed force) and members of

---

[23] Article 19, even if the personnel of the unit or establishment are armed or otherwise protected, article 22. Chapter IV concerns the treatment of medical personnel.

[24] Chapter VII.   [25] Articles 12 and 13. See also Green, *Armed Conflict*, chapter 11.

[26] Chapter III. See, with regard to the use of hospital ships in the Falklands conflict, H. Levie, 'The Falklands Crisis and the Laws of War' in *The Falklands War* (eds. A. R. Coll and A. C. Arend), Boston, 1985, pp. 64, 67–8. Chapter IV deals with medical personnel, Chapter V with medical transports and Chapter VI with the emblem: see above, p. 1170.

[27] See e.g. Dinstein, *Conduct of Hostilities*, pp. 29 ff., and UK, *Manual*, Chapter 8. Note that the Eritrea–Ethiopia Claims Commission in its Partial Award, Prisoners of War, Ethiopia's Claim 4, 1 July 2003, para. 32, has held that this Convention substantially reflected customary international law.

[28] See also the Regulations annexed to the Hague Convention IV on the Laws and Customs of War on Land, 1907, Section I, Chapter II.

other militias and volunteer corps, including those of organised resistance movements, belonging to a party to the conflict providing the following conditions are fulfilled: (a) being commanded by a person responsible for his subordinates; (b) having a fixed distinctive sign recognisable at a distance; (c) carrying arms openly; (d) conducting operations in accordance with the laws and customs of war.[29] This article reflected the experience of the Second World War, although the extent to which resistance personnel were covered was constrained by the need to comply with the four conditions. Since 1949, the use of guerrillas spread to the Third World and the decolonisation experience. Accordingly, pressures grew to expand the definition of combatants entitled to prisoner of war status to such persons, who as practice demonstrated rarely complied with the four conditions. States facing guerrilla action, whether the colonial powers or others such as Israel, objected. Articles 43 and 44 of Protocol I, 1977, provide that combatants are members of the armed forces of a party to an international armed conflict.[30] Such armed forces consist of all organised armed units under an effective command structure which enforces compliance with the rules of international law applicable in armed conflict. Article 44(3) further notes that combatants are obliged to distinguish themselves from the civilian population while they are engaged in an attack or in a military operation preparatory to an attack. When an armed combatant cannot so distinguish himself, the status of combatant may be retained provided that arms are carried openly during each military engagement and during such time as the combatant is visible to the adversary while engaged in a military deployment preceding the launching of an attack. This formulation is clearly controversial and was the subject of many declarations in the vote at the conference producing the draft.[31]

---

[29] These conditions appear in article 1 of the Hague Regulations and have been regarded as part of customary law: see G. I. A. D. Draper, 'The Status of Combatants and the Question of Guerilla Warfare', 45 BYIL, 1971, pp. 173, 186. See also the *Tadić* case, Judgment of the Appeals Chamber of 15 July 1999, IT-94-1-A; 124 ILR, p. 61.

[30] Article 1(4) of Protocol I includes as international armed conflicts 'armed conflicts in which peoples are fighting against colonial domination and alien occupation and against racist regimes in the exercise of their right of self-determination'. Note that there is no provision for prisoner of war status in non-international armed conflicts: see below, p. 1194.

[31] See e.g. H. Verthy, *Guérrilla et Droit Humanitaire*, 2nd edn, Geneva, 1983, and P. Nahlik, 'L'Extension du Statut de Combattant à la Lumière de Protocol I de Genève de 1977', 164 HR, 1979, p. 171. Where a person is a mercenary, there is no right to combatant or prisoner of war status under article 47. See also the International Convention against the Recruitment, Use, Financing and Training of Mercenaries, 1989: Green, *Armed Conflict,*

Article 5 also provides that where there is any doubt as to the status of any person committing a belligerent act and falling into the hands of the enemy, 'such person shall enjoy the protection of the present Convention until such time as their status has been determined by a competent tribunal'.[32] This formulation was changed somewhat in article 45 of Protocol I. This provides that a person who takes part in hostilities and falls into the power of an adverse party 'shall be presumed to be a prisoner of war and therefore shall be protected by the Third Convention'. The term 'unlawful combatant', therefore, refers to a person who fails the tests laid down in articles 43 and 44, after due determination of status, and who would not be entitled to the status of prisoner of war under international humanitarian law. Such a person, who would thus be a civilian, would be protected by the basic humanitarian guarantees laid down in articles 45(3) and 75 of Protocol I and by the general principles of international human rights law in terms of his/her treatment upon capture. However, since such a person would not have the status of a prisoner of war, he would not benefit from the protections afforded by such status and would thus be liable to prosecution under the normal criminal law.[33]

---

pp. 114 ff. However, such persons remain entitled to the basic humanitarian guarantees provided by Protocol I: see articles 45(3) and 75. See also UK, *Manual*, p. 147.

[32] See also the *British Manual of Military Law*, Part III, *The Law of Land Warfare*, London, 1958, para. 132, note 3, and the US Department of Army, *Law of Land Warfare*, Field Manual 27–10, 1956, para. 71(c), (d) detailing what a competent tribunal might be. In the case of the UK, the competent tribunal would be a board of inquiry convened in accordance with the Prisoner of War Determination of Status Regulations 1958: see UK, *Manual*, p. 150. See as to the question of persons captured by the US in Afghanistan in 2001–2 and elsewhere, and detained at the US military base at Guantanamo Bay, Cuba, *Rasul* v. *Bush* 124 S. Ct. 2686 (2004); US Military Commissions Act 2006, 45 ILM, 2006, p. 1246; and *Hamdan* v. *Rumsfeld* 126 S. Ct. 2749 (2006) and see *Boumediene* v. *Bush* 553 US _ (2008). See also above, chapter 12, p. 658 and chapter 20, p. 1165.

[33] See e.g. A. Cassese, *International Law*, 2nd edn, Oxford, 2005, pp. 409–10, cf. Dinstein, *Conduct of Hostilities*, pp. 29 ff.; M. Finaud, 'L'Abus de la Notion de "Combattant Illégal": Une Atteinte au Droit International Humanitaire', 110 RGDIP, 2006, p. 861, and T. M. Franck, 'Criminals, Combatants, or What – An Examination of the Role of Law in Responding to the Threat of Terror', 98 AJIL, 2005, p. 686. Accordingly, captured Taliban fighters who formed part of the army of Afghanistan at the relevant time would have the status of POWs, while captured Al-Qaida operatives would be subject to relevant national criminal law, including war crimes and crimes against humanity. Note that once a civilian takes part in hostilities, he/she loses the protection of the prohibition of attacks upon him/her: see article 51(3), Protocol I. See also *Public Committee Against Torture in Israel* v. *Government of Israel*, Israeli Supreme Court, 13 December 2006, 101 AJIL, 2007, p. 459, *A and B* v. *State of Israel*, Israeli Supreme Court, 11 June 2008 and D. Kretzmer, 'Targeted Killing of Suspected Terrorists: Extra-Judicial Executions or Legitimate Means of Defence?', 16 EJIL, 2005, p. 171.

The framework of obligations covering prisoners of war is founded upon 'the requirement of treatment of POWs as human beings', while 'At the core of the Convention regime are legal obligations to keep POWs alive and in good health.'[34] Article 13 provides that prisoners of war must at all times be humanely treated and must at all times be protected, particularly against acts of violence or intimidation and against 'insults and public curiosity'.[35] This means that displaying prisoners of war on television in a humiliating fashion confessing to 'crimes' or criticising their own government must be regarded as a breach of the Convention.[36] Measures of reprisal against prisoners of war are prohibited. Article 14 provides that prisoners of war are entitled in all circumstances to respect for their persons and their honour.[37]

Prisoners of war are bound only to divulge their name, date of birth, rank and serial number. Article 17 provides that 'no physical or mental torture, nor any other form of coercion, may be inflicted . . . to secure from them information of any kind whatever. Prisoners of war who refuse to answer may not be threatened, insulted, or exposed to unpleasant or disadvantageous treatment of any kind.' Once captured, prisoners of war are to be evacuated as soon as possible to camps situated in an area far enough from the combat zone for them to be out of danger,[38] while article 23 stipulates that 'no prisoner of war may at any time be sent to, or detained in, areas where he may be exposed to the fire of the combat zone, nor may his presence be used to render certain points or areas immune from military operations'.[39] Prisoners of war are subject to the

---

[34] See the Eritrea–Ethiopia Claims Commission in its Partial Award, Prisoners of War, Ethiopia's Claim 4, 1 July 2003, paras. 53 and 64, where the Commission declared that 'customary international law, as reflected in Geneva Conventions I and III, absolutely prohibits the killing of POWs, requires the wounded and sick to be collected and cared for, the dead to be collected, and demands prompt and humane evacuation of POWs'. See also Best, *War and Law*, p. 135, and Y. Dinstein, 'Prisoners of War' in *Encyclopaedia of Public International Law* (ed. R. Bernhardt), Amsterdam, 1982, pp. 146, 148.

[35] See also article 11 of Protocol I.

[36] See e.g. the treatment of allied prisoners of war by Iraq in the 1991 Gulf War, *The Economist*, 26 January 1991, p. 24, and in the 2003 Gulf War: see the report of the condemnation by the International Committee of the Red Cross, http://news.bbc.co.uk/1/hi/world/middle_east/2881187.stm.

[37] See also article 75 of Protocol I.   [38] Article 19.

[39] Thus the reported Iraqi practice during the 1991 Gulf War of sending allied prisoners of war to strategic sites in order to create a 'human shield' to deter allied attacks was clearly a violation of the Convention: see e.g. *The Economist*, 26 January 1991, p. 24. See also UKMIL, 62 BYIL, 1991, pp. 678 ff.

laws and orders of the state detaining them.[40] They may be punished for disciplinary offences and tried for offences committed before capture, for example for war crimes. They may also be tried for offences committed before capture against the law of the state holding them.[41] Other provisions of this Convention deal with medical treatment, religious activities, discipline, labour and relations with the exterior. Article 118 provides that prisoners of war shall be released and repatriated without delay after the cessation of hostilities. The Convention on prisoners of war applies only to international armed conflicts,[42] but article 3 (which is common to the four Conventions) provides that as a minimum 'persons ... including members of armed forces, who have laid down their arms and those placed *hors de combat* by sickness, wounds, detention, or any other cause, shall in all circumstances be treated humanely'.

Protection of civilians and occupation

The Fourth Geneva Convention is concerned with the protection of civilians in time of war and builds upon the Hague Regulations (attached to Hague Convention IV on the Law and Customs of War on Land, 1907).[43] This Geneva Convention, which marked an extension to the pre-1949 rules, is limited under article 4 to those persons, 'who, at a given moment and in any manner whatsoever, find themselves, in case of a conflict or occupation, in the hands of a party to the conflict or occupying power of which they are not nationals'. The Convention comes into operation immediately upon the outbreak of hostilities or the start of an occupation and ends at the general close of military operations.[44] Under article 50(1) of Protocol I, 1977, a civilian is defined as any person not a combatant,[45]

---

[40] Article 82, Geneva Convention III.

[41] Articles 82 and 85. See Green, *Armed Conflict*, p. 210. See also *US* v. *Noriega* 746 F. Supp. 1506, 1529 (1990); 99 ILR, pp. 143, 171.

[42] See below, p. 1190.

[43] See e.g. Green, *Armed Conflict*, chapters 12 and 15; UK, *Manual*, Chapters 9 and 11; E. Benvenisti, *The International Law of Occupation*, Princeton, 2004 (with new preface), and S. Wills, 'Occupation Law and Multi-National Operations: Problems and Perspectives', 77 BYIL, 2006, p. 256. The Hague Regulations have become part of customary international law: see *Construction of a Wall*, ICJ Reports, 2004, pp. 136, 172; 129 ILR, pp. 37, 91.

[44] Article 6.

[45] As defined in article 4 of the Third Geneva Convention, 1949 and article 43, Protocol I, 1977, above, p. 1172. Note, however, the obligation contained in the Optional Protocol to the Convention on the Rights of the Child on the involvement of children in armed conflict, 25 May 2000, to ensure that children under the age of eighteen do not take part in hostilities.

and in cases of doubt a person is to be considered a civilian. The Fourth Convention provides a highly developed set of rules for the protection of such civilians, including the right to respect for person, honour, convictions and religious practices and the prohibition of torture and other cruel, inhuman or degrading treatment, hostage-taking and reprisals.[46] The wounded and sick are the object of particular protection and respect[47] and there are various judicial guarantees as to due process.[48]

The protection of civilians in occupied territories is covered in section III of Part III of the Fourth Geneva Convention,[49] but what precisely occupied territory is may be open to dispute.[50] Article 42 of the Hague Regulations provides that territory is to be considered as occupied 'when it is actually placed under the authority of the hostile army' and that the occupation only extends to the territory 'where such authority has been established and can be exercised',[51] while article 2(2) of the Convention provides that it is to apply to all cases of partial or total occupation 'of the territory of a High Contracting Party, even if the said occupation meets with no resistance'. The International Court in the *Democratic Republic of the Congo* v. *Uganda* case[52] noted that in order to determine whether a state whose forces are present on the territory of another state is an occupying power, one must examine whether there is sufficient evidence to demonstrate that the said authority was in fact established and exercised by the intervening state in the areas in question. The Court understood this to mean in practice in that case that Ugandan forces in the Congo were stationed there in particular areas and that they had substituted their own authority for that of the Congolese government.

The military occupation of enemy territory is termed 'belligerent occupation' and international law establishes a legal framework concerning the legal relations of occupier and occupied. There are two key conditions for the establishment of an occupation in this sense, first, that the former government is no longer capable of publicly exercising its authority in

---

[46] See articles 27–34. The rights of aliens in the territory of a party to a conflict are covered in articles 35–46.
[47] Article 16.   [48] See articles 71–6. See also article 75 of Protocol I, 1977.
[49] See also the Hague Regulations, Section III.
[50] Iraqi-occupied Kuwait in 1990–1 was, of course, a prime example of the situation covered by this Convention: see e.g. Security Council resolution 674 (1990).
[51] See the *Construction of a Wall* case, ICJ Reports, 2004, pp. 136, 167 and *Democratic Republic of the Congo* v. *Uganda*, ICJ Reports, 2005, pp. 168, 229, reaffirming article 42 as part of customary international law.
[52] ICJ Reports, 2005, pp. 168, 230.

the area in question and, secondly, that the occupying power is in a position to substitute its own authority for that of the former government.[53] An occupation will cease as soon as the occupying power is forced out or evacuates the area.[54] Article 43 of the Hague Regulations provides the essential framework of the law of occupation. It notes that, 'The authority of the legitimate power having in fact passed into the hands of the occupant, the latter shall take all the measures in his power to restore and ensure, as far as possible, public order and safety, while respecting, unless absolutely prevented, the laws in force in the country.'[55] This establishes several key elements. First, only 'authority' and not sovereignty passes to the occupier.[56] The former government retains sovereignty and may be deprived of it only with its consent. Secondly, the basis of authority of the occupier lies in effective control. Thirdly, the occupier has both the obligation and the right to maintain public order in the occupied territory. Fourthly, the existing laws of the territory must be preserved as far as possible.

The situation with regard to the West Bank of Jordan (sometimes known as Judaea and Samaria), for example, demonstrates the problems that may arise. Israel has argued that since the West Bank has never been

---

[53] See e.g. UK, *Manual*, p. 275.

[54] *Ibid.*, p. 277. See also *R v. Civil Aviation Authority* [2006] EWHC 2465 (Admin), at para. 15; 132 ILR, p. 713, noting that 'The state of Israel has withdrawn from Gaza [in 2005] so that it is not an occupied Palestinian Territory.' Note that Israel handed over certain powers with regard to parts of the West Bank to the Palestinian Authority following the Oslo agreements of 1993: see generally J. Crawford, *The Creation of States*, 2nd edn, 2006, pp. 442 ff.; *New Political Entities in Public and Private International Law* (eds. A. Shapira and M. Tabory), The Hague, 1999; E. Benvenisti, 'The Israeli–Palestinian Declaration of Principles: A Framework for Future Settlement', 4 EJIL, 1993, p. 542, and P. Malanczuk, 'Some Basic Aspects of the Agreements Between Israel and the PLO from the Perspective of International Law', 7 EJIL, 1996, p. 485. Since one assumes that the Palestinian Authority is not an occupying power, the fact that Israel is not in effective day-to-day control over the whole area must impact upon its responsibilities, but it is unlikely that this has affected its legal status as such as belligerent occupant.

[55] Note that the International Court has emphasised that 'international humanitarian law contains provisions enabling account to be taken of military exigencies in certain circumstances' and that 'the military exigencies contemplated by these texts may be invoked in occupied territories even after the general close of the military operations that lead to their occupation', *Construction of a Wall*, ICJ Reports, 2004, pp. 136, 192. See also M. Sassòli, 'Legislation and Maintenance of Public Order and Civil Life by Occupying Powers', 16 EJIL, 2005, p. 661.

[56] See e.g. *Prefecture of Voiotia v. Germany (Distomo Massacre)*, Court of Cassation, Greece, 4 May 2000, 129 ILR, pp. 514, 519 and *Mara'abe v. The Prime Minister of Israel*, Israel Supreme Court, 15 September 2005, 129 ILR, pp. 241, 252. See also Benvenisti, *International Law of Occupation*, pp. 5-6, and UK, *Manual*, p. 278.

recognised internationally as Jordanian territory,[57] it cannot therefore be regarded as its territory to which the Convention would apply. In other words, to recognise that the Convention applies formally would be tantamount to recognition of Jordanian sovereignty over the disputed land.[58] However, the International Court has stated that the Convention 'is applicable in any occupied territory in the event of an armed conflict arising between two or more High Contracting Parties' so that with regard to the Israel/Palestine territories question, 'the Convention is applicable in the Palestinian territories which before the conflict lay to the east of the Green Line [i.e. the 1949 armistice line] and which, during that conflict, were occupied by Israel, there being no need for any enquiry into the precise legal status of those territories.'[59] The Eritrea–Ethiopia Claims Commission has pointed out that 'These protections [provided by international humanitarian law] should not be cast into doubt because the belligerents dispute the status of territory ... respecting international protections in such situations does not prejudice the status of the territory.'[60] Further, the Commission emphasised that 'neither text [the Hague Regulations and the Fourth Geneva Convention] suggests that only territory the title of which is clear and uncontested can be occupied territory.'[61]

---

[57] It was annexed by the Kingdom of Transjordan, as it then was, in 1949 at the conclusion of the Israeli War of Independence, but this annexation was recognised only by the UK and Pakistan. See e.g. A. Gerson, *Israel, the West Bank and International Law*, London, 1978.

[58] Note that Israel does observe the Convention *de facto*: see e.g. *Mara'abe* v. *The Prime Minister of Israel*, Israeli Supreme Court, 15 September 2005, 129 ILR, pp. 241, 253. This was noted by the International Court in the *Construction of a Wall* case, ICJ Reports, 2004, pp. 136, 174. See also D. Kretzmer, *The Occupation of Justice*, New York, 2002; M. Shamgar, 'The Observance of International Law in the Administered Territories', *Israel Yearbook on Human Rights*, 1977, p. 262; T. Meron, 'West Bank and Gaza', *ibid.*, 1979, p. 108; F. Fleiner-Gerster and H. Meyer, 'New Developments in Humanitarian Law', 34 ICLQ, 1985, p. 267, and E. Cohen, *Human Rights in the Israeli-Occupied Territories*, Manchester, 1985.

[59] *Construction of a Wall* case, ICJ Reports, 2004, pp. 136, 177. It should be noted that Israel has long asserted that it applies the humanitarian parts of the Convention to the occupied territories: see e.g. Shamgar, 'Observance of International Law in the Administered Territories'; and Meron, 'West Bank and Gaza', and *Mara'abe* v. *The Prime Minister of Israel*, Israeli Supreme Court, 15 September 2005, 129 ILR, pp. 241, 252–3. See also M. N. Shaw, 'Territorial Administration by Non-Territorial Sovereigns' in *The Shifting Allocation of Authority in International Law* (eds. Y. Shany and T. Broudie), Oxford, 2008, pp. 369, 385 ff.

[60] Partial Award, Central Front, Ethiopia's Claim 2, 28 April 2004, para. 28.

[61] *Ibid.*, para. 29. Note that article 4 of Protocol I provides that, 'The application of the Conventions and of this Protocol, as well as the conclusion of the agreements provided for therein, shall not affect the legal status of the Parties to the conflict. Neither the occupation of a territory nor the application of the Conventions and this Protocol shall affect the legal status of the territory in question.'

Article 47 provides that persons protected under the Convention cannot be deprived in any case or in any manner whatsoever of the benefits contained in the Convention by any change introduced as a result of the occupation nor by any agreement between the authorities of the occupied territory and the occupying power nor by any annexation by the latter of the whole or part of the occupied territory. Article 49 prohibits 'individual or mass forcible transfers' as well as deportations of protected persons from the occupied territory regardless of motive, while the occupying power 'shall not deport or transfer parts of its own civilian population into the territory it occupies'.[62] Other provisions refer to the prohibition of forced work or conscription of protected persons, and the prohibition of the destruction of real or personal property except where rendered absolutely necessary by military operations, and of any alteration of the status of public or judicial officials.[63] The occupying power also has the responsibility to ensure that the local population has adequate food and medical supplies and, if not, to facilitate relief schemes.[64] Article 70 provides that protected persons shall not be arrested, prosecuted or convicted for acts committed or opinions expressed before the occupation, apart from breaches of the laws of war.[65]

In addition to the traditional rules of humanitarian law, international human rights law is now seen as in principle applicable to occupation situations. The International Court interpreted article 43 of the Hague Regulations to include 'the duty to secure respect for the applicable rules of international human rights law and international humanitarian law, to protect the inhabitants of the occupied territory against acts of violence, and not to tolerate such violence by any third state'.[66] Further, the Court has stated that the protection offered by human rights conventions

---

[62] The International Court has stated that this provision prohibits 'any measures taken by an occupying power in order to organize or encourage transfers of parts of its own population into the occupied territory' and that 'the Israeli settlements in the Occupied Palestinian Territory (including East Jerusalem) have been established in breach of international law', *Construction of a Wall*, ICJ Reports, 2004, pp. 136, 183–4. See also criticisms of Israel's policy of building settlements in territories it has occupied since 1967, UKMIL, 54 BYIL, 1983, pp. 538–9. Note also Kretzmer, *Occupation of Justice*, chapter 5.

[63] Articles 51, 53 and 54. Article 64 stipulates that penal laws remain in force, unless a threat to the occupier's security, while existing tribunals continue to function. See also Security Council resolution 1472 (2003) concerning the March–April 2003 military operation by coalition forces in Iraq.

[64] Articles 55, 56, 59 and 60.

[65] Section IV consists of regulations for the treatment of internees.

[66] *Democratic Republic of the Congo* v. *Uganda*, ICJ Reports, 2005, pp. 168, 231 and 242 ff.

does not cease in case of armed conflict, unless there has been a relevant derogation permitted by the convention in question. The Court has also emphasised that many human rights treaties apply to the conduct of states parties where the state is exercising jurisdiction on foreign territory[67] and that in such cases the matter will fall to be determined by the applicable *lex specialis*, that is international humanitarian law.[68] In *Democratic Republic of Congo* v. *Uganda* the Court reaffirmed that 'international human rights instruments are applicable "in respect of acts done by a state in the exercise of its jurisdiction outside its own territory", particularly in occupied territories'.[69] It was concluded that Uganda was internationally responsible for various violations of international human rights law and international humanitarian law, including those committed by virtue of failing to comply with its obligations as an occupying power.[70]

As part of this general approach, the Court has noted that the principle of self-determination applies to the Palestinian people,[71] and that the construction by Israel of a separation barrier (sometimes termed a wall or a fence) between its territory and the occupied West Bank was unlawful to the extent that it was situated within the occupied territories.[72]

---

[67] *Construction of a Wall*, ICJ Reports, 2004, pp. 136, 178 ff. See also Wills, 'Occupation Law', pp. 265 ff.

[68] *Legality of the Threat or Use of Nuclear Weapons*, ICJ Reports, 1996, pp. 226, 240.

[69] ICJ Reports, 2005, pp. 168, 242–3. A series of international human rights instruments was listed as being applicable with regard to the Congo situation, including the International Covenants on Human Rights, the Convention on the Rights of the Child and the African Charter on Human and Peoples' Rights, *ibid.*, pp. 243–4.

[70] *Ibid.*, pp. 244–5. Reference was also made to the violation of Article 47 of the Hague Regulations and Article 33 of the Fourth Geneva Convention and of the African Charter on Human and Peoples' Rights with regard to the exploitation of the natural resources of Congo, *ibid.*, pp. 252 ff.

[71] The Court relied primarily upon the terms of the Israeli–Palestinian Interim Agreement, 1995 and the reference therein to the 'legitimate rights' of the Palestinian people, which the Court held included the right to self-determination 'as the General Assembly has moreover recognized on a number of occasions (see, for example, resolution 58/163 of 22 December 2003)', *Construction of a Wall*, ICJ Reports, 2004, pp. 136, 183.

[72] This was partly because the Court saw this as creating a fait accompli on the ground which might become permanent and would then be tantamount to *de facto* annexation, and partly because it was seen as severely impeding the exercise by the Palestinian people of its right to self-determination, *ibid.*, p. 184. The Court also noted that it appeared that the construction of the wall was contrary to provisions in the Hague Regulations and the Fourth Geneva Convention concerning requisition of property and liberty of movement, *ibid.*, pp. 185 ff. Israel's argument was that the construction of the barrier commenced after a series of suicide car bombings within its territory emanating from the occupied territories and that the barrier was a temporary security measure, *ibid.*, p. 182. See generally the articles on the case collected in 'Agora', 99 AJIL, 2005, p. 1.

Further, although an occupying power can plead military exigencies and the requirements of national security or public order in the framework of the international law of occupation, the route of the wall could not be so justified.[73]

The Israeli Supreme Court in a judgment rendered shortly before the International Court's advisory opinion emphasised that the authority of a military commander to order the construction of each segment of the separation barrier could not be founded upon political as distinct from military considerations and that the barrier could not be motivated by annexation wishes nor in order to draw a political border. Such military authority was inherently temporary since belligerent occupation was inherently temporary.[74] In a further case, decided one year after the International Court's advisory opinion, the Israeli Supreme Court referred to the balance to be drawn between the legitimate security needs of the state, its military forces and of persons present in the occupied area in question on the one hand, and the human rights of the local population derived from international humanitarian law on the other.[75] The Court also proceeded on the assumption that the international conventions on human rights applied in the area.[76] In addressing the question as to how to achieve what was termed the 'delicate balance' between military necessity and humanitarian considerations, the Court referred to the application of general principles of law, one of these being the principle of proportionality. This principle was based on three sub-tests, the first being a call for a fit between goal and means, the second calling for the application of the least harmful means in such a situation, and the third being that the damage caused to an individual by the means employed must be of appropriate proportion to the benefit stemming from it.[77] Each segment of the route of the barrier had to be assessed in the light of the impact upon the Palestinian residents and whether any impingement was proportional.[78]

---

[73] ICJ Reports, 2004, pp. 192 and 193.

[74] *Beit Sourik* v. *Government of Israel*, Israeli Supreme Court, 30 June 2004, 129 ILR, pp. 189, 205–6.

[75] *Mara'abe* v. *Prime Minister of Israel*, Israeli Supreme Court, 15 September 2005, 129 ILR, pp. 241, 264–5. See also Y. Shany, 'Capacities and Inadequacies: A Look at the Two Separation Barrier Cases', 38 *Israel Law Review*, 2005, p. 230.

[76] *Mara'abe* 129 ILR, pp. 241, 266, but without formally deciding the matter, *ibid.*

[77] *Ibid.*, pp. 266 and 268, reaffirming the decision in *Beit Sourik* v. *Government of Israel*, Israeli Supreme Court, 30 June 2004, 129 ILR, pp. 189, 215 ff.

[78] *Mara'abe* 129, ILR, pp. 241, 286. The Court held that the route of the barrier in the area in question in the case had to be reconsidered as it was not shown that the least injurious means test had been satisfied, *ibid.*, pp. 316 ff. The effect of this would be to reduce the

In relation to the application of international human rights treaties outside the territory of the state concerned, the UK Manual of the Law of Armed Conflict concluded that: 'Where the occupying power is a party to the European Convention on Human Rights the standards of that Convention may, depending on the circumstances, be applicable in the occupied territories.'[79]

Moving further beyond the traditional and passive approach with regard to the law of occupation,[80] the Security Council adopted resolution 1483 (2003) after the coalition military action against Iraq, reaffirming the position of the UK and US as occupying powers in Iraq under international law but placing upon them (and the Coalition Provisional Authority, which included other states) a range of other powers and responsibilities over and above the international law relating to occupation.[81] These included the obligation 'to promote the welfare of the Iraqi people through the effective administration of the territory, including . . . the creation of conditions in which the Iraqi people can freely determine their own political future' and the relevance of the establishment of an internationally recognised, representative government of Iraq. In addition,

---

size of the fenced-in enclave projecting into the West Bank. Note that the Court explained that the difference between its judgment and the advisory opinion of the International Court stemmed from the difference in facts laid before the two courts, particularly the paucity of facts relating to the security–military necessity to erect the fence arising from the phenomenon of suicide bombing inside Israel put before the International Court, *ibid.*, pp. 287–8.

[79] At p. 282. See also *Al-Skeini* v. *Secretary of State for Defence* [2007] UKHL 26; 133 ILR, p. 693, where the House of Lords held that the European Convention applied to British military detention facilities but not to soldiers on patrol in Iraq, and *Al-Jedda* v. *Secretary of State for Defence* [2007] UKHL 58, where the House of Lords held that a binding Security Council resolution authorising the maintenance of public order had precedence over the terms of article 5 of the European Convention. See also *Coard* v. *United States*, Report No. 109/99, 29 September 1999; 123 ILR, p. 156, for the view expressed by the Inter-American Commission on Human Rights that the US was bound by relevant rules of humanitarian law and human rights law in the Grenada intervention.

[80] Note the problems posed by long-lasting occupations and the tension between the traditional law of minimal interference with local life and the need to cope with societal changes: see e.g. A. Roberts, 'Prolonged Military Occupation: The Israeli-Occupied Territories Since 1967', 84 AJIL, 1990, p. 44, and Roberts, 'Transformative Military Occupation: Applying the Laws of War and Human Rights', 100 AJIL, 2006, p. 580.

[81] See generally 'Iraq: Law of Occupation', House of Commons Research Paper 03/51, 2 June 2003; E. Benvenisti, 'Water Conflicts During the Occupation of Iraq', 97 AJIL, 2003, p. 860; M. Hmoud, 'The Use of Force Against Iraq: Occupation and Security Council Resolution 1483', 36 *Cornell International Law Journal*, 2004, p. 435, and D. Scheffer, 'Beyond Occupation Law', 97 AJIL, 2003, p. 842.

a Special Representative for Iraq was appointed, whose functions included the promotion of human rights.

The conduct of hostilities[82]

International law, in addition to seeking to protect victims of armed conflicts, also tries to constrain the conduct of military operations in a humanitarian fashion. In analysing the rules contained in the 'Law of the Hague', it is important to bear in mind the delicate balance to be maintained between military necessity and humanitarian considerations. A principle of long standing, if not always honoured in practice, is the requirement to protect civilians against the effects of hostilities. As far as the civilian population is concerned during hostilities,[83] the basic rule (sometimes termed the principle of distinction)[84] formulated in article 48 of Protocol I is that the parties to the conflict must at all times distinguish between such population and combatants and between civilian and military objectives and must direct their operations only against military objectives.[85] Military objectives are limited in article 52(2) to 'those objects which by their nature, location, purpose or use make an effective contribution to military action and whose total or partial destruction, capture or neutralisation, in the circumstances ruling at the time, offers a definite military advantage'. There is thus a principle of proportionality to be considered. Judge Higgins, for example, in referring to this principle, noted that 'even a legitimate target may not be attacked if the collateral civilian casualties would be disproportionate to the specific military gain from the attack'.[86] Issues have arisen particularly with regard to so-called 'dual use' objects such as bridges, roads and power stations,[87] and care must be taken to

---

[82] See e.g. Dinstein, *Conduct of Hostilities*; UK, *Manual*, chapter 5; Green, *Armed Conflict*, chapters 7 (land), 8 (maritime) and 9 (air). See also Rogers, *Law on the Battlefield*, and Best, *War and Law*, pp. 253 ff. As to armed conflicts at sea, see also *The San Remo Manual on International Law Applicable to Armed Conflicts at Sea* (ed. L. Doswald-Beck), Cambridge, 1995.

[83] Apart from the provisions protecting the inhabitants of occupied territories under the Fourth Geneva Convention. See also Security Council resolution 1674 (2006) on the Protection of Civilians in Armed Conflicts, and Security Council Presidential Statement of 27 May 2008, 5/PRST/2008/18.

[84] See e.g. Dinstein, *Conduct of Hostilities*, p. 55.   [85] *Ibid.*, chapter 4.

[86] Dissenting Opinion, *Legality of the Threat or Use of Nuclear Weapons*, ICJ Reports, 1996, pp. 226, 587; 110 ILR, pp. 163, 536.

[87] Note that in the Eritrea–Ethiopia Claims Commission, Partial Award, Western Front, Aerial Bombardment and Related Claims, Eritrea's Claims 1, 3, 5, 9–13, 14, 21, 25 and 26, 19 December 2005, paras. 113 ff., it was held that article 52(2) constituted a statement of

interpret these so that such objects are not indiscriminately attacked on the one hand, while ensuring that, on the other, such objects or facilities are not used by opposing military forces in an attempt to secure immunity from attack, with the inevitable result that civilians may be endangered.[88] Much will depend upon whether the military circumstances are such that they fall within the definition provided in article 52(2). This will require a balancing of military need and civilian endangerment.

Article 51 provides that the civilian population as such, as well as individual civilians, 'shall not be the object of attack. Acts or threats of violence the primary purpose of which is to spread terror among the civilian population are prohibited.'[89] Additionally, indiscriminate attacks[90] are prohibited.[91] Article 57 provides that in the conduct of military operations, 'constant care shall be taken to spare the civilian population, civilians and civilian objects'.

Although reprisals involving the use of force are now prohibited in international law (unless they can be brought within the framework of

---

customary international law. Whether an aerial attack on a power station fell within the term 'military advantage' could only be understood in the context of military operations between the parties as a whole and not simply in the context of a simple attack, *ibid*. See also UK, *Manual*, pp. 55 ff.

[88] See, as to the Kosovo conflict 1999, e.g. J. A. Burger, 'International Humanitarian Law and the Kosovo Crisis', 82 *International Review of the Red Cross*, 2000, p. 129; P. Rowe, 'Kosovo 1999: The Air Campaign', *ibid*., p. 147, and W. J. Fenrick, 'Targeting and Proportionality during the NATO Bombing Campaign Against Yugoslavia', 12 EJIL, 2001, p. 489. See also the Review of the NATO Bombing Campaign Against the Federal Republic of Yugoslavia by a review committee of the International Criminal Tribunal for the Former Yugoslavia recommending that no investigation be commenced by the Office of the Prosecutor: see www.un.org/icty/pressreal/nato061300.htm, and the attempt to bring aspects of the bombing campaign before the European Court of Human Rights: see *Banković* v. *Belgium*, Judgment of 12 December 2001, 133 ILR, p. 94.

[89] See e.g. the Eritrea–Ethiopia Claims Commission, Partial Award, Western Front, Aerial Bombardment and Related Claims, Eritrea's Claims 1, 3, 5, 9–13, 14, 21, 25 and 26, 19 December 2005, para. 27.

[90] These are defined in article 51(4) as: (a) those which are not directed at a specific military objective; (b) those which employ a method or means of combat which cannot be at a specific military objective; or (c) those which employ a method or means of combat the effects of which cannot be limited as required by Protocol I; and consequently in each such case are of a nature to strike military objectives and civilians or civilian objects without distinction.

[91] See 21(5) *UN Chronicle*, 1984, p. 3 with regard to an appeal by the UN Secretary-General to Iran and Iraq to refrain from attacks on civilian targets. See also Security Council resolution 540 (1983). The above provisions apply to the use by Iraq in the 1991 Gulf War of missiles deliberately fired at civilian targets. The firing of missiles at Israeli and Saudi Arabian cities in early 1991 constituted, of course, an act of aggression against a state not a party to that conflict: see e.g. *The Economist*, 26 January 1991, p. 21.

self-defence),[92] belligerent reprisals during an armed conflict may in certain circumstances be legitimate. Their purpose is to ensure the termination of the prior unlawful act which precipitated the reprisal and a return to legality. They must be proportionate to the prior illegal act.[93] Modern law, however, has restricted their application. Reprisals against prisoners of war are prohibited by article 13 of the Third Geneva Convention, while article 52 of Protocol I provides that civilian objects are not to be the object of attack or of reprisals.[94] Civilian objects are all objects which are not military objectives as defined in article 52(2).[95] Cultural objects and places of worship are also protected,[96] as are objects deemed indispensable to the survival of the civilian population, such as foodstuffs, agricultural areas for the production of foodstuffs, crops, livestock, drinking water installations and supplies, and irrigation works, so long as they are not used as sustenance solely for the armed forces or in direct support of military action.[97] Attacks are also prohibited against works or installations containing dangerous forces, namely dams, dykes and nuclear generating stations.[98]

The right of the parties to an armed conflict to choose methods of warfare is not unconstrained.[99] The preamble of the St Petersburg Declaration of 1868, banning explosives or inflammatory projectiles below 400 grammes in weight, emphasises that the 'only legitimate object which states should endeavour to accomplish during war is to weaken the military forces of the enemy', while article 48 of Protocol I provides that a distinction must at all times be drawn between civilians and combatants. Article 22 of the Hague Regulations points out that the 'right of

---

[92] See above, chapter 20, p. 1131.
[93] See e.g. Green, *Armed Conflict*, p. 123; C. J. Greenwood, 'Reprisals and Reciprocity in the New Law of Armed Conflict' in *Armed Conflict in the New Law* (ed. M. A. Meyer), London, 1989, p. 227, and F. Kalshoven, *Belligerent Reprisals*, Leiden, 1971.
[94] Similarly wounded, sick, shipwrecked, medical and missing persons; also protected against reprisal are the natural environment and works or installations containing dangerous forces: see articles 20 and 53–6.
[95] See above, p. 1176.
[96] See article 53. See also the Hague Convention for the Protection of Cultural Property in the Event of Armed Conflict, 1954 together with the First Protocol, 1954 and the Second Protocol, 1999. The protections as to cultural property are subject to 'military necessity': see article 4 of the 1954 Convention and articles 6 and 7 of the 1999 Protocol. Under articles 3 and 22 of the Protocol, protection is extended to non-international armed conflicts: see R. O'Keefe, *The Protection of Cultural Property in Armed Conflict*, Cambridge, 2006, and below, p. 1194.
[97] Article 54.   [98] Article 56.
[99] See UK, *Manual*, chapter 6, and Dinstein, *Conduct of Hostilities*, chapter 3.

belligerents to adopt means of injuring the enemy is not unlimited',[100] while article 23(e) stipulates that it is especially prohibited to 'employ arms, projectiles or material calculated to cause unnecessary suffering'.[101] Quite how one may define such weapons is rather controversial and can only be determined in the light of actual state practice.[102] The balance between military necessity and humanitarian considerations is relevant here. The International Court in its Advisory Opinion on the *Legality of the Threat or Use of Nuclear Weapons*[103] summarised the situation in the following authoritative way:

> The cardinal principles contained in the texts constituting the fabric of humanitarian law are the following. The first is aimed at the protection of the civilian population and civilian objects and establishes the distinction between combatants and non-combatants; states must never make civilians the object of attack and must consequently never use weapons that are incapable of distinguishing between civilian and military targets. According to the second principle, it is prohibited to cause unnecessary suffering to combatants; it is accordingly prohibited to use weapons causing them such harm or uselessly aggravating their suffering. In application of that second principle, states do not have unlimited freedom of choice of means in the weapons they use.

The Court emphasised that the fundamental rules flowing from these principles bound all states, whether or not they had ratified the Hague and Geneva Conventions, since they constituted 'intransgressible principles of international customary law'.[104] At the heart of such rules and principles lies the 'overriding consideration of humanity'.[105] Whether the

---

[100] This is repeated in virtually identical terms in article 35, Protocol I.

[101] See article 35(2) of Protocol I and the Preamble to the 1980 Convention on Conventional Weapons: see M. N. Shaw, 'The United Nations Convention on Prohibitions or Restrictions on the Use of Certain Conventional Weapons, 1981', 9 *Review of International Studies*, 1983, p. 109 at p. 113. Note that 'employment of poisonous weapons or other weapons calculated to cause unnecessary suffering' is stated to be a violation of the laws and customs of war by article 3(a) of the Statute of the International Criminal Tribunal for the Former Yugoslavia: see Report of the UN Secretary-General, S/25704 and Security Council resolution 827 (1993), and see also article 20(d)e of the Draft Code of Crimes against the Peace and Security of Mankind, Report of the International Law Commission on the Work of its Forty-eighth Session, 1996, A/51/10, pp. 111–12.

[102] See e.g. the United States Department of the Army, *Field Manual, The Law of Land Warfare*, FM 27–10, 1956, p. 18, and regarding the UK, *The Law of War on Land*, Part III of the *Manual of Military Law*, 1958, p. 41.

[103] ICJ Reports, 1996, pp. 226, 257; 110 ILR, p. 163.   [104] *Ibid.*

[105] ICJ Reports, 1996, pp. 226, 257 and 262–3. See also the *Corfu Channel* case, ICJ Reports, 1949, pp. 4, 22; 16 AD, p. 155.

actual possession or threat or use of nuclear weapons would be regarded as illegal in international law has been a highly controversial question,[106] although there is no doubt that such weapons fall within the general application of international humanitarian law.[107] The International Court has emphasised that, in examining the legality of any particular situation, the principles regulating the resort to force, including the right to self-defence, need to be coupled with the requirement to consider also the norms governing the means and methods of warfare itself. Accordingly, the types of weapons used and the way in which they are used are also part of the legal equation in analysing the legitimacy of any use of force in international law.[108] The Court analysed state practice and concluded that nuclear weapons were not prohibited either specifically or by express provision.[109] Nor were they prohibited by analogy with poisoned gases prohibited under the Second Hague Declaration of 1899, article 23(a) of the Hague Regulations of 1907 and the Geneva Protocol of 1925.[110] Nor were they prohibited by the series of treaties[111] concerning the acquisition,

---

[106] See e.g. *Shimoda* v. *Japan* 32 ILR, p. 626.

[107] *Ibid.*, pp. 259–61. See e.g. *International Law, the International Court of Justice and Nuclear Weapons* (eds. L. Boisson de Chazournes and P. Sands), Cambridge, 1999; D. Akande, 'Nuclear Weapons, Unclear Law?', 68 BYIL, 1997, p. 165; *Nuclear Weapons and International Law* (ed. I. Pogany), Aldershot, 1987; Green, *Armed Conflict*, pp. 128 ff., and Green, 'Nuclear Weapons and the Law of Armed Conflict', 17 *Denver Journal of International Law and Policy*, 1988, p. 1; N. Singh and E. McWhinney, *Nuclear Weapons and Contemporary International Law*, Dordrecht, 1988; G. Schwarzenberger, *Legality of Nuclear Weapons*, London, 1957, and H. Meyrowitz, 'Les Armes Nucléaires et le Droit de la Guerre' in *Humanitarian Law of Armed Conflict: Challenges* (eds. A. J. M. Delissen and G. J. Tanja), Dordrecht, 1991.

[108] The Court emphasised, for example, that 'a use of force that is proportionate under the law of self-defence, must, in order to be lawful, also meet the requirements of the law applicable in armed conflict', ICJ Reports, 1996, pp. 226, 245; 110 ILR, p. 163. The Court also pointed to the applicability of the principle of neutrality to all international armed conflicts, irrespective of the type of weaponry used, ICJ Reports, 1996, p. 261. See also the *Nicaragua* case, ICJ Reports, 1986, pp. 3, 112; 76 ILR, pp. 349, 446.

[109] ICJ Reports, 1986, p. 247.

[110] *Ibid.*, p. 248. Nor by treaties concerning other weapons of mass destruction such as the Bacteriological Weapons Treaty, 1972 and the Chemical Weapons Treaty, 1993, *ibid.*, pp. 248–9.

[111] E.g. the Peace Treaties of 10 February 1947; the Austrian State Treaty, 1955; the Nuclear Test Ban Treaty, 1963; the Outer Space Treaty, 1967; the Treaty of Tlatelolco of 14 February 1967 on the Prohibition of Nuclear Weapons in Latin America; the Nuclear Non-Proliferation Treaty, 1968 (extended indefinitely in 1995); the Treaty on the Prohibition of the Emplacement of Nuclear Weapons on the Ocean Floor and Sub-soil, 1971; Treaty of Rarotongo of 6 August 1985 on the Nuclear Weapons-Free Zone of the South Pacific; the Treaty of Final Settlement with Respect to Germany, 1990; the Treaty on the

manufacture, deployment and testing of nuclear weapons and the treaties concerning the ban on such weapons in certain areas of the world.[112] Nor were nuclear weapons prohibited as a consequence of a series of General Assembly resolutions, which taken together fell short of establishing the necessary *opinio juris* for the creation of a new rule to that effect.[113] In so far as the principles of international humanitarian law were concerned, the Court, beyond noting their applicability, could reach no conclusion. The Court felt unable to determine whether the principle of neutrality or the principles of international humanitarian law or indeed the norm of self-defence prohibited the threat or use of nuclear weapons.[114] This rather weak conclusion, however, should be seen in the context of continuing efforts to ban all nuclear weapons testing, the increasing number of treaties prohibiting such weapons in specific geographical areas and the commitment given in 1995 by the five declared nuclear weapons states not to use such weapons against non-nuclear weapons states that are parties to the Nuclear Non-Proliferation Treaty.[115] Nevertheless, it does seem clear that the possession of nuclear weapons and their use *in extremis* and in strict accordance with the criteria governing the right to self-defence are not prohibited under international law.[116]

A number of specific bans on particular weapons has been imposed.[117] Examples would include small projectiles under the St Petersburg formula of 1868, dum-dum bullets under the Hague Declaration of 1899 and asphyxiating and deleterious gases under the Hague Declaration of 1899 and the 1925 Geneva Protocol.[118] Under the 1980 Conventional Weapons Treaty,[119] Protocol I, 1980, it is prohibited to use weapons that cannot be detected by X-rays, while Protocol II, 1980 (minimally amended in 1996), prohibits the use of mines and booby-traps against civilians, Protocol III, 1980, the use of incendiary devices against civilians or against military objectives located within a concentration of civilians where the attack is by

---

South East Asia Nuclear Weapon-Free Zone, 1995 and the Treaty on an African Nuclear Weapon-Free Zone, 1996.

[112] ICJ Reports, 1996, pp. 226, 248–53; 110 ILR, p. 163. [113] ICJ Reports, 1996, pp. 254–5.

[114] *Ibid.*, pp. 262–3 and 266. [115] See Security Council resolution 984 (1995).

[116] See also the UK, *Manual*, pp. 117 ff., and the US *The Law of Land Warfare*, 1956, s. 35.

[117] See e.g. Green, *Armed Conflict*, pp. 133 ff.

[118] See also e.g. the 1972 Convention on the Prohibition of the Development, Production and Stockpiling of Bacteriological Weapons and the 1993 Convention on the Prohibition of the Development, Production, Stockpiling and Use of Chemical Weapons and Their Destruction. See 21(3) *UN Chronicle*, 1984, p. 3 with regard to the use of chemical weapons in the Iran–Iraq war.

[119] See Shaw, 'Conventional Weapons'. Note article 1 was amended in 2001.

air-delivered incendiary weapons, Protocol IV, 1995, the use of blinding laser weapons and Protocol V, 2003, concerns the explosive remnants of war. In 1997, the Ottawa Convention on the Prohibition of the Use, Stockpiling, Production and Transfer of Anti-Personnel Mines and on their Destruction was adopted.[120]

Article 35(3) of Additional Protocol I to the 1949 Conventions provides that it is prohibited to employ methods or means of warfare which are intended, or may be expected, to cause widespread, long-term and severe damage to the natural environment.[121] Article 55 further states that care is to be taken in warfare to protect the natural environment against such damage, which may prejudice the health or survival of the population, while noting also that attacks against the natural environment by way of reprisals are prohibited. The Convention on the Prohibition of Military or Any Other Hostile Use of Environmental Modification Techniques, 1977 prohibits such activities having widespread, long-lasting or severe effects as the means of destruction, damage or injury to any other state party.

Armed conflicts: international and internal

The rules of international humanitarian law apply to armed conflicts. Accordingly, no formal declaration of war is required in order for the Conventions to apply. The concept of 'armed conflict' is not defined in the Conventions or Protocols, although it has been noted that 'any difference arising between states and leading to the intervention of members of the armed forces is an armed conflict' and 'an armed conflict exists whenever there is a resort to armed force between states or protracted armed violence between governmental authorities and organized armed groups within a state'.[122]

---

[120] Note the adoption on 30 May 2008 of a Convention banning the use, stockpiling, production and transfer of cluster munitions.

[121] See, for example, the deliberate spillage of vast quantities of oil into the Persian Gulf by Iraq during the 1991 Gulf War: see *The Economist*, 2 February 1991, p. 20. See also Green, *Armed Conflict*, p. 138, and Rogers, *Law of the Battlefield*, chapter 6.

[122] J. Pictet, *Commentary on the Geneva Conventions of 12 August 1949*, Geneva, 1952, vol. I, p. 29. In the *Tadić* case, IT-94-1, Decision on Jurisdiction, para. 70; 105 ILR, pp. 453, 488, the Appeals Chamber of the International Criminal Tribunal for the Former Yugoslavia stated that, 'an armed conflict exists whenever there is a resort to armed force between states or protracted armed violence between governmental authorities and organised armed groups or between such groups within a state'.

A distinction has historically been drawn between international and non-international armed conflicts,[123] founded upon the difference between inter-state relations, which was the proper focus for international law, and intra-state matters which traditionally fell within the domestic jurisdiction of states and were thus in principle impervious to international legal regulation. However, this difference has been breaking down in recent decades. In the sphere of humanitarian law, this can be seen in the gradual application of such rules to internal armed conflicts.[124] The notion of an armed conflict itself was raised before the Appeals Chamber of the International Criminal Tribunal for the Former Yugoslavia in its decision on jurisdictional issues in the *Tadić* case.[125] It was claimed that no armed conflict as such existed in the Former Yugoslavia with respect to the circumstances of the instant case since the concept of armed conflict covered only the precise time and place of actual hostilities and the events alleged before the Tribunal did not take place during hostilities. The Appeals Chamber of the Tribunal correctly refused to accept a narrow geographical and temporal definition of armed conflicts, whether international or internal. It was stated that:[126]

> International humanitarian law applies from the initiation of such armed conflicts and extends beyond the cessation of hostilities until a general conclusion of peace is reached; or, in the case of internal conflicts, a peaceful settlement is achieved. Until that moment, international humanitarian law continues to apply in the whole territory of the warring states or, in the case of internal conflicts, the whole territory under the control of a party, whether or not actual combat takes place.

This definition arose in the specific context of the Former Yugoslavia, where it was unclear whether an international or a non-international armed conflict or some kind of mixture of the two was involved. This was important to clarify since it would have had an effect upon the relevant applicable law. The Security Council did not as such classify the nature of the conflict, simply condemning widespread violations of international humanitarian law, including mass forcible expulsion and deportation of civilians, imprisonment and abuse of civilians and deliberate attacks upon non-combatants, and calling for the cessation.[127] The Appeals Chamber

---

[123] See e.g. Green, *Armed Conflict*, chapter 3.   [124] See further below, p. 1194.
[125] Case No. IT-94-1-AR 72; 105 ILR, pp. 453, 486 ff.   [126] *Ibid.*, p. 488.
[127] See e.g. Security Council resolution 771 (1992). See also C. Gray, 'Bosnia and Herzegovina: Civil War or Inter-State Conflict? Characterisation and Consequences', 67 BYIL, 1996, p. 155.

concluded that 'the conflicts in the former Yugoslavia have both internal and international aspects'.[128] Since such conflicts could be classified differently according to time and place, a particularly complex situation was created. However, many of the difficulties that this would have created were mitigated by an acceptance of the evolving application of humanitarian law to internal armed conflicts.[129] This development has arisen partly because of the increasing frequency of internal conflicts and partly because of the increasing brutality in their conduct. The growing interdependence of states in the modern world makes it more and more difficult for third states and international organisations to ignore civil conflicts, especially in view of the scope and insistence of modern communications, while the evolution of international human rights law has contributed to the end of the belief and norm that whatever occurs within other states is the concern of no other state or person.[130] Accordingly, the international community is now more willing to demand the application of international humanitarian law to internal conflicts.[131] In the *Tadić* case, the Appeals Chamber (in considering jurisdictional issues) concluded that article 3 of its Statute, which gave it jurisdiction over 'violations of the laws or customs of war',[132] provided it with such jurisdiction 'regardless of whether they occurred within an internal or an international armed conflict'.[133] In its decision, the Appeals Chamber noted that,

> It is indisputable that an armed conflict is international if it takes place between two or more States. In addition, in case of an internal armed conflict breaking out on the territory of a State, it may become international (or, depending upon the circumstances, be international in character alongside

---

[128] Case No. IT-94-1-AR; 105 ILR, pp. 453, 494.   [129] *Ibid.*, pp. 495 ff.

[130] See e.g. General Assembly resolutions 2444 (XXV) and 2675 (XXV), adopted in 1970 unanimously.

[131] See e.g. Security Council resolutions 788 (1992), 972 (1995) and 1001 (1995) with regard to the Liberian civil war; Security Council resolutions 794 (1992) and 814 (1993) with regard to Somalia; Security Council resolution 993 (1993) with regard to Georgia and resolution 1193 (1998) with regard to Afghanistan.

[132] An historic term now subsumed within the concept of international humanitarian law. Article 3 states that such violations shall include, but not be limited to, the employment of poisonous weapons or other weapons calculated to cause unnecessary suffering; wanton destruction of cities, towns or villages or devastation not justified by military necessity; attack or bombardment of undefended towns, villages or buildings; seizure of or destruction or wilful damage done to institutions dedicated to religion, charity and education, the arts and sciences, historic monuments and works of art and science; and plunder of public or private property.

[133] Case No. IT-94-1-AR 72; 105 ILR, pp. 453, 504. See also the *Furundžija* case, Case No. IT-95-17/1 (decision of Trial Chamber II, 10 December 1998); 121 ILR, pp. 213, 253–4.

an internal armed conflict) if (i) another State intervenes in that conflict through its troops, or alternatively if (ii) some of the participants in the internal armed conflict act on behalf of that other State.[134]

The Appeals Chamber concluded that until 19 May 1992 with the open involvement of the Federal Yugoslav Army, the conflict in Bosnia had been international, but the question arose as to the situation when this army was withdrawn at that date. The Chamber examined the legal criteria for establishing when, in an armed conflict which is *prima facie* internal, armed forces may be regarded as acting on behalf of a foreign power thus turning the conflict into an international one. The Chamber examined article 4 of the Third Geneva Convention which defines prisoner of war status[135] and noted that states have in practice accepted that belligerents may use paramilitary units and other irregulars in the conduct of hostilities only on the condition that those belligerents are prepared to take responsibility for any infringements committed by such forces. In order for irregulars to qualify as lawful combatants, control over them by a party to an international armed conflict was required and thus a relationship of dependence and allegiance. Accordingly, the term 'belonging to a party to the conflict' used in article 4 implicitly refers to a test of control.[136]

In order to determine the meaning of 'control', the decision of the International Court in the *Nicaragua* case was examined[137] and rejected, the Appeals Chamber preferring a rather weaker test, concluding that in order to attribute the acts of a military or paramilitary group to a state, it must be proved that the state wields overall control over the group, not only by equipping and financing the group, but also by co-ordinating or helping in the general planning of its military activity. However, it was not necessary that, in addition, the state should also issue, either to the head

---

[134] Judgment of 15 July 1999, para. 84; 124 ILR, p. 96.   [135] See above, p. 1172.

[136] Judgment of 15 July 1999, paras. 94 and 95; 124 ILR, p. 100.

[137] In that case it was held that in order to establish the responsibility of the US over the 'Contra' rebels, it was necessary to show that the state was not only in effective control of a military or paramilitary group, but also that there was effective control of the specific operation in the course of which breaches may have been committed. In order to establish that the US was responsible for 'acts contrary to human rights and humanitarian law' allegedly perpetrated by the Nicaraguan Contras, it was necessary to prove that the US had specifically 'directed or enforced' the perpetration of those acts: see ICJ Reports, 1986, pp. 14, 64–5; 76 ILR, p. 349. The International Court in the *Genocide Convention (Bosnia v. Serbia)* case, ICJ Reports, 2007, reaffirmed its decision in the *Nicaragua* case on this point and distinguished the *Tadić* case: see above, chapter 14, p. 791.

or to members of the group, instructions for the commission of specific acts contrary to international law.[138]

Accordingly, the line between international and internal armed conflicts may be drawn at the point at which it can be shown that a foreign state is either directly intervening within a civil conflict or exercising 'overall control' over a group that is fighting in that conflict.

The Appeals Chamber in the *Kunarac* case discussed the issue of the meaning of armed conflict where the fighting is sporadic and does not extend to all of the territory of the state concerned. The Chamber held that the laws of war would apply in the whole territory of the warring states or, in the case of internal armed conflicts, the whole territory under the control of a party to the conflict, whether or not actual combat takes place there, and continued to apply until a general conclusion of peace or, in the case of internal armed conflicts, a peaceful settlement is achieved. A violation of the laws or customs of war may therefore occur at a time when and in a place where no fighting is actually taking place.[139]

Non-international armed conflict[140]

Although the 1949 Geneva Conventions were concerned with international armed conflicts, common article 3 did provide in cases of non-international armed conflicts occurring in the territory of one of the parties a series of minimum guarantees for protecting those not taking an active part in hostilities, including the sick and wounded.[141] Precisely where this article applied was difficult to define in all cases. Non-international armed conflicts could, it may be argued, range from full-scale civil wars to relatively minor disturbances. This poses problems for the state in question which may not appreciate the political implications of the application of the Geneva Conventions, and the lack of the reciprocity element due to the absence of another state adds to the problems of enforcement.

---

[138] Judgment of 15 July 1999, paras. 131 and 145; 124 ILR, pp. 116 and 121.

[139] Decision of 12 June 2002, Case No. IT-96-23 and IT-96-23/1, para. 57.

[140] See e.g. UK, *Manual*, chapter 15; L. Moir, *The Law of Internal Armed Conflict*, Cambridge, 2002; Green, *Armed Conflict*, chapter 19, and T. Meron, *Human Rights in Internal Strife*, Cambridge, 1987. See also ICRC, *Increasing Respect for International Humanitarian Law in Non-International Armed Conflicts*, Geneva, 2008.

[141] Note that the Court in the *Nicaragua* case, ICJ Reports, 1986, pp. 3, 114; 76 ILR, pp. 349, 448, declared that common article 3 also applied to international armed conflicts as a 'minimum yardstick, in addition to the more elaborate rules which are also to apply to international conflicts'.

Common article 3 lists the following as the minimum safeguards:

1. Persons taking no active part in hostilities to be treated humanely without any adverse distinction based on race, colour, religion or faith, sex, birth or wealth.

To this end the following are prohibited:

 a) violence to life and person, in particular murder, cruel treatment and torture;
 b) hostage-taking;
 c) outrages upon human dignity, in particular humiliating and degrading treatment;
 d) the passing of sentences and the carrying out of executions in the absence of due process.

2. The wounded and the sick are to be cared for.

Common article 3[142] was developed by Protocol II, 1977,[143] which applies by virtue of article 1 to all non-international armed conflicts which take place in the territory of a state party between its armed forces and dissident armed forces. The latter have to be under responsible command and exercise such control over a part of its territory as to enable them to carry out sustained and concerted military operations and actually implement Protocol II. It does not apply to situations of internal disturbances and tensions, such as riots, isolated and sporadic acts of violence and other acts of a similar nature, not being armed conflicts.[144] The Protocol lists a series of fundamental guarantees and other provisions calling for the

---

[142] The International Court in the *Nicaragua* case stated that the rules contained in common article 3 reflected 'elementary considerations of humanity', ICJ Reports, 1986, pp. 14, 114; 76 ILR, p. 349. See also the *Tadić* case, Case No. IT-94-1-AR; 105 ILR, pp. 453, 506.

[143] Note, of course, that by article 1(4) of Protocol I, 1977, international armed conflicts are now deemed to include armed conflicts in which peoples are fighting against colonial domination, alien occupation and racist regimes: see D. Forsyth, 'Legal Management of International War', 72 AJIL, 1978, p. 272. Article 96(3), Protocol I, requires the authority representing such peoples to make a special declaration undertaking to apply the Geneva Conventions and Protocol I. The UK made a declaration on ratification of Protocol I to the effect that it would not be bound by any such special declaration unless the UK has expressly recognised that it has been made by a body 'which is genuinely an authority representing a people engaged in an armed conflict': see UK, *Manual*, p. 384. Note also the UK view that 'a high level of intensity of military operations' is required regarding Protocol I so that the Northern Ireland situation, for example, would not have been covered: see 941 HC Deb., col. 237.

[144] See article 1(2), Protocol II and see article 8(2)d of the Rome Statute of the International Criminal Court, 1998. Article 8(2)e of the Rome Statute lists a series of acts which if committed in internal armed conflicts are considered war crimes.

protection of non-combatants.[145] In particular, one may note the prohibitions on violence to the life, health and physical and mental well-being of persons, including torture; collective punishment; hostage-taking; acts of terrorism; outrages upon personal dignity, including rape and enforced prostitution; and pillage.[146] Further provisions cover the protection of children;[147] the protection of civilians, including the prohibition of attacks on works or installations containing dangerous forces that might cause severe losses among civilians;[148] the treatment of civilians, including their displacement;[149] and the treatment of prisoners and detainees,[150] and the wounded and sick.[151]

The Appeals Chamber in its decision on jurisdiction in the *Tadić* case noted that international legal rules had developed to regulate internal armed conflict for a number of reasons, including the frequency of civil wars, the increasing cruelty of internal armed conflicts, the large-scale nature of civil strife making third-party involvement more likely and the growth of international human rights law. Thus the distinction between inter-state and civil wars was losing its value so far as human beings were concerned.[152] Indeed, one of the major themes of international humanitarian law has been the growing move towards the rules of human rights law and vice versa.[153] There is a common foundation in the principle of respect for human dignity.[154]

---

[145] Note that in non-international armed conflicts the domestic law of the state in which the conflict is taking place continues to apply and that a captured rebel is not entitled to POW status. However, persons captured from either the government or rebel or opposition side are entitled to humane treatment: see e.g. UK, *Manual*, pp. 387 ff.

[146] See article 4.   [147] Article 6.   [148] Article 15.   [149] Article 17.   [150] Article 5.

[151] Article 10. Note that the International Criminal Tribunal for Rwanda has jurisdiction to try violations of common article 3 and Protocol II. These are defined in article 4 of its Statute as including: '(a) Violence to life, health and physical or mental well-being of persons, in particular murder as well as cruel treatment such as torture, mutilation or any form of corporal punishment; (b) Collective punishments; (c) Taking of hostages; (d) Acts of terrorism; (e) Outrages upon personal dignity, in particular humiliating and degrading treatment, rape, enforced prostitution and any form of indecent assault; (f) Pillage; (g) The passing of sentences and the carrying out of executions without previous judgment pronounced by a regularly constituted court, affording all the judicial guarantees which are recognized as indispensable by civilised peoples; and (h) Threats to commit any of the foregoing acts.'

[152] Case No. IT-94-1-AR; 105 ILR, pp. 453, 505 ff. But see Moir, *Internal Armed Conflict*, pp. 188 ff., and Meron, 'The Continuing Role of Custom in the Formation of International Humanitarian Law', 90 AJIL, 1996, pp. 238, 242–3.

[153] See e.g. Moir, *Internal Armed Conflict*, chapter 5, and R. Provost, *International Human Rights and Humanitarian Law*, Cambridge, 2002. See also above, p. 1180.

[154] See the *Furundžija* case, 121 ILR, pp. 213, 271.

The principles governing internal armed conflicts in humanitarian law are becoming more extensive, while the principles of international human rights law are also rapidly evolving, particularly with regard to the fundamental non-derogable rights which cannot be breached even in times of public emergency.[155] This area of overlap was recognised in 1970 in General Assembly resolution 2675 (XXV) which emphasised that fundamental human rights 'continue to apply fully in situations of armed conflict', while the European Commission on Human Rights in the *Cyprus v. Turkey (First and Second Applications)* case declared that in belligerent operations a state was bound to respect not only the humanitarian law laid down in the Geneva Conventions but also fundamental human rights.[156]

The Inter-American Commission of Human Rights in the *La Tablada* case against Argentina noted that the most difficult aspect of common article 3 related to its application at the blurred line at the lower end separating it from especially violent internal disturbances.[157] It was in situations of internal armed conflict that international humanitarian law and international human rights law 'most converge and reinforce each other', so that, for example, common article 3 and article 4 of the Inter-American Convention on Human Rights both protected the right to life and prohibited arbitrary execution. However, there are difficulties in resorting simply to human rights law when issues of the right to life arise in combat situations. Accordingly, 'the Commission must necessarily look to and apply definitional standards and relevant rules of humanitarian law as sources of authoritative guidance in its resolution' of such issues.[158]

The Commission returned to the issue in *Coard v. USA* and noted that there was 'an integral linkage between the law of human rights and the humanitarian law because they share a "common nucleus of non-derogable rights and a common purpose of protecting human life and dignity", and there may be a substantial overlap in the application of these bodies of law'.[159]

However, in addition to the overlap between internal armed conflict principles and those of human rights law in situations where the level of

---

[155] See e.g. article 15 of the European Convention on Human Rights, 1950; article 4 of the International Covenant on Civil and Political Rights, 1966; and article 27 of the Inter-American Convention on Human Rights, 1969. See also above, chapters 6 and 7.

[156] Report of the Commission of 10 July 1976, paras. 509–10.

[157] Report No. 55/97, Case 11.137 and OEA/Ser.L/V/II.98, para. 153.

[158] *Ibid.*, paras. 160–1.   [159] Case No. 10.951; 123 ILR, pp. 156, 169 (footnote omitted).

domestic violence has reached a degree of intensity and continuity, there exists an area of civil conflict which is not covered by humanitarian law since it falls below the necessary threshold of common article 3 and Protocol II.[160] Moves have been underway to bridge the gap between this and the application of international human rights law.[161] The International Committee of the Red Cross has been considering the elaboration of a new declaration on internal strife. In addition, a Declaration of Minimum Humanitarian Standards was adopted by a group of experts in 1990.[162] This Declaration emphasises the prohibition of violence to the life, health and physical and mental well-being of persons, including murder, torture and rape; collective punishment; hostage-taking; practising, permitting or tolerating the involuntary disappearance of individuals; pillage; deliberate deprivation of access to necessary food, drinking water and medicine, and threats or incitement to commit any of these acts.[163] In addition, the Declaration provides *inter alia* that persons deprived of their liberty should be held in recognised places of detention (article 4); that acts or threats of violence to spread terror are prohibited (article 6); that all human beings have the inherent right to life (article 8); that children are to be protected so that, for example, children under fifteen years of age should not be permitted to join armed groups or forces (article 10); that the wounded and sick should be cared for (article 12) and medical, religious and other humanitarian personnel should be protected and assisted (article 14).[164]

---

[160] See A. Hay, 'The ICRC and International Humanitarian Issues', *International Review of the Red Cross*, Jan–Feb 1984, p. 3. See also T. Meron, 'Towards a Humanitarian Declaration on Internal Strife', 78 AJIL, 1984, p. 859; Meron, *Human Rights in Internal Strife*, and Meron, 'On the Inadequate Reach of Humanitarian and Human Rights Law and the Need for a New Instrument', 77 AJIL, 1983, p. 589, and T. Meron and A. Rosas, 'A Declaration of Minimum Humanitarian Standards', 85 AJIL, 1991, p. 375.

[161] As to international human rights law, see generally above, chapter 6. Problems centre upon the situation where humanitarian law does not apply since the threshold criteria for applicability have not been reached; where the state in question is not a party to the relevant instrument; where derogation from the specified standards is involved as a consequence of the declaration of a state of emergency, and where the party concerned is not a government: see A. Eide, A. Rosas and T. Meron, 'Combating Lawlessness in Gray Zone Conflicts Through Minimum Humanitarian Standards', 89 AJIL, 1995, pp. 215, 217.

[162] This was reprinted in the Report of the UN Sub-Commission: see E/CN.4/1995/116 (1995) and UN Commission on Human Rights resolution 1995/29 and E/CN.4/1995/81 and 116. See also T. Meron and A. Rosas, 'Current Development: A Declaration of Minimum Humanitarian Standards', 85 AJIL, 1991, pp. 375, 375–7.

[163] Article 3.

[164] See also the Declaration for the Protection of War Victims, 1993, A/48/742, Annex.

Enforcement of humanitarian law[165]

Parties to the 1949 Geneva Conventions and to Protocol I, 1977, undertake to respect and to ensure respect for the instrument in question,[166] and to disseminate knowledge of the principles contained therein.[167] A variety of enforcement methods also exist, although the use of reprisals has been prohibited.[168] One of the means of implementation is the concept of the Protecting Power, appointed to look after the interests of nationals of one party to a conflict under the control of the other, whether as prisoners of war or occupied civilians.[169] Sweden and Switzerland performed this role during the Second World War. Such a Power must ensure that compliance with the relevant provisions has been effected and that the system acts as a form of guarantee for the protected person as well as a channel of communication for him with the state of which he is a national. The drawback of this system is its dependence upon the consent of the parties involved. Not only must the Protecting Power be prepared to act in that capacity, but both the state of which the protected person is a national and the state holding such persons must give their consent for the system to operate.[170] Since the role is so central to the enforcement and working of humanitarian law, it is a disadvantage for it to be subject to state sovereignty and consent. It only requires the holding state to refuse its cooperation for this structure of implementation to be greatly weakened, leaving only reliance upon voluntary operations. This has occurred on a number of occasions, for example the Chinese refusal to consent to the appointment of a Protecting Power with regard to its conflict with India in 1962, and the Indian refusal, of 1971 and subsequently, with regard to Pakistani prisoners of war in its charge.[171] Protocol I also provides for an International Fact-Finding Commission for competence to inquire into grave breaches[172] of the Geneva Conventions and that Protocol or other

---

[165] See e.g. UK, *Manual*, chapter 16, and Best, *War and Law*, pp. 370 ff.

[166] Common article 1.

[167] See e.g. articles 127 and 144 of the Third and Fourth Geneva Conventions, article 83 of Protocol I and article 19 of Protocol II.

[168] See e.g. articles 20 and 51(6) of Protocol I.

[169] See e.g. Draper, 'Implementation and Enforcement', pp. 13 ff.

[170] See articles 8, 8, 8 and 9 of the Four Geneva Conventions, 1949, respectively.

[171] Note that the system did operate in the Falklands conflict, with Switzerland acting as the Protecting Power of the UK and Brazil as the Protecting Power of Argentina: see e.g. Levie, 'Falklands Crisis', pp. 68–9.

[172] See articles 50, 51, 130 and 147 of the four 1949 Conventions respectively and article 85 of Protocol I, 1977. A Commission of Experts was established in 1992 to investigate violations of international humanitarian law in the territory of the Former Yugoslavia:

serious violations, and to facilitate through its good offices the 'restoration of an attitude of respect' for these instruments.[173] The parties to a conflict may themselves, of course, establish an ad hoc inquiry into alleged violations of humanitarian law.[174]

It is, of course, also the case that breaches of international law in this field may constitute war crimes or crimes against humanity or even genocide for which universal jurisdiction is provided.[175] Article 6 of the Charter of the Nuremberg Tribunal, 1945, for example, includes as war crimes for which there is to be individual responsibility the murder, ill-treatment or deportation to slave labour of the civilian population of an occupied territory; the ill-treatment of prisoners of war; the killing of hostages and the wanton destruction of cities, towns and villages.[176]

A great deal of valuable work in the sphere of humanitarian law has been accomplished by the International Red Cross.[177] This indispensable organisation consists of the International Committee of the Red Cross (ICRC), over 100 national Red Cross (or Red Crescent) societies with a League co-ordinating their activities, and conferences of all these elements every four years. The ICRC is the most active body and has a wide-ranging series of functions to perform, including working for the application of the Geneva Conventions and acting in natural and man-made disasters. It has operated in a large number of states, visiting prisoners of war[178] and otherwise functioning to ensure the implementation of humanitarian law.[179] It operates in both international and internal armed conflict

---

see Security Council resolution 780 (1992). See also the Report of the Commission of 27 May 1994, S/1994/674.

[173] Article 90, Protocol I, 1977.

[174] Articles 52, 53, 132 and 149 of the four 1949 Conventions respectively.

[175] See e.g. Draper, 'Implementation and Enforcement', pp. 35 ff. Note also that grave breaches are to be the subject of sanction.

[176] See further, with regard to the statutes of the various war crimes tribunals, above, chapters 8 and 12. Note also the UN Compensation Commission dealing with compensation for victims of Iraq's invasion of Kuwait in 1990, above, chapter 18, p. 1045.

[177] See e.g. G. Willemin and R. Heacock, *The International Committee of the Red Cross*, The Hague, 1984, and D. Forsythe, 'The Red Cross as Transnational Movement', 30 *International Organisation*, 1967, p. 607. See also Best, *War and Law*, pp. 347 ff.

[178] See e.g. articles 126 and 142 of the Third and Fourth Geneva Conventions respectively.

[179] The International Court in the *Construction of a Wall* case, ICJ Reports, 2004, pp. 136, 175–6; 129 ILR, pp. 37, 94, referred to the 'special position' of the ICRC with regard to the Fourth Geneva Convention, while the Eritrea–Ethiopia Claims Commission in the Partial Award, Prisoners of War, Ethiopia's Claim 4, 1 July 2003, paras. 58 and 61–2, noted that the ICRC had been assigned significant responsibilities in a number of articles of the Third Geneva Convention (with which it was concerned) both as 'a humanitarian organization providing relief and as an organization providing necessary and vital external scrutiny of

situations. One of the largest operations it has undertaken since 1948 related to the Nigerian civil war, and in that conflict nearly twenty of its personnel were killed on duty. The ICRC has since been deeply involved in the Yugoslav situation and indeed, in 1992, contrary to its usual confidentiality approach, it felt impelled to speak out publicly against the grave breaches of humanitarian law taking place. The organisation has also been involved in Somalia (where its activities included visiting detainees held by the UN forces), Rwanda, Afghanistan, Sri Lanka[180] and in Iraq. Due to circumstances, the ICRC must act with tact and discretion and in many cases states refuse their co-operation. It performed a valuable function in the exchange of prisoners after the 1967 and 1973 Middle East wars, although for several years Israel did not accept the ICRC role regarding the Arab territories it occupied.[181]

Conclusion

The ICRC formulated the following principles as a guide to the relevant legal rules:

1. Persons *hors de combat* and those who do not take a direct part in hostilities are entitled to respect for their lives and physical and moral integrity. They shall in all circumstances be protected and treated humanely without any adverse distinctions.
2. It is forbidden to kill or injure an enemy who surrenders or who is *hors de combat.*
3. The wounded and sick shall be collected and cared for by the party to the conflict which has them in its power. Protection also covers medical personnel, establishments, transports and *matériel*. The emblem of the red cross (red crescent, red lion and sun) is the sign of such protection and must be respected.
4. Captured combatants and civilians under the authority of an adverse party are entitled to respect for their lives, dignity, personal rights and convictions. They shall be protected against all acts of violence and

the treatment of POWs' and further emphasised that the provisions requiring scrutiny of the treatment of, and access to, POWs had become part of customary international law.

[180] See e.g. *Challenges of the Nineties: ICRC Special Report on Activities 1990–1995*, Geneva, 1995. Between 1990 and 1994, over half a million prisoners in over sixty countries were visited by ICRC delegates, *ibid.*

[181] See generally *Annual Report of the ICRC*, 1982. See also 'Action by the ICRC in the Event of Breaches of International Humanitarian Law', *International Review of the Red Cross*, March–April 1981, p. 1.

reprisals. They shall have the right to correspond with their families and to receive relief.

5. Everyone shall be entitled to benefit from fundamental judicial guarantees. No one shall be held responsible for an act he has not committed. No one shall be subjected to physical or mental torture, corporal punishment or cruel or degrading treatment.

6. Parties to a conflict and members of their armed forces do not have an unlimited choice of methods and means of warfare. It is prohibited to employ weapons or methods of warfare of a nature to cause unnecessary losses or excessive suffering.

7. Parties to a conflict shall at all times distinguish between the civilian population and combatants in order to spare civilian population and property. Neither the civilian populations as such nor civilian persons shall be the object for attack. Attacks shall be directed solely against military objectives.[182]

In addition, the ICRC has published the following statement with regard to non-international armed conflicts:

A. General Rules

1. The obligation to distinguish between combatants and civilians is a general rule applicable in non-international armed conflicts. It prohibits indiscriminate attacks.

2. The prohibition of attacks against the civilian population as such or against individual civilians is a general rule applicable in non-international armed conflicts. Acts of violence intended primarily to spread terror among the civilian population are also prohibited.

3. The prohibition of superfluous injury or unnecessary suffering is a general rule applicable in non-international armed conflicts. It prohibits, in particular, the use of means of warfare which uselessly aggravate the sufferings of disabled men or render their death inevitable.

4. The prohibition to kill, injure or capture an adversary by resort to perfidy is a general rule applicable in non-international armed conflicts; in a non-international armed conflict, acts inviting the confidence of an adversary to lead him to believe that he is entitled to, or obliged to accord protection under the rules of international law applicable in non-international armed conflicts, with intent to betray that confidence, shall constitute perfidy.

---

[182] See *International Review of the Red Cross*, Sept.–Oct. 1978, p. 247. See also Green, *Armed Conflict*, pp. 355–6.

5. The obligation to respect and protect medical and religious personnel and medical units and transports in the conduct of military operations is a general rule applicable in non-international armed conflicts.

6. The general rule prohibiting attacks against the civilian population implies, as a corollary, the prohibition of attacks on dwellings and other installations which are used only by the civilian population.

7. The general rule prohibiting attacks against the civilian population implies, as a corollary, the prohibition to attack, destroy, remove or render useless objects indispensable to the survival of the civilian population.

8. The general rule to distinguish between combatants and civilians and the prohibition of attack against the civilian population as such or against individual civilians implies, in order to be effective, that all feasible precautions have to be taken to avoid injury, loss or damage to the civilian population.[183]

Suggestions for further reading

I. Detter, *The Law of War*, 2nd edn, Cambridge, 2000

Y. Dinstein, *The Conduct of Hostilities under the Law of International Armed Conflict*, Cambridge, 2004

L. Green, *The Contemporary Law of Armed Conflict*, 2nd edn, Manchester, 2000

UK Ministry of Defence, *Manual on the Law of Armed Conflict*, Oxford, 2004

---

[183] See *International Review of the Red Cross*, Sept.–Oct. 1989, p. 404. See also Green, *Armed Conflict*, p. 356. Part B of this Declaration dealing with Prohibitions and Restrictions on the Use of Certain Weapons has been omitted. It may be found at the above references.

22

The United Nations

The UN system

The United Nations[1] was established following the conclusion of the Second World War and in the light of Allied planning and intentions expressed during that conflict.[2] The purposes of the UN are set out in article 1 of the Charter as follows:

> 1. To maintain international peace and security, and to that end, to take effective collective measures for the prevention and removal of threats to the peace, and for the suppression of acts of aggression or other breaches of the peace, and to bring about by peaceful means, and in conformity with the principles of justice and international law, adjustment or settlement of international disputes or situations which might lead to a breach of the peace;
>
> 2. To develop friendly relations among nations based on respect for the principle of equal rights and self-determination of peoples, and to take other appropriate measures to strengthen universal peace;
>
> 3. To achieve international co-operation in solving international problems of an economic, social, cultural or humanitarian character, and in

---

[1] See e.g. *The Charter of the United Nations* (ed. B. Simma), 2nd edn, Oxford, 2002; J. P. Cot, A. Pellet and M. Forteau, *La Charte des Nations Unies: Commentaire Article par Article*, 3rd edn, Paris, 2005; S. Chesterman, T. M. Franck and D. M. Malone, *Law and Practice of the United Nations*, Oxford, 2008; *La Charte des Nations Unies, Constitution Mondiale?* (eds. R. Chemain and A. Pellet), Paris 2006; B. Conforti, *The Law and Practice of the United Nations*, 2nd edn, The Hague, 2000; *United Nations Legal Order* (eds. O. Schachter and C. C. Joyner), Cambridge, 2 vols., 1995; *Bowett's Law of International Institutions* (eds. P. Sands and P. Klein), 5th edn, London, 2001, chapter 2; *The United Nations and a Just World Order* (eds. R. A. Falk, S. S. Kim and S. H. Mendlovitz), Boulder, 1991; B. Broms, *United Nations*, Helsinki, 1990; E. Luard, *A History of the United Nations*, London, 1982, vol. I; R. Higgins, *The Development of International Law Through the Political Organs of the United Nations*, Oxford, 1963; *United Nations, Divided World* (eds. A. Roberts and B. Kingsbury), 2nd edn, Oxford, 1993; L. M. Goodrich, *The United Nations in a Changing World*, New York, 1974; the *Bertrand Report*, 1985, A/40/988, and L. M. Goodrich, E. Hambro and A. P. Simons, *Charter of the United Nations*, 3rd edn, New York, 1969. See also www.un.org/.

[2] See UNCIO, San Francisco, 15 vols., 1945.

promoting and encouraging respect for human rights and for fundamental freedoms for all without distinction as to race, sex, language, or religion; and

4. To be a centre for harmonizing the actions of nations in the attainment of these common ends.

While the purposes are clearly wide-ranging, they do provide a useful guide to the comprehensiveness of its concerns. The question of priorities as between the various issues noted is constantly subject to controversy and change, but this only reflects the continuing pressures and altering political balances within the organisation. In particular, the emphasis upon decolonisation, self-determination and apartheid mirrored the growth in UN membership and the dismantling of the colonial empires, while increasing concern with economic and developmental issues is now very apparent and clearly reflects the adverse economic conditions in various parts of the world.

The Charter of the United Nations is not only the multilateral treaty which created the organisation and outlined the rights and obligations of those states signing it, it is also the constitution of the UN, laying down its functions and prescribing its limitations.[3] Foremost amongst these is the recognition of the sovereignty and independence of the member states. Under article 2(7) of the Charter, the UN may not intervene in matters essentially within the domestic jurisdiction of any state (unless enforcement measures under Chapter VII are to be applied). This provision has inspired many debates in the UN, and it came to be accepted that colonial issues were not to be regarded as falling within the article 2(7) restriction. Other changes have also occurred, demonstrating that the concept of domestic jurisdiction is not immutable but a principle of international law delineating international and domestic spheres of operations. As a principle of international law it is susceptible of change through international law and is not dependent upon the unilateral determination of individual states.[4]

In addition to the domestic jurisdiction provision, article 2 also lays down a variety of other principles in accordance with which both the UN and the member states are obliged to act. These include the assertion that the UN is based upon the sovereign equality of states and the principles of fulfilment in good faith of the obligations contained in the Charter, the peaceful settlement of disputes and the prohibition on the use of force.

[3] See Chesterman *et al.*, *United Nations*, pp. 4 ff.   [4] See above, chapter 12, p. 647.

It is also provided that member states must assist the organisation in its activities taken in accordance with the Charter and must refrain from assisting states against which the UN is taking preventive or enforcement action.

The UN has six principal organs, these being the Security Council, General Assembly, Economic and Social Council, Trusteeship Council, Secretariat and International Court of Justice.[5]

The Security Council[6]

The Council was intended to operate as an efficient executive organ of limited membership, functioning continuously. It was given primary responsibility for the maintenance of international peace and security.[7] The Security Council consists of fifteen members, five of them being permanent members (USA, UK, Russia, China and France). These permanent members, chosen on the basis of power politics in 1945, have the veto. Under article 27 of the Charter, on all but procedural matters, decisions of the Council must be made by an affirmative vote of nine members, including the concurring votes of the permanent members.

A negative vote by any of the permanent members is therefore sufficient to veto any resolution of the Council, save with regard to procedural questions, where nine affirmative votes are all that is required. The veto was written into the Charter in view of the exigencies of power. The USSR, in particular, would not have been willing to accept the UN as it was envisaged without the establishment of the veto to protect it from the Western bias of the Council and General Assembly at that time.[8] In practice, the veto was exercised by the Soviet Union on a considerable

---

[5] See e.g. *The United Nations at the Millennium* (eds. P. Taylor and A. J. R. Groom), London, 2000. As to the administration of territory by the UN, see above, chapter 5, p. 230.

[6] See e.g. C. Denis, *Le Pouvoir Normatif du Conseil de Sécurité des Nations Unies: Portée et Limites*, Brussels, 2004; M. Hilaire, *United Nations Law and the Security Council*, Aldershot, 2005; *The UN Security Council from the Cold War to the 21st Century* (ed. D. M. Malone), Boulder, 2004; Cot *et al.*, *Charte*, pp. 867 ff.; S. Bailey and S. Daws, *The Procedure of the UN Security Council*, Oxford, 1998; S. Bailey, *Voting in the Security Council*, Oxford, 1969, and Bailey, *The Procedure of the Security Council*, 2nd edn, Oxford, 1988; *Bowett's International Institutions*, p. 39, and R. Higgins, 'The Place of International Law in the Settlement of Disputes by the Security Council', 64 AJIL, 1970, p. 1. See also M. C. Wood, 'Security Council Working Methods and Procedure: Recent Developments', 45 ICLQ, 1996, p. 150.

[7] Articles 23, 24, 25 and 28 of the UN Charter.

[8] See e.g. H. G. Nicholas, *The United Nations as a Political Institution*, Oxford, 1975, pp. 10–13.

number of occasions, and by the USA less frequently, and by the other members fairly rarely. In more recent years, the exercise of the veto by the US has increased. The question of how one distinguishes between procedural and non-procedural matters has been a highly controversial one. In the statement of the Sponsoring Powers at San Francisco, it was declared that the issue of whether or not a matter was procedural was itself subject to the veto.[9] This 'double-veto' constitutes a formidable barrier. Subsequent practice has interpreted the phrase 'concurring votes of the permanent members' in article 27 in such a way as to permit abstentions. Accordingly, permanent members may abstain with regard to a resolution of the Security Council without being deemed to have exercised their veto against it.[10]

It does not, of course, follow that the five supreme powers of 1945 will continue to be the only permanent members of the Council nor the only ones with a veto.[11] However, the complicated mechanisms for amendment of the Charter,[12] coupled with the existence of the veto, make any change difficult. The question of expansion of Council membership has been before the UN for an appreciable period and various proposals have been made.[13] One proposal would provide for six new permanent seats with

---

[9] *Repertory of Practice of UN Organs*, New York, 1955, vol. II, p. 104. See also Simma, *Charter*, p. 489.

[10] See e.g. A. Stavropoulos, 'The Practice of Voluntary Abstentions by Permanent Members of the Security Council under Article 27(3) of the Charter', 61 AJIL, 1967, p. 737. See also the *Namibia* case, ICJ Reports, 1971, pp. 16, 22; 49 ILR, pp. 2, 12, recognising this practice as lawful.

[11] Of the ten non-permanent seats, five are allocated to Afro-Asian states, one to Eastern Europe, two to Latin America, and two to Western European and other powers: see General Assembly resolution 1991 (XVIII).

[12] See articles 108 and 109 of the Charter, which require *inter alia* the consent of all the permanent members to any amendment to or alteration of the Charter. It may indeed be suggested that the speed with which Russia was accepted as the continuance of the former USSR with regard to the permanent seat on the Security Council partly arose out of a desire by the Council to avoid opening up the question of membership for general debate: see F. Kirgis, *International Organisations in their Legal Setting*, 2nd edn, St Paul, 1993, pp. 188 ff. See also above, chapter 17, p. 960.

[13] See e.g. the Report of the High Level Panel on Threats, Challenges and Change, 2004, A/59/565, especially paras. 244 ff. detailing the two proposals made (models A and B respectively) and Secretary-General, *In Larger Freedom*, A/59/2005, paras. 167 ff. The General Assembly has also been considering the question of the 'equitable representation on and increase in the membership of the Security Council' and an open-ended working group was established in 1993 to consider the matter further: see General Assembly resolution 48/26. In 2007, the President of the General Assembly appointed five facilitators, who reported that expansion of the Council needed to be based both on the contribution of member states to the maintenance of international peace and security and to the other

no veto and three new non-permanent seats. Another would provide for no new permanent seats but a new category of eight four-year renewable-term seats and one new two-year non-permanent and non-renewable seat. States usually seen as candidates for permanent positions on the Council include Germany, India, Japan and Brazil, but others are also keen to be considered and no consensus is yet in sight.

The Council has currently three permanent committees, being a Committee of Experts on Rules of Procedure, a Committee on Admission of New Members and a Committee on Council meeting away from Headquarters. There are also a number of ad hoc committees, such as the Governing Council of the United Nations Compensation Commission established by Security Council resolution 692 (1991), the Counter-Terrorism Committee[14] and the Committee established by resolution 1540 (2004), which obliges states *inter alia* to refrain from supporting by any means non-state actors from developing, acquiring, manufacturing, possessing, transporting, transferring or using nuclear, chemical or biological weapons and their delivery systems. There are also a number of sanctions committees covering particular states under sanction as well as the committee established under resolution 1267 (1999) concerning persons and bodies associated with Al-Qaida and the Taliban.[15] Further subsidiary bodies include the Peacebuilding Commission, the UN Compensation Commission and the International Criminal Tribunals for the Former Yugoslavia and for Rwanda.

The Security Council acts on behalf of the members of the organisation as a whole in performing its functions, and its decisions (but not its recommendations)[16] are binding upon all member states.[17] Its powers are concentrated in two particular categories, the peaceful settlement of disputes and the adoption of enforcement measures. By these means, the Council conducts its primary task, the maintenance of international peace

---

purposes of the United Nations and on equitable geographical distribution, while addressing the underrepresentation of developing countries as well as small states, A/61/47, pp. 11 ff. See also Chesterman *et al.*, *United Nations*, chapter 17; A. Blanc Altemir and B. Real, 'La Réforme du Conseil de Sécurité des Nations Unies: Quelle Structure et Quels Membres?', 110 RGDIP, 2006, p. 801, and Y. Blum, 'Proposals for UN Security Council Reform', 99 AJIL, 2005, p. 632.

14 Established under resolution 1373 (2001). See above, chapter 20, p. 1162.

15 As amended by a number of subsequent resolutions, including resolution 1735 (2006): see further above, chapter 20, p. 1163, note 225.

16 Compare, for example, article 36 of the Charter (peaceful settlement) with articles 41, 42 and 44 (enforcement actions).

17 Article 25 of the Charter.

and security. However, the Council also has a variety of other functions. In the case of trusteeship territories, for example, designated strategic areas fall within the authority of the Security Council rather than the General Assembly,[18] while the admission, suspension and expulsion of member states is carried out by the General Assembly upon the recommendation of the Council.[19] Amendments to the UN Charter require the ratification of all the permanent members of the Council (as well as adoption by a two-thirds vote of the Assembly and ratification by two-thirds of UN members).[20] The judges of the International Court are elected by the Assembly and Council.[21]

Until the end of the Cold War, the Council generally did not fulfil the expectations held of it, although resolution 242 (1967) laid down the basis for negotiations for a Middle East peace settlement and is regarded as the most authoritative expression of the principles to be taken into account.[22] With the development of the *glasnost* and *perestroika* policies in the Soviet Union in the late 1980s, increasing co-operation with the US ensued and reached its highest point as the Kuwait crisis evolved.[23] After the attacks on the US of 11 September 2001, further activities ensued, including the adoption of resolutions 1368 and 1373 of 2001 condemning international terrorism, reaffirming the right of self-defence and establishing a Counter-Terrorism Committee. However, the failure of the Council to agree upon measures consequent to resolution 1441 (2002) concerning Iraq's possession of weapons of mass destruction contrary to resolution 687 (1991) and others precipitated a major division within the Council. The US and the UK commenced military operations against Iraq in late March 2003 without express Security Council authorisation and against the opposition of other permanent members.[24] However, despite this crisis, the Council has begun to assume a more proactive role in

---

[18] See articles 82 and 83 of the Charter.

[19] See articles 4, 5 and 6 of the Charter. The restoration of the rights and privileges of a suspended member is by the Council, article 5.

[20] Article 108. A similar requirement operates with regard to alteration of the Charter by a General Conference of Members: see article 109.

[21] Article 4 of the Statute of the International Court of Justice.

[22] Reaffirmed in resolution 338 (1973). See generally I. Pogany, *The Security Council and the Arab–Israeli Conflict*, Aldershot, 1984, chapter 5, and A. Shapira, 'The Security Council Resolution of November 22, 1967 – Its Legal Nature and Implications', 4 *Israel Law Review*, 1969, p. 229.

[23] See below, p. 1243. See also *The Kuwait Crisis: Basic Documents* (eds. E. Lauterpacht, C. Greenwood, M. Weller and D. Bethlehem), Cambridge, 1991.

[24] See further below, p. 1255.

certain areas. The effect of resolutions 1373 (2001) and 1540 (2004) with the establishment of monitoring committees with significant authority, together with the increasing use of sanctions against specific states, has led some to talk of legislative activity.[25]

The failure of the Council in its primary responsibility to preserve world peace stimulated a number of other developments. It encouraged the General Assembly to assume a residual responsibility for maintaining international peace and security, it encouraged the Secretary-General to take upon himself a more active role and it hastened the development of peacekeeping operations. It also encouraged in some measure the establishment of the military alliances, such as NATO and the Warsaw Pact, which arose as a consequence of the onset of the Cold War and constituted, in effect, regional enforcement systems bypassing the Security Council.

The General Assembly[26]

The General Assembly is the parliamentary body of the UN organisation and consists of representatives of all the member states, of which there are currently 192. Membership of the UN, as provided by article 4 of the Charter, is open to:

> all other peace-loving states which accept the obligations contained in the present Charter and, in the judgment of the organisation, are able and willing to carry out these obligations,

and is effected by a decision of the General Assembly upon the recommendation of the Security Council.[27] Other changes in membership may

---

[25] See e.g. J. E. Alvarez, 'Hegemonic International Law Revisited', 97 AJIL, 2003, p. 873, and S. Talmon, 'The Security Council of World Legislature', 99 AJIL, 2005, p. 175. See further as to these resolutions, above, chapter 20, p. 1208.

[26] See e.g. *Bowett's International Institutions*, pp. 27 ff.; Cot *et al.*, *Charte*, pp. 631 ff.; Nicholas, *United Nations*, chapter 5; B. Finley, *The Structure of the United Nations General Assembly*, Dobbs Ferry, 3 vols., 1977, and S. Bailey, *The General Assembly of the United Nations*, London, 1964.

[27] An advisory opinion by the International Court held that only the conditions enumerated in article 4 were to be taken into account in considering a request for membership: the *Conditions of Admission of a State to Membership of the United Nations* case, ICJ Reports, 1948, p. 57; 15 AD, p. 333. See also the *Competence of the General Assembly for the Admission of a State to the United Nations* case, ICJ Reports, 1950, p. 4; 17 ILR, p. 326, where the Court held that the General Assembly alone could not effect membership in the absence of a recommendation by the Security Council. See also Chesterman *et al.*, *United Nations*, chapter 5, and Cot *et al.*, *Charte*, pp. 511 ff.

take place. For example, in 1991, Byelorussia informed the UN that it had changed its name to Belarus, while the Czech and Slovak Federal Republic ceased to exist on 31 December 1992 to be replaced by two new states (the Czech Republic and Slovakia), accepted as UN members on 19 January 1993. The former German Democratic Republic ceased to exist and its territory was absorbed into the Federal Republic of Germany as from 3 October 1990, while 'The Former Yugoslav Republic of Macedonia' was admitted to the UN on 8 April 1993 under that unusual appellation. Russia was regarded as the continuator of the Soviet Union, so no action was required. In November 2000, the Federal Republic of Yugoslavia was admitted as a new member and in February 2003 it changed its name to Serbia and Montenegro. In 2006, Montenegro seceded and became a member of the UN in its own right.[28] Membership of the UN may be suspended under article 5 of the Charter by the General Assembly, upon the recommendation of the Security Council, where the member state concerned is the object of preventive or enforcement action by the Security Council. Article 6 allows for expulsion of a member by the General Assembly, upon the recommendation of the Security Council, where the member state has persistently violated the Principles contained in the Charter.[29]

Voting in the Assembly is governed by article 18, which stipulates that each member has one vote only, despite widespread disparities in populations and resources between states, and that decisions on 'important questions', including the admission of new members and recommendations relating to international peace and security, are to be made by a two-thirds majority of members present and voting.[30]

---

[28] See as to succession issues, Chesterman et al., United Nations, pp. 173 ff. and see further as to Yugoslavia and the UN, above, chapter 17, p. 962.

[29] See article 2. See also as to the question of the refusal of credentials to General Assembly delegations e.g. Chesterman et al., United Nations, pp. 191 ff.; Simma, Charter, pp. 253 ff.; D. Ciobanu, 'Credentials of Delegations and Representation of Member States at the United Nations', 25 ICLQ, 1976, p. 351, and M. Halberstam, 'Excluding Israel from the General Assembly by a Rejection of its Credentials', 78 AJIL, 1984, p. 179.

[30] See e.g. G. Clarke and L. B. Sohn, World Peace Through World Law, Cambridge, 1958, pp. 19–30; The Strategy of World Order (eds. R. A. Falk and S. H. Mendlovitz), New York, 1966, vol. III, pp. 272 ff., and L. B. Sohn, Cases on United Nations Law, 2nd edn, Brooklyn, 1967, pp. 248 ff. Note also the emergence of bloc voting, whereby, for example, the Afro-Asian states agree to adopt a common stance on particular issues, which has been a constant feature of the work of the Assembly.

Except for certain internal matters, such as the budget,[31] the Assembly cannot bind its members. It is not a legislature in that sense, and its resolutions are purely recommendatory. Such resolutions, of course, may be binding if they reflect rules of customary international law and they are significant as instances of state practice that may lead to the formation of a new customary rule, but Assembly resolutions in themselves cannot establish binding legal obligations for member states.[32] The Assembly is essentially a debating chamber, a forum for the exchange of ideas and the discussion of a wide-ranging category of problems. It meets in annual sessions, but special sessions may be called by the Secretary-General at the request of the Security Council or a majority of UN members.[33] Emergency special sessions may also be called by virtue of the Uniting for Peace machinery.[34] Ten such sessions have been convened, covering situations ranging from various aspects of the Middle East situation in 1956, 1958, 1967, 1980 and 1982 and a rolling session commencing in 1997, to Afghanistan in 1980 and Namibia in 1981.

The Assembly has established a variety of organs covering a wide range of topics and activities. It has six main committees that cover respectively disarmament and international security; economic and financial; social, humanitarian and cultural; special political and decolonisation; administrative and budgetary; and legal matters.[35] In addition, there is a procedural General Committee dealing with agenda issues and a Credentials Committee. There are also two Standing Committees dealing with inter-sessional administrative and budgetary questions and contributions, and a number of subsidiary, ad hoc and other bodies dealing with relevant topics, including the International Law Commission, the UN Commission on International Trade Law, the UN Institute for Training and Research, the Council for Namibia and the UN Relief and Works

---

[31] Article 17 of the Charter.   [32] See further above, chapter 3, p. 114.

[33] Article 20 of the Charter. Such special sessions have been held, for example, to discuss the issues of Palestine in 1947–8, Namibia (South West Africa) in 1967, 1978 and 1986, and to debate the world economic order in 1974, 1975 and 1990. Other issues covered include financing the UN Interim Force in Lebanon in 1978, apartheid in 1989, disarmament in 1978, 1982 and 1988, drug abuse in 1990 and 1998, small island developing states in 1999, women in 2000, HIV/AIDS in 2001, children in 2002 and commemoration of the sixtieth anniversary of the liberation of the concentration camps in 2005.

[34] See below, p. 1272.

[35] See e.g. Broms, *United Nations*, pp. 198 ff. Note that in 1993, the Special Political Committee was merged with the Fourth Committee on Decolonisation: see General Assembly resolution 47/233.

Agency.[36] The Human Rights Council, established in 2006, is elected by and reports to the Assembly.[37]

Other principal organs [38]

Much of the work of the United Nations in the economic and social spheres of activity is performed by the Economic and Social Council (ECOSOC). It can discuss a wide range of matters, but its powers are restricted and its recommendations are not binding upon UN member states. It consists of fifty-four members elected by the Assembly for three-year terms with staggered elections, and each member has one vote.[39] The Council may, by article 62, initiate or make studies upon a range of issues and make recommendations to the General Assembly, the members of the UN and to the relevant specialised agencies. It may prepare draft conventions for submission to the Assembly and call international conferences. The Council has created a variety of subsidiary organs, ranging from nine functional commissions,[40] to five regional commissions[41] and a number of standing committees and expert bodies.[42] The Council also runs a variety of programmes including the Environment Programme and the Drug Control Programme, and has established a number of other bodies such as the Office of the UN High Commissioner for Refugees and the UN Conference on Trade and Development. Its most prominent function has been in establishing a wide range of economic, social and human rights bodies.[43]

---

[36] See e.g. *2001 United Nations Handbook*, Wellington, 2001, pp. 27 ff. There is also an Investments Committee and a Board of Auditors.

[37] See above, chapter 6, p. 306.

[38] See e.g. *2001 United Nations Handbook*, pp. 83 ff., and Broms, *United Nations*, chapter 11. See also *Bowett's International Institutions*, p. 55; W. R. Sharp, *The UN Economic Council*, New York, 1969, and above, chapter 6, p. 302.

[39] Article 61 of the Charter. Note that under article 69, any member of the UN may be invited to participate in its deliberations without a vote. See also Cot *et al.*, *Charte*, pp. 1581 ff.

[40] These include the Statistical Commission, the Commission on Human Rights which came to an end in 2006, the Commission on the Status of Women and the Commission on Sustainable Development.

[41] On Africa, Asia and the Pacific, Europe, Latin America and the Caribbean, and Western Asia.

[42] These include the Commission on Transnational Corporations; the Commission on Human Settlements; the Committee on Natural Resources; the Committee on Economic, Social and Cultural Rights and the Committee on New and Renewable Sources of Energy and on Energy for Development.

[43] ECOSOC is considering a range of reforms, including holding annual ministerial substantive reviews (AMR) to assess the progress made in the implementation of the outcomes

The Trusteeship Council[44] was established in order to supervise the trust territories created after the end of the Second World War.[45] Such territories were to consist of mandated territories, areas detached from enemy states as a result of the Second World War and other territories voluntarily placed under the trusteeship system by the administering authority (of which there have been none).[46] The only former mandated territory which was not placed under the new system or granted independence was South West Africa.[47] With the independence of Palau, the last remaining trust territory, on 1 October 1994, the Council suspended operation on 1 November that year.[48]

The Secretariat of the UN[49] consists of the Secretary-General and his staff, and constitutes virtually an international civil service. The staff are appointed by article 101 upon the basis of efficiency, competence and integrity, 'due regard' being paid 'to the importance of recruiting the staff on as wide a geographical basis as possible'. All member states have undertaken, under article 100, to respect the exclusively international character of the responsibilities of the Secretary-General and his staff,

---

of major UN conferences and summits and internationally agreed development goals: see General Assembly resolution 61/16, 2006, and ECOSOC resolution E/2007/274, 2007.

[44] See e.g. Cot et al., Charte, pp. 1887 ff.; Broms, United Nations, chapter 12; Bowett's International Institutions, p. 63, and C. E. Toussaint, The Trusteeship System of the United Nations, New York, 1956.

[45] By article 83 of the Charter, the functions of the UN relating to strategic areas were to be exercised by the Security Council (where each permanent member has a veto) rather than, as normal for trust territories, under article 85 by the General Assembly with the assistance of the Trusteeship Council. The last trust territory was the strategic trust territory of the Pacific Islands, administered by the US.

[46] Article 77 of the Charter.   [47] See above, chapter 5, p. 225.

[48] See e.g. Basic Facts About the United Nations, E.95.I.3.1 and Press Release ORG/1211/Rev.1. Note that the UN Secretary-General has called for its formal termination, but this would require an amendment of the Charter: see A/49/1. See also C. L. Willson, 'Changing the Charter: The United Nations Prepares for the Twenty-First Century', 90 AJIL, 1996, pp. 115, 121–2.

[49] See e.g. Chesterman et al., United Nations, chapter 4; Cot et al., Charte, pp. 2023 ff.; S. Bailey, 'The United Nations Secretariat' in The Evolution of International Organisations (ed. E. Luard), London, 1966, p. 92, and Bailey, The Secretariat of the UN, London, 1962; T. Meron, The UN Secretariat, Lexington, 1977; S. Schwebel, The Secretary-General of the United Nations, Cambridge, MA, 1952, and Schwebel, 'The International Character of the Secretariat of the United Nations' and 'Secretary-General and Secretariat' in Justice in International Law, Cambridge, 1994, pp. 248 and 297 respectively; A. W. Rovine, The First Fifty Years: The Secretary General in World Politics, 1920–1970, Leiden, 1970, and generally Public Papers of the Secretaries-General of the United Nations (eds. A. W. Cordier and W. Foote, and A. W. Cordier and M. Harrelson), New York, 8 vols., 1969–77. See also Simma, Charter, pp. 1191 ff., and below, p. 1222.

who are neither to seek nor receive instructions from any other authority but the UN organisation itself.

Under article 97, the Secretary-General is appointed by the General Assembly upon the unanimous recommendation of the Security Council and constitutes the chief administrative officer of the UN. He (or she) must accordingly be a personage acceptable to all the permanent members and this, in the light of effectiveness, is vital. Much depends upon the actual personality and outlook of the particular office holder, and the role played by the Secretary-General in international affairs has tended to vary according to the character of the person concerned. An especially energetic part was performed by Dr Hammerskjöld in the late 1950s and very early 1960s until his untimely death in the Congo,[50] but since that time a rather lower profile has been maintained by the occupants of that position. The current holder of the office is Ban Ki-Moon of the Republic of Korea.

Apart from various administrative functions,[51] the essence of the Secretary-General's authority is contained in article 99 of the Charter, which empowers him to bring to the attention of the Security Council any matter which he feels may strengthen the maintenance of international peace and security, although this power has not often been used.[52] In practice, the role of Secretary-General has extended beyond the various provisions of the Charter. In particular, the Secretary-General has an important role in exercising good offices in order to resolve or contain international crises.[53] Additionally, the Secretary-General is in an important position to mark or possibly to influence developments. The publication of *An Agenda for Peace*[54] by Dr Boutros-Ghali and of *In Larger Freedom*[55] by Kofi Annan, for instance, constituted particularly significant events.

---

[50] See e.g. Bailey, 'United Nations Secretariat'.

[51] These include servicing a variety of organs, committees and conferences; co-ordinating the activities of the secretariat, the specialised agencies and other inter-governmental organisations; the preparation of studies and reports and responsibility for the preparation of the annual budget of the UN. Note that the Secretary-General also acts as depositary for a wide range of multilateral treaties, and under article 98, submits an annual report on the work of the organisation.

[52] Article 99 was invoked, for example, in 1950 in the Korean war crisis, in 1960 in the Congo crisis and in 1979 with regard to the Iranian hostage issue: see *Yearbook of the UN, 1979*, pp. 307–12. See also S/13646 and S. Schwebel, 'The Origins and Development of Article 99 of the Charter' in *Justice in International Law*, p. 233.

[53] See further below, p. 1222.

[54] The Report of the Secretary-General Pursuant to the Statement Adopted by the Summit Meeting of the Security Council on 31 January 1992, New York, 1992.

[55] A/59/2005.

In many disputes, the functions assigned to the Secretary-General by the other organs of the United Nations have enabled him to increase the influence of the organisation.[56] One remarkable example of this occurred in the Congo crisis of 1960 and the subsequent Council resolution authorising the Secretary-General in very wide-ranging terms to take action.[57] Another instance of the capacity of the Secretary-General to take action was the decision of 1967 to withdraw the UN peacekeeping force in the Middle East, thus removing an important psychological barrier to war, and provoking a certain amount of criticism.

The sixth principal organ of the UN is the International Court of Justice, established in 1946 as the successor to the Permanent Court of International Justice.[58]

The peaceful settlement of disputes[59]

The League of Nations[60]

The provisions set out in the UN Charter are to a large degree based upon the terms of the Covenant of the League of Nations as amended in the light of experience. Article 12 of the Covenant declared that any dispute likely to lead to a conflict between members was to be dealt with in one of three ways: by arbitration, by judicial settlement or by inquiry by the Council of the League. Article 15 noted that the Council was to try to effect a settlement of the dispute in question, but if that failed, it was to publish a report containing the facts of the case and 'the recommendations which are deemed just and proper in regard thereto'. This report was not, however, binding upon the parties, but if it was a unanimous one the League members were not to go to war 'with any party to the dispute

---

[56] Article 98. See also J. Pérez de Cuéllar, 'The Role of the UN Secretary-General' in Roberts and Kingsbury, *United Nations, Divided World*, p. 125.

[57] See below, p. 1226.   [58] See above, chapter 19.

[59] See e.g. M. Raman, *Dispute Settlement through the United Nations*, Oxford, 1977; J. G. Merrills, *International Dispute Settlement*, 4th edn, Cambridge, 2005, chapter 10; United Nations, *Handbook on the Peaceful Settlement of Disputes Between States*, New York, 1992; N. Bar-Yaacov, *The Handling of International Disputes by Means of Inquiry*, London, 1974, chapter 8; B. S. Murty, 'Settlement of Disputes' in *Manual of Public International Law* (ed. M. Sørensen), London, 1968, p. 673; E. Luard, *A History of the United Nations*, London, 1982, vol. I; Falk and Mendlovitz, *Strategy of World Order*, vol. III; *The United Nations* (eds. R. A. Falk and S. Mendlovitz), New York, 1966; Cot *et al.*, *Charte*, pp. 1047 ff.; N. D. White, *Keeping the Peace*, 2nd edn, Manchester, 1998.

[60] See generally, e.g. G. Scott, *The Rise and Fall of the League of Nations*, London, 1973, and Falk and Mendlovitz, *Strategy of World Order*, chapter 1.

which complies with the recommendations of the report'. If the report was merely a majority one, League members reserved to themselves 'the right to take such action as they shall consider necessary for the maintenance of right and justice'. In other words, in the latter case the Covenant did not absolutely prohibit the resort to war by members. Where a member resorted to war in disregard of the Covenant, then the various sanctions prescribed in article 16 might apply, although whether the circumstances in which sanctions might be enforced had actually arisen was a point to be decided by the individual members and not by the League itself. Sanctions were in fact used against Italy in 1935–6, but in a half-hearted manner due to political considerations by the leading states at the time.[61]

The United Nations system

The UN system is founded in constitutional terms upon a relatively clear theoretical distinction between the functions of the principal organs of the organisation. However, due to political conditions in the international order, the system failed to operate as outlined in the Charter and adjustments had to be made as opportunities presented themselves. The Security Council was intended to function as the executive of the UN, with the General Assembly as the parliamentary forum. Both organs could contribute to the peaceful settlement of disputes through relatively traditional mechanisms of discussion, good offices and mediation. Only the Security Council could adopt binding decisions and those through the means of Chapter VII, while acting to restore international peace and security. But the pattern of development has proved rather less conducive to clear categorisation. An influential attempt to detail the methods and mechanisms available to the UN in seeking to resolve disputes was made by the UN Secretary-General in the immediate aftermath of the demise of the Soviet Union and the unmistakable ending of the Cold War.

In *An Agenda for Peace*,[62] the Secretary-General, while emphasising that respect for the fundamental sovereignty and integrity of states constituted the foundation-stone of the organisation,[63] noted the rapid changes affecting both states individually and the international community as a

---

[61] See e.g. Scott, *Rise and Fall*, chapter 15.

[62] This was welcomed by the General Assembly in resolution 47/120. See also the Report of the Secretary-General on the Implementation of the Recommendations in the 1992 Report, A/47/965.

[63] *Ibid.*, p. 9.

whole and emphasised the role of the UN in securing peace. The Report sought to categorise the types of actions that the organisation was undertaking or could undertake. *Preventive Diplomacy* was action to prevent disputes from arising between states, to prevent existing disputes from escalating into conflicts and to limit the spread of the latter when they occur. This included efforts such as fact-finding, good offices and goodwill missions.[64] *Peacemaking* involves action to bring the hostile parties to agreement, utilising the peaceful means elaborated in Chapter VI of the Charter.[65] *Peacekeeping* is the deployment of a UN presence in the field.[66] *Peacebuilding* is action to identify and support structures that will assist peace.[67] *Peace Enforcement* is peacekeeping not involving the consent of the parties, which would rest upon the enforcement provisions of Chapter VII of the Charter.[68]

The attack on the World Trade Center on 11 September 2001 'dramatised the global threat of terrorism', while focusing attention upon 'reconstructing weak or collapsed states'.[69] The Secretary-General has also emphasised the need to replace the culture of reaction by one of prevention and by developing *inter alia* a thirty to ninety-day deployment capability.[70]

The Security Council

The primary objective of the United Nations as stipulated in article 1 of the Charter is the maintenance of international peace and security and disputes likely to endanger this are required under article 33 to be solved 'by negotiation, inquiry, mediation, conciliation, arbitration, judicial settlement, resort to regional agencies or arrangements or other peaceful means'. Indeed, the Charter declares as one of its purposes in article 1, 'to

---

[64] *Ibid.*, pp. 13 ff.   [65] *Ibid.*, pp. 20 ff.   [66] *Ibid.*, pp. 28 ff.

[67] *Ibid.*, pp. 32 ff. See the establishment of the Peacebuilding Commission in 2006, General Assembly resolution 60/180 and Security Council resolution 1645 (2005), intended to bring together all relevant actors, to marshal and sustain resources and advise on the proposed integrated strategies for post-conflict peacebuilding and recovery. See the Report of the Commission on its first session, A/62/137–S/2007/458, 25 July 2007, and Chesterman *et al.*, *United Nations*, chapter 9.

[68] See Report of the Secretary-General on the Work of the Organisation, New York, 1993, p. 96.

[69] See Report of the Secretary-General on the Work of the Organisation, A/57/1, 2002, p. 1. See also the Secretary-General's *Agenda for Further Change*, A/57/387, 9 September 2002.

[70] See the *Road Map Towards Implementation of the United Nations Millennium Declaration*, A/56/326, 6 September 2001. The Millennium Report may be found at www.un.org/millennium/sg/report/.

bring about by peaceful means and in conformity with the principles of justice and international law, adjustment or settlement of international disputes or situations which might lead to a breach of the peace'. By article 24,[71] the members of the UN conferred on the Security Council primary responsibility for the maintenance of international peace and security, and by article 25[72] agreed to accept and carry out the decisions of the Security Council. The International Court in the *Namibia* case[73] drew attention to the fact that the provision in article 25 was not limited to enforcement actions under Chapter VII of the Charter but applied to '"decisions of the Security Council" adopted in accordance with the Charter'. Accordingly a declaration of the Council taken under article 24 in the exercise of its primary responsibility for the maintenance of international peace and security could constitute a decision under article 25 so that member states 'would be expected to act in consequence of the declaration made on their behalf'.[74] Whether a particular resolution adopted under article 24 actually constituted a decision binding all member states (and outside the collective security framework of Chapter VII)[75] was a matter for analysis in each particular case, 'having regard to the terms of the resolution to be interpreted, the discussions leading to it, the Charter provisions invoked and, in general, all circumstances that might assist in determining the legal consequences of the resolution of the Security Council'.[76] Under the Charter, the role of the Security Council when dealing with the pacific settlement of disputes specifically under Chapter VI differs from when the Council is contemplating action relating to threats to or breaches of the peace, or acts of aggression under Chapter VII. In the former instance there is no power as such to make binding decisions with regard to member states.

In pursuance of its primary responsibility, the Security Council may, by article 34, 'investigate any dispute, or any situation which might lead to

---

[71] See e.g. Simma, *Charter*, pp. 442 ff.   [72] *Ibid.*, pp. 452 ff.

[73] ICJ Reports, 1971, pp. 16, 52–3; 49 ILR, pp. 1, 42–3.

[74] This approach is controversial and has not, for example, been accepted by Western states: see e.g. Simma, *Charter*, p. 457. See also R. Higgins, 'The Advisory Opinion on Namibia. Which UN Resolutions are Binding under Article 25 of the Charter?', 21 ICLQ, 1972, p. 270.

[75] See below, p. 1235.

[76] ICJ Reports, 1971, pp. 16, 53; 49 ILR, p. 43. The question as to whether relevant Security Council resolutions on East Timor could be regarded as binding was raised in the *East Timor* case, ICJ Reports, 1995, pp. 90, 103; 105 ILR, p. 226, but the Court concluded that the resolutions cited did not go so far as to impose obligations. But cf. the Dissenting Opinion by Judge Weeramantry, ICJ Reports, 1995, pp. 205–8.

international friction or give rise to dispute, in order to determine whether the continuance of the dispute or situation is likely to endanger the maintenance of international peace and security'. In addition to this power of investigation, the Security Council can, where it deems necessary, call upon the parties to settle their dispute by the means elaborated in article 33.[77] The Council may intervene if it wishes at any stage of a dispute or situation, the continuance of which is likely to endanger international peace and security, and under article 36(1) recommend appropriate procedures or methods of adjustment. But in making such recommendations, which are not binding, it must take into consideration the general principle that legal disputes should be referred by the parties to the International Court of Justice.[78] Where the parties to a dispute cannot resolve it by the various methods mentioned in article 33, they should refer it to the Security Council by article 37. The Council, where it is convinced that the continuance of the dispute is likely to endanger international peace and security, may recommend not only procedures and adjustment methods, but also such terms of settlement as it may consider appropriate.

Once the Council, however, has determined the existence of a threat to, or a breach of, the peace or act of aggression, it may make decisions which are binding upon member states of the UN under Chapter VII, but until that point it can under Chapter VI issue recommendations only.[79] Under article 35(1) any UN member state may bring a dispute or a situation which might lead to international friction or give rise to a dispute before the Council, while a non-member state may bring to the attention of the Council any dispute under article 35(2) provided it is a party to the dispute in question and 'accepts in advance, for the purposes of the dispute, the obligations of pacific settlement provided in the present Charter'.

---

[77] Note that under article 38, the Security Council may make recommendations to the parties with regard to the peaceful settlement of disputes generally if all the parties to the dispute so request.

[78] For example, when the Security Council recommended that the UK and Albania should take their case regarding the *Corfu Channel* incident to the International Court: see Security Council resolution 22 (1947) and SCOR, 2nd yr, 127th meeting, 9 April 1947, p. 727. See also Luard, *History*, pp. 209–12. However, this example proved to be exceptional. See also Security Council resolution 395 (1976) calling for negotiations between Turkey and Greece over the Aegean Sea continental shelf dispute and inviting the parties to refer the question to the International Court.

[79] However, note that under article 37(2) if the Council deems that a continuance of a dispute is likely to endanger international peace and security, it 'shall decide whether to take action under article 36 [i.e. recommend appropriate procedures or methods of adjustment] or to recommend such terms of settlement as it may consider appropriate'.

It is also possible for third parties to bring disputes to the attention of the Council.[80]

In practice, the Security Council has applied all the diplomatic techniques available in various international disputes. This is in addition to open debates and the behind-the-scenes discussions and lobbying that take place. On numerous occasions it has called upon the parties to a dispute to negotiate a settlement and has requested that it be kept informed. The Council offered its good offices in the late 1940s with regard to the Dutch–Indonesian dispute[81] and has had recourse to mediation attempts in many other conflicts, for example with regard to the Kashmir[82] and Cyprus[83] questions.[84] However, the cases where the Council has recommended procedures or methods of adjustment under article 36 have been comparatively rare. Only in the *Corfu Channel* and *Aegean Sea* disputes did the Council recommend the parties to turn to the International Court. Probably the most famous Security Council resolution recommending a set of principles to be taken into account in resolving a particular dispute is resolution 242 (1967) dealing with the Middle East. This resolution pointed to two basic principles to be applied in establishing a just and lasting peace in the Middle East: first, Israeli withdrawal 'from territories occupied in the recent conflict' (i.e. the Six Day War) and, secondly, the termination of all claims of belligerency and acknowledgement of the right of every state in the area to live in peace within secure and recognised frontiers.[85]

The General Assembly[86]

Although the primary responsibility with regard to the maintenance of international peace and security lies with the Security Council, the

---

[80] See the succeeding sections as to the General Assembly and the Secretary-General.

[81] See e.g. Luard, *History*, chapter 9, and S/1156. See also S/514 and S/1234, and Murty, 'Settlement', p. 721.

[82] Murty, 'Settlement', p. 721. See also Luard, *History*, chapter 14.

[83] See e.g. Murty, 'Settlement', p. 721. See also T. Ehrlich, *Cyprus 1958–1967*, Oxford, 1974.

[84] Note also the appointment of Count Bernadotte and Dr Jarring as UN mediators in the Middle East in 1948 and 1967 respectively. See Luard, *History*, chapters 10 and 11, and *The Arab–Israeli Conflict* (ed. J. N. Moore), Princeton, 3 vols., 1974.

[85] Various other points were referred to in resolution 242, including the need to guarantee freedom of navigation through international waterways in the area, achieve a just settlement of the refugee problem and reinforce the territorial inviolability of every state in the area through measures such as the use of demilitarised zones. Resolution 242 (1967) was reaffirmed in Security Council resolution 338 (1973).

[86] See e.g. White, *Keeping the Peace*, part II, and M. J. Peterson, *The General Assembly in World Politics*, Boston, 1986.

General Assembly may discuss any question or matter within the scope of the Charter, including the maintenance of international peace and security, and may make recommendations to the members of the UN or the Security Council,[87] provided the Council is not itself dealing with the same matter.[88] Under similar conditions, the Assembly may under article 14 'recommend measures for the peaceful adjustment of any situation regardless of origin, which it deems likely to impair the general welfare or friendly relations among nations'. In the *Construction of a Wall* case,[89] the International Court emphasised that under article 24 the Security Council had a primary and not necessarily an exclusive competence with regard to the maintenance of international peace and security, while the constraint placed by article 12 on the powers of the Assembly to make recommendations for the peaceful adjustment of situations had been interpreted by evolving practice to permit both the Assembly and the Council to deal in parallel with the same matter concerning the maintenance of international peace and security, with the former often taking a broader view.[90]

In practice, the resolutions and declarations of the General Assembly (which are not binding) have covered a very wide field, from colonial disputes to alleged violations of human rights and the need for justice in international economic affairs. The role of the General Assembly increased after 1945 due to two factors: first, the existence of the veto in the Security Council rendered that organ powerless in many important disputes since the permanent members (USA, UK, USSR (now Russia), France and China) rarely agreed with respect to any particular conflict; and secondly, the vast increase in the membership of the UN had the effect of radicalising the Assembly and its deliberations. More recently the increased role of the Security Council has overshadowed that of the Assembly.

The Secretary-General[91]

Just as the impotence of the Security Council stimulated a growing awareness of the potentialities of the General Assembly, it similarly underlined

---

[87] Articles 10 and 11 of the Charter.   [88] Article 12.

[89] ICJ Reports, 2004, pp. 136, 148–9; 129 ILR, pp. 37, 66.

[90] As to the right of the Assembly to deal with a threat to or breach of the peace or act of aggression if the Security Council fails to act because of the exercise of the veto by a permanent member, see resolution 377(V), the 'Uniting for Peace' resolution, below, p. 1272.

[91] See e.g. Rovine, *First Fifty Years*, and Cordier *et al.*, *Public Papers*.

the role to be played by the United Nations Secretary-General. By article 99 of the Charter, he is entitled to bring to the attention of the Security Council any matter which he thinks may threaten the maintenance of international peace and security and this power is in addition to his function as the chief administrative officer of the United Nations organisation under article 79.[92] In effect, the Secretary-General has considerable discretion and much has depended upon the views and outlook of the person filling the post at any given time, as well as the general political situation.

The good offices role of the Secretary-General has rapidly expanded.[93] In exercising such a role, Secretaries-General have sought to act independently of the Security Council and General Assembly, in the former case, in so far as they have not been constrained by binding resolutions (as for example in the Kuwait situation of 1990–1). The assumption of good offices and mediation activity may arise either because of independent action by the Secretary-General as part of the exercise of his inherent powers[94] or as a consequence of a request made by the Security Council[95] or General Assembly.[96] In some cases, the Secretary-General has acted upon the invitation of the parties themselves,[97] and on other occasions, the Secretary-General has acted in concert with the relevant regional

---

[92] Under article 98, the Secretary-General also performs such other functions as are entrusted to him by the General Assembly, Security Council, Economic and Social Council and the Trusteeship Council.

[93] See e.g. T. M. Franck, *Fairness in International Law and Institutions*, Oxford, 1995, chapter 6; Pérez de Cuéllar, 'Role of the UN Secretary-General', p. 125, and T. M. Franck and G. Nolte, 'The Good Offices Function of the UN Secretary-General' in Roberts and Kingsbury, *United Nations, Divided World*, p. 143.

[94] See e.g. with regard to Abkhazia, Franck, *Fairness*, p. 207, and Central America, *ibid.*

[95] See e.g. Security Council resolutions 242 (1967) regarding the Middle East; 367 (1975) regarding Cyprus; 384 (1975) regarding East Timor; 435 (1978) regarding Namibia and 713 (1991) regarding Yugoslavia.

[96] See e.g. with regard to Afghanistan, General Assembly resolution ES-6/2, 1980, and *The Geneva Accords* published by the United Nations, 1988, DPI/935-40420. As to Cambodia, see Franck, *Fairness*, p. 184.

[97] See e.g. the General Peace Agreement of Rome between the Mozambique government and RENAMO rebels in 1992, which called upon the UN to monitor its implementation. The President of Mozambique called upon the Secretary-General to chair the key implementation commissions and assist in other ways including the dispatch of monitors: see Report of the Secretary-General, S/24635, 1992, and Franck, *Fairness*, p. 188. Note that in his Report on the Work of the Organisation, A/57/1, 2002, the Secretary-General noted that he had used his good offices to facilitate national reconciliation and democratisation in Myanmar (at p. 5), while stating that if requested he 'would positively consider the use of my good offices' in seeking a peaceful solution in Nepal (at p. 4).

organisation.[98] In many cases, the Secretary-General will appoint a Special Representative to assist in seeking a solution to the particular problem.[99]

The development of good offices and mediation activities first arose as a consequence of the severe restrictions imposed upon UN operations by the Cold War. The cessation of the Cold War led to greatly increased activity by the UN and as a consequence the work of the Secretary-General expanded as he sought to bring to fruition the wide range of initiatives undertaken by the organisation. The experiences of Somalia, Rwanda and Bosnia in the mid-1990s and Iraq from 1991 to the 2003 war have been disappointing for the organisation.

Peacekeeping and observer missions[100]

There is no explicit legal basis for peacekeeping activities in the UN Charter. They arose in the absence of the contribution of armed forces and facilities to the UN as detailed in article 43. Accordingly, a series of arrangements and operations have evolved since the inception of the organisation, which taken together have established a clear pattern of acceptable reaction by the UN in particular crisis situations. The broad bases for such activities lie in the general provisions in the Charter governing the powers of the Security Council and General Assembly. The Security Council, for example, may establish such subsidiary organs as it deems necessary for the performance of its functions (article 29) and those functions are laid down in articles 34 (powers of investigation); 36, 37 and 38 (powers to recommend appropriate procedures or methods of dispute settlement); and 39 (powers of recommendation or decision in order to maintain or restore international peace and security). The Security Council may, in particular under article 42, take such action by land, sea or air forces as may be necessary to maintain or restore international peace

---

[98] See e.g. with regard to the Secretary-General of the Organisation of American States concerning the Central American peace process from the mid-1980s, Report of the UN Secretary-General, A/42/127–S/18688, 1987.

[99] See, for the full list, www.un.org/Depts/dpko/SRSG/index.htm.

[100] See e.g. R. Murphy, *UN Peacekeeping in Lebanon, Somalia and Kosovo*, Cambridge, 2007; United Nations, *United Nations Peacekeeping Operations: Principles and Guidelines*, New York, 2008, and UN, *The Blue Helmets: A Review of United Nations Peacekeeping*, 2nd edn, New York, 1990; D. W. Bowett, *UN Forces*, London, 1964; *The Evolution of UN Peacekeeping* (ed. W. J. Durch), London, 1994; White, *Keeping the Peace*; R. Higgins, *United Nations Peacekeeping*, Oxford, 4 vols., 1969–81; S. Morphet, 'UN Peacekeeping and Election Monitoring' in Roberts and Kingsbury, *United Nations, Divided World*, p. 183; A. James, *Peacekeeping in International Politics*, London, 1990, and Simma, *Charter*, pp. 648 ff.

and security. This is the basis for action explicitly taken under Chapter VII of the Charter.[101]

However, the majority of peacekeeping activities have not been so authorised and it is unlikely that article 42 can be seen as the legal basis for all such activities. The Security Council can entrust functions to the Secretary-General under article 98 and this mechanism has proved significant in practice. The General Assembly has wide powers under articles 10 and 11 to discuss and make recommendations on matters within the scope of the UN Charter, including recommendations concerning the maintenance of international peace and security.[102] Under article 14, the Assembly may recommend measures for the peaceful adjustment of any situation regardless of origin which it deems likely to impair the general welfare or friendly relations among nations. It can, however, take no binding decision in such matters.[103] The Assembly may also establish such subsidiary organs as it deems necessary for the performance of its functions (article 22) and entrust functions to the Secretary-General (article 98). It is because such operations fall somewhat between Chapter VI (peaceful settlement) and Chapter VII (enforcement) of the Charter, that the term 'Chapter Six and a Half' has been used.[104]

Essentially peacekeeping involves the deployment of armed forces under UN control to contain and resolve military conflicts. Although originally intended to deal with inter-state conflicts, more recently peacekeeping forces have been used with respect to civil wars and other intra-state conflicts. Again, primarily military deployments have expanded to include civilian personnel as more and more civil functions have been entrusted to such forces. There have been sixty-three peacekeeping missions to date and there are currently seventeen in operation.[105] Peacekeeping and observer missions operate upon a continuum of UN activities and it is helpful to consider these operations together. Indeed, that continuum has in recent years been extended to incorporate elements of enforcement action.[106]

---

[101] The power of the Security Council to resort to force under article 42 is dealt with below, p. 1251.

[102] However, under article 11(2), where action is necessary on any question relating to the maintenance of international peace and security, the matter must be referred to the Security Council.

[103] See further below, p. 1271.

[104] See e.g. T. Franck, *Recourse to Force*, Cambridge, 2002, p. 39. It seems to have been first used by Secretary-General Hammarskjöld: see www.un.org/Depts/dpko/dpko/index.asp.

[105] See www.un.org/Depts/dpko/dpko/index.asp (April 2008).

[106] See below, p. 1257.

The origin of peacekeeping by the UN may be traced to truce supervision activities. The first such activity occurred in Greece, where the UN Special Committee on the Balkans (UNSCOB) was created in 1947.[107] The UN Truce Supervision Organisation (UNTSO) was established in 1948 to supervise the truce in the 1948 Middle East War.[108] Peacekeeping[109] as such arose as a direct consequence of the problems facing the Security Council during the Cold War. The first peacekeeping activity took place in 1956 as a result of the Suez crisis. The UN Emergency Force (UNEF) was established by the General Assembly[110] to position itself between the hostile forces and to supervise the withdrawal of British and French forces from the Suez Canal and Israeli forces from the Sinai peninsula. It was then deployed along the armistice line until May 1967. The second crucial peacekeeping operation took place in the Congo crisis of 1960, which erupted soon after Belgium granted independence to the colony and resulted in mutinies, insurrections and much confused fighting. The Security Council adopted a resolution permitting the Secretary-General to provide military assistance to the Congo government.[111] This was

---

[107] See General Assembly resolution 109. The operation lasted until 1954. See also K. Birgisson, 'United Nations Special Committee on the Balkans' in Durch, *Evolution of UN Peacekeeping*, chapter 5.

[108] See Security Council resolution 50 (1948), and M. Ghali, 'The United Nations Truce Supervision Organisation' in Durch, *Evolution of UN Peacekeeping*, chapter 6. It has expanded to supervise the armistice agreements of 1949 and ceasefire arrangements of June 1967. See also the UN Military Observer Group in India and Pakistan (UNMOGIP) established by Security Council resolution 47 (1948) to supervise the ceasefire in Jammu and Kashmir: see K. Birgisson, 'United Nations Military Observer Group in India and Pakistan' in Durch, *Evolution of UN Peacekeeping*, chapter 16.

[109] This has been defined by the Secretary-General as 'the deployment of a United Nations presence in the field, hitherto with the consent of all the parties concerned, normally involving United Nations military and/or police personnel and frequently civilians as well', *An Agenda for Peace*, p. 11. Another definition was put forward by a former UN Legal Counsel, who noted that peacekeeping operations were 'actions involving the use of military personnel in international conflict situations on the basis of the consent of all parties concerned and without resorting to armed force except in cases of self-defence', E. Suy, 'Peacekeeping Operations' in *A Handbook on International Organisations* (ed. R. J. Dupuy), Dordrecht, 1988, p. 379.

[110] See General Assembly resolutions 997, 998 and 1000 (ES-1). The Security Council was unable to act as two permanent members (the UK and France) were directly involved in the crisis and had vetoed draft resolutions. See e.g. M. Ghali, 'United Nations Emergency Force I' in Durch, *Evolution of UN Peacekeeping*, chapter 7.

[111] S/4387, 14 July 1960. By resolution S/4405, 22 July 1960, the Council requested all states to refrain from action which might impede the restoration of law and order or undermine the territorial integrity and political independence of the Congo. By resolution S/4426, 9 August 1960, the Council confirmed the authority given to the

interpreted by Dr Hammarskjöld, the Secretary-General, as a mandate to set up a peacekeeping force on an analogy with UNEF. The exercise of the veto in the Council left the Secretary-General with little guidance as to how to proceed in the situation. Accordingly, he performed many of the tasks that had in 1956 been undertaken by the General Assembly with respect to the Middle East.[112] The development of the Congo crisis from mutiny to civil war meant that the United Nations force (ONUC) was faced with many difficult decisions and these had in the main to be taken by the Secretary-General. The role that could be played by the Secretary-General was emphasised in the succeeding crises in Cyprus (1964)[113] and the Middle East (1973)[114] and in the consequent establishment of United Nations peacekeeping forces for these areas under the general guidance of the Secretary-General.

The creation of traditional peacekeeping forces, whether in the Middle East in 1967 and again in 1973, in the Congo in 1960 or in Cyprus in 1964, was important in that such forces tended to stabilise particular situations for a certain time. Such United Nations forces are not intended to take enforcement action, but to act as an influence for calm by physically separating warring factions. They are dependent upon the consent of the state upon whose territory they are stationed and can in no way prevent a determined aggression. The various United Nations peacekeeping operations have met with some limited success in temporarily preventing

Secretary-General by earlier resolutions and called on member states to carry out the decisions of the Security Council. See e.g. G. Abi-Saab, *The United Nations Operation in the Congo 1960–1964*, Oxford, 1978; C. Hoskyns, *The Congo Since Independence*, Oxford, 1965; L. Miller, 'Legal Aspects of UN Action in the Congo', 55 AJIL, 1961, p. 1, and W. J. Durch, 'The UN Operation in the Congo' in Durch, *Evolution of UN Peacekeeping*, chapter 19.

[112] See Abi-Saab, *Congo*, pp. 15 ff.

[113] See Security Council resolution 186 (1964). See also Ehrlich, *Cyprus 1958–1967*, J. A. Stegenger, *The United Nations Force in Cyprus*, Columbus, 1968, and K. Birgisson, 'United Nations Peacekeeping Forces in Cyprus' in Durch, *Evolution of UN Peacekeeping*, chapter 13. The force is known as the UN Force in Cyprus (UNICYP).

[114] The Security Council established the UN Emergency Force (UNEF II) to monitor the Israeli–Egyptian disengagement process in 1973: see resolution 340 (1973), and a Disengagement Observer Force with respect to the Israel–Syria disengagement process: see resolution 350 (1974). See generally Pogany, *Arab–Israeli Conflict*, and M. Ghali, 'United Nations Emergency Force II' in Durch, *Evolution of UN Peacekeeping*, chapter 8. Note also the creation of the UN Interim Force in the Lebanon (UNIFIL) established by the Council in resolution 425 (1978) after Israel's incursion into the Lebanon in 1978: see e.g. M. Ghali, 'United Nations Interim Force in Lebanon' in Durch, *The Evolution of UN Peacekeeping*, chapter 10.

major disturbances, but they failed to prevent the 1967 Arab–Israeli war[115] and the 1974 Turkish invasion of Cyprus.[116] One has to be careful not to overestimate their significance in difficult political situations. In addition to the consent of the host state, such forces also require the continuing support of the Security Council and if that is lost or not provided such forces cannot operate.[117] Just as crucial as these factors is the provision of sufficient resources by the UN and its member states in order to fulfil the agreed mandate. Events in Bosnia, for example, demonstrated how the absence of adequate resources impacted severely upon operations.

Nevertheless, peacekeeping and observer operations do have a role to play, particularly as a way of ensuring that conflict situations in the process of being resolved do not flare up as a result of misunderstandings or miscalculations. Some recent UN operations in this area demonstrate this.[118] The UN Good Offices Mission in Afghanistan and Pakistan was established in the context of the Geneva Accords of 14 April 1988 dealing with the withdrawal of Soviet forces from Afghanistan,[119] while the UN Iran–Iraq Military Observer Group was created the same year following the acceptance by the belligerent states of Security Council resolution 598 (1987) calling for a ceasefire.[120] In 1989, in the context of the resolution of the Namibian problem, the UN Angola Verification Mission (UNAVEM I) commenced operation in order to verify the withdrawal of Cuban forces

---

[115] In fact the hasty withdrawal of the UNEF in May 1967 by the Secretary-General following an Egyptian request did much to precipitate the conflict. See generally Special Report of the Secretary-General on Removal of UNEF from Egyptian territory, A/6669, 1967, and T. M. Franck, *Nation Against Nation*, Oxford, 1985.

[116] See e.g. Security Council resolution 359 (1974) criticising the Turkish invasion.

[117] The Israel–Egypt Peace Treaty of 1979 envisaged the deployment of a UN force such as UNEF to supervise the limited forces zones established by the parties but, due to Soviet action, the mandate of UNEF II expired in July 1979: see e.g. M. Akehurst, 'The Peace Treaty Between Egypt and Israel', 7 *International Relations*, 1981, pp. 1035, 1046, and M. N. Shaw, 'The Egyptian–Israeli Peace Treaty, 1979', 2 *Jewish Law Annual*, 1980, pp. 180, 185. As a result, a special Multinational Force and Observers unit was established by the parties and the United States, independently of the UN: see 20 ILM, 1981, pp. 1190 ff. See also M. Tabory, *The Multinational Force and Observers in the Sinai*, Boulder, 1986, and James, *Peacekeeping*, pp. 122 ff.

[118] See generally White, *Keeping the Peace*.

[119] See S/19836 and Security Council resolution 622 (1988). This activity continued until 1990: see Morphet, 'UN Peacekeeping', p. 213. See also K. Birgisson, 'United Nations Good Offices Mission in Afghanistan and Pakistan' in Durch, *Evolution of UN Peacekeeping*, chapter 18.

[120] This was to monitor the ceasefire and lasted until February 1991: see e.g. Morphet, 'UN Peacekeeping', p. 213, and B. Smith, 'United Nations Iran–Iraq Military Observer Group' in Durch, *Evolution of UN Peacekeeping*, chapter 14.

from Angola,[121] while the UN Transition Assistance Group (UNTAG), although originally established in 1978 in Security Council resolution 435 (1978), commenced operations with the Namibian independence process on 1 April 1989.[122] Efforts to hold a referendum in Western Sahara are being assisted by the UN Mission for the Referendum in Western Sahara (MINURSO),[123] while the UN Iraq–Kuwait Observer Mission (UNIKOM) was set up to monitor the demilitarised zone between these two states following the Gulf War.[124]

Further examples of crucial and complex peacekeeping and/or observer activities include observing Eritrea's plebiscite on secession from Ethiopia[125] and South Africa's elections in 1994,[126] supervising the demilitarisation of Eastern Slavonia, Baranja and Western Sirmium (Croatia) and *inter alia* overseeing the return of refugees, training a police force,

---

[121] Security Council resolution 626 (1988). This was completed in 1991. The Security Council then established UNAVEM II to monitor the implementation of the peace accords between the Angolan government and the UNITA rebels: see Security Council resolution 696 (1991), and V. P. Fortna, 'United Nations Angola Verification Mission I' in Durch, *Evolution of UN Peacekeeping*, chapter 21, and Fortna, 'United Nations Angola Verification Mission II' in Durch, *Evolution of UN Peacekeeping*, chapter 22. This ended in February 1995.

[122] Security Council resolution 632 (1989). UNTAG monitored the withdrawal of South African troops, confined SWAPO forces to their bases in Angola and Zaire and assisted in the election process. The operation ended in March 1990. See V. P. Fortna, 'United Nations Transition Assistance Group in Namibia' in Durch, *Evolution of UN Peacekeeping*, chapter 20. In 1992, the UN Operation in Mozambique (ONUMOZ) was established in order to monitor the peace agreement between the Government and RENAMO rebels: see Security Council resolution 797 (1992). The mission ended in December 1994. See also the UN Observer Group for the Verification of Elections in Nicaragua (ONUVEN) sent to monitor elections in that country following the 1987 Esquipulas Agreement. This was the first electoral observer mission to monitor elections in an independent state: see Security Council 637 (1989). See also Morphet, 'UN Peacekeeping', pp. 216 ff., and Franck, *Fairness*, pp. 105 ff.

[123] See e.g. Security Council resolution 690 (1991) and W. J. Durch, 'United Nations Mission for the Referendum in Western Sahara' in Durch, *Evolution of UN Peacekeeping*, chapter 23. See also the UN Observer Mission in El Salvador established to verify that the government and rebels in the El Salvador civil war complied with the 1990 peace accord, including human rights provisions: see resolution 693 (1991).

[124] See Security Council resolution 689 (1991). See also the UN Advance Mission in Cambodia (UNAMIC) established pursuant to peace efforts in the civil war in that country and which was followed by the UN Transitional Authority in Cambodia (UNTAC), which exercised governmental functions in that state: see resolutions 717 (1991) and 745 (1992). See further above, chapter 5, p. 231.

[125] See General Assembly resolution 47/114, 1992, and A/47/544.

[126] See Security Council resolution 894 (1994). Over 1,800 electoral observers were sent: see Franck, *Fairness*, p. 107.

organising elections and facilitating the removal of mines from the area,[127] monitoring the demilitarisation of the Prevlaka Peninsula in Croatia,[128] assisting the Haitian government in the professionalisation of the police and maintaining a secure environment.[129]

The UN Mission in Ethiopia and Eritrea is a more traditional operation, aimed at overseeing a ceasefire between the two states and assisting them in delimiting and demarcating the boundary.[130] The UN Observer Mission in Georgia has since 1993 been trying to resolve the Abkhazia conflict in Georgia. Its mandate has been expanded and extended since that time.[131] The UN played an extensive role in the move to Timor–Leste independence. The establishment of the UN Mission in East Timor in 1999 provided a mandate to oversee a transition period pending implementation of the decision of the people of that territory under Indonesian occupation as to their future. After the elections and the vote for independence, pro-Indonesian militias commenced a campaign of violence and, after an agreement with Indonesia, the UN adopted resolution 1264 (1999) establishing a multinational force under Australian command to restore peace and security. The UN Transitional Administration in East Timor was established by resolution 1272 (1999) with powers to administer the territory until independence. At the time of the independence of the territory of Timor–Leste in May 2002, the UN Mission of Support in East Timor was established to replace UNTAET.[132] A more traditional peacekeeping deployment was that in August 2006 in Lebanon, facilitating

---

[127] The UN Transitional Administration for Eastern Slavonia, Baranja and Western Sirmium (UNTAES): see Security Council resolution 1037 (1996). This mission had both a military and a civilian component.

[128] The UN Mission of Observers in Prevlaka (UNMOP), Security Council resolution 1038 (1996).

[129] The UN Support Mission in Haiti (UNSMIH): see Security Council resolution 1063 (1996). In June 1996, this mission succeeded the UN Mission in Haiti (UNMIH) created by resolution 867 (1993) to assist the military and police forces in that state. However, it was prevented from deploying. In resolution 940 (1994), the Security Council authorised the creation of a Multi-National Force (MNF): see below, p. 1239, and extended the mandate and scope of UNMIH. After the restoration of the ousted President and the subsequent holding of elections, UNMIH took over responsibility from the MNF (March 1995).

[130] See e.g. Security Council resolutions 1312 (2000), 1320 (2000) and 1640 (2005). This mandate has been regularly renewed: see most recently resolution 1798 (2008).

[131] See e.g. Security Council resolutions 849 (1993), 881 (1993), 1077 (1996), 1364 (2001) 1393 (2002), 1427 (2002), 1462 (2003) and 1494 (2003).

[132] See resolution 1410 (2002). See also, with regard to the UN administration of East Timor, above, chapter 5, p. 232. See as to the establishment by the Security Council of a joint UN–African Union force in Darfur in 2007, below, p. 1280.

the withdrawal of Israeli forces and permitting the return of the Lebanese army to southern Lebanon following a period of Hizbollah control in that area.[133]

The legal framework for the actual conduct of peacekeeping and observer activities reflects their status as UN organs, so that they are, for example, subject to the law governing the UN organisations as a whole, such as that concerning the privileges and immunities of UN personnel[134] and responsibility.[135] The UN would be liable for breaches of law committed by members of peacekeeping and observer forces and groups and would, on the other hand, be able to claim compensation for damage and injuries caused to its personnel. Where forces are stationed on the territory of a state, the usual practice is for formal agreements to be entered into between that state and the UN concerning, for example, facilities, logistics, privileges and immunities of persons and property, and dispute settlement procedures. In 1990, the Secretary-General produced a Model Status of Forces Agreement for Peacekeeping Operations,[136] which covers such matters. It notes, for instance, that the peacekeeping operation and its members are to respect all local laws and regulations, while the government in question undertakes to respect the exclusively international nature of the operation. Jurisdictional and military discipline issues are also dealt with. The UN has also adopted the Convention on the Safety of United Nations and Associated Personnel, 1994 in order to deal with the situation where the UN operation is not an enforcement operation authorised under Chapter VII of the Charter, in combat with local forces and operating under the laws of armed conflict.

The Convention lays down that the UN and the host state should conclude as soon as possible an agreement on the status of the UN operation and all personnel engaged in the operation, including privileges and immunities issues (article 4), and stipulates that the UN and its personnel shall respect local laws and regulations and refrain from any action or activity incompatible with the impartial and international nature of their duties (article 6). The Convention provides that the intentional commission of activities such as the murder or kidnapping of UN or associated personnel, attacks on official premises or private accommodation or means of transportation, are to be made criminal offences under

---

[133] See resolution 1701 (2006).
[134] See in particular the General Convention on the Privileges and Immunities of the United Nations, 1946.
[135] See also Simma, *Charter*, pp. 694 ff.   [136] A/45/594.

national law (article 9), while states parties must take such measures as are necessary to establish jurisdiction in such cases when the crime is committed within their territory (or on board a ship or aircraft registered in that state) or when the alleged offender is a national (article 10). In addition, states parties may establish jurisdiction when the crime has been committed by a stateless person whose habitual residence is in the state concerned or with regard to a national of that state or in an attempt to compel that state to do or abstain from doing any act (article 10).[137]

The question as to whether UN forces are subject to the laws of armed conflict or international humanitarian law[138] has proved controversial. Since the UN is bound by general international law, it is also bound by the customary rules concerning armed conflict,[139] although not by the rules contained only in treaties to which the UN is not a party. Can the United Nations in its various operations involving military personnel in either an enforcement or peacekeeping capacity within states be regarded as subject to international humanitarian law? The problem has arisen in the light of whether such UN activities may be properly classified as 'armed conflicts'.[140] The question of the application of international humanitarian law to operations has been a matter of some concern and a model agreement was put forward in 1991. While the issue proved little of a problem with regard to UN enforcement actions, where it has long been accepted that the rules of humanitarian law applied,[141] although there may be a countervailing pressure since article 2(2) of the Convention on the Safety of United Nations Personnel provides that the Convention will not apply to a UN enforcement operation 'to which the law of international armed conflict applies', difficulties have arisen where the UN has become involved in operations of a mixed peacekeeping/enforcement character. However, the Model Agreement prepared by the Secretary-General in May 1991 specified that 'United Nations peacekeeping operations shall observe and respect the principles and spirit of the general international conventions applicable to the conduct of military

---

[137] The Convention also deals with extradition (articles 13–15) and the fair treatment of alleged offenders (article 17).

[138] See above, chapter 21.

[139] See e.g. S. Will, 'Occupation Law and Multi-National Operations: Problems and Perspectives', 77 BYIL, 2006, pp. 256, 277.

[140] See L. Green, *The Contemporary Law of Armed Conflict*, 2nd edn, Manchester, 2000, chapter 20.

[141] See e.g. D. W. Bowett, *United Nations Forces*, London, 1964, p. 56.

operations'[142] and status of forces agreements signed by the UN with host countries usually contain a provision that humanitarian law applies.[143]

On 6 August 1999, the UN Secretary-General addressed the difficulty and issued a statement declaring that

> The fundamental principles and rules of international humanitarian law . . . are applicable to United Nations forces when in situations of armed conflict they are actively engaged therein as combatants, to the extent and for the duration of their engagement. They are accordingly applicable in enforcement actions, or in peacekeeping operations when the use of force is permissible in self-defence.[144]

Conclusion

The functioning of the United Nations system for the preservation and restoration of world peace has not been a tremendous success in the broadest strategic sense. It constitutes merely one additional factor in international disputes management and one often particularly subject to political pressures. The United Nations has played a minimal part in some of the major conflicts and disputes since its inception, whether it be the Cuban missiles crisis of 1962 or the Vietnam war, the Soviet intervention

---

[142] These conventions would include the 1949 Geneva Conventions and the 1977 Protocols as well as the Convention on the Protection of Cultural Property, 1954: see Green, *Armed Conflict*, p. 344; C. Greenwood, 'International Humanitarian Law and United Nations Military Operations', 1 *Yearbook of International Humanitarian Law*, 1998, p. 3, and D. Shraga, 'UN Peacekeeping Operations: Applicability of International Humanitarian Responsibility for Operations-Related Damage', 94 AJIL, 2000, p. 406.

[143] See e.g. the agreement with Rwanda in 1993 on the status of the UN Mission in that country, Shraga, 'UN Peacekeeping Operation', p. 325, footnote 16, and S/26927, 1993, para. 7. Note also the resolutions adopted by the Institut de Droit International stating that the laws of armed conflict apply to the UN, 54 (II) *Annuaire de l'Institut de Droit International*, 1971, p. 465, and 56 *Annuaire de l'Institut de Droit International*, 1975, p. 540.

[144] ST/SGB/1999/13 (Bulletin on the Observance by UN Forces of International Humanitarian Law). According to the official *United Nations Peacekeeping Operations: Principles and Guidance*, pp. 15–16, this statement sets out the 'fundamental principles and rules of international law that may be applicable to United Nations peacekeepers'. See also P. Rowe, 'Maintaining Discipline in United Nations Peace Support Operations', 5 *Journal of Conflict and Security Law*, 2000, pp. 45, 52 ff.; A. J. T. Dörenberg, 'Legal Aspects of Peacekeeping Operations', 28 *The Military Law and Law of War Review*, 1989, p. 113; F. Hampson, 'States' Military Operations Authorised by the United Nations and International Humanitarian Law' in *The United Nations and International Humanitarian Law* (eds. L. Condorelli, A. M. LaRosa and S. Scherrer), Paris, 1996, p. 371; Y. Dinstein, *War, Aggression and Self-Defence*, 4th edn, Cambridge, 2005, pp. 162–3, and Will, 'Occupation Law', pp. 274 ff.

in Czechoslovakia and Afghanistan or the Nigerian and Angolan civil wars.

Nevertheless, the position of the United Nations improved with the ending of the Cold War and the substantial changes in the approach of the USSR, soon to be Russia, in particular.[145] More emphasis was laid upon the importance of the UN in the context of an increased co-operation with the US. This began to have a significant impact upon the work and achievements of the UN. The new co-operative approach led to the agreements leading to the independence of Namibia, while substantial progress was made by the five permanent members of the Security Council in working out a solution to the Cambodian problem. The long-running dispute with Iraq and how to deal with its failure to comply fully with Security Council resolution 687 (1991) appeared to mark a further moment of achievement with the adoption of resolution 1441 (2002). However, the unanimity of the Council fractured and, amid deep division, the US and the UK commenced a military action against Iraq in March 2003.[146]

The range and extent of activities engaged in by the UN is startling by past experience. UN missions may not only be used now to stabilise a tense situation in the traditional exposition of the peacekeeping approach, they may also be utilised in order to carry out key administrative functions; verify peace agreements both international and internal; monitor the implementation of human rights accords; supervise and monitor elections; train and oversee police forces; oversee withdrawal and demilitarisation arrangements, and assist in demining operations.

The Secretary-General has emphasised that there are three particularly important principles of peacekeeping.[147] These are the consent of the parties, impartiality and the non-use of force. While these three may characterise traditional peacekeeping and observer missions, even as these developed during the 1990s, they do not apply necessarily to a new form of peacekeeping that is mandated under Chapter VII of the Charter.[148] To seek to revitalise the structure, the Secretary-General mandated a Panel on UN Peace Operations to conduct a thorough review. In the Panel Report, a series of recommendations were made.[149] These included encouraging

---

[145] See e.g. A. Roberts and B. Kingsbury, 'The UN's Role in International Society since 1945' in Roberts and Kingsbury, *United Nations, Divided World*, p. 1.

[146] See further below, p. 1255.

[147] *Supplement to an Agenda for Peace*, A/50/60, 1995, para. 33. See also UN, *United Nations Peacekeeping Operations: Principles and Guidelines*, chapter 3.

[148] See below, p. 1257.

[149] See A/55/305–S/2000/809, 21 August 2000 and 39 ILM, 2000, p. 1432. The Report is also termed the Brahimi Report after its chair.

a more frequent use by the Secretary-General of fact-finding missions to areas of tension in support of short-term crisis-preventive action and a doctrinal shift in the use of civilian police and related rule of law elements in peace operations that emphasises an increased focus on, and team approach to, upholding the rule of law and human rights.[150] The Panel reaffirmed that consent of the local parties, impartiality and the use of forces only in self-defence constitute the 'bedrock principles of peacekeeping', but noted that consent could sometimes be manipulated and that impartiality must take into account adherence to UN principles. Equal treatment where one party is violating such principles could not be acceptable.[151] The Panel also called for improved standby arrangements to enable forces to 'meet the need for the robust peacekeeping forces that the Panel has advocated'[152] and 'robust rules of engagement against those who renege on their commitments to a peace accord or otherwise seek to undermine it by violence'.[153] A variety of other recommendations have also been made and the implementation process commenced.[154] In 2006 the Secretary-General outlined a 'Peace Operations 2010' reform strategy[155] and a major reform of the support aspects of peacekeeping operations was initiated.[156]

The collective security system[157]

The system established by the United Nations for the maintenance of international peace and security was intended to be comprehensive in its provisions and universal in its application. It has often been termed a

---

[150] *Ibid.*, paras. 29 ff.   [151] *Ibid.*, paras. 48 ff.
[152] *Ibid.*, paras. 86 ff.   [153] *Ibid.*, para. 55.
[154] See e.g. the Secretary-General's Report on Implementation of 20 October 2000, A/55/502 and the Implementation Reports of 1 June and 21 December 2001, A/55/977 and A/56/732.
[155] A/60/696, paras. 6 ff.
[156] See A/62/11, paras. 51 ff. and Press Release GA/SPD/382, 31 October 2007. As of January 2008, over 100,000 personnel were serving in peace operations, with contributions from 119 states with a budget of $7 billion. Pakistan (10,616), Bangladesh (9,717) and India (9,345) were the largest uniformed personnel contributors, with the US (26%), Japan (17%) and Germany (9%) being the largest providers to the budget: see UN Peacekeeping Factsheet, DPI/2429/rev.2, February 2008.
[157] See e.g. Chesterman *et al.*, *United Nations*, chapter 10; Cot *et al.*, *Charte*, pp. 1131 ff.; Denis, *Pouvoir Normatif*; A. Novosseloff, *Le Conseil de Sécurité des Nations Unies et la Maîtrise de la Force Armée*, Brussels, 2003; E. de Wet, *The Chapter VII Powers of the United Nations Security Council*, Oxford, 2004; Franck, *Fairness*, chapter 9; C. Gray, *International Law and the Use of Force*, 2nd edn, Oxford, 2004, chapter 7; D. Sarooshi, *The United Nations and the Development of Collective Security*, Oxford, 1999; R. Higgins, *Problems and Process*, Oxford, 1994, chapter 15; P. M. Dupuy, 'Sécurité Collective et Organisation de la Paix', 97 RGDIP, 1993, p. 617; G. Gaja, 'Réflexions sur le Rôle du Conseil de Sécurité

collective security system, since a wronged state was to be protected by all, and a wrongdoer punished by all. The history of collective security since 1945 demonstrates how flexibility and textual interpretation have prevented the system from failing completely.

The Security Council

The original scheme by which this was achieved laid great stress upon the role of the Security Council, although this has been modified to some extent in practice. By article 24 of the United Nations Charter, the Council was granted primary responsibility for the maintenance of international peace and security, and its decisions are under article 25 binding upon all member states. It was thus intended to fulfil a dynamic, executive function.

While actions adopted by the Security Council in pursuance of Chapter VI of the Charter, dealing with the pacific settlement of disputes, are purely recommendatory, matters concerning threats to, or breaches of, the peace or acts of aggression, under Chapter VII, give rise to decision-making powers on the part of the Council. This is an important distinction and emphasises the priority accorded within the system to the preservation of peace and the degree of authority awarded to the Security Council to achieve this. The system is completed by article 103 which declares that obligations under the Charter prevail over obligations contained in other international agreements.[158]

Determination of the situation

Before the Council can adopt measures relating to the enforcement of world peace, article 39 of the Charter requires that it must first 'determine the existence of any threat to the peace, breach of the peace or act of

dans le Nouvel Ordre Mondial', *ibid.*, p. 297; T. M. Franck and F. Patel, 'UN Police Action in Lieu of War: "The Older Order Changeth"' , 85 AJIL, 1991, p. 63; C. Gray, 'A Crisis of Legitimacy for the UN Collective Security System?', 56 ICLQ, 2007, p. 157; Nguyen Quoc Dinh, P. Daillier and A. Pellet, *Droit International Public*, 7th edn, Paris, 2002, p. 989, and Simma, *Charter*, pp. 701 ff.

[158] See the *Lockerbie* case, ICJ Reports, 1992, p. 3; 94 ILR, p. 478. But see the discussion of article 103 by Judge Lauterpacht in the second provisional measures order in the *Genocide (Bosnia and Herzegovina v. Yugoslavia (Serbia and Montenegro))* case, ICJ Reports, 1993, pp. 325, 440; 95 ILR, pp. 43, 158, and by Judge Bedjaoui in the *Lockerbie* case, ICJ Reports, 1992, pp. 3, 47; 94 ILR, pp. 478, 530. See also Cot *et al.*, *Charte*, pp. 2133 ff., and A. Toublanc, 'L'Article 103 et la Valeur Juridique de la Charte des Nations Unies', 108 RGDIP, 2004, p. 439.

aggression'. This is the key to the collective security system. Once such a determination has been made, which may be done implicitly by the use of the language contained in article 39 of the Charter,[159] the way is clear for the adoption of recommendations or decisions to deal with the situation. The adoption of Chapter VII enforcement action constitutes an exception to the principle stated in article 2(7) of the Charter, according to which the UN is not authorised 'to intervene in matters which are essentially within the domestic jurisdiction of any state'.

The question is thus raised at this juncture as to the definition of a threat to, or breach of, the peace or act of aggression. The answer that has emerged in practice is that it depends upon the circumstances of the case and it also depends upon the relationship of the five permanent members of the Council (United Kingdom, United States of America, Russia, China and France) to the issue under consideration, for a negative vote by any of the permanent members is sufficient to block all but procedural resolutions of the Council.[160]

Threat to the peace is the broadest category provided for in article 39 and the one least susceptible to precise definition. In a sense it constitutes a safety net for Security Council action where the conditions needed for a breach of the peace or act of aggression do not appear to be present. It is also the category which has marked a rapid evolution as the perception as to what amounts to a threat to international peace and security has broadened. In particular, the concept has been used to cover internal situations that would once have been shielded from UN action by article 2(7) of the Charter.

A threat to the peace was first determined in the 1948 Middle East War, when in resolution 54 (1948), the Security Council found that the situation created by the conflict in the former mandated territory of Palestine where neighbouring Arab countries had entered the territory in order to conduct hostilities against the new state of Israel constituted 'a threat to the peace within the meaning of article 39' and demanded a cease-fire. In resolution 221 (1966) the Council determined that the situation of the minority white regime in Rhodesia constituted a threat to the peace.[161]

With the cessation of the Cold War, the Security Council has been able to extend its activities under Chapter VII to a remarkable extent. In resolution 713 (1991) the Council determined that the situation in former

---

[159] Gray, *Use of Force*, p. 197.   [160] Article 27 of the UN Charter.
[161] See also Security Council resolution 217 (1965).

Yugoslavia[162] constituted a threat to the peace and in resolution 733 (1992), it was held that the situation in Somalia amounted to a threat to peace. In resolution 794 (1992), the Council underlined that 'the magnitude of the human tragedy caused by the conflict in Somalia, further exacerbated by the obstacles being created to the distribution of humanitarian assistance, constitutes a threat to international peace and security'.[163] In resolution 788 (1992) the Council decided that the deteriorating civil war situation in Liberia constituted a threat to international peace, while in resolution 955 (1994), it was determined that the genocide in Rwanda constituted a threat to international peace and security. The latter three cases were clearly internal civil war situations and it could be said that the situation in Yugoslavia at the time of the adoption of the 1991 resolution was also a civil war situation, although this is more complex. Further resolutions with regard to former Yugoslavia determined that threats to the peace were involved.[164] In another move of considerable importance, the Council has also determined that 'widespread violations of international humanitarian law' constitute a threat to peace.[165] Resolutions concerning Sierra Leone[166] affirmed that the civil war in that country constituted a threat to international peace, while resolutions concerning the mixed civil war/foreign intervention conflicts in the Democratic Republic of the Congo affirmed that there existed a 'threat to international peace and security in the region'.[167]

A further expansion in the meaning in practice of a threat to international peace and security took place with regard to Libya. In resolution 748 (1992) the Council determined that 'the failure by the Libyan Government to demonstrate by concrete actions its renunciation of terrorism and in particular its continued failure to respond fully and effectively to the requests in resolution 731 (1992),[168] constitute a threat to international peace and security'. Again, in resolution 1070 (1996), the Council determined that the failure of Sudan to comply with earlier resolutions

---

[162] This situation was characterised by fighting 'causing a heavy loss of human life and material damage, and by the consequences for the countries in the region, in particular in the border areas of neighbouring countries', *ibid.*

[163] See also Security Council resolution 751 (1992).

[164] See e.g. Security Council resolutions 743 (992), 757 (1992), 787 (1992) and 827 (1993).

[165] See Security Council resolutions 808 (1993), with regard to former Yugoslavia, and 955 (1994), with regard to Rwanda.

[166] See further below, p. 1263.   [167] See further below, p. 1264.

[168] Which called for the extradition of alleged bombers of an airplane over Lockerbie in 1988 to the US or UK.

demanding that it act to extradite to Ethiopia for prosecution suspects on its territory wanted in connection with an assassination attempt against the President of Egypt,[169] constituted a threat to international peace and security. In both cases references to 'international terrorism' were made in the context of a determination of a threat to the peace. This constitutes an important step in combating such a phenomenon for it paves the way for the adoption of binding sanctions in such circumstances. This has been reinforced by resolutions 1368 (2001) and 1373 (2001) adopted in the wake of the 11 September bombings of the World Trade Center in New York and of the Pentagon.[170]

The Haiti situation similarly marked a development in the understanding by the Council as to what may amount to a threat to international peace and security. UN observers monitored an election in that country in 1990, but on 30 September 1991 the elected President Aristide was ousted. In a process which demonstrates the growing interaction between UN organs in crisis situations, the Secretary-General appointed a Special Representative for Haiti on 11 December 1991, the General Assembly authorised a joint UN–Organisation of American States civilian mission on human rights (MICIVIH) on 20 April 1993,[171] and on 16 June 1993, the Security Council imposed an arms and oil embargo on Haiti with sanctions to enter into force on 23 June unless the Secretary-General and the OAS reported that such measures were no longer warranted.[172] The Security Council referred to the fact that 'the legitimate Government of President Jean-Bernard Aristide' had not been reinstated and noted 'the incidence of humanitarian crises, including mass displacements of population, becoming or aggravating threats to international peace and security'.[173] The Council determined therefore that 'in these unique and exceptional circumstances', the continuation of the situation constituted a threat to international peace and security. Thus although the Security Council did not go so far as to declare that the removal of a legitimate government constituted of itself a threat to peace, it was clearly the precipitating factor that taken together with other matters could enable a determination to be made under article 39 thus permitting the

---

[169] Security Council resolutions 1044 (1996) and 1054 (1996).

[170] See above, chapter 20, p. 1162.   [171] See General Assembly resolution 47/20 B.

[172] Security Council resolution 841 (1993).

[173] Note that in Security Council resolution 688 (1991), it had been determined that the consequences of the Iraqi repression of its civilian population in different parts of the country, including areas populated by Kurds, involving considerable refugee flows over the borders of Turkey and Iran threatened international peace and security.

adoption of binding sanctions. The sanctions were suspended following the Governors Island Agreement of 3 July 1993.[174] However, in resolution 873 (1993), the Council determined that the failure by the military authorities in Haiti to fulfil obligations under that agreement constituted a threat to international peace and security, and sanctions were reimposed.[175] As the Appeal Chamber declared in the *Tadić* case:

> Indeed, the practice of the Security Council is rich with cases of civil war or internal strife which is classified as a 'threat to the peace' and dealt with under Chapter VII... It can thus be said that there is a common understanding, manifested by the 'subsequent practice' of the membership of the United Nations at large, that the 'threat to the peace' of article 39 may include, as one of its species, internal armed conflicts.[176]

Further, in resolution 1540 (2004), the Council affirmed that the proliferation of nuclear, chemical and biological weapons, as well as their means of delivery, constituted a threat to international peace and security and proceeded to establish a sanctions regime monitored by a committee of the Council.

After several decades of discussion and deliberation, a definition of aggression was finally agreed upon by the United Nations General Assembly in 1974.[177] Article 1 provides that aggression is the use of armed force by a state against the sovereignty, territorial integrity or political independence of another state, or in any other manner inconsistent with the United Nations Charter. A number of examples of aggressive acts are given in article 3 and these include the use of weapons by a state against the territory of another state, the blockade of the ports or coasts of a state by the armed forces of another state,[178] and attack by the armed forces of a state on the land, sea or air forces of another state and the sending by, or on behalf of, a state of armed bands to carry out acts of armed force against another state.[179] This elucidation of some of the features of the concept of aggression might prove of some use to the Security Council, but the Council does retain the right to examine all the relevant circumstances,

---

[174] Security Council resolution 861 (1993).
[175] Security Council resolution 873 (1993). Further sanctions were imposed in resolution 917 (1994). Sanctions were finally lifted by resolution 944 (1994), upon the restoration of President Aristide following a US-led operation in Haiti.
[176] 105 ILR, pp. 419, 466.   [177] General Assembly resolution 3314 (XXIX).
[178] As, for example, the blockade of the Israeli port of Eilat in May 1967, above, chapter 20, p. 1138.
[179] See the *Nicaragua* case, ICJ Reports, 1986, pp. 14, 103–4; 76 ILR, pp. 349, 437.

including the gravity of any particular incident, before deciding on the determination to make pursuant to article 39.[180]

Findings as to actual breaches of the peace have occurred four times. In 1950, as a result of the invasion of South Korea by North Korea, the Security Council adopted resolutions determining that a breach of the peace had occurred and calling upon member states to assist South Korea,[181] while in resolution 502 (1982) the Council determined that a breach of the peace in the Falkland Islands region had taken place following the Argentine invasion. The third situation which prompted a finding by the Security Council of a breach of the peace was in resolution 598 (1987) dealing with the Iran–Iraq war, while the fourth occasion was in resolution 660 (1990) in which the Council determined that there existed 'a breach of international peace and security as regards the Iraqi invasion of Kuwait'.

Chapter VII measures[182]

Measures not involving the use of force[183] Once the Security Council has resolved that a particular dispute or situation involves a threat to the peace or act of aggression, the way is open to take further measures. Such further measures may, however, be preceded by provisional action taken to prevent the aggravation of the situation. This action, provided for by article 40 of the Charter,[184] is without prejudice to the rights or claims of the parties, and is intended as a provisional measure to stabilise a crisis situation. Usual examples of action taken by the Security Council under this provision include calls for ceasefires (as in the Middle East in 1967 and 1973)[185] and calls for the withdrawal of troops from foreign territory.[186] However, the adoption of provisional measures by the Council

---

[180] The first finding as to aggression by the Security Council was in 1976 with regard to South African action against Angola, Security Council resolution 387 (1976). See also Security Council resolutions 411 (1977) condemning Rhodesian action against Mozambique, 573 (1985) condemning Israel's action against PLO headquarters in Tunisia and 667 (1990) condemning aggressive acts by Iraq against diplomatic premises and personnel in Kuwait.

[181] Security Council resolution S/1501.

[182] See e.g. P. Conlon, 'Legal Problems at the Centre of United Nations Sanctions', 65 *Nordic Journal of International Law*, 1996, p. 73.

[183] See e.g. M. Doxey, *Economic Sanctions and International Enforcement*, London, 1980; J. Combacau, *Le Pouvoir de Sanction de l'ONU*, Paris, 1974; N. Schrijver, 'The Use of Economic Sanctions by the UN Security Council: An International Perspective' in *International Economic Law and Armed Conflict* (ed. H. Post), Dordrecht, 1994, and *Economic Sanctions: Panacea or Peace-Building in a Post-Cold War World* (eds. D. Cortright and G. Lopez), Boulder, 1995.

[184] See Simma, *Charter*, p. 729, and Cot *et al.*, *Charte*, p. 1171.

[185] See Security Council resolutions 234 (1967) and 338 (1973).

[186] See e.g. Security Council resolution 509 (1982), with regard to Israel's invasion of Lebanon.

often has an effect ranging far beyond the confines of a purely temporary action. They may induce a calmer atmosphere leading to negotiations to resolve the difficulties and they may set in train moves to settle the dispute upon the basis laid down in the Security Council resolution which called for the provisional measures.

The action adopted by the Council, once it has decided that there exists with regard to a situation a threat to the peace, breach of the peace or act of aggression, may fall into either of two categories. It may amount to the application of measures not involving the use of armed force under article 41, such as the disruption of economic relations or the severance of diplomatic relations, or may call for the use of such force as may be necessary to maintain or restore international peace and security under article 42.

The Council has not until recently utilised the powers it possesses under article 41 to any great extent. The first major instance of action not including the use of force occurred with respect to the Rhodesian situation following upon the Unilateral Declaration of Independence by the white minority government of that territory in 1965.[187] In two resolutions in 1965, the Council called upon member states not to recognise or assist the illegal regime and in particular to break all economic and arms relations with it.[188] The next year, the Council went further and imposed selective mandatory economic sanctions upon Rhodesia,[189] which were extended in 1968 and rendered comprehensive,[190] although several states did act in defiance of these resolutions.[191] Sanctions were

---

[187] See e.g. Simma, *Charter*, p. 735; Cot *et al.*, *Charte*, p. 1195; Nguyen Quoc Dinh *et al.*, *Droit International Public*, p. 997; R. Zacklin, *The United Nations and Rhodesia*, New York, 1974; J. E. S. Fawcett, 'Security Council Resolutions on Rhodesia', 41 BYIL, 1965–6, p. 103; M. S. McDougal and W. M. Reisman, 'Rhodesia and the United Nations: The Lawfulness of International Concern', 62 AJIL, 1968, p. 1, and J. Nkala, *The United Nations, International Law and the Rhodesia Independence Crisis*, Oxford, 1985. See also V. Gowlland-Debbas, *Collective Responses to Illegal Acts in International Law*, Dordrecht, 1990, and Gowlland-Debbas, 'Security Council Enforcement Action and Issues of State Responsibility', 43 ICLQ, 1994, p. 55.

[188] Security Council resolutions 216 (1965) and 217 (1965).

[189] Security Council resolution 232 (1966). Note that under Security Council resolution 221 (1966) the Council *inter alia* called upon the UK 'to prevent by the use of force if necessary' the arrival in Mozambique of vessels believed to be carrying oil for Rhodesia.

[190] Security Council resolution 253 (1968). See also Security Council resolution 409 (1977).

[191] See N. Polakas, 'Economic Sanctions: An Effective Alternative to Military Coercion?', 6 *Brooklyn Journal of International Law*, 1980, p. 289. Note also the importation by the United States of Rhodesian chrome and other minerals under the Byrd Amendment between 1972 and 1977: see DUSPIL, 1977, Washington, pp. 830–4.

terminated in 1979 as a result of the agreement leading to the independence of Zimbabwe.[192]

However, the most comprehensive range of economic sanctions thus far imposed by the Security Council was adopted in the wake of the invasion of Kuwait by Iraq on 2 August 1990.[193] Security Council resolution 661 (1990), noting that Iraq had failed to withdraw immediately and unconditionally from Kuwait[194] and acting specifically under Chapter VII of the Charter, imposed a wide range of economic sanctions upon Iraq, including the prohibition by states of all imports from and exports to Iraq and occupied Kuwait,[195] and the transfer of funds to Iraq and Kuwait for such purposes. Additionally, the Security Council decided that states should not make available to the Government of Iraq or to any commercial, industrial or public utility undertaking in Iraq or Kuwait any funds or any other financial or economic resources and should prevent their nationals and persons within their territories from remitting any other funds to persons or bodies within Iraq or Kuwait,[196] notwithstanding any existing contract or licence.

The Security Council also established a Committee consisting of all members of the Council to oversee the implementation of these measures.[197] Under Security Council resolution 666 (1990), the Committee was instructed to keep the situation regarding foodstuffs in Iraq and Kuwait under constant review and to bear in mind that foodstuffs (as permitted under the terms of the previous resolutions) should be provided through the UN in co-operation with the International Committee of the Red Cross or other appropriate humanitarian agencies and distributed by them or under their supervision. The Committee was additionally given the task of examining requests for assistance under

---

[192] Security Council resolution 460 (1979). See also 19 ILM, 1980, pp. 287 ff. Note in addition Security Council resolution 418 (1977), which imposed an arms embargo upon South Africa.

[193] See Lauterpacht et al., Kuwait Crisis: Basic Documents; The Kuwait Crisis: Sanctions and their Economic Consequences (ed. D. Bethlehem), Cambridge, 1991.

[194] As required in Security Council resolution 660 (1990).

[195] Apart from supplies intended strictly for medical purposes and, 'in humanitarian circumstances', foodstuffs, paragraph 3(c).

[196] Except payments exclusively for strictly medical or humanitarian purposes and, in humanitarian circumstances, foodstuffs, paragraph 4.

[197] See e.g. M. Koskenniemi, 'Le Comité des Sanctions Créé par la Résolution 661 (1990) du Conseil de Sécurité', AFDI, 1991, p. 121, and P. Conlon, 'Lessons from Iraq: The Functions of the Iraq Sanctions Committee as a Source of Sanctions Implementation Authority and Practice', 35 Va. JIL, 1995, p. 632.

article 50 of the Charter[198] and making recommendations to the President of the Security Council for appropriate action.[199] The binding economic sanctions imposed on Iraq because of its invasion and purported annexation of Kuwait were tightened in Security Council resolution 670 (1990), in which the Council decided that all states, irrespective of any international agreements or contracts, licences or permits in existence, were to deny permission to any aircraft to take off from their territory if the aircraft was carrying cargo to or from Iraq or Kuwait.[200] In addition, states were to deny permission to any aircraft destined to land in Iraq or Kuwait to overfly their territory.[201]

The economic sanctions were reinforced under Security Council resolution 665 (1990) which authorised those UN member states deploying maritime forces in the area in co-operation with the legitimate government of Kuwait 'to use such measures commensurate to the specific circumstances as may be necessary under the authority of the Security Council' in order to enforce the naval blockade on Iraq. The states concerned were requested to co-ordinate their actions 'using as appropriate mechanisms of the Military Staffs Committee'[202] and after consultation with the UN Secretary-General to submit reports to the Security Council and the Committee established under resolution 661 (1990). It is unclear whether given a substantial period of operation, this impressive range of sanctions would have sufficed to compel Iraq to withdraw from Kuwait, for on 16 January 1991 force was employed.

Having once established a comprehensive set of economic and financial sanctions together with mechanisms of supervision, it has become easier to put in place similar responses to other situations. On 31 March 1992, the Security Council imposed a relatively restricted range of sanctions upon Libya due to the latter's refusal to renounce terrorism and

---

[198] Article 50 provides that if preventive or enforcement measures against any state are taken by the Security Council, any other state which finds itself confronted with special economic problems arising from the carrying out of those measures shall have the right to consult the Security Council with regard to a solution to those problems. Note also the reference to article 50 in Security Council resolution 748 (1992), imposing sanctions upon Libya, and resolution 669 (1990). See e.g. Dinstein, *War*, pp. 283–4; J. Carver and J. Hulsmann, 'The Role of Article 50 of the UN Charter in the Search for International Peace and Security', 49 ICLQ, 2000, p. 528, and Cot *et al.*, *Charte*, p. 1313.

[199] Security Council resolution 669 (1990).

[200] Other than food in humanitarian circumstances subject to authorisation by the Council or the Committee or supplies intended strictly for medical purposes.

[201] Unless the aircraft was landing for inspection or the flight had been approved by the Committee or the flight was certified by the UN as solely for the purposes of the UN Iran–Iraq Military Observer Group (UNIIMOG).

[202] See below, p. 1251.

respond fully and effectively to the call in Security Council resolution 731 (1992) to extradite suspected bombers to the UK or US.[203] These sanctions imposed a mandatory arms and air embargo upon Libya. It also called upon states to reduce significantly the number and the level of staff at Libyan diplomatic missions and diplomatic posts. A Committee was set up to monitor compliance with the sanctions. Resolution 1192 (1998) provided *inter alia* for the suspension of the sanctions upon the certification by the Secretary-General of the arrival of the accused bombers in the Netherlands for trial. This duly occurred[204] and the President of the Council issued a statement on 9 July 1999 noting therefore the suspension of the sanctions.[205]

On 30 May 1992, the Security Council in resolution 757 (1992) imposed a wide range of economic sanctions upon the Federal Republic of Yugoslavia (Serbia and Montenegro), having imposed an arms embargo upon all states within the territory of the former Yugoslavia in resolution 713 (1991).[206] The resolution, adopted under Chapter VII, prohibited the importation of goods from the Federal Republic of Yugoslavia (Serbia and Montenegro) and the export or trans-shipment of such goods by states or their nationals and the sale or supply of any commodities or products to any person or body in the Federal Republic of Yugoslavia or to any person or body for the purposes of any business carried on in or operated from it. In addition, paragraph 5 of this resolution prohibited states from making available to the authorities in the Federal Republic of Yugoslavia (Serbia and Montenegro) or to any commercial, industrial or public utility undertaking there, any funds or any other financial or economic resources. States were also to prevent their nationals and any persons within their territories from providing to anyone within the Federal Republic any funds or resources at all, except for payments exclusively for strictly medical or humanitarian purposes and foodstuffs.[207]

These sanctions were essentially extended by Security Council resolution 820 (1993) to areas of Croatia and Bosnia controlled by the Bosnian Serb forces. In addition, the Danube River was included within the sanctions control system and the transport of all goods (apart from medical

---

[203] Security Council resolution 748 (1992).

[204] See S/1999/726.   [205] See S/PRST/1999/22.

[206] A Sanctions Committee was established under Security Council resolution 724 (1991).

[207] See also resolution 787 (1992), which decided that any vessel in which a majority or a controlling interest was held by a person or undertaking in or operating from the Federal Republic was to be considered for the purpose of the sanctions regime as a Yugoslav vessel, irrespective of the flag flown. Further maritime control measures were also adopted under this resolution.

supplies and foodstuffs) across the land borders to or from the ports of the Federal Republic was prohibited.[208] Resolution 942 (1994) extended sanctions to cover economic activities carried on within states by any entity owned or controlled, directly or indirectly, by any person or entity resident in areas of Bosnia under the control of the Bosnian Serb forces.

As negotiations progressed, the sanctions against the Federal Republic of Yugoslavia were progressively eased.[209] After the Dayton peace agreement was initialled, the arms embargo was lifted[210] and sanctions were suspended indefinitely by resolution 1022 (1995) on 22 November 1995, except with regard to Bosnian Serb forces.[211] Sanctions were fully lifted by resolution 1074 (1996) following the holding of elections in Bosnia as required under the peace agreement and the Sanctions Committee was dissolved. Arms sanctions were reimposed in 1998 due to the Kosovo situation, but lifted in 2001.[212]

Arms sanctions have also been imposed upon Somalia,[213] Rwanda,[214] Liberia[215] and Ethiopia and Eritrea.[216] An arms embargo on Sierra Leone[217]

---

[208] Resolution 820 also decided that states were to impound all vessels, freight vehicles, rolling stock and aircraft in their territories in which a majority or controlling interest was held by a person or undertaking in or operating from the Federal Republic. Paragraph 21 of the resolution called for states to freeze funds of the authorities in the Federal Republic or of commercial, industrial or public utility undertakings there, and of funds controlled directly or indirectly by such authorities or undertakings or by entities, wherever located or organised, owned or controlled by such authorities or undertakings.

[209] See e.g. Security Council resolutions 943 (1994), 988 (1995), 992 (1995), 1003 (1995) and 1015 (1995).

[210] Security Council resolution 1021 (1995).

[211] The resolution also provided for the release of frozen assets, 'provided that any such funds and assets that are subject to any claims, liens, judgments, or encumbrances, or which are the funds of any person, partnership, corporation, or other entity found or deemed insolvent under law or the accounting principles prevailing in such state, shall remain frozen or impounded until released in accordance with applicable law'.

[212] See resolutions 1160 (1998) and 1367 (2001).

[213] See Security Council resolutions 733 (1992), 751 (1992), 1356 (2001), 1407 (2002) ,1425 (2002), 1744 (2007) and 1772 (2007).

[214] See resolutions 918 (1994), 1005 (1995), 1011 (1995), 1013 (1995), 1053 (1996) and 1161 (1998).

[215] See resolutions 788 (1992) and 985 (1995). Sanctions were terminated by resolution 1343 (2001), but reintroduced in resolution 1521 (2003). See also resolutions 1532 (2004) and 1683 (2006). The regime was most recently extended by resolution 1713 (2006).

[216] See resolution 1298 (2000). Sanctions were terminated in pursuance of Presidential Statement S/PRST/2001/14 of 15 May 2001. Note that this was the first time that sanctions had been imposed on both sides in a conflict: see C. Gray, 'From Unity to Polarisation: International Law and the Use of Force against Iraq', 13 EJIL, 2002, pp. 1, 3.

[217] See resolutions 1132 (1997) and 1171 (1998).

was extended to cover the import of rough-cut diamonds other than those controlled by the government under the certificate of origin scheme.[218] An air embargo and a freezing of assets was imposed on the Taliban regime in Afghanistan in 1999.[219] An arms embargo was imposed on all foreign and Congolese armed groups and militias operating in the territory of North and South Kivu and Ituri, and on groups not party to the Global and All-inclusive Agreement in the Democratic Republic of the Congo in resolution 1493 (2003),[220] while in resolution 1718 (2006) an arms embargo was placed on North Korea, which was called upon to suspend all activities related to its ballistic missile programme, and abandon all nuclear weapons and existing nuclear programmes, and all other existing weapons of mass destruction and ballistic missile programmes in a complete, verifiable and irreversible manner. An arms embargo on the Sudan was imposed in 2004 with regard to all non-governmental entities and individuals, including the Janjaweed Arab militia, operating in North, South and West Darfur,[221] while sanctions have also been imposed upon Iran in view of suspicions that it is moving towards the acquisition of nuclear weapons in violation of its obligations under the Nuclear Non-Proliferation Treaty.[222]

---

[218] See resolutions 1306 (2000), 1385 (2001) and 1446 (2002). The diamonds sanctions ended in June 2003: see SC/7778. Note also the sanctions imposed on the Ivory Coast, comprising an arms embargo, travel ban on particular individuals, assets freeze on individuals and designated entities and diamond sanctions: see e.g. resolutions 1572 (2004), 1584 (2005), 1643 (2005) and 172 (2007). Sanctions were also imposed on individuals to be determined with regard to Lebanon following the assassination of former prime minister Hariri and others: see resolution 1636 (2005).

[219] See resolution 1267 (1999). The sanctions regime was intensified in e.g. resolutions 1333 (2000), 1390 (2002), 1455 (2003), 1526 (2004), 1617 (2005) and 1735 (2006). Sanctions currently cover individuals and entities associated with Al-Qaida, Usama bin Laden and/or the Taliban wherever located.

[220] See also resolutions 1533 (2004), 1596 (2005), 1649 (2005) and 1698 (2006), expanding the scope of the arms embargo, imposing additional targeted sanctions measures (travel ban and assets freeze), and broadening the criteria under which individuals could be designated as subject to those measures. In resolution 1807 (2008), the arms embargo was limited to all non-governmental entities and individuals operating in the territory of the Congo, while the travel ban and assets freeze were extended to individuals operating in that country and committing serious violations of international law involving the targeting of women. See also resolution 1804 (2008) affirming the application of sanctions to various Rwandan armed groups operating in the Congo.

[221] See resolution 1556 (2004). The scope of the arms embargo was expanded and additional measures imposed, including a travel ban and an assets freeze on designated individuals, in resolution 1591 (2005).

[222] Sanctions include a proliferation-sensitive nuclear and ballistic missile programmes-related embargo; an export ban on arms and related matériel from Iran; and individual

While measures taken under article 41 have traditionally been economic sanctions, other possibilities exist. The Council may, for example, call for action to be taken to reduce the number and level of diplomatic staff of the target state within other states.[223] More dramatically,
the Council has on two occasions established international tribunals to
prosecute war criminals by the adoption of binding resolutions under
Chapter VII.[224] Further, the Council may adopt a series of determinations concerning legal responsibilities of states that will have considerable
consequences.

Security Council Resolution 687 (1991), adopted under Chapter VII of
the Charter and agreed to by Iraq as part of the ceasefire arrangement,[225]
constitutes the supreme illustration of such a situation. This laid down
a series of conditions for the ending of the conflict in the Gulf. The resolution demanded that Iraq and Kuwait respect the inviolability of the
international boundary as laid down in the Agreed Minutes signed by Iraq
and Kuwait on 4 October 1963. The Council then proceeded to guarantee
the inviolability of this international boundary, a development of great
significance in the history of the UN. The resolution also provided for the
immediate deployment of a UN observer unit to monitor a demilitarised
zone to be established extending 10 kilometres into Iraq and 5 kilometres
into Kuwait from the international boundary.[226] Iraq was called upon to
accept the destruction or removal of all chemical and biological weapons
and all ballistic missiles with a range greater than 150 kilometres. A special
commission was provided for to ensure that this happened.[227] Iraq was
to agree unconditionally not to acquire or develop nuclear weapons. The
Security Council resolution reaffirmed that Iraq was liable under international law for any direct loss, damage, including environmental damage
and the depletion of natural resources, or injury to foreign governments,

targeted sanctions (a travel ban, a travel notification requirement and an assets freeze
on designated persons and entities): see resolutions 1737 (2006), 1747 (2007) and 1803
(2008).

[223] See e.g. Security Council resolution 748 (1992), with regard to Libya.

[224] See Security Council resolutions 808 (1992) and 827 (1992) with regard to former
Yugoslavia, and 955 (1994) with regard to Rwanda. See also the *Milutinović* case before the International Criminal Tribunal for the Former Yugoslavia, IT–99–37–PT, 6 May
2003.

[225] See S/22456, 6 April 1991.   [226] See further above, p. 1229.

[227] See also Security Council resolutions 707 (1991) and 715 (1991) and the Reports of
the Special Commission, e.g. S/23165; S/23268; S/24108 and Corr.1; S/24984; S/25977;
S/26910; S/1994/750; S/1994/1138; S/1994/1422 and S/1994/1422/Add.1.

nationals and corporations, as a result of Iraq's unlawful invasion and occupation of Kuwait.[228]

The scope and extent of this binding resolution amounts to a considerable development of the Security Council's efforts to resolve disputes. The demands that Iraq give up certain types of weapons and the requirement that repudiation of foreign debt is invalidated would appear to mark a new departure for the Council. In this category would also fall the guarantee given to the inviolability of an international border which is still the subject of dispute between the two parties concerned. In addition to the provisions noted above, the Council established a fund to pay compensation for claims[229] and created a UN Compensation Commission.[230]

Sanctions continued after the ceasefire as the Security Council determined that Iraq had failed to comply fully with resolution 687 (1991). Concern centred upon the failure to destroy weapons of mass destruction as required in the resolution. Iraq was also required to place all of its nuclear-weapon-usable materials under the exclusive control of the International Atomic Energy Agency (IAEA) and unconditionally agree not to acquire or develop nuclear weapons or nuclear-weapon-usable materials.[231] The United Nations Special Commission (UNSCOM) was created to implement the non-nuclear provisions of the resolution and to assist the IAEA in the nuclear areas.

Iraq ceased its partial co-operation with UNSCOM in October 1998. The Security Council adopted resolution 1205 (1998) condemning this as a 'flagrant violation' of resolution 687 (1991). The UNSCOM inspectors were withdrawn in December 1998 and the conclusion of its final report was that Iraq had not provided it with the necessary declarations and notifications as required under Security Council resolution.[232] In resolution 1284 (1999), noting that Iraq had not fully carried out Council resolutions so that sanctions could not be lifted, the Security Council

---

[228] In a further interesting but controversial provision, the resolution 'decides that all Iraqi statements made since 2 August 1990, repudiating its foreign debt, are null and void, and demands that Iraq scrupulously adhere to all of its obligations concerning servicing and repayment of its foreign debt'.

[229] See paragraph 18 of resolution 687 (1991).

[230] *Ibid.*, paragraph 16 and see Security Council resolution 692 (1991). See further above, chapter 18, p. 1045.

[231] Paragraph 12.

[232] See S/1999/1037. See also S/1999/94 detailing the problems faced by UNSCOM and Iraq's partial destruction of proscribed weapons coupled with 'a practice of concealment of proscribed items, including weapons, and a cover up of its activities in contravention of Council resolutions', *ibid.*, para. 5.

established the UN Monitoring, Verification and Inspection Commission (UNMOVIC) to replace UNSCOM.[233] In resolution 1441 (2002), adopted unanimously, the Security Council pointed to Iraq's failures to comply with resolution 687 (1991) and decided that Iraq remained in 'material breach' of its obligations under Council resolutions. The sanctions regime that continued in force was mitigated by the adoption of the 'oil-for-food' programme instituted under resolution 986 (1995) and administered by the UN.[234]

The issue generally of the efficacy of sanctions remains open, but the economic damage that sanctions can do to the general population of a state, particularly where the government concerned does not operate in good faith, may be immense, and this has opened a debate as to whether sanctions may be better focused and targeted or made 'smarter'.[235] One manifestation of this has been the increasing resort to sanctions against particular individuals or entities (as determined by the Security Council sanctions committee established to deal with the matter). This has raised the issue as to the ability of the named persons or entities to challenge their inclusion on the relevant list. Different de-listing (removal) procedures have been established by the various sanctions committees monitoring imposed sanctions, but these have not permitted direct approaches by individuals or entities concerned and this has prompted human rights concerns.[236] Accordingly, the Security Council adopted resolution 1730 (2006), which called for the Secretary-General to establish within the Secretariat (Security Council Subsidiary Organs Branch) a focal point to receive de-listing requests from the pertinent individuals or entities.

---

[233] See e.g. C. de Jonge Oudraat, 'UNSCOM: Between Iraq and a Hard Place', 13 EJIL, 2002, p. 139.

[234] See S/1996/356 and, most recently, S/2002/1239. Note that Security Council resolution 1472 (2003), adopted eight days after the military operation against Iraq began, provided for the temporary extension of the oil-for-food arrangements under the changed conditions. The arrangements were also modified in resolutions 1284 (1999) and 1409 (2002). Resolution 1483 (2003) supported the formation of an 'interim administration' for Iraq, following the occupation of that state by the UK and the USA, by the people of Iraq with the help of 'the Authority' (the UK and USA) and all economic sanctions (apart from arms) were lifted: see further below, p. 1256.

[235] See e.g. General Assembly resolution 51/242 and UKMIL, 70 BYIL, 1999, p. 549. See also Gray, Use of Force, p. 209, and Forum, 13 EJIL, 2002, p. 43.

[236] See e.g. E. Rosand, 'The Security Council's Efforts to Monitor the Implementation of Al-Qaida/Taliban Sanctions', 98 AJIL, 2004, p. 745, and B. Fassbender, Targeted Sanctions and Due Process, 2006, a study commissioned by the UN Office of Legal Affairs, www.un.org/law/counsel/Fassbender_study.pdf. See also C. Tomuschat, Human Rights, Oxford, 2003, p. 90, and K. Wellens, Remedies against International Organizations, Cambridge, 2002, p. 89.

Such requests are to be sent to the designating governments concerned (and governments of citizenship and residence), who may approach the sanctions committee directly or through the focal point, proposing that the individuals or entitites be removed from the sanctions list. It will then be for the sanctions committee to take the decision.[237]

Measures involving the use of force   Where the Council feels that the measures short of armed force as prescribed under article 41 have been or would be inadequate, it may take 'such action by air, sea or land forces as may be necessary to maintain or restore international peace and security'. Article 42 also provides that such action may extend to demonstrations, blockades and other armed operations by members of the United Nations. In order to be able to function effectively in this sphere, article 43 provides for member states to conclude agreements with the Security Council to make available armed forces, assistance and facilities, while article 45 provides that member states should hold immediately available national air-force contingents for combined international enforcement action in accordance with article 43 agreements. In this manner it was intended to create a United Nations corps to act as the arm of the Council to suppress threats to, or breaches of, the peace or acts of aggression.

Article 47 provides for the creation of a Military Staffs Committee, composed of the Chiefs of Staff of the five permanent members or their representatives, to advise and assist the Security Council on military requirements and to be responsible for the strategic direction of any armed force placed at the disposal of the Security Council. Indeed, article 46 provides that plans for the application of armed force 'shall be made by the Security Council with the assistance of the Military Staffs Committee'. However, during the Kuwait crisis of 1990–1, the Military Staffs Committee played an important co-ordinating role, while under Security Council resolution 665 (1990) it was given a more general co-ordination function.

---

[237] Where no comments are received within three months, the sanctions committee will be so informed and any member may request de-listing. The Secretary-General informed the Security Council on 30 March 2007 that the focal point had been established, S/2007/178. Note that in the *Yusuf* and *Kadi* cases it was argued that the persons concerned had been wrongly listed and that EU Regulation 881/2002, implementing the UN sanctions, should be annulled with regard to them: see the judgment of 21 September 2005 of the European Court of First Instance, T-306/01 and T/315/01 (which refused to review the Regulation) and the opinion of the advocate-general of the European Court of Justice, C-402/05 P of 16 January 2008, which proposed that the judgment of the Court of First Instance be set aside and the Regulation in so far as it related to the persons concerned annulled. The matter is currently before the European Court of Justice.

Because of great power disputes and other factors, none of the projected agreements has been signed and article 43 remains ineffective. This has weakened article 42 to the extent that the envisaged procedure for its implementation has had to be abandoned. This has meant that the UN through a process of interpretation by subsequent conduct has been obliged to reconfigure the collective security regime.

The first example of enforcement action in practice was the United Nations' reaction to the North Korean invasion of the South in 1950,[238] and this only occurred because of a fortuitous combination of circumstances. In June 1950 North Korean forces crossed the 28th Parallel dividing North from South Korea and thus precipitated armed conflict. Almost immediately the Security Council debated the issue and, after declaring that a breach of the peace had taken place, called upon member states to assist the United Nations in achieving a North Korean withdrawal. Two days later, another resolution was adopted which recommended that United Nations members should furnish all necessary assistance to the South Korean authorities, while the third in the trio of Security Council resolutions on this issue authorised the United States to designate the commander of the unified forces established for the purpose of aiding the South Koreans and permitted the use of the United Nations flag by such forces.[239]

The only reason that these resolutions were in fact passed by the Council was the absence of the USSR in protest at the seating of the Nationalist Chinese delegation.[240] This prevented the exercise of the veto by the Soviet Union and permitted the creation of an authoritative United Nations umbrella for the US-commanded forces combating the North Korean armies. The USSR returned to the Council at the start of August 1950 and effectively blocked further action by the Council on this issue, but they could not reverse what had been achieved, despite claims that the resolutions were not constitutionally valid in view of the Soviet boycott.[241]

However, although termed United Nations forces, the contingents from the sixteen states which sent troops were under effective United States control, pursuant to a series of agreements concluded by that country with each of the contributing states, and were not in any real sense directed by the United Nations other than operating under a general Security

---

[238] See e.g. Dinstein, *War*, pp. 292 ff.; Gray, *Use of Force*, pp. 199 ff., and Franck, *Fairness*, p. 223.

[239] Security Council resolutions 82 (1950), 83 (1950) and 84 (1950).

[240] See e.g. L. Sohn, *Cases on United Nations Law*, 2nd edn, Brooklyn, 1967, pp. 479 ff.

[241] *Ibid.*, pp. 481 ff. See also *ibid.*, pp. 509 ff. with regard to the situation following the Chinese involvement in the conflict.

Council authorisation. This improvised operation clearly revealed the deficiencies in the United Nations system of maintaining the peace since the Charter collective security system as originally envisaged could not operate, but it also demonstrated that the system could be reinterpreted so as to function.[242]

The second example occurred following the invasion of Kuwait by Iraq on 2 August 1990.[243] Resolution 660 (1990), adopted unanimously the same day by the Security Council, condemned the invasion and called for an immediate and unconditional withdrawal. Resolution 662 (1990) declared that the purported Iraqi annexation of Kuwait had no legal validity and was null and void. States and international organisations were called upon to refrain from any action or dealing that might be interpreted as an indirect recognition of the annexation. The Council, specifically acting under Chapter VII of the UN Charter, demanded in resolution 664 (1990) that Iraq permit the immediate departure of the nationals of third countries[244] and in resolution 667 (1990) condemned Iraqi aggressive acts against diplomatic premises and personnel in Kuwait, including the abduction of foreign nationals present in those premises, and demanded the protection of diplomatic premises and personnel.[245] Eventually, the Security Council, feeling that the response of Iraq to all the foregoing resolutions and measures adopted had been unsatisfactory, adopted resolution 678 (1990) on 29 November 1990. This allowed Iraq a further period of grace within which to comply with earlier resolutions and withdraw from Kuwait. This 'final opportunity' was to end on 15 January 1991. After this date, member states co-operating with the Government of Kuwait were authorised to use all necessary means to uphold and implement Security Council resolution 660 (1990) and to restore international peace and security in the area. All states were requested to provide appropriate support for the actions undertaken in pursuance of this resolution. The armed action commenced on 16 January 1991 by a coalition of states[246]

---

[242] Franck has written, referring to the 'adaptive capacity' of the UN, that the 'gradual emancipation of article 42 as a free-standing authority for deploying collective force, ad hoc, had prevented the collapse of the Charter system in the absence of the standby militia envisioned by article 43', Recourse, p. 23.

[243] See Lauterpacht et al., Kuwait Crisis: Basic Documents. See also O. Schachter, 'United Nations Law in the Gulf Conflict', 85 AJIL, 1991, p. 452.

[244] See also Security Council resolution 674 (1990).

[245] See generally Keesing's Record of World Events, pp. 37631 ff. and pp. 37694 ff. (1990).

[246] The following states supplied armed forces and/or warships or aircraft for the enforcement of the UN resolutions: USA, UK, France, Egypt, Syria, Saudi Arabia, Morocco, the Netherlands, Australia, Italy, Spain, Argentina, Belgium, Canada, Pakistan, Norway,

under the leadership of the United States can thus be seen as a legitimate use of force authorised by the UN Security Council under its enforcement powers elaborated in Chapter VII of the UN Charter and binding upon all member states of the UN by virtue of article 25.[247] This is to be seen in the context of the purposes laid down by the Council in binding resolutions, that is the immediate and unconditional withdrawal of Iraq from Kuwait and the restoration of international peace and security in the area, and within the framework of the exercise of enforcement action in the light of the absence of article 43 arrangements.

However, the question has arisen whether the process of reinterpreting the Charter by subsequent conduct has moved beyond the authorisation by the Council to member states to take action in the absence of specifi-cally designated UN forces operating under the aegis of the Military Staffs Committee. In particular, is it possible to argue that in certain situations such authorisation may be implied rather than expressly granted?[248] Fol-lowing the Gulf War, revolts against the central government in Iraq led to widespread repression by Iraqi forces against the Shias in the south and the Kurds in the north of the country. Security Council resolution 688 (1991), which was not adopted under Chapter VII and did not au-thorise the use of force, condemned such repression 'the consequences of which threaten international peace and security' and insisted that Iraq allow immediate access by international humanitarian organisations to those in need in the country. In the light of the repression, the US, UK and France sent troops into northern Iraq to create a safe haven for hu-manitarian operations. They were speedily withdrawn and replaced by a small number of UN Guards operating with the consent of Iraq.[249] In addition, the Western states declared a 'no-fly' zone over southern Iraq in August 1992, having established one over northern Iraq in April 1991. The justification of these zones was argued to be that of supporting res-olution 688.[250] Further, it was maintained that the right of self-defence

Denmark, USSR, Bangladesh, Senegal, Niger, Czechoslovakia and the Gulf Co-operation Council (Kuwait, Qatar, Bahrain, Oman and the United Arab Emirates): see *Sunday Times* 'War in the Gulf' Briefing, 27 January 1991, p. 9.

[247] As well as a legitimate use of force in collective self-defence: see above, chapter 20, p. 1146.

[248] See e.g. Gray, *Use of Force*, pp. 264 ff.

[249] See e.g. White, *Keeping the Peace*, p. 192, and F. L. Kirgis, *International Organisations in their Legal Setting*, 2nd edn, St Paul, 1993, pp. 854 ff.

[250] See e.g. the statement of the Minister of State at the Foreign Office on 27 January 1993, UKMIL, 64 BYIL, 1993, p. 739, and see also *ibid.*, at p. 728 and UKMIL, 65 BYIL, 1994, p. 683. See also the statement of President Bush of the US cited in Kirgis, *International Organisations*, p. 856. Note that on 3 September 1996, in response to the entry of Iraqi

existed with regard to flights over the zones, thus permitting proportionate responses to Iraqi actions.[251] Whether resolution 688 can indeed be so interpreted is unclear. What is clear is that such actions were not explicitly mandated by the UN. It is also to be noted that the UK in particular has also founded such actions upon the need to prevent a humanitarian crisis as supported by resolution 688. In March 2001, for example, it was noted that the no-fly zones were established 'in support of resolution 688' and 'are justified under international law in response to a situation of overwhelming humanitarian necessity'.[252]

More dramatically, the use of force based impliedly on Security Council resolutions occurred in March 2003, when the UK and the US commenced military action against Iraq.[253] The legal basis for this action was deemed to rest upon the 'combined effect of resolutions 678, 687 and 1441'.[254] Resolution 1441 (2002)[255] *inter alia* recognised that Iraq's non-compliance with Council resolutions and proliferation of weapons of mass destruction posed a threat to international peace and security and recalled that resolution 678 authorised member states to use all necessary means to restore international peace and security. Citing Chapter VII, the resolution decided that Iraq was and remained in material breach of resolutions

troops and tanks into the northern 'no-fly' Kurdish zone in order to aid one of the Kurdish groups against another, US aircraft launched a series of air strikes against Iraq and extended the southern 'no-fly' zone from the 32nd to the 33rd parallel. In so doing the US government cited Security Council resolution 688 (1991): see *The Economist*, 7 September 1996, pp. 55–6. See also Gray, 'Unity to Polarisation', p. 9.

[251] UKMIL, 64 BYIL, 1993, pp. 728 and 740 with regard to Western air raids against Iraqi targets on 13 January 1993. See also UKMIL, 69 BYIL, 1998, p. 592 and UKMIL, 70 BYIL, 1999, pp. 565, 568 and 590.

[252] See UKMIL, 72 BYIL, 2001, p. 694. See also above, chapter 20, p. 1156.

[253] Note that in December 1998, UK and US airplanes attacked targets in Iraq in response to the withdrawal by that state of co-operation with UN weapons inspectors and based this action on resolutions 1154 (1998) and 1205 (1998) adopted under Chapter VII. The resolutions did not authorise force, but the former noted that any violation by Iraq of its obligations to accord 'immediate, unconditional and unrestricted access' to UNSCOM and the IAEA would have 'severest consequences' and the latter declared that Iraq's decision to end co-operation with UNSCOM was 'a flagrant violation' of resolution 687 (1991): see UKMIL, 69 BYIL, 1998, pp. 589 ff., and Gray, 'Unity to Polarisation', pp. 11 ff.

[254] See the Attorney General, Hansard, House of Lords, vol. 646, Written Answer, 17 March 2003. This UK position was referred to without demur by the US Secretary of State, Briefing, 17 March, 2003: see www.state.gov/secretary/rm/2003/18771.htm. See also the letters dated 21 March 2003 sent to the President of the Security Council from the Permanent Representatives of the UK, US and Australia, S/2003/350-2. See also 52 ICLQ, 2003, pp. 812 ff.

[255] See, as to resolutions 678 (1990) and 687 (1991), above, pp. 1253 and 1248.

including 687, decided to afford that state a 'final opportunity to comply with its disarmament obligations under relevant resolutions of the Council' and established an enhanced inspection regime. The Council called for declarations from Iraq detailing all aspects of its programmes with regard to weapons of mass destruction and ballistic missiles, noting that false statements or omissions would constitute a further material breach. It decided that Iraq was to provide UNMOVIC and the IAEA with immediate, unimpeded, unconditional and unrestricted access to all relevant sites, records and officials. The Council decided to convene further to 'consider the situation and the need for full compliance with all of the relevant Council resolutions in order to secure international peace and security' and recalled in that context that 'the Council has repeatedly warned Iraq that it will face serious consequences as a result of its continued violations of its obligations'. This resolution was adopted unanimously.

Subsequent events, however, revealed Iraqi deficiencies in complying with the resolution.[256] The Security Council was divided on the need for a follow-up resolution to 1441 in order for force to be used and a draft resolution drawn up by the UK, US and Spain was withdrawn on 17 March once it became clear that one or more permanent members would exercise a veto.[257] On 20 March the military operations commenced. The Security Council can authorise member states to resort to force in order to maintain international peace and security, as in the Kuwait conflict of 1990–1, and the Council did affirm that Iraq's failure to comply with its obligations in resolution 687 to divest itself of weapons of mass destruction constituted a threat to international peace and security. Resolution 1441 was intended as a final opportunity and it was provided that serious consequences would ensue upon Iraq's failure to comply. However, whether this amounts to a justification in international law for the UK and the US to use force in the face of the opposition of other Security Council members remains controversial.[258]

---

[256] See e.g. UNMOVIC Report of 28 February 2003, S/2003/232, pp. 3, 12–13 and UNMOVIC Working Document on Unresolved Disarmament Issues: Iraq's Proscribed Weapons Programme ('Cluster Document'), 6 March 2003.

[257] See US Secretary of State, Briefing, 17 March 2003, www.state.gov/secretary/rm/2003/18771.htm.

[258] See e.g. 'Agora', 97 AJIL, 2003, p. 553; Gray, Use of Force, pp. 270 ff.; Dinstein, War, pp. 297 ff.; E. Papastavridis, 'Interpretation of Security Council Resolutions under Chapter VII in the Aftermath of the Iraqi Crisis', 56 ICLQ, 2007, p. 83; J.-M. Sorel, 'L'ONU et l'Irak: Le Vil Plomb N'Est Pas Transformé en Or Pur', 108 RGDIP, 2004, p. 845; S. Wheatley, 'The Security Council, Democratic Legitimacy and Regime Change in Iraq', 17 EJIL, 2006, p. 531; and C. Greenwood, 'International Law and the Pre-emptive Use of Force:

The use of force in non-enforcement situations

In some recent peacekeeping situations, missions established without reference to Chapter VII of the Charter have later been expanded with mandates wholly or partly referring specifically to Chapter VII and in some cases this has led to the application of force by the UN. The results are variable. In both Bosnia and Somalia the temptation to resort to more robust tactics (often for the best of humanitarian reasons) involving the use of force, but without adequate political or military resources or support, led to severe difficulties.

Former Yugoslavia The outbreak of hostilities in Yugoslavia led the Security Council in resolution 713 (1991), adopted on 25 September 1991, to impose an arms embargo on that country. As the situation deteriorated, the decision was taken to establish a peacekeeping force (the UN Protection Force or UNPROFOR) in order to ensure the demilitarisation of three protected areas in Croatia (inhabited by Serbs).[259] This resolution did not refer to Chapter VII and did specifically note the request of the Government of Yugoslavia for a peacekeeping operation.[260] The full deployment of the force was authorised by resolution 749 (1992). During the following months the mandate of UNPROFOR was gradually extended. By resolution 762 (1992), for example, it was authorised to monitor the situation in areas of Croatia under Yugoslav army control,[261] while by resolution 779 (1992) UNPROFOR assumed responsibility for monitoring the demilitarisation of the Prevlaka peninsula near Dubrovnik.[262] At the same time, the situation in Bosnia and Herzegovina deteriorated. Both Croatia and the Federal Republic of Yugoslavia (Serbia and Montenegro) were criticised for their actions in Bosnia in resolution 757 (1992)[263] and sanctions were imposed upon the latter. In resolution 758 (1992), the Council approved an enlargement of UNPROFOR's mandate and strength and

Afghanistan, Al-Qaida and Iraq', 4 *San Diego Journal of International Law*, 2003, p. 7. See also Sarooshi, *Collective Security*, chapter 4 and pp. 174 ff. with regard to delegation of Chapter VII powers to member states and the limitations thereupon.

[259] Security Council resolution 743 (1992). See also the Report of the Secretary-General, S/23592 and Security Council resolutions 721 (1991) and 724 (1991).

[260] The resolution, however, did mention article 25.

[261] See also Security Council resolution 769 (1992).

[262] Note also Security Council resolution 802 (1993) criticising Croatia for its attacks within or adjacent to the UN protected areas and upon UNPROFOR personnel.

[263] The Security Council in this resolution was explicitly acting under Chapter VII. See also resolution 752 (1992) also criticising outside interference in Bosnia, which did not refer to Chapter VII.

authorised the deployment of military observers and related personnel and equipment to Sarajevo, the capital of Bosnia.[264]

In a further measure responding to the dire situation, the Security Council, acting under Chapter VII, adopted resolution 770 (1992) calling on all states to 'take nationally or through regional agencies or arrangements all measures necessary' to facilitate, in co-ordination with the UN, the delivery of humanitarian assistance to and within Bosnia. The phrase 'all necessary measures', it will be recalled, permits in UN terminology the resort to force.[265] The mandate of UNPROFOR was augmented by resolution 776 (1992) to incorporate support for the humanitarian relief activities of the UN High Commissioner for Refugees (UNHCR) and, in particular, to provide protection where requested. It was noted in the Secretary-General's Report, approved by this resolution, that the normal peacekeeping rules of engagement would be followed, so that force could be used in self-defence, particularly where attempts were made to prevent the carrying out of the mandate.[266] However, resolution 776 (1992) made no mention of either Chapter VII or 'all necessary measures'.

A further stage in the evolution of UNPROFOR's role occurred with the adoption of the 'no-fly' ban imposed on military flights over Bosnia by Security Council resolution 781 (1992). UNPROFOR was given the task of monitoring compliance with this ban.[267]

In order to protect certain Bosnian Moslem areas under siege from Bosnian Serb forces, the Security Council established a number of 'safe

---

[264] Additional elements were deployed to ensure the security of the airport by resolution 761 (1992). Note that neither of these resolutions referred to Chapter VII. See also S/1994/300, with regard to UNPROFOR's mandate relating to Sarajevo airport. The airlift of humanitarian supplies into this airport was the longest lasting such airlift in history and well over 150,000 tons were delivered: see S/1995/444, para. 23.

[265] The Secretary-General was, however, careful to state that this resolution created no additional mandate for UNPROFOR: see S/1995/444, para. 25.

[266] See S/24540. Note that a number of resolutions extended the application of Chapter VII to UNPROFOR's freedom of movement, e.g. resolutions 807 (1993) and 847 (1993), and force was used on a number of occasions in self-defence: see e.g. S/1995/444, para. 55.

[267] See also Security Council resolution 786 (1992). The ban on air activity was expanded in resolution 816 (1993) to cover flights by all fixed-wing and rotary-wing aircraft. At the request of the Secretary-General, the no-fly zone was enforced by aircraft from NATO: see S/1995/444, para. 30. A 'dual key' system was put into operation under which decisions on targeting and execution were to be taken jointly by UN and NATO commanders and the principle of proportionality of response to violations was affirmed: see e.g. Joint Press Statement of 29 October 1994, PKO/32.

areas'.[268] Although Chapter VII was referred to in these resolutions, it was cited only in the context of resolution 815 (1993), which dealt with the security of UNPROFOR personnel. The enforcement of the 'safe areas' was therefore to be attained by UNPROFOR personnel authorised to use force only to protect themselves.[269] Although the Secretary-General stated that approximately 34,000 extra troops would be necessary, only an additional 7,000 were authorised.[270] At the request of the Secretary-General, NATO established a 3-kilometre 'total exclusion zone' and a 20-kilometre 'military exclusion zone' around Gorazde and a 20-kilometre 'heavy weapons exclusion zone' around Sarajevo. These zones were to be enforced by air strikes if necessary, although no Security Council resolutions referred to such zones or created any special regime with regard to them.[271] Relations between UNPROFOR and the Bosnian Serbs led to a series of incidents in the spring of 1995. The latter breached the Sarajevo no-heavy-weapons arrangement. This precipitated NATO airstrikes which provoked the taking hostage of several hundred UNPROFOR soldiers. The 'safe area' of Srebrenica was then captured by Bosnian Serb forces in July 1995, involving major human rights abuses against the population. After incidents involving other 'safe areas' and Sarajevo, NATO with UN approval launched a series of airstrikes.[272] At the same time, Bosnian and Croat forces captured areas held by the Bosnian Serbs. A ceasefire agreement came into force on 12 October 1995.[273]

UN peacekeeping missions in former Yugoslavia were reorganised in March 1995, following the capture by Croatian forces of three of the four protected areas inhabited by Serbs in Croatia. The UN missions therefore comprised UNPROFOR in Bosnia,[274] the UN Confidence Restoration Operation in Croatia (UNCRO)[275] and the UN Preventive Deployment

---

[268] See resolutions 819 (1993) and 824 (1993). These were Srebrenica, Sarajevo, Tuzla, Zepa, Gorazde and Bihac.

[269] See also Security Council resolution 836 (1993).

[270] Security Council resolution 844 (1993). See also S/25939. Note that the Secretary-General called for the demilitarisation of the 'safe areas', S/1994/1389. At the request of the Secretary, UNPROFOR was also given the task of monitoring the ceasefire agreement between the Bosnian and Croatian armies: see Security Council resolution 908 (1994), and given additional responsibilities with regard to Sarajevo: see Security Council resolution 900 (1994).

[271] S/1995/444, paras. 48–9.

[272] See also Security Council resolution 998 (1995) regarding the proposal to establish a rapid reaction force.

[273] See S/1995/987. [274] See also Security Council resolution 1026 (1995).

[275] See also Security Council resolutions 990 (1995) and 994 (1995).

Force (UNPREDEP) in the former Yugoslav Republic of Macedonia.[276] As a consequence of the Dayton peace agreement initialled in November 1995, UNPROFOR was replaced by a multinational implementation force (IFOR)[277] composed primarily of troops from NATO countries. In addition, it was proposed to set up a UN International Police Task Force to carry out a variety of police-related training and assistance missions.[278]

The evolution of the UN role in the complex Yugoslav tragedy may be characterised as a series of impromptu actions taken in response to traumatic events. UNPROFOR was never authorised to use force beyond that required in self-defence while performing their rapidly expanding duties. The UN sought to fulfil its fundamental mandated responsibilities with respect to Sarajevo and the transportation of humanitarian aid in co-operation with the warring parties based on the peacekeeping principles of impartiality and consent. But the situation was far from a normal peacekeeping situation of separating hostile forces that consent to such separation. The use of air power was subsequently authorised both in order to defend UNPROFOR personnel and to deter attacks upon the 'safe areas', which had been proclaimed as such with little in the way of initial enforcement means. Eventually air strikes by NATO were resorted to in the face of fears of further Bosnian Serb capture of 'safe areas'. Whether a peacekeeping mission in the traditional sense can ever really be mounted in the conditions then faced in Bosnia must be seriously in doubt, although the humanitarian efforts undertaken were important. Only a meaningful enforcement mandate could have given the UN a chance to put an end to the fighting. But that required a major political commitment and substantial resources. These states are rarely willing to provide unless their own vital national interests are at stake.

Somalia[279]   The Somali situation marked a similar effort by the UN to resolve a humanitarian crisis arising out of civil war conditions and one that saw a peacekeeping mission drifting into an enforcement one. Following

---

[276] Security Council resolutions 981 (1995), 982 (1995) and 983 (1995). The Security Council had authorised deployment of a preventive force in Macedonia in resolution 795 (1992). See also S/24923, annex.

[277] See Security Council resolution 1031 (1995).

[278] See e.g. S/1995/1031 and Security Council resolution 1026 (1995). The International Police Task Force was established under resolution 1035 (1995).

[279] See e.g. Franck, *Fairness*, pp. 301 ff., and I. Lewis and J. Mayall, 'Somalia' in *The New Interventionism 1991–1994* (ed. J. Mayall), Cambridge, 1996, p. 94. See also J. M. Sorel, 'La Somalie et les Nations Unies', AFDI, 1992, p. 61.

a prolonged period of civil war, the Security Council urged all parties to agree to a ceasefire and imposed an arms embargo. The Secretary-General was requested to organise humanitarian assistance.[280] A UN technical mission was then established to look at mechanisms to provide such aid and to examine peacekeeping options.[281] The UN Operation in Somalia (UNOSOM) was set up shortly thereafter,[282] but this modest operation (of fifty ceasefire observers and a security force) was deemed insufficient to ensure the delivery of humanitarian assistance, and the deployment of additional UN security units in order to protect the distribution centres and humanitarian convoys was authorised.[283] However, the situation continued to deteriorate and few humanitarian supplies arrived where needed due to constant attacks.[284] Accordingly, after the Secretary-General had concluded that Chapter VII action was required,[285] the Security Council determined that the 'magnitude of the human tragedy caused by the conflict in Somalia, further exacerbated by the obstacles being created to the distribution of humanitarian assistance, constitutes a threat to international peace and security'. The use of 'all necessary means to establish as soon as possible a secure environment for humanitarian relief operations' was authorised and the Unified Task Force was created (UNITAF).[286] This comprised troops from over twenty states, including some 30,000 from the US.[287]

This operation was expanded the following spring and UNOSOM II was established with an enlarged mandate with enforcement powers under Chapter VII.[288] UNOSOM II was given the humanitarian mandate of UNITAF, together with 'responsibility for the consolidation, expansion and maintenance of a secure environment throughout Somalia' and the provision of security to assist the repatriation of refugees and the assisted resettlement of displaced persons. The force was also to complete the disarmament of factions, enforce the Addis Ababa agreement of January 1993[289] and help rebuild the country. The authorisation to take all

---

[280] Security Council resolution 733 (1992). See also S/23829, 1992.
[281] Security Council resolution 746 (1992).
[282] Security Council resolution 751 (1992). This was not originally a Chapter VII operation.
[283] Security Council resolution 775 (1992). See also S/244480, 1992. Under resolution 767 (1992) Somalia was divided into four operational zones for the delivery of food aid and ceasefire purposes.
[284] See S/24859, 1992.   [285] S/24868, 1992.   [286] Security Council resolution 794 (1992).
[287] The operation was termed 'Operation Restore Hope' and it arrived in Somalia in December 1992: see S/24976, 1992 and S/25168, 1993.
[288] Security Council resolution 814 (1993). See also S/25354, 1993.
[289] See S/25168, annex III.

necessary measures was reiterated in resolution 837 (1993), following an attack upon UNOSOM II forces. This authorisation was stated to include taking action against those responsible for the attacks and to establish the effective authority of UNOSOM II throughout the country. A series of military incidents then took place involving UN forces.[290] Security Council resolution 897 (1994), while condemning continued violence in the country especially against UN personnel, authorised a reduction in UNOSOM II's force levels to 22,000.[291] And in resolution 954 (1994), the Council decided to terminate the mission at the end of March 1995 and authorised UNOSOM II to take actions necessary to protect the mission and the withdrawal of personnel and assets and to that end called upon member states to provide assistance to aid the withdrawal process. The Secretary-General concluded his report of 14 October 1994 noting that the vacuum of civil authority and of governmental authority severely hampered the work of the UN, while 'the presence of UNOSOM II troops has had limited impact on the peace process and limited impact on security in the face of continuing interclan fighting and banditry'.[292]

Rwanda[293]   Following a civil war between government forces and RPF rebels, the Security Council authorised the deployment of the UN Observer Mission Uganda Rwanda (UNOMUR) on the Ugandan side of the border.[294] A peace agreement was signed between the parties at Arusha and the UN set up the UN Assistance Mission for Rwanda (UNAMIR) with a mandate to ensure the security of the capital, Kigali, monitor the ceasefire agreement and monitor the security situation generally up to the installation of the new government.[295] However, the projected transitional institutions were not set up and the security situation deteriorated. Following the deaths of the Presidents of Rwanda and Burundi in an airplane crash on 5 April 1994, full-scale civil war erupted which led to massacres of Hutu opposition leaders and genocidal actions against members of the Tutsi minority. Faced with this situation, the Security Council rejected the option of strengthening UNAMIR and empowering it

---

[290] See e.g. S/26022, 1993, and Security Council resolutions 865 (1993), 878 (1993), 885 (1993) and 886 (1993).

[291] See also Security Council resolutions 923 (1994) and 946 (1994).

[292] S/1994/1166, Part 2, para. 22.   [293] See e.g. Franck, *Fairness*, pp. 300 ff.

[294] See Security Council resolution 846 (1993). See also resolutions 812 (1993) and 891 (1993). This mission was terminated in resolution 928 (1994).

[295] Security Council resolution 872 (1993). See also resolutions 893 (1994) and 909 (1994).

under Chapter VII in favour of withdrawing most of the mission from the country.[296]

As the situation continued to deteriorate, the Council imposed an arms embargo on the country, authorised the increase of UNAMIR to 5,500 and its redeployment in Rwanda and expanded its mandate to include the establishment and maintenance of secure humanitarian areas.[297] However, delays in implementing this led to a proposal from France to establish a French-commanded force to act under Chapter VII of the Charter and subject to Security Council authorisation in order to protect displaced persons and civilians at risk. This was accepted in resolution 929 (1994) in which the Council, acting under Chapter VII, authorised a two-month operation (Operation Turquoise) until UNAMIR was up to strength. Member states were authorised to use all necessary measures to achieve their humanitarian objectives. The force, therefore acting as the 1990–1 Gulf War Coalition had on the basis of Security Council authorisation under Chapter VII, established a humanitarian protected zone in south-western Rwanda. Gradually UNAMIR built up to strength and it began deploying troops in the protected zone on 10 August 1994, taking over responsibility from the French-led force shortly thereafter and deploying in areas throughout the country. UNAMIR's mandate ended on 6 March 1996.[298]

Sierra Leone   After prolonged fighting, a military junta took power and the Security Council imposed an oil and arms embargo which was terminated upon the return of the democratically elected President.[299] This was followed by the establishment of the UN Observer Mission in Sierra Leone with the function of monitoring the disarmament process and restructuring the security forces.[300] This mandate was increased following further violence.[301] In October 1998, the Security Council, noting the signing of the Lomé Agreement the previous July, set up the UN Mission in Sierra Leone (UNAMSIL) with an initial 6,000 military personnel to replace the previous mission with an enhanced mandate, including establishing a presence at key locations in the country, monitoring the ceasefire and facilitating humanitarian assistance. Specifically acting under

---

[296] Security Council resolution 912 (1994).

[297] Security Council resolution 918 (1994). See also resolutions 925 (1994) and 935 (1994).

[298] See Security Council resolution 1029 (1995).

[299] See resolutions 1132 (1997) and 1156 (1998).   [300] See resolution 1181 (1998).

[301] See resolutions 1220 (1999), 1231 (1999), 1245 (1999) and 1260 (1999).

Chapter VII, paragraph 14 of resolution 1270 (1999), the Council decided that 'in the discharge of its mandate UNAMSIL may take the necessary action to ensure the security and freedom of movement of its personnel and . . . to afford protection to civilians under imminent threat of physical violence'. The force was increased and the mandate revised in resolution 1289 (2000) to include in paragraph 10, specifically citing Chapter VII, the provision of security at key locations and at other sites and to assist the Sierra Leone law enforcement authorities in the discharge of their responsibilities. UNAMSIL was further authorised to 'take the necessary action' to fulfil the additional tasks.[302]

The Democratic Republic of the Congo   The Security Council has also concerned itself with the civil war and foreign interventions in the Democratic Republic of the Congo (the former Zaire). Following fighting involving both internal and external forces, the Lusaka Ceasefire Agreement was signed in July 1999.[303] This was welcomed by the Security Council and the deployment of a small UN military liaison force was authorised.[304] This force was designated the UN Organisation Mission in the Democratic Republic of the Congo (MONUC).[305] The Mission was expanded and extended with a mandate *inter alia* to include monitoring the ceasefire and to supervise and verify the disengagement arrangements.[306] Paragraph 8 of the resolution, specifically citing Chapter VII, states that the Council has decided that MONUC 'may take the necessary action . . . to protect United Nations and co-located JMC [Joint Military Commission] personnel, facilities, installations and equipment, ensure the security and freedom of movement of its personnel, and protect civilians under imminent threat of physical violence'. During the summer of 2000, fighting broke out between Ugandan and Rwandan forces in the Congo and the Security Council in resolution 1304 (2000), acting under Chapter VII, demanded that Uganda and Rwanda withdraw all their forces from the Congo and that all other foreign military presence and activity, direct and indirect, be brought to an end. MONUC was asked to monitor the cessation of hostilities and

---

[302] The mission was further extended and expanded: see e.g. resolutions 1299 (2000), 1346 (2001), 1400 (2002) and 1436 (2002). It ended in 2005 to be succeeded by the UN Integrated Office in Sierra Leone: see resolutions 1562 (2004) and 1610 (2005). See also, as to the role of ECOWAS, below, p. 1278, note 365.

[303] See S/1999/815 and resolution 1234 (1999). See also P. Okawa, 'Congo's War: The Legal Dimensions of a Protracted Conflict', 77 BYIL, 2006, p. 203, and above, chapter 20, p. 1154.

[304] Resolution 1258 (1999).   [305] Resolution 1279 (1999).   [306] Resolution 1291 (2000).

the disengagement of forces and withdrawal of foreign forces.[307] This demand was repeated in resolutions 1341 (2001) and 1355 (2001), again acting under Chapter VII.[308] In resolution 1797 (2008), MONUC was authorised to assist the authorities in organising, preparing and conducting local elections, while in resolution 1804 (2008), the Security Council demanded that armed groups and militias in the eastern part of the country immediately lay down their arms and turn themselves in to Congolese and MONUC authorities for disarmament, demobilisation, repatriation, resettlement and reintegration. In virtually all of these resolutions, the situation was characterised as a 'threat to international peace and security in the region'.[309]

Sudan   Following a long-running civil war in the south of the country, an agreement was signed on 20 July 2002 (the Machakos Protocol) between the parties and this led to subsequent agreements in 2004. In June that year, the UN established a special political mission (UNAMIS) to assist the parties. Faced with a deteriorating situation in Darfur in the western Sudan, the Security Council, acting under Chapter VII of the Charter, adopted resolution 1556 (2004), calling for political talks between the parties, endorsing the dispatch of international monitors, including a protection force envisioned by the African Union, and assigning certain responsibilities to UNAMIS.[310] On 9 January 2005, a full peace agreement (the Comprehensive Peace Agreement) was signed, ending the civil war in the south of Sudan. In resolution 1590 (2005), the Council, acting under Chapter VII, established the UN Mission in Sudan (UNMIS) to support implementation of the Comprehensive Peace Agreement and to take over from UNAMIS, and authorised it to 'take the necessary action' to protect UN and humanitarian personnel. A peaceful solution to the Darfur crisis was also called for in this resolution.[311] African Union efforts to seek a solution to the crisis in Darfur culminated in the signing of the Darfur

---

[307] The mandate of MONUC was further extended in a series of resolutions: 1316 (2000); 1332 (2000); 1493 (2003); 1565 (2004); 1592 (2005); 1635 (2005); 1711 (2006); and 1794 (2007).

[308] See also resolutions 1376 (2001), 1399 (2002), 1417 (2002), 1457 (2003) and 1468 (2003).

[309] See as to the imposition of sanctions, above, p. 1247.

[310] See also resolution 1564 (2004) authorising a human rights presence and resolution 1574 (2004).

[311] Note that on 1 February 2005, a UN Commission of Inquiry into Darfur called for in resolution 1564 (2004) reported that while genocide had not been committed by the Sudan government, its forces and allied Janjaweed militias had carried out 'indiscriminate attacks, including killing of civilians, torture, enforced disappearances, destruction of

Peace Agreement on 5 May 2006. Following a recommendation from the UN Secretary-General,[312] the Security Council adopted resolution 1706 (2006) under Chapter VII, determining that the situation in Darfur constituted a threat to international peace and security and deciding that the UNMIS forces be increased and deployed in Darfur in order to support implementation of the Darfur Peace Agreement, without prejudice to their existing mandate in the south of Sudan. UNMIS was authorised to use all necessary measures to protect UN personnel, to support implementation of the peace agreement, to protect civilians under threat of physical violence and to collect arms.[313]

Following discussions with the African Union in view of the deteriorating situation in Darfur,[314] and in the light of the presence of forces from the African Mission in the Sudan (AMIS),[315] the Security Council, noting that the situation continued to constitute a threat to international peace and security, adopted resolution 1769 (2007) establishing the UN–African Union Hybrid Operation in Darfur (UNAMID) incorporating AMIS personnel to consist of a force of up to 19,555 military personnel. Unity of command and control was provided for, with command and control structures and backstopping provided by the United Nations. The Council, acting under Chapter VII, decided that UNAMID was authorised to take the necessary action to protect its personnel, facilities, installations and equipment, and to ensure the security and freedom of movement of its own personnel and humanitarian workers, to support early and effective implementation of the Darfur Peace Agreement, to prevent the disruption of its implementation and armed attacks, and to protect civilians, without prejudice to the responsibility of the government of Sudan.

The range of UN actions from humanitarian assistance to enforcement – conclusions

The UN has not been able to operate Chapter VII as originally envisaged. It has, however, been able to develop a variety of mechanisms to fill the

---

villages, rape and other forms of sexual violence, pillaging and forced displacement', S/2005/60.

[312] S/2006/591.

[313] The mandate of UNMIS was extended in resolutions 1709 (2006), 1714 (2006) and 1755 (2007).

[314] See S/2007/307/Rev.1. As to the imposition of sanctions, see above, p. 1247, and as to the reference of the Darfur situation to the International Criminal Court, see above, chapter 8, p. 412.

[315] See below, p. 1280.

gap left by the non-implementation of article 43. First and foremost, the Council may delegate its enforcement powers to member states. This occurred in Korea, the Gulf War and to some extent in Rwanda. However, the events concerning Iraq have shown uncertainty as to the extent to which, if at all, such authorisation may be implied from resolutions adopted. The UN has also been able to create peacekeeping forces, whose mandate has traditionally been to separate hostile forces with their consent, such as in the Middle East and in Cyprus. The evolution of peacekeeping activities to include confused civil war situations where fighting has not ended and no lasting ceasefire has been put into operation, although prefigured in the Congo crisis of the 1960s, has really taken place in the last few years. It has brought attendant dangers for, as has been seen, the slippage from peacekeeping to self-defence activities more widely defined and thence to *de facto* enforcement action is sometimes hard to avoid and complicated to justify in legal terms. Consent is the basis of traditional peacekeeping and irrelevant in enforcement activities. In the mandate drift that has been evident in some situations, elements of both consent and imposition have been present in a way that has confused the role of the UN. Nevertheless, behind the difficulties of the UN have lain a dearth of both political will demonstrated by, and material resources provided by, member states for the completion of complex enforcement actions.

Developments that have been seen in recent years have demonstrated an acceptance of a far broader conception of what constitutes a threat to international peace and security, so that not only external aggression but certain purely internal convulsions may qualify, thus constraining further the scope of article 2(7) and the exclusive jurisdiction of states. Secondly, the range of actions taken by the Security Council under Chapter VII has increased to cover a wide variety of missions and the creation of international criminal tribunals to prosecute alleged war criminals for crimes occurring within particular states arising out of civil wars. Not only that, but with regard to Iraq, the Security Council took a range of binding measures of unprecedented scope, from the guaranteeing of a contested boundary to implementing strict controls on certain kinds of armaments and establishing a compensation commission to be funded by a levy on oil exports. Finally, increasing flexibility has been manifested in the creation and use of such forces. The establishment of the hybrid UN–African Union force for Darfur is an interesting development and one that may prefigure a number of similar operations as regions may increasingly wish to marry regional personnel with expertise, equipment and logistical support from outside the region.

The Security Council, international law and the International Court of Justice

The issue of the relationship between binding decisions of the Council and international law generally has arisen with particular force in recent years in view of the rapidly increased range and nature of activity by the Security Council. The issue has involved particular consideration of the role of the International Court.[316] The Security Council is, of course, constrained by the provisions of the Charter itself. It must follow the procedures laid down and act within the confines of its constitutional authority as detailed particularly in Chapters V to VII. Its composition and voting procedures are laid down, as are the conditions under which it may adopt binding enforcement measures. As the International Court has emphasised, '[t]he political character of an organ cannot release it from the observance of the treaty provisions established by the Charter when they constitute limitations on its powers or criteria for its judgment'.[317] In particular, the Council must under article 24(2) act in accordance with the Purposes and Principles of the Charter, article 1(1) of which declares that one of the aims of the organisation is to bring about a resolution

---

[316] See, for example, G. R. Watson, 'Constitutionalism, Judicial Review, and the World Court', 34 *Harvard International Law Journal*, 1993, p. 1; Gowlland-Debbas, 'Security Council Enforcement', p. 55, and Gowlland-Debbas, 'The Relationship between the International Court of Justice and the Security Council in the Light of the *Lockerbie* Case', 88 AJIL, 1994, p. 643; R. St J. Macdonald, 'Changing Relations between the International Court of Justice and the Security Council of the United Nations', Canadian YIL, 1993, p. 3; R. F. Kennedy, '*Libya* v. *United States*: The International Court of Justice and the Power of Judicial Review', 33 Va. JIL, 1993, p. 899; T. M. Franck, 'The "Powers of Appreciation": Who is the Ultimate Guardian of UN Legality?', 86 AJIL, 1992, p. 519, and Franck, *Fairness*, pp. 242 ff.; W. M. Reisman, 'The Constitutional Crisis in the United Nations', 87 AJIL, 1993, p. 83; E. McWhinney, 'The International Court as Emerging Constitutional Court and the Co-ordinate UN Institutions (Especially the Security Council): Implications of the *Aerial Incident at Lockerbie*', Canadian YIL, 1992, p. 261; J. M. Sorel, 'Les Ordonnances de la Cour Internationale de Justice du 14 Avril 1992 dans l'Affaire Relative a des Questions d'Interpretation et d'Application de la Convention de Montreal de 1971 Resultant de l'Incident Aérien de Lockerbie', *Revue Générale de Droit International Public*, 1993, p. 689; M. N. Shaw, 'The Security Council and the International Court of Justice: Judicial Drift and Judicial Function' in *The International Court of Justice* (eds. A. S. Muller, D. Raič and J. M. Thuránszky), The Hague, 1997, p. 219; J. Alvarez, 'Judging the Security Council', 90 AJIL, 1996, p. 1, and D. Akande, 'The International Court of Justice and the Security Council: Is There Room for Judicial Control of Decisions of the Political Organs of the United Nations?', 46 ICLQ, 1997, p. 309.

[317] *Conditions of Admission of a State to Membership in the United Nations*, ICJ Reports, 1948, p. 64; 15 AD, p. 333. See also Judge Bedjaoui, the *Lockerbie* case, ICJ Reports, 1992, pp. 3, 45; 94 ILR, pp. 478, 528.

of international disputes by peaceful means 'and in conformity with the principles of justice and international law'.[318]

The Council has recently not only made determinations as to the existence of a threat to or breach of international peace and security under article 39 in traditional inter-state conflict situations, but also under Chapter VII binding determinations as to the location of boundaries, supervision of destruction of weaponry, liability under international law for loss or damage, methods of compensation, asserted repudiation of foreign debt,[319] the establishment of tribunals to try individual war criminals,[320] and assertions as to the use of force against those responsible for, and those inciting, attacks against UN personnel, including their arrest, prosecution and punishment.[321] In addition, the Council has asserted that particular acts were null and void, demanding non-recognition.[322]

In view of this increased activity and the impact this has upon member states, the issue has arisen as to whether there is a body capable of ensuring that the Council does act in conformity with the Charter and international law. Since the International Court is the 'principal judicial organ' of the UN,[323] it would seem to be the natural candidate, and indeed the problem has been posed in two recent cases. In the *Genocide (Bosnia and Herzegovina v. Yugoslavia (Serbia and Montenegro))* case,[324] it was claimed by Bosnia that the Security Council-imposed arms embargo upon the former Yugoslavia had to be construed in a manner that did not deprive Bosnia of its inherent right of self-defence under article 51 of the Charter and under customary international law.[325] In the *Lockerbie* case,[326] Libya claimed that the UK and US were seeking to compel it to surrender alleged

---

[318] See Judge Weeramantry's Dissenting Opinion in the *Lockerbie* case, ICJ Reports, 1992, p. 65 and that of Judge Bedjaoui, *ibid.*, p. 46; 94 ILR, pp. 548 and 529. See also Judge Fitzmaurice in the *Namibia* case, ICJ Reports, 1971, pp. 17, 294; 49 ILR, pp. 2, 284–5.

[319] See Security Council resolution 687 (1991) with regard to Iraq after the Gulf War.

[320] Security Council resolutions 808 (1993) and 827 (1993) regarding former Yugoslavia and resolution 955 (1994) regarding Rwanda. See also the *Tadić* case decided by the Appeals Chamber of the International Criminal Tribunal for the Former Yugoslavia, Case No. IT-94-1-AR72, pp. 13 ff.; 105 ILR, pp. 419, 428 ff.

[321] Security Council resolution 837 (1993) concerning Somalia.

[322] Security Council resolutions 662 (1990) regarding the purported annexation by Iraq of Kuwait and 541 (1983) terming the purported Turkish Cypriot state 'legally invalid'.

[323] Article 92 of the Charter.   [324] ICJ Reports, 1992, pp. 3, 6; 95 ILR, pp. 1, 21.

[325] See also the second provisional measures order, ICJ Reports, 1993, pp. 325, 327–8; 95 ILR, pp. 43, 45–6. The Court confined itself to the Genocide Convention.

[326] ICJ Reports, 1992, pp. 3, 14; 94 ILR, pp. 478, 497.

bombers contrary to the Montreal Convention, 1971 (which required that a state either prosecute or extradite alleged offenders) and that the Council's actions in resolutions 731 (1992) and 748 (1992)[327] were contrary to international law.

While the question of the compatibility of Security Council resolutions with international law was not discussed by the Court in the *Bosnia* case, the issue assumed central position in the *Lockerbie* case. The Court here affirmed that all member states were obliged to accept and carry out the decisions of the Security Council in accordance with article 25 of the Charter and that *prima facie* this obligation extended to resolution 748 (1992), which imposed sanctions upon Libya for failing to extradite the suspects. Thus, in accordance with article 103 of the Charter, under which obligations under the Charter prevail over obligations contained in other international agreements, the resolution prevailed over the Montreal Convention.[328] Judge Shahabuddeen in his Separate Opinion underlined that the issue in the case was whether a decision of the Council could override the legal rights of states and, if so, whether there were any limitations upon its power to characterise a situation as one justifying the making of the decision importing such consequences.[329]

The issue was raised in the request for provisional measures phase of the *Congo* v. *Uganda* case. Uganda argued that the request by the Congo for interim measures would 'directly conflict with the Lusaka Agreement, and with the Security Council resolutions – including resolution 1304 . . . calling for implementation of the Agreement'.[330] The Court noted that resolution 1304 was adopted under Chapter VII, but concluded after quoting the text of the resolution that the Security Council had taken no decision which would *prima facie* preclude the rights claimed by the Congo from being regarded as appropriate for protection by the indication of provisional measures.[331] While there is no doubt that under the Charter system the Council's discretion to determine the existence of threats to or breaches of international peace and security is virtually absolute, limited only by inherent notions of good faith and non-abuse

---

[327] Calling upon Libya to surrender the suspects and imposing sanctions for failing so to do.
[328] ICJ Reports, 1992, p. 15; 94 ILR, p. 498.
[329] ICJ Reports, 1992, p. 32; 94 ILR, p. 515. Judge Lachs noted that the Court was bound 'to respect' the binding decisions of the Security Council as part of international law, ICJ Reports, 1992, p. 26; 94 ILR, p. 509. See Franck, *Fairness*, p. 243, who emphasised that the verb used, to 'respect', does not mean to 'defer to'. Note that Judge Lachs also pointed to the Court as the 'guardian of legality for the international community as a whole, both within and without the United Nations', *ibid*.
[330] ICJ Reports, Order of 1 July 2000, para. 30.   [331] *Ibid.*, para. 36.

of rights,[332] and its discretion to impose measures consequent upon that determination in order to maintain or restore international peace and security is undoubtedly extensive,[333] the determination of the legality or illegality of particular situations is essentially the Council's view as to the matching of particular facts with existing rules of international law. That view, when adopted under Chapter VII, will bind member states, but where it is clearly wrong in law and remains unrectified by the Council subsequently, a challenge to the system is indubitably posed. While the Court can, and has, examined and analysed UN resolutions in the course of deciding a case or rendering an Advisory Opinion, for it to assert a right of judicial review in the fullest sense enabling it to declare invalid a binding Security Council resolution would equally challenge the system as it operates. Between the striking down of Chapter VII decisions and the acceptance of resolutions clearly embodying propositions contrary to international law, an ambiguous and indeterminate area lies.

The role of the General Assembly[334]

The focus of attention during the 1950s shifted from the Security Council to the General Assembly as the use of the veto by the permanent members led to a perception of the reduced effectiveness of the Council. Since it was never really envisaged that the General Assembly would play a large part in the preservation of international peace and security, its powers as defined in the Charter were vague and imprecise. Articles 10 to 14 provide that the Assembly may discuss any question within the scope of the Charter and may consider the general principles of co-operation in the maintenance of international peace and security. The Assembly may make recommendations with respect to questions relating to international peace to members of the United Nations or the Security Council or both, provided (except in the case of general principles of co-operation, including disarmament) the Council is not dealing with the particular matter. In addition, any

---

[332] See e.g. Gowlland-Debbas, 'Security Council Enforcement', pp. 93–4. See also the *Tadić* case decided by the Appeals Chamber of the International Criminal Tribunal for the Former Yugoslavia, Case No. IT-94-1-AR72, pp. 13 ff.; 105 ILR, pp. 419, 428 ff.

[333] Note that under article 1(1) actions to bring about the adjustment or settlement of international disputes or situations which might lead to a breach of the peace must be in conformity with 'the principles of justice and international law', while there is no such qualification with regard to effective collective measures to prevent and remove threats to the peace and the suppression of breaches of the peace or acts of aggression.

[334] See e.g. Simma, *Charter*, pp. 247 ff., and White, *Keeping the Peace*, part II.

question respecting international peace and security on which action is necessary has to be referred to the Security Council.

The Uniting for Peace resolution was adopted by the Assembly in 1950 and was founded on the view that as the Security Council had the primary responsibility for the maintenance of peace under article 24, it could therefore be argued that the Assembly possessed a secondary responsibility in such matters, which could be activated in the event of obstruction in the Security Council. The resolution[335] declared that where the Council failed to exercise its responsibility upon the occurrence of a threat to the peace, breach of the peace or act of aggression because of the exercise of the veto by any of its permanent members, the General Assembly was to consider the matter at once with a view to making appropriate recommendations to members for collective measures. Such measures could include the use of force when necessary in the case of a breach of the peace or act of aggression, and, if not already in session, the Assembly would be able to meet within twenty-four hours in emergency special session.[336]

However problems soon arose in the context of the creation by the Assembly in 1956 of the United Nations Emergency Force which was to supervise the ceasefire in the Middle East, and by the United Nations Secretary-General in 1960 of the United Nations Force in the Congo. It was argued that since article 11 provides that any question dealing with international peace and security on which action was necessary had to be referred to the Security Council, the constitutionality of such forces was questionable. A number of states refused to pay their share of the expenses incurred, and the matter was referred to the International Court. In the *Certain Expenses* case,[337] the Court took the term 'action'[338] to refer to 'enforcement action', thus permitting action which did not amount to enforcement action to be called for by the General Assembly and the Secretary-General.[339] This opinion, although leading to some interpretive problems, did permit the creation of United

---

[335] General Assembly resolution 377(V). See e.g. J. Andrassy, 'Uniting for Peace', 50 AJIL, 1956, p. 563. See also M. J. Petersen, 'The Uses of the Uniting for Peace Resolution since 1950', 8 *International Organisation*, 1959, p. 219, and F. Woolsey, 'The Uniting for Peace Resolution of the United Nations', 45 AJIL, 1951, p. 129.

[336] The General Assembly under article 20 of the UN Charter meets only in regular annual sessions and in such special sessions as occasion may require.

[337] ICJ Reports, 1962, p. 151; 34 ILR, p. 281.

[338] Article 11(2) of the Charter provides that the General Assembly may discuss any questions relating to the maintenance of international peace and security, but any such question 'on which action is necessary' must be referred to the Security Council.

[339] Accordingly, the UN Emergency Force in the Middle East established in 1956 was not contrary to article 11(2) since it had not been intended to take enforcement action, ICJ

Nations peacekeeping forces in situations where because of superpower rivalry it was not possible for the Security Council to reach a decision, provided such forces were not concerned with enforcement action. The adoption of this kind of action remains firmly within the prerogative of the Security Council.

In practice the hopes raised by the adoption of the Uniting for Peace resolution have not really been fulfilled. The procedure prescribed within the resolution has been used, for example, with regard to the Suez and Hungarian crises of 1956, the Lebanese and Jordanian troubles of 1958, the Congo upheavals of 1960, the Middle East in 1967, the conflict leading to the creation of Bangladesh in 1971, Afghanistan in 1980, Namibia in 1981 and the Palestine question in 1980 and 1982. But it cannot be said that the Uniting for Peace system has in effect exercised any great influence regarding the maintenance of international peace and security. It has provided a method whereby disputes may be aired before the Assembly in a way that might not have otherwise been possible, but as a reserve mechanism for the preservation or restoration of international peace, it has not proved very successful.

The UN and regional arrangements and agencies[340]

The Security Council has increasingly made use of regional organisations in the context of peacekeeping and peace enforcement. Chapter VIII of the UN Charter concerns regional arrangements. Article 52 provides that nothing contained in the Charter precludes the existence of regional arrangements or agencies for dealing with such matters relating to international peace and security as are appropriate for such arrangements or agencies, providing that these are consistent with the Purposes and Principles of the UN itself.[341] Article 53 notes that the Security Council where appropriate shall utilise such arrangements or agencies for enforcement action under its authority. Without the authorisation of the Security

---

Reports, 1962, pp. 151, 165, 171–2. This precipitated a crisis over the arrears of the states refusing to pay their contributions.

[340] See e.g. Simma, *Charter*, pp. 807 ff., and Cot, *et al.*, *Charte*, pp. 1367 ff. See also Gray, *Use of Force*, chapter 9; A. Abass, *Regional Organisations and the Development of Collective Security: Beyond Chapter VIII of the UN Charter*, Oxford, 2004; Sarooshi, *Collective Security*, chapter 6, and O. Schachter, 'Authorised Uses of Force by the United Nations and Regional Organisations' in *The New International Order and the Use of Force* (eds. L. Damrosch and D. J. Scheffer), Boulder, 1991, p. 65.

[341] Note also the relevance of the right of collective self-defence under both customary international law and article 51 of the Charter: see above, chapter 20, p. 1146.

Council, regional enforcement action is not possible.[342] Article 54 provides that the Security Council is to be kept fully informed at all times of activities undertaken or in contemplation by regional organisations. The definition of 'regional arrangements or agencies' is left open, so that a useful measure of flexibility is provided, enabling the term to cover a wide range of regional organisations going beyond those strictly established for defence co-operation.[343]

Several issues arise. First, there is the issue of when regional action may be deemed to be appropriate, and here recent events have demonstrated a broader measure of flexibility akin to the widening definition of what constitutes a threat to international peace and security. Secondly, there is the extent to which regional action is consistent with UN purposes and principles, and here the provisions of article 103, assigning priority to Charter obligations over obligations contained in other international agreements, should be noted. Thirdly, there is the question as to whether a broad or a narrow definition of enforcement action is to be accepted.[344] Fourthly, the important issue is raised as to whether prior approval by the Security Council is required in order for a regional organisation to engage in an activity consistent with Chapter VIII. Practice here recently appears to suggest rather controversially that not only is prior approval not required, but that Security Council authorisation need not occur until substantially after the action has commenced.[345] However, it is clear that the UN is keen to co-ordinate activity with regional organisations.[346]

---

[342] See e.g. M. Akehurst, 'Enforcement Action by Regional Agencies', 42 BYIL, 1967, p. 175; *Les Forces Régionales du Maintien de la Paix* (ed. A. Pellet), Paris, 1982; C. Borgen, 'The Theory and Practice of Regional Organization Intervention in Civil Wars', 26 *New York University Journal of International Law and Politics*, 1994, p. 797, and I. Pogany, 'The Arab League and Regional Peacekeeping', 34 NILR, 1987, p. 54.

[343] A number of organisations specifically self-identify as regional agencies as understood by Chapter VIII, such as the Organisation of American States (see article 1 of the Charter of the OAS, 1948), the Organisation for Security and Co-operation in Europe (see para. 25 of the Helsinki Summit Declaration, 1992 and the Charter for European Security, 2000, 39 ILM, 2000, p. 255 and General Assembly resolution 47/10) and the Commonwealth of Independent States (see 35 ILM, 1996, p. 783). See as to the OSCE role in Bosnia under the Dayton peace arrangements, above, chapter 18, p. 1034.

[344] That is, whether all actions noted in articles 41 and 42 are covered or just those using military force.

[345] Note that the report of the High-Level Panel on Threats, Challenges and Change, A/59/565, 2 December 2004, stated that, 'Authorization from the Security Council should in all cases be sought for regional peace operations, recognizing that in some urgent situations that authorization may be sought after such operations have commenced', *ibid.* at para. 272(a).

[346] See, for example, the Secretary-General, *An Agenda for Peace*, A/47/277, 17 June 1992, p. 37 and Secretary-General, *In Larger Freedom*, A/59/2005, 21 March 2005, para.

Article 52(2) and (3) establishes that peaceful settlement of disputes through regional mechanisms before resort is had to the Security Council is the preferred route and this, on the whole, has been the practice of the UN.[347] Enforcement action is a different matter and here priority lies with the Council under the Charter. However, the reference to the inherent right of collective self-defence in article 51 does detract somewhat from the effect of Chapter VIII, and it also seems clear that regional peacekeeping operations, in the traditional sense of being based on consent of the parties and eschewing the use of force save in self-defence, do not need the authorisation of the Security Council.

Practice in the post-Cold War era has amply demonstrated the increasing awareness by the Security Council of the potentialities of regional organisations. References in resolutions of the Council have varied in this regard. Some have specifically mentioned, commended or supported the work of named regional organisations without mentioning Chapter VIII,[348] others have referred explicitly to Chapter VIII,[349] while others have stated that the Council is acting under Chapter VIII.[350]

A particularly interesting example of the interaction of regional organisations and the UN occurred with regard to Haiti. The OAS adopted sanctions against Haiti upon the overthrow of the elected President Jean-Bertrand Aristide in 1991.[351] Although the General Assembly welcomed

---

213, proposing that the UN should sign memoranda of understanding with regional organisations having a conflict prevention or peacekeeping capacity, linking such organisations with the UN Standby Arrangements System. See also the World Summit Outcome 2005, General Assembly resolution 60/1, and Security Council resolution 1631 (2005) and the subsequent report of the Secretary-General, A/61/204–S/2006/590, 28 July 2006, paras. 94 ff. See also S/25184 (1993).

[347] Although article 52(4) provides that 'this article in no way impairs the application of articles 34 and 35'. See e.g. Simma, *Charter.*, p. 848.

[348] See e.g. Security Council resolutions 743 (1992) commending the work of the European Community and the CSCE in former Yugoslavia and 855 (1993) endorsing the activities of the CSCE in former Yugoslavia; and resolution 865 (1993) noting the efforts of the Arab League, the OAU and the Organisation of the Islamic Conference with regard to Somalia.

[349] E.g. Security Council resolutions 727 (1992) in regard to former Yugoslavia; 795 (1992) in regard to Macedonia; 757 (1992) in regard to former Yugoslavia; 816 (1993) extending the 'no-fly' zone over Bosnia; 820 (1993) in regard to former Yugoslavia; and resolution 751 (1992) with regard to Somalia, 'cognisant of the importance of co-operation between the United Nations and regional organisations in the context of Chapter VIII of the Charter of the United Nations'.

[350] See e.g. Security Council resolution 787 (1992) with regard to the maritime blockade of former Yugoslavia; resolution 794 (1992) with regard to Somalia.

[351] OAS resolutions MRE/RES.1/91, MRE/RES.2/91 and MRE/RES.3/92. See article 19 of the OAS Charter. See also S/23109, 1991.

the actions,[352] the Security Council did not react. Eventually in June 1993, the Council, acting under Chapter VII, imposed an arms and oil embargo on Haiti. Resolution 841 (1993) specifically referred to a series of OAS resolutions,[353] commended the work of the OAS Secretary-General and stressed the need 'for effective co-operation between regional organisations and the United Nations'.[354] In resolution 875 (1993), the Council, acting under Chapters VII and VIII, called upon member states 'acting nationally or through regional agencies or arrangements' in co-operation with the legitimate Government of Haiti to act to ensure the implementation of the arms and oil embargo.[355]

Liberia constitutes another instructive example.[356] A complicated civil war broke out during 1989–90 and, in the absence of any moves by the UN or the OAS, the Economic Community of West African States (ECOWAS) decided to act. This organisation, which consists of sixteen members including Liberia, is aimed at improving living standards in the region.[357] A Protocol on Non-Aggression was signed in 1978 and came into force three years later.[358] This prohibits aggression among member states and does not specifically mention peacekeeping nor provide for the right of unilateral intervention. In May 1990, ECOWAS established a Standing Mediation Committee and this called for an immediate ceasefire in Liberia and for its implementation to be monitored by an ECOWAS monitoring group (ECOMOG). This group, led by Nigeria, landed in Liberia in August 1990 and became involved in actual

---

[352] See General Assembly resolution 46/7, 1991.

[353] Including in addition to those already mentioned, resolutions MRE/RES.4/92, MRE/RES.5/93 and CP/RES.594 (923/92), and declarations CP/Dec. 8 (927/93), CP/Dec. 9 (931/93) and CP/Dec. 10 (934/93).

[354] See also Security Council resolutions 917 (1994) and 933 (1994).

[355] Note also the problematic US argument concerning its invasion of Grenada, claiming that the 1981 treaty establishing the Organisation of Eastern Caribbean States operated as the necessary 'existing' or 'special' treaty which would excuse intervention and a violation of territorial integrity under article 22 of the OAS Charter. However, the OECS Defence Committee could only act unanimously and in cases of external aggression and the landing of troops in order to overthrow the Marxist government on the island would not appear to satisfy the requirements: see e.g. J. N. Moore, *Law and the Grenada Mission*, Charlottesville, 1984, pp. 45–50, and W. C. Gilmore, *The Grenada Intervention*, London, 1984. See also American Bar Association Section of International Law and Practice, Report on Grenada, 1984.

[356] See e.g. G. Nolte, 'Restoring Peace by Regional Action: International Legal Aspects of the Liberian Conflict', 53 ZaöRV, 1993, p. 603.

[357] See article 2 of the ECOWAS Treaty, 1975. See also F. Olonisakin, *Reinventing Peacekeeping in Africa: Conceptual and Legal Issues in ECOMOG Operations*, The Hague, 2000.

[358] See also the Protocol Relating to Mutual Assistance on Defence, 1981.

fighting. It is somewhat unclear whether ECOWAS provides a sufficient legal basis of itself to justify the actions taken, and UN involvement did not occur until January 1991, when the President of the Security Council issued a statement commending the efforts of ECOWAS to promote peace in Liberia and calling upon the parties to the conflict to co-operate fully with ECOWAS.[359] In April 1992, ECOMOG proceeded to secure a buffer zone on the Liberia–Sierra Leone border envisaged by an October 1991 accord (the Yamoussoukro IV Accord) between the Liberian parties, to secure all entry and exit points in the country and to enforce the disarmament of combatants.[360]

The situation, however, continued to deteriorate and the Security Council adopted resolution 788 (1992) in November of that year. This determined that the deterioration of the situation constituted a threat to international peace and security 'particularly in West Africa as a whole' and recalled Chapter VIII of the Charter. The resolution commended ECOWAS for its 'efforts to restore peace, security and stability in Liberia' and, acting under Chapter VII, imposed an arms embargo upon that country. This support was reaffirmed in resolution 813 (1993), which also noted the endorsement of ECOWAS' efforts by the OAU.[361] With the assistance of the special representative of the UN Secretary-General, a new peace agreement was signed at Cotonou on 25 July 1993, which called upon ECOWAS and the UN to assist in its implementation.[362] The UN Observer Mission in Liberia was established to assist in this process.[363] Security Council resolution 866 (1993) in particular noted that 'this would be the first peacekeeping mission undertaken by the United Nations in co-operation with a peacekeeping mission already set up by another organisation, in this case ECOWAS'. Subsequent resolutions continued to commend ECOWAS for its actions and the UNOMIL mission was extended. Eventually elections were held.[364] When ECOWAS sought

---

[359] S/22110/Add.3, 1991.

[360] S/23863, 1992. This was also supported by a statement from the President of the Security Council, S/23886, 1992. See also S/24815, 1993.

[361] See also S/25402, 1993.

[362] The peace agreement provided that ECOMOG would have the primary responsibility of supervising the military provisions of the agreement, with the UN monitoring and verifying the process, S/26200, 1993, and Security Council resolution 866 (1993) preamble.

[363] See Security Council resolutions 856 (1993) and 866 (1993). See also S/26200 and S/26422 and Add. 1, 1993.

[364] See e.g. Security Council resolutions 911 (1994); 950 (1994), which also commended African states sending troops to ECOMOG; 1014 (1995), which also encouraged African

to intervene in Liberia in 2003, the Security Council adopted resolution 1497 (2003) under Chapter VII, authorising the establishment of a multinational force based upon ECOWAS to implement a June 2003 ceasefire. The role of ECOWAS within the context of Chapter VIII was specifically commended. Authority was transferred from the ECOWAS force to a new UN Mission in Liberia in October 2003 by resolution 1509.

The Liberian situation is therefore marked by the following features: first, intervention in a civil war in an attempt to secure a ceasefire by a regional organisation whose authority in this area was far from clear constitutionally; secondly, delayed support by the Security Council in the context of Chapter VIII until 1992; thirdly, the first establishment of a dual UN–regional organisation peacekeeping operation; fourthly, the acceptance by the UN of the responsibility of the regional organisation for military issues with the UN mission possessing a rather indeterminate monitoring and peace-encouraging role. It should also be noted that apart from the imposition of the arms embargo in resolution 788 (1992), Security Council resolutions refrained from referring to Chapter VII. The UN, therefore, adopted very much a secondary role. While it is clear that the Security Council ultimately supported the action taken by ECOWAS, it is questionable whether the spirit and terms of Chapter VIII were fully complied with.[365] Ultimately, the Security Council fully adopted the actions of ECOWAS, authorised further such actions and then subsumed the ECOWAS operation into a UN peacekeeping mission.

The failed UN experience of the early 1990s in Somalia was succeeded by a long period of neglect in practice, during which the UN maintained the arms embargo on that country and expressed support for regional action to seek to resolve the complicated civil war. In a number of

---

states to send troops to join ECOMOG; and resolutions 1020 (1995), 1071 (1996), 1100 (1997) and 1116 (1997) concerning elections. Note also the Security Council Presidential Statement of July 1997 after the elections *inter alia* commending ECOMOG, S/PRST/1997/41. See further as to ECOWAS, above, chapter 18, p. 1029.

[365] Note also ECOWAS involvement in Guinea Bissau under an agreement between the government and the opposing junta: see 38 ILM, 1999, p. 28. Security Council resolution 1233 (1999) welcomed the ECOMOG role. ECOMOG also played a part in the Sierra Leone crisis: see e.g. Security Council resolution 1162 (1998) commending ECOWAS and ECOMOG for playing an important role in restoring international peace and security, and resolutions 1270 (1999) and 1289 (2000).

Security Council resolutions, for example, the Council, acting under Chapter VII, called for continuation of the arms embargo and also commended the efforts of the African Union (AU) and the Intergovernmental Authority on Development in Eastern Africa (IGAD), the relevant subregional organisation, in support of the Transitional Federal Institutions, the claimant Somali government.[366] In resolution 1725 (2006), the Council, acting under Chapter VII, and following decisions taken by IGAD and the AU, authorised IGAD and the member states of the AU to establish 'a protection and training mission' in Somalia with the mandate *inter alia* to monitor progress in talks between the Transitional Federal Institutions and the rival Union of Islamic Courts and to maintain security in Baidoa (the headquarters of the Transitional Federal Institutions). In January 2007, the AU decided to deploy for six months a mission to Somalia (AMISOM) aimed at stabilising the situation and which would evolve into a UN operation for long-term stabilisation and post-conflict restoration of Somalia.[367]

As already noted, the UN in the situation in Bosnia turned to NATO[368] in particular in order to enforce the arms embargo against all the states of the former Yugoslavia and to implement sanctions against the Federal Republic of Yugoslavia (Serbia and Montenegro). NATO airplanes in particular enforced the 'no-fly' zone over Bosnia (Operation Deny Flight) as from April 1993 and on 28 February 1994, four warplanes were shot down by NATO aircraft for violating the zone. NATO airplanes also provided close air support for UNPROFOR activities as from June 1993, and as from April 1994, air support to protect UN personnel in the 'safe areas' was instituted. NATO airstrikes took place at UN request during 1994–5 in a variety of situations.[369] Following the Dayton Peace Agreement initialled in November 1995, a 60,000 troop NATO-led implementation force (IFOR) commenced operations in Bosnia. This was authorised by the Security Council, acting under Chapter VII, in resolution 1031 (1995), under which authority was transferred from UNPROFOR to IFOR. Within a short time, this organisation gave way to SFOR (stabilisation force), which was NATO-led but included non-NATO countries.[370] SFOR was

---

[366] See resolutions 1630 (2005), 1676 (2006) and 1724 (2006).

[367] This was authorised in Security Council resolution 1744 (2007).

[368] With the assistance of the WEU in the maritime activities in the Adriatic under Operation Sharp Guard: see above, p. 1258.

[369] See e.g. S/1995/444, 1995.

[370] See Security Council resolution 1088 (1996). See also www.nato.int/sfor/index.htm.

replaced by an EU force, EUFOR, in December 2004.[371] In Kosovo, an international security presence parallels the international civil presence[372] and this force, KFOR, like SFOR in Bosnia, is NATO-led.[373] Kosovo declared independence in February 2008.[374] In December 2001, the Security Council authorised the establishment of an International Security Assistance Force in Afghanistan (ISAF) pursuant to the Bonn Agreement.[375] In March 2003, the NATO peacekeeping mission in the Former Yugoslav Republic of Macedonia, which had commenced in August 2001, was handed over to the European Union, this being the first such mission for the EU.[376]

The most dramatic and far-reaching co-operation with a regional organisation in the context of peacekeeping and enforcement is the UN–African Union Hybrid Operation in Darfur. The African Mission in Sudan (AMIS) was created in July 2004, as part of a ceasefire monitoring arrangement together with the European Union. In August that year, AU troops were sent to protect the monitors and the force grew from there. Due to the deteriorating situation, including difficulties with the government of Sudan and resource problems, the AU force eventually merged with the UN force to form the hybrid mission (UNAMID) in 2007.[377]

---

[371] As authorised by Security Council resolution 1575 (2004). Note the creation of an Interim Emergency Multinational Force in Bunia (the Democratic Republic of the Congo) in Security Council resolution 1484 on 30 May 2003. By a decision of 5 June 2003, the Council of the European Union authorised the sending of a peacekeeping force pursuant to the Security Council resolution. See also EUFOR operations in the Democratic Republic of the Congo during 2006: see Council Joint Action 2006/319/CFSP (repealed by Council Joint Action 2007/147/CFSP) and Council Decision 2006/412/CFSP as authorised in Security Council resolution 1671 (2006); and in Chad and the Central African Republic since 2007: see Council Joint Action 2007/677/CFSP and Council Decision 2008/101/CFSP as authorised by the Security Council in resolution 1778 (2007).

[372] See Security Council resolution 1244 (1999). See also above, chapter 5, p. 1232.

[373] See e.g. www.nato.int/kfor/welcome.html.

[374] See further above, chapter 9, p. 452.

[375] See resolution 1386 (2001). Its mandate has been regularly extended under different leaders: see e.g. resolutions 1413 (2002), 1444 (2003), 1510 (2003) which extended its role throughout the country, 1563 (2004), 1623 (2005), 1707 (2006) and 1776 (2007). ISAF has been supported and led by NATO since 11 August 2003: see www.nato-otan.org/isaf/topics/history/index.html.

[376] See www.nato-otan.org/issues/nato_fyrom/evolution.html.

[377] See www.africa-union.org/DARFUR/homedar.htm; www.unmis.org/english/au.htm and www.accord.org.za/ct/2005-4/ct4_2005_pgs52_53.pdf. See further as to UNAMID, above, p. 1266.

Suggestions for further reading

Bowett's Law of International Institutions (eds. P. Sands and P. Klein), 5th edn, London, 2001

The Charter of the United Nations (ed. B. Simma), 2nd edn, Oxford, 2002

S. Chesterman, T. M. Franck and D. M. Malone, *Law and Practice of the United Nations*, Oxford, 2008

J. P. Cot, A. Pellet and M. Forteau, *La Charte des Nations Unies: Commentaire Article par Article*, 3rd edn, Paris, 2005

J. G. Merrills, *International Dispute Settlement*, 4th edn, Cambridge, 2005, chapter 10

23

International institutions[1]

Introduction

The evolution of the modern nation-state and the consequent development of an international order founded upon a growing number of independent and sovereign territorial units inevitably gave rise to questions of international co-operation.[2] The first major instance of organised international co-operation occurred with the Peace of Westphalia in 1648, which ended the thirty-year religious conflict of Central Europe and formally established the modern secular nation-state arrangement of European politics.[3] Over a century later the Napoleonic wars terminated with the Congress of Vienna in 1815, marking the first systematic attempt to regulate international affairs by means of regular international

---

[1] Often called 'international organisations'. The terms will be used interchangeably.

[2] See C. F. Amerasinghe, *Principles of the Institutional Law of International Organizations*, 2nd edn, Cambridge, 2005; J. E. Alvarez, *International Organizations as Law-Makers*, Oxford, 2005; D. Sarooshi, *International Organizations and their Exercise of Sovereign Powers*, Oxford, 2005; H. G. Schermers and N. M. Blokker, *International Institutional Law*, 3rd edn, The Hague, 1995; J. Klabbers, *An Introduction to International Institutional Law*, Cambridge, 2002; *Bowett's Law of International Institutions* (eds. P. Sands and P. Klein) 5th edn, London, 2001; N. White, *The Law of International Organizations*, Manchester, 1996; P. Reuter, *International Institutions*, London, 1958; *Encyclopedia of Public International Law* (ed. R. Bernhardt), Amsterdam, 1983, vols. V and VI; G. Schwarzenberger, *International Law*, London, 1976, vol. III; E. Lauterpacht, 'The Development of the Law of International Organizations by the Decisions of International Tribunals', 152 HR, p. 377; F. Kirgis, *International Organizations in their Legal Settings*, 2nd edn, St Paul, 1993; A. El Erian, 'The Legal Organization of International Society' in *Manual of Public International Law* (ed. M. Sørensen), London, 1968, p. 55; M. Whiteman, *Digest of International Law*, Washington, 1968, vol. XIII; *A Handbook of International Organizations* (ed. R. J. Dupuy), Dordrecht, 1988; I. Seidl-Hohenveldern, *Corporations In and Under International Law*, Cambridge, 1987; F. Morgenstern, *Legal Problems of International Organizations*, Cambridge, 1986, and Nguyen Quoc Dinh, P. Daillier and A. Pellet, *Droit International Public*, 7th edn, Paris, 2002, p. 571. See also G. Schiavone, *International Organizations: A Dictionary and Directory*, London, 1992, and Union of International Associations, *Yearbook of International Organizations*, 39th edn, Brussels, 5 vols., 2002–3.

[3] See e.g. L. Gross, 'The Peace of Westphalia, 1648–1948', 42 AJIL, 1948, p. 20.

conferences.[4] The Congress system lasted, in various guises, for practically a century and institutionalised not only the balance of power approach to politics, but also a semi-formal international order.[5]

Until the outbreak of the First World War, world affairs were to a large extent influenced by the periodic conferences that were held in Europe. The Paris conference of 1856 and the Berlin gathering of 1871 dealt with the problems of the Balkans, while the 1884–5 Berlin conferences imposed some order upon the scramble for Africa that had begun to develop. These, and other such conferences, constituted an important prelude to the establishment of international institutions, but became themselves ever more inadequate to fulfil the job they had been intended to do. A conference could only be called into being upon the initiative of one or more of the states involved, usually following some international crisis, and this ad hoc procedure imposed severe delays upon the resolution of the issue. It meant that only states specifically invited could attend and these states made decisions upon the basis of unanimous agreement, a factor which severely restricted the utility of the system.[6]

The nineteenth century also witnessed a considerable growth in international non-governmental associations, such as the International Committee of the Red Cross (founded in 1863) and the International Law Association (founded in 1873). These private international unions[7] demonstrated a wide-ranging community of interest on specific topics, and an awareness that co-operation had to be international to be effective. Such unions created the machinery for regular meetings and many established permanent secretariats. The work done by these organisations was, and remains, of considerable value in influencing governmental activities and stimulating world action.[8]

In addition, there developed during the course of the nineteenth century a series of public international unions. These were functional associations linking together governmental departments or administrations for specific purposes, and were set up by multilateral treaties. The first instances of such inter-governmental associations were provided by the international commissions established for the more efficient functioning of such vital arteries of communication as the Rhine and Danube rivers,

---

[4] See e.g. El Erian, 'Legal Organization', p. 58. See also A. Zamoyski, *Rites of Peace*, London, 2007.

[5] See e.g. Reuter, *Institutions*, pp. 55–6. See also *Bowett's International Institutions*, chapter 1.

[6] *Bowett's International Institutions*, p. 3.   [7] *Ibid.*, pp. 4–65.

[8] See as to the role of the International Committee of the Red Cross in international humanitarian law, above, chapter 21, p. 1200.

and later for other rivers of Central and Western Europe.[9] The powers given to the particular commissions varied from case to case, but most of them performed important administrative and legislative functions. In 1865 the International Telegraphic Union was set up with a permanent bureau or secretariat and nine years later the Universal Postal Union was created. This combined a permanent bureau with periodic conferences, with decisions being taken by majority vote. This marked a step forward, since one of the weaknesses of the political order of ad hoc conferences had been the necessity for unanimity.

The latter half of the nineteenth century was especially marked by the proliferation of such public international unions, covering transportation, communications, health and economic co-operation. These unions restricted themselves to dealing with specific areas and were not comprehensive, but they introduced new ideas which paved the way for the universal organisations of the twentieth century. Such concepts as permanent secretariats, periodic conferences, majority voting, weighted voting and proportionate financial contributions were important in easing administrative co-operation, and they laid the basis for contemporary international institutions.

International organisations (or institutions) have now become indispensable. In a globalised world they facilitate co-operation across state frontiers, allowing for the identification, discussion and resolution of difficulties in a wide range of subjects, from peacekeeping and peace-enforcement to environmental, economic and human rights concerns. This dimension of the international legal system permits the relatively rapid creation of new rules, new patterns of conduct and new compliance mechanisms. Indeed, if there is one paramount characteristic of modern international law, it is the development and reach of international institutions, whether universal or global, regional or subregional.

A brief survey of international institutions

Institutions of a universal character

The innovation of the twentieth century was, of course, the creation of the global, comprehensive organisations of the League of Nations in 1919 and the United Nations in 1945. These were, in many ways, the logical culmination of the pioneering work of the private and public international unions,

---

[9] See *Bowett's International Institutions*, pp. 6–9.

the large numbers of which required some form of central co-ordination. This function both the League[10] and the UN attempted to provide.[11] Associated with the UN are the specialised agencies. These are organisations established by inter-governmental agreement and having wide international responsibilities in economic, social, cultural and other fields that have been brought into relationship with the United Nations.[12] Most of the specialised agencies have devised means whereby the decisions of the particular organisation can be rendered virtually binding upon members. This is especially so with regard to the International Labour Organisation (established in 1919 to protect and extend the rights of workers), UNESCO (the UN Educational, Scientific and Cultural Organisation established to further the increase and diffusion of knowledge by various activities, including technical assistance and co-operative ventures with national governments) and the World Health Organisation (established in 1946 with the aim of unifying the standards of health care).[13] Although such institutions are not able to legislate in the usual sense, they are able to apply pressures quite effectively to discourage non-compliance with recommendations or conventions.[14]

The International Bank for Reconstruction and Development (IBRD – the World Bank) emerged from the Bretton Woods Conference of 1944 to encourage financial investment, and it works in close liaison with the International Monetary Fund (IMF), which aims to assist monetary co-operation and increase world trade. A state can only become a member

---

[10] See e.g. *Bowett's International Institutions*, chapter 2; G. Scott, *Rise and Fall of the League of Nations*, London, 1973; El Erian, 'Legal Organization', pp. 60 ff., and F. P. Walters, *A History of the League of Nations*, Oxford, 2 vols., 1952.

[11] See above, chapter 22.

[12] Article 57 of the Charter. See also articles 62–6 and e.g. J. Harrod, 'Problems of the United Nations Specialised Agencies at the Quarter Century', 28 YBWA, 1974, p. 187, and Klein, in Bernhardt, *Encyclopedia of Public International Law*, vol. V, pp. 349–69. See also El Erian, 'Legal Organization', pp. 55, 96–106.

[13] See also the Food and Agriculture Organisation, created in 1943 to collect and distribute information related to agricultural and nutritional matters: see e.g. R. W. Phillips, *FAO, Its Origins, Formation and Evolution 1945–1981*, Rome, 1981. See also www.fao.org/.

[14] The following specialised agencies should also be noted in passing: the International Civil Aviation Organisation; the Universal Postal Union; the International Telecommunication Union; the World Meteorological Organisation; the International Maritime Organisation; the World Intellectual Property Organisation; the International Fund for Agricultural Development; the UN Industrial Development Organisation and the International Fund for Agricultural Development. The International Atomic Energy Agency exists as an autonomous organisation within the UN. See e.g. L. Henkin, R. C. Pugh, O. Schachter and H. Smit, *International Law: Cases and Materials*, 3rd edn, St Paul, 1993, chapter 18.

of the World Bank if it is an IMF member. The plenary organ of these agencies is the Board of Governors and the executive organs are the Executive Directors. These agencies, based in Washington DC, are assisted by the International Development Association (IDA) and the International Finance Corporation (IFC), which are affiliated to the World Bank and encourage financial investment and the obtaining of loans on easy terms. These financial organisations differ from the rest of the specialised agencies in that authority lies with the Board of Governors, and voting is determined on a weighted basis according to the level of subscriptions made. Very important decisions require the consent of 70 to 85 per cent of the votes. The IBRD, IDA and IFC together with the Multilateral Investment Guarantee Agency constitute the 'World Bank Group'.[15]

A number of international economic arrangements and institutions (not being specialised agencies) of increasing importance have been established The GATT[16] arose out of an international conference held at Havana in 1947–8 at which it was decided to establish an International Trade Organisation. The organisation did not in fact come into being. However, a General Agreement on Tariffs and Trade (GATT) had been agreed shortly before the conference, involving a series of tariff concessions and trade rules, and this originally temporary instrument continued. The arrangement operated on the basis of a bilateral approach to trade negotiations coupled with unconditional acceptance of the most-favoured-nation principle (by which the most favourable benefits obtained by one state are passed on to other states), although there were special conditions for developing states in this respect. A series of tariff and trade negotiating rounds were held under the auspices of the GATT, which thus

---

[15] See e.g. *Bowett's International Institutions*, pp. 87 ff. See also W. M. Scammell, 'The International Monetary Fund' in *The Evolution of International Organizations* (ed. E. Luard), London, 1966, chapter 9; A. Shonfield, 'The World Bank', in *ibid.*, chapter 10; R. Townley, 'The Economic Organs of the United Nations', in *ibid.*, chapter 11, and C. W. Alexandrowicz, *The Law-Making Functions of the Specialised Agencies of the United Nations*, Sydney, 1973, chapter 9. See also www.worldbank.org/.

[16] See e.g. A. F. Lowenfeld, *International Economic Law*, 2nd edn, Oxford, 2008; J. H. Jackson, *Sovereignty, the WTO, and Changing Fundamentals of International Law*, Cambridge, 2006; K. W. Dam, *The GATT, Law and International Economic Relations*, Chicago, 1970; J. H. Jackson, *The World Trading System*, 2nd edn, Cambridge, MA, 1997; T. Flory, 'Les Accords du Tokyo Round du GATT et la Réforme des Procédures de Règlement des Différends dans la Système Commercial Interétatique', 86 RGDIP, 1982, p. 235; A. H. Qureshi, *International Economic Law*, London, 1999, and I. Seidl-Hohenveldern, *International Economic Law*, 2nd edn, Dordrecht, 1992, p. 90.

offered a package approach to trade negotiations, and a wide variety of tariff reductions was achieved, as well as agreement reached on mitigating non-tariff barriers. The eighth such round, termed the Uruguay round, commenced in 1986 and concluded with the signing at Marrakesh on 15 April 1994 of a long and complex agreement covering a range of economic issues. It also provided for the establishment of the World Trade Organisation on 1 January 1995 as a permanent institution with its own secretariat. The organisation consists of a Ministerial Conference, with representatives of all members meeting at least once every two years; a General Council composed of representatives of all members meeting as appropriate and exercising the functions of the Conference between sessions;[17] Councils for Trade in Goods, Trade in Services and Trade Related Aspects of Intellectual Property Rights operating under the general guidance of the General Council; a Secretariat and a Director-General.[18] The organisation's main aims are to administer and implement the multilateral and plurilateral trade agreements together making up the WTO, to act as a forum for multilateral trade negotiations, to try and settle trade disputes and to oversee national trade policies. The GATT of 1947 continued until the end of 1995, when it was effectively subsumed, with changes, as GATT 1994 within the WTO system.[19]

Regional institutions

The proliferation of regional institutions, linking together geographically and ideologically related states, since the close of the Second World War, has been impressive. A number of factors can help explain this. The onset of the Cold War and the failure of the Security Council's enforcement procedures stimulated the growth of regional defence alliances (such as NATO and the Warsaw Pact) and bloc politics. The decolonisation process resulted in the independence of scores of states, most of which were eager to play a non-aligned role between East and West, and the rise of globalisation has meant that all states form part of one economic trading system and can no longer individually function effectively, thus precipating the evolution of regional economic arrangements.

---

[17] The General Council will also meet to discharge the responsibilities of the Dispute Settlement Body and the Trade Policy Review Body: see article IV(3) and (4) of the 1994 Agreement.

[18] See article IV of the Agreement.

[19] See further as to the WTO dispute settlement system, above, chapter 18, p. 1036.

Europe

It is in Europe that regionalism became most developed institutionally. The establishment of the European Economic Community (thereafter European Union), in particular, was intended to lay the basis for a resurgent Europe with meaningful economic and political integration.[20] It has developed to become a major regional organisation with significant supranational components. Consisting originally of three interlocking communities (the European Coal and Steel Community 1951, the European Atomic Energy Community 1957 and the European Economic Community 1957), the European Union aims at establishing a single unified market with common external tariffs and the elimination of internal tariffs and quotas, and it promotes the free movement of capital and labour. The Single European Act, 1986 and the Treaty on European Union, 1992 both introduced significant changes. The Treaty of Lisbon, signed in 2007 and currently awaiting ratification, is intended to streamline the governance of the Union. The membership of the Union has progressively increased and currently stands at twenty-seven. The institutions of the Union comprise primarily the European Parliament, the Council of Ministers, the Commission and the Court of Justice.[21]

The Council of Europe was created in 1949 with wide-ranging co-operative aims.[22] There are currently forty-seven member states. The Council comprises the Committee of Ministers, consisting of governmental representatives, and the Parliamentary Assembly, composed of members representing the Parliaments of the member states. The most important part of the work of the Council of Europe is the preparation and conclusion of conventions and protocols.[23] There are a very large

---

[20] D. Chalmers and A. Tomkins, *European Union Public Law*, Cambridge, 2007; P. Craig and G. De Burca, *EU Law: Text, Cases and Materials*, 4th edn, Oxford, 2007; T. C. Hartley, *The Foundations of European Community Law*, 6th edn, Oxford, 2007; J. Steiner, L. Woods and C. Twigg-Flesner, *EU Law*, 9th edn, Oxford, 2006; *Lasok's Law and Institutions of the European Communities* (eds. D. Lasok and K. P. E. Lasok), 7th edn, London, 2001, and D. Wyatt and A. Dashwood, *European Community Law*, 4th edn, London, 2000.

[21] Note also the Organisation for Economic Co-operation and Development established in 1960 and developed out of the European machinery created to administer the American Marshall Plan, which was aimed at reviving the European economies: see e.g. C. Archer, *Organising Europe*, London, 1994, chapter 3; *Bowett's International Institutions*, pp. 167 ff., and Miller, 'The OECD', YBWA, 1963, p. 80.

[22] See e.g. Archer, *Organising Europe*, chapter 4; A. H. Robertson, *The Council of Europe*, 2nd edn, London, 1961, and T. Ouchterlony, *The Council of Europe in the New Europe*, Edinburgh, 1991. See also above, chapter 7, p. 345, and www.coe.int.

[23] See articles 15 and 16 of the Statute of the Council of Europe.

number of these, including pre-eminently the European Convention for the Protection of Human Rights and Fundamental Freedoms (1950), but including also the European Social Charter (1961) and agreements dealing with cultural and educational questions and conventions covering patents, extradition, migration, state immunity, terrorism and others.

The Organisation for Security and Co-operation in Europe (OSCE)[24] was originally created in 1975 following the Helsinki Conference of European powers (plus the USA and Canada). The Helsinki Final Act was not a binding treaty but a political document, concerned with three areas or 'baskets', being security questions in Europe; co-operation in the fields of economics, science and technology; and co-operation in humanitarian fields. The Conference itself (at the time termed the CSCE) was a diplomatic conference with regular follow-up meetings to review the implementation of the Helsinki Final Act, but after the changes in Eastern Europe in the late 1980s the organisation began to develop. The Charter of Paris for a New Europe signed in 1990 provided for the first standing institutions. The OSCE is essentially a conflict prevention organisation, with an Office for Democratic Institutions and Human Rights, responsible for the promotion of human rights and democracy in the OSCE area. It also monitors elections. Overall responsibility for executive action is exercised by the Chairman-in-Office, who is assisted by the Troika (i.e. the present, preceding and succeeding Chairmen). The High Commissioner on National Minorities was appointed in 1992[25] and there exist a variety of Missions to assist in dispute settlement. The OSCE was also assigned a role in the Bosnia peace arrangements.[26] There are currently fifty-six participating states in the organisation.

The North Atlantic Treaty Organization (NATO)[27] was created in 1949 to counter possible threats from the USSR. It associated the USA and Canada with fourteen European powers for the protection, in essence,

---

[24] See e.g. *The CSCE* (ed. A. Bloed), Dordrecht, 1993; J. Maresca, *To Helsinki – The CSCE 1973–75*, Durham, 1987; *Essays on Human Rights in the Helsinki Process* (eds. A. Bloed and P. Van Dijk), Dordrecht, 1985; A. Bloed and P. Van Dijk, *The Human Dimension of the Helsinki Process*, Dordrecht, 1991, and D. McGoldrick, 'The Development of the Conference on Security and Co-operation in Europe – From Process to Institution' in *Legal Visions of the New Europe* (eds. B. S. Jackson and D. McGoldrick), London, 1993, p. 135. See also www.osce.org/ and above, chapters 7, p. 372, and 18, p. 1032.

[25] See further above, chapter 7, p. 376.   [26] See further above, chapter 18, p. 1034.

[27] See e.g. *The NATO Handbook*, Brussels, 2002 and at www.nato.int/docu/handbook/2001/index.htm; Archer, *Organising Europe*, chapter 9; Bowett's *International Institutions*, pp. 180 ff.; K. Myers, *NATO, The Next Thirty Years*, Boulder, 1980, and L. S. Kaplan and R. W. Clawson, *NATO After Thirty Years*, Wilmington, 1981.

of Western Europe (although Greece and Turkey are also involved). By the Treaty,[28] the parties agreed to consult where the territorial integrity, political independence or security of any of them has been threatened,[29] and accepted that an armed attack against one or more of them in Europe or North America should be considered an attack against all.[30]

The alliance (now comprising twenty-six states) consists of a Council, which is the supreme organ and on which all members are represented,[31] and a NATO parliamentary conference (the North Atlantic Assembly), which acts as an official consultative body. The ending of the Cold War brought about a variety of changes in the organisation. The Euro-Atlantic Partnership Council (EAPC) was established in 1997 (it currently has fifty members, among them NATO states and former members of the Warsaw Pact, including successor states of the USSR).[32] In 1994, the Partnership for Peace programme was inaugurated and this brings together EAPC and other OSCE states into a co-operative framework, which has the potential to provide the mechanism for enlarging the membership of NATO itself. There are currently thirty-four such partners. While the Partnership for Peace focuses upon practical, defence-related and military co-operation, the EAPC constitutes the forum for broad consultation on political and security issues. Countries participating in the Partnership for Peace sign a Framework Document, affirming the commitment to the preservation of democratic societies and the maintenance of the principles of international law, to fulfil in good faith the obligations of the UN Charter and the principles contained in the Universal Declaration of Human Rights and to respect existing borders.[33]

---

[28] 43 AJIL, 1949, Supp., p. 159.

[29] Article 4. Support to Turkey was requested and provided in early 2003 under article 4: see www.nato.int/docu/pr/2003/p030216e.htm.

[30] Article 5. This was invoked for the first time on 12 September 2001, when the Allies declared that the terrorist attack on the US was deemed to constitute an attack on all members of the alliance: see www.nato.int/docu/pr/2003/p030216e.htm.

[31] Article 9.

[32] This replaced the North Atlantic Co-operation Council established in 1991.

[33] See as to NATO's involvement in peacekeeping and peace-enforcement, above, chapter 22, p. 1279. Note also the Western European Union, described by the Treaty on European Union, 1992 as an integral part of the EU and as its defence component to strengthen the European pillar of the Atlantic alliance. It had a role in the Yugoslav crisis, both in enforcing the Security Council sanctions in co-operation with NATO and in forming part of the joint European Union/WEU administration of the city of Mostar in Bosnia in July 1994. It also conducted a police training mission in Albania in 1997 and demining operations in Croatia from 1997: see e.g. Archer, *Organising Europe*, chapter 10, and T. Taylor, *European Defence Co-operation*, London, 1984. See also www.weu.int/.

The Commonwealth of Independent States was established by an Agreement signed by Russia, Belarus and Ukraine in Minsk on 8 December 1991, to which eight other former Republics of the USSR adhered at Alma Ata on 21 December that year. Georgia joined in 1993, so that the organisation now comprises all the former Soviet Republics apart from the three Baltic States. The organisation is based on respect for the territorial integrity of member states and member states agreed to maintain and retain under joint command, a common military and strategic space, including joint control over nuclear weapons. It was also agreed to establish common co-ordinating institutions.[34] The CIS adopted a Charter in Minsk in January 1993.[35] Under this Charter, the Commonwealth is expressed to be based on the sovereign equality of its members, who are independent subjects of international law. It is expressly stated that the CIS is not a state nor does it possess supranational powers.[36] The supreme organ is the Council of Heads of State, while the Council of Heads of Government has a co-ordinating role.[37] Decisions of both Councils are to be achieved by common consent.[38] In 1993, the leaders of the CIS states, apart from Ukraine and Turkmenistan, signed a treaty to create an Economic Union, while in 1995, seven of the twelve member states signed an agreement for the Defence of the CIS External Borders. A large number of agreements have been signed between member states on a variety of subjects, including prevention of drug smuggling and terrorism, but many of these agreements have not been ratified.[39]

The American continent[40]

The Organisation of American States emerged after the Second World War and built upon the work already done by the Pan-American Union and the various inter-American Conferences since 1890. It consists of two basic treaties: the 1947 Inter-American Treaty of Reciprocal Assistance

---

[34] See articles 5, 6 and 7 of the Minsk Agreement, 31 ILM, 1992, pp. 143 ff.
[35] See 4 Finnish YIL, 1993, p. 263.   [36] See article 1.   [37] See articles 21 and 22.
[38] Article 23. There are a number of other councils linking various ministers, see articles 27, 28, 30 and 31, together with an Economic Court and a Commission on Human Rights, see articles 32 and 33.
[39] See www.cis.minsk.by/main.aspx?uid=74.
[40] See e.g. *Bowett's International Institutions*, chapter 7; A. V. W. Thomas and A. J. Thomas, *The Organization of American States*, Dallas, 1963; M. Ball, *The OAS in Transition*, Durham, 1969, and M. Wood, 'The Organization of American States', 33 YBWA, 1979, p. 148. See also www.oas.org/.

(the Rio Treaty), which is a collective self-defence system, and the 1948 Pact of Bogotá, which is the original Charter of the OAS and which was amended in 1967 by the Buenos Aires Protocol, in 1985 by the Cartagena de Indias Protocol and by the 1992 Washington Protocol and the 1993 Managua Protocol. There are currently thirty-five member states. The OAS is a collective security system, an attack on one being deemed an attack on all. The organisation consists of a General Assembly, the supreme organ, which is a plenary organ with wide terms of reference; meetings of consultation of Ministers of Foreign Affairs, which exercise broad powers; a Permanent Council which performs both secretarial supervision and political functions, subject to the authority of the aforementioned institutions, and a number of subsidiary organs. The organisation has adopted a Human Rights Convention[41] and is the most developed of the regional organisations outside Europe, but without any of the supranational powers possessed by the European Union.[42]

The Arab League[43]

The Arab League was created in 1944 and has broad aims. The Council of the League is the supreme organ and performs a useful conciliatory role and various subsidiary organs dealing with economic, cultural and social issues have been set up. Its headquarters are in Tunisia, having been moved there from Egypt after the Israel–Egypt Peace Treaty of 1979. There is also a permanent secretariat and a Secretary-General. The Council of the League has been involved in the peacekeeping operations in Kuwait in 1961, where an Inter-Arab Force was established to deter Iraqi threats, and in Lebanon in 1976 as an umbrella for the operations of the Syrian

---

[41] See above, chapter 7, p. 381.

[42] There exist also a number of other American organisations of limited competence: see e.g. *Bowett's International Institutions*, chapter 7. These include, for example, the Inter-American Bank (1959); the Andean Pact (1969); the Caribbean Community and Common Market or CARICOM (1973); the Latin American Integration Association (1980); the Southern Cone Common Market or MERCOSUR (1991) and the Association of Caribbean States (1994).

[43] See e.g. *Bowett's International Institutions*, p. 237, and R. W. MacDonald, *The League of Arab States*, Princeton, 1965. See also B. Boutros-Ghali, 'La Ligue des États Arabes', 137 HR, 1972, p. 1, and H. A. Hassouna, *The League of Arab States*, Dobbs Ferry, 1975. Note also the existence of the Organisation of Petroleum Exporting Countries, founded in 1960, which obtained the power to fix crude oil prices in 1973: see e.g. I. Seymour, *OPEC, Instrument of Change*, London, 1980, and I. Skeet, *OPEC: Twenty-five Years of Prices and Politics*, Cambridge, 1988. See also www.Arabji.com/ArabGovt/ArabLeague.htm.

troops.[44] It played no meaningful part in the Gulf wars and crises from 1980 to 2003.[45]

Africa[46]

The Organisation of African Unity was established in 1963 in Ethiopia and was replaced by the African Union in 2001. The Constitutive Act of the Union lists a series of objectives in article 3 and these include the achieving of greater unity between African countries; defending the sovereignty, territorial integrity and independence of its member states; the promotion of peace, security and stability on the continent and of human and peoples' rights in accordance with the African Charter on Human and Peoples' Rights and other relevant human rights instruments; and the promotion of sustainable development. Article 4 of the Constitutive Act sets out the Principles of the Union and these include respect of borders existing on achievement of independence; establishment of a common defence policy for the African continent; peaceful resolution of conflicts among member states and the prohibition of the use of force or threat to use force among member states of the Union. Interestingly, in addition to the emphasis on territorial integrity, the Principles also provide for the right of the Union to intervene in a member state pursuant to a decision of the Assembly in respect of grave circumstances, namely war crimes, genocide and crimes against humanity, and the right of member states to request intervention from the Union in order to restore peace and security.[47] Also included are respect for democratic principles, human rights, the rule of law and good governance, and condemnation and rejection of unconstitutional changes of governments. The organs of the Union include an Assembly, the supreme organ of the Union, composed of heads of state or government or their representatives, which sets the common policy of the Union;

---

[44] See e.g. *Bowett's International Institutions*, p. 238, and G. Feuer, 'Le Force Arabe de Securité au Liban', 22 AFDI, 1976, p. 51. See also above, chapter 18, p. 1031.

[45] Note also the existence of the Gulf Co-operation Council: see *Bowett's International Institutions*, p. 240.

[46] *Ibid.*, p. 243; Z. Cervenka, *The Organization of African Unity and Its Charter*, London, 1969, and *The Unfinished Quest for Unity*, London, 1977; B. Andemicael, *The OAU and the UN*, London, 1976; M. Wolfers, *Politics in the Organization of African Unity*, London, 1976; C. A. A. Packer and D. Rukare, 'The New African Union and Its Constitutive Act', 96 AJIL, 2002, p. 365, and K. D. Magliveras and G. J. Naldi, 'The African Union – A New Dawn for Africa?', 51 ICLQ, 2002, p. 415. See also above, chapter 18, p. 1026, and www.africa-union.org/.

[47] See e.g. B. Kioko, 'The Right of Intervention under the African Union's Constitutive Act: From Non-Interference to Non-Intervention', 85 *International Review of the Red Cross*, 2003, p. 807.

an Executive Council, composed of foreign or other ministers, which co-ordinates and takes decisions on policies in areas of common interest to the member states, such as foreign trade, water resources and energy; the Pan-African Parliament and the Court of Justice, the jurisdiction of which comprises the application and interpretation of the Act and which is currently being merged with the African Court of Human Rights.[48]

Asia

The Association of South East Asian Nations (ASEAN) was created in 1967.[49] It possesses economic, political and cultural aims and groups together Brunei, Cambodia, Indonesia, Laos, Malaysia, Myanmar, the Philippines, Singapore, Thailand and Vietnam. In 1976 three agreements were signed: a Treaty of Amity and Co-operation, which reaffirmed the parties' commitment to peace and dealt with the peaceful settlement of disputes; the Declaration of ASEAN Concord, which called for increased political and economic co-ordination and co-operation; and the Agreement of Establishment of the Permanent Secretariat to co-ordinate the national secretariats established under the 1967 ASEAN Declaration. In 1987, the Protocol amending the Treaty of Amity was signed, under which countries outside the ASEAN region could accede to the treaty. A number of economic agreements have also been signed, ranging from the Manila Declaration of 1987 to the Framework Agreement on Enhancing ASEAN Economic Co-operation, 1992 and the decision to establish an ASEAN Free Trade Area within fifteen years utilising a Common Effective Preferential Tariff scheme. In 2003, ASEAN Concord II was signed, establishing the ASEAN Security Community, Economic Community and Socio-Cultural Community,[50] and on 20 November 2007 the ASEAN Charter was adopted.

The supreme policy-making body of ASEAN is the Summit, comprising the Heads of State or Government, with a Co-ordinating Council composed of Foreign Ministers.[51] A variety of community councils and sectorial ministerial bodies were also established.[52] An ASEAN Human

---

[48] As to the peaceful settlement mechanisms and as to other African organisations, see above, chapter 18, p. 1026.

[49] See e.g. *Bowett's International Institutions*, p. 228. See also T. W. Allen, *The ASEAN Report*, Washington, 2 vols., 1979, and *Understanding ASEAN* (ed. A. Broinowski), London, 1982. See also www.aseansec.org/.

[50] See 43 ILM, 2004, p. 18.   [51] See articles 7 and 8 of the Charter.

[52] See articles 9 and 10. There is also a Secretary-General and Secretariat and a Committee of Permanent Representatives: see articles 11 and 12.

Rights Body was proposed under conditions to be determined.[53] Decision-making is in principle to be by consultation and consensus.[54]

Some legal aspects of international organisations[55]

There is no doubt that the contribution to international law generally made by the increasing number and variety of international organisations is marked. In many fields, the practice of international organisations has had an important effect and one that is often not sufficiently appreciated. In addition, state practice within such organisations is an increasingly significant element within the general process of customary law formation. This is particularly true with regard to the United Nations, with its universality of membership and extensive field of activity and interest, although not all such practice will be capable of transmission into customary law, and particular care will have to be exercised with regard to the *opinio juris*, or binding criterion.[56]

As well as the impact of the practice of international organisations upon international law, it is worth noting the importance of international legal norms within the operations of such organisations. The norms in question guide the work and development of international institutions and may act to correct illegal acts.[57] International organisations have in the past been defined in international treaties simply as 'inter-governmental organisations' in order to demonstrate that the key characteristic of such groupings

---

[53] Article 14.

[54] Article 20. Where there is no consensus, it will be for the ASEAN Summit to decide how to proceed in a particular matter. Article 22 calls for the establishment of dispute settlement mechanisms.

[55] See e.g. Amerasinghe, *Principles*; Schermers and Blokker, *International Institutional Law*; *Bowett's International Institutions*, part 3; Klabbers, *Introduction*; A. Reinisch, *International Organizations Before National Courts*, Cambridge, 2000; I. Brownlie, *Principles of Public International Law*, 6th edn, Oxford, 2003, chapter 31, and Reuter, *International Institutions*, pp. 227–64. See also E. Lauterpacht, 'Development' and 'The Legal Effects of Illegal Acts of International Organizations' in *Cambridge Essays in International Law*, Cambridge, 1965, p. 98; K. Skubiszewski, 'Enactment of Law by International Organizations', 4 BYIL, 1965–6, p. 198; Whiteman, *Digest*, vol. XIII; R. Higgins, *The Development of International Law Through the Political Organs of the United Nations*, Oxford, 1963, and generally other sources cited in footnote 2 above.

[56] See above, chapter 3, p. 84.

[57] See e.g. the *IMCO* case, ICJ Reports, 1960, p. 150; 30 ILR, p. 426; the *Conditions of Admission of a State to the United Nations* case, ICJ Reports, 1948, p. 57; 15 AD, p. 333; and the *Certain Expenses of the United Nations* case, ICJ Reports, 1962, p. 151; 34 ILR, p. 281. See also E. Lauterpacht, 'Development', pp. 388–95.

is that their membership comprises states.[58] However, the International Law Commission in article 2 of its Draft Articles on the Responsibility of International Organisations refers to 'an organisation established by a treaty or other instrument governed by international law and possessing its own legal personality', while noting that international organisations 'may include as members, in addition to states, other entitites'.[59] Amerasinghe refers to organisations 'normally created by a treaty or convention to which states are parties and the members of the organisation so created are generally states' and points to basic characteristics such as establishment by international agreement among states, possession of a constitution, possession of organs separate from its members, establishment under international law, and either exclusive or predominant membership of states or governments.[60]

One may therefore distinguish public international organisations that are the subject of this chapter, from private or non-governmental organisations and from international public companies.[61] The former may have a wide-ranging, open or universal membership (such as the UN and the specialised agencies) or may have a limited or closed membership (such as the African Union or the Organisation for Economic Co-operation and Development). Organisations may have a wider or narrower range of functions, depending upon their constitution, with the UN as a good example of the former and the World Health Organisation as a good example of the latter. Whether a grouping will be regarded as an international organisation will depend essentially upon whether it in fact possesses some or all of the criteria noted above.

Personality[62]

The role of international organisations in the world order centres on their possession of international legal personality as distinct from, and

---

[58] See e.g. the Vienna Convention on the Representation of States in their Relations with International Organizations, 1975; the Vienna Convention on Succession of States in Respect of Treaties, 1978 and the Vienna Convention on the Law of Treaties between States and International Organizations, 1986.

[59] Report of the International Law Commission, 2003, A/58/10, pp. 38 ff.

[60] *Principles*, pp. 9 and 10.

[61] See above, chapter 5, p. 248.

[62] See e.g. H. Thirlway, 'The Law and Procedure of the International Court of Justice, 1960–1989 (Part Eight)', 67 BYIL, 1996, p. 1; Klabbers, *Introduction*, chapter 3; *Bowett's International Institutions*, chapter 15; Amerasinghe, *Principles*, chapter 3; Schermers and Blokker, *International Institutional Law*, chapter 11; C. W. Jenks, 'The Legal Personality of

in addition to, personality under domestic law. Once this is established, they become subjects of international law and thus capable of enforcing rights and duties upon the international plane as distinct from operating merely within the confines of separate municipal jurisdictions. Not all arrangements by which two or more states co-operate will necessarily establish separate legal personality. The International Court of Justice in *Nauru* v. *Australia*[63] noted that the arrangements under which Australia, New Zealand and the UK became the joint 'Administering Authority' for Nauru in the Trusteeship Agreement approved by the UN in 1947 did not establish a separate international legal personality distinct from that of the states.

The question of personality will in the first instance depend upon the terms of the instrument establishing the organisation. If states wish the organisation to be endowed specifically with international personality, this will appear in the constituent treaty and will be determinative of the issue.[64] But this actually occurs in only a minority of cases. However, personality on the international plane may be inferred from the powers or purposes of the organisation and its practice.[65] This is the more usual situation and one authoritatively discussed and settled (at least as far as the UN was concerned directly) by the International Court in the *Reparation for Injuries Suffered in the Service of the United Nations* case.[66] The Court held that the UN had international legal personality because this was indispensable in order to achieve the purposes and principles specified in the Charter. In other words, it was a necessary inference from the

International Organizations', 22 BYIL, 1945, p. 267; M. Rama-Montaldo, 'International Legal Personality and Implied Powers of International Organizations', 44 BYIL, 1970, p. 111; M. Sørensen, 'Principes de Droit International Public', 101 HR, 1960, pp. 1, 127 ff.; H. Barberis, 'Nouvelles Questions Concernant la Personalité Juridique Internationale', 179 HR, 1983, p. 145; F. Seyersted, 'Objective International Personality of Intergovernmental Organizations', 34 *Nordisk Tidskrift for International Ret*, 1964, p. 1, and C. Ijalaye, *The Extension of Corporate Personality in International Law*, Dobbs Ferry, 1978. See also above, chapter 5, p. 195.

[63] ICJ Reports, 1992, pp. 240, 258; 97 ILR, pp. 1, 25.

[64] See e.g. article 6 of the European Coal and Steel Community Treaty, 1951, and article 210 of the EEC Treaty, 1957 (now article 281 of the EC Treaty, Consolidated Version). See also *Costa (Flaminio)* v. *ENEL* [1964] ECR 585; 93 ILR, p. 23.

[65] Note also the approach championed by Seyersted that international organisations become *ipso facto* international legal persons where there exists at least one organ with a will distinct from that of the member states: see Seyersted, 'Objective International Personality', and Schermers and Blokker, *International Institutional Law*, p. 978.

[66] ICJ Reports, 1949, p. 174; 16 AD, p. 318.

functions and rights the organisation was exercising and enjoying. The Court emphasised that it had to be:

> acknowledged that its [i.e. UN's] members, by entrusting certain functions to it, with the attendant duties and responsibilities, have clothed it with the competence required to enable those functions to be effectively discharged.[67]

The possession of international personality meant that the organisation was a subject of international law and capable of having international rights and duties and of enforcing them by bringing international claims.

In reaching this conclusion, the Court examined the United Nations Charter and subsequent relevant treaties and practice to determine the constitutional nature of the United Nations and the extent of its powers and duties. It noted the obligations of members towards the organisation, its ability to make international agreements and the provisions of the Charter contained in Articles 104 and 105, whereby the United Nations was to enjoy such legal capacity, privileges and immunities in the territory of each member state as were necessary for the fulfilment of its purposes. The Court emphasised that:

> fifty states, representing the vast majority of the members of the international community, had the power in conformity with international law, to bring into being an entity possessing objective international personality, and not merely personality recognised by them alone.[68]

Accordingly, the Court derived the objective international legal personality of the UN from the intention of the members, either directly or implicitly. Such personality was objective in the sense that it could be maintained as against non-members as well, of course, as against members. Objective personality is not dependent upon prior recognition by the non-member concerned and would seem to flow rather from the nature and functions of the organisation itself. It may be that the number of states members of the organisation in question is relevant to the issue of objective personality, but it is not determinative.[69]

---

[67] ICJ Reports, 1949, p. 179; 16 AD, p. 322.　　[68] ICJ Reports, 1949, p. 185; 16 AD, p. 330.

[69] See the *Third US Restatement of Foreign Relations Law*, St Paul, 1987, vol. I, p. 141, noting that '[a]n international organisation with a substantial membership is a person in international law even in relation to states not members of the organisation. However, a state does not have to recognise the legal personality of an organisation of which it is not a member, which has few members, or which is regional in scope in a region to which the state does not belong.' Cf. Amerasinghe, *Principles*, p. 90. It should be noted that the

The attribution of international legal personality to an international organisation is therefore important in establishing that organisation as an entity operating directly upon the international stage rather than obliging the organisation to function internationally through its member states, who may number in the tens of dozens or more. The latter situation inevitably leads to considerable complication in the reaching of agreements as well as causing problems with regard to enforcing the responsibility or claims of such organisations internationally. The question of the effect of international personality upon the liability of member states for problems affecting the organisation will be referred to later in this chapter.[70] However, one needs to be careful not to confuse international with domestic legal personality. Many constituent instruments of international organisations expressly or impliedly provide that the organisation in question shall have personality in domestic law so as to enable it, for example, to contract or acquire or dispose of property or to institute legal proceedings in the local courts or to have the legal capacity necessary for the exercise of its functions.[71] Article 104 of the United Nations Charter itself provides that the UN 'shall enjoy in the territory of each of its members such legal capacity as may be necessary for the exercise of its functions and the fulfilment of its purposes'. Where such provisions exist, it follows that member states of the organisation have accepted an obligation to recognise such legal personality within their legal systems. How that may be achieved will vary from state to state and will depend upon the domestic legal system.[72]

The issue also arises at this point as to whether states that are not parties to the treaty in question and thus not member states of the particular international organisation are obliged to recognise the personality of such organisation. This can be achieved either directly, by entering into an agreement with the organisation – a headquarters agreement permitting the establishment of the organisation within the jurisdiction is the obvious

---

question of objective personality is not essentially linked to recognition by non-member states as such. What will, however, be important will be patterns of dealing with such organisations by non-member states.

[70] See below, p. 1314.

[71] See e.g. articles IX(2) and VII(2) respectively of the Articles of Agreement of the International Monetary Fund and the International Bank for Reconstruction and Development. See also article 16 of the Constitution of the Food and Agriculture Organisation, article 6h of the Constitution of the World Health Organisation and article 12 of the Constitution of UNESCO.

[72] See also e.g. article 282 of the EC Treaty (Consolidated Version) and Klabbers, *Introduction*, p. 49.

example[73] – or indirectly by virtue of the rules of private international law
(or conflict of laws).

Of course, most international organisations need to operate within
particular states and thus require that their personality be recognised not
only within international law but also within particular domestic law in
order to be able to make and defend claims and generally to perform legal
acts in domestic law. This may be achieved in different ways. In many legal
systems, a domestic court will determine the legal status and capacity of
a legal person by reference to the applicable or proper law, which will in
the case of international organisations be international law. Thus if the
organisation had personality under international law, this would suffice
to establish personality under domestic law.[74] Indeed, in states where
treaties form part of domestic law upon ratification by parliament, then
domestic legal personality would be a consequence of becoming a party
to an international agreement establishing an international organisation
explicitly endowed with legal personality, such as the UN, for example.[75]

However, in the UK, the approach has been rather different since the
UK adopts a dualist approach to international treaties, so that in order
for such agreements to operate within the domestic system, express legislative incorporation is required.[76] The International Organisations Act
1968 grants the legal capacity of a body corporate to any organisation
declared by Order in Council to be an organisation of which the UK and
one or more foreign states are members. The view taken by the House of
Lords in the *Tin* case[77] was that the legal effect of the Order in Council
of 1972 concerning the International Tin Council (ITC) was to create the
ITC as a legal person separate and distinct from its members, since 'as

---

[73] See e.g. *Re Poncet* 15 AD, p. 346 (concerning Switzerland and the UN).

[74] See e.g. *International Tin Council* v. *Amalgamet Inc.* 524 NYS 2d 971 (1988); 80 ILR, p. 30.
See also *UNRAA* v. *Daan* 16 AD, p. 337 and *Branno* v. *Ministry of War* 22 ILR, p. 756.

[75] See e.g. *UN* v. *B* 19 ILR, p. 490 and *International Tin Council* v. *Amalgamet Inc.* 524 NYS
2d 971 (1988). See also Amerasinghe, *Principles*, pp. 69 ff. As to the relationship between
international law and domestic law generally, see above, chapter 4.

[76] See e.g. J. W. Bridge, 'The United Nations and English Law', 18 ICLQ, 1969, p. 689;
G. Marston, 'The Origin of the Personality of International Organizations in United Kingdom Law', 40 ICLQ, 1991, p. 403, and F. A. Mann, 'International Organizations as National
Corporations', 107 LQR, 1991, p. 357. See also R. Higgins, Report on the 'Legal Consequences for Member States of the Non-Fulfilment by International Organizations of their
Obligations toward Third States', *Annuaire de l'Institut de Droit International*, 1995 I,
p. 249.

[77] *J. H. Rayner (Mincing Lane) Ltd* v. *Department of Trade and Industry* [1989] 3 WLR 969,
982 and 1004 ff.; 81 ILR, pp. 670, 678 and 703 ff.

an international legal persona [it] had no status under the laws of the United Kingdom'.[78] In other words, without such legislative action, an international organisation would have no legal existence in the UK. There is an exception to this strict approach and that is where the organisation has been granted legal personality in another country. The case of *Arab Monetary Fund* v. *Hashim (No. 3)*[79] concerned the attempt by the AMF to bring an action before the English courts to recover funds allegedly embezzled. The relevant constituent treaty of 1976 between a number of Arab states gave the AMF 'independent juridical personality' and a decree was adopted in Abu Dhabi giving the organisation independent legal status and the capacity to sue and be sued in United Arab Emirates law. There was, however, no Order in Council under the International Organisations Act 1968 giving the AMF legal personality within the UK. The Court of Appeal took the view that the decision of the House of Lords in the *Tin* case[80] meant that the ordinary conflict of laws rules allowing recognition of an entity created under foreign law could not be applied to an organisation established under international law, since this would apparently circumvent the principle that an international organisation with legal personality created outside the jurisdiction would not have capacity to sue in England without a relevant authorising Order in Council.[81]

The House of Lords, however, by a majority of four to one, expressed the opinion that the majority of the Court of Appeal had felt inhibited by observations made in the *Tin* cases and that the latter cases had not affected the principles that the recognition of a foreign state was a matter for the Crown and that if a foreign state is recognised by the Crown, the courts of the UK would recognise the corporate bodies created by that state. The House of Lords noted that the UK courts could indeed recognise an international organisation as a separate entity by comity provided that the entity was created by one or more of the member states.[82]

In other words, in the UK, an international organisation can be recognised as having personality by one of several methods: first, where Parliament has by legislation incorporated an international treaty

---

[78] [1989] 3 WLR 1008; 81 ILR, p. 708 (per Lord Oliver). But see Lord Templeman in *Arab Monetary Fund* v. *Hashim (No. 3)* [1991] 2 WLR 729, 738; 85 ILR, pp. 1, 11, who noted that no argument based on incorporation by one or more foreign states had been relevant or canvassed in the *Tin* case.

[79] [1991] 2 WLR 729; 85 ILR, p. 1.   [80] [1989] 3 WLR 969; 81 ILR, p. 670.

[81] [1990] All ER 769, 775 (Donaldson MR); 83 ILR, pp. 259–61 and 778 (Nourse LJ); 83 ILR, p. 264.

[82] [1991] 2 WLR 738–9; 85 ILR, pp. 12–13.

establishing such an organisation;[83] secondly, where the executive expressly recognises an international organisation;[84] thirdly, where an Order in Council under the International Organisations Act so provides; and fourthly, where the courts by virtue of comity recognise an international organisation that has personality in one or more of the member states.[85] It is an approach that is not without some difficulty, not least because of the implication that an international organisation not the subject of a UK Order in Council and not incorporated in the domestic law of member states may not be recognised as having personality in the UK, even though there exists an international treaty establishing such an international organisation with international personality. On the other hand, to argue that an international organisation has legal personality solely due to the fact that it has legal personality within the domestic law of another country which is thus to be applied in the UK due to conflict of law rules poses its own problems. However, the court in *Westland Helicopters Ltd* v. *AOI*[86] held that the law governing the status and capacities of such an organisation was international law.

To state that an international organisation has international personality does not dispose of the question of what such personality entails. While the attribution of international personality to an organisation endows it with a separate identity, distinct from its constituent elements, the consequences of such personality will vary according to the circumstances. Whereas all international legal persons will have some rights and duties (and by definition rights and duties distinct from those of the members of the organisation), they will not all have the same capacities.[87] The question of how such rights and duties may be enforced or maintained will also depend upon the circumstances. States are recognised as possessing the widest range of rights and duties, those of international organisations are clearly circumscribed in terms of express powers laid down in the constituent instruments or implied powers necessarily derived therefrom or otherwise evolved through practice.[88] The International Court

---

[83] See [1991] 2 WLR 738; 85 ILR, p. 12, giving the example of the Bretton Woods Agreements Act 1945.

[84] *Ibid.*   [85] *Ibid.*   [86] [1995] 2 WLR 126; 108 ILR, p. 564.

[87] The International Court in the *Reparation* case, ICJ Reports, 1949, pp. 174, 178; 16 AD, p. 330, stated that, 'The subjects of law in any legal system are not necessarily identical in nature or in the extent of their rights, and their nature depends upon the needs of the community.'

[88] The Court in the *Reparation* case took particular care to emphasise that possession of international personality was far from an ascription of statehood or recognition of equal rights and duties, ICJ Reports, 1949, pp. 174, 185; 16 AD, p. 330.

emphasised that the attribution of international personality to the UN, for example, was not the same thing as declaring the UN to be a state nor that its legal personality and rights and duties were the same as those of a state. By the same token it did not mean that the UN was a 'super-state'.[89] The Court declared that UN personality involved the competence to possess and maintain rights and the capacity to enforce them on the international stage.[90] Accordingly, whereas states would possess the total-ity of international rights and duties recognised by international law, 'the rights and duties of an entity such as the [UN] Organisation must depend upon its purposes and functions as specified or implied in its constituent documents and developed in practice'.[91] Precisely which powers and ca-pacities are involved will in reality therefore depend upon a careful analysis of the organisation itself, including the relationship of such powers and capacities to the stated purposes and duties of that organisation.

The constituent instruments[92]

International organisations are expressly created by states by formal de-cision as laid down in their constituent instruments. The very nature, status and authority of such organisations will therefore depend primar-ily upon the terms of the constituent instruments or constitutions under which they are established. Such instruments have a dual provenance. They constitute multilateral treaties, since they are binding agreements entered into by states parties, and as such fall within the framework of the international law of treaties.[93] But such agreements are multilateral treaties possessing a special character since they are also methods of cre-ation of new subjects of international law. This dual nature has an impact most clearly in the realm of interpretation of the basic documents of the organisation.[94] This was clearly brought out in the Advisory Opinion of

---

[89] *Ibid.*, p. 179; 16 AD, p. 322. See also the *WHO* case, ICJ Reports, 1980, pp. 73, 89; 62 ILR, pp. 450, 473.

[90] ICJ Reports, 1949, p. 179.   [91] *Ibid.*, p. 180.

[92] See e.g. Amerasinghe, *Principles*, chapter 2; Schermers and Blokker, *International Institu-tional Law*, pp. 710 ff., and E. P. Hexner, 'Interpretation by International Organizations of their Basic Instruments', 53 AJIL, 1959, p. 341.

[93] As to which see above, chapter 16.

[94] See C. F. Amerasinghe, 'Interpretation of Texts in Open International Organizations', 65 BYIL, 1994, p. 175; M. N. Shaw, *Title to Territory in Africa: International Legal Issues*, Oxford, 1986, pp. 64–73; S. Rosenne, 'Is the Constitution of an International Organi-zation an International Treaty?', 12 *Communicazioni e Studi*, 1966, p. 21, and G. Diste-fano, 'La Pratique Subséquente des États Parties à un Traité', AFDI, 1994, p. 41. See also

the International Court of Justice (requested by the World Health Organisation) in the *Legality of the Use by a State of Nuclear Weapons in Armed Conflict* case. The Court declared that:

> [t]he constituent instruments of international organisations are also treaties of a particular type; their object is to create new subjects of law endowed with a certain autonomy, to which the parties entrust the task of realising common goals. Such treaties can raise specific problems of interpretation owing, *inter alia*, to their character which is conventional and at the same time institutional; the very nature of the organisation created, the objectives which have been assigned to it by its founder, the imperatives associated with the effective performance of its functions, as well as its own practice, are all elements which may deserve special attention when the time comes to interpret these constituent treaties.[95]

Accordingly, one needs to consider the special nature of the constituent instruments as forming not only multilateral agreements but also constitutional documents subject to constant practice, and thus interpretation, both of the institution itself and of member states and others in relation to it. In the first instance, it will usually be for the organs of the institution to interpret the relevant constituent instruments.[96] In some cases, the constituent instruments themselves will determine the organ with the power of interpretation and may provide the methods and mechanisms for resolving interpretation disputes.[97] Occasionally, a court or tribunal will be established with such a competence. For example, the International Tribunal for the Law of the Sea can interpret the Law of the Sea Convention and the European Court of Justice can interpret the EU treaties and instruments. In so far as the UN is concerned, the Security Council and General Assembly may request an advisory opinion from the International Court of Justice, as may other organs of the organisation and specialised agencies where authorised by the General Assembly with regard to a question within the scope of their activities.[98] The constituent instruments of

---

H. Lauterpacht, *The Development of International Law by the International Court*, London, 1958, pp. 267–81, and E. Lauterpacht, 'Development', pp. 414 ff.

[95] ICJ Reports, 1996, pp. 66, 74–5; 110 ILR, pp. 1, 14–15.

[96] See *Certain Expenses of the United Nations*, ICJ Reports, 1962, pp. 151, 168. See also Amerasinghe, *Principles*, pp. 25 ff.

[97] The constitutions of the various international financial institutions, such as the International Monetary Fund and the World Bank, invariably provide for binding determination by the supreme plenary organ: see e.g. Amerasinghe, *Principles*, pp. 28 ff.

[98] See article 96(1) and (2) of the Charter. See further above, chapter 19, p. 1108. Note that there is no provision in the Charter authorising the International Court to review decisions of the UN judicially, but see further above, chapter 22, p. 1268.

some organisations provide for binding final determination by the International Court using advisory proceedings, that is, organisations in such situations agree to accept the advisory opinion as binding.[99] In addition, article XIX, section 32, of the Convention on the Privileges and Immunities of Specialised Agencies, 1947, provides that differences between a specialised agency and a member arising out of the interpretation or the application of the convention are to be submitted to the International Court under the advisory procedure contained in article 96 of the Charter and article 65 of the Statute of the Court and the opinion thus obtained is to be treated as decisive by the parties.[100] In contentious cases, the International Court may need to interpret the constituent instruments of an international organisation, including the UN Charter itself, where this is relevant to the determination of the issue at hand.[101]

The fact that the constituent instruments of international organisations are invariably multilateral agreements means that the process of their interpretation will be governed by articles 31 and 32 of the Vienna Convention on the Law of Treaties, 1969.[102] However, such agreements are of a special nature since they also from the constitutions of international organisations[103] and this argues for a more flexible or purpose-orientated

---

[99] See e.g. article 37 of the International Labour Organisation Constitution. Article XIV of the UNESCO Constitution 1945 provides that, 'Any question or dispute concerning the interpretation of this Constitution shall be referred for determination to the International Court of Justice or to an arbitral tribunal, as the General Conference may determine.' See also Amerasinghe, *Principles*, p. 29.

[100] See also article VIII, section 30, of the Convention on the Privileges and Immunities of the United Nations, 1946, with regard to disputes between the UN and member states as to the interpretation or application of the Convention. Note in addition article VIII, sectioin 21(b) of the UN–US Headquarters Agreement, 1947.

[101] Note that by article 34 of the Statute of the International Court, only states may be parties to a contentious case before the Court.

[102] Note that by virtue of article 5 of the Vienna Convention on the Law of Treaties, 1969, this Convention applies to any treaty which is the constituent instrument of an international organisation and to any treaty adopted within an international organisation, without prejudice to any relevant rules of the organisation. See also the Advisory Opinion on the *Legality of the Use by a State of Nuclear Weapons*, ICJ Reports, 1996, pp. 66, 74, noting that, 'From a formal standpoint, the constituent instruments of international organisations are multilateral treaties, to which the well-established rules of treaty interpretation apply.' See as to the principles of treaty interpretation, above, chapter 16, p. 932.

[103] ICJ Reports, 1996, pp. 66, 74, referring to the institutional character of such organisations and emphasising that, 'the very nature of the organisation created, the objectives which have been assigned to it by its founders, the imperatives associated with the effective performance of its functions, as well as its own practice, are all elements which may deserve special attention when the time comes to interpret these constituent treaties'.

method of interpretation. Rather less attention than would be the case in the interpretation of normal treaties is paid to the intentions of the original framers and the *travaux préparatoires* (negotiating materials) and rather more to the principle of effectiveness in the light of the object and purposes of the agreement in question.[104] Because constitutions are 'living instruments' in constant use in order to carry out the purposes of the organisation in changing and developing circumstances, subsequent practice is of particular importance in the context of interpretation.[105] The International Court has relied upon the subsequent practice of international organisations in a number of cases, although usually to support an interpretation already reached by the Court.[106]

The powers of international institutions[107]

International organisations are unlike states that possess a general competence as subjects of international law.[108] They are governed by the principle of speciality, so that, as the International Court has noted, 'they are invested by the states which create them with powers, the limits of which are a function of the common interests whose promotion those states entrust to them'.[109] Such powers may be expressly laid down in the constituent

---

[104] See Amerasinghe, *Principles*, p. 59. See also the *Reparation* case, ICJ Reports, 1949, pp. 174, 180.

[105] See article 31(3)b of the Vienna Convention. See also E. Lauterpacht, 'Development', p. 420 ff.

[106] See e.g. the *Competence of the General Assembly for the Admission of a State to the United Nations* case, ICJ Reports, 1950, pp. 4, 9; 17 ILR, pp. 326, 329; the *Namibia* case, ICJ Reports, 1971, pp. 17, 22; 49 ILR, pp. 2, 12, and the *IMCO* case, ICJ Reports, 1960, pp. 150, 167–8; 30 ILR, pp. 426, 439–41.

[107] See e.g. Sarooshi, *International Organizations*; Klabbers, *Introduction*, chapter 4; E. Lauterpacht, 'Development', pp. 423–74; Amerasinghe, *Principles*, p. 135; Rama-Montaldo, 'Legal Personality'; A. I. L. Campbell, 'The Limits of Powers of International Organizations', 32 ICLQ, 1983, p. 523; K. Skubiszewski, 'Implied Powers of International Organizations' in *International Law at a Time of Perplexity* (ed. Y. Dinstein), Dordrecht, 1989, p. 855, and Kirgis, *International Organizations*, chapter 3.

[108] See the Advisory Opinion of the International Court on the *Legality of the Use by a State of Nuclear Weapons in Armed Conflict* brought by the World Health Organisation, ICJ Reports, 1996, pp. 66, 78–9.

[109] *Ibid.* The Court here cited the Permanent Court's Advisory Opinion in the *Jurisdiction of the European Commission of the Danube*, PCIJ, Series B, No. 14, p. 64, which noted that, 'As the European Commission is not a state, but an international institution with a special purpose, it only has the functions bestowed upon it by the Definitive Statute with a view to the fulfilment of that purpose, but it has power to exercise those functions to their full extent, in so far as the Statute does not impose restrictions upon it.'

instruments or may arise subsidiarily as implied powers,[110] being those deemed necessary for fulfilment of the functions of the particular organisation. The test of validity for such powers has been variously expressed. The International Court noted in the *Reparation* case that:[111]

> [u]nder international law the organization must be deemed to have those powers which, though not expressly provided in the charter, are conferred upon it by necessary implication as being essential to the performance of its duties.[112]

In the *Effect of Awards of Compensation Made by the UN Administrative Tribunal* case,[113] the Court held that the General Assembly could validly establish an administrative tribunal in the absence of an express power since the capacity to do this arose 'by necessary intendment' out of the Charter, while in the *Certain Expenses of the UN* case,[114] the Court declared that 'when the organisation takes action which warrants the assertion that it was appropriate for the fulfilment of one of the stated purposes of the United Nations, the presumption is that such action is not *ultra vires* the organisation'. The tests posited therefore have ranged from powers arising by 'necessary implication as being essential to the performance' of constitutionally laid down duties, to those arising 'by necessary intendment' out of the constituent instrument, to those deemed 'appropriate for the fulfilment' of constitutionally authorised purposes of the organisation. There are clearly variations of emphasis in such formulations.[115] Nevertheless, although the functional test is determinative, it operates within the framework of those powers expressly conferred by the constitution of the organisation. Thus any attempt to infer a power that was inconsistent with an express power would fail, although there is clearly an area of ambiguity here.[116] In the *Legality of the Use by a State of Nuclear Weapons*

---

[110] See Schermers and Blokker, *International Institutional Law*, pp. 158 ff.

[111] ICJ Reports, 1949, pp. 174, 182; 16 AD, pp. 318, 326.

[112] This passage was cited in the *Legality of the Use by a State of Nuclear Weapons* case, ICJ Reports, 1996, pp. 66, 78–9. Compare also the approach adopted by the International Court in the *Reparation* case with that adopted by Judge Hackworth in his Dissenting Opinion in that case, ICJ Reports, 1949, pp. 196–8; 16 AD, pp. 318, 328. See also G. G. Fitzmaurice, 'The Law and Procedure of the International Court of Justice: International Organizations and Tribunals', 29 BYIL, 1952, p. 1.

[113] ICJ Reports, 1954, pp. 47, 56–7; 21 ILR, pp. 310, 317–18.

[114] ICJ Reports, 1962, pp. 151, 168; 34 ILR, pp. 281, 297.

[115] See also the *Fédéchar* case, Case 8/55, European Court Reports, 1954–6, p. 299.

[116] See also e.g. the *International Status of South-West Africa* case, ICJ Reports, 1950, pp. 128, 136–8; 17 ILR, pp. 47, 53; the *Expenses* case, ICJ Reports, 1962, pp. 151, 167–8; 34 ILR, pp. 281, 296 and the *Namibia* case, ICJ Reports, 1971, pp. 16, 47–9; 49 ILR, pp. 2, 37.

case,[117] the Court noted that the World Health Organisation had under article 2 of its Constitution adopted in 1946 the competence 'to deal with the effects on health of the use of nuclear weapons, or any other hazardous activity, and to take preventive measures aimed at protecting the health of populations in the event of such weapons being used or such activities engaged in'.[118] However, the Court concluded that the question asked of it related not to the effects of the use of nuclear weapons on health, but to the legality of the use of such weapons in view of their health and environmental effects. Whatever those effects might be, the competence of the WHO to deal with them was not dependent upon the legality of the acts that caused them. Accordingly, the Court concluded that in the light of the constitution of the WHO as properly interpreted, the organisation had not been granted the competence to address the legality of the use of nuclear weapons and that therefore the competence to request an advisory opinion did not exist since the question posed was not one that could be considered as arising 'within the scope of . . . activities' of the WHO as required by article 96(2) of the UN Charter.[119]

So far as the International Court itself is concerned, it has held that it possesses 'an inherent jurisdiction enabling it to take such action as may be required, on the one hand to ensure that the exercise of its jurisdiction over the merits, if and when established, shall not be frustrated, and on the other, to provide for the orderly settlement of all matters in dispute, to ensure the observance of the "inherent limitations on the exercise of the judicial function" of the Court, and to "maintain its judicial character"'.[120]

Of great importance is the question of the capacity of international organisations to conclude international treaties.[121] This will primarily

---

[117] ICJ Reports, 1996, pp. 66, 78–9.   [118] *Ibid.*, p. 76.

[119] Article 96(2) of the UN Charter provides that organs of the UN (apart from the Security Council and General Assembly) and specialised agencies which may at any time be so authorised by the General Assembly may request advisory opinions of the International Court on 'legal questions arising within the scope of their activities'.

[120] The *Nuclear Tests* case, ICJ Reports, 1974, pp. 253, 259; 57 ILR, p. 398. See the Appeals Chamber in the *Tadić (Jurisdiction)* case, 105 ILR, pp. 453, 463 ff. See also E. Lauterpacht, '"Partial" Judgments and the Inherent Jurisdiction of the International Court of Justice' in *Fifty Years of the International Court of Justice* (eds. V. Lowe and M. Fitzmaurice), Cambridge, 1996, pp. 465, 476 ff.

[121] See e.g. Klabbers, *Introduction*, chapter 13; Schermers and Blokker, *International Institutional Law*, pp. 1096 ff.; J. W. Schneider, *Treaty-Making Power of International Organizations*, Geneva, 1959, and C. Parry 'The Treaty-Making Power of the UN', 26 BYIL, 1949, p. 147. See also above, chapter 16, p. 953, with regard to the Convention on the Law of Treaties between States and International Organisations. See also *Yearbook of the ILC*, 1982, vol. II, part 2, pp. 9 ff.

depend upon the constituent instrument, since the existence of legal personality is on its own probably insufficient to ground the competence to enter into international agreements.[122] Article 6 of the Vienna Convention on the Law of Treaties between States and International Organisations, 1986 provides that '[t]he capacity of an international organisation to conclude treaties is governed by the rules of that organisation'. This is a wider formulation than reliance solely upon the constituent instrument and permits recourse to issues of implied powers, interpretation and subsequent practice. It was noted in the commentary of the International Law Commission that the phrase 'the rules of the organisation' meant, in addition to the constituent instruments,[123] relevant decisions and resolutions and the established practice of the organisation.[124] Accordingly, demonstration of treaty-making capacity will revolve around the competences of the organisation as demonstrated in each particular case by reference to the constituent instruments, evidenced implied powers and subsequent practice.

The applicable law[125]

International institutions are established by states by means of international treaties. Such instruments fall to be interpreted and applied within the framework of international law. Accordingly, as a general rule, the applicable or 'proper' or 'personal' law of international organisations is international law.[126] In addition, the organisation in question may well have entered into treaty relationships with particular states, for example,

---

[122] See e.g. Hungdah Chiu, *The Capacity of International Organizations to Conclude Treaties and the Special Legal Aspects of the Treaties So Concluded*, The Hague, 1966; *Agreements of International Organizations and the Vienna Convention on the Law of Treaties* (ed. K. Zemanek), Vienna, 1971; G. Nascimento e Silva, 'The 1986 Vienna Convention and the Treaty-Making Power of International Organizations', 29 German YIL, 1986, p. 68, and 'The 1969 and 1986 Conventions on the Law of Treaties: A Comparison' in Dinstein, *International Law at a Time of Perplexity*, p. 461.

[123] See e.g. article 43 and articles 75, 77, 79, 83 and 85 of the UN Charter concerning military assistance arrangements with the Security Council and Trusteeship Agreements respectively.

[124] *Yearbook of the ILC*, 1982, vol. II, part 2, p. 41.

[125] See e.g. Amerasinghe, *Principles*, pp. 20–2 and 227 ff.; F. A. Mann, 'International Corporations and National Law', 42 BYIL, 1967, p. 145; F. Seyersted, 'Applicable Law in Relations Between Intergovernmental Organizations and Private Parties', 122 HR, 1976 III, p. 427, and C. W. Jenks, *The Proper Law of International Organizations*, London, 1961.

[126] Jenks, *Proper Law*, p. 3, wrote that 'if a body has the character of an international body corporate the law governing its corporate life must necessarily be international in character'. See also the *Third US Restatement of Foreign Relations Law*, vol. I, pp. 133 ff.

in the case of a headquarters agreement, and these relationships will also be governed by international law. Those matters that will necessarily (in the absence of express provision to the contrary) be governed by international law will include questions as to the existence, constitution, status, membership and representation of the organisation.[127]

However, the applicable law in particular circumstances may be domestic law. Thus, where the organisation is purchasing or leasing land or entering into contracts for equipment or services, such activities will normally be subject to the appropriate national law. Tortious liability as between the organisation and a private individual will generally be subject to domestic law, but tortious activity may be governed by international law depending upon the circumstances, for example, where there has been damage to the property of an international organisation by the police or armed forces of a state. The internal law of the organisation will cover matters such as employment relations, the establishment and functioning of subsidiary organs and the management of administrative services.[128] The internal law of an organisation, which includes the constituent instruments and subsidiary regulations and norms and any relevant contractual arrangements, may in reality be seen as a specialised and particularised part of international law, since it is founded upon agreements that draw their validity and applicability from the principles of international law.

The responsibility of international institutions[129]

The establishment of an international organisation with international personality results in the formation of a new legal person, separate and distinct from that of the states creating it. This separate and distinct personality necessarily imports consequences as to international responsibility,

---

[127] See also Colman J in *Westland Helicopters Ltd* v. *AOI* [1995] 2 WLR 126, 144 ff., and Millett J in *In re International Tin Council* [1987] Ch. 419, 452, upheld by the Court of Appeal, [1989] Ch. 309, 330.

[128] See e.g. Amerasinghe, *Principles*, chapter 9. See also P. Cahier, 'Le Droit Interne des Organisations Internationales', 67 RGDIP, 1963, p. 563, and G. Balldore-Pallieri, 'Le Droit Interne des Organisations Internationales', 127 HR, 1969 II, p. 1.

[129] See e.g. Klabbers, *Introduction*, chapter 14; Amerasinghe, *Principles*, chapter 12; Schermers and Blokker, *International Institutional Law*, pp. 1166 ff.; *Bowett's International Institutions*, pp. 512 ff.; M. Hirsch, *The Responsibility of International Organizations Towards Third Parties: Some Basic Principles*, Dordrecht, 1995; P. Klein, *La Responsabilité des Organisations Internationales*, Brussels, 1998; C. Eagleton, 'International Organisation and the Law of Responsibility', 76 HR, 1950 I, p. 319; F. V. Garcia Amador, 'State Responsibility: Some New Problems', 94 HR, 1958, p. 410, and M. Perez Gonzalez, 'Les Organisations

both to and by the organisation. The International Court noted in the *Reparation* case, for example, that[130] 'when an infringement occurs, the organisation should be able to call upon the responsible state to remedy its default, and, in particular, to obtain from the state reparation for the damage that the default may have caused' and emphasised that there existed an 'undeniable right of the organization to demand that its members shall fulfil the obligations entered into by them in the interest of the good working of the organization'.[131] Responsibility is a necessary consequence of international personality and the resulting possession of international rights and duties. Such rights and duties may flow from treaties, such as headquarters agreements,[132] or from the principles of customary international law.[133] The precise nature of responsibility will depend upon the circumstances of the case and, no doubt, analogies drawn from the law of state responsibility with regard to the conditions under which responsibility will be imposed.[134] In brief, one can note the following. The basis of international responsibility is the breach of an international obligation[135] and such obligations will depend upon the situation. The Court noted in the *Reparation* case[136] that the obligations entered into by member states to enable the agents of the UN to perform their duties were obligations owed to the organisation. Thus, the organisation has, in the case of a breach of such obligations, 'the capacity to claim adequate reparation, and that in assessing this reparation it is authorised to include the damage suffered by the victim or by persons entitled through him'. Whereas

---

Internationales et le Droit de la Responsabilité', 92 RGDIP, 1988, p. 63. The International Law Commission is currently considering the question of responsibility of international organisations: see e.g. Report of the ILC, 2007, A/62/10, p. 178, and references to draft articles as currently proposed are to those contained in this document. See also above, chapter 14.

[130] ICJ Reports, 1949, pp. 174, 183; 16 AD, pp. 318, 327.

[131] ICJ Reports, 1949, p. 184; 16 AD, p. 328.

[132] See e.g. the *WHO Regional Office* case, ICJ Reports, 1980, p. 73; 62 ILR, p. 450 and the *Case Concerning the Obligation to Arbitrate*, ICJ Reports, 1988, p. 12; 82 ILR, p. 225.

[133] See the *WHO Regional Office* case, ICJ Reports, 1980, pp. 73, 90; 62 ILR, pp. 450, 474, referring to 'general rules of international law'.

[134] See above, chapter 14. See also Report of the ILC, 2007, A/62/10, p. 178.

[135] See e.g. the *Reparation* case, ICJ Reports, 1949, p. 180; 16 AD, p. 323. Article 3 of the ILC draft articles on responsibility of international organisations provides that, 'Every internationally wrongful act of an international organization entails the international responsibility of the international organization' and that, 'There is an internationally wrongful act of an international organization when conduct consisting of an action or omission: (*a*) Is attributable to the international organization under international law; and (*b*) Constitutes a breach of an international obligation of that international organization.'

[136] ICJ Reports, 1949, p. 184; 16 AD, p. 328.

the right of a state to assert a claim on behalf of a victim is predicated upon the link of nationality, in the case of an international organisation, the necessary link relates to the requirements of the organisation and therefore the fact that the victim was acting on behalf of the organisation in exercising one of the functions of that organisation. As the Court noted, 'the organization ... possesses a right of functional protection in respect of its agents'.[137]

Just as a state can be held responsible for injury to an organisation, so can the organisation be held responsible for injury to a state, where the injury arises out of a breach by the organisation of an international obligation deriving from a treaty provision or principle of customary international law.[138] Again, analogies will be drawn from the general rules relating to state responsibility with regard to the conditions under which responsibility is imposed. For example, the conduct of an organ or an agent of an international organisation in the performance of the functions of that organ or agent (including officials and other persons or entities through whom the organisation acts) is considered as an act of the organisation, irrespective of the position actually held by the organ or agent and even if the conduct exceeds the authority of that organ or agent.[139] An international organisation which aids or assists a state or another international organisation in the commission of an internationally wrongful act will itself bear international responsibility where the organisation knew the circumstances of the wrongful act and the act would be internationally wrongful if committed by that organisation.[140] As in

---

[137] ICJ Reports, 1949, p. 184; 16 AD, p. 329. Note that the Court held that there was no rule of law which assigned priority either to the national state of the victim or the international organisation with regard to the bringing of an international claim, ICJ Reports, 1949, p. 185; 16 AD, p. 330.

[138] See e.g. the *WHO Regional Office* case, ICJ Reports, 1980, p. 73; 62 ILR, p. 450. Note that under articles 6 and 13 of the Outer Space Treaty, 1967, international organisations may be subject to the obligations of the treaty without being parties to it.

[139] See articles 4 and 6 of the ILC draft articles on responsibility of international organisations.

[140] Article 12 of the ILC draft articles on the responsibility of international organisations. Note that draft article 25 provides that a state which aids or assists an international organisation in the commission of an internationally wrongful act by the latter is internationally responsible in the same circumstances. But see here *Behrami* v. *France*, European Court of Human Rights, judgment of 2 May 2007, 133 ILR, p. 1, where the Court dismissed as inadmissible an application against a number of NATO states operating with the framework of KFOR (the international security force in Kosovo authorised by the Security Council under Chapter VII of the UN Charter) on the grounds that the actions complained against were 'directly attributable to the UN', whether to KFOR or to UNMIK (the international civil administration in Kosovo): see above, chapter 7, p. 350.

the case of states, international organisations may benefit from the precluding of responsibility in particular circumstances, such as consent by
a state or an international organisation to the commission of the act
or where the act constitutes a lawful measure of self-defence in conformity with international law.[141] An international organisation responsible
for the internationally wrongful act is under an obligation to cease that
act and to offer appropriate assurances and guarantees of non-repetition
(if circumstances so require) and to make full reparation for the injury
caused.[142]

The issue of responsibility has particularly arisen in the context of UN
peacekeeping operations and liability for the activities of the members of
such forces. In such circumstances, the UN has accepted responsibility
and offered compensation for wrongful acts.[143] The crucial issue will be
whether the wrongful acts in question are imputable to the UN and this
has not been accepted where the offenders were under the jurisdiction of
the national state, rather than under that of the UN. Much will depend
upon the circumstances of the operation in question and the nature of the
link between the offenders and the UN. It appears, for example, to have
been accepted that in the Korean (1950) and Kuwait (1990) operations
the relationship between the national forces and the UN was such as to
preclude the latter's responsibility.[144] While responsibility will exist for
internationally unlawful acts attributable to the institution in question,
tortious liability may also arise for injurious consequences caused by lawful activities, for example environmental damage as a result of legitimate
space activities.[145]

---

[141] Articles 17 and 18. Other examples of circumstances precluding wrongfulness include
countermeasures, *force majeure*, distress and necessity: see articles 19–22. However, nothing may preclude the wrongful act of an international organisation which is not in conformity with an obligation arising under a peremptory norm of general international law
(*jus cogens*): article 23 and see above, chapter 3, p. 123.

[142] Articles 33 and 34. Full reparation is to take the form of restitution (re-establishment
of the situation existing before the wrongful act was committed), compensation and
satisfaction, either singly or in combination: see articles 37 to 42.

[143] See e.g. B. Amrallah, 'The International Responsibility of the United Nations for Activities
Carried Out by UN Peace-Keeping Forces', 23 *Revue Égyptienne de Droit International*,
1976, p. 57; D. W. Bowett, *UN Forces*, London, 1964, pp. 149 ff.; F. Seyersted, 'United
Nations Forces: Some Legal Problems', 37 BYIL, 1961, p. 351. See also Amerasinghe,
Principles, pp. 401 ff., and *M v. Organisation des Nations Unies et l'État Belge* 45 ILR,
p. 446.

[144] See Amerasinghe, *Principles*, p. 403. See also *Behrami v. France*, above, note 140.

[145] As to remedies generally, see K. Wellens, *Remedies Against International Organizations*,
Cambridge, 2002.

In the context of often unclear divisions of responsibility between the UN itself and states contributing troops for peacekeeping purposes, particularly serious issues have arisen with regard to allegations of sexual misconduct by UN peacekeepers. Because military members of national contingents are not subject to the criminal jurisdiction of the host state, the model Status of Forces Agreement between the UN and the state where the peacekeeping force was to be stationed envisaged that the Secretary-General would obtain formal assurances from the troop-contributing country concerned that it would exercise jurisdiction with respect to crimes that might be committed by its forces in the mission area. However, this has not been the practice. It has recently been recommended that peacekeeping operations should be accompanied by a memorandum of understanding which would include a provision to this effect.[146]

Liability of member states[147]

The relationship between the member states of an organisation and the organisation itself is often complex. The situation is further complicated upon a consideration of the position of third states (or organisations) prejudiced by the activities of the organisation. The starting point for any analysis is the issue of legal personality. An international organisation created by states that does not itself possess legal personality cannot be the bearer of rights or obligations separate and distinct from those of the member states. It therefore follows that such organisations cannot be interposed as between the injured third parties and the member states of that organisation. In such cases any liability for the debts or delicts attributable to the organisation causing harm to third parties would fall upon the member states.[148] Where, however, the organisation does possess legal personality, the situation is different. Separate personality implies liability for activities entered into. The question of the liability of member states to third parties may arise subsidiarily and poses some difficulty. Such a question falls to be decided by the rules of international law not

---

[146] See the UN Report on Sexual Exploitation and Abuse by UN Peacekeeping Personnel, A/59/710, 24 March 2005, para. 78. See also A/45/594, annex, para. 48.

[147] See e.g. Amerasinghe, *Principles*, chapter 13; Schermers and Blokker, *International Institutional Law*, pp. 990 ff.; Higgins, 'Legal Consequences'; H. Schermers, 'Liability of International Organizations', 1 *Leiden Journal of International Law*, 1988, p. 14; C. F. Amerasinghe, 'Liability to Third Parties of Member States of International Organizations: Practice, Principle and Judicial Precedent', 85 AJIL, 1991, 259.

[148] See e.g. Higgins, 'Legal Consequences', p. 378, and Amerasinghe, *Principles*, p. 412.

least since it is consequential upon a determination of personality which is in the case of international organisations governed by international law.[149] The problem is also to be addressed in the context of the general principle of international law that treaties do not create obligations for third states without their consent (*pacta tertiis nec nocent nec prosunt*).[150] By virtue of this rule, member states would not be responsible for breaches of agreements between organisations and other parties.

The problems faced by the International Tin Council during 1985–6 are instructive in this context.[151] The ITC, created in 1956, conducted its activities in accordance with successive international tin agreements, which aimed to regulate the tin market by virtue of export controls and the establishment of buffer stocks of tin financed by member states. The Sixth International Tin Agreement of 1982 brought together twenty-three producer and consumer states and the EEC. In October 1985, the ITC announced that it had run out of funds and credit and the London Metal Exchange suspended trading in tin. The situation had arisen basically as a result of over-production of the metal and purchasing of tin by the ITC at prices above the market level.

Since the ITC member states refused to guarantee the debts of the organisation and since proposals to create a successor organisation to the ITC collapsed, serious questions were posed as to legal liabilities. The ITC was a corporate entity enjoying a measure of legal immunity in the UK as a result of the International Tin Council (Immunities and Privileges) Order 1972. It had immunity from the jurisdiction of the courts except in cases of enforcement of an arbitral award. The ITC Headquarters Agreement provided that contracts entered into with a person or company resident

---

[149] It is possible for states to create an international organisation under domestic law, for example, the Bank for International Settlements, but this is very rare: see e.g. M. Giovanoli, 'The Role of the Bank for International Settlements in International Monetary Co-operation and Its Tasks Relating to the European Currency Unit', 23 *The International Lawyer*, 1989, p. 841.

[150] See articles 34 and 35 of the Vienna Convention on the Law of Treaties, 1969 and articles 34 and 35 of the Vienna Convention on the Law of Treaties between States and International Organisations or between International Organisations, 1986. See also C. Chinkin, *Third Parties in International Law*, Oxford, 1993. See also above, chapter 16, p. 928.

[151] See e.g. The Second Report from the Trade and Industry Committee, 1985–6, HC 305-I, 1986 and *The Times*, 13 March 1986, p. 21 and *ibid.*, 14 March 1986, p. 17. See also G. Wassermann, 'Tin and Other Commodities in Crisis', 20 *Journal of World Trade Law*, 1986, p. 232; E. Lauterpacht, 'Development', p. 412; I. Cheyne, 'The International Tin Council', 36 ICLQ, 1987, p. 931, *ibid.*, 38 ICLQ, 1989, p. 417 and *ibid.*, 39 ICLQ, 1990, p. 945, and R. Sadurska and C. M. Chinkin, 'The Collapse of the International Tin Council: A Case of State Responsibility?', 30 Va. JIL, 1990, p. 845.

in the UK were to contain an arbitration clause. It was also the case that where a specific agreement provided for a waiver of immunity by the organisation, the courts would have jurisdiction.[152] Accordingly, the immunity from suit of the ITC was by no means unlimited.

A variety of actions were commenced by the creditors, of which the most important was the direct action. Here, a number of banks and brokers proceeded directly against the Department of Trade and Industry of the British government and other members of the ITC on the argument that they were liable on contracts concluded by the ITC.[153] The issues were argued at length in the Court of Appeal and in the House of Lords.[154] The main submission[155] for present purposes was that the members of the ITC and the organisation were liable concurrently for the debts under both English and international law. It was argued that under international law members of an international organisation bear joint and several liability for its debts unless the constituent treaty expressly excludes such liability. Although there had been hints of such an approach earlier[156] and treaty practice had been far from consistent, Lord Templeman noted that 'no plausible evidence was produced of the existence of such a rule of international law'[157] and this, it is believed, correctly

---

[152] See e.g. *Standard Chartered Bank* v. *ITC* [1986] 3 All ER 257; 77 ILR, p. 8.

[153] See also the attempt to have the ITC wound up under Part XXI of the Companies Act 1985, *Re International Tin Council* [1988] 3 All ER 257, 361; 80 ILR, p. 181, and the attempt to appoint a receiver by way of equitable execution over the assets of the ITC following an arbitration award against the ITC (converted into a judgment) which it was argued would enable contributions or an indemnity to be claimed from the members, *Maclaine Watson* v. *International Tin Council* [1988] 3 WLR 1169; 80 ILR, p. 191.

[154] *Maclaine Watson* v. *Department of Trade and Industry* [1988] 3 WLR 1033 (Court of Appeal); 80 ILR, p. 49 and [1989] 3 All ER 523 (House of Lords) sub. nom. *J. H. Rayner Ltd* v. *Department of Trade and Industry*; 81 ILR, p. 671.

[155] One submission was that the relevant International Tin Council (Immunities and Privileges) Order 1972 did not incorporate the ITC under English law but conferred upon it the capacities of a body corporate and thus the ITC did not have legal personality. This was rejected by the House of Lords, [1989] 3 All ER 523, 527–8 and 548–9; 81 ILR, pp. 677, 703. Another submission was that the ITC was only authorised to enter into contracts as an agent for the members under the terms of the Sixth International Tin Agreement, 1982. This was also dismissed, on the basis that the terms of the Order clearly authorised the ITC to enter into contracts as a principal, [1989] 3 All ER 530 and 556–7; 81 ILR, pp. 681, 715.

[156] See e.g. *Westland Helicopters* v. *Arab Organization for Industrialisation* 23 ILM, 1984, 1071; 80 ILR, p. 600. See H. T. Adam, *Les Organismes Internationaux Specialisés*, Paris, 1965, vol. I, pp. 129–30, and Seidl-Hohenveldern, *Corporations*, pp. 119–20.

[157] [1989] 3 All ER 523, 529; 81 ILR, p. 680. This was the view adopted by a majority of the Court of Appeal: see Ralph Gibson LJ, [1988] 3 WLR 1033, 1149 and Kerr LJ, *ibid.*, 1088–9 (but cf. Nourse LJ, *ibid.*, 1129–31); 80 ILR, pp. 49, 170; 101–2; 147–9. It is fair to

represents the current state of international law.[158] The liability of a member state could arise, of course, either through an express provision[159] in the constituent instruments of the organisation providing for the liability of member states or where the organisation was in fact under the direct control of the state concerned or acted as its agent in law and in fact, or by virtue of unilateral undertakings or guarantee by the state in the particular circumstances.[160]

There may, however, be instances where the liability of member states is engaged. For example, in *Matthews* v. *UK*, the European Court of Human Rights stated that the European Convention on Human Rights did not exclude the transfer of competences to international organisations 'provided that Convention rights continue to be "secured". Member states' responsibility therefore continues even after such a transfer.'[161] Similarly, where the member state acts together with an international organisation in the commission of an unlawful act, then it too will be liable.[162]

The accountability of international institutions

The concept of accountability is broader than the principles of responsibility and liability for internationally wrongful acts and rests upon the notion that the lawful application of power imports accountability for its exercise. Such accountability will necessarily range across legal, political, administrative and financial forms and essentially create a

---

emphasise that the approach of the Court, in effect, was primarily focused upon domestic law and founded upon the perception that without the relevant Order in Council the ITC had no legal existence in the law of the UK. An international organisation had legal personality in the sphere of international law and it did not thereby automatically acquire legal personality within domestic legal systems. For that, at least in the case of the UK, specific legislation was required.

[158] See e.g. the 1991 Partial Award on Liability of the ICC Tribunal in the *Westland Helicopters* case: see Higgins, 'Legal Consequences', p. 393. See also I. F. I. Shihata, 'Role of Law in Economic Development: The Legal Problems of International Public Ventures', 25 *Revue Égyptienne de Droit International*, 1969, pp. 119, 125; Schermers and Blokker, *International Institutional Law*, p. 992, and Amerasinghe, *Principles*, pp. 431 ff.

[159] Or indeed a provision demonstrating such an intention.

[160] See articles 7 and 8 of the Resolution of the Institut de Droit International, *Annuaire de l'Institut de Droit International*, 1995 I, pp. 465, 467.

[161] Judgment of 18 February 1999, para. 32; 123 ILR, p. 13. However, see also *Bosphorus Airways* v. *Ireland*, Judgment of 30 June 2005 and *Behrami* v. *France*, Judgment of 2 May 2007; 133 ILR, p. 1.

[162] See above, p. 1312.

regulatory and behavioural framework. In such a context, particular attention should be devoted to the principle of good governance, which concerns the benchmarks of good administration and transparent conduct and monitoring; the principle of good faith; the principle of constitutionality and institutional balance, including acting within the scope of functions; the principle of supervision and control with respect to subsidiary organs; the principle of stating reasons for decisions; the principle of procedural regularity to prevent *inter alia* abuse of discretionary powers and errors of fact or law; the principle of objectivity and impartiality, and the principle of due diligence.[163]

Privileges and immunities[164]

In order to carry out their functions more effectively, states and their representatives benefit from a variety of privileges and immunities. International organisations will also be entitled to the grant of privileges and immunities for their assets, properties and representatives. The two situations are not, of course, analogous in practice, since, for example, the basis of state immunities may be seen in terms of the sovereign equality of states and reciprocity, while this is not realistic with regard to organisations, both because they are not in a position of 'sovereign

---

[163] See e.g. A. Momirov, *Accountability of International Organizations in Post-Conflict Governance Missions*, The Hague, 2005, and K. Wellens, 'The Primary Model Rules of Accountability of International Organizations: The Principles and Rules Governing Their Conduct or the Yardsticks for Their Accountability', in *Proliferation of International Organizations* (eds. N. M. Blokker and H. G. Schermers), Leiden, 2001, p. 433. See also the Recommended Rules and Practices drafted by the Committee on the Accountability of International Organisations and adopted in 2004 at the Berlin Conference of the International Law Association.

[164] See e.g. Klabbers, *Introduction*, chapter 8; Reinisch, *International Organizations*, pp. 127 ff.; Amerasinghe, *Principles*, chapter 10; E. Gaillard and I. Pingel-Lenuzza, 'International Organizations and Immunity from Jurisdiction: To Restrict or To Bypass', 51 ICLQ, 2002, p. 1; M. Singer, 'Jurisdictional Immunity of International Organizations: Human Rights and Functional Necessity Concerns', 36 Va. JIL, 1995, p. 53; C. W. Jenks, *International Immunities*, London, 1961; J. F. Lalive, 'L'Immunité de Juridiction et d'Execution des Organisations Internationales', 84 HR, 1953 III, p. 205; C. Dominicé, 'Le Nature et l'Étendue de l'Immunité des Organisations' in *Festschrift Ignaz Seidl-Hohenveldern* (ed. K. H. Böckstiegel), Cologne, 1988, p. 11; Nguyen Quoc Dinh, 'Les Privilèges et Immunités des Organisations Internationales d'après les Jurisprudences Nationales Depuis 1945', AFDI, 1957, p. 55; D. B. Michaels, *International Privileges and Immunities*, The Hague, 1971; Kirgis, *International Organizations*, pp. 26 ff.; *Yearbook of the ILC*, 1967, vol. II, pp. 154 ff.; DUSPIL, 1978, pp. 90 ff. and *ibid.*, 1979, pp. 189 ff., and Morgenstern, *Legal Problems*, pp. 5–10.

equality'[165] and because they are unable to grant (or withdraw) immunities as a reciprocal gesture. It is also the case that the immunities of states have been restricted in the light of the distinction between transactions *jure imperii* and *jure gestionis*,[166] while any such distinction in the case of international organisations would be inappropriate.[167] The true basis for the immunities accorded to international organisations is that they are necessitated by the effective exercise of their functions. This, of course, will raise the question as to how one is to measure the level of immunities in the light of such functional necessity.

As far as the UN itself is concerned, article 105 of the Charter notes that:

(1) The Organization shall enjoy in the territory of each of its members such privileges and immunities as are necessary for the fulfilment of its purposes.

(2) Representatives of the members of the United Nations and officials of the Organization shall similarly enjoy such privileges and immunities as are necessary for the independent exercise of their functions in connection with the Organization.[168]

These general provisions have been supplemented by the General Convention on the Privileges and Immunities of the United Nations, 1946, and by the Convention on Privileges and Immunities of the Specialised Agencies, 1947.[169] These general conventions, building upon provisions in the relevant constituent instruments, have themselves been supplemented by bilateral agreements, particularly the growing number of headquarters and host agreements. The UN, for example, has concluded headquarters agreements with the United States for the UN Headquarters in New

---

[165] The reference, for example, in *Branno* v. *Ministry of War* 22 ILR, p. 756, to the 'sovereignty of NATO' is misleading.

[166] See above, chapter 13, p. 708.

[167] See R. Higgins, *Problems and Process*, Oxford, 1994, p. 93.

[168] Note that the provisions dealing with privileges and immunities of international financial institutions tend to be considerably more detailed: see e.g. article VII of the Articles of Agreement of the International Bank for Reconstruction and Development, article IX of the Articles of Agreement of the International Monetary Fund and articles 46 to 55 of the Constitution of the European Bank for Reconstruction and Development.

[169] This also contains separate draft annexes relating to each specialised agency. See also the Agreement on the Privileges and Immunities of the Organisation of American States, 1949; the General Agreement on the Privileges and Immunities of the Council of Europe, 1949 and the Protocol Concerning the Privileges and Immunities of the European Communities, 1965.

York and with Switzerland for the UN Office in Geneva in 1947.[170] Such agreements, for example, provide for the application of local laws within the headquarters area subject to the application of relevant staff administrative regulations; the immunity of the premises and property of the organisation from search, requisition and confiscation and other forms of interference by the host state; exemption from local taxes except for utility charges and freedom of communication.[171]

The International Court noted in the *Applicability of the Obligation to Arbitrate* case,[172] which concerned US anti-terrorism legislation necessitating the closure of the PLO Observer Mission to the UN in New York, that the US was obliged to respect the obligation contained in section 21 of the UN Headquarters Agreement to enter into arbitration where a dispute had arisen concerning the interpretation and application of the Agreement. This was despite the US view that it was not certain a dispute had arisen, since the existence of an international dispute was a matter for objective determination.[173] The Court emphasised in particular that the provisions of a treaty prevail over the domestic law of a state party to that treaty.[174]

It is clearly the functional approach rather than any representational argument that forms the theoretical basis for the recognition of privileges and immunities with respect to international organisations. This point has been made in cases before domestic courts, but it is important to note that this concept includes the need for the preservation of the independence of the institution as against the state in whose territory it is operating. In *Mendaro* v. *World Bank*,[175] for example, the US Court of Appeals held that the reason for the granting of immunities to international organisations was to enable them to pursue their functions more effectively and in particular to permit organisations to operate free from unilateral control by a member state over their activities within its territory. In *Iran–US Claims Tribunal* v.

---

[170] See also the agreements with Austria, 1979, regarding the UN Vienna Centre; with Japan, 1976, regarding the UN University, and with Kenya, 1975, regarding the UN Environment Programme. Note also the various Status of Forces Agreements concluded by the UN with, for example, Egypt in 1957, the Congo in 1961 and Cyprus in 1964, dealing with matters such as the legal status, facilities, privileges and immunities of the UN peacekeeping forces.

[171] Similar agreements may cover regional offices of international organisations: see e.g. the Agreement between the World Health Organisation and Egypt, 1951 concerning a regional office of the organisation in that state.

[172] ICJ Reports, 1988, p. 12; 82 ILR, p. 225.

[173] ICJ Reports, 1988, pp. 27–30; 82 ILR, p. 245.

[174] ICJ Reports, 1988, pp. 33–4; 82 ILR, p. 251.

[175] 717 F.2d 610, 615–17 (1983); 99 ILR, pp. 92, 97–9.

$AS,^{176}$ the Dutch Supreme Court pointed to the 'interest of the international organisation in having a guarantee that it will be able to perform its tasks independently and free from interferences under all circumstances' and noted that 'an international organisation is in principle not subject to the jurisdiction of the courts of the host state in respect of all disputes which are immediately connected with the performance of the tasks entrusted to the organisation in question'. The Italian Court of Cassation in *FAO* v. *INPDAI*[177] held that activities closely affecting the institutional purposes of the international organisation qualified for immunity, while the Employment Appeal Tribunal in *Mukuro* v. *European Bank for Reconstruction and Development*[178] stated that immunity from suit and legal process was justified on the ground that it was necessary for the fulfilment of the purposes of the bank in question, for the preservation of its independence and neutrality from control by or interference from the host state and for the effective and uninterrupted exercise of its multinational functions through its representatives. The Swiss Labour Court in *ZM* v. *Permanent Delegation of the League of Arab States to the UN* held that 'customary international law recognised that international organisations, whether universal or regional, enjoy absolute jurisdictional immunity... This privilege of international organisations arises from the purposes and functions assigned to them. They can only carry out their tasks if they are beyond the censure of the courts of member states or their headquarters.'[179]

The issue of the immunity of international organisations came before the European Court of Human Rights in *Waite and Kennedy* v. *Germany*, where the applicants complained that by granting immunity to an international organisation in an employment dispute, Germany had violated the Convention right of free access to a court under article 6(1). The European Court, however, declared that the attribution of privileges and immunities to international organisations was 'an essential means of ensuring the proper functioning of such organisations free from unilateral interference

---

[176] 94 ILR, pp. 321, 329. See also *Eckhardt* v. *Eurocontrol (No. 2), ibid.*, pp. 331, 337–8, where the District Court of Maastricht held that since an international organisation had been created by treaty by states, such organisation was entitled to immunity from jurisdiction on the grounds of customary international law to the extent necessary for the operation of its public service.

[177] 87 ILR, pp. 1, 6–7. See also *Mininni* v. *Bari Institute, ibid.*, p. 28 and *Sindacato UIL* v. *Bari Institute, ibid.*, p. 37.

[178] [1994] ICR 897, 903. See also the *European Molecular Biology Laboratory Arbitration* 105 ILR, p. 1.

[179] 116 ILR, pp. 643, 647.

by individual governments' and that the requirements of article 6 would be satisfied where there existed reasonable alternative means to protect effectively the rights in question under the Convention and a satisfactory system of dispute settlement in the relevant international instruments.[180] It may be that such alternative dispute settlement requirements are not essential where the relevant international agreement providing for the immunities in question pre-dated the European Convention on Human Rights, but this should be regarded as controversial.[181]

Immunities may be granted to the representatives of states to the organisation, to the officials of the organisation and to the organisation itself. As far as the position of representatives of states to international organisations is concerned, article IV, section 11, of the UN General Convention, 1946 provides for the following privileges and immunities:

(a) immunity from personal arrest or detention and from seizure of their personal baggage, and in respect of words spoken or written and all acts done by them in their capacity as representatives, immunity from legal process of every kind;

(b) inviolability for all papers and documents;

(c) the right to use codes and to receive papers or correspondence by courier or in sealed bags;

(d) exemption in respect of themselves and their spouses from immigration restrictions, alien registration or national service obligations in the state they are visiting or through which they are passing in the exercise of their functions;

(e) the same facilities in respect of currency or exchange restrictions as are accorded to representatives of foreign governments on temporary official missions;

(f) the same immunities and facilities in respect of their personal baggage as are accorded to diplomatic envoys; and also

(g) such other privileges, immunities and facilities not inconsistent with the foregoing as diplomatic envoys enjoy, except that they shall have no right to claim exemption from customs duties on goods imported (otherwise than as part of their personal baggage) or from excise duties or sales taxes.

---

[180] Judgment of 18 February 1999, paras. 63 and 67 ff.; 116 ILR, pp. 121, 134, and see *Beer and Regan* v. *Germany*, European Court of Human Rights, Judgment of 18 February 1999, paras. 53 ff. See also *Consortium X* v. *Swiss Federal Government*, Swiss Federal Supreme Court, 1st Civil Law Chamber, 2 July 2004 and *Entico Corporation* v. *UNESCO* [2008] EWHC 531 (Comm).

[181] See e.g. *Entico Corporation* v. *UNESCO* [2008] EWHC 531 (Comm).

Article IV, section 14 provides that such privileges and immunites are accorded

> in order to safeguard the independent exercise of their functions in connection with the United Nations. Consequently a Member not only has the right but is under a duty to waive the immunity of its representative in any case where in the opinion of the Member the immunity would impede the course of justice, and it can be waived without prejudice to the purpose for which the immunity is accorded.[182]

One particular issue that has arisen and appears to have received no definitive determination relates to the competence of the host state under customary international law to seek unilaterally to withdraw the immunities of a state representative to an international organisation where relevant international agreements are unclear.[183] The matter was the subject of an application to the International Court of Justice by the Commonwealth of Dominica against Switzerland in 2006, complaining that the latter state had terminated the appointment of a Head of Mission accredited by the applicant to the UN and specialised agencies (but not to Switzerland).[184] However, the application was subsequently withdrawn.[185]

The question of the privileges and immunities of representatives, however, is invariably addressed in headquarters agreements between

---

[182] Article IV, section 16 provides that the term 'representatives' is deemed to include 'all delegates, deputy delegates, advisers, technical experts and secretaries of delegations'. The question of the representation of states to international organisations is also dealt with in the 1975 Vienna Convention on the Representation of States in their Relations with International Organisations of a Universal Character, which is closely modelled on the 1961 Vienna Convention on Diplomatic Relations, although it has been criticised by a number of host states for permitting more extensive privileges and immunities than is required in the light of functional necessity. See DUSPIL, 1975, pp. 38 ff. Article 30 of the Convention, in particular, provides that the head of mission and the members of the diplomatic staff of the mission shall enjoy immunity from the criminal jurisdiction of the host state and immunity from its civil and administrative jurisdiction, except in cases of real action relating to private immovable property situated in the host state (unless held on behalf of the sending state for the purposes of the mission); actions relating to succession and actions relating to any professional or commercial activity exercised by the person in question in the host state outside his official functions. See also above, chapter 13, p. 764.

[183] Note that some conventions permit this: see, for example, article VII, section 25 of the Convention on the Immunities of Specialised Agencies. See also Amerasinghe, *Principles*, pp. 338 ff.

[184] This application dated 26 April 2006 was precipitated by the case of *A* v. *B*, Swiss Federal Supreme Court, 1st Civil Law Chamber, 8 April 2004, no. 4C.140/2003.

[185] See ICJ, Order of 9 June 2006. The case was entitled 'case concerning the status vis-à-vis the host state of a diplomatic envoy to the United Nations'.

international organisations and host states. Article V, section 15 of the UN Headquarters Agreement, 1947, for example, states that representatives[186] are entitled in the territory of the US 'to the same privileges and immunities, subject to corresponding conditions and obligations, as it accords to diplomatic envoys accredited to it'.[187]

Secondly, privileges and immunities are granted to the officials of the organisation. Article V, section 18 of the UN Convention provides that officials of the UN are immune from legal process in respect of words spoken or written and all acts performed by them in their official capacity; exempt from taxation on the salaries and emoluments paid to them by the United Nations; immune from national service obligations; and immune, together with their spouses and relatives dependent on them, from immigration restrictions and alien registration. They also have the right to import free of duty their furniture and effects at the time of first taking up their post in the country in question. In addition, the Secretary-General and all Assistant Secretaries-General are accorded in respect of themselves, their spouses and minor children, the privileges and immunities exemptions and facilities accorded to diplomatic envoys, in accordance with international law.[188] Further, section 20 provides that privileges and immunities are granted to officials in the interests of the United Nations and not for the personal benefit of the individuals themselves. The Secretary-General has the right and the duty to waive the immunity of any official in any case where, in his opinion, the immunity would impede the course of justice and can be waived without prejudice to the interests of the United Nations. In the case of the Secretary-General, the Security Council shall have the right to waive immunity.

Experts performing missions for the UN are also granted a range of privileges and immunities, such as are necessary for the independent exercise of their functions during the period of their missions, including the time spent on journeys in connection with their missions. In particular they are accorded immunity from personal arrest or detention and from seizure of their personal baggage; immunity from legal process in respect of words spoken or written and acts done by them in the course of the performance of their mission; inviolability for all papers and documents; for the purpose of their communications with the United Nations, the right to use codes and to receive papers or correspondence by courier or

---

[186] These are defined in article V, section 15(1)–(4).
[187] See also *Third US Restatement of Foreign Relations Law*, pp. 518 ff.
[188] Section 19.

in sealed bags; and the same immunities and facilities in respect of their personal baggage as are accorded to diplomatic envoys.[189]

The question of the immunities of persons on mission for the UN has come before the International Court in a couple of cases. The International Court delivered an advisory opinion concerning the applicability of provisions in the UN General Convention to special rapporteurs appointed by the Sub-Commission on the Prevention of Discrimination and the Protection of Minorities.[190] As noted above, article VI, section 22, of the Convention provides that experts performing missions for the United Nations are to be accorded such privileges and immunities as are necessary for the independent exercise of their functions during the periods of their missions. The International Court noted that such privileges and immunities could indeed be invoked against the state of nationality or of residence[191] and that special rapporteurs for the Sub-Commission were to be regarded as experts on missions within the meaning of section 22.[192] The privileges and immunities that would apply would be those that were necessary for the exercise of their functions, and in particular for the establishment of any contacts which may be useful for the preparation, the drafting and the presentation of their reports to the Sub-Commission.[193]

The issue was revisited in the *Immunity from Legal Process* advisory opinion of the International Court which concerned the question of the immunity from legal process in Malaysia of Mr Cumaraswamy, a Special Rapporteur of the UN Commission of Human Rights on the Independence of Judges and Lawyers.[194] The Court confirmed that article VI, section 22 applied to Mr Cumaraswamy who, as Special Rapporteur, had been entrusted with a mission by the UN and was therefore an expert

---

[189] Article VI, section 22. Section 23 provides that privileges and immunities are granted in the interests of the United Nations and not for the personal benefit of the individuals themselves and the Secretary-General has the right and the duty to waive the immunity of any expert in any case where, in his opinion, the immunity would impede the course of justice and it can be waived without prejudice to the interests of the United Nations.

[190] *Applicability of Article VI, Section 22, of the Convention on the Privileges and Immunities of the United Nations*, ICJ Reports, 1989, p. 177; 85 ILR, p. 300. This opinion was requested by the Economic and Social Council, its first request for an Advisory Opinion under article 96(2) of the UN Charter.

[191] In the absence of a reservation by the state concerned, ICJ Reports, 1989, pp. 195–6; 85 ILR, pp. 322–3.

[192] This applied even though the rapporteur concerned was not, or was no longer, a member of the Sub-Commission, since such a person is entrusted by the Sub-Commission with a research mission, ICJ Reports, 1989, pp. 196–7; 85 ILR, pp. 323–4.

[193] *Ibid.*   [194] ICJ Reports, 1999, p. 62; 121 ILR, p. 405.

within the terms of the section. The Court held that he was entitled to immunity with regard to the words spoken by him during the course of an interview that was published in a journal and that, in deciding whether an expert on mission was entitled to immunity in particular circumstances, the UN Secretary-General had a 'pivotal role'.[195] The Court concluded by stating that the government of Malaysia had an obligation under article 105 of the Charter and under the General Convention to inform its courts of the position taken by the Secretary-General. Failure to do so rendered the state liable under international law.[196]

Thirdly, privileges and immunities are granted to the organisation itself. The range of privileges and immunities usually extended includes immunity from jurisdiction; inviolability of premises and archives; currency and fiscal privileges and freedom of communications.[197] In the case of immunity from jurisdiction, article II, section 2 of the UN General Convention, 1946 provides that:

> The United Nations, its property and assets wherever located and by whomsoever held, shall enjoy immunity from every form of legal process except insofar as in any particular case it has expressly waived its immunity. It is, however, understood that no waiver of immunity shall extend to any measure of execution.[198]

One question that has arisen is whether such immunity is absolute or, as is the case now with state immunity, a distinction between sovereign or public acts (*jure imperii*) on the one hand and private acts (*jure gestionis*) on the other can be drawn. However, the analogy with state immunity is inappropriate. International organisations do not exercise sovereign power nor is the theoretical basis of reciprocity arguable. International organisations are not states, but entities created in order to perform particular functions. In any event, relevant treaties do not make a distinction between sovereign or public acts and private acts in the case of international organisations and such a distinction cannot be inferred. Amerasinghe has, indeed, concluded that such a distinction is not justified and

---

[195] ICJ Reports, 1999, pp. 84 and 87.
[196] *Ibid.*, pp. 87–8. The Court also affirmed that questions of immunity were preliminary issues to be decided expeditiously *in limine litis*, *ibid.*, p. 88. This is the same position as immunity claims before domestic courts: see above, chapter 13, p. 700.
[197] In all cases, the relevant agreements need to be examined as particular privileges and immunities may vary.
[198] See also article III, section 4 of the Specialised Agencies Convention, 1947. See Amerasinghe, *Principles*, pp. 320 ff.

that the key to immunity for international organisations is whether the immunity is necessary for the fulfilment of the organisation's functions and purposes.[199] It should also be noted that international organisations benefit from immunity from execution or enforcement, which means that their property or other assets cannot be seized, while a waiver of immunity from jurisdiction, which must be express, does not encompass a waiver of immunity from execution which would have to be given separately and expressly.[200]

Immunity will also cover inviolability of premises and archives.[201] This is particularly important for the effective operation of international organisations. Article II, section 3 of the UN Convention, for example, provides that,

> The premises of the Untied Nations shall be inviolable. The property and assets of the United Nations, wherever located and by whomsoever held, shall be immune from search, requisition, confiscation, expropriation and any other form of interference, whether by executive, administrative, judicial or legislative action,

while section 4 provides that, 'The archives of the United Nations, and in general all documents belonging to it or held by it, shall be inviolable wherever located.'[202] Similar provisions exist in all relevant agreements concerning international organisations. The inviolability of premises means that the authorities of a state cannot enter without the permission of the administrative head of the organisation even where a crime has been committed there or in order to arrest a person. Further, the host state is under

---

[199] *Principles*, p. 322. Note, however, that many international financial institutions, such as the International Bank for Reconstruction and Development, known as the World Bank (but not the International Monetary Fund), expressly qualify immunity and permit actions to be brought against them, particularly with regard to applications founded on loan agreements in the case of the World Bank: see article VII of the Articles of Agreement of the International Bank for Reconstruction and Development and *Lutcher SA* v. *Inter-American Development Bank* 382 F.2d 454 (1967) and *Mendaro* v. *World Bank* 717 F.2d 610 (1983); 92 ILR, p. 92. Note also article 6 of the Headquarters Agreement between the UK and the International Maritime Satellite Organisation, 1980. See also Amerasinghe, *Principles*, pp. 320 ff.

[200] See e.g. article II, section 2 of the UN Convention. See also Singer, 'Jurisdictional Immunity', pp. 72 ff.

[201] See Amerasinghe, *Principles*, pp. 330 ff.

[202] See also article II, section 5 of the Convention on the Privileges and Immunities of Specialised Agencies, 1947. Note that in *Shearson Lehman* v. *Maclaine Watson (No. 2)* [1988] 1 WLR 16; 77 ILR, p. 145, the House of Lords held that the inviolability of official documents could be lost as a result of communication to third parties.

a duty of due diligence with regard to the protection of the premises in question. However, the premises remain under the general jurisdiction of the host state, subject to the immunity described. Accordingly, a crime committed on the premises may be prosecuted in the local courts.[203]

Immunity also includes certain currency and fiscal privileges, such as exemption from direct taxation with regard to the assets, income and property of the organisation and from customs dues. Organisations may also be permitted to hold and transfer funds and other financial assets freely.[204] Freedom of official communications equal to that provided to foreign governments is also usually stipulated with regard to international organisations, including freedom from censorship, while the right to send and receive correspondence by courier and bag, on the same basis as diplomatic couriers and diplomatic bags, is also provided for.[205]

International agreements concerning privileges and immunities have been implemented into domestic law by specific legislation in a number of states where there is no automatic incorporation of ratified treaties, examples being the UK International Organisations Act 1968[206] and the US International Organisations Immunities Act 1945.[207] The usual pattern under such legislation is for the general empowering provisions contained in those Acts to be applied to named international organisations by specific secondary acts. In the case of the International Organisations Act 1968, for example, a wide variety of organisations have had privileges and immunities conferred upon them by Order in Council.[208] In the case of

---

[203] See Amerasinghe, *Principles*, pp. 330 ff.

[204] *Ibid.*, p. 335. See also article II, sections 5 and 7 of the UN Convention and article III, sections 7 and 9 of the Specialised Agencies Convention.

[205] See article III, sections 9 and 10 of the UN Convention and article IV, sections 11 and 12 of the Specialised Agencies Convention. See also Amerasinghe, *Principles*, pp. 335 ff.

[206] Replacing the International Organisations (Immunities and Privileges) Act 1950. The International Organisations Act 1981 *inter alia* extended the 1968 Act to commonwealth organisations and to international commodity organisations and permitted the extension of privileges and immunities to states' representatives attending conferences in the UK. See also the International Organisations Act 2005.

[207] See also *Legislative Texts and Treaty Provisions Concerning the Legal Status, Privileges and Immunities of International Organizations*, ST/LEG/SER.B/10 and 11.

[208] See e.g. the African Development Bank, SI 1983/142; Council of Europe, SI 1960/442; European Patent Organisation, SI 1978/179 and SI 1980/1096; International Maritime and Satellite Organisation, SI 1980/187; NATO, SI 1974/1257 and SI 1975/1209, and the UN, SI 1974/1261 and SI 1975/1209. An examination of Orders in Council would demonstrate the following privileges and immunities: immunity from suit and legal process; inviolability of official archives and premises; exemption or relief from taxes and rates, but not import taxes except where the goods or publications are imported or exported for official use; various reliefs with regard to car tax and VAT (value added tax) with regard to cars or

the US Act, the same process is normally conducted by means of Executive Orders.[209]

Dissolution[210]

The constitutions of some international organisations contain express provisions with regard to dissolution. Article VI(5) of the Articles of Agreement of the International Bank for Reconstruction and Development (the World Bank), for example, provides for dissolution by a vote of the majority of Governors exercising a majority of total voting, and detailed provisions are made for consequential matters. Payment of creditors and claims, for instance, will have precedence over asset distribution, while the distribution of assets will take place on a proportional basis to shareholding. Different organisations with such express provisions take different positions with regard to the type of majority required for dissolution. In the case of the European Bank for Reconstruction and Development, for example, a majority of two-thirds of the members and three-quarters of the total voting power is required. A simple majority vote is sufficient in the case of the International Monetary Fund, and a majority of member states coupled with a majority of votes is necessary in the case of the International Bank for Reconstruction and Development. Where an organisation has been established for a limited period, the constitution will invariably provide for dissolution upon the expiry of that period.[211] Where there are no specific provisions concerning dissolution,

---

goods destined for official use, and priority to be given to telecommunications to and from the UN Secretary-General, the heads of principal organs of the UN and the President of the International Court: see also the International Organisations Act 1968, Schedule I. See also sections 2–7 of the US International Organisations Immunities Act 1945.

[209] See e.g. the Executive Order 12359 of 22 April 1980 designating the Multi-National Force and Observers as a public international organisation under s. 1 of the 1945 Act entitled to enjoy the privileges, exemptions and immunities conferred by that Act. See also Executive Order 12403 of 8 February 1983 with regard to the African Development Bank; Executive Order 12467 of 2 March 1984 with regard to the International Boundary and Water Commission, US and Mexico; Executive Order 12628 of 8 March 1988 with regard to the UN Industrial Development Organisation, and Executive Order 12647 of 2 August 1988 with regard to the Multilateral Investment Guarantee Agency. See further Cumulative DUSPIL 1981–8, Washington, 1993, vol. I, pp. 330 ff.

[210] See e.g. Amerasinghe, *Principles*, chapter 15; Klabbers, *Introduction*, chapter 15, and Schermers and Blokker, *International Institutional Law*, pp. 1015 ff. See also C. W. Jenks, 'Some Constitutional Problems of International Organizations', 22 BYIL, 1945, p. 11, and *Bowett's International Institutions*, pp. 526 ff.

[211] This applies particularly to commodity organisations: see e.g. the International Tin Agreement, 1981; the Natural Rubber Agreement, 1987 and the International Sugar Agreement, 1992.

it is likely that an organisation may be dissolved by the decision of its highest representative body.[212] The League of Nations, for example, was dissolved by a decision taken by the Assembly without the need for individual assent by each member[213] and a similar process was adopted with regard to other organisations.[214] It is unclear whether unanimity is needed or whether the degree of majority required under the constitution of the particular organisation for the determination of important questions[215] would suffice.[216] The actual process of liquidating the assets and dealing with the liabilities of dissolved organisations is invariably laid down by the organisation itself, either in the constitutional documents or by special measures adopted on dissolution.

Succession[217]

Succession between international organisations takes place when the functions and (usually) the rights and obligations are transferred from one organisation to another. This may occur by way of straightforward replacement,[218] or by absorption,[219] or by merger, or by effective secession of part of an organisation, or by simple transfer of certain functions from one organisation to another.[220] This is achieved by agreement and is dependent upon the constitutional competence of the successor organisation

---

212 See Amerasinghe, *Principles*, p. 468, and Schermers and Blokker, *International Institutional Law*, p. 1024.

213 In fact the decision was taken unanimously by the thirty-five members present, ten members being absent: see e.g. H. McKinnon Wood, 'Dissolution of the League of Nations', 23 BYIL, 1946, p. 317.

214 See e.g. the dissolutions of the International Meteorological Organisation; the UN Relief and Rehabilitation Administration; the International Refugee Organisation; the International Commission for Air Navigation; the South East Asian Treaty Organisation and the Latin American Free Trade Association: see Schermers and Blokker, *International Institutional Law*, pp. 1024–5.

215 E.g. the two-thirds majority required under article 18 of the UN Charter for the General Assembly's determination of important questions.

216 Organisations may be dissolved where the same parties to the treaty establishing the organisations enter a new agreement or possibly by disuse or more controversially as a result of changed circumstances (*rebus sic stantibus*): see Schermers and Blokker, *International Institutional Law*, pp. 1021–8.

217 See Amerasinghe, *Principles*, pp. 473 ff.; Schermers and Blokker, *International Institutional Law*, pp. 1015 ff.; H. Chiu, 'Succession in International Organizations', 14 ICLQ, 1965, p. 83, and P. R. Myers, *Succession between International Organizations*, London, 1993.

218 Such as the replacement of the League of Nations by the United Nations.

219 E.g. the absorption of the International Bureau of Education by UNESCO.

220 See Amerasinghe, *Principles*, pp. 474 ff.

to perform the functions thus transferred of the former organisation. In certain circumstances, succession may proceed by way of implication in the absence of express provision.[221] The precise consequences of such succession will depend upon the agreement concerned between the parties in question.[222] In general, assets of the predecessor organisation will go to the successor organisation, as well as archives.[223] Whether the same rule applies to debts is unclear.[224]

Suggestions for further reading

J. E. Alvarez, *International Organizations as Law-Makers*, Oxford, 2005

C. F. Amerasinghe, *Principles of the Institutional Law of International Organizations*, 2nd edn, Cambridge, 2005

Bowett's Law of International Institutions (eds. P. Sands and P. Klein), 5th edn, London, 2001

J. Klabbers, *An Introduction to International Institutional Law*, Cambridge, 2002

D. Sarooshi, *International Organizations and their Exercise of Sovereign Powers*, Oxford, 2005

H. G. Schermers and N. M. Blokker, *International Institutional Law*, 3rd edn, The Hague, 1995

---

[221] The International Court in the *Status of South-West Africa* case, ICJ Reports, 1950, pp. 128, 134–7; 17 ILR, pp. 47, 51–5, held that the supervisory responsibilities of South Africa under the mandate to administer the territory of South West Africa/Namibia continued beyond the dissolution of the League of Nations and were in essence succeeded to by the UN. This was in the context of the fact that the mandate itself constituted an international status for the territory which therefore continued irrespective of the existence of the League and partly because the resolution of the Assembly of the League dissolving the League of Nations had declared that the supervisory functions of the League were ending, not the mandates themselves. It was emphasised that the obligation to submit to supervision did not disappear merely because the supervisory organ had ceased to exist as the UN performed similar, though not identical, supervisory functions. The Court concluded that the UN General Assembly was legally qualified to exercise these supervisory functions, in the light *inter alia* of articles 10 and 80 of the UN Charter. This was reaffirmed by the Court in the *Namibia* case, ICJ Reports, 1971, pp. 16, 37; 49 ILR, pp. 2, 26–34.

[222] See Schermers and Blokker, *International Institutional Law*, p. 1017 with regard to the relationship between the World Trade Organisation and the General Agreement on Tarrifs and Trade (GATT) arrangements.

[223] See e.g. *PAU* v. *American Security and Trust Company*, US District Court for the District of Columbia, 18 ILR, p. 441.

[224] See e.g. Klabbers, *Introduction*, pp. 329–30.

SOME USEFUL INTERNATIONAL LAW WEBSITES

See also web references in chapter footnotes

General sites (with links to relevant materials)

www.washlaw.edu/forint/forintmain.html   The foreign and international law web of the Washburn University School of Law Library

www.asil.org/resource/home.htm   Electronic resource guide of the American Society of International Law

www.llrx.com/international law.html   Web journal research guide

www.lib.uchicago.edu/~llou/forintlaw.html   LyonetteLouis-Jacques guide to international law research, University of Chicago

www.law.ecel.uwa.edu.au/intlaw/   University of Western Australia guide to international law resources

www2.spfo.unibo.it/spolfo/ILMAIN.htm   University of Bologna research guide to international law

www.law.cam.ac.uk/RCIL/home.htm   Lauterpacht Research Centre for International Law

www.worldlii.org/catalog/   World Law site

www.hg.org/govt.html   Hieros Gamos law links

library.ukc.ac.uk/library/lawlinks/international.htm   University of Kent law links

www.bibl.ulaval.ca/ress/droit/bouton8.html   University of Laval, French Canadian site on international law

www.ridi.org/   French resource for international law generally

This listing excludes subscription services. The links were correct at the date of writing. No responsibility is undertaken as to their continued existence or accuracy.

www.un.org/law   United Nations site dealing with international law generally

www4.worldbank.org/legal/lawlibrary.html   World Bank Law Library, including links to international organisations, treaties and legal topics

www.un.org/law/ilc/   International Law Commission

www.icc-cpi.int/legaltools   ICC Legal Tools (these deal mostly with international criminal law, but also with general international law, human rights law, humanitarian law and national implementation)

www.asil.org/resource/home.htm   ASIL Guide for Electronic Resources for International Law

www.llrx.com/international_law.html   Law & Technology Resources for Legal Professions (International Law Guide)

www2.lib.uchicago.edu/~llou/forintlaw.html   University of Chicago Library (Legal Research on International Law Issues Using the Internet)

www2.spfo.unibo.it/spolfo/ILMAIN.htm   University of Bologna (Research Guide to International Law on the Internet)

www.lcil.cam.ac.uk/   The Lauterpacht Centre for International Law, University of Cambridge

www.worldlii.org/catalog/   World Law

www.hg.org/govt.html   HG.org Worldwide Legal Directories

www.bibl.ulaval.ca/mieux/chercher/portails/droit/ droit_international Université Laval

www.ridi.org/   Réseau Internet pour le Droit International

www.un.org/law/   United Nations (International Law)

History of international law

www.yale.edu/lawweb/avalon/avalon.htm   Yale University Avalon Project – historical documents

Sources

Treaties (see also Treaties)

http://untreaty.un.org/   UN treaty site

Cases (see also International courts and tribunals)

www.virtual-institute.de/en/wcd/wcd.cfm   Max Planck Institute World Court digest

www.jura.uni-duesseldorf.de/rave/e/englhome.asp   Index to court decisions and journal articles

Sources and evidence of custom/state practice/development of international law (see also International law and municipal law)

www.un.org/law/ilc/   International Law Commission

www.uncitral.org/en-index.htm   UN Commission on International Trade Law

www.gksoft.com/govt/en/   Links to government websites

Writings

www.jura.uni-duesseldorf.de/rave/e/englhome.asp   Index to court decisions and journal articles

www.ejil.org/ and www3.oup.co.uk/ejilaw/   European Journal of International Law

http://stu.findlaw.com/journals/international.html   International law journals

www.srdi.ws/   Summary of international law journals (French)

International law and municipal law

National constitutions and legislation

www.oefre.unibe.ch/law/icl/index.html   International constitutional law site from University of Berne

www.findlaw.com/01topics/06constitutional/03forconst/ index.html World constitutions

www.legislation.hmso.gov.uk/   UK legislation

www.hmso.gov.uk/stat.htm   UK statutory instruments

www.bailii.org/   British and Irish legal information – cases and legislation

http://thomas.loc.gov/   US legislation

www.canlii.org/   Canadian legal materials

www.llrx.com/features/canadian3.htm   Canadian law

www.journal-officiel.gouv.fr/   French legislation

www.llrx.com/features/frenchlaw.htm   French law

www.austlii.org/   Australian legal materials

www.worldlii.org/   Materials from other jurisdictions

http://jurist.law.pitt.edu/world/index.htm   Links to national laws

National cases

www.courtserve2.net/index.htm   UK cases

www.bailii.org/   British and Irish legal information – cases and legislation

www.scotcourts.gov.uk/   Scottish cases

http://supct.law.cornell.edu/supct/index.php   US Supreme Court cases

http://europa.eu.int/comm/justice_home/ejn/index_en.htm   European Judicial Network in civil and commercial law

www.coe.fr/venice/links-e.htm   Venice Commission links to national constitutional courts

Human rights (See also International humanitarian law)

International human rights

www.un.org/rights/index.html   UN human rights

www.unhchr.ch/   UN High Commissioner for Human Rights

www1.umn.edu/humanrts/   University of Minnesota human rights library

http://humanrights.britishcouncil.org/newsite2/frameset.asp?CatID=1& CatName=News&GroupID=3&GroupName=World&UserID=   British Council's human rights network

www.law-lib.utoronto.ca/diana/   Women's human rights resources

www.amnesty.org/   Amnesty International

www.un.org/law/icc/   International Criminal Court

www.iccnow.org/   International Criminal Court materials

www.icty.org/   International Criminal Tribunal for the Former Yugoslavia

www.ictr.org/   International Criminal Tribunal for Rwanda

Regional human rights

www.echr.coe.int/   European Court of Human Rights

www.cpt.coe.int/en/   European Committee for the Prevention of Torture

www.coe.int/t/E/human rights/ecri/   European Commission against Racism and Intolerance

www.ecmi.de/doc/index.html   European Centre for Minority Issues

www.achpr.org/   African Commission for Human and Peoples' Rights

www1.umn.edu/humanrts/africa/comcases/allcases.html   Decisions of African Commission

www1.umn.edu/humanrts/cases/commissn.htm   Inter-American Commission on Human Rights

www1.umn.edu/humanrts/iachr/iachr.html   Inter-American Court of Human Rights

www.corteidh.or.cr/   Official site for Inter-American Court of Human Rights

www.cidh.oas.org/   Official site for Inter-American Commission

www.gwdg.de/~ujvr/hrch/hrch.htm   Human Rights Chamber, Bosnia

Territory

www-ibru.dur.ac.uk/   International Boundaries Research Unit, University of Durham

http://garnet.acns.fsu.edu/~phensel/territory.html   general boundary links

www.antdiv.gov.au/default.asp?casid=76   Antarctica site of Australian government

Air and space law

www.iasl.mcgill.ca/   McGill University Institute of Air and Space Law

www.icao.int/   International Civil Aviation Organisation

www.oosa.unvienna.org/SpaceLaw/spacelaw.htm   UN international space law site

www.fas.org/spp/civil/russia/pol docs.htm   Russian space policy documents

www.nasa.gov/   NASA

www.esa.int/export/esaCP/index.html   European Space Agency

Law of the sea

www.un.org/Depts/los/index.htm   UN site dealing with law of the sea issues

www.oceanlaw.org/   Council on Ocean Law site

Treaties

www.yale.edu/lawweb/avalon/avalon.htm   University of Yale Avalon Project

http://fletcher.tufts.edu/multilaterals.html   University of Tufts Fletcher School Multilaterals Project

http://untreaty.un.org/   UN treaty site

http://conventions.coe.int/   Council of Europe treaty site

www.state.gov/s/l/c8455.htm   US treaties in force site

www.fco.gov.uk/servlet/Front?pagename=OpenMarket/Xcelerate/ShowPage&c=Page&cid=1007029396014   UK Foreign Office treaty site

www.austlii.edu.au/au/other/dfat/   Australian Treaties Library

International environmental law

www.ipcc.ch/   Intergovernmental Panel on Climate Change, established by WMO and UNEP

http://unfccc.int/   UN Framework Convention on Climate Change www.internationalwaterlaw.org/   International Water Law Project

www.iaea.org/worldatom/   IAEA

www.nea.fr/   OECD Nuclear Energy Agency

www.un.org/esa/sustdev/   UN Commission on Sustainable Development

http://iisdl.iisd.ca/   International Institute for Sustainable Development

International courts and tribunals (see also Human rights)

www.pict-pcti.org/home.html   International Courts and Tribunals Project site

www.icj-cij.org/   International Court of Justice

www.itlos.org/   International Tribunal for the Law of the Sea

http://pca-cpa.org/   Permanent Court of Arbitration

http://europa.eu.int/cj/en/index.htm   European Court of Justice and Court of First Instance

www.eca.eu.int/EN/menu.htm   European Court of Auditors

http://wbln0018.worldbank.org/ipn/ipnweb.nsf   World Bank Inspection Panels

www.bicusa.org/mdbs/wbg/inspectionpanel/   World Bank Inspection Panel

http://untreaty.un.org/ola-internet/unat.htm   UN Administrative Tribunal

www.worldbank.org/icsid/   International Centre for the Settlement of Investment Disputes

www.iccwbo.org/index court.asp   International Chamber of Commerce dispute resolution

www.iusct.org/index-english.html   Iran–US Claims Tribunal

www.unog.ch/uncc/   UN Compensation Commission (Iraq)

www.tas-cas.org/   Court of Arbitration for Sport

www.ccj.org.ni/   Central American Court of Justice

www.wto.org/english/tratop_e/dispu_e/dispu_e.htm   WTO dispute settlement

International terrorism

http://jurist.law.pitt.edu/terrorism.htm   terrorism

www.un.org/terrorism   UN website on terrorism

www.undcp.org/odccp/terrorism.html   UN Office on Drugs and Crime terrorism programme

www.un.org/Docs/sc/committees/1373/   Counter-Terrorism Committee of the Security Council

http://europa.eu.int/comm/justice home/news/terrorism/documents/ index en.htm   EU and terrorism materials

International humanitarian law

www.ihlresearch.org/portal/ihli/portalhome.php   International humanitarian law research site

www.icrc.org/   International Committee of the Red Cross

www1.umn.edu/humanrts/instree/auoy.htm   University of Minnesota international humanitarian law

www.yale.edu/lawweb/avalon/lawofwar/lawwar.htm   University of Yale Avalon Project laws of war

www.yale.edu/lawweb/avalon/imt/imt.htm   Nuremberg war crimes trials

http://fas-www.harvard.edu/~hsp/   Chemical and biological weapons site

www.sipri.se/   Stockholm International Peace Research Institute

http://ourworld.compuserve.com/homepages/Aspals/Homepage.htm Military law site

International institutions

General

www.uia.org/extlinks/pub.php   Links to international organisations

www.un.org/   United Nations

www.wto.org   WTO

Specialised agencies

www.imo.org/home.asp   International Maritime Organisation

http://ilo.org/   ILO

http://who.org/   WHO

www.fao.org/   Food and Agriculture Organisation

Regional organisations

www.nato.int/sfor/index.htm   SFOR

www.nato.int/kfor/welcome.html   KFOR

www.weu.int/   WEU

www.oecd.org/   OECD

www.coe.int/   Council of Europe

http://europa.eu.int/   EU

www.arableagueonline.org/arableague/index en.jsp   Arab League

www.africa-union.org/   African Union

www.aseansec.org/   Association of South East Asian Nations (ASEAN)

www.sadc.int/index.php?lang=english&path=&page=index SADC

www.ecowas.int/   ECOWAS

www.iss.co.za/AF/RegOrg/unity_to_union/ecowas.html   ECOWAS documents

www.oas.org/default.htm   OAS

www.al-bab.com/arab/docs/league.htm   Arab League

www.nato.int/   NATO

www.osce.org/   OSCE

www.nafta-sec-alena.org/english/index.htm   NAFTA

www.mercosur.org.uy/   Mercosur

www.ohr.int/   High Representative of Bosnia and Herzegovina

International Criminal Law

www.icc-cpi.int   International Criminal Court

www.un.org/icty   International Criminal Tribunal for the Former Yugoslavia

www.sc-sl.org   Special Court for Sierra Leone

www.eccc.gov.kh   Extraordinary Chambers in the Courts of Cambodia

INDEX